2020
CHASE'S
Calendar of Events

ROWMAN & LITTLEFIELD
Lanham • Boulder • New York • London

Published by Rowman & Littlefield
A wholly owned subsidiary of The Rowman & Littlefield Publishing Group, Inc.
4501 Forbes Boulevard, Suite 200, Lanham, Maryland 20706
www.rowman.com
800-865-3457

6 Tinworth Street, London SE11 5AL, United Kingdom

NOTICE
Events listed herein are not necessarily endorsed by the editors or publisher. Every effort has been made to assure the correctness of all entries, but neither the editors nor the publisher can warrant their accuracy. IT IS IMPERATIVE, IF FINANCIAL PLANS ARE TO BE MADE IN CONNECTION WITH THE DATES OR EVENTS LISTED HEREIN, THAT PRINCIPALS BE CONSULTED FOR FINAL INFORMATION.

About the Companion Website:
The companion website to *Chase's Calendar of Events 2020* is available only to purchasers of this edition. Please see page 752 for more details.

Note: The companion website will be available to users only from October 14, 2019, through December 31, 2020.

ISBN: 978-1-64143-315-0
E-ISBN: 978-1-64143-316-7
ISSN: 0740-5286

♾️™ The paper used in this publication meets the minimum requirements of American National Standard for Information Sciences—Permanence of Paper for Printed Library Materials, ANSI/NISO Z39.48-1992.

◆ Contents ◆

◆ Introduction ◆

We are pleased to welcome you to *Chase's Calendar of Events 2020*, the 63rd edition of this publication. *Chase's* was first published by brothers William D. and Harrison Chase on Dec 4, 1957, as a 32-page pamphlet with 364 entries, meant to be, as Bill Chase has said, "A reliable guide to known events of the forthcoming year [1958]." That first edition was enthusiastically embraced by libraries, teachers, newspapers, broadcasters and planners in almost every conceivable branch of human activity, from hospitals and nursing homes to charitable organizations to federal government agencies and officials. Not to mention the general public.

In 1958, the US Chamber of Commerce invited the Chases to incorporate their publication, *Special Days, Weeks and Months*, which listed commercial promotions. The content grew and matured to have an international scope. In 1987, celebrity birthdays were added—a popular feature. Through the years, the extended Chase's clan had helped prepare each edition, among them Helen Chase, wife of William, and their children. Harrison retired from the book in 1969, and the rest of the Chases retired in 1987 but have remained consultants and a treasured resource to the current *Chase's* staff based in Chicago, IL.

Today, *Chase's* is a combination book/searchable website with 12,500 entries in a range of subject areas—plus exhaustive appendices. All entries are updated and thoroughly fact-checked, making *Chase's* the most respected and comprehensive reference available on holidays, special events, international days of celebration, federal and state observances, historic and birth anniversaries and special days, weeks and months. *Chase's* strives to deliver interesting facts every day of the year.

What's New in 2020

2020 is both the International Year of Plant Health (as sponsored by the United Nations) and the Year of the Nurse and Midwife (occasioned by the 200th birth anniversary of Florence Nightingale, the founder of modern nursing). This year marks the 75th anniversary of the end of World War II and the 100th anniversary of US women gaining the right to vote. In Tokyo, Japan, the Games of the XXXII Olympiad take place—where they took place in 1964. Tokyo promises a historic Olympics marrying tradition from the past with innovation of the future.

There are other anniversary milestones in 2020. The 250th birth anniversary of Ludwig van Beethoven is being observed around the world in a series of musical events. The 400th anniversary of the *Mayflower* landing in North America reflects how the destinies of English, Wampanoag and Dutch intertwined just as the 250th anniversary of Captain James Cook's exploration of what is now Australia investigates how Cook's arrival affected the Guugu Yimithirr people. The 75th anniversary of the atomic bombings of Hiroshima and Nagasaki will also be observed around the world. All of these and much more are discussed more fully in the "Spotlight" section.

New special days, weeks and months can be found throughout the main calendar section. New observances include National Cheesy Sock Day (Jan 21), National Goat Yoga Month (February), Words Matter Week (Mar 1–7), National Catch and Release Day (Apr 11), International Go Kart Week (Sept 20–26), Random Acts of Poetry Day (Oct 7) and much more.

Types of Entries in *Chase's Calendar of Events*

Astronomical Phenomena

Information about eclipses, equinoxes and solstices, moon phases and other astronomical phenomena is calculated from data prepared by the US Naval Observatory and Her Majesty's Nautical Almanac Office. **Please note: In *Chase's*, Universal Time has been converted to Eastern Time.**

Religious Observances

Principal observances of the Christian, Jewish, Muslim and Baha'i faiths are presented with background information from their respective calendars. We include anticipated dates for Muslim holidays. When known, religious events of China, Japan and India are also listed. There is no single Hindu calendar and different sects define the Hindu lunar month differently. There is no single lunar calendar that serves as a model for all Buddhists, either. Therefore, we are not able to provide the dates of many religious holidays for these faiths.

National and International Observances and Civic Holidays

Chase's features independence days, national days and public holidays from around the world. Technically, there are no national holidays in the US: holidays proclaimed by the president only apply to federal employees and to the District of Columbia. State governors proclaim holidays for their states. In practice, federal holidays are usually proclaimed by governors as well. Some governors proclaim commemorative days that are unique to their state.

Special Days, Weeks and Months

Whether it's Black History Month, National Police Week or National Grandparents' Day, the annual calendar has myriad special days, weeks and months. Since 1957, *Chase's* has been the most comprehensive and authoritative reference of these. Until January 1995, Congress had been active in seeing that special observances were commemorated. Members of the Senate and House could introduce legislation for a special observance to commemorate people, events and other activities they thought worthy of national recognition. Because these bills took up a disproportionate amount of time on the part of congressmen and their staffs, Congress decided to discontinue this process in January 1995 when it reviewed and reformed its rules and practices.

Today, Congress does from time to time issue commemorative resolutions, which do not have the force of law. The president of the US has the authority to declare any commemorative event by proclamation, but this is done infrequently. (Some state legislatures and governors proclaim special days, weeks and months, as do mayors of cities.)

So where do all these special days, weeks and months come from? The majority come from national organizations that use their observances for public outreach and to plan specific events. For special months regarding health issues, for example, you can expect to see more information disseminated, special commemorative walks and medical screenings during that month. The *Chase's* editorial staff includes a special day, week or month in the annual reference based on the authority of the organization observing it, how many years it has been observed, the amount of promotion and activities that are a part of it, its uniqueness and a variety of other factors. (We also include a list of 2020 special months in our appendix section.)

Presidential Proclamations

As we noted above, the president has the authority to declare any commemorative event by proclamation. A good number of these will be proclamations for which there has been legislation giving continuing authority for a proclamation to be issued each year. Mother's Day, for example, has been proclaimed since 1914 by public resolution. The White House Clerk's Office initiates the issuing of these proclamations each year, since they are mandated by authorizing legislation. Of course, there will be new ones: Patriot Day (in the wake of the Sept 11, 2001, terrorist attacks) is an example. In *Chase's* we list proclamations that have continuing authority and those that have been issued consistently since 2008 in the main calendar of the book. In our text, ★ indicates a presidential proclamation. In our appendix, we also offer a complete list of proclamations issued from Jan 1, 2018, to June 15, 2019.

Events and Festivals

Chase's includes national and international special events as well as festivals defined by their uniqueness and their finite brief length of time. Sporting events; book, film, food and other festivals; seasonal celebrations; folkloric events (Up Helly Aa or Carnival, for example); music outings and more make up these types of entries. These entries are usually sponsored: they have contact information for the general public and all information in the entry comes from the sponsor (see below on sponsored events).

Anniversaries

Anniversaries include historic (creation of nations or states, battles, inventions, publications of note, popular culture events, famous firsts, etc.) and biographical (birth or death anniversaries of notable personages) milestones.

Birthdays Today

Living celebrities in politics, the arts, sports and popular culture are included in the "Birthdays Today" section following each calendar day. If there is a question about the birth day or year, this is noted. **Be aware that national and international political leaders (US president, US governors and senators, prime ministers, cabinet officials, etc) listed are current as of July 2019.**

Spotlight

The tinted pages starting off *Chase's Calendar of Events* form the "Spotlight" section. In a book as packed as *Chase's*, the reader may need a little help picking out significant anniversaries and events for the current year, and "Spotlight" is the answer to that need. We cover significant 2020 historical and birth anniversaries as well as major events with a little more depth than in the main calendar section. In Spotlight on the Past, the years 1920, 1945, 1970 and 1995 are presented with major events, artistic and scientific milestones, sports highlights and more.

New Style Versus Old Style Dates

Please note that dates for historic events can be assumed to be Gregorian calendar (New Style) dates unless "(OS)" appears after the date. This annotation means that the date in question is an Old Style, or Julian calendar, date. Most of America's founders were born before 1752, when Great Britain and its colonies adopted the Gregorian calendar. As an example of this, we list George Washington's birthday as Feb 22, 1732, which is the Gregorian or New Style date. However, when he was born Great Britain and its colonies began the year on Mar 25, not Jan 1, so his Julian birthdate was Feb 11, 1731.

About Sponsored Events

Events for which there is individual or organizational sponsorship are listed with the name of the event, inclusive dates of observance, a brief description, estimated attendance figures and the sponsor's name and contact information. We obtain information for these events directly from the sponsors. There is no fee to be listed in *Chase's* and sponsors submit events to be chosen at the discretion of the *Chase's* editors. Neither the editors nor the publisher necessarily endorse these events.

About the Companion Website

Purchasers of *Chase's Calendar of Events 2020* have access to an exclusive companion website from October 2019 to Dec 31, 2020. This website offers many ways to search 2020 content digitally. Please go to page 752 to get the URL (the website's address) and the password as well as more information on certain features. (Please note that www.chases.com is still the general marketing website for *Chase's Calendar of Events*—it is not the companion website.)

Acknowledgments

A book the size of *Chase's* comes about through the care and attention of many organizations and people. The editors and publisher would like to thank the event sponsors; CVBs; chambers of commerce; tourism agencies; nonprofit organizations; publicists; festival organizers; state fair administrative staffs; historians; museum directors; librarians; National Park Service employees; the American Library Association; embassy and cultural affairs staffs; astronomers; national, state and local government officials and many others who help us put together this reference every year.

Bill Chase and his family are ongoing consultants for and supporters of *Chase's*. In Bill Chase there's no better advocate of holidays and celebrations—he led the way for the "democratization" of special days, weeks and months. Bill Chase and the Chase family are also sponsors of many special days.

We offer grateful thanks to the researchers, writers and fact-checkers who helped us to assemble the 2020 edition: Rob Walton, Loretta Ullrich Ferguson, Joel Super, Johnny Loftus, Sandy Whiteley, Peter Ericksen, James Foster and Gigi Grajdura.

Thank you to our editorial and production colleagues at Bernan Press and Rowman & Littlefield: Patricia Stevenson, Emily Eastridge, Karen Ackermann, Chloe Batch, Joyce Culley, Ira Sumarno, Al Hinds and Cecil Richards. Thank you also to Mary Meghan Ryan, Kicheko Driggins and Veronica Dove at Bernan Press; Paul Konowitch, publisher, Bernan Press; and Jed Lyons, president and CEO of Rowman & Littlefield.

Holly McGuire, *Editor in Chief*
July 2019

Spotlight on the Past

1920

100 YEARS AGO

Landmark World Events

Jan 10 The Treaty of Versailles, signed on June 28, 1919, went into effect—ending World War I.

Jan 10 The League of Nations came into existence. Fifty nations entered into a covenant designed to avoid war. The United States never joined.

Feb 2 In the Tartu Peace Treaty, Soviet Russia recognized the independence of Estonia.

March The Franco-Syrian War began.

May 16 Joan of Arc (1412–31) was canonized.

May 21 Mexican president Venustiano Carranza was assassinated in Tlaxcalantongo.

June 28–July The Connaught Rangers, a division of the British Army, mutinied in Jalandhar, India, in protest of British actions in Ireland.

July 24 The French army deposed king Faisal I of Syria, who had only ruled since March, ending the Franco-Syrian War.

Aug 10 The Treaty of Sèvres was signed, beginning the process of dismantling the Ottoman Empire after World War I.

Oct 17 War correspondent and communist activist John Reed, who penned *Ten Days That Shook the World* (1919) about the Russian Revolution, died in Moscow of typhus. He was given an honored internment at the Kremlin Wall Necropolis.

Oct 25 Alexander, the 27-year-old king of Greece, died of sepsis—he had been bitten by a monkey three weeks earlier.

Nov 11 In England and France, "Unknown Warriors" of the Great War were laid to rest.

Dec 1 Álvaro Obregón, elected president of Mexico in October, took office.

■ The Nobel Prize for Peace was awarded to Léon Bourgeois, French politician and former prime minister of France, for his foundational work on the League of Nations.

■ Around the world, armed conflicts continued: the Russian Revolution, the Polish-Soviet War, the Irish War of Independence and the Franco-Syrian War. The Mexican Revolution came to an end.

Landmark US Events

Jan 2 The Palmer Raids, an initiative targeting leftists, labor activists, anarchists and communists (especially of immigrant status) by US attorney general A. Mitchell Palmer, began in 1919 and culminated in a huge and aggressive effort in the New Year. Starting on this date, more than 3,000 people were arrested and detained in more than 30 cities. The raids were headed by J. Edgar Hoover.

Jan 16 The 18th Amendment took effect and the sale and manufacture of alcoholic beverages became illegal in the United States, with the Volstead Act providing enforcement.

Feb 14 The League of Women Voters was formed. With the vote for women just a few months away, the new organization was created to help American women exercise their new political rights and responsibilities.

Aug 18 The 19th Amendment was ratified, extending the right to vote to US women. See "Spotlight on American Anniversaries."

Sept 16 The J.P. Morgan Bank at Wall and Broad streets was bombed by unknown assailants. A horse-drawn cart was filled with dynamite and 500 pounds of iron sash weights. The explosion killed 38 people and injured more than 140 people seriously. Hundreds more were slightly injured, including Joe Kennedy, a young stock broker who later established the Kennedy political dynasty, and J.P. Morgan's grandson, Junius. No one was ever caught in the terrorist act, but Italian anarchists were suspected.

Nov 2 The only surviving attendee of the 1848 Seneca Falls Women's Rights Convention, Charlotte Woodward, voted in the general election.

Nov 2 Republican candidate Warren G. Harding, US senator for Ohio, won the 1920 presidential election, defeating Democrat James Cox in a rout. Harding carried 37 states and won 60 percent of the vote.

■ The American Civil Liberties Union was founded by Roger Baldwin, Crystal Eastman and Albert DeSilver.

Culture

Literary Arts

■ Norwegian author Knut Hamsun received the Nobel Prize in Literature "for his monumental work, *Growth of the Soil.*"

Fiction

Mar 26 F. Scott Fitzgerald's first novel, *This Side of Paradise*, was published by Charles Scribner's Sons to immediate success. It was edited by the famed Maxwell Perkins. Fitzgerald was able to marry Zelda Sayre on Apr 3—she had told him that publication would win her hand.

October Belgian detective Hercule Poirot first exercised his "little grey cells" with the publication in the United States of *The Mysterious Affair at Styles*, by Agatha Christie. (The mystery was published in Britain in 1921.)

■ D.H. Lawrence, *Women in Love*

■ John Galsworthy, *In Chancery* (book two of the Forsyte Saga)

■ Marcel Proust, *The Guermantes Way*, Part I (book three of *In Search of Lost Time*)

■ Colette, *Chéri*

■ Sinclair Lewis, *Main Street*

■ Edith Wharton, *The Age of Innocence* (winner of the 1921 Pulitzer Prize for Fiction)

Nonfiction

■ The renowned and influential Dutch American editor, Edward Bok, who helmed *Ladies Home Journal* for 30 years, published his memoir, *The Americanization of Edward Bok: The Autobiography of a Dutch Boy Fifty Years After*. This work received a Pulitzer Prize in 1921.

■ H.G. Wells's *Outline of History*, originally released in installments in 1919, was published in a single volume.

■ *Beyond the Pleasure Principle*, by Sigmund Freud, described the death instinct.

Poetry

■ Edna St. Vincent Millay, *A Few Figs from Thistles*

■ Wilfred Owen, *Poems* (published posthumously)

■ Carl Sandburg, *Smoke and Steel*

■ Ezra Pound, *Hugh Selwyn Mauberley*

Children's Literature

Oct 22 *The Western Pennsylvania Scholastic* was first published. It was a four-page newspaper for high-school students in the Pittsburgh, PA, area. In 1922, the company became The Scholastic and is today the world's largest provider of children's books and educational media.

■ *The Little Engine That Could*, by Mabel Caroline Bragg, was published in *My Book House*. It was one of many incarnations of the plucky, never-say-die train engine.

■ Hugh Lofting published *The Story of Doctor Dolittle*, the first book in a beloved series.

Journalism

April *Black Mask*, the influential pulp magazine that would popularize such authors as Dashiell Hammett, Raymond Chandler and Erle Stanley Gardner, was launched by H.L. Mencken and George Jean Nathan.

May 22 Henry Ford's *The Dearborn Independent*'s front-page article was "The International Jew: The World's Problem." This article signaled Ford's intent to make the newspaper (which was distributed to Ford dealerships) into a mouthpiece for his anti-Semitic views.

Theater and Opera

Nov 1 Eugene O'Neill's *The Emperor Jones* premiered at the Provincetown Playhouse in New York City. Charles S. Gilpin portrayed Brutus Jones. The play was a major critical and financial success for O'Neill.

Dec 21 Jerome Kern's musical *Sally*, produced by Flo Ziegfeld, premiered on Broadway. It featured a 1919 song, "Look for the Silver Lining," that became popular in 1920. P.G. Wodehouse contributed lyrics to some of the songs.

■ Czech author and playwright Karel Capek wrote and published the futuristic play *R.U.R.*, which featured "robots" as characters. It premiered in Czechoslovakia the next year.

■ J.M. Barrie, *Mary Rose*

Film

Feb 26 *The Cabinet of Dr. Caligari* premiered in Berlin, Germany. Directed by Robert Weine and starring Conrad Veidt as a murderous sleepwalker, the film is considered the epitome of German Expressionism.

Aug 2 During night filming in Los Angeles, CA, for a stunt in *The Skywayman*, stunt pilot/leading actor Ormer Locklear was disoriented by arc lights left on and crashed, killing himself and his copilot. Fox released the film (with the crash scene) the next month. The film is now lost, but Locklear is regarded as a pioneer for filmed aviation stunts.

■ *Way Down East*, directed by D.W. Griffith and starring Lillian Gish

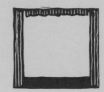

- *The Mark of Zorro*, starring Douglas Fairbanks
- *Pollyanna*, starring Mary Pickford
- *Something to Think About*, with Gloria Swanson, was the most popular film of 1920
- *The Golem*, directed by and starring Paul Wegener
- "One Week," starring and cowritten by Buster Keaton

Radio

Aug 20 The *Detroit News* founded a radio station (call sign "8MK") to broadcast the "Detroit News Radiophone." In 1922, the station was given the call sign WWJ. It is still in operation today.

Sept 6 The first radio broadcast of a prize fight: Jack Dempsey knocked out Billy Miske in the third round.

Nov 2 The first scheduled radio broadcast: Pittsburgh, PA's KDKA broadcast the results of the presidential election.

Music

Feb 14 Okeh Records in New York City released the first record ("That Thing Called Love") to feature a black singer—Mamie Smith.

Aug 10 "Crazy Blues," performed by Mamie Smith and Her Jazz Hounds on Okeh Records, sold one million copies.

Nov 15 The London Symphony Orchestra gave Gustav Holst's *The Planets* its first public premiere. The now-popular orchestral suite was written during WWI.

Dec 12 Maurice Ravel's *La valse* premiered in Paris, France.

- Russian physicist Lev Sergeyevich Termen invented the theremin, an electronic musical instrument that he patented in 1928.

The instrument was used later to eerie effect in film and television soundtracks—most famously, those for *Spellbound*, *The Day the Earth Stood Still* and *Lost Weekend*.

Popular Songs

- "Crazy Blues"
- Al Jolson, "Avalon"
- Nora Bayes, "(I'll Be with You) in Apple Blossom Time"
- "Look for the Silver Lining"

Art

Nov 11 In Westminster, London, England, Sir Edwin Lutyens's war memorial, The Cenotaph, was unveiled on Remembrance Day.

- *The Table (Still Life with Rabbit)*, by Joan Miró
- *Republican Automatons* and "*The Convict*" *Monteur John Heartfield After Franz Jung's Attempt to Get Him Up on His Feet*, by George Grosz
- *Composition C*, by Piet Mondrian

Science and Technology

- Charles Edouard Guillaume received the Nobel Prize in Physics "in recognition of the service he has rendered to precision measurements in Physics by his discovery of anomalies in nickel steel alloys."
- The Nobel Prize in Chemistry was awarded to Walther Nernst "in recognition of his work in thermochemistry."
- August Krogh received the Nobel Prize in Physiology or Medicine "for his discovery of the capillary motor regulating mechanism."

Jan 13 In an editorial, *The New York Times* ridiculed engineer and physicist Robert Goddard and his now-foundational text, *A Method of*

Reaching Extreme Altitudes, which had been published in 1919 by the Smithsonian. The *Times* charged that Goddard seemed "to lack the knowledge ladled out daily in high schools." (On July 17, 1969, one day after *Apollo 11* launched, the newspaper apologized for its editorial, but Goddard had died in 1945.)

- In his Bakerian Medal lecture before the Royal Society, physicist Ernest Rutherford posited the existence of the neuron (discovered in 1932 by James Chadwick).
- German neuropathologist Hans Gerhard Creutzfeldt first described the fatal brain disease that now bears his name: Creutzfeldt–Jakob disease. (German neurologist Alfons Maria Jakob later independently also described the disease, hence the hyphenate designation.)
- The pain-relieving opioid hydrocodone was first synthesized in Germany.

Commerce and New Products

January Italian immigrant Charles Ponzi set up the Security Exchange Company in Boston, MA. Ponzi promised high returns to investors—the first 18 were paid promptly—but with money that came from new investors. Soon, shares were selling like wildfire and Ponzi was living a luxurious life. Authorities and journalists began asking pressing questions in July, and by August Ponzi could not pay investors. He surrendered to authorities Aug 12, went to prison and eventually died penniless in 1949. His name lives on as a term for a fraudulent pyramid investing scheme, the Ponzi Scheme.

Jan 16 As the 18th Amendment took effect, breweries had to retool, some making "near" beer, others making ice cream. Prohibition started a boom in illegal business activities, as gangsters saw a growth opportunity in clandestine alcohol supply.

■ Published in December 1919, *The Economic Consequences of the Peace*, by economist John Maynard Keynes, was a bestseller in 1920, although many critics savaged it. The book criticized the harsh terms of the Treaty of Versailles and correctly predicted Germany's economic collapse paired with instability in Europe—presaging World War II. The book thrust Keynes into the spotlight as an important economist and thinker until his death in 1946.

■ Radios were first offered in retail stores for $10.

■ Although not invented in 1920, handheld hair dryers began to be sold this year.

■ Band-Aid adhesive bandages were first sold to the public by Johnson & Johnson.

■ The Snap-On Wrench Company was founded in Milwaukee, WI, and featured tools with interchangeable handles and sockets.

Sports

Auto Racing

May 31 Indianapolis 500: Gaston Chevrolet

Nov 25 During a race at the Beverly Hills Speedway in Los Angeles, CA, driver Gaston Chevrolet crashed and died. An Indy 500 winner and the brother of Louis Chevrolet, who founded the automobile company that bears his name, Chevrolet nonetheless was still posthumously National Champion of 1920.

Games of the VII Olympiad

The Olympics, which had not been contested since 1912 due to World War I, were held in Antwerp, Belgium. The nations who lost World War I—Germany, the Ottoman Empire, Austria, Hungary, Bulgaria—were excluded. For the first time, the Olympic flag with the iconic five interlocking rings was flown for the games (the design had been adopted in 1914). In total medal count and most gold medals, the United States was the victor. Among US athletes was swimmer Duke Kahanamoku, who repeated his 1912 gold medal performance in the 100 meters and won gold with the US relay team.

Baseball

Jan 3 Boston Red Sox owner and theatrical producer Harry Frazee sold pitcher-outfielder Babe Ruth to the New York Yankees for $125,000 and a $300,000 loan. The "Curse of the Bambino" began. Frazee used the loan several years later to produce *No, No, Nanette*, a hit musical.

Feb 13 Rube Foster cofounded the Negro National League, which mainly operated in the Midwest. The League lasted through 1930.

Apr 14 After being sold by the Boston Red Sox, Babe Ruth played his first game for the New York Yankees. He got two singles against the Philadelphia Athletics but made an error in the outfield, giving the A's two runs and a 3–1 victory.

May 14 Pitcher Walter Johnson of the Washington Senators, considered by some to be the greatest pitcher of all time and the fastest, won the 300th game of his career, beating the Detroit Tigers, 9–8.

Aug 16 Cleveland Indians shortstop Ray Chapman was hit by a pitch during a game with the New York Yankees. Chapman collapsed with a fractured skull and died the next day. He is the only major league player to have received a fatal injury during play.

Sept 28 Eight members of the 1919 Chicago White Sox were indicted by a grand jury at Chicago on charges that they conspired to fix the 1919 World Series and allowed the Cincinnati Reds to win. The eight players were Eddie Cicotte, Oscar ("Happy") Felsch, Charles ("Chick") Gandil, ("Shoeless") Joe Jackson, Fred McMullin, Charles ("Swede") Risberg, George ("Buck") Weaver and Claude ("Lefty") Williams. White Sox owner Charles Comiskey immediately suspended the eight. They were acquitted but nevertheless banned from baseball for life.

Oct 2 In the only major league tripleheader played in the 20th century, the Cincinnati Reds took two games from the Pittsburgh Pirates before the Pirates won the nightcap, called by darkness after six innings.

Oct 10 The Cleveland Indians defeated the Brooklyn Dodgers, 8–1, in the fifth game of the 1920 World Series. The Indians' Elmer Smith hit the first grand slam in World Series play in the first inning, and winning pitcher Jim Bagby hit the first World Series homer by a pitcher in the fourth inning. But the most famous play in the game was the unassisted triple play recorded by Cleveland second baseman Bill Wambsganss in the fifth inning. "Wamby" caught a line drive hit by Clarence Mitchell, touched second to double off Pete Kilduff and tagged Otto Miller before he could return safely to first base.

Nov 12 In the wake of the growing scandal surrounding accusations that members of the Chicago White Sox conspired to fix the 1919 World Series, baseball owners appointed federal judge Kenesaw Mountain Landis the game's first commissioner with extremely broad powers. Landis replaced the National Commission, a three-man governing board, and served until his death in 1944.

Football

Sept 17 After a preliminary meeting on Aug 20, at which the owners of four teams formed the American Professional Football Conference, a second meeting at Canton, OH, brought together these teams and others, and the APFC changed its name to the American Professional Football Conference. This league, which played its first games in the fall, later became the National Football League. See "Spotlight on American Anniversaries."

Oct 3 The Dayton Triangles defeated the Columbus Panhandles, 14–0, in the first game played in the American Professional Football Association. The APFA became the National Football League in 1922, but this game is considered the NFL's first game. Lou Partlow of Dayton scored what is regarded as the NFL's first touchdown.

Golf

■ Scottish golfer George Duncan won the Open Championship.

Hockey

■ The Ottawa Senators won the Stanley Cup, defeating the Seattle Metropolitans.

Horse Racing

Oct 3 Comrade won the inaugural edition of the Prix de l'Arc de Triomphe thoroughbred horse race in Paris, France.

Oct 11 The legendary Man o' War ended his two-year racing career at Windsor, ON, Canada, winning the Kenilworth Park Gold Cup. He had only lost one race. He retired and lived until 1947.

■ Paul Jones, ridden by Ted Rice, won the Kentucky Derby.

■ Man o' War, ridden by Charles Kummer, won the Preakness and the Belmont Stakes (he had not been entered in the Kentucky Derby).

Soccer

■ Aston Villa defeated Huddersfield to win the storied FA Cup in England.

Tennis

July 1 Suzanne Lenglen of France became the first woman tennis player to win three Wimbledon championships in the same year. She won the singles title, the doubles and the mixed doubles.

■ Bill Tilden of the United States won the men's title at Wimbledon, defeating Gerald Patterson, the previous year's champion.

1920 Deaths

■ Alexander, king of Greece

■ Grand Duchess Maria Alexandrovna, Russian noble, aunt of Tsar Nicholas II

■ Madeline McDowell Breckinridge, American suffragette leader

■ Max Bruch, German composer

■ Venustiano Carranza, president of Mexico

■ Ray Chapman, American baseball player

■ Gaston Chevrolet, Swiss-French auto racer

■ "Big Jim" Colosimo, Italian-American gangster based in Chicago

■ Eugénie de Montijo, last empress of France

■ John Dodge, American automobile magnate (Dodge Brothers Company)

■ Peter Carl Fabergé, founder of the House of Fabergé, Russian jeweler

■ Benito Pérez Galdós, Spanish author

■ George "The Gipper" Gip, American college football star

■ William Crawford Gorgas, American army surgeon who successfully battled malaria and yellow fever

■ Evelina Haverfield, British suffragette

■ William Heinemann, English publisher

■ William Dean Howells, American author

■ Edward D. Jones, cofounder of Dow Jones & Company, the *Wall Street Journal* and the Dow Jones Industrial Average

■ Ormer Locklear, American stunt pilot and actor

■ Norman Lockyer, British scientist (codiscoverer of helium) and founder of the journal *Nature*

■ William Chester Minor, American surgeon, convicted murderer and major contributor to the *Oxford English Dictionary*

■ Amedeo Modigliani, Italian artist

■ Levi Parsons Morton, 22nd US vice president

■ Robert Peary, American naval officer and polar explorer

■ John Reed, American journalist and author of *Ten Days That Shook the World*

■ Max Weber, German philosopher and sociologist

1945

75 YEARS AGO

Landmark World Events

Jan 25 As the Battle of the Bulge concluded, the Allies emerged victorious.

Jan 27 Soviet troops liberated Auschwitz in Poland. Among the survivors was 16-year-old Elie Wiesel. Jan 27 is now observed worldwide as International Holocaust Remembrance Day.

February (or March) Sisters Margot and Anne Frank died of typhus at the Bergen-Belsen concentration camp.

Feb 3 The Battle of Manila began. By Mar 3, the allies, led by US general Douglas MacArthur, were victorious and Japanese occupation of the Philippines ended.

Feb 4–11 US president Franklin Roosevelt, Soviet premier Josef Stalin and British prime minister Winston Churchill meet at Yalta, USSR.

Feb 5 Nazi SS officers executed four female Allied secret (SOE) agents at Ravensbrück concentration camp (which was exclusively for female prisoners): Violette Szabo, Denise Bloch, Lilian Rolfe and Cecily Lefort (who may have been killed later in the month). All four were posthumously awarded France's Croix de Guerre.

Feb 13 Allied air power bombed Dresden, Germany, which resulted in a firestorm that killed 25,000 people.

Feb 19–Mar 16 Battle of Iwo Jima: US forces recaptured the island. The press photograph of the US flag being raised on Mount Suribachi is one of the iconic images of WWII.

Mar 9–10 US bombers attacked Tokyo, Japan, killing more than 90,000 people.

Apr 1 Battle of Okinawa began— the biggest amphibious operation in the Pacific War.

Apr 11 US troops liberated Buchenwald concentration camp: inmates within had sent coded messages for help on Apr 8 and attacked their guards.

Apr 15 British troops liberated Bergen-Belsen concentration camp.

Apr 16 Fall of Berlin began. On May 2, the Soviets announced the city taken.

Apr 25 US and Soviet troops met, completing a link that cut Germany in two.

Apr 28 Italian dictator Benito Mussolini and his mistress were executed after attempting to flee to Switzerland.

Apr 29 Dachau concentration camp was liberated.

Apr 30 German dictator Adolf Hitler killed himself in his bunker complex in Berlin, Germany. Soviet troops secured the bunker on May 2.

May 8 Victory in Europe Day: Germany unconditionally surrendered.

June 21 Battle of Okinawa ended.

June 26 United Nations charter was signed.

July 17–Aug 2 The Potsdam Conference: new US president Harry S Truman joined Stalin and Churchill and Clement Attlee. They issued the Potsdam Declaration calling for Japan's unconditional surrender on July 26, which Japan rejected.

July 26 Clement Attlee became prime minister of the United Kingdom after Winston Churchill's Conservative Party suffered losses in the general election earlier in the month.

Aug 6 The United States dropped an atomic bomb, nicknamed "Little Boy," on the city of Hiroshima, Japan. See "Spotlight on World Anniversaries."

Aug 9 The United States dropped a second atomic bomb, nicknamed "Fat Man," on the city of Nagasaki, Japan.

Aug 15 Emperor Hirohito, in a prerecorded message over the radio, announced Japan's unconditional surrender.

Aug 15 The terms of Japan's surrender meant the independence of Korea.

Sept 2 Representatives from Japan officially and unconditionally surrendered to the Allied powers on board the USS *Missouri*, which was docked in Tokyo Bay. World War II was over. See "Spotlight on World Anniversaries."

Oct 16 The Food and Agriculture Organization (FAO) of the United Nations was founded. Oct 16 is observed as World Food Day today in honor of the FAO's founding.

Oct 24 With ratification of its charter, the United Nations was founded.

Nov 20 At Nuremberg, Germany, war crimes trials of Nazi leaders began.

■ The Nobel Prize for Peace was awarded to former US secretary of state Cordell Hull as one of the architects of the United Nations.

Landmark US Events

Jan 2 Japanese Americans were allowed to return to the West Coast.

Jan 20 Franklin Delano Roosevelt took the oath of office as president of the United States for a fourth time—at the White House rather than the Capitol. He gave a brief address and vowed, "In the days and in the years that are to come we shall work for a just and honorable peace, a durable peace, as today we work and fight for total victory in war."

Jan 25 Grand Rapids, MI, began fluoridating its water supply in a study to test its positive effect on teeth. This was the first instance of water fluoridation in the world. Eleven years later, scientists found that tooth decay among children had decreased 60 percent.

Jan 31 Private Eddie Slovik was executed for desertion in France—the first such execution since the Civil War.

Apr 12 President Roosevelt died of a cerebral hemorrhage at the "Little White House," in Warm Springs, GA. Vice president Harry Truman became US president.

July 13 The War Relocation Authority announced that 9 out 10 internment camps would close during October to December.

July 28 Hampered by a thick fog, a B-25 bomber crashed into the 79th and 80th floors of the Empire State Building, killing 14. Miraculously, Betty Lou Oliver, one of the building's elevator operators, survived a 75-floor plunge in a damaged car.

July 30 USS *Indianapolis* was sunk by the Japanese after delivering materials for an atomic bomb at Tinian Island. Of almost 1,200 crew members, only 318 were rescued on Aug 2. It is still the US Navy's worst loss.

Aug 8 The United States joined the newly formed United Nations.

Sept 8 Miss New York, Bess Myerson, became the first Jewish Miss America. She was subjected to anti-Semitic abuse during her subsequent US tour.

November The United Automobile Workers (UAW) began a 113-day strike against GM.

Dec 28 The US Congress officially recognized the Pledge of Allegiance (originally composed in 1892) and urged its frequent recitation in America's schools. (The phrase "Under God" was not added until 1954.)

Culture

Literary Arts

■ Chilean poet Gabriela Mistral received the Nobel Prize in Literature. On Dec 10, in his presentation speech, Swedish Academy member Hjalmar Gullberg noted, "This poet gives us a drink which tastes of the earth and which appease the thirst of the heart."

■ Future author Kurt Vonnegut survived the Dresden firestorm as a German prisoner of war—that experience became the inspiration for his 1969 novel *Slaughterhouse-Five*.

Fiction

Aug 17 In London, England, Secker and Warburg published George Orwell's *Animal Farm*, a dystopian satire of the Russian Revolution and Stalinist USSR.

■ Agatha Christie, *Sparkling Cyanide*

■ Chester Himes, *If He Hollers, Let Him Go*

■ Nancy Mitford, *The Pursuit of Love*

■ John Steinbeck, *Cannery Row*

■ C.S. Lewis, *That Hideous Strength*

■ Evelyn Waugh, *Brideshead Revisited*

Nonfiction

■ Carlo Levi, *Christ Stopped at Eboli*

■ Betty MacDonald, *The Egg and I*

■ Richard Wright, *Black Boy*

Poetry

May Poet Ezra Pound, who had made pro-Fascist, anti-Semitic radio broadcasts during the war, turned himself in to US military authorities in Italy as the war ended in Europe. He was placed in isolation in an outdoor, 6-foot-by-6-foot cage for three weeks, which prompted a nervous breakdown and the genesis of his *Pisan Cantos*.

Children's Literature

November Astrid Lindgren's *Pippi Longstocking* was published in Sweden.

■ Maud and Miska Petersham, *The Rooster Crows: A Book of American Rhymes and Jingles* (winner of the 1946 Caldecott Medal)

■ Lois Lenski, *Strawberry Girl* (winner of the 1946 Newbery Medal)

■ Ruth Krauss, *The Carrot Seed*

■ E.B. White, *Stuart Little*

Journalism

Apr 18 Celebrated American war correspondent Ernie Pyle was killed by Japanese fire during the Battle of Okinawa.

Nov 1 The first issue of *Ebony* magazine was published by Chicago-based entrepreneur John H. Johnson, who had introduced *Negro Digest* three years earlier. The 25,000-copy first printing sold out in hours.

Theater and Opera

Apr 19 *Carousel*, a musical by Rodgers and Hammerstein, premiered at the Majestic Theatre in New York City and ran for two years. The song "You'll Never Walk Alone" featured in it.

July 6 J.B. Priestley's now-classic play skewering Edwardian morality, *An Inspector Calls*, premiered in Moscow, Russia. It didn't open in the United Kingdom until 1946.

Film

Jan 6 Undaunted romantic Pepé Le Pew made his screen debut in the Warner Bros' cartoon "Odorable Kitty." Creator Chuck Jones

based the skunk on a friend; voice artist Mel Blanc used Charles Boyer as an inspiration for the accent.

Nov 29 *Lost Weekend*, starring Ray Milland and directed by Billy Wilder, was released. The dramatic portrait of alcoholism won four Oscars—including for Milland's performance.

■ Basil Rathbone appeared in three Sherlock Holmes films in 1945 with costar Nigel Bruce: *The House of Fear*, *The Woman in Green*, *Pursuit to Algiers*.

■ *Thunderhead: Son of Flicka*, starred Roddy McDowall.

■ *Spellbound*, directed by Alfred Hitchcock, starred Gregory Peck and Ingrid Bergman.

■ *And Then There Were None*, directed by Rene Clair, brought Agatha Christie's thriller to life.

Notable Films

■ *A Tree Grows in Brooklyn*

■ *The Bells of St Mary's*

■ *Son of Lassie*

■ *Christmas in Connecticut*

■ *Rome: Open City*

■ *Brief Encounter*

■ *The Body Snatcher*

■ *Anchors Away*

■ *State Fair*

■ *I Know Where I'm Going!*

■ *The Thin Man Goes Home*

■ *They Were Expendable*

■ *The Story of GI Joe*

Academy Awards

(18th, Awarded in 1946 for 1945 achievement)

■ Best Picture: *Lost Weekend*

■ Best Actor: Ray Milland, *Lost Weekend*

■ Best Actress: Joan Crawford, *Mildred Pierce*

■ Best Supporting Actor: James Dunn, *A Tree Grows in Brooklyn*

■ Best Supporting Actress: Anne Revere, *National Velvet*

■ Best Director: Billy Wilder, for *Lost Weekend*

Radio

■ "*American Mercury* Presents: Meet the Press" debuted. It moved to television in 1947 and remains the longest running television program.

■ "The Saint" debuted on the NBC radio network. It was based on the successful thriller novels by Leslie Charteris.

Music

January Bing Crosby and the Andrews Sisters recorded the Johnny Mercer/Harold Arlen song "Ac-Cent-Tchu-Ate the Positive," and it reached number one in January 1945.

January Dizzy Gillespie, who had left the Billy Eckstine band the month before, began recording as the leader of his own band. His brand of jazz was bebop and marked jazz's evolution from large swing bands to smaller bebop outfts.

Feb 29 Dizzy Gillespie and Charlie Parker recorded together for the first time.

■ The Andrews Sisters released their version of the calypso song "Rum and Coca-Cola." It was a smash number one for weeks on *Billboard*.

■ Doris Day had her first number-one hit with "Sentimental Journey," recorded with Les Brown and His Band of Renown.

■ "It's Been a Long, Long Time," written by Jule Styne and Sammy Cahn, was a hit in November and December 1945 for Kitty Kallen and Harry James, then Bing Crosby with Les Paul.

■ Mel Tormé and Robert Wells wrote "The Christmas Song," which would gain fame when Nat King Cole recorded it the next year (and many times over the years).

■ "Till the End of Time" was Perry Como's first number-one hit.

Popular Songs

■ Bing Crosby and the Andrews Sisters, "Ac-Cent-Tchu-Ate the Positive" (recorded in December 1944)

■ Louis Jordan and His Tympany Five, "Caldonia"

■ Gene Autry, "Have I Told You Lately That I Love You?"

■ Joe Liggins, "The Honeydripper"

■ Duke Ellington, "I'm Just a Lucky So-and-So"

■ Vaughn Monroe, "Let It Snow! Let It Snow! Let It Snow!" and "There! I've Said It Again"

■ Tex Ritter, "You Two-Timed Me One Time Too Often"

■ "You'll Never Walk Alone," from *Carousel*

Art

■ *The Charnel House*, by Pablo Picasso

■ *Apocalypse in Lilac, Capriccio*, by Marc Chagall

■ *Without Hope* and *Moses*, by Frida Kahlo

■ *Lunar Bird* was modeled by Joan Miró (and cast in bronze 20 years later)

Science and Technology

■ The Nobel Prize in Physiology or Medicine was awarded to Sir Alexander Fleming, Ernst Boris Chain and Sir Howard Walter Florey "for

the discovery of penicillin and its curative effect in various infectious diseases."

■ The Nobel Prize in Physics was awarded to Austrian Wolfgang Pauli for his postulation of the Exclusion Principle.

■ Finnish scientist Artturi Ilmari Virtanen received the Nobel Prize in Chemistry for his work on nutrition, especially in agricultural applications: more nutritional fodder for cows.

July 16 In the Trinity Test, the US successfully exploded the first atomic bomb near Socorro, NM.

■ Scientists at Oak Ridge National Laboratory in Tennessee produced the rare chemical element promethium (atomic number 61). The discovery was not announced until 1947.

Commerce and New Products

July The World Bank was founded—it was theorized at the 1944 Bretton Woods Conference.

Sept 21 Henry Ford II, 28 years old, became president of the Ford Motor Company, taking over for his ailing grandfather Henry Ford.

Oct 6 A variation on the "biro" ballpoint ink pen, developed by Hungarian Laszlo Biro in the 1930s, began production in the United States by Milton Reynolds. By the end of October the pens were offered for sale at Gimbels for $12.50 and were a great success.

Nov 27 Richard and Betty James demonstrated their "Slinky" toy at Philadelphia, PA's Gimbels department store to roaring success: 400 $1 toys sold in 90 minutes. Richard James, a mechanical engineer, was originally working on industrial application of springs before he was inspired to consider their playful aspects.

■ Percy Spencer, an American physicist working for Raytheon, devised the first microwave oven to cook food. Raytheon patented it Oct 8, 1945. The "Radarange" was first sold in 1946.

Sports

■ Many sporting events were not held due to the war—including the Indianapolis 500, the Wimbledon championships and the US Open (golf).

Baseball

Aug 1 Outfielder Mel Ott of the New York Giants hit the 500th home run of his career in a 9–2 win over the Boston Braves at the Polo Grounds. At this point in baseball history, Ott stood third on the all-time home run list behind Babe Ruth with 714 and Jimmie Foxx with 531. Ott finished with 511 homers.

Oct 5–12 Detroit Tigers won the World Series, defeating the Brooklyn Dodgers.

Basketball

Mar 27 Oklahoma A&M defeated NYU to take the NCAA national championship in a final at Madison Square Garden.

Football

Dec 4 Fullback Felix ("Doc") Blanchard of Army became the first junior to win the Heisman Trophy. "Mr Inside" to teammate Glenn Davis's "Mr Outside," Blanchard also won the Sullivan Award, given to the country's best overall athlete.

Dec 16 The Cleveland Rams nosed the Washington Redskins 15–14 to win the 1945 NFL championship. The temperature was -8 degrees F.

■ Army, undefeated in the 1945 college football season, were voted national champions.

Hockey

■ The Toronto Maple Leafs defeated the Detroit Red Wings to take the Stanley Cup.

Horse Racing

■ Hoop, Jr, ridden by Eddie Arcaro, won the Kentucky Derby.

■ Polynesian, ridden by W.D. Wright, won the Preakness.

■ Pavot, ridden by Eddie Arcaro, won the Belmont Stakes.

Sailing

■ The first Sydney to Hobart Yacht Race took place. The 628-nautical-mile race between Australia and Tasmania in the Tasman Sea was won by *Rani* with a time of six days, 14 hours.

1945 Deaths

■ Béla Bartók, Hungarian composer

■ Robert Benchley, American humorist, actor

■ John Birch, American missionary and soldier

■ Denise Bloch, French secret agent executed by the Germans

■ Dietrich Bonhoeffer, German theologian and member of the German resistance

■ Eva Braun, German companion/wife to Adolf Hitler

■ Edgar Cayce, American psychic and mystic

■ William Darby, American solder and leader of Darby's Rangers

■ Dwight Davis, American tennis player and creator of the Davis Cup, former secretary of war

■ Lord Alfred "Bosie" Douglas, poet, editor, former lover of Oscar Wilde

■ Theodore Dreiser, American author

■ Anne Frank, German schoolgirl, victim of the Holocaust and posthumously famed diarist

■ Hans Geiger, German physicist and co-creator of the radiation detector that bears his name

■ Robert Goddard, American rocket scientist

■ Joseph Goebbels, German Minister of Propaganda

■ Milton S. Hershey, American chocolate magnate

■ Heinrich Himmler, German head of the SS

■ Adolf Hitler, Führer of Nazi Germany

■ Jerome Kern, American composer

■ Lucille La Verne, American actress and voice of the Evil Queen in *Snow White and the Seven Dwarfs* (1937)

■ Pierre Laval, former French prime minister and leader in the Vichy government, by execution

■ Eric Liddell, Scottish missionary and Olympic gold medal runner (depicted in the film *Chariots of Fire*)

■ David Lloyd George, former British prime minister

■ John S. McCain Sr, American admiral

■ Thomas McGuire, American WWII hero

■ Benito Mussolini, fascist dictator of Italy

■ George S. Patton, American general

■ Ernie Pyle, American journalist

■ Vidkun Quisling, Norwegian politician, by execution

■ Élise Rivet, French Roman Catholic nun and WWII hero

■ Lilian Rolfe, British secret agent executed by the Germans

■ Franklin D. Roosevelt, president of the United States

■ Eddie Slovik, American soldier executed for desertion

■ Violette Szabo, French secret agent executed by the Germans

■ Henrietta Szold, American teacher, social worker and founder of Hadassah

■ Paul Valéry, French poet

■ N.C. Wyeth, American artist

1970

50 YEARS AGO

Landmark World Events

Jan 5 A massive earthquake struck Tonghai County at Yunnan Province, southwest China, killing at least 10,000 and causing damages in the millions. Tremors from the quake were felt at Hanoi, Vietnam, nearly 300 miles from its epicenter.

Jan 15 The three-year Nigerian Civil War ended with the capitulation of Biafra, the southern Nigerian state whose people felt misrepresented by the northern-controlled Nigerian government. The violence and unrest surrounding the war caused widespread famine in the Biafra region, starving millions.

Feb 23 The South American country of Guyana became a sovereign republic within the British Commonwealth.

Mar 1 After a contentious period of growing pains, racial disharmony and attempts to extricate itself from the grip of colonialism, Rhodesia finally severed all ties to Great Britain, established a new constitution and declared itself a republic.

Mar 5 The Nuclear Non-Proliferation Treaty officially went into effect. The treaty had been opened for signature in 1968, with 56 nations ratifying the document.

Mar 15 The Expo '70 World's Fair opened at Suita, Osaka, Japan. There were major architectural pavilions from Canada, West Germany, the United States, Korea, the USSR and the Netherlands; other installations included the Tower of the Sun, designed by Japanese artist Taro Okamoto, which was restored and preserved to remain standing in Expo Commemoration Park at Osaka.

Mar 31 Japan Airlines Flight 351 from Tokyo to Fukuoka was hijacked by the Japanese Communist League Red Army Faction, who were armed with Samurai swords and pipe bombs.

May 31 The Ancash earthquake struck in the Pacific Ocean 35 miles off the coast of Peru. The quake and the massive landslide it caused killed more than 65,000.

June 18 The Conservative Party ousted the Labour Party of Harold Wilson, bringing Edward Heath to power as new prime minister of the United Kingdom.

July 21 The Aswan High Dam was completed across the Nile River at Aswan, Egypt. The dam regulated the cycle of annual flooding of the Nile River valley and resulting employment for farming that had occurred in Egypt since ancient times.

Sept 4 Socialist senator Salvador Allende won the Chilean presidency. Allende would preside over the country for three years, until he was forcibly ousted by a military coup backed by the Central Intelligence Agency (CIA).

Sept 17 "Black September": Under the leadership of King Hussein, Jordanian Armed Forces (JAF) engaged in a series of attacks and skirmishes with forces of the Palestinian Liberation Organization (PLO), led by Yasser Arafat.

Sept 28 With the death in office of Gamal Abdel Nasser, vice president Anwar Sadat was named temporary president of Egypt. Sadat officially became president on Oct 15.

Oct 5 At Quebec, Canada, a Marxist-Leninist separatist group known as the Front de Liberation du Quebec (FLQ) kidnapped provincial deputy premier Pierre Luporte and British diplomat James Cross. Luporte was eventually murdered by his captors.

Oct 9 The pro-US Khmer Republic was proclaimed at Cambodia, sparking a civil war with the Communist-leaning Khmer Rouge.

Nov 13 The Bhola cyclone struck the Ganges delta region of East Pakistan (now Bangladesh) with 120-mile-per-hour winds, killing almost 500,000.

Dec 3 At Quebec, the October Crisis culminated with the negotiated release of British diplomat James Cross, and the exile to Cuba of five FLQ members. The killers of deputy premier Luporte remained at large until Dec 28, when they were apprehended at Montreal.

Dec 8 The United Nations General Assembly voted to support the isolation of South Africa over its policy of Apartheid.

■ Nobel Peace Prize: Norman E. Borlaug, for his contributions to fostering the growth of the world food supply. In his Nobel lecture, Borlaug said "When the Nobel Peace Prize committee designated me the recipient of the 1970 award for my contribution to the 'green revolution,' they were in effect, I believe, selecting an individual to symbolize the vital role of agriculture and food production in a world that is hungry, both for bread and for peace."

Landmark US Events

Jan 1 The National Environmental Policy Act was enacted. The law established the Council on Environmental Quality and made environmental protection an expressed policy of the federal government.

Feb 18 In the culmination of their trial that had begun in September 1969, the "Chicago Seven"—Abbie Hoffman, Tom Hayden, Jerry Rubin, David Dellinger, Rennie Davis, John Froines, and Lee Weiner—were acquitted of conspiracy charges stemming from their arrest at the 1968 Democratic National Convention at Chicago, and five of the defendants were convicted of crossing state lines with intent to incite a riot. These convictions were eventually overturned on appeal.

Mar 6 At Greenwich Village in New York City, in a townhouse where they were assembling a bomb, three members of the leftist radical group The Weather Underground died when the device accidentally went off. The blast leveled the structure, but two other members of the group, Cathlyn Wilkerson and Kathy Boudin, managed to get free of the rubble and escape.

Apr 22 Earth Day was observed for the very first time. This event was the brainchild of senator Gaylord Nelson (D, WI), and designed as a national teach-in exploring environmental issues. See "Spotlight on World Anniversaries."

Apr 30 President Richard Nixon announced that the United States would invade Cambodia in an effort to eradicate Viet Cong safe havens, sparking widespread domestic protest, particularly on college campuses.

May 4 At Kent State University, four students were killed by the Ohio National Guard during protests over Nixon's planned incursion into Cambodia. They were Allison Krause, 19; Sandra Lee Scheuer, 20; Jeffrey Glenn Miller, 20; and William K. Schroeder, 19. See "Spotlight on American Anniversaries."

June 22 President Nixon signed into a law a series of amendments to the 1965 Voting Rights Act, including the lowering of the legal voting age to 18 for all federal, state and local elections.

June 24 The US Senate voted to repeal the Gulf of Tonkin Resolution, wishing to curtail the "blank check" war powers the resolution had granted the executive branch during the United States' initial forays into the conflict in Vietnam.

Sept 5 Vietnam War: Operation Jefferson Glenn began at Thura Thien Province, South Vietnam. This was the last major ground offensive for US forces in the country, and for which the 101st Airborne Division joined forces with the Army of the Republic of Vietnam (ARVN).

Oct 12 President Nixon announced plans to withdraw 40,000 more US troops from Vietnam before Christmas 1970.

Nov 3 Ronald Reagan was reelected governor of California, Jimmy Carter was elected governor of Georgia.

Nov 10 Vietnam War: For the first time in five years, no combat fatalities for US forces were reported for an entire week.

Nov 17 The trial of Lieutenant William Calley over the My Lai Massacre began.

Dec 2 The US Environmental Protection Agency was officially launched.

Dec 21 At the White House, president Richard M. Nixon met Elvis Presley. The two shared a cordial meeting, and shook hands for a legendary photo-op.

Culture

Literary Arts

■ Nobel Prize in Literature: Aleksandr Isayevich Solzhenitsyn "for the ethical force with which he has pursued the indispensable traditions of Russian literature."

Nov 25 Japanese author Yukio Mishima committed seppuku during a coup attempt in Tokyo, Japan.

Fiction

■ Erich Segal, *Love Story*

■ Joan Didion, *Play It as It Lays*

■ Saul Bellow, *Mr. Sammler's Planet*

■ Helene Hanff, *84 Charing Cross Road*

■ Dee Brown, *Bury My Heart at Wounded Knee*

■ Richard Bach, *Jonathan Livingston Seagull*

■ Toni Morrison, *The Bluest Eye*

■ J.G. Farrell, *Troubles*

■ Louis L'Amour, *The Man Called Noon*

■ Donald E. Westlake, *The Hot Rock* (Dortmunder #1)

■ Ernest Hemingway, *Islands in the Stream* (posthumously)

■ Arkady Strugatsky and Boris Strugatsky, *The Dead Mountaineer's Hotel*

Nonfiction

■ Hannah Arendt, *On Violence*

■ Phillip Slater, *The Pursuit of Loneliness: American Culture at the Breaking Point*

■ Charles Breunig, *The Age of Revolution and Reaction, 1789–1850*

■ Robert Townshend, *Up the Organization: How to Stop the Corporation from Stifling People and Strangling Profits*

■ Charles A. Reich, *The Greening of America*

Poetry

■ W.S. Merwin, *The Carrier of Ladders* (winner of the 1971 Pulitzer Prize)

■ Michael Ondaatje, *The Collected Works of Billy the Kid: Left-Handed Poems*

■ Derek Mahon, *Beyond Howth Head*

■ C. Day-Lewis, *The Whispering Roots*

■ Ted Hughes, *Crow*

■ Gwendolyn Brooks, *Family Pictures*

■ John Ashbery, *The Double Dream of Spring*

Children's Literature

■ Judith Kerr, *Mog, the Forgetful Cat*

■ Judy Blume, *Are You There, God? It's Me, Margaret*

■ Roald Dahl, *Fantastic Mr Fox*

■ Zilpha Keatley Snyder, *The Changeling*

■ Russell Hoban, *A Bargain for Frances*

■ John Christopher, *The Guardians*

■ Al Perkins, *The Nose Book*

Theater and Opera

Apr 26 *Company*, a musical by Stephen Sondheim, opened at the Alvin Theatre in New York City. It was an unconventional work in Broadway terms: composed of vignettes and taking as its subject adult relationships. Dean Jones originated the lead role of Robert, but withdrew after opening night. It wound up winning six Tony Awards out of 14 nominations, collecting statues for Best Musical, Best Book of a Musical, Best Original Score, Best Direction of a Musical (Hal Prince), Best Lyrics and Best Scenic Design. It also won five Drama Desk Awards.

The 25th Tony Awards

(Awarded in 1971 for 1970 achievement)

■ Best Play: *Sleuth*

■ Best Musical: *Company*

■ Best Performance by a Leading Actor in a Play: Brian Bedford, *The School for Wives*

■ Best Performance by a Leading Actress in a Play: Maureen Stapleton, *The Gingerbread Lady*

■ Best Performance by a Leading Actor in a Musical: Hal Linden, *The Rothschilds*

■ Best Performance by a Leading Actress in a Musical: Helen Gallagher, *No, No Nanette*

Film

Academy Awards

(Awarded in 1971 for 1970 achievement)

■ Best Picture: *Patton*

■ Best Director: Franklin J. Schaffner, *Patton*

■ Best Actor: George C. Scott, *Patton*

■ Best Actress: Glenda Jackson, *Women in Love*

■ Best Supporting Actor: John Mills, *Ryan's Daughter*

■ Best Supporting Actress: Helen Hayes, *Airport*

■ George C. Scott turned down his nomination, explaining to the Academy that he did not believe in competition among actors. He did not appear at the ceremony. *Patton* producer Frank McCarthy gave Scott's Best Actor Oscar to the George C. Marshall Foundation Library at the Virginia Military Institute, where Patton and members of his family studied.

■ Best Original Song Score: *Let It Be*—Music and Lyrics by The Beatles: John Lennon, Paul McCartney, George Harrison and Ringo Starr

■ Best Foreign Language Film: *Investigation of a Citizen Above Suspicion*

Notable films

■ *Airport*

■ *Patton*

■ *Love Story*

■ *M*A*S*H*

■ *Tora! Tora! Tora!*

- *Five Easy Pieces*
- *Ryan's Daughter*
- *Scrooge*
- *Women in Love*
- *Darling Lili*
- *I Never Sang for My Father*
- *Lovers and Other Strangers*
- *Performance*
- *The Great White Hope*
- *Myra Breckinridge*
- *On a Clear Day You Can See Forever*
- *Little Big Man*
- *Kelly's Heroes*
- *Let It Be*
- *The Aristocats*
- *A Man Called Horse*
- *The Molly Maguires*
- *Catch-22*
- *Diary of a Mad Housewife*
- *Beyond the Valley of the Dolls*
- *The Boys in the Band*
- *Brewster McCloud*
- *Gimme Shelter*
- *Zabriskie Point*

Television

Jan 5 "All My Children" premiered on ABC.

Mar 7 CBS broadcast in color the total solar eclipse that passed across the southeastern United States.

July 5 "Evening at Pops" premiered on PBS, with conductor Arthur Fiedler heading the Boston Pops Orchestra.

July 31 Retiring television news broadcaster Chet Huntley anchored his final newscast with David Brinkley. "The Huntley-Brinkley Report" was renamed "NBC Nightly News" and expanded to seven nights a week.

Sept 19 "The Mary Tyler Moore Show" premiered on CBS.

Sept 21 "Monday Night Football" premiered on ABC. Howard Cosell, Keith Jackson and Don Meredith called the debut game, a 31–21 Cleveland Browns victory over the New York Jets.

Sept 24 "The Odd Couple" debuted on ABC.

Sept 25 "The Partridge Family" debuted on ABC.

Oct 5 Public Broadcasting Service (PBS) debuted, replacing its predecessor, National Educational Television (NET).

Radio

July 4 Casey Kasem's pop music countdown show "American Top 40" premiered on a broadcast over seven US AM stations.

Music

The 13th Annual Grammy Awards (Awarded in 1971 for 1970 achievement)

- Record of the Year: Simon & Garfunkel for "Bridge over Troubled Water"
- Album of the Year: *Bridge over Troubled Water*; Roy Halee, Art Garfunkel and Paul Simon (producers)
- Song of the Year: Paul Simon (songwriter) for "Bridge over Troubled Water"
- Best New Artist: The Carpenters
- Best Contemporary Vocal Performance, Female: Dionne Warwick for "I'll Never Fall in Love Again"
- Best Contemporary Vocal Performance, Male: Ray Stevens for "Everything Is Beautiful"
- Best Contemporary Vocal Performance by a Duo, Group or Chorus: The Carpenters for "Close to You"
- Best R&B Vocal Performance, Female: Aretha Franklin for "Don't Play That Song"
- Best R&B Vocal Performance, Male: B.B. King for "The Thrill Is Gone"
- Best R&B Performance by a Duo or Group, Vocal or Instrumental: The Delfonics for "Didn't I"
- Best Country Vocal Performance, Female: Lynn Anderson, "Rose Garden"
- Best Country Vocal Performance, Male: Ray Price for "For the Good Times"
- Best Country Vocal Performance by a Duo or Group: Johnny Cash and June Carter for "If I Were a Carpenter"

Jan 14 Diana Ross & the Supremes performed for the last time together at the Frontier Hotel at Las Vegas, NV.

July 27 Van Morrison's *Moondance* was issued in the United Kingdom and was an immediate critical and commercial success. It was rated triple platinum by 1996 and today ranks 65 on *Rolling Stone*'s 500 greatest albums list.

Feb 13 British trio Black Sabbath issued its self-titled debut, marking the beginning of the heavy metal genre.

Mar 6 In the wake of Charles Manson and his followers' 1969 killing spree, *Lie: The Love and Terror Cult* was released independently on vinyl by Paul Kaufman, a Manson associate. The album included a version of the song "Cease to Exist," which Manson had originally recorded with Brian Wilson and the Beach Boys when he was still an itinerant ex-convict with delusions of becoming a singer-songwriter.

Mar 28 The Vietnam Moratorium Concert was held at Madison Square Garden at New York City. Among the performers and stars who donated their time to the seven-hour event were Jimi Hendrix, Harry Belafonte, Dave Brubeck, Judy Collins, Peter, Paul & Mary, the Rascals, Blood, Sweat & Tears and the Broadway cast of *Hair*.

Apr 10 The Beatles were no more. Announcing his departure from the group via a press release accompanying his eponymous debut solo record (released Apr 17), Paul McCartney cited "personal differences, business differences, musical differences" as grounds for his exit. Making it official, McCartney sued to dissolve The Beatles on Dec 31.

May 8 *Let It Be*, the Beatles' final album recorded as a band, was issued in the United Kingdom.

Aug 26 The Isle of Wight Festival, held on farmland at the island off England's south coast, drew 600,000 music fans to the still new phenomenon of a large-scale music festival. The stacked lineup included The Who, Jimi Hendrix, The Doors, Richie Havens, Miles Davis, Leonard Cohen, The Moody Blues, Jethro Tull, Ten Years After, Joan Baez and Emerson, Lake & Palmer.

Sept 16 Jimi Hendrix performed in public for the last time, appearing with Eric Burdon & War at the Ronnie Scott's Jazz Club at London, England. Hendrix died Sept 18 from a drug overdose. He was 27.

Sept 19 The first Glastonbury Festival took place at Worthy Farm, Pilton, England. T. Rex and Al Stewart were among the performers.

Oct 4 Janis Joplin was found in her hotel room at Hollywood, dead of a heroin overdose. She was 27.

Popular Songs

- Mungo Jerry, "In the Summertime"
- Diana Ross, "Ain't No Mountain High Enough"
- The Beatles, "Let It Be" and "The Long and Winding Road"
- Eric Clapton, "After Midnight"
- Simon & Garfunkel, "Bridge over Troubled Water" and "Cecilia"
- The Carpenters, "Close to You" and "We've Only Just Begun"
- The Guess Who, "American Woman"
- The Jackson Five, "ABC," "I'll Be There" and "I Want You Back"
- Rare Earth, "Get Ready"
- Freda Payne, "Band of Gold"
- Three Dog Night, "Mama Told Me (Not to Come)"
- Ray Stevens, "Everything Is Beautiful"
- Sly & the Family Stone, "Thank You (Falettinme Be Mice Elf Again)"
- Eric Burdon & War, "Spill the Wine"
- Five Stairsteps, "O-o-h Child"
- The Temptations, "Ball of Confusion (That's What the World Is Today)"
- Free, "All Right Now"
- Stevie Wonder, "Signed, Sealed, Delivered I'm Yours"
- John Lennon, "Instant Karma!"
- The Hollies, "He Ain't Heavy, He's My Brother"
- Badfinger, "Come and Get It"
- The Kinks, "Lola"
- Chicago, "25 or 6 to 4"
- James Taylor, "Fire and Rain"
- Ike & Tina Turner, "I Want to Take You Higher"

Notable Albums

- Simon & Garfunkel, *Bridge over Troubled Water*
- Joni Mitchell, *Ladies of the Canyon*
- Chicago, *Chicago*
- Van Morrison, *Moondance*
- The Guess Who, *American Woman*
- James Taylor, *Sweet Baby James*
- Black Sabbath, *Black Sabbath*
- The Doors, *Morrison Hotel*
- Funkadelic, *Funkadelic*
- The Temptations, *Psychedelic Shack*
- Crosby, Stills, Nash & Young, *Deja Vu*
- Jimi Hendrix, *Band of Gypsies*
- Miles Davis, *Bitches Brew*
- Three Dog Night, *It Ain't Easy*
- Elton John, *Elton John*
- Paul McCartney, *McCartney*
- The Jackson Five, *ABC*
- Grateful Dead, *Workingman's Dead* and *American Beauty*
- The Stooges, *Fun House*
- Supertramp, *Supertramp*
- Traffic, *John Barleycorn Must Die*
- Stevie Wonder, *Signed, Sealed & Delivered*
- Eric Clapton, *Eric Clapton*
- Neil Young, *After the Gold Rush*

- Santana, *Abraxas*
- Curtis Mayfield, *Curtis*
- Pink Floyd, *Atom Heart Mother*
- Led Zeppelin, *Led Zeppelin III*
- David Bowie, *The Man Who Sold the World*
- Cat Stevens, *Tea for the Tillerman*
- George Harrison, *All Things Must Pass*
- John Lennon, *John Lennon/Plastic Ono Band*
- T. Rex, *T. Rex*

Art

Jan 16 Twenty-four hours after it opened, Bag One, John Lennon's gallery showing at London, was shut down by Scotland Yard for displaying "erotic lithographs."

April Robert Smithson constructed *Spiral Jetty*, a large, coiling earthwork sculpture at the Great Salt Lake, UT. It is visible today during periods of drought.

- Robert Indiana recreated his famous 1965 popart *LOVE* design into a steel sculpture in Indianapolis, IN.
- *Three People*, by Rufino Tamayo (the painting was stolen in 1977 and resurfaced in a New York City trash heap in 2007)
- *Who's Afraid of Red, Yellow and Blue IV*, by Barnett Newman
- *Reclining Figure* and *Two-Piece Reclining Figure: Points*, by Henry Moore

Science and Technology

- Nobel Prize in Chemistry: Luis F. Leloir, "for his discovery of sugar nucleotides and their role in the biosynthesis of carbohydrates."

- Nobel Prize in Physics: Hannes Olof Gosta Alfven, "for fundamental work and discoveries in magnetohydro-dynamics with fruitful applications in different parts of plasma physics," and Louis Eugene Felix Neel, "for fundamental work and discoveries concerning antiferromagnetism and ferrimagnetism which have led to important applications in solid state physics."

- Nobel Prize in Medicine: Awarded jointly to Sir Bernard Katz, Ulf von Euler and Julius Axelrod "for their discoveries concerning the humoral transmittors in the nerve terminals and the mechanism for their storage, release and inactivation."

Jan 1 Unix time began (00:00:00 UTC Thursday, 1 Jan 1970). This technological expression of an encoded point in time was represented as both a real number and its sequenced or decimal counterpart, and formed the foundational language of the Unix operating system. ("Unix" was coined by the operating system's designers as shorthand for "Uniplexed Information and Computer Services.")

Feb 11 Japan became the fourth nation to send a satellite into space with the successful launch of *Osumi*, tasked with an earth science mission.

Mar 31 *Explorer 1* (US) reentered Earth's atmosphere after twelve

years and 58,000 orbits in space. The satellite was the first orbiting object to return scientific data to Earth, and its activity and lifespan while in orbit imparted valuable lessons for future efforts toward satellite design and implementation.

Apr 11 *Apollo 13* was successfully launched from Kennedy Space Center at Florida. Its mission to land on the moon was scrubbed two days later when an oxygen tank exploded aboard the mission's support module, forcing the crew to improvise emergency repairs. *Apollo 13* returned safely to Earth six days later.

Apr 24 China joined the space race, now five countries strong, with the successful launch of *Dong Fang Hong 1* into orbit.

May 24 Drilling of the Kola Superdeep Borehole began at Pechengsky District, Kola Peninsula, USSR, with the goal of drilling as deep as possible into Earth's crust. At its deepest point, the bore hole reached 40,230 feet, or 7.619 miles, and was the deepest artificial point on Earth.

Aug 17 The USSR successfully launched *Venera 7*, the latest in a series of Soviet space probes designed to explore the surface of Venus ("Venera" meaning "Venus" in Russian). *Venera 7* entered the Venusian atmosphere on Dec 15. It became the first spacecraft to transmit data back to Earth from the surface of another planet.

Nov 10 The USSR successfully launched *Luna 17*, and unmanned spacecraft that landed on the lunar surface and released *Lunakhod 1*, an eight-wheeled, remotely operated research vehicle.

- In 1970 Italian physicist and inventor Federico Faggin brought his pioneering work in metal-oxide-semiconductor (MOS) technology to Intel, where he led the team that designed the first widely used microprocessor. This innovative technology quickly became industry standard on a global scale, revolutionizing the design and usage of commercial electronics forever.

Commerce and New Products

■ The Sveriges Riksbank Prize in Economic Sciences in Memory of Alfred Nobel: Paul A. Samuelson, "for the scientific work through which he has developed static and dynamic economic theory and actively contributed to raising the level of analysis in economic science."

January Pan American World Airways announced direct service to London from New York City via its new Boeing 747 "jumbo jet." (The 747 debuted in 1969.) This was followed by additional direct routes for the 747 from San Francisco and Los Angeles to Honolulu, HI, Tokyo, Japan, and Hong Kong, China.

Apr 1 President Richard Nixon signed legislation banning the broadcast of advertisements for cigarettes over television and radio. The legislation would go into effect in 1971.

■ Automobiles introduced to the consumer market in 1970 included the Ford Pinto, the Toyota Celica, the Dodge Colt, the Chevrolet Monte Carlo, the AMC Gremlin, the Range Rover Classic, the Plymouth Duster and the Ford Maverick.

Sports

Auto Racing

■ Indianapolis 500: Al Unser, Sr.

■ NASCAR Grand National Series: Bobby Isaac (This was the final year of the Grand National Series, as NASCAR transitioned to the Winston Cup Series.)

Baseball

■ World Series: The Baltimore Orioles defeated the Cincinnati Reds four games to one.

Apr 1 After one year as an American League expansion team, the Seattle Pilots moved to Milwaukee, WI, to become the Brewers.

May 10 Hoyt Wilhelm of the Atlanta Braves became the first MLB pitcher to appear in 1,000 games. He entered a game in relief against the St. Louis Cardinals, gave up three runs, and the Braves lost 6–5.

May 12 Ernie Banks of the Chicago Cubs hit the 500th home run of his career off Pat Jarvis of the Atlanta Braves in a 5–3 Cubs victory.

May 17 Henry "Hank" Aaron hit a scratch single off Wayne Simpson of the Cincinnati Reds to tally his 3,000th hit.

June 30 The Cincinnati Reds christened their new home of Riverfront Stadium with an 8–2 losing effort against Hank Aaron and the visiting Atlanta Braves.

July 16 The Pittsburgh Pirates debuted their new home of Three Rivers Stadium with a 3–2 loss to the Cincinnati Reds.

July 18 Willie Mays of the San Francisco Giants got the 3,000th hit of his career with a single off of the Montreal Expos' Mike Wegener.

Aug 11 Pitching for the Philadelphia Phillies, Jim Bunning defeated the Houston Astros 6–5, becoming the second pitcher (after Cy Young) ever to notch 100 wins in each major league. Bunning had started his career with the Detroit Tigers.

Sept 3 Chicago Cubs outfielder Billy Williams's streak of consecutive games played ended at 1,117, a National League record that stood until Steve Garvey broke it in 1983.

Basketball

■ NBA Finals: The New York Knicks won their first NBA title, defeating the Los Angeles Lakers four games to three.

Football

■ Super Bowl IV: The Kansas City Chiefs defeated the Minnesota Vikings 23–7.

■ Heisman Trophy winner: Jim Plunkett, Quarterback, Stanford University

Jan 4 The Minnesota Vikings became the first expansion team to win the NFL title when they defeated the Cleveland Browns 27–7. The Vikings would lose to the Kansas City Chiefs in Super Bowl IV.

Jan 4 The Kansas City Chiefs won the last-ever American Football League championship game, defeating the Oakland Raiders 17–7. The Chiefs would go on to beat the Minnesota Vikings in Super Bowl IV.

June 8 The American Football League and the National Football League announced that they would merge, ending a protracted battle over players, fans, and TV ratings. Teams from the AFL were joined by the Cleveland Browns, the Pittsburgh Steelers and the Baltimore Colts to become the American Football Conference, while the remaining NFL teams became the National Football Conference.

Oct 2 Fourteen members of the Wichita State University football team were killed when their plane crashed in the Rocky Mountains.

Nov 14 Thirty-seven members of the Marshall University football team were killed when their plane crashed at Kenova, WV.

Golf

- The Master's Tournament: Billy Caspar
- PGA Championship: Dave Stockton
- US Open: Tony Jacklin
- The Open Championship: Jack Nicklaus
- LPGA Championship: Shirley Engelhorn
- US Women's Open Golf Championship: Donna Caponi

Hockey

- Stanley Cup: The Boston Bruins defeated the St. Louis Blues four games to none.

Oct 29 Chicago Red Wings right winger Gordie Howe became the first player to record 1,000 assists in a 5–3 victory over the Boston Bruins.

Dec 12 Chicago Blackhawks left winger Bobby Hull got the 1,000th point of his NHL career with an assist in the first period of a 5–3 victory over the Minnesota North Stars.

Horse Racing

- Kentucky Derby: Dust Commander, ridden by Mike Manganello

- Preakness Stakes: Personality, ridden by Eddie Belmonte
- Belmont Stakes: High Echelon, ridden by John L. Rotz

Sept 7 Jockey Willie Shoemaker won the 6,033rd race of his career at Del Mar at California, surpassing the previous career wins record holder Johnny Longden.

Soccer

- 1970 FIFA World Cup: Brazil claimed its third World Cup title, beating Italy 4–1 in the final at Mexico City. The 1970 tournament was the first World Cup held in North America.
- Chelsea defeated Leeds United to win the FA Cup.

Tennis

- Australian Open
- Men's Singles: Arthur Ashe
- Women's Singles: Margaret Court

French Open

- Men's Singles: Jan Kodes
- Women's Singles: Margaret Court

Wimbledon

- Men's Singles: John Newcombe
- Women's Singles: Margaret Court

US Open

- Men's Singles: Ken Rosewall
- Women's Singles: Margaret Court

July 24 The International Lawn Tennis Association changed tennis history with its adoption of a nine-point tie-breaker on sets tied 6–6.

Miscellaneous

Sept 13 The first-ever New York City Marathon drew 127 runners, 55 of whom finished the course.

Gary Muhrcke won the race with a time of 2:31:38.2.

1970 Deaths

- S. Y. Agnon, Polish author, recipient of the 1966 Nobel Prize in Literature
- Abe Attell, American boxer, World Featherweight Champion (1906–12)
- Albert Ayler, American jazz musician
- Ed Begley, American actor
- Max Born, German physicist, recipient of the 1954 Nobel Prize in Physics
- Vera Brittain, English nurse, pacifist and writer
- Billie Burke, American actress
- James Anthony "Ripper" Collins, American baseball lifer
- James G. Conzelman, American pro football Hall of Fame player and coach
- Emmett J. Culligan, American businessman—water treatment entrepreneur
- Edgar Allen "Uncle Ed" Diddle, Sr, American basketball player and Hall of Fame coach
- John Dos Passos, American author
- Frances Farmer, American actress
- E.M. Forster, English author (*A Room with a View*, *Howards End*)
- Arnold "Chick" Gandil, American baseball player
- Erle Stanley Gardner, American author and creator of Perry Mason
- Charles de Gaulle, French military and political leader
- Rube Goldberg, American cartoonist

- Leslie Groves, American army officer and engineer, director of the Manhattan Project

- Alice Hamilton, American pathologist

- Slim Harpo, American blues musician

- Jimi Hendrix, American rock musician

- Eva Hesse, German-American artist

- Hirsch Jacobs, American thoroughbred trainer and owner

- William H. Johnson, American artist

- Janis Joplin, American musician

- Joseph Bohomiel Lapchick, American basketball player and coach

- Gypsy Rose Lee (Rose Louise Hovick), American ecdysiast and vaudeville performer

- Charles "Sonny" Liston, American boxer

- Vince Lombardi, American football coach

- Anita Louise, American actress

- Abraham Maslow, American psychologist ("Maslow's hierarchy of needs")

- François Mauriac, French author, 1952 Nobel Prize in Literature recipient

- Emmett Branch McCracken, American basketball player and coach

- Bruce McLaren, New Zealand race car driver and designer

- Yukio Mishima, Japanese author, poet and playwright

- Chester Morris, American actor, portrayer of Boston Blackie

- Gamal Abdel Nasser, Egyptian politician

- Richard Neutra, Austrian modernist architect

- Alfred Newman, American composer

- Barnett Newman, American painter

- Louis Brian Piccolo, American football player

- Vladimir Propp, Russian folklorist and scholar

- C.V. Raman, Indian physicist, recipient of the 1930 Nobel Prize in Physics

- Walter Philip Reuther, American labor leader

- Edward Aloysious Rommel, American baseball player and umpire

- Charles Henry Root, American baseball player

- Mark Rothko, American painter

- Bertrand Russell, English philosopher

- Nelly Sachs, German-Swedish poet, 1966 Nobel Prize in Literature recipient

- Raymond William Schalk, American Hall of Fame baseball player

- John T. Scopes, American educator at the center of the 1925 Scopes Trial that challenged the teaching of evolution in Tennessee

- Clark D. Shaughnessy, American football player and coach

- Inger Stevens, Swedish-American actress

- Maurice "Mo" Stokes, American basketball Hall of Fame player

- Sukarno, first president of Indonesia

- Tammi Terrell, American recording artist

- Preston Rudolph York, American baseball player

- Abraham Zapruder, Ukrainian-American tailor who filmed the John Kennedy assassination

1995

25 YEARS AGO

Landmark World Events

Jan 17 A massive earthquake struck the southern region of Hyogo Prefecture, Japan, its epicenter occurring just over 12 miles outside the major city of Kobe. Some 6,434 people lost their lives in the Great Hanshin, or Kobe Earthquake, infrastructure was severely damaged, and thousands of fires raged. It was the most destructive quake to hit Japan in more than 70 years.

Jan 31 US president Bill Clinton secured a $20 billion loan for Mexico, then in a currency crisis, from Congress and additional emergency funding was pumped in from the International Monetary Fund (IMF), G7 countries and the Bank for International Settlements (BIS).

Feb 13 The United Nations' International Criminal Tribunal formally charged 21 Bosnian Serb military commanders with crimes against humanity and genocide for the widespread human rights abuses that had occurred during ongoing warfare in the Balkans.

Feb 26 At London, Barings Bank, the United Kingdom's oldest merchant bank, completely collapsed after rogue securities broker Nick Leeson lost $1.4 billion speculating on the Tokyo Stock Exchange.

Mar 3 United Nations Operation in Somalia II (UNOSOM II) officially ended. The UN peace-keeping force, with its US military majority and contributions from other countries such as France, Sweden and Italy, had completely withdrawn from direct action by this time.

Mar 20 Members of the Japanese doomsday cult Aum Shinrikyo carried out a shocking act of domestic terrorism when, in coordinated attacks, its members released deadly sarin gas on three different lines of the Tokyo Metro system during rush hour. Twelve people died in the attacks and hundreds took sick.

Apr 7 At Samashki in western Chechnya, shock units within the MVD (Russian Ministry of Internal Affairs) massacred hundreds of innocent, unarmed civilians in the small border village.

May 6 Health officials in the country and the US Embassy at Zaire notified the Centers for Disease Control (CDC) of an outbreak of Ebola at Kikwit, a city of 400,000 located 240 miles east of Kinshasha.

May 7 After two rounds of voting on Apr 23 and May 7 Jacques Chirac was elected president of France.

May 11 Reaffirming its establishment in 1968, more than 170 countries agreed to extend the Nuclear Nonproliferation Treaty indefinitely and without conditions.

May 16 Sarin Gas Attack: Tokyo police besieged and raided Aum Shinrikyo headquarters, where they discovered and took into custody the doomsday cult's leader, Shoko Asahara.

May 28 At Sakhalin Island off of Russia's far Eastern shore, at 1:04 a.m. local time, the Neftegorsk earthquake struck with sudden and extreme violence (7.1 on the Mercalli intensity scale). Some 2,040 of Neftegorsk's 3,977 citizens were killed and hundreds were injured.

June 2 A Bosnian Serb Army 2K12 Kub surface-to-air missile site shot down US Air Force pilot Scott O'Grady's F-16, where he was patrolling the NATO-enforced no-fly zone over Mrkonjic Grad. O'Grady, who had safely ejected from his aircraft, survived for six days on the ground in hostile territory before being rescued by US Marines.

June 29 The Sampoong Department Store at Seoul, South Korea, collapsed, killing 502 people and injuring over 900.

July 1 In response to evidence obtained by the United Nations Special Commission (UNSCOM), Iraq admitted for the first time that it was pursuing an offensive biological weapons program, but denied any weaponization.

July 4 John Major, prime minister of the United Kingdom, was reelected as leader of the Conservative Party.

July 11–22 The Srebrenica Massacre: Over 8,000 Bosniaks, an ethnic group living in the Drina Valley area of Northeastern Bosnia and Herzegovina, were indiscriminately murdered by forces of the Bosnian Serb Army of Republika Srpska (VRS). The killings and accompanying violence against citizens occurred despite UN peacekeeping forces operating in the region.

Aug 4 Operation Storm: The Croation Army attacked and subdued forces of the rogue Republic of Serbian Krajina, regaining 4,000 miles of contested territory and enabling the end to hostilities that diplomacy and a failed UN peace-keeping mission had sought.

Aug 30 A NATO bombing campaign began against Bosnian Serb artillery positions in Bosnia and Herzegovina.

Oct 17 At 120 years 238 days, Frenchwoman Jean Calment seized the title as World's Oldest Person.

Oct 28 At Baku, Azerbaijan, an electrical fire swept through a portion of the downtown Baku subway system, killing 289 people and injuring almost 300.

Oct 30 With the pro-independence Parti Quebecois back in power, a referendum on independence was once again on the ballot at the Canadian province of Quebec. (A similar 1980 referendum had failed.) This time around the vote was astonishingly close: 50.6% NO to 49.4% YES, and included the largest voter turnout in Quebec history with 93.52% of eligible voters participating.

Nov 4 Israeli prime minister Yitzhak Rabin was assassinated at a peace rally at Tel Aviv, Israel, held in support of the Oslo Accords, which endeavored to establish peace between Israel and Palestine.

Nov 2–7 Typhoon Angela slammed into the Philippines and Vietnam with wind speeds of over one hundred miles-per-hour. Almost 900 people were killed.

Nov 16 At the United Nations, a tribunal charged Bosnian Serb politician Radovan Karadzic and VRS warlord Ratko Mladic with genocide during the Bosnian War.

Dec 14 The signing of the Dayton Agreement at Paris, France, officially ended the Bosnian War. Brokered by the United States, Russia, and other international players, the agreement's participants were president Slobodan Milosevic, representing Republic of Serbia; Croatian president Franjo Tudman; and Alija Izetbegovic, president of Bosnia and Herzegovina.

■ Nobel Peace Prize: Awarded jointly to Joseph Rotblat and the Pugwash Conferences on Science and World Affairs for their efforts to diminish the role of nuclear arms in international politics and to further efforts toward eliminating such weapons entirely. Rotblat was a Polish-born physicist who worked on the Manhattan Project.

Landmark US Events

Jan 4 The 104th United States Congress convened. It marked the first time the Republican Party had controlled both houses since 1953.

Jan 24 President Bill Clinton delivered the State of the Union address to the 104th US Congress. At 1 hour and 25 minutes and 9,190 words, it was the longest State of the Union speech in US history.

Jan 24 The O.J. Simpson murder trial began at Los Angeles, and was broadcast to America via Court TV. Simpson was accused of the double-murder of his wife, Nicole Brown, and her friend, Los Angeles-area waiter Ron Goldman. Simpson's high-profile legal representation included Robert Shapiro,

Johnnie Cochran, F. Lee Bailey and Alan Dershowitz; Deputy District Attorney Marcia Clark was the lead prosecutor.

Feb 7 At Islamabad, Pakistan, agents of the US Diplomatic Security Service and Pakistan's Inter-Services Intelligence (ISI) apprehended Ramzi Yousef, a known terrorist wanted by the FBI for his role in the planning and execution of the 1993 World Trade Center bombing.

Feb 21 American businessman and adventurer Steve Fossett became the first person to successfully pilot a balloon solo across the Pacific Ocean when he landed his 150-foot tall helium balloon in a farmer's field at Leader, Saskatchewan, Canada after a four-day, 5,800-mile flight from South Korea.

Mar 16 Mississippi ratified the 13th Amendment to the US Constitution, becoming the last state to approve the abolition of slavery.

Apr 3 Supreme Court Justice Sandra Day O'Connor became the first woman to preside over the high court when she sat in for Chief Justice William Rehnquist.

Apr 5 The Republican-controlled Congress voted 246–188 on a $189 billion, five-year tax cut package for individuals and corporations.

Apr 19 At 9:02 AM, a truck bomb detonated outside the Alfred P. Murrah Federal Building at Oklahoma City, OK, killing 168 people, including 19 children, and wounding more than 680 others. See "Spotlight on American Anniversaries."

Apr 24 Gilbert Brent Murray, a forestry industry lobbyist, was killed at his Sacramento, CA, office when the bomb inside a package he opened exploded. This mail bomb

had been addressed to William N. Dennison, former president of the California Forestry Association, and later identified as the intended target of the Unabomber, Ted Kaczynski. Murray was his last victim.

May 17 Disgruntled ex-plumber Shawn Nelson stole an M60A3 Patton tank from the California Army National Guard Armory at Kearny Mesa, San Diego, and proceeded to lead authorities on a 30-minute, low-speed, high-destruction chase through suburban San Diego. Though its onboard weapons weren't active, the 57-ton Patton easily crushed cars, utility poles and fire hydrants along the wayward route of Nelson's angry trundle. Police reached the tank when it became stuck on a highway median. When Nelson wouldn't comply with police demands to shut down the M60, he was shot and killed.

May 20 At Washington, DC, in a direct response to the Oklahoma City bombing, the two-block stretch of Pennsylvania Avenue passing in front of the White House was barricaded and closed.

June 15 "If it doesn't fit, you must acquit": Johnnie Cochran's enduring quip was uttered at the Simpson trial as the defendant tried on a pair of gloves believed to have been worn by Brown and Goldman's murderer. The gloves appeared to fit Simpson's hand too tightly.

July 11 A dangerous heat wave struck the Midwest, with its epicenter at Chicago, IL. Temperatures topped 90 degrees on the 11th; by July 14 they were over 100. A volatile high-pressure system had parked itself over the city, with constantly high humidity, no respite from the heat at night and almost no wind to agitate the meteorological status quo. Urban heat islands and faltering technology and emergency service logistics contributed to the official death toll of 739 Chicagoans over the course of five days; the extreme conditions were found to have adversely affected the city's poor.

July 27 The Korean War Memorial was dedicated at its site near the Lincoln Memorial at Washington, DC.

Sept 19 The Unabomber had written letters to numerous media outlets pushing for his manifesto to be published, promising to cease his terrorist acts were it to appear. With the encouragement of Attorney General Janet Reno, who hoped its appearance would lead to the bomber's identification by a member of the public, *The New York Times* and *Washington Post* published *Industrial Society and Its Future* in full, and David Kaczynski noticed similarities in its grammar and polemicist tone to the writings of his brother, Ted, who had departed academia for life off the grid as a survivalist.

Oct 3 O.J. Simpson was acquitted of the double murder of his wife, Nicole Brown, and her friend Ron Goldman.

Oct 9 An Amtrak train was forcibly derailed near Palo Verde, AZ, killing a railroad worker and causing four of its cars to fall 30 feet off a trestle bridge. Though typewritten notes from a group called "Sons of the Gestapo" were discovered near the wreck that criticized the federal government's role in the incidents at Ruby Ridge and Waco, the derailment case remains unsolved.

Oct 16 Hundreds of thousands of African-American men united at Washington, DC, for the Million Man March. Organized by Nation of Islam leader Louis Farrakhan, the marchers pledged to take responsibility for themselves, their families and their communities.

Nov 1 The US House of Representatives passed the Partial-Birth Abortion Ban, which outlawed intact dilation and extraction abortion procedures. The act was vetoed by President Clinton in 1996.

Nov 14 Partisan bickering between President Bill Clinton and the Republican Congress over allocations in the federal budget forced a government shutdown that would last five days.

Dec 16 The federal government fell into another shutdown due to partisan budget acrimony; this time around, the shutdown extended into early 1996.

Culture

Literary Arts

- Nobel Prize in Literature: Seamus Heaney

- Pulitzer Prize for Fiction: Carol Shields, *The Stone Diaries*

- Pulitzer Prize for Biography or Autobiography: Joan D. Hedrick, *Harriet Beecher Stowe: A Life*

- Pulitzer Prize for General Non-Fiction: Jonathan Weiner, *The Beak of the Finch: A Story of Evolution in Our Time*

- Pulitzer Prize for History: Doris Kearns Goodwin, *No Ordinary Time: Franklin and Eleanor Roosevelt: The Home Front in World War II*

Fiction

- Nick Hornby, *High Fidelity*
- Michael Crichton, *The Lost World*
- John Grisham, *The Rainmaker*
- Douglas Coupland, *Microserfs*
- Rohinton Mistry, *A Fine Balance*
- Richard Ford, *Independence Day*

- Bernhard Schlink, *The Reader*
- Anne Rice, *Memnoch the Devil*
- Nicholas Evans, *The Horse Whisperer*
- Pat Conroy, *Beach Music*
- Sue Grafton, *"L" Is for Lawless*
- Martin Amis, *The Information*
- Umberto Eco, *The Island of the Day Before*
- T.C. Boyle, *The Tortilla Curtain*
- Carlos Fuentes, *The Crystal Frontier*
- Jane Smiley, *Moo*
- Jose Saramago, *Blindness*
- Billie Letts, *Where the Heart Is*
- Stephen King, *Rose Madder*
- David Baldacci, *Absolute Power*
- Neal Stephenson, *The Diamond Age: Or, A Young Lady's Illustrated Primer*
- Alice Hoffman, *Practical Magic*
- Jodi Picoult, *Picture Perfect*
- Michael Chabon, *Wonder Boys*
- Mary McGarry Morris, *Songs in Ordinary Time*

Nonfiction

- Barack Obama, *Dreams from My Father: A Story of Race and Inheritance*
- Thomas Cahill, *How the Irish Saved Civilization*
- Tina Rosenberg, *The Haunted Land: Facing Europe's Ghosts after Communism*
- Anatoly Dobrynin, *In Confidence*

- David Herbert Donald, *Lincoln*
- Shirley MacLaine, *My Lucky Stars*
- Glenn Loury, *One by One from the Inside Out: Essays and Reviews on Race and Responsibility in America*
- Andrew Weil, *Spontaneous Healing: How to Discover and Embrace Your Body's Natural Ability to Heal Itself*
- John Loewen, *Lies My Teacher Told Me: Everything Your American History Textbook Got Wrong*
- Daniel Goleman, *Emotional Intelligence: Why It Can Matter More Than IQ*
- Carl Sagan, *The Demon-Haunted World: Science as a Candle in the Dark*
- Mary Karr, *The Liars' Club*
- John E. Douglas, *Mindhunter: Inside the FBI's Elite Serial Crime Unit*
- Oliver Sachs, *An Anthropologist on Mars: Seven Paradoxical Tails*
- Temple Grandin, *Thinking in Pictures: My Life with Autism*
- George G. Blackburn, *The Guns of Normandy: A Soldier's Eye View, France 1944*
- Doris Kearns Goodwin, *No Ordinary Time: Franklin and Eleanor Roosevelt: The Home Front in World War II*
- Leonard Nimoy, *I Am Spock*
- Ibn Warraq, *Why I Am Not a Muslim*
- Howard Stern, *Miss America*

Children's Literature

- Jim Murphy, *The Great Fire*
- Phillip Pullman, *The Golden Compass* (the first book in the His Dark Materials trilogy)

Theater and Opera

Oct 25 *Victor/Victoria* opened on Broadway's Marquis Theatre at New York City. When star Julie Andrews later received the show's lone Tony nomination, she declined, stating "I have searched my conscience and my heart and find that I cannot accept this nomination. I stand instead with the egregiously overlooked" cast and crew of the show. Andrews further declined to perform at the Tony Awards ceremony. While ratings for that broadcast suffered, the controversy surrounding Andrew's decision did boost ticket sales for *Victor/Victoria*.

Film

May 27 *Superman* actor Christopher Reeve was paralyzed from the neck down after a fall from his horse during a riding competition at Culpepper, VA.

Nov 13 The 14th James Bond film, *GoldenEye*, premiered at Los Angeles, CA, and featured a new 007: Irish actor Pierce Brosnan.

The 68th Academy Awards (Awarded in 1996 for 1995 achievement)

- Best Picture: *Braveheart*
- Best Director: Mel Gibson, *Braveheart*
- Best Actor: Nicolas Cage, *Leaving Las Vegas*
- Best Actress: Susan Sarandon, *Dead Man Walking*
- Best Supporting Actor: Kevin Spacey, *The Usual Suspects*
- Best Supporting Actress: Mira Sorvino, *Mighty Aphrodite*

Notable Films

- *Apollo 13*
- *Babe*
- *Sense and Sensibility*
- *Dead Man Walking*
- *Il Postino (The Postman)*
- *The Bridges of Madison County*
- *Die Hard with a Vengeance*
- *Casino*
- *Heat*
- *Leaving Las Vegas*
- *Nixon*
- *Mr. Holland's Opus*
- *Rob Roy*
- *12 Monkeys*
- *Pocahontas*
- *The American President*
- *Batman Forever*

"To Infinity and Beyond!"

1995's smash hit *Toy Story* was the first feature-length film to be entirely computer animated. It marked a rousing debut for Pixar, Hollywood's first computer animation film studio, and was the first film of a $26 million, three-picture deal Pixar signed with Walt Disney Animation Studios. It eventually grossed over $373 million in worldwide box office revenues, trading top-grossing spots for 1995 as home media receipts were added in with the year's other big earner, *Die Hard with a Vengeance*. At the Academy Awards, *Toy Story* was nominated for Best Screenplay Written Directly for the Screen, and director John Lasseter received a Special Achievement Award. Composer Randy Newman was nominated in the Best Original Musical or Comedy Score category as well as for Best Original Song, the year's seemingly omnipresent "You've Got a Friend in Me." As debuts go, *Toy Story* went to infinity, and beyond.

- Crimson Tide
- Waterworld
- Richard III
- A Little Princess
- Seven
- GoldenEye
- Ace Ventura: When Nature Calls
- Jumanji
- Get Shorty
- A Walk in the Clouds
- Mighty Aphrodite
- Before Sunrise
- Billy Madison
- The Quick and the Dead
- Outbreak
- Tank Girl
- Tommy Boy
- Bad Boys
- The Basketball Diaries
- While You Were Sleeping
- French Kiss
- The City of Lost Children
- Species
- Clueless
- The Brothers McMullen
- Dangerous Minds
- To Wong Foo, Thanks for Everything! Julie Newmar
- Hackers
- The Usual Suspects
- Showgirls
- Empire Records
- Strange Days
- Mallrats
- Waiting to Exhale
- Cry, the Beloved Country
- Dolores Claiborne
- The Net

Television

Jan 5 The venerable soap opera "All My Children" celebrated its 25th anniversary with a prime-time special on ABC.

Jan 11 The WB Network launched on 70 network affiliates and directly on the WGN-TV superstation feed. The WB's initial programming run featured "The Wayans Bros," "The Parent 'Hood," "Unhappily Ever After" and the short-lived workout gym comedy "Muscles."

Jan 16 Not willing to let the freshly launched WB hog the spotlight, the United Paramount Network launched with a two-hour premiere of "Star Trek: Voyager." "Voyager" was the only property on UPN to ever enjoy even limited success.

Jan 16 "Hercules: The Legendary Journeys" with star Kevin Sorbo debuted in syndication. It would run for six seasons.

Jan 24 With the start of the O.J. Simpson murder trial and its accompanying daily broadcasts, network soap operas braced for a prolonged period of preemptions and cancellations.

May 12 "As the World Turns" broadcast its 10,000th episode on CBS.

July 31 The Walt Disney Company announced its plan to purchase ABC and cable sports network ESPN.

Sept 4 "Xena: Warrior Princess" with star Lucy Lawless premiered in syndication. It would enjoy a six-season run and develop a strong cult following.

- Will Ferrell, Cheri Oteri and Darryl Hammond joined the cast of "Saturday Night Live."

Notable 1995 debuts

- "Taxicab Confessions"
- "NewsRadio"
- "Sliders"
- "Dr. Katz, Professional Therapist"
- "Aeon Flux"
- "WCW Monday Nitro"
- "The Drew Carey Show"
- "Murder One"
- "Caroline in the City"
- "The Single Guy"
- "JAG"
- "Mad TV"

Music

The 38th Annual Grammy Awards

- Record and Song of the Year: "Kiss from a Rose," Seal (songwriter)
- Album of the Year: *Jagged Little Pill*, Alanis Morissette
- Best New Artist: Hootie & the Blowfish
- Best Country Album: Robert John "Mutt" Lange (producer) and Shania Twain, *The Woman in Me*
- Best Female Pop Vocal Performance: Annie Lennox for "No More I Love You's"
- Best Male Pop Vocal Performance: Seal, "Kiss from a Rose"
- Best Pop Album: Larry Klein (producer) & Joni Mitchell (producer and artist) for *Turbulent Indigo*
- Best Female R&B Vocal Performance: Anita Baker, "I Apologize"
- Best Male R&B Vocal Performance: Stevie Wonder for "For Your Love"
- Best R&B Performance by a Duo or Group with Vocal: TLC for "Creep"
- Best R&B Album: TLC for *CrazySexyCool*

- Best Rap Solo Performance: Coolio, "Gangsta's Paradise"

- Best Rap Performance by a Duo or Group: Method Man featuring Mary J. Blige, "I'll Be There for You/You're All I Need to Get By"

- Best Rap Album: Naughty by Nature, *Poverty's Paradise*

- Best Female Rock Vocal Performance: Alanis Morissette for "You Oughta Know"

- Best Male Rock Vocal Performance: Tom Petty for "You Don't Know How It Feels"

- Best Rock Performance by a Duo or Group with Vocal: Blues Traveler for "Run-Around"

- Best Hard Rock Performance: Pearl Jam for "Spin the Black Circle"

- Best Metal Performance: Nine Inch Nails for "Happiness in Slavery"

- Best Rock Song: Alanis Morissette and Glen Ballard (songwriters) for "You Oughta Know" performed by Alanis Morissette

- Best Rock Album: Glen Ballard (producer), Alanis Morissette for *Jagged Little Pill*

Feb 19 A beach at Cancun, Mexico, became the site of Motley Crue drummer Tommy Lee and *Baywatch* star Pamela Anderson's marriage after an impulsive, party-fueled 96-hour courtship.

Mar 1 R.E.M. drummer Bill Berry suffered a brain aneurysm and collapsed on stage while performing with the band in Switzerland. Berry received treatment and recovered, but he would later cite the health

scare as one of the reasons for his departure from R.E.M. in 1997.

Mar 14 *Me Against the World* (Interscope) debuted at number one on the *Billboard 200* as its creator, Tupac Shakur, sat in Clinton Correctional Facility at New York State, serving a prison sentence on sexual assault charges. It was the first time an artist had an album at the top of the charts while at the same time being incarcerated.

Mar 31 At a motel in Corpus Christi, TX, Tejano superstar Selena was shot and killed by Yolanda Saldivar, the manager of her chain of fashion boutiques and a former president of the Selena fan club. In the weeks before the shooting, Saldivar had been accused of financial improprieties by Abraham Quintanella, Jr, Selena's father and manager.

July 9 The Grateful Dead performed its final concert with Jerry Garcia at Chicago's Soldier Field. On Aug 9, Garcia, the band's lead guitarist and vocalist, died of a heart attack at 53.

Sept 1 The Rock and Roll Hall of Fame opened its doors at Cleveland, OH.

Sept 27 Time Warner sold its 50 percent share of Interscope Records, caving under pressure from conservative groups over the explicit lyrics of rap artists who recorded for the imprint.

Oct 21 Shannon Hoon, singer of the band Blind Melon, was found dead of a cocaine overdose at New Orleans, LA. He was 28.

Oct 23 Def Leppard successfully orchestrated an arena rock, travel and time zone high-wire act, performing three concerts on three continents on the very same day. The jaunt began at Tangier,

Morocco; made its way to London; and culminated at Vancouver, BC, Canada.

Dec 4 The Beatles released new material. "Free as a Bird" was originally written recorded as a demo by John Lennon in 1977 but remained unreleased. As part of the Beatles' *Anthology I*, issued that November, surviving Beatles Paul McCartney, George Harrison and Ringo Starr added their contributions to "Free as a Bird," and it became the promotional single for the retrospective.

Popular Songs

- TLC, "Creep"

- Alanis Morissette, "You Oughta Know"

- Dionne Farris, "I Know"

- Seal, "Kiss from a Rose"

- Luniz, "I Got 5 on It"

- Skee-Lo, "I Wish"

- Rancid, "Ruby Soho"

- Hootie & the Blowfish, "Only Wanna Be with You"

- Mariah Carey, "Fantasy"

- Bryan Adams, "Have You Ever Really Loved a Woman?"

- Sophie B. Hawkins, "As I Lay Me Down"

- Des'Ree, "You Gotta Be"

- Bjork, "Hyperballad"

- Radiohead, "Fake Plastic Trees" and "High and Dry"

- Del Amitri, "Roll to Me"

- Blues Traveler, "Run-Around"

- Montell Jordan, "This Is How We Do It"

- Monica, "Don't Take It Personal (Just One of Dem Days)"

- Shaggy, "Boombastic/In the Summertime"

- 2Pac, "Dear Mama/Old School"

- Oasis, "Wonderwall"
- Dr. Dre, "Keep Their Heads Ringin'"
- Coolio Featuring L.V., "Gangsta's Paradise (From *Dangerous Minds*)"
- LL Cool J, "Hey Lover"
- Rancid, "Roots Radicals"
- Michael Jackson, "You Are Not Alone"
- Whitney Houston, "Exale (Shoop Shoop) (From *Waiting to Exhale*)"
- Shania Twain, "Any Man of Mine/Whose Bed Have Your Boots Been Under?"
- Tim McGraw, "I Like It, I Love It"
- Trisha Yearwood, "Thinkin' About You"
- Reba McEntire, "The Heart Is a Lonely Hunter"
- John Michael Montgomery, "I Can Love You Like That"
- Clint Black, "Summer's Comin'"
- Annie Lennox, "No More I Love You's"
- U2, "Hold Me, Thrill Me, Kiss Me, Kill Me"

Notable Albums

- Radiohead, *The Bends*
- Alanis Morissette, *Jagged Little Pill*
- Mariah Carey, *Daydream*
- Bjork, *Post*
- Oasis, *(What's the Story) Morning Glory?*
- The Smashing Pumpkins, *Mellon Collie and the Infinite Sadness*
- Tricky, *Maxinquaye*
- Pulp, *Different Class*
- GZA, *Liquid Swords*
- Blur, *The Great Escape*
- Elastica, *Elastica*
- 2Pac, *Me Against the World*

- Alice in Chains, *Alice in Chains*
- D'Angelo, *Brown Sugar*
- Foo Fighters, *Foo Fighters*
- No Doubt, *Tragic Kingdom*
- Michael Jackson, *HIStory: Past, Present and Future*
- Emmylou Harris, *Wrecking Ball*
- Ol' Dirty Bastard, *Return to the 36 Chambers: The Dirty Version*
- LL Cool J, *Mr. Smith*
- Ben Folds Five, *Ben Folds Five*
- The Roots, *Do You Want More?!!!??!*
- Shania Twain, *The Woman in Me*
- Trisha Yearwood, *Thinkin' About You*
- PJ Harvey, *To Bring You My Love*
- Jewel, *Pieces of You*
- Collective Soul, *Collective Soul*
- Annie Lennox, *Medusa*
- Matthew Sweet, *100% Fun*
- Wilco, *A.M.*
- The Highwaymen, *The Road Goes on Forever*
- Montell Jordan, *This Is How We Do It*
- Pavement, *Wowee Zowee*
- Naughty by Nature, *Poverty's Paradise*
- Jamiroquai, *Return of the Space Cowboy*
- The Rembrandts, *LP*
- Everclear, *Sparkle & Fade*
- All-4-One, *And the Music Speaks*
- The Verve, *A Northern Soul*
- Neil Young, *Mirror Ball*
- Shaggy, *Boombastic*
- Elliott Smith, *Elliott Smith*
- Bone Thugs-n-Harmony, *E 1999 Eternal*
- Garbage, *Garbage*

- Faith Evans, *Faith*
- Lenny Kravitz, *Circus*
- Red Hot Chili Peppers, *One Hot Minute*
- Green Day, *Insomniac*
- Melissa Etheridge, *Your Little Secret*
- Bruce Springsteen, *The Ghost of Tom Joad*
- Stevie Wonder, *Natural Wonder*

Science and Technology

- Nobel Prize in Physiology or Medicine: Awarded jointly to Edward B. Lewis, Christiane Nusslein-Volhard and Eric F. Wieschaus "for their discoveries the genetic control of early embryonic development."

- Nobel Prize in Chemistry: Paul Crutzen, Mario Molina, and F. Sherwood Rowland "for their work in atmospheric chemistry, particularly concerning the formation and decomposition of ozone."

- Nobel Prize in Physics: Martin L. Perl ("for the discovery of the tau lepton") and Frederick Reines ("for the detection of the neutrino").

Mar 14 Astronaut Norman Thagard became the first American to reach space aboard a Russian launch vehicle—and thereby America's first cosmonaut—when the Soyuz T M-21 lifted off from Baikonur Cosmodrome at Kazakhstan en route to *Mir*. Thagard would break NASA's space endurance record during his time spent on the space station.

Mar 22 Russian cosmonaut Valery Polyakov returned to Earth after spending a record 438 days in space aboard the *Mir* modular space station.

Apr 30 US government funding for the National Science Foundation Network (NSFNET) ended, making the Internet a wholly private enterprise.

June 29 American Space Shuttle *Atlantis* docked with the Russian space station *Mir*, forming while docked together the largest spacecraft ever in orbit and fostering the cooperation that would lead to the construction of the International Space Station.

Sept 30 NASA terminated regular contact with the *Pioneer 11* robotic space probe. Launched in 1973, *Pioneer* was the first probe to encounter Saturn and the second to fly through the asteroid belt between Mars and Jupiter.

Dec 7 Launched from Space Shuttle *Atlantis* in 1989, the space probe *Galileo* arrived at its mission's research goal, Jupiter and its moons.

Commerce and New Products

■ The Sveriges Riksbank Prize in Economic Sciences: Robert E. Lucas, Jr., "for having developed and applied the hypothesis of rational expectations, and thereby having transformed macroeconomic analysis and deepened our understanding of economic policy."

Jan 1 The World Trade Organization (WTO) officially replaced the General Agreement on Tariffs and Trade (GATT), which had functioned as the de facto international instrument on trade cooperation since its signing in 1947.

Feb 28 Denver International Airport opened northeast of Denver, CO. The largest airport in North America by total landmass (52.4 sq miles), DIA ultimately came on line over a year behind schedule, and at a cost of $4.8 billion, or more than $2 billion over budget.

Mar 2 A few short months after establishing its yahoo.com domain name, Yahoo! was incorporated by its founders, Jerry Yang and David Filo, and on Apr 5 Yahoo! entered two rounds of venture capital funding, raising $3 million. An initial public offering followed in 1996.

Mar 6 Netscape announced that Version 1.1 of its popular Navigator web browser—which was itself the early leader in the marketplace new web browsers—would not be free for all, as had originally been planned, but free only for academic and non-profit organizational use.

July 16 Amazon.com was first incorporated as an online bookstore by founder Jeff Bezos at Seattle, WA.

Aug 24 Microsoft released its Windows 95 operating system to the general public.

Nov 21 The Dow Jones Industrial Average topped the 5,000 mark for the first time in its history.

■ In 1995, under the leadership of ex-Viacom/VH-1 executive Edward Bennett, Prodigy became the first of the early-generation dialup services to offer consumers full access to the World Wide Web and the ability to host Web pages for its members.

■ Notoriously straight-laced IBM began relaxing its dress code. Business attire before 1995 was white shirt, tie, suit and wingtips. Casual attire (no tie) and occasional "dress-down" days made an appearance.

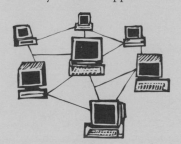

Sports
Auto Racing

■ Indianapolis 500: Jacques Villeneuve

Baseball

■ World Series: The Atlanta Braves defeated the Cleveland Indians four games to two.

Apr 2 The strike that decimated the 1994 Major League Baseball season ended on this date after 232 days, making it the longest work stoppage in MLB history.

June 3 Pedro Martinez pitched nine perfect innings for the Montreal Expos before Leon "Bip" Roberts opened the 10th frame with a double. Mel Rojas relieved Martinez and secured the last three outs for a 1–0 Expos victory.

June 30 Eddie Murray of the Cleveland Indians got the 3,000th hit of his major league career, a single off Mike Trombley of the Minnesota Twins, on the way to 4–1 Indians victory.

Sept 6 Baltimore Orioles third-baseman Cal Ripken passed Lou Gehrig's record for consecutive games played. Ripken's streak began on May 30, 1982, and ended on Sept 30, 1998, at 2,632 consecutive games played.

Sept 16, 17 and 19 San Diego Padres switch-hitter Ken Caminiti launched home runs from both sides of the plate in three games (two in a row and three out of four).

Sept 29 A New York court upheld the injunction that had ended the player strike in April. Baseball owners' appeal was rejected, and the three-judge panel said they had indeed illegally attempted to eliminate free agency and salary arbitration.

Basketball

- NBA Finals: The Houston Rockets defeated the Orlando Magic four games to none.

Jan 6 Lenny Wilkins became the winningest coach in NBA history when his Atlanta Hawks defeated the Washington Bullets 112–90.

Mar 18 Michael Jordan announced his historic return to professional basketball. After a 17-month break from the game that had made him a legend, a hiatus that found him dabbling in professional baseball as an offensive talent in the Chicago White Sox minor league system and mourning the loss of his father James Jordan, MJ returned to the hardwood and led the Chicago Bulls through three more NBA World Championship seasons.

Sept. 12 The Harlem Globetrotters lost a game 91–85 to a team led by Kareem Abdul-Jabbar, ending their winning streak at 8,829.

Football

- Super Bowl XXIX: The San Francisco 49ers defeated the San Diego Chargers 49–26.

- Heisman Trophy: Eddie George, Running Back, Ohio State University

Golf

- The Master's Tournament: Ben Crenshaw

- PGA Championship: Steve Elkington

- US Open: Corey Pavin

- The Open Championship: John Daly

- The US Womens' Open Championship: Annika Sorenstam

- Women's PGA Championship: Kelly Robbins

- The Evian Championship (as a Ladies' European Tour event): Laura Davies

- Women's British Open: Karrie Webb

Hockey

- Stanley Cup: The New Jersey Devils defeated the Detroit Red Wings four games to none.

Feb 7 Pittsburgh Penguins right winger Joey Mullen got the 1,000th point of his NHL career with an assist in a 7–3 victory over the Florida Panthers.

Mar 8 New York Rangers right winger Steve Larmer got the 1,000th point of his NHL career with an assist in a 6–4 victory over the New Jersey Devils.

Dec 23 Toronto Maple Leafs center Doug Gilmore tallied the 1,000th point of his NHL career with an assist in a 6–1 win over the Edmonton Oilers.

Horse Racing

- The Kentucky Derby: Thunder Gulch, ridden by Gary Stevens

- Preakness Stakes: Timber Country, ridden by Pat Day

- Belmont Stakes: Thunder Gulch, ridden by Pat Stevens

Sailing

May 14 Yacht Racing: Dennis Conner and his Stars & Stripes yacht team lost to Team New Zealand in the America's Cup final.

Soccer

May 24 AFC Ajax won the UEFA Champions League with the defeat of AC Milan 1–0 at Ernst Happel Stadium, Vienna.

- Everton defeated Manchester United to win the FA Cup.

Tennis

Australian Open
- Men's Singles: Andre Agassi
- Women's Singles: Mary Pierce

French Open
- Men's Singles: Thomas Muster
- Women's Singles: Steffi Graf

Wimbledon
- Men's Singles: Pete Sampras
- Women's Singles: Steffi Graf

US Open
- Men's Singles: Pete Sampras
- Women's Singles: Steffi Graf

1995 Deaths

- William Robert Allison, American baseball player

- Kingsley Amis, British writer, author of *Lucky Jim*

- Richard William Bartell, American baseball player

- Earl W. Bascom, American rodeo showman

- David Russell "Gus" Bell, American baseball player

- Robert Bolt, Oscar-winning English playwright

- Ernest L. Boyer, American educator

- Cheyenne Brando, Tahitian model

- Jeremy Brett, English actor famed for his interpretation of Sherlock Holmes

- Warren E. Burger, American lawyer and chief justice of the United States
- Glenn Lawrence Burke, American baseball player
- Rosalind Cash, American actress
- Florence May Chadwick, American swimmer
- Don Cherry, American jazz musician
- Peter Cook, English actor
- Elisha Cook, Jr, American actor
- Howard Cosell, American broadcaster
- Anthony Francis Cuccinello, American baseball player and coach
- Gilles Deleuze, French philosopher
- Eazy-E (Eric Lynn Wright), American musician
- John Presper Eckert, American electrical engineer and computer pioneer
- Alfred Eisenstaedt, American photojournalist
- Stanley Elkin, American teacher and author
- Ed Flanders, American actor
- William J. Fulbright, US senator
- Eva Gabor, Hungarian-American actress
- Jerry Garcia, American musician (Grateful Dead)
- Alexander Godunov, Russian dancer and actor
- Richard Alonzo "Pancho" Gonzalez, American tennis player
- Gale Gordon, American actor
- Charles Gordone, American playwright

- Harry Guardino, American actor
- James Herriot, English veterinarian and author
- Patricia Highsmith, American writer
- Nathan Holman, American basketball Hall of Famer
- Michael Hordern, English actor
- Leslie Horvath, American football player
- Burl Ives, American actor and singer
- Rose Kennedy, American philanthropist, matriarch of the Kennedy political family
- Margaret Kuhn, American age discrimination opponent
- William Kunstler, American lawyer
- Priscilla Lane, American actress
- Ida Lupino, English actress
- Louis Malle, French director
- Mickey Mantle, American baseball player
- Dean Martin, American singer, entertainer and actor
- Doug McClure, American actor
- Elizabeth Montgomery, American actress
- Lindsey Nelson, American broadcaster
- Hugh O'Connor, American actor
- Fred Perry, British athlete
- Vada Edward Pinson, American baseball player
- Donald Pleasence, English actor
- Selena Quintanilla-Perez, American singer

- Yitzhak Rabin, Israeli political leader
- Orville Redenbacher, American popcorn entrepreneur
- James Reston, American journalist
- Charlie Rich, American musician
- Bobby Riggs, American tennis player
- Ginger Rogers, American actress
- Saul Walter Rogovin, American baseball player
- Bob Ross, American painter and TV personality
- Jonas Salk, American medical researcher
- Joe Slovo, South African politician
- John Smith, American actor and singer
- Margaret Chase Smith, American politician
- Robert Stephens, English actor
- John Cameron Swayze, American television journalist
- Lana Turner, American actress
- Margaret Wade, American basketball Hall of Fame coach
- David Wayne, American actor
- Mary Wickes, American actor
- Eugene Wigner, Hungarian-American theoretical physicist
- Harold Wilson, British politician
- Woodrow Wilson Williams, American baseball player
- Wolfman Jack (Robert Weston Smith), American actor and disc jockey

Spotlight on World Anniversaries

James Cook Exploration of Australia

1770 * 250 YEARS

James Cook, born 1728 in North Yorkshire, England, was a British naval officer, explorer, surveyor, navigator and cartographer. Based on his detailed maps of Newfoundland made during the Seven Years' War, Lt. Cook was commissioned as commander of the HMS *Endeavour*, embarking from England on Aug 26, 1768, on a Pacific voyage to chart the transit of Venus across the sun at the equator and to search for the existence of, and to chart, the theoretical continent Terra Australis.

Cook became the first recorded European to circumnavigate New Zealand in 1769–70 and map its complete coastline. On Apr 20, 1770, he made first sight of Australia at Point Hicks, then the first recorded European contact with the eastern coast of Australia on Apr 29, 1770, when the *Endeavour* landed on the Kurnell Peninsula, in what the locals called "Kamay" and Cook christened "Botany Bay" for the rich flora collected and catalogued by the expedition's botanists. On June 11, the *Endeavour* ran aground on the Great Barrier Reef near Cooktown, and the voyage was delayed for 48 days while repairs were made. The ship then rounded Cape York, landing at Possession Island in the Torres Strait on Aug 22 before returning to England.

Cook's exploration of the Pacific Ocean has left a legacy of scientific investigation, including the first large-scale hydrographic surveys and a significant contribution to the measurement of longitude. Cook's legacy is contested for its disregard for indigenous peoples, who, today, characterize his encounters as colonial invasions. The 250th anniversary of Cook's Pacific voyages is commemorated around the world and began in 2018.

Such 250th anniversary "Meeting" commemorations are being planned with sensitivity. The National Museum of Australia in Canberra presents a 250th anniversary virtual exhibition representing the perspectives of both non-Indigenous and First Australians by counterpointing the "view from the ship" with the "view from the shore." In Sydney, the Kamay Botany Bay National Park is being restored and upgraded to increase visitor access, including new piers and ferry service, and recognition of Aboriginal significance with balanced storytelling that includes both Indigenous and European history. The Australian National Maritime Museum invites nautical buffs to sail and live aboard the replica ship HMS *Endeavour* as it circumnavigates Australia from March 2020 to May 2021, berthing in a variety of ports to connect with as many Australians as possible. From June 17 through Aug 4, Queensland hosts Cooktown 2020, a 48-day festival celebrating Cook's arrival, the scientific discoveries recorded during his 48 days on shore and the interactions that occurred between the crew and the Guugu Yimithirr people. During the festival, a time capsule buried in 1970 at the Cook Cairn monument dedication in Childers will be opened.

For information:

James Cook 250

E-mail: jamescook250@gmail.com
Web: http://jamescook250.org

The Captain Cook Society

E-mail: President@
 CaptainCookSociety.com
Web: www.captaincooksociety.com

NSW Government Office of Environment & Heritage

PO Box A290
Sydney South, NSW 1232
Australia
Phone: (02) 9995 5347
E-mail: media@environment.nsw.
 gov.au

National Museum of Australia

GPO Box 1901
Canberra ACT 2601
Australia
E-mail: media@nma.gov.au or
 information@nma.gov.au
Web: www.nma.gov.au

Australian National Maritime Museum

Communication & Public Affairs
Publicist: Tim O'Halloran
Phone: (61) 2 9298 3645
E-mail: media@sea.museum
Web: www.sea.museum

Cooktown 2020

Cook Shire Council
10 Furneaux St
Cooktown QLD 4895,
Australia
Phone: (07) 4069 5444
E-mail: info@cooktown2020.com
Web: www.cooktown2020.com

Ludwig van Beethoven

BAPTIZED DEC 17, 1770 * 250 YEARS

Widely ranked first in the pantheon of musical gods, German composer Ludwig van Beethoven dominated the transitional period between the Classical and Romantic eras, moving from the traditions of Joseph Haydn and Mozart toward musical forms embodying the growing focus on humanist, nationalist and egalitarian ideals that would characterize the Romantic worldview. Perhaps Beethoven's greatest achievement was to help move instrumental music onto the highest plane of seriousness from its previous status as an accompaniment to text-based forms like the cantata, opera and oratorio, making possible late-Romantic critic Walter Pater's comment that "All arts aspire to the condition of music."

Born into a musical family at Bonn, Germany, Beethoven had a reputation as a piano virtuoso before moving to Vienna, where he spent the majority of his career, supporting himself largely from the sale and publication of his work. Though lonely, quarrelsome and often miserable as an adult, his achievements as an innovator in musical forms including the sonata, symphony, concerto and quartet are unmatched. These included the Third Symphony, the *Eroica*; *Piano Sonata in F Minor*, "the *Appassionata*"; the *Piano Concerto No. 4 in G Major*; the three *Razumovsky Quartets*; the *Fourth Symphony*; and the *Ninth Symphony, "Ode to Joy,"* which combined vocal and instrumental music in a hitherto untried way and is considered his towering achievement, though composed after he had gone completely deaf. Beethoven also composed one opera, *Fidelio*, and his *Missa Solemnis* is generally considered one of the composer's supreme achievements. By sheer repetition, the famous openings to his Fifth Symphony and the piano piece *Fur Elise* (Bagatelle No. 25) are modern testaments to his enduring influence, while the attendance at his funeral—20,000 people—attest to his fame in his own time.

Beethoven died at the age of 56—famously, during a thunderstorm—on Mar 26, 1827, at Vienna, Austria. For the many commemorations of his 250th birth anniversary, see "Spotlight on 2020 Events."

Lady with the Lamp: Florence Nightingale

BORN MAY 12, 1820 * 200 YEARS

Synonymous in the public imagination with the image of nurses as angels of mercy, Florence Nightingale was, in addition, a formidable social reformer, statistician and health care administrator. Considered the foundational philosopher of modern nursing, Nightingale, classically educated child of affluent English parents, brought to her profession her facility in mathematics as well as important social connections.

Despite her family's objections, she eschewed marriage in pursuit of a life in service to the suffering, having experienced "calls from God" to this path as early as age 16. Her calling may have become clearer during a visit to Egypt in 1847, where she encountered the Sisters of Saint Vincent de Paul, whose order had been active in military hospital nursing since the 17th century. In 1851, she trained for three months in Prussia at the Institute for Protestant Deaconesses at Kaiserwerth before becoming superintendent of London's Institution for the Care of Sick Gentlewomen in 1853. She assumed oversight in 1854 of British field hospitals during the Crimean War. Nightingale, with 38 nurses, oversaw four miles of beds and worked 20-hour days. From her nightly ward rounds, she earned the sobriquet "Lady with the Lamp" and became a national hero for reducing mortality rates through improvements in hospital management, sanitation, food, water supplies, and hospital ward design. Basing these reforms on record keeping and data collection that she established, she demonstrated that soldiers were seven times more likely to die of diseases caused by poor sanitation than in battle.

Nightingale established the first scientifically based nursing school—the Nightingale School of Nursing—and wrote *Notes on Nursing* (1860), a bestseller still in print. She returned from the Crimean War with broken health and was an invalid for the last 30 years of her life. Nevertheless, Nightingale remained influential in social reform in health care and nursing; she was the first woman awarded the British Order of Merit (1907). Born at Florence, Italy (the source of her given name), Nightingale died at London, England, on Aug 13, 1910.

In honor of the bicentenary of her birth, nursing organizations and the World Health Organization has designated 2020 as "The Year of the Nurse and Midwife." Many health, nursing and historical organizations are celebrating with conferences, exhibitions and even a walking tour of Nightingale's country retreat, Lea Hurst. Partners to bicentennial events are the Florence Nightingale Foundation, the British Library, the University of Nottingham, the Arts and Humanities

Research Council, the Guild of Nurses and many others.

For information:

Florence Nightingale Foundation

Nightingale2020

Deans Mews
11-13 Cavendish Square
London W1G 0AN
England
E-mail: admin@ florence-nightingale-foundation.org.uk
Web: https://florence-nightingale-foundation.org.uk

Florence Nightingale 2020

The Guild of Nurses
Web: http://guildofnurses.co.uk/florencenightingale-202/

Vladimir Lenin

BORN APR 10, 1870 * 150 YEARS

Born Vladimir Ilyich Ulyanov Apr 10, 1870, at Simbursk, Russia (later renamed Ulyanovsk in his honor), the man widely regarded as history's greatest revolutionary leader adopted the pseudonym Lenin while writing for *Iskra* (*The Spark*), the periodical he cofounded following a Siberian exile. Influenced by Marx's *Das Kapital*, which he read in 1887 after both his expulsion from Kazan Imperial University for illegal protest and eldest brother Aleksandr's execution for conspiracy to assassinate Tsar Alexander III, Lenin became a Marxist in 1889 and was a lifelong adherent to revolutionary social democracy.

His work as a lawyer in early adulthood influenced his developing views on classist biases. First espoused in his book *What's to Be Done?* (1902), Lenin's theories of party as vanguard of the proletariat guided by democratic centralism and absolute party discipline, together with his view of revolutionary defeatism—the belief that only the overthrow of capitalism could end imperialist war—presented in *Imperialism, the Highest Stage of Capitalism* (1917), laid the foundations for modern-day communist political theory. His political beliefs were posthumously dubbed Leninism and, coupled with Marxism, became the leading philosophy of 20th-century communism.

Between the failed revolution of 1905 and the February Revolution of 1917, Lenin's Bolshevik Party, in opposition to rival faction the Mensheviks, slowly emerged independent of the Russian Social-Democratic Workers' Party. His unpublished pamphlet *The State and Revolution* proposed the revolutionary idea of dictatorship of the proletariat. Written while in hiding, this ideal, which he proposed achieving through an armed deposing of the provisional government by the Bolsheviks' Red Guard, propelled him to party leadership in October 1917.

Lenin famously said, "Give us an organization of revolutionaries and we will overturn Russia!" The October Revolution (1917), coordinated by Lenin and Leon Trotsky, was a bloodless coup d'etat that established Soviet rule with Lenin as first Soviet head of state. Anti-Soviet forces retaliated, resulting in the Russian Civil War (1918–21) between Lenin's Red Army and the Anti-Soviet White Army, comprised of former tsarist military leaders and funded by Allied forces. Despite

overwhelming odds, the Red Army succeeded; many credit this victory to Lenin's political and military leadership. During this period, Lenin founded the Third or Communist International (1919), but despite Soviet military success, the nascent country was on the precipice of economic disaster. In response, Lenin instituted the New Economic Policy (NEP, 1921), a stopgap policy that permitted capitalist economic gains in an effort to stabilize the economy.

A surgery to remove bullets from a 1918 assassination attempt resulted in a stroke in 1922, which led to an ensuing precipitous physical decline. Despite this, Lenin worked tirelessly to establish the Union of Soviet Socialist Republics (USSR), which he strongly preferred to Stalin's proposed unitary organization. He feared for the USSR's future with disparate leaders Stalin and Trotsky; he saw the former, his successor, as a grave threat, a belief espoused in his posthumously (and ultimately fruitless) published *Testament*. Thoroughly incapacitated in early 1923, Lenin remained the nominal Soviet figurehead until his death on Jan 21, 1924, at Moscow, USSR. Despite the brutal Russian winter, tens of thousands of Soviets attended his funeral in Red Square, where his embalmed body remains on display in his eponymous tomb.

Anne Frank: 75th Death Anniversary

FEBRUARY/MARCH 1945 * 75 YEARS

German-Jewish teenager known worldwide for her chronicle of life in hiding following the Nazi occupation of The Netherlands during WWII, she was born Annelise Marie Frank in Frankfurt am Main, Germany, on June 12, 1929, and perished in Bergen-Belsen concentration camp just weeks before the Allied liberation.

Soon after the Nazis came to power in 1933, Frank's father, Otto, a well-to-do banker, moved his wife and two daughters to Amsterdam, where he became managing director of a food company with a warehouse and office on the Prinsengracht. It was there he set up two secret apartments in a hidden rear annex where the Franks moved on July 6, 1942, following Anne's sister Margot's deportation order. They were joined by Otto's coworker, Mr. van Daan, with his wife and 16-year-old son, Peter, as well as an elderly Jewish dentist named Dussel. All except Otto died in death camps following their arrest by the Gestapo in 1944.

The annex became the setting for the book—originally published in Dutch (1947) and later in English (1952)—as *Anne Frank: Diary of a Young Girl*, often called *The Diary of Anne Frank*. The *Diary*, now translated into dozens of languages, is widely held to be the most read personal journal of the Holocaust. Frank herself is one of the best-known Holocaust victims, thanks to the book; a 1955 Broadway play, *The Diary of Anne Frank*; a 1959 film of the same title; an Academy Award–winning 1996 documentary, *Anne Frank Remembered*; a radio play; an opera; a traveling exhibition "Anne Frank in the World"; many television productions worldwide over decades; and the hundreds of thousands of people who visit Amsterdam's Anne Frank House museum yearly. There is even a Japanese anime film *Ann no Nikki* (1995).

The manuscript from which these works descended came into Otto Frank's hands thanks to friends who saved papers not confiscated by the Gestapo. He was the work's first

editor and has been criticized for "universalizing" Anne by expunging details about his daughter's Jewish identity, her hatred of the Germans, her femininity, her sexuality and her complicated relationships with other Annex residents. A new English translation (1995) restored some of the material her father deleted. Although Frank wrote a few short stories and started a novel during her period in hiding, she will be remembered as the accomplished, insightful writer of a work that has touched millions of people.

For information:

Anne Frank House

Westermarkt 20
1016 DK Amsterdam
Netherlands
Phone: (31) 20 556 71 05
E-mail: services@annefrank.nl
Web: www.annefrank.org

Bombing of Hiroshima and Nagasaki

AUG 6 AND 9, 1945 * 75 YEARS

On Monday, Aug 6, 1945, at 8:15am, in the final chapter of WWII, American B-29 bomber *Enola Gay* dropped a uranium-enriched atomic bomb, code-named "Little Boy," on Hiroshima—a manufacturing center in western Japan—instantly killing 80,000 people, including more than 20,000 combatants, more than 50,000 Japanese civilians and 2,000 Korean slave laborers, and leveling 90 percent of the city's buildings and homes. Three days later, in a radio address, President Harry S. Truman urged Japanese civilians to evacuate industrial cities to avoid another attack; on Aug 9, the US military

dropped a second atomic bomb, nicknamed "Fat Man," on the port city of Nagasaki, instantly killing 40,000. This was the first-ever deployment of nuclear weapons against human beings, and it hastened the end of the war; citing the devastating power of "a new and most cruel bomb," Emperor Hirohito announced Japan's unconditional surrender to Allied forces on Aug 15, bringing an end to WWII.

Earlier, in May 1945, with war in Europe over after Germany's surrender, Truman had been eager to end the war in the Pacific, but Japan's militarist government rejected the Allied demand for surrender. Top American military commanders, including General Douglas MacArthur, wanted to continue the traditional bombing that was already in effect, but in an effort to prevent massive American casualties expected to result from an invasion of Japan, Truman approved the dropping of the A-bombs on Hiroshima and Nagasaki, which remains one of the most controversial and highly debated wartime decisions to this day. By the end of 1945, the death toll reached 140,000 resulting from burns and radiation exposure, with countless more survivors succumbing to leukemia and other cancers over the following decades. The events of 1945 ushered in the Nuclear Age, wherein nuclear energy emerged as a dominant military, industrial and sociopolitical factor, sparking a worldwide nuclear arms race and igniting the cold war with the Soviet Union.

On Aug 6, 2020, as it has annually since 1947, the city of Hiroshima will honor those killed and remember its destruction at the Hiroshima Peace Memorial—a UNESCO World Heritage site at the Genbaku Dome, the only structure left standing on the site where the bomb exploded—with testimonials from *hibakusha* (A-bomb survivors), lantern-floating ceremonies on the Motoyasu River and the recitation of a Peace Declaration by the mayor and prime minister. A similar ceremony happens yearly on Aug 9 in Nagasaki. In collaboration with the Hiroshima Peace Memorial Museum, an A-bomb exhibit, comprising personal artifacts, photographs, artwork and a paper crane booth, is planned for the USS *Arizona* Memorial at Pearl Harbor and other US locations in 2020. Although details are kept secret, the closing ceremonies of the Games of the XXXII Olympiad, the 2020 Summer Olympics in Japan, coincide with the 75th anniversaries of the nuclear bombings of Nagasaki and will likely include a commemoration of the Hiroshima and Nagasaki bombings.

For information:

Hiroshima Peace Memorial Museum

1-2 Nakajima-cho, Naka-ku
Hiroshima
Japan 730-0811
E-mail: hpcf@pcf.city.hiroshima.jp
Web: http://hpmmuseum.
jp/?lang=eng

Atomic Bomb Heritage Section

Nagasaki City Hall
7-8 Hiranomachi
Nagasaki
Japan 852-8117
E-mail: hibaku@city.nagasaki.
lg.jp
Web: www.pcf.city.hiroshima.
jp/AbombExhibition/english/
activities_eOS/index.html

City of Hiroshima

Peace Promotion Division
1-6-34 Kokutaiji-machi, Naka-ku
Hiroshima City
Japan 730-8586
E-mail: peace@city.hiroshima.lg.jp
Web: www.city.hiroshima.lg.jp/
english/

Pearl Harbor Visitor Center

1845 Wasp Blvd., #176
Honolulu, HI 96818
Phone: (808) 725-6145
Web: www.nps.gov/valr

The End of World War II

SEPT 2, 1945 * 75 YEARS

In late January 1945, American and British troops depleted the German army's resources and defeated the exhausted German soldiers at the Battle of the Bulge in Belgium, enabling Allied forces to sweep across Europe into Germany by April, taking 1.5 million prisoners along the way. At the same time Russian troops rolled in from the east, taking Warsaw and Krakow in the Vistula-Oder Offensive before closing in on Berlin. On Apr 20, Hitler's birthday, the Red Army invaded Berlin and, at the Battle of Nuremburg, US forces took that city. On Apr 28, as Allied forces closed in on Milan, Italian partisans executed duce of fascism Benito Mussolini. To avoid Mussolini's fate, Hitler committed suicide in Berlin on Apr 30, two days before the city garrison surrendered to Russia. The British took the last Nazi stronghold on May 3 at the Battle of Hamburg. Germany signed its official surrender in front of Soviet, US, British and French delegations at Eisenhower's headquarters at Reims and, at midnight on May 8, 1945 (May 9, Russian time), the war in Europe was officially over. Spontaneous celebrations broke out around the world, with millions of celebrants taking to Trafalgar Square and Times Square.

But the war still raged in the Pacific. Allied forces had firebombed Tokyo, Nagoya, Ōsaka, Kōbe, Yokohama and Toyama in March 1945, killing hundreds of thousands and rendering millions homeless, but Japan would not capitulate. It was after the United States dropped nuclear bombs on Hiroshima and Nagasaki on Aug 6 and 9 that Japan surrendered to the Allies on Aug 14. When President Truman announced the war was over, jubilation erupted in cities around the globe, including in Times Square, where Alfred Eisenstaedt's famous photograph of a sailor kissing a nurse was snapped. The war's end was made official on Sept 2 when US General Douglas MacArthur accepted Japan's formal surrender aboard the USS *Missouri* in Tokyo Bay.

Around the world, May 8 is celebrated as Victory in Europe Day, or V-E Day. Victory over Japan Day, or V-J Day, is commemorated on Aug 13 in the United States and Sept 2 in Europe. In Russia, the Kremlin is planning several events for May 9, 2020, to mark 75 years since the end of what Russians call the Great Patriotic War.

In January 2019, US president Donald Trump signed into law the 75th Anniversary of WWII Commemoration Act, intended to thank and honor veterans of World War II; educate the public about the history of the war; pay tribute to the contributions made on the home front by the people of the United States; recognize the contributions and sacrifices made by the Allies; and remember the Holocaust. On May 8, 2020, V-E Day, the Frank Gehry–designed Dwight D. Eisenhower Memorial—a national monument to the supreme commander who led Allied Forces to victory in WWII and became the 34th US president—will be dedicated on its four-acre site at the base of Capitol Hill, a ceremony for veterans will take place at the National World War II Memorial and 100

WWII-era vintage aircraft will fly along the Potomac River and across the National Mall in 24 formations in the Arsenal of Democracy 75th WW II Victory Commemoration Flyover.

Beyond Washington, DC, the Spirit of '45 Coalition is encouraging the public to participate in commemorative events such as wreath-laying ceremonies at memorials and other appropriate venues in their local communities the V-J Day weekend of Aug 14–16. The USS *Missouri*, now permanently docked in Pearl Harbor, will commemorate the end of the war in the Pacific with programs highlighting the transition from war to global commitment to peace and friendship Aug 29–Sept 2. A special exhibit of historic artifacts tied to the landmark ceremony on loan from Japan will be on display at the USS *Missouri* Memorial in 2020 to help tell the story of how history's most destructive war came to an end. The year's 75th anniversary commemoration will conclude with a wreath-laying at the V-J Day 75th Anniversary Commemoration at the WWII Memorial on Sept 2.

For information:

National World War II Memorial

National Park Service
900 Ohio Dr SW
Washington, DC 20024
Phone: (202) 245-4676
E-mail: Mike_Litterst@nps.gov,
Web: www.nps.gov/nwwm

Dwight D. Eisenhower Memorial Commission

Joyce Jacobson, Director of
 Operations & Programs
1629 K St NW, Ste 801
Washington, DC 20007
Phone: (202) 296-0004
E-mail: jjacobson@
 eisenhowermemorial.gov
Web: www.EisenhowerMemorial.gov

Arsenal of Democracy Flyover

Sarah McCann, Director of
 Communications
General Aviation Manufacturers
 Association
Phone: (202) 393-1500
Web: www2flyover@gmail.com

Spirit of '45 Coalition

300 E 40th St
St. 23 X
New York, NY 10004
E-mail: info@Spiritof45.org

USS *Missouri* Memorial Association

Jaclyn Hawse
Phone: (808) 455-1600, ext. 246
E-mail: JaclynH@ussmissouri.org
Web: www.ussmissouri.org

Earth Day

APR 22, 1970 * 50 YEARS

Created in response to numerous environmental issues that captured public consciousness in the 1960s— such as Rachel Carson's *Silent Spring* (1962), the Santa Barbara, CA, oil spill (1969) and a *TIME* magazine article on repeated Cuyahoga River fires (1969)—Earth Day was initially a US-based national teach-in on the state of the environment and the importance of environmental conservation. Hoping to harness a similar fervor to the student-led antiwar movement, Senator Gaylord Nelson (WI), with assistance from Rep Pete McCloskey (CA) and Harvard graduate student organizer Denis Hayes—later dubbed "Mr Earth Day" by *TIME* (1999)—selected Apr 22 for the teach-ins because it was a Wednesday, the middle of the week when students were unlikely to have competing plans, after the northern winter thaw but early enough that it didn't interfere with the first day of final exams for students. More than 20 million people, many at universities and

colleges, participated in numerous teach-ins across the United States; the largest gatherings were at the Washington Monument in Washington, DC (10,000 participants), and New York City, where cars were banned from Fifth Avenue for the gathering.

The event was a catalyst for environmental awareness and activism. In the 1970 general election, activists identified the "Dirty Dozen" politicians with abysmal environmental records; seven lost their reelection campaigns. Within five years, sweeping environmental changes were implemented; the Nixon-created EPA (1970), the Clean Air Act Extension (1970), National Environmental Policy Act (1970), Mammal Protection Act (1972), Endangered Species Act (1973), Marine Safe Water Drinking Act (1974) and Resource Conservation and Recovery Act (1976) were all implemented, and the Clean Water Act was amended (1972) following the first Earth Day.

More than 200 million people in 140 countries participated in the 20th anniversary celebration in 1990, including over a million people in New York City's Central Park and 350,000 on the National Mall in Washington, DC. In the ensuing years, contemporary celebrations focus on raising awareness of climate change and the importance of renewable energy. Earth Day Network's Global Advisory Committee is currently planning 50th-anniversary events, including Earth Challenge 2020, which is working to collect over a billion citizen-scientist-provided environmental data points.

For information:

Earth Day Network

1616 P St NW, Ste 340
Washington, DC 20036
Phone: (202) 518-0044
Web: www.earthday.org

Spotlight on American Anniversaries

The *Mayflower* Landing and the Mayflower Compact

NOV 21–DEC 26, 1620 * 400 YEARS

The 1620 *Mayflower* landing and its eponymous Compact are among the most iconic events in American history. Forty Protestant-Separatist Englishmen, calling themselves Saints and seeking to create a religious safe haven without government interference or worldly distractions, and a larger group of 62 non-Separatists (whom the Saints called Strangers) journeyed together to the New World; collectively, they are now known as the Pilgrims.

The *Mayflower* was originally part of a twin voyage: her sister craft, the *Speedwell*, which left the Netherlands (a place of refuge for the Saints after their initial departure from England in 1608) on July 22, 1620, was abandoned due to issues of seaworthiness. After the ships' consolidation of passengers, the *Mayflower* departed Plymouth, England, on Sept 16, 1620.

Their original destination was the northern Virginia Colony

(modern-day New York). The delayed departure resulted in treacherous travel conditions at the height of Atlantic storm season; following a near shipwreck, the Pilgrims opted to stop north of their destination. After a 66-day journey, the ship landed Nov 21, 1620, on the tip of Cape Cod in what is now Provincetown, MA. On that date, 41 of the ship's male travelers—including Captain Myles Standish, William Bradford and first governor John Carver—signed the 200-word Mayflower Compact, which created "Civil Body Politick" and the first set of European laws and self-governance enacted in what would later become the United States.

Most of the ship's travelers stayed aboard while scouts surveyed the area looking for the best location in which to situate a permanent settlement. On Dec 26, they christened the location of their new settlement Plymouth, the first permanent colony in New England. Due to the harsh weather conditions, the travelers actually continued to live on the ship until after the winter passed. Only 53 passengers and about half the crew survived that brutal winter. Official disembarkation and construction of the Plymouth Colony began on Mar 21, 1621. The colony—eventually absorbed into the Massachusetts Bay Colony—celebrated its survival with the indigenous Wampanoag in 1621. This celebration is the basis for contemporary US Thanksgiving celebrations.

There are many planned 400th-anniversary celebrations—in the United States as well as in England, the Netherlands and the Wampanoag Nation. In the United States, celebrations center on Plymouth and Provincetown. Plymouth 400 commemorations include a *Mayflower* replica visit to Provincetown Harbor, a Mayflower Compact Gala, the Embarkation Festival and a Statehouse Salute, as well as "Our Story: 400 Years of Wampanoag History." The General Society of Mayflower Descendants, with more than 30,000 members, will expand its annual conference, among other special events. The New England Historic Genealogical Society is sponsoring spring and summer 2020 tours to the Netherlands and England. Plymouth's Plymouth Memorial State Park encompasses a waterfront museum as well as the Plymouth Rock—the famous granite boulder that was identified in 1741 as a marker of the original landing place (probably apocryphal). The park offers educational tours from spring through autumn.

For information:

Plymouth 400

6 Main St Extension
Post Office Square
Plymouth, MA 02360
Phone: (508) 812-2020
Web: https://plymouth400inc.org

Provincetown 400

1 High Pole Hill Rd
Provincetown, MA 02657
E-mail: dcappuccio@pilgrim-monument.org
Web: https://provincetown400.com

Plymouth Memorial State Park

79 Water St
Plymouth, MA 02360
Phone: (508) 747-5360
Web: www.mass.gov/locations/pilgrim-memorial-state-park

General Society of Mayflower Descendants

PO Box 3297
Plymouth, MA 02361-3297
Web: www.themayflowersociety.org

New England Historic Genealogical Society

99-101 Newbury St
Boston, MA 02116
Phone: (888) 296-3447
Web: www.americanancestors.org/
heritage-tours

The Boston Massacre

MAR 5, 1770 * 250 YEARS

In a confrontation on Mar 5, 1770, between British troops and a crowd in front of Boston, MA's Customs House, eight soldiers fired on the people, killing three immediately and wounding eight, two of whom later died. Initially called "The Bloody Massacre Perpetrated in King Street" after the title of an engraving by Paul Revere, it later became known as the Boston Massacre. Depictions, reports and propaganda heightened tensions throughout the 13 colonies and helped build support for the American Revolution.

The skirmish began when seven soldiers with fixed bayonets arrived to support the sentry posted outside the Customs House where a crowd of 50–60 people had gathered, taunting the soldiers, daring them to shoot and throwing snow, ice and oyster shells. One soldier, amid the confusion, was jostled and fired his musket. Others, believing the order to fire had been given, also fired. Acting colonial governor Thomas Hutchinson, who had been called to the scene, eventually persuaded the crowd to disperse with the promise that justice would be done.

Defended by a team including John Adams, the commanding officer and six enlisted men were acquitted; two were convicted of manslaughter. In the days that followed, British troops were moved to an island in Boston Harbor. The massacre had antecedents in the Townsend Acts of 1767–68 and the resulting occupation of Boston by British troops in 1768. Tensions were high, due in part to popular resentment of the Acts, which levied tariffs on glass, lead, paints, paper and tea imported from Britain. Colonists saw the import duties as violations of their rights as British subjects, and the Massachusetts House of Representatives started a campaign against the Acts, including calling for boycotting merchants importing these goods. The duties exemplified a slogan adopted by the colonists: "No taxation without representation."

Commemoration events are planned at Boston, MA, centering on the Old State House (the former Customs House and now a museum). The Old State House plans fresh interpretive programming for the 250th anniversary.

For information:

The Bostonian Society

Old State House
206 Washington St
Boston, MA 02109-1773
Web: www.bostonhistory.org

Susan B. Anthony Birth Anniversary

FEB 15, 1820 * 200 YEARS

Born at Adams, MA, abolitionist and temperance activist Susan Brownell Anthony is best known for her foundational contributions to the US women's suffrage movement. She famously said, "Men, their rights and nothing more; women, their rights and nothing less."

Born to a Quaker family, Anthony's parents, Daniel and Lucy, signers of the Seneca Falls Declaration of Sentiments, instilled in her a strong sense of morality and social justice. In her adopted hometown of Rochester, NY, she collaborated with famed abolitionist and lifelong, albeit at times contentious, friend Frederick Douglass. Her most renowned partnership was with Elizabeth Cady Stanton, to whom she was introduced by reformer Amelia Bloomer.

The Anthony-Stanton partnership propelled the fledgling women's suffrage movement into a robust, flourishing one, with Stanton as writer and Anthony as orator. They formed the American Equal Rights Association (AERA, 1866), the National Women's Suffrage Association (1869), and National American Women's Suffrage Association (NAWSA, 1890), edited the weekly *The Revolution* (1868–70), wrote the first three volumes of *History of Women's Suffrage* (1881, 1882, 1886), as well as wrote and presented numerous speeches and articles and organized many rallies, protests and events in their ceaseless advocacy for women's enfranchisement. Notably, Anthony was arrested for attempting to vote in the 1872 presidential election. Of the 16 women arrested for this violation, only Anthony was tried for civil disobedience. Her 1873 trial was a

predetermined farce, wherein the presiding judge prohibited her from testifying, ordered the jury to find her guilty and immediately ended the trial. Her appeal was denied, and she was ordered to pay a $100 fine. Refusing, she never paid a penny.

Although she once stated, "The older I get, the greater power I seem to have in the world; I am like a snowball—the farther I am rolled the more I gain," Anthony eventually retired in 1900, passing NAWSA leadership to Carrie Chapman Catt. She died on Mar 13, 1906, at Rochester, NY, before seeing her lifelong work fulfilled; the 19th Amendment granting women suffrage was ratified in 1920, 14 years after her death. Anthony was the first woman immortalized on US currency: her dollar coin was introduced in 1979.

Maine Statehood Bicentennial

MAR 15, 1820 * 200 YEARS

Though confirmed as part of Massachusetts in the treaty ending the Revolutionary War, the people of Maine formally won secession and became the 23rd state Mar 15, 1820.

Originally home to the Penobscot and Passamaquoddy peoples, the land later saw an influx of Scotch-Irish Protestants (source of the dour, industrious Yankee stereotype), French peoples driven from Nova Scotia by the British in the 18th century and, later, Quebecois. French is the primary language in much of the St. John Valley, and the second language in Maine's industrial cities. Sparsely populated—only three cities have greater than 25,000 inhabitants—the total estimated 2018 population was 1,338,404, with more than 500,000 living in the Portland metropolitan area. The state's racial mix is low: 94.7% white, and per

capita income is the lowest in New England. Maine's traditional industries have declined substantially, including fishing; paper and paper product manufacturing; and textile, shoe and electronic manufacture. The service and tourism industries, however, have grown and lobster production increased. Historically, the state was a shipbuilding center and continues the tradition in producing next-generation naval warships. In addition to its famous picturesque rocky coastline (part of a 3,500-mile total) and extensive forests, Maine has the Appalachian Trail, which starts on Mt. Katahdin. Birthplace of disparate literary giants Henry Wadsworth Longfellow and Stephen King, the state also counts among its achievers film director John Ford and politician Margaret Chase Smith, the first woman to serve in both houses of the US Congress and the first woman to represent Maine in either.

Bicentennial events are kicked off with Statehood Day on Mar 15 and are followed by conferences and other educational events, the Great Schooner Race and a time capsule creation for the future.

For information:

Maine200: Leading the Way

Maine Bicentennial Commission
Business Manager: Bradley Sawyer
Media contact: Kristen Muszynski
   at Kristen.Muszynski@maine.gov
323 State St
Augusta, ME 04330
Phone: (207) 441-2713
E-mail: info@maine200.org
Web: www.maine200.org

> Two states celebrate their 175th statehood anniversaries in 2020: Florida ("The Sunshine State"), admitted to the Union on Mar 3, 1845, as the 27th state; and Texas ("The Lone Star State"), admitted to the Union on Dec 29, 1845, as the 28th state. Both states previously had been part of the Spanish Empire.

US Women Get the Vote

AUG 18, 1920 * 100 YEARS

Arguably the greatest achievement of the US women's rights movement, the ratification on Aug 18, 1920, of the 19th Amendment to the Constitution granting women the right to vote marked the end of a lengthy, contentious struggle lasting more than 70 years. This period, also known as the first wave of feminism, focused on securing women's legal rights, including property ownership, contractual and custodial rights and, most importantly, suffrage, for, as Susan B. Anthony said, "There will never be complete equality until women themselves help make laws and elect lawmakers."

The women's suffrage movement emerged in conjunction with broader social justice efforts of the era. At London, England's 1840 World Anti-Slavery Convention, female attendees, including Elizabeth Cady Stanton and Lucretia Mott, were denied participation. In response, the two coordinated the Seneca Falls Convention on Women's Rights (July 19–20, 1848), where women's suffrage was first formally espoused in the convention's eponymous Declaration of Sentiments. The document mimicked the Declaration of Independence in its articulation of the nascent movement's varied goals; its most contentiously debated resolution was the 9th, which stated, "*Resolved*, That it is the duty of the women of this country to secure to themselves their sacred right to the elective franchise." Many attendees were initially opposed; following a heated debate—including, crucially, Frederick Douglass's impassioned speech—a majority voted for its inclusion.

The Civil War redirected suffragists' attention; many focused on supporting the war's effort to end slavery. At war's end, Stanton and Anthony, the movement's seminal figures, formed the American Equal Rights Association (AERA, 1866), which advocated for universal suffrage regardless of sex or race. Subsequent debates over the 14th and 15th amendments caused a huge rift among supporters. Gender was explicitly stated in the Constitution for the first time in the 14th Amendment, Section II (1868), which identified citizens as male; in response, some pushed for the inclusion of the word *sex* in the 15th Amendment, while others resisted. This schism resulted in the disbanding of the AERA and the formation of two competing organizations: the more progressive National Women's Suffrage Association led by Stanton and Anthony and the more conservative American Women's Suffrage Association led by Lucy Stone and her husband, Harry Brown Blackwell (1869). Ultimately, the 15th Amendment (1870) did not enshrine women's suffrage, stating, "The rights of citizens of the United States to vote shall not be denied or abridged by the United States or by any State on the account of race, color or previous condition of servitude," which resulted in a lengthy hostility between the two groups. The factions did not reunite until merging into the National American Women's Suffrage Association (NAWSA) in 1890.

In 1878, Congress first introduced a women's suffrage amendment;

thereafter, the amendment, verbatim, was introduced annually until its eventual passage. The text is identical to the 15th Amendment but replaces "race, color, or previous condition of servitude" with "sex." In the intervening years between the amendment's first congressional introduction and its passage, much occurred. Sixteen territories and states extended the electoral franchise to women, starting with Wyoming (1869) and Utah (1870). Anthony was arrested for attempting to vote in the 1872 presidential election and fined $100, which she refused to pay. Frances E. Willard's Women's Christian Temperance Union began actively supporting women's suffrage, much like early suffragists who advocated abolitionism. Leadership changes in the NAWSA after Anthony's retirement (1900) revitalized the organization. President Carrie Chapman Catt's grassroots reorganizations increased support. NAWSA's congressional committee chair Alice Paul's suffrage march on the eve of Woodrow Wilson's inauguration led to the formation of the National Women's Party (NWP), the movement's radical arm. In 1917, Paul, Lucy Burns and other protestors were imprisoned; their protests, picketing, imprisonment, hunger strikes and subsequent mistreatment increased sympathy for the movement.

In 1919, the 19th Amendment was finally passed by both houses

of Congress. Some credit women's involvement in both the workplace and war efforts during WWI for the change in congressional inclination. On Aug 18, 1920, Tennessee, by one vote from formerly opposed Rep. Harry Burn upon the urging of his mother to vote yea, became the 36th state to ratify the amendment; on Aug 26, 1920, Secretary of State Bainbridge Colby officially proclaimed the 19th Amendment part of the Constitution. Following its ratification, the NAWSA became the League of Women Voters. The Sheppard-Towner Act, which provided federal funding for maternity care, was passed in 1921 to appeal to newly enfranchised women voters. In 1923, the NWP first proposed the Equal Rights Amendment (as yet unratified). As with all waves of feminism, the movement declined in the years following their crowning achievement and did not reemerge in force until the 1960s.

Founding of the National Football League

AUG 20, 1920 ∗ 100 YEARS

Professional football emerged as an increasingly popular spectator sport in the early 1900s, and its star was 1912 Olympic decathlon gold medalist Jim Thorpe, who played for the Ohio League, drawing huge crowds to Canton and creating a market for the game. With able-bodied men being shipped off to war in 1917, teams began to recruit available players from neighboring communities and adjacent states.

Wanting to regulate recruitment and schedules, seven team investors gathered at the Jordan and Hupmobile Auto Showroom in Canton, OH, on Aug 20, 1920, to form the new

America Professional Football Conference. Thorpe was elected its first president on Sept 17, and a new league was born, comprising 14 teams, from Ohio and surrounding states: the Canton Bulldogs, the Cleveland Tigers, the Dayton Triangles, the Akron Professionals, the Rochester (NY) Jeffersons, the Rock Island (IL) Independents, the Muncie (IN) Flyers, the Decatur (IL) Staleys, the Chicago (IL) Cardinals, the Buffalo (NY) All-Americans, the Chicago (IL) Tigers, the Columbus Panhandles, the Detroit (MI) Heralds and the Hammond (IN) Pros.

In 1922, after a series of name changes, the conference was renamed the National Football League and today has 32 teams. Dubbed its "Fantennial," the NFL's yearlong NFL100 initiative began during Super Bowl LIII in 2019 with the airing of the immensely popular "The 100 Year Game" commercial starring 34 gridiron greats. The NFL kicked off its 100th season of play on Sept 5, 2019, when the Chicago Bears (née the Decatur Staleys) hosted the Green Bay Packers in a matchup of the only two current franchises that were around in 1920.

NFL100 initiatives continue at Super Bowl LIV, on Feb 2, 2020, in Miami, FL. In Canton, the Pro Football Hall of Fame estimates that between 5,000 and 10,000 legends will attend its Centennial Celebration on Sept 16–21, 2020, kicking off with a splashy ceremony akin to the Olympics opening ceremony, with former players parading together, organized by team. Every former NFL player is invited to the Centennial Celebration.

For information:

National Football League
Alex Riethmiller, Vice President of
    Communications
Phone: (310) 840-4635
E-mail: alex.riethmiller@nfl.com
Web: www.nfl.com/100

Pro Football Hall of Fame
Pete Fierle, Chief of Staff and
    Senior VP of Communications
2121 George Halas Dr NW
Canton, OH 44708
Phone: (330) 588-3622
E-mail: Pete.Fierle@
    ProFootballHOF.com
Web: www.profootballhof.com

The Kent State Shootings

MAY 4, 1970 * 50 YEARS

On this day in northeastern Ohio, members of the Ohio National Guard fired M-1 military rifles at unarmed protestors on the campus of Kent State University, killing four students aged 19 to 20.

Antiwar activism, particularly among college students whose peers and siblings were being drafted, had swelled across the country in the preceding days since President Richard Nixon announced US troops were being sent into Cambodia. On May 2, protesters set fire to the Kent State ROTC building. By May 3, 1,200 National Guardsmen occupied the campus and, with bayonets and teargas, drove back students who were blocking traffic. The governor banned all demonstrations. Regardless, nearly 3,000 people congregated on the university commons to hear antiwar speakers at a scheduled rally at noon on May 4. Kent State police ordered the assembly to disperse and were met with chants and rock throwing.

The guard effectively drove away the crowd with teargas and bayonets.

For unknown reasons, 28 guardsmen who had retreated up a hill fired their weapons into the crowd, killing two demonstrators and two bystanders and wounding nine others in the Prentice Hall parking lot. Allison Krause, Jeffrey Miller, Sandra Scheuer and William Knox Schroeder were the fatalities. The shootings—captured by John Filo's Pulitzer Prize–winning photograph of a 14-year-old girl wailing over the body of a victim who had been shot in the mouth—gelled the cultural rift in the United States, sparking more national protests and a four-million-student strike that closed hundreds of colleges and universities across the country. At the same time, it rallied conservatives, dubbed the "Silent Majority," to elect Nixon to a second term in 1972. Moreover, the incident confronted Americans' ideas of what it means to be patriotic.

Kent State University's yearlong 50th commemoration began in 2019 and continues with educational programs and events that will culminate May 4, 2020, with a midnight-to-noon candlelight vigil in the parking lot where the students fell followed by a noontime 50th commemoration program on the commons with nationally known speakers, musicians and poets.

For information:

50th Commemoration
Ron Flauhaus
May 4th, 50th Commemoration
    Project Manager
Office of the President
800 E Summit St
Kent, OH 44242
Phone: (330) 672-2423
E-mail: rflauha1@kent.edu
Web: www.kent.edu/may4kentstate50

Oklahoma City Bombing

APR 19, 1995 * 25 YEARS

In the worst domestic terrorism incident since the 1920 Wall Street bombing, a truck bomb exploded outside the Alfred P. Murrah Federal Building at Oklahoma City, OK, at 9:02 am, killing 168 people, 19 of them children at a day care center; a nurse died of head injuries sustained while helping in rescue efforts. The injured numbered almost 700. The bomb was comprised of 13 barrels packed with ammonium nitrate fertilizer and explosives and was estimated to have weighed 5,000 pounds. It was contained in a rented truck. The blast ripped off the north face of the nine-story building, leaving a 20-foot-wide crater and debris two stories high. (Structurally unsound and increasingly dangerous, the bombed building was razed May 23.)

The perpetrators were Timothy J. McVeigh and Terry L. Nichols, disaffected army vets and white nationalists. McVeigh was a decorated Gulf War army vet who claimed to have acted in retaliation to federal law enforcement actions at the fatal Ruby Ridge stand-off in August 1992 and the Branch Davidian compound stand-off and conflagration at Waco, TX, exactly two years before. McVeigh was convicted of the bombing and executed June 11, 2001. Nichols was convicted of murder and conspiracy charges and was sentenced to life in prison.

The nation and the world reached out to Oklahoma City with rescue workers, aid and compassion. And many were moved by the famous photo of firefighter Chris Fields cradling mortally injured infant Baylee Almon. The photo, taken by Charles Porter, won a 1996 Pulitzer Prize. The Oklahoma City National Memorial was constructed on the site of the demolished Alfred P. Murrah Federal Building and was put on the National Register of Historic Places upon completion. The memorial includes 168 empty chairs to represent the victims, a reflecting pool, the Survivors' Wall constructed out of reclaimed slabs from the Murrah building and the Survivor Tree—a 100-plus-year-old tree that survived the bombing. Each year, on the anniversary of the bombing, a remembrance event is held, with names of the 168 killed read and 168 seconds of silence observed. The annual commemorations will be expanded for the 25th anniversary.

For information:

Oklahoma City National Memorial and Museum

MaryAnn Eckstein, Director of Media
620 N Harvey Ave
Oklahoma City, OK 73102
Phone: (405) 235-3313
E-mail: mae@oklahomacity nationalmemorial.org
Web: https://oklahomacitynational memorial.org

Spotlight on People

This portion of Spotlight presents a selection of notables observing a major birth or death anniversary in 2020. Several are covered more fully in "Spotlight on World Anniversaries" and "Spotlight on American Anniversaries": Ludwig van Beethoven, Florence Nightingale, Vladimir Lenin, Anne Frank and Susan B. Anthony. And see the main text for even more historic birth anniversaries.

World History

Tomás de Torquemada

Birth * Oct 14, 1420 * 600 years

Dominican monk, confessor to Isabella I, who was appointed Grand Inquisitor of Spain in 1483. As Grand Inquisitor, Torquemada expanded the Spanish Inquisition, establishing tribunals all over the country. His remit was to eradicate heresy, and the austere zeal with which he pursued this aim made his name feared at the time and hated throughout the centuries since. Once the Muslims, who supported religious tolerance, left Spain in 1492, Torquemada pushed for expulsion of Jews, which King Ferdinand and Queen Isabella accomplished with their Alhambra Decree on Mar 31, 1492, soon after. Torquemada, who himself was of Jewish background, sought those remaining Jews who had converted to Catholicism—*conversos*—as he was suspicious of the genuineness of their conversion. Estimates vary of the numbers tortured and/or executed under Torquemada's authority. As many as 2,000 people may have been executed. Torquemada was born at Valladolid, Kingdom of Castile, and died at Ávila, Spain, Sept 16, 1498.

Guy Fawkes

Birth * Apr 13, 1570 * 450 years

Englishman who, along with a small group of fellow Catholics, conspired to blow up England's Houses of Parliament and kill its Protestant members—including King James I—on Nov 5, 1605. The "Gunpowder Plot" was foiled the night before, and Nov 5 is commemorated as a day of delivery each year with bonfires, fireworks and burning of life-size Fawkes effigies (called "guys"—origin of the English word). Born to a wealthy Protestant family in York, England, Fawkes converted to Catholicism later in life. After several days of torture in November 1605—in which he broke down and named co-conspirators, Fawkes was put on trial Jan 27, 1606, and found guilty of high treason. His sentence was to be half-hung, disemboweled and then decapitated. On Jan 31, 1606, at London, Fawkes leapt off the scaffold, breaking his neck and thus escaping the full course of his execution.

Friedrich Engels

Birth * Nov 28, 1820 * 200 years

German philosopher and social theorist best known for his lifelong collaboration with Karl Marx, Engels was born at Barmen, Prussia (Germany). With Marx, Engels cofounded the German Workers' Society (1847) and cowrote *The Holy Family* (1845), *The German Ideology* (1846), and, famously, *The Communist Manifesto* (1848); following Marx's death, Engels served as the foremost authority on Marxism, editing the second and third posthumously published volumes of *Das Kapital*. A widely published journalist and social critic in his own right, works such as *The Condition of the Working Class in England* (1844/5) and *Anti-Dühring* (1878) firmly established Engels's place in in the pantheon of great social theorists. His oeuvre, particularly *Anti-Dühring*'s commentary on Marxian thought, profoundly influenced Soviet Marxist-Leninist ideology. He died Aug 5, 1895, at London, England.

Mietek Pemper

Birth * Mar 24, 1920 * 100 years

In his position as personal typist to Amon Goeth, commandant of the Plaszow forced labor camp in Poland, Pemper learned that all labor camp inmates not engaged in work on the war effort would be liquidated. He persuaded industrialist Oskar Schindler to convert his enamel works to the production of grenade parts. He then falsified records to suggest that certain Plaszow inmates had essential manufacturing skills and compiled lists of inmates to be transferred to Schindler's factory. These, along with names compiled by Itzhak Stern, later became known as "Schindler's list." The scheme saved the lives of 1,200 people. Born at Krakow, Poland, Pemper died at Augsburg, Germany, on June 7, 2011.

American History

Crispus Attucks

Death * Mar 5, 1770 * 250 years

Little can definitively be ascertained about Attucks, save that he was the first victim of the Boston Massacre, credited (or blamed, depending upon the perspective) with leading the event. Born around 1723, Attucks was most likely a sailor and was generally held to be of mixed racial ancestry—African, Native American and white. Attucks may once have been a slave from Framingham, MA. Black abolitionists inaugurated "Crispus Attucks Day" in 1858, and a monument to Attucks and his compatriots was erected on the Boston Common in 1888 amid controversy over their status as villains or martyrs, "the first to defy, the first to die."

William Clark

Birth * Aug 1, 1770 * 250 years

The soldier, explorer and public servant was born at Caroline County, VA. He served seven years in the US Army and then gained his lasting fame when Meriwether Lewis asked him to join an expedition exploring the Louisiana Territory (1803–06). Clark was an able leader and contributed detailed maps and animal illustrations on the journey. A grateful president Thomas Jefferson made Clark brigadier general of militia for the Louisiana Territory (1807–13) and superintendent of Indian Affairs (1807–38). Clark was also governor of the Missouri Territory (1813–20) and surveyor general for Illinois, Missouri and Arkansas (1824–25). Clark foresaw the tension between US interests and the native peoples of the western United States, and he urged the United States to treat native tribes with respect. Clark died at St. Louis, MO, on Sept 1, 1838.

James K. Polk

Birth * Nov 2, 1795 * 225 years

The 11th president of the United States was born at Mecklenburg County, NC. A compromise candidate at the 1844 Democratic Party convention, Polk was awarded the nomination on the ninth ballot. He served one term of office: Mar 4, 1845–Mar 3, 1849, but those four years were eventful and productive. Controversially, the United States waged war on Mexico from 1846 to 1848, and the victory gained land that would become Nevada, California and Utah, along with most of Arizona and parts of Colorado and New Mexico. (In 1848, the US House of Representatives formally censured Polk for going to war without congressional approval.) And during his administration the Oregon Territory was established (and the northern border of the United States was set at the 49th Parallel). This expansive growth to the Pacific Ocean is Polk's major legacy. He declined to be a candidate for a second term and declared himself "exceedingly relieved" at the completion of his presidency. He died shortly thereafter at Nashville, TN, June 15, 1849.

William Tecumseh Sherman

Birth * Feb 8, 1820 * 200 years

West Point–educated Union general during the Civil War, Sherman was an early practitioner of psychological warfare, infamous in the South and popular in the North for his "March to the Sea," the invasion of Georgia in 1864 aimed at destroying southern infrastructure and popular support for the war. While serving as commanding general of the army from 1869 to 1884, he declined the Republican presidential nomination twice but enjoyed a reputation in retirement as a public speaker and writer in defense of the Union cause. His observations in a letter deriding the glories of battle were famously shortened to "war is hell." Born at Lancaster, OH, Sherman died at New York, NY, Feb 14, 1891.

J. Edgar Hoover

Birth * Jan 1, 1895 * 125 years

The legendary law enforcement officer was born John Edgar Hoover at Washington, DC. He led the Palmer Raids in 1919–20 and was director of the FBI from 1924 to 1972. During his time as director, Hoover practiced modern investigative techniques, improved FBI agent training and increased FBI funding from Congress. His legacy was marred, however, by harassment, surveillance and illegal wiretapping of public figures he deemed undesirable, from civil rights leaders like Martin Luther King, Jr, to pop stars like John Lennon. Hoover died May 2, 1972, at Washington, DC.

James Farmer

Birth * Jan 12, 1920 * 100 years

Civil rights leader, born at Marshall, TX. Farmer was one of the founders of CORE, the Congress of Racial Equality, a volunteer organization established in 1942 in Chicago, IL, to improve race relations and eliminate discriminatory practices. A student of Gandhian principles, Farmer led the nonviolent fight to desegregate buses and terminals in the South in 1961, known as the Freedom Rides. He received the Presidential Medal of Freedom in 1998. Farmer died at Fredericksburg, VA, July 9, 1999. US representative John Lewis, a fellow civil rights leader, said of Farmer, "He was one of the founding fathers not just of the New South, but of the New America."

John Paul Stevens

Birth * Apr 20, 1920 * 100 years

Named to the Supreme Court in 1975 (retired 2010), many considered him its liberal anchor, although he can be characterized as a judicial centrist. Born at Chicago, IL, Stevens graduated from the University of Chicago (1941) and, after WWII naval service, Northwestern University's School of Law (1947) followed by a Supreme Court clerkship. In private practice, he specialized in litigation and antitrust law before being appointed in 1970 to the US Seventh Circuit Court of Appeals. His significant majority opinions include *Chevron v. Natural Resources Defense Council* and *Hamdan v. Rumsfeld*; he is known for dissents in *Bush v. Gore* and *Citizens United v. FEC*. He died July 16, 2019, at Fort Lauderdale, FL.

Major Thomas McGuire, Jr

Birth * Aug 1, 1920 * 100 years

WWII flying ace killed in action over the Philippines on Jan 7, 1945. Posthumously awarded the Congressional Medal of Honor, he also received the Distinguished Service Cross with three silver stars, six Distinguished Flying Crosses, and 15 Air Medals. He survived being shot down once and holds the record for the second highest number of US "kills" in the war: 38. Born at Ridgewood, NJ, he attended Georgia Institute of Technology but left in 1941 to enlist in the US Army Air Corps. Assigned in 1942 to fly patrols in the Aleutian Islands, he requested transfer to see combat action and was sent to the South Pacific in 1943.

Timothy Leary

Birth * Oct 22, 1920 * 100 years

Timothy Francis Leary was born at Springfield, MA. Prominent psychologist and professor at Harvard, Leary became an icon of the countercultural movement in the 1960s. He lost his professorship after giving a hallucinogenic drug, psilocybin, to students. Leary was arrested numerous times, and on one occasion, while being held at a California prison, he was forced to submit to a personality test that he had designed himself several years earlier. He continued to advocate the use of LSD in the pursuit of spiritual and political freedom and simply for the fun of it, until his death, of prostate cancer, May 31, 1996, at Beverly Hills, CA. Ten months after his death, Leary's ashes were rocketed into space to orbit Earth.

Literature

William Wordsworth

Birth * Apr 7, 1770 * 250 years

Born at Cockermouth, Cumberland, England, Wordsworth was one of the world's greatest lyric poets. Known for his short, dramatic poems, he collaborated with Samuel Taylor Coleridge on the initially anonymously published *Lyrical Ballads* (1798), which opened with Coleridge's "The Rime of the Ancient Mariner" and ended with Wordsworth's "Tintern Abbey." Later editions listed Wordsworth as author. The compilation presented a new literary style distinct from the diction and forms of 18th-century poetry, one based on the real language of people and that explored the relationship between the person and the natural world. It is widely regarded the first and one of the greatest pieces of the Romantic literary era. Wordsworth's magnum opus *The Prelude*, a semi-autobiographical collection, first completed in 1805 and later revised and expanded over several decades, was published posthumously in 1850. Britain's poet laureate from 1843 until his death, Wordsworth died of pleurisy Apr 23, 1850, at Rydal Mount, Westmoreland, England. "Poetry," he said, "is the spontaneous overflow of powerful feelings: it takes its origin from emotion recollected in tranquility."

John Keats

Birth * Oct 31, 1795 * 225 years

The Romantic poet was born at London, England. He was a struggling medical student when he embarked on his poetic career. Despite financial worries and increasing debility due to tuberculosis, Keats was able to pen a significant body of work—most famously, his odes. "Ode on a Grecian Urn" ("'Beauty is truth, truth beauty,'—that is all/Ye know on earth, and all ye need to know.") and "Ode to a Nightingale" are especially remembered. Keats wrote to his betrothed, Fanny Brawne, in 1820: "If I should die . . . I have left no immortal work behind me—nothing to make my friends proud of my memory—but I have loved the principle of beauty in all things, and if I had had time I would have made myself remembered." Keats died at the age of 25 at Rome, Italy, Feb 23, 1821, believing that he had no audience, but he is now considered one of the greatest English poets.

Anne Brontë

Birth * Jan 17, 1820 * 200 years

Author of *Agnes Grey* (1847) and *The Tenant of Wildfell Hall* (1848) published under the pseudonym Acton Bell, Anne was the youngest of the famous and successful Brontë sisters, Charlotte (*Jane Eyre*) and Emily (*Wuthering Heights*). Well-educated sixth child of an Anglican clergyman, she grew up on the Yorkshire moors, briefly attending boarding school before working as a governess, experiences that doubtless provided her with novelistic background material. Her interest and talents as a writer were cultivated early in collaborations with siblings on tales of imaginary lands. Contemporary critical assessment has lauded her work for its strongly feminist perspective. Born at Thornton, England, Anne died of tuberculosis May 28, 1849, at Scarborough, England, just a few months after Emily and brother Branwell died of the same affliction.

John Bartlett

Birth * June 14, 1820 * 200 years

American editor and compiler (*Bartlett's Familiar Quotations* [1855]) was born at Plymouth, MA. Though he had little formal education, he created one of the most-used reference works of the English language. No quotation of his own is among the more than 25,000 listed today, but in the preface to the first edition he wrote that the object of this work "originally made without any view of publication" was to show "the obligation our language owes to various authors for numerous phrases and familiar quotations which have become 'household words.'" Bartlett died at Cambridge, MA, Dec 3, 1905.

Isaac Asimov

Birth * Jan 2, 1920 * 100 years

Although Isaac Asimov was one of the world's best-known writers of science fiction, his almost 500 books dealt with subjects as diverse as the Bible, works for preschoolers, college course work, mysteries, chemistry, biology, limericks, Shakespeare, Gilbert and Sullivan and modern history. During his prolific career he helped to elevate science fiction from pulp magazines to a more intellectual level. A self-taught reader, he sold his first story at the age of 18 to *Amazing Stories*: "Marooned off Vesta" (October 1938). His works include the influential *Foundation* trilogy, *The*

Robots of Dawn, Robots and Empire, Nemesis, Murder at the ABA (in which he himself was a character), *The Gods Themselves* and *I, Robot*, in which he posited the famous Three Laws of Robotics. His *The Clock We Live On* is an accessible explanation of the origins of calendars. Asimov was born near Smolensk, Russia, and died at New York, NY, Apr 6, 1992. After his death, Gerard Piel, former publisher of *Scientific American*, eulogized in *The New York Times*: "What H.G. Wells did for public appreciation and understanding of science in the first half of the 20th century, Isaac Asimov did in the second half."

Howard Nemerov

Birth * Feb 29, 1920 * 100 years

Nemerov was the third poet laureate of the US, from 1988 to 1990. Among his works are 26 books, including five novels. He won a Pulitzer Prize and the National Book Award for his *Collected Works* in 1978. He was also a recipient of the National Medal of the Arts. As poet laureate he penned verses commemorating the 200th anniversary of the US Congress and the launch of the space shuttle *Atlantis*. Nemerov was born at New York, NY, and died July 5, 1991, at St. Louis, MO.

P.D. James

Birth * Aug 3, 1920 * 100 years

Born at Oxford, England, Phyllis Dorothy James is considered one of the best crime novelists of the late 20th century—creating in-depth psychological dramas in such works as *Cover Her Face* and *Original Sin*. Her early career in medical administration and at the Office of Home Affairs lent medical and procedural credence to her novels. Most of her

canon features poet and Scotland Yard detective Adam Dalgliesh. In an interview late in her career, she averred, "Detective stories do affirm the sanctity of each individual life and the possibility of human justice." James was a member of the Royal Society of Literature (1987) and Royal Society of the Arts (1983). Inducted into the Order of the British Empire (1983) and made a baroness (1991) and Commander of the British Empire (1992), James died Nov 27, 2014, at Oxford.

Ray Bradbury

Birth * Aug 22, 1920 * 100 years

Born at Waukegan, IL, Ray Bradbury was one of the preeminent science fiction/fantasy writers of the 20th century. His body of work, which critiqued social mores and depicted the consequences of unfettered technology, is considered timeless and transcends generations. Notable works include *Something Wicked This Way Comes*, *The Body Electric* and *Fahrenheit 451*, his most famous novel. Awarded a Special Citation by the Pulitzer Board (2007) for his oeuvre, Bradbury died June 5, 2012, at Los Angeles, CA. He once wrote, "Re-create the world in your own image and make it better for your having been here."

Frank Herbert

Birth * Oct 8, 1920 * 100 years

A writer who started his career as a journalist, Herbert published his first

story in 1945 and went on to write the phenomenally successful science fiction novel *Dune* (1965) and its five sequels. Initially refused by numerous publishers, *Dune* eventually sold more than 12 million copies during Herbert's lifetime; won the Hugo and the Nebula, science fiction's highest awards; and spurred a franchise in screen adaptations, comics and board, video and role-play games. Readers admire Herbert's creation of a complex, detailed world and the novels' reflection of his deep interest in ecology and the intersection of religious demagoguery and personal charisma. Born at Tacoma, WA, Herbert died Feb 11, 1986, at Madison, WI.

Children's Literature

Anna Sewell

Birth * Mar 30, 1820 * 200 years

Anna Sewell's legacy resides in the only book she ever wrote, a book she didn't live to see blossom as a classic beloved for more than 100 years. Born at Great Yarmouth, England, into a family of Quakers, Anna Sewell taught and engaged in charitable activities. She became lame as a teenager, and her health in general disintegrated over the years due to an unknown affliction. As a result of her lameness, she relied on horses and developed excellent equestrian

skills. She noted with alarm the abuses and injustices horses suffered. This abuse prompted her to author *Black Beauty*—dictated to her mother off and on over six years. *Black Beauty: The Autobiography of a Horse* was published in December 1877 and sold 12,000 in its first year. Sewell, though, died at Old Catton, Norfolk, England, Apr 25, 1878. *Black Beauty*, actually intended for adults, is now a children's classic and one of the bestselling English novels ever published. (Tragically, in 1984, the Quaker graveyard where Sewell and her family were buried was destroyed for private development. Their headstones were recovered and mounted on an adjoining wall.)

Christopher Robin Milne

Birth * Aug 21, 1920 * 100 years

A bookseller by trade, Milne was the inspiration for the character of Christopher Robin in the Winnie-the-Pooh books authored by his father, A.A. Milne. Christopher Milne was enamored of Winnipeg the black bear at the London Zoo, and this "Winnie" along with Milne's stuffed toy animals (including Eeyore, Piglet and Roo) came to life first in a poem in *When We Were Very Young* (1924) and then in a series of beloved books. The stories were set in a fictionalized Ashdown Forest, where A.A. Milne had bought a country retreat in 1925. Christopher Milne was born at London, England, and died Apr 20, 1996, at Totnes, England.

Journalism

David Brinkley

Birth * July 10, 1920 * 100 years

Born at Wilmington, NC, David Brinkley was one of the most recognizable faces in American broadcast

journalism for more than 50 years. He was NBC's first White House correspondent, and his outstanding coverage of the 1956 Democratic and Republican national conventions landed him the anchor job on NBC's nightly TV newscast, paired with Chet Huntley until 1970. In 1981 Brinkley moved to ABC, creating a Sunday morning interview show called "This Week with David Brinkley." His 1995 memoir was titled *David Brinkley: 11 Presidents, 4 Wars, 22 Political Conventions, 1 Moon Landing, 3 Assassinations, 2,000 Weeks of News and Other Stuff on Television, and 18 Years of Growing Up in North Carolina*. He died on June 12, 2003, at Houston, TX.

Ernest Taylor (Ernie) Pyle

Death * Apr 18, 1945 * 75 years

Ernie Pyle was born at Dana, IN, Aug 3, 1900, and began his career in journalism in 1923. After serving as managing editor of the *Washington Daily News*, in 1935 he returned to his first journalistic love of working as a roving reporter. His column was syndicated by nearly 200 newspapers and often focused on figures behind the news. His reports of the bombing of London in 1940 and subsequent reports from Africa, Sicily, Italy and France earned him a Pulitzer Prize in 1944. But he was also admired by the GIs he reported on. General Omar Bradley said, "My men always fight better when Ernie's around." Pyle was killed by a Japanese sniper at the Pacific island of Ie Shima, Apr 18, 1945, during the Battle of Okinawa, and was buried with his helmet on. His death stunned the soldiers he was embedded with as well as the nation, and the slain journalist received warm eulogies from president Harry Truman, former first lady Eleanor Roosevelt, general Dwight D. Eisenhower and others. In his honor, the unit he was with erected a monument with the words, "On this spot the 77th Infantry Division lost a Buddy. Ernie Pyle, 18 April 1945." The monument is tended today by US Marines.

Comics

Hank Ketcham

Birth * Mar 14, 1920 * 100 years

Born at Seattle, WA, Henry King Ketcham dropped out of the University of Washington in 1938 to try his hand at cartoon animation. He worked with Walter Lantz Productions ("Woody Woodpecker") and Walt Disney. After World War II, during which he created the comic strip "Half Hitch," he became a freelancer and created the tow-headed, mischievous imp known as "Dennis the Menace." Dennis was based on Ketcham's own son Dennis. The comic strip began on Mar 14, 1951, and soon took American newspapers and the public by a storm. The strip inspired a television show and a movie and is still read today in more than 1,000 newspapers around the world. Ketcham retired in 1994 and died June 1, 2001, at Carmel, CA.

Art, Architecture and Design

Maxfield Parrish

Birth * July 25, 1870 * 150 years

Born at Philadelphia, PA, Frederick Maxfield Parrish become one of the most beloved and popular illustrators of the first half of the twentieth century, creating fantastical dreamscapes for children's books, calendars, magazine covers and bestselling prints and posters. After training at the Pennsylvania Academy of the Arts and the Drexel Institute of Art, Parrish became an in-demand cover illustrator to the top magazines of the day—especially *Scribners*. His ethereally cyan blue skies would win such notice that "Maxfield Parrish blue" became a universally recognized color. He illustrated such classic children's books as *Poems of Childhood* (1904), *The Arabian Nights* (1909) and *The Knave of Hearts* (1925). In the 1920s, his prints and calendar art (not to mention his hotel lobby murals such as "Old King Cole" in the bar of the same name at the St. Regis Hotel in New York City) made him the bestselling artist of the day. His painting *Daybreak* (1922) sold more than 200,000 prints and remains his most popular work. In his later years, Parrish almost exclusively painted quiet landscapes. He died at Plainfield, NH, on Mar 10, 1966.

Josef Hoffmann

Birth * Dec 15, 1870 * 150 years

The acclaimed architect and designer was born at Pirnitz, Austria-Hungary. He moved to Vienna, Austria, in 1892 to complete his schooling and in 1899 was appointed professor in that city's school of applied arts—the Kunstgewerbeschule. He was a cofounder of the Vienna Secession and the Wiener Werkstätte. With Gustav Klimt and Koloman Moser, Hoffmann articulated an influential, avant-garde modernist style that synthesized architecture, art and crafts. Against the prevailing flowery and ornate art nouveau style, Hoffman prioritized straight lines and cubes, earning the nickname "Little Square." The work of the Vienna Secession and Wiener Werkstätte was ahead of its time. Many Hoffmann designs in furniture and domestic items are still in production. He died May 7, 1956, at Vienna.

Saul Bass

Birth * May 8, 1920 * 100 years

The graphic designer and creator of film title sequences was born at New York, NY. His first work in Hollywood was in marketing, designing film posters, but a dramatic opening credit sequence for *The Man with the Golden Arm* (1955) soon made him in demand for that craft. Bass was able with concise, arresting graphics to immediately signal the tone and theme of a film (opening credits before the 1950s being prosaic efforts). Title sequences in his hands became an integral part of the film. Bass is known for work with Alfred Hitchcock (in *Vertigo*, a startling close-up of a woman's face followed by a mesmerizing run of colored spirals and mandalas) and later in his career for Martin Scorsese. He received an Oscar for the documentary short "Why Man Creates" in 1968. As an in-demand graphic designer, Bass continued to create iconic film posters as well as logos for the YMCA, Kleenex, AT&T, Warner Communications and others. Bass died Apr 25, 1996, at Los Angeles, CA.

Spotlight on People

Fashion

Cristóbal Balenciaga Eizaguirre

Birth * Jan 21, 1895 * 125 years

The couturier's couturier was born at Getaria, Spain, the son of a fisherman and a seamstress. His first boutique opened in 1914 at the resort city of San Sebastián, Spain, and he soon expanded to Madrid and Barcelona. The Spanish Civil War forced his move to Paris, France, where he founded the House of Balenciaga in 1937 and became a critical and popular success. After WWII, perfectionist Balenciaga moved away from the hour-glass "New Look" offered by Christian Dior—his silhouette was more fluid and streamlined. Key Balenciaga pieces—all expertly tailored and flattering—were the cocoon coat (with only one seam), the bubble skirt and the chemise/sack dress. Key elements were the bracelet sleeve and the use of black lace over pink fabric. The "King of Fashion" closed his firm in 1968 and died Mar 23, 1972, at Valencia, Spain, universally mourned. His pupils included Oscar de la Renta, Andre Courreges and Hubert de Givenchy. The House of Balenciaga was revived in 1986.

Music

Ravi Shankar

Apr 7, 1920 * 100 years

Sitar player and composer who introduced Indian music to the Western world, born at Varanasi, India. He began performing music and dance as a child and was soon recognized and trained by the head musician of the Maihar court. A key figure in the movement to bring world music to the attention of mass audiences, he toured extensively and taught around the world—influencing such musicians as George Harrison and The Beatles, John Coltrane and Philip Glass. Shankar also used his music to bring attention to the plight of the poor around the world, especially in Bangladesh. He died at Long Beach, CA, Dec 12, 2012.

Carmen McRae

Birth * Apr 8, 1920 * 100 years

After winning an amateur contest at Harlem's legendary Apollo Theatre in her hometown of New York City, McRae went on to become a noted and influential jazz singer who toured the world. Inspired by Billie Holiday, she sang and/or collaborated with jazz greats such as Mercer Ellington, George Shearing, Dave Brubeck, Benny Carter and, later, a young Harry Connick Jr. McRae recorded more than 60 albums and was nominated seven times for a Grammy. The recipient of a Jazz Master Award from the National Endowment of the Arts in 1994, she died later that year on Nov 10, at Beverly Hills, CA.

Peggy Lee

Birth * May 26, 1920 * 100 years

Singer, songwriter and actress Peggy Lee was born Norma Deloris Egstrom at Jamestown, ND. She got her start singing on a Fargo, ND, radio station and was soon hired by Benny Goodman to sing with his band. Known for her simple, jazzy style as well as her sex appeal. Her biggest hits were "Fever" (1958) and "Is That All There Is?" (1969). She is perhaps best remembered for the songs that she cowrote and performed in Disney's *Lady and the Tramp*. She continued to perform until the 1990s, when poor health forced her to retire. She died Jan 21, 2002, at Los Angeles, CA.

Charlie Parker

Birth * Aug 29, 1920 * 100 years

Jazz giant Charlie "Yardbird" Parker was born at Kansas City, KS. The man who later became known simply as "Bird" was mostly self-taught—on an alto saxophone his mother gave him when he was 11. His career took him from jam sessions in Kansas City to New York (in 1939), where he met Dizzy Gillespie and others who were creating an innovative style of jazz that would become known as bop or bebop. Influential to other jazz artists, instrumentalists and the Beat Generation, Parker was a master improviser dubbed "the cool one" by producer Norman Granz. Parker struggled with mental health issues (especially when his young daughter died in 1954) as well as with alcohol and heroin. He died at Rochester, NY, Mar 12, 1955, at age 34, and was honored in Harlem with a wake and memorial concert before being sent back to Kansas City for burial. The popular New York City jazz club Birdland (established in 1949) was named for Parker, a frequent headliner.

Dave Brubeck

Birth * Dec 6, 1920 * 100 years

With his innovative and forever intuitive sound as both a pianist and composer, Dave Brubeck became one of the biggest stars of American jazz in the 1950s and '60s, at a time when rock and roll was the dominant force in popular music. Legendary records like his 1955 Columbia debut, *Brubeck Time*, and the ambitious *Time Out* (1959)—featuring the hit "Take Five" and the first million-selling jazz album—remain as hallmarks of jazz, and document how Brubeck and his collaborators defined the contours of American cool. A recipient of the National Medal of Arts, he was also the first modern jazz musician to be featured on the cover of *Time* magazine. Born at Concord, CA, Brubeck died Dec 5, 2012, at Norwalk, CT.

Entertainment

John Ford

Birth * Feb 1, 1895 * 125 years

Prolific and influential American film director, born at Cape Elizabeth, ME. Winner of five Oscars—for *The Informer* (1936), *The Grapes of Wrath* (1941), *How Green Was My Valley* (1942), *The Quiet Man* (1953) and the documentary *The Battle of Midway* (1942)—Ford is strongly associated with the western and its most iconic setting, Monument Valley. His famous westerns include *Stagecoach*, *My Darling Clementine*, *The Searchers* and *The Man Who Shot Liberty Valance*. Popular with audiences and venerated by French auteur critics of the '50s, Ford himself said, "The secret is to make films that please the public and that also allow the director to reveal his personality." He died Aug 31, 1973, at Palm Desert, CA.

Rudolph Valentino

Birth * May 6, 1895 * 125 years

Rodolfo Alfonso Raffaello Pierre Filibert Guglielmi di Valentina d'Antonguella, whose professional name was Rudolph Valentino, was born at Castellaneta, Italy. The biggest male star of the silent film era started his career in New York City as a dancer. He journeyed to Hollywood in 1917. The silent films that catapulted Rudolph Valentino into stardom were *The Four Horsemen of the Apocalypse* (1921) and *The Sheik*, released on Nov 20, 1921. The latter film, a romantic melodrama

about a prince of the desert's obsession with an Englishwoman, was a hit that actually had women fainting in theaters. The film was scandalously frank for the times about sexual desire. "Sheik" even became slang for a man whom women couldn't resist. While the film made Valentino a reluctant sex symbol, it also typecast him—to his frustration. A sequel, *The Son of the Sheik*, was released in Sept 1926 a few weeks after Valentino's sudden death of a perforated ulcer in New York, NY, on Aug 23, 1926. His death was greeted with widespread grief among his fans, and in the decades since a succession of veiled women in black have brought flowers to his tomb at Hollywood Memorial Park annually on this death anniversary.

Oscar Hammerstein II

Birth * July 12, 1895 * 125 years

Master of the "musical play" form, Oscar Hammerstein II was a titan of the theater. Born Oscar Greeley Clendenning Hammerstein at New York, NY, the lyricist, playwright and producer worked with such collaborators as Jerome Kern and—most famously—Richard Rodgers. The partnerships produced *Oklahoma!*, *Show Boat*, *Carousel*, *The King and I*, *South Pacific* and *Sound of Music*, among other well-known shows. Many of Hammerstein's songs have settled permanently into the repertoires of

vocalists everywhere. The recipient of two Academy Awards, the Pulitzer Prize for Drama and eight Tony Awards, Hammerstein died Aug 23, 1960, at Doylestown, PA. Following his death, lights at Times Square, New York City, and the West End of London, England, were dimmed in his honor.

Buster Keaton

Birth * Oct 4, 1895 * 125 years

Born Joseph Francis Keaton at Piqua, KS, Buster Keaton (supposedly nicknamed by Harry Houdini) was one of America's greatest filmmakers. He became a star on the vaudeville stage by age six, in a family show with his parents, but moved on to films at age 21, costarring in several comic shorts with Roscoe "Fatty" Arbuckle and then starring in, writing, directing and producing his own shorts—which featured improbable stunts and physical gags punctuated with Keaton's deadpan expression. His full-length silent films are regarded as masterpieces of American comedy, especially *Sherlock, Jr* (1924) and the Civil War epic *The General* (1927)—both of which are on the Library of Congress's National Film Registry. Alcoholism and troubled relations with the MGM studio sidelined his career in the 1930s and '40s, but he later began a quieter career writing gags, making comic cameos in such films as *Around the World in Eighty*

🔍 Buster's Porkpie Hat

Charlie Chaplin had his derby, Harold Lloyd had his straw boater. Buster Keaton picked the porkpie hat as his signature head gear. Actually, he made his own out of a cut-down, felt Stetson whose brim he stiffened with sugar water. In a 1964 interview, Keaton mused that he went through thousands of hats during his long career: some destroyed in water stunts, others snatched off his head by eager fans.

Days, appearing on TV's "Candid Camera" and even performing as a clown in Paris's Cirque Medrano. Keaton died on Feb 1, 1966, at Los Angeles, CA.

Federico Fellini

Birth * Jan 20, 1920 * 100 years

Director and screenwriter Federico Fellini was born at Rimini, Italy. Four of Fellini's movies won Oscars for best foreign language film: *La Strada* (1956), *Nights of Cabiria* (1957), 8½ (1963) and *Amarcord* (1974). He received an honorary Oscar in 1993 in recognition of his cinematic accomplishments. Of his work, *New York Times* critic Vincent Canby said, "[Fellini's world is] a place whose spectacularly grand, studio-built artificiality makes us see the interior truth of what is taken to be the 'real' world outside, which is a circus." Fellini died Oct 31, 1993, at Rome.

Tony Randall

Birth * Feb 26, 1920 * 100 years

Born Leonard Rosenberg at Tulsa, OK, actor Tony Randall had a career that spanned five decades. He was a successful film actor, starring in 1957's *Will Success Spoil Rock Hunter?* and 1959's *Pillow Talk*, and performed extensively on the stage. He launched the National Actors Theatre, a company dedicated to performing classic works of theater. He is perhaps best remembered for his role opposite Jack Klugman in television's "The Odd Couple," playing Felix Unger, the tidy, hypochondriac photographer forced by circumstance to share an apartment with slob sportswriter Oscar Madison. The wildly popular series ran from 1970 to 1975. Randall died at New York, NY, May 17, 2004.

Toshiro Mifune

Birth * Apr 1, 1920 * 100 years

Japanese actor known worldwide for his collaboration with renowned director Akira Kurosawa in films including *Rashomon*, *Seven Samurai*, *Throne of Blood*, and *Yojimbo*. Mifune was born in Qingdao, China, and grew up in Manchuria before being drafted into the Imperial Japanese Army in 1940, where he served as an aerial photographer. He appeared in his first film in 1947, but his performance in *Rashomon* (1950) made him an international star. Celebrated for his good looks, screen-idol magnetism and broad acting range, he may be most familiar to American audiences for his role as Lord Toranga in the 1980 television miniseries *Shogun*. Mifune died Dec 24, 1997, at Tokyo, Japan.

Hilda Sims

Birth * Apr 15, 1920 * 100 years

American stage and film actress, born Hilda Moses at Minneapolis, MN. She joined the American Negro Theater at Harlem, NY, in 1943 and was given the title role in *Anna Lucasta*. When the production moved to Broadway in 1944, it became the first all-black production to be performed on Broadway without a racial theme. Simms was the creative arts director of New York State's human rights division, through which she was instrumental in bringing discrimination against black actors to public attention during the 1960s. She died at Buffalo, NY, Feb 6, 1994.

Maureen O'Hara

Birth * Aug 17, 1920 * 100 years

The actress with the flaming red hair was born Maureen FitzSimons at Ranelagh, Dublin, Ireland. She pursued drama while still a child and appeared on the Dublin stage in small parts. Famed actor Charles Laughton developed her early film career and starred with her in Alfred Hitchcock's thriller *Jamaica Inn* (1939). She was just 18 during filming. She appeared—often as an independent, outspoken woman—in countless films over six decades. Her last film was *Only the Lonely* in 1991. She appeared in many John Ford films and often with John Wayne—most famously, in *The Quiet Man* (1952). Other famous films include *The Hunchback of Notre Dame*, *How Green Was My Valley*, *Miracle on 34th Street* and *The Parent Trap*. Awarded an honorary Oscar in 2014, O'Hara died Oct 24, 2015, at Boise, ID.

Mickey Rooney

Birth * Sept 23, 1920 * 100 years

An outsized personality in a pint-size package, entertainer Mickey Rooney had a career that spanned nine decades in vaudeville, film, television and Broadway. Born Joseph Yule Jr at Brooklyn, NY, Rooney became a teen movie idol in the Depression. He was Hollywood's number-one box office star in 1939, 1940 and 1941. Famous for the Andy Hardy films, *Babes in Arms*, *Boys Town* and *National Velvet*. In 1979 he had a career revival in the Broadway show *Sugar Babies*. The recipient of two honorary Oscars (in 1939 and 1983), Rooney died Apr 6, 2014, at Los Angeles, CA.

Walter Matthau

Birth * Oct 1, 1920 * 100 years

The acclaimed actor of stage and screen was born in New York City. He won two Tony Awards—one as best actor in a play for his portrayal of slob Oscar Madison in *The Odd Couple* (1965), a role he repeated in the 1968 film. A frequent film collaborator was Jack Lemmon, first in Billy Wilder's *The Fortune Cookie* (1966), in which Matthau won the Best Supporting Actor Oscar as "Whiplash Willie" Gingrich. Notable film work for Matthau included *Charade*, *Cactus Flower*, *Hello Dolly!*, *The Front Page*, *The Sunshine Boys*, *The Taking of Pelham One Two Three*, *The Bad News Bears*, *Grumpy Old Men* and *Kotch*. He died July 1, 2000, at Santa Monica, CA.

Melina Mercouri

Birth * Oct 18, 1920 * 100 years

Greek actress and politician Melina Mercouri was born Maria Amalia Mercouri at Athens, Greece. She appeared in more than 70 films and plays. She is best known for her role in *Never on Sunday* (1960), for which she won the best actress award at Cannes. Other acclaimed roles were in *Stella*, *Phaedra*, *Promise at Dawn* and the crime caper *Topkapi*. In 1977 she was elected to Greece's parliament; she became the first woman in Greece's senior cabinet when appointed by premier Andreas Papandreou to the position of minister of culture in 1981. She died Mar 6, 1994, at New York, NY.

Education

Maria Montessori

Birth * Aug 31, 1870 * 150 years

Physician and educator born at Chiaravalle, Italy. In 1894, Montessori became the first Italian woman in the modern era to get a medical degree. Her areas of specialty were psychiatry and the treatment of children. While working with mentally disabled children at the Orthophrenic School in Rome, she experimented with ways of engaging the children and developed what is now called the Montessori method. She believed that children should work at tasks that interested them, and if they were given the right materials and tasks, they learn through self-motivation—teachers would only intercede if the children needed help. Her method provided a system of education whereby children learned and developed skills at their own pace. Montessori set up a preschool—which included her specially designed child-size furniture—in Rome and it proved successful. Her books—*The Montessori Method* (1912) and *The Secret of Childhood* (1936)—made her famous. Montessori schools now operate all over the world for preschoolers to secondary schoolers. Montessori died May 6, 1952, at Noordwijk, Netherlands.

Religion and Philosophy

Georg Wilhelm Friedrich Hegel

Birth * Aug 27, 1770 * 250 years

Born at Stuttgart, Germany, Hegel was the last of the great German Idealist philosophers. Influenced by religion, Hegel's philosophy posited the idea that an abstract spirit, the Absolute, underlay all experience, which together formed the reality of experience. In *Phenomenology of Spirit* (1807), his most discussed work, Hegel develops his eponymous dialectical method; the three editions of *Encyclopedia of Philosophical Sciences* (1817, 1827, 1830) presents his entire mature philosophy. A prolific writer, his oeuvre is widely regarded as one of philosophy's most challenging. A response to Kantian philosophy, Hegelian philosophy influenced Kierkegaard, Sartre and Existentialism, Marxism and the Positivists. Hegel died of cholera Nov 14, 1831, at Berlin, Germany.

Sun Myung Moon

Birth * Feb 25, 1920 * 100 years

Business mogul, self-proclaimed Messiah, and founder, in 1954, of the Unification Church. His followers are popularly known as "Moonies" and infamous for mass wedding ceremonies. Born in North Korea, Moon became a Presbyterian as a child but later developed a theology that mixed Eastern philosophy, biblical teachings and what he called God's revelations to him. He began organizing on a large scale in the United States in the 1970s, where his church was widely considered a cult and his business dealings suspect. At its height, the church claimed a worldwide following of 3 million, but experts estimate a membership of 50,000. Born at Chongju in what is now North Korea, Moon died Sept 3, 2012, at Gapyeong, South Korea.

Pope John Paul II

Birth * May 18, 1920 * 100 years

Karol Wojtyla, 264th pope of the Roman Catholic Church, was born at Wadowice, Poland. Elected pope Oct 16, 1978, he was the first non-Italian to be elected pope in 456 years and the first Polish pope. His theology was conservative and traditional, and he was known for his worldwide travels to bring the message of the Catholic Church to people around the world. He survived an assassination attempt in 1981 and died at Vatican City on Apr 2, 2005. He was beatified May 1, 2011.

Science and Technology

Jeannette Ridlon Piccard

Birth * Jan 5, 1895 * 125 years

On Oct 23, 1934, at Dearborn, MI, Piccard piloted the balloon "Century of Progress" 57,579 feet into the stratosphere with her husband, Jean-Felix Piccard. Besides being a record-setting ascent, the feat almost made Piccard the first woman in space. Born Jeannette Ridlon at Chicago, IL, she earned degrees from Bryn Mawr and the University of Chicago and a PhD in education from the University of Minnesota. She was the first woman to qualify as a free-balloon pilot (1934). She was an identical twin married to an identical twin. The scientific couple researched advances in plastic film and polyethylene balloon materials, which eventually lead to ascents of more than 100,000 feet. Jeannette Piccard served for many years at NASA as a manned-flight consultant. In 1976 she became one of the first women to be ordained as an Episcopal priest. Piccard died at Minneapolis, MN, May 17, 1981. The Piccard Gondola is a part of the permanent collection at Chicago's Museum of Science and Industry.

Henry Heimlich, M.D.

Birth * Feb 3, 1920 * 100 years

Best known for the Heimlich maneuver, a procedure introduced in 1974 to save choking victims, Heimlich, a surgeon by training, also developed and held patents on many medical innovations and devices. The Heimlich maneuver involves wrapping arms around the victim from behind, making a fist just above the navel and thrusting up sharply to eject a throat obstruction. Although initially criticized by professionals as unscientific and possibly unsafe, the AMA accepted it in 1975, and it is credited with saving thousands of lives annually. Some question Heimlich's claim as sole developer of the technique, but none question his talent at self-promotion. Born at Wilmington, DE, he died Dec 17, 2016, at Cincinnati, OH.

Economics, Business and Labor

John Graunt

Birth * Apr 24, 1620 * 400 years

Graunt was a prosperous draper and merchant in London, England, but his fame today rests on the fact that he was the first demographer. In the 1660s Graunt began to study death records of London parishes and began to see patterns (for example, urban death rates exceeded rural death rates). He saw the value such statistics and data of the populace could have. In 1662, he published *Natural and Political Observations Made upon the Bills of Mortality*, a well-received work that enabled his being elected a fellow in the Royal Society. His work is the foundation of mortality tables, a tool of modern insurance. Born at London, he died there Apr 16, 1674.

Sports

Alexander Joy Cartwright, Jr.

Birth * Apr 17, 1820 * 200 years

This baseball innovator was born at New York, NY. Cartwright helped to organize the Knickerbocker Base Ball Club in 1845 and wrote the game's first rule book. He joined the California gold rush and eventually wound up in Hawaii, spreading the gospel of baseball all the way. He died at Honolulu, HI, July 12, 1892.

Bill Pickett

Birth * Dec 5, 1870 * 150 years

The great American rodeo cowboy was born in Williamson County, TX, the son of a former slave and one of 13 children. He was the creator of "bulldogging" (an early form of steer wrestling in the modern rodeo) where a cowboy leaps off his mount and wrestles a runaway steer to the ground by grappling its horns. Pickett developed this skill as a ranch hand in the 1890s by watching ranch dogs at work. His own special twist involved biting the lip of the steer. He left ranch work to form the successful touring show The Pickett Brothers Bronco Busters and Rough Riders Association. He then joined the 101 Ranch Wild West Show in 1907 (as "The Dusky Demon"), which featured film star Tom Mix. Pickett himself appeared on film to demonstrate his rodeo skills. He died 11 days after a bronco kicked him in the head at the 101 Ranch on Apr 2, 1932, at Tulsa, OK. He is buried at the White Eagle Monument near Marland, OK. He was the first African American to be inducted in the Rodeo Hall of Fame of the National Cowboy and Western Heritage Museum (in 1971). He is also in the Pro Rodeo Hall of Fame (1989) and has been featured on a US postage stamp designed after one of his film posters.

George Halas

Birth * Feb 2, 1895 * 125 years

George "Papa Bear" Halas, Pro Football Hall of Fame coach and team owner, born at Chicago, IL. After playing football at the University of Illinois and baseball with the New York Yankees, Halas helped to found the National Football League and the

Chicago Bears in 1920. As coach of the Bears for 40 years, he compiled a record of 324 wins, 151 losses and 31 ties. Halas was a charter member of the Hall of Fame, 1963. He died at Chicago, Oct 31, 1983.

George "Babe" Ruth

Birth * Feb 6, 1895 * 125 years

One of baseball's greatest heroes and a bigger-than-life character, George Herman "Babe" Ruth was born at Baltimore, MD. He was sent to St Mary's Industrial School for Boys at age 7 for unknown reasons (as his parents were living), and didn't emerge for 12 years. 1914 was the beginning of his illustrious baseball career. The "Sultan of Swat" (who was also a left-handed pitcher) hit 714 home runs in 22 major league seasons and played in 10 World Series. Fourteen of his pro seasons were spent with the New York Yankees. The "Bambino" retired June 2, 1935, and was inducted as a charter member of the Baseball Hall of Fame in 1936. Diagnosed with cancer in November 1946, he died at New York, NY, Aug 16, 1948. His body lay in state at the main entrance of Yankee Stadium ("The House That Ruth Built"), where people waited in line for hours to march past the coffin. On Aug 19 countless people surrounded St Patrick's Cathedral for the funeral mass and lined the streets along the route to the cemetery.

Jack Dempsey

Birth * June 24, 1895 * 125 years

William Harrison "Jack" Dempsey, boxer, was born at Manassa, CO. Dempsey boxed under several pseudonyms in western mining camps, then came east and picked up Jack "Doc" Kearns as his manager. After defeating all available heavyweights, Dempsey took on champion Jess

Ruth Calls His Shot?

It was Oct 1, 1932, the fifth inning of game three of the 1932 World Series. With a count of two balls and two strikes and with hostile Cubs fans shouting "epithets" at him, Babe Ruth pointed to the center field bleachers in Chicago's Wrigley Field and followed up by hitting a soaring home run high above the very spot to which he had just gestured. With that homer Ruth squashed the Chicago Cubs' hopes of winning the game, and the Yankees went on to sweep the Series with four straight victories.

Did Ruth actually call his shot that day? Even eyewitnesses disagree. Joe Williams of the *New York Times* wrote, "In no mistaken motions, the Babe notified the crowd that the nature of his retaliation would be a wallop right out of the confines of the park." But Cubs pitcher Charlie Root said, "Ruth did *not* point at the fence before he swung. If he'd made a gesture like that, I'd have put one in his ear and knocked him on his ass." Ruth's daughter has said that he denied it. But then the Babe himself also claimed he did it.

Willard at Toledo, OH, July 4, 1919. The fight, which drew fans from as far away as New York, was held outdoors in a specially built arena outside Toledo, OH. Dempsey won when Willard failed to answer the bell for the fourth round. He reigned as champ for seven years but defended his title only six times, losing to Gene Tunney in 1926. Following his boxing career, he became a successful New York restaurateur. The "Manassa Mauler" died at New York, NY, May 31, 1983.

Stan Musial

Birth * Nov 21, 1920 * 100 years

Legendary left-handed hitter for the St. Louis Cardinals, dubbed "Stan the Man" and famous for his concentration at bat and for his unique "corkscrew" stance. Musial played 22 major league seasons including three World Series championships, won three Most Valuable Player awards and was inducted into the baseball Hall of Fame in 1969. At retirement, Musial held several National League career batting records, including the most hits (3,630) to go with his 331 batting average and 475 home runs. While

first in his league to earn a $100,000 salary, Musial was widely held to be the nicest guy in baseball. Musial died Jan 19, 2013, in Ladue, MO.

Sammy Lee

Birth * Aug 1, 1920 * 100 years

Born to Korean immigrants in Fresno, CA, Lee faced decades of discrimination before he became the first Asian-American man to win an Olympic gold medal. As a child, he could only practice at his local pool one day a week, due to restrictions on nonwhite swimmers. He competed at the 1948 Olympic games in London, England, winning gold for the 10-meter platform and bronze for the springboard. He also became the first man to grab consecutive golds in diving when he conquered the platform at the 1952 Helsinki Olympics. He was a medical doctor and served in the Korean War. Later, he was a coach and an ambassador for the United States in the Olympics and for the sport of diving. Lee was elected to the International Swimming Hall of Fame in 1968 and the United States Olympic Hall of Fame in 1990. Lee died Dec 2, 2016, at Newport Beach, CA.

Spotlight on 2020 Events

Beethoven 250

Jan 1–Dec 31, 2020

Born in December 1770 and baptized Dec 17, 1770, the great German composer Ludwig van Beethoven is the focus of the 250th birth anniversary celebrations all through 2020—and all over the world. Aficionados can expect concerts, music festivals, exhibitions, seminars and more. A selection of events follows.

GERMANY

BTHVN2020 is the catchy name that Germany's Beethoven Anniversary Society has come up with as an umbrella brand for the various projects taking place in honor of the composer. On Dec 16–17, it will not just be the city of Bonn, regular host of the annual Beethovenfest, but the entire region of North Rhine–Westphalia that bustles with events—from historical to contemporary, from static to mobile, from interactive to traditional events. The BTHVN2020 website serves as a clearinghouse for scores of events (Web: www. bthvn2020.de/en/program/ calendar-of-events).

In Bonn is the birthplace of Beethoven at Bonngasse 20. It is now a museum and the headquarters of the Beethoven House association, which is actually a complex of buildings, including a chamber music hall and library. See their website for exhibition, performance and other info: www.beethoven.de.

AUSTRIA

Centered in Vienna, there are concert events for the 250th jubilee. At the State Opera House (Staatsoper, www.wiener-staatsoper.at) major performances of Beethoven's opera, *Fidelio* (including in the original "Leonore" version), are planned Jan 19; Feb 1, 5, 8, 11, 14; April 22, 25 and 28; and May 2. The Feb 1 performance will be livestreamed.

Vienna's historic Theater an der Wien opera house, built in 1801, was a favorite with Beethoven, who premiered many works there (and actually lived on the premises for a time). In March 2020, there will be special performances of Beethoven's *Fidelio* there, directed by Oscar winner Christoph Waltz (Web: www.theater-wien.at/de/ home).

"Resound Beethoven" is a project of the Orchester Wiener Akademie and Martin Haselböck (www. wienerakademie.at) performing Beethoven's works on original instruments and in original venues around Vienna. Various dates are planned for 2020.

From May 4 to May 14, the University of Music and Performing Arts hosts the 16th International Beethoven Piano Competition for young pianists. The 2020 version has a first prize of €10,000 and a Bösendorfer grand piano. See www. beethoven-comp.at.

LONDON, ENGLAND

In London, the Southbank Centre has a year-long celebration of Beethoven beginning in January

2020 that includes Beethoven rarities and historic recreations alongside famous symphonic works, outstanding chamber concerts and contemporary reflections and reinterpretations of Beethoven's music. See their website at www. southbankcentre.co.uk/whats-on/ festivals-series/classical-season/ beethoven-250.

The *Barbican* Centre's "Beethoven 250" presents his complete symphonies, piano concertos and recitals as well as less familiar works. Talks, films and exhibitions round out the offerings that began in September 2019 and conclude May 28, 2020. See www.barbican.org.uk/whats-on/2019/series/beethoven-250. And in February 2020, the London Philharmonic performs his first six symphonies plus concerts of works for strings, piano and lesser known works (www. lpo.org.uk/what-s-on/beethoven. html).

AROUND THE WORLD

Major music institutions around the world will join in the celebrations. These include the Philharmonie de Paris, the Chicago Symphony Orchestra and the National Symphony Orchestra in Washington, DC. Carnegie Hall in New York City plans "one of the largest explorations of the great master's music in our time" with such outstanding artists as Evgeny Kissin, Emanuel Ax, Yo-Yo Ma and Anne-Sophie Mutter (www.carnegiehall. org/Events/Season-Highlights/ Beethoven).

The American Beethoven Society is also a source for jubilee events,

International Year of Plant Health and Year of the Nurse and Midwife

2020 will see two special years. The United Nations has designated 2020 as International Year of Plant Health per a resolution adopted on Dec 20, 2018. The year seeks to raise awareness of the importance of plant health and the economic, social and environmental impact of plant health on food security and ecosystem functions.

The Year of the Nurse and Midwife is an observance promoted by nursing and midwife organizations around the world. It is anchored on the 200th birth anniversary of modern nursing pioneer Florence Nightingale (1820–1910; see "Spotlight on World Anniversaries"). The World Health Organization—the public health agency of the United Nations—has endorsed the year.

"Beethoven@250." Planning is still in progress. See their website at http://americanbeethovensociety.org.

Glastonbury 50

Pilton, Somerset, England
June 24–28

On Sept 19, 1970—the day after rock star Jimi Hendrix was found dead—1,500 rock and blues fans gathered at Worthy Farm in Pilton, England, near Glastonbury, for music, camping and free milk from the farm. Headliners were T. Rex and Al Stewart and admission was £1. Today, the Glastonbury Festival is the largest greenfield festival in the world and at peak times sees 175,000 fans *each day* over a five-day period.

The originator of the festival is dairy farmer Michael Eavis, who has turned his farm and the festival into an iconic cultural, political and environmental event not to be missed. The festival was moved from September to the June Summer Solstice and now covers 900 acres in the Vale of Avalon (legendary burial site of King Arthur). The festival site is more than a mile and a half

across and has a perimeter of eight and a half miles. Such enormity means that for five days in June a mini city pops up, divided into neighborhoods and a complicated infrastructure. To give the land (and organizers/volunteers) a rest, there are "fallow years" periodically when the festival is suspended. Proceeds go to various charitable organizations.

Glastonbury is committed to green initiatives: lights (low-energy LEDs) are only on at night, power is supplied by biodiesel generators run on more than 60,000 liters of hydro-treated vegetable oil, 1,200 compost toilets handle biological needs and festival goers are urged to take public transportation (which is augmented during festival days).

Headliners in recent years have included Radiohead, Kanye West, Motörhead, Metallica, Coldplay, Adele, Dolly Parton, Arcade Fire, Arctic Monkeys, U2 and many others. Headliners perform on the famous Pyramid Stage, which was first constructed in 1971 above the Glastonbury-Stonehenge ley line, and then was reconstructed in a more permanent form in 1981.

Organizers are promising an exciting lineup for the 50th anniversary, dubbed "Glastonbury 50."
For information:

Glastonbury Festival
Web: www.glastonburyfestivals.co.uk

Games of the XXXII Olympiad— Tokyo 2020

16th SUMMER PARALYMPIC GAMES

Tokyo, Japan
July 24–Aug 9; Aug 25–Sept 6

Tokyo, Japan, site of the 1964 Olympics, returns as host for the XXXII Olympiad and XVI Paralympiad. It is the first city to host a second paralympiad. The motto for these games is "Discover Tomorrow." Organizers, inspired by the 1964 event, "which completely transformed Japan," hope that the 2020 games will be the most innovative in Olympic history and be a catalyst for world peace. An example of the innovative spirit behind these games is the commitment to creating medals with 100 percent recycled content. Citizens across Japan have donated old cell phones and other discarded small electronics in order to extract gold and precious metals for the 5,000 medals needed for the Olympic winners.

More than five million Japanese schoolchildren participated in

choosing and naming the Olympic mascots—Miraitowa (Olympics) and Someity (Paralympics). *Miraitowa* was a name created from the Japanese words for future and eternity. *Someity* is derived from the "Someiyoshino" variety of cherry blossom.

The beloved and historic torch relay begins Mar 26 in Fukushima and passes through all of Japan's 47 prefectures as well as 857 local municipalities for 121 days. The torch relay route is designed so that it is within one-hour commuting/driving distance for most of the nation's citizenry. The relay passes world historic sites as well as regions still recovering from the 2011 earthquake and tsunami.

For the 2020 summer games, there will be 33 sports, broken into 50 disciplines and 339 events. In 2016, the International Olympic Committee (IOC) announced five new sports for 2020: baseball/ softball, karate, skateboard, sport

climbing and surfing. Said the IOC president, Thomas Bach, "The five sports are an innovative combination of established and emerging, youth-focused events that are popular in Japan and will add to the legacy of the Tokyo Games." At the Paralympics, there will be 540 events in 22 sports. New events are badminton and taekwondo. Sailing and 7-a-side football (soccer) have been dropped.

Tokyo, with a population of at least 9.2 million, has created two main zones for Olympic events: the Heritage Zone, which includes venues used in 1964, and the Tokyo Bay Zone, situated at the bay and representing the future and innovation. The Athlete's Village sits at the intersection of the two zones, and the whole venue area resembles the outline of an infinity symbol. Again, the organizers are embedding the Olympics and

Paralympics with innovation and deep symbolism.

For information:

The Tokyo Organising Committee of the Olympic and Paralympic Games

Tokyo 2020 Press Office
Toranomon Hills Mori Tower, 8th Fl
1-23-1 Toranomon, Minato-ku
Tokyo 105-6308
Japan
E-mail: pressoffice@tokyo2020.jp
Web: https://tokyo2020.org

International Olympic Committee

Château de Vidy
Case postale 356
1001 Lausanne
Switzerland
Phone: (41) (21) 621-61-11
E-mail: pressoffice@olympic.org (media)
Web: www.olympic.org

◆ January ◆

January 1 — Wednesday

DAY 1   **365 REMAINING**

WEDNESDAY, JANUARY ONE, 2020. Jan 1. First day of the first month of the Gregorian calendar year, Anno Domini 2020, being a leap year, and (until July 4) 244th year of American independence. 2020 will be year 6733 of the Julian Period, a time frame consisting of 7,997 years that began at noon, universal (Greenwich) time, Jan 1, 4714 BC. Astronomers will note that Julian Day number 2,452,658 begins at noon, universal time (representing the number of days since the beginning of the Julian Period). New Year's Day is a public holiday in the US and in many other countries. Traditionally, it is a time for personal stocktaking, for making resolutions for the coming year and sometimes for recovering from the festivities of New Year's Eve. Financial accounting begins anew for businesses and individuals whose fiscal year is the calendar year. Jan 1 has been observed as the beginning of the year in most English-speaking countries since the British Calendar Act of 1751, prior to which the New Year began Mar 25 (approximating the vernal equinox). Earth begins another orbit of the sun, during which it, and we, will travel some 583,416,000 miles in 365.2422 days. New Year's Day has been called "Everyman's Birthday," and in some countries a year is added to everyone's age on Jan 1 rather than on the anniversary of each person's birth.

ALLSTATE SUGAR BOWL. Jan 1. Mercedes-Benz Superdome, New Orleans, LA. 86th annual. Now part of the College Football Playoff series. The Sugar Bowl originated in 1935. Est attendance: 72,500. For info: Allstate Sugar Bowl Office, Louisiana Superdome, 1500 Sugar Bowl Dr, New Orleans, LA 70112. Phone: (504) 828-2440. E-mail: info@sugarbowl.org. Web: www.allstatesugarbowl.org.

AUSTRALIA: COMMONWEALTH FORMED: ANNIVERSARY. Jan 1, 1901. On this day the six colonies of Victoria, New South Wales, Queensland, South Australia, Western Australia and Northern Territory were united into one nation. The British Parliament had passed the Commonwealth Constitution Bill in the spring of 1900, and Queen Victoria signed the document Sept 17, 1900.

BE KIND TO FOOD SERVERS MONTH. Jan 1–31. Start the New Year off with a resolution to be kind to your hardworking waiter or waitress. This month's goal is to establish a positive relationship between food servers and the dining public. Proclaimed by the State of Tennessee. For info: Sybil Presley, 1056 Linden Ave, #608, Memphis, TN 38104. Phone: (901) 643-1982. E-mail: sybilpresley@bellsouth.net.

BONZA BOTTLER DAY®. Jan 1. (also Feb 2, Mar 3, Apr 4, May 5, June 6, July 7, Aug 8, Sept 9, Oct 10, Nov 11 and Dec 12). A day to celebrate when the number of the day is the same as the number of the month. Bonza Bottler Day® is an excuse to have a party at least once a month. Created by the late Elaine Fremont and continued by her family, Bonza Bottler Day is now celebrated not only in the US but also in many other countries. See the website for info on Bonza Bottler Day stickers, mugs, notecards and more. For info: Gail Berger, Bonza Bottler Day. Phone: (864) 201-3988. E-mail: bonza@bonzabottlerday.com. Web: www.bonzabottlerday.com.

BOOK BLITZ MONTH. Jan 1–31. Focuses attention on improving authors' relationships with the media in order to create a bestselling book. Free book PR evaluation available. For info: Barbara Gaughen, Media 21, 7456 Evergreen Dr, Santa Barbara, CA 93117. Phone: (805) 680-9445. E-mail: bgaughenmu@aol.com.

CANADA: POLAR BEAR SWIM 2020. Jan 1. English Bay Beach, Vancouver, BC. 100th annual. The Vancouver Polar Bear Swim Club is one of the largest and oldest Polar Bear Clubs in the world. Its initial swim was in 1920 when a small number of hardy swimmers took the plunge into English Bay on New Year's Day. Led by their founder, Peter Pantages, the swim has grown from about 10 swimmers in that year to the record number of 2,550 official entries in 2014. Today, the swim takes place at 2:30 PM on the first day of each new year. Costumes and the Peter Pantages Memorial 100-yard swim race are the highlights of this event. For info: Vancouver Aquatic Centre, 1050 Beach Ave, Vancouver, BC V6E 1T7, Canada. Web: www.vancouver.ca/parks-recreation-culture/polar-bear-swim.aspx.

CAPITAL ONE ORANGE BOWL. Jan 1. Hard Rock Stadium, Miami Gardens, FL. 87th edition. Storied college bowl game. Est attendance: 65,000. For info: Larry Wahl, VP of Communications, Orange Bowl Committee, 14360 NW 77th Ct, Miami Lakes, FL 33016. Phone: (305) 341-4700. E-mail: info@orangebowl.org. Web: www.orangebowl.org.

CHILDREN IMPACTED BY A PARENT'S CANCER MONTH. Jan 1–31. There are more than five million children in the United States who have been impacted by a parent's cancer (lost a parent, has a parent undergoing treatment or has a parent who is a survivor). These children—sometimes overlooked in a parent's cancer journey—suffer real (and lifelong) consequences, including isolation from peers, lower academic scores and assumption of adult roles. This month's goal is to bring a heightened understanding of their needs (and tips to support these children) to school counselors, teachers and mental health professionals as well as families and friends of children impacted by a parent's cancer. Since 2000. For info: Kesem, 10586 W Pico Blvd, #196, Los Angeles, CA 90064. Web: www.kesem.org.

CIRCUMCISION OF CHRIST. Jan 1. Holy day in many Christian churches. Celebrates Jesus's submission to Jewish law; on the octave day of Christmas. See also: "Solemnity of Mary, Mother of God" (Jan 1) for Roman Catholic observance since 1969 calendar reorganization.

COPYRIGHT REVISION LAW SIGNED: ANNIVERSARY. Jan 1, 1976. The first major revision since 1909 of laws governing intellectual property in the US was signed by President Ford. It took effect two years later on Jan 1, 1978. The act (Public Law 94–553) contains substantial revisions of the principles governing acquisition and duration of copyright and deals with issues that have been raised in recent years concerning photocopying and the use of copyrighted works by public broadcasting and cable television systems.

CUBA: ANNIVERSARY OF THE REVOLUTION. Jan 1. National holiday celebrating the overthrow of the government of Fulgencio Batista in 1959 by the revolutionary forces of Fidel Castro, which had begun a civil war in 1956.

CUBA: LIBERATION DAY. Jan 1. A national holiday that celebrates the end of Spanish rule in 1899. Cuba, the largest island of the West Indies, was a Spanish possession from its discovery by Columbus (Oct 27, 1492) until 1899. Under US military control during 1899–1902 and 1906–09; a republican government took over Jan 28, 1909, and controlled the island until overthrown Jan 1, 1959, by Fidel Castro's revolutionary movement.

CZECH-SLOVAK DIVORCE: ANNIVERSARY. Jan 1, 1993. As Dec 31, 1992, gave way to Jan 1, 1993, the 74-year-old state of Czechoslovakia separated into two nations—the Czech Republic and Slovakia. The Slovaks held a celebration through the night in the streets of Bratislava amid fireworks, bell ringing, singing of the new country's national anthem and the raising of the Slovak flag. In the new Czech Republic no official festivities took place, but later in the day the Czechs celebrated with a solemn oath by their parliament. The nation of Czechoslovakia ended peacefully though polls showed that most Slovaks and Czechs would have preferred that it survive. Before the split Czech prime minister Vaclav Klaus and Slovak prime minister Vladimir Meciar reached an agreement on dividing everything from army troops and gold reserves to the art on government building walls.

ELLIS ISLAND OPENED: ANNIVERSARY. Jan 1, 1892. Ellis Island was opened on New Year's Day in 1892. Over the years more than 20 million individuals were processed through the stations. The island was used as a point of deportation as well: in 1932 alone, 20,000 people were deported from Ellis Island. When the US entered WWII in 1941, Ellis Island became a Coast Guard station. It closed Nov 12, 1954, and was declared a national park in 1956. After years of disuse it was restored, and in 1990 it was reopened as a museum.

EMANCIPATION PROCLAMATION TAKES EFFECT: ANNIVERSARY. Jan 1, 1863. Abraham Lincoln, by executive proclamation of Sept 22, 1862, declared that on this date "all persons held as slaves within any state or designated part of a state, the people whereof shall then be in rebellion against the United States, shall be then, thenceforward, and forever, free." Slaves in the four slave states that had not seceded from the Union (Delaware, Maryland, Kentucky and Missouri) were not freed until the passage of the 13th Amendment in 1865. See also: "Thirteenth Amendment to the US Constitution Ratified: Anniversary" (Dec 6).

ENGLAND: LNYDP—LONDON'S NEW YEAR'S DAY PARADE. Jan 1. London. 34th annual. The biggest parade of its kind in the world. The event, which attracts huge crowds to the streets of the capital, runs from the Ritz Hotel, Piccadilly, to Piccadilly Circus, lower Regent St, Pall Mall, Trafalgar Square, along Whitehall to Parliament Square. All the pageantry, glitz and razzmatazz remain: dozens of massive marching bands, cheerleaders, mayors of London boroughs, vintage cars, clowns and street performers. The event also includes a spectacular series of orchestral and choral concerts in majestic historic settings. Est attendance: 650,000. For info: LNYDP—London's New Year's Day Parade. Phone: (44) (20) 3275-0190. E-mail: info@LNYDP.com. Web: www.LNYDP.com.

EURO INTRODUCED: ANNIVERSARY. Jan 1, 1999. The euro, the common currency of members of the European Union, was introduced for use by financial institutions. The value of the currencies of the original 11 nations (Austria, Belgium, Finland, France, Germany, Ireland, Italy, Luxembourg, The Netherlands, Portugal and Spain) was locked in at a permanent conversion rate to the euro. Estonia, Latvia, Lithuania, Greece, Slovenia, Cyprus, Malta and Slovakia joined the eurozone in subsequent years. On Jan 1, 2002, euro bills and coins began circulating; other currencies were phased out as of Feb 28, 2002.

FIRST BABY BOOMER BORN: ANNIVERSARY. Jan 1, 1946. Kathleen Casey Wilkens, born at one minute after midnight at Philadelphia, PA, was the first of the almost 78 million baby boomers born between 1946 and 1964.

FORSTER, E.M.: BIRTH ANNIVERSARY. Jan 1, 1879. Edward Morgan Forster, English author born at London, England, is remembered for his six novels: *Where Angels Fear to Tread* (1905), *The Longest Journey* (1907), *A Room with a View* (1908), *Howard's End* (1910), *A Passage to India* (1924) and the posthumously published *Maurice* (1971). He also achieved eminence for his short stories and essays, and he collaborated on the libretto for an opera, Benjamin Britten's *Billy Budd* (1951). Forster died at Coventry, England, June 7, 1970.

***FRANKENSTEIN* PUBLISHED: ANNIVERSARY.** Jan 1, 1818. Mary Shelley's classic, groundbreaking horror novel *Frankenstein; or, The Modern Prometheus* was published anonymously by Lackington, Allen & Company in London, England. The tale of scientist-inventor Victor Frankenstein and his creature has enthralled readers for generations and spawned countless adaptations in many mediums.

GET ORGANIZED MONTH. Jan 1–31. Is your New Year's resolution to get more organized? This month is an opportunity to streamline your life, create more time, lower your stress and increase your productivity. For info: National Assn of Professional Organizers (NAPO), 1120 Route 73, Ste 200, Mount Laurel, NJ 08054. Phone: (856) 380-6828. E-mail: napo@napo.net. Web: www.napo.net/gomonth.

GREENBERG, HANK: BIRTH ANNIVERSARY. Jan 1, 1911. Henry Benjamin (Hank) Greenberg, Hall of Fame first baseman and outfielder, born at New York, NY. One of the game's most prodigious sluggers, Greenberg hit 331 home runs and drove in 1,276 runs in only nine full seasons. Baseball's first Jewish superstar, Greenberg entered the army after playing just 19 games in 1941 and did not return to the Detroit Tigers until midway through the 1945 season. His grand slam on that season's last day won the pennant for the Tigers and propelled them toward a World Series triumph. He was inducted into the Hall of Fame in 1956 and died at Beverly Hills, CA, Sept 4, 1986.

HAITI: INDEPENDENCE DAY. Jan 1. A national holiday commemorating the proclamation of independence in 1804. Haiti, occupying the western third of the island Hispaniola (second largest of the West Indies), was a Spanish colony from its discovery by Columbus in 1492 until 1697. Then it was a French colony until the proclamation of independence in 1804.

HANGOVER HANDICAP RUN. Jan 1. Veteran's Park, Klamath Falls, OR. Two-mile fun run at 9 AM, New Year's Day. The first-place male and female finishers each take home a beer-can trophy. Est attendance: 100. For info: Hangover Handicap, 1800 Fairmount, Klamath Falls, OR 97601. Phone: (541) 882-6922. Fax: (541) 883-6481.

HOOVER, J. EDGAR: 125th BIRTH ANNIVERSARY. Jan 1, 1895. John Edgar Hoover was born at Washington, DC. He led the Palmer Raids and was director of the FBI, 1924–72. During his time as director, Hoover practiced modern investigative techniques, improved FBI agent training and increased FBI funding from Congress. His legacy was marred by harassment and surveillance of public figures he deemed undesirable, from civil rights leaders to pop stars like John Lennon. Hoover died May 2, 1972, at Washington, DC.

INTERNATIONAL CHILD-CENTERED DIVORCE MONTH. Jan 1–31. Dedicated to reminding parents about how children are affected by divorce and how to create the most positive outcome during and after divorce. The month is commemorated by divorce professionals and professional associations around the world through free public seminars, webinars, interviews, special website offerings and complimentary services. For info: Rosalind Sedacca. Phone: (561) 385-4205. E-mail: rosalind@childcentereddivorce.com. Web: www.divorcedparentsupport.com.

INTERNATIONAL CREATIVITY MONTH. Jan 1–31. A month to remind individuals and organizations around the globe to capitalize on the power of creativity. Unleashing creativity and innovation is vital for personal and business success in this age of

January 2020	S	M	T	W	T	F	S
				1	2	3	4
	5	6	7	8	9	10	11
	12	13	14	15	16	17	18
	19	20	21	22	23	24	25
	26	27	28	29	30	31	

accelerating change. The first month of the year provides an opportunity to take a fresh approach to problem-solving and renew confidence in our creative capabilities. For info: Randall Munson, Pres, Creatively Speaking, 508 Meadow Run Dr SW, Rochester, MN 55902-2337. Phone: (507) 286-1331. E-mail: Creativity@CreativelySpeaking.com. Web: www.CreativityMonth.com.

INTERNATIONAL YEAR OF PLANT HEALTH (UNITED NATIONS). Jan 1–Dec 31. Per Resolution 73/252 adopted on Dec 20, 2018, by the General Assembly, the United Nations has declared 2020 the International Year of Plant Health. This year seeks to raise awareness of the importance of plant health and the economic, social and environmental impact of plant health on food security and ecosystem functions. For info: United Nations. Web: www.un.org.

MUMMERS PARADE. Jan 1. Philadelphia, PA. World-famous New Year's Day parade of 20,000 spectacularly costumed Mummers in a colorful parade that goes on all day. This celebration has taken place since before the American Revolution. Est attendance: 100,000. For info: Mummers Parade. Web: http://phillymummers.com.

NATIONAL CLEAN UP YOUR COMPUTER MONTH. Jan 1–31. Dedicated to the education of computer users with simple tips and methods to increase the efficiency of their systems. For info: Denise Hoyle, 4565 Deerfield Dr, Pensacola, FL 32526. Phone: (251) 943-3315. E-mail: denise@specterweb.com.

NATIONAL ENVIRONMENTAL POLICY ACT: 50th ANNIVERSARY. Jan 1, 1970. The National Environmental Policy Act of 1969 established the Council on Environmental Quality and made it a federal government policy to protect the environment. It went into effect on this day in 1970.

NATIONAL GLAUCOMA AWARENESS MONTH. Jan 1–31. More than two million Americans aged 40 and older suffer from glaucoma. Nearly half do not know they have the disease—it causes no early symptoms. Prevent Blindness provides valuable information about this "sneak thief of sight." Organizations are encouraged to educate the community through screenings, forums and programs. For info: Prevent Blindness, 211 W Wacker Dr, Ste 1700, Chicago, IL 60606. Phone: (800) 331-2020. E-mail: info@preventblindness.org. Web: www.preventblindness.org.

NATIONAL HOT TEA MONTH. Jan 1–31. To celebrate one of nature's most popular, soothing and relaxing beverages; the only beverage in America commonly served hot or iced, anytime, anywhere, for any occasion. For info: The Tea Council of the USA, 362 Fifth Ave, Ste 1002, New York, NY 10001. Phone: (212) 986-9415. Fax: (212) 697-8658. E-mail: info@teausa.org. Web: www.teausa.org.

NATIONAL MENTORING MONTH. Jan 1–31. Goals include raising awareness of mentoring in its various forms; recruiting individuals to mentor, especially in programs that have a waiting list of young people; and promoting the rapid growth of mentoring by recruiting organizations to help find mentors for young people. Each January, this monthlong campaign provides nationwide publicity and information about mentoring programs in various communities that need volunteers. The National Mentoring Summit is the culminating event and takes place Feb 1–3 in Washington, DC. Sponsors: Harvard T.H. Chan School of Public Health, the Highland Street Foundation and MENTOR: The National Mentoring Partnership. For info: MENTOR/National Mentoring Partnership, 201 South St, Ste 615, Boston, MA 02111. Phone: (617) 303-4600. E-mail: info@mentoring.org. Web: www.mentoring.org.

NATIONAL PERSONAL SELF-DEFENSE AWARENESS MONTH. Jan 1–31. To educate women and teens about realistic self-defense options that could very well save their lives. Sponsored by the National Self-Defense Institute, Inc, a not-for-profit 501(c)(3) corporation. NSDI/SAFE Program™ seminars and related events nationally emphasize total preparation, realizing that awareness + risk reduction = 90 percent of self-defense while the other 10 percent is physical. For info: National Self-Defense Institute, Inc, PO Box 398355, Miami Beach, FL 33239-8355. Phone: (305) 868-NSDI. Fax: (305) 867-6634. E-mail: nsdi@att.net. Web: www.nsdi.org.

NATIONAL POVERTY IN AMERICA AWARENESS MONTH. Jan 1–31. To promote public awareness of the continuing existence of poverty and social injustice in America. Individuals are encouraged to support efforts to eradicate poverty by increasing their understanding of the causes and practical solutions and by active participation and support for antipoverty programs. Sponsored by the Catholic Campaign for Human Development, one of the largest non-governmental funders of self-help programs for the poor and disenfranchised in the US regardless of religion, race or ethnic origin. For info: US Conference of Catholic Bishops. Web: www.povertyusa.org.

NATIONAL RADON ACTION MONTH. Jan 1–31. To increase the public's awareness of the effects of radon, a colorless, odorless, tasteless and chemically inert radioactive gas. Radon is formed by the natural radioactive decay of uranium in rock, soil and water. It can be found in all 50 states. Testing for it is the only way of telling how much is present. For info: Environmental Protection Agency. Radon Hotline: (800) SOS-RADON (767-7236). E-mail: radon@ksu.edu. Web: www.epa.gov/radon or www.sosradon.org.

NATIONAL SKATING MONTH. Jan 1–31. This month is an opportunity for rinks and local programs to celebrate skating, alert local media and invite members to perform and host activities that will attract new families to the wonderful world of skating. Through a series of organized on- and off-ice activities, everyone enjoys a fun-filled day at the rink! For info: US Figure Skating, 20 First St, Colorado Springs, CO 80906. Phone: (719) 635-5200. E-mail: info@usfigureskating.org. Web: www.usfsa.org.

★NATIONAL SLAVERY AND HUMAN TRAFFICKING PREVENTION MONTH. Jan 1–31. To acknowledge that forms of slavery still exist in the modern era and to recommit American efforts to stop the human traffickers who ply this horrific trade. First proclaimed in 2010 by the Obama administration.

NATIONAL VOLUNTEER BLOOD DONOR MONTH. Jan 1–31. Since 1970. A time to highlight the importance of giving life through the donation of blood—and to honor past and present donors. For info: American Red Cross. Web: www.redcross.org/blood.

NEW YEAR'S DAY. Jan 1. Legal holiday in all states and territories of the US and in most other countries. The world's most widely celebrated holiday.

NHL WINTER CLASSIC. Jan 1. Cotton Bowl Stadium, Dallas, TX. Since 2008, a regular-season NHL game held outdoors on New Year's Day. For 2020, the Dallas Stars battle the Nashville Predators. For info: National Hockey League. Web: www.nhl.com.

OATMEAL MONTH. Jan 1–31. Oatmeal is an affordable, delicious and nutritious way to start the day, and it is also a versatile ingredient for cooking and baking your favorite recipes. When eaten daily as part of a diet low in saturated fat and cholesterol, three grams of soluble fiber from oatmeal may reduce the risk of heart disease. For delicious, sweet and savory recipes and more info: Quaker Oats. Web: www.QuakerOats.com.

OUTBACK BOWL. Jan 1. Raymond James Stadium, Tampa, FL. 34th edition. The Outback Bowl brings together college football teams from the SEC and the Big Ten. In addition, the bowl is highlighted by a variety of special events, sports activities and private functions. Est attendance: 55,000. For info: Tampa Bay Bowl Assn.

Phone: (813) 874-BOWL. E-mail: info@outbackbowl.com. Web: www.outbackbowl.com.

PHILBY, KIM: BIRTH ANNIVERSARY. Jan 1, 1912. Born at Ambala, India, Harold Adrian Russell Philby was the most successful Soviet double agent of the cold war. Recruited by the KGB while still a student at Cambridge University, Philby first worked as a journalist, but he later joined British Intelligence. Philby held a number of sensitive posts at MI-6, including head of counterespionage and liaison to US intelligence. These posts afforded Philby many opportunities to pass secret information to Moscow and to manipulate British and US intelligence activities. Suspicion mounted against Philby after two of his associates in the intelligence service defected to the USSR. He was dismissed from the service in 1955 and fled to Moscow in 1963. He died May 11, 1988, at Moscow, USSR.

PHILIPPINES: BLACK NAZARENE FIESTA. Jan 1–9. Manila. This traditional nine-day fiesta honors Quiapo district's patron saint. Cultural events, fireworks and parades culminate in a procession with the life-size statue of the Black Nazarene. Procession begins at the historic Quiapo Church.

***PROFILES IN COURAGE* PUBLISHED: ANNIVERSARY.** Jan 1, 1956. Senator John F. Kennedy of Massachusetts published his book (written in collaboration with his speechwriter Ted Sorensen) to great praise and sales. It won a Pulitzer Prize in 1957.

REVERE, PAUL: BIRTH ANNIVERSARY. Jan 1, 1735. American patriot, silversmith and engraver; maker of false teeth, eyeglasses, picture frames and surgical instruments. Best remembered for his famous ride Apr 18, 1775, celebrated in Longfellow's poem "The Midnight Ride of Paul Revere." Born at Boston, MA; died there May 10, 1818. See also: "Paul Revere's Ride: Anniversary" (Apr 18).

ROSE BOWL GAME. Jan 1. Pasadena, CA. Presented by Northwestern Mutual. The Rose Bowl football game has been a New Year's event since 1902. Michigan defeated Stanford 49–0 in what was the first postseason football game. Called the Rose Bowl since 1923, it is preceded each year by the Tournament of Roses Parade. Features champions from the Big Ten and Pac-12 conferences. (If the conference champion is selected to participate in the College Football Playoff Semifinal, the Rose Bowl Game will select the next best team in the conference.) Est attendance: 93,000. For info: Tournament of Roses. Web: www.tournamentofroses.com/rose-bowl.

THE ROSE PARADE PRESENTED BY HONDA. Jan 1. Pasadena, CA. 131st annual parade. The Tournament of Roses has been an annual New Year's event since 1890, with the parade featuring amazing flower-bedecked floats as well as marching bands and equestrian groups. The Rose Parade starts at 8 AM, PST, and is broadcast live across the nation. The 2020 theme: "The Power of Hope." Est attendance: 700,000. For info: Tournament of Roses Association. Web: www.tournamentofroses.com.

ROSS, BETSY: BIRTH ANNIVERSARY. Jan 1, 1752. (Old Style date.) According to legend based largely on her grandson's revelations in 1870, needleworker Betsy Ross created the first Stars and Stripes flag in 1775, under instructions from George Washington. Her sewing and her making of flags were well known, but there is little corroborative evidence of her role in making the first Stars and Stripes. The account is generally accepted, however, in the absence of any documented claims to the contrary. She was born Elizabeth Griscom at Philadelphia, PA, and died there Jan 30, 1836.

RUSSIA: NEW YEAR'S DAY OBSERVANCE. Jan 1–2. National holiday. Modern tradition calls for setting up New Year's trees in homes, halls, clubs, palaces of culture and the hall of the Kremlin Palace. Children's parties with Granddad Frost and his granddaughter,

Snow Girl. Games, songs, dancing, special foods, family gatherings and exchange of gifts and New Year's cards.

SAINT BASIL'S DAY. Jan 1. St. Basil's or St. Vasily's feast day observed by Eastern Orthodox churches. Special traditions for the day include serving St. Basil cakes, each of which contains a coin. Feast day observed Jan 14 by those churches using the Julian calendar.

SALINGER, JEROME DAVID (J.D.): BIRTH ANNIVERSARY. Jan 1, 1919. Reclusive author, born at New York City. Wrote 13 short stories mostly for *The New Yorker*. In 1951 he published his only novel, *The Catcher in the Rye*—one of the great books of the 20th century. In 1953 he retreated to Cornish, NH, where he lived until his death on Jan 27, 2010.

SOLEMNITY OF MARY, MOTHER OF GOD. Jan 1. Holy day of obligation in the Roman Catholic Church since calendar reorganization of 1969, replacing the Feast of the Circumcision, which had been recognized for more than 14 centuries. See also: "Circumcision of Christ" (Jan 1).

STIEGLITZ, ALFRED: BIRTH ANNIVERSARY. Jan 1, 1864. Arguably the most important photographer of his time, Stieglitz was also a publisher, art dealer and advocate for the Modernist movement, particularly artist Georgia O'Keeffe, who was his lover and, later, wife. He was convinced photography should be considered a fine art and cofounded the Photo-Secessionist organization, which advocated the Pictorialist style, an approach to photography that emphasizes beauty of subject matter, tonality and composition rather than documentation of reality. Born at Hoboken, NJ, he died July 13, 1946, at New York, NY.

STOCK EXCHANGE HOLIDAY (NEW YEAR'S DAY). Jan 1. The holiday schedules for the various exchanges are subject to change if relevant rules, regulations or exchange policies are revised. If you have questions, contact: CME Group (CME, CBOT, NYMEX, COMEX) (www.cmegroup.com), Chicago Board Options Exchange (www.cboe.com), NASDAQ (www.nasdaq.com), NYSE (www.nyse.com).

SUDAN: INDEPENDENCE DAY. Jan 1. National holiday. Sudan was proclaimed a sovereign independent republic in 1956, ending its status as an Anglo-Egyptian condominium (since 1899).

TAIWAN: FOUNDATION DAYS. Jan 1–2. Public holiday. Commemorates the founding of the Republic of China on Jan 1, 1912.

WALKER, DOAK: BIRTH ANNIVERSARY. Jan 1, 1927. Ewell Doak Walker, Jr, Hall of Fame and Heisman Trophy running back, was born at Dallas, TX. Walker won the Heisman Trophy in 1948, playing for SMU, and went on to an outstanding pro career with the Detroit Lions. He was a handsome, humble player during a time when football players could become national heroes. Inducted into the Hall of Fame in 1986. Died at Steamboat Springs, CO, Sept 27, 1998.

WAYNE, "MAD ANTHONY": 275th BIRTH ANNIVERSARY. Jan 1, 1745. (Old Style date.) American Revolutionary War general whose daring, sometimes reckless, conduct earned him the nickname "Mad." His courage and shrewdness as a soldier made him a key figure in capturing Stony Point, NY (1779), preventing Benedict Arnold's "delivery" of West Point to the British and subduing hostile Indians of the Northwest Territory (1794). He was born at Waynesboro, PA, and died at Presque Isle, PA, Dec 15, 1796.

WORLDWIDE RISING STAR MONTH. Jan 1–31. A month urging everyone to reach for the stars by designing a personal life plan. It takes place in January because that is the month when people can review the past year and design, revise or redesign their life

	S	M	T	W	T	F	S
January					1	2	3	4
	5	6	7	8	9	10	11
2020	12	13	14	15	16	17	18
	19	20	21	22	23	24	25
	26	27	28	29	30	31	

plans for the current year. "Remember to reach for the stars by designing your life plan!" For info: Deborah Le Bouf Kulkkula, PhD, 381 Billings Rd, Fitchburg, MA 01420. Phone: (978) 343-4009 or (978) 808-8084 (cell). E-mail: DebKulkkula@gmail.com. Web: www.RisingStarMonth.com.

YEAR OF THE NURSE AND MIDWIFE. Jan 1–Dec 31. An observance promoted for 2020 by nursing and midwife organizations around the world. It is anchored on the 200th birth anniversary of modern nursing pioneer Florence Nightingale (1820–1910).

Z DAY. Jan 1. To give recognition on the first day of the year to all persons and places whose names begin with the letter *Z* and who are always listed or thought of last in any alphabetized list. For info: Tom Zager. E-mail: tom_zager@yahoo.com.

🎂 BIRTHDAYS TODAY

Glen "Big Baby" Davis, 34, basketball player, born Baton Rouge, LA, Jan 1, 1986.

Meryl Davis, 33, Olympic ice dancer, born Royal Oak, MI, Jan 1, 1987.

Holliday Grainger, 32, actress ("The Borgias," *Jane Eyre*), born Didsbury, Manchester, England, Jan 1, 1988.

Michael Imperioli, 54, actor ("The Sopranos"), born Mount Vernon, NY, Jan 1, 1966.

Helmut Jahn, 80, architect, born Nuremberg, Germany, Jan 1, 1940.

Frank Langella, 80, actor (Tonys for *Frost/Nixon* and *The Father*; *The Twelve Chairs, Lolita*), born Bayonne, NJ, Jan 1, 1940.

Robert Menendez, 66, US Senator (D, New Jersey), born New York, NY, Jan 1, 1954.

Don Novello, 77, comedian ("Saturday Night Live"), born Ashtabula, OH, Jan 1, 1943.

January 2 — Thursday

DAY 2	364 REMAINING

ASIMOV, ISAAC: 100th BIRTH ANNIVERSARY. Jan 2, 1920. Although Isaac Asimov was one of the world's best-known writers of science fiction, his almost 500 books dealt with subjects as diverse as the Bible, works for preschoolers, college course work, mysteries, chemistry, biology, limericks, Shakespeare, Gilbert and Sullivan and modern history. During his prolific career he helped to elevate science fiction from pulp magazines to a more intellectual level. His works include the Foundation trilogy, *The Robots of Dawn, Robots and Empire, Nemesis, Murder at the A.B.A.* (in which he himself was a character), *The Gods Themselves* and *I, Robot*, in which he posited the famous Three Laws of Robotics. His *The Clock We Live On* is an accessible explanation of the origins of calendars. Asimov was born near Smolensk, Russia, and died at New York, NY, Apr 6, 1992.

DISTINGUISHED SERVICE MEDAL: ANNIVERSARY. Jan 2, 1918. With US troops fighting in the trenches in France during WWI, President Woodrow Wilson authorized the creation of a new bronze, beribboned medal to be given to US Army personnel who performed "exceptionally meritorious service."

55-MPH SPEED LIMIT: ANNIVERSARY. Jan 2, 1974. President Richard Nixon signed a bill requiring states to limit highway speeds to a maximum of 55 mph. This measure was meant to conserve energy during the crisis precipitated by the embargo imposed by the Arab oil-producing countries. A plan, used by some states, limited sale of gasoline to odd-numbered days for cars whose plates ended in odd numbers and even-numbered days for even-numbered plates. Some states limited purchases to $2–$3 per auto, and lines as long as six miles resulted in some locations. See also: "Arab Oil Embargo Lifted: Anniversary" (Mar 13).

FRANKLIN, JOHN HOPE: BIRTH ANNIVERSARY. Jan 2, 1915. Historian, educator and author Dr. John Hope Franklin was born in the all-black town of Rentiesville, OK. A son of segregation, he received a doctorate from Harvard. Franklin's bestselling 1947 book *From Slavery to Freedom: A History of African-Americans* recast the telling of American history. Franklin was a consultant on 1954's *Brown v Board of Education* Supreme Court case. In 1995, President Bill Clinton awarded him the Medal of Freedom. Franklin died Mar 25, 2009, at Durham, NC.

GEORGIA: RATIFICATION DAY. Jan 2, 1788. By unanimous vote, Georgia became the fourth state to ratify the Constitution.

HAITI: ANCESTORS' DAY. Jan 2. Commemoration of the ancestors. Also known as Hero's Day. Public holiday.

HAPPY MEW YEAR FOR CATS DAY. Jan 2. Felines, ever above mere humans in the great chain of being, have a day unto themselves to celebrate the "mewness" of a new time. Annually, Jan 2. (©2006 by WH.) For info: Thomas & Ruth Roy, Wellcat Holidays, 2418 Long Ln, Lebanon, PA 17046. Phone: (717) 279-0184. E-mail: info@wellcat.com. Web: www.wellcat.com.

JAPAN: KAKIZOME. Jan 2. Traditional Japanese festival gets under way when the first strokes of the year are made on paper with the traditional brushes.

MILLER, ROGER: BIRTH ANNIVERSARY. Jan 2, 1936. Country and western singer, songwriter and musician ("King of the Road"), Roger Miller was born at Fort Worth, TX. Miller won 11 Grammy Awards and a Tony Award (1986 for the score to the Broadway play *Big River*). He died Oct 25, 1992, at Los Angeles, CA.

MOON PHASE: FIRST QUARTER. Jan 2. Moon enters First Quarter phase at 11:45 PM, EST.

SCOTLAND: NEW YEAR'S BANK HOLIDAY. Jan 2. Public holiday. The first working day after New Year's Day.

"SOMEDAY WE'LL LAUGH ABOUT THIS" WEEK. Jan 2–8. 43rd annual. We've all used the expression, "Someday we'll laugh about this!" Why wait? It usually takes less than seven days for people to violate 90 percent of their New Year's resolutions. This week helps us to remember the art of laughing at ourselves and tickles the joke of perfectionism while encouraging people to strive for excellence. Laughing at the humorous human condition is a great way to start the New Year. For info: Dr. Joel Goodman, The Humor Project, Inc, 10 Madison Ave, Saratoga Springs, NY 12866. Phone: (518) 587-8770. E-mail: info@HumorProject.com. Web: www.HumorProject.com.

SPACE MILESTONE: *LUNA 1* (USSR). Jan 2, 1959. Launch of robotic moon probe that missed the moon and became the first spacecraft from Earth to orbit the sun.

SPAIN CAPTURES GRANADA: ANNIVERSARY. Jan 2, 1492. Spaniards took the city of Granada from the Moors, ending seven centuries of Muslim rule in Spain.

SWITZERLAND: BERCHTOLDSTAG. Jan 2. Holiday in many cantons. Commemorates the founding of the city of Bern by Duke Berchtold V in the 12th century. Now mainly a children's holiday.

TAFT, HELEN HERRON: BIRTH ANNIVERSARY. Jan 2, 1861. Wife of William Howard Taft, 27th president of the US, born at Cincinnati, OH. Died at Washington, DC, May 22, 1943.

WOLFE, JAMES: BIRTH ANNIVERSARY. Jan 2, 1727. English general who commanded the British army's victory over Montcalm's French forces on the Plains of Abraham at Quebec City in 1759. As a result, France surrendered Canada to England. Wolfe was born at Westerham, Kent, England. He died at the Plains of Abraham of battle wounds, Sept 13, 1759.

WORLD INTROVERT DAY. Jan 2. Since 2011. On this day introverts take time to relax and recharge after the busy holiday season. It's also a day to bring awareness to the strengths and contributions of introverts. "Quiet ones" make up 30–50 percent of the population, yet they continue to be overlooked and misunderstood. Celebrate World Introvert Day by spending time alone or doing something that recharges your energy. Annually, Jan 2. For info: IntrovertDear.com, 500 Westover Dr, #12657, Sanford, NC 27330. E-mail: jenn@introvertdear.com. Web: https://introvertdear.com.

🎂 BIRTHDAYS TODAY

Jim Bakker, 81, former television evangelist, born James Orsen at Muskegon, MI, Jan 2, 1939.

Kate Bosworth, 37, actress ("SS-GB," *21, Superman Returns, Blue Crush*), born Los Angeles, CA, Jan 2, 1983.

Brian Boucher, 43, former hockey player, born Woonsocket, RI, Jan 2, 1977.

Tia Carrere, 53, actress (*Wayne's World, True Lies*), born Honolulu, HI, Jan 2, 1967.

David Cone, 57, former baseball player, born Kansas City, MO, Jan 2, 1963.

Taye Diggs, 48, actor ("Private Practice," *Rent, How Stella Got Her Groove Back*), born Rochester, NY, Jan 2, 1972.

Christopher Durang, 71, playwright (Tony Award for *Vanya and Sonia and Masha and Spike*), actor, born Montclair, NJ, Jan 2, 1949.

Cuba Gooding, Jr, 52, actor (Oscar for *Jerry Maguire*; "The People v O.J. Simpson"), born the Bronx, NY, Jan 2, 1968.

Todd Haynes, 59, film director (*Carol, Far from Heaven, Velvet Goldmine, Safe*), screenwriter, born Los Angeles, CA, Jan 2, 1961.

Edgar Martinez, 57, Hall of Fame baseball player, born New York, NY, Jan 2, 1963.

Wendy Phillips, 68, actress ("Big Love," "Homefront"), born Brooklyn, NY, Jan 2, 1952.

Dax Shepard, 45, actor, comedian (*Baby Mama, When in Rome*, "Parenthood," "Punk'd"), born Milford, MI, Jan 2, 1975.

Christy Turlington, 51, model, born Walnut Creek, CA, Jan 2, 1969.

January 3 — Friday

DAY 3   **363 REMAINING**

ALASKA: ADMISSION DAY: ANNIVERSARY. Jan 3, 1959. Alaska, which had been purchased from Russia in 1867, became the 49th state. The area of Alaska is nearly one-fifth the size of the rest of the US.

January 2020	S	M	T	W	T	F	S
				1	2	3	4
	5	6	7	8	9	10	11
	12	13	14	15	16	17	18
	19	20	21	22	23	24	25
	26	27	28	29	30	31	

AMERICAN HISTORICAL ASSOCIATION: ANNUAL MEETING. Jan 3–6. New York, NY. 134th annual. Approximately 400 sessions will be held covering a wide range of scholarly, professional and pedagogical topics dealing with all areas of history. Est attendance: 5,500. For info: American Historical Assn. Phone: (202) 544-2422. E-mail: info@historians.org. Web: www.historians.org.

"THE ARSENIO HALL SHOW" TV PREMIERE: ANNIVERSARY. Jan 3, 1989. Arsenio Hall became the first African American to host a successful, syndicated late-night talk show. The show attracted a younger audience than that of Johnny Carson's "The Tonight Show" and effectively limited the impact of CBS's 1989 late-night entry, "The Pat Sajak Show." Hall was able to book soul and rap music acts that had rarely been seen on other shows. His was also the show on which presidential candidate Bill Clinton appeared, playing the saxophone in dark glasses. Hall was named by *TV Guide* (June 1990) as its first "TV Person of the Year."

ATTLEE, CLEMENT RICHARD: BIRTH ANNIVERSARY. Jan 3, 1883. English leader of the Labour Party and prime minister (July 1945–October 1951). Born at London, England; died there Oct 8, 1967.

CONGRESS ASSEMBLES. Jan 3. The Constitution provides that "the Congress shall assemble at least once in every year . . . ," and the 20th Amendment specifies "and such meeting shall begin at noon on the third day of January, unless they shall by law appoint a different day." If Jan 3 happens to fall on a weekend, Congress by resolution will meet on the following Monday or Tuesday.

COOLIDGE, GRACE ANNA GOODHUE: BIRTH ANNIVERSARY. Jan 3, 1879. Wife of Calvin Coolidge, 30th president of the US, born at Burlington, VT. Died at Northampton, MA, July 8, 1957.

"CURSE OF THE BAMBINO" BEGINS: 100th ANNIVERSARY. Jan 3, 1920. Boston Red Sox owner and theatrical producer Harry Frazee sold pitcher-outfielder Babe Ruth to the New York Yankees for $125,000 and a $300,000 loan. The "Curse of the Bambino" began: the Red Sox, who had won the World Series in 1903, 1912, 1915, 1916 and 1918, faced a drought—until victory in 2004. Sportswriters began blaming the drought on Ruth's sale in the 1980s and 1990s. Red Sox fans were famous for the unique ways they used to attempt to "reverse the curse."

DAVIES, MARION: BIRTH ANNIVERSARY. Jan 3, 1897. Born at Brooklyn, NY, Marion Cecilia Douras became Marion Davies and made her first appearance on film in 1917. Her romantic and professional involvement with newspaper magnate William Randolph Hearst ensured the type of publicity that would launch her to stardom. Her films include *When Knighthood Was in Flower, The Patsy* and *Show People*. Davies died at Hollywood, CA, Sept 23, 1961.

MEMENTO MORI. Jan 3. *Memento, mori*, Latin for "Remember, you die," is also the title of a novel by Muriel Spark. We suggest posting the words at home and at work, not to be morbid, but to remind us to cherish all that we have today . . . for tomorrow may never arrive. (©2006 by WH.) For info: Thomas & Ruth Roy, Wellcat Holidays, 2418 Long Ln, Lebanon, PA 17046. Phone: (717) 279-0184. E-mail: info@wellcat.com. Web: www.wellcat.com.

MOTT, LUCRETIA (COFFIN): BIRTH ANNIVERSARY. Jan 3, 1793. American teacher, minister, antislavery leader and (with Elizabeth Cady Stanton) one of the founders of the women's rights movement in the US. Born at Nantucket, MA, she died near Philadelphia, PA, Nov 11, 1880.

RAUH, JOSEPH L., JR: BIRTH ANNIVERSARY. Jan 3, 1911. Political activist Joseph L. Rauh, Jr, was born at Cincinnati, OH. In 1947 he cofounded Americans for Democratic Action (ADA), which supports liberal causes. Rauh helped create the minority civil rights plank at the 1948 Democratic National Convention—a foundation for the federal civil rights legislation in the 1960s. He served on the executive board of the NAACP and was general counsel to the Leadership Conference on Civil Rights. He died Sept 3, 1992, at Washington, DC.

SAINT GENEVIÈVE: FEAST DAY. Jan 3. The patron saint of Paris, St. Geneviève is credited with rallying Parisian resistance to Attila's Huns as they moved west into France in 451. Following her death, a reliquary containing her remains was carried at the head of a parade every Jan 3 and at times of peril and privation in Paris, until the reliquary was melted down during the Revolutionary Terror. She lived from about 422 to about 500.

SPACE MILESTONE: *MARS EXPLORATION ROVER SPIRIT* **(US).** Jan 3, 2004. After traveling 302.6 million miles from its June 10, 2003, launch at Cape Canaveral Air Force Station, FL, the *Mars Exploration Rover Spirit* landed at Gusev Crater on Mars. The robotic rover's mission was to examine the soil and environment of the red planet. By Jan 6, *Spirit* had taken the sharpest color photograph of Mars ever achieved. *Spirit*'s twin rover, *Opportunity*, landed Jan 24, 2004. In 2009, *Spirit* became stuck in soft soil and, after sending data from its stationary position, ended communication with NASA on Mar 22, 2010. NASA announced the mission complete on May 24, 2011.

TOLKIEN, J.R.R.: BIRTH ANNIVERSARY. Jan 3, 1892. Author, professor, medieval scholar and philologist John Ronald Reuel Tolkien was born at Bloemfontein, in what is now South Africa. He is best known for his sagas of Middle Earth: *The Hobbit* (1937) and *The Lord of the Rings* (published in three volumes from 1954 to 1955), which introduced the world to hobbits, elves, orcs and more. These novels are some of the most influential fantasies of the 20th century. Tolkien's works have been translated into more than 60 languages and remain bestsellers. Made a Commander of the British Empire in 1972, he died at Bournemouth, England, Sept 2, 1973.

🎂 BIRTHDAYS TODAY

Joan Walsh Anglund, 94, author, illustrator of children's books (*Crocus in the Snow, Bedtime Book*), born Hinsdale, IL, Jan 3, 1926.

Nicole Beharie, 35, actress ("Sleepy Hollow," *42, American Violet*), born West Palm Beach, FL, Jan 3, 1985.

Dabney Coleman, 88, actor ("Buffalo Bill," *Nine to Five, Tootsie*), born Austin, TX, Jan 3, 1932.

Mel Gibson, 64, actor (*Braveheart, Lethal Weapon*), director (Oscar for *Braveheart*; *Hacksaw Ridge, The Passion of the Christ*), born Peekskill, NY, Jan 3, 1956.

Robert Marvin (Bobby) Hull, 81, Hall of Fame hockey player, born Point Anne, ON, Canada, Jan 3, 1939.

Ned Lamont, 66, Governor of Connecticut (D), born Washington, DC, Jan 3, 1954.

Eli Manning, 39, football player, born New Orleans, LA, Jan 3, 1981.

Danica McKellar, 45, actress ("The Wonder Years," *Sidekicks*), born La Jolla, CA, Jan 3, 1975.

Victoria Principal, 70, actress ("Dallas"), born Fukuoka, Japan, Jan 3, 1950.

Florence Pugh, 24, actress (*Lady Macbeth, Outlaw King*, "The Little Drummer Girl"), born Oxford, England, Jan 1, 1996.

Stephen Stills, 75, musician, songwriter, born Dallas, TX, Jan 3, 1945.

January 4 — Saturday

DAY 4   **362 REMAINING**

AMNESTY FOR POLYGAMISTS: ANNIVERSARY. Jan 4, 1893. President Benjamin Harrison issued a proclamation granting full amnesty and pardon to all persons who had since Nov 1, 1890, abstained from unlawful cohabitation in a polygamous marriage. This was intended in the main for a specific group of elderly Mormons who had continued in the practice of contracting serial marriages. Amnesty was based on the condition that those pardoned must obey the law in the future or be "vigorously prosecuted." The practice of polygamy was a factor interfering with attainment of statehood for Utah.

BRAILLE, LOUIS: BIRTH ANNIVERSARY. Jan 4, 1809. The inventor of a widely used touch system of reading and writing for blind people was born at Coupvray, France. Permanently blinded at the age of three by a leatherworking awl in his father's saddle-making shop, Braille developed a system of writing that used, ironically, an awl-like stylus to punch marks in paper that could be felt and interpreted by people who are blind. The system was largely ignored until after Braille died in poverty, suffering from tuberculosis, at Paris, Jan 6, 1852.

COLOMBIA: CARNIVAL OF BLACKS AND WHITES. Jan 4–6. Pasto. Annual multicultural festival of parades, arts, music and costumes—an outgrowth of ancient Indian harvest rituals. During the Jan 5 Carnival of Blacks, revelers dance to African music and streak their bodies with black paint, signifying the day of freedom to granted slaves by the Spanish Crown. At the Jan 6 Carnival of Whites, festivalgoers throw white talcum powder at one another to symbolize equality and integrate all citizens through a celebration of ethnic and cultural differences. See the official site at www.carnavaldepasto.org.

DIMPLED CHAD DAY. Jan 4. This is a day to commemorate all the dimpled chads of the world, left over from various and sundry contested elections. Chads, roasted in garlic, make an excellent sprinkle topping for salads. (©2006 by WII.) For info: Thomas & Ruth Roy, Wellcat Holidays, 2418 Long Ln, Lebanon, PA 17046. Phone: (717) 279-0184. E-mail: info@wellcat.com. Web: www.wellcat.com.

DOW JONES TOPS 25,000: ANNIVERSARY. Jan 4, 2018. Continuing a record-setting pace that started in 2009 and accelerated in 2017, the Dow Jones industrial average (including 30 publicly traded companies) topped 25,000 points for the first time, closing at 25,075.

GENERAL TOM THUMB: BIRTH ANNIVERSARY. Jan 4, 1838. Charles Sherwood Stratton, perhaps the most famous little person in history, was born at Bridgeport, CT. He eventually reached a height of three feet, four inches and a weight of 70 pounds. Discovered by P.T. Barnum in 1842, Stratton, as "General Tom Thumb," became an internationally known entertainer and performed before Queen Victoria and other heads of state. On Feb 10, 1863, he married another little person, Lavinia Warren. Stratton died at Middleborough, MA, July 15, 1883.

GRIMM, JACOB: BIRTH ANNIVERSARY. Jan 4, 1785. Librarian, mythologist and philologist, born at Hanau, Germany. Best remembered for *Grimm's Fairy Tales* (in collaboration with his brother Wilhelm). Died at Berlin, Germany, Sept 20, 1863.

HOLLOWAY, STERLING: BIRTH ANNIVERSARY. Jan 4, 1905. Actor Sterling Holloway prospered in films and television, but he is

probably best remembered as the voice of Winnie the Pooh. He provided the voices for characters in several full-length animated features, including *Alice in Wonderland* (the Cheshire Cat), *The Aristocats* and *The Jungle Book*. Born at Cedartown, GA, he died Nov 22, 1992, at Los Angeles, CA.

MYANMAR: INDEPENDENCE DAY. Jan 4. National Day. The British controlled the country from 1826 until 1948, when it was granted independence. The country's name was changed from Burma to the Union of Myanmar in 1989 to reflect that the population is made up not just of the Burmese but of many other ethnic groups as well.

NEWTON, ISAAC: BIRTH ANNIVERSARY. Jan 4, 1643. Sir Isaac Newton was the chief figure of the scientific revolution of the 17th century, a physicist and mathematician who laid the foundations of calculus, studied the mechanics of planetary motion and discovered the law of gravitation. Born at Woolsthorpe, England, he died at London, England, Mar 31, 1727. Newton was born before Great Britain adopted the Gregorian calendar. His Julian (Old Style) birth date is Dec 25, 1642.

PATTERSON, FLOYD: 85th BIRTH ANNIVERSARY. Jan 4, 1935. Dominant heavyweight boxer of the 1950s and early '60s, born at Waco, NC. Patterson was the gold middleweight medalist at the 1952 Helsinki Olympics (winning all his matches by knockouts), and in 1956 he became the youngest-ever world heavyweight champion. In 1960 he became the first boxer to regain the title (after he had lost it in 1959). Shy and good-natured, Patterson was admired by sportswriters and fans. He died May 11, 2006, at New Paltz, NY.

POP MUSIC CHART INTRODUCED: ANNIVERSARY. Jan 4, 1936. *Billboard* magazine published the first list of bestselling pop records, covering the week that ended Dec 30, 1935. On the list were recordings by the Tommy Dorsey and the Ozzie Nelson orchestras.

RUSH, BENJAMIN: BIRTH ANNIVERSARY. Jan 4, 1746. Physician, patriot and humanitarian of the American Revolution, born on a plantation at Byberry, PA. Rush was a signer of the Declaration of Independence and his writings on mental illness earned him the title "Father of Psychiatry." His tract *Inquiry* attacked the common wisdom of the time that alcohol was beneficial. He was the first American to call alcoholism a chronic disease. Benjamin Rush died at Philadelphia, PA, Apr 19, 1813.

SETON, ELIZABETH ANN BAYLEY: FEAST DAY. Jan 4. First American-born saint (beatified Mar 17, 1963; canonized Sept 14, 1975). Born at New York, NY, Aug 28, 1774, Seton was the founder of the American Sisters of Charity, the first American order of Roman Catholic nuns. She died at Baltimore, MD, Jan 4, 1821.

TRIVIA DAY. Jan 4. In celebration of those who know all sorts of facts and/or have doctorates in uselessology. (Created by Robert L. Birch, Pun Corps.)

January 2020	S	M	T	W	T	F	S
				1	2	3	4
	5	6	7	8	9	10	11
	12	13	14	15	16	17	18
	19	20	21	22	23	24	25
	26	27	28	29	30	31	

UTAH: ADMISSION DAY: ANNIVERSARY. Jan 4. Utah became the 45th state in 1896.

WORLD BRAILLE DAY. Jan 4. Observed on the birth anniversary of Louis Braille and commemorating his life and work. Braille created a simple, effective and revolutionary tactile system of communication in 1824, publishing information about his system in 1829.

WORLD'S TALLEST BUILDING: 10th DEDICATION ANNIVERSARY. Jan 4, 2010. On this date, United Arab Emirates (UAE) member Dubai unveiled Burj Khalifa—a 2,717-foot tower that, upon opening, became the world's tallest building. Taiwan's Taipei 101 was the previous record holder at 1,667 feet. Dubbed Burj Dubai during its construction, the skyscraper was surprisingly renamed to honor UAE president Sheikh Khalifa bin Zayed, who, in 2009, provided Dubai with $25 billion in bailout funds.

🧁 BIRTHDAYS TODAY

Kris Bryant, 28, baseball player, born Las Vegas, NV, Jan 4, 1992.

Dyan Cannon, 83, actress (*Heaven Can Wait, Bob and Carol and Ted and Alice*), born Tacoma, WA, Jan 4, 1937.

Harlan Coben, 58, author (*Don't Let Go, Tell No One*), born Newark, NJ, Jan 4, 1962.

Dave Foley, 58, actor ("NewsRadio"), comedian (Kids in the Hall), born Toronto, ON, Canada, Jan 4, 1962.

Doris Kearns Goodwin, 77, historian (*No Ordinary Time, Team of Rivals*), born Brooklyn, NY, Jan 4, 1943.

Derrick Henry, 26, football player, 2015 Heisman Trophy winner, born Yulee, FL, Jan 4, 1994.

Ann Magnuson, 64, performance artist, actress ("Anything but Love," *Clear and Present Danger*), born Charleston, WV, Jan 4, 1956.

Julia Ormond, 55, actress (*Temple Grandin, Legends of the Fall, Sabrina*), born Surrey, England, Jan 4, 1965.

Barbara Rush, 93, actress ("7th Heaven," "Peyton Place," *Hombre*), born Denver, CO, Jan 4, 1927.

Donald Francis (Don) Shula, 90, Hall of Fame football coach and player, born Painesville, OH, Jan 4, 1930.

Michael Stipe, 60, singer (REM), born Decatur, GA, Jan 4, 1960.

January 5 — Sunday

DAY 5   **361 REMAINING**

AILEY, ALVIN: BIRTH ANNIVERSARY. Jan 5, 1931. Born at Rogers, TX, Alvin Ailey began his noted career as a choreographer in the late 1950s after a successful career as a dancer. He founded the Alvin Ailey American Dance Theater, drawing from classical ballet, jazz, Afro-Caribbean and modern dance idioms to create the 79 ballets of the company's repertoire. He and his work played a central part in establishing a role for blacks in the world of modern dance. Ailey died Dec 1, 1989, at New York, NY.

"ALL MY CHILDREN" TV PREMIERE: 50th ANNIVERSARY. Jan 5, 1970. This ABC show, created by Agnes Nixon, became TV's top-rated soap opera by the 1978–79 season. Set in Pine Valley, PA, the show originally focused on the Tyler and Martin families. The story included Erica Kane (Susan Lucci), one of daytime TV's most popular characters. The show garnered more than 150 Daytime Emmy Awards, including one for Lucci (in 1999)—she was nominated a record 21 times. Other award-winning or longtime cast members included Ruth Warrick as Phoebe Tyler Wallingford, Julia Barr as Brooke English, Michael E. Knight as Tad Martin and David Canary as twin brothers Adam and Stuart Chandler. The show also launched the careers of Kim Delaney, Sarah Michelle Gellar, Eva LaRue and Kelly Ripa. The 10,000th episode aired Nov 12, 2008. ABC canceled the show in 2011 (the finale aired Sept 23, 2011) but sold rights for an online version, which lasted another year.

CARVER, GEORGE WASHINGTON: DEATH ANNIVERSARY. Jan 5, 1943. Black American agricultural scientist, author, inventor and teacher. Born into slavery at Diamond Grove, MO, probably in 1864. His research led to the creation of synthetic products made from peanuts, potatoes and wood. Carver died at Tuskegee, AL. His birthplace became a national monument in 1953.

DAKAR RALLY 2020: SAUDI ARABIA. Jan 5–17. 42nd edition. Held since 1978, when it was the Paris–Dakar Rally, the Dakar Rally, the legendary event of the off-road rally discipline, continues in Saudi Arabia. The 2020 edition starts in Jeddah and finishes in Al Qiddiya. Midway through the race there is a rest day in Riyadh. Est attendance: 1,000,000. For info: Amaury Sport Organisation. E-mail: garriola@aso.fr. Web: www.dakar.com or www.aso.fr.

DATING AND LIFE COACH RECOGNITION WEEK. Jan 5–11. Coaches love to help people lead joyful, purposeful, successful lives. Whether the goals are to find love, pursue passions, embrace challenges, cultivate a career or achieve personal gratification, a coach's job is to empower, guide and inform. This week is a time to recognize the contributions dating and life coaches make to the well-being of society. For info: Robin Gorman Newman, 44 Somerset Dr N, Great Neck, NY 10020. Phone: (516) 773-0911. E-mail: rgnewman@optonline.net. Web: www.lovecoach.com.

DECATUR, STEPHEN: BIRTH ANNIVERSARY. Jan 5, 1779. American naval officer (whose father and grandfather, both also named Stephen Decatur, were also seafaring men) born at Sinepuxent, MD. In a toast at a dinner in Norfolk, VA, in 1815, Decatur spoke his most famous words: "Our country! In her intercourse with foreign nations may she always be in the right; but our country, right or wrong." Mortally wounded in a duel with Commodore James Barron, at Bladensburg, MD, on the morning of Mar 22, 1820, Decatur was carried to his home in Washington, DC, where he died a few hours later.

EARTH AT PERIHELION. Jan 5. At approximately 2:48 AM, EST, planet Earth will reach perihelion, that point in its orbit when it is closest to the sun (about 91,400,000 miles). Earth's mean distance from the sun (mean radius of its orbit) is reached early in the months of April and October. Note that Earth is closest to the sun during the Northern Hemisphere winter. See also: "Earth at Aphelion" (July 4).

FIVE-DOLLAR-A-DAY MINIMUM WAGE: ANNIVERSARY. Jan 5, 1914. Henry Ford announced that all worthy Ford Motor Company employees would receive a minimum wage of $5 a day. Ford explained the policy as "profit sharing and efficiency engineering." The more cynical attributed it to an attempt to prevent unionization and to obtain a docile workforce that would accept job speed-ups. To obtain this minimum wage, an employee had to be of "good personal habits." Whether an individual fit these criteria was determined by a new office created by Ford Motor Company—the Sociological Department.

GOLDEN GLOBE AWARDS. Jan 5. Beverly Hilton Hotel, Beverly Hills, CA. 77th annual. Presented by the Hollywood Foreign Press Association and honoring achievement in film and television. Aired live on NBC. (Nominations are Dec 9, 2019.) For info: The Hollywood Foreign Press Assn. E-mail: info@hfpa.org. Web: www.goldenglobes.com.

ITALY: EPIPHANY FAIR. Jan 5. Piazza Navona, Rome. On the eve of Epiphany a fair of toys, sweets and presents takes place among the beautiful Bernini Fountains.

NATIONAL BIRD DAY. Jan 5. 18th annual. The survival and well-being of the world's birds depends upon public education and support for conservation. Birds are sentinel species whose plight serves as a barometer of ecosystem health and an alert system for detecting global environmental ills. Today, nearly 12 percent of the world's 9,800 bird species may face extinction within the next century, including nearly one-third of the world's 330 parrot species. This is a day to celebrate birds and learn how to protect them. Annually, Jan 5. For info: Avian Welfare Coalition, PO Box 40212,

St. Paul, MN 55104. E-mail: info@avianwelfare.org. Web: www.avianwelfare.org/nationalbirdday.

PICCARD, JEANNETTE RIDLON: 125th BIRTH ANNIVERSARY. Jan 5, 1895. First American woman to qualify as a free-balloon pilot (1934). Later, one of the first women to be ordained as an Episcopal priest (1976). Pilot for record-setting balloon ascent (57,579 feet) into the stratosphere (from Dearborn, MI, Oct 23, 1934) with her husband, Jean Felix Piccard. Identical twin married to identical twin. Born at Chicago, IL, she died at Minneapolis, MN, May 17, 1981. See also: "Piccard, Jean Felix: Birth Anniversary" (Jan 28).

REEVES, GEORGE: BIRTH ANNIVERSARY. Jan 5, 1914. The boxer turned actor was born George Keefer Brewer at Woodstock, IA. Active in the 1940s in minor Hollywood roles (including a small part in *Gone with the Wind*), Reeves found stardom on the small screen as Superman/Clark Kent in "The Adventures of Superman," which ran from 1952 to 1957. Reeves did his own stunts as the "Man of Steel" and was popular with children all over. To his frustration, though, Reeves saw his serious acting career suffer due to his being typecast as a cartoon superhero. He died June 16, 1959, of an apparently self-inflicted gunshot wound at his Beverly Hills, CA, home.

ROMAN CATHOLIC/EASTERN ORTHODOX MEETING: ANNIVERSARY. Jan 5, 1964. Pope Paul VI and Patriarch Athenagoras of Jerusalem traveled to the Holy Land for the first meeting in five centuries between a Roman Catholic pontiff and an Eastern Orthodox patriarch.

RUFFIN, EDMUND: BIRTH ANNIVERSARY. Jan 5, 1794. Born at Prince George County, VA, Edmund Ruffin was an American agriculturist whose discoveries about crop rotation and fertilizer were influential in the early agrarian culture of the US. He published the *Farmer's Register* from 1833 to 1842, a journal that promoted scientific agriculture. A noted politician as well as a farmer, he was an early advocate of Southern secession whose views were widely circulated in pamphlets. As a member of the Palmetto Guards of Charleston, he was given the honor of firing the first shot on Fort Sumter on Apr 12, 1861. According to legend, after the South's defeat he became despondent and, wrapping himself in the Confederate flag, took his own life on June 18, 1865, at Amelia County, VA.

TWELFTH NIGHT. Jan 5. Evening before Epiphany (Jan 6). Twelfth Night marks the end of medieval Christmas festivities. Also called Twelfth Day Eve. See also: "Epiphany or Twelfth Day" (Jan 6).

WILSON, KEMMONS: BIRTH ANNIVERSARY. Jan 5, 1913. The "father of the modern hotel," Wilson revolutionized the travel industry by creating the first standardized chain of clean, air-conditioned hotels with swimming pools and ice machines. In 1951 Wilson became angered by the conditions and costs of hotels he encountered during what he called "the most miserable vacation trip of my life." From this family vacation, the idea for the Holiday Inn chain was born. Named after the 1942 Bing Crosby film, Holiday Inns were strategically located next to the burgeoning interstate highway system, where growing numbers of post-WWII families could travel from one to the next, knowing there would be no unsavory surprises. Today, there are Holiday Inns in every state and in more than 50 countries worldwide. Born at Osceola, AR, Wilson died at his home at Memphis, TN, on Feb 12, 2003.

WYOMING INAUGURATES FIRST WOMAN GOVERNOR IN US: 95th ANNIVERSARY. Jan 5, 1925. Nellie Tayloe (Mrs William B.) Ross became the first woman to serve as governor upon her inauguration in Wyoming. She had previously finished out the term of her husband, who had died in office. In 1974 Ella Grasso of Connecticut became the first woman to be elected governor in her own right.

🧁 BIRTHDAYS TODAY

Bradley Cooper, 45, actor (*American Sniper, Silver Linings Playbook, The Hangover*), born Philadelphia, PA, Jan 5, 1975.

Mike DeWine, 73, Governor of Ohio (R), born Yellow Springs, OH, Jan 5, 1947.

Warrick Dunn, 45, former football player, born Baton Rouge, LA, Jan 5, 1975.

Robert Duvall, 89, actor (Oscar for *Tender Mercies*; *Get Low, A Civil Action, Lonesome Dove, The Godfather*), born San Diego, CA, Jan 5, 1931.

Carrie Ann Inaba, 52, choreographer, television personality ("Dancing with the Stars"), born Honolulu, HI, Jan 5, 1968.

January Jones, 42, actress ("Mad Men," *Unknown*), born Sioux Falls, SD, Jan 5, 1978.

Diane Keaton, 74, actress (*Something's Gotta Give, Looking for Mr Goodbar, Reds*, Oscar for *Annie Hall*), born Diane Hall at Los Angeles, CA, Jan 5, 1946.

Pamela Sue Martin, 66, actress (*The Poseidon Adventure*, "The Nancy Drew Mysteries," "Dynasty"), born Westport, CT, Jan 5, 1954.

Walter Frederick (Fritz) Mondale, 92, 42nd vice president of the US, former senator, born Ceylon, MN, Jan 5, 1928.

Charlie Rose, 78, former newscaster, television host ("CBS This Morning"), born Henderson, NC, Jan 5, 1942.

January 6 — Monday

DAY 6   **360 REMAINING**

ARMENIAN CHRISTMAS. Jan 6. Christmas is observed in the Armenian Church, the oldest Christian national church.

BUSH, GEORGE H.W. AND BARBARA, WEDDING: 75th ANNIVERSARY. Jan 6, 1945. George Herbert Walker Bush was 20 and Barbara Pierce was 19 when they married. They had four sons and two daughters (one of whom died in childhood). Bush served as the 41st president of the US. Their son George W. Bush became the 43rd president of the US.

CARNIVAL SEASON. Jan 6–Feb 25. A secular festival preceding Lent. A time of merrymaking and feasting before the austere days of Lenten fasting and penitence (40 weekdays between Ash Wednesday and Easter Sunday). The word *carnival* probably is derived from the Latin *carnem levare*, meaning "to remove meat." Depending on local custom, the carnival season may start any time between Nov 11 and Shrove Tuesday. Conclusion of the season is much less variable, being the close of Shrove Tuesday in most places. Celebrations vary considerably, but the festival often includes many theatrical aspects (masks, costumes and songs) and has given its name (in the US) to traveling amusement shows that may be seen throughout the year. Observed traditionally in Roman Catholic countries from Epiphany through Shrove Tuesday.

EPIPHANY OR TWELFTH DAY. Jan 6. Known also as Old Christmas Day and Twelfthtide. On the 12th day after Christmas, Christians celebrate the visit of the Magi, the first Gentile recognition of Christ. Epiphany of Our Lord, one of the oldest Christian feasts, is observed in Roman Catholic churches in the US on a Sunday between Jan 2 and 8. Theophany of the Eastern Orthodox Church is observed in churches using the Gregorian calendar (Jan 19 in those churches using the Julian calendar). This feast day celebrates the manifestation of the divinity of Jesus at the time of his baptism in the Jordan River by John the Baptist. Note: In centuries past, the day began at sunset. This custom has often led to confusion between Twelfth Night and Twelfth Day.

GIBRAN, KAHLIL: BIRTH ANNIVERSARY. Jan 6, 1883. Lebanese-American poet (*The Prophet*) and artist. Born at Bsharri, Lebanon, he died Oct 10, 1931, at New York, NY.

"HALLMARK HALL OF FAME" TV PREMIERE: ANNIVERSARY. Jan 6, 1952. Carried at different times by ABC, CBS, NBC and PBS, this was a top-quality dramatic anthology series. Originally titled "Hallmark Television Playhouse," the program was sponsored by Hallmark Cards and hosted by Sarah Churchill until 1955. A few of the presentations were *Hamlet*, with Maurice Evans and Ruth Chatterton (Apr 26, 1953); *Moby Dick*, with Victor Jory (May 16, 1954); *Macbeth*, with Maurice Evans, Dame Judith Anderson and House Jameson (Nov 28, 1954); and *Alice in Wonderland*, with Eva LeGallienne, Elsa Lanchester and Reginald Gardiner (Oct 23, 1955). The list goes on with splendid performances by many highly acclaimed actors and actresses.

ITALY: LA BEFANA. Jan 6. Epiphany festival in which the "Befana," a kindly witch, bestows gifts on children—toys and candy for those who have been good, but a lump of coal or a pebble for those who have been naughty. The festival begins on the night of Jan 5 with much noise and merrymaking (when the Befana is supposed to come down the chimneys on her broom, leaving gifts in children's stockings) and continues with joyous fairs, parades and other activities throughout Jan 6.

JAMAICA: MAROON FESTIVAL. Jan 6. Commemorates the 18th-century Treaty of Cudjoe. While Jamaica was a Spanish colony, its native inhabitants (Arawaks) were exterminated. The Spanish then imported African slaves to work on their plantations. When the Spanish were driven out (1655), the black slaves fled to the mountains. The "Maroons" (fugitive slaves) were permitted to settle in the north of the island in 1738.

JOAN OF ARC: BIRTH ANNIVERSARY. Jan 6, 1412. Born at the village of Domrémy, in the Meuse River Valley of France (probably in 1412), the teenage Jeanne d'Arc heard the voice of God commanding her to take up arms against the English during the Hundred Years War. She led a French army—dressed in men's armor—to try to oust the English from France. After some initial victories, she was captured in 1431 and turned over to a French ecclesiastical court by the British. The court found her guilty of heresy. Joan was burned at the stake May 30, 1431, at age 19, in Rouen, France.

MIX, TOM: BIRTH ANNIVERSARY. Jan 6, 1880. American motion picture actor, especially remembered for cowboy films. Born at Driftwood, PA. Died near Florence, AZ, Oct 12, 1940.

MONTGOLFIER, JACQUES ETIENNE: 275th BIRTH ANNIVERSARY. Jan 6, 1745. Merchant and inventor, born at Annonay, Ardèche, France. With his older brother, Joseph Michel, in November 1782, conducted experiments with paper and fabric bags filled with smoke and hot air, which led to the invention of the hot-air balloon and a human's first flight. Died at Serrieres, France, Aug 2, 1799. See also: "First Balloon Flight: Anniversary" (June 5); "Aviation History Month" (Nov 1).

January 2020	S	M	T	W	T	F	S
				1	2	3	4
	5	6	7	8	9	10	11
	12	13	14	15	16	17	18
	19	20	21	22	23	24	25
	26	27	28	29	30	31	

NATIONAL THANK GOD IT'S MONDAY! DAY. Jan 6. Besides holidays, such as Presidents' Day, being celebrated on Mondays, people everywhere start new jobs, have birthdays, celebrate promotions and begin vacations on Mondays. A day in recognition of this first day of the week. For info: Dorothy Zjawin, 61 W Colfax Ave, Roselle Park, NJ 07204.

NEW MEXICO: ADMISSION DAY: ANNIVERSARY. Jan 6, 1912. Became 47th state in 1912.

PAN AM CIRCLES EARTH: ANNIVERSARY. Jan 6, 1942. A Pan American Airways plane arrived in New York to complete the first around-the-world trip by a commercial aircraft.

SALOMON, HAYM: DEATH ANNIVERSARY. Jan 6, 1785. American Revolutionary War patriot and financier was born at Lissa, Poland, in 1740 (exact date unknown). Salomon died at Philadelphia, PA.

SANDBURG, CARL: BIRTH ANNIVERSARY. Jan 6, 1878. The bard of the American heartland, Sandburg was poet, biographer of Lincoln, historian and folklorist, born at Galesburg, IL. He was the recipient of two Pulitzer Prizes. In "Chicago" (1916), Sandburg gave that city the nickname it still bears: "City of Big Shoulders." He wrote in 1936, "Sometime they'll give a war and nobody will come." Sandburg died at Flat Rock, NC, July 22, 1967.

SCRUGGS, EARL: BIRTH ANNIVERSARY. Jan 6, 1924. Born at Flint Hill, NC, Earl Scruggs was a legendary bluegrass banjo musician. As a youth, Scruggs developed a trademark three-fingered style and joined the band of the "father of bluegrass," Bill Monroe, in 1945. His innovative syncopation provided the melodic glue in the Blue Grass Boys' sound, and he honed a role for his instrument that eschewed its past as a novelty and revealed its true beauty. "Foggy Mountain Breakdown," his Grammy Award–winning 1949 recording with guitarist Lester Flatt, is now a bluegrass standard as well as the technical mark by which all banjo players are judged. Scruggs also brought bluegrass to a wider audience with "The Ballad of Jed Clampett," the theme song for "The Beverly Hillbillies" (1962–71), a television show on which he regularly appeared. Scruggs died on Mar 28, 2012, at Nashville, TN.

SMITH, JEDEDIAH STRONG: BIRTH ANNIVERSARY. Jan 6, 1799. Mountain man, fur trader and one of the first explorers of the American West, Smith helped develop the Oregon Trail. He was the first American to reach California by land and the first to travel by land from San Diego up the West Coast to the Canadian border. Smith was born at Jericho (now Bainbridge), NY, and was killed by Comanche Indians along the Santa Fe Trail in what is now Kansas on May 27, 1831.

SPACE MILESTONE: *LUNAR EXPLORER* (US). Jan 6, 1998. NASA headed back to the moon for the first time since the *Apollo 17* flight 25 years before. This unmanned probe searched for evidence of frozen water on the moon and found evidence of ice in late 1998.

THOMAS, DANNY: BIRTH ANNIVERSARY. Jan 6, 1912. Comedian Danny Thomas was born Muzyad Yakhoob, later Amos Jacobs, at Deerfield, MI. Thomas began his entertainment career as a radio actor and nightclub comedian and then went on to movies in the late 1940s and early 1950s. His greatest fame came from his television show "Make Room for Daddy" (1953–64) and later as a television producer. He was also a tireless philanthropist who founded St. Jude Children's Research Hospital at Memphis, TN. Thomas died Feb 6, 1991, at Los Angeles, CA.

THREE KINGS DAY. Jan 6. Major festival of the Christian Church observed in many parts of the world with gifts, feasting, last lighting of Christmas lights and burning of Christmas greens. Twelfth and last day of the Feast of the Nativity. Commemorates the visit of the Three Wise Men (Kings or Magi) to Bethlehem.

"WHEEL OF FORTUNE" TV PREMIERE: 45th ANNIVERSARY. Jan 6, 1975. This quiz show, created by Merv Griffin, is the longest-running syndicated game show in television history. Players spin a wheel and guess letters in a word puzzle, winning money for every correct guess. Originally hosted by Chuck Woolery and first airing on NBC. Current hosts Pat Sajak and Vanna White took over in 1981, and the show went into syndication in 1983. There are scores of international versions of this show.

YOUNG, LORETTA: BIRTH ANNIVERSARY. Jan 6, 1913. Gretchen Michaela Young was born at Salt Lake City, UT. Initially a child extra, Young scooped a role from her unavailable older sister in *Naughty but Nice* (1927) and launched her film career as "Loretta." After a prolific career that saw her navigate from silents to talkies and from ingenue to leading lady, Young won an Oscar as Best Actress in 1947 for *The Farmer's Daughter*. She began a second career on television in 1953, winning three Emmy Awards for her television show, "The Loretta Young Show" (1953–61), becoming one of the first actors to win both an Oscar and Emmy. She died Aug 12, 2000, at Los Angeles, CA.

🎂 BIRTHDAYS TODAY

Joey Lauren Adams, 49, actress (*Chasing Amy, Big Daddy*), born Little Rock, AR, Jan 6, 1971.

Gilbert Arenas, 38, former basketball player, born Los Angeles, CA, Jan 6, 1982.

Rowan Atkinson, 65, actor (*Maigret in Montmartre, Johnny English,* "Mr Bean," "Blackadder"), born Newcastle-upon-Tyne, England, Jan 6, 1955.

Louis Leo (Lou) Holtz, 83, sportscaster, former football coach, born Follansbee, WV, Jan 6, 1937.

Howard M. (Howie) Long, 60, sportscaster, Hall of Fame football player, born Somerville, MA, Jan 6, 1960.

Nancy Lopez, 63, Hall of Fame golfer, born Torrance, CA, Jan 6, 1957.

Kate McKinnon, 36, actress, comedienne ("Saturday Night Live," *Ghostbusters*), born Kathryn McKinnon Berthold at Sea Cliff, NY, Jan 6, 1984.

Eddie Redmayne, 38, actor (Oscar for *The Theory of Everything; Fantastic Beasts and Where to Find Them, The Danish Girl*), born London, England, Jan 6, 1982.

Gabrielle Reece, 50, volleyball player, sportscaster, model, born La Jolla, CA, Jan 6, 1970.

Norman Reedus, 51, actor (*The Boondock Saints,* "The Walking Dead"), born Hollywood, FL, Jan 6, 1969.

Ndamukong Suh, 33, football player, born Portland, OR, Jan 6, 1987.

Jameis Winston, 26, football player, 2013 Heisman Trophy winner, born Bessemer, AL, Jan 6, 1994.

January 7 — Tuesday

DAY 7   **359 REMAINING**

ADDAMS, CHARLES: BIRTH ANNIVERSARY. Jan 7, 1912. The prolific cartoonist with a macabre sense of humor was born at Westfield, NJ. He became a full-time staff member of *The New Yorker* in 1935 and stayed there for his entire career, producing some 1,300 cartoons. His most famous creation was the ghoulish "Addams Family," who escaped print into television and film. Author of numerous bestselling cartoon collections and the *Charles Addams Mother Goose* (1967), Addams died Sept 29, 1988, at New York,

NY. See also: "'The Addams Family' TV Premiere: Anniversary" (Sept 18).

ASARAH B'TEVET. Jan 7. Hebrew calendar date: Tevet 10, 5780. The Fast of the 10th of Tevet begins at first morning light and commemorates the beginning of the Babylonian siege of Jerusalem in the sixth century BC. Begins at dawn.

FILLMORE, MILLARD: BIRTH ANNIVERSARY. Jan 7, 1800. 13th president of the US (July 10, 1850–Mar 3, 1853). Fillmore succeeded to the presidency upon the death of Zachary Taylor, but he did not get the hoped-for nomination from his party in 1852. He ran for president in 1856 as candidate of the Know-Nothing Party, whose platform demanded, among other things, that every government employee (federal, state and local) be a native-born citizen. Fillmore was born at Summerhill, NY, and died at Buffalo, NY, Mar 8, 1874. Now his birthday is often used as an occasion for parties for which there is no other reason.

FIRST BALLOON FLIGHT ACROSS ENGLISH CHANNEL: ANNIVERSARY. Jan 7, 1785. Dr. John Jeffries, a Boston physician, and Jean-Pierre François Blanchard, French aeronaut, crossed the English Channel from Dover, England, to Calais, France, landing in a forest after being forced to throw overboard all ballast, equipment and even most of their clothing to avoid a forced landing in the icy waters of the English Channel. Blanchard's trousers are said to have been the last article thrown overboard.

FIRST US COMMERCIAL BANK: ANNIVERSARY. Jan 7, 1782. The first commercial bank in the US, the Bank of North America, was opened at Philadelphia, PA.

GERMANY: MUNICH FASCHING CARNIVAL. Jan 7–Feb 25. Munich. From Jan 7 through Shrove Tuesday is Munich's famous carnival season. Costume balls are popular throughout carnival. The high points of the festival occur on Fasching Sunday (Feb 23) and Shrove Tuesday (Feb 25), with great carnival revelry outside at the Viktualienmarkt and on Pedestrian Mall.

HARLEM GLOBETROTTERS PLAY FIRST GAME: ANNIVERSARY. Jan 7, 1927. Basketball promoter Abe Saperstein's "New York Globetrotters" took the floor on this date at Hinckley, IL. Despite the "New York" in their name, the Globetrotters (who included Inman Jackson, Lester Johnson and Walter Wright) hailed from Chicago's South Side. The talented African-American players—unable to play in white professional leagues—barnstormed the nation in serious basketball promotional events. They changed to "Harlem Globetrotters" in the 1930s and added humor to their games in the 1940s.

HURSTON, ZORA NEALE: BIRTH ANNIVERSARY. Jan 7, 1891. One of the most important African-American writers of the 20th century was born at Notasulga, AL, to a preacher and former schoolteacher. After a childhood in Eatonville, FL, Hurston attended Barnard College and then became an integral part of the Harlem Renaissance of the 1920s and 1930s. Hurston published four novels in her lifetime, including the classic *Their Eyes Were Watching God* (1937), as well as important anthropological works, short stories, plays and a moving memoir. She was a trailblazer in collecting regional black folklore. Hurston died at Fort Pierce, FL, on Jan 28, 1960.

INTERNATIONAL CONSUMER ELECTRONICS SHOW. Jan 7–10. Las Vegas, NV. The world's largest annual trade show for consumers and America's largest annual trade show of any kind. Exhibitors are manufacturers, developers and suppliers of consumer technology hardware, content, technology delivery systems and related products and services. Attendees representing more than 160 countries include manufacturers, retailers, content providers and creators, broadband developers, wireless carriers, cable and satellite TV providers, installers, engineers, corporate buyers,

government leaders, financial analysts and the media from around the world. Held since 1967. Est attendance: 182,000. For info: Consumer Technology Assn. Phone: (866) 233-7968. E-mail: media@CTA.tech. Web: www.cesweb.org.

INTERNATIONAL PROGRAMMERS' DAY. Jan 7. A day to recognize and thank programmers for their contributions to our lives. Programmers are ultimately responsible for many of the conveniences we enjoy today, such as direct deposit and online bill paying, apps, cell phones and more. Annually, Jan 7. For info: Dan Loomis. Web: www.internationalprogrammersday.org.

JAPAN: NANAKUSA. Jan 7. Festival dates back to the seventh century and recalls the seven plants served to the emperor that are believed to have great medicinal value—shepherd's purse, chickweed, parsley, cottonweed, radish, hotoke-no-za and aona.

JAPAN: USOKAE (BULLFINCH EXCHANGE FESTIVAL). Jan 7. Dazaifu, Fukuoka Prefecture. "Good Luck" gilded-wood bullfinches, mixed among many plain ones, are sought after by the throngs as priests of the Dazaifu Shrine pass them out in the dim light of a small bonfire.

MARIAN ANDERSON PERFORMS WITH THE METROPOLITAN OPERA: 65th ANNIVERSARY. Jan 7, 1955. Contralto Marian Anderson made her debut with New York's Metropolitan Opera in Verdi's *Un ballo in maschera*, becoming the first African American to perform with that organization. She was 57 years old. The audience gave her repeated ovations.

NATIONAL BOBBLEHEAD DAY. Jan 7. Since 2015, a day to celebrate the awesomeness of bobbleheads! Annually, Jan 7. For info: Natl Bobblehead Hall of Fame and Museum. E-mail: info@bobbleheadhall.com. Web: www.bobbleheadhall.com.

NATIONAL NO-TILLAGE CONFERENCE. Jan 7–10. St. Louis, MO. Attracts innovative farmers interested in reducing tillage to protect the environment and boost profits. Est attendance: 1,000. For info: Dallas Ziebell, Natl No-Tillage Conference, PO Box 624, Brookfield, WI 53008-0624. Phone: (262) 777-2412. Fax: (262) 782-1252. E-mail: info@no-tillfarmer.com. Web: www.NoTillConference.com.

ORTHODOX CHRISTMAS. Jan 7. Observed by those churches using the Julian calendar.

POL POT OVERTHROWN: ANNIVERSARY. Jan 7, 1979. Pol Pot's Cambodian government fell to combined forces of Cambodian rebels and Vietnamese soldiers.

RUSSIA: CHRISTMAS OBSERVANCE. Jan 7. National holiday.

TRANSATLANTIC PHONING: ANNIVERSARY. Jan 7, 1927. Commercial transatlantic telephone service between New York and London was inaugurated. There were 31 calls made the first day.

🎂 BIRTHDAYS TODAY

Nicolas Cage, 56, actor (Oscar for *Leaving Las Vegas*; *National Treasure, Adaptation, Moonstruck*), born Nicolas Coppola at Long Beach, CA, Jan 7, 1964.

David Caruso, 64, actor ("NYPD Blue," "CSI: Miami"), born Forest Hills, NY, Jan 7, 1956.

Katie Couric, 63, journalist ("The CBS Evening News," "The Today Show"), born Arlington, VA, Jan 7, 1957.

Brett Dalton, 37, actor ("Agents of S.H.I.E.L.D."), born San Jose, CA, Jan 7, 1983.

Eric Gagne, 44, former baseball player, born Montreal, QC, Canada, Jan 7, 1976.

	S	M	T	W	T	F	S
January				1	2	3	4
	5	6	7	8	9	10	11
2020	12	13	14	15	16	17	18
	19	20	21	22	23	24	25
	26	27	28	29	30	31	

Erin Gray, 70, actress ("Buck Rogers in the 25th Century," "Silver Spoons"), born Honolulu, HI, Jan 7, 1950.

Lewis Hamilton, 35, Formula One racing driver, born Stevenage, England, Jan 7, 1985.

Lamar Jackson, 23, football player, 2016 Heisman Trophy winner, born Pompano Beach, FL, Jan 7, 1997.

Kenny Loggins, 72, singer, songwriter, born Everett, WA, Jan 7, 1948.

Ruth Negga, 38, actress (*Loving*, "Preacher," "Agents of S.H.I.E.L.D."), born Addis Ababa, Ethiopia, Jan 7, 1982.

Rand Paul, 57, US Senator (R, Kentucky), born Pittsburgh, PA, Jan 7, 1963.

Jeremy Renner, 49, actor (*Wind River, Arrival, The Avengers, The Hurt Locker*), born Modesta, CA, Jan 7, 1971.

Alfonso Soriano, 42, former baseball player, born San Pedro de Macoris, Dominican Republic, Jan 7, 1978.

John R. Thune, 59, US Senator (R, South Dakota), born Pierre, SD, Jan 7, 1961.

Jann Wenner, 73, journalist, publisher, *Rolling Stone* magazine, born New York, NY, Jan 7, 1947.

January 8 — Wednesday

DAY 8   **358 REMAINING**

ARGYLE DAY. Jan 8. 12th annual. Bring some brightness to winter by wearing an argyle print—not just socks: anything with the diagonal diamond pattern. The more argyle, the better! For info: Keely McAleer, 515 N 162nd Ave, Ste 202, Omaha, NE 68118. Phone: (402) 334-8899. Fax: (403) 334-5599. E-mail: kmcaleer@mheginc.com.

AT&T DIVESTITURE: ANNIVERSARY. Jan 8, 1982. In the most significant antitrust suit since the breakup of Standard Oil in 1911, American Telephone and Telegraph agreed to give up its 22 local Bell System companies ("Baby Bells"). These companies represented 80 percent of AT&T's assets. This ended the corporation's virtual monopoly on US telephone service.

BATTLE OF NEW ORLEANS: ANNIVERSARY. Jan 8, 1815. British forces suffered crushing losses (more than 2,000 casualties) in an attack on New Orleans, LA. Defending US troops were led by General Andrew Jackson, who became a popular hero as a result of the victory. Neither side knew that the War of 1812 had ended two weeks previously with the signing of the Treaty of Ghent, Dec 24, 1814. Battle of New Orleans Day is observed in Louisiana.

BOWIE, DAVID: BIRTH ANNIVERSARY. Jan 8, 1947. A relentless creative who explored rock, folk, electronic music, film and visual art in a career that spanned five decades, David Bowie (born David Jones at London, England) defined pop stardom as a chameleonic innovator. From his hit debut, 1969's "Space Oddity," through his outsized Ziggy Stardust persona of 1972, and onward to numerous experiments in spectacle and showmanship, Bowie's work shapeshifted freely for more than three decades. He explored photography and post-modernist painting, acted in films, mounted ambitious world tours and retained his status as a pop icon well into the 21st century. *Blackstar*, his last album, was issued two days before his death, at New York, NY, Jan 10, 2016.

COLLINS, WILLIAM WILKIE: BIRTH ANNIVERSARY. Jan 8, 1824. English novelist, author of *The Moonstone* (one of the first examples of detective fiction), *The Woman in White* and *The Dead Secret*. Born at London, England, he died there Sept 23, 1889.

EARTH'S ROTATION PROVED: ANNIVERSARY. Jan 8, 1851. In his Paris home using a device now known as Foucault's pendulum, physicist Jean Foucault demonstrated that Earth rotates on its axis.

ELVIS PRESLEY'S BIRTHDAY CELEBRATION. Jan 8–11. Graceland, Memphis, TN. Special birthday celebration on Jan 8 as well as other events at Graceland. For info: Graceland, 3734 Elvis Presley Blvd, Memphis, TN 38116. Phone: (800) 238-2000 or (901) 332-3322. E-mail: media@graceland.com. Web: www.graceland.com.

FERRER, JOSE: BIRTH ANNIVERSARY. Jan 8, 1912. Award-winning actor, producer, writer and director was born at Santurce, Puerto Rico. Nominated three times for an Academy Award, he won Best Actor for his role in *Cyrano de Bergerac*. In addition, Ferrer was awarded Tonys and Critics' Circle prizes during half a century in the entertainment world. He died Jan 26, 1992, at Coral Gables, FL.

GREECE: MIDWIFE'S DAY OR WOMEN'S DAY. Jan 8. Midwife's Day or Women's Day is celebrated Jan 8 each year to honor midwives and all women. "On this day women stop their housework and spend their time in cafés, while the men do all the housework chores and look after the children." In some villages, men caught outside "will be stripped . . . and drenched with cold water."

HAWKING, STEPHEN W.: BIRTH ANNIVERSARY. Jan 8, 1942. World-renowned physicist and author, born at Oxford, England. Hawking came to prominence in the early 1970s through his groundbreaking work on black holes, in which he suggested that the properties of black holes must be governed by the laws of both quantum theory and general relativity (that is, by the physics of very small and very massive objects). He authored several books, including the bestselling *A Brief History of Time* (1988), and founded and directed the Centre for Theoretical Cosmology at Cambridge, England, from 2007 until his death. He died at Cambridge on Mar 14, 2018, of amyotrophic lateral sclerosis—he was the longest-living person with the disease. His life encompassed academic highs—Hawking was awarded the 2006 Copley Medal among many other honors—and popular culture fandom—he "appeared" as himself on "The Simpsons."

NATIONAL JOYGERM DAY. Jan 8. 39th annual. A reawakening to the need to fill yourself to the brim with kindness and courtesy, self-respect (not self-centeredness), responsibility, encouragement and civility; then gently and freely sharing those traits with the "world out there"—our extended family of humanity. Free Joygerm membership cards and hug coupons for added incentive. For info: Joygerm Joan E. White, Founder/"Cheer"leader, Joygerms Unltd. Phone: (315) 472-2779. E-mail: joygerms@gmail.com.

PRESLEY, ELVIS AARON: 85th BIRTH ANNIVERSARY. Jan 8, 1935. Popular American rock singer, born at Tupelo, MS. Although his middle name was spelled incorrectly as "Aron" on his birth certificate, Elvis had it legally changed to "Aaron," which is how it is spelled on his gravestone. Died at Memphis, TN, Aug 16, 1977.

SAINT GUDULA: FEAST DAY. Jan 8. Virgin, patron saint of the city of Brussels. Died Jan 8, probably in the year 712. Her relics were transferred to the church of St. Michael in Brussels.

SHOW-AND-TELL DAY AT WORK. Jan 8. Students have show-and-tell at school, so adults should get to do the same. (©2006 by WH.) For info: Thomas & Ruth Roy, Wellcat Holidays, 2418 Long Ln, Lebanon, PA 17046. Phone: (717) 279-0184. E-mail: info@wellcat.com. Web: www.wellcat.com.

WAR ON POVERTY: ANNIVERSARY. Jan 8, 1964. President Lyndon Johnson declared a War on Poverty in his State of the Union address. He stressed improved education as one of the cornerstones of the program. The following Aug 20, he signed a $947.5 million antipoverty bill designed to assist more than 30 million citizens.

🎂 BIRTHDAYS TODAY

Shirley Bassey, 83, singer, born Cardiff, Wales, Jan 8, 1937.

Betsy DeVos, 62, US Secretary of Education (Trump administration), born Holland, MI, Jan 8, 1958.

Bob Eubanks, 83, game show host ("The Newlywed Game"), born Flint, MI, Jan 8, 1937.

Vladimir Feltsman, 68, pianist, born Moscow, USSR (now Russia), Jan 8, 1952.

Jeff Francoeur, 36, baseball player, born Atlanta, GA, Jan 8, 1984.

Jason Giambi, 49, former baseball player, born West Covina, CA, Jan 8, 1971.

Ron Cephas Jones, 63, actor ("This Is Us," "Luke Cage"), born Paterson, NJ, Jan 8, 1957.

Kathleen Noone, 74, actress ("All My Children," "Sunset Beach"), born Hillsdale, NJ, Jan 8, 1946.

Charles Osgood, 87, journalist, born New York, NY, Jan 8, 1933.

January 9 — Thursday

DAY 9   **357 REMAINING**

AVIATION IN AMERICA: ANNIVERSARY. Jan 9, 1793. A Frenchman, Jean-Pierre François Blanchard, made the first manned free-balloon flight in America's history at Philadelphia, PA. The event was watched by President George Washington and many other high government officials. The hydrogen-filled balloon rose to a height of about 5,800 feet, traveled some 15 miles and landed 46 minutes later in New Jersey. Reportedly Blanchard had one passenger on the flight—a little black dog.

BEAUVOIR, SIMONE DE: BIRTH ANNIVERSARY. Jan 9, 1908. French author who wrote both novels and treatises on ethics and feminism. Along with her companion and fellow philosopher Jean-Paul Sartre, Beauvoir was known as one of the foremost Existentialist writers of the 20th century. Her novel *The Mandarins* (1954) won the highest literary award in France. *The Second Sex* lays out her theories of feminism. Born at Paris, France; she died there on Apr 15, 1986.

CATT, CARRIE LANE CHAPMAN: BIRTH ANNIVERSARY. Jan 9, 1859. American women's rights leader, founder (in 1919) of National League of Women Voters. Born at Ripon, WI, she died at New Rochelle, NY, Mar 9, 1947.

CHICAGO SKETCH COMEDY FESTIVAL. Jan 9–19. Chicago, IL. 19th annual event that celebrates the best in local and national sketch comedy. Over two weeks audiences can take in more than 100 events, including performances and discussions. This is the world's largest sketch comedy festival, with hundreds of funny people in one convenient location—laughter guaranteed. For info: Chicago Sketch Comedy Festival. E-mail: info@stage773.com. Web: www.stage773.com.

CONNECTICUT RATIFIES CONSTITUTION: ANNIVERSARY. Jan 9, 1788. By a vote of 128 to 40, Connecticut became the fifth state to ratify the Constitution.

DENVER, BOB: 85th BIRTH ANNIVERSARY. Jan 9, 1935. Television actor born at New Rochelle, NY. He worked as a mailman and a high school teacher before landing the role—Maynard G. Krebs—that made him famous on "The Many Loves of Dobie Gillis" in 1959. Krebs was one of the first beatniks portrayed on television.

When that series ended in 1963, Denver took on the memorable lead character in "Gilligan's Island." That series is one of the most popular in television history. Denver died at Winston-Salem, NC, on Sept 2, 2005.

NIXON, RICHARD MILHOUS: BIRTH ANNIVERSARY. Jan 9, 1913. Richard Nixon served as 36th vice president of the US (under President Dwight D. Eisenhower) Jan 20, 1953–Jan 20, 1961. He was the 37th president of the US, serving Jan 20, 1969–Aug 9, 1974, when he resigned the presidency while under the threat of impeachment. First US president to resign that office. He was born at Yorba Linda, CA, and died at New York, NY, Apr 22, 1994.

PANAMA: MARTYRS' DAY. Jan 9. Public holiday.

PHILIPPINES: FEAST OF THE BLACK NAZARENE. Jan 9. Culmination of a nine-day fiesta. Manila's largest procession takes place in the afternoon of Jan 9, in honor of the Black Nazarene, whose shrine is at the Quiapo Church.

"RAWHIDE" TV PREMIERE: ANNIVERSARY. Jan 9, 1959. CBS western that kept them dogies (cattle) rollin' home from northern Texas to Sedalia, KS, for seven years. The series featured Eric Fleming as trail boss Gil Favor; Clint Eastwood as Rowdy Yates, ramrod and trail boss after Fleming's departure from the show; Jim Murdock as Mushy; Paul Brinegar as the cook, Wishbone; Steve Raines as Quince; Rocky Shahan as Joe Scarlett; Sheb Wooley as scout Pete Nolan; Robert Cabal as Hey Soos; John Ireland as Jed Colby; David Watson as Ian Cabot; and Raymond St. Jacques as Solomon King. Also remembered for its rollicking theme song.

ST. PETERSBURG MASSACRE: ANNIVERSARY. Jan 9, 1905. Guards at St. Petersburg's Winter Palace opened fire on some 150,000 unarmed protesting workers, killing at least 200. This event was the major catalyst for revolution in Russia that year, prompting more strikes and uprisings.

ULTIMATE FISHING SHOW—DETROIT. Jan 9–12. Suburban Collection Showplace, Novi, MI. This event brings together buyers and sellers of boating, fishing and outdoor sporting products. US and Canadian fishing trips, as well as other vacation travel destinations, are featured. Detroit is the largest freshwater fishing market in the nation. Est attendance: 30,000. For info: ShowSpan, Inc. Phone: (616) 447-2860. Fax: (616) 447-2861. E-mail: events@showspan.com. Web: www.showspan.com.

US LANDING ON LUZON: 75th ANNIVERSARY. Jan 9, 1945. US forces began the final push to retake the Philippines by attacking at the same location where the Japanese had begun their invasion nearly four years earlier. General Douglas MacArthur landed 67,000 troops in the Gulf of Lingayen on the western coast of the big island of Luzon. The Japanese offered little opposition to the landing itself but fought fiercely against Allied advancement, particularly around Clarke Field, the major air base in the islands.

VAN CLEEF, LEE: 95th BIRTH ANNIVERSARY. Jan 9, 1925. Actor Lee Van Cleef was born at Somerville, NJ. He appeared in many westerns and action films including *High Noon* (1952), *The Man Who Shot Liberty Valance* (1962), *The Good, the Bad and the Ugly* (1967) and *Escape from New York* (1981). Van Cleef died on Dec 16, 1989, at Oxnard, CA.

YOUNG, MURAT BERNARD "CHIC": BIRTH ANNIVERSARY. Jan 9, 1901. The comic strip "Blondie" was created by Murat Bernard "Chic" Young in 1930. Originally about a jazz-age flapper who marries a playboy from a socially prominent family, "Blondie" soon changed its direction: two children and a dog were added to the cast, Dagwood became a working stiff, and the strip focused on

January 2020	S	M	T	W	T	F	S
				1	2	3	4
	5	6	7	8	9	10	11
	12	13	14	15	16	17	18
	19	20	21	22	23	24	25
	26	27	28	29	30	31	

middle-class family situations and problems. "Blondie" introduced America to the "dagwood," an enormous sandwich made during Dagwood's late-night forays in the refrigerator. Chic Young was born at Chicago, IL, and died at St. Petersburg, FL, Mar 14, 1973.

YOUTH WINTER OLYMPIC GAMES: LAUSANNE 2020. Jan 9–22. Lausanne, Switzerland. A recent initiative by the International Olympic Committee to engage youth through an integrated sport, culture and education program. Representing 70 countries, athletes between the ages of 15 and 18 compete in 16 disciplines. Yodli—a goat-cow-Saint Bernard mash-up—is the official mascot. For info: Lausanne 2020 Youth Olympic Games. Web: www.lausanne2020.sport. Est attendance: 500,000.

🎂 BIRTHDAYS TODAY

Joan Baez, 79, folksinger, born Staten Island, NY, Jan 9, 1941.

Matt Bevin, 53, Governor of Kentucky (R), born Denver, CO, Jan 9, 1967.

Tyrone Curtis "Muggsy" Bogues, 55, former basketball player, born Baltimore, MD, Jan 9, 1965.

Catherine, Duchess of Cambridge, 38, wife of Prince William, born Catherine Middleton at Reading, Berkshire, England, Jan 9, 1982.

Nina Dobrev, 31, actress ("The Vampire Diaries," "Degrassi: The Next Generation"), born Nikolina Konstantinova Dobreva at Sofia, Bulgaria, Jan 9, 1989.

Sergio Garcia, 40, golfer, born Borriol, Spain, Jan 9, 1980.

Crystal Gayle, 69, singer, born Brenda Gayle Webb at Paintsville, KY, Jan 9, 1951.

Mat Hoffman, 48, BMX bike racer, born Oklahoma City, OK, Jan 9, 1972.

Dave Matthews, 53, singer, musician (Dave Matthews Band), born Johannesburg, South Africa, Jan 9, 1967.

Joely Richardson, 55, actress (*The Girl with the Dragon Tattoo*, "The Tudors," "Nip/Tuck"), born London, England, Jan 9, 1965.

J.K. Simmons, 65, actor (Oscar for *Whiplash*; "Law & Order," *The Snowman, Spiderman*), born Detroit, MI, Jan 9, 1955.

Imelda Staunton, 64, actress (*Pride, Harry Potter and the Order of the Phoenix, Vera Drake*), born London, England, Jan 9, 1956.

January 10 — Friday

DAY 10　　　　　　　　　　　**356 REMAINING**

COMMON SENSE PUBLISHED: ANNIVERSARY. Jan 10, 1776. More than any other publication, *Common Sense* influenced the authors of the Declaration of Independence. Thomas Paine's 50-page pamphlet sold 150,000 copies within a few months of its first printing.

FIRST UNITED NATIONS GENERAL ASSEMBLY: ANNIVERSARY. Jan 10, 1946. On the 26th anniversary of the establishment of the unsuccessful League of Nations, delegates from 51 nations met at London, England, for the first meeting of the UN General Assembly.

HENRIED, PAUL: BIRTH ANNIVERSARY. Jan 10, 1908. Actor Paul Henried once estimated that he had played in or directed more than 300 films. Though he was a staunch anti-Nazi, his early film parts included a number of German roles, including those in *Goodbye, Mr Chips* and *Night Train to Munich*. He eventually moved away from the German stereotype in such films as *Of Human Bondage* and *The Four Horsemen of the Apocalypse* and as Victor Laslo in *Casablanca*. His film career cut short by the anti-Communist blacklist in Hollywood during the 1940s, Henried found a second calling as a director, with more than 80 episodes of TV's "Alfred Hitchcock Presents" to his credit. Born at Trieste, Austria, he died Mar 29, 1992, at Pacific Palisades, CA.

JEFFERS, ROBINSON: BIRTH ANNIVERSARY. Jan 10, 1887. American poet and playwright. Born at Pittsburgh, PA, he died at Carmel, CA, Jan 20, 1962.

LEAGUE OF NATIONS FOUNDING: 100th ANNIVERSARY. Jan 10, 1920. Through the Treaty of Versailles, the League of Nations came into existence. Fifty nations entered into a covenant designed to avoid war. The US never joined the League of Nations, which was dissolved Apr 18, 1946.

LEVINE, PHILIP: BIRTH ANNIVERSARY. Jan 10, 1928. Born at Detroit, MI, poet Levine is renowned for his focus on working-class life; he is regarded as "a large, ironic Whitman of the industrial heartland." Starting at age 14, Levine worked in Detroit's auto factories; he later said, "The irony is, going to work every day became the subject of probably my best work." Recipient of many accolades, including the National Book Award for poetry (1980), the Pulitzer Prize (1994) and the American Academy of Poets' Wallace Stevens Award (2013), Levine was named US poet laureate in 2011 and died Feb 14, 2015, at Fresno, CA.

LUNAR ECLIPSE. Jan 10. Penumbral eclipse of the moon. Visible in Africa, Indian Ocean, Asia, Europe.

"MASTERPIECE THEATRE" TV PREMIERE: ANNIVERSARY. Jan 10, 1971. PBS's long-running anthology series consists of highly acclaimed original and adapted dramatizations. Many are produced by the BBC. Alistair Cooke, Russell Baker and Laura Linney have hosted the program. The first presentation was "The First Churchills." Other notable programs include "The Six Wives of Henry VIII" and "Elizabeth R" (1972); "Upstairs Downstairs" (1974–77); "I, Claudius" (1978); "The Jewel in the Crown" (1984); "White Teeth" (2002) and "Downton Abbey" (2011–16). The title of the series is now "Masterpiece."

MOON PHASE: FULL MOON. Jan 10. Moon enters Full Moon phase at 2:21 PM, EST.

US AND VATICAN REESTABLISH DIPLOMATIC RELATIONS: ANNIVERSARY. Jan 10, 1984. The US and the Vatican established full diplomatic relations after a break of 117 years.

WOLF MOON. Jan 10. So called by Native American tribes of New England and the Great Lakes because at this time of winter, the wolves howl in hunger. The January Full Moon.

WOMEN'S SUFFRAGE AMENDMENT INTRODUCED IN CONGRESS: ANNIVERSARY. Jan 10, 1878. Senator A.A. Sargent of California, a close friend of Susan B. Anthony's, introduced into the US Senate a women's suffrage amendment known as the Susan B. Anthony Amendment. It wasn't until Aug 26, 1920, 42 years later, that the amendment was signed into law.

🎂 BIRTHDAYS TODAY

Pat Benatar, 67, singer, born Patricia Andrejewski at Brooklyn, NY, Jan 10, 1953.

Roy Blunt, 70, US Senator (R, Missouri), born Niangua, MO, Jan 10, 1950.

Jemaine Clement, 46, actor, comedian (*What We Do in the Shadows, Moana*, "Legion," "Flight of the Conchords"), musician, born Masterton, New Zealand, Jan 10, 1974.

George Foreman, 71, former boxer, entrepreneur, born Marshall, TX, Jan 10, 1949.

Evan Handler, 59, actor ("Californication," "Sex and the City"), born New York, NY, Jan 10, 1961.

Jared Kushner, 39, presidential adviser, real estate developer, former newspaper executive, born Livingston, NJ, Jan 10, 1981.

Rod Stewart, 75, singer, born London, England, Jan 10, 1945.

William Anthony (Bill) Toomey, 81, Olympic decathlete, born Philadelphia, PA, Jan 10, 1939.

Chris Van Hollen, 61, US Senator (D, Maryland), born Karachi, Pakistan, Jan 10, 1959.

January 11 — Saturday

DAY 11   **355 REMAINING**

CUCKOO DANCING WEEK. Jan 11–17. To honor the memory of Laurel and Hardy, whose theme, "The Dancing Cuckoos," shall be heard throughout the land as their movies are seen and their antics greeted with laughter by old and new fans of these unique masters of comedy. (Originated by the late William T. Rabe of Sault Ste. Marie, MI.)

FIRST BLACK SOUTHERN LIEUTENANT GOVERNOR: ANNIVERSARY. Jan 11, 1986. L. Douglas Wilder was sworn in as lieutenant governor of Virginia. He was the first black elected to statewide office in the South since Reconstruction. He later served as governor of Virginia.

HAMILTON, ALEXANDER: BIRTH ANNIVERSARY. Jan 11, 1755. American founding father, diplomat, soldier and coauthor of *The Federalist* papers, born at Charlestown, Nevis, British West Indies. George Washington appointed Hamilton the first secretary of the Treasury in 1789, and in that position, Hamilton established the basis for all future American fiscal policy. Engaged in a duel with Aaron Burr the morning of July 11, 1804, at Weehawken, NJ. Mortally wounded there and died July 12, 1804.

HOSTOS, EUGENIO MARÍA: BIRTH ANNIVERSARY. Jan 11, 1839. Puerto Rican patriot, scholar and author of more than 50 books. Born at Ríuo Cañas, Puerto Rico, he died at Santo Domingo, Dominican Republic, Aug 11, 1903.

JAMES, WILLIAM: BIRTH ANNIVERSARY. Jan 11, 1842. American psychologist and philosopher of the pragmatist school. Considered the father of American psychology. Key works include *The Principles of Psychology, Essays in Radical Empiricism* and *The Will to Believe.* "There is no worse lie," he wrote in *Varieties of Religious Experience* (1902), "than a truth misunderstood by those who hear it." Born at New York City of the distinguished family that included his brother, novelist Henry James, he died at Chocorua, NH, Aug 26, 1910.

LEOPOLD, ALDO: BIRTH ANNIVERSARY. Jan 11, 1887. Considered by many to be the father of wildlife ecology, Leopold was a scholar, writer, teacher and philosopher. Born at Burlington, IA, Leopold is best known for his posthumously published book *A Sand County Almanac* (1949), in which he lyrically described putting his ecological theories into practice at a run-down farm in Wisconsin. He died at Madison, WI, on Apr 26, 1948.

MACDONALD, JOHN A.: BIRTH ANNIVERSARY. Jan 11, 1815. Canadian statesman, first prime minister of Canada. Born at Glasgow, Scotland, he died June 6, 1891, at Ottawa. His birth anniversary is observed in Canada.

January 2020	S	M	T	W	T	F	S
				1	2	3	4
	5	6	7	8	9	10	11
	12	13	14	15	16	17	18
	19	20	21	22	23	24	25
	26	27	28	29	30	31	

MOROCCO: INDEPENDENCE DAY. Jan 11. National holiday. Commemorates the date in 1944 when the Independence Party submitted a memo to the Allied authorities asking for independence under a constitutional regime. Morocco gained independence from France in 1956.

NEPAL: NATIONAL UNITY DAY. Jan 11. Celebration paying homage to King Prithvi Narayan Shah (1723–75), founder of the present house of rulers of Nepal and creator of the unified Nepal of today.

PAUL, ALICE: BIRTH ANNIVERSARY. Jan 11, 1885. Women's rights leader and founder of the National Woman's Party in 1913, advocate of an equal rights amendment to the US Constitution. Born at Moorestown, NJ, she died there July 10, 1977.

THEODOSIUS I: BIRTH ANNIVERSARY. Jan 11, 347. Roman emperor known as Theodosius the Great was born at Cauca, Gallaecia, in Spain. In 379 Theodosius was summoned by the emperor Gratian to become emperor of the East. On Feb 28, 380, without consulting religious authorities, he issued the edict that made the Nicene Creed (in which God the Father, the Son and the Holy Spirit are all of the same substance) binding on all subjects. Only those who accepted it would be considered Christians; this was the first recorded use of that designation. Theodosius engaged in a continuing struggle with the West for power. He prohibited pagan worship, but the emperors of the West had strong connections with pagan aristocracy. The two sides came to blows in 394. His final victory in September of that year was seen as a divine victory in which the Christian god had triumphed over the Roman gods. Theodosius died in January 395.

US SURGEON GENERAL DECLARES CIGARETTES HAZARDOUS: ANNIVERSARY. Jan 11, 1964. US Surgeon General Luther Terry issued the first government report saying that smoking may be hazardous to one's health.

🎂 BIRTHDAYS TODAY

Mary J. Blige, 49, singer, actress (*Mudbound*), born the Bronx, NY, Jan 11, 1971.

Jean Chretien, 86, 20th prime minister of Canada (1993–2003), born Shawinigan, QC, Canada, Jan 11, 1934.

Ben Daniel Crenshaw, 68, golfer, born Austin, TX, Jan 11, 1952.

Jim Hightower, 77, columnist, author (*There's Nothing in the Middle of the Road but Yellow Stripes and Dead Armadillos*), born Denison, TX, Jan 11, 1943.

Naomi Judd, 74, country singer (The Judds), born Ashland, KY, Jan 11, 1946.

Christine Kaufmann, 75, actress (*Taras Bulba, Bagdad Café*), born Lansdorf Graz, Austria, Jan 11, 1945.

Phyllis Logan, 64, actress ("Downton Abbey"; *Another Time, Another Place; Secrets and Lies*), born Paisley, Scotland, Jan 11, 1956.

Amanda Peet, 48, actress ("Brockmire," *Melinda and Melinda, Something's Gotta Give*), born New York, NY, Jan 11, 1972.

Kailash Satyarthi, 66, children's rights advocate, Nobel Peace Prize recipient, born Kailash Sharma at Vidisha, India, Jan 11, 1954.

Cody Simpson, 23, singer, born Gold Coast, Australia, Jan 11, 1997.

Stanley Tucci, 60, actor (*The Hunger Games, The Devil Wears Prada, Big Night*), director, born Katonah, NY, Jan 11, 1960.

January 12 — Sunday

DAY 12   **354 REMAINING**

"ALL IN THE FAMILY" TV PREMIERE: ANNIVERSARY. Jan 12, 1971. Based on the success of the British comedy "Till Death Us Do Part," Norman Lear created CBS's controversial sitcom "All in the Family." The series was the first of its kind to realistically portray the prevailing issues and taboos of its time with a wickedly humorous bent. From bigotry to birth control, few topics were considered too sacred to discuss on air. Ultraconservative Archie Bunker (played by Carroll O'Connor) held court from his recliner, spewing invective at any who disagreed with him. Jean Stapleton portrayed Archie's dutiful wife, Edith. Sally Struthers and Rob Reiner rounded out the cast as Archie's liberal daughter and son-in-law, Gloria and Mike "Meathead" Stivic. The series had a 12-year run.

"BATMAN" TV PREMIERE: ANNIVERSARY. Jan 12, 1966. Based on the DC Comics characters created by Bob Kane in 1939, ABC's crime-fighting show gained a place in Nielsen's top 10 ratings in its first season. Adam West starred as millionaire Bruce Wayne and his superhero alter ego, Batman. Burt Ward costarred as Dick Grayson/Robin, the Boy Wonder. An assortment of villains guest-starred each week, including Cesar Romero as the Joker, Eartha Kitt and Julie Newmar as Catwoman, Burgess Meredith as the Penguin and Frank Gorshin as the Riddler. Other stars making memorable appearances included Liberace, Vincent Price, Milton Berle, Tallulah Bankhead and Ethel Merman. The series played up its comic-strip roots with innovative and sharply skewed camera angles, bright bold colors and wild graphics. Although the last telecast was Mar 14, 1968, the show's memorable theme song, composed by Neal Hefti, can be heard today with some 120 episodes in syndication.

BURKE, EDMUND: BIRTH ANNIVERSARY. Jan 12, 1729. British orator, politician and philosopher, born at Dublin, Ireland. "Superstition is the religion of feeble minds," he wrote in 1790, but best remembered is "The only thing necessary for the triumph of evil is for good men to do nothing," not found in his writings but almost universally attributed to Burke. Died at Beaconsfield, England, July 9, 1797.

CONGRESS AUTHORIZED USE OF FORCE AGAINST IRAQ: ANNIVERSARY. Jan 12, 1991. The US Congress passed a resolution authorizing the president of the US to use force to expel Iraq from Kuwait. This was the sixth congressional vote in US history declaring war or authorizing force on another nation.

"DYNASTY" TV PREMIERE: ANNIVERSARY. Jan 12, 1981. The popular ABC prime-time serial focused on the high-flying exploits of the Denver-based Carrington family. The series had a weekly wardrobe budget of $10,000, with many elegant costumes designed by Nolan Miller. In addition to following the juicy story lines, many people tuned in worldwide to view the palatial mansions and lavish sets. John Forsythe played patriarch Blake Carrington, with Linda Evans as his wife, Krystle. Joan Collins played Alexis, Blake's scheming ex-wife and arch business rival.

FARMER, JAMES: 100th BIRTH ANNIVERSARY. Jan 12, 1920. Civil rights leader, born at Marshall, TX. Farmer was one of the founders of CORE, the Congress of Racial Equality, a volunteer organization established in 1942 to improve race relations and eliminate

discriminatory practices. Farmer led the nonviolent fight to desegregate buses and terminals in 1961, known as the Freedom Rides. He received the Presidential Medal of Freedom in 1998. Died at Fredericksburg, VA, July 9, 1999.

FIRST ELECTED WOMAN SENATOR: ANNIVERSARY. Jan 12, 1932. Hattie W. Caraway, a Democrat from Arkansas, was the first woman elected to the US Senate. Born in 1878, Caraway was appointed to the Senate on Nov 13, 1931, to fill out the term of her husband, Senator Thaddeus Caraway, who had died a few days earlier. On Jan 12, 1932, she won a special election to fill the remaining months of his term. Subsequently elected to two more terms, she served in the Senate until January 1945. She was an adept and tireless legislator (once introducing 43 bills on the same day) who worked for women's rights (once cosponsoring an equal rights amendment) and supported New Deal policies. She died Dec 21, 1950, at Falls Church, VA. The first woman appointed to the Senate was Mrs W.H. Felton, who in 1922 served for two days. The first woman to be elected to the Senate without having been appointed first was Margaret Chase Smith of Maine, who had served first in the House. She was elected to the Senate in 1948.

HAITI EARTHQUAKE: 10th ANNIVERSARY. Jan 12, 2010. An earthquake of magnitude 7.0 struck the impoverished nation of Haiti, resulting in more than 200,000 deaths and leaving more than one million homeless. The epicenter was only 25 km from the capital, Port-au-Prince, which was reduced to rubble.

HAYES, IRA HAMILTON: BIRTH ANNIVERSARY. Jan 12, 1922. Ira Hayes was one of six US Marines who raised the American flag on Iwo Jima's Mount Suribachi, Feb 23, 1945, following a US assault on the Japanese stronghold. The event was immortalized by AP photographer Joe Rosenthal's famous photo and later by a Marine War Memorial monument at Arlington, VA. Hayes was born on a Pima Indian Reservation at Arizona. He returned home after WWII a much celebrated hero but was unable to cope with fame. He was found dead of "exposure to freezing weather and overconsumption of alcohol" on the Sacaton Indian Reservation at Arizona, Jan 24, 1955.

LONDON, JACK: BIRTH ANNIVERSARY. Jan 12, 1876. American author of more than 50 books: short story collections, novels and travel tales of the sea and the Far North, many marked by brutal realism. His most widely known work is *The Call of the Wild*, the great dog story published in 1903. London was born at San Francisco, CA. He died of gastrointestinal uremia on Nov 22, 1916, near Santa Rosa, CA.

MISSION SANTA CLARA DE ASIS: FOUNDING ANNIVERSARY. Jan 12, 1777. California mission built by followers of Father Junipero Serra to educate the Indians. In the 1850s the mission became Santa Clara University, the oldest university in California. The current building, used by the university as its chapel, is a replica of an older building that was destroyed by fire in 1926.

NATIONAL HOT TEA DAY. Jan 12. 5th annual. An ancient beverage—nearly 5,000 years old—tea is enjoyed worldwide and has become a favorite drink among Americans. On any given day, more than half of the American population drinks tea. This day is the perfect occasion to celebrate the many reasons to drink tea: diverse flavors, rich culture and history, health benefits and soothing qualities. Annually, Jan 12. For info: Tea Council of the USA, 362 Fifth Ave, Ste 1002, New York, NY 10001. E-mail: info@teausa.org. Web: www.teausa.org.

RAINER, LUISE: BIRTH ANNIVERSARY. Jan 12, 1910. Film actress born in Dusseldorf, Germany. Rainer was the first person to win consecutive Oscars, in 1936 for *The Great Ziegfeld*, and again in 1937 for *The Good Earth*. Rainer was also the inaugural victim of the so-called, career-deflating "Oscar Curse." Rainer was less cursed than stricken by disputes over script quality; the death of her studio champion, Irving Thalberg; and her dislike of the studio system. Unable to control her projects, she walked out on her MGM contract, abruptly ending her career. She did not make another film until *The Gambler* in 1997. She died Dec 30, 2014, in London, England.

SARGENT, JOHN SINGER: BIRTH ANNIVERSARY. Jan 12, 1856. Born in Florence, Italy, of American parents, Sargent became one of the most famous portrait artists of the late Victorian and Edwardian ages in Britain and the US. His best-known paintings include *Madame X* (1884); *Carnation, Lily, Lily, Rose* (1885–86) and *Ellen Terry as Lady Macbeth* (1889). Sargent died Apr 15, 1925, at London, England.

SWITZERLAND: MEITLISUNNTIG. Jan 12. On Meitlisunntig, the second Sunday in January, the girls of Meisterschwanden and Fahrwangen, in the Seetal district of Aargau, Switzerland, stage a procession in historical uniforms and a military parade before a female General Staff. According to tradition, the custom dates from the Villmergen War of 1712, when the women of both communes gave vital help that led to victory. Popular festival follows the procession.

TANZANIA: ZANZIBAR REVOLUTION DAY. Jan 12. National Day. Zanzibar became independent in December 1963, under a sultan; the sultan was overthrown on this day in 1964.

WINTHROP, JOHN: BIRTH ANNIVERSARY. Jan 12, 1588. (Old Style date.) Born at Edwardstone, Suffolk, England, Puritan John Winthrop is renowned for his leadership in the migration to the Massachusetts Bay Colony and the key role he played in developing its character and its relationship with neighboring colonies and indigenous people. Father of 16 children, most notably son John, who was governor of the Connecticut Colony. Winthrop served 13 annual terms as governor of the Massachusetts Bay Colony from his arrival in 1630 to his death on Mar 26, 1649, at Boston, MA. While alive he kept a detailed journal, which is now considered the foremost historical record of the era.

🎂 BIRTHDAYS TODAY

Kirstie Alley, 65, actress ("Cheers," "Veronica's Closet," *Look Who's Talking*), born Wichita, KS, Jan 12, 1955.

Jeff Bezos, 56, founder, Amazon.com, born Albuquerque, NM, Jan 12, 1964.

HAL, 28, computer in *2001: A Space Odyssey*, by Arthur C. Clarke, "born" Urbana, IL, Jan 12, 1992.

Marián Hossa, 41, hockey player, born Stará Lubovna, Czechoslovakia (now Slovakia), Jan 12, 1979.

Rush Limbaugh, 69, talk show host ("The Rush Limbaugh Show"), author, born Cape Girardeau, MO, Jan 12, 1951.

Zayn Malik, 27, singer (formerly in One Direction), born Zain Javadd Malik at Bradford, England, Jan 12, 1993.

David Mitchell, 51, author (*Cloud Atlas, number9dream*), born Southport, England, Jan 12, 1969.

Walter Mosley, 68, author (*Devil in a Blue Dress, A Little Yellow Dog*), born Los Angeles, CA, Jan 12, 1952.

Haruki Murakami, 71, author (*Norwegian Wood, The Wind-Up Bird Chronicle, 1Q84*), born Kyoto, Japan, Jan 12, 1949.

Oliver Platt, 60, actor ("Chicago Med," "The Big C," "Huff"), born Windsor, ON, Canada, Jan 12, 1960.

Issa Rae, 35, producer ("Insecure," "The Choir"), actress ("Insecure"), born Los Angeles, CA, Jan 12, 1985.

Howard Stern, 66, radio and television personality ("The Howard Stern Show"), born Queens, NY, Jan 12, 1954.

Dominique Wilkins, 60, Hall of Fame basketball player, born Paris, France, Jan 12, 1960.

January 2020	S	M	T	W	T	F	S
				1	2	3	4
	5	6	7	8	9	10	11
	12	13	14	15	16	17	18
	19	20	21	22	23	24	25
	26	27	28	29	30	31	

January 13 — Monday

ALGER, HORATIO, JR: BIRTH ANNIVERSARY. Jan 13, 1834. American clergyman and author of more than 100 popular books for boys (some 20 million copies sold). Honesty, frugality and hard work assured that the heroes of his books would find success, wealth and fame. Born at Revere, MA, he died at Natick, MA, July 18, 1899.

CHASE, SALMON PORTLAND: BIRTH ANNIVERSARY. Jan 13, 1808. American statesman, born at Cornish, NH. US senator, secretary of the Treasury and chief justice of the US. Salmon P. Chase spent much of his life fighting slavery (he was popularly known as "attorney general for runaway Negroes"). He was one of the founders of the Republican Party, and his hopes of becoming candidate for president of the US in 1856 and 1860 were dashed because his unconcealed antislavery views made him unacceptable. Died at New York, NY, May 7, 1873.

COLLEGE FOOTBALL PLAYOFF NATIONAL CHAMPIONSHIP GAME. Jan 13. Mercedes-Benz Superdome, New Orleans, LA. NCAA Division I college football champion will be decided in this game, with the combatants determined by the College Football Playoff system. For info: College Football Playoff. Web: www.collegefootballplayoff.com.

ENGLAND: PLOUGH MONDAY. Jan 13. Work on the farm is resumed after the festivities of the 12 days of Christmas. On the preceding Sunday, ploughs may be blessed in churches. Celebrated with dances and plays. Annually, the Monday after Twelfth Day.

FULLER, ALFRED CARL: BIRTH ANNIVERSARY. Jan 13, 1885. Founder of the Fuller Brush Company, born at Kings County, NS, Canada. In 1906 the young brush salesman went into business on his own, making brushes at a bench between the furnace and the coal bin in his sister's basement. Died at Hartford, CT, Dec 4, 1973.

JAPAN: COMING-OF-AGE DAY. Jan 13. National holiday for youth of the country who reached adulthood during the preceding year. Annually, the second Monday in January.

JOHNNY CASH AT FOLSOM PRISON: ANNIVERSARY. Jan 13, 1968. In a landmark concert, country music star Johnny Cash performed in front of 2,000 inmates at Folsom Prison at Folsom, CA. Backed by the Tennessee Three and accompanied by June Carter, Carl Perkins and the Statler Brothers, Cash performed in the prison cafeteria. The concert was recorded as a live album and was a worldwide hit. Cash's choice to play for prisoners cemented his reputation as a hero to the downtrodden.

NATIONAL CLEAN-OFF-YOUR-DESK DAY. Jan 13. To provide one day early each year for every desk worker to see the top of the desk and prepare for the following year's paperwork. Annually, the second Monday in January. For info: A.C. Vierow, Box 71, Clio, MI 48420-0071.

NORWAY: TYVENDEDAGEN. Jan 13. "Twentieth Day" is the traditional end of the Christmas season, marked by festivities. The Christmas tree is taken down and burned.

RADIO BROADCASTING: ANNIVERSARY. Jan 13, 1910. Radio pioneer and electron tube inventor Lee De Forest arranged the world's first radio broadcast to the public at New York, NY. He succeeded

in broadcasting the voice of Enrico Caruso along with other stars of the Metropolitan Opera to several receiving locations in the city where listeners with earphones marveled at wireless music from the air. Though only a few were equipped to listen, it was the first broadcast to reach the public and the beginning of a new era in which wireless radio communication became almost universal. See also: "First Scheduled Radio Broadcast: Anniversary" (Nov 2).

RUSSIA: OLD NEW YEAR'S EVE. Jan 13. Although Jan 1 is the official New Year's Day in Russia, some Russians still celebrate on the old Julian date of Jan 13–14. Also celebrated in Belarus and Ukraine.

"THE SOPRANOS" TV PREMIERE: ANNIVERSARY. Jan 13, 1999. The thinking viewer's mob drama, "The Sopranos" featured James Gandolfini as Tony Soprano, whose panic attacks drove him to seek out a psychiatrist (Lorraine Bracco). The HBO drama revolved around Tony's home and crime lives. *TV Guide* named the series one of the greatest TV shows of all time. The final episode aired June 10, 2007.

STACK, ROBERT: BIRTH ANNIVERSARY. Jan 13, 1919. Actor, born at Los Angeles, CA, best known for his Emmy Award–winning portrayal of Eliot Ness in the television series "The Untouchables" (1959–63). On the big screen, Stack was a matinee idol in the 1940s (he gave Deanna Durbin her first on-screen kiss), had an Oscar-nominated turn in *Written on the Wind* (1956) and then spoofed his good-guy roles in *Airplane!* (1980) and other film comedies in his later years. He was the trenchcoat-clad host of "Unsolved Mysteries," one of the first reality television programs, which aired on various networks from 1987 to 2002. Stack died May 14, 2003, at Beverly Hills, CA.

SWEDEN: ST. KNUT'S DAY. Jan 13. St. Knut's Day (Tjugondag Knut, or "The 20th Day of Knut") marks the end of the Christmas season in Sweden—with parties, song and the dismantling of the yule tree (which traditionally is thrown out the window). Named for Knut (or Canute) IV, also Knut the Holy, former king and patron saint of Denmark. Although St. Knut's feast day is Jan 19, Sweden and Finland have conflated observances of Knut IV with that of his nephew and saint Knut Lavard (feast day is Jan 7).

TOGO: LIBERATION DAY. Jan 13. National holiday. Commemorates 1967 uprising.

VERDON, GWEN: BIRTH ANNIVERSARY. Jan 13, 1926. One of Broadway's premier female dancers and actresses; many of her most successful roles were choreographed by her husband, Bob Fosse. She won Tony Awards for *Can-Can, Damn Yankees, New Girl in Town* and *Redhead*. She also acted in movies, including *Cocoon* and the film adaptation of *Damn Yankees*. Born at Los Angeles, CA, she died Oct 18, 2000, at Woodstock, VT.

🎂 BIRTHDAYS TODAY

Trace Adkins, 58, country singer, born Sarepta, LA, Jan 13, 1962.

Orlando Bloom, 43, actor (*Pirates of the Caribbean*, the Lord of the Rings film trilogy), born Canterbury, Kent, England, Jan 13, 1977.

Keith Coogan, 50, actor (*Adventures in Babysitting, Cousins*), born Palm Springs, CA, Jan 13, 1970.

Patrick Dempsey, 54, actor ("Grey's Anatomy," *Enchanted, Sweet Home Alabama*), born Lewiston, ME, Jan 13, 1966.

Nicole Eggert, 48, actress ("Baywatch," "Charles in Charge"), born Glendale, CA, Jan 13, 1972.

Frank Gallo, 87, artist, sculptor, born Toledo, OH, Jan 13, 1933.

Liam Hemsworth, 30, actor (*The Hunger Games, The Last Song*), born Melbourne, Australia, Jan 13, 1990.

Nikolai Khabibulin, 47, former hockey player, born Sverdlovsk, USSR (now Russia), Jan 13, 1973.

Julia Louis-Dreyfus, 59, actress (Emmys for "Veep" and "Seinfeld"; *Enough Said*), born New York, NY, Jan 13, 1961.

Jay McInerney, 65, writer (*Bright Lights, Big City*), born Hartford, CT, Jan 13, 1955.

Penelope Ann Miller, 56, actress (*Adventures in Babysitting, The Freshman, Carlito's Way*), born Los Angeles, CA, Jan 13, 1964.

Richard Moll, 77, actor ("Night Court," *Wicked Stepmother, The Flintstones*), born Pasadena, CA, Jan 13, 1943.

Lorrie Moore, 63, author (*Birds of America, A Gate at the Stairs*), born Glens Falls, NY, Jan 13, 1957.

Mark O'Meara, 63, Hall of Fame golfer, born Goldsboro, NC, Jan 13, 1957.

Shonda Rhimes, 50, television producer, creator, writer ("Grey's Anatomy," "Scandal"), born Chicago, IL, Jan 13, 1970.

Joannie Rochette, 34, Olympic figure skater, born Montreal, QC, Canada, Jan 13, 1986.

Nate Silver, 42, statistician, author (*The Signal and the Noise*), born East Lansing, MI, Jan 13, 1978.

Frances Sternhagen, 90, actress ("Cheers," *Misery*; stage: *The Good Doctor, The Heiress*), born Washington, DC, Jan 13, 1930.

January 14 — Tuesday

DAY 14   **352 REMAINING**

ARNOLD, BENEDICT: BIRTH ANNIVERSARY. Jan 14, 1741. Born at Norwich, CT, Arnold was an American officer who deserted to the British during the Revolutionary War. When the Revolutionary War began in 1775, Arnold was commissioned a colonel and led forces in the capture of Fort Ticonderoga. His service was distinguished, but a major leg injury prohibited further command in the field. Arnold resented being passed over for promotion and became disillusioned with the American leadership. When he was given command of West Point in New York by General George Washington, he entered into a secret deal to sell the fort to the British. The plot was discovered and, branded a traitor, Arnold fled. He defected to the British and settled in Canada with his wife, Peggy Shippen. His name has since become synonymous with treachery. He died June 14, 1801, at London, England.

FIRST CAESAREAN SECTION: ANNIVERSARY. Jan 14, 1794. Dr. Jesse Bennett, of Edom, VA, performed the first successful caesarean section. The patient was his wife.

MAURY, MATTHEW FONTAINE: BIRTH ANNIVERSARY. Jan 14, 1806. Naval officer, born at Fredericksburg, VA. Maury established oceanography as a branch of science and revolutionized the recording of oceanographic data as a superintendent of the Naval Observatory. Died at Lexington, VA, Feb 1, 1873.

OUTCAULT, RICHARD FELTON: BIRTH ANNIVERSARY. Jan 14, 1863. When Richard Felton Outcault was asked by the *New York World*'s Sunday editor to submit drawings for use with the paper's new color printing process, the "funny papers" were born. Outcault's first color drawing, titled "Origin of a New Species," was published Nov 18, 1894. The first regular colored cartoon, "Hogan's Alley," drawn by Outcault, began appearing with its main character's blustery comments written across his yellow nightshirt—thus making him the "Yellow Kid." The term "yellow journalism" was coined for newspapers featuring the Kid. Outcault's strip "Buster Brown" brought him celebrity and fortune. Outcault was born at Lancaster, OH, and died Sept 25, 1928, at Flushing, NY.

POETRY AT WORK DAY. Jan 14. 8th annual. Celebrates the power of poetry in the workplace. It also remembers the many poets who led an ordinary life working and writing in tandem. People will be encouraged to embrace their work lives and the potential for poetry to flourish alongside—even inside—work itself. Annually, the second Tuesday in January. For info: Laura Barkat, TweetSpeak Poetry. E-mail: editor@tspoetry.com. Web: www.tweetspeakpoetry.com/poetry-at-work-day.

RATIFICATION DAY. Jan 14, 1784. Anniversary of the act that officially ended the American Revolution and established the US as a sovereign power. On Jan 14, 1784, the Continental Congress, meeting at Annapolis, MD, ratified the Treaty of Paris, thus fulfilling the Declaration of Independence of July 4, 1776.

ROACH, HAL: BIRTH ANNIVERSARY. Jan 14, 1892. American film writer, director and producer Harold Eugene (Hal) Roach was born at Elmira, NY. He pioneered film comedy as chief of his own studio for nearly 40 years. During that time he produced, and sometimes directed and wrote, nearly 1,000 movies. Roach is noted for originating the *Our Gang* comedies in 1922 and for introducing Laurel and Hardy to film audiences. He won Academy Awards for the short films "The Music Box" (1932) and "Bored of Education" (1936). Roach produced the film version of Steinbeck's novel *Of Mice and Men* in 1939. In 1984 he won an honorary Academy Award for career achievement. Roach died Nov 2, 1992, at Los Angeles, CA.

SCHWEITZER, ALBERT: BIRTH ANNIVERSARY. Jan 14, 1875. The Alsatian philosopher, musician, physician and winner of the 1952 Nobel Peace Prize was born at Kayserberg, Upper Alsace, and died at Lambarene, Gabon, Sept 4, 1965.

SPACE MILESTONE: *SOYUZ 4* (USSR). Jan 14, 1969. First docking of two-manned spacecraft (with *Soyuz 5*) and first interchange of spaceship personnel in orbit by means of space walks.

"TODAY" TV PREMIERE: ANNIVERSARY. Jan 14, 1952. NBC program that started the morning news format we know today. Captained by Dave Garroway, the show was segmented with bits and pieces of news, sports, weather, interviews and other features that were repeated so that viewers did not have to stop their morning routine to watch. The segments were brief and to the point. Sylvester Weaver devised this concept to capitalize on television's unusual qualities. What used to take three hours to broadcast live across the country was done in two with videotape on a delayed basis. The addition of chimpanzee J. Fred Muggs in 1953 helped push ratings up. There have been a number of hosts over the years, from John Chancellor and Hugh Downs to Tom Brokaw, Bryant Gumbel, Matt Lauer, Al Roker and Carson Daly. Female hosts (originally called "Today Girls") have included Betsy Palmer, Florence Henderson, Barbara Walters, Jane Pauley, Katie Couric, Meredith Viera, Savannah Guthrie, Natalie Morales and Jenna Bush Hager.

UZBEKISTAN: ARMY DAY. Jan 14. National holiday.

WHIPPLE, WILLIAM: BIRTH ANNIVERSARY. Jan 14, 1730. American patriot and signer of the Declaration of Independence. Born at Kittery, ME, he died at Portsmouth, NH, Nov 10, 1785.

🎂 BIRTHDAYS TODAY

Jason Bateman, 51, actor ("Arrested Development," *Horrible Bosses, Bad Words*), born Rye, NY, Jan 14, 1969.

Kristin Cavallari, 33, actress ("Laguna Beach: The Real Orange County"), born Chicago, IL, Jan 14, 1987.

Faye Dunaway, 79, actress (Oscar for *Network*; *Bonnie and Clyde, Chinatown*), born Bascom, FL, Jan 14, 1941.

Grant Gustin, 30, actor ("The Flash"), born Norfolk, VA, Jan 14, 1990.

David Hall, 50, Hall of Fame wheelchair tennis player, born Sydney, Australia, Jan 14, 1970.

Lawrence Kasdan, 71, filmmaker (*The Bodyguard, The Big Chill, Mumford*), born Miami Beach, FL, Jan 14, 1949.

LL Cool J, 52, actor ("NCIS: Los Angeles," "In the House," *SWAT*), singer, born James Todd Smith at Bay Shore, NY, Jan 14, 1968.

Shannon Lucid, 77, former astronaut, born Shanghai, China, Jan 14, 1943.

Shepard Smith, 56, news anchor, born David Shepard Smith, Jr, at Holly Springs, MS, Jan 14, 1964.

Steven Soderbergh, 57, filmmaker (*Magic Mike, Traffic, Ocean's Eleven, Erin Brockovich*), born Atlanta, GA, Jan 14, 1963.

Holland Taylor, 77, actress ("The Practice," *The Truman Show*), born Philadelphia, PA, Jan 14, 1943.

Nina Totenberg, 76, broadcast journalist, correspondent ("Nightline"), born New York, NY, Jan 14, 1944.

Emily Watson, 53, actress ("Little Women," *Gosford Park, Angela's Ashes, Hilary and Jackie*), born London, England, Jan 14, 1967.

Carl Weathers, 72, actor (*Rocky, Happy Gilmore*), born New Orleans, LA, Jan 14, 1948.

January 15 — Wednesday

DAY 15   **351 REMAINING**

ALPHA KAPPA ALPHA SORORITY FOUNDED: ANNIVERSARY. Jan 15, 1908. Founded at Howard University at Washington, DC, by Ethel Hedgeman Lyle, Alpha Kappa Alpha was the first organization of its type for black women. It was incorporated Jan 29, 1913.

BLACK DAHLIA MURDER: ANNIVERSARY. Jan 15, 1947. On this day, the body of Elizabeth Short was found in an empty lot in Los Angeles, CA. Short, nicknamed the Black Dahlia for her striking looks, had been murdered and mutilated, and her body's discovery sparked a media frenzy. Although dozens of men (and women) confessed to the crime, those confessions were discounted. The murder remains LA's most famous unsolved murder and one that evokes the noirish aura of postwar LA's corruption and crime problems.

BRITISH MUSEUM: ANNIVERSARY. Jan 15, 1759. On this date, the British Museum opened its doors at Montague House in London. Incorporated by an act of Parliament in 1753, following the death of British medical doctor and naturalist Sir Hans Sloane, who had bequeathed his personal collection of books, manuscripts, coins, medals and antiquities to Britain. As the national museum of the United Kingdom, the British Museum houses many of the world's most prized treasures. The national library moved to separate facilities in 1997.

DESERT CLASSIC. Jan 15–19. La Quinta, CA. 61st annual. Sponsored by Workday. Established in 1960, formerly known as the Bob Hope Classic—winners now receive the Bob Hope Memorial Trophy. The nation's largest sports event for charity. It features PGA Tour

	S	M	T	W	T	F	S
January				1	2	3	4
2020	5	6	7	8	9	10	11
	12	13	14	15	16	17	18
	19	20	21	22	23	24	25
	26	27	28	29	30	31	

pros, celebrities and amateurs. Est attendance: 110,000. For info: Desert Classic. Phone: (888) 672-4673. E-mail: tickets@desert-classic.com. Web: www.desert-classic.com.

FIRST SUPER BOWL: ANNIVERSARY. Jan 15, 1967. The Green Bay Packers won the first NFL–AFL World Championship Game, defeating the Kansas City Chiefs, 35–10, at the Los Angeles Memorial Coliseum. Packers quarterback Bart Starr was named the game's Most Valuable Player. Pro football's title game later became known as the Super Bowl.

"HAPPY DAYS" TV PREMIERE: ANNIVERSARY. Jan 15, 1974. This nostalgic comedy set in Milwaukee in the 1950s starred Ron Howard as teenager Richie Cunningham with Anson Williams and Don Most as his friends "Potsie" Weber and Ralph Malph. Tom Bosley and Marion Ross played Richie's parents, and his sister, Joanie, was played by Erin Moran. The most memorable character was The Fonz—Arthur "Fonzie" Fonzarelli—played by Henry Winkler. "Happy Days" remained on the air until July 12, 1984. "Laverne and Shirley" was a spin-off.

"HILL STREET BLUES" TV PREMIERE: ANNIVERSARY. Jan 15, 1981. Immensely popular NBC police series created by Steven Bochco and Michael Kozoll that focused more on police officers than crime. The realistic show was highly praised by actual police officers. It won a slew of Emmys and ran for seven seasons. The cast featured Daniel J. Travanti as Captain Frank Furillo, Veronica Hamel as public defender Joyce Davenport and Michael Conrad as Sergeant Phil "Let's be careful out there" Esterhaus. Other cast members included Barbara Bosson, Bruce Weitz, Taurean Blacque, Joe Spano, James B. Sikking, Michael Warren, Betty Thomas, Ed Marinaro and Charles Haid. The last telecast was on May 19, 1987.

KING, MARTIN LUTHER, JR: BIRTH ANNIVERSARY. Jan 15, 1929. Black civil rights leader, minister, advocate of nonviolence and recipient of the Nobel Peace Prize (1964). Born at Atlanta, GA, he was assassinated at Memphis, TN, Apr 4, 1968. After his death many states and territories observed his birthday as a holiday. In 1983 Congress approved HR 3706, "A bill to amend Title 5, United States Code, to make the birthday of Martin Luther King, Jr, a legal public holiday." Signed by the president on Nov 2, 1983, it became Public Law 98–144. The law sets the third Monday in January for observance of King's birthday. First observance was Jan 20, 1986. See also: "King, Martin Luther, Jr: Birthday Observed" (Jan 20).

LIVINGSTON, PHILIP: BIRTH ANNIVERSARY. Jan 15, 1716. Merchant and signer of the Declaration of Independence, born at Albany, NY. Died at York, PA, June 12, 1778.

MOLIÈRE DAY: BAPTISM ANNIVERSARY. Jan 15, 1622. Most celebrated of French authors and dramatists, Jean Baptiste Poquelin, baptized at Paris, France, Jan 15, 1622, took the stage name Molière when he was about 22 years old. While playing in a performance of his last play, *Le Malade Imaginaire* (about a hypochondriac afraid of death), Molière became ill and died within a few hours at Paris, Feb 17, 1673.

NATIONAL BAGEL DAY. Jan 15. Bagels have earned their day in the spotlight, with the chewy circular bread first debuting in 1610 in Krakow, Poland. Bagels continue to be a popular breakfast staple, with more than 350 million bagels sold in 2018 alone. Join sponsor Thomas' Bagels (the number one grocery bagel in the United States) in toasting the bagel. Annually, since 2014. For info: Thomas' Bagels, PO Box 976, Horsham, PA 19044. Web: www.thomasbreads.com.

PENTAGON COMPLETED: ANNIVERSARY. Jan 15, 1943. The world's largest office building with 6.5 million square feet of usable space, the Pentagon is located in Virginia across the Potomac River from Washington, DC, and serves as headquarters for the Department of Defense.

QUARTERLY ESTIMATED FEDERAL INCOME TAX PAYERS' DUE DATE. Jan 15. For those individuals whose fiscal year is the calendar year and who make quarterly estimated federal income tax payments, today would be one of the due dates (Jan 15, Apr 15, June 15 and Sept 15, 2020).

SIEGMEISTER, ELIE: BIRTH ANNIVERSARY. Jan 15, 1909. American composer Elie Siegmeister was born at New York, NY. He composed eight symphonies and eight operas and a number of concertos, chamber pieces and orchestral works using folk, jazz and street songs to create a contemporary American classical music. He died Mar 10, 1991, at Manhasset, NY.

TELLER, EDWARD: BIRTH ANNIVERSARY. Jan 15, 1908. Born at Budapest, Hungary, Edward Teller was a physicist who worked on the Manhattan Project at Los Alamos, NM, in the 1940s. He promoted the first hydrogen fusion bomb, work that was considered secondary to the atomic bomb research taking place at the same time. He was a vocal critic of Robert Oppenheimer, director of the Manhattan Project, and his comments eventually destroyed Oppenheimer's career. Teller's hydrogen bomb research ultimately proved feasible but was never used in wartime. Throughout his life he remained a profound influence on America's defense and energy policies. He died at Stanford, CA, Sept 9, 2003.

TRAIN FOR PARIS: 75th ANNIVERSARY. Jan 15, 1945. The civilian populations of England and France had their first direct contact since May 1940 when a boat train left London's Victoria Station headed for Paris.

🎂 BIRTHDAYS TODAY

Drew Brees, 41, football player, born Austin, TX, Jan 15, 1979.

Ernest J. Gaines, 87, author (*The Autobiography of Miss Jane Pittman, A Lesson Before Dying*), born Oscar, LA, Jan 15, 1933.

David Ige, 63, Governor of Hawaii (D), born Pearl City, HI, Jan 15, 1957.

Regina King, 49, actress (Oscar for *If Beale Street Could Talk*, Emmys for "Seven Seconds" and "American Crime"), born Los Angeles, CA, Jan 15, 1971.

Chad Lowe, 52, actor ("Now and Again," "Life Goes On," *Nobody's Perfect*), born Dayton, OH, Jan 15, 1968.

Andrea Martin, 73, actress (Tonys for *My Favorite Year* and *Pippin*; *My Big Fat Greek Wedding*, "SCTV"), born Portland, ME, Jan 15, 1947.

Margaret O'Brien, 83, actress (*Little Women, Meet Me in St. Louis*), born San Diego, CA, Jan 15, 1937.

Pitbull, 39, rapper, record producer, born Armando Christian Pérez at Miami, FL, Jan 15, 1981.

Mario Van Peebles, 63, actor (*Love Kills, Judgment Day*), director, born Mexico City, Mexico, Jan 15, 1957.

January 16 — Thursday

DAY 16　　　　　**350 REMAINING**

APPRECIATE A DRAGON DAY. Jan 16. A day to celebrate the many dragons in popular literature. A great opportunity for libraries—public and school—to create activities where children can share their enthusiasm for the dragon of their choice. (Created by Donita K. Paul.)

AUSTRALIA: SANTOS TOUR DOWN UNDER. Jan 16–26. Adelaide. 21st annual. The world's best cycling teams light up South Australia in the first race of the prestigious UCI ProTour calendar. From beaches to vineyards, through the city of Adelaide and iconic South Australian towns—the six-stage Santos Tour Down Under is truly a world-class event that showcases the speed, skill and spectacle that is professional cycling. For info: Santos Tour Down Under. E-mail: tourdownunder@sa.gov.au. Web: www.tour-downunder.com.au.

BRITISH AIR RAID ON BERLIN: ANNIVERSARY. Jan 16, 1943. In the first bombing of Germany since the Casablanca Conference, the British Royal Air Force began heavy bombing of Germany by day and night to bring about "the progressive destruction and dislocation of the German military, industrial and economic system, and for the undermining of the morale of the German people." The RAF used their new "target indicator" bombs to mark targets for their bombers.

CIVIL SERVICE CREATED: ANNIVERSARY. Jan 16, 1883. The US Congress passed a bill creating the civil service.

DEAN, DIZZY: BIRTH ANNIVERSARY. Jan 16, 1911. Jay Hanna "Dizzy" Dean, major league pitcher (St. Louis Cardinals) and Hall of Fame member, was born at Lucas, AR. Following his baseball career, Dean established himself as a radio and TV sports announcer and commentator, becoming famous for his innovative delivery. "He slud into third," reported Dizzy, who on another occasion explained that "Me and Paul [baseball player brother Paul "Daffy" Dean] . . . didn't get much education." Died at Reno, NV, July 17, 1974.

EISENHOWER ASSUMES COMMAND: ANNIVERSARY. Jan 16, 1944. General Dwight D. Eisenhower arrived in London to assume command of the Supreme Headquarters Allied Expeditionary Forces in Europe (SHAEF). Having demonstrated his organizational abilities in North Africa as well as his strength as an arbitrator of inter-Allied rivalries, Eisenhower was charged with the most far-reaching push of the war—the invasion of France.

EL SALVADOR: NATIONAL DAY OF PEACE. Jan 16. A peace treaty was signed in Mexico City on this date in 1992 ending the 12-year civil war that had claimed 75,000 lives. On Feb 1, a cease-fire went into effect.

FOSSEY, DIAN: BIRTH ANNIVERSARY. Jan 16, 1932. Born at San Francisco, CA, Fossey went to the Virunga Mountains at Rwanda, Africa, to study the endangered mountain gorillas. Her work, conducted in isolation among the primates, was groundbreaking in terms of increasing our understanding of the gorillas' social world. Fossey was a vigorous crusader against the poachers who decimate the gorilla population, and she was probably murdered by them. Her body was discovered on Dec 26, 1985, at Mount Visoke, Rwanda.

GET TO KNOW YOUR CUSTOMER DAY. Jan 16 (also Apr 16, July 16 and Oct 15). Set aside the third Thursday of each quarter to get to know your customers even better. For example, salespeople might plan to take a customer out to lunch, not to sell, but to learn more about the customer's needs and why the customer likes doing business with them. Executives could get out from behind the desk and go into the field. For info: Shep Hyken, Shepard Presentations, LLC, 200 S Hanley Rd, Ste 509, St. Louis, MO 63105. Phone: (314) 692-2200. E-mail: Shep@hyken.com. Web: www.GetToKnowYourCustomerDay.com.

GULF WAR BEGINS: ANNIVERSARY. Jan 16, 1991. Allied forces launched a major air offensive against Iraq to begin the Gulf War. The strike was designed to destroy Iraqi air defenses and command, control and communication centers. As Desert Shield became Desert Storm, the world was able to see and hear for the first time an initial engagement of war as CNN broadcasters, stationed at Baghdad, covered the attack live.

JAPAN: HARU-NO-YABUIRI. Jan 16. Employees and servants who have been working over the holidays are given a day off.

MALAWI: JOHN CHILEMBWE DAY. Jan 16. National holiday. Honors a leader for independence who led an uprising against the British in 1915.

MERMAN, ETHEL: BIRTH ANNIVERSARY. Jan 16, 1909. Musical comedy star famous for her belting voice and brassy style. Born Ethel Agnes Zimmerman on Jan 16, 1909 (or 1912—the date changed the older she got, but most sources say 1909), at Queens, NY. Died Feb 15, 1984, at New York, NY.

MICHELIN, ANDRÉ: BIRTH ANNIVERSARY. Jan 16, 1853. French industrialist who, along with his brother Édouard, started the Michelin Tire Company in 1888, manufacturing bicycle tires. They were the first to use demountable pneumatic tires on cars. Born at Paris, France; died there Apr 4, 1931.

MONACO: INTERNATIONAL CIRCUS FESTIVAL OF MONTE CARLO. Jan 16–26. Chapiteau de Fontvieille, Monte Carlo. 44th annual. The best circus acts and performers from five continents compete for the Golden Clown Award at this storied festival. For info: Monte Carlo Festivals. Web: www.montecarlofestivals.com.

NATIONAL NOTHING DAY: ANNIVERSARY. Jan 16, 1973. Anniversary of National Nothing Day, an event created by newspaperman Harold Pullman Coffin and first observed "to provide Americans with one national day when they can just sit without celebrating, observing or honoring anything." Since 1975, though many other events have been listed on this day, lighthearted traditional observance of Coffin's idea has continued. Coffin, a native of Reno, NV, died at Capitola, CA, Sept 12, 1981, at the age of 76.

NATIONAL QUINOA DAY. Jan 16. A day celebrating the rich history and health benefits of quinoa. This interesting "new" grain (actually seeds from a plant in the amaranth family) came to the United States in 1983 but has been cultivated for more than 4,000 years in the Andes. Discover quinoa today with fun facts and new recipes. Annually, Jan 16. For info: Ancient Harvest, PO Box 4240, Boulder, CO 80306.

PROHIBITION (EIGHTEENTH) AMENDMENT: ANNIVERSARY. Jan 16, 1919. When Nebraska became the 36th state to ratify the prohibition amendment, the 18th Amendment became part of the US Constitution. One year later, Jan 16, 1920, the 18th Amendment took effect and the sale of alcoholic beverages became illegal in the United States, with the Volstead Act providing for enforcement. This was the first time that an amendment to the Constitution dealt with a social issue. The 21st Amendment, repealing the 18th, went into effect on Dec 6, 1933.

★**RELIGIOUS FREEDOM DAY.** Jan 16. Commemorates the adoption of a religious freedom statute by the Virginia legislature in 1786. Annually, Jan 16.

RELIGIOUS FREEDOM DAY. Jan 16, 1786. The legislature of Virginia adopted a religious freedom statute that protected Virginians against any requirement to attend or support any church and against discrimination. This statute, which had been drafted by Thomas Jefferson and introduced by James Madison, later was the model for the First Amendment to the US Constitution.

SERVICE, ROBERT WILLIAM: BIRTH ANNIVERSARY. Jan 16, 1874. Canadian poet, born at Preston, England. Lived in the Canadian Northwest for many years and perhaps is best remembered for such ballads as "The Shooting of Dan McGrew" and "The Cremation of Sam McGee" and for such books as *Songs of a Sourdough, Rhymes of a Rolling Stone* and *The Spell of the Yukon*. Died at France, Sept 11, 1958.

January 2020	S	M	T	W	T	F	S
				1	2	3	4
	5	6	7	8	9	10	11
	12	13	14	15	16	17	18
	19	20	21	22	23	24	25
	26	27	28	29	30	31	

🎂 BIRTHDAYS TODAY

Alex Acosta, 51, former US secretary of labor (Trump administration), born Miami, FL, Jan 16, 1969.

Debbie Allen, 70, dancer, choreographer, singer, actress ("Fame"), born Houston, TX, Jan 16, 1950.

John Carpenter, 72, director (*Halloween, The Thing*), born Carthage, NY, Jan 16, 1948.

Joe Flacco, 35, football player, born Audubon, NJ, Jan 16, 1985.

Anthony Joseph (A.J.) Foyt, Jr, 85, former auto racer, born Houston, TX, Jan 16, 1935.

Marilyn Horne, 86, opera singer, born Bradford, PA, Jan 16, 1934.

William Kennedy, 92, author (*Ironweed, Roscoe*), born Albany, NY, Jan 16, 1928.

James May, 57, television personality ("The Grand Tour," "Top Gear"), born Bristol, England, Jan 16, 1963.

Jack Burns McDowell, 54, former baseball player, born Van Nuys, CA, Jan 16, 1966.

Ronnie Milsap, 76, Hall of Fame country singer, born Robbinsville, NC, Jan 16, 1944.

Lin-Manuel Miranda, 40, composer, lyricist, performer (Pulitzer and Tony for *Hamilton*, Tony for *In the Heights*), born New York, NY, Jan 16, 1980.

Kate Moss, 46, model, designer, born Croyden, Surrey, England, Jan 16, 1974.

Albert Pujols, 40, baseball player, born Santo Domingo, Dominican Republic, Jan 16, 1980.

January 17 — Friday

DAY 17   **349 REMAINING**

ALI, MUHAMMAD: BIRTH ANNIVERSARY. Jan 17, 1942. Born Cassius Clay at Louisville, KY, boxing's "The Greatest" lived up to his nickname: winning the gold medal in the light heavyweight division at the 1960 Rome Olympics and winning the world heavyweight title three times (1964, 1974, 1978). Ali was also nicknamed the "Louisville Lip"—always ready with a quote-worthy quip or challenge. He converted to Islam in 1964 (under Malcolm X's mentorship) and dropped his "slave name" for that of Muhammad Ali. Later, as a conscientious objector, he refused to be drafted to fight in the Vietnam War—he was arrested and stripped of his title. In a battle that went to the US Supreme Court in 1971, Ali saw his conviction overturned. Ali's refusal to bow to the establishment, his civil rights beliefs and leadership and his outsize personality made him one of the great iconic figures—in sports and otherwise—of the 20th century. After battling Parkinson's disease (diagnosed in 1984) for 30 years, Ali died at Scottsdale, AZ, on June 3, 2016.

ARBOR DAY IN FLORIDA. Jan 17. The third Friday in January is Arbor Day in Florida, a ceremonial day.

ART DECO WEEKEND. Jan 17–19. Miami Beach, FL. 43rd annual. Features parade, jazz entertainment, antique furniture expo and plenty of food. This event celebrates the Miami Beach visionaries and includes art deco antiques, vendors and artists, from national and local talent. Est attendance: 300,000. For info: Art Deco Weekend, Miami Design Preservation League, 1001 Ocean Dr, Miami Beach, FL 33139. Phone: (305) 672-2014. E-mail: info@mdpl.org. Web: www.artdecoweekend.com.

BRONTË, ANNE: 200th BIRTH ANNIVERSARY. Jan 17, 1820. Author of *Agnes Grey* (1847) and *The Tenant of Wildfell Hall* (1848) published under the pseudonym Acton Bell, Anne was the youngest of the famous and successful Brontë sisters, Charlotte (*Jane Eyre*) and Emily (*Wuthering Heights*). Well-educated sixth child of an Anglican clergyman, she grew up on the Yorkshire moors, briefly attending boarding school before working as a governess, experiences which doubtless provided her with novelistic background material. Contemporary critical assessment has lauded her work for its strongly feminist perspective. Born at Thornton, England, Anne died of tuberculosis May 28, 1849, at Scarborough, England.

BRONTË200. Jan 17 (and whole of 2020). Brontë Parsonage Museum, Haworth, West Yorkshire, England—and other locations. A multiyear celebration of the 200th birth anniversaries of the Brontë siblings: Charlotte (2016), Branwell (2017) and Emily (2018). Anne's celebration is in 2020. Anne, the author of *Agnes Grey* and *The Tenant of Wildfell Hall*, was born Jan 17, 1820, and died of tuberculosis on May 28, 1849. Throughout 2020 there will be special exhibitions, events and celebrations. For info: Brontë Society, Brontë Parsonage Museum, Church St, Haworth, West Yorkshire, United Kingdom BD22 8DR. Web: www.bronte200.org or www.bronte.org.uk.

THE BUSINESS OF AMERICA QUOTATION: 95th ANNIVERSARY. Jan 17, 1925. President Calvin Coolidge, in a speech to the American Society of Newspaper Editors, described America in a way that was to define the country in the 20th century and beyond—not just for the prosperous 1920s. "The chief business of the American people," he said, "is business."

CABLE CAR PATENT: ANNIVERSARY. Jan 17, 1871. Andrew Hallikie received a patent for a cable car system that began service in San Francisco in 1873.

CAPONE, AL: BIRTH ANNIVERSARY. Jan 17, 1899. Gangster Alphonse "Scarface" Capone was born this date at Brooklyn, NY, to immigrants from Naples, Italy. Capone dominated organized crime in Chicago throughout Prohibition. Targeted by the "Untouchables" after 1929's St. Valentine's Day Massacre (which he allegedly ordered), Capone was finally imprisoned on tax evasion charges. He died Jan 25, 1947, at Miami, FL, after suffering from syphilis.

EISENHOWER'S FAREWELL ADDRESS: ANNIVERSARY. Jan 17, 1961. President Dwight D. Eisenhower, in his farewell address to the nation on national radio and television, spoke the sentences that would be the most quoted and remembered of his presidency. In a direct warning, he said, "In the councils of government, we must guard against the acquisition of unwarranted influence, whether sought or unsought, by the military-industrial complex. The potential for the disastrous rise of misplaced power exists and persists."

ENGLAND: WHITTLESEA STRAW BEAR FESTIVAL. Jan 17–19. Whittlesey. 41st annual. Since 1980, a revival of old Plough Monday festivities: on the weekend after Plough Monday, a straw bear leads a merry procession of more than 250 musicians, dancers and other performers through the streets of Whittlesey. Procession also includes a decorated plough. The festival concludes with a "bear burning" on Sunday. For info: Whittlesea Straw Bear Festival, 119 Eastrea Rd, Whittlesey, Peterborough, United Kingdom PE7 2AJ. E-mail: info@strawbear.org.uk. Web: www.strawbear.org.uk.

FIRST NUCLEAR-POWERED SUBMARINE VOYAGE: 65th ANNIVERSARY. Jan 17, 1955. At 11 AM, EST, the commanding officer of the world's first nuclear-powered submarine, the *Nautilus*, ordered all lines cast off and sent the historic message: "Under way on nuclear power." Highlights of the *Nautilus*: keel laid by President Harry S Truman June 14, 1952; christened and launched by Mrs Dwight D. Eisenhower Jan 21, 1954; commissioned to the US Navy Sept 30, 1954. It now forms part of the *Nautilus* Memorial Submarine Force Library and Museum at the Naval Submarine Base New London at Groton, CT.

FORT WORTH STOCK SHOW AND RODEO. Jan 17–Feb 8. Fort Worth, TX. Western extravaganza. "World's original indoor rodeo" began in 1918 (45 acres under one roof). Professional rodeo, prize livestock (more than 29,000 head) shows, horse shows, carnival midway, shopping and quality family-oriented entertainment. Est attendance: 1,200,000. For info: Fort Worth Stock Show and Rodeo, 3400 Burnett-Tandy Dr, Fort Worth, TX 76107. Phone: (817) 877-2400. E-mail: contact@fwssr.com. Web: www.fwssr.com.

FRANKLIN, BENJAMIN: BIRTH ANNIVERSARY. Jan 17, 1706. "Elder statesman of the American Revolution," oldest signer of both the Declaration of Independence and the Constitution, scientist, diplomat, author, printer, publisher, philosopher, philanthropist and self-made, self-educated man. Author, printer and publisher of *Poor Richard's Almanack* (1733–58). Born at Boston, MA, Franklin died at Philadelphia, PA, Apr 17, 1790. His birthday is commemorated each year by the Poor Richard Club of Philadelphia with graveside observance. In 1728 Franklin wrote a premature epitaph for himself. It first appeared in print in Ames's 1771 almanac: "The Body of BENJAMIN FRANKLIN/Printer/Like a Covering of an old Book/Its contents torn out/And stript of its Lettering and Gilding,/Lies here, Food for Worms;/But the work shall not be lost,/It will (as he believ'd) appear once more/In a New and more beautiful Edition/Corrected and amended/By the Author."

"FRONTLINE" TV PREMIERE: ANNIVERSARY. Jan 17, 1983. PBS hour-long independently produced documentaries. The programs often create controversy, focusing on a variety of political, military and social issues.

"THE GOLDBERGS" TV PREMIERE: ANNIVERSARY. Jan 17, 1949. Originally broadcast by CBS, this show was one of the earliest TV sitcoms. The show centered around a Jewish mother and her family living in the Bronx and later in the suburbs. Gertrude Berg created the hit radio show before she wrote, produced and starred as Molly Goldberg in the television version. Contributing actors and actresses included Philip Loeb, Arlene McQuade, Tom Taylor, Eli Mintz, Menasha Skulnik and Arnold Stang.

HUTCHINS, ROBERT MAYNARD: BIRTH ANNIVERSARY. Jan 17, 1899. American educator, foundation executive and civil liberties activist, born at Brooklyn, NY. He was president and later chancellor of the University of Chicago, where he introduced many educational concepts, including the Great Books program. Died at Santa Barbara, CA, on May 14, 1977.

INTERNATIONAL FETISH DAY. Jan 17. A day belonging to everyone with a fetish. First observed in 2009 in the United Kingdom. Annually, the third Friday in January.

INTERNATIONAL MENTORING DAY. Jan 17. Since 2017, observed during National Mentoring Month and on the birthday of boxing legend and global humanitarian Muhammad Ali. A day of international conversation on social media where photos, videos and messages of powerful mentoring stories are shared. Ali's legacy is inspiration for the day—specifically his six core principles of confidence, conviction, dedication, respect, giving and spirituality. For info: MENTOR: The National Mentoring Partnership. Web: www.mentoring.org.

JAPAN SUFFERS MAJOR EARTHQUAKE: 25th ANNIVERSARY. Jan 17, 1995. Japan suffered its second most deadly earthquake in the 20th century when a 20-second temblor left 5,500 people dead and more than 21,600 injured. The epicenter was six miles beneath Awaji Island at Osaka Bay. This was just 20 miles west of Kobe, Japan's sixth-largest city and a major port that accounted for 12 percent of the country's exports. Measuring 7.2 on the Richter scale, the quake collapsed or badly damaged more than 30,400 buildings and left 275,000 people homeless.

JUDGMENT DAY. Jan 17. No need to wait 'til it's too late. All you need to do to see how you measure up to the standards of your God is simple: look in the mirror. There's your judgment. (©2006 by WH.) For info: Thomas & Ruth Roy, Wellcat Holidays, 2418 Long Ln, Lebanon, PA 17046. Phone: (717) 279-0184. E-mail: info@wellcat.com. Web: www.wellcat.com.

KID INVENTORS' DAY. Jan 17. Water skis. Earmuffs. The Popsicle. What do these have in common? All were invented by kids! Some 500,000 children and teens invent gadgets and games each year to make our lives easier—and more fun. Celebrate the ingenuity and value of these young brainstormers on the birthday of Benjamin Franklin, who invented the first swim fins at age 12. Teachers' guides, book lists and links, and information about inventor contests, camps and clubs for kids available. For info: Lee Wardlaw. E-mail: author@leewardlaw.com. Web: www.kidinventorsday.com.

LAEMMLE, CARL: BIRTH ANNIVERSARY. Jan 17, 1867. Considered the father of Hollywood, Laemmle was born at Laupheim, Germany. He came to the US in 1884 and opened his first nickelodeon theater at Chicago, IL, in 1906. He founded the Independent Motion Picture Company (IMP) in 1909, which had produced more than 100 silent films by 1910. Laemmle's pioneering move of listing stars, beginning with Mary Pickford, in film credits gave birth to the Hollywood star system. In 1912, IMP merged with several smaller independent film companies to form Universal Pictures; in 1920, Laemmle assumed sole control of the company, which he retained until its sale to a syndicate in 1935. He died Sept 24, 1939, at Beverly Hills, CA.

LEE-JACKSON DAY IN VIRGINIA. Jan 17. Annually, the Friday in January that precedes Martin Luther King Day. To commemorate the January birthdays of Robert E. Lee and Thomas Jonathan "Stonewall" Jackson.

LLOYD GEORGE, DAVID: BIRTH ANNIVERSARY. Jan 17, 1863. Powerful statesman who guided Britain through the tumult of WWI as prime minister (1916–22). After the war, Lloyd George helped shape the Treaty of Versailles at the Paris Peace Conference of 1919. Born at Manchester, England, he died at Llanystumdwy, Caernarvonshire, Wales, Mar 26, 1945.

LOOP ICE CARNIVAL. Jan 17–19. St. Louis, MO. 15th annual. Winter frolics galore: ice slides, zip line rides, ice carving demos, ice sculptures, frozen turkey bowling, Friday night Snow Ball, 5k and 10k "Frozen Buns" runs, $1,000 in ice cubes, music, shopping and more. Est attendance: 15,000. For info: Loop Ice Carnival, 6504 Delmar in The Loop, St. Louis, MO 63130. Web: www.VisitThe-Loop.com.

MEXICO: BLESSING OF THE ANIMALS AT THE CATHEDRAL. Jan 17. Church of San Antonio at Mexico City or Xochimilco provide best

	S	M	T	W	T	F	S
January				1	2	3	4
	5	6	7	8	9	10	11
2020	12	13	14	15	16	17	18
	19	20	21	22	23	24	25
	26	27	28	29	30	31	

sights of chickens, cows and household pets gaily decorated with flowers. (Saint's day for San Antonio Abad, patron saint of domestic animals.)

MILWAUKEE BOAT SHOW. Jan 17–19 (also Jan 22–26). Wisconsin Expo Center at State Fair Park, Milwaukee, WI. This event brings together buyers and sellers of powerboats, including fishing boats, pontoons and boating accessories, as well as vacation property and travel destinations. Est attendance: 25,000. For info: ShowSpan, Inc. Phone: (616) 447-2860. Fax: (616) 447-2861. E-mail: events@showspan.com. Web: www.showspan.com.

MOON PHASE: LAST QUARTER. Jan 17. Moon enters Last Quarter phase at 7:58 AM, EST.

PALOMARES HYDROGEN BOMB ACCIDENT: ANNIVERSARY. Jan 17, 1966. At 10:16 AM, according to villagers, fire fell from the sky over Palomares, Spain. An American B-52 bomber carrying four hydrogen bombs collided with its refueling plane, spilling the bombs (two of which had "chemical explosions," scattering radioactive plutonium over the area). In a cleanup, American soldiers burned crops, slaughtered animals and removed tons of topsoil (which was sent to South Carolina for burial). More than 19 years later, in November 1985, the Nuclear Energy Board permitted villagers to see their medical reports for the first time.

PGA OF AMERICA FOUNDED: ANNIVERSARY. Jan 17, 1916. Golf great Walter Hagen and 34 New York–area golf professionals met at the Taplow Club for a luncheon hosted by department store magnate Rodman Wanamaker. They discussed forming a national organization that promoted interest in the game and elevated the status of the professional golfer. An organizing committee was appointed and a constitution was approved on Apr 16, 1916, to form the Professional Golfers' Association of America. This golfing luncheon also inspired the idea for a national championship. Wanamaker provided the trophy and the $2,580 purse for the first PGA Championship, which was played Apr 10, 1916, at the Siwanoy course at Bronxville, NY.

POLAND: LIBERATION DAY. Jan 17. Celebration of 1945 liberation of the city of Warsaw from Nazi oppression on this day by Soviet troops. Special ceremonies at the Monument to the Unknown Soldier in Warsaw's Victory Square (which had been called Adolf Hitler Platz during the German occupation).

POPEYE DEBUTS: ANNIVERSARY. Jan 17, 1929. In E.C. Segar's newspaper comic strip "Thimble Theatre," a new character, Popeye, appeared on the scene and was an immediate success. Olive Oyl quickly dumped her beau, Ham Gravy, for the colorful sailor. Popeye's signature line was to be "Tha's all I can stands, 'cause I can't stands no more!"

QUEEN LILIUOKALANI DEPOSED: ANNIVERSARY. Jan 17, 1893. Queen Liliuokalani, the last monarch of Hawaii, lost her throne when the monarchy was abolished by the "Committee of Safety," with the foreknowledge of US minister John L. Stevens, who encouraged the revolutionaries. The queen's supporters were intimidated by the 300 US Marines sent to protect American lives and property. Judge Sanford B. Dole became president of the republic and later was Hawaii's first governor after the US annexed it by joint resolution of Congress on July 7, 1898. Hawaii held incorporated territory status for 60 years. President Dwight D. Eisenhower signed the proclamation making Hawaii the 50th state on Aug 21, 1959.

RUSH, WILLIAM: DEATH ANNIVERSARY. Jan 17, 1833. First American-born sculptor. William Rush's work in wood and clay included busts of many notables, American and European alike; carved wooden female figureheads for ships; the masks of Tragedy and Comedy seen at the Actor's House outside Philadelphia, PA; and the *Spirit of Schuylkill* in Fairmount Park in Philadelphia. In 1805 Rush and others founded the Pennsylvania Academy of the Fine Arts. Rush was born at Philadelphia in 1756.

SAINT ANTHONY'S DAY. Jan 17. Feast day honoring Egyptian hermit who became the first Christian monk and who established communities of hermits; patron saint of domestic animals and patriarch of all monks. Lived about AD 251–354.

SASSOON, VIDAL: BIRTH ANNIVERSARY. Jan 17, 1928. Born into poverty at London, England, this future hairdresser to the stars was raised partly in an orphanage and apprenticed to a beauty shop at age 14. He opened his first salon in 1954 and was soon experimenting with geometric styles and angular cuts. He moved to New York in 1965, where his groundbreaking new styles worn by women like Mary Quant, Grace Coddington and Mia Farrow made him into a superstar. His chain of salons and line of affordable hair care products made him a household name among American women. "If you don't look good, we don't look good" was the signature line for his brand. He died at Los Angeles, CA, May 9, 2012.

SOUTHERN CALIFORNIA EARTHQUAKE: ANNIVERSARY. Jan 17, 1994. An earthquake measuring 6.6 on the Richter scale struck the Los Angeles area about 4:20 AM. The epicenter was at Northridge in the San Fernando Valley, about 20 miles northwest of downtown Los Angeles. A death toll of 51 was announced Jan 20. Sixteen of the dead were killed in the collapse of one apartment building. More than 25,000 people were made homeless by the quake and 680,000 lost electric power. Many buildings were destroyed and others made uninhabitable due to structural damage. A section of the Santa Monica Freeway, part of the Simi Valley Freeway and three major overpasses collapsed. Hundreds of aftershocks occurred in the following several weeks. Costs to repair the damage were estimated at $15–30 billion.

🎂 BIRTHDAYS TODAY

Naveen Andrews, 51, actor ("Lost," *The English Patient*), born London, England, Jan 17, 1969.

Cuauhtémoc Blanco, 47, former soccer player, born Mexico City, Mexico, Jan 17, 1973.

Jim Carrey, 58, actor (*I Love You Phillip Morris, Dumb and Dumber, The Truman Show*), comedian ("In Living Color"), born Newmarket, ON, Canada, Jan 17, 1962.

Maksim Chmerkovskiy, 40, dancer, choreographer, instructor, television personality ("Dancing with the Stars"), born Odessa, USSR (now Ukraine), Jan 17, 1980.

Zooey Deschanel, 40, actress ("The New Girl," *[500] Days of Summer*), born Los Angeles, CA, Jan 17, 1980.

Calvin Harris, 36, DJ, singer, music producer, composer, born Adam Richard Wiles at Dumfries, Scotland, Jan 17, 1984.

James Earl Jones, 89, actor (Tonys for *The Great White Hope* and *Fences*; *Gabriel's Fire*), born Arkabutla, MS, Jan 17, 1931.

Newton Minow, 94, attorney, former head of the Federal Communications Commission (1961–63), born Milwaukee, WI, Jan 17, 1926.

Michelle Obama, 56, former first lady, wife of Barack Obama, 44th president of the US, born Michelle Robinson at Chicago, IL, Jan 17, 1964.

Maury Povich, 81, talk show host, born Washington, DC, Jan 17, 1939.

Dwyane Wade, 38, former basketball player, born Chicago, IL, Jan 17, 1982.

Betty White, 98, actress ("The Mary Tyler Moore Show," "The Golden Girls," "Hot in Cleveland"), animal rights activist, born Oak Park, IL, Jan 17, 1922.

January 18 — Saturday

DAY 18   **348 REMAINING**

BALD EAGLE APPRECIATION DAYS. Jan 18–19. River City Mall, Keokuk, IA. Features trained personnel stationed at observation points for viewing the American bald eagle. Indoor activities include a woodcarver's show and Native American activities. Also featuring live eagle/raptor demonstrations from the World Bird Sanctuary of St. Louis and Insect Zoo from Iowa State University. Est attendance: 8,000. For info: Keokuk Area Convention and Tourism Bureau, 428 Main St, Keokuk, IA 52632. Phone: (319) 524-5599. E-mail: info@keokukiowatourism.org. Web: www.keokukiowatourism.org.

CORRIDOR OF DEATH: ANNIVERSARY. Jan 18, 1943. The suffering of the people of Leningrad (now St. Petersburg) during the German siege of that city was one of the greatest tragedies of WWII. More than half the population of Russia's second-largest city died during the winter of 1942. On Jan 18, 1943, in Operation Iskra, Soviet troops broke through German lines and opened a 10-mile-wide corridor south of Lake Ladoga. Within a week supplies were arriving in the city by way of this narrow opening. Because fierce German bombardment of the passage continued for another year, the pass came to be called the "Corridor of Death." The siege finally ended Jan 27, 1944, after 880 days.

DARÍO, RUBÉN: BIRTH ANNIVERSARY. Jan 18, 1867. The great Nicaraguan poet was born in Metapa. Influenced by French and Asian literary and artistic works, Darío was to become the leader of the Latin American *modernista* movement. Darío's rich and opulent poetry was tremendously influential in all of the Spanish-speaking literary world and beyond. His breakthrough book was *Azul . . .* (1888). In his later years, Darío served his native Nicaragua in various diplomatic posts. He died at Léon, Nicaragua, on Feb 6, 1916.

FIRST BLACK US CABINET MEMBER: ANNIVERSARY. Jan 18, 1966. Robert Clifton Weaver was sworn in as secretary of housing and urban development, becoming the first black cabinet member in US history. He was nominated by President Lyndon Johnson.

FLOOD, CURT: BIRTH ANNIVERSARY. Jan 18, 1938. Curtis Charles (Curt) Flood, baseball player, born at Houston, TX. Flood was one of baseball's best center fielders in the 1960s, batting .293 over 15 seasons and playing spectacular defense. After the 1969 season, he refused to accept a trade from the St. Louis Cardinals to the Philadelphia Phillies. "I am not a piece of property to be bought and sold irrespective of my wishes," he said in a letter to Commissioner Bowie Kuhn. The resulting lawsuit went to the Supreme Court, where Flood lost. But his stand, taken because he did not want to switch teams, paved the way for the end of baseball's reserve clause and the advent of free agency. Died at Los Angeles, CA, Jan 20, 1997.

GRANT, CARY: BIRTH ANNIVERSARY. Jan 18, 1904. Known as a romantic leading actor, Grant was born Archibald Leach at Bristol, England. For more than three decades Grant entertained with his wit, charm, sophistication and personality. His films include *Topper, The Awful Truth, Bringing Up Baby, His Girl Friday, North by Northwest* and *Charade.* Died at Davenport, IA, Nov 29, 1986.

HARDY, OLIVER: BIRTH ANNIVERSARY. Jan 18, 1892. Stan Laurel's rotund comedy partner was born Norvell Hardy at Harlem, GA. He took "Oliver" as a first name in honor of his father. Hardy played a heavy in the silents but found comedy gold with Englishman Laurel after Leo McCarey, noting their contrasting physiques, urged their partnership in 1926. Their 1927 silent film *The Battle*

of the Century is notable for depicting the largest-ever pie-in-the-face battle. The team made their first talkie in 1929, with *Unaccustomed as We Are,* and the team continued to delight audiences on film and stage until 1955. Their 1932 short, "The Music Box," directed by Hal Roach, won an Oscar. Hardy died at Hollywood, CA, Aug 7, 1957.

HOGGETOWNE MEDIEVAL FAIRE. Jan 18–19 (also Jan 25–26; Jan 31–Feb 2). Alachua County Fairgrounds, Gainesville, FL. 34th annual. Cheer on jousting knights and watch battles unfold during the living chess match. Nine stages of entertainment featuring gypsy dancing, full-flight falconry and armored combat. A village marketplace with hundreds of artisans selling their medieval wares. Games, rides, food and more. Est attendance: 40,000. For info: Sunshine Andrei, Faire Coordinator, City of Gainesville, Dept of Cultural Affairs, PO Box 490 Station 30, Gainesville, FL 32627. Phone: (352) 393-8536. E-mail: andreisv@cityofgainesville.org. Web: www.hoggetownefaire.com.

"THE JEFFERSONS" TV PREMIERE: 45th ANNIVERSARY. Jan 18, 1975. CBS sitcom about an African-American family (formerly neighbors of the Bunkers on "All in the Family") who moved to Manhattan's East Side, thanks to the success of George Jefferson's chain of dry-cleaning stores. Having a format similar to "All in the Family," the show featured a black bigot, George Jefferson. Cast included Sherman Hemsley as George Jefferson, Isabel Sanford as Louise Jefferson and Marla Gibbs as maid Florence. The last episode aired July 23, 1985.

KAYE, DANNY: BIRTH ANNIVERSARY. Jan 18, 1913. American entertainer Danny Kaye was born David Daniel Kaminski at Brooklyn, NY. Kaye became a star in films, international stage performances and television. His most notable films are *The Secret Life of Walter Mitty* (1947) and *Hans Christian Andersen* (1952), as well as the classic *White Christmas* (1954). He hosted the television show "The Danny Kaye Show" in the 1960s. In addition, Kaye helped raise millions of dollars for the United Nations International Children's Emergency Fund (UNICEF) and musicians' pension plans. He died Mar 3, 1987, at Los Angeles, CA.

LEWIS AND CLARK EXPEDITION COMMISSIONED: ANNIVERSARY. Jan 18, 1803. Seeking information on what lay west of the young US, President Thomas Jefferson sent a confidential letter to Congress on Jan 18, 1803, requesting funds for an exploratory expedition to be led by Captain Meriwether Lewis and Lieutenant William Clark. After the Louisiana Purchase was signed on Apr 30, 1803, the expedition's mission changed: it became a survey of new American land. The Corps of Discovery set off May 14 from St. Louis and returned on Sept 23, 1806, with much information about the land, flora and fauna and peoples there. See also Lewis and Clark anniversaries on May 14, Sept 23 and Nov 16.

NATIONAL USE YOUR GIFT CARD DAY. Jan 18. 1st annual. This "public service" call-to-action day is a reminder to American consumers to use their gift cards, and will incorporate events, social media and publicity. The news-of-the-day will revolve around tips and tactics to maximize gift card use. Two percent of the $25.9 billion spent annually on gift cards goes unused—that's more than $500 million of hard-earned American dollars going to waste. Timing this day to post-holiday is ideal because 44 percent of gift cards sold annually are bought for the December holidays. Annually, the third Saturday in January. For info: Tracy Tilson, Tilson PR, 1001 Yamato Rd, Ste 300, Boca Raton, FL 33431. Web: https://useyourgiftcard.com.

POOH DAY: A.A. MILNE: BIRTH ANNIVERSARY. Jan 18, 1882. Anniversary of the birth of Alan Alexander Milne, English author, especially remembered for his children's stories: *Winnie the Pooh* and *The House at Pooh Corner.* Also the author of *Mr Pim Passes By, When We Were Very Young* and *Now We Are Six.* Born at London, England; died at Hartfield, England, Jan 31, 1956.

ROGET, PETER MARK: BIRTH ANNIVERSARY. Jan 18, 1779. English physician, best known as author of Roget's *Thesaurus of English Words and Phrases,* first published in 1852. Roget was also the inventor of the "log-log" slide rule. He was born at London and died at West Malvern, Worcestershire, England, Sept 12, 1869.

January 2020	S	M	T	W	T	F	S
				1	2	3	4
	5	6	7	8	9	10	11
	12	13	14	15	16	17	18
	19	20	21	22	23	24	25
	26	27	28	29	30	31	

RUFFIN, DAVIS ELI (DAVID): BIRTH ANNIVERSARY. Jan 18, 1941. American popular singer David Ruffin was born at Meridian, MS. He was one of the original members of the Motown singing group the Temptations, which began in Detroit in the 1960s. Ruffin left the group in 1968 to pursue a solo career. He and the other original members of the Temptations were inducted into the Rock & Roll Hall of Fame in 1989. Ruffin died June 1, 1991, at Philadelphia, PA.

VERSAILLES PEACE CONFERENCE: ANNIVERSARY. Jan 18, 1919. French president Raymond Poincare formally opened the (WWI) peace conference at Versailles, France. It proceeded under the chairmanship of Georges Clemenceau. In May the conference disposed of Germany's colonies and delivered a treaty to the German delegates on May 7, 1919, fourth anniversary of the sinking of the *Lusitania*. Final treaty-signing ceremonies were completed at the palace at Versailles, June 28, 1919.

WEBSTER, DANIEL: BIRTH ANNIVERSARY. Jan 18, 1782. American statesman and orator who said, on Apr 6, 1830, "The people's government, made for the people, made by the people and answerable to the people." Born at Salisbury, NH; died at Marshfield, MA, Oct 24, 1852.

WEEK OF CHRISTIAN UNITY. Jan 18–25. From the Conversion of St. Peter (Jan 18) to the Conversion of St. Paul (Jan 25).

🎂 BIRTHDAYS TODAY

John Boorman, 87, filmmaker (*Deliverance, Excalibur*), born Shepperton, England, Jan 18, 1933.

Kevin Costner, 65, actor, director (*Field of Dreams, Dances with Wolves, Bull Durham*), born Lynwood, CA, Jan 18, 1955.

Jane Horrocks, 56, actress (*Little Voice*, "Absolutely Fabulous"), born Lancashire, England, Jan 18, 1964.

Jesse L. Martin, 51, actor ("Law & Order," "Ally McBeal"), born Rocky Mountain, VA, Jan 18, 1969.

Mark Messier, 59, former hockey player, born Edmonton, AB, Canada, Jan 18, 1961.

Mark Rylance, 60, actor (Oscar for *Bridge of Sighs*; "Wolf Hall," Tonys for *Twelfth Night, Jerusalem* and *Boeing-Boeing*), born David Mark Waters at Ashford, England, Jan 18, 1960.

Jason Segel, 40, actor (*Forgetting Sarah Marshall*, "Freaks and Geeks," "How I Met Your Mother"), born Los Angeles, CA, Jan 18, 1980.

Philippe Starck, 71, designer, born Paris, France, Jan 18, 1949.

January 19 — Sunday

DAY 19   **347 REMAINING**

CÉZANNE, PAUL: BIRTH ANNIVERSARY. Jan 19, 1839. Post-Impressionist painter, born at Aix-en-Provence, France. Seeking to "treat nature by the cylinder, the sphere, the cone," Cézanne's portraits, still lifes and landscapes are a seminal bridge from the Romantics and Impressionists to the Fauves, Cubists and later Modernists. He created such masterpieces as *The Bathers* (1875), *The Card Players* (1892) and *Compotier, Pitcher and Fruit* (1892–94). Cézanne died Oct 23, 1906, at Aix, from pneumonia after painting outside in the rain.

CHEVRON HOUSTON MARATHON. Jan 19. Houston, TX. 48th annual citywide race. The race weekend also features Aramco Houston Half Marathon (Jan 19) and We Are Houston 5k run (Jan 18). Est attendance: 27,000. For info: Houston Marathon Committee, 720 N Post Oak Rd, #200, Houston, TX 77024. Phone: (713) 957-3453. Fax: (713) 957-3406. E-mail: marathon@houstonmarathon.com. Web: www.chevronhoustonmarathon.com.

CONFEDERATE HEROES DAY IN TEXAS. Jan 19. Also called Confederate Memorial Day, observed on anniversary of Robert E. Lee's birthday. Official holiday in Texas.

ETHIOPIA: TIMKET. Jan 19. National holiday. Epiphany in the Ethiopian and Coptic churches. Occurs some years on Jan 20. Also a holiday in Eritrea.

"48 HOURS" TV PREMIERE: ANNIVERSARY. Jan 19, 1988. CBS prime-time newsmagazine program airing each week with first Dan Rather as host and then Leslie Stahl. After 15 years, the program changed format to focus on crime mysteries presented by a revolving stable of reporters, who include Erin Moriarty, Peter Van Sant, Richard Schlesinger and others.

HELMS, EDGAR J.: BIRTH ANNIVERSARY. Jan 19, 1863. Preacher and philanthropist born near Malone, NY. Helms ministered to a parish of poor immigrants in Boston, MA's South End. He developed the philosophy and organization and founded in 1902 the program that eventually became Goodwill Industries. By 1920 there were 15 Goodwills in the US. Helms died Dec 23, 1942, at Boston.

JOHNSON, JOHN H.: BIRTH ANNIVERSARY. Jan 19, 1918. Born at Arkansas City, AR, the grandson of a slave, John H. Johnson rose from abject poverty to become one of the most influential black businessmen in America. In 1942 he launched the first of his successful magazines, *Negro Digest*, which reached a circulation of 50,000 within eight months. In 1945 came *Ebony*, followed by *Jet* in 1951. By the time of his death at Chicago, IL, on Aug 8, 2005, Johnson's company was the world's largest African-American owned-and-operated publishing operation. He served the US as goodwill ambassador and received numerous honors, the most important of which was the Presidential Medal of Freedom in 1996 for "building self-respect in the black community."

JOPLIN, JANIS: BIRTH ANNIVERSARY. Jan 19, 1943. Possibly the most highly regarded white female blues singer of all time, Janis Joplin was born at Port Arthur, TX. Joplin's appearance with Big Brother and the Holding Company at the Monterey International Pop Festival in August 1967 launched her to superstar status. Among her recording hits were "Get It While You Can," "Piece of My Heart" and "Ball and Chain." She died of a heroin overdose Oct 4, 1970, at Hollywood, CA, at the age of 27.

LEE, ROBERT E.: BIRTH ANNIVERSARY. Jan 19, 1807. Greatest military leader of the Confederacy, son of Revolutionary War general Henry (Light-Horse Harry) Lee. His surrender Apr 9, 1865, to Union general Ulysses S. Grant brought an end to the Civil War. Born at Westmoreland County, VA, he died at Lexington, VA, Oct 12, 1870. His birthday is observed in Florida, Kentucky, Louisiana, South Carolina and Tennessee. Observed on third Monday in January in Alabama, Arkansas and Mississippi.

NATIONAL POPCORN DAY. Jan 19. Celebrate the goodness of one of America's oldest and most beloved snacks—as a healthy start to the New Year, big game-day crowd pleaser, or signature snack of the movie industry award shows. Annually, Jan 19. For info: The Popcorn Board, 330 N Wabash Ave, Ste 2000, Chicago, IL 60611. Phone: (312) 644-6610. E-mail: info@popcorn.org. Web: www.popcorn.org.

POE, EDGAR ALLAN: BIRTH ANNIVERSARY. Jan 19, 1809. American poet and story writer, called "America's most famous man of letters." Born at Boston, MA, he was orphaned in dire poverty in 1811 and was raised by Virginia merchant John Allan. In 1836 he married his 13-year-old cousin, Virginia Clemm. A magazine

editor of note, he is best remembered for his poetry (especially "The Raven") and for his tales of suspense. Died at Baltimore, MD, Oct 7, 1849.

SNOWCARE FOR TROOPS AWARENESS WEEK. Jan 19–25. Snow-removal contractors, able-bodied veterans and anyone with a shovel are encouraged to volunteer this week to help out the families of currently deployed military personnel with snow and ice removal. This week is more than clearing driveways and sidewalks of snow and ice; it is a means to allow military families to maintain their independence and go about their daily routines taking care of family and going to work. For info: Project EverGreen, 8500 Station St, Ste 230, Mentor, OH 44060. Phone: (888) 611-2955. Web: www.ProjectEverGreen.org.

STEPHEN FOSTER DAY. Jan 19. Stephen Foster Folk Culture Center State Park, White Springs, FL. A musical program and carillon recital in honor of the legendary American composer Stephen Foster. For info: Stephen Foster Day, PO Box G, White Springs, FL 32096. Phone: (386) 397-4408. Fax: (386) 397-4262. E-mail: patricia.cromer@dep.state.fl.us. Web: www.floridastateparks.org/stephenfoster.

WATT, JAMES: BIRTH ANNIVERSARY. Jan 19, 1736. (Old Style date.) Mechanical engineer and inventor, born at Greenock, Scotland. Watt's tireless efforts to improve the steam engine resulted in a more efficient machine that powered the Industrial Revolution. He died at Heathfield, England, Aug 25, 1819.

🎂 BIRTHDAYS TODAY

Desi Arnaz, Jr, 67, singer, actor, born Los Angeles, CA, Jan 19, 1953.

Frank Caliendo, 46, comedian ("MadTV," "FrankTV"), born Chicago, IL, Jan 19, 1974.

Damien Chazelle, 35, director (Oscar for *La La Land*; *Whiplash*), screenwriter, born Providence, RI, Jan 19, 1985.

Michael Crawford, 78, actor, singer (*The Phantom of the Opera*), born Salisbury, Wiltshire, England, Jan 19, 1942.

Drea de Matteo, 48, actress ("The Sopranos," "Joey"), born Queens, NY, Jan 19, 1972.

Paula Deen, 73, chef, cookbook author, born Albany, GA, Jan 19, 1947.

Shelley Fabares, 78, actress ("The Donna Reed Show," "Coach"), born Santa Monica, CA, Jan 19, 1942 (some sources say 1944).

Shawn Johnson, 28, Olympic gymnast, born West Des Moines, IA, Jan 19, 1992.

Richard Lester, 88, director (*The Four Musketeers, Superman II, Superman III*), born Philadelphia, PA, Jan 19, 1932.

Robert MacNeil, 89, broadcast journalist, born Montreal, QC, Canada, Jan 19, 1931.

Simone Missick, 38, actress ("Luke Cage," "The Defenders"), born Simone Cook at Detroit, MI, Jan 19, 1982.

Dolly Parton, 74, singer, actress (*Nine to Five*), born Sevier County, TN, Jan 19, 1946.

Jay Robert "J.B." Pritzker, 55, Governor of Illinois (D), born Atherton, CA, Jan 19, 1965.

William Ragsdale, 59, actor ("Brother's Keeper," "Herman's Head"), born El Dorado, AR, Jan 19, 1961.

Simon Rattle, 65, orchestra conductor, born Liverpool, England, Jan 19, 1955.

Cindy Sherman, 66, artist, photographer (*Untitled Film Stills*), born Glen Ridge, NJ, Jan 19, 1954.

January 2020	S	M	T	W	T	F	S
				1	2	3	4
	5	6	7	8	9	10	11
	12	13	14	15	16	17	18
	19	20	21	22	23	24	25
	26	27	28	29	30	31	

Bitsie Tulloch, 39, actress ("Grimm," *The Artist*), born San Diego, CA, Jan 19, 1981.

Jeff Van Gundy, 58, basketball coach, born Inkster, MI, Jan 19, 1962.

Shawn Wayans, 49, actor (*Scary Movie*, "In Living Color"), born New York, NY, Jan 19, 1971.

January 20 — Monday

DAY 20   **346 REMAINING**

ADAMSON, JOY: BIRTH ANNIVERSARY. Jan 20, 1910. A conservationist and author who championed the preservation of African wildlife, Adamson was born Friederike Victoria Gessner at Troppau, Silesia, Austria-Hungary, or what is now the Czech Republic. In 1939 she moved to Kenya, where she met and married George Adamson, a British game warden. The couple raised Elsa, a lion cub, and eventually released her back into the wild, chronicling the events in a bestselling book, *Born Free* (1960), and two sequels. In 1961 Adamson founded the Elsa Conservation Trust, an international group that financed conservation and education projects. Both Joy and George Adamson met tragic ends: she was murdered by an employee Jan 3, 1980 (Shaba National Reserve, Kenya), and he was killed by animal poachers in 1989.

AQUARIUS, THE WATER CARRIER. Jan 20–Feb 19. In the astronomical/astrological zodiac, which divides the sun's apparent orbit into 12 segments, the period Jan 20–Feb 19 is traditionally identified as the sun sign of Aquarius, the Water Carrier. The ruling planet is Uranus or Saturn.

AUSTRALIA: AUSTRALIAN OPEN. Jan 20–Feb 2. Melbourne Park, Melbourne. Part of the Grand Slam of tennis tournaments. First held in 1905. For info: Australian Open. Web: www.ausopen.com.

AZERBAIJAN: MARTYRS' DAY. Jan 20. National holiday. Commemorates the Azeris killed by Soviet troops, Jan 20, 1990, as they fought for independence.

BRAZIL: NOSSO SENHOR DO BONFIM FESTIVAL. Jan 20–30. Salvador, Bahia. Our Lord of the Happy Ending Festival is one of Salvador's most colorful religious feasts. Climax comes with people carrying water to pour over church stairs and sidewalks to cleanse them of impurities.

BRAZIL: SAN SEBASTIAN'S DAY. Jan 20. Patron saint of Rio de Janeiro.

"BREAKING BAD" TV PREMIERE: ANNIVERSARY. Jan 20, 2008. Bryan Cranston won four Lead Actor Emmys for the AMC network's seriocomic morality play about an Albuquerque high school chemistry teacher with inoperable cancer who turns to making meth to secure his family's financial future. He recruits a former student and petty criminal (Aaron Paul) to introduce him to the crime world. The series ran for five seasons. More than 10 million viewers watched the series finale on Sept 29, 2013. One of the most-watched cable TV series in history, "Breaking Bad" also holds the Guinness World Record for being the most critically

acclaimed show of all time. In 2015, a spin-off prequel, "Better Call Saul," centered on crooked lawyer Saul Goodman (Bob Odenkirk), debuted on AMC.

BURNS, GEORGE: BIRTH ANNIVERSARY. Jan 20, 1896. Comedian George Burns was born at New York City. He began in vaudeville without much success until he teamed up with Gracie Allen, who became his wife. As Burns and Allen, the two had a long career on radio, in film and with their hit TV show, "The George Burns and Gracie Allen Show." Later he played the roles of God and the Devil in the *Oh, God!* movies. He lived to be 100 and died Mar 9, 1996, at Los Angeles, CA.

FELLINI, FEDERICO: 100th BIRTH ANNIVERSARY. Jan 20, 1920. Director and screenwriter Federico Fellini was born at Rimini, Italy. Four of Fellini's movies won Oscars for best foreign-language film: *La Strada* (1956), *Nights of Cabiria* (1957), 8½ (1963) and *Amarcord* (1974). He received an honorary Oscar in 1993 in recognition of his cinematic accomplishments. Fellini died Oct 31, 1993, at Rome.

"FINAL SOLUTION": ANNIVERSARY. Jan 20, 1942. At the Wannsee Conference (held in the Berlin suburb of Wannsee), chaired by Reinhard Heydrich and attended by 15 German government officials, the Nazis decided on the Final Solution: to send all Jews to death camps. The official minutes were edited and sanitized of specific language about killing. The resulting mass murder took the lives of at least six million Jews.

GUINEA-BISSAU: NATIONAL HEROES DAY. Jan 20. National holiday.

JOHN MARSHALL APPOINTED CHIEF JUSTICE: ANNIVERSARY. Jan 20, 1801. John Marshall was appointed the fourth chief justice of the US.

KELLEY, DEFOREST: 100th BIRTH ANNIVERSARY. Jan 20, 1920. Character actor with a long career on film and television who became famous for his portrayal of Dr. Leonard "Bones" McCoy on the original "Star Trek" television series and the later films. Born Jackson DeForest Kelley at Toccoa, GA, he died June 11, 1999, at Los Angeles, CA.

KING, MARTIN LUTHER, JR: BIRTHDAY OBSERVED. Jan 20. Public Law 98–144 designates the third Monday in January as an annual legal public holiday observing the birth of Martin Luther King, Jr. First observed in 1986. In New Hampshire, this day is designated Civil Rights Day. See also: "King, Martin Luther, Jr: Birth Anniversary" (Jan 15).

LEDBETTER, HUDDIE "LEAD BELLY": BIRTH ANNIVERSARY. Jan 20, 1889. Born on a plantation in Mooringsport, LA, on Jan 20, 1889 (some sources say 1888), Huddie "Lead Belly" Ledbetter learned guitar while working as a farmer and sharecropper. He got his start in the music business as a collaborator with Blind Lemon Jefferson, playing his 12-string at juke joints and dances. In the 1930s, while serving time in Angola Prison, Lead Belly met folklorists and researchers John and Alan Lomax, who first recorded his most famous song, "Goodnight Irene," as well as early versions of the eventual standards "Rock Island Line" and "Midnight Special." Lead Belly worked off and on with the Lomaxes over the next several years and also cut sides for Capitol and the pioneering Folkways label. He died of ALS Dec 6, 1949, at New York, NY.

LEE, RICHARD HENRY: BIRTH ANNIVERSARY. Jan 20, 1732. Signer of the Declaration of Independence. Born at Westmoreland County, VA, he died June 19, 1794, at his birthplace.

LESOTHO: ARMY DAY. Jan 20. Lesotho.

★MARTIN LUTHER KING, JR, FEDERAL HOLIDAY. Jan 20. Presidential Proclamation has been issued without request each year for the third Monday in January since 1986.

PHILIPPINES: ATI-ATIHAN FESTIVAL. Jan 20–25. Kalibo, Aklan. One of the oldest and most colorful celebrations in the Philippines, the Ati-Atihan Festival commemorates the peace pact between the Ati of Panay (pygmies) and the Malays, who were early migrants in the islands. The townspeople blacken their bodies with soot, don

colorful and bizarre costumes and sing and dance in the streets. The festival also celebrates the Feast Day of Santo Niño (the infant Jesus). Annually, the third week in January (beginning on Monday).

STOCK EXCHANGE HOLIDAY (MARTIN LUTHER KING DAY). Jan 20. The holiday schedules for the various exchanges are subject to change if relevant rules, regulations or exchange policies are revised. For info: CME Group (CME, CBOT, NYMEX, COMEX) (www.cmegroup.com), Chicago Board Options Exchange (www.cboe.com), NASDAQ (www.nasdaq.com), NYSE (www.nyse.com).

US HOSTAGES IN IRAN RELEASED: ANNIVERSARY. Jan 20, 1981. The Iran hostage crisis ended with the release of 52 US citizens after 444 days of captivity. The deal was announced minutes after the swearing in of President Ronald Reagan.

US REVOLUTIONARY WAR: CESSATION OF HOSTILITIES: ANNIVERSARY. Jan 20, 1783. The British and US commissioners signed a preliminary "Cessation of Hostilities," which was ratified by England's King George III Feb 14 and led to the treaties of Paris and Versailles, Sept 3, 1783, ending the war.

🎂 BIRTHDAYS TODAY

Edwin "Buzz" Aldrin, 90, former astronaut, one of the first two men on moon, born Montclair, NJ, Jan 20, 1930.

Tom Baker, 86, actor ("Doctor Who," "Little Britain"), born Liverpool, England, Jan 20, 1934.

Kellyanne Conway, 53, counselor to the president (Trump administration), political strategist, born Kellyanne Fitzpatrick at Camden, NY, Jan 20, 1967.

James Denton, 57, actor ("The Pretender," "Desperate Housewives"), born Nashville, TN, Jan 20, 1963.

Nick Foles, 31, football player (Super Bowl LII MVP), born Austin, TX, Jan 20, 1989.

Nikki Haley, 48, former US ambassador to the United Nations, former governor of South Carolina (R), born Bamberg, SC, Jan 20, 1972.

Arte Johnson, 86, comedian, actor (Emmy for "Rowan & Martin's Laugh-In"), born Benton Harbor, MI, Jan 20, 1934 (some sources say 1929).

Lorenzo Lamas, 62, actor ("Falcon Crest," "Renegade"), born Los Angeles, CA, Jan 20, 1958.

David Lynch, 74, director ("Twin Peaks," *Blue Velvet*), writer, producer, born Missoula, MT, Jan 20, 1946.

Bill Maher, 64, comedian, television host ("Real Time with Bill Maher"), born New York, NY, Jan 20, 1956.

Questlove, 49, musician (The Roots), television personality ("The Tonight Show Starring Jimmy Fallon"), born Ahmir-Khalib Thompson at Philadelphia, PA, Jan 20, 1971.

Geovany Soto, 37, baseball player, born San Juan, Puerto Rico, Jan 20, 1983.

Skeet Ulrich, 50, actor ("Jericho," *Scream*), born New York, NY, Jan 20, 1970 (some sources say 1969).

Rainn Wilson, 52, actor ("The Office," "Six Feet Under," *The Last Mimzy*), born Seattle, WA, Jan 20, 1968.

January 21 — Tuesday

DAY 21   **345 REMAINING**

ALLEN, ETHAN: BIRTH ANNIVERSARY. Jan 21, 1738. Revolutionary War hero and leader of the Vermont "Green Mountain Boys," born at Litchfield, CT. He is best remembered for his capture of British Fort Ticonderoga at Lake Champlain, NY, on May 10, 1775, which was the first major American victory of the Revolutionary War. He was captured by British forces on Sept 25, 1775, while attempting to capture Montreal and was a prisoner of war until 1778, when his release was secured in exchange for a British officer. Upon his return, Allen was an ardent supporter of Vermont's separation from New York for independent statehood, although this goal was not achieved until 1791, two years after his death at Burlington, VT, on Feb 12, 1789.

BALDWIN, ROGER NASH: BIRTH ANNIVERSARY. Jan 21, 1884. Founder of the American Civil Liberties Union, called the "country's unofficial agitator for, and defender of, its civil liberties." Born at Wellesley, MA, he died Aug 26, 1981, at Ridgewood, NJ.

BALENCIAGA, CRISTOBÁL: 125th BIRTH ANNIVERSARY. Jan 21, 1895. The couturier's couturier was born at Getaria, Spain, the son of a fisherman and a seamstress. His first boutique opened in 1914 at the resort city of San Sebastián, Spain, and he soon expanded to Madrid and Barcelona. The Spanish Civil War forced his move to Paris, France, where he founded the House of Balenciaga in 1937 and became a critical and popular success. After WWII, perfectionist Balenciaga moved away from the hour-glass "New Look" offered by Christian Dior—his silhouette was more fluid and streamlined. Key Balenciaga pieces—all expertly tailored and flattering—were the cocoon coat (with only one seam), the bubble skirt and the chemise/sack dress. Key elements were the bracelet sleeve and the use of black lace over pink fabric. The "King of Fashion" closed his firm in 1968 and died Mar 23, 1972, at Valencia, Spain, universally mourned. His pupils included Oscar de la Renta, Andre Courreges and Hubert de Givenchy. The House of Balenciaga was revived in 1986.

BRECKINRIDGE, JOHN CABELL: BIRTH ANNIVERSARY. Jan 21, 1821. 14th vice president of the US (1857–61), serving under President James Buchanan. Born at Lexington, KY; died there May 17, 1875.

BROWNING, JOHN MOSES: BIRTH ANNIVERSARY. Jan 21, 1855. The world-famous gun maker and inventor who was taught gunsmithing by his Mormon pioneer father, Jonathan Browning, was born at Ogden, UT. Starting the J.M. & M.S. Browning Arms Company with his brother, he designed guns for Winchester, Remington, Stevens and Colt arms companies, as well as American and European armies. Browning had more gun patents than any other gunsmith in the world. He is best known for inventing the machine gun in 1890 and the automatic pistol in 1896. He died suddenly Nov 26, 1926, at age 71, while at Belgium on business. The company he founded, known now as Browning Arms Company, is located at Morgan, UT.

DIOR, CHRISTIAN: BIRTH ANNIVERSARY. Jan 21, 1905. Influential French fashion designer who was the world's premier style maker after WWII up until the 1950s. He was also one of the first designers to utilize licensing to help create his own brand. Born at Granville, France, Dior died on Oct 24, 1957, at Montecatini, Italy.

FIRST CONCORDE FLIGHT: ANNIVERSARY. Jan 21, 1976. The supersonic Concorde airplane was put into service by Britain and France. The Concorde ended flights on Oct 24, 2003—bringing an end to supersonic air travel.

January 2020	S	M	T	W	T	F	S
				1	2	3	4
	5	6	7	8	9	10	11
	12	13	14	15	16	17	18
	19	20	21	22	23	24	25
	26	27	28	29	30	31	

JACKSON, THOMAS JONATHAN "STONEWALL": BIRTH ANNIVERSARY. Jan 21, 1824. Confederate general and one of the most famous soldiers of the American Civil War, best known as "Stonewall" Jackson. Born at Clarksburg, VA (now WV). He died of wounds received in battle near Chancellorsville, VA, May 10, 1863.

KITCHEN AND BATH INDUSTRY SHOW (KBIS). Jan 21–23. Las Vegas, NV. KBIS, in conjunction with the National Kitchen and Bath Association (NKBA), is an inspiring, interactive platform that showcases the latest industry products, trends and technologies. More than 600 brands are featured. KBIS is the voice of the kitchen and bath industry and has been for 50 years. For info: Natl Kitchen and Bath Assn. Phone: (800) 843-6522 (THE-NKBA). Web: www.kbis.com or www.nkba.org.

KIWANIS INTERNATIONAL: ANNIVERSARY. Jan 21, 1915. First Kiwanis Club chartered at Detroit, MI.

NATIONAL CHEESY SOCK DAY™. Jan 21. The day raises awareness of homeless and foster children who often go without a good pair of socks. The goal is to raise funds to provide unaccompanied homeless youth and foster children with a fun and functional care package during the winter months. The package includes warm socks, cheese popcorn and toiletry items, along with a "cheesy" joke and heartfelt note. Annually, Jan 21. For info: Fill a Heart 4 Kids, 400 E Illinois Rd, Lake Forest, IL 60045. Web: www.filla-heart4kids.org.

NATIONAL HUG YOUR PUPPY DAY. Jan 21. Since 2019, a day to show love and kindness to dogs—who bring so much joy to our lives. Give 'em a gentle hug! For info: The Elking Family, 410 Chesterfield Shores CT, Wildwood, MO 63040.

NATIONAL HUGGING DAY™. Jan 21. Because hugging is something everyone can do and because it is a healthful form of touching, this day should be spent hugging anyone who will accept a hug, especially family and friends. The most "Huggable People" of the year will be announced. Nominations accepted through Jan 10. Official events around the world. For info, please send SASE to: Kevin C. Zaborney, 2023 Vickory Rd, Caro, MI 48723. Phone: (989) 673-6696. E-mail: kevin@nationalhuggingday.com. Web: www.nationalhuggingday.com.

WOLFMAN JACK: BIRTH ANNIVERSARY. Jan 21, 1938. Wolfman Jack was born Robert Smith at Brooklyn, NY. He became famous as a disc jockey for radio stations at Mexico in the 1960s. Wolfman Jack was influential as a border radio voice because the Mexican station broadcast at 250,000 watts, five times the legal limit for American stations at the time, and therefore he was heard over a vast part of the US. During his night shift he played blues, hillbilly and other black and white music that wasn't getting a lot of exposure. He later appeared on American radio, in movies and on television as an icon of 1960s radio. Wolfman Jack died July 1, 1995, at Belvidere, NC.

🎂 BIRTHDAYS TODAY

Robby Benson, 64, actor ("Search for Tomorrow," *Ode to Billie Joe*), born Robin Segal at Dallas, TX, Jan 21, 1956.

Kevin Cramer, 59, US Senator (R, North Dakota), born Rolette, ND, Jan 21, 1961.

Geena Davis, 63, actress (*Thelma and Louise*, Oscar for *The Accidental Tourist*), born Ware, MA, Jan 21, 1957.

Mac Davis, 78, singer, actor ("The Mac Davis Show," *North Dallas Forty*), born Lubbock, TX, Jan 21, 1942.

Plácido Domingo, 79, opera singer, one of the "Three Tenors," born Madrid, Spain, Jan 21, 1941.

Ashton Eaton, 32, Olympic decathlete and heptathlete, born Portland, OR, Jan 21, 1988.

Jill Eikenberry, 73, actress ("LA Law"), born New Haven, CT, Jan 21, 1947.

Eric H. Holder, Jr, 69, former US attorney general (Obama administration), born the Bronx, NY, Jan 21, 1951.

Jeff Koons, 65, artist (*Balloon Dog [Orange]*), born York, PA, Jan 21, 1955.

Jack William Nicklaus, 80, golfer, born Columbus, OH, Jan 21, 1940.

Billy Ocean, 70, musician, songwriter, born Leslie Charles at Trinidad, West Indies, Jan 21, 1950.

Hakeem Abdul Olajuwon, 57, Hall of Fame basketball player, born Lagos, Nigeria, Jan 21, 1963.

Martin Shaw, 75, actor ("Inspector George Gently," "Judge John Deed," "The Professionals"), born Birmingham, England, Jan 21, 1945.

January 22 — Wednesday

DAY 22 **344 REMAINING**

ALLIES TAKE NEW GUINEA: ANNIVERSARY. Jan 22, 1943. In the first land victory over the Japanese in WWII, American and Australian soldiers overcame the last pockets of resistance west and south of Sanananda on New Guinea. Three thousand Allies were killed in the battle. The Japanese lost 7,000. Of the 350 prisoners taken, most were Chinese and Korean laborers attached to the Japanese forces. Almost no Japanese allowed themselves to be taken prisoner, preferring to commit hari-kiri.

AMPÈRE, ANDRÉ: BIRTH ANNIVERSARY. Jan 22, 1775. Physicist, student of electrical and magnetic phenomena and founder of the science of electrodynamics. Born at Lyons, France. From his early childhood, tragedy and depression pursued him. His father was executed during the French Revolution. Ampère died at Marseilles, France, June 10, 1836. The epitaph he selected for his tombstone was *tandem felix* ("happy at last"). The ampere, a unit of electrical current, is named for him.

ANSWER YOUR CAT'S QUESTION DAY. Jan 22. If you will stop what you are doing and take a look at your cat, you will observe that the cat is looking at you with a serious question. Meditate upon the question, and then answer it! Annually, Jan 22. (©2006 by WH.) For info: Thomas & Ruth Roy, Wellcat Holidays, 2418 Long Ln, Lebanon, PA 17046. Phone: (717) 279-0184. E-mail: info@wellcat.com. Web: www.wellcat.com.

BACON, FRANCIS: BIRTH ANNIVERSARY. Jan 22, 1561. (Old Style date.) The lawyer, statesman, philosopher and author was born at London, England. Bacon's fame rests on his philosophical works, including *Advancement of Learning* (1605) and *Novum Organum* (1620). Bacon is considered the father of the scientific method, and he was a hero to scientists later in the century. Bacon died at London, Apr 9, 1626.

BALANCHINE, GEORGE: BIRTH ANNIVERSARY. Jan 22, 1904. Born Georgi Militonovitch Balanchivadze at St. Petersburg, Russia, George Balanchine became one of the leading influences in 20th-century ballet. He choreographed more than 200 ballets including *Concerto Barocco, Apollo, Orpheus, Firebird, Swan Lake, Waltz Academy* and *The Nutcracker*. In 1933 he was invited to the US by Boston philanthropist Lincoln Kirstein to establish a school for American dancers. Together they founded the School of American Ballet in 1934 and then formed several ballet companies, including the New York City Ballet, which was led by Balanchine. Died at New York, NY, Apr 30, 1983.

BYRON, GEORGE GORDON: BIRTH ANNIVERSARY. Jan 22, 1788. Born at London, England, flamboyant Romantic poet Lord Byron was one of the first literary celebrities in the modern sense. His works—*Childe Harold's Pilgrimage, The Corsair, Manfred*—often sold out within days of publication. Described as "Mad, bad and dangerous to know" by Lady Caroline Lamb, Byron died of fever at Missolonghi, Greece, Apr 19, 1824, while fighting for Greek independence.

GRIFFITH, DAVID (LLEWELYN) WARK: BIRTH ANNIVERSARY. Jan 22, 1875. D.W. Griffith, pioneer producer-director in the American motion picture industry, best remembered for his film *Birth of a Nation* (1915). Born at LaGrange, KY. Died at Hollywood, CA, July 23, 1948.

HOWARD, ROBERT E.: BIRTH ANNIVERSARY. Jan 22, 1906. Born at Peaster, TX, Howard was to become one of the great and prolific pulp fiction writers of the 1920s and 1930s. He is most famous for creating Conan the Barbarian. Committed suicide at Cross Plains, TX, Jan 11, 1936.

"LAUGH-IN" TV PREMIERE: ANNIVERSARY. Jan 22, 1968. Actually the name of this NBC comedy was "Rowan & Martin's Laugh-In." Funny men Dan Rowan and Dick Martin hosted the show, but they seemed staid next to the show's other regulars, most of whom were young unknowns, including Dennis Allen, Chelsea Brown, Judy Carne, Ruth Buzzi, Ann Elder, Richard Dawson, Teresa Graves, Arte Johnson, Goldie Hawn, Alan Sues, Jo Anne Worley and Lily Tomlin. The show moved fast from gag to gag, with heads popping out of bushes or doors in the big wall. The show brought a new energy to comedy as well as new phrases to our vocabulary ("You bet your sweet bippy," "Sock it to me"). The last telecast was May 14, 1973.

PONSELLE, ROSA: BIRTH ANNIVERSARY. Jan 22, 1897. Formerly Rosa Melba Ponzilla, soprano Ponselle was born at Meriden, CT. Her career changed direction from vaudeville to opera when she was discovered by Enrico Caruso at the age of 21. Ponselle made her operatic debut at the Met in Verdi's *La forza del destino*. Her career spanned 19 seasons at the Met and included performances at London and Florence. Ponselle died May 25, 1981, at Baltimore, MD.

QUEEN VICTORIA: DEATH ANNIVERSARY. Jan 22, 1901. Queen Victoria died at age 82 after a reign of 63 years, seven months, the longest in British history until the reign of Queen Elizabeth II. She had ruled over the one-quarter of the world that was the British Empire. Born May 24, 1819, at London, she died at Osborne, England.

***ROE V WADE* DECISION: ANNIVERSARY.** Jan 22, 1973. In the case of *Roe v Wade*, the US Supreme Court struck down state laws restricting abortions during the first six months of pregnancy. In the following decades debate has continued to rage between those who believe a woman has a right to choose whether to continue a pregnancy and those who believe that aborting such a pregnancy is murder of an unborn child.

SAINT VINCENT: FEAST DAY. Jan 22. Spanish deacon and martyr who died in AD 304. Patron saint of winegrowers. Old weather lore says if there is sun on this day, good wine crops may be expected in the ensuing season.

STRINDBERG, AUGUST: BIRTH ANNIVERSARY. Jan 22, 1849. Swedish novelist and dramatist often called Sweden's greatest

playwright. Born at Stockholm and died there of cancer on May 14, 1912, at age 63.

UKRAINE: UKRAINIAN DAY. Jan 22. National holiday. Commemorates the proclamation of the Ukrainian National Republic, Jan 22, 1918. Independence was short lived, however; by 1921 Ukraine had become part of the Soviet Union. It gained its independence from the Soviet Union in 1991.

UPJOHN, RICHARD: BIRTH ANNIVERSARY. Jan 22, 1802. American architect and founder of the American Institute of Architects in 1857. A Gothic revivalist, he designed many churches. Among his works were Trinity Chapel, New York, NY; Corn Exchange Bank Building, New York, NY; and Central Congregational Church, Boston, MA. Born at Shaftesbury, England, he died Aug 17, 1878, at Garrison, NY.

VINSON, FRED M.: BIRTH ANNIVERSARY. Jan 22, 1890. The 13th chief justice of the US, born at Louisa, KY. Served in the House of Representatives, appointed director of war mobilization during WWII and secretary of the Treasury under Harry Truman. Nominated by Truman to succeed Harlan F. Stone as chief justice of the US. Died at Washington, DC, Sept 8, 1953.

ZEHNDER'S SNOWFEST (WITH ICE AND SNOW CARVING COMPETITIONS). Jan 22–27. Frankenmuth, MI. Annual festival includes ice carving demonstrations; world-class, state and high school snow sculpting competitions; fireworks; entertainment and food; and many children's activities such as a petting zoo, pony rides, carousel and more. Est attendance: 130,000. For info: Linda Kelly, Zehnder's of Frankenmuth, 730 S Main St, Frankenmuth, MI 48734. Phone: (800) 863-7999. Fax: (989) 652-3544. Web: www.zehnders.com.

🎂 BIRTHDAYS TODAY

Linda Blair, 61, actress (*The Exorcist, Airport*), born Westport, CT, Jan 22, 1959.

Olivia D'Abo, 53, actress ("The Wonder Years," "The Single Guy"), born London, England, Jan 22, 1967.

Guy Fieri, 52, television personality ("Diners, Drive-Ins and Dives"), restaurant executive, born Columbus, OH, Jan 22, 1968.

Balthazar Getty, 45, actor ("Brothers & Sisters," "Alias," *Lost Highway*), born Los Angeles, CA, Jan 22, 1975.

Diane Lane, 55, actress (*Unfaithful, A Walk on the Moon, A Little Romance*), born New York, NY, Jan 22, 1965.

Piper Laurie, 88, actress (*Fighting for My Daughter,* "Twin Peaks"), born Rosetta Jacobs at Detroit, MI, Jan 22, 1932.

Gabriel Macht, 48, actor (*The Spirit,* "Suits"), born New York, NY, Jan 22, 1972.

Christopher Masterson, 40, actor ("Malcolm in the Middle"), born Long Island, NY, Jan 22, 1980.

Greg Oden, 32, basketball player, born Buffalo, NY, Jan 22, 1988.

Steve Perry, 71, singer (Journey), born Hanford, CA, Jan 22, 1949.

Joseph Wambaugh, 83, former police officer, author (*The Onion Field, The Choir Boys*), born East Pittsburgh, PA, Jan 22, 1937.

January 2020	S	M	T	W	T	F	S
				1	2	3	4
	5	6	7	8	9	10	11
	12	13	14	15	16	17	18
	19	20	21	22	23	24	25
	26	27	28	29	30	31	

January 23 — Thursday

DAY 23   **343 REMAINING**

"BARNEY MILLER" TV PREMIERE: 45th ANNIVERSARY. Jan 23, 1975. This ABC sitcom about a New York precinct captain starred Hal Linden as Captain Barney Miller. The 12th Precinct gang included Barbara Barrie as Miller's wife, Abe Vigoda as Detective Phil Fish, Max Gail as Sergeant Stan Wojciehowicz, Gregory Sierra as Sergeant Chano Amenguale, Jack Soo as Sergeant Nick Yemana, Ron Glass as Detective Ron Harris and a host of others. The last episode aired in 1982.

BLACKWELL, ELIZABETH, AWARDED MD: ANNIVERSARY. Jan 23, 1849. Dr. Elizabeth Blackwell became the first woman to receive an MD degree. The native of Bristol, England, was awarded her degree by the Medical Institution of Geneva, NY.

BULGARIA: BABIN DEN. Jan 23. Celebrated throughout Bulgaria as Day of the Midwives or Grandmother's Day. Traditional festivities.

HANCOCK, JOHN: BIRTH ANNIVERSARY. Jan 23, 1737. American patriot and statesman, first signer of the Declaration of Independence. Hancock served as president of the Continental Congress (1775–77) and served as Massachusetts governor for nine terms beginning in 1780. Because of his conspicuous signature on the Declaration, Hancock's name has become part of the American language, referring to any handwritten signature. Born at Braintree, MA, he died at Quincy, MA, Oct 8, 1793. (Some sources cite Hancock's Old Style birth date of Jan 12, 1736/7.)

HEWES, JOSEPH: BIRTH ANNIVERSARY. Jan 23, 1730. Signer of the Declaration of Independence. Born at Princeton, NJ, he died Nov 10, 1779, at Philadelphia, PA.

KOVACS, ERNIE: BIRTH ANNIVERSARY. Jan 23, 1919. Comedian and television pioneer, born at Trenton, NJ. Throughout the '40s and '50s Ernie Kovacs made a name for himself hosting his own shows, including "The Ernie Kovacs Show" and "Ernie In Kovacsland" and a variety of quiz shows. He died in an automobile accident at Los Angeles, CA, Jan 13, 1962.

MANET, ÉDOUARD: BIRTH ANNIVERSARY. Jan 23, 1832. Painter, born at Paris, France. Among his best-known paintings are *Olympia* and *Déjeuner sur l'herbe*. Manet died Apr 30, 1883, at Paris.

NATIONAL HANDWRITING DAY. Jan 23. Popularly observed on the birthday of John Hancock to encourage more legible handwriting. (Some sources cite Hancock's Old Style birth date of Jan 12, 1736/7.)

NATIONAL PIE DAY. Jan 23. First observed in 1975 as a day to set aside and celebrate pie! Today is a day to maintain America's pie heritage, pass on the tradition of pie making and promote America's love affair with pie. Annually, Jan 23. For info: Linda Hoskins, Executive Director, American Pie Council, PO Box 523, Bonita Springs, FL 34133. Phone: (847) 687-2722. E-mail: piecouncil@aol.com. Web: www.piecouncil.org.

SAINT PAUL WINTER CARNIVAL. Jan 23–Feb 2. St. Paul, MN. One of Minnesota's largest tourist attractions and the nation's oldest and largest winter festival (first celebrated in 1886). The Saint Paul Winter Carnival provides the "Coolest Celebration on Earth" with many indoor and outdoor events celebrating the thrills and chills of wintertime fun. Est attendance: 200,000. For info: Saint Paul Festival and Heritage Foundation, 429 Landmark Ctr, 75 W 5th St, St. Paul, MN 55102. Phone: (651) 223-7400. E-mail: info@wintercarnival.com. Web: www.wintercarnival.com.

SNOWPLOW MAILBOX HOCKEY DAY. Jan 23. It's wintertime and time for snowplow drivers everywhere to see how many rural mailboxes they can knock over. Twenty extra points for boosting one into the next township! (©2006 by WH.) For info: Thomas & Ruth Roy, Wellcat Holidays, 2418 Long Ln, Lebanon, PA 17046. Phone: (717) 279-0184. E-mail: info@wellcat.com. Web: www.wellcat.com.

STENDHAL: BIRTH ANNIVERSARY. Jan 23, 1783. French author Marie-Henri Beyle, whose best-known pseudonym was Stendhal. Best remembered are his novels *The Red and the Black* (1831) and *The Charterhouse of Parma* (1839). Born at Grenoble, France, he died at Paris, Mar 23, 1842.

STEWART, POTTER: BIRTH ANNIVERSARY. Jan 23, 1915. Associate justice of the US, nominated by President Eisenhower Jan 17, 1959. (Oath of office, May 15, 1959.) Born at Jackson, MI, he retired in July 1981 and died Dec 7, 1985, at Putney, VT, five days after suffering a stroke. Buried at Arlington National Cemetery.

SUNDANCE FILM FESTIVAL. Jan 23–Feb 2. Park City, UT. Since 1985. "The premier US festival for independent filmmakers." More than 120 feature-length films and more than 80 short films screened. Est attendance: 40,000. For info: Sundance Institute, PO Box 684429, Park City, UT 84068. Phone: (435) 658-3456. E-mail: press@sundance.org or institute@sundance.org. Web: www.sundance.org/festival.

TWENTIETH AMENDMENT TO US CONSTITUTION RATIFIED: ANNIVERSARY. Jan 23, 1933. The 20th Amendment was ratified, fixing the date of the presidential inauguration at the current Jan 20 instead of the previous Mar 4. It also specified that were the president-elect to die before taking office, the vice president–elect would succeed to the presidency. In addition, it set Jan 3 as the official opening date of Congress each year.

TWENTY-FOURTH AMENDMENT TO US CONSTITUTION RATIFIED: ANNIVERSARY. Jan 23, 1964. Poll taxes and other taxes were eliminated as a prerequisite for voting in all federal elections by the 24th Amendment.

USS *PUEBLO* SEIZED BY NORTH KOREA: ANNIVERSARY. Jan 23, 1968. North Korea seized the USS *Pueblo* in the Sea of Japan, claiming the ship was on a spy mission. The crew was held for 11 months. The vessel was confiscated. Accompanying the crew when released—on Dec 22, 1968—was the body of Seaman Duane D. Hodges, the only crewman killed.

WALCOTT, DEREK: 90th BIRTH ANNIVERSARY. Jan 23, 1930. Born at Castries, Santa Lucia, Walcott published his first poem at 14. He found international recognition with *In a Green Night* (1962) and won the Nobel Prize for Literature in 1992 for "a poetic oeuvre of great luminosity." Admired for its technical mastery and lyrical beauty, his poetry deployed both Caribbean patois and a literary English that plumbed the complexities of Caribbean colonial identity. Also a playwright, Walcott founded Trinidad Theatre Workshop in 1959 and Boston Playwright's Theater in 1981, and he won an Obie Award for *Dream on Monkey Mountain* (1971). Other notable awards include a MacArthur Foundation Fellowship (1981), the Queen's Medal for Poetry (1988) and the T.S. Eliot Prize (2011). He died Mar 17, 2017, at Gros Islet, Santa Lucia.

🎂 **BIRTHDAYS TODAY**

Richard Dean Anderson, 70, actor ("Stargate SG-1," "MacGyver"), born Minneapolis, MN, Jan 23, 1950.

Princess Caroline, 63, born Monte Carlo, Monaco, Jan 23, 1957.

Tom Carper, 73, US Senator (D, Delaware), born Beckley, WV, Jan 23, 1947.

Gil Gerard, 77, actor ("Buck Rogers," "Sidekicks"), born Little Rock, AR, Jan 23, 1943.

Patrick Capper (Pat) Haden, 67, college football executive, former player, born Westbury, NY, Jan 23, 1953.

Mariska Hargitay, 56, actress ("Law & Order: SVU"), born Los Angeles, CA, Jan 23, 1964.

Norah O'Donnell, 46, broadcast anchor, journalist, born Washington, DC, Jan 23, 1974.

Gail O'Grady, 57, actress ("NYPD Blue"), born Detroit, MI, Jan 23, 1963.

Tito Ortiz, 45, mixed martial artist, born Santa Ana, CA, Jan 23, 1975.

Chita Rivera, 87, singer, actress (Tonys for *The Kiss of the Spider Woman* and *The Rink*), born Conchita del Rivero at Washington, DC, Jan 23, 1933.

Tiffani Thiessen, 46, actress ("Beverly Hills 90210," "Saved by the Bell"), born Long Beach, CA, Jan 23, 1974.

January 24 — Friday

DAY 24   **342 REMAINING**

ACHELIS, ELISABETH: BIRTH ANNIVERSARY. Jan 24, 1880. Calendar reform advocate, author of *The World Calendar*, born at Brooklyn, NY. Her proposed calendar made every year the same, with equal quarters, each year beginning on Sunday, Jan 1, and each date falling on the same day of the week every year. Died at New York, NY, Feb 11, 1973.

BELLY LAUGH DAY. Jan 24. Belly Laugh Day is a day to celebrate the great gift of laughter. Smiling and laughing are encouraged and celebrated. How? Smile, throw your arms in the air and laugh out loud. Join the Belly Laugh Bounce Around the World, as people from Antarctica to Hawaii in kitchens, schools, hospitals, offices, plants and stores stop at 1:24 PM (local time) to bounce a smile and a laugh around the world. #bellylaughday. For info: Elaine Helle. E-mail: jan24@bellylaughday.com. Web: www.bellylaughday.com.

BELUSHI, JOHN: BIRTH ANNIVERSARY. Jan 24, 1949. Actor, comedian ("Saturday Night Live," *Animal House*, *The Blues Brothers*), born at Chicago, IL. Died Mar 5, 1982, at Hollywood, CA.

BLACK HILLS STOCK SHOW AND RODEO. Jan 24–Feb 2. Rapid City, SD. Events include rodeos, ranch rodeo, timed sheepdog trials, ranch horse competition, saddle bronc match, livestock shows and sales, buffalo show and sale, team penning, bucking horse and bull sale, AQHA show, stockman banquet and ball and commercial exhibits. Est attendance: 300,000. For info: Black Hills Stock Show and Rodeo, 800 San Francisco, Rapid City, SD 57701. Phone: (605) 355-3861. Web: www.blackhillsstockshow.com.

BOLIVIA: ALASITAS FESTIVAL. Jan 24. La Paz. Annual celebration combining both Catholic and ancient Andean beliefs. The principal festivities focus on Ekeko, the god of abundance, to whom the Aymara Indians offer prayers and gifts. Although the festival is ancient, the current date was chosen to acknowledge the 1781 anniversary of a battle between Bolivians and the Spanish colonizers.

BRICKHOUSE, JACK: BIRTH ANNIVERSARY. Jan 24, 1916. John Beasley (Jack) Brickhouse was born at Peoria, IL. A legend in Chicago broadcasting, Brickhouse was the play-by-play voice for the first baseball game televised by WGN, an exhibition game between the Cubs and the White Sox on Apr 16, 1948. The dominant sports voice on Chicago radio and television, he broadcast Cubs games for 40 years, Chicago Bears football games for 24 years and some Chicago Bulls and White Sox games. In 1983 he received the Ford C. Frick Award. Brickhouse died at Chicago, IL, Aug 6, 1998.

CALIFORNIA GOLD DISCOVERY: ANNIVERSARY. Jan 24, 1848. James W. Marshal, an employee of John Sutter, accidentally discovered gold while building a sawmill near Coloma, CA. Efforts to keep the discovery secret failed, and the gold rush of 1849 was under way.

FDR'S "UNCONDITIONAL SURRENDER" STATEMENT: ANNIVERSARY. Jan 24, 1943. At the end of the Casablanca Conference, 1943, Franklin D. Roosevelt and Winston Churchill held a press conference. Roosevelt stated, "Peace can come to the world only by the total elimination of German and Japanese war power. That means the unconditional surrender of Germany, Italy and Japan." This position calling for "unconditional surrender" has subsequently been criticized by some as having prolonged the war.

FIRST CANNED BEER: 85th ANNIVERSARY. Jan 24, 1935. Canned beer went on sale for the first time at Richmond, VA. The American Can Company and the Gottfried Krueger Brewing Company collaborated to package 2,000 cans of Krueger's Finest Beer and Krueger's Cream Ale. It was an immediate success, and by the end of 1935, most major breweries had begun using cans. More than 200 million cans sold that first year.

HEINKEL, ERNST: BIRTH ANNIVERSARY. Jan 24, 1888. Aeronautical engineer, born in Grunbach, Germany. Founder of Heinkel-Flugzeugwerke, which built the military aircraft that powered Germany's early success in WWII. Heinkel built the first jet airplane, the He-178, in 1939. Heinkel died in Stuttgart, West Germany, on Jan 30, 1958.

MOON PHASE: NEW MOON. Jan 24. Moon enters New Moon phase at 4:42 PM, EST.

NATIONAL COMPLIMENT DAY. Jan 24. This day is set aside to compliment at least five people. Not only are compliments appreciated by the receiver, but also they lift the spirit of the giver. Compliments provide a quick and easy way to connect positively with those you come in contact with. Giving compliments forges bonds, dispels loneliness and just plain feels good. (Originated by Debby Hoffman and Kathy Chamberlin.)

SPACE MILESTONE: *COSMOS 954* (USSR) FALLS. Jan 24, 1978. Nuclear-equipped reconnaissance satellite launched Sept 18, 1977, fell into Earth's atmosphere and burned over northern Canada. Some radioactive debris reached ground on Jan 24, 1978.

SPACE MILESTONE: *DISCOVERY* (US). Jan 24, 1985. Space shuttle *Discovery* launched from Kennedy Space Center, FL. On its secret, all-military mission, Jan 24–27, 1985, it deployed an eavesdropping satellite.

SWITZERLAND: ST. MORITZ POLO WORLD CUP ON SNOW. Jan 24–26. St. Moritz. Since 1985, spectacular winter polo on the frozen lake of St. Moritz 1,800 meters above sea level. Est attendance: 20,000. For info: Evviva Polo St. Moritz. E-mail: info@snowpolo-stmoritz.com or media@snowpolo-stmoritz.com. Web: www.snowpolo-stmoritz.com.

UNITED NATIONS: INTERNATIONAL DAY OF EDUCATION. Jan 24. First observed in 2019. The United Nations General Assembly proclaimed this day in celebration of the role of education for peace and development (Res 73/25). UNESCO calls on governments and all partners to make universal quality education a leading priority. For info: United Nations. Web: www.un.org.

WHARTON, EDITH: BIRTH ANNIVERSARY. Jan 24, 1862. Born at New York, NY, author Edith Wharton in her stories and novels specialized in intense examinations of upper-class Manhattan society at the end of the 19th century. Major novels include *The House of Mirth* (1905) and *The Age of Innocence* (1920), which won a Pulitzer Prize. *Ethan Frome* (1911) departed from the upper-class society milieu to depict a grim New England love triangle and its tragic consequences. Wharton died at Pavilion Colombe, Saint-Brice-sous-Forĕt, France, Aug 11, 1937.

🎂 BIRTHDAYS TODAY

Mischa Barton, 34, actress ("The O.C."), born London, England, Jan 24, 1986.

Neil Diamond, 79, Rock and Roll Hall of Fame singer, composer (Grammy for *Jonathan Livingston Seagull*), born Coney Island, NY, Jan 24, 1941.

Ed Helms, 46, actor (*The Hangover*, "The Daily Show," "The Office"), writer, born Atlanta, GA, Jan 24, 1974.

January 2020	S	M	T	W	T	F	S
				1	2	3	4
	5	6	7	8	9	10	11
	12	13	14	15	16	17	18
	19	20	21	22	23	24	25
	26	27	28	29	30	31	

Laura Kelly, 70, Governor of Kansas (D), born New York, NY, Jan 24, 1950.

Nastassja Kinski, 60, actress (*Tess*; *Cat People*; *Paris, Texas*), born Berlin, Germany, Jan 24, 1960.

Matthew Lillard, 50, actor (*Scream, Scooby-Doo*), born Lansing, MI, Jan 24, 1970.

Aaron Neville, 79, singer, songwriter, born New Orleans, LA, Jan 24, 1941.

Michael Ontkean, 74, actor ("Twin Peaks," *Slap Shot*), born Vancouver, BC, Canada, Jan 24, 1946.

Mary Lou Retton, 52, Olympic gymnast, born Fairmont, WV, Jan 24, 1968.

Kristen Schaal, 42, actress ("Bob's Burgers"), comedienne, television personality ("The Daily Show"), born Longmont, CO, Jan 24, 1978.

Yakov Smirnoff, 69, comedian, born Odessa, USSR (now Ukraine), Jan 24, 1951.

Nik Wallenda, 41, aerialist, acrobat, stunt performer, born Sarasota, FL, Jan 24, 1979.

January 25 — Saturday

DAY 25 **341 REMAINING**

AFRMA FANCY RAT AND MOUSE ANNUAL SHOW. Jan 25. Riverside, CA. Annual show where trophies are awarded to the winners. Rats and mice are emerging as ideal pets: they provide all the pleasure and satisfaction of a warm, cuddly, intelligent and friendly pet companion. The American Fancy Rat and Mouse Association (AFRMA) was founded in 1983 to promote the breeding and exhibition of fancy rats and mice, to educate the public on their positive qualities as companion animals and to provide information on their proper care. Est attendance: 100. For info: AFRMA (CAE), 9230 64th St, Riverside, CA 92509-5924. Phone: (951) 685-2350 or (818) 992-5564. E-mail: afrma@afrma.org. Web: www.afrma.org.

AMHERST RAILWAY SOCIETY RAILROAD HOBBY SHOW. Jan 25–26. West Springfield, MA. Nearly 8½ acres in four buildings featuring dealers, displays, art, manufacturers, more than 40 operating layouts and railroads including Shortline, Tourist, Class 1 and more. Special clinics open on Thursday and Friday (Jan 23–24). Est attendance: 26,000. For info: Amherst Railway Society, PO Box 247, Monson, MA 01057-0247. Phone: (413) 267-4555. E-mail: showoffice@amherstrail.org. Web: www.amherstrail.org or www.railroadhobbyshow.com.

AROUND THE WORLD IN 72 DAYS: ANNIVERSARY. Jan 25, 1890. Newspaper reporter Nellie Bly (pen name used by Elizabeth Cochrane Seaman) set off from Hoboken, NJ, Nov 14, 1889, to attempt to break Jules Verne's imaginary hero Phileas Fogg's record of voyaging around the world in 80 days. She did beat Fogg's record, taking 72 days, 6 hours, 11 minutes and 14 seconds to make the trip, arriving back in New Jersey on Jan 25, 1890.

BOYLE, ROBERT: BIRTH ANNIVERSARY. Jan 25, 1627. Irish physicist, chemist and author who formulated Boyle's law in 1662. Born at Lismore, Ireland, he died at London, England, on Dec 30, 1691.

BROOKFIELD ICE HARVEST. Jan 25. Brookfield, VT. 41st annual. Demonstrations of ice harvesting using the original equipment near the Brookfield Floating Bridge, one of only two such bridges remaining in the US today. Annually, the last Saturday in January. Est attendance: 1,000. For info: Jon Binhammer, 553 Ridge Rd, Brookfield, VT 05036. Phone/fax: (802) 276-3260.

BURNS, ROBERT: BIRTH ANNIVERSARY. Jan 25, 1759. Farmer, lover of women, father of at least 11 children, freemason, songwriter and beloved poet who wove the folk traditions and dialects of Scotland into lovely lyrics and ballads. Poems and songs include "Tam O'Shanter," "To a Mouse," "Green Grow the Rushes, O" and most of "Auld Lang Syne." "Oh wad some power the giftie gie us/To see oursels as others see us!" Born at Ayrshire, Scotland, he died at Dumfries, Scotland, July 21, 1796. His birthday is widely celebrated as Burns Night, especially in Scotland, England and Newfoundland.

CHINESE NEW YEAR. Jan 25. Traditional Chinese Lunar Year begins at sunset on the day of the second New Moon following the winter solstice—the Year of the Rat. Outside China, the date of the New Year may differ by a day. The New Year can begin anytime from Jan 21 through Feb 21. Generally celebrated until the Lantern Festival 15 days later, but merchants usually reopen their stores and places of business on the fifth day of the first lunar month. This holiday is celebrated as Tet in Vietnam. See also: "China: Lantern Festival" (Feb 8).

CURTIS, CHARLES: BIRTH ANNIVERSARY. Jan 25, 1860. The 31st vice president of the US (1929–33). Born at Topeka, KS, he died at Washington, DC, Feb 8, 1936.

EGYPTIAN REVOLUTION BEGINS: ANNIVERSARY. Jan 25, 2011. Encouraged by the Tunisian Revolution of December 2010 to January 2011, tens of thousands of protesters took to the streets of Cairo and other Egyptian cities to demand legal and social rights as well as regime change. The "Day of Revolt" on Jan 25 was the spark, catalyzing further protests—both on the streets and in cyberspace through social media—that eventually led to President Hosni Mubarak resigning on Feb 11, 2011, after 30 years in power. On June 30, 2012, Mohamed Morsi was sworn in as new Egyptian president after the first contested elections since before 1981.

FIRST SCHEDULED TRANSCONTINENTAL FLIGHT: ANNIVERSARY. Jan 25, 1959. American Airlines opened the jet age in the US with the first scheduled transcontinental flight—on a Boeing 707 nonstop from California to New York.

FIRST TELEVISED PRESIDENTIAL NEWS CONFERENCE: ANNIVERSARY. Jan 25, 1961. Beginning a tradition that survives to this day, John F. Kennedy held the first televised presidential news conference five days after being inaugurated the 35th president.

FIRST WINTER OLYMPICS: ANNIVERSARY. Jan 25, 1924. The first Winter Olympic Games opened at Chamonix, France, with athletes representing 16 nations. The ski jump, previously unknown, thrilled spectators. The Olympics offered a boost to skiing, which became enormously popular in the next decade.

JAMES, ETTA: BIRTH ANNIVERSARY. Jan 25, 1938. Dynamic singer, born Jamesetta Hawkins at Los Angeles, CA. Etta James was one of the greats of rhythm and blues music. Enduring hits like "At Last" (1961) harnessed her R&B influences to the stately drama of jazz, but James also led a life of itinerant hustle and struggled with addiction, abusive relationships and career missteps. She recorded with legendary labels like Chess, won four Grammys and continued performing into the 21st century. A member of the Rock & Roll Hall of Fame and Blues Hall of Fame, Etta James died on Jan 20, 2012, at Riverside, CA.

LOCAL QUILT SHOP DAY. Jan 25. An annual celebration for independently owned quilt shops worldwide. If you love fabric and quilting, plan to make a special connection with your favorite local quilt shop on this day. Annually, the fourth Saturday in January. For info: Laurie Harsh, The Fabric Shop Network, Inc, PO Box 820128, Vancouver, WA 98682. Phone: (360) 666-2392. Fax: (360) 666-2863. E-mail: info@quiltshopday.com. Web: www.quiltshopday.com.

MACINTOSH DEBUTS: ANNIVERSARY. Jan 25, 1984. Apple's Macintosh computer went on sale this day for $2,495. It wasn't until mid-1985, however, that sales began to take off and this computer began to replace the Apple II model.

MAUGHAM, W. SOMERSET: BIRTH ANNIVERSARY. Jan 25, 1874. English short-story writer, novelist and playwright, born at Paris, France. Among his best-remembered books: *Of Human Bondage, Cakes and Ale* and *The Razor's Edge*. Died at Cap Ferrat, France, Dec 16, 1965.

MILLS, FLORENCE: BIRTH ANNIVERSARY. Jan 25, 1896. The leading black American singer and dancer of the Jazz Age and the Harlem Renaissance was born Florence Winfree at Washington, DC. She appeared in Langston Hughes's *Shuffle Along* in 1921 and *Plantation Review* on Broadway in 1922, and then at the London Pavilion in *Dover Street to Dixie* in 1923. Offered a spot in the *Ziegfeld Follies*, she turned it down and joined in creating a rival show with an all-black cast. Mills was the first black woman to appear as a headliner at the Palace Theatre. She was so revered for her efforts to create opportunities for black entertainers and to bring the unique culture of blacks to Broadway that more than 150,000 people filled the streets of Harlem to mourn her when she died at New York City, Nov 1, 1927, at age 31.

NATIONAL SEED SWAP DAY. Jan 25. Washington, DC. Bring your extra seeds and swap them with other gardeners. Everyone will leave with a bag full of seeds, new garden friends and expert planting advice. Seed swap categories include natives, edibles, herbs, exotics, annuals, perennials and woodies (trees/shrubs). Learn, network and prepare for next year's seed collecting! If you are outside of the DC area, celebrate seed swapping by setting up an event in your area. Annually, the last Saturday in January. For info: *Washington Gardener*, 826 Philadelphia Ave, Silver Spring, MD 20910. Phone: (301) 588-6894. E-mail: kathyjentz@gmail.com. Web: www.seedswapday.com.

ORANGE CITY BLUE SPRING MANATEE FESTIVAL. Jan 25–26. Valentine Park, Orange City, FL. Now in its 35th year, this festival was created to raise awareness of the endangered West Indian manatee. It features a free shuttle to see manatees in the wild. In addition, nearly 100 exhibitors honor the manatee in a variety of mediums. Children's games and rides, family entertainment, environmental exhibits and food vendors round out the event. For info: Orange City Blue Spring Manatee Festival. E-mail: info@themanateefestival.com. Web: www.themanateefestival.com.

"ROBOT" ENTERS WORLD LEXICON: ANNIVERSARY. Jan 25, 1921. On this date, the play *R.U.R.* premiered at the National Theater in Prague, Czechoslovakia. "R.U.R." stood for "Rossum's Universal Robots," and the play concerned artificial human workers who

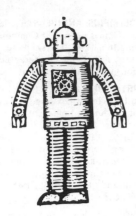

rebel against their human masters. Czech dramatist Karel Capek and his brother, Josef Capek, derived *robot* from the Czech noun *robota*, which means "labor" and "servitude." As the play became a hit worldwide (with an English translation published in 1923), the concept of the robot took hold. Capek's robots were chemically created; today's real and fictional robots are metallic machines.

A ROOM OF ONE'S OWN DAY. Jan 25. For anyone who knows or longs for the sheer bliss and rightness of having a private place, no matter how humble, to call one's own. (©2006 by WH.) For info: Thomas & Ruth Roy, Wellcat Holidays, 2418 Long Ln, Lebanon, PA 17046. Phone: (717) 279-0184. E-mail: info@wellcat.com. Web: www.wellcat.com.

SAINT DWYNWEN'S DAY. Jan 25. Patron saint of friendship and love in Wales. Dwynwen was a fifth-century saint (died AD 460) who lived in seclusion at Llanddwyn Island. The church there (the ruins of which still stand today) was a medieval pilgrimage site and supposedly featured a magic well. Saint Dwynwen's Day is not officially recognized in the Catholic and Anglican liturgical calendars, but its celebration has become a popular custom in Wales for lovers.

STERN, ITZHAK: BIRTH ANNIVERSARY. Jan 25, 1901. An accountant for industrialist Oskar Schindler, Stern advised Schindler to take advantage of the availability of forced labor from the Nazi concentration camps. In collaboration with Schindler and Mietek Pemper, an inmate and assistant to the commandant of Plaszow forced labor camp in Poland, Stern helped to compile lists of Jews who would otherwise be sent to their deaths and to create work histories that would justify their being transferred to Schindler's Krakow plant. In the movie *Schindler's List* the character Itzhak Stern is a composite of Stern and Pemper. Stern, born at Poland, emigrated to Israel after WWII. He died there in 1969. See also: "Pemper, Mietek: Birth Anniversary" (Mar 24).

US NATIONALS SNOW SCULPTING COMPETITION. Jan 25–Feb 2. Lake Geneva, WI. 24th annual. Snow sculpting competition where each three-person team creates a work of art out of a 7-foot × 9-foot block of snow. Several awards given. Est attendance: 40,000. For info: US Nationals Snow Sculpting Competition. Web: www.visitlakegeneva.com/winterfest.

WATER FLUORIDATION BEGINS IN UNITED STATES: 75th ANNIVERSARY. Jan 25, 1945. Grand Rapids, MI, began fluoridating its water supply in a study to test its positive effect on teeth. This was the first instance of water fluoridation in the world. Eleven years later, scientists found that tooth decay among children had decreased 60 percent.

January 2020	S	M	T	W	T	F	S
				1	2	3	4
	5	6	7	8	9	10	11
	12	13	14	15	16	17	18
	19	20	21	22	23	24	25
	26	27	28	29	30	31	

WOOLF, VIRGINIA: BIRTH ANNIVERSARY. Jan 25, 1882. Modernist writer and critic, member of the Bloomsbury artistic circle, author of *Mrs Dalloway, Orlando* and *To the Lighthouse.* Born at London, England. Cofounder of the Hogarth Press with her husband, Leonard Woolf. After completing her last novel, *Between the Acts,* she collapsed under the strain and drowned herself in the River Ouse near Rodmell, England, on Mar 28, 1941.

🎂 BIRTHDAYS TODAY

Vince Carter, 43, basketball player, born Daytona Beach, FL, Jan 25, 1977.

Chris Chelios, 58, former hockey player, born Chicago, IL, Jan 25, 1962.

Alicia Keys, 39, musician, singer, television personality ("The Voice"), born Harlem, NY, Jan 25, 1981.

Dinah Manoff, 62, actress ("Soap," "Empty Nest," Tony for *I Ought to Be in Pictures*), born New York, NY, Jan 25, 1958.

Ana Ortiz, 49, actress ("Ugly Betty"), born New York, NY, Jan 25, 1971.

Leigh Taylor-Young, 75, actress ("Peyton Place," "Dallas," *I Love You, Alice B. Toklas*), born Washington, DC, Jan 25, 1945.

Xavi, 40, soccer manager and former player, born Xavi Hernández i Creus at Terrassa, Spain, Jan 25, 1980.

January 26 — Sunday

DAY 26 **340 REMAINING**

AUSTRALIA: AUSTRALIA DAY. Jan 26, 1788. Day commemorating the anniversary of the first British settlement in Australia: a shipload of convicts arrived briefly at Botany Bay (which proved to be unsuitable) and then at Port Jackson (later the site of the city of Sydney). Establishment of an Australian prison colony was to relieve crowding of British prisons. Australia Day, formerly known as Foundation Day or Anniversary Day, has been observed since about 1817 and has been a public holiday since 1838.

AUSTRALIA: AUSTRALIA DAY COCKROACH RACES. Jan 26. Brisbane, Queensland. 39th annual. "The greatest gathering of thoroughbred cockroaches in the known universe." Cockroach race enthusiasts celebrate Australia Day at the Story Bridge Hotel, where icky insects (such as Cocky Balboa, Lord of the Drains and others) compete. Race includes steeplechase. Also: music, "Miss Cocky" pageant, "Best Dressed" contest and more. Proceeds benefit charity. For info: Story Bridge Hotel, 200 Main St, Kangaroo Point, Brisbane, Queensland 4169 Australia. Phone: (61) (7) 3391-2266. Web: www.storybridgehotel.com.au.

CATHOLIC SCHOOLS WEEK. Jan 26–Feb 1. Since 1974, the annual celebration of Catholic education in the US. The focus is on the value Catholic education provides to young people and its contributions to our church, our communities and our schools. Annually, the week beginning on the last Sunday in January. For info: Natl Catholic Educational Assn, 1005 N Glebe Rd, Ste 525, Arlington, VA 22201. Phone: (800) 711-6232. E-mail: nceaadmin@ncea.org. Web: www.ncea.org/csw.

CLEAN OUT YOUR INBOX WEEK. Jan 26–31. 13th annual. This week, observed annually the last business week of January, urges businesses and individuals to cure their e-mail "e-ddictions" and clean out their e-mail inboxes. A new year brings new beginnings—it's a great time to adopt healthy e-mail habits, which make life stress-free and work more productive. People across the world have benefited from COYIW, which has been recognized by countless media outlets internationally. For info: Marsha Egan, The Egan Group, 23 Cato Ln, Nantucket, MA 02554. Phone: (610) 780-1640. E-mail: Marsha@MarshaEgan.com.

COLEMAN, BESSIE: BIRTH ANNIVERSARY. Jan 26, 1892. Born at Atlanta, TX, Bessie Coleman would not take no for an answer, especially where it concerned her dreams of flying. Because of her race and gender, she was denied admission to aviation school programs in the US. She therefore worked as a manicurist, earning her way to Paris. There she received an international pilot's license from the Fédération Aéronautique Internationale in 1921. Upon return, "Queen Bess" took part in numerous acrobatic air exhibitions where her stunt flying and "figure eights" won her many admirers. She avidly encouraged others to follow in her footsteps. Coleman, however, perished in a plane crash during a practice session, at Jacksonville, FL, Apr 30, 1926.

DENTAL DRILL PATENT: ANNIVERSARY. Jan 26, 1875. George F. Green, of Kalamazoo, MI, patented the electric dental drill.

DOMINICAN REPUBLIC: NATIONAL HOLIDAY. Jan 26. An official public holiday celebrates the birth anniversary of Juan Pablo Duarte, one of the fathers of the republic.

FRANKLIN PREFERS TURKEY: ANNIVERSARY. Jan 26, 1784. In a letter to his daughter, Benjamin Franklin expressed his unhappiness over the choice of the eagle as the symbol of America. He preferred the turkey.

THE GRAMMY AWARDS. Jan 26. Staples Center, Los Angeles, CA. 62nd annual. Celebrating the best in recording arts and sciences, the Grammys cover more than 100 categories—from classical to jazz to pop and rock. Awarded by and to artists and technical professionals. For info: National Academy of Recording Arts & Sciences. Web: www.grammy.com.

GRANT, JULIA DENT: BIRTH ANNIVERSARY. Jan 26, 1826. Wife of Ulysses Simpson Grant, 18th president of the US. Born at St. Louis, MO; died at Washington, DC, Dec 14, 1902.

INDIA: REPUBLIC DAY. Jan 26. National holiday. Anniversary of Proclamation of the Republic, Basant Panchmi. In 1929 the Indian National Congress resolved to work for establishment of a sovereign republic, a goal that was realized Jan 26, 1950, when India became a democratic republic and its constitution went into effect.

INDIAN EARTHQUAKE: ANNIVERSARY. Jan 26, 2001. An earthquake that struck the state of Gujarat in India left more than 15,000 dead. The quake was estimated to be 7.7 on the Richter scale. India's largest port at Kandla suffered severe damage.

MACARTHUR, DOUGLAS: BIRTH ANNIVERSARY. Jan 26, 1880. US general and supreme commander of Allied forces in Southwest Pacific during WWII. Born at Little Rock, AR, he served as commander of the Rainbow Division's 84th Infantry Brigade in WWI, leading it in the St. Mihiel, Meuse-Argonne and Sedan offensives. Remembered for his "I shall return" prediction when forced out of the Philippines by the Japanese during WWII, a promise he fulfilled. Relieved of Far Eastern command by President Harry Truman on Apr 11, 1951, during the Korean War. MacArthur died at Washington, DC, Apr 5, 1964.

MICHIGAN: ADMISSION DAY: ANNIVERSARY. Jan 26. Became 26th state in 1837.

NEWMAN, PAUL: 95th BIRTH ANNIVERSARY. Jan 26, 1925. Blue-eyed actor, director, race car driver and philanthropist born at Cleveland, OH. Appeared in 65 films, including *Butch Cassidy and the Sundance Kid*, *The Sting*, *Hud* and *Cool Hand Luke*. Received a Best Actor Oscar for *The Color of Money* (1986). Newman was also a successful entrepreneur, establishing in 1982 Newman's Own, a specialty foods company whose proceeds were donated to charity. He died Sept 26, 2008, at Westport, CT.

***PHANTOM OF THE OPERA* BROADWAY PREMIERE: ANNIVERSARY.** Jan 26, 1988. This multiple-award-winning musical, based on the classic Gaston Leroux novel about the tortured soul haunting the Paris Opera House, premiered in London on Oct 9, 1986. Its music and lyrics are by Andrew Lloyd Webber and Charles Hart, with book by Lloyd Webber and Richard Stilgoe. It premiered on Broadway in 1988 and in January 2006 became the longest-running show in Broadway history. On Feb 11, 2012, it reached its 10,000th performance—an unprecedented feat.

ROCKY MOUNTAIN NATIONAL PARK ESTABLISHED: ANNIVERSARY. Jan 26, 1915. Under President Woodrow Wilson, the area covering more than 1,000 square miles in Colorado became a national park.

SCREEN ACTORS GUILD AWARDS. Jan 26. Los Angeles, CA. 26th annual. Lauded by critics for its style, simplicity and genuine warmth, the Screen Actors Guild Awards®, which made its debut in 1995, has become one of the industry's most prized honors. It presents 13 awards for acting in film and television. It airs live on TNT and TBS. For info: Screen Actors Guild (SAG). Web: www.sagawards.org.

2020 PRO BOWL. Jan 26. Location TBA. The best football players from the AFC and NFC battle it out. Annually, the Sunday before the Super Bowl. For info: National Football League. Web: www.nfl.com/probowl.

VAN HEUSEN, JIMMY: BIRTH ANNIVERSARY. Jan 26, 1913. Jimmy Van Heusen was born Edward Chester Babcock at Syracuse, NY. He was a composer of many popular songs with his lyricist partners Johnny Burke and Sammy Cahn. One of his 76 songs that Frank Sinatra recorded was "My Kind of Town." Van Heusen won four Academy Awards for songs in movies such as *Going My Way* (1944). He was inducted into the Songwriters Hall of Fame when it was founded in 1971. Van Heusen died Feb 7, 1990, at Rancho Mirage, CA.

WORLD LEPROSY DAY. Jan 26 (or Jan 30). Observed since 1953, a day to bring awareness to this misunderstood but curable disease. More than 225,000 new cases of Hansen's disease are reported each year—usually among the poorest of the poor. In 1991, the World Health Organization passed a resolution to eliminate leprosy and there have been dramatic results worldwide. Annually, on the last Sunday in January—originally scheduled to be the third Sunday after Epiphany. World Leprosy Day is also observed by some on Jan 30—in remembrance of Mohandas Gandhi, assassinated on Jan 30, 1948, who cared for leprosy patients and sought its end. For info: World Health Organization. Web: www.who.int/lep/en. Also for info: Lepra. E-mail: lepra@lepra.org.uk. Web: www.lepra.org.uk/world-leprosy-day.

🎂 BIRTHDAYS TODAY

Anita Baker, 62, singer, born Toledo, OH, Jan 26, 1958.

W. Kamau Bell, 47, comedian, television host ("United Shades of America"), born Walter Kamau Bell at Palo Alto, CA, Jan 26, 1973.

Father George Harold Clements, 88, Roman Catholic priest, civil rights leader, born Chicago, IL, Jan 26, 1932.

Angela Davis, 76, political activist, born Birmingham, AL, Jan 26, 1944.

Ellen DeGeneres, 62, comedienne, actress ("Ellen"), television personality ("The Ellen DeGeneres Show"), born New Orleans, LA, Jan 26, 1958.

Jules Feiffer, 91, cartoonist, writer, born New York, NY, Jan 26, 1929.

Scott Glenn, 78, actor (*The Bourne Ultimatum, The Silence of the Lambs, The Right Stuff*), born Pittsburgh, PA, Jan 26, 1942.

Wayne Gretzky, 59, Hall of Fame hockey player, born Brantford, ON, Canada, Jan 26, 1961.

José Mourinho, 57, soccer manager, born José Mário dos Santos Mourinho Félix at Setúbal, Portugal, Jan 26, 1963.

Andrew Ridgeley, 57, singer, musician (Wham!), born Bushey, England, Jan 26, 1963.

David Strathairn, 70, actor (*Good Night, and Good Luck; LA Confidential*), born San Francisco, CA, Jan 26, 1950.

Robert George (Bob) Uecker, 85, sportscaster, former baseball player, actor ("Mr Belvedere"), born Milwaukee, WI, Jan 26, 1935.

Eddie Van Halen, 65, Rock and Roll Hall of Fame guitarist, born Nijmegen, Netherlands, Jan 26, 1955.

January 27 — Monday

DAY 27   **339 REMAINING**

APOLLO I: **SPACECRAFT FIRE: ANNIVERSARY.** Jan 27, 1967. Three American astronauts, Virgil I. Grissom, Edward H. White and Roger B. Chaffee, died when fire suddenly broke out at 6:31 PM, EST, in *Apollo I* during a launching simulation test, as it stood on the ground at Cape Kennedy, FL. First launching in the Apollo program had been scheduled for Feb 27, 1967.

AUSCHWITZ LIBERATED: 75th ANNIVERSARY. Jan 27, 1945. The Soviet army liberated about 6,000 prisoners of the Nazi concentration camp Auschwitz. It is estimated that 1.5 million inmates were killed at Auschwitz between 1941 and liberation—95 percent of them were Jewish.

BUBBLE WRAP® APPRECIATION DAY. Jan 27. A day to celebrate the joy that Bubble Wrap® brings to our lives. A day to learn the history and snapping etiquette and to gain a new appreciation of the country's favorite shipping material (invented in 1960). Also, a day to snap and share Bubble Wrap® with coworkers, classmates and loved ones. Annually, the last Monday in January. (Created by Jim Webster.)

CANADIAN CAPER/OPERATION ARGO: 40th ANNIVERSARY. Jan 27, 1980. On Nov 4, 1979, during the siege of the US embassy in Tehran, Iran, six American embassy employees were able to slip away—and took refuge in the home of Kenneth Taylor, Canadian diplomat. Canada and the CIA, under the leadership of agent Tony Mendez, came up with an escape plan that was implemented on this day: The six employees were disguised as a Canadian film crew working on a science fiction film entitled *Argo* and flown out of Tehran in the very early morning. The 52 hostages at the embassy were released Jan 20, 1981.

DODGSON, CHARLES LUTWIDGE (LEWIS CARROLL): BIRTH ANNIVERSARY. Jan 27, 1832. The English mathematician and author, better known by his pseudonym, Lewis Carroll, creator of *Alice's Adventures in Wonderland*, was born at Cheshire, England. *Alice* was written for Alice Liddell, daughter of a friend, and first published in 1865. *Through the Looking-Glass*, an 1871 sequel, and *The Hunting of the Snark* (1876) followed. Dodgson's books for children proved equally enjoyable to adults, and they overshadowed his serious works on mathematics. Dodgson died at Guildford, Surrey, England, Jan 14, 1898.

January 2020	S	M	T	W	T	F	S
				1	2	3	4
	5	6	7	8	9	10	11
	12	13	14	15	16	17	18
	19	20	21	22	23	24	25
	26	27	28	29	30	31	

GERMANY: DAY OF REMEMBRANCE FOR VICTIMS OF NAZISM. Jan 27. Since 1996 commemorated on this day, the date in 1945 that Soviet soldiers liberated the Auschwitz concentration camp in Poland.

GOMPERS, SAMUEL: BIRTH ANNIVERSARY. Jan 27, 1850. Labor leader, first president of the American Federation of Labor, born at London, England. Died Dec 13, 1924, at San Antonio, TX.

KERN, JEROME: BIRTH ANNIVERSARY. Jan 27, 1885. American composer born at New York City; died there Nov 11, 1945. In addition to scores for stage and screen, Kern wrote many memorable songs, including "Ol' Man River," "Smoke Gets in Your Eyes," "I Won't Dance," "The Way You Look Tonight," "All the Things You Are" and "The Last Time I Saw Paris."

"LAVERNE AND SHIRLEY" TV PREMIERE: ANNIVERSARY. Jan 27, 1976. This ABC sitcom was a spin-off of the popular TV show "Happy Days" that was also set during the late '50s in Milwaukee, WI. Penny Marshall (sister of series cocreator Garry Marshall) starred as Laverne DeFazio with Cindy Williams as Shirley Feeney. The two friends worked at a brewery and shared a basement apartment. Also featured in the cast were Phil Foster as Laverne's father, Frank DeFazio; David L. Lander as Andrew "Squiggy" Squiggman; Michael McKean as Lenny Kosnowski; Betty Garrett as landlady Edna Babish; and Eddie Mekka as Carmine Ragusa, Shirley's sometime boyfriend.

LENINGRAD LIBERATED: ANNIVERSARY. Jan 27, 1944. The siege of Leningrad (now St. Petersburg) began with German bombing of the city on Sept 4, 1941. The bombing continued for 430 hours. The suffering of the people of Leningrad during the 880-day siege was one of the greatest tragedies of WWII. More than half the population of Russia's second-largest city died during the winter of 1942. The siege finally ended on Jan 27, 1944.

MOZART, WOLFGANG AMADEUS: BIRTH ANNIVERSARY. Jan 27, 1756. One of the world's greatest music makers. Born at Salzburg, Austria, into a gifted musical family, Mozart began performing at age three and composing at age five. Some of the best known of his more than 600 compositions are the operas *Marriage of Figaro*, *Don Giovanni*, *Cosi fan tutte* and *The Magic Flute*; his unfinished Requiem Mass; his C major symphony known as the "Jupiter"; and many of his quartets and piano concertos. He died at Vienna, Austria, Dec 5, 1791.

NATIONAL GEOGRAPHIC SOCIETY FOUNDED: ANNIVERSARY. Jan 27, 1888. The largest nonprofit scientific and educational institution in the world was incorporated on this date after an initial meeting on Jan 13, 1888, in which a group of 33 geographers, explorers, cartographers, teachers and other professionals met at the Cosmos Club in Washington, DC, to discuss organizing a "a society for the increase and diffusion of geographical knowledge." The first president was Gardiner Greene Hubbard. The first *National Geographic Magazine* was published nine months later in October 1888.

RICKOVER, HYMAN GEORGE: BIRTH ANNIVERSARY. Jan 27, 1900. American naval officer, known as the "Father of the Nuclear Navy." Admiral Rickover directed development of nuclear reactor–powered submarines, the first of which was the *Nautilus*, launched in 1954. Rickover was noted for his blunt remarks: "To increase the efficiency of the Department of Defense," he said, "you must first abolish it." The four-star admiral retired (unwillingly) at the age of 81, after 63 years in the navy. Born in Russia, Rickover died at Arlington, VA, July 9, 1986, and was buried at Arlington National Cemetery.

THOMAS CRAPPER DAY: DEATH ANNIVERSARY. Jan 27, 1910. Born at Thorne, Yorkshire, England, in 1836 (exact date unknown), Crapper is often described as the prime developer of the flush toilet mechanism as it is known today. The flush toilet had been in use for more than 100 years; Crapper perfected it. Founder, London, 1861, of Thomas Crapper & Co, later patentees and manufacturers of sanitary appliances.

UNITED KINGDOM: HOLOCAUST MEMORIAL DAY. Jan 27. Commemorates the day in 1945 that Soviet troops liberated the Auschwitz concentration camp.

UNITED NATIONS: INTERNATIONAL DAY OF COMMEMORATION IN MEMORY OF THE VICTIMS OF THE HOLOCAUST. Jan 27. On Nov 1, 2005, the General Assembly designated Jan 27 as an annual day in memory of the victims of the Holocaust conducted during the Second World War by the Nazi regime (Res 60/7). In doing so, the UN rejected any denial of the Holocaust as a historical event, either in full or in part. On Jan 26, 2007, the Assembly condemned without any reservation any denial of the Holocaust and urged all Member States unreservedly to reject any denial of the Holocaust as a historical event, either in full or in part, or any activities to that end (Res 61/255). Annually, Jan 27. For info: United Nations, Dept of Public Info, New York, NY, 10017. Web: www.un.org.

VIETNAM PEACE AGREEMENT SIGNED: ANNIVERSARY. Jan 27, 1973. The US and North Vietnam, along with South Vietnam and the Viet Cong, signed an "Agreement on ending the war and restoring peace in Vietnam." Signed at Paris, France, to take effect Jan 28 at 8 AM Saigon time, thus ending the US combat role in a war that had involved American personnel stationed in Vietnam since defeated French forces departed under terms of the Geneva Accords in 1954. This was the longest war in US history, with more than one million combat deaths (US: 47,366). However, within weeks of the departure of American troops, the war between North and South Vietnam resumed. For the Vietnamese, the war didn't end until Apr 30, 1975, when Saigon fell to Communist forces.

VON SACHER-MASOCH, LEOPOLD: BIRTH ANNIVERSARY. Jan 27, 1836. Author, born at Lemberg, Austrian Galicia (now Lviv, Ukraine), best known for his 1870 novella *Venus in Furs*, a semi-autobiographical tale of psychosexual perversion and supplication that led the psychiatric field to name the practice of masochism after its author. Von Sacher-Masoch died at Lindheim, Germany, on Mar 9, 1895.

🎂 BIRTHDAYS TODAY

Mikhail Baryshnikov, 72, ballet dancer, actor (*White Nights, The Turning Point*), born Riga, USSR (now Latvia), Jan 27, 1948.

(Anthony) Cris Collinsworth, 61, sportscaster, former football player, born Dayton, OH, Jan 27, 1959.

James Cromwell, 78, actor (*The People vs Larry Flynt, Babe, LA Confidential*), born Los Angeles, CA, Jan 27, 1942.

Alan Cumming, 55, actor (*Macbeth*, Tony for *Cabaret*; "The Good Wife"), director, born Perthshire, Scotland, Jan 27, 1965.

Bridget Fonda, 56, actress (*Single White Female, Lake Placid*), born Los Angeles, CA, Jan 27, 1964.

Julie Foudy, 49, sportscaster, Hall of Fame soccer player, born San Diego, CA, Jan 27, 1971.

Liu Wen, 32, model, born Yongzhou, China, Jan 27, 1988.

Mairead Corrigan Maguire, 76, pacifist, Nobel Peace Prize recipient, born Belfast, Northern Ireland, Jan 27, 1944.

Keith Olbermann, 61, journalist, political commentator, born New York, NY, Jan 27, 1959.

Patton Oswalt, 51, comedian, actor (*Young Adult, Big Fan*, "The King of Queens"), born Portsmouth, VA, Jan 27, 1969.

John G. Roberts, Jr, 65, Chief Justice of the US, born Buffalo, NY, Jan 27, 1955.

Mimi Rogers, 64, actress (*The Doors, The Rapture*), born Coral Gables, FL, Jan 27, 1956.

January 28 — Tuesday

DAY 28   **338 REMAINING**

***CHALLENGER* SPACE SHUTTLE EXPLOSION: ANNIVERSARY.** Jan 28, 1986. At 11:39 AM, EST, the space shuttle *Challenger STS-51L* exploded, 74 seconds into its flight and about 10 miles above the earth. Hundreds of millions around the world watched television replays of the horrifying event that killed seven people. The billion-dollar craft was destroyed, all shuttle flights suspended and much of the US manned space flight program temporarily halted. Killed were teacher Christa McAuliffe (who was to have been the first ordinary citizen in space) and six crew members: Francis R. Scobee, Michael J. Smith, Judith A. Resnik, Ellison S. Onizuka, Ronald E. McNair and Gregory B. Jarvis.

DATA PRIVACY DAY. Jan 28. Since 2008. All online participants, from home computer users to multinational corporations, need to be aware of the personal data others have entrusted to them and remain vigilant about protecting it. Good online citizenship means practicing conscientious data stewardship. Data Privacy Day is an effort to empower and educate people to protect their privacy, control their digital footprint and make the protection of privacy and data a great priority in their lives. Annually, Jan 28—the anniversary of the 1981 signing of Convention 108, the first legally binding international treaty dealing with privacy and data protection. For info: National CyberSecurity Alliance. Web: www.staysafeonline.org.

"FANTASY ISLAND" TV PREMIERE: ANNIVERSARY. Jan 28, 1978. Ricardo Montalbán starred as the prescient guide, Mr Roarke, with Hervé Villechaize as his faithful assistant, Tattoo. Each week, guest stars played characters eager to live out their fantasies in camp splendor. The show's run of 130 episodes, ending on Aug 18, 1984, was produced by Aaron Spelling and Leonard Goldberg. Best remembered is Tattoo's opening line each week: "De plane, de plane!"

GREAT SEAL OF THE US: AUTHORIZATION ANNIVERSARY. Jan 28, 1782. Congress resolved that the secretary of the Congress should "keep the public seal, and cause the same to be affixed to every act, ordinance or paper, which Congress shall direct . . . ." Although the Great Seal did not exist yet, the Congress recognized the need for it. See also: "Great Seal of the US Proposed: Anniversary" (July 4 and Sept 16).

ISRAELI SIEGE OF SUEZ CITY ENDS: ANNIVERSARY. Jan 28, 1974. The Israeli army lifted its siege of Suez City, freed encircled Egyptian troops and turned over 300,000 square miles of Egyptian territory to the UN, thereby ending the occupation that started during the October 1973 war.

MACKENZIE, ALEXANDER: BIRTH ANNIVERSARY. Jan 28, 1822. The man who became the first Liberal prime minister of Canada (1873–78) was born at Logierait, Perth, Scotland. He died at Toronto, Apr 17, 1892.

MARTÍ, JOSÉ JULIAN: BIRTH ANNIVERSARY. Jan 28, 1853. Cuban author and political activist, born at Havana, Martí was exiled to Spain, where he studied law before coming to the US in 1890. He was killed in battle at Dos Rios, Cuba, May 19, 1895.

PICCARD, AUGUSTE: BIRTH ANNIVERSARY. Jan 28, 1884. Scientist and explorer, born at Basel, Switzerland. Made a record-setting balloon ascent into the stratosphere on May 27, 1931, and also ocean-depth descents and explorations. Twin brother of Jean Felix Piccard. Died at Lausanne, Switzerland, Mar 24, 1962. See also: "Piccard, Jean Felix: Birth Anniversary" (Jan 28).

PICCARD, JEAN FELIX: BIRTH ANNIVERSARY. Jan 28, 1884. Scientist, engineer, explorer, born at Basel, Switzerland. Noted for cosmic-ray research and record-setting balloon ascensions into the stratosphere. Reached 57,579 feet in a sealed gondola piloted by his wife, Jeannette, in 1934. Twin brother of Auguste Piccard. Died at Minneapolis, MN, Jan 28, 1963. See also: "Piccard, Jeannette Ridlon: Birth Anniversary" (Jan 5); "Piccard, Auguste: Birth Anniversary" (Jan 28).

POLLOCK, JACKSON: BIRTH ANNIVERSARY. Jan 28, 1912. Abstract Expressionist born at Cody, WY. In postwar New York, Pollock placed his canvases on the floor and developed signature "drip" paintings, controversially incorporating the ideas of gravity and chance into the creation process. Pollock was killed in an automobile accident Aug 11, 1956, at East Hampton, NY.

***PRIDE AND PREJUDICE* PUBLISHED: ANNIVERSARY.** Jan 28, 1813. Jane Austen's second novel was published on this date by Thomas Egerton, in London, England. The author was 37 years old. Of her six published novels, *Pride and Prejudice* became her most famous and beloved. Its opening line is often quoted: "It is a truth universally acknowledged, that a single man in possession of a good fortune must be in want of a wife." The novel was an immediate success, selling out its first printing before autumn.

SCOTLAND: UP HELLY AA. Jan 28. Lerwick, Shetland Islands. Norse galley burned in impressive ceremony symbolizing sacrifice to the sun. Old Viking custom. A festival marking the end of Yule. Annually, the last Tuesday in January. For info: Visit Shetland. Web: www.shetland.org.

STANLEY, HENRY MORTON: BIRTH ANNIVERSARY. Jan 28, 1841. Explorer and journalist, born John Rowlands at Denbigh, Wales. Stanley immigrated to the US as a teenager and took the name of a mentor; he served in the Civil War and then became an overseas correspondent writing exclusively for the *New York Herald*. The newspaper tasked Stanley with finding the missing missionary-explorer David Livingstone, who had not been heard from for more than two years. Stanley led the expedition that began in Africa on Mar 21, 1871. They finally found the explorer at Ujiji, near Lake Tanganyika, on Nov 10, 1871, whereupon Stanley asked the now famous question: "Dr. Livingstone, I presume?" After some years exploring the Congo and engaging in relief work, Stanley died at London, England, on May 10, 1904.

🎂 BIRTHDAYS TODAY

Alan Alda, 84, actor (*Paper Lion*, *The Four Seasons*, "M*A*S*H"), director, born Alphonso D'Abruzzo at New York, NY, Jan 28, 1936.

John Beck, 77, actor ("Dallas," *Sleeper*, *The Big Bus*), born Chicago, IL, Jan 28, 1943.

Jessica Ennis, 34, Olympic heptathlete, born Sheffield, England, Jan 28, 1986.

Susan Howard, 77, actress ("Dallas"), born Jeri Lynn Mooney at Marshall, TX, Jan 28, 1943.

Harley Jane Kozak, 63, actress (*When Harry Met Sally*, *Parenthood*), born Wilkes-Barre, PA, Jan 28, 1957.

Sarah McLachlan, 52, singer, born Halifax, NS, Canada, Jan 28, 1968.

Kathryn Morris, 51, actress (*Mindhunters*, "Cold Case"), born Cincinnati, OH, Jan 28, 1969.

January 2020	S	M	T	W	T	F	S
				1	2	3	4
	5	6	7	8	9	10	11
	12	13	14	15	16	17	18
	19	20	21	22	23	24	25
	26	27	28	29	30	31	

Claes Oldenburg, 91, artist, sculptor, born Stockholm, Sweden, Jan 28, 1929.

Rick Ross, 44, rapper, born William Leonard Roberts II at Coahoma County, MS, Jan 28, 1976.

Nicolas Sarkozy, 65, former president of France, born Paris, France, Jan 28, 1955.

Jeanne Shaheen, 73, US Senator (D, New Hampshire), former governor of New Hampshire, born St. Charles, MO, Jan 28, 1947.

Elijah Wood, 39, actor (the Lord of the Rings film trilogy, *The Ice Storm*), born Cedar Rapids, IA, Jan 28, 1981.

January 29 — Wednesday

DAY 29 **337 REMAINING**

CHEKHOV, ANTON PAVLOVICH: BIRTH ANNIVERSARY. Jan 29, 1860. Russian playwright and short-story writer, especially remembered for *The Sea Gull*, *The Three Sisters* and *The Cherry Orchard*. Born at Taganrog, Russia; died July 15, 1904, at the Black Forest spa at Badenweiler, Germany.

CURMUDGEONS DAY. Jan 29. An annual celebration of the crusty, yet insightful, wags who consistently apply the needle of truth to the balloons of hypocrisy and social norms. Annually, Jan 29, the birthday of W.C. Fields, one of America's most beloved curmudgeons. For info: Michael Montgomery, 4701 D'Adrian Dr, Godfrey, IL 62035. Phone: (618) 466-4188. E-mail: hdprof@sbcglobal.net.

FIELDS, W.C.: BIRTH ANNIVERSARY. Jan 29, 1880. Stage and motion picture actor (*My Little Chickadee*), screenwriter and expert juggler. Born Claude William Dukenfield at Philadelphia, PA; died Dec 25, 1946, at Pasadena, CA. He wrote his own epitaph: "On the whole, I'd rather be in Philadelphia."

KANSAS: ADMISSION DAY: ANNIVERSARY. Jan 29. Became the 34th state in 1861.

LUBITSCH, ERNST: BIRTH ANNIVERSARY. Jan 29, 1892. The popular filmmaker, born at Berlin, Germany, is known for his effervescent, witty and sexy comedies. His best-known films include *Design for Living* (1933), *The Merry Widow* (1934), *Ninotchka* (1939, with Greta Garbo), *The Shop Around the Corner* (1940, with Jimmy Stewart), *To Be or Not to Be* (1942, with Jack Benny and Carole Lombard) and *Heaven Can Wait* (1943). The recipient of a Lifetime Achievement Academy Award in March 1947, Lubitsch died Nov 30, 1947, at Hollywood, CA.

MCKINLEY, WILLIAM: BIRTH ANNIVERSARY. Jan 29, 1843. 25th president of the US (1897–1901), born at Niles, OH. Died in office, at Buffalo, NY, Sept 14, 1901, as the result of a gunshot wound by an anarchist assassin Sept 6, 1901, while he was attending the Pan-American Exposition.

MORMON BATTALION ARRIVAL IN CALIFORNIA: ANNIVERSARY. Jan 29, 1847. The 500 men of the US Mormon Battalion, along with 50 women and children, arrived at San Diego, CA, on this date, having marched 2,000 miles—the longest march in modern military history—since leaving Council Bluffs, IA, on July 16, 1846, to fight in the war against Mexico. In the course of their trek they established the first wagon route from Santa Fe to southern California. Their historic arrival is commemorated each year with a military parade in San Diego's Old Town.

PAINE, THOMAS: BIRTH ANNIVERSARY. Jan 29, 1737. American Revolutionary leader, a corset maker by trade, author of *Common Sense*, *The Age of Reason* and many other influential works, was born at Thetford, England. "These are the times that try men's souls" are the well-known opening words of his inspirational tract *The Crisis*. Paine died at New York, NY, June 8, 1809, but 10 years later his remains were moved to England by William Cobbett for

reburial there. Reburial was refused, however, and the location of Paine's bones, said to have been distributed, is unknown.

"THE RAVEN" PUBLISHED: 175th ANNIVERSARY. Jan 29, 1845. One of the most famous poems in American literature was published on this date in New York's *Evening Mirror* newspaper. The author was anonymous, but the poem was such a sensation (it would be reprinted at least 16 times in various periodicals and books that year) that soon the author was revealed as literary critic and author Edgar Allan Poe. Despite the celebrity status Poe enjoyed as a result of "The Raven," it did not relieve his poverty: Poe received $15 for the poem. The classic lines "Once upon a midnight dreary" and "Quoth the Raven, 'Nevermore'" resound in countless anthologies and dramatic readings as well as in parodies.

THE SEEING EYE ESTABLISHED: ANNIVERSARY. Jan 29, 1929. The Seeing Eye, North America's first guide dog school, was incorporated on this date at Nashville, TN. The first Seeing Eye dog was Buddy, a German shepherd. The Seeing Eye was the first program in the US that enabled people with disabilities to be full participants in society. Its mission is to enhance the independence, self-confidence and dignity of people who are blind through the use of Seeing Eye dogs. Since its founding, The Seeing Eye has matched more than 17,000 specially bred dogs with blind people from the US and Canada. In 1931, the school moved to New Jersey, where it continues to breed, raise and train Seeing Eye dogs and instruct blind and visually impaired people in the use and care of their dogs. For info: The Seeing Eye. E-mail: info@seeingeye.org. Web: www.seeingeye.org.

SWEDENBORG, EMANUEL: BIRTH ANNIVERSARY. Jan 29, 1688. Born at Stockholm, Sweden, Swedenborg is remembered as a scientist, inventor, writer and religious leader. Swedenborg made plans for machine guns, submarines and airplanes and published Sweden's first scientific journal. His study of human anatomy and his search for the soul led him to begin thinking about religion. His writings interpreting the Scriptures formed the basis of the Church of the New Jerusalem, which was established by his devotees soon after his death. He died at London, England, Mar 29, 1772.

🎂 BIRTHDAYS TODAY

Marc Gasol, 35, basketball player, born Barcelona, Spain, Jan 29, 1985.

Sara Gilbert, 45, actress ("The Big Bang Theory," "Roseanne"), television personality ("The Talk"), born Santa Monica, CA, Jan 29, 1975.

Heather Graham, 50, actress (*The Hangover, From Hell, Boogie Nights*), born Milwaukee, WI, Jan 29, 1970.

Germaine Greer, 81, author (*Daddy We Hardly Knew You, The Female Eunuch*), born Melbourne, Australia, Jan 29, 1939.

Justin Hartley, 43, actor ("This Is Us," "The Young and the Restless," "Smallville"), born Knoxville, IL, Jan 29, 1977.

Dominik Hasek, 55, former hockey player, born Pardubice, Czechoslovakia (now the Czech Republic), Jan 29, 1965.

Sam Jaeger, 43, actor ("Parenthood," "Eli Stone"), born Perrysburg, OH, Jan 29, 1977.

Ann Jillian, 69, actress ("It's a Living," *The Ann Jillian Story*), born Cambridge, MA, Jan 29, 1951.

Andrew Keegan, 41, actor (*Independence Day*), born Los Angeles, CA, Jan 29, 1979.

Stacey King, 53, sportscaster, former basketball player, born Lawton, OK, Jan 29, 1967.

Adam Lambert, 38, singer, television personality ("American Idol"), born Indianapolis, IN, Jan 29, 1982.

Gregory Efthimios (Greg) Louganis, 60, actor, Olympic diver, born San Diego, CA, Jan 29, 1960.

Bobbie Phillips, 52, actress ("Murder One," *Red Shoe Diaries*), born Charleston, SC, Jan 29, 1968 (some sources say 1972).

Katharine Ross, 77, actress (*The Graduate*), born Los Angeles, CA, Jan 29, 1943.

Tom Selleck, 75, actor ("Blue Bloods," "Magnum, P.I.," *Three Men and a Baby*), born Detroit, MI, Jan 29, 1945.

Olga Tokarczuk, 58, author (Man Booker International for *Flights*), psychologist, born Sulechów, Poland, Jan 29, 1962.

Nick Turturro, 58, actor ("Blue Bloods," "NYPD Blue"), born Queens, NY, Jan 29, 1962.

Oprah Winfrey, 66, media entrepreneur, television talk show host ("The Oprah Winfrey Show"), actress (*A Wrinkle in Time, The Color Purple*), producer, born Kosciusko, MS, Jan 29, 1954.

January 30 — Thursday

DAY 30   **336 REMAINING**

ANGOULÊME INTERNATIONAL COMICS FESTIVAL. Jan 30–Feb 2. Angoulême, France. Since 1974, Europe's largest comics show set in the Bordeaux region of France. It attracts fans, critics, publishers, artists, cartoonists, writers and the general public. The highlight of the festival is the presentation of the Grand Prize, a lifetime achievement award given to a master who then becomes the festival's president the following year. Other prizes honor best albums, new talent, heritage comics and more. Est attendance: 200,000. For info: Angoulême: Festival International de la Bande Desinée, 71, rue Hergé, 16000 Angoulême, France. E-mail: info@bdangouleme.com. Web: www.bdangouleme.com.

THE BEATLES' LAST CONCERT: ANNIVERSARY. Jan 30, 1969. On this day The Beatles performed together in public for the last time. The show took place on the roof of their Apple Studios in London, England, but it was interrupted by police after they received complaints from the neighbors about the noise.

BLOODY SUNDAY: ANNIVERSARY. Jan 30, 1972. In Londonderry, Northern Ireland, 14 Roman Catholics were shot dead by British troops during a banned civil rights march. During 1972, the first year of British direct rule, 467 people were killed in the fighting. On June 15, 2010, after a 12-year investigation, the 5,000-page Saville Report was issued that strongly condemned the soldiers who fired and exonerated the victims. As a result, prime minister David Cameron issued an apology on behalf of the British government.

CHARLES I: EXECUTION ANNIVERSARY. Jan 30, 1649. English king beheaded by order of Parliament under Oliver Cromwell on this date; considered a martyr by some.

FIRST BRAWL IN THE US HOUSE OF REPRESENTATIVES: ANNIVERSARY. Jan 30, 1798. The first brawl to break out on the floor of the US House of Representatives occurred at Philadelphia, PA. The fight was precipitated by an argument between Matthew Lyon of Vermont and Roger Griswold of Connecticut. Lyon spat in Griswold's face. Although a resolution to expel Lyon was introduced, the measure failed and Lyon maintained his seat.

GANDHI ASSASSINATED: ANNIVERSARY. Jan 30, 1948. Indian religious and political leader, assassinated at New Delhi, India. The assassin was a Hindu extremist. See also: "Gandhi, Mohandas Karamchand (Mahatma): Birth Anniversary" (Oct 2).

INANE ANSWERING MESSAGE DAY. Jan 30. Annually, the day set aside to change, shorten, replace or delete those ridiculous and/or annoying answering machine messages that waste the time of anyone who must listen to them. (©2006 by WH.) For info:

Thomas & Ruth Roy, Wellcat Holidays, 2418 Long Ln, Lebanon, PA 17046. Phone: (717) 279-0184. E-mail: info@wellcat.com. Web: www.wellcat.com.

JORDAN: KING'S BIRTHDAY. Jan 30. National holiday. Honors King Abdullah II, son of the late King Hussein, who was born Jan 30, 1962, and assumed the throne June 9, 1999.

MARYLAND ADOPTS ARTICLES OF CONFEDERATION: ANNIVERSARY. Jan 30, 1781. Maryland became the last of the 13 original states to adopt the Articles of Confederation.

MICHIGAN INTERNATIONAL AUTO SHOW. Jan 30–Feb 2. DeVos Place, Grand Rapids, MI. Hundreds of the latest-model cars, trucks, vans, SUVs, hybrids and sports cars from all the major manufacturers will be joined by concept cars and preproduction displays. For info: ShowSpan, Inc. Phone: (616) 447-2860. Fax: (616) 447-2861. E-mail: events@showspan.com. Web: www.showspan. com.

NATIONAL CROISSANT DAY. Jan 30. A day to celebrate this delicate, crescent-shaped puff pastry (*croissant* means "crescent" in French). Although associated with France, the flaky pastry originated in the Austrian kipfel and was introduced to France in the mid-19th century. Annually, Jan 30.

OSCEOLA: DEATH ANNIVERSARY. Jan 30, 1838. Osceola was a leader during the Second Seminole War (1835–42). During the first two years of the war, he led the fight against removal of the Florida Seminoles to Indian territory. He was captured under a flag of truce in 1837 and imprisoned at Fort Marion in St. Augustine, FL. He was moved to Fort Moultrie at Charleston Harbor, SC, where he died. He was born near present-day Tuskegee, AL, circa 1804.

ROOSEVELT, FRANKLIN DELANO: BIRTH ANNIVERSARY. Jan 30, 1882. 32nd president of the US (Mar 4, 1933–Apr 12, 1945). The only president to serve more than two terms, FDR was elected four times. He supported the Allies in WWII before the US entered the struggle by supplying them with war materials through the Lend-Lease Act; he became deeply involved in broad decision making after the Japanese attack on Pearl Harbor Dec 7, 1941. Born at Hyde Park, NY, he died a few months into his fourth term at Warm Springs, GA, Apr 12, 1945.

TET OFFENSIVE BEGINS: ANNIVERSARY. Jan 30, 1968. After calling for a cease-fire during the Tet holiday celebrations, North Vietnam and the National Liberation Front launched a major offensive throughout South Vietnam on that holiday. Attacks erupted in 36 of the 44 provincial capitals and five of the six major cities. In addition, the Viet Cong attacked the US embassy in Saigon, Tan Son Nhut Air Base, the presidential palace and South Vietnamese general staff headquarters. Costing as many as 40,000 battlefield deaths, the offensive was a tactical defeat for the Viet Cong and North Vietnam. The South Vietnamese held their ground, and the

US was able to airlift troops into the critical areas and quickly regain control. However, the offensive is credited as a strategic success in that it continued the demoralization of Americans. After Tet, American policy toward Vietnam shifted from winning the war to seeking an honorable way out.

THOMAS, ISAIAH: BIRTH ANNIVERSARY. Jan 30, 1749. American printer, editor, almanac publisher, historian and founder of the American Antiquarian Society. Born at Boston, MA; died Apr 4, 1831, at Worcester, MA.

🎂 BIRTHDAYS TODAY

Christian Bale, 46, actor (*The Big Short, American Hustle, Batman Begins*, Oscar for *The Fighter*), born Pembrokeshire, West Wales, Jan 30, 1974.

Brett Butler, 62, comedienne, actress ("Grace Under Fire"), born Montgomery, AL, Jan 30, 1958.

Richard (Dick) Cheney, 79, 46th vice president of the US, born Lincoln, NE, Jan 30, 1941.

Phil Collins, 69, musician, singer, songwriter, born Chiswick, England, Jan 30, 1951.

Olivia Colman, 46, actress (Oscar for *The Favourite*, "The Night Manager," "Broadchurch"), born Norwich, England, Jan 30, 1974.

Charles S. Dutton, 69, actor ("Roc," *Mississippi Masala, Menace II Society*), born Baltimore, MD, Jan 30, 1951.

Felipe VI of Bourbon and Greece, 52, King of Spain, born Madrid, Spain, Jan 30, 1968.

Gene Hackman, 90, actor (Oscars for *The French Connection* and *Unforgiven*; *The Royal Tenenbaums*), born San Bernardino, CA, Jan 30, 1930.

Johnathan Lee Iverson, 44, circus ringmaster, born New York, NY, Jan 30, 1976.

Davey Johnson, 77, baseball manager and former player, born Orlando, FL, Jan 30, 1943.

Vanessa Redgrave, 83, actress (Tony for *Long Day's Journey into Night*; Oscar for *Julia*; Emmys for *Playing for Time* and *If These Walls Could Talk 2*), born London, England, Jan 30, 1937.

Jalen Rose, 47, sportscaster, former basketball player, born Detroit, MI, Jan 30, 1973.

Boris Spassky, 83, former chess player, journalist, born Leningrad, USSR (now St. Petersburg, Russia), Jan 30, 1937.

Curtis Strange, 65, golfer, born Norfolk, VA, Jan 30, 1955.

Jody Watley, 61, singer, born Chicago, IL, Jan 30, 1959.

January 31 — Friday

DAY 31   **335 REMAINING**

BANKS, ERNIE: BIRTH ANNIVERSARY. Jan 31, 1931. Born at Dallas, TX, "Mr Cub" began his career in the Negro Leagues at age 19 and debuted as the first African-American player for the Chicago Cubs at Wrigley Field on Sept 17, 1953. He went on to become 1954's Rookie of the Year and win numerous Golden Glove, MVP and All-Star honors as his club's shortstop for the next 17 years. After his retirement as a player in 1971, he served as the team's ambassador, famous for his relentless love and support, even in losing years, and for his catchphrase: "It's a beautiful day . . . Let's play two!" His uniform number (14) was the first ever to be retired by the Cubs organization, and he was elected to the Baseball Hall of Fame in 1977 on his first ballot. Banks died Jan 23, 2015, at Chicago, IL.

CANADA: WINTERLUDE. Jan 31–Feb 17. Ottawa, ON, and Gatineau, QC. 42nd edition. Annual celebration of Canadian winter and traditions for the whole family. Skating on the Rideau Canal, the

		S	M	T	W	T	F	S
January						1	2	3	4
		5	6	7	8	9	10	11
2020		12	13	14	15	16	17	18
		19	20	21	22	23	24	25
		26	27	28	29	30	31	

world's largest skating rink; snow and ice sculptures; huge snow playground; winter sporting events; arts, culture and food. Est attendance: 695,000. For info: Winterlude, Canadian Heritage. Phone: (819) 994-9101. E-mail: pch.media-media.pch@canada.ca. Web: www.canada.ca/en/canadian-heritage/campaigns/winter-lude.html.

FIRST SOCIAL SECURITY CHECK ISSUED: 80th ANNIVERSARY. Jan 31, 1940. Ida May Fuller of Ludlow, VT, received the first monthly retirement check—in the amount of $22.54. Fuller had worked for three years under the Social Security program (which had been established by legislation in 1935). The accumulated taxes on her salary over those three years were $24.75. She lived to be 100 years old, collecting $22,888 in Social Security benefits. See also: "Social Security Act: Anniversary" (Aug 14).

GOLDWYN, SAMUEL: DEATH ANNIVERSARY. Jan 31, 1974. Motion picture producer and industry pioneer Goldwyn died at Los Angeles, CA. He was born Samuel Goldfish, at Warsaw, Poland, probably in July 1879 (although he always claimed Aug 27, 1882, as his birthday). Famous for his confusing outbursts, Goldwyn is claimed to have said such things as "Anybody who goes to see a psychiatrist ought to have his head examined."

GREY, ZANE: BIRTH ANNIVERSARY. Jan 31, 1872. Zane Grey (original name Pearl Grey), American dentist and prolific author of tales of the Old West, was born at Zanesville, OH. Grey wrote more than 80 books that were translated into many languages and sold more than 10 million copies. The novel *Riders of the Purple Sage* (1912) was the most popular. Grey died Oct 23, 1939, at Altadena, CA.

INSPIRE YOUR HEART WITH THE ARTS DAY. Jan 31. A day to experience art in your life. Food sustains you as a human; art inspires you to be divine. Go to an art museum, browse through an art book at the library, enroll in an art class or commission an artist. Read your favorite poem out loud. Go to a concert or play. Sign up for dance lessons. Today is a day to inspire your heart with the arts! For info: Rev Jayne Howard Feldman, Angel Heights, PO Box 95, Upperco, MD 21155. Phone: (410) 833-6912. E-mail: earthangel4peace@aol.com.

JAPAN: SAPPORO SNOW FESTIVAL. Jan 31–Feb 11. Sapporo, Hokkaido. 71st annual. Every winter, a large number of splendid snow statues and ice sculptures line Odori Park, the grounds at Community Dome Tsudome and the main street in Susukino. For seven days in February, these statues and sculptures (both large and small) turn Sapporo into a winter dreamland of crystal-like ice and white snow. Odori and Susukino sites, Feb 4–11; Tsudome site Jan 31– Feb 11. Est attendance: 2,000,000. For info: Sapporo Snow Festival. Web: www.snow-fes.com/english.

MARSHALL ISLANDS LANDINGS: ANNIVERSARY. Jan 31, 1944. After two months of saturation bombing (the heaviest to precede an attack thus far in the Pacific), the 23rd and 24th Marine Regiments attacked the Marshall Islands. In four days Kwajalein was taken, providing the Allies with a major staging area. The dead numbered 8,122 Japanese and 356 Americans.

MORRIS, ROBERT: BIRTH ANNIVERSARY. Jan 31, 1734. Signer of the Declaration of Independence, the Articles of Confederation and the Constitution. He was one of only two men who signed all three documents. He was born at Liverpool, England, and died May 7, 1806, at Philadelphia, PA.

NATIONAL PRESCHOOL FITNESS DAY. Jan 31. Daycare centers throughout the US. A day promoting healthy lifestyle habits of physical education and healthy eating in preschool children. Annually, the last Friday in January. For info: Michele Silence, Kid-Fit, 135 W Maple Ave, Monrovia, CA 91016. Phone: (626) 848-2950. E-mail: michele@kid-fit.com. Web: www.kid-fit.com.

NAURU: NATIONAL HOLIDAY. Jan 31. Republic of Nauru. Commemorates independence in 1968 from a UN trusteeship administered by Australia, New Zealand and the UK.

ROBINSON, JACKIE: BIRTH ANNIVERSARY. Jan 31, 1919. Jack Roosevelt Robinson, athlete and business executive, first black to enter professional major league baseball (Brooklyn Dodgers, 1947–56). Voted National League's Most Valuable Player in 1949 and elected to the Baseball Hall of Fame in 1962. Born at Cairo, GA, Jackson died at Stamford, CT, Oct 24, 1972.

SARANAC LAKE WINTER CARNIVAL. Jan 31–Feb 9. Saranac Lake, NY. 123rd annual. Since 1897—the oldest winter festival in the eastern United States. This 10-day festival includes sports, performances, two parades and three sets of spectacular fireworks. The centerpiece of the carnival is the Ice Palace, built by volunteers on the shore of Lake Flower's Pontiac Bay at the state boat launch. 2020 theme: "Myths and Legends." For info: Society for Promotion of Winter Carnival. Web: www.saranaclakewintercarnival.com.

SCHUBERT, FRANZ: BIRTH ANNIVERSARY. Jan 31, 1797. Composer, born at Vienna, Austria, and died there of typhus Nov 19, 1828, at age 31. Buried, at his request, near the grave of Beethoven. Schubert last worked on his "Unfinished Symphony" (No. 8) in 1822. On the 100th anniversary of his death in 1928, a $10,000 prize was offered to "finish" the work. The protests were so great that the offer was withdrawn.

SLOVIK, EDDIE D.: 75th EXECUTION ANNIVERSARY. Jan 31, 1945. Anniversary of execution by firing squad of 24-year-old Private Eddie D. Slovik at Sainte-Marie-aux-Mines, France. Born at Detroit, MI, Feb 18, 1920, Slovik was assigned to Company G, 109th Infantry, 28th Division, US Army. His death sentence, the first for desertion since the Civil War, has been a subject of controversy. First buried in France, Slovik's remains were exhumed in 1987 for reburial beside his wife, Antoinette, who died in 1979, after years of effort to clear Slovik's name and have his body returned to the US.

SPACE MILESTONE: *APOLLO 14* (US). Jan 31, 1971. Launch date of *Apollo 14*. Five days later on Feb 5, astronauts Alan B. Shepard, Jr, and Edgar D. Mitchell landed on the moon (lunar module *Antares*). Command module *Kitty Hawk* was piloted by Stuart A. Roosa. Pacific splashdown on Feb 9.

SPACE MILESTONE: *EXPLORER 1* (US). Jan 31, 1958. The first successful US satellite. Although launched four months later than the Soviet Union's *Sputnik*, *Explorer* reached a higher altitude and detected a zone of intense radiation inside Earth's magnetic field. This was later named the Van Allen radiation belts. More than 65 subsequent *Explorer* satellites were launched through 1984.

SPACE MILESTONE: *LUNA 9* (USSR). Jan 31, 1966. Launch of unmanned mission that accomplished the first soft landing on the moon three days later on Feb 3. Relayed TV photos of the lunar surface.

SPACE MILESTONE: PROJECT MERCURY TEST (US). Jan 31, 1961. A test of Project Mercury spacecraft accomplished the first US recovery of a large animal from space. Ham, the chimpanzee, successfully performed simple tasks in space.

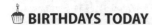 **BIRTHDAYS TODAY**

Princess Beatrix of the Netherlands, 82, former queen of the Netherlands, born Sostdijk, Netherlands, Jan 31, 1938.

Portia de Rossi, 47, actress ("Ally McBeal," "Arrested Development"), born Geelong, Australia, Jan 31, 1973.

Minnie Driver, 49, actress (*Return to Zero, Good Will Hunting*, "Speechless," "The Riches"), born London, England, Jan 31, 1971.

Philip Glass, 83, composer, born Baltimore, MD, Jan 31, 1937.

John Lydon, 64, singer ("Johnny Rotten," Sex Pistols), composer, born near London, England, Jan 31, 1956.

Kelly Lynch, 61, actress (*Drugstore Cowboy*), born Minneapolis, MN, Jan 31, 1959.

Stuart Margolin, 80, actor, director, writer ("The Rockford Files," *The Big Blue*), born Davenport, IA, Jan 31, 1940.

Marcus Mumford, 33, singer (Mumford & Sons), born Anaheim, CA, Jan 31, 1987.

(Lynn) Nolan Ryan, 73, Hall of Fame baseball player, born Refugio, TX, Jan 31, 1947.

Justin Timberlake, 39, singer, actor (*Alpha Dog, Black Snake Moan*), born Memphis, TN, Jan 31, 1981.

Jessica Walter, 79, actress ("Arrested Development," *Play Misty for Me, The Flamingo Kid*), born Brooklyn, NY, Jan 31, 1941.

Kerry Washington, 43, actress ("Scandal," *Django Unchained, Ray*), born the Bronx, NY, Jan 31, 1977.

February 1 — Saturday

DAY 32   **334 REMAINING**

AFRICAN-AMERICAN CULTURAL HERITAGE MONTH. Feb 1–29. Jamestown Settlement, Williamsburg, VA, and American Revolution Museum at Yorktown, Yorktown, VA. Through monthlong activities and demonstrations, visitors can learn about the culture, society and technology of west central Africans, who comprised the first recorded arrival of Africans to Virginia in 1619. At the American Revolution Museum at Yorktown, periodic lectures throughout the month and daily programming explore the role and impact of African Americans on both sides of the war. For info: Jamestown-Yorktown Foundation, PO Box 1607, Williamsburg, VA 23187. Phone (757) 253-4838 or (888) 593-4682. Fax: (757) 253-5299. Web: www.historyisfun.org.

AMD/LOW VISION AWARENESS MONTH. Feb 1–29. Macular degeneration is a leading cause of vision loss. Low-vision aids can make the most of remaining vision. Information on eye disease warning signs and on low-vision aids will be available. For info: Prevent Blindness, 211 W Wacker Dr, Ste 1700, Chicago, IL 60606. Phone: (800) 331-2020. E-mail: info@preventblindness.org. Web: www.preventblindness.org.

★AMERICAN HEART MONTH. Feb 1–29. Presidential Proclamation issued each year for February since 1964. (PL 88–254 of Dec 30, 1963.)

AMERICAN HEART MONTH. Feb 1–29. During this month, the American Heart Association will focus on women with "Go Red for Women," an educational movement about women and cardiovascular disease. Each year cardiovascular diseases claim the lives of nearly 500,000 women. For all of the women you know who have been affected by cardiovascular disease, participate in National Wear Red Day on Friday, Feb 7. For info: American Heart Association. Web: www.heart.org or www.goredforwomen.org.

CAR INSURANCE FIRST ISSUED: ANNIVERSARY. Feb 1, 1898. Travelers Insurance Company issued the first car insurance against accidents with horses.

CARAWAY, HATTIE WYATT: BIRTH ANNIVERSARY. Feb 1, 1878. Born at Bakersville, TN, Hattie Caraway became a US senator from Arkansas in 1931 when her husband died and she was appointed to fill out his term. The following year, she ran for the seat herself and became the first woman elected to the US Senate. She served 14 years there, becoming an adept and tireless legislator (once introducing 43 bills on the same day) who worked for women's rights (once cosponsoring an equal rights amendment), supported New Deal policies as well as Prohibition and opposed the increasing influence of lobbyists. Caraway died at Falls Church, VA, Dec 21, 1950. See also: "First Elected Woman Senator: Anniversary" (Jan 12).

FELINE FIX BY FIVE MONTH. Feb 1–29. A month encouraging pet owners and veterinarians to spay cats before the first heat. The goal is to prevent unwanted litters and decrease the number of animals abandoned and euthanized. For info: Feline Fix by Five Month, Marian's Dream, PO Box 365, Brunswick, ME 04011. Phone: (207) 751-9591. E-mail: esther@mariansdream.org. Web: www.felinefixbyfive.org.

FIRST SESSION OF SUPREME COURT: ANNIVERSARY. Feb 1, 1790. The Supreme Court of the US met for the first time in New York City, with Chief Justice John Jay presiding.

FORD, JOHN: 125th BIRTH ANNIVERSARY. Feb 1, 1895. Prolific and influential American film director, born at Cape Elizabeth, ME. Winner of five Oscars—for *The Informer* (1936), *The Grapes of Wrath* (1941), *How Green Was My Valley* (1942), *The Quiet Man* (1953) and the documentary *The Battle of Midway* (1942)—Ford is strongly associated with the western and its most iconic setting, Monument Valley. His famous westerns include *Stagecoach, My Darling Clementine, The Searchers* and *The Man Who Shot Liberty Valance*. Popular with audiences and venerated by French auteur critics of the 50s, Ford himself said, "The secret is to make films that please the public and that also allow the director to reveal his personality." He died Aug 31, 1973, at Palm Desert, CA.

FREEDOM DAY: ANNIVERSARY. Feb 1, 1865. Anniversary of President Abraham Lincoln's approval of the 13th Amendment to the US Constitution (abolishing slavery): "1. Neither slavery nor involuntary servitude, except as a punishment for crime whereof the party shall have been duly convicted, shall exist within the United States or any place subject to their jurisdiction. 2. Congress shall have power to enforce this article by appropriate legislation." The amendment had been proposed by Congress Jan 31, 1865; ratification was completed Dec 6, 1865.

GABLE, CLARK: BIRTH ANNIVERSARY. Feb 1, 1901. Actor William Clark Gable's first film was *The Painted Desert* in 1931, when talking films were replacing silent films. He won an Academy Award for his role in the comedy *It Happened One Night*, which established him as a romantic screen idol. Other films include *China Seas, Mutiny on the Bounty, Saratoga* and *Gone with the Wind*, for which his casting as Rhett Butler seemed a foregone conclusion due to his popularity as the acknowledged "King of Movies." Gable was born at Cadiz, OH, and died Nov 16, 1960, at Hollywood, CA, shortly after completing his last film, Arthur Miller's *The Misfits*, in which he starred with Marilyn Monroe.

G.I. JOE INTRODUCED: ANNIVERSARY. Feb 1, 1964. This toy action figure was introduced by Hasbro and sold for $2.49. It was the first mass-market doll intended for boys and was a great success. The figure's name came from a film, *The Story of G.I. Joe* (1945), that starred Robert Mitchum and Burgess Meredith.

"GOOD TIMES" TV PREMIERE: ANNIVERSARY. Feb 1, 1974. A CBS spin-off of "Maude," which was a spin-off of "All in the Family," "Good Times" featured an African-American family living in the housing projects of Chicago and struggling to improve their lot. The cast featured Esther Rolle and John Amos as Florida and James Evans, Jimmie Walker as son J.J., BernNadette Stanis as daughter Thelma, Ralph Carter as son Michael, Johnny Brown as janitor Mr Bookman, Ja'Net DuBois as neighbor Willona Woods, Janet Jackson as Willona's adopted daughter, Penny, and Ben Powers as Thelma's husband, Keith Anderson.

GREENSBORO SIT-IN: 60th ANNIVERSARY. Feb 1, 1960. Commercial discrimination against blacks and other minorities provoked a nonviolent protest. At Greensboro, NC, four students from the Agricultural and Technical College (Ezell Blair, Jr; Franklin McCain; Joseph McNeill and David Richmond) sat down at an F.W. Woolworth store lunch counter and ordered coffee. Refused service, they remained all day. In the following days similar sit-ins took place at Woolworth's lunch counter. Before the week was over, they were joined by a few white students. The protest spread rapidly, especially in the South. More than 1,600 people were arrested before the year was over for participating in sit-ins. Civil rights for all became a cause for thousands of students and activists. In response, equal accommodation regardless of race became the rule at lunch counters, hotels and business establishments in thousands of places.

HERBERT, VICTOR: BIRTH ANNIVERSARY. Feb 1, 1859. Born at Dublin, Ireland, Herbert was a cellist, conductor and prolific composer of operettas who dominated the popular American music scene in the late 19th and early 20th centuries. Among his many popular operettas were *Babes in Toyland* (1903) and *Naughty Marietta* (1910). Herbert also helped found the American Society of Composers, Artists and Publishers (ASCAP), which protects artists' intellectual property rights. Herbert died May 26, 1924, at New York, NY.

HUGHES, LANGSTON: BIRTH ANNIVERSARY. Feb 1, 1902. African-American poet and author, born at Joplin, MO. Among his works are the poetry collection *Montage of a Dream Deferred*, plays, a novel, memoirs and short stories. He wrote, "My soul has grown deep like the rivers," and asked, "What happens to a dream deferred?" Hughes died May 22, 1967, at New York, NY.

ICE FISHING DERBY. Feb 1 (or Feb 8). Fort Peck, MT. 24th annual contest held on Fort Peck Lake. Entry fee of $50 per hole or three holes for $100. Subject to cancellation if no ice. For info: Glasgow Area Chamber of Commerce, PO Box 832, Glasgow, MT 59230. Phone: (406) 228-2222. Fax: (406) 228-2244. E-mail: chamber@nemont.net. Web: www.glasgowchamber.net.

"LATE NIGHT WITH DAVID LETTERMAN" TV PREMIERE: ANNIVERSARY. Feb 1, 1982. "Late Night" premiered on NBC as a talk/variety show appearing after "The Tonight Show with Johnny Carson." Host David Letterman was known for his irreverent sense of humor and daffy antics and guests: stupid pet tricks, stupid human tricks and the legendary top 10 lists. The show also featured bandleader-sidekick Paul Shaffer. In 1993 Letterman made a highly publicized exit from NBC and began hosting "The Late Show" on CBS, where he continued to revitalize the late-night talk show format at the Ed Sullivan Theater (kept at a chilly 58° for his studio audience to stay alert). Letterman announced his retirement for 2015, and the last show aired May 20, 2015. Out of 97 nominations, Letterman's show garnered 16 Emmys, including six for Outstanding Variety, Music or Comedy Series.

LIBRARY LOVERS' MONTH. Feb 1–29. A monthlong celebration of school, public and private libraries of all types. This is a time for everyone, especially library support groups, to recognize the value of libraries and to work to ensure that the nation's libraries will continue to serve.

MARFAN SYNDROME AWARENESS MONTH. Feb 1–29. Volunteers across the country distribute educational information and raise funds for Marfan syndrome and related connective-tissue disorders that can result in life-threatening cardiovascular problems as well as orthopedic and ophthalmologic handicaps. Marfan affects one in 5,000. Annually, the month of February. For info: The Marfan Foundation. Web: www.marfan.org.

MOON PHASE: FIRST QUARTER. Feb 1. Moon enters First Quarter phase at 8:42 PM, EST.

★NATIONAL AFRICAN-AMERICAN HISTORY MONTH. Feb 1–29. A month "to honor the significant contributions African Americans have made to our great nation—contributions that stand as a testament to their resolve, resilience and courage."

NATIONAL BIRD-FEEDING MONTH. Feb 1–29. This national event was created to advance and publicize the wild-bird-feeding and wild-bird-watching hobby. Each February, the National Bird-Feeding Society promotes a new theme to help celebrate this month. For info: National Bird-Feeding Society, 7370 MacArthur Blvd, Glen Echo, MD 20812. Phone: (301) 841-6404. Web: www.facebook.com/birdfeedingsociety.

NATIONAL BLACK HISTORY MONTH. Feb 1–29. Traditionally the month containing Abraham Lincoln's birthday (Feb 12) and Frederick Douglass's presumed birthday (Feb 14). Observance of a special period to recognize achievements and contributions by African Americans dates from February 1926, when it was launched by Dr. Carter G. Woodson. Variously designated Negro History, Black History, Afro-American History, African-American History, the observance period was initially one week, but since 1976 the entire month of February. 2020 theme: "African Americans and the Vote." For info: Assn for the Study of African American Life and History, Inc. Phone: (202) 238-5910. E-mail: info@asalh.org. Web: www.asalh.org.

NATIONAL CANDY-MAKING DAY. Feb 1. Make all your confectionary dreams come true. Try your hand at making homemade chocolates, swirled candy bark topped with sprinkles or candy lollipops with candy melts. Celebrate and share with your friends. Find all inspiration and instructions on our website. Annually, Feb 1. For info: Desiree Smith, Wilton Enterprises, 535 E Diehl Rd, Naperville, IL 60563. Phone: (630) 810-2254. E-mail: dsmith@wilton.com. Web: www.wilton.com.

NATIONAL CHERRY MONTH. Feb 1–29. Celebrate tart cherries and enjoy them year-round in dried, frozen and juice forms. For info: Cherry Marketing Institute. E-mail: info@choosecherries.com. Web: www.choosecherries.com.

NATIONAL CONDOM MONTH. Feb 1–29. To educate consumers, patients, students and professionals about the prevention of sexually transmitted diseases, AIDS and unwanted pregnancies. National Condom Week is Feb 14–21. Sponsored by the American College of Apothecaries/Pharmacists Planning Service, Inc (PPSI). For info: ACA/PPSI, 2830 Summer Oaks Dr, Bartlett, TN 38134. E-mail: info@ppsinc.org. Web: www.ppsinc.org.

NATIONAL GOAT YOGA MONTH. Feb 1–29. Since 2015. This month, diverse communities of goat-loving yogis come together to celebrate the humble beginnings of combining goats and exercise. This ever-growing fitness craze naturally increases strength, flexibility and mindfulness through therapeutic elements of adorable baby goats jumping on and all around you. For info: April Gould, Arizona Goat Yoga. Phone: (480) 269-4144. E-mail: april@goatyoga.com. Web: www.goatyoga.com.

NATIONAL PARENT LEADERSHIP MONTH®. Feb 1–29. In order to recognize, honor and celebrate parents for their vital leadership roles in their homes and communities and in state, national and international arenas, Parents Anonymous® Inc has designated the month of February as National Parent Leadership Month®. This annual event acknowledges the strengths of parents as leaders and generates awareness about the important roles parents play in shaping the lives of their families and communities. Founded in 1969, Parents Anonymous® Inc is dedicated to strengthening families around the world. For info: Dr. Lisa Pion-Berlin, Parents Anonymous Inc, 250 W First St, Ste 250, Claremont, CA 91711. Phone: (909) 575-4211. E-mail: lpion-berlin@parentsanonymous.org. Web: www.parentsanonymous.org.

NATIONAL PET DENTAL HEALTH MONTH. Feb 1–29. To address the significance of oral health care for pets, the American Veterinary Medical Association and several veterinary groups sponsor National Pet Dental Health Month in February. Use this month to learn more

	S	M	T	W	T	F	S
February							1
	2	3	4	5	6	7	8
2020	9	10	11	12	13	14	15
	16	17	18	19	20	21	22
	23	24	25	26	27	28	29

about good pet dental health. For info: American Veterinary Medical Assn. Phone: (800) 248-2862. Web: www.avma.org.

NATIONAL TIME MANAGEMENT MONTH. Feb 1–29. This is the month when those noble plans made in January start to go awry. This observance is dedicated to renewing those best-laid plans; breaking out those new calendars that have yet to be opened; and reevaluating and reprioritizing over-scheduled, out-of-balance lives—making specific commitments to achieve greater balance. For info: Sylvia Henderson, 3570 Olney-Laytonsville Rd, Ste 588, Olney, MD 20832. Phone: (301) 260-1538. E-mail: sylvia@springboardtraining.com. Web: www.ideasuccessnetwork.com.

PLANT THE SEEDS OF GREATNESS MONTH. Feb 1–29. Think globally—build for the future—Plant the Seeds of Greatness. If you're unhappy with your present situation, discover how you can remove the barriers and make a change in your life for the better. Use this month to put to use your own unique prosperity consciousness and "plant the seeds" for your new career, life objectives or goals. Make a difference for yourself, your family, your business or your community. Get outside of your comfort zone and take action on your ideas and dreams. For info: Lorrie Walters Marsiglio, PO Box 284-CC, Wasco, IL 60183-0284. Phone: (630) 584-9368.

RETURN SHOPPING CARTS TO THE SUPERMARKET MONTH. Feb 1–29. A monthlong opportunity to return stolen shopping carts, milk crates and bread trays to supermarkets and to avoid the increased food prices that these thefts cause. Annually, the month of February. (Originated by Anthony A. Dinolfo and the Illinois Food Retailers Association.)

ROBINSON CRUSOE DAY. Feb 1, 1709. (Old Style date.) Anniversary of the rescue of Alexander Selkirk, a Scottish sailor who had been put ashore (in September 1704) on the uninhabited island Juan Fernández, at his own request, after a quarrel with his captain. His adventures formed the basis for Daniel Defoe's book *Robinson Crusoe*. A day to be adventurous and self-reliant.

ST. LAURENT, LOUIS STEPHEN: BIRTH ANNIVERSARY. Feb 1, 1882. Canadian lawyer and prime minister, born at Compton, QC, Canada. Died at Quebec City, July 25, 1973.

SIX NATIONS CHAMPIONSHIP (RBS 6 NATIONS). Feb 1–Mar 14. Annual rugby union championship among England, Wales, Scotland, Ireland, France and Italy, with several individual competitions taking place under the umbrella of the tournament (Calcutta Cup, Millennium Trophy, Giuseppe Garibaldi Trophy). Each team plays every other team once, with home field advantage alternating from one year to the next. The Six Nations grew out of the Home International Championship in 1883, with France's membership creating the Five Nations in 1910 and Italy's membership creating the current Six Nations in 2000. For info: Six Nations Rugby Ltd. Web: www.rbs6nations.com.

SPACE SHUTTLE *COLUMBIA* DISASTER: ANNIVERSARY. Feb 1, 2003. Minutes before space shuttle *Columbia* was due to land after a successful 16-day scientific mission, it disintegrated 40 miles above the state of Texas, killing its seven-member crew. Commander Rick Husband, pilot William McCool, Michael Anderson, David Brown, Kalpana Chawla (first woman astronaut from India), Laurel Clark and Ilan Ramon (first Israeli astronaut) lost their lives and were mourned worldwide. *Columbia* was the first shuttle to fly in space (1981).

SPARK, MURIEL: BIRTH ANNIVERSARY. Feb 1, 1918. The novelist, critic, dramatist and editor was born Muriel Camberg at Edinburgh, Scotland. Author of *Memento Mori* (1959), *The Prime of Miss Jean Brodie* (1961) and other works. Spark received many awards and honors (including Dame Commander of the Order of the British Empire) for her tart, crisp novels that often explored intelligent, independent women in the postwar era. She died at Florence, Italy, on Apr 13, 2006.

SPAY/NEUTER AWARENESS MONTH. Feb 1–29. Globally, roaming pets and community animals contribute to the problem of street animal overpopulation. Often local authorities and individuals

use brutal methods to kill unwanted animals—methods that are not effective long-term solutions to street animal overpopulation. They may also accidentally harm the environment or kill other animals in the community. The message of this month is that by spaying or neutering your pet, by supporting spay/neuter efforts in your community and by informing others of the importance of spay/neuter, you become an important part of the solution! When we spay or neuter pets, feral cats and other street animals, we ensure those animals and their offspring will not add to the millions of already suffering animals. For info: Humane Society International. Web: www.worldspayday.org.

SPUNKY OLD BROADS MONTH. Feb 1–29. A monthlong celebration for all women over 50 who are interested in living a regret-free life. For info: Gayle Carson, SOB, 7910 Harbor Island Dr, #1208B, North Bay Village, FL 33141. Phone: (305) 310-9954. E-mail: gaylecarson13@gmail.com. Web: www.spunkyoldbroad.com.

TAKE YOUR CHILD TO THE LIBRARY DAY. Feb 1. Parents are encouraged to visit the public library with their children to participate in special events and learn about all the wonderful materials and services the library has to offer for families. Annually, the first Saturday in February. For info: Caitlin Augusta, Children's Librarian, Stratford Library, 2203 Main St, Stratford, CT 06615. Phone: (203) 385-4165. Fax: (203) 381-2079. E-mail: caugusta@stratfordlibrary.org.

WISE HEALTH CARE CONSUMER MONTH. Feb 1–29. Teaching consumers to make better healthcare decisions is a proven way to reduce healthcare costs. For this reason, companies, hospitals and MCOs are offering medical self-care programs for employees, subscribers and patients. Wise Health Care Consumer Marketing packet available. For info: American Institute for Preventive Medicine, 30445 Northwestern Hwy, Ste 350, Farmington Hills, MI 48334. Phone: (248) 539-1800. Fax: (248) 539-1808. E-mail: aipm@healthylife.com. Web: www.healthylife.com/wise.

WORLDWIDE RENAISSANCE OF THE HEART MONTH. Feb 1–29. This month is dedicated to compassionately thinking with your heart as well as your intellect. During this month, you are asked to take a heartfelt look at the way you think. On the first Saturday of this month, the Worldwide Renaissance of the Heart Tea takes place at noon all around the world. This informal tea is dedicated to heartfelt thinking. "Remember to give your heart a renaissance!" For info: Deborah Le Bouf Kulkkula, PhD, 381 Billings Rd, Fitchburg, MA 01420-1407. Phone: (978) 343-4009 or (978) 808-8084 (cell). E-mail: DebKulkkula@gmail.com. Web: www.RenaissanceoftheHeart.com.

YELTSIN, BORIS: BIRTH ANNIVERSARY. Feb 1, 1931. First president of the Russian Federation, born at Butka, Sverdlovsk, Russia. He worked in construction in his youth and rose through the Communist Party ranks to become mayor of Moscow. Estranged from the party for his criticism of Mikhail Gorbachev but popular with the people, he was elected president by the Russian parliament in 1989, and in 1991, after the breakup of the Soviet Union, he was reelected in the first popular election to take place in that nation's history. His work focused on transforming the Russian economy and on establishing a constitution and revising systems of parliament within the Russian government. His administration was fraught with controversy, and he survived two impeachment attempts before he resigned on Dec 31, 1999, appointing Vladimir Putin as his successor. Yeltsin died at Moscow, Apr 23, 2007.

YOUTH LEADERSHIP MONTH. Feb 1–29. This month is dedicated to celebrating young people who take on leadership roles in their lives. It is also focused on encouraging those who have not yet done so to consider a leadership role because they can. Programs that focus on youth leadership opportunities and effective leadership skill building are appropriate for this month. For info: Sylvia Henderson, Springboard Training, 3570 Olney-Laytonsville Rd, Ste 588, Olney, MD 20832. Phone: (301) 260-1538. E-mail: sylvia@springboardtraining.com.

🧁 BIRTHDAYS TODAY

Michelle Akers, 54, Hall of Fame soccer player, born Santa Clara, CA, Feb 1, 1966.

Big Boi, 45, singer, musician (Outkast), born Antwan Patton at Savannah, GA, Feb 1, 1975.

Lauren Conrad, 34, television personality ("The Hills," "Laguna Beach"), born Laguna Beach, CA, Feb 1, 1986.

Michael B. Enzi, 76, US Senator (R, Wyoming), born Bremerton, WA, Feb 1, 1944.

Don Everly, 83, singer, musician (The Everly Brothers), born Brownie, KY, Feb 1, 1937.

Sherilyn Fenn, 55, actress ("Twin Peaks," *Wild at Heart*), born Detroit, MI, Feb 1, 1965.

Leymah Gbowee, 48, women's rights activist, Nobel Peace Prize recipient, born Monrovia, Liberia, Feb 1, 1972.

Michael C. Hall, 49, actor ("Six Feet Under," "Dexter"), born Raleigh, NC, Feb 1, 1971.

Terry Jones, 78, actor, director ("Monty Python's Flying Circus"), born Colwyn Bay, Wales, Feb 1, 1942.

Garrett Morris, 83, comedian ("Saturday Night Live"), born New Orleans, LA, Feb 1, 1937.

Bill Mumy, 66, actor ("Lost in Space," "Babylon 5"), composer, born El Centro, CA, Feb 1, 1954.

Lisa Marie Presley, 52, singer, born Memphis, TN, Feb 1, 1968.

Ronda Rousey, 33, former UFC women's bantamweight champion, Olympic medalist (judo), mixed martial artist, judoka, actress, born Riverside County, CA, Feb 1, 1987.

Pauly Shore, 50, comedian, actor, born Los Angeles, CA, Feb 1, 1970.

Harry Styles, 26, singer (formerly of One Direction), born Redditch, England, Feb 1, 1994.

Stuart Whitman, 91, actor ("Cimarron Strip," *The Seekers*), born San Francisco, CA, Feb 1, 1929.

February 2 — Sunday

DAY 33	**333 REMAINING**

AFRICAN HERITAGE AND HEALTH WEEK. Feb 2–8. Coinciding with Black History Month, African Heritage and Health Week commemorates the foods, flavors and healthy cooking techniques that were core to the well-being of African ancestors from Africa, South America, the Caribbean and the American South. The foods that have sustained cultures are an important part of history.

February 2020	S	M	T	W	T	F	S
							1
	2	3	4	5	6	7	8
	9	10	11	12	13	14	15
	16	17	18	19	20	21	22
	23	24	25	26	27	28	29

What better time to dedicate a week to African heritage and health and learn about the healthy culinary side of history than during Black History Month? Annually, the first full week in February. For info: Oldways, 266 Beacon St, Boston, MA 02116. Phone: (617) 421-5500. E-mail: media@oldwayspt.org. Web: https://oldwayspt.org/programs/african-heritage-health.

BASEBALL HALL OF FAME'S CHARTER MEMBERS: ANNIVERSARY. Feb 2, 1936. The five charter members of the brand-new Baseball Hall of Fame at Cooperstown, NY, were announced. Of 226 ballots cast, Ty Cobb was named on 222, Babe Ruth on 215, Honus Wagner on 215, Christy Mathewson on 205 and Walter Johnson on 189. A total of 170 votes were necessary to be elected to the Hall of Fame.

BENÉT, WILLIAM ROSE: BIRTH ANNIVERSARY. Feb 2, 1886. American poet and critic. Born at Fort Hamilton, NY; died at New York, NY, May 4, 1950.

BONZA BOTTLER DAY®. Feb 2. To celebrate when the number of the day is the same as the number of the month. Bonza Bottler Day® is an excuse to have a party at least once a month. For more information see Jan 1. For info: Gail Berger, Bonza Bottler Day. Phone: (864) 201-3988. E-mail: bonza@bonzabottlerday.com. Web: www.bonzabottlerday.com.

CANDLEMAS DAY OR PRESENTATION OF THE LORD. Feb 2. Observed in the Roman Catholic Church. Commemorates presentation of Jesus in the Temple and the purification of Mary 40 days after his birth. Candles have been blessed since the 11th century. This marks the end of the Christmas liturgical season. Formerly called the Feast of Purification of the Blessed Virgin Mary. Old Scottish couplet proclaims: "If Candlemas is fair and clear/There'll be two winters in the year."

DUMP YOUR "SIGNIFICANT JERK" WEEK. Feb 2–8. It's time to take out the garbage and get rid of that "jerk" boyfriend or girlfriend. This year will be the 26th annual call to arms. Annually, the week before Valentine's Day. For info: Marcus P. Meleton, Jr, PO Box 940159, Houston, TX 77094. Phone: (832) 851-4400. E-mail: sharkbaitp@aol.com.

ENGLAND: GRIMALDI MEMORIAL SERVICE/CLOWN CHURCH SERVICE. Feb 2. All Saints Church, Haggerston, London. Church service (since 1946) celebrating Joseph Grimaldi (1778–1837), England's greatest clown. Also commemorates clowns who have died during the past year. Clowns—in dress and not—attend and entertain afterward. Annually, the first Sunday in February.

FAWCETT, FARRAH: BIRTH ANNIVERSARY. Feb 2, 1947. Actress and '70s pop-culture icon, born at Corpus Christi, TX. Almost as famous for her feathered hairstyle as for her acting, she was the star of television's "Charlie's Angels" and later earned several Emmy and Golden Globe nominations for her dramatic roles in made-for-television movies such as *The Burning Bed* and *Small Sacrifices*. Fawcett's 1976 swimsuit poster is the bestselling pinup of all time. She died at Santa Monica, CA, June 25, 2009.

GERMAN SURRENDER AT STALINGRAD: ANNIVERSARY. Feb 2, 1943. Two pockets of starving German soldiers remained in Stalingrad, USSR, on this date. They had received few supplies since Soviet soldiers had encircled the city the previous November. Friedrich Paulus, whom Hitler had promoted to field marshal only the day before, was forced to seek surrender terms, thereby becoming the first German marshal to surrender. Hitler was furious with

Paulus, believing he should have preferred suicide to surrender. Approximately 160,000 Germans died in the Stalingrad Battle; 34,000 were evacuated by air. Of the 90,000 captured and sent to Siberia on foot, tens of thousands died on the way. This Allied victory is generally considered the psychological turning point of WWII.

GETZ, STAN: BIRTH ANNIVERSARY. Feb 2, 1927. American jazz saxophonist Stan Getz was born at Philadelphia, PA. He introduced the cool-jazz style, which became a major movement in the 1950s, and the bossa nova (new wave) style of the 1960s. Getz received 11 Grammy Awards and was the first jazz musician to win the Grammy Award for Record of the Year (1965), for "The Girl from Ipanema." Died at Malibu, CA, June 6, 1991.

GROUNDHOG DAY. Feb 2. Old belief that if the sun shines on Candlemas Day, or if the groundhog sees his shadow when he emerges on this day, six weeks of winter will ensue.

GROUNDHOG DAY IN PUNXSUTAWNEY, PENNSYLVANIA. Feb 2. Punxsutawney, PA. Widely observed traditional annual Candlemas Day event at which "Punxsutawney Phil, king of the weather prophets," is the object of a search. Tradition is said to have been established by early German settlers. The official trek (which began in 1887) is followed by a weather prediction for the next six weeks. Phil made his dramatic film debut with Bill Murray in *Groundhog Day*.

HALAS, GEORGE: 125th BIRTH ANNIVERSARY. Feb 2, 1895. George "Papa Bear" Halas, Pro Football Hall of Fame coach and team owner, born at Chicago, IL. After playing football at the University of Illinois and baseball with the New York Yankees, Halas helped to found the National Football League and the Chicago Bears in 1920. As coach of the Bears for 40 years, he compiled a record of 324 wins, 151 losses and 31 ties. Charter member of the Hall of Fame, 1963. Died at Chicago, Oct 31, 1983.

HEDGEHOG DAY. Feb 2. This ancient Roman tradition was an inspiration for Groundhog Day in the US. Romans observed whether a hedgehog emerging from hibernation could see its shadow in the moonlight—if it could, then six more weeks of winter were expected. Later observed as a folk holiday in Europe and the British Isles.

IMBOLC. Feb 2. (Also called Imbolg, Candlemas, Lupercalia, Feast of Pan, Feast of Torches, Feast of Waxing Light, Brigit's Day and Oimelc.) One of the "Greater Sabbats" during the Wiccan year, Imbolc marks the recovery of the Goddess (after giving birth to the Sun, or the God, at Yule) and celebrates the anticipation of spring. Annually, Feb 2.

JOYCE, JAMES: BIRTH ANNIVERSARY. Feb 2, 1882. Irish novelist and poet, author of *Dubliners*, *A Portrait of the Artist as a Young Man*, *Ulysses* and *Finnegans Wake*, born at Dublin, Ireland. "A man of genius," he wrote in *Ulysses*, "makes no mistakes. His errors are volitional and are portals of discovery." Of *Finnegans Wake*, Joyce is reported to have replied to an academic whose letter had asked for clues to its meaning, "If I can throw any obscurity on the subject, let me know." Joyce died at the age of 58 of peritonitis Jan 13, 1941, at Zurich, Switzerland, and was buried there.

LUXEMBOURG: CANDLEMAS. Feb 2. Traditional observance of Candlemas. At night children sing a customary song wishing health and prosperity to their neighbors and receive sweets in return. They carry special candles called *Lichtebengel*, symbolizing the coming of spring.

MEXICO: DIA DE LA CANDELARIA. Feb 2. "Day of the Light." All Mexico celebrates. Dances, processions, bullfights.

NEW AMSTERDAM (NEW YORK) INCORPORATED AS CITY: ANNIVERSARY. Feb 2, 1653. The magistrates of the Dutch colony on Manhattan Island signed a municipal charter making New Amsterdam a city. This was the official birth of New York City, as New Amsterdam was renamed in August 1664, when the English took over the colony. New York was named in honor of James, the Duke of York, brother to the English king Charles II.

RAND, AYN: BIRTH ANNIVERSARY. Feb 2, 1905. Novelist (*The Fountainhead*, *Atlas Shrugged*), born Alyssa Rosenbaum at St. Petersburg, Russia. Founded the Objectivism school of philosophy. Died Mar 6, 1982, at New York, NY.

"THE RECORD OF A SNEEZE": ANNIVERSARY. Feb 2, 1893. One day after Thomas Edison's "Black Maria" studio was completed at West Orange, NJ, a studio cameraman took the first "close-up" in film history. "The Record of a Sneeze," starring Edison's assistant Fred P. Ott, was also the first motion picture to receive a copyright (1894).

SLED DOGS SAVE NOME: 95th ANNIVERSARY. Feb 2, 1925. When a diphtheria outbreak was diagnosed in Nome, AK (population 1,500), on Jan 21, the nearest large amount of antitoxin serum was in Anchorage. Bitter winter temperatures made air delivery impossible, so a heroic dog sled relay was set up. Some 300,000 units of serum were delivered by train to Nenana, AK, and on Jan 27—in temperatures of 40–50 degrees below zero (Fahrenheit)—20 mushers drove scores of dogs on a 674-mile journey to Nome in 127 hours. Togo was the lead dog for the first 350 miles, and Balto was the lead dog on the final 53 miles. The frozen serum arrived at 5:30 AM, and once it was thawed and administered, there were no more diphtheria deaths. Balto became a national hero, and a statue was erected in his honor in New York City's Central Park.

STRITCH, ELAINE: 95th BIRTH ANNIVERSARY. Feb 2, 1925. Actress, singer born at Detroit, MI. Sometimes called the First Lady of Broadway. Stritch's career spanned seven decades on stage, film and television. Her Broadway highlights include roles in *Bus Stop* (1956), *Pal Joey* (1952) and *Company* (1970), which gave her a signature song, "The Ladies Who Lunch." A long-awaited Tony Award came with her one-woman show, *Elaine Stritch at Liberty* (2002). Her acerbic off-stage persona was as famous as her onstage cabaret presence, where she showcased her legs wearing a long cream blouse over black stockings. She died July 17, 2014, at Birmingham, MI.

SUPER BOWL LIV. Feb 2. Hard Rock Stadium, Miami Gardens, FL. Football's legendary battle between NFC and AFC champions. For info: The National Football League. Web: www.nfl.com or https://nflonlocation.com/superbowl-tickets.

SWITZERLAND: HOMSTROM. Feb 2. Scuol. Burning of straw men on poles as a symbol of winter's imminent departure. Annually, the first Sunday in February.

TREATY OF GUADALUPE HIDALGO: ANNIVERSARY. Feb 2, 1848. The war between Mexico and the US formally ended with the Treaty of Guadalupe Hidalgo, signed in the village for which it was named. The treaty provided for Mexico's cession to the US of the territory that became the states of California, Nevada and Utah; most of Arizona; and parts of New Mexico, Colorado and Wyoming in exchange for $15 million from the US. In addition, Mexico relinquished all rights to Texas north of the Rio Grande. The Senate ratified the treaty Mar 10, 1848.

WALTON, GEORGE: DEATH ANNIVERSARY. Feb 2, 1804. Signer of the Declaration of Independence. Born at Prince Edward County, VA, 1749 (exact date unknown). Died at Augusta, GA.

"WHAT'S MY LINE?" TV PREMIERE: 70th ANNIVERSARY. Feb 2, 1950. This popular game show premiered on CBS and ran for 17 years in primetime. A panel of four celebrities figured out the professions of the contestants and the identities of the mystery guests by asking yes-or-no questions. The first panel consisted of poet Louis Untermeyer, columnist Dorothy Kilgallen, former New Jersey governor Harold Hoffman and psychiatrist Dr. Richard Hoffman. Yankee Phil Rizzuto was the first mystery guest. John Daly hosted.

🎂 BIRTHDAYS TODAY

Christie Brinkley, 67, model, born Monroe, MI, Feb 2, 1953.

John Cornyn, 68, US Senator (R, Texas), born Houston, TX, Feb 2, 1952.

Ina Garten, 72, chef, cookbook author, television personality ("The Barefoot Contessa"), born Brooklyn, NY, Feb 2, 1948.

Bo Hopkins, 78, actor, born Greenwood, SC, Feb 2, 1942.

Zosia Mamet, 32, actress ("Girls," "United States of Tara," "Mad Men"), born Randolph, VT, Feb 2, 1988.

Graham Nash, 78, Rock and Roll Hall of Fame musician, singer, born Blackpool, England, Feb 2, 1942.

Tom Smothers, 83, comedian ("The Smothers Brothers Comedy Hour"), folksinger, born New York, NY, Feb 2, 1937.

Michael T. Weiss, 58, actor ("The Pretender"), born Chicago, IL, Feb 2, 1962.

February 3 — Monday

DAY 34   **332 REMAINING**

BLACKWELL, ELIZABETH: BIRTH ANNIVERSARY. Feb 3, 1821. First woman physician. Born near Bristol, England, she and several other members of her family were active abolitionists, women's suffrage advocates and pioneers in women's medicine. Her family moved to New York State in 1832, and she received a medical doctor's degree at Geneva, NY, in 1849. She established a hospital in New York City with an all-woman staff, where she recruited nurses and trained them for service in the Civil War. Returning to England in 1869, she continued to teach and practice medicine until her death at Hastings, England, May 31, 1910.

"THE DAY THE MUSIC DIED": ANNIVERSARY. Feb 3, 1959. The anniversary of the death of rock-and-roll legend Charles Hardin "Buddy" Holly. "The Day the Music Died," so called in singer Don McLean's song "American Pie," is the date on which Holly was killed in a plane crash in a cornfield near Mason City, IA, along with J.P. Richardson (otherwise known as "The Big Bopper") and Richie Valens. Holly was born Sept 7, 1936, at Lubbock, TX.

FIFTEENTH AMENDMENT TO US CONSTITUTION RATIFIED: 150th ANNIVERSARY. Feb 3, 1870. The 15th Amendment granted that the right of citizens to vote shall not be denied on account of race, color or previous condition of servitude.

FOUR CHAPLAINS MEMORIAL DAY. Feb 3, 1943. Commemorates four chaplains (George Fox, Alexander Goode, Clark Poling, John Washington) who sacrificed their life belts and lives when the SS *Dorchester* was torpedoed off Greenland during WWII.

GREELEY, HORACE: BIRTH ANNIVERSARY. Feb 3, 1811. Newspaper editor, born at Amherst, NH. Founder of the *New York Tribune*

and one of the organizers of the Republican Party, Greeley was an outspoken opponent of slavery. Best remembered for his saying, "Go West, young man." Died Nov 29, 1872, at New York City.

INCOME TAX BIRTHDAY: SIXTEENTH AMENDMENT TO US CONSTITUTION RATIFIED. Feb 3, 1913. The 16th Amendment was ratified, granting Congress the authority to levy taxes on income. (Church bells did not ring throughout the land, and no dancing in the streets was reported.)

JAPAN: BEAN-THROWING FESTIVAL (SETSUBUN). Feb 3. Setsubun marks the last day of winter according to the lunar calendar. Throngs at temple grounds throw beans to drive away imaginary devils.

JOHNSTON, JOSEPH: BIRTH ANNIVERSARY. Feb 3, 1807. Born near Farmville, VA, and died Mar 21, 1891, at Washington, DC. Confederate general in the Civil War whose troops were never directly defeated. Long-standing differences with Jefferson Davis, president of the Confederacy, prevented him from reaching his full potential as a military leader.

LINCOLN, ABRAHAM: OREGON BIRTHDAY OBSERVANCE. Feb 3. Observed annually in Oregon on the first Monday in February. See also: "Lincoln, Abraham: Birth Anniversary" (Feb 12).

MICHENER, JAMES: BIRTH ANNIVERSARY. Feb 3, 1907. American author, born at New York, NY. His *Tales of the South Pacific* was the basis for the popular musical *South Pacific*. A prolific author; his works include *Sayonara, Iberia, Hawaii, Centennial* and *Texas.* Died at Austin, TX, Oct 17, 1997.

MOZAMBIQUE: HEROES' DAY. Feb 3. National holiday. Honors all heroic citizens, especially Eduardo Mondlane, leader of the fight for independence, assassinated on Feb 3, 1969.

NAUVOO LEGION CHARTERED: ANNIVERSARY. Feb 3, 1841. Created by Illinois charter and composed of 5,000 Mormon men under the command of Lieutenant General Joseph Smith, the Nauvoo Legion was considered the "largest trained soldiery in the US" except for the US Army.

NISSEN, GEORGE: BIRTH ANNIVERSARY. Feb 3, 1914. Champion teenage gymnast Nissen invented the trampoline and trademarked the name in 1937. After WWII, he was an indefatigable marketer of the portable jumping station that he also manufactured. He lived to see trampoline gymnastics become an Olympic event in 2000. Born at Blairstown, IA, Nissen died at San Diego, CA, Apr 7, 2010.

ROCKWELL, NORMAN: BIRTH ANNIVERSARY. Feb 3, 1894. American artist and illustrator especially noted for his realistic and homey magazine cover art for the *Saturday Evening Post*. Born at New York, NY, he died at Stockbridge, MA, Nov 8, 1978.

SPACE MILESTONE: *CHALLENGER STS-10* **(US).** Feb 3, 1984. Shuttle *Challenger* launched from Kennedy Space Center, FL, with a crew of five—Vance Brand, Robert Gibson, Ronald McNair, Bruce McCandless and Robert Stewart. On Feb 7 McCandless and Stewart became the first to fly freely in space (propelled by their backpack jets), untethered to any craft. Landed at Cape Canaveral, FL, Feb 11.

STEIN, GERTRUDE: BIRTH ANNIVERSARY. Feb 3, 1874. Avant-garde expatriate American writer, perhaps best remembered for her poetic declaration (in 1913): "Rose is a rose is a rose is a rose." Born at Allegheny, PA; died at Paris, France, July 27, 1946.

VIETNAM: NATIONAL HOLIDAY. Feb 3. National holiday. Anniversary of the founding of the Vietnamese Communist Party, Feb 3, 1930.

WEIL, SIMONE: BIRTH ANNIVERSARY. Feb 3, 1909. French philosopher and social activist whose impact came posthumously with the publication of her many notebooks. Born at Paris, France, Weil died at Ashford, England, on Aug 24, 1943. Her 20 volumes of writings include these thoughts: "What a country calls its vital economic interests are not the things which enable its citizens to live, but the things which enable it to make war. Gasoline is much more likely than wheat to be a cause of international conflict."

February 2020	S	M	T	W	T	F	S
							1
	2	3	4	5	6	7	8
	9	10	11	12	13	14	15
	16	17	18	19	20	21	22
	23	24	25	26	27	28	29

🎂 BIRTHDAYS TODAY

Paul Auster, 73, author (*The New York Trilogy, Moon Palace, The Brooklyn Follies*), screenwriter, born Newark, NJ, Feb 3, 1947.

Thomas Calabro, 61, actor ("Melrose Place"), born Brooklyn, NY, Feb 3, 1959.

Blythe Danner, 77, actress (*Butterflies Are Free, Brighton Beach Memoirs*), born Philadelphia, PA, Feb 3, 1943.

Dave Davies, 73, singer, musician (The Kinks), born London, England, Feb 3, 1947.

Vlade Divac, 52, former basketball player, born Prijepolje, Yugoslavia (now Serbia), Feb 3, 1968.

Morgan Fairchild, 70, actress ("Dallas," "Falcon Crest," "Flamingo Road"), born Patsy McClenny at Dallas, TX, Feb 3, 1950.

Isla Fisher, 44, actress (*Wedding Crashers, The Lookout*), born Muscat, Oman, Feb 3, 1976.

Keith Gordon, 59, actor (*Dressed to Kill, A Midnight Clear*), director, born New York, NY, Feb 3, 1961.

Robert Allen (Bob) Griese, 75, sportscaster, Hall of Fame football player, born Evansville, IN, Feb 3, 1945.

Nathan Lane, 64, actor (Tonys for *Angels in America, A Funny Thing Happened on the Way to the Forum* and *The Producers*; *The Birdcage*), born Jersey City, NJ, Feb 3, 1956.

Francis Asbury (Fran) Tarkenton, 80, Hall of Fame football player, born Richmond, VA, Feb 3, 1940.

Maura Tierney, 55, actress ("The Affair," "NewsRadio," "ER"), born Boston, MA, Feb 3, 1965.

February 4 — Tuesday

DAY 35   **331 REMAINING**

AFRICAN-AMERICAN COACHES DAY. Feb 4. To provide a day each year to educate the African-American community about the value of working with a personal or business coach and to provide an opportunity for coaches and their clients to acknowledge the results and progress made through the coaching process. Annually, the first Tuesday in February. For info: Monique Belton, PhD, 35 Dix Hills Rd, Huntington, NY 11743. Phone: (631) 549-7314. E-mail: drbelton@wisefellows.com.

ANGOLA: ARMED STRUGGLE DAY. Feb 4. National holiday. Commemorates the beginning of the struggle for independence from Portugal in 1961.

APACHE WARS BEGIN: ANNIVERSARY. Feb 4, 1861. The period of conflict known as the Apache Wars began at Apache Pass, AZ, when army lieutenant George Bascom arrested Apache chief Cochise and other tribe members for raiding a ranch. Bascom killed Cochise's brother, but Cochise escaped and declared war. The wars lasted 25 years under the leadership of Cochise and, later, Geronimo.

FACEBOOK LAUNCHES: ANNIVERSARY. Feb 4, 2004. Mark Zuckerberg and fellow Harvard students Dustin Moskovitz, Chris

Hughes and Eduardo Saverin launched "TheFacebook" as a social networking site. Facebook, later dropping "The," quickly became an Internet sensation, reaching 901 million users by March 2012. The site currently has 2 billion monthly active users and is offered in 70 languages. On May 18, 2012, Facebook went public, with a volume of 567 million shares trading that day.

FRIEDAN, BETTY: BIRTH ANNIVERSARY. Feb 4, 1921. The cofounder and first president of the National Organization for Women (NOW) was born Bettye Naomi Goldstein at Peoria, IL. She was an outspoken feminist who spent her entire career crusading for women's rights. Her book *The Feminine Mystique* chronicled the frustrations of the 1960s American housewife, to which she referred as "the problem that has no name." The book struck a chord with millions of women and is widely regarded as one of the most influential books of the 20th century. Friedan died at Washington, DC, on Feb 4, 2006, her 85th birthday.

KOŚCIUSZKO, TADEUSZ: BIRTH ANNIVERSARY. Feb 4, 1746. Polish patriot and American Revolutionary War figure. Born at Lithuania, he died at Solothurn, Switzerland, Oct 15, 1817.

LINDBERGH, CHARLES AUGUSTUS: BIRTH ANNIVERSARY. Feb 4, 1902. American aviator Charles "Lucky Lindy" Lindbergh was the first to fly solo and nonstop over the Atlantic Ocean, New York to Paris, May 20–21, 1927. Born at Detroit, MI; died at Kipahulu, Maui, HI, Aug 27, 1974. See also: "Lindbergh Flight: Anniversary" (May 20).

MEDJOOL DATE DAY. Feb 4. Eighty percent of the Medjool dates consumed in North America are produced by the Bard Valley Medjool Date Growers Association. The association has officially proclaimed Feb 4 as National Medjool Date Day, dedicated to the celebration of Medjool dates as the perfect healthy snack, while also serving as a "naturally sweet, perfectly healthy" addition to salads, appetizers, entrees and smoothies. For info: Natural Delights Medjool Dates, Bard Valley Date Growers, 538 E 16th St, Ste 201, Yuma, AZ 85365. Phone: (928) 248-5647. E-mail: info@naturaldelights.com. Web: www.naturaldelights.com.

NELSON, BYRON: BIRTH ANNIVERSARY. Feb 4, 1912. "Lord Byron" was the premier golfer of the 1930s and '40s, whose spectacular play in 1945 enshrined him as one of the legendary sportsmen of all time. In 1945 Nelson won 11 consecutive tournaments, with the season's total coming to 18. That single-season victory record has never been equaled. In all, Nelson had 52 PGA victories in a professional career that began in 1932. He retired from full-time play in 1946. Nelson's golf swing is still considered the one to emulate today. Born John Byron Nelson, Jr, near Waxahachie, TX, he died Sept 26, 2006, at Roanoke, TX.

PARKS, ROSA: BIRTH ANNIVERSARY. Feb 4, 1913. Born Rosa Louise McCauley in Tuskegee, AL, Rosa Parks was a seamstress who was active with the NAACP. On a fateful day in Montgomery, AL, in 1955, a time when African Americans were obligated by law to ride in the back of a bus, she refused to give up her seat to a white man during a ride home from work. Parks was subsequently arrested, found guilty of disorderly conduct and fined $14. This simple act sparked the modern civil rights movement, leading to a 381-day boycott of the Montgomery bus system, lawsuits and an eventual Supreme Court decision decreeing segregation to be unconstitutional. A hero to blacks and whites alike, Parks continued work on civil rights until her death on Oct 25, 2005, at Detroit, MI. She was awarded the Presidential Medal of Freedom and the Congressional Gold Medal, and she is the only American woman to lie in state at the US Capitol Rotunda. Many municipalities consider Dec 1, the day of her arrest in 1955, a holiday: Rosa Parks Day.

SRI LANKA: INDEPENDENCE DAY. Feb 4. Democratic Socialist Republic of Sri Lanka observes National Day. Public holiday. On Feb 4, 1948, Ceylon (as it was then known) obtained independence from Great Britain. The country's name was changed to Sri Lanka in 1972.

USO FOUNDED: ANNIVERSARY. Feb 4, 1941. This civilian agency was founded in 1941 to provide support worldwide for US service people and their families. The United Service Organizations

(USO) centers have served as a home away from home for hundreds of thousands of Americans.

WORLD CANCER DAY. Feb 4. An international observance that seeks to take a positive and proactive approach to the fight against cancer, highlighting that solutions do exist across the continuum of cancer and they are within our reach. Annually, Feb 4. For info: Union for International Cancer Control. E-mail: press@worldcancerday.org. Web: www.worldcancerday.org.

🧁 BIRTHDAYS TODAY

Gabrielle Anwar, 49, actress (*Scent of a Woman*, "The Tudors," "Burn Notice"), born Laleham, England, Feb 4, 1971.

Clint Black, 58, country singer, songwriter, born Katy, TX, Feb 4, 1962.

Gary Conway, 84, actor ("Burke's Law," *I Was a Teenage Frankenstein*), born Boston, MA, Feb 4, 1936.

Alice Cooper, 72, singer, songwriter, born Vincent Damon Furnier at Detroit, MI, Feb 4, 1948.

Rob Corddry, 49, comedian ("The Daily Show," *Hot Tub Time Machine*), writer, born Weymouth, MA, Feb 4, 1971.

Oscar De La Hoya, 47, former boxer, born Los Angeles, CA, Feb 4, 1973.

Lisa Eichhorn, 68, actress (*The Vanishing, King of the Hill*), born Reading, PA, Feb 4, 1952.

Jerome Powell, 67, Chairman of the Federal Reserve, born Washington, DC, Feb 4, 1953.

J. Danforth (Dan) Quayle, 73, 44th vice president of the US (1989–93), born Indianapolis, IN, Feb 4, 1947.

John Schuck, 80, actor ("McMillan and Wife," *McCabe and Mrs Miller, Dick Tracy*), born Boston, MA, Feb 4, 1940.

Lawrence Taylor, 61, Hall of Fame football player, born Williamsburg, VA, Feb 4, 1959.

February 5 — Wednesday

DAY 36	330 REMAINING

BURROUGHS, WILLIAM S.: BIRTH ANNIVERSARY. Feb 5, 1914. Renowned Beat author born at St. Louis, MO. His novels, notably *Naked Lunch* (1959), pushed fiction to the outermost limits and explored previously taboo subjects such as drug use, homosexuality and systems of control, and his books were frequently banned. Burroughs once stated, "all fiction is autobiographical and all autobiography is fiction." He died Aug 2, 1997, at Lawrence, KS.

February 2020	S	M	T	W	T	F	S
							1
	2	3	4	5	6	7	8
	9	10	11	12	13	14	15
	16	17	18	19	20	21	22
	23	24	25	26	27	28	29

CARRADINE, JOHN: BIRTH ANNIVERSARY. Feb 5, 1906. American film actor John Carradine was born Richmond Reed Carradine at Greenwich Village, NY. He appeared in more than 200 films. Frequently observed wandering the streets in a velvet suit and satin cape while reciting Shakespeare, he became known as "the Bard of the Boulevard." Died Nov 27, 1988, at Milan, Italy.

FAMILY LEAVE BILL: ANNIVERSARY. Feb 5, 1993. President William Clinton signed legislation requiring companies with 50 or more employees (and all government agencies) to allow employees to take up to 12 weeks of unpaid leave in a 12-month period to deal with the birth or adoption of a child or to care for a relative with a serious health problem. The bill became effective Aug 5, 1993.

LONGEST WAR IN HISTORY ENDS: 35th ANNIVERSARY. Feb 5, 1985. The Third Punic War, between Rome and Carthage, started in the year 149 BC. It culminated in the year 146 BC, when Roman soldiers led by Scipio razed Carthage to the ground. The desolated site was cursed and rebuilding forbidden. On this date, 2,131 years after the war began, Ugo Vetere, mayor of Rome, and Chedli Klibi, mayor of Carthage, met at Tunis to sign a treaty of friendship officially ending the Third Punic War.

MEXICO: CONSTITUTION DAY. Feb 5. National holiday. On Feb 5, 1917, Mexico's Constitutional Congress approved a new constitution that was proclaimed by President Venustiano Carranza. Reflecting the aims of the still ongoing Mexican Revolution (1910–20), the constitution promised wide-ranging reforms.

MOVE HOLLYWOOD & BROADWAY TO LEBANON, PENNSYLVANIA, DAY. Feb 5. There's lots of room, friendly folks and Amish farms. Lebanon is a haven for residents and tourists to serenely indulge in the city's world-famous bologna and the Wertz family homemade candies. (©2006 by WH.) For info: Thomas & Ruth Roy, Wellcat Holidays, 2418 Long Ln, Lebanon, PA 17046. Phone: (717) 279-0184. E-mail: info@wellcat.com. Web: www.wellcat.com.

NATIONAL GIRLS AND WOMEN IN SPORTS DAY. Feb 5. Celebrates and honors all girls and women participating in sports. Recognizes the passage of Title IX in 1972, the law that guarantees gender equity in federally funded school programs, including athletics. Sponsored by the Women's Sports Foundation and many other organizations. Annually, the first Wednesday in February.

NATIONAL SIGNING DAY (COLLEGE FOOTBALL). Feb 5. This day—eagerly followed by the press and fans—marks the earliest day a prospective high school student-athlete can sign a national letter of intent with an NCAA Division I and II football program. Annually, the first Wednesday in February. For info: NCAA/National Letter of Intent. Web: www.nationalletter.org.

PEEL, ROBERT: BIRTH ANNIVERSARY. Feb 5, 1788. English Tory statesman, born at Bury, Lancashire, England, who twice served as prime minister (1834–35; 1841–46). As chief secretary for Ireland (1812), Peel established the Irish constabulary known as the "Peelers." In June 1829, Greater London's Metropolitan Police were established by an act of parliament at the request of Peel, then home secretary. London police officers, who first took to the streets in September 1829, became affectionately known as "bobbies." As prime minister, he oversaw the repeal of the Corn Laws in 1846 in an effort to address the then-raging Irish potato famine. Sir Robert Peel died July 2, 1850, at London from injuries received in a fall from his horse.

STEVENSON, ADLAI EWING, II: BIRTH ANNIVERSARY. Feb 5, 1900. American statesman, governor of Illinois, Democratic candidate for president in 1952 and 1956, US representative to the UN, 1961–65. Born at Los Angeles, CA. Died at London, England, July 14, 1965. Not to be confused with his grandfather, Vice President Adlai Ewing Stevenson. See also: "Stevenson, Adlai Ewing: Birth Anniversary" (Oct 23).

WEATHERPERSON'S DAY. Feb 5. Commemorates the birth of one of America's first weathermen, John Jeffries, a Boston physician who kept detailed records of weather conditions, 1774–1816. Born at Boston, MA, Feb 5, 1744, and died there Sept 16, 1819.

WITHERSPOON, JOHN: BIRTH ANNIVERSARY. Feb 5, 1723. Clergyman, signer of the Declaration of Independence and reputed coiner of the word *Americanism* (in 1781). Born near Edinburgh, Scotland. Died at Princeton, NJ, Nov 15, 1794.

🎂 BIRTHDAYS TODAY

Henry Louis (Hank) Aaron, 86, Hall of Fame baseball player, baseball executive, 755 career home-run hitter, born Mobile, AL, Feb 5, 1934.

Roberto Alomar, 52, Hall of Fame baseball player, born Ponce, Puerto Rico, Feb 5, 1968.

Bobby Brown, 51, singer, born Roxbury, MA, Feb 5, 1969.

Sara Evans, 49, country singer, born Boonville, MO, Feb 5, 1971.

Christopher Guest, 72, writer, comedian (Emmy for writing *Lily Tomlin; This Is Spinal Tap, Best in Show*), born New York, NY, Feb 5, 1948.

Barbara Hershey, 72, actress (*Hannah and Her Sisters*), born Barbara Hertzstein at Los Angeles, CA, Feb 5, 1948.

David Alan Ladd, 73, actor, producer (*A Dog of Flanders, The Day of the Locust*), born Los Angeles, CA, Feb 5, 1947.

Jennifer Jason Leigh, 58, actress (*The Hateful Eight, Margot at the Wedding, Georgia, Mrs Parker and the Vicious Circle*), born Los Angeles, CA, Feb 5, 1962.

Laura Linney, 56, actress (*The Savages, You Can Count on Me, Kinsey*, "John Adams," "The Big C"), born New York, NY, Feb 5, 1964.

Neymar, 28, soccer player, born Neymar da Silva Santos, Jr, at Mogi das Cruzes, Brazil, Feb 5, 1992.

Jane Bryant Quinn, 79, financial writer (*Everyone's Money Book*), born Niagara Falls, NY, Feb 5, 1941.

Charlotte Rampling, 74, actress (*45 Years, Swimming Pool, The Night Porter*), born Sturmer, England, Feb 5, 1946.

Cristiano Ronaldo, 35, soccer player, born Funchal, Portugal, Feb 5, 1985.

David Selby, 79, actor ("Falcon Crest," *Rich and Famous*), born Morgantown, WV, Feb 5, 1941.

Michael Sheen, 51, actor ("Good Omens," "Masters of Sex," *Frost/Nixon, The Queen*), born Newport, Gwent, Wales, Feb 5, 1969.

Roger Thomas Staubach, 78, Hall of Fame football player, born Cincinnati, OH, Feb 5, 1942.

Carlos Tévez, 36, soccer player, born Buenos Aires, Argentina, Feb 5, 1984.

Darrell Waltrip, 73, auto racer, born Owensboro, KY, Feb 5, 1947.

February 6 — Thursday

DAY 37   **329 REMAINING**

ACCESSION OF QUEEN ELIZABETH II: ANNIVERSARY. Feb 6, 1952. Princess Elizabeth Alexandra Mary succeeded to the British throne (becoming Elizabeth II, Queen of the United Kingdom of Great Britain and Northern Ireland and Head of the Commonwealth) upon the death of her father, King George VI, Feb 6, 1952. Her coronation took place June 2, 1953, at Westminster Abbey at London.

BURR, AARON: BIRTH ANNIVERSARY. Feb 6, 1756. Third vice president of the US (Mar 4, 1801–Mar 3, 1805). While vice president, Burr challenged political enemy Alexander Hamilton to a duel and mortally wounded him July 11, 1804, at Weehawken, NJ. Indicted for the challenge and for murder, he returned to Washington to complete his term of office (during which he presided over the impeachment trial of Supreme Court Justice Samuel Chase). In 1807 Burr was arrested, tried for treason (in an alleged scheme to invade Mexico and set up a new nation in the West) and acquitted. Born at Newark, NJ, he died at Staten Island, NY, Sept 14, 1836.

FLORIDA STATE FAIR. Feb 6–17. Florida State Fairgrounds, Tampa, FL. 116th annual. The fair features the best arts, crafts, competitive exhibits, equestrian shows, livestock, entertainment, midway rides and food found in Florida. Also not to be missed is Cracker Country, a rural-history living museum where cultural and architectural history has been preserved. Est attendance: 500,000. For info: Florida State Fair. Phone: (813) 621-7821 or (800) 345-FAIR. Web: www.floridastatefair.com.

LEAKEY, MARY: BIRTH ANNIVERSARY. Feb 6, 1913. Born Mary Douglas Nicol at London, England, archaeologist and paleoanthropologist Mary Leakey made several remarkable discoveries instrumental in the scientific understanding of the pattern of human evolution. For 50 years she worked at various excavation sites in eastern Africa, with the majority of her research taking place at Olduvai Gorge, Tanzania. Her fastidious excavatory techniques resulted in the discovery of the skull of *Proconsul africanus*—a 25-million-year-old common ancestor of both early humans and apes—and a 3.5-million-year-old preserved trail of hominid footprints that conclusively proved human bipedalism at that date. For much of her career Leakey collaborated with her husband, Louis Leakey, who interpreted and published much of her research. Mary Leakey died Dec 9, 1996, at Nairobi, Kenya.

MARLEY, BOB: 75th BIRTH ANNIVERSARY. Feb 6, 1945. With his group, the Wailers, Bob Marley was one of the most popular and influential performers of reggae music. Marley was born at Rhoden Hall in northern Jamaica. Died of cancer at Miami, FL, May 11, 1981.

MASSACHUSETTS RATIFIES CONSTITUTION: ANNIVERSARY. Feb 6, 1788. By a vote of 187 to 168, Massachusetts became the sixth state to ratify the Constitution.

NEW ZEALAND: WAITANGI DAY. Feb 6. National Day. Commemorates signing of the Treaty of Waitangi in 1840 (at Waitangi, Chatham Islands, New Zealand). The treaty, between the native Maori and the European peoples, provided for development of New Zealand under the British Crown.

RAVENSCROFT, THURL: BIRTH ANNIVERSARY. Feb 6, 1914. Singer and voice artist known worldwide for his Tony the Tiger cereal commercials ("They're grrrrreat!"). Ravenscroft's distinctive bass was in demand for backup singing (for Bing Crosby and Elvis Presley, among many), Disney movies (and theme parks) and, most famously, the song "He's a Mean One, Mr Grinch" in the popular TV cartoon "How the Grinch Stole Christmas" (1966). Born at Norfolk, NE, Ravenscroft died May 22, 2005, at Fullerton, CA.

REAGAN, RONALD WILSON: BIRTH ANNIVERSARY. Feb 6, 1911. 40th president of the US (1981–89). Former sportscaster, motion picture actor, governor of California (1967–74); he was the oldest and the first divorced person to become US president. Born at Tampico, IL. Married actress Jane Wyman in 1940 (divorced in 1948); married actress Nancy Davis, Mar 4, 1952. The "Great Communicator" ushered in a decade of conservative policies upon his election in 1980 and was an indefatigable critic of Communist states: he famously challenged Soviet president Mikhail Gorbachev to "tear down this wall!" at the Berlin Wall in 1987. He died at his Los Angeles, CA, home on June 5, 2004.

RUTH, "BABE": 125th BIRTH ANNIVERSARY. Feb 6, 1895. One of baseball's greatest heroes and a bigger-than-life character, George Herman "Babe" Ruth was born at Baltimore, MD. 1914 was the beginning of his illustrious baseball career. The "Sultan of Swat" (who was also a left-handed pitcher) hit 714 home runs in 22 major league seasons and played in 10 World Series. Fourteen of his pro

seasons were spent with the New York Yankees. The "Bambino" retired June 2, 1935, and was inducted as a charter member of the Baseball Hall of Fame in 1936. Diagnosed with cancer in November 1946, he died at New York, NY, Aug 16, 1948.

TRUFFAUT, FRANÇOIS: BIRTH ANNIVERSARY. Feb 6, 1932. Born at Paris, France, Truffaut was the most popular and successful French film director of his time. His films include *The 400 Blows*, *Jules and Jim*, *The Last Metro* and *The Story of Adele H.* He died at Paris, Oct 21, 1984.

UNITED NATIONS: INTERNATIONAL DAY OF ZERO TOLERANCE FOR FEMALE GENITAL MUTILATION. Feb 6. Recognizing that injury to the female genital organs for nonmedical reasons is a violation of the human rights of girls and women and violates a person's rights to health, security and physical integrity; the right to be free from torture and cruel, inhuman or degrading treatment; and the right to life when the procedure results in death, the General Assembly designated Feb 6 as an annual day of zero tolerance for this practice. The UN urges that this day promote awareness-raising campaigns and concrete actions against female genital mutilations (Res 67/146 of Mar 5, 2013). For info: United Nations, Dept of Public Info, New York, NY 10017. Web: www. un.org.

🎂 BIRTHDAYS TODAY

Tom Brokaw, 80, journalist, author, born Yankton, SD, Feb 6, 1940.

Fabian, 77, singer, actor, born Fabian Forte at Philadelphia, PA, Feb 6, 1943.

Mike Farrell, 81, actor ("M*A*S*H," "Providence"), born St. Paul, MN, Feb 6, 1939.

Gayle Hunnicutt, 77, actress ("Dallas," *The Wild Angels*, *Marlowe*), born Fort Worth, TX, Feb 6, 1943.

Barry Miller, 62, stage and screen actor (Tony for *Biloxi Blues*; *Saturday Night Fever*, *The Last Temptation of Christ*), born Los Angeles, CA, Feb 6, 1958.

Kathy Najimy, 63, actress ("Veronica's Closet," *Sister Act*), born San Diego, CA, Feb 6, 1957.

Gigi Perreau, 79, actress (*Bonzo Goes to College*, *Tammy Tell Me True*), born Los Angeles, CA, Feb 6, 1941.

Robert Townsend, 63, actor, director (*The Five Heartbeats*, *The Mighty Quinn*), born Chicago, IL, Feb 6, 1957.

Michael Tucker, 76, actor ("LA Law"), born Baltimore, MD, Feb 6, 1944.

Mamie Van Doren, 87, actress (*High School Confidential*, *Three Nuts in Search of a Bolt*), born Rowena, SD, Feb 6, 1933.

February 7 — Friday

DAY 38   **328 REMAINING**

BALLET INTRODUCED TO THE US: ANNIVERSARY. Feb 7, 1827. Renowned French danseuse Mme Francisquy Hutin introduced ballet to the US with a performance of *The Deserter*, staged at the Bowery Theater, New York, NY. A minor scandal erupted when the ladies in the lower boxes left the theater upon viewing the light and scanty attire of Mme Hutin and her troupe.

February 2020	S	M	T	W	T	F	S
							1
	2	3	4	5	6	7	8
	9	10	11	12	13	14	15
	16	17	18	19	20	21	22
	23	24	25	26	27	28	29

BLAKE, EUBIE: BIRTH ANNIVERSARY. Feb 7, 1883. James Hubert "Eubie" Blake, American composer and pianist, writer of nearly 1,000 songs (including "I'm Just Wild About Harry" and "Memories of You"). Born at Baltimore, MD. Recipient of the Presidential Medal of Freedom in 1981. Last professional performance was in January 1982. Died at Brooklyn, NY, five days after his 100th birthday, Feb 12, 1983.

BUBBLE GUM DAY. Feb 7. Imagine being able to chew bubble gum at school while helping a worthy cause! Today children around the world will be doing just that. Kids who donate 50 cents or more get to chew gum at school. The money collected is donated to a charity chosen by the school. Don't forget to get your principal's permission! If your school or business plans to celebrate and is willing to be interviewed by the media, please notify the organizers in advance so that we can match media requests with local celebrations. Annually, the first Friday in February. For info: Ruth Spiro, PO Box 1023, Deerfield, IL 60015. Web: www.bubblegum-day.com.

CHAPLIN'S "TRAMP" DEBUTS: ANNIVERSARY. Feb 7, 1914. Charlie Chaplin, vaudeville star-turned-comedic actor, debuted a new character in *Kid Auto Races at Venice*, a Keystone Studios short released on this date. The mischievous but romantic "Tramp," sporting a tiny mustache, twirling a cane and wearing a little derby, a tight-fitting jacket, baggy trousers and floppy shoes, was an immediate success with audiences. Soon mass-produced Tramp dolls were selling all over the US and the world.

DICKENS, CHARLES: BIRTH ANNIVERSARY. Feb 7, 1812. English novelist, publisher and social critic, born at Portsmouth, England. Among his most successful books: *Oliver Twist*, *The Posthumous Papers of the Pickwick Club*, *A Tale of Two Cities*, *David Copperfield* and *A Christmas Carol*. Died at Gad's Hill, England, June 9, 1870, and was buried at Westminster Abbey.

ELEVENTH AMENDMENT TO US CONSTITUTION (SOVEREIGNTY OF THE STATES): RATIFICATION ANNIVERSARY. Feb 7, 1795. The 11th Amendment to the Constitution was ratified, curbing the powers of the federal judiciary in relation to the states. The amendment reaffirmed the sovereignty of the states by prohibiting suits against them.

GRENADA: INDEPENDENCE DAY. Feb 7. National Day. Commemorates independence from Great Britain in 1974.

LEWIS, SINCLAIR: BIRTH ANNIVERSARY. Feb 7, 1885. American novelist and social critic. Recipient of Nobel Prize for Literature (1930). Among his novels: *Main Street*, *Babbitt* and *It Can't Happen Here*. Born Harry Sinclair Lewis at Sauk Center, MN. Died at Rome, Italy, Jan 10, 1951.

MORE, SIR THOMAS: BIRTH ANNIVERSARY. Feb 7, 1478. Anniversary of the birth of the lawyer, scholar, author, lord chancellor of England, martyr and saint at London, England. Refusing to recognize Henry VIII's divorce from Queen Catherine, the "Man for All Seasons" was found guilty of treason and imprisoned in the Tower of London, Apr 17, 1534. He was beheaded at Tower Hill on July 6, 1535, and his head displayed from Tower Bridge. Canonized in 1935. Memorial observed on June 22.

MURRAY, JAMES AUGUSTUS: BIRTH ANNIVERSARY. Feb 7, 1837. Lexicographer born at Denholm, Roxburghshire, England. Best known as the third editor of the *Oxford English Dictionary*, a post that he took over in 1879. With the goal of compiling a definitive history of the English language from the 12th century on, Murray and his successors sought to define each word and provide an example of how it was used. During his lifetime, Murray, who was primarily self-educated, edited approximately half of the dictionary with the help of several assistants. And after dedicating 40 years to working on the unfinished publication, Murray died on July 26, 1915, at Oxford, Oxfordshire, England, while working on the letter *T*.

NATIONAL BLACK HIV/AIDS AWARENESS DAY. Feb 7. This day was first observed in 1999 as a national response to the growing HIV and AIDS epidemic in African-American communities. Its focus is fourfold: education, testing, treatment and involvement in prevention. Annually, Feb 7.

NATIONAL WEAR RED DAY. Feb 7. During American Heart Month in February, the American Heart Association will focus on women with "Go Red for Women," a national movement about women and cardiovascular disease. Each year cardiovascular diseases claim the lives of nearly 500,000 women. For all of the women you know who have been affected by cardiovascular disease, participate in Wear Red Day. Annually, the first Friday in February. For info: American Heart Assn. Web: www.heart.org or www.goredforwomen.org.

SPACE MILESTONE: *STARDUST* (US). Feb 7, 1999. *Stardust* began its 3-billion-mile journey to collect comet dust on this date. The unmanned mission met up with *Comet Wild-2* on Jan 2, 2004, and returned to Earth on Jan 15, 2006, with a 100-pound canister of comet dust samples. This was the first US mission devoted solely to a comet.

WAVE ALL YOUR FINGERS AT YOUR NEIGHBORS DAY. Feb 7. After all the challenges our neighbors and we have faced, it's time to put it all aside for at least one day. Wave "hello" to everybody and mean it. Annually, Feb 7. (©2006 by WH.) For info: Thomas & Ruth Roy, Wellcat Holidays, 2418 Long Ln, Lebanon, PA 17046. Phone: (717) 279-0184. E-mail: info@wellcat.com. Web: www.wellcat.com.

WILDER, LAURA INGALLS: BIRTH ANNIVERSARY. Feb 7, 1867. One of the 20th century's most beloved, bestselling children's authors, Wilder was born at Lake Pepin, WI. She is known for her *Little House on the Prairie* book series, an autobiographical recollection of coming of age in the American frontier in the 1800s that celebrates the American spirit and independence. Five *Little House* novels were Newbery Honor books, and the series was the basis for the popular eponymous TV shows in the 1970s/'80s. Wilder died Feb 10, 1958, at Mansfield, MO.

🎂 BIRTHDAYS TODAY

Garth Brooks, 58, country singer, born Tulsa, OK, Feb 7, 1962.

Juwan Howard, 47, former basketball player, coach, born Chicago, IL, Feb 7, 1973.

Eddie Izzard, 58, performer, actor ("The Riches"), born Edward John Izzard at Aden, Yemen, Feb 7, 1962.

Tawakkol Karman, 41, women's rights activist, Nobel Peace Prize recipient, born Ta'izz, Yemen, Feb 7, 1979.

Ashton Kutcher, 42, actor ("Two and a Half Men," "That '70s Show," *Jobs, New Year's Eve*), born Cedar Rapids, IA, Feb 7, 1978.

Steve Nash, 46, former basketball player, born Johannesburg, South Africa, Feb 7, 1974.

Chris Rock, 54, actor, comedian, born Brooklyn, NY, Feb 7, 1966.

James Spader, 60, actor ("The Blacklist," "Boston Legal," *Secretary*), born Boston, MA, Feb 7, 1960.

Gay Talese, 88, author (*The Kingdom and the Power, Unto the Sons*), born Ocean City, NJ, Feb 7, 1932.

February 8 — Saturday

DAY 39   **327 REMAINING**

ARIZONA RENAISSANCE FESTIVAL. Feb 8–Mar 29. (Saturdays, Sundays and Presidents' Day only.) Gold Canyon, AZ. Enjoy your best day out in history. Find yourself surrounded by medieval merriment with knights, a king and queen, maidens, mermaids and minstrels. Stroll through 30 acres of amusements, shoppes and nonstop revelry as you join the village celebration. The official sister event to the Robin Hood Festival in Sherwood Forest, England. Est attendance: 265,000. For info: Arizona Renaissance Festival, 12601 E US Hwy 60, Gold Canyon, AZ 85118. Phone: (520) 463-2600. Web: www.renfestinfo.com.

BISHOP, ELIZABETH: BIRTH ANNIVERSARY. Feb 8, 1911. Award-winning poet and author born at Worcester, MA. She published numerous volumes of poetry, including the acclaimed *Geography III* (1976), and during her career received the Pulitzer Prize, National Book Award and National Book Critics Circle Award. Bishop died Oct 6, 1979, at Boston, MA.

BOY SCOUTS OF AMERICA FOUNDED: ANNIVERSARY. Feb 8, 1910. The Boy Scouts of America was founded at Washington, DC, by William Boyce, based on the work of Sir Robert Baden-Powell with the British Boy Scout Association.

CAMEX. Feb 8–11. Ernest N. Morial Convention Center, New Orleans, LA. The only national conference and trade exhibit designed exclusively for collegiate retailers. College store buyers and suppliers gather at CAMEX to preview products to be seen on college campuses in the coming year. Est attendance: 7,000. For info: Natl Assn of College Stores (NACS), 500 E Lorain St, Oberlin, OH 44074. Phone: (800) 622-7498. E-mail: info@nacs.org. Web: www.camex.org or nacs.org.

CHINA, TAIWAN, KOREA: LANTERN FESTIVAL. Feb 8. Traditional Chinese festival falls on the 15th day of the first month of the Chinese lunar calendar year. Lantern processions mark the end of the Chinese New Year holiday season. Date in other countries may differ. See also: "Chinese New Year" (Jan 25).

CHINESE NEW YEAR PARADE IN SAN FRANCISCO. Feb 8. San Francisco, CA. First celebrated in the 1860s. North America's largest Chinese community salutes the Year of the Rat. A crowd favorite is the spectacular 288-foot Golden Dragon ("Gum Lung"). It takes a team of more than 180 men and women from the martial arts group White Crane to carry the Golden Dragon through the streets of San Francisco. Sponsored by Southwest Airlines. For info: Chinese Chamber of Commerce, 730 Sacramento St, San Francisco, CA 94108. Phone: (415) 982-3000. Web: www.chinese-parade.com.

DEAN, JAMES: BIRTH ANNIVERSARY. Feb 8, 1931. American stage, film and television actor who achieved immense popularity during a brief career. Born at Fairmount, IN. Best remembered for his role in *Rebel Without a Cause*. Died in an automobile accident near Cholame, CA, Sept 30, 1955, at age 24.

JAPAN: HARI-KUYO (FESTIVAL OF BROKEN NEEDLES). Feb 8. For Hari-Kuyo, a Needle Mass, observed on Feb 8, women gather their old and broken needles and take them to their temples to offer a prayer of thanks for their hard work. Girls pray to Awashima Myozin (their protecting deity) that their needlework, symbolic of love and marriage, will be good. Girls hope that participation in the Needle Mass will lead to a happy marriage.

LEMMON, JACK: 95th BIRTH ANNIVERSARY. Feb 8, 1925. Stage, screen and television actor, born John Uhler Lemmon III at Boston, MA. Often paired with actor Walter Matthau, he starred in such films as *The Odd Couple, The Fortune Cookie* and *The Front Page*. He was nominated for seven Academy Awards, winning in 1955 for his supporting role in *Mister Roberts* and in 1974 for his leading role in *Save the Tiger*. Other films include *Some Like It Hot, Days of Wine and Roses* and *Grumpy Old Men*. He also starred in television versions of *Inherit the Wind* and *Twelve Angry Men* and won an Emmy in 2000 for the TV movie *Tuesdays with Morrie*. He died at Los Angeles, CA, June 27, 2001.

LOVE MAY MAKE THE WORLD GO 'ROUND, BUT LAUGHTER KEEPS US FROM GETTING DIZZY WEEK. Feb 8–14. 43rd annual. This week is dedicated to Victor Borge's notion that "Laughter is the shortest distance between two people" and Joel Goodman's notion that "Seven days without laughter makes one weak." Here is a chance to lighten your relationships and to reinforce the connection between "heart" and "hearty laughter." Annually, the week leading up to and including Valentine's Day. For info: Joel Goodman, The HUMOR Project, Inc, 10 Madison Ave, Saratoga Springs, NY 12866. Phone: (518) 587-8770. E-mail: info@HumorProject. com. Web: www.HumorProject.com.

MARY, QUEEN OF SCOTS: EXECUTION ANNIVERSARY. Feb 8, 1587. Mary Stuart, the queen regent of Scotland, was beheaded at Fotheringhay, England, after being accused of plotting Queen Elizabeth I's death. Mary, the daughter of James V of Scotland by his second wife, Mary of Guise, was born Dec 7 or 8, 1542, at Linlithgow, Scotland, and became queen a week later upon the death of her father, although she did not begin governing until after her mother's death in 1561. Accused of knowingly marrying the alleged murderer of her second husband, Lord Darnley, she was forced to abdicate in favor of her son (James VI) and fled to England for protection, only to find herself a prisoner for the rest of her life—a victim of Elizabethan political intrigue.

OPERA DEBUT IN THE COLONIES: ANNIVERSARY. Feb 8, 1735. The first opera produced in the colonies was performed at the Courtroom, at Charleston, SC. The opera was *Flora; or the Hob in the Well*, written by Colley Cibber.

PORTLAND, OREGON: BIRTHDAY. Feb 8, 1851. The "City of Roses" was incorporated.

SHERMAN, WILLIAM TECUMSEH: 200th BIRTH ANNIVERSARY. Feb 8, 1820. West-Point educated Union general during the Civil War, Sherman was an early practitioner of psychological warfare, infamous in the South and popular in the North for his "March to the Sea," the invasion of Georgia in 1864 aimed at destroying Southern infrastructure and popular support for the war. While serving as Commanding General of the Army from 1869–1884, he declined the Republican presidential nomination twice but enjoyed a reputation in retirement as a public speaker and writer in defense of the Union cause. His observations in a letter deriding the glories of battle was famously shortened to "war is hell." Born at Lancaster, OH, Sherman died at New York, NY, Feb 14, 1891.

February 2020	S	M	T	W	T	F	S
							1
	2	3	4	5	6	7	8
	9	10	11	12	13	14	15
	16	17	18	19	20	21	22
	23	24	25	26	27	28	29

SLOVENIA: CULTURE DAY. Feb 8. National holiday. Honors France Preseren, Slovenia's national poet, who died Feb 8, 1849.

SPACE MILESTONE: *ARABSAT-1* AND *BRASILSAT-1*: 35th ANNIVERSARY. Feb 8, 1985. League of Arab States and Brazilian communications satellites launched into geosynchronous orbit from Kourou, French Guiana, by the European Space Agency.

VERNE, JULES: BIRTH ANNIVERSARY. Feb 8, 1828. French writer, sometimes called "the father of science fiction," born at Nantes, France. Author of *Around the World in Eighty Days, Twenty Thousand Leagues Under the Sea* and many other novels. Died at Amiens, France, Mar 24, 1905.

🎂 BIRTHDAYS TODAY

Brooke Adams, 71, actress (*Days of Heaven, Invasion of the Body Snatchers*), born New York, NY, Feb 8, 1949.

Seth Green, 46, actor ("Family Guy," "Greg the Bunny," *Austin Powers*), born Overbrook Park, PA, Feb 8, 1974.

John Grisham, 65, author (*The Firm, The Client*), born Jonesboro, AR, Feb 8, 1955.

Robert Klein, 78, comedian, actor ("Comedy Tonight," *They're Playing Our Song*), born New York, NY, Feb 8, 1942.

Ted Koppel, 80, journalist, born Lancashire, England, Feb 8, 1940.

Alonzo Mourning, 50, Hall of Fame basketball player, born Chesapeake, VA, Feb 8, 1970.

Nick Nolte, 79, actor (*Affliction; The Prince of Tides; Rich Man, Poor Man*), born Omaha, NE, Feb 8, 1941.

Dawn Olivieri, 39, actress ("House of Lies," "The Vampire Diaries," "Heroes"), born Seminole, FL, Feb 8, 1981.

Mary Steenburgen, 67, actress (Oscar for *Melvin and Howard; Elf, Parenthood, Cross Creek*), born Newport, AR, Feb 8, 1953.

Klay Thompson, 30, basketball player, born Los Angeles, CA, Feb 8, 1990.

John Williams, 88, pianist, conductor (formerly with Boston Pops), composer (Oscars for *Jaws, Star Wars, E.T. The Extraterrestrial* and *Schindler's List*), born New York, NY, Feb 8, 1932.

February 9 — Sunday

DAY 40   **326 REMAINING**

ACADEMY AWARDS PRESENTATION. Feb 9. Dolby Theatre, Hollywood and Highland Center, Los Angeles, CA. 92nd annual. Honoring film achievements of the previous year. Televised live on ABC. For info: Academy of Motion Picture Arts and Sciences, 8949 Wilshire Blvd, Beverly Hills, CA 90211-1972. Phone: (310) 247-3000. Web: www.oscars.org.

ALLIES RETAKE GUADALCANAL: ANNIVERSARY. Feb 9, 1943. In a major strategic victory of WWII, the American 161st and 132nd Regiments retook Guadalcanal in the Solomon Islands on this date

after a six-month-long battle. More than 9,000 Japanese and 2,000 Americans were killed. The fierce resistance by the Japanese was an indication to the Allies of things to come. Guadalcanal put the Allies within striking distance of Rabaul, the major Japanese base in the area.

THE BEATLES APPEAR ON "THE ED SULLIVAN SHOW": ANNIVERSARY. Feb 9, 1964. British pop phenomenon The Beatles began the "British Invasion" of America with their appearance on America's top television variety show. They performed five songs before a screaming studio audience of 728. The estimated viewership for that night's show was 73 million people—making it the most-viewed US TV program in history up to that time. See also: "Beatles Take Over Music Charts" (Apr 4).

BEHAN, BRENDAN: BIRTH ANNIVERSARY. Feb 9, 1923. Playwright (*The Quare Fellow, The Hostage*), poet and author (*Borstal Boy*), born at Dublin, Ireland. Died there Mar 20, 1964.

GYPSY ROSE LEE: BIRTH ANNIVERSARY. Feb 9, 1914. American ecdysiast and author whose real name was Rose Louise Hovick, born at Seattle, WA. Her autobiography, *Gypsy*, was made into a Broadway musical and a motion picture. Died at Los Angeles, CA, Apr 26, 1970.

HARRISON, WILLIAM HENRY: BIRTH ANNIVERSARY. Feb 9, 1773. Ninth president of the US (Mar 4–Apr 4, 1841). His term of office was the shortest in America's history—30½ days. He was the first president to die in office and the last to have been born a British subject. As a military officer, he gained hero status for his leadership in the Battle of Tippecanoe (1811) and the Battle of the Thames (1813). His famous campaign slogan was "Tippecanoe and Tyler, Too." Born at Berkeley, VA, he died at Washington, DC, Apr 4, 1841. His grandson, Benjamin Harrison, was the 23rd president of the US.

INTERNATIONAL FLIRTING WEEK. Feb 9–15. Celebrating the ancient art of flirting and recognizing the role it plays in the lives of singles seeking a mate, couples looking to sustain their love and those simply exchanging a playful glance with a stranger, acquaintance, colleague, etc. For info: Robin Gorman Newman, 44 Somerset Dr N, Great Neck, NY 11020. Phone: (516) 773-0911. E-mail: rgnewman@optonline.net. Web: www.lovecoach.com.

LEBANON: SAINT MARON'S DAY. Feb 9. Holiday of Lebanon's Maronite Christian community. Saint Maron was a Syrian hermit of the fourth–fifth centuries.

LOVE A MENSCH WEEK. Feb 9–15. Mensches are decent, responsible men or women. During this week, singles look to meet a mensch as well as take time to appreciate how mensches enhance our lives. For info: Robin Gorman Newman, 44 Somerset Dr N, Great Neck, NY 11020. Phone: (516) 773-0911. E-mail: rgnewman@optonline.net. Web: www.lovecoach.com.

LOWELL, AMY: BIRTH ANNIVERSARY. Feb 9, 1874. American imagist poet, critic and editor, born at Brookline, MA. Awarded the 1926 Pulitzer Prize (posthumously) for *What O'Clock*. She died at Brookline May 12, 1925.

MAN DAY. Feb 9. A day for celebration by friends, family and associates of the men of the world. Annually, the Sunday before Valentine's Day. (©2002 C. Daniel Rhodes.) For info: C. Daniel Rhodes,

1900 Crossvine Rd, Hoover, AL 35244. Phone: (205) 908-6781. E-mail: rhodan@charter.net.

MOON PHASE: FULL MOON. Feb 9. Moon enters Full Moon phase at 2:33 AM, EST.

NATIONAL PIZZA DAY. Feb 9. A day to celebrate America's favorite pie. The first known pizzeria opened in Naples, Italy, in 1738 as a snack stall serving mostly working-class residents. Pizza has since become a worldwide favorite, with pizzerias and Italian pizza and pasta restaurants comprising 14 percent of all US restaurants. Many pizza parlors offer special deals on this day. Annually, Feb 9.

READ IN THE BATHTUB DAY. Feb 9. Set aside a day each year to be spent in the bathtub reading a novel. (Created by Christine Rogers.)

RUSK, (DAVID) DEAN: BIRTH ANNIVERSARY. Feb 9, 1909. US diplomat Dean Rusk was born at Cherokee County, GA. He served as US secretary of state from 1961 to 1969, during which time he supported US involvement in the Vietnam War. He died Dec 20, 1994, at Athens, GA.

SNOW MOON. Feb 9. So called by Native American tribes of New England and the Great Lakes because this time of year sees heavy snowfalls. Also called the Hunger Moon, because of the meager hunting at this time of winter. The February Full Moon.

TUBB, ERNEST: BIRTH ANNIVERSARY. Feb 9, 1914. Country and western singer, born at Crisp, TX. Ernest Tubb was the sixth member to be elected to the Country Music Hall of Fame and the headliner on the first country music show ever to be presented at Carnegie Hall. His first major hit, "Walking the Floor over You," gained him his first appearance at the Grand Ole Opry in 1942, and he attained regular membership in 1943. He died Sept 6, 1984, at Nashville, TN.

UNION OFFICERS ESCAPE LIBBY PRISON: ANNIVERSARY. Feb 9, 1864. On this date 109 Union officers escaped from Libby Prison at Richmond, VA, in the largest and most dramatic prisoner of war escape of the Civil War. The Libby Prison was the former Libby and Sons candle factory. Forty-eight of the men were recaptured, two drowned and fifty-nine successfully made it back to Federal lines.

VEECK, BILL: BIRTH ANNIVERSARY. Feb 9, 1914. William Louis (Bill) Veeck, Jr, Baseball Hall of Fame executive born at Chicago, IL. Veeck was baseball's premier promoter and showman as an owner of several teams. He integrated the American League and sought to provide fans with entertainment in addition to baseball. Inducted into the Hall of Fame in 1991. Died at Chicago, Jan 2, 1986.

BIRTHDAYS TODAY

Mia Farrow, 75, actress ("Peyton Place," *Rosemary's Baby, Hannah and Her Sisters*), born Maria de Lourdes Villers at Los Angeles, CA, Feb 9, 1945.

Vladimir Guerrero, 44, Hall of Fame baseball player, born Nizao Bani, Dominican Republic, Feb 9, 1976.

Tom Hiddleston, 39, actor ("The Night Manager," *Kong, The Avengers, Thor*), born London, England, Feb 9, 1981.

Jay Inslee, 69, Governor of Washington (D), born Seattle, WA, Feb 9, 1951.

Michael B. Jordan, 33, actor (*Black Panther, Creed, Fruitvale Station*), born Santa Ana, CA, Feb 9, 1987.

Carole King, 78, singer, songwriter, born Brooklyn, NY, Feb 9, 1942.

Judith Light, 71, actress ("Ugly Betty," "One Life to Live," "Who's the Boss?"), born Trenton, NJ, Feb 9, 1949.

Roger Mudd, 92, journalist, born Washington, DC, Feb 9, 1928.

Jameer Nelson, 38, basketball player, born Chester, PA, Feb 9, 1982.

Joe Pesci, 77, actor (*Raging Bull, Goodfellas, My Cousin Vinny*), born Newark, NJ, Feb 9, 1943.

Gerhard Richter, 88, artist (*Abstraktes Bild*), born Dresden, Germany, Feb 9, 1932.

Shakira, 43, singer, television personality ("The Voice"), born Shakira Isabelle Mebarak Ripoll at Barranquilla, Colombia, Feb 9, 1977.

Charles Shaughnessy, 65, actor ("Days of Our Lives," "The Nanny"), born London, England, Feb 9, 1955.

Mena Suvari, 41, actress (*American Beauty, Loser*), born Newport, RI, Feb 9, 1979.

Janet Suzman, 81, actress (*Nicholas and Alexandra, A Dry White Season*), born Johannesburg, South Africa, Feb 9, 1939.

Travis Tritt, 57, country singer, born Marietta, GA, Feb 9, 1963.

Alice Walker, 76, author (*The Color Purple*), born Eatonton, GA, Feb 9, 1944.

Ziyi Zhang, 41, actress (*Crouching Tiger, Hidden Dragon; House of Flying Daggers*), born Beijing, China, Feb 9, 1979.

February 10 — Monday

DAY 41   **325 REMAINING**

"ALL THE NEWS THAT'S FIT TO PRINT": ANNIVERSARY. Feb 10, 1897. The familiar slogan "All the News That's Fit to Print" has appeared on page one of the *New York Times* since Feb 10, 1897. It had first appeared on the editorial page on Oct 25, 1896. Although in 1896 a $100 prize was offered for a slogan, owner Adolph S. Ochs concluded that his own slogan was best.

ANDERSON, DAME JUDITH: BIRTH ANNIVERSARY. Feb 10, 1898. Film and stage actress born Frances Margaret Anderson at Adelaide, Australia. She was nominated for an Academy Award in 1941 for her role in Alfred Hitchcock's film *Rebecca*. In 1960 she was made Dame Commander of the Order of the British Empire by Queen Elizabeth II. She died Jan 3, 1992, at Santa Barbara, CA.

BRECHT, BERTOLT: BIRTH ANNIVERSARY. Feb 10, 1898. German playwright, born at Augsburg, Germany. His plays, such as *Mother Courage*, reflect his Marxist and antimilitary worldview. Also wrote *The Threepenny Opera* in collaboration with composer Kurt Weill. Died at East Berlin, Aug 14, 1956.

"BRIDGE OF SPIES" PRISONER SWAP: ANNIVERSARY. Feb 10, 1962. In the first prisoner exchange of the Cold War, U-2 spy plane pilot Francis Gary Powers (imprisoned in the USSR for espionage) and graduate student Frederic Power of the US were swapped for Soviet spy Vilyam Fisher (known as Rudolf Abel) on the Glienicke Bridge at Berlin, Germany. The bridge, later termed the "Bridge of Spies" by the media for being the locale of many later such swaps, spanned the Havel River and at the time connected West Berlin and East Germany—a Soviet satellite.

***DEATH OF A SALESMAN* PREMIERE: ANNIVERSARY.** Feb 10, 1949. Arthur Miller's postwar dramatic masterpiece opened at Broadway's Morosco Theater on this day. Elia Kazan was the director, and Lee J. Cobb (Willy Loman), Arthur Kennedy (Biff) and Cameron Mitchell (Happy) starred. The play garnered six Tony Awards and was also awarded the 1949 Pulitzer Prize for Drama.

DURANTE, JIMMY: BIRTH ANNIVERSARY. Feb 10, 1893. "The Schnozz," Jimmy Durante, was born at New York City. His break into show biz came when he was 17 and got a regular job playing ragtime at a saloon at Coney Island. Later his friend Eddie Cantor urged him to try comedy. Durante developed a unique comedic style as a short-tempered but lovable personage. His shtick included slamming down his hat and flapping his arms. His clothing, enormous nose, craggy face, gravelly singing voice and mispronunciations were all part of the persona. Durante, whose career spanned six decades, appeared on TV, stage and screen. His television sign-off, "Good night, Mrs Calabash, wherever you are!" became a trademark. Jimmy Durante died at Santa Monica, CA, Jan 29, 1980.

FIRST COMPUTER CHESS VICTORY OVER HUMAN: ANNIVERSARY. Feb 10, 1996. IBM's Deep Blue computer defeated world champion Garry Kasparov in 34 moves on this date in Philadelphia, PA—the first such victory by a computer in tournament conditions. Kasparov, however, went on to win the tournament, defeating the computer three times (the other two matches were draws). In May 1997, in a six-game rematch, Deep Blue emerged the overall victor. Deep Blue, an RS/6000 supercomputer, can evaluate 200 million chess positions a second but is not capable of using artificial intelligence to "learn." Kasparov was reigning World Chess Champion from 1985 to 2000.

FIRST WORLD WAR II MEDAL OF HONOR: ANNIVERSARY. Feb 10, 1942. Second Lieutenant Alexander Ramsey "Sandy" Nininger, Jr, was posthumously awarded WWII's first Medal of Honor for heroism at the Battle of Bataan. He had graduated from West Point in 1941 and was on his first assignment after being commissioned.

FREELANCE WRITERS APPRECIATION WEEK. Feb 10–15. Freelance writers do more than query editors and write and submit articles and books (nonfiction and fiction). They provide overworked editors with material, as well as inform and entertain readers. Annually, the second week in February. For info: Dorothy Zjawin, 61 W Colfax Ave, Roselle Park, NJ 07204.

LAMB, CHARLES: BIRTH ANNIVERSARY. Feb 10, 1775. Literary critic, poet and essayist, born at London, England. "The greatest pleasure I know," he wrote in 1834, "is to do a good action by stealth, and to have it found out by accident." Died at Edmonton, England, Dec 27, 1834.

MALTA: FEAST OF SAINT PAUL'S SHIPWRECK. Feb 10. Valletta. Holy day of obligation. Commemorates the shipwreck of Saint Paul on the north coast of Malta in AD 60.

PASTERNAK, BORIS LEONIDOVICH: BIRTH ANNIVERSARY. Feb 10, 1890. Foremost poet and writer of the Soviet era, Pasternak was born at Moscow, Russia. While renowned for his translations, particularly of Goethe, Rilke, Shakespeare, Keats and Shelley, Pasternak is best known for his capstone novel *Dr. Zhivago*. The novel follows the eponymous protagonist's personal conflicts during the emergence of the Soviet Union; it was banned in Soviet Russia until 1987 for its perceived critique of the October Revolution and Soviet governance. Awarded the Nobel Prize for Literature in 1958, Pasternak was forced to decline the award due to significant opposition in the USSR. Officially scorned in his homeland, Pasternak died in isolation, May 30, 1960, at Peredelkino, Russia.

PLIMSOLL DAY (SAMUEL PLIMSOLL BIRTH ANNIVERSARY). Feb 10, 1824. A day to remember Samuel Plimsoll, "the Sailor's Friend," a coal merchant–turned–reformer and politician, who was elected to the British parliament in 1868. He attacked the practice of

February	S	M	T	W	T	F	S
							1
2020	2	3	4	5	6	7	8
	9	10	11	12	13	14	15
	16	17	18	19	20	21	22
	23	24	25	26	27	28	29

overloading heavily insured ships, calling them "coffin ships." His persistence brought about amendment of Britain's Merchant Shipping Act. The Plimsoll Line, named for him, is a line on the side of ships marking maximum load allowed by law. Born at Bristol, England; died at Folkestone, England, June 3, 1898.

TILDEN, BILL: BIRTH ANNIVERSARY. Feb 10, 1893. William Tatem (Bill) Tilden, Jr, tennis player, born at Philadelphia, PA. Generally considered one of the greatest players of all time, Tilden won more tournaments than the record books can count. A nearly flawless player, he was also an egotistical showman on the court with an interest in show business. He turned pro in 1930 and continued to win regularly. Died at Hollywood, CA, June 5, 1953.

TREATY OF PARIS ENDS FRENCH AND INDIAN WAR: ANNIVERSARY. Feb 10, 1763. Known in Europe as the Seven Years' War, this conflict ranged from North America to India, with many European nations involved. In North America, French expansion in the Ohio River Valley in the 1750s led to conflict with Great Britain. Some Indians fought alongside the French; a young George Washington fought for the British. As a result of the signing of the Treaty of Paris, France lost all claims to Canada and had to cede Louisiana to Spain. Fifteen years later, bitterness over the loss of its North American colonies to Britain contributed to France's supporting the colonists in the American Revolution.

TU B'SHVAT. Feb 10. Hebrew calendar date: Shebat 15, 5780. The 15th day of the month of Shebat in the Hebrew calendar year is set aside as Hamishah Asar (New Year of the Trees, or Jewish Arbor Day), a time to show respect and appreciation for trees and plants. Began at sundown on Feb 9.

TWENTY-FIFTH AMENDMENT TO US CONSTITUTION RATIFIED (PRESIDENTIAL SUCCESSION, DISABILITY): ANNIVERSARY. Feb 10, 1967. Procedures for presidential succession were further clarified by the 25th Amendment, along with provisions for continuity of power in the event of a disability or illness of the president.

UNITED NATIONS: WORLD PULSES DAY. Feb 10. First observed in 2019. Following the success of the International Year of Pulses 2016, World Pulses Day was created (Res 73/251) to heighten public awareness of the nutritional benefits of eating pulses. Pulses are more than just nutritious seeds—they contribute to sustainable food systems. Annually, Feb 10. For info: United Nations. Web: www.un.org or www.fao.org/world-pulses-day.

WESTMINSTER KENNEL CLUB DOG SHOW. Feb 10–11. Madison Square Garden, New York, NY. 144th annual. Established in 1877, the Westminster Kennel Club is America's oldest organization dedicated to the sport of purebred dogs. Westminster's influence has been felt for more than a century through its famous all-breed, benched dog show held annually at New York City's Madison Square Garden. Today, America's dog show has expanded into Westminster Week, which also includes the Agility Championship (Feb 8). More than 3,000 dogs from the US and abroad make Westminster Week like no other. For info: Westminster Kennel Club, 149 Madison Ave, Ste 402, New York, NY 10016. Web: westminsterkennelclub.org.

🎂 BIRTHDAYS TODAY

Elizabeth Banks, 46, actress (*The Hunger Games*, "30 Rock," "Scrubs"), born Pittsfield, MA, Feb 10, 1974.

Jim Cramer, 65, financial analyst, television personality ("Mad Money with Jim Cramer"), born Wyndmoor, PA, Feb 10, 1955.

Laura Dern, 53, actress (*Wild, Blue Velvet, Rambling Rose*), born Los Angeles, CA, Feb 10, 1967.

Donovan, 74, singer, songwriter, born Donovan P. Leitch at Glasgow, Scotland, Feb 10, 1946.

Leonard Kyle (Lenny) Dykstra, 57, former baseball player, born Santa Ana, CA, Feb 10, 1963.

Roberta Flack, 81, singer, born Black Mountain, NC, Feb 10, 1939.

Justin Gatlin, 38, sprinter, born Brooklyn, NY, Feb 10, 1982.

Keeley Hawes, 44, actress ("The Durrells," "Bodyguard," "Ashes to Ashes," "Spooks," *The Bank Job*), born London, England, Feb 10, 1976.

Frances Moore Lappé, 76, author (*Diet for a Small Planet, Rediscovering America's Values*), born Pendleton, OR, Feb 10, 1944.

Chloe Grace Moretz, 23, actress (*Let Me In, Dark Shadows, Hugo*), born Atlanta, GA, Feb 10, 1997.

Gregory John (Greg) Norman, 65, golfer, born Melbourne, Australia, Feb 10, 1955.

Leontyne Price, 93, opera singer, born Laurel, MS, Feb 10, 1927.

Mark Andrew Spitz, 70, Olympic swimmer, born Modesto, CA, Feb 10, 1950.

Robert Wagner, 90, actor (*Austin Powers, The Pink Panther*, "It Takes a Thief," "Hart to Hart"), born Detroit, MI, Feb 10, 1930.

February 11 — Tuesday

DAY 42   **324 REMAINING**

BOCUSE, PAUL: BIRTH ANNIVERSARY. Feb 11, 1926. Bocuse, named "chef of the century" by the Culinary Institute of America in 2011, was born at Collonges-au-Mont-d'Or, near Lyon, France. As a leading figure in nouvelle cuisine, Bocuse became one of the world's biggest celebrity chefs in the 1960s and '70s, stressing fresh ingredients, lighter sauces, unusual flavor combinations and radical innovation—such as lobster mousse stuffed sea bass encased in pastry scales and fins. His restaurant in Lyon, L'Auberge du Pont de Collonges, rates three Michelin stars. The Bocuse d'Or, the biennial cooking competition he founded in 1987, is regarded as the culinary equivalent of the Olympics. Bocuse died Jan 20, 2018, age 91, at Collonges-au-Mont-d'Or, in the same bedroom where he was born.

CAMEROON: YOUTH DAY. Feb 11. Public holiday.

CHILD, LYDIA MARIA: BIRTH ANNIVERSARY. Feb 11, 1802. Writer whose works include *Hobomok*, about early Salem and Plymouth life, and *The Rebels*, which describes pre-Revolutionary Boston. In addition, she produced several practical works, including *The Frugal Housewife*, which enjoyed 21 editions, and *The Mother's Book*. In 1833 she and her husband, David Lee Child, published the controversial abolitionist document "An Appeal in Favor of That Class of Americans Called Africans," which called for educating slaves. Their work for abolition continued with the weekly newspaper *The National Anti-Slavery Standard*, which they published at New York City during 1840–44. Born at Medford, MA, Child died Oct 20, 1880, at Wayland, MA.

EDISON, THOMAS ALVA: BIRTH ANNIVERSARY. Feb 11, 1847. American inventive genius and holder of more than 1,200 patents (including the incandescent electric lamp, the phonograph, the electric dynamo and key parts of many now-familiar devices such as the movie camera and the telephone transmitter). Edison said, "Genius is 1 percent inspiration and 99 percent perspiration." His birthday is now widely observed as Inventor's Day. Born at Milan, OH, and died at Menlo Park, NJ, Oct 18, 1931.

EXTRATERRESTRIAL CULTURE DAY. Feb 11. A day "to celebrate and honor all past, present and future extraterrestrial visitors in ways to enhance relationships among all citizens of the cosmos, known and unknown." Originally passed as a memorial (not law) by the New Mexico state legislature to acknowledge that ever since the Roswell UFO incident of 1947, New Mexico has been recognized

worldwide as a nexus of sightings and unexplained mysteries. Annually, the second Tuesday in February.

FIRST WOMAN EPISCOPAL BISHOP: ANNIVERSARY. Feb 11, 1989. The presiding bishop of the Episcopal Church, Bishop Edmond L. Browning, consecrated the Reverend Barbara Clementine Harris as a bishop of the Episcopal Church.

"THE FRENCH CHEF" TV PREMIERE: ANNIVERSARY. Feb 11, 1963. Beginning on this date, Julia Child demystified French cooking and entertained viewers as "The French Chef" on WGBH-TV, Boston, MA. The show was a great success in syndication on PBS stations, and Child filmed 200 programs—always with her trademark trilling voice and at times slapping around the poultry—signing off with a cheery "Bon appétit!" Child's show, along with her book *Mastering the Art of French Cooking* (1961, authored with Simone Beck and Louisette Bertholle), are credited with awakening Americans to the joy of continental cuisine. See also: "Child, Julia: Birth Anniversary" (Aug 15).

FULLER, MELVILLE WESTON: BIRTH ANNIVERSARY. Feb 11, 1833. Eighth chief justice of the US. Born at Augusta, ME, he died at Sorrento, ME, July 4, 1910.

GET OUT YOUR GUITAR DAY. Feb 11. 8th annual. Chances are today is a cold, gloomy day—so get out your guitar. If your guitar (or other instrument) has been put away for a while, this is the day to take it out and play it. For info: Arthur Bargar. E-mail: abargar@hotmail.com.

IRAN: VICTORY OF ISLAMIC REVOLUTION. Feb 11. National holiday. Commemorates the revolution that overthrew the shah in 1979.

JAPAN: NATIONAL FOUNDATION DAY. Feb 11. Marks the founding of the Japanese nation. In 1872 the government officially set Feb 11, 660 BC, as the date of accession to the throne of the Emperor Jimmu (said to be Japan's first emperor) and designated the day Empire Day, a national holiday. The holiday was abolished after WWII but was revived as National Foundation Day in 1966. Ceremonies are held with Their Imperial Majesties the Emperor and Empress, the prime minister and other dignitaries attending.

MANDELA, NELSON: PRISON RELEASE: 30th ANNIVERSARY. Feb 11, 1990. After serving more than 27 years of a life sentence (convicted, with eight others, of sabotage and conspiracy to overthrow the government), South Africa's Nelson Mandela, 71 years old, walked away from the Victor Verster prison farm at Paarl, South Africa, a free man. He had survived the governmental system of apartheid. Mandela greeted a cheering throng of well-wishers, along with hundreds of millions of television viewers worldwide, with demands for an intensification of the struggle for equality for blacks, who make up nearly 75 percent of South Africa's population.

MANKIEWICZ, JOSEPH L.: BIRTH ANNIVERSARY. Feb 11, 1909. Oscar-winning American film writer, director and producer, born at Wilkes-Barre, PA. He coined the famous W.C. Fields phrase "my little chickadee" in his screenplay for the 1932 film *If I Had a Million*. In 1935 he turned to producing and subsequently made *The Philadelphia Story* and *Woman of the Year*. He began directing in 1946, and his stature grew with such films as *The Late George Apley, The Ghost and Mrs Muir, A Letter to Three Wives, All About Eve, Guys and Dolls, Cleopatra* and *Sleuth*. Mankiewicz won four Academy Awards for directing and screenwriting. He died Feb 5, 1993, at Mount Kisco, NY.

NATIONAL SHUT-IN VISITATION DAY. Feb 11. Visit and entertain those unable to leave their homes or residences. Created by the late Monsignor Losito of Reading, PA.

February 2020	S	M	T	W	T	F	S
							1
	2	3	4	5	6	7	8
	9	10	11	12	13	14	15
	16	17	18	19	20	21	22
	23	24	25	26	27	28	29

PRO SPORTS WIVES DAY. Feb 11. This national day of observance will give polite recognition to nearly half a million active and retired sports wives throughout the country for their public service in the estimated $213 billion professional sports industry. Unknown generally to the public, pro sports wives are the household managers and silent partners who keep their favorite athletes motivated, focused and determined to win and create the feeling of being a winner within us all. Annually, Feb 11. For info: Gena Pitts, PSWA, Inc, 11877 Douglas Rd, Ste 102178, Johns Creek, GA 30005-4325. E-mail: info@prosportswives.com. Web: www.prosportswives.com.

REYNOLDS, BURT: BIRTH ANNIVERSARY. Feb 11, 1936. Burton Leon Reynolds, Jr, born at Lansing, MI, and raised in Florida, was one of the top movie stars of the '70s and '80s, whose breakthrough came in 1972's *Deliverance*, the same year he posed for a nude centerfold in *Cosmopolitan*. The actor's box office hits include *Smokey and the Bandit*, football drama *The Longest Yard* and *Cannonball Run*. He showed his range in the movie musical *The Best Little Whorehouse in Texas* and the romantic comedy *Starting Over*. On television he found success, and an Emmy, with the '90s sitcom "Evening Shade." Reynolds earned an Oscar nomination for late-career comeback, *Boogie Nights*. His memoir *But Enough about Me* was published three years before his death on Sept 6, 2018, in Jupiter, FL.

SATISFIED STAYING SINGLE DAY. Feb 11. As Valentine's Day approaches, some single folks would like to point out that they're quite content buying candy and flowers for no one but themselves. Live it up. Shadow dance! (©2006 by WH.) For info: Thomas & Ruth Roy, Wellcat Holidays, 2418 Long Ln, Lebanon, PA 17046. Phone: (717) 279-0184. E-mail: info@wellcat.com. Web: www.well-cat.com.

SHELDON, SIDNEY: BIRTH ANNIVERSARY. Feb 11, 1917. Writer, born Sidney Schectel at Chicago, IL. After his college years at Northwestern University, he moved to Hollywood and found work as a screenwriter. B movies led to Broadway musicals, and by the mid-1940s he was one of the most prolific and successful writers of his generation. He earned an Academy Award for *The Bachelor and the Bobby Soxer* in 1947 and a Tony Award for *Redhead* in 1959. He also wrote for television, creating several successful series, including "The Patty Duke Show" and "I Dream of Jeannie." In 1969 he moved to writing novels and shortly became one of the bestselling novelists in history, as titles such as *Rage of Angels, Windmills of the Gods* and *The Other Side of Midnight* were translated into 51 languages, adapted as made-for-TV movies and in all sold more than 300 million copies. He died at Rancho Mirage, CA, Jan 30, 2007.

SPACE MILESTONE: *ENDEAVOUR* MAPPING MISSION (US): 20th ANNIVERSARY. Feb 11, 2000. This manned flight spent 11 days in space creating a 3-D map of more than 70 percent of Earth's surface—the most accurate and complete topographic map of Earth ever produced.

SPACE MILESTONE: FIRST SOVIET COMMERCIAL SATELLITE MISSION. Feb 11, 1990. Anatoly Solovyov and Aleksandr Balandin departed the Baikonur launching site on the Soviet Union's first satellite mission designed for profit—by producing industrial crystals in the weightlessness of space. The craft arrived at the *Mir* orbital space station on Feb 13. Launching of the *Soyuz TM-9* capsule was witnessed by four American astronauts and televised live. The mission was hailed as initiating a new level of openness of information about Soviet space projects.

SPACE MILESTONE: *OSUMI* (JAPAN). Feb 11, 1970. First Japanese satellite launched. Japan became the fourth nation to send a satellite into space.

UNITED NATIONS: INTERNATIONAL DAY OF WOMEN AND GIRLS IN SCIENCE. Feb 11. On Dec 22, 2015 (Res 70/212), the General Assembly designated Feb 11 as an international day urging "commitment to end bias, greater investments in science, technology, engineering and math education for all women and girls as well as opportunities for their careers and longer-term professional advancement so that all can benefit from their ground-breaking future contributions." For info: United Nations, Dept of Public Info, New York, NY 10017. Web: www.un.org.

VATICAN CITY: INDEPENDENCE ANNIVERSARY. Feb 11, 1929. The Lateran Treaty, signed by Pietro Cardinal Gasparri and Benito Mussolini, guaranteed the independence of the State of Vatican City and recognized the sovereignty of the Holy See over it. Area is about 109 acres.

WHITE SHIRT DAY: ANNIVERSARY. Feb 11, 1937. Anniversary of UAW-GM agreement following 44-day sit-down strike at General Motors' Flint, MI, factories. Blue-collar workers traditionally wear white shirts to work on this day, symbolic of workingman's dignity won. Has been observed by proclamation at Flint.

WORLD AG EXPO. Feb 11–13. Tulare, CA. 53rd annual. Attendees and exhibitors from all over the United States and around the world come to the show grounds to join in the largest annual outdoor agricultural expo in the world, which spans more than 2.6 million square feet of exhibit space. Est attendance: 106,000. For info: World Ag Expo, International Agri Center, 4500 S Laspina St, Tulare, CA 93274. Phone: (800) 999-9186 or (559) 688-1030. E-mail: info@farmshow.org. Web: www.worldagexpo.com.

YALTA AGREEMENT SIGNED: 75th ANNIVERSARY. Feb 11, 1945. President Franklin D. Roosevelt, British prime minister Winston Churchill and Soviet leader Joseph Stalin signed an agreement at Yalta, a Soviet city on the Black Sea in the Crimea. The agreement contained plans for new blows at the heart of Germany and for occupying Germany at the end of the war. It also called for a meeting in San Francisco to draft a charter for the United Nations.

🎂 BIRTHDAYS TODAY

Jennifer Aniston, 51, actress (*Horrible Bosses, Marley & Me, The Good Girl*, "Friends"), born Sherman Oaks, CA, Feb 11, 1969.

Tammy Baldwin, 58, US Senator (D, Wisconsin), born Madison, WI, Feb 11, 1962.

Brandy, 41, singer, actress ("Cinderella," "Moesha"), born Brandy Norwood at McComb, MS, Feb 11, 1979.

Sheryl Crow, 58, singer, musician, born Kennett, MO, Feb 11, 1962.

Natalie Dormer, 38, actress ("Game of Thrones," "The Tudors"), born Reading, England, Feb 11, 1982.

Taylor Lautner, 28, actor (*Twilight*), born Grand Rapids, MI, Feb 11, 1992.

Damian Lewis, 49, actor ("Billions," "Wolf Hall," "Homeland"), born St. John's Wood, Westminster, England, Feb 11, 1971.

Tina Louise, 86, actress ("Gilligan's Island," *The Stepford Wives*), born New York, NY, Feb 11, 1934.

Carey Lowell, 59, actress ("Law & Order," *Licence to Kill*), born New York, NY, Feb 11, 1961.

Sergio Mendes, 79, musician, bandleader, born Niteroi, Brazil, Feb 11, 1941.

Sarah Palin, 56, 2008 vice presidential candidate, former governor of Alaska (R), television personality, born Sandpoint, ID, Feb 11, 1964.

February 12 — Wednesday

DAY 43   **323 REMAINING**

ADAMS, LOUISA CATHERINE JOHNSON: BIRTH ANNIVERSARY. Feb 12, 1775. Wife of John Quincy Adams, sixth president of the US. Born at London, England. Died at Washington, DC, May 14, 1852.

BENEKE, "TEX": BIRTH ANNIVERSARY. Feb 12, 1914. Popular big band–era tenor saxophonist and vocalist, born Gordon Beneke at Fort Worth, TX. A member of Glenn Miller's band (Miller dubbed Beneke "Tex"), he was voted most popular sax player in 1941 and 1942 by music journalists. After Miller's WWII death, Beneke became leader of the Glenn Miller Orchestra, then eventually headed his own Tex Beneke and His Orchestra. Best known for vocals (with Miller) for "I've Got a Gal in Kalamazoo" and "Chattanooga Choo Choo"—the latter a million-copy hit. Beneke died at Costa Mesa, CA, May 30, 2000.

DANA, JAMES DWIGHT: BIRTH ANNIVERSARY. Feb 12, 1813. Geologist, naturalist, author, explorer born at New Utica, NY. Made important contributions to the understanding of mountain building, volcanic activity, ocean basins, coral reefs, mineralogy and more. Was the preeminent American geologist of his time, although illness shadowed his career. Among other honors, was awarded the Copley Medal by the Royal Society in 1877. Dana died Apr 14, 1895, at New Haven, CT.

DARWIN, CHARLES ROBERT: BIRTH ANNIVERSARY. Feb 12, 1809. Author and naturalist, born at Shrewsbury, England. Best remembered for his books *On the Origin of Species by Means of Natural Selection, or the Preservation of Favoured Races in the Struggle for Life* and *The Descent of Man, and Selection in Relation to Sex*. Died at Down, Kent, England, Apr 19, 1882.

DARWIN DAY. Feb 12. Darwin Day is an international celebration of science and humanity. Events are coordinated around the world to commemorate the life and work of Charles Darwin and the theory of evolution by natural selection and to recognize the contributions and achievements of science and reason. On a broad scale, the program is an effort to advance science literacy, champion the efforts to humanize science and celebrate the adventurous spirit. Events are held on or near Feb 12, the anniversary of Darwin's birth. For info: International Darwin Day Foundation and American Humanist Association. E-mail: darwinday@americanhumanist.org. Web: https://americanhumanist.org/what-we-do/darwin-day.

DRACULA PREMIERE: ANNIVERSARY. Feb 12, 1931. The horror film classic starring Bela Lugosi premiered on this day at the Roxy Theatre in New York City. It had been slated to premiere on Friday, Feb 13, but director Tod Browning, confessing to a superstitious nature, asked for the opening to be moved up a day. *Dracula* made the Hungarian actor Lugosi a star, but at a price: he was offered only horror film roles the rest of his career.

HARRIS, ROY: BIRTH ANNIVERSARY. Feb 12, 1898. Born at Chandler, OK, Harris was one of the most important composers of the 20th century. He was known for his use of Anglo-American folk tunes. He composed more than 200 works, including 13 symphonies, several ballet scores and much chamber and choral music. His best-known work is his Third Symphony (1939). He died at Santa Monica, CA, Oct 1, 1979.

LEWIS, JOHN LLEWELLYN: BIRTH ANNIVERSARY. Feb 12, 1880. American labor leader, born near Lucas, IA. His parents came to the US from Welsh mining towns, and Lewis left school in the seventh grade to become a miner himself. Became leader of United Mine Workers of America and champion of all miners' causes. Died at Washington, DC, June 11, 1969.

LINCOLN, ABRAHAM: BIRTH ANNIVERSARY. Feb 12, 1809. 16th president of the US (Mar 4, 1861–Apr 15, 1865) and the first to be assassinated (on Good Friday, Apr 14, 1865, at Ford's Theatre at Washington, DC). His presidency encompassed the tragic Civil War. Especially remembered are his Emancipation Proclamation (Jan 1, 1863), his Gettysburg Address (Nov 19, 1863) and his proclamation establishing the last Thursday of November as Thanksgiving Day. Born at Hardin County, KY, he died at Washington, DC, Apr 15, 1865. Lincoln's birthday is observed as part of Presidents' Day in many states but is a legal holiday in Illinois on Feb 12. See also: "Presidents' Day" (Feb 17).

LINCOLN'S BIRTHPLACE CABIN WREATH LAYING. Feb 12. Abraham Lincoln Birthplace National Historical Park, Hodgenville, KY. A wreath is placed at the door of the symbolic "Birthplace Cabin" in commemoration of the birth of Abraham Lincoln. For info: Abraham Lincoln Birthplace NHP, 2995 Lincoln Farm Rd, Hodgenville, KY 42748. Phone: (270) 358-3137. Web: www.nps.gov/abli.

MATHER, COTTON: BIRTH ANNIVERSARY. Feb 12, 1663. Puritan minister, scholar and author born at Boston, MA. With his father, Increase Mather, he led a congregation at Old North Church. A staunch believer in mystical forces, he published *Wonders of the Invisible World* in 1692—a treatise supporting the prosecution of the Salem "witches." The last of a Puritan dynasty, Mather died Feb 13, 1728, at Boston.

MYANMAR: UNION DAY. Feb 12. National holiday. Commemorates the founding of the Union of Burma, Feb 12, 1947. The country changed its name to Union of Myanmar in 1989.

NAACP FOUNDED: ANNIVERSARY. Feb 12, 1909. The National Association for the Advancement of Colored People was founded by W.E.B. Du Bois and Ida Wells-Barnett, among others, to wage a militant campaign against lynching and other forms of racial oppression. Its legal wing brought many lawsuits that successfully challenged segregation in the 1950s and '60s.

OGLETHORPE DAY. Feb 12. General James Edward Oglethorpe (born at London, England, Dec 22, 1696), with some 100 other Englishmen, landed at what is now Savannah, GA, on Feb 12, 1733. Naming the new colony Georgia for England's King George II, Oglethorpe was organizer and first governor of the colony and founder of the city of Savannah. Oglethorpe Day and Georgia Day observed on this date.

PAVLOVA, ANNA: BIRTH ANNIVERSARY. Feb 12, 1881. Russian ballerina Anna Pavlova, thought by some to have been the greatest dancer of all time, was born at St. Petersburg, Russia. After performing with much success with the Ballet Russe and other companies, she formed her own company in 1910 and performed on tour for enthusiastic audiences in nearly every country in the world. Pavlova died at The Hague, Netherlands, Jan 23, 1931.

SAFETYPUP®'S BIRTHDAY. Feb 12. This year Safetypup®, created by the National Child Safety Council, joyously celebrates his birthday by bringing safety awareness/educational messages to children and their parents in a positive, nonthreatening manner. Age-appropriate

materials available through local law enforcement departments on topics including bike safety, drug abuse prevention, child abduction prevention and bullying. For info: NCSC, Box 1368, Jackson, MI 49204-1368. Phone: (517) 764-6070. Web: www.nationalchildsafety-council.org.

SENATE ACQUITS CLINTON: ANNIVERSARY. Feb 12, 1999. After President William Clinton was impeached by the US House of Representatives, the Senate began a January trial on the charges of perjury and obstruction of justice. On this date the Senate acquitted Clinton. See also: "Clinton Impeachment Proceedings: Anniversary" (Dec 20).

SIMENON, GEORGES: BIRTH ANNIVERSARY. Feb 12, 1903. Simenon was the top bestselling author of the 20th century, selling more than 500 million copies of his novels in more than 50 languages. The prodigious Simenon wrote up to six novels per year, specializing in dark, intellectual crime works. He garnered worldwide acclaim for his Inspector Maigret novels. He also gained worldwide notoriety in 1977 when he claimed to have had sexual relations with at least 10,000 women. Simenon, born at Liège, Belgium, died at Lausanne, France, on Sept 4, 1989.

UTAH WOMEN GIVEN THE VOTE: 150th ANNIVERSARY. Feb 12, 1870. The women in the Utah Territory were granted the right to vote in political elections—50 years before the 19th Amendment was ratified.

🎂 BIRTHDAYS TODAY

Maud Adams, 75, actress (*Killer Force, Octopussy*), born Lulea, Sweden, Feb 12, 1945.

Joe Don Baker, 84, actor (*Charlie Varrick, Cool Hand Luke*), born Groesbeck, TX, Feb 12, 1936.

Ehud Barak, 78, former Israeli prime minister, born Mishmar, Hasharon, Israel, Feb 12, 1942.

Judy Blume, 82, author (*Blubber, Superfudge*), born Elizabeth, NJ, Feb 12, 1938.

Josh Brolin, 52, actor (*Deadpool 2, Avengers: Infinity War, Sicario, Milk, No Country for Old Men*), born Los Angeles, CA, Feb 12, 1968.

Costa-Gavras, 87, film director (*Z, Missing, Amen*), screenwriter (Oscar with Donald Stewart for *Missing*), born Konstantinos Gavras at Loutra-Iraias, Greece, Feb 12, 1933.

Cliff De Young, 73, actor (*Blue Collar, F/X*), born Inglewood, CA, Feb 12, 1947.

Robert Griffin III, 30, football player, 2011 Heisman Trophy winner, born Okinawa Prefecture, Japan, Feb 12, 1990.

Arsenio Hall, 65, comedian, actor (*Coming to America*), former television talk show host, born Cleveland, OH, Feb 12, 1955.

Brett Kavanaugh, 55, Associate Justice of the United States, born Washington, DC, Feb 12, 1965.

Joanna Kerns, 67, actress ("Growing Pains"), former gymnast, born San Francisco, CA, Feb 12, 1953.

Chynna Phillips, 52, singer (Wilson Phillips), born Los Angeles, CA, Feb 12, 1968.

Christina Ricci, 40, actress ("Z: The Beginning of Everything," *Sleepy Hollow, Ice Storm*), born Santa Monica, CA, Feb 12, 1980.

February 2020	S	M	T	W	T	F	S
							1
	2	3	4	5	6	7	8
	9	10	11	12	13	14	15
	16	17	18	19	20	21	22
	23	24	25	26	27	28	29

William Felton (Bill) Russell, 86, Hall of Fame basketball player and former coach, born Monroe, LA, Feb 12, 1934.

Jesse Spencer, 41, actor ("Chicago Fire," "House"), born Melbourne, Australia, Feb 12, 1979.

Jacqueline Woodson, 57, author (National Book Award for *Brown Girl Dreaming*), National Ambassador for Young People's Literature (2018–19), born Columbus, OH, Feb 12, 1963.

February 13 — Thursday

DAY 44   **322 REMAINING**

AMERICAN ASSOCIATION FOR THE ADVANCEMENT OF SCIENCE ANNUAL MEETING. Feb 13–16. Washington State Convention Center, Seattle, WA. 186th meeting. 2020 theme: "Envisioning Tomorrow's Earth." The 2020 meeting theme focuses on drawing on our current understanding of the world, and bravely experimenting with forward-thinking visions. The scientific community needs to respond with discoveries and developments to help solve many pressing problems. Est attendance: 9,000. For info: AAAS, 1200 New York Ave NW, Washington, DC 20005. Phone: (202) 326-6450. E-mail: meetings@aaas.org. Web: www.aaas.org/meetings.

DRESDEN FIREBOMBING: 75th ANNIVERSARY. Feb 13, 1945. Dresden, Germany. Allied firebombing caused a firestorm that destroyed the city and killed 25,000 people.

EMPLOYEE LEGAL AWARENESS DAY. Feb 13. A day emphasizing the importance of legal education for employees so that large and small businesses reduce their risk of legal problems. For info: Paul Brennan, PO Box 27, Mooloolaba, Queensland 4557, Australia. E-mail: paul.brennan@brennanlaw.com.au.

FIRST MAGAZINE PUBLISHED IN AMERICA: ANNIVERSARY. Feb 13, 1741. (Old Style date.) Andrew Bradford published *The American Magazine* just three days ahead of Benjamin Franklin's *General Magazine*.

FORD, TENNESSEE ERNIE: BIRTH ANNIVERSARY. Feb 13, 1919. The Country Hall of Fame singer, radio personality and actor was born Ernest Jennings Ford at Bristol, TN. On Oct 17, 1955, Capitol Records released his version of "Sixteen Tons"—actually a b side—to tremendous reception: it was Capitol's fastest-selling record ever and sold more than one million copies in less than a month. After popular appearances as "Cousin Ernie" on "I Love Lucy" in 1954, Ford went on to have his own variety show for five years. A recipient of the Presidential Medal of Freedom and a Grammy Award winner for *Great Gospel Songs*, Ford died at Reston, VA, on Oct 17, 1991, the release anniversary of his biggest hit.

GET A DIFFERENT NAME DAY. Feb 13. For the pity of the millions of us who hate our birth names. On this day we may change our names to whatever we wish and have the right to expect colleagues, family and friends to so address us. (©2006 by WH.) For info: Thomas & Ruth Roy, Wellcat Holidays, 2418 Long Ln, Lebanon, PA 17046. Phone: (717) 279-0184. E-mail: info@wellcat.com. Web: www.wellcat.com.

IRWIN EARNS FIRST MEDAL OF HONOR: ANNIVERSARY. Feb 13, 1861. Colonel Bernard Irwin distinguished himself while leading troops in a battle with Chiricahua Apache Indians at Apache Pass, AZ (at that time, part of the territory of New Mexico). For those actions Irwin later became the first person awarded the new US Medal of Honor, although he didn't actually receive it until three years later (Jan 24, 1864).

NATIONAL WINGMAN'S DAY. Feb 13. 5th annual. Wingmen are the unsung, self-sacrificing, supporting actors, the sidekicks, the true heroes who robustly support their friends in the tricky navigation of love. Tomorrow, on Valentine's Day, our lovestruck friends will reap the harvest, while the wingmen will be left to forlornly contemplate the mysteries of the heart. Wingmen everywhere deserve a day of recognition, a day when their hormones can rage

unchecked. On National Wingman's Day, celebrated strategically on Feb 13, the day before Valentine's Day, the wingmen can at last come first. For info: Bruce J. Novotny, PO Box 1270, Bandon, OR 97411. E-mail: novovet@gmail.com.

ROBINSON, EDDIE: BIRTH ANNIVERSARY. Feb 13, 1919. One of the winningest coaches in college football history, born at Jackson, LA. As the head coach at Grambling State University in Grambling, LA, he led the Tigers to more than 400 victories during his 56-year tenure (1941–97). Considered a civil rights pioneer for his leadership in an era when doors were not always open for black athletes, he battled segregation and ultimately sent more than 200 players to the NFL. He was elected to the College Football Hall of Fame immediately upon his retirement in 1997 and was diagnosed with Alzheimer's that same year. He died at Ruston, LA, Apr 3, 2007.

TORK, PETER: BIRTH ANNIVERSARY. Feb 13, 1942. Musician Peter Halsten Thorkelson, born at Washington, DC, became Peter Tork while a banjo player in Greenwich Village's folk music scene of the early '60s. He was cast as the bass player in "The Monkees," a 1966 NBC sitcom about a Beatles-esque pop-rock quartet. The actors' musical ability transcended the program, and the foursome became a real band, writing music, releasing best-selling albums and touring beyond the series' two seasons. Tork left The Monkees in 1969 after their sixth album, but reunited with the band several times over the years. He died Feb 21, 2019, at Mansfield, CT.

TRUMAN, ELIZABETH VIRGINIA (BESS) WALLACE: BIRTH ANNIVERSARY. Feb 13, 1885. Wife of Harry S Truman, 33rd president of the US. Born at Independence, MO, and died there Oct 18, 1982.

WOOD, GRANT: BIRTH ANNIVERSARY. Feb 13, 1891. American artist, especially noted for his powerful realism and satirical paintings of the American scene, born near Anamosa, IA. He was a printer, sculptor, woodworker and high school and college teacher. Among his best-remembered works are *American Gothic, Fall Plowing* and *Stone City*. Died at Iowa City, IA, Feb 12, 1942.

WORLD RADIO DAY. Feb 13. Since 2012, a global observance celebrating radio: why we love it and why we need it today more than ever. A day to remember the unique power of radio to touch lives and bring people together across every corner of the globe. Hundreds of radio stations and media organizations take part in the celebrations—which take place in more than 80 countries on every single continent. Annually, Feb 13. For info: UNESCO, World Radio Day. Web: www.diamundialradio.org.

🎂 BIRTHDAYS TODAY

Richard Blumenthal, 74, US Senator (D, Connecticut), born Brooklyn, NY, Feb 13, 1946.

Stockard Channing, 76, actress (Tony for *Joe Egg*; *Six Degrees of Separation*, *The House of Blue Leaves*, "The West Wing"), born Susan Stockard at New York, NY, Feb 13, 1944.

Peter Gabriel, 70, singer, songwriter, born London, England, Feb 13, 1950.

Kelly Hu, 53, actress ("Martial Law," "Nash Bridges"), born Honolulu, HI, Feb 13, 1967.

Carol Lynley, 78, actress (*Harlow, Bunny Lake Is Missing*), born New York, NY, Feb 13, 1942.

Randy Moss, 43, Hall of Fame football player, born Rand, WV, Feb 13, 1977.

David Naughton, 69, singer, actor (*An American Werewolf in London, Overexposed*), born Hartford, CT, Feb 13, 1951.

Kim Novak, 87, actress (*Bell, Book and Candle*; *Vertigo*), born Marilyn Novak at Chicago, IL, Feb 13, 1933.

George Segal, 86, actor (*A Touch of Class*, "Just Shoot Me"), born Great Neck, NY, Feb 13, 1934.

Jerry Springer, 76, television host ("The Jerry Springer Show"), born London, England, Feb 13, 1944.

Bo Svenson, 79, actor (*North Dallas Forty, Heartbreak Ridge*), born Gothenburg, Sweden, Feb 13, 1941.

Chuck Yeager, 97, pilot who broke sound barrier, born Myra, WV, Feb 13, 1923.

February 14 — Friday

DAY 45   **321 REMAINING**

ALLEN, MEL: BIRTH ANNIVERSARY. Feb 14, 1913. Born Melvin Allen Israel at Birmingham, AL, he began broadcasting baseball and other sporting events for the CBS radio network in 1936. He became the Yankees' lead announcer after World War II and was nationally famous for two phrases: "How about that!" to describe a fine play and "Going, going, gone," his home run call. After being fired by the Yankees in 1963, Allen attracted a new generation of listeners with his weekly television show, "This Week in Baseball." He died at Greenwich, CT, June 16, 1996.

ARIZONA: ADMISSION DAY: ANNIVERSARY. Feb 14. Became 48th state in 1912.

BENNY, JACK: BIRTH ANNIVERSARY. Feb 14, 1894. American comedian. Born Benjamin Kubelsky, Jack Benny entered vaudeville at Waukegan, IL, at age 17, using the violin as a comic stage prop. His radio show first aired in 1932 and continued for 20 years with little change in format. He also had a long-running television show. One of his most well-known comic gimmicks was his purported stinginess. Benny was born at Chicago, IL, and died Dec 26, 1974, at Los Angeles, CA.

BULGARIA: VITICULTURISTS' DAY (TRIFON ZAREZAN). Feb 14. Celebrated since Thracian times. Festivities are based on the cult of Dionysus, god of merriment and wine.

DOUGLASS, FREDERICK: BIRTH ANNIVERSARY. Feb 14, 1818. One of the preeminent social justice activists of the 19th century, Frederick Douglass was born into slavery as Frederick Augustus Washington Bailey in Tuckahoe, MD. His exact birthdate is unknown, although it is widely regarded as sometime in February 1818. Douglass adopted Feb 14 as his birthdate, explaining that his mother called him her "valentine." He escaped slavery in 1838 (after having taught himself to read and write) and changed his surname to Douglass. Many credit the Emancipation Proclamation as well as the passage of the 13th, 14th and 15th Amendments to Douglass's tireless advocacy. Douglass was the first African American to hold several politically appointed US government positions: US marshal of Washington DC, recorder of deeds for Washington, DC, and minister and general counsel to Haiti. After

speaking to the National Council of Women, Douglass suffered a heart attack and died Feb 20, 1895, at Washington, DC.

ENIAC COMPUTER INTRODUCED: ANNIVERSARY. Feb 14, 1946. J. Presper Eckert and John W. Mauchly demonstrated the Electronic Numerical Integrator and Computer (ENIAC) for the first time at the University of Pennsylvania. This was the first electronic digital computer. It occupied a room the size of a gymnasium and contained nearly 18,000 vacuum tubes. The army commissioned the computer to speed the calculation of firing tables for artillery. By the time the computer was ready, WWII was over. However, ENIAC prepared the way for future generations of computers.

FERRIS WHEEL DAY: GEORGE FERRIS'S BIRTH ANNIVERSARY. Feb 14, 1859. Anniversary of the birth of George Washington Gale Ferris, American engineer and inventor, at Galesburg, IL. Among his many accomplishments as a civil engineer, Ferris is best remembered as the inventor of the Ferris wheel, which he developed for the World's Columbian Exposition at Chicago, IL, in 1893. Built on the Midway Plaisance, the 250-foot-diameter Ferris wheel (with 36 coaches, each capable of carrying 40 passengers) proved one of the greatest attractions of the fair. It was America's answer to the Eiffel Tower of the Paris International Exposition of 1889. Ferris died at Pittsburgh, PA, Nov 22, 1896.

FIRST AFRICAN-AMERICAN TO BE RECORDED ON VINYL: 100th ANNIVERSARY. Feb 14, 1920. Okeh Records in New York City released the first record ("That Thing Called Love") to feature a black singer—Mamie Smith. Smith's recordings for Okeh were a huge success.

FIRST PRESIDENTIAL PHOTOGRAPH: ANNIVERSARY. Feb 14, 1849. President James Polk became the first US president to be photographed while in office. The photographer was Mathew B. Brady, who would become famous for his photography during the American Civil War.

GREAT BACKYARD BIRD COUNT. Feb 14–17. 23rd annual. Thousands of volunteers nationwide track the number and types of birds that live near their homes. Results help researchers monitor species in trouble. Cosponsored by the National Audubon Society, the Cornell University Lab of Ornithology and Bird Studies Canada. For info: National Audubon Society or The Cornell Lab, Cornell University. E-mail: gbbc@cornell.edu or citizenscience@audubon.org. Web: http://gbbc.birdcount.org or www.audubon.org.

HANCOCK, WINFIELD SCOTT: BIRTH ANNIVERSARY. Feb 14, 1824. Born at Montgomery, PA; died Feb 9, 1886, at Governor's Island, NY. After his service as a Union general in the Civil War, his command of the military division of Texas and Louisiana won him much favor from the Democratic Party because he allowed local civil authorities to retain their power. He pleased the Democrats so well that they made him their presidential candidate in 1880. He lost to James A. Garfield by a narrow margin.

LEAGUE OF WOMEN VOTERS FORMED: 100th ANNIVERSARY. Feb 14, 1920. While meeting in Chicago, IL, to celebrate the imminent ratification of the 19th Amendment to the Constitution, leaders of the National American Woman Suffrage Association (NAWSA) approved the formation of a new organization—the League of Women Voters. With the vote for women just a few months away, the new organization was created to help American women exercise their new political rights and responsibilities. For info: League of Women Voters. Web: www.lwv.org.

February 2020	S	M	T	W	T	F	S
							1
	2	3	4	5	6	7	8
	9	10	11	12	13	14	15
	16	17	18	19	20	21	22
	23	24	25	26	27	28	29

***THE MALTESE FALCON* PUBLISHED: 90th ANNIVERSARY.** Feb 14, 1930. Former Pinkerton agent–turned author Dashiell Hammett's crime novel introducing Sam Spade was published on this day by Alfred A. Knopf in New York, NY. (The novel had been serialized in *Black Mask* magazine in the fall of 1929, but Hammett revised the text.) The novel was a milestone in American literature, offering the model that all "hard-boiled" crime fiction would follow. And in terse tough-guy Sam Spade (who "looked rather pleasantly like a blond satan"), the world found a new pop icon. The notably dark-haired Humphrey Bogart played Spade in the 1941 film version directed by John Huston.

NATIONAL DATE FESTIVAL. Feb 14–23. Riverside County Fairgrounds, Indio, CA. 74th annual. America's most exotic county fair features Arabian Nights theme, musical pageant, date exhibits and sampling, thousands of competitive exhibits and carnival. Headliner entertainment included with admission. Est attendance: 280,000. For info: Riverside County Fair and National Date Fest. Web: www.datefest.org.

NATIONAL DONOR DAY. Feb 14. Valentine's Day is the day of love, and organ donation is the gift of life. Make Feb 14 the day to join thousands of Americans in making the donation decision. National Donor Day was started in 1998 by the Saturn Corporation and its United Auto Workers partners with the support of the US Department of Health and Human Services and many nonprofit health organizations. For info: US Dept of Health and Human Services. Web: www.organdonor.gov.

OREGON: ADMISSION DAY: ANNIVERSARY. Feb 14. Became 33rd state in 1859.

PARKLAND SCHOOL SHOOTING: ANNIVERSARY. Feb 14, 2018. On Valentine's Day, 2018, a former student entered Stoneman Douglas High School in the Miami exurb of Parkland, FL, and opened fire with an AK-15 assault rifle, killing 14 students and three staff members. Both the FBI and the Broward County Sheriff's Office had received warnings about the shooter and disregarded them. In the aftermath, surviving Stoneman Douglas students utilized social media to coalesce the youth-led #NeverAgain movement calling for stricter gun laws. Schools worldwide participated in a 17-minute National School Walkout on Mar 14, 2018, in solidarity and hundreds of thousands of supporters convened on Mar 24 for the March for Our Lives in Washington, DC, with millions more participating in 800 sibling events around the world.

PROUT, MARY ANN ("AUNT MARY PROUT"): BIRTH ANNIVERSARY. Feb 14, 1801. It is believed most likely that Mary Prout—social activist, humanitarian, educator—was born free on this date at Baltimore, MD. Prout became a teacher and in 1830 founded a day school. Actively involved in her church, she founded a secret society that became the Independent Order of St. Luke to help with the cost of medical care and burial services for needy blacks, an organization that grew to 1,500 chapters across the nation by 1900. Prout died at Baltimore in 1884.

RACE RELATIONS DAY. Feb 14. A day designated by some churches to recognize the importance of interracial relations. Formerly was observed on Abraham Lincoln's birthday or on the Sunday preceding it. Since 1970 observance has generally been Feb 14.

REENACTMENT OF THE BATTLE OF OLUSTEE. Feb 14–16. Olustee Battlefield Historic State Park, Olustee, FL. Join us for the 155th anniversary of the largest Civil War battle fought in Florida. Est attendance: 25,000. For info: Elaine McGrath, Special Events Coordinator, Stephen Foster Folk Culture Center State Park, PO Box G, White Springs, FL 32096. Phone: (386) 397-4462. Fax: (386) 397-4262. E-mail: elaine.mcgrath@dep.state.fl.us. Web: www.floridastateparks.org/olustee.

SAINT VALENTINE'S DAY. Feb 14. Saint Valentine's Day celebrates the feasts of two Christian martyrs of this name. One, a priest and physician, was beaten and beheaded on the Flaminian Way at Rome, Italy, Feb 14, AD 269, during the reign of Emperor Claudius II. Another Valentine, the bishop of Terni, is said to have been beheaded, also on the Flaminian Way at Rome, Feb 14 (possibly in a later year). Both history and legend are vague and contradictory about details of the Valentines, and some say that Feb 14 was selected for the celebration of Christian martyrs as a diversion from the ancient pagan observance of Lupercalia. An old legend has it that birds choose their mates on Valentine's Day. Now it is one of the most widely observed unofficial holidays. It is an occasion for the exchange of gifts (usually books, flowers or sweets) and greeting cards with affectionate or humorous messages. See also: "Lupercalia" (Feb 15).

SAINT VALENTINE'S DAY MASSACRE: ANNIVERSARY. Feb 14, 1929. Anniversary of gangland executions at Chicago, IL, when gunmen posing as police shot seven members of the George "Bugs" Moran gang.

SALMAN RUSHDIE'S DEATH SENTENCE: ANNIVERSARY. Feb 14, 1989. Iranian leader Ayatollah Ruhollah Khomeini, offended by *The Satanic Verses*, called on Muslims to kill the book's British author, Salman Rushdie. On the following day the ayatollah offered a $1 million reward for execution of his sentence. Rushdie, fearful for his life, went into hiding. Worldwide protests against the efforts to abridge academic and literary freedoms, countered by protests of Muslim and other religious fundamentalists, stimulated the sales of *The Satanic Verses*, but Rushdie remained virtually a prisoner, unable to resume a public life. In 1998 the Iranian government rescinded the death sentence.

SPACE MILESTONE: *NEAR* ORBITS ASTEROID: 20th ANNIVERSARY. Feb 14, 2000. The robot spacecraft *Near Earth Asteroid Rendezvous* (now called *NEAR Shoemaker*) finished circling the asteroid Eros for the first time on this day. Eros is called a near-Earth asteroid because its orbit crosses that of Earth and poses a potential collision danger. *NEAR* continued orbiting the asteroid for a year, moving closer to the surface to make more precise measurements and transmit thousands of pictures. In October 2000 it passed within three miles of Eros. Though it was never designed for landing, on Feb 12, 2001, *NEAR* touched down on Eros, history's first landing of an object on an asteroid. *NEAR* was launched from Cape Canaveral, FL, Feb 17, 1996.

SPACE MILESTONE: 100th SPACE WALK. Feb 14, 2001. Two astronauts from the space shuttle *Atlantis* took the 100th space walk; the first had been taken by American Edward White in 1965. On their excursion Thomas Jones and Robert Curbeam, Jr, put the finishing touches on the International Space Station's new science lab, *Destiny*. See also: "Space Milestone: *Gemini 4*" (June 3).

TOYODA, SAKICHI: BIRTH ANNIVERSARY. Feb 14, 1867. Hailed as Japan's Thomas Edison, inventor Toyoda was born at Kosai, Japan. His most notable invention was an automatic loom that ceased work immediately if a thread broke, ensuring defect-free fabric; with it, he founded the Toyoda Automatic Loom Works, Ltd. The commitment to product excellence was continued when his son Kiichiro moved the family business into the automotive industry, founding the Toyota Motor Company in 1933. He was the recipient of 40 Japanese and 62 international patents. Toyoda died Oct 30, 1930, at Tokyo, Japan.

WALLET, SKEEZIX: "BIRTHDAY". Feb 14, 1921. Comic strip character in "Gasoline Alley," by Frank King. First cartoon character to grow and age with the years of publication. Foundling

child of Walt Wallet, discovered on his doorstep Feb 14, 1921. Skeezix grew through childhood, marriage and military service in WWII, returning home to parenthood and business after the war. Comic strip began in the *Chicago Tribune*, Aug 23, 1919.

WASHINGTON'S BIRTHDAY AT MOUNT VERNON. Feb 14–17. Mount Vernon, VA. George Washington's home is the site of a variety of events in honor of his birthday. Each day of the celebration is kicked off by "George Washington's Surprise Birthday Party" on Mount Vernon's Bowling Green. Visitors can partake of the first president's favorite breakfast on Saturday and Sunday: hoecakes swimming in butter and honey. On Monday, Feb 17, there will be a wreath-laying ceremony at Washington's tomb as well as military demonstrations. Admission is free on Washington's birthday (federal observance). For info: Mount Vernon, 3200 Mount Vernon Memorial Hwy, Mount Vernon, VA 22121. Phone: (703) 780-2000. E-mail: tickets@mountvernon.org. Web: www. MountVernon.org.

BIRTHDAYS TODAY

Carl Bernstein, 76, journalist, author (*All the President's Men* with Bob Woodward), born Washington, DC, Feb 14, 1944.

Drew Bledsoe, 48, former football player, born Ellensburg, WA, Feb 14, 1972.

Michael Bloomberg, 78, former mayor of New York City, business executive, born Brighton, MA, Feb 14, 1942.

Jadeveon Clowney, 27, football player, born Rock Hill, SC, Feb 14, 1993.

Enrico Colantoni, 57, actor ("Person of Interest," "Just Shoot Me," "Veronica Mars"), born Toronto, ON, Canada, Feb 14, 1963.

Hugh Downs, 99, broadcaster ("The Today Show," "20/20"), born Akron, OH, Feb 14, 1921.

Renée Fleming, 61, opera singer, born Rochester, NY, Feb 14, 1959.

Zach Galligan, 56, actor (*Gremlins*), born New York, NY, Feb 14, 1964.

Danai Gurira, 42, actress (*Black Panther, The Visitor*, "The Walking Dead"), playwright (*Eclipsed, The Convert*), born Grinnell, IA, Feb 14, 1978.

Richard Hamilton, 42, former basketball player, born Coatesville, PA, Feb 14, 1978.

Milan Hejduk, 44, hockey player, born Usti-nad-Labem, Czechoslovakia (now the Czech Republic), Feb 14, 1976.

Freddie Highmore, 28, actor ("The Good Doctor," "Bates Motel"), born London, England, Feb 14, 1992.

Simon Pegg, 50, actor (*Shaun of the Dead, Hot Fuzz, Star Trek* films), born Simon John Beckingham at Brockworth, Gloucestershire, England, Feb 14, 1970.

Andrew Prine, 84, actor (*The Miracle Worker, Chisum*), born Jennings, FL, Feb 14, 1936.

Teller, 72, magician (Penn and Teller), born Raymond Joseph Teller at Philadelphia, PA, Feb 14, 1948.

Meg Tilly, 60, actress (*Agnes of God, The Two Jakes*), born Long Beach, CA, Feb 14, 1960.

Jessica Yu, 54, filmmaker, born Los Altos Hills, CA, Feb 14, 1966.

February 2020	S	M	T	W	T	F	S
							1
	2	3	4	5	6	7	8
	9	10	11	12	13	14	15
	16	17	18	19	20	21	22
	23	24	25	26	27	28	29

February 15 — Saturday

DAY 46   **320 REMAINING**

ANTHONY, SUSAN BROWNELL: 200th BIRTH ANNIVERSARY. Feb 15, 1820. American reformer, abolitionist and militant advocate of women's suffrage born into a Quaker family at Adams, MA. Susan B. Anthony was arrested on Nov 18, 1872, for voting in the US presidential election. In the short federal trial that followed in 1873, Justice Ward Hunt found her guilty and ordered her to pay a fine. She refused. Anthony was integral in the founding of the International Council of Women (1888). She was the first American woman to have her likeness on coinage (1979, Susan B. Anthony dollar). She died at Rochester, NY, Mar 13, 1906.

ARLEN, HAROLD: BIRTH ANNIVERSARY. Feb 15, 1905. American composer and songwriter, born at Buffalo, NY. Arlen wrote many popular songs, including "Over the Rainbow" (for which he won the 1939 Oscar for Best Song), "That Old Black Magic," "Blues in the Night" and "Stormy Weather." Died at New York, NY, Apr 23, 1986.

ASTEROID NEAR MISS: ANNIVERSARY. Feb 15, 2013. In a stunning coincidence, on the same day that a huge meteor exploded over Chelyabinsk, Russia, the asteroid 2012 DA14 passed Earth at a distance of less than 18,000 miles. The asteroid, more than 150 feet across, came so close to Earth that it passed inside the belt of man-made geostationary weather and communications satellites surrounding the planet. The near-miss was the closest approach by any object of its size in recorded history.

BARRYMORE, JOHN: BIRTH ANNIVERSARY. Feb 15, 1882. American actor of famous acting family, brother of Ethel and Lionel. Born John Blythe at Philadelphia, PA, and died at Los Angeles, CA, May 29, 1942.

CANADA: MAPLE LEAF FLAG ADOPTED: 55th ANNIVERSARY. Feb 15, 1965. The new Canadian national flag was raised at Ottawa, Canada's capital, on this day. The red-and-white flag with a red maple leaf in the center replaced the Red Ensign flag, which had the British Union Jack in the upper left-hand corner.

CERMAK, ANTON J.: ASSASSINATION ANNIVERSARY. Feb 15, 1933. At Bay Front Park, Miami, FL, an assassin shooting at President-elect Franklin D. Roosevelt had his aim deflected by a spectator. Anton Cermak, mayor of Chicago, IL, born May 9, 1873, at Kladno, Bohemia, Austria-Hungary, was struck and killed instead. Giuseppe (Joe) Zangara, the 32-year-old assassin, who had emigrated from Italy in 1923, was electrocuted at the Raiford, FL, state prison Mar 20, 1933.

CHELYABINSK METEOR EXPLOSION: ANNIVERSARY. Feb 15, 2013. Moving at approximately 40,000 miles per hour, a meteor measuring more than 50 feet in diameter and weighing about 7,000 tons exploded in a massive fireball over Chelyabinsk, Russia. The explosion, captured from dozens of angles in amateur video footage, injured more than 1,500 people and was detected by Comprehensive Nuclear Test Ban monitoring stations from Greenland to

Antarctica. At an estimated 450–500 kilotons, it is thought to be the most powerful such event since the Tunguska incident in Siberia in 1908.

CLARK, ABRAHAM: BIRTH ANNIVERSARY. Feb 15, 1726. Signer of the Declaration of Independence, farmer and lawyer. Born at Elizabethtown, NJ, and died there Sept 15, 1794.

LA FIESTA DE LOS VAQUEROS AND TUCSON RODEO. Feb 15–23. Tucson, AZ. 95th annual. Tucson celebrates its Old West heritage with a parade, a PRCA rodeo and other related rodeo events, including an Extreme bull-riding event. Est attendance: 55,000. For info: Tucson Rodeo Committee, Inc, PO Box 11006, Tucson, AZ 85734. Phone: (520) 741-2233 or (800) 964-5662. E-mail: info@tucsonrodeo.com. Web: www.tucsonrodeo.com.

FRANCE: NICE CARNIVAL. Feb 15–29. Nice. Dates from the 14th century. Derived from ancient rites of spring, the carnival offers parades, floats, battles of flowers and confetti and a fireworks display lighting up the entire Baie des Anges. King Carnival is burned on his pyre at the end of the event. 2020 theme: "Roi de la Mode" ("King of Fashion"). For info: Nice Carnival. E-mail: presse@otc-nice.com. Web: www.nicecarnaval.com.

GALILEI, GALILEO: BIRTH ANNIVERSARY. Feb 15, 1564. Physicist and astronomer who helped overthrow medieval concepts of the world, born at Pisa, Italy. He proved the theory that all bodies, large and small, descend at equal speed and gathered evidence to support Copernicus's theory that Earth and other planets revolve around the sun. In 1632 Galileo was tried by the Inquisition and found "vehemently suspect of heresy" because his *Dialogue Concerning the Two Chief World Systems* argued in favor of heliocentrism in contradiction to literal readings of scripture. Galileo remained under house arrest until his death at Florence, Italy, on Jan 8, 1642. The *Dialogue* was finally published in an uncensored form in 1835, and the Catholic Church issued an official apology to Galileo in 2000.

GIES, MIEP: BIRTH ANNIVERSARY. Feb 15, 1909. Dutch woman, born Hermine Santrouschitz at Vienna, Austria-Hungary, who with her husband, Jan Gies, helped hide the Otto Frank family from the Nazis in Amsterdam during WWII. After the Franks were arrested, Gies discovered the now-famous diary of their youngest daughter, Anne. Following the war, Gies returned the diary to Anne's father, who had it published in 1947. Gies died Jan 11, 2010, at the age of 100 at Hoorn, Netherlands.

LOVE RESET DAY. Feb 15. A day for celebrating self love and for deciding to make better romantic choices after a disappointing Valentine's Day. Annually, the day after Valentine's Day. For info: Carla Lynne Hall, 286 Fort Washington Ave, Ste 6CC, New York, NY 10032. Phone: (347) 317-4957. E-mail: Carla@DatingRelating.com. Web: www.DatingRelating.com/LoveResetDay.

LUPERCALIA. Feb 15. Anniversary of ancient Roman fertility festival. Thought by some to have been established by Romulus and Remus, who, legend says, were suckled by a she-wolf at Lupercal (a cave in Palestine). Goats and dogs were sacrificed. Lupercalia celebrations persisted until the fifth century of the Christian era. Possibly a forerunner of Valentine's Day customs.

MCCORMICK, CYRUS H.: BIRTH ANNIVERSARY. Feb 15, 1809. Inventor of the reaper, born at Rockbridge County, VA. It is said that Cyrus McCormick's invention of the reaper rates second only to the railroad in the development of the US. Continuing the dream of his father, McCormick constructed a horse-operated reaper, which was demonstrated for the first time in a Virginia wheat field in July 1831. He moved his operation to Chicago, IL, in 1847 in order to be closer to the Midwest's expanding wheat fields. His business prospered despite two decades of constant litigation over patent rights. He died May 13, 1884, at Chicago. In 1902–03, his McCormick Harvesting Machine Company was consolidated with other firms to become the International Harvester Company.

MENENDEZ DE AVILES, PEDRO: BIRTH ANNIVERSARY. Feb 15, 1519. Spanish explorer and naval adventurer. Explored Florida coastal regions for the king of Spain and established a fort at St. Augustine in September 1565. Died Sept 17, 1574, at Santander, Spain.

MOON PHASE: LAST QUARTER. Feb 15. Moon enters Last Quarter phase at 5:17 PM, EST.

NEW ENGLAND MID-WINTER SURFING CHAMPIONSHIP. Feb 15. Narragansett Town Beach, Narragansett, RI. 52nd annual. Competition in all age categories and specialty events with prizes and trophies. Est attendance: 125. For info: Peter Panagiotis, ESA Dir, 31 Othmar St, Narragansett, RI 02882. E-mail: bicsurf@hotmail.com.

REMEMBER THE *MAINE* DAY: ANNIVERSARY. Feb 15, 1898. The American battleship *Maine* was blown up while at anchor in Havana Harbor, at 9:40 PM, on this day in 1898. The ship, under the command of Captain Charles G. Sigsbee, sank quickly, and 260 members of its crew were lost. Inflamed public opinion in the US ignored the lack of evidence to establish responsibility for the explosion. "Remember the *Maine*" became the war cry, and a formal declaration of war against Spain followed on Apr 25, 1898.

SENDLER, IRENA: BIRTH ANNIVERSARY. Feb 15, 1910. Polish social worker who at great personal risk headed a rescue effort to smuggle some 2,500 Jewish children out of the Warsaw Ghetto in WWII. Sendler, a Roman Catholic, recognized early in the war the Nazi threat to Jews and used her bureaucratic contacts to bring medicine and food into the ghetto and then faced the heartbreaking task of separating children from parents in order to save them. Recognized by Yad Vashem in 1965 as Righteous Among the Nations, Sendler died May 12, 2007, at Warsaw, Poland, which was also her birthplace.

SERBIA: NATIONAL DAY. Feb 15.

SHACKLETON, ERNEST: BIRTH ANNIVERSARY. Feb 15, 1874. The Antarctic explorer was born at Kilkea, Ireland. His fame rests not on reaching the South Pole (he tried three times), but on his leadership and bravery. During the British Imperial Trans-Arctic expedition of 1914, the icy seas crushed his ship, *Endurance*, but Shackleton protected his men and buoyed their morale for the two years they were marooned. In 1916 he led a six-man team in a lifeboat on a 17-day, 800-mile journey (without sleep) in search of help. Upon arrival at South Georgia Island, he initiated a rescue effort, and three months later all his men were rescued without a death. Shackleton died Jan 5, 1922, at Grytviken, South Georgia Island, while beginning a fourth expedition to the South Pole.

SPANISH WAR MEMORIAL DAY AND *MAINE* MEMORIAL DAY. Feb 15. Massachusetts.

SUTTER, JOHN AUGUSTUS: BIRTH ANNIVERSARY. Feb 15, 1803. Born at Kandern, Germany, Sutter established the first Anglo settlement on the site of Sacramento, CA, in 1839. He owned a large tract of land there, which he named New Helvetia. The first great gold strike in the US was on his property, at Sutter's Mill, Jan 24, 1848. His land was soon overrun by gold seekers who, he claimed, slaughtered his cattle and stole or destroyed his property. Sutter was bankrupt by 1852. Died at Washington, DC, June 18, 1880.

TIFFANY, CHARLES LEWIS: BIRTH ANNIVERSARY. Feb 15, 1812. American jeweler whose name became synonymous with high standards of quality. Born at Killingly, CT, and died at New York, NY, Feb 18, 1902. Father of artist Louis Comfort Tiffany. See also: "Tiffany, Louis Comfort: Birth Anniversary" (Feb 18).

WORLD PANGOLIN DAY. Feb 15. 9th annual. A day to raise awareness for pangolins: the most illegally traded mammal in the world. The pangolin is also known as a scaly anteater and resides in Africa and Asia. All eight species of pangolins are in danger, and the two most-endangered pangolin species may go extinct within only 10 years. Annually, the third Saturday in February. For info: Annamiticus. Web: www.pangolins.org/world-pangolin-day.

🧁 BIRTHDAYS TODAY

Adolfo, 87, fashion designer, born Adolfo F. Sardina at Havana, Cuba, Feb 15, 1933.

Marisa Berenson, 72, actress (*Cabaret, Barry Lyndon*), model, born New York, NY, Feb 15, 1948.

Claire Bloom, 89, actress (*A Doll's House, The Spy Who Came In from the Cold*), born London, England, Feb 15, 1931.

Susan Brownmiller, 85, author, feminist (*Against Our Will, Femininity*), born Brooklyn, NY, Feb 15, 1935.

Matt Groening, 66, cartoonist ("The Simpsons"), born Portland, OR, Feb 15, 1954.

Jaromir Jagr, 48, hockey player, born Kladno, Czechoslovakia (now the Czech Republic), Feb 15, 1972.

Brad Little, 66, Governor of Idaho (R), born Emmett, ID, Feb 15, 1954.

Melissa Manchester, 69, singer, born the Bronx, NY, Feb 15, 1951.

Amber Riley, 34, actress ("Glee"), born Los Angeles, CA, Feb 15, 1986.

Jane Seymour, 69, actress ("Dr. Quinn, Medicine Woman"; *Live and Let Die, East of Eden*), born Joyce Frankenberg at Hillingdon, England, Feb 15, 1951.

February 16 — Sunday

DAY 47   **319 REMAINING**

BUILD A BETTER TRADE SHOW IMAGE WEEK. Feb 16–22. For companies that exhibit at trade shows, this week is set aside to evaluate and improve exhibit strategies for the upcoming trade show season. "10 Steps to a Better Trade Show Image" tip sheet available. Annually, the third full week in February. For info: Marlys K. Arnold, ImageSpecialist, PO Box 901808, Kansas City, MO 64190-1808. Phone: (816) 746-7888. E-mail: marnold@imagespecialist.com. Web: www.exhibitmarketerscafe.com/free-resources.

DAYTONA 500. Feb 16. Daytona International Speedway, Daytona Beach, FL. 62nd annual running of the "Great American Race." The world's top drivers compete in NASCAR's biggest, richest and most prestigious motorsports event. Est attendance: 100,000. For info: Daytona International Speedway. Phone: (800) PIT-SHOP. Web: www.daytonainternationalspeedway.com.

FLAHERTY, ROBERT JOSEPH: BIRTH ANNIVERSARY. Feb 16, 1884. American filmmaker, explorer and author, called "father of the

February 2020	S	M	T	W	T	F	S
							1
	2	3	4	5	6	7	8
	9	10	11	12	13	14	15
	16	17	18	19	20	21	22
	23	24	25	26	27	28	29

documentary film." Films include *Nanook of the North, Moana of the South Seas* and *Man of Aran*. Born at Iron Mountain, MI; died at Dunnerston, VT, July 23, 1951.

HAMILTON, SLIDING BILLY: BIRTH ANNIVERSARY. Feb 16, 1866. William Robert ("Sliding Billy") Hamilton, Baseball Hall of Fame outfielder, born at Newark, NJ. Hamilton was the leading base stealer of the 19th century, with 912–937 steals (sources differ). With Ed Delahanty and Sam Thompson, he formed one of baseball's greatest outfields for the Philadelphia Phillies throughout the 1890s. Inducted into the Hall of Fame in 1961. Died at Worcester, MA, Dec 15, 1940.

KENNAN, GEORGE: BIRTH ANNIVERSARY. Feb 16, 1904. US diplomat who coined the phrase "containment policy." Kennan was born at Milwaukee, WI. He served as a diplomat during WWII and was briefly arrested by the Nazis. After the war, he wrote an article for *Foreign Affairs* magazine that had a significant influence on America's Cold War policy. The article, entitled "The Sources of Soviet Conduct" and submitted under the pseudonym "Mr. X," called upon the US and its allies to prevent the territorial spread of communism, either by shows of military force or by economic and technological intervention in at-risk nations. Both the Marshall Plan and the Truman Doctrine were heavily influenced by the ideas expressed in the article. Kennan later had a controversial turn as ambassador to the Soviet Union. He died at Princeton, NJ, at the age of 101, Mar 17, 2005.

KREWE OF CARROLLTON PARADE. Feb 16. New Orleans, LA. Founded in 1924, the Krewe of Carrollton is the fourth-oldest marching krewe and kicks off the New Orleans carnival season with this popular parade in the Carrollton neighborhood. Annually, two Sundays before Mardi Gras. For info: Krewe of Carrollton. Web: www.kreweofcarrollton.org.

LITHUANIA: INDEPENDENCE DAY. Feb 16. National day. The anniversary of Lithuania's declaration of independence in 1918 is observed as the Baltic state's Independence Day. In 1940 Lithuania became a part of the Soviet Union under an agreement between Joseph Stalin and Adolf Hitler. On Mar 11, 1990, Lithuania declared its independence from the Soviet Union, the first of the Soviet republics to do so. After demanding independence, Lithuania set up a border police force and aided young men in efforts to avoid the Soviet military draft, prompting then Soviet leader Mikhail Gorbachev to send tanks into the capital of Vilnius and impose oil and gas embargoes. In the wake of the failed coup attempt in Moscow, Aug 19, 1991, Lithuanian independence finally was recognized.

MYSTIC KREWE OF BARKUS PARADE. Feb 16. French Quarter, New Orleans, LA. Popular 15-block walking parade of costumed dogs (and a few cats) held annually two Sundays before Ash Wednesday. The Krewe of Barkus (Barkus is the dog equivalent of Bacchus) is a licensed Mardi Gras Krewe and nonprofit organization. All proceeds of the parade registration fees, merchandise sales and ball profits are donated to worthy animal welfare groups. For info: Mystic Krewe of Barkus. E-mail: info@barkus.org. Web: www.barkus.org.

NATIONAL ENGINEERS WEEK. Feb 16–22. The 69th annual observance, cosponsored by more than 140 national engineering societies, federal agencies and major corporations, will feature classroom programs in elementary and secondary schools throughout the US, hands-on activities in science centers and museums, engineering workplace tours, the Future City Competition (www.futurecity.org) and the annual

"Introduce a Girl to Engineering Day." Annually, the week that includes George Washington's birthday. For info: DiscoverE. E-mail: Info@DiscoverE.org. Web: discovere.org/our-programs/engineers-week.

NBA ALL-STAR GAME 2020. Feb 16. United Center, Chicago, IL. 69th annual. The NBA All-Star Game features the greatest professional basketball athletes in an action-packed weekend. The All-Star Weekend kicks off Feb 14. Est attendance: 100,000. For info: National Basketball Assn. Web: https://nbaevents.com or www.unitedcenter.com/events/2020/02/16/nba-all-star-game.

SURRENDER OF FORT DONELSON: ANNIVERSARY. Feb 16, 1862. With Confederate troops evacuating Bowling Green, KY, and other points along the Kentucky line, General Ulysses S. Grant's forces encircled Fort Donelson, KY. After hard fighting on land and on the Cumberland River, Grant requested surrender of Fort Donelson, stating that "No terms except unconditional and immediate surrender can be accepted." This earned him the nickname "Unconditional Surrender" Grant. Confederate general Simon Buckner surrendered the fort, in essence giving the Union army control of Tennessee and Kentucky and the Tennessee and Cumberland Rivers. Disruption ensued and civilians attempted to flee the area occupied by Federal troops.

WILSON, HENRY: BIRTH ANNIVERSARY. Feb 16, 1812. 18th vice president of the US (1873–75). Born at Farmington, NH; died at Washington, DC, Nov 22, 1875.

🧁 BIRTHDAYS TODAY

Mahershala Ali, 46, actor (Oscars for *Green Book* and *Moonlight*; "True Detective," "Luke Cage," "House of Cards"), born Mahershalalhashbaz Gilmore at Oakland, CA, Feb 16, 1974.

Jerome Bettis, 48, Hall of Fame football player, born Detroit, MI, Feb 16, 1972.

LeVar Burton, 63, actor, host (*Roots*, "Star Trek: The Next Generation," "Reading Rainbow"), born Landsthul, Germany, Feb 16, 1957.

Christopher Eccleston, 56, actor ("Doctor Who," "Heroes," *Shallow Grave*), born Salford, Lancashire, England, Feb 16, 1964.

Lupe Fiasco, 38, rapper, music executive, born Wasalu Muhammad Jaco at Chicago, IL, Feb 16, 1982.

Richard Ford, 76, author (*Independence Day, The Sportswriter*), born Jackson, MS, Feb 16, 1944.

Carl Icahn, 84, business magnate, philanthropist, born New York, NY, Feb 16, 1936.

Ice T, 61, rapper, actor ("Law & Order: SVU," *New Jack City*), born Tracy Morrow at Newark, NJ, Feb 16, 1959.

William Katt, 69, actor ("The Greatest American Hero," *Perry Mason Returns, Carrie*), born Los Angeles, CA, Feb 16, 1951.

Eric Laden, 42, actor ("The Killing," "Mad Men"), born Houston, TX, Feb 16, 1978.

John Patrick McEnroe, Jr, 61, sportscaster, Hall of Fame tennis player, born Wiesbaden, West Germany (now Germany), Feb 16, 1959.

Barry Primus, 82, actor ("Cagney and Lacey," *Absence of Malice, Down and Out in Beverly Hills*), born New York, NY, Feb 16, 1938.

The Weeknd, 30, singer, songwriter, producer, born Abel Makkonen Tesfaye at Toronto, ON, Canada, Feb 16, 1990.

February 17 — Monday

DAY 48   **318 REMAINING**

BARBER, WALTER LANIER "RED": BIRTH ANNIVERSARY. Feb 17, 1908. One of the first broadcasters inducted into the Baseball Hall of Fame, Red Barber was born at Columbus, MS. Barber's first professional play-by-play experience was announcing the Cincinnati Reds' opening day on radio in 1934. That game was also the first major league game he had ever seen. He broadcast baseball's first night game (in Brooklyn) on Aug 26, 1939, the 1947 game in which Jackie Robinson broke the color barrier and Roger Maris's 61st home run in 1961. Red Barber died Oct 22, 1992, at Tallahassee, FL.

CANADA: FAMILY DAY (SELECTED PROVINCES). Feb 17. Statutory (not federal) holiday observed in Prince Edward Island, Nova Scotia, Ontario, Manitoba, Saskatchewan and Alberta. Annually, the third Monday in February. (Other provinces have a different observance on the third Monday in February. British Columbia observes Family Day on the second Monday in February.)

COLUMBIA SURRENDERS TO SHERMAN: ANNIVERSARY. Feb 17, 1865. On this morning city officials of the capital city of South Carolina, Columbia, rode out to Union lines to surrender the city to Union general William Tecumseh Sherman. The city was occupied during the day by the Union forces, and during the night fires broke out, which eventually consumed two-thirds of the city. Although Sherman blamed retreating Southern soldiers for the fires, the symbol of a burning Columbia stands in Southern memory as a testament to the cruelty of Sherman's army.

CORELLI, ARCANGELO: BIRTH ANNIVERSARY. Feb 17, 1653. Italian composer and virtuoso violinist, born at Fusignano, Italy. From his home in Rome, Corelli made extensive and popular concert tours throughout much of Europe. Died at Rome, Jan 8, 1713.

CRABBE, BUSTER: BIRTH ANNIVERSARY. Feb 17, 1908. Clarence Linden "Buster" Crabbe, Olympic gold medal swimmer, born at Oakland, CA. Crabbe's first-place finish in the 400-meter freestyle was the only swimming medal won by an American at the 1932 Olympic Games at Los Angeles, CA. After his swimming career was over, he played Tarzan, Flash Gordon and Buck Rogers in the movies. Died at Scottsdale, AZ, Apr 23, 1983.

FORT SUMTER RETURNED TO UNION CONTROL: ANNIVERSARY. Feb 17, 1865. After a siege that lasted almost a year and a half, Fort Sumter in South Carolina returned to Union hands on this date. The site of the first shots fired in the American Civil War on Apr 12, 1861, the fort had become a symbol for both sides. As Union attempts to retake it by shelling diminished the fort's capacity with large bombardments, Southern forces managed to hold out with few casualties.

GEORGE WASHINGTON BIRTHDAY PARADE. Feb 17. Alexandria, VA. Nation's largest parade honoring George Washington, staged by his hometown. Floats, bands, antique cars, equestrian and military units and bagpipers. Route goes through historic district. Annually, the third Monday in February. Est attendance: 50,000. For info: George Washington Birthday Celebration Committee. Phone: (703) 829-6640. E-mail: gwparade@gmail.com. Web: www.washingtonbirthday.net.

GERONIMO: DEATH ANNIVERSARY. Feb 17, 1909. American Indian of the Chiricahua (Apache) tribe, born about 1829 in Arizona. He was the leader of a small band of warriors whose devastating raids in Arizona, New Mexico and Mexico caused the US Army to send 5,000 men to recapture him after his first escape. He was confined at Fort Sill, OK, where he died after dictating the story of his life for publication.

LAENNEC, RENE THEOPHILE HYACINTHE: BIRTH ANNIVERSARY. Feb 17, 1781. Famed French physician, author and inventor of the stethoscope, called "the father of chest medicine." He wrote extensively about respiratory and heart ailments. Born at Quimper, France, he died there Aug 13, 1826.

LEAGUE OF UNITED LATIN AMERICAN CITIZENS (LULAC) FOUNDED: ANNIVERSARY. Feb 17, 1929. Delegates from the Corpus Christi Order of the Sons of America, the Knights of America of San Antonio and the League of Latin America Citizens from the Rio Grande Valley met at Obreros Hall, Corpus Christi, TX, to form LULAC. It is now the oldest and largest Hispanic civic organization.

LEARNING DISABILITIES ASSOCIATION OF AMERICA INTERNATIONAL CONFERENCE. Feb 17–20. Orlando, FL. 57th annual. LDA's mission is to create opportunities for success for all individuals affected by learning disabilities and to reduce the incidence of learning disabilities in future generations. LDA believes everyone can succeed at school, at work, in relationships and in the community—if given the right opportunities and supports as needed. The annual conference is a time of learning and discovering how we can advocate and work together to create new opportunities for children and adults with learning disabilities. Est attendance: 900. For info: Learning Disabilities Assn of America, PO Box 10369, Pittsburgh, PA 15234. Phone: (412) 341-1515. Fax: (412) 344-0224. E-mail: info@ldaamerica.org. Web: www.ldaamerica.org.

***MADAMA BUTTERFLY* PREMIERE: ANNIVERSARY.** Feb 17, 1904. Giacomo Puccini's *Madama Butterfly* was performed for the first time in Milan, Italy. The sold-out crowd, restive at what they saw as Puccini's lack of originality, responded with boos, moos, groans and heckling to the extent that the performers couldn't hear the orchestra. Rosina Storchio, the soprano portraying Madama Butterfly, began crying on stage. Puccini, enraged at the opera's reception (saying the opera was "daisies thrown to swine"), nevertheless revised the work, and it had a successful performance on May 24.

MALTHUS, THOMAS: BIRTH ANNIVERSARY. Feb 17, 1766. English scholar, demographer and author, born near Dorking, England. Malthusian population theories (especially that population growth exceeds growth of production) provoked great controversy when published in 1798. Malthus died near Bath, England, Dec 23, 1834.

MY WAY DAY. Feb 17. Hundreds of people have their opinions as to who we are. Today is the day we decide who's right. Today we determine our identities all by ourselves. (©2006 by WH.) For info: Thomas & Ruth Roy, Wellcat Holidays, 2418 Long Ln, Lebanon, PA 17046. Phone: (717) 279-0184. E-mail: info@wellcat.com. Web: www.wellcat.com.

NATIONAL PTA FOUNDERS' DAY: ANNIVERSARY. Feb 17, 1897. Founders' Day is a reminder of the substantial role that the PTA has played locally, regionally and nationally in supporting parent involvement and working on behalf of all children and families. It honors the PTA's founders Phoebe Apperson Hearst and Alice McLellan Birney, and the founder of Georgia's Congress of Colored Parents and Teachers, Selena Sloan Butler. For info: National PTA. E-mail: info@pta.org. Web: www.pta.org.

"A PRAIRIE HOME COMPANION" PREMIERE: ANNIVERSARY. Feb 17, 1979. This popular live variety show debuted locally on Minnesota Public Radio in 1974 and was first broadcast nationally on Feb 17, 1979, as part of National Public Radio's Folk Festival USA. It became a regular Saturday-night program in early 1980. Host Garrison Keillor's monologues about the mythical Lake Wobegon and his humorous ads for local businesses such as Bertha's Kitty Boutique, Powdermilk Biscuits and the Chatterbox Cafe were accompanied by various musical groups. Broadcast from the World Theater in St. Paul, MN, the show went off the air in 1986. A series of programs were done for cable TV, and Keillor continues to write works of fiction (*Lake Wobegon Days*). In 1994 "A Prairie Home Companion" went back on the air on Public Radio International.

PRESIDENTS' DAY. Feb 17. Presidents' Day observes the birthdays of George Washington (Feb 22) and Abraham Lincoln (Feb 12). With the adoption of the Monday Holiday Law (which moved the observance of George Washington's birthday from Feb 22 to the third Monday in February), some of the specific significance of the event was lost and added impetus was given to the popular description of that holiday as Presidents' Day. Present usage often regards Presidents' Day as a day to honor all former presidents of the US, though the federal holiday is still Washington's Birthday. Annually, the third Monday in February. See also: "Washington, George: Birthday Observance" this date.

RANDOM ACTS OF KINDNESS DAY. Feb 17. A day to raise awareness about kindness and to invite people to give and receive kindness. Annually, Feb 17. For info: Random Acts of Kindness Foundation. Phone: (303) 297-1964. E-mail: info@randomactsofkindness.org. Web: www.randomactsofkindness.org.

STOCK EXCHANGE HOLIDAY (WASHINGTON'S BIRTHDAY). Feb 17. The holiday schedules for the various exchanges are subject to change if relevant rules, regulations or exchange policies are revised. If you have questions, contact: CME Group (CME, CBOT, NYMEX, COMEX) (www.cmegroup.com), Chicago Board Options Exchange (www.cboe.com), NASDAQ (www.nasdaq.com), NYSE (www.nyse.com).

WASHINGTON, GEORGE: BIRTHDAY OBSERVANCE (LEGAL HOLIDAY). Feb 17. Legal public holiday. (Public Law 90–363 sets Washington's birthday observance on the third Monday in February each year—applicable to federal employees and to the District of Columbia.) Observed in all states. See also: "Washington, George: Birth Anniversary" (Feb 22).

🎂 BIRTHDAYS TODAY

Vanessa Atler, 38, former gymnast, born Valencia, CA, Feb 17, 1982.

James Nathaniel (Jim) Brown, 84, Hall of Fame football player, activist, actor, born St. Simons Island, GA, Feb 17, 1936.

Ronald DeVoe, 53, singer (Bell Biv DeVoe), born Boston, MA, Feb 17, 1967.

Michelle Forbes, 53, actress ("Homicide: Life on the Street," "Prison Break"), born Austin, TX, Feb 17, 1967.

Brenda Fricker, 75, actress (Oscar for *My Left Foot*; *The Field*), born Dublin, Ireland, Feb 17, 1945.

Joseph Gordon-Levitt, 39, actor (*Inception, [500] Days of Summer*, "3rd Rock from the Sun"), born Los Angeles, CA, Feb 17, 1981.

Paris Hilton, 39, socialite, television personality ("The Simple Life"), born New York, NY, Feb 17, 1981.

Hal Holbrook, 95, actor (Tony for *Mark Twain Tonight!*; *Magnum Force, All the President's Men*), born Harold Rowe Holbrook, Jr, at Cleveland, OH, Feb 17, 1925.

Barry Humphries, 86, actor, comedian, aka Dame Edna Everidge, born Melbourne, Australia, Feb 17, 1934.

February 2020	S	M	T	W	T	F	S
							1
	2	3	4	5	6	7	8
	9	10	11	12	13	14	15
	16	17	18	19	20	21	22
	23	24	25	26	27	28	29

Michael Jordan, 57, Hall of Fame basketball player, basketball executive, born Brooklyn, NY, Feb 17, 1963.

Richard Karn, 61, actor ("Home Improvement"), game show host ("Family Feud"), born Seattle, WA, Feb 17, 1959.

Lou Diamond Phillips, 58, actor (*La Bamba, Stand and Deliver*), born Corpus Christi, TX, Feb 17, 1962.

Denise Richards, 49, actress (*Wild Things, The World Is Not Enough*), born Downers Grove, IL, Feb 17, 1971.

Jason Ritter, 40, actor ("Parenthood," "The Event," "Joan of Arcadia"), born Los Angeles, CA, Feb 17, 1980.

Rene Russo, 66, actress (*The Thomas Crown Affair, Tin Cup, Get Shorty*), born Burbank, CA, Feb 17, 1954.

Ed Sheeran, 29, singer, composer, born Halifax, England, Feb 17, 1991.

February 18 — Tuesday

DAY 49   **317 REMAINING**

ALEICHEM, SHOLEM: BIRTH ANNIVERSARY. Feb 18, 1859. (Old Style date.) Pen name of Russian-born author and humorist Solomon Rabinowitz. The musical *Fiddler on the Roof* drew from Aleichem's short stories about Tevye the Milkman. Affectionately known in the US as "the Jewish Mark Twain." Died at New York, NY, May 13, 1916.

BROWN, HELEN GURLEY: BIRTH ANNIVERSARY. Feb 18, 1922. Longtime editor in chief of *Cosmopolitan* magazine and groundbreaking feminist, born at Green Forest, AR. After a successful career in copywriting, she published the book *Sex and the Single Girl* in 1962 and became an outspoken advocate for sexual freedom, breaking the mythology that women had to be "good girls" who saved themselves till marriage. At *Cosmo* she steered women toward careers, dating, beauty, diet and ultimately marriage, telling them that they really could "have it all." She did have it all, married for more than 50 years to film and TV producer David Brown. She died Aug 13, 2012, at New York, NY.

COW MILKED WHILE FLYING IN AN AIRPLANE: 90th ANNIVERSARY. Feb 18, 1930. Elm Farm Ollie became the first cow to fly in an airplane. During the flight, which was attended by reporters, she was milked, and the milk was sealed in paper containers and parachuted over St. Louis, MO.

DAVIS, JEFFERSON: INAUGURATION ANNIVERSARY. Feb 18, 1861. In the years before the Civil War, Senator Jefferson Davis was the acknowledged leader of the Southern bloc and a champion of states' rights, but he had little to do with the secessionist movement until after his home state of Mississippi joined the Confederacy Jan 9, 1861. Davis withdrew from the Senate that same day. He was unanimously chosen as president of the Confederacy's provisional government and was inaugurated at Montgomery, AL, Feb 18. Within the next year he was elected to a six-year term by popular vote and inaugurated a second time Feb 22, 1862, at Richmond, VA.

GAMBIA: INDEPENDENCE DAY. Feb 18, 1965. National holiday. Independence from Britain granted. Referendum in April 1970 established Gambia as a republic within the Commonwealth.

HUGHES, JOHN: 70th BIRTH ANNIVERSARY. Feb 18, 1950. Born at Lansing, MI, this film director and screenwriter created some of the most iconic works of the 1980s and '90s. His "Brat Pack" films, including *Sixteen Candles* (1984) and *The Breakfast Club* (1985), provided hilarious insight into the lives of American teenagers, and his broad comedies *Home Alone* (1990) and *Planes, Trains and Automobiles* (1987) were also huge commercial successes. Hughes died at New York, NY, Aug 11, 2009.

NEPAL: NATIONAL DEMOCRACY DAY. Feb 18. National holiday. Anniversary of the 1952 constitution.

PALANCE, JACK: BIRTH ANNIVERSARY. Feb 18, 1919. This tall, rugged, hard working actor was born Volodymyr Palahniuk to Ukrainian immigrant parents at Hazleton, PA. After a short boxing career and WWII, Palance began an acting career that spanned from 1947 to 2004. He became a household name for his role as Jack Wilson in *Shane* (1953), for which he was nominated for a supporting actor Oscar. He won the supporting actor Oscar for his comic turn in *City Slickers* (1991)—he startled the Academy Awards audience by performing one-armed push-ups on stage. Palance died Nov 10, 2006, at Montecito, CA.

PEABODY, GEORGE: 225th BIRTH ANNIVERSARY. Feb 18, 1795. American merchant and philanthropist, born at South Danvers, MA. He endowed the Peabody Institute at Baltimore, MD, museums at Harvard and Yale and the George Peabody College for Teachers at Nashville, TN. Died at London, England, Nov 4, 1869.

PLUTO DISCOVERY: 90th ANNIVERSARY. Feb 18, 1930. Pluto was discovered by astronomer Clyde Tombaugh at the Lowell Observatory at Flagstaff, AZ. It was given the name of the Roman god of the underworld. It was considered the ninth planet of the solar system until 2006, when astronomers reclassified it as a dwarf planet. See also: "Pluto Demoted: Anniversary" (Aug 24).

TIFFANY, LOUIS COMFORT: BIRTH ANNIVERSARY. Feb 18, 1848. American artist, son of famed jeweler Charles L. Tiffany. Best remembered for his remarkable work with decorative iridescent "favrile" glass. Born at New York, NY; died there Jan 17, 1933. See also: "Tiffany, Charles Lewis: Birth Anniversary" (Feb 15).

WILLKIE, WENDELL LEWIS: BIRTH ANNIVERSARY. Feb 18, 1892. American lawyer, author, public utility executive and politician, born at Elwood, IN. Presidential nominee of the Republican Party in 1940. Remembered for his book *One World*, published in 1943. Died at New York, NY, Oct 8, 1944.

🎂 BIRTHDAYS TODAY

Len Deighton, 91, author (*SS-GB, The Ipcress File, Bomber*), born London, England, Feb 18, 1929.

Matt Dillon, 56, actor (*Crash, There's Something About Mary, Drugstore Cowboy*), born Westchester, NY, Feb 18, 1964.

Dr. Dre, 55, rapper, record producer, born Andre Romelle Young at Compton, CA, Feb 18, 1965.

J-Hope, 26, rapper (BTS), born Jung Ho-seok at Gwangju, South Korea, Feb 18, 1994.

Jillian Michaels, 46, personal trainer, television personality ("The Biggest Loser"), born Los Angeles, CA, Feb 18, 1974.

Toni Morrison, 89, Nobel Prize–winning novelist (*Beloved, Jazz, Tar Baby, Sula*), born Lorain, OH, Feb 18, 1931.

Juice Newton, 68, singer, born Judy Cohen at Virginia Beach, VA, Feb 18, 1952.

Yoko Ono, 87, artist, musician, born Tokyo, Japan, Feb 18, 1933.

Molly Ringwald, 52, actress (*Sixteen Candles, The Breakfast Club, Pretty in Pink*), born Roseville, CA, Feb 18, 1968.

Greta Scacchi, 60, actress (*White Mischief, Presumed Innocent*), born Milan, Italy, Feb 18, 1960.

Cybill Shepherd, 70, actress (*The Last Picture Show*, "Moonlighting," "Cybill"), born Memphis, TN, Feb 18, 1950.

John Travolta, 65, actor (*Hairspray, Get Shorty, Pulp Fiction, Grease, Saturday Night Fever*, "Welcome Back, Kotter"), born Englewood, NJ, Feb 18, 1955.

John William Warner, 93, retired US senator (R, Virginia), born Washington, DC, Feb 18, 1927.

Vanna White, 63, television personality ("Wheel of Fortune"), born Conway, SC, Feb 18, 1957.

February 19 — Wednesday

DAY 50 **316 REMAINING**

CARNAVAL DE PONCE. Feb 19–25. Ponce, PR. First held in 1858. Carnival, artisans, parade with floats and colorfully dressed people with papier-mâché masks (*vejigantes*). Also featuring kiosks with typical Puerto Rican foods and drinks. Festivities end with the Burial of the Sardine on Shrove Tuesday. Annually, the Wednesday before Ash Wednesday through Shrove Tuesday. Est attendance: 100,000.

COPERNICUS, NICOLAUS: BIRTH ANNIVERSARY. Feb 19, 1473. Polish astronomer and priest who revolutionized scientific thought with what came to be called the Copernican theory, which placed the sun instead of Earth at the center of our planetary system. Considered the founder of modern astronomy. Born at Torun, Poland, he died at East Prussia, May 24, 1543.

"EASTENDERS" TV PREMIERE: 35th ANNIVERSARY. Feb 19, 1985. This popular UK soap opera features the residents of Albert Square in the East End of London. More than 30 million viewers tuned in Dec 25, 1986, to make that episode the highest rated in UK soap history. It has won several awards, including BAFTAs.

***THE FEMININE MYSTIQUE* PUBLISHED: ANNIVERSARY.** Feb 19, 1963. Betty Friedan's *The Feminine Mystique* was a call for women to achieve their full potential. The book generated enormous response and revitalized the women's movement in the US.

FIRST BOLLINGEN PRIZE: ANNIVERSARY. Feb 19, 1949. On this date the first Bollingen Prize for poetry was awarded to Ezra Pound for his collection *The Pisan Cantos*. This first award was steeped in controversy because Pound had been charged with treason after making pro-Fascist broadcasts in Italy during WWII.

GARRICK, DAVID: BIRTH ANNIVERSARY. Feb 19, 1717. Foremost 18th-century English stage actor and author of nearly two dozen plays, Garrick was born at Hereford, England. An instantaneous success from his first major role in *Richard III* (1741), Garrick is thought to have had the greatest range of any Shakespearean performer, which, along with his direction and adaptations, helped elevate the Bard's oeuvre to its long-standing cultural prominence and centrality. Comanager of the famed Drury Lane Theatre, he established a new style of natural, interpretive acting that presaged legion Shakespearean actors who followed in his wake. Garrick died Jan 20, 1779, at London, England; in 1831 the Garrick Club for actors was established in his honor.

GRAND RAPIDS BOAT SHOW. Feb 19–23. DeVos Place, Grand Rapids, MI. This event brings together buyers and sellers of powerboats ranging from 16 to 50 feet, fishing boats, ski boats, pontoons and motor yachts and boating accessories, docks, dockominiums and vacation properties. Est attendance: 30,000. For info: ShowSpan, Inc. Phone: (616) 447-2860. Fax: (616) 447-2861. E-mail: events@showspan.com. Web: www.showspan.com.

JAPANESE INTERNMENT: ANNIVERSARY. Feb 19, 1942. As a result of President Franklin Roosevelt's Executive Order 9066, some 110,000 Japanese Americans living in coastal Pacific areas were placed in concentration camps in remote areas of Arizona, Arkansas, inland California, Colorado, Idaho, Utah and Wyoming. The interned Japanese Americans (two-thirds of whom were US citizens) lost an estimated $400 million in property. They were allowed to return to their homes Jan 2, 1945.

KNIGHTS OF PYTHIAS: FOUNDING ANNIVERSARY. Feb 19, 1864. The social and fraternal order of the Knights of Pythias was founded at Washington, DC.

MCCULLERS, CARSON: BIRTH ANNIVERSARY. Feb 19, 1917. Born Lula Carson Smith at Columbus, GA, McCullers was a renowned 20th-century author whose works are emblematic of the Southern Gothic literary tradition. Her first novel, *The Heart Is a Lonely Hunter* (1940), deals with themes of inner loneliness and isolation, both of which run through McCullers's other work. McCullers was inducted into the National Institute of Arts and Letters in 1952 and died Sept 29, 1967, at Nyack, NY, after a long-suffering battle with rheumatic fever.

US LANDING ON IWO JIMA: 75th ANNIVERSARY. Feb 19, 1945. Beginning at dawn, the landing of 30,000 American troops took place on the barren 12-square-mile island of Iwo Jima. Initially there was little resistance, but 21,500 Japanese stood ready underground to fight to the last man to protect massive strategic fortifications linked by tunnels. See also: "Iwo Jima Day: Anniversary" (Feb 23).

🎂 BIRTHDAYS TODAY

Prince Andrew, 60, Duke of York, born London, England, Feb 19, 1960.

Justine Bateman, 54, actress ("Family Ties," "Men Behaving Badly"), born Rye, NY, Feb 19, 1966.

Millie Bobby Brown, 16, actress ("Stranger Things," "Intruders"), born Málaga, Spain, Feb 19, 2004.

Lou Christie, 77, singer, born Glen Willard, PA, Feb 19, 1943.

Jeff Daniels, 65, actor ("The Newsroom," *The Purple Rose of Cairo, Dumb and Dumber*), born Chelsea, MI, Feb 19, 1955.

Benicio Del Toro, 53, actor (Oscar for *Traffic; Sicario, Che, The Usual Suspects*), born Santurce, Puerto Rico, Feb 19, 1967.

Haylie Duff, 35, actress ("7th Heaven," *Napoleon Dynamite*), born Houston, TX, Feb 19, 1985.

February 2020	S	M	T	W	T	F	S
							1
	2	3	4	5	6	7	8
	9	10	11	12	13	14	15
	16	17	18	19	20	21	22
	23	24	25	26	27	28	29

Roger Goodell, 61, Commissioner of the National Football League, born Jamestown, NY, Feb 19, 1959.

Jeff Kinney, 49, author (Diary of a Wimpy Kid series), born Fort Washington, MD, Feb 19, 1971.

Jonathan Lethem, 56, author (*Motherless Brooklyn, Fortress of Solitude*), born Brooklyn, NY, Feb 19, 1964.

Hana Mandlikova, 57, Hall of Fame tennis player, born Prague, Czechoslovakia (now the Czech Republic), Feb 19, 1963.

Marta, 34, soccer player, born Marta Vieira da Silva at Dois Riachas, Brazil, Feb 19, 1986.

Stephen Nichols, 69, actor ("Days of Our Lives," "General Hospital"), born Cincinnati, OH, Feb 19, 1951.

Smokey Robinson, 80, Rock and Roll, Songrwriters and Rhythm & Blues halls of fame singer, songwriter, born William Robinson, Jr, at Detroit, MI, Feb 19, 1940.

Seal, 57, singer, songwriter, born Sealhenry Samuel at London, England, Feb 19, 1963.

Andrew Shue, 53, actor ("Melrose Place"), born South Orange, NJ, Feb 19, 1967.

Amy Tan, 68, author (*The Joy Luck Club*), born Oakland, CA, Feb 19, 1952.

Ray Winstone, 63, actor (*Indiana Jones and the Kingdom of the Crystal Skull, The Departed, Sexy Beast*), born London, England, Feb 19, 1957.

February 20 — Thursday

DAY 51 **315 REMAINING**

ADAMS, ANSEL: BIRTH ANNIVERSARY. Feb 20, 1902. American photographer, known for his photographs of Yosemite National Park, born at San Francisco, CA. Adams died at Monterey, CA, Apr 22, 1984.

ALTMAN, ROBERT: 95th BIRTH ANNIVERSARY. Feb 20, 1925. This iconoclastic filmmaker was master of satire, ensemble casts and the long take. His long and lauded career included such classic films as *M*A*S*H* (1970), *McCabe and Mrs Miller* (1971), *Nashville* (1975), *The Player* (1992) and *Gosford Park* (2001). Altman received a Lifetime Achievement Oscar in 2006. Born at Kansas City, MO, Altman died Nov 20, 2006, at Los Angeles, CA.

CANADA: MONTREAL HUNTING, FISHING & CAMPING SHOW. Feb 20–23. Palais des Congrè de Montreal, Montreal, QC. 59th annual. Manufacturers' representatives, distributors and retailers of the outdoors, including camping, fishing, ATVs, hunting, marine (fishing boats, canoes, kayaks, etc), tourism offices, outfitters (lodges), RVs and entertainment. For info: Canadian National Sportsmen's Shows, 8150 E Metropolitan Blvd, Ste 330, Anjou, QC, H1K 1A1, Canada. Phone: (514) 866-5409. Fax: (514) 866-4092. Web: www.salonpleinairmontreal.ca.

CLOSEST APPROACH OF A COMET TO EARTH: ANNIVERSARY. Feb 20, 1491. An unnamed comet came within 860,000 miles (.0094 AU) of Earth on this date. By comparison, the closest approach that Halley's comet made to Earth was on Apr 10, AD 837, at 3 million miles.

DOUGLASS, FREDERICK: 125th DEATH ANNIVERSARY. Feb 20, 1895. American journalist, orator and antislavery leader. Born at Tuckahoe, MD, probably in February 1818, he died at Anacostia Heights, DC. He was buried at Mount Hope Cemetery, Rochester, NY. His original name before his escape from slavery was Frederick Augustus Washington Bailey.

GERMANY: BERLIN INTERNATIONAL FILM FESTIVAL. Feb 20–Mar 1. Potsdamer Platz, Berlin. The 70th festival. One of the premier international film festivals since its inaugural opening in 1951. Includes film competition, children's film festival and other special programs. The awarding of Golden and Silver Bears by the international jury marks the conclusion of the festival. Est attendance: 300,000. For info: Internationale Filmfestspiele Berlin, Potsdamer Strasse 11, 10785 Berlin, Germany. Phone: (49) 30-25920-0. E-mail: info@berlinale.de. Web: www.berlinale.de.

INTRODUCE A GIRL TO ENGINEERING DAY (DISCOVERE GIRL DAY). Feb 20. 19th annual. On the Thursday of National Engineers Week, the engineering community is asked to mobilize women and men engineers to reach more than one million girls and encourage them to pursue the fields that lead to engineering careers. Website includes links for teachers. For info: DiscoverE. E-mail: Info@DiscoverE.org. Web: www.discovere.org/our-programs/girl-day.

ITALY: FEAST OF THE INCAPPUCCIATI. Feb 20. Gradoli (near Viterbo). On the Thursday before Ash Wednesday, the members of the Confraternity of Purgatory make the rounds of the town dressed in traditional hooded robes, bearing a banner and walking to the beat of a drum. They stop at every house to collect foodstuffs in the name of the souls in purgatory; the food is then served at the banquet on Ash Wednesday.

JEFFERSON, JOSEPH: BIRTH ANNIVERSARY. Feb 20, 1829. Distinguished American actor, born at Philadelphia, PA, into a family of actors. Jefferson made his stage debut at the age of three in Kotzebue's *Pizarro*. After many successes, his search for a character both humorous and pathetic centered on Rip van Winkle, about whom he wrote a short play. Later revised by Dion Boucicault, the play opened in 1865 with Jefferson in the leading role at London, England, and was an immediate success. Rip van Winkle became the signature role for which he was known. Jefferson died at Palm Beach, FL, Apr 23, 1905. He is remembered each year in Chicago, IL, when the Joseph Jefferson (Jeff) Awards are presented to recognize excellence in theatrical productions.

NORTHERN HEMISPHERE HOODIE-HOO DAY. Feb 20. At high noon (local time) citizens are asked to go outdoors and yell, "Hoodie-Hoo" to chase away winter and make ready for spring, one month away. (©2006 by WH.) For info: Thomas & Ruth Roy, Wellcat Holidays, 2418 Long Ln, Lebanon, PA 17046. Phone: (717) 279-0184. E-mail: info@wellcat.com. Web: www.wellcat.com.

PISCES, THE FISH. Feb 20–Mar 20. In the astronomical/astrological zodiac, which divides the sun's apparent orbit into 12 segments, the period Feb 20–Mar 20 is traditionally identified as the sun sign of Pisces, the Fish. The ruling planet is Neptune.

PRESCOTT, WILLIAM: BIRTH ANNIVERSARY. Feb 20, 1726. American Revolutionary soldier, born at Groton, MA. Died at Pepperell, MA, Oct 13, 1795. Credited with the order "Don't one of you fire until you see the whites of their eyes," at the Battle of Bunker Hill, June 17, 1775.

SPACE MILESTONE: *FRIENDSHIP 7* (US): FIRST AMERICAN TO ORBIT EARTH. Feb 20, 1962. John Herschel Glenn, Jr, became the first American and the third person to orbit Earth. Aboard the capsule *Friendship 7*, he made three orbits of Earth. Spacecraft was *Mercury-Atlas 6*. In 1998 the 77-year-old Glenn went into space again on the space shuttle *Discovery* to test the effects of aging.

SPACE MILESTONE: *MIR* **SPACE STATION (USSR).** Feb 20, 1986. A "third-generation" orbiting space station, *Mir* (Peace), was launched without crew from the Baikonur space center at Leninsk, Kazakhstan. Believed to be 40 feet long, weigh 47 tons and have six docking ports. Both Russian and American crews used the station. After many equipment failures and financial problems, the Russians took *Mir* out of service Mar 23, 2001. See also: "Space Milestone: *Mir* Abandoned (USSR)" (Mar 23).

STOTZ, CARL E.: 100th BIRTH ANNIVERSARY. Feb 20, 1920. Carl E. Stotz shaped the summers of millions of kids as the founder of Little League Baseball. Born at Williamsport, PA, he organized the first three-team league there in 1939. Stotz served as Little League commissioner until 1955. He died at Williamsport, June 4, 1992.

UNITED NATIONS: WORLD DAY FOR SOCIAL JUSTICE. Feb 20. Observance of this day should support efforts of the international community in poverty eradication, the promotion of full employment and decent work, gender equity and access to social well-being and justice for all. (Res 62/10 of Nov 26, 2007.) Annually, Feb 20. For info: United Nations. Web: www.un.org.

🎂 BIRTHDAYS TODAY

Charles Barkley, 57, sportscaster, Hall of Fame basketball player, born Leeds, AL, Feb 20, 1963.

Brenda Blethyn, 74, actress ("Vera," *Secrets and Lies*, *A River Runs Through It*), born Ramsgate, England, Feb 20, 1946.

Gordon Brown, 69, former prime minister of Great Britain (2007–10), born Glasgow, Scotland, Feb 20, 1951.

Cindy Crawford, 54, model, actress, born DeKalb, IL, Feb 20, 1966.

Sandy Duncan, 74, actress (*Funny Face*, "The Hogan Family," *Peter Pan*), born Henderson, TX, Feb 20, 1946.

Ron Eldard, 57, actor ("Men Behaving Badly," "ER"), born Long Island, NY, Feb 20, 1963.

Philip Anthony (Phil) Esposito, 78, hockey executive, former hockey coach, Hall of Fame hockey player, born Sault Ste. Marie, ON, Canada, Feb 20, 1942.

Stephon Marbury, 43, basketball player, born New York, NY, Feb 20, 1977.

Mitch McConnell, 78, US Senator (R, Kentucky), born Colbert County, AL, Feb 20, 1942.

Trevor Noah, 36, talk show host ("The Daily Show"), comedian, born Johannesburg, South Africa, Feb 20, 1984.

Jennifer O'Neill, 72, actress (*The Summer of '42*, "Cover-Up"), born Rio de Janeiro, Brazil, Feb 20, 1948.

Sidney Poitier, 93, actor (Oscar for *Lilies of the Field*; *In the Heat of the Night*), born Miami, FL, Feb 20, 1927.

Rihanna, 32, singer, born Robyn Rihanna Fenty at St. Michael, Barbados, Feb 20, 1988.

Buffy Sainte-Marie, 79, folksinger, born Craven, SK, Canada, Feb 20, 1941.

Patty Hearst Shaw, 66, newspaper heiress, kidnap victim, actress (*Cry-Baby*), born San Francisco, CA, Feb 20, 1954.

French Stewart, 56, actor ("3rd Rock from the Sun"), born Albuquerque, NM, Feb 20, 1964.

Peter Strauss, 73, actor (*Rich Man, Poor Man*; *Soldier Blue*), born Croton-on-Hudson, NY, Feb 20, 1947.

Lili Taylor, 53, actress ("Six Feet Under," *I Shot Andy Warhol*, *Ransom*, *Mystic Pizza*), born Glencoe, IL, Feb 20, 1967.

Miles Teller, 33, actor (*Whiplash*, *Divergent* series), born Downingtown, PA, Feb 20, 1987.

Robert William (Bobby) Unser, 86, auto racer, born Albuquerque, NM, Feb 20, 1934.

Justin Verlander, 37, baseball player, born Manakin Sabot, VA, Feb 20, 1983.

February 21 — Friday

DAY 52   **314 REMAINING**

AUDEN, W.H.: BIRTH ANNIVERSARY. Feb 21, 1907. The Pulitzer Prize–winning, Anglo-American poet was born Wystan Hugh Auden at York, England. "Some books," he wrote in *The Dyer's Hand* (1962), "are undeservedly forgotten; none are undeservedly remembered." Died at Vienna, Austria, Sept 28, 1973.

BANGLADESH: MARTYRS DAY. Feb 21. National mourning day in memory of martyrs of the Bengali Language Movement in 1952. Mourners gather at the Azimpur graveyard.

BATTLE OF VERDUN: ANNIVERSARY. Feb 21–Dec 18, 1916. The German High Command launched an offensive on the Western Front at Verdun, France, which became WWI's single longest battle. It is estimated that more than 300,000 troops died out of 750,000 total casualties (350,000 German and 400,000 French).

BOMBECK, ERMA: BIRTH ANNIVERSARY. Feb 21, 1927. Humorist and writer, born at Dayton, OH. Authored many books, including *The Grass Is Always Greener over the Septic Tank*. Bombeck died at San Francisco, CA, Apr 22, 1996.

CIA AGENT ARRESTED AS SPY: ANNIVERSARY. Feb 21, 1994. Aldrich Hazen Ames and his wife, Maria del Rosario Casas Ames, were arrested on charges they had spied for the Soviet Union beginning in 1985 and had continued to spy for Russia after the Soviet collapse in 1991. Aldrich Ames had worked as a counterintelligence officer for the CIA at its headquarters at Langley, VA. Prosecutors said that the pair had been paid about $2.5 million for their activities and were probably responsible for the deaths of at least 10 CIA agents whom Ames had identified for the Soviets. The government considered this to be one of the most serious spy cases ever uncovered in the US. On Apr 28 Aldrich Ames was sentenced to life in prison. Rosario Ames was sentenced to a 63-month prison term in return for her husband's promise to cooperate with authorities.

MALCOLM X ASSASSINATED: 55th ANNIVERSARY. Feb 21, 1965. Just as he began a speech to his newly formed Organization of Afro-American Unity, black activist leader Malcolm X was gunned down by several men standing among the 400-plus crowd in the Audubon Ballroom at Harlem, New York City. The assassination occurred barely a week after Malcolm X's Queens home was fire-bombed. Three men were convicted of the murder in 1966 and sentenced to life in prison (two were released in the 1980s and the third won parole in 2010). See also: "Malcolm X: Birth Anniversary" (May 19).

February 2020	S	M	T	W	T	F	S
							1
	2	3	4	5	6	7	8
	9	10	11	12	13	14	15
	16	17	18	19	20	21	22
	23	24	25	26	27	28	29

THE NEW YORKER PUBLISHED: 95th ANNIVERSARY. Feb 21, 1925. First issue of the magazine published on this date.

NIXON'S TRIP TO CHINA: ANNIVERSARY. Feb 21, 1972. Richard Nixon became the first US president to visit any country not diplomatically recognized by the US when he went to the People's Republic of China for meetings with Chairman Mao Tse-tung and Premier Chou En-lai. Nixon arrived at Peking on this date and departed China on Feb 28. The "Shanghai Communiqué" was issued Feb 27. See also: "Shanghai Communiqué: Anniversary" (Feb 27).

PALMER, ALICE FREEMAN: BIRTH ANNIVERSARY. Feb 21, 1855. Born at Colesville, NY, Alice Freeman Palmer became president of Wellesley College at the age of 27. Under her leadership the school grew into one of the leading women's colleges. She was also instrumental in bringing the women's school Radcliffe College into its association with Harvard University. One of the organizers of the American Association of University Women, she served as its president for two terms. She was appointed the first dean of women at the University of Chicago when it opened in 1892. Palmer died Dec 6, 1902, at Paris, France.

SANDINO, CESAR AUGUSTO: ASSASSINATION ANNIVERSARY. Feb 21, 1934. Nicaraguan guerrilla leader after whom the Sandinistas are named. Sandino, born in 1893 (exact date unknown), was murdered along with his brother and several aides at Managua on this date. He and his followers had eluded the occupying force of US Marines as well as the Nicaraguan National Guard from 1927 until 1933. Regarded by the US as an outlaw and a bandit, he is revered as a martyred patriot hero by many Nicaraguans. His successful resistance and the resulting widespread anti-US feeling were largely responsible for inauguration of a US counteraction—the Good Neighbor Policy—toward Latin American nations during the administration of President Franklin Roosevelt.

SIMONE, NINA: BIRTH ANNIVERSARY. Feb 21, 1933. The blues and jazz singer was born Eunice Waymon at Tryon, NC. Initially determined to become a concert pianist, Simone instead found a career as a singer of a wide range of musical genres in which she could put her uniquely raw and emotional voice on display. Simone was an ardent supporter of the 1950s and '60s civil rights movement. She died at Carry-le-Rouet, France, on Apr 21, 2003.

SPAIN: JEREZ FLAMENCO FESTIVAL (FESTIVAL DE JEREZ). Feb 21–Mar 7 (tentative). Jerez de la Frontera, Cadiz, Andalusia. 24th annual. Celebration of flamenco and Spanish dance. The greatest performers of flamenco from around the world take over the city of Jerez for two weeks to showcase both traditional and contemporary expressions of the passionate dance. Events take place around the city—from grand theaters to smoky secluded bars. Festival includes classes for all ability levels. For info: Ayuntamiento de Jerez. Web: www.jerez.es/webs_municipales/festival_jerez.

UNITED NATIONS: INTERNATIONAL MOTHER LANGUAGE DAY. Feb 21. Since 2000, a day to promote linguistic and cultural diversity and multilingualism. Observed on the anniversary of the day in 1952 when students demonstrating for recognition of their language, Bangla, as one of the two national languages of the then Pakistan, were shot and killed by police in Dhaka, the capital of what is now Bangladesh. Annually, Feb 21. For info: United Nations/UNESCO. Web: www.un.org.

WASHINGTON MONUMENT DEDICATED: ANNIVERSARY. Feb 21, 1885. Monument to the first US president was dedicated at Washington, DC.

🎂 BIRTHDAYS TODAY

Christopher Atkins, 59, actor ("Dallas," *The Blue Lagoon*), born Rye, NY, Feb 21, 1961.

William Baldwin, 57, actor ("Dirty Sexy Money," *Born on the Fourth of July*, *Backdraft*), born Massapequa, NY, Feb 21, 1963.

Corbin Bleu, 31, singer, actor (*High School Musical*), born Brooklyn, NY, Feb 21, 1989.

Tituss Burgess, 41, actor ("Unbreakable Kimmy Schmidt"), born Athens, GA, Feb 21, 1979.

Mary Chapin Carpenter, 62, singer, musician, born Princeton, NJ, Feb 21, 1958.

Charlotte Church, 34, singer, born Cardiff, Wales, Feb 21, 1986.

Jack Coleman, 62, actor ("Heroes," "Dynasty"), born Easton, PA, Feb 21, 1958.

Tyne Daly, 73, actress ("Judging Amy," Emmy for "Cagney and Lacey"; *Gypsy*), born Madison, WI, Feb 21, 1947.

Christine Ebersole, 67, actress (Tonys for *Grey Gardens* and *42nd Street*; *War Paint*, *Amadeus*), born Chicago, IL, Feb 21, 1953.

David Geffen, 76, record company executive (Geffen Records), born New York, NY, Feb 21, 1944.

Kelsey Grammer, 65, actor (Golden Globe for "Boss," Golden Globe and Emmys for "Frasier"; "The Last Tycoon," "The Simpsons"), born St. Thomas, US Virgin Islands, Feb 21, 1955.

Ashley Greene, 33, actress (*Twilight*), born Jacksonville, FL, Feb 21, 1987.

Jennifer Love Hewitt, 41, actress ("Ghost Whisperer," "Party of Five," "Time of My Life"), born Waco, TX, Feb 21, 1979.

Gary Lockwood, 83, actor (*Splendor in the Grass*, *2001: A Space Odyssey*), born Van Nuys, CA, Feb 21, 1937.

Kumail Nanjiani, 42, comedian, actor (*The Big Sick*, "Silicon Valley"), screenwriter, born Karachi, Pakistan, Feb 21, 1978.

Ellen Page, 33, actress (*Juno*, *X-Men: The Last Stand*), born Halifax, NS, Canada, Feb 21, 1987.

Jordan Peele, 41, director (*Us*, *Get Out*), screenwriter (Oscar for *Get Out*), actor, comedian (*Keanu*, "Key & Peele"), born New York, NY, Feb 21, 1979.

William Petersen, 67, actor ("CSI," *Manhunter*, *To Live and Die in LA*), born Evanston, IL, Feb 21, 1953.

February 22 — Saturday

DAY 53   **313 REMAINING**

ANDERSON, SPARKY: BIRTH ANNIVERSARY. Feb 22, 1934. American baseball manager, born George Lee Anderson at Bridgewater, SD. After an unremarkable playing career, he began managing the Cincinnati Reds in 1970 and with that team won five division titles, three National League Championships and two World Series Championships. After being fired by the Reds, he won another World Series title with Detroit in 1984 and remained with the Tigers until his retirement in 1995. First manager to win a World Series in both the National and American Leagues, Anderson was elected to the Baseball Hall of Fame in 2000. Died Nov 4, 2010, at Thousand Oaks, CA.

BADEN-POWELL, ROBERT: BIRTH ANNIVERSARY. Feb 22, 1857. British army officer who founded the Boy Scouts and Girl Guides. Born at London, England, he died at Kenya, Africa, Jan 8, 1941.

BRAZIL: CARNIVAL. Feb 22–25. Especially in Rio de Janeiro, this carnival is said to be one of the last great folk festivals and the big annual event in the life of Brazilians. Begins on Saturday night before Ash Wednesday and continues through Shrove Tuesday.

CHURCH, FRANCIS PHARCELLUS: BIRTH ANNIVERSARY. Feb 22, 1839. Born at Rochester, NY, journalist and editor best known for writing the most famous editorial in history. As editor of the *New York Sun*, Church responded to the summer 1897 letter of eight-year-old Virginia O'Hanlon, who desperately asked whether Santa Claus existed. On Sept 21, 1897, she saw the unsigned editorial response: "Yes, Virginia, there is a Santa Claus. . . ." Church died Apr 11, 1906, at New York, NY. After his death, the *New York Sun* revealed that he had been the author of its most famous opinion piece.

FLORIDA ACQUIRED BY US: ANNIVERSARY. Feb 22, 1819. Secretary of State John Quincy Adams signed the Florida Purchase Treaty, under which Spain ceded Florida to the US. As payment, the US assumed $5 million of claims by US citizens against Spain. Florida became a state in 1845.

FRENCH WEST INDIES: CARNIVAL. Feb 22–26. Martinique. For five days ending on Ash Wednesday, business comes to a halt. Streets spill over with parties and parades. A Carnival Queen is elected. On Dimanche Gras, or Fat Sunday, revelers dressed as red devils parade in the streets. King Carnival is "buried" on Ash Wednesday.

***IT HAPPENED ONE NIGHT* FILM RELEASE: ANNIVERSARY.** Feb 22, 1934. Frank Capra's romantic screwball comedy, starring Claudette Colbert as a spoiled runaway heiress and Clark Gable as a cocky reporter on to a good story, was the first film to sweep all the major Academy Awards, winning Best Picture, Best Director, Best Actor, Best Actress and Best Screenplay. (A scene in which Clark Gable leans on a fence munching a carrot inspired the Warner Bros. animation team when they were creating Bugs Bunny.)

KENNEDY, EDWARD: BIRTH ANNIVERSARY. Feb 22, 1932. The youngest brother of the Kennedy political dynasty, this elder statesman of American politics was born at Boston, MA. Elected to his brother John's former seat in the US Senate in 1962, he served almost 47 years representing the state of Massachusetts and was a tireless crusader for liberal causes. For years he battled alcoholism and various family scandals, including responsibility for the death of a young woman in a car accident in 1969. As a legislator Kennedy worked with both sides of the political aisle to enact legislative reforms in health care, civil rights, education and voting rights. He was diagnosed with a brain tumor in May 2008 but remained at work until his death at Hyannis Port, MA, Aug 25, 2009.

February 2020	S	M	T	W	T	F	S
							1
	2	3	4	5	6	7	8
	9	10	11	12	13	14	15
	16	17	18	19	20	21	22
	23	24	25	26	27	28	29

KREWE OF ENDYMION PARADE. Feb 22. New Orleans, LA. Formed in 1966, the Krewe of Endymion puts on a spectacular carnival parade the Saturday before Mardi Gras. Features more than 3,000 riders on 37 floats—many of which are multivehicle units. For info: Krewe of Endymion. Web: https://endymion.org.

LOWELL, JAMES RUSSELL: BIRTH ANNIVERSARY. Feb 22, 1819. American essayist, Romantic poet, editor and diplomat. Author of the bestselling *Biglow Papers* (1848). Lowell was the first editor of *The Atlantic Monthly* upon its founding in 1857. Born at Cambridge, MA, he died there Aug 12, 1891.

MALTA: CARNIVAL. Feb 22–25. Valletta. Festival dates from 1535 when Knights of St. John of Jerusalem introduced Carnival at Malta. Dancing (featuring the sword dance, or *Il Parata*, and other national dances), bands, decorated trucks and grotesque masks. Annually, the Saturday through Tuesday before Ash Wednesday.

MILLAY, EDNA ST. VINCENT: BIRTH ANNIVERSARY. Feb 22, 1892. The poet, dramatist, feminist Millay was born at Rockland, ME. Her work, noted for its ardent and frank explorations of desire, was acclaimed (she won the Pulitzer Prize in 1923) and bestselling during the interwar period. Her sonnet sequence of a love affair, *Fatal Interview* (1931), sold more than 50,000 copies in its first year of publication. She is well known for her lyric, "My candle burns at both ends. . . ." Millay died Oct 19, 1950, at Austerlitz, NY.

MILLS, JOHN: BIRTH ANNIVERSARY. Feb 22, 1908. Popular actor, born at North Elmham, England, who played stalwart, everyman heroes. His career ranged from 1932 to 2004, and his memorable films include *In Which We Serve* (1942), *Great Expectations* (1946), *Tunes of Glory* (1960) and *Ryan's Daughter* (1970)—for which he received a Best Supporting Actor Oscar. Mills was knighted in 1976. He died Apr 23, 2005, at Denham, England.

MIRACLE ON ICE: US HOCKEY TEAM DEFEATS USSR: ANNIVERSARY. Feb 22, 1980. The US Olympic hockey team upset the team from the Soviet Union, 4–3, at the Lake Placid Winter Games to earn a victory often called the "Miracle on Ice." Led by coach Herb Brooks, the Americans went on to defeat Finland two days later and win the gold medal.

MONTGOMERY BOYCOTT ARRESTS: ANNIVERSARY. Feb 22, 1956. On Feb 20 white city leaders of Montgomery, AL, issued an ultimatum to black organizers of the three-month-old Montgomery bus boycott. They said if the boycott ended immediately, there would be "no retaliation whatsoever." If it did not end, it was made clear they would begin arresting black leaders. Two days later, 80 well-known boycotters, including Rosa Parks, Martin Luther King, Jr. and E.D. Nixon, marched to the sheriff's office in the county courthouse, where they gave themselves up for arrest. They were booked, fingerprinted and photographed. The next day the story was carried by newspapers all over the world.

NATIONAL MARGARITA DAY. Feb 22. A day to celebrate the sweet, tangy and refreshing margarita. A margarita is mixture of tequila, orange liqueur and lime juice served frozen or over ice. *Margarita* means "daisy flower" in Spanish, and it is rumored that the drink was invented in the 1930s when a bartender in Tijuana, Mexico, accidentally put tequila instead of brandy in an American news editor's Brandy Daisy cocktail. Observed since 2009. Annually, Feb 22. For info: Todd McCalla. E-mail: sponsors@nationalmargaritaday.com. Web: www.nationalmargaritaday.com.

NIXON, MARNI: 90th BIRTH ANNIVERSARY. Feb 22, 1930. Soprano and playback singer, born Margaret Nixon McEathron at Alladena, CA. Called the "ghostess with the mostest" by *Time* in 1964, Marni Nixon was the uncredited singing voice of Deborah Kerr in *The King and I* (1956), Natalie Wood in *West Side Story* (1961) and Audrey Hepburn in *My Fair Lady* (1964). Other actresses she dubbed include Marilyn Monroe, Janet Leigh and Margaret O'Brien. She died July 24, 2016, at New York, NY.

SAINT LUCIA: INDEPENDENCE DAY. Feb 22. National holiday. Commemorates independence of the island in the West Indies from Britain in 1979.

SCHOPENHAUER, ARTHUR: BIRTH ANNIVERSARY. Feb 22, 1788. German philosopher and author born at Danzig, Prussia (now Gdansk, Poland). Dubbed "the philosopher of pessimism," Schopenhauer was one of the first in his field to suggest that humankind should suppress their natural desires in order to achieve harmony, both cerebrally and universally, in an irrational world. He was a contemporary of many German Idealists, and his philosophical works directly challenged idealism in favor of rationalism and influenced later scholars such as Nietzsche and Freud, as well as artists Dvorak, Brahms, Borges and Tolstoy, among others. He died at Frankfurt am Main, Germany, Sept 21, 1860.

WADLOW, ROBERT PERSHING: BIRTH ANNIVERSARY. Feb 22, 1918. Tallest man in recorded history, born at Alton, IL. Though only 9 pounds at birth, by age 10 Wadlow already stood more than 6 feet tall and weighed 210 pounds. When Wadlow died at age 22, he was a remarkable 8 feet 11.1 inches tall, 490 pounds. His gentle, friendly manner in the face of constant public attention earned him the name "Gentle Giant." Wadlow died July 15, 1940, at Manistee, MI, of complications resulting from a foot infection.

WASHINGTON, GEORGE: BIRTH ANNIVERSARY. Feb 22, 1732. First president of the US ("first in war, first in peace, and first in the hearts of his countrymen" in the words of Henry "Light-Horse Harry" Lee). Born at Westmoreland County, VA, Feb 22, 1732 (New Style). However, the Julian (Old Style) calendar was still in use in the colonies when he was born, and the year began in March, so the date on the calendar when he was born was Feb 11, 1731. He died at Mount Vernon, VA, Dec 14, 1799. See also: "Washington, George: Birthday Observance (Legal Holiday)" (Feb 17) and "Washington, George: Death Anniversary" (Dec 14).

WOOLWORTH'S FIRST OPENED: ANNIVERSARY. Feb 22, 1879. First chain store, F.W. Woolworth, opened at Utica, NY. In 1997 the closing of the chain was announced.

🎂 BIRTHDAYS TODAY

Amy Strum Alcott, 64, Hall of Fame golfer, born Kansas City, MO, Feb 22, 1956.

Drew Barrymore, 45, actress ("Santa Clarita Diet," *Whip It, Charlie's Angels, Never Been Kissed, E.T. The Extra-Terrestrial*), producer, born Los Angeles, CA, Feb 22, 1975.

James Blunt, 43, singer, born Tidworth, Wiltshire, England, Feb 22, 1977.

Michael Te Pei Chang, 48, Hall of Fame tennis player, born Hoboken, NJ, Feb 22, 1972.

Paul Dooley, 92, actor (*Slap Shot, Breaking Away, The Player*), born Parkersburg, WV, Feb 22, 1928.

Julius Winfield "Dr. J" Erving, 70, Hall of Fame basketball player, born Roosevelt, NY, Feb 22, 1950.

Kyle MacLachlan, 61, actor ("Twin Peaks," *Blue Velvet, The Flintstones*), born Yakima, WA, Feb 22, 1959.

Miou-Miou, 70, actress (*Entre Nous, La Lectrice*), born Paris, France, Feb 22, 1950.

Rajon Rondo, 34, basketball player, born Louisville, KY, Feb 22, 1986.

Jeri Ryan, 52, actress ("Shark," "Boston Public," "Star Trek: Voyager"), born Munich, Germany, Feb 22, 1968.

Ben Sasse, 48, US Senator (R, Nebraska), born Plainview, NE, Feb 22, 1972.

Vijay Singh, 57, golfer, born Lautoka, Fiji, Feb 22, 1963.

Julie Walters, 70, actress (*Calendar Girls, Billy Elliot, Educating Rita*), born Birmingham, England, Feb 22, 1950.

February 23 — Sunday

DAY 54   **312 REMAINING**

BELGIUM: CARNIVAL OF BINCHE. Feb 23–25. Binche. This famous carnival dates back to the 16th century and is on the UNESCO Heritage List. Events include giants parade, children's parade, fireworks, orange tossing and more. Annually, Shrove Sunday to Shrove Tuesday.

BRUNEI DARUSSALAM: NATIONAL DAY. Feb 23. National holiday observed in Brunei Darussalam, located on the island of Borneo. Commemorates independence from Britain, Feb 23, 1984.

CURLING IS COOL DAY. Feb 23. Offer up a worldwide embrace for an Olympic sport the entire family can play! If you don't get it, you ain't cool. (©2006 by WH.) For info: Thomas & Ruth Roy, Wellcat Holidays, 2418 Long Ln, Lebanon, PA 17046. Phone: (717) 279-0184. Fax: (240) 332-4886. E-mail: info@wellcat.com. Web: www.wellcat.com.

DIESEL ENGINE PATENTED: ANNIVERSARY. Feb 23, 1893. Rudolf Diesel received a patent in Germany for the engine that bears his name. The diesel engine burns fuel oil rather than gasoline and is used in trucks and heavy industrial machinery.

DU BOIS, W.E.B.: BIRTH ANNIVERSARY. Feb 23, 1868. William Edward Burghardt Du Bois, American educator and leader of the movement for black equality. Born at Great Barrington, MA, he died at Accra, Ghana, Aug 27, 1963. "The cost of liberty," he wrote in 1909, "is less than the price of repression."

FASCHING SUNDAY. Feb 23. Germany and Austria. The last Sunday before Lent.

FIRST CLONING OF AN ADULT ANIMAL: ANNIVERSARY. Feb 23, 1997. Researchers in Scotland announced the first cloning of an adult animal, a lamb they named Dolly with a genetic makeup identical to that of her mother. This led to worldwide speculation about the possibility of human cloning. On Mar 4, 1997, President William Clinton imposed a ban on the federal funding of human cloning research.

FLEMING, VICTOR LONZO: BIRTH ANNIVERSARY. Feb 23, 1889. Film director, born at Pasadena, CA (some sources say 1883). His directorial talents are manifest in two of Hollywood's most popular and enduring movies: *The Wizard of Oz* (1939) and *Gone with the Wind* (1939), for which he won an Academy Award. He died Jan 6, 1949, at Cottonwood, AZ.

GROUND WAR AGAINST IRAQ BEGINS: DESERT STORM: ANNIVERSARY. Feb 23, 1991. After an air campaign lasting slightly more than a month, allied forces launched the ground offensive against Iraqi forces as part of Desert Storm.

GUYANA: ANNIVERSARY OF REPUBLIC. Feb 23. National holiday. Guyana in South America became a republic within the British Commonwealth, Feb 23, 1970.

HANDEL, GEORGE FREDERICK: BIRTH ANNIVERSARY. Feb 23, 1685. Born at Halle, Saxony, Germany. Handel and Bach, born the same year, were perhaps the greatest masters of Baroque music. Handel's

most frequently performed work is the oratorio *Messiah*, which was first heard in 1742. He died at London, England, Apr 14, 1759. See also: "Premiere of Handel's *Messiah*: Anniversary" (Apr 13).

HUSTLE CHICAGO. Feb 23 (tentative). 875 N Michigan Ave, Chicago, IL. Chicago's premier winter fitness event raises funds for the Respiratory Health Association's lung disease and clean air education, research and policy change efforts. There are two stair climb categories, the full climb (94 floors) and the half climb (52 floors), held simultaneously in two separate stairwells. Est attendance: 4,000. For info: Respiratory Health Association, 1440 W Washington Blvd, Chicago, IL 60607. Phone: (312) 628-0223. E-mail: hustle@resphealth.org. Web: https://resphealth.org/specialevents/hustle-chicago.

ITALY: CARNIVAL WEEK. Feb 23–29. Milan. Carnival week is held according to local tradition, with shows and festive events for children on Tuesday and Thursday. Parades of floats, figures in the costume of local folk characters Meneghin and Cecca, parties and more traditional events are held on Saturday. Annually, the Sunday–Saturday of Ash Wednesday week.

IWO JIMA DAY: 75th ANNIVERSARY. Feb 23, 1945. Anniversary of the day that the US flag was raised on the Pacific island of Iwo Jima by US Marines. Almost 20,000 American soldiers lost their lives before the island was finally taken from the Japanese on Mar 16, 1945.

JAPAN: BIRTHDAY OF THE EMPEROR. Feb 23. National Day. Holiday honoring Emperor Naruhito, born in 1960.

JAPANESE ATTACK US MAINLAND: ANNIVERSARY. Feb 23, 1942. In the first attack on the US mainland, a Japanese submarine fired 25 shells at an oil refinery at the edge of Ellwood Oil Field, 12 miles west of Santa Barbara, CA. One shell made a direct hit of the rigging, causing minor damage. President Franklin Roosevelt was giving a fireside chat at the time of the attack.

KREWE OF BACCHUS PARADE. Feb 23. New Orleans, LA. This legendary social club, formed in 1968, throws one of the highlight parades of carnival season. Annually, the Sunday before Mardi Gras. For info: Krewe of Bacchus. Web: www.kreweofbacchus.org.

MOON PHASE: NEW MOON. Feb 23. Moon enters New Moon phase at 10:32 AM, EST.

ORTHODOX MEATFARE SUNDAY. Feb 23. In preparation for the Great Lent, no meat is eaten after Meatfare Sunday.

PEPYS, SAMUEL: BIRTH ANNIVERSARY. Feb 23, 1633. (Old Style date.) Diarist, born at London, England. Wrote Pepys in his diary (Mar 10, 1666): "The truth is, I do indulge myself a little the more in pleasure, knowing that this is the proper age of my life to do it; and, out of my observation that most men that do thrive in the world do forget to take pleasure during the time that they are getting their estate, but reserve that till they have got one, and

then it is too late for them to enjoy it." Died at London, May 26, 1703.

RUSSIA: DEFENDER OF THE FATHERLAND DAY. Feb 23. Commemorates the 1918 birth of the Red Army (when the first drafts took place) and the Red Army's initial combat against invading German troops. Formerly known as Army and Navy Day. Observed with parades and processions. Wreaths are laid at the Tomb of the Unknown Soldier. Also observed on different dates in the former Soviet republics.

SHIRER, WILLIAM L.: BIRTH ANNIVERSARY. Feb 23, 1904. American journalist and author William L. Shirer was born at Chicago, IL. As the European correspondent from 1927 to 1934 for the *Chicago Tribune*, he became a friend of Mohandas K. Gandhi, the leader of India's independence movement. As a result of this he published *Gandhi: A Memoir* in 1980. His best-known book is *The Rise and Fall of the Third Reich* (1960), in which he used his experiences in Europe with the *New York Herald Tribune*, the Universal News Service and CBS Radio. He died Dec 28, 1993, at Boston, MA.

SHROVETIDE. Feb 23–25. The three days before Ash Wednesday: Shrove Sunday, Monday and Tuesday—a time for confession and festivity before the beginning of Lent.

SINGLE-TASKING DAY. Feb 23. Multitasking does not work: it reduces productivity and increases stress. Today, do only one thing at a time without feeling guilty. Annually, Feb 23. For info: Theresa Gabriel, 2914 E 38th St, Columbus, NE 68601. Phone: (402) 910-4563. E-mail: tree.gabriel@gmail.com.

TAYLOR, GEORGE: DEATH ANNIVERSARY. Feb 23, 1781. Signer of the Declaration of Independence. Born 1716 at British Isles (exact date unknown). Died at Easton, PA.

WILLARD, EMMA HART: BIRTH ANNIVERSARY. Feb 23, 1787. Pioneer in higher education for women, born at Berlin, CT. Intent on improving educational opportunities for women, she sent her *Plan for Improving Female Education* to the governor of New York. In it she described her ideal for a girls' school, including the instruction usually offered the girls of her day (music, drawing, penmanship, dancing), as well as adding religious and moral instruction, natural philosophy and domestic science. The New York legislature granted her a charter for the Waterford Academy for Young Ladies. The school later moved to Troy, NY, where it was first named the Troy Female Seminary and later the Emma Willard School. She assisted in the founding of a teachers' training school for girls at Athens, Greece, in 1832. She began the Willard Association for the Mutual Improvement of Female Teachers in 1837, and she authored several textbooks on geography, history and astronomy. Willard died at Troy, Apr 15, 1870.

🎂 BIRTHDAYS TODAY

Aziz Ansari, 37, comedian, actor ("Master of None," "Parks and Recreation"), author (*Modern Romance*), born Columbia, SC, Feb 23, 1983.

Emily Blunt, 37, actress (*Mary Poppins Returns, A Quiet Place, The Girl on the Train, Sicario*), born London, England, Feb 23, 1983.

Roberto Martin Antonio (Bobby) Bonilla, 57, former baseball player, born New York, NY, Feb 23, 1963.

Dakota Fanning, 26, actress ("The Alienist," *American Pastoral, War of the Worlds, I Am Sam*), born Conyers, GA, Feb 23, 1994.

Peter Fonda, 81, actor (*Easy Rider, Ulee's Gold*), born New York, NY, Feb 23, 1939.

Josh Gad, 39, actor (*Beauty and the Beast, The Book of Mormon*, "The Comedians"), comedian, born Hollywood, FL, Feb 23, 1981.

Edward Lee "Too Tall" Jones, 69, former football player and boxer, born Jackson, TN, Feb 23, 1951.

Howard Jones, 65, singer, born Southampton, England, Feb 23, 1955.

Kelly Macdonald, 44, actress ("Boardwalk Empire," *No Country for Old Men, Trainspotting*), born Glasgow, Scotland, Feb 23, 1976.

February 2020	S	M	T	W	T	F	S
							1
	2	3	4	5	6	7	8
	9	10	11	12	13	14	15
	16	17	18	19	20	21	22
	23	24	25	26	27	28	29

Joe-Max Moore, 49, Hall of Fame soccer player, born Tulsa, OK, Feb 23, 1971.

Naruhito, 60, Emperor of Japan, born Tokyo, Japan, Feb 23, 1960.

Niecy Nash, 50, comedienne, actress ("Claws," "The Soul Man," "Reno 911!"), born Palmdale, CA, Feb 23, 1970.

Patricia Richardson, 69, actress ("Double Trouble," "Home Improvement"), born Bethesda, MD, Feb 23, 1951.

February 24 — Monday

DAY 55   **311 REMAINING**

CARNIVAL. Feb 24–25. Period of festivities, feasts, foolishness and gaiety immediately before Lent begins on Ash Wednesday. Ordinarily Carnival includes only Fasching (the Feast of Fools), which is the Monday and Tuesday immediately preceding Ash Wednesday. The period of Carnival may be extended in some areas.

ESTONIA: INDEPENDENCE DAY. Feb 24. National holiday. Commemorates declaration of independence from Soviet Union in 1918. Independence was brief, however; Estonia was again under Soviet control from 1940 until 1991.

FASCHING. Feb 24–25. In Germany and Austria, Fasching—also called Fasnacht, Fasnet or Feast of Fools—is a Shrovetide festival with processions of masked figures, both beautiful and grotesque. Always the two days (Rose Monday and Shrove Tuesday) between Fasching Sunday and Ash Wednesday.

GREGORIAN CALENDAR DAY: ANNIVERSARY. Feb 24, 1582. Pope Gregory XIII, enlisting the expertise of distinguished astronomers and mathematicians, issued a bull correcting the Julian calendar, which was then 10 days in error. The correction was a minor one, changing the rule about leap years. The new calendar named for him, the Gregorian calendar, became effective Oct 4, 1582, in most Catholic countries; in 1752 in Britain and the American colonies; in 1918 in Russia and in 1923 in Greece. It is the most widely used calendar in the world today. See also: "Calendar Adjustment Day: Anniversary" (Sept 2) and "Gregorian Calendar Adjustment: Anniversary" (Oct 4).

GRIMM, WILHELM CARL: BIRTH ANNIVERSARY. Feb 24, 1786. Mythologist and author, born at Hanau, Germany. Best remembered for *Grimm's Fairy Tales,* in collaboration with his brother, Jacob. Died at Berlin, Germany, Dec 16, 1859. See also: "Grimm, Jacob: Birth Anniversary" (Jan 4).

HADASSAH FOUNDED: ANNIVERSARY. Feb 24, 1912. Twelve members of the Daughters of Zion Study Circle met at New York City under the leadership of Henrietta Szold. A constitution was drafted to expand the study group into a national organization called Hadassah (Hebrew for *myrtle* and the biblical name of Queen Esther) to foster Jewish education in America and to create public health nursing and nurses' training in Palestine. Hadassah is now the largest women's volunteer organization in the US, with 1,500 chapters rooted in healthcare delivery, education and vocational training, children's villages and services, and land reclamation in Israel.

HOMER, WINSLOW: BIRTH ANNIVERSARY. Feb 24, 1836. Born at Boston, MA, Homer made the transition from commercial illustrator to acclaimed artist while working in a variety of media. "Look at nature, work independently and solve your own problems," was his advice to another artist, but it also served as his motto. Specializing in rural and nautical landscapes and seascapes, he was noted for the realism of his work, from gentle country life scenes to brutal scenes of nature—a dichotomy that can be observed in two of his famous paintings: *Breezing Up* (1876) and *Gulf Stream* (1899). Somewhat of a recluse in his later years and always struggling financially, Homer died at his home at Prouts Neck, ME, on Sept 29, 1910.

ICELAND: BUN DAY. Feb 24. Children invade homes in the morning with colorful sticks and receive gifts of whipped cream buns. On Shrove Monday.

JOBS, STEVE: 65th BIRTH ANNIVERSARY. Feb 24, 1955. CEO, tech innovator, visionary Steve Jobs, the cocreator of Apple, Inc, and 39th on the Forbes Richest People in America list when he died of cancer at age 56, was also a college dropout who once searched for enlightenment in rural India. In 1976, Jobs founded Apple with Steve Wozniak in order to sell the Apple I personal computer Wozniak had invented. Next came the Apple II, which Jobs made as the first PC housed in consumer-friendly plastic, and in 1984 came the Macintosh, which together with its iconic ad campaign solidified the Apple brand as charismatic, quirky and intuitive, traits that also applied to Jobs himself. A respected leader who was also fired from his own company before returning in 1996—the "Think Different" era—Jobs changed personal computing again with the iPod, iPhone and iPad, devices that forever transformed how society interacts with technology. Born at San Francisco, CA, Jobs died Oct 5, 2011, at Palo Alto, CA.

JOHNSON IMPEACHMENT PROCEEDINGS: ANNIVERSARY. Feb 24, 1868. In a showdown over reconstruction policy following the Civil War, the House of Representatives voted to impeach President Andrew Johnson. Congress had passed the Tenure of Office Act, which required Senate approval before Johnson could remove any official whose appointment was originally approved by the Senate. Johnson vetoed this act, but the veto was overridden by Congress. To test the constitutionality of the act, Johnson dismissed Secretary of War Edwin Stanton, triggering the impeachment vote. On Mar 5, 1868, the Senate convened as a court to hear the charges against the president. The Senate vote of 35–19 fell one vote short of the two-thirds majority needed for impeachment.

MEXICO: FLAG DAY. Feb 24. *El Día de la Bandera.* National holiday honoring the Mexican flag, which was created in 1821 after Mexico achieved independence.

NIMITZ, CHESTER: BIRTH ANNIVERSARY. Feb 24, 1885. Commander of all Allied naval, land and air forces in the southwest Pacific during a portion of WWII, Admiral Chester William Nimitz was born at Fredericksburg, TX. During the final assault on Japan in April 1945, Nimitz resumed command of the entire naval operation in the Pacific, which he had shared with General Douglas MacArthur for some time. Nimitz was one of the signers of the Japanese document of surrender Sept 2, 1945, aboard the USS *Missouri* in Tokyo Bay. Nimitz died Feb 20, 1966, at Treasure Island, San Francisco Bay, CA. The USS *Nimitz* was named in his honor.

SHROVE MONDAY. Feb 24. The Monday before Ash Wednesday. In Germany and Austria, this is called Rose Monday.

TRINIDAD AND TOBAGO: CARNIVAL. Feb 24–25. Port of Spain. This national festival is widely acclaimed as "the mother" of more than 100 carnivals worldwide. The parade of costumed bands and competitions prior to Carnival feature the world's most celebrated calypsonians, steel band players, costume designers and

masqueraders. Annually, the two days before Ash Wednesday. For info: Natl Carnival Commission of Trinidad and Tobago. Phone: (868) 622-1670. E-mail: info@ncctt.org. Web: www.ncctt.org.

WAGNER, HONUS: BIRTH ANNIVERSARY. Feb 24, 1874. American baseball great, born John Peter Wagner at Carnegie, PA. Nicknamed "the Flying Dutchman," Wagner was among the first five players elected to the Baseball Hall of Fame in 1936. Died at Carnegie, Dec 6, 1955.

🎂 BIRTHDAYS TODAY

Wilson Bethel, 36, actor ("Hart of Dixie," "The Young and the Restless"), born Hillsborough, NH, Feb 24, 1984.

Barry Bostwick, 75, actor (*The Rocky Horror Picture Show*, "Spin City"), born San Mateo, CA, Feb 24, 1945.

Jeff Garcia, 50, former football player, born Gilroy, CA, Feb 24, 1970.

Lleyton Hewitt, 39, former tennis player, born Adelaide, Australia, Feb 24, 1981.

Rupert Holmes, 73, musician, songwriter, born Tenafly, NJ, Feb 24, 1947.

Daniel Kaluuya, 31, actor (*Get Out*, *Black Panther*), born London, England, Feb 24, 1989.

Joseph I. Lieberman, 78, former US senator (I, Connecticut), born Stamford, CT, Feb 24, 1942.

Floyd Mayweather, Jr, 43, boxer, quintuple champion, born Grand Rapids, MI, Feb 24, 1977.

Eddie Clarence Murray, 64, Hall of Fame baseball player, born Los Angeles, CA, Feb 24, 1956.

Edward James Olmos, 73, actor (*Stand and Deliver*, "Battlestar Galactica," Emmy for "Miami Vice"), born East Los Angeles, CA, Feb 24, 1947.

Bob Sanders, 39, football player, born Erie, PA, Feb 24, 1981.

Renata Scotto, 84, soprano, born Savona, Italy, Feb 24, 1936.

Helen Shaver, 69, actress (*Desert Hearts*, *The Color of Money*), born St. Thomas, ON, Canada, Feb 24, 1951.

Paula Zahn, 64, television journalist, born Naperville, IL, Feb 24, 1956.

Billy Zane, 54, actor (*Titanic*, *The Phantom*), born Chicago, IL, Feb 24, 1966.

February 25 — Tuesday

DAY 56	**310 REMAINING**

BACKUS, JIM: BIRTH ANNIVERSARY. Feb 25, 1913. Born James Gilmore Backus at Cleveland, OH. An actor whose career encompassed radio, television and film, Jim Backus is most remembered as the voice behind the nearsighted bumbler Mr Magoo and for his portrayal of Thurston Howell III on the popular TV show "Gilligan's Island." Backus died July 3, 1989, at Santa Monica, CA.

BASCOM, "TEXAS ROSE": BIRTH ANNIVERSARY. Feb 25, 1922. A Cherokee-Choctaw Indian born at Covington County, MS, Rose Flynt married rodeo cowboy Earl Bascom and learned trick roping, becoming known as the greatest female trick roper in the world. She appeared on stage, in movies and on early TV. She

February 2020	S	M	T	W	T	F	S
							1
	2	3	4	5	6	7	8
	9	10	11	12	13	14	15
	16	17	18	19	20	21	22
	23	24	25	26	27	28	29

toured with the USO during WWII, performing at every military base and military hospital in the US. After the war she entertained servicemen stationed overseas. In 1981 she was inducted into the National Cowgirl Hall of Fame (located at Fort Worth, TX). She died Sept 23, 1993, at St. George, UT.

BURGESS, ANTHONY: BIRTH ANNIVERSARY. Feb 25, 1917. The composer, literary critic and novelist was born John Anthony Burgess Wilson at Manchester, England. Burgess wrote a great variety of novels, but he is best known for his 1962 dystopian novella *A Clockwork Orange*, which introduced the world to *droogs* and a curious pseudo Russian-inflected slang featuring words like *horrorshow*. Burgess died Nov 22, 1993, at London, England.

CARUSO, ENRICO: BIRTH ANNIVERSARY. Feb 25, 1873. Operatic tenor of legendary voice and fame, born at Naples, Italy. Died there Aug 2, 1921.

CLAY BECOMES HEAVYWEIGHT CHAMP: ANNIVERSARY. Feb 25, 1964. Twenty-two-year-old Cassius Clay (later Muhammad Ali) became world heavyweight boxing champion by defeating Sonny Liston. At the height of his athletic career Ali was well known for both his fighting ability and personal style. His most famous saying was "I am the greatest!" Ali is the only fighter to win the heavyweight fighting title three separate times. He defended that title nine times.

DULLES, JOHN FOSTER: BIRTH ANNIVERSARY. Feb 25, 1888. American statesman born at Washington, DC. In 1953, President Dwight Eisenhower appointed Dulles secretary of state. Dulles was the architect of Eisenhower's cold war foreign policy that promised "massive retaliatory power" in response to Soviet aggression. He helped create the Southeast Asia Treaty Organization (1954) and the Baghdad Pact Organization (1955) in order to bolster NATO and isolate the USSR. Dulles died May 24, 1959, at Washington, DC.

ENGLAND: SHROVETIDE PANCAKE RACE. Feb 25. Olney, Buckinghamshire. The pancake race at Olney has been run since 1445. Competitors must be women over 16 years of age, wearing a traditional housewife's costume, including apron and head covering. With a toss and flip of the pancake on the griddle that each must carry, the women dash from the marketplace to the parish church, where the winner receives a kiss from the ringer of the Pancake Bell. Shriving service follows. Annually, on Shrove Tuesday.

FENWICK, MILLICENT HAMMOND: BIRTH ANNIVERSARY. Feb 25, 1910. Fashion model, author, member of the New Jersey General Assembly and US congresswoman, Millicent Fenwick was born at New York, NY. A champion of liberal causes, Fenwick pointed to her sponsorship of the resolution creating the commission to monitor the 1975 Helsinki accords on human rights as her proudest achievement. She fought for civil rights, peace in Vietnam, aid for the poor, reduction of military programs, gun control and restrictions on capital punishment. Fenwick, the inspiration for Garry Trudeau's "Doonesbury" character Lacey Davenport, died at Bernardsville, NJ, Sept 16, 1992.

FIRST NATIONAL BANK CHARTERED BY CONGRESS: ANNIVERSARY. Feb 25, 1791. The First Bank of the US at Philadelphia, PA, was chartered. Proposed as a national bank by Alexander Hamilton, it lost its charter in 1811. The Second Bank of the US received a charter in 1816, which expired in 1836. Since that time, the US has had no central bank. Central banking functions are carried out by the Federal Reserve System, established in 1913. See also: "Federal Reserve System: Anniversary" (Dec 23).

HARRISON, GEORGE: BIRTH ANNIVERSARY. Feb 25, 1943. Musician and singer born at Liverpool, England, Harrison was the lead guitarist and co-songwriter for The Beatles, alongside John Lennon, Paul McCartney and Ringo Starr. The band is considered the most influential rock-and-roll group of all time. Harrison is credited with introducing Eastern musical styles and instrumentation to Western pop. After the breakup of The Beatles, Harrison embarked on a successful solo career, became an independent film producer (*Time Bandits*) and created one of the first charity rock concerts with his Concert for Bangladesh, which brought relief to flood victims of that country. He died at Los Angeles, CA, on Nov 29, 2001.

HEBRON MASSACRE: ANNIVERSARY. Feb 25, 1994. An American-born Jewish settler in Hebron, Israel, Baruch Goldstein, opened fire with an assault rifle in a crowded mosque, part of a complex sacred to both Jews and Muslims because it is believed to contain the tomb of Abraham and his wife Sarah. Of the more than 400 Muslims gathered for early-morning prayers during the holy month of Ramadan, 29 were killed immediately and 150 were wounded. Others, including Goldstein, were crushed in the panic to flee or during subsequent rioting.

ICELAND: BURSTING DAY. Feb 25. Feasts with salted mutton and thick pea soup. On Shrove Tuesday.

KREWE OF REX MARDI GRAS PARADE. Feb 25. New Orleans, LA. The Krewe of Rex parade is the main event of New Orleans's Mardi Gras festivities. The parade passes through the Garden District and downtown New Orleans. King Rex presides and is considered the King of New Orleans's Carnival. The Rex motto is "Pro bono publico." Annually, Mardi Gras day.

KUWAIT: NATIONAL DAY. Feb 25. National holiday. Commemorates the 1978 accession of King Shaykh Sir 'abdullah Al-Salim al-Sabah.

MARDI GRAS. Feb 25. Last feast before Lent. Although Mardi Gras (Fat Tuesday, literally) is properly limited to Shrove Tuesday, it has come to be popularly applied to the preceding two weeks of celebration. Celebrated especially at New Orleans, LA; Mobile, AL; and certain Mississippi and Florida cities. State holiday in Louisiana.

PACZKI DAY. Feb 25. Food lovers pick this day to enjoy these round, sugarcoated, fruit-filled, Polish pre-Lenten pastries, pronounced "poonch-kee," available in bakeries nationwide. Paczki Day coincides with Shrove Tuesday or Fat Tuesday, the day before Ash Wednesday.

RENOIR, PIERRE-AUGUSTE: BIRTH ANNIVERSARY. Feb 25, 1841. Artist born at Limoges, France. Renoir's paintings are known for their joy and sensuousness as well as the light techniques he employed. With contemporaries Monet, Pissarro, Sisley and others, he formed the Impressionist school of painting, characterized by small yet visible brushstrokes, unusual visual angles and ordinary subject matter. In his later years he was crippled by arthritis and would paint with the brush strapped to his hand. He died at Cagnes-sur-Mer, Provence, France, on Dec 3, 1919.

SHROVE TUESDAY. Feb 25. Always the day before Ash Wednesday. Sometimes called Pancake Tuesday. This day is a legal holiday in some counties in Florida.

SPACE MILESTONE: *SOYUZ 32* (USSR). Feb 25, 1979. Launched from Baikonur space center in Soviet Central Asia. Cosmonauts Vladimir Lyakhov and Valery Ryumin docked at *Salyut 6* space station Feb 26. Returned to Earth in *Soyuz 34* after what was then a record 175 days in space Aug 19, 1979.

WORLD SPAY DAY. Feb 25. 26th annual. Worldwide campaign of The Humane Society of the United States, Humane Society International and the Humane Society Veterinary Medical Association. Highlighting the importance of saving animal lives by spaying or neutering, particularly pets in underserved communities, community cats and street dogs. Veterinary clinics, humane societies/shelters, businesses and animal advocates are encouraged to participate. Annually, the last Tuesday in February, with events in honor of World Spay Day taking place on the day and throughout the month. For info: World Spay Day Coordinator, The Humane Society of the United States, 700 Professional Dr, Gaithersburg, MD 20879. E-mail: spayday@hsi.org. Web: www.worldspayday.org.

"YOUR SHOW OF SHOWS" TV PREMIERE: 70th ANNIVERSARY. Feb 25, 1950. Sid Caesar and Imogene Coca starred in the NBC 90-minute variety program along with Carl Reiner and Howard Morris. The show included monologues, improvisations, parodies, pantomimes and sketches of varying length. Some of its writers were Mel Tolkin, Lucille Kallen, Mel Brooks, Larry Gelbart, Neil Simon and Woody Allen.

ZULU MARDI GRAS PARADE. Feb 25. New Orleans, LA. The Zulu Social Aid and Pleasure Club, one of New Orleans's oldest social clubs (formally established in 1916), has one of the most anticipated parades of the Mardi Gras season in the city. Annually, Mardi Gras day. For info: Zulu Social Aid and Pleasure Club, Inc. Web: www.kreweofzulu.com.

🎂 BIRTHDAYS TODAY

Sean Astin, 49, actor (the Lord of the Rings film trilogy, *The Goonies, Rudy, Courage Under Fire*), born Santa Monica, CA, Feb 25, 1971.

Diane Baker, 82, actress (*Mirage, Marnie, Silence of the Lambs*), born Hollywood, CA, Feb 25, 1938.

Tom Courtenay, 83, actor (*45 Years, The Dresser, The Loneliness of the Long Distance Runner*), born Hull, England, Feb 25, 1937.

Ric Flair, 71, former professional wrestler, born Richard Fliehr at Memphis, TN, Feb 25, 1949.

Karen Grassle, 76, actress ("Little House on the Prairie"), born Berkeley, CA, Feb 25, 1944.

Chelsea Handler, 45, author, television personality ("Chelsea Lately"), born Livingston, NJ, Feb 25, 1975.

Rashida Jones, 44, actress ("Angie Tribeca," "Parks and Recreation"), born Los Angeles, CA, Feb 25, 1976.

Neil Jordan, 70, director, writer (*The Crying Game, Interview with the Vampire*), born County Sligo, Ireland, Feb 25, 1950.

Tea Leoni, 54, actress ("Madam Secretary," *Jurassic Park III, Deep Impact*), born New York, NY, Feb 25, 1966.

Joakim Noah, 35, basketball player, born New York, NY, Feb 25, 1985.

Nancy O'Dell, 54, television personality ("Entertainment Tonight"), born Nancy Humphries at Sumter, NC, Feb 25, 1966.

Sally Jessy Raphael, 77, talk show host, born Easton, PA, Feb 25, 1943.

Bob Schieffer, 83, television journalist, born Austin, TX, Feb 25, 1937.

February 26 — Wednesday

DAY 57   **309 REMAINING**

ASH WEDNESDAY. Feb 26. Marks the beginning of Lent. Forty weekdays and six Sundays (Saturday considered a weekday) remain until Easter Sunday. Named for use of ashes in ceremonial penance.

CASH, JOHNNY: BIRTH ANNIVERSARY. Feb 26, 1932. The iconic country music star was born J.R. Cash at Kingsland, AR. His career spanned the 1950s through the year he died, and he recorded more than 1,500 songs, including such hits as "I Walk the Line," "Ring of Fire," "Folsom Prison Blues" and "A Boy Named Sue." He was called "the Man in Black" because he wore a black, long-tailed suit in sympathy for those who suffered. The recipient of numerous awards and honors, Cash died at Nashville, TN, on Sept 12, 2003. Cash was inducted into both the Country Music and Rock & Roll Halls of Fame.

CODY, WILLIAM FREDERICK "BUFFALO BILL": BIRTH ANNIVERSARY. Feb 26, 1846. American frontiersman born at Scott County, IA, who claimed to have killed more than 4,000 buffalo. Subject of many heroic Wild West yarns, Cody became successful as a showman, taking his acts across the US and to Europe. Died Jan 10, 1917, at Denver, CO.

***COMMUNIST MANIFESTO* PUBLISHED: ANNIVERSARY.** Feb 26, 1848. Written by Karl Marx and Friedrich Engels on the eve of the revolutions of 1848, the *Manifesto* provided ideas for Socialist and Communist movements.

DAUMIER, HONORÉ: BIRTH ANNIVERSARY. Feb 26, 1808. French painter and caricaturist famous for his satirical and comic lithographs. Once spent six months in prison for a caricature of Louis Philippe shown as Gargantua consuming the heavy taxes of the citizens. Born at Marseilles, France, he died Feb 11, 1879, at Valmondois, France.

FEDERAL COMMUNICATIONS COMMISSION CREATED: ANNIVERSARY. Feb 26, 1934. President Franklin Roosevelt ordered the creation of a Communications Commission, which became the FCC. It was established by Congress June 19, 1934, to oversee communication by radio, wire or cable. TV and satellite communication later became part of its charge.

FOR PETE'S SAKE DAY. Feb 26. A world wonders: after all these years, who is Pete and why do we do or not do things for his sake? (©2006 by WH.) For info: Thomas & Ruth Roy, Wellcat Holidays, 2418 Long Ln, Lebanon, PA 17046. Phone: (717) 279-0184. E-mail: info@wellcat.com. Web: www.wellcat.com.

GLEASON, JACKIE: BIRTH ANNIVERSARY. Feb 26, 1916. American musician, comedian and actor, Herbert John "Jackie" Gleason was born at Brooklyn, NY. Best known for his role as Ralph Kramden in the long-running television series "The Honeymooners," which began as a recurring sketch on "Cavalcade of Stars" in 1951. Iconic

February 2020	S	M	T	W	T	F	S
							1
	2	3	4	5	6	7	8
	9	10	11	12	13	14	15
	16	17	18	19	20	21	22
	23	24	25	26	27	28	29

film roles include that of pool shark Minnesota Fats in *The Hustler,* for which he earned an Oscar nomination, and Sheriff Buford T. Justice in the *Smokey and the Bandit* franchise. Gleason died at Fort Lauderdale, FL, June 24, 1987.

GRAND CANYON NATIONAL PARK ESTABLISHED: ANNIVERSARY. Feb 26, 1919. By an act of Congress, Grand Canyon National Park was established. An immense gorge cut through the high plateaus of northwest Arizona by the raging Colorado River and covering 1,218,375 acres, Grand Canyon National Park is considered one of the most spectacular natural phenomena in the world.

GRAND TETON NATIONAL PARK ESTABLISHED: ANNIVERSARY. Feb 26, 1929. Grand Teton, in Wyoming, was established as a national park and preserve by Congress. On Sept 14, 1950, Congress authorized enlarging the park to include areas of Jackson Hole National Monument.

HUGO, VICTOR: BIRTH ANNIVERSARY. Feb 26, 1802. One of the most popular 19th-century authors, born at Besançon, France. His most well-known work is the novel *Les Misérables,* and his most famous character is Quasimodo, the Hunchback of Notre Dame. "An invasion of armies can be resisted," Hugo wrote in 1852, "but not an idea whose time has come." He died at Paris, France, May 22, 1885, and more than 2 million people thronged to his state funeral.

ITALY: PURGATORY BANQUET. Feb 26. Gradoli (near Viterbo). On Ash Wednesday, gourmands are on hand for the banquet of penitence for the souls in purgatory, held on the premises of the cooperative winery.

KUWAIT: LIBERATION DAY. Feb 26. Public holiday commemorating the liberation of Kuwait from Iraqi occupation by allied forces in 1991. Annually, Feb 26.

LENT. Feb 26–Apr 11. Most Christian churches observe a period of fasting and penitence (40 weekdays and six Sundays—Saturday considered a weekday) beginning on Ash Wednesday and ending on the Saturday before Easter.

MARLOWE, CHRISTOPHER: BIRTH ANNIVERSARY. Feb 26, 1564. Great Elizabethan dramatist and poet, born at Canterbury, England (baptism date used as birth date). Made popular the use of blank verse in drama. Major works include *Doctor Faustus* and *Tamburlaine the Great.* Most famous poem is "The Passionate Shepherd to His Love." Killed in mysterious circumstances (perhaps connected to his working as a spy) on May 30, 1593, at Deptford, London, England.

RANDALL, TONY: 100th BIRTH ANNIVERSARY. Feb 26, 1920. Born Leonard Rosenberg at Tulsa, OK, actor Tony Randall had a career that spanned five decades. He was a successful film actor, starring in 1957's *Will Success Spoil Rock Hunter?* and 1959's *Pillow Talk,* and performed extensively on the stage. He launched the National Actors Theatre, a company dedicated to performing classic works of theater. He is perhaps best remembered for his role opposite Jack Klugman in television's "The Odd Couple," playing Felix Unger, the tidy, hypochondriac photographer forced by circumstance to share an apartment with slob sportswriter Oscar Madison. The wildly popular series ran from 1970 to 1975. Randall died at New York, NY, May 17, 2004.

STRAUSS, LEVI: BIRTH ANNIVERSARY. Feb 26, 1829. Bavarian immigrant Levi Strauss created the world's first pair of jeans—Levi's 501 jeans—for California's gold miners in 1850. Born at Buttenheim, Bavaria, Germany, he died in 1902, at San Francisco, CA.

TRAYVON MARTIN SHOOTING: ANNIVERSARY. Feb 26, 2012. In the Orlando-area town of Sanford, an armed neighborhood watch captain of mixed Hispanic race called in "a suspicious person" to the police when he observed an African-American high school student wearing a hoodie. The dispatcher instructed George Zimmerman not to approach the person, but he disregarded the instruction and chased down 17-year-old Trayvon Martin, who was returning to his father's nearby townhouse in the gated community. Zimmerman shot the unarmed Martin in the chest, killing him. Police found Zimmerman moments later with a broken nose and a scalp wound. Authorities initially declined to press charges, citing Florida's "Stand Your Ground" statute. The apparent mishandling of the investigation ignited racial tensions across the United States. A petition calling for Zimmerman's arrest collected 2.2 million signatures. Zimmerman was eventually charged and tried; an all-female jury found him not guilty.

UCI TRACK CYCLING WORLD CHAMPIONSHIPS. Feb 26–Mar 1. Berlin, Germany. Presented by Tissot. Sponsored by the Union Cycliste Internationale (UCI), a nonprofit organization founded on Apr 14, 1900. For info: Union Cycliste Internationale, Chemin de la Mêlée 12, 1860 Aigle, Switzerland. E-mail: admin@uci.ch. Web: www.uci.ch or www.trackcycling-berlin.com.

WORLD TRADE CENTER BOMBING OF 1993: ANNIVERSARY. Feb 26, 1993. A 1,210-pound bomb packed in a van exploded in the underground parking garage of the World Trade Center in New York City, killing six people and injuring more than 1,000 (mostly from smoke inhalation). The powerful blast left a crater 200 feet wide and several stories deep. The cost for damage to the building and disruption of business for the 350 companies with offices in the Center exceeded $591 million. Fifteen people—the fundamentalist Muslim cleric Sheik Omar Abdul Rahman and 14 of his followers—were indicted for the bombing. Rahman was given a life sentence, and the others received prison terms of up to 240 years each.

🎂 BIRTHDAYS TODAY

Erykah Badu, 48, singer, born Dallas, TX, Feb 26, 1972.

Michael Bolton, 67, singer, born New Haven, CT, Feb 26, 1953.

Recep Tayyip Erdogan, 66, President of Turkey, born Istanbul, Turkey, Feb 26, 1954.

Marshall Faulk, 47, sportscaster, Hall of Fame football player, born New Orleans, LA, Feb 26, 1973.

Elizabeth George, 71, author (Inspector Lynley mysteries, *A Great Deliverance*), born Warren, OH, Feb 26, 1949.

Tim Kaine, 62, US Senator (D, Virginia), former chair of the Democratic National Committee, former governor of Virginia, born St. Paul, MN, Feb 26, 1958.

Teresa Palmer, 34, actress ("A Discovery of Witches," *Hacksaw Ridge, Berlin Syndrome*), born Adelaide, Australia, Feb 26, 1986.

February 27 — Thursday

DAY 58   **308 REMAINING**

AFRICAN BURIAL GROUND NATIONAL MONUMENT ESTABLISHED: ANNIVERSARY. Feb 27, 2006. On this date President George W. Bush signed a proclamation declaring a seven-acre plot at the corners of Duane and Elk Streets in Lower Manhattan, New York, to be a national monument. From the 1690s to the 1790s, this land served as a cemetery for both free and enslaved Africans and is believed to be the resting place of more than 15,000 people.

ANDERSON, MARIAN: BIRTH ANNIVERSARY. Feb 27, 1897. Born at Philadelphia, PA (some sources say in 1899 or 1902). Anderson's talent was evident at an early age. Her career stonewalled by the prejudice she encountered in the US, she moved to Europe, where

the magnificence of her voice and her versatility as a performer began to establish her as one of the world's finest contraltos. Preventing Anderson's performance at Washington's Constitution Hall in 1939 on the basis of her color, the Daughters of the American Revolution unintentionally secured for her the publicity that would lay the foundation for her success in the states. Her performance was rescheduled, and on Apr 9 (Easter Sunday), 75,000 people showed up to hear her sing from the steps of the Lincoln Memorial. The performance was simultaneously broadcast by radio. In 1955 Anderson became the first African American to perform with the New York Metropolitan Opera. The following year President Dwight Eisenhower named her a delegate to the United Nations. She performed at President John F. Kennedy's inauguration and in 1963 received the Presidential Medal of Freedom. Anderson died Apr 8, 1993, at Portland, OR.

BLACK, HUGO LA FAYETTE: BIRTH ANNIVERSARY. Feb 27, 1886. Born in rural Alabama, Black was a lawyer, New Deal evangelist and US senator before serving on the US Supreme Court 1937–71. Black died on Sept 25, 1971, at Bethesda, MD, only one week after retiring from the bench.

DOMINICAN REPUBLIC: INDEPENDENCE DAY. Feb 27. National Day. Independence gained in 1844 with the withdrawal of Haitians, who had controlled the area for 22 years.

FARRELL, JAMES THOMAS: BIRTH ANNIVERSARY. Feb 27, 1904. American author, novelist and short-story writer, best known for his Studs Lonigan trilogy. Born at Chicago, IL, he died at New York, NY, Aug 22, 1979.

HAMILTON, ALICE: BIRTH ANNIVERSARY. Feb 27, 1869. American pathologist Alice Hamilton was born at New York, NY. She contributed to the workmen's compensation laws by reporting on the dangers to workers of industrial toxic substances. She taught at Harvard Medical School from 1919 until 1935. Hamilton died Sept 22, 1970, at Hadlyme, CT.

INTERNATIONAL POLAR BEAR DAY. Feb 27. The polar bear, *Ursus maritimus* (sea bear), is the only bear classified as a marine mammal by most countries within its range. These impressive animals (males can reach 10 feet tall and weigh 1,300 pounds) are threatened by habitat loss and reduced access to their seal prey due to climate change. International Polar Bear Day draws attention to the challenges polar bears face in a warming Arctic—and how we each can help. Annually, Feb 27. For info: Polar Bears International—US, PO Box 3008, Bozeman, MT 59772. E-mail: media@pbears.org. Web: www.polarbearsinternational.org.

KUWAIT LIBERATED AND 100-HOUR WAR ENDS: ANNIVERSARY. Feb 27, 1991. Allied troops entered Kuwait City, Kuwait, four days after launching a ground offensive (Feb 23) against the Iraqi forces who had invaded the country. President George H.W. Bush declared Kuwait to be liberated and ceased all offensive military operations in the Gulf War. The end of military operations at midnight EST came 100 hours after the beginning of the land attack. Feb 26 is commemorated as Liberation Day in Kuwait.

LONGFELLOW, HENRY WADSWORTH: BIRTH ANNIVERSARY. Feb 27, 1807. American poet and writer, born at Portland, ME. He is best remembered for his classic narrative poems, such as *The Song of Hiawatha, Paul Revere's Ride* and *The Wreck of the Hesperus*. Died at Cambridge, MA, Mar 24, 1882.

NATIONAL CHILI DAY. Feb 27. A day to recognize chili as an American staple and to celebrate our love for a great bowl of red—especially in the cold winter months. Annually, the last Thursday in February. Created by Doug Welsh of the Hard Times Cafe.

NATIONAL MONEY SHOW. Feb 27–29. Cobb Galleria Centre, Atlanta, GA. Numismatic education programs, exhibits and family activities. Buy, sell and trade coins, paper money, medals and tokens. For info: American Numismatic Assn, 818 N Cascade Ave, Colorado Springs, CO 80903. Phone: (800) 367-9723. E-mail: ana@money.org. Web: www.nationalmoneyshow.com.

SARAZEN, GENE: BIRTH ANNIVERSARY. Feb 27, 1902. Gene Sarazen, golfer, born Eugenio Saraceni at Harrison, NY. Sarazen was one of the game's foremost players and in his later years one of its popular goodwill ambassadors. The inventor of the sand wedge, Sarazen was also the first to win the modern grand slam (the Masters, US Open, British Open and PGA), although not in the same year. During the 1935 Masters, he hit one of golf's most famous shots, a four-wood for a double eagle on the par-5 15th hole of the final round. The shot enabled him to tie Craig Wood for the lead and defeat him in a play-off. Sarazen's last shot was the traditional ceremonial tee shot to open the 1999 Masters. Died at Marco Island, FL, May 13, 1999.

SARNOFF, DAVID: BIRTH ANNIVERSARY. Feb 27, 1891. Influential media executive born at Uzlyany, Russian Empire (now Belarus). After his family moved to New York in 1900, Sarnoff worked his way from office boy to president at the Marconi Wireless Telegraph of America, which was later renamed Radio Corporation of America (RCA). RCA not only manufactured radio sets but also provided programming; the company bought its first radio station in 1926 and expanded rapidly thereafter, calling its network the National Broadcasting Company (NBC). Sarnoff established AM broadcasting as a viable standard and led his companies into the era of television. During WWII he served on General Eisenhower's communications staff, transmitting the news from the European front across Europe on a channel he called "Radio Free Europe." Sarnoff died Dec 12, 1971, at New York, NY.

SHANGHAI COMMUNIQUÉ: ANNIVERSARY. Feb 27, 1972. On this day President Richard Nixon and Premier Chou En-lai released a joint communiqué (the Shanghai Communiqué) after Nixon's weeklong visit to the People's Republic of China. The two nations agreed to work toward normalizing relations. Stopping short of establishing diplomatic relations, this was the first step in that direction. The two nations entered full diplomatic relations on Jan 1, 1979, during the Carter administration.

STEINBECK, JOHN: BIRTH ANNIVERSARY. Feb 27, 1902. Born at Salinas, CA, American author of such classics as *Of Mice and Men* (1937) and *The Grapes of Wrath* (1938), winner of the National Book Award and the Pulitzer Prize for Fiction. Steinbeck received the Nobel Prize for Literature in 1962. He died at New York, NY, Dec 20, 1968.

TAYLOR, ELIZABETH: BIRTH ANNIVERSARY. Feb 27, 1932. Child star, film actress, international sex symbol and legendary philanthropist, born at London, England, to American parents. Taylor's talent as an actress was apparent early on with roles in several Lassie films, and her breakthrough part was in *National Velvet* (1944) at the age of 12. She became an enormously popular film star, winning Best Actress Oscars for *Butterfield 8* (1960) and *Who's Afraid of Virginia Woolf?* (1966), and earning nominations for three other roles. Her great beauty assured her a permanent place in the public eye, and her multiple romances, affairs, marriages and divorces were fuel for the tabloids for decades. In her later years, Taylor launched very successful perfume and jewelry lines modeled on her great love of diamonds, and was known as a tireless campaigner for AIDS fundraising and research. She died at Los Angeles, CA, Mar 23, 2011.

TERRY, ELLEN: BIRTH ANNIVERSARY. Feb 27, 1847. Popular English actress Alice Ellen Terry was born at Coventry, Warwickshire. Terry was best known for her portrayal of Shakespeare's heroines, especially Portia, and as theatrical partner of English actor Henry Irving. Together she and Irving dominated both the British and American theater of their day. She died at Small Hythe, Kent, July 21, 1928.

TWENTY-SECOND AMENDMENT TO US CONSTITUTION (TWO-TERM LIMIT) RATIFICATION: ANNIVERSARY. Feb 27, 1951. After the four successive presidential terms of Franklin Roosevelt, the 22nd Amendment limited the tenure of presidential office to two terms.

🎂 BIRTHDAYS TODAY

Adam Baldwin, 58, actor ("Firefly," *My Bodyguard, Full Metal Jacket*), born Chicago, IL, Feb 27, 1962.

Chelsea Clinton, 40, philanthropist, fund-raiser, born Little Rock, AR, Feb 27, 1980.

Josh Groban, 39, singer, born Los Angeles, CA, Feb 27, 1981.

Alan Guth, 73, physicist, born New Brunswick, NJ, Feb 27, 1947.

Maggie Hassan, 62, US Senator (D, New Hampshire), born Margaret Wood at Boston, MA, Feb 27, 1958.

Howard Hesseman, 80, actor ("WKRP in Cincinnati," "Head of the Class"), born Salem, OR, Feb 27, 1940.

Charlayne Hunter-Gault, 78, broadcast journalist, born Due West, SC, Feb 27, 1942.

Donal Logue, 54, actor ("Gotham," "Grounded for Life," *The Tao of Steve*), born Ottawa, ON, Canada, Feb 27, 1966.

Ralph Nader, 86, consumer advocate, lawyer, former presidential candidate, born Winsted, CT, Feb 27, 1934.

Grant Show, 57, actor ("Swingtown," "Melrose Place," "Ryan's Hope"), born Detroit, MI, Feb 27, 1963.

Joanne Woodward, 90, actress (Oscar for *The Three Faces of Eve*; *Mr and Mrs Bridge*), born Thomasville, GA, Feb 27, 1930.

James Ager Worthy, 59, Hall of Fame basketball player, born Gastonia, NC, Feb 27, 1961.

February 2020	S	M	T	W	T	F	S
							1
	2	3	4	5	6	7	8
	9	10	11	12	13	14	15
	16	17	18	19	20	21	22
	23	24	25	26	27	28	29

February 28 — Friday

DAY 59   **307 REMAINING**

BLONDIN, CHARLES: BIRTH ANNIVERSARY. Feb 28, 1824. Daring French acrobat and aerialist (whose real name was Jean François Gravelet), born at St. Omer, France. Especially remembered for his conquest of Niagara Falls on a tightrope. Died Feb 19, 1897, at London, England. See also: "Charles Blondin's Conquest of Niagara Falls: Anniversary" (June 30).

CANIFF, MILTON: BIRTH ANNIVERSARY. Feb 28, 1907. Creator of the comic strips "Terry and the Pirates®" and "Steve Canyon," Milton Caniff was born at Hillsboro, OH. His strips were noted for their fine draftsmanship and action/adventure story lines. Caniff died Apr 3, 1988, at New York City.

CHICAGO COMIC & ENTERTAINMENT EXPO (C2E2). Feb 28–Mar 1. McCormick Place, Chicago, IL. A convention spanning the latest and greatest from the worlds of comics, movies, television, toys, anime, manga and video games. From a show floor packed with hundreds of exhibitors, to panels and autograph sessions giving fans a chance to interact with their favorite creators, to screening rooms featuring sneak peeks at films and television shows months before they hit either the big or small screen. For info: C2E2. Phone: (800) 354-4003. E-mail: Inquiry@c2e2.com. Web: www.c2e2.com.

FLORAL DESIGN DAY. Feb 28. A day to commemorate floral designing as an art form. Annually, Feb 28. For info: Dr. Stephen Rittner, Rittners School of Floral Design, 345 Marlborough St, Boston, MA 02115. Phone: (617) 267-3824. E-mail: steve@floralschool.com. Web: www.floralschool.com/floral-design-day.htm.

HECHT, BEN: BIRTH ANNIVERSARY. Feb 28, 1894. In the course of his career Ben Hecht wrote in many genres. His newspaper column, "1,001 Afternoons in Chicago," popularized human interest sketches. His play *The Front Page*, written with Charles MacArthur, was a hit on Broadway (1928) and on film (1931). He was a successful reporter and his first novel, *Eric Dorn*, resulted partly from his time reporting from Berlin after WWI. Hecht wrote or cowrote a number of successful movie scripts, including *Notorious* and *Wuthering Heights*. Born at New York City, he died there Apr 18, 1964.

LYON, MARY: BIRTH ANNIVERSARY. Feb 28, 1797. Mary Lyon, born near Buckland, MA, became a pioneer in the field of higher education for women. She founded Mount Holyoke Seminary (forerunner of Mount Holyoke College) in South Hadley, MA, in 1837 at a time when American women were educated primarily by ministers in classes held in their homes. Mount Holyoke was one of the first permanent women's colleges. Lyon died Mar 5, 1849, at South Hadley.

"M*A*S*H": THE FINAL EPISODE: ANNIVERSARY. Feb 28, 1983. Concluding a run of 255 episodes, this 2½-hour finale was the most-watched television show at that time—77 percent of the viewing public was tuned in. The show premiered in 1972. See also: "'M*A*S*H' TV Premiere: Anniversary" (Sept 17).

MINNELLI, VINCENTE: BIRTH ANNIVERSARY. Feb 28, 1903. Minnelli, director of the classic film musicals *Meet Me in St. Louis* (1944), *Gigi* (1958) and *An American in Paris* (1951), was born at Chicago, IL. He died July 25, 1986, at Beverly Hills, CA.

MONTAIGNE, MICHEL DE: BIRTH ANNIVERSARY. Feb 28, 1533. French essayist and philosopher, born at Périgord, France. "And if you have lived a day," he wrote in Book I of his *Essays*, "you have seen everything. One day is equal to all days. There is no other light, no other night. This sun, this moon, these stars, the way they are arranged, all is the very same your ancestors enjoyed and that will entertain your grandchildren." Died at Montaigne, France, Sept 13, 1592.

NATIONAL CUSTOMIZED WHEEL AND TIRE DAY. Feb 28. A day to remember that even vehicles of transportation can be outlets of creative self-expression. This day, show off your customized wheels and tires—or switch up your wheels for the first time. For info: Stephen Wong, Velocity Wheel, 1000 E Garvey Ave, Monterey Park, CA 91755.

NATO PLANES DOWN SERB JETS: ANNIVERSARY. Feb 28, 1994. In the first military action by the North Atlantic Treaty Organization (NATO) in the two-year-old Bosnian civil war and the first combat action by NATO in its 45-year history, UN-designated American fighter planes shot down four of six Bosnian Serb jets operating in a no-fly zone.

PALME, OLOF: ASSASSINATION ANNIVERSARY. Feb 28, 1986. The popular prime minister of Sweden was shot to death as he left a movie theater in Stockholm with his wife. A courageous and dominant figure in Swedish politics, Palme, an aristocrat turned Socialist, had earned international respect. On the day of his death he had signed (with five other world leaders) an appeal to the leaders of the US and the Soviet Union to forgo nuclear testing until the next summit meeting. Born on Jan 30, 1927, Palme was the third European head of government to be assassinated since the beginning of WWII (the others: Prime Minister Armand Calinescu of Romania in 1939 and Prime Minister Luis Carrero Blanco of Spain in 1973).

SHABBAT ACROSS AMERICA AND CANADA. Feb 28. 24th annual. More than 400 participating synagogues and Jewish centers (Conservative, Orthodox, Reform and Reconstructionist) encourage Jews to observe the Sabbath on this Friday night. For info: Natl Jewish Outreach Program, 989 Sixth Ave, 10th Fl, New York, NY 10018. Phone: (888) SHA-BBAT or (646) 871-4444. E-mail: info@njop.org. Web: www.njop.org.

TAIWAN: 228 MEMORIAL DAY (PEACE MEMORIAL DAY). Feb 28. A day of remembrance for those killed in a government crackdown following a popular protest that began Feb 27–28, 1947.

TENNIEL, JOHN: 200th BIRTH ANNIVERSARY. Feb 28, 1820. Illustrator and cartoonist, born at London, England. Best remembered for his illustrations for Lewis Carroll's *Alice's Adventures in Wonderland*. Died at London, Feb 25, 1914.

228 INCIDENT: ANNIVERSARY. Feb 28, 1947. On Feb 27, 1947, Chinese agents confiscated the merchandise and life savings of a Taiwanese cigarette vendor because she was violating the state monopoly on tobacco, sparking a riot that left at least one dead. The following day Chinese troops turned machine guns on a peaceful demonstration against the corruption of the Chinese administration of Taiwan. In the ensuing days several cities and towns were taken over by native Taiwanese groups. A week later a large force of Chinese troops arrived to retake control of the island through a campaign of rape and summary public executions. Between 10,000 and 20,000 Taiwanese were killed. Called the "228 Incident" because of the date of the initial massacre, this grim episode in Taiwan's history is commemorated every Feb 28.

US LANDING ON PUERTO PRINCESA: 75th ANNIVERSARY. Feb 28, 1945. Having retaken the big Philippine island of Luzon, American forces began "mopping-up" activities in the southern islands with the landing of troops at Puerto Princesa on Palawan Island. By mid-July at least 13,000 American lives had been lost in the series of 38 attacks, needed to overcome 450,000 Japanese remaining in the islands.

USS *PRINCETON* EXPLOSION: ANNIVERSARY. Feb 28, 1844. The newly built "war steamer," USS *Princeton*, cruising on the Potomac River with top government officials as its passengers, fired one of its guns (known, ironically, as the "Peacemaker") to demonstrate the latest in naval armament. The gun exploded, killing Abel P. Upshur, secretary of state; Thomas W. Gilmer, secretary of the navy; David Gardiner, of Gardiners Island, NY; and several others. Many were injured. The president of the US, John Tyler, was on board and narrowly escaped death.

🧁 BIRTHDAYS TODAY

Jason Aldean, 43, country singer, born Macon, GA, Feb 28, 1977.

Mario Gabrielle Andretti, 80, former auto racer, born Montona, Trieste, Italy, Feb 28, 1940.

Frank Gehry, 91, architect, born Toronto, ON, Canada, Feb 28, 1929.

Jelena Janković, 35, tennis player, born Belgrade, Yugoslavia (now Serbia), Feb 28, 1985.

Ali Larter, 44, actress ("Heroes," *Final Destination*), born Cherry Hill, NJ, Feb 28, 1976.

Robert Sean Leonard, 51, actor ("House," *The Manhattan Project, Dead Poets Society*), born Westwood, NJ, Feb 28, 1969.

Eric Lindros, 47, former hockey player, born London, ON, Canada, Feb 28, 1973.

Bernadette Peters, 76, singer, actress (Tonys for *Song and Dance* and *Annie Get Your Gun*; *Gypsy, Sunday in the Park with George, Into the Woods*), born Queens, NY, Feb 28, 1944.

Tommy Tune, 81, actor, singer, dancer, director, choreographer (winner of 11 Tony Awards; *My One and Only, Grand Hotel, The Will Rogers Follies, Nine*), born Wichita Falls, TX, Feb 28, 1939.

John Turturro, 63, actor (*O Brother, Where Art Thou?; Quiz Show*), born Brooklyn, NY, Feb 28, 1957.

February 29 — Saturday

DAY 60 **306 REMAINING**

BACHELORS DAY. Feb 29. Observed only in Leap Years. A day of supposed immunity for unmarried men during Leap Year, a year during which bachelors are traditionally regarded as "fair game" for dates and proposals of marriage by women.

February 2020	S	M	T	W	T	F	S
							1
	2	3	4	5	6	7	8
	9	10	11	12	13	14	15
	16	17	18	19	20	21	22
	23	24	25	26	27	28	29

DEERFIELD MASSACRE: ANNIVERSARY. Feb 29, 1704. The garrison at Deerfield, MA, was surprised by French and Native American forces from Canada on this date. The town was burned, with 47 persons killed and 120 captured. The object of the raid was to recover a bell that had been shipped from France intended for a Native American village church in Canada. The Deerfield congregation had bought the bell without knowing of its intended destination or that a privateer had taken it from a captured ship and offered it for sale in Boston.

FIRST SALEM WITCHES ARRESTED: ANNIVERSARY. Feb 29, 1692. After several Salem girls exhibited strange behavior and accused three women witches of causing their ailments, arrest warrants were issued for Sarah Good, Sarah Osborne and Tituba, a West Indian slave. The next day, Tituba broke down under examination and admitted to witchcraft—and to there being other witches in the Massachusetts Bay Colony village. Tituba's testimony and that of the afflicted girls sparked hysteria that claimed 24 lives. Good was hanged, Osborne died in jail and Tituba was imprisoned for one year. Upon her release, she continued life as a slave. See also: "Salem Witch Hysteria Begins: Anniversary" (Mar 1).

INTERNATIONAL UNDERLINGS DAY. Feb 29. Since 1984, a date to recognize everyone who is neither a boss nor a professional assistant (both of whom have annual days already!). Recognized quadrennially on Feb 29—in keeping with the esteemed position of an Underling. For info: Peter Morris. E-mail: pdmorris@mail.com. Web: www.facebook.com/109219019117982.

LEAP YEAR DAY. Feb 29. In 2020 we add one day, Feb 29, to bring our calendar more nearly into accord with the seasons. Under the Julian calendar of 46 BC every fourth year was a leap year, on the assumption that it took Earth 365.25 days to orbit the sun. However, Earth's orbital period is actually 365.24219 days. For the more than 1,600 years that the Julian calendar was used, the calendar got out of sync with the seasons. The Gregorian calendar made just one small change: a leap day is added to the calendar once every four years except for century years that are not exactly divisible by 400.

LEE, ANN: BIRTH ANNIVERSARY. Feb 29, 1736. The founder of Shakerism in America was born at Manchester, England. She joined the Shaking Quakers, or Shakers, in 1758, and came to the US in 1774, forming a Shaker group near Albany. She became known for the gift of tongues and ability to work miracles and to cure diseases. Pacifists, the Shakers refused to bear arms in the American Revolution. Branded a British sympathizer, Lee was charged with high treason and jailed for 4½ months. Known as "Ann the Word" or "Mother Ann," she died at Watervliet, NY, Sept 8, 1784, at age 48.

NEMEROV, HOWARD: 100th BIRTH ANNIVERSARY. Feb 29, 1920. Howard Nemerov was the third poet laureate of the US, from 1988 to 1990. Among his works are 26 books, including five novels. He won a Pulitzer Prize and the National Book Award for his *Collected Works* in 1978. He was also a recipient of the National Medal of the Arts. As poet laureate he penned verses commemorating the 200th anniversary of the US Congress and the launch of the

space shuttle *Atlantis*. Nemerov was born at New York, NY, and died July 5, 1991, at St. Louis, MO.

OPEN THAT BOTTLE NIGHT. Feb 29. 21st annual. A night to finally drink that bottle of wine that you've been saving for a special occasion that never seems to come. Annually, the last Saturday in February. Originated by Dorothy J. Gaiter and John Brecher.

PHS PHILADELPHIA FLOWER SHOW. Feb 29–Mar 8. PA Convention Center, Philadelphia, PA. Held since 1829. The largest flower show in the US and the premier event of its kind in the world. Display gardens, plant competitions, floral design, educational areas and much more. 2020 theme: "Riviera Holiday." Est attendance: 250,000. For info: Pennsylvania Horticultural Society, 100 N 20th St, 5th Fl, Philadelphia, PA 19103-1495. Phone: (215) 988-8800. E-mail: phs-info@pennhort.org. Web: www.theflowershow.com.

SAINT OSWALD OF WORCESTER FEAST DAY. Feb 29. Bishop of Worcester, England, from 961 and archbishop of York from 972. Oswald died Feb 29, 992, but Feb 28 is generally celebrated as his feast day—except on leap years.

US LANDING ON THE ADMIRALTY ISLANDS: ANNIVERSARY. Feb 29, 1944. General Douglas MacArthur accompanied the first units to land on Los Negros Island, in the Admiralty Islands. The Momote airfield was taken with little resistance but was not held, and the beachhead was reduced overnight. MacArthur visited the fields personally and gave orders that the position had to be held. In spite of a Japanese counterattacks, the beachhead was maintained.

WORLD SWORD SWALLOWERS DAY. Feb 29. 14th annual. A day to celebrate 4,000 years of doing the impossible! Sword swallowers have been risking their lives for 4,000 years. On the last Saturday in February, sword swallowers around the world honor this ancient art by doing what they do best: swallowing swords! For info: Sword Swallowers Assn Intl. E-mail: ssai@swordswallow.org. Web: www.swordswallow.org.

🎂 BIRTHDAYS TODAY

Joss Ackland, 92, actor (*The Hunt for Red October*, *The Sicilian*), born London, England, Feb 29, 1928.

Patriarch Bartholomew I, 80, Ecumenical Patriarch, Archbishop of Constantinople—New Rome, spiritual leader of Eastern Orthodox Communion, born Demetrios Archondonis at Imvros (now Gökçeada), Turkey, Feb 29, 1940.

Phyllis Frelich, 76, actress (Tony for *Children of a Lesser God*; *Love Is Never Silent*), born Devil's Lake, ND, Feb 29, 1944.

Simon Gagne, 40, hockey player, born Ste-Foy, QC, Canada, Feb 29, 1980.

Jack Lousma, 84, retired astronaut, born Grand Rapids, MI, Feb 29, 1936.

Antonio Sabato, Jr, 48, actor ("General Hospital," "Earth 2"), born Rome, Italy, Feb 29, 1972.

Taylor Twellman, 40, sportscaster, former soccer player, born St. Louis, MO, Feb 29, 1980.

Cam Ward, 36, hockey player, born Saskatoon, SK, Canada, Feb 29, 1984.

March 1 — Sunday

DAY 61   **305 REMAINING**

ALPORT SYNDROME AWARENESS MONTH. Mar 1–31. Scheduled in March to coincide with National Kidney Month, this month raises awareness of Alport Syndrome, the risks of kidney disease and the benefits of organ donation. Members of the Alport Syndrome community plan various activities and talk about Alport Syndrome, kidney disease and organ donation with family, friends, neighbors, coworkers, physicians, etc. For info: Alport Syndrome Foundation, PO Box 4130, Scottsdale, AZ 85261-4130. Phone: (480) 800-3510. E-mail: info@alportsyndrome.org. Web: www.alportsyndrome.org.

★**AMERICAN RED CROSS MONTH.** Mar 1–31. Presidential Proclamation for Red Cross Month issued each year for March since 1943. Issued as American Red Cross Month since 1987.

THE ARRIVAL OF MARTIN PINZON: ANNIVERSARY. Mar 1, 1493. Martin Alonzo Pinzon (1440–1493), Spanish shipbuilder, navigator and co-owner of the *Niña* and the *Pinta*, accompanied Christopher Columbus on his first voyage, as commander of the *Pinta*. Storms separated the ships on their return voyage, and the *Pinta* first touched land at Bayona, Spain, where Pinzon gave Europe its first news of the discovery of the New World (before Columbus's landing at Palos). Pinzon's brother, Vicente Yanez Pinzon, was commander of the third caravel of the expedition, the *Niña*.

ARTICLES OF CONFEDERATION RATIFIED: ANNIVERSARY. Mar 1, 1781. This compact made among the original 13 states had been adopted by Congress Nov 15, 1777, and submitted to the states for ratification Nov 17, 1777. Maryland was the last state to approve, Feb 27, 1781, but Congress named Mar 1, 1781, as the day of formal ratification. The Articles of Confederation remained the supreme law of the nation until Mar 4, 1789, when the US Constitution went into effect.

BABY SLEEP DAY. Mar 1. 4th annual. This day brings attention to the importance of a good night's sleep—a critical part of development for young children and, in turn, a better rest for their families. Annually, Mar 1. For info: Pediatric Sleep Council. Web: www.babysleep.com/pediatric-sleep-council.

BOSNIA AND HERZEGOVINA: INDEPENDENCE DAY. Mar 1. Commemorates independence in 1992.

BRADFORD, WILLIAM: BIRTH ANNIVERSARY. Mar 1, 1590. Born at Austerfield, Yorkshire, England, Bradford is best known as a Pilgrim Father and governor of Plymouth Colony. "Saint" on the *Mayflower* in 1620, he signed the Mayflower Compact and was elected second governor of the colony after John Carver died; he was subsequently reelected 30 times. Active and vigorous, Bradford was responsible for the financial burdens of the colony until his death at Plymouth, MA, May 9, 1657. His book *Of Plymouth Plantation*, posthumously published in 1856, is a seminal primary source document of the colony's history.

CARAY, HARRY: BIRTH ANNIVERSARY. Mar 1, 1914. Born Harry Christopher Carabina at St. Louis, MO. Caray began his baseball broadcasting career with the St. Louis Cardinals in 1945. He then was the announcer for the Oakland A's, the Chicago White Sox and finally the Chicago Cubs. He became a legend at Wrigley Field with his seventh-inning stretch "Take Me Out to the Ball Game" and his quirky phrase "Holy Cow!" Caray was inducted into the Broadcasters Hall of Fame in 1989. Died at Rancho Mirage, CA, Feb 18, 1998.

CELEBRATE YOUR NAME WEEK! Mar 1–7. Who would you be if you didn't have a name? Your name identifies you to the world. Celebrate Your Name Week is about honoring your name. It's about making sure your name is a respected part of your personhood. Use this week to connect to your name! See also related events each day this week. Annually, the first full week in March. For info: Jerry Hill. E-mail: CYNW2011@gmail.com. Web: www.namesuniverse.com.

CHASE'S DEADLINE APPROACHING. Mar 1. Time to plan ahead. Schedule 2021 celebrations and observances and submit information to *Chase's Calendar of Events 2021* by Apr 1, 2020. Sponsors/information suppliers of events in this book should have received confirmation/revision forms for the 2021 edition by this time. To submit new entries for consideration, go to www.chases.com. Send to: Editor, *Chase's Calendar of Events*, Bernan Press, 4501 Forbes Blvd, Ste 200, Lanham, MD 20706. E-mail: chases@rowman.com.

CHOPIN, FRÉDÉRIC: BIRTH ANNIVERSARY. Mar 1, 1810. Pianist and influential composer of gorgeous piano works, born at Warsaw, Poland. He died at Paris, France, on Oct 17, 1849, after a 10-year battle with tuberculosis.

CLAP 4 HEALTH MONTH. Mar 1–31. This campaign provides a unique way to prevent cardiovascular disease and obesity using clapping to educate children, families, seniors and communities about healthier lifestyles. Clapping can improve motor and spatial skills, lead to better socialization skills and elevate moods through increased endorphin levels. (Formerly observed in January.) For info: Jyl Steinback, Shape Up US, Inc. Phone: (602) 996-6300. E-mail: Jyl@ShapeUpUS.org. Web: www.ShapeUpUS.org.

COLORECTAL CANCER EDUCATION AND AWARENESS MONTH. Mar 1–31. To educate consumers, patients and professionals regarding the need for early diagnosis, education and treatment of colorectal cancer. Sponsored by the American College of Apothecaries (ACA)/Pharmacists Planning Service, Inc (PPSI). For info: ACA/PPSI, 2830 Summer Oaks Dr, Bartlett, TN 38134. E-mail: info@ppsinc.org. Web: www.ppsinc.org.

CREDIT EDUCATION MONTH. Mar 1–31. Sponsored by Credit Professionals International and the Credit Education Resources Foundation, this event is designed to remind consumers and educators, as well as business and government leaders, of the importance of developing the skills needed to manage their finances efficiently and effectively. For info: Credit Professionals Intl. E-mail: creditpro@creditprofessionals.org. Web: www.creditprofessionals.org.

ELLISON, RALPH WALDO: BIRTH ANNIVERSARY. Mar 1, 1914. American writer and educator, born at Oklahoma City, OK. Author of the acclaimed novel *Invisible Man* (1952), the story of a young black man's struggle for his own identity in the face of rejection from both whites and blacks. Quickly recognized as a classic of 20th-century literature, it won the National Book Award in 1953. While only one of his novels was published, Ellison published collections of his essays, reviews and stories in *Shadow and Act* (1964) and *Going to the Territory* (1986). He died Apr 16, 1994, at New York City.

EMPLOYEE SPIRIT MONTH. Mar 1–31. This month seeks to inspire the most vital part of any organization: the employees. Motivate your employees this month—create employee spirit. Annually, the month of March. For info: Harriet Meyerson. E-mail: Harriet@ConfidenceCenter.com.

GAINES, WILLIAM M.: BIRTH ANNIVERSARY. Mar 1, 1922. The magazine *Mad*, especially popular in the 1960s and 1970s, was founded and published by William Gaines. Alfred E. Neuman, the loony, freckle-faced mascot of the publication, became a pop-culture hero. The magazine, known for its parodies of movies, comic strips and celebrities as well as its satire of politics and social mores, greatly influenced dozens of humorists. Gaines was born at the Bronx, NY. He died June 3, 1992, at New York City.

HUMORISTS ARE ARTISTS MONTH (HAAM). Mar 1–31. To recognize the important contributions made by various types of humorists to the high art of living. For info: Lone Star Publications of Humor, 8452 Fredericksburg Rd, PMB 103, San Antonio, TX 78229. E-mail: lspubs@aol.com.

ICELAND: BEER DAY. Mar 1. Reykjavik. This event began on Mar 1, 1989, when a 75-year prohibition of beer was lifted. Features celebrations in pubs and restaurants all over Reykjavik.

INTERNATIONAL BLACK WOMEN IN JAZZ MONTH. Mar 1–31. This month honors African-American female artists in jazz, including fine, visual, performing and auditory arts—artists currently in the spotlight and those who may have gotten lost in the haze of time. Through various networking events, education and training, seminars, workshops, award galas, features and interviews, concerts and more, we want to ensure that women are honored as a vital part of the past, present and future of jazz and the arts on a global level. Annually, the month of March (formerly a day on Mar 1). For info: Black Women in Jazz, 1544 Wellborn Rd, Ste 1015, Redan, GA 30074. E-mail: info@blackwomeninjazz.com. Web: www.blackwomeninjazz.com.

INTERNATIONAL IDEAS MONTH. Mar 1–31. Everybody has ideas! Many people need to be encouraged or motivated or need to build skills in order to communicate and get their ideas out in the open for consideration and/or action. This month is dedicated to all ideas—large, small, great, not-so-great, past and current as well as ideas yet to come. Without constant new ideas, progress and people stagnate. For info: Sylvia Henderson, 3570 Olney-Laytonsville Rd, Ste 588, Olney, MD 20832. Phone: (301) 260-1538. E-mail: sylvia@springboardtraining.com. Web: www.ideasuccessnetwork.com.

INTERNATIONAL MIRTH MONTH. Mar 1–31. The merry month of March is set aside to encourage more mirthful moments. Its focus is to show people how to use humor to deal with not-so-funny stuff. Mirth Month was founded by Allen Klein, professional speaker and past president of the Association for Applied and Therapeutic Humor (www.aath.org). Free monthly mirth e-mail memo available; request via e-mail. For info: Allen Klein. E-mail: humor@allenklein.com. Web: www.allenklein.com.

★**IRISH-AMERICAN HERITAGE MONTH.** Mar 1–31. Presidential Proclamation called for by House Joint Resolution 401 (PL 103–379).

JAPAN: OMIZUTORI (WATER-DRAWING FESTIVAL). Mar 1–14. Todaiji, Nara. At midnight, a solemn rite is performed in the flickering light of pine torches. People rush for sparks from the torches, which are believed to have magic power against evil. Most spectacular on the night of Mar 12. The ceremony of drawing water is observed at 2 AM on Mar 13, to the accompaniment of ancient Japanese music.

KOREA: SAMILJOL OR INDEPENDENCE MOVEMENT DAY. Mar 1. Koreans observe the anniversary of the independence movement against Japanese colonial rule in 1919.

LAND MINE BAN: ANNIVERSARY. Mar 1, 1999. The Ottawa Treaty, a United Nations treaty banning land mines, took effect on this date. To date 164 nations have signed the treaty; the US, Russia, India and China (among 33 nations) have not. For info: International Committee to Ban Landmines. Web: www.icbl.org.

LINDBERGH KIDNAPPING: ANNIVERSARY. Mar 1, 1932. Twenty-month-old Charles A. Lindbergh, Jr, the son of Charles A. and Anne Morrow Lindbergh, was kidnapped from their home at Hopewell, NJ. Even though the Lindberghs paid a $50,000 ransom, their child's body was found in a wooded area less than five miles from the family home on May 12. Bruno Richard Hauptmann was charged with the murder and kidnapping. He was executed in the electric chair Apr 3, 1936. As a result of the kidnapping and murder, the Crime Control Act was passed on May 18, 1934, authorizing the death penalty for kidnappers who take their victims across state lines.

LOWELL, ROBERT: BIRTH ANNIVERSARY. Mar 1, 1917. This important 20th-century poet and professor was born at Boston, MA, into one of the city's prominent families. He received Pulitzer Prizes for *Lord Weary's Castle* (1946) and *The Dolphin* (1973) and the National Book Award for *Life Studies* (1959). Lowell served as the sixth US poet laureate (1947–48) and was chancellor of the Academy of American Poets (1962–70). Lowell died Sept 12, 1977, at New York City.

LUXEMBOURG: BÜRGSONNDEG. Mar 1. Young people build a huge bonfire on a hill to celebrate the victorious sun, marking the end of winter. A tradition dating to pre-Christian times. On the Sunday after Ash Wednesday.

MILLER, GLENN: BIRTH ANNIVERSARY. Mar 1, 1904. American bandleader and composer Alton Glenn Miller was born at Clarinda, IA. He enjoyed great popularity preceding and during WWII. His hit recordings include "Moonlight Serenade," "String of Pearls," "Jersey Bounce" and "Sleepy Lagoon." Major Miller, leader of the US Army Air Force band, disappeared Dec 15, 1944, over the English Channel, on a flight to Paris, where he was scheduled to give a show. There were many explanations of his disappearance, but 41 years later, in December 1985, crew members of an aborted RAF bombing said they believed they had seen Miller's plane go down, the victim of bombs being jettisoned by the RAF over the English Channel.

MUSIC IN OUR SCHOOLS MONTH. Mar 1–31. To raise awareness of the importance of music education for all children—and to remind citizens that school is where all children should have access to music. MIOSM is an opportunity for music teachers to bring their music programs to the attention of the school and the community, and to display the benefits that school music brings to students of all ages. Additional information and awareness items are available. For info: Natl Assn for Music Education, 1806 Robert Fulton Dr, Reston, VA 20191. Phone: (800) 336-3768. Web: www.nafme.org.

NAMESAKE DAY. Mar 1. Today, ponder your name, and think about why you were given the name you have. Were you named after someone? Explore the history of your name, and have fun discovering whether you have a name twin! You may even be inspired to reach out to a namesake. Annually, the Sunday of Celebrate Your Name Week. For info: Jerry Hill. E-mail: CYNW2011@gmail.com. Web: www.namesuniverse.com.

NATIONAL CHEERLEADING WEEK. Mar 1–7. Various cheer activities conducted on a daily basis throughout the week. Annually, Mar 1–7. For info: Linda Lundy, 120 Walker Dr, Cleveland, TX 77328. Phone: (832) 221-0145. E-mail: linda@cheerintegrity.com. Web: www.ncwinfo.com or www.nationalcheerleadingweek.co.

NATIONAL CLEAN UP YOUR IRS ACT MONTH. Mar 1–31. Special month to focus on resolving problems with the IRS. Specialists offer "clean-up" gifts to taxpayers in need of assistance. Sponsored by the American Society of Tax Problem Solvers, a national nonprofit professional organization. For info: Lawrence Lawler, American Society of Tax Problem Solvers, 2250 Wehrle Dr, Ste 3, Williamsville, NY 14221. Phone: (716) 630-1650. Fax: (716) 630-1651. E-mail: larry@astps.org. Web: www.astps.org.

NATIONAL COLORECTAL CANCER AWARENESS MONTH. Mar 1–31. To generate widespread awareness about colorectal cancer and to encourage people to learn more about how to prevent the disease through a healthy lifestyle and regular screening. Observed since 1999, founding partners include the Prevent Cancer Foundation, the American Society for Gastrointestinal Endoscopy, the National Colorectal Cancer Roundtable and The Foundation for Digestive Health and Nutrition. For info: Colorectal Cancer Alliance, 1025 Vermont Ave NW, Ste 1066, Washington, DC 20005. Phone: (877) 422-2030. Web: www.ccalliance.org. Or Centers for Disease Control and Prevention. Web: www.cdc.gov/cancer/colorectal.

★**NATIONAL CONSUMER PROTECTION WEEK.** Mar 1–7 (tentative). A week for "government officials, industry leaders, and consumer advocates across [the] nation to share information about consumer protection." Also, a time for "all Americans to learn more about marketing and business, whether they are shopping at their local store or in the global online marketplace."

NATIONAL HORSE PROTECTION DAY (WORLD HORSE DAY). Mar 1. A day to raise awareness through public education about the plight of horses in America—the abuse, neglect, homelessness and slaughter. This day also encourages adoption events around the nation to help unwanted horses find a forever home. For info: Colleen Paige. Web: www.worldhorseday.com.

NATIONAL KIDNEY MONTH. Mar 1–31. When it comes to vital organs, hearts get all the love and kidneys get the short end of the stick. So this Mar 14, on World Kidney Day, we're asking you to heart your kidneys for a change! Make kidney health part of everyday conversations with the same urgency as heart disease, cancer or diabetes. Because if your kidneys stop working, so do you. For info: National Kidney Foundation, 30 E 33rd St, New York, NY 10016. Phone: (800) 622-9010. E-mail: info@kidney.org. Web: www.kidney.org.

NATIONAL MULTIPLE SCLEROSIS EDUCATION AND AWARENESS MONTH. Mar 1–31. This month focuses on raising awareness of and compassion for those diagnosed with multiple sclerosis. A series of national events takes place, and educational materials and publications are circulated upon request from the Multiple Sclerosis Foundation. For info: Multiple Sclerosis Foundation, 6520 N Andrews Ave, Fort Lauderdale, FL 33309-2132. Phone: (800) 225-6495. Fax: (954) 938-8708. E-mail: awareness@msfocus.org. Web: www.msfocus.org.

NATIONAL NUTRITION MONTH®. Mar 1–31. This month focuses on the importance of making informed food choices and developing sound eating and physical activity habits. For info: Academy of Nutrition and Dietetics, 120 S Riverside Plaza, Ste 2190, Chicago, IL 60606-6995. Phone: (800) 877-1600 or (312) 899-0040. E-mail: nnm@eatright.org. Web: www.eatright.org.

NATIONAL PEANUT MONTH. Mar 1–31. This month celebrates one of America's favorite foods! Roasted in the shell for a ballpark snack, ground into peanut butter or tossed in a salad or stir-fry, peanuts find their way into everything from breakfast to dessert. National Peanut Month had its beginnings as National Peanut Week in 1941. It was expanded into a monthlong celebration in 1974. For info: Southern Peanut Growers. Web: www.peanutbutterlovers.com.

NATIONAL PIG DAY. Mar 1. To accord to the pig its rightful, though generally unrecognized, place as one of humankind's most intelligent and useful domesticated animals. Annually, Mar 1. For further information send a SASE to: Ellen Stanley, 7006 Miami Ave, Lubbock, TX 79413.

NATIONAL UMBRELLA MONTH. Mar 1–31. In honor of one of the most versatile and underrated inventions of the human race, this month is dedicated to the purchase of, use of and conversation about umbrellas. Annually, the month of March. (Originated by Thomas Edward Knibb.)

NATIONAL WOMEN'S HISTORY MONTH. Mar 1–31. A time for reexamining and celebrating the wide range of women's contributions and achievements that are too often overlooked in the telling of US history. Every year in March, the NWHA coordinates observances of National Women's History Month throughout the country. The NWHA originated this widely recognized celebration and sets the annual theme, produces educational materials, and chooses particular women to honor nationally for their work. Women's History Month programs, community events, plays, essay contests, and related projects often have wide-ranging effects. 2020 theme: "Valiant Women of the Vote." For info: Natl Women's History Alliance, PO Box 469, Santa Rosa, CA 95402. Phone: (707) 636-2888. Fax: (707) 636-2909. E-mail: info@nationalwomenshistoryalliance.org. Web: www.nwhp.org.

NEBRASKA: ADMISSION DAY: ANNIVERSARY. Mar 1. Became 37th state in 1867.

OHIO: ADMISSION DAY: ANNIVERSARY. Mar 1. Became 17th state in 1803.

OPTIMISM MONTH. Mar 1–31. To encourage people to boost their optimism. Research proves optimists achieve better health, greater prosperity and more happiness than pessimists. Use this monthlong celebration to practice optimism and turn it into a delightful, permanent habit. For info: Dr. Michael Mercer and Dr. Mary Ann Mercer, 2700 Las Vegas Blvd S, Ste 4108, Las Vegas, NV 89109. Phone: (847) 382-0690. E-mail: drmercer@positivelifeanswers.com.

ORTHODOX FORGIVENESS SUNDAY (CHEESEFARE SUNDAY). Mar 1. The last day for dairy and fish before Clean Monday, which begins Great Lent in the Eastern Orthodox Church. Traditionally a day when neighbors, families and friends ask forgiveness of each other.

PARAGUAY: NATIONAL HEROES' DAY. Mar 1. National holiday. Honors those who have died for the country, especially Mariscal Francisco Solano López, who died Mar 1, 1870.

PAWS TO READ MONTH. Mar 1–31. 5th annual. Recent studies reveal dog-gone grrreat news: Children who read aloud to therapy dogs or shelter cats on a regular basis demonstrate drastic improvement in their reading skills! Our furry friends provide a safe, nonjudgmental presence for struggling readers, giving them the opportunity to sustain concentration, expand vocabulary, increase comprehension, boost confidence and cultivate a higher motivation for learning. Paws to Read Month connects parents, educators and animal lovers to local, state and national organizations that offer these programs. Recommended reading lists and suggested activities are also available to help schools and libraries celebrate Paws to Read Month all year long! For info: Lee Wardlaw, Paws to Read Month, 2319 Foothill Ln, Santa Barbara, CA 93105. E-mail: author@leewardlaw.com. Web: www.pawstoread.com.

PEACE CORPS FOUNDED: ANNIVERSARY. Mar 1, 1961. President John F. Kennedy signed an executive order officially establishing the Peace Corps on this date. The Peace Corps has sent more than 220,000 volunteers to 140 countries to help people help themselves. The volunteers assist in projects such as health, education, water sanitation, agriculture, nutrition and forestry.

	S	**M**	**T**	**W**	**T**	**F**	**S**
March		1	2	3	4	5	6	7
	8	9	10	11	12	13	14
2020	15	16	17	18	19	20	21
	22	23	24	25	26	27	28
	29	30	31				

PLAN A SOLO VACATION DAY. Mar 1. Wanderlust stirring? Tired of waiting for friends' timetables to coincide with yours? Unable to agree with your spouse on the perfect vacation? This is the day to follow the lead of millions of adults who have taken a vacation by themselves. Indulge yourself by spending the day checking out your growing opportunities for solo travel, including tours, cruises and travel clubs that either match roommates or charge little or no supplement. Annually, Mar 1. (Created by Marya Alexander.)

PLAY-THE-RECORDER MONTH. Mar 1–31. During the month of March since 1993, American Recorder Society members all over the continent will celebrate the organization's annual Play-the-Recorder Month by performing in public places such as libraries, bookstores, museums and shopping malls. Some will offer workshops on playing the recorder or demonstrations in schools. Founded in 1939, the ARS is the membership organization for all recorder players, from amateurs to leading professionals. Annually, the month of March. For info: American Recorder Society, PO Box 480054, Charlotte, NC 28269-5300. Phone: (844) 509-1422. E-mail: director@americanrecorder.org. Web: www.americanrecorder.org.

POISON PREVENTION AWARENESS MONTH. Mar 1–31. To educate parents, grandparents, schoolchildren and PTAs about accidental poisoning and how to prevent it. Sponsored by the American College of Apothecaries (ACA)/Pharmacists Planning Service, Inc (PPSI). Annually, the month of March. For info: ACA/PPSI, 2830 Summer Oaks Dr, Bartlett, TN 38134. E-mail: info@ppsinc.org. Web: www.ppsinc.org.

RED CROSS MONTH. Mar 1–31. To make the public aware of American Red Cross service in the community. There are nearly 600 Red Cross offices nationwide; each local office plans its own activities. For activities in your area, contact your local Red Cross. For blood donation info, see www.redcrossblood.org. For info: American Red Cross. Web: www.redcross.org.

REFIRED, NOT RETIRED, DAY. Mar 1. This is a day for retirees (or those soon to be retired) to decide that this is the beginning of "Life, Part II," and to commit to making this an exciting adventure. Annually, Mar 1. For info: Phyllis May, 1800 Atlantic Blvd, Ste A-312, Key West, FL 33040. Phone: (305) 295-7501. E-mail: pmaykeys@bellsouth.net. Web: www.refiredretired.com.

RETURN THE BORROWED BOOKS WEEK. Mar 1–7. To remind you to make room for those precious old volumes that will be returned to you by cleaning out all that worthless trash that your friends are waiting for. Created by the late Al Kaelin. Annually, the first full week in March.

ROZELLE, PETE: BIRTH ANNIVERSARY. Mar 1, 1926. Alvin Ray ("Pete") Rozelle, commissioner of the National Football League, born at South Gate, CA. Rozelle began his career in the public relations department of the Los Angeles Rams, became general manager and in 1960 was elected commissioner. He built the NFL into a sporting power through the use of television. He helped engineer the NFL's merger with the American Football League, created the Super Bowl as America's greatest sports extravaganza, conceived the idea for Monday Night Football and persuaded NFL owners to accept revenue sharing. Died at Rancho Santa Fe, CA, Dec 6, 1996.

SAINT-GAUDENS, AUGUSTUS: BIRTH ANNIVERSARY. Mar 1, 1848. Sculptor, born at Dublin, Ireland. His works include the statue of Lincoln in Lincoln Park, Chicago, and of Admiral Farragut in Madison Square, New York. Saint-Gaudens died at Cornish, NH, Aug 3, 1907.

SALEM WITCH HYSTERIA BEGINS: ANNIVERSARY. Mar 1, 1692. The Massachusetts Bay Colony village of Salem had experienced a strange February in which several teenaged girls exhibited bizarre behavior and attributed their ailments to witches. Three women were then arrested on Feb 29, 1692. One of the accused, Tituba, a West Indian slave, broke down under questioning on Mar 1 and admitted to being a witch. Soon the teenaged girls accused four other residents, and by the end of April, 19 women had been accused of witchcraft and were languishing in jail—including a four-year-old child. Massachusetts governor Sir William Phips, seeking to control the growing terror, ordered trials held. In October, the special court was dissolved after growing protests of the trials' unjust proceedings. By then, 19 people had been hanged, 5 had died in jail, 1 had been tortured to death and more than 150 had been imprisoned. Two dogs were also executed. On Jan 14, 1697, Judge Samuel Sewall publicly apologized and a court-ordered day of atonement began. In 1711, all those accused of witchcraft were pardoned by the colony's legislature. See also: "Salem Witch Trials Begin: Anniversary" (June 2).

SAVE THE VAQUITA MONTH. Mar 1–31. This month celebrates the beautiful, rare and critically endangered porpoise, the vaquita. Fewer than 100 vaquita survive in their only home, the Gulf of California. Most people are unaware of this porpoise—yet it is the most endangered marine mammal in the world. Celebrate vaquita during March and learn how to save these important whales from extinction. For info: Oregon Coast Aquarium, Oceanscape Network. Web: http://oceanscape.aquarium.org. Also for info: Southwest Fisheries Science Center, NOAA Fisheries. Web: https://swfsc.noaa.gov.

SAVE YOUR VISION MONTH. Mar 1–31. To remind Americans of the importance of eye health and regular exams. For info: American Optometric Assn, 243 N Lindbergh Blvd, 1st Fl, St. Louis, MO 63141. Phone: (800) 365-2219. E-mail: slthomas@aoa.org. Web: www.aoa.org.

SHORE, DINAH: BIRTH ANNIVERSARY. Mar 1, 1917. American radio and television personality Dinah Shore was born Frances Rose Shore at Winchester, TN. In addition to recording many hit songs in the 1930s and 1940s, she was one of the first women to be successful as a television host, beginning in the 1950s with the "Dinah Shore Chevy Show." She received 10 Emmys before she died Feb 24, 1994, at Beverly Hills, CA.

SLAYTON, DONALD K. "DEKE": BIRTH ANNIVERSARY. Mar 1, 1924. Deke Slayton, longtime chief of flight operations at the Johnson Space Center, was born at Sparta, WI. Slayton was a member of the Mercury Seven, the original group of young military aviators chosen to inaugurate America's sojourn into space. Unfortunately, a heart problem prevented him from participating in any of the Mercury flights. When in 1971 the heart condition mysteriously went away, Slayton flew on the last Apollo mission. The July 1975 flight, involving a docking with a Soviet *Soyuz* spacecraft, symbolized a momentary thaw in relations between the two nations. During his years as chief of flight operations, Slayton directed astronaut training and selected the crews for nearly all missions. He died June 13, 1993, at League City, TX.

SOCIAL WORK MONTH. Mar 1–31. First commissioned by President Ronald Reagan, the National Association of Social Workers and its members spend this month celebrating the accomplishments of social workers and the services they provide to vulnerable populations. For info: Natl Assn of Social Workers. Phone: (800) 742-4089. E-mail: media@naswdc.org. Web: www.naswdc.org.

SWITZERLAND: CHALANDRA MARZ. Mar 1. Engadine. Springtime traditional event when costumed young people, ringing bells and cracking whips, drive away the demons of winter.

TELECOMMUTER APPRECIATION WEEK. Mar 1–7. Sponsored by the American Telecommuting Association, this week is designed to call attention to the benefits of telecommuting: the individual and family as well as the employer and society benefit in a win-win-win situation. For info: American Telecommuting Assn, 827 Second St #104, Santa Monica, CA 90403. Phone: (800) ATA-4-YOU. E-mail: YourATA@YourATA.com.

WALES: SAINT DAVID'S DAY. Mar 1. Celebrates patron saint of Wales (Dewi Sant). Welsh tradition calls for the wearing of a leek on this day.

WILL EISNER WEEK. Mar 1–7. Since 2010, an annual national and international celebration promoting graphic novel literacy, free speech awareness and the legacy of legendary graphic artist and storyteller Will Eisner (1917–2005). Annually, Mar 1–7, which encompasses Eisner's birthday on Mar 6. For info: Will Eisner Studios, Inc. E-mail: info@willeisner.com. Web: www.willeisner.com.

★**WOMEN'S HISTORY MONTH.** Mar 1–31. Proclamation urging Americans to observe this month and learn more about the generations of women who have left enduring imprints on history. Also urges celebration of International Women's Day on Mar 8.

WORDS MATTER WEEK. Mar 1–7. Since 2009, a week designed to wipe out verbal slop and drivel. Words are the basis for communication, no matter the language spoken. Annually, the first week in March. For info: April Michelle Davis, Executive Director, National Assn of Independent Writers and Editors, PO Box 412, Montpelier, VA 23192. Phone: (804) 476-4484. E-mail: director@naiwe.com. Web: www.wordsmatterweek.com.

WORKPLACE EYE WELLNESS MONTH. Mar 1–31. Can you see the dangers at your workplace? Accidents at work are a major cause of preventable blindness. For info: Prevent Blindness, 211 W Wacker Dr, Ste 1700, Chicago, IL 60606. Phone: (800) 331-2020. E-mail: info@preventblindness.org. Web: www.preventblindness.org.

WORLD COMPLIMENT DAY. Mar 1. Most positive day in the year! Appreciate with words instead of gifts—brighten everyone's day. Nobody wins commercially, but everyone wins emotionally. First celebration in 2011 was observed by participants from more than 50 nations. Annually, Mar 1. For info: Hans Poortvliet, Apartado de Correos 101, 03727 Xaló/Jalon—Alicante, Spain. E-mail: hans@withcompliments.com. Web: www.worldcomplimentday.com.

WORLDWIDE HOME SCHOOLING AWARENESS MONTH. Mar 1–31. Promoted since 2009 to bring awareness to the general population and especially to parents of school-age children about the benefits of homeschooling. "Remember to include the homeschooling community." (Formerly observed in May.) For info: Deborah Le Bouf Kulkkula, PhD, or Jane K. Andrews, BEd., 381 Billings Rd, Fitchburg, MA 01420-1407. Phone: (978) 343-4009 or (978) 808-8084 (cell). E-mail: DebKulkkula@gmail.com. Web: www.HomeSchoolingAwarenessMonth.com.

YELLOWSTONE NATIONAL PARK ESTABLISHED: ANNIVERSARY. Mar 1, 1872. The first area in the world to be designated a national park, most of Yellowstone is in Wyoming, with small sections in Montana and Idaho. It was established by an act of Congress.

YOUTH ART MONTH. Mar 1–31. Since 1961. To emphasize the value and importance of art and art education in the development of all children and young people. Sponsored by the Council for Art Education and the Art And Creative Materials Institute (ACMI) with the cooperation of the National Art Education Association (NAEA). For info: National Art Education Association, 901 Prince St, Alexandria, VA 22314. Phone: (800) 299-8321. E-mail: info@arteducators.org. Web: www.arteducators.org/news/yam.

ZERO DISCRIMINATION DAY. Mar 1. Sponsored by the Joint United Nations Programme on HIV/AIDS (UNAIDS) since 2014, this annual global observance seeks solidarity to end discrimination

of all kinds, which remains widespread. A day to celebrate diversity and to call on governments to make greater efforts to realize and protect human rights and eliminate discrimination. Annually, Mar 1. For info: UNAIDS. Web: www.unaids.org.

🎂 BIRTHDAYS TODAY

Jensen Ackles, 42, actor ("Supernatural"), born Dallas, TX, Mar 1, 1978.

Catherine Bach, 66, actress ("The Dukes of Hazzard"), born Warren, OH, Mar 1, 1954.

Javier Bardem, 51, actor (Oscar for *No Country for Old Men*; *Skyfall, Before Night Falls*), born Las Palmas de Gran Canaria, Canary Islands, Spain, Mar 1, 1969.

Harry Belafonte, 93, singer, born New York, NY, Mar 1, 1927.

Justin Bieber, 26, singer, born Stratford, ON, Canada, Mar 1, 1994.

Robert Conrad, 85, actor ("The Wild Wild West," "Black Sheep Squadron," *Centennial*), born Chicago, IL, Mar 1, 1935.

Roger Daltrey, 76, singer (The Who), born London, England, Mar 1, 1944.

Timothy Daly, 64, actor ("Madam Secretary," "Private Practice," "Wings"), born New York, NY, Mar 1, 1956.

George Eads, 53, actor ("MacGyver," "CSI"), born Fort Worth, TX, Mar 1, 1967.

Deb Fischer, 69, US Senator (R, Nebraska), born Lincoln, NE, Mar 1, 1951.

Ron Francis, 57, former hockey player, born Sault Ste. Marie, ON, Canada, Mar 1, 1963.

Mark-Paul Gosselaar, 46, actor ("Franklin & Bash," "NYPD Blue," "Saved by the Bell"), born Panorama City, CA, Mar 1, 1974.

Yolanda Griffith, 50, former basketball player, born Chicago, IL, Mar 1, 1970.

Ron Howard, 66, director (*In the Heart of the Sea, Apollo 13*, Oscar for *A Beautiful Mind*), actor, born Duncan, OK, Mar 1, 1954.

Ke$ha, 33, singer, born Kesha Rose Sebert at Los Angeles, CA, Mar 1, 1987.

Lupita Nyong'o, 37, actress (Oscar for *12 Years a Slave*; *Us, Black Panther, Queen of Katwe*), born Mexico City, Mexico, Mar 1, 1983.

Chris Webber, 47, former basketball player, born Detroit, MI, Mar 1, 1973.

March 2 — Monday

DAY 62	304 REMAINING

ARNAZ, DESI: BIRTH ANNIVERSARY. Mar 2, 1917. Born at Santiago, Cuba, as Desidero Alberto Arnaz y Acha III, to a wealthy family. The 1933 revolution sent them (now impoverished) to Miami, FL, and the young Arnaz sought a music career. Arnaz led his own band and introduced the conga line to America. He had several musical hits including "Babalu." He moved into acting, meeting his future wife, Lucille Ball, at RKO. Ball and Arnaz created one of the great TV comedies, "I Love Lucy" (1951–57), and started the innovative Desilu TV production company. Ball and Arnaz divorced in 1960. Arnaz died on Dec 2, 1986, at Del Mar, CA.

AUSTRALIA: EIGHT HOUR DAY OR LABOR DAY. Mar 2. Western Australia and Tasmania. Parades and celebrations commemorate trade union efforts during the 19th century to limit working hours. Their slogan: "Eight hours labor, eight hours recreation, eight hours rest!" Annually, the first Monday in March.

BATTLE OF BISMARCK SEA: ANNIVERSARY. Mar 2–4, 1943. Protected by American and Australian fighters, 137 American Flying Fortress and Liberator bombers attacked a Japanese convoy en route from its base at Rabaul to New Guinea on Mar 2, 1943. In the convoy were

March 2020	S	M	T	W	T	F	S
							1	2	3	4	5	6	7
	8	9	10	11	12	13	14
	15	16	17	18	19	20	21
	22	23	24	25	26	27	28
	29	30	31				

eight transports carrying 7,000 reinforcements, which were escorted by eight destroyers. All the transports and four of the destroyers were sunk and 3,500 Japanese troops were drowned. Of the 150 Japanese aircraft involved in the fighting, 102 were shot down. The battle of Bismarck Sea was a major victory for the Allies, ending any efforts by the Japanese to send reinforcements to New Guinea.

ETHIOPIA: ADWA DAY. Mar 2. Ethiopian forces under Menelik II inflicted a crushing defeat on the invading Italians at Adwa in 1896.

FUN FACTS ABOUT NAMES DAY. Mar 2. Celebrate names today by looking up interesting tidbits about names. Get started with fun facts about names on our website. Or maybe you already know the name of Santa's brother? Surprise, entertain, enlighten and amaze others by sharing what you find. Ask others to share the stories of their names. Discuss the exotic names some celebrities give their children. Annually, the Monday of Celebrate Your Name Week. For info: Jerry Hill. E-mail: CYNW2011@gmail.com. Web: www.namesuniverse.com.

GEISEL, THEODOR "DR. SEUSS": BIRTH ANNIVERSARY. Mar 2, 1904. Theodor Seuss Geisel, creator of *The Cat in the Hat* and *How the Grinch Stole Christmas*, was born at Springfield, MA. Known to children and parents as Dr. Seuss. His books have sold more than 200 million copies and have been translated into 20 languages. His career began with *And to Think That I Saw It on Mulberry Street*, which was turned down by 27 publishing houses before being published by Vanguard Press. His books included many messages, from environmental consciousness in *The Lorax* to the dangers of pacifism in *Horton Hatches the Egg* and *Yertle the Turtle*'s thinly veiled references to Hitler as the title character. He was awarded a Pulitzer Prize in 1984 "for his contribution over nearly half a century to the education and enjoyment of America's children and their parents." He died Sept 24, 1991, at La Jolla, CA.

GUAM: DISCOVERY DAY OR MAGELLAN DAY. Mar 2. Commemorates discovery of Guam in 1521 by Ferdinand Magellan. Annually, the first Monday in March.

HIGHWAY NUMBERS INTRODUCED: 95th ANNIVERSARY. Mar 2, 1925. A joint board of state and federal highway officials created the first system of interstate highway numbering in the US. Standardized road signs identifying the routes were also introduced. Later the system would be improved with the use of odd and even numbers that distinguish between north-south and east-west routes, respectively.

HOUSTON, SAM: BIRTH ANNIVERSARY. Mar 2, 1793. American soldier and politician, born at Rockbridge County, VA, is remembered for his role in Texas history. Houston was a congressman (1823–27) and governor (1827–29) of Tennessee. He resigned his office as governor in 1829 and rejoined the Cherokee Indians (with whom he had lived for several years as a teenage runaway), who accepted him as a member of their tribe. Houston went to Texas in 1832 and became commander of the Texan army in the War for Texan Independence, which was secured when Houston routed the much larger Mexican forces led by Santa Anna, Apr 21, 1836, at the Battle of San Jacinto. After Texas's admission to the Union, Houston served as US senator and later as governor of the state. He was deposed in 1861 when he refused to swear allegiance to the Confederacy. Houston, the only person to have been elected governor of two different states, failed to serve his full term of office in either. The city of Houston, TX, was named for him. He died July 26, 1863, at Huntsville, TX.

KING KONG FILM PREMIERE: ANNIVERSARY. Mar 2, 1933. One of the greatest adventure movies of all time premiered on this date at New York City's Radio City Music Hall and the RKO Roxy. It was to be an immediate hit—the biggest film blockbuster up to that time. Directed by Merian Cooper and Ernest Schoedsack, *King Kong* was a variation of "Beauty and the Beast," with the Beast being the 50-foot ape (actually, an 18-inch model) and Beauty portrayed by actress Fay Wray, who became known as the "Queen of Scream" after this film. Kong climbing the newly completed Empire State Building clutching Wray as biplanes attack him is one of the iconic images of cinema. Technician Willis O'Brien used state-of-the-art, stop-motion photography for the film's special effects.

MOON PHASE: FIRST QUARTER. Mar 2. Moon enters First Quarter phase at 2:57 PM, EST.

MOUNT RAINIER NATIONAL PARK ESTABLISHED: ANNIVERSARY. Mar 2, 1899. Located in the Cascade Mountains of Washington State, this is the fourth-oldest national park.

NATIONAL SCHOOL BREAKFAST WEEK. Mar 2–6. Since 1989. To focus on the importance of a nutritious breakfast served in the schools, giving children a good start to their day. Annually, the first full week in March, Monday to Friday. For info: School Nutrition Association, 2900 S Quincy St, Ste 700, Arlington, VA 22206. Phone: (703) 824-3000. E-mail: servicecenter@schoolnutrition.org. Web: www.schoolnutrition.org.

NEA'S READ ACROSS AMERICA DAY. Mar 2. Get ready to grab your hat and read with the Cat in the Hat for Read Across America Day. The Seussical celebration will kick off a week of reading across the nation as NEA members gather students, parents and community members together to share their love of reading. Annually, on or near Dr. Seuss's birthday (Mar 2). For info: Natl Education Assn, 1201 16th St NW, Washington, DC 20036-3290. Phone: (202) 833-4000. Web: www.nea.org/readacross.

ORTHODOX GREEN MONDAY. Mar 2. Green, or Clean, Monday is the first Monday of Lent on the Orthodox Christian calendar. Lunch in the fields, with bread, olives and uncooked vegetables and no meat or dairy products.

ORTHODOX LENT. Mar 2–Apr 10. Great Lent, or Easter Lent, observed by Eastern Orthodox churches, lasts 40 days. The first day is known as Clean Monday, which begins the Great Fast, when Orthodox Christians abstain from eating meat, dairy and fish. (Fasting continues on Lazarus Saturday [Apr 11] and a stricter fast is kept during Holy Week [Apr 12–18].)

OTT, MELVIN (MEL): BIRTH ANNIVERSARY. Mar 2, 1909. Baseball Hall of Fame outfielder, born at Gretna, LA. Playing for the New York Giants, Ott hit 511 home runs, a National League record until Willie Mays surpassed it in 1966. Inducted into the Hall of Fame in 1951. Died at New Orleans, LA, Nov 21, 1958.

POPE LEO XIII: BIRTH ANNIVERSARY. Mar 2, 1810. Giocchino Vincenzo Pecci, 256th pope of the Roman Catholic Church, born at Carpineto, Italy. Elected pope Feb 20, 1878. Died July 20, 1903, at Rome, Italy.

POPE PIUS XII: BIRTH ANNIVERSARY. Mar 2, 1876. Eugenio Maria Giovanni Pacelli, 260th pope of the Roman Catholic Church, born at Rome, Italy. Elected pope Mar 2, 1939. Died at Castel Gandolfo, near Rome, Oct 9, 1958.

PULASKI DAY IN ILLINOIS. Mar 2. Celebrates the Polish and American Revolutionary hero Casimir Pulaski (1747–79) on the first Monday in March.

SCHURZ, CARL: BIRTH ANNIVERSARY. Mar 2, 1829. American journalist, political reformer and army officer in Civil War. Born near Cologne, Germany, he died at New York, NY, May 14, 1906.

***THE SOUND OF MUSIC* FILM PREMIERE: 55th ANNIVERSARY.** Mar 2, 1965. The perennially popular family film musical, starring Julie Andrews as Maria Von Trapp, premiered on this date at New York City. Nominated for 10 Academy Awards, the film won five Oscars, including awards for Best Picture and Best Director (Robert Wise).

SPACE MILESTONE: PIONEER 10 (US). Mar 2, 1972. This unmanned probe began a journey on which it passed and photographed Jupiter and its moons, 620 million miles from Earth, in December 1973. It crossed the orbit of Pluto and then in 1983 became the first known Earth object to leave our solar system. On Sept 22, 1987, *Pioneer 10* reached another space milestone at 4:19 PM, when it reached a distance 50 times farther from the sun than the sun is from Earth.

SPACE MILESTONE: *SOYUZ 28* (USSR). Mar 2, 1978. Cosmonauts Alexi Gubarev and Vladimir Remek linked with *Salyut 6* space station Mar 3, visiting crew of *Soyuz 26*. Returned to Earth Mar 10. Remek, from Czechoslovakia, was the first person in space from a country other than the US or USSR.

TEXAS INDEPENDENCE DAY. Mar 2, 1836. Texas adopted declaration of independence from Mexico.

TRIAL OF THE TWENTY-ONE: ANNIVERSARY. Mar 2–13, 1938. Third and last of the Moscow show trials that were part of Stalin's Great Purge. Notable for the prominence of the defendants, including the former head of the Communist International, Nikolai Bukharin, the trial convinced many Communist observers of the failure and moral bankruptcy of the Stalin regime. Tortured and coerced with threats to family, the defendants confessed to counterrevolutionary activity and conspiracy to murder Stalin and others. Eighteen of the defendants were sentenced to death and executed on Mar 15. The other three were sent to prison, but all three were killed in a prisoner massacre in September 1941.

WILT CHAMBERLAIN SCORES 100: ANNIVERSARY. Mar 2, 1962. In one of sport's greatest nights, Wilt Chamberlain of the Philadelphia Warriors scored 100 points against the New York Knicks in an NBA game in Hershey, PA. Chamberlain scored 41 points by halftime and the crowd roared for him to take all shots for the rest of the game. Philadelphia won 169 to 147. It was and still is the single-game scoring record.

🎂 BIRTHDAYS TODAY

Jon Bon Jovi, 58, singer, songwriter, actor, born John Bongiovi at Sayreville, NJ, Mar 2, 1962.

Reggie Bush, 35, football player, born Spring Valley, CA, Mar 2, 1985.

Daniel Craig, 52, actor (*Spectre*, *The Girl with the Dragon Tattoo* [US], *Casino Royale*, *Munich*), born Chester, England, Mar 2, 1968.

John Cullum, 90, actor (*Shenandoah*, *On the Twentieth Century*, "Northern Exposure"), born Knoxville, TN, Mar 2, 1930.

Mikhail Sergeyvich Gorbachev, 89, former Soviet political leader, born Privolnoye, Stavropol, Russia, Mar 2, 1931.

Bryce Dallas Howard, 39, actress (*Jurassic World*, *Terminator Salvation*, *Lady in the Water*), born Los Angeles, CA, Mar 2, 1981.

John Irving, 78, author (*The Cider House Rules*, *The World According to Garp*), born Exeter, NH, Mar 2, 1942.

Henrik Lundqvist, 38, hockey player, born Are, Sweden, Mar 2, 1982.

Chris Martin, 43, singer, songwriter (Coldplay), born Exeter, Devon, England, Mar 2, 1977.

Method Man, 49, rapper (Wu-Tang Clan), actor, television personality ("Drop the Mic"), born Clifford Smith at Hempstead, Long Island, NY, Mar 2, 1971.

Eddie Money, 71, musician, born Brooklyn, NY, Mar 2, 1949.

Laraine Newman, 68, comedienne ("Saturday Night Live"), born Los Angeles, CA, Mar 2, 1952.

Rebel Wilson, 40, actress (*How to Be Single*, *Pitch Perfect*), born Melanie Elizabeth Bownds at Sydney, Australia, Mar 2, 1980.

March 2020	S	M	T	W	T	F	S
	1	2	3	4	5	6	7
	8	9	10	11	12	13	14
	15	16	17	18	19	20	21
	22	23	24	25	26	27	28
	29	30	31				

March 3 — Tuesday

DAY 63 **303 REMAINING**

BELL, ALEXANDER GRAHAM: BIRTH ANNIVERSARY. Mar 3, 1847. Inventor of the telephone, born at Edinburgh, Scotland, Bell acquired his interest in the transmission of sound from his father, Melville Bell, a teacher of the deaf. Bell's use of visual devices to teach articulation to the deaf contributed to the theory from which he derived the principle of the vibrating membrane used in the telephone. On Mar 10, 1876, Bell spoke the first electrically transmitted sentence to his assistant in the next room: "Mr Watson, come here, I want you." Bell's other accomplishments include a refinement of Edison's phonograph, the first successful phonograph record and the audiometer. He also continued exploring the nature and causes of deafness. He died near Baddeck, NS, Canada, Aug 2, 1922.

BONZA BOTTLER DAY®. Mar 3. To celebrate when the number of the day is the same as the number of the month. Bonza Bottler Day® is an excuse to have a party at least once a month. For more information see Jan 1. For info: Gail Berger, Bonza Bottler Day. Phone: (864) 201-3988. E-mail: bonza@bonzabottlerday.com. Web: www.bonzabottlerday.com.

BULGARIA: LIBERATION DAY. Mar 3. Grateful tribute to the Russian, Romanian and Finnish soldiers and Bulgarian volunteers who, in the Russo-Turkish War, 1877–78, liberated Bulgaria from five centuries of Ottoman rule.

DOOHAN, JAMES: 100th BIRTH ANNIVERSARY. Mar 3, 1920. Actor, best known for his portrayal of Montgomery "Scotty" Scott on the iconic television and film series *Star Trek*. Crew members of the USS *Enterprise* frequently asked his character, "Beam me up, Scotty"—now a pop culture catchphrase. Born at Vancouver, BC, Canada, World War II veteran Doohan died at Redmond, WA, July 20, 2005. In 2012, a portion of his ashes were flown into space (after two other failed attempts).

EMANCIPATION OF THE SERFS: ANNIVERSARY. Mar 3, 1861. On this day, Czar Alexander II emancipated the serfs of Russia. The 20 million serfs represented one-third of that nation's population.

FLORIDA: ADMISSION DAY: 175th ANNIVERSARY. Mar 3. Became 27th state in 1845.

GRAPES OF WRATH EVENING: GUTHRIE MEETS SEEGER: 80th ANNIVERSARY. Mar 3, 1940. Historic evening where actor Will Geer put together a "hootenanny" featuring famous and soon-to-be-famous folk musicians. On this night, at the Forrest Theater in New York City, the "Grapes of Wrath Evening" benefited the John Steinbeck Fund for Migrant Workers. Performers included Lead Belly, Aunt Molly, Woody Guthrie and Pete Seeger in his public debut. This was also when Guthrie and Seeger first met.

HARLOW, JEAN: BIRTH ANNIVERSARY. Mar 3, 1911. Born Harlean Carpenter at Kansas City, MO. Harlow's platinum blonde hair, arresting beauty and flair for comedy made her a star in 1930s Hollywood. Following her big break in Howard Hughes's 1930 war epic *Hell's Angels* ("Would you be shocked if I put on something more comfortable?"), Harlow became a superstar at MGM, where she starred in six films with Clark Gable. Harlow's meteoric rise was cut short, however, when she collapsed on the set during the filming of *Saratoga*. She died at Los Angeles, CA, June 7, 1937—she was 26.

HIN-MAH-TOO-YAH-LAT-KEKT (CHIEF JOSEPH): BIRTH ANNIVERSARY. Mar 3, 1840. Nez Percé chief, whose name means "Thunder Rolling Down the Mountain," born at Wallowa Valley, Oregon Territory. Faced with war or resettlement to a reservation, Chief Joseph led 700 of his people (of which only 200 were warriors) in a dramatic attempt to escape to Canada. After three months and more than 1,400 miles, during which the tribe held off larger US forces in four battles and many skirmishes, he and his people were surrounded 40 miles from Canada. On Oct 5, 1877, he surrendered and uttered the legendary words: "From where the sun now stands I will fight no more forever." They were sent to a reservation at Oklahoma. Though a few survivors were later allowed in 1885 to relocate to another reservation at Washington, they never regained their ancestral lands. He died—his physician said of a broken heart—on Sept 21, 1904, on the Colville Reservation at Washington.

HOUSTON LIVESTOCK SHOW AND RODEO™. Mar 3–22. NRG Park, Houston, TX. First held in 1932, this is the world's largest livestock show and rodeo. Rodeo action and top-name musical entertainment. More than 34,000 livestock and horse entries. Est attendance: 2,500,000. For info: Houston Livestock Show and Rodeo, PO Box 20070, Houston, TX 77225-0070. Phone: (832) 667-1000. E-mail: questions@rodeohouston.com. Web: www.rodeohouston.com.

INTERNATIONAL EAR CARE DAY. Mar 3. This day aims to raise awareness and promote ear and hearing care across the world. The WHO estimates that more than five percent of the world's population—360 million people—has disabling hearing loss. About half of all cases of hearing loss worldwide are easily prevented or treated. For info: World Health Organization. Web: www.who.int/pbd/deafness/news/IECD.

JAPAN: HINA MATSURI (DOLL FESTIVAL). Mar 3. This special festival for girls is observed throughout Japan. Dolls are displayed. Annually, Mar 3.

MALAWI: MARTYR'S DAY. Mar 3. Public holiday in Malawi.

MISSOURI COMPROMISE: 200th ANNIVERSARY. Mar 3, 1820. In February 1819 a bill was introduced into Congress that would admit Missouri to the Union as a state that prohibited slavery. At the time there were 11 free states and 10 slave states. Southern congressmen feared this would upset the balance of power between North and South. As a compromise, on this date Missouri was admitted as a slave state, but slavery was forever prohibited in the northern part of the Louisiana Purchase. In 1854 this act was repealed when Kansas and Nebraska were allowed to decide on slave or free status by popular vote.

NATIONAL ANTHEM DAY. Mar 3, 1931. The bill designating "The Star-Spangled Banner" as our national anthem was adopted by the US Senate and went to President Herbert Hoover for signature. The president signed it the same day.

PEACE CORPS DAY. Mar 3. Commemorates the founding of the Peace Corps on Mar 1, 1961, by President John F. Kennedy. Observed on the first Tuesday in March.

PULLMAN, GEORGE: BIRTH ANNIVERSARY. Mar 3, 1831. Born at Brocton, NY, George Mortimer Pullman was an inventor and industrialist who became famous for his design and production of the "Pullman" railroad sleeping car. His first attempt at improving railroad sleeping accommodations began in 1858, while he was working as a contractor for the Chicago & Alton Railroad at Chicago, IL. His initial model was not adopted, but in 1863 a new design was enthusiastically received. He secured a patent for the folding upper berth design in 1864 and one for the lower berth design in 1865. By 1867 Pullman and his partner organized the Pullman Palace Car Company, which became the greatest railroad car-building organization in the world. In 1881 the town of Pullman, IL, south of Chicago, was formed by Pullman to house his

employees. Because rents were not lowered when wages were cut, a strike was initiated against Pullman's company in May 1894. Pullman was eventually forced to give up control of all property in the town not directly required for manufacturing. Pullman died Oct 19, 1897, at Chicago.

RIDGWAY, MATTHEW BUNKER: 125th BIRTH ANNIVERSARY. Mar 3, 1895. American army officer Matthew Bunker Ridgway was born at Fort Monroe, VA. As major general commanding the newly formed 82nd Airborne Division, he led it in the invasion of Sicily in July 1943 and the invasion of the Italian mainland in 1944. Ridgway replaced MacArthur as commander of the US Eighth Army in Korea in 1951 and succeeded Eisenhower as supreme allied commander of the North Atlantic Treaty Organization in 1952. He became US army chief of staff in 1953. Ridgway died at Fox Chapel, PA, July 26, 1993.

SIMPLIFY-YOUR-LIFE DAY. Mar 3. Since 2011. For busy people who want to calm the chaos, Simplify-Your-Life Day™ encourages participants to choose three steps (on the third day of the third month) to cut clutter, save time and money and simplify. Annually, Mar 3. For info: Carmen Coker, International Association of Virtual Organizers, 2308 Mt Vernon Ave, Ste 322, Alexandria, VA 22301. Phone: (800) 821-3071. Web: simplifyyourlifeday.com.

***TIME* MAGAZINE FIRST PUBLISHED: ANNIVERSARY.** Mar 3, 1923. The first issue of *Time* bore this date. The magazine was founded by Henry Luce and Briton Hadden.

TOWN MEETING DAY. Mar 3. Vermont. The first Tuesday in March is an official state holiday in Vermont. Nearly every town elects officers, approves budget items and deals with a multitude of other items in a daylong public meeting of the voters.

UNIQUE NAMES DAY. Mar 3. This is the day to salute friends, acquaintances and loved ones who have unique names. Let's appreciate them for going through life without seeing their names on things such as ready-made key chains. If you or anyone you know has a unique name, discuss it today! Celebrate it! Annually, the Tuesday of Celebrate Your Name Week. For info: Jerry Hill. E-mail: CYNW2011@gmail.com. Web: www.namesuniverse.com.

UNITED NATIONS: WORLD WILDLIFE DAY. Mar 3. This day seeks to celebrate the many beautiful and varied forms of wild fauna and flora, recall the privileged interactions between wildlife and populations across the globe and raise awareness of the urgent need to step up the fight against wildlife crime, which has wide-ranging economic, environmental and social impacts. Annually, Mar 3, the anniversary date of the adoption of the Convention on International Trade in Endangered Species of Wild Fauna and Flora. For info: United Nations. Web: www.wildlifeday.org.

WARD, MONTE: BIRTH ANNIVERSARY. Mar 3, 1860. John Montgomery (Monte) Ward, Baseball Hall of Fame infielder, born at Bellefonte, PA. Ward helped to organize the Brotherhood of Professional Base Ball Players, the original players' union that led to the creation of the Players League, a third major league that played only one season, 1890. Inducted into the Hall of Fame in 1964. Died at Augusta, GA, Mar 4, 1925.

WATSON, DOC: BIRTH ANNIVERSARY. Mar 3, 1923. Folk guitar virtuoso and prolific songwriter Arthel Lane Watson was born at Deep Gap, NC. Watson lost his sight as an infant but was still raised to work hard on the family property and be self-sufficient. A natural musical talent led him to embrace that career. He possessed a rich baritone, an innovative style of flatpicking, and bluegrass guitar play that mimicked the frenzy of a country fiddle. Watson brought to his songwriting a ranging knowledge of American musical tradition—especially from the Appalachia region. He was a great influence on the thriving folk scene of the 1960s. Awarded a National Medal of Arts in 1997, Watson died at Winston-Salem, NC, on May 29, 2012.

WHAT IF CATS AND DOGS HAD OPPOSABLE THUMBS DAY. Mar 3. We are grateful today that the infinite wisdom of the universe has not allowed cats and dogs to have thumbs. Imagine the cat able to operate the can opener! Imagine the dog able to open the

refrigerator door! (©2006 by WH.) For info: Thomas & Ruth Roy, Wellcat Holidays, 2418 Long Ln, Lebanon, PA 17046. Phone: (717) 279-0184. E-mail: info@wellcat.com. Web: www.wellcat.com.

WOMAN SUFFRAGE PARADE ATTACKED: ANNIVERSARY. Mar 3, 1913. A parade held by the National American Woman Suffrage Association at Washington, DC, on the day before Woodrow Wilson's inauguration turned into a near riot when people in the crowd began jeering and shoving the marchers. The 5,000 women and their supporters were spit upon, struck in the face and pelted with burning cigar stubs while police looked on and made no effort to intervene. Secretary of War Henry Stimson was forced to send soldiers from Fort Myer to restore order.

WORLD BIRTH DEFECTS DAY. Mar 3. More than eight million babies worldwide are born each year with a serious birth defect. Birth defects are a leading cause of death in the first year of life, and babies who survive may be physically or mentally disabled, taking a costly toll on their families, communities and nations. This day seeks to raise awareness of this serious global problem and advocate for more surveillance, prevention, care and research to help babies and children. Sponsored by the March of Dimes and more than 50 other international organizations. Annually, Mar 3. For info: March of Dimes. Web: www.worldbirthdefectsday.org.

🎂 BIRTHDAYS TODAY

Jessica Biel, 38, actress (*Hitchcock, The Illusionist*, "7th Heaven"), born Ely, MN, Mar 3, 1982.

Julie Bowen, 50, actress ("Modern Family," "Ed"), born Baltimore, MD, Mar 3, 1970.

Bob Bradley, 62, Hall of Fame soccer coach, born Montclair, NJ, Mar 3, 1958.

David Faustino, 46, actor ("Married . . . With Children"), born Los Angeles, CA, Mar 3, 1974.

Ira Glass, 61, radio host ("This American Life"), born Baltimore, MD, Mar 3, 1959.

Santonio Holmes, 36, former football player, born Belle Glade, FL, Mar 3, 1984.

Jacqueline (Jackie) Joyner-Kersee, 58, Olympic heptathlete, born East St. Louis, IL, Mar 3, 1962.

Tim Kazurinsky, 70, actor, comedian, writer ("Saturday Night Live"), born Johnstown, PA, Mar 3, 1950.

Brian Leetch, 52, Hall of Fame hockey player, born Corpus Christi, TX, Mar 3, 1968.

Miranda Richardson, 62, actress ("And Then There Were None," *An Inspector Calls, The Crying Game, Enchanted April*), born Lancashire, England, Mar 3, 1958.

Herschel Walker, 58, former football player, 1982 Heisman Trophy winner, born Wrightsville, GA, Mar 3, 1962.

	S	M	T	W	T	F	S
March	1	2	3	4	5	6	7
	8	9	10	11	12	13	14
2020	15	16	17	18	19	20	21
	22	23	24	25	26	27	28
	29	30	31				

March 4 — Wednesday

DAY 64   **302 REMAINING**

ADAMS, JOHN QUINCY: RETURN TO CONGRESS: ANNIVERSARY. Mar 4, 1830. On this day, John Quincy Adams returned to the House of Representatives to represent the district of Plymouth, MA. He was the first former president to do so and served for eight consecutive terms.

ASSOCIATION OF WRITERS AND WRITING PROGRAMS CONFERENCE AND BOOKFAIR. Mar 4–7. Henry B. Gonzalez Convention Center, San Antonio, TX. AWP's mission is to foster literary achievement, foster the art of writing as essential to good education and to serve the makers, teachers, students and readers of contemporary writing. The annual conference—the largest literary conference in North America—hosts more than 2,000 presenters and 550 readings, lectures and panel discussions. The conference attracts more than 12,000 attendees. The bookfair showcases 800 presses, journals and literary organizations from around the world. Est attendance: 13,000. For info: Assn of Writers and Writing Programs, 5700 Rivertech Ct, Ste 225, Riverside Park, MD 20737-1250. Phone: (240) 696-7700. E-mail: events@awpwriter.org. Web: www.awpwriter.org.

CITY OF CHICAGO INCORPORATED: ANNIVERSARY. Mar 4, 1837. The Illinois state legislature enacted into law a city charter for Chicago on this date. William B. Ogden became the first mayor of this city of 4,170 people. Chicago had been incorporated as a town on Aug 12, 1833. The name *Chicago* was formed from a Native American word, but its meaning is disputed. It probably means "strong" or "great."

CLEVELAND'S SECOND PRESIDENTIAL INAUGURATION: ANNIVERSARY. Mar 4, 1893. Grover Cleveland was inaugurated for a second but nonconsecutive term as president. In 1885 he had become the 22nd president of the US and in 1893 the 24th. Originally a source of some controversy, the Congressional Directory for some time listed him only as the 22nd president. The directory now lists him as both the 22nd and 24th presidents though some historians continue to argue that one person cannot be both. Benjamin Harrison served during the intervening term, defeating Cleveland in electoral votes, though not in the popular vote.

CONGRESS: ANNIVERSARY OF FIRST MEETING UNDER CONSTITUTION. Mar 4, 1789. The first Congress met at New York, NY. A quorum was obtained in the House Apr 1 and in the Senate Apr 5, and the first Congress was formally organized Apr 6. Electoral votes were counted, and George Washington was declared president (69 votes) and John Adams vice president (34 votes).

DISCOVER WHAT YOUR NAME MEANS DAY. Mar 4. There are many sources, online and otherwise, about names and naming. To discover the (traditional/conventional) meaning of names, possibly yours, consider any of the available sources on the subject. Also try this: Give your name its own meaning that reflects who you are. Make your definition uniquely yours; decide for yourself what your own name means! Annually, the Wednesday of Celebrate Your Name Week. For info: Jerry Hill. E-mail: CYNW2011@gmail.com. Web: www.namesuniverse.com.

NATIONAL BACKCOUNTRY SKI DAY. Mar 4. Since 2016. Skiers and riders around the country get together to enjoy a day in the backcountry. Backcountry skiing is one of the fastest growing sports in the outdoor industry and we want to ensure that everyone is having fun and staying safe. Organizers of individual groups are encouraged to emphasize avalanche awareness and to approach terrain that is manageable by skiers and riders of all skill levels. Annually, Mar 4. For info: Peter Arlein, Mountainflow Eco-Wax. E-mail: peter@mountainflowecowax.com. Web: www.mountainflowecowax.com/national-backcountry-ski-day.

NATIONAL GRAMMAR DAY. Mar 4. On National Grammar Day, we honor our language and its rules, which help us communicate clearly with each other. In turn, clear communication helps us understand each other—a critical component of peaceful relations.

The day is sponsored by the Quick and Dirty Tips network and Grammar Girl (Mignon Fogarty), a *New York Times* bestselling author and host of the top English language podcast in the world. Annually, Mar 4th—both a date and an imperative. For info: Karen Hertzberg and Mignon Fogarty, Quick and Dirty Tips, Macmillan Publishers, 120 Broadway, 22nd Fl, New York, NY 10271. Phone: (602) 307-5045. E-mail: editor@quickanddirtytips.com. Web: www.nationalgrammarday.com.

OLD INAUGURATION DAY. Mar 4. Anniversary of the date set for beginning the US presidential term of office, 1789–1933. Although the Continental Congress had set the first Wednesday of March 1789 as the date for the new government to convene, a quorum was not present to count the electoral votes until Apr 6. Though George Washington's term of office began on Mar 4, he did not take the oath of office until Apr 30, 1789. All subsequent presidential terms (except successions following the death of an incumbent), until Franklin D. Roosevelt's second term, began Mar 4. The 20th Amendment (ratified Jan 23, 1933) provided that "the terms of the President and Vice President shall end at noon on the 20th day of January . . . and the terms of their successors shall then begin."

PENNSYLVANIA DEEDED TO WILLIAM PENN: ANNIVERSARY. Mar 4, 1681. To satisfy a debt of £16,000, King Charles II of England granted a royal charter, deed and governorship of Pennsylvania to William Penn.

PEOPLE **MAGAZINE: ANNIVERSARY.** Mar 4, 1974. The popular magazine highlighting celebrities was officially launched with the Mar 4, 1974, issue featuring a cover photo of Mia Farrow.

PERKINS, FRANCES: CABINET APPOINTMENT: ANNIVERSARY. Mar 4, 1933. Frances Perkins became the first woman appointed to the president's cabinet when she was appointed secretary of labor by President Franklin D. Roosevelt.

PULASKI, CASIMIR: BIRTH ANNIVERSARY. Mar 4, 1747. American Revolutionary hero, General Kazimierz (Casimir) Pulaski, born at Winiary, Mazovia, Poland, the son of a count. He was a patriot and military leader in Poland's fight against Russia of 1770–71 and went into exile at the partition of Poland in 1772. He came to America in 1777 to join the Revolution, fighting with General Washington at Brandywine and also serving at Germantown and Valley Forge. He organized the Pulaski Legion to wage guerrilla warfare against the British. Mortally wounded in a heroic charge at the siege of Savannah, GA, he died aboard the warship *Wasp* Oct 11, 1779. In Illinois, Pulaski Day is celebrated as a holiday on the first Monday in March.

ROCKNE, KNUTE: BIRTH ANNIVERSARY. Mar 4, 1888. Football coach, born at Voss, Norway. Rockne played end at the University of Notre Dame and then in 1918 was appointed head coach at his alma mater. Over 13 seasons, Rockne became a living legend, and Notre Dame football rose to a position of unprecedented prominence. His teams won 105 games (and three national championships) against only 12 losses and 5 ties. Rockne died in a plane crash at Bazaar, KS, Mar 31, 1931; he was 43 years old.

TELEVISION ACADEMY HALL OF FAME: FIRST INDUCTEES ANNOUNCED: ANNIVERSARY. Mar 4, 1984. The Television Academy of Arts and Sciences announced the formation of the Television Academy Hall of Fame at Burbank, CA. The first inductees were Lucille Ball, Milton Berle, Paddy Chayefsky, Norman Lear, Edward R. Murrow, William S. Paley and David Sarnoff.

VERMONT: ADMISSION DAY: ANNIVERSARY. Mar 4. Became 14th state in 1791.

🎂 BIRTHDAYS TODAY

Chaz Bono, 51, author, television personality, born Chastity Sun Bono at Los Angeles, CA, Mar 4, 1969.

Landon Donovan, 38, soccer executive and former player, born Redlands, CA, Mar 4, 1982.

James Ellroy, 72, author (*LA Confidential, Perfidia*), born Los Angeles, CA, Mar 4, 1948.

Emilio Estefan, 67, musician, born Havana, Cuba, Mar 4, 1953.

Draymond Green, 30, basketball player, born Saginaw, MI, Mar 4, 1990.

Patricia Heaton, 61, actress ("The Middle," "Everybody Loves Raymond"), born Bay Village, OH, Mar 4, 1959.

Kevin Johnson, 54, politician, former basketball player, born Sacramento, CA, Mar 4, 1966.

Patsy Kensit, 52, actress (*The Great Gatsby, Blame It on the Bellboy*), born London, England, Mar 4, 1968.

James Lankford, 52, US Senator (R, Oklahoma), born Dallas, TX, Mar 4, 1968.

Kay Lenz, 67, actress (*Rich Man, Poor Man*), born Los Angeles, CA, Mar 4, 1953.

Ray "Boom Boom" Mancini, 59, Hall of Fame boxer, born Youngstown, OH, Mar 4, 1961.

Catherine O'Hara, 66, comedienne, writer ("SCTV Network 90"), actress (*Home Alone*), born Toronto, ON, Canada, Mar 4, 1954.

Rick Perry, 70, US Secretary of Energy (Trump administration), former governor of Texas (R), born Haskell, TX, Mar 4, 1950.

Paula Prentiss, 81, actress ("He & She"; *The Stepford Wives; What's New, Pussycat?*), born Paula Ragusa at San Antonio, TX, Mar 4, 1939.

Tina Smith, 62, US Senator (D, Minnesota), born Albuquerque, NM, Mar 4, 1958.

Steven Weber, 59, actor ("NCIS: New Orleans," "Wings," "Studio 60 on the Sunset Strip"), born Queens, NY, Mar 4, 1961.

Mary Wilson, 76, singer (the Supremes), born Detroit, MI, Mar 4, 1944.

March 5 — Thursday

DAY 65   **301 REMAINING**

BOSTON MASSACRE: 250th ANNIVERSARY. Mar 5, 1770. A skirmish between British troops and a crowd at Boston, MA, became widely publicized and contributed to the unpopularity of the British regime in the colonies before the American Revolution. Five men were killed and six more were injured by British troops commanded by Captain Thomas Preston.

CHE GUEVARA PHOTOGRAPH: 60th ANNIVERSARY. Mar 5, 1960. During a protest march in Havana, Cuba, photojournalist Alberto Korda snapped the famous head and shoulders shot of Cuban revolutionary Che Guevara that was later used on banners, posters, Cuban currency and—in contemporary times—T-shirts.

CRISPUS ATTUCKS DAY: 250th DEATH ANNIVERSARY. Mar 5, 1770. Honors Crispus Attucks, possibly a runaway slave, who was the first to die in the Boston Massacre.

ENGLAND: CRUFTS DOG SHOW. Mar 5–8. National Exhibition Centre, Birmingham, West Midlands. The World's Greatest Dog Show where more than 23,000 top pedigree dogs compete to achieve the title of "Best in Show," the most prestigious award in the world of dogs. Held since 1891. Est attendance: 140,000. For info: The Kennel Club. E-mail: crufts@thekennelclub.org.uk. Web: www.crufts.org.uk.

HARRISON, REX: BIRTH ANNIVERSARY. Mar 5, 1908. Born Reginald Carey at Huyton, England. Rex Harrison's career as an actor encompassed more than 40 films and scores of plays. He won both a Tony and an Oscar for the role of Henry Higgins in *My Fair Lady*, perhaps his most famous role. Among other films, he appeared in *Dr. Dolittle*, *Cleopatra*, *Blithe Spirit* and *Major Barbara*. He claimed he would never retire from acting, and he was appearing in a Broadway revival of Somerset Maugham's *The Circle* three weeks before his death June 2, 1990, at his home at New York, NY.

IRON CURTAIN SPEECH: ANNIVERSARY. Mar 5, 1946. Winston Churchill, speaking at Westminster College, Fulton, MO, established the cold war boundary with these words: "From Stettin in the Baltic to Trieste in the Adriatic an iron curtain has descended across the continent." Though Churchill was not the first to use the phrase *iron curtain*, his speech gave it a new currency and its usage persisted.

KATYN FOREST MASSACRE ORDERED: 80th ANNIVERSARY. Mar 5, 1940. In a bid to cripple the Polish army and intelligentsia, on this date Stalin ordered the killings of more than 21,000 Polish prisoners, including more than 8,000 officers captured in the Soviet invasion of Poland. In early April the killings began at sites across Russia, with the largest mass graves in Katyn Forest. Soviet and pro-Soviet Polish governments denied the massacre until Mikhail Gorbachev admitted in 1990 that Stalin had ordered the killings.

MERCATOR, GERHARDUS: BIRTH ANNIVERSARY. Mar 5, 1512. Cartographer-geographer Mercator was born at Rupelmonde, Belgium. His Mercator projection for maps provided an accurate ratio of latitude to longitude and is still used today. He also introduced the term *atlas* for a collection of maps. He died at Duisberg, Germany, Dec 2, 1594.

NAMETAG DAY. Mar 5. Today's celebration of names stipulates that wherever you are, whatever you're doing, you wear a "Hello, I'm [your name here]" nametag. (Note: this event is not for unsupervised children.) Annually, the Thursday of Celebrate Your Name Week. For info: Jerry Hill. E-mail: CYNW2011@gmail.com. Web: www.namesuniverse.com.

NATIONAL POUTINE DAY. Mar 5. 7th annual. Today is the day to lose your poutinnocence or shamelessly partake of the gustatorial guilty pleasure of poutine, a culinary experience imported from Quebec, Canada, featuring fries topped with cheese curds and gravy. Celebrate National Poutine Day with those you love to get dirty with. Annually, Mar 5. (Created by Danny Rodriguez.)

SAINT PIRAN'S DAY. Mar 5. Celebrates the birthday of Saint Piran, the patron saint of Cornish tinners. Cornish worldwide celebrate this day.

UNITED KINGDOM AND IRELAND: WORLD BOOK DAY. Mar 5. 23rd annual. World Book Day is the biggest annual celebration of books and reading in the UK and Ireland. (Most other countries hold World Book Day on Apr 23.) A main aim of this day is to encourage children to explore the pleasures of books and reading by providing them with the opportunity to have a book of their own. Annually, the first Thursday in March. For info: World Book Day. E-mail: wbd@education.co.uk. Web: www.worldbookday.com

UNITED STATES BANK HOLIDAY: ANNIVERSARY. Mar 5, 1933. On his first full day in office (Sunday, Mar 5, 1933), President Franklin Roosevelt proclaimed a national "Bank Holiday" to help save the nation's faltering banking system. Most banks were able to reopen after the 10-day "holiday" (Mar 4–14), but in the meantime, "scrip" had temporarily replaced money in many American households.

March 2020	S	M	T	W	T	F	S
	1	2	3	4	5	6	7
	8	9	10	11	12	13	14
	15	16	17	18	19	20	21
	22	23	24	25	26	27	28
	29	30	31				

🧁 BIRTHDAYS TODAY

Kevin Connolly, 46, actor ("Entourage"), born New York, NY, Mar 5, 1974.

Samantha Eggar, 81, actress ("Samantha and the King," *The Collector*), born London, England, Mar 5, 1939.

Penn Jillette, 65, magician, born Greenfield, MA, Mar 5, 1955.

Eva Mendes, 46, actress (*Hitch*, *The Place Beyond the Pines*), singer, model, born Miami, FL, Mar 5, 1974.

Joel Osteen, 57, preacher, author, born Houston, TX, Mar 5, 1963.

Paul Sand, 76, actor ("St. Elsewhere," Tony for *Story Theatre*), born Paul Sanchez at Los Angeles, CA, Mar 5, 1944.

Dean Stockwell, 84, actor (*The Boy with Green Hair*, "Quantum Leap"), born Los Angeles, CA, Mar 5, 1936.

Marsha Warfield, 66, actress ("Night Court," "Empty Nest"), born Chicago, IL, Mar 5, 1954.

Michael Warren, 74, actor ("Paris," "Hill Street Blues"), born South Bend, IN, Mar 5, 1946.

Fred Williamson, 82, actor ("Julia," "Half Nelson"), former football player, born Gary, IN, Mar 5, 1938.

March 6 — Friday

DAY 66   **300 REMAINING**

ALDO LEOPOLD WEEKEND. Mar 6–8. Statewide, Wisconsin. Communities across Wisconsin come together to demonstrate their individual and combined commitment to the "Land Ethic" put forth by renowned environmentalist Aldo Leopold in his famous book, *A Sand County Almanac*. He wrote, "That land is a community is the basic concept of ecology, but that land is to be loved and respected is an extension of ethics." Annually, the first full weekend in March. For info: The Aldo Leopold Foundation, E13701 Levee Rd, Baraboo, WI 53913. Phone: (608) 355-0279. E-mail: mail@aldoleopold.org. Web: www.aldoleopold.org.

BROWNING, ELIZABETH BARRETT: BIRTH ANNIVERSARY. Mar 6, 1806. English poet, author of *Sonnets from the Portuguese*, wife of poet Robert Browning and subject of the play *The Barretts of Wimpole Street*, was born near Durham, England. She died at Florence, Italy, June 29, 1861.

COSTELLO, LOU: BIRTH ANNIVERSARY. Mar 6, 1906. Born at Paterson, NJ, partner with Bud Abbott in the legendary comedy duo Abbott and Costello. The team formed in 1936 and was popular on radio, TV and film. Films include *Buck Privates* and *Abbott and Costello Meet Frankenstein*. "Who's on First?" was their legendary comedy routine. Costello died Mar 3, 1959, at East Los Angeles, CA.

DRED SCOTT DECISION: ANNIVERSARY. Mar 6, 1857. This was the most famous US Supreme Court decision during the prewar slavery controversy. Dred Scott, a slave, had successfully petitioned for his freedom based on his previous residence in a free state and territory. On this date, the Supreme Court overturned Missouri's Supreme Court decision and declared the 1820 Missouri Compromise unconstitutional. Chief Justice Roger Taney wrote that slaves were property, not citizens, and that Congress had no power to restrict slavery in the territories.

DRESS IN BLUE DAY. Mar 6. 12th annual. Observed on the first Friday in March, the Dress in Blue Day program promotes awareness about colon cancer and encourages people to get their colon checked. Part of National Colorectal Cancer Awareness Month since 2006. For info: Colorectal Cancer Alliance, 1025 Vermont Ave NW, Ste 1066, Washington, DC 20005. Phone: (877) 422-2030. Web: www.ccalliance.org/about/awareness-month/dress-in-blue-day.

EISNER, WILL: BIRTH ANNIVERSARY. Mar 6, 1917. One of the greatest comic book/graphic artists, William Erwin Eisner was born at Brooklyn, NY, to Jewish immigrant parents. In a career spanning eight decades, Eisner created the popular and innovative *Spirit* comic book, started an educational comic book business, taught legions of students graphic narrative techniques and created the first graphic novel, *A Contract with God* (1978). He brought cinematic touches—including German Expressionist style—to comics. The Eisner Awards were created in his honor in 1988 to recognize other bright lights in the field. Eisner died Jan 3, 2005, at Fort Lauderdale, FL.

ENGLAND: WORDS BY THE WATER: A FESTIVAL OF WORDS AND IDEAS. Mar 6–15. Lake District. The Theatre by the Lake at Keswick, sitting on the banks of Derwentwater, is the perfect setting for this lively festival. More than 100 speakers and performers participate in lectures, interviews, discussions and readings. For info: Ways with Words, Droridge Farm, Dartington, Totnes, Devon, England TQ9 6JG. Phone: (44) (1803) 86-73-73. Web: www.wayswithwords.co.uk.

FALL OF THE ALAMO: ANNIVERSARY. Mar 6, 1836. Anniversary of the fall of the Texan fort, the Alamo. The siege, led by Mexican general Santa Anna, began Feb 23 and reached its climax Mar 6, when the last of the defenders was slain. Texans, under General Sam Houston, rallied with the war cry "Remember the Alamo" and, at the Battle of San Jacinto, Apr 21, defeated and captured Santa Anna, who signed a treaty recognizing Texas's independence.

GARCÍA MÁRQUEZ, GABRIEL: BIRTH ANNIVERSARY. Mar 6, 1927. Acclaimed author, whose novel *One Hundred Years of Solitude* (1967) made him a worldwide sensation and ambassador of the magic realism genre. García Márquez received the Nobel Prize in Literature in 1982. Other works include *Chronicle of a Death Foretold, Love in the Time of Cholera*, memoirs and screenplays. Born at Aracataca, Colombia, he died Apr 17, 2014, at Mexico City, Mexico.

GHANA: INDEPENDENCE DAY. Mar 6. National holiday. Commemorates independence from Great Britain in 1957.

INTERNATIONAL FESTIVAL OF OWLS. Mar 6–8. Houston, MN. Immerse yourself in owls at this all-owl family event. Kids will delight in the owl face painting, owl crafts and owl pellet dissection. Adults will enjoy presentations by prominent "owlologists," including a banquet address and the presentation of the World Owl Hall of Fame awards. Live owl presentations with five or more species of owls, hooting contest, owl prowls, medallion hunt, owl merchandise and owl-themed food. Annually, the first full weekend in March. Est attendance: 2,000. For info: Karla Bloem, International Owl Center, 126 E Cedar St, PO Box 536, Houston, MN 55943. Phone: (507) 896-6957. E-mail: karla@internationalowlcenter.org. Web: www.festivalofowls.com.

LARDNER, RING: BIRTH ANNIVERSARY. Mar 6, 1885. Ringgold Wilmer "Ring" Lardner, sportswriter, born at Niles, MI. Lardner wrote about sports for a variety of newspapers, mostly in Chicago. In both his columns and his short stories, he reproduced ballplayers' vernacular speech patterns with great success, thereby laying the groundwork for generations of baseball fiction to come. Lardner abandoned baseball after the Black Sox scandal was exposed. He wrote songs, plays and magazine articles but never the novel that some of his friends thought he should. Taciturn and solemn with a biting sense of humor, Lardner drank and smoked to excess,

even after contracting tuberculosis in 1926. Posthumously given the J.G. Taylor Spink Award in 1963 for his baseball writing. Died at East Hampton, NY, Sept 25, 1933.

MICHELANGELO: BIRTH ANNIVERSARY. Mar 6, 1475. Anniversary of the birth, at Caprese, Italy, of Michelangelo di Lodovico Buonarroti Simoni, a prolific Renaissance painter, sculptor, architect and poet who had a profound impact on Western art. Michelangelo's fresco painting on the ceiling of the Sistine Chapel at the Vatican at Rome, Italy, is often considered the pinnacle of his achievement in painting, as well as the highest achievement of the Renaissance. Also among his works are the sculptures *David* and *The Pieta*. Appointed architect of St. Peter's in 1542, a post he held until his death on Feb 18, 1564, at Rome.

MIDDLE NAME PRIDE DAY. Mar 6. Today's name celebration requires honesty and possibly some courage. Tell three people who don't already know it what your middle name is (even if it's Egbert). Annually, the Friday of Celebrate Your Name Week. For info: Jerry Hill. E-mail: CYNW2011@gmail.com. Web: www.namesuniverse.com.

NATIONAL DAY OF UNPLUGGING. Mar 6–7 (tentative). The National Day of Unplugging is sponsored by Reboot, a nonprofit organization that aims to reinvent the cultures, traditions and rituals of Jewish life. The day is guided by Reboot's Sabbath Manifesto, a project that is encouraging hyperconnected and frequently frantic people to re-embrace the ancient beauty of a day of rest. Reboot encourages people of all backgrounds to recharge their spiritual and personal lives by not using computers, cell phones or any technology for 24 hours—from sundown on Friday, Mar 6, to sundown on Saturday, Mar 7. For info: Reboot. Phone: (415) 322-0981. E-mail: josh@rebooters.net. Web: www.rebooters.net or www.nationaldayofunplugging.com.

NORWAY: FINNMARKSLØPET. Mar 6. Alta, Finnmark County. First taking place in 1981, the Finnmarksløpet is the world's northernmost sled dog race. Hosted by Alta Sled Dog Club, the Finnmarksløpet is in fact two races: a 500-km race with up to eight dogs and a 1,200-km race with a maximum of 14 dogs. For info: Finnmarksløpet. Web: www.finnmarkslopet.no.

SPACE MILESTONE: *DAWN* ORBITS DWARF PLANET CERES: 5th ANNIVERSARY. Mar 6, 2015. NASA's *Dawn* spacecraft, which was launched Sept 27, 2007, with the mission to orbit and explore protoplanet Vesta and dwarf planet Ceres, reached Ceres on this date. *Dawn* had reached Vesta in July 2011. In reaching Ceres, *Dawn* achieved two milestones: first spacecraft to orbit two extraterrestrial targets and first spacecraft to orbit a main-belt asteroid (Vesta). The spacecraft, part of the Discovery program, is 5.4 feet long, 4.2 feet wide and 5.8 feet high, with a wingspan of almost 65 feet. In traveling from Earth to Vesta to Ceres, *Dawn* has trekked 3.1 billion miles.

WILLS, BOB: BIRTH ANNIVERSARY. Mar 6, 1905. The Father of Western Swing was born at Kosse, TX. Originally a performer (fiddler) with the Light Crust Doughboys, Wills later formed the popular Texas Playboys. Bob Wills and the Texas Playboys appeared on film and at the Grand Ole Opry and made Western swing popular with such hits as "San Antonio Rose." Wills died May 13, 1975, at Fort Worth, TX.

🧁 BIRTHDAYS TODAY

Tom Arnold, 61, actor ("Roseanne," *McHale's Navy, True Lies*), born Ottumwa, IA, Mar 6, 1959.

Jake Arrieta, 34, baseball player, born Farmington, MO, Mar 6, 1986.

Connie Britton, 52, actress ("Nashville," "Friday Night Lights," "Spin City"), born Boston, MA, Mar 6, 1968.

Dave Gilmour, 76, singer, guitarist (Pink Floyd), born Cambridge, England, Mar 6, 1944.

Alan Greenspan, 94, economist, former chair of the Federal Reserve Board, born New York, NY, Mar 6, 1926.

D.L. Hughley, 57, comedian, actor ("The Hughleys," *The Original Kings of Comedy*), born Los Angeles, CA, Mar 6, 1963.

Kiri Te Kanawa, 76, opera singer, born Gisborne, New Zealand, Mar 6, 1944.

Ben Murphy, 78, actor ("Alias Smith and Jones," *Yours, Mine and Ours*), born Jonesboro, AR, Mar 6, 1942.

Ryan Nyquist, 41, BMX bike racer, born Los Gatos, CA, Mar 6, 1979.

Shaquille Rashan O'Neal, 48, former basketball player, born Newark, NJ, Mar 6, 1972.

Amy Pietz, 51, actress ("Caroline in the City"), born Oakcreek, WI, Mar 6, 1969.

Rob Reiner, 73, actor ("All in the Family"), director (*When Harry Met Sally, This Is Spinal Tap*), born New York, NY, Mar 6, 1947.

Valentina Tereshkova-Nikolaeva, 83, cosmonaut, born Maslennikovo, USSR (now Russia), Mar 6, 1937.

March 7 — Saturday

DAY 67   **299 REMAINING**

BURBANK, LUTHER: BIRTH ANNIVERSARY. Mar 7, 1849. Anniversary of the birth of American naturalist and author, creator and developer of many new varieties of flowers, fruits, vegetables and trees. Burbank's birthday is observed in California as Bird and Arbor Day. Born at Lancaster, MA, he died at Santa Rosa, CA, Apr 11, 1926.

GENEALOGY DAY. Mar 7. Climb into your family tree. Jiggle a few branches. Start piecing together your personal history today via one of the world's fastest-growing hobbies, genealogy, a puzzle waiting to be put together. Annually, the Saturday of Celebrate Your Name Week. For info: Jerry Hill. E-mail: CYNW2011@gmail.com. Web: www.namesuniverse.com.

HOPKINS, STEPHEN: BIRTH ANNIVERSARY. Mar 7, 1707. Colonial governor (Rhode Island) and signer of the Declaration of Independence. Born at Providence, RI, and died there July 13, 1785.

IDITAROD TRAIL SLED DOG RACE. Mar 7–22. 48th running of "The Last Great Race on Earth"® (first run on Mar 3, 1973), 1,000 miles through Alaskan wilderness from Anchorage to Nome, AK, along the historic Iditarod Trail. More than 60 16-dog teams competing. Finishers' banquet on Sunday, Mar 22. Est attendance: 25,000. For info: Iditarod Trail Committee, 2100 S Knik-Goose Bay Rd, Wasilla, AK 99654. Phone: (907) 376-5155. Fax: (907) 373-6998. E-mail: media@iditarod.com. Web: www.iditarod.com.

REMAGEN BRIDGE CAPTURE: 75th ANNIVERSARY. Mar 7, 1945. On this date in 1945, a small advance force of the US First Army captured the Ludendorff railway bridge across the Rhine River at Remagen (between Bonn and Coblenz)—the only bridge across the Rhine that had not been blown up by the German defenders—thus acquiring the first bridgehead onto the east bank and the beginning of the Allied advance into Germany, a turning point in WWII.

March 2020	S	M	T	W	T	F	S
							1
	1	2	3	4	5	6	7
	8	9	10	11	12	13	14
	15	16	17	18	19	20	21
	22	23	24	25	26	27	28
	29	30	31				

BIRTHDAYS TODAY

Bryan Cranston, 64, actor (*Trumbo, Argo*, Tony for *All the Way*, Emmys for "Breaking Bad"), born San Fernando Valley, CA, Mar 7, 1956.

Taylor Dayne, 58, singer, born Long Island, NY, Mar 7, 1962.

Michael Eisner, 78, media executive, born Mount Kisco, NY, Mar 7, 1942.

Jenna Fischer, 46, actress ("The Office," *Walk Hard: The Dewey Cox Story*), born Fort Wayne, IN, Mar 7, 1974.

Denyce Graves, 56, opera singer, born Washington, DC, Mar 7, 1964.

Janet Guthrie, 82, former auto racer, born Iowa City, IA, Mar 7, 1938.

Franco Harris, 70, Hall of Fame football player, born Fort Dix, NJ, Mar 7, 1950.

Robert Harris, 63, author (*The Ghost, Pompeii, Fatherland*), born Nottingham, England, Mar 7, 1957.

Jeff Kent, 52, former baseball player, born Bellflower, CA, Mar 7, 1968.

Ivan Lendl, 60, Hall of Fame tennis player, born Ostrava, Czechoslovakia (now the Czech Republic), Mar 7, 1960.

Tobias Menzies, 46, actor ("Outlander," "Rome"), born London, England, Mar 7, 1974.

Laura Prepon, 40, actress ("Orange Is the New Black," "That '70s Show"), born Watchung, NJ, Mar 7, 1980.

Ricky Rosselló, 41, former governor of Puerto Rico (PNP, 2017–19), biomedical engineer, born Ricardo Antonio Rosselló Nevares at San Juan, Puerto Rico, Mar 7, 1979.

Willard Herman Scott, 86, retired weatherman ("The Today Show"), friend of centenarians, born Alexandria, VA, Mar 7, 1934.

Nick Searcy, 61, actor ("Justified," *Moneyball*), born Cullowhee, NC, Mar 7, 1959.

Daniel J. Travanti, 80, actor ("Hill Street Blues"), born Kenosha, WI, Mar 7, 1940.

Rachel Weisz, 49, actress (Oscar for *The Constant Gardener; Denial, The Bourne Legacy*), born London, England, Mar 7, 1971.

Peter Wolf, 74, singer (J. Geils Band), born Boston, MA, Mar 7, 1946.

March 8 — Sunday

DAY 68   **298 REMAINING**

BACH, CARL PHILIPP EMANUEL: BIRTH ANNIVERSARY. Mar 8, 1714. Musically the most important and influential of Johann Sebastian Bach's sons. German composer, keyboard performer and theorist, C.P.E. Bach was born at Weimar, Germany. He was a contributor to the Viennese classical style and pioneer of the sonata-allegro musical form. The publication of *Essay on the True Art of Playing Keyboard Instruments* (1753), which remains one of the principal monuments of 18th-century musical thought and practice, made him the most renowned authority of the 18th century on keyboard pedagogy and composition. Influential to Haydn and Beethoven, he died Dec 15, 1788, at Hamburg, Germany.

BEAVERS, LOUISE: BIRTH ANNIVERSARY. Mar 8, 1902. The Hollywood career of Louise Beavers spanned 30 years and more than 125 films. Though she was forced to play stereotypical roles, such as those of maids, her authentic talent was always apparent. Her starring role in the film *Imitation of Life* earned her high praise. Beavers was a member of the Black Filmmakers Hall of Fame. She also played the title role in the TV series "Beulah" (1951–53). Born at Cincinnati, OH; died at Los Angeles, CA, Oct 26, 1962.

CAXTON'S *MIRROR OF THE WORLD* TRANSLATION: ANNIVERSARY. Mar 8, 1481. William Caxton, England's first printer, completed the translation from French into English of *Mirror of the World*, a popular account of astronomy and other sciences. In print soon afterward, *Mirror of the World* became the first illustrated book printed in England.

CHECK YOUR BATTERIES DAY. Mar 8. A day set aside for checking the batteries in your smoke detector, carbon monoxide detector, HVAC thermostat, audio/visual remote controls and other electronic devices. This could save your life! Annually, the second Sunday in March (with daylight saving time).

DAYLIGHT SAVING TIME BEGINS. Mar 8–Nov 1. Daylight saving time begins at 2 AM. The Energy Policy Act of 2005 extended the period of daylight saving time as originally outlined in the Uniform Time Act of 1966 (amended in 1986 by Public Law 99–359). Standard time in each zone is advanced one hour from 2 AM on the second Sunday in March until 2 AM on the first Sunday in November (except where state legislatures provide exemption). Prior to 1986, daylight saving time began on the last Sunday in April. Many use the popular rule "spring forward, fall back" to remember which way to turn their clocks. See also: "Daylight Saving Time Ends; Standard Time Resumes" (Nov 1).

GRAHAME, KENNETH: BIRTH ANNIVERSARY. Mar 8, 1859. Scottish author, born at Edinburgh. His children's book *The Wind in the Willows* has as its main characters a mole, a rat, a badger and a toad. He died July 6, 1932, at Pangbourne, Berkshire, England.

HOLMES, OLIVER WENDELL, JR: BIRTH ANNIVERSARY. Mar 8, 1841. "The Great Dissenter," Holmes was born at Boston, MA, and began his career in jurisprudence in the 1860s. He became a law professor at Harvard and was appointed to the Massachusetts Supreme Court, where he was serving as chief justice when he was appointed to the US Supreme Court by President Theodore Roosevelt in 1902. Holmes quickly became known for his pithy opinions and is best remembered for his writings on cases like *Otis v Parker*, which guaranteed due process of law; the landmark case on free speech, *Schenck v United States*, in which he noted a "clear and present danger" to limiting speech and suggested a litmus test equating the severity of a crime to "shouting fire in a crowded theater"; and *Silverthorne Lumber Co v United States*, which prohibited any illegally obtained evidence from being used at trial. He retired from the Supreme Court in 1932 at the age of 90 and died at Washington, DC, on Mar 6, 1935.

INTERNATIONAL (WORKING) WOMEN'S DAY. Mar 8. A day to honor women, especially working women. Said to commemorate an 1857 march and demonstration at New York, NY, by female garment and textile workers. Believed to have been first proclaimed for this date at an international conference of women held at Helsinki, Finland, in 1910, "that henceforth Mar 8 should be declared International Women's Day." The 50th anniversary observance, at Peking, China, in 1960, cited Clara Zetkin (1857–1933) as "initiator of Women's Day on Mar 8." This is perhaps the most widely observed holiday of recent origin and is unusual among holidays originating in the US in having been widely adopted and observed in other nations, including socialist countries. In Russia it is a national holiday, and flowers or gifts are presented to women workers.

MALAYSIA AIRLINES FLIGHT 370 DISAPPEARS: ANNIVERSARY. Mar 8, 2014. Not long after takeoff on a flight from Kuala Lumpur, Malaysia, to Beijing, China, Malaysia Airlines Flight 370 disappeared from air traffic control and military radar over the

South China Sea—in the midst of making a sharp deviation from the planned route. Further analysis of satellite communication data seemed to indicate that the plane crashed into the Indian Ocean, but despite a massive multinational search and rescue effort, the plane has never been found. Lost were 239 passengers and crew.

NATIONAL PROOFREADING DAY. Mar 8. Do typos (typographical errors) make you cringe? Strive for 100 percent accuracy in all documents and messages on National Proofreading Day. Grab a red pen or red pencil on Mar 8 to correct misspelled words; misused words; typos; grammatical errors; and missing, overused and misused punctuation marks. For info: Judy Beaver, National Proofreading Day, 26W112 Klein Creek Dr, Winfield, IL 60190. Phone: (630) 917-1015. E-mail: Judy@NationalProofreadingDay.com. Web: www.NationalProofreadingDay.com.

RUSSIA: INTERNATIONAL WOMEN'S DAY. Mar 8. National holiday.

SYRIAN ARAB REPUBLIC: REVOLUTION DAY. Mar 8. Official public holiday commemorating assumption of power by Revolutionary National Council on Mar 8, 1963.

TERMITE AWARENESS WEEK. Mar 8–14. Termites feed on the cellulose found in wood and paper products and cause more than $5 billion in property damage every year. With termite season upon us, homeowners should be on the lookout for swarmers (winged termites), which serve as a warning that a colony may have already settled inside. The National Pest Management Association (NPMA) launched this week to spread awareness, promote public vigilance and provide essential prevention advice. For info: National Pest Management Assn, 10460 North St, Fairfax, VA 22030. Phone: (703) 352-6762. Fax: (703) 352-3031. E-mail: NPMATeam@vaultcommunications.com. Web: www.pestworld.org.

UNITED NATIONS: INTERNATIONAL WOMEN'S DAY. Mar 8. An international day observed by the organizations of the United Nations system. In some years, known as International Day for Women's Rights and International Peace. Annually, Mar 8. For info: United Nations, Dept of Public Info, New York, NY 10017. Web: www.un.org.

UNITED STATES INCOME TAX: ANNIVERSARY. Mar 8, 1913. The Internal Revenue Service began to levy and collect income taxes. The 16th Amendment to the Constitution, ratified Feb 3, 1913, gave Congress the authority to tax income. The US had also levied an income tax during the Civil War. See also: "Lincoln Signs Income Tax: Anniv" (July 1).

VAN BUREN, HANNAH HOES: BIRTH ANNIVERSARY. Mar 8, 1783. Wife of Martin Van Buren, 8th president of the US. Born at Kinderhook, NY, she died at Albany, NY, Feb 5, 1819.

🎂 BIRTHDAYS TODAY

Susan Clark, 80, actress ("Webster," *Babe*), born Sarnia, ON, Canada, Mar 8, 1940.

Micky Dolenz, 75, singer, actor ("The Monkees"), director, born Los Angeles, CA, Mar 8, 1945.

Lester Holt, 61, journalist, anchor ("NBC Nightly News"), born Marin County, CA, Mar 8, 1959.

Kathy Ireland, 57, model, born Santa Barbara, CA, Mar 8, 1963.

Petra Kvitova, 30, tennis player, born Bílovec, Czechoslovakia (now the Czech Republic), Mar 8, 1990.

Camryn Manheim, 59, actress ("Ghost Whisperer," "The Practice"), born Caldwell, NJ, Mar 8, 1961.

John McPhee, 89, author (Pulitzer Prize for *Annals of the Former World*; *Oranges, The Founding Fish*), professor, born Princeton, NY, Mar 8, 1931.

Freddie Prinze, Jr, 44, actor (*Scooby-Doo, She's All That*), born Albuquerque, NM, Mar 8, 1976.

Aidan Quinn, 61, actor ("Elementary," *Eclipse, Desperately Seeking Susan;* stage: *A Streetcar Named Desire*), born Chicago, IL, Mar 8, 1959.

James Edward (Jim) Rice, 67, Hall of Fame baseball player, born Anderson, SC, Mar 8, 1953.

Carole Bayer Sager, 73, singer, songwriter, born New York, NY, Mar 8, 1947.

Raynoma Gordy Singleton, 83, cofounder of Motown Records, born Detroit, MI, Mar 8, 1937.

James Van Der Beek, 43, actor ("CSI: Cyber," "Dawson's Creek"), born Cheshire, CT, Mar 8, 1977.

March 9 — Monday

DAY 69   **297 REMAINING**

BARBIE DEBUTS: ANNIVERSARY. Mar 9, 1959. The popular girls' doll, created by Ruth Handler for Mattel from a German toy, debuted at the International American Toy Fair in New York City. A brunette at first, Barbie was named for Handler's daughter and her full name is Barbara Millicent Roberts. More than 1 billion dolls have been sold—with an estimated sale every three seconds around the world today.

BATTLE OF HAMPTON ROADS: ANNIVERSARY. Mar 9, 1862. In a Civil War battle that changed the face of naval warfare, two iron-clad vessels, the CSS *Virginia* and the USS *Monitor*, engaged in an exchange of fire for two hours. Neither vessel suffered much damage, but injuries forced both commanders to pull back without a clear victory. On the previous day, the heavily armored *Virginia* had succeeded in severely damaging three Union vessels prior to the arrival of the *Monitor*.

BELIZE: BARON BLISS DAY. Mar 9. Official public holiday. Celebrated in honor of Sir Henry Edward Ernest Victor Bliss, a great benefactor of Belize.

GAGARIN, YURI ALEXSEYEVICH: BIRTH ANNIVERSARY. Mar 9, 1934. Russian cosmonaut Yuri Gagarin, the first person to travel in space, was born at Gzhatsk, USSR. The 27-year-old Soviet Air Force major made his flight Apr 12, 1961, lasting 108 minutes and orbiting Earth in a rocket-propelled, five-ton space capsule 187 miles above Earth's surface. Gagarin was killed in an airplane crash near Moscow, USSR, Mar 27, 1968. After his death the town in which he was born was renamed Gagarin, and the Gagarin Museum was established in the frame house where he spent his childhood.

GRANT COMMISSIONED COMMANDER OF ALL UNION ARMIES: ANNIVERSARY. Mar 9, 1864. At Washington, DC, Ulysses S. Grant accepted his commission as lieutenant general, becoming the commander of all the Union armies.

MOLOTOV, VYACHESLAV MIKHAILOVICH: BIRTH ANNIVERSARY. Mar 9, 1890. Soviet people's commissar for foreign affairs, Molotov negotiated the German-Soviet nonaggression pact of 1939. An active participant in the Stalinist Great Purge, he signed numerous orders of execution. Molotov's claim that Russian forces were dropping food, and not incendiary bombs, on Finnish forces during the Winter War led the Finns to christen their improvised gasoline bombs "Molotov cocktails." Born Mar 9, 1890 (NS; Feb 25 OS) at Kukarka, Russia, he died Nov 8, 1986, at Moscow, Russia, at the age of 96.

	S	**M**	**T**	**W**	**T**	**F**	**S**
March	1	2	3	4	5	6	7
	8	9	10	11	12	13	14
2020	15	16	17	18	19	20	21
	22	23	24	25	26	27	28
	29	30	31				

MOON PHASE: FULL MOON. Mar 9. Moon enters Full Moon phase at 1:48 PM, EDT.

NATIONAL NAPPING DAY. Mar 9. Since 1999, a day for employees to "lie down and be counted" in support of napping at the workplace. This day occurs on the Monday following the advent of daylight saving time. (Created by Dr. William and Camille Anthony.)

PANIC DAY. Mar 9. Run around all day in a panic, telling others you can't handle it anymore. (©2006 by WH.) For info: Thomas & Ruth Roy, Wellcat Holidays, 2418 Long Ln, Lebanon, PA 17046. Phone: (717) 279-0184. E-mail: info@wellcat.com. Web: www.wellcat.com.

SACKVILLE-WEST, VITA: BIRTH ANNIVERSARY. Mar 9, 1892. Born at Sevenoaks, England, Sackville-West was an award-winning author, lecturer, broadcaster and landscape architect; she is now arguably best known for her love affair with Virginia Woolf and her gardens at Sissinghurst. Her two greatest passions, writing and gardening, are married in *The Land* (1926), "a poetic saga of the land and the beauties of the changing seasons." Recipient of the Hawthornden Prize (1927) and the Heinemann Prize (1946), Sackville-West was made a Companion of Honour in 1948 for her work. She died June 2, 1962, at Cranbrook, England.

SAINT FRANCES OF ROME: FEAST DAY. Mar 9. Patron of motorists and model for housewives and widows (1384–1440). After 40 years of marriage she was widowed in 1436 and later joined the community of Benedictine Oblates. Canonized in 1608.

SPILLANE, MICKEY: BIRTH ANNIVERSARY. Mar 9, 1918. Author of hard-boiled detective novels featuring tough guy Mike Hammer. Spillane, born Frank Morrison Spillane, at Brooklyn, NY, introduced Hammer in 1947's *I, The Jury*, which was an immediate hit and prompted a film version and, later, a television series. Spillane's books upped the sex and violence quotient in the hard-boiled genre and prompted both admiration and outrage in their time. Spillane died at Murrells Inlet, SC, on July 17, 2006.

TA'ANIT ESTHER (FAST OF ESTHER). Mar 9. Hebrew calendar date: Adar 13, 5780. Commemorates Queen Esther's fast, in the sixth century BC, to save the Jews of ancient Persia. Begins at dawn.

TOKYO BLANKET BOMBING: 75th ANNIVERSARY. Mar 9, 1945. The Japanese capital of Tokyo was bombed by 343 Superfortresses carrying all the incendiary bombs they could hold. Within the targeted areas of the city, population densities were four times greater than those of most American cities, and homes were made primarily of wood and paper. Carried by the wind, the fires leveled 16 square miles. More than a quarter million buildings were destroyed. The death toll was more than 90,000; 41,000 were injured. For the balance of WWII, American strategic bombing followed this pattern.

UNITED KINGDOM: COMMONWEALTH DAY. Mar 9. Replaces Empire Day observance recognized until 1958. Observed on second Monday in March. Also observed in the British Virgin Islands, Gibraltar and Newfoundland, Canada.

VESPUCCI, AMERIGO: BIRTH ANNIVERSARY. Mar 9, 1454. Italian navigator, merchant and explorer for whom the Americas were named. Born at Florence, Italy (some sources cite his birth year as 1451). He participated in at least two expeditions between 1499 and 1502, which took him to the coast of South America, where he discovered the Amazon and Plata rivers. Vespucci's expeditions were of great importance because he believed that he had discovered a new continent, not just a new route to the Orient. Neither Vespucci nor his exploits achieved the fame of Columbus, but the New World was to be named for Amerigo Vespucci by an obscure German geographer and mapmaker, Martin Waldseemuller. Ironically, in his work as an outfitter of ships, Vespucci had been personally acquainted with Christopher Columbus. Vespucci died at Seville, Spain, Feb 22, 1512. See also: "Waldseemuller, Martin: Remembrance Day" (Apr 25).

VILLA RAIDS COLUMBUS, NEW MEXICO: ANNIVERSARY. Mar 9, 1916. Mexican revolutionary Francisco "Pancho" Villa led 484 "Villistas" in a raid for supplies on Columbus, NM. Townspeople and the nearby 13th Cavalry fought the band and pursued them into Mexico. Eighteen townspeople and US soldiers were killed, while Villa lost 90 men. On Mar 16, General John Pershing led 50,000 US troops in an unsuccessful punitive invasion of Mexico to get Villa dead or alive.

WORM MOON. Mar 9. So called by Native American tribes of New England and the Great Lakes because at this time of year there are signs of earthworms as the ground thaws in preparation for spring. The March Full Moon.

🧁 BIRTHDAYS TODAY

Juliette Binoche, 56, actress (Oscar for *The English Patient*; *Let the Sunshine In, Chocolat*), born Paris, France, Mar 9, 1964.

Linda Fiorentino, 60, actress (*Men in Black, The Last Seduction*), born Philadelphia, PA, Mar 9, 1960.

Mickey Gilley, 84, singer, musician, born Natchez, MS, Mar 9, 1936.

Oscar Isaac, 41, actor (*Ex-Machina, A Most Violent Year, Inside Llewyn Davis*), born Oscar Isaac Hernandez at Guatemala, Mar 9, 1979 (some sources say 1980).

David Hume Kennerly, 73, photographer, journalist, born Rosenburg, OR, Mar 9, 1947.

Emmanuel Lewis, 49, actor ("Webster"), born Brooklyn, NY, Mar 9, 1971.

Terence John (Terry) Mulholland, 57, former baseball player, born St. Paul, MN, Mar 9, 1963.

Jeffrey Osborne, 72, musician, songwriter, born Providence, RI, Mar 9, 1948.

Benito Santiago, 55, former baseball player, born Ponce, Puerto Rico, Mar 9, 1965.

Suga, 27, rapper (BTS), born Min Yoon-gi at Daegu, South Korea, Mar 9, 1993.

Trish Van Devere, 77, actress (*Where's Poppa?, One Is a Lonely Number*), born Tenafly, NJ, Mar 9, 1943.

Joyce Van Patten, 86, actress (*Monkey Shines*, "The Goodbye Guys"), born Queens, NY, Mar 9, 1934.

March 10 — Tuesday

DAY 70   **296 REMAINING**

"BUFFY THE VAMPIRE SLAYER" TV PREMIERE: ANNIVERSARY. Mar 10, 1997. The popular WB show mixed B-movie horror with teen drama. Buffy Summers, played by Sarah Michelle Gellar, is a chosen slayer of vampires, but she still has to get through high school. The witty series was a spin-off of the 1992 film of the same name. After changing networks, the series ended in May 2003.

ENGLAND: CHELTENHAM FESTIVAL. Mar 10–13. Cheltenham Racecourse, Cheltenham, Gloucestershire. Four days of jump racing magic, madness and magnificence, played out on a stage framed by the breathtaking vista of the Cotswold Hills. First race on Tuesday is Champion Day, followed by Ladies Day, St. Patrick's Thursday and then the grand finale of Cheltenham Gold Cup Day. Presented by Magners. Est attendance: 230,000. For info: Cheltenham Racecourse, Cheltenham, Gloucestershire, England GL50 4SH. Web: www.thejockeyclub.co.uk/cheltenham.

FITZGERALD, BARRY: BIRTH ANNIVERSARY. Mar 10, 1888. Actor, born William Joseph Shields, at Dublin, Ireland. He performed with the Abbey Theatre before moving to Hollywood, CA, in 1936. Fitzgerald won a Best Supporting Actor Oscar for his role as Father Fitzgibbon in *Going My Way* (1944)—while also being nominated as Best Actor for the same role. Fitzgerald died Jan 14, 1961, at Dublin.

INDIA: HOLI. Mar 10. In this spring "Festival of Color," people run through the streets throwing brightly hued powders and colored water at each other in celebration of the end of winter and also for the triumph of good over evil. Huge bonfires are built on the eve of Holi. Because there is no one universally accepted Hindu calendar, this holiday may be celebrated on a different date in some parts of India, but it usually falls in March around the full moon in the lunar month of Phalguna. Holika Dahum begins the evening before.

INTERNATIONAL BAGPIPE DAY. Mar 10. 9th annual. A day to celebrate the world's bagpipes and piping traditions. There are more than 130 different kinds of bagpipes played worldwide. On this day pipers everywhere organize local events—talks, lectures, school visits, museum events, pipers' picnics, concerts, gigs and ceilidhs. Annually, Mar 10. For info: The Bagpipe Society. E-mail: info@bagpipesociety.org.uk. Web: www.bagpipesociety.org.uk.

LONDON BOOK FAIR. Mar 10–12. Olympia London, London, England. The London Book Fair is the global marketplace for rights negotiation and the sale and distribution of content across print, audio, TV, film and digital channels. Taking place every spring in the world's premier publishing and cultural capital, it is a unique opportunity to explore, understand and capitalize on the innovations shaping the publishing world of the future. Est attendance: 23,000. For info: London Book Fair. Web: www.londonbookfair.co.uk.

LUCE, CLARE BOOTHE: BIRTH ANNIVERSARY. Mar 10, 1903. Playwright and politician Clare Boothe Luce was born at New York City. Luce wrote for and edited *Vogue* and *Vanity Fair*. She also wrote plays, three of which were later adapted into motion pictures—*The Women* (1936), *Kiss the Boys Goodbye* (1938) and *Margin of Error* (1939). She served in the US House of Representatives (1943–47) and as ambassador to Italy (1953–56)—the first woman appointed ambassador to a major country. Luce died Oct 9, 1987, at Washington, DC.

MARIO DAY. Mar 10. A day for all persons named Mario. Using the abbreviation for the month of March, i.e., MAR, with the day, i.e., 10, you get the name spelled out: MAR10. Annually, Mar 10. Created by Mario Fascitelli.

NATIONAL WOMEN AND GIRLS HIV/AIDS AWARENESS DAY. Mar 10. NWGHAAD is an annual observance that sheds light on the impact of HIV and AIDS on women and girls. Every year on Mar 10, and throughout the month of March, federal, national and community organizations come together to show support for women and girls impacted by HIV and AIDS. For info: Office on Women's Health, US Department of Health and Human Services. Web: www.womenshealth.gov/nwghaad.

***THE ODD COUPLE* PREMIERE: 55th ANNIVERSARY.** Mar 10, 1965. Neil Simon's classic play of mismatched roommates premiered at the Plymouth Theatre, New York, NY. Art Carney portrayed neatnik Felix Unger and Walter Matthau played slob Oscar Madison. The play ran for 964 performances and was nominated for five Tony Awards and received four, including direction (Mike Nichols), actor (Matthau), scene design (Oliver Smith) and author (Simon). It failed to take home the Tony

for best play but inspired a popular movie adaptation and hit TV series.

PURIM. Mar 10. Hebrew calendar date: Adar 14, 5780. Feasts, gifts, charity and the reading of the Book of Esther mark this joyous commemoration of Queen Esther's intervention, in the sixth century BC, to save the Jews of ancient Persia. Haman's plot to exterminate the Jews was thwarted, and he was hanged on the very day he had set for execution of the Jews. Began at sundown Mar 9.

SALVATION ARMY IN THE US: ANNIVERSARY. Mar 10, 1880. Commissioner George Scott Railton and seven women officers landed at New York to officially begin the work of the Salvation Army in the US.

TELEPHONE INVENTION: ANNIVERSARY. Mar 10, 1876. Alexander Graham Bell transmitted the first telephone message to his assistant in the next room: "Mr Watson, come here, I want you," at Cambridge, MA. See also: "Bell, Alexander Graham: Birth Anniversary" (Mar 3).

TUBMAN, HARRIET: DEATH ANNIVERSARY. Mar 10, 1913. American abolitionist, Underground Railroad leader, born a slave at Bucktown, Dorchester County, MD, about 1822. She escaped from a Maryland plantation in 1849 and later helped more than 300 slaves reach freedom. Died at Auburn, NY.

US PAPER MONEY ISSUED: ANNIVERSARY. Mar 10, 1862. After the Legal Tender Act of 1862 passed Feb 25, 1862, the first paper money was issued in the US on this date. The denominations were $5 (Hamilton), $10 (Lincoln) and $20 (Liberty).

 BIRTHDAYS TODAY

Joseph (Sepp) Blatter, 84, former president of FIFA, born Visp, Switzerland, Mar 10, 1936.

Edie Brickell, 54, singer, born Oak Cliff, TX, Mar 10, 1966.

Kim Campbell, 73, 19th prime minister of Canada (1993), first female prime minister, born Vancouver Island, BC, Canada, Mar 10, 1947.

Prince Edward, 56, third son of Queen Elizabeth II, born London, England, Mar 10, 1964.

Bob Greene, 73, journalist, born Columbus, OH, Mar 10, 1947.

Jasmine Guy, 56, singer, actress ("A Different World"), born Boston, MA, Mar 10, 1964.

Jon Hamm, 49, actor (Golden Globe and Emmy for "Mad Men"; *Beirut, Baby Driver*), born St. Louis, MO, Mar 10, 1971.

Thomas Middleditch, 38, actor ("Silicon Valley"), born Nelson, BC, Canada, Mar 10, 1982.

Shannon Miller, 43, Olympic gymnast, born Rolla, MO, Mar 10, 1977.

Chuck Norris, 80, actor (*Missing in Action*, "Walker, Texas Ranger"), born Ryan, OK, Mar 10, 1940.

Pam Oliver, 59, sportscaster, born Dallas, TX, Mar 10, 1961.

David Rabe, 80, playwright (Tony for *Sticks and Bones*; *Hurlyburly, Streamers*), born Dubuque, IA, Mar 10, 1940.

Emeli Sandé, 33, singer, born Sunderland, England, Mar 10, 1987.

Sharon Stone, 62, actress (*Basic Instinct, The Specialist, Casino*), born Meadville, PA, Mar 10, 1958.

Timbaland, 49, music producer, born Timothy Zachery Mosley at Norfolk, VA, Mar 10, 1971.

Shannon Tweed, 63, actress ("Pacific Blue," *Detroit Rock City*), born St. John's, NF, Canada, Mar 10, 1957.

	S	M	T	W	T	F	S
		1	2	3	4	5	6	7
March	8	9	10	11	12	13	14
2020	15	16	17	18	19	20	21
	22	23	24	25	26	27	28
	29	30	31				

Carrie Underwood, 37, singer ("American Idol"), born Muskogee, OK, Mar 10, 1983.

Olivia Wilde, 36, actress ("Vinyl," "House," *Tron: Legacy*), born Olivia Cockburn at New York, NY, Mar 10, 1984.

March 11 — Wednesday

DAY 71   **295 REMAINING**

BUREAU OF INDIAN AFFAIRS ESTABLISHED: ANNIVERSARY. Mar 11, 1824. The US War Department created the Bureau of Indian Affairs.

DREAM 2020 DAY. Mar 11. To focus attention on our millennium—so that all humans, nations and institutions devote every year to unparalleled dreams for a better world and thought, action, inspiration, determination and love to solve the remaining problems and to achieve a peaceful, united human family on Earth. As envisioned by Robert Muller, called the Millennium Man. For info: Barbara Gaughen-Muller, Gaughen Global Public Relations, 7456 Evergreen Dr, Santa Barbara, CA 93117. Phone: (805) 680-9445. E-mail: bgaughenmu@aol.com.

JAPAN EARTHQUAKE AND TSUNAMI OF 2011: ANNIVERSARY. Mar 11, 2011. With an epicenter near Sendai, Japan, this 9.0 earthquake struck the northeast side of Japan's Honshu island. The earthquake triggered a massive tsunami that caused widespread devastation. The dead and missing were estimated at 24,500. The disaster also caused a level 7 emergency at nuclear power plants at Fukushima when cooling systems failed at three reactors, releasing radiation. This was the worst natural disaster in Japan's recorded history.

JOHNNY APPLESEED DAY (JOHN CHAPMAN'S 175th DEATH ANNIVERSARY). Mar 11, 1845. Anniversary of the death of John Chapman, better known as Johnny Appleseed, believed to have been born at Leominster, MA, Sept 26, 1774. The planter of orchards and friend of wild animals was regarded by the Indians as a great medicine man. He died at Allen County, IN. See also: "Appleseed, Johnny: Birth Anniversary" (Sept 26).

KEY DEER AWARENESS DAY. Mar 11. Since 2016. Key deer, a smaller version of white tail deer, have been on the endangered species list since 1967; yet most people are unaware of their existence. Today they are threatened by sea level rise, habitat loss and parasites. Annually, Mar 11—when their endangered status was published in 1967 to the Federal Register. For info: Madison Metz. Web: www.keydeerday.com.

LITHUANIA: RESTITUTION OF INDEPENDENCE DAY. Mar 11. National holiday. Commemorates independence from the Soviet Union in 1990. Lithuania had initially declared its independence in 1918 but lost it to the Soviet Union in 1940.

MADRID TRAIN BOMBINGS: ANNIVERSARY. Mar 11, 2004. Ten terrorist bombs exploded on four commuter trains in Spain's busy capital on this date, killing 191 people and injuring 1,800. It was the worst loss of life by violence in Europe since WWII. Nations around the world expressed their sorrow, and demonstrations against terrorism were held in Brussels, Paris, Helsinki, Geneva, Berlin and Stockholm. Spain observed a three-minute period of silence at noon on Mar 15 in order to remember the wounded and slain. Several European countries arrested suspects in the case, and seven militants considered major suspects blew themselves up at Madrid to avoid capture on Apr 3. The terrorists responsible were believed to be allied with Al Qaeda.

NATIONAL COLLEGIATE MEN'S AND WOMEN'S SKIING CHAMPIONSHIPS. Mar 11–14. Montana State University, Bozeman, MT. 67th annual. For info: NCAA, PO Box 6222, Indianapolis, IN 46206-6222. Phone: (317) 917-6222. Fax: (317) 917-6826. Web: www.NCAA.com.

PAINE, ROBERT TREAT: BIRTH ANNIVERSARY. Mar 11, 1731. Jurist and signer of the Declaration of Independence. Born at Boston, MA; died there May 11, 1814.

PANDEMIC OF 1918 HITS US: ANNIVERSARY. Mar 11, 1918. The first cases of the "Spanish" influenza were reported in the US when 107 soldiers became sick at Fort Riley, KS. By the end of 1920 nearly 25 percent of the US population had been infected. As many as 500,000 civilians died from the virus, exceeding the number of US troops killed abroad in WWI. Worldwide, more than 1 percent of the global population, or 22 million people, had died by 1920 because of the virus. The origin of the virus was never determined absolutely, though it was probably somewhere in Asia. The name "Spanish" influenza came from the relatively high number of cases in that country early in the epidemic. Due to the panic, cancellation of public events was common, and many public service workers wore masks on the job. Emergency tent hospitals were set up in some locations due to overcrowding.

REGISTERED DIETITIAN NUTRITIONIST DAY. Mar 11. This day commemorates the dedication of RDNs as advocates for advancing the nutritional status of Americans and people around the world. Annually, the second Wednesday in March. For info: Academy of Nutrition and Dietetics, 120 S Riverside Plaza, Ste 2190, Chicago, IL 60606. Phone: (800) 877-1600. E-mail: nnm@eatright.org. Web: www.eatright.org.

SCALIA, ANTONIN: BIRTH ANNIVERSARY. Mar 11, 1936. Born at Trenton, NJ, Scalia was Associate Justice of the US (appointed by President Ronald Reagan) from 1986 to 2016. At times caustic but usually displaying an audience-entertaining wit, Scalia was the leading conservative on the bench and the leading promulgator of the originalism school of constitutional theory (focusing on the intent of the document's creators). At the time of his death, at Shafter, TX, Feb 13, 2016, Scalia was the longest-serving justice on the court.

TASSO, TORQUATO: BIRTH ANNIVERSARY. Mar 11, 1544. Poet of the late Renaissance, born at Sorrento, Italy. His violent outbursts and acute sensitivity to criticism led to his imprisonment for seven years, during which the "misunderstood genius" continued his literary creativity. Died at Rome, Italy, Apr 25, 1595.

TURKEY VULTURES RETURN TO THE LIVING SIGN. Mar 11–17. Entire Canisteo Valley, Canisteo, NY. Traditionally turkey vultures return on St. Pat's Day to their roosting sites in and around the world-famous Living Sign, as mentioned in "Ripley's Believe It or Not." The sign spells out "Canisteo" using 250 trees on a ridge above Greenwood Street. For info: Bill Berry, 6950 Lain Rd, Hornell, NY 14843-9419. Phone: (607) 661-5500. E-mail: thepaperwolf@gmail.com.

WELK, LAWRENCE: BIRTH ANNIVERSARY. Mar 11, 1903. Bandleader Lawrence Welk was born at Strasburg, ND. He learned to play the accordion and at 17 formed his first band. After playing all over the Midwest, he moved to Los Angeles, where in 1955 his show began its nationwide television broadcast of "Champagne Music." The longest-running primetime program in TV history, "The Lawrence Welk Show" played each Saturday on ABC from 1955 until 1971, when it was dropped because sponsors thought its audience was too old. Welk kept the show on a network of more than 250 independent stations for 11 more years, and it still can be seen in reruns. Welk's entertainment empire included the purchase of royalty rights to songs, among them the entire collection of songs by Jerome Kern. Welk died at Santa Monica, CA, May 17, 1992.

WILSON, HAROLD: BIRTH ANNIVERSARY. Mar 11, 1916. British statesman and twice prime minister (1964–70 and 1974–76), leader of the Labour Party. Born at Huddersfield, Yorkshire, England. He died May 24, 1995, at London, England.

🎂 BIRTHDAYS TODAY

John Barrowman, 53, actor ("Arrow," "Torchwood," "Doctor Who"), born Glasgow, Scotland, Mar 11, 1967.

Elton Brand, 41, former basketball player, born Peekskill, NY, Mar 11, 1979.

Curtis Brown, Jr, 64, astronaut, born Elizabethtown, NC, Mar 11, 1956.

Jodie Comer, 27, actress ("Killing Eve," "Doctor Foster"), born Liverpool, England, Mar 11, 1993.

Anthony Davis, 27, basketball player, born Chicago, IL, Mar 11, 1993.

Sam Donaldson, 86, journalist, born El Paso, TX, Mar 11, 1934.

Didier Drogba, 42, soccer executive and player, born Abidjan, Ivory Coast, Mar 11, 1978.

Terrence Howard, 51, actor ("Empire," *Iron Man, Hustle & Flow*), born Chicago, IL, Mar 11, 1969.

Alex Kingston, 57, actress ("Doctor Who," "ER," *Macbeth*), born London, England, Mar 11, 1963.

Elias Koteas, 59, actor ("Chicago P.D.," "The Killing," *The Curious Case of Benjamin Button, The Thin Red Line*), born Montreal, QC, Canada, Mar 11, 1961.

Bobby McFerrin, 70, jazz musician, singer, songwriter, conductor, born New York, NY, Mar 11, 1950.

Rupert Murdoch, 89, media executive, born Melbourne, Australia, Mar 11, 1931.

Jerry Zucker, 70, writer, (*Naked Gun* movies with brother David), producer (*Airplane!*), born Milwaukee, WI, Mar 11, 1950.

March 12 — Thursday

DAY 72   **294 REMAINING**

ALBEE, EDWARD: BIRTH ANNIVERSARY. Mar 12, 1928. American modernist playwright and director, born in Virginia. He was adopted as an infant by an uncaring mother and distant father. Albee's plays have a recognizable autobiographical emotional landscape where barbed language and caustic wit delve into the dark side of personality and family life. His first success was *The Zoo Story* in 1959, but it was the picture of alcohol-fueled marital discord and stifling middle-class American values in the 1963 Tony Award–winning *Who's Afraid of Virginia Woolf?* that brought Albee fame and lasting critical recognition. Alcoholism almost destroyed his own career, but despite plays like *Tiny Alice* (1964) that sometimes failed spectacularly, Albee won two more Tonys, for *Seascape* (1975) and *The Goat, or Who Is Sylvia?* (2008), and Pulitzer Prizes for *A Delicate Balance* (1967), *Seascape* and *Three Tall Women* (1994). He died Sept 16, 2016, in Montauk, NY.

ATATÜRK, MUSTAFA KEMAL: BIRTH ANNIVERSARY. Mar 12, 1881. The founder of modern Turkey was born at Salonika, Greece (then part of the Ottoman Empire). After a distinguished army career, he led the Turkish revolution after WWI and was elected Turkey's first president. He died at Istanbul, Nov 10, 1938.

AUSTRIA INVADED BY NAZI GERMANY: ANNIVERSARY. Mar 12, 1938. As a test of its own war readiness and of the response of the other major powers, Germany occupied Austria. A year later Germany invaded Czechoslovakia and, in September 1939, Poland, beginning WWII.

BERMUDA COLONIZED BY ENGLISH: ANNIVERSARY. Mar 12, 1609. The ship of Admiral Sir George Somers, taking settlers to Virginia, was wrecked on the reefs of Bermuda. The islands had been discovered in the early 1500s but were uninhabited until 1609.

BOYCOTT, CHARLES CUNNINGHAM: BIRTH ANNIVERSARY. Mar 12, 1832. Charles Cunningham Boycott, born at Norfolk, England, has been immortalized by having his name become part of the English language. In County Mayo, Ireland, the Tenants' "Land League" in 1880 asked Boycott, an estate agent, to reduce

rents (because of poor harvest and dire economic conditions). Boycott responded by serving eviction notices on the tenants, who retaliated by refusing to have any dealings with him. Charles Stewart Parnell, then president of the National Land League and agrarian agitator, retaliated against Boycott by formulating and implementing the method of economic and social ostracism that came to be called a "boycott." Boycott died at Suffolk, England, June 19, 1897.

CHURCH OF ENGLAND ORDAINS WOMEN PRIESTS: ANNIVERSARY. Mar 12, 1994. The Church of England for the first time ordained 32 women at Bristol Cathedral. About 700 male members of the clergy and unknown thousands of lay members indicated they would leave the Church of England and join the Roman Catholic Church. The Catholic Church responded to the ordination by saying that it "constitutes a profound obstacle to every hope of reunion between the Catholic Church and the Anglican Communion." This day's ordinations were not the first. Earlier that year about 1,380 women priests were ordained in churches of the Anglican Communion outside of Great Britain.

DE KOONING, ELAINE: BIRTH ANNIVERSARY. Mar 12, 1918. Noted American artist and teacher, born Elaine Fried at Brooklyn, NY. She worked in the Abstract Expressionist genre. Married fellow artist Willem de Kooning in 1943. De Kooning died Feb 1, 1989, at Southhampton, NY.

EMERALD CITY COMIC CON. Mar 12–15. Washington State Convention Center, Seattle, WA. The largest comic book and pop culture convention in the Pacific Northwest! With hundreds of comic book guests, celebrity guests and more. Est attendance: 90,000. For info: Emerald City Comic Con. E-mail: ECCCinfo@reedexpo.com. Web: www.emeraldcitycomiccon.com.

FDR'S FIRST FIRESIDE CHAT: ANNIVERSARY. Mar 12, 1933. President Franklin Delano Roosevelt made the first of his Sunday evening "fireside chats" to the American people. Speaking by radio from the White House, he reported rather informally on the economic problems of the nation and on his actions to deal with them.

GABON: NATIONAL DAY. Mar 12. Observes founding of Gabonese Democratic Party on Mar 12, 1968.

GIRL SCOUTS OF THE USA FOUNDING: ANNIVERSARY. Mar 12, 1912. Juliette Low founded the Girl Scouts of the USA at Savannah, GA.

GREAT BLIZZARD OF '88: ANNIVERSARY. Mar 12, 1888. One of the most devastating blizzards to hit the northeastern US began in the early hours of Monday, Mar 12, 1888. A snowfall of 40–50 inches, accompanied by gale-force winds, left drifts as high as 30–40 feet. More than 400 persons died in the storm (200 at New York City alone). Some survivors of the storm, "The Blizzard Men of 1888," held annual meetings at New York City as late as 1941 to recount personal recollections of the event.

March 2020	S	M	T	W	T	F	S
				1	2	3	4	5	6	7
	8	9	10	11	12	13	14
	15	16	17	18	19	20	21
	22	23	24	25	26	27	28
	29	30	31				

KEROUAC, JACK: BIRTH ANNIVERSARY. Mar 12, 1922. American poet and novelist Jack (Jean-Louis) Kerouac, leader of and spokesman for the Beat movement, was born at Lowell, MA. Kerouac is best known for his novel *On the Road*, published in 1957, which celebrates the Beat ideal of nonconformity. Kerouac published *The Dharma Bums* in 1958, followed by *The Subterraneans* the same year, *Doctor Sax* and its sequel, *Maggie Cassidy*, in 1959, *Lonesome Traveler* in 1960, *Big Sur* in 1962 and *Desolation Angels* in 1965. Kerouac died at St. Petersburg, FL, at age 47, Oct 21, 1969. A previously unpublished part of *On the Road* called *Visions of Cody* was published posthumously in 1972.

LESOTHO: MOSHOESHOE'S DAY. Mar 12. National holiday. Commemorates the great leader Chief Moshoeshoe I, who unified the Basotho people, beginning in 1820.

MAURITIUS: INDEPENDENCE DAY. Mar 12. National holiday commemorates attainment of independent nationhood (within the British Commonwealth) on Mar 12, 1968.

NEWCOMB, SIMON: BIRTH ANNIVERSARY. Mar 12, 1835. Astronomer, born at Wallace, NS, Canada. Newcomb investigated the orbits of Uranus, Neptune and the inner planets and devised planetary tables that were used universally by observatories. Died at Washington, DC, July 11, 1909.

PIERCE, JANE MEANS APPLETON: BIRTH ANNIVERSARY. Mar 12, 1806. Wife of Franklin Pierce, 14th president of the US. Born at Hampton, NH. Died at Concord, NH, Dec 2, 1863.

RIO GRANDE VALLEY LIVESTOCK SHOW. Mar 12–22. Mercedes, TX. 81st annual. PRCA rodeo, open cattle show and carnival. For the youth of the four counties in the valley to exhibit their projects. Est attendance: 200,000. For info: Rio Grande Valley Livestock Show Inc, 1000 North Texas, Mercedes, TX 78570. Phone: (956) 565-2456. E-mail: info@rgvls.com. Web: www.rgvls.com.

SCHIRRA, WALLY: BIRTH ANNIVERSARY. Mar 12, 1923. One of the original seven *Mercury* astronauts, born Walter Marty Schirra, Jr, at Hackensack, NJ. A US Navy pilot during WWII and the Korean conflict, Schirra entered the US space program in 1959. He was the only man to fly all three of the first manned space missions (*Mercury, Gemini* and *Apollo*), logging a total of 295 hours, 15 minutes in space. He won an Emmy Award for the footage he sent back from *Apollo 7*, the first televised pictures from space, and later worked with Walter Cronkite on broadcasts of other NASA missions. He died at La Jolla, CA, May 3, 2007.

SPAIN: FIESTA DE LAS FALLAS. Mar 12–19. Valencia. This festival of burning effigies and fireworks has been celebrated for more than 150 years.

SUN YAT-SEN: 95th DEATH ANNIVERSARY. Mar 12, 1925. The heroic leader of China's 1911 revolution is remembered on the anniversary of his death at Peking, China. Observed as Arbor Day in Taiwan.

WORLD KIDNEY DAY. Mar 12. The purpose of this day is to raise awareness about the importance of our kidneys—amazing organs that play a crucial role in keeping us alive and well—and to spread the message that kidney disease is common, harmful and treatable. Observed since 2006—now in 100 countries. Annually, the second Thursday in March. For info: World Kidney Day. E-mail: info@worldkidneyday.org. Web: www.worldkidneyday.org.

🎂 BIRTHDAYS TODAY

Jaimie Alexander, 36, actress ("Blindspot," *Thor* films), born Greenville, SC, Mar 12, 1984.

Jason Beghe, 60, actor ("Chicago P.D.," "Californication," *G.I. Jane*), born New York, NY, Mar 12, 1960.

Rob Cohen, 71, producer (*Bird on a Wire*), director (*Dragonheart*), born Cornwall-on-Hudson, NY, Mar 12, 1949.

Tammy Duckworth, 52, US Senator (D, Illinois), born Bangkok, Thailand, Mar 12, 1968.

Aaron Eckhart, 52, actor (*Olympus Has Fallen*, *The Dark Knight*, *Thank You for Smoking*), born Cupertino, CA, Mar 12, 1968.

Barbara Feldon, 79, actress ("Get Smart," *Smile*), born Pittsburgh, PA, Mar 12, 1941.

Marlon Jackson, 63, singer (Jackson 5), born Gary, IN, Mar 12, 1957.

Liza Minnelli, 74, singer, actress (Oscar for *Cabaret*; Tonys for *The Act* and *Flora, The Red Menace*; *The Sterile Cuckoo, Arthur*), born Los Angeles, CA, Mar 12, 1946.

Dale Murphy, 64, former baseball player, born Portland, OR, Mar 12, 1956.

Mitt Romney, 73, US Senator (R, Utah), 2012 presidential candidate, former governor of Massachusetts (R), born Detroit, MI, Mar 12, 1947.

Darryl Strawberry, 58, former baseball player, born Los Angeles, CA, Mar 12, 1962.

Jake Tapper, 51, journalist, anchor ("The Lead with Jake Tapper," "State of the Union"), born New York, NY, Mar 12, 1969.

James Taylor, 72, singer, musician, born Boston, MA, Mar 12, 1948.

Courtney B. Vance, 60, actor ("The People v O.J. Simpson," "Law & Order: Criminal Intent," *Lucky Guy, Fences*), born Detroit, MI, Mar 12, 1960.

Titus Welliver, 59, actor ("Bosch," "The Good Wife," "Lost," "Deadwood"), born New Haven, CT, Mar 12, 1961.

Andrew Young, 88, civil rights leader, born New Orleans, LA, Mar 12, 1932.

March 13 — Friday

DAY 73 **293 REMAINING**

ANNENBERG, WALTER: BIRTH ANNIVERSARY. Mar 13, 1908. Publisher, philanthropist and ambassador, Walter Annenberg was born at Milwaukee, WI. He inherited the *Philadelphia Inquirer* from his father and built the newspaper into the cornerstone of a publishing empire that included newspapers, magazines, and radio and television stations. He founded many enduring publications, including *Seventeen* (1944) and *TV Guide* (1953). He served as US ambassador to the United Kingdom during 1969–76. As a philanthropist, Annenberg gave billions to charities. He died at Wynnewood, PA, on Oct 1, 2002.

ARAB OIL EMBARGO LIFTED: ANNIVERSARY. Mar 13, 1974. The oil-producing Arab countries agreed to lift their five-month embargo on petroleum sales to the US. During the embargo, prices went up 300 percent and a ban was imposed on Sunday gasoline sales. The embargo was in retaliation for US support of Israel during the October 1973 Middle East War.

BLAME SOMEONE ELSE DAY. Mar 13. To share the responsibility and the guilt for the mess we're in. Blame someone else! Annually, the first Friday the 13th of the year. For info: A.C. Vierow, Box 71, Clio, MI 48420-0071.

CLARENCE DARROW DEATH COMMEMORATION. Mar 13. Jackson Park, Chicago, IL. Annually, on the anniversary of his death, a wreath is tossed from the Jackson Park Clarence Darrow Bridge, named in honor of the famed lawyer and civil libertarian at 10 AM. At 11 AM a discussion follows in the Columbian Room of the Museum of Science and Industry, Chicago.

DEAF HISTORY MONTH. Mar 13–Apr 15. Observance of three important American anniversaries: Mar 13, 1988, first Deaf Civil Rights Victory Day following the deaf movement at Gallaudet University; Apr 8, 1864, charter signed by President Abraham Lincoln authorizing the Board of Directors of what is today Gallaudet University to grant college degrees to deaf students; Apr 15, 1817, opening of the first public school for deaf students in Hartford,

CT. For info: Library for Deaf Action, 2930 Craiglawn Rd, Silver Spring, MD 20904-1816. Web: www.foldadeaf.net.

DELMONICO, LORENZO: BIRTH ANNIVERSARY. Mar 13, 1813. Famed restaurateur and gastronomic authority born at Marengo, Switzerland. Immigrating to New York in 1831, he joined his uncle in the family's small wine, confectionery and catering business and quickly became a junior partner before assuming complete ownership in 1842. The opening of the first of several Delmonico restaurants in New York, NY, revolutionized American eating habits and the standard American diet by turning the preparation and eating of food into an art form. The restaurants specialized in native foods, much of which was grown on the Delmonicos' privately owned 200-acre farm in Brooklyn. Nicknamed "Lorenzo the Great," Delmonico was the preeminent American epicure of his era and a noted philanthropist until his death at Sharon Springs, NY, on Sept 3, 1881.

EARMUFFS PATENTED: ANNIVERSARY. Mar 13, 1887. Chester Greenwood of Maine received a patent for earmuffs.

FILLMORE, ABIGAIL POWERS: BIRTH ANNIVERSARY. Mar 13, 1798. First wife of Millard Fillmore, 13th president of the US. Born at Stillwater, NY. It is said that the White House was without any books until Abigail Fillmore, formerly a teacher, made a room on the second floor into a library. Within a year, Congress appropriated $250 for the president to spend on books for the White House. Died at Washington, DC, Mar 30, 1853.

FRIDAY THE THIRTEENTH. Mar 13. Variously believed to be a lucky or an unlucky day. Every year has at least one Friday the 13th, but never more than three. There are two Friday the 13ths in 2020 (the second one falls in November). Fear of the number 13 is known as triskaidekaphobia. Fear of Friday the 13th is known as paraskavedekatriaphobia.

GENOVESE MURDER: ANNIVERSARY. Mar 13, 1964. Catherine (Kitty) Genovese was stabbed to death in the Kew Gardens neighborhood of Queens, NY. The crime became infamous as it appeared (and was reported in major media outlets) that numerous neighbors did nothing to help her when they heard her screams. The case prompted studies of what is now called the bystander effect, which describes a phenomenon whereby the greater the number of bystanders present at a crime or crisis the less likely any one of them will offer aid.

GOOD SAMARITAN INVOLVEMENT DAY. Mar 13. A day to emphasize the importance of unselfish aid to those who need it. Recognized on the anniversary of the killing of Catherine (Kitty) Genovese, Mar 13, 1964, in Kew Gardens, Queens, NY.

HOLY SEE: NATIONAL DAY. Mar 13. The State of Vatican City and the Holy See observe Mar 13 as a national holiday (on the anniversary of the election of the current pope).

HUBBARD, L. RON: BIRTH ANNIVERSARY. Mar 13, 1911. Lafayette Ronald Hubbard, science fiction writer, recluse and founder of the Church of Scientology, was born at Tilden, NE. His best-known book is *Dianetics: The Modern Science of Mental Health*. Died at San Luis Obispo County, CA, Jan 24, 1986.

LOWELL, PERCIVAL: BIRTH ANNIVERSARY. Mar 13, 1855. American astronomer, founder of the Lowell Observatory at Flagstaff, AZ. Born at Boston, MA, he died at Flagstaff, Nov 12, 1916. Lowell was initiator of the search that resulted (25 years after the search began and 14 years after his death) in discovery of Pluto. The discovery was announced on Lowell's birthday, Mar 13, 1930, by the Lowell Observatory.

NATIONAL OPEN AN UMBRELLA INDOORS DAY. Mar 13. The purpose of this day is for people to open umbrellas indoors and note whether they have any bad luck. Annually, Mar 13. (Originated by Thomas Edward Knibb.)

NCAA DIVISION I MEN'S & WOMEN'S INDOOR TRACK AND FIELD CHAMPIONSHIPS. Mar 13–14. University of New Mexico, Albuquerque, NM. Annually, the second weekend in March. For info: NCAA, PO Box 6222, Indianapolis, IN 46206-6222. Phone: (317) 917-6222. Fax: (317) 917-6888. Web: www.NCAA.com.

NCAA DIVISION I RIFLE CHAMPIONSHIPS. Mar 13–14. University of Kentucky, Lexington, KY. 22nd annual. For info: NCAA, PO Box 6222, Indianapolis, IN 46206-6222. Web: www.NCAA.com.

O'HARE, EDWARD "BUTCH": BIRTH ANNIVERSARY. Mar 13, 1914. Born in St. Louis, MO, O'Hare attended the US Naval Academy and later trained as an aviator. He earned the first Congressional Medal of Honor in World War II after shooting down five Japanese planes in an air battle to save the USS *Lexington* aircraft carrier from damage. He did not return from a later mission on Nov 26, 1943, after losing radio contact and was presumed shot down or crashed over the Pacific. In September 1949 O'Hare International Airport in Chicago, IL, was named in his honor.

OPERATION FLASH: ANNIVERSARY. Mar 13, 1943. Disillusioned German officers planned to take the life of Adolf Hitler on this date. Hitler was traveling by plane from Vinnitsa, USSR, to Rastenburg, Germany, with a scheduled stop at Smolensk, USSR. At Smolensk, the crew was given what appeared to be two bottles of liquor as a gift. These bottles contained incendiary materials and were designed to detonate in midair to create the appearance of an accident. "Flash" was the code word to indicate success and to begin creating a new government. But the detonator failed to work and Hitler arrived safely in Rastenburg. See also: "Gersdorff Hitler Assassination Attempt: Anniversary" (Mar 21).

PLANET URANUS DISCOVERY: ANNIVERSARY. Mar 13, 1781. German-born English astronomer Sir William Herschel discovered the seventh planet from the sun, Uranus.

POPE FRANCIS: ELECTION ANNIVERSARY. Mar 13, 2013. Argentine cardinal and Archbishop of Buenos Aires Jorge Mario Bergoglio was elected 266th pope of the Roman Catholic Church by a papal conclave after the resignation of Pope Benedict XVI. Pope Francis is the first pope chosen from the Americas, the first from the Southern Hemisphere and the first Jesuit. He was born Dec 17, 1936, at Buenos Aires, Argentina.

PRIESTLY, JOSEPH: BIRTH ANNIVERSARY. Mar 13, 1733. (Old Style date.) English clergyman and scientist, discoverer of oxygen, born at Fieldhead, England. He and his family narrowly escaped an angry mob attacking their home because of his religious and political views. They moved to the US in 1794. Died at Northumberland, PA, Feb 6, 1804.

SAINT AUBIN, HELEN "CALLAGHAN" CANDAELE: BIRTH ANNIVERSARY. Mar 13, 1929. Helen Candaele Saint Aubin, known as Helen Callaghan during her baseball days, was born at Vancouver, BC, Canada. Saint Aubin and her sister, Margaret Maxwell, were recruited for the All-American Girls Professional Baseball League, which flourished in the 1940s when many major league players were off fighting WWII. She first played at age 15 for the Minneapolis Millerettes, an expansion team that moved to Indiana and became the Fort Wayne Daisies. For the 1945 season the left-handed outfielder led the league with a .299 average and 24 extra-base hits. In 1946 she stole 114 bases in 111 games. Her son Kelly Candaele's documentary on the women's baseball league inspired the film *A League of Their Own*. Saint Aubin, known as the "Ted Williams of women's baseball," died Dec 8, 1992, at Santa Barbara, CA.

SHERLOCK HOLMES WEEKEND. Mar 13–15 (also Oct 30–Nov 1, Nov 6–8). Cape May, NJ. A weekend of mystery and intrigue awaits amateur sleuths when Cape May celebrates the works of Sir Arthur Conan Doyle, creator of Sherlock Holmes. Offered three times annually. Est attendance: 600. For info: Mid-Atlantic Center for the Arts and Humanities, 1048 Washington St, Cape May, NJ 08204. Phone: (609) 884-5404 or (800) 275-4278. Fax:

(609) 884-0574. E-mail: info@capemaymac.org. Web: www.cape-maymac.org.

SOUTH BY SOUTHWEST (SXSW). Mar 13–22. Austin, TX. Annual, internationally recognized music, film and new media conference. Hundreds of events, performances and panels. Est attendance: 170,000. For info: SXSW, PO Box 685289, Austin, TX 78768. Phone: (512) 467-7979). Web: www.sxsw.com.

🎂 BIRTHDAYS TODAY

Thomas Andrew (Andy) Bean, 67, golfer, born Lafayette, GA, Mar 13, 1953.

Caron Butler, 40, basketball player, born Racine, WI, Mar 13, 1980.

Charo, 69, singer, actress ("Chico and the Man"), born Maria Martinez at Murcia, Spain, Mar 13, 1951.

Adam Clayton, 60, musician (U2), born Dublin, Ireland, Mar 13, 1960.

Dana Delany, 64, actress ("Body of Proof," "Desperate Housewives," "China Beach"), born New York, NY, Mar 13, 1956.

Emile Hirsch, 35, actor (*Speed Racer, Into the Wild, Alpha Dog*), born Palms, CA, Mar 13, 1985.

John Hoeven, 63, US Senator (R, North Dakota), born Bismarck, ND, Mar 13, 1957.

William H. Macy, 70, actor ("Shameless," *Door to Door, Fargo*, "ER"), born Miami, FL, Mar 13, 1950.

Neil Sedaka, 81, singer, songwriter, born Brooklyn, NY, Mar 13, 1939.

March 14 — Saturday

DAY 74	292 REMAINING

CERNAN, EUGENE ANDREW (GENE): BIRTH ANNIVERSARY. Mar 14, 1934. Born in Chicago, IL, Cernan was a US Navy captain who became both the youngest American in space and the second to exit a spacecraft in orbit on the *Gemini 9A* mission. He was the lunar module pilot for *Apollo 10*, a test run for *Apollo 11*'s historic first moon landing, and commander of *Apollo 17*, NASA's last moon mission, where he spent a record 73 hours on the moon's surface. The last man to leave footprints on the moon, he stated before returning to Earth, "America's challenge of today has forged man's destiny of tomorrow." Cernan died Jan 16, 2017, in Houston, TX.

EINSTEIN, ALBERT: BIRTH ANNIVERSARY. Mar 14, 1879. Theoretical physicist best known for his theory of relativity. Born at Ulm, Germany, he won the Nobel Prize in 1921. Died at Princeton, NJ, Apr 18, 1955.

FOOTE, HORTON: BIRTH ANNIVERSARY. Mar 14, 1916. National Medal of Arts–winning American writer who wrote more than 60

March 2020	S	M	T	W	T	F	S
	1	2	3	4	5	6	7
	8	9	10	11	12	13	14
	15	16	17	18	19	20	21
	22	23	24	25	26	27	28
	29	30	31				

films and plays. Foote's screenplays for *To Kill a Mockingbird* and *Tender Mercies* both won Academy Awards. His play *The Young Man from Atlanta* also earned him the Pulitzer Prize. Born at Wharton, TX, Foote died Mar 4, 2009, at Hartford, CT.

HIGHLAND COUNTY MAPLE FESTIVAL. Mar 14–15 (also Mar 21–22). Highland County, VA. 62nd annual. Each year, tens of thousands of visitors are drawn to this unspoiled, rural region of Virginia to celebrate the "opening" of the trees and observe the process of maple syrup-making. Sugar camp tours provide a unique and educational experience that portrays a rapidly vanishing way of American life. Designated a "Local Legacy" by the Library of Congress in 1999. Est attendance: 50,000. For info: Highland County Chamber of Commerce, PO Box 223, Monterey, VA 24465. Phone: (540) 468-2550. E-mail: director@highlandcounty.org. Web: www.highlandcounty.org.

INTERNATIONAL FANNY PACK DAY. Mar 14. Over the centuries a form of the fanny pack has been used to carry items for easy access. Today, pay tribute to this fashion essential. Annually, the second Saturday in March. Use this day as a reminder to end hunger locally and give to a food bank—wearing your fanny pack! For info: Nick Yates, International Fanny Pack Day, 6614 W Baron Dr, Boise, ID 83714. Phone: (208) 863-1414. E-mail: setaykcin@gmail.com.

JONES, CASEY: BIRTH ANNIVERSARY. Mar 14, 1864. The railroad engineer—real name John Luther Jones—was born near Cayce, KY, the source of his nickname. He died in the crash of the Cannonball Express near Vaughn, MS, Apr 30, 1900, and was memorialized as a hero in Wallace Saunders's eponymous ballad.

KETCHAM, HANK: 100th BIRTH ANNIVERSARY. Mar 14, 1920. Born at Seattle, WA, Henry King Ketcham dropped out of the University of Washington in 1938 to try his hand at cartoon animation. He worked with Walter Lantz Productions ("Woody Woodpecker") and Walt Disney. After World War II, he became a freelancer and created the tow-headed, mischievous imp known as "Dennis the Menace." Dennis was based on Ketcham's own son Dennis. The comic strip began on Mar 14, 1951, and soon took American newspapers and the public by a storm. The strip inspired a television show and a movie and is still read today in more than 1,000 newspapers around the world. Ketcham retired in 1994 and died June 1, 2001, at Carmel, CA.

MARSHALL, THOMAS RILEY: BIRTH ANNIVERSARY. Mar 14, 1854. 28th vice president of the US (1913–21). Born at North Manchester, IN, he died at Washington, DC, June 1, 1925.

MOTH-ER DAY. Mar 14. A day set aside to honor moth collectors and specialists. Celebrated in museums or libraries with moth collections. (Created by Robert L. Birch, Pun Corps.)

NATIONAL SKI-JORING FINALS. Mar 14–15. Red Lodge Rodeo Grounds, Red Lodge, MT. Since 1980. Horsemen and skiers provide action entertainment. Derived from the Scandinavian sport of pulling a skier behind a horse, ski-joring has evolved from a leisure winter diversion into lively, regulated competition. Annually, the second weekend in March. Est attendance: 4,000. For info: Red Lodge Ski-Joring Assn, Box 1704, Red Lodge, MT 59068. Web: http://redlodgeskijoring.com.

NETHERLANDS: THE EUROPEAN FINE ART FAIR (MAASTRICHT 2020). Mar 14–22. MECC, Maastricht. Since 1988. Old Master paintings, antiques, textile arts, modern paintings and sculptures, antiquities, books and prints. Discover "7,000 years of art history." Est attendance: 75,000. For info: The European Fine Art Foundation. E-mail: info@tefaf.com. Web: www.tefaf.com.

PI DAY. Mar 14. A day to celebrate pi—the ratio of a circle's circumference to its diameter. Since that mathematical constant is about 3.14, Mar 14 became the day to observe it.

SAINT PATRICK'S DAY PARADE. Mar 14. Downtown Hornell, NY. 33rd annual. It's a "come as you are" line of march, open to anyone, with no entry fee, no judges, no prizes. Hornell's parade is designed as purely a fun affair, especially for those people who've always wanted to be in a parade but never had the

opportunity. It's larger and longer every year, with more and more "would-be Irish" strolling down Main Street. Est attendance: 9,000. For info: Wolf Berry, 6950 Laine Rd, Hornell, NY 14843-9419. Phone: (607) 661-5500. E-mail: thepaperwolf@gmail.com.

SAINT PATRICK'S DAY PARADE: "THE WEARIN' OF THE GREEN". Mar 14. Baton Rouge, LA. 35th annual parade includes more than 70 floats, dignitaries, precision marching bands and bagpipers. Largest St. Patrick's Day celebration in the region rolls through historic Hundred Oaks area in the heart of the city starting at 10 AM. EST attendance: 180,000. Shamrock Run (5k) takes place Mar 14. For info: Parade Group, LLC. E-mail: bririshparade@gmail.com. Web: www.wearinofthegreen.com.

SEOUL RECAPTURED BY UN FORCES: ANNIVERSARY. Mar 14, 1951. Seoul, Korea, which had fallen to Chinese forces in January 1951, was retaken by United Nations troops during the Korean War.

TAYLOR, LUCY HOBBS: BIRTH ANNIVERSARY. Mar 14, 1833. Lucy Beaman Hobbs, first woman in America to receive a degree in dentistry (Ohio College of Dental Surgery, 1866) and to be admitted to membership in a state dental association. Born at Franklin County, NY. In 1867 she married James M. Taylor, who also became a dentist (after she instructed him in the essentials). Active women's rights advocate. Died at Lawrence, KS, Oct 3, 1910.

"10 MOST WANTED" LIST DEBUTS: 70th ANNIVERSARY. Mar 14, 1950. The Federal Bureau of Investigation instituted the "10 Most Wanted Fugitives" list in an effort to publicize particularly dangerous criminals who were at large. From 1950 to 2019, 521 fugitives have appeared on the list; 488 have been located or apprehended. Generally, the only way to get off the list is to die or be captured. In the summer of 2011, the two top fugitives exited the list: terrorist Osama Bin Laden was killed in a raid in May and gangster James "Whitey" Bulger was arrested in June.

🎂 BIRTHDAYS TODAY

Simone Biles, 23, Olympic gymnast, born Columbus, OH, Mar 14, 1997.

Frank Borman, 92, former astronaut, airline executive, born Gary, IN, Mar 14, 1928.

Michael Caine, 87, actor (Oscars for *The Cider House Rules* and *Hannah and Her Sisters*; *Batman Begins, Alfie*), born Maurice Micklewhite at London, England, Mar 14, 1933.

Billy Crystal, 73, actor (*Analyze This, When Harry Met Sally, City Slickers*, "Soap"), born Long Beach, NY, Mar 14, 1947.

Stephen Curry, 32, basketball player, born Akron, OH, Mar 14, 1988.

Rick Dees, 69, DJ, comedian, born Jacksonville, FL, Mar 14, 1951.

Ansel Elgort, 26, actor (*Baby Driver, The Fault in Our Stars, Divergent* films), singer, born New York, NY, Mar 14, 1994.

Mark Gordon, 63, Governor of Wyoming (R), born New York, NY, Mar 14, 1957.

Bobby Jenks, 39, former baseball player, born Mission Hills, CA, Mar 14, 1981.

Quincy Jones, 87, composer, producer (27 Grammys), born Chicago, IL, Mar 14, 1933.

Grace Park, 46, actress ("Battlestar Galactica," "Hawaii Five-0"), born Los Angeles, CA, Mar 14, 1974.

Antoni Porowski, 36, television personality ("Queer Eye"), chef, born Montreal, QC, Canada, Mar 14, 1984.

Tamara Tunie, 61, actress ("24," "Law & Order: SVU," "As the World Turns"), born McKeesport, PA, Mar 14, 1959.

Rita Tushingham, 78, actress (*Dr. Zhivago, A Taste of Honey*), born Liverpool, England, Mar 14, 1942.

March 15 — Sunday

DAY 75   **291 REMAINING**

BEAN, ALAN: BIRTH ANNIVERSARY. Mar 15, 1932. Naval jet pilot, astronaut, spacecraft commander, born at Wheeler, TX. Bean, on *Apollo 12*, was the fourth human to walk on the moon. He later commanded *Skylab 3* in 1973. After retiring, Bean became an author and artist. He died at Houston, TX, May 26, 2018.

BELARUS: CONSTITUTION DAY. Mar 15. National holiday. Commemorates the adoption of the constitution on Mar 15, 1994.

BRUTUS DAY. Mar 15. No matter where you work, you must admit there's as much intrigue, plotting and backstabbing as was found in ancient Rome or is found today inside the Washington Beltway. (©2006 by WH.) For info: Thomas & Ruth Roy, Wellcat Holidays, 2418 Long Ln, Lebanon, PA 17046. Phone: (717) 279-0184. E-mail: info@wellcat.com. Web: www.wellcat.com.

THE GODFATHER FILM PREMIERE: ANNIVERSARY. Mar 15, 1972. Francis Ford Coppola directed what many consider the greatest American film—perhaps challenged only by the sequel released two years later. Based on the Mario Puzo novel that traced the fortunes of the Corleone crime family, *The Godfather* was nominated for 11 Oscars, picking up three for Best Picture, Best Adapted Screenplay and Best Actor (Marlon Brando in a legendary performance). Costars Al Pacino, James Caan and Robert Duvall were all nominated for Best Supporting Actor. *The Godfather Part II*, which premiered in New York City on Dec 12, 1974, was also nominated for 11 Oscars and won 6, including Best Picture. A third film was released on Dec 25, 1990.

HUNGARY: ANNIVERSARY OF THE 1848 REVOLUTION. Mar 15. National day. Commemorates when the country briefly attained autonomy from Austria.

IDES OF MARCH. Mar 15. In the Roman calendar the days of the month were not numbered sequentially. Instead, each month had three division days: kalends, nones and ides. Days were numbered from these divisions: e.g., IV Nones or III Ides. The ides occurred on the 15th of the month (or on the 13th in months that had fewer than 31 days). Julius Caesar was assassinated on this day in 44 BC. This system was used in Europe well into the Renaissance. When Shakespeare wrote "Beware the ides of March" in *Julius Caesar*, his audience knew what he meant.

INTERNATIONAL DAY OF ACTION FOR THE SEALS. Mar 15. Also known as International Day of Action against Seal Slaughter. This day calls attention to and urges action against the commercial slaughter of seal pups. A similar observance that celebrates the seal in general is International Day of the Seal on Mar 22.

JACKSON, ANDREW: BIRTH ANNIVERSARY. Mar 15, 1767. Seventh president of the US (Mar 4, 1829–Mar 3, 1837), born in a log cabin at Waxhaw, SC. A military hero in the War of 1812, the self-educated Jackson was the first president since George Washington who had not attended college and the first president elected by direct appeal to the mass of voters as opposed to an affiliation with a political party. He sought greater democracy for the common man by extending voting rights to all white men, nullifying government-granted bank monopolies and advocating for decentralizing the government in recognition of states' rights. During his first term, Jackson defiantly refused to support the Supreme Court's rulings to preserve the Cherokee Nation in Georgia, resulting in the brutal displacement of 15,000 Native Americans, thousands of whom perished on the deadly Trail of Tears to the Oklahoma Territory. Jackson died at Nashville, TN, June 8, 1845.

March 2020	S	M	T	W	T	F	S
				1	2	3	4	5	6	7
	8	9	10	11	12	13	14
	15	16	17	18	19	20	21
	22	23	24	25	26	27	28
	29	30	31				

LIBERIA: J.J. ROBERTS DAY. Mar 15. National holiday. Commemorates the birth in 1809 of the country's first president.

MAINE: ADMISSION DAY: 200th ANNIVERSARY. Mar 15. Became 23rd state in 1820. Prior to this date, Maine had been part of Massachusetts.

NATIONAL ANIMAL POISON PREVENTION WEEK. Mar 15–21. In conjunction with National Poison Prevention Week, the ASPCA sponsors this important week to educate Americans about common household products, plants and foods that can be dangerous or even deadly to pets. For info: Media & Communications Dept, ASPCA, 520 8th Ave, 7th Fl, New York, NY 10018. Phone: (212) 876-7700, ext 4655. E-mail: press@aspca.org. Web: www.aspca.org.

★NATIONAL POISON PREVENTION WEEK. Mar 15–21. Presidential Proclamation issued each year for the third week in March since 1962 (PL 87–319 of Sept 26, 1961).

NATIONAL POISON PREVENTION WEEK. Mar 15–21. To aid in encouraging the American people to learn of the dangers of unintentional poisoning and to take preventive measures against it. Annually, the third full week in March. For info: American Assn of Poison Control Centers, 515 King St, Ste 510, Alexandria, VA 22314. Phone: (800) 222-1222. Web: www.aapcc.org/prevention/nppw.

NATIONAL VO DAY. Mar 15. This day celebrates the voices behind the scenes, those voice talents that transform audio into something truly special. It celebrates the training, recording, editing and release of vocal performances by experienced actors and newcomers alike. From commercials to IVR to e-learning, VO is to be celebrated! Annually, Mar 15. For info: John J. Grace, 27 El Cencerro, Rancho Santa Margarita, CA 92688.

TRUE CONFESSIONS DAY. Mar 15. Confession is good for the soul. Go into work today and tell all. If you plan to stay home, make an appointment with your mirror. (©2006 by WH.) For info: Thomas & Ruth Roy, Wellcat Holidays, 2418 Long Ln, Lebanon, PA 17046. Phone: (717) 279-0184. E-mail: info@wellcat.com. Web: www.wellcat.com.

VAN BROCKLIN, NORM: BIRTH ANNIVERSARY. Mar 15, 1926. Norman Van Brocklin, Pro Football Hall of Fame quarterback and coach, born at Eagle Butte, SD. Van Brocklin played college football at Oregon and then signed with the Los Angeles Rams. He helped the Rams win their only NFL title in 1951. After finishing his playing career with the Philadelphia Eagles, he coached the Minnesota Vikings and the Atlanta Falcons. Inducted into the Pro Football Hall of Fame in 1979. Died at Social Circle, GA, May 2, 1983.

WASHINGTON'S ADDRESS TO CONTINENTAL ARMY OFFICERS: ANNIVERSARY. Mar 15, 1783. George Washington addressed a meeting at Newburgh, NY, of Continental army officers who were dissatisfied and rebellious for want of back pay, food, clothing and pensions. General Washington called for patience, opening his speech with the words "I have grown gray in your service. . . ." Congress later acted to satisfy most of the demands.

WORLD FOLK TALES AND FABLES WEEK. Mar 15–21. To encourage children and adults to explore the cultural background and lessons learned from folktales, fables, myths and legends from around the world. For info: Anneke Forzani, Language Lizard, PO Box 421, Basking Ridge, NJ 07920. Phone: (888) 554-9273. Fax: (908) 762-4786. E-mail: info@LanguageLizard.com. Web: www.LanguageLizard.com.

🎂 BIRTHDAYS TODAY

Harold Baines, 61, former baseball player, born St. Michael's, MD, Mar 15, 1959.

Mary Carillo, 63, sportscaster, former tennis player, born Queens, NY, Mar 15, 1957.

Fabio, 59, model, born Fabio Lanzoni at Milan, Italy, Mar 15, 1961.

Ruth Bader Ginsburg, 87, Associate Justice of the US, born Brooklyn, NY, Mar 15, 1933.

Judd Hirsch, 85, actor (Emmy for "Taxi"; "Numb3rs," *Ordinary People*), born New York, NY, Mar 15, 1935.

Eva Longoria, 45, actress ("Desperate Housewives," "The Young and the Restless"), born Corpus Christi, TX, Mar 15, 1975.

Mike Love, 79, singer, musician (The Beach Boys), born Los Angeles, CA, Mar 15, 1941.

Kellan Lutz, 35, actor (*Twilight*, "90210"), born Dickinson, ND, Mar 15, 1985.

Mark McGrath, 52, singer (Sugar Ray), born Newport Beach, CA, Mar 15, 1968.

Bret Michaels, 57, musician, television personality ("Rock of Love," "Celebrity Apprentice"), born Butler, PA, Mar 15, 1963.

Park Overall, 63, actress ("Empty Nest," *Mississippi Burning*), born Nashville, TN, Mar 15, 1957.

Kim Raver, 51, actress ("Grey's Anatomy," "Third Watch," "24"), born New York, NY, Mar 15, 1969.

Dee Snider, 65, singer (Twisted Sister), composer, born Massapequa, NY, Mar 15, 1955.

Sly Stone, 76, singer, musician (Sly & the Family Stone), born Sylvester Stewart at Dallas, TX, Mar 15, 1944.

Craig Wasson, 66, actor ("Phyllis," *Body Double, Malcolm X*), born Ontario, OR, Mar 15, 1954.

March 16 — Monday

DAY 76   **290 REMAINING**

AUSTRALIA: CANBERRA DAY. Mar 16. Australian Capital Territory. Public holiday the third Monday in March.

BLACK PRESS DAY: ANNIVERSARY OF THE FIRST BLACK NEWSPAPER. Mar 16, 1827. Anniversary of the founding of the first black newspaper in the US, *Freedom's Journal*, on Varick Street at New York, NY.

BONHEUR, ROSA: BIRTH ANNIVERSARY. Mar 16, 1822. Painter and sculptor best known for her paintings of animals, Rosa (Marie-Rosalie) Bonheur was born at Bordeaux, France. With the income from the sale of her art, she purchased the castle of By near Fontainebleau at Melun, France, where she died May 25, 1899. Bonheur's *The Horse Fair*, which she painted in 1853, was purchased by the American millionaire Cornelius Vanderbilt for $53,600, a record price at the time. In 1865 Bonheur was awarded the Grand Cross of the Légion d'Honneur, the first woman so honored. An early Bohemian and feminist, Bonheur defied female convention of the day by dressing in pants and smoking cigarettes.

BRAIN AWARENESS WEEK. Mar 16–22. Brain Awareness Week is the global campaign to increase public awareness of the progress and benefits of brain research. The Dana Alliance is joined in the campaign by partners in the US and around the world, including medical and research organizations; patient advocacy groups; government agencies; service groups; hospitals and universities; K–12 schools and professional organizations. For info: Dana Alliance for Brain Initiatives, 505 Fifth Ave, 6th Fl, New York, NY 10017. Phone: (212) 223-4040. E-mail: bawinfo@dana.org. Web: www. dana.org/baw.

CLYMER, GEORGE: BIRTH ANNIVERSARY. Mar 16, 1739. Signer of the Declaration of Independence and of the US Constitution. Born at Philadelphia, PA, and died there Jan 24, 1813.

CURLEW DAY. Mar 16. Traditional arrival date for the long-billed curlew at the Umatilla (Oregon) National Wildlife Refuge. More than 500 of the long-billed curlews have been reported at this location during their nesting season.

FREEDOM OF INFORMATION DAY. Mar 16. The American Library Association supports free and open access to government information created at taxpayer expense. On or near the birthday of James Madison (Mar 16), ALA urges libraries and librarians to join in celebrating the public's "right to know" by sponsoring activities to educate their communities about the importance of promoting and protecting freedom of information. Sponsored by the Freedom Forum and the American Library Association. For info: American Library Assn. E-mail: jmcgilvray@alawash.org or alawash@alawash.org. Web: www.districtdispatch.org.

GODDARD DAY: LAUNCH OF FIRST LIQUID-FUELED ROCKET: ANNIVERSARY. Mar 16, 1926. Commemorates first liquid-fuel-powered rocket flight launched by Robert Hutchings Goddard (1882–1945) at Auburn, MA.

"THE GUMBY SHOW" TV PREMIERE: ANNIVERSARY. Mar 16, 1957. This kids' show was a spin-off from "Howdy Doody," where the character of Gumby was first introduced in 1956. Gumby and his horse, Pokey, were clay figures whose adventures were filmed using the process of "claymation." "The Gumby Show," created by Art Clokey, was first hosted by Bobby Nicholson and later by Pinky Lee. It was syndicated in 1966 and again in 1988.

INTERNATIONAL TEACH MUSIC WEEK. Mar 16–22. 6th annual. Each year during the third week in March, musicians, music schools and music stores offer free lessons to new students—both children and adults. The goal is to see more kids and adults reaping the educational, therapeutic and social benefits of playing music. In 2019, more than 750 music schools and music retail sites in 15 countries participated. For info: Vincent James, Keep Music Alive, PO Box 1299, Brookhaven, PA 19015. Phone: (610) 874-6312. E-mail: vincent@KeepMusicAlive.org. Web: www.TeachMusicWeek.org.

LIPS APPRECIATION DAY. Mar 16. Where would all those lovely teeth we paid a bundle for be without a lovely frame? Do something nice for your lips today. Buy a lip balm. Better yet, kiss somebody! (©2006 by WH.) For info: Thomas & Ruth Roy, Wellcat Holidays, 2418 Long Ln, Lebanon, PA 17046. Phone: (717) 279-0184. E-mail: info@wellcat.com. Web: www.wellcat. com.

MADISON, JAMES: BIRTH ANNIVERSARY. Mar 16, 1751. Fourth president of the US (Mar 4, 1809–Mar 3, 1817), born at Port Conway, VA. He was president when British forces invaded Washington, DC, requiring Madison and other high officials to flee while the British burned the Capitol, the president's residence and most other public buildings (Aug 24–25, 1814). Died at Montpelier, VA, June 28, 1836.

MCKERN, LEO: 100th BIRTH ANNIVERSARY. Mar 16, 1920. Prolific actor best known for his portrayal of irascible and contrary English barrister Horace Rumpole in the "Rumpole of the Bailey" television series. Born Reginald McKern at Sydney, Australia, McKern died July 23, 2002, at Bath, England.

MOON PHASE: LAST QUARTER. Mar 16. Moon enters Last Quarter phase at 5:34 AM, EDT.

MY LAI MASSACRE: ANNIVERSARY. Mar 16, 1968. Most-publicized atrocity of the Vietnam War. According to findings of the US Army's investigating team, approximately 300 noncombatant Vietnamese villagers (at My Lai and Mykhe, near the South China Sea) were killed by infantrymen of the American Division.

NATIONAL PANDA DAY. Mar 16. Created by concerned conservationists, National Panda Day aims to educate about and celebrate this shy and sedentary mammal. In the wild, the giant panda lives in China's mountain habitats of bamboo forests. The IUCN Red List of Threatened Species identifies this species (*Ailuropoda melanoleuca*) as "vulnerable." Annually, Mar 16.

NIXON, THELMA CATHERINE PATRICIA (PAT) RYAN: BIRTH ANNIVERSARY. Mar 16, 1912. Wife of Richard Milhous Nixon, 37th president of the US. Born at Ely, NV, she died at Park Ridge, NJ, June 22, 1993.

NO SELFIES DAY. Mar 16. Every day millions take a self-portrait with their cell phone cameras and post the pictures on social networks. No one knows why. Here is just one day where nobody takes a "selfie." Observed on the birthday of Philippe Kahn, the inventor of the cell phone camera and the first person known to transmit a photo: a birth picture of his daughter taken in 1997 with his cell phone. Annually on Mar 16. (Created by Rick Allen and the readers of the *Ocala Star-Banner*.)

OHM, GEORG SIMON: BIRTH ANNIVERSARY. Mar 16, 1789. German physicist lauded for his eponymous law, which states the exact relationship of potential and current in electric conduction. Ohm's Law made it possible for scientists to calculate the amount of current, voltage and resistance in circuitry, establishing the science of electrical engineering. Lord Kelvin recognized Ohm's contribution by dubbing the unit of resistance the "ohm" and its reciprocal, the unit of conductance, the "mho." Born at Erlangen, Germany, Ohm died July 7, 1854, at Munich, Germany.

SPACE MILESTONE: *GEMINI 8* (US). Mar 16, 1966. Launched on this day, *Gemini 8* executed the first docking of orbiting spacecraft when it connected with *Agena*. A malfunction caused a scare when the craft began to spin uncontrollably and pilot Neil Armstrong immediately disengaged, but the craft did eventually land safely.

UNITED KINGDOM: SHAKESPEARE WEEK. Mar 16–23. This week seeks to bring Shakespeare to life vividly for the nation's children and is celebrated in schools, theaters, historic sites, museums, galleries, cinemas and libraries all over the UK. Every child will be given the chance to be inspired by Shakespeare's stories, language and heritage. For info: Shakespeare Birthplace Trust. E-mail: info@shakespeare.org.uk. Web: www.shakespeare.org.uk or www.shakespeareweek.org.uk.

US MILITARY ACADEMY FOUNDED: ANNIVERSARY. Mar 16, 1802. President Thomas Jefferson signed legislation establishing the US Military Academy to train officers for the army. The college is located at West Point, NY, on the site of the oldest continuously occupied military post in America. Women were admitted to West Point in 1976. The academy's motto is "Duty, Honor, Country." For info: www.usma.edu.

🎂 BIRTHDAYS TODAY

Erik Estrada, 71, actor ("CHiPs," *Honey Boy*), born New York, NY, Mar 16, 1949.

Judah Friedlander, 51, actor ("30 Rock," *American Splendor*), born Gaithersburg, MD, Mar 16, 1969.

Victor Garber, 71, actor (*Argo, Godspell*, "Alias"), born London, ON, Canada, Mar 16, 1949.

Lauren Graham, 53, actress ("Parenthood," "Gilmore Girls"), born Honolulu, HI, Mar 16, 1967.

Blake Griffin, 31, basketball player, born Oklahoma City, OK, Mar 16, 1989.

Todd Heap, 40, former football player, born Mesa, AZ, Mar 16, 1980.

Alice Hoffman, 68, writer (*Practical Magic, Aquamarine*), born New York, NY, Mar 16, 1952.

Isabelle Huppert, 65, actress (*Elle, Violette, The Piano Teacher*), born Paris, France, Mar 16, 1955.

Kate Nelligan, 69, actress (*Eye of the Needle, Frankie and Johnny, The Prince of Tides*), born London, ON, Canada, Mar 16, 1951.

Alan Tudyk, 49, actor ("Firefly," "Dollhouse," *Abraham Lincoln: Vampire Hunter*), born El Paso, TX, Mar 16, 1971.

Chuck Woolery, 78, game show host ("Love Connection," "Scrabble"), born Ashland, KY, Mar 16, 1942.

March 2020	S	M	T	W	T	F	S
				1	2	3	4	5	6	7
	8	9	10	11	12	13	14
	15	16	17	18	19	20	21
	22	23	24	25	26	27	28
	29	30	31				

March 17 — Tuesday

BAUGH, SAMMY ADRIAN: BIRTH ANNIVERSARY. Mar 17, 1914. Born at Temple, TX, "Slinging Sammy" was one of the top quarterbacks of the 1930s and '40s. Baugh (whose nickname actually referred to his prowess in baseball) was a first-round draft pick (sixth overall) for the Washington Redskins in 1937, and he stayed with the franchise his entire career—until 1952. He was a star quarterback, tailback and punter. Uniquely, in 1943, he led the league in passing, punting and pass interceptions. Baugh's impact on the pro game was making the forward pass (before then little used) an integral part of the offensive tool kit. He was inducted (charter member) into the Pro Football Hall of Fame on Sept 7, 1963. Baugh died Dec 17, 2008, at Rotan, TX.

BRIDGER, JIM: BIRTH ANNIVERSARY. Mar 17, 1804. American fur trader, frontiersman and scout, born at Richmond, VA, and died July 17, 1881, near Kansas City, MO. Believed to be the first white man to visit (in 1824) the Great Salt Lake, he also established Fort Bridger in southwestern Wyoming as a fur-trading post and as a way station for pioneers heading west on the Oregon Trail. Bridger National Forest in western Wyoming is named for him.

CAMP FIRE: ANNIVERSARY. Mar 17, 1910. To commemorate the anniversary of the founding of Camp Fire and the service given to children and youth across the nation. Founded in 1910 as Camp Fire Girls. For info: Camp Fire, 1801 Main St, Ste 200, Kansas City, MO 64108. Phone: (816) 285-2010. E-mail: info@campfire.org. Web: www.campfire.org.

COLE, NAT "KING" (NATHANIEL ADAMS COLE): BIRTH ANNIVERSARY. Mar 17, 1919. Nat King Cole was born at Montgomery, AL, and began his musical career at an early age, playing the piano at age four. He was the first black entertainer to host a national television show. His many songs include "The Christmas Song," "Nature Boy," "Mona Lisa," "Ramblin' Rose" and "Unforgettable." Although he was dogged by racial discrimination throughout his career, including the cancellation of his television show because opposition from Southern white viewers decreased advertising revenue, Cole was criticized by prominent black newspapers for not joining other black entertainers in the civil rights struggle. Cole contributed more than $50,000 to civil rights organizations in response to the criticism. Nat King Cole died Feb 15, 1965, at Santa Monica, CA.

CORBETT-FITZSIMMONS TITLE FIGHT: ANNIVERSARY. Mar 17, 1897. In one of boxing's greatest fights—and the first heavyweight title fight to be filmed—"Gentleman Jim" Corbett lost the world title to "Ruby Robert" Fitzsimmons at Carson City, NV. Fitzsimmons, seemingly a long shot at 34 years of age, hung on for 13 rounds before landing the "solar plexus punch" that felled Corbett. Western legends in attendance were Bat Masterson (overseeing security) and Wyatt Earp.

EVACUATION DAY: ANNIVERSARY. Mar 17, 1776. A public holiday at Boston and Suffolk County, MA, celebrates the anniversary of the evacuation from Boston of British troops.

FEMALE RELIEF SOCIETY OF NAUVOO ORGANIZED: ANNIVERSARY. Mar 17, 1842. Twenty Mormon women formally initiated this organization at Nauvoo, IL, which is now known as the Relief Society and has grown to more than five and a half million members.

HOWARD, SHEMP: 125th BIRTH ANNIVERSARY. Mar 17, 1895. A member of the original Three Stooges (with Moe Howard and Larry Fine), Howard was born Samuel Horwitz at Brooklyn, NY. He teamed with brother Moe as comic relief with vaudeville entertainer Ted Healy in the early 1920s. In 1925, Larry Fine joined them to create the Three Stooges. Shemp left the trio in 1932—little brother Curly replaced him—and had roles in many films. Upon Curly's retirement in 1946, Shemp rejoined the Stooges until his death on Nov 23, 1955, at Hollywood, CA.

IRELAND: NATIONAL DAY. Mar 17. St. Patrick's Day is observed in the Republic of Ireland as a legal national holiday.

JONES, BOBBY: BIRTH ANNIVERSARY. Mar 17, 1902. Golfing great Robert Tyre Jones, Jr, first golfer to win the grand slam (the four major British and American tournaments in one year). Born at Atlanta, GA, he died there Dec 18, 1971.

LEVINE, CHARLES A.: BIRTH ANNIVERSARY. Mar 17, 1897. Charles A. Levine, whose efforts to beat Charles Lindbergh across the Atlantic by plane were stymied by a lawsuit, nevertheless became the first air passenger to cross the Atlantic Ocean. Levine's 225-horsepower plane, *The Columbia*, was grounded when one of his copilots filed a suit hours after Lindbergh took off from Roosevelt Field. Not to be overshadowed by Lindbergh's success, Levine announced that his flight, leaving June 4, 1927, would fly beyond Paris to Berlin, with himself as a passenger. Piloted by Clarence Chamberlin, the plane exhausted its fuel and landed at Eisleben, Germany, June 6, 100 miles short of his goal. The flight set a new record of 3,911 miles in 43 hours of nonstop flight, besting Lindbergh by approximately 300 miles. Levine was born at North Adams, MA, and died at Washington, DC, on Dec 6, 1991.

NJCAA DIVISION II MEN'S BASKETBALL NATIONAL CHAMPION-SHIPS. Mar 17–21. Danville Area Community College, Danville, IL. Junior College Division II national men's basketball championship tournament. Est attendance: 8,000. For info: Danville Area CVB, 100 W Main St, #146, Danville, IL 61832. Phone: (800) 383-4386. Fax: (217) 442-2137. E-mail: info@danvilleareainfo.com.

NORTHERN IRELAND: SAINT PATRICK'S DAY HOLIDAY. Mar 17. National holiday.

NUREYEV, RUDOLF HAMETOVICH: BIRTH ANNIVERSARY. Mar 17, 1938. Rudolf Nureyev, one of the most charismatic ballet stars of the 20th century, was born on a train in southeastern Siberia, USSR. Nureyev's defection from the Soviet Union on June 17, 1961, while on tour with the Kirov Ballet, made headlines worldwide. The dancer was known for his ability to combine passion with a high level of perfectionism. His long partnership with Dame Margot Fonteyn of the Royal Ballet was legendary, and he performed frequently with the Martha Graham Dance Company. Nureyev also choreographed and restaged many classics and served as the Paris Opera Ballet's artistic director. He died Jan 6, 1993, at Levallois, France, a suburb of Paris.

PARKER, GEORGE: DEATH ANNIVERSARY. Mar 17, 1764. George Parker, the second Earl of Macclesfield, was born in 1697 (exact date unknown). The eminent English astronomer was president of the Royal Society from 1752 until his death. He was one of the principal authors of the Bill for Regulating the Commencement of the Year (British Calendar Act of 1751), which was introduced in parliament by Lord Chesterfield. That act caused the adoption, in 1752, of the "New Style" Gregorian calendar, which is still in use today. Parker died at Shirburn Castle, England.

RUSTIN, BAYARD: BIRTH ANNIVERSARY. Mar 17, 1912. Black pacifist and civil rights leader, Bayard Rustin was an organizer of and participant in many of the great social protest marches—for jobs, freedom and nuclear disarmament. He was arrested and imprisoned more than 20 times for his civil rights and pacifist activities. Born at West Chester, PA, Rustin died at New York, NY, Aug 24, 1987.

SAINT PATRICK'S DAY. Mar 17. Commemorates the patron saint of Ireland, Bishop Patrick (AD 387?–493?), who, about AD 432, left his home in the Severn Valley, England, and introduced Christianity into Ireland. Feast day in the Roman Catholic Church. A national holiday in Ireland and Northern Ireland.

SAINT PATRICK'S DAY PARADE. Mar 17. New York, NY. One of New York City's greatest traditions, held for the first time on Mar 17, 1762. Today it is the largest parade in the world featuring up to 250,000 marchers. Held in honor of the Patron Saint of Ireland and the Archdiocese of New York, the parade is reviewed from the steps of Saint Patrick's Cathedral by the current Archbishop of New York. Members of the National Guard's 69th Regiment proudly lead the way up Fifth Avenue, followed by members of various Irish societies of the city, the 32 Irish County Societies, various schools, colleges, Emerald societies, Irish-language and nationalist societies. The parade remains true to its roots as a traditional marchers' parade by not allowing floats, automobiles and other commercial aspects to participate. Annually, Mar 17, except when the 17th falls on a Sunday—in which case it is celebrated the day before. Est attendance: 2,000,000. For info: St. Patrick's Day Parade and Celebration Committee, PO Box 295, Woodlawn Station, Bronx, NY 10470. Phone: (718) 231-4400. E-mail: info@nycstpatricksparade.org. Web: www.nycstpatricksparade.org.

SOUTH AFRICAN WHITES VOTE TO END MINORITY RULE: ANNIVERSARY. Mar 17, 1992. A referendum proposing ending white minority rule through negotiations was supported by a whites-only ballot. The vote of 1,924,186 (68.6 percent) whites in support of President F.W. de Klerk's reform policies was greater than expected.

SPACE MILESTONE: *VANGUARD 1* (US). Mar 17, 1958. Established "pear shape" of Earth. At only three pounds it was the first solar-powered satellite.

TANEY, ROGER B.: BIRTH ANNIVERSARY. Mar 17, 1777. Fifth chief justice of the US, born at Calvert County, MD. Served as attorney general under President Andrew Jackson. Nominated as secretary of the treasury, he became the first presidential nominee to be rejected by the Senate. His rejection centered on his strong stance against the Bank of the United States as a central bank and his role in urging President Jackson to veto the congressional bill extending its charter. A year later, he was nominated to the Supreme Court as an associate justice by Jackson, but his nomination was stalled until the death of Chief Justice John Marshall July 6, 1835. Taney was nominated to fill Marshall's place on the bench and, after much resistance, was sworn in as chief justice in March 1836. His tenure on the Supreme Court is most remembered for the Dred Scott decision. He died at Washington, DC, Oct 12, 1864.

🎂 BIRTHDAYS TODAY

Daniel Ray (Danny) Ainge, 61, basketball coach, former basketball and baseball player, born Eugene, OR, Mar 17, 1959.

John Boyega, 28, actor (*Star Wars: The Force Awakens*, *The Circle*, *Attack the Block*), born London, England, Mar 17, 1992.

Lesley-Anne Down, 66, actress ("Upstairs, Downstairs," *The Pink Panther Strikes Again*), born London, England, Mar 17, 1954.

Patrick Duffy, 71, actor ("Step by Step," "Dallas"), born Townsend, MT, Mar 17, 1949.

Hozier, 30, singer, songwriter, born Andrew Hozier-Byrne at Bray, County Wicklow, Ireland, Mar 17, 1990.

Kyle Korver, 39, basketball player, born Lakewood, CA, Mar 17, 1981.

Katie Ledecky, 23, Olympic swimmer, born Washington, DC, Mar 17, 1997.

Vicki Lewis, 60, actress ("NewsRadio," *Godzilla*), born Cincinnati, OH, Mar 17, 1960.

Rob Lowe, 56, actor ("Brothers & Sisters," "The West Wing," *St. Elmo's Fire*), born Charlottesville, VA, Mar 17, 1964.

Kurt Russell, 69, actor (*The Hateful Eight, Executive Decision, Captain Ron, The Thing, Elvis*), born Springfield, MA, Mar 17, 1951.

Gary Sinise, 65, actor (*Forrest Gump, Apollo 13*, "CSI: New York"), director (*True West, Buried Child*), born Chicago, IL, Mar 17, 1955.

Natalie Zea, 45, actress ("Passions," "The Following," "Dirty Sexy Money," "Justified"), born Harris County, TX, Mar 17, 1975.

March 18 — Wednesday

DAY 78   288 REMAINING

ARUBA: FLAG DAY. Mar 18. Aruba national holiday. Display of flags, national music and folkloric events.

CALHOUN, JOHN CALDWELL: BIRTH ANNIVERSARY. Mar 18, 1782. American statesman and first vice president of the US to resign that office (Dec 28, 1832). Born at Abbeville District, SC, died at Washington, DC, Mar 31, 1850.

CLEVELAND, GROVER: BIRTH ANNIVERSARY. Mar 18, 1837. The 22nd and 24th president of the US was born Stephen Grover Cleveland at Caldwell, NJ. Terms of office as president: Mar 4, 1885–Mar 3, 1889, and Mar 4, 1893–Mar 3, 1897. He ran for president for the intervening term and received a plurality of votes cast but failed to win electoral college victory. Only president to serve two nonconsecutive terms. Also the only president to be married in the White House. He married 21-year-old Frances Folsom, his ward. Their daughter, Esther, was the first child of a president to be born in the White House. Died at Princeton, NJ, June 24, 1908.

DIESEL, RUDOLPH: BIRTH ANNIVERSARY. Mar 18, 1858. German engineer and inventor of the Diesel oil-burning internal combustion engine (about 1897), born at Paris, France. Diesel drowned in the English Channel, Sept 29, 1913.

FORGIVE MOM AND DAD DAY. Mar 18. Is there a parent alive who has not made mistakes? It's time to let Mom and Dad down off the wedding cake and into the world of mere humans. Besides, you're an alleged grown-up now, and it's time to stop living your life as a reaction to what used to be. (©2006 by WH.) For info: Thomas & Ruth Roy, Wellcat Holidays, 2418 Long Ln, Lebanon, PA 17046. Phone: (717) 279-0184. E-mail: info@wellcat.com. Web: www.wellcat.com.

JOHNSON, WILLIAM H.: BIRTH ANNIVERSARY. Mar 18, 1901. African-American artist born at Florence, SC, he died Apr 13, 1970, at Islip, NY. Johnson spent many years in Europe painting Expressionist works. He was strongly influenced by the vivid styles and brushstrokes of Henry O. Tanner, Vincent van Gogh, Paul Gauguin, Edvard Munch and Otto Dix. He left Europe when Hitler began destroying art that had primitivist or African themes. Back in the US, Johnson developed a new, flatter style and delved into subjects of his own experience as well as historical African-American figures and events. *Going to Church* (1940–41) and *Mom and Dad* (1944) are examples of his later work.

NATIONAL BIODIESEL DAY. Mar 18. Birthday of Rudolph Diesel, who invented the diesel engine and unveiled it at the World's Fair in 1900. Diesel originally designed the engine to run on peanut oil and was a big believer in the role plant oils could play in fueling America. Biodiesel is a cleaner-burning, petroleum-free alternative to diesel that can be made from any fat or vegetable oil. This day honors the man whose vision comes full circle as biodiesel becomes an increasingly popular fuel. For info: National Biodiesel Board, PO Box 104898, Jefferson City, MO 65110-4898.

March 2020	S	M	T	W	T	F	S
				1	2	3	4	5	6	7
	8	9	10	11	12	13	14
	15	16	17	18	19	20	21
	22	23	24	25	26	27	28
	29	30	31				

Phone: (573) 635-3893. Fax: (573) 635-7913. E-mail: info@biodiesel.org. Web: www.biodiesel.org.

NCAA DIVISION I WOMEN'S SWIMMING AND DIVING CHAMPIONSHIPS. Mar 18–21. Ramsey Center, Athens, GA. Est attendance: 3,000. For info: NCAA, 700 W Washington St, PO Box 6222, Indianapolis, IN 46206-6222. Phone: (317) 917-6222. Fax: (317) 917-6888. Web: www.ncaa.org.

NEW LONDON SCHOOL EXPLOSION: ANNIVERSARY. Mar 18, 1937. The London School at New London, TX, exploded from a catastrophic natural gas leak, killing 295 students and teachers.

PITTSBURGH INCORPORATED: ANNIVERSARY. Mar 18, 1816. Founded in 1758, the city of Pittsburgh, PA, was incorporated on this date.

PLIMPTON, GEORGE: BIRTH ANNIVERSARY. Mar 18, 1927. Born at New York, NY, writer and editor George Plimpton called himself a "participatory" journalist, going to great lengths to research his narratives. After training with the 1963 Detroit Lions, he wrote *Paper Lion* based on his experiences; the book is widely considered one of the best pieces of sports writing ever published. He also founded *The Paris Review*, a highly regarded literary quarterly that published the first works of such writers as Philip Roth and Jack Kerouac. The American Academy of Arts and Letters called him a "central figure in American letters" when they inducted him in 2002. He died at New York, NY, Sept 25, 2003.

SPACE MILESTONE: *VOSKHOD 2* (USSR): FIRST SPACE WALK: 55th ANNIVERSARY. Mar 18, 1965. Colonel Alexei Leonov stepped out of the capsule for 20 minutes in a special space suit, the first man to leave a spaceship. It was two months prior to the first US space walk. See also: "Space Milestone: *Gemini 4* (US)" (June 3).

UPDIKE, JOHN: BIRTH ANNIVERSARY. Mar 18, 1932. Pulitzer Prize-winning writer who authored more than 50 books, as well as hundreds of short stories, essays and poems. Updike often wrote of mundane life in Middle America and is best known for his novels about Harry "Rabbit" Angstrom. Born at Reading, PA, Updike died Jan 27, 2009, at Danvers, MA.

🎂 BIRTHDAYS TODAY

Bonnie Blair, 56, Olympic speed skater, born Cornwall, NY, Mar 18, 1964.

Irene Cara, 61, singer ("Fame," "The Dream"), actress (*Ain't Misbehavin'*), born the Bronx, NY, Mar 18, 1959.

Lily Collins, 31, actress ("The Last Tycoon," *Rules Don't Apply, Mirror Mirror*), born Guildford, England, Mar 18, 1989.

Dane Cook, 48, comedian, actor (*Good Luck Chuck*), born Boston, MA, Mar 18, 1972.

Frederik Willem de Klerk, 84, former president of South Africa, born Johannesburg, South Africa, Mar 18, 1936.

Kevin Dobson, 76, actor ("Kojak," "Knots Landing"), born New York, NY, Mar 18, 1944.

Brad Dourif, 70, actor (*One Flew over the Cuckoo's Nest, Blue Velvet, Jungle Fever*), born Huntington, WV, Mar 18, 1950.

John Kander, 93, composer (Tonys [with lyricist Fred Ebb] for *Cabaret, Woman of the Year* and *Kiss of the Spider Woman; Chicago*), born Kansas City, MO, Mar 18, 1927.

Adam Levine, 41, singer (Maroon 5), television personality ("The Voice"), born Los Angeles, CA, Mar 18, 1979.

Charley Pride, 82, singer, former minor league baseball player, born Sledge, MS, Mar 18, 1938.

Reinhold Richard "Reince" Priebus, 48, former White House chief of staff (Trump administration), former Republican National Committee chair, born Dover, NJ, Mar 18, 1972.

Queen Latifah, 50, singer, actress (*Bringing Down the House, Chicago*), born Dana Owens at East Orange, NJ, Mar 18, 1970.

Vanessa Williams, 57, singer, actress ("Ugly Betty," *Bye Bye Birdie, Kiss of the Spider Woman*), born New York, NY, Mar 18, 1963.

Alexei Yagudin, 40, figure skater, born Leningrad, Russia, Mar 18, 1980.

March 19 — Thursday

DAY 79   **287 REMAINING**

ABSOLUTELY INCREDIBLE KID DAY. Mar 19. 24th annual. Camp Fire, one of the nation's leading youth development organizations, sponsors this day of appreciation for America's youth. Adults and teens are asked to write, post and tweet notes of encouragement and inspiration. Annually, the third Thursday of March. For info: Camp Fire, 1801 Main St, Ste 200, Kansas City, MO 64108. Phone: (816) 285-2010. E-mail: info@campfire.org. Web: www.campfire.org.

BRYAN, WILLIAM JENNINGS: BIRTH ANNIVERSARY. Mar 19, 1860. American political leader, member of Congress, Democratic presidential nominee (1896), "free silver" advocate, assisted in prosecution at Scopes trial, known as "the Silver-Tongued Orator." Born at Salem, IL, he died at Dayton, TN, July 26, 1925.

EARP, WYATT: BIRTH ANNIVERSARY. Mar 19, 1848. Born at Monmouth, IL, and died Jan 13, 1929, at Los Angeles, CA. A legendary figure of the Old West, Earp worked as a railroad hand, saloonkeeper, gambler, lawman, gunslinger, miner and real estate investor at various times. Best known for the gunfight at the O.K. Corral Oct 26, 1881, at Tombstone, AZ.

IRAN: NATIONAL DAY OF OIL. Mar 19. National holiday. Commemorates the nationalization of Iran's oil fields in 1963.

JAPAN: VERNAL EQUINOX DAY. Mar 19. National holiday in Japan.

LIVINGSTONE, DAVID: BIRTH ANNIVERSARY. Mar 19, 1813. Physician, missionary and explorer born at Blantyre, Scotland. From 1841 until his death, Livingstone was in Africa, evangelizing, seeking to end slavery and making important geographic observations of the African interior. During a search for the origins of the Nile (1866 to 1871), an ailing Livingstone lost touch with the Western world, occasioning the famous search by journalist Henry M. Stanley. Stanley found him at Ujiji, near Lake Tanganyika in Africa, on Nov 10, 1871. Dr. Livingstone died at Chitambo (now Zambia), May 1, 1873.

MCKEAN, THOMAS: BIRTH ANNIVERSARY. Mar 19, 1734. Signer of the Declaration of Independence, governor of Pennsylvania and chief justice of Pennsylvania. Born at Chester County, PA, he died June 24, 1817, at Philadelphia, PA.

NCAA DIVISION I FENCING CHAMPIONSHIPS. Mar 19–22. Detroit, MI. For info: NCAA, PO Box 6222, Indianapolis, IN 46206-6222. Phone: (317) 917-6222. Web: www.NCAA.com.

NCAA DIVISION I WRESTLING CHAMPIONSHIPS. Mar 19–21. US Bank Stadium, Minneapolis, MN. 92nd annual. For info: NCAA, PO Box 6222, Indianapolis, IN 46206-6222. Phone: (317) 917-6222. Web: www.NCAA.com.

OPERATION IRAQI FREEDOM: ANNIVERSARY. Mar 19, 2003. At 9:30 PM, EST, two hours past a deadline for Iraqi dictator Saddam Hussein to step down from power, US and British forces began air strikes against his regime. A ground campaign (adding Australian forces) followed quickly, and by Apr 9, Baghdad was under the control of allied forces. Hussein was captured by US forces on Dec 13, 2003. On June 28, 2004, Iraq regained its sovereignty. On Dec 15, 2005, 70 percent of Iraq's registered voters turned out for parliamentary elections—one of the freest elections on record in the Arab world. Sectarian and terrorist violence prevented the withdrawal of US and other national combat troops until Aug 18, 2010.

OSTARA. Mar 19. (Also called Alban Eilir.) One of the "Lesser Sabbats" during the Wiccan year, Ostara is a fire and fertility festival that marks the beginning of spring. Annually, on the spring equinox.

PROPOSAL DAY!® Mar 19 (also Sept 22). The biannual Proposal Day!® provides a pleasant opportunity for single adults who are ready to marry to gracefully inform compatible potential marriage partners that they're ready on the days of the vernal equinox and the autumnal equinox. For info: John Michael O'Loughlin, 3124 Chisholm Trail, Irving, TX 75062. Phone: (972) 258-4996. E-mail: lldjohn@aol.com. Web: www.proposalday.com.

ROGERS, EDITH NOURSE: BIRTH ANNIVERSARY. Mar 19, 1881. Edith Nourse Rogers was a YMCA and Red Cross volunteer in France during WWI. In 1925 she was elected to the US Congress to fill the vacancy left by the death of her husband. An able legislator, she was reelected to the House of Representatives 17 times and became the first woman to have her name attached to major legislation. She was a major force in the legislation creating the Women's Army Auxiliary Corps (May 14, 1942) during WWII. Rogers was born at Saco, ME, and died Sept 10, 1960, at Boston, MA.

ROTH, PHILIP. Mar 19, 1933. Philip Roth, born at Newark, NJ, was the best-selling author who came to fame in 1959 with National Book Award-winning short-story collection *Goodbye, Columbus*, the first of many works chronicling family life in Jewish America. His semi-autobiographical 1969 novel *Portnoy's Complaint* exemplified his preoccupation with male lust. He won the Pulitzer Prize for the historical novel *American Pastoral* and became only the third living writer to have books preserved in the Library of America. In 2013, a caucus of 30 authors empaneled by *New York* magazine declared Roth America's greatest living novelist. He died in New York, City, May 22, 2018, having never won the Nobel Prize.

RUSSELL, CHARLES M.: BIRTH ANNIVERSARY. Mar 19, 1864. Born at St. Louis, MO, Charles Marion Russell moved to Montana at age 16 and became a horse wrangler and cow herder with his horse Redbird. In the off hours, he sketched the people and country of the Montana Territory. Today Russell is considered one of the greatest Western artists. He died Oct 26, 1926, at Great Falls, MT.

SAINT JOSEPH'S DAY. Mar 19. Feast day of Joseph, husband of the Virgin Mary and foster father of Jesus. Patron of the Catholic Church, fathers and carpenters.

SIRICA, JOHN JOSEPH: BIRTH ANNIVERSARY. Mar 19, 1904. John Sirica, "the Watergate Judge," was born at Waterbury, CT. During two years of trials and hearings, Sirica relentlessly pushed for the names of those responsible for the June 17, 1972, burglary of the Democratic National Committee headquarters in Washington's Watergate complex. His unwavering search for the truth ultimately resulted in the toppling of the Nixon administration. Judge John Sirica died Aug 15, 1992, at Washington, DC.

SPRING. Mar 19–June 20. In the Northern Hemisphere, spring begins today with the vernal equinox, at 11:50 PM, EDT. Note that in the Southern Hemisphere today is the beginning of autumn. Sun rises due east and sets due west everywhere on Earth (except near poles), and the daylight length (interval between sunrise and sunset) is virtually the same everywhere today: 12 hours, 8 minutes.

SWALLOWS RETURN TO SAN JUAN CAPISTRANO. Mar 19. Traditional date (St. Joseph's Day), since 1776, for swallows to return to the old mission of San Juan Capistrano, CA. See also: "Saint John of Capistrano: Death Anniversary" (Oct 23).

ULTIMATE SPORT SHOW—GRAND RAPIDS. Mar 19–22. DeVos Place, Grand Rapids, MI. This event brings together buyers and sellers of hunting and fishing-boat equipment and accessories, as well as other outdoor sporting goods. US and Canadian hunting and fishing trips and other vacation travel destinations are featured. All aspects of fishing, including tackle boats, seminars, demonstrations and displays, are emphasized. Est attendance: 35,000. For info: ShowSpan, Inc. Phone: (616) 447-2860. Fax: (616) 447-2861. E-mail: events@showspan.com. Web: www.showspan.com.

US STANDARD TIME ACT: ANNIVERSARY. Mar 19, 1918. Anniversary of passage by Congress of the Standard Time Act, which authorized the Interstate Commerce Commission to establish standard time zones for the US. The act also established "daylight saving time," to save fuel and to promote other economies in a country at war. Daylight saving time first went into operation on Easter Sunday, Mar 31, 1918. The Uniform Time Act of 1966, as amended in 1986 and again in 2005, now governs standard time in the US. See also: "Daylight Saving Time Begins" (Mar 8).

WARREN, EARL: BIRTH ANNIVERSARY. Mar 19, 1891. One of the most influential jurists in American law, Warren was born at Los Angeles, CA. He was elected governor of California in 1942 and served three terms before being chosen by President Eisenhower as chief justice of the US in 1953. He guided the court during the Civil Rights era and through a time of shifting social policies in the United States, and many of his decisions are considered the cornerstones of contemporary law and civil procedure. *Gideon v Wainwright* provided for legal assistance for all defendants regardless of ability to pay. *Miranda v Arizona* established the Miranda warning, which requires police to inform arrestees of their "right to remain silent." *Brown v Board of Education* called for the desegregation of American public schools, a first step to eliminating racist policies by decrying the concept of "separate but equal." Fellow justice Abe Fortas called the Warren Court "the most profound and pervasive revolution ever achieved by substantially peaceful means." Warren retired in 1969 and died at Washington, DC, on July 9, 1974.

🎂 BIRTHDAYS TODAY

Ursula Andress, 84, actress (*Dr. No*; *What's New, Pussycat?*), born Bern, Switzerland, Mar 19, 1936.

Michael Bergin, 51, actor ("Baywatch"), born Naugatuck, CT, Mar 19, 1969.

Glenn Close, 73, actress (*Fatal Attraction*, Emmy for "Damages"; Tonys for *Sunset Boulevard*, *Death and the Maiden* and *The Real Thing*), born Greenwich, CT, Mar 19, 1947.

Brent Scowcroft, 95, business executive, consultant, born Ogden, UT, Mar 19, 1925.

Renee Taylor, 85, actress ("The Nanny," *The Producers*, *A New Leaf*), born New York, NY, Mar 19, 1935.

Hidayet "Hedo" Türkoğlu, 41, former basketball player, born Istanbul, Turkey, Mar 19, 1979.

Bruce Willis, 65, actor (*Sin City*, *The Sixth Sense*, *Die Hard*), born Idar-Oberstein, West Germany (now Germany), Mar 19, 1955.

March 20 — Friday

DAY 80   **286 REMAINING**

AMERICAN CROSSWORD PUZZLE TOURNAMENT. Mar 20–22. Stamford Marriott Hotel, Stamford, CT. Eight hundred solvers from the US and Canada compete on eight puzzles during this 43rd annual event. Points are awarded for accuracy and speed. The final puzzle is played on giant white boards for everyone to watch. Prizes are awarded in 22 skill, age and geographic categories, and the grand prize is $5,000. The weekend also includes group word games, guest speakers and appearances by celebrity crossword solvers. Solvers can compete at home for fun, either online or by mail, and receive a ranking in all their solving categories. Est attendance: 1,000. For info: Will Shortz, Director, American Crossword Puzzle Tournament, 55 Great Oak Ln, Pleasantville, NY 10570. Phone: (215) 266-2802. Web: www.crosswordtournament.com.

IBSEN, HENRIK: BIRTH ANNIVERSARY. Mar 20, 1828. Norwegian playwright born at Skien, Norway. Among his best-remembered plays are *Peer Gynt*, *The Pillars of Society*, *The Wild Duck*, *An*

Enemy of the People and *Hedda Gabler*. Died at Oslo, Norway, May 23, 1906.

IRANIAN NEW YEAR: NORUZ. Mar 20. National celebration for all Iranians, this is the traditional Persian New Year. (In Iran, spring comes Mar 20 or 21.) It is a celebration of nature's rebirth. Every household spreads a special cover with symbols for the seven good angels on it. These symbols are sprouts, wheat germ, apples, hyacinth, fruit of the jujube, garlic and sumac heralding life, rebirth, health, happiness, prosperity, joy and beauty. A fishbowl is also customary, representing the end of the astrological year, and wild rue is burned to drive away evil and bring about a happy New Year. This pre-Islamic holiday, a legacy of Zoroastrianism, is also celebrated as Navruz, Nau-Roz or Noo Roz in Afghanistan, Albania, Azerbaijan, Kazakhstan, Kyrgyzstan, Tajikistan, Turkmenistan and Uzbekistan. For info: Stuart A. Schaeffer, Reference Librarian, Farmingdale Public Library, 116 Merritts Rd, Farmingdale, NY 11735. Phone: (516) 249-9090. Fax: (516) 694-9697. Or Yassaman Djalali, Librarian, West Valley Branch Library, 1243 San Tomas Aquino Rd, San Jose, CA 95117. Phone: (408) 244-4766.

NAW-RUZ. Mar 20. Baha'i New Year's Day, which falls on the spring equinox. One of the nine days of the year when Baha'is suspend work. Naw-Ruz is an ancient Persian festival celebrating the "new day" and for Baha'is it marks the end of the annual 19-Day Fast. For info: Baha'is of the US, Office of Communications, 1233 Central St, Evanston, IL 60201. Phone: (847) 733-3584. E-mail: ooc@usbnc.org. Web: www.bahai.us.

NCAA DIVISION I WOMEN'S ICE HOCKEY CHAMPIONSHIP (FROZEN FOUR). Mar 20–22. Boston University, Boston, MA. For info: NCAA, PO Box 6222, Indianapolis, IN 46206-6222. Web: www.NCAA.com.

NERVE GAS ATTACK ON JAPANESE SUBWAY: 25th ANNIVERSARY. Mar 20, 1995. Twelve people were killed and 5,000 injured in a nerve gas attack on the Tokyo subway system during rush hour. Suspected in the attack was the Japanese religious sect Aum Shinrikyo, founded and led by Shoko Asahara (real name Chizuo Matsumoto). The group, which professes belief in a hybrid of Buddhist-Hindu teachings, predicts an apocalypse. In a raid conducted against the sect's main compound in Kamikuishiki on Mar 25, police seized literature that predicted 90 percent of the people in the world would be killed by poison gas. Also seized were two tons of chemicals for making sarin, the poison used in the Mar 20 attack. This cache was reported to contain enough material to kill five million people. In a second raid, Asahara was arrested.

ROGERS, FRED: BIRTH ANNIVERSARY. Mar 20, 1928. Born Fred McFeely Rogers at Latrobe, PA, Rogers began producing television for children in 1953. His first program, "The Children's Hour," was the precursor to "Mister Rogers' Neighborhood," which premiered in Canada in 1966 and the US in 1968. The show ran on public television until Rogers's death, and he became known worldwide for his dedication to the well-being of children and for his demonstrations of the importance of kindness, compassion and learning. He authored a number of books for parents and children, wrote more than 200 songs and won dozens of awards, including Emmys, Peabodys and the Presidential Medal of Freedom. He died Feb 27, 2003, at his home in Pittsburgh, PA.

SKINNER, B.F.: BIRTH ANNIVERSARY. Mar 20, 1904. American psychologist Burrhus Frederic Skinner was born at Susquehanna, PA. He was a pioneer in behaviorism and is best known for developing

March 2020	S	M	T	W	T	F	S
				1	2	3	4	5	6	7
	8	9	10	11	12	13	14
	15	16	17	18	19	20	21
	22	23	24	25	26	27	28
	29	30	31				

the "Skinner box" (an enclosed experimental environment). He died Aug 18, 1990, at Cambridge, MA.

SNOWMAN BURNING. Mar 20 (tentative). Reading of poetry heralding the end of winter and the arrival of spring, followed by sacrifice in effigy, toasts and cheers. Annually, on or near the first day of spring. Est attendance: 300. For info: Public Relations Office, Lake Superior State University, Sault Ste. Marie, MI 49783. Phone: (906) 635-2315 or (906) 635-2314. Web: www.lssu.edu/snowman.

TAYLOR, FREDERICK WINSLOW: BIRTH ANNIVERSARY. Mar 20, 1856. Vilified and praised, Frederick Winslow Taylor changed the face of business forever as the "Father of Scientific Management." Born at Philadelphia, PA, Taylor was a chief engineer at Philadelphia's Midvale Steel Company, when he introduced time-and-motion studies in 1881, which helped companies find efficiencies in worker movement and drive out time wasting on the assembly lines. Henry Ford, in particular, put Taylor's theories to work. Taylor died at Philadelphia, Mar 21, 1915.

TUNISIA: INDEPENDENCE DAY. Mar 20. Commemorates treaty in 1956 by which France recognized Tunisian autonomy.

UNITED NATIONS: FRENCH LANGUAGE DAY. Mar 20. French, along with English, is one of the two working languages of the United Nations Secretariat, and one of the organization's six official and working languages (English, French, Arabic, Chinese, Russian, Spanish). This day celebrates the diversity of the Francophone world—French is spoken on five continents. Annually, Mar 20. For info: United Nations. Web: www.un.org/fr/events/frenchlanguageday.

UNITED NATIONS: INTERNATIONAL DAY OF HAPPINESS. Mar 20. The General Assembly of the United Nations proclaimed this day recognizing the relevance of happiness and well-being as universal goals and aspirations in the lives of human beings around the world and the importance of their recognition in public policy objectives. (Res 66/281 of July 12, 2012.) Annually, Mar 20. For info: United Nations. Web: www.un.org.

WON'T YOU BE MY NEIGHBOR DAY. Mar 20. An annual day celebrating Fred Rogers (born today in 1928) and his legacy of neighborliness on his birthday. Neighbors everywhere are encouraged to wear a favorite sweater and promote neighborliness in their neighborhood. For info: The Fred Rogers Company. Web: www.fredrogers.org.

🎂 BIRTHDAYS TODAY

Holly Hunter, 62, actress (Oscar for *The Piano*; "Top of the Lake," "Saving Grace," *The Big Sick, Broadcast News*), born Conyers, GA, Mar 20, 1958.

William Hurt, 70, actor (*Too Big to Fail, The Accidental Tourist, Broadcast News*), born Washington, DC, Mar 20, 1950.

Spike Lee, 63, director, producer, writer (Oscar for *BlacKkKlansman, She's Gotta Have It, Do the Right Thing, Malcolm X*), actor, born Atlanta, GA, Mar 20, 1957.

Hal Linden, 89, actor ("Barney Miller," "Blacke's Magic"), born Harold Lipshitz at the Bronx, NY, Mar 20, 1931.

Ronna Romney McDaniel, 47, Chair of the Republican National Committee, born Austin, TX, Mar 20, 1973.

Brian Mulroney, 81, 18th prime minister of Canada (1984–93), born Baie Comeau, QC, Canada, Mar 20, 1939.

Robert Gordon (Bobby) Orr, 72, Hall of Fame hockey player, born Parry Sound, ON, Canada, Mar 20, 1948.

Carl Reiner, 98, actor ("The Dick Van Dyke Show," "Your Show of Shows"), writer, director, born the Bronx, NY, Mar 20, 1922.

Patrick James (Pat) Riley, 75, basketball coach and former player, born Schenectady, NY, Mar 20, 1945.

Mary Roach, 61, author (*Grunt, Gulp, Packing for Mars, Stiff*), journalist, born Hanover, NH, Mar 20, 1959.

Theresa Russell, 63, actress (*Straight Time, Black Widow*), born San Diego, CA, Mar 20, 1957.

David Thewlis, 57, actor (*War Horse, Besieged*, Harry Potter films), born Blackpool, Lancashire, England, Mar 20, 1963.

Fernando Torres, 36, soccer player, born Fuenlabrada, Spain, Mar 20, 1984.

Louis (Louie) Vito, 32, Olympic snowboarder, born Columbus, OH, Mar 20, 1988.

March 21 — Saturday

DAY 81　　　　　　　　　　　　　　　　**285 REMAINING**

ARIES, THE RAM. Mar 21–Apr 19. In the astronomical/astrological zodiac, which divides the sun's apparent orbit into 12 segments, the period Mar 21–Apr 19 is traditionally identified as the sun sign of Aries, the Ram. The ruling planet is Mars.

BACH, JOHANN SEBASTIAN: BIRTH ANNIVERSARY. Mar 21, 1685. Organist and composer, one of the most influential composers in musical history. Born at Eisenach, Germany, he died at Leipzig, Germany, July 28, 1750.

BURKE, SOLOMON: 80th BIRTH ANNIVERSARY. Mar 21, 1940. American musician and singer, born at Philadelphia, PA, widely considered to be one of the greatest soul singers of all time. Burke's hits include 1962's "Cry to Me" and 1964's "Everybody Needs Somebody to Love." He was a flamboyant showman, performing from a throne in keeping with his self-styled King of Rock and Soul persona. Burke's personal life was outsized as well: he weighed more than 400 pounds at the time of his death and he fathered at least 21 children. He died at an airport in Amsterdam, Netherlands, on Oct 10, 2010.

ENGLAND: HEAD OF THE RIVER RACE. Mar 21. Thames Championship Course, Mortlake to Putney, London. Processional race over 4½ miles on the River Thames for 400 eight-oared crews, starting at 10-second intervals. The previous year's winner starts first. The first race was held in 1926 and 21 crews took part. Est attendance: 7,000. For info: Head of the River Race. Web: www.horr.co.uk.

FIRST ROUND-THE-WORLD BALLOON FLIGHT: ANNIVERSARY. Mar 21, 1999. Swiss psychiatrist Bertrand Piccard and British copilot Brian Jones landed in the Egyptian desert on this date, having flown 29,056 miles nonstop around the world in a hot-air balloon. Leaving from Chateau d'Oex in the Swiss Alps on Mar 1, the trip took 19 days, 21 hours and 55 minutes. Piccard is the grandson of balloonist Auguste Piccard, who was the first to ascend into the stratosphere in a balloon. See also: "First Solo Round-the-World Balloon Flight: Anniversary" (July 2) and "Piccard, Auguste: Birth Anniversary" (Jan 28).

GALLO, JULIO: BIRTH ANNIVERSARY. Mar 21, 1910. American vintner Julio Gallo was born at Oakland, CA. He is best known for his role in the Ernest and Julio Gallo Winery, of Modesto, CA, which at one time claimed about 26 percent of the US wine industry. He died May 2, 1993, near Tracy, CA.

GERSDORFF HITLER ASSASSINATION ATTEMPT: ANNIVERSARY. Mar 21, 1943. In a suicide/assassination attempt planned for this date, Major General Baron von Gersdorff was to carry a bomb in the pocket of his greatcoat to the "Heroes Memorial Day" annual dedication to the dead of the First World War. Hitler was to attend this event to inspect some weaponry taken from captured Russian soldiers. The bomb was to go off within 10 minutes of Hitler's arrival at the event, as he was not expected to be there for very long. The conspirators were unable to locate the necessary short time fuse and the attempt had to be called off. This was the second serious plan to assassinate Hitler in 1943.

INDIA: NEW YEAR'S DAY. Mar 21. This is the first day of the New Year on the Saka calendar adopted by India after independence from Great Britain. The Saka calendar is a solar calendar with the same leap year schedule as the Gregorian calendar. In common years, the New Year is Mar 22; in leap years, the New Year falls on Mar 21.

JUAREZ, BENITO: BIRTH ANNIVERSARY. Mar 21, 1806. A Zapotec Indian, Benito Pablo Juarez was born at Oaxaca, Mexico, and grew up to become that country's president. He learned Spanish at age 12. Juarez became judge of the civil court in Oaxaca in 1842, a member of congress in 1846 and governor in 1847. In 1858, following a rebellion against the constitution, the presidency was passed to Juarez. He died at Mexico City, Mexico, July 18, 1872. In recognition of Juarez as a symbol of liberation and of Mexican resistance to foreign intervention, his birthday is a public holiday in Mexico.

LESOTHO: NATIONAL TREE PLANTING DAY. Mar 21. Lesotho.

LEWIS, FRANCIS: BIRTH ANNIVERSARY. Mar 21, 1713. Signer of the Declaration of Independence, born at Wales. Died Dec 31, 1802, at Long Island, NY.

LUNSFORD, BASCOM LAMAR: BIRTH ANNIVERSARY. Mar 21, 1882. Songwriter and folklorist who authored the song "Mountain Dew," Lunsford started the first folk music festival in 1928 at Asheville, NC. This event, which led to the formation of the National Clogging and Hoedown Council, is held to this day. He was known as the "father of clogging dance" and the "king of folk music." He recorded some 320 folk songs, tunes and stories for the Library of Congress. Born at Mars Hill, NC, Lunsford died Sept 4, 1973, at South Turkey Creek, NC.

MEMORY DAY. Mar 21. To encourage awareness of the traditional memory system using pattern t,d = 1; n = 2; m = 3; r = 4; l = 5; j,ch = 6; k,q,g-hard = 7; f,v = 8; b,p = 9. Study historic examples of the use of the memory system in the writings of Milton, Thomas Gray, Longfellow, Lincoln and others. (Created by Robert L. Birch, Pun Corps.)

MILITARY THROUGH THE AGES. Mar 21–22. Jamestown Settlement, Williamsburg, VA. Re-enactors and modern-day units show how uniforms, weapons and military tactics evolved through the centuries. For info: Jamestown-Yorktown Foundation, PO Box 1607, Williamsburg, VA 23187. Phone: (757) 253-4838 or (888) 593-4682. Fax: (757) 253-5299. Web: www.historyisfun.org.

MUSSORGSKY, MODEST: BIRTH ANNIVERSARY. Mar 21, 1839. Romantic composer, born at Karevo, Russia. A military officer and, later, a civil servant, he joined The Five, a group of other amateur Russian composers passionate about creating a Russian music free from European musical conventions. Best-known works are *Boris Godunov* (1874) and *Pictures at an Exhibition* (1874). He died Mar 28, 1881, at St. Petersburg, Russia.

NAMIBIA: INDEPENDENCE DAY: 30th ANNIVERSARY OF INDEPENDENCE. Mar 21. National Day. Commemorates independence from South Africa in 1990.

NATIONAL HEALTHY FATS DAY. Mar 21. This day is a celebration of traditional, healthy animal fats—pure lard, beef tallow, duck fat, goose fat and the like—that are now enjoying a resurgence within America's food culture, in restaurants, fast-food operations and home kitchens. Artificial trans fats are out, and minimally processed animal fats—for superior baking, frying and a host of other cooking applications—are making a comeback. The color, texture and flavor that healthy animal fats impart make them a vastly superior alternative to heavily processed, industrially produced substitutes. Annually, Mar 21—around the first day of spring. For info: Healthy Fats Coalition. Web: www.healthy-fatscoalition.org.

	S	**M**	**T**	**W**	**T**	**F**	**S**
March	1	2	3	4	5	6	7
	8	9	10	11	12	13	14
2020	15	16	17	18	19	20	21
	22	23	24	25	26	27	28
	29	30	31				

NATIONAL QUILTING DAY. Mar 21. This day unites quilters and quilt lovers everywhere, not only in this country, but also around the world. Individuals, groups of quilters, shop owners, publishers, quilting organizations and the entire quiltmaking community are invited to recognize and promote the tradition of quiltmaking. Annually, the third Saturday in March. (Created by the National Quilting Association [now dissolved] in 1992.)

NORWAY: BIRKEBEINERRENNET. Mar 21. Rena and Lillehammer. Since 1932, ski marathon of 54 km between the cities of Rena and Lillehammer in which competitors carry a backpack weighing 3.5 kg. The race and the backpack commemorate an epic journey in Norwegian history: On Christmas Day in 1205, in the midst of a power struggle for the Norwegian throne, two birkebeiners (warriors who wore birch-bark leg coverings) smuggled infant prince Hakon Hakonsson by ski over mountainous terrain to safety away from a rival faction. The baby survived to become King Hakon Hakonsson IV, and he ended the civil war. For info: Birken, Fabrikkveien 2, 2450 Rena, Norway. Phone: (47) (41) 77-29-00. E-mail: info@birkebeiner.no. Web: www.birkebeiner.no.

PLAY-THE-RECORDER DAY. Mar 21. This day, first observed in 1992, celebrates the recorder, an end-blown woodwind instrument with no reed that dates to the Middle Ages. Recorder consorts featuring the entire family (sopranino to contrabass) of "fipple flutes," or flutes with a beak, were common in Renaissance musical life. The recorder saw its popularity revived in the 20th century as a relatively inexpensive, portable instrument. Annually, the third Saturday in March. For info: American Recorder Society. Web: www.americanrecorder.org.

POCAHONTAS (REBECCA ROLFE): DEATH ANNIVERSARY. Mar 21, 1617. Pocahontas, daughter of Powhatan, born about 1595, near Jamestown, VA, leader of the Indian union of Algonquin nations, helped to foster goodwill between the colonists of the Jamestown settlement and her people. Pocahontas converted to Christianity, was baptized with the name Rebecca and married John Rolfe Apr 5, 1614. In 1616, she accompanied Rolfe on a trip to his native England, where she was regarded as an overseas "ambassador." Pocahontas's stay in England drew so much attention to the Virginia Company's Jamestown settlement that lotteries were held to help support the colony. Shortly before she was scheduled to return to Jamestown, Pocahontas died at Gravesend, Kent, England, of either smallpox or pneumonia.

SAVE THE FLORIDA PANTHER DAY. Mar 21. Florida. A ceremonial holiday on the third Saturday in March.

SELMA CIVIL RIGHTS MARCH: 55th ANNIVERSARY. Mar 21, 1965. More than 3,000 civil rights demonstrators led by Dr. Martin Luther King, Jr, began a four-day march from Selma, AL, to Montgomery, AL, to demand federal protection of voting rights. There were violent attempts by local police, using fire hoses and dogs, to suppress the march. A march two weeks before on Mar 7, 1965, was called "Bloody Sunday" because of the use of nightsticks, chains and electric cattle prods against the marchers by the police.

SHARPEVILLE MASSACRE: 60th ANNIVERSARY. Mar 21, 1960. During protests against South Africa's pass laws in the township of Sharpeville, police opened fire on the crowd (estimated at about 7,000 or more), killing 69 people and injuring 180. The anniversary is observed in South Africa and by the United Nations.

SOUTH AFRICA: HUMAN RIGHTS DAY. Mar 21. National holiday. Commemorates the Mar 21, 1960, massacre at Sharpeville and all those who lost their lives in the struggle for equal rights as citizens of South Africa.

SPRING OFFENSIVE: ANNIVERSARY. Mar 21–Apr 4, 1918. General Erich Ludendorff launched the Michael offensive, the biggest German offensive of 1918, on Mar 21 with a five-hour artillery barrage. The Central Powers' objective was to drive a wedge between the British and French forces and drive the British to the sea. Although they did not accomplish this objective, in the south they captured Montdidier and advanced to a depth of 40 miles. They managed to create a bulge in the front south of Somme and end what had effectively been a stalemate. The Allies lost nearly 230,000 men and the Germans lost almost as many.

STRANG, JAMES JESSE (KING STRANG): BIRTH ANNIVERSARY. Mar 21, 1813. Perhaps America's only crowned king was born at Scipio, NY, and christened Jesse James Strang (which he later changed to James Jesse Strang). He was crowned king of Mormons at Beaver Island, MI, July 8, 1850, and ruled his kingdom until his death. Elected to the Michigan legislature in 1852 and 1854. Wounded by assassins June 16, 1856, at Beaver Island, and died June 19, 1856, at Voree, WI.

TWITTER CREATED: ANNIVERSARY. Mar 21, 2006. Jack Dorsey sent the first "tweet"—"just setting up my twttr"—in the now immensely popular microblogging and social networking platform. Twitter enables users to post 280-character public messages. Dorsey, Evan Williams and Biz Stone of Odeo launched Twitter to the public on July 15, 2006.

UNITED NATIONS: INTERNATIONAL DAY FOR THE ELIMINATION OF RACIAL DISCRIMINATION. Mar 21. Initiated by the United Nations General Assembly in 1966 to be observed annually Mar 21, the anniversary of the killing of 69 African demonstrators at Sharpeville, South Africa, in 1960, as a day to remember "the victims of Sharpeville and those countless others in different parts of the world who have fallen victim to racial injustice" and to promote efforts to eradicate racial discrimination worldwide. For info: United Nations, Dept of Public Info, New York, NY 10017. Web: www.un.org.

UNITED NATIONS: INTERNATIONAL DAY OF FORESTS. Mar 21. This global celebration of forests provides a platform to raise awareness of the importance of all types of forests and of trees outside forests. Forests are the most biologically diverse ecosystems on land, home to more than 80 percent of the terrestrial species of animals, plants and insects. They also provide shelter, jobs and security for forest-dependent communities. Forests contribute to the balance of oxygen, carbon dioxide and humidity in the air. They protect watersheds, which supply 75 percent of freshwater worldwide. Annually, Mar 21. For info: United Nations. Web: www.un.org.

UNITED NATIONS: INTERNATIONAL NOWRUZ DAY. Mar 21. Nowruz is an ancestral festivity marking the first day of spring and the renewal of nature. It promotes values of peace and solidarity between generations and within families as well as reconciliation and neighborliness, thus contributing to cultural diversity and friendship among peoples and different communities. Proclaimed by the United Nations General Assembly, in its resolution A/RES/64/253 of 2010, at the initiative of several countries that share this holiday—Afghanistan, Albania, Azerbaijan, the Former Yugoslav Republic of Macedonia, India, Iran (Islamic Republic of), Kazakhstan, Kyrgyzstan, Tajikistan, Turkey and Turkmenistan. For info: United Nations. Web: www.un.org/en/events/nowruzday.

UNITED NATIONS: WEEK OF SOLIDARITY WITH THE PEOPLES STRUGGLING AGAINST RACISM AND RACIAL DISCRIMINATION. Mar 21–27. Annual observance initiated by the UN General Assembly as part of its program of the Decade for Action to Combat Racism and Racial Discrimination. For info: United Nations, Dept of Public Info, New York, NY 10017. Web: www.un.org.

UNITED NATIONS: WORLD POETRY DAY. Mar 21. First proclaimed in 1999 to recognize the unique ability of poetry to capture the creative spirit of the human mind. One of the main objectives of the day is to support linguistic diversity through poetic expression and to offer endangered languages the opportunity to be heard within their communities. World Poetry Day also seeks to encourage a return to the oral tradition of poetry recitals, to promote the teaching of poetry, to restore a dialogue between poetry and the other arts such as theater, dance, music and painting and to support small publishers and create an attractive image of poetry in the media. Annually, Mar 21. For info: UNESCO. Web: www.un.org/en/events/poetryday.

WALK IN THE SAND DAY. Mar 21. This is a day to gather at the beaches around the world and take a walk in a global effort to raise awareness to the problems facing our beaches and the need to protect this beautiful natural land. Annually, on the Saturday after the March Equinox (start of spring in the Northern Hemisphere and autumn in the Southern Hemisphere). For info: Patti Jewel, Walk in the Sand Day, 5840 Red Bug Lake Rd, #1514, Winter Springs, FL 32708. E-mail: beaches@walkinthesand.com. Web: https://walkinthesand.com/day.

WORLD DOWN SYNDROME DAY. Mar 21. 14th annual. A global awareness day (officially observed by the United Nations since 2012) raising awareness of what Down syndrome is, what it means to have Down syndrome and how people with Down syndrome play a vital role in our lives and communities. Join the cause to create a single global voice for advocating for the rights, inclusion and well-being of people with Down syndrome. Annually, Mar 21. For info: Down Syndrome International. E-mail: contact@ds-int.org. Web: www.worlddownsyndromeday.org.

ZIEGFELD, FLORENZ: BIRTH ANNIVERSARY. Mar 21, 1867. The theater impresario, born at Chicago, IL, was creator of the world-famous *Ziegfeld Follies*, lavish annual Broadway spectacles (from 1907 to 1931) that were a mix of vaudeville variety and chorus girl beauty pageant. The "Ziegfeld Girls," bedecked in ornament, moved in strict synchronization accompanied (after 1919) by the Irving Berlin song "A Pretty Girl Is Like a Melody." The Great Ziegfeld also produced the Jerome Kern–Oscar Hammerstein II musical *Show Boat* in 1927. Ziegfeld died July 32, 1932, at Hollywood, CA.

🎂 BIRTHDAYS TODAY

Marit Bjørgen, 40, Olympic cross-country skier, born Trondheim, Norway, Mar 21, 1980.

Jair Messias Bolsonaro, 65, President of Brazil, born Gilcério, São Paulo, Brazil, Mar 21, 1955.

Matthew Broderick, 58, actor (*Godzilla, Inspector Gadget, Election*; stage: *The Producers*), born New York, NY, Mar 21, 1962.

Peter Brook, 95, theater director, born London, England, Mar 21, 1925.

Timothy Dalton, 74, actor ("Penny Dreadful," *Hot Fuzz, The Living Daylights, Centennial*), born Colwyn Bay, Wales, Mar 21, 1946.

Scott Eastwood, 34, actor (*The Longest Ride*), born Scott Reeves at Monterey, CA, Mar 21, 1986.

Kevin Federline, 42, dancer, born Fresno City, CA, Mar 21, 1978.

Sonequa Martin-Green, 35, actress ("Star-Trek: Discovery," "The Walking Dead"), born Russellville, AL, Mar 21, 1985.

Rosie O'Donnell, 58, actress (*A League of Their Own*), television personality ("The Rosie O'Donnell Show"), born Commack, NY, Mar 21, 1962.

Gary Oldman, 62, actor (Oscar for *Darkest Hour*; *Tinker Tailor Soldier Spy, Sid and Nancy*, Harry Potter films), director, born South London, England, Mar 21, 1958.

Adrian Peterson, 35, football player, born Palestine, TX, Mar 21, 1985.

Ronaldinho, 40, former soccer player, born Ronaldo de Assis Moreira at Porto Alegre, Brazil, Mar 21, 1980.

March 22 — Sunday

DAY 82   **284 REMAINING**

AS YOUNG AS YOU FEEL DAY. Mar 22. Now more than ever you are as young as you feel. So stop acting your chronological age and get out there and start feeling peppy! (©2006 by WH.) For info: Thomas & Ruth Roy, Wellcat Holidays, 2418 Long Ln, Lebanon, PA 17046. Phone: (717) 279-0184. E-mail: info@wellcat.com. Web: www.wellcat.com.

BRUSSELS TERRORIST ATTACK: ANNIVERSARY. Mar 22, 2016. At Brussels, Belgium, three terrorist bombs exploded at the city airport and one of its metro stations, killing 32 and injuring 300. The perpetrators (three of whom died in the attacks) were members of the Islamic State.

ENGLAND: MOTHERING SUNDAY. Mar 22. Fourth Sunday of Lent, formerly occasion for attending services at Mother Church, family gatherings and visits to parents. Now popularly known as Mother's Day and a time for visiting and taking gifts to mothers.

EQUAL RIGHTS AMENDMENT SENT TO STATES FOR RATIFICATION: ANNIVERSARY. Mar 22, 1972. The Senate passed the 27th Amendment, prohibiting discrimination on the basis of sex, sending it to the states for ratification. Hawaii led the way as the first state to ratify, and by the end of the year, 22 states had ratified it. On Oct 6, 1978, the deadline for ratification was extended to June 30, 1982, by Congress. The amendment still lacked three of the required 38 states for ratification. This was the first extension granted since Congress set seven years as the limit for ratification. The amendment failed to achieve ratification as the deadline came and passed and no additional states ratified the measure.

FIRST WOMEN'S COLLEGIATE BASKETBALL GAME: ANNIVERSARY. Mar 22, 1893. The first women's collegiate basketball game was played at Smith College at Northampton, MA. Senda Berenson, then Smith's director of physical education and "mother of women's basketball," supervised the game, in which Smith's sophomore team beat the freshman team 5–4.

INTERNATIONAL DAY OF THE SEAL. Mar 22. In 1982 Congress declared an International Day of the Seal to draw attention to the cruelty of seal hunts and the virtual inevitability of these creatures' extinction. Zoos and aquariums around the world observe this day with special programs and activities. The International Day of Action for the Seals (urging action against seal-pup slaughter) is Mar 15.

ISRA AL MI'RAJ: ASCENT OF THE PROPHET MUHAMMAD. Mar 22. Islamic calendar date: evening after Rajab 26, 1441 (some use the date of Rajab 27). Commemorates the journey of the Prophet Muhammad from Mecca to Jerusalem, his ascension into the Seven Heavens and his return on the same night. Muslims believe that on that night Muhammad prayed together with Abraham, Moses and Jesus in the area of the Al-Aqsa Mosque in Jerusalem. The rock from which he is believed to have ascended to heaven to speak with God is the one inside the Dome of the Rock. Different methods for "anticipating" the visibility of the new moon crescent at Mecca are used by different Muslim groups, so date can vary one to two days.

L'AMOUR, LOUIS: BIRTH ANNIVERSARY. Mar 22, 1908. Popular author Louis Dearborn LaMoore was born at Jamestown, ND. He began writing stories in the 1930s, initially selling them to pulp magazines. Despite an interruption by military service during WWII, L'Amour was quite a successful writer of adventure stories, Westerns and scripts for television and film. He eventually authored 116 Western novels that sold 20 million copies in 20 different languages. He was the first novelist to be awarded the Congressional Medal of Freedom (1983) and was also given the Presidential Medal of Freedom (1984). L'Amour died June 10, 1988, at Los Angeles, CA.

LASER PATENTED: 60th ANNIVERSARY. Mar 22, 1960. The first patent for a laser (light amplification by stimulated emission of radiation) granted to Arthur Schawlow and Charles Townes.

LUXEMBOURG: BRETZELSONNDEG. Mar 22. The fourth Sunday of Lent is an occasion for boys to give pretzel-shaped cakes to sweethearts, who may respond, on Easter Sunday, with a gift of a decorated egg or sweet.

MARDI GRAS INDIANS SUPER SUNDAY. Mar 22. New Orleans, LA. In a tradition dating back to the 19th century, the Crescent City's Mardi Gras Indian tribes don their colorful and weighty (up to 150 pounds) costumes for parades on the Sunday closest to St. Joseph's Day, Mar 19. (The St. Joseph's Day Indians come out only on the actual holiday.) This is the only time other than Mardi Gras that the tribes don their costumes. The 50 tribes engage in neighborhood processions and "strut their stuff." St. Joseph is patron saint of fathers and laborers, and his feast day is an important observance in New Orleans.

MARX, CHICO: BIRTH ANNIVERSARY. Mar 22, 1887. Known for his sly wisecracks and put-on Italian accent, Chico Marx—born Leonard Marx in New York City—was the oldest of the five Marx brothers. The brothers, in various combinations, performed first as a singing group and later as a comedy act featuring music. After honing their act on the vaudeville circuit, they mounted three successful shows on Broadway, two of which were made into movies, *The Cocoanuts* and *Animal Crackers*. After the team disbanded in 1941, Chico led his own big band before settling into semiretirement until his death at age 74, Oct 11, 1961, at Hollywood, CA.

NATIONAL GOOF-OFF DAY. Mar 22. First observed in 1976. A day of relaxation and a time to be oneself; a day for some good-humored silliness and fun. Everyone needs one special day each year to goof off. Annually, Mar 22. (Originated by Monica A. Dufour.)

NATIONAL PROTOCOL OFFICERS WEEK. Mar 22–28. 14th annual. Recognizes protocol officers—the trusted advisers who plan and orchestrate international VIP visits, meetings, ceremonies and special events for the military, government, academia and business world. This week acknowledges those who influence worldwide diplomacy by understanding and embracing customs such as forms of address, flag etiquette, titles and more. Annually, the last week in March. For info: The Protocol School of Washington, PO Box 676, Columbia, SC 29202. Phone: (877) 766-3757. E-mail: info@psow.edu. Web: www.psow.edu.

NEUHARTH, AL: BIRTH ANNIVERSARY. Mar 22, 1924. Flamboyant, innovative media executive who transformed the American media landscape first as chief executive of the Gannett Company and then as the founder of *USA Today*. Neuharth grew Gannett from a regional news group into the nation's largest newspaper chain. *USA Today*, founded in 1982 and the only major daily established in the US after WWII, brought color, lifestyle coverage, shorter articles and other innovations to media. *USA Today* was embraced by the public and forced other journals to make changes. Born at Eureka, SD, Al Neuharth died Apr 19, 2013, at Cocoa Beach, FL.

PUERTO RICO: EMANCIPATION DAY. Mar 22. Holiday commemorates the end of slavery on Mar 22, 1873.

TUSKEGEE AIRMEN ACTIVATED: ANNIVERSARY. Mar 22, 1941. This pioneering and highly decorated WWII African-American aviator unit gained their name during training at the US Army airfield near Tuskegee, AL, and at the Tuskegee Institute. They were activated as the 99th Pursuit Squadron and later formed the 332nd Fighter Group (with the 100th, 301st and 302nd squadrons). A total of 992 black pilots emerged from training to fly P-39, P-40, P-47 and P-51 aircraft in more than 15,000 sorties in North Africa, Sicily and Europe. On escort missions, they were the only unit that never lost a US bomber. They shot down 111 enemy planes and destroyed 273 planes on the ground. Lieutenant Colonel Benjamin

March 2020	S	M	T	W	T	F	S
	1	2	3	4	5	6	7
	8	9	10	11	12	13	14
	15	16	17	18	19	20	21
	22	23	24	25	26	27	28
	29	30	31				

O. Davis, Jr—later the US Air Force's first black general—was their commander. When President Harry Truman integrated the US military, the all-black group was deactivated. See also: "Davis, Benjamin O., Jr: Birth Anniversary" (Dec 18).

UNITED NATIONS: WORLD WATER DAY. Mar 22. The General Assembly declared this observance (Res 47/193) to promote public awareness of how water resource development contributes to economic productivity and social well-being. Annually, on Mar 22.

🎂 BIRTHDAYS TODAY

George Benson, 77, singer, guitarist, born Pittsburgh, PA, Mar 22, 1943.

Robert Quinlan (Bob) Costas, 68, sportscaster, born New York, NY, Mar 22, 1952.

Orrin Grant Hatch, 86, former US senator (R, Utah), born Pittsburgh, PA, Mar 22, 1934.

Keegan-Michael Key, 49, actor, comedian (*Keanu, Don't Think Twice*, "Key & Peele"), born Detroit, MI, Mar 22, 1971.

Andrew Lloyd Webber, 72, composer (*Cats, The Phantom of the Opera*), born London, England, Mar 22, 1948.

Martha McSally, 54, US Senator (R, Arizona), born Warwick, RI, Mar 22, 1966.

Matthew Modine, 61, actor ("Stranger Things," *Full Metal Jacket*, "And the Band Played On"), born Loma Linda, CA, Mar 22, 1959.

James Patterson, 73, author (*Kiss the Girls, Along Came a Spider*), born Newburgh, NY, Mar 22, 1947.

Pat Robertson, 90, television evangelist, born Lexington, VA, Mar 22, 1930.

William Shatner, 89, actor ("Star Trek," "Boston Legal"), author (*Tek* novels), born Montreal, QC, Canada, Mar 22, 1931.

Stephen Sondheim, 90, Tony Award–winning composer and lyricist (*Follies, A Little Night Music, Into the Woods, Sunday in the Park with George*), born New York, NY, Mar 22, 1930.

Elvis Stojko, 48, former figure skater, born Newmarket, ON, Canada, Mar 22, 1972.

M. Emmet Walsh, 85, actor (*Serpico, Blood Simple, Raising Arizona*), born Ogdensburg, NY, Mar 22, 1935.

Justin James (J.J.) Watt, 31, football player, born Waukesha, WI, Mar 22, 1989.

Reese Witherspoon, 44, actress (Oscar for *Walk the Line*; "Big Little Lies," *Wild, Legally Blonde*), born Nashville, TN, Mar 22, 1976.

Constance Wu, 38, actress (*Crazy Rich Asians*, "Fresh off the Boat"), born Richmond, VA, Mar 22, 1982.

March 23 — Monday

DAY 83 **283 REMAINING**

"BEAT THE CLOCK" TV PREMIERE: 70th ANNIVERSARY. Mar 23, 1950. On this game show from the team of Mark Goodson and Bill Todman, couples performed stunts within a specified time, with the winners being given a chance to try a special stunt. Special stunts were very difficult, and the same one was attempted every week until a couple got it right. In 1952, James Dean got his first TV job testing stunts and warming up the audience. Bud Collyer was the host, assisted by Roxanne (real name Dolores Rosedale). A 1969 syndicated version hosted by Jack Narz and then by Gene Wood had celebrities who helped the contestants. A 1979 revival was hosted by Monty Hall.

"BIG BERTHA" PARIS GUN: ANNIVERSARY. Mar 23, 1918. Germany initiated use of a terrifying new weapon—the Paris Gun—so called because it was first used against that city. The great gun, with a 25-foot carriage, was first used in combat when it was fired from

a wooded location near Laon on Mar 23, 1918. It took 176 seconds for a shell to reach the city from a distance of 75 miles. On that first day, 15 shots killed 16 individuals. Ridiculing the designers and manufacturers of the weapon, Parisians nicknamed it "Big Bertha" after the wife of the head of the munitions corporation. On Good Friday, Mar 29, a shell from the armament struck the church of Saint Gervais, which was crowded with worshippers. The casualty toll was 88 dead and 68 injured.

COLFAX, SCHUYLER: BIRTH ANNIVERSARY. Mar 23, 1823. 17th vice president of the US (1869–73). Born at New York, NY. Died Jan 13, 1885, at Mankato, MN.

CRAWFORD, JOAN: BIRTH ANNIVERSARY. Mar 23, 1904 (some sources say 1905 or 1908). Actress, born Lucille Fay LeSueur at San Antonio, TX. Crawford became a Hollywood star with her performance in *Our Dancing Daughters*. She won an Oscar in 1945 for her role in *Mildred Pierce*. Events of Crawford's life are chronicled in *Mommie Dearest*. Other films include *The Women, What Ever Happened to Baby Jane?* and *Twelve Miles Out*. She died at New York, NY, May 10, 1977.

KUROSAWA, AKIRA: BIRTH ANNIVERSARY. Mar 23, 1910. Acclaimed filmmaker (*Rashomon, The Seven Samurai, Kagemusha, Ran*), born at Tokyo, Japan. The ambassador of Japanese cinema to the West, Kurosawa is considered one of the greatest film directors of all time. Died at Tokyo, Sept 6, 1998.

LIBERTY DAY: ANNIVERSARY. Mar 23, 1775. Anniversary of Patrick Henry's speech for arming the Virginia militia at St. John's Church, Richmond, VA. "I know not what course others may take, but as for me, give me liberty or give me death."

NATIONAL PUPPY DAY. Mar 23. To celebrate puppies for all the joy they bring to our lives. This day also seeks to educate the public about the horrors of puppy mills and to encourage adoption: adopt—don't shop. For info: Colleen Paige. Web: www.nationalpuppyday.com.

NATIONAL TAMALE DAY. Mar 23. This spring day is a day to enjoy flavorful and unique tamales—which date back more than 5,000 years to the Aztecs and Mayans. Tamales can be enjoyed any time of the year, so order a tamale at your favorite local restaurant or have friends over to celebrate with a homemade tamale dinner. Visit the website for recipes, information on tamale festivals and more. Annually, Mar 23. For info: Richard Lambert, Chairman, National Tamale Day, 6605 SE 69th Ave, Portland, OR 97206. Web: www.nationaltamaleday.com.

NEAR MISS DAY. Mar 23, 1989. A mountain-sized asteroid passed within 500,000 miles of Earth, a very close call according to NASA. Impact would have equaled the strength of 40,000 hydrogen bombs, created a crater the size of the District of Columbia and devastated everything for 100 miles in all directions.

NEW ZEALAND: OTAGO AND SOUTHLAND PROVINCIAL ANNIVERSARY. Mar 23. In addition to the statutory public holidays of New Zealand, there is in each provincial district a holiday for the provincial anniversary. This day is observed in Otago and Southland.

"OK" FIRST APPEARANCE IN PRINT: ANNIVERSARY. Mar 23, 1839. *The Boston Morning Post* printed the first known "ok"

on this day in 1839. It derived from a jovial misspelling of "all correct": "oll korrect." Etymologist Allen Read doggedly tracked down the word's origin in the 1960s. "OK" is now used in most languages.

PAKISTAN: REPUBLIC DAY. Mar 23, 1940. National holiday. In 1940 the All-India-Muslim League adopted a resolution calling for a Muslim homeland. On the same day in 1956 Pakistan declared itself a republic.

RALLY FOR DECENCY: ANNIVERSARY. Mar 23, 1969. Anita Bryant, Jackie Gleason and Kate Smith rallied with 30,000 others in Miami on this day in reaction to Jim Morrison's arrest for indecent exposure.

SPACE MILESTONE: *MIR* ABANDONED (USSR). Mar 23, 2001. The 140-ton *Mir* space station, launched in 1986, was brought down into the South Pacific near Fiji, about 1,800 miles east of New Zealand, just before 1 AM, EST. Two-thirds of the station burned up during its controlled descent. *Mir*'s core component had been aloft for more than 15 years and orbited Earth 86,330 times. Nearly 100 people, seven of them American, had spent some time on *Mir*. See also: "Space Milestone: *Mir* Space Station (USSR)" (Feb 20).

UNITED NATIONS: WORLD METEOROLOGICAL DAY. Mar 23. An international day observed by meteorological services throughout the world and by the organizations of the UN system. Annually, Mar 23. For info: United Nations, Dept of Public Info, New York, NY 10017. Web: www.un.org.

🎂 BIRTHDAYS TODAY

Louie Anderson, 67, comedian, actor ("Life with Louie"), born Minneapolis, MN, Mar 23, 1953.

Mo Farah, 37, Olympic runner, born Mogadishu, Somalia, Mar 23, 1983.

Richard Grieco, 55, actor (*Ultimate Deception, Blackheart*), born Watertown, NY, Mar 23, 1965.

Gordon Hayward, 30, basketball player, born Indianapolis, IN, Mar 23, 1990.

Perez Hilton, 42, gossip columnist, blogger, born Mario Lavandeira at Miami, FL, Mar 23, 1978.

Kyrie Irving, 28, basketball player, born Melbourne, Australia, Mar 23, 1992.

Chaka Khan, 67, singer, born Yvette Marie Stevens at Chicago, IL, Mar 23, 1953.

Jason Kidd, 47, former basketball player, born San Francisco, CA, Mar 23, 1973.

Amanda Plummer, 63, actress (Tony for *Agnes of God*; *The Fisher King*), born New York, NY, Mar 23, 1957.

March 2020	S	M	T	W	T	F	S
	1	2	3	4	5	6	7
	8	9	10	11	12	13	14
	15	16	17	18	19	20	21
	22	23	24	25	26	27	28
	29	30	31				

Keri Russell, 44, actress ("The Americans," "Felicity," *Waitress, Mission: Impossible III*), born Fountain Valley, CA, Mar 23, 1976.

Rex Tillerson, 68, former US secretary of state (Trump administration), former oil executive (ExxonMobil), born Wichita Falls, TX, Mar 23, 1952.

March 24 — Tuesday

DAY 84   **282 REMAINING**

AMERICAN DIABETES ASSOCIATION ALERT DAY. Mar 24. A one-day "wake-up call" to raise awareness about the seriousness of diabetes and its risk factors. The centerpiece of the alert is the diabetes risk test, which is distributed and promoted through national and local media. Annually, the fourth Tuesday in March. For info: American Diabetes Assn. Phone: (800) DIABETES (800-342-2383). Web: www.diabetes.org.

ARGENTINA: NATIONAL DAY OF MEMORY FOR TRUTH AND JUSTICE. Mar 24. Public holiday since 2002 commemorating victims of the military coup d'état of 1976.

BARBERA, JOE: BIRTH ANNIVERSARY. Mar 24, 1911. Joseph Roland Barbera, born at New York, NY, was one-half of one of the world's most prolific and beloved animation teams: Hanna-Barbera. Working with Bill Hanna, Barbera created the Tom and Jerry theatrical shorts for MGM that garnered seven Oscars. Moving to television, Hanna-Barbera produced some 100 cartoon series, including the groundbreaking sitcom-style shows "The Flintstones" and "The Jetsons." Barbera continued working in animation almost to his death, creating a Tom and Jerry short in 2005. He died at Los Angeles, CA, on Dec 18, 2006.

***EXXON VALDEZ* OIL SPILL: ANNIVERSARY.** Mar 24, 1989. The tanker *Exxon Valdez* ran aground at Prince William Sound, AK, leaking 11 million gallons of oil into one of nature's richest habitats.

FO, DARIO: BIRTH ANNIVERSARY. Mar 24, 1926. Playwright, director, performer, born in Sangiano, Italy. Best remembered for *Accidental Death of an Anarchist* (1970), Fo and his wife and collaborator, Franca Rame, founded several theater companies, all vehicles for their "unofficial leftism," which attacked capitalism, church authority and political corruption. Fo created absurd satires, often deploying commedia dell'arte types and farcical events, which were presented on national television (where he was banned) and in theaters, community centers and factories. Italy's most translated author, Fo was arrested 47 times and endured death threats, and Rame was brutally abducted in 1974. Accepting the 1997 Nobel Prize in Literature, he observed, "Laughter does not please the mighty." Fo died Oct 13, 2016, in Milan, Italy.

HEIGHT, DOROTHY: BIRTH ANNIVERSARY. Mar 24, 1912. African-American civil rights leader and champion of education and women's causes, born at Richmond, VA. She was an active member of the National Council of Negro Women, serving as its president for 40 years, and was a consultant to several governmental offices and presidential administrations on education and civil rights issues. Height died at Washington, DC, Apr 20, 2010.

HOUDINI, HARRY: BIRTH ANNIVERSARY. Mar 24, 1874. Magician and escape artist. Born Erik Weisz at Budapest, Hungary, died at Detroit, MI, Oct 31, 1926. Lecturer, athlete, author, expert on the history of magic, exposer of fraudulent mediums and motion picture actor. He was best known for his ability to escape from locked restraints (handcuffs, straitjackets, coffins, boxes and milk cans). The anniversary of his death (Halloween) has been the occasion for meetings of magicians and attempts at communication by mediums.

"LETTER FROM AMERICA" RADIO PREMIERE: ANNIVERSARY. Mar 24, 1946. Acclaimed news correspondent and broadcaster Alistair Cooke began his weekly observations on American life on this date, with a story about British war brides traveling to America on the *Queen Mary*. Broadcast from Radio 4 and the BBC World Service, "Letter from America" would become the world's longest continuously running radio talk program. Cooke created 2,869 "letters." His last broadcast was Feb 20, 2004, and the BBC announced his retirement on Mar 2, 2004.

MOON PHASE: NEW MOON. Mar 24. Moon enters New Moon phase at 5:28 AM, EDT.

MORRIS, WILLIAM: BIRTH ANNIVERSARY. Mar 24, 1834. English poet, artist and social reformer. Born at Walthamstow, England; died at Hammersmith, London, Oct 3, 1896.

NATIONAL AGRICULTURE DAY. Mar 24 (tentative). A day when producers, agricultural associations, corporations, universities, government agencies and countless others across the country gather to recognize and celebrate the abundance provided by American agriculture. For info: Agriculture Council of America. E-mail: info@agday.org. Web: www.agday.org.

PEMPER, MIETEK: 100th BIRTH ANNIVERSARY. Mar 24, 1920. In his position as personal typist to Amon Goeth, commandant of the Plaszow forced labor camp in Poland, Pemper learned that all labor camp inmates not engaged in work on the war effort would be liquidated. He persuaded industrialist Oskar Schindler to convert his enamel works to the production of grenade parts. He then falsified records to suggest that certain Plaszow inmates had essential manufacturing skills and compiled lists of inmates to be transferred to Schindler's factory. These, along with names compiled by Itzhak Stern, later became known as "Schindler's list." The scheme saved the lives of 1,200 people. Born at Krakow, Poland, Pemper died at Augsburg, Germany, on June 7, 2011. See also: "Stern, Itzhak: Birth Anniversary" (Jan 25).

PHILIPPINE INDEPENDENCE: ANNIVERSARY. Mar 24, 1934. President Franklin Roosevelt signed a bill granting independence to the Philippines. The bill, which took effect July 4, 1946, brought to a close almost half a century of US control of the islands.

POWELL, JOHN WESLEY: BIRTH ANNIVERSARY. Mar 24, 1834. American geologist, explorer, ethnologist. He is best known for his explorations of the Grand Canyon by boat on the Colorado River. Born at Mount Morris, NY, he died at Haven, ME, Sept 23, 1902.

PRESLEY INDUCTED INTO THE ARMY: ANNIVERSARY. Mar 24, 1958. Teenagers across the US mourned as rock idol Elvis Presley was inducted into the US Army on this date at Memphis, TN. Presley completed basic training and then was posted overseas to Germany. He left active service on Mar 5, 1960.

RHODE ISLAND VOTERS REJECT CONSTITUTION: ANNIVERSARY. Mar 24, 1788. In a popular referendum, Rhode Island rejected the new Constitution by a vote of 2,708 to 237. The state later ratified the Constitution (May 29, 1790) and the Bill of Rights (June 7, 1790).

SAINT GABRIEL: FEAST DAY. Mar 24. Saint Gabriel the Archangel, patron saint of postal, telephone and telegraph workers.

STRATTON, DOROTHY CONSTANCE: BIRTH ANNIVERSARY. Mar 24, 1899. Dorothy Constance Stratton, born at Brookfield, MO, was instrumental during WWII in organizing the SPARS, the women's branch of the US Coast Guard (authorized Nov 23, 1942). Under Lieutenant Commander Stratton's command, some 10,000 women were trained for supportive noncombat roles in the Coast Guard. SPARS was dissolved in 1946 after the war ended. Stratton worked with many women's organizations, including the Girl Scouts as national executive director in the '50s. Stratton died at age 107 on Sept 17, 2006, at West Lafayette, IN.

WESTON, EDWARD: BIRTH ANNIVERSARY. Mar 24, 1886. One of the greatest photographers of the 20th century, Weston was born at Highland Park, IL. Weston's work gradually changed from a self-described pictorial style to one that was more realistic yet abstract. He created a great body of work that included nudes, barren landscapes (especially in California and Mexico) and natural still lifes. Weston died on Jan 1, 1958, at Carmel, CA.

WORLD TUBERCULOSIS DAY. Mar 24. Designed to promote awareness about the serious health consequences of tuberculosis throughout the world. Observed on the anniversary of Dr. Robert Koch's 1882 announcement that he had discovered the bacillus that causes TB. Sponsored by the World Health Organization, the International Union Against Tuberculosis and Lung Disease and other international health agencies. Annually, Mar 24. For info: Stop TB Partnership. Web: www.stoptb.org.

ZARAGOZA, IGNACIO SEGUÍN: BIRTH ANNIVERSARY. Mar 24, 1829. Born at Bahía del Espíritu Santo, Coahuila y Texas, Mexico (now Goliad, TX), General Ignacio Zaragoza was the hero of the daylong Battle of Puebla on May 5, 1862. He led the Mexican army to victory over invading French forces under the command of General Charles Latrille Lorencez. The French lost about 500–1,000 personnel (estimates have varied); the Mexican army lost fewer than 100. Zaragoza, acclaimed as a hero, tragically succumbed to typhoid fever at Puebla on Sept 8. A grateful President Benito Juarez honored Zaragoza with a state funeral and on Sept 11 declared Cinco de Mayo a national holiday that has been celebrated since.

🎂 BIRTHDAYS TODAY

Mary Berry, 85, cookbook author, television personality ("The Great British Baking Show"), born Bath, England, Mar 24, 1935.

Chris Bosh, 36, basketball player, born Dallas, TX, Mar 24, 1984.

Lara Flynn Boyle, 50, actress ("Twin Peaks," "The Practice," *Dead Poets Society*), born Davenport, IA, Mar 24, 1970.

Mike Braun, 66, US Senator (R, Indiana), born Jasper, IN, Mar 24, 1954.

Jessica Chastain, 43, actress (*Molly's Game, Zero Dark Thirty, The Help, The Tree of Life*), born Sacramento, CA, Mar 24, 1977.

Lawrence Ferlinghetti, 101, Beat poet, author (*Coney Island of the Mind*), born Yonkers, NY, Mar 24, 1919.

Byron Janis, 92, pianist, born Byron Yanks at McKeesport, PA, Mar 24, 1928.

Star Jones, 58, television personality, born Badin, NC, Mar 24, 1962.

Bob Mackie, 80, costume and fashion designer, born Monterey Park, CA, Mar 24, 1940.

Peyton Manning, 44, former football player, born New Orleans, LA, Mar 24, 1976.

Jim Parsons, 47, actor (Emmy for "The Big Bang Theory"; *The Normal Heart*), born Houston, TX, Mar 24, 1973.

Donna Pescow, 66, actress (*Saturday Night Fever*, "Angie"), born Brooklyn, NY, Mar 24, 1954.

Annabella Sciorra, 56, actress (*The Hand That Rocks the Cradle, Jungle Fever*), born Wethersfield, CT, Mar 24, 1964.

March 25 — Wednesday

DAY 85　　　　　　　　　　**281 REMAINING**

BARTOK, BELA: BIRTH ANNIVERSARY. Mar 25, 1881. Hungarian composer, born at Nagyszentmiklos (now in Romania). Died at New York, NY, Sept 26, 1945.

BED-IN FOR PEACE: ANNIVERSARY. Mar 25–31, 1969. After their Mar 20 wedding, John Lennon (of The Beatles) and Yoko Ono celebrated their honeymoon with a "happening": a bed-in for peace at their hotel room. In Room 902 of the Hilton Hotel in Amsterdam, pajama-clad Lennon and Ono received the world's print, radio and TV media while sitting up in bed, singing and talking for seven days encouraging the world to choose peace. The couple held another bed-in May 26–June 2 in Montreal, during which "Give Peace a Chance" was recorded.

BORGLUM, GUTZON: BIRTH ANNIVERSARY. Mar 25, 1867. American sculptor who created the huge sculpture of four American presidents (Washington, Jefferson, Lincoln and Theodore Roosevelt) at Mount Rushmore National Memorial in the Black Hills of South Dakota. Born John Gutzon de la Mothe Borglum at Bear Lake, ID, the son of Mormon pioneers, he worked the last 14 years of his life on the Mount Rushmore sculpture. He died at Chicago, IL, Mar 6, 1941.

BORLAUG, NORMAN: BIRTH ANNIVERSARY. Mar 25, 1914. Agricultural scientist, plant pathologist and geneticist, born at Saude, IA. Won 1970 Nobel Prize for Peace for the "Green Revolution" initiated in Mexico, Pakistan and India, where he engineered high-yield, disease-resistant, climate-specific grain hybrids that could theoretically end world hunger. Borlaug established the annual World Food Prize and received the Presidential Medal of Freedom. Died Sept 12, 2009, at Dallas, TX.

"CAGNEY & LACEY" TV PREMIERE: ANNIVERSARY. Mar 25, 1982. "Cagney & Lacey" broke new ground as the first TV crime show in which the central characters were both female. The series was based on a made-for-TV movie that aired Oct 8, 1981, starring Loretta Swit and Tyne Daly. When the show became a weekly series, Meg Foster played Swit's character, Chris Cagney, but after one season she was replaced by Sharon Gless. Daly and Gless together won six Emmys for their roles. The last telecast aired on Aug 25, 1988.

CHURCHILL ENTERS GERMANY: 75th ANNIVERSARY. Mar 25, 1945. Winston Churchill briefly crossed to the eastern bank of the Rhine, the first British leader to enter Germany since Chamberlain signed the Munich Pact in September 1938. Churchill later wrote to Montgomery, "The Rhine and all its fortress lines lie behind the 21st Group of Armies. A beaten army, not long ago Master of Europe, retreats before its pursuers."

COSELL, HOWARD: BIRTH ANNIVERSARY. Mar 25, 1918. Howard Cosell, broadcaster, born at New York, NY. After earning a law degree, Cosell began his broadcasting career as the host of "Howard Cosell Speaking of Sports." He achieved national prominence and a great deal of notoriety for his support of Muhammad Ali's stand against the Vietnam War and then as cohost of ABC's "Monday Night Football." Died at New York, Apr 23, 1995.

COXEY'S ARMY MARCH ON WASHINGTON: ANNIVERSARY. Mar 25, 1894. Anniversary of a march on the nation's Capitol. Jacob S. Coxey, businessman, economic reformer, advocate of interest-free government bonds, left Massillon, OH, on foot with an "army" of about 100 followers. Arrived at Washington, DC, May 1. His hope to influence Congress was thwarted when he and part of his army were arrested for trespassing on government property. Fifty years later he spoke from the Capitol steps, reiterating his belief in non-interest-bearing government bonds.

FEAST OF THE ANNUNCIATION. Mar 25. Celebrated in the Roman Catholic Church in commemoration of the message of the Angel Gabriel to Mary that she was to be the mother of Christ.

FORD, EILEEN: BIRTH ANNIVERSARY. Mar 25, 1922. Founder of the prestigious and influential Ford Modeling Agency, Eileen Ford was born at New York, NY. Her agency's business model set new standards for industry practices and launched the careers of many supermodels, including Christie Brinkley and Brooke Shields; the latter signed with Ford at age eight after the agency expanded to include children and male models. Ford's preference for tall, slender, blond, light-eyed, long-necked models "determined the American standard of beauty for a generation." Recipient of Woman of the Year in Advertising Award in 1983, Ford died July 9, 2014, at Morristown, NJ.

		S	M	T	W	T	F	S
March								1
		1	2	3	4	5	6	7
March		8	9	10	11	12	13	14
2020		15	16	17	18	19	20	21
		22	23	24	25	26	27	28
		29	30	31				

GREECE: INDEPENDENCE DAY. Mar 25. National holiday. Celebrates the beginning of the Greek revolt for independence from the Ottoman Empire, Mar 25, 1821 (OS). Greece attained independence in 1829.

★GREEK INDEPENDENCE DAY: A NATIONAL DAY OF CELEBRATION OF GREEK AND AMERICAN DEMOCRACY. Mar 25. "On Greek Independence Day, we honor the deep connections between our two nations and celebrate the democratic ideals at the heart of our shared history." Annually, Mar 25.

LEAN, SIR DAVID: BIRTH ANNIVERSARY. Mar 25, 1908. Film director Sir David Lean was born at London, England. He directed 16 films and won two Best Director Academy Awards. His films include *The Bridge on the River Kwai* (1957), *Lawrence of Arabia* (1962) and *Dr. Zhivago* (1965). He died Apr 16, 1991, at London.

LITTLE RED WAGON DAY. Mar 25. This day celebrates the power of imagination on wheels as children of all ages take flight with their little red wagons. Annually, the last Wednesday in March. For info: Radio Flyer. Web: www.radioflyer.com/little-red-wagon-day.

MANATEE APPRECIATION DAY. Mar 25. The manatee, or sea cow, is an herbivorous marine mammal (*Trichechus* sp.) only occurring in the Gulf of Mexico/Caribbean Sea, the Amazon River and West Africa. This is a day to appreciate these "gentle giants" and raise awareness of efforts to save this threatened species. Observed since 2013. Annually, the last Wednesday in March.

MARYLAND DAY. Mar 25. Commemorates arrival of Lord Baltimore's first settlers at Maryland in 1634.

NATIONAL MEDAL OF HONOR DAY. Mar 25. Annual day honoring the heroic recipients of the Medal of Honor, the highest award that can be given by the president, in the name of Congress, to members of the armed forces who have distinguished themselves beyond the call of duty. Created by congressional resolution (PL 101–564) in 1991.

NATO FORCES ATTACK YUGOSLAVIA: ANNIVERSARY. Mar 25, 1999. After many weeks of unsuccessful negotiations with Serb leader Slobodan Milosevic over the treatment of ethnic Albanians by Serb forces in the Kosovo Province of Yugoslavia, NATO forces began bombing Serbia and Kosovo. In response, the Serb army forced hundreds of thousands of ethnic Albanians to flee Kosovo for neighboring Albania, Macedonia and Montenegro. On June 10, 1999, NATO and Yugoslav officials signed an agreement providing for withdrawal of Serb troops from Kosovo, the end of Allied air strikes and the return of Kosovo refugees.

NCAA DIVISION I MEN'S SWIMMING AND DIVING CHAMPIONSHIPS. Mar 25–28. IU Natatorium, Indianapolis, IN. For info: NCAA, 700 W Washington St, PO Box 6222, Indianapolis, IN 46206-6222. Phone: (317) 917-6222. Fax: (317) 917-6888. Web: www.ncaa.org.

OLD NEW YEAR'S DAY. Mar 25. In Great Britain and its North American colonies this was the beginning of the new year up through 1751, when with the adoption of the Gregorian calendar the beginning of the year was changed to Jan 1.

PECAN DAY. Mar 25, 1775. Anniversary of the planting by George Washington of pecan trees (some of which still survive) at Mount Vernon, VA. The trees were a gift to Washington from Thomas Jefferson, who had planted a few pecan trees from the southern US at Monticello, VA. The pecan, native to southern North America, is sometimes called "America's own nut." First cultivated by Native Americans, it has been transplanted to other continents but has failed to achieve wide use or popularity outside the US.

ROME EXECUTIONS: ANNIVERSARY. Mar 25, 1944. Nazis occupying Rome during WWII executed 300 Italian priests, Jews and women, including two 14-year-old boys. The executions were in retaliation for the deaths of 33 German soldiers who had been killed by Italian partisans. Hitler demanded 50 Italian lives for each German life that had been taken, but German officials in Italy lowered the number.

SLAVE TRADE ABOLISHED BY ENGLAND: ANNIVERSARY. Mar 25, 1807. The English parliament abolished the slave trade after a long campaign against it.

TENNESSEE WILLIAMS/NEW ORLEANS LITERARY FESTIVAL. Mar 25–29. French Quarter, New Orleans, LA. 34th annual. Founded in 1986, the festival celebrates the region's rich cultural heritage as well as the special bond between Williams (born Mar 26, 1911) and the adopted city he called his "spiritual home." Events include theater, food and music events; celebrity interviews; a scholars' conference; a poetry slam, writing marathon and breakfast book club; French Quarter literary walking tours; a book fair; short fiction, poetry and one-act play competitions; and special evening events and parties. The riotous closing ceremony is the "Stanley and Stella Shouting Contest," a playful homage to the bellowing mates in *A Streetcar Named Desire.* Annually, the last weekend of March (subject to change). Est attendance: 10,000. For info: Tennessee Williams / New Orleans Literary Festival, 938 Lafayette St, Ste 514, New Orleans, LA 70113. Phone: (504) 581-1144. E-mail: info@tennesseewilliams. net. Web: www.tennesseewilliams.net.

TOLKIEN READING DAY. Mar 25. A day dedicated to reading the works of J.R.R. Tolkien, including *The Hobbit* and *The Lord of the Rings.* Celebrated on the fictional anniversary of the downfall of Sauron, the shape-shifting antagonist in the *Rings.* The event exists to encourage the use of Tolkien's works in education and to get schoolteachers and library staff to participate in reading Tolkien to their classes and in their libraries. Public readings are performed and online communities have discussions and debates. For info: The Tolkien Society. Web: www.tolkiensociety.org.

TOSCANINI, ARTURO: BIRTH ANNIVERSARY. Mar 25, 1867. Italian opera and symphony conductor Arturo Toscanini was born at Parma, Italy. He had an all-encompassing repertoire but was famous primarily for the operas of Verdi and the symphonies of Beethoven. Toscanini died at New York City, Jan 16, 1957.

TRIANGLE SHIRTWAIST FIRE: ANNIVERSARY. Mar 25, 1911. At about 4:45 PM, fire broke out at the Triangle Shirtwaist Company at New York, NY, minutes before the seamstresses were to go home. Some workers were fatally burned while others leaped to their deaths from the windows of the 10-story building. The fire lasted only 18 minutes but left 146 workers dead, most of them young immigrant women. Some of the deaths were a direct result of workers being trapped on the ninth floor by a locked door. Labor law forbade locking factory doors while employees were at work, and owners of the company were indicted on charges of first- and second-degree manslaughter. The tragic fire became a turning point in labor history, bringing about reforms in health and safety laws.

UNITED NATIONS: INTERNATIONAL DAY OF REMEMBRANCE FOR THE VICTIMS OF SLAVERY AND THE TRANSATLANTIC SLAVE TRADE. Mar 25. Recognizing how little is known about the 400-year-long transatlantic slave trade and its lasting consequences, felt throughout the world, the General Assembly has designated Mar 25 as an annual day of remembrance (Res 62/122, Dec 17, 2007). For info: United Nations, Dept of Public Info, New York, NY, 10017. Web: www.un.org.

UNITED NATIONS: INTERNATIONAL DAY OF SOLIDARITY WITH DETAINED AND MISSING STAFF MEMBERS. Mar 25. A day to mobilize action, demand justice and strengthen our resolve to protect UN staff and peacekeepers, as well as our colleagues in the nongovernmental community and the press. Observed on the anniversary of the 1985 abduction by armed men of Alec Collett, a former journalist who was working for the United Nations Relief and Works Agency for Palestine Refugees in the Near East (UNRWA). His body was finally found in Lebanon's Bekaa Valley in 2009. Annually, Mar 25. For info: United Nations, Dept of Public Info, New York, NY 10017. Web: www.un.org.

WHOLE GRAIN SAMPLING DAY. Mar 25. Whole grains are certainly healthy—but some people may not realize how delicious they can be. On Whole Grain Sampling Day, you'll find opportunities to try delicious whole grains everywhere you go. Supermarkets, restaurants and schools will be offering samples of whole grains, and you'll find special deals on social media. It's all coordinated by the nonprofit Oldways and its Whole Grains Council, with creative and original events across the US. Annually, the last Wednesday in March. For info: Oldways Whole Grains Council, 266 Beacon St, Boston, MA 02116. Phone: (617) 421-5500. E-mail: media@oldwayspt.org. Web: www.wholegrainscouncil.org.

🎂 BIRTHDAYS TODAY

Bonnie Bedelia, 72, actress ("Parenthood," "The Division," *Die Hard*), born New York, NY, Mar 25, 1948.

Anita Bryant, 80, singer ("The George Gobel Show"), former Miss America, born Barnsdall, OK, Mar 25, 1940.

Marcia Cross, 58, actress ("Melrose Place," "Everwood," "Desperate Housewives"), born Marlborough, MA, Mar 25, 1962.

Paul Michael Glaser, 77, actor ("Starsky and Hutch"), director (*Butterflies Are Free*), born Cambridge, MA, Mar 25, 1943.

Tom Glavine, 54, Hall of Fame baseball player, born Concord, MA, Mar 25, 1966.

Cammi Granato, 49, former hockey player, born Maywood, IL, Mar 25, 1971.

Mary Gross, 67, comedienne, actress ("Saturday Night Live"), born Chicago, IL, Mar 25, 1953.

Elton John, 73, musician, singer, songwriter, born Reginald Kenneth Dwight at Pinner, England, Mar 25, 1947.

Avery Johnson, 55, basketball coach and former player, born New Orleans, LA, Mar 25, 1965.

Ryan Lewis, 32, music producer, DJ, musician (Macklemore & Ryan Lewis), born Puyallup, WA, Mar 25, 1988.

James Lovell, 92, former astronaut, born Cleveland, OH, Mar 25, 1928.

Katharine McPhee, 36, actress ("Scorpion," "Smash"), singer, television personality ("American Idol"), born Los Angeles, CA, Mar 25, 1984.

Lee Pace, 41, actor (*Guardians of the Galaxy, The Hobbit,* "Pushing Daisies," "Wonderfalls"), born Chickasha, OK, Mar 25, 1979.

Sarah Jessica Parker, 55, actress (*Sex and the City, Honeymoon in Vegas,* "Divorce," "Sex and the City"), born Nelsonville, OH, Mar 25, 1965.

Danica Patrick, 38, race car driver, born Beloit, WI, Mar 25, 1982.

Gloria Steinem, 85, feminist (original publisher of *Ms* magazine), journalist, author, born Toledo, OH, Mar 25, 1935.

John Stockwell, 59, actor, writer, director (*Top Gun, Under Cover*), born Galveston, TX, Mar 25, 1961.

Sheryl Swoopes, 49, basketball coach and former player, US Olympic basketball team member (1996, 2000, 2004), born Brownfield, TX, Mar 25, 1971.

March 26 — Thursday

DAY 86   **280 REMAINING**

BANGLADESH: INDEPENDENCE DAY. Mar 26. Commemorates East Pakistan's independence in 1971 as the state of Bangladesh. Celebrated with parades, youth festivals and symposia.

BOWDITCH, NATHANIEL: BIRTH ANNIVERSARY. Mar 26, 1773. American mathematician and astronomer, author of the *New American Practical Navigator*. Born at Salem, MA, he died at Boston, MA, Mar 16, 1838.

CAMP DAVID ACCORD SIGNED: ANNIVERSARY. Mar 26, 1979. Israeli prime minister Menachem Begin and Egyptian president Anwar Sadat signed the Camp David peace treaty, ending 30 years of war between their two countries. The agreement was fostered by President Jimmy Carter.

DELANO, JANE: BIRTH ANNIVERSARY. Mar 26, 1862. Jane Arminda Delano, dedicated American nurse and teacher, superintendent of the US Army Nurse Corps, chair of the American Red Cross Nursing Service and recipient (posthumously) of the Distinguished Service Medal of the US, was born near Townsend, NY. While on an official visit to review Red Cross activities, she died Apr 15, 1919, in an army hospital at Savenay, France. Her last words: "What about my work? I must get back to my work." Originally buried at Loire, France, her remains were reinterred at Arlington National Cemetery in 1920.

FROST, ROBERT LEE: BIRTH ANNIVERSARY. Mar 26, 1874. American poet who tried his hand at farming, teaching, shoemaking and editing before winning acclaim as a poet. Pulitzer Prize winner. Born at San Francisco, CA, he died at Boston, MA, Jan 29, 1963.

INTERNATIONAL LISTENING ASSOCIATION ANNUAL CONVENTION. Mar 26–28. Seattle, WA. Convention dedicated to learning more about the impact that listening has on all human activity. To promote the study, development and teaching of effective listening in all settings. For info: International Listening Assn, 943 Park Dr, Belle Plaine, MN 56011. Phone: (952) 594-5697. Fax: (952) 856-5100. E-mail: info@listen.org. Web: www.listen.org.

LEGAL ASSISTANTS DAY. Mar 26. A day recognizing the many contributions made to the legal profession by legal assistants. For info: Claudia Evart, 30 Park Ave, #2-P, New York, NY 10016. Phone: (212) 779-2227. E-mail: ms.dia326@gmail.com.

LIVE LONG AND PROSPER DAY. Mar 26. 4th annual. Inspired by Spock's famous Vulcan blessing from the television series "Star Trek," this day encourages you to do something for yourself (or others) that will increase happiness, longevity and prosperity. Annually, Mar 26, actor Leonard Nimoy's birthday. For info: Matt McCarthy. E-mail: llapday@gmail.com. Web: llapday.com.

MAKE UP YOUR OWN HOLIDAY DAY. Mar 26. This day is a day you may name for whatever you wish. Reach for the stars! Make up a holiday! Annually, Mar 26. (©2006 by WH.) For info: Thomas & Ruth Roy, Wellcat Holidays, 2418 Long Ln, Lebanon, PA 17046. Phone: (717) 279-0184. E-mail: info@wellcat.com. Web: www.wellcat.com.

NIMOY, LEONARD: BIRTH ANNIVERSARY. Mar 26, 1931. Actor, director, photographer, singer, poet and pop culture icon born at Boston, MA. Nimoy is best known for his portrayal of half-human, half-Vulcan Spock in the science fiction television-film franchise *Star Trek*. Nimoy died Feb 27, 2015, at Los Angeles, CA.

PRINCE JONAH KUHIO KALANIANA'OLE DAY. Mar 26. Hawaii. Commemorates the man who, as Hawaii's delegate to the US Congress, introduced the first bill for statehood in 1919. Not until 1959 did Hawaii become a state.

SOVIET COSMONAUT RETURNS TO NEW COUNTRY: ANNIVERSARY. Mar 26, 1992. After spending 313 days in space in the Soviet *Mir* space station, cosmonaut Serge Krikalev returned to Earth and to what was for him a new country. He left Earth May 18, 1991, a citizen of the Soviet Union, but during his stay aboard the space station, the Soviet Union crumbled and became the Commonwealth of Independent States. Originally scheduled to return in October 1991, Krikalev was delayed by five months due to his country's disintegration and the ensuing monetary problems.

WILLIAMS, TENNESSEE: BIRTH ANNIVERSARY. Mar 26, 1911. Tennessee Williams was born at Columbus, MS. He was one of America's most prolific playwrights, producing such works as *The Glass Menagerie*; *A Streetcar Named Desire* and *Cat on a Hot Tin Roof*, both of which won Pulitzer Prizes; *Night of the Iguana*; *Summer and Smoke*; *The Rose Tattoo*; and *Sweet Bird of Youth*. Williams died at New York, NY, Feb 25, 1983.

"THE YOUNG AND THE RESTLESS" TV PREMIERE: ANNIVERSARY. Mar 26, 1973. This daytime serial is generally thought of as TV's most artistic soap and has won numerous Emmys for outstanding daytime drama series. Its original storylines revolved around the Brooks and Foster families, but by the early '80s most of them were gone and the Abbott and Williams families were highlighted. The serial's very large and changing cast has included now-famous actors David Hasselhoff, Tom Selleck, Wings Hauser, Deidre Hall and Michael Damian. In 1980, "Y&R" expanded from a half-hour to an hour. Its theme music is well known as "Nadia's Theme," as it was played during Nadia Comaneci's routine at the 1976 Olympics.

🎂 BIRTHDAYS TODAY

Marcus Allen, 60, former football player, sportscaster, born San Diego, CA, Mar 26, 1960.

Alan Arkin, 86, actor (*Argo, Catch-22, Little Miss Sunshine*), director (*Little Murders*), born New York, NY, Mar 26, 1934.

James Caan, 80, actor (*Elf, Misery, Thief, The Godfather*), born New York, NY, Mar 26, 1940.

Elaine Chao, 67, US Secretary of Transportation (Trump administration), former US secretary of labor (George W. Bush administration), former US secretary of transportation (George H.W. Bush administration), born Taipei, Taiwan, Mar 26, 1953.

Kenny Chesney, 52, country singer, born Knoxville, TN, Mar 26, 1968.

Leeza Gibbons, 63, television personality, born Hartsville, SC, Mar 26, 1957.

Jennifer Grey, 60, actress (*Dirty Dancing*), born New York, NY, Mar 26, 1960.

Erica Jong, 78, author, poet (*Fear of Flying, Becoming Light*), born New York, NY, Mar 26, 1942.

March 2020	S	M	T	W	T	F	S
							1
	1	2	3	4	5	6	7
	8	9	10	11	12	13	14
	15	16	17	18	19	20	21
	22	23	24	25	26	27	28
	29	30	31				

Catherine Keener, 60, actress (*Get Out, Capote, The 40-Year-Old Virgin, Being John Malkovich*), born Miami, FL, Mar 26, 1960.

T.R. Knight, 47, actor ("Grey's Anatomy"), born Minneapolis, MN, Mar 26, 1973.

Keira Knightley, 35, actress (*The Imitation Game, Atonement, Pirates of the Caribbean*), born Teddington, Middlesex, England, Mar 26, 1985.

Vicki Lawrence, 71, singer, actress ("The Carol Burnett Show," "Mama's Family"), born Inglewood, CA, Mar 26, 1949.

Josh Lucas, 48, actor (*Sweet Home Alabama, American Psycho*), born Little Rock, AR, Mar 26, 1972.

Leslie Mann, 48, actress (*Knocked Up, Big Daddy*), born San Francisco, CA, Mar 26, 1972.

Von Miller, 31, football player, born Dallas, TX, Mar 26, 1989.

Sandra Day O'Connor, 90, former associate justice of the US, born El Paso, TX, Mar 26, 1930.

Nancy Pelosi, 80, US Congresswoman (D, California), Speaker of the US House of Representatives, born Baltimore, MD, Mar 26, 1940.

Diana Ross, 76, singer, actress (*Lady Sings the Blues, The Wiz*), born Detroit, MI, Mar 26, 1944.

Martin Short, 70, comedian, actor (*Martin Short: Fame Becomes Me, Captain Ron*, "Primetime Glick"), born Hamilton, ON, Canada, Mar 26, 1950.

John Stockton, 58, Hall of Fame basketball player, born Spokane, WA, Mar 26, 1962.

Steven Tyler, 72, singer (Aerosmith), television personality ("American Idol"), born Steven Victor Tallarico at Yonkers, NY, Mar 26, 1948.

Bob Woodward, 77, journalist, author (*All the President's Men* with Carl Bernstein, *Plan of Attack*), born Geneva, IL, Mar 26, 1943.

March 27 — Friday

DAY 87   **279 REMAINING**

CANARY ISLANDS PLANE DISASTER: ANNIVERSARY. Mar 27, 1977. The worst accident in the history of civil aviation. Two Boeing 747s collided on the ground; 570 people lost their lives—249 on the KLM Airlines plane and 321 on the Pan Am plane.

CURRIER, NATHANIEL: BIRTH ANNIVERSARY. Mar 27, 1813. Lithographer born at Roxbury, MA. With James Merritt Ives, established the immensely popular and successful Currier & Ives printing firm, which produced millions of prints from an inventory of 7,500 scenes. Very few American parlors were without a Currier & Ives print in the mid-19th century. Currier died Nov 20, 1888, at Amesbury, MA. The printing firm survived until 1907—although its images remain popular today.

EARTHQUAKE STRIKES ALASKA: ANNIVERSARY. Mar 27, 1964. The strongest earthquake in North American history (8.4 on the Richter scale) struck Alaska, east of Anchorage; 117 people were killed. This was the world's second-worst earthquake of the 20th century in terms of magnitude.

FDA APPROVES VIAGRA: ANNIVERSARY. Mar 27, 1998. The US Food and Drug Administration approved the drug Viagra for treatment of male impotence on this date. It had been patented in 1996.

"FUNKY WINKERBEAN": ANNIVERSARY. Mar 27, 1972. Anniversary of the nationally syndicated comic strip. For info: Tom Batiuk, Creator, 2750 Substation Rd, Medina, OH 44256. Phone: (330) 304-6095.

HILL, PATTY SMITH: BIRTH ANNIVERSARY. Mar 27, 1868. Patty Smith Hill, schoolteacher, author and education specialist, was born at Anchorage (suburb of Louisville), KY. She was author of the lyrics of the song "Good Morning to All," which later became known as "Happy Birthday to You." Her older sister, Mildred J. Hill, composed the melody for the song, which was first published in 1893 as a classroom greeting in the book *Song Stories for the Sunday School*. A stanza beginning "Happy Birthday to You" was added in 1924, and the song became arguably the most frequently sung song in the world. Hill died at New York, NY, May 25, 1946. See also: "Happy Birthday to 'Happy Birthday to You'" (June 27).

LUXEMBOURG: OSWEILER. Mar 27. Blessing of horses, tractors and cars.

MIES VAN DER ROHE, LUDWIG: BIRTH ANNIVERSARY. Mar 27, 1886. Born Maria Ludwig Michael Mies at Aachen, Germany, Mies van der Rohe was recognized by peers, critics, casual observers and the scope of history as one of the most influential architects of the 20th century. His profound, simple and resolutely powerful works represented a shift in style, technique and appreciation for material structure that defined the look and feel of the modern industrial era. From 1938 to 1958, he served as chair of the school of architecture at Illinois Institute of Technology in Chicago; the campus contains 20 of his buildings. Mies van der Rohe died at Chicago, IL, Aug 17, 1969.

MYANMAR: RESISTANCE DAY. Mar 27. National holiday. Commemorates the day in 1945 when Burma officially joined the Allies in WWII. Also called Armed Forces Day.

NATIONAL GEOGRAPHIC GEOBEE, STATE LEVEL. Mar 27. Site is different in each state—many are in the state capital. Winners of school-level competitions who scored in the top 100 in their state on a written test compete in the State GeoBees. The winner of each state competition will go to Washington, DC, for the national level in May. For info: Natl Geographic GeoBee, Natl Geographic Society. E-mail: ngbee@ngs.org. Web: www.natgeobee.org.

NORTH SEA OIL RIG DISASTER: 40th ANNIVERSARY. Mar 27, 1980. The Alexander L. Kielland Oil Rig capsized during a heavy storm in the Norwegian sector of the North Sea. The pentagon-type, French-built oil rig had about 200 persons aboard, and 123 lives were lost.

QUIRKY COUNTRY MUSIC SONG TITLES DAY. Mar 27. We love those old country music quirky song titles, and it's time to create some new ones. How about "Put Me Out at the Curb, Darlin', 'Cause the Recycling Truck's A-comin', and You Done Throwed Me Out," for starters? (©2006 by WH.) For info: Thomas & Ruth Roy, Wellcat Holidays, 2418 Long Lane, Lebanon, PA 17046. Phone: (717) 279-0184. E-mail: info@wellcat.com. Web: www.wellcat.com.

RÖNTGEN, WILHELM CONRAD: 175th BIRTH ANNIVERSARY. Mar 27, 1845. German scientist who discovered x-rays (1895) and won a Nobel Prize in 1901. Born at Lennep, Prussia, he died at Munich, Germany, Feb 10, 1923.

ROSTROPOVICH, MSTISLAV: BIRTH ANNIVERSARY. Mar 27, 1927. Russian composer and conductor, perhaps the finest cellist of the 20th century. Born at Baku, USSR (now Azerbaijan), to parents who were also musicians, he studied under Shostakovich and

Prokofiev and was performing all over the world by the early 1950s. Fiercely dedicated to human rights and freedom of speech and expression, he was forced to flee the Soviet Union in the early 1970s when the government attempted to interfere with his travels due to his support of dissident writer Alexander Solzhenitsyn. Rostropovich became an American citizen and was named the musical director of the US National Symphony Orchestra in 1977, a job he held until 1994. He is also remembered for his impromptu performance at the Berlin Wall in 1989 and his trip to Moscow in 1991 to support the new Russian government. He died at Moscow, Russia, Apr 27, 2007.

ROYCE, HENRY: BIRTH ANNIVERSARY. Mar 27, 1863. Industrialist and pioneering automotive manufacturer born at Alwalton, Huntingtonshire, England. In 1906 his successful engineering business, Royce Ltd, merged with C.S. Rolls's company to form Rolls-Royce Ltd. Royce's insistence on perfection and attention to detail, as well as his refusal to reduce the quality of his product to make his prices more competitive, made the company's automobile and airplane engines legendary. Awarded the Order of the British Empire (1918) and created a baronetcy (1930), Royce died at West Wittering, Sussex, England, on Apr 22, 1933.

SAINTS AND SINNERS LITERARY FESTIVAL. Mar 27–29. New Orleans, LA. Founded in 2003, this internationally recognized literary event brings together a who's who of LGBTQ publishers, writers and readers from throughout the United States and beyond. SASFest features panel discussions, readings, master classes and special events that provide a forum for authors, editors and publishers to talk about their work for the benefit of emerging writers and the enjoyment of fans of LGBTQ literature. Held in conjunction with the Tennessee Williams/New Orleans Literary Festival. For info: Saints and Sinners Literary Festival, 938 Lafayette St, Ste 514, New Orleans, LA 70113. Web: www.sasfest.org.

***SINGIN' IN THE RAIN* FILM PREMIERE: ANNIVERSARY.** Mar 27, 1952. MGM's joyous, comic film musical premiered on this date at New York, NY. Starring Gene Kelly, Debbie Reynolds and Donald O'Connor and featuring the songs "Singin' in the Rain," "Good Morning" and "Make 'Em Laugh," *Singin' in the Rain* depicted a Hollywood romance at the time the talkies arrived. Directed by Kelly and Stanley Donen and written by Betty Comden and Adolph Green, the film was only nominated for two Oscars, yet is now regarded as one of the greatest movie musicals.

SMITH, THORNE: BIRTH ANNIVERSARY. Mar 27, 1892. Perhaps the most critically neglected popular author of the 20th century, he was born James Thorne Smith, Jr, at Annapolis, MD, educated at Dartmouth and died at Sarasota, FL, June 21, 1934. Author of many humorous supernatural fantasy novels, including *Rain in the Doorway*, *The Stray Lamb* and *Topper*, he was the master of the pointless conversation. The "Thorne Smith touch" has inspired several motion pictures and television series, including "Bewitched." For info: George H. Scheetz, Exec Secy, The Thorne Smith Society, 406 Wolcott Ln, Batavia, IL 60510-2838.

SPACE MILESTONE: *VENERA 8* (USSR). Mar 27, 1972. Launched on this date, this unmanned probe made a soft landing on Venus July 22 and sent back radio transmissions of surface data.

STEICHEN, EDWARD: BIRTH ANNIVERSARY. Mar 27, 1879. Celebrated American photographer. Co-published the groundbreaking *Camera Work* magazine, was a pioneering fashion photographer, directed the documentary *The Fighting Lady* (1945 Academy Award–winner) and curated the photography holdings at the

Museum of Modern Art. A recipient of the Presidential Medal of Freedom. Born at Bivange, Luxembourg, Steichen died Mar 25, 1973, at his farm near West Redding, CT.

SUGARLOAF CRAFTS FESTIVAL. Mar 27–29. Dulles Expo Center, Chantilly, VA. This show, now in its 22nd year, features more than 300 nationally recognized craft designers and fine artists displaying and selling their original creations. Includes craft demonstrations, music, specialty foods, gift certificate drawings and more. Est attendance: 17,600. For info: Sugarloaf Mountain Works, 13225 Executive Park Terrace, Germantown, MD 20874. Phone: (800) 210-9900. Fax: (301) 253-9620. E-mail: sugarloafinfo@sugarloaffest.com. Web: www.sugarloafcrafts.com.

SWANSON, GLORIA: BIRTH ANNIVERSARY. Mar 27, 1899. American film actress (*Sunset Boulevard*) and businesswoman. Born Gloria May Josephine Svensson at Chicago, IL. Author of an autobiography, *Swanson on Swanson*, published in 1980. Died at New York, NY, Apr 4, 1983.

VAUGHAN, SARAH: BIRTH ANNIVERSARY. Mar 27, 1924. Legendary jazz singer, born at Newark, NJ, renowned for her melodic improvising, wide vocal range and extraordinary technique. She began her career by winning an amateur contest at New York's Apollo Theater in 1943. She was hired by Earl Hines to accompany his band as his relief pianist as well as singer. She was given the nickname "The Divine One" by Chicago disc jockey Dave Garroway, a moniker that would remain with her the rest of her life. Died at Los Angeles, CA, Apr 3, 1990.

🎂 BIRTHDAYS TODAY

Mariah Carey, 50, singer, born Long Island, NY, Mar 27, 1970.

Randall Cunningham, 57, former football player, born Santa Barbara, CA, Mar 27, 1963.

Stephen Dillane, 63, actor ("The Tunnel," "Game of Thrones," *Darkest Hour, The Hours*), born London, England, Mar 27, 1957.

Fergie, 45, singer, musician (The Black-Eyed Peas), born Stacy Ferguson at Hacienda Heights, CA, Mar 27, 1975.

Nathan Fillion, 49, actor ("Castle," "Firefly," *Serenity*), born Edmonton, AB, Canada, Mar 27, 1971.

Kimbra, 30, musician, born Kimbra Johnson at Hamilton, New Zealand, Mar 27, 1990.

Austin Pendleton, 80, actor (*Mr and Mrs Bridge, Guarding Tess*), director, born Warren, OH, Mar 27, 1940.

Pauley Perrette, 51, actress ("NCIS"), singer, born New Orleans, LA, Mar 27, 1969.

Quentin Tarantino, 57, director (*The Hateful Eight, Reservoir Dogs*), screenwriter (Oscars for *Django Unchained* and *Pulp Fiction*), born Knoxville, TN, Mar 27, 1963.

William Caleb (Cale) Yarborough, 80, former auto racer, born Timmonsville, SC, Mar 27, 1940.

Michael York, 78, actor (*Austin Powers, Cabaret, The Three Musketeers*), born Fulmer, England, Mar 27, 1942.

March 2020	S	M	T	W	T	F	S
				1	2	3	4	5	6	7
	8	9	10	11	12	13	14
	15	16	17	18	19	20	21
	22	23	24	25	26	27	28
	29	30	31				

March 28 — Saturday

DAY 88   **278 REMAINING**

BARTHOLOMEW, FREDDIE: BIRTH ANNIVERSARY. Mar 28, 1924. Child star of the 1930s, Freddie Bartholomew was born Frederick Llewellyn at Great Britain. He appeared in 24 films and became the second-highest-paid child star after Shirley Temple. He died Jan 23, 1992, at Sarasota, FL.

BATTLE OF LA GLORIETTA PASS: ANNIVERSARY. Mar 28, 1862. At Pigeon's Ranch, a stagecoach stop on the Santa Fe Trail (about 19 miles southeast of Santa Fe, NM), Confederate forces briefly prevailed over Union troops in what some have called the most important battle of the Civil War in the Southwest. It was feared that if Union troops failed to hold here, the Confederate forces would proceed to Fort Union and on to control the rich gold fields of Colorado and California.

"BIG BANG" COINED: ANNIVERSARY. Mar 28, 1949. On BBC Radio's "Third Programme," British astronomer Fred Hoyle, searching for language to explain to listeners one theory to describe the universe, coined the term "big bang." Hoyle, in fact, favored what he called a "steady state" theory of the universe (the universe being unchanging and eternal). The "big bang" theory, originally proposed by Belgian astronomer and priest Georges Lemaître, described an expanding universe that originated at a single point. It took several decades for the term to take hold in scientific circles.

CZECH REPUBLIC: TEACHERS' DAY. Mar 28. Celebrates birth on this day of Jan Amos Komensky (Comenius), Moravian educational reformer (1592–1671).

EARTH HOUR. Mar 28. This event reaches more than one billion people in 187 countries and territories around the world, inviting communities, businesses and governments to switch off lights for one hour at 8:30 PM, local time—sending a powerful global message that we care enough about climate change to take action. For info: World Wildlife Fund. Web: www.worldwildlife.org or www.earthhour.org.

GORKY, MAXIM: BIRTH ANNIVERSARY. Mar 28, 1868. Social realist author, playwright and poet born Alexei Maximovich Peshkov at Nizhny Novgorod, Russia. Gorky was a political activist and supported the nascent movements intent on toppling the czarist regime—meaning that his life was marked with periods of imprisonment and exile. His works include *The Lower Depths, The Mother* and *Children of the Sun*. After a period in exile, Gorky returned to what was then the Soviet Union, where he died in Moscow on June 18, 1936.

"GREATEST SHOW ON EARTH" FORMED: ANNIVERSARY. Mar 28, 1881. P.T. Barnum and James A. Bailey merged their circuses to form the "Greatest Show on Earth."

LIBYA: BRITISH BASES EVACUATION DAY. Mar 28. National holiday. Commemorates the closing of British bases on this day in 1970.

SAINT JOHN NEPOMUCENE NEUMANN: BIRTH ANNIVERSARY. Mar 28, 1811. The first male saint from the US was born at Prachitiz, Bohemia (now the Czech Republic). After seminary school, he immigrated to the US, arriving at Manhattan, NY, in 1836. Neumann took a post in a rural area, walking miles from farm to farm to meet settlers from many countries. His facility with languages (he spoke 12 fluently) allowed him to minister to a wide variety of people. He joined an order called the Redemptionists at Pittsburgh, PA, in 1840 and became bishop of Philadelphia in 1852 (affectionately known as the "Little Bishop"). During his tenure, a cathedral was begun, 50 churches were built, almost 100 schools were opened and the number of parochial students grew from 500 to 9,000. He died at Philadelphia, PA, on Jan 5, 1860. Beatified on Oct 13, 1963, Neumann was canonized on June 19, 1977.

SAINT TERESA OF ÁVILA: BIRTH ANNIVERSARY. Mar 28, 1515. Founder of the discalced Carmelites, Doctor of the Catholic Church, born at Ávila, Spain. Creating a rule of silence, poverty and separation from the world, Teresa founded 17 reformed Carmelite convents, called discalced from their practice of wearing sandals. She befriended Saint John of the Cross, with whom she established the first Carmelite community of friars. Her writings include *The Way of Perfection* (1573) and *The Interior Castle* (1577). She died October 4, 1582, at Alba de Tormes. Canonized Mar 12, 1622, by Pope Gregory XV.

THREE MILE ISLAND NUCLEAR POWER PLANT ACCIDENT: ANNIVERSARY. Mar 28, 1979. A series of accidents, beginning at 4 AM, EST, at Three Mile Island on the Susquehanna River about 10 miles southeast of Harrisburg, PA, was responsible for extensive reevaluation of the safety of existing nuclear power–generating operations. Equipment and other failures reportedly brought Three Mile Island close to a meltdown of the uranium core, threatening extensive radiation contamination.

VIETNAM MORATORIUM CONCERT: 50th ANNIVERSARY. Mar 28, 1970. A seven-hour concert at Madison Square Garden at New York City featured many stars who donated their services for the antiwar cause. Among them were Jimi Hendrix; Dave Brubeck; Harry Belafonte; Peter, Paul and Mary; Judy Collins; the Rascals; Blood, Sweat and Tears; and the Broadway cast of *Hair*.

🎂 BIRTHDAYS TODAY

Conchata Ferrell, 77, actress ("Two and a Half Men"), born Charleston, WV, Mar 28, 1943.

Kate Gosselin, 45, television personality ("Jon & Kate Plus 8"), author, born Wernersville, PA, Mar 28, 1975.

Laura Harrier, 30, actress (*BlacKkKlansman, Spider-Man: Homecoming*), model, born Chicago, IL, Mar 28, 1990.

Lady Gaga, 34, singer, actress ("American Horror Story: Hotel"), born Stefani Germanotta at Yonkers, NY, Mar 28, 1986.

Reba McEntire, 65, singer, actress ("Reba," *Annie Get Your Gun*), born Chockie, OK, Mar 28, 1955.

Byron Scott, 59, basketball coach and former player, born Ogden, UT, Mar 28, 1961.

Jerry Sloan, 78, former basketball coach and player, born McLeansboro, IL, Mar 28, 1942.

Julia Stiles, 39, actress (*The Prince & Me, The Bourne Identity, Save the Last Dance, O*), born New York, NY, Mar 28, 1981.

Keith Tkachuk, 48, hockey player, born Melrose, MA, Mar 28, 1972.

Jonathan Van Ness, 33, television personality ("Queer Eye," "Gay of Thrones"), podcaster, hairdresser, born Quincy, IL, Mar 28, 1987.

Vince Vaughn, 50, actor (*Wedding Crashers, Old School, Swingers*), born Minneapolis, MN, Mar 28, 1970.

Dianne Wiest, 72, actress (Oscars for *Hannah and Her Sisters* and *Bullets over Broadway*; "Law & Order"), born Kansas City, MO, Mar 28, 1948.

March 29 — Sunday

DAY 89 **277 REMAINING**

BAILEY, PEARL MAE: BIRTH ANNIVERSARY. Mar 29, 1918. American singer and Broadway musical star Pearl Bailey was born at Newport News, VA. She began her career in vaudeville and won a special Tony Award in 1968 and the Presidential Medal of Freedom in 1988. Bailey died Aug 17, 1990, at Philadelphia, PA.

CANADA: BRITISH NORTH AMERICA ACT: ANNIVERSARY. Mar 29, 1867. This act of the British parliament established the Dominion of Canada, uniting Ontario, Quebec, Nova Scotia and New Brunswick. The remaining colonies in Canada were still ruled directly by Great Britain until Manitoba joined the Dominion in 1870, British Columbia in 1871, Prince Edward Island in 1873, Alberta and Saskatchewan in 1905 and Newfoundland in 1949. Union was proclaimed July 1, 1867. See also: "Canada: Canada Day" (July 1).

CENTRAL AFRICAN REPUBLIC: BOGANDA DAY. Mar 29. National holiday. Commemorates the death of Barthélemy Boganda, the first president, in 1959.

COMMITTEE ON ASSASSINATIONS REPORT: ANNIVERSARY. Mar 29, 1979. The House Select Committee on Assassinations released on this day its final report on its investigation into the assassinations of President John F. Kennedy; Martin Luther King, Jr; and Robert Kennedy. Based on available evidence, the committee concluded that President Kennedy was assassinated as a result of a conspiracy, although no trail of a conspiracy could be established. They also concluded that on the basis of scientific acoustical evidence two gunmen fired at the president, although no second gunman could be identified. (Note: In December 1980, the FBI released a report discounting the two-gunmen theory, stating that the distinguishable sounds of two separate guns were not proven scientifically.) In addition the committee concluded that the possibility of conspiracy did exist in the cases of Dr. King and Robert Kennedy, although no specific individuals or organizations could be pinpointed as being involved. See also: "Warren Commission Report: Anniversary" (Sept 27).

CONSIDER CHRISTIANITY WEEK. Mar 29–Apr 4. A week to encourage Christians to examine the evidence and reasons for their faith and for non-Christians to take another look at the faith that has played such an important role in shaping the history and culture in which we live. Annually, beginning two Sundays before Easter. For info: Hanna Hushbeck, PR, Aletheia, 3675 N 108th Ave, Wausau, WI 54401. Phone: (715) 675-7361. E-mail: hanna@consider.org. Web: www.consider.org.

DOW JONES TOPS 10,000: ANNIVERSARY. Mar 29, 1999. The Dow Jones Index of 30 major industrial stocks topped the 10,000 mark for the first time.

ENGLAND: CARE SUNDAY. Mar 29. The fifth Sunday of Lent, also known as Carling Sunday and Passion Sunday. First day of Passiontide, remembering the sorrow and passion of Christ.

EUROPEAN UNION: DAYLIGHT SAVING TIME (SUMMER TIME) BEGINS. Mar 29. All members of the European Union observe daylight saving (summer) time from the last Sunday in March until the last Sunday in October. See also: "European Union: Daylight Saving Time (Summer Time) Ends" (Oct 25).

HOOVER, LOU HENRY: BIRTH ANNIVERSARY. Mar 29, 1875. Wife of Herbert Clark Hoover, 31st president of the US. Born at Waterloo, IA, she died at Palo Alto, CA, Jan 7, 1944.

MADAGASCAR: COMMEMORATION DAY. Mar 29. Memorial Day for those who died in the 1947 rebellion against the French.

MCCARTHY, EUGENE: BIRTH ANNIVERSARY. Mar 29, 1916. Born at Watkins, MN, the longtime congressman and senator from Minnesota is best remembered for his campaign for the 1968 Democratic presidential nomination. McCarthy ran on a strong antiwar platform, garnering support from those opposed to American involvement in the Vietnam conflict, but ultimately lost the nomination to Hubert Humphrey. McCarthy never held public office again, despite four more tries at the presidency, and died at Washington, DC, Dec 10, 2005.

NATIONAL MOM AND POP BUSINESS OWNERS DAY. Mar 29. A day recognizing those very special husband-and-wife business owner teams that work and commune together. Take this day to strike a balance between business and love. For info: Rick and Margie Segel, 268 Hamrick Dr, Kissimmee, FL 34759. Phone: (863) 852-8227. E-mail: rick@ricksegel.com.

NIAGARA FALLS RUNS DRY: ANNIVERSARY. Mar 29, 1848. A massive assemblage of ice blocks formed upstream of Niagara Falls late on Mar 29, 1848, and by midnight had stopped water flow over the falls (which are actually three falls: the American, the Horseshoe [or Canadian] and the Bridal Veil). The ice jam held until Apr 1, when the waters of Lake Erie punched through and things got back to normal. Until that happened, hundreds of the curious swarmed into the now-waterless gorge to hunt for geologic souvenirs while thousands of spectators watched from above. Although the American Falls had stopped flowing before, this 1848 stoppage was the first and only time the entire falls was affected.

PASSION WEEK. Mar 29–Apr 4. The week beginning on the fifth Sunday of Lent; the week before Holy Week.

PASSIONTIDE. Mar 29–Apr 11. The last two weeks of Lent (Passion Week and Holy Week), beginning with the fifth Sunday of Lent (Passion Sunday) and continuing through the day before Easter (Holy Saturday or Easter Even).

QUINLAN, KAREN ANN: BIRTH ANNIVERSARY. Mar 29, 1954. Born at Scranton, PA, Karen Ann Quinlan became the center of a legal, medical and ethical controversy over the right to die. She became irreversibly comatose on Apr 14, 1975. A petition filed by her adoptive parents in New Jersey's Superior Court, Sept 12, 1975, sought permission to discontinue use of a respirator, allowing her to die "with grace and dignity." In 1976 the petition was upheld by New Jersey's Supreme Court. Quinlan lived nearly a decade without the respirator, until June 11, 1985. Her plight brought into focus the ethical dilemmas of advancing medical technology—the need for a new understanding of life and death; the right to die; and the role of judges, doctors and hospital committees in deciding when not to prolong life.

TAIWAN: YOUTH DAY. Mar 29. Honors the young revolutionaries killed during a revolt against the Qing government on Mar 29, 1911.

TEXAS LOVE THE CHILDREN DAY. Mar 29. A day recognizing every child's right and need to be loved. Promoting the hope that one day all children will live in loving, safe environments and will be given proper health care and equal learning opportunities. Precedes the start of National Child Abuse Prevention Month (April). Think SHELL: Safety, Health, Education, Laughter, Love. For info: Patty

March 2020	S	M	T	W	T	F	S
				1	2	3	4	5	6	7
	8	9	10	11	12	13	14
	15	16	17	18	19	20	21
	22	23	24	25	26	27	28
	29	30	31				

Murphy, 1509 Elizabeth St, Arlington, TX 76013. Phone: (817) 980-9591. E-mail: MURPH0@swbell.net.

TWENTY-THIRD AMENDMENT TO US CONSTITUTION RATIFIED: ANNIVERSARY. Mar 29, 1961. District of Columbia residents were given the right to vote in presidential elections under the 23rd Amendment.

TYLER, JOHN: BIRTH ANNIVERSARY. Mar 29, 1790. Tenth president of the US (Apr 6, 1841–Mar 3, 1845). Born at Charles City County, VA, Tyler succeeded to the presidency upon the death of William Henry Harrison—this was the first such succession in US history. Tyler's first wife died while he was president, and he remarried before the end of his term in office, becoming the first president to marry while in office. Fifteen children were born of the two marriages. During his administration, he worked to bring Texas into the Union. In 1861 he was elected to the Congress of the Confederate States, but he died at Richmond, VA, Jan 18, 1862, before being seated. His death received no official tribute from the US government—the only instance to date of a US president not receiving national honors.

UNITED KINGDOM: SUMMER TIME. Mar 29–Oct 25. "Summer Time" (one hour in advance of standard time), similar to daylight saving time, is observed from the last Sunday in March until the last Sunday in October.

WALTON, SAM: BIRTH ANNIVERSARY. Mar 29, 1918. Pioneering, charismatic business executive who caused a seismic shift in the retail landscape with his discount mega-store chain Walmart, started in 1962. Born on a farm at Kingfisher, OK, he died a multibillionaire at Little Rock, AR, Apr 5, 1992.

YOUNG, DENTON TRUE (CY): BIRTH ANNIVERSARY. Mar 29, 1867. Baseball Hall of Fame pitcher, born at Gilmore, OH. Young is baseball's all-time winningest pitcher, having accumulated 511 victories in his 22-year career. The Cy Young Award is given each year in his honor to Major League Baseball's best pitcher. Inducted into the Hall of Fame in 1937. Died at Newcomerstown, OH, Nov 4, 1955.

🎂 BIRTHDAYS TODAY

Earl Christian Campbell, 65, Hall of Fame football player, born Tyler, TX, Mar 29, 1955.

Jennifer Capriati, 44, Hall of Fame tennis player, born New York, NY, Mar 29, 1976.

Ernest Cline, 48, author (*Ready Player One, Armada*), born Ashland, OH, Mar 29, 1972.

Bud Cort, 72, actor (*Harold and Maude, Brewster McCloud*), born New Rochelle, NY, Mar 29, 1948 (some sources say 1950).

Catherine Cortez Masto, 56, US Senator (D, Nevada), born Las Vegas, NV, Mar 29, 1964.

Michel Hazanavicius, 53, director (*The Artist*; *OSS 117: Cairo, Nest of Spies*), born Paris, France, Mar 29, 1967.

Megan Hilty, 39, actress ("Smash"), born Bellevue, WA, Mar 29, 1981.

Eric Idle, 77, actor ("Monty Python's Flying Circus," "Suddenly Susan"), composer/lyricist (*Spamalot*), born Durham, England, Mar 29, 1943.

Christopher Lambert, 63, actor (*Highlander*; *Greystoke: The Legend of Tarzan, Lord of the Apes*), born New York, NY, Mar 29, 1957.

Lucy Lawless, 52, actress ("Xena"), born Mount Albert, Auckland, New Zealand, Mar 29, 1968.

Elle Macpherson, 56, model, actress (*Sirens*), born Sydney, Australia, Mar 29, 1964.

John Major, 77, former British prime minister (1990–97), born Brixton, England, Mar 29, 1943.

Jo Nesbø, 60, author (Harry Hole books, *Headhunters, The Snowman*), journalist, musician, born Oslo, Norway, Mar 29, 1960.

Kurt Thomas, 64, Olympic gymnast, born Miami, FL, Mar 29, 1956.

March 30 — Monday

DAY 90   **276 REMAINING**

ANESTHETIC FIRST USED IN SURGERY: ANNIVERSARY. Mar 30, 1842. Dr. Crawford W. Long, having seen the use of nitrous oxide and sulfuric ether at "laughing gas" parties, observed that individuals under their influence felt no pain. On this date, he removed a tumor from the neck of a man who was under the influence of ether.

DOCTORS' DAY. Mar 30. Traditional annual observance since 1933 to honor America's physicians on the anniversary of the occasion when Dr. Crawford W. Long became the first acclaimed physician to use ether as an anesthetic agent in a surgical technique, Mar 30, 1842. The red carnation has been designated the official flower of Doctors' Day.

GOYA, FRANCISCO JOSE DE: BIRTH ANNIVERSARY. Mar 30, 1746. Spanish painter and etcher. It is estimated that he executed more than 1,800 paintings, drawings and lithographs during his lifetime. Born at Aragon, Spain; died at Bordeaux, France, Apr 16, 1828.

GRASS IS ALWAYS BROWNER ON THE OTHER SIDE OF THE FENCE DAY. Mar 30. A day to honor all of those who did not jump ship, did not quit the same old job or did not leave the same old relationship because things appeared to look better somewhere else. (©2006 by WH.) For info: Thomas & Ruth Roy, Wellcat Holidays, 2418 Long Ln, Lebanon, PA 17046. Phone: (717) 279-0184. E-mail: wellcat@comcast.net. Web: www.wellcat.com.

INTERNATIONAL LAUNDRY FOLDING DAY. Mar 30. Re-organizing our closets is something we do at least twice a year between summer and winter. But folding laundry is a daily task that is both tedious and at the same time underappreciated. So on this day, we *appreciate* all of the laundry folding in our life and the people who help us. Just one day to look anew at this task. Annually, Mar 30, when seasons change and closets are rearranged. For info: Folimate. E-mail: Debbie@folimate.com.

ITALY: BOLOGNA CHILDREN'S BOOK FAIR. Mar 30–Apr 2. Bologna Fair Centre, Bologna. 57th edition. The most important international event dedicated to the children's publishing and multimedia industry. Here authors, illustrators, literary agents, licensors and licensees, packagers, distributors, printers, booksellers and librarians meet to sell and buy copyright, find the very best of children's publishing and multimedia production, generate and gather new contacts while strengthening professional relationships, discover new business opportunities, discuss and debate the latest sector trends. The year 2018 saw 1,400 exhibitors coming from more than 80 countries. Est attendance: 28,000. For info: Bologna Children's Book Fair, Piazza Costituzione, 6, 40128 Bologna, Italy. E-mail: bookfair@bolognafiere.it. Web: www.bookfair.bolognafiere.it.

"JEOPARDY!" TV PREMIERE: ANNIVERSARY. Mar 30, 1964. The "thinking person's" game show, "Jeopardy" has a reputation as an intelligent and classy program. Art Fleming was the original host of the show, in which three contestants won cash by giving the correct questions to answers in six different categories. Contestants go through two rounds and "final jeopardy," where they can wager up to all their earnings on one question. The series returned in 1984 with Alex Trebek as the popular host.

MULE DAY. Mar 30–Apr 5. Columbia, TN. Started in 1934 as Breeders Day when mules were brought into town to be sold and traded. Today this homecoming is celebrated with arts and crafts, a flea market, Mule Day Pageant, a huge parade and several mule shows. Est attendance: 40,000. For info: Mule Day, PO Box 66, Columbia, TN 38402. Phone: (931) 381-9557. E-mail: info@muleday.com. Web: www.muleday.com.

O'CASEY, SEAN: BIRTH ANNIVERSARY. Mar 30, 1880. Born John Casey into an impoverished Irish Protestant family at Dublin, Ireland, this playwright received only three years of formal schooling. He became an Irish nationalist, changing his name to the Irish form. O'Casey produced several plays set during key moments in Irish history. *The Shadow of a Gunman* was produced by the Abbey Theatre in 1923, and *Juno and the Paycock* and *The Plough and the Stars* soon followed. Disillusioned with Ireland, he moved to England in the late 1920s. O'Casey died at Torquay, Devon, England, on Sept 18, 1964.

PENCIL PATENTED: ANNIVERSARY. Mar 30, 1858. First pencil with the eraser top was patented by Hyman Lipman.

REAGAN, RONALD: ASSASSINATION ATTEMPT: ANNIVERSARY. Mar 30, 1981. President Ronald Reagan was shot in the chest by a 25-year-old gunman at Washington, DC. Three other persons were wounded (press secretary James Brady was wounded and died of his injuries on Aug 8, 2014—33 years later). John W. Hinckley, Jr, the accused attacker, was arrested at the scene. On June 21, 1982, a federal jury in the District of Columbia found Hinckley not guilty by reason of insanity, and he was committed to St. Elizabeth's Hospital at Washington, DC, until 2016.

SEWARD'S DAY. Mar 30. Observed in Alaska near the anniversary of its acquisition from Russia in 1867. The treaty of purchase was signed between the Russians and the Americans Mar 30, 1867, and ratified by the Senate May 28, 1867. The territory was formally transferred Oct 18, 1867. Annually, the last Monday in March.

SEWELL, ANNA: 200th BIRTH ANNIVERSARY. Mar 30, 1820. Born at Great Yarmouth, England, Anna Sewell is the author of *Black Beauty*, published in December 1877 and one of the bestselling English novels of all time. It describes the abuse and injustices horses—especially working horses—suffered in Victorian England. Sewell died at Old Catton, Norfolk, England, Apr 25, 1878, not realizing the impact her novel would have.

SPACE MILESTONE: FALCON 9 RELAUNCHED (SPACEX). Mar 30, 2017. SpaceX—the aerospace company founded by Tesla Motors CEO Elon Musk—made history by launching a used rocket into orbit. The Falcon 9, previously deployed in a 2016 mission to the International Space Station, was (re)launched from Cape Canaveral to deliver a communications satellite into orbit 22,000 miles into space; a few minutes after takeoff, the first stage—the 14-story core that contains the main engines and launch fuel—separated from the top of the rocket and made a controlled descent back to a platform in the Atlantic Ocean. This marked the first time in the history of spaceflight that the same rocket has been used on two separate missions to orbit. The rocket

	S	M	T	W	T	F	S
March	1	2	3	4	5	6	7
	8	9	10	11	12	13	14
2020	15	16	17	18	19	20	21
	22	23	24	25	26	27	28
	29	30	31				

originally cost $62 million to manufacture; reuse greatly reduces the cost of a single launch, increasing the feasibility of future commercial space travel.

TRINIDAD AND TOBAGO: SPIRITUAL/SHOUTER BAPTIST LIBERATION DAY. Mar 30. Public holiday. Celebrates the 1951 repeal of the Shouter Prohibition Ordinance of 1917.

VAN GOGH, VINCENT: BIRTH ANNIVERSARY. Mar 30, 1853. Dutch post-Impressionist painter, especially known for his bold and powerful use of color. Born at Groot Zundert, Holland, he died at Auvers-sur-Oise, France, July 29, 1890.

WILLIAMSON, SONNY BOY: BIRTH ANNIVERSARY. Mar 30, 1914. Legendary and influential harmonica player, born John Lee Curtis Williamson near Jackson, TN. Helped make the harmonica a blues staple. "Good Morning, School Girl" is one of his best-remembered hits. Murdered during a robbery on June 1, 1948, at Chicago, IL.

WORLD BIPOLAR DAY. Mar 30. First observed in 2014, World Bipolar Day seeks through international collaboration to bring the world population information about bipolar disorders that will educate and improve sensitivity toward the illness. Annually, Mar 30—the birth anniversary of Vincent van Gogh, who was posthumously diagnosed as probably having bipolar disorder. For info: World Bipolar Day. Web: www.worldbipolarday.org.

🎂 BIRTHDAYS TODAY

John Astin, 90, actor ("The Addams Family"; stage: *The Three Penny Opera*), director, born Baltimore, MD, Mar 30, 1930.

Warren Beatty, 82, actor (*Bonnie and Clyde*), director (*Reds, Dick Tracy*), producer, born Richmond, VA, Mar 30, 1938.

Tracy Chapman, 56, singer, born Cleveland, OH, Mar 30, 1964.

Eric Clapton, 75, singer, songwriter, guitarist, born Ripley, England, Mar 30, 1945.

Robbie Coltrane, 70, actor (*GoldenEye*, Harry Potter films, "Cracker"), born Anthony Robert McMillan at Rutherglen, Scotland, Mar 30, 1950.

Celine Dion, 52, singer, born Charlemagne, QC, Canada, Mar 30, 1968.

Jason Dohring, 38, actor ("Veronica Mars," *Black Cadillac*), born Dayton, OH, Mar 30, 1982.

M.C. Hammer, 57, rapper, born Stanley Kirk Burrell at Oakland, CA, Mar 30, 1963.

Norah Jones, 41, singer, born New York, NY, Mar 30, 1979.

Peter Marshall, 93, television host, actor, born Pierre La Cock at Huntington, WV, Mar 30, 1927.

Paul Reiser, 63, actor (*Diner*, "Mad About You"), author, born New York, NY, Mar 30, 1957.

March 31 — Tuesday

DAY 91   **275 REMAINING**

BUNSEN BURNER DAY: BIRTH ANNIVERSARY OF ROBERT BUNSEN. Mar 31. A day to honor the inventor of the Bunsen burner, Robert Wilhelm Eberhard von Bunsen, who provided chemists and chemistry students with one of their most indispensable instruments. The Bunsen burner allows the user to regulate the proportions of flammable gas and air to create the most efficient flame. Bunsen was born at Gottingen, Germany, on Mar 31, 1811, and was a professor of chemistry at the universities at Kassel, Marburg, Breslau and Heidelberg. He died at Heidelberg, Germany, Aug 16, 1899.

CESAR CHAVEZ DAY. Mar 31. A tribute day to Cesar Chavez (1927–93), on his birth anniversary. Celebrating one of America's greatest champions of social justice. Often observed as a community day of service. State holiday in California, unofficial holiday in Colorado and Texas. Widely observed across the US.

CHAVEZ, CESAR ESTRADA: BIRTH ANNIVERSARY. Mar 31, 1927. Labor leader who organized migrant farmworkers in support of better working conditions. Chavez initiated the National Farm Workers Association in 1962, attracting attention to the migrant farmworkers' plight by organizing boycotts of products including grapes and lettuce. He was born at Yuma, AZ, and died Apr 23, 1993, at San Luis, AZ. His birthday is a holiday in California.

DALAI LAMA FLEES TIBET: ANNIVERSARY. Mar 31, 1959. The Dalai Lama fled Chinese suppression and was granted political asylum in India. In 1950 Tibet had been invaded by China, and in 1951 an agreement was signed under which Tibet became a "national autonomous region" of China. Tibetans suffered under China's persecution of Buddhism, and after years of scattered protest a full-scale revolt broke out in 1959. The Dalai Lama fled, and with the beginning of the Chinese Cultural Revolution the Chinese took brutal repressive measures against the Tibetans, with the practice of religion banned and thousands of monasteries destroyed. The ban was lifted in 1976 with the end of the Cultural Revolution. The Dalai Lama received the Nobel Peace Prize in 1989 for his commitment to the nonviolent liberation of his country.

DESCARTES, RENE: BIRTH ANNIVERSARY. Mar 31, 1596. French philosopher and mathematician, known as the "father of modern philosophy," born at La Haye, Touraine, France. Cartesian philosophical precepts are often remembered because of his famous proposition "I think, therefore I am" (*Cogito ergo sum . . .*). Died of pneumonia at Stockholm, Sweden, Feb 11, 1650.

EIFFEL TOWER: ANNIVERSARY. Mar 31, 1889. Built for the Paris Exhibition of 1889, the tower was named for its architect, Alexandre Gustave Eiffel, and is one of the world's best-known landmarks.

FITZGERALD, EDWARD: BIRTH ANNIVERSARY. Mar 31, 1809. English author, born at Bredfield, England, perhaps best known for his translation of Omar Khayyam's *Rubaiyat*. Died at Merton, Norfolk, England, June 14, 1883.

GOGOL, NIKOLAI VASILEVICH: BIRTH ANNIVERSARY. Mar 31, 1809. Russian author of plays, novels and short stories. Born at Sorochinsk, Russia, he died at Moscow, Russia, Mar 4, 1852. Gogol's most famous work is the novel *Dead Souls*.

HAYDN, FRANZ JOSEPH: BIRTH ANNIVERSARY. Mar 31, 1732. "Father of the symphony," born at Rohrau, Austria-Hungary. Composed about 120 symphonies, more than a hundred works for chamber groups, a dozen operas and hundreds of other musical works. Died at Vienna, Austria, May 31, 1809.

INTERNATIONAL HUG A MEDIEVALIST DAY. Mar 31. Since 2011, a day of appreciation and celebration of these hardworking historians. Created by Sarah Laseke.

JOHNSON, JOHN (JACK) ARTHUR: BIRTH ANNIVERSARY. Mar 31, 1878. In 1908 Jack Johnson became the first black to win the heavyweight boxing championship when he defeated Tommy Burns at Sydney, Australia. Unable to accept a black man's triumph, the boxing world tried to find a white challenger. Jim Jeffries, former heavyweight title holder, was badgered out of retirement. On July

4, 1910, at Reno, NV, the "battle of the century" proved to be a farce when Johnson handily defeated Jeffries. Race riots swept the US, and plans to exhibit the film of the fight were canceled. Johnson was born at Galveston, TX, and died in an automobile accident June 10, 1946, at Raleigh, NC. He was inducted into the Boxing Hall of Fame in 1990. In 2018, President Donald Trump granted Johnson a posthumous presidential pardon for an unjust 1913 conviction that had caused Johnson to go into exile and then serve a short prison term.

MARVELL, ANDREW: BIRTH ANNIVERSARY. Mar 31, 1621. English poet. Born at Winestead, Yorkshire, England. From his poem "To His Coy Mistress": "Had we but world enough and time/this coyness, lady, were no crime. . . . But at my back I always hear/time's winged chariot drawing near. . . ." Died at London, England, Aug 18, 1678.

OKLAHOMA! BROADWAY PREMIERE: ANNIVERSARY. Mar 31, 1943. Rodgers and Hammerstein's landmark musical (their first collaboration) opened at the St. James Theatre on this date in 1943. (It had its world premiere under the title *Away We Go* at the Shubert Theatre in New Haven, CT, on Mar 11, 1943.) *Oklahoma!* is considered significant because it was the first musical in which songs, music, characterization and story were integrated into an emotional whole. It changed musicals forever. It was also the first musical to run more than 2,000 performances and to have a cast album recorded. Agnes de Mille was the choreographer. It received a special Pulitzer Prize for drama on May 2, 1944. In May 1953, "Oklahoma!" became that state's official song.

PAZ, OCTAVIO: BIRTH ANNIVERSARY. Mar 31, 1914. Poet, diplomat, translator, critic, professor and journal editor born at Mexico City, Mexico. His seminal prose work is *The Labyrinth of Solitude* (1950), an examination of the Mexican psyche. The prodigious Paz was awarded the Miguel de Cervantes Prize in 1981 and the Nobel Prize in Literature in 1990 "for impassioned writing with wide horizons, characterized by sensuous intelligence and humanistic integrity." He died in Mexico City, Apr 19, 1998.

PEARSE, RICHARD: ANNIVERSARY OF MONOPLANE FLIGHT. Mar 31, 1903. Richard Pearse, a farmer and inventor, flew a monoplane of his own design several hundred yards along a road near Temuka, New Zealand, and then landed it on top of a 12-foot-high hedge. Pearse had built the craft, which consisted of a steerable tricycle undercarriage and an internal combustion engine. A Pearse commemorative medal was issued on Sept 19, 1971, by the Museum of Transport and Technology, Auckland, New Zealand.

SELENA: 25th DEATH ANNIVERSARY. Mar 31, 1995. At a motel in Corpus Christi, TX, Tejano superstar Selena was shot and killed by Yolanda Saldivar, the manager of her chain of fashion boutiques and a former president of the Selena fan club. The state of Texas declared a day of mourning afterward.

SOVIET GEORGIA VOTES FOR INDEPENDENCE: ANNIVERSARY. Mar 31, 1991. On this date the Soviet Republic of Georgia voted to declare its independence from the Soviet Union. Georgia followed the Baltic states of Lithuania, Estonia and Latvia by becoming the fourth republic to reject Mikhail Gorbachev's new vision of the Soviet Union as espoused in a new Union Treaty. Totals revealed that 98.9 percent of those voting favored independence from Moscow. Hours after the election, troops were dispatched from Moscow to Georgia under a state of emergency.

US VIRGIN ISLANDS: TRANSFER DAY. Mar 31. Commemorates transfer resulting from purchase of the Virgin Islands by the US from Denmark, Mar 31, 1917, for $25 million.

WORLD BACKUP DAY. Mar 31. World Backup Day is a day for people to learn about the increasing role of data in our lives and the importance of regular backups. Annually, Mar 31. For info: World Backup Day. E-mail: hello@worldbackupday.com. Web: www.worldbackupday.com.

🎂 BIRTHDAYS TODAY

Herb Alpert, 85, musician (Tijuana Brass), born Los Angeles, CA, Mar 31, 1935.

Pavel Bure, 49, former hockey player, born Moscow, USSR (now Russia), Mar 31, 1971.

Richard Chamberlain, 85, actor ("Dr. Kildare," *Shogun*), born Los Angeles, CA, Mar 31, 1935.

William Daniels, 93, actor (Emmy for "St. Elsewhere"; "Boy Meets World," *1776*), born Brooklyn, NY, Mar 31, 1927.

David Eisenhower, 72, author (*Eisenhower at War*), lawyer, professor, born West Point, NY, Mar 31, 1948.

Albert (Al) Gore, Jr, 72, 45th vice president of the US (1993–2001), environmental activist, author, documentary filmmaker (*An Inconvenient Truth*), born Washington, DC, Mar 31, 1948.

John Jakes, 88, author (*North and South*, the Kent Family Chronicles), born Chicago, IL, Mar 31, 1932.

James Earl (Jimmy) Johnson, 82, Hall of Fame football player, born Dallas, TX, Mar 31, 1938.

Shirley Jones, 86, actress (Oscar for *Elmer Gantry*; *The Music Man, Oklahoma!*, "The Partridge Family"), born Smithton, PA, Mar 31, 1934.

Gabe Kaplan, 74, actor ("Welcome Back, Kotter"), born Brooklyn, NY, Mar 31, 1946.

Angus King, Jr, 76, US Senator (I, Maine), former governor of Maine, born Alexandria, VA, Mar 31, 1944.

Patrick J. Leahy, 80, US Senator (D, Vermont), born Montpelier, VT, Mar 31, 1940.

Edward Francis (Ed) Marinaro, 70, actor ("Hill Street Blues," "Sisters"), former football player, born New York, NY, Mar 31, 1950.

Marc McClure, 63, actor (*Freaky Friday, Back to the Future*), born San Mateo, CA, Mar 31, 1957.

Ewan McGregor, 49, actor ("Fargo," *Beauty and the Beast, Moulin Rouge, Trainspotting, Star Wars* films), born Crieff, Scotland, Mar 31, 1971.

Rhea Perlman, 72, actress ("Cheers," *Carpool*), born Brooklyn, NY, Mar 31, 1948.

Steve Smith, 51, former basketball player, born Highland Park, MI, Mar 31, 1969.

Christopher Walken, 77, actor (*Hairspray, Catch Me If You Can, The Deer Hunter*), born Queens, NY, Mar 31, 1943.

April 1 — Wednesday

DAY 92   **274 REMAINING**

ADOPT A FERRET MONTH. Apr 1–30. Since 2007, this month promotes awareness of ferret shelters and adoptable ferrets. "Adopt, not shop." For info: Support Our Shelters, 100 Walsh Rd, Lansdowne, PA 19050. Web: www.supportourshelters.org/Adopt_a_Ferret.html.

ALCOHOL AWARENESS MONTH. Apr 1–30. Since 1987, a month to help raise awareness among community prevention leaders and citizens about the problem of underage drinking. Concentrates on community grassroots activities. For info: Facing Addiction with NCADD, 217 Broadway, Ste 712, New York, NY 10007. Phone: (212) 269-7797. Web: www.ncadd.org.

APRIL FOOLS' OR ALL FOOLS' DAY. Apr 1. April Fools' Day seems to have begun in France in 1564. Apr 1 used to be New Year's Day, but the New Year was changed to Jan 1 that year. People who insisted on celebrating the "old" New Year became known as April fools, and it became common to play jokes and tricks on them. The general concept of a feast of fools is, however, an ancient one. The Romans had such a day, and medieval monasteries also had days when the abbot or bishop was replaced for a day by a common monk, who would order his superiors to do the most menial or ridiculous tasks. According to Brady's *Clavis Calendaria* (1812): "The joke of the day is to deceive persons by sending them upon frivolous and nonsensical errands; to pretend they are wanted when they are not, or, in fact, any way to betray them into some supposed ludicrous situation, so as to enable you to call them 'An April Fool.'"

BATTLE OF OKINAWA BEGINS: 75th ANNIVERSARY. Apr 1, 1945. On Easter Sunday, the US 10th Army began Operation Iceberg, the invasion of the Ryukyu Islands of Okinawa. Ground troops numbering 180,000 plus 368,000 men in support services made a total of 548,000 troops involved—the biggest amphibious operation of the Pacific war.

BISMARCK, OTTO VON: BIRTH ANNIVERSARY. Apr 1, 1815. The "Iron Chancellor" was born into nobility at Schönhausen, Prussia (Germany). He was appointed minister president of Prussia by King Wilhelm I and later became architect and first chancellor of Europe's leading military and industrial power, the German Empire. After leading Prussia through three wars prior to the creation of Germany, he waged peace in Europe for two decades to secure its supremacy. Known for his political method of realpolitik, Bismarck also created Europe's first comprehensive social welfare program, which included state-mandated health, worker accident and old-age insurance programs and disability. Died July 30, 1898, at Friedrichsruh, Germany.

BRIDGE OVER THE NEPONSET: ANNIVERSARY. Apr 1, 1634. The first bridge built in the US spanned the Neponset River between Milton and Dorchester, MA. The authority to build the bridge and an adjoining mill was issued to Israel Stoughton on this date by the Massachusetts General Court.

BULGARIA: SAINT LASARUS'S DAY. Apr 1. Ancient Slavic holiday of young girls, in honor of the goddess of spring and love.

CANADA: NUNAVUT INDEPENDENCE: ANNIVERSARY. Apr 1, 1999. Nunavut became Canada's third independent territory. This self-governing territory with an Inuit majority was created from the eastern half of the Northwest Territories.

CHANEY, LON: BIRTH ANNIVERSARY. Apr 1, 1883. The "Man of a Thousand Faces" was born Leonidas Chaney at Colorado Springs, CO. One of the biggest box office stars of the silent era, Chaney was a master of disguise and makeup (he kept his transformation tools and methods a closely guarded secret). He specialized in playing tortured, tragic and often menacing characters. He is best known for his gripping portrayals of Quasimodo in *The Hunchback of Notre Dame* (1923) and the Phantom in *The Phantom of the Opera* (1925). Chaney died of cancer on Aug 26, 1930, at Hollywood, CA—only one month after his first sound film was released. His impact on films was such that all Hollywood studios observed a moment of silence in his honor to commemorate his death.

COMMUNITY SPIRIT DAYS. Apr 1–30. Any town may observe this period by doing a special project to help those in need or by having a ceremony to present that community's Spirit of America Foundation Tribute for outstanding volunteerism. For info: Spirit of America Foundation, PO Box 5637, Augusta, ME 04332.

DEFEAT AT FIVE FORKS: ANNIVERSARY. Apr 1, 1865. After withdrawing to Five Forks, VA, Confederate troops under George Pickett were defeated and cut off by Union troops. This defeat, according to many military historians, sealed the immediate fate of Robert E. Lee's armies at Petersburg and Richmond. On Apr 2, Lee informed Confederate president Jefferson Davis that he would have to evacuate Richmond. Davis and his cabinet fled by train to Danville, VA.

DISTRACTED DRIVING AWARENESS MONTH. Apr 1–30. Since 2010, Distracted Driving Awareness Month informs people on the dangers of cell phone use while driving and furthers understanding of cognitive distraction to the brain. The National Safety Council saves lives by preventing injuries and deaths at work, in homes and communities and on the road through leadership, research, education and advocacy. For info: National Safety Council, Communications Department, 1121 Spring Lake Dr, Itasca, IL 60143. Phone: (800) 621-7615. E-mail: media@nsc.org. Web: www.nsc.org/cellfree.

"GENERAL HOSPITAL" TV PREMIERE: ANNIVERSARY. Apr 1, 1963. "General Hospital," ABC's longest-running soap, revolves around the denizens of fictional Port Charles, NY. "GH" was created by Doris and Frank Hursley. John Beradino, who was with the show from the beginning until his death in May 1996, played the role of Dr. Steve Hardy, upstanding director of medicine and pillar of the community. In the '80s, story lines became unusual with plots involving international espionage, mob activity and aliens. The wedding of supercouple Luke and Laura (Anthony Geary and Genie Francis) was a ratings topper. By the '90s, stories moved away from high-powered action to more conventional romance. Many actors received their big break on the show, including Demi Moore, Janine Turner, Jack Wagner, Richard Dean Anderson, Rick Springfield, John Stamos, Emma Samms, Mark Hamill, Finola Hughes, Ricky Martin and Tia Carrere.

GLOBAL ASTRONOMY MONTH. Apr 1–30. Since 2010. Global Astronomy Month (GAM), organized each April by Astronomers Without Borders, is the world's largest global celebration of

astronomy. Each year a broad range of 30 to 40 programs fills the month, with GAM events taking place around the world. Includes the Global Star Party and much more. GAM brings enthusiasts together worldwide to celebrate Astronomers Without Borders' motto: "One People, One Sky." For info: Astronomers Without Borders, 26500 W Agoura Rd, Ste 102-618, Calabasas, CA 91302. Phone: (818) 597-0223. Web: www.astronomerswithoutborders. org.

GRANGE MONTH. Apr 1–30. State and local recognition for Grange's contribution to rural/urban America. Celebrated at National Headquarters at Washington, DC, and in all states with local, county and state Granges. Begun in 1867, the National Grange is the oldest US rural community-service, family-oriented organization with a special interest in agriculture. Annually, the month of April. For info: The National Grange of the Patrons of Husbandry, 1616 H St NW, Washington, DC 20006. Phone: (888) 4-GRANGE. E-mail: info@nationalgrange.org. Web: www.nationalgrange.org.

HARVEY, WILLIAM: BIRTH ANNIVERSARY. Apr 1, 1578. (Old Style date.) Physician, born at Folkestone, England. The first to discover the mechanics of the circulation of the blood. Died at Roehampton, England, June 3, 1657 (OS).

HITLER MOVES TO BUNKER: 75th ANNIVERSARY. Apr 1, 1945. With the Red Army relentlessly approaching Berlin, Adolf Hitler moved his headquarters to a bunker 50 feet below the Reich Chancellery. Here he committed suicide on Apr 30, 1945.

HOLY HUMOR MONTH. Apr 1–30. To recognize the healing power of Christian joy, humor and celebration; to celebrate "Holy Humor Sunday," the Sunday after Easter (Apr 19), and to be "Fools for Christ" on April Fools' Day (Apr 1). Churches and prayer groups nationwide participate. For info: Cal Samra, The Joyful Noiseletter, PO Box 895, Portage, MI 49081-0895. Phone: (269) 324-0990. E-mail: joyfulnz@aol.com. Web: www.joyfulnoiseletter.com.

INFORMED WOMAN MONTH. Apr 1–30. Are you taking control of your life, or are you letting things control you? Don't live with regrets, feel limited in your opportunities or have unfulfilled goals and dreams. Starting today, and for the next 30 days, determine what to do, how to do it and where to go, then make a list of the resources available. Discover how to enjoy a better life for yourself, and learn how to become a more informed and aware individual. For info: Lorrie Walters Marsiglio, PO Box 284-CC, Wasco, IL 60183-0284. Phone: (630) 584-9368.

INTERNATIONAL BLACK WOMEN'S HISTORY MONTH. Apr 1–30. 6th annual. This month embraces the achievements, seeks to build understanding and awareness and celebrates the rich history of the past, present and future generations of not only black women but also minority women who are the descendants of Africa. It is about unifying communities by promoting visibility, empowerment and achievements. Previously proclaimed by the State of Georgia and the City of Atlanta, GA. For info: Sha Battle, Founder/President/CEO, 1544 Wellborn Rd, Ste 1055, Redan, GA 30074. E-mail: blackwomenshistorymonth@mail.com or info@blackwomeninjazz.com. Web: www.blackwomenshistorymonth.com.

INTERNATIONAL CUSTOMER LOYALTY MONTH. Apr 1–30. We highlight this month to honor and generate customer loyalty! Even though building customer loyalty should be a year-round thing, not just a month, take this month to strategize on how you can improve on relationships with your customers through better service, higher quality, etc. For info: Shep Hyken, Shepard Presentations, LLC, 200 S Hanley Rd, Ste 509, St. Louis, MO 63105. Phone: (314) 696-2200. E-mail: Shep@hyken.com. Web: www.CustomerLoyaltyMonth.com.

INTERNATIONAL TWIT AWARD MONTH. Apr 1–30. Any famous name (celebrity with the worst sense of humor) is eligible to be designated most Tiresome Wit (TWIT) of the year. For info: Lone Star Publications of Humor, 8452 Fredericksburg Rd, PMB 103, San Antonio, TX 78229. E-mail: lspubs@aol.com.

IRAN: ISLAMIC REPUBLIC DAY. Apr 1. National holiday. Commemorates the approval of the new constitution of the Islamic Republic of Iran in 1979.

JAZZ APPRECIATION MONTH. Apr 1–30. Every April, Jazz Appreciation Month (JAM) highlights the glories of jazz as both a historical and a living treasure. Here is one special month to draw greater public attention to the extraordinary heritage and history of jazz and its importance to American culture. Musicians, concert halls, schools, colleges, museums, libraries and public broadcasters are encouraged to offer special programs during this month. The Smithsonian Institution's National Museum of American History (which operates the world's most comprehensive set of jazz programs) leads this initiative in concert with a distinguished roster of federal agencies, nongovernmental organizations and broadcasting networks. For info: The Smithsonian Institution, National Museum of American History. Web: http://americanhistory.si.edu/smithsonian-jazz/jazz-appreciation-month.

LAUGH AT WORK WEEK. Apr 1–7. Laughter and humor are vital to a healthy, productive workplace. Benefits of laughing at work include improved productivity, teamwork, communication, stress relief, job satisfaction and employee retention. This week, which begins on April Fools' Day, focuses on the very serious business of humor. For info: Randall Munson, Creatively Speaking, 508 Meadow Run Dr SW, Rochester, MN 55902-2337. Phone: (507) 286-1331. E-mail: humor@CreativelySpeaking.com. Web: www.LaughAtWorkWeek.com.

LIBRARY SNAPSHOT DAY. Apr 1–30. The American Library Association encourages all libraries to choose a day during the month of April and record what happens in that single day in their libraries. How many books are checked out? How many people receive help finding a job? Doing their taxes? Doing their homework? This initiative provides an easy means to collect statistics, photos and stories that will enable library advocates to prove the value of their libraries to decision makers and increase public awareness. The ALA provides free wiki software to help libraries publish their statistics for their community. For info: American Library Assn, 50 E Huron St, Chicago, IL 60611. Phone: (312) 280-5044. E-mail: pio@ala.org. Web: www.ala.org/advocacy/snapshotday.

MATHEMATICS AND STATISTICS AWARENESS MONTH. Apr 1–30. The goal of this month is to increase public understanding of and appreciation for mathematics and statistics. Mathematics and Statistics Awareness Month began in 1986 as Mathematics Awareness Week with a proclamation by President Ronald Reagan. Activities are organized by college and university departments, institutional public information offices, student groups and related associations and interest groups. They have included a wide variety of workshops, competitions, exhibits, festivals, lectures and symposia. For info: Joint Policy Board for Mathematics (JPBM). Web: www.mathstatmonth.org/mathstatmonth/msamhome.

MEDICAL CANNABIS EDUCATION AND AWARENESS MONTH. Apr 1–30. A month for education about the use of medical cannabis. Sponsored by the American College of Apothecaries (ACA)/Pharmacists Planning Service, Inc (PPSI). For info: ACA/PPSI, 2830

	S	M	T	W	T	F	S
April				1	2	3	4
	5	6	7	8	9	10	11
2020	12	13	14	15	16	17	18
	19	20	21	22	23	24	25
	26	27	28	29	30		

Summer Oaks Dr, Bartlett, TN 38134. E-mail: info@ppsinc.org. Web: www.ppsinc.org.

MIFUNE, TOSHIRO: 100th BIRTH ANNIVERSARY. Apr 1, 1920. Japanese actor known worldwide for his collaboration with renowned director Akira Kurosawa in films including *Rashomon, Seven Samurai, Throne of Blood* and *Yojimbo*. Mifune was born in Qingdao, China, and grew up in Manchuria before being drafted into the Imperial Japanese Army in 1940, where he served as an aerial photographer. He appeared in his first film in 1947 but his performance in *Rashomon* (1950) made him an international star. Celebrated for his good looks, screen-idol magnetism and broad acting range, he may be most familiar to American audiences for his role as Lord Toranga in the 1980 television miniseries *Shogun*. Mifune died Dec 24, 1997, at Tokyo, Japan.

MOON PHASE: FIRST QUARTER. Apr 1. Moon enters First Quarter phase at 6:21 AM, EDT.

MYLESDAY. Apr 1. A day to celebrate the life and works of Irish writer Brian O'Nolan (also known as Flann O'Brien and Myles na gCopaleen). The author of *At Swim-Two-Birds* and countless satiric newspaper columns was born Oct 5, 1911, and died Apr 1, 1966. First observed at the Palace Bar, Dublin, Ireland, in 2011, the year of his birth centennial. See also: "O'Brien, Flann: Birth Anniversary" (Oct 5).

NATIONAL AFRICAN-AMERICAN WOMEN'S FITNESS MONTH. Apr 1–30. A national event designed to encourage health awareness through physical activity for African-American women. The event will increase awareness of the health risks associated with a sedentary lifestyle and promote the benefits of an active lifestyle. For info: Sheila Madison, Natl African-American Women's Fitness Month, PO Box 2733, Washington, DC 20013-2733. Phone: (281) 750-2767. E-mail: info@sheilamadison.com. Web: www.sheilamadison.com.

NATIONAL AUTISM AWARENESS MONTH. Apr 1–30. In order to highlight the growing need for concern and awareness about autism, the Autism Society has been celebrating National Autism Awareness Month since the 1970s. This month creates a special opportunity for people to educate themselves and others about autism and issues within the autism community. For info: Autism Society, 4340 East-West Hwy, Ste 350, Bethesda, MD 20814. Phone: (800) 328-8476. Web: www.autism-society.org.

★NATIONAL CANCER CONTROL MONTH. Apr 1–30.

NATIONAL CARD AND LETTER WRITING MONTH. Apr 1–May 10. An annual effort to promote literacy and celebrate the art of letter writing. The writing, sending and receiving of letters, postcards and greeting cards is a tradition that has preserved our nation's history and changed lives. Unlike other forms of communications, card and letter writing is timeless, personal and immediately tangible. Annually, from Apr 1 until Mother's Day.

★NATIONAL CHILD ABUSE PREVENTION MONTH. Apr 1–30.

NATIONAL CHILD ABUSE PREVENTION MONTH. Apr 1–30. A time to recognize that we each can play a part in promoting the social and emotional well-being of children and families in communities. For info: Administration for Children and Families, US Dept of Health and Human Services. Web: www.childwelfare.gov/preventing/preventionmonth.

★NATIONAL DONATE LIFE MONTH. Apr 1–30.

NATIONAL EXCHANGE CLUB CHILD ABUSE PREVENTION MONTH. Apr 1–30. In 1979 The National Exchange Club adopted the prevention of child abuse as its National Project. The National Exchange Club Foundation is a chartered nonprofit corporation in Ohio. Exchange has established Exchange Club Child Abuse Prevention Centers throughout the US. For info: The Natl Exchange Club Foundation. E-mail: info@nationalexchangeclub.org. Web: www.nationalexchangeclub.org/cap.

NATIONAL FROG MONTH. Apr 1–30. Longtime observance celebrating frogs and toads. This is a chance to learn about these amphibians—how important they are to their ecosystems—and perhaps create a frog- or toad-friendly habitat in your own yard. Annually, April.

NATIONAL HEARTWORM AWARENESS MONTH. Apr 1–30. This is a month to be sure pet owners understand the risks of heartworm disease. Heartworm disease is caused by foot-long worms that live in the heart, lungs and associated blood vessels of affected pets. Known as heartworms, these worms can cause severe lung disease, heart failure and organ damage. Some instances of heartworm infection may even prove fatal. Pet owners should test their pets for heartworm every 12 months. For info: American Heartworm Society. Web: www.heartwormsociety.org.

NATIONAL HUMOR MONTH. Apr 1–30. 45th anniversary. A month focusing on the pleasures of humor in all its forms as well as recognition of the value of humor to help us lighten up instead of tighten up. Ideas and resources available. For info: Steve Wilson, Director, Psychologist, The Joyologist, 5691 Asherton Woods Dr, Westerville, OH 43081. Phone: (800) NOW-LAFF. E-mail: steve@worldlaughtertour.com. Web: www.humormonth.com.

NATIONAL LAWN CARE MONTH. Apr 1–30. Since 1992, this month is dedicated to heightening public awareness of the many environmental and health benefits of natural grass, and educating consumers about how to best care for their lawns so they can maximize their enjoyment of the outdoors. Annually, the month of April. For info: National Association of Landscape Professionals, 12500 Fair Lakes Circle, Ste 200, Fairfax, VA 22033. E-mail: info@landscapeprofessionals.org. Web: www.LoveYourLandscape.org.

NATIONAL 9-1-1 EDUCATION MONTH. Apr 1–30. Since 2008, this month promotes ongoing, age-appropriate 9-1-1 education that can save lives. The National 9-1-1 Education Coalition provides resources and materials to support public education about the optimal use of 9-1-1 services nationwide. For info: Natl Assn of State 911 Administrators (NASNA). Web: www.know911.org.

NATIONAL OCCUPATIONAL THERAPY MONTH. Apr 1–30. Since 1980, a month to recognize the services and accomplishments of occupational therapy practitioners and promote awareness of the benefits of occupational therapy. For info: The American Occupational Therapy Assn, Inc, 4720 Montgomery Ln, Ste 200, Bethesda, MD 20814-3449. Phone: (301) 652-6611. Web: www.aota.org.

NATIONAL PECAN MONTH. Apr 1–30. A celebration of the great taste, health benefits and versatility of pecans. This delicious tree nut native to North America adds unmistakable flavor, crunch and texture to just about any meal or snack. Pecans have proven cholesterol-lowering properties and contain more than 19 important vitamins and minerals. Almost 90 percent of the fats in pecans are of the heart-healthy, unsaturated variety. For info: National Pecan Shellers Assn, 3200 Windy Hill Rd SE, Ste 600 West, Atlanta, GA 30339. Phone: (678) 298-1189. E-mail: npsa@kellencompany.com. Web: www.ilovepecans.org.

NATIONAL PEST MANAGEMENT MONTH. Apr 1–30. For more than 40 years, April has been celebrated as National Pest Management Month, recognizing the professional pest management industry for its role in protecting public health and property from significant pest threats. For info: Natl Pest Management Assn, 10460 North St, Fairfax, VA 22030. Phone: (703) 352-6762. Fax: (703) 352-3031. E-mail: NPMATeam@vaultcommunications.com. Web: www.pestworld.org.

NATIONAL POETRY MONTH. Apr 1–30. Since 1996, annual observance to pay tribute to the great legacy and ongoing achievement of American poets and the vital place of poetry in American culture. In a proclamation issued in honor of the first observance, President Bill Clinton called it "a welcome opportunity to celebrate

not only the unsurpassed body of literature produced by our poets in the past, but also the vitality and diversity of voices reflected in the works of today's American poetry." Spearheaded by the Academy of American Poets, this is the largest and most extensive celebration of poetry in American history. For info: Academy of American Poets, 75 Maiden Ln, Ste 901, New York, NY 10038. Phone: (212) 274-0343. E-mail: mcampagna@poets.org. Web: www.poets.org.

NATIONAL REBUILDING MONTH. Apr 1–30. 7th annual. A month-long call to service during the entire month of April, culminating with National Rebuilding Day, held on the last Saturday in April. Nearly 50,000 volunteers are in service on more than 1,700 affiliate-led rebuild projects on National Rebuilding Day across the country. Volunteers come together to rehabilitate the homes of low-income, elderly or disabled people and nonprofit facilities. For info: Rebuilding Together, 999 N Capitol St NE, Ste 701, Washington, DC 20002. Phone: (800) 473-4229. E-mail: info@rebuildingtogether.org. Web: www.rebuildingtogether.org.

★**NATIONAL SEXUAL ASSAULT AWARENESS AND PREVENTION MONTH.** Apr 1–30. First proclaimed by President Barack Obama in 2009 to urge Americans to respond to sexual assault by establishing policies at work and school, by engaging in discussions with family and friends and by making the prevention of sexual assault a priority in their communities.

NATIONAL SEXUAL ASSAULT AWARENESS MONTH. Apr 1–30. This month seeks to raise public awareness about sexual violence and to educate communities and individuals on how to prevent sexual violence. Each year during the month of April, state, territory, tribal and community-based organizations, rape crisis centers, government agencies, businesses, campuses and individuals plan events and activities to highlight sexual violence as a public health, human rights and social justice issue and reinforce the need for prevention efforts. The theme, slogan, resources and materials for the national SAAM campaign are coordinated by the National Sexual Violence Resource Center each year with assistance from anti-sexual assault organizations throughout the country. For info: National Sexual Violence Resource Center, 2101 N Front St, Governor's Plaza North, Building #2, Harrisburg, PA 17110. Phone: (877) 739-3895. E-mail: media@nsvrc.org. Web: www.nsvrc.org/saam.

NATIONAL SEXUALLY TRANSMITTED DISEASES (STDS) EDUCATION AND AWARENESS MONTH. Apr 1–30. To educate consumers, patients, students and professionals about the prevention of sexually transmitted diseases. Sponsored by the American College of Apothecaries (ACA)/Pharmacists Planning Service, Inc (PPSI). For info: ACA/PPSI, 2830 Summer Oaks Dr, Bartlett, TN 38134. E-mail: info@ppsinc.org. Web: www.ppsinc.org.

NATIONAL YOUTH SPORTS SAFETY MONTH. Apr 1–30. Bringing public attention to the prevalent problem of injuries in youth sports. This event promotes safety in sports activities and is supported by more than 60 national sports and medical organizations.

PET FIRST AID AWARENESS MONTH. Apr 1–30. Founded in 1999 by Pet Tech Productions, Inc, the first international training center for pet CPR, first aid and care. The goal of this annual month is to prevent one million pet ER visits by helping pet parents understand the importance of knowing the skills and techniques of CPR, first aid and care for their pets. For info: Pet Tech Productions, Inc, PO Box 2285, Carlsbad, CA 92018. Phone: (760) 930-0309. E-mail: pfaam@pettech.net. Web: www.PetTech.net.

PHARMACISTS' WAR ON DIABETES. Apr 1–30. To educate consumers, patients and healthcare professionals about prevention of diabetes, especially focusing on "Know Your Numbers for Diabetes"

and screening along with awareness and interest in the diabetes epidemic. Sponsored by the American College of Apothecaries (ACA)/Pharmacists Planning Service, Inc (PPSI). For info: ACA/PPSI, 2830 Summer Oaks Dr, Bartlett, TN 38134. E-mail: info@ppsinc.org. Web: www.ppsinc.org.

PREVENTION OF CRUELTY TO ANIMALS MONTH. Apr 1–30. Sponsored by the ASPCA, this crucial month is designed to educate Americans about animal cruelty and to urge them to report instances of violence toward animals. For info: Media & Communications Dept, ASPCA, 520 8th Ave, 7th Fl, New York, NY 10018. Phone: (212) 876-7700, ext 4655. E-mail: press@aspca.org. Web: www.aspca.org.

RAM, JAGJIVAN: BIRTH ANNIVERSARY. Apr 1, 1908. Indian political leader and coworker with Mohandas K. Gandhi and Jawaharlal Nehru in the fight for Indian independence. Born into a family of "untouchables" at the village of Chandwa, Bihar, India, Ram was one of the first of that class to attend school and university. Known as the champion and spokesman for India's 100 million untouchables, he overcame most of the handicaps of caste. He served in a number of ministerial cabinet posts and twice was a candidate for prime minister. Ram died at New Delhi, India, July 6, 1986.

REYNOLDS, DEBBIE: BIRTH ANNIVERSARY. Apr 1, 1932. Actress, born Mary Frances Reynolds in El Paso, TX. Reynolds rose to fame when her sultry voice and girl-next-door beauty lit up the *Singin' in the Rain* set in 1952. She starred in numerous films, including *The Tender Trap* (1955) and *How the West Was Won* (1962) and earned an Oscar nomination for *The Unsinkable Molly Brown* (1964). Her private life became front-page tabloid news when husband Eddie Fisher left her and their two children for Elizabeth Taylor in 1955. The demise of the musical did not derail her career; she continued working in film, on TV and on stage into her 80s. She was known for her volunteer work, receiving a Jean Hersholt Humanitarian Award in 2015 as well as a Screen Actors Guild Lifetime Achievement Award. Reynolds died Dec 28, 2016, one day after her daughter, actress Carrie Fisher, in Los Angeles, CA.

ROBERT THE HERMIT: DEATH ANNIVERSARY. Apr 1, 1832. One of the most famous hermits in American history died in his hermitage at Seekonk, MA. Robert was a bonded slave, the son of an African mother and probably an Anglo-Saxon father. After obtaining his freedom, he was swindled out of it and shipped to a foreign slave market, then later escaped to America. He was separated from his first wife by force and rejected by his second wife after a long sea voyage, before withdrawing from society.

ROSACEA AWARENESS MONTH. Apr 1–30. Rosacea Awareness Month has been designated by the National Rosacea Society to raise awareness and understanding of this increasingly common disease. Rosacea is a facial skin condition that can cause significant physical and psychological problems if it is not diagnosed and treated. For info: Natl Rosacea Society, 196 James St, Barrington, IL 60010. Phone: (847) 382-8971 or (888) NO-BLUSH. Fax: (847) 382-5567. E-mail: rosaceas@aol.com. Web: www.rosacea.org.

SCHOOL LIBRARY MONTH. Apr 1–30. First celebrated in 1985, School Library Month (SLM) is the American Association of School Librarians' (AASL) celebration of school librarians and their programs. Every April school librarians are encouraged to create activities to help their school and local community celebrate the essential role that strong school library programs play in a student's educational career. For info: American Assn of School Librarians, 50 E Huron

	S	M	T	W	T	F	S
April				1	2	3	4
	5	6	7	8	9	10	11
2020	12	13	14	15	16	17	18
	19	20	21	22	23	24	25
	26	27	28	29	30		

St, Chicago, IL 60611. Phone: (800) 545-2433, ext 4382. E-mail: aasl@ala.org. Web: www.ala.org/aasl/advocacy/slm.

SKAGIT VALLEY TULIP FESTIVAL. Apr 1–30. Skagit County, La Conner, Mount Vernon and Burlington, WA. To celebrate and share the spectacular beauty of more than 1,000 acres of blooming daffodils and tulips that herald the arrival of spring in the Skagit Valley of Washington State. Est attendance: 350,000. For info: Cindy Verge, SVTF Exec Dir, PO Box 1784, Mount Vernon, WA 98273. Phone: (360) 428-5959. Fax: (360) 428-6753. E-mail: info@tulipfestival.org. Web: www.tulipfestival.org.

STRAW HAT MONTH. Apr 1–30. A month of celebration during which the felt hat is put aside in favor of the straw or fabric hat by both men and women. Local businesses and the media are encouraged to plan hat-related activities. Originally sponsored by Casey Bush and the Headwear Information Bureau.

STRESS AWARENESS MONTH. Apr 1–30. To promote public awareness of what stress is, what causes it to occur and what can be done about it. A monthlong focus on the dangers of stress, successful coping strategies and the myths about stress that are prevalent in our society. For info: National Stress Awareness Month. Web: www.stressawarenessmonth.com.

TESTICULAR CANCER AWARENESS WEEK. Apr 1–7. This public awareness and education program was conceived in 1997 to create a better public understanding of the dangers of undetected testicular cancer in young men aged 15–34. The campaign is designed to promote the importance of early detection, which saves hundreds of young men's lives each year. Information is made available to high school and college health centers to ensure correct diagnosis. Annually, Apr 1–7. For info: Gordon Clay, TCAW, PO Box 12-CH, Brookings, OR 97415-0001. Web: www.menstuff.org/tcaw.

US AIR FORCE ACADEMY ESTABLISHED: ANNIVERSARY. Apr 1, 1954. President Dwight Eisenhower signed the bill this day that created the US Air Force Academy to train officers for the US Air Force. Construction on the Colorado Springs, CO, academy began July 11, 1955, and ended in 1958. The academy was accredited in 1959. Women were admitted in 1976. For info: www.usafa.edu.

US HOUSE OF REPRESENTATIVES ACHIEVES A QUORUM: ANNIVERSARY. Apr 1, 1789. First session of Congress was held Mar 4, 1789, but not enough representatives arrived to achieve a quorum until Apr 1.

WOMEN'S EYE HEALTH AND SAFETY MONTH. Apr 1–30. Women often manage family health concerns. Do women know how to protect their sight? Hormonal changes, age and smoking can endanger sight. Information on women's and family eye-health issues will be provided. For info: Prevent Blindness, 211 W Wacker Dr, Ste 1700, Chicago, IL 60606. Phone: (800) 331-2020. E-mail: info@preventblindness.org. Web: www.preventblindness.org.

WORKPLACE CONFLICT AWARENESS MONTH. Apr 1–30. At today's harried pace, workplace conflict is increasing. Many of us try to avoid this conflict, and instead we take it home with us. This month was created to make people aware that trying to avoid conflict is futile; we must learn to deal with it and manage it. For info: Richard Brenner, Chaco Canyon Consulting, 2455 Eaton Rd, University Heights, OH 44118. Phone: (650) 787-6475. E-mail: rbrenner@ChacoCanyon.com.

WORLD LANDSCAPE ARCHITECTURE MONTH. Apr 1–30. This month is an international celebration of landscape architecture. WLAM

introduces the profession to the public by showcasing landscape architect-designed spaces around the world. From the High Line in New York to your favorite local park, WLAM celebrates the work of ASLA's members and landscape architects around the globe. Annually, during April, as Apr 26 is the birth anniversary of Frederick Law Olmsted. Olmsted is widely regarded as the founder of the profession of landscape architecture. For info: ASLA, 636 Eye St NW, Washington, DC 20001-3736. Phone: (202) 898-2444 or (888) 999-2752. E-mail: info@asla.org. Web: www.asla.org.

WORLDWIDE BEREAVED SPOUSES AWARENESS MONTH. Apr 1–30. A month to promote support for bereaved spouses. Often people don't know what to say to or do for grieving spouses. So sometimes they turn away and do nothing. We encourage people to turn back and begin to reach out to bereaved spouses by listening to them without advising them; offering a shoulder to cry on; and hugging them when appropriate and needed. "Remember to reach out to the bereaved so they won't have to grieve alone." For info: Deborah Le Bouf Kulkkula, PhD, or Jane Guimares, MEd, 381 Billings Rd, Fitchburg, MA 01420-1407. Phone: (978) 343-4009 or (978) 808-8084 (cell). E-mail: DebKulkkula@gmail.com. Web: www.bereavementawareness.com.

🎂 BIRTHDAYS TODAY

Samuel A. Alito, Jr, 70, Associate Justice of the US, born Trenton, NJ, Apr 1, 1950.

Asa Butterfield, 23, actor (*Ender's Game*, *Hugo*), born Islington, London, England, Apr 1, 1997.

Taran Killam, 38, actor, comedian ("Saturday Night Live"), born Culver City, CA, Apr 1, 1982.

Ali MacGraw, 81, actress (*Goodbye, Columbus*; *Love Story*), born Pound Ridge, NY, Apr 1, 1939.

Rachel Maddow, 47, political commentator, born Castro Valley, CA, Apr 1, 1973.

Dan Mintz, 39, actor, writer ("Bob's Burgers," "Crank Yankers"), born Anchorage, AK, Apr 1, 1981.

Randy Orton, 40, professional wrestler, born Knoxville, TN, Apr 1, 1980.

Annette O'Toole, 67, actress (*Smile*, *48 Hrs*), born Houston, TX, Apr 1, 1953.

David Oyelowo, 44, actor (*Selma*, *Queen of Katwe*, *A United Kingdom*, "Spooks" ["MI-5"]), born Oxford, England, Apr 1, 1976.

Jane Powell, 91, actress (*Seven Brides for Seven Brothers*), born Suzanne Burce at Portland, OR, Apr 1, 1929.

Libby Riddles, 64, first woman to win the 1,135-mile Iditarod Alaskan dogsled race, born Madison, WI, Apr 1, 1956.

Hillary Scott, 34, country singer (Lady Antebellum), born Nashville, TN, Apr 1, 1986.

Daniel Joseph "Rusty" Staub, 76, former baseball player, born New Orleans, LA, Apr 1, 1944.

Jesmyn Ward, 43, author (National Book Awards for *Salvage the Bones* and *Sing, Unburied, Sing*), born Berkeley, CA, Apr 1, 1977.

April 2 — Thursday

DAY 93   **273 REMAINING**

ANDERSEN, HANS CHRISTIAN: BIRTH ANNIVERSARY. Apr 2, 1805. Author chiefly remembered for his more than 150 fairy tales, many of which are regarded as classics of children's literature. Andersen was born at Odense, Denmark, and died at Copenhagen, Denmark, Aug 4, 1875.

ARGENTINA: MALVINAS DAY. Apr 2. Public holiday. Full name is Day of the War Veterans and the Fallen in the Malvinas Islands. Commemorates the Argentine dead and wounded as a result of the attempt to regain the Falkland Islands in 1982. Observed since 2001.

"AS THE WORLD TURNS" TV PREMIERE: ANNIVERSARY. Apr 2, 1956. One of the longest-running soaps to air on television, "ATWT" premiered on CBS. The series was set in midwestern Oakdale and revolved around the Hughes family and their neighbors. Irna Phillips was the show's creator and head writer. Some of its famous former cast members are Meg Ryan, Julianne Moore, Steven Weber and Swoosie Kurtz. The final episode aired on Sept 17, 2010.

BARTHOLDI, FRÉDÉRIC AUGUSTE: BIRTH ANNIVERSARY. Apr 2, 1834. French sculptor who created *Liberty Enlightening the World* (better known as the Statue of Liberty), which stands at New York Harbor. Also remembered for the *Lion of Belfort* at Belfort, France. Born at Colman, at Alsace, France. Died at Paris, Oct 4, 1904.

CASANOVA, GIOVANNI GIACOMO GIROLAMO: BIRTH ANNIVERSARY. Apr 2, 1725. Celebrated Italian writer-librarian and, by his own account, philanderer, adventurer, rogue, seminarian, soldier and spy, born at Venice, Italy. As the Chevalier de Seingalt, he died at Dux, Bohemia, June 4, 1798, while serving as librarian and working on his lively and frank *History of My Life*, a brilliant picture of 18th-century life.

"DALLAS" TV PREMIERE: ANNIVERSARY. Apr 2, 1978. Oil tycoons battled for money, power and prestige in this prime-time CBS drama that ran for nearly 13 years. The Ewings and Barneses were Texas's modern-day Hatfields and McCoys. Larry Hagman starred as the devious, scheming womanizer J.R. Ewing. When J.R. was shot in the 1980 season-ending cliffhanger, the revelation of the mystery shooter was the single most-watched episode of its time (it was Kristin, J.R.'s sister-in-law, played by Mary Crosby). Cast members included Jim Davis, Barbara Bel Geddes, Donna Reed, Ted Shackelford, Joan Van Ark, Patrick Duffy, Linda Gray, Charlene Tilton, David Wayne, Keenan Wynn, Ken Kercheval, Victoria Principal and Steve Kanaly. A spin-off show was "Knots Landing." "Dallas" was revived in 2012 with many of the original cast as well as a new generation of troublemakers.

EBSEN, BUDDY: BIRTH ANNIVERSARY. Apr 2, 1908. Born Christian Rudolph Ebsen, Jr, at Belleville, IL. Buddy Ebsen started his career as a vaudeville "song-and-dance" man, then was popular throughout the 1930s on film as well. He almost played the Tin Man in *The Wizard of Oz* (1939) but had a serious allergic reaction to the makeup and was forced to stop filming. In the 1950s, he played Davy Crockett's sidekick on television and in film. He played Jed Clampett in "The Beverly Hillbillies" (1962–71) and starred as "Barnaby Jones" (1973–80). He died at Torrance, CA, July 6, 2003.

ENGLAND: GRAND NATIONAL. Apr 2–4. Aintree Racecourse, Liverpool. 173rd annual. First held in 1839. Often called the world's greatest steeplechase, the Grand National is one of the most famous steeplechases in the world. It is a unique test of horsemanship for the rider and also a test of great significance for a horse. The course is nearly two and a quarter miles in length and has 16 unique fences. Apr 2 is Grand National Thursday, Apr 3 is Ladies Day and Apr 4 is Grand National Day. Sponsored by Randox Health. Est attendance: 150,000. For info: Grand National, Aintree Racecourse, Ormskirk Rd, Aintree, Liverpool L9 5AS, England. Web: www.aintree.co.uk or www.randoxhealthgrandnational.co.uk.

FALKLAND ISLANDS WAR: ANNIVERSARY. Apr 2–June 15, 1982. Argentina, claiming sovereignty over the nearby Falkland Islands (called the Malvinas by Argentina), invaded and occupied the British Crown colony on Apr 2, 1982. British forces defeated the Argentinians on June 15, 1982. About 250 British and 600

Argentine lives were lost in the conflict. In 1986 three military officers, including General Leopoldo Galtieri (who was president of Argentina at the time of the invasion), were convicted and sentenced for the military crime of negligence. Commemorative ceremonies are observed as Malvinas Day in Argentina.

FIRST WHITE HOUSE EASTER EGG ROLL: ANNIVERSARY. Apr 2, 1878. The first White House Easter Egg Roll took place during the administration of Rutherford B. Hayes. The traditional event was discontinued by President Franklin D. Roosevelt in 1942 and reinstated Apr 6, 1953, by President Dwight D. Eisenhower.

FRENCH QUARTER FESTIVAL. Apr 2–5. New Orleans, LA. 37th annual. This festival focuses on all that makes the Quarter special—food, music and people. Free concerts on 23 stages featuring 1,700 local musicians, parade and children's and other activities. Est attendance: 730,000. For info: French Quarter Festivals. Phone: (504) 522-5730 E-mail: info@fqfi.org. Web: www.fqfi.org.

GUINNESS, SIR ALEC: BIRTH ANNIVERSARY. Apr 2, 1914. One of Britain's greatest stage and screen actors, born at London, England. He received an Academy Award for his performance in *The Bridge on the River Kwai* (1957). Other important films include the Star Wars initial trilogy, *Great Expectations, Oliver Twist, The Ladykillers, Kind Hearts and Coronets* and *A Passage to India*. Knighted in 1959, he died at West Sussex, England, Aug 5, 2000.

LOVE YOUR PRODUCE MANAGER DAY®. Apr 2. Since 2012, a day to honor exemplary customer service in US supermarket produce departments. These hardworking produce staff are the unsung heroes of the healthy eating revolution, quietly playing a key role in increasing fruit and vegetable consumption just by helping us take home the freshest produce. Say hello and thank you to your produce manager or give a shout-out on social media #LYPM. Annually, Apr 2. For info: Frieda's. E-mail: news.bureau@friedas.com. Web: www.friedas.com/LYPM.

NATIONAL FERRET DAY. Apr 2. A day to educate the public to respect this lively and intelligent companion animal—the domesticated ferret. This day is also a time to focus on such ferret issues as welfare, care, nutrition and responsible ownership. Annually, Apr 2 (in the United States). For info: American Ferret Assn, PO Box 554, Frederick, MD 21705-0554. Phone: (888) FERRET-1. E-mail: afa@ferret.org. Web: www.ferret.org/nationalferretday.

NICKELODEON DEBUT: ANNIVERSARY. Apr 2, 1979. Nickelodeon, the cable TV channel for kids owned by MTV Networks, debuted on this date.

PASCUA FLORIDA DAY. Apr 2. A legal holiday in Florida, designated as State Day. When it falls on a Saturday or Sunday, the governor may declare either the preceding Friday or the following Monday as State Day. Commemorates the sighting of Florida by Ponce de León in 1513. He named the land Pascua Florida because of its discovery at Easter, the "Feast of the Flowers."

PONCE DE LEÓN DISCOVERS FLORIDA: ANNIVERSARY. Apr 2, 1513. Juan Ponce de León discovered Florida, landing at the site that became the city of St. Augustine. He claimed the land for the king of Spain.

POPE JOHN PAUL II: 15th DEATH ANNIVERSARY. Apr 2, 2005. Karol Wojtyla, 264th pope of the Roman Catholic Church, elected Oct 16, 1978, died at Vatican City.

April 2020	S	M	T	W	T	F	S
				1	2	3	4
	5	6	7	8	9	10	11
	12	13	14	15	16	17	18
	19	20	21	22	23	24	25
	26	27	28	29	30		

RECONCILIATION DAY. Apr 2. Columnist Ann Landers wrote, "Since 1989, I have suggested that Apr 2 be set aside to write that letter or make that phone call and mend a broken relationship. Life is too short to hold grudges. To forgive can be enormously life-enhancing."

SWITZERLAND: NÄFELS PILGRIMAGE. Apr 2. Canton Glarus. Commemoration of the battle of Näfels, fought on Apr 9, 1388. Observed annually on the first Thursday in April, with processions, prayers, sermon and a reading out of the names of those killed in the battle.

***2001: A SPACE ODYSSEY* PREMIERE: ANNIVERSARY.** Apr 2, 1968. Directed by Stanley Kubrick, this influential film has elicited many different interpretations. Sci-fi novelist Arthur C. Clarke based the screenplay on his 1968 book, which was prescient in several ways. Writing before men had landed on the moon, Clarke describes an expedition launched to Jupiter to track a mysterious signal emanating from the moon. Clarke gave the world's population as six billion (achieved in 1999) and described a space station. During flight, a character reads the news on his electronic news pad. The film starred Keir Dullea, William Sylvester, Gary Lockwood, Daniel Richter and HAL 9000, the creepy computer that had human emotions. The theme music was Richard Strauss's *Also Sprach Zarathustra*.

UNITED NATIONS: WORLD AUTISM AWARENESS DAY. Apr 2. Deeply concerned by the prevalence and high rate of autism in children in all regions of the world, the General Assembly designated Apr 2 as World Autism Awareness Day on Dec 18, 2007 (Res 62/139). Autism affects children in all regions, irrespective of gender, race or socioeconomic status. It poses challenges to long-term health care, education, training and intervention programs, and it has a tremendous impact on children, families, communities and societies. For info: United Nations, Dept of Public Info, New York, NY, 10017. Web: www.un.org.

US MINT: ANNIVERSARY. Apr 2, 1792. The first US Mint was established at Philadelphia, PA, as authorized by an act of Congress.

WEBB, JACK: 100th BIRTH ANNIVERSARY. Apr 2, 1920. "Just the facts, ma'am"—this no-nonsense request meant that Sgt Joe Friday (badge 714) was on the case in the influential, documentary-style cop drama, "Dragnet." Friday portrayer Jack Webb was the brains behind "Dragnet" and other law-enforcement television series (among them "Adam-12"). He was also a director and producer. Born John Randolph Webb at Santa Monica, CA, he saw service in WWII, then worked in radio, the medium in which he first launched "Dragnet." Webb died Dec 23, 1982, at West Hollywood, CA.

WHITE, CHARLES: BIRTH ANNIVERSARY. Apr 2, 1918. Renowned African-American artist, born at Chicago, IL; died Oct 3, 1979. Charles White began his professional career by painting murals for the WPA during the Depression. He was influenced by Mexican muralists Diego Rivera and David Alfaro Siqueiros. Among his most notable creations are *J'Accuse* (1966), a series of charcoal drawings depicting a variety of African Americans from all ages and walks of life; the *Wanted* posters (c. 1969), a series of paintings based on old runaway slave posters; and *Homage to Langston Hughes* (1971).

ZOLA, ÉMILE: BIRTH ANNIVERSARY. Apr 2, 1840. Journalist and novelist of the naturalist school whose scores of novels made him wealthy and a key figure in France's literary establishment. Émile Edouard Charles Antoine Zola was born at Paris, France. Some of his notable novels are *Therese Raquin* (1867), *The Belly of Paris* (1873), *Nana* (1880) and *Germinal* (1885). He is also remembered for his role in the Dreyfus case, with his Jan 13, 1898, newspaper indictment entitled "J'Accuse . . .!" His efforts exposed a military cover-up and resulted in the retrial and ultimate vindication of Alfred Dreyfus. Defective venting of a stove flue in his bedroom (which some believed to be the work of political enemies) resulted in his death from carbon monoxide poisoning at Paris, Sept 28, 1902. In 1908, his remains were removed from their burial place to the Pantheon.

🎂 BIRTHDAYS TODAY

Michael Fassbender, 43, actor (*Steve Jobs, 12 Years a Slave, Prometheus, X-Men: First Class*), born Heidelberg, Germany, Apr 2, 1977.

Clark Gregg, 58, actor ("Agents of S.H.I.E.L.D.," *Iron Man*), born Boston, MA, Apr 2, 1962.

Emmylou Harris, 73, singer, born Birmingham, AL, Apr 2, 1947.

Linda Hunt, 75, actress ("NCIS: Los Angeles," "The Practice," Oscar for *The Year of Living Dangerously*), born Morristown, NJ, Apr 2, 1945.

Bethany Joy Lenz, 39, actress, musician ("One Tree Hill," "Guiding Light"), born Hollywood, FL, Apr 2, 1981.

Christopher Meloni, 59, actor ("True Blood," "Law & Order: SVU," "Oz"), born Washington, DC, Apr 2, 1961.

Camille Paglia, 73, literature professor and literary and cultural critic, born Endicott, NY, Apr 2, 1947.

Pamela Reed, 67, actress (*The Right Stuff, Bob Roberts*), born Tacoma, WA, Apr 2, 1953 (some sources say 1949).

April 3 — Friday

DAY 94   **272 REMAINING**

BIRMINGHAM RESISTANCE: ANNIVERSARY. Apr 3, 1962. In retaliation against a black boycott of downtown stores, the Birmingham, AL, city commission voted not to pay the city's $45,000 share of a $100,000 county program that supplied surplus food to the needy. More than 90 percent of the recipients of aid were black. When the NAACP protested the commission's decision, Birmingham mayor Arthur J. Hanes dismissed the complaint as a "typical reaction from New York Socialist radicals."

BLACKS RULED ELIGIBLE TO VOTE: ANNIVERSARY. Apr 3, 1944. The US Supreme Court, in an 8–1 ruling, declared that blacks could not be barred from voting in the Texas Democratic primaries. The high court repudiated the contention that political parties are private associations and held that discrimination against blacks violated the 15th Amendment.

BOSTON PUBLIC LIBRARY: ANNIVERSARY. Apr 3, 1848. The Massachusetts legislature passed legislation enabling Boston to levy a tax for a public library. This created the funding model for all public libraries in the US. The Boston Public Library opened its doors in 1854.

BRANDO, MARLON: BIRTH ANNIVERSARY. Apr 3, 1924. Born at Omaha, NE, Marlon Brando was perhaps the most influential film actor of his generation. Using the Method style of acting as taught by Stella Adler, his powerful performances in *A Streetcar Named Desire* (1951) and *Viva Zapata!* (1952) established his presence as a star, and *On the Waterfront* (1953) earned him an Academy Award. Later films include *Last Tango in Paris* (1972) and

Apocalypse Now (1979), but he is perhaps best remembered for his role as Vito Corleone from *The Godfather* (1972), for which he won his second Oscar. Somewhat of a recluse later in his life, he died July 1, 2004, at Los Angeles, CA.

BURROUGHS, JOHN: BIRTH ANNIVERSARY. Apr 3, 1837. American naturalist and author, born at Roxbury, NY. "Time does not become sacred to us until we have lived it," he wrote in 1877. Died en route from California to New York, Mar 29, 1921.

FALL OF RICHMOND: ANNIVERSARY. Apr 3, 1865. After the withdrawal of Robert E. Lee's troops, the Confederate capital of Richmond and nearby Petersburg surrendered to Union forces on this day. Richmond had survived four years of continuous threats from the North. On Apr 4, the city was toured by President Abraham Lincoln.

GRAHAM, CALVIN "BABY VET": 90th BIRTH ANNIVERSARY. Apr 3, 1930. The man who became known as WWII's "baby vet," Calvin Graham was born at Canton, TX, and enlisted in the navy at the age of 12. As a gunner on the USS *South Dakota*, he was struck by shrapnel during the battle of Guadalcanal in 1942 but still helped pull fellow crew members to safety. The navy gave Graham a dishonorable discharge, revoked his disability benefits and stripped him of his decorations, including a Purple Heart and Bronze Star, after discovering his age. Eventually, through congressional efforts, he was granted an honorable discharge and won back all but the Purple Heart. His benefits were restored in 1988. Graham died Nov 6, 1992, at Fort Worth, TX.

GUINEA: ANNIVERSARY OF THE SECOND REPUBLIC. Apr 3. National holiday. Commemorates the establishment of the Second Republic in 1984.

HOWARD, LESLIE: BIRTH ANNIVERSARY. Apr 3, 1893. Romantic actor of Hollywood's golden age who became a casualty of WWII. During the return trip from a British government–sponsored tour of Spain, a plane transporting Leslie Howard was shot down by German raiders. Howard's most-remembered film role is that of Ashley Wilkes in *Gone with the Wind*. Born at London, England; died at sea June 1, 1943.

INAUGURATION OF PONY EXPRESS: ANNIVERSARY. Apr 3, 1860. The Pony Express began when the first rider left St. Joseph, MO, heading west. The following day another rider headed east from Sacramento, CA. For $5 an ounce, letters were delivered within 10 days. There were 190 way stations between 10 and 15 miles apart, and each rider had a "run" of between 75 and 100 miles. The Pony Express lasted less than two years, ceasing operation in October 1861, when the overland telegraph was completed.

INTERNATIONAL KIDS' YOGA DAY. Apr 3. 5th annual. A special day whose mission is to raise awareness of and ignite a passion for fitness and yoga in children around the world. On this day, tens of thousands of children from all 50 states and all over the globe do a simple, five-minute routine according to age and physical ability. (No cost to participate.) Help change the world, one pose at a time. Annually, the first Friday in April. For info: Teresa Power, International Kids Yoga Day, PO Box 291, Pacific Palisades, CA 90272. E-mail: info@kidsyogaday.com. Web: kidsyogaday.com.

IRVING, WASHINGTON: BIRTH ANNIVERSARY. Apr 3, 1783. American author, attorney and onetime US minister to Spain, Irving was born at New York, NY. Creator of *Rip van Winkle* and *The Legend of Sleepy Hollow*, he was also the author of many historical and biographical works, including *A History of the Life and Voyages of Christopher Columbus* and the *Life of Washington*. Died at Tarrytown, NY, Nov 28, 1859.

"I'VE BEEN TO THE MOUNTAINTOP" SPEECH: ANNIVERSARY. Apr 3, 1968. Martin Luther King, Jr's last speech was given at Mason Temple in Memphis, TN, in support of striking black sanitation workers. After urging continued nonviolent protest as well as economic boycotts, King seemed to prophesy his death the next day by assassination: "I've seen the Promised Land. I may not get there with you. But I want you to know tonight, that we, as a people, will get to the promised land!"

LUCE, HENRY: BIRTH ANNIVERSARY. Apr 3, 1898. American editor and publisher, born to missionary parents at Penglai, China. He built his publishing empire with *Time, Fortune, Life* and *Sports Illustrated*. Luce also was involved in broadcasting. Died at Phoenix, AZ, Feb 28, 1967.

MARSHALL PLAN: ANNIVERSARY. Apr 3, 1948. Suggested by Secretary of State George C. Marshall in a speech at Harvard, June 5, 1947, the legislation for the European Recovery Program, popularly known as the Marshall Plan, was signed by President Truman on Apr 3, 1948. After distributing more than $12 billion, the program ended in 1952.

MEDIEVAL FAIR. Apr 3–5. Reaves Park, Norman, OK. Arts and crafts and living-history fair. The Middle Ages come alive with dancers, music, theater, jousting, knights in combat and a human chess match. Feasts and follies include games and food "fit for a king." Meet such characters as King Arthur, Sir Lancelot and Merlin. Admission is free. Est attendance: 325,000. For info: Ann Marie Eckart, Medieval Fair, 1700 Asp Ave, Norman, OK 73072-6400. Phone: (405) 325-8610. Fax: (405) 325-0860. Web: www.medievalfair.org.

NCAA DIVISION I WOMEN'S BASKETBALL CHAMPIONSHIP (WOMEN'S FINAL FOUR). Apr 3 and 5. New Orleans, LA. 39th annual. For info: NCAA, PO Box 6222, Indianapolis, IN 46206-6222. Phone: (317) 917-6222. Web: www.NCAA.com/womens-final-four.

RAND, SALLY: BIRTH ANNIVERSARY. Apr 3, 1904. American actress, ecdysiast and inventor of the fan dance, which gained fame at the 1933 Chicago World's Fair. Born Helen Gould Beck at Hickory County, MO. Died at Glendora, CA, Aug 31, 1979.

TAIWAN: CHILDREN'S DAY. Apr 3. Public holiday observed before or on Tomb-Sweeping Day. Reinstated holiday starting in 2011.

TWEED DAY: BIRTH ANNIVERSARY OF WILLIAM TWEED. Apr 3, 1823. Day to consider the cost of political corruption. Birthday of William March Tweed, New York City political boss, whose "Tweed Ring" is said to have stolen $30 million to $200 million from the city. Born at New York, NY, Apr 3, 1823, he died in his cell at New York's Ludlow Street Jail, Apr 12, 1878. Cartoonist Thomas Nast deserves much credit for Tweed's arrests and convictions.

WOMAN PRESIDES OVER US SUPREME COURT: 25th ANNIVERSARY. Apr 3, 1995. Supreme Court Justice Sandra Day O'Connor became the first woman to preside over the US high court when she sat in for Chief Justice William H. Rehnquist and second-in-seniority Justice John Paul Stevens when both were out of town.

🎂 BIRTHDAYS TODAY

Alec Baldwin, 62, actor ("30 Rock," *Blue Jasmine, The Cooler, The Hunt for Red October*), born Massapequa, NY, Apr 3, 1958.

Jamie Bamber, 47, actor ("Battlestar Galactica"), born Hammersmith, London, England, Apr 3, 1973.

Rachel Bloom, 33, actress ("Crazy Ex-Girlfriend"), comedienne, born Los Angeles, CA, Apr 3, 1987.

April	S	M	T	W	T	F	S
				1	2	3	4
	5	6	7	8	9	10	11
	12	13	14	15	16	17	18
2020	19	20	21	22	23	24	25
	26	27	28	29	30		

Sofia Boutella, 38, actress (*The Mummy, Atomic Blonde, Star Trek: Beyond*), born Bab el Oued, Algeria, Apr 3, 1982.

Amanda Bynes, 34, actress (*Big Fat Liar*, "What I Like About You"), born Thousand Oaks, CA, Apr 3, 1986.

Max Frankel, 90, journalist, born Gera, Germany, Apr 3, 1930.

Jennie Garth, 48, actress ("Beverly Hills 90210"), born Champaign, IL, Apr 3, 1972.

Jane Goodall (Baroness Van Lawick-Goodall), 86, anthropologist known for study of chimpanzees, born London, England, Apr 3, 1934.

Matthew Goode, 42, actor ("A Discovery of Witches," "Death Comes to Pemberley," *Stoker, A Single Man*), born Exeter, England, Apr 3, 1978.

Leona Lewis, 35, singer, born Islington, London, England, Apr 3, 1985.

Jonathan Lynn, 77, writer, actor, director (*Into the Night, Nuns on the Run, My Cousin Vinny*), born Bath, England, Apr 3, 1943.

Marsha Mason, 78, actress (*The Goodbye Girl, Cinderella Liberty*), born St. Louis, MO, Apr 3, 1942.

Eddie Murphy, 59, comedian ("Saturday Night Live"), actor (*Dreamgirls, Trading Places, Beverly Hills Cop*), born Brooklyn, NY, Apr 3, 1961.

Wayne Newton, 78, singer, born Norfolk, VA, Apr 3, 1942.

Tony Orlando, 76, singer (Tony Orlando and Dawn), born Michael Orlando Cassivitis at New York, NY, Apr 3, 1944.

Bernie Parent, 75, Hall of Fame hockey player, born Montreal, QC, Canada, Apr 3, 1945.

David Hyde Pierce, 61, actor (Tony for *Curtains*; Emmys for "Frasier"), born Albany, NY, Apr 3, 1959.

Adam Scott, 47, actor (*Krampus*, "Ghosted," "Big Little Lies," "Parks and Recreation"), born Santa Cruz, CA, Apr 3, 1973.

Cobie Smulders, 38, actress ("How I Met Your Mother," "The L Word"), born Vancouver, BC, Canada, Apr 3, 1982.

Picabo Street, 49, Olympic skier, born Triumph, ID, Apr 3, 1971.

April 4 — Saturday

DAY 95　　　　　**271 REMAINING**

ANGELOU, MAYA: BIRTH ANNIVERSARY. Apr 4, 1928. The acclaimed poet, civil rights activist and memoirist, best known as the author of *I Know Why the Caged Bird Sings* (1969), was born Marguerite Johnson at St. Louis, MO. She delivered the inaugural poem, "On the Pulse of the Morning," in 1993 for incoming US president William Clinton. She received the Presidential Medal of Freedom in 2011. Angelou, who was also a Tony Award–nominated actress, died May 28, 2014, at Winston-Salem, NC.

BEATLES TAKE OVER MUSIC CHARTS: ANNIVERSARY. Apr 4, 1964. On this date The Beatles held the top five positions of the Billboard Hot 100 chart: "Can't Buy Me Love" was number one, followed by (in order) "Twist and Shout," "She Loves You," "I Want to Hold Your Hand" and "Please, Please Me." The Beatles had made their first US appearance barely two months before. In the same week, they held the top six places on the Australian music chart.

BONZA BOTTLER DAY®. Apr 4. To celebrate when the number of the day is the same as the number of the month. Bonza Bottler Day® is an excuse to have a party at least once a month. For more information see Jan 1. For info: Gail Berger, Bonza Bottler Day. Phone: (864) 201-3988. E-mail: bonza@bonzabottlerday.com. Web: www.bonzabottlerday.com.

CANADA: ELMIRA MAPLE SYRUP FESTIVAL. Apr 4. Elmira, ON. 56th annual. Tours of maple bush by hay wagon, sugaring-off shanties in operation, pancakes with local maple syrup, other varieties of food on the mall, handcrafted goods, arts and crafts, antiques, toy show, Old MacDonald's Farm and performances. Fun for the whole family! Recognized by Guinness World Records as the "world's largest one-day maple syrup festival." Est attendance: 80,000. For info: Woolwich Visitor Services, 24 Church St W, Elmira, ON, Canada N3B 2Z6. Phone: (519) 669-6000 or (877) 969-0094. E-mail: info@elmiramaplesyrup.com. Web: www.elmiramaplesyrup.com.

CHINA AND TAIWAN: QING MING FESTIVAL OR TOMB-SWEEPING DAY. Apr 4. This Confucian festival was traditionally celebrated on the fourth or fifth day of the third month but is now on fixed dates (Apr 4 or 5) in China and Taiwan. It is observed by the maintenance of ancestral graves, the presentation of food, wine and flowers as offerings and the burning of paper money at gravesides to help ancestors in the afterworld. People also picnic and gather for family meals.

DIX, DOROTHEA LYNDE: BIRTH ANNIVERSARY. Apr 4, 1802. American social reformer and author, born at Hampden, ME. Left home at age 10, was teaching at age 14 and founded a home for girls at Boston, MA, while still in her teens. In spite of frail health, she was a vigorous crusader for humane conditions in insane asylums, jails and almshouses and for the establishment of state-supported institutions to serve those needs. Named superintendent of women nurses during the Civil War. Died at Trenton, NJ, July 17, 1887.

DURAS, MARGUERITE: BIRTH ANNIVERSARY. Apr 4, 1914. Novelist, playwright, screenwriter and filmmaker Duras was one of France's most prolific, popular writers after WWII. Best-known works are her screenplay for *Hiroshima, Mon Amour* (1959) and her novel *The Lover* (1984). Duras said, "Even when my books are completely invented, even when I think they have come from elsewhere, they are always personal." Born Marguerite Donnadieu at Saigon (now Ho Chi Minh City), Vietnam, she died Mar 3, 1996, at Paris, France.

FLAG ACT OF 1818: ANNIVERSARY. Apr 4, 1818. During the presidency of James Monroe, Congress approved the first flag of the US, designating that after the next July 4 (1818), the flag would have 13 alternating stripes of red and white and that there would be 20 stars on a blue field. In section two, it specified that "on the admission of every new state into the Union, one star be added to the union of the flag; and that such addition shall take effect on the fourth day of July then next succeeding such admission."

HARRISON, WILLIAM HENRY: DEATH ANNIVERSARY. Apr 4, 1841. Just over 30 days after being inaugurated as the ninth president of the US, William Henry Harrison died at Washington, DC. He was 68 years old. Doctors at the time diagnosed the cause of death as pneumonia and blamed his two-hour inaugural address given Mar 4, 1841, in dismal, cold weather. It is more likely that he died of typhus. Harrison was the first US president to die in office.

HATE WEEK. Apr 4–10. Recognizes the day on which the fictional character Winston Smith started his secret diary and wrote the words "DOWN WITH BIG BROTHER," Wednesday, Apr 4, 1984. From George Orwell's dystopian novel, *1984*, portraying the end of human privacy and the destruction of the individual in a totalitarian state (first published in 1949). "Hates" varied from the daily two-minute concentrated hate to the grand culmination observed during Hate Week.

INTERNATIONAL PILLOW FIGHT DAY. Apr 4. Since 2008, a day to participate in a massive pillow fight! Observed in cities all over the world. Rules: soft pillows only, light swings, no glasses and only with obvious participants. And it truly is better with feather

pillows. All participants clean up afterward. Annually, the first Saturday in April. For info: The Urban Playground Movement. Web: www.pillowfightday.com.

KING, MARTIN LUTHER, JR: ASSASSINATION: ANNIVERSARY. Apr 4, 1968. The Reverend Dr. Martin Luther King, Jr, was shot at Memphis, TN, while standing on the balcony of the Lorraine Motel. He was in that city to support striking sanitation workers. Assassin James Earl Ray died in prison in 1998 while serving a 99-year sentence for the crime. See also: "King, Martin Luther, Jr: Birth Anniversary" (Jan 15).

NATIONAL ROBOTICS WEEK. Apr 4–12. Since 2010, this observance encompasses a series of grassroots events and activities aimed at increasing public awareness of the strength and importance of the US robotics industry and of the tremendous social and cultural impact that robotics will have on the future. Activities come in all shapes and sizes from a robot block party to a university open house or a robotics competition. The mission of "RoboWeek" is simple: to inspire students in STEM-related fields and to share the excitement of robotics with audiences of all ages. For info: iRobot. E-mail: press@nationalroboticsweek.org. Web: www.nationalroboticsweek.org.

NCAA DIVISION I MEN'S BASKETBALL CHAMPIONSHIP (MEN'S FINAL FOUR). Apr 4 and 6. Mercedes-Benz Stadium, Atlanta, GA. 82nd annual. For info: NCAA, 700 W Washington St, PO Box 6222, Indianapolis, IN 46206-6222. Phone: (317) 917-6222. Web: www.NCAAsports.com/finalfour.

NORTH ATLANTIC TREATY RATIFIED: ANNIVERSARY. Apr 4, 1949. The North Atlantic Treaty Organization was created by this treaty, which was signed by 12 nations, including the US. (Other countries joined later.) The NATO member nations are united for common defense. The treaty went into effect Apr 24, 1949, and the first session of the North Atlantic Council was held Sept 17, 1949.

PERKINS, ANTHONY: BIRTH ANNIVERSARY. Apr 4, 1932. American actor Anthony Perkins was born at New York, NY. Best known for his movie role as homicidal innkeeper Norman Bates in the film *Psycho* (1960), Perkins appeared in many Broadway plays in addition to his numerous film roles. He received an Oscar nomination for his supporting role in *Friendly Persuasion* (1956). Perkins died Sept 12, 1992, at Hollywood, CA.

SALTER ELECTED FIRST WOMAN MAYOR IN US: ANNIVERSARY. Apr 4, 1887. The first woman elected mayor in the US was Susanna Medora Salter, who was elected mayor of Argonia, KS. Her name had been submitted for election without her knowledge by the Women's Christian Temperance Union, and she did not know she was a candidate until she went to the polls to vote. She received a two-thirds majority vote and served one year for the salary of $1.

SENEGAL: INDEPENDENCE DAY: 60th ANNIVERSARY OF INDEPENDENCE. Apr 4. National holiday. Commemorates independence from France in 1960.

	S	M	T	W	T	F	S
April				1	2	3	4
	5	6	7	8	9	10	11
2020	12	13	14	15	16	17	18
	19	20	21	22	23	24	25
	26	27	28	29	30		

SMOTHERS BROTHERS FIRED: ANNIVERSARY. Apr 4, 1969. CBS canceled the brothers' popular comedy series on this date. The hour-long show strongly influenced television humor during the two years it aired. Tom and Dick, however, frequently found themselves at odds with the censors over material that would be considered tame today. Guests and cast members frequently knocked the Vietnam War and the Nixon administration. Acts featuring antiwar protestors such as Harry Belafonte were often cut.

SPEAKER, TRIS: BIRTH ANNIVERSARY. Apr 4, 1888. Tristram E. Speaker, Baseball Hall of Fame outfielder, was born at Hubbard City, TX. Known as "the Gray Eagle," Speaker was one of the greatest center fielders of all time. He started his career with the Boston Red Sox, where he was part of the Hooper-Speaker-Lewis outfield, and then achieved stardom in a second city, playing for the Cleveland Indians. Inducted into the Hall of Fame in 1937, he died at Lake Whitney, TX, Dec 8, 1958.

SPRING SWING CITY ELECTRA-QUANAH-WIDE GARAGE SALE. Apr 4. Electra, TX. More than 50 miles of garage sales throughout the Electra area. Chamber of commerce will provide free coffee and maps at 7 AM; sales start at 8 AM. The chamber of commerce office will close at 8 AM so that we too may enjoy all of the bargains. Est attendance: 500. For info: Sherry Strange, Electra Chamber of Commerce, 112 W Cleveland, Electra, TX 76360. Phone: (940) 495-3577. E-mail: electracoc@electratel.net. Web: www.electratexas.org.

SUBARU CHERRY BLOSSOM FESTIVAL OF GREATER PHILADELPHIA. Apr 4–5. Philadelphia, PA. Welcome to the world of the cherry blossoms (*sakura*). A program of the Japan America Society of Greater Philadelphia, this festival is an initiative to encourage a better understanding of the cultural, social and educational customs of Japan and the United States. For hundreds of years, Japan has been celebrating the beauty of the elegant pink cherry blossom with picnics under the trees accompanied by traditional music and dance. Set under the blossoming canopy of Philadelphia's cherry trees, the festival is a chance to experience a centuries-old tradition that celebrates the fleeting splendor of spring like no other. Sakura Sunday is the festival's major event. Est attendance: 50,000. For info: Japan America Society of Greater Philadelphia. Web: www.subarucherryblossom.org.

SWAYZE, JOHN CAMERON: BIRTH ANNIVERSARY. Apr 4, 1906. Pioneering television journalist whose catchphrase was "hopscotching the world for news." Swayze was one of the first reporters to do on-air interviews and report on breaking news stories. Born at Wichita, KS, he died at Sarasota, FL, Aug 15, 1995.

UNITED NATIONS: INTERNATIONAL DAY FOR MINE AWARENESS AND ASSISTANCE IN MINE ACTION. Apr 4. Calling for continued efforts by member states, with the assistance of the United Nations and relevant organizations, to foster the establishment and development of national mine-action capacities in countries where mines and explosive remnants of war constitute a serious threat to the safety, health and lives of the civilian population or an impediment to social and economic development at the national and local levels. (Res 60/97 of Dec 8, 2005.) Annually, Apr 4. For info: United Nations, Dept of Public Info, New York, NY 10017. Web: www.un.org.

VITAMIN C ISOLATED: ANNIVERSARY. Apr 4, 1932. Vitamin C was first isolated by C.C. King at the University of Pittsburgh.

WATERS, MUDDY: BIRTH ANNIVERSARY. Apr 4, 1915. Born McKinley Morganfield at Rolling Fork, MS (some sources say in 1913 or 1914), American blues guitarist and singer Muddy Waters played a significant part in developing the modern electric rhythm and blues that came to be known as Chicago, or urban, blues. It was predominantly from this music that later forms such as rock and roll and soul sprang. His songs include "Hoochie Coochie Man," "Mannish Boy," "Got My Mojo Working" and many others. "They say my blues is the hardest blues in the world to play," he said once in an interview. Muddy Waters died at Westmont, IL, Apr 30, 1983.

YALE, LINUS: BIRTH ANNIVERSARY. Apr 4, 1821. The American portrait painter and inventor of the lock that is named for him was born at Salisbury, NY. He was creator of the Yale Infallible Bank Lock and developer of the cylinder lock. Yale died at New York, NY, Dec 25, 1868.

YAMAMOTO, ISOROKU: BIRTH ANNIVERSARY. Apr 4, 1884. Considered Japan's greatest naval strategist, Admiral Isoroku Yamamoto, who planned the attack on Pearl Harbor, was born at Nagaoka, Honshu. Yamamoto also devised the complex attack on Midway Island, which ended in defeat for the Japanese because the Allies had the key to the Imperial fleet code and were prepared for the June 4, 1942, attack. The US intercepted reports of Yamamoto's proposed 1943 tour of the Western Solomons and shot down his plane Apr 18, while he was touring Japanese installations in the area.

🎂 BIRTHDAYS TODAY

David Blaine, 47, magician, born Brooklyn, NY, Apr 4, 1973.

Robert Downey, Jr, 55, actor (*Iron Man* films, *The Avengers, Sherlock Holmes, Zodiac, Chaplin*), born New York, NY, Apr 4, 1965.

Kitty Kelley, 78, author (*Jackie Oh!, Nancy Reagan*), born Hartford, CT, Apr 4, 1942.

Christine Lahti, 70, actress (Emmys for "Chicago Hope"; *Swing Shift*), director (Oscar for the short film "Lieberman in Love"), born Birmingham, MI, Apr 4, 1950.

Austin Mahone, 24, singer, born San Antonio, TX, Apr 4, 1996.

Nancy McKeon, 54, actress ("The Facts of Life," "The Division"), born Westbury, NY, Apr 4, 1966.

Craig T. Nelson, 74, actor ("Parenthood," "Coach," "The District," *The Family Stone, Poltergeist*), born Spokane, WA, Apr 4, 1946.

Barry Pepper, 50, actor (*The Kennedys, True Grit, Saving Private Ryan*), born Campbell River, BC, Canada, Apr 4, 1970.

Scott Rolen, 45, former baseball player, born Evansville, IN, Apr 4, 1975.

Jill Scott, 48, musician, actress ("The No. 1 Ladies' Detective Agency"), born Philadelphia, PA, Apr 4, 1972.

April 5 — Sunday

DAY 96   **270 REMAINING**

DAVIS, BETTE: BIRTH ANNIVERSARY. Apr 5, 1908. American actress Bette Davis was born Ruth Elizabeth Davis at Lowell, MA. In addition to acting in more than 80 films, earning 10 Academy Award nominations and winning the Academy Award twice, for Best Actress in *Dangerous* (1935) and *Jezebel* (1938), Davis claimed to have nicknamed the Academy Award "Oscar" after her first husband, Harmon Oscar Nelson, Jr. She died Oct 6, 1989, at Neuilly-sur-Seine, France.

★**EDUCATION AND SHARING DAY.** Apr 5 (tentative). Proclaimed annually each year on the Jewish calendar date of 11 Nissan, in honor of Rabbi Menachem Mendel Schneerson, an advocate for youth around the world.

FIRST US CHAMBER OF COMMERCE FOUNDED: ANNIVERSARY. Apr 5, 1768. The first chamber of commerce in the US was founded at New York City.

GOLD STAR SPOUSES DAY. Apr 5. Since 2010, a day to honor and pay respect to the surviving husbands and wives of fallen armed forces members. Annually, Apr 5.

GREECE: DUMB WEEK. Apr 5–11. The week preceding Holy Week on the Orthodox calendar is known as Dumb Week, as no services are held in churches throughout this period except on Friday, eve of the Saturday of Lazarus.

HELEN KELLER'S MIRACLE: ANNIVERSARY. Apr 5, 1887. Anne Sullivan went to Tuscumbia, AL, in March 1887 to teach the "unteachable" deaf and blind Helen Keller. Although Keller was resistant, Sullivan was determined, and after only one month she succeeded in reaching her: she placed Keller's hand under a gushing water pump and used sign language to spell "w-a-t-e-r" into her palm. Helen grasped the meaning—spelling the word back into Sullivan's palm—and excitedly learned 30 more words that day. Keller's life changed at that breakthrough moment, as she recalled later: "As the cool stream gushed over one hand . . . I felt a misty consciousness as of something forgotten, a thrill of returning thought, and somehow the mystery of language was revealed to me." Keller would go on to become the first deaf and blind person to graduate from college, write books and crusade for the disabled. See also: "Keller, Helen: Birth Anniversary" (June 27).

HOLY WEEK. Apr 5–11. Christian observance dating from the fourth century, known also as Great Week. The seven days beginning on the sixth and final Sunday of Lent (Palm Sunday), consisting of Palm Sunday, Monday of Holy Week, Tuesday of Holy Week, Spy Wednesday (or Wednesday of Holy Week), Maundy Thursday, Good Friday and Holy Saturday (or Great Sabbath or Easter Even). A time of solemn devotion to and memorializing of the suffering (passion), death and burial of Christ. Formerly a time of strict fasting.

LISTER, JOSEPH: BIRTH ANNIVERSARY. Apr 5, 1827. English physician who was the founder of aseptic surgery, born at Upton, Essex, England. Died at Walmer, England, Feb 10, 1912.

"MARRIED . . . WITH CHILDREN" TV PREMIERE: ANNIVERSARY. Apr 5, 1987. This raunchy FOX TV show premiered as the antidote to Cosby-style family shows. Ed O'Neill starred as boorish, luckless shoe salesman Al Bundy; Katey Sagal portrayed Al's big-haired, spandex-clad, sex-starved wife, Peggy; Christina Applegate played their airheaded bombshell daughter, Kelly; and David Faustino played their hormone-driven son, Bud. The last episode aired Apr 20, 1997.

MEXICO: PASSION PLAY IN IZTAPALAPA (SEMANA SANTA EN IZTAPALAPA). Apr 5–11. Iztapalapa, Mexico City. One of the largest and most amazing religious passion plays in the world, where the small community of Iztapalapa has acted out the Way of the Cross since 1843 (the original *Semana Santa*, or Holy Week, play was given in gratitude after a devastating cholera epidemic finally dissipated). A cast of thousands—none of whom are professional actors—performs. Annually, from Palm Sunday to Good Saturday. Est attendance: 1,000,000. For info: COSSIAC (Comité Organizador de Semana Santa en Iztapalapa AC). Web: www.iztapalapa.gob.mx.

NATIONAL DEEP DISH PIZZA DAY. Apr 5. To celebrate Chicago deep dish pizza—originated by Uno's—and the efforts by UNO Pizzeria & Grill to bring deep dish pizza to the entire United States. The original restaurant, which opened in 1943, began serving deep dish as a way to make sure hungry families could get a "real meal" when it came to pizza. Up to that point, pizza was hardly more than a snack. Annually celebrated on the anniversary of the day (Apr 5, 1979) that the first restaurant outside Chicago opened (in Boston, MA). For info: Uno Restaurants, 100 Charles Park Rd, West Roxbury, MA 02132. Phone: (617) 323-9200. Web: www.unos.com.

PALM SUNDAY. Apr 5. Commemorates Christ's last entry into Jerusalem, when his way was covered with palms by the multitudes. Beginning of Holy (or Great) Week in Western Christian churches.

PECK, GREGORY: BIRTH ANNIVERSARY. Apr 5, 1916. Born Eldred Gregory Peck at La Jolla, CA, Gregory Peck was one of Hollywood's most popular and likable leading men. Nominated five times for Best Actor, he finally won the Oscar for his role as Atticus Finch in 1962's *To Kill a Mockingbird*. Other popular films include *Roman Holiday*, *Gentlemen's Agreement* and Alfred Hitchcock's *Spellbound*. He also founded the La Jolla Playhouse with Dorothy McGuire and Mel Ferrer in 1947 and appeared there throughout his career. He died at his home in La Jolla on June 12, 2003.

PHILIPPINES: HOLY WEEK. Apr 5–11. National observance. Flagellants in the streets, *cenaculos* (passion plays) and other colorful and solemn rituals mark the country's observance of Holy Week.

RESNIK, JUDITH A.: BIRTH ANNIVERSARY. Apr 5, 1949. Dr. Judith A. Resnik, the second American woman in space (1984), was born at Akron, OH. The 36-year-old electrical engineer was mission specialist on space shuttle *Challenger*. She perished with all others aboard when *Challenger* exploded Jan 28, 1986. See also: "*Challenger* Space Shuttle Explosion: Anniversary" (Jan 28).

"SECRET AGENT" TV PREMIERE: ANNIVERSARY. Apr 5, 1961. Before Patrick McGoohan became the star of "The Prisoner," he played the role of intelligence agent John Drake on this CBS adventure series. Produced in England by ATV, it also aired there as "Danger Man."

TRACY, SPENCER: BIRTH ANNIVERSARY. Apr 5, 1900. Born at Milwaukee, WI, Spencer Tracy was one of the most respected actors in film history. He won Academy Awards for Best Actor for 1937's *Captains Courageous* and 1938's *Boys Town* and was nominated seven other times. In 1942, he met actress Katharine Hepburn, and they shared a relationship that lasted until his death, although they never married. Together, they starred in nine films, including *Adam's Rib* in 1949 and *Guess Who's Coming to Dinner* in 1967. Tracy died June 10, 1967, at Hollywood Hills, CA.

WASHINGTON, BOOKER TALIAFERRO: BIRTH ANNIVERSARY. Apr 5, 1856. Black educator and leader born at Franklin County, VA. "No race can prosper," he wrote in *Up from Slavery*, "till it learns that there is as much dignity in tilling a field as in writing a poem." Died at Tuskegee, AL, Nov 14, 1915.

WORLD IRISH DANCING CHAMPIONSHIPS. Apr 5–12. Dublin, Ireland. 50th anniversary. This event attracts more than 5,000 dancers accompanied by more than 15,000 family members, friends, teachers and supporters to cheer them on. These talented contestants represent Irish dance schools from 32 countries around the globe. Est attendance: 25,000. For info: An Coimisiún le Rincí Gaelacha. Web: www.clrg.ie.

🎂 BIRTHDAYS TODAY

Hayley Atwell, 38, actress ("Agent Carter," *Captain America* films, *The Pillars of the Earth*), born London, England, Apr 5, 1982.

Sterling K. Brown, 44, actor (Emmys for "The People v O.J. Simpson" and "This is Us"), born St. Louis, MO, Apr 5, 1976.

Roger Corman, 94, filmmaker (*House of Usher*, *The Wild Angels*), born Detroit, MI, Apr 5, 1926.

Max Gail, 77, actor ("Barney Miller," *Pearl*), born Grosse Pointe, MI, Apr 5, 1943.

Lily James, 31, actress (*Darkest Hour*, *Baby Driver*, *Cinderella*, "War and Peace," "Downton Abbey"), born Lily Thomson at Esher, England, Apr 5, 1989.

April 2020	S	M	T	W	T	F	S
				1	2	3	4
	5	6	7	8	9	10	11
	12	13	14	15	16	17	18
	19	20	21	22	23	24	25
	26	27	28	29	30		

Michael Moriarty, 78, actor (*The Last Detail*, *Bang the Drum Slowly*, "Law & Order"), born Detroit, MI, Apr 5, 1942.

Mitch Pileggi, 68, actor ("The X-Files"), born Portland, OR, Apr 5, 1952.

Colin Luther Powell, 83, former US secretary of state, general, former chairman of the US Joint Chiefs of Staff, born New York, NY, Apr 5, 1937.

Pharrell Williams, 47, singer, producer, songwriter, born Virginia Beach, VA, Apr 5, 1973.

April 6 — Monday

DAY 97   **269 REMAINING**

ASSOCIATION OF AMERICAN GEOGRAPHERS ANNUAL MEETING. Apr 6–10. Denver, CO. 116th annual national meeting of members with workshops, paper and poster sessions and field trips. Est attendance: 7,000. For info: Assn of American Geographers, 1710 16th St NW, Washington, DC 20009-3198. Phone: (202) 234-1450. E-mail: meeting@aag.org. Web: www.aag.org.

BATTLE OF SHILOH: ANNIVERSARY. Apr 6, 1862. General Ulysses S. Grant's Union forces at Shiloh, or Pittsburg Landing, TN, were attacked by a large force under General Albert Sidney Johnston on this date. After heavy fighting, the first day of the battle ended without a conclusive victory for either side. Grant was reinforced before the Confederates on the second day, and Confederate general P.G.T. Beauregard, in command after Johnston's death the previous day, ordered a retreat back to Corinth, MS, leaving the Federal troops in a stronger position in Tennessee than before the battle. Losses on both sides totaled more than 23,000.

CAPITOL RECORDS BUILDING OPENS: ANNIVERSARY. Apr 6, 1956. The world's first circular office building, located near the famous Hollywood and Vine intersection in Los Angeles, CA, was dedicated on this day. Designed by Louis Naidorf of Welton Becket and Associates, the Capitol Tower (official name) was not actually meant to resemble a stack of vinyl records—Naidorf designed the mid-century modern classic without knowing who his client was. The 13-story building, completed at a cost of $2 million, housed the headquarters of Capitol Records and state-of-the-art studios. "The House That Nat [King Cole] Built" is topped by a spire that blinks out "Hollywood" in Morse code at night.

CHURCH OF JESUS CHRIST OF LATTER-DAY SAINTS: ANNIVERSARY. Apr 6, 1830. Under the leadership of Joseph Smith, Jr, The Church of Jesus Christ of Latter-day Saints was founded with six members in a log cabin at Fayette, NY.

DROWSY DRIVER AWARENESS DAY. Apr 6. Annual memorial for people who have died in collisions related to drowsy driving. This is an official state-recognized "day" in the state of California. Annually, on Apr 6. For info: Phil Konstantin, PO Box 17515, San Diego, CA 92177-7515.

EXPLORE YOUR CAREER OPTIONS WEEK. Apr 6–10. Maybe you're aspiring to a new career or merely interested in more opportunities in your present career. Get a fresh start by taking stock of all available options. For info: Dorothy Zjawin, Dir, 61 W Colfax Ave, Roselle Park, NJ 07204.

FIRST MODERN OLYMPICS: ANNIVERSARY. Apr 6, 1896. The first modern Olympics formally opened at Athens, Greece, after a 1,500-year hiatus. Thirteen nations participated, represented by 235 male athletes.

FIRST TONY AWARDS PRESENTED: ANNIVERSARY. Apr 6, 1947. The American Theatre Wing bestowed the first annual Tony Awards for distinguished service to the theater.

GANDHI MAKES SALT: 90th ANNIVERSARY. Apr 6, 1930. Mohandas Gandhi, frustrated by British indifference to Indian civil rights demands, planned a symbolic, peaceful protest by conducting a 241-mile march from Sabarmati Ashram to the coast at Dandi. Leaving on Mar 12, Gandhi and his followers arrived at Dandi on Apr 5, and on Apr 6, he made salt by boiling seawater—a violation of the salt law, which granted royal monopoly in its manufacture and levied heavy taxes on its purchasers. His peaceful act and the two-mile-long procession that accompanied it gained worldwide headlines. Besides Gandhi, thousands of Indians were arrested as they, too, made salt in protest.

INDIA: MAHAVIR JAYANTI. Apr 6 (or Apr 9). Jain holiday. The birth anniversary of Mahavira, the founder of Jainism, in 615 BC. This holiday may be celebrated on different dates in different parts of India, but it always falls in March or April.

LALIQUE, RENÉ: BIRTH ANNIVERSARY. Apr 6, 1860. Born at Ay, France, Lalique was a goldsmith, jeweler, glass artist and interior designer known for his Art Nouveau and Art Deco works. He died on May 5, 1945, at Paris.

THE MASTERS TOURNAMENT. Apr 6–12. Augusta National Golf Club, Augusta, GA. Prestigious golf tournament, first held Mar 22, 1934, created by Bobby Jones and Clifford Roberts. Champions don the fabled green jackets that members of Augusta began wearing in 1937. Sam Snead was the first Masters champion to be given the green jacket. For info: Augusta National Golf Club. Web: www.masters.com or www.augusta.com.

MULLIGAN, GERRY: BIRTH ANNIVERSARY. Apr 6, 1927. American jazz saxophonist Gerry Mulligan was born at New York, NY. He performed with many great jazz musicians, including Miles Davis, Dave Brubeck, Chet Baker and Duke Ellington, and is credited with helping create the cool-jazz movement with Miles Davis. Mulligan died Jan 20, 1996, at Darien, CT.

NORTH POLE DISCOVERED: ANNIVERSARY. Apr 6, 1909. Robert E. Peary reached the North Pole after several failed attempts. The team consisted of Peary, leader of the expedition; Matthew A. Henson, a black man who had served with Peary since 1886 as ship's cook, carpenter and blacksmith, and then as Peary's coexplorer and valuable assistant; and four Eskimo guides—Coquesh, Ootah, Eginwah and Seegloo. They sailed July 17, 1908, on the ship *Roosevelt*, wintering on Ellesmere Island. After a grueling trek with dwindling food supplies, Henson and two of the Eskimos were first to reach the Pole. An exhausted Peary arrived 45 minutes later and confirmed their location. Dr. Frederick A. Cook, surgeon on an earlier expedition with Peary, claimed to have reached the Pole first, but that could not be substantiated and the National Geographic Society credited the Peary expedition.

RAPHAEL: BIRTH ANNIVERSARY. Apr 6, 1483. Raffaello Santi (Sanzio), Italian painter and architect. Probably born Apr 6, 1483, at Urbino, Italy. Died on his birthday, at Rome, Italy, Apr 6, 1520.

SCHNEIDERMAN, ROSE: BIRTH ANNIVERSARY. Apr 6, 1882. A pioneer in the battle to increase wages and improve working conditions for women, Rose Schneiderman was born at Saven, Poland, and her family immigrated to the US six years later. At age 16 she began factory work in New York City's garment district and quickly became a union organizer. Opposed to the open-shop policy, which permitted nonunion members to work in a unionized shop, Schneiderman organized a 1913 strike of 25,000 women shirtwaist makers. She worked as an organizer for the International Ladies Garment Workers Union (ILGWU) and for the Women's Trade Union League (WTUL), serving as president for more than 20 years. During the Great Depression, President Roosevelt appointed her to his Labor Advisory Board—the only woman member. Died Aug 11, 1972, at New York, NY.

SCOTTSBORO TRIAL: ANNIVERSARY. Apr 6, 1931. In what became a cause célèbre, nine black youths went on trial at Scottsboro, AL, accused of raping two white women on a freight train. All were convicted in a hasty trial and, on Apr 9, sentenced to death. A series of appeals and reexaminations began soon after and by 1950 all were either free on parole or because the charges were dropped.

TARTAN DAY. Apr 6. Groups and societies throughout North America take the anniversary of the Declaration of Arbroath (1320) as the day to celebrate their Scottish roots.

TEFLON INVENTED: ANNIVERSARY. Apr 6, 1938. Polytetrafluoroethylene resin was invented by Roy J. Plunkett while he was employed by E.I. du Pont de Nemours & Co. Commonly known as Teflon, it revolutionized the cookware industry. This substance or something similar coated three-quarters of the pots and pans in America at the time of Plunkett's death in 1994.

THAILAND: CHAKRI DAY. Apr 6. Commemorates the foundation of the present dynasty by King Rama I (reigned 1782–1809), who also established Bangkok as the country's capital.

THOMAS, LOWELL: BIRTH ANNIVERSARY. Apr 6, 1892. World traveler, reporter, editor and radio newscaster, whose broadcasts spanned more than half a century, 1925–76. His radio sign-off, "So long until tomorrow," was known to millions of listeners, and he is said to have been the first to broadcast from a ship, an airplane, a submarine and a coal mine. Born at Woodington, OH, he died at Pawling, NY, Aug 29, 1981.

TRAGEDY IN RWANDA: ANNIVERSARY. Apr 6, 1994. A plane carrying the presidents of Rwanda and Burundi was shot down near Kigali, the Rwandan capital, exacerbating a brutal ethnic war that led to the massacre of hundreds of thousands. Presidents Juvenal Habyarimana of Rwanda and Cyprien Ntaryamira of Burundi were returning from a summit in Tanzania where they discussed ways of ending the killing in their countries sparked by ethnic rivalries between the Hutu and Tutsi tribes. Following the attack on the two leaders, Rwanda descended into chaos as the two tribes began killing each other in a genocidal battle for power, leading to a mass exodus of civilians caught in the maelstrom.

TWINKIES CREATED: 90th ANNIVERSARY. Apr 6, 1930. Continental Baking manager James Dewar created the Twinkie on this day in River Forest, IL, by filling extra shortcakes with sweet cream (at first, banana). He named the treat after Twinkle Toe Shoes.

UNITED NATIONS: INTERNATIONAL DAY OF SPORT FOR DEVELOPMENT AND PEACE. Apr 6. Sports can foster peace and contribute to an atmosphere of tolerance and understanding. The United Nations system and, in particular, the United Nations Office on Sport for Development and Peace; states; international, regional and national sports organizations; and others are invited to observe and raise awareness of this international day. Annually, Apr 6. For info: United Nations, Dept of Public Info, New York, NY, 10017. Web: www.un.org.

US ENTERS WORLD WAR I: ANNIVERSARY. Apr 6, 1917. Congress approved a declaration of war against Germany and the US entered WWI, which had begun in 1914. The first US "doughboys" landed in France June 25, 1917.

US SENATE ACHIEVES A QUORUM: ANNIVERSARY. Apr 6, 1789. The US Senate was formally organized after achieving a quorum.

🧁 BIRTHDAYS TODAY

Michele Bachmann, 64, former US congresswoman (R, Minnesota), born Waterloo, IA, Apr 6, 1956.

Bert Blyleven, 69, Hall of Fame baseball player, born Rik Aalbert Blijleven at Zeist, Netherlands, Apr 6, 1951.

Bret Boone, 51, former baseball player, born El Cajon, CA, Apr 6, 1969.

Zach Braff, 45, actor ("Scrubs," *Garden State*), director (*Going in Style*), born South Orange, NJ, Apr 6, 1975.

Candace Cameron Bure, 44, actress ("Full House"), born Canoga Park, CA, Apr 6, 1976.

Jerrod Carmichael, 32, comedian, actor ("The Carmichael Show," *Neighbors*), writer, born Winston-Salem, NC, Apr 6, 1988.

Marilu Henner, 68, actress ("Taxi," "Evening Shade"), born Chicago, IL, Apr 6, 1952.

Olaf Kolzig, 50, former hockey player, born Johannesburg, South Africa, Apr 6, 1970.

Barry Levinson, 78, director, producer, writer, actor ("The Carol Burnett Show," *Rain Man, Avalon, Bugsy*), born Baltimore, MD, Apr 6, 1942.

John Ratzenberger, 73, actor ("Cheers," *Toy Story* films), born Bridgeport, CT, Apr 6, 1947.

Paul Rudd, 51, actor (*Ant Man, Anchorman, Clueless*), born Passaic, NJ, Apr 6, 1969.

Roy Thinnes, 82, actor ("The Invaders," "The Outer Limits"), born Chicago, IL, Apr 6, 1938.

Tim Walz, 56, Governor of Minnesota (DFL), born West Point, NE, Apr 6, 1964.

James Watson, 92, discoverer (with Francis Crick) of the structure of DNA, born Chicago, IL, Apr 6, 1928.

Billy Dee Williams, 83, actor (*Brian's Song, Lady Sings the Blues, Return of the Jedi*), born New York, NY, Apr 6, 1937.

April 7 — Tuesday

DAY 98   **268 REMAINING**

BATTLE OF LYS RIVER: ANNIVERSARY. Apr 7, 1918. Having failed to break through Allied lines at the Somme in March, General Erich Ludendorff made another attempt by attacking Flanders along the Lys River. On the hot, misty, sticky mornings of Apr 7 and 8, 1918, the Germans released mustard gas. On Apr 9 the Central Powers began a high-explosive bombardment along the 12-mile front from La Bassée to Armentières. The British managed to avoid a break in their line, and finally General Ferdinand Foch sent nine French divisions to take over a portion of it. On Apr 30, realizing that "further attacks promised no success," Ludendorff ended the offensive. As a result of this battle the British were unable to initiate an offensive for three months. The Allies suffered 240,000 casualties while the German losses exceeded 348,000.

CAMP, WALTER: BIRTH ANNIVERSARY. Apr 7, 1859. Walter Chauncey Camp, college athlete, coach and administrator, was born at New Britain, CT. Camp played football and several other sports at Yale, but he gained prominence for helping to reshape the rules of rugby football into American football. Among his innovations were reducing the number of players on a side from

April 2020	S	M	T	W	T	F	S
				1	2	3	4
	5	6	7	8	9	10	11
	12	13	14	15	16	17	18
	19	20	21	22	23	24	25
	26	27	28	29	30		

15 to 11, introducing the scrimmage, giving one team definite possession of the ball and proposing the downs system. He served as a volunteer coach at Yale and became a national figure as a promoter of football. He selected an All-American team member from 1889 until his death. Died at New York, NY, Mar 14, 1925.

CHANNING, WILLIAM ELLERY: BIRTH ANNIVERSARY. Apr 7, 1780. Well-known abolitionist and leader of the Unitarian movement in the US, born at Newport, RI. He stood for religious liberalism and influenced such people as Longfellow, Bryant, Emerson, Lowell and Holmes. Died at Bennington, VT, Oct 2, 1842.

DULLES, ALLEN: BIRTH ANNIVERSARY. Apr 7, 1893. Diplomat, lawyer and director of the Central Intelligence Agency (CIA) from 1953 to 1961. He was the first civilian to head the CIA. Dulles also served in the OSS during World War II. Born at Watertown, NY, he died at Washington, DC, on Jan 29, 1969.

HOLIDAY, BILLIE: BIRTH ANNIVERSARY. Apr 7, 1915. Billie Holiday (born Eleanora Fagan, nicknamed "Lady Day") is considered by many jazz critics to have been the greatest jazz singer ever recorded. In her 26-year career, despite having received no formal training, she demonstrated a unique style with sophisticated and dramatic phrasing. Among her best-known songs are "Lover Man," "God Bless the Child," "Don't Explain" and "Strange Fruit." Holiday was born at Philadelphia, PA. She died at New York, NY, July 17, 1959.

INTERNATIONAL BEAVER DAY. Apr 7. Observed around the world, this day celebrates the species that restores the most valuable terrestrial ecosystem—wetlands. Annually, Apr 7 (with other events throughout April, Beaver Awareness Month). For info: Beavers: Wetlands & Wildlife, 146 Van Dyke Rd, Dolgeville, NY 13329. Phone: (518) 568-2077. E-mail: castor@frontiernet.net. Web: www.BeaversWW.org/about-us/international-beaver-day/.

INTERNATIONAL SNAILPAPERS DAY. Apr 7. A day to celebrate hardcopy media. Pick up a print newspaper today and read it! Annually, Apr 7. (Created by Danny Bloom.)

KING, WILLIAM RUFUS DEVANE: BIRTH ANNIVERSARY. Apr 7, 1786. The 13th vice president of the US died on Apr 18, 1853, the 46th day after taking the oath of office, of tuberculosis, at Cahaba, AL. The oath of office had been administered to King at Havana, Cuba, as authorized by a special act of Congress (the only presidential or vice presidential oath to be administered outside the US). Born on this day at Sampson County, NY, King was the only vice president who had served in both the House of Representatives and the Senate. King's term as vice president was Mar 4–Apr 18, 1853.

McGRAW, JOHN: BIRTH ANNIVERSARY. Apr 7, 1873. John Joseph McGraw, Baseball Hall of Fame third baseman and manager, born at Truxton, NY. Generally regarded as the best manager ever or close to it, McGraw ran the New York Giants with an iron hand from 1902 to 1932. A scrappy ballplayer with the Baltimore Orioles in the 1890s, McGraw demanded and got total effort from his players. Inducted into the Hall of Fame in 1937. Died at New Rochelle, NY, Feb 25, 1934.

METRIC SYSTEM: 225th ANNIVERSARY. Apr 7, 1795. The metric system was adopted in France, where it had been developed.

MISTRAL, GABRIELA: BIRTH ANNIVERSARY. Apr 7, 1889. Chilean educator, poet and diplomat born Lucila Godoy Alcayaga at Vicuña, Chile. Diplomatic work was extensive: she was Chilean consul in many nations, served as a League of Nations and UN representative, and was notably on the Subcommittee on the Status of Women and promoting UNICEF. Mistral was the first Latin

American to be awarded the Nobel Prize for Literature in 1945. Called "the spiritual mentor of the Spanish American world in a degree rarely equaled before by any man and never by a woman," she died Jan 10, 1957, at Hempstead, NY.

MOON PHASE: FULL MOON. Apr 7. Moon enters Full Moon phase at 10:35 PM, EDT.

NATIONAL BEER DAY. Apr 7. When the Cullen-Harrison Act went into effect at 12:01 AM on Apr 7, 1933, thirsty customers could buy a beer that was 3.2 percent alcohol by weight instead of the "near beer" they had suffered with all through Prohibition. The public lined up on "New Beer's Eve" (Apr 6) at breweries in 20 states and Washington, DC, and purchased 1.5 million barrels. Apr 7 has remained an unofficial holiday celebrating beer in the US.

NATIONAL MAKING THE FIRST MOVE DAY. Apr 7. This is an advocacy day when kids, families and all "start making the first move towards bullying prevention and recovery in all forms"—including shaming, abuse and criminal victimization. Though everyone's first move may not be the same, all positive change starts with "making the first move." Extensively covered in major media outlets, this day has also been proclaimed/recognized by four mayors and two celebrities.#mtfmoveday Annually, Apr 7. For info: Greshun De Bouse, MA/DM, PLC, First Move Life Coaching LLC. E-mail: pr@mtfmoveday.com. Web: www.mtfmoveday.com.

NEW YORK SLAVE REVOLT: ANNIVERSARY. Apr 7, 1712. Nine whites were killed in a slave revolt in New York City. Planned by 27 slaves, the rebellion was begun by setting fire to an outhouse; as whites came to put the fire out, they were shot. The state militia was called out to capture the rebels, and the city of New York responded to the event by strengthening its slave codes. Twenty-one blacks were executed as participants, and six alleged participants committed suicide. New York outlawed slavery in 1799, though the last slaves were not freed until 1827.

NO HOUSEWORK DAY. Apr 7. No trash. No dishes. No making of beds or washing of laundry. And no guilt. Give it a rest. (©2006 by WH.) For info: Thomas & Ruth Roy, Wellcat Holidays, 2418 Long Ln, Lebanon, PA 17046. Phone: (717) 279-0184. E-mail: info@wellcat.com. Web: www.wellcat.com.

PINK MOON. Apr 7. So called by Native American tribes of New England and the Great Lakes because at this time of the season wildflowers—especially the pink ground phlox—herald the newly arrived spring. The April Full Moon.

RWANDA: GENOCIDE REMEMBRANCE DAY. Apr 7. National holiday. Commemorates massacres of 1994.

SHANKAR, RAVI: 100th BIRTH ANNIVERSARY. Apr 7, 1920. Sitar player and composer who introduced Indian music to the Western world, born at Varanasi, India. He began performing music and dance as a child and was soon recognized and trained by the head musician of the Maihar court. A key figure in the movement to bring world music to the attention of mass audiences, he toured extensively and taught around the world—influencing such musicians as George Harrison, John Coltrane and Philip Glass. Shankar also used his music to bring attention to the plight of the poor around the world, especially in Bangladesh. He died at Long Beach, CA, Dec 12, 2012.

SPACE MILESTONE: *MARS ODYSSEY* **(US).** Apr 7, 2001. *Odyssey* was launched on this day and successfully entered Mars's orbit on Oct 23, 2001. The one-way trip was 286 million miles. The two-and-one-half-year mission monitored space radiation, sought out underground water and identified minerals on the Red Planet.

UNITED NATIONS: INTERNATIONAL DAY OF REFLECTION ON THE GENOCIDE IN RWANDA. Apr 7. On Dec 23, 2003, the United Nations General Assembly (Res 58/234) designated Apr 7, the start date of the 1994 genocide in Rwanda, as the International Day of Reflection on the Genocide in Rwanda. Every year, on or around that date, the United Nations organizes commemorative events at its headquarters in New York and at United Nations offices around the world. For info: United Nations, Dept of Public Info, New York, NY, 10017. Web: www.un.org.

UNITED NATIONS: WORLD HEALTH DAY. Apr 7. A UN observance commemorating the establishment of the World Health Organization in 1948. For info: United Nations, Dept of Public Info, New York, NY 10017. Web: www.un.org.

WINCHELL, WALTER: BIRTH ANNIVERSARY. Apr 7, 1897. Journalist, broadcaster, reporter and gossip columnist Walter Winchell was born at New York, NY, and died at Los Angeles, CA, Feb 20, 1972. He was admired for his way with turning a phrase. His show business columns were voraciously read by millions of Americans between 1924 and 1963.

WORDSWORTH, WILLIAM: 250th BIRTH ANNIVERSARY. Apr 7, 1770. Born at Cockermouth, Cumberland, England, Wordsworth was one of the world's greatest lyric poets. Known for his short, dramatic poems, he collaborated with Samuel Taylor Coleridge on *Lyrical Ballads* (1798), a compilation now widely regarded as one of the greatest pieces of the Romantic literary era. Wordsworth's magnum opus *The Prelude*, a semi-autobiographical collection, first completed in 1805 and later revised and expanded over several decades, was published posthumously in 1850. Britain's poet laureate from 1843 until his death, Wordsworth died of pleurisy Apr 23, 1850, at Rydal Mount, Westmoreland, England. "Poetry," he said, "is the spontaneous overflow of powerful feelings: it takes its origin from emotion recollected in tranquility."

WORLD HEALTH ORGANIZATION: ANNIVERSARY. Apr 7, 1948. This agency of the UN was founded to coordinate international health systems. It is headquartered at Geneva, Switzerland. Among its achievements is the elimination of smallpox.

YAMATO **SUICIDE MISSION: 75th ANNIVERSARY.** Apr 7, 1945. The 72,000-ton Japanese battleship *Yamato* set sail for Okinawa carrying only enough fuel for a one-way trip—a suicide mission against the American transport fleet. But she failed to reach her target: struck 19 times by American aerial torpedoes, she sank with 2,498 of her crew aboard.

🧁 BIRTHDAYS TODAY

Hodding Carter III, 85, television and newspaper journalist, born New Orleans, LA, Apr 7, 1935.

Jackie Chan, 66, actor (*The Forbidden Kingdom, Rush Hour, Shanghai Noon*), born Hong Kong, Apr 7, 1954.

Francis Ford Coppola, 81, filmmaker (*Godfather* films, *Apocalypse Now*), born Detroit, MI, Apr 7, 1939.

Russell Crowe, 56, actor (Oscar for *Gladiator*; *Cinderella Man, LA Confidential, A Beautiful Mind*), born Auckland, New Zealand, Apr 7, 1964.

Anthony Drew (Tony) Dorsett, 66, Hall of Fame football player, born Rochester, PA, Apr 7, 1954.

Daniel Ellsberg, 89, author (released the "Pentagon Papers" to the *New York Times*), born Chicago, IL, Apr 7, 1931.

John Oates, 72, singer (Hall and Oates), born New York, NY, Apr 7, 1948.

Sandy Powell, 60, costume designer (Oscars for *The Young Victoria*, *The Aviator* and *Shakespeare in Love*), born London, England, Apr 7, 1960.

Gerhard Schröder, 76, former chancellor of Germany, born Mossenberg, Germany, Apr 7, 1944.

April 8 — Wednesday

DAY 99   **267 REMAINING**

ANNAN, KOFI: BIRTH ANNIVERSARY. Apr 8, 1938. Kofi Annan, born in Kumasi, colonial Ghana, succeeded Dr. Boutros Boutros-Ghali to become Secretary-General of the United Nations in 1996. Annan and the UN were jointly awarded the Nobel Peace Prize in 2001 "for their work for a better organized and more peaceful world." Annan opposed Iran's nuclear program in 2003 and said the Iraq War did not conform to the UN charter and was illegal. While assistant secretary-general of Peacekeeping Operations for the UN, Annan was accused of being overly passive to the 1994 Rwanda genocide in which 800,000 were killed. Annan died Aug 18, 2018, in Bern, Switzerland.

BLACK SENATE PAGE APPOINTED: 55th ANNIVERSARY. Apr 8, 1965. Sixteen-year-old Lawrence Bradford of New York City was the first black page appointed to the US Senate.

FEDERAL GOVERNMENT SEIZURE OF STEEL MILLS: ANNIVERSARY. Apr 8, 1952. On this date President Harry S Truman seized control of the nation's steel mills by presidential order in an attempt to prevent a shutdown by strikers. On Apr 29, a US district court declared the seizure unconstitutional and workers immediately walked out. Production dropped from 300,000 tons a day to less than 20,000. The strike ended July 24, with steelworkers receiving a 16-cent hourly wage raise plus a 5.4-cent hourly increase in fringe benefits.

FORD, BETTY: BIRTH ANNIVERSARY. Apr 8, 1918. Former first lady, wife of Gerald Ford, 38th president of the US, born Elizabeth Ann Bloomer at Chicago, IL. She spoke openly on policy issues, was a strong advocate for women's rights and endorsed legalized abortion. Ford used her 1974 mastectomy as an opportunity to educate women on breast cancer, and after her own struggles with alcohol and prescription drugs, she opened an addiction-treatment clinic to help others. The Betty Ford Center opened in 1982 and is still one of the premier treatment facilities in the US. She and President Ford were married for 58 years until his death in 2006, and she died at Rancho Mirage, CA, July 8, 2011.

HENIE, SONJA: BIRTH ANNIVERSARY. Apr 8, 1912. Sonja Henie, Olympic gold medal figure skater, born at Oslo, Norway. Henie competed in the 1924 Winter Olympics when she was just 11 but finished last in ladies' singles. She won gold medals at the Winter Games of 1928, 1932 and 1936. She became a professional skater and an actress (*Sun Valley Serenade*). Died Oct 13, 1969.

HOME RUN RECORD SET BY HANK AARON: ANNIVERSARY. Apr 8, 1974. Henry "Hammerin' Hank" Aaron hit the 715th home run of his career, breaking the record set by Babe Ruth in 1935. Playing for the Atlanta Braves, Aaron broke the record at Atlanta in a game against the Los Angeles Dodgers. He finished his career in 1976 with a total of 755 home runs. At the time of his retirement, Aaron also ranked first in RBIs, second in at bats and runs scored and third in base hits. On Aug 7, 2007, Barry Bonds of the San Francisco Giants hit his 756th home run to break Aaron's record.

INTERNATIONAL ROMA DAY. Apr 8. A day to celebrate Roma culture and history and the contributions of Roma to our societies. Also a day to acknowledge historical and systemic discrimination against this population, one of the largest minority groups in Europe (at 10 to 12 million Roma). Originally declared on Apr 8, 1971, at the Fourth Romani World Congress.

JAPAN: FLOWER FESTIVAL (HANA MATSURI). Apr 8. Commemorates Buddha's birthday. Ceremonies in all temples.

		S	M	T	W	T	F	S
April					1	2	3	4
		5	6	7	8	9	10	11
2020		12	13	14	15	16	17	18
		19	20	21	22	23	24	25
		26	27	28	29	30		

KNIGHT, O. RAYMOND: BIRTH ANNIVERSARY. Apr 8, 1872. The "Father of Canadian Rodeo," O. Raymond Knight was born at Payson, UT. His father, the Utah mining magnate Jesse Knight, founded the town of Raymond, AB, Canada, in 1901. In 1902, Knight produced Canada's first rodeo, the "Raymond Stampede." He also built rodeo's first grandstand and first chute in 1903. Knight died Feb 7, 1947.

MCRAE, CARMEN: 100th BIRTH ANNIVERSARY. Apr 8, 1920. After winning an amateur contest at Harlem's legendary Apollo Theatre in her hometown of New York City, McRae went on to become a noted jazz singer, singing with the Earl Hines, Mercer Ellington and Benny Carter bands, among others, and recording more than 20 albums. She died Nov 10, 1994, at Beverly Hills, CA.

MORRIS, LEWIS: BIRTH ANNIVERSARY. Apr 8, 1726. Signer of the Declaration of Independence, born at Westchester County, NY. Died Jan 22, 1798, at Morrisania Manor at NY.

NATIONAL DOGFIGHTING AWARENESS DAY. Apr 8. A day to raise awareness of the prevalence of dogfighting in the US, reveal little-known truths about the blood sport and encourage animal lovers nationwide to act against this brutal form of animal cruelty. The ASPCA continues to tackle the illegal underground world of dog-fighting rings through investigations, law enforcement training, legislation, advocacy and rehabilitation of dogs seized during dog-fighting raids. Annually, Apr 8. For info: ASPCA, 520 8th Ave, 7th Fl, New York, NY 10018. Phone: (212) 876-7700. Fax: (212) 423-9813. E-mail: press@aspca.org. Web: www.aspca.org/dogfighting.

PASSOVER BEGINS AT SUNDOWN. Apr 8. See "Pesach" (Apr 9).

PICKFORD, MARY: BIRTH ANNIVERSARY. Apr 8, 1892. Born Gladys Louise Smith at Toronto, ON, Canada, Pickford, known as "America's sweetheart" for her acting roles in films such as *Rebecca of Sunnybrook Farm, Pollyanna* and *Poor Little Rich Girl*, was the world's first movie star. She cofounded United Artists (1919) with Charlie Chaplin, D.W. Griffith and second husband Douglas Fairbanks and was one of the original 39 founders of the Academy of Motion Picture Arts and Sciences. Winner of the second Academy Award for Best Actress for her role in *Coquette* (1929), Pickford also received an honorary Academy Award in 1976. She died May 29, 1979, at Santa Monica, CA.

SEVENTEENTH AMENDMENT TO US CONSTITUTION RATIFIED: ANNIVERSARY. Apr 8, 1913. Prior to the 17th Amendment, members of the Senate were elected by each state's respective legislature. The advent and popularity of primary elections during the last decade of the 19th century and the early 20th century and a string of senatorial scandals, most notably a scandal involving William Lorimer, an Illinois political boss in 1909, forced the Senate to end its resistance to a constitutional amendment requiring direct popular election of senators.

WILLIAMS, WILLIAM: BIRTH ANNIVERSARY. Apr 8, 1731. Signer of the Declaration of Independence, born at Lebanon, CT. Died there Aug 2, 1811.

🧁 BIRTHDAYS TODAY

Patricia Arquette, 52, actress (Oscar for *Boyhood*; "CSI: Cyber," "Medium"), born Chicago, IL, Apr 8, 1968.

William D. Chase, 98, librarian and chronicler of contemporary civilization as cofounder and coeditor of *Chase's Annual Events*, born Lakeview, MI, Apr 8, 1922.

Shecky Greene, 95, comedian, actor, born Chicago, IL, Apr 8, 1925.

Seymour Hersh, 83, journalist, born Chicago, IL, Apr 8, 1937.

Ron Johnson, 65, US Senator (R, Wisconsin), born Mankato, MN, Apr 8, 1955.

Barbara Kingsolver, 65, author (*The Bean Trees, The Poisonwood Bible, The Lacuna*), born Annapolis, MD, Apr 8, 1955.

Julian Lennon, 57, musician, singer, born Liverpool, England, Apr 8, 1963.

Stuart Pankin, 74, actor ("Not Necessarily the News," *Irreconcilable Differences, Arachnophobia*), born Philadelphia, PA, Apr 8, 1946.

Katee Sackhoff, 40, actress ("Battlestar Galactica," "The Bionic Woman"), born Portland, OR, Apr 8, 1980.

John Schneider, 60, actor ("Smallville," "The Dukes of Hazzard"), singer, born Mount Kisco, NY, Apr 8, 1960.

Vivienne Westwood, 79, designer, born Vivienne Isabel Swire at Glossop, England, Apr 8, 1941.

Robin Wright, 54, actress ("House of Cards," *White Oleander, Forrest Gump, The Princess Bride*), born Dallas, TX, Apr 8, 1966.

April 9 — Thursday

DAY 100   **266 REMAINING**

AFRICAN METHODIST EPISCOPAL CHURCH ORGANIZED: ANNIVERSARY. Apr 9, 1816. The first all-black US religious denomination, the AME Church was organized at Philadelphia, PA, with Richard Allen, a former slave who had bought his freedom, as the first bishop.

BATAAN DEATH MARCH BEGINS: ANNIVERSARY. Apr 9, 1942. On this morning American and Filipino prisoners were herded together by Japanese soldiers on Mariveles Airfield at Bataan (in the Philippine islands) and forced to march 61 miles to Camp O'Donnell, near Cabanatuan. During the march they were given only one bowl of rice. Approximately 10,000 Americans and Filipinos lost their lives in the course of the trek.

BLACK PAGE APPOINTED TO US HOUSE OF REPRESENTATIVES: 55th ANNIVERSARY. Apr 9, 1965. Fifteen-year-old Frank Mitchell of Springfield, IL, was the first black page appointed to the US House of Representatives.

CIVIL RIGHTS BILL OF 1866: ANNIVERSARY. Apr 9, 1866. The Civil Rights Bill of 1866, passed by Congress over the veto of President Andrew Johnson, granted blacks the rights and privileges of American citizenship and formed the basis for the 14th Amendment to the US Constitution.

CIVIL WAR ENDING: ANNIVERSARY. Apr 9, 1865. At 1:30 PM General Robert E. Lee, commander of the Army of Northern Virginia, surrendered to General Ulysses S. Grant, commander in chief of the Union Army, ending four years of civil war. The meeting took place in the house of Wilmer McLean at the village of Appomattox Court House, VA. Confederate soldiers were permitted to keep their horses and go free to their homes, while Confederate officers were allowed to retain their swords and sidearms as well. Grant wrote the terms of surrender. Formal surrender took place at the courthouse on Apr 12. Death toll for the Civil War is estimated at 500,000 men.

DENMARK: OBSERVATION OF NAZI OCCUPATION. Apr 9. Flag-flying day to observe the anniversary of the 1940 Nazi invasion and occupation of the country.

ECKERT, J(OHN) PRESPER, JR: BIRTH ANNIVERSARY. Apr 9, 1919. Coinventor with John W. Mauchly of ENIAC (Electronic Numerical Integrator and Computer), which was first demonstrated at the Moore School of Electrical Engineering at the University of Pennsylvania at Philadelphia Feb 14, 1946. This is generally considered the birth of the computer age. Originally designed to process artillery calculations for the army, ENIAC was also used in the Manhattan Project. Eckert and Mauchly formed Electronic Control Company, which later became Unisys Corporation. Eckert was born at Philadelphia and died at Bryn Mawr, PA, June 3, 1995.

ITALY: PROCESSION OF THE ADDOLORATA AND PROCESSION OF THE MYSTERIES. Apr 9–10. Taranto. Procession of the Addolorata is held on Holy Thursday, and the Procession of the Mysteries takes place on Good Friday. Both processions have in common the very slow pace of the participants and their unusual costumes.

JENKINS'S EAR DAY: ANNIVERSARY. Apr 9, 1731. Spanish *guardacosta* boarded and plundered the British ship *Rebecca* off Jamaica, and among other outrages, they cut off the ear of English master mariner Robert Jenkins. Little notice was taken until seven years later, when Jenkins exhibited the detached ear and described the atrocity to a committee of the House of Commons. In consequence, Britain declared war on Spain in October 1739, a war that lasted until 1743 and is still known as the "War of Jenkins's Ear." Nothing else is known of him.

JUMBO THE ELEPHANT ARRIVES IN AMERICA: ANNIVERSARY. Apr 9, 1882. The most famous elephant in history was captured as a calf near Lake Chad, Africa, in 1861. He was a tremendously popular part of the London Zoo from 1865 to 1882. At London, he gained the name Jumbo (from a West African word for elephant). In 1882, American circus impresario P.T. Barnum bought the 11½-foot-tall and seven-ton animal for $10,000. Jumbo arrived at Manhattan, NY, on Easter Sunday. In an amazing spectacle, Jumbo paraded up Broadway in a crate pulled by 16 horses. Jumbo was just as popular in the US as he was in Britain, and his name entered the English language to describe anything oversized.

KING, FRANK: BIRTH ANNIVERSARY. Apr 9, 1883. Influential comic strip artist who created "Gasoline Alley" in 1919. Originally about men's interest in autos, "Gasoline Alley" had a notable jump in popularity in 1921 when its main character, Walt, adopted a foundling called Skeezix. Devoid of melodrama, this strip sympathetically described the day-to-day lives of Walt, Skeezix and their friends and family, and it was the first American cartoon in which the characters actually aged. Frank King was born at Cashton, WI, and died at Winter Park, FL, June 24, 1969.

MARIAN ANDERSON EASTER CONCERT: ANNIVERSARY. Apr 9, 1939. On this Easter Sunday, black American contralto Marian Anderson sang an open-air concert from the steps of the Lincoln Memorial at Washington, DC, to an audience of 75,000, after having been denied use of the Daughters of the American Revolution (DAR) Constitution Hall. The event became an American anti-discrimination cause célèbre and led First Lady Eleanor Roosevelt to resign from the DAR.

MAUNDY THURSDAY OR HOLY THURSDAY. Apr 9. The Thursday before Easter, originally "dies mandate," celebrates Christ's injunction to love one another, "Mandatus novum do vobis. . . ." ("A new commandment I give to you. . . .")

MUYBRIDGE, EADWEARD: BIRTH ANNIVERSARY. Apr 9, 1830. English photographer famed for his studies of animals in motion. Born

Edward James Muggeridge, at Kingston-on-Thames, England. Died there May 8, 1904.

★NATIONAL FORMER PRISONER OF WAR RECOGNITION DAY. Apr 9.

NCAA DIVISION I MEN'S ICE HOCKEY CHAMPIONSHIP (FROZEN FOUR). Apr 9–11. Little Caesars Arena, Detroit, MI. 73rd annual. For info: NCAA, PO Box 6222, Indianapolis, IN 46206-6222. Web: www.NCAA.com.

PESACH OR PASSOVER. Apr 9–16. Hebrew calendar dates: Nisan 15–22, 5780. The first day of Passover begins an eight-day celebration of the delivery of the Jews from slavery in Egypt. Unleavened bread (matzo) is eaten at this time. Began at sundown Apr 8.

PHILIPPINES: ARAW NG KAGITINGAN. Apr 9. Day of Valor. National observance to commemorate the fall of Bataan in 1942. The infamous "Death March" is reenacted at the Mount Samat Shrine, the Dambana ng Kagitingan.

PHILIPPINES: MORIONE'S FESTIVAL. Apr 9–12. Marinduque Island. Provincewide masquerade, Lenten plays and celebrations. Annually, Holy Thursday through Easter Sunday.

ROBESON, PAUL BUSTILL: BIRTH ANNIVERSARY. Apr 9, 1898. Paul Robeson, born at Princeton, NJ, was an All-American football player at Rutgers University and received his law degree from Columbia University in 1923. After being seen by Eugene O'Neill in an amateur stage production, he was offered a part in O'Neill's play *The Emperor Jones.* His performance in that play with the Provincetown Players established him as an actor. Without ever having taken a voice lesson, he also became a popular singer. His stage credits include *Show Boat, Porgy and Bess, The Hairy Ape* and *Othello,* which enjoyed the longest Broadway run of a Shakespeare play. In 1950 he was denied a passport by the US for refusing to sign an affidavit stating whether he was or ever had been a member of the Communist Party. The action was overturned by the Supreme Court in 1958. His film credits include *Emperor Jones, Show Boat, King Solomon's Mines* and *Song of Freedom.* Robeson died at Philadelphia, PA, Jan 23, 1976.

SPACE MILESTONE: *SOYUZ 35* (USSR): 40th ANNIVERSARY. Apr 9, 1980. Two cosmonauts (Valery Ryumin and Leonid Popov) were launched from Baikonur space center at Kazakhstan, USSR. Docked at *Salyut 6* Apr 10. Ryumin and Popov returned to Earth Oct 11, 1980, after setting a new space endurance record of 185 days.

TEXAS PANHANDLE TORNADO: ANNIVERSARY. Apr 9, 1947. A monster tornado clearing a 1.5-mile-long path struck through at least 12 towns in Texas, Oklahoma and Kansas, killing 169 people and causing more than $15 million in damage. The tornado traveled 221 miles across the three states.

TUNISIA: MARTYRS' DAY. Apr 9. Commemorates the day in 1938 when citizens protesting for freedom from France and against the arrest of their leader were fired upon by French police. More than 20 protesters were killed and scores were wounded.

WINSTON CHURCHILL DAY. Apr 9. Anniversary of enactment of legislation in 1963 that made the late British statesman an honorary citizen of the US.

THE WRESTLING PRESIDENT: ANNIVERSARY. Apr 9, 1904. In a letter to his son Kermit, President Theodore Roosevelt wrote, "I am wrestling with two Japanese wrestlers three times a week. I am not the age or build one would think to be whirled lightly over an opponent's head and batted down on a mattress without damage. But they are so skillful that I have not been hurt at all." Roosevelt was 46 years old. An avid sportsman, he had given up boxing because "it seems rather absurd for a President to appear with a black eye or a swollen nose or a cut lip."

April 2020	S	M	T	W	T	F	S
				1	2	3	4
	5	6	7	8	9	10	11
	12	13	14	15	16	17	18
	19	20	21	22	23	24	25
	26	27	28	29	30		

🎂 BIRTHDAYS TODAY

Doug Ducey, 56, Governor of Arizona (R), born Toledo, OH, Apr 9, 1964.

Elle Fanning, 22, actress (*20th Century Women, Maleficent*), born Conyers, GA, Apr 9, 1998.

Marc Jacobs, 57, fashion designer, born New York, NY, Apr 9, 1963.

Taylor Kitsch, 39, actor (*John Carter, Savages,* "Friday Night Lights"), born Kelowna, BC, Canada, Apr 9, 1981.

Paul Krassner, 88, editor, journalist, born Brooklyn, NY, Apr 9, 1932.

Michael Learned, 81, actress ("The Waltons"), born Washington, DC, Apr 9, 1939.

Tom Lehrer, 92, songwriter, pianist, mathematician, born New York, NY, Apr 9, 1928.

Leighton Meester, 34, actress ("Gossip Girl," *Country Strong*), born Marco Island, FL, Apr 9, 1986.

Cynthia Nixon, 54, actress ("Sex and the City," *Amadeus*), born New York, NY, Apr 9, 1966.

Keshia Knight Pulliam, 41, actress ("The Cosby Show"), born Newark, NJ, Apr 9, 1979.

Dennis Quaid, 66, actor (*Far from Heaven, The Rookie, Traffic*), born Houston, TX, Apr 9, 1954.

Kristen Stewart, 30, actress (*Twilight Saga* films, *Snow White and the Huntsman, On the Road*), born Los Angeles, CA, Apr 9, 1990.

Jacques Villeneueve, 49, race car driver, born St. Jean d'Iberville, QC, Canada, Apr 9, 1971.

April 10 — Friday

DAY 101   **265 REMAINING**

ASPCA INCORPORATED: ANNIVERSARY. Apr 10, 1866. American diplomat Henry Bergh, angry at the widespread abuse of animals (cockfighting, whipping of cart horses, starving of working dogs and more) sought its end through the creation of the American Society for the Prevention of Cruelty to Animals in the New York State legislature. On this day, the charter was passed, and on Apr 19, 1866, the first animal cruelty laws were passed. Bergh based the formation of the ASPCA on Britain's Royal Society for the Prevention of Cruelty to Animals, which had been founded in 1840. "It is a moral question in all its aspects," Bergh persuasively argued.

THE BEATLES BREAK UP: 50th ANNIVERSARY. Apr 10, 1970. In a press release accompanying promotional copies of his new solo album, Paul McCartney announced that he had no plans for working with The Beatles because of "personal differences, business differences, musical differences." He stated that he didn't know if the break was temporary or permanent, but the years-long tension in the group coupled with the musicians' solo work brought about the end of the band that year. McCartney sued to dissolve The Beatles on Dec 31, 1970, and the group was formally dissolved four years later.

BERMUDA: GOOD FRIDAY KITE FLYING. Apr 10. Horseshoe Bay Beach. In a longtime Good Friday tradition, Bermudans take to the beach to fly kites after 3 PM. It is thought that the tradition began when a local preacher used a cross-framed kite to represent the Ascension. Annually, Good Friday.

BOOTH, WILLIAM: BIRTH ANNIVERSARY. Apr 10, 1829. General William Booth, founder of the movement that became known, in 1878, as the Salvation Army, was born at Nottingham, England. Apprenticed to a pawnbroker at the age of 13, Booth experienced firsthand the misery of poverty. He broke with conventional church religion and established a quasi-military religious organization with military uniforms and ranks. Recruiting from the poor, from converted criminals and from many other social outcasts, his organization grew rapidly and its influence spread from England to the US and to other countries. At revivals in slum areas the itinerant evangelist offered help for the poor, homes for the homeless, sobriety for alcoholics, rescue homes for women and girls, training centers and legal aid. Booth died at London, England, Aug 20, 1912. See also: "Salvation Army Founder's Day" (Apr 10).

CHINCOTEAGUE ISLAND EASTER DECOY SHOW. Apr 10–11. Chincoteague Island, VA. One hundred local and national carvers and artists exhibit their work. Awards are given in various carving categories, art and photography. Special awards are given for best carving display and best art display. There is also a Children's Choice Award given for a favorite artist. The Curtis Merritt Award of Excellence is awarded to the exhibitor who displays excellence as an individual as well as an artist and/or carver. This award is voted on by the exhibitors. There are hand-carved and/or painted wooden Easter eggs designed by various exhibitors, which will be offered in a silent auction. An auction of pre-loved treasures benefiting a local nonprofit has been a festival highlight in recent years. Annually, Easter weekend. Est attendance: 1,000. For info: Chincoteague Chamber of Commerce, 6733 Maddox Blvd, Chincoteague Island, VA 23336. Phone: (757) 336-6161. Fax: (757) 336-1242. E-mail: joanne@chincoteaguechamber.com. Web: www.chincoteaguechamber.com or www.chincoteaguedecoyshow.com.

COACHELLA VALLEY MUSIC AND ARTS FESTIVAL. Apr 10–12 (and Apr 17–19). Empire Polo Grounds, Indio, CA. Since 1999, annual music and arts festival held in the California Desert. Features established and emerging artists on multiple stages—and usually a major band reunion. Rain or shine. Camping available; carpooling encouraged. Est attendance: 200,000. For info: Coachella. E-mail: info@coachella.com. Web: www.coachella.com.

COMMODORE PERRY DAY: BIRTH ANNIVERSARY. Apr 10, 1794. Birth anniversary of Matthew Calbraith Perry, commodore in the US Navy, negotiator of first treaty between US and Japan (Mar 31, 1854). Born at South Kingston, RI. Died Mar 4, 1858, at New York, NY.

CONNORS, CHUCK (KEVIN JOSEPH): BIRTH ANNIVERSARY. Apr 10, 1921. "The Rifleman" of television fame, Chuck Connors played that title role from 1958 to 1963. His portrayal of a slave owner in the miniseries *Roots* won him an Emmy nomination. Connors acted in more than 45 films and appeared on many TV series and specials. He played professional basketball and baseball before becoming an actor. Born at Brooklyn, NY; died Nov 10, 1992, at Los Angeles, CA.

ENGLAND: BRITISH AND WORLD MARBLES CHAMPIONSHIP. Apr 10. Greyhound Public House, Tinsley Green, West Sussex. Since 1932, more than 100 competitors have vied for team and individual titles in the marbles tournament. Annually, on Good Friday. For info: Greyhound Public House. Web: www.greyhoundmarbles.com.

ENGLAND: DEVIZES TO WESTMINSTER INTERNATIONAL CANOE RACE. Apr 10–13. 72nd year. Starts from Wharf Car Park, Wharf St, Devizes, Wiltshire. Canoes race along 125 miles of the Kennet and Avon canals and the River Thames, ending at County Hall Steps, Westminster Bridge Rd, London. Annually, Good Friday to Easter Monday. Est attendance: 6,000. For info: DW Organisation Ltd. E-mail: publicity@dwrace.co.uk. Web: www.dwrace.co.uk.

GOOD FRIDAY. Apr 10. Oldest Christian celebration—commemorates the Crucifixion. Possible corruption of "God's Friday." Observed in some manner by most Christian sects. Public holiday in many nations. In the US, a public or part holiday in Connecticut,

Delaware, Florida, Hawaii, Indiana, Kentucky, Louisiana, New Jersey, North Carolina, North Dakota, Tennessee and Texas.

GOOD FRIDAY PEACE AGREEMENT IN NORTHERN IRELAND: ANNIVERSARY. Apr 10, 1998. Protestant and Catholic factions reached a power-sharing agreement on Good Friday, 1998. It was endorsed by referenda in Northern Ireland and the Republic of Ireland on May 22, 1998. As a result, a provincial government was established in Northern Ireland to replace direct rule by Britain. The Northern Ireland Assembly met for the first time June 5, 2000.

GROTIUS, HUGO: BIRTH ANNIVERSARY. Apr 10, 1583. (Old Style date.) Anniversary of the birth of Hugo Grotius, the Dutch theologian, attorney, scholar and statesman whose beliefs profoundly influenced American thinking, especially with regard to the conscience of humanity. Born at Delft, Holland, he died at Rostock, Germany, Aug 28, 1645 (OS).

NATIONAL SIBLINGS DAY. Apr 10. A commemorative day to honor, appreciate and celebrate all brothers and sisters and, in cases of deceased siblings, hold them in memory. Recognizing the bond between siblings for the special gift it is. Founded by Claudia Evart of New York City through her 501(C)(3) nonprofit, Siblings Day Foundation, to honor the memories of her sister Lisette and brother Alan; they both died from accidents early in their lives. Since 1998, 49 states' governors have officially recognized this day. Presidents Clinton (2000), Bush (2008) and Obama (2016) have also issued presidential messages acknowledging this day. Annually, Apr 10. For info: Claudia Evart, Siblings Day Foundation. E-mail: april10@siblingsday.org. Web: www.siblingsday.org.

ODESSA RETAKEN: ANNIVERSARY. Apr 10, 1944. The Red Army retook the Ukrainian city of Odessa, a port on the northwest coast of the Black Sea that had been in the hands of the Nazis since October 1941.

PERKINS, FRANCES: BIRTH ANNIVERSARY. Apr 10, 1880. First woman member of a US presidential cabinet. Born at Boston, MA, she was married in 1915 to Paul Caldwell Wilson but used her maiden name in public life. She was appointed secretary of labor by President Franklin D. Roosevelt in 1933, a post in which she served until 1945. Died at New York, NY, May 14, 1965.

PULITZER, JOSEPH: BIRTH ANNIVERSARY. Apr 10, 1847. American journalist and newspaper publisher, founder of the Pulitzer Prizes, born at Budapest, Hungary. Died at Charleston, SC, Oct 29, 1911. Pulitzer Prizes awarded annually since 1917.

SALVATION ARMY FOUNDER'S DAY. Apr 10, 1829. Birth anniversary of William Booth, a Methodist minister who began an evangelical ministry in the East End of London, England, in 1865 and established mission stations to feed and house the poor. In 1878 he changed the name of the organization to the Salvation Army. Booth was born at Nottingham, England; he died at London, Aug 20, 1912. See also: "Booth, William: Birth Anniversary" (Apr 10).

STOCK EXCHANGE HOLIDAY (GOOD FRIDAY). Apr 10. The holiday schedules for the various exchanges are subject to change if relevant rules, regulations or exchange policies are revised. If you have questions, contact: CME Group (CME, CBOT, NYMEX, COMEX) (www.cmegroup.com), Chicago Board Options Exchange (www.cboe.com), NASDAQ (www.nasdaq.com), NYSE (www.nyse.com).

UNITED KINGDOM: GOOD FRIDAY BANK HOLIDAY. Apr 10. Bank and public holiday in England, Wales, Scotland and Northern Ireland.

🧁 BIRTHDAYS TODAY

Kenneth "Babyface" Edmonds, 63, singer, songwriter, born Indianapolis, IN, Apr 10, 1957.

David Harbour, 45, actor ("Stranger Things," *Black Mass*), born New York, NY, Apr 10, 1975.

Dolores Huerta, 90, cofounder, with Cesar Chavez, of the United Farm Workers of America labor union, born Dawson, NM, Apr 10, 1930.

Chyler Leigh, 38, actress ("Grey's Anatomy," "The Practice"), born Charlotte, NC, Apr 10, 1982.

Peter MacNicol, 66, actor ("Numb3rs," "Ally McBeal," *Ghostbusters II*), born Dallas, TX, Apr 10, 1954.

John Madden, 84, sportscaster, Hall of Fame football coach, video game namesake, born Austin, MN, Apr 10, 1936.

Mandy Moore, 36, actress ("This Is Us," *Tangled, A Walk to Remember*), singer, born Amanda Leigh Moore at Nashua, NH, Apr 10, 1984.

Haley Joel Osment, 32, actor (*The Sixth Sense, Bogus*), born Los Angeles, CA, Apr 10, 1988.

Michael Pitt, 39, actor ("Boardwalk Empire," *Last Days*), born West Orange, NJ, Apr 10, 1981.

Daisy Ridley, 28, actress (*Star Wars: The Last Jedi, Murder on the Orient Express, Star Wars: The Force Awakens*), born London, England, Apr 10, 1992.

Steven Seagal, 69, actor, producer (*Hard to Kill, On Deadly Ground*), born Lansing, MI, Apr 10, 1951.

Paul Theroux, 79, author (*The Mosquito Coast, The Great Railway Bazaar, Dark Star Safari*), born Medford, MS, Apr 10, 1941.

Max Von Sydow, 91, actor (*The Seventh Seal, The Emigrants*), born Lund, Sweden, Apr 10, 1929.

April 11 — Saturday

DAY 102	264 REMAINING

BARBERSHOP QUARTET DAY. Apr 11. Commemorates the gathering of 26 persons at Tulsa, OK, Apr 11, 1938, and the founding there of the Society for the Preservation and Encouragement of Barbershop Quartet Singing in America.

BOLIN, JANE MATILDA: BIRTH ANNIVERSARY. Apr 11, 1908. Jane Matilda Bolin, born at Poughkeepsie, NY, was the first black woman to graduate from the Yale School of Law (1931) and went on to become the first black woman judge in the US. She served as assistant corporation counsel for the city of New York before

	S	M	T	W	T	F	S
April				1	2	3	4
	5	6	7	8	9	10	11
2020	12	13	14	15	16	17	18
	19	20	21	22	23	24	25
	26	27	28	29	30		

being appointed to the city's Domestic Relations Court and the Family Court of the State of New York. Bolin died Jan 8, 2007, at New York, NY.

CIVIL RIGHTS ACT OF 1968: ANNIVERSARY. Apr 11, 1968. Exactly one week after the assassination of Martin Luther King, Jr, the Civil Rights Act of 1968 (protecting civil rights workers, expanding the rights of Native Americans and providing antidiscrimination measures in housing) was signed into law by President Lyndon B. Johnson, who said: "[T]he proudest moments of my presidency have been times such as this when I have signed into law the promises of a century."

COSTA RICA: JUAN SANTAMARÍA DAY. Apr 11. National holiday. Commemorates the 1856 Battle of Rivas.

CYPRUS: THE PROCESSION OF ICON OF SAINT LAZARUS. Apr 11. Larnaca. The tomb of Lazarus (the man raised from the dead by Christ) resides in the Church of Saint Lazarus built by Emperor Leo VI in the ninth century. Eight days before the Orthodox Easter Sunday, his icon is taken through the streets of Larnaca.

EASTER EVEN. Apr 11. The Saturday before Easter. Last day of Holy Week and of Lent.

HAROLD WASHINGTON ELECTED FIRST BLACK MAYOR OF CHICAGO: ANNIVERSARY. Apr 11, 1983. Harold Washington defeated Bernard Epton and became the first black mayor of Chicago, IL. Of the city's 1.6 million voters, a record 82 percent voted. Washington won 51 percent of the votes, which split along racial lines. He was reelected in April 1987 but died suddenly seven months later at his office, Nov 25, 1987.

HUGHES, CHARLES EVANS: BIRTH ANNIVERSARY. Apr 11, 1862. Prominent American conservative, born at Glens Falls, NY, who served his country in a variety of roles. Hughes was governor of New York (1907–10), associate justice of the US (1910–16), US secretary of state (1921–25) and 11th chief justice of the US (1930–41). He also was the 1916 Republican candidate for president who was defeated by Woodrow Wilson. Hughes died at Osterville, MA, Aug 27, 1948.

INTERNATIONAL "LOUIE LOUIE" DAY. Apr 11. A day to celebrate what has been called the greatest party song of all time. "Louie Louie" has been recorded more times than any other rock song in history and was very nearly declared the official state song of Washington. Annually, Apr 11, the birthday of composer Richard Berry in 1935, who first released the song as a B-side in 1957. Created by the Louie Louie Advocacy and Music Appreciation Society (LLAMAS).

JULIAN, PERCY: BIRTH ANNIVERSARY. Apr 11, 1899. Percy Julian, producer of a synthetic progesterone using soybeans, was born at Montgomery, AL. He also developed a cheaper method of producing cortisone, as well as a drug to treat glaucoma and a chemical foam to fight petroleum fires. Julian died Apr 19, 1975, at Waukegan, IL.

LAZARUS SATURDAY. Apr 11. Orthodox celebration of Christ raising Lazarus from the dead. Only time the Resurrection liturgy is used on a day other than Sunday. Occurs eight days before Pascha.

LIBERATION OF BUCHENWALD CONCENTRATION CAMP: 75th ANNIVERSARY. Apr 11, 1945. Buchenwald, north of Weimar, Germany, was entered by US troops and liberated at 3:15 PM. It had been established in 1937, and about 56,000 people died there.

NATIONAL CATCH AND RELEASE DAY. Apr 11. A day of no judgments for every angler—regardless of his or her fishing habits. Also, a day to promote and celebrate the practice of catch and release fishing. Annually, the second Saturday in April. For info: Kevin Hulit, By the Bay Media, LLC, 85 Aberdeen Rd, Matawan, NJ 07747. E-mail: kevin@bythebaymedia.com.

NATIONAL PET DAY. Apr 11. Founded in 2006, a day to celebrate the unconditional love and bond between humans and their pets—as well as to encourage adoption. Founded by Colleen Paige, who also founded National Dog Day and National Cat Day. For info: The Holiday Guild. Phone: (323) 285-2148. E-mail: k.kelly@the-holidayguild.com. Web: www.nationalpetday.co.

PARKINSON, JAMES: BIRTH ANNIVERSARY. Apr 11, 1755. The remarkable English physician and paleontologist first described the "shaking palsy" and later had it named for him—Parkinson's disease. He was the author of numerous books and articles on a variety of subjects. His *Organic Remains of a Former World* is called the first attempt to give a scientific account of fossils. Under oath, Parkinson declared that he was a member of the group that hatched the "Pop-gun Plot" to assassinate King George III in a theater, using a poisoned dart for the deed. Parkinson was born at London, England, and died there, Dec 21, 1824.

SPACE MILESTONE: *APOLLO 13* LAUNCHED (US). Apr 11, 1970. Fifty-six hours into flight, astronauts James Lovell (commander), Fred Haise and John Swigert were endangered when an oxygen tank ruptured. The planned moon landing was canceled, and details of the accident were made public. The entire world shared concern for the crew, who splashed down successfully in the Pacific Apr 17.

SPELMAN COLLEGE ESTABLISHED: ANNIVERSARY. Apr 11, 1881. Spelman College, with funding from the Rockefeller family, opened its doors for the first time with the purpose of educating young African-American women. The institution, located at Atlanta, GA, was dubbed "the Radcliffe for Negro women."

UGANDA: LIBERATION DAY. Apr 11. Republic of Uganda celebrates anniversary of overthrow of Idi Amin's dictatorship in 1979.

WORLD PARKINSON'S DAY. Apr 11. This world awareness day is observed on the birth anniversary of James Parkinson (1755–1824), the English physician who first described the disease now named for him. In "An Essay on the Shaking Palsy" (1817) he noted the disease's attributes in several patients. This observance day seeks to educate about the disease and empower those who have it. Annually, Apr 11.

🎂 BIRTHDAYS TODAY

Tony Brown, 87, television journalist, born Charleston, WV, Apr 11, 1933.

Steve Bullock, 54, Governor of Montana (D), born Missoula, MT, Apr 11, 1966.

Jeremy Clarkson, 60, television personality ("The Grand Tour," "Top Gear"), born Doncaster, South Yorkshire, England, Apr 11, 1960.

Ellen Goodman, 72, Pulitzer Prize–winning columnist, born Newton, MA, Apr 11, 1948.

Joel Grey, 88, actor (Oscar for *Cabaret*; *The Seven-Per-Cent Solution*), born Joel Katz at Cleveland, OH, Apr 11, 1932.

Tricia Helfer, 46, actress ("Battlestar Galactica"), born Donalda, AB, Canada, Apr 11, 1974.

Bill Irwin, 70, actor (Tony Award for *Who's Afraid of Virginia Woolf?*; "Legion," *Rachel Getting Married*), clown, mime, born Santa Monica, CA, Apr 11, 1950.

Ethel Kennedy, 92, human rights activist, widow of Robert Kennedy, born Greenwich, CT, Apr 11, 1928.

Louise Lasser, 81, actress ("Mary Hartman, Mary Hartman"), born New York, NY, Apr 11, 1939.

Peter Riegert, 73, actor (*Local Hero*, *Crossing Delancey*), born New York, NY, Apr 11, 1947.

Bret William Saberhagen, 56, former baseball player, born Chicago Heights, IL, Apr 11, 1964.

April 12 — Sunday

DAY 103   **263 REMAINING**

ATTACK ON FORT SUMTER: ANNIVERSARY. Apr 12, 1861. After months of escalating tension, Major Robert Anderson refused to evacuate Fort Sumter at Charleston, SC. Confederate troops under the command of General P.G.T. Beauregard opened fire on the harbor fort at 4:30 AM and continued until Major Anderson surrendered on Apr 13. No lives were lost despite the firing of some 40,000 shells in the first major engagement of the American Civil War.

THE BIG WIND: ANNIVERSARY. Apr 12, 1934. The highest-velocity natural wind ever recorded occurred in the morning at the Mount Washington, NH, observatory. Three weather observers, Wendell Stephenson, Alexander McKenzie and Salvatore Pagliuca, observed and recorded the phenomenon in which gusts reached 231 mph—"the strongest natural wind ever recorded on the earth's surface." The 50th anniversary was observed at the site in 1984, with the three original observers participating in the ceremony.

CLAY, HENRY: BIRTH ANNIVERSARY. Apr 12, 1777. Statesman, born at Hanover County, VA. Served as the Speaker of the House of Representatives and later became the leader of the new Whig Party. He was defeated for the presidency three times. Clay died at Washington, DC, June 29, 1852.

EASTER SUNDAY. Apr 12. Commemorates the Resurrection of Christ. Most joyous festival of the Christian year. The date of Easter, a movable feast, is derived from the lunar calendar: the first Sunday following the first ecclesiastical full moon on or after Mar 21—always between Mar 22 and Apr 25. The Council of Nicaea (AD 325) prescribed that Easter be celebrated on the Sunday after Passover, as that feast's date had been established in Jesus's time. After 1582, when Pope Gregory XIII introduced the Gregorian calendar, Orthodox Christians continued to use the Julian calendar, so Easter can sometimes be as much as five weeks apart in the Western and Eastern churches. Easter in 2021 will be Apr 4; in 2022 it will be Apr 17; in 2023 it will be Apr 9. Many other dates in the Christian year are derived from the date of Easter. See also: "Orthodox Easter Sunday or Pascha" (Apr 19).

FDR COMMEMORATIVE CEREMONY. Apr 12. Little White House, Warm Springs, GA. Annual ceremony honoring Franklin Delano Roosevelt on the anniversary of his death in Warm Springs. Est attendance: 1,000. For info: Little White House, 401 Little White House Rd, Warm Springs, GA 31830. Phone: (706) 655-5870. Web: gastateparks.org/littlewhitehouse.

HALIFAX INDEPENDENCE DAY: ANNIVERSARY. Apr 12, 1776. North Carolina. Anniversary of the resolution adopted by the Provincial Congress of North Carolina at Halifax, NC, authorizing the delegates from North Carolina to the Continental Congress to vote for a Declaration of Independence.

HALL, LYMAN: BIRTH ANNIVERSARY. Apr 12, 1724. Signer of the Declaration of Independence. Born at Wallingford, CT, he died at Burke County, GA, Oct 19, 1790.

ITALY: EXPLOSION OF THE CART. Apr 12. Florence. At noon on Easter Sunday in Piazza del Duomo a cart full of fireworks is exploded, perpetuating a ceremony of ancient origin and recalling the fire that was kindled during the *Gloria* at Easter mass and then distributed to all of Florence's households. The tradition is held to date back to the time of the First Crusade, when the valorous Pazzino dei Pazzi was awarded some pieces of flint from the Holy Sepulcher. After his return to Florence the holy fire was kindled with these flints, now preserved in the church of Santi Apostoli.

MASSACRE AT FORT PILLOW: ANNIVERSARY. Apr 12, 1864. After surrounding Fort Pillow, TN, Confederate general Nathan Bedford Forrest attacked the stronghold on this date. The ensuing Confederate victory led to many casualties, many of them black Union soldiers. Although Forrest claimed that the large number of casualties was a result of the fort's refusal to surrender, most believe that Forrest's men massacred the defenseless troops after the fort was surrendered. The action inflamed Northern sentiments and is considered one of the most controversial events of the Civil War.

MERRIE MONARCH FESTIVAL WITH WORLD'S LARGEST HULA COMPETITION. Apr 12–18. Hilo, HI. Cultural event honoring King David Kalakaua. Festival culminates with the world's largest hula competition. Hawaii's finest hula schools compete in ancient and modern divisions. Annually, beginning on Easter Sunday. Est attendance: 6,000. For info: Merrie Monarch Office, 865 Piilani St, Hilo, HI 96720. Phone: (808) 935-9168. Web: www.merriemonarch.com.

NATIONAL D.E.A.R. DAY—NATIONAL DROP EVERYTHING AND READ DAY. Apr 12. A special reading celebration to remind and encourage families to make reading together on a daily basis a family priority. Annually, Apr 12, the birthday of author Beverly Cleary. For info: American Library Assn. Web: www.ala.org.

NATIONAL DOG BITE PREVENTION WEEK. Apr 12–18. With an estimated population of 78 million dogs living in US households, millions of people—most of them children—are bitten by dogs every year. The majority of these bites, if not all, are preventable. This week focuses on education and prevention. Annually, second full week in April. Sponsored by the National Dog Bite Prevention Week® Coalition. For info: AVMA. Web: www.avma.org/Events/pethealth/Pages/Dog-Bite-Prevention-Week.aspx.

NATIONAL LICORICE DAY. Apr 12. Celebrating black licorice, including its history, health benefits and world renown as a delightful confection. Throughout the entire month of April (which is also National Licorice Month), Licorice International offers tours and free samples to the public. For info: Erin Burianek, Licorice International. Phone: (402) 488-2230. E-mail: licorice-news@licoriceinternational.com. Web: www.licoriceinternational.com or www.ilovelicorice.com.

ORTHODOX HOLY WEEK. Apr 12–18.

ORTHODOX PALM SUNDAY. Apr 12. Celebration of Christ's entry into Jerusalem, when his way was covered with palms by the multitudes. Beginning of Holy Week in the Orthodox Church.

★PAN-AMERICAN WEEK. Apr 12–18. Presidential Proclamation customarily issued as "Pan-American Day and Pan-American Week." Always issued for the week including Apr 14 (except from 1946 through 1948, 1955 through 1977 and 1979).

POLIO VACCINE: 65th ANNIVERSARY. Apr 12, 1955. Anniversary of announcement that the polio vaccine developed by American physician Dr. Jonas E. Salk was "safe, potent and effective." Incidence of the dreaded infantile paralysis, or poliomyelitis, declined by 95 percent following introduction of preventive vaccines. The first mass inoculations of children with the Salk vaccine had begun in Pittsburgh, PA, Feb 23, 1954.

ROOSEVELT, FRANKLIN DELANO: 75th DEATH ANNIVERSARY. Apr 12, 1945. With the end of WWII only months away, the nation and the world were stunned by the sudden death of the president shortly into his fourth term of office. Roosevelt, 32nd president of the US (Mar 4, 1933–Apr 12, 1945), was the only president to serve more than two terms—he was elected to four consecutive terms. He died at Warm Springs, GA.

SPACE MILESTONE: *COLUMBIA STS-1* (US) FIRST SHUTTLE FLIGHT. Apr 12, 1981. First flight of shuttle *Columbia*. Two astronauts (John Young and Robert Crippen), on first manned US space mission since *Apollo-Soyuz* in July 1976, spent 54 hours in space (36 orbits of Earth) before landing at Edwards Air Force Base, CA, Apr 14.

	S	M	T	W	T	F	S
April				1	2	3	4
	5	6	7	8	9	10	11
2020	12	13	14	15	16	17	18
	19	20	21	22	23	24	25
	26	27	28	29	30		

SPACE MILESTONE: *VOSTOK I*, FIRST MAN IN SPACE. Apr 12, 1961. Yuri Gagarin became the first man in space when he made a 108-minute voyage, orbiting Earth in a 10,395-pound vehicle, *Vostok I*, launched by the USSR.

TRUANCY LAW: ANNIVERSARY. Apr 12, 1853. The first truancy law was enacted at New York. A $50 fine was charged against parents whose children between the ages of 5 and 15 were absent from school.

UNITED NATIONS: INTERNATIONAL DAY OF HUMAN SPACE FLIGHT. Apr 12. Marking the anniversary of the flight of Russian cosmonaut Yuri Gagarin on Apr 12, 1961, this day reaffirms the important contribution of space science and technology in achieving sustainable development goals. The General Assembly has designated Apr 12 each year as the International Day of Human Space Flight (Res 65/271 of Apr 7, 2010). For info: United Nations, Dept of Public Info, New York, NY 10017. Web: www.un.org.

WALK ON YOUR WILD SIDE DAY. Apr 12. Time's wasting, friends. It's high time you went out and did some things no one expects you to do. Be unpredictable for once. Go to work dressed like a gorilla, get a master's degree—do something "they" said you'd never ever do. (©2006 by WH.) For info: Thomas & Ruth Roy, Wellcat Holidays, 2418 Long Ln, Lebanon, PA 17046. Phone: (717) 279-0184. E-mail: info@wellcat.com. Web: www.wellcat.com.

YURI'S NIGHT. Apr 12. Worldwide celebration of space and human spaceflight, observed on the anniversary of USSR cosmonaut Yuri Gargarin's flight of Apr 12, 1961, and the first launch of NASA's space shuttle on the same day in 1981.

🎂 BIRTHDAYS TODAY

Beverly Cleary, 104, author (the Ramona Quimby series, Newbery Medal for *Dear Mr Henshaw*), born McMinnville, OR, Apr 12, 1916.

Claire Danes, 41, actress ("Homeland," *Temple Grandin, Shopgirl, The Hours*), born New York, NY, Apr 12, 1979.

Shannen Doherty, 49, actress ("Beverly Hills 90210," "Charmed," *Heathers*), born Memphis, TN, Apr 12, 1971.

Andy Garcia, 64, actor (*Ocean's Eleven, The Untouchables*), born Havana, Cuba, Apr 12, 1956.

Herbie Hancock, 80, musician, born Chicago, IL, Apr 12, 1940.

Dan Lauria, 73, actor ("The Wonder Years," *Stakeout*), born Brooklyn, NY, Apr 12, 1947.

David Letterman, 73, comedian, former television talk show host ("Late Show with David Letterman"), born Indianapolis, IN, Apr 12, 1947.

Sarah Jane Morris, 43, actress ("Brothers & Sisters," "Felicity"), born Memphis, TN, Apr 12, 1977.

Ed O'Neill, 74, actor ("Modern Family," "Married . . . With Children," *Wayne's World*), born Youngstown, OH, Apr 12, 1946.

Saoirse Ronan, 26, actress (*Lady Bird, Brooklyn, The Lovely Bones*), born New York, NY, Apr 12, 1994.

April 13 — Monday

DAY 104   **262 REMAINING**

BECKETT, SAMUEL: BIRTH ANNIVERSARY. Apr 13, 1906. Author, critic and playwright, born at Foxrock, County Dublin, Ireland. Beckett is best remembered for his plays, including *Waiting for Godot, Endgame, Krapp's Last Tape* and *Happy Days*. Beckett settled at Paris, France, in 1937 and served with an underground resistance group during the early years of WWII. In the years following the war, he wrote the challenging novels *Molloy, Malone Dies* and *The Unnamable* and two plays, *Eleutheria* and *Waiting for Godot*. *Waiting for Godot* received an acclaimed production at Paris in January 1953, and with it Beckett achieved worldwide renown. Awarded the Nobel Prize for Literature in 1969, he died Dec 22, 1989, at Paris.

CASSIDY, BUTCH: BIRTH ANNIVERSARY. Apr 13, 1866. Notorious outlaw who robbed banks and trains throughout the American West during the late 1800s. Born Robert LeRoy Parker at Beaver, UT, Cassidy formed "the Wild Bunch"—a gang that teamed him with Harry Longabaugh ("the Sundance Kid"). Under pressure from Pinkerton agents, Cassidy and Sundance fled to South America in the early 1900s. Details of Cassidy's death are uncertain, but many believe he was killed in San Vicente, Bolivia, in 1908, while attempting to rob a mine station.

DYNGUS DAY USA. Apr 13. Dyngus Day celebrates the end of Lent and the joy of Easter. "Dyngus" comes from a medieval Polish word for "worthy, proper." Over the decades, the day has become a wonderful way to celebrate Polish-American culture, heritage and traditions. With the largest concentration of festival locations, live polka music and authentic traditions, Buffalo, NY, is the "Dyngus Day Capital of the World!" Many parties begin during the midmorning with a large buffet of traditional Easter foods (kielbasa, ham, fresh breads, eggs). The most important tradition of Dyngus Day is the exchange of pussy willow branches and water as a playful form of flirting. Men and women tap each other with the pussy willows and squirt each other with water to attract attention. Annually, the Monday after Easter. For info: Dyngus Day USA. E-mail: dyngusdayusa@yahoo.com. Web: www.DyngusDay.com.

EASTER MONDAY. Apr 13. Holiday or bank holiday in many places, including England, Northern Ireland, Wales and Canada.

ENGLAND: HALLATON BOTTLE KICKING. Apr 13. Hallaton, Leicestershire. Ancient custom dating back at least 600 years. Annually, Easter Monday.

FAWKES, GUY: 450th BIRTH ANNIVERSARY. Apr 13, 1570. Englishman who, along with a small group of fellow Catholics, conspired to blow up England's Houses of Parliament and kill its Protestant members—including King James I—on Nov 5, 1605. The "Gunpowder Plot" was foiled the night before, and Nov 5 is commemorated as a day of delivery each year with bonfires, fireworks and burning of life-size Fawkes effigies (called "guys"—origin of the English word). Born to a wealthy Protestant family in York, England, Fawkes converted to Catholicism later in life. He was executed Jan 31, 1606, at London. See also: "England: Guy Fawkes Day" (Nov 5).

HEANEY, SEAMUS: BIRTH ANNIVERSARY. Apr 13, 1939. Poet born at Mossbawn, Northern Ireland. Heaney began writing poetry seriously after graduating from Queen's University, Belfast, in 1962. Though he was a teacher by training, his career was marked by increasing critical and popular notice of his work, leading to posts of professor of poetry at both Oxford (1989–94) and Harvard (1984–95). A 1995 Nobel Prize Laureate in Literature, Heaney called his work "poetry that doesn't fancy itself up to be poetry." His works include *Death of a Naturalist* (1966), *Wintering Out* (1973), *The Spirit Level* (1996) and various essays and translations, notably *Beowulf* (2000). Heaney died Aug 30, 2013, at Dublin, Ireland.

JEFFERSON, THOMAS: BIRTH ANNIVERSARY. Apr 13, 1743. Third president of the US (Mar 4, 1801–Mar 3, 1809), second vice president (1797–1801), born at Shadwell, VA. Jefferson, who died at Charlottesville, VA, July 4, 1826, wrote his own epitaph: "Here was buried Thomas Jefferson, author of the Declaration of American Independence, of the statute of Virginia for religious freedom, and father of the University of Virginia." A holiday in Alabama and Oklahoma. See also: "Adams, John, and Jefferson, Thomas: Death Anniversary" (July 4).

LUXEMBOURG: EMAISHEN. Apr 13. Luxembourg (city). Popular traditional market and festival at the "Marche-aux-Poissons." Young lovers present each other with earthenware articles, sold only on this day. Annually, Easter Monday.

PREMIERE OF HANDEL'S *MESSIAH*: ANNIVERSARY. Apr 13, 1742. In a charity performance at the New Musick Hall on Fishamble Street, Dublin, Ireland, George Frederick Handel sat at the harpsichord and conducted the first concert of his masterpiece, *Messiah*. This sacred oratorio became Handel's most popular work and has been performed every year since 1742. Newspapers of the day anticipated the popularity of the first performance and asked ladies not to wear hoops under their skirts and gentlemen not to wear swords so that 700 people could fit into a hall designed for 600. Some years later, King George II stood up in admiration of the Hallelujah Chorus, starting a tradition still followed by audiences to this day.

***SILENT SPRING* PUBLISHED: ANNIVERSARY.** Apr 13, 1962. Rachel Carson's *Silent Spring* warned humankind that for the first time in history every person is subjected to contact with dangerous chemicals from conception until death. Carson painted a vivid picture of how chemicals—used in many ways but particularly in pesticides—have upset the balance of nature, undermining the survival of countless species. This enormously popular and influential book was a soft-spoken battle cry to protect our natural surroundings. Its publication signaled the beginning of the environmental movement.

SOUTH AFRICA: FAMILY DAY. Apr 13. National holiday. Annually, Easter Monday.

SRI LANKA: SINHALA AND TAMIL NEW YEAR. Apr 13–14. This New Year festival includes traditional games, the wearing of new clothes in auspicious colors and special foods. Public holiday.

SWITZERLAND: EGG RACES. Apr 13. Rural northwest Swiss Easter Monday custom. Race among competitors carrying large numbers of eggs while running to neighboring villages.

THAILAND: SONGKRAN FESTIVAL. Apr 13–15. Public holiday. Thai New Year festival (also known as the "Water Festival"). To welcome the new year, the image of Buddha is bathed with holy or fragrant water and lustral water is sprinkled on celebrants. Joyous event, especially observed at Buddhist temples.

UNITED KINGDOM: EASTER MONDAY BANK HOLIDAY. Apr 13. Bank and public holiday in England, Wales and Northern Ireland. (Scotland not included.)

WELTY, EUDORA: BIRTH ANNIVERSARY. Apr 13, 1909. Great novelist and short-story writer whose characters lived in the rural South. Her short stories are considered the zenith of the art. Wrote *The Ponder Heart* (1954), among other works. Lived her entire life in Jackson, MS, and died there July 23, 2001.

WHITE HOUSE EASTER EGG ROLL. Apr 13. Traditionally held at executive mansion's south lawn on Easter Monday.

🎂 BIRTHDAYS TODAY

Peabo Bryson, 69, singer, born Greenville, SC, Apr 13, 1951.

Jack Casady, 76, musician (Jefferson Airplane), born Washington, DC, Apr 13, 1944.

Robert Casey, 60, US Senator (D, Pennsylvania), born Scranton, PA, Apr 13, 1960.

Bill Conti, 78, composer (Oscar for *The Right Stuff*), born Providence, RI, Apr 13, 1942.

Tony Dow, 75, actor ("Leave It to Beaver"), born Hollywood, CA, Apr 13, 1945.

Sergei Gonchar, 46, hockey coach and former player, born Chelyabinsk, USSR (now Russia), Apr 13, 1974.

Al Green, 74, Rock and Roll, Songwriters and Gospel Music halls of fame singer, songwriter, born Forrest City, AR, Apr 13, 1946.

Garry Kasparov, 57, International Grandmaster chess player, born Baku, Azerbaijan, Apr 13, 1963.

Davis Love III, 56, golfer, born Charlotte, NC, Apr 13, 1964.

Ron Perlman, 70, actor (*Hellboy*, "Sons of Anarchy," "Beauty and the Beast"), born New York, NY, Apr 13, 1950.

Saundra Santiago, 63, actress ("Miami Vice"), born the Bronx, NY, Apr 13, 1957.

Rick Schroder, 50, actor ("Silver Spoons," "NYPD Blue," *The Champ*), born Staten Island, NY, Apr 13, 1970.

Paul Sorvino, 81, actor ("Law & Order"), born Brooklyn, NY, Apr 13, 1939.

Lyle Waggoner, 85, actor ("The Carol Burnett Show," "Wonder Woman"), born Kansas City, KS, Apr 13, 1935.

Max M. Weinberg, 69, musician (E Street Band), bandleader ("Late Night with Conan O'Brien"), born South Orange, NJ, Apr 13, 1951.

April 14 — Tuesday

DAY 105   **261 REMAINING**

CHILDREN WITH ALOPECIA DAY. Apr 14. If you are a child (or have a child) who is losing hair because of the autoimmune hair-loss disease alopecia areata, today is your day to stand up and be proud of not having hair while still being you! For info: Jeffery Woytovich, The Children's Alopecia Project, 906 Penn Ave, Ste 1, Wyomissing, PA 19610. Phone: (610) 468-1011. E-mail: Jeff.Woytovich@childrensalopeciaproject.org. Web: www.childrensalopeciaproject.org.

CHILDREN'S DAY IN FLORIDA. Apr 14. A legal holiday in Florida commemorated on the second Tuesday in April.

FIRST AMERICAN ABOLITION SOCIETY FOUNDED: ANNIVERSARY. Apr 14, 1775. The first abolition organization formed in the US was The Society for the Relief of Free Negroes Unlawfully Held in Bondage, founded at Philadelphia, PA.

FIRST DICTIONARY OF AMERICAN ENGLISH PUBLISHED: ANNIVERSARY. Apr 14, 1828. Noah Webster published his *American Dictionary of the English Language*.

GIELGUD, SIR JOHN: BIRTH ANNIVERSARY. Apr 14, 1904. Director and actor, born at London, England. A legend of the stage, he played the role of Hamlet more than 500 times. He made his professional film debut in *Who Is the Man?* in 1924. Other film credits include *Arthur, Murder on the Orient Express* and *Plenty*. He won

April 2020	S	M	T	W	T	F	S
				1	2	3	4
	5	6	7	8	9	10	11
	12	13	14	15	16	17	18
	19	20	21	22	23	24	25
	26	27	28	29	30		

the Tony Award for Best Director in 1961 for *Big Fish Little Fish*. He died at Buckinghamshire, England, May 21, 2000.

***GRAPES OF WRATH* PUBLISHED: ANNIVERSARY.** Apr 14, 1939. John Steinbeck's novel of the Great Depression, *Grapes of Wrath*, won the National Book Award and the 1940 Pulitzer Prize. It chronicled the mass migration of dispossessed farmers from the Dust Bowl region of the Great Plains to California.

HONDURAS: DIA DE LAS AMERICAS. Apr 14. Pan-American Day, a national holiday.

HUYGENS, CHRISTIAAN: BIRTH ANNIVERSARY. Apr 14, 1629. Scientist, born at the Hague, Netherlands. He discovered the rings of Saturn and formulated the wave theory, or pulse theory, of light. In 1656 he invented the pendulum clock. He died at the Hague, June 8, 1695.

INTERNATIONAL BE KIND TO LAWYERS DAY. Apr 14. Lawyers are perhaps the most reviled and ridiculed profession in the world today, and yet people flock to lawyers the moment they need help writing a will, running a business or avoiding jail time. This is the one day out of the year to give an ounce or two of respect to the men and women who daily tip the scales of justice. Whether you take your favorite attorney out to lunch or simply refrain from telling lawyer jokes for 24 hours, this is the day to give a little love to the attorneys in your life. Annually, the second Tuesday in April. For info: Steve Hughes, 1001 Alsace Ct, St. Louis, MO 63017. Phone: (314) 821-8700. E-mail: Steve@hityourstride.com. Web: www.BeKindToLawyers.com.

INTERNATIONAL MOMENT OF LAUGHTER DAY. Apr 14. Laughter is a potent and powerful way to deal with the difficulties of modern living. Since the physical, emotional and spiritual benefits of laughter are widely accepted, this day is set aside for everyone to take the necessary time to experience the power of laughter. For info: Izzy Gesell, Head Honcho of Wide Angle Humor, PO Box 962, Northampton, MA 01061. Phone: (413) 222-4142. E-mail: izzy@izzyg.com. Web: www.izzyg.com.

LINCOLN, ABRAHAM: ASSASSINATION ANNIVERSARY. Apr 14, 1865. President Abraham Lincoln was shot while watching a performance of *Our American Cousin* at Ford's Theatre, Washington, DC. He died the following day. The assassin was John Wilkes Booth, a young actor.

MOON PHASE: LAST QUARTER. Apr 14. Moon enters Last Quarter phase at 6:56 PM, EDT.

NATIONAL CATHOLIC EDUCATIONAL ASSOCIATION CONVENTION AND EXPO. Apr 14–16. Baltimore Convention Center, Baltimore, MD. This meeting is for NCEA members and anyone else working in, or interested in the welfare of, Catholic and faith-based education. Annually, in the week after Easter Sunday. Est attendance: 7,000. For info: Natl Catholic Educational Assn, 1005 N Glebe Rd, Ste 525, Arlington, VA 22201. Phone: (571) 257-0010. Web: www.ncea.org/convention.

★PAN-AMERICAN DAY. Apr 14. Presidential Proclamation 1912, of May 28, 1930, covers every Apr 14 (required by Governing Board of Pan-American Union). Proclamation issued each year since 1948. Commemorates the first International Conference of American States in 1890.

PAN-AMERICAN DAY IN FLORIDA. Apr 14. A ceremonial day in Florida that is observed in the public schools as a day honoring the republics of Latin America. When Apr 14 does not fall on a

school day, the governor may designate the preceding Friday or the following Monday as Pan-American Day.

PATHOLOGISTS' ASSISTANT DAY. Apr 14. A pathologists' assistant is an intensively trained allied healthcare professional who provides surgical and autopsy pathology services under the direction and supervision of a pathologist. This day honors these professionals. Annually, on Apr 14 (the day the AAPA's Articles of Incorporation were received and filed in 1972). For info: American Assn of Pathologists' Assistants, 2345 Rice St, Ste 220, St. Paul, MN 55113. E-mail: info@pathassist.org. Web: www.pathassist.org.

PRESIDENT TAFT OPENS BASEBALL SEASON: ANNIVERSARY. Apr 14, 1910. President William Howard Taft began a sports tradition by throwing out the first baseball of the season at an American League game between Washington and Philadelphia. Washington won, 3–0.

SEWARD ATTACK: ANNIVERSARY. Apr 14, 1865. As part of the conspiracy to assassinate President Lincoln and cause chaos in the US, Lewis Powell broke into the home of Secretary of State William Seward and stabbed him in his bed several times. Five others in the house were also injured. Seward recovered but his face was disfigured.

SULLIVAN, ANNE: BIRTH ANNIVERSARY. Apr 14, 1866. Anne Sullivan, born at Feeding Hills, MA, became well known for "working miracles" with Helen Keller, who was blind and deaf. Nearly blind herself, Sullivan used a manual alphabet communicated by the sense of touch to teach Keller to read, write and speak and then to help her go on to higher education. Anne Sullivan died Oct 20, 1936, at Forest Hills, NY.

VAN CLIBURN CONQUERS MOSCOW: ANNIVERSARY. Apr 14, 1958. Young Texan pianist Van Cliburn won the first International Tchaikovsky Competition in Moscow, USSR (now Russia)—sparking a music frenzy that brought a brief thaw to the cold war. Embraced by Muscovites, Cliburn was also treated to a ticker tape parade in New York City (the only musician so honored). His subsequent recording of Tchaikovsky's Piano Concerto No. 1 was the first classical music album to go platinum.

🎂 BIRTHDAYS TODAY

Abigail Breslin, 24, actress (*Little Miss Sunshine, Signs*), born New York, NY, Apr 14, 1996.

Adrien Brody, 47, actor (Oscar for *The Pianist*; *The Grand Budapest Hotel, King Kong*), born New York, NY, Apr 14, 1973.

Peter Capaldi, 62, actor ("Doctor Who," "The Thick of It," Oscar for "Kranz Kafka's It's a Wonderful Life"), born Glasgow, Scotland, Apr 14, 1958.

Robert Carlyle, 59, actor ("Once Upon a Time," *Angela's Ashes, The Full Monty*), born Glasgow, Scotland, Apr 14, 1961.

Julie Christie, 80, actress (*Dr. Zhivago, Shampoo, Away from Her*), born Chukua, India, Apr 14, 1940.

Cynthia Cooper, 57, former basketball player, born Chicago, IL, Apr 14, 1963.

Brad Garrett, 60, comedian, actor ("Everybody Loves Raymond"), born Woodland Hills, CA, Apr 14, 1960.

Sarah Michelle Gellar, 43, actress (*Scooby-Doo*, "Buffy the Vampire Slayer"), born New York, NY, Apr 14, 1977.

Anthony Michael Hall, 52, actor, comedian ("The Dead Zone," *Sixteen Candles, The Breakfast Club*), born Boston, MA, Apr 14, 1968.

David Christopher Justice, 54, former baseball player, born Cincinnati, OH, Apr 14, 1966.

Loretta Lynn, 85, Country Music and Songwriters halls of fame singer/songwriter, born Butcher's Hollow, KY, Apr 14, 1935.

Greg Maddux, 54, Hall of Fame baseball player, born San Angelo, TX, Apr 14, 1966.

Baker Mayfield, 25, football player, 2017 Heisman Trophy winner, born Austin, TX, Apr 14, 1995.

Pete Rose, 79, former baseball manager and player, born Cincinnati, OH, Apr 14, 1941.

April 15 — Wednesday

DAY 106   **260 REMAINING**

ASTRONOMERS FIND NEW SOLAR SYSTEM: ANNIVERSARY. Apr 15, 1999. Astronomers from San Francisco State University working at an observatory in Arizona announced the discovery of the first multiplanet system ever found orbiting around a star other than our own. Three planets orbit the star Upsilon Andromedae, which can be seen with the naked eye. This suggests that the Milky Way probably teems with similar planetary systems.

BENTON, THOMAS HART: BIRTH ANNIVERSARY. Apr 15, 1889. Born at Neosho, MO, Thomas Hart Benton studied art in Paris and New York. But he left the metropolitan art world in 1935, traveling to Kansas, determined to create work that reacted against European trends and reflected what was felt to be the integrity of the American heartland. He became one of the foremost artists of the populist art movement known as American Regionalism. He died at Kansas City, MO, Jan 19, 1975.

BOSTON MARATHON BOMBINGS: ANNIVERSARY. Apr 15, 2013. At 2:49 PM in the midst of the running of the Boston Marathon, Boston, MA, two pressure-cooker bombs exploded in short succession near the finish line, killing three people and wounding more than 260. As the city of Boston faced an unprecedented manhunt, during the late evening of Apr 18 and into Apr 19, authorities accosted the bombers, two brothers of Chechen ethnicity from Russia. The brothers had murdered a police officer on Apr 18. The manhunt left one bomber dead, the other arrested and 16 police officers wounded. On May 15, 2015, Dzhokhar Tsarnaev was sentenced to death for his actions.

CHINA: CANTON SPRING TRADE FAIR. Apr 15–May 15. The Guangzhou (Canton) Spring Trade Fair is held on the same dates each year.

FDA APPROVES BOTOX: ANNIVERSARY. Apr 15, 2002. The US Food and Drug Administration approved the cosmetic use of Botox (an injected preparation of purified botulism) on this date.

FIRST MCDONALD'S OPENS: 65th ANNIVERSARY. Apr 15, 1955. The first franchised McDonald's was opened at Des Plaines, IL, by Ray Kroc, who had gotten the idea from a hamburger joint at San Bernardino, CA, run by the McDonald brothers. On opening day a hamburger was 15 cents. The Big Mac was introduced in 1968 for 49 cents and the Quarter Pounder in 1971 for 53 cents. By the 21st century, there were more than 31,000 McDonald's in 119 countries.

FIRST SCHOOL FOR DEAF FOUNDED: ANNIVERSARY. Apr 15, 1817. Thomas Hopkins Gallaudet and Laurent Clerc founded the first US public school for the deaf, Connecticut Asylum for the Education and Instruction of Deaf and Dumb Persons (now the American School for the Deaf), at Hartford, CT.

HILLSBOROUGH TRAGEDY: ANNIVERSARY. Apr 15, 1989. During a soccer match between Liverpool and Nottingham Forest at Hillsborough Stadium, Sheffield, England, unprepared local police and stadium staff made what proved to be fatal and criminal mistakes regarding crowd control and funneled fans into a too-small area. As a result, 96 Liverpool supporters died after being crushed against metal barriers that separated fans from the field and 766 people were injured. Later investigations also found that local police and municipal officials colluded to blame the victims for the tragedy. On Apr 6, 2016, after one of the longest trials in British history, a jury returned a verdict of unlawful killing in each of the 96 deaths.

"IN LIVING COLOR" TV PREMIERE: 30th ANNIVERSARY. Apr 15, 1990. FOX's sketch comedy series, created by Keenen Ivory Wayans, was modeled after "Saturday Night Live." The show featured Wayans, his brothers Damon, Marlon and Shawn and his sister Kim. Between skits, the Fly Girls would entertain the studio audience with hip-hop dance. The dance segments of the show helped launch the careers of celebrities including Rosie Perez, Carrie Ann Inaba and Jennifer Lopez, and many comedians including David Alan Grier, Jamie Foxx, Kim Coles and Jim Carrey also began their careers on the show. Some of the most popular recurring characters were Homey, the embittered clown, the flammable Fire Marshall Bill and the effeminate movie critics of "Men on Film."

INCOME TAX PAY DAY. Apr 15. A day all Americans need to know—the day by which taxpayers are supposed to make their accounting of the previous year and pay their share of the cost of government. The US Internal Revenue Service provides free forms.

JAMES, HENRY: BIRTH ANNIVERSARY. Apr 15, 1843. Influential novelist and critic, born at New York, NY. Among his best-known works are *The Portrait of a Lady, Washington Square, The Turn of the Screw* and *The Ambassadors.* James died Feb 28, 1916, at London, England.

KIM IL SUNG: BIRTH ANNIVERSARY. Apr 15, 1912. President Kim Il Sung, first leader of North Korea, was born at Man'gyandae, Korea. A Stalinist-styled dictator, Kim created a godlike personality cult surrounding himself and his son and heir, Kim Jong Il. He died July 8, 1994—just a few weeks before a historic summit with the president of South Korea was to take place, at Pyongyang, North Korea. His death came at a crucial time in world politics: North Korea and the US had recently cooled rhetoric regarding North Korea's nuclear program and had begun further talks just hours prior to the announcement of Kim's death. The North-South Summit and the US–North Korean talks were postponed.

LIBERATION OF BELSEN CONCENTRATION CAMP: 75th ANNIVERSARY. Apr 15, 1945. British troops reached the concentration camp at Belsen, Germany. They counted approximately 35,000 corpses there.

NATIONAL TAKE A WILD GUESS DAY. Apr 15. The day honoring guesses, hunches, inspirations, speculations and other forms of "intuitive intelligence." For info: Jim Barber, 1101 Marcano Blvd, Fort Lauderdale, FL 33322. Phone: (954) 476-9252. E-mail: wildguessday@thebarbershop.com. Web: www.thebarbershop.com/wildguessday.

NATIONAL THAT SUCKS DAY. Apr 15. Income tax pay day, quarterly estimated federal income tax payers' due date and the anniversary of the sinking of the *Titanic* all fall on Apr 15. These events and more support a designation for a National That Sucks Day. Visit our website's history of things that suck. Annually, Apr 15. For info: Bruce Novotny, PO Box 1270, Bandon, OR 97411. Phone: (541) 347-5468. Fax: (541) 347-4252. E-mail: novovet@gmail.com. Web: www.thatsucks.net.

QUARTERLY ESTIMATED FEDERAL INCOME TAX PAYERS' DUE DATE. Apr 15. For those individuals whose fiscal year is the calendar year and who make quarterly estimated federal income tax payments, today is one of the due dates (Jan 15, Apr 15, June 15 and Sept 15, 2020).

ROBINSON BREAKS BASEBALL COLOR LINE: ANNIVERSARY. Apr 15, 1947. Jackie Robinson became the first African American to play in the major leagues in the 20th century when he made his debut for the Brooklyn Dodgers against the Boston Braves. Robinson went 0-for-3 but scored the deciding run as the Dodgers prevailed, 5–3. He was later voted 1947's Rookie of the Year.

ROGER EBERT'S FILM FESTIVAL (EBERTFEST). Apr 15–18. Virginia Theatre, Champaign, IL. Spring film festival founded by the late Roger Ebert, University of Illinois journalism graduate and Pulitzer Prize–winning film critic. The festival presents 12 films representing a cross section of important cinematic works. Each film is introduced, then a panel—often composed of the film's producers, writers, actors or directors as well as scholars—discusses it on stage afterward. For general audiences, distributors and international critics. Sponsored by the College of Media, University of Illinois. For info: Roger Ebert's Film Festival. Web: www.ebertfest.com.

SIMMS, HILDA: 100th BIRTH ANNIVERSARY. Apr 15, 1920. American stage and film actress, born Hilda Moses at Minneapolis, MN. She joined the American Negro Theater at Harlem, NY, in 1943 and was given the title role in *Anna Lucasta.* When the production moved to Broadway in 1944, it became the first all-black production to be performed on Broadway without a racial theme. Simms was the creative arts director of New York State's human rights division, through which she was instrumental in bringing discrimination against black actors to public attention during the 1960s. She died at Buffalo, NY, Feb 6, 1994.

SINKING OF THE *TITANIC*: ANNIVERSARY. Apr 15, 1912. The "unsinkable" luxury liner *Titanic* on its maiden voyage from Southampton, England, to New York, NY, struck an iceberg just before midnight Apr 14, and sank at 2:27 AM, Apr 15. The *Titanic* had 2,224 persons aboard. Of these, more than 1,500 were lost. About 700 people were rescued from the icy waters off Newfoundland by the liner *Carpathia,* which reached the scene about two hours after the *Titanic* went down. See also: "*Titanic* Discovered: Anniversary" (Sept 1).

SMITH, BESSIE: BIRTH ANNIVERSARY. Apr 15, 1894. The "Empress of the Blues," Bessie Smith, was born at Chattanooga, TN (year varies as late as 1900). She was assisted in her efforts to break into show business by Ma Rainey, the first great blues singer. Her first recording was made in February 1923. Smith died of injuries she sustained in an automobile accident at Clarksdale, MS, Sept 26, 1937.

WASHINGTON, HAROLD: BIRTH ANNIVERSARY. Apr 15, 1922. Illinois legislator and mayor of Chicago (1983–87). Born at Chicago, IL, and died there Nov 25, 1987. Harold Washington was one of the first African Americans to head a major US city. He was instrumental in tearing down Chicago's famed Democratic machine, a holdover from the many decades of domination by the Richard J. Daley administration.

April 2020	S	M	T	W	T	F	S
				1	2	3	4
	5	6	7	8	9	10	11
	12	13	14	15	16	17	18
	19	20	21	22	23	24	25
	26	27	28	29	30		

🧁 BIRTHDAYS TODAY

Evelyn Ashford, 63, Olympic track athlete, born Shreveport, LA, Apr 15, 1957.

Linda Bloodworth-Thomason, 73, producer, writer ("Designing Women," "Evening Shade"), born Poplar Bluff, MO, Apr 15, 1947.

Heloise Cruse Evans, 69, newspaper columnist ("Hints from Heloise"), born Waco, TX, Apr 15, 1951.

Luke Evans, 41, actor ("The Alienist," *Beauty and the Beast, The Girl on the Train, The Fast and the Furious* films), born Pontypool, Wales, Apr 15, 1979.

Ilya Kovalchuck, 37, hockey player, born Tver, Russia, Apr 15, 1983.

Madeleine Martin, 27, actress ("Californication"), born New York, NY, Apr 15, 1993.

Seth Rogen, 38, actor (*This Is the End, Knocked Up, Pineapple Express*), screenwriter, born Vancouver, BC, Canada, Apr 15, 1982.

Jason Sehorn, 49, former football player, born Mount Shasta, CA, Apr 15, 1971.

Emma Thompson, 61, actress (Oscar for *Howards End*; *Wit, Sense and Sensibility*), screenwriter (Oscar for *Sense and Sensibility*), born London, England, Apr 15, 1959.

Emma Watson, 30, actress (Harry Potter films, *Beauty and the Beast, The Bling Ring*), born Paris, France, Apr 15, 1990.

Amy Wright, 70, actress (*Breaking Away, Wise Blood, The Accidental Tourist*), born Chicago, IL, Apr 15, 1950.

April 16 — Thursday

DAY 107   **259 REMAINING**

AMIS, KINGSLEY: BIRTH ANNIVERSARY. Apr 16, 1922. Author (*The Old Devils, Lucky Jim*), poet, critic, editor, born at London, England, and died there Oct 22, 1995.

CHAPLIN, CHARLES SPENCER: BIRTH ANNIVERSARY. Apr 16, 1889. Actor, comedian, director, producer, screenwriter and composer born at London, England. He suffered through extreme poverty as a child but escaped the workhouses as a touring music hall dancer and comic. He joined Mack Sennett's Keystone film company and with Keystone and on his own created funny and poignant film masterpieces beginning in 1914—many featuring his "Little Tramp." The derby-hatted Little Tramp—a bit of a dreamer and a bit of a scamp—was a worldwide sensation. Chaplin was knighted in 1975 and died Dec 25, 1977, at Vevey, Switzerland. See also: "Chaplin's 'Tramp' Debuts: Anniversary" (Feb 7).

DENMARK: QUEEN MARGRETHE II'S BIRTHDAY. Apr 16. Thousands of children gather to cheer the queen (born 1940) at Amalienborg Palace, and the Royal Guard wears scarlet gala uniforms.

DIEGO, JOSÉ DE: BIRTH ANNIVERSARY. Apr 16, 1866. Puerto Rican patriot and political leader José de Diego was born at Aguadilla, PR. His birthday is a holiday in Puerto Rico. He died July 16, 1918, at New York, NY.

EMANCIPATION DAY. Apr 16. Legal public holiday in the District of Columbia commemorating President Abraham Lincoln's signing of the Compensated Emancipation Act on Apr 16, 1862. This act freed 3,100 slaves in Washington, DC. When it falls during a weekend, will be observed either the Friday before or Monday after.

FIESTA SAN ANTONIO. Apr 16–26. San Antonio, TX. Eleven days of culture, heritage, beauty and remembrance. Parades, carnivals, sports, fireworks, music, ethnic feasts, art exhibits, dances—more than 100 events. This colorful fiesta originated in 1891 with the Battle of Flowers parade honoring the memory of Texas heroes who fought against General Santa Anna for Texan independence at the Alamo and San Jacinto. Est attendance: 3,500,000. For info: Fiesta San Antonio Commission, Inc, 2611 Broadway St, San Antonio, TX 78215-1022. Phone: (210) 227-5191. Web: www.fiesta-sa.org.

FRANKLIN, JOHN: BIRTH ANNIVERSARY. Apr 16, 1786. Born at Spilsby, Lincolnshire, England, John Franklin was a British naval officer, administrator and explorer. His four Arctic expeditions to map the Northwest Passage solidified his name in history. Three were successes; the fourth was a disaster. Setting sail from England in May 1845, Franklin's outfit was locked in thick ice off the Canadian archipelago by the autumn of 1846. The entire party died there, detached from civilization and suffering from a host of horrible ailments, including hypothermia, starvation and lead poisoning. Franklin himself died June 11, 1847, near King William Island, Canada.

MANCINI, HENRY: BIRTH ANNIVERSARY. Apr 16, 1924. Born at Cleveland, OH, Mancini made his mark in Hollywood composing film scores and songs. He won 20 Grammy Awards and four Oscars (song "Moon River" and score for *Breakfast at Tiffany's*; song "Days of Wine and Roses" for the same-titled film; score for *Victor/Victoria*). He also composed *The Pink Panther*, "Peter Gunn" and "Mr Lucky" themes. Died June 14, 1994, at Beverly Hills, CA.

NATIONAL HIGH FIVE DAY. Apr 16. 19th annual. National High Five Day is as simple as it sounds—a day devoted to giving and receiving high-fives. The organization National High Five Project runs an annual National High-5-A-Thon for charity that anyone, anywhere can participate in. Past causes include cancer research, victims of the Boston Marathon bombings and college scholarships. Annually, the third Thursday in April. For info: National High Five Project. E-mail: nationalhighfiveproject@gmail.com. Web: www.nationalhighfiveproject.org.

NATIONAL STRESS AWARENESS DAY. Apr 16. To focus public awareness on one of the leading health problems in the world today. Health-related organizations throughout the country are encouraged to sponsor stress education programs and events. Annually, the first workday after income taxes are due. For info: The Health Resource Network. Web: www.stressawarenessmonth.com.

NATURAL BRIDGES NATIONAL MONUMENT: ANNIVERSARY. Apr 16, 1908. Utah. Natural Bridges National Monument was established on this date.

SELENA: BIRTH ANNIVERSARY. Apr 16, 1971. Popular Grammy Award–winning Tejana singer, born Selena Quintanilla at Lake Jackson, TX. Her hits include "Como La Flor," "Bidi Bidi Bom Bom" and "Dreaming of You." The "Queen of Tejano Music" died Mar 31, 1995, at Corpus Christi, TX; she was murdered by the president of her fan club. Selena was inducted into the Billboard Latin Music Hall of Fame in 1995.

SLAVERY ABOLISHED IN DISTRICT OF COLUMBIA: ANNIVERSARY. Apr 16, 1862. Congress abolished slavery in the District of Columbia. One million dollars was appropriated to compensate owners of freed slaves, and $100,000 was set aside to pay district slaves who wished to emigrate to Haiti, Liberia or any other country outside the US.

SLOANE, HANS: BIRTH ANNIVERSARY. Apr 16, 1660. British medical doctor and naturalist whose personal collection became the nucleus of the British Museum, born at County Down, Ireland. Upon his death at Chelsea, England, Jan 11, 1753, his collections of books, manuscripts, medals and antiquities were bequeathed

to Britain and accepted by an act of Parliament that incorporated the British Museum. It was opened to the public at London, England, Jan 15, 1759. It is the national museum of the United Kingdom.

SPACE MILESTONE: *APOLLO 16* (US). Apr 16, 1972. Astronauts John W. Young, Charles M. Duke, Jr, and Thomas K. Mattingly II (command module pilot) began an 11-day mission that included 71-hour exploration of moon (Apr 20–23). Landing module named *Orion.* Splashdown in Pacific Ocean within a mile of target, Apr 27.

SYNGE, JOHN MILLINGTON: BIRTH ANNIVERSARY. Apr 16, 1871. Irish dramatist and poet, most of whose plays were written in the brief span of six years before his death at age 37 of lymphatic sarcoma. His best-known work is *The Playboy of the Western World* (1907), which caused protests and rioting at early performances. Synge (pronounced "Sing") was born near Dublin, Ireland, and died there Mar 24, 1909.

TEXAS CITY DISASTER: ANNIVERSARY. Apr 16–17, 1947. The worst industrial disaster in US history. The French-owned *Grandcamp,* docked at the oil and port town of Texas City, TX, and carrying a load of ammonium nitrate, was discovered to have a smoldering fire in the hold. At 9:12 AM, as onlookers gathered and a small firefighting team attempted to extinguish the blaze, the ship exploded with tremendous force, immediately killing everyone at the dock area. The resulting fires destroyed the nearby Monsanto Chemical Company and spread through oil pipelines into the city. At 1 AM, another ship, the *High Flyer,* exploded. The city was left defenseless due to the deaths of almost the entire fire department. There were 576 known casualties, but most estimate that at least 100 more died in the conflagrations. Thousands were injured. The fires burned for a week. The disaster prompted new regulations on handling chemicals. With thousands of lawsuits, the US Congress passed a special act to settle claims in 1956.

USTINOV, PETER: BIRTH ANNIVERSARY. Apr 16, 1921. British actor and playwright born at London, England, Peter Ustinov wrote his first play at age 19. He performed on stage, television and the screen, winning two Oscars (for 1961's *Spartacus* and 1965's *Topkapi*) and several Emmys. He wrote dozens of plays, screenplays and novels and also directed several films, including the highly regarded 1962 version of *Billy Budd.* He played Agatha Christie's detective Hercule Poirot in several screen adaptations. He was knighted by Queen Elizabeth II and dedicated many years to fundraising for UNICEF. He died at Geneva, Switzerland, Mar 28, 2004.

VIRGINIA TECH SHOOTINGS: ANNIVERSARY. Apr 16, 2007. In the second-worst shooting in US history, a disturbed college student shot and killed 32 people on the Virginia Tech University campus at Blacksburg, VA.

WRIGHT, WILBUR: BIRTH ANNIVERSARY. Apr 16, 1867. Aviation pioneer, born at Millville, IN. Died at Dayton, OH, May 30, 1912. See also: "Wright Brothers First Powered Flight: Anniversary" (Dec 17).

🎂 BIRTHDAYS TODAY

Kareem Abdul-Jabbar, 73, Hall of Fame basketball player, born Lewis Ferdinand Alcindor, Jr, at New York, NY, Apr 16, 1947.

Akon, 47, singer, born Aliaune Damala Badara Akon Thiam at St. Louis, MO, Apr 16, 1973.

April 2020	S	M	T	W	T	F	S
				1	2	3	4
	5	6	7	8	9	10	11
	12	13	14	15	16	17	18
	19	20	21	22	23	24	25
	26	27	28	29	30		

Ellen Barkin, 66, actress (Tony for *The Normal Heart;* "Animal Kingdom," *Sea of Love, The Big Easy, Diner*), born New York, NY, Apr 16, 1954.

Benedict XVI, Pope Emeritus, 93, retired; born Joseph Ratzinger at Marktl Am Inn, Germany, Apr 16, 1927.

Chance the Rapper, 27, singer, rapper, songwriter, born Chancelor Bennett at Chicago, IL, Apr 16, 1993.

Jon Cryer, 55, actor ("Two and a Half Men," *Pretty in Pink, Hot Shots!*), born New York, NY, Apr 16, 1965.

Luol Deng, 35, basketball player, born Wow, Sudan, Apr 16, 1985.

Claire Foy, 36, actress ("The Crown," "Wolf Hall," "Little Dorrit"), born Stockport, England, Apr 16, 1984.

Lukas Haas, 44, actor (*Witness, Rambling Rose*), born West Hollywood, CA, Apr 16, 1976.

Martin Lawrence, 55, comedian, actor (*Wild Hogs, Bad Boys, Big Momma's House*), born Frankfurt, Germany, Apr 16, 1965.

Freddie Ljungberg, 43, former soccer player, born Vittsjo, Sweden, Apr 16, 1977.

Jay O. Sanders, 67, actor ("Crime Story," "Person of Interest," *JFK, The Day after Tomorrow*), born Austin, TX, Apr 16, 1953.

Tracy K. Smith, 48, former poet laureate of the US (2017–19), poet (Pulitzer for *Life on Mars*), born Falmouth, MS, Apr 16, 1972.

Anya Taylor-Joy, 24, actress ("The Miniaturist," *Split, The Witch*), born Miami, FL, Apr 16, 1996.

Bobby Vinton, 85, singer, born Canonsburg, PA, Apr 16, 1935.

April 17 — Friday

DAY 108　　　　　　　　　　　　　　　**258 REMAINING**

AMERICAN SAMOA: FLAG DAY. Apr 17. National holiday commemorating first raising of American flag in what was formerly Eastern Samoa in 1900. Public holiday with singing, dancing, costumes and parades.

ANSON, CAP: BIRTH ANNIVERSARY. Apr 17, 1852. Adrian Constantine "Cap" Anson, Baseball Hall of Fame player and manager, born at Marshalltown, IA. Anson played professional baseball from 1871 through 1897 and is considered one of the game's greatest first basemen. As a manager, he piloted the Chicago White Stockings (today's Cubs) to five National League pennants and a .575 winning percentage. Inducted into the Hall of Fame in 1939. Died at Chicago, IL, Apr 18, 1922.

BAY OF PIGS INVASION LAUNCHED: ANNIVERSARY. Apr 17, 1961. More than 1,500 Cuban exiles invaded Cuba in an ill-fated attempt to overthrow Fidel Castro.

BLAH BLAH BLAH DAY. Apr 17. Today's the day to do any of the following, or whatever. Stop smoking, take out the trash, empty the cat litter, lose weight, pick up your clothes, put dirty dishes in the sink, get a job or quit your job. Annually, Apr 17. (©2006 by WH.) For info: Thomas & Ruth Roy, Wellcat Holidays, 2418 Long Ln, Lebanon, PA 17046. Phone: (717) 279-0184. E-mail: info@wellcat.com. Web: www.wellcat.com.

CAMBODIA FALLS TO THE KHMER ROUGE: 45th ANNIVERSARY. Apr 17, 1975. Cambodia fell when its capital, Phnom Penh, was captured by the Khmer Rouge. The Pol Pot regime inaugurated "Year One," and the wholesale slaughter of intellectuals, political enemies and peasants began. As many as two million Cambodians perished. See also: "Pol Pot Overthrown: Anniversary" (Jan 7).

CHASE, SAMUEL: BIRTH ANNIVERSARY. Apr 17, 1741. Signer of the Declaration of Independence. Associate justice of the United States (1796–1811). Only Supreme Court judge to be impeached (1803). He was acquitted Mar 1, 1805. Born at Somerset County, MD, he died June 19, 1811, at Baltimore, MD.

GIBBS, MIFFLIN WISTAR: BIRTH ANNIVERSARY. Apr 17, 1823. Mifflin Wistar Gibbs was born at Philadelphia, PA. In 1873 he became the first black man to be elected a judge in the US, winning an election for city judge at Little Rock, AR. He died July 11, 1915, at Little Rock.

HERBALIST DAY. Apr 17. Herbalists are known for generously sharing knowledge about herbalism with those around them, helping to empower others to tend to their own wellness. From the seemingly small actions of showing someone how to brew a cup of tea or make a comforting herbal bath to more formal instruction of students in a classroom or writing an informative book, herbalists teach those around them every day how to use and enjoy herbs. Since 2014, Apr 17 is a day to celebrate and thank the herbalists in our lives. For info: Herbal Academy, 24 South Rd, Bedford, MA 01730. Web: www.theherbalacademy.com.

HOLDEN, WILLIAM: BIRTH ANNIVERSARY. Apr 17, 1918. William Holden's first starring role was in *Golden Boy*. The actor, born at O'Fallon, IL, won an Oscar for his role in *Stalag 17* in 1953. He was found dead at Los Angeles, CA, Nov 16, 1981.

INTERNATIONAL HAIKU POETRY DAY. Apr 17. A celebration of the genre of haiku, whose origins date back a millennium in Japan, and which is now written in more than 50 countries and cultures around the world. This day is observed in the heart of National Poetry Month (United States), under the auspices of The Haiku Foundation. In addition to various public events, readings, exhibitions and competitions around the world, the foundation hosts on this day the HaikuLife Haiku Film Festival and the Earthrise Rolling Haiku Collaboration. For info: The Haiku Foundation. E-mail: jim.kacian@thehaikufoundation.org. Web: www.thehaikufoundation.org.

MORGAN, JOHN PIERPONT: BIRTH ANNIVERSARY. Apr 17, 1837. American financier and corporation director, born at Hartford, CT. Morgan died Mar 31, 1913, at Rome, Italy, leaving an estate valued at more than $70 million.

NATIONAL COLLEGIATE MEN'S GYMNASTICS CHAMPIONSHIP. Apr 17–18. Ann Arbor, MI. Host is University of Michigan. For info: NCAA, PO Box 6222, Indianapolis, IN 46206-6222. Web: www.NCAA.com.

NATIONAL COLLEGIATE WOMEN'S GYMNASTICS. Apr 17–18. Fort Worth, TX. 39th annual. Host is Texas Woman's University. For info: NCAA, PO Box 6222, Indianapolis, IN 46206-6222. Phone: (317) 917-6222. Fax: (317) 917-6837. Web: www.NCAA.com.

NEEDHAM, THERESA: BIRTH ANNIVERSARY. Apr 17, 1912. Owner of Chicago's legendary South Side blues bar Theresa's Lounge, Theresa Needham was born at Meridian, MS. Especially memorable at the bar were "Blue Monday" all-day jams at which the city's top blues performers locked horns in musical battles. Needham, who was bartender, bouncer and talent agent, came to be known as "the Godmother of Chicago Blues." Died at Chicago, IL, Oct 16, 1992.

NETHERLANDS AND SCILLY ISLES PEACE: ANNIVERSARY. Apr 17, 1986. The 335-year "state of war" that had existed between The Netherlands and the Scilly Isles came to an end on this date when Dutch ambassador Jonkheer Huydecoper flew to the Scilly Isles to deliver a proclamation terminating the war that had started in 1651. Though hostilities had ceased three centuries earlier, a standing joke in the islands was that no one had bothered to declare an end to the war.

SOLIDARITY GRANTED LEGAL STATUS: ANNIVERSARY. Apr 17, 1989. After nearly a decade of struggle and suppression, the Polish labor union Solidarity was granted legal status, clearing the way for the downfall of the Polish Communist Party. Solidarity and the Polish people surprised the government by winning 99 of the 100 parliamentary seats in the election. General Wojciech Jaruzelski was elected president on July 19 and nominated Czelaw Kiszczak prime minister, enraging the Lech Walesa–led Solidarity. On Aug 7 Walesa swayed the traditional allies of the Communist Party—the United Peasant and Democratic parties—to switch sides. Kiszczak resigned as prime minister a week later after failing to form a government, forcing Jaruzelski to accept the principle of a government led by Solidarity.

STEIGER, ROD: 95th BIRTH ANNIVERSARY. Apr 17, 1925. The magnetic character actor was born at Westhampton, NY. In a 50-year career, Steiger played a wide range of roles for some of the best directors of the day. He won a Best Actor Oscar for *In the Heat of the Night* and was also nominated for *On the Waterfront* and *The Pawnbroker*. He died at Los Angeles, CA, July 9, 2002.

SUGARLOAF CRAFTS FESTIVAL. Apr 17–19. Montgomery County Fairgrounds, Gaithersburg, MD. This show, now in its 45th year, features 300 nationally recognized craft designers and fine artists displaying and selling their original creations. Craft demonstrations, music, gift certificate drawings, specialty foods and more! Est attendance: 12,600. For info: Sugarloaf Mountain Works, Inc, 13225 Executive Park Terrace, Germantown, MD 20874. Phone: (800) 210-9900. E-mail: sugarloafinfo@sugarloaffest.com. Web: www.sugarloafcrafts.com.

SYRIAN ARAB REPUBLIC: INDEPENDENCE DAY. Apr 17. Official holiday. Proclaimed independence from League of Nations mandate under French administration in 1946.

VERRAZANO DAY: ANNIVERSARY. Apr 17, 1524. Celebrates discovery of New York harbor by Giovanni Verrazano, Florentine navigator, 1485–1527.

WILDER, THORNTON: BIRTH ANNIVERSARY. Apr 17, 1897. Pulitzer Prize–winning American playwright (*Our Town*) and novelist, born at Madison, WI. Died at Hamden, CT, Dec 7, 1975.

🎂 BIRTHDAYS TODAY

Sean Bean, 62, actor ("Game of Thrones," *The Lord of the Rings: Fellowship of the Ring, Patriot Games*), born Sheffield, Yorkshire, England, Apr 17, 1958.

Victoria Beckham, 45, designer, singer (Spice Girls), born Hertfordshire, England, Apr 17, 1975.

Norman Julius "Boomer" Esiason, 59, sportscaster, former football player, born West Islip, NY, Apr 17, 1961.

Jennifer Garner, 48, actress (*Dallas Buyers Club, Juno,* "Alias"), born Houston, TX, Apr 17, 1972.

Nick Hornby, 63, author (*High Fidelity, About a Boy, Fever Pitch*), screenwriter, critic, born Redhill, England, Apr 17, 1957.

Olivia Hussey, 69, actress (*Romeo and Juliet*), born Buenos Aires, Argentina, Apr 17, 1951.

Rooney Mara, 35, actress (*Carol, The Social Network, The Girl with the Dragon Tattoo* [US]), born Bedford, NY, Apr 17, 1985.

Cynthia Ozick, 92, feminist, writer, born New York, NY, Apr 17, 1928.

Liz Phair, 53, rock singer/songwriter, born New Haven, CT, Apr 17, 1967.

Lela Rochon, 54, actress (*Waiting to Exhale, Boomerang*), born Los Angeles, CA, Apr 17, 1966.

April 18 — Saturday

DAY 109	257 REMAINING

AMERICA'S OLDEST BREWERY DAY. Apr 18. Yuengling Brewery, Pottsville, PA. Yuengling is America's oldest brewery, certified by the National Register of Historic Places. In 1829, David G. Yuengling arrived from Württemberg, Germany, and settled in the coal-mining town of Pottsville, PA. He established the Eagle Brewery, which was later destroyed by a fire and rebuilt to become Yuengling Brewery. This day commemorates Yuengling's rich history over the past 190 years. Fans can tour the historic brewery, including its iconic hand-dug fermentation caves used for refrigeration in the 1800s, for free. For info: D.G. Yuengling & Son, Inc. Web: www.yuengling.com.

CANADA: CONSTITUTION ACT OF 1982: ANNIVERSARY. Apr 18, 1982. Replacing the British North America Act of 1867, the Canadian Constitution Act of 1982 provided Canada with a new set of fundamental laws and civil rights. Signed by Queen Elizabeth II, at Parliament Hill, Ottawa, Canada, on Apr 17, it went into effect at 12:01 AM, Sunday, Apr 18, 1982.

CRAWFORD, SAMUEL EARL "WAHOO SAM": BIRTH ANNIVERSARY. Apr 18, 1880. Major league baseball player with the Detroit Tigers, born at Wahoo, NE. Wahoo Sam played pro ball for 20 years, racking up a career batting average of .309. His record of 309 career triples still stands. He was inducted into the Baseball Hall of Fame in 1957. Crawford died June 15, 1968, at Hollywood, CA.

DARROW, CLARENCE SEWARD: BIRTH ANNIVERSARY. Apr 18, 1857. American attorney often associated with unpopular causes, from the Pullman strike in 1894 to the Leopold and Loeb trial in 1924, born at Kinsman, OH. At the Scopes trial, July 13, 1925, Darrow said: "I do not consider it an insult, but rather a compliment, to be called an agnostic. I do not pretend to know where many ignorant men are sure—that is all that agnosticism means." Darrow died at Chicago, IL, Mar 13, 1938.

	S	**M**	**T**	**W**	**T**	**F**	**S**
April				1	2	3	4
	5	6	7	8	9	10	11
2020	12	13	14	15	16	17	18
	19	20	21	22	23	24	25
	26	27	28	29	30		

HISTORIC GARDEN WEEK IN VIRGINIA. Apr 18–25. This annual statewide event, celebrating its 87th anniversary, is billed as "America's Largest Open House." Showcases more than 250 of Virginia's finest homes, gardens, plantations and landmark properties on more than 30 separate tours on different days of the week. Est attendance: 30,000. For info: Karen Ellsworth, State Director, Garden Club of Virginia, Attention: Historic Garden Week, 12 E Franklin St, Richmond, VA 23219. Phone: (804) 644-7776. E-mail: karen@vagardenweek.org. Web: www.vagardenweek.org.

INTERNATIONAL RAW MILK CHEESE APPRECIATION DAY. Apr 18. Raw milk cheeses are unique in flavor and history, and they tell the story of traditional cheesemaking practices. Producers who make them are passionate about craftsmanship and animal husbandry, and their cheeses represent years, even decades, of knowledge and thoughtful innovation to better their products. This day recognizes cheeses made with raw milk as part of our collective culinary heritage and is the perfect opportunity to try a new cheese, visit a farm, engage with a producer or cheesemonger and even write your elected officials to encourage them to protect and promote artisanal cheese producers. Annually, the third Saturday in April. For info: Oldways Cheese Coalition, Oldways, 266 Beacon St, Ste 1, Boston, MA 02116. Phone: (617) 421-5500. E-mail: media@oldwayspt.org. Web: https://oldwayspt.org/cheese.

JUST PRAY NO! WORLDWIDE WEEKEND OF PRAYER AND FASTING. Apr 18–19. 30th annual. Churches throughout the world participate. Concerts of prayer, fasting, street rallies and marches to gain media attention. Bible studies and sermons concerning alcoholism and drug abuse and revival meetings aimed at those bound by addiction. For info: Just Pray No, Ltd, 1875 Sunset Point Rd, #704, Clearwater, FL 33765. E-mail: justprayno@aol.com. Web: www. justprayno.org.

NAB 2020/NATIONAL BROADCASTERS CONVENTION. Apr 18–22. Las Vegas Convention Center, Las Vegas, NV. World's largest convention of radio, television and other types of multimedia. The awards for the National Broadcasting Hall of Fame are also presented at the convention. Est attendance: 95,000. For info: Natl Assn of Broadcasters. E-mail: dlemle@nab.org. Web: www.nab-show.com.

★NATIONAL PARK WEEK. Apr 18–26 (tentative). Proclamation encouraging Americans to visit their national parks and be reminded of these unique blessings we share as a nation. (Annually, nine days beginning on a Saturday.)

OCLOO, ESTHER AFUA: BIRTH ANNIVERSARY. Apr 18, 1919. Ghanaian pioneer of microlending and, as cofounder of Women's World Banking, activist who sought to improve women's economic opportunities. Born Esther Afua Nkulenu in British Togoland (now part of Ghana), she died at Accra, Ghana, Feb 8, 2002.

PAUL REVERE'S RIDE: ANNIVERSARY. Apr 18, 1775. The "Midnight Ride" of Paul Revere and William Dawes started at about 10 PM to warn American patriots between Boston, MA, and Concord, MA, of the approaching British.

PET OWNERS INDEPENDENCE DAY. Apr 18. Dog and cat owners take the day off from work, and the pets go to work in their place, since most pets are jobless, sleep all day and do not even take out the trash. (©2006 by WH.) For info: Thomas & Ruth Roy, Wellcat Holidays, 2418 Long Ln, Lebanon, PA 17046. Phone: (717) 279-0184. E-mail: info@wellcat.com. Web: www.wellcat.com.

RECORD STORE DAY. Apr 18. 13th annual. Hundreds of independently owned music stores across the country will celebrate Record Store Day. On this day, all of these stores will simultaneously link and act as one with the purpose of celebrating the culture and unique place that they occupy both in their local communities and nationally. Check your local record store for special events—including artist appearances. Annually, the third Saturday in April (except for Easter weekends). For info: Record Store Day. E-mail: information@recordstoreday.com. Web: www.recordstoreday.com.

SAN FRANCISCO 1906 EARTHQUAKE: ANNIVERSARY. Apr 18, 1906. Business section of San Francisco, some 10,000 acres, destroyed by earthquake. First quake at 5:13 AM, followed by fire. Nearly 4,000 lives lost.

"THIRD WORLD" DAY: 65th ANNIVERSARY. Apr 18, 1955. Anniversary of the first use of the phrase "third world," which was by Indonesia's President Sukarno in his opening speech at the Bandung Conference. Representatives of nearly 30 African and Asian countries (2,000 attendees) heard Sukarno praise the American war of independence, "the first successful anticolonial war in history." More than half the world's population, he said, was represented at this "first intercontinental conference of the so-called colored peoples, in the history of mankind." The phrase and the idea of a "third world" rapidly gained currency, generally signifying the aggregate of nonaligned peoples and nations—the nonwhite and underdeveloped portion of the world.

***TITAN 34-D* ROCKET FAILURE: ANNIVERSARY.** Apr 18, 1986. Launched from Vandenberg Air Force Base, CA, the $65 million *Titan* exploded when it was only a few hundred feet into flight, destroying the $500 million *KH-11* reconnaissance satellite payload. Poisonous fumes were released by the explosion, causing concern for the safety of people in nearby communities.

TOKYO RAID: ANNIVERSARY. Apr 18, 1942. Also known as the Doolittle Raid. For the first time during WWII, the mainland of Japan was bombed. Brigade General James Doolittle led a squadron of B-25s from the US carrier *Hornet*. Cities bombed included Tokyo, Yokohama, Kobe and Nagoya. Doolittle said they flew so low that "one of our party observed a ball game in progress." Although the bombers did little damage, the psychological victory was enormous.

WORLD CIRCUS DAY. Apr 18. Created by the Fédération Mondiale du Cirque in 2009, this day celebrates traditional circus arts all over the world. Annually, the third Saturday in April. For info: Fédération Mondiale du Cirque. Web:ww.circusfederation.org.

WORLD HERITAGE DAY/INTERNATIONAL DAY FOR MONUMENTS AND SITES. Apr 18. Established and approved by UNESCO in 1983, this day celebrates our shared cultural heritage. This is a day to visit monuments and sites, encourage the restoration of monuments and sites, sponsor a talk, raise awareness among schoolchildren and much more. Annually, Apr 18. For info: International Council on Monuments and Sites (ICOMOS). Web: www.icomos.org/en/focus/18-april-international-day-for-monuments-and-sites.

ZIMBABWE: INDEPENDENCE DAY: 40th ANNIVERSARY. Apr 18. National holiday commemorates the recognition by Great Britain of Zimbabwean independence on this day in 1980. Prior to this, the country had been the British colony of Southern Rhodesia.

🎂 BIRTHDAYS TODAY

Chloe Bennet, 28, actress ("Agents of S.H.I.E.L.D.," "Nashville"), born Chloe Wang at Chicago, IL, Apr 18, 1992.

America Ferrera, 36, actress ("Superstore," "Ugly Betty," *The Sisterhood of the Traveling Pants*), born Los Angeles, CA, Apr 18, 1984.

Melissa Joan Hart, 44, actress ("Sabrina the Teenage Witch"), born Long Island, NY, Apr 18, 1976.

Michael D. Higgins, 79, president of Ireland, born Limerick, Ireland, Apr 18, 1941.

Robert Hooks, 83, actor, director, producer (*Star Trek III: The Search for Spock*; stage: *Day of Absence*), born Washington, DC, Apr 18, 1937.

John James, 64, actor ("Search for Tomorrow," "Dynasty"), born Minneapolis, MN, Apr 18, 1956.

Jane Leeves, 59, actress ("Murphy Brown," "Frasier," "Hot in Cleveland"), born East Grinstead, England, Apr 18, 1961.

Dorothy Lyman, 73, actress ("All My Children," "Mama's Family"), director, born Minneapolis, MN, Apr 18, 1947.

Eric McCormack, 57, actor ("Lonesome Dove," "Will & Grace"), born Toronto, ON, Canada, Apr 18, 1963.

Hayley Mills, 74, actress (*Pollyana, The Parent Trap, The Moon Spinners*), born London, England, Apr 18, 1946.

Rick Moranis, 66, actor, writer (*Ghostbusters*; *Honey, I Shrunk the Kids*), born Toronto, ON, Canada, Apr 18, 1954.

Conan O'Brien, 57, television talk show host, born Brookline, MA, Apr 18, 1963.

John Pankow, 66, actor ("Episodes," "Mad About You"), born St. Louis, MO, Apr 18, 1954.

Eric Roberts, 64, actor (*Runaway Train, Star 80*), born Biloxi, MS, Apr 18, 1956.

Eli Roth, 48, actor (*Inglourious Basterds, Death Proof*), director, born Boston, MA, Apr 18, 1972.

David Tennant, 49, actor ("Broadchurch," "Doctor Who," *Richard II, Hamlet*), born Bathgate, West Lothian, Scotland, Apr 18, 1971.

James Woods, 73, actor (*Holocaust, The Onion Field*), born Vernal, UT, Apr 18, 1947.

April 19 — Sunday

DAY 110   **256 REMAINING**

BATTLE OF LEXINGTON AND CONCORD: ANNIVERSARY. Apr 19, 1775. Massachusetts. Start of the American Revolution as the British fired the "shot heard 'round the world."

BRANCH DAVIDIAN FIRE AT WACO: ANNIVERSARY. Apr 19, 1993. After a 51-day standoff between the Branch Davidians and law-enforcement groups, the compound of the religious cult burned to the ground with 86 of its members inside, near Waco, TX, after federal agents began battering the compound with armored vehicles. Nine people escaped, but the 86 who perished included 17 children and the cult's leader, David Koresh.

CHEMISTS CELEBRATE EARTH WEEK. Apr 19–25. First observed in 2003. To celebrate the contributions of chemistry to modern life and to help the public understand that chemistry affects every part of our lives. The American Chemical Society provides activities that include open houses, contests, workshops, exhibits and classroom visits around the United States and Puerto Rico. Ten million participants worldwide. For info: Office of Science Outreach, American Chemical Society, 1155 16th St NW, Washington, DC 20036. E-mail: outreach@acs.org. Web: www.acs.org/chasesCCEW.

EXPLOSION ON THE USS *IOWA*: ANNIVERSARY. Apr 19, 1989. In one of the worst naval disasters since the war in Vietnam, a freak explosion rocked the battleship USS *Iowa*, killing 47 sailors. The explosion occurred in the number 2 gun turret as the *Iowa* was participating in gunnery exercises about 300 miles northeast of Puerto Rico.

GARFIELD, LUCRETIA RUDOLPH: BIRTH ANNIVERSARY. Apr 19, 1832. Wife of James Abram Garfield, 20th president of the US, born at Hiram, OH. Died at Pasadena, CA, Mar 14, 1918.

JOHN PARKER DAY. Apr 19. Remembering John Parker's order, at Lexington Green, MA, Apr 19, 1775: "Stand your ground. Don't fire unless fired upon; but if they mean to have a war, let it begin here." Parker, Revolutionary soldier, captain of minutemen, was born at Lexington, MA, July 13, 1729. He died Sept 17, 1775.

NATIONAL COIN WEEK. Apr 19–25. 98th annual. Discover the world of money and the hobby of coin collecting. Annually, the third full week of April, Sunday through Saturday. For info: American Numismatic Assn. Phone: (800) 367-9723. E-mail: ana@money.org. Web: www.money.org/numismatic-events/national-coin-week.

★**NATIONAL CRIME VICTIMS' RIGHTS WEEK.** Apr 19–25.

NATIONAL CRIME VICTIMS' RIGHTS WEEK. Apr 19–25. During this week, the Office for Victims of Crime and communities across the country raise awareness of victims' rights and services, highlight local programs, celebrate progress achieved and honor victims and the professionals who serve them. For info: Office for Victims of Crime, 810 Seventh St NW, Washington, DC 20531. Web: https://ovc.ncjrs.gov/ncvrw.

NATIONAL HANGING OUT DAY. Apr 19. National Hanging Out Day was created to demonstrate how it is possible to save money and energy by using a clothesline. Annually, Apr 19. (Created by Project Laundry List.)

NATIONAL LIBRARY WEEK. Apr 19–25. National Library Week is a time to celebrate the contributions of our nation's libraries and librarians and to promote library use and support. All types of libraries—school, public, academic and special—participate. For info: American Library Assn, Public Info Office, 50 E Huron St, Chicago, IL 60611. Phone: (312) 280-5041. Fax: (312) 280-5274. E-mail: pao@ala.org. Web: www.ala.org/nlw.

★**NATIONAL VOLUNTEER WEEK.** Apr 19–25.

NATIONAL VOLUNTEER WEEK. Apr 19–25. National Volunteer Week has become the official time to recognize and celebrate the efforts of volunteers at the local, state and national levels. It began in 1974 when President Richard Nixon signed an executive order establishing the week as an annual celebration of volunteering. Every president since has signed a proclamation promoting National Volunteer Week, as have governors, mayors and other elected officials. For info: Points of Light Institute. E-mail: info@pointsoflight.org. Web: www.pointsoflight.org.

NESS, ELIOT: BIRTH ANNIVERSARY. Apr 19, 1903. The legendary Prohibition-era lawman was born at Chicago, IL. He gained lasting fame as the leader of the "Untouchables": young, dedicated federal agents handpicked by Ness who could not be bribed by the mobsters they were targeting. Ness especially went after Chicago gangster Al Capone's bootlegging business, which was finally brought down in 1931. After stints in other federal and municipal agencies, Ness died May 7, 1957, at Coudersport, PA—just before publication of his memoirs, *The Untouchables*, which went on to inspire a TV series and later a film.

NETHERLANDS–US DIPLOMATIC RELATIONS: ANNIVERSARY. Apr 19, 1782. Anniversary of establishment of America's oldest continuously peaceful diplomatic relations. On this date, the States General of the Netherlands United Provinces admitted John Adams (later to become second president of the US) as minister plenipotentiary of the young American republic. This was the second diplomatic recognition of the US as an independent nation.

	S	M	T	W	T	F	S
April				1	2	3	4
	5	6	7	8	9	10	11
2020	12	13	14	15	16	17	18
	19	20	21	22	23	24	25
	26	27	28	29	30		

Within six months Adams had succeeded in bringing about the signing of the first Treaty of Amity and Commerce between the two countries (Oct 8, 1782).

OKLAHOMA CITY BOMBING: 25th ANNIVERSARY. Apr 19, 1995. A truck bomb exploded outside the Alfred P. Murrah Federal Building at Oklahoma City, OK, at 9:02 AM, killing 168 people, 19 of them children at a day-care center; a nurse died of head injuries sustained while helping in rescue efforts. The bomb, estimated to have weighed 5,000 pounds, had been placed in a rented truck. The blast ripped off the north face of the nine-story building, leaving a 20-foot-wide crater and debris two stories high. Structurally unsound and increasingly dangerous, the bombed building was razed May 23. Timothy J. McVeigh, a decorated Gulf War army vet who is alleged to have been angered by the Bureau of Alcohol, Tobacco and Firearms (ATF) attack on the Branch Davidian compound at Waco, TX, exactly two years before, was convicted of the bombing and was executed June 11, 2001. The ATF had offices in the federal building. Terry L. Nichols, an army buddy of McVeigh's, was convicted of murder and conspiracy charges and was sentenced to life in prison.

OKLAHOMA CITY BOMBING REMEMBRANCE. Apr 19. Oklahoma City National Memorial and Museum, Oklahoma City, OK. Annual observance honoring the victims and survivors of the 1995 bombing. The names of the 168 killed are read and 168 seconds of silence are observed. For info: Oklahoma City National Memorial and Museum, 620 N Harvey Ave, Oklahoma City, OK 73102. Phone: (405) 235-3313. Web: www.oklahomacitynationalmemorial.org.

ORTHODOX EASTER SUNDAY OR PASCHA. Apr 19. Observed by Eastern Orthodox churches on this date. Normally Easter falls on different Sundays in the Eastern and Western churches. See also: "Easter Sunday" (Apr 12).

PATRIOTS' DAY IN FLORIDA. Apr 19. A ceremonial day to commemorate the first blood shed in the American Revolution at Lexington and Concord in 1775.

SHERMAN, ROGER: BIRTH ANNIVERSARY. Apr 19, 1721. (Old Style date.) American statesman, member of the Continental Congress (1774–81 and 1783–84), signer of the Declaration of Independence and of the Constitution, born at Newton, MA. He also calculated astronomical and calendar information for an almanac. Sherman died at New Haven, CT, July 23, 1793.

SIERRA LEONE: NATIONAL HOLIDAY. Apr 19. Sierra Leone became a republic in 1971.

SPACE MILESTONE: *SALYUT* **(USSR).** Apr 19, 1971. The Soviet Union launched *Salyut*, the first manned, orbiting space laboratory. It was replaced in 1986 by *Mir*, a manned space station and laboratory.

SWAZILAND: KING'S BIRTHDAY. Apr 19. National holiday. Commemorates the birth of King Mswati III, born Apr 19, 1968.

URUGUAY: LANDING OF THE 33 PATRIOTS DAY. Apr 19. National holiday. Commemorates the arrival in 1825 of Juan Lavalleja, an anticolonial leader, and his 33 fighters. This landing marked the first stage in the fight for independence from Brazil in 1828.

WARSAW GHETTO REVOLT: ANNIVERSARY. Apr 19, 1943. A prolonged revolt began at Warsaw, Poland, when German troops tried to resume deportation of Jewish residents of the Warsaw Ghetto to the Treblinka concentration camp. With only 17 rifles and handmade grenades, for almost a month 1,200 Jewish fighters resisted 2,100 German troops who were armed with machine guns. When the uprising ended on May 16, 300 Germans and 7,000 Jews had died and the Warsaw Ghetto lay in ruins.

🎂 BIRTHDAYS TODAY

Hayden Christensen, 39, actor (*Shattered Glass, Star Wars* films), born Vancouver, BC, Canada, Apr 19, 1981.

Tim Curry, 74, actor (*The Rocky Horror Picture Show*; stage: *Spamalot, Amadeus, My Favorite Year*), born Cheshire, England, Apr 19, 1946.

Elinor Donahue, 83, actress ("Father Knows Best," "The Andy Griffith Show"), born Tacoma, WA, Apr 19, 1937.

James Franco, 42, actor (*Oz the Great and Powerful, Rise of the Planet of the Apes, 127 Hours*), born Palo Alto, CA, Apr 19, 1978.

Joanna Gaines, 42, television personality ("Fixer Upper"), interior designer, housewares designer, born Joanna Stevens at Wichita, KS, Apr 19, 1978.

Kate Hudson, 41, actress (*Fool's Gold; Almost Famous; You, Me and Dupree*), born Los Angeles, CA, Apr 19, 1979.

Ashley Judd, 52, actress (*High Crimes, Double Jeopardy, Kiss the Girls*), born Los Angeles, CA, Apr 19, 1968.

Tony Plana, 66, actor ("Ugly Betty," "Resurrection Boulevard"), born Havana, Cuba, Apr 19, 1954.

Alan Price, 78, singer, songwriter, born Fairfield, England, Apr 19, 1942.

Maria Sharapova, 33, tennis player, born Nyagan, Russia, Apr 19, 1987.

Al Unser, Jr, 58, race car driver, born Albuquerque, NM, Apr 19, 1962.

April 20 — Monday

DAY 111   **255 REMAINING**

ADMINISTRATIVE PROFESSIONALS WEEK. Apr 20–24. Since 1952. Acknowledgment of the contributions of all administrative professionals and their vital roles in business, industry, education and government. Annually, the last full week (Monday–Sunday) in April. Administrative Professionals Day is observed on Wednesday of this week (Apr 22 in 2020). For info: Intl Assn of Administrative Professionals, 10502 N Ambassador Dr, Ste 100, Kansas City, MO 64153-1291. Phone: (816) 891-6600. E-mail: geninfo@iaap-hq.org. Web: www.iaap-hq.org.

BOSTON MARATHON—123rd RUNNING. Apr 20. Boston, MA. The marathon begins in the rural New England town of Hopkinton, winds through eight cities and towns and finishes near downtown Boston. Always the third Monday in April. More than 27,000 participants. Athletes qualify by meeting time standards

that correspond to age. Est attendance: 500,000. For info: Boston Athletic Assn, 185 Dartmouth St, 6th Fl, Boston, MA 02116. Phone: (617) 236-1652. E-mail: info@baa.org. Web: www.baa.org.

COLUMBINE HIGH SCHOOL KILLINGS: ANNIVERSARY. Apr 20, 1999. At this high school at Littleton, CO, students Eric Harris and Dylan Klebold killed 12 other students, a teacher and then themselves.

DEEPWATER HORIZON OIL RIG EXPLOSION: 10th ANNIVERSARY. Apr 20, 2010. On this day, an oil rig run by British Petroleum (BP) exploded in the Gulf of Mexico about 50 miles off the Louisiana coast, resulting in the largest offshore oil spill in US history. The fire and explosions on the platform—perhaps caused by escaping methane gas—killed 11 workers and injured 17. The rig eventually sank, and the damage to the drilling equipment resulted in an unrelenting flow of oil from the well directly into the gulf. Several attempts to staunch the flow were unsuccessful, primarily because of the difficulty in working at such depths (approximately 5,000 feet below sea level). At the height of the disaster, the well was pouring as much as 60,000 barrels of oil per day into the Gulf of Mexico, and the damage to marine wildlife and the surrounding coastal areas was immeasurable.

FESTIVAL OF RIDVAN. Apr 20–May 1. Annual Baha'i festival commemorating the 12 days (in 1863) when Baha'u'llah, the prophet-founder of the Baha'i Faith, resided in a garden called Ridvan (Paradise) in Baghdad, at which time he publicly proclaimed his mission as God's messenger for this age. The first, ninth and twelfth days are celebrated as holy days and are three of the nine days of the year when Baha'is suspend work. For info: Baha'is of the US, Office of Communications, 1233 Central St, Evanston, IL 60201. Phone: (847) 733-3584. E-mail: ooc@usbnc.org. Web: www.bahai.us.

4/20 DAY. Apr 20. A longtime and—until recent years—underground celebration of marijuana and cannabis culture. Often observed with festivals and smoking events. The origin of "4/20" has been lost to time and is vigorously debated. Annually, Apr 20.

FRENCH, DANIEL CHESTER: BIRTH ANNIVERSARY. Apr 20, 1850. American sculptor, born at Exeter, NH. One of the most important artists of the 19th and early 20th centuries as a sculptor of public monuments, French is best known for his 1875 *Minute Man* statue at Concord, MA, and his 1922 statue of the seated Abraham Lincoln in the Lincoln Memorial at Washington, DC. French died at Stockbridge, MA, Oct 7, 1931.

HAMPTON, LIONEL: BIRTH ANNIVERSARY. Apr 20, 1908. The jazz great was born at Louisville, KY. Hampton started out on piano and drums, but Louis Armstrong urged him to take up the vibraphone in 1930. Hampton went on to make that his signature instrument. He recorded and played with Armstrong, Benny Goodman, Dizzy Gillespie, Benny Carter and other legends before becoming a bandleader himself. He played almost up until his death on Aug 31, 2002, at New York, NY.

HITLER, ADOLF: BIRTH ANNIVERSARY. Apr 20, 1889. German dictator, born at Braunau am Inn, Austria. Despite a brief time in prison—during which he wrote *Mein Kampf* (published in 1925 and 1926)—Hitler quickly rose in politics as leader of the Nazis, feeding on German anger over the economy and WWI defeat. He also fanned violent anti-Semitism, which later resulted in millions of Jewish deaths in concentration camps. A German plebiscite vested sole executive power in Führer Adolf Hitler Aug 19, 1934. In seeking to increase German power, he started WWII in 1939. Facing certain defeat by the Allied forces, he shot himself Apr 30, 1945, in a Berlin bunker where he had been hiding for more than three months.

LLOYD, HAROLD: BIRTH ANNIVERSARY. Apr 20, 1893. A comic genius of early American film, Harold Lloyd frequently played the boy next door whose distinguishing feature was his round horn-rimmed spectacles. This character thrilled audiences in "daredevil" comedy featuring dangerous stunts (Lloyd never used a double). Lloyd's hits include *Safety Last* (1923), where he dangled from a building's clock face, *The Freshman* (1925) and *Speedy*

(1928). The biggest box-office star of the 1920s, Lloyd survived with lesser success in the talkie 1930s. He was given an honorary Oscar in 1953 for being a "master comedian and good citizen." Born at Burchard, NE, Lloyd died on Mar 8, 1971, at Hollywood, CA.

LUDLOW MINE INCIDENT: ANNIVERSARY. Apr 20, 1914. Miners struggling for recognition of their United Mine Workers Union were attacked at Ludlow, CO, by National Guard troops. The guardsmen were paid by the mining company. A tent colony was destroyed, five men and one boy were killed by machine-gun fire, and 11 children and two women were burned to death.

MIRÓ, JOAN: BIRTH ANNIVERSARY. Apr 20, 1893. Internationally acclaimed artist born at Barcelona, Spain. He often drew on his Catalan heritage and used idiosyncratic visual codes in his colorful, surrealistic works. Miró died at Palma, Majorca, Spain, on Dec 25, 1983.

PATRIOTS' DAY IN MASSACHUSETTS AND MAINE. Apr 20. Commemorates battles of Lexington and Concord, 1775. Annually, the third Monday in April.

PUENTE, TITO: BIRTH ANNIVERSARY. Apr 20, 1923. The King of the Mambo—or "El Rey"—was born Ernesto Antonio Puente, Jr, at Spanish Harlem, New York City, to Puerto Rican parents. The legendary Puente had a career that spanned more than six decades, starting in 1937. He popularized the timbal but played many other percussion instruments and was also a composer, arranger and bandleader. His album *Dance Mania* (1958) was an international bestseller, and he released more than 100 albums. His song "Oye Como Va" was covered by Carlos Santana and has become a classic. Puente won five Grammys, was inducted into the Jazz and Hispanic halls of fame and received a Smithsonian Lifetime Achievement Award. President Jimmy Carter pronounced him "the Goodwill Ambassador of Latin American Music." Puente died on May 31, 2000, at New York, NY.

SMITH, HOLLAND: BIRTH ANNIVERSARY. Apr 20, 1882. Considered the father of amphibious warfare, Holland "Howling Mad" Smith was born at Hatchechubbee, AL. Smith developed techniques for amphibious assaults that involved coordination of land, sea and air forces. During WWII he led troops in assaults in the Marshall and Mariana Islands and also directed forces at Guam, Iwo Jima and Okinawa. Smith died Jan 12, 1967, at San Diego, CA.

TAURUS, THE BULL. Apr 20–May 20. In the astronomical/astrological zodiac that divides the sun's apparent orbit into 12 segments, the period Apr 20–May 20 is traditionally identified as the sun sign of Taurus, the Bull. The ruling planet is Venus.

UNDERGRADUATE RESEARCH WEEK. Apr 20–24. Annual week celebrating the achievements of students and faculty participating in collaborative research. Sponsored by the Council on Undergraduate Research (CUR), a not-for-profit organization whose mission is to support and promote high-quality student-faculty collaborative research and creative inquiry. All academic institutions are invited to submit their related events for posting with CUR and to participate in CUR-sponsored webinars, receptions and research presentations. For info: The Council on Undergraduate Research, 734 15th St NW, Ste 850, Washington, DC 20005. Phone: (202) 783-4810. Fax: (202) 783-4811. E-mail: robin@cur.org. Web: www.cur.org.

UNITED NATIONS: CHINESE LANGUAGE DAY. Apr 20. Chinese is one of the United Nations Secretariat's six official and working languages (English, French, Arabic, Chinese, Russian, Spanish). Chinese is one of the oldest languages in the world, and it is also the most used language in the world. This day celebrates the grace, history and culture of Chinese. Observed since 2010. Annually, Apr 20. For info: United Nations. Web: www.un.org/zh/events/chineselanguageday.

🎂 BIRTHDAYS TODAY

Felix Baumgartner, 51, skydiver, daredevil, BASE jumper, born Salzburg, Austria, Apr 20, 1969.

Miguel Díaz-Canel, 60, President of Cuba, born Miguel Díaz-Canel Bermúdez at Placetas, Villa Clara, Cuba, Apr 20, 1960.

Carmen Electra, 47, actress ("Baywatch," "Singled Out"), born Cincinnati, OH, Apr 20, 1973.

Tanweer Wasim "Tan" France, 37, television personality ("Queer Eye"), fashion designer, born Doncaster, England, Apr 20, 1983.

Crispin Glover, 56, actor (*Willard, Back to the Future, The People vs Larry Flynt*), born New York, NY, Apr 20, 1964.

Danny Granger, 37, basketball player, born New Orleans, LA, Apr 20, 1983.

Miranda Kerr, 37, model, born Sydney, Australia, Apr 20, 1983.

Jessica Lange, 71, actress (Oscars for *Tootsie* and *Blue Sky*; "American Horror Story," *Frances*), born Cloquet, MN, Apr 20, 1949.

Joey Lawrence, 44, actor ("Blossom," "Brotherly Love"), born Strawbridge, PA, Apr 20, 1976.

David Leland, 73, actor (*Time Bandits*), writer, director (*Mona Lisa, Wish You Were Here*), born Cambridge, England, Apr 20, 1947.

Don Mattingly, 59, former baseball player, manager, born Evansville, IN, Apr 20, 1961.

Shemar Moore, 50, actor ("SWAT," "Criminal Minds," "The Young and the Restless," *The Brothers*), born Oakland, CA, Apr 20, 1970.

Ryan O'Neal, 79, actor ("Peyton Place," *Love Story, Paper Moon*), born Los Angeles, CA, Apr 20, 1941.

Pat Roberts, 84, US Senator (R, Kansas), born Topeka, KS, Apr 20, 1936.

Steve Spurrier, 75, football coach and former player, born Miami Beach, FL, Apr 20, 1945.

April 21 — Tuesday

DAY 112   **254 REMAINING**

AGGIE MUSTER. Apr 21. Texas A&M University, College Station, TX, and around the world. A ceremony where current and former students (Aggies) of Texas A&M University gather together to recall their days at the university and to honor fellow Aggies who have died in the past year. During the ceremony, a Roll Call for the Absent is read and a comrade answers "here" for the deceased. The school's most sacred and time-honored tradition. First held in 1883, but in 1903 the Muster date was moved to Apr 21—San Jacinto Day. Celebrated on the school campus and at more than

	S	**M**	**T**	**W**	**T**	**F**	**S**
April				1	2	3	4
	5	6	7	8	9	10	11
2020	12	13	14	15	16	17	18
	19	20	21	22	23	24	25
	26	27	28	29	30		

400 locations around the world. Annually, Apr 21. Est attendance: 100,000. For info: The Association of Former Students, 505 George Bush Dr, College Station, TX 77840-2918. E-mail: aggienetwork@aggienetwork.com. Web: www.aggienetwork.com.

BRASÍLIA INAUGURATED: 60th ANNIVERSARY. Apr 21, 1960. At 9:30 AM, Brazil's new federal capital, Brasília, was inaugurated. The futuristic-looking city, located on the country's central plain and featuring the bold architecture of Oscar Niemeyer and others, was built in four years under the master plan of Lúcio Costa, who won a national contest to create a plan. The former capital was Rio de Janeiro.

BRAZIL: TIRADENTES DAY. Apr 21. National holiday commemorating execution of national hero, dentist José da Silva Xavier, nicknamed Tiradentes (tooth-puller), a conspirator in revolt against the Portuguese in 1789.

BRONTË, CHARLOTTE: BIRTH ANNIVERSARY. Apr 21, 1816. Novelist, born at Hartshead, Yorkshire, England, into a family of six children headed by strict clergyman father Patrick. Charlotte and her younger siblings (Emily, Anne and brother Branwell) lived an isolated existence, during which they imagined and wrote elaborate stories of fantasy. Brontë worked as a governess and teacher but continued writing. Her first novel, published under the name Currer Bell, was *Jane Eyre: An Autobiography* (August 1847). It drew on her life experiences and is considered a cornerstone of British literature. "Conventionality," she wrote in the preface to *Jane Eyre*, "is not morality. Self-righteousness is not religion. To attack the first is not to assail the last." Brontë died Mar 31, 1855, at Haworth, Yorkshire.

FROEBEL, FRIEDRICH: BIRTH ANNIVERSARY. Apr 21, 1782. German educator and author Friedrich Froebel, who believed that play is an important part of a child's education, was born at Oberwiessbach, Thuringia. Froebel invented the kindergarten, founding the first one at Blankenburg, Germany, in 1837. Froebel also invented a series of toys that he intended to stimulate learning. (The American architect Frank Lloyd Wright as a child received these toys [maplewood blocks] from his mother and spoke throughout his life of their value.) Froebel's ideas about the role of directed play, toys and music in children's education had a profound influence in England and the US, where the nursery school became a further extension of his ideas. Froebel died at Marienthal, Germany, June 21, 1852.

INDIA: VAISAKHI. Apr 21 (or 27). Sikh holiday (also known as Khalsa Day) that commemorates the founding of the brotherhood of the Khalsa in 1699. This harvest festival is regarded as the Sikh New Year.

INDONESIA: KARTINI DAY. Apr 21. Honors the birth in 1879 of Raden Adjeng Kartini, pioneer in the emancipation of the women of Indonesia.

ISRAEL: HOLOCAUST DAY (YOM HASHOAH). Apr 21. Hebrew calendar date: Nisan 27, 5780. A day established by Israel's Knesset as a memorial to the Jewish dead of WWII. Anniversary in Jewish calendar of Nisan 27, 5705 (corresponding to Apr 10, 1945, in the Gregorian calendar), the day on which Allied troops liberated the first Nazi concentration camp, Buchenwald, north of Weimar, Germany, where about 56,000 prisoners, many of them Jewish, perished. Began at sundown Apr 20.

ITALY: BIRTHDAY OF ROME. Apr 21. Celebration of the founding of Rome, traditionally thought to be in 753 BC.

KINDERGARTEN DAY. Apr 21. A day to recognize the importance of play, games and "creative self-activity" in children's education and to note the history of the kindergarten. Observed on the anniversary of the birth of Friedrich Froebel, in 1782, who established the first kindergarten in 1837. German immigrants brought Froebel's ideas to the US in the 1840s. The first kindergarten in a public school in the US was started in 1873, at St. Louis, MO.

MUIR, JOHN: BIRTH ANNIVERSARY. Apr 21, 1838. Scottish-American naturalist, explorer, conservationist and author for whom the 550-acre Muir Woods National Monument (near San Francisco, CA) is named. Muir, born at Dunbar, Scotland, immigrated to the US in 1849, eventually settling out west, where he was instrumental in the creation of numerous national parks, including Yosemite, Sequoia, Mount Rainier and Grand Canyon. His writings and his work in the Sierra Club (founded in 1892) created public support for his belief that national parks should be federally protected and their resources left untapped. Muir died at Los Angeles, CA, Dec 24, 1914.

NATIONAL BULLDOGS ARE BEAUTIFUL DAY. Apr 21. In addition to recognizing the beauty in our portly pets, National Bulldogs Are Beautiful Day celebrates people's differences whether they're big, small, short, tall, skinny or stout or have names like Stinky or Lulu. For info: Jackie Valent, 3250 Pleasant View Ct, Brookfield, WI 53045. Phone: (414) 232-8271. E-mail: stinkythebulldog@sbcglobal.net.

NATIONAL LIBRARY WORKERS DAY. Apr 21. First celebrated in 2004, this day is designated to honor and recognize all library workers, including librarians, support staff and others who make library service possible every day. Annually, on the Tuesday of National Library Week. For info: American Library Assn, 50 E Huron St, Chicago, IL 60611. E-mail: pao@ala.org. Web: http://ala-apa.org/nlwd.

QUINN, ANTHONY: BIRTH ANNIVERSARY. Apr 21, 1915. Actor, sculptor and painter, Anthony Rodolfo Oaxaca Quinn was born at Chihuahua, Mexico, and moved to the US as a child. He became a US citizen in 1947. He won Academy Awards for Best Supporting Actor in 1952 for *Viva Zapata!* and in 1956 for *Lust for Life*. His best-remembered role is that of the title character in *Zorba the Greek*, for which he was nominated for Best Actor in 1964. He died at Boston, MA, on June 3, 2001.

RED BARON SHOT DOWN: ANNIVERSARY. Apr 21, 1918. Lethal WWI Prussian flying ace Baron Manfred von Richthofen—known as the "Red Baron" for the color of his Fokker triplane—was shot and killed during the Battle of the Somme. The shot that mortally wounded him probably came from Allied ground gunners as von Richthofen flew unusually low. The Red Baron was able to land, but died almost immediately. Royal Flying Corps pilots recovered his body, and the Allies buried him with full military honors. See also: "The Red Baron: Birth Anniversary" (May 2).

SAN JACINTO DAY. Apr 21. Texas. Commemorates Battle of San Jacinto in 1836, in which Texas won independence from Mexico. A 570-foot monument, dedicated on the 101st anniversary of the battle, marks the site on the banks of the San Jacinto River, about 20 miles from present-day Houston, TX, where General Sam Houston's Texans decisively defeated the Mexican forces led by Santa Anna in the final battle between Texas and Mexico.

SPACE MILESTONE: *COPERNICUS, OAO 4* (US). Apr 21, 1972. Launch of Orbiting Astronomical Observer, named in honor of the Polish astronomer.

WEBER, MAX: BIRTH ANNIVERSARY. Apr 21, 1864. Born at Erfurt, Germany, Weber was a founder of modern sociological thought. His historical and comparative studies of the sociocultural processes of great civilizations, notably *The Protestant Ethic and the Spirit of Capitalism*, are pivotal in sociological history. Weber's ethical themes are foundational in existentialist philosophical thought. He died June 14, 1920, at Munich, Germany.

🧁 BIRTHDAYS TODAY

Ed Belfour, 55, former hockey player, born Carman, MB, Canada, Apr 21, 1965.

Dylan Bruce, 40, actor ("Orphan Black," *Flowers in the Attic*), born Vancouver, BC, Canada, Apr 21, 1980.

Tony Danza, 69, actor ("Taxi," "Who's the Boss?"), born Brooklyn, NY, Apr 21, 1951.

Queen Elizabeth II, 94, Queen of the United Kingdom, born London, England, Apr 21, 1926.

Charles Grodin, 85, actor (*Midnight Run, Beethoven*), director, talk show host ("The Charles Grodin Show"), born Pittsburgh, PA, Apr 21, 1935.

Patti LuPone, 71, singer, stage and screen actress (Tonys for *Gypsy, Sweeney Todd* and *Evita*), born Northport, NY, Apr 21, 1949.

Andie MacDowell, 62, actress (*Harrison's Flowers, Four Weddings and a Funeral, Groundhog Day*), born Gaffney, SC, Apr 21, 1958.

Elaine May, 88, actress, writer, director (*A New Leaf*), born Philadelphia, PA, Apr 21, 1932.

James McAvoy, 41, actor (*X-Men* films, *Atonement, The Last King of Scotland*), born Glasgow, Scotland, Apr 21, 1979.

Iggy Pop, 73, singer, born James Newell Osterberg, Jr, at Ann Arbor, MI, Apr 21, 1947.

Tony Romo, 40, former football player, sportscaster, born San Diego, CA, Apr 21, 1980.

April 22 — Wednesday

DAY 113   **253 REMAINING**

ADMINISTRATIVE PROFESSIONALS DAY. Apr 22. A day to show appreciation to all administrative professionals. Annually, the Wednesday of Administrative Professionals Week. For info: Intl Assn of Administrative Professionals, 10502 N Ambassador Dr, Ste 100, Kansas City, MO 64153-1291. Phone: (816) 891-6600. E-mail: geninfo@iaap-hq.org. Web: www.iaap-hq.org.

BABE RUTH'S PITCHING DEBUT: ANNIVERSARY. Apr 22, 1914. Babe Ruth made his professional pitching debut, playing for the Baltimore Orioles in his hometown. Allowing just six hits and contributing two singles himself, Ruth shut out the Buffalo Bisons, 6–0.

BRAZIL: DISCOVERY OF BRAZIL DAY. Apr 22. Commemorates discovery by Pedro Álvares Cabral in 1500.

COINS STAMPED "IN GOD WE TRUST": ANNIVERSARY. Apr 22, 1864. By act of Congress, the phrase "In God We Trust" began to be stamped on all US coins.

EARTH DAY: 50th ANNIVERSARY CELEBRATION. Apr 22. 2020 marks Earth Day's 50th Anniversary! As the global coordinator of Earth Day, Earth Day Network is working to make sure that Earth Day 2020 is the most diverse global mobilization in defense of the environment in world history. We work year-round with more than 50,000 partner organizations in 190 countries, and our global campaigns and programs bring hundreds of thousands of new voices—representing youth and faculty, the faith community, minority groups, women, teachers, students and others—into the environmental movement. Check our site for events. For info: Earth Day Network, 1616 P St NW, Ste 340, Washington, DC 20036. Phone: (202) 518-0044. E-mail: info@earthday.org. Web: www.earthday.org.

April 2020	S	M	T	W	T	F	S
				1	2	3	4
	5	6	7	8	9	10	11
	12	13	14	15	16	17	18
	19	20	21	22	23	24	25
	26	27	28	29	30		

FIRST SOLO TRIP TO NORTH POLE: ANNIVERSARY. Apr 22, 1994. Norwegian explorer Børge Ousland became the first person to make the trip to the North Pole alone. The trip took 52 days, during which he pulled a 265-pound sled. Departing from Cape Atkticheskiy at Siberia Mar 2, he averaged about 18½ miles per day over the 630-mile journey. Ousland had traveled to the Pole on skis with Erling Kagge in 1990.

LENIN, NIKOLAI: 150th BIRTH ANNIVERSARY. Apr 22, 1870. Russian Socialist and revolutionary leader (real name: Vladimir Ilyich Ulyanov), ideological follower of Karl Marx, born at Simbirst, on the Volga, Russia. Leader of the Great October Socialist Revolution of 1917. Died at Gorky, near Moscow, Jan 21, 1924. His embalmed body, in a glass coffin at the Lenin Mausoleum, has been viewed by millions of visitors to Moscow's Red Square.

MENUHIN, YEHUDI: BIRTH ANNIVERSARY. Apr 22, 1916. Born at New York, NY, Menuhin is regarded as one of the greatest classical violinists of all time. He began lessons at the age of four and at seven made his debut as a soloist with the San Francisco Symphony. He performed for Allied soldiers during WWII and for concentration camp survivors at Bergen-Belsen in 1945. During his 70-year career as a soloist and chamber musician, he performed and recorded essentially all major works of the 18th- and 19th-century classical violin repertoire with all of the most significant artists and ensembles of the day. He played some of the most significant historical violins ever made, including a Guarnerius, a Stradivarius and a Guarneri del Jesu. He died on Mar 12, 1999, at Munich, Germany.

MOON PHASE: NEW MOON. Apr 22. Moon enters New Moon phase at 10:26 PM, EDT.

NATIONAL BOOKMOBILE DAY. Apr 22. An annual celebration of the contributions of our nation's bookmobiles and the dedicated professionals who make quality bookmobile outreach possible in their communities. First celebrated in 2010 by the American Library Association Office for Literacy and Outreach Services (OLOS), the Association of Bookmobile and Outreach Service (ABOS) and the Association for Rural and Small Libraries (ARSL). Annually, the Wednesday of National Library Week. For info: American Library Assn, 50 E Huron St, Chicago, IL 60611. Phone: (312) 280-5044. E-mail: pao@ala.org. Web: www.ala.org/aboutala/bookmobileday.

NATIONAL JELLY BEAN DAY. Apr 22. A day to celebrate the colorful candy that has been around since biblical times. For info: National Confectioners Association, 1101 30th St NW, Ste 200, Washington, DC 20007. Phone: (202) 534-1440. E-mail: info@CandyUSA.org. Web: www.CandyUSA.org.

OKLAHOMA LAND RUSH: ANNIVERSARY. Apr 22, 1889. At noon a gunshot signaled the start of the Oklahoma land rush as thousands of settlers rushed into the territory to claim land. Under pressure from cattlemen, the federal government opened 1,900,000 acres of central Oklahoma that had been bought from the Creek and Seminole tribes.

SECOND BATTLE OF YPRES: ANNIVERSARY. Apr 22, 1915. At the Second Battle of Ypres, Germany used poisonous chlorine gas for the first time on the Western Front. A survivor described it as a "low cloud of yellow-grey smoke or vapour."

UNITED NATIONS: INTERNATIONAL MOTHER EARTH DAY. Apr 22. Acknowledging that Earth and its ecosystems are our home, and convinced that to achieve a just balance among the economic, social and environmental needs of present and future generations,

it is necessary to promote harmony with nature and Earth, the UN General Assembly has proclaimed Apr 22 to be celebrated annually as International Mother Earth Day. (Res 63/278 of Apr 22, 2009.) For info: United Nations, Dept of Public Info, New York, NY 10017. Web: www.un.org.

🧁 BIRTHDAYS TODAY

Byron Allen, 59, comedian, television host ("The Byron Allen Show," "Real People"), actor (*Case Closed*), born Detroit, MI, Apr 22, 1961.

Peter Frampton, 70, singer, guitarist, born Beckenham, England, Apr 22, 1950.

Amber Heard, 34, actress (*3 Days to Kill, Pineapple Express, The Informers*), born Austin, TX, Apr 22, 1986.

Kaká, 38, soccer player, born Ricardo Izecson dos Santos Leite at Brasília, Brazil, Apr 22, 1982.

Marshawn Lynch, 34, football player, born Oakland, CA, Apr 22, 1986.

Eric Mabius, 49, actor ("Ugly Betty," "The L Word"), born Harrisburg, PA, Apr 22, 1971.

Chris Makepeace, 56, actor (*My Bodyguard*), born Montreal, QC, Canada, Apr 22, 1964.

Jeffrey Dean Morgan, 54, actor ("The Good Wife," "Grey's Anatomy," *Watchmen*), born Seattle, WA, Apr 22, 1966.

Jack Nicholson, 84, actor (Oscars for *One Flew over the Cuckoo's Nest, Terms of Endearment* and *As Good as It Gets*), born Neptune, NJ, Apr 22, 1936.

Sherri Shepard, 53, actress, television personality ("30 Rock," "The View"), born Chicago, IL, Apr 22, 1967.

Ryan Stiles, 61, actor ("The Drew Carey Show," "Whose Line Is It Anyway?"), born Seattle, WA, Apr 22, 1959.

John Waters, 74, filmmaker (*Hairspray, Pink Flamingoes*), actor, born Baltimore, MD, Apr 22, 1946.

April 23 — Thursday

DAY 114   **252 REMAINING**

"BAYWATCH" TV PREMIERE: ANNIVERSARY. Apr 23, 1989. Set on a California beach, this program starred David Hasselhoff and a changing cast of nubile young men and women as lifeguards. Later the program was moved to Hawaii; the last episode was made in 2001. The most widely viewed TV series in the world, the program aired in 142 countries with an estimated weekly audience of 1.1 billion.

BERMUDA: PEPPERCORN CEREMONY. Apr 23. St. George. Commemorates the payment of one peppercorn in 1816 to the governor of Bermuda for rental of Old State House by the Masonic Lodge.

BLACK, SHIRLEY TEMPLE: BIRTH ANNIVERSARY. Apr 23, 1928. Born at Santa Monica, CA, Temple was a child star in hit films in the Depression Era. She had unprecedented appeal and popularity; her likeness and name were merchandised decades before film-product marketing's heyday. She was awarded a special Academy Award "in grateful recognition of her outstanding contribution to screen entertainment during the year" (1934), the only Oscar ever awarded based on the film-going public rather than Academy member votes. Her post-film life focused on public service: Black cofounded the National Foundation of Multiple Sclerosis Societies, was ambassador to Czechoslovakia and Ghana and served as the US's UN ambassador. She died Feb 10, 2014, at Woodside, CA.

BUCHANAN, JAMES: BIRTH ANNIVERSARY. Apr 23, 1791. 15th president of the US, born at Cove Gap, PA. Buchanan was the only president who never married. Prior to becoming president, he had

served in both houses of Congress and was secretary of state under President James Polk. As secretary of state, he helped to negotiate the Oregon Treaty, which set the northern boundary of the US. Buchanan served one term in office, Mar 4, 1857–Mar 3, 1861, declined to run for reelection and died at Lancaster, PA, June 1, 1868.

CANADA: NEWFOUNDLAND: SAINT GEORGE'S DAY. Apr 23. Not a statutory holiday but a cultural observance in Newfoundland and Labrador.

CERVANTES SAAVEDRA, MIGUEL DE: DEATH ANNIVERSARY. Apr 23, 1616. Spanish poet, playwright and novelist, died at Madrid, Spain. The exact date of his birth at Alcala de Henares is unknown, but he was baptized Oct 9, 1547. As soldier and tax collector, Cervantes traveled widely. He spent more than five years in prisons in Spain, Italy and North Africa. His greatest creation was Don Quixote, the immortal Knight of La Mancha whose profession was chivalry. Riding his nag, Rozinante, and accompanied by squire Sancho Panza, Don Quixote tilts at windmills of the mind in the world's best-known novel. Nearly a thousand editions of *Don Quixote* (a bestseller since its first appearance in 1605) have been published, and it has been translated into more languages than any other book except the Bible.

DOUGLAS, STEPHEN A.: BIRTH ANNIVERSARY. Apr 23, 1813. Famous for his oratorical skills, American politician Stephen A. Douglas was born at Brandon, VT. Upon adulthood, he moved to the Illinois frontier, where he rose to prominence in the Democratic Party while serving in various elected positions in both the Illinois and US legislatures. Douglas's US Senate reelection campaign of 1858 is renowned for its seven debates with Abraham Lincoln. Despite winning the Senate contest, Douglas was soundly defeated by Abraham Lincoln two years later in the 1860 presidential race, due in large part to the disaffection of Southern Democrats. Following Lincoln's inauguration Douglas argued vigorously against secession. He died June 3, 1861, at Chicago, IL.

ENGLAND: HARROGATE SPRING FLOWER SHOW. Apr 23–26. Great Yorkshire Showground, Harrogate, North Yorkshire. Beautiful show gardens, 100 plant nurseries, Britain's biggest exhibition of floral art, spectacular spring blooms. Est attendance: 60,000. For info: Harrogate Flower Shows, North of England Horticultural Society, Regional Agricultural Centre, Great Yorkshire Showground, Harrogate, North Yorkshire, England HG2 8NZ. Phone: (44) (1423) 546-157. E-mail: info@flowershow.org.uk. Web: www.flowershow.org.uk.

FIDDLER'S FROLICS. Apr 23–26. Knights of Columbus Hall, Hallettsville, TX. First held in 1971, competition to determine the Texas state champion fiddler and inductees to the Texas Fiddlers Hall of Fame. Includes jam sessions, dances, concerts. Up to $25,000 in prize money awarded during the weekend. There's also the Gone To Texas contest, with competitors from all over the US and world. Est attendance: 15,000. For info: Kenneth Henneke, Cochair, Fiddler's Frolics, PO Box 46, Hallettsville, TX 77964. Phone: (361) 798-5934 or (361) 798-2311. Fax: (361) 798-9555. E-mail: kchall2006@sbcglobal.net. Web: www.kchall.com.

FIRST MOVIE THEATER OPENS: ANNIVERSARY. Apr 23, 1896. The first movie was shown at Koster and Bials Music Hall at New York City. Up until this time, people saw films individually by looking into a kinetoscope, a boxlike "peep show." This was the first time in the US that an audience sat in a theater and watched a movie together. See also: "First Cinema: Anniversary" (Dec 28).

FIRST PUBLIC SCHOOL IN AMERICA: ANNIVERSARY. Apr 23, 1635. (New Style date.) The Boston Latin School opened—America's oldest public school.

HITLER TAKES COMMAND OF BERLIN: 75th ANNIVERSARY. Apr 23, 1945. Enlisting the police force, members of the Hilter youth and old men and women to defend the city against the approaching Red Army, Adolf Hitler took personal command of Berlin's defense. A week later, he would commit suicide.

ICELAND: "FIRST DAY OF SUMMER". Apr 23. A national public holiday, *Sumardagurinn fyrsti*, where general festivities, processions and much street dancing, especially at Reykjavik, greet the coming of summer. Flags are flown. Annually, the Thursday between Apr 19 and 25.

NATIONAL ENGLISH MUFFIN DAY. Apr 23. 6th annual. English baker Samuel Bath Thomas created his original English muffin using a secret process that included griddle baking to create a muffin filled with "nooks and crannies." He later opened his own bakery, the Muffin House, in New York City in 1880. "English" was added to the muffin name in 1902. This is a day to celebrate the creation of the English muffin and the legacy of his company, Thomas' English Muffins—and to eat some, of course. Annually, Apr 23. For info: Thomas' English Muffins, Bimbo Bakeries USA, PO Box 976, Horsham, PA 19044. Web: www.thomasbreads.com.

NEW ORLEANS JAZZ & HERITAGE FESTIVAL. Apr 23–May 3. New Orleans, LA. A two-weekend festival with hundreds of musicians playing. Evening concerts, outdoor daytime activities, Louisiana specialty foods and handmade crafts. Est attendance: 500,000. For info: New Orleans Jazz & Heritage Festival, 1205 N Rampart St, New Orleans, LA 70116. Phone: (504) 558-6100. Web: www.nojazzfest.com.

PEARSON, LESTER B.: BIRTH ANNIVERSARY. Apr 23, 1897. 14th prime minister of Canada, born at Toronto, Canada. He was Canada's chief delegate at the San Francisco conference where the UN charter was drawn up and later served as president of the General Assembly. He wrote the proposal that resulted in the formation of the North Atlantic Treaty Organization (NATO). He was awarded the Nobel Peace Prize. Died at Rockcliffe, Canada, Dec 27, 1972.

PHYSICISTS DISCOVER TOP QUARK: ANNIVERSARY. Apr 23, 1994. Physicists at the Department of Energy's Fermi National Accelerator Laboratory found evidence for the existence of the subatomic particle called the top quark, the last undiscovered quark of the six predicted to exist by current scientific theory. The discovery provides strong support for the quark theory of the structure of matter. Quarks are subatomic particles that make up protons and neutrons found in the nuclei of atoms. The five other quark types that had already been proven to exist are the up quark, down quark, strange quark, charm quark and bottom quark. Further experimentation over many months confirmed the discovery, and it was publicly announced Mar 2, 1995.

PLANCK, MAX: BIRTH ANNIVERSARY. Apr 23, 1858. Formulator of the quantum theory, which revolutionized physics, born at Kiel, Germany. Einstein's application of quantum theory to light led to the theories of relativity. Planck died at Göttingen, Germany, Oct 3, 1947.

SAINT GEORGE: FEAST DAY. Apr 23. Martyr and patron saint of England, who died Apr 23, AD 303. Hero of the St. George and the Dragon legend. The story says that his faith helped him slay a vicious dragon that demanded daily sacrifice after the king's daughter became the intended victim.

SHAKESPEARE, WILLIAM: BIRTH (AND DEATH) ANNIVERSARY. Apr 23, 1564/1616. Author of at least 38 plays and 154 sonnets, the dramatist, actor, poet and theater manager Shakespeare created the most influential and lasting body of work in the English language, an extraordinary exploration of human nature. Shakespeare contributed thousands of words to the English language and expanded the dramatic possibilities of blank verse, making it mimic the rhythm of speech even as he elevated speech to poetry. He was born at Stratford-on-Avon, England, Apr 23, 1564, was baptized there three days later and died there on his birthday, Apr 23, 1616.

SPAIN: BOOK DAY AND LOVER'S DAY. Apr 23. Barcelona. Saint George's Day and the anniversary of the death of Spanish writer Miguel de Cervantes have been observed with special ceremonies in the Palacio de la Disputacion and throughout the city since 1714. Book stands are set up in the plazas and on street corners. This is Spain's equivalent of Valentine's Day. Women give books to men; men give roses to women.

TAKE OUR DAUGHTERS AND SONS TO WORK® DAY. Apr 23. 27th annual. A national public education campaign sponsored by the Take Our Daughters and Sons to Work Foundation in which children aged 8–18 go to work with adult hosts—parents, grandparents, cousins, aunts, uncles and friends. More than 36 million youth and 10 million adults participate at more than 3 million workplaces across the country. Annually, the fourth Thursday in April. For info: Take Our Daughters and Sons to Work Foundation, 209 E Fearing St, Ste 1, Elizabeth City, NC 27909. Phone: (800) 676-7780. E-mail: todastw@mindspring.com. Web: www.DaughtersandSonstoWork.org.

TURKEY: NATIONAL SOVEREIGNTY AND CHILDREN'S DAY. Apr 23. Commemorates Grand National Assembly's inauguration in 1923.

UNITED NATIONS: ENGLISH LANGUAGE DAY. Apr 23. English, along with French, is one of the two working languages of the United Nations Secretariat, and one of the organization's six official and working languages (English, French, Chinese, Arabic, Russian, Spanish). Beginning in 2010, this day has been celebrated on the date traditionally observed as the birthday of William Shakespeare. For info: United Nations, Dept of Public Info, New York, NY 10017. Web: www.un.org.

UNITED NATIONS: SPANISH LANGUAGE DAY. Apr 23. Spanish is one of the United Nations Secretariat's six official and working languages (English, French, Arabic, Chinese, Russian, Spanish). This day is observed on the death anniversary (1616) of the great genius of Spanish letters, Miguel de Cervantes Saavedra. Annually, Apr 23. For info: United Nations. Web: www.un.org/es/events/spanishlanguageday.

UNITED NATIONS: WORLD BOOK AND COPYRIGHT DAY. Apr 23. By celebrating this day throughout the world, UNESCO seeks to promote reading, publishing and the protection of intellectual property through copyright. It was a natural choice for UNESCO's General Conference to pay a worldwide tribute to books and authors on Apr 23, because on this date and in the same year of 1616, Cervantes, Shakespeare and Inca Garcilaso de la Vega all died. It is also the date of birth or death of other prominent authors such as Maurice Druon, Halldor Laxness, Josep Pla, Manuel Mejía Vallejo and William Wordsworth. Observed throughout the United Nations system. For info: United Nations, Dept of Public Info, New York, NY 10017. Web: www.un.org.

April 2020	S	M	T	W	T	F	S
				1	2	3	4
	5	6	7	8	9	10	11
	12	13	14	15	16	17	18
	19	20	21	22	23	24	25
	26	27	28	29	30		

WILKINSON, BUD: BIRTH ANNIVERSARY. Apr 23, 1915. Charles "Bud" Wilkinson, football player and coach and broadcaster, was born at Minneapolis, MN. Wilkinson became head coach at Oklahoma in 1947 and remained through 1964. During his tenure, the Sooners compiled a record 47-game winning streak. He headed the President's Physical Fitness Council and, after retiring from coaching, analyzed football games on ABC television. Died at Oklahoma City, OK, Feb 9, 1994.

WOODS, GRANVILLE T.: BIRTH ANNIVERSARY. Apr 23, 1856. Granville T. Woods was born at Columbus, OH. He invented the Synchronous Multiplex Railway Telegraph, which allowed communication between dispatchers and trains while the trains were in motion, which decreased the number of train accidents. In addition, Woods is credited with several other electrical inventions. Died Jan 30, 1910, at New York, NY.

WORLD BOOK NIGHT. Apr 23. This night is a celebration of books and reading held on Apr 23—World Book and Copyright Day—when passionate volunteers around the world hand out books within their communities to those who don't regularly read. World Book Night was first celebrated in the UK and Ireland in 2011. In 2012, World Book Night was celebrated in the US, the UK, Ireland and Germany and saw more than 80,000 people gift more than 2.5 million books. (US operations are suspended now.) For info: World Book Night, The Reading Agency, Free Word Centre, 60 Farringdon Rd, London EC1R 3GA, England. E-mail: worldbooknight@readingagency.org.uk. Web: www.worldbooknight.org.

🎂 BIRTHDAYS TODAY

Valerie Bertinelli, 60, actress ("One Day at a Time," "Hot in Cleveland"), born Wilmington, DE, Apr 23, 1960.

David Birney, 80, actor ("Love Is a Many Splendored Thing," "Bridget Loves Bernie"), born Washington, DC, Apr 23, 1940.

John Cena, 43, professional wrestler, actor (*The Marine, Trainwreck*), born West Newbury, MA, Apr 23, 1977.

Judy Davis, 65, actress ("Life with Judy Garland," *Husbands and Wives, A Passage to India, My Brilliant Career*), born Perth, Australia, Apr 23, 1955.

Joyce Dewitt, 71, actress ("Three's Company"), born Wheeling, WV, Apr 23, 1949.

Gigi Hadid, 25, model, born Jelena Noura Hadid at Los Angeles, CA, Apr 23, 1995.

Andruw Jones, 43, former baseball player, born Willemstad, Curaçao, Netherlands Antilles, Apr 23, 1977.

Melina Kanakaredes, 53, actress ("CSI: New York," "Providence," "Guiding Light"), born Akron, OH, Apr 23, 1967.

Chloe Kim, 20, Olympic gold medal snowboarder, born Long Beach, CA, Apr 23, 2000.

Jaime King, 41, actress (*Sin City, Pearl Harbor,* "Hart of Dixie"), born Omaha, NE, Apr 23, 1979.

George Lopez, 59, comedian, actor (*Beverly Hills Chihuahua,* "George Lopez"), born Mission Hills, CA, Apr 23, 1961.

Lee Majors, 80, actor ("The Six Million Dollar Man," "The Fall Guy"), born Wyandotte, MI, Apr 23, 1940.

Bernadette Devlin McAliskey, 73, political activist, born Cookstown, Northern Ireland, Apr 23, 1947.

Michael Moore, 66, author (*Dude, Where's My Country?*), filmmaker (Oscar for *Bowling for Columbine; Sicko, Fahrenheit 9/11*), born Flint, MI, Apr 23, 1954.

John Oliver, 43, comedian, writer, television personality ("Last Week Tonight"), born Birmingham, England, Apr 23, 1977.

Dev Patel, 30, actor (*Lion,* "The Newsroom," *The Best Exotic Marigold Hotel, Slumdog Millionaire*), born Harrow, England, Apr 23, 1990.

Kal Penn, 43, actor (*The Namesake, Harold & Kumar Go to White Castle,* "House"), born Montclair, NJ, Apr 23, 1977.

Jesse Lee Soffer, 36, actor ("Chicago P.D.," "As the World Turns," *The Brady Bunch Movie*), born Ossining, NY, Apr 23, 1984

April 24 — Friday

DAY 115   **251 REMAINING**

AFRMA DISPLAY AT AMERICA'S FAMILY PET EXPO. Apr 24–26 (tentative). Costa Mesa, CA. Rats and mice are emerging as ideal pets: they provide all the pleasure and satisfaction of a warm, cuddly, intelligent and friendly pet companion. The American Fancy Rat and Mouse Association (AFRMA) was founded in 1983 to promote the breeding and exhibition of fancy rats and mice, to educate the public on their positive qualities as companion animals and to provide information on their proper care. For info: AFRMA (CAE), 9230 64th St, Riverside, CA 92509-5924. Phone: (951) 685-2350 or (818) 992-5564. E-mail: afrma@afrma.org. Web: www.afrma.org.

ARBOR DAY IN ARIZONA. Apr 24. The last Friday in April is proclaimed as Arbor Day in Arizona. It is not a legal holiday.

ARMENIA: ARMENIAN MARTYRS DAY. Apr 24. Commemorates the massacre and deportations of Armenians under the Ottoman Turks in 1915. Also called Armenian Genocide Memorial Day.

ARMENIAN GENOCIDE BEGINS: ANNIVERSARY. Apr 24, 1915. Fearing that the long-oppressed Armenian subjects would side with Russia and the Allies in WWI, authorities in the Central Powers–aligned Ottoman Empire rounded up and imprisoned 250 Armenian intellectuals and community leaders in the capital of Constantinople on Apr 24, 1915, Red Sunday, a date recognized as the start of the Armenian Genocide. Over the next six years, through 1921, beyond the end of the war, between 500,000 and 1.5 million Armenians and other minorities were systematically killed through mass burnings, drowning, toxic gas, lethal inoculations, extermination camps and death marches into the Syrian desert.

GRAUNT, JOHN: 400th BIRTH ANNIVERSARY. Apr 24, 1620. Graunt was a prosperous draper and merchant in London, England, but his fame today rests on the fact that he was the first demographer. In the 1660s Graunt began to study death records of London parishes and began to see patterns. In 1662, he published *Natural and Political Observations Made upon the Bills of Mortality*, a well-received work that enabled his being elected a fellow in the Royal Society. His work is the foundation of mortality tables, a tool of modern insurance. Born at London, he died there Apr 16, 1674.

IRELAND: EASTER RISING: ANNIVERSARY. Apr 24, 1916. Irish nationalists seized key buildings in Dublin and proclaimed an Irish republic. The rebellion collapsed, however, and it wasn't until 1922 that the Irish Free State, the predecessor of the Republic of Ireland, was established.

LIBRARY OF CONGRESS: ANNIVERSARY. Apr 24, 1800. Congress approved an act providing "for the purchase of such books as may be necessary for the use of Congress . . . and for fitting up a suitable apartment for containing them." Thus began one of the world's greatest libraries.

NATIONAL ARBOR DAY. Apr 24. Since 1872, a day to honor and plant trees. Observed the last Friday in April (although some states have different dates), which is generally a good planting date throughout the country. First observance of Arbor Day was in Nebraska, Apr 10, 1872, where it is still a state holiday. For info: Arbor Day Foundation, 100 Arbor Ave, Nebraska City, NE 68410. Phone: (888) 448-7337. Web: www.arborday.org/celebrate.

NATIONAL HAIRBALL AWARENESS DAY. Apr 24. A day to recognize and take steps to eliminate hairballs in cats. Hairballs are more than an inconvenience for cat owners: they cause great discomfort and irritation in our cat companions. Take steps now to stop this injustice of nature for our feline friends. Annually, the last Friday in April. For info: Dr. Blake Hawley, Motega Health, Inc, 1738 Lake Alvamar Dr, Ste M, 2029, Lawrence, KS 66047. Phone: (785) 260-1094. E-mail: blake@motegahealth.com. Web: www.motega-health.com.

NATIONAL PIE CHAMPIONSHIPS. Apr 24–25. Renaissance Orlando SeaWorld, Orlando, FL. This is the official national pie championships for pie makers competing in the amateur, professional and commercial divisions. For info: Linda Hoskins, Executive Director, American Pie Council, PO Box 523, Bonita Springs, FL 34133. Phone: (847) 687-2722. E-mail: piecouncil@aol.com. Web: www.piecouncil.org.

NATIONAL TEACH CHILDREN TO SAVE DAY. Apr 24. Since 1997, more than 170,000 banker volunteers across America teach children of all ages the importance of saving and making fiscal fitness a lifetime habit. For info: American Bankers Assn Community Engagement Foundation, 1120 Connecticut Ave NW, Washington, DC 20036. Phone: (202) 663-5453 or (800) BAN-KERS. E-mail: communityengagement@aba.com. Web: www.aba.com/teach.

POLK COUNTY RAMP TRAMP FESTIVAL. Apr 24–25. Polk County 4-H Camp, Camp McCroy, near Benton, TN. Since 1958, a tribute to the ramp, a wild leek that grows in the Appalachian Mountains. Spend the day enjoying bluegrass and gospel music and old-time fellowship while enjoying a meal of fried ramps in eggs, fried potatoes, streaked meat, white beans and cornbread. Local craftsman have handmade articles for sale. The festival is the fourth Saturday

in April, with the Friday before (preceded by days of digging and preparing ramps). Est attendance: 800. For info: Polk County Ramp Tramp Festival, Box 189, Benton, TN 37307. Phone: (423) 338-4503. Web: www.ramptrampfestival.com.

RAMADAN: THE ISLAMIC MONTH OF FASTING. Apr 24–May 23. Begins on Islamic lunar calendar date Ramadan 1, 1441. Ramadan, the ninth month of the Islamic calendar, is holy because it was during this month that the Holy Qur'an (Koran) was revealed. All adults of sound body and mind fast from dawn (before sunrise) until sunset to achieve spiritual and physical purification and self-discipline, abstaining from food, drink and intimate relations. It is a time for feeling a common bond with people who are poor and needy, a time of piety and prayer. Different methods for "anticipating" the visibility of the new moon crescent at Mecca are used by different Muslim groups, so date can vary one to two days. Began at sunset the preceding day.

SPACE MILESTONE: *CHINA 1* (PEOPLE'S REPUBLIC OF CHINA). Apr 24, 1970. China became the fifth nation to orbit a satellite with the launch of its own rocket. The satellite broadcast the Chinese song "Tang Fang Hung" ("The East Is Red") and telemetric signals.

SUGARLOAF CRAFTS FESTIVAL. Apr 24–26. Maryland State Fairgrounds, Timonium, MD. This show, now in its 43rd year, features more than 250 nationally recognized craft designers and fine artists displaying and selling their original creations. Includes craft demonstrations, music, specialty food, gift certificate drawings and more. Est attendance: 15,000. For info: Sugarloaf Mountain Works, Inc, 13225 Executive Park Terrace, Germantown, MD 20874. Phone: (800) 210-9900. E-mail: sugarloafinfo@sugarloaffest.com. Web: www.sugarloafcrafts.com.

THOMAS, ROBERT BAILEY: BIRTH ANNIVERSARY. Apr 24, 1766. Founder and editor of *The Farmer's Almanac* (first issued in 1792 for 1793), born at Grafton, MA. Thomas died May 19, 1846, at West Boylston, MA, while working on the 1847 edition.

TROLLOPE, ANTHONY: BIRTH ANNIVERSARY. Apr 24, 1815. Author born at London, England, known for his portrayals of English life, political life and the social structures of Victorian England. Trollope wrote more than 50 books over the course of his career while also working as a postal inspector. His works include *The Way We Live Now* (1875), the Barchester Chronicles and the Palliser novels. "There must be love in a novel," he once stated. He died at London on Dec 6, 1882.

US ATTEMPT TO FREE IRAN HOSTAGES: 40th ANNIVERSARY. Apr 24, 1980. US Marines attempted to stage a surprise raid to free citizens held at the US embassy in Tehran, Iran, but their helicopters collided at the desert staging area. Eight were killed and five were wounded. No further military rescues were attempted, and the hostages were later released in January 1981 after 444 days of captivity.

WARD WORLD CHAMPIONSHIP WILDFOWL CARVING COMPETITION AND ART FESTIVAL. Apr 24–26. Roland E. Powell Convention Center, Ocean City, MD. 50th annual. Life-size, miniature, interpretive wildfowl carving and sculpture competitions. Festival includes vendors selling carvings, folk art, paintings, home decorating items and art supplies. Est attendance: 6,000. For info: Ward Museum of Wildfowl Art, 909 S Schumaker Dr, Salisbury, MD 21804. Phone: (410) 742-4988. Fax: (410) 742-3107. E-mail: wardevents@salisbury.edu. Web: www.wardmuseum.org.

WARREN, ROBERT PENN: BIRTH ANNIVERSARY. Apr 24, 1905. American poet, novelist, essayist and critic. America's first official poet laureate, 1986–88, Robert Penn Warren was born at Guthrie, KY. Warren was awarded the Pulitzer Prize for his novel *All the King's Men* (1947), as well as for his poetry in 1958 and 1979. He died of cancer Sept 15, 1989, at Stratton, VT.

WASHMO BBQ, BIKES & BLUES. Apr 24–26. Washington, MO. A KCBS-sanctioned barbecue competition, featuring 50 barbecue teams. People's Choice tasting, live blues music, Vintage Market vendor event and a full food court. For info: Downtown Washington, Inc, 123 Lafayette St, PO Box 144, Washington, MO 63090.

April 2020	S	M	T	W	T	F	S
				1	2	3	4
	5	6	7	8	9	10	11
	12	13	14	15	16	17	18
	19	20	21	22	23	24	25
	26	27	28	29	30		

Phone: (636) 239-1743. Fax: (636) 239-4832. E-mail: events@downtownwashmo.org. Web: www.downtownwashmo.org.

WORLD IMMUNIZATION WEEK. Apr 24–30. Immunization currently averts an estimated 2 to 3 million deaths every year, but millions of infants worldwide are still missing out on basic vaccines. This is a week to bring attention to global vaccination and keep it on track. Annually, Apr 24–30 (dates may vary around the world, but all fall toward the end of April). For info: World Health Organization. Web: www.who.int.

🎂 BIRTHDAYS TODAY

Eric Balfour, 43, actor (*Rescue Me, No One Would Tell*), musician, born Los Angeles, CA, Apr 24, 1977.

Ashleigh Barty, 24, tennis player, born Ipswich, Australia, Apr 24, 1996.

Eric Bogosian, 67, actor, playwright (*Talk Radio*), performance artist, born Boston, MA, Apr 24, 1953.

Cedric the Entertainer, 56, comedian, actor (*Street Kings, Barbershop, Be Cool*), born Cedric Kyles at Jefferson City, MO, Apr 24, 1964.

Kelly Clarkson, 38, singer, born Fort Worth, TX, Apr 24, 1982.

Richard M. Daley, 78, former mayor of Chicago, born Chicago, IL, Apr 24, 1942.

Jean-Paul Gaultier, 68, fashion designer, born Paris, France, Apr 24, 1952.

Djimon Hounsou, 56, actor (*Blood Diamond, In America*), born Cotonou, Benin, Apr 24, 1964.

Chipper Jones, 48, Hall of Fame baseball player, born DeLand, FL, Apr 24, 1972.

Shirley MacLaine, 86, author, actress (Oscar for *Terms of Endearment*; *The Turning Point, Being There*), born Richmond, VA, Apr 24, 1934.

Michael O'Keefe, 65, actor (*The Great Santini, Caddyshack*; stage: *Mass Appeal*), born Larchmont, NY, Apr 24, 1955.

Barbra Streisand, 78, singer, actress (Oscar for *Funny Girl*; *The Way We Were, Yentl*), director (*The Prince of Tides*), born Brooklyn, NY, Apr 24, 1942.

April 25 — Saturday

DAY 116	250 REMAINING

ABORTION FIRST LEGALIZED: ANNIVERSARY. Apr 25, 1967. The first law legalizing abortion in the US was signed by Colorado governor John Arthur Love. The law allowed therapeutic abortions in cases in which a three-doctor panel unanimously agreed.

ANZAC DAY. Apr 25. Australia, New Zealand and Samoa. Memorial day and veterans' observance, especially to mark WWI ANZAC (Australia and New Zealand Army Corps) landing at Gallipoli, Turkey, in 1915.

BATTLE OF GALLIPOLI: ANNIVERSARY. Apr 25, 1915, to January 1916. During WWI the Gallipoli Expedition, or the Dardanelles Campaign, combined Allied naval and military forces tried to capture the Gallipoli peninsula in Turkey in order to effect an open route to Russia via the Black Sea. One French and four British divisions were forced back by a strong Turkish-German defense after almost nine months of fighting. The Australian and New Zealand Army Corps (ANZAC) took much of the brunt of the battle.

BRENNAN, WILLIAM: BIRTH ANNIVERSARY. Apr 25, 1906. US Supreme Court associate justice William J. Brennan was appointed to the Supreme Court in 1956 by President Dwight Eisenhower. His liberal leanings and judicial activism raised the ire of many conservatives. He was responsible for many landmark decisions, including the decision requiring the Little Rock, AR, schools to desegregate. His legacy also includes major decisions upholding affirmative action, a losing battle to declare the death penalty unconstitutional, decisions broadening free speech and free press guarantees, expansion of the due process guarantees under the 14th Amendment and protection of flag burning as a form of expression. Brennan was born at Newark, NJ; he died at Arlington, VA, July 25, 1997.

CATTUS ISLAND NATURE FESTIVAL. Apr 25. Cattus Island County Park, Toms River, NJ. Annual celebration full of exciting activities such as nature walks, lectures and crafts. Live music and a variety of exhibitors and food vendors make this a great day out. Est attendance: 1,500. For info: Cattus Island County Park, 1170 Cattus Island Blvd, Toms River, NJ 08753. Phone: (732) 270-6960. E-mail: jkline@co.ocean.nj.us.

COSMOGRAPHIAE INTRODUCTIO PUBLISHED: ANNIVERSARY. Apr 25, 1507. Little is known about the obscure scholar now called "the godfather of America," the German geographer and mapmaker Martin Waldseemuller, who gave America its name. In a book titled *Cosmographiae Introductio*, published Apr 25, 1507, Waldseemuller wrote: "Inasmuch as both Europe and Asia received their names from women, I see no reason why any one should justly object to calling this part Amerige, i.e., the land of Amerigo, or America, after Amerigo, its discoverer, a man of great ability." Believing it was the Italian navigator and merchant Amerigo Vespucci who had discovered the new continent, Waldseemuller sought to honor Vespucci by placing his name on his map of the world, published in 1507. First applied only to the South American continent, it soon was used for both the American continents. Waldseemuller did not learn about the voyage of Christopher Columbus until several years later. Of the thousand copies of his map that were printed, only one is known to have survived. Waldseemuller probably was born at Radolfzell, Germany, about 1470. He died at St. Die, France, about 1517–20. See also: "Vespucci, Amerigo: Birth Anniversary" (Mar 9).

CRUYFF, JOHAN: BIRTH ANNIVERSARY. Apr 25, 1947. Hendrik Johannes (Johan) Cruijff was an influential soccer star and coach born at Amsterdam, The Netherlands. Cruyff elevated Dutch football to international prestige with his dynamic play and cerebral approach to the game. At the 1974 World Cup, he executed a feint against a Swedish defender now known as the "Cruyff Turn"; it remains a universally taught dribbling technique. In addition to his lifelong association with Ajax in his homeland, in Spain Cruyff led FC Barcelona to La Liga victories as a player and returned to coach the club in 1988. Stricken with lung cancer, Cruyff died March 24, 2016, at Barcelona, Spain.

EGYPT: SINAI DAY. Apr 25. National holiday celebrating the return of Sinai to Egypt in 1982 after the peace treaty between Egypt and Israel.

FARRAGUT CAPTURES NEW ORLEANS: ANNIVERSARY. Apr 25, 1862. Union forces under the command of Flag Officer David Farragut seized the city of New Orleans, LA, resulting in the surrender of several Confederate forts along the Mississippi in subsequent days. This action removed any Confederate resistance to Northern action on the Mississippi River as far north as New Orleans. General Benjamin Butler arrived on Apr 27 and took command of the management of the captured city.

FIRST LICENSE PLATES: ANNIVERSARY. Apr 25, 1901. New York began requiring license plates on automobiles, the first state to do so.

FITZGERALD, ELLA: BIRTH ANNIVERSARY. Apr 25, 1917. Born at Newport News, VA, but raised in Yonkers, NY, Ella Fitzgerald was a regular at Harlem's Apollo Theater by the time she was 15. After getting her start as a singer on the big band circuit, Fitzgerald transitioned to bebop and developed her famous "scat" singing style. She worked with all the greats, including Duke Ellington, Louie Armstrong, Nat King Cole, Dizzy Gillespie, Frank Sinatra and Benny Goodman, recorded more than 200 albums, won 13

Grammy Awards and continued to perform into the 1980s. She died at Beverly Hills, CA, June 15, 1996.

FOXFIELD RACES. Apr 25 (also Sept 27). Charlottesville, VA. Since 1978 the Foxfield Races have presented to attendees spectacular steeplechase horse racing. The spring race is always held the last Saturday in April while the fall race, known as "Family Day," is held on the last Sunday in September. The fall race also hosts a variety of activities for children and families. Est attendance: 25,000. For info: W. Patrick Butterfield, Racing Mgr, Foxfield Racing Assn, PO Box 5187, Charlottesville, VA 22905. Phone: (434) 293-9501. Fax: (434) 293-8169. E-mail: wpbutterfield@foxfieldraces.com. Web: www.foxfieldraces.com.

HIGH POINT MARKET (SPRING). Apr 25–29. High Point, NC. The largest wholesale home furnishings market in the world. (Not open to the general public.) Est attendance: 75,000. For info: High Point Market Authority, 164 S Main St, Ste 700, High Point, NC 27260. Phone: (336) 869-1000. E-mail: info@highpointmarket.org. Web: www.highpointmarket.org.

INDEPENDENT BOOKSTORE DAY. Apr 25. A one-day national party at and honoring more than 500 independent bookstores. Independent bookstores are not just stores; they're community centers and local anchors run by passionate readers. They are entire universes of ideas that contain the possibility of real serendipity. In addition to authors, live music, cupcakes, scavenger hunts, kids events, art tables, readings, barbecues, contests and other fun stuff, there are exclusive books and literary items that you can get only on that day. Annually, the last Saturday in April. For info: Independent Bookstore Day. E-mail: IBD@NCIBA.com. Web: www.indiebookstoreday.com.

ITALY: LIBERATION DAY. Apr 25. National holiday. Commemorates the liberation of Italy from German troops in 1945.

LEIBER, JERRY: BIRTH ANNIVERSARY. Apr 25, 1933. An influential lyricist, songwriter and record producer, Jerry Leiber and his longtime composing partner Mike Stoller wrote such iconic songs of the early rock 'n' roll era as "Hound Dog," "Jailhouse Rock," "Yakety Yak" and "Stand by Me." Born at Baltimore, MD, Leiber met Stoller as a high schooler in Los Angeles, where the two combined Leiber's ear for street-smart lyrics with Stoller's love of rhythm and blues, a formula that would prove successful for the next three decades. Leiber died Aug 22, 2011, at Los Angeles, CA.

LLOYD, POP: BIRTH ANNIVERSARY. Apr 25, 1884. John Henry "Pop" Lloyd, Baseball Hall of Fame shortstop, born at Palatka, FL. Lloyd was often compared to Honus Wagner and considered one of the best shortstops ever. He played with and managed black teams and made quite a career in Cuba, where the fans nicknamed him "Cuchara" (scoop or shovel) for his big hands. Inducted into the Hall of Fame in 1977. Died at Atlantic City, NJ, Mar 19, 1965.

MARCONI, GUGLIELMO: BIRTH ANNIVERSARY. Apr 25, 1874. Inventor of wireless telegraphy (1895), born at Bologna, Italy. Died at Rome, Italy, July 20, 1937.

MURROW, EDWARD R.: BIRTH ANNIVERSARY. Apr 25, 1908. Among the greatest journalists in American history, Edward R. Murrow was born at Greensboro, NC. He was a European war correspondent for CBS during WWII and rose to prominence with his dramatic and vivid radio broadcasts. After the war, CBS moved him to television, where he was the trusted host of "See It Now," a newsmagazine show spotlighting hot-button issues of the day. He died at Pawling, NY, Apr 27, 1965.

NATIONAL DANCE DAY. Apr 25. Participants across America organize events in every community to celebrate the spirit and diversity of dance of all kinds. For info: Sharon King Hoge, 480 Park Ave, Apt 3D, New York, NY 10022. Phone: (212) 750-6168.

NATIONAL REBUILDING DAY. Apr 25. There are millions of limited-income home owners who live in deteriorating, physically inadequate homes that threaten their well-being. This day is the culmination of National Rebuilding Month and sees neighbors helping neighbors with critical home repairs: thousands of volunteers repaint, fix, improve accessibility and more. Annually, the last Saturday in April. For info: Rebuilding Together. E-mail: info@rebuildingtogether.org. Web: www.rebuildingtogether.org.

PET TECH CPR DAY®. Apr 25. 3rd annual. The mission of this day is to teach pet parents and pet care professionals how to better care for their pets in an emergency, so that they have a healthier, happier and longer relationship with their furry four-legged family members. Our 2020 goal is 300 classes scheduled and more than 3,000 pet parents and pet care professionals trained—around the world. Come join us in our mission of "Preventing 1 Million Pet ER Visits." Annually, the last Saturday in April. For info: Pet Tech Productions, PO Box 2285, Carlsbad, CA 92018. Phone: (760) 930-0309. E-mail: CPRDay@PetTech.net. Web: www.PetTech.net.

PORTUGAL: LIBERTY DAY. Apr 25. Public holiday. Anniversary of the 1974 revolution.

REDBUD TRAIL RENDEZVOUS. Apr 25–26. Rochester, IN. Reenactment of a pre-1865 gathering to trade furs on the Tippecanoe River, featuring tepee and wigwam villages, traditional music and crafts, pioneer and Indian dances and foods cooked over wood fires. Seven Years' War field day. Museum, round barn and Living History Village at north end of grounds. For frontier fun, follow the redbuds blooming along the Tippecanoe River. Est attendance: 2,000. For info: Fulton County Historical Society, 37 E 375 N, Rochester, IN 46975. Phone: (574) 223-4436. E-mail: fchs@rtcol.com. Web: www.fultoncountyhistory.org.

SPACE MILESTONE: HUBBLE SPACE TELESCOPE DEPLOYED (US): 30th ANNIVERSARY. Apr 25, 1990. Deployed by *Discovery*, the telescope is the largest on-orbit observatory to date and is capable of imaging objects up to 14 billion light-years away. The resolution of images was expected to be seven to ten times greater than images from Earth-based telescopes, since the Hubble Space Telescope is not hampered by Earth's atmospheric distortion. Launched Apr 12, 1990, from Kennedy Space Center, FL. Unfortunately, the telescope's lenses were defective, so the anticipated high quality of imaging was not possible. In 1993, however, the world watched as a shuttle crew successfully retrieved the Hubble from orbit, executed the needed repair and replacement work and released it into orbit once more. Further repairs were completed in 1997, 1999, 2002 and 2009, and the telescope remains functional today.

SWAZILAND: NATIONAL FLAG DAY. Apr 25. National holiday.

US WOMEN'S AMATEUR FOUR-BALL (GOLF) CHAMPIONSHIP. Apr 25–29. Quail Creek Country Club, Naples, FL. For info: USGA, Golf House, Championship Dept, PO Box 708, Far Hills, NJ 07931. Phone: (908) 234-2300. E-mail: champs@usga.org. Web: www.usga.org.

WORLD HEALING DAY. Apr 25. A day to focus on personal and global healing, inspired by research from the Global Consciousness Project, which evolved from preliminary research at Princeton University on how human consciousness affects the physical world. This day is globally observed in hundreds of cities in more than 80 nations. There are also many allied events under the

April 2020	S	M	T	W	T	F	S
				1	2	3	4
	5	6	7	8	9	10	11
	12	13	14	15	16	17	18
	19	20	21	22	23	24	25
	26	27	28	29	30		

umbrella event of World Healing Day, including World Healing Meditation Day, World Art Day, World Tai Chi Day, World Yoga Day, World Qigong Day, World Sufi Dance Day, World Native Aboriginal Sacred Dance Day and several others. Annually, the last Saturday in April. For info: World Healing Day. E-mail: bill-douglas@worldtaichiday.org. Web: www.worldtaichiday.org.

WORLD MALARIA DAY. Apr 25. A day to provide education and understanding of malaria as a global scourge that is preventable and a disease that is curable. Annually, April 25.

WORLD PENGUIN DAY. Apr 25. A day of awareness for these amazing creatures, celebrated by many conservation groups. Penguins spend 75 percent of their life at sea. They can dive to 1,850 feet. There are 17 species of these flightless birds. Annually, on Apr 25, the date that Adelie penguins begin their northward migration in Antarctica.

WORLD TAI CHI AND QIGONG DAY. Apr 25. World Tai Chi and Qigong Day (also spelled T'ai Chi and Ch'i Kung) is an annual event held in 80 countries the last Saturday in April each year since 1999 to promote the related disciplines of tai chi and qigong. The mission of this multinational effort is ongoing: to expose people to the growing body of medical research related to traditional Chinese medicine and direct them to teachers in their hometowns. For info: Bill Douglas, World Tai Chi and Qigong Day, 10100 Roe Ave, Overland Park, KS 66207. Phone: (913) 648-2256. E-mail: billdouglas@worldtaichiday.org. Web: www.worldtaichiday.org.

WORLD VETERINARY DAY. Apr 25. World Veterinary Day was instigated by the World Veterinary Association (WVA) in 2000 to be celebrated annually on the last Saturday in April. Apart from their well-known role as animal doctors, veterinarians create prevention and control programs against infectious diseases, including those transmissible to humans. Much more than that, be it for food security, poverty alleviation, prevention and management of risks at the animal-human interface, animal welfare, scientific research or political commitment, veterinarians operate in all sectors of the society. For info: World Veterinary Assn. E-mail: secretariat@worldvet.org. Web: www.worldvet.org.

WORLD WAR II: EAST MEETS WEST: 75th ANNIVERSARY. Apr 25, 1945. US Army lieutenant Albert Kotzebue encountered a single Soviet soldier near the German village of Lechwitz, 75 miles south of Berlin. Patrols of US general Leonard Gerow's Fifth Corps saluted the advance guard of Marshall Ivan Konev's Soviet 58th Guards Division. Soldiers of both nations embraced and exchanged toasts. The Allied armies of East and West had finally met.

🎂 BIRTHDAYS TODAY

Hank Azaria, 56, actor ("Brockmire," "Huff," *The Birdcage*, many voices on "The Simpsons"), born Forest Hills, NY, Apr 25, 1964.

Emily Bergl, 45, actress ("Men in Trees"), born Milton Keynes, Buckinghamshire, England, Apr 25, 1975.

Jeffrey DeMunn, 73, actor ("The Walking Dead," *Citizen X, The Green Mile*), born Buffalo, NY, Apr 25, 1947.

Tim Duncan, 44, former basketball player, born St. Croix, Virgin Islands, Apr 25, 1976.

Gwen Jorgensen, 34, Olympic triathlete, born Waukesha, WI, Apr 25, 1986.

Jason Lee, 50, actor ("My Name Is Earl," *Almost Famous, Chasing Amy*), born Orange, CA, Apr 25, 1970.

Al Pacino, 80, actor (Oscar for *Scent of a Woman*; *Dog Day Afternoon, Godfather* films), born New York, NY, Apr 25, 1940.

Talia Shire, 74, actress (*Godfather* films, *Rocky* films), born Jamaica, NY, Apr 25, 1946.

Gina Torres, 51, actress ("Suits," "Firefly"), born New York, NY, Apr 25, 1969.

Renée Zellweger, 51, actress (Oscar for *Cold Mountain*; *Miss Potter, Chicago, Bridget Jones's Diary*), born Katy, TX, Apr 25, 1969.

April 26 — Sunday

DAY 117 **249 REMAINING**

AUDUBON, JOHN JAMES: BIRTH ANNIVERSARY. Apr 26, 1785. The great artist and naturalist was born at Les Cayes, Santo Domingo (now Haiti), the illegitimate son of a French trader and plantation owner. Audubon led a peripatetic life—escaping the slave revolts of Santo Domingo to return to Nantes, France, only to face the Revolution. His father sent him to America in 1803 in order to avoid conscription in Napoleon's army. In America, Audubon set out in 1820 along the Ohio and Mississippi rivers to document and paint all the birds of America. His lively and idiosyncratic paintings made him a great success in America and Europe. His *Birds of America*, published in several volumes from 1827 to 1838, is a landmark of art and printing. He died on his New York farm, Jan 27, 1851.

CHERNOBYL NUCLEAR REACTOR DISASTER: ANNIVERSARY. Apr 26, 1986. At 1:23 AM, local time, an explosion occurred at the Chernobyl atomic power station at Pripyat in the Ukraine. The resulting fire burned for days, sending radioactive material into the atmosphere. More than 100,000 persons were evacuated from a 300-square-mile area around the plant. Three months later 31 people were reported to have died and thousands exposed to dangerous levels of radiation. Estimates projected an additional 1,000 cancer cases in nations downwind of the radioactive discharge. The plant was encased in a concrete tomb in an effort to prevent the still-hot reactor from overheating again and to minimize further release of radiation.

CONFEDERATE MEMORIAL DAY IN FLORIDA AND GEORGIA. Apr 26. Observed on the anniversary of Confederate general Joseph E. Johnston's surrender to General William T. Sherman at Durham, NC, in 1865. Other Southern states observe this day on different dates.

ENGLAND: VIRGIN MONEY LONDON MARATHON. Apr 26. London. Held since 1981 and awarded a road race Gold Label by the International Association of Athletics Federations, the London Marathon hosts more than 37,000 participants in 26.2 miles from Greenwich to The Mall. For info: Virgin Money London Marathon. Web: www.virginmoneylondonmarathon.com.

FAUSET, JESSIE REDMON: BIRTH ANNIVERSARY. Apr 26, 1882. African-American poet, editor and novelist, born at Fredericksville, NJ, and died in 1961. Fauset, as literary editor of *Crisis* (a publication of the NAACP), was a patron to so many writers of the Harlem Renaissance that her efforts prompted Langston Hughes to dub her the "midwife of the so-called New Negro Literature." Along with W.E.B. Du Bois, Fauset also published and edited the children's magazine *The Brownie Book*. Her novels about the African-American middle-class experience dealt with issues of identity, autonomy and struggles for fulfillment. Her most recognized works include *The Chinaberry Tree* (1931) and *Comedy, American Style* (1933).

GUERNICA MASSACRE: ANNIVERSARY. Apr 26, 1937. Late in the afternoon, the ancient Basque town of Guernica, in northern Spain, was attacked without warning by German-made airplanes. Three hours of intensive bombing left the town in flames, and citizens who fled to the fields and ditches around Guernica were machine-gunned from the air. This atrocity inspired Pablo Picasso's mural *Guernica*. Responsibility for the bombing was never officially established, but the suffering and anger of the victims and their survivors are still evident at anniversary demonstrations. Intervention by Nazi Germany in the Spanish Civil War has been described as practice for WWII.

HESS, RUDOLF: BIRTH ANNIVERSARY. Apr 26, 1894. One of the most bizarre figures of WWII Germany, Walter Richard Rudolf Hess was born at Alexandria, Egypt. He was a close friend, confidant and personal secretary to Adolf Hitler, who had dictated much of *Mein Kampf* to Hess while both were prisoners at Landsberg Prison. Third in command in Nazi Germany, Hess surprised the world on May 10, 1941, by flying alone to Scotland and parachuting from his plane on what he called a "mission of humanity": offering peace to Britain if it would join Germany in attacking the Soviet Union. He was immediately taken prisoner of war. At the Nuremberg Trials (1946), after questions about his sanity, he was convicted and sentenced to life imprisonment at Spandau Allied War Crimes Prison at Berlin, Germany. Outliving all other prisoners there, he was the only inmate from 1955 until he succeeded (in his fourth attempt) in committing suicide. He died at West Berlin, Germany, Aug 17, 1987.

HUG AN AUSTRALIAN DAY. Apr 26. To show our great appreciation for all the love and support the Aussies have given us over the years. (©2006 by WH.) For info: Thomas & Ruth Roy, Wellcat Holidays, 2418 Long Ln, Lebanon, PA 17046. Phone: (717) 279-0184. E-mail: info@wellcat.com. Web: www.wellcat.com.

LOOS, ANITA: BIRTH ANNIVERSARY. Apr 26, 1893. American author and playwright, born at Sisson, CA. She is best remembered for her book *Gentlemen Prefer Blondes*, published in 1925. Loos, a brunette, died at New York, NY, Aug 18, 1981.

MALAMUD, BERNARD: BIRTH ANNIVERSARY. Apr 26, 1914. Pulitzer Prize–winning novelist, born to Russian-Jewish immigrant parents at Brooklyn, NY. Works include *The Natural* (1952) and *The Fixer* (1966). Also a two-time recipient of the National Book Award, he died Mar 18, 1986, at New York, NY.

MONTGOMERY WARD SEIZED: ANNIVERSARY. Apr 26, 1944. Montgomery Ward chairman Sewell Avery was physically removed from his office when federal troops seized Ward's Chicago offices after the company refused to obey President Franklin D. Roosevelt's order to recognize a CIO union. Government control ended May 9, shortly before the National Labor Relations Board announced the United Mail Order Warehouse and Retail Employees Union had won an election to represent the company's workers.

NATIONAL HELP A HORSE DAY. Apr 26. Horses have been central to the ASPCA's work since its founding, with the first successful arrest for the mistreatment of a horse on Apr 26, 1866, when ASPCA founder Henry Bergh stopped a cart driver from beating his horse. The protection of horses has been a core part of the ASPCA mission ever since, which includes working with partners in animal welfare and equine industries to ensure equines nationwide have good welfare. On this day, be a voice for horses and help raise awareness about the year-round lifesaving work that equine rescues, shelters and sanctuaries do to find homes for the horses in their care. Annually, Apr 26. For info: ASPCA, Media and Communications Dept, 520 8th Ave, 7th Fl, New York, NY 10018. Phone: (212) 876-7700. E-mail: press@aspca.org. Web: www.aspca.org.

NATIONAL PRETZEL DAY. Apr 26. A celebration of the beloved entwined bakery snack, originally proclaimed nationally in 1983, then later proclaimed by Pennsylvania governor Ed Rendell in 2003. The hard pretzel is thought to have originated in the US in 1850 at Lititz, PA, with baker Julius Sturgis.

	S	M	T	W	T	F	S
April				1	2	3	4
	5	6	7	8	9	10	11
2020	12	13	14	15	16	17	18
	19	20	21	22	23	24	25
	26	27	28	29	30		

OKLAHOMA CITY MEMORIAL MARATHON. Apr 26. Oklahoma City, OK. More than a race, it's a run to remember those impacted by the 1995 bombing of the Murrah Federal Building in Oklahoma City. 2020 marks the 25th anniversary of the Oklahoma City bombing and the 20th anniversary of the running of the Memorial Marathon. There's a race for everyone: marathon, half marathon, relay, 5K and kids marathon. Look for course changes, a new finish line and a great Finish Line Festival and concert in the new Scissortail Park downtown. Annually, the last Sunday in April. Est attendance: 30,000. For info: Oklahoma City National Memorial & Museum, 620 N Harvey Ave, Oklahoma City, OK 73102. Phone: (405) 235-3313. Web: www.oklahomacitynationalmemorial.org.

OLMSTED, FREDERICK LAW: BIRTH ANNIVERSARY. Apr 26, 1822. Known as "the father of landscape architecture in America," Olmsted participated in the designing of Yosemite National Park, New York City's Central Park and parks for Boston, MA; Hartford, CT; and Louisville, KY. Born at Hartford, died at Waverly, MA, Aug 28, 1903. Olmsted's home and studio, Fairsted Estate, outside of Boston, is now preserved as a National Historic Site and is open to the public: 99 Warren St, Brookline, MA 02146.

PRESERVATION WEEK. Apr 26–May 2. Some 630 million items in collecting institutions require immediate attention and care, with no budget or staff allocated. Some 2.6 billion items are not protected by an emergency plan. As natural disasters of recent years have taught us, these resources are in jeopardy should a disaster strike. Personal, family and community collections are equally at risk. The ALA encourages libraries and other institutions to use this week to connect our communities through events, activities and resources that highlight what we can do, individually and together, to preserve our personal and shared collections. For info: Assn for Library Collections and Technical Services (ALCTS), American Library Assn. E-mail: alcts@ala.org. Web: www.ala.org/alcts/preservationweek.

RAINEY, MA (GERTRUDE BRIDGET): BIRTH ANNIVERSARY. Apr 26, 1886. Known as "the Mother of the Blues," Gertrude "Ma" Rainey was born at Columbus, GA. She made her stage debut at the Columbus Opera House in 1900 in a talent show called "The Bunch of Blackberries." After touring together as "Rainey and Rainey, the Assassinators of the Blues," she and her husband eventually separated, and she toured on her own. She made her first recording in 1923 and her last on Dec 28, 1928, after being told that the rural Southern blues she sang had gone out of style. She died Dec 22, 1939, at Columbus.

RICHTER SCALE DAY. Apr 26. A day to recognize the importance of Charles Francis Richter's research and his work in development of the earthquake magnitude scale that is known as the Richter scale. Richter, an American author, physicist and seismologist, was born Apr 26, 1900, near Hamilton, OH. An Earthquake Awareness Week was observed in recognition of his work. Richter died at Pasadena, CA, Sept 30, 1985.

ROLFE, LILIAN: BIRTH ANNIVERSARY. Apr 26, 1914. Born at Paris, France, to British parents, Rolfe was a WWII secret agent (Special Operations Executive) who transmitted details on Nazi troop movements to the Allies and assisted the French Resistance in occupied France. She was arrested July 31, 1944, and tortured for months before being executed at Ravensbrück (a women's concentration camp), Germany, on Feb 5, 1945. Awarded the Croix de Guerre among many posthumous honors.

SIRK, DOUGLAS: BIRTH ANNIVERSARY. Apr 26, 1900. Film director Douglas Sirk was born Detlef Sierck at Hamburg, Germany. His films include *Magnificent Obsession* (1954), *Written on the Wind* (1956) and *Imitation of Life* (1959). He died Jan 14, 1987, at Lugano, Switzerland.

SOUTH AFRICAN MULTIRACIAL ELECTIONS: ANNIVERSARY. Apr 26–29, 1994. For the first time in the history of South Africa, the nation's approximately 18 million blacks voted in multiparty elections. This event marked the definitive end of apartheid, the system of racial separation that had kept blacks and other minorities out of the political process. The election resulted in Nelson Mandela of the African National Congress being elected president and F.W. de Klerk (incumbent president) of the National Party vice president.

STEWARDSHIP WEEK. Apr 26–May 3. This week is one of the largest national programs to promote natural resource conservation. Celebrated annually since 1955 between the last Sunday in April and the first Sunday in May, NACD Stewardship Week reminds us of our individual responsibilities to care for natural resources. For info: Natl Assn of Conservation Districts, 509 Capitol Ct NE, Washington, DC 20002-4937. Phone: (202) 547-6223. E-mail: info@nacdnet.org. Web: www.nacdnet.org.

SWITZERLAND: LANDSGEMEINDE. Apr 26. In one of the last examples of direct democracy, the citizens of Switzerland's smallest canton, Appenzell Innerrhoden, gather annually on the last Sunday in April to vote. Uniquely, they don't cast secret ballots but raise their arms in full view of their neighbors. About 2,000 to 3,000 voters of 18 years and older come to the square of the canton capital, Appenzell, after attending a morning church service. Once affairs of the canton are voted on, festivities begin. As part of the tradition, which dates back to the 14th century, men wear swords.

TANZANIA: UNION DAY. Apr 26. Celebrates union between mainland Tanzania (formerly Tanganyika) and the islands of Zanzibar and Pemba, in 1964.

UNITED NATIONS: INTERNATIONAL CHERNOBYL DISASTER REMEMBRANCE DAY. Apr 26. On Dec 8, 2016, the General Assembly designated this international day, recognizing that three decades after the Chernobyl disaster, there are still-persistent serious long-term consequences—and continuing related needs of the affected communities and territories. For info: United Nations, Dept of Public Info, New York, NY 10017. Web: www.un.org.

UNITED NATIONS: WORLD INTELLECTUAL PROPERTY DAY. Apr 26. Since 2000, a day to promote discussion of the role of intellectual property in encouraging innovation and creativity. Annually, Apr 26—the day in 1970 on which the WIPO Convention came into force. For info: United Nations, Dept of Public Info, New York, NY 10017. Web: www.wipo.int/ip-outreach/en/ipday or www.un.org.

WITTGENSTEIN, LUDWIG: BIRTH ANNIVERSARY. Apr 26, 1889. One of the most influential analytic and linguistic philosophers of the 20th century, born at Vienna, Austria. Wittgenstein had a fundamental influence on logical positivism, linguistic analysis and semantics. He theorized that philosophical problems were fundamentally problems of language, and studying "ordinary language" would enable one to solve many of these problems. Died Apr 29, 1951, at Cambridge, England.

🎂 BIRTHDAYS TODAY

Carol Burnett, 84, actress ("The Carol Burnett Show," *The Four Seasons*), born San Antonio, TX, Apr 26, 1936.

Joan Chen, 59, actress ("Twin Peaks," "Golden Gate"), born Shanghai, China, Apr 26, 1961.

Joe Crede, 42, former baseball player, born Jefferson City, MO, Apr 26, 1978.

Michael Damian, 58, actor ("The Young and the Restless"; stage: *Joseph and the Amazing Technicolor Dreamcoat*), born San Diego, CA, Apr 26, 1962.

Duane Eddy, 82, musician, born Corning, NY, Apr 26, 1938.

Giancarlo Esposito, 62, actor ("Revolution," "Breaking Bad," *Do the Right Thing, King of New York*), born Copenhagen, Denmark, Apr 26, 1958.

Kosuke Fukudome, 43, baseball player, born Osaki, Japan, Apr 26, 1977.

Kevin James, 55, actor (*Pixels, Grown Ups, Hitch,* "The King of Queens"), born Stony Brook, NY, Apr 26, 1965.

Stana Katic, 42, actress ("Absentia," "Castle"), born Hamilton, ON, Canada, Apr 26, 1978.

Jemima Kirke, 35, actress (*Tiny Furniture,* "Girls"), born London, England, Apr 26, 1985.

Jet Li, 57, actor (*The Forbidden Kingdom, Hero, Kiss of the Dragon*), former martial arts champion, born Li Lian Jie at Beijing, China, Apr 26, 1963.

Boyd Matson, 73, television journalist ("National Geographic Explorer"), born Oklahoma City, OK, Apr 26, 1947.

Bobby Rydell, 78, singer, born Philadelphia, PA, Apr 26, 1942.

Natasha Trethewey, 54, poet, former poet laureate of the US (2012–14), born Gulfport, MS, Apr 26, 1966.

Melania Trump, 50, First Lady, wife of Donald Trump, 45th president of the US, born Melanija Knavs at Novo Mesto, Yugoslavia (now Slovenia), Apr 26, 1970.

Tom Welling, 43, actor ("Smallville"), born New York, NY, Apr 26, 1977.

Gary Wright, 77, musician, born Englewood, NJ, Apr 26, 1943.

April 27 — Monday

DAY 118   **248 REMAINING**

BABE RUTH DAY: ANNIVERSARY. Apr 27, 1947. Babe Ruth Day was celebrated in every ballpark in organized baseball in the US as well as Japan. Mortally ill with throat cancer, Ruth appeared at Yankee Stadium to thank his former club for the honor.

CONFEDERATE MEMORIAL DAY IN ALABAMA. Apr 27. On the fourth Monday in April. Other Southern states observe Confederate Memorial Day on different dates.

CONFEDERATE MEMORIAL DAY IN MISSISSIPPI. Apr 27. Annually, on the last Monday in April. Observed on other dates in some states.

DENNIS, SANDY: BIRTH ANNIVERSARY. Apr 27, 1937. American actress Sandy Dennis was born Sandra Dale Dennis at Hastings, NE. In addition to two Tony Awards, she won an Academy Award for her supporting role in *Who's Afraid of Virginia Woolf?* (1966). She died Mar 2, 1992, at Westport, CT.

GIBBON, EDWARD: BIRTH ANNIVERSARY. Apr 27, 1737. (Old Style date.) English historian and author. His *History of the Decline and Fall of the Roman Empire* remains a model of historical writing. From his description of the Roman emperor Gordianus II: "Twenty-two acknowledged concubines, and a library of sixty-two thousand volumes, attested the variety of his inclinations; and from the productions which he left behind him, it appears that the former as well as the latter were designed for use rather than for ostentation." Born at Putney, Surrey, England, Gibbon died at London, Jan 16, 1794.

GRANT, ULYSSES SIMPSON: BIRTH ANNIVERSARY. Apr 27, 1822. 18th president of the US (Mar 4, 1869–Mar 3, 1877), born Hiram Ulysses Grant at Point Pleasant, OH. He graduated from the US Military Academy in 1843. President Lincoln promoted Grant to lieutenant general in command of all the Union armies Mar 9, 1864. On Apr 9, 1865, Grant received General Robert E. Lee's surrender, at Appomattox Court House, VA, which he announced to the secretary of war as follows: "General Lee surrendered the Army of Northern Virginia this afternoon on terms proposed by myself. The accompanying additional correspondence will show the conditions fully." Nicknamed "Unconditional Surrender Grant," he died at Mount McGregor, NY, July 23, 1885, just four days after completing his memoirs. He was buried at Riverside Park, New York, NY, where Grant's Tomb was dedicated in 1897.

KING, CORETTA SCOTT: BIRTH ANNIVERSARY. Apr 27, 1927. The wife of Dr. Martin Luther King, Jr, was born on a farm near Heiberger, AL. She picked cotton as a child but was able to go to college, where she met and married the young minister-turned-civil-rights-activist. She worked by his side, establishing Freedom Concerts and other social-change movements, while also raising the couple's four children. After King's 1968 assassination, she took on his mission, founding the Martin Luther King Jr Center for Nonviolent Social Change in Atlanta (now called The King Center), and also spearheading the efforts to have a national holiday established in her late husband's honor. The American Library Association established a prestigious children's literature award for African-American writers and illustrators in her name in 1970, and in her later years she was a tireless advocate for gay and lesbian rights. She died at Rosarito, Mexico, Jan 30, 2006.

LANTZ, WALTER: BIRTH ANNIVERSARY. Apr 27, 1900. Originator of Universal Studios' animated opening sequence for their first major musical film, *The King of Jazz*. Walter Lantz is best remembered as the creator of Woody Woodpecker, the bird with the wacky laugh and the taunting ways. Lantz received a Lifetime Achievement Academy Award for his animation in 1979. He was born at New Rochelle, NY, and died Mar 22, 1994, at Burbank, CA.

MAGELLAN, FERDINAND: DEATH ANNIVERSARY. Apr 27, 1521. Portuguese explorer Ferdinand Magellan was probably born near Oporto, Portugal, about 1480, but neither the place nor the date is certain. Usually thought of as the first man to circumnavigate the earth, he died before completing the voyage; thus, his coleader, Basque navigator Juan Sebastian de Elcano, became the world's first circumnavigator. The westward, round-the-world expedition began Sept 20, 1519, with five ships and about 250 men. Magellan was killed by natives of the Philippine island of Mactan.

MATANZAS MULE DAY. Apr 27, 1898. In one of the first naval actions of the Spanish-American War, US naval forces bombarded the Cuban village of Matanzas. It was widely reported that the only casualty of the bombardment was one mule. The "Matanzas Mule" became instantly famous and remains a footnote in the history of the Spanish-American War.

MORSE, SAMUEL FINLEY BREESE: BIRTH ANNIVERSARY. Apr 27, 1791. The American artist and inventor, after whom the Morse code is named, was born at Charlestown, MA, and died at New York, NY, Apr 2, 1872. Graduating from Yale University in 1810, he went to the Royal Academy of London to study painting. After returning to America, he achieved success as a portraitist. Morse conceived the idea of an electromagnetic telegraph while on shipboard, returning from art instruction in Europe in 1832, and he proceeded to develop his idea. With financial assistance approved by Congress, the first telegraph line in the US was constructed, between Washington, DC, and Baltimore, MD. The first message tapped out by Morse from the Supreme Court Chamber at the US Capitol building on May 24, 1844, was "What hath God wrought?"

MOST TORNADOES IN A DAY (US): ANNIVERSARY. Apr 27–28, 2011. The 24-hour period from 8 AM, Apr 27, to 8 AM, Apr 28, saw more tornadoes in a day—226—than in any other period in US history. Striking in the southeast US, this was part of a larger outbreak from Apr 25–28, called the "2011 Super Outbreak," that was one of the most deadly systems of extreme weather that the US has ever seen. In Alabama, 50 tornadoes struck. During this 24-hour period 334 people died.

NATIONAL LITTLE PAMPERED DOG DAY. Apr 27. A day to remember that it's okay to pamper your loved ones—including your dog. Taking your dogs places, dressing them up (but only if they like it) and giving them all of the love that they deserve is wonderful. This day was created to celebrate those owners who truly care for and love their dogs but also to bring attention to the fact that not all dogs are so lucky. Give a bit of your time and/or resources to a local animal rescue or shelter. Annually, Apr 27. For info: Lourdes Welhaven, Little Pampered Dog, 4101 S Indian River Dr, Fort Pierce, FL 34982. Phone: (800) 359-3193, ext 1. Web: www.nationallittlepampereddogday.com.

NETHERLANDS: KING'S DAY. Apr 27. National holiday celebrating the birth of King Willem-Alexander, who was born Apr 27, 1967. The holiday was formerly observed on Apr 30 (in honor of Queen Juliana [1909–2004] and Queen Beatrix [1938–]). The whole country parties as young and old participate in free markets, theater, music, games and *Oranjegekte* ("orange fever").

PROKOFIEV, SERGEI: BIRTH ANNIVERSARY. Apr 27, 1891. Born at Sontsovka, Russia (now Sontsivka, Ukraine), Prokofiev is regarded as one of the most significant composers of the 20th century. He created a wide array of music, including symphonies; ballets; operas; orchestral suites; concertos for piano, violin and cello and works for solo piano. His best-known works include the ballet *Romeo and Juliet*, the opera *The Love for Three Oranges* and the popular orchestral piece (with narration) *Peter and the Wolf*. Prokofiev left Russia in 1918 to avoid the upheaval of the Russian Revolution. He composed, performed as a pianist and conducted extensively in the United States and Europe before returning to the Soviet Union in 1936. He had conflicts with Soviet authorities, which, in 1948, banned several of his works for allegedly having renounced "the basic principles of classical music." Prokofiev died Mar 5, 1953, at Moscow, USSR.

SIERRA LEONE: INDEPENDENCE DAY. Apr 27. National Day. Commemorates independence from Britain in 1961.

SLOVENIA: INSURRECTION DAY. Apr 27. National holiday. Commemorates the founding of the Liberation Front in 1941 to resist Slovenia's occupation by the Axis powers.

SOUTH AFRICA: FREEDOM DAY. Apr 27. National holiday. Commemorates the day in 1994 when, for the first time, all South Africans had the opportunity to vote.

***SULTANA* STEAMSHIP EXPLOSION: ANNIVERSARY.** Apr 27, 1865. Early in the morning on this day, America's worst steamship disaster occurred. The *Sultana*, heavily overloaded with an estimated 2,300 passengers, exploded in the Mississippi River, just north of Memphis, TN, en route to Cairo, IL. Most of the passengers were Union soldiers who had been prisoners of war and were eagerly returning to their homes. Although there was never an accurate accounting of the dead, estimates range from 1,450 to nearly 2,000. Cause of the explosion was not determined, but the little-known event is unparalleled in US history.

TOGO: INDEPENDENCE DAY: 60th ANNIVERSARY OF INDEPENDENCE. Apr 27. National holiday. In 1960 Togo gained its independence from French administration under a UN trusteeship.

WOLLSTONECRAFT, MARY: BIRTH ANNIVERSARY. Apr 27, 1759. Writer and advocate of equality for women, Mary Wollstonecraft was born at London, England. Rebelling against her father, she left

April 2020	S	M	T	W	T	F	S
				1	2	3	4
	5	6	7	8	9	10	11
	12	13	14	15	16	17	18
	19	20	21	22	23	24	25
	26	27	28	29	30		

home at age 18 and served as a lady's companion, opened a school and worked as a governess. Beginning with *Thoughts on the Education of Daughters* in 1787, Wollstonecraft attracted notice as a writer in favor of women's rights. Her *A Vindication of the Rights of Woman* (1792) argued that women should be given an education that would allow them to gain economic independence. She died at London on Sept 10, 1797, 11 days after giving birth to her second daughter (Mary Wollstonecraft Shelley, the author of *Frankenstein*).

🎂 BIRTHDAYS TODAY

Anouk Aimée, 86, actress (*A Man and a Woman*, *8½*, *La Dolce Vita*), born Paris, France, Apr 27, 1934.

Nigel Barker, 48, television personality ("The Face," "America's Next Top Model"), photographer, born London, England, Apr 27, 1972.

Cory Booker, 51, US Senator (D, New Jersey), born Washington, DC, Apr 27, 1969.

Francis Capra, 37, actor ("Veronica Mars," *A Bronx Tale*), born New York, NY, Apr 27, 1983.

Jenna Coleman, 34, actress ("Victoria," "Doctor Who," "Emmerdale"), born Blackpool, England, Apr 27, 1986.

Sheena Easton, 61, singer, born Sheena Shirley Orr at Bellshill, Scotland, Apr 27, 1959.

Sally Hawkins, 44, actress (*The Shape of Water*, *Blue Jasmine*, *Happy-Go-Lucky*, *Persuasion*), born London, England, Apr 27, 1976.

Jim Justice, 69, Governor of West Virginia (R), born Charleston, WV, Apr 27, 1951.

King Willem-Alexander, 53, King of the Netherlands, born Utrecht, Netherlands, Apr 27, 1967.

April 28 — Tuesday

DAY 119 **247 REMAINING**

BARRYMORE, LIONEL: BIRTH ANNIVERSARY. Apr 28, 1878. Famed actor of the celebrated acting family, Lionel Barrymore was born Lionel Blythe, at Philadelphia, PA. Brother of actors Ethel and John Barrymore, he was a prolific actor who was not slowed down by partial paralysis sustained in 1938. Barrymore won a Best Actor Oscar for *A Free Soul* (1931) and appeared in *You Can't Take It with You, Young Dr. Kildare, It's a Wonderful Life* and *Key Largo*, among many others. He died at Van Nuys, CA, Nov 15, 1954.

BIOLOGICAL CLOCK GENE DISCOVERED: ANNIVERSARY. Apr 28, 1994. Northwestern University announced that the so-called biological clock, that gene governing the daily cycle of waking and sleeping called the circadian rhythm, had been found in mice. Never before pinpointed in a mammal, the biological clock gene was found on mouse chromosome 5.

CANADA: NATIONAL DAY OF MOURNING. Apr 28. A national day of mourning for workers killed or injured on the job in Canada. The Canadian Labour Congress first officially recognized the day in 1986. Pointing to the nearly one million workplace injuries each year in Canada, the CLC has called for stricter health and safety regulations and for annual recognition of this day throughout Canada. Federal legislation (Bill D–223) first recognized this day in 1991.

ISRAEL: REMEMBRANCE DAY (YOM HA'ZIKKARON). Apr 28. Honors the more than 23,000 soldiers killed in battle since the start of the nation's war for independence in 1947. Hebrew calendar date: Iyar 4, 5780. Began at sundown Apr 27. See also: "Israel: Independence Day (Yom Ha'atzma'ut)."

JAMES MONROE BIRTHDAY CELEBRATION. Apr 28. Highland, Charlottesville, VA. Highland, the home of James Monroe, commemorates the fifth president's birthday with topics relevant to Monroe's participation in important aspects of early American history, including the Revolutionary War, the expansion of the United States, national defense and the establishment of American foreign policy. For info: Highland, 2050 James Monroe Pkwy, Charlottesville, VA 22902. Phone: (434) 293-8000. E-mail: info@ highland.org. Web: www.highland.org.

LEE, HARPER: BIRTH ANNIVERSARY. Apr 28, 1926. The author of easily the best-loved American novel of the 20th century—*To Kill a Mockingbird* (1960)—was born Nelle Harper Lee at Monroeville, AL. Her father, respected attorney Amasa Coleman Lee, was the model for *Mockingbird*'s Atticus Finch. *To Kill a Mockingbird*, which received the 1961 Pulitzer Prize, was Lee's only published novel—until 2015, when an early version/draft of *Mockingbird*, *Go Set a Watchman*, was published. She told an interviewer in 1964, "All I want to be is the Jane Austen of South Alabama." A recipient of the Presidential Medal of Freedom in 2007, Lee died at her hometown Feb 19, 2016.

MARYLAND CONSTITUTION RATIFICATION: ANNIVERSARY. Apr 28, 1788. Maryland became the seventh state to ratify the Constitution, by a vote of 63 to 11.

MONROE, JAMES: BIRTH ANNIVERSARY. Apr 28, 1758. The fifth president of the US was born at Westmoreland County, VA, and served two terms in that office (Mar 4, 1817–Mar 3, 1825). Monrovia, the capital city of Liberia, is named after him, as is the Monroe Doctrine, which he enunciated at Washington, DC, Dec 2, 1823. The last of three presidents to die on US Independence Day, Monroe died at New York, NY, July 4, 1831.

MUSSOLINI EXECUTED: 75th ANNIVERSARY. Apr 28, 1945. Italian partisans shot Benito Mussolini near the lakeside village of Dongo. Leaders of the Fascist Party, several of his friends and his mistress, Clara Petacci, also were executed. The 23-year-long Fascist rule of Italy was ended.

MUTINY ON THE *BOUNTY*: ANNIVERSARY. Apr 28, 1789. The most famous of all naval mutinies occurred on board HMS *Bounty*. Captain of the *Bounty* was Lieutenant William Bligh, an able seaman and a mean-tempered disciplinarian. The ship, with a load of breadfruit tree plants from Tahiti, was bound for Jamaica. Fletcher Christian, leader of the mutiny, put Bligh and 18 of his loyal followers adrift in a 23-foot open boat. Miraculously, Bligh and all of his supporters survived a 47-day voyage of more than 3,600 miles, before landing on the island of Timor, June 14, 1789. In the meantime, Christian had put all of the remaining crew (except 8 men and himself) ashore at Tahiti, where he picked up 18 Tahitians (6 men and 12 women) and set sail again. Landing in 1790 at Pitcairn Island (probably uninhabited at the time), they burned the *Bounty* and remained undiscovered for 18 years, when an American whaler, the *Topaz*, called at the island (1808) and found only one member of the mutinous crew surviving. However,

the little colony had thrived and, when counted by the British in 1856, numbered 194 persons.

SCHINDLER, OSKAR: BIRTH ANNIVERSARY. Apr 28, 1908. German industrialist Oskar Schindler was born Apr 28, 1908, at Svitavy, Moravia, Austria-Hungary (now Zwittau, Czech Republic). For his role in saving over 1,200 Jews during WWII, Schindler was declared a "Righteous Gentile" by Israel in 1962. Although financial opportunism initiated Schindler's employment of Polish Jews in his enamel factory, by 1944 he embraced his part in saving many of them from execution. Despised by many of his countrymen for his actions during and following WWII, he died Oct 9, 1974, at Frankfurt am Main, Germany. He was buried in Jerusalem, Israel—more than 500 *Schindlerjuden* were in attendance at his funeral. Schindler was later immortalized in the 1982 novel *Schindler's Ark* and 1993 film *Schindler's List*.

SPACE MILESTONE: FIRST TOURIST IN SPACE. Apr 28, 2001. Millionaire US businessman Dennis Tito reportedly paid the Russian space agency $20 million to accompany *Soyuz TM* to the International Space Station. The rocket with Tito and two Russian cosmonauts was launched this day from the Baikonur launch site in Kazakhstan and arrived at the ISS on Apr 30, 2001. The crew returned to Earth in a week. NASA initially objected to the inclusion of the 60-year-old tycoon on the mission but dropped its opposition.

UNITED NATIONS: WORLD DAY FOR SAFETY AND HEALTH AT WORK. Apr 28. Annual international campaign to promote safe, healthy and decent work, observed by the International Labour Organization (ILO) since 2003. Annually, Apr 28. For info: United Nations, Dept of Public Info, New York, NY 10017. Web: www.un.org.

WORKERS MEMORIAL DAY. Apr 28. First proclaimed in 1970 by the AFL-CIO to commemorate the founding of the Occupational Safety and Health Administration (OSHA). Now observed internationally.

🎂 BIRTHDAYS TODAY

Jessica Alba, 39, actress (*Good Luck Chuck, Fantastic Four, Into the Blue, Sin City*, "Dark Angel"), born Pomona, CA, Apr 28, 1981.

Ann-Margret, 79, actress (*Carnal Knowledge, Tommy, Grumpy Old Men*), born Ann-Margaret Olsson at Stockholm, Sweden, Apr 28, 1941.

Penelope Cruz, 46, actress (Oscar for *Vicky Cristina Barcelona; Nine, Volver, Bandidas*), born Madrid, Spain, Apr 28, 1974.

John Daly, 54, golfer, born Carmichael, CA, Apr 28, 1966.

Jorge Garcia, 47, actor ("Hawaii Five-0," "Lost," "Becker"), born Omaha, NE, Apr 28, 1973.

	S	M	T	W	T	F	S
April				1	2	3	4
	5	6	7	8	9	10	11
2020	12	13	14	15	16	17	18
	19	20	21	22	23	24	25
	26	27	28	29	30		

Paul Guilfoyle, 71, actor (*Spotlight*, "CSI"), born Boston, MA, Apr 28, 1949.

Elena Kagan, 60, Associate Justice of the US, born New York, NY, Apr 28, 1960.

Barry Larkin, 56, Hall of Fame baseball player, born Cincinnati, OH, Apr 28, 1964.

Jay Leno, 70, comedian, former television talk show host ("The Tonight Show"), born New Rochelle, NY, Apr 28, 1950.

Nicklas Lidstrom, 50, former hockey player, born Vasteras, Sweden, Apr 28, 1970.

Mary McDonnell, 68, actress ("Battlestar Galactica," *Independence Day, Dances with Wolves*), born Wilkes-Barre, PA, Apr 28, 1952.

Ian Rankin, 60, author (*Black and Blue, The Hanging Garden*), born Cardenden, Fife, Scotland, Apr 28, 1960.

Tony Revolori, 24, actor (*The Grand Budapest Hotel*), born Anaheim, CA, Apr 28, 1996.

Drew Scott, 42, television personality ("Property Brothers"), real estate entrepreneur, born Vancouver, BC, Canada, Apr 28, 1978.

Jonathan Silver Scott, 42, television personality ("Property Brothers"), real estate entrepreneur, born Vancouver, BC, Canada, Apr 28, 1978.

Marcia Strassman, 72, actress ("Welcome Back, Kotter"; *Honey, I Shrunk the Kids*), born New York, NY, Apr 28, 1948.

Jenna Ushkowitz, 34, actress ("Glee"), born Seoul, South Korea, Apr 28, 1986.

Alice Waters, 76, chef, restaurateur (Chez Panisse), author, born Chatham Borough, NJ, Apr 28, 1944.

Bradley Wiggins, 40, cyclist, born Ghent, Belgium, Apr 28, 1980.

April 29 — Wednesday

DAY 120   **246 REMAINING**

EARNHARDT, DALE: BIRTH ANNIVERSARY. Apr 29, 1952. Stock car racer, born at Kannapolis, NC. Dale Earnhardt was one of NASCAR's most popular personalities, winning the Winston Cup seven times. He was killed while driving in the Daytona 500 at Daytona Beach, FL, Feb 18, 2001.

ELLINGTON, "DUKE" (EDWARD KENNEDY): BIRTH ANNIVERSARY. Apr 29, 1899. Duke Ellington, one of the most influential individuals in jazz history, was born at Washington, DC. Ellington's professional career began when he was 17, and by 1923 he was leading a small group of musicians at the Kentucky Club at New York City who became the core of his big band. Ellington is credited with being one of the founders of big band jazz. He used his band as an instrument for composition and orchestration to create big band pieces, film scores, operas, ballets, Broadway shows and religious music. Ellington was responsible for more than 1,000 musical pieces. He drew together instruments from different sections of the orchestra to develop unique and haunting sounds such as that of his famous "Mood Indigo." Ellington died May 24, 1974, at New York City.

ELLSWORTH, OLIVER: 275th BIRTH ANNIVERSARY. Apr 29, 1745. (Old Style date.) Third chief justice of the US, born at Windsor, CT. Died there, Nov 26, 1807.

***HAIR* BROADWAY OPENING: ANNIVERSARY.** Apr 29, 1968. The controversial rock musical *Hair*, produced by Michael Butler, opened at the Biltmore Theatre at New York City, after playing off-Broadway. For those who opposed the Vietnam War and the "Establishment," this was a defining piece of work—as evidenced by some of its songs, such as "Aquarius," "Hair" and "Let the Sunshine In."

HEARST, WILLIAM RANDOLPH: BIRTH ANNIVERSARY. Apr 29, 1863. Media magnate of the late 19th and early 20th centuries, who, starting with the *San Francisco Examiner* in 1887 and the *New York Morning Journal* in 1895, built an empire consisting of 28 dailies, 18 magazines, radio stations and other outlets. The Hearst brand of journalism—stoked by vicious competition with other chains—tended to be sensational and truculent. It was dubbed "yellow journalism" by detractors. The film classic *Citizen Kane* was loosely based on his life. Born at San Francisco, CA, Hearst died at Beverly Hills, CA, Aug 14, 1951.

HIROHITO MICHI-NO-MIYA, EMPEROR: BIRTH ANNIVERSARY. Apr 29, 1901. Former emperor of Japan, born at Tokyo. Hirohito's death, Jan 7, 1989, ended the reign of the world's longest-ruling monarch. He became the 124th in a line of monarchs when he ascended to the Chrysanthemum Throne in 1926. Hirohito presided over perhaps the most eventful period in the 2,500 years of recorded Japanese history, including the attempted military conquest of Asia; the attack on the US that brought that country into WWII, leading to Japan's ultimate defeat after the US dropped atomic bombs on Hiroshima and Nagasaki; and the amazing economic restoration following the war, which led Japan to a preeminent position of economic strength.

ISRAEL: INDEPENDENCE DAY (YOM HA'ATZMA'UT). Apr 29. Celebrates proclamation of independence from British mandatory rule by Palestinian Jews and establishment of the state of Israel and the provisional government May 14, 1948 (Hebrew calendar date: Iyar 5, 5708). Dates in the Hebrew calendar vary from their Gregorian equivalents from year to year. Hebrew calendar date: Iyar 5, 5780. Began at sundown Apr 28.

JAPAN: GOLDEN WEEK HOLIDAYS. Apr 29–May 5. National holidays. This period includes Showa Day (Apr 29), Constitution Memorial Day (May 3), Greenery Day (May 4) and Children's Day (May 5).

JAPAN: SHOWA DAY. Apr 29. Formerly celebrated as Greenery Day until 2007. Honors Emperor Hirohito (1901–89) and is observed on his birthday. "Showa" refers to Japan's postwar era. Part of the Golden Week Holidays.

LIBERATION OF DACHAU: 75th ANNIVERSARY. Apr 29, 1945. The Charlie Battery of the 522nd Field Artillery Battalion liberated the concentration camp at Dachau, Germany. The 522nd, part of the legendary 442nd (Go for Broke) regimental combat team, was made up of nisei—second-generation Japanese Americans. Dachau was the first concentration camp opened in Germany, and more than 200,000 prisoners were housed there throughout the course of WWII. An estimated 35,000 people lost their lives in the camp, and more than 32,000 were liberated when the Americans arrived beginning on this date.

LOS ANGELES RIOTS: ANNIVERSARY. Apr 29, 1992. A jury in Simi Valley, CA, failed to convict four Los Angeles police officers accused in the videotaped beating of Rodney King in 1991, providing the spark that set off rioting, looting and burning at South Central Los Angeles, CA, and other areas across the country. The anger unleashed during and after the violence was attributed to widespread racism, lack of job opportunities and the resulting hopelessness of inner-city poverty.

"PEACE" ROSE INTRODUCED TO WORLD: 75th ANNIVERSARY. Apr 29, 1945. The 20th century's most popular rose was publicly released by the Pacific Rose Society at Pasadena, CA, just as Berlin, Germany, was falling to the Allies. The history of "Peace" is interwoven with events of WWII, and for many the hybrid tea rose has symbolized the hope that grew out of terrible conflict. French rose grower Francis Meilland bred the cream and pink rose (then called "Mme A. Meilland") in the late 1930s and knew he had something extraordinary. A seedling was smuggled out of France in an American diplomatic pouch on one of the last planes to leave that country before Nazi occupation. American rose company Conrad-Pyle carefully cultivated it. To note Germany's surrender, "Peace" blooms were presented to all delegates during the first United Nations Conference that May of 1945.

SAINT CATHERINE OF SIENA: FEAST DAY. Apr 29, 1347. St. Catherine of Siena was born at Tuscany, Italy. Patron saint of Italy. She died Apr 29, 1380, at Rome, Italy.

ZIPPER PATENTED: ANNIVERSARY. Apr 29, 1913. Gideon Sundback of Hoboken, NJ, received a patent for the zipper.

🎂 BIRTHDAYS TODAY

Andre Agassi, 50, former tennis player, born Las Vegas, NV, Apr 29, 1970.

Megan Boone, 37, actress ("The Blacklist"), born Petoskey, MI, Apr 29, 1983.

Bob Bryan, 42, Olympic gold medal tennis player (multiple Grand Slam titles for doubles with Mike Bryan), born Camarillo, CA, Apr 29, 1978.

Mike Bryan, 42, Olympic gold medal tennis player (multiple Grand Slam titles for doubles with Bob Bryan), born Camarillo, CA, Apr 29, 1978.

Daniel Day-Lewis, 63, actor (Oscars for *Lincoln, There Will Be Blood* and *My Left Foot*), born London, England, Apr 29, 1957.

Nora Dunn, 68, comedienne, actress (*Three Kings*, "Saturday Night Live"), born Chicago, IL, Apr 29, 1952.

Robert Gottlieb, 89, editor, born New York, NY, Apr 29, 1931.

Zubin Mehta, 84, conductor, born Bombay (now Mumbai), India, Apr 29, 1936.

Kate Mulgrew, 65, actress ("Orange Is the New Black," "Star Trek: Voyager," "Ryan's Hope"), born Dubuque, IA, Apr 29, 1955.

Michelle Pfeiffer, 62, actress (*What Lies Beneath, Batman Returns, Dangerous Liaisons*), born Santa Ana, CA, Apr 29, 1958.

Eve Plumb, 62, actress ("The Brady Bunch," "Fudge"), born Burbank, CA, Apr 29, 1958.

Jerry Seinfeld, 66, comedian, actor ("Seinfeld"), born Brooklyn, NY, Apr 29, 1954.

Debbie Stabenow, 70, US Senator (D, Michigan), born Clare, MI, Apr 29, 1950.

Uma Thurman, 50, actress (Kill Bill films, *Gattaca, Pulp Fiction*), born Boston, MA, Apr 29, 1970.

Jonathan Toews, 32, hockey player, born Winnipeg, MB, Canada, Apr 29, 1988.

Carnie Wilson, 52, singer, born Bel Air, CA, Apr 29, 1968.

April 30 — Thursday

DAY 121   **245 REMAINING**

BELTANE. Apr 30. (Also called Bealtaine, May Eve, Walpurgis Night, Cyntefyn, Roodmass and Cethsamhain.) One of the "Greater Sabbats" during the Wiccan year, Beltane celebrates the union or marriage of the Goddess and God. In Scotland, Beltane was one of the quarter days, or terms when rents were due and debts settled. On the eve of Beltane, two fires were built close together and cattle were driven between them to ward off disease prior to putting the stock out to pasture for the new season. Annually, on Apr 30.

BUGS BUNNY'S DEBUT: ANNIVERSARY. Apr 30, 1938. Warner Bros.' "wascally wabbit" first appeared on screen in the theatrical short "Porky's Hare Hunt," directed by Ben "Bugs" Hardaway and released on this date. Chuck Jones and Tex Avery further developed him into the character we know now—in such cartoons as "A Wild Hare" (1940), in which Bugs asks, "What's up, Doc?" for the first time and first kisses perennial foe Elmer Fudd. The rabbit's noisy carrot munching was based on Clark Gable's carrot chewing in the film *It Happened One Night* (1934).

CAMBODIA INVADED BY US: 50th ANNIVERSARY. Apr 30, 1970. President Richard Nixon announced the US was sending troops into Cambodia in an attempt to destroy the "sanctuaries" from which men and materiel were infiltrated into South Vietnam. This sparked widespread protests on the home front, including a march on Washington and the closure of many American colleges and universities. See also: "Kent State Students' Memorial Day: Anniversary" (May 4).

CHINA: BIRTHDAY OF LORD BUDDHA. Apr 30. Religious observances are held in Buddhist temples, offerings of flowers and incense are made and Buddha's statue is bathed. Annually, eighth day of fourth lunar month. Date in other countries may differ from China's.

DÍA DE LOS NIÑOS/DÍA DE LOS LIBROS. Apr 30. A celebration of children, families and reading, held annually on Apr 30, emphasizing the importance of advocating literacy for every child regardless of linguistic and cultural background. Originally proclaimed by the National Association to Promote Library and Information Services to Latinos and the Spanish Speaking (REFORMA) as an enhancement of Children's Day, which began in 1925. In 1996, nationally acclaimed children's book author Pat Mora proposed linking the celebration of childhood and children with literacy, to found this unique day. Est attendance: 15,000. For info: American Library Assn, Association for Library Service to Children (ALSC), 50 E Huron St, Chicago, IL 60611. Phone: (312) 280-5044. E-mail: dia@ala.org. Web: dia.ala.org.

FIRST NORTH AMERICAN THEATRICAL PERFORMANCE: ANNIVERSARY. Apr 30, 1598. On the banks of the Rio Grande, near present-day El Paso, TX, the first North American theatrical performance took place. The play was a Spanish commedia featuring an expedition of soldiers. On July 10 of the same year, the same group produced *Moros y Los Cristianos* (*Moors and Christians*), by an anonymous playwright.

FIRST PRESIDENTIAL TELECAST: ANNIVERSARY. Apr 30, 1939. Franklin D. Roosevelt became the first president to appear on television when he was televised at the New York World's Fair. However, the appearance was beamed to only 200 TV sets in a 40-mile radius. See also: "First Scheduled Television Broadcast: Anniversary" (July 1).

HARRISON, MARY SCOTT LORD DIMMICK: BIRTH ANNIVERSARY. Apr 30, 1858. Second wife of Benjamin Harrison, 23rd president of the US, born at Honesdale, PA. Died at New York, NY, Jan 5, 1948.

INTERNATIONAL JAZZ DAY. Apr 30. In November 2011, the United Nations Educational, Scientific and Cultural Organization (UNESCO) officially designated Apr 30 as International Jazz Day in order to highlight jazz and its diplomatic role of uniting people in all corners of the globe. This special day brings together communities, schools, artists, historians, academics and jazz enthusiasts worldwide to celebrate and learn about jazz and its roots, future and impact; raise awareness of the need for intercultural dialogue and mutual understanding; and reinforce international cooperation and communication. UNESCO and United Nations missions, embassies, government outposts, universities, libraries, schools, community centers and performing arts venues around the world will present special events for the eighth annual International Jazz Day on Apr 30, 2020, with a spectacular culminating celebration in Global Host City Sydney, Australia. More than one billion people around the world are reached annually through International Jazz Day programs and media coverage. Produced by the Thelonious Monk Institute of Jazz. For info: Thelonious Monk Institute of Jazz, 5225 Wisconsin Ave NW, Ste 605, Washington, DC 20015. E-mail: outreach@jazzday.com. Web: www.jazzday.com.

KANSAS BARBED WIRE SWAP/SELL AND FESTIVAL. Apr 30–May 3. La Crosse, KS. Barbed Wire Collectors Association show and meeting. Est attendance: 200. For info: Kansas Barbed Wire Collectors Assn, PO Box 578, La Crosse, KS 67548. Phone: (785) 222-9900. E-mail: barbedwiremuseum@rushcounty.org. Web: www.rushcounty.org/wireshow.

LILLY, WILLIAM: BIRTH ANNIVERSARY. Apr 30, 1602. (Old Style date.) English astrologer, author and almanac compiler, born at Diseworth, Leicestershire, England. His almanacs were among the most popular in Britain from 1644 until his death, June 9, 1681 (OS), at Hersham, Surrey, England.

LOUISIANA: ADMISSION DAY: ANNIVERSARY. Apr 30. Became 18th state in 1812.

LOUISIANA PURCHASE DAY: ANNIVERSARY. Apr 30, 1803. One of the greatest real estate deals in history was completed in 1803, when more than 820,000 square miles of the Louisiana Territory was turned over to the US by France, for $15 million. This almost doubled the size of the US, extending its western border to the Rocky Mountains.

MOON PHASE: FIRST QUARTER. Apr 30. Moon enters First Quarter phase at 4:38 PM, EDT.

MUHAMMAD ALI STRIPPED OF TITLE: ANNIVERSARY. Apr 30, 1967. Muhammad Ali was stripped of his world heavyweight boxing championship when he refused to be inducted into military service. Said Ali, "I have searched my conscience, and I find I cannot be true to my belief in my religion by accepting such a call." He had claimed exemption as a minister of the Black Muslim religion. He was convicted of violating the Selective Service Act, but the Supreme Court reversed this decision in 1971.

NATIONAL ANIMAL ADVOCACY DAY. Apr 30. The ASPCA's Government Relations department works closely with lawmakers and citizen advocates to secure the strongest possible protections for animals through the passage of humane legislation and regulations. We encourage all animal advocates to get involved in the legislative process and make a real difference for the animals in their community. Help the ASPCA enact meaningful protections for animals at the federal, state and local levels by celebrating National Animal Advocacy Day and being an effective voice for animals in the lawmaking process. Annually, Apr 30. For info: ASPCA, Media and Communications Dept, 520 8th Ave, 7th Fl, New York, NY 10018. Phone: (212) 876-7700. E-mail: press@aspca.org. Web: www.aspca.org.

NATIONAL HONESTY DAY (WITH HONEST ABE AWARDS). Apr 30. To celebrate honesty and those who are honest and honorable in their dealings with others. Nominations accepted for most honest people and companies. Winners to be acknowledged with "Honest Abe" awards and given "Abies" on National Honesty Day. Also presented are dishonorable mentions for notables who have been less than honest. Schools, religious organizations and the media are encouraged to make honesty a subject of discussion on or near this day. Annually, Apr 30. For info: M. Hirsh Goldberg, 3103

		S	M	T	W	T	F	S
April					1	2	3	4
		5	6	7	8	9	10	11
2020		12	13	14	15	16	17	18
		19	20	21	22	23	24	25
		26	27	28	29	30		

Szold Dr, Baltimore, MD 21208. Phone: (410) 486-4150 or (443) 286-5106. E-mail: mhgoldberg@comcast.net.

NATIONAL RAISIN DAY. Apr 30. The sweet, nutritious dried grape has been celebrated on Apr 30 since the early 1900s. For info: California Raisin Marketing Board, 2445 Capitol St, Ste 200, Fresno, CA 93721. Web: https://calraisins.org.

ORGANIZATION OF AMERICAN STATES FOUNDED: ANNIVERSARY. Apr 30, 1948. The OAS regional alliance was founded by 21 nations of the Americas at Bogotá, Colombia. Its purpose is to further economic development and integration among nations of the Western Hemisphere, to promote representative democracy and to help overcome poverty. The Pan-American Union, with offices at Washington, DC, serves as the General Secretariat for the OAS.

RANSOM, JOHN CROWE: BIRTH ANNIVERSARY. Apr 30, 1888. Influential and award-winning poet, professor and critic, born at Pulaski, TN. Part of the 1920–30s "New Criticism" movement, which gained its name from his book *The New Criticism*, published in 1941. Founded and edited *The Kenyon Review*. His *Selected Poems* received the National Book Award. Ransom died July 3, 1974, at Gambier, OH.

SOUTH VIETNAM FALLS TO VIETCONG: 45th ANNIVERSARY. Apr 30, 1975. The president of South Vietnam announced the country's unconditional surrender to the Vietcong. Communist troops moved into Saigon, and 1,000 Americans in the city were hastily evacuated. Thousands of South Vietnamese also tried to flee. The surrender announcement came 21 years after the 1954 Geneva agreements divided Vietnam into North and South. The last American troops had left South Vietnam in March 1973.

SWEDEN: FEAST OF VALBORG. Apr 30. An evening celebration in which Sweden "sings in the spring" by listening to traditional hymns to the spring, often around community bonfires. Also known as Walpurgis Night, the Feast of Valborg occurs annually Apr 30.

VIETNAM: LIBERATION DAY. Apr 30. National holiday. Commemorates the fall of Saigon to the Communists in 1975, ending the Vietnam War.

WALPURGIS NIGHT. Apr 30. The eve of May Day, which is the feast day of St. Walpurgis, the protectress against the magic arts. According to German legend, witches gather this night and celebrate their Sabbath on the highest peak in the Harz Mountains. Celebrated particularly by university students in northern Europe.

WASHINGTON, GEORGE: PRESIDENTIAL INAUGURATION ANNIVERSARY. Apr 30, 1789. George Washington was inaugurated as the first president of the US under the new Constitution at New York, NY. Robert R. Livingston administered the oath of office to Washington on the balcony of Federal Hall, at the corner of Wall and Broad streets.

WILSON, ELLIS: BIRTH ANNIVERSARY. Apr 30, 1899. African-American artist born at Mayfield, KY, and died at New York, NY, Jan 1, 1977. Wilson painted realistic portrayals of African Americans at work and at play. In 1944 he was awarded a Guggenheim fellowship. He visited South Carolina, painting city scenes and fishing towns. In the 1950s, Wilson took a revelatory trip to Haiti, which changed the way he painted. Unable to note any facial features on the Haitians he painted from a distance, Wilson began painting flat, stylized silhouettes. *Haitian Funeral Procession* remains Wilson's most popular and accessible painting.

BIRTHDAYS TODAY

Dianna Agron, 34, actress ("Glee," "Heroes"), born Savannah, GA, Apr 30, 1986.

Jane Campion, 66, director/screenwriter ("Top of the Lake," *The Piano*), born Wellington, New Zealand, Apr 30, 1954.

Carl XVI Gustaf, 74, King of Sweden, born Solna, Sweden, Apr 30, 1946.

Kirsten Dunst, 38, actress (*Spider-Man* films, *Marie Antoinette*, *The Cat's Meow*), born Point Pleasant, NJ, Apr 30, 1982.

Gal Gadot, 35, actress (*Wonder Woman*, *Batman v Superman*, *Furious 7*), born Rosh Ha'ayin, Israel, Apr 30, 1985.

Johnny Galecki, 45, actor ("The Big Bang Theory," "Roseanne," *Suicide Kings*), born Bree, Belgium, Apr 30, 1975.

António Guterres, 71, Secretary-General of the United Nations (2017–), born António Manuel de Oliveira Guterres at Lisbon, Portugal, Apr 30, 1949.

Stephen Harper, 61, 22nd prime minister of Canada (2006–15), born Toronto, ON, Canada, Apr 30, 1959.

Sam Heughan, 40, actor ("Outlander"), born New Galloway, Scotland, Apr 30, 1980.

Perry King, 72, actor (*Slaughterhouse Five*, *The Lords of Flatbush*, *Switch*), born Alliance, OH, Apr 30, 1948.

Cloris Leachman, 90, actress ("Raising Hope," "Phyllis," Oscar for *The Last Picture Show*), born Des Moines, IA, Apr 30, 1930.

Kunal Nayyar, 39, actor ("The Big Bang Theory"), born London, England, Apr 30, 1981.

Willie Nelson, 87, singer, actor (*Honeysuckle Rose*), born Abbott, TX, Apr 30, 1933.

Adrian Pasdar, 55, actor ("Heroes," "Judging Amy"), born Pittsfield, MA, Apr 30, 1965.

Isiah Thomas, 59, basketball coach and Hall of Fame player, born Chicago, IL, Apr 30, 1961.

Burt Young, 80, writer, actor (*Chinatown*, *Rocky*, *Once upon a Time in America*), born New York, NY, Apr 30, 1940.

May 1 — Friday

DAY 122	244 REMAINING

ADDISON, JOSEPH: BIRTH ANNIVERSARY. May 1, 1672. (Old Style date.) English essayist born at Milston, Wiltshire, England. Died at London, June 17, 1719 (OS). "We are," he wrote in *The Spectator*, "always doing something for Posterity, but I would fain see Posterity do something for us."

AMTRAK: ANNIVERSARY. May 1, 1971. Amtrak, the national rail service that combined the operations of 18 passenger railroads, went into service.

★ASIAN-AMERICAN AND PACIFIC ISLANDER HERITAGE MONTH. May 1–31. Presidential Proclamation issued honoring Asian/Pacific Americans each year since 1979. Public Law 102-450 of Oct 28, 1992, designated the observance for the month of May each year.

ASTHMA AWARENESS MONTH. May 1–31. Asthma is a chronic lung disease that makes it difficult to breathe. More than 25 million people in America have asthma—including more than seven million kids. Asthma is the third-leading cause of hospitalization among children under the age of 15 and is a leading cause of school absences. During May, the American Lung Association has set out to bring greater awareness of this disease, with information and resources people with asthma need to manage their asthma to live active, healthy lives. Join the effort to make a difference for people living with asthma. For info: American Lung Association. Phone: (800) LUNG-USA. Web: www.lung.org/asthma.

BATMAN DEBUTS: ANNIVERSARY. May 1, 1939. In the May 1 issue of *Detective Comics #27*, which appeared on newsstands a few days earlier, a new crime fighter, the "Batman," debuted, created by Bob Kane (collaborating with Bill Finger). The caped hero was an immediate success. See also: "Superman Debuts: Anniversary" (June 1).

CARPENTER, SCOTT: 95th BIRTH ANNIVERSARY. May 1, 1925. One of the original seven astronauts for NASA's Project Mercury, born at Boulder, CO. Carpenter trained to be a navy pilot during the final days of WWII, and then returned to the navy in 1949 to serve in Korea. He became a test pilot, then an intelligence officer, and then in 1959 was chosen to work for NASA. He was John Glenn's backup pilot on the first *Mercury* mission to orbit Earth in 1962 and then flew into orbit himself on May 24, 1962. He was the first astronaut to eat solid food in space, and his reentry proved nerve-racking when he had to use manual controls and landed 250 miles off course. At first he was feared dead, but was quickly discovered in a life raft by the USS *Intrepid*. In later years he worked for the Navy on SEALAB II as an aquanaut and deep-sea diver, and founded a company to utilize ocean resources. Carpenter died at Denver, CO, Oct 10, 2013.

CHOOSE PRIVACY WEEK. May 1–7. An initiative that invites library users into a national conversation about privacy rights in a digital age. The campaign gives libraries the tools they need to educate and engage users and gives citizens the resources to think critically and make more-informed choices about their privacy. Annually, May 1–7. For info: American Library Assn, Office of Intellectual Freedom. E-mail: oif@ala.org. Web: https://chooseprivacyweek.org or www.ala.org.

CITIZEN KANE FILM PREMIERE: ANNIVERSARY. May 1, 1941. Orson Welles's directorial masterpiece premiered at New York City's RKO Palace. The premiere had been delayed almost three months due to studio jitters about what media magnate William Randolph Hearst's reaction would be—since the film was a thinly disguised version of his life. The film's multiple points of view, deep-focus photography and witty script made it a favorite with critics at the time. John O'Hara in *Newsweek* said, "Your faithful bystander reports that he has just seen a picture which he thinks must be the best picture he ever saw." Nominated for nine Academy Awards, *Citizen Kane* won for Best Original Screenplay by Herman J. Mankiewicz and Welles. The film did not perform well commercially (due in part to Hearst's influence) but is now regarded as the greatest American film.

CLARK, MARK: BIRTH ANNIVERSARY. May 1, 1896. US general who served in both World Wars, Mark Clark was born at Madison Barracks, NY. In November 1942 he commanded the US forces taking part in the invasion of North Africa, and in January 1943 he became commander of the US Fifth Army, which invaded Italy in September 1943, taking Rome in June 1944. After the Germans capitulated in Italy, Clark was appointed commander of US occupation forces in Austria. He died at Charleston, SC, Apr 17, 1984.

COLUMBIAN EXPOSITION OPENING: ANNIVERSARY. May 1, 1893. At 12:08 PM President Grover Cleveland, in the presence of nearly a quarter of a million people, placed his finger on a golden key opening the Columbian Exposition at Chicago, IL. Amid the unfurling of thousands of flags, sounding of trumpets and booming of cannons, the key activated an electromagnetic valve, steam rushed into great cylinders and an immense pump began its enormous burden of pumping 15 million gallons of water a day to provide the 685-acre fair and its visitors with an ample water supply.

DANDELION MAY FEST. May 1–2. Dover, OH. Old-fashioned festival includes cooking demonstrations, live entertainment and food booths featuring dishes made from dandelions, such as dandelion coffee ice cream, dandelion pizza and dandelion gravy. Also, dandelion wine and jelly tasting, dandelion picking contests for the kids, family entertainment and 5k fun run. Est attendance: 15,000. For info: Anita Davis, Coord, Der Marktplatz-Breitenbach Wine Cellars, 5773 Old Rte 39 NW, Dover, OH 44622. Phone: (330) 343-3603. Fax: (330) 343-8290. E-mail: info@breitenbachwine.com. Web: www.dandelionfestival.com.

ENGLAND: MITSUBISHI MOTORS BADMINTON HORSE TRIALS. May 1–5. Badminton, Gloucestershire. First held in 1949. Famous international horse trials consisting of show jumping, cross-country and dressage. Est attendance: 180,000. For info: Box Office, Badminton Horse Trials, Badminton, Glos, England GL9 1DF. Phone: (44) (1454) 218272. E-mail: info@badminton-horse.co.uk. Web: www.badminton-horse.co.uk.

FIBROMYALGIA EDUCATION AND AWARENESS MONTH. May 1–31. To promote education and awareness of the dangers of fibromyalgia, which is also known as fibromyalgia syndrome, fibrositis or chronic muscle pain syndrome. Fibromyalgia affects more than 12 million American women. Sponsored by the American College of Apothecaries (ACA)/Pharmacists Planning Service, Inc (PPSI). For info: ACA/PPSI, 2830 Summer Oaks Dr, Bartlett, TN 38134. E-mail: info@ppsinc.org. Web: www.ppsinc.org.

FIRST SKYSCRAPER: ANNIVERSARY. May 1, 1884. Construction was begun on the Home Insurance Company building on this date in Chicago, IL. The 10-story building was completed in 1885. Designed by William Le Baron Jenney, it had a steel frame that carried the weight of the building. The walls provided no support but hung like curtains on the metal frame. This method of construction revolutionized American architecture and allowed architects to build taller and taller buildings. The Home Insurance Building was demolished in 1931.

FORD, GLENN: BIRTH ANNIVERSARY. May 1, 1916. Born at Sainte-Christine, QC, Canada, Ford was a popular Hollywood actor who appeared in more than 100 films. Important films include *Gilda* with Rita Hayworth, *Blackboard Jungle* with Sidney Poitier, *3:10 to Yuma* and *The Rounders*. He won a Golden Globe Award in 1962 for his leading role in Frank Capra's *Pocketful of Miracles*. He died at Hollywood, CA, Aug 30, 2006.

GARDENING FOR WILDLIFE MONTH. May 1–31. Be it an apartment balcony or a 20-acre farm, any space can accommodate a garden that attracts beautiful wildlife and helps restore habitat in commercial and residential areas. By providing food, water, cover and a place for wildlife to raise their young, not only do you help wildlife, but also your garden may qualify to become an official Certified Wildlife Habitat. During May, the National Wildlife Federation sponsors this month to inspire and assist all who are passionate about wildlife to make a difference right in their own backyard. For info: National Wildlife Federation. Web: www.nwf.org.

GEORGE MALLORY FOUND ON EVEREST: ANNIVERSARY. May 1, 1999. On June 8, 1924, British mountaineers George Mallory and Andrew Irvine began their final ascent of Mount Everest in Nepal—Mallory hoping to become the first human to reach the top. But both men disappeared in a snowstorm and were never seen again. On this date in 1999, Conrad Anker of the Mallory and Irvine Research Expedition (an endeavor sponsored by the BBC) found the remains of a frozen, mummified body wearing antique clothing that bore labels of "G.L. Mallory." The evidence—broken bones and contusions—indicated Mallory died in a fall, but unknown is whether Mallory (and Irvine) died on the way up the summit or on the way down. After a simple Anglican service, the expedition team covered Mallory with rocks and scree. Irvine has never been found.

GET CAUGHT READING MONTH. May 1–31. Launched in 1999, this month is a nationwide campaign to remind people of all ages how much fun it is to read. Because of research indicating that early language experience actually stimulates a child's brain to grow and that reading to children gives them a huge advantage when they start school, we hope to encourage people of all ages to enjoy books and magazines and to share that pleasure with the young children in their lives. For info: Every Child a Reader, 54 W 39th St, 14th Fl, New York, NY 10018. E-mail: carl.lennertz@cbcbooks.org. Web: www.getcaughtreading.org.

GIFTS FROM THE GARDEN MONTH. May 1–31. May is the month to celebrate the many ways gardens and gardening benefit people. From flowers and fitness to color and conversation, many treasures are growing in your own backyard. For info: C.L. Fornari, PO Box 355, Osterville, MA 02655. Phone: (508) 428-5895. E-mail: clfornari@yahoo.com. Web: www.gardenlady.com.

GLOBAL CIVILITY AWARENESS MONTH. May 1–31. Champion civility with 31 days of considerate conduct by practicing behavior and communication to inspire, involve and impact campuses, corporations and communities worldwide. Inspire civility because civility counts. For info: Image Impact International, 474 W 238th St, #6I, Riverdale, NY 10463. Phone: (718) 530-3500. Web: www.image-impact.org.

GREAT BRITAIN FORMED: ANNIVERSARY. May 1, 1707. (Old Style date.) A union between England and Scotland resulted in the formation of Great Britain. (Wales had been part of England since the 1500s.) Today's United Kingdom consists of Great Britain and Northern Ireland.

HUG YOUR CAT DAY. May 1. Cats act as if they don't want or need attention—but they do. Apricat, the pampered star of her own book series, has created a special day for humans to hug their cats without fear of scratches or hisses. Annually, May 1—May Day. For info: Marisa D'Vari, NewOak, 575 Fifth Ave, 15th Fl, New York, NY 10017. E-mail: mdvari@newoak.com.

HUNTINGTON'S DISEASE AWARENESS MONTH. May 1–31. Sponsored by the Huntington's Disease Society of America, a month spotlighting this devastating hereditary, degenerative brain disorder for which there is, at present, no cure. For info: Huntington's Disease Society of America, 505 Eighth Ave, Ste 902, New York, NY 10018. Phone: (212) 242-1968. E-mail: hdsainfo@hdsa.org. Web: www.hdsa.org.

INTERNATIONAL MEDITERRANEAN DIET MONTH. May 1–31. Traditional diets from the lands surrounding the Mediterranean Sea abound in olive oil, vegetables, fish, whole grains and other healthy foods. Decades of scientific research have shown that the Mediterranean Diet ("Med Diet") is one of the world's healthiest ways to eat. During International Mediterranean Diet Month, Oldways and the Mediterranean Foods Alliance offer education and promotions to consumers, retailers and health professionals to celebrate a way of eating that is both delicious and healthy. For info: Oldways, 266 Beacon St, Boston, MA 02116. Phone: (617) 421-5500. E-mail: media@oldwayspt.org. Web: https://oldwayspt.org/programs/mediterranean-program.

INTERNATIONAL VICTORIOUS WOMAN MONTH. May 1–31. Celebrating every woman who has shaped her challenges into victories. Events during this month include the 21-Day Victory Challenge, International Victorious Woman Contest and The Victorious Woman Project's annual celebration, The Girlfriend Gala (May 20, 2020). For info: Annmarie Kelly, The Victorious Woman Project. E-mail: info@victoriouswoman.com. Web: www.victorious-woman.com.

ISLE OF EIGHT FLAGS SHRIMP FESTIVAL. May 1–3. Fernandina Beach, FL, on beautiful Amelia Island. Festival commemorates Fernandina's role as the birthplace of the modern shrimping industry. Events include juried fine arts and crafts show, entertainment, antiques/vintage items, pirates, Kids Fun Zone and lots of food and shrimp. Pirate Parade is Apr 30. Est attendance: 150,000. For info: Isle of Eight Flags Shrimp Festival, PO Box 6146, Fernandina Beach, FL 32035. E-mail: 4info@shrimpfestival.com. Web: www.shrimpfestival.com.

ITALY: FESTIVAL OF SAINT EFISIO. May 1–4. Cagliari, Sardinia. Dating from 1656, this is one of the biggest and most colorful religious processions in the world. Several thousand pilgrims on foot, in carts and on horseback in traditional costume accompany the statue of the saint through the streets. The festival honors Saint Efisio for saving the city of Cagliari from the plague that in the 1650s took more than 10,000 lives.

JAPAN: REIWA ERA BEGINS: ANNIVERSARY. May 1, 2019. After the abdication of Emperor Akihito on Apr 30, 2019, Crown Prince Naruhito became emperor. The Heisei Era ended and the Reiwa ("Fortunate Harmony") began.

★**JEWISH-AMERICAN HERITAGE MONTH.** May 1–31. Formerly celebrated as Jewish Heritage Week.

JONES, MARY HARRIS (MOTHER JONES): BIRTH ANNIVERSARY. May 1, 1830. Irish-born American labor leader. After the death of her husband and four children (during the Memphis yellow fever epidemic of 1867) and loss of her belongings in the Chicago Fire in 1871, Jones devoted her energies and her life to organizing and advancing the cause of labor. It seemed she was present wherever there were labor troubles. She gave her last speech on her 100th birthday. Born at Cork, Ireland, she died Nov 30, 1930, at Silver Spring, MD.

KEEP KIDS ALIVE—DRIVE 25® DAY. May 1. 13th annual. Keep Kids Alive—Drive 25® Day is a call to action on the part of citizens in communities of all sizes across the US to commit to safe driving behaviors on neighborhood streets. Communities develop activities to educate and engage citizens in the effort through neighborhoods, schools, businesses and civic organizations. In many communities law enforcement and public officials take the lead. Annually, May 1. For info: Keep Kids Alive—Drive 25. E-mail: kkad25@kkad25.org. Web: www.KeepKidsAliveDrive25.org.

LABOR DAY. May 1. In 140 countries, May 1 is observed as a workers' holiday. When it falls on a Saturday or Sunday, the following Monday is observed as a holiday. Bermuda, Canada and the US are the only countries that observe Labor Day in September. The Bahamas observe Labor Day in June.

★**LAW DAY, USA.** May 1. Presidential Proclamation issued each year for May 1 since 1958 at request. (Public Law 87–20 of Apr 7, 1961.)

LAW ENFORCEMENT APPRECIATION MONTH IN FLORIDA. May 1–31. Law Enforcement Appreciation Day is May 15 in Florida, a ceremonial day.

LEI DAY. May 1. Hawaii. On this special day—the Hawaiian version of May Day—leis are made, worn, given, displayed and entered in lei-making contests. One of the most popular Lei Day celebrations takes place at Honolulu at Kapiolani Park at Waikiki. Includes the state's largest lei contest, the crowning of the Lei Day Queen, Hawaiian music, hula and flowers galore.

★**LOYALTY DAY.** May 1. Presidential Proclamation issued annually for May 1 since 1959 at request. (Public Law 85–529 of July 18, 1958.) An earlier proclamation was issued in 1955.

MARSHALL ISLANDS, REPUBLIC OF THE: CONSTITUTION DAY. May 1. National holiday.

MAY DAY. May 1. The first day of May has been observed as a holiday since ancient times. Spring festivals, maypoles and maying are still common, but the political importance of May Day has grown since the 1880s, when it became a workers' day in the US. Now widely observed in countries as a workers' holiday or as Labor Day. (Bermuda, Canada and the US observe Labor Day in September.) In most European countries, when May Day falls on Saturday or Sunday, the Monday following is observed as a holiday, with bank and store closings, parades and other festivities.

MAY ONE DAY. May 1. Since 2016, May One Day is an annual celebration for children to "Choose a dream, take a step, make a reality." A day of encouragement for schoolchildren and their parents. Observance includes book drives, art projects, author visits and more. Annually, May 1. For info: Lenora Riegel, Coordinator, May One Day, 466 Glen Mary Dr, Owego, NY 13827. Web: www.mayoneday.org.

MENTAL HEALTH MONTH. May 1–31. Mental Health Month was created in 1949 by Mental Health America to raise awareness about mental health conditions and the importance of mental wellness and promoting good mental health for all. One in five American adults lives with a diagnosable, treatable mental health condition. For info: Mental Health America, 500 Montgomery St, Ste 820, Alexandria, VA 22314. Phone: (800) 969-6642 or (703) 684-7722. Web: www.mentalhealthamerica.net/may.

MISSION SAN ANTONIO DE VALERO FOUNDED: ANNIVERSARY. May 1, 1718. This mission (later known as the Alamo) was founded by Franciscans in the state of Coahuila and Texas, New Spain. The mission and four later ones formed the community that became San Antonio, TX.

MOTHER GOOSE DAY. May 1. To reappreciate the old nursery rhymes. Motto: "Either alone or in sharing, read childhood nursery favorites and feel the warmth of Mother Goose's embrace." Annually, May 1. (Created by Gloria T. Delamar.)

MOTORCYCLE SAFETY MONTH. May 1–31. This month is dedicated to encouraging safe motorcycle-riding practices. Learn safe riding practices through state and local motorcycle-safety courses and continue improving skills through advanced riding courses. Set a safe environment this month to prepare for a safe riding season. For info: Sylvia Henderson, 3570 Olney-Laytonsville Rd, Ste 588, Olney, MD 20832. Phone: (301) 260-1538. E-mail: motosylvia@aol.com.

MYSTERY MONTH. May 1–31. 10th annual. A month dedicated to the mystery genre in literature and its authors. Sponsored by *Booklist Reader* and celebrated by libraries all over with special programming, including author visits, book-group discussions, displays and more. If you haven't read a mystery lately, investigate this month for criminally good fiction! For info: *The Booklist Reader*, 50 E Huron St, Chicago, IL 60611. Web: www.booklistreader.com.

NATIONAL ALLERGY/ASTHMA AWARENESS MONTH. May 1–31. The change of season to spring reminds us that it's not only time to venture out again, but also time for spring cleaning to reduce allergic triggers that cause stuffy noses and asthma flare-ups. Layers of dust, mildew and other allergen-harboring substances may cling to upholstered furniture and bedding in tightly closed and insulated homes. Furnaces, air conditioners and heating/cooling ducts can harbor dust, mold and bacteria, while carpets collect pet dander, dirt and dust mites. Sponsored by the American College of Apothecaries (ACA)/Pharmacists Planning Service, Inc (PPSI). For info: ACA/PPSI, 2830 Summer Oaks Dr, Bartlett, TN 38134. E-mail: info@ppsinc.org. Web: www.ppsinc.org.

NATIONAL ARTHRITIS AWARENESS MONTH. May 1–31. An annual observance founded by Presidential Proclamation in 1972, this month aims to focus attention on the nation's leading cause of disability—one that affects more than 50 million adults and nearly 300,000 children in the US. Arthritis costs the US economy $128 billion each year and is a more frequent cause of activity limitation than heart disease, cancer or diabetes. During the month of May, the Arthritis Foundation hosts the Walk to Cure Arthritis in more than 100 cities nationwide to raise funds for programs, research and advocacy initiatives to find a cure. For info: Arthritis Foundation, 1355 Peachtree St NE, Ste 600, Atlanta, GA 30309. Phone: (404) 872-7100. Web: www.arthritis.org.

NATIONAL BARBECUE MONTH. May 1–31. May is the beginning of peak grilling season as home cooks take to their backyards to fire

May 2020	S	M	T	W	T	F	S
						1	2
	3	4	5	6	7	8	9
	10	11	12	13	14	15	16
	17	18	19	20	21	22	23
	24	25	26	27	28	29	30
	31						

up a quick weeknight meal or a low and slow weekend feast with friends and family. Seven in 10 US adults own a grill or smoker, and in Canada, ownership is 8 in 10. Annually, the month of May. For info: Hearth, Patio & Barbecue Assn, 1901 N Moore St, Ste 600, Arlington, VA 22209. Phone: (703) 522-0086. Web: www.hpba.org.

NATIONAL BIKE MONTH. May 1–31. Since 1956, a celebration of bicycling for fun, fitness and transportation. Local activities sponsored by bicycling organizations, environmental groups, PTAs, police departments, health organizations and civic groups. About 5 million participants nationwide. Annually, the month of May. For info: League of American Bicyclists, 1612 K St NW, Ste 1102, Washington, DC 20006. Phone: (202) 822-1333. E-mail: stevetaylor@bikeleague.org. Web: www.bikeleague.org/bikemonth.

NATIONAL BUBBA DAY. May 1. Comedian T. Bubba Bechtol has created a holiday for Bubbas and Bubbettes everywhere. Annually, May 1. For info: T. Bubba Bechtol, 339 Panferio Dr, Pensacola Beach, FL 32561. Phone: (850) 572-4119. E-mail: tbubba@tbubba.com. Web: www.tbubba.com.

NATIONAL FOSTER CARE MONTH. May 1–31. A time to renew our commitment to ensuring a bright future for the more than 400,000 children and youth in foster care and celebrate all those who make a meaningful difference in their lives. For info: Children's Bureau, Administration for Children and Families, US Department of Health and Human Services. Web: www.childwelfare.gov/fostercaremonth.

NATIONAL GOOD CAR-KEEPING MONTH. May 1–31. To promote increased safety and value through good car maintenance. For info: A.B. Allen, Good Car-Keeping Institute, 1313 Oak Ave, #2L, Evanston, IL 60201-4245. Phone: (847) 869-9755. E-mail: adrienne@adbridon.com.

NATIONAL HAMBURGER MONTH. May 1–31. Sponsored by White Castle, the original fast-food hamburger chain (founded in 1921), to pay tribute to one of America's favorite foods. With or without condiments, on or off a bun or bread, hamburgers have grown in popularity since the early 1920s and are now an American meal mainstay. For info: White Castle Management Co, Marketing Dept, 555 W Goodale St, Columbus, OH 43215-1158. Phone: (614) 228-5781. Web: www.whitecastle.com.

NATIONAL HEPATITIS AWARENESS MONTH. May 1–31. A month to raise awareness of and increase research on viral hepatitis, while also promoting prevention through schools, health departments, churches, community organizations and other groups. Hepatitis Testing Day is May 19. For info: Centers for Disease Control and Prevention. Web: www.cdc.gov/hepatitis/heppromoresources.htm.

NATIONAL MEDITATION MONTH. May 1–31. A monthlong campaign to educate the public about the physical, emotional and mental benefits of meditation. Sponsored by The Deep Calm, an organization committed to creating awareness about meditation and its link to inner peace and peace in the world. Annually, in May. For info: Elesa Commerse, The Deep Calm, 4258 W High Bridge Ln, Ste 100, Chicago, IL 60646-6041. Phone: (773) 777-7754. E-mail: info@thedeepcalm.com. Web: www.thedeepcalm.com.

NATIONAL MILITARY APPRECIATION MONTH. May 1–31. This month honors, remembers, recognizes and appreciates all military personnel—those men and women who have served throughout our history and all who now serve in uniform and their families as well as those Americans who have given their lives in defense of the freedoms we all enjoy today.

NATIONAL OSTEOPOROSIS MONTH. May 1–31. Osteoporosis is not a natural part of aging. Find out what you can do to prevent, diagnose and treat it by joining the NOF family. For info: Natl Osteoporosis Foundation, 251 18th St S, Ste 630, Arlington, VA 22202. Phone: (800) 231-4222. E-mail: info@nof.org. Web: www.nof.org.

NATIONAL PHYSICAL FITNESS AND SPORTS MONTH. May 1–31. Get moving in May! This month encourages individuals and organizations to promote fitness activities and programs. Popularly known as "May Month," it was established by the President's Council on Physical Fitness and Sports in 1983. #MoveInMay. For info: President's Council on Fitness, Sports and Nutrition. Phone: (240) 276-9567. E-mail: fitness@hhs.gov. Web: www.fitness.gov or www.presidentschallenge.org.

NATIONAL PRESERVATION MONTH. May 1–31. To draw public attention to historic preservation, including neighborhoods, districts, landmark buildings, open space and maritime heritage. The National Trust for Historic Preservation encourages preservation and Main Street organizations to use this month to showcase how they are celebrating and saving historic places year-round. For info: Natl Trust for Historic Preservation, 2600 Virginia Ave NW, Ste 1100, Washington, DC 20037. Phone: (202) 588-6000. E-mail: info@savingplaces.org. Web: www.savingplaces.org.

NATIONAL READ TO YOUR BABY BUMP MONTH. May 1–31. A preliteracy initiative to encourage mothers-to-be to read to their babies in the womb. Inclusive in this initiative is an educational movement, service projects and, ultimately, a world record with the most mothers-to-be reading to their baby bumps. For info: Corletia Dunlap-Banks. E-mail: nyobee472@gmail.com. Web: https://readtoyourbabybump.blogspot.com.

NATIONAL SALAD MONTH. May 1–31. Since 1992. Celebrate healthy eating and good nutrition with salads and salad dressing in May and all year long. For info: Association for Dressings and Sauces.. E-mail: ads@kellencompany.com. Web: www.dressings-sauces.org.

NATIONAL VINEGAR MONTH. May 1–31. Celebrate the season of cooking and cleaning with one of the home's most versatile products. For info: The Vinegar Institute, 3200 Windy Hill Rd, Ste 600 W, Atlanta, GA 30339. Phone: (404) 252-3663. E-mail: info@versatilevinegar.org. Web: www.versatilevinegar.org.

NEW HOME OWNER'S DAY. May 1. You have faced all the challenges—now take the time as a new home owner to stand back and reflect on your new home and savor the feeling. For info: Dorothy Zjawin, 61 W Colfax Ave, Roselle Park, NJ 07204.

★OLDER AMERICANS MONTH. May 1–31. Presidential Proclamation; from 1963 through 1973 this was called "Senior Citizens Month." In May 1974 it became Older Americans Month. In 1980 the title included Senior Citizens Day, which was observed May 8, 1980. Issued annually since 1963.

ORANGEBURG FESTIVAL OF ROSES. May 1–3. Edisto Memorial Gardens, Orangeburg, SC. 49th annual. This annual event celebrates the blooming of Orangeburg's beautiful roses and the beginning of a yearlong opportunity to enjoy the natural setting of the Edisto Memorial Gardens along the banks of the Edisto River, the longest black-water river in the world. Est attendance: 30,000. For info: Orangeburg Festival of Roses Committee, PO Box 328, Orangeburg, SC 29116-0328. Phone: (803) 534-6821 or (800) 545-6153. E-mail: chamber@orangeburgsc.net.

PAAR, JACK: BIRTH ANNIVERSARY. May 1, 1918. Radio personality, actor and humorist Jack Paar began hosting "The Tonight Show" on NBC in 1957. With his catchphrase "I kid you not," he revolutionized late-night television, changing the format of traditional late shows from variety hours to talk shows and charming his audience and celebrity guests with a witty interviewing style. Paar introduced dozens of new stars to the American public, including Bill Cosby, Woody Allen, Carol Burnett and the Smothers Brothers. He left the show in 1962, handing it over to Johnny Carson,

and retired from show business a few years later. Born at Canton, OH, he died at Greenwich, CT, Jan 27, 2004.

PHILIPPINES: FEAST OF OUR LADY OF PEACE AND GOOD VOYAGE. May 1–31. Pilgrimage to the shrine of Nuestra Sra de la Paz y Buen Viaje at Antipolo, Rizal.

PHILIPPINES: SANTACRUZAN. May 1–31. Maytime pageant-procession that recalls the quest of Queen Helena and Prince Constantine for the Holy Cross.

REACT MONTH. May 1–31. Celebrates the radio safety efforts of volunteer REACT Teams worldwide. REACT monitors receive emergency radio calls from motorists, boaters, hikers, etc, and relay them to authorities. REACTers also teach correct emergency radio procedure to the public. REACT Teams provide two-way radio safety communications for local events, parades, walkathons, etc, on request. REACT also offers speakers on radio safety to community groups. REACT Teams welcome new members keen to help authorities and serve their communities with two-way radio. No experience needed. REACT will train you. For info: REACT International, Inc, PO Box 21064, Glendale, CA 91221-5164. Phone: (301) 316-2900 or (866) 732-2899. E-mail: RI.HQ@REACTintl.org. Web: www.REACTintl.org.

RICHMOND'S MUSHROOM FESTIVAL. May 1–2. Richmond, MO. Parade, arts and crafts, carnival, food vendors, car show, bands and stage shows. Est attendance: 15,000. For info: Richmond Area Chamber of Commerce, 104 W North Main St, Richmond, MO 64085. Phone: (816) 776-6916. Fax: (816) 776-6917. E-mail: director@richmondchamber.org. Web: www.richmondchamber.org.

RUSSIA: INTERNATIONAL LABOR DAY. May 1–2. Public holiday in Russian Federation. Official May Day demonstrations of working people.

SAVE YOUR TOOTH MONTH. May 1–31. This month enables endodontists (specialty dentists who provide root canal treatment) to proactively talk, educate the community and build relationships with other partners to emphasize that your natural teeth are worth saving. Endodontists provide a relaxing and virtually pain-free experience that saves natural teeth. For info: American Assn of Endodontists, 180 N Stetson Ave, Ste 1500, Chicago, IL 60601. Phone: (800) 872-3636. E-mail: info@aae.org. Web: www.aae.org.

SCHOOL PRINCIPALS' DAY. May 1. A day of recognition for all elementary, middle and high school principals for their leadership and dedication in providing the best education possible for their students. Annually, May 1. For info: Janet M. Dellaria, PhD, PO Box 39, Trout Creek, MI 49967. Phone: (808) 987-1908. E-mail: janshine@yahoo.com.

SKIN CANCER AWARENESS MONTH. May 1–31. A month to focus on skin cancer. Current estimates are that one in five Americans will develop skin cancer. You can prevent and detect skin cancer with (1) prevention: seek shade, cover up and wear sunscreen; (2) detection: look for new or changing spots on your skin; and (3) awareness: see a dermatologist if you notice anything changing, itching or bleeding. For info: American Academy of Dermatology, PO Box 1968, Des Plaines, IL 60017. Web: www.aad.org.

SMITH, KATE: BIRTH ANNIVERSARY. May 1, 1909. One of America's most popular singers, Kate Smith, who never took a formal music lesson, recorded more songs than any other performer (more than 3,000), made more than 15,000 radio broadcasts and received more than 25 million fan letters. On Nov 11, 1938, she introduced a new song during her regular radio broadcast, written especially for her by Irving Berlin: "God Bless America." It soon became the unofficial national anthem. Born Kathryn Elizabeth Smith at Greenville, VA, she began her radio career May 1, 1931, with "When the

Moon Comes over the Mountain," a song identified with her throughout her career. She died at Raleigh, NC, June 17, 1986.

SPIRITUAL LITERACY MONTH. May 1–31. Promoting respect for and among the world's religions and spiritual traditions by encouraging people to read the "book of the world" for sacred meaning. Practice Circles are set up in libraries, community centers, houses of worship, homes and online sites. For info: Mary Ann Brussat, Spiritual Literacy Project, 223 W Foothill Blvd, 2nd Fl, Claremont, CA 91711. Phone: (917) 447-8800. E-mail: brussat@spiritualityandpractice.com.

STRIKE OUT STROKES MONTH. May 1–31. Dedicated to the prevention of strokes. Factors resulting from heredity or natural processes can't be changed, but with proper medical treatment, early detection and healthful lifestyle adjustments, some risk factors can be eliminated. Sponsored by the American College of Apothecaries (ACA)/Pharmacists Planning Service, Inc (PPSI). For info: ACA/PPSI, 2830 Summer Oaks Dr, Bartlett, TN 38134. E-mail: info@ppsinc.org. Web: www.ppsinc.org.

U-2 INCIDENT: 60th ANNIVERSARY. May 1, 1960. On the eve of a summit meeting between US president Dwight D. Eisenhower and Soviet premier Nikita Khrushchev, a U-2 espionage plane flying at about 60,000 feet was shot down over Sverdlovsk, in central USSR. The pilot, CIA agent Francis Gary Powers, survived the crash, as did large parts of the aircraft, a suicide kit and sophisticated surveillance equipment. The sensational event, which US officials described as a weather reconnaissance flight gone astray, resulted in cancellation of the summit meeting. Powers was tried, convicted and sentenced to 10 years in prison by a Moscow court. In 1962 he was returned to the US in exchange for an imprisoned Soviet spy. See also: "'Bridge of Spies' Prisoner Swap: Anniversary" (Feb 10) and "Powers, Francis Gary: Birth Anniversary" (Aug 17).

ULTRAVIOLET AWARENESS MONTH. May 1–31. Exposure to UV rays can burn delicate eye tissue and raise the risk of developing cataracts and cancers of the eye. Protecting your eyes from UV dangers by choosing the right sunglasses is the message of this month. For info: Prevent Blindness, 211 W Wacker Dr, Ste 1700, Chicago, IL 60606. Phone: (800) 331-2020. E-mail: info@preventblindness.org. Web: www.preventblindness.org.

WILLIAMS, ARCHIE: BIRTH ANNIVERSARY. May 1, 1915. Archie Williams, along with Jesse Owens and others, debunked Hitler's theory of the superiority of Aryan athletes at the 1936 Berlin Olympics. As a black member of the US team, Williams won a gold medal by running the 400-meter in 46.5 seconds (0.4 second slower than his own record of earlier that year). Williams, who was born at Oakland, CA, earned a degree in mechanical engineering from the University of California–Berkeley in 1939 but had to dig ditches for a time because companies weren't hiring black engineers. He became an airplane pilot and for 22 years trained Tuskegee Institute pilots, including the black air corps of WWII. When asked during a 1981 interview about his treatment by the Nazis during the 1936 Olympics, he replied, "I didn't have to ride in the back of the bus over there." Archie Williams died June 24, 1993, at Fairfax, CA.

WOMEN'S HEALTH CARE MONTH. May 1–31. To initiate a public education campaign devoted to increasing awareness of the many health concerns unique to women. Focus will be on the prevention

		S	M	T	W	T	F	S
May							1	2
		3	4	5	6	7	8	9
2020		10	11	12	13	14	15	16
		17	18	19	20	21	22	23
		24	25	26	27	28	29	30
		31						

of the major causes of death and poor health among women—heart disease, cancer, arthritis, osteoporosis and bone fractures—as well as on depression and alcoholism in women. Annually, the month of May. Sponsored by the American College of Apothecaries (ACA)/Pharmacists Planning Service, Inc (PPSI). For info: ACA/PPSI, 2830 Summer Oaks Dr, Bartlett, TN 38134. E-mail: info@ppsinc.org. Web: www.ppsinc.org.

YOUNG ACHIEVERS/LEADERS OF TOMORROW MONTH. May 1–31. International Leadership Network's Young Achievers/Leaders of Tomorrow Program recognizes and encourages positive achievement, behavior, leadership and service. Community and national recognition events honor more than a thousand student leaders in grades 5–11. Annually, the month of May. For info: Tom Eichhorst, PO Box 190216, St. Louis, MO 63119-6216. Phone: (314) 961-5978. E-mail: ilnleadnet@aol.com. Web: www.ilnleadnet.com.

🎂 BIRTHDAYS TODAY

Wes Anderson, 51, director, screenwriter (*Isle of Dogs*, *The Grand Budapest Hotel*, *The Royal Tenenbaums*), born Houston, TX, May 1, 1969.

Steve Cauthen, 60, former jockey, born Walton, KY, May 1, 1960.

Judy Collins, 81, singer, born Seattle, WA, May 1, 1939.

Rita Coolidge, 75, singer, born Nashville, TN, May 1, 1945.

Jamie Dornan, 38, actor (*Fifty Shades of Grey*, "The Fall"), model, born Holywood, Northern Ireland, May 1, 1982.

Curtis Martin, 47, former football player, born Pittsburgh, PA, May 1, 1973.

Bobbie Ann Mason, 80, writer (*In Country*, *The Girl in the Blue Beret*), born Mayfield, KY, May 1, 1940.

Tim McGraw, 53, country singer, born Delhi, LA, May 1, 1967.

Shahar Peer, 33, former tennis player, born Jerusalem, Israel, May 1, 1987.

Charlie Schlatter, 54, actor ("Diagnosis Murder"), born Englewood, NJ, May 1, 1966.

Paul Teutul, Sr, 71, motorcycle designer, television personality ("American Chopper"), born Yonkers, NY, May 1, 1949.

May 2 — Saturday

DAY 123   **243 REMAINING**

BERLIN SURRENDERS: 75th ANNIVERSARY. May 2, 1945. At 6:45 AM, Soviet marshal Georgi Zhukov accepted the surrender of Berlin, the German capital. The victory came at a terrible cost for the Red Army, with 304,887 men killed, wounded or missing—10 percent of its soldiers. About 125,000 Berliners died in the siege, many by suicide.

CHINCOTEAGUE SEAFOOD FESTIVAL. May 2. Toms Cove Park, Chincoteague Island, VA. 52nd annual. This festival promotes the seafood industry on Virginia's Eastern Shore. Enjoy fresh, local seafood. Renowned festival cooks, volunteers and professionals prepare exciting offerings and signature dishes from local restaurants as well as old and new Eastern Shore favorites. Littleneck steamed clams, a long-time festival staple, are available along with clam chowder, fried fish, steamed shrimp, clam strips, raw clams and oysters, grilled chicken and boardwalk fries, corn bread, hush puppies and more. Tickets will sell out. Annually, the first Saturday in May. Est attendance: 3,000. For info: Chincoteague Chamber of Commerce, 6733 Maddox Blvd, Chincoteague, VA 23336. Phone: (757) 336-6161. Fax: (757) 336-1242. E-mail: info@chincoteaguechamber.com. Web: www.chincoteaguechamber.com.

COTTON PICKIN' FAIR. May 2–3 (also Oct 3–4). Gay Family Farmstead, Gay, GA. The Cotton Pickin' Fair is a national award–winning festival held continuously since 1972. Some 350 exhibits provide an exciting range of art, antiques and crafts nestled in and around interesting farm buildings dating from 1891. Delicious southern foods cooked on site and excellent regional entertainment combine to make a truly unique family outing and a historic farm country experience. Est attendance: 35,000. For info: Cotton Pickin' Fair, PO Box 1, Gay, GA 30218. Phone: (706) 538-6814. E-mail: info@cpfair.org. Web: www.cpfair.org.

FREE COMIC BOOK DAY. May 2. Since 2002, thousands of independent comic book stores around the world give out free comic books to children. Annually, the first Saturday in May. For info: Diamond Comic Distributors. E-mail: gashton@diamondcomics.com (press). Web: www.freecomicbookday.com.

GALVESTON HISTORIC HOMES TOUR. May 2–3 (also May 9–10). Galveston Island, TX. 46th annual. Discover Galveston Island's great treasures of Victorian and post-Victorian architecture as privately owned homes are opened to the public for tours. Annually, the first two full weekends in May. Est attendance: 5,000. For info: Galveston Historical Foundation, 2228 Broadway, Galveston, TX 77550. Phone: (409) 765-3404. E-mail: foundation@galveston-history.org. Web: www.galvestonhistory.org.

GEHRIG'S STREAK ENDS: ANNIVERSARY. May 2, 1939. New York Yankees first baseman Lou Gehrig asked manager Joe McCarthy to take him out of the lineup for the game against the Detroit Tigers. By his sitting out, Gehrig's record streak of consecutive games played, begun May 25, 1925, stopped at 2,130. The slugger complained of fatigue, but he was really suffering from ALS, amyotrophic lateral sclerosis, a condition later known as Lou Gehrig's disease. Gehrig never played again.

KENTUCKY DERBY. May 2. Churchill Downs, Louisville, KY. The 146th running of America's premier Thoroughbred horse race, inaugurated in 1875. First jewel in the Triple Crown, traditionally followed by the Preakness (second Saturday after the Derby) and the Belmont Stakes (fifth Saturday after the Derby). Annually, the first Saturday in May. Est attendance: 150,000. For info: Churchill Downs, 700 Central Ave, Louisville, KY 40208. Phone: (502) 636-4400. Web: kentuckyderby.com.

KING JAMES BIBLE PUBLISHED: ANNIVERSARY. May 2, 1611. King James I had appointed a committee of learned men to produce a new translation of the Bible in English. This version, popularly called the King James Version, is known in England as the Authorized Version.

LEARN TO RIDE A BIKE DAY. May 2. Since 2018, a day to encourage children and adults to learn how to ride a bicycle—for health, fitness and fun. Part of National Bike Month. Annually, the first Saturday in May. For info: City Bike Coach, LLC, PO Box 250570, New York, NY 10025. Phone: (917) 536-6120. E-mail: ridebetter@citybikecoach.com. Web: www.citybikecoach.com.

LEONARDO DA VINCI: DEATH ANNIVERSARY. May 2, 1519. Legendary Renaissance painter, sculptor and inventor, Leonardo was the illegitimate son of an Italian notary. He is famous for the now iconic portrait of a silk merchant's wife, the *Mona Lisa*, for the often-reproduced mural of *The Last Supper* and for the drawing of the "Vitruvian Man." Born at Vinci, Italy, in 1452 (exact date unknown), he died at Amboise, France.

LOWCOUNTRY SHRIMP FESTIVAL AND BLESSING OF THE FLEET. May 2. McClellanville, SC. 44th annual. Seafood, arts, crafts, civic

display, entertainment and blessing of the fleet. Annually, the first Saturday in May. Est attendance: 8,000. For info: CREECS, 1011 Old Cemetery Rd, McClellanville, SC 29458. Phone: (843) 887-3323. E-mail: jmcclellan@creecs.org. Web: www.lowcountryshrimpfestival.com.

NATIONAL AUCTIONEERS DAY. May 2. Recognizes the auction profession and its contribution to American commerce. Annually, the first Saturday in May. For info: Natl Auctioneers Assn, 8880 Ballentine St, Overland Park, KS 66214. E-mail: eshipps@auctioneers.org. Web: www.auctioneers.org.

NATIONAL FITNESS DAY. May 2. Since 2017, this is a single day to celebrate strength and empowerment through fitness. People are encouraged to observe this day by working out, sharing what fitness means to them on social media or hosting their own workout classes and events. Annually, the first Saturday in May. For info: Kim Bielak, National Fitness Co, 160 Waverly Pl, #15, New York, NY 10014. Phone: (805) 558-1644. E-mail: kim@nationalfitnessday.org. Web: www.nationalfitnessday.org.

OSAMA BIN LADEN KILLED: ANNIVERSARY. May 2, 2011. US Navy SEAL Team Six raided a large compound in Abbottabad, Pakistan, and killed Al Qaeda terrorist leader Osama Bin Laden. Bin Laden's body was buried at sea in accordance with Islamic rites later that day. Bin Laden was born Mar 10, 1957, at Riyadh, Saudi Arabia. Bin Laden was the world's most-wanted terrorist.

RAY, SATYAJIT: BIRTH ANNIVERSARY. May 2, 1921. Film director Satyajit Ray was born at Calcutta (now Kolkata), India. Possibly India's best-known film director, he made more than 30 films and won numerous international awards, including an Academy Award for lifetime achievement. His films include the trilogy *Pather Panchali* (1956), *Aparajito* (1956) and *The World of Apu* (1959). Ray died Apr 23, 1992, at Calcutta.

ROBERT'S RULES DAY: ROBERT, HENRY: BIRTH ANNIVERSARY. May 2, 1837. Anniversary of the birth of Henry M. Robert (General, US Army), author of *Robert's Rules of Order*, a standard parliamentary guide. Born at Robertville, SC. Died at Hornell, NY, May 11, 1923.

SPOCK, BENJAMIN: BIRTH ANNIVERSARY. May 2, 1903. Pediatrician and author, born at New Haven, CT. His book on child rearing, *Common Sense Book of Baby and Child Care* (later called *Baby and Child Care*), has sold more than 30 million copies. In 1955 he became professor of child development at Western Reserve University at Cleveland, OH. He resigned from this position in 1967 to devote his time to the pacifist movement. Spock died at San Diego, CA, Mar 15, 1998.

SPRING ASTRONOMY DAY. May 2. To take astronomy to the people. Spring Astronomy Day is observed on a Saturday near the first-quarter moon between mid-April and mid-May. Cosponsored by 14 astronomical organizations. For info: Gary E. Tomlinson, Astronomy Day Headquarters, 30 Stargazer Ln, Comstock Park, MI 49321. Phone: (616) 784-9518. E-mail: gtomlins@sbcglobal.net. Web: www.astroleague.org.

UNITED NATIONS: WORLD TUNA DAY. May 2. On Dec 7, 2016, the General Assembly designated this day (Res 71/124), recognizing that many countries depend heavily on tuna resources for food security and nutrition, economic development, employment, government revenue, livelihoods, culture and recreation. This day highlights the importance of sustainably managed fish stocks in achieving the 2030 Agenda for Sustainable Development. For info: United Nations, Dept of Public Info, New York, NY 10017. Web: www.un.org.

VON RICHTHOFEN, MANFRED—THE "RED BARON": BIRTH ANNIVERSARY. May 2, 1892. Baron Manfred von Richthofen, the most lethal ace of WWI, was born at Breslau, German Empire (now Wroclaw, Poland), into an aristocratic family of military men. "Baron" was a title conferred on male family members. He entered training to be a fighter pilot in the fall of 1915, and by the time of his death he was credited with 80 aerial victories—including 21 in April 1917—making him notorious in his homeland and to his enemies. He painted his airplane red in January 1917, an act that gave him the nicknames "Red Baron" and *Der Rote Kampfflieger* (the Red Air Fighter). Recipient of 24 military decorations, including the Blue Max, von Richthofen became a massive propaganda symbol for the German WWI effort. He was shot down over the Somme River Valley on Apr 21, 1918. See also: "Red Baron Shot Down: Anniversary" (Apr 21).

🎂 BIRTHDAYS TODAY

Christine Baranski, 68, actress (Tonys for *The Real Thing* and *Rumors*; "The Good Fight," "The Good Wife"), born Buffalo, NY, May 2, 1952.

David Beckham, 45, soccer executive and former player, born Leytonstone, London, England, May 2, 1975.

Elizabeth Berridge, 58, actress (*Amadeus*, "The John Larroquette Show"), born Westchester, NY, May 2, 1962.

Larry Gatlin, 71, singer, songwriter, born Odessa, TX, May 2, 1949.

Paul George, 30, basketball player, born Palmdale, CA, May 2, 1990.

Eric Holcomb, 52, Governor of Indiana (R), born Indianapolis, IN, May 2, 1968.

Sarah Hughes, 35, Olympic figure skater, born Manhasset, NY, May 2, 1985.

Bianca Jagger, 75, actress, political activist, born Managua, Nicaragua, May 2, 1945.

Ellie Kemper, 40, actress ("Unbreakable Kimmy Schmidt," "The Office"), born Kansas City, MO, May 2, 1980.

Tina Maze, 37, Olympic skier, born Slovenj Gradec, Slovenia, May 2, 1983.

David Suchet, 74, actor ("The Way We Live Now," "Hercule Poirot Mysteries"), born London, England, May 2, 1946.

Jenna Von Oy, 43, actress ("Blossom"), born Newtown, CT, May 2, 1977.

May 3 — Sunday

DAY 124   **242 REMAINING**

BE KIND TO ANIMALS WEEK®. May 3–9. First held in 1915, this week promotes kindness and humane care toward animals. Annually, the first full week in May, beginning on Sunday. For info: American Humane. E-mail: info@americanhumane.org. Web: www.americanhumane.org.

May 2020	S	M	T	W	T	F	S
						1	2
	3	4	5	6	7	8	9
	10	11	12	13	14	15	16
	17	18	19	20	21	22	23
	24	25	26	27	28	29	30
	31						

BROWN, JAMES: BIRTH ANNIVERSARY. May 3, 1933. Singer and songwriter born at Barnwell, SC. Brown began singing gospel while in reform school. He quickly moved into pop music and by the early 1960s was a hugely successful performer. Transcending musical genres, he called himself the "Godfather of Soul" but was equally prominent in rock, gospel and rhythm and blues. He was a spectacular dancer and showman, known for outlandish costumes and energy-filled performances. The "hardest working man in show business" died Dec 25, 2006, at Atlanta, GA.

"CBS EVENING NEWS" TV PREMIERE: ANNIVERSARY. May 3, 1948. The news program began as a 15-minute telecast with Douglas Edwards as anchor. Walter Cronkite succeeded him in 1962 and expanded the show to 30 minutes; Eric Sevareid served as commentator. Dan Rather anchored the newscasts upon Cronkite's retirement from 1981 to 2005. Katie Couric assumed the anchor seat in 2006; Scott Pelley came to the helm in 2011. Jeff Glor was replaced in 2019 with Norah O'Donnell and the show moved to Washington, DC.

CROSBY, HARRY LILLIS "BING": BIRTH ANNIVERSARY. May 3, 1903. Bing Crosby, born at Tacoma, WA, was the bestselling artist, most popular radio star and biggest box office draw in his day—even beyond the emergence of rock in the mid-1950s. His "White Christmas" was one of the bestselling single records of the 20th century. He appeared in numerous comedic and dramatic film roles. He earned an Oscar for his performance in *Going My Way* (1944) and was also known for his *Road* films with Bob Hope. Crosby died on Oct 14, 1977, directly after shooting an 85 on 18 holes at La Moraleja Golf Course in Madrid, Spain.

DOW JONES TOPS 11,000: ANNIVERSARY. May 3, 1999. The Dow Jones Index of 30 major industrial stocks topped the 11,000 mark for the first time.

GARDEN MEDITATION DAY. May 3. Let go of your concerns and center your full attention on the garden for even a few minutes today. Focusing on weeding, tilling the soil or cleaning up the garden is a relaxing way to direct your concentration to just one thing. Annually, May 3. For info: C.L. Fornari, PO Box 355, Osterville, MA 02655. Phone: (508) 428 5895. E-mail: clfornari@yahoo.com. Web: www.gardenlady.com.

INGE, WILLIAM: BIRTH ANNIVERSARY. May 3, 1913. Award-winning American playwright, much of whose work was turned into successful Hollywood films. Best known for *Come Back, Little Sheba* (1950), *Picnic* (1953) and *Bus Stop* (1955). Inge received a Pulitizer Prize for *Picnic* and an Oscar for his original screenplay of *Splendor in the Grass* (1960). Born at Independence, KS, Inge committed suicide at Hollywood, CA, on June 10, 1973.

KENT STATE COMMEMORATION. May 3–4. Kent State University, Kent, OH. 50th annual commemoration remembering the victims of the May 4, 1970, shootings at Kent State during an antiwar rally. Candlelight vigil and march begin at 10:30 PM on May 3 and continue through the night until the afternoon of May 4. May 4 ceremony includes ringing the Victory Bell at 12:24 PM, the time of the shootings. For info: May 4th, 50th Commemoration, Office of the President, 800 E Summit St, Kent, OH 44242. Phone: (330) 672-2423. Web: www.kent.edu/may4kentstate50.

LUMPY RUG DAY. May 3. To encourage the custom of teasing bigots and trigots for shoving unwelcome facts under the rug. When many cans of worms have been shoved under the rug, the defenders of the status quo obtain a new rug high enough to cover the unwanted facts. (Created by Robert L. Birch, Pun Corps.)

MACHIAVELLI, NICCOLÒ: BIRTH ANNIVERSARY. May 3, 1469. Writer, statesman and political philosopher, Machiavelli worked within the patronage system common in his day. His personal, political and intellectual relationship with his patrons, the powerful Florentine Medici family, informed his writing and career, especially *The Prince* (published in 1532), which prescribes strong, absolute government. The tenor of his advice inspired the adjective "Machiavellian," meaning cunning, scheming and unscrupulous in political or career advancement. Born at Florence, Republic of Florence, Machiavelli died there June 21, 1527.

MEIR, GOLDA: BIRTH ANNIVERSARY. May 3, 1898. Born Goldie Mabovitch at Kiev, Russia, Meir was prime minister of Israel during 1969–74. She died at Jerusalem, Dec 8, 1978.

MEXICO: DAY OF THE HOLY CROSS. May 3. Celebrated especially by construction workers and miners, a festive day during which anyone who is building must give a party for the workers. A flower-decorated cross is placed on every piece of new construction in the country.

MOTORCYCLE CLUB MASS AND BLESSING OF THE BIKES. May 3. Paterson, NJ. 50th annual. Since 1969, a blessing of motorcycles, their riders and friends. Annually, the first Sunday in May. Est attendance: 2,000. For info: Cathedral of St. John the Baptist, 381 Grand St, Paterson, NJ 07505. Web: cathedralofstjohnthebaptist.org.

NATIONAL FAMILY WEEK. May 3–9. Traditionally the first Sunday and the first full week in May are observed as National Family Week in many Christian churches.

NATIONAL HUG HOLIDAY WEEK. May 3–9. Huggers of all ages are invited to make a difference one hug at a time! Send SASE for a "Hugger's Package." For info: Hugs 4 Health, PO Box 896, Seal Beach, CA 90740-0896. E-mail: hugs4health@yahoo.com. Web: www.facebook.com/hugs4health.

★NATIONAL HURRICANE PREPAREDNESS WEEK. May 3–9 (tentative). Presidential Proclamation, issued annually in May since 2006, calling upon government agencies, private organizations, schools and the media to share information about hurricane preparedness. Americans living in vulnerable coastal areas are also urged to take appropriate measures and precautions to protect themselves, their homes and their communities against the effects of hurricanes.

NATIONAL HURRICANE PREPAREDNESS WEEK. May 3–9. History teaches that a lack of hurricane awareness and preparation are common threads among all major hurricane disasters. By knowing your vulnerability and what actions you should take, you can reduce the effects of a hurricane disaster. Hurricane hazards come in many forms, including storm surge, heavy rainfall, inland flooding, high winds, tornadoes and rip currents. The National Weather Service is responsible for protecting life and property through issuance of timely watches and warnings, but it is essential that everyone be ready before a storm approaches. Furthermore, mariners should be aware of special safety precautions when confronted with a hurricane. Annually, the first full week in May. For info: National Hurricane Center. Web: www.weather.gov/wrn/hurricane-preparedness.

NATIONAL INFERTILITY SURVIVAL DAY®. May 3. Beat the Mother's Day blues the week *before* Mother's Day. Here is the chance for infertile women and those who love them to celebrate themselves, too! Infertility survivors also are encouraged to reach out to those struggling to find resolution to their challenges, through friendship, fundraising and other supportive and creative endeavors. National Infertility Survival Day® is for those who want to use their experiences to attain positive outcomes for themselves and others. Annually, the first Sunday in May. For info: Beverly Barna. E-mail: infertilitysucks@aol.com. Web: www.infertilitysurvival-day.com.

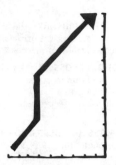

NATIONAL PUBLIC RADIO FIRST BROADCAST: ANNIVERSARY. May 3, 1971. National noncommercial radio network, financed by the Corporation for Public Broadcasting, began programming.

NATIONAL SMALL BUSINESS WEEK. May 3–9. This week is the Small Business Administration's annual celebration of entrepreneurship and innovation. Events include awards, conferences, hackathons and more. For info: Small Business Administration. E-mail: smallbusinessweek@sba.gov. Web: www.sba.gov/national-small-business-week.

NATIONAL SPECIALLY ABLED PETS DAY. May 3. Celebrated on May 3 annually, with events around the nation, this day helps educate the public about caring for disabled pets, features disabled animals looking for a home and encourages animal lovers to consider choosing a disabled pet when looking to bring home a new furry family member. For info: Colleen Paige. Web: www.specially-abledpetsday.org.

NATIONAL TWO DIFFERENT COLORED SHOES DAY. May 3. A day to recognize and celebrate the uniqueness and diversity of humanity. The simple and lighthearted act of purposely wearing two different colored shoes demonstrates the courage to take a risk and step outside of one's daily routine. Annually, May 3. For info: Arlene Kaiser, EdD, 3424 Spring Creek Ln, Milpitas, CA 95035. Phone: (408) 946-4444. E-mail: drarlenekaiser@mac.com. Web: www.NTDCSD.com.

POLAND: CONSTITUTION DAY (SWIETO TRZECIEGO MAJA). May 3. National day. Celebrates ratification of Poland's first constitution, 1791.

ROBINSON, SUGAR RAY: BIRTH ANNIVERSARY. May 3, 1921. Ray "Sugar Ray" Robinson, boxer, born Walker Smith, Jr, at Detroit, MI. Generally considered "pound for pound the greatest boxer of all time," Robinson was a welterweight and middleweight champion who won 175 professional fights and lost only 19. A smooth and precise boxer, he fought until he was 45, dabbled in show business and established the Sugar Ray Robinson Youth Foundation to counter juvenile delinquency. Died at Los Angeles, CA, Apr 12, 1989.

SEEGER, PETE: BIRTH ANNIVERSARY. May 3, 1919. Legendary American folksinger/songwriter and political activist born at New York City, NY, Seeger is credited with saving folk music—and his signature instrument, the five-string banjo—from obscurity. Notable works include "If I Had a Hammer" and "Where Have All the Flowers Gone?" A social justice activist, he popularized "We Shall Overcome," which later became the civil rights movement's anthem. Blacklisted for decades for a McCarthy-era conviction of contempt of Congress (eventually overturned), Seeger was awarded the National Medal of Arts (1994), was inducted into the Rock and Roll Hall of Fame (1996) and received two Grammys before his death on Jan 27, 2014, at New York City.

★**SMALL BUSINESS WEEK.** May 3–9. This week we recognize the ingenuity of the American spirit and the renewed promise of the American Dream. Small businesses are at the heart of our nation.

	S	M	T	W	T	F	S
May						1	2
	3	4	5	6	7	8	9
2020	10	11	12	13	14	15	16
	17	18	19	20	21	22	23
	24	25	26	27	28	29	30
	31						

Our country's 30 million small businesses employ nearly 58 million Americans—48 percent of the labor force.

TD BANK FIVE BORO BIKE TOUR. May 3. New York, NY. 43rd anniversary. The country's largest bike ride draws 32,000 cyclists from every state in the nation and 65 countries around the globe for an experience unlike any other: a 40-mile, traffic-free journey through Manhattan, the Bronx, Queens, Brooklyn and across the Verrazano-Narrows Bridge into Staten Island. Proceeds from the tour fund Bike New York's free bike education programs. In 2017, they taught bike skills to more than 25,000 kids and adults. Pre-registration required. Annually, the first Sunday in May. Est attendance: 40,000. For info: Bike New York, 475 Riverside Dr, 13th Fl, New York, NY 10115. Phone: (212) 870-2080. E-mail: info@bike.nyc. Web: www.bike.nyc.

UNITED NATIONS: WORLD PRESS FREEDOM DAY. May 3. A day to recognize that a free, pluralistic and independent press is an essential component of any democratic society and to promote press freedom in the world. Annually, May 3. For info: United Nations, Dept of Public Info, New York, NY 10017. Web: www.un.org.

UPDATE YOUR REFERENCES WEEK. May 3–9. A reminder to all job seekers to update their references annually because people are always moving or changing jobs. Additionally, it reminds former supervisors, etc, of who you are. Keeping an updated list of references means job seekers can be ready when an opportunity presents itself. For info: Laura DeCarlo, Career Directors International, 1665 Clover Circle, Melbourne, FL 32935. Phone: (321) 752-0442. E-mail: info@careerdirectors.com.

🎂 BIRTHDAYS TODAY

Joseph Addai, 37, football player, born Houston, TX, May 3, 1983.

Bobby Cannavale, 50, actor ("Vinyl," "Boardwalk Empire," *Blue Jasmine*), born Union City, NJ, May 3, 1970.

Greg Gumbel, 74, television personality, sportscaster, born New Orleans, LA, May 3, 1946.

Christina Hendricks, 45, actress (*Crooked House*, "Good Girls," "Mad Men"), born Knoxville, TN, May 3, 1975.

Dulé Hill, 46, actor ("The West Wing," "Psych"), born Orange, NJ, May 3, 1974.

Engelbert Humperdinck, 84, singer, born Gerry Dorsey at Madras, India, May 3, 1936.

Jim Risch, 79, US Senator (R, Idaho), born Milwaukee, WI, May 3, 1941.

Frankie Valli, 83, singer, born Newark, NJ, May 3, 1937.

Ron Wyden, 71, US Senator (D, Oregon), born Wichita, KS, May 3, 1949.

May 4 — Monday

DAY 125   **241 REMAINING**

CHINA: YOUTH DAY. May 4. Annual public holiday recalls the demonstration on May 4, 1919, by thousands of patriotic students in Beijing's Tiananmen Square to protest imperialist aggression in China.

CURAÇAO: MEMORIAL DAY. May 4. Victims of WWII are honored on this day. Military ceremonies at the War Monument. Not an official public holiday.

DISCOVERY OF JAMAICA BY CHRISTOPHER COLUMBUS: ANNIVERSARY. May 4, 1494. Christopher Columbus discovered Jamaica. The Arawak Indians were its first inhabitants.

FELIX, MARIA: BIRTH ANNIVERSARY. May 4, 1914. The goddess of Mexico's golden age of cinema (1930s–50s), "La Dona" appeared in more than 45 films and was awarded the first Mexico City Prize for a lifetime of distinguished achievement. Born at Alamos, Mexico, Felix died Apr 8, 2002, at Mexico City, Mexico.

FIRST WOMAN BRITISH PRIME MINISTER: ANNIVERSARY. May 4, 1979. With the Conservative Party victory in the British election of May 3, 1979, Margaret Thatcher accepted Queen Elizabeth's appointment as prime minister on May 4. She thus became the first woman prime minister in 700 years of English parliamentary history. Thatcher, dubbed the "Iron Maiden" by a Soviet journalist for her toughness, held the office until forced to resign on Nov 22, 1990.

FREEDOM RIDES BEGIN: ANNIVERSARY. May 4, 1961. Civil rights advocates joined James Farmer of the Congress of Racial Equality (CORE) to conduct "freedom rides" on buses from Washington, DC, across the Deep South to New Orleans. The trips were intended to test Supreme Court decisions and Interstate Commerce Commission regulations prohibiting discrimination in interstate travel. (The rides were patterned after a similar challenge to segregation, the 1947 Journey of Reconciliation.) In several places riders were brutally beaten by local people and policemen. On May 14 members of the Ku Klux Klan attacked the Freedom Riders in Birmingham, AL, while local police watched. In Mississippi, Freedom Riders were jailed. They never made it to New Orleans.

HAYMARKET SQUARE RIOT: ANNIVERSARY. May 4, 1886. Labor union unrest at Chicago, IL, led to violence when a crowd of unemployed men tried to enter the McCormick Reaper Works, where a strike was underway. Although no one was killed, anarchist groups called a mass meeting in Haymarket Square to avenge the "massacre." When the police advanced on the demonstrators, a bomb was thrown and several policemen were killed. Four leaders of the demonstration were hanged, and another committed suicide in jail. Three others were given jail terms. The case aroused considerable controversy around the world. See also: "Haymarket Pardon: Anniversary" (June 26).

HEPBURN, AUDREY: BIRTH ANNIVERSARY. May 4, 1929. Audrey Hepburn, whose first major movie role in *Roman Holiday* (1953) won her an Academy Award as Best Actress, was born Edda Van Heemstra Hepburn-Ruston near Brussels, Belgium. She made 26 movies during her career and received four additional Oscar nominations. During the latter years of her life, Hepburn served as spokesperson for the United Nations Children's Fund, traveling worldwide raising money for the organization. Audrey Hepburn died Jan 20, 1993, at Tolochenaz, Switzerland.

INTERNATIONAL RESPECT FOR CHICKENS DAY. May 4. Launched in 2005, International Respect for Chickens Day (IRCD) is a project of United Poultry Concerns, a nonprofit organization that promotes the compassionate and respectful treatment of domestic fowl. IRCD is a day to celebrate chickens throughout the world by encouraging people to do an "action" for chickens on May 4, showing the world that chickens matter. Ideas include arranging a library display/video presentation, an IRCD school celebration, letters to the editor, radio talk show participation, a local mall exhibit, etc. UPC supplies posters, brochures, videos and event ideas. For info: United Poultry Concerns, PO Box 150, Machipongo, VA 23405. Phone: (757) 678-7875. E-mail: karen@upc-online.org. Web: www.upc-online.org.

IRELAND: MAY DAY BANK HOLIDAY. May 4. Bank holiday in the Republic of Ireland on the first Monday in May.

JAPAN: GREENERY DAY. May 4. National holiday. Celebrates nature. Formerly observed on Apr 29, but moved to May 4 in 2007.

KENT STATE STUDENTS SHOT: 50th ANNIVERSARY. May 4, 1970. Four students (Allison Krause, 19; Sandra Lee Scheuer, 20; Jeffrey Glenn Miller, 20; and William K. Schroeder, 19) were killed by the National Guard during demonstrations against the Vietnam War at Kent (Ohio) State University.

MANN, HORACE: BIRTH ANNIVERSARY. May 4, 1796. The American educator, author and public servant, known as the "father of public education in the US," was born at Franklin, MA. Founder of Westfield (MA) State College, president of Antioch College and editor of the influential *Common School Journal*. Mann died at Yellow Springs, OH, Aug 2, 1859.

MELANOMA MONDAY. May 4. Also known as National Skin Self-Examination Day. People are encouraged to spot skin cancer and to examine their skin. Annually, the first Monday in May. For info: American Academy of Dermatology, PO Box 1968, Des Plaines, IL 60017. Web: www.aad.org or www.spotskincancer.org.

METROPOLITAN MUSEUM OF ART COSTUME INSTITUTE BENEFIT. May 4. New York, NY. First held in 1948, the "Met Gala" is an invitation-only, black-tie fundraising event benefiting the Costume Institute—and the social event of the season. Designers, models and celebrities in attendance set the fashion pace in spectacular formal dress. Annually, the first Monday in May. Est attendance: 600. For info: Metropolitan Museum of Art Costume Institute. Web: www.metmuseum.org.

NATIONAL PET WEEK. May 4–10. Since 1981, a week to honor the many important roles pets have in our lives and to encourage responsible pet ownership. Annually, the first full week in May. For info: The American Veterinary Medical Assn, 1931 N Meacham Rd, Ste 100, Schaumburg, IL 60173-4360. Phone: (800) 248-2862. Web: www.petweek.org.

RHODE ISLAND: INDEPENDENCE DAY. May 4. Rhode Island abandoned allegiance to Great Britain in 1776.

SPACE MILESTONE: *ATLANTIS* (US). May 4, 1989. First American planetary expedition in 11 years. Space shuttle *Atlantis* was launched, its major objective to deploy the *Magellan* spacecraft on its way to Venus to map the planet's surface. The shuttle was on its 65th orbit when it landed May 8, mission accomplished.

STAR WARS DAY. May 4. A day celebrated worldwide by fans of the Star Wars series. Fans greet each other by saying "May the 4th be with you," have lightsaber fights and indulge in other fun connected to the sci-fi world created by George Lucas.

TEACHER APPRECIATION WEEK. May 4–8. PTAs across the country conduct activities to strengthen respect and support for teachers and the teaching profession. Founded in 1984. Annually, Monday through Friday of the first full week in May. For info: National PTA or NEA. E-mail: info@pta.org. Web: www.pta.org or www.nea.org.

TYLER, JULIA GARDINER: 200th BIRTH ANNIVERSARY. May 4, 1820. Second wife of John Tyler, 10th president of the US, born at Gardiners Island, NY. Died at Richmond, VA, July 10, 1889.

UNITED KINGDOM: MAY DAY BANK HOLIDAY. May 4. Bank and public holiday in England, Wales, Scotland and Northern Ireland. Annually, the first Monday in May.

WADE-DAVIS RECONSTRUCTION BILL PASSES THE HOUSE: ANNIVERSARY. May 4, 1864. Over the objections of President Abraham Lincoln, the House of Representatives on this date passed the Wade-Davis Reconstruction Bill, containing stiff punitive measures against the South that if put into law would have destroyed Lincoln's more moderate reconstruction aims. The bill was also adamantly opposed by radical Republicans led by Thaddeus Stevens, for whom it was insufficiently severe in its treatment of the Southern rebels. Lincoln eventually killed the bill by using the pocket veto.

🎂 BIRTHDAYS TODAY

Erin Andrews, 42, sportscaster, born Lewiston, ME, May 4, 1978.

Francesc (Cesc) Fàbregas, 33, soccer player, born Vilessoc de Mar, Spain, May 4, 1987.

David Guterson, 64, author (*Snow Falling on Cedars*), born Seattle, WA, May 4, 1956.

Jackie Jackson, 69, singer (Jackson 5), born Sigmund Esco Jackson at Gary, IN, May 4, 1951.

Richard Jenkins, 73, actor (*The Shape of Water*, *The Visitor*, "Berlin Station," "Six Feet Under"), born DeKalb, IL, May 4, 1947.

Doug Jones, 66, US Senator (D, Alabama), former federal prosecutor, born Fairfield, AL, May 4, 1954.

Rory McIlroy, 31, golfer, born Holywood, Northern Ireland, May 4, 1989.

Dawn Staley, 50, former basketball player, born Philadelphia, PA, May 4, 1970.

Randy Travis, 61, country musician, born Marshville, NC, May 4, 1959.

George F. Will, 79, editor, columnist, baseball executive, born Champaign, IL, May 4, 1941.

Pia Zadora, 64, actress, singer, dancer, born Hoboken, NJ, May 4, 1956.

May 5 — Tuesday

DAY 126   **240 REMAINING**

AMERICAN MEDICAL ASSOCIATION FOUNDED: ANNIVERSARY. May 5, 1847. The American Medical Association was organized at a meeting at Philadelphia, PA, attended by 250 delegates. This was the first national medical convention in the US.

BATTLE OF PUEBLA: ANNIVERSARY. May 5, 1862. Mexican troops under General Ignacio Zaragoza, outnumbered three to one, defeated invading French forces of Napoleon III at the city of Puebla. This day is commemorated as a national holiday in Mexico.

BATTLE OF THE WILDERNESS: ANNIVERSARY. May 5, 1864. The Battle of the Wilderness was the first major encounter between opposing troops under Robert E. Lee and Ulysses S. Grant. So named for the area of dense forest and underbrush of northern Virginia where it occurred. The engagement was especially fierce, with opposing armies often fighting at point-blank range as the battle lines became obscured in the smoke-filled forest. Both sides suffered heavy casualties totaling more than 28,000, and after the fighting had ceased on the second day, more than 200 wounded Federal troops were trapped and killed by the flames of fires started by the battle.

BEARD, JAMES: BIRTH ANNIVERSARY. May 5, 1903. The "father of American cooking" was born at Portland, OR. In a long and busy culinary career, he penned more than 20 classic cookbooks, appeared on television's first cooking show in 1946 and was an enthusiastic ambassador for American regional cooking. He died Jan 21, 1985. His Greenwich Village brownstone is America's only culinary historic landmark and serves as the headquarters of the James Beard Foundation.

BLY, NELLIE: BIRTH ANNIVERSARY. May 5, 1864. Born at Cochran's Mills, PA. "Nellie Bly" was the pseudonym used by pioneering American journalist Elizabeth Cochrane Seaman. Like her namesake in a Stephen Foster song, Nellie Bly was a social reformer and human rights advocate. As a journalist, she is best known for her exposé of conditions in what were then popularly called "insane asylums," where she posed as an "inmate." As an adventurer, she is best known for her 1889–90 around-the-world tour in 72 days,

in which she bettered the time of Jules Verne's fictional character Phileas Fogg by eight days. She died at New York, NY, Jan 27, 1922.

BONZA BOTTLER DAY®. May 5. To celebrate when the number of the day is the same as the number of the month. Bonza Bottler Day® is an excuse to have a party at least once a month. For more information see Jan 1. For info: Gail Berger, Bonza Bottler Day. Phone: (864) 201-3988. E-mail: bonza@bonzabottlerday.com. Web: www.bonzabottlerday.com.

CARTOONISTS DAY. May 5. To honor all cartoonists in the industry: animation, magazines, comic strips, etc. For info: Polly Keener, 400 W Fairlawn Blvd, Akron, OH 44313. Phone: (330) 836-4448. E-mail: pollytoon@aol.com.

DENMARK: OBSERVATION OF 1945 LIBERATION. May 5. Flag-flying day to commemorate the 1945 liberation of Denmark from the Nazi occupation.

ETHIOPIA: PATRIOTS VICTORY DAY. May 5. National holiday. Commemorates the 1941 liberation of Addis Ababa by British and Ethiopian forces.

INTERNATIONAL DAY OF THE MIDWIFE. May 5. Since 1992, a day for highlighting the work of midwives. The day is an occasion for every individual midwife to think about the many others in the profession, to make new contacts within and outside midwifery and to widen the knowledge of what midwives do for the world. Annually, May 5. For info: International Confederation of Midwives, Koninginnegracht 60, The Hague 2514 AE, The Netherlands. Web: www.internationalmidwives.org.

JAPAN: CHILDREN'S DAY. May 5. National holiday. Observed on the fifth day of the fifth month each year.

JOHNSON, AMY: 90th FLIGHT ANNIVERSARY. May 5, 1930. Yorkshire-born Amy Johnson began the first successful solo flight by a woman from England to Australia. Leaving Croydon Airport in a de Havilland Tiger Moth named *Jason*, she flew 9,960 miles to Port Darwin, Australia, arriving May 28. The song "Amy, Wonderful Amy" celebrated the fame of this "wonder girl of the air," who became a legend in her own lifetime. Serving as an air ferry pilot during WWII, she was lost over the Thames Estuary in 1941.

KIERKEGAARD, SØREN: BIRTH ANNIVERSARY. May 5, 1813. Philosopher and Christian apologist born at Copenhagen, Denmark. Kierkegaard's philosophy was a major influence on both existentialism and modern theology. A central idea is his "leap of faith"—taking the risk to believe in the face of doubt. His major works include *Fear and Trembling* (1843), *Either/Or: A Fragment of Life* (1843), *Stages on Life's Way* (1845) and *Sickness unto Death* (1849). These works deal with the subjectivity of truth and the despair and suffering inherent in life. He also crafted polemics against the conventional institutions of the time, especially the protestant Church of Denmark. Kierkegaard died at Copenhagen on Nov 11, 1855.

MARX, KARL: BIRTH ANNIVERSARY. May 5, 1818. German Socialist, founder and father of modern communism, author of *Das Kapital* and (with Friedrich Engels) the *Communist Manifesto*. Born at Treves, Germany, he died at London, England, Mar 14, 1883, at age 64.

MEXICO: CINCO DE MAYO. May 5. Mexican national holiday recognizing the anniversary of the Battle of Puebla in 1862. Anniversary is observed by Mexicans everywhere with parades, festivals, dances and speeches.

May 2020	S	M	T	W	T	F	S
						1	2
	3	4	5	6	7	8	9
	10	11	12	13	14	15	16
	17	18	19	20	21	22	23
	24	25	26	27	28	29	30
	31						

NATIONAL TEACHER DAY. May 5. To pay tribute to American educators, sponsored by the National Education Association, Teacher Day falls during the National PTA's Teacher Appreciation Week. Local communities and organizations are encouraged to use this opportunity to honor those who influence and inspire the next generation through their work. Annually, the Tuesday of the first week in May. For info: Natl Education Assn, 1201 16th St NW, Washington, DC 20036-3290. Phone: (202) 833-4000. Web: www.nea.org.

NETHERLANDS: LIBERATION DAY. May 5. Marks liberation of The Netherlands from Nazi Germany in 1945.

POWER, TYRONE: BIRTH ANNIVERSARY. May 5, 1914. American actor, born at Cincinnati, OH, into a theatrical family, who was one of the most popular romantic and swashbuckling leads in Hollywood during the 1930s and '40s. Best known for his roles in *Suez, The Mark of Zorro, Blood and Sand, The Razor's Edge* and *Nightmare Alley.* Tyrone Power died Nov 15, 1958, at Madrid, Spain, during a film shoot.

SOUTH KOREA: CHILDREN'S DAY. May 5. A time for families to take their children on excursions. Parks and children's centers throughout the country are packed with excited and colorfully dressed children. A national holiday since 1975.

SPACE MILESTONE: *FREEDOM 7* (US). May 5, 1961. First US astronaut in space, second man in space, Alan Shepard, Jr, projected 115 miles into space in suborbital flight reaching a speed of more than 5,000 mph. This was the first piloted Mercury mission.

STOCK MARKET CRASH OF 1893: ANNIVERSARY. May 5, 1893. Wall Street stock prices took a sudden drop. By the end of the year, 600 banks had closed. The Philadelphia and Reading, the Erie, the Northern Pacific, the Union Pacific and the Atchison, Topeka and Santa Fe railroads had gone into receivership; 15,000 other businesses went into bankruptcy. Other than the Great Depression of the 1930s, this was the worst economic crisis in US history; 15–20 percent of the workforce was unemployed.

WORLD ASTHMA DAY. May 5. This day is organized by the Global Initiative for Asthma (GINA) in collaboration with healthcare groups and asthma educators to raise awareness about asthma and improve asthma care throughout the world. The first day, in 1998, was celebrated in more than 35 countries in conjunction with the first World Asthma Meeting held in Barcelona, Spain. Participation has increased with each World Asthma Day held since then, and the day has become one of the world's most important asthma awareness and education events. Annually, the first Tuesday in May. For info: Global Initiative for Asthma. Web: www.ginasthma.org.

🎂 BIRTHDAYS TODAY

Adele, 32, singer, born Adele Laurie Blue Adkins at Tottenham, England, May 5, 1988.

Chris Brown, 31, singer, born Tappahannock, VA, May 5, 1989.

Pat Carroll, 93, actress (Emmy for "Caesar's Hour"; "The Ted Knight Show"), born Shreveport, LA, May 5, 1927.

Henry Cavill, 37, actor (*Batman v Superman, Man of Steel,* "The Tudors"), born Jersey, Channel Islands, May 5, 1983.

Mike Dunleavy, 59, Governor of Alaska (R), born Scranton, PA, May 5, 1961.

Richard E. Grant, 63, actor (*Can You Ever Forgive Me?, Dom Hemingway, Gosford Park, Withnail and I*), born Richard Grant Esterhuysen at Mbabane, Swaziland, May 5, 1957.

Lance Henriksen, 80, actor ("Millennium," *Aliens, Dog Day Afternoon, Near Dark*), born New York, NY, May 5, 1940.

Paul Konerko, 44, former baseball player, born Providence, RI, May 5, 1976.

Jean-Pierre Léaud, 76, actor (*The 400 Blows, Stolen Kisses, Bed and Board*), born Paris, France, May 5, 1944.

Michael Murphy, 82, actor (*Nashville, Manhattan, Salvador*), born Los Angeles, CA, May 5, 1938.

Ziggy Palffy, 48, former hockey player, born Skalica, Czechoslovakia (now Slovakia), May 5, 1972.

Michael Palin, 77, actor, comedian ("Monty Python's Flying Circus," *Life of Brian*), author, born Sheffield, Yorkshire, England, May 5, 1943.

Brian Williams, 61, journalist, anchor, born Elmira, NY, May 5, 1959.

Tina Yothers, 47, singer, actress ("Family Ties"), born Whittier, CA, May 5, 1973.

May 6 — Wednesday

DAY 127   **239 REMAINING**

BANNISTER BREAKS FOUR-MINUTE MILE: ANNIVERSARY. May 6, 1954. Running for the British Amateur Athletic Association in a meet at Oxford University, Roger Bannister broke the four-minute barrier with a time of 3:59.4. Four minutes for a mile at the time was considered not only a physical barrier but also a psychological one.

FREUD, SIGMUND: BIRTH ANNIVERSARY. May 6, 1856. Austrian physician, born at Freiberg, Moravia. Founder of psychoanalysis. Freud died at London, England, Sept 23, 1939.

***HINDENBURG* DISASTER: ANNIVERSARY.** May 6, 1937. At 7:20 PM, the dirigible *Hindenburg* exploded as it approached the mooring mast at Lakehurst, NJ, after a transatlantic voyage. Of its 97 passengers and crew, 36 died in the accident, which ended the dream of mass transportation via dirigible.

INTERNATIONAL MANAGEMENT ACCOUNTING DAY. May 6. Since 2012, the Institute of Management Accountants (IMA) has observed this day to recognize the accountants and finance professionals who work in business. These professionals do their part to uphold the highest ethical business practices, enabling value-driven organizations to serve the public interest. Annually, May 6. For info: Morgan Del Rio, Marketing and Social Media Manager, IMA, 10 Paragon Dr, Ste 1, Montvale, NJ 07645. Phone: (800) 638-4427. E-mail: morgan.delrio@imanet.org. Web: www.imanet.org.

JAPAN: CONSTITUTION MEMORIAL DAY (OBSERVED). May 6. National holiday commemorating adoption of the constitution in 1947. Part of the Golden Week Holidays. Normally observed on May 3, in 2020 it is observed on May 6 since May 3 falls on a Sunday.

JARRELL, RANDALL: BIRTH ANNIVERSARY. May 6, 1914. Poet, author and incisive literary critic, born at Nashville, TN. Jarrell served in the US Army during World War II and the experience greatly influenced his early work, including his most well-known poem, "The Death of the Ball Turret Gunner." He was struck by a car and died Oct 14, 1965, near Chapel Hill, NC.

JOSEPH BRACKETT DAY. May 6. Day honoring the Shaker religious leader, born May 6, 1797, at Cumberland, ME. In 1848 he composed the popular Shaker song "Simple Gifts" (also known as "'Tis the Gift to Be Simple") while at the Shaker community in Alfred, ME. This Shaker dance song became known worldwide after Aaron Copland used it in his score for the ballet *Appalachian*

Spring in 1944. Elder Joseph Brackett died at New Gloucester, ME, July 4, 1882. For info: PineTree Productions, 235 Prospect St, Stoughton, MA 02072. E-mail: pinetreepro@aol.com. Web: www.americanmusicpreservation.com/JosephBrackettSimpleGifts.htm.

NATIONAL BIKE TO SCHOOL DAY. May 6. Since 2012, a day providing an opportunity for schools across the country to join together and to build on the energy of National Bike Month. Held in coordination with the League of American Bicyclists. For info: National Center for Safe Routes to School, 730 Martin Luther King, Jr, Blvd, Ste 300, Campus Box 3430, Chapel Hill, NC 27599-3430. E-mail: info@walkbiketoschool.org. Web: www.walkbiketoschool.org.

NATIONAL NURSES WEEK. May 6–12. A week to honor the outstanding efforts of nurses everywhere to strengthen the health of the nation. Annually, beginning May 6, National Nurses Day, and ending May 12, Florence Nightingale's birthday. For info: American Nurses Assn. Web: www.nursingworld.org.

NATIONAL SCHOOL NURSE DAY. May 6. Established to foster a better understanding of the role of school nurses in the educational setting. Annually, the Wednesday of National Nurses Week (May 6–12). For info: NASN, 1100 Wayne Ave, Ste 925, Silver Spring, MD 20910. Phone: (240) 821-1130. E-mail: nasn@nasn.org. Web: www.nasn.org.

NO DIET DAY. May 6. Since 1992, a day to stop dieting and hazardous weight-loss attempts. No Diet Day celebrates a paradigm shift to diet-free, healthful living and to acceptance and respect for oneself and others. Annually, May 6. Created by Mary Evans Young.

NO HOMEWORK DAY. May 6. Millions of kids, all of them overloaded with homework, get a much-needed night off tonight. Give 'em a break, teachers! These young folks are working harder than Mom 'n' Dad. (©2006 by WH.) For info: Thomas & Ruth Roy, Wellcat Holidays, 2418 Long Ln, Lebanon, PA 17046. Phone: (717) 279-0184. E-mail: info@wellcat.com. Web: www.wellcat.com.

PEARY, ROBERT E.: BIRTH ANNIVERSARY. May 6, 1856. Born at Cresson, PA. Peary served as a cartographic draftsman in the US Coast and Geodetic Survey for two years and then joined the US Navy's Corps of Civil Engineers in 1881. He first worked as an explorer in tropical climates as he served as subchief of the Inter-Ocean Canal Survey in Nicaragua. After reading about the inland ice of Greenland, Peary became attracted to the Arctic. He organized and led eight Arctic expeditions and is credited with the verification of Greenland's island formation, proving that the polar ice cap extended beyond 82° north latitude, and the discovery of the Melville meteorite on Melville Bay, in addition to his famous discovery of the North Pole, Apr 6, 1909. Peary died Feb 20, 1920, at Washington, DC.

	S	M	T	W	T	F	S
May						1	2
	3	4	5	6	7	8	9
2020	10	11	12	13	14	15	16
	17	18	19	20	21	22	23
	24	25	26	27	28	29	30
	31						

PENN, JOHN: BIRTH ANNIVERSARY. May 6, 1740. Signer of the Declaration of Independence, born at Caroline County, VA. Died Sept 14, 1788.

SACK OF ROME: ANNIVERSARY. May 6, 1527. The Renaissance ended with the Sack of Rome, which began on this date. As part of a series of wars between the Hapsburg Empire and the French monarchy, German troops killed some 4,000 inhabitants of Rome and looted works of art and libraries. Pope Clement VII, who supported the French, was imprisoned at the Castel St. Angelo. Nearly a year passed before order could be restored in the city.

STOVER, RUSSELL: BIRTH ANNIVERSARY. May 6, 1888. Entrepreneur, born in a sod house at Alton, KS, who became the founder of a candy company whose products can now be found in more than 20 countries around the world. Stover and his wife, Clara, launched their candy business from their home in Denver, CO, in 1923, with Clara as the sole production team and Russell the sales force. The venture was practically an overnight success with the Stovers opening their first factory the following year. At the time of his death at Kansas City, MO, on May 11, 1954, Russell Stover Candies was selling 11 million pounds of candy each year.

TAGORE, RABINDRANATH: BIRTH ANNIVERSARY. May 6, 1861. Hindu poet, mystic and musical composer born at Calcutta (now Kolkata), India. A prolific author, he wrote some 50 volumes of poetry besides his other work. He received the Nobel Prize in Literature in 1913. Died at Calcutta, Aug 7, 1941. His birthday is observed in Bangladesh on the 25th day of the Bengali month of Baishakha (second week of May), when the poet laureate is honored with songs, dances and discussions of his works.

VALENTINO, RUDOLPH: 125th BIRTH ANNIVERSARY. May 6, 1895. Rodolfo Alfonso Raffaello Pierre Filibert Guglielmi di Valentina d'Antonguella, whose professional name was Rudolph Valentino, was born at Castellaneta, Italy. Popular cinema actor. For years press reports claimed that "at least one weeping veiled woman in black brought flowers to his tomb" (at Hollywood Memorial Park) every year on the anniversary of his death at New York, NY, Aug 23, 1926.

WELLES, ORSON: BIRTH ANNIVERSARY. May 6, 1915. Actor, director; radio, stage and film writer, born at Kenosha, WI. Saying, "I always have to be bigger than life. It's a fault in my nature," Welles created experimental and larger-than-life works, including *The War of the Worlds*, his panic-inducing 1938 radio broadcast about alien invasion (from his innovative Mercury Theatre, founded in 1937), and his films, *Citizen Kane* (1941), *The Lady from Shanghai* (1947) and *Touch of Evil* (1958). Financially unsuccessful, his films initially garnered growing critical admiration outside Hollywood for their innovative narrative style and cinematography, and he has since been recognized as arguably one of cinema's greatest directors. Died Oct 10, 1985, at Los Angeles, CA.

🎂 BIRTHDAYS TODAY

José Altuve, 30, baseball player (2017 AP Athlete of the Year), born Maracay, Venezuela, May 6, 1990.

Tom Bergeron, 65, television personality and host ("Hollywood Squares," "America's Funniest Home Videos," "Dancing with the Stars"), born Haverhill, MA, May 6, 1955.

Tony Blair, 67, former British prime minister (1997–2007), born Edinburgh, Scotland, May 6, 1953.

Martin Brodeur, 48, former hockey player, born Montreal, QC, Canada, May 6, 1972.

George Clooney, 59, actor (Oscar for *Syriana*; *The Descendants, Ocean's Eleven, Michael Clayton*), born Lexington, KY, May 6, 1961.

Alan Dale, 73, actor ("Dynasty," "NCIS," "Ugly Betty," "The OC"), born Dunedin, South Island, New Zealand, May 6, 1947.

Roma Downey, 56, actress ("Touched by an Angel"), born Derry, Northern Ireland, May 6, 1964.

Leslie Hope, 55, actress ("24," *Talk Radio*), born Halifax, NS, Canada, May 6, 1965.

Ben Masters, 73, actor (*All That Jazz, Making Mr Right*), born Corvallis, OR, May 6, 1947.

Willie Mays, 89, Hall of Fame baseball player, born Westfield, AL, May 6, 1931.

Chris Paul, 35, basketball player, born Winston-Salem, NC, May 6, 1985.

Bob Seger, 75, singer, musician, born Ann Arbor, MI, May 6, 1945.

Richard C. Shelby, 86, US Senator (R, Alabama), born Birmingham, AL, May 6, 1934.

Gabourey Sidibe, 37, actress (*Precious: Based on the Novel "Push" by Sapphire*, "The Big C"), born Brooklyn, NY, May 6, 1983.

Lynn Whitfield, 67, actress (*Stepmom, Eve's Bayou*), born Baton Rouge, LA, May 6, 1953.

May 7 — Thursday

DAY 128   **238 REMAINING**

BEAUFORT SCALE DAY (FRANCIS BEAUFORT BIRTH ANNIVERSARY). May 7, 1774. A day to honor the British naval officer, Sir Francis Beaufort, who in 1806 devised a scale of wind force from 0 (calm) to 12 (hurricane) that was based on observation, not requiring any special instruments. The scale was adopted for international use in 1874 and has since been enlarged and refined. Beaufort was born at Flower Hill, Meath, Ireland, and died at Brighton, England, Dec 17, 1857.

BEETHOVEN'S NINTH SYMPHONY PREMIERE: ANNIVERSARY. May 7, 1824. Beethoven's Ninth Symphony in D Minor was performed for the first time at Vienna, Austria. Known as the *Choral* because of his use of voices in symphonic form for the first time, the Ninth was his musical interpretation of Schiller's "Ode to Joy." Beethoven was completely deaf when he composed it, and it was said a soloist had to tug on his sleeve when the performance was over to get him to turn around and see the enthusiastic response he could not hear.

BIRTHDAY OF THE BUDDHA (DAY OF VESAK). May 7. Among Buddhist holidays, this day is the most important, as it commemorates the birthday of the Buddha. It is also known as the Day of Vesak. The founder of Buddhism had the given name Siddhartha, the family name Gautama and the clan name Shaka. He is commonly called the Buddha, meaning in Sanskrit "the enlightened one." He is thought to have lived in India from circa 563 BC to 483 BC. Some countries celebrate this holiday on the lunar calendar, so the date changes from year to year, but it usually occurs in either April or May. This day is a holiday in India, Indonesia, Korea, Singapore and Thailand. This is also a holiday in China, but the date differs on the Chinese calendar.

BRAHMS, JOHANNES: BIRTH ANNIVERSARY. May 7, 1833. Regarded as one of the greatest composers of 19th-century music, Johannes Brahms was born at Hamburg, Germany. His works were firmly rooted in traditional classical principles and truly Romantic in spirit. When Brahms was 17, his talent was discovered and promoted by the Hungarian violinist Eduard Reményi, who took him on a national concert tour. During this tour Brahms met composer Robert Schumann and his wife, Clara Schumann. The

endorsement and support of the Schumanns quickly established his musical reputation. Brahms completed his most important work, *Ein Deutsches Requiem (The German Requiem)*, after his mother's death in 1865. It is considered one of the best examples of 19th-century choral music and was presented with much success throughout Germany. Brahms died at Vienna, Austria, Apr 3, 1897.

BROWNING, ROBERT: BIRTH ANNIVERSARY. May 7, 1812. The great Victorian poet, born at Camberwell, London, England, was known for his use of dramatic monologues. Browning created memorable portraits in verse of figures throughout history. His most acclaimed work, *The Ring and the Book* (1868–69), features 12 books of varying viewpoints concerning a 17th-century love triangle and murder in Rome. Browning's dramatic 1845 courtship of and 1846 marriage to fellow poet Elizabeth Barrett have been often chronicled in popular culture. Barrett died in 1861, and Browning died at Venice, Italy, Dec 12, 1889.

COOPER, GARY: BIRTH ANNIVERSARY. May 7, 1901. Frank James Cooper was born at Helena, MT. He changed his name to Gary at the start of his movie career. He is best known by baseball fans for his portrayal of Lou Gehrig in *The Pride of the Yankees*. Other films include *Wings, The Virginian, The Plainsman, Beau Geste, Sergeant York* (for which he won his first Academy Award), *High Noon* (winning his second Oscar for Best Actor), *The Court Martial of Billy Mitchell* and *Friendly Persuasion*. He died May 13, 1961, at Hollywood, CA.

CYSTINOSIS AWARENESS DAY. May 7. 3rd annual. This day is aimed at educating the general population about cystinosis. Cystinosis is a rare genetic metabolic disease that causes an amino acid, cystine, to accumulate in various organs of the body. Without specific treatment, children with cystinosis develop end-stage kidney failure at approximately age nine. It is estimated that 2,000 individuals worldwide have cystinosis, though exact numbers are difficult to obtain because the disease is often undiagnosed and/or misdiagnosed. Now is the time to improve diagnosis, improve treatments, advocate for our children and ourselves, and become relentless in our mission until a cure becomes reality. Annually, May 7. For info: Cystinosis Research Network, 302 Whytegate Ct, Lake Forest, IL 60045. Phone: (866) 276-3669. E-mail: info@cystinosis.org. Web: www.cystinosis.org.

DIEN BIEN PHU FALLS: ANNIVERSARY. May 7, 1954. Vietnam's victory over France at Dien Bien Phu ended the Indochina War.

DOW JONES TOPS 15,000: ANNIVERSARY. May 7, 2013. The Dow Jones Index of major industrial stocks closed above 15,000 for the first time (15,009.59). On May 3, 2013, it had briefly surpassed 15,000 before closing at 14,974.

EL SALVADOR: DAY OF THE SOLDIER. May 7. National holiday. Anniversary of the founding of the country's armed forces in 1824.

FIRST PRESIDENTIAL INAUGURAL BALL: ANNIVERSARY. May 7, 1789. Celebrating the inauguration of George Washington, the first Presidential Inaugural Ball was held at New York, NY.

FLOWER MOON. May 7. So called by Native American tribes of New England and the Great Lakes because by this time of the year, flowers are everywhere. The May Full Moon.

GERMANY: HAMBURG HARBOR BIRTHDAY. May 7, 1189. "Hafengeburtstag" celebrates establishment of Hamburg as a free city.

GERMANY'S FIRST SURRENDER: 75th ANNIVERSARY. May 7, 1945. Russian, American, British and French ranking officers crowded into a second-floor recreation room of a small redbrick schoolhouse (which served as General Dwight Eisenhower's headquarters) at Reims, Germany. Representing Germany, Field Marshal Alfred Jodl signed an unconditional surrender of all German fighting forces. After a signing that took almost 40 minutes, Jodl was ushered into Eisenhower's presence. The American general asked the German if he fully understood what he had signed and informed Jodl that he would be held personally responsible for any deviation from the terms of the surrender, including the

requirement that German commanders sign a formal surrender to the USSR at a time and place determined by that government.

HUME, DAVID: BIRTH ANNIVERSARY. May 7, 1711. Scottish Enlightenment philosopher born at Edinburgh (Old Style date, Apr 26, 1711). Hume's ideas present the culmination of the philosophical movement of empiricism. Hume addressed such questions as the limits of knowledge. He rejected metaphysical questions and stated that we should be skeptical of all conclusions reached by the use of reason. A prolific author, Hume wrote the six-volume *History of England* (1754–62), as well as other essays and historical work. Today, his *A Treatise of Human Nature* is seen as his most important work. Hume died on Aug 25, 1776, at Edinburgh.

"KRAFT TELEVISION THEATRE" TV PREMIERE: ANNIVERSARY. May 7, 1947. Live theatrical programs appearing on both the NBC and ABC networks. The show was a gold mine for discovering new talent. Among the playwrights getting their big breaks were Rod Serling, Paddy Chayefsky and Tad Mosel. Some of the show's most notable plays were "The Easy Mark" (1951) with Jack Lemmon, "Double in Ivory" (1953) with Lee Remick, "To Live in Peace" (1953) with Anne Bancroft, "The Missing Years" (1954) with Anthony Perkins and Mary Astor and "A Profile in Courage" (1956) with James Whitmore. The latter play was based on a book by Senator John F. Kennedy, who appeared on the program to introduce the drama.

***LUSITANIA* SINKING: ANNIVERSARY.** May 7, 1915. British passenger liner *Lusitania*, on its return trip from New York to Liverpool, carrying nearly 2,000 passengers, was torpedoed by a German submarine off the coast of Ireland, sinking within minutes; 1,198 lives were lost. US president Woodrow Wilson sent a note of protest to Berlin on May 13, but Germany, which had issued a warning in advance, pointed to *Lusitania*'s cargo of ammunition for Britain. The US maintained its neutrality for the time being.

MACLEISH, ARCHIBALD: BIRTH ANNIVERSARY. May 7, 1892. American poet and librarian of Congress (1939–44), born at Glencoe, IL. MacLeish was also a playwright, screenwriter, political activist, diplomat, UNESCO member, editor, lawyer, professor and farmer. He received the Pulitzer Prize three times: for two books of poetry—*Conquistador* and *Collected Poems*—and for the drama *J.B.* (1958). An Academy Award winner for his screenplay of *The Eleanor Roosevelt Story* (1965), he died at Boston, MA, Apr 20, 1982.

MOON PHASE: FULL MOON. May 7. Moon enters Full Moon phase at 6:45 AM, EDT.

★**NATIONAL DAY OF PRAYER.** May 7. Presidential Proclamation always issued for the first Thursday in May since 1981. (Public Law 100–307 of May 5, 1988.) Beginning in 1957, a day in October was designated, except in 1972 and 1975–77.

	S	M	T	W	T	F	S
May						1	2
	3	4	5	6	7	8	9
2020	10	11	12	13	14	15	16
	17	18	19	20	21	22	23
	24	25	26	27	28	29	30
	31						

NATIONAL DAY OF REASON. May 7. A day to celebrate reason and to raise public awareness about the persistent threat to religious liberty posed by government intrusion into the private sphere of worship. This day also exists to inspire the secular community to be visible and active on this day to set the right example for how to effect positive change. Local organizations might use "Day of Reason" to label their events, or they might choose labels such as Day of Action, Day of Service or Rational Day of Care. The important message is to provide a positive, useful, constitutional alternative to the exclusionary National Day of Prayer. Annually, the first Thursday in May. For info: American Humanist Assn, 1821 Jefferson Pl NW, Washington, DC 20036. Web: www.NationalDayOfReason.org.

NCAA DIVISION I MEN'S VOLLEYBALL CHAMPIONSHIP. May 7–9. EagleBank Arena, Fairfax, VA. Host is George Mason. For info: NCAA, PO Box 6222, Indianapolis, IN 46206-6222. Web: www.NCAA.com.

PERÓN, EVA: BIRTH ANNIVERSARY. May 7, 1919. Born María Eva Duarte at Los Toldos, Argentina, "Evita" had already made a name for herself in the theater before marrying army officer Juan Perón and shortly thereafter becoming Argentina's first lady in 1946. Her advocacy of women's suffrage, labor rights and social welfare programs endeared her to *los descamisados* ("the shirtless ones"). During her tenure as first lady, women gained the right to vote (1947), many new hospitals were built and infection rates of communicable disease fell dramatically under her unofficial supervision of the departments of labor and health. Her untimely death from cancer on July 26, 1952, at Buenos Aires thrust the nation into profound grief, and her funeral was attended by an estimated three million people.

TCHAIKOVSKY, PETER ILYICH: BIRTH ANNIVERSARY. May 7, 1840. (New Style date.) One of the outstanding composers of all time, Peter Ilyich Tchaikovsky was born at Votkinsk, Russia. Among his famous works are the symphony *Pathétique*; the opera *Eugene Onegin*; and the ballets *Swan Lake*, *Sleeping Beauty* and *The Nutcracker*. He was the first to turn the ballet into a sustained dramatic expression. Tchaikovsky died of cholera during an epidemic at St. Petersburg, Russia, Nov 6, 1893—nine days after conducting his *Pathétique* symphony for the first time.

TWENTY-SEVENTH AMENDMENT RATIFIED: ANNIVERSARY. May 7, 1992. The 27th Amendment to the Constitution was ratified, prohibiting Congress from giving itself midterm pay raises.

UNITAS, JOHNNY: BIRTH ANNIVERSARY. May 7, 1933. Born at Pittsburgh, PA, Johnny Unitas played football for the University of Louisville. After college, he went to work as a construction worker but continued to play football (for $6 per game) for the Bloomfield Rams, a semipro team that played on dirt, not grass. Based on a fan's letter, the Baltimore Colts gave him a conditional contract, and soon he was a star. He played 17 seasons for the Colts, was the MVP three times, went to 10 Pro Bowls and led his team to three NFL championships. He was inducted into the Pro Football Hall of Fame in 1979 and has often been called the greatest quarterback ever to play the game. He died at Baltimore, MD, Sept 11, 2002.

🎂 BIRTHDAYS TODAY

Peter Carey, 77, author (Booker Prizes for *Oscar and Lucinda* and *True History of the Kelly Gang*), born Bacchus Marsh, Australia, May 7, 1943.

Amy Heckerling, 66, filmmaker (*Fast Times at Ridgemont High*, *Look Who's Talking*), born New York, NY, May 7, 1954.

Gary R. Herbert, 73, Governor of Utah (R), born American Fork, UT, May 7, 1947.

Alexander Ludwig, 28, actor ("Vikings," *Lone Survivor*), born Vancouver, BC, Canada, May 7, 1992.

Shawn Marion, 42, former basketball player, born Waukegan, IL, May 7, 1978.

Peter Reckell, 65, actor ("Days of Our Lives"), born Elkhart, IN, May 7, 1955.

May 8 — Friday

DAY 129 **237 REMAINING**

BASS, SAUL: 100th BIRTH ANNIVERSARY. May 8, 1920. The graphic designer and creator of film title sequences was born at New York, NY. His first work in Hollywood was in marketing, designing film posters, but a dramatic opening credit sequence for *The Man with the Golden Arm* (1955), soon made him in-demand for that craft. Bass was able with concise, arresting graphics to immediately signal the tone and theme of a film (opening credits before the 1950s being prosaic efforts). Title sequences in his hands became an integral part of the film. Bass is known for work with Alfred Hitchcock and later in his career for Martin Scorsese. He received an Oscar for the documentary short "Why Man Creates" in 1968. As an in-demand graphic designer, Bass continued to create iconic film posters as well as logos for the YMCA, Kleenex, AT&T, Warner Communications and others. Bass died Apr 25, 1996, at Los Angeles, CA.

BLUEBERRY HILL OPEN DART TOURNAMENT. May 8–10. St. Louis, MO. 48th annual. America's oldest and largest pub dart tournament open to everyone. Est attendance: 375. For info: Joe Edwards, Blueberry Hill, 6504 Delmar in The Loop, St. Louis, MO 63130. Phone: (314) 727-4444. Web: www.BlueberryHill.com.

CZECH REPUBLIC: LIBERATION DAY. May 8. Commemorates the liberation of Czechoslovakia from the Germans in 1945.

DENMARK: COMMON PRAYER DAY. May 8. Public holiday. The fourth Friday after Easter, known as "Store Bededag," is a day for prayer and festivity.

DUNANT, JEAN-HENRI: BIRTH ANNIVERSARY. May 8, 1828. Author and philanthropist, founder of the Red Cross, born at Geneva, Switzerland. His book *Un Souvenir de Solferino* (1862) is both a firsthand recounting of one of the bloodiest battles of the 19th century and a proposal to establish relief aid to wartime wounded. The conference that resulted as a response to its call to action had two significant results: the founding of the Red Cross and the implementation of the international treaty known as the Geneva Convention. Dunant was awarded the first Nobel Peace Prize in 1901. Died at Heiden, Switzerland, Oct 30, 1910.

ENGLAND: HELSTON FURRY DANCE/FLORA DAY. May 8. Helston, Cornwall. The world-famous Helston Furry Dance is held each year on Flora Day, May 8 (except when the 8th is a Sunday or Monday, in which case it is held on the preceding Saturday). Dancing around the streets begins early in the morning and continues throughout the day. The dance leaves Guildhall at the stroke of noon and winds its way into and out of many of the larger buildings.

FINTASTIC FRIDAY: GIVING SHARKS A VOICE!. May 8. Everyone needs a special day, especially sharks! Fintastic Friday celebrates sharks and encourages kids to find ways to change public opinion from hatred to love and from fear to appreciation. Sharks need our help. People kill as many as 100 million sharks a year. Populations are dropping at catastrophic rates. WhaleTimes is confident kids can change the tide for sharks in a positive way. Throughout the world, kids celebrate Fintastic Friday in all kinds of ways, such as making their home a shark conservation zone or having a "Sharks in the Park" rally. Annually, the second Friday in May. For info: WhaleTimes, Inc, 19190 SW 90th, #2702, Tualatin, OR 97062. E-mail: fintasticfriday@whaletimes.org. Web: www.whaletimes.org.

FRANCE: VICTORY DAY. May 8. Commemorates the surrender of Germany to Allied forces and the cessation of hostilities in 1945.

GERMANY'S SECOND SURRENDER: 75th ANNIVERSARY. May 8, 1945. Stalin refused to recognize the document of unconditional surrender signed at Reims, Germany, the previous day, so a second signing was held near Berlin. The event was turned into an elaborate formal ceremony by the Soviets, who had lost some 20 million lives during the war. As in the Reims document, the end of hostilities was set for 12:01 AM local time on May 9.

GOTTSCHALK, LOUIS MOREAU: BIRTH ANNIVERSARY. May 8, 1829. American pianist of international fame who toured the US during the Civil War. Gottschalk composed for the piano, combining American and Creole folk themes and rhythms in his work. Born at New Orleans, LA, he died Dec 18, 1869, at Rio de Janeiro, Brazil.

HIDALGO Y COSTILLA, MIGUEL: BIRTH ANNIVERSARY. May 8, 1753. Father of Mexican independence and Catholic priest, born at Corralejo, New Spain (now Mexico). Famously, on Sept 16, 1810, he rang the church bell at Dolores calling for the people to fight for independence from Spain. Defeated at the Battle of Calderón Bridge on Jan 17, 1811, Hidalgo tried to lead his depleted revolutionary forces to the US but was captured. He was executed on July 30, 1811, at Chihuahua.

JOHNSON, ROBERT: BIRTH ANNIVERSARY. May 8, 1911. Born at Hazlehurst, MS, and murdered at age 27, Aug 16, 1938, at Greenwood, MS (poisoned by a jealous husband), Johnson was a master blues guitarist, singer and songwriter of broad influence. He developed a unique guitar style of such skill that it was said he acquired his ability by selling his soul to the devil. Johnson's only two recording sessions captured the classics "Sweet Home Chicago," "Cross Road Blues," "Me and the Devil Blues" and others. Johnson was inducted into the Blues Hall of Fame in 1980 and the Rock and Roll Hall of Fame in 1986.

LAVOISIER, ANTOINE-LAURENT: EXECUTION ANNIVERSARY. May 8, 1794. French chemist and the "father of modern chemistry." Especially noted for having first explained the real nature of combustion and for showing that matter is not destroyed in chemical reactions. Born at Paris, France, Aug 26, 1743, Lavoisier was guillotined at the Place de la Révolution for his former position as a tax collector. The Revolutionary Tribunal is reported to have responded to a plea to spare his life with the statement: "We need no more scientists in France."

LISTON, SONNY: BIRTH ANNIVERSARY. May 8, 1932. Charles "Sonny" Liston, boxer born at St. Francis County, AR. Liston rose above a record of criminal activity to defeat Floyd Patterson for the heavyweight title on Sept 25, 1962. He defeated Patterson in a rematch but then lost the title to Cassius Clay, who later changed his name to Muhammad Ali. In a rematch Ali knocked Liston out with a punch few observers saw. Died at Las Vegas, NV, Dec 30, 1970.

★MILITARY SPOUSE APPRECIATION DAY. May 8. First proclaimed by President Ronald Reagan in 1984 to recognize and honor the contributions and sacrifices of military spouses. Annually, the Friday before Mother's Day.

MILITARY SPOUSE APPRECIATION DAY. May 8. Observed on US military posts worldwide, this day celebrates the strength and patriotism of the spouses of members of the military. Annually on the Friday before Mother's Day, events are commonly sponsored to recognize the spouses of men and women in uniform for their support, contributions and sacrifices.

MOUNT PELÉE ERUPTION: ANNIVERSARY. May 8, 1902. In the worst volcanic disaster of the 20th century, Mount Pelée erupted on the tiny French Caribbean island of Martinique. In minutes a cloud of ashes, gases and rocks destroyed the thriving port city of Saint-Pierre, killing all but one of its 30,000 inhabitants.

NCAA DIVISION I WOMEN'S WATER POLO CHAMPIONSHIP. May 8–10. Chris Kjeldsen Pool Complex, Stockton, CA. For info: NCAA, PO Box 6222, Indianapolis, IN 46206-6222. Web: www.NCAA.com.

NO SOCKS DAY. May 8. If we give up wearing socks for one day, it will mean a little less laundry, thereby contributing to the betterment of the environment. Besides, we will all feel a bit freer, at least for one day. Annually, May 8. (©2006 by WH.) For info: Thomas & Ruth Roy, Wellcat Holidays, 2418 Long Ln, Lebanon, PA 17046. Phone: (717) 279-0184. E-mail: info@wellcat.com. Web: www.wellcat.com.

OUIMET, FRANCIS DESALES: BIRTH ANNIVERSARY. May 8, 1893. American amateur golfer who is credited with establishing the popularity of golf in the US. Born at Brookline, MA, he began his golfing career as a caddy. In 1913, at age 20, he generated national enthusiasm for the game when he became the first American and first amateur to win the US Open Golf Championship. He won the US Amateur Championship in 1914 and 1931 and was a member of the US Walker Cup team from its first tournament in 1922 until 1949, serving as its nonplaying captain for six of those years. In 1951 he became the first American to be elected captain of the Royal and Ancient Golf Club of St. Andrews, Scotland. Ouimet died at Newton, MA, Sept 2, 1967.

ROCHESTER LILAC FESTIVAL. May 8–17. Highland Park, Rochester, NY. The only 10-day free festival of its kind in North America. Visitors experience the incredible beauty and intense fragrance of more than 500 varieties of lilacs on 1,200 plants—the largest lilac collection in the US. Visitors enjoy nonstop entertainment at Center Stage, Craft Beer Expo, Wine Tasting Expo, Bloody Mary Tasting Expo, a wide variety of foods, art and craft shows and one-of-a-kind shopping. Special events include Lilac Parade, Seniors Day and Lilac 10k and 5k Fun Run. Free admission. Est attendance: 500,000. For info: Rochester Lilac Festival. Phone: (585) 473-4482. E-mail: info@rochesterevents.com. Web: www.rochesterevents.com.

SLOVAKIA: LIBERATION DAY. May 8. Commemorates the liberation of Czechoslovakia from the Germans in 1945.

TRUMAN, HARRY S: BIRTH ANNIVERSARY. May 8, 1884. The 33rd president of the US, succeeded to that office upon the death of Franklin D. Roosevelt, Apr 12, 1945, and served until Jan 20, 1953. Born at Lamar, MO, Truman was the last of the nine US presidents who did not attend college. Affectionately nicknamed "Give 'em Hell Harry" by admirers. Truman died at Kansas City, MO, Dec 26, 1972. His birthday is a holiday in Missouri.

UNITED NATIONS: TIME OF REMEMBRANCE AND RECONCILIATION FOR THOSE WHO LOST THEIR LIVES DURING THE SECOND WORLD WAR. May 8–9. In 2004, the General Assembly declared May 8–9 as a time of remembrance and reconciliation and invited member states, United Nations bodies, nongovernmental organizations and individuals to observe annually either one or both of those days in an appropriate manner to pay tribute to all those who lost their lives in WWII. (Res 59/26 of Nov 22, 2004.) For info: United Nations, Dept of Public Info, New York, NY 10017. Web: www.un.org.

May 2020	S	M	T	W	T	F	S
						1	2
	3	4	5	6	7	8	9
	10	11	12	13	14	15	16
	17	18	19	20	21	22	23
	24	25	26	27	28	29	30
	31						

V-E DAY: 75th ANNIVERSARY. May 8, 1945. Victory in Europe Day commemorates unconditional surrender of Germany to Allied forces. The surrender document was signed by German representatives at General Dwight D. Eisenhower's headquarters at Reims, Germany, to become effective, and hostilities to end, at one minute past midnight May 9, 1945, which in the United States was 9:01 PM, EDT, on May 8. President Harry S Truman on May 8 declared May 9, 1945, to be "V-E Day," but it later came to be observed on May 8. A separate German surrender to the USSR was signed at Karlshorst, near Berlin, May 8. See also: "Russia: Victory Day" (May 9).

WORLD RED CROSS RED CRESCENT DAY. May 8. A day for commemorating the 1828 birth of Jean-Henri Dunant, the Swiss founder of the International Red Cross Movement in 1863, and for recognizing the humanitarian work of the Red Cross and Red Crescent around the world. For info: International Committee of the Red Cross. Web: www.icrc.org or www.redcross.org.

🎂 BIRTHDAYS TODAY

Stephen Amell, 39, actor (*Justice for Natalee Holloway*, "Arrow," "Hung"), born Toronto, ON, Canada, May 8, 1981.

David Attenborough, 94, author, naturalist (*Life on Earth, Trials of Life*), born London, England, May 8, 1926.

Joe Bonamassa, 43, guitarist, born New Hartford, NY, May 8, 1977.

Bill Cowher, 63, sportscaster, former football coach and player, born Pittsburgh, PA, May 8, 1957.

Bill de Blasio, 59, Mayor of New York City (D), born Warren Wilhelm, Jr, at New York, NY, May 8, 1961.

Elyes Gabel, 37, actor ("Scorpion," "Casualty," *A Most Violent Year*), born London, England, May 8, 1983.

Melissa Gilbert, 56, actress ("Little House on the Prairie," *The Miracle Worker*), born Los Angeles, CA, May 8, 1964.

Enrique Iglesias, 45, singer, born Madrid, Spain, May 8, 1975.

David Keith, 66, actor (*The Great Santini, An Officer and a Gentleman*), director, born Knoxville, TN, May 8, 1954.

Bobby Labonte, 56, race car driver, born Corpus Christi, TX, May 8, 1964.

Ronald Mandel (Ronnie) Lott, 61, Hall of Fame football player, born Albuquerque, NM, May 8, 1959.

Thomas Pynchon, 83, author (*Vineland, V, Gravity's Rainbow*), born Glen Cove, NY, May 8, 1937.

Toni Tennille, 77, singer (Captain & Tennille), born Montgomery, AL, May 8, 1943.

May 9 — Saturday

DAY 130   **236 REMAINING**

ADAMS, RICHARD: 100th BIRTH ANNIVERSARY. May 9, 1920. Award-wining novelist, author of *Watership Down, Shardik, The Plague Dogs* and many others. Born at Newbury, England, he died Dec 24, 2016, at Oxford, England.

BARRIE, JAMES M.: BIRTH ANNIVERSARY. May 9, 1860. Playwright and author, born at Kirriemuir, Angus, Scotland. Barrie is best known for his play *Peter Pan, or the Boy Who Would Not Grow Up*, which was first performed in 1904 and published in 1928. Barrie died June 19, 1937, at London, England.

BRITISH CAPTURE ENIGMA MACHINE: ANNIVERSARY. May 9, 1941. During WWII, when a German U-110 submarine attacked a British convoy, two British vessels, the *Bulldog* and *Aubretia*, were able to retaliate so quickly with depth charges that the submarine was disabled and unable to dive. With the submarine captured, British sailors investigated the radio room and discovered the typewriter-like Enigma, a ciphering machine that enabled safe German communication, and documents of tables that helped explain how it worked. The U-110's capture was kept secret, and British cryptographers used this break to begin unraveling German code during the war.

BROWN, JOHN: BIRTH ANNIVERSARY. May 9, 1800. Abolitionist leader born at Torrington, CT, and hanged Dec 2, 1859, at Charles Town, WV. Leader of attack on Harpers Ferry, VA, Oct 16, 1859, which was intended to give impetus to the movement for escape and freedom of slaves. His aim was frustrated and in fact resulted in increased polarization and sectional animosity. Legendary martyr of the abolitionist movement.

EUROPEAN UNION: 70th ANNIVERSARY OBSERVANCE. May 9, 1950. Member countries of the European Union commemorate the announcement by French statesman Robert Schuman of the "Schuman Plan" for establishing a single authority for production of coal, iron and steel in France and Germany. The European Coal and Steel Community was founded in 1952. This organization was a forerunner of the European Economic Community, founded in 1958, which later became the European Union. At the European Summit at Milan, Italy, in 1985, this day was proclaimed the Day of Europe.

GONZALES, PANCHO: BIRTH ANNIVERSARY. May 9, 1928. Richard Alonzo "Pancho" Gonzales, tennis player born at Los Angeles, CA. A self-taught player, Gonzales won the 1948 US National Singles Championship and repeated in 1949. He turned pro and won the world championship from 1954 through 1962. Gonzales was an aggressive, temperamental player who rarely trained. Died at Las Vegas, NV, July 3, 1995.

INTERNATIONAL MIGRATORY BIRD DAY. May 9. To educate the public about migratory birds and the preservation of their habitats in the US and Central America. Annually, the second Saturday in May.

INVICTUS GAMES—THE HAGUE 2020. May 9–16. The Hague, The Netherlands. 5th edition. The Invictus Games use the power of sport to inspire recovery, support rehabilitation and generate a wider understanding of and respect for wounded, injured and sick servicemen and servicewomen. The inaugural Invictus Games were held in London in September 2014 and were attended by more than 400 competitors from 13 nations. Invictus Games competitors are the men and women who put their lives on the line and suffered life-changing injuries for their country. For info: Invictus Games Foundation. E-mail: info@invictusgames2020.nl. Web: www.invictusgames2020.nl.

ITALY: GIRO D'ITALIA. May 9–31. 103rd edition. One of world cycling's three Grand Tours, the Giro d'Italia was organized in 1909 as a way to boost circulation of *La Gazzetta dello Sport*, a Milan-based daily newspaper covering sports. Modeled on the Tour de France, the Giro is held annually over the last three weeks of May on a course that changes from year to year. The race is broadcast in 198 countries with an estimated global viewing audience of 775 million. In 2020, the race starts outside Italy in Budapest, Hungary, with two more stages in Hungary. Est attendance: 12,500,000. For info: RCS Sport SpA or Union Cycliste Internationale. Web: www.gazzetta.it or www.giroditalia.it/it.

JAMESTOWN DAY. May 9. Jamestown Settlement and Historic Jamestowne, Williamsburg, VA. Salute the 413th anniversary of the 1607 founding of Jamestown, America's first permanent English colony, with maritime and interpretive demonstrations, archaeology programs and tours. Separate site admission. For info: Jamestown-Yorktown Foundation, PO Box 1607, Williamsburg, VA 23187. Phone: (757) 253-4838 or (888) 593-4682. Fax: (757) 253-5299. Web: www.historyisfun.org.

LETTER CARRIERS' "STAMP OUT HUNGER" FOOD DRIVE. May 9. 28th annual. Every year since 1993, on the second Saturday in May, letter carriers in more than 10,000 cities and towns across the 50 states, the District of Columbia, Puerto Rico, the Virgin Islands and Guam collect nonperishable food items left by mailboxes and in post offices from their postal customers. The National Association of Letter Carriers' "Stamp Out Hunger" Food Drive is the largest one-day food drive in the nation. In 2018, the food drive gathered more than 71.6 million pounds of food. For info: Stamp Out Hunger, Natl Association of Letter Carriers, 100 Indiana Ave NW, Washington, DC 20001-2144. Phone: (202) 662-2489. Web: www.nalc.org.

MARSTON, WILLIAM MOULTON: BIRTH ANNIVERSARY. May 9, 1893. Born at Cliftondale, MA. Psychologist and author William Marston's legacy continues to have a profound impact on contemporary criminal science and popular culture. While an undergraduate at Harvard he created the Marston Deception Test—now known as the lie detector—and was its most ardent advocate. Marston was also a prolific writer, penning many academic and popular texts, although his most well-known work, the Wonder Woman comic book series, which depicted the first female superhero, was written under the pseudonym Charles Moulton. Ahead of his time, Marston foresaw the increasing empowerment of women in the future, famously writing, "I fully believe I am hitting a great movement now under way, the growth in power of women." He died of cancer May 2, 1947, at Rye, NY.

NATIONAL BABYSITTERS DAY. May 9. To give babysitters across the nation appreciation and special recognition for their quality child care. Annually, the Saturday before Mother's Day. For info: Barbara Baldwin, RN, Safety Whys, PO Box 1177, Helotes, TX 78023-1177. Phone: (210) 695-9838. E-mail: bbaldwin@satx.rr.com. Web: www.safetywhys.com.

NETHERLANDS: NATIONAL WINDMILL DAY. May 9. About 1,200 windmills survive, and some 300 are used occasionally and have been designated national monuments by the government. As many windmills as possible are in operation on National Windmill Day for the benefit of tourists. Annually, the second Saturday in May.

RENO, NEVADA: ANNIVERSARY. May 9, 1868. First known as Fullers Crossing, and then Lakes Crossing, on this date it officially became Reno, known today as "the Biggest Little City in the World." Its six-week residency requirement for divorce became law on May 1, 1931.

RUSSIA: VICTORY DAY. May 9. National holiday observed annually to commemorate the 1945 Allied forces' defeat of Nazi Germany in WWII and to honor the 20 million Soviet people who died in that war. Hostilities ceased and the German surrender became effective at one minute after midnight on May 9, 1945. See also: "V-E Day: Anniversary" (May 8).

SNOW, HANK: BIRTH ANNIVERSARY. May 9, 1914. Country Hall of Fame singer born at Brooklyn, Nova Scotia, Canada. Snow, whose career spanned six decades, was most popular in the 1950s. His first hit among many was 1950's "I'm Moving On"—it stayed on top of the charts for 21 weeks. Snow, a regular at the Grand Ole Opry, was instrumental in getting Elvis Presley on the bill there. Snow died Dec 20, 1999, at Madison, TN.

STAY UP ALL NIGHT NIGHT. May 9. A night when people are encouraged to stay awake through the night, reliving the excitement of staying up late as a child. It's a chance to catch up on chores, do some cleaning, watch films, read, cook, drink or chat with friends. There is something incredibly satisfying in staying up to see the sun rise—and everyone should do it at least once a year. Annually,

the second Saturday in May. For info: George Mahood. E-mail: george@georgemahood.com. Web: www.georgemahood.com/stayupallnight.

UZBEKISTAN: DAY OF MEMORY AND HONOR. May 9. Honors Uzbek citizens killed in WWII. Formerly Victory Day when Uzbekistan was part of the Soviet Union.

"VAST WASTELAND" SPEECH: ANNIVERSARY. May 9, 1961. Speaking before the bigwigs of network TV at the annual convention of the National Association of Broadcasters, Newton Minow, the new chairman of the Federal Communications Commission, exhorted those executives to sit through an entire day of their own programming. He suggested that they "will observe a vast wasteland." Further, he urged them to try for "imagination in programming, not sterility; creativity, not imitation; experimentation, not conformity; excellence, not mediocrity."

WALLACE, MIKE: BIRTH ANNIVERSARY. May 9, 1918. With a career of more than 60 years as a journalist and broadcaster, Mike Wallace was known for his tireless work ethic and strident interviewing style, firing probing questions at his subjects in a relentless quest for the real story. Born Myron Leon Wallace to Russian immigrants at Brookline, MA, Wallace got his start as a radio announcer, game show host and pitchman but by 1960 had developed his hard-hitting style. He brought that tenacity to "60 Minutes" when it debuted in 1968, helping to shape the style and substance of the long-running CBS newsmagazine, and in the process became a star in his own right. Wallace won 21 Emmys. He died Apr 7, 2012, at New Canaan, CT.

WORLD FAIR TRADE DAY. May 9. Since 2001, a day to promote Fair Trade as an alternative economic model. "Fair Trade" means that trading partnerships are based on reciprocal benefits and mutual respect; prices paid to producers reflect the work they do; workers have the right to organize; national health, safety and wage laws are enforced; and products are environmentally sustainable and conserve natural resources. Celebrated worldwide in 70 countries with a variety of events from live music to symposia. Annually, the second Saturday in May. For info: World Fair Trade Organization, Godfried Bomansstraat 8-3, 4103 WR Culemborg, The Netherlands. Phone: (31) (345) 53-64-87. E-mail: info@wfto.com. Web: www.wfto.com.

🎂 BIRTHDAYS TODAY

Candice Bergen, 74, actress (*Starting Over*, "Murphy Brown," "Boston Legal"), born Beverly Hills, CA, May 9, 1946.

James L. Brooks, 80, director, producer, screenwriter (Oscar for *Terms of Endearment*; *As Good as It Gets*, "Taxi," "The Mary Tyler Moore Show"), born Brooklyn, NY, May 9, 1940.

Nina Campbell, 75, interior designer, born London, England, May 9, 1945.

Rosario Dawson, 41, actress (*He Got Game, Sin City*), born New York, NY, May 9, 1979.

Nicolas Ghesquière, 49, fashion designer, director of Louis Vuitton, born Comines, France, May 9, 1971.

Joy Harjo, 69, Poet Laureate of the US (2019–), poet, professor, born Joy Foster at Tulsa, OK, May 9, 1951.

Glenda Jackson, 83, actress (Oscars for *Women in Love* and *A Touch of Class*), born Cheshire, England, May 9, 1937.

Billy Joel, 71, singer, composer, born Hicksville, NY, May 9, 1949.

Charles Simic, 82, former US poet laureate (2007–8), born Belgrade, Yugoslavia (now Serbia), May 9, 1938.

Steve Yzerman, 55, hockey executive and Hall of Fame player, born Cranbrook, BC, Canada, May 9, 1965.

May 2020	S	M	T	W	T	F	S
						1	2
	3	4	5	6	7	8	9
	10	11	12	13	14	15	16
	17	18	19	20	21	22	23
	24	25	26	27	28	29	30
	31						

May 10 — Sunday

ASTAIRE, FRED: BIRTH ANNIVERSARY. May 10, 1899. Actor, dancer and choreographer, born at Omaha, NE. Astaire began dancing with his sister, Adele, and in the mid-1930s began dancing with Ginger Rogers. After Astaire's first Hollywood screen test, a producer noted of him: "Can't act. Slightly bald. Can dance a little." Despite this, Astaire starred in more than 40 films, including *Holiday Inn, The Gay Divorcée, Silk Stockings* and *Easter Parade*. Died at Los Angeles, CA, June 22, 1987.

ASTOR PLACE RIOT: ANNIVERSARY. May 10, 1849. A riot erupted outside the Astor Place Opera House at New York, NY, where the British actor William Charles Macready was performing. Led by the American actor Edwin Forrest, angry crowds revolted against dress requirements for admission and against Macready's public statements on the vulgarity of American life. On May 8 Macready's performance of *Macbeth* was stopped by Forrest's followers. Two days later, a mob led by Ned Buntline shattered the windows of the theater during a performance. Troops were summoned and ordered to fire, killing 22 and wounding 26.

BARTH, KARL: BIRTH ANNIVERSARY. May 10, 1886. The most influential Protestant theologian of the 20th century, Barth was born at Basel, Switzerland. Among his scores of works are *The Epistle to the Romans* (1918) and the 13-volume *Church Dogmatics* (1932–67). In 1934, Barth lost his teaching position at the University of Bonn when he did not sign the oath of allegiance to German chancellor Adolf Hitler. He explained afterward that he refused "to begin a commentary on the Sermon on the Mount with 'Heil Hitler.'" He died on Dec 10, 1968, at Basel.

BOOTH, JOHN WILKES: BIRTH ANNIVERSARY. May 10, 1838. Born near Bel Air, MD, into a famous theatrical family, Booth was himself a well-known actor when he assassinated President Abraham Lincoln. Fanatically opposed to abolition, Booth was present at the hanging of the abolitionist John Brown in 1859. During the Civil War, he outspokenly supported the South and denounced Lincoln, whom he regarded as a tyrant. As leader of a small group of conspirators, on the evening of Apr 14, 1865, Booth entered the presidential box at Ford's Theatre in Washington, DC, and shot the president in the back of the head. Shouting "Sic semper tyrannis!" he jumped to the stage, injuring his leg, and escaped on horseback. Tracked to a farm near Port Royal, VA, Booth was shot evading capture on Apr 26, 1865, and died from his wounds.

CARTER, MAYBELLE: BIRTH ANNIVERSARY. May 10, 1909. The guitar/banjo-playing cofounder of the singing Carter Family was born at Nickelsville, VA. The Carter Family were the first country music stars in America, reigning from 1927 to the 1950s and combining the influences of folk, bluegrass, rural country and gospel. Their hits include "Wabash Cannonball" and "Will the Circle Be Unbroken." Carter died Oct 23, 1978, at Nashville, TN.

CONFEDERATE MEMORIAL DAY IN NORTH AND SOUTH CAROLINA. May 10. Observed on the anniversary of the capture of Jefferson Davis by Union troops in 1865. Other Southern states observe Confederate Memorial Day on different dates.

GAUMONT, LÉON: BIRTH ANNIVERSARY. May 10, 1864. Important early film entrepreneur and inventor born at Paris, France. He established

the Gaumont Film Production Company in 1895 to capitalize on the growing new entertainment medium. Gaumont's technical work included a camera-projector, an early sound-synchronizing system and an early color process. Gaumont's company produced France's first "talkie"—*Eau de Nil* (1928). The Gaumont Company also comprised studios and a theater chain. Gaumont retired in 1929, and he died Aug 10, 1946, at Sainte-Maxime, Var, France.

GOLDEN SPIKE DRIVING: ANNIVERSARY. May 10, 1869. Anniversary of the meeting of Union Pacific and Central Pacific railways at Promontory Point, UT. On that day a golden spike was driven by Leland Stanford, president of the Central Pacific, to celebrate the linkage. The golden spike was promptly removed for preservation. Long called the final link in the ocean-to-ocean railroad, this event cannot be accurately described as completing the transcontinental railroad, but it did complete continuous rail tracks between Omaha and Sacramento. See also: "Transcontinental US Railway Completion: Anniversary" (Aug 15).

JEFFERSON DAVIS CAPTURED: ANNIVERSARY. May 10, 1865. Confederate president Jefferson Davis, his wife and cabinet officials were captured at Irwinville, GA, by the Fourth Michigan Cavalry. The prisoners were taken to Nashville, TN, and later sent to Richmond, VA.

MANDELA INAUGURATION: ANNIVERSARY. May 10, 1994. In a dramatic and historic exchange of power, former political prisoner Nelson Mandela was inaugurated as president of South Africa. Long the focal point of apartheid foes' attempts to end the enforced policy of discrimination in South Africa, Mandela handily won the first free election in South Africa despite many attempts by various political factions to either stop the electoral process or alter the outcome.

MICRONESIA, FEDERATED STATES OF: CONSTITUTION DAY. May 10. Proclamation of the Federated States of Micronesia in 1979. National holiday.

★**MOTHER'S DAY.** May 10. Presidential Proclamation always issued for the second Sunday in May. (Pub Res No. 2 of May 8, 1914.)

MOTHER'S DAY. May 10. Observed first in 1907 at the request of Anna Jarvis of Philadelphia, PA, who asked her church to hold a service in memory of all mothers on the anniversary of her mother's death. In 1909, two years after her mother's death, Jarvis and friends began a letter-writing campaign to create a Mother's Day observance. Congress passed legislation in 1914 designating the second Sunday in May as Mother's Day. Some say the predecessor of Mother's Day was the ancient spring festival dedicated to mother goddesses: Rhea (Greek) and Cybele (Roman).

MOTHER'S DAY AT THE WALL. May 10. Washington, DC. Annual observance at the Vietnam Veterans Memorial since 2000 honoring the mothers of those who died in combat. Area schoolchildren offer cards.

NATIONAL GEOGRAPHIC GEOBEE: NATIONAL FINALS. May 10–13. National Geographic Society Headquarters, Washington, DC. The first-place winner from each state-level competition (that took place on Mar 27) advances to the national level. Contestants compete for scholarships and prizes totaling more than $85,000. For info: Natl Geographic GeoBee, Natl Geographic Society. E-mail: ngbee@ngs.org. Web: www.natgeobee.org.

NATIONAL POLICE WEEK. May 10–16. Every 57 hours a police officer is killed in the line of duty somewhere in America. During this week and on Peace Officer Memorial Day, the American Police Hall of Fame and Museum honors those lost with memorial services and outreach to surviving family. See also: "Peace Officer Memorial Day" (May 15). For info: American Police Hall of Fame and Museum, 6350 Horizon Dr, Titusville, FL 32780. Phone: (321) 264-0911. E-mail: policeinfo@aphf.org. Web: www.aphf.org.

★**NATIONAL TRANSPORTATION WEEK.** May 10–16. Presidential Proclamation issued for week including third Friday in May since 1960. (PL 86–475 of May 20, 1960, first requested; PL 87–449 of May 14, 1962, requested an annual proclamation.)

★**POLICE WEEK.** May 10–16. Presidential Proclamation 3537 of May 4, 1963, covers all succeeding years. (Public Law 87–726 of Oct 1, 1962.) Since 1962, the week including May 15.

ROSS, GEORGE: BIRTH ANNIVERSARY. May 10, 1730. Signer of the Declaration of Independence. Born at New Castle, DE, he died July 14, 1779, at Philadelphia, PA.

SALUTE TO 35+ MOMS WEEK. May 10–16. Motherhood is challenging at any age, and if you become a mom when you're 35 or older, it can be quite an adjustment. This week is dedicated to moms with more life experience than baby experience. Now, and throughout the year, it is empowering to connect with peers and share the joys and the trials and tribulations that childrearing may encompass when you parent later in life. For info: Robin Gorman Newman, 44 Somerset Dr N, Great Neck, NY 11020. Phone: (516) 773-0911. E-mail: rgnewman@optonline.net. Web: www.motherhoodlater.com.

STEINER, MAX: BIRTH ANNIVERSARY. May 10, 1888. Composer, born Maximilian Raoul Steiner at Vienna, Austria-Hungary. A musical prodigy who studied under Gustav Mahler as well as a conductor, he went to Hollywood in 1929 and became one of the top film composers of the 20th century. Nominated 20 times for an Academy Award, he received the Oscar three times—for *The Informer; Now, Voyager;* and *Since You Went Away.* Other famous scores include those for *King Kong, Gone with the Wind, Casablanca* and *The Treasure of the Sierra Madre.* Steiner died Dec 28, 1971, at Los Angeles, CA.

TAIWAN: BIRTHDAY OF BUDDHA. May 10. National holiday since 1999. Originally observed on the eighth day of the fourth lunar month (as it is in China), this religious holiday was moved to the second Sunday in May (in alignment with Mother's Day) in 1999. Celebrates the birth of Prince Siddhartha, founder of Buddhism, with offerings of food, incense, flowers and light.

WORLD LUPUS DAY. May 10. 17th annual. An international call to action has been issued by more than 100 lupus organizations based in countries around the world. Goal is to call attention to the confusing characteristics of this potentially fatal autoimmune disease that mimics other, less serious illnesses. In addition, observing World Lupus Day offers lupus patients the comfort of knowing their condition is recognized and being addressed on a global level. For info: World Lupus Federation, c/o Lupus Foundation of America, 2121 K St NW, Ste 200, Washington, DC 20037. Phone: (202) 349-1155. E-mail: info@lupus.org. Web: www.lupus.org or www.worldlupusday.org.

🧁 BIRTHDAYS TODAY

Bono, 60, singer (U2), humanitarian activist, born Paul Hewson at Dublin, Ireland, May 10, 1960.

Barbara Taylor Bradford, 87, author (*A Woman of Substance, Hold the Dream*), born Upper Armley, Leeds, Yorkshire, England, May 10, 1933.

Jason Brooks, 54, actor ("Days of Our Lives"), born Colorado Springs, CO, May 10, 1966.

Missy Franklin, 25, Olympic swimmer, born Pasadena, CA, May 10, 1995.

Cindy Hyde-Smith, 61, US Senator (R, Mississippi), born Brookhaven, MS, May 10, 1959.

Dave Mason, 74, singer, musician, songwriter, born Worcester, England, May 10, 1946.

Salvador Pérez, 30, baseball player, born Valencia, Venezuela, May 10, 1990.

Kenan Thompson, 42, comedian, actor ("All That," "Saturday Night Live," *Good Burger*), born Atlanta, GA, May 10, 1978.

May 11 — Monday

DAY 132 **234 REMAINING**

BATTLE OF HAMBURGER HILL: ANNIVERSARY. May 11, 1969. Beginning of one of the most infamous battles that signified the growing frustration with America's involvement in the Vietnam War. Attempting to seize Dong Ap Bia mountain, American troops repeatedly scaled the hill over a 10-day period, often engaging in bloody hand-to-hand combat with the North Vietnamese. After finally securing the objective, American military decision makers chose to abandon it, and the North Vietnamese retook it shortly thereafter. The heavy casualties in the struggle to take the hill inspired the name "Hamburger Hill."

BERLIN, IRVING: BIRTH ANNIVERSARY. May 11, 1888. Songwriter born Israel Isidore Baline at Tyumen, Russia. Irving Berlin moved to New York, NY, with his family when he was four years old. After the death of his father, he began singing in saloons and on street corners in order to help his family and worked as a singing waiter as a teenager. Berlin became one of America's most prolific songwriters, authoring such songs as "Alexander's Ragtime Band," "White Christmas," "God Bless America," "There's No Business like Show Business," "Doin' What Comes Naturally," "Puttin' on the Ritz," "Blue Skies" and "Oh! How I Hate to Get Up in the Morning," among others. He could neither read nor write musical notation. Berlin died Sept 22, 1989, at New York.

BUNKER, CHANG AND ENG: BIRTH ANNIVERSARY. May 11, 1811. Conjoined twins born in Meklong, Siam (now Thailand), Chang and Eng found worldwide fame as the Siamese Twins, their rare condition and flair for showmanship wowing royalty and regular folk alike. The twins settled on a plantation in Wilkesboro, NC; bought slaves; were naturalized as American citizens; and in 1843 married a pair of local sisters. The couples eventually had 21 children between them. Chang and Eng died hours apart at Wilkesboro, Jan 17, 1874. They were never separated.

DALI, SALVADOR: BIRTH ANNIVERSARY. May 11, 1904. A leading painter in the surrealist movement, Salvador Dali was equally well known for his baffling antics and attempts to shock his audiences. The largest collection of his works resides in the Salvador Dali Museum at St. Petersburg, FL. Born at Figueres, Spain, Dali died there Jan 23, 1989.

EAT WHAT YOU WANT DAY. May 11. Here's a day you may actually enjoy yourself. Ignore all those on-again, off-again warnings. (©2006 by WH.) For info: Thomas & Ruth Roy, Wellcat Holidays, 2418 Long Ln, Lebanon, PA 17046. Phone: (717) 279-0184. E-mail: info@wellcat.com. Web: www.wellcat.com.

FAIRBANKS, CHARLES WARREN: BIRTH ANNIVERSARY. May 11, 1852. 26th vice president of the US (1905–09), born at Unionville Center, OH. Died at Indianapolis, IN, June 4, 1918.

FEYNMAN, RICHARD: BIRTH ANNIVERSARY. May 11, 1918. Renowned physicist born at Far Rockaway, Queens, NY. He assisted with the Manhattan Project as a young man, then became a research professor in the areas of quantum mechanics, quantum electrodynamics and subatomic particles (in 1948 he introduced the Feynman Diagrams). He received the 1965 Nobel Prize in Physics (with Julian Schwinger and Shinichiro Tomonaga). His three-volume *Feynman Lectures on Physics* (1964) remains an important foundation text in undergraduate physics. Feynman died Feb 15, 1988, at Los Angeles, CA.

GRAHAM, MARTHA: BIRTH ANNIVERSARY. May 11, 1894. Martha Graham was born at Allegheny, PA, and became one of the giants of the modern dance movement in the US. She began her dance career at the comparatively late age of 22 and joined the Greenwich Village Follies in 1923. Her new ideas began to surface in the late '20s and '30s, and by the mid-1930s she was incorporating the rituals of southwestern Native Americans in her work. She is credited with bringing a new psychological depth to modern dance by exploring primal emotions and ancient rituals in her work. She performed until the age of 75 and premiered her 180th ballet, *The Maple Leaf Rag*, in the fall of 1990. Died Apr 1, 1991, at New York, NY.

HART, JOHN: DEATH ANNIVERSARY. May 11, 1779. Signer of the Declaration of Independence, farmer and legislator, born about 1711 (exact date unknown), at Stonington, CT; died at Hopewell, NJ.

JAPAN: CORMORANT FISHING FESTIVAL. May 11–Oct 15. Cormorant fishing on the Nagara River, Gifu. This ancient method of catching ayu, a troutlike fish, with trained cormorants takes place nightly under the light of blazing torches.

MINNESOTA: ADMISSION DAY: ANNIVERSARY. May 11. Became 32nd state in 1858.

NATIONAL ETIQUETTE WEEK. May 11–15. National Etiquette Week is the national recognition of etiquette and protocol in all areas of American life—business, social, dining, travel, technology, wedding and international protocol. The week is designated to raise awareness of all people to act with courtesy, civility, kindness, respect and manners as well as rally people to act with good manners in their everyday lives. Annually, the workweek beginning with the second Monday in May. For info: Debra Lassiter, The Etiquette and Leadership Institute, PO Box 6073, Athens, GA 30604. Phone: (706) 769-5150. E-mail: debral@etiquetteleadership.com. Web: www.etiquetteleadership.com.

NATIONAL STUTTERING AWARENESS WEEK. May 11–17. This week offers an opportunity to focus public attention on a complex disorder that touches 70 million people around the world and more than 3 million in the US alone. Annually, the second week in May, Monday to Sunday. For info: Stuttering Foundation of America, PO Box 11749, Memphis, TN 38111-0749. Phone: (800) 992-9392 or (901) 761-0343. E-mail: info@stutteringhelp.org. Web: www.stutteringhelp.org or www.tartamudez.org in Spanish.

	S	M	T	W	T	F	S
May						1	2
	3	4	5	6	7	8	9
2020	10	11	12	13	14	15	16
	17	18	19	20	21	22	23
	24	25	26	27	28	29	30
	31						

PGA CHAMPIONSHIP. May 11–17. TPC Harding Park, San Francisco, CA. The 102nd championship conducted by the Professional Golfers' Association of America. Est attendance: 150,000. For info: PGA of America, 100 Ave of the Champions, Palm Beach Gardens, FL 33418. Phone: (561) 624-8400. Web: www.pga.com.

SUTTON HOO SHIP BURIAL DISCOVERED: ANNIVERSARY. May 11, 1939. On this date in a large mound at Sutton Hoo in rural Suffolk, England, archaeologist Basil Brown discovered an undisturbed royal Anglo-Saxon ship burial. The ship—the largest ever found—was 90 feet long and 14 feet wide (the wood had rotted away, leaving only an outline and rivets). Also discovered were gold, bronze, silver and gemmed artifacts and weapons. The buried ship is believed to be that of King Raedwald of East Anglia, who ruled in the early AD 600s.

UNITED NATIONS: WORLD MIGRATORY BIRD DAY. May 11. Since 2006, an annual awareness-raising campaign highlighting the need for the conservation of migratory birds and their habitats. Marked by bird-watching excursions, festivals, educational programs and more. For info: United Nations, Dept of Public Info, New York, NY 10017. Web: www.migratorybirdday.org or www.un.org.

WORK AT HOME MOMS WEEK. May 11–17. The challenge of motherhood and working at home can be a balancing act. All women who do it every day: you are applauded this week and always. For info: Robin Gorman Newman, 44 Somerset Dr N, Great Neck, NY 11020. Phone: (516) 773-0911. E-mail: rgnewman@optonline.net. Web: www.motherhoodlater.com.

🎂 BIRTHDAYS TODAY

Louis Farrakhan, 87, Nation of Islam leader, born New York, NY, May 11, 1933.

Boyd Gaines, 67, actor (Tonys for *Gypsy, Contact, She Loves Me* and *The Heidi Chronicles*), born Atlanta, GA, May 11, 1953.

Jonathan Jackson, 38, actor ("Nashville," "General Hospital"), born Orlando, FL, May 11, 1982.

Robert Jarvik, 74, physician, inventor of artificial heart, born Midland, MI, May 11, 1946.

John F. Kelly, 70, former White House chief of staff (Trump administration), born Boston, MA, May 11, 1950.

Matt Leinart, 37, sports analyst, former football player, 2004 Heisman Trophy winner, born Santa Ana, CA, May 11, 1983.

Cam Newton, 31, football player, 2010 Heisman Trophy winner, born Atlanta, GA, May 11, 1989.

Mort Sahl, 93, comic actor (*Don't Make Waves; Doctor, You've Got to Be Kidding*), born Montreal, QC, Canada, May 11, 1927.

May 12 — Tuesday

DAY 133   **233 REMAINING**

BATTLE OF SPOTSYLVANIA: ANNIVERSARY. May 12, 1864. After the Battle of the Wilderness, Grant and Lee next engaged at the Battle of Spotsylvania (VA). Lee had positioned his troops in breastworks along a horseshoe formation, utilizing the natural features of the landscape. During Grant's attack on this strong defensive position, both sides suffered losses of more than 12,000 in what became known as "the Bloody Angle." Lee was forced to use every available man in order to protect the position and so ordered his troops to pull back during the night.

BERRA, YOGI: 95th BIRTH ANNIVERSARY. May 12, 1925. The baseball great and all-around character was born Lawrence Peter Berra to Italian immigrants at St. Louis, MO. As a Yankees catcher, Berra helped lead his club to 10 World Series victories. After his career as a player ended, he had tumultuous spells managing the Yankees and the Mets. Berra is almost better known for his "Yogi-isms": humorous non sequiturs that induced head scratching in his listeners—such as "Ninety percent of the game is half mental." Berra was inducted into the Baseball Hall of Fame in 1972. He died Sept 22, 2015, at West Caldwell, NJ.

CANNES FILM FESTIVAL. May 12–23. Cannes, France. 73rd annual. Premier international film festival, with hundreds of screenings (in competition and out), critical panels, director spotlights, Cannes Market for film distribution and numerous other cultural and artistic activities. Palme d'Or, Caméra d'Or, Grand Prix and other awards presented on the last day of the festival. The festival was first held in September 1946, and there have been only three cancellations since then, in 1948, 1950 and 1968. For info: Festival de Cannes. E-mail: festival@festival-cannes.fr. Web: www.festival-cannes.fr.

FRANK, OTTO: BIRTH ANNIVERSARY. May 12, 1889. Decorated for bravery as a German officer after WWI, Frank is best remembered as the father of Anne, whose diary he published in 1947 in hope of preventing future genocides. Born in Frankfurt, Germany, Frank moved his family to Holland in 1933 as anti-Semitism erupted in his homeland. His wife and two daughters died in concentration camps, but Frank was liberated from Auschwitz in 1945. In 1963, he established the Anne Frank Foundation, which undertakes charitable works and social activities in the spirit of Anne Frank. Frank devoted his life to Holocaust education until his death on Aug 19, 1980, at Basel, Switzerland.

GEORGE VI'S CORONATION: ANNIVERSARY. May 12, 1937. George VI was crowned at Westminster Abbey at London, England, following the abdication of his brother, Edward VIII. Born Dec 14, 1895, King George died Feb 6, 1952. He was succeeded by his daughter Elizabeth, the current reigning monarch.

HEPBURN, KATHARINE: BIRTH ANNIVERSARY. May 12, 1907. American actress Katharine Houghton Hepburn was born at Hartford, CT. Nominated for 12 Oscars over the course of her career, she won four times: for 1933's *Morning Glory,* 1967's *Guess Who's Coming to Dinner,* 1968's *The Lion in Winter* and 1981's *On Golden Pond.* She is best remembered for her on- and offscreen pairing with Spencer Tracy. Together, they made nine films, including *Adam's Rib* and *Woman of the Year,* and enjoyed a 27-year personal relationship. There is often confusion regarding her date of birth: in her 1991 autobiography, *Me: Stories of My Life,* she confirmed the May date and admitted often giving out a late brother's birth date as her own. She died at Old Saybrook, CT, June 29, 2003.

LAG B'OMER. May 12. Hebrew calendar date: Iyar 18, 5780. Literally, the 33rd day of the omer (harvest time), the 33rd day after the beginning of Passover. Traditionally a joyous day for weddings, picnics and outdoor activities. Began at sundown May 11.

LEAR, EDWARD: BIRTH ANNIVERSARY. May 12, 1812. English artist and author, best remembered for his light verse and limericks. Lear published *A Book of Nonsense* in 1846. His most famous poem, "The Owl and the Pussycat," appeared in 1867. Lear was born at Highgate, England, and died at San Remo, Italy, Jan 29, 1888. See also: "Limerick Day" (below).

LIMERICK DAY. May 12. Observed on the birthday of one of its champions, Edward Lear. The limerick, which dates from the early 18th century, has been described as the "only fixed verse form

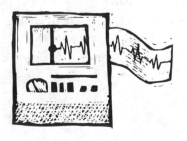

indigenous to the English language." It gained its greatest popularity following the publication of Edward Lear's *A Book of Nonsense* (and its sequels). Example: "There was a young poet named Lear/ Who said, it is just as I fear/Five lines are enough/For this kind of stuff/Make a limerick each day of the year." See also: "Lear, Edward: Birth Anniversary" (above).

NATIVE AMERICAN RIGHTS RECOGNIZED: ANNIVERSARY. May 12, 1879. When the US tried to forcibly remove the Poncas from their homeland in Nebraska to an Oklahoma reservation, their chief, Standing Bear, brought suit to prevent it. The US claimed that Standing Bear could not bring suit because as a Native American he had no legal standing in US law. In *Standing Bear v George Crook* at US District Court, Judge J. Dundy ruled on this day that "an Indian is a PERSON within the meaning of the laws of the United States." This landmark decision was appealed by the US to the Supreme Court, which dismissed it. Standing Bear was not forced to move his tribe, but other Native Americans were unable to use the decision to their advantage in other disputes with the US.

NIGHTINGALE, FLORENCE: 200th BIRTH ANNIVERSARY. May 12, 1820. English nurse and public health activist who, through her unselfish devotion to nursing, contributed perhaps more than any other single person to the development of modern nursing procedures and the dignity of nursing as a profession. Founder of the Nightingale training school for nurses. Author of *Notes on Nursing* (1860). Born at Florence, Italy. Died at London, England, Aug 13, 1910.

ODOMETER INVENTED: ANNIVERSARY. May 12, 1847. Anniversary of the invention of the odometer by Mormon pioneer William Clayton while crossing the plains in a covered wagon. Previous to this, mileage was calculated by counting the revolutions of a rag tied to a spoke of a wagon wheel.

PORTUGAL: PILGRIMAGE TO FATIMA. May 12–13. Commemorates first appearance of the Virgin of the Rosary to little shepherd children May 13, 1917. Pilgrims come to Cova da Iria—religious center, candlelit procession, mass of the sick—for annual observance.

SMITH, HOWARD K.: BIRTH ANNIVERSARY. May 12, 1914. Born at Ferriday, LA, Smith was an acclaimed and opinionated war correspondent, broadcast journalist, anchor and author who was one of "Murrow's Boys" (those who worked closely with Edward R. Murrow—especially during WWII). Smith had long stints at CBS and ABC. He also moderated the first televised US presidential debate between Richard Nixon and John F. Kennedy in 1960. Smith died Feb 15, 2002, at Bethesda, MD.

🎂 BIRTHDAYS TODAY

MacKenzie Astin, 47, actor (*The Last Days of Disco*), born Los Angeles, CA, May 12, 1973.

May 2020	S	M	T	W	T	F	S
						1	2
	3	4	5	6	7	8	9
	10	11	12	13	14	15	16
	17	18	19	20	21	22	23
	24	25	26	27	28	29	30
	31						

Burt Bacharach, 92, composer (six Grammys, three Oscars, core-cipient of the 2012 Gershwin Prize for Popular Song), born Kansas City, MO, May 12, 1928.

Stephen Baldwin, 54, actor (*The Usual Suspects*), born Massapequa, NY, May 12, 1966.

Jason Biggs, 42, actor ("Orange Is the New Black," *American Pie*), born Pompton Plains, NJ, May 12, 1978.

Clare Bowen, 31, actress (*Dead Man's Burden*, "Nashville"), born Minnamurra, Australia, May 12, 1989 (some sources say 1984).

Bruce Boxleitner, 69, actor (*How the West Was Won*, "Babylon 5," "Scarecrow and Mrs King"), born Elgin, IL, May 12, 1951.

Cheryl Burke, 36, professional dancer, television personality ("Dancing with the Stars"), born San Francisco, CA, May 12, 1984.

Gabriel Byrne, 70, actor ("In Treatment," *The Usual Suspects*), born Dublin, Ireland, May 12, 1950.

Christian Campbell, 48, actor ("Malibu Shores," *Cold Hearts*), born Toronto, ON, Canada, May 12, 1972.

Lindsay Crouse, 72, actress (*House of Games, The Verdict, Places in the Heart*), born New York, NY, May 12, 1948.

Emilio Estevez, 58, actor (*The Breakfast Club, Repo Man*), born New York, NY, May 12, 1962.

Kim Fields, 51, actress ("The Facts of Life," "Living Single"), born Los Angeles, CA, May 12, 1969.

Domhnall Gleeson, 37, actor (*Ex Machina, Star Wars: The Force Awakens, About Time*), born Dublin, Ireland, May 12, 1983.

Kim Greist, 62, actress (*Brazil, Throw Momma from the Train*), born Stamford, CT, May 12, 1958.

Tony Hawk, 51, skateboarder, born Carlsbad, CA, May 12, 1969.

Jamie Luner, 49, actress ("Melrose Place," "Profiler"), born Los Angeles, CA, May 12, 1971.

Rami Malek, 39, actor (Oscar for *Bohemian Rhapsody*, "Mr Robot," *Papillon*), born Los Angeles, CA, May 12, 1981.

Millie Perkins, 82, actress ("Knots Landing," *The Diary of Anne Frank, Wall Street*), born Passaic, NJ, May 12, 1938.

Jared Polis, 45, Governor of Colorado (D), born Boulder, CO, May 12, 1975.

Ving Rhames, 59, actor ("Kojak," "Don King: Only in America," *Mission: Impossible* films, *Pulp Fiction*), born New York, NY, May 12, 1961.

Frank Stella, 84, artist, born Malden, MA, May 12, 1936.

Emily VanCamp, 34, actress ("Brothers & Sisters," "Everwood"), born Port Perry, ON, Canada, May 12, 1986.

Steve Winwood, 72, musician, singer, born Birmingham, England, May 12, 1948.

May 13 — Wednesday

DAY 134   **232 REMAINING**

CHILDREN OF FALLEN PATRIOTS DAY. May 13. 6th annual. This day seeks to raise awareness for military children who have lost a parent in the line of duty. It honors the bravery of surviving children while also creating awareness for our foundation's mission: to ensure a college education for all children of the fallen. Annually, May 13—the founding date of Arlington National Cemetery in 1864. For info: Children of Fallen Patriots Foundation, 44900 Prentice Dr, Dulles, VA 20166. Web: http://fallenpatriots.org.

DONATE A DAY'S WAGES TO CHARITY DAY. May 13. 19th annual. All working people are asked to donate the money they make today to charity. If unable to afford the donation, they are then asked to take off the day from work and donate their time to

charity. Annually, the second Wednesday in May. For info: Donate a Day's Wages To Charity Day. E-mail: donatetocharity@ yahoo.com.

ENGLAND: ROYAL WINDSOR HORSE SHOW. May 13–17. Home Park, Private Windsor, Berkshire. International driving, show jumping, dressage, endurance and national showing. Est attendance: 65,000. For info: Penelope Henderson, Sec'y, Royal Windsor Horse Show, The Royal Mews, Windsor Castle, Windsor, Berkshire, England SL4 1NG. E-mail: info@rwhs.co.uk. Web: www.rwhs.co.uk.

EVANS, GIL: BIRTH ANNIVERSARY. May 13, 1912. A true jazz innovator, Gil Evans was a pianist, composer and arranger who started out in big bands but went on to help shape the sound of modal and free jazz, particularly with his work as an arranger and bandleader for Miles Davis (*Miles Ahead, Porgy and Bess, Sketches of Spain*). Evans worked steadily throughout the 1970s and '80s as well, releasing music under his own name and collaborating with artists as varied as Astrud Gilberto and Sting. Born at Toronto, ON, Canada, Evans died at Cuernavaca, Mexico, on Mar 20, 1988.

LOUIS, JOE: BIRTH ANNIVERSARY. May 13, 1914. World heavyweight boxing champion, 1937–49, nicknamed the "Brown Bomber," Joseph Louis Barrow was born near Lafayette, AL. He died Apr 12, 1981, at Las Vegas, NV. Buried at Arlington National Cemetery. (Louis's burial there, by presidential waiver, was the 39th exception ever to the eligibility rules for burial in Arlington National Cemetery.)

MEXICAN WAR DECLARED: ANNIVERSARY. May 13, 1846. Although fighting had begun days earlier, Congress officially declared war on Mexico on this date. The struggle cost the lives of 11,300 American soldiers and resulted in the annexation by the US of land that became parts of Oklahoma, New Mexico, Arizona, Nevada, California, Utah and Colorado. The war ended in 1848. See also: "Treaty of Guadalupe Hidalgo: Anniversary" (Feb 2).

NATIONAL HUMMUS DAY. May 13. Since 2013, a day to celebrate all things hummus! Hummus originates from the Middle East and dates to at least the 13th century. The main ingredients are chickpeas (the legumes sometimes referred to as garbanzos), which are blended to a smooth consistency and then combined with tahini, a Mediterranean paste made from ground sesame seeds. Olive oil, garlic, lemon juice and herbs and spices are added to traditional preparations. Annually, May 13. For info: Sabra Dipping Company. Phone: (804) 518-2000. E-mail: news@sabra.com. Web: www.Sabra.com.

NATIONAL NIGHTSHIFT WORKERS DAY. May 13. To honor those workers who reverse their natural circadian rhythm to keep business running 24 hours a day. Annually, the second Wednesday in May. (Originally sponsored by Velcea Kae.)

NATIONAL RECEPTIONISTS DAY. May 13. Celebrated in the US, UK, Canada and Australia, this is a day of recognition for the frontline personnel in business, the Directors of First Impressions. You only get one chance to make a good first impression and that is the unique job of a receptionist. This day was inaugurated in 1991 by Jennifer Alexander to recognize the special role that receptionists play and to distinguish their skills from that of an administrative

assistant or secretary. According to the Bureau of Labor Statistics there are more than one million receptionists in the US, most heavily employed in legal and medical offices. Annually, the second Wednesday in May.

PHILADELPHIA POLICE BOMBING: 35th ANNIVERSARY. May 13, 1985. During the siege of the radical group MOVE at Philadelphia, PA, police in a helicopter reportedly dropped a bomb containing the powerful military plastic explosive C-4 on the building in which the group was housed. The bomb and the resulting fire left 11 persons dead (including four children) and destroyed 61 homes.

SAINT LAWRENCE SEAWAY ACT: ANNIVERSARY. May 13, 1954. President Dwight D. Eisenhower signed legislation authorizing US–Canadian construction of a waterway that would make it possible for oceangoing ships to reach the Great Lakes.

SPACE MILESTONE: *ENDEAVOUR* (US). May 13, 1992. Three astronauts from the shuttle *Endeavour* simultaneously walked in space for the first time.

SULLIVAN, ARTHUR: BIRTH ANNIVERSARY. May 13, 1842. English composer best known for light operas (with Sir William Gilbert), born at London, England. Died there Nov 22, 1900.

WELLS, MARY: BIRTH ANNIVERSARY. May 13, 1943. Motown's first big star, Mary Wells was born at Detroit, MI. She was known for such hits as "You Beat Me to the Punch," "Two Lovers" and her signature song, "My Guy." She was one of a group of black artists of the '60s who helped end musical segregation by having their work played on white radio stations. Mary Wells died July 26, 1992, at Los Angeles, CA.

 BIRTHDAYS TODAY

Franklyn Ajaye, 71, actor ("Deadwood," *Car Wash*), born Brooklyn, NY, May 13, 1949.

Frances Barber, 63, actress (*Sammy and Rosie Get Laid, We Think the World of You*), born Wolverhampton, England, May 13, 1957.

Mike Bibby, 42, former basketball player, born Cherry Hill, NJ, May 13, 1978.

Stephen Colbert, 56, television talk show host ("The Late Show"), comedian ("The Daily Show," "The Colbert Report"), author, born Charlestown, SC, May 13, 1964.

Tom Cotton, 43, US Senator (R, Arkansas), born Dardanelle, AR, May 13, 1977.

Lena Dunham, 34, writer, actress (*Tiny Furniture*, "Girls"), born New York, NY, May 13, 1986.

Harvey Keitel, 81, actor (*Reservoir Dogs, The Piano, Bugsy, Taxi Driver*), born Brooklyn, NY, May 13, 1939.

Scott Morrison, 52, Prime Minister of Australia, born Sydney, Australia, May 13, 1968.

Robert Pattinson, 34, actor (*Twilight Saga* films, *Water for Elephants, Harry Potter and the Goblet of Fire*), born London, England, May 13, 1986.

Julianne Phillips, 58, actress (*Allie & Me*, "Sisters"), born Lake Oswego, OR, May 13, 1962.

Dennis Rodman, 59, Hall of Fame basketball player, born Trenton, NJ, May 13, 1961.

Darius Rucker, 52, singer (Hootie and the Blowfish), born Charleston, SC, May 13, 1968.

Bobby Valentine, 70, baseball manager, former player and broadcaster, born Stamford, CT, May 13, 1950.

Stevie Wonder, 70, singer, musician, born Steveland Morris Hardaway at Saginaw, MI, May 13, 1950.

May 14 — Thursday

DAY 135   **231 REMAINING**

CARLSBAD CAVERNS NATIONAL PARK ESTABLISHED: 90th ANNIVERSARY. May 14, 1930. Located in southwestern New Mexico, Carlsbad Caverns was proclaimed a national monument, Oct 25, 1923, and was later established as a national park and preserve.

FAHRENHEIT, GABRIEL DANIEL: BIRTH ANNIVERSARY. May 14, 1686. German physicist born at Danzig, Prussia (now Gdansk, Poland). Fahrenheit introduced the use of mercury in thermometers and markedly improved their accuracy. He devised the Fahrenheit temperature scale (based on 32° for the freezing/melting point of water/ice) that is still used in the US (the Celsius scale is used more universally). He died at Amsterdam, The Netherlands, on Sept 16, 1736.

FREEDOM RIDERS ATTACKED: ANNIVERSARY. May 14, 1961. On Mother's Day, a Greyhound bus of Freedom Riders—challenging segregation on interstate travel—was attacked in Anniston, AL, by Ku Klux Klan members and townspeople with rocks, bats and metal bars. The mob attempted to burn the riders alive with gas incendiaries, but they escaped—only to be refused medical care. Later that day, Freedom Riders in a Trailways bus were beaten by Klansmen passengers trying to enforce Jim Crow seating. A mob met this bus when it arrived at the Birmingham, AL, bus station and attacked Freedom Riders who went into the whites-only waiting room. The mob also attacked journalists attempting to document the violence.

GAINSBOROUGH, THOMAS: BAPTISM ANNIVERSARY. May 14, 1727. (Old Style date.) English landscape and portrait painter. Among his most remembered works: *The Blue Boy*, *The Watering Place* and *The Market Cart*. Born at Sudbury, Suffolk, England, he was baptized on May 14, 1727 (OS), and he died at London, England, Aug 2, 1788.

JAMESTOWN, VIRGINIA: FOUNDING ANNIVERSARY. May 14, 1607. (Old Style date.) The first permanent English settlement in what is now the US took place at Jamestown, VA (named for England's King James I), on this date. Captains John Smith and Christopher Newport were among the leaders of the group of royally chartered Virginia Company settlers who had traveled from Plymouth, England, in three small ships: *Susan Constant*, *Godspeed* and *Discovery*.

LEWIS AND CLARK EXPEDITION SETS OUT: ANNIVERSARY. May 14, 1804. Charged by President Thomas Jefferson with finding a route to the Pacific, Captain Meriwether Lewis and Lieutenant William Clark left St. Louis, MO, with a 33-member group skilled in botany, zoology, outdoor survival and other scientific skills. They arrived at the Pacific coast of Oregon in November 1805 and returned to St. Louis on Sept 23, 1806.

MILES CITY BUCKING HORSE SALE. May 14–17. Miles City, MT. Miles City is real "Lonesome Dove" country, and its annual bucking horse sale is where rodeo stock operators from around the nation and Canada head to purchase their bucking horses for the coming rodeo season. A festive event, the sale not only involves cowboys trying to ride some of the wildest horses in the country but also includes Western artists displaying and creating works in a weekend art show, a Western trade show featuring practical and gift items, a Saturday morning parade and Miles City's Western attractions such as the Range Riders Museum. (Miles City is the community featured in the novel and two television miniseries about "Lonesome Dove.") Est attendance: 10,000. For info:

	S	M	T	W	T	F	S
May						1	2
	3	4	5	6	7	8	9
2020	10	11	12	13	14	15	16
	17	18	19	20	21	22	23
	24	25	26	27	28	29	30
	31						

Bucking Horse Sale Office, PO Box 1027, Miles City, MT 59301. Phone: (406) 874-BUCK. Web: www.buckinghorsesale.com.

MOON PHASE: LAST QUARTER. May 14. Moon enters Last Quarter phase at 10:03 AM, EDT.

NCAA DIVISION I MEN'S AND WOMEN'S TENNIS CHAMPIONSHIPS. May 14–23. Stillwater, OK. 83rd annual for men and 38th annual for women. For info: Natl Collegiate Athletic Assn, PO Box 6222, Indianapolis, IN 46206-6222. Phone: (317) 917-6222. Web: www.NCAA.com.

NORWAY: MIDNIGHT SUN AT NORTH CAPE. May 14–July 30. North Cape. First day of the season with around-the-clock sunshine. At North Cape the sun never dips below the horizon from May 14 to July 30, but the night is bright long before and after these dates.

OWEN, ROBERT: BIRTH ANNIVERSARY. May 14, 1771. English progressive owner of spinning works, philanthropist, utopian socialist, founder of New Harmony, IN, born at Newtown, Wales. Died there Nov 17, 1858.

PHILIPPINES: CARABAO FESTIVAL. May 14–15. Pulilan, Bulacan; Nueva Ecija; Angono, Rizal. Parade of farmers to honor their patron saint, San Isidro, with hundreds of "dressed-up" *carabaos* (water buffalo) participating.

SMALLPOX VACCINE DISCOVERED: ANNIVERSARY. May 14, 1796. In the 18th century smallpox was a widespread and often fatal disease. Edward Jenner, a physician in rural England, heard reports of dairy farmers who apparently became immune to smallpox as a result of exposure to cowpox, a related but milder disease. After two decades of studying the phenomenon, Jenner injected cowpox into a healthy eight-year-old boy, who subsequently developed cowpox. Six weeks later, Jenner inoculated the boy with smallpox. He remained healthy. Jenner called this new procedure *vaccination*, from *vaccinia*, another term for cowpox. Within 18 months, 12,000 people in England had been vaccinated and the number of smallpox deaths dropped by two-thirds.

SPACE MILESTONE: *SKYLAB 1*(US). May 14, 1973. The US launched *Skylab*, its first manned orbiting laboratory.

"THE STARS AND STRIPES FOREVER" DAY. May 14, 1897. Anniversary of the first public performance of John Philip Sousa's march "The Stars and Stripes Forever," at Philadelphia, PA. The occasion was the unveiling of a statue of George Washington, and President William McKinley was present.

UNDERGROUND AMERICA DAY. May 14. 44th annual. Underground America Day is one man's (the late Malcolm Wells's) attempt to get others to think of designing and building structures underground. Wells published illustrations and humorous suggestions for celebrating Underground America Day. Annually, May 14. For info: Karen North Wells, 673 Satucket Rd, Brewster, MA 02631. Web: www.malcolmwells.com.

WAAC: ANNIVERSARY. May 14, 1942. During WWII, women became eligible to enlist for noncombat duties in the Women's Auxiliary Army Corps (WAAC) by an act of Congress. Women also served through Women Accepted for Voluntary Emergency Service (WAVES), Women's Auxiliary Ferrying Squadron (WAFS) and Coast Guard or Semper Paratus Always Ready Service (SPARS), the Women's Reserve of the Marine Corps.

🧁 BIRTHDAYS TODAY

Cate Blanchett, 51, actress (Oscars for *Blue Jasmine* and *The Aviator*; *Elizabeth*, *Babel*), born Melbourne, Australia, May 14, 1969.

David Byrne, 68, singer, composer, born Dumbarton, Scotland, May 14, 1952.

Sofia Coppola, 49, filmmaker (*The Bling Ring*, *Lost in Translation*), born New York, NY, May 14, 1971.

Meg Foster, 72, actress ("Cagney and Lacey," *The Emerald Forest*, *They Live*), born Reading, PA, May 14, 1948.

Rob "Gronk" Gronkowski, 31, former football player, born Amherst, NY, May 14, 1989.

Suzy Kolber, 56, sportscaster, born Philadelphia, PA, May 14, 1964.

George Lucas, 76, filmmaker (*Star Wars* films), born Modesto, CA, May 14, 1944.

Jose Dennis Martinez, 65, former baseball player, born Granada, Nicaragua, May 14, 1955.

Atanasio (Tony) Perez, 78, Hall of Fame baseball player, born Camaguey, Cuba, May 14, 1942.

Tim Roth, 59, actor (*The Hateful Eight*, *Planet of the Apes*, *Rob Roy*, *Pulp Fiction*), born London, England, May 14, 1961.

Amber Tamblyn, 37, actress (*The Sisterhood of the Traveling Pants*, "Joan of Arcadia"), born Santa Monica, CA, May 14, 1983.

Ronan Tynan, 60, opera singer (The Irish Tenors), born Dublin, Ireland, May 14, 1960.

Robert Zemeckis, 68, director (Oscar for *Forrest Gump*; *Flight*, *Cast Away*, *Back to the Future*), screenwriter, born Chicago, IL, May 14, 1952.

Mark Zuckerberg, 36, computer programmer, founder of Facebook, born White Plains, NY, May 14, 1984.

May 15 — Friday

DAY 136   **230 REMAINING**

ART FAIR AND WINEFEST. May 15–17. Washington, MO. This unique festival in the heart of wine country features tastings from 14 Missouri wineries as well as a juried art show featuring 30 Midwestern artists. Art fair is free. Admission to the wine pavilion includes a commemorative wine glass. Est attendance: 20,000. For info: Downtown Washington, Inc, PO Box 144, Washington, MO 63090. Phone: (636) 239-1743. Fax: (636) 239-4832. E-mail: events@downtownwashmo.org. Web: www.downtownwashmo.org.

AVEDON, RICHARD: BIRTH ANNIVERSARY. May 15, 1923. Influential photographer born at New York, NY. Avedon began his career with the merchant marines, taking personnel identification photos and images of shipwrecks. Later, he worked for *Harper's Bazaar* and *Vogue*, where his artistic style of shooting fashion models against famous backgrounds revolutionized that industry's approach to fashion layouts. He was known for taking memorable, while not necessarily flattering, portraits and was honored with retrospectives and exhibits at many museums. He received the National Medal for the Arts in 2003 and died at New York, Oct 1, 2004.

BAUM, LYMAN FRANK: BIRTH ANNIVERSARY. May 15, 1856. The American newspaperman who wrote the Wizard of Oz stories was born at Chittenango, NY. Although *The Wonderful Wizard of Oz* is the most famous, Baum also wrote many other books for children, including more than a dozen about Oz. He died at Hollywood, CA, May 6, 1919.

BULGAKOV, MIKHAIL: BIRTH ANNIVERSARY. May 15, 1891. Novelist and playwright born at Kiev, Russian Empire (now Ukraine). Bulgakov left the medical profession to become a writer in 1919. He published satirical works of fiction and science fiction, and his plays caught the attention of Joseph Stalin, who established him at the Moscow Art Theater. Despite Stalin's initial support, Bulgakov struggled with government censorship and by 1929, his writing career was over. Bulgakov's masterwork is the novel *The Master and Margarita*, published years after his death at Moscow on Mar 10, 1940.

COTTEN, JOSEPH: BIRTH ANNIVERSARY. May 15, 1905. Stage and screen star Joseph Cotten was born at Petersburg, VA. Among Cotten's movie credits are *Citizen Kane*, *The Magnificent Ambersons* and *The Third Man*. Among his most noted performances on Broadway were *The Philadelphia Story* and *Once More with Feeling*. Joseph Cotten died Feb 6, 1994, at Los Angeles, CA.

CURIE, PIERRE: BIRTH ANNIVERSARY. May 15, 1859. Born at Paris, France, Curie was one of the founders of modern physics. His research had already brought important results (in heat waves, crystals, magnetism, symmetry) and the formulation of Curie's law before he married Marie Sklodowska in 1895. Together, the Curies discovered polonium and radium while conducting research in radioactivity. With Henri Becquerel, the Curies were awarded the Nobel Prize in Physics in 1903. Tragically, Pierre Curie was struck by a dray in Paris and died Apr 19, 1906.

EASTERN PACIFIC HURRICANE SEASON. May 15–Nov 30. Eastern Pacific defined as coast to 140° west longitude.

ELECTRA GOAT BBQ COOK-OFF. May 15–16. Electra Goat Grounds, Electra, TX. Goat brisket, pork ribs, chicken cook-off, live band, Jackpot Steak & Beans Competition, children's games and crafts. Friday night dance and salsa contest. Est attendance: 2,000. For info: Sherry Strange, Electra Chamber of Commerce, 112 W Cleveland, Electra, TX 76360. Phone: (940) 495-3577. E-mail: electra-coc@electratel.net. Web: www.electratexas.org.

ENDANGERED SPECIES DAY. May 15. 15th annual. Observed by many conservation and wildlife organizations, Endangered Species Day was first proclaimed by the US Congress in 2006. It is a celebration of the nation's wildlife and wild places and is an opportunity for people to learn about the importance of protecting endangered species, as well as everyday actions they can take to help protect them. Annually, the third Friday in May. For info: Endangered Species Coalition. Web: www.endangered.org/campaigns/endangered-species-day. Also for info: US Fish and Wildlife Service. Web: www.fws.gov/midwest/endangered/esday.

FIRST FLIGHT ATTENDANT: 90th ANNIVERSARY. May 15, 1930. Ellen Church became the first airline stewardess (today's flight attendant), flying on a United Airlines flight from San Francisco, CA, to Cheyenne, WY.

FISHING HAS NO BOUNDARIES—HAYWARD EVENT. May 15–16. Lake Chippewa Campgrounds, Hayward, WI. 33rd annual two-day fishing experience for disabled persons. Any disability, age, sex, race, etc, eligible. Fishing with experienced guides on one of the best fishing waters in Wisconsin, attended by 150 participants and 350 volunteers. Est attendance: 500. For info: Fishing Has No Boundaries, PO Box 375, Hayward, WI 54843. Phone: (715) 634-3185. Fax: (715) 634-1305. E-mail: hayfhnb@cheqnet.net. Web: www.haywardFHNB.org.

JAPAN: AOI MATSURI (HOLLYHOCK FESTIVAL). May 15. Kyoto. The festival features a pageant reproducing imperial processions of ancient times that paid homage to the shrine of Shimogamo and Kamigamo.

MEXICO: SAN ISIDRO DAY. May 15. Day of San Isidro Labrador celebrated widely in farming regions to honor St. Isidore, the Plowman. Livestock gaily decorated with flowers. Celebrations usually begin about May 13 and continue for about a week.

NAKBA DAY. May 15. Palestinian day of mourning (roughly translated as "Day of Catastrophe"), observed on the day after the anniversary of Israeli independence (Gregorian date: May 14, 1948). Since Israeli Independence Day is observed on the Jewish calendar, it can differ from Gregorian dates by up to 11 days.

NATIONAL BIKE TO WORK DAY. May 15. At the state or local level, Bike to Work events are conducted by small and large businesses, city governments, bicycle clubs and environmental groups. Bike To Work Week is May 11–17. Annually, the third Friday in May. Est attendance: 2,000,000. For info: League of American Bicyclists, 1612 K St NW, Ste 1102, Washington, DC 20006. Phone: (202) 822-1333. E-mail: communications@bikeleague.org. Web: www.bikeleague.org/bikemonth.

★**NATIONAL DEFENSE TRANSPORTATION DAY.** May 15. Presidential Proclamation customarily issued as "National Defense Transportation Day and National Transportation Week." Issued each year for the third Friday in May since 1957. (PL 85–32 of May 16, 1957.)

NATIONAL PIZZA PARTY DAY. May 15. As the school year winds down, students and parents should celebrate with pizza parties! Local promotions support the day within classrooms and at home. Annually, the third Friday in May. (Created by Ross Marzolf and Garlic Jim's Famous Gourmet Pizza.)

NATIONAL SLIDER DAY. May 15. 6th annual. During National Hamburger Month, a day to honor the iconic, petit, steamed-grilled-on-a-bed-of-onions hamburger. The term "slider" originated with White Castle—America's first fast-food hamburger chain (founded in 1921)—because the little hamburgers were dubbed so easy to eat. Today, restaurants and chefs around the world use the term to describe their two-by-two-inch burgers. After more than 99 years, signature sliders are sure to satisfy any craving. Annually, May 15. For info: White Castle Management Company, Marketing Department, 555 W Goodale St, Columbus, OH 43215-1185. Phone: (614) 228-5781. Web: www.whitecastle.com.

NORGAY, TENZING: BIRTH ANNIVERSARY. May 15, 1914. Sherpa co-conqueror of Mount Everest, born as Namgyal Wangdi, at Tshechu, Tibet. Raised in Nepal, Tenzing began mountaineering as a porter. Having participated in six previous attempts at scaling Mount Everest, he was the most experienced Everest climber on the British expedition of 1953, and on May 29, he and New Zealander Edmund Hillary were the first two men atop the world's highest mountain. Died May 9, 1983, at Darjeeling, India.

NYLON STOCKINGS: 80th ANNIVERSARY. May 15, 1940. Nylon hose went on sale at stores throughout the country. Competing producers bought their nylon yarn from E.I. du Pont de Nemours and Company (later DuPont). W.H. Carothers, of DuPont, developed nylon, called "Polymer 66," in 1935. It was the first totally man-made fiber and over time was substituted for other materials and came to have widespread application.

PARAGUAY: INDEPENDENCE DAY. May 15. Commemorates independence from Spain, attained in 1811.

★**PEACE OFFICER MEMORIAL DAY.** May 15. Presidential Proclamation 3537, of May 4, 1963, covers all succeeding years. (PL 87–726 of Oct 1, 1962.) May 15 of each year since 1963; however, first issued in 1962 for May 14.

PEACE OFFICER MEMORIAL DAY. May 15. An event honored by police departments nationwide. Memorial ceremonies are held at the American Police Hall of Fame and Museum. See also: "National Police Week" (May 10–16). For info: American Police Hall of Fame and Museum, 6350 Horizon Dr, Titusville, FL 32780. Phone: (321) 264-0911. E-mail: policeinfo@aphf.org. Web: www.aphf.org.

PORTER, KATHERINE ANNE: BIRTH ANNIVERSARY. May 15, 1890. Author, born Callie Russell Porter, at Indian Creek, TX. Best known for short stories and novellas (among them, *Pale Horse, Pale Rider* [1939]) for most of her literary career, in 1962 Porter published her one novel, *Ship of Fools*, a work that had taken 20 years to write. It was an instant public and critical success. Porter won the Pulitzer Prize and the National Book Award in 1966 for *Collected Stories*. She died Sept 18, 1980, at Silver Spring, MD.

SPACE MILESTONE: *FAITH 7* **(US).** May 15, 1963. Launched with Major Gordon Leroy Cooper and orbited Earth 22 times.

TEACHER'S DAY IN FLORIDA. May 15. A ceremonial day observed on the third Friday in May.

UNITED NATIONS: INTERNATIONAL DAY OF FAMILIES. May 15. Since 1994, an international day to promote awareness of issues relating to families and to increase knowledge of the social, economic and demographic processes affecting families. (Res 47/237 of Sept 20, 1993.) Annually, May 15. For info: United Nations, Dept of Public Info, New York, NY 10017. Web: www.un.org.

THE WACO HORROR: JESSE WASHINGTON LYNCHING: ANNIVERSARY. May 15, 1916. Jesse Washington, a black teenager on trial for murdering a white woman, was grabbed from a Waco, TX, courtroom by a mob who tortured him and then burned him alive outside the courtroom while thousands watched. The atrocity, which was photographed by many witnesses, caused an international outcry. No one was prosecuted.

WILSON, ELLEN LOUISE AXSON: BIRTH ANNIVERSARY. May 15, 1860. First wife of Woodrow Wilson, 28th president of the US. Born at Savannah, GA; died at Washington, DC, Aug 6, 1914.

🎂 BIRTHDAYS TODAY

Anna Maria Alberghetti, 84, singer, actress (*Cinderfella, Carnival*), born Pesaro, Italy, May 15, 1936.

Madeleine Albright, 83, former US secretary of state (Clinton administration), born Prague, Czechoslovakia (now the Czech Republic), May 15, 1937.

George Brett, 67, Hall of Fame baseball player, executive, born Glen Dale, WV, May 15, 1953.

David Charvet, 48, singer, actor ("Melrose Place," "Baywatch"), born Lyon, France, May 15, 1972.

David Cronenberg, 77, filmmaker (*Eastern Promises, A History of Violence, The Fly*), born Toronto, ON, Canada, May 15, 1943.

Brian Eno, 72, avant-garde musician, producer, born Woodbridge, England, May 15, 1948.

Giselle Fernandez, 59, television host, actress, born Mexico City, Mexico, May 15, 1961.

	S	M	T	W	T	F	S
May						1	2
	3	4	5	6	7	8	9
2020	10	11	12	13	14	15	16
	17	18	19	20	21	22	23
	24	25	26	27	28	29	30
	31						

Lee Horsley, 65, actor ("Nero Wolfe," "Matt Houston"), born Muleshoe, TN, May 15, 1955.

Jasper Johns, 90, artist, born Augusta, GA, May 15, 1930.

Lainie Kazan, 78, singer, actress (*My Big Fat Greek Wedding, My Favorite Year, Beaches*), born New York, NY, May 15, 1942.

David Krumholtz, 42, actor ("Numb3rs," *The Santa Clause*), born New York, NY, May 15, 1978.

Trini Lopez, 83, singer, actor (*Marriage on the Rocks, The Dirty Dozen*), born Dallas, TX, May 15, 1937.

Justin Morneau, 39, baseball player, born New Westminster, BC, Canada, May 15, 1981.

Andy Murray, 33, tennis player, born Dunblane, Scotland, May 15, 1987.

Chazz Palminteri, 69, actor (*Bullets over Broadway*), playwright, screenwriter (*A Bronx Tale*), born the Bronx, NY, May 15, 1951.

Dan Patrick, 64, sportscaster, radio personality, born Zanesville, OH, May 15, 1956.

Kathleen Sebelius, 72, former US secretary of health and human services (Obama administration), former governor of Kansas (D), born Cincinnati, OH, May 15, 1948.

Jamie-Lynn Sigler, 39, actress ("The Sopranos"), born Jericho, NY, May 15, 1981.

Emmitt Smith, 51, Hall of Fame football player, born Pensacola, FL, May 15, 1969.

John Smoltz, 53, broadcaster, Hall of Fame baseball player, born Warren, MI, May 15, 1967.

Sam Trammell, 49, actor ("True Blood"), born New Orleans, LA, May 15, 1971.

Nicola Walker, 50, actress ("Spooks" ["MI-5"], "Last Tango in Halifax," Olivier Award for *The Curious Incident of the Dog in the Night-Time*), born London, England, May 15, 1970.

May 16 — Saturday

DAY 137   **229 REMAINING**

★**ARMED FORCES DAY.** May 16. Presidential Proclamation 5983, of May 17, 1989, covers the third Saturday in May in all succeeding years. Originally proclaimed as "Army Day" for Apr 6, beginning in 1936 (S.Con.Res. 30 of Apr 2, 1936). S.Con.Res. 5 of Mar 16, 1937, requested annual Apr 6 issuance, which was done through 1949. Always the third Saturday in May since 1950. Traditionally issued once by each administration.

BIOGRAPHERS DAY. May 16. Anniversary of the meeting, at London, England, May 16, 1763, of James Boswell and Samuel Johnson, beginning history's most famous biographer-biographee relationship. Boswell's *Journal of a Tour to the Hebrides* (1785) and his *Life of Samuel Johnson* (1791) are regarded as models of biographical writing. Thus this day is recommended as one on which to start reading or writing a biography.

FIRST ACADEMY AWARDS: ANNIVERSARY. May 16, 1929. About 270 people attended a dinner at the Hollywood Roosevelt Hotel at which the first Academy Awards were given in 12 categories. The silent film *Wings* won Best Picture. A committee of only 20 members selected the winners that year. By the third year the entire membership of the Academy voted. The Academy Awards were first televised in 1953.

FIRST WOMAN TO CLIMB MOUNT EVEREST: 45th ANNIVERSARY. May 16, 1975. Japanese climber Junko Tabei, leading an all-woman expedition to Mount Everest, became the first woman to reach the summit on this date in 1975. Taking the South-East Ridge route, Tabei was delayed by an avalanche before her last leg up the mountain. "Even after reaching the peak," she later recalled, "instead of shouting with excitement, I was simply happy that I didn't have to go any higher!"

FISHING HAS NO BOUNDARIES. May 16–17. Freeman Lake, Monticello, IN. A two-day event for people with disabilities to experience fishing on the lake. Any disability, sex, age, race, etc, eligible. For info: Fishing Has No Boundaries of Mid-North Indiana, PO Box 325, Battle Ground, IN 47920. Phone: (765) 567-2567. E-mail: smlinder3000@gmail.com.

FONDA, HENRY: BIRTH ANNIVERSARY. May 16, 1905. American stage, TV and screen actor (*The Grapes of Wrath, Mister Roberts*), Academy Award winner, born Henry Jaynes Fonda at Grand Island, NE. Began his acting career at the Omaha (NE) Playhouse. Fonda died at Los Angeles, CA, Aug 12, 1982.

GETTYSBURG OUTDOOR ANTIQUE SHOW. May 16 (and Sept 26). Gettysburg, PA. Features 150 dealers in antiques with exhibits and displays. Est attendance: 25,000. For info: Gettysburg Antiques Show, PO Box 4070, Gettysburg, PA 17325. Phone: (717) 253-5750. E-mail: gettysburgantiqueshow@comcast.net. Web: gettysburgretailmerchants.com.

GWINNETT, BUTTON: DEATH ANNIVERSARY. May 16, 1777. Signer of the Declaration of Independence, born at Down Hatherley, Gloucestershire, England, about 1735 (exact date unknown). Died following a duel at St. Catherines Island, south of Savannah, GA.

HERMAN, WOODY: BIRTH ANNIVERSARY. May 16, 1913. The legendary jazz clarinetist, saxophonist, singer and bandleader was born at Milwaukee, WI. After cutting his teeth playing with bands led by others in Chicago, IL, Herman formed his first band in 1936. For the next 50 years he continued to form and front talented ensembles that played in a variety of jazz styles—from blues and improvisation to bop and jazz-rock. Herman died Oct 29, 1987, at Los Angeles, CA.

INTERNATIONAL LEARN TO SWIM DAY. May 16. 9th annual. A nationwide campaign designed to raise awareness about the importance of teaching children to swim. It takes place annually on the Saturday the week before the unofficial start of summer: Memorial Day weekend. Families nationwide are invited to participate by attending a local event, teaching their children to swim with at-home instruction, visiting a community pool as a family or enrolling children in swim lessons at a local facility. For info: SwimWays Corp, 5816 Ward Ct, Virginia Beach, VA 23455. E-mail: mjones@swimways.com. Web: www.teachmetoswim.com.

LIBERACE: BIRTH ANNIVERSARY. May 16, 1919. Wladziu Valentino Liberace, concert pianist who began with a piano, a candelabra, a brother named George and a huge engaging smile, threw in extravagant clothes and jewels and became a Las Vegas headliner and the winner of two Emmy Awards, six gold albums and two stars on the Hollywood Walk of Fame. Liberace was born at West Allis, WI; he died Feb 4, 1987, at Palm Springs, CA.

MARTIN, BILLY: BIRTH ANNIVERSARY. May 16, 1928. Baseball player and manager born at Berkeley, CA. Billy Martin's baseball career included managerial stints with five major league teams: the New York Yankees, Minnesota Twins, Detroit Tigers, Texas Rangers and Oakland Athletics. After a successful playing career, he compiled a record of 1,258 victories to 1,018 losses in his 16 seasons as a manager. His combative style both on and off the field kept him in the headlines, and he will long be remembered for his on-again, off-again relationship with Yankees owner George Steinbrenner, for whom he managed the Yankees five different times. Martin died in an auto accident near Fenton, NY, Dec 25, 1989.

MOREL MUSHROOM FESTIVAL. May 16–17. Muscoda, WI. 38th annual. Wisconsin's "Morel Mushroom Capital" celebrates the end of the morel mushroom's two-week peak season. The celebration includes the buying and selling of morels, wine tasting, food vendors, softball tournament, bounce houses, arts and crafts, flea market and many fun activities for the whole family. Saturday evening is the annual Fireman's Steak Feed followed by music and fireworks; Sunday brings a large parade. Annually, the weekend after Mother's Day. Est attendance: 3,000. For info: Village of Muscoda, Morel Mushroom Fest, PO Box 206, Muscoda, WI 53573-0206. Phone: (608) 739-3182. Fax: (608) 739-3183. E-mail: cljohnson@wppienergy.org. Web: www.muscoda.com.

MORTON, LEVI PARSONS: BIRTH ANNIVERSARY. May 16, 1824. 22nd vice president of the US (1889–93), born at Shoreham, VT. Died at Rhinebeck, NY, May 16, 1920.

NATIONAL FOUL BALL WEEK. May 16–21. On May 16, 1921, during a Reds–Giants game, Reuben Berman kept a caught foul ball—for which he was ushered out of the Polo Grounds. Berman sued for emotional distress and was awarded the ball and $100. Because of him, baseball fans are allowed to keep foul balls hit into the stands. This event celebrates the court ruling by having fans who catch foul balls during the week proudly show their #foulballweeksnag to the world by tweeting it. Annually, May 16–21. For info: Ed Comber, FoulBallz.com. E-mail: ed@foulballz.com. Web: www. FoulBallz.com.

★**NATIONAL SAFE BOATING WEEK.** May 16–22. Presidential Proclamation during May since 1995. From 1958 through 1977, issued for a week including July 4 (PL 85–445 of June 4, 1958). From 1981 through 1994, issued for the first week in June (PL 96–376 of Oct 3, 1980). From 1995, issued for a seven-day period ending on the Friday before Memorial Day. Not issued 1978–80.

NATIONAL SAFE BOATING WEEK. May 16–22. Brings boating safety to the public's attention, decreases the number of boating fatalities and makes the waterways safer for all boaters. Sponsors: National Safe Boating Council and US Coast Guard. Annually, seven days ending on the Friday before Memorial Day. For info: Natl Safe Boating Council, 6985 Gateway Ct, Manassas, VA 20109. Phone: (703) 361-4294. E-mail: outreach@safeboatingcouncil.org. Web: www.safeboatingcouncil.org.

PEABODY, ELIZABETH PALMER: BIRTH ANNIVERSARY. May 16, 1804. Born at Billerica, MA, Peabody was an innovative educator, author and publisher. She opened her first school at Lancaster, MA, when only 16. In 1839 Peabody opened a bookstore that quickly became the intellectuals' hangout. With her own printing press Peabody became the first woman publisher in Boston, MA, and possibly the US. She published three of her brother-in-law Nathaniel Hawthorne's books. For two years she published and wrote for *The Dial*, the literary magazine and voice of the transcendental movement. Peabody's enduring accomplishment was the establishment of the first kindergarten in the US, in 1860 at Boston. She created a magazine, *Kindergarten Messenger*, in 1873. Died Jan 3, 1894, at Jamaica Plain, MA.

PREAKNESS STAKES. May 16. Pimlico Race Course, Baltimore, MD. The Preakness Stakes, the middle jewel in Thoroughbred racing's Triple Crown, was inaugurated in 1873. Annually, the third Saturday in May—two Saturdays after the Kentucky Derby—and followed, three Saturdays later, by the Belmont Stakes. Est attendance: 140,000. For info: Maryland Jockey Club, Pimlico Race Course, 5201 Park Heights Ave, Baltimore, MD 21215. Phone: (410) 542-9400. E-mail: info@marylandracing.com. Web: www.preakness.com.

REY, MARGARET: BIRTH ANNIVERSARY. May 16, 1906. Children's author, born at Hamburg, Germany. Together with her illustrator husband, H.A. Rey, she produced the Curious George series. Rey died at Cambridge, MA, Dec 21, 1996.

RICH, ADRIENNE: BIRTH ANNIVERSARY. May 16, 1929. Born at Baltimore, MD, Adrienne Rich was one of the preeminent poets and feminist theorists of her era. She famously wrote, "The most notable fact our culture imprints on women is the sense of our limits. The most important thing one woman can do for another is to illuminate and expand her sense of actual possibilities." Rich's extensive body of work critiques many social systems—most prominently, patriarchy—and exhibits her progression as a poet, migrating from more formal and structured form earlier in her career to a looser, more personal and intimate form later. Distinguished works include *Of Woman Born: Motherhood as Experience and Institution* (1976) and *Diving into the Wreck: Poems 1971–1972* (1973), for which she received the National Book Award. Rich died Mar 27, 2012, at Santa Cruz, CA.

SEWARD, WILLIAM HENRY: BIRTH ANNIVERSARY. May 16, 1801. American statesman, secretary of state under Lincoln and Andrew Johnson. Seward negotiated the purchase of Alaska from Russia for $7,200,000. At the time some felt the price was too high and referred to the purchase as "Seward's Folly." Seward was governor of New York, 1839–43, and a member of the US Senate, 1848–60. On the evening of Lincoln's assassination, Apr 14, 1865, Seward was stabbed in the throat by Lewis Posell, a fellow conspirator of John Wilkes Booth. Seward recovered and maintained his cabinet position under President Andrew Johnson until 1869. Born at Florida, NY, he died at Auburn, NY, Oct 10, 1872.

TERKEL, STUDS: BIRTH ANNIVERSARY. May 16, 1912. The Chicago-based radio interviewer–turned–oral historian was born Louis Terkel on this date at New York City. Terkel was a self-described "guerrilla journalist" who authored dozens of books, including the Pulitzer Prize–winning *The Good War: An Oral History of World War II* (1984), as well as the similarly structured *Working* (1974). Good interviewing was, Terkel said, listening with respect. He died Oct 31, 2008, at Chicago, IL.

WRIGHT PLUS HOUSEWALK. May 16. Oak Park, IL. The Frank Lloyd Wright Trust's annual housewalk features rare interior tours of privately owned homes and public buildings designed by Frank Lloyd Wright and his contemporaries. For info: Frank Lloyd Wright Trust, 209 S LaSalle St, Ste 118, Chicago, IL 60604. Phone: (312) 994-4000. E-mail: info@flwright.org. Web: www.flwright.org.

🧁 BIRTHDAYS TODAY

David Boreanaz, 49, actor ("Bones," "Angel," "Buffy the Vampire Slayer"), born Philadelphia, PA, May 16, 1971.

Pierce Brosnan, 67, actor (*The Ghost Writer*, *The Thomas Crown Affair*, "Remington Steele," James Bond films), born County Meath, Ireland, May 16, 1953.

Jean-Sébastien Giguère, 43, former hockey player, born Montreal, QC, Canada, May 16, 1977.

Tracey Gold, 51, actress ("Growing Pains"), born New York, NY, May 16, 1969.

	S	M	T	W	T	F	S
May						1	2
	3	4	5	6	7	8	9
2020	10	11	12	13	14	15	16
	17	18	19	20	21	22	23
	24	25	26	27	28	29	30
	31						

Janet Jackson, 54, singer (five Grammys), actress, born Gary, IN, May 16, 1966.

Olga Korbut, 65, Olympic gymnast, born Grodno, USSR (now Belarus), May 16, 1955.

Kirstin Maldonado, 28, singer (Pentatonix), born Fort Worth, TX, May 16, 1992.

John Scott (Jack) Morris, 65, former baseball player, born St. Paul, MN, May 16, 1955.

Matt Ryan, 35, football player, born Exton, PA, May 16, 1985.

Gabriela Sabatini, 50, Hall of Fame tennis player, born Buenos Aires, Argentina, May 16, 1970.

Joan (Benoit) Samuelson, 63, Olympic runner, born Cape Elizabeth, ME, May 16, 1957.

Bill Smitrovich, 73, actor ("Crime Story," *Splash, Manhunter*), born Bridgeport, CT, May 16, 1947.

Tori Spelling, 47, television personality ("Tori & Dean"), actress ("Beverly Hills 90210"), author, born Beverly Hills, CA, May 16, 1973.

Jim Sturgess, 39, actor (*Across the Universe, 21*), born London, England, May 16, 1981.

Mare Winningham, 61, actress (*Mildred Pierce, St. Elmo's Fire*), born Phoenix, AZ, May 16, 1959.

May 17 — Sunday

DAY 138 **228 REMAINING**

BELL, JAMES "COOL PAPA": BIRTH ANNIVERSARY. May 17, 1903. Negro League baseball player James "Cool Papa" Bell was born at Starkville, MS. He played 25 seasons from 1922 to 1946 (one year before Jackie Robinson broke the "color barrier" in major league baseball) with a career average of .338. Regarded as the fastest man ever to play the game—he could round the bases in 13 seconds—he was inducted into the Baseball Hall of Fame in 1974. Bell died Mar 7, 1991, at St. Louis, MO.

***BROWN V BOARD OF EDUCATION* DECISION: ANNIVERSARY.** May 17, 1954. The US Supreme Court ruled unanimously that segregation of public schools "solely on the basis of race" denied black children "equal educational opportunity" even though "physical facilities and other 'tangible' factors may have been equal. Separate educational facilities are inherently unequal." The case was argued before the Court by Thurgood Marshall, who would go on to become the first African American appointed to the Supreme Court.

FIRST KENTUCKY DERBY: ANNIVERSARY. May 17, 1875. The first running of the Kentucky Derby took place at Churchill Downs, Louisville, KY. Jockey Oliver Lewis rode the horse Aristides to a winning time of 2:37.25.

FIRST US SAME-SEX MARRIAGES: ANNIVERSARY. May 17, 2004. Massachusetts became the first US state to sanction gay marriage on this date. Hundreds of gay and lesbian couples received licenses and were married.

INTERNATIONAL NEW FRIENDS, OLD FRIENDS WEEK. May 17–23. A week to celebrate and make time for old friends and new friends and remember how vital friends are for our emotional and physical health and well-being and even professional or career success. *Friendshifts* is the word coined by author and sociologist Jan Yager to denote the way our ideas about friendships as well as who our friends are may change as we go through different stages of life. But at every stage, friendship is crucial for children, teenagers, young adults, singles, couples, new mothers, the middle-aged and especially those who are older, retired or widowed. For info: Jan Yager, PhD, 1127 High Ridge Rd, #110, Stamford, CT 06905. E-mail: jyager@aol.com.

JENNER, EDWARD: BIRTH ANNIVERSARY. May 17, 1749. English physician, born at Berkeley, England. He was the first to establish a scientific basis for vaccination with his work on smallpox. Jenner died at Berkeley, Jan 26, 1823.

LOCKYER, JOSEPH NORMAN: BIRTH ANNIVERSARY. May 17, 1836. Born at Rugby, England, this astronomer discovered a new element in 1868 that he called "helium." He was observing a solar eclipse through electromagnetic spectroscopy when he noticed this element in the sun's atmosphere (this observation was made simultaneously by French scientist Pierre Janssen, who shared credit for the discovery). Another term coined by Lockyer is *chromosphere*. In 1869, he founded the prestigious scientific journal *Nature*. Lockyer died at Salcombe Regis, England, on Aug 16, 1920.

NATIONAL UNICYCLE WEEK. May 17–23. This week gives riders around the country an opportunity to share their love of the sport, promote the benefits of riding and encourage new riders to give it a try. Annually, the week beginning with the third Sunday in May. For info: Unicycling Society of America, 41557 Fallbrook Rd, Northville, MI 48167. E-mail: president@uniusa.org. Web: www.uniusa.org.

NEW YORK STOCK EXCHANGE ESTABLISHED: ANNIVERSARY. May 17, 1792. Some two dozen merchants and brokers agreed to establish what is now known as the New York Stock Exchange. In fair weather they operated under a buttonwood tree on Wall St, at New York, NY. In bad weather they moved to the shelter of a coffeehouse to conduct their business.

NILSSON, BIRGIT: BIRTH ANNIVERSARY. May 17, 1918. The preeminent dramatic soprano of the mid-20th century was born Märta Birgit Svensson at Västra Karup, Sweden. She made her professional debut in 1946 and her Metropolitan Opera debut in 1959 in a headline-making turn. Once, when she sang a high C in *Turandot* at an outdoor venue in Verona, Italy, the residents outside the arena thought a fire alarm had gone off. Nilsson was showered with awards and commendation. She died at Bjärlöv, Sweden, on Dec 25, 2005.

NORWAY: CONSTITUTION DAY OR INDEPENDENCE DAY. May 17. National holiday. Constitution signed and Norway separated from Denmark in 1814. Parades and children's festivities.

O'SULLIVAN, MAUREEN: BIRTH ANNIVERSARY. May 17, 1911. This MGM star was born at Boyle, Ireland, and was discovered at Dublin in 1930 when a visiting Hollywood film director spotted her. Although she had a long (1930–88) and varied film career, O'Sullivan's lasting fame comes from the many Tarzan films she made as Jane Parker opposite Johnny Weissmuller and Cheetah (a costar she was not fond of). Her first film in the Tarzan series was *Tarzan the Ape Man* (1932) and her last was *Tarzan's New York Adventure* (1942). O'Sullivan died on June 23, 1998, at Scottsdale, AZ.

RIDE A UNICYCLE DAY. May 17. The kickoff to National Unicycle Week is Ride a Unicycle Day, a challenge to everyone, young and old, to take to one wheel, perhaps for the very first time! Annually, the third Sunday in May. For info: Unicycling Society of America. E-mail: president@uniusa.org. Web: www.uniusa.org.

ROGATION SUNDAY. May 17. The fifth Sunday after Easter is the beginning of Rogationtide (Rogation Sunday and the following three days before Ascension Day). Rogation Day rituals date from the fifth century.

RURAL LIFE SUNDAY. May 17. With an increase in ecological and environmental concerns, Rural Life Sunday emphasizes the concept that Earth belongs to God, who has granted humanity the use of it, along with the responsibility of caring for it wisely. At the suggestion of the International Association of Agricultural Missions, Rural Life Sunday was first observed in 1929. The day is observed annually by churches of many Christian denominations and includes pulpit exchanges by rural and urban pastors. Traditionally, Rural Life Sunday is Rogation Sunday, the Sunday preceding Ascension Day.

UNITED NATIONS: WORLD TELECOMMUNICATION AND INFORMATION SOCIETY DAY. May 17. On Mar 27, 2006, the UN General Assembly proclaimed this annual day to help raise awareness of the possibilities that the Internet and other information and communication technology can bring to societies and economies, as well as ways to bridge the digital divide (Res 60/252). Annually, May 17. For info: United Nations, Dept of Public Info, New York, NY 10017. Web: www.un.org.

★**WORLD TRADE WEEK.** May 17–23. Presidential Proclamation has been issued each year since 1948 for the third week in May with three exceptions: 1949, 1955 and 1966.

🎂 BIRTHDAYS TODAY

Craig Ferguson, 58, comedian, actor ("The Drew Carey Show"), television talk show host ("The Late Late Show with Craig Ferguson"), author, born Glasgow, Scotland, May 17, 1962.

Thom Filicia, 51, interior designer, television personality, born Syracuse, NY, May 17, 1969.

Mia Hamm, 48, Hall of Fame soccer player, born Selma, AL, May 17, 1972.

Christian Lacroix, 70, fashion designer, born Arles, France, May 17, 1950.

Ray Charles "Sugar Ray" Leonard, 64, Hall of Fame boxer, born Washington, DC, May 17, 1956.

Tony Parker, 38, basketball player, born Bruges, Belgium, May 17, 1982.

Gina Raimondo, 49, Governor of Rhode Island (D), born Smithfield, RI, May 17, 1971.

Sendhil Ramamurthy, 46, actor ("Heroes"), born Chicago, IL, May 17, 1974.

Nikki Reed, 32, actress (*Thirteen, Twilight*), born Los Angeles, CA, May 17, 1988.

Trent Reznor, 55, singer (Nine Inch Nails), born Mercer, PA, May 17, 1965.

	S	M	T	W	T	F	S
May						1	2
	3	4	5	6	7	8	9
2020	10	11	12	13	14	15	16
	17	18	19	20	21	22	23
	24	25	26	27	28	29	30
	31						

Bob Saget, 64, actor ("Full House"), host ("America's Funniest Home Videos"), born Philadelphia, PA, May 17, 1956.

Debra Winger, 65, actress (*Terms of Endearment, Shadowlands*), born Columbus, OH, May 17, 1955.

May 18 — Monday

DAY 139   **227 REMAINING**

ALLIES CAPTURE MONTE CASSINO: ANNIVERSARY. May 18, 1944. Between Oct 12, 1943, and Jan 17, 1944, there were five Allied attempts to take the German position at the Benedictine abbey at Monte Cassino. Although the abbey had been reduced to rubble, it served as a bunker for the Germans. In the spring of 1944 Marshal Alphonse Pierre Juin devised an operation that crossed the mountainous regions behind the fortresslike structure, using Moroccan troops of the French Expeditionary Force. Specially trained for mountain operations, they climbed 4,850 feet to locate a pass. On May 15, 1944, they attacked the Germans from behind. On May 18, Polish troops attached to this force took Monte Cassino.

BAKUNIN, MIKHAIL ALEKSANDROVICH: BIRTH ANNIVERSARY. May 18, 1814. Revolutionary agitator born at Premukhino, Russia. Bakunin advocated completely dismantling the state and in 1842 wrote, "The passion for destruction is also a creative passion," which became the motto of international anarchism. Involved in various European insurrections, Bakunin espoused liberation of Slav peoples and was exiled to Siberia before escaping to Western Europe, where he died at Bern, Switzerland, July 1, 1876.

CANADA: VICTORIA DAY. May 18. Commemorates the birth of Queen Victoria May 24, 1819. Observed annually on the Monday preceding May 25.

CAPRA, FRANK: BIRTH ANNIVERSARY. May 18, 1897. Academy Award–winning director whose movies were suffused with affectionate portrayals of the common man and the strengths and foibles of American democracy. Capra was born at Palermo, Sicily. He bluffed his way into silent movies in 1922 and, despite total ignorance of moviemaking, directed and produced a profitable one-reeler. He was the first to win three directorial Oscars—for *It Happened One Night* (1934), *Mr Deeds Goes to Town* (1936) and *You Can't Take It with You* (1938). The Motion Picture Academy voted the first and third of these as Best Picture. Capra said his favorite of the films he made was *It's a Wonderful Life* (1946). He died at La Quinta, CA, Sept 3, 1991.

FONTEYN, MARGOT: BIRTH ANNIVERSARY. May 18, 1919. Born Margaret Hookham at Reigate, Surrey, England, Dame Margot Fonteyn thrilled ballet audiences for 45 years. She emerged from the Sadler's Wells company during the 1930s and 1940s as a solo artist and followed those successes by partnering with Soviet exile Rudolph Nureyev in the 1960s. She died Feb 21, 1991, at Panama City, Panama.

FRANCE: ROLAND GARROS 2020 (FRENCH OPEN TENNIS TOURNAMENT). May 18–June 7. Roland-Garros Stadium, Paris. Storied clay-court international tournament—part of the Grand Slam of Tennis—played annually since 1925. For info: Fédération Française de Tennis, 2 avenue Gordon Bennett, 75016 Paris, France. E-mail: fft@fft.fr. Web: www.fft.fr or www.rolandgarros.com.

HAITI: FLAG AND UNIVERSITY DAY. May 18. Public holiday.

INTERNATIONAL MUSEUM DAY. May 18. To pay tribute to museums of the world. "Museums are an important means of cultural exchange, enrichment of cultures and development of mutual understanding and peace among people." Recently observed by more than 37,000 museums in more than 158 countries and territories. Observed annually on May 18 since 1977. Sponsor: International Council of Museums (ICOM), Paris, France. For info:

ICOM General Secretariat, Maison de l'UNESCO, 1 rue Miollis, 75732 Paris Cedex 15, France. Web: https://icom.museum.

MOUNT SAINT HELENS ERUPTION: 40th ANNIVERSARY. May 18, 1980. A major eruption of Mount Saint Helens volcano, in southwestern Washington, blew steam and ash more than 11 miles into the sky. First major eruption of Mount Saint Helens since 1857, though on Mar 26, 1980, there had been a warning eruption of smaller magnitude.

POPE JOHN PAUL II: 100th BIRTH ANNIVERSARY. May 18, 1920. Karol Wojtyla, 264th pope of the Roman Catholic Church, born at Wadowice, Poland. Elected pope Oct 16, 1978, he was the first non-Italian to be elected pope in 456 years and the first Polish pope. His theology was conservative and traditional, and he was known for his worldwide travels to bring the message of the Catholic Church to people around the world. He survived an assassination attempt in 1981 and died at Vatican City on Apr 2, 2005. He was beatified May 1, 2011.

SPACE MILESTONE: *APOLLO 10* (US). May 18, 1969. Launched with astronauts Colonel Thomas Stafford and Commander Eugene Cernan, who brought lunar module "Snoopy" within nine miles of the moon's surface on May 22. *Apollo 10* circled the moon 31 times and returned to Earth May 26.

SUPPLY CHAIN PROFESSIONALS DAY. May 18. 3rd annual. This day celebrates the individuals responsible for the buy, make, move and sell activities that define our modern lifestyle. The idea for a professional organization of distribution managers (later referred to as logistics managers) was first conceived in May 1962 in order to meet an urgent need for continuing education and to provide an opportunity for an interchange of ideas in this rapidly growing profession—a profession known today as supply chain management. Annually, the third Monday in May. For info: Nichole Mumford, Vice President, Council of Supply Chain Management Professionals (CSCMP), 333 E Butterfield Rd, Ste 140, Lombard, IL 60148. Phone: (630) 645-3476. E-mail: nmumford@cscmp.org. Web: www.cscmp.org.

SWITZERLAND: PACING THE BOUNDS. May 18. Liestal. Citizens set off at 8 AM and march along boundaries to the beating of drums and firing of pistols and muskets. Occasion for fetes. Annually, the Monday before Ascension Day.

TURKMENISTAN: REVIVAL AND UNITY DAY. May 18. National holiday. Commemorates the 1992 adoption of the constitution.

TURNER, BIG JOE: BIRTH ANNIVERSARY. May 18, 1911. The "boss of the blues" and "grandfather of rock and roll" was born Joseph Vernon Turner, Jr, at Kansas City, MO. After a lengthy career singing blues, swing and jazz, Turner helped usher in the rock-and-roll era with his 1954 hit "Shake, Rattle and Roll" (later covered with cleaner lyrics by Bill Haley and His Comets). Turner died Nov 24, 1985, at Inglewood, CA. He was inducted into the Blues Hall of Fame in 1983 and the Rock & Roll Hall of Fame in 1987.

URUGUAY: BATTLE OF LAS PIEDRAS DAY. May 18. National holiday. Commemorates battle fought for independence from Spain in 1811.

VISIT YOUR RELATIVES DAY. May 18. A day to renew family ties and joys by visiting often-thought-of-seldom-seen relatives. Annually, May 18. For info: A.C. Vierow, Box 71, Clio, MI 48420-0071.

WILLSON, MEREDITH: BIRTH ANNIVERSARY. May 18, 1902. American musician, playwright and composer best known for *The Music Man.* Born at Mason City, IA, Willson received Oscar nominations for *The Little Foxes* and *The Great Dictator.* Many of his songs, including "It's Beginning to Look a Lot like Christmas," "Seventy-Six Trombones" and "Till There Was You," have become standards. Willson died at Santa Monica, CA, June 15, 1984.

🎂 **BIRTHDAYS TODAY**

Chow Yun-Fat, 65, actor (*Crouching Tiger, Hidden Dragon; Anna and the King; Bulletproof Monk*), born Lamma Island, Hong Kong, May 18, 1955.

Tina Fey, 50, actress, comedienne ("30 Rock," *Whiskey Tango Foxtrot, Sisters, Mean Girls*), writer, born Upper Darby, PA, May 18, 1970.

Brad Friedel, 49, Hall of Fame soccer player and coach, born Lakewood, OH, May 18, 1971.

Dwayne Hickman, 86, actor ("The Many Loves of Dobie Gillis"), born Los Angeles, CA, May 18, 1934.

Reginald Martinez (Reggie) Jackson, 74, Hall of Fame baseball player, born Wyncote, PA, May 18, 1946.

Luke Kleintank, 30, actor ("The Man in the High Castle," "Pretty Little Liars"), born Cincinnati, OH, May 18, 1990.

Jari Kurri, 60, Hall of Fame hockey player, born Helsinki, Finland, May 18, 1960.

Yannick Noah, 60, Hall of Fame tennis player, born Sedan, France, May 18, 1960.

Brooks Robinson, 83, Hall of Fame baseball player, born Little Rock, AR, May 18, 1937.

James Stephens, 69, actor ("The Paper Chase"), born Mount Kisco, NY, May 18, 1951.

George Strait, 68, country singer, musician, born Poteet, TX, May 18, 1952.

Tom Udall, 72, US Senator (D, New Mexico), born Tucson, AZ, May 18, 1948.

Vince Young, 37, football player, born Houston, TX, May 18, 1983.

May 19 — Tuesday

DAY 140   **226 REMAINING**

AKELEY, CARL: BIRTH ANNIVERSARY. May 19, 1864. Born near Clarendon, NY, the "father of modern taxidermy" was unhappy with the "upholsterer's method of mounting animals" and spent his life elevating taxidermy to a science. Akeley's research led to many inventions and innovations that benefited museums worldwide. Akeley survived a leopard attack, charging rhinos and an elephant stampede during his many African expeditions to collect specimens, many of which are still on display in the naturalistic settings he created. Regret over killing a mountain gorilla led him to petition King Albert I of Belgium to create a sanctuary, later Africa's first national park. Akeley died Nov 18, 1926, from a fever near Mount Mkeno, Congo.

BOLEYN, ANNE: EXECUTION ANNIVERSARY. May 19, 1536. Born around 1501, Anne Boleyn captured the eye of England's King Henry VIII in 1527. Her demand that he make her a wife, not a mistress, caused the married Henry's break with the Catholic Church (which didn't allow divorce), which in turn led to decades of religious turmoil in England. Henry had his marriage to Catherine of Aragon annulled and wed Boleyn in 1533. Boleyn's inability to bear a male heir (although her daughter with Henry was the future Queen Elizabeth I) and court intrigue caused her arrest on charges of adultery. She was executed by sword at the Tower of London. The morning of her execution she said, "I heard say the executioner was very good, and I have a little neck."

BOYS' CLUBS FOUNDED: ANNIVERSARY. May 19, 1906. The Federated Boys' Clubs, which later became the Boys' and Girls' Clubs of America, was founded.

DARK DAY IN NEW ENGLAND: ANNIVERSARY. May 19, 1780. At midday near-total darkness unaccountably descended on much of New England. Candles were lit, fowls went to roost and many fearful persons believed that doomsday had arrived. At New Haven, CT, Colonel Abraham Davenport opposed adjournment of the town council in these words: "I am against adjournment. The day of judgment is either approaching or it is not. If it is not, there is no cause for an adjournment. If it is, I choose to be found doing my duty. I wish therefore that candles may be brought." No scientifically verifiable cause for this widespread phenomenon was ever discovered.

HANSBERRY, LORRAINE: 90th BIRTH ANNIVERSARY. May 19, 1930. American playwright Lorraine Hansberry was born at Chicago, IL. For her now classic play *A Raisin in the Sun*, she became the youngest American and first black writer to win the Best Play Award from the New York Critics' Circle. The play, titled after the Langston Hughes poem, deals with issues such as racism, cultural pride and self-respect and was the first stage production written by a black woman to appear on Broadway (1959). *To Be Young, Gifted, and Black*, a book of excerpts from her journals, letters, speeches and plays, was published posthumously in 1969. Lorraine Hansberry died of cancer Jan 12, 1965, at New York, NY.

HEPATITIS TESTING DAY. May 19. May is National Hepatitis Awareness Month and May 19 is Hepatitis Testing Day. Millions of Americans have chronic viral hepatitis and most of them do not know they are infected. This day is an opportunity to remind healthcare providers and the public who should be tested for viral hepatitis. For info: Centers for Disease Control and Prevention. Web: www.cdc.gov/hepatitis/heppromoresources.htm.

HO CHI MINH: BIRTH ANNIVERSARY. May 19, 1890. Vietnamese revolutionary leader and first president of the Democratic Republic of Vietnam, born at Kim Lien, a central Vietnamese village (Nghiem An Province), probably May 19, 1890. His original name was Nguyen That Than. A Communist, he led the independence movement and defeated the French (colonial overlords) at Dien Bien Phu. As president, he ruled from 1945 to 1969. Saigon was officially renamed Ho Chi Minh City in his honor. He died at Hanoi, Vietnam, Sept 3, 1969. The anniversary of his birth is a national holiday in Vietnam, as is the anniversary of his death.

MALCOLM X: 95th BIRTH ANNIVERSARY. May 19, 1925. Black nationalist and civil rights activist Malcolm X was born Malcolm Little at Omaha, NE. While serving a prison term, he resolved to transform his life. On his release in 1952 he changed his name to Malcolm X and worked for the Nation of Islam until he was suspended by Black Muslim leader Elijah Muhammad on Dec 4, 1963. Malcolm X later made the pilgrimage to Mecca and became an orthodox Muslim. He was assassinated as he spoke to a meeting at the Audubon Ballroom at New York, NY, Feb 21, 1965.

MARILYN MONROE SERENADES JFK: ANNIVERSARY. May 19, 1962. Hollywood star Marilyn Monroe serenaded President John F. Kennedy at his 45th birthday celebration at Madison Square Garden in New York City on this date (Kennedy's actual birthday was May 29). Her sheer, sparkling dress (which she had to be sewn into) and breathily seductive version of "Happy Birthday to You" (which Ken-

nedy joked was "sweet and wholesome") became a pop culture legend. The dress was auctioned in 1999 and sold for $1.26 million.

SPACE MILESTONE: *MARS 2* AND *MARS 3* (USSR). May 19 and 28, 1971. Entered Martian orbits on Nov 27 and Dec 2, respectively. *Mars 3* sent down a TV-equipped capsule that soft-landed and transmitted pictures for 20 seconds.

TURKEY: YOUTH AND SPORTS DAY. May 19. Public holiday commemorating the beginning of a national movement for independence in 1919, led by Mustafa Kemal Ataturk.

🎂 BIRTHDAYS TODAY

James Fox, 81, actor (*A Passage to India, The Russia House, Patriot Games*), born London, England, May 19, 1939.

Kevin Garnett, 44, basketball player, born Mauldin, SC, May 19, 1976.

David Hartman, 83, actor, broadcaster (Emmy for "Good Morning America"), born Pawtucket, RI, May 19, 1937.

Grace Jones, 68, model, singer, actress (*A View to a Kill*), born Spanish Town, Jamaica, May 19, 1952.

William (Bill) Laimbeer, Jr, 63, former basketball player and coach, born Boston, MA, May 19, 1957.

Jim Lehrer, 86, journalist, political analyst, former anchor ("PBS NewsHour"), author (*Viva Max!*), born Wichita, KS, May 19, 1934.

Eric Lloyd, 34, actor ("Jesse," *Dunston Checks In, The Santa Clause*), born Glendale, CA, May 19, 1986.

Archie Manning, 71, former football player, born Drew, MS, May 19, 1949.

Sam Smith, 28, singer, songwriter (Oscar with Jimmy Napes for "Writing's on the Wall"), born London, England, May 19, 1992.

Pete Townshend, 75, musician (The Who), born London, England, May 19, 1945.

May 20 — Wednesday

DAY 141   **225 REMAINING**

AMELIA EARHART ATLANTIC CROSSING: ANNIVERSARY. May 20, 1932. Leaving Harbor Grace, Newfoundland, Canada, at 7 PM, Amelia Earhart landed near Londonderry, Ireland. The 2,026-mile flight took 13 hours and 30 minutes. She was the first woman to fly solo across the Atlantic.

BALZAC, HONORÉ DE: BIRTH ANNIVERSARY. May 20, 1799. French author of a huge cycle of stories and novels known as *The Human Comedy*, born at Tours, France. "It is easier," Balzac wrote in 1829, "to be a lover than a husband for the simple reason that it is more difficult to be witty every day than to say pretty things from time to time." Died at Paris, Aug 18, 1850.

CAMEROON: NATIONAL HOLIDAY. May 20. Republic of Cameroon. Commemorates adoption of constitution in 1972.

COUNCIL OF NICAEA I: ANNIVERSARY. May 20–Aug 25, 325. First ecumenical council of Christian Church, called by Constantine I, first Christian emperor of Roman Empire. Nearly 300 bishops are said to have attended this first of 21 ecumenical councils (latest,

May 2020	S	M	T	W	T	F	S
						1	2
	3	4	5	6	7	8	9
	10	11	12	13	14	15	16
	17	18	19	20	21	22	23
	24	25	26	27	28	29	30
	31						

Vatican II, began Sept 11, 1962), which was held at Nicaea, in Asia Minor (today's Turkey). The council condemned Arianism (which denied the divinity of Christ), formulated the Nicene Creed and fixed the day of Easter—always on a Sunday.

EAST TIMOR: ANNIVERSARY OF INDEPENDENCE. May 20, 2002. East Timor became fully independent from Indonesia on this day. Indonesia had controlled the tiny nation since 1975. It had previously been a colony of Portugal for 450 years.

ELIZA DOOLITTLE DAY. May 20. To honor Miss Doolittle (heroine of George Bernard Shaw's *Pygmalion*) for demonstrating the importance and the advantage of speaking one's native language properly. (Created by William and Helen Chase.)

FLEET WEEK NEW YORK 2020. May 20–26. New York, NY. Held nearly every year since 1984, Fleet Week New York is the city's celebration of the sea services. Fleet Week New York provides an opportunity for the citizens of New York City and the surrounding tri-state area to meet sailors, marines and coast guardsmen, as well as see, firsthand, the latest capabilities of today's maritime services. For info: Fleet Week New York. Phone: (757) 322-2853. Web: www.fleetweeknewyork.com.

HERZL, THEODOR: BIRTH ANNIVERSARY. May 20, 1860. Founder of the modern Zionist movement, born at Budapest, Hungary. Herzl died at Edlach, Austria, July 3, 1904.

HEWLETT, WILLIAM: BIRTH ANNIVERSARY. May 20, 1913. Born at Ann Arbor, MI, engineer and businessman William Hewlett started the Hewlett-Packard Company with cofounder David Packard in 1939. Hewlett served the company in various capacities as president, CEO, chairman and vice chairman of the board, and director emeritus. The recipient of numerous honorary degrees, he was awarded the prestigious National Medal of Science in 1983. Packard died Jan 12, 2001, at Palo Alto, CA, one of the richest people in the world with an estate valued at more than $9 billion.

HOMESTEAD ACT: ANNIVERSARY. May 20, 1862. President Abraham Lincoln signed the Homestead Act opening millions of acres of government-owned land in the West to settlers, or "homesteaders," who had to reside on the land and cultivate it for five years.

LINDBERGH FLIGHT: ANNIVERSARY. May 20–21, 1927. Anniversary of the first solo transatlantic flight. Captain Charles Augustus Lindbergh, 25-year-old aviator, departed from rainy, muddy Roosevelt Field, Long Island, NY, alone at 7:52 AM, May 20, 1927, in a Ryan monoplane named *Spirit of St. Louis*. He landed at Le Bourget airfield, Paris, France, at 10:24 PM, Paris time (5:24 PM, NY time), May 21, winning a $25,000 prize offered by Raymond Orteig for the first nonstop flight between New York City and Paris (3,600 miles). The "flying fool," as he had been dubbed by some doubters, became "Lucky Lindy," an instant world hero. See also: "Lindbergh, Charles Augustus: Birth Anniversary" (Feb 4).

MADISON, DOLLEY (DOROTHEA) DANDRIDGE PAYNE TODD: BIRTH ANNIVERSARY. May 20, 1768. Wife of James Madison, fourth president of the US, born at Guilford County, NC. Died at Washington, DC, July 12, 1849.

MECKLENBURG DAY. May 20. North Carolina. Commemorates claimed signing of a declaration of independence from England by citizens of Mecklenburg County on this day, 1775.

MIKITA, STAN: 80th BIRTH ANNIVERSARY. May 20, 1940. Stan "Stosh" Mikita, born Stanislaus Guoth May 20, 1940, in the Slovak Republic, was one of the most successful forwards in National Hockey League history. Signed to the Chicago Blackhawks at age 18, Mikita led all goal scorers during his sophomore season and, with his 100-mile-per-hour slap slot, helped Chicago win its first Stanley Cup since 1938. During a career that spanned four decades—the late 1950s through 1980, all with the Blackhawks—Mikita won awards in numbers unmatched until Wayne Gretzky. He retired in 1980 as one of most popular stars and all-time leading scorers in NHL history with 541 goals and nearly 1,500 points over 22 seasons. A nine-time All-Star, Mikita was elected to the Hockey Hall of Fame in 1983. He died on Aug 7, 2018, at Chicago, IL.

ROUSSEAU, HENRI JULIEN FELIX: BIRTH ANNIVERSARY. May 20, 1844. Henri Rousseau, nicknamed "Le Douanier" (customs officer) because of his onetime post as customs tollkeeper, was a celebrated French painter born at Laval, Mayenne, France. Painted deceptively "primitive" pictures of exotic foliage, flowers and fruit of the jungle, with stilted human and animal figures. Died at Hospital Necker, Paris, Sept 4, 1910.

SPACE MILESTONE: *PIONEER VENUS I* (US). May 20, 1978. Launched this date, became first Venus orbiter the following Dec 4.

STEWART, JIMMY: BIRTH ANNIVERSARY. May 20, 1908. Film actor born James Stewart at Indiana, PA. Best known for his everyman roles and work with directors Frank Capra and Alfred Hitchcock. Starred in *Mr Smith Goes to Washington*, *It's a Wonderful Life*, *Rear Window* and many classic Westerns. Stewart won a Best Actor Oscar for *The Philadelphia Story*. He died July 2, 1997, at Beverly Hills, CA.

WEIGHTS AND MEASURES DAY. May 20. Anniversary of international treaty, signed May 20, 1875, providing for the establishment of an International Bureau of Weights and Measures. The bureau was founded on international territory at Sèvres, France.

WORLD AIARTHRITIS DAY. May 20. This day seeks to raise awareness about autoimmune and autoinflammatory diseases with arthritis as a major component. Observed since 2012 (formerly, World Autoimmune Arthritis Day). Annually, May 20. For info: International Foundation for Autoimmune and Autoinflammatory Arthritis. E-mail: info@aiarthritis.org. Web: https://www.facebook.com/AIArthritisDay.

🧁 BIRTHDAYS TODAY

Ted Allen, 55, television personality ("Chopped," "Queer Eye for the Straight Guy"), author, journalist, born Columbus, OH, May 20, 1965.

John Carney, 64, Governor of Delaware (D), born Wilmington, DE, May 20, 1956.

Iker Casillas, 39, soccer player, born Madrid, Spain, May 20, 1981.

Cher, 74, singer, actress (Oscar for *Moonstruck*; *Mask, Silkwood*), born Cherilyn Sarkisian at El Centro, CA, May 20, 1946.

Michael Crapo, 69, US Senator (R, Idaho), born Idaho Falls, ID, May 20, 1951.

Matt Czuchry, 39, actor ("The Good Wife"), born Manchester, NH, May 20, 1977.

Chris Froome, 35, cyclist, born Nairobi, Kenya, May 20, 1985.

Tony Goldwyn, 60, actor ("Scandal," *Ghost, Kiss the Girls*), born Los Angeles, CA, May 20, 1960.

Timothy Olyphant, 52, actor ("Justified," "Damages"), born Honolulu, HI, May 20, 1968.

Tahmoh Penikett, 45, actor ("Battlestar Galactica," "Dollhouse"), born Whitehorse, YT, Canada, May 20, 1975.

Bronson Pinchot, 61, actor ("Perfect Strangers," "Step by Step"), born New York, NY, May 20, 1959.

Ronald Prescott Reagan, 62, television host, commentator, born Los Angeles, CA, May 20, 1958.

Anthony Zerbe, 84, actor ("Harry-O," *American Hustle, Papillon*), born Long Beach, CA, May 20, 1936.

May 21 — Thursday

DAY 142   **224 REMAINING**

AMERICAN RED CROSS FOUNDED: ANNIVERSARY. May 21, 1881. Commemorates the founding of the American Red Cross by Clara Barton, its first president. The Red Cross had been founded in Switzerland in 1864 by representatives from 16 European nations. It is a not-for-profit organization governed and directed by volunteers and provides disaster relief at home and abroad. Its 1.1 million volunteers are involved in community services such as collecting and distributing donated blood and blood products, teaching health and safety classes and acting as a medium for emergency communication between Americans and their armed forces.

ASCENSION DAY. May 21. Commemorates Christ's ascension into heaven. Observed since AD 68. Ascension Day is the 40th day after the Resurrection, counting Easter as the first day.

BELGIUM: PROCESSION OF THE HOLY BLOOD. May 21. Religious historical procession. Recalls adventurous crusaders, including Count Thierry of Alsace, who carried back relics of the Holy Blood. Always on Ascension Day.

BURR, RAYMOND WILLIAM STACY: BIRTH ANNIVERSARY. May 21, 1917. Stage, film and TV actor best known for the role of lawyer/sleuth Perry Mason in the long-running hit television series of the same name (1957–66) and 26 made-for-TV movies. He was also the star of "Ironside" (1967–75), playing a paraplegic investigative consultant. His films include *Rear Window* and *Godzilla* (in the US edit). Burr received two Best Actor Emmy Awards for playing Mason (1959 and 1961). Born at New Westminster, BC, Canada, Burr died near Healdsburg, CA, Sept 12, 1993.

CHILE: BATTLE OF IQUIQUE DAY. May 21. Commemorates a naval battle in 1879, part of the War of the Pacific with Peru and Bolivia.

CURTISS, GLENN HAMMOND: BIRTH ANNIVERSARY. May 21, 1878. American inventor and aviator, born at Hammondsport, NY. The aviation pioneer died at Buffalo, NY, July 23, 1930.

DÜRER, ALBRECHT: BIRTH ANNIVERSARY. May 21, 1471. German painter and engraver, one of the foremost artists of the Renaissance, was born at Nuremberg, Germany, and died there Apr 6, 1528.

GEMINI, THE TWINS. May 21–June 20. In the astronomical/astrological zodiac, which divides the sun's apparent orbit into 12 segments, the period May 21–June 20 is traditionally identified as the sun sign of Gemini, the Twins. The ruling planet is Mercury.

HERRINFESTA ITALIANA. May 21–25. Herrin Civic Center, Herrin, IL. Top-name entertainment, bocce tournaments, Grand Parade, grape stomp, pasta sauce contest, Italian food, triathlon, road races, carnival and more. Est attendance: 55,000. For info: Herrinfesta Italiana, PO Box 2005, Herrin, IL 62948. Phone: (800) ITF-ESTA. Web: www.herrinfesta.com.

HUMMEL, SISTER MARIA INNOCENTIA: BIRTH ANNIVERSARY. May 21, 1909. Born at Massing, Bavaria, Sister Maria Innocentia Hummel attended Munich's Academy of Fine Arts. She entered Siessen Convent, run by the Sisters of the Third Order of St. Francis, and began teaching art to kindergarten children. In 1934 Franz Goebel obtained an exclusive license to translate her drawings into three-dimensional figurines. The first M.I. Hummel figurines were displayed at the Leipzig Trade Fair in 1935; they made their first appearance in the American market in May 1935. She died Nov 6, 1946, at Siessen, Germany.

May **2020**	S	M	T	W	T	F	S
						1	2
	3	4	5	6	7	8	9
	10	11	12	13	14	15	16
	17	18	19	20	21	22	23
	24	25	26	27	28	29	30
	31						

"I NEED A PATCH FOR THAT" DAY. May 21. They have patches for nicotine and they have patches for heart patients. How about a patch for runny noses or bad hair? (©2006 by WH.) For info: Thomas & Ruth Roy, Wellcat Holidays, 2418 Long Ln, Lebanon, PA 17046. Phone: (717) 279-0184. E-mail: info@wellcat.com. Web: www.wellcat.com.

MONACO: GRAND PRIX DE MONACO. May 21–24. Monte Carlo. 78th edition. One of the premier sporting events in the world. Thrilling Formula 1 race: 77 laps through the streets of Monte Carlo, held since Apr 14, 1929. For info: Automobile Club de Monaco, 23 bd Albert 1er, BP 464, Monaco. E-mail: info@acm.mc. Web: www.acm.mc.

NATIONAL EAT MORE FRUITS AND VEGETABLES DAY. May 21. Only 27 percent of US adults eat enough fruit and vegetables, and more than 33 percent of US children eat less than one serving of fresh produce a day. To encourage the public to adopt a healthier diet and lifestyle, this day celebrates the extraordinary health, taste and convenience benefits of fresh fruits and vegetables—and is part of a larger initiative to make the world healthier. On this day, Dole offers new fruit and vegetable recipes, nutritional tips and education from the Dole Nutrition Institute and an interactive, healthy-eating pledge. Annually, the Thursday before Memorial Day. For info: Dole Food Company, One Dole Dr, Westlake Village, CA 91362. Web: www.dole.com.

NATIONAL WAITSTAFF DAY. May 21. A day for restaurant managers and patrons to recognize and to express their appreciation for the many fine and dedicated waitresses and waiters. (Created by Gaylord F. Ward.)

POPE, ALEXANDER: BIRTH ANNIVERSARY. May 21, 1688. Poet, critic, translator (of Homer), satirist born at London, England. *The Rape of the Lock* (1712–14) firmly established Pope as the foremost poet of the time and remains his most popular work. Also author of the unfinished *An Essay on Man*, which features the line "Hope springs eternal in the human breast." He died at Twickenham, England, May 30, 1744.

SAKHAROV, ANDREI DMITRIYEVICH: BIRTH ANNIVERSARY. May 21, 1921. Soviet physicist, human rights activist and environmentalist Andrei Sakharov was born at Moscow, Russia. A collaborator in producing the first Soviet atomic bomb and later the hydrogen bomb, Sakharov denounced shortcomings of his country's government and was exiled to Gorky, Russia, 1980–86. He helped create the reform and restructuring concept known as *perestroika* and of *glasnost* (freedom). He was named to the Soviet Congress of People's Deputies eight months before his death at Moscow on Dec 14, 1989. As a physicist, he was the developer of destructive weapons; as a humanitarian, he was courageous as a dissident from militarism and an advocate of human rights.

UNITED NATIONS: WORLD DAY FOR CULTURAL DIVERSITY FOR DIALOGUE AND DEVELOPMENT. May 21. Recognizing the need to enhance the potential of culture as a means of achieving prosperity, sustainable development and global peaceful coexistence, the General Assembly, on Dec 20, 2002, proclaimed May 21 to serve as this day. The Assembly acknowledged the close link between protecting cultural diversity and the larger framework of the dialogue among civilizations. For info: United Nations, Dept of Public Info, New York, NY 10017. Web: www.un.org.

🎂 BIRTHDAYS TODAY

Bobby Cox, 79, baseball manager, former executive and player, born Tulsa, OK, May 21, 1941.

Lisa Edelstein, 53, actress ("House," "Felicity"), born Boston, MA, May 21, 1967.

Al Franken, 69, former US senator (D, Minnesota), comedian, actor, writer (*Lies and the Lying Liars Who Tell Them*), born New York, NY, May 21, 1951.

Gotye, 40, musician, born Wouter De Backer at Bruges, Belgium, May 21, 1980.

Josh Hamilton, 39, baseball player, born Raleigh, NC, May 21, 1981.

Heinz Holliger, 81, oboist, composer, conductor, born Langenthal, Switzerland, May 21, 1939.

Loretta E. Lynch, 61, former US attorney general (Obama administration), born Greensboro, NC, May 21, 1959.

Ian McEwan, 72, author (*On Chesil Beach, Atonement, Amsterdam*), born Aldershot, Hampstead, England, May 21, 1948.

Sarah Ramos, 29, actress ("Parenthood," "American Dreams"), born Los Angeles, CA, May 21, 1991.

Judge Reinhold, 63, actor (*Beverly Hills Cop*), born Wilmington, DE, May 21, 1957.

Leo Sayer, 72, singer, songwriter, born Shoreham, England, May 21, 1948.

Mr T, 68, actor (*Rocky III*, "The A-Team"), born Lawrence Tureaud at Chicago, IL, May 21, 1952.

Jeffrey Toobin, 60, legal commentator, journalist, author (*The Run of His Life: The People v O.J. Simpson, The Nine, American Heiress*), former attorney, born New York, NY, May 21, 1960.

May 22 — Friday

DAY 143   **223 REMAINING**

AZNAVOUR, CHARLES: BIRTH ANNIVERSARY. May 22, 1924. The international singer-songwriter and actor, born Sharmouz Varenagh Aznavourian at Paris, France, was one of the most famous French performers of his day. Over an 80-year career, he composed more than 1,000 songs sung in eight different languages, sold more than 100 million albums and appeared in more than 80 films, including the lead in François Truffaut's *Shoot the Piano Player*. A master of the *chanson française*, Aznavour sang ballads of wounded souls, including his signature song "La Bohème," an ode to lost artistic inspiration. A world citizen of Armenian heritage, he resided in a number of countries during his lifetime. In 2008, he was given Armenian citizenship and served as that country's ambassador to Switzerland and Representative to UNESCO. He still toured internationally until his death on Oct 1, 2018, in southern France at age 94. He received a state funeral in France.

BEST, GEORGE: BIRTH ANNIVERSARY. May 22, 1946. Mercurial soccer star of the 1960s and '70s. Beginning his professional career at 17, Best played mainly for Manchester United, for which he scored 178 goals in 466 appearances. His playboy lifestyle off field was as famous as his quicksilver brilliance on it. Born at Belfast,

Northern Ireland, Best died at London, England, on Nov 22, 2005. More than 100,000 mourners lined the streets of Belfast for his funeral procession, and at British soccer matches a minute of silence (or applause) was observed in his honor.

CASSATT, MARY: BIRTH ANNIVERSARY. May 22, 1844. Leading American artist of the Impressionist school, Mary Cassatt was born May 22, 1844 (some sources say 1845), at Allegheny City, PA (now part of Pittsburgh). She settled in Paris, France, in 1874, where she was influenced by Degas and the Impressionists. She was later instrumental in their works becoming well known in the US. The majority of her paintings and pastels were based on the theme of mother and child. After 1900 her eyesight began to fail, and by 1914 she was no longer able to paint. Cassatt died at Chateau de Beaufresne near Paris, June 14, 1926.

DOYLE, SIR ARTHUR CONAN: BIRTH ANNIVERSARY. May 22, 1859. British physician Sir Arthur Conan Doyle is best remembered as a mystery author and the creator of Sherlock Holmes and Dr. Watson. Doyle was born at Edinburgh, Scotland. He was deeply interested in and lectured on the subject of spiritualism. Died at Crowborough, Sussex, England, July 7, 1930.

FLORIDA FOLK FESTIVAL. May 22–24. Stephen Foster Folk Culture Center State Park, White Springs, FL. To celebrate Florida's folk heritage with music, song, dance and stories. Est attendance: 20,000. For info: Stephen Foster Folk Culture Center State Park, PO Box G, White Springs, FL 32096. Phone: (877) 6FL-FOLK. E-mail: Elaine.Mcgrath@dep.state.fl.us. Web: www.FloridaFolk-Festival.com.

ISRAEL: JERUSALEM DAY (YOM YERUSHALAYIM). May 22. Hebrew calendar date: Iyar 28, 5780. Commemorates the liberation of the old city, June 7, 1967. Began at sundown May 21.

JOPLIN, MO, TORNADO: ANNIVERSARY. May 22, 2011. Beginning about 5:40 PM in the evening an EF-5 tornado, with wind speeds in excess of 200 miles per hour, struck the southern end of Joplin, MO, a city of about 50,000 residents. The storm resulted in the deaths of 161 people, injured more than 1,100 people and caused an estimated $2.8 billion in damage. The unusually large and slow-moving twister destroyed about a third of the city, including hundreds of homes, a high school and a hospital.

MANCHESTER CONCERT TERRORIST BOMBING: ANNIVERSARY. May 22, 2017. A 22-year-old suicide bomber detonated a home-made explosive as crowds exited an Ariana Grande concert in the UK's Manchester Arena. The Manchester-born terrorist detonated the device in the foyer between the main arena and neighboring Victoria Station, killing 22 concertgoers and waiting parents and physically injuring 119 others. Mancunians came together overnight providing free taxi rides home; hotels and temples offered free shelter. It was the deadliest attack in Britain since the 7/7 London subway bombings in 2005. Grande's remorseful tweet "broken. From the bottom of my heart, I am so so sorry. I don't have words" became the most liked tweet in history at the time.

"MISTER ROGERS' NEIGHBORHOOD" TV PREMIERE: ANNIVERSARY. May 22, 1967. Presbyterian minister Fred Rogers hosted this long-running PBS children's program. Puppets and human characters interacted in the Neighborhood of Make-Believe. Rogers voiced many of the puppets and educated young viewers on a variety of important subjects. The last episodes of the program were made in 2001. Almost 1,000 episodes were produced over the show's history. Rogers died in 2003. See also: "Rogers, Fred: Birth Anniversary" (Mar 20).

MOON PHASE: NEW MOON. May 22. Moon enters New Moon phase at 1:39 PM, EDT.

★NATIONAL MARITIME DAY. May 22. Presidential Proclamation issued for May 22 since 1933. (Pub Res No. 7 of May 20, 1933.)

NATIONAL MARITIME DAY. May 22. Anniversary of departure for first steamship crossing of Atlantic from Savannah, GA, to Liverpool, England, by steamship *Savannah* in 1819.

NATIONAL POLKA FESTIVAL. May 22–24. Ennis, TX. 54th anniversary. A Czech-heritage festival for the entire family in a small-city atmosphere. Kicks off Friday evening with the King and Queen Dance Contest, where everyone is encouraged to wear traditional Czech *kroj* (costumes). Saturday morning features a colorful parade twisting through historic downtown Ennis with polka bands, floats, the Shriners, motorcycles, horseback riders, clowns and more. Other events: Polkafest Run, horseshoe tourney and more. Experience "a little bit of the Czech Lands" and enjoy a weekend of polka dancing, Czech foods and 14 sensational live polka bands. Annually, Memorial Day weekend. For info: Ennis CVB, PO Box 1237, Ennis, TX 75120. Phone: (972) 878-4748. E-mail: ennis4u@swbell.net. Web: www.nationalpolkafestival.com.

NCAA DIVISION I WOMEN'S LACROSSE CHAMPIONSHIP. May 22–24. Johns Hopkins, Baltimore, MD. For info: NCAA, 700 W Washington St, Indianapolis, IN 46206-6222. Phone: (317) 917-6222. Web: www.NCAAsports.com.

NIXON FIRST AMERICAN PRESIDENT TO VISIT MOSCOW: ANNIVERSARY. May 22, 1972. President Richard Nixon became the first American president to visit Moscow. Four days later on May 26, Nixon and Soviet leader Leonid Brezhnev signed a treaty on antiballistic missile systems and an interim agreement on limitation of strategic missiles.

OLIVIER, LAURENCE: BIRTH ANNIVERSARY. May 22, 1907. Actor, director and theater manager, born at Dorking, England. Thought by many to be the most influential actor of the 20th century. Olivier's theatrical and film career shaped the art forms in which he participated. Honored with nine Academy Award nominations, three Oscars and five Emmy Awards, his repertoire included most of the prime Shakespearean roles and roles in such films as *Rebecca, Pride and Prejudice, Marathon Man* and *Wuthering Heights*. Olivier was an innovative theater manager with London's Old Vic company and the National Theatre of Great Britain. The National Theatre's largest auditorium and Britain's equivalent of Broadway's Tony Awards carry his name. He was knighted in 1947 and made a peer of the throne in 1970. Olivier died at Ashurst, England, July 11, 1989.

PORTLAND ROSE FESTIVAL. May 22–June 7. (Weekends and Memorial Day.) Portland, OR. Annual celebration includes more than 50 events and features three parades, dragon boat races, a CityFair with amusement rides and US Navy fleet visits. Est attendance: 2,000,000. For info: Portland Rose Festival Foundation, 1020 SW Naito Pkwy, Portland, OR 97204. Phone: (503) 227-2681. Fax: (503) 227-6603. E-mail: info@rosefestival.org. Web: www.rosefestival.org.

RA, SUN: BIRTH ANNIVERSARY. May 22, 1914. Born Herman (Sonny) Blount, Sun Ra was a pioneering and innovative jazz musician whose avant-garde performances mixed elements of theater with his surreal composition and performance style. He once said, "I wanted to give God something he's never heard before." Ra was born at Birmingham, AL, and died there May 30, 1993.

SPACE MILESTONE: SPACEX *DRAGON* LAUNCHES. May 22, 2012. In the first commercial mission to the International Space Station, this free-flying, reusable spacecraft delivered food, clothing, computer equipment and supplies for science experiments, and returned with trash, scientific research and samples. A Falcon 9 rocket launched the capsule into space from Cape Canaveral, FL, and it splashed down May 31, 2012, in the Pacific Ocean off the coast of Baja California, Mexico. The *Dragon* is owned by SpaceX, a private American transportation company.

SPOLETO FESTIVAL USA. May 22–June 7. Charleston, SC. Comprehensive arts festival with a mix of more than 150 performances of opera, dance, theater, jazz and chamber and symphonic music set in one of America's most beautiful and historic cities. For info: Spoleto Festival USA, 14 George St, Charleston, SC 29401. Phone: (843) 579-3100. Web: www.spoletousa.org.

SRI LANKA: NATIONAL HEROES DAY. May 22. Commemorates the struggle of the leaders of the National Independence Movement to liberate the country from colonial rule in 1971. Public holiday.

STRONGEST EARTHQUAKE OF THE 20th CENTURY: 60th ANNIVERSARY. May 22, 1960. An earthquake of magnitude 9.5 struck southern Chile, killing 2,000 people and leaving 2 million homeless. The earthquake also caused damage in Hawaii, Japan and the Philippines. While 20th-century earthquakes in Mexico City, Japan and Turkey resulted in far more deaths, this earthquake in Chile was of the greatest magnitude.

SUMNER ATTACKED IN THE SENATE: ANNIVERSARY. May 22, 1856. Two days after he decried the "Crime Against Kansas," US senator Charles Sumner of Massachusetts was attacked with a walking cane by South Carolina congressman Preston Brooks in the Senate Chamber (the Senate was not in session). Abolitionist Sumner needed three years to recuperate.

TRUMAN DOCTRINE: ANNIVERSARY. May 22, 1947. Congress approved the Truman Doctrine on this day. In order to contain communism after WWII, it provided for US aid to Greece and Turkey. A corollary of this doctrine was the Marshall Plan, which began sending aid to war-torn European countries in 1948.

UNITED NATIONS: INTERNATIONAL DAY FOR BIOLOGICAL DIVERSITY. May 22. This day is an opportunity to strengthen people's commitment and actions for the conservation of the world's biological diversity. (The General Assembly proclaimed this observance originally for Dec 29, the date of entry into force of the Convention on Biological Diversity [Res 49/119 of Dec 19, 1994]. But in 2000 the date was changed to May 22.) For info: United Nations, Dept of Public Info, New York, NY 10017. Web: www.un.org.

US COLORED TROOPS FOUNDERS DAY. May 22. African American Civil War Memorial Freedom Foundation and Museum, Washington, DC. On May 22, 1863, Congress established the Bureau of United States Colored Troops with the express purpose of providing uniforms and training to and deploying soldiers of African descent. By the end of the Civil War the United States Colored Troops (USCT) had more than 200,000 soldiers of African descent, but also employed Native Americans, Hawaiians, Latinos and Anglos. While most of the USCT officers were white, there were more than 120 African-American officers—and some of Latino descent. Each year the African American Civil War Memorial Freedom Foundation and Museum commemorates the founding of the Bureau of United States Colored Troops with public and educational programming. Annually, May 22. For info: African American Civil War Memorial Freedom Foundation and Museum, 1925 Vermont Ave NW, Washington, DC 20001. Phone: (202) 667-2667. Web: www.afroamcivilwar.org.

WAGNER, RICHARD: BIRTH ANNIVERSARY. May 22, 1813. German composer born at Leipzig who made revolutionary changes in the structure of opera. Best known for his Ring Cycle (*Der Ring des Nibelungen*). Died at Italy, Feb 13, 1883.

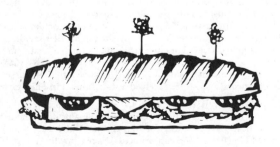

May		S	M	T	W	T	F	S
							1	2
		3	4	5	6	7	8	9
		10	11	12	13	14	15	16
2020		17	18	19	20	21	22	23
		24	25	26	27	28	29	30
		31						

WORLD GOTH DAY. May 22. A day when the goth scene gets to celebrate its own being and to make its presence known to the rest of the world. First observed in the UK in 2009. Annually, May 22. For info: World Goth Day. Web: www.worldgothday.com.

YEMEN: NATIONAL DAY. May 22. Public holiday. Commemorates the reunification of Yemen in 1990.

🎂 BIRTHDAYS TODAY

Richard Benjamin, 82, director, actor (*Goodbye Columbus, Diary of a Mad Housewife*, "He & She"), born New York, NY, May 22, 1938.

Naomi Campbell, 50, model, actress ("Empire"), born London, England, May 22, 1970.

Frank Converse, 82, actor ("Movin' On," *Hurry Sundown*), born St. Louis, MO, May 22, 1938.

Novak Djokovic, 33, tennis player, born Belgrade, Yugoslavia (now Serbia), May 22, 1987.

Ginnifer Goodwin, 42, actress ("Big Love," "Once Upon a Time"), born Memphis, TN, May 22, 1978.

Thomas Edward (Tommy) John, 77, former baseball player, born Terre Haute, IN, May 22, 1943.

A.J. Langer, 46, actress ("My So-Called Life," "Brooklyn South"), born Columbus, OH, May 22, 1974.

Lisa Murkowski, 63, US Senator (R, Alaska), born Ketchikan, AK, May 22, 1957.

Peter Nero, 86, conductor, composer, pianist, born Brooklyn, NY, May 22, 1934.

Mick Tingelhoff, 80, Hall of Fame football player, born Lexington, NE, May 22, 1940.

Tatiana Volosozhar, 34, Olympic figure skater, born Dnipropetrovsk, USSR (now Ukraine), May 22, 1986.

Garry Wills, 86, author (*John Wayne's America, Lincoln at Gettysburg*), born Atlanta, GA, May 22, 1934.

May 23 — Saturday

DAY 144   **222 REMAINING**

ALMA HIGHLAND FESTIVAL AND GAMES. May 23–24. Alma College, Alma, MI. 53rd annual. Old-world pageantry honoring Scottish traditions—Highland dancing, piping, drumming, athletic competitions, clan tents and grand parade. Annually, Memorial Day weekend. Est attendance: 12,000. For info: Alma Highland Festival, 110 W Superior St, PO Box 516, Alma, MI 48801. Phone: (989) 463-8979. Fax: (989) 463-6588. E-mail: highland@almahighlandfestival.com. Web: www.almahighlandfestival.com.

BONNIE AND CLYDE: DEATH ANNIVERSARY. May 23, 1934. The two-year crime spree of Bonnie Parker and Clyde Barrow, bank robbers accused of at least 12 murders, came to an end when a law enforcement posse led by Frank Hamer opened fire on the couple in an ambush at Gibsland, LA. The couple had operated in Texas, Oklahoma, Missouri, Louisiana and other states, and had sent ballads to local newspapers chronicling their exploits, making them two of the most notorious—and romanticized—of many Depression-era gangsters. Some 20,000 people lined up to see the body of Clyde Barrow put on display in a mortuary in downtown Dallas, TX.

CLOONEY, ROSEMARY: BIRTH ANNIVERSARY. May 23, 1928. The beloved pop and jazz singer was born at Maysville, KY. She became popular in the 1950s for singing the novelty song "Come-on-a-My House" and pop standards. She also starred in the holiday film *White Christmas* (1954). She died June 29, 2002, at Beverly Hills, CA.

DECLARATION OF THE BAB. May 23. Baha'i commemoration of May 23, 1844, when the Bab, the prophet-herald of the Baha'i Faith, announced in Shiraz, Persia, that he was the herald of a new messenger of God. One of the nine days of the year when Baha'is suspend work. For info: Baha'is of the US, Office of Communications, 1233 Central St, Evanston, IL 60201. Phone: (847) 733-3584. E-mail: ooc@usbnc.org. Web: www.bahai.us.

ENGLAND: THE EMIRATES FA CUP. May 23. Wembley Stadium, London, England. Established in 1871, the oldest cup competition in the world. Teams in the leagues of England's Football Association compete in single-elimination games leading up to this cup final. For info: Football Association. Web: www.thefa.com/competitions/thefacup.

FAIRBANKS, DOUGLAS ELTON: BIRTH ANNIVERSARY. May 23, 1883. Douglas Fairbanks was born at Denver, CO. He made his professional debut as an actor at Richmond, VA, Sept 10, 1900, in *The Duke's Jester*. His theatrical career turned to Hollywood, and he became a movie idol, appearing in such films as *The Mark of Zorro, The Three Musketeers, Robin Hood, The Thief of Bagdad, The Black Pirate* and *The Gaucho*. He married "America's Sweetheart," Mary Pickford, in 1918, and in 1919 they joined with D.W. Griffith and Charlie Chaplin to form the production company United Artists. He died at Santa Monica, CA, Dec 12, 1939.

FIRST BLACK RECEIVES CONGRESSIONAL MEDAL OF HONOR: ANNIVERSARY. May 23, 1900. Sergeant William H. Carney, of the 54th Massachusetts Colored Infantry, was the first black person to win the Congressional Medal of Honor. He was cited for his efforts, although wounded twice, during the Battle of Fort Wagner, SC, June 18, 1863.

FULLER, MARGARET: BIRTH ANNIVERSARY. May 23, 1810. Journalist and author Sarah Margaret Fuller, born at Cambridgeport, MA, began reading Virgil at age six. Her conversational powers won her the admiration of students at Harvard University, and she was befriended by Ralph Waldo Emerson. She shared editorial duties with Emerson on the transcendentalist quarterly *The Dial* and was hired by Horace Greeley as literary critic for the *New York Tribune*. Her book *Women in the Nineteenth Century*, the first feminist statement by an American writer, brought her international acclaim. In 1846, as a foreign correspondent for the *Tribune*, she became caught up in the Italian revolutionary movement and secretly married a young Roman nobleman, the Marquis Giovanni Angelo Ossoli. En route to the US, Fuller and her husband and child died July 19, 1850, when their ship was wrecked off Fire Island near New York, NY.

INTERNATIONAL WORLD TURTLE DAY®. May 23. An observance sponsored by American Tortoise Rescue to help people celebrate and protect turtles and tortoises, as well as their habitats around the world. For info: Susan Tellem, American Tortoise Rescue, 30745 Pacific Coast Hwy #243, Malibu, CA 90265. E-mail: info@tortoise.com. Web: www.worldturtleday.org.

ITALY: BIENNALE ARCHITETTURA 2020 (VENICE BIENNALE OF ARCHITECTURE). May 23–Nov 29. Venice. 17th edition. Held on even-numbered years since 1980, when the first edition was held as a spin-off of the acclaimed Venice Biennale. Each session has

its own curators and theme, accompanied by exhibits, educational programs, seminars, collateral events and more. The goals include to "interrogate" the profession and promote a "desire" for architecture. For info: La Biennale di Venezia, Architecture Press Office. E-mail: infoarchitettura@labiennale.org. Web: www.labiennale.org.

LORENZ, EDWARD NORTON: BIRTH ANNIVERSARY. May 23, 1917. Award-winning and influential mathematician, meteorologist and father of chaos theory who formulated the idea of the "butterfly effect"—that a small, seemingly insignificant act or disturbance can actually have huge consequences. His famous 1972 talk, "Predictability: Does the Flap of a Butterfly's Wings in Brazil Set Off a Tornado in Texas?" helped popularize the notion. Born at West Hartford, CT, Lorenz died Apr 16, 2008, at Cambridge, MA.

MANSFIELD, ARABELLA: BIRTH ANNIVERSARY. May 23, 1846. Arabella Mansfield, born Belle Aurelia Babb near Burlington, IA, was the first woman admitted to the legal profession in the US. In 1869 while teaching at Iowa Wesleyan College, Mansfield was certified as an attorney and admitted to the Iowa bar. According to the examiners, "she gave the very best rebuke possible to the imputation that ladies cannot qualify for the practice of law." Mansfield never did practice law, however, continuing her career as an educator. She joined the faculty of DePauw University, at Greencastle, IN, where she became dean of the schools of art and music. One of the first woman college professors and administrators in the US, Mansfield was also instrumental in the founding of the Iowa Woman Suffrage Society in 1870. She died Aug 2, 1911, at Aurora, IL.

MESMER, FRANZ ANTON: BIRTH ANNIVERSARY. May 23, 1734. German physician after whom mesmerism was named. Magnetism and hypnotism were used by him in treating disease. Born at Iznang, Swabia, Germany. Died Mar 5, 1815, at Meersburg, Swabia.

MOROCCO: NATIONAL DAY. May 23. National holiday. Commemorates referendum on the majority of the king in 1980.

NATIONAL BEST FRIEND-IN-LAW DAY. May 23. This day celebrates those who come into our intimate friendship circles by marriage—the best friends of our spouses. Annually, May 23. For info: Kristen Healy and Mike Mochan. E-mail: khealyslp@gmail.com.

NCAA DIVISION I MEN'S LACROSSE CHAMPIONSHIP. May 23–25. Lincoln Financial Field, Philadelphia, PA. For info: NCAA, PO Box 6222, Indianapolis, IN 46206-6222. Web: www.NCAA.com.

NEW YORK PUBLIC LIBRARY: 125th ANNIVERSARY. May 23, 1895. New York's then governor Samuel J. Tilden was the driving force that resulted in the combining of the private Astor and Lenox libraries with a $2 million endowment and 15,000 volumes from the Tilden Trust to become the New York Public Library. The main branch of the library opened to the public on this day in 1911.

SOUTH CAROLINA CONSTITUTION RATIFICATION: ANNIVERSARY. May 23, 1788. By a vote of 149 to 73, South Carolina became the eighth state to ratify the Constitution.

SWEDEN: LINNAEUS DAY. May 23, 1707. Stenbrohult. Commemorates birth of Carolus Linnaeus (Carl von Linné), Swedish naturalist, born May 23, 1707 (OS), and died at Uppsala, Sweden, Jan 10, 1778.

TAPPAN, LEWIS: BIRTH ANNIVERSARY. May 23, 1788. Abolitionist and merchant born at Northampton, MA. Best known for his vigorous participation in the US antislavery movement. Helped found the American Anti-Slavery Society (1833) and led the efforts to aid the Mendi people who revolted against their captors on the slave ship *Amistad*. Tappan also created the first credit-rating service in the US in 1841. The Mercantile Service's success enabled Tappan to retire a wealthy man and to focus on abolition and philanthropy. (In 1858, the Mercantile Service was bought by Graham Dun and evolved into Dun & Bradstreet.) Tappan died June 21, 1873, at Brooklyn, NY.

UNITED NATIONS: INTERNATIONAL DAY TO END OBSTETRIC FISTULA. May 23. Obstetric fistula is a preventable and treatable childbearing injury—the result of prolonged, obstructed labor. It leaves women incontinent, ashamed and often isolated from their communities. A debilitating condition, obstetric fistula is perhaps one of the most telling examples of inequitable access to maternal health care and, until recently, one of the most hidden. Generally accepted estimates suggest that 2–3.5 million women live with obstetric fistula in the developing world, and between 50,000 and 100,000 new cases develop each year. (Res 67/147.) For info: United Nations, Dept of Public Info, New York, NY 10017. Web: www.un.org.

US AMATEUR FOUR-BALL (GOLF) CHAMPIONSHIP. May 23–27. Philadelphia Cricket Club, Philadelphia, PA. For info: USGA, Golf House, Championship Dept, PO Box 708, Far Hills, NJ 07931. Phone: (908) 234-2300. E-mail: champs@usga.org. Web: www.usga.org.

🎂 BIRTHDAYS TODAY

Mitch Albom, 62, journalist, author (*Tuesdays with Morrie, The Five People You Meet in Heaven*), born Passaic, NJ, May 23, 1958.

William Barr, 70, US Attorney General (Trump administration and previously George H.W. Bush administration), born New York, NY, May 23, 1950.

Barbara Barrie, 89, actress ("Suddenly Susan"; *One Potato, Two Potato; Breaking Away*), born Chicago, IL, May 23, 1931.

H. Jon Benjamin, 54, actor ("Bob's Burgers," "Archer," "Family Guy"), born Worcester, MA, May 23, 1966.

Brian Campbell, 41, hockey player, born Strathroy, ON, Canada, May 23, 1979.

Drew Carey, 59, actor ("The Drew Carey Show"), host ("The Price Is Right"), born Cleveland, OH, May 23, 1961 (some sources say 1958).

Joan Collins, 87, actress ("Dynasty"), born London, England, May 23, 1933.

David Graham, 74, Hall of Fame golfer, born Windsor, Australia, May 23, 1946.

"Marvelous" Marvin Hagler, 66, former boxer, born Newark, NJ, May 23, 1954.

Jewel, 46, singer, born Jewel Kilcher at Payson, UT, May 23, 1974.

Charles Kimbrough, 84, actor ("Murphy Brown"), born St. Paul, MN, May 23, 1936.

Robert A.M. Stern, 81, architect, professor, author, born Brooklyn, NY, May 23, 1939.

	S	M	T	W	T	F	S
May						1	2
	3	4	5	6	7	8	9
2020	10	11	12	13	14	15	16
	17	18	19	20	21	22	23
	24	25	26	27	28	29	30
	31						

May 24 — Sunday

DAY 145   **221 REMAINING**

ANDERSONVILLE MEMORIAL DAY CEREMONIES. May 24. Andersonville, GA. The Andersonville National Historic Site hosts a series of activities to commemorate Memorial Day and to pay tribute to our country's men and women who paid for our freedom with their lives. Annually, the Sunday of Memorial Day weekend. For info: Park Ranger, Andersonville National Historic Site. Phone: (229) 924-0343. Web: www.nps.gov/ande.

BELIZE: COMMONWEALTH DAY. May 24. Public holiday.

BROOKLYN BRIDGE OPENED: ANNIVERSARY. May 24, 1883. Nearly 14 years in construction, the $16 million Brooklyn Bridge over the East River opened. Designed by John A. Roebling, the steel suspension bridge has a span of 1,595 feet.

BROTHER'S DAY. May 24. Celebration of brotherhood for biological brothers, fraternity brothers and brothers bonded by union affiliation or lifetime experiences. Annually, May 24. (©2001 C. Daniel Rhodes.) For info: C. Daniel Rhodes, 1900 Crossvine Rd, Hoover, AL 35244. Phone: (205) 908-6781. E-mail: rhodan@charter.net.

BULGARIA: CULTURE DAY. May 24. National holiday festively celebrated by schoolchildren, students and people of science and art.

CAPE MAY MUSIC FESTIVAL. May 24–June 12. Cape May, NJ. 31st annual. Enjoy world-class orchestral and chamber music performances. Also features brass band, jazz music and more. Est attendance: 5,000. For info: Mid-Atlantic Center for the Arts and Humanities, 1048 Washington St, Cape May, NJ 08204. Phone: (800) 275-4278 or (609) 884-5404. Fax: (609) 884-0574. E-mail: info@capemaymac.org. Web: www.capemaymac.org.

ECUADOR: BATTLE OF PICHINCHA. May 24. National holiday. Commemorates battle in 1822 that marked the final defeat of Spain in Ecuador.

EID-AL-FITR: CELEBRATING THE FAST. May 24. Islamic calendar date: Shawwal 1, 1441. This feast/festival celebrates the completion of the Ramadan fasting and usually lasts for several days. Everyone wears new clothes; children receive gifts from parents and relatives; children are allowed to stay up late and participate in games, folktales, plays, puppet shows and trips to amusement parks. This holiday is known as Seker Bayram in Turkey and Hari Raya Puasa in Southeast Asia. Different methods for "anticipating" the visibility of the new moon crescent at Mecca are used by different Muslim groups, so date can vary one to two days. Began at sunset the preceding day.

ERITREA: INDEPENDENCE DAY. May 24. National Day. Gained independence from Ethiopia in 1993 after 30-year civil war.

INDIANAPOLIS 500-MILE RACE. May 24. Indianapolis, IN. 104th running. Recognized as the world's largest single-day sporting event. First race was in 1911. Annually, the Sunday of Memorial Day weekend. For info: Indianapolis Motor Speedway. Web: www.indy500.com.

INTERNATIONAL TIARA DAY. May 24. A day when all women embrace and celebrate their powers of leadership. Real or virtual tiara-wearing is encouraged. Annually, May 24—Queen Victoria's birthday. For info: International Tiara Day. Web: www.internationaltiaraday.com.

ITALY: WEDDING OF THE SEA. May 24. Venice. The feast of the Ascension is the occasion of the ceremony recalling the "Wedding of the Sea," performed by Venice's doge, who cast his ring into the sea from the ceremonial ship known as the *Bucintoro* to symbolize eternal dominion. Annually, on the Sunday following Ascension.

MORSE OPENS FIRST US TELEGRAPH LINE: ANNIVERSARY. May 24, 1844. The first US telegraph line was formally opened between Baltimore, MD, and Washington, DC. Samuel F.B. Morse sent the first officially telegraphed words—"What hath God wrought?"—from the Capitol building to Baltimore. Earlier messages had been sent along the historic line during testing, and one, sent May 1 from a meeting in Baltimore, contained the news that Henry Clay had been nominated as president by the Whig Party. This message reached Washington one hour prior to a train carrying the same news.

NATIONAL AFRICAN VIOLET WEEK. May 24–30. Little Rock Marriott, Little Rock, AR. The African Violet Society of America (AVSA) is hosting its 74th Annual Convention. The highlight of the convention is the AVSA-judged show, where growers from around the nation showcase their best African violets and compete for top awards. This is an opportunity to see unique varieties, mingle with growers and hybridizers and share a passion for these beloved houseplants. Registered attendees can learn more about growing and showing African violets from the speakers, presentations and tours. For info: African Violet Society of America, 1310 IH-10 S, Ste 100, Beaumont, TX 77707. Phone: (844) 400-AVSA. Web: www.avsa.org.

NEWHOUSE, SAMUEL I.: 125th BIRTH ANNIVERSARY. May 24, 1895. Multimillionaire businessman who built a family publishing and communications empire. Born to immigrant parents in a New York City tenement, Newhouse became "America's most profitable publisher." He accumulated 31 newspapers, seven magazines, six television stations, five radio stations and 20 cable television systems. He died at New York, NY, Aug 29, 1979.

QUEEN VICTORIA: BIRTH ANNIVERSARY. May 24, 1819. Born at Kensington Palace, London, England, Queen Victoria of Great Britain and Ireland, Empress of India, was one of the British Empire's most influential monarchs. Victoria's ascension to the throne on June 20, 1837, marked a period of scientific, industrial, political, cultural and military change so significant that it is called the Victorian Age. The last ruler of the house of Hanover, she died Jan 22, 1901, at Osborne House, Isle of Wight.

SPACE MILESTONE: *AURORA 7* MERCURY SPACE CAPSULE (US). May 24, 1962. With this launch Scott Carpenter became the second American to orbit Earth, circling it three times.

🎂 BIRTHDAYS TODAY

Jim Broadbent, 71, actor (*Moulin Rouge, Topsy-Turvy*, Oscar for *Iris*), born Lincoln, Lincolnshire, England, May 24, 1949.

Gary Burghoff, 77, actor (Emmy for "M*A*S*H"), born Bristol, CT, May 24, 1943.

Michael Chabon, 57, author (*Wonder Boys, The Adventures of Kavalier & Clay*; Hugo Award for *The Yiddish Policemen's Union*), born Washington, DC, May 24, 1963.

Tommy Chong, 82, actor (*Up in Smoke, The Corsican Brothers*), born Edmonton, AB, Canada, May 24, 1938.

Eric Close, 53, actor ("Nashville," "Without a Trace"), born Staten Island, NY, May 24, 1967.

Bob Dylan, 79, Rock and Roll and Songwriters halls of fame composer, singer, 2016 Nobel Prize in Literature recipient, born Robert Zimmerman at Duluth, MN, May 24, 1941.

Alyson Hannigan, 46, actress ("How I Met Your Mother," "Buffy the Vampire Slayer," *American Pie*), born Washington, DC, May 24, 1974.

Patti LaBelle, 76, singer, born Patricia Louise Holte at Philadelphia, PA, May 24, 1944.

Tracy McGrady, 41, basketball player, born Bartow, FL, May 24, 1979.

Alfred Molina, 67, actor (*An Education, Frida, Chocolat*), born London, England, May 24, 1953.

Frank Oz, 76, director, puppeteer, born Hereford, England, May 24, 1944.

Priscilla Beaulieu Presley, 75, actress ("Dallas," *Naked Gun* films), born Brooklyn, NY, May 24, 1945.

Kristin Scott Thomas, 60, actress (*Darkest Hour, Gosford Park, The English Patient, The Horse Whisperer*), born Cornwall, England, May 24, 1960.

May 25 — Monday

DAY 146   **220 REMAINING**

AFRICAN FREEDOM DAY. May 25. Public holiday in Chad, Zambia and some other African nations. Members of the Organization for African Unity (formed May 25, 1963) commemorate their independence from colonial rule. Sports contests, political rallies and tribal dances.

AMERICAN FLIGHT CRASHES AT O'HARE: ANNIVERSARY. May 25, 1979. An American Airlines DC-10 lost an engine upon takeoff and crashed seconds later, killing all 272 aboard and three people on the ground.

ARGENTINA: REVOLUTION DAY. May 25. National holiday. Commemoration of revolt against Spanish rule in 1810.

CARVER, RAYMOND: BIRTH ANNIVERSARY. May 25, 1938. American poet and short story writer who chronicled the lives of America's working poor. Born at Clatskanie, OR, he died Aug 2, 1988, at his home at Port Angeles, WA, soon after finishing a book of poetry titled *A New Path to the Waterfall.*

CONSTITUTIONAL CONVENTION: ANNIVERSARY. May 25, 1787. At Philadelphia, PA, delegates from seven states, forming a quorum, opened the Constitutional Convention, which had been proposed by the Annapolis Convention held Sept 11–14, 1786. Among those who were in attendance: George Washington, Benjamin Franklin, James Madison, Alexander Hamilton and Elbridge Gerry. See also: "1786 Annapolis Convention: Anniversary" (Sept 11).

DAVID, HAL: BIRTH ANNIVERSARY. May 25, 1921. Together with composer Burt Bacharach, lyricist Hal David produced a sophisticated string of songs that have become not only standards but also pop music legends. Romance, sensuality and a profound intimacy were hallmarks of David's lyrical style, on display in such classics as "Walk on By," "What the World Needs Now Is Love" and the Carpenters' "Close to You." The pair won a 1970 Best Song Oscar for "Raindrops Keep Falling on My Head." In the 1970s David and Bacharach's partnership dissolved into acrimony, but by then their pop music legacy was set in stone. Born at New York, NY, David died Sept 1, 2012, at Los Angeles, CA.

DAVIS, MILES: BIRTH ANNIVERSARY. May 25, 1926. Jazz trumpeter Miles Davis was born at Alton, IL. He was influenced by the bebop music style of Charlie Parker and Dizzy Gillespie and ended up leaving the Juilliard School of Music to join Parker's quintet in 1945. He experimented with different styles throughout his career,

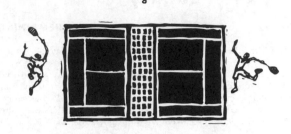

exploring new voicings in jazz with arranger Gil Evans and musicians John Coltrane and Red Garland, delving into modal music with Tony Williams and Wayne Shorter and moving into a fusion sound in the '60s. His career was beset with bouts of drug addiction, but in the 1970s his return to the music scene found him creating a sound that melded his bebop origins, modal chord progressions and driving rock rhythms. He died Sept 28, 1991, at Santa Monica, CA.

EMERSON, RALPH WALDO: BIRTH ANNIVERSARY. May 25, 1803. American author and philosopher born at Boston, MA, and died there Apr 27, 1882. It was Emerson who wrote (in his essay "Self-Reliance," 1841), "A foolish consistency is the hobgoblin of little minds, adored by little statesmen and philosophers and divines. With consistency a great soul has simply nothing to do."

ENGLAND: GLOUCESTERSHIRE CHEESE ROLLING. May 25. Cooper's Hill, near Gloucester, Stroud and Cheltenham in the Cotswolds. Ancient tradition dating to pre-Roman times. Held continuously for the last 200 years, an event in which contestants race down a steep, 300-yard hill after a seven- to nine-pound wheel of double Gloucester cheese. The races (four in total, with 10–15 participants) begin at noon, with a top-hatted master of ceremonies beginning the countdown: "One to be ready, two to be steady, three to prepare and four to be off!" Spectators lining the hill chant, "Roll that cheese!" The unusual festival is marked by many injuries of racers and spectators. The winner gets the cheese. Annually, the last Monday in May—the second May bank holiday. Est attendance: 4,000.

GREATEST DAY IN TRACK AND FIELD: JESSE OWENS'S REMARKABLE RECORDS: 85th ANNIVERSARY. May 25, 1935. During the Big Ten Championships at the University of Michigan at Ann Arbor, Jesse Owens, representing Ohio State University, broke three world records and tied a fourth in the space of 45 minutes—from 3:15 PM to 4:00 PM. The "Buckeye Bullet" (who was suffering from an injured back) set records in the running broad jump, the 220-yard dash and the 220-yard hurdles and tied the record for the 100-yard dash. See also: "Owens, Jesse: Birth Anniversary" (Sept 12).

JORDAN: INDEPENDENCE DAY. May 25. National holiday. Commemorates treaty in 1946, proclaiming independence from Britain and establishing a monarchy.

MEMORIAL DAY. May 25. Legal public holiday. (PL 90–363 sets Memorial Day on the last Monday in May. Applicable to federal employees and District of Columbia.) Also known as Decoration Day because of the tradition of decorating the graves of service people. An occasion for honoring those who have died in battle. (Observance dates from Civil War years in US: first documented observance at Waterloo, NY, May 5, 1866.)

MEMORIAL DAY PARADE AND CEREMONIES. May 25. Gettysburg, PA. The parade starts at 2 PM at Lefever St and concludes at the Soldiers' National Cemetery. The ceremony begins at 3 PM at the rostrum in the Soldiers' National Cemetery. Est attendance: 20,000. For info: Destination Gettysburg. E-mail: info@destinationgettysburg.com. Web: www.destinationgettysburg.com.

MURRAY, PHILIP: BIRTH ANNIVERSARY. May 25, 1886. The American labor leader and founder of the Congress of Industrial Organizations, also active in and a leader of the United Mine Workers,

May 2020	S	M	T	W	T	F	S
						1	2
	3	4	5	6	7	8	9
	10	11	12	13	14	15	16
	17	18	19	20	21	22	23
	24	25	26	27	28	29	30
	31						

was born near Blantyre, Scotland. Murray died at San Francisco, CA, Nov 9, 1952.

NATIONAL BACKYARD GAMES WEEK. May 25–June 1. Observance to celebrate the unofficial start of summer by fostering social interaction and family togetherness through backyard games. Get outside and be both physically and mentally stimulated, playing classic games of the past while discovering and creating new ways to be active and interact with friends and neighbors. For info: Beth Muehlenkamp, Playmonster, 1400 E Inman Pkwy, Beloit, WI 53511. Phone: (608) 362-6896. Fax: (608) 362-8178. E-mail: bethm@playmonster.com. Web: www.playmonster.com.

NATIONAL MISSING CHILDREN'S DAY. May 25. To promote awareness of the problem of missing children, to offer a forum for change and to offer safety information for children in school and the community. Annually, May 25. For info: Child Find of America, Inc, PO Box 277, New Paltz, NY 12561-0277. Phone: (845) 883-6060 or (800) I-AM-LOST. E-mail: information@childfindofamerica.org. Web: www.childfindofamerica.org.

NATIONAL TAP DANCE DAY. May 25. To celebrate this unique American art form that represents a fusion of African and European cultures and to transmit tap to succeeding generations through documentation and archival and performance support. Held on the anniversary of the birth of Bill "Bojangles" Robinson to honor his outstanding contribution to the art of tap dancing on stage and in films through the unification of diverse stylistic and racial elements.

POETRY DAY IN FLORIDA. May 25. In 1947 the legislature decreed this day to be "Poetry Day in all of the public schools of Florida."

★PRAYER FOR PEACE, MEMORIAL DAY. May 25. Presidential Proclamation issued each year since 1948. PL 81–512 of May 11, 1950, asks the president to proclaim annually this day as a day of prayer for permanent peace. PL 90–363 of June 28, 1968, requires that beginning in 1971 it will be observed the last Monday in May. Often titled "Prayer for Peace Memorial Day," and traditionally requests the flying of the flag at half-staff "for the customary forenoon period."

ROBINSON, BILL "BOJANGLES": BIRTH ANNIVERSARY. May 25, 1878. Born at Richmond, VA, the grandson of a slave, Robinson is considered one of the greatest tap dancers—and was one of the most successful African-American entertainers of the first half of the 20th century. He is best known for a routine in which he tap-danced up and down a staircase. He appeared in several films with Shirley Temple and starred in *Stormy Weather* (1943). Robinson died at New York, NY, Nov 25, 1949.

SCRIPPS NATIONAL SPELLING BEE FINALS. May 25–28. Gaylord National Resort and Convention Center, National Harbor, MD. Newspapers and other sponsors across the country send 500 youngsters to the national finals near Washington, DC. RSVBee, an invitational program, brings an additional 250 spellers to compete with regional winners. Bee Week is May 24–29; competition is May 25–28. Annually, Tuesday through Thursday of Memorial Day week. Est attendance: 2,000. For info: Scripps Natl Spelling Bee. Web: www.spellingbee.com.

SIKORSKY, IGOR: BIRTH ANNIVERSARY. May 25, 1889. Aeronautical engineer best remembered for his development of the first successful helicopter in 1939. The first to design and fly a multiengine airplane in 1913, Sikorsky also produced multiengine airplanes and large flying boats, called "clippers," that made transoceanic air transportation possible. Born at Kiev, Russia (now Ukraine), he died Oct 26, 1972, at Easton, CT.

SILLS, BEVERLY: BIRTH ANNIVERSARY. May 25, 1929. The acclaimed coloratura soprano was born Belle Silverman at Brooklyn, NY. Signature roles were the title roles in *Lucia di Lammermoor* and *Anna Bolena*, as well as Queen Elizabeth I in *Roberto Devereux*. She was a dedicated ambassador of opera in America and was instrumental in making it accessible both as a singer and later as a television personality and opera executive. She died July 2, 2007, at New York, NY.

SPACE MILESTONE: *SKYLAB 2* (US) LAUNCHED. May 25, 1973. Joseph P. Kerwin, Paul J. Weitz and Charles (Pete) Conrad, Jr, were aboard *Skylab 2*—the first manned mission to the orbiting space laboratory. During 28 days, the three made repairs on this space station, which had been launched May 14, 1973, sustaining some damage, which included space walks. Pacific splashdown occurred June 22.

***STAR WARS* RELEASED: ANNIVERSARY.** May 25, 1977. "May the Force be with you" entered the modern lexicon as a new kind of science fiction film opened at 32 theaters. George Lucas's space epic, starring Mark Hamill as Luke Skywalker, Harrison Ford as Han Solo and Carrie Fisher as Princess Leia, featured stunning special effects and was a smash hit worldwide. It went on to win six Academy Awards out of 10 nominations—plus an additional special Academy Award for sound effects. The film was part of a larger saga and in later years was retitled *Star Wars—Episode IV: A New Hope* as prequels were released.

STOCK EXCHANGE HOLIDAY (MEMORIAL DAY). May 25. The holiday schedules for the various exchanges are subject to change if relevant rules, regulations or exchange policies are revised. For info: CME Group (CME, CBOT, NYMEX, COMEX) (www.cmegroup.com), Chicago Board Options Exchange (www.cboe.com), NASDAQ (www.nasdaq.com), NYSE (www.nyse.com).

TITO (JOSIP BROZ): BIRTH ANNIVERSARY. May 25, 1892. Josip Broz, Yugoslavian soldier and political leader, born near Zagreb, Yugoslavia. Died May 4, 1980, at Ljubljana, Yugoslavia (now Slovenia), and was interred in the garden of his home at Belgrade. Tito, a Croat, had managed to keep the many nationalities and religions that made up Yugoslavia in one state, but in the early 1990s the nation broke up as Croats, Serbs and others went to war against each other.

TOWEL DAY. May 25. In honor of Douglas Adams, author of *The Hitchhiker's Guide to the Galaxy*, carry a towel on this day and make sure that it is conspicuous. Wrap it around your head, use it as a weapon or sleep on it beneath the stars. For info: Towel Day. E-mail: info@towelday.org. Web: www.towelday.org.

TUNNEY, JAMES JOSEPH (GENE): BIRTH ANNIVERSARY. May 25, 1898. Heavyweight boxing champion, business executive. The famous "long count" occurred in the seventh round of the Jack Dempsey–Gene Tunney world championship fight, Sept 22, 1927, at Soldier Field, Chicago, IL. Tunney was born at New York, NY, and died Nov 7, 1978, at Greenwich, CT.

UNITED KINGDOM: SPRING BANK HOLIDAY. May 25. Bank and public holiday in England, Wales, Scotland and Northern Ireland. Observed on the last Monday in May.

UNITED NATIONS: WEEK OF SOLIDARITY WITH THE PEOPLES OF NON-SELF-GOVERNING TERRITORIES. May 25–31. On Dec 6, 1999 (Res 54/91), the General Assembly requested the Special Committee on Decolonization to observe this week beginning on May 25, Africa Liberation Day. For info: United Nations, Dept of Public Info, New York, NY 10017. Web: www.un.org.

🎂 BIRTHDAYS TODAY

Jessi Colter, 73, singer, songwriter, born Miriam Johnson at Phoenix, AZ, May 25, 1947.

Tom T. Hall, 84, Country Music Hall of Fame singer, songwriter, born Olive Hill, KY, May 25, 1936.

Anne Heche, 51, actress ("Men in Trees," *Wag the Dog, Volcano*), born Aurora, OH, May 25, 1969.

Justin Henry, 49, actor (*Kramer vs Kramer, Sixteen Candles*), born Rye, NY, May 25, 1971.

Lauryn Hill, 45, singer, actress (*Sister Act 2*), born South Orange, NJ, May 25, 1975.

Larry Hogan, 64, Governor of Maryland (R), born Washington, DC, May 25, 1956.

K.C. Jones, 88, Hall of Fame basketball player, former coach, born Tyler, TX, May 25, 1932.

Jamie Kennedy, 50, actor ("JKX: The Jamie Kennedy Experiment," *Malibu's Most Wanted*), born Upper Darby, PA, May 25, 1970.

Amy Klobuchar, 60, US Senator (D, Minnesota), born Plymouth, MN, May 25, 1960.

Sir Ian McKellen, 81, actor (Tony for *Amadeus*; Lord of the Rings films, The Hobbit, X-Men films), born Burnley, England, May 25, 1939.

Cillian Murphy, 44, actor ("Peaky Blinders," *Dunkirk, The Dark Knight Rises, 28 Days Later*), born Douglas, Ireland, May 25, 1976.

Mike Myers, 57, comedian, actor ("Saturday Night Live," *Wayne's World, Austin Powers: International Man of Mystery* and sequels), born Scarborough, ON, Canada, May 25, 1963.

Aly Raisman, 26, Olympic gymnast, born Needham, MA, May 25, 1994.

Connie Sellecca, 65, actress ("Hotel," *While My Pretty One Sleeps*), born the Bronx, NY, May 25, 1955.

Ethan Suplee, 44, actor ("My Name Is Earl," "Boy Meets World," *Art School Confidential*), born New York, NY, May 25, 1976.

Leslie Uggams, 77, actress (Tony for *Hallelujah, Baby!*; "Sing Along with Mitch," *Roots*), singer, born New York, NY, May 25, 1943.

Brian Urlacher, 42, former football player, born Lovington, NM, May 25, 1978.

Karen Valentine, 73, actress ("Room 222"), born Sebastopol, CA, May 25, 1947.

May 26 — Tuesday

DAY 147 **219 REMAINING**

AUSTRALIA: SORRY DAY. May 26. A day to express sorrow for the forced removal of aboriginal children from their families.

DUNKIRK EVACUATED: 80th ANNIVERSARY. May 26, 1940. The British Expeditionary Force had become trapped by advancing German armies near this port on the northern coast of France. On this date the evacuation of 200,000 British and 140,000 French and Belgian soldiers began. Sailing on every kind of transport available, including fishing boats and recreational craft, these men were safely brought across the English Channel by June 2.

FEAST OF SAINT AUGUSTINE OF CANTERBURY. May 26. Pope Gregory sent Augustine to convert the pagan English. Augustine became the first archbishop of Canterbury. He died May 26, AD 604.

GEORGIA: INDEPENDENCE DAY. May 26. National Day. Commemorates declaration of independence from Russia in 1918. Was absorbed by the Soviet Union in 1922 (until 1991).

	S	M	T	W	T	F	S
May						1	2
	3	4	5	6	7	8	9
	10	11	12	13	14	15	16
2020	17	18	19	20	21	22	23
	24	25	26	27	28	29	30
	31						

GOULD, JAY: BIRTH ANNIVERSARY. May 26, 1836. American financier, seen by some as a robber baron, born at Roxbury, NY. In 1867, he joined the board of the Erie Railroad and made millions manipulating Erie stock. In 1869, he conspired to control the price of gold by buying up all the gold in New York City, causing the Black Friday Panic of Sept 24, in which thousands of investors sustained losses and Gould made a fortune. He began developing railroads in the West in 1872; by 1880, he controlled more than 8,000 miles of railroad track. He also gained control of the Western Union Telegraph Co and several elevated railroads in New York City. Gould died on Dec 2, 1892, at New York City.

HELM, LEVON: 80th BIRTH ANNIVERSARY. May 26, 1940. Born at Marvell, AR, Levon Helm grew up listening to Grand Ole Opry radio shows and early rock and roll, sounds that informed his long career as a drummer, bandleader and respected singer-songwriter. Helm formed The Band in the late 1950s and played drums with the roots rock outfit on legendary albums such as *Songs from Big Pink* and *The Last Waltz* (1978). As a bandleader he issued a string of solo records in the 1980s and '90s and continued to work steadily; the folky *Dirt Farmer* (2007) was a late critical favorite. Helm died of cancer Apr 19, 2012, at New York City.

JOLSON, AL: BIRTH ANNIVERSARY. May 26, 1886. "You ain't heard nothin' yet" was the famous catchphrase of the world's first full-length talkie, *The Jazz Singer* (1927). It starred the legendary entertainer Al Jolson, who by that time already had decades of showbiz experience behind him. Born Asa Yoelson at St. Petersburg, Russia, Jolson first appeared in front of an audience as a child singing in the synagogue where his father was cantor. But he yearned for a show business career, quickly becoming a star in minstrel-type shows in vaudeville and then on Broadway. He was also a successful recording star before moving on to film, where he made several melodramatic shorts and features. Jolson died at San Francisco, CA, on Oct 23, 1950.

LEE, PEGGY: 100th BIRTH ANNIVERSARY. May 26, 1920. Singer, songwriter and actress Peggy Lee was born Norma Deloris Egstrom at Jamestown, ND. She got her start singing on a Fargo, ND, radio station and was soon hired by Benny Goodman to sing with his band. Known for her simple, jazzy style as well as her sex appeal. Her biggest hits were "Fever" (1958) and "Is That All There Is?" (1969). She is perhaps best remembered for the songs that she cowrote and performed in Disney's *Lady and the Tramp*. She continued to perform until the 1990s, when poor health forced her to retire. She died Jan 21, 2002, at Los Angeles, CA.

MANNING, FRANKIE: BIRTH ANNIVERSARY. May 26, 1914. Dancer famed for his innovations and ambassadorship of the Lindy hop (or the jitterbug). Born at Jacksonville, FL, but living in New York City since age three, Manning danced at the Savoy Ballroom in Harlem, NYC, as a teenager, then was lead dancer and chief choreographer of the touring troupe Whitey's Lindy Hoppers, followed by his own post–World War II troupe, the Congaroo Dancers. Appeared in numerous films, including *Hellzapoppin'*. His choreography for the Broadway musical *Black and Blue* earned him a Tony Award in 1989. The recipient of an NEA National Heritage Fellowship Award in 2000, Manning died Apr 27, 2009, at New York, NY.

MONTAGU, LADY MARY WORTLEY: BAPTISM ANNIVERSARY. May 26, 1689. English author, scholar and "scientific lady" known for her wit and verse, Wortley was born at London, England. Her diaries and letters, including the preeminent *Turkish Embassy Letters*, are considered to be among the most significant literary works of 18th-century England. A proponent of smallpox inoculation, Montagu directed experiments that proved the vaccine's efficacy, although her work was disregarded by the British medical establishment because of her sex. She wrote, "True knowledge consists in knowing things, not words." Died Aug 21, 1762, at London.

RIDE, SALLY KRISTEN: BIRTH ANNIVERSARY. May 26, 1951. Dr. Sally Ride, one of the first women in the US astronaut corps and the first American woman in space, was born at Encino, CA. Her flight aboard the space shuttle *Challenger* was launched from Cape Canaveral, FL, June 18, 1983, and landed at Edwards Air Force Base, CA, June 24. The six-day flight was termed "nearly a perfect mission." She died July 23, 2012, at La Jolla, CA.

SILVERHEELS, JAY: BIRTH ANNIVERSARY. May 26, 1912. Best known as Tonto, the faithful companion of the Lone Ranger on the long-running television series, Jay Silverheels was born Harold Smith at the Six Nations Indian Reserve, a Mohawk reservation at Brantford, ON, Canada. He excelled at athletics as a young man and found work as an itinerant boxer and lacrosse player before landing in Hollywood, where he was a stuntman and bit player in films. He attained the defining role of his career as Tonto in 1949. Silverheels died of a stroke at Calabasas, CA, on Mar 5, 1980.

SPACE MILESTONE: *PHOENIX* LANDS ON MARS (US). May 26, 2008. NASA's *Phoenix* spacecraft landed successfully on the northern plains of Mars. Designed to be stationary, *Phoenix* analyzed soil and permafrost samples and transmitted photographs back to Earth.

VIETNAM AND US RESUME RELATIONS: ANNIVERSARY. May 26, 1994. Nearly 20 years after the end of the Vietnam War, the US and Vietnam agreed to resume diplomatic relations. In the early 1990s Vietnam had become one of the fastest-growing economies in Asia after giving up Communist controls and allowing economic reform. Earlier in 1994 President William Clinton had lifted the American embargo that hindered Americans from doing business in Vietnam.

WAYNE, JOHN: BIRTH ANNIVERSARY. May 26, 1907. American motion picture actor, born Marion Michael Morrison, at Winterset, IA. The quintessential Western actor for five decades. Among his films are *Stagecoach* (1939), *Red River* (1948), *The Searchers* (1956) and *True Grit* (1969), for which he won a Best Actor Oscar. He died at Los Angeles, CA, June 11, 1979. "Talk low, talk slow and don't say too much" was his advice on acting.

WORLD LINDY HOP DAY. May 26. A day celebrating this exuberant African-American social dance. Originating at the Savoy Ballroom at Harlem, New York City, in the 1920s and 1930s, the Lindy hop (aka swing dancing or jitterbug) is usually danced to the big band jazz of the era. Lindy hop features creative and exhilarating movements that allow partners to connect in a way that uplifts the spirit, promotes human connection and develops generosity. Annually, May 26—the birth anniversary of Frankie Manning (1914–2009), one of the most important ambassadors and innovators of the Lindy hop.

🎂 BIRTHDAYS TODAY

Simon Armitage, 57, Poet Laureate of the United Kingdom (2019–), born Huddersfield, England, May 26, 1963.

Helena Bonham Carter, 54, actress (Harry Potter films, *The King's Speech, Sweeney Todd, A Room with a View*), born London, England, May 26, 1966.

Genie Francis, 58, actress ("General Hospital"), born Englewood, NJ, May 26, 1962.

Alex Garland, 50, author (*The Beach*), film director (*Ex Machina, Annihilation*), screenwriter (*Ex Machina, 28 Days Later, Never Let Me Go*), born London, England, May 26, 1970.

Pam Grier, 71, actress (*Jackie Brown, Ghosts of Mars, Foxy Brown*), born Winston-Salem, NC, May 26, 1949.

Lenny Kravitz, 56, actor, singer, musician, songwriter, born New York, NY, May 26, 1964.

Brent Musburger, 81, former sportscaster, born Portland, OR, May 26, 1939.

Stevie Nicks, 72, singer (Fleetwood Mac), songwriter, born Phoenix, AZ, May 26, 1948.

Philip Michael Thomas, 71, actor ("Miami Vice," *Hair*), born Los Angeles, CA, May 26, 1949.

Hank Williams, Jr, 71, singer, born Shreveport, LA, May 26, 1949.

May 27 — Wednesday

DAY 148 **218 REMAINING**

BENNETT, ARNOLD: BIRTH ANNIVERSARY. May 27, 1867. English novelist, playwright and critic Enoch Arnold Bennett was born at Hanley, in the pottery-manufacturing district of North Staffordshire, England. Best known of his novels is *The Old Wives' Tale* (1908). His *Journals* from 1896 until near the time of his death in 1931 provide insight into Bennett's thought. "The price of justice," Bennett wrote, "is eternal publicity." He contracted typhoid fever in France and died at London, England, May 27, 1931.

BLOOMER, AMELIA JENKS: BIRTH ANNIVERSARY. May 27, 1818. American social reformer and women's rights advocate, born at Homer, NY. Her name is remembered especially because of her work for more sensible dress for women and her recommendation of a costume that had been introduced about 1849 by Elizabeth Smith Miller but came to be known as the "Bloomer Costume" or "bloomers." Amelia Bloomer died at Council Bluffs, IA, Dec 30, 1894.

BOOKEXPO AMERICA TRADE EXHIBIT. May 27–29. Javits Center, New York, NY. Publishers display fall titles for booksellers and all interested in reaching the retail bookseller. Book-related items also on display. For info: BookExpo America. Web: www.bookexpoamerica.com.

CANADA: ANNAPOLIS VALLEY APPLE BLOSSOM FESTIVAL. May 27–June 1. Windsor to Digby, NS. Since 1933, annual festival with barbecues, sports events, art show, coronation ceremonies, concerts, fireworks, children's parade, Grand Street Parade and "Family Fun Day at Scotian Gold." Est attendance: 100,000. For info: Annapolis Valley Apple Blossom Festival, 325 Main St. Unit 8, Kentville, NS, B4N 1K5 Canada. Phone: (902) 678-8322. Fax: (902) 678-3710. E-mail: info@appleblossom.com. Web: www.appleblossom.com.

CARSON, RACHEL LOUISE: BIRTH ANNIVERSARY. May 27, 1907. American scientist and author, born at Springdale, PA. Author of *Silent Spring* (1962), a book that provoked widespread controversy over the use of pesticides. Died Apr 14, 1964, at Silver Spring, MD.

CELLOPHANE TAPE PATENTED: 90th ANNIVERSARY. May 27, 1930. Richard Gurley Drew received a patent for his adhesive tape, later manufactured by 3M as Scotch tape.

DUNCAN, ISADORA: BIRTH ANNIVERSARY. May 27, 1878. American-born interpretive dancer who revolutionized the entire concept of dance. Barefooted, freedom-loving, liberated woman and rebel against tradition, she experienced worldwide professional success and profound personal tragedy (her two children drowned, her marriage failed and she met a bizarre death when the long scarf she was wearing caught in a wheel of the open car in which she was riding, strangling her). Born at San Francisco, CA; died at Nice, France, Sept 14, 1927.

FIRST FLIGHT INTO THE STRATOSPHERE: ANNIVERSARY. May 27, 1931. In a balloon launched from Augsburg, Germany, Paul Kipfer and Auguste Piccard became the first to reach the stratosphere. In a pressurized cabin they rose almost 10 miles during their flight.

FIRST RUNNING OF PREAKNESS: ANNIVERSARY. May 27, 1873. The first running of the Preakness Stakes at Pimlico, MD, was won by Survivor with a time of 2:43. The winning jockey was G. Barbee.

GOLDEN GATE BRIDGE OPENED: ANNIVERSARY. May 27, 1937. Some 200,000 people crossed San Francisco's Golden Gate Bridge on its opening day.

HAMMETT, DASHIELL: BIRTH ANNIVERSARY. May 27, 1894. The man who brought realism to the genre of mystery writing, Samuel Dashiell Hammett was born at St. Mary's County, MD. His first two novels, *Red Harvest* (1929) and *The Dain Curse* (1929), were based on his eight years spent as a Pinkerton detective. Hammett is recognized as the founder of the "hard-boiled" school of detective fiction. Three of his novels have been made into films: *The Maltese Falcon* (1930), considered by many to be his finest work; *The Thin Man* (1932), which provided the basis for a series of five movies starring William Powell and Myrna Loy; and *The Glass Key* (1931). Hammett was called to testify but refused to name members of an alleged subversive organization during House Un-American Activities Committee hearings. He died Jan 10, 1961, at New York City.

HICKOK, WILD BILL: BIRTH ANNIVERSARY. May 27, 1837. Born at Troy Grove, IL, and died Aug 2, 1876, at Deadwood, SD. American frontiersman, legendary marksman, lawman, army scout and gambler. Hickok's end came when he was shot dead at a poker table by a drunk in the Number Ten saloon.

HOWE, JULIA WARD: BIRTH ANNIVERSARY. May 27, 1819. American author, feminist, social activist and orator Julia Ward Howe was born at New York, NY. Famous for "Battle Hymn of the Republic," composed after visiting military camps during the Civil War (1862), Howe was a prolific author and, with husband Samuel Gridley Howe, edited the antislavery paper *The Commonwealth*. Her social activism extended beyond the abolition movement to the women's suffrage and peace movements. Howe was president of the American Branch of the Women's International Peace Association and organized the New England Women's and American Women's Suffrage Associations. The first woman elected to the American Academy of Arts and Letters (1908), Howe died Oct 17, 1910, at Newport, RI.

HUMPHREY, HUBERT HORATIO: BIRTH ANNIVERSARY. May 27, 1911. The 38th vice president of the US (1965–69) was born at Wallace, SD. As mayor of Minneapolis, MN (1945–48), Humphrey successfully led the fight for a strong party stand on civil rights at the 1948 Democratic National Convention. He was elected to the US Senate in 1948, the first Democratic senator to come from Minnesota since the Civil War. He served five terms; in 1961 he was the Senate Democratic whip. In 1964 he was elected vice president under Lyndon Johnson. As the Democratic nominee for president he was narrowly defeated by Richard Nixon in 1968. Humphrey died on Jan 13, 1978, at Waverly, MN.

PRICE, VINCENT: BIRTH ANNIVERSARY. May 27, 1911. This silken-voiced actor—best known for his portrayal of sinister villains in horror films—was born at St. Louis, MO. After graduating from Yale, Price first sought theater work but was successful in film, especially in Roger Corman's series of Edgar Allan Poe adaptations in the 1960s. A noted art historian, Price was also an epicure who authored several cookbooks. In his later years, he was a host of the PBS anthology series "Mystery!" and had a moving part in

Tim Burton's *Edward Scissorhands* (1990). Price died at Los Angeles, CA, on Oct 25, 1993.

RMS *QUEEN MARY* MAIDEN VOYAGE: ANNIVERSARY. May 27, 1936. Anniversary of the maiden voyage from Southampton, England, to New York Harbor. In 1967 the ship sailed to Long Beach, CA, where it is permanently berthed and used as a hotel.

SAINT PETERSBURG FOUNDED: ANNIVERSARY. May 27, 1703. Czar Peter the Great founded the city of Saint Petersburg on the banks of the Neva River by laying the first stone of the Peter and Paul Fortress. It became the capital of Russia in 1712.

SNEAD, SAM: BIRTH ANNIVERSARY. May 27, 1912. The winningest US Tour golfer of the 20th century was born at Hot Springs, VA. He turned pro in 1934 and went on to become the only golfer to win tournaments in six different decades. He won 84 US Tour events and 182 tournaments in total. Snead always wore a snappy straw hat and was a favorite on the Tour. He was one of the founders of the US Senior Tour. Snead died at Hot Springs, on May 23, 2002.

WORLD OTTER DAY. May 27. Since 2014, a day to raise awareness about how important otters are to the environment, how they suffer as part of the illegal wildlife trade and how much they need our help. There are 13 species of otter, and all of them are listed in the IUCN Red List. More than 20 countries take part in this global awareness day. Annually, the last Wednesday in May. For info: International Otter Survival Fund. E-mail: enquiries@otter.org. Web: www.otter.org.

🎂 BIRTHDAYS TODAY

Jeff Bagwell, 52, former baseball player, born Boston, MA, May 27, 1968.

John Barth, 90, author (*Giles Goat-Boy, Chimera, The Floating Opera*), born Cambridge, MD, May 27, 1930.

André Benjamin, 45, singer, musician (André 3000, Outkast), actor, born Atlanta, GA, May 27, 1975.

Todd Bridges, 55, actor ("Diff'rent Strokes"), born San Francisco, CA, May 27, 1965.

Pat Cash, 55, former tennis player, born Melbourne, Australia, May 27, 1965.

Chris Colfer, 30, actor ("Glee"), born Fresno, CA, May 27, 1990.

Joseph Fiennes, 50, actor ("American Horror Story," *Enemy at the Gates, Shakespeare in Love*), born Salisbury, England, May 27, 1970.

Peri Gilpin, 59, actress ("Frasier"), born Waco, TX, May 27, 1961.

Louis Gossett, Jr, 84, actor (Emmy for *Roots*; Oscar for *An Officer and a Gentleman*), born Brooklyn, NY, May 27, 1936.

Henry Kissinger, 97, former US secretary of state, author, born Fuerth, Germany, May 27, 1923.

Ramsey Lewis, 85, jazz musician, born Chicago, IL, May 27, 1935.

Jack McBrayer, 47, actor ("30 Rock"), born Macon, GA, May 27, 1973.

Henry McMaster, 73, Governor of South Carolina (R), born Columbia, SC, May 27, 1947.

Lee Meriwether, 85, actress ("Barnaby Jones," "Batman"), former Miss America (1955), born Los Angeles, CA, May 27, 1935.

Jamie Oliver, 45, chef, television personality ("The Naked Chef"), born Clavering, Essex, England, May 27, 1975.

May 2020	S	M	T	W	T	F	S
						1	2
	3	4	5	6	7	8	9
	10	11	12	13	14	15	16
	17	18	19	20	21	22	23
	24	25	26	27	28	29	30
	31						

Richard Schiff, 65, actor ("The West Wing"), born Bethesda, MD, May 27, 1955.

Frank Thomas, 52, Hall of Fame baseball player, born Columbus, GA, May 27, 1968.

Bruce Weitz, 77, actor ("Hill Street Blues"), born Norwalk, CT, May 27, 1943.

May 28 — Thursday

DAY 149   **217 REMAINING**

AGASSIZ, LOUIS: BIRTH ANNIVERSARY. May 28, 1807. Professor of zoology and geology at Harvard, born at Môtier, Switzerland. He was a major influence in spawning American interest in natural history and helped to establish the Harvard Museum of Comparative Zoology. "The eye of the trilobite," Agassiz wrote in 1870, "tells us that the sun shone on the old beach where he lived; for there is nothing in nature without a purpose, and when so complicated an organ was made to receive the light, there must have been light to enter it." Died at Cambridge, MA, Dec 14, 1873.

AMNESTY INTERNATIONAL FOUNDED: ANNIVERSARY. May 28, 1961. This Nobel Prize–winning human rights organization was founded by London lawyer Peter Benenson after he read about two Portuguese students arrested simply for drinking a toast to freedom. He realized that people around the world were at risk daily for peacefully expressing their views. AI currently has more than 3 million members in every corner of the world. Its mission is to undertake research and action focused on preventing and ending grave abuses of the rights of physical and mental integrity, freedom of conscience and expression and freedom from discrimination, within the context of its work to promote all human rights. For info: Amnesty International Secretariat. Web: www.amnesty. org.

ASCENSION OF BAHA'U'LLAH. May 28. Baha'i observance of the anniversary of the death in 1892 of Baha'u'llah (the prophet-founder of the Baha'i Faith). One of the nine days of the year when Baha'is suspend work. For info: Baha'is of the US, Office of Communications, 1233 Central St, Evanston, IL 60201-1611. Phone: (847) 733-3584. E-mail: ooc@usbnc.org. Web: www.bahai.us.

AZERBAIJAN: DAY OF THE REPUBLIC. May 28. Public holiday. Commemorates the declaration of the Azerbaijan Democratic Republic in 1918.

DIONNE QUINTUPLETS: BIRTHDAY. May 28, 1934. Five daughters (Marie, Cecile, Yvonne, Emilie and Annette) were born to Oliva and Elzire Dionne, near Callander, ON, Canada. They were the first quints known to have lived for more than a few hours after birth. Emilie died in 1954, Marie in 1970, Yvonne in 2001. The other two sisters are still living.

END OF THE PARIS COMMUNE: ANNIVERSARY. May 28, 1871. On Mar 18, 1871, a revolt of the Parisian workers' parties against the policies of the national government erupted. It ended just over two months later in a hail of buildings in flames, frustrated social foment in the streets and harsh reprisals from Versailles. In the violence that followed, 147 members of the Commune were murdered, their bodies dumped in a trench along a wall beside Père Lachaise Cemetery. May 28 is a date still considered sacred by the French Left.

ETHIOPIA: NATIONAL DAY. May 28. National holiday. Commemorates the downfall of the Dergue, the military government that ruled Ethiopia from 1974 to 1991.

FISCHER-DIESKAU, DIETRICH: 95th BIRTH ANNIVERSARY. May 28, 1925. Born at Berlin, Germany, preeminent baritone Fischer-Dieskau was perhaps the world's most recorded classical singer. He made hundreds of recordings that set the standard for lieder (German art song) performance and also recorded a wider ranging repertoire than any other singer, performing selections from Bach to Wagner to Stravinsky to Schumann, among others. After an abrupt retirement from performing in 1992, Fischer-Dieskau continued to teach and conduct for many years thereafter until his death on May 18, 2012, at Berg, Bavaria.

FLEMING, IAN: BIRTH ANNIVERSARY. May 28, 1908. English journalist, novelist, creator of the James Bond series, beginning with *Casino Royale* in 1953. Fleming also penned the children's classic *Chitty Chitty Bang Bang*. Born at London, died Aug 12, 1964, at Sandwich, England.

GUILLOTIN, JOSEPH-IGNACE: BIRTH ANNIVERSARY. May 28, 1738. French physician and member of the Constituent Assembly who urged the use of a machine that was sometimes called the Maiden for the execution of death sentences—a less painful, more certain way of dispatching those sentenced to death. The guillotine was first used on Apr 25, 1792, for the execution of a highwayman, Nicolas Jacques Pelletier. Other machines for decapitation had been in use in other countries since the Middle Ages. Guillotin was born at Saintes, France, and died at Paris, Mar 26, 1814.

MEMORY DAYS. May 28–31. Grayson, KY. Parade, art show and live shows. Est attendance: 10,000. For info: Maggie Duncan, Grayson Area Chamber of Commerce, PO Box 612, Grayson, KY 41143-1341. Phone: (606) 474-4401. E-mail: graysonchamber41143@ windstream.net.

NEPAL: REPUBLIC DAY. May 28. Public holiday. Commemorates the anniversary of Nepal's becoming a democratic republic in 2008 after years of being a monarchy.

ORTHODOX ASCENSION DAY. May 28. Observed by Eastern Orthodox churches. Falls on the sixth Thursday after Pascha.

PITT, WILLIAM: BIRTH ANNIVERSARY. May 28, 1759. British prime minister from 1783 to 1801 and from 1804 to 1806, Pitt was influenced by Adam Smith's economic theories and reduced England's large national debt caused by the American Revolution. Born at Hayes, Kent, England, he died Jan 23, 1806, at Putney. He was the son of William Pitt, first earl of Chatham, for whom the city of Pittsburgh was named.

SAINT BERNARD OF MONTJOUX: FEAST DAY. May 28. Patron saint of mountain climbers, founder of Alpine hospices of the Great and Little St. Bernard, died at age 85, probably on May 28, 1081.

SHAVUOT BEGINS AT SUNDOWN. May 28. Jewish Pentecost. See also: "Shavuot" (May 29).

SIERRA CLUB FOUNDED: ANNIVERSARY. May 28, 1892. Founded by famed naturalist John Muir, the Sierra Club promotes conservation of the natural environment by influencing public policy. It has been especially important in the founding and protection of our national parks.

SLUGS RETURN FROM CAPISTRANO DAY. May 28. It's a little-known secret that slimy slugs spend their winters in lovely Capistrano and return to our patios and gardens on this date. Bare feet are not a good idea now through first frost. (©2006 by WH.) For info: Thomas & Ruth Roy, Wellcat Holidays, 2418 Long Ln, Lebanon, PA 17046. Phone: (717) 279-0184. E-mail: info@wellcat. com. Web: www.wellcat.com.

THORPE, JAMES FRANCIS (JIM): BIRTH ANNIVERSARY. May 28, 1888. Olympic gold medal track athlete, baseball player and football player, born at Prague, OK. Thorpe, a Native American, won the pentathlon and the decathlon at the 1912 Olympic Games but later lost his medals when Olympic officials declared that an earlier stint as a minor league baseball player besmirched his amateur standing. He later played professional baseball and football and was acclaimed the greatest male athlete of the first half of the 20th century. Died at Lomita, CA, Mar 28, 1953. (Thorpe's medals were returned to his family many years after his death when the earlier decision was reversed.)

🧁 BIRTHDAYS TODAY

Carroll Baker, 89, actress (*Baby Doll, Harlow*), born Johnstown, PA, May 28, 1931.

Alexa Davalos, 38, actress ("The Man in the High Castle," *Clash of the Titans*), born Paris, France, May 28, 1982.

Kirk Gibson, 63, baseball manager, former player, born Pontiac, MI, May 28, 1957.

Rudolph Giuliani, 76, former mayor of New York City, born Brooklyn, NY, May 28, 1944.

Elisabeth Hasselbeck, 43, television personality ("The View," "Survivor"), born Cranston, RI, May 28, 1977.

Jake Johnson, 42, actor ("New Girl"), born Evanston, IL, May 28, 1978.

Gladys Knight, 76, singer, born Atlanta, GA, May 28, 1944.

Christa Miller, 56, actress ("The Drew Carey Show," "Scrubs"), born New York, NY, May 28, 1964.

Carey Mulligan, 35, actress (*Suffragette, Far from the Madding Crowd, The Great Gatsby*), born Greater London, England, May 28, 1985.

Marco Rubio, 49, US Senator (R, Florida), born Miami, FL, May 28, 1971.

May 29 — Friday

DAY 150   216 REMAINING

AMNESTY ISSUED FOR SOUTHERN REBELS: ANNIVERSARY. May 29, 1865. President Andrew Johnson issued a proclamation giving a general amnesty to all who participated in the rebellion against the US. High-ranking members of the Confederate government and military and those who owned more than $20,000 worth of property were excepted and had to apply individually to the president for a pardon. Once an oath of allegiance was taken, all former property rights, except those in slaves, were returned to the former owners.

CENTRALIA ANCHOR FESTIVAL. May 29–31. City Square, Centralia, MO. Continuous entertainment, crafts, concessions, carnival, 3-on-3 basketball, tractor show, car show, fun run, anchor driving and parade. Est attendance: 20,000. For info: Centralia Anchor Festival, PO Box 235, Centralia, MO 65240. Phone: (573) 682-2272. Fax: (573) 682-1111. E-mail: ginny@centraliamochamber.com. Web: www.centraliamochamber.com.

CHARLES II: RESTORATION ANNIVERSARY. May 29, 1660. Restoration of Charles II to English throne. Also his birthday (May 29, 1630). English monarchy restored after Commonwealth period under Oliver Cromwell.

CHESTERTON, GILBERT KEITH: BIRTH ANNIVERSARY. May 29, 1874. Author, journalist, critic born at London, England. Chesterton created beloved mysteries featuring the gentle sleuth and Catholic priest Father Brown, who debuted in 1910. Chesterton is also the author of the surrealistic thriller *The Man Who Was Thursday* (1908). He died June 14, 1936, at Beaconsfield, Buckinghamshire, England.

CONSTANTINOPLE FALLS TO THE TURKS: ANNIVERSARY. May 29, 1453. The city of Constantinople was captured by the Turks, who later renamed it Istanbul. This conquest marked the end of the

Byzantine Empire; the city became the capital of the Ottoman Empire.

HENRY, PATRICK: BIRTH ANNIVERSARY. May 29, 1736. American Revolutionary leader and orator, born at Studley, VA, and died near Brookneal, VA, June 6, 1799. Especially remembered for his speech (Mar 23, 1775) for arming the Virginia militia, at St. Johns Church, Richmond, VA, when he declared: "I know not what course others may take, but as for me, give me liberty or give me death."

HEYSEL STADIUM TRAGEDY: 35th ANNIVERSARY. May 29, 1985. Soccer fans attending the European Cup Final, between Liverpool and Juventus of Turin, at Heysel Stadium, Brussels, Belgium, clashed before the match started. As fans fled the riot, many were crushed against a barrier. There were 39 people killed and 600 injured. The incident was televised and viewed by millions throughout Europe. More than two years later, Sept 2, 1987, the British government announced that 26 British soccer fans (identified from television tapes) would be extradited to Belgium for trial. Hooliganism at soccer matches became the target of increased security measures for England's professional teams following the 1985 tragedy.

HOPE, BOB: BIRTH ANNIVERSARY. May 29, 1903. The comedic actor was born Leslie Townes Hope at Eltham, England. Hope had a long career in vaudeville, stage, radio, film and TV. His first film appearance was in *The Big Broadcast of 1938* (in which he sang his signature song, "Thanks for the Memory"). Hope went on to appear in more than 75 films—most memorably with crooner Bing Crosby in their series of *Road* movies. He received five honorary Oscars (among them the Jean Hersholt Humanitarian Award) and numerous other honors. Hope tirelessly entertained US troops during every war from WWII to the Gulf War. President Lyndon Johnson presented him with the Medal of Freedom, and he was knighted in 1998. Hope died July 27, 2003, at Toluca Lake, CA.

KENNEDY, JOHN FITZGERALD: BIRTH ANNIVERSARY. May 29, 1917. 35th president of the US (1961–63), born at Brookline, MA. Assassinated while riding in an open automobile at Dallas, TX, Nov 22, 1963. (Accused assassin Lee Harvey Oswald was killed at the Dallas police station by a gunman, Jack Ruby, two days later.) Kennedy was the youngest man ever elected to the presidency, the first Roman Catholic and the first president to have served in the US Navy. He was the fourth US president to be killed by an assassin and the second to be buried at Arlington National Cemetery (first was William Howard Taft).

MOON PHASE: FIRST QUARTER. May 29. Moon enters First Quarter phase at 11:30 PM, EDT.

MOSCOW COMMUNIQUÉ: ANNIVERSARY. May 29, 1972. President Richard Nixon and Soviet Party leader Leonid Brezhnev released a joint communiqué after Nixon's weeklong visit to Moscow. During the visit the two men acknowledged their major differences on the Vietnam War and signed a treaty on antiballistic missile systems, as well as an interim agreement on limitation of strategic missiles and an agreement for a joint space flight in 1975. This was the first visit ever to Moscow by a US president (May 22–30, 1972).

MOUNT EVEREST SUMMIT REACHED: ANNIVERSARY. May 29, 1953. New Zealand explorer Sir Edmund Hillary and Tenzing Norgay, a Sherpa guide, became the first team to reach the summit of Mount Everest, the world's highest mountain.

NCAA DIVISION I WOMEN'S ROWING CHAMPIONSHIP. May 29–31. Melton Lake, Oak Ridge, TN. For info: NCAA, PO Box 6222, Indianapolis, IN 46206-6222. Web: www.NCAA.com.

May 2020	S	M	T	W	T	F	S
						1	2
	3	4	5	6	7	8	9
	10	11	12	13	14	15	16
	17	18	19	20	21	22	23
	24	25	26	27	28	29	30
	31						

RHODE ISLAND: RATIFICATION DAY. May 29. The last of the 13 original states to ratify the Constitution in 1790.

***THE RITE OF SPRING* PREMIERE AND RIOT: ANNIVERSARY.** May 29, 1913. In the most notorious world premiere in any of the arts, Igor Stravinsky's *The Rite of Spring* received a rough reception at the Théâtre des Champs-Élysées at Paris, France, on this date. Performed by Sergey Diaghilev's Ballets Russes and choreographed by the legendary Vaslav Nijinsky, the ballet and music presented scenes from pagan Russia. The audience began to boo at Stravinsky's challenging and dissonant music, and before long fistfights between different camps of music lovers broke out. The police were called to restore order. Despite its inauspicious beginning, *The Rite of Spring* is now regarded as a masterpiece.

SHAVUOT OR FEAST OF WEEKS. May 29–30. Jewish Pentecost holy days. Hebrew dates, Sivan 6–7, 5780. Celebrates giving of Torah (the Law) to Moses on Mount Sinai. Began at sundown May 28.

SOJOURNER TRUTH'S "AIN'T I A WOMAN" SPEECH: ANNIVERSARY. May 29, 1851. During the Women's Rights Convention held at Akron, OH, from May 28 to May 29, 1851, former slave Sojourner Truth delivered an impassioned speech that is now titled after its common refrain: "I have ploughed, and planted, and gathered into barns, and no man could head me! And ain't I a woman? I could work as much and eat as much as a man—when I could get it—and bear the lash as well! And ain't I a woman? And when I cried out with my mother's grief, none but Jesus heard me. And ain't I a woman?"

UNITED NATIONS: INTERNATIONAL DAY OF UNITED NATIONS PEACEKEEPERS. May 29. A day to pay tribute to all the men and women who have served in United Nations peacekeeping operations for their high level of professionalism, dedication and courage, and to honor the memory of those who have lost their lives in the cause of peace (Res 57/129, Dec 11, 2002). Annually, May 29. For info: United Nations, Dept of Public Info, New York, NY 10017. Web: www.un.org.

VIRGINIA PLAN PROPOSED: ANNIVERSARY. May 29, 1787. Just five days after the Constitutional Convention met at Philadelphia, PA, the "Virginia Plan" was proposed. It called for establishment of a new governmental organization consisting of a legislature with two houses, an executive branch (chosen by the legislature) and a judicial branch.

WISCONSIN: ADMISSION DAY: ANNIVERSARY. May 29. Became 30th state in 1848.

🧁 BIRTHDAYS TODAY

Carmelo Anthony, 36, basketball player, born New York, NY, May 29, 1984.

Annette Bening, 62, actress (*20th Century Women, American Beauty, The Kids Are All Right*), born Topeka, KS, May 29, 1958.

Kevin Conway, 78, actor (*When You Comin' Back, Red Ryder?*; *Of Mice and Men*; *Other People's Money*), born New York, NY, May 29, 1942.

Laverne Cox, 36, actress ("Orange Is the New Black"), born Robert Laverne Cox at Mobile, AL, May 29, 1984.

Eric Davis, 58, former baseball player, born Los Angeles, CA, May 29, 1962.

Paul Ehrlich, 88, population biologist, born Philadelphia, PA, May 29, 1932.

Melissa Etheridge, 59, singer, guitarist, born Leavenworth, KS, May 29, 1961.

Rupert Everett, 61, actor (*An Ideal Husband, My Best Friend's Wedding*), born Norfolk, England, May 29, 1959.

Anthony Geary, 72, actor ("General Hospital"), born Coalville, UT, May 29, 1948.

Riley Keough, 31, actress (*The Runaways, Magic Mike*), model, born Los Angeles, CA, May 29, 1989.

Jerry Moran, 66, US Senator (R, Kansas), born Great Bend, KS, May 29, 1954.

Adrian Paul, 61, actor ("Highlander"), born London, England, May 29, 1959.

Alfred (Al) Unser, Sr, 81, former auto racer, born Albuquerque, NM, May 29, 1939.

Francis Thomas (Fay) Vincent, Jr, 82, former commissioner of baseball, born Waterbury, CT, May 29, 1938.

Lisa Whelchel, 57, actress ("The Facts of Life"), born Fort Worth, TX, May 29, 1963.

May 30 — Saturday

DAY 151 **215 REMAINING**

BATTLE OF THE ALEUTIAN ISLANDS: ANNIVERSARY. May 30, 1943. The islands of Kiska and Attu in the Aleutian Islands off the coast of Alaska were retaken by the US 7th Infantry Division. The battle (Operation Landgrab) began when an American force of 11,000 landed on Attu May 12. In three weeks of fighting, US casualties numbered 552 killed and 1,140 wounded. Only 28 wounded Japanese were taken prisoner. Japan's dead amounted to 2,352, of whom 500 committed suicide.

BLANC, MEL: BIRTH ANNIVERSARY. May 30, 1908. The greatest voice artist in history, Mel Blanc was born at San Francisco, CA. He performed more than 400 voices in his career, but he is best remembered for "Looney Tunes" and "Merrie Melodies," in which he performed the voices of Bugs Bunny, Elmer Fudd, Porky Pig, Sylvester, Tweetie Pie and Road Runner. He died on June 10, 1989, at Los Angeles, CA.

BOOKCON 2020. May 30–31. Javits Center, New York, NY. 7th annual. BookCon is the event where storytelling and pop culture collide. Book consumers experience the origin of the story in all its forms by interacting with the authors, publishers, celebrities and creators of content that influence everything we read, hear and see. Est attendance: 20,000. For info: ReedPOP. Web: www.thebookcon.com.

CULLEN, COUNTEE: BIRTH ANNIVERSARY. May 30, 1903. One of the leading poets of the Harlem Renaissance. A key work is his first book, *Color* (1925). Born at New York City, Cullen died there Jan 9, 1946.

FABERGÉ, CARL: BIRTH ANNIVERSARY. May 30, 1846. Goldsmith, designer and jeweler Peter Carl Fabergé was born on this date at St. Petersburg, Russia. He made the House of Fabergé an internationally known name with fantastical bejeweled decorative objects. His workshop began creating the famous imperial Easter eggs for czars Alexander III and Nicholas II in 1885. After the Russian Revolution, the Bolsheviks shut down the House of Fabergé, and the family fled the country. Fabergé died at Lausanne, France, on Sept 24, 1920. (His birth date was May 18 on the Old Style [Julian] calendar.)

FIRST AMERICAN DAILY NEWSPAPER PUBLISHED: ANNIVERSARY. May 30, 1783. *The Pennsylvania Evening Post* became the first daily

newspaper published in the US. The paper was published at Philadelphia, PA, by Benjamin Towne.

GOODMAN, BENNY: BIRTH ANNIVERSARY. May 30, 1909. Jazz clarinetist and bandleader, born Benjamin David Goodman at Chicago, IL. The "King of Swing" reigned in popularity, especially in the 1930s and 1940s. His band was the first to play jazz at New York's Carnegie Hall. He died June 13, 1986, at New York, NY.

INDIANAPOLIS 500: ANNIVERSARY. May 30, 1911. Ray Harroun won the first Indy 500, averaging 74.6 mph. The race was created by Carl Fisher, who in 1909 replaced the stone surface of his 2.5-mile racetrack with a brick one—hence the nickname "The Brickyard."

ISLE OF MAN: TOURIST TROPHY. May 30–June 12. For two weeks of every year the eyes of the world focus on the Isle of Man as the finest road racers on the planet pit their skills against the 37¾ miles of public roads that form the legendary TT circuit. Starting at the capital, Douglas, up to 600 competitors rocket around the "Jewel of the Irish Sea" at speeds of up to 200 mph. First held in 1907. Est attendance: 35,000. For info: Isle of Man Tourist Trophy. Web: www.iomtt.com.

LINCOLN MEMORIAL DEDICATION: ANNIVERSARY. May 30, 1922. The memorial is made of marble from Colorado and Tennessee and limestone from Indiana. It stands in West Potomac Park at Washington, DC. The memorial was designed by architect Henry Bacon, and its cornerstone was laid in 1915. A skylight lets light into the interior where the compelling statue *Seated Lincoln*, by sculptor Daniel Chester French, is situated.

LOOMIS DAY. May 30. To honor Mahlon Loomis, a Washington, DC, dentist who received a US patent on wireless telegraphy in 1872 (before Marconi was born). Titled "An Improvement in Telegraphing," the patent described how to do without wires; this patent was backed up by experiment on the Massanutten Mountains of Virginia. (Created by Robert L. Birch, Pun Corps.)

MEMORIAL DAY (TRADITIONAL). May 30. This day honors the tradition of making memorial tributes to the dead, especially remembering those who have died in battle. Observed as a legal public holiday on the last Monday in May.

***ONE HUNDRED YEARS OF SOLITUDE* PUBLISHED: ANNIVERSARY.** May 30, 1967. Colombian Gabriel García Márquez's blockbuster magic realist novel, *Cien años de soledad*, was published in Buenos Aires, Argentina, by Editorial Sudamericana. The epic chronicles seven generations of the Buendía family in the fictional and magical city of Macondo, Colombia. Hailed as a landmark novel in any language, *One Hundred Years of Solitude* has sold more than 30 million copies.

PETER I: BIRTH ANNIVERSARY. May 30, 1672. Peter I (Peter the Great), Czar and Emperor of all the Russias. His primary aim was to make Russia a major power equal to its size and potential, and the way he saw to do this was through education and technology. He established printing presses and published translations of foreign books, particularly scientific and technical material. The Russian alphabet was simplified, and Arabic numerals were introduced. Peter encouraged trade with foreign countries, mercantilism within Russia and the entrepreneurial skills of resident foreigners; he allowed industrialists to own serfs, a right previously limited to landholders. He completely overhauled the government, the Russian Orthodox Church, the military system and the structure of taxes, ultimately increasing the power of the monarchy at the expense of the nobility and the national church. Upon his death, Jan 28, 1725, he was succeeded by his wife, Catherine.

RIPKEN STREAK BEGINS: ANNIVERSARY. May 30, 1982. Baltimore Oriole Cal Ripken took to the baseball field on this date and began a consecutive-games-played streak that lasted for 2,632 games—a major league record. His streak ended Sept 19, 1998.

SAINT JOAN OF ARC: FEAST DAY. May 30. French heroine and martyr, known as the "Maid of Orleans," led the French against the English invading army. Captured, found guilty of heresy and burned at the stake in 1431 (at age 19). Innocence declared in 1456. Canonized in 1920.

SPACE MILESTONE: *MARINER 9* (US). May 30, 1971. Unmanned spacecraft was launched, entering Martian orbit the following Nov 13. The craft relayed temperature and gravitational field information and sent back spectacular photographs of both the surface of Mars and its two moons. First spacecraft to orbit another planet.

TRINIDAD AND TOBAGO: INDIAN ARRIVAL DAY. May 30. Public holiday. Commemorates the 1845 arrival of the first Indian laborers to Trinidad.

UEFA CHAMPIONS LEAGUE FINAL 2020. May 30. Atatürk Olympic Stadium, Istanbul, Turkey. The prestigious Champions League tournament comes to a close with this final match featuring the two European professional teams who outplayed their opponents beginning in summer 2019. Est attendance: 76,000. For info: UEFA. Web: www.uefa.com.

🧁 BIRTHDAYS TODAY

Keir Dullea, 84, actor (*David and Lisa*, *2001: A Space Odyssey*), born Cleveland, OH, May 30, 1936.

Steven Gerrard, 40, soccer manager and former player, born Liverpool, England, May 30, 1980.

Jared Gilmore, 20, actor ("Once Upon a Time," "Mad Men"), born San Diego, CA, May 30, 2000.

Cee Lo Green, 46, singer, rapper, record producer, born Thomas DeCarlo Callaway at Atlanta, GA, May 30, 1974.

Wynonna Judd, 56, singer, born Ashland, KY, May 30, 1964.

Ted McGinley, 62, actor ("Married . . . With Children," *Revenge of the Nerds*), born Newport Beach, CA, May 30, 1958.

Colm Meaney, 67, actor ("Star Trek: Deep Space Nine," *Layer Cake*, *The Snapper*), born Dublin, Ireland, May 30, 1953.

Trey Parker, 48, director, creator ("South Park"), born Auburn, AL, May 30, 1972.

Michael J. Pollard, 81, actor (*Bonnie and Clyde*), born Passaic, NJ, May 30, 1939.

Manny Ramirez, 48, former baseball player, born Santo Domingo, Dominican Republic, May 30, 1972.

Gale Sayers, 77, Hall of Fame football player, born Wichita, KS, May 30, 1943.

Stephen Tobolowsky, 69, actor ("Deadwood," *The Grifters*, *Groundhog Day*), born Dallas, TX, May 30, 1951.

		S	M	T	W	T	F	S
May							1	2
		3	4	5	6	7	8	9
2020		10	11	12	13	14	15	16
		17	18	19	20	21	22	23
		24	25	26	27	28	29	30
		31						

May 31 — Sunday

DAY 152   **214 REMAINING**

BATTLE OF JUTLAND: ANNIVERSARY. May 31–June 1, 1916. The largest naval battle of WWI—involving 250 ships, including battleships—took place in the North Sea near Jutland, Denmark. The combatants were Britain's Grand Fleet and Germany's High Seas Fleet. The outcome was inconclusive, but the cost was great: 8,600 lives were lost and 25 ships sunk.

BAY TO BREAKERS. May 31. San Francisco, CA. Established in 1912, the Bay to Breakers is the largest footrace in the world, attracting 50,000 runners each year, from world-class athletes to fun runners. Includes a post-race festival with music, food and beverages. Sponsored by Alaska Airlines. Est attendance: 110,000. For info: Bay to Breakers. Phone: (415) 231-3130. E-mail: info@baytobreakers.com. Web: www.baytobreakers.com.

COPYRIGHT LAW PASSED: ANNIVERSARY. May 31, 1790. President George Washington signed the first US copyright law. It gave protection for 14 years to books written by US citizens. In 1891 the law was extended to cover books by foreign authors as well.

HAITI: MOTHER'S DAY. May 31. Celebration observed on the last Sunday in May.

HARRIS, PATRICIA ROBERTS: BIRTH ANNIVERSARY. May 31, 1924. Born at Mattoon, IL. The first African-American woman to serve in an ambassadorial post, the first African American to hold a cabinet position (secretary of housing and urban development) and the first woman to serve as dean of a law school—at Howard University. Died Mar 23, 1985, at Washington, DC.

ITALY: PALIO DEI BALESTRIERI (PALIO OF THE ARCHERS). May 31. Gubbio. The last Sunday in May is set aside for a crossbow contest that has been held since medieval times between the neighboring towns of Gubbio and Sansepolcro. Participants wear medieval costumes and bear medieval arms. Sansepolcro hosts the second part of the contest on the second Sunday in September. The colorful event is accompanied by a parade.

JOHNSTOWN FLOOD: ANNIVERSARY. May 31, 1889. Heavy rains caused the Connemaugh River Dam to burst. At nearby Johnstown, PA, the resulting flood killed more than 2,300 people and destroyed the homes of thousands more. Nearly 800 unidentified drowning victims were buried in a common grave at Johnstown's Grandview Cemetery. So devastating was the flood and so widespread the sorrow for its victims that "Johnstown Flood" entered the language as a phrase to describe a disastrous event. The valley city of Johnstown, in the Allegheny Mountains, has been damaged repeatedly by floods. Floods in 1936 (25 deaths) and 1977 (85 deaths) were the next most destructive.

PEALE, NORMAN VINCENT: BIRTH ANNIVERSARY. May 31, 1898. American religious leader Norman Vincent Peale was born at Bowersville, OH. He is best known for his book *The Power of Positive Thinking* (1952), which combines religion and psychology. He was a minister at the Marble Collegiate Church at New York, NY. He died Dec 24, 1993, at Pawling, NY.

PENTECOST. May 31. The Christian feast of Pentecost commemorates the descent of the Holy Spirit unto the Apostles, 50 days after Easter. Observed on the seventh Sunday after Easter. Recognized since the third century. See also: "Whitsunday" (below).

POPE PIUS XI: BIRTH ANNIVERSARY. May 31, 1857. Ambrogio Damiano Achille Ratti, 259th pope of the Roman Catholic Church, born at Desio, Italy. Elected pope Feb 6, 1922. Died Feb 10, 1939, at Rome, Italy.

"SEINFELD" TV PREMIERE: 30th ANNIVERSARY. May 31, 1990. "Seinfeld"—the show about nothing—premiered on NBC to wide acclaim. The show revolved around the everyday lives of its four main leads, whose story lines intertwined for some surprising plot twists. Some of the programs concerned relationships, valet parking, annoying dogs and waiting for Chinese food. The cast featured Jerry Seinfeld as himself; Michael Richards as his neighbor, Cosmo Kramer; Julia Louis-Dreyfus as his ex-girlfriend, Elaine Benes; and Jason Alexander as his best friend, George Costanza. The series ended with the May 14, 1998, episode.

"SURVIVOR" TV PREMIERE: 20th ANNIVERSARY. May 31, 2000. On this immensely popular reality show, 16 people were sequestered on a deserted island in Malaysia for 39 days. They competed for the right to remain on the island, with the final survivor winning $1 million. Hosted by Jeff Probst, the show drew a total audience of 51 million people. The show has consistently ranked in the top of the Nielsen ratings.

UNITED NATIONS: WORLD NO-TOBACCO DAY. May 31. A day to raise awareness of the global tobacco epidemic's massive toll of death, sickness and misery. For info: United Nations, Dept of Public Info, New York, NY 10017. Web: www.un.org.

WHAT YOU THINK UPON GROWS DAY. May 31. A day to remind people of the power of positive thinking. For info: Stephanie West Allen, 1376 S Wyandot St, Denver, CO 80223. Phone: (303) 935-8866. E-mail: stephanie@westallen.com.

WHITMAN, WALT: BIRTH ANNIVERSARY. May 31, 1819. Poet and journalist, born at West Hills, Long Island, NY. Whitman's best-known work, *Leaves of Grass* (1855), is a classic of American poetry. His poems celebrated all of modern life, including subjects that were considered taboo at the time. Died Mar 26, 1892, at Camden, NJ.

WHITSUNDAY. May 31. Whitsunday, the seventh Sunday after Easter, is a popular time for baptism. "White Sunday" is named for the white garments formerly worn by the candidates for baptism and occurs at the Christian feast of Pentecost. See also: "Pentecost" (above).

"WITH ALL DELIBERATE SPEED": 65th ANNIVERSARY. May 31, 1955. In an instruction one year after its *Brown v Board of Education of Topeka* decision, the US Supreme Court ordered recalcitrant states to begin school integration "with all deliberate speed."

🎂 BIRTHDAYS TODAY

Svetlana Alexievich, 72, journalist, author (*Voices from Chernobyl*), Nobel Prize in Literature recipient, born Stanislaviv, USSR (now Ivano-Frankivsk, Ukraine), May 31, 1948.

Tom Berenger, 70, actor (*Born on the Fourth of July, Major League, Gettysburg*), born Chicago, IL, May 31, 1950.

Clint Eastwood, 90, actor, director (Oscars for *Unforgiven* and *Million Dollar Baby*), born San Francisco, CA, May 31, 1930.

Chris Elliott, 60, writer, comedian, actor ("Get a Life"), born New York, NY, May 31, 1960.

Colin Farrell, 44, actor (*Total Recall, In Bruges, Minority Report, Tigerland*), born Castleknock, Dublin, Ireland, May 31, 1976.

Sharon Gless, 77, actress ("Burn Notice," Emmy for "Cagney and Lacey"), born Los Angeles, CA, May 31, 1943.

Gregory Harrison, 70, actor ("Logan's Run," "Trapper John, MD"), born Avalon, Catalina Island, CA, May 31, 1950.

Phil Keoghan, 53, television personality, host ("The Amazing Race"), born Christchurch, New Zealand, May 31, 1967.

Kenny Lofton, 53, former baseball player, born East Chicago, IN, May 31, 1967.

Roma Maffia, 62, actress ("Chicago Hope," "Nip/Tuck"), born New York, NY, May 31, 1958.

Joseph William (Joe) Namath, 77, Hall of Fame football player, former sportscaster, actor, born Beaver Falls, PA, May 31, 1943.

Archie Panjabi, 48, actress (Emmy for "The Good Wife"; *San Andreas, Bend It like Beckham*), born London, England, May 31, 1972.

Kyle Secor, 62, actor ("Homicide: Life on the Street"), born Tacoma, WA, May 31, 1958.

Brooke Shields, 55, actress (*Pretty Baby, The Blue Lagoon*, "Suddenly Susan"), born New York, NY, May 31, 1965.

Lea Thompson, 59, actress ("Caroline in the City," *Back to the Future, Howard the Duck*), born Rochester, MN, May 31, 1961.

Terry Waite, 81, Church of England special envoy, former hostage in Lebanon (1987–91), born Bollington, Cheshire, England, May 31, 1939.

Peter Yarrow, 82, composer, singer (Peter, Paul and Mary), born New York, NY, May 31, 1938.

June

June 1 — Monday

ADOPT-A-SHELTER-CAT MONTH. June 1–30. To promote the adoption of cats from local shelters, the ASPCA sponsors this important observance. "Make Pet Adoption Your First Option®" is a message the organization promotes throughout the year in an effort to end the euthanasia of all adoptable animals. For info: ASPCA, 520 8th Ave, 7th Fl, New York, NY 10018. Phone: (212) 876-7700, ext 4655. E-mail: press@aspca.org. Web: www.aspca.org.

★**AFRICAN-AMERICAN MUSIC APPRECIATION MONTH.** June 1–30. Proclaimed annually since 2009 to honor the rich musical traditions of African-American musicians and their gifts to our country and our world and to celebrate the legacy of African-American music and its enduring power to bring life to the narrative of our nation.

ALZHEIMER'S AND BRAIN AWARENESS MONTH. June 1–30. Worldwide, 50 million people are living with Alzheimer's and other dementias. Join the Alzheimer's Association in going purple and raising awareness this month. The more people know about Alzheimer's, the more action we inspire. On June 21—the summer solstice—people across the world will participate in a fundraising activity on The Longest Day. For info: Alzheimer's Assn, 225 N Michigan Ave, Ste 1700, Chicago, IL 60601-7633. Phone: (800) 272-3900. E-mail: advocate@alz.org. Web: www.alz.org.

ATLANTIC, CARIBBEAN AND GULF HURRICANE SEASON. June 1–Nov 30. For info: National Oceanic and Atmospheric Administration. Web: www.noaa.gov.

AUDIOBOOK APPRECIATION MONTH. June 1–30. To encourage new listeners to learn more about the fascinating history and current status of audiobooks in the United States. Audiobooks are one of the fastest-growing areas of the publishing industry. For info: Audio Publishers Association, 333 Hudson St, Ste 503, New York, NY 10013. Phone: (646) 688-3044. E-mail: info@audiopub.org. Web: www.audiopub.org.

BABY BOOMERS RECOGNITION DAY. June 1. As baby boomers, we'll never forget The Beatles, the Vietnam War and other sixties events. However, many of us accomplished a great deal, becoming successful in business, education, medicine and other fields. This special day commemorates our contributions. For info: Dorothy Zjawin, 61 W Colfax Ave, Roselle Park, NJ 07204.

CANADA: NATIONAL INDIGENOUS HISTORY MONTH. June 1–30. Since 1996, Canadians have celebrated this month to honor the history, heritage and diversity of indigenous peoples in Canada. It is also an opportunity to recognize the strength of present-day indigenous communities. For info: Government of Canada. Web: www.canada.ca.

CANCER FROM THE SUN MONTH. June 1–30. To promote education and awareness of the dangers of skin cancer from too much exposure to the sun. Sponsored by the American College of Apothecaries (ACA)/Pharmacists Planning Service, Inc (PPSI). For info: ACA/PPSI, 2830 Summer Oaks Dr, Bartlett, TN 38134. E-mail: info@ppsinc.org. Web: www.ppsinc.org.

★**CARIBBEAN-AMERICAN HERITAGE MONTH.** June 1–30. To pay tribute to the diverse cultures and immeasurable contributions of all Americans who trace their heritage to the Caribbean.

CATARACT AWARENESS MONTH. June 1–30. Cataracts are the leading cause of blindness in the world. There are more than 25 million Americans age 40 and older with cataracts. More than half of all Americans will have cataracts by age 80. Prevent Blindness offers tips about prevention and information about surgery. For info: Prevent Blindness, 211 W Wacker Dr, Ste 1700, Chicago, IL 60606. Phone: (800) 331-2020. E-mail: info@preventblindness.org. Web: www.preventblindness.org.

CENTRAL PACIFIC HURRICANE SEASON. June 1–Oct 31. Central Pacific is defined as 140° west longitude to the International Date Line (180° west longitude). For info: National Oceanic and Atmospheric Administration. Web: www.noaa.gov.

CHILD VISION AWARENESS MONTH. June 1–30. To better educate and counsel the public on children's vision problems and detection of eye diseases in infants and children, to increase the number of school-aged children who have an eye exam by an eye doctor and to increase the number of children with learning disabilities who have a developmental vision exam to rule out vision problems. Sponsored by the American College of Apothecaries (ACA)/Pharmacists Planning Service, Inc (PPSI). For info: ACA/PPSI, 2830 Summer Oaks Dr, Bartlett, TN 38134. E-mail: info@ppsinc.org. Web: www.ppsinc.org.

CHINA: INTERNATIONAL CHILDREN'S DAY. June 1. Shanghai.

CNN DEBUT: 40th ANNIVERSARY. June 1, 1980. The Cable News Network, TV's first all-news service, went on the air.

DEMENTIA CARE PROFESSIONALS MONTH. June 1–30. Since 2016, a month to recognize the individuals who tirelessly care for people with dementia. For info: Alzheimer's Foundation of America, 322 Eighth Ave, New York, NY 10001. Web: www.alzfdn.org.

EFFECTIVE COMMUNICATIONS MONTH. June 1–30. The most important cog in the wheel of interpersonal relationships is communication. Active listening, verbal language, paralanguage, body language and written communication skills are the essence of how humans relate to each other personally and professionally. This month is dedicated to learning how to communicate more effectively. For info: Sylvia Henderson, Springboard Training, 3570 Olney-Laytonsville Rd, Ste 588, Olney, MD 20832. Phone: (301) 260-1538. E-mail: sylvia@springboardtraining.com. Web: www.ideasuccessnetwork.com.

ENGLAND: DICING FOR BIBLES. June 1. An old Whitmonday ceremony at All Saints Church, St. Ives, Huntingdonshire. A bequest (in 1675) with the intent of providing Bibles for poor children of the parish required winning them at a dice game played in the church. In recent years the dicing has been moved from the altar to a "more suitable" place. Six Bibles are given on Whitmonday each year.

ENTREPRENEURS "DO IT YOURSELF" MARKETING MONTH. June 1–30. Discover and apply creative and effective problem-solving marketing ideas that will help you gain the competitive edge. Act now and remove the barriers that are stopping you from achieving your goals. For info: Lorrie Walters Marsiglio, Lorimar Communications, PO Box 284-CC, Wasco, IL 60183-0284. Phone: (630) 584-9368.

FIREWORKS SAFETY MONTHS. June 1–July 31. Activities during this period will alert parents and children about the dangers of playing with fireworks. Prevent Blindness will offer suggestions for safer ways to celebrate the Fourth of July. For info: Prevent Blindness, 211 W Wacker Dr, Ste 1700, Chicago, IL 60606. Phone: (800) 331-2020. E-mail: info@preventblindness.org. Web: www.preventblindness.org.

GAY AND LESBIAN PRIDE MONTH. June 1–30. Observed this month because on June 28, 1969, the clientele of a gay bar at New York City rioted after the club was raided by the police. President

Clinton issued presidential proclamations for this month, but President Bush did not declare it during his administration. President Obama resumed proclaiming this month as Lesbian, Gay, Bisexual and Transgender Pride Month in 2009. See also: "Stonewall Riot: Anniversary" (June 28).

GENERAL MOTORS CORPORATION BANKRUPTCY: ANNIVERSARY. June 1, 2009. The 100-year-old automaker filed for Chapter 11 bankruptcy protection on this date. In response, the US federal government invested $57 billion in the company, making the US Treasury GM's majority shareholder, owning a 60 percent stake. The reorganized GM, now General Motors Company, exited bankruptcy July 10, 2009, eliminating 13 US plants, 2,000 dealerships and 20,000 jobs.

★**GREAT OUTDOORS MONTH.** June 1–30. To celebrate the rich blessings of our nation's natural beauty and to renew our commitment to protecting the environment and keeping our country's open spaces beautiful and accessible to our citizens.

HEIMLICH MANEUVER INTRODUCED: ANNIVERSARY. June 1, 1974. The June issue of the journal *Emergency Medicine* published an article by Dr. Henry Heimlich outlining a better method for aiding choking victims. Instead of the prevailing method of backslaps (which merely pushed foreign objects farther into the airways), Dr. Heimlich advocated "subdiaphragmatic pressure" to force objects out. Three months later, the method was dubbed "the Heimlich Maneuver" by the *Journal of the American Medical Association*.

INTERNATIONAL IGBO DAY. June 1. 2nd annual. A day to commemorate, celebrate and educate others about the Igbo people, language, culture and contribution to society. The Igbo people comprise a population of approximately 42 million people and are one of the largest tribal groups in Nigeria. Unfortunately, the Igbo language is on the brink of extinction as many people are not preserving the language and not teaching it to children. Annually, June 1. For info: LIGO Foundation. E-mail: internationaligboday@gmail.com. Web: www.internationaligboday.com.

INTERNATIONAL MEN'S MONTH. June 1–30. This program was initiated in 1996 to increase media and local community awareness of the many unique issues that impact men's lives and that are of concern to the people who love them. In an effort to promote positive changes in male roles and relationships, a different issue is addressed each day of the month during June, and information and resources on that issue are provided on the website. For info: Gordon Clay, PO Box 12-CH, Brookings, OR 97415-0001. E-mail: menstuff@aol.com. Web: www.menstuff.org/calendar/intmensmonth.html.

INTERNATIONAL SURF MUSIC MONTH. June 1–30. 12th annual. Surf instrumental music, born in the US in the 1960s, reflects the freedom and joy of surf culture. This month celebrates that music and the bands the world over that inject local flavors into it. Concerts take place around the world. For info: Sandy Rosado, NESMA, 653 Browns Rd, Storrs Mansfield, CT 06268. E-mail: sandy9thwave@yahoo.com. Web: www.nesmasurf.org.

IRELAND: JUNE BANK HOLIDAY. June 1. National holiday in the Republic of Ireland on the first Monday in June.

JUNE DAIRY MONTH. June 1–30. Observed since 1937. Promotes national awareness of the quality and nutritional benefits of refrigerated dairy foods. For info: Natl Frozen & Refrigerated Foods Assn, 4755 Linglestown Rd, Ste 300, Harrisburg, PA 17112. Phone: (717) 657-8601. E-mail: nfra@nfraweb.org. Web: www.nfraweb.org.

KENTUCKY: ADMISSION DAY: ANNIVERSARY. June 1. Became 15th state in 1792.

KENYA: MADARAKA DAY. June 1. Madaraka Day (Self-Rule Day) is observed as a national public holiday. Commemorates attainment of self-government in 1963.

MARQUETTE, JACQUES: BIRTH ANNIVERSARY. June 1, 1637. Father Jacques Marquette (Père Marquette) was a Jesuit missionary-explorer of the Great Lakes region. Born at Laon, France; died at Ludington, MI, May 18, 1675.

MEN'S HEALTH EDUCATION AND AWARENESS MONTH. June 1–30. A month to keep informed about health concerns for men—and to learn how to prevent heart disease, prostate cancer, COPD, osteoporosis, ED, BPH, HIV, STDs and other diseases. Sponsored by the American College of Apothecaries (ACA)/Pharmacists Planning Service, Inc (PPSI). For info: ACA/PPSI, 2830 Summer Oaks Dr, Bartlett, TN 38134. E-mail: info@ppsinc.org. Web: www.ppsinc.org.

MIGRAINE AND HEADACHE AWARENESS MONTH. June 1–30. To educate the public on the personal and societal costs of migraines and headaches while providing resources for the 37 million migraine patients and their families. For info: National Headache Foundation. E-mail: info@headaches.org. Web: www.headaches.org.

MONROE, MARILYN: BIRTH ANNIVERSARY. June 1, 1926. American actress and sex symbol of the '50s, born at Los Angeles, CA, as Norma Jean Mortensen or Baker. She had an unstable childhood in a series of orphanages and foster homes. Her film career came to epitomize Hollywood glamour. In 1954 she wed New York Yankees legend "Jolting Joe" DiMaggio, but the marriage didn't last. Monroe was troubled by the pressures of Hollywood life. Her death from a drug overdose Aug 5, 1962, at Los Angeles shocked the world. Among her films: *The Seven Year Itch, Bus Stop, Some Like It Hot, Gentlemen Prefer Blondes* and *The Misfits*.

NATIONAL APHASIA AWARENESS MONTH. June 1–30. More than one million Americans have acquired aphasia, a language-processing disorder that impairs a person's ability to speak or understand speech. The mission of the National Aphasia Association (NAA) is to reduce the social and emotional consequences of aphasia by raising awareness of and giving a voice to people who cannot use their own. Annually, the month of June. For info: National Aphasia Association, PO Box 87, Scarsdale, NY 10583. Phone: (800) 922-4622. E-mail: naa@aphasia.org. Web: www.aphasia.org.

NATIONAL BATHROOM READING MONTH. June 1–30. Since 1988, the Bathroom Readers Institute has led the movement to stand up for those who sit down and read in the bathroom. National Bathroom Reading Month celebrates the 66 percent of Americans who proudly admit to this time-honored pastime. For info: Portable Press. E-mail: mail@bathroomreader.com. Web: www.bathroomreader.com.

NATIONAL CANDY MONTH. June 1–30. A whole month to celebrate your favorite candy. Celebrated throughout the confectionary industry. Candy is good food and can definitely be enjoyed as part of a balanced diet. For info: National Confectioners Association. Web: www.candyusa.com.

NATIONAL CARIBBEAN-AMERICAN HERITAGE MONTH. June 1–30. Since the 16th century, the destinies of the peoples of the Caribbean and the American continent have been inextricably linked. Through the commemoration of this month, we hope to ensure that America is reminded that its greatness lies in its diversity. Caribbean immigrants from founding father Alexander Hamilton to journalist Malcolm Gladwell have shaped the American dream. For info: Institute of Caribbean Studies, 1629 K St NW, Ste 300,

June 2020	S	M	T	W	T	F	S
		1	2	3	4	5	6
	7	8	9	10	11	12	13
	14	15	16	17	18	19	20
	21	22	23	24	25	26	27
	28	29	30				

Washington, DC 20006. Phone: (202) 638-0460. E-mail: icsdcorg@gmail.com. Web: www.caribbeanamericanmonth.org.

NATIONAL FOSTER A PET MONTH. June 1–30. If less than two percent of pet-owning households in the United States fostered one pet a year, we could eliminate unnecessary euthanasia in America's animal shelters tomorrow. Fostering saves animal lives and is highly rewarding to the foster family. To create awareness and inspire more people to foster pets, the Petco Foundation created this month for June each year, starting in 2019. Throughout the month, the Petco Foundation shares information and stories about how fostering can have a significant impact on helping the United States become a lifesaving nation. For info: Petco Foundation, 654 Richland Hills Dr, San Antonio, TX 78245.

NATIONAL GLBT BOOK MONTH™. June 1–30. Created to celebrate books about gay, lesbian, bisexual and transgender people as well as to promote GLBT authors. Begun in 1992 by The Publishing Triangle, June was selected in honor of the anniversary of the 1969 Stonewall Riot in New York City. Libraries, bookstores, publishers and readers are invited to recognize and promote GLBT books and authors. For info: Gay Lesbian Bisexual Transgender Roundtable, American Library Association. E-mail: diversity@ala.org. Web: www.ala.org/rt/glbtrt/glbt-book-month.

NATIONAL ICED TEA MONTH. June 1–30. To celebrate one of the most widely consumed beverages in the world and one of nature's most perfect beverages, and to encourage Americans to refresh themselves with this all-natural, low-calorie, refreshing thirst-quencher. For info: The Tea Council of the USA, 362 Fifth Ave, Ste 1002, New York, NY 10001. Phone: (212) 986-6998. Fax: (212) 697-8658. E-mail: info@teausa.org. Web: www.teausa.org.

★**NATIONAL OCEANS MONTH.** June 1–30. This month is an opportunity to show our gratitude toward all those who work to protect the oceans, to learn more about the vital role oceans play in the life of our country and to discover ways we can conserve their many natural treasures. Originally proclaimed as a week in 2006, this became a month in 2007.

NATIONAL POLLINATOR MONTH. June 1–30. A month to learn about, promote and protect pollinators—the bees, birds, butterflies, bats and beetles so important for home gardens and agriculture. Observed by several organizations as part of a national initiative to reverse declining habitats and pollinator populations. For info: National Wildlife Federations, Pollinator Partnership, USFWS, National Recreation and Park Association and others.

NATIONAL RIVERS MONTH. June 1–30. Commemorated by local groups in many states.

NATIONAL ROSE MONTH. June 1–30. A month to celebrate roses—originally sponsored by rose growers and the International Cut Flower Growers Association to recognize American-grown roses and the billions of fresh-cut roses sold at retail each year. Annually, the month of June.

NATIONAL SAFETY MONTH. June 1–30. Join NSC and thousands of organizations across the country as we work to raise awareness of what it takes to stay safe. Observed annually in June, National Safety Month focuses on reducing leading causes of injury and death at work, on the road and in our homes and communities. For info: Natl Safety Council, 1121 Spring Lake Dr, Itasca, IL 60143-3201. Phone: (800) 621-7615. E-mail: media@nsc.org. Web: www.nsc.org.

NATIONAL SOUL FOOD MONTH. June 1–30. A month to recognize, convey and celebrate the heritage and history of the foods and foodways of African Americans and peoples from the African diaspora. The culinary contributions of this group have had an indelible impact on the American menu and on mainstream American life and culture. For info: Culinary Historians of Chicago. E-mail: chc2001@att.net. Web: www.culinaryhistorians.org.

NATIONAL ZOO AND AQUARIUM MONTH. June 1–30. A national celebration to focus public attention on the role of zoos and aquariums in wildlife education and conservation. June is a great time to explore your local zoo and aquarium. For info: American Zoo and Aquarium Association or your local zoo or aquarium. Web: www.aza.org.

OUTDOOR MARKETING MONTH. June 1–30. Could you imagine a world without signs spotlighting where you enter, banners signaling a sale or special event, festivals without pennants or flags welcoming guests, signs or door wraps that welcome you to an open house, sporting events without team tents or team spirit motivators? There are more than 20,000 practitioners who provide outdoor marketing products to businesses, causes and consumers. Outdoor Marketing Day is June 13. For info: Quinn, Inc, 640 Boundary Ave, Hanover, PA 17331-3807. E-mail: info@OutdoorMarketingMonth.com.

PERENNIAL GARDENING MONTH. June 1–30. June is the perfect month to celebrate the versatility and beauty of perennial garden plants. During this month the Perennial Plant Assn offers gardening tips on how to keep your perennial garden beautiful all season long and highlight many individual perennials that bloom for the month of June. For info: Perennial Plant Association. Web: https://perennialplant.org/page/PerennialGardenMonth.

PHARMACISTS DECLARE WAR ON ALCOHOLISM. June 1–30. To encourage pharmacists, healthcare professionals and consumers to better educate and counsel the public on alcoholism and other substance abuse illnesses. Sponsored by the American College of Apothecaries (ACA)/Pharmacists Planning Service, Inc (PPSI). For info: ACA/PPSI, 2830 Summer Oaks Dr, Bartlett, TN 38134. E-mail: info@ppsinc.org. Web: www.ppsinc.org.

PTSD AWARENESS MONTH. June 1–30. Post-traumatic stress disorder (PTSD) is a mental health problem that can occur after someone goes through a traumatic event like war, assault, an accident or a disaster. The National Center for PTSD promotes awareness of PTSD and effective treatments throughout the year. Starting in 2010, Congress named June 27 PTSD Awareness Day (S. Res. 455). For the second consecutive year in 2014, the Senate designated the full month of June for National PTSD Awareness (S. Res. 481). Annually, the month of June. For info: National Center for PTSD. Veterans Crisis Line: (800) 273-8255. Web: www.ptsd.va.gov.

SAMOA: INDEPENDENCE DAY. June 1. National holiday. Commemorates independence from New Zealand in 1962. The former Western Samoa changed its name in 1997.

SAY SOMETHING NICE DAY. June 1. This is a day to say thank you to those who make our lives better just by being a part of them. A day to recognize those who contribute to our lives in specific ways. And a day to apologize for words spoken in frustration, anger or disappointment. One day is one day, but perhaps we can stretch it to two, and then just maybe if we encourage one another, we might change the world! For info: Mitch Carnell, 2444 Birkenhead Dr, Charleston, SC 29414. Phone: (843) 556-2310. E-mail: mitch@mitchcarnell.com. Web: www.mitchcarnell.com or www.fbcharleston.org.

***SGT PEPPER'S LONELY HEARTS CLUB BAND* RELEASED: ANNIVERSARY.** June 1, 1967. After 700 hours of studio work, The Beatles released what many consider one of the greatest rock albums of the 20th century. No singles were released, but the album included such popular tracks as "Lucy in the Sky with Diamonds," "With a Little Help from My Friends," "When I'm Sixty-Four" and "A Day in the Life."

SKYSCRAPER MONTH. June 1–30. Skyscraper Month celebrates the evolution of the high-rise building and the oldest commercial real

estate association, the Building Owners and Managers Association (BOMA) International. BOMA will observe this month at its annual conference June 27–30, at the Pennsylvania Convention Center, Philadelphia, PA. For info: BOMA International, 1101 15th St NW, Ste 800, Washington, DC 20005. Phone: (202) 326-6300. Web: www.boma.org or www.bomaconvention.org.

STUDENT SAFETY MONTH. June 1–30. To heighten the awareness of safety and of making sound decisions following graduations, parties, senior proms and other special events. Encourages young people everywhere not to drink and drive and to use good judgment while celebrating throughout the month. For info: Carole Copeland Thomas, 6 Azel Rd, Lakeville, MA 02347. Phone: (508) 947-5755. E-mail: TellCarole@mac.com. Web: www.TellCarole.com.

SUPERMAN DEBUTS: ANNIVERSARY. June 1, 1938. Ohio teenagers Joe Shuster and Jerry Siegel wowed the comic book world with a new kind of pulp hero: Superman. Superman, a refugee with superpowers from the planet Krypton, appeared in the June issue of *Action Comics* #1. Now a pop culture icon, Superman was then a smash hit who ushered in many more fantastical superheroes. (The comic book's actual release date was earlier, either Apr 18 or May 3.) See also: "Batman Debuts: Anniversary" (May 1).

TENNESSEE: ADMISSION DAY: ANNIVERSARY. June 1. Became 16th state in 1796. Observed as a holiday in Tennessee.

UNITED NATIONS: GLOBAL DAY OF PARENTS. June 1. This day honors parents throughout the world. (Res 66/292 in 2012.) Annually, June 1. For info: United Nations, Dept of Public Info, New York, NY 10017. Web: www.un.org.

WESTERN PACIFIC HURRICANE SEASON. June 1–Oct 1. Most hurricanes occur from June 1 through Oct 1, though the season lasts all year. (Western Pacific: west of the International Date Line.)

WHITMONDAY. June 1. The day after Whitsunday is observed as a public holiday in some countries.

YOUNG, BRIGHAM: BIRTH ANNIVERSARY. June 1, 1801. Mormon church leader born at Whitingham, VT. Known as "the American Moses," having led thousands of religious followers across 1,000 miles of wilderness to settle more than 300 towns in the West. He died at Salt Lake City, UT, Aug 29, 1877, and was survived by 17 wives and 47 children. Utah observes, as a state holiday, the anniversary of his entrance into the Salt Lake Valley, July 24, 1847.

🎂 BIRTHDAYS TODAY

René Auberjonois, 80, actor (*M*A*S*H*, "Boston Legal," "Benson," Tony for *Coco*), born New York, NY, June 1, 1940.

Lisa Hartman Black, 64, actress ("Tabitha," "Knots Landing"), born Houston, TX, June 1, 1956.

June 2020	S	M	T	W	T	F	S
		1	2	3	4	5	6
	7	8	9	10	11	12	13
	14	15	16	17	18	19	20
	21	22	23	24	25	26	27
	28	29	30				

Pat Boone, 86, singer, actor (*State Fair*), author, born Jacksonville, FL, June 1, 1934.

Sarah Wayne Callies, 43, actress ("The Walking Dead," "Prison Break"), born La Grange, IL, June 1, 1977.

Mark Curry, 56, comedian, actor ("Hangin' with Mr Cooper"), born Oakland, CA, June 1, 1964.

Morgan Freeman, 83, stage and film actor (Oscar for *Million Dollar Baby*; *The Shawshank Redemption*, *Driving Miss Daisy*), born Memphis, TN, June 1, 1937.

Justine Henin, 38, former tennis player, born Liege, Belgium, June 1, 1982.

Javier "Chicharito" Hernández, 32, soccer player, born Guadalajara, Mexico, June 1, 1988.

Tom Holland, 24, actor (*Spider-Man: Homecoming, Pilgrimage*), "Wolf Hall"), born Kingston-upon-Thames, England, June 1, 1996.

Heidi Klum, 47, fashion model, television personality ("Project Runway"), born Bergisch-Gladbach, Germany, June 1, 1973.

Alexi Lalas, 50, sportscaster, Hall of Fame soccer player, born Detroit, MI, June 1, 1970.

Alanis Morissette, 46, singer, born Ottawa, ON, Canada, June 1, 1974.

Jonathan Pryce, 73, actor (*Glengarry Glen Ross*; stage: *Miss Saigon*, Tony for *Hamlet*), born Holywell, North Wales, June 1, 1947.

Amy Schumer, 39, comedienne, actress (*Trainwreck*), born New York, NY, June 1, 1981.

Frederica von Stade, 75, opera singer, born Somerville, NJ, June 1, 1945.

Ron Wood, 73, musician (Rolling Stones), born London, England, June 1, 1947.

Carlos Zambrano, 39, baseball player, born Puerto Cabello, Venezuela, June 1, 1981.

June 2 — Tuesday

DAY 154   **212 REMAINING**

BELGIUM: PROCESSION OF THE GOLDEN CHARIOT. June 2. Mons. Horse-drawn coach carrying a reliquary of St. Waudru circles the town of Mons. Procession commemorates delivery of Mons from the plague in 1349. In the town square, in the afternoon, St. George fights the dragon.

BHUTAN: CORONATION DAY. June 2. National holiday. Commemorates the crowning of the fourth king in 1974.

BULGARIA: HRISTO BOTEV DAY. June 2. Poet and national hero Hristo Botev fell fighting Turks, 1876.

GERMANY: WALDCHESTAG (FOREST DAY). June 2. Frankfurt. For centuries Frankfurters have spent the Tuesday after Whitsunday in their city forest (Am Oberforsthaus).

HAMLISCH, MARVIN: BIRTH ANNIVERSARY. June 2, 1944. Composer and conductor of film and Broadway scores, born at New York, NY. A child prodigy accepted to Juilliard at age seven, Hamlisch composed his first hit song before he turned 21. Famous film scores include *The Sting* (1973) and *The Way We Were* (1973), and his best-known Broadway work includes *A Chorus Line* (1975) and *They're Playing Our Song* (1979). Winner of multiple Emmy, Grammy, Oscar and Tony Awards, as well as the 1976 Pulitzer Prize for Drama for *A Chorus Line*, he died at Los Angeles, CA, Aug 6, 2012.

HARDY, THOMAS: BIRTH ANNIVERSARY. June 2, 1840. Novelist, dramatist and poet, Hardy was born at Higher Bockhampton, England. Renowned for his novels, most notably *Tess of the d'Urbervilles* and *Jude the Obscure*. Hardy's oeuvre mirrors both his personal and broader societal changes, including the decline in Christianity, the movement from reticence to openness about sexuality, the shift from agricultural to modern economy and the contrast between the universe and the individual. He died Jan 11, 1928, at Dorchester, England.

ITALY: REPUBLIC DAY. June 2. National holiday. Commemorates 1946 referendum in which republic status was selected instead of return to monarchy.

MARQUIS DE SADE: BIRTH ANNIVERSARY. June 2, 1740. Donatien-Alphonse-François de Sade was born at Paris, France. Military man, governor-general, playwright and author, he spent much of his life in prison or asylums because of his acts of cruelty and violence, outrageous behavior and debauchery. As early as 1772, his effigy was burned in response to his crimes. His infamous and obscene *120 Days of Sodom* was written in the Bastille, where he was incarcerated during 1784–89 (he was transferred to an asylum 10 days before the storming of the prison). As late as 1957, French publishers were found guilty of obscenity for publishing his work. The word *sadism* was created from his name to describe gratification in inflicting pain. "Citizen Sade," as he termed himself during the Revolution, died near Paris, at the Charenton lunatic asylum, Dec 2, 1814.

NATIONAL GUN VIOLENCE AWARENESS DAY. June 2. 6th annual. A nationwide movement to honor lives cut short by gun violence. Observed on the birth date of Hadiya Pendleton, who was killed by gunfire on Jan 21, 2013, at 15 years of age. Observers are asked to wear orange. Sponsored by Everytown for Gun Safety and many other community organizations. For info: Everytown for Gun Safety. Web: www.wearorange.org.

RUTH RETIRES: 85th ANNIVERSARY. June 2, 1935. Three days after he benched himself from his last game (May 30), George Herman "Babe" Ruth announced his retirement from major league baseball.

SAINT ERASMUS DAY. June 2. Feast day of Erasmus, also known as Elmo, bishop of Formiae, Campagna, Italy, who was martyred around AD 303. Patron saint of sailors. The blue light seen around ship masts that marks atmospheric electricity is popularly called St. Elmo's fire from the ancient belief that it signifies the saint's protection of sailors during storms.

SAINT PIUS X: BIRTH ANNIVERSARY. June 2, 1835. Giuseppe Melchiorre Sarto, 257th pope of the Roman Catholic Church, born at Riese, Italy. Elected pope Aug 4, 1903. Died Aug 20, 1914, at Rome, Italy. Canonized May 29, 1954.

SALEM WITCH TRIALS BEGIN: ANNIVERSARY. June 2, 1692. As the village of Salem was gripped by terror of witches, Massachusetts Bay Colony governor Sir William Phips ordered a special court created on May 27, 1692, to expedite judgment of the more than 150 people accused of witchcraft. Unpopular resident Bridget Bishop, originally accused in April, was the first of the jailed brought to trial on June 2. At her April examination her accusers—teenaged girls—had collapsed in fits as she appeared, but Bishop adamantly denied the charges: "I am no witch—I know not what a witch is." She was convicted June 2 and hanged June 10. See also: "Salem Witch Hysteria Begins: Anniversary" (Mar 1).

UNITED KINGDOM: CORONATION DAY. June 2. Commemorates the crowning of Queen Elizabeth II in 1953.

WASHINGTON, MARTHA DANDRIDGE CUSTIS: BIRTH ANNIVERSARY. June 2, 1731. Wife of George Washington, first president of the US, born at New Kent County, VA. Died at Mount Vernon, VA, May 22, 1802.

WEISSMULLER, JOHNNY: BIRTH ANNIVERSARY. June 2, 1904. Peter John (Johnny) Weissmuller, actor and Olympic gold medal swimmer, born at Friedorf, Romania (although he later adopted Windber, PA, as his hometown). Weissmuller won three gold medals at the 1924 Olympics and two more at the 1928 games. He set 24 world records and in 1950 was voted the best swimmer of the first half of the 20th century. After retiring from amateur competition, he appeared as Tarzan in a dozen movies and as "Jungle Jim" in the movies and on television. Died at Acapulco, Mexico, Jan 20, 1984.

"THE WIRE" TV PREMIERE: ANNIVERSARY. June 2, 2002. HBO's gritty, Baltimore-set series created by former *Baltimore Sun* police reporter David Simon is commonly cited as the greatest TV drama of all time from sources as diverse as *Entertainment Weekly, Rolling Stone, Slate, TIME, Chicago Tribune, San Francisco Chronicle, The Guardian* and the BBC. Seasoned actors Wendell Pierce, Dominic West, Idris Elba and Sonja Sohn were cast alongside real-life Baltimore personalities and gang members. Each of "The Wire"'s five 12-episode seasons focuses knowingly on a different institution of the city as it relates to law enforcement: S1: illegal drugs; S2: unions; S3: City Hall; S4: public education; S5: the media. While it attracted negligible viewership during its original run, the Peabody Award–winning series later developed a cult following through home video and is credited with raising the bar for the storytelling possibilities of television.

YELL "FUDGE" AT THE COBRAS IN NORTH AMERICA DAY. June 2. Anywhere north of the Panama Canal. In order to keep poisonous cobra snakes out of North America, all citizens are asked to go outdoors at noon, local time, and yell "Fudge." Fudge makes cobras gag and the mere mention of it makes them skedaddle. Annually, June 2. (©2006 by WH.) For info: Thomas & Ruth Roy, Wellcat Holidays, 2418 Long Ln, Lebanon, PA 17046. Phone: (717) 279-0184. E-mail: info@wellcat.com. Web: www.wellcat.com.

🎂 BIRTHDAYS TODAY

Awkwafina, 32, actress (*Crazy Rich Asians, Oceans 8*), rap artist, born Nora Lum at Forest Hills, NY.

Morena Baccarin, 41, actress (*Deadpool*, "Gotham," "Homeland," "V"), born Rio de Janeiro, Brazil, June 2, 1979.

Diana Canova, 67, actress ("Soap," "I'm a Big Girl Now"), born West Palm Beach, FL, June 2, 1953.

Dana Carvey, 65, comedian, actor (*Wayne's World*, "Saturday Night Live"), born Missoula, MT, June 2, 1955.

Dominic Cooper, 42, actor ("Preacher," *Need for Speed, The Devil's Double, The History Boys*), born Greenwich, England, June 2, 1978.

Nikolay Davydenko, 39, tennis player, born Severodonetsk, Ukraine, June 2, 1981.

Gary Grimes, 65, actor (*Summer of '42, Class of '44*), born San Francisco, CA, June 2, 1955.

Charles Haid, 77, actor ("Hill Street Blues," "Delvecchio"), producer, born San Francisco, CA, June 2, 1943.

Dennis Haysbert, 66, actor ("24," *Waiting to Exhale, Major League*), born San Mateo, CA, June 2, 1954.

Stacy Keach, Jr, 79, actor (*Conduct Unbecoming*, "Mickey Spillane's Mike Hammer"), born Savannah, GA, June 2, 1941.

Sally Kellerman, 84, actress (*M*A*S*H, Back to School*), born Long Beach, CA, June 2, 1936.

Justin Long, 42, actor (*Dodgeball, Live Free or Die Hard*, "Ed"), born Fairfield, CT, June 2, 1978.

Jerry Mathers, 72, actor ("Leave It to Beaver"), born Sioux City, IA, June 2, 1948.

Wentworth Miller, 48, actor ("Prison Break," *The Human Stain*), born Chipping Norton, Oxfordshire, England, June 2, 1972.

Zachary Quinto, 43, actor (*Star Trek* films, "NOS4A2," "Heroes," "24"), born Pittsburgh, PA, June 2, 1977.

Charlie Watts, 79, musician (Rolling Stones), born Islington, England, June 2, 1941.

June 3 — Wednesday

DAY 155	211 REMAINING

BAKER, JOSEPHINE: BIRTH ANNIVERSARY. June 3, 1906. The sensation of 1920s Paris, Baker was born into poverty at St. Louis, MO. She began working as a dancer at age 16 and went to Paris in 1925, where her seminude "danse sauvage" became a hit. She was the first American-born woman to be awarded the Croix de Guerre and the Legion of Honor, in recognition for her Red Cross work during WWII. Baker performed up until her death on Apr 12, 1975, at Paris, France.

BATTLE OF COLD HARBOR: ANNIVERSARY. June 3, 1864. Although Confederate general Robert E. Lee had placed his troops behind considerable breastworks, Union general Ulysses S. Grant launched an all-out attack on the Southern army in Virginia. More than 7,000 Union troops were killed within one-half hour of battle on the first attack. After a second unsuccessful attack, Grant's orders for a third assault were all but ignored. Battlefield tradition held that the first commander who sought a truce in order to tend to the wounded was the loser. Grant refused to admit defeat by seeking such a truce, and the wounded were left on the ground for three days following the battle. As a consequence, all but two of the thousands of wounded men died from either their wounds, hunger, thirst or exposure.

BRINKER, NORMAN: BIRTH ANNIVERSARY. June 3, 1931. Restaurant entrepreneur, born at Denver, CO. Lauded as "the most influential person in the restaurant industry" by *Nation's Restaurant News*. Innovator of casual-dining concept of full service for middle-class customers. Mainstreamed the salad bar. Created Steak & Ale (1966), conceived Bennigan's (1978) and grew Chili's from 28 restaurants to a 1,000-location chain from 1984 to 2001 under Brinker International, which also includes Maggiano's Little Italy and On the Border Mexican Grill. Initial funder and board member of the Susan G. Komen Breast Cancer Foundation, created by his wife and named for her sister in 1982. Died June 9, 2009, at Colorado Springs, CO.

CHIMBORAZO DAY. June 3. To bring the shape of Earth into focus by publicizing the fact that Mount Chimborazo, Ecuador, near the equator, pokes farther out into space than any other mountain on Earth, including Mount Everest. (The distance from sea level at the equator to the center of Earth is 13 miles greater than the radius to sea level at the North Pole. This means that New Orleans is about six miles farther from the center of Earth than is Lake Itasca at the headwaters of the Mississippi, so the Mississippi flows uphill.) (Created by Robert L. Birch, Pun Corps.)

CONFEDERATE MEMORIAL DAY IN KENTUCKY, LOUISIANA AND TENNESSEE. June 3. Ceremonial holiday on the birthday of Jefferson Davis. Also observed as Jefferson Davis Day in Kentucky and Confederate Decoration Day in Tennessee.

CURTIS, TONY: 95th BIRTH ANNIVERSARY. June 3, 1925. Film star from Hollywood's Golden Age, born Bernard Schwartz at the Bronx, NY. He was a master of both dramatic and comedic roles, garnering acclaim for such films as *The Defiant Ones* (1958), *Some Like It Hot* (1959) and *The Boston Strangler* (1968). He died at Henderson, NV, Sept 29, 2010.

DAVIS, JEFFERSON: BIRTH ANNIVERSARY. June 3, 1808. American statesman, US senator, only president of the Confederate States of America. Imprisoned May 10, 1865–May 13, 1867, but never brought to trial, deprived of rights of citizenship after the Civil War. Davis was born at Todd County, KY, and died at New Orleans, LA, Dec 6, 1889. His citizenship was restored, posthumously, Oct 17, 1978, when President Carter signed an amnesty bill. This bill, he said, "officially completes the long process of reconciliation that has reunited our people following the tragic conflict between the states." Davis's birth anniversary is observed in Florida, Kentucky and South Carolina on this day; in Alabama on the first Monday in June and in Mississippi on the last Monday in May. Davis's birth anniversary is observed as Confederate Decoration Day in Tennessee.

DEWHURST, COLLEEN: BIRTH ANNIVERSARY. June 3, 1924. Colleen Dewhurst was born at Quebec, Canada. Her 40-year career as an actress spanned stage, screen and television. After making her Broadway debut in Eugene O'Neill's *Desire Under the Elms* in 1952, she became the actress most associated with O'Neill's works in the later part of the 20th century, also performing in *Long Day's Journey into Night; Mourning Becomes Electra; Ah, Wilderness!* and *A Moon for the Misbegotten*, for which she won her second Tony Award. At the time of her death, she was president of Actor's Equity Association, the union for professional actors. She won three Emmy Awards. She died Aug 22, 1991, at South Salem, NY.

DREW, CHARLES RICHARD: BIRTH ANNIVERSARY. June 3, 1904. African-American physician who discovered how to store blood plasma and who organized the blood bank system in the US and UK during WWII. Born at Washington, DC, he was killed in an automobile accident near Burlington, NC, Apr 1, 1950.

GINSBERG, ALLEN: BIRTH ANNIVERSARY. June 3, 1926. Poet of the Beat Generation, social activist, born at Newark, NJ. Best known for "Howl" (published 1956) and "Kaddish" (published 1961). The sexual content of "Howl" caused the book to be impounded and Ginsberg to be charged with obscenity until a judge ruled that the work was not without "redeeming social importance." Recipient of the National Book Award, the Robert Frost Medal and the American Book Award, Ginsberg died Apr 5, 1997, at New York, NY.

GLOBAL RUNNING DAY. June 3. Since 2009, a day when runners everywhere declare their passion for running. The country's foremost running organizations work together with thousands of participants to celebrate the sport. Runners join in by planning a run, spreading the running bug to a friend, signing up for a race or setting a new goal. Annually, the first Wednesday in June. For info: Global Running Day. E-mail: runningday@nyrr.org. Web: www.runningday.org.

HOBART, GARRET AUGUSTUS: BIRTH ANNIVERSARY. June 3, 1844. 24th vice president of the US (1897–99), born at Long Branch, NJ. Died at Paterson, NJ, Nov 21, 1899.

JACK JOUETT'S RIDE: ANNIVERSARY. June 3, 1781. Jack Jouett made a heroic 45-mile ride on horseback during the night of June 3–4, 1781, to warn Virginia governor Thomas Jefferson and the Virginia legislature that the British were coming. Jouett rode from

	S	M	T	W	T	F	S
June		1	2	3	4	5	6
2020	7	8	9	10	11	12	13
	14	15	16	17	18	19	20
	21	22	23	24	25	26	27
	28	29	30				

a tavern in Louisa County to Charlottesville, VA, in about 6½ hours, arriving at Jefferson's home at dawn on June 4. Lieutenant Colonel Tarleton's British forces raided Charlottesville, but Jouett's warning gave the Americans time to escape. Jouett was born at Albemarle County, VA, Dec 7, 1754, and died at Bath, KY, in 1822 (exact date unknown).

KHOMEINI, AYATOLLAH RUHOLLAH: DEATH ANNIVERSARY. June 3, 1989. The Ayatollah Ruhollah Khomeini, leader of the Islamic Revolution, first Supreme Leader of Iran (1979–89), died at Tehran, Iran. The anniversary of his death is a national holiday in Iran.

"MIGHTY CASEY HAS STRUCK OUT": ANNIVERSARY. June 3, 1888. The famous comic baseball ballad "Casey at the Bat" was printed in the Sunday *San Francisco Examiner*. Appearing anonymously, it was written by Ernest L. Thayer. Recitation of "Casey at the Bat" became part of the repertoire of actor William DeWolf Hopper. The recitation took 5 minutes and 40 seconds. Hopper claimed to have recited it more than 10,000 times, the first being at Wallack's Theatre at New York, NY, in 1888. See also: "Thayer, Ernest Lawrence: Birth Anniversary" (Aug 14).

MISSION SAN CARLOS BORROMEO DE CARMELO: FOUNDING ANNIVERSARY. June 3, 1770. California mission to the Indians founded on this date.

OLDS, RANSOM: BIRTH ANNIVERSARY. June 3, 1864. American automobile inventor and manufacturer Olds was born at Geneva, OH. Founded the Olds Motor Works, which made Oldsmobile, the first affordable, mass-produced American car. It was also the first automobile produced in quantity with a progressive assembly system and composed of interchangeable parts. In a marketing innovation, Olds also introduced the policy of insisting that dealers pay cash for cars delivered to them, a practice that became standard and provided much-needed immediate capital for the fledgling automotive industry. Died Aug 26, 1950, at Lansing, MI.

SPACE MILESTONE: *GEMINI 4* (US). June 3, 1965. James McDivitt and Edward White made 66 orbits of Earth. White took the first space walk by an American and maneuvered 20 minutes outside the capsule.

UNITED NATIONS: WORLD BICYCLE DAY. June 3. First observed in 2018, this celebrates the bicycle as a simple, affordable, reliable, clean and environmentally fit sustainable means of transportation that can serve as a tool for development and as a means not just of transportation but also of access to education, health care and sport. (Res 72/272). For info: United Nations. Web: www.un.org/en/events/bicycleday.

ZOOT SUIT RIOTS: ANNIVERSARY. June 3–8, 1943. In Los Angeles, CA, simmering racial unease exploded as 200 white sailors stormed into East LA and began beating Hispanics in response to an earlier altercation between a few sailors and some street kids. The sailors targeted Zoot Suiters—youths outfitted in the defiant, exaggerated suit of their community (long jackets, wide trousers and ankle-length watch chains). The rioting grew as police either stood by or arrested the victims. The media, antagonistic to the Hispanic community, spurred on the violence with sensational headlines. Finally, military brass declared Los Angeles off-limits to its personnel and the LA City Council banned zoot suits. There were no deaths, but the injuries and mayhem were such that a special state committee was convened and First Lady Eleanor Roosevelt wrote in her newspaper column that the riots were symptomatic of a problem with deep roots.

BIRTHDAYS TODAY

Raúl Castro, 89, former president of Cuba (2008–18), born Holguín, Cuba, June 3, 1931.

Anderson Cooper, 53, journalist, television personality ("Anderson Cooper 360"), born New York, NY, June 3, 1967.

Hale S. Irwin, 75, golfer, born Joplin, MO, June 3, 1945.

Larry McMurtry, 84, author (*Terms of Endearment, Lonesome Dove, The Last Picture Show*), screenwriter (Oscar for *Brokeback Mountain*), born Wichita Falls, TX, June 3, 1936.

Rafael Nadal, 34, tennis player, born Manacor, Spain, June 3, 1986.

James Purefoy, 56, actor ("The Following," *Rome*), born Taunton, Somerset, England, June 3, 1964.

Scott Valentine, 62, actor ("Family Ties"), born Saratoga Springs, NY, June 3, 1958.

Jodie Whittaker, 38, actress ("Doctor Who," "Broadchurch," *Venus*), born Skelmanthorpe, England, June 3, 1982.

Deniece Williams, 69, singer, born Gary, IN, June 3, 1951.

Penelope Wilton, 74, actress ("Downton Abbey," "Doctor Who," *Shaun of the Dead*), born Scarborough, North Yorkshire, England, June 3, 1946.

June 4 — Thursday

DAY 156　　　　　　　　　　　　　　**210 REMAINING**

BATTLE OF MIDWAY: ANNIVERSARY. June 4–7, 1942. A Japanese task force attempted to capture Midway Island in the Central Pacific, but American bombers from Midway and from two nearby aircraft carriers sent the Japanese into retreat. The Japanese lost four carriers, two large cruisers and three destroyers. Midway was one of the most decisive naval battles of WWII. Japan never regained its margin in carrier strength, and the Central Pacific was made safe for American troops.

CHINA: TIANANMEN SQUARE MASSACRE: ANNIVERSARY. June 4, 1989. After almost a month and a half of student demonstrations for democracy, the Chinese government ordered its troops to open fire on the unarmed protestors at Tiananmen Square in Beijing. Under the cover of darkness, early June 4, troops opened fire on the assembled crowds, and armored personnel carriers rolled into the square, crushing many of the students as they lay sleeping in their tents. Although the government claimed that few died in the attack, estimates range from several hundred to several thousand casualties. In the following months thousands of demonstrators were rounded up and jailed.

FENDER, FREDDY: BIRTH ANNIVERSARY. June 4, 1937. Born Baldemar Huerta at San Benito, TX, to migrant farmworkers, Fender was a Grammy-winning balladeer who worked in country, R&B and Tex-Mex music styles—singing in both Spanish and English. In the 1970s, Fender had several number-one country hits, including "Before the Next Teardrop Falls" and "Wasted Days and Wasted Nights." He died Oct 14, 2006, at Corpus Christi, TX.

FINLAND: FLAG DAY. June 4. Finland's armed forces honor the June 4, 1867, birth anniversary of Carl Gustaf Mannerheim, military leader and sixth president of Finland.

FIRST FREE FLIGHT BY A WOMAN: ANNIVERSARY. June 4, 1784. Marie Thible, of Lyons, France, accompanied by a pilot (Monsieur Fleurant), became the first woman in history to fly in a free balloon. She drifted across Lyons in a balloon named *Le Gustave* (for King Gustav III of Sweden, who was watching the ascent). The balloon reached a height of 8,500 feet in a flight that lasted about 45 minutes. The event occurred one day short of a year after the first flight in history by a man. See also: "First Balloon Flight: Anniversary" (June 5).

GEORGE III: BIRTH ANNIVERSARY. June 4, 1738. As king of Great Britain and Ireland from 1760 to 1820, George III was also elector and, later, king of Hanover. His reign was uneven, marked by political instability and popularity that wavered. He alienated parliament and populace when he lost the American colonies in a costly war but was embraced as the embodiment of England during its war with France in 1793. Often called "The Mad King," George III suffered from periods of insanity, possibly from porphyria. After 1811 he was permanently insane. Born at London, England, he died Jan 29, 1820, at Windsor.

NEVADA STATE FAIR. June 4–7. Carson City, NV. Originally founded in 1874. Four days of fun, entertainment, carnival rides, culture, music and so much more in Nevada's great capital.. Est attendance: 60,000. For info: Nevada State Fair, 112 N Curry St, Carson City, NV 89703. Phone: (877) 916-FAIR. E-mail: Info@NevadaStateFair.org. Web: www.NevadaStateFair.org.

PULITZER PRIZES FIRST AWARDED: ANNIVERSARY. June 4, 1917. The first Pulitzer Prizes were awarded on this date: for biography, *Julia Ward Howe* by Laura E. Richards and Maude H. Elliott assisted by Florence H. Hall, and for history, *With Americans of Past and Present Days* by Jean Jules Jusserand, the French ambassador to the US. Prizes were also awarded for journalistic achievement.

ROME LIBERATED: ANNIVERSARY. June 4, 1944. The US 9th Army, commanded by General Mark Clark, entered the southern suburbs of Rome as the last of the German rear guard retreated from Mussolini's former capital. Fearful of a last-ditch effort by the Germans to hold the city, the populace remained behind closed doors as Clark's forces entered the Eternal City.

TONGA: EMANCIPATION DAY. June 4. National holiday. Commemorates independence from Britain in 1970.

UNITED NATIONS: INTERNATIONAL DAY OF INNOCENT CHILDREN VICTIMS OF AGGRESSION. June 4. On Aug 19, 1982, the General Assembly decided to commemorate June 4 of each year as a day to call attention to the urgent need to protect the rights of children. It reminds people that throughout the world there are many children suffering from different forms of abuse. Annually, June 4. For info: United Nations, Dept of Public Info, New York, NY 10017. Web: www.un.org.

US WOMEN'S OPEN (GOLF) CHAMPIONSHIP. June 4–7. Champions Golf Club, Houston, TX. For info: USGA, Golf House, Championship Dept, PO Box 708, Far Hills, NJ 07931-0708. Phone: (908) 234-2300. E-mail: champs@usga.org. Web: www.usga.org.

🎂 BIRTHDAYS TODAY

Cecilia Bartoli, 54, opera singer, born Rome, Italy, June 4, 1966.

Russell Brand, 45, comedian, actor (*Forgetting Sarah Marshall, Bedtime Stories*), born Grays, Essex, England, June 4, 1975.

James Callis, 49, actor ("Battlestar Galactica," *Bridget Jones's Diary*), born London, England, June 4, 1971.

Keith David, 64, actor (*Platoon, Barbershop,* "Jazz"), born New York, NY, June 4, 1956.

Eldra DeBarge, 59, musician, born Grand Rapids, MI, June 4, 1961.

Bruce Dern, 84, actor (*The Hateful Eight, Nebraska, Coming Home, That Championship Season*), born Chicago, IL, June 4, 1936.

Joe Hill, 48, author (*The Fireman, Horns, 20th Century Ghosts*), comic book writer ("Locke & Key"), born Joseph Hillstrom King at Bangor, ME, June 4, 1972.

Andrea Jaeger, 55, former tennis player, born Chicago, IL, June 4, 1965.

Angelina Jolie, 45, actress (Oscar for *Girl, Interrupted; The Tourist, Mr & Mrs Smith, Lara Croft: Tomb Raider*), director, born Los Angeles, CA, June 4, 1975.

Mike Lee, 49, US Senator (R, Utah), born Mesa, AZ, June 4, 1971.

Evan Lysacek, 35, Olympic figure skater, born Chicago, IL, June 4, 1985.

T.J. Miller, 39, actor ("Silicon Valley," *Office Christmas Party, Cloverfield*), comedian, born Denver, CO, June 4, 1981.

Michelle Phillips, 75, singer (The Mamas and the Papas), actress ("Knots Landing"), born Long Beach, CA, June 4, 1945.

Parker Stevenson, 67, actor ("Falcon Crest," "Baywatch," *Lifeguard*), born Philadelphia, PA, June 4, 1953.

Robin Lord Taylor, 42, actor ("Gotham"), born Shueyville, IA, June 4, 1978.

Dr. Ruth Westheimer, 91, television and radio host for shows on sexual relationships, born Frankfurt, Germany, June 4, 1929.

Scott Wolf, 52, actor ("Party of Five," *The Evening Star*), born Boston, MA, June 4, 1968.

Noah Wyle, 49, actor ("Falling Skies," "ER," *The Librarian*), born Hollywood, CA, June 4, 1971.

June 5 — Friday

DAY 157	209 REMAINING

AIDS FIRST NOTED: ANNIVERSARY. June 5, 1981. The Centers for Disease Control first described a new illness striking gay men in a newsletter on June 5, 1981. On July 27, 1982, the CDC adopted Acquired Immune Deficiency Syndrome as the official name for the new disease. The virus that causes AIDS was identified in 1983 and in May 1985 was named Human Immunodeficiency Virus (HIV) by the International Committee on the Taxonomy of Viruses. The first person killed by this disease in the developed world died in 1959. More than 678,500 Americans have died of AIDS. Worldwide, more than 39 million people have died of AIDS. About 36.9 million people worldwide are living with HIV/AIDS.

APPLE II COMPUTER RELEASED: ANNIVERSARY. June 5, 1977. The Apple II computer, with 4K of memory, went on sale for $1,298. Its predecessor, the Apple I, was sold largely to electronics hobbyists the previous year. Apple released the Macintosh computer Jan 24, 1984.

BAHAMAS: LABOR DAY. June 5. Public holiday. First Friday in June celebrated with parades, displays and picnics.

June 2020	S	M	T	W	T	F	S
		1	2	3	4	5	6
	7	8	9	10	11	12	13
	14	15	16	17	18	19	20
	21	22	23	24	25	26	27
	28	29	30				

BOYD, WILLIAM: BIRTH ANNIVERSARY. June 5, 1895. Born at Hendrysburg, OH, Boyd went to Hollywood in 1919 and got a job as a film extra. In 1935 he got the role of Hopalong Cassidy in a series of popular Westerns. He made 66 of these films between 1935 and 1948. Some of them were edited and shown on television; Boyd then made some episodes especially for TV. Died at Hollywood, CA, Sept 12, 1972. See also: "'Hopalong Cassidy' TV Premiere: Anniversary" (June 24).

DENMARK: CONSTITUTION DAY. June 5. National holiday. Commemorates Denmark's becoming a constitutional monarchy in 1849 and the new constitution adopted in 1953.

ENGLAND: INVESTEC DERBY FESTIVAL. June 5–6. Epsom Downs, Surrey. Ladies' Day is June 5 and Derby Day is June 6. The Derby dates back to 1780 and is still ranked the greatest flat race in the world. With winnings of 1.25 million pounds, the Investec Derby has one of the biggest prizes in UK racing, matched only by the prestige that victory brings. It remains the race that everyone wants to win, as horses and riders push themselves to the limit around the unique and challenging course. For info: Investec Derby Festival. Web: www.epsomderby.co.uk.

FIRST BALLOON FLIGHT: ANNIVERSARY. June 5, 1783. The first public demonstration of a hot-air balloon flight took place at Annonay, France, where brothers Joseph and Jacques Montgolfier succeeded in launching the 33-foot-diameter *globe aerostatique* that they had invented. The unmanned balloon rose an estimated 1,500 feet and traveled, wind-borne, about 7,500 feet before landing after a 10-minute flight—the first sustained flight of any object achieved by man.

HARVARD MILK DAYS™ FESTIVAL. June 5–7. Harvard, IL. This salute to the dairy farmer includes a parade, evening entertainment, business expo, milk-drinking contest, antique farm tractor display, golf outing, carnival, fireworks, 10k milk run, 5k run, kids dash, junior dairy cattle show, talent show, food and wee farm. Annually, the first full weekend in June. Est attendance: 30,000. For info: Harvard Milk Days, Inc, PO Box 325, Harvard, IL 60033-0325. Phone: (815) 943-4614. E-mail: info@milkdays.com. Web: www.milkdays.com.

HIV LONG-TERM SURVIVORS AWARENESS DAY. June 5. Created in 2014 by Tez Anderson, this day celebrates those who have defied the odds by living with HIV for decades. June 5 is a national day of storytelling—the stories of survivors' lives and resilience. Annually, June 5—the date in 1981 when the CDC first noted the disease. For info: Let's Kick ASS—AIDS Survivor Syndrome. Web: https://medium.com/hiv-long-term-survivors-awareness-day-hltsad/2019/home.

IRAN: FIFTEENTH OF KHORDAD. June 5. National holiday. Commemorates the deaths of Islamic clerics in a clash with the shah's forces in 1963.

KENNEDY, ROBERT F.: ASSASSINATION ANNIVERSARY. June 5, 1968. Senator Kennedy was shot while campaigning for the Democratic presidential nomination at Los Angeles, CA; he died the following day. Sirhan Sirhan was convicted of his murder.

KEYNES, JOHN MAYNARD: BIRTH ANNIVERSARY. June 5, 1883. British economist born at Cambridge, England. Author of *Treatise on Money* and *The General Theory of Employment, Interest and Money*, which focused on "expansionist" economic policy. Died at Firle, England, Apr 21, 1946.

LUNAR ECLIPSE. June 5. Penumbral eclipse of the moon. Visible in Africa, Indian Ocean, Asia.

MOON PHASE: FULL MOON. June 5. Moon enters Full Moon phase at 3:12 PM, EDT.

NATIONAL DONUT DAY. June 5. Founded in 1938 by the Salvation Army for fundraising during the Great Depression, National Donut Day is now an annual tradition. During WWI, doughnuts were served to doughboys by the Salvation Army. Later, symbolic paper "donuts" were given to charitable contributors. This day now celebrates the doughnut itself. Annually, the first Friday in June.

OLD TIME MUSIC OZARK HERITAGE FESTIVAL. June 5–6. West Plains, MO. Celebrate the distinctive culture of the Ozark Highlands. Old-time music performances (with headliners), artisans in action, exhibits and activities. Jig dance competition, mule jumping competition, cooking stage, Brush Arbor, youth talent competition and musical workshops. For info: Ozark Heritage Welcome Center, 2999 Porter Wagoner Blvd, West Plains, MO 65775. Phone: (888) 256-8835. E-mail: tourism@westplains.net. Web: www.oldtimemusic.org.

SCARRY, RICHARD MCCLURE: BIRTH ANNIVERSARY. June 5, 1919. Author and illustrator of children's books born at Boston, MA. Two widely known books of the more than 250 authored by Scarry are *Richard Scarry's Best Word Book Ever* (1965) and *Richard Scarry's Please & Thank You* (1973). The pages are crowded with small animal characters that live like humans. More than 100 million copies of his books have sold worldwide. Died Apr 30, 1994, at Gstaad, Switzerland.

SIX-DAY WAR: ANNIVERSARY. June 5–11, 1967. The Six-Day War between Israel and its Arab neighbors (Egypt, Syria and Jordan) resulted in Israeli control of the Sinai Peninsula, Gaza Strip, Golan Heights and the West Bank (with East Jerusalem). The United Nations mediated a cease-fire on June 11.

SMITH, ADAM: BIRTH ANNIVERSARY. June 5, 1723. (Old Style date.) Scottish economist and philosopher, author of *An Enquiry into the Nature and Causes of the Wealth of Nations* (1776), born at Kirkcaldy, Fifeshire, Scotland. Died at Edinburgh, Scotland, July 17, 1790. "Consumption," he wrote, "is the sole end and purpose of production; and the interest of the producer ought to be attended to only so far as it may be necessary for promoting that of the consumer."

STRAWBERRY MOON. June 5. So called by Native American tribes of New England and the Great Lakes because at this time of the year the strawberry ripened. The June Full Moon.

SUMMER FARM TOY SHOW. June 5–6. National Farm Toy Museum and Beckman High School, Dyersville, IA. 35th annual. This two-day show attracts farm toy dealers and collectors from all over the country who buy, sell and trade in farm toys. Thousands of farm toy collectibles and farm machinery memorabilia can be found for purchase. Annual show events include a 50-mile tractor ride, farm toy model contest and diorama display contest, colorful tractor parade through downtown and kids' pedal pull. Est attendance: 2,500. For info: National Farm Toy Museum, 1110 16th Ave Ct SE, Dyersville, IA 52040. Phone: (563) 875-2727. E-mail: farmtoys@dyersville.com. Web: www.summerfarmtoyshow.com.

TEXAS FOLKLIFE FESTIVAL. June 5–7. San Antonio, TX. Provides an entertaining and historic understanding of the crafts, art, food, music, history and heritage of the more than 40 different cultures and ethnic groups that settled and developed the state of Texas. Est attendance: 50,000. For info: Texas Folklife Festival, Institute of Texan Cultures, 801 E Cesar E. Chavez Blvd, San Antonio, TX 78205-3296. Phone: (210) 458-2224. Fax: (210) 458-2113. Web: www.texasfolklifefestival.org.

UNITED NATIONS: WORLD ENVIRONMENT DAY. June 5. Observed annually June 5, the anniversary of the opening of the UN Conference on the Human Environment held in Stockholm in 1972, which led to establishment of the UN Environment Programme, based in Nairobi. The General Assembly has urged marking the day with activities reaffirming concern for the preservation and

enhancement of the environment. For info: United Nations, Dept of Public Info, New York, NY 10017. Web: www.un.org.

WINDSURFING REGATTA MUSIC FESTIVAL. June 5–7. Worthington, MN. Windsurfing on Lake Okabena. Regatta, surfing instruction, music on the beach. Beer garden and food vendors. Est attendance: 8,000. For info: Worthington Okabena Windsurfers, 1121 Third Ave, Worthington, MN 56187. Phone: (507) 372-2919. E-mail: info@worthingtonwindsurfing.net. Web: www.worthingtonwind-surfing.net.

🎂 BIRTHDAYS TODAY

Chad Allen, 46, actor ("Dr. Quinn, Medicine Woman"), born Cerritos, CA, June 5, 1974.

Jill Biden, 69, wife of former US vice president Joseph R. Biden, Jr, born Hammonton, NJ, June 5, 1951.

Margaret Drabble, 81, author (*Jerusalem the Golden, The Millstone*), born Sheffield, Yorkshire, England, June 5, 1939.

Ken Follett, 71, author (*The Pillars of the Earth, The Eye of the Needle*), born Cardiff, Wales, June 5, 1949.

Kathleen Kennedy, 67, film producer (*Lincoln, Jurassic Park, Schindler's List*), film executive (president of Lucasfilm), born Berkeley, CA, June 5, 1953.

Brian McKnight, 51, singer, born Buffalo, NY, June 5, 1969.

Bill Moyers, 86, journalist ("Bill Moyers' Journal"), born Hugo, OK, June 5, 1934.

Suze Orman, 69, author, television personality, speaker, born Chicago, IL, June 5, 1951.

Rick Riordan, Jr, 56, author (*The Lightning Thief*, Percy Jackson series, *The Maze of Bones*), born San Antonio, TX, June 5, 1964.

Mark Wahlberg, 49, actor (*The Fighter, The Departed, Boogie Nights*), former rapper, born Dorchester, MA, June 5, 1971.

June 6 — Saturday

DAY 158   208 REMAINING

BELMONT STAKES. June 6. Belmont Park, NY. 152nd annual. Final race of the "Triple Crown" was inaugurated in 1867. Traditionally run on the fifth Saturday after Kentucky Derby (third Saturday after Preakness). Est attendance: 90,000. For info: Press Office, New York Racing Assn, PO Box 90, Jamaica, NY 11417. Phone: (718) 659-2244. E-mail: info@nyrainc.com. Web: www.belmontstakes.com.

BONZA BOTTLER DAY®. June 6. To celebrate when the number of the day is the same as the number of the month. Bonza Bottler Day® is an excuse to have a party at least once a month. For more information see Jan 1. For info: Gail Berger, Bonza Bottler Day. Phone: (864) 201-3988. E-mail: bonza@bonzabottlerday.com. Web: www.bonzabottlerday.com.

CASTROVILLE ARTICHOKE FESTIVAL. June 6–7. Monterey County Fair and Event Center, Monterey, CA. 61st annual. Annually, in the Artichoke Capital of the World. Events include artichoke eating contest, wine tasting, chef demos, agro-art contest, canasta contest, live entertainment and field tours. Est attendance: 32,000. For info: Castroville Artichoke Festivals, Inc, PO Box 1041,

Castroville, CA 95012. Phone: (888) 808-7707 or (831) 633-2465. E-mail: info@artichokefestival.org. Web: www.artichokefestival.org.

D-DAY: ANNIVERSARY. June 6, 1944. In the early morning hours Allied forces landed in Normandy on the north coast of France. In an operation that took months of planning, a fleet of 2,727 ships of every description converged from British ports from Wales to the North Sea. Operation *Overlord* involved 2,000,000 tons of war materials, including more than 50,000 tanks, armored cars, jeeps, trucks and half-tracks. The US alone sent 1,700,000 fighting men. The Germans believed the invasion would not take place under the adverse weather conditions of this early June day. But as the sun came up, the village of Saint Mère Église was liberated by American parachutists, and by nightfall the landing of 155,000 Allies attested to the success of D-Day. The long-awaited second front had at last materialized.

DENMARK: EEL FESTIVAL. June 6–7. Jyllinge (near Roskilde). Festival celebrated since 1968. Every restaurant and pub in town serves delicious fried eel. Other entertainments include theater, sports, tattoo bands, sailing competitions, flea markets and fireworks. Annually, the first weekend in June.

FIRST DRIVE-IN MOVIE OPENS: ANNIVERSARY. June 6, 1933. Richard M. Hollingshead, Jr, opened America's first drive-in movie theater in Camden, NJ, on this date. At the height of their popularity in 1958, there were more than 4,000 drive-ins across America. Today there are only 330 open.

HALE, NATHAN: BIRTH ANNIVERSARY. June 6, 1755. American patriot Nathan Hale was born at Coventry, CT. During the battles for New York in the American Revolution, he volunteered to seek military intelligence behind enemy lines and was captured on the night of Sept 21, 1776. In an audience before General William Howe, Hale admitted he was an American officer and was ordered hanged the following morning. Although some question them, his dying words, "I only regret that I have but one life to lose for my country," have become a symbol of American patriotism. He was hanged Sept 22, 1776, at Manhattan, NY.

INTERNATIONAL CLOTHESLINE WEEK. June 6–13. The public is asked to join together to save energy by hanging clothes to dry instead of using their electric dryers. Annually, the week beginning the first Saturday in June, Saturday to Saturday. (Created by Gary Drisdelle.)

KHACHATURIAN, ARAM (ILICH): BIRTH ANNIVERSARY. June 6, 1903. Armenian musician and composer, noted for compositions based on folk music and legend, born at Tbilisi, Georgia, USSR. Died at Moscow, USSR, May 1, 1978.

KOREA: MEMORIAL DAY. June 6. Nation pays tribute to the war dead, and memorial services are held at the National Cemetery in Seoul. Legally recognized Korean holiday.

MALAYSIA: HEAD OF STATE'S OFFICIAL BIRTHDAY. June 6. National holiday. The Yang di-Pertuan Agong's official birthday is observed on the first Saturday in June (not on the elected ruler's actual birthday).

NATIONAL TRAILS DAY. June 6. National Trails Day is the only nationally coordinated event designed to unite all muscle-powered trail activities with the goal of connecting more people to

June 2020	S	M	T	W	T	F	S
		1	2	3	4	5	6
	7	8	9	10	11	12	13
	14	15	16	17	18	19	20
	21	22	23	24	25	26	27
	28	29	30				

trails. Each year, on the first Saturday in June, American Hiking Society and the trails community invite Americans of all ages and abilities to find their own adventure at one of the thousands of events hosted in every state. Events include guided hikes, bike and equestrian rides, trail races, paddling trips, trail stewardship projects, special exhibits and more. For info: Program Outreach, American Hiking Society, 8605 Second Ave, Silver Spring, MD 20910. Phone: (800) 972-8608. E-mail: info@americanhiking.org. Web: www.americanhiking.org.

NATIONAL YO-YO DAY. June 6. A celebration of yo-yos and yo-yo playing held on the birth anniversary of Donald F. Duncan (1892–1971), the entrepreneur (founder of the Duncan Toys Company) who was the great popularizer of the toy. A day to practice the sleeper, walk the dog, skin the cat, rock the baby or around the world. Created by Daniel Volk, a former yo-yo demonstrator, in 1990.

PRINTERS ROW LIT FEST. June 6–7. South Dearborn Street between Congress and Polk, Chicago, IL. Since 1985. More than 200 booksellers and publishers from all over the US and Canada fill the streets with new, used, rare and antiquarian books for sale; demonstrations of paper making, paper marbling and book binding; author readings, panel discussions, poetry tent and an elaborate children's program are all part of the free programs. Food, music and much more at the largest free book event in the Midwest. Est attendance: 125,000. For info: Printers Row Book Fair. E-mail: printersrowlitfestival@gmail.com. Web: www.printersrowlitfest.org.

PROPOSITION 13: ANNIVERSARY. June 6, 1978. California voters (65 percent of them) supported a primary election ballot initiative to cut property taxes 57 percent. Regarded as a possible omen of things to come across the country—a taxpayers' revolt against high taxes and government spending.

PUSHKIN, ALEXANDER: BIRTH ANNIVERSARY. June 6, 1799. Nobleman, poet and author born at Moscow, Russia. During periods of exile created some of his greatest work, notably his "novel in verse," *Eugene Onegin*. Other well-known works include *Boris Godunov, Queen of Spades, Tales of Belkin* and *The Bronze Horseman*. Goaded into a duel by an admirer of his wife on Jan 27, 1837, Pushkin died of his injury on Jan 29, 1837, at St. Petersburg, Russia. His birthday is widely observed in Russia.

SCOTT, ROBERT FALCON: BIRTH ANNIVERSARY. June 6, 1868. British naval officer and polar explorer, born at Devonport, England. Led the ill-starred expedition to the South Pole that arrived on Jan 18, 1912—one month after Norwegian Roald Amundsen's team became the first humans to set foot on the South Pole. Scott and four team members died on the return journey and their bodies were found in November 1912. Scott's diary, with a final entry of Mar 29, 1912, had a message to the public: "Had we lived, I should have had a tale to tell of the hardihood, endurance, and courage of my companions which would have stirred the heart of every Englishman. These rough notes and our dead bodies must tell the tale."

SECURITIES AND EXCHANGE COMMISSION CREATED: ANNIVERSARY. June 6, 1934. President Franklin D. Roosevelt signed the Securities Exchange Act, which established the SEC. Wall Street had operated almost unfettered since the end of the 18th century. However, the stock market crash of 1929 necessitated regulation of the exchanges. The SEC is composed of five members appointed by the president of the US.

"SEX AND THE CITY" TV PREMIERE: ANNIVERSARY. June 6, 1998. HBO's modern comedy of manners focused on four fashionable women navigating the perilous waters of New York City's dating scene. Starred Sarah Jessica Parker (Carrie Bradshaw), Kristin Davis (Charlotte York), Kim Cattrall (Samantha Jones) and Cynthia Nixon (Miranda Hobbes). More than 10 million viewers tuned in to watch the 94th and final episode on Feb 22, 2004.

SPACE MILESTONE: *SOYUZ 11* (USSR). June 6, 1971. Launched with cosmonauts G.T. Dobrovolsky, V.N. Volkov and V.I. Patsayev, who died during the return landing June 30, 1971, after a 24-day space flight. *Soyuz 11* had docked at *Salyut* orbital space station June 7–29; the cosmonauts entered the space station for the first time and conducted scientific experiments. First humans to die in space.

SWEDEN: NATIONAL DAY. June 6. Public holiday since 2005. Commemorates two key dates in Swedish sovereignty—both falling on June 6: the day Gustavus I (Gustavus Vasa) ascended the throne of Sweden in 1523 and the day in 1809 when Sweden adopted a new constitution—one that established civil rights and liberties. Originally observed as Flag Day beginning in 1916, then changed to National Day in 1983.

"20/20" TV PREMIERE: ANNIVERSARY. June 6, 1978. An hourly newsmagazine developed by ABC to compete with CBS's "60 Minutes." Its original hosts, Harold Hayes and Robert Hughes, were cut after the first show and replaced by Hugh Downs. Barbara Walters became coanchor in 1984. The show consisted of investigative and background reports. Contributors to the show have included Tom Jarriel, Sylvia Chase, Geraldo Rivera, Thomas Hoving, John Stossel, Lynn Sherr and Stone Phillips.

UNITED NATIONS: RUSSIAN LANGUAGE DAY. June 6. Russian is one of the United Nations Secretariat's six official and working languages (English, French, Arabic, Chinese, Russian, Spanish). This celebratory day is observed on the birth anniversary of Alexander Pushkin (June 6, 1799 [NS, May 26 OS]), founder of modern Russian literature. Annually, June 6. For info: United Nations. Web: www.un.org/ru/events/russianlanguageday.

YMCA FOUNDED: ANNIVERSARY. June 6, 1844. In London, England, George Williams, the head of a draper's shop who was concerned about the vice and squalor of the urban city, founded the Young Men's Christian Association to offer an alternative, safe, Christian social environment for young men. (The YWCA was founded independently in 1855.) Williams was later knighted for his efforts. The YMCA is now an international organization.

🎂 BIRTHDAYS TODAY

Maria Alyokhina, 32, political activist, musician (Pussy Riot), born Moscow, USSR (now Russia), June 6, 1988.

Sandra Bernhard, 65, actress (*The King of Comedy*), performer, born Flint, MI, June 6, 1955.

Marsha Blackburn, 68, US Senator (R, Tennessee), born Marsha Wedgeworth at Laurel, MS, June 6, 1952.

Gary U.S. Bonds, 81, singer, songwriter, born Gary Anderson at Jacksonville, FL, June 6, 1939.

Bjorn Borg, 64, Hall of Fame tennis player, born Sodertalje, Sweden, June 6, 1956.

Marian Wright Edelman, 81, President of the Children's Defense Fund, civil rights activist, born Bennettsville, SC, June 6, 1939.

Harvey Fierstein, 66, actor/playwright (Tonys for *Hairspray, La Cage aux Folles* and *Torch Song Trilogy*), born Brooklyn, NY, June 6, 1954.

Kenny G, 64, saxophone player, born Kenny Gorelick at Seattle, WA, June 6, 1956.

Paul Giamatti, 53, actor ("Billions," "John Adams," *Sideways, American Splendor*), born New York, NY, June 6, 1967.

Jason Isaacs, 57, actor (Harry Potter films, "Case Histories," "Brotherhood"), born Liverpool, England, June 6, 1963.

Amanda Pays, 61, actress ("Max Headroom," *Exposure*), born Berkshire, England, June 6, 1959.

June 7 — Sunday

DAY 159   **207 REMAINING**

APGAR, VIRGINIA: BIRTH ANNIVERSARY. June 7, 1909. Dr. Apgar developed the simple assessment method that permits doctors and nurses to evaluate newborns while they are still in the delivery room to identify those in need of immediate medical care. The Apgar score was first published in 1953, and the Perinatal Section of the American Academy of Pediatrics is named for Dr. Apgar. Born at Westfield, NJ, Apgar died Aug 7, 1974, at New York, NY.

BED BUG AWARENESS WEEK. June 7–13. Bed bugs continue to plague Americans as they infest hotels, schools, college dorms, residences and other places where people gather. A 2013 survey conducted by the NPMA and the University of Kentucky found that nearly 100 percent of pest professionals had encountered bed bugs in the past year, a number that has steadily risen over a 10-year period. In an effort to encourage public education about this resilient pest, NPMA launched this week to spread awareness, promote public vigilance and provide essential prevention advice. For info: National Pest Management Assn, 10460 North St, Fairfax, VA 22030. Phone: (703) 352-6762. Fax: (703) 352-3031. E-mail: NPMATeam@vaultcommunications.com. Web: www.pestworld.org.

BOONE DAY. June 7. Each year on June 7, the Kentucky Historical Society celebrates the anniversary of the day in 1767 when Daniel Boone, America's most famous frontiersman, reportedly first sighted the land that would become Kentucky. The June 7 date is taken from the book *The Discovery, Settlement and Present State of Kentucky*, by John Filson, published in 1784, with an appendix titled "The Adventures of Colonel Daniel Boone." The information in the appendix supposedly originated with Boone, although Filson is the actual author. The work is not considered completely reliable by historians.

BRADDOCK, JAMES: BIRTH ANNIVERSARY. June 7, 1906. James Walter Braddock, boxer, born at New York, NY. Braddock rose from the ranks of undistinguished fighters to win three key bouts in 1934 and 1935 that propelled him to a match for the heavyweight title. He upset the defending champion, Max Baer, on June 13, 1935, remained inactive for two years and then lost his first title defense to Joe Louis. Died at North Bergen, NJ, Nov 29, 1974.

BROOKS, GWENDOLYN: BIRTH ANNIVERSARY. June 7, 1917. Famed African-American poet Brooks was born at Topeka, KS. Her poems and novels portrayed ordinary urban black life and commented on racism, poverty, social protest and revolution, the latter of which reflect her pivotal role in the Black Arts Movement. Experimentation with form, technique and language give a breadth to her oeuvre (notably *Maud Martha* [1953], *The Bean Eaters* [1960]) to which few others can attest. The first black writer, male or female, to win the Pulitzer Prize (*Annie Allen*, 1950), Brooks was Library of Congress' Poet Laureate during 1985–86 and received the National Endowment for the Arts' Lifetime Achievement Award in 1989. She died at Chicago, IL, on Dec 3, 2000.

CELEBRATION OF THE ARTS. June 7. Hurless Barton Park, Yorba Linda, CA. A fine arts and music festival for all ages. More than 100 exhibitors, art demonstrations and hands-on activities. Continuous entertainment includes dance, drama, bands and choirs. Free event. Annually, the first Sunday in June. Est attendance: 3,000. For info: Yorba Linda Arts Alliance, PO Box 1037, Yorba Linda, CA 92885. Phone: (714) 996-1960. E-mail: ylartsalliance@aol.com. Web: www.artsyl.org.

GAUGUIN, (EUGENE HENRI) PAUL: BIRTH ANNIVERSARY. June 7, 1848. French painter born at Paris, France. Formerly a stockbroker, he became a painter in his middle age and three years later renounced his life at Paris to move to Tahiti. He is remembered best for his broad, flat tones and bold colors. Gauguin died May 8, 1903, at Atoana on the island of Hiva Oa in the Marquesas.

ITALY: GIOCO DEL PONTE. June 7. Pisa. The first Sunday in June is set aside for the Battle of the Bridge, a medieval parade and a contest for possession of the bridge.

JAPAN: DAY OF THE RICE GOD. June 7. Chiyoda. Annual rice-transplanting festival observed on the first Sunday in June. Centuries-old rural folk ritual revived in 1930s and celebrated with colorful costumes, parades, music, dancing and prayers to the Shinto rice god Wbai-sama.

MACKINTOSH, CHARLES RENNIE: BIRTH ANNIVERSARY. June 7, 1868. Born at Glasgow, Scotland, Mackintosh was an influential architect and designer. He developed a distinct style that was highly influenced by Japanese art and architecture blended with Art Nouveau designs. Along with his wife, artist Margaret MacDonald, he also developed styles for interior design, furniture, textiles and other household items. He died at London, England, Dec 10, 1928.

MALTA: NATIONAL DAY. June 7. National Day, or (in Maltese) Sette Giugno.

MARTIN, DEAN: BIRTH ANNIVERSARY. June 7, 1917. Actor/singer Dean Martin was born Dino Paul Crocetti, at Steubenville, OH. Martin's career was barely moving in 1946, when he met Jerry Lewis. Together they formed an unforgettable comedy act that carried them to dizzying heights of success. When the team broke up, Martin found continued success as a singer as well as a Hollywood film and TV star. Signature songs include "Everybody Loves Somebody," "That's Amore" and "Volare." He died Dec 25, 1995, at Beverly Hills, CA.

NATIONAL BUSINESS ETIQUETTE WEEK. June 7–13. 14th annual. A week to recognize the need for the proper business etiquette necessary to compete in the growing global marketplace. Review everything from how to network to the proper handshake to how to remember names. Check the proper forms of address in business as well as government, military and academic areas. Annually, the first full week in June. For info: The Protocol School of Washington, PO Box 676, Columbia, SC 29202. Phone: (877) 766-3757. E-mail: info@psow.edu. Web: www.psow.edu.

NATIONAL CANCER SURVIVORS DAY. June 7. The 33rd annual celebration of life. Hundreds of communities nationwide honor survivors who are living with and beyond cancer. Annually, the first Sunday in June. For info: Natl Cancer Survivors Day Foundation, PO Box 682285, Franklin, TN 37068-2285. Phone: (615) 794-3006. E-mail: info@ncsd.org. Web: www.ncsd.org.

ORTHODOX PENTECOST. June 7. Observed by Eastern Orthodox churches.

PRINCE: BIRTH ANNIVERSARY. June 7, 1958. The prolific, stylish music artist and dynamic guitarist was born Prince Rogers Nelson at Minneapolis, MN. The "Purple One" released 39 studio albums and such chart-topping singles as "When Doves Cry," "Let's Go Crazy," "Kiss" and many more. Besides ruling the music charts in the 1990s and beyond with his infectious pop-funk, Prince was a savvy businessman, establishing his own label, building a recording studio and leading the way for artists to retain their creative

June 2020	S	M	T	W	T	F	S
		1	2	3	4	5	6
	7	8	9	10	11	12	13
	14	15	16	17	18	19	20
	21	22	23	24	25	26	27
	28	29	30				

rights. Prince died at his Paisley Park home/studio at Chanhassen, MN, on Apr 21, 2016.

SUPREME COURT STRIKES DOWN CONNECTICUT LAW BANNING CONTRACEPTION: 55th ANNIVERSARY. June 7, 1965. In *Griswold v Connecticut*, the Supreme Court guaranteed the right to privacy, including the freedom from government intrusion into matters of birth control.

TANDY, JESSICA: BIRTH ANNIVERSARY. June 7, 1909. Born at London, England, Tandy was an acclaimed stage actress who often collaborated with her husband, Hume Cronyn. She originated the role of Blanche DuBois in Tennessee Williams's *A Streetcar Named Desire* (1947) and was awarded a Tony. Her other Tony Awards came for her work in *The Gin Game* (1977) and *Foxfire* (1982). Also a frequent film actress, she won an Academy Award for her leading role in *Driving Miss Daisy* (1989). She continued to work up until her death on Sept 11, 1994, at Easton, CT.

TRINITY SUNDAY. June 7. Christian Holy Day on the Sunday after Pentecost commemorates the Holy Trinity, the three divine persons—Father, Son and Holy Spirit—in one God. See also: "Pentecost" (May 31).

🧁 BIRTHDAYS TODAY

Roberto Alagna, 57, opera singer, born Clichy-sous-Bois, Seine-Saint-Denis, France, June 7, 1963.

Michael Cera, 32, actor (*Scott Pilgrim vs the World, Juno*, "Arrested Development"), born Brompton, ON, Canada, June 7, 1988.

Louise Erdrich, 66, author (*Love Medicine, The Beet Queen*), born Little Falls, MN, June 7, 1954.

Bear Grylls, 46, television personality ("Man vs Wild"), author, born Isle of Wight, England, June 7, 1974.

Bill Hader, 42, comedian, actor ("Barry," "Saturday Night Live," *Trainwreck, Adventureland*), born Tulsa, OK, June 7, 1978.

Damien Hirst, 55, artist (*The Physical Impossibility of Death in the Mind of Someone Living*), born Bristol, England, June 7, 1965.

Allen Iverson, 45, former basketball player, born Hampton, VA, June 7, 1975.

James Ivory, 92, film director (*The Remains of the Day, Howards End, A Room with a View*), screenwriter (Oscar for *Call Me by Your Name*), producer, born Berkeley, CA, June 7, 1928.

Jenny Jones, 74, talk show host, born London, ON, Canada, June 7, 1946.

Tom Jones, 80, singer, born Thomas Woodward at Pontypridd, Wales, June 7, 1940.

Anna Kournikova, 39, former tennis player, born Moscow, USSR (now Russia), June 7, 1981.

Bill Kreutzmann, Jr, 74, drummer, singer, cofounder of The Grateful Dead, born Palo Alto, CA, June 7, 1946.

Mike Modano, 50, former hockey player, born Livonia, MI, June 7, 1970.

Liam Neeson, 68, actor (*Taken, Kinsey, Ethan Frome, Schindler's List*), born Ballymena, Northern Ireland, June 7, 1952.

Orhan Pamuk, 68, author (*My Name Is Red*), Nobel Prize in Literature recipient, professor, born Istanbul, Turkey, June 7, 1952.

Mike Pence, 61, 48th Vice President of the US, former governor of Indiana (R), born Columbus, IN, June 7, 1959.

John Napier Turner, 91, 17th prime minister of Canada (1984), born Richmond, Surrey, England, June 7, 1929.

June 8 — Monday

DAY 160   **206 REMAINING**

AMERICAN HEROINE REWARDED: ANNIVERSARY. June 8, 1697. On Mar 16, 1697, in an attack on Haverhill, MA, Indians captured Hannah Duston and killed her baby, also killing or capturing 39 others. After being taken to an Indian camp, she escaped on Apr 29 after killing 10 Indians with a tomahawk and scalping them as proof of her deed. On June 8 her husband was awarded, on her behalf, the sum of 25 pounds for her heroic efforts, the first public award to a woman in America.

ATTACK ON THE USS *LIBERTY*: ANNIVERSARY. June 8, 1967. At 2 PM local time, the unescorted US intelligence ship USS *Liberty*, sailing in international waters off the Egyptian coast, was attacked without warning by Israeli jet planes and three Israeli torpedo boats. It was strafed and hit repeatedly by rockets, cannon, napalm and finally a torpedo. Out of a crew of 294 Americans, there were 34 dead and 171 wounded. Israel apologized, claiming mistaken identity, but surviving crew members charged that it was a deliberate attack by Israel and cover-up by US authorities.

BILL OF RIGHTS PROPOSED: ANNIVERSARY. June 8, 1789. The Bill of Rights, which led to the first 10 amendments to the US Constitution, was first proposed by James Madison.

BUSH, BARBARA: 95th BIRTH ANNIVERSARY. June 8, 1925. Barbara Pierce was born at New York City and was the popular and self-deprecating wife of 41st president George Herbert Walker Bush (1989–93) and mother of 43rd president George W. Bush. In contrast to predecessor Nancy Reagan, Barbara Bush as first lady was indifferent to glamour (except for her signature strands of pearls) and its trappings. Her key project was child literacy: she created the Barbara Bush Foundation for Family Literacy and authored several children's books. Her compassion and tenderness for children with HIV/AIDS generated much publicity in 1989, a time when such children were shunned. The Bush family matriarch died Apr 17, 2018, in Houston, TX, survived by her husband, five children, 17 grandchildren and seven great-grandchildren.

COCHISE: DEATH ANNIVERSARY. June 8, 1874. Born around 1810 in northern Mexico (now Arizona), Cochise was a fierce and courageous leader of the Chiricahua Apache. As a chief, Cochise maintained a delicate peace with Mexican and American authorities, but in 1861, American military murdered his brother, and Cochise launched the Apache Wars, which lasted until 1872. He died near his stronghold in southeastern Arizona.

CRICK, FRANCIS: BIRTH ANNIVERSARY. June 8, 1916. Born at Northampton, England, Crick was a molecular biologist who credited his background in physics as enabling him to be more daring in his scientific pursuits. He changed his focus to biology in 1947 and was soon analyzing theories of helix patterns and x-ray diffraction. He met James (J.D.) Watson at Cavendish Laboratory at the University of Cambridge, and the two scientists developed a model for the physical structure of deoxyribonucleic acid (DNA), the molecule that encodes a person's genetic characteristics and is often referred to as the "building block of all life." For their work, Crick and Watson received the 1962 Nobel Prize in Physiology or Medicine. Crick died at San Diego, CA, on July 28, 2004.

LAKI VOLCANO ERUPTION: ANNIVERSARY. June 8, 1783. One of the most violent and important volcanic eruptions of recorded history began on this date. Laki, or Skafta, volcano in southern Iceland continued erupting for eight months, expelling an estimated 4½ cubic miles of lava, ultimately causing a famine and the deaths of nearly 10,000 persons. Acid rain reached Western Europe, and other climatic and atmospheric changes were worldwide. English naturalist Gilbert White described some of the "horrible phenomena" of the summer of 1783, including the "peculiar haze, or smokey fog . . . Unlike anything known within the memory of man." The effects of this volcanic eruption and its possible long-term consequences are still being studied by scientists.

MCKINLEY, IDA SAXTON: BIRTH ANNIVERSARY. June 8, 1847. Wife of William McKinley, 25th president of the US, born at Canton, OH. She died there May 26, 1907.

***1984* PUBLISHED: ANNIVERSARY.** June 8, 1949. "It was a bright cold day in April, and the clocks were striking thirteen." George Orwell's influential dystopian novel, set in the superstate of Oceania and introducing Big Brother, was published in England by Secker & Warburg.

QUEEN'S OFFICIAL BIRTHDAY (SELECTED NATIONS). June 8. A holiday in Australia (except for Western Australia), Belize, Cayman Islands, Fiji and Papua New Guinea on the second Monday in June. (In New Zealand and Tuvalu it is commemorated on the first Monday in June.) Celebrating Queen Elizabeth II's "official" birthday, not the day she was actually born (which is Apr 21).

SPACE MILESTONE: *VENERA 9* AND *10* (USSR): 45th ANNIVERSARY. June 8 and 14, 1975. Launched on these dates, unmanned exploration vehicles landed on Venus Oct 22 and 25, respectively. Sent first pictures ever transmitted from Venus, atmospheric analysis and other data.

UNITED NATIONS: WORLD OCEANS DAY. June 8. The UN General Assembly has designated June 8 annually as World Oceans Day (Res 63/111 of Dec 8, 2008). The Assembly noted that ecosystem approaches to ocean management should be focused on managing human activities in order to maintain and, where needed, restore ecosystem health. The aim would be to sustain goods and environmental services, provide social and economic benefits for food security, sustain livelihoods in support of international development goals and conserve marine biodiversity. For info: United Nations, Dept of Public Info, New York, NY 10017. Web: www.un.org.

UPSY DAISY DAY. June 8. A day to remind people to get up gloriously, gratefully and gleefully each morning. For info: Stephanie West Allen, 1376 S Wyandot St, Denver, CO 80223. Phone: (303) 935-8866. E-mail: stephanie@westallen.com.

WHITE, BYRON RAYMOND: BIRTH ANNIVERSARY. June 8, 1917. One of the longest-serving justices of the Supreme Court of the US, Byron White was born at Fort Collins, CO. He was a football star in college (College Football Hall of Fame) and in the National Football League, as well as an academic standout: he was a Rhodes Scholar among other honors. A graduate of Yale Law School, White was a successful lawyer and director of the Justice Department before being nominated by President Kennedy for the highest court on Apr 3, 1962. White took the oath of office Apr 16, 1962, and served 31 years before retiring in 1993. He died on April 15, 2002, at Denver, CO.

WORLD OCEANS DAY. June 8. This day was first proposed in 1992 by Canada at the Earth Summit in Rio de Janeiro, Brazil, and was officially recognized by the United Nations in 2008. Coordinated since 2002 by The Ocean Project, this day is recognized by an increasing number of countries each year as an opportunity to celebrate our world ocean and our personal connection to the sea. It is also a day to think about solutions to the challenges facing society and our shared ocean. The Ocean Project partners with all types of organizations and business to expand the reach and impact of World Oceans Day: a growing community of aquariums,

zoos, museums, schools, youth groups, universities, businesses, recreational stakeholders, maritime interests, faith communities, conservation organizations and many more participate by holding events or recognizing the day in some way. Millions of people become involved onsite and online via social media. Annually, June 8. For info: The Ocean Project, PO Box 2506, Providence, RI 02906. Phone: (401) 709-4071. E-mail: bmott@theoceanproject. org. Web: www.worldoceansday.org.

WRIGHT, FRANK LLOYD: BIRTH ANNIVERSARY. June 8, 1867. One of the greatest and most influential of modern architects, born at Richland Center, WI. Wright fathered the uniquely American "Prairie School," embodied by single-story structures with low, pitched roofs and long rows of casement windows, using locally available materials and unpainted wood, aesthetically mimicking the Midwest prairie landscape. His self-described "organic architecture," marked by its horizontal emphasis and expansive, open interior spaces, referred to buildings that harmonize both with their inhabitants and with their environment. In his autobiography Wright wrote: "No house should ever be *on* any hill or on anything. It should be *of* the hill, belonging to it, so hill and house could live together each the happier for the other." Wright died at Phoenix, AZ, Apr 9, 1959.

WYTHE, GEORGE: DEATH ANNIVERSARY. June 8, 1806. Signer of the Declaration of Independence. Born at Elizabeth County, VA, about 1726 (exact date unknown). Died at Richmond, VA.

🎂 BIRTHDAYS TODAY

Scott Adams, 63, cartoonist ("Dilbert"), born Windham, NY, June 8, 1957.

Kathy Baker, 70, actress ("Picket Fences," *The Right Stuff*), born Midland, TX, June 8, 1950.

Tim Berners-Lee, 65, inventor of the World Wide Web, born London, England, June 8, 1955.

Bernie Casey, 81, former football player, actor (*I'm Gonna Git You Sucka!*), born Wyco, WV, June 8, 1939.

Kim Clijsters, 37, tennis player, born Bilzen, Belgium, June 8, 1983.

James Darren, 84, singer, actor (*Gidget*), born Philadelphia, PA, June 8, 1936.

Lindsay Davenport, 44, former tennis player, sportscaster, born Palos Verdes, CA, June 8, 1976.

Griffin Dunne, 65, actor (*After Hours, An American Werewolf in London*), director, producer, born New York, NY, June 8, 1955.

Gabrielle Giffords, 50, former US congresswoman (R, Arizona), born Tucson, AZ, June 8, 1970.

Julianna Margulies, 54, actress (Emmy and Golden Globe for "The Good Wife"; Emmy for "ER"), born Spring Valley, NY, June 8, 1966.

Sara Paretsky, 73, author (*Killing Orders, Burn Marks*), born Ames, IA, June 8, 1947.

Boz Scaggs, 76, singer, musician, songwriter (*Silk Degrees, Middle Man*), born Dallas, TX, June 8, 1944.

Nancy Sinatra, 80, singer, born Jersey City, NJ, June 8, 1940.

Jerry Stiller, 91, comedian, actor (*Hairspray*, "Seinfeld," "The King of Queens"), born Brooklyn, NY, June 8, 1929.

Keenen Ivory Wayans, 62, actor ("In Living Color"), born New York, NY, June 8, 1958.

Andrew Weil, MD, 78, physician and writer on natural healing, born Philadelphia, PA, June 8, 1942.

Kanye West, 43, singer, producer, born Atlanta, GA, June 8, 1977.

June 2020	S	M	T	W	T	F	S
		1	2	3	4	5	6
	7	8	9	10	11	12	13
	14	15	16	17	18	19	20
	21	22	23	24	25	26	27
	28	29	30				

June 9 — Tuesday

DAY 161   **205 REMAINING**

DONALD DUCK: BIRTHDAY. June 9, 1934. Donald Duck made his screen debut on this date with the release of "The Wise Little Hen," a short film in the Disney series of "Silly Symphonies."

HONG KONG: LEASE SIGNING ANNIVERSARY. June 9, 1898. Hong Kong, consisting of about 400 square miles (islands and mainland) with more than five million persons, was administered as a British Crown Colony after a 99-year lease was signed on June 9, 1898. In 1997 Hong Kong's sovereignty reverted to the People's Republic of China.

INTERNATIONAL ARCHIVES DAY. June 9. A day to raise awareness of the importance of records and archives, in order to make it understood that records and archives provide the foundation for people's rights and identity. Also a time to raise the private and public sectors' awareness of the necessity of preserving archives for the long term and of providing access to them. This day is observed all over the world. Annually, June 9. For info: International Council on Archives. Web: www.ica.org.

JORDAN: ACCESSION DAY. June 9. National holiday. Commemorates the accession to the throne of King Abdullah II in 1999, following the death of his father, King Hussein.

KUTNER, LUIS: BIRTH ANNIVERSARY. June 9, 1908. Human rights attorney Luis Kutner was born at Chicago, IL. Responsible for the release of many unjustly confined prisoners, he came to be known as "The Springman." He helped free Hungarian cardinal József Mindszenty, poet Ezra Pound and former Congo president Moïse Tshombe. He was the author of the living will and founded the World Habeas Corpus. Kutner was nominated nine times for the Nobel Peace Prize. He died Mar 1, 1993, at Chicago.

LOLOMA, CHARLES: BIRTH ANNIVERSARY. June 9, 1921. Charles Loloma was a major influence on modern Native American art and was famous for changing the look of American Indian jewelry. A painter, sculptor and potter, he was best known for his jewelry, which broke tradition with previous Indian styles in using materials such as coral, fossilized ivory, pearls and diamonds. Loloma was born at Hotevilla-Bacavi on the Hopi Indian Reservation in Arizona and died June 9, 1991, at Scottsdale, AZ.

MCNAMARA, ROBERT: BIRTH ANNIVERSARY. June 9, 1916. Former US secretary of defense (1961–68) and chief architect of the Vietnam War. McNamara's handling of the conflict in Vietnam made him a much-maligned public figure. Born at San Francisco, CA, McNamara graduated from the Harvard Business School and was president of the Ford Motor Company before serving under presidents Kennedy and Johnson. Years later, in the Oscar-winning documentary *The Fog of War* (2003) and elsewhere, McNamara publicly acknowledged his failures in judgment and execution with regard to Vietnam. He died July 6, 2009, at Washington, DC.

MUSEUM MILE FESTIVAL. June 9. New York, NY. 42nd annual. On the second Tuesday in June each year, 10 of the country's finest museums—all ones that call Fifth Avenue home—collectively open their doors from 6 PM to 9 PM for free to visitors for a mile-long block party and visual art celebration. Festivities begin at the steps of the landmark National Academy Museum building at 5:45 PM. Participating museums: National Academy Museum, Museum of the City of New York, Metropolitan Museum of Art, Museum for African Art, El Museo del Barrio New York, The Jewish Museum, Cooper-Hewitt, Guggenheim, Neue Galerie and Goethe Institute. Twenty-three car-free blocks, family activities, art in the street, live music. Rain or shine. For info: Museum Mile Festival, Culture Partners. Web: www.museummilefestival.org.

NATIONAL CALL YOUR DOCTOR DAY. June 9. 5th annual. A day (falling near the halfway point of the year) to encourage young women to schedule their annual Well-Woman Exam. According to a recent study, "80 percent of Americans admit they are delaying or forgoing preventive care. The issue is worse for Millennials, with 9 in 10 (93 percent) not scheduling doctor visits."

Call Your Doctor Day rallies together young women all over the country to set aside five minutes to call their doctor and make an appointment that puts them on the path to maintained breast and ovarian health. Sponsored by Bright Pink, a women's health nonprofit organization. Annually, the second Tuesday in June. For info: Bright Pink, 670 N Clark St, Fl 2, Chicago, IL 60654. E-mail: brightpink@brightpink.org. Web: www.brightpink.org.

NORTH AMERICAN INTERNATIONAL AUTO SHOW. June 9–20. Cobo Center, Detroit, MI. The premier auto show in North America, the NAIAS is a showcase for the world's vehicle introductions. An estimated 70 introductions will take place during the show. Est attendance: 815,000. For info: NAIAS, 1900 W Big Beaver, Ste 100, Troy, MI 48084. Phone: (248) 643-0250. Fax: (248) 637-0784. Web: www.naias.com.

PAUL, LES: BIRTH ANNIVERSARY. June 9, 1915. Legendary American musician, born at Waukesha, WI, who designed one of the first solid-body electric guitars. Though best known for the guitars that bear his name, Paul also made groundbreaking contributions in guitar effects and recording techniques (such as multitrack recording). A performer into his 90s, Paul died Aug 13, 2009, at the age of 94 at White Plains, NY.

PAYNE, JOHN HOWARD: BIRTH ANNIVERSARY. June 9, 1791. American author, actor and diplomat, born at New York, NY, and died at Tunis, Tunisia, Apr 9, 1852. Author of opera libretto (*Clari, or The Maid of Milan*) that contained the song "Home, Sweet Home."

PORTER, COLE: BIRTH ANNIVERSARY. June 9, 1891. Cole Porter published his first song, "The Bobolink Waltz," at the age of 10. His career as a composer and lyricist for Broadway was launched in 1928 when five of his songs were used in the musical play *Let's Do It*. His prolific contributions to the Broadway stage include *Fifty Million Frenchmen, Wake Up and Dream, The Gay Divorcée, Anything Goes, Leave It to Me, Du Barry Was a Lady, Something for the Boys, Kiss Me Kate, Can Can* and *Silk Stockings*. Porter was born at Peru, IN, and died at Santa Monica, CA, Oct 15, 1964.

SITKA SUMMER MUSIC FESTIVAL. June 9–July 5. Sitka, AK. Sitka hosts a highly acclaimed chamber music festival that attracts performers and spectators from around the world. Est attendance: 5,000. For info: Sitka Summer Music Festival, PO Box 3333, Sitka, AK 99835. Phone: (907) 747-6774. E-mail: director@sitkamusicfestival.org. Web: www.alaskaclassics.org.

STEPHENSON, GEORGE: BIRTH ANNIVERSARY. June 9, 1781. English inventor, developer of the steam locomotive, born near Newcastle, England. Died near Chesterfield, England, Aug 12, 1848.

THAYER, SYLVANUS: BIRTH ANNIVERSARY. June 9, 1785. A military engineer and educator, born at Braintree, MA. He was appointed superintendent of West Point at 32 and became known as the "Father of the Military Academy." Thayer died at Braintree, MA, Sept 7, 1872.

🎂 BIRTHDAYS TODAY

Tedy Bruschi, 47, sportscaster, former football player, born San Francisco, CA, June 9, 1973.

Patricia Cornwell, 64, author (*All That Remains, Postmortem*), born Miami, FL, June 9, 1956.

Johnny Depp, 57, actor (*Pirates of the Caribbean* films, *Black Mass, Alice in Wonderland, Edward Scissorhands*), born Owensboro, KY, June 9, 1963.

Michael J. Fox, 59, actor ("Family Ties," "Spin City," Back to the Future films), born Edmonton, AB, Canada, June 9, 1961.

Marvin Kalb, 90, educator, journalist, born New York, NY, June 9, 1930.

Miroslav Klose, 42, soccer coach and former player, born Opole, Poland, June 9, 1978.

Jackie Mason, 86, comedian ("Chicken Soup," *The World According to Me*), born Yacov Moshe Maza at Sheboygan, WI, June 9, 1934.

Dave Parker, 69, former baseball player, born Calhoun, MS, June 9, 1951.

Natalie Portman, 39, actress (Oscar for *Black Swan*; *Jackie, Thor, Closer*), born Natalie Hershlag at Jerusalem, Israel, June 9, 1981.

Ashley Postell, 34, former gymnast, born Cheverly, MD, June 9, 1986.

Gloria Reuben, 56, actress ("ER"), born Toronto, ON, Canada, June 9, 1964.

Peja Stojakovic, 43, basketball executive and former player, born Predrag Stojakovic at Belgrade, Yugoslavia (now Serbia), June 9, 1977.

Dick Vitale, 81, sportscaster, born East Rutherford, NJ, June 9, 1939.

Mae Whitman, 32, actress ("Arrested Development," "Parenthood," *One Fine Day*), born Los Angeles, CA, June 9, 1988.

June 10 — Wednesday

DAY 162   **204 REMAINING**

ALCOHOLICS ANONYMOUS FOUNDED: 85th ANNIVERSARY. June 10, 1935. On this day at Akron, OH, Dr. Robert Smith completed his first day of permanent sobriety. "Doctor Bob" and William G. Wilson are considered to have founded Alcoholics Anonymous on that day.

BELLOW, SAUL: BIRTH ANNIVERSARY. June 10, 1915. Born at Lachine, QC, Canada, Bellow would become one of America's great postwar authors, examining the urban antiheroes at war with the society they live in. His novels include *The Adventures of Augie March* (1953), *Herzog* (1964) and *Mr Sammler's Planet* (1970). Garnered numerous National Book Awards as well as a Pulitzer. Winner of the Nobel Prize in Literature in 1976. Died at Brookline, MA, Apr 5, 2005.

CONGO (BRAZZAVILLE): DAY OF NATIONAL RECONCILIATION. June 10. National holiday. Commemorates official conference in 1991.

FIRST MINT IN AMERICA: ANNIVERSARY. June 10, 1652. In defiance of English colonial law, John Hull, a silversmith, established

June 2020	S	M	T	W	T	F	S
		1	2	3	4	5	6
	7	8	9	10	11	12	13
	14	15	16	17	18	19	20
	21	22	23	24	25	26	27
	28	29	30				

the first mint in America. The first coin issued was the Pine Tree Shilling, designed by Hull.

GARLAND, JUDY: BIRTH ANNIVERSARY. June 10, 1922. American actress and singer born Frances Gumm at Grand Rapids, MN. While Garland played in many films and toured widely as a singer, she is probably most remembered for her portrayal of Dorothy Gale in the now-classic *The Wizard of Oz*. Died June 22, 1969, at London, England.

JORDAN: GREAT ARAB REVOLT AND ARMY DAY. June 10. National holiday. Commemorates the beginning of the Great Arab Revolt in 1916.

MCDANIEL, HATTIE: BIRTH ANNIVERSARY. June 10, 1893. Hattie McDaniel, born at Wichita, KS, to former slaves, was a trailblazer in a variety of ways. She began her career as a singer and was the first African-American woman to sing on radio. As she moved into film in the 1930s and '40s, she was the first African American to win an Academy Award, winning it in 1940 for her role as Mammy in the 1939 film blockbuster *Gone with the Wind*. She appeared in *I'm No Angel, Alice Adams, The Little Colonel, Show Boat* and *Saratoga*, among others. A veteran of vaudeville, the concert hall, radio, television and film, she died Oct 26, 1952, at Los Angeles, CA.

NATIONAL ICED TEA DAY. June 10. Take a time out to enjoy summer's most refreshing beverage! Annually, June 10. For info: For info: The Tea Council of the USA. E-mail: info@teausa.org. Web: www.teausa.org.

NCAA DIVISION I MEN'S & WOMEN'S OUTDOOR TRACK & FIELD CHAMPIONSHIPS. June 10–13. Mike A. Myers Stadium, Austin, TX. Host is University of Texas. Est attendance: 20,000. For info: NCAA, PO Box 6222, Indianapolis, IN 46206-6222. Phone: (317) 917-6222. Fax: (317) 917-6826. Web: www.NCAA.com.

PORTUGAL: DAY OF PORTUGAL. June 10. National holiday. Anniversary of the death in 1580 of Portugal's national poet, Luís Vaz de Camões (Camoens), born in 1524 (exact date unknown) at either Lisbon or Coimbra. Died at Lisbon, Portugal.

RAPE OF LIDICE: ANNIVERSARY. June 10, 1942. Nazi German troops executed, by shooting, all male inhabitants of the Czechoslovakian village of Lidice (total population about 500 persons), burned every house and deported the women and children to Germany for "reeducation." (In New Jersey, June 10 is observed as Lidice Memorial Day.)

SENDAK, MAURICE: BIRTH ANNIVERSARY. June 10, 1928. Author and illustrator born at Brooklyn, NY. In a career spanning more than half a century, Sendak wrote and illustrated many notable children's books, including *In the Night Kitchen, Kenny's Window* and, his most famous work, *Where the Wild Things Are*. Widely regarded as the first picture book artist to deal openly with children's emotions, Sendak received numerous awards for his work, notably the Caldecott Medal (1964), the Hans Christian Andersen Award (1970) and the Laura Ingalls Wilder Medal (1983). "The picture book is where I put down those fantasies that have been with me all my life, and where I give them a form that means something," he once said. "I live inside the picture book; it's where I fight all my battles, and where, hopefully, I win my wars." He died May 8, 2012, at Danbury, CT.

🎂 BIRTHDAYS TODAY

F. Lee Bailey, 87, lawyer, born Waltham, MA, June 10, 1933.

John Edwards, 67, former US senator (D, North Carolina), born Seneca, SC, June 10, 1953.

Linda Evangelista, 55, model, born St. Catharines, ON, Canada, June 10, 1965.

Jeff Greenfield, 77, author, journalist, born New York, NY, June 10, 1943.

Elizabeth Hurley, 55, actress ("The Royals," *Austin Powers: International Man of Mystery*), model, designer, born Basingstoke, England, June 10, 1965.

Tara Lipinski, 38, sportscaster, Olympic figure skater, born Philadelphia, PA, June 10, 1982.

Doug McKeon, 54, actor (*On Golden Pond*), born Pompton Plains, NJ, June 10, 1966.

Prince Philip, 99, Duke of Edinburgh, husband of Queen Elizabeth II, born Corfu, Greece, June 10, 1921.

Leelee Sobieski, 38, actress (*Joan of Arc, A Soldier's Daughter Never Cries*), born New York, NY, June 10, 1982.

Jeanne Tripplehorn, 57, actress ("Big Love," *Grey Gardens, The Firm, Basic Instinct*), born Tulsa, OK, June 10, 1963.

Kate Upton, 28, model, born St. Joseph, MI, June 10, 1992.

June 11 — Thursday

DAY 163   **203 REMAINING**

"AMERICAN IDOL" TV PREMIERE: ANNIVERSARY. June 11, 2002. FOX's phenomenally successful talent show was based on a British program. Talented singers competed for a major-label record deal while being judged by a panel of highly critical music experts: initially—and for many seasons—Simon Cowell, Paula Abdul and Randy Jackson; later, by other entertainment stars. The audience voted for favorites (online or by phone). Ryan Seacrest hosted. The first "American Idol" was Kelly Clarkson, who has gone on to chart-topping success and Grammys. After a few seasons of declining ratings, FOX announced on May 11, 2015, that the 2016 season was the final one. In 2018, ABC revived the series with Seacrest and new judges Katy Perry, Luke Bryan and Lionel Richie.

BONNAROO MUSIC AND ARTS FESTIVAL. June 11–14. Manchester, TN. 18th annual. An escape into excitement, music, art, discoveries, trees, fresh air, green grass. Bonnaroo is a four-day, multi-stage camping festival held on a beautiful 700-acre farm. Bonnaroo brings together some of the best performers in rock and roll, along with dozens of artists in jazz, Americana, hip-hop and electronica. The festival's 100-acre entertainment village buzzes around the clock with attractions and activities including a classic arcade, on-site cinema, silent disco, comedy club, theater performers, a beer festival and a music technology area. Annually, the second weekend in June. Est attendance: 80,000. For info: Bonnaroo Music and Arts Festival. E-mail: info@bonnaroo.com. Web: www.bonnaroo.com.

CONSTABLE, JOHN: BIRTH ANNIVERSARY. June 11, 1776. English landscape painter. Born at East Bergholt, Suffolk, England, he died at London, England, Mar 31, 1837.

CORPUS CHRISTI. June 11. Roman Catholic festival celebrated in honor of the Eucharist. A solemnity observed on the Thursday following Trinity Sunday since 1246. In the US Corpus Christi is celebrated on the Sunday following Trinity Sunday. See also: "Corpus Christi (US Observance)" (June 14).

COUSTEAU, JACQUES: BIRTH ANNIVERSARY. June 11, 1910. French undersea explorer, writer and filmmaker born at St.

André-de-Cubzac, France. He invented the Aqua-Lung™, which allowed him and his colleagues to produce more than 80 documentary films about undersea life, two of which won Oscars. This scientist and explorer was awarded the French Legion of Honor for his work in the Resistance in WWII. He died June 25, 1997, at Paris, France.

GERMANY: LEIPZIG BACH FESTIVAL. June 11–21. Leipzig. Since 1904, the festival has been held in Leipzig, where Johann Sebastian Bach lived in his later years and composed some of his best-known works. Est attendance: 75,000. For info: Bach-Archiv Leipzig. E-mail: bachfest@bach-leipzig.de. Web: www.bachfestleipzig.de.

JONSON, BEN: BIRTH ANNIVERSARY. June 11, 1572. (Old Style date.) English playwright and poet. "Talking and eloquence," he wrote, "are not the same: to speak and to speak well, are two things." Born at London, England, he died there Aug 6, 1637 (OS). The epitaph written on his tombstone in Westminster Abbey: "O rare Ben Jonson."

KING KAMEHAMEHA I DAY. June 11. Designated state holiday in Hawaii honors memory of Hawaiian monarch (1737–1819). Governor appoints state commission to plan annual celebration.

LIBYA: EVACUATION DAY. June 11. National Day. Commemorates the closing of US base in 1970.

LOMBARDI, VINCE: BIRTH ANNIVERSARY. June 11, 1913. Vincent Thomas Lombardi, Pro Football Hall of Fame coach, born at New York, NY. Lombardi played football for Fordham's famed "Seven Blocks of Granite" line in the mid-1930s, became a teacher and began to coach high school football. He became offensive line coach at West Point in 1949 and moved to the New York Giants in 1954. Five years later, he was named head coach of the Green Bay Packers. His Packers won five NFL titles and two Super Bowls in nine years, and Lombardi was generally regarded as the greatest coach and the finest motivator in pro football history. He retired in 1968 but was lured back to coach the Washington Redskins a year later. Inducted into the Pro Football Hall of Fame posthumously in 1971. Died at Washington, DC, Sept 3, 1970.

NATIONAL COTTON CANDY DAY. June 11. A day for folks to reconnect with childhood memories of fairs, circuses and carnivals. Cotton candy is the original interactive candy in terms of the way it magically disappears when placed in your mouth! Annually, June 11. For info: Fun Sweets. Web: www.funsweets.net.

RANKIN, JEANNETTE: BIRTH ANNIVERSARY. June 11, 1880. First woman elected to the US Congress, a reformer, feminist and pacifist, was born at Missoula, MT. She was the only member of Congress to vote against a declaration of war against Japan in December 1941. Died May 18, 1973, at Carmel, CA.

RED ARMY DEPARTS BERLIN: ANNIVERSARY. June 11, 1994. After 49 years, the Russian military occupation of the region once called East Germany ended. At one time there had been 337,800 Soviet troops stationed in Germany. The departure was celebrated with a parade in Wünsdorf, south of Berlin, which was the Soviet Union's military headquarters in the former German Democratic Republic.

ROYALL, ANNE: BIRTH ANNIVERSARY. June 11, 1769. America's first woman journalist was born Anne Newport in New Baltimore, MD. After the death of her husband, William, left her penniless at age 54, Royall traveled across the United States, writing her observations to support herself; those ten publications remain a valuable source of American social history. Her acerbic observations won her many enemies: in 1829 she was successfully prosecuted as a "common scold"—quarrelsome nuisance—for her unrelenting criticism of a Washington, DC, Presbyterian church. She became a Washington, DC-based reporter and editor who exposed the abuses of government first in *Paul Pry* (1831–36; a newspaper typeset by orphans) and then *The Huntress* (1836–54). Royall died at Washington, DC, on Oct 1, 1854.

STRAUSS, RICHARD GEORG: BIRTH ANNIVERSARY. June 11, 1864. German Romantic composer, musician and conductor born at Munich. Some of his best-remembered operas are *Salome* (1905), *Elektra* (1909) and *Der Rosenkavalier* (1911), and his acclaimed symphonic, or tone, poems include *Don Juan* (1889) and *Don Quixote* (1898). Strauss died at Garmisch-Partenkirchen, Germany, on Sept 8, 1949.

STYRON, WILLIAM: 95th BIRTH ANNIVERSARY. June 11, 1925. Winner of both the National Book Award and the Pulitzer Prize in Literature, Styron was born at Newport News, VA. His acclaimed 1967 novel, *The Confessions of Nat Turner*, a fictionalized memoir of the leader of an 1831 slave rebellion, drew upon his knowledge of Virginia. *Sophie's Choice* (1979) chronicled the life of a non-Jewish Nazi victim. He also chronicled his own struggles with debilitating depression in *Darkness Visible* (1990). Styron died at Martha's Vineyard, MA, Nov 1, 2006.

SUPERMAN CELEBRATION. June 11–14. Metropolis, IL. 42nd annual. Weekend full of "super" activities. See 15-foot Superman statue, live entertainment, celebrity appearances, Super Museum, costume contest, road race, carnival, Supertrek bicycle ride, super car show, washer pitch tournament, weight lifting, children's games and food fair. Est attendance: 50,000. For info: Metropolis Area Chamber of Commerce, 516 Market St, Metropolis, IL 62960. Phone: (618) 524-2714. Fax: (618) 524-4780. E-mail: office@metropolischamber.com. Web: www.supermancelebration.net.

🎂 BIRTHDAYS TODAY

Adrienne Barbeau, 75, actress (*Escape from New York*, "Maude"), born Sacramento, CA, June 11, 1945.

Peter Bergman, 67, actor ("All My Children," "The Young and the Restless"), born Guantanamo Bay, Cuba, June 11, 1953.

Peter Dinklage, 51, actor ("Game of Thrones," *The Station Agent*), born Morristown, NJ, June 11, 1969.

Joshua Jackson, 42, actor ("The Affair," "Fringe," "Dawson's Creek," *Scream 2*), born Vancouver, BC, Canada, June 11, 1978.

Hugh Laurie, 61, actor ("The Night Manager," "House," "Jeeves and Wooster"), born Oxford, England, June 11, 1959.

Joseph C. (Joe) Montana, Jr, 64, Hall of Fame football player, born New Eagle, PA, June 11, 1956.

Mehmet Öz, 60, surgeon, television personality, author, born Cleveland, OH, June 11, 1960.

Jackie Stewart, 81, former auto racer, born Dunbartonshire, Scotland, June 11, 1939.

June 2020	S	M	T	W	T	F	S
		1	2	3	4	5	6
	7	8	9	10	11	12	13
	14	15	16	17	18	19	20
	21	22	23	24	25	26	27
	28	29	30				

June 12 — Friday

BASEBALL'S FIRST PERFECT GAME: ANNIVERSARY. June 12, 1880. Lee Richmond of the Worcester Ruby Legs (National League) pitched baseball's first perfect game (not allowing a single opposing player to reach first base), 1–0, against the Cleveland Indians.

BIG BEND NATIONAL PARK ESTABLISHED: ANNIVERSARY. June 12, 1944. Area on the "big bend" of the Rio Grande in western Texas along the Mexican border was established as a national park (authorized June 20, 1935). For info: Big Bend Natl Park, PO Box 129, Big Bend Natl Park, TX 79834.

BUSH, GEORGE H.W.: BIRTH ANNIVERSARY. June 12, 1924. George Herbert Walker Bush, born at Milton, MA, was 41st president of the United States (1989–93) and father of 43rd president George W. Bush. At 18, Bush became the youngest pilot in the Navy during World War II and earned the Distinguished Flying Cross. After graduating Yale, Bush found success in the Texas oil industry before turning to public service. He was US Representative for Texas, United Nations ambassador, head of the Republican National Committee and Director of the CIA before becoming 43rd vice president (1981–89) under Ronald Reagan. At the time of his death on Nov 30, 2018, at Houston, TX—seven months after the passing of wife Barbara—he was the longest living president in American history.

CHICAGO BLUES FESTIVAL. June 12–14 (tentative). Millennium Park, Chicago, IL. Since 1984. The Chicago Blues Festival is the largest free blues festival in the world and remains the largest of Chicago's music festivals. During three days on five stages, more than 500,000 blues fans prove that Chicago is the "Blues Capital of the World." Performers through the years have included Bonnie Raitt, Ray Charles, B.B. King, Bo Diddley, Buddy Guy and Koko Taylor. Est attendance: 500,000. For info: Chicago Department of Cultural Affairs and Special Events. Web: www.chicagobluesfestival.us.

COPA AMÉRICA. June 12–July 12. Argentina and Colombia. 47th edition. Multinational soccer tournament (American Cup). Twelve to 16 teams battle it out: 10 from the CONMEBOL federation of South America and two to four squads invited from other federations. The final will be contested in Argentina. For info: CONMEBOL. Web: www.conmebol.com.

CURTIS CUP (WOMEN'S INTERNATIONAL CUP). June 12–14. Conway Golf Club, Caernarvonshire, Wales. 41st edition. Biennial competition (officially named "The Women's International Cup") between teams of women amateur golfers from the US and the UK and Ireland. Named after British golfing sisters Harriot and Margaret Curtis. Contested in even-numbered years since 1932 (except during WWII). Sponsored by the USGA and Ladies' Golf Union. For info: Curtis Cup, USGA, Phone: (908) 234-2300. E-mail: champs@usga.org. Web: www.usga.org or www.curtiscup.org.

EURO 2020 (UEFA EUROPEAN SOCCER CHAMPIONSHIP). June 12–July 12. First held in 1958, this two-year-long tournament pits 53 national European soccer teams against each other, with the final 24 battling it out June 12–July 12, 2020. The tournament is held in 12 cities across Europe: London, Munich, Rome, Baku, Bucharest, Saint Petersburg, Amsterdam, Bilbao, Glasgow, Budapest, Copenhagen and Dublin. The opening match is held at Stadio Olimpico in Rome, Italy, and the final match takes place at Wembley Stadium in London, England. More than one million spectators should be in attendance. Matches are broadcast live in 200 territories. Est attendance: 1,400,000. For info: UEFA, Route de Genève 46, CH-1260 Nyon 2, Switzerland. Web: www.uefa.com.

FIRST MAN-POWERED FLIGHT ACROSS ENGLISH CHANNEL: ANNIVERSARY. June 12, 1979. Bryan Allen, 26-year-old Californian, pedaled the 70-pound *Gossamer Albatross* 22 miles across the English Channel, from Folkestone, England, to Cape Gris-Nez, France, in 2 hours, 49 minutes, winning (with the craft's designer, Paul MacCready of Pasadena, CA) the £100,000 prize offered by

British industrialist Henry Kremer for the first man-powered flight across the English Channel.

FRANK, ANNE: BIRTH ANNIVERSARY. June 12, 1929. Born Annelise Marie Frank at Frankfurt, Germany. This Jewish girl is remembered today as the accomplished, insightful writer of a work that has touched millions of people. Anne Frank and her family moved to Amsterdam to escape the Nazis, but after The Netherlands was invaded by Germany, they had to go into hiding. In 1942 Anne began to keep a diary. She died with her sister Margot at the Bergen-Belsen concentration camp in either February or March of 1945. After the war, her father published her diary, on which a stage play and movie were later based. See also: "Diary of Anne Frank: The Last Entry: Anniversary" (Aug 1).

LOVING V VIRGINIA: **ANNIVERSARY.** June 12, 1967. The US Supreme Court decision in *Loving v Virginia* swept away all 16 remaining state laws prohibiting interracial marriages.

NATIONAL BASEBALL HALL OF FAME DEDICATED: ANNIVERSARY. June 12, 1939. The National Baseball Hall of Fame and Museum was dedicated at Cooperstown, NY. More than 200 individuals have been honored for their contributions to the game of baseball by induction into the hall. The first players chosen for membership (1936) were Ty Cobb, Honus Wagner, Babe Ruth, Christy Mathewson and Walter Johnson. Relics and memorabilia from the history of baseball are housed at this shrine of America's national sport.

ORLANDO NIGHTCLUB MASSACRE: ANNIVERSARY. June 12, 2016. In the second-worst mass shooting by a single perpetrator in US history—and the deadliest instance of anti-LGBT violence—a gunman shot and killed 49 patrons of the Pulse nightclub at Orlando, FL. An additional 53 people were injured. Police killed the self-proclaimed terrorist during the rampage.

PARAGUAY: PEACE WITH BOLIVIA DAY. June 12. Commemorates the end of the Chaco War in 1935.

PHILIPPINES: INDEPENDENCE DAY. June 12. National holiday. Declared independence from Spain in 1898.

RUSSIA: RUSSIA DAY. June 12. National holiday. Commemorates the date—June 12, 1990—when the First Congress of People's Deputies of the Russian Federation adopted the Declaration of State Sovereignty of the Russian Soviet Federative Socialist Republic. Observed since 1992.

SPACE MILESTONE: *VENERA 4* (USSR). June 12, 1967. Launched on this date, this instrumental capsule landed on Venus by parachute on Oct 18 and reported a temperature of 536°F.

"TEAR DOWN THIS WALL" SPEECH: ANNIVERSARY. June 12, 1987. US president Ronald Reagan, standing at the Brandenburg Gate and the Berlin Wall, gave one of the most powerful speeches of his career when he challenged Soviet president Mikhail Gorbachev to give liberalization in the Eastern Bloc more than lip service: "General Secretary Gorbachev, if you seek peace, if you seek prosperity for the Soviet Union and Eastern Europe, if you seek liberalization: Come here to this gate! Mr Gorbachev, open this gate! Mr Gorbachev, tear down this wall!" The speech was audible to East Berliners, but East German police made a gathering crowd at the wall disperse. The State Department had sought to make the speech more conciliatory, but Reagan and his speechwriter, Peter

Robinson, refused. The wall was finally opened in 1989. See also: "Berlin Wall Opened: Anniversary" (Nov 9).

UNITED NATIONS: WORLD DAY AGAINST CHILD LABOR. June 12. The International Labour Organization (ILO) launched this day in 2002 to focus attention on the global extent of child labor and the action and efforts needed to eliminate it. Annually, June 12. For info: United Nations, Dept of Public Info, New York, NY 10017. Web: www.un.org.

🎂 BIRTHDAYS TODAY

Marv Albert, 77, sportscaster, born Marvin Philip Aufrichtig at New York, NY, June 12, 1943.

Timothy Busfield, 63, actor ("thirtysomething," *Field of Dreams*), born Lansing, MI, June 12, 1957.

Chick Corea, 79, musician, born Chelsea, MA, June 12, 1941.

Rick Hoffman, 50, actor ("Suits," "The Bernie Mac Show," *Battleship*), born New York, NY, June 12, 1970.

Adriana Lima, 39, model, born Salvador, Bahia, Brazil, June 12, 1981.

Hideki Matsui, 46, former baseball player, born Ishikawa, Japan, June 12, 1974.

Frances O'Connor, 51, actress (*The Importance of Being Earnest*, *Mansfield Park*), born Oxford, England, June 12, 1969.

June 13 — Saturday

DAY 165   **201 REMAINING**

"THE CLOSER" TV PREMIERE: 15th ANNIVERSARY. June 13, 2005. This original cable (TNT) series featured Kyra Sedgwick as Deputy Police Chief Brenda Leigh Johnson, a former Atlanta detective brought to Los Angeles to head a special LAPD homicide unit. The premiere telecast set a record for an ad supported cable original series, and Sedgwick won a Golden Globe for her performance.

ENGLAND: TROOPING THE COLOUR—THE QUEEN'S OFFICIAL BIRTHDAY PARADE. June 13 or 20. Horse Guards Parade, Whitehall, London. Colorful ceremony with music and pageantry during which Her Majesty The Queen takes the salute from her Household Division. Observance dates from 1805 in the reign of King George III. Starts at 11 AM. When requesting info, send SASE. Trooping the Colour is always the second or third Saturday in June; The Queen's real birthday is Apr 21. For info: The Ticket Office, HQ Household Division, Horse Guards, Whitehall, London, England SW1A 2AX. Web: www.royal.gov.uk.

FIRST ROLLER COASTER OPENS: ANNIVERSARY. June 13, 1884. The world's first roller coaster opened on this day in 1884 at Coney Island, Brooklyn, NY. Built and later patented by LaMarcus Thompson, the "Gravity Pleasure Switchback Railway" boasted two parallel 600-foot tracks that descended from 50 feet. The cars traveled at six miles per hour. Riders paid five cents each for their rides. The roller coaster was a sensation, and soon amusement parks all over the US and the world featured them.

FRANCE: 24 HOURS OF LE MANS. June 13–14. Le Mans. 88th annual. Organized on a regular basis since 1923, it is the biggest sporting challenge for car manufacturers because it is based on "being the best over 24 hours." More than 55 teams compete in this storied road test. Est attendance: 250,000. For info: Automobile Club de l'Ouest, Circuit des 24 Heures, 72019 Le Mans, France. Web: www.lemans.org.

GRANGE, RED: BIRTH ANNIVERSARY. June 13, 1903. Harold Edward "Red" Grange, Pro Football Hall of Fame halfback and broadcaster, born at Forksville, PA. Perhaps the most famous football player of all time, Grange had a spectacular college career at the University of Illinois, being named an All-American in 1923,

1924 and 1925. When Illinois dedicated its Memorial Stadium on Oct 18, 1924, Grange scored four touchdowns against Michigan in the game's first 12 minutes. Known as the "Galloping Ghost," Grange joined the Chicago Bears in 1925 for what amounted to a barnstorming tour, the start of a professional career dictated by Grange and his manager, Charles C. "Cash and Carry" Pyle. He retired in 1934 following a knee injury, having put pro football on the sports map. Grange entered business and did announcing work on radio and television. In retirement, he lived quietly and humbly. Inducted into the Hall of Fame as a charter member in 1963. Died at Lake Wales, FL, Jan 28, 1991.

HERITAGE DAYS FESTIVAL. June 13–14. Cumberland, MD. 52nd annual. Held in historic Cumberland, the festival showcases more than 100 arts and crafts booths. Also, music, entertainment, children's activities, carnivals, tours of historic homes and buildings and historic reenactments. Annually, the second weekend in June. Est attendance: 10,000. For info: Heritage Days Festival, PO Box 984, Cumberland, MD 21501-0984. Phone: (301) 722-0037. E-mail: info@heritagedaysfestival.com. Web: www.heritagedaysfestival.com.

MEDGAR EVERS ASSASSINATED: ANNIVERSARY. June 13, 1963. Civil rights leader Medgar Wiley Evers was active in seeking integration of schools and voter registration. He was assassinated by Byron de la Beckwith. The public outrage following his death was one of the factors that led President John F. Kennedy to propose a comprehensive civil rights law.

MIRANDA **DECISION: ANNIVERSARY.** June 13, 1966. The US Supreme Court rendered a 5–4 decision in the case of *Miranda v Arizona*, holding that the Fifth Amendment of the Constitution "required warnings before valid statements could be taken by police." The decision has been described as "providing basic legal protections to persons who might otherwise not be aware of their rights." Ernesto Miranda, the 23-year-old whose name became nationally known, was retried after the Miranda Decision, convicted and sent back to prison. Miranda was stabbed to death in a card game dispute at Phoenix, AZ, in 1976. A suspect in the killing was released by police after he had been read his "Miranda rights." Police procedures now routinely require the reading of a prisoner's constitutional ("Miranda") rights before questioning.

MISSION SAN LUIS REY DE FRANCIA: FOUNDING ANNIVERSARY. June 13, 1798. California mission to the Indians founded on this date. Abandoned by 1846; restoration began in 1892.

MOON PHASE: LAST QUARTER. June 13. Moon enters Last Quarter phase at 2:24 AM, EDT.

NATIONAL HERMIT WEEK. June 13–20. This week, take an adventure in solitude. Discover yourself by journeying within or going off-the-grid. Celebrate the contributions of others who have indulged their need to hermit. Whether you seek inner peace, spiritual release or a moment's peace, this eight-day week is just for you. Annually, June 13–20. Observed since 1996. For info: The Hermit Project, PO Box 2628, Spotsylvania, VA 22553-2628. E-mail: seh2@nyu.edu.

SAINT ANTHONY OF PADUA: FEAST DAY. June 13. Born at Lisbon, Portugal, Aug 15, 1195, Saint Anthony is patron of the illiterate and the poor. Died at Padua, Italy, June 13, 1231. Public holiday, Lisbon.

SAYERS, DOROTHY: BIRTH ANNIVERSARY. June 13, 1893. Renowned crime novelist Sayers was born at Oxford, England. A graduate of Oxford University (1915) and first published as a poet, she toiled some years as an advertising copywriter before she turned her hand to detective fiction. Her first novel, *Whose Body?* (1923), introduced the character of Lord Peter Wimsey, an aristocrat who stumbles onto murder scenes in 11 novels and many short stories.

Sayers is regarded as a primary member of the Golden Age mystery writers, alongside Agatha Christie and Ngaio Marsh. A cofounder of the Detection Club, she served as its president from 1949 until her death at Witham, Essex, England, Dec 17, 1957.

SCOTT, WINFIELD: BIRTH ANNIVERSARY. June 13, 1786. Through five wars and more than 50 years as an officer, Winfield Scott was the early US Army's most enduring influence. A hero of both the War of 1812 and the Mexican-American War (1846–48), he also led the Cherokee nation out of Georgia on the infamous Trail of Tears. As brilliant a tactician as he was an infamous clotheshorse, Scott developed the Anaconda Plan, which the Union employed in its defeat of the Confederacy. Scott retired from active duty in 1861, when he was removed as lieutenant general of the US forces by Abraham Lincoln. The Whig Party chose Scott as their presidential nominee in 1848 and 1852, but he was never elected to office. Born at Petersburg, VA, he died at West Point, NY, on May 29, 1866.

UNITED NATIONS: INTERNATIONAL ALBINISM AWARENESS DAY. June 13. Albinism is a rare, noncontagious, genetically inherited difference present at birth. It is still profoundly misunderstood, socially and medically, and, as a result, people with albinism face many forms of discrimination worldwide. This day encourages UN member states and communities worldwide to protect and preserve the rights of persons with albinism to life, dignity and security, as well as their right not to be subject to torture and degrading treatment or punishment, and to ensure equal access to employment, education, justice and health services. Annually, June 13. (Res 69/170 of Dec 18, 2014.) For info: United Nations, Dept of Public Info, New York, NY 10017. Web: www.un.org.

YEATS, WILLIAM BUTLER: BIRTH ANNIVERSARY. June 13, 1865. Nobel Prize–winning Irish poet and dramatist, born at Dublin, Ireland. He once wrote: "If an author interprets a poem of his own, he limits its suggestibility." Yeats died at France, Jan 28, 1939. After WWII his body was returned, as he had wished, for reburial in a churchyard at Drumcliff, Ireland.

🎂 BIRTHDAYS TODAY

Tim Allen, 67, comedian, actor ("Last Man Standing," "Home Improvement," *The Santa Clause, Galaxy Quest*), born Denver, CO, June 13, 1953.

Ban Ki-Moon, 76, former secretary-general of the UN (2007–16), born Eumseong, Korea (now South Korea), June 13, 1944.

Christo, 85, conceptual artist (*Running Fence, Valley Curtain*), born Christo Javacheff at Gabrovo, Bulgaria, June 13, 1935.

Roy Cooper, 63, Governor of North Carolina (D), born Nash County, NC, June 13, 1957.

Kat Dennings, 34, actress ("Two Broke Girls," *Nick and Norah's Infinite Playlist*), born Bryn Mawr, PA, June 13, 1986.

Chris Evans, 39, actor (*The Avengers, Captain America: The First Avenger*), born Boston, MA, June 13, 1981.

Malcolm McDowell, 77, actor (*A Clockwork Orange, O Lucky Man!*), born Leeds, England, June 13, 1943.

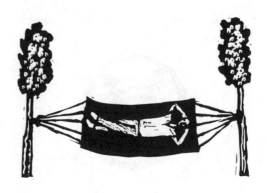

June 2020	S	M	T	W	T	F	S
		1	2	3	4	5	6
	7	8	9	10	11	12	13
	14	15	16	17	18	19	20
	21	22	23	24	25	26	27
	28	29	30				

Ashley Olsen, 34, fashion designer, actress ("Full House," "Two of a Kind"), born Los Angeles, CA, June 13, 1986.

Mary-Kate Olsen, 34, fashion designer, actress ("Weeds," "Full House," "Two of a Kind"), born Los Angeles, CA, June 13, 1986.

Ally Sheedy, 58, actress (*St. Elmo's Fire, The Breakfast Club*), born New York, NY, June 13, 1962.

Stellan Skarsgard, 69, actor (*Our Kind of Traitor, The Avengers, The Girl with the Dragon Tattoo* [US]), born Gothenburg, Sweden, June 13, 1951.

Richard Thomas, 69, actor ("The Waltons," *Roots: The Next Generations*), born New York, NY, June 13, 1951.

June 14 — Sunday

DAY 166   **200 REMAINING**

ALZHEIMER, ALOIS: BIRTH ANNIVERSARY. June 14, 1864. The German psychiatrist and pathologist Alois Alzheimer was born at Marktbreit am Mainz, Germany. In 1907 an article by Alzheimer appeared in *Allgemeine Zeitschrift für Psychiatrie* first describing the disease that was named for him. It was thought of as a kind of presenile dementia, usually beginning at age 40–60. Alzheimer died Dec 19, 1915, at Breslau, Germany.

BARTLETT, JOHN: 200th BIRTH ANNIVERSARY. June 14, 1820. American editor and compiler (*Bartlett's Familiar Quotations* [1855]) was born at Plymouth, MA. Though he had little formal education, he created one of the most-used reference works of the English language. No quotation of his own is among the more than 25,000 listed today, but in the preface to the first edition he wrote that the object of this work "originally made without any view of publication" was to show "the obligation our language owes to various authors for numerous phrases and familiar quotations which have become 'household words.'" Bartlett died at Cambridge, MA, Dec 3, 1905.

BOURKE-WHITE, MARGARET: BIRTH ANNIVERSARY. June 14, 1904. Margaret Bourke was born at New York City. One of the original photojournalists, she developed her personal style while photographing the Krupp Iron Works in Germany and the Soviet Union during the first Five-Year Plan. Bourke-White was one of the four original staff photographers for *Life* magazine in 1936. The first woman attached to the US armed forces during WWII, she covered the Italian campaign, siege of Moscow and American soldiers' crossing of the Rhine into Germany, and she shocked the world with her photographs of the concentration camps. Bourke-White photographed Mahatma Gandhi and covered the migration of millions of people after the Indian subcontinent was divided into Hindu India and Muslim Pakistan. She served as a war correspondent during the Korean War. Among her several books, the most famous is her collaboration with her second husband, novelist Erskine Caldwell, a study of rural poverty in the American South called *You Have Seen Their Faces*. She died Aug 27, 1971, at Stamford, CT.

CHILDREN'S DAY IN MASSACHUSETTS. June 14. Annually, the second Sunday in June. The governor proclaims this day each year.

CHILDREN'S SUNDAY. June 14. Traditionally the second Sunday in June is observed as Children's Sunday in many Christian churches.

CORPUS CHRISTI (US OBSERVANCE). June 14. A movable Roman Catholic celebration commemorating the institution of the Holy Eucharist. The solemnity has been observed around the world on the Thursday following Trinity Sunday since 1246, except in the US, where it is observed on the Sunday following Trinity Sunday.

FAMILY HISTORY DAY. June 14. Every summer, family reunions are so busy with games and activities that most of us forget the true purpose: to share the folklore, legends and myths that bind us together. Each participant should share at least one good recollection (fact or fiction). Don't forget the hot dogs and lemonade. (©2006 by WH.) For info: Thomas & Ruth Roy, Wellcat Holidays, 2418 Long Ln, Lebanon, PA 17046. Phone: (717) 279-0184. E-mail: info@wellcat.com. Web: www.wellcat.com.

FIRST NONSTOP TRANSATLANTIC FLIGHT: ANNIVERSARY. June 14–15, 1919. Captain John Alcock and Lieutenant Arthur W. Brown flew a Vickers Vimy bomber 1,900 miles nonstop from St. Johns, Newfoundland, to Clifden, County Galway, Ireland. In spite of their crash landing in an Irish peat bog, their flight inspired public interest in aviation. See also: "Lindbergh Flight: Anniversary" (May 20).

FIRST US BREACH OF PROMISE SUIT: ANNIVERSARY. June 14, 1623. The first breach of promise suit in the US was filed in the Virginia Council of State, at Charles City, VA. Reverend Greville Pooley brought suit against Cicely Jordan, who had jilted him in favor of another man. (Jordan won the suit.)

★FLAG DAY. June 14. Presidential Proclamation issued each year for June 14. Proclamation 1335, of May 30, 1916, covers all succeeding years. Has been issued annually since 1941 (PL 81–203 of Aug 3, 1949). Customarily issued as "Flag Day and National Flag Week," as in 1986; the president usually mentions "a time to honor America," Flag Day to Independence Day (89 Stat. 211).

FLAG DAY: ANNIVERSARY OF THE STARS AND STRIPES. June 14, 1777. John Adams introduced the following resolution before the Continental Congress, meeting at Philadelphia, PA: "Resolved, That the flag of the thirteen United States shall be thirteen stripes, alternate red and white; that the union be thirteen stars, white on a blue field, representing a new constellation." Legal holiday in Pennsylvania.

FLAG DAY AT FORT MCHENRY: PAUSE FOR THE PLEDGE. June 14. Fort McHenry National Monument and Historic Shrine, Baltimore, MD. Celebration of the Stars and Stripes at the site that inspired Francis Scott Key to write the lyrics to "The Star-Spangled Banner" in 1814. Evening programs present music, military displays and Pledge of Allegiance and conclude with fireworks.

GREENCARE FOR TROOPS AWARENESS WEEK. June 14–20. GreenCare for Troops is a nationwide outreach program to care for lawns and landscapes of families of deployed military personnel. This week is the national observance of the program whose goal is to raise awareness with military families about the complimentary services available as well as to recruit additional volunteers to provide these valuable services. For info: Project EverGreen, 8500 Station St, Ste 230, Mentor, OH 44060. Phone: (888) 611-2955. Web: www.ProjectEverGreen.org.

IVES, BURL: BIRTH ANNIVERSARY. June 14, 1909. American singer and actor Burl Icle Ivanhoe Ives was born at Hunt, IL. He helped to reintroduce Anglo-American folk music in the '40s and '50s. Ives won an Academy Award for his supporting role in *The Big Country* (1958), and he is well known for his role as Big Daddy in both the film and Broadway productions of *Cat on a Hot Tin Roof*. He died Apr 14, 1995, at Anacortes, WA.

JAPAN: RICE PLANTING FESTIVAL. June 14. Osaka. Ceremonial transplanting of rice seedlings in paddy field at Sumiyoshi Shrine, Osaka.

MALAWI: FREEDOM DAY. June 14. National holiday. Commemorates free elections in 1994.

MUNICH FOUNDED: ANNIVERSARY. June 14, 1158. Traditional date of the founding of Munich (or "Home of the Monks"), when a marketplace was founded on the banks of the Isar River by Benedictine monks with the blessing of Henry the Lion, Duke of Bavaria.

★**NATIONAL FLAG WEEK.** June 14–20. Presidential Proclamation issued each year since 1966 for the week including June 14 (PL 89–443 of June 9, 1966). In addition, the president often calls upon the American people to participate in public ceremonies in which the Pledge of Allegiance is recited.

ORTHODOX FESTIVAL OF ALL SAINTS. June 14. Observed by Eastern Orthodox churches on the Sunday following Orthodox Pentecost (June 7 in 2020). Marks the end of the 18-week Triodion cycle.

RACE UNITY DAY. June 14. Baha'i-sponsored observance promoting racial harmony and understanding and the essential unity of humanity. Annually, the second Sunday in June. Established in 1957 by the Baha'is of the US. For info: Baha'is of the US, Office of Communications, 1233 Central St, Evanston, IL 60201. Phone: (847) 733-3584. E-mail: ooc@usbnc.org. Web: www.bahai.us.

SPACE MILESTONE: *MARINER 5* (US). June 14, 1967. Launched on this date, interplanetary probe established that 72.5–87.5 percent of Venus's atmosphere is carbon dioxide on Oct 18 flyby of the planet.

SPAIN: BABY JUMPING FESTIVAL (EL SALTO DEL COLACHO). June 14. Castrillo de Murcia (near Burgos). Annual festival dating back to 1620 where babies of the village are laid out on pallets in the lanes and men dressed as devils leap over them. Annually, the Sunday after Corpus Christi (June 11).

STOWE, HARRIET BEECHER: BIRTH ANNIVERSARY. June 14, 1811. American writer Harriet Beecher Stowe, daughter of the Reverend Lyman Beecher and sister of Henry Ward Beecher. Author of *Uncle Tom's Cabin* (1850), an antislavery novel that provoked a storm of protest and notoriety. It sold 300,000 copies in its first year alone. The reaction to *Uncle Tom's Cabin* and its profound political impact are without parallel in American literature. It is said that during the Civil War, when Harriet Beecher Stowe was introduced to President Abraham Lincoln, his words to her were, "So you're the little woman who wrote the book that made this great war." Stowe was born at Litchfield, CT, and died at Hartford, CT, July 1, 1896.

SUMMITT, PATRICIA SUE HEAD: BIRTH ANNIVERSARY. June 14, 1952. College basketball coach, born at Clarksville, TN. A college basketball star and member of the 1976 silver-medal Olympic basketball team, Summitt was head coach of the University of Tennessee's Lady Volunteers between 1974 and 2012. She led the team to eight NCAA championship titles, capping her career with a 1,098–208 record, giving her the most wins of any Division I NCAA coach. Showered with accolades, she said her personal barometer of success was that every player who completed her NCAA eligibility on her team graduated. She continued to inspire players and spectators when she carried on coaching for a year after being diagnosed with dementia. She was awarded a Presidential Medal of Freedom in 2012. Summitt died June 28, 2016, at Knoxville, TN.

UNIVAC COMPUTER: ANNIVERSARY. June 14, 1951. Univac 1, the world's first commercial computer, designed for the US Bureau of the Census, was unveiled, demonstrated and dedicated at Philadelphia, PA. Though this milestone of the computer age was the first commercial electronic computer, it had been preceded by ENIAC (Electronic Numeric Integrator and Computer). Univac was completed under the supervision of J. Presper Eckert, Jr, and John W. Mauchly at the University of Pennsylvania in 1946.

US ARMY ESTABLISHED BY CONGRESS: ANNIVERSARY. June 14, 1775. Anniversary of resolution of the Continental Congress establishing the army as the first US military service.

	June 2020					
S	**M**	**T**	**W**	**T**	**F**	**S**
	1	2	3	4	5	6
7	8	9	10	11	12	13
14	15	16	17	18	19	20
21	22	23	24	25	26	27
28	29	30				

WARREN G. HARDING BECOMES FIRST PRESIDENT TO BROADCAST ON RADIO: ANNIVERSARY. June 14, 1922. Warren G. Harding became the first president to broadcast a message over the radio. The event was the dedication of the Francis Scott Key Memorial at Baltimore, MD. The first official government message was broadcast Dec 6, 1923.

WORLD BLOOD DONOR DAY. June 14. This day seeks to raise awareness of the need for safe blood and blood products and to thank voluntary unpaid blood donors for their lifesaving gifts of blood. Give the gift of life: donate blood. Annually, June 14. For info: World Health Organization. Web: www.who.int/campaigns.

🎂 BIRTHDAYS TODAY

Yasmine Bleeth, 52, actress ("Baywatch," "Nash Bridges"), born New York, NY, June 14, 1968.

Boy George, 59, singer (Culture Club), born George Alan O'Dowd at London, England, June 14, 1961.

Diablo Cody, 42, screenwriter (*Juno*, "United States of Tara"), born Chicago, IL, June 14, 1978.

Marla Gibbs, 89, actress ("227," "The Jeffersons"), born Margaret Bradley at Chicago, IL, June 14, 1931.

Stephanie Maria (Steffi) Graf, 51, Hall of Fame tennis player, born Bruhl, West Germany (now Germany), June 14, 1969.

Eric Arthur Heiden, 62, Olympic speed skater, born Madison, WI, June 14, 1958.

Traylor Howard, 54, actress ("Monk," "Two Guys and a Girl"), born Orlando, FL, June 14, 1966.

Kevin McHale, 32, actor ("Glee," "Zoey 101"), born Plano, TX, June 14, 1988.

Eddie Mekka, 68, actor ("Laverne & Shirley"), born Worcester, MA, June 14, 1952.

Will Patton, 66, actor ("The Agency," *Remember the Titans*, *Armageddon*, *No Way Out*), born Charleston, SC, June 14, 1954.

Donald Trump, 74, 45th President of the US, real estate mogul, television personality ("The Apprentice"), born New York, NY, June 14, 1946.

June 15 — Monday

DAY 167   **199 REMAINING**

ARKANSAS: ADMISSION DAY: ANNIVERSARY. June 15. Became 25th state in 1836.

FIRST FATAL AVIATION ACCIDENT: ANNIVERSARY. June 15, 1785. Two French aeronauts, Jean François Pilatre de Rozier and P.A. de Romain, attempting to cross the English Channel from France to England in a balloon, were killed when their balloon caught fire and crashed to the ground—the first fatal accident in aviation history. Pilatre de Rozier was the first man to fly.

GREAT SMOKY MOUNTAINS NATIONAL PARK ESTABLISHED: ANNIVERSARY. June 15, 1934. Area along southern section of Tennessee–North Carolina boundary was authorized May 22, 1926; established for administration and protection on Feb 6, 1930; and finally established for full development as a national park in 1934.

GRIEG, EDVARD: BIRTH ANNIVERSARY. June 15, 1843. Pianist, composer, conductor and teacher, the first Scandinavian to compose nationalistic music. His incidental music for Henrik Ibsen's *Peer Gynt*, including ""In the Hall of the Mountain King," is his best known. Born at Bergen, Norway, Grieg died there Sept 4, 1907.

"HEE HAW" TV PREMIERE: ANNIVERSARY. June 15, 1969. "Hee Haw" has been described as a country-western version of "Laugh-In," composed of fast-paced sketches, silly jokes and songs. Though critics didn't like it, it had popular appeal and did well as a syndicated show. It was cohosted by Buck Owens and Roy Clark, alternating with guest hosts. Regular performers included Louis M. "Grandpa" Jones, Junior Samples, Jeannine Riley, Lulu Roman, David "Stringbean" Akeman, Sheb Wooley, Marianne Gordon, Minnie Pearl and Gordie Tapp.

JACKSON, RACHEL DONELSON ROBARDS: BIRTH ANNIVERSARY. June 15, 1767. Wife of Andrew Jackson, seventh president of the US, born at Halifax County, NC. Died at Nashville, TN, Dec 22, 1828.

MAGNA CARTA: ANNIVERSARY. June 15, 1215. Anniversary of King John of England's sealing of the Magna Carta "in the meadow called Ronimed between Windsor and Staines on the fifteenth day of June in the seventeenth year of our reign." Continually reinterpreted, the Magna Carta influenced the rise of England's constitutional monarchy and lent historical weight to 18th-century ideas about inalienable natural laws. It is still invoked popularly and in jurisprudence as a symbol of the written law's power to subdue tyranny. Four original copies of the 1215 charter survive.

MEET A MATE WEEK. June 15–21. To inspire singles seeking a mate to take advantage of summer by pursuing warm-weather meeting opportunities. Options include singles travel, sports activities, New Blood parties and volunteer work. For info: Robin Gorman Newman, 44 Somerset Dr N, Great Neck, NY 11020. Phone: (516) 773-0911. E-mail: rgnewman@optonline.com. Web: www.lovecoach.com/events.html.

MOUNT PINATUBO ERUPTS: ANNIVERSARY. June 15, 1991. Dormant for almost 500 years, Philippines volcano Mount Pinatubo erupted with a violent explosion, spewing ash and gases that could be seen for more than 60 miles. The surrounding areas were covered with ash and mud created by rainstorms. It was the second-largest eruption of the 20th century, killing nearly 1,000 people. On July 6, 1992, Ellsworth Dutton of the National Oceanic and Atmospheric Administration's Climate Monitoring and Diagnostics Laboratory announced that a layer of sulfuric acid droplets released into Earth's atmosphere by the eruption had cooled the planet's average temperature by about 1°F. The greatest difference was noted in the Northern Hemisphere with a drop of 1.5°. Although the temperature drop was temporary, the climate trend made determining the effect of greenhouse warming on Earth more difficult.

NATIONAL PRUNE DAY. June 15. Since 1988, a day to honor the prune for its health benefits as well as its delicious goodness. Celebrate the prune with festivals, cancer awareness workshops, school nutrition days and educational cooking events. Annually, June 15. For info: Rhayne Thomas, The Prune Whisperer, Prunes Are Sexy, LLC, 2251 N Rampart Blvd, Ste 242, Las Vegas, NV 89128. E-mail: PrunesAreSexy@hotmail.com.

NATIVE AMERICAN CITIZENSHIP DAY. June 15. Commemorates the day in 1924 when the US Congress passed legislation recognizing the citizenship of Native Americans.

NATURE PHOTOGRAPHY DAY. June 15. A day to promote the art and science of nature photography as a medium of communication, inspiration, nature appreciation and environmental protection. Annually, June 15. For info: North American Nature Photography Association, 6382 Charleston Rd, Alma, IL 62807. Phone: (618) 547-7616. Fax: (618) 547-7438. E-mail: info@nanpa.org. Web: www.nanpa.org.

NORWAY: CELEBRATION OF EDVARD GRIEG'S BIRTH ANNIVERSARY. June 15. Special celebrations at Lofthus on the Hardanger fjord where Grieg's cabin still stands.

QUARTERLY ESTIMATED FEDERAL INCOME TAX PAYERS' DUE DATE. June 15. For those individuals whose fiscal year is the calendar year and who make quarterly estimated federal income tax payments, today is one of the due dates (Jan 15, Apr 15, June 15 and Sept 15, 2020).

STEINBERG, SAUL: BIRTH ANNIVERSARY. June 15, 1914. Artist, born at Râmnicu Sarat, Romania, who immigrated to the US in the 1940s to escape anti-Semitism in Italy. Most famous for his work for the *New Yorker* magazine, for which he completed 90 covers and 1,200 drawings. Steinberg said of his work, "Drawing makes up its own syntax as it goes along. The line can't be reasoned in the mind. It can only be reasoned on paper." He died May 12, 1999, at New York, NY.

TWELFTH AMENDMENT TO US CONSTITUTION RATIFIED: ANNIVERSARY. June 15, 1804. The 12th Amendment to the Constitution was ratified. It changed the method of electing the president and vice president after a tie in the electoral college during the election of 1800. Rather than each elector voting for two candidates, with the candidate receiving the most votes elected president and the second-place candidate elected vice president, each elector was now required to designate his or her choice for president and vice president, respectively.

UNITED NATIONS: WORLD ELDER ABUSE AWARENESS DAY. June 15. Elder abuse is a global social issue that affects the health and human rights of millions of older persons around the world, and an issue that deserves the attention of the international community. The General Assembly has designated June 15 as World Elder Abuse Awareness Day (Res 66/127 of Mar 9, 2012). It represents the one day in the year when the whole world voices its opposition to the abuse and suffering inflicted on some of our older citizens. For info: United Nations, Dept of Public Info, New York, NY 10017. Web: www.un.org.

US LANDING ON SAIPAN: ANNIVERSARY. June 15, 1944. In a continued effort to penetrate the Japanese inner defenses, US amphibious forces invaded the Mariana Islands. A huge fleet of 800 ships from Guadalcanal and Hawaii carried the 2nd and 4th Marine Divisions, consisting of 162,000 men. By the end of the day 20,000 of these men had established a 5½-mile-long beachhead on the island of Saipan. Though the American forces suffered heavy losses during an overnight counterattack, on the morning of June 16 the Marines still held the area they had taken the day before.

US VIRGIN ISLANDS: ORGANIC ACT DAY. June 15. Commemorates the enactment by the US Congress, July 22, 1954, of the Revised Organic Act, under which the government of the Virgin Islands is organized. Observed annually on the third Monday in June.

🧁 BIRTHDAYS TODAY

Jay Ajayi, 27, football player, born London, England, June 15, 1993.
Jim Belushi, 66, actor ("Saturday Night Live," "According to Jim"), born Chicago, IL, June 15, 1954.
Wade Boggs, 62, Hall of Fame baseball player, born Omaha, NE, June 15, 1958.

Simon Callow, 71, actor (*A Room with a View, Howards End*), author, born London, England, June 15, 1949.

Courteney Cox, 56, actress ("Friends," "Cougar Town," *Scream*), born Birmingham, AL, June 15, 1964.

Julie Hagerty, 65, actress (*Airplane!, Lost in America, Reversal of Fortune*), born Cincinnati, OH, June 15, 1955.

Neil Patrick Harris, 47, actor (Tony for *Hedwig and the Angry Inch*; "How I Met Your Mother"), born Albuquerque, NM, June 15, 1973.

Mike Holmgren, 72, football executive, former coach, born San Francisco, CA, June 15, 1948.

Helen Hunt, 57, actress (*The Sessions, Cast Away*, Oscar for *As Good as It Gets*; "Mad About You"), born Los Angeles, CA, June 15, 1963.

Justin Leonard, 48, golfer, born Dallas, TX, June 15, 1972.

Nicola Pagett, 75, actress ("Upstairs, Downstairs," *There's a Girl in My Soup*), born Cairo, Egypt, June 15, 1945.

Leah Remini, 50, actress ("The King of Queens," "Saved by the Bell"), born Brooklyn, NY, June 15, 1970.

Mohamed Salah, 28, soccer player, born Mohamed Salah Ghaly at Nagrig, Egypt, June 15, 1992.

Anna Torv, 42, actress ("Fringe"), born Melbourne, Australia, June 15, 1978.

Xi Jinping, 67, President of the People's Republic of China, born Beijing, China, June 15, 1953.

June 16 — Tuesday

DAY 168	198 REMAINING

BLOOMSDAY: ANNIVERSARY. June 16, 1904. Anniversary of events in Dublin, Ireland, recorded in James Joyce's *Ulysses*, whose central character is Leopold Bloom.

ENGLAND: ROYAL ASCOT. June 16–20 (tentative). Ascot, Berkshire. There are few sporting venues that can match the rich heritage and history of Ascot Racecourse. Since 1711, Royal Ascot has established itself as a national institution and the centerpiece of the British social calendar as well as being the ultimate stage for the best racehorses in the world. There are a total of 18 "Group" races over the five days. Est attendance: 300,000. For info: Enquiry Office, Ascot Racecourse, Ascot, Berkshire SL5 7JX, England. Web: www.ascot.co.uk.

GRAHAM, KATHARINE: BIRTH ANNIVERSARY. June 16, 1917. Born at New York, NY, Graham is acclaimed for her role as the most powerful woman in publishing during her tenure as publisher of the *Washington Post*. Under her direction, the *Post* gained status until it was regarded as one of the nation's two best and most prestigious newspapers. As owner and chair of the paper, Graham controlled the fifth-largest publishing company in the US. A Pulitzer Prize winner in her own right for her autobiography (*Personal History*, 1997), Graham died July 17, 2001, at Boise, ID, and was posthumously inducted into the National Women's Hall of Fame in 2002.

GRIFFIN, JOHN HOWARD: 100th BIRTH ANNIVERSARY. June 16, 1920. American author and photographer deeply concerned about racial problems in the US. To better understand blacks in the American South, Griffin blackened his skin by the use of chemicals and ultraviolet light, keeping a journal as he traveled through

the South, resulting in his best-known book, *Black Like Me*. Born at Dallas, TX. Died at Fort Worth, TX, Sept 9, 1980.

HOUSE DIVIDED SPEECH: ANNIVERSARY. June 16, 1858. Political newcomer Abraham Lincoln, beginning his campaign for the Illinois US Senate seat, addressed the Republican State Convention at Springfield, IL, and made a controversial speech that has come to be known as the House Divided speech. Attacking the Kansas-Nebraska Act of 1854, Lincoln said, "A house divided against itself cannot stand. I believe this government cannot endure, permanently, half slave and half free. I do not expect the Union to be dissolved; I do not expect the house to fall; but I do expect it will cease to be divided. It will become all one thing, or all the other."

LADIES' DAY INITIATED IN BASEBALL: ANNIVERSARY. June 16, 1883. The New York Giants hosted the first Ladies' Day baseball game. Both escorted and unescorted ladies were admitted to the game free.

LAUREL, STAN: BIRTH ANNIVERSARY. June 16, 1890. Born Arthur Stanley Jefferson at Ulverston, England. Laurel's career began on the vaudeville stage before moving to motion pictures; he appeared in nearly 200 short and feature-length films. He is known for his 25-year partnership with Oliver Hardy. The comedic duo—Laurel, the creative force, played the thin foil to rotund Hardy—began in silent films and successfully transitioned to "talkies." Awarded a special Oscar for "creative pioneering in comedy" (1961), Laurel died Feb 23, 1965, at Santa Monica, CA.

MONTEREY INTERNATIONAL POP FESTIVAL: ANNIVERSARY. June 16–18, 1967. Taking place in Monterey, CA, with more than 55,000 fans, the festival featured performances from Jimi Hendrix, the Byrds, Jefferson Airplane, Simon & Garfunkel, the Animals, The Who, Ravi Shankar and many others. Monterey was the world's first outdoor rock concert pitched on a grand scale.

PETIT JEAN ANTIQUE AUTO SHOW AND SWAP MEET. June 16–20. Petit Jean Mountain, Morrilton, AR. 62nd annual show and meet with more than 125 antique and classic cars competing for awards, from turn-of-the-century to 25-year-old models. Also, a separate open car show. More than 1,500 vendor spaces filled with antique cars, parts and arts and crafts. Est attendance: 85,000. For info: Mark Hoelzeman, Museum of Automobiles, 8 Jones Ln, Morrilton, AR 72110. Phone: (501) 727-5427. E-mail: info@motaa.com. Web: www.motaa.com.

***PSYCHO* FILM PREMIERE: 60th ANNIVERSARY.** June 16, 1960. Millions of filmgoers (and star Janet Leigh) avoided the shower after this thriller's debut in 1960. Alfred Hitchcock's shocker, punctuated by shrieking violins and sudden knife attacks, juxtaposed the old-time horror of the dark gothic mansion with a new locus of fear: the isolated postwar roadside motel. *Psycho* led the way to the "slasher" films of the 1970s and later. Anthony Perkins starred as motel proprietor and bird lover Norman Bates.

***THE RISE AND FALL OF ZIGGY STARDUST AND THE SPIDERS FROM MARS* RELEASED: ANNIVERSARY.** June 16, 1972. David Bowie introduced a new persona—Ziggy Stardust, the alien rock star—with the release of this classic album. Featuring the single "Starman," the album entered the UK music charts at number 15 on July 1 and eventually reached number 5. The album carried this directive: "To be played at maximum volume."

SOUTH AFRICA: YOUTH DAY. June 16. National holiday. Commemorates a student uprising in Soweto against "Bantu Education" and the enforced teaching of Afrikaans in 1976.

	S	M	T	W	T	F	S
June		1	2	3	4	5	6
	7	8	9	10	11	12	13
2020	14	15	16	17	18	19	20
	21	22	23	24	25	26	27
	28	29	30				

SPACE MILESTONE: *VOSTOK 6* (USSR): FIRST WOMAN IN SPACE. June 16, 1963. Valentina Tereshkova, 26, former cotton-mill worker, born on a collective farm near Yaroslavl, USSR, became the first woman in space when her spacecraft, *Vostok 6*, took off from the Tyuratam launch site. She manually controlled *Vostok 6* during the 70.8-hour flight through 48 orbits of Earth and landed by parachute (separate from her cabin) June 19, 1963. In November 1963 she married cosmonaut Andrian Nikolayev, who had piloted *Vostok 3* through 64 Earth orbits, Aug 11–15, 1962. Their child, Yelena (1964), was the first born to space-traveler parents.

🎂 BIRTHDAYS TODAY

Sonia Braga, 70, actress ("American Family," *Kiss of the Spider Woman*), born Maringá, Paraná, Brazil, June 16, 1950.

Daniel Brühl, 42, actor ("The Alienist," *Rush, Good Bye Lenin!*), born Barcelona, Spain, June 16, 1978.

John Cho, 48, actor (*Star Trek, Harold & Kumar Go to White Castle*), born Seoul, South Korea, June 16, 1972.

Roberto Durán, 69, former boxer, born Chorrillo, Panama, June 16, 1951.

Abby Elliott, 33, comedienne, actress ("Saturday Night Live"), born Wilton, CT, June 16, 1987.

Cobi Jones, 50, Hall of Fame soccer player, born Westlake Village, CA, June 16, 1970.

Laurie Metcalf, 65, actress (Tony for *A Doll's House, Part 2*; Emmy for "Roseanne"; "The Norm Show"), born Edwardsville, IL, June 16, 1955.

Phil Mickelson, 50, golfer, born San Diego, CA, June 16, 1970.

Joyce Carol Oates, 82, writer (*The Gravedigger's Daughter, Blonde, What I Lived For, Black Water*), born Lockport, NY, June 16, 1938.

Joan Van Ark, 77, actress ("Knots Landing"), born New York, NY, June 16, 1943.

Kerry Wood, 43, former baseball player, born Irving, TX, June 16, 1977.

June 17 — Wednesday

DAY 169   **197 REMAINING**

BATTLE OF BUNKER HILL: ANNIVERSARY. June 17, 1775. Early battle in the American Revolutionary War fought on Bunker and Breed's hills near Charleston, MA. Although the British were victorious in negating the colonial attack, they lost more than 1,000 killed or wounded while the colonists only lost 450 killed or wounded. Famously—or mythically—the order was given: "Don't fire until you see the whites of their eyes."

BELLAMY, RALPH: BIRTH ANNIVERSARY. June 17, 1904. American actor Ralph Rexford Bellamy was born at Chicago, IL. He appeared in more than 100 films and was best known for his stage and film

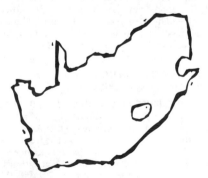

portrayals of President Franklin D. Roosevelt. He was a founder of the Screen Actors Guild and president of Actors' Equity. Bellamy was awarded an honorary Academy Award in 1987. He died Nov 29, 1991, at Los Angeles, CA.

BRONCO CHASE: ANNIVERSARY. June 17, 1994. Facing arrest in connection with the June 12 murders of his ex-wife, Nicole Brown Simpson, and Ronald Goldman, football great O.J. Simpson fled his home and joined friend Al Cowlings in Simpson's white Ford Bronco vehicle. After leading police on a lengthy, low-speed car chase over Los Angeles's freeways, the pair eventually arrived back at Simpson's home, where he was apprehended. The drama was carried live on television nationwide; an estimated 90 million people watched.

BUNKER HILL DAY. June 17. Suffolk County, MA. Legal holiday in the county in commemoration of the Battle of Bunker Hill that took place in 1775.

CHARLESTON CHURCH SHOOTING: 5th ANNIVERSARY. June 17, 2015. At the historic Emanuel African Methodist Episcopal Church (the oldest AME church in the South) at Charleston, SC, a white-supremicist gunman fired on a prayer group, killing nine people and injuring one.

FAIN, SAMMY: BIRTH ANNIVERSARY. June 17, 1902. American composer Sammy Fain was born Samuel Feinberg at New York, NY. He won an Academy Award for his song "Secret Love" from *Calamity Jane* (1953) and for "Love Is a Many-Splendored Thing" from the film of the same name (1955). He died Dec 6, 1989, at Los Angeles, CA.

HERSEY, JOHN: BIRTH ANNIVERSARY. June 17, 1914. American novelist, born at Tientsin, China, who wrote *A Bell for Adano*, which won the Pulitzer Prize in 1945. *The Wall* and *Hiroshima* are both based on fact and set in Poland and Japan, respectively, during WWII. Died at Key West, FL, Mar 24, 1993.

HOOPER, WILLIAM: BIRTH ANNIVERSARY. June 17, 1742. Signer of the Declaration of Independence, born at Boston, MA. Died Oct 14, 1790, at Hillsboro, NC.

ICELAND: INDEPENDENCE DAY. June 17. National holiday. Anniversary of founding of republic and independence from Denmark in 1944, a major festival, especially in Reykjavik. Parades, competitions and street dancing.

MISS TENNESSEE VOLUNTEER PAGEANT. June 17–20. Carl Perkins Civic Center, Jackson, TN. Part of the Miss America Organization. For info: Miss Tennessee Volunteer Pageant, PO Box 998, Jackson, TN 38302. Phone: (731) 425-8590. Fax: (731) 668-2758. E-mail: MissTNED@gmail.com. Web: www.misstennessee.org.

SOUTH AFRICA REPEALS LAST APARTHEID LAW: ANNIVERSARY. June 17, 1991. The parliament of South Africa repealed the Population Registration Act, removing the law that was the foundation of apartheid. The law, first enacted in 1950, required the classification by race of all South Africans at birth. It established four compulsory racial categories: white, mixed race, Asian and black. Although this marked the removal of the last of the apartheid laws, blacks in South Africa still could not vote.

STRAVINSKY, IGOR FYODOROVICH: BIRTH ANNIVERSARY. June 17, 1882. Russian composer and author, born at Oranienbaum (near Leningrad). Among his best-known music: the ballets *The Firebird, Petrushka* and *The Rite of Spring*; the choral work *Symphony of Psalms*; and *Abraham and Isaac, A Sacred Ballet*. Died at New York, NY, Apr 6, 1971.

UNITED NATIONS: WORLD DAY TO COMBAT DESERTIFICATION AND DROUGHT. June 17. Proclaimed by the General Assembly Dec 19, 1994 (Res 49/115). States were invited to promote public awareness of the need for international cooperation to combat desertification and the effects of drought and the implementation of the UN Convention to Combat Desertification. For info: United Nations, Dept of Public Info, New York, NY 10017. Web: www.un.org.

WATERGATE ARRESTS: ANNIVERSARY. June 17, 1972. Anniversary of arrests at Democratic Party Headquarters (in Watergate complex, Washington, DC) that led to revelations of political espionage, threats of imminent impeachment of the president and, on Aug 9, 1974, the resignation of President Richard M. Nixon.

WESLEY, JOHN: BIRTH ANNIVERSARY. June 17, 1703. Born at Epworth, England. Wesley, along with his younger brother, Charles, was the founder of Methodism. John Wesley died Mar 2, 1791.

🎂 BIRTHDAYS TODAY

K.J. Apa, 23, actor ("Riverdale," *A Dog's Purpose*), born Kenati James Fitzgerald at Auckland, New Zealand, June 17, 1997.

Alex Azar, 53, US Secretary of Health and Human Services (Trump administration), born Johnstown, PA, June 17, 1967.

Tory Burch, 54, fashion designer, born Tory Robinson at Valley Forge, PA, June 17, 1966.

Thomas Haden Church, 60, actor (*Sideways*, "Divorce," "Wings"), born Thomas McMillen at El Paso, TX, June 17, 1960.

Tom Corbett, 71, former governor of Pennsylvania (R), born Philadelphia, PA, June 17, 1949.

Will Forte, 50, comedian, actor (*Nebraska*, "The Last Man on Earth," "Saturday Night Live"), born Alameda County, CA, June 17, 1970.

Tommy R. Franks, 75, retired general, US Army, born Wynnewood, OK, June 17, 1945.

Newt Gingrich, 77, former Speaker of the US House of Representatives, consultant, born Harrisburg, PA, June 17, 1943.

Dan Jansen, 55, Olympic speed skater, sportscaster, born West Allis, WI, June 17, 1965.

Greg Kinnear, 57, actor (*Little Miss Sunshine*, *The Matador*, *As Good as It Gets*), born Logansport, IN, June 17, 1963.

Kendrick Lamar, 33, rapper (12 Grammys, one Pulitzer), born Kendrick Lamar Duckworth at Compton, CA, June 17, 1987.

Mark Linn-Baker, 67, actor ("Perfect Strangers," *My Favorite Year*), born St. Louis, MO, June 17, 1953.

Barry Manilow, 74, Songwriters Hall of Fame singer, songwriter, producer, born Brooklyn, NY, June 17, 1946.

Joe Piscopo, 69, comedian ("Saturday Night Live"), born Passaic, NJ, June 17, 1951.

Venus Williams, 40, tennis player, born Lynwood, CA, June 17, 1980.

June 18 — Thursday

DAY 170	196 REMAINING

BATTLE OF WATERLOO: ANNIVERSARY. June 18, 1815. Date of the decisive defeat of Emperor Napoleon and his army of 74,000 soldiers by a combined Anglo-Allied (68,000 troops) and Prussian army (70,000 troops) led by the Duke of Wellington and Marshal Blücher. The bloody battle in a gentle valley near Waterloo—a municipality then annexed to the French Republic, now part of French-speaking Belgium—ended the French First Empire and the career of Napoleon Bonaparte, one of the greatest commanders

	S	M	T	W	T	F	S
June		1	2	3	4	5	6
	7	8	9	10	11	12	13
2020	14	15	16	17	18	19	20
	21	22	23	24	25	26	27
	28	29	30				

and statesmen in history, and ushered in half a century of international peace and stability in Europe.

CAHN, SAMMY: BIRTH ANNIVERSARY. June 18, 1913. Tin Pan Alley legend Sammy Cahn was born Samuel Cohen at New York City. He was nominated for 26 Academy Awards and won four times, for "Three Coins in the Fountain" (1954), "All the Way" (1957), "High Hopes" (1959) and "Call Me Irresponsible" (1963). In the late 1940s he began working with composer Jimmy Van Heusen, and the two in essence were the personal songwriting team for Frank Sinatra. Cahn wrote the greatest number of Sinatra hits, including "Love and Marriage," "The Second Time Around" and "The Tender Trap." Died Jan 15, 1993, at Los Angeles, CA.

EGYPT: EVACUATION DAY. June 18. Public holiday celebrating the anniversary of the withdrawal of the British army from the Suez Canal area of Egypt in 1954.

FOLGER, HENRY CLAY, JR: BIRTH ANNIVERSARY. June 18, 1857. American businessman and industrialist who amassed one of the finest collections of Shakespeareana in the world and bequeathed it (The Folger Shakespeare Library, Washington, DC) to the American people. Born at New York, NY. Died June 11, 1930, at Brooklyn, NY.

LITTLE BIGHORN DAYS. June 18–20 (tentative). Hardin, MT. To celebrate the history of the Old West. This annual celebration of Custer's Last Stand includes such activities as Custer's Last Stand Reenactment (sponsored by the Real Bird family), the Fort Custer and Plains Indian Exhibit, two parades, a historic book fair, musical show, rodeo, street dance, arm wrestling and more. Est attendance: 2,500. For info: Dorothy Stenerson, Secretary, Hardin Area Chamber of Commerce & Agriculture, PO Box 446, Hardin, MT 59034. Phone: (406) 665-1672. E-mail: hardinchamber@gmail.com. Web: www.thehardinchamber.com.

MALLORY, GEORGE LEIGH: BIRTH ANNIVERSARY. June 18, 1886. English explorer and mountain climber born at Mobberley, Cheshire, England. Last seen climbing through the mists toward the summit of the highest mountain in the world, Mount Everest, on the morning of June 8, 1924. Best remembered for his answer when asked why he wanted to climb Mount Everest: "Because it is there." In 1999 Mallory's body was found by an expedition to Mount Everest, 75 years after his death at age 37.

RECESS AT WORK DAY. June 18. Seeking productive, creative, happier and healthier employees? Take a break from the norm this month—make time for recess. Take an hour for some teambuilding. Play some games. Seek out a creativity or innovation exercise. Work on improving morale. Just make sure you make it fun. Annually, the third Thursday in June. (Or, commit to happier employees throughout the year on the third Thursday of each month.) RECESSitate your team before you need to resuscitate them! For info: Rich DiGirolamo. Phone: (203) 470-3388. E-mail: rich@RichDiGirolamo.com. Web: www.recessatworkday.com.

SEYCHELLES: CONSTITUTION DAY. June 18. National holiday commemorating adoption of constitution in 1993.

SPACE MILESTONE: FIRST AMERICAN WOMAN IN SPACE. June 18, 1983. Dr. Sally Ride, 32-year-old physicist and pilot, functioned as a "mission specialist" and became the first American woman in space when she began a six-day mission aboard the space shuttle *Challenger*. The "near-perfect" mission was launched from Cape Canaveral, FL, and landed June 24, 1983, at Edwards Air Force Base, CA. See also: "Space Milestone: *Vostok 6* (USSR): First Woman in Space" (June 16).

UNITED NATIONS: SUSTAINABLE GASTRONOMY DAY. June 18. On Dec 21, 2016, the General Assembly designated this day (Res 71/246), recognizing that "gastronomy is a cultural expression related to the natural and cultural diversity of the world, and reaffirming that all cultures and civilizations can contribute to and are crucial enablers of sustainable development." This day seeks "to focus the world's attention on the role that sustainable gastronomy can play in achieving the Sustainable Development Goals, including by promoting agricultural development, food security, nutrition, sustainable food production and the conservation of biodiversity." For info: United Nations. Web: www.un.org.

US OPEN (GOLF) CHAMPIONSHIP. June 18–21. Winged Foot Golf Club, Mamaroneck, NY. Since 1895, golf's greatest players have competed at this major world championship. For info: USGA, Golf House, Championship Dept, PO Box 708, Far Hills, NJ 07931. Phone: (908) 234-2300. E-mail: champs@usga.org. Web: www.usga.org.

WAR OF 1812: DECLARATION ANNIVERSARY. June 18, 1812. After much debate in Congress between "hawks" such as Henry Clay and John Calhoun and "doves" such as John Randolph, Congress issued a declaration of war on Great Britain. The action was prompted primarily by Britain's violation of America's rights on the high seas and British incitement of Native American warfare on the frontier. War was seen by some as a way to acquire Florida and Canada. The hostilities ended with the signing of the Treaty of Ghent on Dec 24, 1814, at Ghent, Belgium.

🎂 BIRTHDAYS TODAY

Barbara Broccoli, 60, film producer (James Bond films; BAFTA [shared] for *Skyfall*), born Los Angeles, CA, June 18, 1960.

Lou Brock, 81, Hall of Fame baseball player, born El Dorado, AR, June 18, 1939.

Eddie Cibrian, 47, actor ("Third Watch"), born Burbank, CA, June 18, 1973.

David Giuntoli, 40, actor ("Grimm"), born Milwaukee, WI, June 18, 1980.

Willa Holland, 29, model, actress (*Tiger Eyes*, "Arrow," "The O.C."), born Los Angeles, CA, June 18, 1991.

Carol Kane, 68, actress (*Hester Street*, "Gotham," "Taxi"), born Cleveland, OH, June 18, 1952.

Donald Keene, 98, literary critic, translator, educator, born New York, NY, June 18, 1922.

Richard Madden, 34, actor ("Bodyguard," "Game of Thrones," *Birdsong*), born Elderslie, Scotland, June 18, 1986.

Paul McCartney, 78, singer, songwriter (The Beatles, Wings), born Liverpool, England, June 18, 1942.

Richard Powers, 63, author (*The Overstory*, *The Echo Maker*, *Galatea 2.2*), born Evanston, IL, June 18, 1957.

Isabella Rossellini, 68, model, actress (*Blue Velvet*, *Cousins*), born Rome, Italy, June 18, 1952.

Blake Shelton, 44, country singer, television personality ("The Voice"), born Ada, OK, June 18, 1976.

June 19 — Friday

DAY 171	195 REMAINING

BASCOM, EARL W.: BIRTH ANNIVERSARY. June 19, 1906. Rodeo showman and pioneer, Earl W. Bascom was born at Vernal, UT. During his career he developed the first side-delivery rodeo chute (1916), the first hornless bronc saddle (1922) and the first one-handed bareback rigging (1924). He produced the first rodeo in Mississippi and also produced the first rodeo performed at night under electric lights (1935). Bascom died Aug 28, 1995, at Victorville, CA.

BATTLE OF PHILIPPINE SEA: ANNIVERSARY. June 19–20, 1944. Determined to prevent any further advancement by the Allies in Japan's area of inner defense, Vice Admiral Jisaburō Ozawa ordered the imperial fleet to the Mariana Islands. Admiral Raymond Spruance, possibly the US's greatest and most successful naval commander, ordered a strike force against the Japanese fleet in the Philippine Sea. A furious battle developed in the skies between US carrier-borne aircraft and Japanese aircraft from their carriers and land bases on the Marianas. The Japanese lost three aircraft carriers (*Shokaku, Taiho* and *Hiyo*), two destroyers and one tanker. Three carriers, one battleship, three cruisers, one destroyer and three tankers were seriously damaged. The Japanese lost at least 400 aircraft.

DALESBURG MIDSUMMER FESTIVAL. June 19. Dalesburg Lutheran Church, rural Vermillion, SD. Celebration of Scandinavian and rural heritage. Programs, dances to raise the Midsummer Pole, a supper, children's activities and more. Est attendance: 600. For info: Ronald Johnson, Midsummer Committee, Dalesburg Midsummer Festival, 30595 University Rd, Vermillion, SD 57069-6507. Phone: (605) 253-2575. Web: www.dalesburg.org.

DENMARK: FREDERIKSSUND VIKING GAMES. June 19–July 12 (tentative). Frederikssund. Famous, long-running cultural festival featuring outdoor theater based on Viking legends and mythology. Also features an authentic reimagining of a Viking market with plenty of mead. Begins on the Friday near the summer solstice. For info: Vikingespil Frederikssund. Web: www.vikingespil.dk.

EMANCIPATION DAY IN TEXAS: ANNIVERSARY. June 19, 1865. In honor of the 1865 emancipation of the slaves in Texas. See also: "Juneteenth" (below).

FIRST RUNNING OF THE BELMONT STAKES: ANNIVERSARY. June 19, 1867. The first running of the Belmont Stakes took place at Jerome Park, NY. The team of jockey J. Gilpatrick and his horse, Ruthless, finished in a time of 3:05. The Belmont Stakes continued at Jerome Park until 1889; moved to Morris Park, NY, 1890–1905; and in 1906 settled at Belmont Park, NY, where it has continued to the present day. The Belmont Stakes is the oldest event of horse racing's Triple Crown.

FORTAS, ABE: BIRTH ANNIVERSARY. June 19, 1910. Abe Fortas was born at Memphis, TN. He was appointed to the Supreme Court by President Lyndon Johnson in 1965. Prior to his appointment he was known as a civil libertarian, having argued cases for government employees and other individuals accused by Senator Joe McCarthy of having Communist affiliations. He argued the 1963 landmark Supreme Court case of *Gideon v Wainwright*, which established the right of indigent defendants to free legal aid in criminal prosecutions. In 1968 he was nominated by Johnson to succeed Chief Justice Earl Warren, but his nomination was withdrawn after much conservative opposition in the Senate. In 1969 Fortas became the first Supreme Court justice to be forced to resign after revelations about questionable financial dealings were made public. He died Apr 5, 1982, at Washington, DC.

GEHRIG, LOU: BIRTH ANNIVERSARY. June 19, 1903. Henry Louis (Lou) Gehrig, Baseball Hall of Fame first baseman, born Ludwig Heinrich Gehrig at New York, NY, June 19, 1903. Gehrig played baseball at Columbia and then signed with the New York Yankees, making his major league debut in 1923. Together with Babe Ruth, he personified the powerful Yankees lineup that came to be called "Murderers' Row." Gehrig played first base and hit .340 over 17

seasons with 493 home runs, 23 of them grand slams. He drove in 184 runs in 1931 and won the American League Triple Crown in 1934. He earned the nickname "the Iron Horse" for playing in a record 2,130 consecutive games, a streak stopped only by illness. Stricken with amyotrophic lateral sclerosis, a disease later called Lou Gehrig's disease, he retired abruptly in May 1939. Inducted into the Hall of Fame in 1939 by special election. Died at New York, NY, on June 2, 1941.

HOWARD, MOE: BIRTH ANNIVERSARY. June 19, 1897. The head stooge in the Three Stooges, Moe Howard was born Moses Horwitz at Bensonhurst, NY. He died May 4, 1975, at Hollywood, CA. Howard began his show business career at age 12 by running errands at Vitagraph studios. He worked with Ted Healy in various comedy and singing acts, and together they teamed with Shemp Howard and Larry Fine in the mid-1920s for an early Stooges act. In 1930 the Stooges made their film debut in *Soup to Nuts.* Howard appeared in four feature films without the other Stooges, including *Doctor Death, Seeker of Souls.*

JUNETEENTH. June 19. Celebrated in Texas to commemorate the day in 1865 when Union general Gordon Granger proclaimed the slaves of Texas free. Also proclaimed as Emancipation Day by the Florida legislature. Juneteenth has become an occasion for commemoration by African Americans in many parts of the US.

PASCAL, BLAISE: BIRTH ANNIVERSARY. June 19, 1623. French philosopher, physicist and mathematician born at Clermont-Ferrand and died at Paris, Aug 19, 1662. It was Pascal who said, "Had Cleopatra's nose been shorter, the whole history of the world would have been different." And, in his *Provincial Letters,* he wrote, "I have made this letter longer than usual because I lack the time to make it short."

ROSENBERG EXECUTION: ANNIVERSARY. June 19, 1953. Anniversary of the electrocution of the only married couple ever executed together in the US. Julius (35) and Ethel (37) Rosenberg were executed for espionage at Sing Sing Prison, Ossining, NY. Time for the execution was advanced several hours to avoid conflict with the Jewish sabbath. Their conviction has been a subject of controversy over the years.

SLAVES IN TEXAS EMANCIPATED (JUNETEENTH): ANNIVERSARY. June 19, 1865. On this date, at Galveston, TX, Union general and commander of the Department of Texas (June 10–Aug 6) Gordon Granger issued General Order Number 3, which informed 250,000 slaves in the state of the Emancipation Proclamation of 1863 that freed them. "This involves an absolute equality of personal rights and rights of property between former masters and slaves, and the connection heretofore existing between them becomes that between employer and hired labor." Although it took months for all Texas slaves to hear the news, the date of Granger's alert, June 19, became a statewide date of celebration that continues nationwide today.

SPACE MILESTONE: *ARIANE* (ESA). June 19, 1981. Launched from Kourou, French Guiana, by the European Space Administration, *Ariane* carried two satellites into orbit: *Meteostat 2,* an ESA weather satellite, and *Apple,* a geostationary communications satellite for India, to be stationed over Sumatra.

UNITED NATIONS: INTERNATIONAL DAY FOR THE ELIMINATION OF SEXUAL VIOLENCE IN CONFLICT. June 19. First observed in 2016. A day to raise awareness of the need to put an end to conflict-related sexual violence, to honor the victims and survivors of sexual violence around the world and to pay tribute to all those who have courageously devoted their lives to and lost their lives in standing up for the eradication of these crimes. Annually, June 19. (Res 69/293 adopted June 19, 2015.) For info: United Nations, Dept of Public Info, New York, NY 10017. Web: www.un.org.

URUGUAY: ARTIGAS DAY. June 19. National holiday. Commemorates the birth in 1764 of General José Gervasio Artigas, the father of Uruguayan independence.

"WAR IS HELL": ANNIVERSARY. June 19, 1879. Addressing the graduating class at Michigan Military Academy, General William Tecumseh Sherman uttered his famous words on war—more than a decade after the Civil War had ended. He said, "War is at best barbarism. . . . Its glory is all moonshine. It is only those who have neither fired a shot nor heard the shrieks and groans of the wounded who cry aloud for blood, more vengeance, more desolation. War is hell."

WORLD SAUNTERING DAY. June 19. A day to revive the lost art of Victorian sauntering and to discourage jogging, lollygagging, sashaying, fast walking and trotting. (Originated by the late W.T. Rabe of Sault Ste Marie, MI.)

🎂 BIRTHDAYS TODAY

Paula Abdul, 58, singer, dancer, choreographer, television personality ("American Idol"), born Los Angeles, CA, June 19, 1962.

Aung San Suu Kyi, 75, Nobel Peace Prize recipient, born Rangoon, Burma (now Myanmar), June 19, 1945.

Hugh Dancy, 45, actor (*Elizabeth I, Ella Enchanted,* "Hannibal," "The Big C"), born Stoke-on-Trent, Staffordshire, England, June 19, 1975.

Jean Dujardin, 48, actor (Oscar for *The Artist*), born Rueil-Malmaison, France, June 19, 1972.

Boris Johnson, 56, Prime Minister of the United Kingdom (2019–), born New York, NY, June 19, 1964.

Andy Lauer, 55, actor ("Caroline in the City," *I'll Be Home for Christmas*), born Santa Monica, CA, June 19, 1965.

Macklemore, 37, rapper, born Ben Haggerty at Seattle, WA, June 19, 1983.

Brian McBride, 48, Hall of Fame soccer player, born Arlington Heights, IL, June 19, 1972.

Poppy Montgomery, 48, actress ("Unforgettable," "Without a Trace"), born Sydney, Australia, June 19, 1972.

Dirk Nowitzki, 42, former basketball player, born Wurzburg, West Germany (now Germany), June 19, 1978.

Phylicia Rashad, 72, actress ("The Cosby Show"), born Houston, TX, June 19, 1948.

Gena Rowlands, 90, actress ("Peyton Place," *A Woman Under the Influence*), born Cambria, WI, June 19, 1930.

Salman Rushdie, 73, author (*The Satanic Verses, Midnight's Children*), born Mumbai, India, June 19, 1947.

Zoe Saldana, 42, actress (*Guardians of the Galaxy, Avatar, Star Trek*), born Passaic, NJ, June 19, 1978.

Aiden Turner, 37, actor ("Poldark," The Hobbit films), born Clondalkin, Ireland, June 19, 1983.

Kathleen Turner, 66, actress (*Body Heat, Peggy Sue Got Married, Romancing the Stone*), born Springfield, MO, June 19, 1954.

Ann Wilson, 69, musician (Heart), born San Diego, CA, June 19, 1951.

June		S	M	T	W	T	F	S
2020			1	2	3	4	5	6
		7	8	9	10	11	12	13
		14	15	16	17	18	19	20
		21	22	23	24	25	26	27
		28	29	30				

June 20 — Saturday

DAY 172   **194 REMAINING**

ANNE AND SAMANTHA DAY. June 20 (also Dec 21). Celebrated worldwide, this twice-yearly holiday is meant for reflection on Anne Frank's and Samantha Smith's contributions to our world and to promote them as subjects worthy to be honored on official American postage stamps, as well as the stamps of all nations. Annually, on the solstice each June and December. For info: John O'Loughlin, 3124 Chisholm Trail, Irving, TX 75062. Phone: (972) 258-4996. E-mail: lldjohn@aol.com. Web: www.anneandsamantha.com.

ARGENTINA: FLAG DAY. June 20. National holiday. Commemorates the death in 1820 of Manuel Belgrano, the designer of the Argentine flag.

BELGIUM: BATTLE OF WATERLOO REENACTMENT. June 20–21 (tentative). Waterloo. To commemorate the anniversary of the Battle of Waterloo (June 18, 1815), an immense reenactment takes place, featuring 1,000 troops in period uniform on the historical battlefield. For info: The Napoleonic Association. Web: www.napoleonicassociation.org.

CHESNUTT, CHARLES W.: BIRTH ANNIVERSARY. June 20, 1858. Born at Cleveland, OH, Chesnutt was considered by many as the first important black novelist. His collections of short stories include *The Conjure Woman* (1899) and *The Wife of His Youth and Other Stories of the Color Line* (1899). *The Colonel's Dream* (1905) dealt with the struggles of the freed slave. His work has been compared to that of later writers such as William Faulkner, Richard Wright and James Baldwin. He died Nov 15, 1932, at Cleveland.

"THE ED SULLIVAN SHOW" ("TOAST OF THE TOWN") TV PREMIERE: ANNIVERSARY. June 20, 1948. "The Ed Sullivan Show" was officially titled "Toast of the Town" until 1955. It was the longest-running variety show (through 1971) and the most popular for decades. Sullivan, the host, signed all types of acts, both well-known and new, trying to have something to please everyone. Thousands of performers appeared, many making their television debut, such as Irving Berlin, Victor Borge, Hedy Lamarr, Walt Disney, Fred Astaire and Jane Powell. Two acts attracted the largest audience of the time: Elvis Presley and The Beatles.

FIRST BALLOON HONEYMOON: ANNIVERSARY. June 20, 1909. Roger Burnham and Eleanor Waring took the first balloon honeymoon, ascending at 12:40 PM in the balloon *Pittsfield*. They began their trip at Woods Hole, Cape Cod, MA, and landed at 4:30 PM in an orchard at Holbrook, MA.

FIRST DOCTOR OF SCIENCE DEGREE EARNED BY A WOMAN: ANNIVERSARY. June 20, 1895. Caroline Willard Baldwin became the first woman to earn a doctor of science degree, at Cornell University, Ithaca, NY.

FULTON COUNTY HISTORICAL POWER SHOW. June 20–21. Rochester, IN. This show features a different tractor each year. Power show includes antique tractors, hit 'n' miss engines, farm equipment and antique trucks. Also features vendors of swap parts, crafts, food, trading post in the Round Barn and toy show. Contests held for exhibitors. Admission fee. Annually, the third weekend in June. Est attendance: 6,000. For info: Fulton County Historical Power Assn, c/o Fulton County Historical Society, 37 E 375 N, Rochester, IN 46975. Phone: (574) 223-4436. E-mail: melinda@rtcol.com. Web: www.fultoncountyhistory.org.

HELLMAN, LILLIAN: BIRTH ANNIVERSARY. June 20, 1905. One of the 20th century's important playwrights, author of such works as *The Children's Hour* (1934), *The Little Foxes* (1939) and *Toys in the Attic* (1960). One of many artists blacklisted by Hollywood in the 1950s. Hellman was the companion for 30 years of novelist Dashiell Hammett. Born at New Orleans, LA, Hellman died June 30, 1984, at Martha's Vineyard, MA.

***JAWS* FILM RELEASE: 45th ANNIVERSARY.** June 20, 1975. With its tagline "Don't go in the water" and its ominous cello music, the Steven Spielberg–directed thriller shocked audiences on this date. Adapted from a Peter Benchley bestseller, *Jaws* showed a great white shark preying on the beachgoers of a New England town. It won three Oscars—best editing, best sound and best original score (by John Williams)—and was a blockbuster success.

LIZZIE BORDEN VERDICT: ANNIVERSARY. June 20, 1893. Spectators at her trial cheered when the "not guilty" verdict was read by the jury foreman in the murder trial of Lizzie Borden on this date. Elizabeth Borden had been accused of and tried for the hacking deaths of her father and stepmother in their Fall River, MA, home, Aug 4, 1892.

LONGEST DAM RACE. June 20. Fort Peck, MT. The run crosses Fort Peck Dam. The 5k is flat. Both distances finish running downhill grade from the top of the dam. Included in the events is a 10-mile novice bike race. There are also a 5k run/walk, 1-mile timed competitive race and 1-mile casual event. Professional timing for the races. Online registration at www.runsignup.com. Annually, the third weekend in June. Est attendance: 750. For info: Glasgow Chamber of Commerce and Agriculture, Box 832, Glasgow, MT 59230. Phone: (406) 228-2222. Fax: (406) 228-2244. E-mail: chamber@nemont.net. Web: www.glasgowchamber.net.

THE MERMAID PARADE. June 20. Surf Ave, Coney Island, New York, NY. Founded in 1983, the Mermaid Parade is the nation's largest art parade and one of New York City's greatest summer events. It pays homage to Coney Island's forgotten Mardi Gras (1903–54) and draws from a host of other sources to create a wonderful and wacky event. The parade celebrates the sand, the sea, the salt air and the beginning of summer, as well as the history and mythology of Coney Island. Participants dress as mermaids, Neptune, various sea creatures or the occasional wandering lighthouse. Viewers also get to see antique cars, marching bands, drill teams and the odd yacht pulled on flatbed. A different celebrity King Neptune and Queen Mermaid rule over the proceedings. Past royalty have included David Byrne, Queen Latifah, Lou Reed and Laurie Anderson. Annually, the third Saturday in June. For info: Coney Island USA, 1208 Surf Ave, Brooklyn, NY 11224-2816. Phone: (718) 372 5159. E-mail: info@coneyisland.com. Web: www.coneyisland.com.

MIDSUMMER. June 20. (Also called Litha.) One of the "Lesser Sabbats" during the Wiccan year, celebrating the peak of the Sun God in his annual cycle. Annually, on the summer solstice.

MURPHY, AUDIE: BIRTH ANNIVERSARY. June 20, 1924. Born at Kingston, TX, Murphy was the most decorated soldier in WWII. He later became an actor in Western and war movies. He died May 28, 1971, in a plane crash near Roanoke, VA.

OFFENBACH, JACQUES: BIRTH ANNIVERSARY. June 20, 1819. Composer, born Jacob Offenbach in Cologne, Germany. Originally a cellist in the Opera Comique, he became a conductor and then composer. Opening his own theater, the Bouffes-Parisiens, in 1855, Offenbach pioneered the French comic opera. His operettas include *Orphée aux enfers* (*Orpheus in the Underworld*, 1858), which gave the world the music for the can-can; *La belle Hélène* (1864) and a final unfinished grand opera, *The Tales of Hoffmann*, finished and produced after his death. Offenbach died at Paris, France, Oct 5, 1880.

ROCHESTERFEST. June 20–28. Rochester, MN. This community festival includes children's and seniors' events, gigantic street parade, street vendors with exotic foods, Party in the Park, ice cream social and breakfast on the farm. Est attendance: 150,000. For info: Brent Ackerman, Executive Director, Rochesterfest, Box 007, Rochester, MN 55903. Phone: (507) 285-8769. E-mail: director@rochesterfest.com. Web: www.rochesterfest.com.

SPANISH-AMERICAN WAR SURRENDER OF GUAM TO US: ANNIVERSARY. June 20, 1898. Not knowing that a war was in progress and having no ammunition on the island, the Spanish commander of Guam surrendered to Captain Glass of the USS *Charleston*.

SPIRIT OF THE WOODS FOLK FESTIVAL. June 20. Dickson Township Park, Brethren, MI. A one-day free outdoor festival of folk music, dance and handcrafts. Family friendly, this event features two stages, children's activities and good food. Annually, the third Saturday in June since 1978. For info: Spirit of the Woods Music Assn, 11171 Kerry Rd, Brethren, MI 49619. Phone: (231) 477-5381. E-mail: spiritofthewoodsmusic@gmail.com. Web: www.spiritofthewoods.org.

SUMMER. June 20–Sept 22. In the Northern Hemisphere, summer begins today with the summer solstice, at 5:44 PM, EDT. Note that in the Southern Hemisphere today is the beginning of winter. Anywhere between the equator and the Arctic Circle, the sun rises and sets farthest north on the horizon for the year and length of daylight is maximum (12 hours, 8 minutes at equator, increasing to 24 hours at the Arctic Circle).

UNITED NATIONS: WORLD REFUGEE DAY. June 20. A day to bring attention to the situation of refugees—their rights, as well as their suffering. First observed on June 20, 2001, the 50th anniversary of the 1951 Convention on the Status of Refugees. Date chosen to coincide with Africa Refugee Day. For info: United Nations, Dept of Public Info, New York, NY 10017. Web: www.un.org.

WEST VIRGINIA: ADMISSION DAY: ANNIVERSARY. June 20, 1863. Became 35th state in 1863. Observed as a holiday in West Virginia. The state of West Virginia is a product of the Civil War. Originally part of Virginia, West Virginia became a separate state when Virginia seceded from the Union.

WORLD JUGGLING DAY. June 20. Juggling clubs all over the world hold local festivals to demonstrate, teach and celebrate their art. Annually, the Saturday on or closest to June 17 (June 17, 1947, was the founding date of the International Jugglers' Association). For info: Intl Jugglers' Assn, PO Box 580005, Kissimmee, FL 34758. Web: www.juggle.org.

June 2020	S	M	T	W	T	F	S
		1	2	3	4	5	6
	7	8	9	10	11	12	13
	14	15	16	17	18	19	20
	21	22	23	24	25	26	27
	28	29	30				

🎂 BIRTHDAYS TODAY

Danny Aiello, Jr, 87, actor (*The Last Don, Hudson Hawke, Do the Right Thing*), born New York, NY, June 20, 1933.

Olympia Dukakis, 89, actress (Oscar for *Moonstruck; Steel Magnolias*), theatrical director, born Lowell, MA, June 20, 1931.

John Goodman, 68, actor ("Roseanne"; *The Big Lebowski; O Brother, Where Art Thou?*), born Afton, MO, June 20, 1952.

Nicole Kidman, 53, actress (Oscar for *The Hours*; "Big Little Lies," *Cold Mountain, Moulin Rouge*), born Honolulu, HI, June 20, 1967.

Frank Lampard, 42, former soccer player, born Romford, England, June 20, 1978.

Michael Landon, Jr, 56, actor ("Bonanza: The Return," "Bonanza: The Ghosts"), born Encino, CA, June 20, 1964.

Cyndi Lauper, 67, singer, composer (Tony for score of *Kinky Boots*), born Brooklyn, NY, June 20, 1953.

Anne Murray, 75, singer, born Springhill, NS, Canada, June 20, 1945.

Lionel Richie, 71, singer, Songwriters Hall of Fame songwriter (Oscar for "Say You, Say Me"), born Tuskegee, AL, June 20, 1949.

Robert Rodriguez, 52, director, screenwriter (*Sin City, Spy Kids, Desperado*), born San Antonio, TX, June 20, 1968.

James Tolkan, 89, actor (*Serpico, Back to the Future, Dick Tracy*), born Calumet, MI, June 20, 1931.

Bob Vila, 74, handyman, television personality ("This Old House"), born Miami, FL, June 20, 1946.

Abby Wambach, 40, former soccer player, born Rochester, NY, June 20, 1980.

Andre Watts, 74, pianist, born Nuremburg, Germany, June 20, 1946.

Brian Wilson, 78, singer (The Beach Boys), songwriter, born Hawthorne, CA, June 20, 1942.

June 21 — Sunday

DAY 173   **193 REMAINING**

BATTLE OF OKINAWA ENDS: 75th ANNIVERSARY. June 21, 1945. With American grenades exploding in the background, inside the Japanese command cave at Mabuni the battle for Okinawa was ended when Major General Isamu Cho and Lieutenant General Mitsuru Ushijima killed themselves in the ceremonial rite of seppuku. In the long battle that had begun Apr 1, the American death toll reached enormous proportions by Pacific battle standards—7,613 died on land and 4,907 in the air or from kamikaze attacks. A total of 36 US warships were sunk. More than 70,000 Japanese and 80,000 civilian Okinawans died in the course of the battle.

BHUTTO, BENAZIR: BIRTH ANNIVERSARY. June 21, 1953. The first woman democratically elected to lead a Muslim nation, born at Karachi, Sindh, Pakistan. She served as that nation's prime minister during 1988–90 and 1993–96, and she accomplished much national reform, especially on women's issues. However, during both of her terms, she was ejected from office under charges of corruption in Pakistan's turbulent and often violent political climate. She was assassinated by a suicide bomber as she tried to mount her third campaign for prime minister, Dec 27, 2007, at Rawalpindi, Punjab, Pakistan.

CANADA: NATIONAL INDIGENOUS PEOPLES DAY. June 21. Today all Canadians to recognize and celebrate the unique heritage, diverse cultures and outstanding contributions of First Nations, Inuit and Métis peoples. Although these groups share many similarities, they each have their own distinct heritage, language, cultural practices and spiritual beliefs. In cooperation with indigenous organizations, the Government of Canada chose June 21, the summer solstice, for National Aboriginal Day, now known as National

Indigenous Peoples Day. For info: Government of Canada. Web: www.canada.ca.

CANCER, THE CRAB. June 21–July 22. In the astronomical/astrological zodiac, which divides the sun's apparent orbit into 12 segments, the period June 21–July 22 is traditionally identified as the sun sign of Cancer, the Crab. The ruling planet is the moon.

CRAFT SPIRITS WEEK. June 21–27. Craft Spirits Week is a national celebration of the craft spirits movement. From artisanal gin to small-batch whiskey, single estate rum to barrel-finished vodka, aged brandy and more, we raise a glass to the craft distillers making extraordinary libations from locally sourced ingredients, family recipes and hands-on production techniques. Annually, the third week in June. For info: National Craft Spirits Week, 9852 Katella Ave, Ste 332, Anaheim, CA 92804. E-mail: contact@nationalcraftspiritsweek.com. Web: www.nationalcraftspiritsweek.com.

★FATHER'S DAY. June 21. Presidential Proclamation issued for third Sunday in June in 1966 and annually since 1971 (PL 92–278 of Apr 24, 1972).

FATHER'S DAY. June 21. Recognition of the third Sunday in June as Father's Day occurred first at the request of Mrs John B. Dodd of Spokane, WA, on June 19, 1910. It was proclaimed for that date by the mayor of Spokane and recognized by the governor of Washington. The idea was publicly supported by President Calvin Coolidge in 1924 but not presidentially proclaimed until 1966. It was assured of annual recognition by PL 92–278 of April 1972. Also celebrated on this day in Britain.

GO SKATEBOARDING DAY. June 21. This day, held on June 21 annually since 2004, is the official holiday of skateboarding. Founded by the International Association of Skateboard Companies (IASC), this day gives passionate skateboarders as well as those who are simply inspired by skateboarding the opportunity to drop everything and get on a skateboard. A cooperative of decentralized events that take place around the globe. In the years since the first observance, this day continues to grow, but the mission remains the same: Have fun, go skateboarding! For info: International Association of Skateboard Companies. Web: www.theiasc.org.

GREENLAND: NATIONAL DAY. June 21. National holiday.

HIRSCHFELD, AL: BIRTH ANNIVERSARY. June 21, 1903. Caricature artist known for his inimitable sketches of Broadway and Hollywood stars, Al Hirschfeld was born at St. Louis, MO. His first cartoon appeared in 1926 in the now-defunct *New York Herald Tribune*. Later moving to the *New York Times*, his drawings appeared on the drama page for seven decades. He was known for hiding "Nina" (his daughter's name) somewhere in every caricature that he created after 1945. His art is found in many museums, including the Metropolitan Museum of Art in New York City. He died Jan 20, 2003, at New York, NY.

HURRICANE AGNES: ANNIVERSARY. June 21–26, 1972. Hurricane Agnes hit the eastern seaboard wreaking havoc across seven Atlantic Coast states. Casualties included 118 lives and 116,000 homes, leaving more than 200,000 homeless after Agnes dumped 28.1 trillion gallons of water over 5,000 square miles.

LIGHTNING SAFETY AWARENESS WEEK. June 21–27 (tentative). First observed in 2001, this annual safety campaign seeks to educate people about the danger of lightning and to reduce the number of deaths caused by lightning each year. Annually, the last full week in June. For info: National Lightning Safety Council. Web: www.lightningsafetycouncil.org.

MATHER, INCREASE: BIRTH ANNIVERSARY. June 21, 1639. Puritan minister, author, college administrator (Harvard) and influential

colonial citizen, born at Dorchester, Massachusetts Bay Colony. Father of Cotton Mather. Author of *Case of Conscience Concerning Evil Spirits Personating Men* (1693), in which he expressed concern over the Salem Witch Trials. Mather died Aug 23, 1723, at Boston.

MCCARTHY, MARY: BIRTH ANNIVERSARY. June 21, 1912. Acerbic novelist, critic and essayist born at Seattle, WA. Her 28 published fiction and nonfiction books include *Memories of a Catholic Girlhood*, *The Group*, *Birds of America*, *The Mask of State* and *How I Grew*. She died Oct 25, 1989, at New York, NY.

MIDSUMMER DAY/EVE CELEBRATIONS. June 21. Celebrate the beginning of summer with maypoles, music, dancing and bonfires. Observed mainly in northern Europe, including Finland, Latvia and Sweden. Day of observance is sometimes St. John's Day (June 24), with celebration on St. John's Eve (June 23) as well, or June 19. Time approximates the summer solstice. See also: "Summer" (June 20).

MOON PHASE: NEW MOON. June 21. Moon enters New Moon phase at 2:41 AM, EDT.

NEW HAMPSHIRE RATIFIES CONSTITUTION: ANNIVERSARY. June 21, 1788. By a vote of 57 to 47, New Hampshire became the ninth state to ratify the Constitution. With this ratification, the Constitution became effective for all ratifying states; approval of nine states was required for the Constitution to go into effect.

NIEBUHR, REINHOLD: BIRTH ANNIVERSARY. June 21, 1892. Born at Wright City, MO, Niebuhr was a prominent American theologian whose liberal political and conservative theological beliefs helped shape the field of Christian social ethics. Widely regarded one of Protestantism's most influential social critics. Niebuhr's ideas provided philosophical justification for the New Deal and post-WWII foreign policy. An advocate for the social justice movements of his era, particularly labor and civil rights, Niebuhr helped found Americans for Democratic Action, the Fellowship of Christian Socialists and New York's Liberal Party. He once remarked, "Man's capacity for justice makes democracy possible, but man's inclination to injustice makes democracy necessary." Niebuhr died June 1, 1971, at Stockbridge, MA.

SARTRE, JEAN-PAUL: BIRTH ANNIVERSARY. June 21, 1905. French philosopher, "father of existentialism," born at Paris, France. In 1964 Sartre rejected the Nobel Prize in Literature when it was awarded to him. He died at Paris, Apr 15, 1980. In *Being and Nothingness*, he wrote: "Man can will nothing unless he has first understood that he must count on no one but himself; that he is alone, abandoned on earth in the midst of his infinite responsibilities, without help, with no other aim than the one he sets for himself, with no other destiny than the one he forges for himself on this earth."

SOLAR ECLIPSE. June 21. Annular eclipse of the sun. Visible in Africa, southeastern Europe and Asia.

SPACE MILESTONE: FIRST MANNED PRIVATE SPACEFLIGHT. June 21, 2004. Michael Melvill, flying the privately financed *SpaceShipOne*, flew 62 miles in altitude on this date, leaving Earth's atmosphere. The spacecraft was designed by Burt Rutan and was financed by Paul Allen, philanthropist and Microsoft cofounder. *SpaceShipOne* made the flight from Mojave Airport at Mojave, CA.

TANNER, HENRY OSSAWA: BIRTH ANNIVERSARY. June 21, 1859. Tanner was one of the first black artists to have works exhibited in galleries in the US. He was born at Pittsburgh, PA, and died May 25, 1937, at Paris, France.

TOMPKINS, DANIEL D.: BIRTH ANNIVERSARY. June 21, 1774. Sixth vice president of the US (1817–25), born at Fox Meadows, NY. Died at Staten Island, NY, June 11, 1825.

UNITED NATIONS: INTERNATIONAL DAY OF YOGA. June 21. A day to raise awareness worldwide of the many benefits of practicing yoga. The day was proposed by India and Prime Minister Narendra Modi and endorsed by a record 175 member states. Prime Minister Modi said: "Yoga is an invaluable gift from our ancient tradition. Yoga is not just about exercise; it is a way to discover the sense of oneness with yourself, the world and nature." (Res 69/131 adopted Dec 11, 2014.) Annually, June 21—chosen because it is the summer solstice. For info: United Nations, Dept of Public Info, New York, NY 10017. Web: www.un.org and http://idayofyoga.org.

WINDJAMMER DAYS. June 21–27. Boothbay Harbor, ME. The premier maritime event along the coast of Maine. Parades, concerts, waterfront food, interactive children's activities, live music, fireworks and much more. Windjammers sail into the harbor under full sail on June 24 during the Gathering of the Fleet. Fun for the whole family. Est attendance: 20,000. For info: Friends of Windjammer Days, PO Box 101, Boothbay Harbor, ME 04538. E-mail: windjammerdays@gmail.com. Web: www.boothbayharborwindjammerdays.org.

WORLD MUSIC DAY/FÊTE DE LA MUSIQUE. June 21. Originated in 1982 by composer Maurice Fleuret within the auspices of France's Department of Culture, World Music Day celebrates music on the summer solstice by encouraging free outdoor concerts—by anyone, amateur or professional. The day has been embraced by more than 100 nations around the world. Annually, on June 21.

🎂 BIRTHDAYS TODAY

Kris Allen, 35, singer, television personality ("American Idol"), born Jacksonville, AR, June 21, 1985.

Meredith Baxter, 73, actress ("Bridget Loves Bernie," "Family," "Family Ties"), born Los Angeles, CA, June 21, 1947.

Berkeley Breathed, 63, author, cartoonist ("Bloom County"), born Encino, CA, June 21, 1957.

Kate Brown, 60, Governor of Oregon (D), born Torrejón de Ardoz, Spain, June 21, 1960.

Thomas Doane (Tom) Chambers, 61, former basketball player, born Ogden, UT, June 21, 1959.

Ray Davies, 76, singer, musician (The Kinks), born London, England, June 21, 1944.

Sammi Davis-Voss, 56, actress ("Homefront," *Hope and Glory*), born Kidderminster, Worcestershire, England, June 21, 1964.

Lana Del Rey, 35, singer, born Elizabeth Woolridge Grant at New York, NY, June 21, 1985.

Joe Flaherty, 80, comedian, actor ("SCTV," "Freaks and Geeks"), born Pittsburgh, PA, June 21, 1940.

Michael Gross, 73, actor ("Family Ties"), born Chicago, IL, June 21, 1947.

Mariette Hartley, 79, actress ("Peyton Place," *Ride the High Country*), born New York, NY, June 21, 1941.

Richard Jefferson, 40, basketball player, born Los Angeles, CA, June 21, 1980.

Bernie Kopell, 87, actor ("Get Smart," "The Love Boat," "When Things Were Rotten"), born New York, NY, June 21, 1933.

Juliette Lewis, 47, singer, actress (*Kalifornia*, *Natural Born Killers*), born Los Angeles, CA, June 21, 1973.

Nils Lofgren, 69, musician, singer, songwriter, born Chicago, IL, June 21, 1951.

Chris Pratt, 41, actor (*Jurassic World*, *Guardians of the Galaxy*, "Parks and Recreation"), born Virginia, MN, June 21, 1979.

Doug Savant, 56, actor ("Melrose Place," "Desperate Housewives"), born Burbank, CA, June 21, 1964.

Jussie Smollett, 37, actor ("Empire"), singer, born Santa Rosa, CA, June 21, 1983.

Edward Snowden, 37, computer professional, released classified NSA documents, born Elizabeth City, NC, June 21, 1983.

Rick Sutcliffe, 64, sportscaster, former baseball player, born Independence, MO, June 21, 1956.

Lana Wachowski, 55, filmmaker with sibling Lilly Wachowski (*The Matrix*), born Larry Wachowski at Chicago, IL, June 21, 1965.

Benjamin Walker, 38, actor (*Abraham Lincoln: Vampire Hunter*, *Flags of Our Fathers*), born Cartersville, GA, June 21, 1982.

Prince William (William Arthur Philip Louis), 38, son of Prince Charles and Princess Diana, born London, England, June 21, 1982.

June 22 — Monday

DAY 174	192 REMAINING

BLASS, BILL: BIRTH ANNIVERSARY. June 22, 1922. Born at Fort Wayne, IN, William Ralph Blass moved to New York at 17 to study fashion design. After service in WWII, he returned to New York and went to work for Anne Klein. By 1970 he had his own company and put American fashion on the map—favoring a sporty yet classy silhouette. His client list soon included Jacqueline Kennedy, Barbra Streisand and Gloria Vanderbilt, and he became one of the most successful fashion designers in history. He was known as a philanthropist in his later years and died soon after retirement at New Preston, CT, June 12, 2002.

BRADLEY, ED: BIRTH ANNIVERSARY. June 22, 1941. Television journalist Edward Rudolph Bradley, Jr, was born at Philadelphia, PA. His career began with battlefield reporting as he covered the fall of Saigon, and he was the first African-American television correspondent to cover the White House. He spent his entire career with CBS and worked on the venerable "60 Minutes" for 26 years. Highly respected for his journalistic integrity, he earned 19 Emmy Awards and four George Peabody Awards in the course of his career. He died at New York, NY, Nov 7, 2006.

BUTLER, OCTAVIA: BIRTH ANNIVERSARY. June 22, 1947. African-American science fiction author, born at Pasadena, CA. Significant works include *The Parable of the Sower* and the Patternist series, featuring *Wild Seed* and *Clay's Ark*. Winner of multiple Hugo and Nebula awards, in 1995, she became the first science fiction writer to be awarded a MacArthur Foundation fellowship, and in 2000 she received a PEN Award for lifetime achievement. She died Feb 24, 2006, at Seattle, WA.

CANADA: DISCOVERY DAY (NEWFOUNDLAND AND LABRADOR). June 22. Commemorates the discovery of Newfoundland by John Cabot, June 24, 1497. Commemorated on the Monday nearest June 24.

CHESAPEAKE-LEOPARD AFFAIR: ANNIVERSARY. June 22, 1807. One of the events leading to the War of 1812 occurred about 40 miles east of Chesapeake Bay. The US frigate *Chesapeake* was fired upon and boarded by the crew of the British man-of-war *Leopard*. The *Chesapeake*'s commander, James Barron, was court-martialed and convicted of not being prepared for action. Later Barron killed

June 2020	S	M	T	W	T	F	S
		1	2	3	4	5	6
	7	8	9	10	11	12	13
	14	15	16	17	18	19	20
	21	22	23	24	25	26	27
	28	29	30				

one of the judges (Stephen Decatur) in a duel fought at Bladensburg, MD, Mar 22, 1820.

CROATIA: ANTIFASCIST STRUGGLE DAY. June 22. National holiday. Commemorates uprising against Fascist invaders in 1941.

FALL OF FRANCE: 80th ANNIVERSARY. June 22, 1940. WWII's Battle of France, which began May 12 with German forces crossing into the nation at Sedan and the Meuse River, reached its conclusion with France surrendering. Previously, the British Expeditionary Force had evacuated via Dunkirk on May 27 to June 4, and Paris had been declared an open city on June 13. On June 22, France and Germany signed a second armistice agreement at the Compiègne Forest—the same location as the 1918 armistice of WWI. Adolf Hitler made a point of signing the 1940 compact in the same railway carriage as the 1918 document.

HUXLEY, JULIAN: BIRTH ANNIVERSARY. June 22, 1887. Evolutionary biologist, scholar and educator; brother of author Aldous Huxley. He segued easily from his early work as an ornithologist to establishing the biology department at Rice University, Houston, TX; later, he was a professor of zoology at King's College London, and an author (with H.G. Wells) of the multivolume study of biology *The Science of Life*. Huxley was the first director of UNESCO, as well as a cofounder of the World Wildlife Fund, and coined the phrase "evolutionary synthesis" to describe the discipline of evolution. He died at London, England (his birthplace), on Feb 14, 1975.

JOE LOUIS V MAX SCHMELING FIGHT: ANNIVERSARY. June 22, 1938. Joe Louis won the World Heavyweight Championship by knocking out James J. Braddock on June 22, 1937. Exactly one year later, Louis met Germany's Max Schmeling, at New York City's Yankee Stadium. Louis knocked out Schmeling in the first round. He retained his title until his retirement in 1949.

LINDBERGH, ANNE MORROW: BIRTH ANNIVERSARY. June 22, 1906. American author and aviator, born at Englewood, NJ. Wife of aviator Charles A. Lindbergh, she served as his copilot and navigator when he broke the transatlantic speed record in 1930. A prolific author and poet, in *Gift from the Sea* she wrote: "By and large, mothers and housewives are the only workers who do not have regular time off. They are the great vacationless class." She died Feb 7, 2001, at Passumpsic, VT.

MALTA: MNARJA. June 22–23. Buskett Gardens. A folk-cum-harvest festival. An all-night traditional Maltese "festa" with folk music, dancing and impromptu Maltese folksinging (ghana). This festival originated in the Middle Ages, and the word *Mnarja* is derived from *luminarja*, because the countryside and the bastions around Mdina, Malta's ancient capital, used to be illuminated by "Fjakkoli" (torches made of sand mixed with oil and animal fat) on the eve of and on the feast day itself.

MARADONA'S "HAND OF GOD" GOAL: ANNIVERSARY. June 22, 1986. Argentine superstar Diego Maradona scored one of the most controversial goals in soccer history when, in a World Cup win over England, he used his fist to punch the ball into England's net. Though obvious to many, the official missed the illegal act and allowed the goal. After the game, Maradona said the goal was scored, "A little with the head of Maradona, and a little with the hand of God."

NATIONAL OLDTIME FIDDLERS' CONTEST® AND FESTIVAL. June 22–27. Weiser, ID. Since 1953, the largest event in the world dedicated to perpetuate old-time fiddling. Includes national competition old-time divisions as well as twin fiddling and swing fiddling. Est attendance: 50,000. For info: National Oldtime Fiddlers' Contest, PO Box 447, Weiser, ID 83672. Phone: (208) 414-0255. E-mail: admin@fiddlecontest.com. Web: www.fiddlecontest.org.

NATIONAL POLLINATOR WEEK. June 22–28. An international celebration of the valuable ecosystem services provided by bees, birds, butterflies, bats and beetles. Pollinators positively affect all our lives, supporting wildlife, healthy watersheds and more. This week let's save and celebrate them. Annually, the week beginning on the Monday after Father's Day. For info: Pollinator Partnership, 423 Washington St, 5th FL, San Francisco, CA 94111. Phone: (415) 362-1137. E-mail: info@pollinator.org. Web: www.pollinator.org.

O'BRIEN, DAVEY: BIRTH ANNIVERSARY. June 22, 1917. Robert David (Davey) O'Brien, football player, born at Dallas, TX. O'Brien backed up quarterback Sammy Baugh in his sophomore year at Texas Christian University and became a starter the next year. In 1937, his senior season, he led TCU to the national championship and won several awards, including the Heisman Trophy, as the nation's best player. He played pro football for two years and then retired to join the FBI. Each year, the Davey O'Brien Educational and Charitable Trust of Fort Worth presents the Davey O'Brien National Quarterback Award to the nation's top college quarterback. O'Brien died at Fort Worth, TX, Nov 18, 1977.

PAPP, JOSEPH: BIRTH ANNIVERSARY. June 22, 1921. Born Yosl Papirofsky at Brooklyn, NY, Joe Papp became one of the leading figures in American theater. At the helm of the New York Public Theatre, Papp produced a wide range of works from the classical to that of the newest American dramatists, including *Hair, Two Gentlemen of Verona, The Pirates of Penzance, The Mystery of Edwin Drood, That Championship Season* and *A Chorus Line*. He began in 1954 with the Shakespeare Theatre Workshop, taking touring productions around the city on a flatbed truck. When the truck broke down in Central Park, Papp turned his touring company into Shakespeare-in-the-Park. Producing and directing more than 400 productions, Papp garnered three Pulitzer Prizes, six New York Critics Circle Awards and 28 Tonys. He died Oct 31, 1991, at New York, NY.

SOVIET UNION INVADED: ANNIVERSARY. June 22, 1941. German troops invaded the Soviet Union in Operation Barbarossa, beginning a conflict that left 27 million Soviet citizens dead. Ceremonies are held this day in Russia, Belarus and Ukraine, the areas of the former Soviet Union that bore the brunt of the initial invasion.

STUPID GUY THING DAY. June 22. Women are always talking about it, so here's the day to commemorate it! Women everywhere are to make a list of "stupid guy things" and pass it on! (©2006 by WH.) For info: Thomas & Ruth Roy, Wellcat Holidays, 2418 Long Ln, Lebanon, PA 17046. Phone: (717) 279-0184. E-mail: info@wellcat.com. Web: www.wellcat.com.

SWITZERLAND: MORAT BATTLE ANNIVERSARY. June 22, 1476. The little walled town of Morat played a decisive part in Swiss history. There, the Confederates were victorious over Charles the Bold of Burgundy, laying the basis for French-speaking areas to become Swiss. Now an annual children's festival.

UNITED KINGDOM: NATIONAL INSECT WEEK. June 22–28. Diversity isn't just about wildlife in exotic locations. Get involved in National Insect Week and you'll discover that insect diversity is just as relevant and fascinating to explore in your garden or local countryside as it is in the savannas, deserts, wetlands and rain forests of the tropics. Lots of events all over the UK for all ages: beastie hunts, pond surveys, bughouse building, special exhibits, photo competition and more. For info: Royal Entomological Society, The Mansion House, Chiswell Green Lane, St Albans AL2 3NS, England. Web: www.nationalinsectweek.co.uk or www.royensoc.co.uk.

US DEPARTMENT OF JUSTICE: 150th ANNIVERSARY. June 22, 1870. Established by an act of Congress, the Department of Justice is headed by the attorney general. Prior to 1870, the attorney general (whose office had been created Sept 24, 1789) had been a member of the president's cabinet but had not been the head of a department.

VANCOUVER, GEORGE: BIRTH ANNIVERSARY. June 22, 1757. English navigator, explorer and author for whom Vancouver Island and the cities of Vancouver (British Columbia and Washington) are named. Born at Norfolk, England, he joined the navy at the age of 13. He surveyed the coasts of Australia, New Zealand and western North America and sailed with Captain James Cook to the Arctic in 1780. Vancouver died at Petersham, Surrey, England, May 10, 1798, just as he was correcting the final pages of his *Journal*, which was published at London later that year.

WILDER, BILLY: BIRTH ANNIVERSARY. June 22, 1906. One of the greatest directors of Hollywood's Golden Age was born Samuel Wilder at Sucha Beskidzka in the Austro-Hungarian Empire. After a short career in Berlin, Wilder fled Germany in 1933 and eventually landed in Hollywood, where he directed and cowrote some of the 20th century's foremost films. His classics include the film noir works *Double Indemnity* and *Sunset Boulevard*, the searing dramas *Stalag 17* and *The Lost Weekend* and the comic gem *Some Like It Hot*. He received six Oscars (out of 21 nominations), and Best Film Oscars went to *The Lost Weekend* and *The Apartment*. Wilder died at Los Angeles, CA, on Mar 27, 2002.

🎂 BIRTHDAYS TODAY

Darrell Armstrong, 52, basketball coach and former player, born Gastonia, NC, June 22, 1968.

Klaus Maria Brandauer, 76, actor (*Out of Africa*, *White Fang*), born Altaussee, Austria, June 22, 1944.

Amy Brenneman, 56, actress ("Private Practice," "Judging Amy"), born Glastonbury, CT, June 22, 1964.

Dan Brown, 56, author (*The Da Vinci Code, Angels & Demons*), born Exeter, NH, June 22, 1964.

Randy Couture, 57, mixed martial artist, born Everett, WA, June 22, 1963.

Carson Daly, 47, host ("The Today Show," "Last Call with Carson Daly"), born Santa Monica, CA, June 22, 1973.

Clyde Drexler, 58, basketball coach and Hall of Fame player, born Houston, TX, June 22, 1962.

Dianne Feinstein, 87, US Senator (D, California), born San Francisco, CA, June 22, 1933.

Kris Kristofferson, 84, singer, actor (*Alice Doesn't Live Here Anymore, A Star Is Born*), born Brownsville, TX, June 22, 1936.

Michael Lerner, 79, actor (*The Candidate, Eight Men Out, Barton Fink*), born Brooklyn, NY, June 22, 1941.

Tracy Pollan, 60, actress (*Bright Lights, Big City*; "Family Ties"), born New York, NY, June 22, 1960.

Todd Rundgren, 72, singer, producer, born Upper Darby, PA, June 22, 1948.

Meryl Streep, 71, actress (*August: Osage County, The Devil Wears Prada*, Oscars for *Kramer vs Kramer* and *Sophie's Choice*), born Summit, NJ, June 22, 1949.

Kurt Wagner, 49, former football player, born Burlington, IA, June 22, 1971.

Lindsay Wagner, 71, actress ("The Bionic Woman," *The Paper Chase*), born Los Angeles, CA, June 22, 1949.

Elizabeth Warren, 71, US Senator (D, Massachusetts), born Oklahoma City, OK, June 22, 1949.

June 2020	S	M	T	W	T	F	S
		1	2	3	4	5	6
	7	8	9	10	11	12	13
	14	15	16	17	18	19	20
	21	22	23	24	25	26	27
	28	29	30				

June 23 — Tuesday

AKHMATOVA, ANNA: BIRTH ANNIVERSARY. June 23, 1889. Born at Odessa, Russia, Akhmatova was one of the most beloved and renowned Russian poets of the 20th century. Part of the Acmeist literary group devoted to tactile, concrete, material images in poetry, her poems are like photographs or sketches of real life. Her work reflects the historical and spiritual experience of her generation and references many of her poetic predecessors. She wrote, "It could be that poetry itself is one great quotation." Outcast from Soviet literary society for her unwillingness to write about the new socialist order, Akhmatova died Mar 6, 1966, at Moscow, Soviet Union.

"THE BREAKFAST CLUB" RADIO PREMIERE: ANNIVERSARY. June 23, 1933. "The Breakfast Club with Don McNeil," which hit radio airwaves on this date, had a 35-year run. It was carried by 400 affiliates, and tickets became as sought-after as those for a taping of "The Tonight Show" are today. The hour-long show included celebrities such as Fran Allison of "Kukla, Fran and Ollie" fame. Its popularity, however, stemmed mainly from regular features such as "Memory Time," when McNeil read poems and letters from listeners. During WWII, "Prayer Time" was started. McNeil's "Call to Breakfast," which was announced every 15 minutes, invited listeners to get up and march around the breakfast table. McNeil died in 1996.

CASH, JUNE CARTER: BIRTH ANNIVERSARY. June 23, 1929. Grammy-winning country-western star born Valerie June Carter at Maces Springs, VA. As a member of the Carter Family, a group that included her mother, sisters and various cousins, she toured as a performer from childhood. She met Johnny Cash on the road in 1961. She cowrote his hit song "Ring of Fire," and they began recording together. They married in 1968 and won two Grammys for their duets. She died May 15, 2004, at Nashville, TN.

DENMARK: MIDSUMMER EVE. June 23. Celebrated all over the country with bonfires and merrymaking.

ESTONIA: VICTORY DAY. June 23. National holiday. Commemorates victory against Germany in 1919.

FOSSE, ROBERT LOUIS (BOB): BIRTH ANNIVERSARY. June 23, 1927. Bob Fosse was born at Chicago, IL. The son of a vaudeville singer, he began his show business career at the age of 13. He was the only director in history to win an Oscar, an Emmy and a Tony for his work. As a choreographer he was known for his unique dance style that focused on explosive angularity of the human body in its movement. His body of work includes the plays *Pippin, Sweet Charity, Pajama Game, Chicago* and *Damn Yankees* and the films *Cabaret, Lenny* and *All That Jazz*. Fosse died Sept 23, 1987, at Washington, DC.

INDIA: RATHA YATRA. June 23. In this festival, wooden images of Lord Jagannath, the Lord of the Universe, his sister Balabhadra and his sister Subhadra are taken out in procession in immense temple chariots, or raths. The main chariot with its striped yellow awning is more than 14 meters high and 10 meters square with 16 wheels. Because there is no one universally accepted Hindu calendar, the date of this holiday may vary in different parts of India but it always falls in June or July.

KINSEY, ALFRED: BIRTH ANNIVERSARY. June 23, 1894. Born at Hoboken, NJ, Kinsey was a professor of zoology who moved into the study of human sexual behavior in the 1940s at Indiana University's Institute for Sex Research (later renamed after him). Kinsey published two controversial books based on his research: *Sexual Behavior in the Human Male* (1948) and *Sexual Behavior in the Human Female* (1953). Kinsey died Aug 25, 1956, at Bloomington, IN.

LAST FORMAL SURRENDER OF CONFEDERATE TROOPS: ANNIVERSARY. June 23, 1865. The last formal surrender of Confederate troops took place in the Oklahoma Territory. Cherokee leader and Confederate brigadier general Waite surrendered his command of a battalion formed by Indians.

LET IT GO DAY. June 23. Whatever it is that's bugging you, drop it! It's only eating away at you and providing nothing positive. (©2006 by WH.) For info: Thomas & Ruth Roy, Wellcat Holidays, 2418 Long Ln, Lebanon, PA 17046-1708. Phone: (717) 279-0184. E-mail: info@wellcat.com. Web: www.wellcat.com.

LUXEMBOURG: NATIONAL HOLIDAY. June 23. Official birthday of His Royal Highness Grand Duke Jean in 1921. Also, Luxembourg's independence is celebrated June 23.

NATIONAL COLUMNISTS' DAY. June 23. Newspaper columnists, who bring you joy all year long, deserve to be celebrated by their readers at least once a year. Now you can send your favorite columnists, local or nationally syndicated, your own wishes for a Happy Columnists' Day and make them feel wonderful. Annually, the fourth Tuesday in June. (Created by Jim Six, Columnist, *South Jersey Times*.)

RUDOLPH, WILMA: 80th BIRTH ANNIVERSARY. June 23, 1940. Olympic gold medal sprinter, born at Bethlehem, TN. She won the 100-, 200- and 400-meter relays at the 1960 Rome games, thus becoming the first woman to win three gold medals at the same Olympics. She overcame polio as a child and went on to Tennessee State University to become an athlete. Rudolph won the Sullivan Award in 1961. Died at Brentwood, TN, Nov 12, 1994.

RUNNER'S SELFIE DAY. June 23. A day for runners worldwide to take selfies while on a run and connect with the running community. Create a photo that celebrates the traits of a runner: resilience, focus, strength, vision, openness, trust and awesomeness! Annually, June 23. For info: Wendy Lee. E-mail: runnersselfie@gmail.com. Web: www.facebook.com/runnersselfie.

SWEDEN: MIDSUMMER. June 23–24. Celebrated throughout Sweden with maypole dancing, games and folk music.

SWEDISH DAYS—A MIDSOMMAR FESTIVAL. June 23–28. Geneva, IL. This granddaddy of all Illinois festivals commemorates Swedish heritage. Visitors will discover a host of family-friendly activities, with live entertainment, music competitions, Sweden Väst, carnival, kid's day activities and a Grand Parade. Foodstands throughout the historic downtown area tempt visitors with Swedish and American menus. Begins annually on the Tuesday after Father's Day. Est attendance: 200,000. For info: Geneva Chamber of Commerce, 8 S Third St, Geneva, IL 60134. Phone: (630) 232-6060. E-mail: chamberinfo@genevachamber.com. Web: www.genevachamber.com.

TURING, ALAN: BIRTH ANNIVERSARY. June 23, 1912. British mathematician, logician and cryptographer, recognized as the father of modern computer science and artificial intelligence. Born at London, England, Alan Mathison Turing conceived in 1936 the "Turing Machine," an abstract information-processing mathematical model that foreshadowed digital computers. During WWII, he was a member of the top-secret code-breaking team at England's Bletchley Park. The decoding team saved incalculable Allied lives. Turing was made a member of the Order of the British Empire for his wartime service. In 1945, Turing designed the Automatic Computing Engine—what would have been the first digital computer had it been built. In the 1950s, Turing devised the "Turing Test" that would determine the success of an artificial intelligence machine (of whether it was thinking). Turing was stripped of his government security clearance after being convicted in 1952 for "gross indecency"—Turing was openly gay, and homosexuality was a crime in England. He committed suicide June 7, 1954, at Wilmslow, England. On Dec 24, 2013, Queen Elizabeth II granted Turing a posthumous royal pardon for his criminal conviction.

UNITED NATIONS: INTERNATIONAL WIDOWS' DAY. June 23. Abuse of widows and their children constitutes one of the most serious violations of human rights and obstacles to development today. Millions of the world's widows endure extreme poverty, ostracism, violence, homelessness, ill health and discrimination in law and custom. To give special recognition to the situation of widows of all ages and across regions and cultures, the General Assembly has declared this day to be observed annually on June 23. For info: United Nations, Dept of Public Info, New York, NY 10017. Web: www.un.org.

UNITED NATIONS: PUBLIC SERVICE DAY. June 23. The General Assembly designated June 23 of each year as United Nations Public Service Day (Res 57/277). Member states are encouraged to organize special events on that day to highlight the contribution of public service in the development process. For info: United Nations, Dept of Public Info, New York, NY 10017. Web: www.un.org.

WESTERN DAYS. June 23–27. Elgin, TX. Events include a parade, horseshoe contest, volleyball tournament, Miss Western Days contest, live music, arts and crafts and carnival. Est attendance: 20,000. For info: Gena Carter, Elgin Chamber of Commerce, PO Box 408, Elgin, TX 78621. Phone: (512) 285-4515. Web: www.elgintxchamber.com.

🎂 BIRTHDAYS TODAY

Bryan Brown, 73, actor (*A Town like Alice, Breaker Morant, F/X*), born Sydney, Australia, June 23, 1947.

Joel Edgerton, 46, actor (*Black Mass, The Gift, The Great Gatsby*), director, born Blacktown, Australia, June 23, 1974.

Randy Jackson, 64, musician, television personality ("American Idol"), born Baton Rouge, LA, June 23, 1956.

James Levine, 77, pianist, conductor (formerly with Metropolitan Opera of New York City), born Cincinnati, OH, June 23, 1943.

Frances McDormand, 63, actress (Oscars for *Three Billboards Outside Ebbing, Missouri* and *Fargo*; *Moonrise Kingdom, Almost Famous*), born Chicago, IL, June 23, 1957.

Chellsie Memmel, 32, Olympic gymnast, born West Allis, WI, June 23, 1988.

Ted Shackelford, 74, actor ("Knots Landing," "Dallas"), born Oklahoma City, OK, June 23, 1946.

Bridget Sloan, 28, Olympic gymnast, born Cincinnati, OH, June 23, 1992.

Clarence Thomas, 72, Associate Justice of the US, born Pinpoint, GA, June 23, 1948.

LaDainian Tomlinson, 41, Hall of Fame football player, born Waco, TX, June 23, 1979.

Louis Van Amstel, 48, professional dancer, television personality ("Dancing with the Stars"), born Amsterdam, Netherlands, June 23, 1972.

Zinedine Zidane, 48, soccer coach and former player, born Marseille, France, June 23, 1972.

June 24 — Wednesday

DAY 176   **190 REMAINING**

BATTLE OF BANNOCKBURN: ANNIVERSARY. June 24, 1314. Decisive battle for Scottish independence in which a smaller force of Scots (mainly pikemen) under Robert the Bruce defeated the English (with 3,000 horses) under King Edward II. The battle took place by the strategically important Stirling Castle at the Bannock Burn stream and the River Forth. The battle began June 23 and ended June 24 in a rout—the worst English defeat since the Battle of Hastings.

BEECHER, HENRY WARD: BIRTH ANNIVERSARY. June 24, 1813. Famous clergyman and orator, brother of Harriet Beecher Stowe, born at Litchfield, CT. From the pulpit at Plymouth Church, Beecher advocated for many controversial issues of his era, including temperance, women's suffrage, Darwinian evolution and—most notably—abolition. Beecher's tactics in support of abolition were often sensational and contentious, as was the case when he raised money to provide rifles—widely dubbed "Beecher's Bibles"—to antislavery settlers in Kansas in 1856. In the 1870s Beecher was the subject of one of the biggest scandals of the century—the Beecher-Tilton Affair—when he was accused of adultery by a parishioner and sued in civil court. The trial resulted in a hung jury, and although Beecher was exonerated by two ecclesiastical courts, public opinion about his innocence was divided. Died Mar 8, 1887, at Brooklyn, NY. His dying words were, "Now comes the mystery."

BERLIN AIRLIFT: ANNIVERSARY. June 24, 1948. In the early days of the cold war, the Soviet Union challenged the West's right of access to Berlin. The Soviets created a blockade, and an airlift to supply some 2,250,000 people resulted. The airlift lasted a total of 321 days and brought into Berlin 1,592,787 tons of supplies. Joseph Stalin finally backed down and the blockade ended May 12, 1949.

BIERCE, AMBROSE: BIRTH ANNIVERSARY. June 24, 1842. American critic, journalist, short story author and creator of the satirical and misanthropic *Devil's Dictionary*, born at Horse Cave Creek, Meigs County, OH. Best-known story is "An Occurrence at Owl Creek Bridge." Disappeared in January 1914 after professing an interest in going to Mexico to observe the ongoing revolution there. He wrote to his niece in October 1913: "Civilization be dinged!—It is the mountains and the desert for me."

CANADA: SAINT JEAN-BAPTISTE DAY. June 24. Public holiday in Quebec.

CELEBRATION OF THE SENSES. June 24. Treat yourself to a stimulation of the five senses—taste, touch, scent, sight and sound—and you may experience the elevation known to many mystics as the elusive sixth sense. (©2006 by WH.) For info: Thomas & Ruth Roy, Wellcat Holidays, 2418 Long Ln, Lebanon, PA 17046. Phone: (717) 279-0184. E-mail: info@wellcat.com. Web: www.wellcat.com.

CHINA: MACAU DAY. June 24. Celebrates defeat of the Dutch invasion forces of 1622 and pays homage to patron saint of Macau, Saint John the Baptist. Macau is a former Portuguese colony that is now part of China.

DEMPSEY, JACK: 125th BIRTH ANNIVERSARY. June 24, 1895. William Harrison Dempsey, known as the "Manassa Mauler," was world heavyweight boxing champion from 1919 to 1926. Following his boxing career Dempsey became a successful New York restaurant operator. Born at Manassa, CO, Dempsey died May 31, 1983, at New York, NY.

	S	M	T	W	T	F	S
June		1	2	3	4	5	6
	7	8	9	10	11	12	13
2020	14	15	16	17	18	19	20
	21	22	23	24	25	26	27
	28	29	30				

ENGLAND: GLASTONBURY FESTIVAL: 50th ANNIVERSARY. June 24–28. Worthy Farm, Pilton, Somerset. The world's largest greenfield music and performing arts festival. The 1,000-acre festival offers music, theater, circus, cabaret, markets, children's activities and more. 2020 marks Glastonbury's 50th anniversary: the festival was first held Sept 19, 1970 (with T. Rx and Al Stewart). Annually, the Wednesday through Sunday after the summer solstice. For info: Glastonbury Festival. Web: www.glastonburyfestivals.co.uk.

"FLYING SAUCER" DAY: SIGHTING ANNIVERSARY. June 24, 1947. Pilot Kenneth Arnold of Boise, ID, reported seeing pie-plate-shaped unidentified flying objects (UFOs) over Mount Rainier, WA. Flying at more than 9,000 feet, Arnold saw flashes of light and then nine "saucer-like" objects flying at incredible speeds. The term "flying saucer" came into currency soon after to describe a UFO.

HOMESTEAD DAYS®. June 24–28 (tentative). Beatrice, NE. This community-wide celebration recognizes the importance of the Homestead Act of 1862 to the settlement of Nebraska. Entertainment, parades and special museum exhibits. Est attendance: 30,000. For info: Homestead Days, Beatrice Area Chamber of Commerce, 218 N 5th St, Beatrice, NE 68310. Phone: (402) 223-2338. E-mail: info@beatricechamber.com. Web: www.beatricechamber.com.

ITALY: CALCIO FIORENTINO. June 24–28. Florence. Revival of a 16th-century football match in medieval costumes.

LATVIA: JOHN'S DAY (MIDSUMMER NIGHT DAY). June 24. The festival of Jani, which commemorates the summer solstice and the name day of (Janis) John, is one of Latvia's most ancient as well as joyous rituals. This festival is traditionally celebrated in the countryside, as it emphasizes fertility and the beginning of summer. Festivities begin June 23.

NATIONAL ENERGY SHOPPING DAY. June 24. An important facet of America's culture and history is the right to choose. But when it comes to energy, not all Americans enjoy this right. Currently, only 13 states and Washington, DC, allow for energy choice. National Energy Shopping Day celebrates the freedom to choose. It encourages shopping for the best energy plan for lifestyle, families and the environment. Annually, the first Monday of Summer. For info: Retail Energy Supply Assn, PO Box 6089, Harrisburg, PA 17112.

PERU: COUNTRYMAN'S DAY. June 24. Half-day public holiday.

SAINT JOHN THE BAPTIST DAY. June 24. Celebrates the birth of the saint.

SUMMERFEST. June 24–July 5 (closed June 29, tentative). Milwaukee, WI. First held in 1968, Summerfest is the world's largest music festival. For 11 days, more than 800 bands play across the 11 stages featured on the permanent 75-acre festival site. On any given day, attendees can enjoy national, alternative, rock, country, R&B, pop, EDM and more. Est attendance: 1,000,000. For info: Milwaukee World Festival, Inc, Summerfest, 200 N Harbor Dr, Milwaukee, WI 53202. E-mail: summerfestinfo@summerfest.com. Web: www.summerfest.com.

SWIFT, GUSTAVUS: BIRTH ANNIVERSARY. June 24, 1839. American industrialist known for revolutionizing the meatpacking industry. He commissioned the development of the refrigerator car, which allowed the transportation of processed meat for the first time, and his company was one of the first in modern history to implement "vertical integration": it had departments for purchasing, production, shipping, sales and marketing. Swift was also a pioneer in using by-products of animal parts previously discarded for products like glue, fertilizer and soap; this efficiency was the model for the contemptuous fictional Durham Company in Upton Sinclair's *The Jungle*. Born at Sandwich, MA, Swift died Mar 29, 1903, at Chicago, IL.

THORNTON, MATTHEW: DEATH ANNIVERSARY. June 24, 1803. Signer of the Declaration of Independence. Born at Ireland about 1714, he died at Newburyport, MA.

VENEZUELA: BATTLE OF CARABOBO DAY. June 24. National holiday. Commemorates a victory in 1821 that assured Venezuelan independence from Spain.

🎂 BIRTHDAYS TODAY

Nancy Allen, 70, actress (*Carrie, Blow Out, Robocop*), born New York, NY, June 24, 1950.

Mick Fleetwood, 78, musician (Fleetwood Mac), born Cornwall, England, June 24, 1942.

Phyllis George, 71, former sportscaster, former Miss America, born Denton, TX, June 24, 1949.

Juli Inkster, 60, golfer, born Santa Cruz, CA, June 24, 1960.

Mindy Kaling, 41, actress ("The Office," "The Mindy Project"), author (*Is Everyone Hanging Out Without Me?*), born Vera Mindy Chokalingam at Cambridge, MA, June 24, 1979.

Solange Knowles, 34, singer, model, dancer, born Houston, TX, June 24, 1986.

Michele Lee, 78, actress ("Knots Landing"), born Los Angeles, CA, June 24, 1942.

Lionel Messi, 33, soccer player, born Rosario, Argentina, June 24, 1987.

Sherry Stringfield, 53, actress ("NYPD Blue," "ER"), born Colorado Springs, CO, June 24, 1967.

Lotte Verbeek, 38, actress ("The Borgias"), born Venlo, Limburg, Netherlands, June 24, 1982.

Peter Weller, 73, actor (*Robocop, Naked Lunch*), born Stevens Point, WI, June 24, 1947.

June 25 — Thursday

DAY 177   **189 REMAINING**

AMERICAN LIBRARY ASSOCIATION ANNUAL CONFERENCE. June 25–30. Chicago, IL. The American Library Association (ALA), the oldest and largest library association in the world, holds its annual conference each summer. Its attendees include librarians, educators, writers, publishers, friends of libraries, trustees and special guests. More than 2,000 meetings, discussion groups, tours, special events and awards ceremonies are spread throughout the weeklong conference. Est attendance: 25,000. For info: American Library Assn, 50 E Huron St, Chicago, IL 60611. Phone: (800) 545-2433. E-mail: ala@ala.org. Web: www.ala.org.

ARNOLD, HENRY H. "HAP": BIRTH ANNIVERSARY. June 25, 1886. US general and commander of the Army Air Force in all theaters throughout WWII, Arnold was born at Gladwyne, PA. Although no funds were made available, as early as 1938 Arnold was persuading the US aviation industry to step up manufacturing of airplanes. Production grew from 6,000 to 262,000 per year from 1940 to 1944. He supervised pilot training and by 1944 Air Force personnel strength had grown to two million from a prewar high of 21,000. Made a full general in 1944, he became the US Air Force's first five-star general when the Air Force was made a separate military branch equal to the Army and Navy. Arnold died Jan 15, 1950, at Sonoma, CA.

BATTLE OF LITTLE BIGHORN: ANNIVERSARY. June 25, 1876. Lieutenant Colonel George Armstrong Custer, leading military forces of more than 200 men, attacked an encampment of 2,000 Sioux

Indians led by Chiefs Sitting Bull and Crazy Horse near Little Bighorn River, MT. Custer and all men in his immediate command were killed in the brief battle (about two hours) of Little Bighorn.

BHUTAN: NATIONAL DAY. June 25. National holiday observed.

CANADA'S FIRST WOMAN PRIME MINISTER: ANNIVERSARY. June 25, 1993. After winning the June 13 election to the leadership of the ruling Progressive-Conservative Party, Kim Campbell became Canada's 19th prime minister and its first woman prime minister. However, in the general election held Oct 25, 1993, the Liberal Party routed the Progressive-Conservatives in the worst defeat for a governing political party in Canada's 126-year history, reducing the former government's seats in the House of Commons from 154 to 2. Campbell was among those who lost their seats.

CBS SENDS FIRST COLOR TV BROADCAST OVER THE AIR: ANNIVERSARY. June 25, 1951. Columbia Broadcasting System broadcast the first color television program. The four-hour program was carried by stations at New York City, Baltimore, Philadelphia, Boston and Washington, DC, although no color sets were owned by the public. At the time, CBS itself owned fewer than 40 color receivers.

CHINA: DRAGON BOAT FESTIVAL. June 25. An important Chinese observance, the Dragon Boat Festival commemorates a hero of ancient China, poet Qu Yuan, who drowned himself in protest against injustice and corruption. It is said that rice dumplings were cast into the water to lure fish away from the body of the martyr, and this is remembered by the eating of *zhong zi*, glutinous rice dumplings filled with meat and wrapped in bamboo leaves. Dragon boat races are held on rivers. The Dragon Boat Festival is observed in many countries by their Chinese populations (date may differ from China's). Also called Fifth Month Festival or Summer Festival. Annually, the fifth day of the fifth lunar month.

CIVIL WAR IN YUGOSLAVIA: ANNIVERSARY. June 25, 1991. In an Eastern Europe freed from the iron rule of communism and the USSR, separatist and nationalist tensions suppressed for decades rose to a violent boiling point. The republics of Croatia and Slovenia declared their independence, sparking a fractious and bitter war that spread throughout what was formerly Yugoslavia. Ethnic rivalries between Serbians and Croatians began the military conflicts that spread to Slovenia, and in 1992 fighting began in Bosnia-Herzegovina between Serbians and ethnic Muslims. Although the new republics were recognized by the UN and sanctions passed to stop the fighting, it raged on through 1995 despite the efforts of UN peacekeeping forces.

HARRY THAW SHOOTS STANFORD WHITE: ANNIVERSARY. June 25, 1906. Wealthy playboy Harry Thaw shot celebrated architect Stanford White dead at Madison Square Garden's rooftop theater in front of horrified theater patrons. Thaw claimed to be avenging the assault of his wife, showgirl Evelyn Nesbit, who was White's former mistress. Later, Thaw pled guilty by reason of temporary insanity in what newspapers dubbed the "Trial of the Century."

HELEN KELLER FESTIVAL. June 25–28. Tuscumbia, AL. Commemorates the remarkable life of Helen Keller with stage shows for all ages, arts and crafts fair, free musical entertainment, races, historic tours of Helen Keller's birthplace and other beautiful homes and much more. Est attendance: 105,000. For info: Hellen Keller Festival. E-mail: info@helenkellerfestival.com. Web: www.helenkellerfestival.com.

KOREA: TANO DAY. June 25. Fifth day of fifth lunar month. Summer food offered at the household shrine of the ancestors. Also known as Swing Day, since girls, dressed in their prettiest clothes, often compete in swinging matches. The Tano Festival usually lasts from the third through eighth day of the fifth lunar month.

KOREAN WAR BEGINS: 70th ANNIVERSARY. June 25, 1950. Forces from northern Korea invaded southern Korea, beginning a civil war. US ground forces entered the conflict June 30. An armistice was signed at Panmunjom July 27, 1953, formally dividing the country in two—North Korea and South Korea.

LUMET, SIDNEY: BIRTH ANNIVERSARY. June 25, 1924. Acclaimed film director, born at Philadelphia, PA. Lumet's remarkable list of films directed includes *Long Day's Journey into Night, Fail-Safe* and *Serpico*. He was Oscar-nominated as best director for *12 Angry Men, Dog Day Afternoon, Network* and *The Verdict*, although he never took home the prize. Lumet was awarded an honorary Lifetime Achievement Academy Award in 2005. Died Apr 9, 2011, at New York, NY.

MONTSERRAT: VOLCANO ERUPTS: ANNIVERSARY. June 25, 1997. After lying dormant for 400 years, the Soufriere Hills volcano began to come to life in July 1995. It finally erupted, wiping out the capital city of Plymouth and two-thirds of the rest of this lush Caribbean island on June 25, 1997. Two-thirds of the population relocated to other islands or to Great Britain.

MOZAMBIQUE: INDEPENDENCE DAY. June 25. National holiday. Commemorates independence from Portugal in 1975.

NATIONAL HANDSHAKE DAY. June 25. Get a grip on a professional handshake today! The handshake is an important part of corporate America and can make or break a business deal, interview or other encounter. Take this day to perfect your own handshake and put it into practice. Learn how to avoid the 10 nightmare handshakes. Annually, the last Thursday in June. For info: Miryam S. Roddy, BRODY Professional Development, 115 West Ave, Ste 114, Jenkintown, PA 19046. Phone: (215) 886-1688. E-mail: mroddy@BrodyPro.com.

O'NEILL, ROSE CECIL: BIRTH ANNIVERSARY. June 25, 1874. Rose O'Neill was born at Wilkes-Barre, PA. Her career included work as an illustrator, author and doll designer, the latter gaining her commercial success with the Kewpie Doll. In 1910 *The Ladies' Home Journal* devoted a full page to her Kewpie Doll designs, which were a marketing phenomenon for three decades. Died at Springfield, MO, Apr 6, 1944.

ORWELL, GEORGE: BIRTH ANNIVERSARY. June 25, 1903. The journalist, essayist and novelist was born Eric Arthur Blair in Motihari, India. He adopted the pen name George Orwell for the publication of the autobiographical *Down and Out in Paris and London*(1933). Orwell participated briefly in the Spanish Civil War, and from 1941 to 1943 worked at the BBC. In 1945, he published his devastating political allegory *Animal Farm* (1945).

Fighting a losing battle with tuberculosis, Orwell was able to finish *1984* during 1948 (it was published in 1949). He died Jan 21, 1950, at London, England,

REVERE, ANNE: BIRTH ANNIVERSARY. June 25, 1903. American actress Anne Revere was born at New York, NY. She won an Academy Award for her supporting role in *National Velvet* (1944) but was barred from films for 20 years after she refused to testify before the House Committee on Un-American Activities in the 1950s. In 1960 she won a Tony Award for her role in *Toys in the Attic*. Revere died Dec 18, 1990, at Locust Valley, NY.

SEVEN DAYS CAMPAIGN: ANNIVERSARY. June 25–July 1, 1862. In an effort to prevent an attack on Richmond, VA, Confederate general Robert E. Lee launched a series of engagements that became known as the Seven Days Campaign. Battles at Oak Grove, Gaine's Mills, Garnett's Farm, Golding's Farm, Savage's Station, White Oak Swamp and, finally, Malvern Hill left more than 35,000 casualties on both sides. Despite losing the final assault at Malvern Hill, the Confederates succeeded in preventing the Union army from taking Richmond.

SLOVENIA: NATIONAL DAY. June 25. Public holiday. Commemorates independence from the former Yugoslavia in 1991.

SUPREME COURT BANS SCHOOL PRAYER: ANNIVERSARY. June 25, 1962. The Supreme Court ruled, 6–3, that a prayer read aloud in public schools violated the First Amendment's separation of church and state. The court again struck down a law pertaining to the First Amendment when it disallowed an Alabama law that permitted a daily one-minute period of silent meditation or prayer in public schools June 1, 1985.

SUPREME COURT UPHOLDS RIGHT TO DIE: 30th ANNIVERSARY. June 25, 1990. In the case *Cruzan v Missouri*, the Supreme Court, in a 5–4 ruling, upheld the constitutional right of a person whose wishes are clearly known to refuse life-sustaining medical treatment.

TWO YUGOSLAV REPUBLICS DECLARE INDEPENDENCE: ANNIVERSARY. June 25, 1991. The republics of Slovenia and Croatia formally declared independence from Yugoslavia. The two northwestern republics did not, however, secede outright.

UNITED NATIONS: DAY OF THE SEAFARER. June 25. A day to recognize the unique contribution made by seafarers to international seaborne trade, the world economy and civil society as a whole. A day to say thank you to the people who bring us 90 percent of our household goods. Annually, June 25. For info: United Nations/International Maritime Organization. Web: www.imo.org.

US SENIOR OPEN (GOLF) CHAMPIONSHIP. June 25–28. Newport Country Club, Newport, RI. For info: USGA, Golf House, Championship Dept, PO Box 708, Far Hills, NJ 07931. Phone: (908) 234-2300. E-mail: champs@usga.org. Web: www.usga.org.

VIRGINIA: RATIFICATION DAY. June 25. 10th state to ratify the Constitution in 1788.

🎂 BIRTHDAYS TODAY

Linda Cardellini, 45, actress (*Scooby-Doo, Legally Blonde*), born Redmond City, CA, June 25, 1975.

Carlos Delgado, 48, former baseball player, born Mayaguez, Puerto Rico, June 25, 1972.

Ricky Gervais, 59, actor, comedian ("The Office" [UK], "Extras"), born Reading, Berkshire, England, June 25, 1961.

John Benjamin Hickey, 57, actor ("The Big C"; stage: *The Normal Heart*), born Plano, TX, June 25, 1963.

June Lockhart, 95, actress ("Lassie," "Lost in Space," Tony for *For Love or Money*), born New York, NY, June 25, 1925.

Dikembe Mutombo, 54, former basketball player, humanitarian, born Kinshasa, Zaire, June 25, 1966.

Willis Reed, Jr, 78, Hall of Fame basketball player, basketball executive and former coach, born Hico, LA, June 25, 1942.

June 2020	S	M	T	W	T	F	S
		1	2	3	4	5	6
	7	8	9	10	11	12	13
	14	15	16	17	18	19	20
	21	22	23	24	25	26	27
	28	29	30				

Carly Simon, 75, singer, songwriter, born New York, NY, June 25, 1945.

Sonia Sotomayor, 66, Associate Justice of the US, born the Bronx, NY, June 25, 1954.

Billy Wagner, 49, former baseball player, born Tannersville, VA, June 25, 1971.

Jimmie Walker, 72, actor, comedian ("Good Times," "B.A.D. Cats"), born New York, NY, June 25, 1948.

June 26 — Friday

DAY 178   **188 REMAINING**

BAR CODE INTRODUCED: ANNIVERSARY. June 26, 1974. A committee formed in 1970 by US grocers and food manufacturers recommended in 1973 a Universal Product Code (i.e., a bar code) for supermarket items that would allow electronic scanning of prices. On this day in 1974 a pack of Wrigley's gum was swiped across the first checkout scanner at a supermarket in Troy, OH. Today bar codes are used to keep track of everything from freight cars to cattle.

BORDEN, SIR ROBERT LAIRD: BIRTH ANNIVERSARY. June 26, 1854. Statesman and eighth prime minister of Canada (1911–20), born at Grand Pre, NS, Canada. Died at Ottawa, ON, Canada, June 10, 1937.

BUCK, PEARL SYDENSTRICKER: BIRTH ANNIVERSARY. June 26, 1892. American author, humanitarian and authority on China. Her premier novel, *The Good Earth* (1931), first in the House of Earth trilogy, won the Pulitzer Prize, and Buck became the first American woman—fourth overall—to win the Nobel Prize in Literature (1938). Born at Hillsboro, WV. Died Mar 6, 1973, at Danby, VT.

CLARKSON CZECH FESTIVAL. June 26–28. Main St, Clarkson, NE. Czech food, entertainment, music, polkas, cooking demonstrations, carnival and arts and crafts. Annually, the fourth full weekend in June. Sponsor: Clarkson Commercial Club. Est attendance: 10,000. For info: Robert Brabec, 515 Elm St, Clarkson, NE 68629. Phone: (402) 892-3331. Fax: (402) 892-3318. E-mail: cphtvh@gmail.com.

CN TOWER OPENED: ANNIVERSARY. June 26, 1976. Birthday of the world's second-tallest building and freestanding structure, the CN Tower, 1,815 feet, 5 inches high, at Toronto, ON, Canada. It was the world's tallest building until the Burj Khalifa in Dubai (dedicated in 2010).

DOUBLEDAY, ABNER: BIRTH ANNIVERSARY. June 26, 1819. Abner Doubleday served in the US Army during the Mexican War and the Seminole War in Florida prior to his service in the American Civil War. His service found him at the battles of Second Bull Run, Antietam and Fredericksburg, and as a major general he commanded a division at Gettysburg. A commission set up by sporting goods manufacturer Albert Spalding to investigate the origins of baseball credited Doubleday with inventing the game in 1839. Subsequent research has debunked the commission's finding. Doubleday was born at Ballston Spa, NY, and died at Mendham, NJ, Jan 26, 1893.

FEDERAL CREDIT UNION ACT: ANNIVERSARY. June 26, 1934. Commemorates signing by President Franklin Delano Roosevelt of the Federal Credit Union Act, thus enabling the formation of credit unions anywhere in the US.

"GUIDING LIGHT" TV PREMIERE: ANNIVERSARY. June 26, 1952. "Guiding Light," previously on radio, holds the title of longest-lasting daytime show and longest-lasting series. Set in the fictional Midwestern town of Springfield, this soap ended on Sept 18, 2009, after a 72-year run.

HARRY POTTER AND THE PHILOSOPHER'S STONE PUBLISHED: ANNIVERSARY. June 26, 1997. Bloomsbury published this acclaimed children's fantasy book by Joanne (J.K.) Rowling in the United Kingdom with an initial hardcover print run of 500 copies. The first book in a seven-title series, it became a smash hit almost overnight. The seventh title, *Harry Potter and the Deathly Hallows*, was published July 21, 2007. The books—which became a blockbuster film series—have been translated into 69 languages and have sold more than 450 million copies.

HAYMARKET PARDON: ANNIVERSARY. June 26, 1893. Illinois governor John Peter Altgeld pardoned Samuel Fielden, Michael Schwab and Oscar Neebe, three of the anarchists who had been convicted in the violence connected with the Haymarket Riot on May 4, 1886. At a protest meeting at Haymarket Square an unknown individual threw a bomb that caused the death of several policemen. Eight anarchists were tried and convicted of the bombing. Of those, one committed suicide the day before he was to be hanged; three were hanged; and Fielden, Schwab and Neebe were imprisoned. In 1893 the newly elected Altgeld, at the urging of Clarence Darrow, reviewed the transcripts of the trial of these men and concluded that they had been railroaded. The pardon was widely criticized. It was an act of political suicide for Altgeld.

HUMAN GENOME MAPPED: 20th ANNIVERSARY. June 26, 2000. Biologists J. Craig Venter and Francis S. Collins announced that their research groups had mapped the human genome, a strand of DNA with three billion parts that spell out our genetic code.

"THE LOTTERY" PUBLISHED: ANNIVERSARY. June 26, 1948. Shirley Jackson's chilling story of a small-town ritual appeared in *The New Yorker*. No other story in the magazine's history has generated more response—much of it negative.

MADAGASCAR: INDEPENDENCE DAY: 60th ANNIVERSARY OF INDEPENDENCE. June 26. National holiday. Commemorates independence from France in 1960.

MIDDLETON, ARTHUR: BIRTH ANNIVERSARY. June 26, 1742. American Revolutionary leader and signer of the Declaration of Independence, born near Charleston, SC. Died at Goose Creek, SC, Jan 1, 1787.

NATIONAL EAT AT A FOOD TRUCK DAY. June 26. 4th annual. A day to get outside, enjoy the weather, eat at a food truck and support local small businesses. Food trucks nationwide are participating by offering deals to entice foodies to get out and eat. Annually, the fourth Friday in June. For info: Roaming Hunger, 8228 W Sunset Blvd, West Hollywood, CA 90046.

PURPLEHULL PEA FESTIVAL AND WORLD CHAMPIONSHIP ROTARY TILLER RACE. June 26–27. Emerson, AR. 31st annual festival. World Cup purplehull pea–shelling competition, rotary tiller race; concessions, arts, crafts, entertainment, children's games, the Great Purplehull Peas and Cornbread Cook-off, Queen's pageant (various ages) and more. Est attendance: 5,000. For info: Bill Dailey, Pea-R Guy, Purplehull Pea Fest, PO Box 1, Emerson, AR 71740. Phone: (501) 416-4657. E-mail: purplehull@juno.com. Web: www.purplehull.com.

SAINT LAWRENCE SEAWAY DEDICATION: ANNIVERSARY. June 26, 1959. President Dwight D. Eisenhower and Queen Elizabeth II jointly dedicated the St. Lawrence Seaway in formal ceremonies held at St. Lambert, QC, Canada. A project undertaken jointly by

Canada and the US, the waterway (which provides access between the Atlantic Ocean and the Great Lakes) had been opened to traffic Apr 25, 1959.

SUPREME COURT STRIKES DOWN DEFENSE OF MARRIAGE ACT: ANNIVERSARY. June 26, 2013. In *United States v Windsor*, by a vote of five to four, the US Supreme Court struck down the federal Defense of Marriage Act, ruling that same-sex couples were entitled to federal benefits.

TAKE YOUR DOG TO WORK DAY®. June 26. Since 1999. A day to celebrate the great companions dogs make and to encourage adoptions from animal shelters. Annually, the first Friday after Father's Day. For info: Beth Stultz, Pet Sitters Intl, 201 E King St, King, NC 27021. Phone: (336) 983-9222, ext 23230. E-mail: takeyourdog@petsit.com. Web: www.takeyourdog.com.

UNITED NATIONS CHARTER SIGNED: 75th ANNIVERSARY. June 26, 1945. The UN Charter was signed at San Francisco by representatives of 50 nations.

UNITED NATIONS: INTERNATIONAL DAY AGAINST DRUG ABUSE AND ILLICIT TRAFFICKING. June 26. Following a recommendation of the 1987 International Conference on Drug Abuse and Illicit Trafficking, the General Assembly (Res 42/112) expressed its determination to strengthen action and cooperation for an international society free of drug abuse and proclaimed June 26 as an annual observance to raise public awareness. For info: United Nations, Dept of Public Info, Public Inquiries Unit, RM GA-57, New York, NY 10017. Phone: (212) 963-4475. E-mail: inquiries@un.org.

UNITED NATIONS: INTERNATIONAL DAY IN SUPPORT OF VICTIMS OF TORTURE. June 26. For info: United Nations, Dept of Public Info, New York, NY 10017. Web: www.un.org.

ZAHARIAS, MILDRED "BABE" DIDRIKSON: BIRTH ANNIVERSARY. June 26, 1911. Born Mildred Ella Didrikson at Port Arthur, TX, the great athlete was nicknamed "Babe" after legendary baseball player Babe Ruth. She was named to the women's All-America basketball team when she was 16. At the 1932 Olympic Games, she won two gold medals and also set world records in the javelin throw and the 80-meter high hurdles; only a technicality prevented her from obtaining the gold in the high jump. Didrikson married professional wrestler George Zaharias in 1938, six years after she began playing golf casually. In 1946 Babe won the US Women's Amateur tournament, and in 1947 she won 17 straight golf championships and became the first American winner of the British Ladies' Amateur tournament. Turning professional in 1948, she won the US Women's Open in 1950 and 1954, the same year she won the All-American Open. Babe also excelled in softball, baseball, swimming, figure skating, billiards—even football. In a 1950 Associated Press poll she was named the woman athlete of the first half of the 20th century. She died of cancer on Sept 27, 1956, at Galveston, TX.

	S	M	T	W	T	F	S
June		1	2	3	4	5	6
	7	8	9	10	11	12	13
2020	14	15	16	17	18	19	20
	21	22	23	24	25	26	27
	28	29	30				

🧁 BIRTHDAYS TODAY

Paul Thomas Anderson, 50, director, screenwriter (*Phantom Thread, Punch-Drunk Love, Magnolia, Boogie Nights*), born Studio City, CA, June 26, 1970.

Rudy Gobert, 28, basketball player, born Saint-Quentin, France, June 26, 1992.

Ariana Grande, 27, actress ("Sam & Cat"), singer, born Ariana Grande-Butera at Boca Raton, FL, June 26, 1993.

Sean P. Hayes, 50, actor ("Will & Grace"), born Glen Ellyn, IL, June 26, 1970.

Chris Isaak, 64, singer, musician, actor ("The Chris Isaak Show"), born Stockton, CA, June 26, 1956.

Derek Jeter, 46, former baseball player, born Pequannock, NJ, June 26, 1974.

Greg LeMond, 59, former cyclist, born Lakewood, CA, June 26, 1961.

Jeanette McCurdy, 28, actress ("Sam & Cat," "I Carly"), singer, born Long Beach, CA, June 26, 1992.

Chris O'Donnell, 50, actor ("NCIS: Los Angeles," *Batman Forever, Scent of a Woman*), born Winnetka, IL, June 26, 1970.

Nick Offerman, 50, actor ("Parks and Recreation," "Children's Hospital"), born Joliet, IL, June 26, 1970.

Chad Pennington, 44, former football player, born Knoxville, TN, June 26, 1976.

Aubrey Plaza, 36, actress ("Legion," "Parks and Recreation," *Scott Pilgrim vs the World*), born Wilmington, DE, June 26, 1984.

Jason Schwartzman, 40, actor (*The Darjeeling Limited, Rushmore*), born Los Angeles, CA, June 26, 1980.

Shannon Sharpe, 52, sportscaster, Hall of Fame football player, born Chicago, IL, June 26, 1968.

Gretchen Wilson, 47, country singer, born Granite City, IL, June 26, 1973.

June 27 — Saturday

DAY 179   **187 REMAINING**

ARRL FIELD DAY. June 27–28. Amateur radio's weekend-long "open house" across North America. Communicate globally with the internet or cell phone networks. "Ham" radio operators set up temporary, portable communications stations in public places and run on battery or solar power in order to demonstrate the science, skill and service amateur radio provides their communities and country. Amateur radio is everybody's gateway into science, electronics and community service. Sponsored by the ARRL, the National Association for Amateur Radio. Annually, the fourth full weekend in June. Est attendance: 100,000. For info: ARRL, 225 Main St, Newington, CT 06111. Phone: (888) 277-5289. E-mail: hq@arrl.org. Web: www.arrl.org/fieldday.

"DARK SHADOWS" TV PREMIERE: ANNIVERSARY. June 27, 1966. This soap opera was completely different from all others because it featured vampires as main characters and had a dark, Gothic feel to it. The show focused on the Collins family living at Collinsport, ME, particularly Barnabas Collins (Jonathan Frid), a 200-year-old vampire. Other cast members included David Selby, Kate Jackson, Lara Parker and Jerry Lacy. Action shifted between the 1800s and the 1960s. This show was very popular with teenagers and was remade as a short-lived series in 1991.

DECIDE TO BE MARRIED DAY. June 27. To focus attention on the joy of couples deciding to get married. Based on the poem "Decide to Be Married": "It's in the deciding to be united in love, to express your joyful oneness to every person you meet, and in every action you take and together a perfect marriage you'll make." For info: Barbara Gaughen-Muller, Gaughen Global Public Relations, 7456

Evergreen Dr, Santa Barbara, CA 93117. Phone: (805) 680-9445. E-mail: bgaughenmu@aol.com.

DJIBOUTI: INDEPENDENCE DAY. June 27. National Day. Commemorates independence from France in 1977.

GREAT AMERICAN CAMPOUT. June 27. The National Wildlife Federation encourages people of all ages to get outside and camp. Participants register their campsites online and receive exclusive information regarding activities, recipes, wildlife and more. More than 40,000 campers have participated in past events. Annually, the fourth Saturday in June. For info: National Wildlife Federation. E-mail: media@nwf.org. Web: www.nwf.org/Great-American-Campout.aspx.

HAPPY BIRTHDAY TO "HAPPY BIRTHDAY TO YOU". June 27, 1859. The melody of probably the most-often-sung song in the world, "Happy Birthday to You," was composed by Mildred J. Hill, a schoolteacher born at Louisville, KY, on this date. Her younger sister, Patty Smith Hill, was the author of the lyrics, which were first published in 1893 as "Good Morning to All," a classroom greeting published in the book *Song Stories for the Sunday School*. The lyrics were amended in 1924 to include a stanza beginning "Happy Birthday to You." Now it is sung somewhere in the world every minute of the day. Although the authors are believed to have earned very little from the song, reportedly it later generated about $1 million a year for its copyright owner. Mildred Hill died at Chicago, IL, June 5, 1916, without knowing that her melody would become the world's most popular song. See also: "Hill, Patty Smith: Birth Anniversary" (Mar 27).

HEARN, LAFCADIO: BIRTH ANNIVERSARY. June 27, 1850. Author, born on the Greek island of Santa Maura. Hearn, who had been a newspaper reporter at Cincinnati, OH, and at New Orleans, LA, went to Japan in 1890 as a magazine writer. Deeply attracted to the country and to the Japanese people, he stayed there as a writer and teacher until his death at Okubo, Japan, Sept 26, 1904. Though his writings are little remembered in America, he remains a popular figure in Japan, where his books are still used, especially in language classes. His home at Matsue is a tourist shrine.

INDUSTRIAL WORKERS OF THE WORLD FOUNDED: ANNIVERSARY. June 27, 1905. With the slogan "One Big Union for All," 43 labor groups merged together to found the IWW at Chicago, IL. Eventually known as the Wobblies, the IWW had a tremendous impact on US labor history.

KEESHAN, BOB: BIRTH ANNIVERSARY. June 27, 1927. Beloved by generations of American children as Captain Kangaroo, Robert J. Keeshan was born at Lynbrook, NJ. He made his acting debut at age 21 as the original Clarabell, the ever-silent clown, sidekick to Buffalo Bob Smith on "The Howdy Doody Show." He was eventually fired from the show, but his future as a children's entertainer was secure. On Oct 3, 1955, "Captain Kangaroo" premiered on CBS, and it remained on the air for 38 years. Captain Kangaroo was joined by characters Mr Green Jeans, Grandfather Clock, Bunny Rabbit and Mr Moose. His gentle, patient wisdom entertained and educated millions of children over the years. Keeshan died in Vermont on Jan 23, 2004.

KELLER, HELEN: BIRTH ANNIVERSARY. June 27, 1880. Born at Tuscumbia, AL, Helen Keller was left deaf and blind by a disease she contracted at 18 months of age. With the help of her teacher, Anne Sullivan, Keller graduated from college and had a career as an author and lecturer. She died June 1, 1968, at Westport, CT.

NATIONAL HIV TESTING DAY. June 27. Since 1995, a nationwide campaign encouraging education, voluntary HIV testing and counseling to people at risk for HIV. Annually, June 27. For info: National HIV Testing Day. Web: www.hiv.gov.

NED KELLY'S LAST STAND: ANNIVERSARY. June 27–29, 1880. Australian folk hero and outlaw Ned Kelly, escaping with his gang from pursuing law officers, made a last stand at Glenrowan—rounding up the townspeople and holing up in a hotel. There he and his mates constructed 90-pound iron body armor. The armor hampered more than it helped, and Kelly's gang—including his brother Dan—were all killed. Kelly was captured and hanged on

Nov 11, 1880, at Melbourne. The Kelly Gang in their grim armor offered an antihero image that Australians have embraced in film and art.

PARNELL, CHARLES STEWART: BIRTH ANNIVERSARY. June 27, 1846. Irish nationalist leader and home-rule advocate born at Avondale, County Wicklow, Ireland. Politically ruined as a result of an affair with Katherine O'Shea, the estranged wife of a member of parliament. O'Shea was divorced by her husband (who named Parnell co-respondent), and on June 25, 1891, she married Parnell. Less than a month later Parnell was defeated in a by-election. He made his last public speech Sept 27, 1891, and died in the arms of his wife, at Brighton, Oct 6, 1891. Reportedly he was given "a magnificent funeral" by the city of Dublin, where he was buried. The anniversary of Parnell's death is observed by some as Ivy Day, when a sprig of ivy is worn on the lapel to remember him. See also: "Ireland: Ivy Day" (Oct 6).

PERRY, ANTOINETTE: BIRTH ANNIVERSARY. June 27, 1888. Esteemed actress, producer and director born at Denver, CO. She starred in numerous theater productions before a stroke in 1927 ended her onstage career. She then became a successful stage director. Perry died June 16, 1946, at New York, NY. In 1947 the American Theater Wing established the annual Antoinette Perry Awards—the Tony Awards—for outstanding accomplishments in theater.

PTSD AWARENESS DAY. June 27. Post-traumatic stress disorder (PTSD) is a mental health problem that can occur after someone goes through a traumatic event like war, assault, an accident or a disaster. The National Center for PTSD promotes awareness of PTSD and effective treatments throughout the year. Starting in 2010, Congress named June 27 PTSD Awareness Day (S. Res. 455). Annually, June 27. For info: National Center for PTSD. Veterans Crisis Line: (800) 273-8255. Web: www.ptsd.va.gov.

SAN FRANCISCO PRIDE CELEBRATION AND PARADE. June 27–28. San Francisco, CA. 50th annual. The annual Pride Celebration commemorates the rebellion of LGBT patrons of the Stonewall Inn in New York City's Greenwich Village in response to a routine police raid on June 27, 1969. On June 27, 1970, a "Gay-In" took place that was the early progenitor of the current Pride Celebration. Since 1972, the event has been held every year and is now one of the largest and most well-known Pride events in the world. Annually, the last full weekend in June. For info: SF Pride, 1841 Market St, 4th Fl, San Francisco, CA 94103-1112. Phone: (415) 864-0831. E-mail: info@sfpride.org. Web: www.sfpride.org.

SMITH, JOSEPH, JR, AND HYRUM SMITH: DEATH ANNIVERSARY. June 27, 1844. The founding prophet of The Church of Jesus Christ of Latter-day Saints and his brother Hyrum were shot to death by an armed mob in Carthage, IL. At the time, Joseph Smith was the presidential candidate of the National Reform Party, the first US presidential candidate to be assassinated. Joseph Smith was born at Sharon, VT, Dec 23, 1805; Hyrum Smith was born at Tunbridge, VT, Feb 9, 1800.

SMITHSON, JAMES: DEATH ANNIVERSARY. June 27, 1829. Scientist and founder of the Smithsonian Institution, James Smithson was born at Paris, France, in 1765 (exact date unknown) and died at Genoa, Italy. His will, dated Oct 23, 1826, bequeathed his great wealth to a nation he had never visited, to found "at Washington under the name of the Smithsonian Institution, establishment for

the increase and diffusion of knowledge among men." In spite of opposition, the Congress approved, on Aug 10, 1846, an act to establish the Smithsonian Institution. Most of Smithson's personal documents, books and collections were destroyed by fire in 1865. Smithson's remains were removed from Italy to Washington, DC, in 1904.

SMITHSONIAN FOLKLIFE FESTIVAL. June 27–29 (tentative). National Mall, Washington, DC. The Smithsonian Folklife Festival, established in 1967, honors contemporary living cultural traditions and celebrates those who practice and sustain them. Produced annually by the Smithsonian Center for Folklife and Cultural Heritage on the National Mall, the Festival has featured participants from all fifty states and more than 100 countries. Est attendance: 450,000. For info: Center for Folklife and Cultural Heritage, c\o Folklife Festival, Smithsonian Institution, PO Box 37012, MRC 520, Washington, DC 20013-7012. Phone: (202) 633-6440. E-mail: folklife@si.edu. Web: www.festival.si.edu.

TOUR DE FRANCE. June 27–July 19. 107th edition. One of the great sporting events in the world. Cycling's best compete for more than 3,500 kilometers in 21 stages in the country of France. Stages are flat-terrain races, mountain races and time trials. For 2020, the Grand Dèpart takes place in Nice. Like every year since beginning in 1903, the last stage will arrive in Paris at Champs Elysees. Est attendance: 5,000,000. For info: Amaury Sport Organisation. Web: www.letour.fr.

UNITED NATIONS: MICRO-, SMALL AND MEDIUM-SIZED ENTERPRISES DAY. June 27. Day designated on Apr 6, 2017 (Res 71/279), to raise awareness of the contribution of such enterprises to sustainable development. Member states are encouraged to promote this day by fostering research presentations, policy discussions, practitioner workshops and business owner testimonials from around the world, in collaboration with public, private and non-profit organizations. For info: United Nations. Web: www.un.org.

🎂 BIRTHDAYS TODAY

J.J. Abrams, 54, television executive ("Lost"), film director (*Star Trek, Mission: Impossible III*), born New York, NY, June 27, 1966.

Isabelle Adjani, 65, actress (*The Story of Adele H., Camille Claudel*), born Paris, France, June 27, 1955.

Julia Duffy, 69, actress ("Newhart," "Designing Women"), born St. Paul, MN, June 27, 1951.

Shirley-Anne Field, 82, actress (*Alfie, My Beautiful Laundrette, Getting It Right*), born London, England, June 27, 1938.

Norma Kamali, 75, fashion designer, born New York, NY, June 27, 1945.

Svetlana Kuznetsova, 35, tennis player, born Leningrad, USSR (now St. Petersburg, Russia), June 27, 1985.

Tobey Maguire, 45, actor (*Spider-Man, Seabiscuit, The Cider House Rules*), born Santa Monica, CA, June 27, 1975.

Jason Patric, 54, actor (*Speed 2, Sleepers*), born Queens, NY, June 27, 1966.

Chuck Connors Person, 56, former basketball player, born Brantley, AL, June 27, 1964.

Chandler Riggs, 21, actor ("The Walking Dead"), born Atlanta, GA, June 27, 1999.

Ed Westwick, 33, actor ("Gossip Girl," *Son of Rambow*), born Stevenage, Hertfordshire, England, June 27, 1987.

June 2020	S	M	T	W	T	F	S
		1	2	3	4	5	6
	7	8	9	10	11	12	13
	14	15	16	17	18	19	20
	21	22	23	24	25	26	27
	28	29	30				

June 28 — Sunday

DAY 180   **186 REMAINING**

"AMOS 'N' ANDY" TV PREMIERE: ANNIVERSARY. June 28, 1951. This show was based on the popular radio show about black characters played by white dialecticians Freeman Gosden and Charles Correll. In fact, it was the first dramatic series with an all-black cast. The cast included Tim Moore, Spencer Williams, Alvin Childress, Ernestine Wade, Amanda Randolph, Johnny Lee, Nick O'Demus and Jester Hairston. The series was widely syndicated until pressure from civil rights groups, who claimed the show was stereotypical and prejudicial, caused CBS to withdraw it from syndication.

COMECON AND WARSAW PACT DISBAND: ANNIVERSARY. June 28, 1991. The last vestiges of the cold war–era Soviet bloc, the Council for Mutual Economic Assistance (COMECON) and the Warsaw Pact, formally disbanded on June 28 and July 1, 1991, respectively.

CYPRUS: SAINT PAUL'S FEAST. June 28–29. Kato Paphos. Religious festivities at Kato Paphos at which the archbishop officiates. Procession of the icon of Saint Paul through the streets.

GAY/LESBIAN/BI/TRANS PRIDE PARADE. June 28. Chicago, IL. Chicago's 51st annual parade begins at 12 noon. Est attendance: 1,000,000. For info: GLBT Pride Parade, 3712 N Broadway, PMB #544, Chicago, IL 60613. Phone: (773) 348-8243. E-mail: pridechgo@aol.com. Web: www.chicagopridecalendar.org.

GOEPPERT-MAYER, MARIA: BIRTH ANNIVERSARY. June 28, 1906. German-American physicist Maria Goeppert-Mayer was born at Kattowitz, Germany. A participant in the Manhattan Project, she worked on the separation of uranium isotopes for the atomic bomb. Goeppert-Mayer became the first American woman to win the Nobel Prize when she shared the 1963 prize in physics with J. Hans Daniel Jensen and Eugene P. Wigner for their explanation of the atomic nucleus, known as the nuclear shell theory. Goeppert-Mayer died Feb 20, 1972, at San Diego, CA.

INDEPENDENCE SUNDAY IN IOWA. June 28. Sunday preceding July 4, by proclamation of the governor.

LOG CABIN DAY. June 28. 34th annual. Commemorates log cabins with tours, open houses and special festivities throughout the state of Michigan. Est attendance: 1,500. For info: Virginia Handy, Sec/Treas, Log Cabin Society of Michigan, 3503 Rock Edwards Dr, Sodus, MI 49126. Phone: (269) 925-3836. E-mail: handyvirginia2@gmail.com. Web: www.qtm.net/logcabincrafts.

MAASS, CLARA: BIRTH ANNIVERSARY. June 28, 1876. Clara Louise Maass was born at East Orange, NJ. After serving as a nurse in Cuba and the Philippines during the Spanish-American War, she returned to Cuba to volunteer in a study to determine the cause of yellow fever. After permitting herself to be bitten by an infected mosquito, she developed yellow fever and succumbed. Maass died at Havana, Cuba, Aug 24, 1901.

MONDAY HOLIDAY LAW: ANNIVERSARY. June 28, 1968. President Lyndon B. Johnson approved PL 90–363, which amended section 6103(a) of Title 5, United States Code, establishing Monday observance of Washington's Birthday, Memorial Day, Labor Day, Columbus Day and Veterans Day. The new holiday law took effect Jan 1, 1971. Veterans Day observance subsequently reverted to

its former observance date, Nov 11. See individual holidays for further details.

MOON PHASE: FIRST QUARTER. June 28. Moon enters First Quarter phase at 4:16 AM, EDT.

PIRANDELLO, LUIGI: BIRTH ANNIVERSARY. June 28, 1867. Among the greatest Italian playwrights and 20th-century dramatists, Pirandello was born at Agrigento, Sicily. Notable works include *Six Characters in Search of an Author* and *Henry IV.* Recipient of the Nobel Prize in Literature in 1934, Pirandello was made Commander of the Crown by the Italian government and a member of the French Légion d'Honneur before his death on Dec 10, 1936, at Rome, Italy.

PUNXSUTAWNEY GROUNDHOG FESTIVAL. June 28–July 4. Punxsutawney, PA. Provides residents and visitors a festive week of free entertainment. Music, crafts, food, entertainers and contests. No admission charge. Est attendance: 28,000. For info: Roger Steele, Chairman, Groundhog Festival Committee, PO Box 1001, Punxsutawney, PA 15767. Phone: (814) 938-2947. Web: www.groundhogfestival.com.

ROUSSEAU, JEAN-JACQUES: BIRTH ANNIVERSARY. June 28, 1712. Philosopher, born at Geneva, Switzerland. Died July 2, 1778, at Ermenonville, France. "Man is born free," he wrote in *The Social Contract,* "and everywhere he is in chains."

RUBENS, PETER PAUL: BIRTH ANNIVERSARY. June 28, 1577. Flemish painter and diplomat born at Siegen, Westphalia. Died of gout at Antwerp, Belgium, May 30, 1640.

SIEGE OF VICKSBURG: ANNIVERSARY. June 28, 1862. The siege of the Confederate city of Vicksburg, MS, began in earnest when Admiral David Farragut succeeded in taking a fleet past the Mississippi River stronghold on this date. The siege continued for over a year.

SINGING ON THE MOUNTAIN. June 28. Grandfather Mountain, Linville, NC. 96th annual sing. Modern and traditional gospel music featuring top groups and nationally known speakers. Annually, the fourth Sunday in June. Free admission. Est attendance: 5,000. For info: Ken Hartley, Singing on the Mountain Foundation, Inc, 531 Brentwood Rd, Ste 209, Denver, NC 28037. E-mail: chair@singingonthemountain.org. Web: www.singingonthemountain.org.

STONEWALL RIOT: ANNIVERSARY. June 28, 1969. Early in the morning of June 28, 1969, the clientele of a gay bar, the Stonewall Inn at New York City, rioted after the club was raided by police. The riot was followed by several days of demonstrations. This event is now recognized as the start of the gay liberation movement.

TREATY OF VERSAILLES: ANNIVERSARY. June 28, 1919. The signing of the Treaty of Versailles at Versailles, France, formally ended WWI.

🧁 BIRTHDAYS TODAY

Kathy Bates, 72, actress (Oscar for *Misery; Failure to Launch, Fried Green Tomatoes*), born Memphis, TN, June 28, 1948.

Danielle Brisebois, 51, actress ("All in the Family," "Knots Landing"), born Brooklyn, NY, June 28, 1969.

Mel Brooks, 92, actor, director (*The Producers, Blazing Saddles*), born Melvin Kaminsky at New York, NY, June 28, 1928.

John Cusack, 54, actor (*High Fidelity, Say Anything, The Grifters, Bullets over Broadway*), born Chicago, IL, June 28, 1966.

Bruce Davison, 74, actor (*Ulzana's Raid, Longtime Companion, Six Degrees of Separation*), born Philadelphia, PA, June 28, 1946.

John Elway, 60, football executive and Hall of Fame player, born Port Angeles, WA, June 28, 1960.

Mark Grace, 56, sportscaster, former baseball player, born Winston-Salem, NC, June 28, 1964.

Thomas Hampson, 65, opera singer, born Elkhart, IN, June 28, 1955.

Alice Krige, 66, actress (*Chariots of Fire, Barfly*), born Upington, South Africa, June 28, 1954.

Mary Stuart Masterson, 54, actress (*Fried Green Tomatoes, Benny & Joon*), born New York, NY, June 28, 1966.

Elon Musk, 49, entrepreneur, inventor, cofounder of PayPal, cofounder of Tesla Motors, CEO of SpaceX, born Pretoria, South Africa, June 28, 1971.

June 29 — Monday

DAY 181   **185 REMAINING**

DEATH PENALTY BANNED: ANNIVERSARY. June 29, 1972. In a decision that spared the lives of 600 individuals then sitting on death row, the US Supreme Court, in a 5–4 vote, found capital punishment a violation of the Eighth Amendment, which prohibits "cruel and unusual punishment." Later overruling themselves, the court determined on July 2, 1976, that the death penalty was not cruel and unusual punishment and on Oct 4, 1976, lifted the ban on the death penalty in murder cases. On Jan 15, 1977, Gary Gilmore became the first individual executed in the US in more than 10 years.

ENGLAND: LAWN TENNIS CHAMPIONSHIPS AT WIMBLEDON. June 29–July 12. Wimbledon, London. Contested since 1877. World-famous men's and women's singles and doubles championships for the most coveted titles in tennis. Tickets are allocated via public ballot. Est attendance: 490,000. For info: All England Lawn Tennis Club, Church Road, Wimbledon, London, England SW19 5AE. Web: www.wimbledon.com.

GOETHALS, GEORGE WASHINGTON: BIRTH ANNIVERSARY. June 29, 1858. American engineer and army officer, chief engineer of the Panama Canal and first civil governor of the Canal Zone, born at Brooklyn, NY. Died at New York, NY, Jan 21, 1928.

HARRYHAUSEN, RAY: 100th BIRTH ANNIVERSARY. June 29, 1920. Hollywood's special effects wizard was born at Los Angeles, CA. Harryhausen perfected the stop-motion animation he learned from mentor Willis O'Brien and created what he called "Dynamation." He thrilled moviegoers in the 1950s and '60s with realistic, rampaging monsters and alarming skeletal warriors in such films as *The Beast From 20,000 Fathoms, The 7th Voyage of Sinbad* and *Jason and the Argonauts.* An influence to many current filmmakers, Harryhausen died May 7, 2013, at London, England.

HERRMANN, BERNARD: BIRTH ANNIVERSARY. June 29, 1911. Herrmann was a pioneering film composer, working with such directors as Alfred Hitchcock, Orson Welles and Martin Scorsese. He introduced the theremin in his score for *The Day the Earth Stood Still* (1951). Other notable credits include Hitchcock's *Psycho* (1960), Welles's *Citizen Kane* (1941) and Scorsese's *Taxi Driver* (1976) as well as the TV shows "The Twilight Zone" and "Lost in Space." Born at New York City, Herrmann died on Dec 24, 1975, at Hollywood, CA.

INTERSTATE HIGHWAY SYSTEM BORN: ANNIVERSARY. June 29, 1956. President Dwight Eisenhower signed a bill providing $33.5 billion for highway construction. It was the biggest public works program in history.

LATHROP, JULIA C.: BIRTH ANNIVERSARY. June 29, 1858. A pioneer in the battle to establish child-labor laws, Julia C. Lathrop was the first woman member of the Illinois State Board of Charities and in 1900 was instrumental in establishing the first juvenile court in the US. In 1912 President Taft named Lathrop chief of the newly created Children's Bureau, then part of the US Department of Commerce and Labor. In 1925 she became a member of the Child Welfare Committee of the League of Nations. Born at Rockford, IL, she died there Apr 15, 1932.

MAYO, WILLIAM JAMES: BIRTH ANNIVERSARY. June 29, 1861. American surgeon, one of the Mayo brothers, establishers of the Mayo Foundation, born at Le Sueur, MN. Died July 28, 1939, at Rochester, MN.

SAINT PETER AND PAUL DAY. June 29. Feast day for Saint Peter and Saint Paul. Commemorates dual martyrdom of Christian apostles Peter (by crucifixion) and Paul (by beheading) during persecution by Roman emperor Nero. Observed since third century.

SAINT PETER'S DAY. June 29. Antakya, Turkey. Peter first preached Christianity at this place. Ceremonies at Saint Peter's Grotto, early Christian cave near Antakya.

SEYCHELLES: INDEPENDENCE DAY. June 29. National holiday. Gained independence from Great Britain in 1976.

SPACE MILESTONE: *ATLANTIS* (US) AND *MIR* (USSR) DOCK: 25th ANNIVERSARY. June 29, 1995. An American space shuttle docked with a Russian space station for the first time, resulting in the biggest craft ever assembled in space. The cooperation involved in this linkup was to serve as a stepping-stone to building the International Space Station.

UNITED NATIONS: INTERNATIONAL DAY OF THE TROPICS. June 29. This day celebrates the extraordinary diversity of the tropics (the area between the tropic of Cancer and the tropic of Capricorn) while highlighting unique challenges—climate change, deforestation, logging, urbanization and demographic changes—and opportunities nations of the tropics face. The tropics account for 40 percent of the world's total surface area and are host to approximately 80 percent of the world's biodiversity and much of its language and cultural diversity (Res 70/267). For info: United Nations. Web: www.un.org/en/events/tropicsday.

		S	M	T	W	T	F	S
June			1	2	3	4	5	6
		7	8	9	10	11	12	13
2020		14	15	16	17	18	19	20
		21	22	23	24	25	26	27
		28	29	30				

VANDERZEE, JAMES: BIRTH ANNIVERSARY. June 29, 1886. This pioneering African-American photographer, born at Lenox, MA, set up a portrait studio at Harlem, NY, in 1916, just as that black community was exploding culturally, politically and materially. VanDerZee was the semiofficial photographer of the Harlem Renaissance (1920s to WWII), capturing such luminaries as poet Countee Cullen and Jamaican leader Marcus Garvey, but also dancers, soldiers, street preachers and prosperous middle-class residents. He died May 15, 1983, at Washington, DC.

🎂 BIRTHDAYS TODAY

Gary Busey, 76, actor (*Under Siege, The Buddy Holly Story*), musician, born Goose Creek, TX, June 29, 1944.

Theo Fleury, 52, former hockey player, born Oxbow, SK, Canada, June 29, 1968.

Fred Grandy, 72, former congressman (R, Iowa), actor ("The Love Boat"), born Sioux City, IA, June 29, 1948.

Joe Johnson, 39, basketball player, born Little Rock, AR, June 29, 1981.

Sharon Lawrence, 58, actress ("Fired Up," "NYPD Blue"), born Charlotte, NC, June 29, 1962.

Kawhi Leonard, 29, basketball player, born Los Angeles, CA, June 29, 1991.

Bret McKenzie, 44, actor, comedian ("Flight of the Conchords"), musician (Oscar for "Man or Muppet"), born Wellington, New Zealand, June 29, 1976.

June 30 — Tuesday

DAY 182   **184 REMAINING**

ASTEROID DAY. June 30. Asteroid Day is a global awareness campaign where people from around the world come together to learn about asteroids, the impact hazard they may pose and what we can do to protect our planet, families, communities and future generations from future asteroid impacts. Asteroid Day is held each year on the anniversary of the largest impact in recent history, the 1908 Tunguska event in Siberia. Launched in 2015. Annually, June 30. For info: Asteroid Foundation, 18, Rue Robert Stümper, L-2557, Luxembourg. Web: asteroidday.org.

BRITAIN CEDES CLAIM TO HONG KONG: ANNIVERSARY. June 30, 1997. The crested flag of the British Crown Colony was officially lowered at midnight and replaced by a new flag (marked by the bauhinia flower) representing China's sovereignty and the official transfer of power. Though Britain owned Hong Kong in perpetuity, the land areas surrounding the city were leased from China and the lease expired July 1, 1997. Rather than renegotiate a new lease, Britain ceded its claim to Hong Kong.

CHARLES BLONDIN'S CONQUEST OF NIAGARA FALLS: ANNIVERSARY. June 30, 1859. Charles Blondin, a French acrobat and aerialist (whose real name was Jean François Gravelet), in view of a crowd estimated at more than 25,000, walked across Niagara Falls on a tightrope. The walk required only about five minutes. On separate occasions he crossed blindfolded, pushing a wheelbarrow, carrying a man on his back and even on stilts. Blondin was born Feb 28, 1824, at St. Omer, France, and died at London, England, Feb 19, 1897.

CONGO (DEMOCRATIC REPUBLIC OF THE): INDEPENDENCE DAY: 60th ANNIVERSARY OF INDEPENDENCE. June 30. National holiday. Democratic Republic of the Congo was previously known as Zaire. Commemorates independence from Belgium in 1960.

***GONE WITH THE WIND* PUBLISHED: ANNIVERSARY.** June 30, 1936. Margaret Mitchell's epic novel of the Civil War South was published on this date. It would be awarded the Pulitzer Prize and National Book Award as best novel of 1936. It has been a bestseller

since publication, and 40 countries have published translations. See also: "*Gone with the Wind* Film Premiere: Anniversary" (Dec 15).

GUATEMALA: ARMED FORCES DAY. June 30. Public holiday.

HORNE, LENA: BIRTH ANNIVERSARY. June 30, 1917. Born at Brooklyn, NY, Horne began singing with the chorus line at the Cotton Club in Harlem at age 16. A career on Broadway and in Hollywood followed in rapid succession and she soon became the symbol for African-American actors and singers trying to break the color barrier. She found success with both black and white audiences, although she did face her share of racial prejudice throughout her lifetime. Best remembered for her nightclub and Broadway performances of torch songs, jazz standards and classics such as her signature "Stormy Weather," she died at New York, NY, on May 9, 2010.

LEAP SECOND ADJUSTMENT TIME. June 30. This day is one of the times that have been favored for the addition or subtraction of a second to or from our clock time to coordinate atomic and astronomical time. The determination to adjust is made by the International Earth Rotation Service of the International Bureau of Weights and Measures, at Paris, France. See also: "Note About Leap Seconds" in appendixes.

MILOSZ, CZESLAW: BIRTH ANNIVERSARY. June 30, 1911. The great Polish-American poet, author and teacher was born at Szetejnie, Lithuania (then part of Russia). He lived in Warsaw during WWII and participated in the Polish Resistance. Milosz was a diplomat after the war but defected to France in 1951. In 1960, he moved to the US as a teacher of Slavic languages and literature at the University of California at Berkeley, eventually becoming a US citizen. He was awarded the Nobel Prize in Literature in 1980. Milosz died on Aug 14, 2004, at Krakow, Poland.

MONROE, ELIZABETH KORTRIGHT: BIRTH ANNIVERSARY. June 30, 1768. Wife of James Monroe, fifth president of the US, born at New York, NY. Died at their Oak Hill estate at Loudoun County, VA, Sept 23, 1830.

NOW FOUNDED: ANNIVERSARY. June 30, 1966. The National Organization for Women was founded at Washington, DC, by people attending the Third National Conference on the Commission on the Status of Women. NOW's purpose is to take action to bring women into full partnership in the mainstream of American society, exercising all privileges and responsibilities in equal partnership with men.

SIBERIAN EXPLOSION (TUNGUSKA EVENT): ANNIVERSARY. June 30, 1908. Early in the morning, a spectacular explosion occurred over central Siberia, near the Stony Tunguska River. The seismic shock, firestorm, ensuing "black rain" and illumination that was reportedly visible for hundreds of miles led to speculation that a meteorite was the cause. Forests for more than 800 square miles were flattened. The largest impact/explosion in recorded history.

SUDAN: REVOLUTION DAY. June 30. National holiday. Commemorates a bloodless coup in 1989.

WHEELER, WILLIAM ALMON: BIRTH ANNIVERSARY. June 30, 1819. 19th vice president of the US (1877–81), born at Malone, NY. Died there June 4, 1887.

🎂 BIRTHDAYS TODAY

Fantasia Barrino, 36, singer ("American Idol"), born High Point, NC, June 30, 1984.

Lizzy Caplan, 38, actress ("Masters of Sex," *Cloverfield, Mean Girls*), born Los Angeles, CA, June 30, 1982.

Vincent D'Onofrio, 61, actor ("Law & Order: Criminal Intent," *Men in Black*), born Brooklyn, NY, June 30, 1959.

Nancy Dussault, 84, actress ("Too Close for Comfort," "The Ted Knight Show"), born Pensacola, FL, June 30, 1936.

Rupert Graves, 57, actor ("Sherlock," *A Room with a View, Maurice*), born Weston-Super-Mare, England, June 30, 1963.

David Alan Grier, 65, actor ("The Carmichael Show," "In Living Color," *A Soldier's Story*), born Detroit, MI, June 30, 1955.

Monica Potter, 49, actress (*Along Came a Spider*, "Parenthood," "Boston Legal"), born Cleveland, OH, June 30, 1971.

Patricia Schroeder, 80, former president of the Association of American Publishers, former congresswoman (D, Colorado), born Portland, OR, June 30, 1940.

Cole Swindell, 37, country singer, born Glennville, GA, June 30, 1983.

Michael Gerard (Mike) Tyson, 54, former heavyweight champion boxer, born New York, NY, June 30, 1966.

◆ July ◆

July 1 — Wednesday

DAY 183   **183 REMAINING**

ALOPECIA MONTH FOR WOMEN, INTERNATIONAL. July 1–31. Let's empower women and girls living with autoimmune alopecia areata. Nonprofit sponsor Bald Girls Do Lunch supports events during this month to raise public awareness, foster camaraderie and build self-confidence for women with hair loss diseases. For info: Thea Chassin, Bald Girls Do Lunch Inc, PO Box 9122, Scarborough, NY 10510. Phone: (800) 578-5332. E-mail: info@BaldGirlsDoLunch.org. Web: www.BaldGirlsDoLunch.org.

BATTLE OF GETTYSBURG: ANNIVERSARY. July 1–3, 1863. After the Southern success at Chancellorsville, VA, Confederate general Robert E. Lee led his forces on an invasion of the North, initially targeting Harrisburg, PA. As Union forces moved to counter the invasion, the battle lines were eventually formed at Gettysburg, PA, in one of the Civil War's most crucial battles. On the climactic third day of the battle (July 3), Lee ordered an attack on the center of the Union line, later to be known as Pickett's Charge. The 15,000 rebels were repulsed, ending the Battle of Gettysburg. After the defeat, Lee's forces retreated back to Virginia, listing more than one-third of the troops as casualties in the failed invasion. Union general George Meade initially failed to pursue the retreating rebels, allowing Lee's army to escape across the rain-swollen Potomac River. With more than 50,000 casualties, this was the worst battle of the Civil War.

BIOTERRORISM/DISASTER EDUCATION AND AWARENESS MONTH. July 1–31. To educate consumers, healthcare professionals, nonprofit organizations and healthcare facilities about being prepared for natural disasters, emergency care, bioterrorism and acts of God. Sponsored by the American College of Apothecaries (ACA)/Pharmacists Planning Service, Inc (PPSI). For info: ACA/PPSI, 2830 Summer Oaks Dr, Bartlett, TN 38134. E-mail: info@ppsinc.org. Web: www.ppsinc.org.

BLERIOT, LOUIS: BIRTH ANNIVERSARY. July 1, 1872. Louis Bleriot, aviation pioneer and first man to fly an airplane across the English Channel (July 25, 1909), was born at Cambrai, France. He died at Paris, Aug 2, 1936.

BOTSWANA: SIR SERETSE KHAMA DAY. July 1. National holiday. Commemorates the birth in 1921 of the first president of Botswana.

BUREAU OF INTERNAL REVENUE ESTABLISHED: ANNIVERSARY. July 1, 1862. The Bureau of Internal Revenue was established by an act of Congress.

BURUNDI: INDEPENDENCE DAY. July 1. National holiday. Anniversary of establishment of independence from Belgian administration in 1962. Had been part of Ruanda-Urundi.

CAIN, JAMES M.: BIRTH ANNIVERSARY. July 1, 1892. The journalist turned bestselling author and screenwriter was born at Annapolis, MD. His first novel, *The Postman Always Rings Twice* (1934), sold more than one million copies. Subsequent novels include *Double Indemnity* and *Mildred Pierce*. Cain died Oct 27, 1977, at Hyattsville, MD.

CANADA: CANADA DAY. July 1. Canada's National Day, formerly known as Dominion Day. Commemorates the confederation of Upper and Lower Canada and some of the Maritime Provinces into the Dominion of Canada in 1867. Observed on the following day when July 1 is a Sunday. (Observed as Memorial Day in Newfoundland and Labrador.)

CANADA: CANADA DAY CELEBRATION. July 1. Ottawa, ON, and Gatineau, QC. Annual event celebrating Canada's birthday. The heart of the capital comes alive with shows, street performers, concerts, games and activities for the whole family. In the evening a spectacular show featuring top Canadian performers is staged on Parliament Hill and culminates with a fireworks display. Est attendance: 350,000. For info: Canadian Heritage. Web: www.canada.ca/en/canadian-heritage/campaigns/canada-day.html.

CELL PHONE COURTESY MONTH. July 1–31. Ninety percent of American adults have cell phones. This month is dedicated to encouraging the increasingly unmindful corps of cell phone users to be more respectful of their surroundings and those around them. Annually, the month of July. For info: Jacqueline Whitmore, Etiquette Expert, PO Box 1135, Mount Dora, FL 32756. Phone: (561) 309-9674. E-mail: info@etiquetteexpert.com. Web: www.etiquetteexpert.com.

CHINA: HALF-YEAR DAY. July 1. National holiday in China. Midyear Day in Thailand.

CLEVELAND'S SECRET SURGERY: ANNIVERSARY. July 1, 1893. President Grover Cleveland boarded the yacht *Oneida* for surgery to be performed in secret on a cancerous growth in his mouth. As this was during the 1893 depression, secrecy was thought desirable to avoid further panic by the public. The whole left side of Cleveland's jaw was removed as well as a small portion of his soft palate. A second, less extensive operation was performed July 17. He was later fitted with a prosthesis of vulcanized rubber that he wore until his death on June 24, 1908. A single leak of the secret was plugged by Cleveland's secretary of war, Daniel Lamont, the only member of the administration to know about the surgery. The illness did not become public knowledge until an article appeared Sept 22, 1917, in the *Saturday Evening Post*, written by William W. Keen, who assisted in the surgery.

DIANA, PRINCESS OF WALES: BIRTH ANNIVERSARY. July 1, 1961. Former wife of Charles, Prince of Wales, and mother of Prince William and Prince Harry. Born Lady Diana Spencer at Sandringham, England, she died in an automobile accident at Paris, France, Aug 31, 1997.

DIXON, WILLIE: BIRTH ANNIVERSARY. July 1, 1915. Blues legend Willie Dixon was born at Vicksburg, MI. He moved to Chicago, IL, in 1936 and began his career as a musician with the Big Three Trio. With the advent of instrument amplification Dixon migrated away from his acoustic upright bass into producing and songwriting with Chess Studios, where he became one of the primary architects of the classic Chicago sound in the 1950s. His songs were performed by Elvis Presley, the Everly Brothers, the Rolling Stones, Led Zeppelin, the Doors, Cream, the Yardbirds, Aerosmith, Jimi Hendrix and the Allman Brothers, among others. Dixon died Jan 29, 1992, at Burbank, CA.

DORSEY, THOMAS A.: BIRTH ANNIVERSARY. July 1, 1899. Thomas A. Dorsey, the father of gospel music, was born at Villa Rica, GA. Originally a blues composer, Dorsey eventually combined blues and sacred music to develop gospel music. It was Dorsey's composition "Take My Hand, Precious Lord" that the Reverend Dr. Martin Luther King, Jr, had asked to have performed just moments before his assassination. Dorsey, who composed more than 1,000 gospel songs and hundreds of blues songs in his lifetime, died Jan 23, 1993, at Chicago, IL.

ENGLAND: HENLEY ROYAL REGATTA. July 1–5. Henley-on-Thames, Oxfordshire. International rowing event that is one of the big social events of the year. More than 575 crews compete. Annually since 1839. Est attendance: 330,000. For info: The Secretary,

Henley Royal Regatta, Regatta Headquarters, Henley-on-Thames, Oxfordshire, England RG9 2LY. Phone: (44) (1491) 572153. Web: www.hrr.co.uk.

FIRST BATTLE OF THE SOMME: ANNIVERSARY. July 1–Nov 13, 1916. The First Battle of the Somme began, with three million men on a 20-mile front along the Somme River in northeastern France. The battle, which became metaphorical for futile and indiscriminate slaughter, was the first British offensive of WWI. It was also the first time tanks were employed in modern warfare, though their effect was negligible due largely to mechanical unreliability. More than one million were wounded or killed in the bloodiest battle in history.

FIRST PHOTOGRAPHS USED IN A NEWSPAPER REPORT: ANNIVERSARY. July 1, 1848. The first instance of photojournalism occurred during the Paris Riots of 1848, when an enterprising French photographer known only as Thibault scrambled to a rooftop to chronicle the events. Taken on June 25 and 26, the two resulting daguerreotypes show first a deserted street, the rue St. Maur, with barricades, and then the same street with insurgents and the military in combat. Wood engravings were made of the daguerreotypes, and on July 1, 1848, the images appeared in the weekly newspaper *L'Illustration Journal Universel.* More than 3,000 Parisians lost their lives during the June revolt.

FIRST SCHEDULED TELEVISION BROADCAST: ANNIVERSARY. July 1, 1941. The National Broadcasting Company (NBC) began broadcasting from the Empire State Building on this day. The Federal Communications Commission had granted the first commercial TV licenses to 10 stations on May 2, 1941.

FIRST US POSTAGE STAMPS ISSUED: ANNIVERSARY. July 1, 1847. The first US postage stamps were issued by the US Postal Service, a five-cent stamp picturing Benjamin Franklin and a 10-cent stamp honoring George Washington. Stamps had been issued by private postal services in the US prior to this date.

FIRST US ZOO: ANNIVERSARY. July 1, 1874. The Philadelphia Zoological Society, the first US zoo, opened. Three thousand visitors traveled by foot, horse and carriage and steamboat to visit the exhibits. Price of admission was 25 cents for adults and 10 cents for children. There were 1,000 animals in the zoo on opening day.

GHANA: REPUBLIC DAY. July 1. National holiday. Commemorates the inauguration of the republic in 1960.

HALFWAY POINT OF 2020. July 1. Because 2020 is a leap year, when July 1, 2020, ends at midnight, 183 days will remain before Jan 1, 2021.

HERBAL/PRESCRIPTION INTERACTION AWARENESS MONTH. July 1–31. To educate health professionals, patients and consumers on dietary supplements, herbs and nutritionals along with mixing those products with prescription drugs. Sponsored by the American College of Apothecaries (ACA)/Pharmacists Planning Service, Inc (PPSI). For info: ACA/PPSI, 2830 Summer Oaks Dr, Bartlett, TN 38134. E-mail: info@ppsinc.org. Web: www.ppsinc.org.

LAUDER, ESTÉE: BIRTH ANNIVERSARY. July 1, 1908 (some sources say 1906). The cosmetics magnate was born Josephine Esther Mentzer at Corona, Queens, NY. In high school she took an interest in the work of her uncle, John Schotz, a Hungarian-born chemist who made beauty products for women. She began a business at her kitchen table in 1946 that went on to become one of the world's largest, most successful cosmetics companies. The introduction of her breakthrough formula for the bath oil Youth Dew in the 1950s led the way to a company currently worth more than $10 billion. At the time of her death on Apr 24, 2004, at New York, NY, Lauder was among the 500 richest women in the world.

"THE LIBERACE SHOW" TV PREMIERE: ANNIVERSARY. July 1, 1952. A pianist known for his outrageous style and a candelabra on his piano, Liberace hosted popular shows in the '50s and '60s. The first premiered on KLAC-TV in Los Angeles, CA, and went national in 1953. That did so well that he began a half-hour syndicated series that featured his brother George as violinist and orchestra leader. After a brief leave, he returned to TV in 1958 with a half-hour show. Liberace also hosted a British series and a summer series produced in London, England.

LINCOLN SIGNS INCOME TAX BILL: ANNIVERSARY. July 1, 1862. President Abraham Lincoln signed into law a bill levying a 3 percent income tax on annual incomes of $600–$10,000 and 5 percent on incomes of more than $10,000. The revenues were to help pay for the Civil War. This tax law actually went into effect, unlike an earlier law passed Aug 5, 1861, making it the first income tax levied by the US. It was rescinded in 1872.

"MAMA" TV PREMIERE: ANNIVERSARY. July 1, 1949. One of TV's first popular sitcoms, "Mama" told the story of a Norwegian family living in San Francisco, CA, in 1917. The show aired live through 1956; after it was canceled, a second, filmed version lasted only 13 weeks. Cast members included Peggy Wood, Judson Laire, Rosemary Rice, Dick Van Patten, Iris Mann, Robin Morgan, Ruth Gates, Malcolm Keen, Carl Frank, Alice Frost, Patty McCormack and Kevin Coughlin. Toni Campbell replaced Robin Morgan in the revival.

MEDICARE GOES INTO EFFECT: ANNIVERSARY. July 1, 1968. Medicare, the US health insurance program for senior citizens, went into effect. The legislation authorizing the program had been signed by President Lyndon Johnson July 30, 1965. Former president Harry Truman and his wife, Bess, received the first Medicare cards.

MORRILL LAND GRANT ACT PASSED: ANNIVERSARY. July 1, 1862. This federal legislation led to the creation of the land grant universities and agricultural experiment stations in each state.

NATIONAL DELI SALAD MONTH. July 1–31. Since 2014, a promotional month to educate consumers and encourage the purchase of convenient, high-quality, ready-to-eat deli salads. For info: Refrigerated Foods Assn, 3823 Roswell Rd, Ste 208, Marietta, GA 30062. E-mail: info@refrigeratedfoods.org. Web: www.refrigeratedfoods.org.

NATIONAL "DOGHOUSE REPAIRS" MONTH. July 1–31. Celebrate "Doghouse Repairs" Month by staying out of trouble with those you love and care about by doing something extra special. For info: Heidi Richards Mooney, PO Box 550856, Fort Lauderdale, FL 33355-0856. Phone: (954) 625-6606. E-mail: heidi@redheadmarketinginc.com.

NATIONAL GRILLING MONTH. July 1–31. The sizzle, the smoke and the mouthwatering aromas that come from a grill can be yours if you take the time out this month and enjoy the fun and ease of cooking on a grill—indoor or out!

NATIONAL HORSERADISH MONTH. July 1–31. What 3,000-year-old plant has been used as a bitter herb for Passover seders and a flavorful accompaniment for beef, chicken and seafood? If you guessed horseradish, you're right. This month, celebrate the healthful and hot horseradish, which has been praised for its numerous food uses for centuries. For info: Horseradish Information Council, 3200 Windy Hill Rd SE, Ste 600W, Atlanta, GA 30339. Phone: (404) 252-3663. Web: www.horseradish.org.

NATIONAL HOT DOG MONTH. July 1–31. Celebrates one of America's favorite and most patriotic foods with fun facts and new recipes. From Memorial Day to Labor Day—hot dog season—Americans typically consume 7 billion hot dogs. On Independence Day itself, Americans typically enjoy 150 million hot dogs, enough to stretch from D.C. to L.A. more than five times. For info: Natl Hot Dog and

Sausage Council, 1150 Connecticut Ave NW, 12th Fl, Washington, DC 20036. Phone: (202) 587-4200. Web: www.hot-dog.org.

NATIONAL ICE CREAM MONTH. July 1–31. First designated by President Ronald Reagan in 1984, this month celebrates ice cream as a fun and nutritious food that is enjoyed by 90 percent of the nation's population. For info: Intl Dairy Foods Assn, 1250 H Street NW, Ste 900, Washington, DC 20005. Phone: (202) 737-4332. Web: www.idfa.org.

NATIONAL MAKE A DIFFERENCE TO CHILDREN MONTH. July 1–31. To remind us of the many ways adults can make a positive difference to children. Create opportunities for kids during this midsummer month when most children are not in school by doing three things: 1. Commit to do one special thing with a child in July—make some kind of positive difference for that child. 2. Support an organization that focuses on children—there are many to choose from. 3. Communicate with your elected leaders to make children a priority in policy and budget issues they address. For info: Kim Ratz, 3665 Woody Ln, Minnetonka, MN 55305. Phone: (952) 938-4472. E-mail: kimratz@aol.com. Web: www.kimratz.com/madtc.html.

NATIONAL MINORITY MENTAL HEALTH AWARENESS MONTH. July 1–31. The US House of Representatives proclaimed July as Bebe Moore Campbell National Minority Mental Health Awareness Month in 2008, aiming to improve access to mental health treatment and services for multicultural communities through increased public awareness. Since then, individuals and organizations around the country have joined the National Alliance on Mental Illness in celebrating the month and increasing awareness. For info: NAMI. Web: www.nami.org.

NATIONAL PARK AND RECREATION MONTH. July 1–31. Since 1985, America has celebrated July as the nation's official Park and Recreation Month. Throughout July, people everywhere should visit their local parks and recreation facilities and celebrate why parks and recreation are so vital in our lives. For info: Natl Recreation and Park Assn, 22377 Belmont Ridge Rd, Ashburn, VA 20148-4501. Phone: (800) 626-6772. E-mail: customerservice@nrpa.org. Web: www.nrpa.org/july.

NATIONAL TOM SAWYER DAYS (WITH FENCE PAINTING CONTEST). July 1–5. Hannibal, MO. 65th annual. Frog jumping, mud volleyball, Tom and Becky Contest, parade, Tomboy Sawyer Contest, 10k run, arts and crafts show and fireworks launched from the banks of the Mississippi River. Highlight is the National Fence Painting Contest. Sponsor: Hannibal Jaycees. Est attendance: 100,000.

July 2020	S	M	T	W	T	F	S
				1	2	3	4
	5	6	7	8	9	10	11
	12	13	14	15	16	17	18
	19	20	21	22	23	24	25
	26	27	28	29	30	31	

For info: Hannibal CVB, 505 N 3rd St, Hannibal, MO 63401. Phone: (573) 221-2477. Web: www.hannibaljaycees.org or www.VisitHannibal.com.

NATIONAL WATERMELON MONTH. July 1–31. Take a whole month to enjoy this refreshing melon, which is packed with vitamins, potassium and water (92 percent). National Watermelon Month occurs annually in July and National Watermelon Day falls Aug 3. For info: National Watermelon Promotion Board, 1321 Sundial Point, Winter Springs, FL 32708. Phone: (407) 657-0261. E-mail: info@watermelon.org. Web: www.watermelon.org.

RESOLUTION RENEWAL DAY. July 1. How are you doing on your New Year's resolutions? July 1 is your midyear checkpoint. Celebrate accomplishments, look at what you did not complete and why, or set new goals. This is a day to help people stay on track and achieve healthier, happier and more successful lives. For info: Cindy Kubica, 414 Parish Pl, Franklin, TN 37067. Phone: (615) 771-3800. E-mail: cindykubica@gmail.com.

RIVERFEST. July 1–4. Riverside Park, La Crosse, WI. 38th annual Riverfest—the city's premier summer event! River activities, four stages to provide continuous entertainment, a children's area with games, face painting, food pavilion featuring 16 different vendors, beverage tent and an arts and crafts area. July 4 features a fireworks display. Est attendance: 40,000. For info: Riverfest, Inc, PO Box 1745, La Crosse, WI 54602. Phone: (608) 782-6000. E-mail: info@riverfestlacrosse.com. Web: www.riverfestlacrosse.com.

RWANDA: INDEPENDENCE DAY. July 1. National holiday. Commemorates independence from Belgium in 1962.

SAND, GEORGE: BIRTH ANNIVERSARY. July 1, 1804. French novelist, author of more than 100 volumes, whose real name was Amandine Aurore Lucile (Dupin) Dudevant, was born at Paris, France. Died at Nohant, France, June 8, 1876. She is better remembered for having been a liberated woman during a romantic epoch than for her literary works.

SMART IRRIGATION MONTH. July 1–31. Most home owners over-irrigate their lawns by 30 percent—not only wasting water but also washing nutrients into rivers and streams and away from the root zone where the plants can use them. Evaluate your irrigation system this month. For smart irrigation, consider adding a "smart" controller (one that uses weather, plant and soil data to determine when to water) or a rain-sensor shutoff device. To find out where your system might be wasting water, seek an irrigation system audit by a qualified irrigation auditor. For info: The Irrigation Assn, 8280 Willow Oaks Corporate Dr, Ste 400, Fairfax, VA 22031. Phone: (703) 536-7080. E-mail: info@irrigationshow.org. Web: www.smartirrigationmonth.com.

SOMALIA DEMOCRATIC REPUBLIC: NATIONAL DAY. July 1. Anniversary of the merger of newly independent British Somaliland and Italian Somaliland on July 1, 1960.

SPACE MILESTONE: *CASSINI-HUYGENS* REACHES SATURN. July 1, 2004. Launched on Oct 15, 1997, the *Cassini-Huygens* spacecraft, a joint venture of NASA, the European Space Agency (ESA) and the Italian Space Agency (ISA), reached Saturn on this date and maneuvered into orbit. The ESA's *Huygens* probe touched down on Saturn's moon Titan on Jan 14, 2005. The purpose of the multibillion-dollar NASA/ESA/ISA mission is to explore the Saturnian system.

SPACE MILESTONE: *KOSMOS 1383* (USSR). July 1, 1982. First search-and-rescue satellite—equipped to hear distress calls from aircraft and ships—launched in cooperative project with the US and France.

SURINAME: LIBERATION DAY. July 1. National holiday. Commemorates the 1863 abolition of slavery in Dutch territory.

TWENTY-SIXTH AMENDMENT RATIFIED: ANNIVERSARY. July 1, 1971. The 26th Amendment to the Constitution granted the right to vote in all federal, state and local elections to all persons 18 years or older. On the date of ratification the US gained an additional 11 million voters. Up until this time, the minimum voting age was set by the states; in most states it was 21.

WOMEN'S MOTORCYCLE MONTH. July 1–31. This month is dedicated to honoring women who ride, co-ride or wish they could ride motorcycles or their derivatives (sidecar rigs, trikes, etc). For info: Sylvia Henderson, 3570 Olney-Laytonsville Rd, Ste 588, Olney, MD 20832. Phone: (301) 260-1538. E-mail: motosylvia@aol.com.

WORLDWIDE BEREAVED PARENTS AWARENESS MONTH. July 1–31. This month seeks to promote support for bereaved parents. Often people don't know what to say to or do for grieving parents. This observance encourages people to reach out to bereaved parents and their families by listening to them without advising them, giving them a shoulder to cry on and giving them a hug when appropriate and needed. Basically, this month seeks to inspire people to "be there" for the bereaved individuals. "Remember to reach out to the bereaved so they won't have to grieve alone." For info: Deborah Le Bouf Kulkkula, PhD, or Peter Kulkkula, 381 Billings Rd, Fitchburg, MA 01420-1407. Phone: (978) 343-4009 or (978) 808-8084 (cell phone). E-mail: DebKulkkula@gmail.com. Web: www.BereavementAwareness.com.

ZIP CODES INAUGURATED: ANNIVERSARY. July 1, 1963. The US Postal Service introduced the five-digit zip code on this day.

🎂 BIRTHDAYS TODAY

Pamela Anderson, 53, model, actress ("V.I.P.," "Baywatch"), born Ladysmith, BC, Canada, July 1, 1967.

Dan Aykroyd, 68, actor (*Ghostbusters, Trading Places, The Blues Brothers*), born Ottawa, ON, Canada, July 1, 1952.

Andre Braugher, 58, actor ("Brooklyn Nine-Nine," "Homicide: Life on the Street," "Thief"), born Chicago, IL, July 1, 1962.

Geneviève Bujold, 78, actress (*Choose Me, Trouble in Mind, Dead Ringers*), born Montreal, QC, Canada, July 1, 1942.

Hilarie Burton, 38, actress ("One Tree Hill"), host (MTV's "TRL"), born Sterling, VA, July 1, 1982.

Leslie Caron, 89, actress (*Gigi, Lili, An American in Paris*), dancer, born Paris, France, July 1, 1931.

Olivia de Havilland, 104, actress (Oscars for *To Each His Own* and *The Heiress; Gone with the Wind*), born Tokyo, Japan, July 1, 1916.

Missy Elliott, 49, singer, born Portsmouth, VA, July 1, 1971.

Joni Ernst, 50, US Senator (R, Iowa), born Joni Culver at Red Oak, IA, July 1, 1970.

Jamie Farr, 86, actor ("M*A*S*H," *The Blackboard Jungle*), born Jameel Farah at Toledo, OH, July 1, 1934.

Debbie Harry, 75, singer (Blondie), born Miami, FL, July 1, 1945.

Jarome Iginla, 43, hockey player, born Edmonton, AB, Canada, July 1, 1977.

Frederick Carlton (Carl) Lewis, 59, Olympic track athlete, born Birmingham, AL, July 1, 1961.

Jean Marsh, 86, actress ("Upstairs, Downstairs"), writer, born Stoke Newington, England, July 1, 1934.

Alan Ruck, 64, actor ("Spin City," *Ferris Bueller's Day Off*), born Cleveland, OH, July 1, 1956.

Adelina Sotnikova, 24, Olympic figure skater, born Moscow, Russia, July 1, 1996.

Twyla Tharp, 79, dancer, choreographer (Tony for *Movin' Out*), born Portland, IN, July 1, 1941.

Liv Tyler, 43, actress (Lord of the Rings film trilogy, *Armageddon*), born Portland, ME, July 1, 1977.

July 2 — Thursday

DAY 184 **182 REMAINING**

AMELIA EARHART DISAPPEARS: ANNIVERSARY. July 2, 1937. In 1937 aviatrix Amelia Earhart planned an around-the-world trip via the equatorial route that would be the longest ever made. Having completed 22,000 miles of her journey, Earhart, accompanied by navigator Fred Noonan, took off on this date from Lae, New Guinea, for the final 7,000 miles over the Pacific. About 800 miles into their flight to tiny Howland Island, radio contact was lost with her craft. Despite a massive search by the US Navy and US Coast Guard, Earhart, Noonan and their plane were never found.

CIVIL RIGHTS ACT OF 1964: ANNIVERSARY. July 2, 1964. President Lyndon Johnson signed the Civil Rights Act of 1964 into law, prohibiting discrimination on the basis of race in public accommodations, in publicly owned or operated facilities, in employment and union membership and in the registration of voters. The bill included Title VI, which allowed for the cutoff of federal funding in areas where discrimination persisted.

CONSTITUTION OF THE US TAKES EFFECT: ANNIVERSARY. July 2, 1788. Cyrus Griffin of Virginia, the president of the Congress, announced that the Constitution had been ratified by the required nine states (the ninth being New Hampshire June 21, 1788), and a committee was appointed to make preparations for the change of government.

CRANMER, THOMAS: BIRTH ANNIVERSARY. July 2, 1489. English clergyman, reformer and martyr, born at Aslacton, Nottinghamshire, England. Archbishop of Canterbury and spearhead of the English Reformation. One of the principal authors of *The English Book of Common Prayer*. Tried for treason, Cranmer temporarily recanted his Protestantism, but then publicly rejected his recantation at his execution, calling it "the great thing that troubleth my conscience more than any other thing that I ever said or did in my life." Burned at the stake at Oxford, England, Mar 21, 1556.

DECLARATION OF INDEPENDENCE RESOLUTION: ANNIVERSARY. July 2, 1776. Anniversary of adoption by the Continental Congress, Philadelphia, PA, of a resolution introduced June 7, 1776, by Richard Henry Lee of Virginia: "Resolved, That these United Colonies are, and of right ought to be, free and independent States, that they are absolved from all allegiance to the British Crown, and that all political connection between them and the State of Great Britain is, and ought to be, totally dissolved. That it is expedient forthwith to take the most effectual measures for forming foreign Alliances. That a plan of confederation be prepared and transmitted to the respective Colonies for their consideration and approbation." This resolution prepared the way for adoption, July 4, 1776, of the Declaration of Independence. See also: "Declaration of Independence Approval and Signing: Anniversary" (July 4).

ESSENCE FESTIVAL. July 2–5 (tentative). Ernest N. Morial Convention Center and the New Orleans Mercedes Benz Superdome, New Orleans, LA. Held since 1995, this is one of the nation's largest live events. Each year, the festival draws nearly 500,000 attendees who gather for three days of music, entertainment, empowerment and culture. Featured are some of the biggest names in entertainment and the nation's most influential speakers, authors and leaders. Annually, July 4th weekend. Est attendance: 500,000. For info: Essence Festival. Web: www.essence.com/festival.

FIRST SOLO ROUND-THE-WORLD BALLOON FLIGHT: ANNIVERSARY. July 2, 2002. In his sixth attempt, Steve Fossett became the first person to circumnavigate the world nonstop and in a nonmotorized craft. In his "Spirit of Freedom" balloon, Fossett traveled 19,400 miles. He began his odyssey on June 18, 2002, at Northam, Australia, and arrived at his starting longitude (117° east) on July 2. (The first balloon flight around the world was accomplished by

a two-man team in 1999. See also: "First Round-the-World Balloon Flight: Anniversary" [Mar 21].)

GARFIELD, JAMES ABRAM: ASSASSINATION ANNIVERSARY. July 2, 1881. President James A. Garfield was shot as he entered the railway station at Washington, DC. He died Sept 19, 1881, never having recovered from the wound. The assassin, Charles J. Guiteau, was hanged June 30, 1882.

ITALY: SIENA PALIO. July 2 (also Aug 16). Siena. Colorful medieval horse race, competing for the banner (Palio).

LACOSTE, RENÉ: BIRTH ANNIVERSARY. July 2, 1904. Jean René Lacoste, tennis player and clothier, born at Paris, France. Lacoste, known as the Crocodile, was one of the four great French tennis players in the 1920s known as the Four Musketeers. He won Wimbledon and the US championship twice each, won the French Open three times and was ranked number one in the world in 1926–27. He designed the first shirt specifically for tennis, a loose-fitting cotton polo shirt that soon became the standard. He adorned the Lacoste shirt with a small crocodile, the first apparel logo. Died at St. Jean-de-Luz, France, Oct 12, 1996.

"THE LAWRENCE WELK SHOW" TV PREMIERE: 65th ANNIVERSARY. July 2, 1955. This musical series, hosted by accordionist and bandleader Lawrence Welk, lasted for almost three decades. In its early years it was known as "The Dodge Dancing Party." Regulars included the Lennon Sisters, Alice Lon, Norma Zimmer, Tanya Falan, Arthur Duncan, Joe Feeney, Guy Hovis, Jim Roberts, Ralna English, Larry Hooper, Jerry Burke and Bobby Burgess. During 1956–59 this show was on concurrently with either "Lawrence Welk's Top Tunes and New Talent" or "The Plymouth Show Starring Lawrence Welk (Lawrence Welk's Little Band)."

MARSHALL, THURGOOD: BIRTH ANNIVERSARY. July 2, 1908. Thurgood Marshall, the first African American on the US Supreme Court, was born at Baltimore, MD. For more than 20 years, he served as director-counsel of the NAACP Legal Defense and Educational Fund. He experienced his greatest legal victory May 17, 1954, when the Supreme Court decision on *Brown v Board of Education* declared an end to the "separate but equal" system of racial segregation in public schools in 21 states. Marshall argued 32 cases before the Supreme Court, winning 29 of them, before becoming a member of the high court himself. Nominated by President Lyndon Johnson, he began his 24-year career on the high court Oct 2, 1967, becoming a voice of dissent in an increasingly conservative court. Marshall announced his retirement June 27, 1991, and he died Jan 24, 1993, at Washington, DC.

SAINT LOUIS RACE RIOTS: ANNIVERSARY. July 2, 1917. Between 75 and 200 blacks were killed in a race riot in St. Louis, MO; hundreds more were injured and thousands were left homeless. To protest this violence against blacks, W.E.B. Du Bois and James Weldon Johnson of the NAACP led a silent march down Fifth Avenue at New York City.

VESEY, DENMARK: DEATH ANNIVERSARY. July 2, 1822. Planner of what would have been the biggest slave revolt in US history, Denmark Vesey was executed at Charleston, SC. He was born around 1767, probably in the West Indies, where he was sold at about age 14 to Joseph Vesey, captain of a slave ship. He purchased his freedom in 1800. In 1818 Vesey and others began to plot an uprising; he held secret meetings, collected disguises and firearms and chose a date in June 1822. But authorities were warned, and police and the military were out in full force. Over the next two months 130 blacks were taken into custody; 35, including Vesey, were hanged and 31 were exiled. As a result of the plot, Southern legislatures passed more rigorous slave codes.

July 2020	S	M	T	W	T	F	S
				1	2	3	4
	5	6	7	8	9	10	11
	12	13	14	15	16	17	18
	19	20	21	22	23	24	25
	26	27	28	29	30	31	

WESTMORELAND ARTS AND HERITAGE FESTIVAL. July 2–5. Twin Lakes Park, Greensburg, PA. 46th annual festival celebrating four decades of arts and humanities. Multicultural celebration including food booths, children's area, crafts, fine art exhibition and continuous entertainment on four stages. Est attendance: 125,000. For info: WAHF, 252 Twin Lakes Rd, Latrobe, PA 15650. Phone: (724) 834-7474. E-mail: info@artsandheritage.com. Web: www.artsandheritage.com.

🧁 BIRTHDAYS TODAY

José Canseco, Jr, 56, former baseball player, born Havana, Cuba, July 2, 1964.

Sean Casey, 46, former baseball player, born Willingboro, NJ, July 2, 1974.

Vicente Fox Quesada, 78, former president of Mexico, born Mexico City, Mexico, July 2, 1942.

Polly Holliday, 83, actress ("Alice," "Home Improvement"), born Jasper, AL, July 2, 1937.

Lindsay Lohan, 34, actress (*The Canyons, Freaky Friday, Mean Girls*), born New York, NY, July 2, 1986.

Alex Morgan, 31, soccer player, born San Dimas, CA, July 2, 1989.

Richard Petty, 83, former race car driver, born Level Cross, NC, July 2, 1937.

Margot Robbie, 30, actress (*I, Tonya; Suicide Squad; The Legend of Tarzan; The Wolf of Wall Street*), born Dalby, Australia, July 2, 1990.

Joe Thornton, 41, hockey player, born London, ON, Canada, July 2, 1979.

Ashley Tisdale, 35, actress, singer ("The Suite Life of Zach and Cody," *High School Musical*), born West Deal, NJ, July 2, 1985.

Johnny Weir, 36, television personality, Olympic figure skater, born Coatesville, PA, July 2, 1984.

July 3 — Friday

DAY 185   **181 REMAINING**

AIR-CONDITIONING APPRECIATION DAYS. July 3–Aug 15. Northern Hemisphere. During Dog Days, the hottest time of the year in the Northern Hemisphere, to acknowledge the contribution of air-conditioning to a better way of life. Annually, July 3–Aug 15. (Originated by John C. Nash.)

BELARUS: INDEPENDENCE DAY. July 3. National holiday. Commemorates liberation of Minsk in 1944.

BENNETT, RICHARD BEDFORD: 150th BIRTH ANNIVERSARY. July 3, 1870. Former Canadian prime minister, born at Hopewell Hill, NB, Canada. Died at Mickleham, England, June 26, 1947.

CANADA: CALGARY STAMPEDE. July 3–12. Calgary, AB. "The Greatest Outdoor Show on Earth." Since 1912, the Calgary Stampede is made up of sights, sounds, tastes and feelings that create a lifetime of memories. More than a century of tradition is distilled into 10 days of music, food, excitement, education, friendship and community. Includes the world's richest tournament-style rodeo,

Rangeland Derby, Grandstand Show, Stampede Parade, Heavy Horse Show, World Championship Blacksmith's Competition, North American Sheep Shearing Challenge, carnival, food and much more. Est attendance: 1,218,000. For info: Calgary Exhibition and Stampede, PO Box 1060, Station M, Calgary, AB, T2P 2K8, Canada. Phone: (403) 261-0101 or (800) 661-1260. E-mail: info@calgarystampede.com. Web: www.calgarystampede.com.

COMPLIMENT-YOUR-MIRROR DAY. July 3. Participation consists of complimenting your mirror on having such a wonderful owner and keeping track of whether other mirrors you meet during the day smile at you. (Created by Robert L. Birch, Pun Corps.)

COPLEY, JOHN SINGLETON: BIRTH ANNIVERSARY. July 3, 1738. Born to Irish immigrants in Boston, MA, perhaps on July 3, 1738, Copley was the most important American painter of the 18th century. After rapid early success in Boston as an in-demand portrait painter (among his subjects was Paul Revere), Copley moved to London, England, in 1774 and traveled in Europe to study further. Copley's best-known painting is *Watson and the Shark* (1782), depicting a youth saved from the jaws of the approaching predator in the Bay of Havana, Cuba. Copley died at London on Sept 9, 1815.

DOG DAYS. July 3–Aug 11. Hottest days of the year in Northern Hemisphere. Usually about 40 days, but variously reckoned at 30–54 days. Popularly believed to be an evil time "when the sea boiled, wine turned sour, dogs grew mad, and all creatures became languid, causing to man burning fevers, hysterics and phrensies" (from Brady's *Clavis Calendarium*, 1813). Originally the days when Sirius, the Dog Star, rose just before or at about the same time as sunrise (no longer true owing to precession of the equinoxes). Ancients sacrificed a brown dog at the beginning of Dog Days to appease the rage of Sirius, believing that star was the cause of the hot, sultry weather.

ENNIS RODEO AND PARADE. July 3–4. Ennis, MT. Billed as the fastest two-day rodeo in Montana, this is a nonstop rodeo of excitement. Parade with clowns, bucking broncos and everything imaginable. Annually, July 3–4. Est attendance: 6,000. For info: Ennis Rodeo Club, Ennis Chamber of Commerce. Phone: (406) 682-4388. Web: www.ennischamber.com/rodeo-parade.asp.

FISHER, M.F.K.: BIRTH ANNIVERSARY. July 3, 1908. The prolific author Mary Frances Kennedy Fisher was born at Albion, MI. With the publication of her first book, *Serve It Forth* (1937), she essentially invented a new genre: essays about food. Her other titles include *The Gastronomical Me* (1943) and *With Bold Knife and Fork* (1969). Fisher died at Glen Ellen, CA, June 22, 1992.

HUNTINGTON, SAMUEL: BIRTH ANNIVERSARY. July 3, 1731. President of the Continental Congress, governor of Connecticut, signer of the Declaration of Independence, born at Windham, CT, and died at Norwich, CT, Jan 5, 1796.

IDAHO: ADMISSION DAY: ANNIVERSARY. July 3. Became 43rd state in 1890.

IRAN AIR FLIGHT 655 DISASTER: ANNIVERSARY. July 3, 1988. At 10:54 AM in the Persian Gulf, the US Navy warship *Vincennes* fired two surface-to-air missiles at Iran Air Flight 655, which destroyed the airbus, killing all 290 passengers aboard. The *Vincennes*, boasting the world's most sophisticated radar-detection equipment, reportedly misread radio signals of the airbus, mistaking it for a hostile F-14 fighter plane. A self-conducted military inquiry blamed human failure—stress on the tense crew rather than equipment malfunction—for the disaster. In the summer of 1992 the public learned that the ship had been in Iranian waters at the time in the course of an operation aimed at preventing Iranian boats from laying mines.

"MR PEEPERS" TV PREMIERE: ANNIVERSARY. July 3, 1952. This sitcom was broadcast live and focused on mild-mannered, junior high school science teacher Robinson J. Peepers (Wally Cox). The cast also included Tony Randall, Georgann Johnson, Marion Lorne, Reta Shaw, Jack Warden and Ernest Truex. This half-hour series was a summer replacement, but it earned such positive reviews that it was brought back as a regular series. In 1954 *TV Guide* wrote that "'Mr Peepers' . . . comes close to being the perfect TV show."

QUÉBEC FOUNDED: ANNIVERSARY. July 3, 1608. French explorer Samuel de Champlain founded a settlement called Québec, from the Algonquin word *kébec*, meaning "where the river narrows." Québec City is thus one of the oldest settlements of European origin in North America.

RAID ON ENTEBBE: ANNIVERSARY. July 3, 1976. An Israeli commando unit staged a raid on the Entebbe airport in Uganda and rescued 103 hostages on a hijacked Air France airliner. Three of the hostages, seven hijackers and 20 Ugandan soldiers were killed in the raid. The plane had been en route from Tel Aviv to Paris when it was taken over by the pro-Palestinian guerrillas.

STAY OUT OF THE SUN DAY. July 3. For health's sake, give your skin a break today. (©2006 by WH.) For info: Thomas & Ruth Roy, Wellcat Holidays, 2418 Long Ln, Lebanon, PA 17046. Phone: (717) 279-0184. E-mail: info@wellcat.com. Web: www.wellcat.com.

STOCK EXCHANGE HOLIDAY (INDEPENDENCE DAY OBSERVED). July 3. The holiday schedules for the various exchanges are subject to change if relevant rules, regulations or exchange policies are revised. If you have questions, contact: CME Group (CME, CBOT, NYMEX, COMEX) (www.cmegroup.com), Chicago Board Options Exchange (www.cboe.com), NASDAQ (www.nasdaq.com), NYSE (www.nyse.com).

US VIRGIN ISLANDS: DANISH WEST INDIES EMANCIPATION DAY. July 3, 1848. Commemorates freeing of slaves in the Danish West Indies. Ceremony at Frederiksted, St. Croix, where actual proclamation was first read by Governor-General Peter Von Scholten.

VICKSBURG SURRENDERS: ANNIVERSARY. July 3, 1863. After weeks of immediate siege at the end of a yearlong campaign, Vicksburg, MS, surrendered to General Ulysses S. Grant. Formal surrender was consummated on July 4, and on July 8 the besieged city of Port Hudson also surrendered, giving the Union complete control of the Mississippi River. This move cut off the western Confederacy from the rest of the South.

WASHINGTON TAKES COMMAND OF THE CONTINENTAL ARMY: ANNIVERSARY. July 3, 1775. George Washington took command of the Continental Army at Cambridge, MA.

🎂 BIRTHDAYS TODAY

Lamar Alexander, 80, US Senator (R, Tennessee), born Maryville, TN, July 3, 1940.

Moises Alou, 54, former baseball player, born Atlanta, GA, July 3, 1966.

Julian Assange, 49, journalist, publisher (www.WikiLeaks.ch), born Townsville, Australia, July 3, 1971.

Dave Barry, 73, humorist, author, born Brooklyn, NY, July 3, 1947.

Betty Buckley, 73, actress (Tony for *Cats*; *Sunset Boulevard*, "Eight Is Enough"), born Fort Worth, TX, July 3, 1947.

Tom Cruise, 58, actor (*Mission: Impossible* films, *Collateral*, *Jerry Maguire*, *Top Gun*), born Thomas Cruise Mapother IV at Syracuse, NY, July 3, 1962.

Thomas Gibson, 58, actor ("Criminal Minds," "Dharma & Greg"), born Charleston, SC, July 3, 1962.

Audra McDonald, 50, actress (six-time Tony winner, including for *Lady Day at Emerson's Bar and Grill* and *The Gershwins' Porgy and Bess*), born Berlin, Germany, July 3, 1970.

Teemu Selänne, 50, former hockey player, born Helsinki, Finland, July 3, 1970.

Kurtwood Smith, 78, actor ("That '70s Show," *Robocop*), born New Lisbon, WI, July 3, 1942.

Tom Stoppard, 83, playwright (Tonys for *The Coast of Utopia*, *The Real Thing*, *Travesties* and *Rosencrantz and Guildenstern Are Dead*), screenwriter (Oscar for *Shakespeare in Love*), born Thomas Straussler at Zlín, Czechoslovakia (now the Czech Republic), July 3, 1937.

Sebastian Vettel, 33, Formula One racing driver, born Heppenheim, West Germany (now Germany), July 3, 1987.

Montel Williams, 64, talk show host ("The Montel Williams Show"), born Baltimore, MD, July 3, 1956.

July 4 — Saturday

DAY 186　　　　　　　　　　　　　　**180 REMAINING**

ADAMS, JOHN, AND JEFFERSON, THOMAS: DEATH ANNIVERSARY. July 4, 1826. Former US presidents John Adams and Thomas Jefferson died on the same day, July 4, 1826, the 50th anniversary of adoption of the Declaration of Independence. Adams had once written to Jefferson (1813): "You and I ought not to die before we have explained ourselves to each other." They thus began a spirited correspondence until their deaths. Adams's last words: "Thomas Jefferson still survives." Jefferson's last words: "This is the Fourth?"

AJC PEACHTREE ROAD RACE. July 4. Atlanta, GA. 51st running. The largest 10k in the world. 60,000-runner limit; advance registration only. Online registration begins in March; see website for details. Est attendance: 200,000. For info: Atlanta Track Club, 201 Armour Dr NE, Atlanta, GA 30324. Phone: (404) 231-9064. E-mail: atc@atlantatrackclub.org. Web: www.atlantatrackclub.org.

"AMERICA THE BEAUTIFUL" PUBLISHED: 125th ANNIVERSARY. July 4, 1895. The poem "America the Beautiful" by Katherine Lee Bates, a Wellesley College professor, was first published in the *Congregationalist*, a church publication.

"AMERICAN TOP 40" RADIO PREMIERE: 50th ANNIVERSARY. July 4, 1970. Casey Kasem's hit-parade music countdown radio program, "American Top 40," was first broadcast on seven AM stations in the US on July 4, 1970. It is now heard in hundreds of markets around the world. For info: Pete Battistini, 6576 Lake Forest Dr, Avon, IN 46123. Phone: (317) 839-1421. E-mail: at40@aol.com.

ANDREWS FOURTH OF JULY FESTIVITIES. July 4. Pioneer Park, Andrews, TX. Features fun-filled family activities including a horse shoe tournament, 52nd annual turtle races, sack races and more. Vendors, food and live musical entertainment. Est

attendance: 2,500. For info: Andrews Chamber of Commerce, 700 W Broadway, Andrews, TX 79714. Phone: (432) 523-2695. Fax: (432) 523-2375. E-mail: achamber@andrewstx.com. Web: www.andrewstx.com.

ANVIL MOUNTAIN RUN. July 4. Nome, AK. 43rd annual. At 8 AM the 17k run up 1,134-foot Anvil Mountain and return to the City of Nome starts the day's celebratory activities. Record time: 1 hour, 11 minutes, 23 seconds. Second-oldest continuous running event in Alaska. Annually, July 4. Est attendance: 1,500. For info: Rasmussen's Music Mart, 675 Sparrow Ct, Fairbanks, AK 99709-6658. Phone: (907) 304-2573. E-mail: leaknome@gmail.com.

BOOM BOX PARADE. July 4. Willimantic, CT. 35th annual. Connecticut's unique people's parade. Anyone can march, enter a float or watch; only requirement: bring a radio. No "real" bands allowed. Marching music broadcast on WILI (1400 AM and 95.3 FM) radio and played by "boom boxes" along the parade route. Begins at 11 AM. Est attendance: 10,000. For info: WILI-AM, 720 Main St, Willimantic, CT 06226. Web: www.wili.com.

BRISTOL FOURTH OF JULY CELEBRATION. July 4. Bristol, RI. 235th annual. The nation's oldest continuous Fourth of July parade and celebration. Features floats, bands, veteran and patriotic organizations and military units. Patriotic exercises, a tradition dating to 1785, are held prior to the parade. Annually, July 4 except when July 4 is a Sunday, then the parade is held Monday, July 5. Est attendance: 100,000. For info: Bristol Fourth of July Celebration, PO Box 561, Bristol, RI 02809. Web: www.july4thbristolri.com.

CALITHUMPIAN PARADE. July 4. Biwabik, MN. Funny parade, clowns and bands; Biwabik's population of 1,000 jumps to more than 15,000 for a day. Annually, on the Fourth of July. Est attendance: 15,000. For info: 4th of July, Biwabik Area Civic Assn, Box 449, Biwabik, MN 55708. Phone: (218) 865-4183.

COOLIDGE, CALVIN: BIRTH ANNIVERSARY. July 4, 1872. The 30th president of the US was born John Calvin Coolidge at Plymouth, VT. He succeeded to the presidency Aug 3, 1923, following the death of Warren G. Harding. Coolidge was elected president once, in 1924, but did "not choose to run for president in 1928." Nicknamed Silent Cal, he is reported to have said, "If you don't say anything, you won't be called on to repeat it." Coolidge died at Northampton, MA, Jan 5, 1933.

DECLARATION OF INDEPENDENCE APPROVAL AND SIGNING: ANNIVERSARY. July 4, 1776. The Declaration of Independence was approved by the Continental Congress: "Signed by Order and in Behalf of the Congress, John Hancock, President, Attest, Charles Thomson, Secretary." The official signing occurred Aug 2, 1776. The manuscript journals of the Congress for that date state: "The declaration of independence being engrossed and compared at the table was signed by the members."

EARTH AT APHELION. July 4. At approximately 7:35 AM, EDT, planet Earth will reach aphelion, that point in its orbit when it is farthest from the sun (about 94,510,000 miles). Earth's mean distance from the sun (mean radius of its orbit) is reached early in the months of April and October. Note that Earth is farthest from the sun during Northern Hemisphere summer. See also: "Earth at Perihelion" (Jan 5).

FOSTER, STEPHEN: BIRTH ANNIVERSARY. July 4, 1826. Stephen Collins Foster, one of America's most famous and best-loved

July 2020	S	M	T	W	T	F	S
				1	2	3	4
	5	6	7	8	9	10	11
	12	13	14	15	16	17	18
	19	20	21	22	23	24	25
	26	27	28	29	30	31	

songwriters, was born at Lawrenceville, PA. Among his nearly 200 songs: "Oh! Susanna," "Camptown Races," "Old Folks at Home" ("Swanee River"), "Jeanie with the Light Brown Hair" and "Beautiful Dreamer." Foster died in poverty at Bellevue Hospital at New York, NY, Jan 13, 1864.

GOLDBERG, RUBE: BIRTH ANNIVERSARY. July 4, 1883. The cartoonist with an engineering degree who put his education to work inventing elaborate machines with involved steps to accomplish ludicrously simple tasks. He is best remembered for the creative inventions of his cartoon character Lucifer Gorgonzola Butts. Born at San Francisco, CA, Goldberg died Dec 7, 1970, at New York City.

GREAT SEAL OF THE US PROPOSED: ANNIVERSARY. July 4, 1776. The Continental Congress, meeting at Philadelphia, PA, after voting to adopt the Declaration of Independence, went on to approve the following: "Resolved, that Dr. Franklin, Mr J. Adams and Mr Jefferson, be a committee, to bring in a device for a seal for the United States of America," thus beginning the history of the Great Seal of the US on the first day of independence. The seal wasn't designed and used until 1782.

HAWTHORNE, NATHANIEL: BIRTH ANNIVERSARY. July 4, 1804. Novelist and short-story writer, born at Salem, MA. Works include *The Scarlet Letter*, *The House of the Seven Gables* and *The Blithedale Romance*. Hawthorne died at Plymouth, NH, May 19, 1864.

INDEPENDENCE DAY. July 4, 1776. The US commemorates adoption of the Declaration of Independence by the Continental Congress. The nation's birthday. Legal holiday in all states and territories.

INDEPENDENCE DAY CELEBRATION. July 4. Mystic Seaport Museum, Mystic, CT. Visitors can participate in a re-creation of an 1870s Fourth of July with costumed staff. There are patriotic ceremonies and a children's parade. Kids' old-fashioned spelling bee and 19th-century games on the Green. Est attendance: 3,500. For info: Mystic Seaport Museum, 75 Greenmanville Ave, Box 6000, Mystic, CT 06355. Phone: (860) 572-0711. Web: www.mysticseaport.org.

INDEPENDENCE DAY CELEBRATION AND ANVIL SHOOT. July 4. Museum of Appalachia, Norris, TN. An old-fashioned celebration highlighted by launching a gunpowder-filled anvil high into the sky. "Anvil shooting" was once a common way for pioneers to celebrate special events. Also featured: musicians, patriotic ceremonies and demonstrations of old-time activities including sassafras tea brewing, spinning, rail splitting and more! For info: Museum of Appalachia, 2819 Andersonville Hwy, Clinton, TN 37716. Phone: (865) 494-7680. E-mail: museum@museumofappalachia.org. Web: www.museumofappalachia.org.

INTERNATIONAL CHERRY PIT SPITTING CHAMPIONSHIP. July 4. Tree-Mendus Fruit Farm, Eau Claire, MI. 47th annual. A nutritious sport—is there a better way to dispose of the pits once you have eaten the cherry? Entrants eat a cherry and then spit the pit as far as possible on a blacktop surface. The entrant who spits the pit the farthest including the roll is the champ. Youth through adult categories. Annually, the first Saturday in July. Est attendance: 300. For info: Tree-Mendus Fruit Farm, 9351 E Eureka Rd, Eau Claire, MI 49111. Phone: (269) 782-7101. Fax: (269) 782-7166. E-mail: contactus@treemendus-fruit.com. Web: www.treemendus-fruit.com.

JACK JOHNSON V JIM JEFFRIES: ANNIVERSARY. July 4, 1910. Boxers Johnson, heavyweight champion of the world, and Jeffries, "the Great White Hope," met in Reno, NV, in what was billed as "the Battle of the Century." More than 20,000 people (whites mostly) were on hand to see Johnson—a 10-to-4 underdog going into the bout—dominate Jeffries from start to finish. Jeffries's brawling style was no match for Johnson, who smiled and talked to spectators ringside as he landed and slipped punches round after round. Finally, in the 15th round, Jeffries's corner threw in the towel before Johnson could knock the former champion out. Afterward, spontaneous celebrations by blacks were marred by white attackers and devolved into race riots in 50 cities in 25 states, leaving 25 dead and hundreds injured.

KOKO THE GORILLA: BIRTH ANNIVERSARY. July 4, 1971. Koko, a lowland gorilla (full name: Hanabi-Ko, or "Fireworks Child" in Japanese), was born this day at the San Francisco Zoo. She is probably the most famous gorilla in the world due to her participation in the longest continuous experiment to teach language to animals. She was taught sign language beginning when she was about a year old, and she had a vocabulary of 1,000 signs. Koko died June 19, 2018, at Woodside, CA, at the age of 46.

LANDERS, ANN: BIRTH ANNIVERSARY. July 4, 1918. Born Esther Pauline Friedman at Sioux City, IA, the advice columnist was beloved worldwide. In 1955 she won a contest to be the new "Ann Landers" columnist for the *Chicago Sun-Times*. For 47 years, with spunky yet compassionate replies that were a refreshing change from prior columnists' styles, she helped everyday people overcome their problems. A trademark admonishment was "40 lashes with a wet noodle." (Her twin sister, Pauline Friedman, followed in her footsteps with a "Dear Abby" column.) By 2002 her column was carried in more than 1,200 newspapers worldwide and had a readership of 30 million. She died June 22, 2002, at Chicago, IL.

LIBERTY CELEBRATION. July 4. American Revolution Museum at Yorktown, Yorktown, VA. Salute the 244th anniversary of the Declaration of Independence. Observe tactical and artillery drills, take part in military exercises and learn about the challenges that faced our nation's founders, including those who signed the historic document. See a rare July 1776 broadside of the Declaration of Independence in exhibition galleries. For info: Jamestown-Yorktown Foundation, PO Box 1607, Williamsburg, VA 23187. Phone: (757) 253-4838 or (888) 593-4682. Fax: (757) 253-5299. Web: www.historyisfun.org.

LOU GEHRIG DAY: ANNIVERSARY. July 4, 1939. After retiring from baseball, Lou Gehrig returned to the New York Yankees for Lou Gehrig Day. In his famous farewell speech he said, "Today I consider myself the luckiest man on the face of the earth."

MACKINAW CITY'S FOURTH OF JULY FIREWORKS. July 4. Mackinaw City, MI. Starting at 1:30 PM on the marina lawn, fun and games for all ages. One of the largest fireworks displays in the North is shot off over the harbor at dusk. For info: Mackinaw City Chamber of Commerce, PO Box 856, Mackinaw City, MI 49701. Phone: (231) 436-5574. Web: www.mackinawchamber.com.

PHILIPPINES: FIL-AMERICAN FRIENDSHIP DAY. July 4. Formerly National Independence Day, when the Philippines were a colony of the US, now celebrated as Fil-American Friendship Day.

SAPERSTEIN, ABE: BIRTH ANNIVERSARY. July 4, 1902. Abraham Michael (Abe) Saperstein, Basketball Hall of Fame executive, born at London, England. Saperstein came to the US in 1905, played and coached basketball at Chicago and organized the Harlem Globetrotters in 1927. Originally a barnstorming professional team, the Globetrotters evolved into the sport's premier entertainment, playing thousands of games around the world and almost never losing. Saperstein died at Chicago, IL, Mar 15, 1966, and was inducted into the Hall of Fame in 1970.

SIMON, NEIL: BIRTH ANNIVERSARY. July 4, 1927. Marvin Neil Simon, born at the Bronx, NY, was a radio and TV comedy writer who went on to win Tony Awards for his plays *The Odd Couple*, *Biloxi Blues* and *Lost in Yonkers*, the latter winning the Pulitzer Prize for Drama in 1991. His screen adaptations of *The Odd Couple* and *The Sunshine Boys* earned Oscar nominations, as did his original screenplay for *The Goodbye Girl*. In 1983, Simon became the first living playwright to have a Broadway theater named after him. In 2006 he was awarded the Mark Twain Prize for American Humor. Simon died Aug 26, 2018, in New York City.

SPACE MILESTONE: *DEEP IMPACT* SMASHES INTO TEMPEL 1 (US): 15th ANNIVERSARY. July 4, 2005. After a six-month journey and 83 million miles, the *Deep Impact* spacecraft smashed—as planned—into the comet Tempel 1. The purpose of the 820-pound, barrel-shaped craft's mission is to give scientists more information about comets.

SPACE MILESTONE: *MARS PATHFINDER* (US). July 4, 1997. Unmanned spacecraft landed on Mars after a seven-month flight. Carried *Sojourner*, a roving robotic explorer that sent back photographs of the landscape. One of its missions was to ascertain whether life ever existed on Mars. See also: "Space Milestone: *Mars Global Surveyor*" (Sept 11).

STEINBRENNER, GEORGE: 90th BIRTH ANNIVERSARY. July 4, 1930. Baseball executive and longtime owner of the New York Yankees. Nicknamed "the Boss," George Michael Steinbrenner III was born at Rocky River, OH, and died at Tampa, FL, July 13, 2010.

TUSKEGEE INSTITUTE OPENING: ANNIVERSARY. July 4, 1881. Booker T. Washington's famed agricultural-industrial institution was built from the ground up by dedicated students seeking academic and vocational training. The institute started in a shanty before Washington purchased an abandoned plantation at Tuskegee, AL. The students built the dormitories, classrooms and chapel from bricks out of their own kiln.

UNITED NATIONS: INTERNATIONAL DAY OF COOPERATIVES. July 4. On Dec 16, 1992, the General Assembly proclaimed this observance for the first Saturday in July 1995 (Res 47/60). On Dec 23, 1994, recognizing that cooperatives were becoming an indispensable factor of economic and social development, the Assembly invited governments, international organizations, specialized agencies and national and international cooperative organizations to observe this day (Res 49/155). Annually, the first Saturday in July. For info: United Nations, Dept of Public Info, New York, NY 10017. Web: www.un.org.

VAN BUREN, ABIGAIL: BIRTH ANNIVERSARY. July 4, 1918. Influential advice columnist ("Dear Abby") born Pauline Esther Friedman at Sioux City, IA. She was a housewife (married name Phillips) who had never held a job when, in 1955, she approached the *San Francisco Chronicle* and declared that she could write better advice than the current columnist. A few sample responses later and a career was born. Van Buren engaged in a personal and professional rivalry with her identical twin sister, Ann Landers, then an already established advice columnist for the *Chicago Sun-Times*. The columns quickly entered the realm of pop culture and journalism history as they ran in competing papers for decades. Van Buren was known for her outspoken, snappy answers and quick wit. Her daughter Jeanne Phillips began to assist with the column in 1987 and took over in an official capacity in 2000 as her mother battled Alzheimer's. Van Buren died at Minneapolis, MN, Jan 16, 2013.

🎂 BIRTHDAYS TODAY

Signy Coleman, 60, actress ("The Young and the Restless"), born Bolinas, CA, July 4, 1960.
Horace Grant, 55, former basketball player, born Augusta, GA, July 4, 1965.

	S	M	T	W	T	F	S
July				1	2	3	4
	5	6	7	8	9	10	11
2020	12	13	14	15	16	17	18
	19	20	21	22	23	24	25
	26	27	28	29	30	31	

Gina Lollobrigida, 92, actress (*Belles de Nuit*; *Bread, Love and Dreams*), born Subiaco, Italy, July 4, 1928.
Becki Newton, 42, actress ("Ugly Betty"), born New Haven, CT, July 4, 1978.
Geraldo Rivera, 77, journalist, talk show host ("Geraldo," *Exposing Myself*), born New York, NY, July 4, 1943.
Eva Marie Saint, 96, actress (Oscar for *On the Waterfront*; *North by Northwest, Exodus*), born Newark, NJ, July 4, 1924.
Pamela Howard (Pam) Shriver, 58, sportscaster, Hall of Fame tennis player, born Baltimore, MD, July 4, 1962.
Mike "The Situation" Sorrentino, 38, television personality ("Jersey Shore"), born New Brighton, NY, July 4, 1982.

July 5 — Sunday

DAY 187   **179 REMAINING**

ALGERIA: INDEPENDENCE DAY. July 5. National holiday. Commemorates the day in 1962 when Algeria gained independence from France.

BARNUM, PHINEAS TAYLOR: BIRTH ANNIVERSARY. July 5, 1810. Promoter of the bizarre and unusual. Barnum's American Museum opened in 1842, promoting unusual acts including the Feejee Mermaid, Chang and Eng (the original Siamese twins) and General Tom Thumb. In 1850 he began his promotion of Jenny Lind, "the Swedish Nightingale," and parlayed her singing talents into a major financial success. Barnum also cultivated a keen interest in politics. A founder of the newspaper *Herald of Freedom*, he wrote outspoken editorials that resulted not only in lawsuits but also in at least one jail sentence. In 1852 he declined the Democratic nomination for governor of Connecticut but did go on to serve two terms in the Connecticut legislature beginning in 1865. He was defeated in a bid for US Congress in 1866 but served as mayor of Bridgeport, CT, from 1875 to 1876. In 1871 "The Greatest Show on Earth" opened at Brooklyn, NY; Barnum merged with his rival J.A. Bailey in 1881 to form the Barnum and Bailey Circus. P.T. Barnum was born at Bethel, CT, and died at Bridgeport, CT, Apr 7, 1891.

BE NICE TO NEW JERSEY WEEK. July 5–11. A time to recognize the assets of the state most maligned by American comedians. Annually, the first full week in July. For info: Lone Star Publications of Humor, 8452 Fredericksburg Rd, PMB 103, San Antonio, TX 78229. E-mail: lspubs@aol.com.

BIKINI DEBUT: ANNIVERSARY. July 5, 1946. The skimpy two-piece bathing suit created by Louis Réard debuted at a fashion show in Paris, France. It was named after an atoll in the Pacific where the hydrogen bomb was first tested.

BUCK MOON. July 5. So called by Native American tribes of New England and the Great Lakes because at this time of year the new antlers of buck deer begin to appear. Also called Thunder Moon, for summer thunderstorms. The July Full Moon.

CAPE VERDE: NATIONAL DAY. July 5. Public holiday. Commemorates independence from Portugal in 1975.

COCTEAU, JEAN: BIRTH ANNIVERSARY. July 5, 1889. French novelist, poet, director, actor and artist, born at Maisons-Laffitte, near Paris. His notable works include the play *Orpheus* (1926), the novel *The Infernal Machine* (1934) and the films *The Blood of a Poet* (1930) and *Beauty and the Beast* (1946). Remembered as an avant-garde icon, Cocteau influenced several generations of French artists. He died Oct 11, 1963, at Milly-la-Forêt, near Paris.

DUCKTONA 500. July 5. River Park, Sheboygan Falls, WI. Duck race along with dunk tank, car show, antique boat show, Big Wheel races, Kids Zone, pony rides, kids safety area, junior firefighter challenge, vendor fair, live music, food court and pancake breakfast. Annually, the first Sunday in July. Est attendance: 8,000. For info: Shirl Breunig, Sheboygan Falls Chamber Main St Office, 504 Broadway,

Sheboygan Falls, WI 53085. Phone: (920) 467-6206. E-mail: chambermnst@sheboyganfalls.org. Web: www.sheboyganfalls.org.

FARRAGUT, DAVID: BIRTH ANNIVERSARY. July 5, 1801. Born near Knoxville, TN, and died Aug 14, 1870, at Portsmouth, NH. Admiral in the American Civil War who was famous for his naval victories. At Mobile Bay, AL, in a disastrous attack on his entire fleet by the Confederates' Fort Morgan, Farragut proclaimed the famous cry, "Damn the torpedoes—full speed ahead!" They escaped the attack, and Mobile Bay surrendered.

LUNAR ECLIPSE. July 5. Partial eclipse of the moon. Visible in the Americas, eastern Africa and Antarctica.

MOON PHASE: FULL MOON. July 5. Moon enters Full Moon phase at 12:44 AM, EDT.

NATIONAL LABOR RELATIONS ACT (THE WAGNER ACT): 85th ANNIVERSARY. July 5, 1935. This bill guaranteed workers the right to organize and bargain collectively with their employers. It also prohibited the formation of company unions. An enforcement agency, the National Labor Relations Board, was created by the Act.

NUDE RECREATION WEEK. July 5–12. Looking for a way to relax this summer? Why not go barefoot all over? Give nude recreation a try this week by attending special events at a clothing-optional beach, campground or resort near you. For info: The Naturist Society, 627 Bay Shore Dr, Ste 100, Oshkosh, WI 54901. Phone: (800) 886-7230. Fax: (920) 426-5184. E-mail: nickyh@naturistsociety.com. Web: www.naturistsociety.com.

RAFFLES, STAMFORD: BIRTH ANNIVERSARY. July 5, 1781. Sir Stamford Raffles, English colonial official, founder of Singapore, where he is supposed to have landed Jan 29, 1819, was born at sea, off Jamaica. He discovered with Joseph Arnold an East Indian fungus that is named after them, *Rafflesia arnoldii*. Raffles died near London, England, on his birthday, July 5, 1826.

RHODES, CECIL JOHN: BIRTH ANNIVERSARY. July 5, 1853. English-born South African millionaire politician. Said to have controlled at one time 90 percent of the world's diamond production. His will founded the Rhodes Scholarships at Oxford University for superior scholastic achievers. Rhodesia (now Zimbabwe) was named for him. Born at Bishop's Stortford, Hertfordshire, England, Rhodes died Mar 26, 1902, at Cape Town, South Africa.

SLOVAKIA: SAINT CYRIL AND METHODIUS DAY. July 5. This day is dedicated to the Greek priests and scholars from Thessaloniki, who were invited by Prince Rastislav of Great Moravia to introduce Christianity and the first Slavic alphabet to the pagan people of the kingdom in AD 863.

STAFFORDSHIRE HOARD DISCOVERED: ANNIVERSARY. July 5, 2009. The most valuable treasure ever discovered in the United Kingdom, the Staffordshire Hoard, was found by metal-detector hobbyist Terry Herbert near Lichfield, England. The Anglo-Saxon hoard, probably warriors' loot, dates to the seventh century and includes 1,500 pieces of gold and silver sword hilts, shield bosses, helmets, crosses and more.

VENEZUELA: INDEPENDENCE DAY. July 5. National holiday. Commemorates proclamation of independence from Spain in 1811. Independence was not achieved until 1821.

ZETKIN, CLARA: BIRTH ANNIVERSARY. July 5, 1857. Women's rights advocate, born at Wiederau, Germany. Zetkin has been credited with being the initiator of International Women's Day, which has been observed on Mar 8 at least since 1910. She died at Arkhangelskoye, Russia, June 20, 1933. See also: "International (Working) Women's Day" (Mar 8).

🎂 BIRTHDAYS TODAY

François Arnaud, 35, actor ("The Borgias"), born Montreal, QC, Canada, July 5, 1985.

Edie Falco, 57, actress ("The Sopranos," "Nurse Jackie"), born Brooklyn, NY, July 5, 1963.

Eliot Feld, 78, choreographer, dancer, born Brooklyn, NY, July 5, 1942.

Richard Michael "Goose" Gossage, 69, Hall of Fame baseball player, born Colorado Springs, CO, July 5, 1951.

Eva Green, 40, actress ("Penny Dreadful," *Miss Peregrine's Home for Peculiar Children, Casino Royale*), born Paris, France, July 5, 1980.

Shirley Knight, 84, stage and screen actress (Tony for *Kennedy's Children*; *Sweet Bird of Youth, Petulia*), born Goessel, KS, July 5, 1936.

Huey Lewis, 70, singer (Huey Lewis and the News), born Hugh Anthony Cregg III at New York, NY, July 5, 1950.

Amélie Mauresmo, 41, Hall of Fame tennis player, born Saint-Germain-en-Laye, France, July 5, 1979.

Megan Rapinoe, 35, soccer player, born Reading, CA, July 5, 1985.

Robbie Robertson, 76, singer, musician, born Toronto, ON, Canada, July 5, 1944.

Gary Shteyngart, 48, author (*Russian Debutante's Handbook, Super Sad True Love Story*), born Igor Semyonovich Shteyngart at Leningrad, USSR (now St. Petersburg, Russia), July 5, 1972.

Michael Stuhlbarg, 52, actor (*Call Me by Your Name, The Shape of Water, A Serious Man*, "The Looming Tower"), born Long Beach, CA, July 5, 1968.

Roger Wicker, 69, US Senator (R, Mississippi), born Pontotoc, MS, July 5, 1951.

July 6 — Monday

DAY 188　　　　　　　　　　　　　　　**178 REMAINING**

ALTHEA GIBSON WINS WIMBLEDON: ANNIVERSARY. July 6, 1957. Althea Gibson became the first black to win a Wimbledon tennis title when she defeated fellow American Darlene Hard in the women's singles final. New York City celebrated her win with a ticker-tape parade on July 11. Gibson went on to win the US Nationals later that season.

BUSH, GEORGE W.: BIRTHDAY. July 6, 1946. 43rd president of the US (2001–09). Born at New Haven, CT.

CARIBBEAN DAY OR CARICOM DAY. July 6. The anniversary of the treaty establishing the Caribbean Community (also called the Treaty of Chaguaramas), signed by the prime ministers of Barbados, Guyana, Jamaica and Trinidad and Tobago July 4, 1973. Observed as a public holiday in Guyana and St. Vincent. Annually, the first Monday in July.

COMOROS: INDEPENDENCE DAY. July 6. Federal and Islamic Republic of Comoros commemorates declaration of independence from France in 1975.

CZECH REPUBLIC: COMMEMORATION DAY OF BURNING OF JOHN HUS. July 6. National holiday. In honor of Bohemian religious reformer John Hus, who was condemned as a heretic and burned at the stake July 6, 1415.

FIRST AIRSHIP CROSSING OF ATLANTIC: ANNIVERSARY. July 6, 1919. The first airship crossing of the Atlantic was completed as a British dirigible landed at New York's Roosevelt Field.

FIRST SUCCESSFUL ANTIRABIES INOCULATION: ANNIVERSARY. July 6, 1885. Louis Pasteur gave the first successful antirabies inoculation to a boy who had been bitten by an infected dog.

GRIFFIN, MERV: 95th BIRTH ANNIVERSARY. July 6, 1925. Born at San Mateo, CA, Mervyn Edward Griffin, Jr, began his career as a nightclub singer who happened by chance to land a film role that would launch a legendary career. He moved from film to television in 1958, working as a game show host, and in 1962 was given his own daytime talk show at NBC. "The Merv Griffin Show" ran for more than 21 years in syndication and won 11 Emmy Awards. He created and produced two of the most successful game shows in television history, "Jeopardy!" and "Wheel of Fortune," and also composed the iconic "Jeopardy!" theme music. He was a real estate mogul and at the time of his death was worth an estimated $1.6 billion. He died at Los Angeles, CA, Aug 12, 2007.

ISLE OF MAN: TYNWALD DAY. July 6. For more than 1,000 years, the people of the Isle of Man have gathered at Tynwald Hill at St. John's to hear new laws read out, to present petitions and to swear in the island's four coroners. Tynwald (a word of Norse extraction) is the name of the Manx parliament, which is the world's oldest continually held parliament. Held annually on July 5, unless that date falls on a weekend, in which case the event occurs on the following Monday.

JONES, JOHN PAUL: BIRTH ANNIVERSARY. July 6, 1747. (Old Style date.) American naval officer born at Kirkbean, Scotland. Remembered for his victory in the battle of his ship, the *Bonhomme Richard*, with the British frigate *Serapis*, Sept 23, 1779. When Jones was queried: "Do you ask for quarter?" he made his famous reply: "I have not yet begun to fight!" Jones was victorious, but the *Bonhomme Richard*, badly damaged, sank two days later. Jones died at Paris, France, July 18, 1792.

KAHLO, FRIDA: BIRTH ANNIVERSARY. July 6, 1907. The great surrealist painter was born Magdalena Carmen Frida Kahlo Calderón at Coyoacán, Mexico. In 1925 she endured severe injuries in a bus accident that would plague her for the rest of her life (and become artistic subject matter). She turned to art at about this time, encouraged by the master muralist Diego Rivera, whom she married in 1929 (and 1941). She is known almost as much for her tumultuous life (she had an affair with Soviet exile Leon Trotsky and was active in leftist politics) as for her vibrant art works filled with symbols and the flora and fauna of her beloved Mexico. She was one of the first women painters to sell a work to the Louvre. She died at her Casa Azul family home in Coyoacán on July 13, 1954.

LEIGH, JANET: BIRTH ANNIVERSARY. July 6, 1927. Born Jeanette Helen Morrison at Merced, CA, Leigh was signed to a contract by MGM while still a teenager. She starred in *Touch of Evil* with Orson Welles (1958), *The Manchurian Candidate* with Frank Sinatra (1962) and *Bye Bye Birdie* (1963) with Dick Van Dyke. She is best remembered for the scene where she was attacked in the shower by Norman Bates, in Alfred Hitchcock's 1960 classic, *Psycho*. She died Oct 3, 2004, at Los Angeles, CA.

LENNON MEETS MCCARTNEY: ANNIVERSARY. July 6, 1957. On this day in Liverpool, England, 15-year-old Paul McCartney watched a band called the Quarrymen led by the almost 17-year-old John Lennon. The two teens met later that day and before long created one of the most popular rock groups of the 20th century—The Beatles.

LITHUANIA: DAY OF STATEHOOD. July 6. National holiday. Commemorates the 1252 crowning of Mindaugas, who united Lithuania.

LUXEMBOURG: ETTELBRUCK REMEMBRANCE DAY. July 6. In honor of US general George Patton, Jr, liberator of the Grand-Duchy of Luxembourg in 1945, who is buried at the American Military Cemetery at Hamm, Germany, among 5,100 soldiers of his famous Third Army.

July 2020	S	M	T	W	T	F	S
				1	2	3	4
	5	6	7	8	9	10	11
	12	13	14	15	16	17	18
	19	20	21	22	23	24	25
	26	27	28	29	30	31	

MAJOR LEAGUE BASEBALL HOLDS FIRST ALL-STAR GAME: ANNIVERSARY. July 6, 1933. The first midsummer All-Star Game was held at Comiskey Park, Chicago, IL. Babe Ruth led the American League with a home run, as they defeated the National League, 4–2. Prior to the summer of 1933, All-Star contests consisted of pre- and postseason exhibitions that often found teams made up of a few stars playing beside journeymen and even minor leaguers.

MALAWI: REPUBLIC DAY. July 6. National holiday. Commemorates attainment of independence from Britain in 1964. Malawi was formerly known as Nyasaland.

OPERATION OVERCAST: 75th ANNIVERSARY. July 6, 1945. As the end of the war approached, the US Army had begun to move German scientists and scientific equipment from the German territory designated for Russian occupation. On this date the American Joint Chiefs of Staff authorized Operation Overcast, under which 350 German and Austrian scientists were transported to the US in a matter of months.

REAGAN, NANCY: BIRTH ANNIVERSARY. July 6, 1921. Born Anne Frances Robbins at New York, NY, Nancy Davis (she took the name of her beloved stepfather) was an actress with MGM in the 1940s and '50s who married then-actor Ronald Reagan in 1952. Thereafter, she was a vital companion to his political aspirations, which ultimately led to the presidency of the United States (1981–89). When she became first lady, Nancy Reagan's major project was the "Just Say No" campaign against drug abuse. After Ronald Reagan's diagnosis of Alzheimer's disease in 1994, Nancy Reagan devoted herself to his care until his death in 2004. Reagan died Mar 6, 2016, at Los Angeles, CA.

REPUBLICAN PARTY FORMED: ANNIVERSARY. July 6, 1854. The Republican Party originated at a convention at Ripon, WI, on Feb 28, 1854. A state convention meeting in Michigan formally adopted the name Republican on July 6.

SPACE MILESTONE: *SOYUZ 21* (USSR). July 6, 1976. Launched this date. Two cosmonauts, Colonel B. Volynov and Lieutenant Colonel V. Zholobov, traveled to *Salyut 5* space station (launched June 22, 1976) to study Earth's surface and conduct zoological-botanical experiments. Their stay was 48 days. Return landing on Aug 24.

TAKE YOUR WEBMASTER TO LUNCH DAY. July 6. Keep the person running your website happy by making sure he or she is well fed. It makes your webmaster feel loved and gives him or her the energy to fix all the typos that you have on your site. (©2006 by WH.) For info: Thomas & Ruth Roy, Wellcat Holidays, 2418 Long Ln, Lebanon, PA 17046. Phone: (717) 279-0184. E-mail: info@wellcat.com. Web: www.wellcat.com.

ZAMBIA: HEROES DAY. July 6. First Monday in July is a Zambian national holiday—a memorial day for Zambians who died in the struggle for independence. Political rallies stress solidarity. See also: "Zambia: Unity Day" (July 7).

🎂 BIRTHDAYS TODAY

Allyce Beasley, 66, actress ("Moonlighting"), born Brooklyn, NY, July 6, 1954.

Ned Beatty, 83, actor ("Homicide: Life on the Street," *Hear My Song, Deliverance*), born Louisville, KY, July 6, 1937.

George W. Bush, 74, 43rd president of the US, former governor of Texas (R), born New Haven, CT, July 6, 1946.

Dalai Lama, 85, Tibetan Buddhist spiritual leader, Nobel Peace Prize recipient, born Lhamo Dondrub (now Taktser, China), July 6, 1935.

Pau Gasol, 40, basketball player, born Barcelona, Spain, July 6, 1980.

Grant Goodeve, 68, actor ("Eight Is Enough," "Dynasty"), born New Haven, CT, July 6, 1952.

Kevin Hart, 40, comedian, actor (*Ride Along, About Last Night, Laugh at My Pain*), born Philadelphia, PA, July 6, 1980.

Manny Machado, 28, baseball player, born Hialeah, FL, July 6, 1992.

Hilary Mantel, 68, author (*Wolf Hall, Beyond Black*), born Glossop, Derbyshire, England, July 6, 1952.

Geoffrey Rush, 69, actor (*Pirates of the Caribbean, The King's Speech*, Oscar for *Shine*), born Toowoomba, Australia, July 6, 1951.

Sylvester Stallone, 74, actor (*Creed, Rocky* and *Rambo* films), director, born New York, NY, July 6, 1946.

Burt Ward, 75, actor ("Batman"), born Los Angeles, CA, July 6, 1945.

July 7 — Tuesday

DAY 189 **177 REMAINING**

BONZA BOTTLER DAY®. July 7. To celebrate when the number of the day is the same as the number of the month. Bonza Bottler Day® is an excuse to have a party at least once a month. For more information see Jan 1. For info: Gail Berger, Bonza Bottler Day. Phone: (864) 201-3988. E-mail: bonza@bonzabottlerday.com. Web: www.bonzabottlerday.com.

CHAGALL, MARC: BIRTH ANNIVERSARY. July 7, 1887. Born at Vitebsk, Russian Empire (in what is now Belarus), Chagall was one of the most important artists of the 20th century, blending a modern sense of the abstract, surreal or magical with a very personal and emotive style. He was an accomplished master in many mediums, including painting, etching, engraving, set design and stained glass. Chagall died Mar 28, 1985, at Saint-Paul, Alpes-Maritimes, France.

FATHER-DAUGHTER TAKE A WALK TOGETHER DAY. July 7. A special time in the summer for fathers and daughters of all ages to spend time together in the beautiful weather. Annually, July 7. For info: Janet Dellaria, PhD, PO Box 39, Trout Creek, MI 49967. Phone: (808) 987-1908. E-mail: janshine@yahoo.com.

HAWAII ANNEXED BY US: ANNIVERSARY. July 7, 1898. President William McKinley signed a resolution annexing Hawaii. No change in government took place until 1900, when Congress passed an act making Hawaii an "incorporated" territory of the US. This act remained in effect until Hawaii became a state in 1959.

JAPAN: TANABATA (STAR FESTIVAL). July 7. As an offering to the stars, children set up bamboo branches to which colorful strips of paper bearing poems are tied.

KUNSTLER, WILLIAM: BIRTH ANNIVERSARY. July 7, 1919. Radical attorney, defense lawyer for the Chicago Seven, born at New York, NY. Died Sept 4, 1995, at New York, NY.

LINCOLN ASSASSINATION CONSPIRATORS HANGING: ANNIVERSARY. July 7, 1865. Four persons convicted of complicity with John Wilkes Booth in the assassination of President Abraham Lincoln on Apr 14, 1865, were hanged at Washington, DC. The four: Mary E. Surratt, Lewis Powell, David E. Herold and George A. Atzerodt. Mary Surratt became the first woman executed for a crime in the US. Her conviction was and is a subject of controversy, as the only crime she appeared to have committed was to own the boardinghouse where John Wilkes Booth planned the assassination.

LONDON TERRORIST BOMBINGS: 15th ANNIVERSARY. July 7, 2005. In the most violent attack on London, England, since WWII, terrorists exploded four bombs in quick succession on three subway cars and one bus, killing more than 50 people and injuring 700. A splinter group of Al Qaeda claimed responsibility.

MENOTTI, GIAN CARLO: BIRTH ANNIVERSARY. July 7, 1911. Composer, born at Cadegliano-Viconago, Italy, who wrote his first opera at age 11. He won two Pulitzer Prizes—for popular operas *The Consul* (1950) and *The Saint of Bleecker Street* (1955). His *Amahl and the Night Visitors* is a Christmas favorite. He died at Monte Carlo, Monaco, on Feb 1, 2007.

MOTHER FRANCES XAVIER CABRINI CANONIZED: ANNIVERSARY. July 7, 1946. Pope Pius XII presided over the canonization ceremonies for Mother Frances Xavier Cabrini as she became the first American to be canonized. She was the founder of the Missionary Sisters of the Sacred Heart of Jesus, and her principal shrine is at Mother Cabrini High School, New York, NY. Cabrini was born at Lombardy, Italy, July 15, 1850, and died at Chicago, IL, Dec 22, 1917. Her feast day is celebrated on Dec 22.

PAIGE, LEROY ROBERT "SATCHEL": BIRTH ANNIVERSARY. July 7, 1906. Baseball Hall of Fame pitcher born at Mobile, AL. Paige was the greatest attraction in the Negro Leagues and was also, at age 42, the first black pitcher in the American League. Inducted into the Hall of Fame in 1971. Died at Kansas City, MO, June 8, 1982.

"RYAN'S HOPE" TV PREMIERE: 45th ANNIVERSARY. July 7, 1975. This ABC soap ran until 1989 and was set mostly at the fictional Ryan's Tavern or Riverside Hospital at New York City. The show depicted the lives of the ardently Irish Ryan family. The original cast included Faith Catlin, Justin Deas, Bernard Barrow, Helen Gallagher, Michael Hawkins, Ilene Kristen, Malcolm Groome and Kate Mulgrew. Marg Helgenberger, Nell Carter, Yasmine Bleeth, Gloria DeHaven, Corbin Bernsen and Grant Show were among the show's other regulars.

SOLOMON ISLANDS: INDEPENDENCE DAY. July 7. National holiday. Commemorates independence from Britain in 1978.

SPAIN: RUNNING OF THE BULLS. July 7–14. Pamplona. Event made famous by Hemingway in his novel *The Sun Also Rises*, in which young men dressed in white with red scarves run through the streets of Pamplona chased by bulls from the bullring. Part of the festival of San Fermín.

TANZANIA: SABA SABA DAY. July 7. Tanzania's mainland ruling party, TANU, was formed on this day in 1954. *Saba Saba* means "Seven-Seven."

ZAMBIA: UNITY DAY. July 7. Memorial day for Zambians who died in the struggle for independence. Political rallies stressing solidarity throughout country. Annually, the first Tuesday in July.

🎂 BIRTHDAYS TODAY

Bérénice Bejo, 44, actress (*The Artist*), born Buenos Aires, Argentina, July 7, 1976.

Billy Campbell, 61, actor ("Cardinal," "The 4400," "Once and Again," *The Rocketeer*), born Charlottesville, VA, July 7, 1959.

Pierre Cardin, 98, fashion designer, born Venice, Italy, July 7, 1922.

Shelley Duvall, 71, actress (*Popeye, Nashville, Roxanne*), born Houston, TX, July 7, 1949.

Jorja Fox, 52, actress ("CSI," "ER"), born New York, NY, July 7, 1968.

Michelle Kwan, 40, Olympic figure skater, born Torrance, CA, July 7, 1980.

Lisa Leslie, 48, Hall of Fame basketball player, born Inglewood, CA, July 7, 1972.

Joe Sakic, 51, former hockey player, born Burnaby, BC, Canada, July 7, 1969.

Ralph Lee Sampson, 60, former basketball player, born Harrisonburg, VA, July 7, 1960.

Doc Severinsen, 93, composer, conductor, musician (former bandleader on "The Tonight Show"), born Arlington, OR, July 7, 1927.

Ringo Starr, 80, singer, musician (The Beatles), born Richard Starkey at Liverpool, England, July 7, 1940.

July 8 — Wednesday

DAY 190   **176 REMAINING**

ASPINWALL CROSSES US ON HORSEBACK: ANNIVERSARY. July 8, 1911. Nan Jane Aspinwall rode into New York City carrying a letter to Mayor William Jay Gaynor from San Francisco mayor Patrick Henry McCarthy, becoming the first woman to cross the US on horseback. She began her trip in San Francisco, CA, on Sept 1, 1910, and covered 4,500 miles in 301 days.

DE SILHOUETTE, ÉTIENNE: BIRTH ANNIVERSARY. July 8, 1709. Born at Limoges, France, de Silhouette was briefly the French controller general of finances in 1759 under Louis XV. De Silhouette drew public scorn for his severe economic measures, and "silhouette" was coined to describe a figure reduced to its simplest form. The word evolved to describe black profile cutouts. He died Jan 20, 1767.

DECLARATION OF INDEPENDENCE FIRST PUBLIC READING: ANNIVERSARY. July 8, 1776. Colonel John Nixon read the Declaration of Independence to the assembled residents at Philadelphia's Independence Square in Pennsylvania.

ECKSTINE, BILLY: BIRTH ANNIVERSARY. July 8, 1914. Bandleader and bass-baritone singer Billy Eckstine was born William Clarence Eckstein at Pittsburgh, PA. After performing with the Earl Hines band for almost 20 years, Eckstine formed his own band in 1944. At one time or another the band's ranks included Charlie Parker, Dizzy Gillespie, Miles Davis, Fats Navarro, Dexter Gordon, Gene Ammons, Art Blakey and vocalist Sarah Vaughan—some of the greatest bebop musicians of all time. Among Eckstine's hits are "Fools Rush In," "Everything I Have Is Yours," "My Foolish Heart," "Blue Moon" and "Body and Soul." Billy Eckstine died Mar 8, 1993, at Pittsburgh.

JOHNSON, PHILLIP: BIRTH ANNIVERSARY. July 8, 1906. Postmodern architect who promoted the International Style. He was director of the Department of Architecture of New York's Museum of Modern Art, worked with Mies van der Rohe on the Seagram Building at New York City and designed his own "Glass House" at New Canaan, CT. Born at Cleveland, OH, and died Jan 25, 2005, in his home at New Canaan.

JORDAN, LOUIS: BIRTH ANNIVERSARY. July 8, 1908. "The King of the Jukebox" was born at Brinkley, AR. The bandleader-vocalist-saxophonist performed from the mid-1920s through the 1950s. A pioneer in American jazz, he was one of the most successful and influential African-American musicians of his era. *Rolling Stone*

		S	**M**	**T**	**W**	**T**	**F**	**S**
July								
					1	**2**	**3**	**4**
		5	**6**	**7**	**8**	**9**	**10**	**11**
2020		**12**	**13**	**14**	**15**	**16**	**17**	**18**
		19	**20**	**21**	**22**	**23**	**24**	**25**
		26	**27**	**28**	**29**	**30**	**31**	

magazine proclaimed Jordan number 59 on its list of the "100 Greatest Artists of All Time." He died Feb 4, 1975, at Los Angeles, CA.

OLIVE BRANCH PETITION: ANNIVERSARY. July 8, 1775. Representatives of New Hampshire, Massachusetts Bay, Rhode Island, Providence, Connecticut, New York, New Jersey, Pennsylvania, Delaware, Maryland, Virginia, North Carolina and South Carolina signed a petition from the Congress to King George III, a final attempt by moderates in the Second Continental Congress to avoid a complete break with England.

ROCKEFELLER, JOHN D.: BIRTH ANNIVERSARY. July 8, 1839. Oil magnate, industrialist and philanthropist, born at Richford, NY. From an austere background, Rockefeller brought his love of discipline and frugality to bear on his business dealings, acquiring his first oil refinery in 1863. By 1870, Rockefeller had created Standard Oil, the world's largest refining operations. He perfected the company's vertical integration, quietly buying out competitors and buying up pipelines, train cars, forests (fuel and barrels) and warehouses. Waste by-products like kerosene and gasoline become profitable side businesses. Standard Oil was declared a monopoly in 1911 and broken into 33 subsidiaries, ironically making Rockefeller richer. At his death, his fortune was $1.4 billion. From the 1880s onward he made philanthropy his business. His gifts were foundational to many institutions, including the University of Chicago, Spelman College and Denison University. The Rockefeller Foundation, originally funded to eradicate hookworm, remains a major humanitarian philanthropy. At his death on May 23, 1937, at Ormond Beach, FL, Rockefeller had given away more than $550 million.

ROCKEFELLER, NELSON ALDRICH: BIRTH ANNIVERSARY. July 8, 1908. Born at Bar Harbor, ME. Governor of New York (1958–73). Nominated as vice president by President Gerald R. Ford, Aug 20, 1974, under provisions of the 25th Amendment. Sworn in Dec 19, 1974, after confirmation by the Senate and served until Jan 20, 1977. Died at New York, NY, Jan 26, 1979. Rockefeller was the second person to become vice president without having been elected (Ford was the first).

SCUD DAY (SAVOR THE COMIC, UNPLUG THE DRAMA). July 8. A day to remind people of the benefits of spending more time in the Comic Zone and less in the Drama Zone. For info: Stephanie West Allen, 1376 S Wyandot St, Denver, CO 80223. Phone: (303) 935-8866. E-mail: stephanie@westallen.com.

SPACE MILESTONE: LAST MISSION OF THE SPACE SHUTTLE PROGRAM. July 8, 2011. Space shuttle *Atlantis* took off from Kennedy Space Center, FL, for the 135th and last mission of the space shuttle program. *Atlantis* was carrying supplies for the International Space Station, and its 12-day mission included an investigation into robotically refueling spacecraft. The first flight of a space shuttle was Apr 12, 1981. Robert L. Crippen, commander on the first flight, was among the attendees for the final launch. The shuttle returned safely to Kennedy Space Center on July 21, 2011.

ZEPPELIN, FERDINAND: BIRTH ANNIVERSARY. July 8, 1838. Born at Konstanz, Baden, Germany, into a noble family, Ferdinand Adolf August Heinrich, Count von Zeppelin, invented the rigid airship (or dirigible) that now bears his name. A military officer, he journeyed to the US during the American Civil War as an observer for the Union army. In that capacity in 1863, he took his first balloon flight in St. Paul, MN—a flight that inspired his postmilitary career as airship innovator. The zeppelin is a cylindrical, framed balloon held aloft by internal gas cells. In July 2, 1900, at Lake

Konstanz, Germany, Zeppelin's craft became the first to make a human-directed flight—the cigar-shaped frame held a motor-controlled gondola, propellers and steering controls. By WWI, more than 100 such zeppelins were being used for military purposes. Zeppelin himself died at Charlottenburg near Berlin on Mar 8, 1917, before he could see transcontinental flight achieved.

ZIEGFELD FOLLIES OF 1907: ANNIVERSARY. July 8, 1907. Theater impresario Florenz Ziegfeld staged the first of his extravagant musical revues in New York City. The show's slogan was "Glorifying the American Girl." The last *Follies* closed in 1957.

🎂 BIRTHDAYS TODAY

Kevin Bacon, 62, actor ("The Following," *Mystic River, Apollo 13, Footloose*), born Philadelphia, PA, July 8, 1958.

Sophia Bush, 38, actress ("Chicago P.D.," "One Tree Hill," *The Hitcher*), born Pasadena, CA, July 8, 1982.

Raffi Cavoukian, 72, children's singer and songwriter, born Cairo, Egypt, July 8, 1948.

Billy Crudup, 52, actor (Tony for *The Coast of Utopia: Voyage*; *Stage Beauty, Big Fish, Almost Famous*), born Manhasset, NY, July 8, 1968.

Kim Darby, 72, actress (*Rich Man, Poor Man*; *True Grit*), born Los Angeles, CA, July 8, 1948.

Cynthia Gregory, 74, former ballerina, choreographer, teacher, born Los Angeles, CA, July 8, 1946.

Beck Hansen, 50, rock singer, songwriter, born Beck David Campbell at Los Angeles, CA, July 8, 1970.

Anjelica Huston, 69, actress (Oscar for *Prizzi's Honor*; *The Royal Tenenbaums, The Addams Family*), born Los Angeles, CA, July 8, 1951.

Toby Keith, 59, country singer, born Clinton, OK, July 8, 1961.

Steve Lawrence, 85, singer, born Sidney Liebowitz at New York, NY, July 8, 1935.

Jeffrey Tambor, 76, actor ("Transparent," "Arrested Development," "The Larry Sanders Show"), born San Francisco, CA, July 8, 1944.

Milo Ventimiglia, 43, actor ("This Is Us," "Heroes," "Gilmore Girls"), born Anaheim, CA, July 8, 1977.

Alyce Faye Wattleton, 77, former executive director of Planned Parenthood Federation, born St. Louis, MO, July 8, 1943.

Michael Weatherly, 52, actor ("Bull," "NCIS," "Dark Angel"), born New York, NY, July 8, 1968.

July 9 — Thursday

DAY 191   **175 REMAINING**

ARGENTINA: INDEPENDENCE DAY. July 9. Anniversary of establishment of independent republic, with the declaration of independence from Spain in 1816.

FAST OF TAMMUZ. July 9. Shiva Asar B'Tammuz begins at first light of day and commemorates the first-century Roman siege that breached the walls of Jerusalem. Begins a three-week time of mourning. Hebrew calendar date: Tammuz 17, 5780.

FIRST OPEN-HEART SURGERY: ANNIVERSARY. July 9, 1893. In Provident Hospital on the South Side of Chicago, IL, black surgeon Dr. Daniel Hale Williams performed the first successful open-heart surgery.

FOURTEENTH AMENDMENT TO US CONSTITUTION RATIFIED: ANNIVERSARY. July 9, 1868. The 14th Amendment defined US citizenship and provided that no state shall have the right to abridge the rights of any citizen without due process and equal protection under the law. Coming three years after the Civil War, the 14th Amendment also included provisions for barring individuals who assisted in any rebellion or insurrection against the US from

holding public office, and releasing federal and state governments from any financial liability incurred in the assistance of rebellion or insurrection against the US.

HIGHEST TSUNAMI IN RECORDED HISTORY: ANNIVERSARY. July 9, 1958. An earthquake registering 8.3 on the Richter scale caused a massive landslide at the head of Lituya Bay, AK, which in turn created a tsunami of 1,700 feet—higher than the Willis Tower in Chicago, IL (which is 1,450 feet). A 300-foot wave immediately followed, scouring bare about four to five square miles of land on both sides of the bay. Of three boats anchored at this remote spot, one was sunk, with the loss of two lives; miraculously, the other two boats with their passengers survived the powerful waves.

HOWE, ELIAS: BIRTH ANNIVERSARY. July 9, 1819. Born at Spencer, MA, Howe patented a sewing machine in 1846, notable for its double-thread stitch and the innovation of placing the eye of the needle near its point. After unsuccessfully trying to develop a market in England, he returned to the United States penniless and discovered others were producing machines that infringed on his patent. He sued successfully and thereafter earned royalties on every machine made, making him a wealthy man as a ready-to-wear garment industry developed around the use of his machine. He died Oct 3, 1867, at Brooklyn, NY.

MARTYRDOM OF THE BAB. July 9. Baha'i observance of the anniversary of the execution by a firing squad in 1850, at Tabriz, Persia, of the 30-year-old Siyyid Ali Muhammed, the Bab (prophet-herald of the Baha'i Faith). One of the nine days of the year when Baha'is suspend work. For info: Baha'is of the US, Office of Communications, 1233 Central St, Evanston, IL 60201. Phone: (847) 733-3584. E-mail: ooc@usbnc.org. Web: www.bahai.us.

MONTANA GOVERNOR'S CUP WALLEYE TOURNAMENT. July 9–11. Fort Peck, MT. Two-person team event, limited to 200 teams. More than $95,000 in cash and prizes awarded. There is a 100 percent payback of $300 entry fee. Kids' fishing event also. Friday fish fry open to the public. Est attendance: 1,500. For info: Glasgow Area Chamber of Commerce and Agriculture, Box 832, Glasgow, MT 59230. Phone: (406) 228-2222. Fax: (406) 228-2244. E-mail: chamber@nemont.net. Web: www.montanagovcup.com.

MOROCCO: YOUTH DAY. July 9. National holiday. On the birthday in 1929 of King Hassan II.

RADCLIFFE, ANN WARD: BIRTH ANNIVERSARY. July 9, 1764. English author considered the most original and distinguished Gothic romance novelist, she brought poetry to the genre through her lush scenic descriptions. Among her works are *The Romance of the Forest* (1791), *The Mysteries of Udolpho* (1794) and *The Italian* (1797). She was born at London, England, and died there Feb 7, 1823.

RESPIGHI, OTTORINO: BIRTH ANNIVERSARY. July 9, 1879. Italian composer (*The Fountains of Rome*), born at Bologna, Italy. He died at Rome, Apr 18, 1936.

RUSSELL-EINSTEIN MANIFESTO: 65th ANNIVERSARY. July 9, 1955. Philosopher Bertrand Russell released this plea, signed by 11 prominent scientists, three months after Albert Einstein's death. Einstein had agreed to put his name to it in his final days. The manifesto urged nations to find peaceful ways to settle differences and to renounce the use of nuclear weapons, which only promised "universal death."

SOUTH SUDAN: INDEPENDENCE DAY. July 9. After almost 50 years of civil war resulting in millions of casualties, South Sudan broke away from Sudan and declared its independence on July 9, 2011.

SOVIET ROCKET THREAT: 60th ANNIVERSARY. July 9, 1960. Soviet premier Nikita Khrushchev threatened military action against the US if Washington were to attempt an overthrow of the Castro regime in Cuba.

US SENIOR WOMEN'S OPEN (GOLF) CHAMPIONSHIP. July 9–12. Brooklawn Country Club, Fairfield, CT. For info: USGA, Golf House, Championship Dept, PO Box 78, Far Hills, NJ 07931. Phone: (908) 234-2300. E-mail: champs@usga.org. Web: www. usga.org.

🧁 BIRTHDAYS TODAY

Brian Dennehy, 82, actor (Tony for *Long Day's Journey into Night*), born Bridgeport, CT, July 9, 1938.

Margaret Gillis, 67, dancer, choreographer, born Montreal, QC, Canada, July 9, 1953.

Lindsey Graham, 65, US Senator (R, South Carolina), born Pickens County, SC, July 9, 1955.

Tom Hanks, 64, actor (*Bridge of Spies, Saving Private Ryan*, Oscars for *Philadelphia* and *Forrest Gump*), born Concord, CA, July 9, 1956.

David Hockney, 83, artist, born Bradford, England, July 9, 1937.

Mathilde Krim, 94, medical researcher, philanthropist (amfAR), born Como, Italy, July 9, 1926.

Courtney Love, 55, singer, actress (*The People vs Larry Flynt*), born San Francisco, CA, July 9, 1965.

Kelly McGillis, 63, actress (*Witness, Top Gun, The Accused*), born Newport Beach, CA, July 9, 1957.

Richard Roundtree, 78, actor ("Being Mary Jane," *Shaft, City Heat, Q, Roots*), born New Rochelle, NY, July 9, 1942.

Fred Savage, 44, actor ("The Wonder Years," "Working," *The Princess Bride*), born Highland Park, IL, July 9, 1976.

Orenthal James (O.J.) Simpson, 73, former sportscaster and actor, Hall of Fame football player, born San Francisco, CA, July 9, 1947.

Jimmy Smits, 65, actor (*Glitz*, "LA Law," "NYPD Blue"), born New York, NY, July 9, 1955.

John Tesh, 68, television host ("Entertainment Tonight"), composer, born Garden City, NY, July 9, 1952.

Jack White, 45, singer, guitarist (The White Stripes, The Raconteurs, The Dead Weather), producer, born John Anthony Gillis at Detroit, MI, July 9, 1975.

	S	M	T	W	T	F	S
July					1	2	3	4
	5	6	7	8	9	10	11
2020	12	13	14	15	16	17	18
	19	20	21	22	23	24	25
	26	27	28	29	30	31	

July 10 — Friday

DAY 192   **174 REMAINING**

ALLIED INVASION OF SICILY: ANNIVERSARY. July 10, 1943. Operation Husky, the Allied infantry attack on Italy, began on the island of Sicily. The British entry into Syracuse was the first Allied success in Europe in WWII. General Dwight D. Eisenhower, the Allied commander in chief, described the invasion as "the first page in the liberation of the European Continent."

ASHE, ARTHUR: BIRTH ANNIVERSARY. July 10, 1943. Born at Richmond, VA, Arthur Ashe became a legend for his list of firsts as a black tennis player. Chosen for the US Davis Cup team in 1963, he became captain in 1980. He won the US men's singles championship and US Open in 1968 and in 1975 the men's singles at Wimbledon. Ashe won a total of 33 career titles. In 1985 he was inducted into the International Tennis Hall of Fame. He helped create inner-city tennis programs for youths and wrote the three-volume *A Hard Road to Glory: A History of the African-American Athlete*. Ashe announced Apr 8, 1992, that he had contracted HIV, probably through a transfusion during bypass surgery in 1983. In September 1992 he began a $5 million fund-raising effort on behalf of the Arthur Ashe Foundation for the Defeat of AIDS and campaigned for public awareness regarding the AIDS epidemic. He died at New York, NY, Feb 6, 1993, from pneumonia.

BAHAMAS: INDEPENDENCE DAY. July 10. Public holiday. At 12:01 AM in 1973 the Bahamas gained its independence after 250 years as a British Crown colony.

"BASEBALL'S SAD LEXICON" PUBLISHED: ANNIVERSARY. July 10, 1910. Journalist Franklin P. Adams created the second best-known baseball poem (after "Casey at the Bat") for the *New York Evening Mail*. Adams extolled the double-play trio of Chicago Cubs Joe Tinker (shortstop), Johnny Evers (second base) and Frank Chance (first base): "These are the saddest of possible words/'Tinker to Evers to Chance.'/Trio of bear cubs, and fleeter than birds,/Tinker and Evers and Chance./Ruthlessly pricking our gonfalon bubble,/Making a Giant hit into a double—/Words that are heavy with nothing but trouble:/'Tinker to Evers to Chance.'" See also: "Mighty Casey Has Struck Out: Anniversary" (June 3) and "Tinker to Evers to Chance: First Double Play Anniversary" (Sept 15).

BETHUNE, MARY MCLEOD: BIRTH ANNIVERSARY. July 10, 1875. Mary Jane McLeod Bethune was born at Mayesville, SC, the first in her family to be born free. Bethune became a teacher and in 1904 founded her own school in Florida, the Daytona Normal and Industrial School for Negro Girls. In 1931 the school merged with a local men's college, Cookman Institute, and was renamed Bethune-Cookman College. An adviser on minority affairs under President Franklin D. Roosevelt, she directed the Division of Negro Affairs of the National Youth Administration. She died May 18, 1955, at Daytona Beach, FL.

BORIS YELTSIN INAUGURATED AS RUSSIAN PRESIDENT: ANNIVERSARY. July 10, 1991. Boris Yeltsin took the oath of office as the first popularly elected president in Russia's 1,000-year history. He defeated the Communist Party candidate resoundingly, establishing himself as a powerful political counterpoint to Mikhail Gorbachev, the president of the Soviet Union, of which Russia was the largest republic. Yeltsin had been dismissed from the Politburo in 1987 and resigned from the Communist Party in 1989. His popularity forced Gorbachev to make concessions to the republics in the new union treaty forming the Confederation of Independent States. Suffering from poor health, Yeltsin resigned as president at the end of 1999.

BRINKLEY, DAVID: 100th BIRTH ANNIVERSARY. July 10, 1920. Born at Wilmington, NC, David Brinkley was one of the most recognizable faces in American broadcast journalism for more than 50 years. He was NBC's first White House correspondent, and his outstanding coverage of the 1956 Democratic and Republican national conventions landed him the anchor job on NBC's nightly TV newscast, paired with Chet Huntley until 1970. In 1981 Brinkley moved to ABC, creating a Sunday-morning interview show called "This Week with David Brinkley." He died on June 12, 2003, at Houston, TX.

CALIFORNIA STATE FAIR. July 10–26 (tentative, subject to change). Sacramento, CA. Top-name entertainment, fireworks, live stage shows, California counties exhibits, animals, culinary delights, carnival rides and award-winning wines and microbrews. For info: California State Fair, 1600 Exposition Blvd, Sacramento, CA 95815. Phone: (916) 263-FAIR or (877) CAL-EXPO. E-mail: info@calexpo.com. Web: www.castatefair.org.

CALVIN, JOHN: BIRTH ANNIVERSARY. July 10, 1509. Theologian, born at Noyon, France. Reformer and founder of Presbyterianism. Calvin died at Geneva, Switzerland, May 27, 1564.

CLERIHEW DAY. July 10. A day recognized in remembrance of Edmund Clerihew Bentley, journalist and author of the celebrated detective thriller *Trent's Last Case* (1912), but perhaps best known for his invention of a popular humorous verse form, the clerihew, consisting of two rhymed couplets of unequal length: "Edmund's middle name was Clerihew/A name possessed by very few,/But verses by Mr Bentley/Succeeded eminently." Bentley was born at London, England, July 10, 1875, and died there, Mar 30, 1956.

DALLAS, GEORGE MIFFLIN: BIRTH ANNIVERSARY. July 10, 1792. 11th vice president of the US (1845–49), born at Philadelphia, PA. Died there, Dec 31, 1864.

DON'T STEP ON A BEE DAY. July 10. Wellcat Holidays reminds kids and grown-ups that now is the time of year when going barefoot can mean getting stung by a bee. If you get stung, tell Mom. (©2006 by WH.) For info: Michael Roy, Wellcat Holidays, 2418 Long Ln, Lebanon, PA 17046. Phone: (717) 279-0184. E-mail: info@wellcat.com. Web: www.wellcat.com.

GILBERT, JOHN: BIRTH ANNIVERSARY. July 10, 1897. Silent film star John Gilbert was born John Pringle at Logan, UT. In 1916 he had his billed screen debut in *Bullets and Brown Eyes.* In the early 1920s Gilbert had leading roles in several films, such as *The Merry Widow* and *The Big Parade.* Although he was a popular leading man, he was unable to succeed when sound came to movies, and MGM released him from his contract in 1934. He died Jan 9, 1936, at Los Angeles, CA.

GWYNNE, FREDERICK HUBBARD: BIRTH ANNIVERSARY. July 10, 1926. Stage, screen and TV actor, best known for the TV roles Herman Munster in "The Munsters" and Officer Muldoon in "Car 54, Where Are You?" Gwynne was born at New York, NY, and died at Taneytown, MD, July 2, 1993.

NATIONAL MOTORCYCLE DAY. July 10. 5th annual. A day celebrating all things motorcycle, including the riders and the industry that supports them. The motorcycle heritage and culture that has developed over time is unique—with a spirit of adventure, freedom, fellowship and community. Sponsored by Dairyland Insurance. Annually, the second Friday in July. For info: National Motorcycle Day. Web: www.nationalmotorcycleday.com.

***NEWS OF THE WORLD* CEASES PUBLICATION: ANNIVERSARY.** July 10, 2011. Once the bestselling newspaper in English, the *News of the World* was closed by its parent company, News International, in an attempt to quell a scandal over journalistic ethics. The 168-year-old tabloid had been the subject of police and government inquiries into allegations that reporters accessed the voice-mail boxes of celebrities, royals and other public figures. Several of the paper's reporters and editors had already been arrested when it came to light that reporters had accessed and deleted some of the contents of the voice mail of a 13-year-old murder victim. At the time the paper ceased publication, its circulation was 2.6 million.

PROUST, MARCEL: BIRTH ANNIVERSARY. July 10, 1871. Famed author, born at Auteuil, France. He gained an international reputation for his 13-volume masterpiece, *A la Recherche du Temps Perdu* (*Remembrance of Things Past*). "Happiness," he wrote in *The Past Recaptured*, "is beneficial for the body but it is grief that develops the powers of the mind." Proust died Nov 19, 1922, at Paris, France.

SHRIVER, EUNICE KENNEDY: BIRTH ANNIVERSARY. July 10, 1921. Philanthropist, born at Brookline, MA. Sister of US president John F. Kennedy; mother of journalist Maria Shriver. Eponym of National Institute of Child Health and Human Development (1961). As advocate for mentally disabled, founded Special Olympics in 1968. Received Presidential Medal of Freedom in 1984. Died Aug 11, 2009, at Hyannis, MA.

SHUSTER, JOE: BIRTH ANNIVERSARY. July 10, 1914. Shuster, born at Toronto, ON, Canada, but raised in Cleveland, OH, teamed with friend Jerry Siegel to create the comic book superhero Superman, who debuted in *Action Comics* in June 1938. Shuster, the artist of the team, based a bit of Superman's alter ego, Clark Kent, on himself: "I was mild-mannered, wore glasses, was very shy with women." Despite Superman's runaway success, Siegel and Shuster never profitted greatly, having sold the rights to their character in 1938 (although later legal action ensured a modest stipend and creative credit). Shuster died July 30, 1992, at Los Angeles, CA.

SPACE MILESTONE: *TELSTAR* (US). July 10, 1962. First privately owned satellite (American Telephone and Telegraph Company) and first satellite to relay live TV pictures across the Atlantic was launched.

WAYNE CHICKEN SHOW. July 10–12. Wayne, NE. 40th annual. To allow humankind to pay tribute to chickenkind (without laying the proverbial egg). National Cluck-Off, Hard-Boiled Egg Eating Contest, Cement Chicken Auction, parade, car show, food and craft vendors, games, contests and musical entertainment. Est attendance: 10,000. For info: Wayne Area Chamber of Commerce, 108 W 3rd St, Wayne, NE 68787. Phone: (402) 375-2240. E-mail: info@wayneworks.org. Web: www.chickenshow.com.

WHISTLER, JAMES ABBOTT MCNEILL: BIRTH ANNIVERSARY. July 10, 1834. American painter especially known for *Arrangement in Grey and Black: The Artist's Mother* (1871, also known as *Whistler's Mother*), born at Lowell, MA. Died at London, England, July 17, 1903. When a woman declared that a landscape reminded her of Whistler's paintings, he reportedly said, "Yes, madam, Nature is creeping up."

WYOMING: ADMISSION DAY: ANNIVERSARY. July 10. Became 44th state in 1890.

🎂 BIRTHDAYS TODAY

Andre Dawson, 66, Hall of Fame baseball player, born Miami, FL, July 10, 1954.

David Norman Dinkins, 93, former and first black mayor of New York City (D), born Trenton, NJ, July 10, 1927.

Chiwetel Ejiofor, 43, actor (*12 Years a Slave, Kinky Boots*), born London, England, July 10, 1977.

Cary Joji Fukunaga, 43, producer, writer, director (Emmy for "True Detective"; *Jane Eyre, Beasts of No Nation*), born Alameda, CA, July 10, 1977.

Adrian Grenier, 44, actor ("Entourage"), born Brooklyn, NY, July 10, 1976.

Arlo Guthrie, 73, singer, born Brooklyn, NY, July 10, 1947.

Jerry Herman, 87, composer, lyricist, born New York, NY, July 10, 1933.

Sue Lyon, 74, actress (*Lolita, The Flim-Flam Man*), born Davenport, IA, July 10, 1946.

Alice Munro, 89, Nobel Prize–winning author (*Dance of the Happy Shades, Dear Life*), born Wingham, ON, Canada, July 10, 1931.

Lawrence Pressman, 81, actor ("Doogie Howser, MD," *The Hanoi Hilton*), born Cynthiana, KY, July 10, 1939.

Karen Russell, 39, author (*Swamplandia!*), born Miami, FL, July 10, 1981.

Jessica Simpson, 40, singer, actress (*The Dukes of Hazzard*), born Abilene, TX, July 10, 1980.

Sofía Vergara, 48, actress ("Modern Family," *Chef*), born Barranquilla, Colombia, July 10, 1972.

Virginia Wade, 75, Hall of Fame tennis player, born Bournemouth, England, July 10, 1945.

July 11 — Saturday

DAY 193   **173 REMAINING**

ADAMS, JOHN QUINCY: BIRTH ANNIVERSARY. July 11, 1767. The sixth president of the US and the son of the second president, John Quincy Adams was born at Braintree, MA. After his single term as president, he served 17 years as a member of Congress from Plymouth, MA. He died Feb 23, 1848, at the House of Representatives (in the same room in which he had taken the presidential oath of office on Mar 4, 1825). John Quincy Adams was the only US president whose father had also been president until George W. Bush became president in January 2001.

BALD IS IN! DAY. July 11. Annual celebration of the bald look for women, men and children with medical hair loss. Bald Is In! inspires people of all ages to choose bald. This day of awareness affirms that being bald is not only just okay—bald is in! Annually, the second Saturday in July. For info: Thea Chassin, Bald Girls Do Lunch, PO Box 9122, Scarborough, NY 10510. Phone: (800) 578-5332. E-mail: info@baldgirlsdolunch.org. Web: www.baldgirlsdolunch.org.

BOWDLER'S DAY. July 11. A day to remember the prudish medical doctor, Thomas Bowdler, born near Bath, England, on July 11, 1754. He gave up the practice of medicine and undertook the cleansing of the works of Shakespeare by removing all the words and expressions he considered to be indecent or impious. His *Family Shakespeare*, in 10 volumes, omitted all those words that "cannot with propriety be read aloud in a family." He also "purified" Edward Gibbon's *History of the Decline and Fall of the Roman Empire* and selections from the Old Testament. His name became synonymous with self-righteous expurgation, and the word *bowdlerize* has become part of the English language. Bowdler died at Rhyddings, in South Wales, Feb 24, 1825.

BRYNNER, YUL: 100th BIRTH ANNIVERSARY. July 11, 1920. The charismatic stage and screen actor was born Yuliy Borisovich Briner at Vladivostok, Russia. Before acting, Brynner was a circus performer on the trapeze. His big break was the title role of King Mongkut in the acclaimed and popular musical *The King and I* (1951). He won a Tony Award for his portrayal and then an Oscar in the film version of 1956. Brynner shaved his head for the role and then continued shaving it for a distinctive look. Other films include *The Ten Commandments, The Magnificent Seven* and *Westworld*. Brynner continued to play Mongkut for a total of 4,625 performances, a feat

that was honored with a special Tony Award in 1985. He was also a director, photographer and activist for refugees, serving as special consultant to the United Nations High Commissioner on Refugees. Brynner died Oct 10, 1985, at New York, NY.

BURR-HAMILTON DUEL: ANNIVERSARY. July 11, 1804. US vice president Aaron Burr shot and mortally wounded former secretary of the Treasury (and primary author of *The Federalist* papers) Alexander Hamilton in a duel at Weehawken, NJ, on this date. Hamilton had insulted Burr and refused to make a public apology. Hamilton died the next day. Although Burr returned to Washington, DC, to execute his duties as vice president, the duel ended his political career.

CARVER DAY. July 11. George Washington Carver National Monument, Diamond, MO. 77th annual. A celebration of the man that features ranger-led programs interpreting the life of Carver. Guest speakers, music groups, storytellers, junior ranger station and exhibits. Annually, the second Saturday in July. For info: George Washington Carver National Monument, 5646 Carver Rd, Diamond, MO 64840. Phone: (417) 325-4151. Fax: (417) 325-4231. E-mail: GWCA_interpretation@nps.gov. Web: www.nps.gov/gwca.

DAY OF THE FIVE BILLION: ANNIVERSARY. July 11, 1987. An eight-pound baby boy, Matej Gaspar, born at 1:35 AM, EST, at Zagreb, Yugoslavia, was proclaimed the five billionth inhabitant of Earth. The United Nations Fund for Population Activities, hoping to draw attention to population growth, proclaimed July 11 as "Day of the Five Billion," noting that 150 babies are born each minute. See also: "Day of the Six Billion: Anniversary" (Oct 12).

MAKE YOUR OWN SUNDAE DAY. July 11. Since 1992, a day to gather friends and family to create custom ice cream sundaes. Each attendee selects two candy toppings and one fruit topping, and then all toppings are made available. Creating themed or artistic sundaes is encouraged. Started by the Cooper family in Baltimore, MD, and now celebrated all over. Annually, July 11. For info: Jonathan Cooper, 5604 Roxbury Pl, Baltimore, MD 21209.

MONGOLIA: NAADAM NATIONAL HOLIDAY. July 11. Public holiday. Commemorates overthrow of the feudal monarch in 1921.

NAPALM USED: 75th ANNIVERSARY. July 11, 1945. The US dropped several thousand pounds of the recently developed weapon napalm on Japanese forces still holed up on Luzon in the Philippines during WWII. Napalm, which was later used heavily as a defoliant in Vietnam, was a thickener consisting of a mixture of aluminum soaps used to jell gasoline.

"THE NEWLYWED GAME" TV PREMIERE: ANNIVERSARY. July 11, 1966. Four newly married couples compete for prizes on this game show created by the inimitable Chuck Barris. The winners are the husband and wife who best predict each other's responses. Bob Eubanks served as host for three incarnations of the show.

NIAGARA MOVEMENT FOUNDED: ANNIVERSARY. July 11, 1905. Led by W.E.B. Du Bois, 29 black intellectuals and activists founded the Niagara Movement at Niagara Falls, ON, Canada. The name of their movement alluded both to the location of their founding and to the "mighty current" of protest they hoped to undam. The movement disbanded in 1910, and the NAACP took over its goals.

SMITH, JAMES: DEATH ANNIVERSARY. July 11, 1806. Signer of the Declaration of Independence, born at Ireland about 1719 (exact date unknown). Died at York, PA.

July 2020	S	M	T	W	T	F	S
				1	2	3	4
	5	6	7	8	9	10	11
	12	13	14	15	16	17	18
	19	20	21	22	23	24	25
	26	27	28	29	30	31	

SPACE MILESTONE: *SKYLAB* (US) FALLS TO EARTH. July 11, 1979. The 82-ton spacecraft launched May 14, 1973, reentered Earth's atmosphere. Expectation was that 20–25 tons probably would survive to hit Earth, including one piece of about 5,000 pounds. This forecast generated intense international public interest in where it would fall. The chance that some person would be hit by a piece of *Skylab* was calculated at one in 152. Targets were drawn and *Skylab* parties were held, but *Skylab* broke up and fell to Earth in a shower of pieces over the Indian Ocean and Australia, with no known casualties.

***TO KILL A MOCKINGBIRD* PUBLISHED: 60th ANNIVERSARY.** July 11, 1960. Harper Lee's evocative novel of tomboy Scout Finch coming of age in a Depression-era Alabama town was published this day by J.B. Lippincott. A bestseller almost immediately, it earned Lee a Pulitzer Prize on May 1, 1961. Librarians voted it the best novel of the 20th century.

UNITED NATIONS: WORLD POPULATION DAY. July 11. In June 1989 the Governing Council of the United Nations Development Programme recommended that July 11 be observed by the international community as World Population Day. An outgrowth of the Day of the Five Billion (July 11, 1987), this day seeks to focus public attention on the urgency and importance of population issues, particularly in the context of overall development plans and programs and the need to create solutions to these problems. For info: United Nations, Dept of Public Info, Public Inquiries Unit, RM GA-57, New York, NY 10017. Phone: (212) 963-4475. E-mail: inquiries@un.org.

WANAMAKER, JOHN: BIRTH ANNIVERSARY. July 11, 1838. Entrepreneur best known for creating a new kind of retail establishment in Philadelphia, PA, by combining specialty shops underneath one roof to form a department store—indeed, what would become one of the largest in the nation. Wanamaker cofounded a clothing firm with Nathan Brown in 1861, which led to his department store creation, John Wanamaker and Company, in 1869. From 1889 to 1893 he also held the position of US postmaster general. Born July 11, 1838, at Philadelphia, Wanamaker died there on Dec 12, 1922.

WHITE, E.B.: BIRTH ANNIVERSARY. July 11, 1899. Versatile author of books for adults and children (*Charlotte's Web, Stuart Little*) and editor at *The New Yorker*. Coauthor of *The Elements of Style*, one of the most acclaimed (and used) English-language style guides. Born at Mount Vernon, NY, White died at North Brooklyn, ME, Oct 1, 1985.

🎂 BIRTHDAYS TODAY

Giorgio Armani, 84, fashion designer, born Romagna, Italy, July 11, 1936.

Harold Bloom, 90, literary critic, born New York, NY, July 11, 1930.

Justin Chambers, 50, actor ("Grey's Anatomy," *The Wedding Planner*), born Springfield, OH, July 11, 1970.

Greg Grunberg, 54, actor ("Heroes," "Alias," "Felicity"), born Los Angeles, CA, July 11, 1966.

John Henson, 53, television personality ("Wipeout," "Talk Soup"), born Stamford, CT, July 11, 1967.

Jacoby Jones, 36, football player, born New Orleans, LA, July 11, 1984.

Stephen Lang, 68, actor (*Avatar, Public Enemies, Tombstone*), born Queens, NY, July 11, 1952.

Al MacInnis, 57, hockey executive and former player, born Inverness, NS, Canada, July 11, 1963.

Ed Markey, 74, US Senator (D, Massachusetts), born Malden, MA, July 11, 1946.

Bonnie Pointer, 69, singer (Pointer Sisters), born East Oakland, CA, July 11, 1951.

Michael Rosenbaum, 48, actor ("Smallville," *Sweet November*), born Oceanside, NJ, July 11, 1972.

Richie Sambora, 60, musician (Bon Jovi), born Amboy, NJ, July 11, 1960.

Joan Smalls, 32, model, born Joan Smalls Rodriguez at Hatillo, Puerto Rico, July 11, 1988.

Leon Spinks, 67, former boxer, born St. Louis, MO, July 11, 1953.

Beverly Todd, 74, actress, director, producer (*Baby Boom, Clara's Heart*), born Chicago, IL, July 11, 1946.

Suzanne Vega, 61, singer, born Santa Monica, CA, July 11, 1959.

Sela Ward, 64, actress ("CSI: New York," "Sisters," "Once and Again"), born Meridian, MS, July 11, 1956.

Caroline Wozniacki, 30, tennis player, born Odenske, Denmark, July 11, 1990.

July 12 — Sunday

DAY 194   **172 REMAINING**

BATTLE OF KURSK: ANNIVERSARY. July 12–Aug 23, 1943. The largest tank battle in history took place during WWII outside the small village of Prokhorovka, Russia. Nine hundred Russian tanks attacked an equal number of German Panther and Porsche tanks. Though the German equipment was larger, that advantage was lost in a close-range battle where the tanks lacked maneuverability. When Hitler ordered a cease-fire, 300 German tanks remained strewn over the field.

BERLE, MILTON: BIRTH ANNIVERSARY. July 12, 1908. His nickname was "Mr Television," but Milton Berle had a long career as a vaudeville, film, radio and theater comedian as well. He was born Mendel Berlinger at Harlem, NY. He was popular before becoming the host of NBC's "Texaco Star Theater" in 1948, but that variety show made him a huge national star. Dressing in drag, rattling off corny jokes and drawing the day's biggest stars, "Uncle Miltie" made the show a television event until its end in 1953. He was one of the first seven inductees into the Academy of Television Arts and Sciences' TV Hall of Fame. Berle died Mar 27, 2002, at Los Angeles, CA.

CLIBURN, VAN: BIRTH ANNIVERSARY. July 12, 1934. Internationally acclaimed pianist whose musical genius briefly thawed the cold war after he won the first Tchaikovsky Competition in 1958. Born Harvey Lavan Cliburn, Jr, at Shreveport, LA, Cliburn was taught piano by his mother as a child and made his concert debut in 1947. He thrilled Muscovites with his interpretation of the romantics at the Tchaikovsky Competition, and surprised competition officials asked Soviet premier Nikita Khrushchev's permission before awarding an American first prize. Cliburn subsequently embarked on a successful concert career and founded the Van Cliburn International Piano Competition to aid young pianists. He died Feb 27, 2013, at Fort Worth, TX, his longtime home. See also: "Van Cliburn Conquers Moscow: Anniversary" (Apr 14).

DIFFERENT COLORED EYES DAY. July 12. A day to celebrate the unique qualities of people—especially those with heterochromia iridis—two differently colored eyes. For info: Jeanne Quinn, B. Able, Inc, 1842 Fox Run Terrace, Warrington, PA 18976. E-mail: kwinzz@yahoo.com.

ENGLAND: THE OPEN. July 12–19. Royal St. George's, Sandwich, Kent. 149th open. One of the sporting world's greatest events, first held at Prestwick Golf Club, Scotland, in 1860. For info: The Open Ticket Office, The R&A, St. Andrews, Fife, Scotland KY16 9JD.

Phone: (44) (1334) 460000. E-mail: tickets@TheOpen.com. Web: www.TheOpen.com.

EURO 2020 FINAL (UEFA EUROPEAN SOCCER CHAMPIONSHIP). July 12. Wembley Stadium, London, England. Final crowns the European soccer champion of the two-year-long tournament of 53 national teams. For info: UEFA, Route de Geneve 46, CH-1260 Nyon 2, Switzerland. Web: www.uefa.com.

"EVENING AT POPS" TV PREMIERE: 50th ANNIVERSARY. July 12, 1970. PBS's popular concert series premiered with conductor Arthur Fiedler heading the Boston Pops Orchestra. Conductor/composer John Williams took over the post upon Fiedler's death in 1979; Keith Lockhart followed. The program concluded in 2005.

"FAMILY FEUD" TV PREMIERE: ANNIVERSARY. July 12, 1976. From the production team of Mark Goodson and Bill Todman, this game show sets two families against each other to accumulate the greater number of points. The contestants have to predict the most common answers to a given survey question. Richard Dawson (TV's famous kissing host), Ray Combs, Louie Anderson, Richard Karn, John O'Hurley and Steve Harvey have been hosts.

FULLER, BUCKMINSTER: 125th BIRTH ANNIVERSARY. July 12, 1895. Architect, inventor, engineer and philosopher, born Richard Buckminster Fuller at Milton, MA. His geodesic dome was one of the most important structural innovations of the 20th century. He died July 1, 1983, at Los Angeles, CA.

HAMMERSTEIN, OSCAR: 125th BIRTH ANNIVERSARY. July 12, 1895. Master of the "musical play" form, Oscar Hammerstein II was a titan of the theater. Born Oscar Greeley Clendenning Hammerstein at New York, NY, the lyricist, playwright and producer worked with such collaborators as Jerome Kern and—most famously—Richard Rodgers. The partnerships produced *Oklahoma!, Show Boat, Carousel, The King and I, South Pacific* and *Sound of Music,* among other well-known shows. Many of Hammerstein's songs have settled permanently into the repertoires of vocalists everywhere. The recipient of two Academy Awards, the Pulitzer Prize for Drama and eight Tony Awards, Hammerstein died Aug 23, 1960, at Doylestown, PA. Following his death, lights at Times Square, New York City, and the West End of London, England, were dimmed in his honor.

JONES WINS FIRST GRAND SLAM OF GOLF: 90th ANNIVERSARY. July 12, 1930. Bobby Jones won the US Open Championship by two strokes over Macdonald Smith at the Interlachen Country Club at Hopkins, MN. Having already won the British Open, the British Amateur and the US Amateur, Jones became the only golfer to win the Grand Slam (the four major tournaments in one calendar year)—a usage that had to be invented by sportswriters, since no one had achieved that feat before.

KIRIBATI: INDEPENDENCE DAY. July 12. Republic of Kiribati attained independence from Britain in 1979. Formerly known as the Gilbert Islands.

MOON PHASE: LAST QUARTER. July 12. Moon enters Last Quarter phase at 7:29 PM, EDT.

NATIONAL FARRIERS WEEK. July 12–18. A salute from the hoof-care community to the men and women who keep their horses shod and equine feet and legs in top-notch condition. Annually, the second week in July. For info: Michelle Drewek, *American Farriers Journal,* PO Box 624, Brookfield, WI 53008-0624. Phone: (262) 777-2435. Fax: (262) 782-1252. E-mail: mdrewek@lessitermedia.com.

NIGHT OF NIGHTS. July 12. Point Reyes Station, Point Reyes National Seashore, CA. Annual event held by the Maritime Radio Historical Society (MRHS) to commemorate the history of maritime radio and the closing of commercial Morse operations in the USA on July 12, 1999. These on-the-air events are intended to honor the men and women who followed the radiotelegraph trade on ships and at coast stations around the world and made it one of honor and skill. For Night of Nights stations KPH, KSM and KFS return to the air. Other stations including WLO, KLB, NMC and NOJ often join in. Calls from ships at sea make the event seem as if the golden age of maritime radio has returned. The transmitters are located in Bolinas, CA, at the transmitting station established in 1913 by the American Marconi Co. The original KPH transmitters, receivers and antennas are used to activate frequencies in all the commercial maritime HF bands and on MF as well. For info: MRHS, PO Box 392, Point Reyes Station, CA 94956. E-mail: info@radiomarine.org. Web: www.radiomarine.org.

"NORTHERN EXPOSURE" TV PREMIERE: 30th ANNIVERSARY. July 12, 1990. In CBS's comedy-drama Dr. Joel Fleischman (Rob Morrow) was forced to practice medicine in remote Cicely, AK, to pay off his student loans. He gradually accepted his lot with the help of the town's quirky citizens, who needed him because he was the only doctor in town. The show's cast included Janine Turner as bush pilot Maggie O'Connell and John Corbett as DJ Chris Stevens. The last episode aired in 1995.

SÃO TOMÉ AND PRÍNCIPE: INDEPENDENCE DAY. July 12. National holiday observed. Gained independence from Portugal in 1975.

SPACE MILESTONE: *PHOBOS 2* (USSR). July 12, 1988. Sent back the first close-up photos of Phobos, one of two small moons of Mars. Launched from Soviet space probe in central Asia on July 12, 1988.

SPORTS CLICHÉ WEEK. July 12–18. This week honors the use of sports clichés by fans, athletes, sports announcers and sportswriters. Annually, the week of the Major League Baseball All-Star Game. For info: Don Powell, PhD, 30445 Northwestern Hwy, Ste 350, Farmington Hills, MI 48334. Phone: (248) 539-1800, ext 235. Fax: (248) 539-1808. E-mail: dpowell@healthylife.com.

THOREAU, HENRY DAVID: BIRTH ANNIVERSARY. July 12, 1817. American author, teacher and philosopher, major figure of the transcendentalism movement, born at Concord, MA. He died at Concord on May 6, 1862. In his influential masterpiece *Walden* (1854) he wrote, "I frequently tramped eight or ten miles through the deepest snow to keep an appointment with a beechtree, or a yellow birch, or an old acquaintance among the pines."

WEDGWOOD, JOSIAH: BIRTH ANNIVERSARY. July 12, 1730. Famed pottery designer and manufacturer, born at Burslem, Staffordshire, England. Died at Etruria, Staffordshire, Jan 3, 1795.

🎂 BIRTHDAYS TODAY

Lisa Nicole Carson, 51, actress ("ER," "Ally McBeal"), born Brooklyn, NY, July 12, 1969.

Bill Cosby, 82, comedian, actor (Emmys for "I Spy" and "The Cosby Show"), born Philadelphia, PA, July 12, 1938.

Anna Friel, 44, actress ("Pushing Daisies," *Our Mutual Friend*), born Rochdale, Lancashire, England, July 12, 1976.

Jeff Glor, 45, broadcast anchor, journalist, born Buffalo, NY, July 12, 1975.

Mel Harris, 63, actress ("Something So Right," "thirtysomething"), born Bethlehem, PA, July 12, 1957.

July 2020	S	M	T	W	T	F	S
				1	2	3	4
	5	6	7	8	9	10	11
	12	13	14	15	16	17	18
	19	20	21	22	23	24	25
	26	27	28	29	30	31	

Cheryl Ladd, 68, actress ("Charlie's Angels"), born Huron, SD, July 12, 1952.

Brock Lesnar, 43, wrestler, mixed martial artist, born Webster, SD, July 12, 1977.

Christine McVie, 77, singer, musician (Fleetwood Mac), born Birmingham, England, July 12, 1943.

Denise Nicholas, 75, actress ("Room 222," "In the Heat of the Night," *Let's Do It Again*), born Detroit, MI, July 12, 1945.

Jamey Sheridan, 69, actor ("Law & Order: Criminal Intent," *The House on Carroll Street*), born Pasadena, CA, July 12, 1951.

Richard Simmons, 72, television personality, weight-loss guru, author, born New Orleans, LA, July 12, 1948.

Kyrsten Sinema, 44, US Senator (D, Arizona), born Tucson, AZ, July 12, 1976.

Erik Per Sullivan, 29, actor ("Malcolm in the Middle," *The Cider House Rules*), born Worcester, MA, July 12, 1991.

Rolonda Watts, 61, talk show host ("Rolonda"), born Winston-Salem, NC, July 12, 1959.

Jordyn Wieber, 25, Olympic gymnast, born Dewitt, MI, July 12, 1995.

Kristi Tsuya Yamaguchi, 49, Olympic figure skater, born Hayward, CA, July 12, 1971.

Malala Yousafzai, 23, activist for female education, Nobel Peace Prize recipient, born Mingora, Pakistan, July 12, 1997.

July 13 — Monday

DAY 195   **171 REMAINING**

DEMOCRATIC NATIONAL CONVENTION. July 13–16. Fiserv Forum, Milwaukee, WI. The Democratic Party meets to select its nominees for president and vice president in the 2020 election. Est attendance: 50,000. For info: Democratic National Committee, 430 S Capitol St SE, Washington, DC 20003. Phone: (202) 863-8000. Web: www.democrats.org.

EMBRACE YOUR GEEKNESS DAY. July 13. Into dungeon games, comic books and vampire dress-up? Spend endless hours going strange places on the Internet? You're a geek, and this is the day to roar! (©2006 by WH.) For info: Thomas & Ruth Roy, Wellcat Holidays, 2418 Long Ln, Lebanon, PA 17046. Phone: (717) 279-0184. E-mail: info@wellcat.com. Web: www.wellcat.com.

FORREST, NATHAN BEDFORD: BIRTH ANNIVERSARY. July 13, 1821. Confederate cavalry commander who specialized in fast-paced, mobile warfare. He was also one of the founders of the short-lived original Ku Klux Klan (1866–69). Forrest was born at Bedford County, TN, and died Oct 29, 1877, at Memphis, TN. His birthday is a special observance day in Tennessee.

FRANCE: NIGHT WATCH (LA RETRAITE AUX FLAMBEAUX). July 13. Celebration on the eve of Bastille Day with parades and fireworks.

GRUNTLED WORKERS DAY. July 13. There's so much news about disgruntled workers that today's the day for gruntled workers to unite! Drive to a fast-food restaurant and say, "Thanks. Your service is fast. Have a nice day." (©2006 by WH.) For info: Thomas & Ruth Roy, Wellcat Holidays, 2418 Long Ln, Lebanon, PA 17046. Phone: (717) 279-0184. E-mail: info@wellcat.com. Web: www.wellcat.com.

INTERNATIONAL TOWN CRIERS DAY. July 13. A day recognizing the ancient and honorable art and tradition of town crying and the significant contribution town criers make to promoting their respective towns and cities. Annually, the second Monday in July. For info: Doug Turvey, Official Town Crier, Township of Zorra and Town of Ingersoll, 784119 Rd 78, RR #5, Embro, ON, Canada N0J 1J0. Phone: (519) 537-9037. E-mail: zoringtowncrier@xplornet.com.

"LIVE AID" CONCERTS: 35th ANNIVERSARY. July 13, 1985. Concerts at Philadelphia, PA, and London, England (Kennedy and Wembley stadiums), were seen by 162,000 attendees and an estimated 1.5 billion television viewers. Organized to raise funds for African famine relief; the musicians performed without a fee, and nearly $100 million was pledged toward aid to the hungry.

NATIONAL BEEF TALLOW DAY. July 13. This day is a celebration of a traditional healthy animal fat—pure beef tallow shortening—that is now enjoying a resurgence within America's food culture, in restaurants, fast-food operations and home kitchens. Minimally processed animal fats like beef tallow make superior french fries and excel in a host of other cooking and frying applications. Annually, July 13. For info: Healthy Fats Coalition, Ken Greenberg, Edge Communications, Inc, 5417 Hollywood Blvd, C-727, Los Angeles, CA 90027. Web: www.healthyfatscoalition.org.

NATIONAL FRENCH FRY DAY. July 13. A day to celebrate and eat the crispy fried potato. Observed by many restaurants and fast-food chains. This food day's origin is unknown, but it has proven to be very popular beginning in the 2000s.

NATIONAL NITROGEN ICE CREAM DAY. July 13. Using nitrogen in the ice cream process results in a creamy, delicious product. Today, ice cream shops and their customers celebrate this innovative summer treat on the July 13, 1909, anniversary of Gustav Robert Paalen receiving a patent for the double-walled vessel—necessary for liquid nitrogen. Annually, July 13. For info: The Freezing Point. E-mail: info@freezingpoint.co. Web: www.nitrogenicecreamday.com.

NORTHERN IRELAND: ORANGEMEN'S DAY (OBSERVED). July 13. National holiday commemorates Battle of Boyne, July 1 (OS), 1690, in which the forces of King William III of England, Prince of Orange, defeated those of James II, at Boyne River in Ireland. Ordinarily observed on July 12, but if that date falls on a weekend, as it does in 2020, the holiday is celebrated on the following Monday.

REPUBLIC OF MONTENEGRO: NATIONAL DAY. July 13.

US GIRLS' JUNIOR (GOLF) CHAMPIONSHIP. July 13–18. Eisenhower Golf Course, Colorado Springs, CO. For info: USGA, Golf House, Championship Dept, PO Box 708, Far Hills, NJ 07931. Phone: (908) 234-2300. E-mail: champs@usga.org. Web: www.usga.org.

WORLD CUP INAUGURATED: 90th ANNIVERSARY. July 13, 1930. The first World Cup soccer competition was held at Montevideo, Uruguay, with 14 countries participating. On July 30 Uruguay defeated Argentina by a score of 4–2 to take the Cup.

🎂 BIRTHDAYS TODAY

Cameron Crowe, 63, director, screenwriter (*Fast Times at Ridgemont High, Jerry Maguire,* Oscar for *Almost Famous*), born Palm Springs, CA, July 13, 1957.

Harrison Ford, 78, actor (*Witness, The Fugitive, Star Wars* films, *Indiana Jones* films), born Chicago, IL, July 13, 1942.

Robert Forster, 79, actor ("Banyon," *Diamond Men, Jackie Brown*), born Rochester, NY, July 13, 1941.

Jane Hamilton, 63, author (*A Map of the World, The Book of Ruth*), born Oak Park, IL, July 13, 1957.

Ken Jeong, 51, comedian, actor (*Crazy Rich Asians, The Hangover,* "Community"), physician, born Kendrick Kang-Joh Jeong at Detroit, MI, July 13, 1969.

Louise Mandrell, 66, country singer, born Corpus Christi, TX, July 13, 1954.

Cheech Marin, 74, writer, actor (Cheech and Chong films, "Nash Bridges"), born Los Angeles, CA, July 13, 1946.

Roger McGuinn, 78, musician (The Byrds), born James Joseph McGuinn at Chicago, IL, July 13, 1942.

Erno Rubik, 76, inventor of the Rubik's Cube, born in a hospital air raid shelter, Budapest, Hungary, July 13, 1944.

Wole Soyinka, 86, Nobel Prize–winning author (*The Lion and the Jewel, The Strong Breed*), born Abeokuta, Nigeria, July 13, 1934.

Michael Spinks, 64, former boxer, born St. Louis, MO, July 13, 1956.

Patrick Stewart, 80, actor ("Star Trek: The Next Generation," *X-Men* films, *A Christmas Carol*), born Mirfield, England, July 13, 1940.

David Storey, 87, author (*This Sporting Life, Saville*), playwright, born Wakefield, England, July 13, 1933.

July 14 — Tuesday

DAY 196	170 REMAINING

BASCOM, FLORENCE: BIRTH ANNIVERSARY. July 14, 1862. After receiving her third bachelor's degree from the University of Wisconsin in 1884 and a master's degree in 1887, Florence Bascom entered Johns Hopkins University and received a doctorate in 1893. She taught at Ohio State and became a professor at Bryn Mawr College. She also was the first woman appointed a geologist with the US Geological Survey, was associate editor of *American Geologist* (1890–1905) and became the first woman elected a Fellow of the Geological Society of America. Born at Williamstown, MA; died at Northampton, MA, June 18, 1945.

BERGMAN, INGMAR: BIRTH ANNIVERSARY. July 14, 1918. One of the most influential filmmakers of the 20th century, Bergman directed such classics as *Fanny and Alexander, Wild Strawberries* and *Cries and Whispers.* He wrote or directed 62 films and more than 170 stage plays, mainly in his native Sweden, but was renowned all over the world and was nominated for nine Academy Awards. Born at Uppsala, Sweden, he died July 30, 2007, at Faro, Sweden.

BIRMINGHAM RIOTS: ANNIVERSARY. July 14, 1791. A dinner celebrating the second anniversary of the fall of the Bastille proved the spark to kindle into fire riots of angry anti–French Revolution mobs at Birmingham, England. The main target of their wrath was scientist (discoverer of oxygen) Joseph Priestley, who approved of the American and French revolutionary causes and who held unpopular religious views. The mob ruled Birmingham for three days, burning Priestley's home and laboratory as well as the homes of his friends. Priestley, in disguise, and his family narrowly escaped with their lives. See also: "Priestley, Joseph: Birth Anniversary" (Mar 13).

CHANCELLOR, JOHN: BIRTH ANNIVERSARY. July 14, 1927. Television broadcast journalist John Chancellor was born at Chicago, IL. He rose through the ranks at the *Chicago Sun-Times*, from copyboy to feature writer. Chancellor spent more than four decades with the NBC network, beginning in 1950. During that time he took a two-year respite from journalism to serve President Lyndon Johnson as director of the Voice of America. Chancellor retired in 1993. He died July 12, 1996, at Princeton, NJ.

EDWARDS, DOUGLAS: BIRTH ANNIVERSARY. July 14, 1917. American television journalist Douglas Edwards was born at Ada, OK. He began his career in radio, but in 1947 he became the first major announcer to move to television. He was anchor for CBS's first nightly news program, "Douglas Edwards with the News" (1948–62), where he gave memorable on-scene coverage of such events as the sinking of the *Andrea Doria* in 1956. Edwards worked for CBS until his retirement, two years before he died on Oct 13, 1990, at Sarasota, FL.

July 2020	S	M	T	W	T	F	S
				1	2	3	4
	5	6	7	8	9	10	11
	12	13	14	15	16	17	18
	19	20	21	22	23	24	25
	26	27	28	29	30	31	

FORD, GERALD RUDOLPH: BIRTH ANNIVERSARY. July 14, 1913. 38th president of the US (1974–77). Born Leslie King at Omaha, NE, Ford became 41st vice president of the US on Dec 6, 1973, by appointment, following the resignation of Spiro T. Agnew from that office on Oct 10, 1973. Ford became president on Aug 9, 1974, following the resignation from that office on that day of Richard M. Nixon. He was the first nonelected vice president and president of the US. He died at Rancho Mirage, CA, Dec 26, 2006.

FRANCE: BASTILLE DAY OR FÉTE NATIONALE. July 14. Public holiday commemorating the fall of the Bastille prison at the beginning of the French Revolution, July 14, 1789. Also celebrated or observed in many other countries.

GUTHRIE, WOODROW WILSON "WOODY": BIRTH ANNIVERSARY. July 14, 1912. American folksinger, songwriter (more than 3,000 songs) born at Okemah, OK. He traveled the country—a figure of hope to others suffering in the Great Depression. He wrote in 1944, "I hate a song that makes you think that you are just born to lose. . . . I am out to fight those kinds of songs to my very last breath of air and my last drop of blood." Guthrie wrote one of America's unofficial national anthems, "This Land Is Your Land," in 1940 and recorded it in 1944—it is now in the Library of Congress's National Recording Registry. He was diagnosed in 1954 with Huntington's chorea and was hospitalized for the rest of his life. Guthrie died Oct 3, 1967, at Creedmoor State Hospital, in Queens, NY.

HANNA, WILLIAM: BIRTH ANNIVERSARY. July 14, 1910. Born at Melrose, NM, William Hanna was the cocreator of such popular animated characters as Tom and Jerry, Yogi Bear, Snagglepuss and Magilla Gorilla. With partner Joe Barbera, he won seven Academy Awards for his Tom and Jerry cartoon shorts, and eight other works were nominated. The Hanna-Barbera team created the first animated TV sitcom for adults, *The Flintstones* (1960), and such favorites as *The Jetsons* and *Scooby-Doo, Where Are You!* Hanna died at Los Angeles, CA, on Mar 22, 2001.

ITALY DECLARES WAR ON JAPAN: 75th ANNIVERSARY. July 14, 1945. Italy, no longer in the control of the Fascists, dramatically ended its Axis partnership by declaring war on Japan.

MAJOR LEAGUE BASEBALL ALL-STAR GAME. July 14. Dodger Stadium, Los Angeles, CA. 91st annual All-Star Game. For info: Major League Baseball. Web: www.mlb.com/all-star.

MISSION SAN ANTONIO DE PADUA: FOUNDING ANNIVERSARY. July 14. California. Mission to the Indians founded July 14, 1771.

SPACE MILESTONE: *NEW HORIZONS* REACHES PLUTO. July 14, 2015. Though it took a 3.6-billion-mile trip and more than a decade, we now have the clearest pictures of Pluto to date. NASA's *New Horizons* spacecraft completed its planned flyby of Pluto, at one point coming just 7,750 miles above the dwarf planet's surface. The spacecraft has begun sending both images and data back to Earth as part of the mission's goal of helping us understand the formation and transformation of the early solar system.

🧁 BIRTHDAYS TODAY

Matthew Fox, 54, actor ("Lost," "Party of Five"), born Crowheart, WY, July 14, 1966.

Missy Gold, 50, actress ("Benson"), born Great Falls, MT, July 14, 1970.

Roosevelt (Rosey) Grier, 88, inspirational speaker, actor, former football player, born Cuthbert, GA, July 14, 1932.

Jackie Earle Haley, 59, actor (*Breaking Away, The Bad News Bears, Little Children*), born Northridge, CA, July 14, 1961.

Maulana Karenga, 79, scholar, author, creator of holiday of Kwanzaa, born Ronald Everett at Parsonsburg, MD, July 14, 1941.

Jane Lynch, 60, actress ("Glee," "The Cleveland Show," *The 40-Year-Old Virgin*), born Dolton, IL, July 14, 1960.

Conor McGregor, 32, mixed martial artist, former UFC featherweight and lightweight champion, born Dublin, Ireland, July 14, 1988.

Scott Porter, 41, actor ("Hart of Dixie," "Friday Night Lights"), born Omaha, NE, July 14, 1979.

Joel Silver, 68, producer (*Lethal Weapon, Die Hard*), born South Orange, NJ, July 14, 1952.

Steve Stone, 73, sportscaster, former baseball player, born Euclid, OH, July 14, 1947.

Robin Ventura, 53, baseball manager and former player, born Santa Maria, CA, July 14, 1967.

Phoebe Waller-Bridge, 35, actress ("Fleabag"), playwright (*Fleabag*), writer, born London, England, July 14, 1985.

July 15 — Wednesday

DAY 197   **169 REMAINING**

BATTLE OF GRUNWALD: ANNIVERSARY. July 15, 1410. (Also known as the Battle of Tannenberg.) Poland and Lithuania joined forces to halt the aggressive advance of the Knights of the Teutonic Order, and they emerged victorious after a 10-hour battle near the villages of Tannenberg and Grunwald in Poland. The political and military power of the Teutonic Knights was severely diminished after this defeat.

DERRIDA, JACQUES: 90th BIRTH ANNIVERSARY. July 15, 1930. Influential French philosopher; proponent of deconstruction. Born at El Biar, Algeria, Derrida died Oct 8, 2004, at Paris, France.

FAIRFEST. July 15–19. Adams County Fairgrounds, Hastings, NE. Annual county fair featuring midway; open-class competitions in culinary arts, needlework, floral culture, woodworking and the visual arts; Adams County 4-H competition; livestock show; strolling acts and live entertainment. Est attendance: 60,000. For info: Jolene Laux, 947 S Baltimore, Hastings, NE 68901. Phone: (402) 462-3247. Fax: (402) 462-4731. Web: www.adamscountyfairgrounds.com.

FOWLER, JOHN: BIRTH ANNIVERSARY. July 15, 1817. Born at Sheffield, England, Fowler was an engineer renowned for his work on British bridges and railways. He constructed Victoria Station (1860) and the Grosvenor Bridge across the Thames River (the first railway bridge across that river, 1860) and was chief engineer of the 8,000-foot-long cantilever Forth Bridge (1890) over the Firth of Forth near Edinburgh, Scotland, which is now a UNESCO World Heritage Site. He was the engineer of the London Metropolitan Railway—now known as the London Underground—which was the world's first underground subway system. President of the Institute of Civil Engineers, Fowler died Nov 20, 1898, at Bournemouth, England.

JAPAN: BON FESTIVAL (FEAST OF LANTERNS). July 15 (also Aug 15). Religious rites throughout Japan in memory of the dead, who, according to Buddhist belief, revisit Earth during this period. During a three-day period centered on July 15, lanterns are lighted for the souls. Spectacular bonfires in the shape of the character *dai* are burned on hillsides on the last day of the Bon (or O-Bon) Festival, bidding farewell to the spirits of the dead. (Some regions celebrate around Aug 15.)

MOORE, CLEMENT CLARKE: BIRTH ANNIVERSARY. July 15, 1779. American author and teacher, best remembered for his popular verse "A Visit from Saint Nicholas" ("'Twas the Night Before Christmas"), which was first published anonymously and without Moore's knowledge in a newspaper, Dec 23, 1823. Moore was born at New York, NY, and died at Newport, RI, July 10, 1863. (In recent years Moore's authorship of the poem has been challenged, with Henry Livingston, Jr, offered as the creator.)

"ONE LIFE TO LIVE" TV PREMIERE: ANNIVERSARY. July 15, 1968. Set in a fictional Pennsylvania town, this Agnes Nixon drama originally depicted the class and ethnic struggles of the town's denizens, and the initial cast featured many Jewish, Polish and African-American characters. The show departed from interethnic storytelling in the 1980s for more fantastic adventures set in heaven, the Old West and a futuristic mountain silo called Eternia. After that phase, the show returned to its strengths of traditional storytelling by featuring Latino and African-American actors as integral characters. Award-winning actress Erika Slezak headed the cast as the venerable Viki Lord Riley Buchanan Carpenter, the town's matron with five alternate personalities. Among those who appeared on "OLTL" were Tom Berenger, Judith Light, Tommy Lee Jones, Laurence Fishburne, Jameson Parker, Phylicia Rashad, Christine Ebersole, Richard Grieco, Blair Underwood, Joe Lando, Audrey Landers, Christian Slater and Yasmine Bleeth. Although canceled in 2011—with the final episode airing Jan 13, 2012—the show returned in a new incarnation as a Web series in 2013.

REMBRANDT: BIRTH ANNIVERSARY. July 15, 1606. Dutch painter and etcher, born Rembrandt Harmenszoon van Rijn at Leiden, Netherlands. One of the undisputed giants of Western art. Known for *The Night Watch* and many portraits and self-portraits. He died at Amsterdam, Netherlands, Oct 4, 1669.

SAINT FRANCES XAVIER CABRINI: BIRTH ANNIVERSARY. July 15, 1850. First American saint, founder of schools, orphanages, convents and hospitals, born at Lombardy, Italy. Died of malaria at Chicago, IL, Dec 22, 1917. Canonized July 7, 1946.

SAINT SWITHIN'S DAY. July 15. Swithin (or Swithun), bishop of Winchester (AD 852–862), died July 2, 862. Little is known of his life, but his relics were transferred into Winchester Cathedral July 15, 971, a day on which there was a heavy rainfall. According to old English belief, it will rain for 40 days thereafter when it rains on this day. "St. Swithin's Day, if thou dost rain, for 40 days it will remain; St. Swithin's Day, if thou be fair, for 40 days, will rain nea mair."

SECOND BATTLE OF THE MARNE: ANNIVERSARY. July 15, 1918. General Erich Ludendorff launched Germany's fifth, and last, offensive to break through the Chateau-Thierry salient in WWI. This all-out effort involved three armies branching out from Reims, France, to cross the Marne River. The Germans were successful in crossing the Marne near Chateau-Thierry before American, British and Italian divisions stopped their progress. On

July 18 General Ferdinand Foch, commander in chief of the Allied troops, launched a massive counteroffensive that resulted in a German retreat that continued for four months until Germany sued for peace in November.

TAKE YOUR POET TO WORK DAY. July 15. 8th annual. Why should kids have all the fun? Poets want to be taken to the workplace too. Take Your Poet to Work Day is a quirky, celebration-style day to do just that: take your poet to work. But not the way you might think. Tweetspeak Poetry provides the custom illustration cutouts; employees all over the world provide the scissors, markers, glue and popsicle sticks—so they can take their poets of choice to work. From Australia to Russia, Turkey to France, people share their pictures of how they take their poets to work on a stick. Tweetspeak Poetry features the creative, beautiful or just plain fun (Emily Dickinson has shown up in Goth, Donne sent airport pictures and Eliot was seen tucked into a matchbox bed). Annually, third Wednesday in July. For info: Tweetspeak Poetry. Phone: (914) 944-9036. E-mail: editor@tspoetry.com. Web: www.tweetspeakpoetry.com.

UNITED NATIONS: WORLD YOUTH SKILLS DAY. July 15. A day to draw attention to the need for education and training for the world's youth. Young people are almost three times more likely to be unemployed than adults and continuously exposed to lower quality of jobs, greater labor market inequalities and longer and more insecure school-to-work transitions. In addition, young women are more likely to be underemployed and underpaid and to undertake part-time jobs or work under temporary contracts. For info: United Nations. Web: www.un.org/en/events/youthskillsday.

🎂 BIRTHDAYS TODAY

Willie Aames, 60, actor ("Eight Is Enough," "Charles in Charge"), born Newport Beach, CA, July 15, 1960.

Kim Alexis, 60, model, born Lockport, NY, July 15, 1960.

Julian Bream, 87, musician (classical guitar, lute), born London, England, July 15, 1933.

Jonathan Cheechoo, 40, hockey player, born Moose Factory, ON, Canada, July 15, 1980.

Clive Cussler, 89, author (*Raise the Titanic!, Sahara, Inca Gold*), marine historian, born Aurora, IL, July 15, 1931.

Lolita Davidovich, 59, actress (*Indictment, Cobb*), born London, ON, Canada, July 15, 1961.

Brian Austin Green, 47, actor ("Beverly Hills 90210"), singer, born Van Nuys, CA, July 15, 1973.

Arianna Huffington, 70, author, journalist (*The Huffington Post*), born Athens, Greece, July 15, 1950.

Irene Jacob, 54, actress (*Red, Othello*), born Paris, France, July 15, 1966.

Taylor Kinney, 39, actor ("Chicago Fire," "The Vampire Diaries"), born Lancaster, PA, July 15, 1981.

Damian Lillard, 30, basketball player, born Oakland, CA, July 15, 1990.

Angela Merkel, 66, Chancellor of Germany (2005–), born Hamburg, Germany, July 15, 1954.

Terry O'Quinn, 68, actor ("Lost," "The West Wing," "Alias"), born Newberry, MI, July 15, 1952.

Lana Parrilla, 43, actress ("Once Upon a Time," "Swingtown"), born Brooklyn, NY, July 15, 1977.

Linda Ronstadt, 74, singer, songwriter, born Tucson, AZ, July 15, 1946.

Richard Russo, 71, author (*Empire Falls, Straight Man, Nobody's Fool*), born Johnstown, NY, July 15, 1949.

July 2020	S	M	T	W	T	F	S
				1	2	3	4
	5	6	7	8	9	10	11
	12	13	14	15	16	17	18
	19	20	21	22	23	24	25
	26	27	28	29	30	31	

Adam Savage, 53, television personality, host ("MythBusters"), born New York, NY, July 15, 1967.

Jesse Ventura, 69, former professional wrestler, former governor of Minnesota (I), born Minneapolis, MN, July 15, 1951.

Forest Whitaker, 59, actor (Oscar for *The Last King of Scotland*; "The Shield," *Bird, The Crying Game*), director (*Waiting to Exhale*), born Longview, TX, July 15, 1961.

July 16 — Thursday

DAY 198 **168 REMAINING**

AMAZON INCORPORATED: 25th ANNIVERSARY. July 16, 1995. Amazon.com was first incorporated as an online bookstore by founder Jeff Bezos at Seattle, WA.

AMUNDSEN, ROALD: BIRTH ANNIVERSARY. July 16, 1872. Norwegian explorer born near Oslo, Norway, Roald Amundsen was the first man to sail from the Atlantic Ocean to the Pacific Ocean via the Northwest Passage (1903–05). He discovered the South Pole (Dec 14, 1911) and flew over the North Pole in a dirigible in 1926. He flew, with five companions, from Norway on June 18, 1928, in a daring effort to rescue survivors of an Italian Arctic expedition. No trace of the rescue party or the airplane was ever located. See also: "South Pole Discovery: Anniversary" (Dec 14).

ATOMIC BOMB TESTED: 75th ANNIVERSARY. July 16, 1945. In the New Mexican desert at Alamogordo Air Base, 125 miles southeast of Albuquerque, the experimental atomic bomb was set off at 5:30 AM. Dubbed "Fat Boy" by its creator, the plutonium bomb vaporized the steel scaffolding holding it as the immense fireball rose 8,000 feet in a fraction of a second—ultimately creating a mushroom cloud to a height of 41,000 feet. At ground zero the bomb emitted heat three times the temperature of the interior of the sun. All plant and animal life for a mile around ceased to exist. When informed by President Truman at Potsdam, Germany, of the successful experiment, Winston Churchill responded, "It's the Second Coming in wrath!"

BOLIVIA: LA PAZ DAY. July 16. Founding of city, now capital of Bolivia, on this day, 1548.

COMET CRASHES INTO JUPITER: ANNIVERSARY. July 16, 1994. The first fragment of the comet Shoemaker-Levy crashed into the planet Jupiter, beginning a series of spectacular collisions, each unleashing more energy than the combined effect of an explosion of all our world's nuclear arsenal. Video imagery from earthbound telescopes as well as the Hubble telescope provided vivid records of the explosions and their aftereffects. In 1993 the comet had shattered into a series of about a dozen large chunks that resembled "pearls on a string" after its orbit brought it within the gravitational effects of our solar system's largest planet.

DISTRICT OF COLUMBIA ESTABLISHING LEGISLATION: ANNIVERSARY. July 16, 1790. George Washington signed legislation that selected the District of Columbia as the permanent capital of the US. Boundaries of the district were established in 1792. Plans called for the government to remain housed at Philadelphia, PA, until 1800, when the new national capital would be ready for occupancy.

EARTHQUAKE JOLTS PHILIPPINES: 30th ANNIVERSARY. July 16, 1990. An earthquake measuring 7.7 on the Richter scale struck the Philippines, killing an estimated 1,621 persons and leaving approximately 1,000 missing. The quake struck in an area north of Manila, and heavy damage was reported at Cabanatuan, at Baguio and on Luzon island. The quake was the worst in the Philippines in 14 years.

EDDY, MARY BAKER: BIRTH ANNIVERSARY. July 16, 1821. Founder of Christian Science; born near Concord, NH, she died at Chestnut Hill, MA, Dec 3, 1910.

MISSION SAN DIEGO DE ALCALA: FOUNDING ANNIVERSARY. July 16, 1769. First of 21 California missions to the Indians.

RAFLE DU VÉLODROME D'HIVER: ANNIVERSARY. July 16, 1942. In the largest roundup of Jews in occupied France to date, nearly 13,000 Jews, mainly foreign-born, were arrested and held at the Vélodrome d'Hiver, an indoor cycling track. After five days, men, women and children were separated for transport to a holding camp and then to Auschwitz. The raids were conducted by French police, with the help of volunteers from the PPF, France's largest Fascist party. French president Jacques Chirac admitted and apologized for French complicity in the deportations on July 16, 1995.

REYNOLDS, JOSHUA: BIRTH ANNIVERSARY. July 16, 1723. (Old Style date.) English portrait painter whose paintings of 18th-century English notables are among the best of the time. Born at Plympton, Devon, England, Sir Joshua died at London, Feb 23, 1792, at age 68. "He who resolves never to ransack any mind but his own," Reynolds told students of the Royal Academy in 1774, "will be soon reduced, from mere barrenness, to the poorest of all imitations; he will be obliged to imitate himself, and to repeat what he has before often repeated."

ROGERS, GINGER: BIRTH ANNIVERSARY. July 16, 1911. Born Virginia Katherine McMath at Independence, MO, Ginger Rogers won a Charleston contest when she was 15, a feat that began a six-decade career in vaudeville, Broadway and film. She became a star of the silver screen as Fred Astaire's dance partner in 10 romantic musicals, including *Top Hat* (1935) and *Swing Time* (1936). Rogers was a versatile actress who appeared in 70 films, winning an Oscar for her performance in *Kitty Foyle* (1940). She died on Apr 25, 1995, at Rancho Mirage, CA.

SPACE MILESTONE: *APOLLO 11* **(US): MAN SENT TO THE MOON.** July 16, 1969. This launch resulted in man's first moon landing, the first landing on any extraterrestrial body. See also: "Space Milestone: Moon Day" (July 20).

STANWYCK, BARBARA: BIRTH ANNIVERSARY. July 16, 1907. Actress Barbara Stanwyck was born Ruby Stevens at the Flatbush section of Brooklyn, NY. At the age of 18 she won a leading role in the Broadway melodrama *Noose*, appearing for the first time as Barbara Stanwyck. She appeared in 82 films including *Stella Dallas*, *Double Indemnity* and *The Lady Eve* and in the television series "The Big Valley." In 1944 the government listed her as the nation's highest-paid woman, earning $400,000 per year. Stanwyck died at Santa Monica, CA, Jan 21, 1990.

WELLS, IDA B.: BIRTH ANNIVERSARY. July 16, 1862. African-American journalist and antilynching crusader Ida B. Wells was born the daughter of slaves at Holly Springs, MS, and grew up as Jim Crow and lynching were becoming prevalent. Wells argued that lynchings occurred not to defend white women but because of whites' fear of economic competition from blacks. She traveled extensively, founding antilynching societies and black women's clubs. Wells's *Red Record* (1895) was one of the first published accounts of lynchings in the South. She died Mar 25, 1931, at Chicago, IL.

🎂 BIRTHDAYS TODAY

Gareth Bale, 31, soccer player, born Cardiff, Wales, July 16, 1989.

Ruben Blades, 72, singer, actor (*Crossover Dreams, The Milagro Beanfield War*), born Panama City, Panama, July 16, 1948.

Phoebe Cates, 57, actress (*Fast Times at Ridgemont High, Gremlins*), born New York, NY, July 16, 1963.

Stewart Copeland, 68, composer, musician (The Police), born Alexandria, VA, July 16, 1952.

Corey Feldman, 49, actor (*Stand by Me, The Lost Boys*), born Reseda, CA, July 16, 1971.

Will Ferrell, 53, comedian, actor (*Semi-Pro, Blades of Glory, Stranger than Fiction, Anchorman*), born Irvine, CA, July 16, 1967.

Michael Flatley, 62, dancer (*Lord of the Dance, Feet of Flames*), born Chicago, IL, July 16, 1958.

Mark Indelicato, 26, actor ("Ugly Betty"), born Philadelphia, PA, July 16, 1994.

Jayma Mays, 41, actress ("Glee," "Heroes," "Ugly Betty"), born Grundy, VA, July 16, 1979.

Barry Sanders, 52, Hall of Fame football player, born Wichita, KS, July 16, 1968.

Pinchas Zukerman, 72, violinist, born Tel Aviv, Israel, July 16, 1948.

July 17 — Friday

DAY 199   **167 REMAINING**

ABBOTT, BERENICE: BIRTH ANNIVERSARY. July 17, 1898. Berenice Abbott was born at Springfield, OH, and went on to become a pioneer of American photography. She is best remembered for her black-and-white photographs of New York City in the 1930s, many of which appeared in the book *Changing New York*. After publishing this collection, she began photographing scientific experiments that illustrated the laws and processes of physics. She died at Monson, ME, Dec 11, 1991.

ASTOR, JOHN JACOB: BIRTH ANNIVERSARY. July 17, 1763. Founder of what is considered the first American business monopoly—the American Fur Company (1808)—Astor broke into the fur trade in 1786 by starting a fur-goods store in New York City. He made considerable transactions in Canada and the Great Lakes region as well as China, through special permission from the British East India Company. Astor was born near Waldorf, Germany, the son of a poor butcher, but by the time he died Mar 29, 1848, at New York, NY, he was the wealthiest person in the United States and had established an Astor dynasty.

BELGIUM: TOMORROWLAND. July 17–19 and July 24–26 (tentative). Boom. Since 2005. Largest electronic music festival in the world, taking place in Boom, near Antwerp. Tickets frequently sell out in minutes. Annually, the third and fourth weekends in July. Est attendance: 180,000. For info: Tomorrowland. Web: www.tomorrowland.com.

BIG SKY STATE GAMES. July 17–19. Billings, MT. An Olympic-style festival for Montana citizens. This statewide, multisport program is designed to inspire people of all ages and skill levels to develop their physical and competitive abilities to the height of their potential through participation in fitness activities. There are 10,000 participants in 36 sports. Est attendance: 30,000. For info: Big Sky State Games, Box 7136, Billings, MT 59103-7136. Phone: (406) 254-7426. Fax: (406) 254-7439. E-mail: info@bigskygames.org. Web: www.bigskygames.org.

CZAR NICHOLAS II AND FAMILY EXECUTED: ANNIVERSARY. July 17, 1918. Russian czar Nicholas II; his wife, Alexandra; son and heir, Alexis; and daughters, Anastasia, Tatiana, Olga and Marie, were executed by firing squad on this date. The murder of the last of the 300-year-old Romanov dynasty occurred at Yekaterinburg, in the Ural Mountains of Siberia, where Nicholas had been imprisoned since his abdication in 1917. Local Soviet officials, concerned about advancing promonarchist forces, executed the royal family rather than have them serve as a rallying point for the White Russians. In 1992 two of nine skeletons dug up the previous summer from a pit at Yekaterinburg were identified as the remains of the czar and czarina.

DILLER, PHYLLIS: BIRTH ANNIVERSARY. July 17, 1917. "Burt Reynolds once asked me out. I was in his room." With her incisive wit, legendary verve and singularly female presence in the standup comedy boys' club, Phyllis Diller broke ground and busted guts for more than 60 years. Born Phyllis Ada Driver July 17, 1917, at Ada, OH, Diller made her standup debut at San Francisco, CA, as a 37-year-old housewife. Appearances on "The Tonight Show" and "The Ed Sullivan Show" raised her profile, and a series of successful comedy albums appeared throughout the 1960s. Diller acted in films alongside mentor Bob Hope and was a regular on American television, often lending her trademark cackle to comedy and variety programs. She was also a successful author. Diller died Aug 20, 2012, at Los Angeles, CA.

DISNEYLAND OPENED: 65th ANNIVERSARY. July 17, 1955. Disneyland, America's first theme park, opened at Anaheim, CA.

GARDNER, ERLE STANLEY: BIRTH ANNIVERSARY. July 17, 1889. American author of detective fiction, born at Malden, MA. Best remembered for his smash-hit series featuring lawyer-detective Perry Mason, who debuted in *The Case of the Velvet Claws* in 1933. Perry Mason is probably the most famous lawyer in popular culture: he was featured in 82 novels as well as on TV and film. At the height of their popularity, Mason novels sold 20,000 copies a day. Gardner died at Temecula, CA, Mar 11, 1970.

GERRY, ELBRIDGE: BIRTH ANNIVERSARY. July 17, 1744. The fifth vice president of the US (1813–14), born at Marblehead, MA. Died at Washington, DC, Nov 23, 1814. His name became part of the language (gerrymander) after he signed a redistricting bill favoring his party while governor of Massachusetts in 1812.

KANSAS CITY HOTEL DISASTER: ANNIVERSARY. July 17, 1981. Anniversary of the collapse of aerial walkways at the Hyatt Regency Hotel at Kansas City, MO. About 1,500 people were attending the popular weekly tea dance when, at about 7 PM, two concrete and steel skywalks that were suspended from the ceiling of the hotel's atrium broke loose and fell on guests in the crowded lobby, killing 114 people. In 1986 a state board revoked the licenses of two engineers convicted of gross negligence for their part in designing the hotel.

July 2020	S	M	T	W	T	F	S
				1	2	3	4
	5	6	7	8	9	10	11
	12	13	14	15	16	17	18
	19	20	21	22	23	24	25
	26	27	28	29	30	31	

KOREA: CONSTITUTION DAY. July 17. Legal national holiday. Commemorates the proclamation of the constitution of the Republic of Korea in 1948. Ceremonies at Seoul's capitol plaza and all major cities.

MALAYSIA AIRLINES FLIGHT 17 SHOT DOWN: ANNIVERSARY. July 17, 2014. An international flight from Amsterdam to Kuala Lumpur was shot down by pro-Russian Ukrainian separatists, killing all 298 passengers and crew. The plane crashed near the Russian-Ukrainian border, during the military conflict that has engulfed the region.

MINIMUM LEGAL DRINKING AGE AT 21: ANNIVERSARY. July 17, 1984. Mothers Against Drunk Driving (MADD) helped pass the 21 Minimum Legal Drinking Age (MLDA) law because it makes sense and saves lives. President Ronald Reagan signed MLDA federal legislation making it illegal for anyone under 21 to purchase or publicly possess alcohol. An estimated 1,000 lives are saved each year as a result. For info: MADD. Phone: (877) 275-6233. E-mail: media@madd.org. Web: www.madd.org.

NORTH DAKOTA STATE FAIR. July 17–25. Minot, ND. The North Dakota State Fair features the best in big-name entertainment, farm and home exhibits, displays, midway and rodeo."Where Summer Shines." Est attendance: 300,000. For info: North Dakota State Fair, PO Box 1796, Minot, ND 58702. Phone: (701) 857-7620. Web: www.ndstatefair.com.

POTSDAM CONFERENCE: 75th ANNIVERSARY. July 17–Aug 2, 1945. The Allied Big Three (the US, Soviet Union and Great Britain) met in a palace at Potsdam, Germany, to discuss Germany's future. On Aug 1 they issued a 6,000-word communiqué laying out how Germany would be disarmed, the Nazi Party abolished and the country divided into four sectors (with France designated the fourth country to occupy a zone). Reparations were set, with the Soviet Union, as the country that suffered the greatest under Germany's hand, receiving the greatest share. Trials were set for Nazi leaders charged with authorizing or committing war crimes. Territorial claims, where directly addressed, were particulary favorable to the Soviet Union.

PUERTO RICO: MUÑOZ-RIVERA DAY. July 17. Public holiday on the anniversary of the birth of Luis Muñoz-Rivera. The Puerto Rican patriot, poet and journalist was born at Barranquitas, Puerto Rico, in 1859. He died at Santurce, a suburb of San Juan, Puerto Rico, Nov 15, 1916.

SHERWOOD ROBIN HOOD FESTIVAL. July 17–18. Sherwood, OR. Renaissance group; knighting ceremony; kids and family area; parade; world's only archery contest between Sherwood and Nottingham, England; castle contest; teen dance; music; food and crafts vendors and much more! Est attendance: 20,000. For info: Robin Hood Festival Assn, PO Box 496, Sherwood, OR 97140. Phone: (503) 625-4233. E-mail: robinhoodfestival@gmail.com. Web: www.robinhoodfestival.org.

SPACE MILESTONE: *APOLLO-SOYUZ* TEST PROJECT (US, USSR): 45th ANNIVERSARY. July 17, 1975. After three years of planning, negotiation and preparation, the first US-USSR joint space project reached fruition with the linkup in space of *Apollo 18* (crew: T. Stafford, V. Brand, D. Slayton; landed in Pacific Ocean July 24, during 136th orbit) and *Soyuz 19* (crew: A.A. Leonov, V.N. Kubasov; landed July 21, after 96 orbits). *Apollo 18* and *Soyuz 19* were linked for 47 hours (July 17–19) while joint experiments and transfer of personnel and materials back and forth between crafts took place. Launch date was July 15, 1975.

SPACE MILESTONE: FIRST WOMAN TO WALK IN SPACE: *SOYUZ T-12* (USSR). July 17, 1984. Cosmonaut Svetlana Savitskaya became the first woman to walk in space (July 25) and the first woman to make more than one space voyage. Docked at *Salyut 7* July 18 and returned to Earth July 29.

SPANISH CIVIL WAR BEGINS: ANNIVERSARY. July 17, 1936. General Francisco Franco led an uprising of army troops based in North Africa against the elected government of the Spanish Republic. Spain was quickly divided into a Nationalist and a Republican zone. Franco's Nationalists drew support from Fascist Italy and Nazi Germany. On Apr 1, 1939, the Nationalists won a complete victory when they entered Madrid. Franco ruled as dictator in Spain until his death in 1975.

STEALTH BOMBER FLIGHT: ANNIVERSARY. July 17, 1989. The B-2 Stealth bomber airplane was flown successfully over the desert near Palmdale, CA, for almost two hours. A decade of work and $22 billion reportedly were spent on the project prior to the first flight. Designed to penetrate Soviet radar, the B-2 Stealth bomber was said to be capable of delivering up to 25 tons of nuclear or other bombs. Average cost of each of the 132 bombers requested by the US Air Force was estimated to be $530 million. On this first test flight the plane flew at speeds of up to 180 knots (200 mph) and was put through several types of turns. Higher speeds and retraction of the landing gear were left for subsequent test flights.

WORLD EMOJI DAY. July 17. A day to celebrate emojis: have a party, correspond only with emojis, sing the official anthem and more. Created by Jeremy Burge, founder of Emojipedia in 2014—noting that the iOS calendar emoji features that date. Annually, July 17. For info: Emojipedia. E-mail: info@emojipedia.org. Web: www.worldemojiday.com.

"WRONG WAY" CORRIGAN DAY: ANNIVERSARY. July 17, 1938. Douglas Groce Corrigan, an unemployed airplane mechanic, left Brooklyn, NY's Floyd Bennett Field, ostensibly headed for Los Angeles, CA, in a 1929 Curtiss Robin monoplane. He landed 28 hours, 13 minutes later at Baldonnell Airport in Dublin, Ireland, after a 3,150-mile nonstop flight without radio or special navigation equipment and in violation of American and Irish flight regulations. Born at Galveston, TX, Jan 22, 1907, Corrigan received a hero's welcome home; he was nicknamed "Wrong Way" Corrigan because he claimed he accidentally followed the wrong end of his compass needle. Died at Santa Ana, CA, Dec 9, 1995.

🎂 BIRTHDAYS TODAY

Lucie Arnaz, 69, actress ("Here's Lucy," "The Lucie Arnaz Show," *Lost in Yonkers*), born Los Angeles, CA, July 17, 1951.

Luke Bryan, 44, country singer, born Leesburg, GA, July 17, 1976.

Diahann Carroll, 85, singer, actress ("Julia," "Dynasty"), born Carol Diahann Johnson at New York, NY, July 17, 1935.

Jason Clarke, 52, actor (*Everest, Zero Dark Thirty, Public Enemies*, "Brotherhood"), born Winton, Australia, July 17, 1968.

David Hasselhoff, 68, actor ("Knight Rider," "Baywatch"), born Baltimore, MD, July 17, 1952.

Aaron Lansky, 65, founder of the National Yiddish Book Center, born New Bedford, MA, July 17, 1955.

Donald Sutherland, 85, actor (The Hunger Games films, *Space Cowboys, M*A*S*H, Klute*), born St. John, NB, Canada, July 17, 1935.

Dawn Upshaw, 60, opera singer, born Nashville, TN, July 17, 1960.

Alex Winter, 55, actor (*Bill & Ted's Excellent Adventure*), born London, England, July 17, 1965.

July 18 — Saturday

DAY 200   **166 REMAINING**

BANNACK DAYS. July 18–19. Bannack, MT. Montana's first territorial capital, now a well-preserved ghost town, comes to life with a celebration of Montana's mining and pioneer history. Wagon rides, Main Street gunfights, old-time dancing, lots of music and fun are provided during this two-day celebration along Grasshopper Creek each year. Bannack State Park allows visitors to explore the old town and imagine what life was like in the mid-1800s. It is open year-round to the public. Special event fee. Est attendance: 5,000. For info: Bannack State Park, 4200 Bannack Rd, Dillon, MT 59725. Phone: (406) 834-3413. E-mail: bannack@smtel.com.

CHAPPAQUIDDICK INCIDENT: ANNIVERSARY. July 18, 1969. Late this night, Senator Edward Kennedy (D, MA) accidentally drove off a bridge at Chappaquiddick Island, MA. While Kennedy swam away and survived, he didn't report the accident for more than ten hours, and his passenger, campaign worker Mary Jo Kopechne, died in the vehicle. The resulting scandal quashed Kennedy's intentions of a presidential run in 1972.

COLTON COUNTRY DAY. July 18. Colton, NY. Annual flea market, live entertainment, museum exhibits. Fireworks at dusk. Sponsor: Colton Historical Society. Est attendance: 1,500. For info: Dennis Eickhoff, Town Historian, PO Box 95, Colton, NY 13625. Phone: (315) 262-2800. Fax: (315) 262-2182. E-mail: collib@ncls.org.

FIRST PERFECT SCORE IN OLYMPIC HISTORY: ANNIVERSARY. July 18, 1976. At the Montreal Olympics, Romanian gymnast Nadia Comaneci scored the first "10" in Olympic history with her flawless performance of the compulsory exercise on the uneven bars. The scoreboard displayed a "1.00" because it couldn't go up to "10." Comaneci had seven total perfect scores and won five medals, including the gold for all-around performance. Four months previous to the Olympics, Comaneci had earned the first perfect score in international gymnastics competition history.

GLENN, JOHN: BIRTH ANNIVERSARY. July 18, 1921. US Marine pilot, astronaut, US senator, born at Cambridge, Ohio. A Marine fighter pilot, Glenn flew more than 149 missions in both World War II and the Korean War, earning the Distinguished Flying Cross six times. One of America's original "Mercury 7" astronauts in 1959, he became the first American in orbit, circling Earth three times and stepping out of his spacecraft an American hero, having helped the US gain lost ground during a tense space race with the Soviet Union. He later served four terms as a US senator from Ohio, advocating for weapons nonproliferation and further space exploration. He became the oldest person to go into space in 1998, aboard the space shuttle *Discovery* on a nine-day mission. He was awarded the Presidential Medal of Freedom in 2012. Glenn died Dec 8, 2016, at Columbus, OH, and was buried in Arlington National Cemetery.

HAYAKAWA, SAMUEL ICHIYE: BIRTH ANNIVERSARY. July 18, 1906. S.I. Hayakawa was born at Vancouver, BC, Canada, and came to the US in 1927. An academic, in 1968 he was appointed acting president of San Francisco State College. During student demonstrations on his first day in office, he climbed atop a sound truck and disconnected the wires, silencing the demonstrators. His actions gained him enormous popularity among conservatives, and he was promoted to permanent president by Governor Ronald Reagan. As his popularity grew, he switched from the Democratic to the Republican Party and in 1976 was elected to the US Senate. He led the successful California initiative to declare English the state's official language in 1986. Hayakawa wrote nine textbooks on language and semantics. He died Feb 27, 1992, at Greenbrae, CA.

MANDELA, NELSON: BIRTH ANNIVERSARY. July 18, 1918. Former South African president Nelson Rolihlahla Mandela was born the son of a Tembu tribal chieftain at Qunu, near Umtata, in the Transkei territory of South Africa. Giving up his hereditary rights, Mandela chose to become a lawyer and earned his degree at the University of South Africa. He joined the African National Congress (ANC) in 1944, eventually becoming deputy national president in 1952. His activities in the struggle against apartheid resulted in his conviction for sabotage in 1964. During his 28 years in jail, Mandela remained a symbol of hope to South Africa's non-white majority, the demand for his release a rallying cry for civil rights activists. That release finally came Feb 11, 1990, as millions watched via satellite television. He was the 1993 recipient of the Nobel Peace Prize. In 1994 Mandela was elected president of South Africa in the first all-race election there. He died Dec 5, 2013, at Johannesburg, South Africa.

MANDELA DAY. July 18. First observed in 2009, this day is a celebration of Nelson Mandela's life and a global call to action for people to recognize their individual ability to make an imprint and change the world around them. The hope is to inspire people from every corner of the earth to embrace the values of Nelson Mandela as they seek to improve their lives through service to their communities. Annually, on Nelson Mandela's birthday, July 18. For info: Nelson Mandela Centre of Memory. E-mail: mandeladay@nelsonmandela.org. Web: www.mandeladay.com.

NATIONAL BRIDAL SALE DAY. July 18. 5th annual. More than 1,000 independent, locally owned bridal retailers in the United States and Canada participate in this day meant to offer brides, bridesmaids and wedding guests an unprecedented opportunity for substantial savings while supporting local bridal retailers. A great way for a bride to get her dream dress at a bargain price. The "Black Friday" of the bridal industry. Organizations supporting this event include *Vows* magazine, The Knot, Wedding Wire, Bridal Guide, BrideClick, My Wedding, Brides.com, International Bridal Manufacturers Association (IBMA) and more. Annually, the third Saturday in July. For info: Jay West Bridal, 151 Kings Hwy E, Haddonfield, NJ 08033. E-mail: nationalbridalsale@gmail.com. Web: www.nationalbridalsaleevent.com.

NATIONAL MOTH WEEK. July 18–26. 9th annual. First observed in 2012, National Moth Week shines a spotlight on moths and their ecological importance, biodiversity and beauty. Citizen scientists of all ages as well as experienced "moth-ers" around the world are invited to register their events for free at nationalmothweek.org. Typical events include moth nights in parks, camps and wooded areas; educational programs at museums and libraries; and daytime caterpillar hunts. Participants are encouraged to share their photos and observations with NMW's partner websites. Annually, the last full week in July for nine days, including two full weekends. For info: Friends of the East Brunswick (NJ) Environmental Commission. E-mail: info@nationalmothweek.org. Web: www.nationalmothweek.org.

NATIONAL WOODIE WAGON DAY. July 18. The "woodie wagon," made famous in the 1940s and '50s, romanticized the American outing. From Route 66 to the surfer lifestyle, the woodie wagon was there. This national day will be celebrated in individual cities and towns across the US and will pay homage to this great American symbol of freedom and the casual lifestyle. Annually, the third Saturday in July. For info: Historic Preservations, Inc, 14011 Blue River Tr, Broomfield, CO 80023-3911. Phone: (303) 949-5964. E-mail: gregoryaraymer@yahoo.com.

ODETS, CLIFFORD: BIRTH ANNIVERSARY. July 18, 1906. Clifford Odets began his writing career as a poet before turning to acting. He helped found the Group Theatre in 1931. In 1935 he returned to writing with works for the Group Theatre such as *Waiting for Lefty, Awake and Sing!* and *Golden Boy.* His proletarian views helped make him a popular playwright during the Depression

years. Odets was born at Philadelphia, PA; he died at Los Angeles, CA, Aug 15, 1963.

PRESIDENTIAL SUCCESSION ACT: ANNIVERSARY. July 18, 1947. President Harry S Truman signed an executive order determining the line of succession should the president be temporarily incapacitated or die in office. The speaker of the House and president pro tem of the Senate are next in succession after the vice president. This line of succession became the 25th Amendment to the Constitution, which was ratified Feb 10, 1967.

QUISLING, VIDKUN: BIRTH ANNIVERSARY. July 18, 1887. Born at Fyresdal, Norway, Vidkun Quisling was military attaché and minister of defense for Norway. He left the government in 1933 to form the fascist National Union Party. After personally urging Hitler to invade his home country (April 1940), Quisling served first as head of the Norwegian puppet state and then as "minister president" of the occupying government, in which capacity Quisling facilitated the deportation of nearly a thousand Jews to concentration camps. Following Norway's liberation Quisling was convicted of treason and executed on Oct 24, 1945, at Oslo, Norway. The name Quisling has come to mean "traitor" or "collaborator" in a number of languages, including English, due to Quisling's collaboration with the Nazis.

RACE TO MACKINAC. July 18 (end date varies). Navy Pier, Chicago, IL, to Mackinac Island, MI. A race like no other: more than 350 boats leave Chicago every July for a 333-statute-mile dash to Mackinac Island. First held in 1898, it is the oldest annual freshwater distance race in the world. The boats cross the finish line between the lighthouse on Round Island and the race committee trailer on Mackinac Island. Participation is by invitation only from the Chicago Yacht Club. For info: Chicago Yacht Club. Web: www.cycracetomackinac.com.

RESTLESS LEG SYNDROME (RLS) EDUCATION AND AWARENESS WEEK. July 18–25. More than 12 million Americans have severe leg pains called restless leg syndrome (RLS), and this education and awareness week, sponsored by the Pharmacy Council on Women's Health, is a means to educate and to call attention to various treatments and diagnoses to assist patients with this problem. Sponsored by the American College of Apothecaries (ACA)/ Pharmacists Planning Service, Inc (PPSI). For info: ACA/PPSI, 2830 Summer Oaks Dr, Bartlett, TN 38134. E-mail: info@ppsinc.org. Web: www.ppsinc.org.

RUTLEDGE, JOHN: DEATH ANNIVERSARY. July 18, 1800. American statesman, associate justice on the Supreme Court, born at Charleston, SC, in September 1739. Nominated second chief justice of the US to succeed John Jay and served as acting chief justice until his confirmation was denied because of his opposition to the Jay Treaty. He died at Charleston.

SKELTON, RED: BIRTH ANNIVERSARY. July 18, 1913. Pantomimist, radio and television comedian, vaudeville performer and artist, born Richard Bernard Skelton at Vincennes, IN, who appeared in nearly 30 movies and whose own eponymous television show ran for 20 years on CBS (1951–71). Best known for his pratfalls, one-liners and comic characterizations (Freddie the Freeloader, Clem Kaddiddlehopper, Sheriff Deadeye, the Mean Widdle Kid). He died Sept 17, 1997, at Rancho Mirage, CA.

SPACE MILESTONE: *ROHINI 1* (INDIA): 40th ANNIVERSARY. July 18, 1980. First successful launch from India, orbited 77-pound satellite.

July 2020	S	M	T	W	T	F	S
				1	2	3	4
	5	6	7	8	9	10	11
	12	13	14	15	16	17	18
	19	20	21	22	23	24	25
	26	27	28	29	30	31	

THACKERAY, WILLIAM MAKEPEACE: BIRTH ANNIVERSARY. July 18, 1811. Author, best remembered for his novels *Vanity Fair* (1848) and *Pendennis* (1850). In his time, Thackeray was second only to Charles Dickens in the hearts of British book lovers. Born at Calcutta (now Kolkata), India, he died at London, England, Dec 23, 1863.

THOMPSON, HUNTER S.: BIRTH ANNIVERSARY. July 18, 1939. Journalist and author born at Louisville, KY, Thompson was one of the first practitioners of "New," or "Gonzo," journalism, a style that featured first-person accounts and scathing criticism of contemporary American society. His most famous work, "Fear and Loathing in Las Vegas," published in *Rolling Stone* magazine in 1972, featured an alter-ego character in search of the American Dream via use of hallucinogenic drugs. Other works include *Hell's Angels, The Great Shark Hunt* and *The Proud Highway*. Long hailed as a hero of counterculture, Thompson committed suicide at his home in Woody Creek, CO, Feb 21, 2005.

TOSS AWAY THE "COULD HAVES" AND "SHOULD HAVES" DAY. July 18. On this day people write down their "could haves" and "should haves" on a piece of paper and then throw that list into the trash. Then they make this resolution: "From this day forward, I choose not to live in the past—the past is history that I can't change. I can do something about the present—I choose to live in the present." Annually, the third Saturday in July. For info: Martha Ross-Rodgers, 1410 Poindexter St, Chesapeake, VA 23324. Phone: (757) 543-9290. E-mail: drmarthajrossrodgers@aol.com.

UNITED NATIONS: NELSON MANDELA INTERNATIONAL DAY. July 18. Recognizing Nelson Rolihlahla Mandela's leading role in Africa's struggle for liberation and unity, his dedication to the service of humanity as a humanitarian and his contribution to the struggle for democracy internationally and in promoting a culture of peace worldwide, the General Assembly has designated July 18 (his birthday) each year as Nelson Mandela International Day (Res 64/13 of Nov 10, 2009). For info: United Nations, Dept of Public Info, New York, NY 10017. Web: www.un.org.

URUGUAY: CONSTITUTION DAY. July 18. National holiday. Commemorates the country's first constitution in 1830.

WHITE, GILBERT: 300th BIRTH ANNIVERSARY. July 18, 1720. Born at Selborne, Hampshire, England, Gilbert White has been called the father of British naturalists. His book *The Natural History of Selborne*, published in 1788, enjoyed immediate success and is said never to have been out of print. White died near his birthplace, June 26, 1793. His home survives as a museum.

WOMEN'S DIVE DAY. July 18. 5th annual. Sponsored by PADI® (Professional Association of Diving Instructors), this day is a global celebration of shared adventure and passion for the ocean. Each year, dive centers across the globe host more than 1,000 dive events designed to get more people actively diving and to create more stewards for the ocean. Annually, the third Saturday in July. For info: PADI Americas. E-mail: womendive@padi.com or media@padi.com. Web: www.padi.com/women.

🧁 BIRTHDAYS TODAY

Kristen Bell, 40, actress (*You Again, Forgetting Sarah Marshall*, "Veronica Mars," "House of Lies"), born Detroit, MI, July 18, 1980.

James Brolin, 79, actor (Emmy for "Marcus Welby, MD"; "Hotel"), born Los Angeles, CA, July 18, 1941.

Richard Totten (Dick) Button, 91, sportscaster, Olympic figure skater, born Englewood, NJ, July 18, 1929.

Priyanka Chopra, 38, actress ("Quantico," *Mary Kom, Fashion*), former Miss World (2000), born Jamshedpur, India, July 18, 1982.

Chace Crawford, 35, actor ("Gossip Girl"), born Lubbock, TX, July 18, 1985.

Vin Diesel, 53, actor (*XXX, The Fast and the Furious, Pitch Black*), born Mark Vincent at New York, NY, July 18, 1967.

Dion DiMucci, 81, singer (Dion and the Belmonts), born the Bronx, NY, July 18, 1939.

Nick Faldo, 63, golfer, born Welwyn Garden City, England, July 18, 1957.

Steve Forbes, 73, publisher, chairman, Forbes Newspapers, born Morristown, NJ, July 18, 1947.

Anfernee "Penny" Hardaway, 48, former basketball player, born Memphis, TN, July 18, 1972.

Margo Martindale, 69, actress ("The Millers," "The Americans," "Justified," "Dexter"), born Jacksonville, TX, July 18, 1951.

Elizabeth McGovern, 59, actress ("Downton Abbey," *Racing with the Moon*), born Evanston, IL, July 18, 1961.

James Norton, 35, actor ("McMafia," "Grantchester," "Happy Valley," "War and Peace"), born London, England, July 18, 1985.

Martha Reeves, 79, singer (Martha and the Vandellas), born Detroit, MI, July 18, 1941.

Ricky Skaggs, 66, musician (bluegrass guitar), singer, born Cordell, KY, July 18, 1954.

Joe Torre, 80, baseball executive, Hall of Fame manager and former player, born New York, NY, July 18, 1940.

July 19 — Sunday

DAY 201   **165 REMAINING**

ATTACK ON FORT WAGNER: ANNIVERSARY. July 19, 1863. In a second attempt to capture Fort Wagner, outside Charleston, SC, Union troops were repulsed after losing 1,515 men as opposed to Southern losses of only 174. The attack was led by the 54th Massachusetts Colored Infantry, commanded by Colonel Robert Gould Shaw, who was killed in the action. This was the first use of black troops in the war. The film *Glory* was based on the Massachusetts 54th, and this was the attack featured in the film. Fort Wagner was never taken by the Union.

★**CAPTIVE NATIONS WEEK.** July 19–25. Presidential proclamation issued each year since 1959 for the third week in July. (Public Law 86–90 of July 17, 1959.)

COLT, SAMUEL: BIRTH ANNIVERSARY. July 19, 1814. Born at Hartford, CT, inventor and manufacturer Colt is best known for developing the multishot pistol, which he patented in 1836. Before the revolver gained popularity, he was also involved in developing waterproof telegraph cables. His company, still currently operational, supplied both the North and South with weaponry during the US Civil War, and at the time of his death on Jan 10, 1862, at Hartford, he was one of the wealthiest men in the US.

CONCOURS D'ELEGANCE. July 19. Forest Grove, OR. Set among the beauty of the Pacific University campus, this is one of the premier car shows on the West Coast, with 300-plus beautifully restored vintage autos. A great family event. Annually, the third Sunday in July. Est attendance: 6,000. For info: Forest Grove Rotary Club,

PO Box 387, Forest Grove, OR 97116. Phone: (503) 357-2300. Web: www.forestgroveconcours.org.

DEGAS, EDGAR: BIRTH ANNIVERSARY. July 19, 1834. The French Impressionist painter, especially noted for his paintings of dancers in motion, was born at Paris, France, and died there Sept 26, 1917.

ELVIS PRESLEY'S FIRST SINGLE RELEASED: ANNIVERSARY. July 19, 1954. "That's All Right (Mama)" backed by "Blue Moon of Kentucky" was released on this date by Sun Records of Memphis, TN. It was 19-year-old Elvis Presley's first professional record. Presley recorded it with guitarist Scotty Moore and bassist Bill Black. Memphis DJ Dewey Phillips previewed the single on July 7—literally two days after it was recorded—on his radio show and his listeners went crazy, demanding that Phillips play it again and again. See also: "Elvis Presley's First Concert Appearance: Anniversary" (July 30).

FIRST UNASSISTED TRIPLE PLAY: ANNIVERSARY. July 19, 1909. Cleveland Blues shortstop Neal Ball recorded the first unassisted triple play in American League history in a game against the Boston Pilgrims. Ball caught a line drive hit by Amby McConnell, stepped on second base to double off Heine Wagner and tagged Jake Stahl before Stahl could get back to first base. Ball also hit a home run as Cleveland won, 6–1.

FIRST WOMAN VICE-PRESIDENTIAL CANDIDATE: ANNIVERSARY. July 19, 1984. Congresswoman Geraldine Ferraro was nominated to run with presidential candidate Walter Mondale on the Democratic ticket. They were defeated by the Republican ticket headed by Ronald Reagan.

ITALY: FEAST OF THE REDEEMER. July 19. Venice. Procession of gondolas and other craft commemorating the end of the epidemic of 1575. Annually, the third Sunday in July.

LINKLETTER, ART: BIRTH ANNIVERSARY. July 19, 1912. Television and radio personality born Gordon Arthur Kelly at Moose Jaw, SK, Canada. He is remembered for his mainly unscripted programs "People Are Funny" and "House Party." Died May 26, 2010, at Los Angeles, CA.

LUXEMBOURG: BEER FESTIVAL. July 19. At Diekirch an annual beer festival is held on the third Sunday in July.

"MAD MEN" TV PREMIERE: ANNIVERSARY. July 19, 2007. In AMC's period drama set in a Madison Avenue advertising agency in the 1960s, the ad men smoke, drink and womanize in the workplace. "Mad Men" explored the cultural morés of the time through the characters of mysterious ad executive Don Draper (Jon Hamm) and ambitious secretary Peggy Olsen (Elisabeth Moss). Praised for its period authenticity, the show painstakingly re-created the fashions, furniture, graphic design and architecture of the era; its popularity is credited with a resurgence in interest in mid-century modern furniture, classic craft cocktails and retro men's fashions. In 2008, "Mad Men" became the first basic cable series to win an Emmy for Outstanding Drama Series, an award it won for three consecutive years, and it tops critics' lists of the best TV series of all time.

MAYO, CHARLES HORACE: BIRTH ANNIVERSARY. July 19, 1865. American surgeon, one of the Mayo brothers, founders of the Mayo Clinic and Mayo Foundation, born at Rochester, MN. Died at Chicago, IL, May 26, 1939.

MCGOVERN, GEORGE: BIRTH ANNIVERSARY. July 19, 1922. US politician and WWII hero, born at Mitchell, SD. McGovern began his career in public service in 1956. Representing South Dakota in both houses of Congress, he was a voice in support of civil rights and social issues throughout the 1960s—as well as a vocal opponent of American involvement in the Vietnam War. The Democratic presidential candidate in 1972, McGovern and his party were targeted by operatives of the Nixon administration in the form of illegal information gathering and wiretapping—the Watergate scandal. He lost the election to Richard Nixon in a crushing defeat, and later he returned to the Senate. His work with UN hunger causes earned him the Presidential Medal of Freedom in 2000. McGovern died at Sioux Falls, SD, Oct 21, 2012.

NATIONAL ICE CREAM DAY. July 19. A day celebrating America's favorite dessert, ice cream. In 1984, President Ronald Reagan designated July as National Ice Cream Month and the third Sunday of the month as National Ice Cream Day. He recognized ice cream as a fun and nutritious food that is enjoyed by over 90 percent of the nation's population. Annually, the third Sunday in July. For info: International Dairy Foods Assn. Web: www.idfa.org.

NICARAGUA: NATIONAL LIBERATION DAY. July 19. Following the National Day of Joy (July 17—anniversary of date in 1979 when dictator Anastasio Somoza Debayle fled Nicaragua) is the annual July 19 observance of National Liberation Day, anniversary of day the National Liberation Army claimed victory over the Somoza dictatorship.

RAGBRAI®—THE *REGISTER'S* ANNUAL GREAT BICYCLE RIDE ACROSS IOWA™. July 19–25. A seven-day, leisurely tour from the western border of Iowa to the Mississippi River enjoying wonderful Iowa scenery and hospitality. RAGBRAI® is the largest, longest and oldest bicycle touring event in the world. The *Des Moines Register* has coordinated this ride, which attracts 10,000 riders from across the country (and around the world). Annually, the last full week in July. Est attendance: 10,000. For info: RAGBRAI. Phone: (515) 284-8074. E-mail: info@ragbrai.com. Web: www.ragbrai.com.

SAINT VINCENT DE PAUL: OLD FEAST DAY. July 19. A day remembering the founder of the Vincentian Congregation and the Sisters of Charity, born at Pouy, France, Apr 24, 1581. He died Sept 27, 1660, at Paris, France. His feast day was formerly observed on July 19 but is now observed on the anniversary of his death, Sept 27.

TURKEY: BOSPHORUS CROSS-CONTINENTAL SWIM. July 19 (or July 26, tentative). Istanbul. First held in 1989, this annual sporting event features 750 athletes swimming across the Bosphorus Strait from Asia to Europe. Sponsored by Samsung. Usually held the third or fourth Sunday in July. For info: National Olympic Committee of Turkey. Web: http://bogazici.olimpiyatkomitesi.org.tr.

WOMEN IN BASEBALL WEEK. July 19–25. Since 2017, an annual worldwide event recognizing the value, diversity and cultural significance of women in baseball. Whether behind the scenes or on the field, women play a vital role in the sport around the globe, and this week was established to celebrate each one! Tournaments, teams, libraries, museums and individuals join the International Women's Baseball Center in observing this week. Annually, the last week in July. For info: The International Women's Baseball Center. E-mail: info@womeninbaseballweek.org. Web: www.womeninbaseballweek.org or www.internationalwomensbaseballcenter.org.

WOMEN'S RIGHTS CONVENTION AT SENECA FALLS: ANNIVERSARY. July 19, 1848. A convention concerning the rights of women, called by Lucretia Mott and Elizabeth Cady Stanton, was held at Seneca Falls, NY, July 19–20, 1848. The issues discussed included voting, property rights and divorce. The convention drafted a

		S	M	T	W	T	F	S
July					1	2	3	4
		5	6	7	8	9	10	11
2020		12	13	14	15	16	17	18
		19	20	21	22	23	24	25
		26	27	28	29	30	31	

"Declaration of Sentiments" that paraphrased the Declaration of Independence, addressing man instead of King George, and called for women's "immediate admission to all the rights and privileges which belong to them as citizens of the United States." This convention was the beginning of an organized women's rights movement in the US. The most controversial issue was Stanton's demand for women's right to vote.

YALOW, ROSALYN: BIRTH ANNIVERSARY. July 19, 1921. Medical physicist born at New York City. Along with Andrew V. Schally and Roger Guillemin, in 1977 Yalow was awarded the Nobel Prize in Physiology or Medicine. Through her research on medical applications of radioactive isotopes, Yalow developed RIA, a sensitive and simple technique used to measure minute concentrations of hormones and other substances in blood or other body fluids. First applied to the study of insulin concentration in the blood of people with diabetes, RIA was soon used in hundreds of other applications. She died May 30, 2011, at the Bronx, NY.

🎂 BIRTHDAYS TODAY

Trai Byers, 37, actor ("Empire," *Selma*), born Kansas City, KS, July 19, 1983.

Benedict Cumberbatch, 44, actor ("Sherlock," *Doctor Strange, The Imitation Game, Star Trek into Darkness*), born London, England, July 19, 1976.

Anthony Edwards, 58, actor ("ER," *Fast Times at Ridgemont High, Top Gun*), born Santa Barbara, CA, July 19, 1962.

Topher Grace, 42, actor (*Spider-Man 3, In Good Company, Traffic*, "That '70s Show"), born New York, NY, July 19, 1978.

Clea Lewis, 55, actress ("Ellen," *The Rich Man's Wife*), born Cleveland Heights, OH, July 19, 1965.

Ilie Nastase, 74, Hall of Fame tennis player, born Bucharest, Romania, July 19, 1946.

Jared Padalecki, 38, actor ("Supernatural"), born San Antonio, TX, July 19, 1982.

Campbell Scott, 58, actor (*Roger Dodger, Singles*), born Westchester County, NY, July 19, 1962.

Nicola Sturgeon, 50, First Minister of Scotland, born Irvine, Scotland, July 19, 1970.

July 20 — Monday

DAY 202   **164 REMAINING**

ATTEMPT ON HITLER'S LIFE: ANNIVERSARY. July 20, 1944. During the daily staff meeting at German headquarters at Rastenburg, an attempt was made to assassinate Adolf Hitler. Count Claus Schenk von Stauffenberg, chosen from a group of German military and civil servants involved in the plot, left a briefcase containing a bomb only six feet from Hitler under the staff table in the briefing room. Four people were killed in the blast, but Hitler's life was saved, probably because Colonel Heinz Brandt (who was among those killed) had found the briefcase in his way and moved it farther from the German dictator.

AURORA THEATER SHOOTING: ANNIVERSARY. July 20, 2012. A heavily armed man opened fire at a midnight show at the Century 16 multiplex theater in Aurora, CO. Standing at the front of the theater, he discharged tear gas and a variety of weapons into the panicked crowd, killing 12 and wounding 58. It was the fourth and largest of the seven mass shootings in the US in 2012.

COLOMBIA: INDEPENDENCE DAY. July 20. National holiday. Commemorates the beginning of the independence movement with an uprising against Spanish officials in 1810 at Bogotá. Colombia gained independence from Spain in 1819 when Simon Bolívar decisively defeated the Spanish.

EAA AIRVENTURE OSHKOSH. July 20–26. Wittman Regional Airport, Oshkosh, WI. World's largest sport aviation event. More than 10,000 airplanes annually fly in for this Experimental Aircraft Association gathering. Daily air shows; special programs; more than 1,000 forums, workshops and seminars. Est attendance: 500,000. For info: Dick Knapinski, Director of Communications, Experimental Aircraft Assn, PO Box 3086, Oshkosh, WI 54903-3086. Phone: (920) 426-4800. E-mail: communications@eaa.org. Web: www.eaa.org.

ENGLAND: FARNBOROUGH INTERNATIONAL AIRSHOW. July 20–24. Farnborough Airfield, Farnborough. Held since 1948, this is the world's largest and most important air show—open to the trade for one week and to the public for two days. Some 1,300 exhibiting companies from 35 countries attend the show. Over the decades dozens of new aircraft have made their debut at Farnborough, including the Comet, Concorde and Airbus A380. Est attendance: 270,000. For info: Farnborough Intl Airshow, ShowCentre, ETPS Rd, Farnborough, Hampshire, England GU14 6FD. Phone: (44) (1252) 532-800. E-mail: enquiries@farnborough.com. Web: www.farnborough.com.

GENEVA ACCORDS: ANNIVERSARY. July 20, 1954. An agreement covering cessation of hostilities in Vietnam, signed at Geneva, Switzerland, on behalf of the commanders in chief of French forces at Vietnam and the People's Army of Vietnam. A further declaration of the Geneva Conference was released July 21, 1954. Partition, foreign troop withdrawal and elections for a unified government within two years were among provisions.

HILLARY, SIR EDMUND PERCIVAL: BIRTH ANNIVERSARY. July 20, 1919. Explorer, mountaineer, born at Tuakau, New Zealand. With Tenzing Norgay, a Sherpa guide, became first to ascend summit of highest mountain in the world, Mount Everest (29,035 feet), at 11:30 AM, May 29, 1953. "We climbed because nobody climbed it before," he said. Hillary, who also listed his occupation as beekeeper, died Jan 11, 2008, at Auckland.

HUTCHINSON, ANNE: BAPTISM ANNIVERSARY. July 20, 1591. Puritan midwife Anne Marbury was born at Alford, England, and in 1633 immigrated to Boston with her husband, William Hutchinson, and their children. Due to her religious views, she was banished from the Massachusetts Bay Colony in 1637. She was cofounder of the city of Portsmouth, in present-day Rhode Island. Forced to flee to New Netherland (now the Bronx, New York City), Hutchinson was killed along with six of her children and others in the household by the Siwanoy people in August 1643. Hutchinson is considered a martyr for civil liberty and religious tolerance.

KARLFELDT, ERIK AXEL: BIRTH ANNIVERSARY. July 20, 1864. Poet, born at Folkärna, Sweden, who was posthumously awarded the Nobel Prize in Literature in 1931. Karlfeldt's lyrical poems celebrated nature and the rustic roots of Swedish culture. He had turned down the Nobel in 1918 because he was also secretary at the Swedish Academy. But when he died Apr 8, 1931, at Stockholm, the Academy honored him despite seeming to go against the purpose of the prize (to aid living artists).

LOCUST PLAGUE OF 1874: ANNIVERSARY. July 20–30, 1874. The Rocky Mountain locust, long a pest in the American Midwest, became an even bigger threat in the summer of 1874. Beginning in late July, the largest recorded swarm of this insect descended on the Great Plains. It is estimated that 124 billion insects formed a swarm 1,800 miles long and 110 miles wide that ranged from Canada and the Dakotas down to Texas. Contemporary accounts said that the

locusts blocked out the sun and devastated farms in mere minutes. The swarms continued in smaller size for the next several years and caused an estimated $200 million in crop destruction.

MOON PHASE: NEW MOON. July 20. Moon enters New Moon phase at 1:33 PM, EDT.

NATIONAL GET OUT OF THE DOGHOUSE DAY. July 20. In trouble with someone you know and care about? This is the day when anyone can "Get out of the doghouse!" Annually, the third Monday in July. For info: Heidi Richards Mooney, Redhead Marketing, Inc, PO Box 550856, Fort Lauderdale, FL 33355. Phone: (954) 625-6606. E-mail: heidi@redheadmarketinginc.com.

O'HANLON, VIRGINIA: BIRTH ANNIVERSARY. July 20, 1889. O'Hanlon (married name Douglas), born at New York, NY, was a teacher and principal who is today best known as the disheartened eight-year-old who asked the staff of the *New York Sun* whether Santa Claus existed. In a famous 1897 editorial Francis P. Church answered her question and reassured Virginia that yes, indeed "there is a Santa Claus." Douglas died at Valatie, NY, at the age of 81 on May 13, 1971.

RIOT ACT: ANNIVERSARY. July 20, 1715. To "read the riot act" now usually means telling children to be quiet or less boisterous, but in 18th-century England reading the riot act was a more serious matter. On July 20, 1715, the Riot Act took effect. By law in England, if 12 or more persons were unlawfully assembled to the disturbance of the public peace, an authority was required "with a loud voice" to command silence and read the riot act proclamation: "Our sovereign lord the king chargeth and commandeth all persons, being assembled, immediately to disperse themselves, and peaceably to depart to their habitations, or to their lawful business, upon the pains contained in the act made in the first year of King George, for preventing tumults and riotous assemblies. God save the king." Any persons who failed to obey within one hour were to be seized, apprehended and carried before a justice of the peace.

SPACE MILESTONE: MOON DAY. July 20, 1969. Anniversary of man's first landing on the moon. Two US astronauts (Neil Alden Armstrong and Edwin Eugene Aldrin, Jr) landed lunar module *Eagle* at 4:17 PM, EDT, and remained on the lunar surface 21 hours, 36 minutes and 16 seconds. The landing was made from the *Apollo XI*'s orbiting command-and-service module, code-named *Columbia*, whose pilot, Michael Collins, remained aboard. Armstrong was first to set foot on the moon. Armstrong and Aldrin were outside the spacecraft, walking on the moon's surface, approximately 2¼ hours. The astronauts returned to Earth July 24, bringing photographs and rock samples.

SPECIAL OLYMPICS: ANNIVERSARY. July 20, 1968. Official anniversary of the first-ever International Special Olympics Competition, held at Soldier Field, Chicago, IL. Special Olympics is an international year-round program of sports training and competition for individuals with intellectual disabilities. More than 3.5 million athletes in more than 170 countries train and compete in 32 Olympic-style summer and winter sports. Founded in 1968 by Eunice Kennedy Shriver, Special Olympics provides people with intellectual disabilities continuing opportunities to develop fitness, demonstrate courage and experience joy as they participate in the sharing of gifts and friendship with other athletes, their families and the community. For info: Special Olympics, Inc. Web: www.specialolympics.org.

US JUNIOR AMATEUR (GOLF) CHAMPIONSHIP. July 20–25. Hazeltine National Golf Club, Chaska MN. For info: USGA, Golf House, Championship Dept, PO Box 708, Far Hills, NJ 07931. Phone: (908) 234-2300. E-mail: champs@usga.org. Web: www.usga.org.

🎂 BIRTHDAYS TODAY

Ray Allen, 45, basketball player, born Merced, CA, July 20, 1975.

Gisele Bündchen, 40, model, born Horizontina, Brazil, July 20, 1980.

Kim Carnes, 74, singer, songwriter, born Hollywood, CA, July 20, 1946.

Judy Chicago, 81, artist, feminist, born Judy Cohen at Chicago, IL, July 20, 1939.

John Daley, 35, actor ("Freaks and Geeks"), born New York, NY, July 20, 1985.

Pavel Datsyuk, 42, hockey player, born Sverdlovsk, Russia, July 20, 1978.

Donna Dixon, 63, actress ("Bosom Buddies," *Dr. Detroit*), born Alexandria, VA, July 20, 1957.

Peter Forsberg, 47, hockey manager and former player, born Örnsköldsvik, Sweden, July 20, 1973.

Josh Holloway, 51, actor ("Colony," "Intelligence," "Lost"), born San Jose, CA, July 20, 1969.

Sally Ann Howes, 90, actress (*Brigadoon, Chitty Chitty Bang Bang, Fools Rush In*), singer, born London, England, July 20, 1930.

Cormac McCarthy, 87, author (*The Road, No Country for Old Men, All the Pretty Horses*), born Providence, RI, July 20, 1933.

Enrique Peña Nieto, 54, former president of Mexico (2012–18), born Atlacomulco, State of Mexico, Mexico, July 20, 1966.

Claudio Reyna, 47, Hall of Fame soccer player, born Livingston, NJ, July 20, 1973.

Diana Rigg, 82, actress (Tony for *Medea*; *King Lear, Bleak House*, "The Avengers"), born Doncaster, Yorkshire, England, July 20, 1938.

Carlos Santana, 73, musician, born Autlan, Mexico, July 20, 1947.

Dean Winters, 56, actor ("Battle Creek," "Rescue Me," "Oz"), born New York, NY, July 20, 1964.

July 21 — Tuesday

DAY 203   **163 REMAINING**

BATTLE OF BULL RUN: ANNIVERSARY. July 21, 1861. Union general Irvin McDowell was defeated by Confederate troops led by General Joseph E. Johnston at the first Battle of Bull Run at Manassas, VA. It was the first major engagement of the Civil War. It was during this battle that Confederate general T.J. Jackson won the nickname "Stonewall." In the second Battle of Bull Run, Aug 29–30, 1862, Union general John Pope was badly defeated by General Robert E. Lee.

BELGIUM: INDEPENDENCE DAY. July 21. Public holiday. Marks accession of first Belgian king, Leopold I, in 1831, after independence from Netherlands.

	S	M	T	W	T	F	S
July				1	2	3	4
	5	6	7	8	9	10	11
2020	12	13	14	15	16	17	18
	19	20	21	22	23	24	25
	26	27	28	29	30	31	

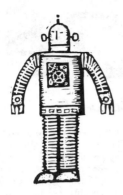

CLEVELAND, FRANCES FOLSOM: BIRTH ANNIVERSARY. July 21, 1864. Wife of Grover Cleveland, 22nd and 24th president of the US, born at Buffalo, NY. She was the youngest first lady at age 21 and the first to marry a president in the White House (June 2, 1886). Cleveland was a popular first lady who championed higher education for women. Died at Baltimore, MD, Oct 29, 1947.

EVERS, JOHNNY: BIRTH ANNIVERSARY. July 21, 1881. John Joseph (Johnny) Evers, Baseball Hall of Fame second baseman, born at Troy, NY. Evers was a member of the Tinker-to-Evers-to-Chance double-play combination for the Chicago Cubs, which first took the field on Sept 13, 1902. Inducted into the Hall of Fame (with Tinker and Chance) in 1946. Evers died at Albany, NY, Mar 28, 1947.

FIRST ROBOT KILLING: ANNIVERSARY. July 21, 1984. The first reported killing of a human by a robot occurred at Jackson, MI. A robot turned and caught a 34-year-old worker between it and a safety bar, crushing him. He died of the injuries July 26, 1984. According to the National Institute for Occupational Safety and Health, it was "the first documented case of a robot-related fatality in the US."

GUAM: LIBERATION DAY. July 21. National holiday. Commemorates US forces' return to Guam in 1944, freeing the island from the Japanese.

HEMINGWAY, ERNEST: BIRTH ANNIVERSARY. July 21, 1899. American author born at Oak Park, IL. Made his name with such works as *The Sun Also Rises* (1926), *A Farewell to Arms* (1929), *For Whom the Bell Tolls* (1940) and *The Old Man and the Sea* (1952). He was awarded the Nobel Prize in 1954 and wrote little thereafter. Hemingway shot himself July 2, 1961, at Ketchum, ID, having been seriously ill for some time.

HEMINGWAY BIRTHDAY CELEBRATION. July 21. Hemingway Museum, Oak Park, IL. Annual celebration of Ernest Hemingway's birth. Includes a lecture and reception. For info: The Ernest Hemingway Foundation of Oak Park, 339 N Oak Park Ave, Oak Park, IL 60302. Phone: (708) 445-3071. E-mail: info@ehfop.org. Web: www.ehfop.org.

LOWEST RECORDED TEMPERATURE: ANNIVERSARY. July 21, 1983. At the USSR's Vostok Station in Antarctica, a temperature of 128.6 degrees below zero Fahrenheit (89.2 degrees below zero Celsius) was recorded on this date.

MCLUHAN, MARSHALL: BIRTH ANNIVERSARY. July 21, 1911. Herbert Marshall McLuhan, university professor and author—called "the Canadian sage of the electronic age"—was born at Edmonton, AB, Canada. His *Understanding Media, The Medium Is the Massage* (not to be confused with his widely quoted aphorism: "The medium is the message") and other books were widely acclaimed for their fresh view of communication. McLuhan is reported to have said: "Most people are alive in an earlier time, but you must be alive in our own time." He died at Toronto, ON, Canada, Dec 31, 1980.

NATIONAL WOMEN'S HALL OF FAME: ANNIVERSARY. July 21, 1979. Seneca Falls, NY. Founded to honor American women whose contributions "have been of the greatest value in the development of their country" and located in the community known as the "birthplace of women's rights," where the first Women's Suffrage Movement convention was held in 1848, the Hall of Fame was dedicated with 23 inductees. An earlier National Women's Hall of Fame, honoring "Twenty Outstanding Women of the Twentieth Century," was dedicated at the New York World's Fair, on May 27, 1965.

NO PET STORE PUPPIES DAY. July 21. Most pet shop puppies come from puppy mills, and so do most dogs sold over the Internet. The ASPCA's national "Barred From Love" campaign raises awareness about puppy mill cruelty and encourages dog lovers to adopt from a local shelter or rescue group or learn how to sniff out the good from the cruel when it comes to finding a dog breeder. Help celebrate this day by joining the fight for love and speak out against the cruel puppy breeding industry. Annually, July 21. For info: Media and Communications, ASPCA, 520 8th Ave, 7th Fl, New York, NY 10018. Phone: (212) 876-7700. E-mail: press@aspca.org. Web: www.barredfromlove.org.

REUTER, PAUL JULIUS: BIRTH ANNIVERSARY. July 21, 1816. Pioneering media executive born Israel Beer Josaphat at Kassel, Germany. He later converted to Christianity and changed his name to Paul Julius Reuter. He worked for a German firm publishing political pamphlets and news translations in Europe in the 1840s, and in 1850, he started a carrier pigeon service called Reuters News Agency to deliver news between Brussels, Belgium, and Aachen, Germany. He opened a telegraph office in London in 1851 and persuaded several publishers to subscribe to a service by which he would transmit important news over the wire virtually as it was happening. The expansion of telegraph cables under the English Channel helped him grow his territory, and his news agency grew to be indispensable across Europe. Reuter was created a baron by the Duke of Saxe-Coburg-Gotha in 1871 and was given similar honors by Queen Victoria. He died Feb 25, 1899 at Nice, France.

SLOPPY JOE'S HEMINGWAY® LOOK-ALIKE CONTEST. July 21–26. Key West, FL. 40th annual. Sloppy Joe's Annual Hemingway® Look-Alike Contest is one of many events in Key West celebrating the birthday of Ernest Hemingway and honoring his work as author and sportsman. Preliminary rounds are Thursday and Friday. The final round is Saturday, when Papa 2020 is announced. Judging is handled by former Look-Alike winners. Contestants arrive in "Hemingway Garb": safari outfits, khakis and such. Many bring their own cheering squad. Saturday at noon is photos with Papas followed by "The Running of the Bulls." The event wraps up Sunday with the Annual Arm Wrestling Contest. For info: Sloppy Joe's, 201 Duval St, Key West, FL 33040. Phone: (305) 296-2388. E-mail: donna@sloppyjoes.com. Web: www.sloppyjoes.com.

🎂 BIRTHDAYS TODAY

John Barrasso, 68, US Senator (R, Wyoming), born Casper, WY, July 21, 1952.

Justin Bartha, 42, actor (*National Treasure, The Hangover*), born West Bloomfield, MI, July 21, 1978.

Brandi Chastain, 52, sportscaster, Hall of Fame soccer player, born San Jose, CA, July 21, 1968.

Michael Connelly, 64, author (Harry Bosch novels), born Philadelphia, PA, July 21, 1956.

Lance Guest, 60, actor ("Lou Grant," *The Last Starfighter*), born Saratoga, CA, July 21, 1960.

Josh Hartnett, 42, actor ("Penny Dreadful," *Pearl Harbor*), born San Francisco, CA, July 21, 1978.

Norman Jewison, 94, producer, director (*Moonstruck, Fiddler on the Roof*), born Toronto, ON, Canada, July 21, 1926.

Jon Lovitz, 63, actor (*A League of Their Own*, "NewsRadio"), born Tarzana, CA, July 21, 1957.

Matt Mulhern, 60, actor ("Major Dad," *Biloxi Blues*), born Philadelphia, PA, July 21, 1960.

C.C. Sabathia, 40, baseball player, born Vallejo, CA, July 21, 1980.

Cat Stevens, 72, singer, songwriter, chosen Muslim name is Yusuf Islam, born Stephen Demetri Georgiou at London, England, July 21, 1948.

Garry Trudeau, 71, political cartoonist ("Doonesbury"), born New York, NY, July 21, 1949.

Sarah Waters, 54, author (*Tipping the Velvet, The Night Watch*), born Neyland, Pembrokeshire, Wales, July 21, 1966.

July 22 — Wednesday

DAY 204   **162 REMAINING**

CALDER, ALEXANDER: BIRTH ANNIVERSARY. July 22, 1898. Internationally acclaimed American abstract artist who invented the mobile. Born at Lawnton, PA, Calder took a degree in mechanical engineering but turned to art in the 1920s. By the 1930s he was the most famous American artist in the world. Calder created the mobile, a delicate hanging kinetic sculpture whose form changed continuously due to air currents or motors. His stationary abstract sculptures were termed "stabiles," and they influenced many generations of artists to turn to industrial materials and monumental scope for expression as he had (with works like *Flamingo* [1974]). Calder died Nov 11, 1976, at New York, NY.

DILLINGER, JOHN: DEATH ANNIVERSARY. July 22, 1934. Bank robber, murderer, prison escapee and the first person to receive the FBI's appellation "Public Enemy Number 1" (July 1934). After nine years in prison (1924–33), Dillinger traveled through the Midwest, leaving a path of violent crimes. He was killed in Illinois by FBI agents led by Melvin Purvis as he left Chicago's Biograph movie theater (where he had watched *Manhattan Melodrama*, starring Clark Gable and Myrna Loy). He was born at Indianapolis, IN, June 28, 1902.

HOOD RIVER COUNTY FAIR. July 22–25. Hood River, OR. From 4-H activities to the excitement of the carnival, this annual old-fashioned country fair is bustling with things to do! Est attendance: 25,000. For info: Hood River County Fair, PO Box 385, Odell, OR 97044. Phone: (541) 354-2865. Fax: (541) 354-2875. E-mail: hrfair@hrecn.net. Web: www.hoodriverfair.org.

MENDEL, GREGOR JOHANN: BIRTH ANNIVERSARY. July 22, 1822. Botanist Gregor Mendel was born of peasant parents at Heinzendorf, Austria. His pioneering work in genetics became the basis for the modern science of genetics and heredity. Around 1856 Mendel began experiments in his small monastery garden, crossing different varieties of the garden pea. The import of Mendel's work was not seen until many years after his death, Jan 6, 1884, at Brünn, Austria. In 1900 other European botanists discovered his papers and confirmed and extended his theories.

OREGON BREWERS FESTIVAL. July 22–25. Tom McCall Waterfront Park, Portland, OR. The Oregon Brewers Festival is one of the nation's longest-running and best-loved craft beer festivals. At least 90 independent craft breweries offer more than two-dozen styles of handcrafted beers to 70,000 beer lovers during the four-day event. There's also food, live music, beer-oriented vendors and a soda garden. Annually, beginning the Wednesday to the last Saturday in July. Est attendance: 70,000. For info: Chris Crabb. E-mail: chris@oregonbrewfest.com. Web: www.oregonbrewfest.com.

PIED PIPER OF HAMELIN: ANNIVERSARY—MAYBE. July 22, 1376. According to legend, the German town of Hamelin, plagued with

rats, bargained with a piper who promised to, and did, pipe the rats out of town and into the Weser River. Refused payment for his work, the piper then piped the children out of town and into a hole in a hill, never to be seen again. More recent historians suggest that the event occurred in 1284 when young men of Hamelin left the city on colonizing adventures.

RAT-CATCHERS DAY. July 22. A day to recognize the rat-catchers who labor to exterminate members of the genus *Rattus*, disease-carrying rodents that infest most of the "civilized" world. Observed on the anniversary of the legendary feat of the Pied Piper of Hamelin on July 22, 1376 (according to 16th-century chronicler Richard Rowland Verstegen).

SPACE MILESTONE: *SOYUZ TM-3* (USSR). July 22, 1987. Two Soviet cosmonauts, Aleksandr Viktorenko and Aleksandr Aleksandrov, along with the first Syrian space traveler, Mohammed Faris, were launched on a projected 10-day mission. Launched from the Baikonur base in central Asia, the spacecraft orbited Earth for two days before linking with Soviet space station *Mir*. The *Soyuz TM-3* spacecraft was used as a shuttle to *Mir* into the 1990s.

SPOONER'S DAY (WILLIAM SPOONER: BIRTH ANNIVERSARY). July 22. A day named for the Reverend William Archibald Spooner (born at London, England, July 22, 1844, warden of New College, Oxford, 1903–24, died at Oxford, England, Aug 29, 1930), whose frequent slips of the tongue led to coinage of the term *spoonerism* to describe them. A day to remember the scholarly man whose accidental transpositions gave us *blushing crow* (for crushing blow), *tons of soil* (for sons of toil), *queer old dean* (for dear old queen), *swell foop* (for fell swoop) and *half-warmed fish* (for half-formed wish).

VANDERBILT, AMY: BIRTH ANNIVERSARY. July 22, 1908. American journalist and etiquette expert, born at New York, NY. Her *Amy Vanderbilt's Complete Book of Etiquette* (1952) became the bible for manners of courtesy and society. Vanderbilt also hosted the television program "It's in Good Taste" from 1954 to 1960. She died at New York City on Dec 27, 1974.

🎂 BIRTHDAYS TODAY

Orson Bean, 92, actor ("To Tell the Truth," "Mary Hartman, Mary Hartman"), born Dallas Frederick Burroughs at Burlington, VT, July 22, 1928.

Irene Bedard, 53, actress ("Grand Avenue," "Crazy Horse"), born Anchorage, AK, July 22, 1967.

Albert Brooks, 73, comedian, director, actor (*Finding Nemo, Broadcast News, Mother*), born Albert Lawrence Einstein at Los Angeles, CA, July 22, 1947.

Tim Brown, 54, Hall of Fame football player, born Dallas, TX, July 22, 1966.

Willem Dafoe, 65, actor (*The Florida Project, Spider-Man, Shadow of the Vampire, Platoon*), born Appleton, WI, July 22, 1955.

Scott Dixon, 40, race car driver, born Brisbane, Australia, July 22, 1980.

Robert J. Dole, 97, former US senator (R, Kansas), born Russell, KS, July 22, 1923.

Ezekiel "Zeke" Elliott, 25, football player, born St. Louis, MO, July 22, 1995.

Rob Estes, 57, actor ("Melrose Place," "Silk Stalkings"), born Norfolk, VA, July 22, 1963.

Danny Glover, 73, actor (*Honeydripper, Beloved, Lethal Weapon, The Color Purple*), born San Francisco, CA, July 22, 1947.

July 2020	S	M	T	W	T	F	S
				1	2	3	4
	5	6	7	8	9	10	11
	12	13	14	15	16	17	18
	19	20	21	22	23	24	25
	26	27	28	29	30	31	

Selena Gomez, 28, singer, actress ("Wizards of Waverly Place," *Spring Breakers, Ramona and Beezus*), born Grand Prairie, TX, July 22, 1992.

Don Henley, 73, musician (The Eagles), songwriter, born Linden, TX, July 22, 1947.

Rhys Ifans, 53, actor (*Anonymous, Notting Hill, Dancing at Lughnasa*), born Ruthin, Wales, July 22, 1967.

Keyshawn Johnson, 48, sportscaster, former football player, born Los Angeles, CA, July 22, 1972.

Josh Lawson, 39, actor (*The Wedding Party, The Campaign*, "House of Lies"), born Brisbane, Australia, July 22, 1981.

John Leguizamo, 56, actor, performer (stage: *Mambo Mouth, Freak, Ghetto Klown*; *Moulin Rouge!, Summer of Sam*), born Bogotá, Colombia, July 22, 1964.

Kristine Lilly, 49, Hall of Fame soccer player, born New York, NY, July 22, 1971.

Alan Menken, 71, film score composer (*Pocahontas, Aladdin*), born New Rochelle, NY, July 22, 1949.

Bobby Sherman, 75, singer, actor, born Santa Monica, CA, July 22, 1945.

David Spade, 55, actor ("Rules of Engagement," "Just Shoot Me," *Tommy Boy*), born Birmingham, MI, July 22, 1965.

Terence Stamp, 81, actor (*The Limey, Alien Nation, The Collector*), born London, England, July 22, 1939.

Keith Sweat, 59, R&B singer, born New York, NY, July 22, 1961.

Alex Trebek, 80, game show host ("Concentration," "Jeopardy!"), born Sudbury, ON, Canada, July 22, 1940.

July 23 — Thursday

DAY 205   **161 REMAINING**

BANGOR STATE FAIR. July 23–Aug 1 (subject to change). Bass Park Complex, Bangor, ME. Fun for the whole family with eating contests, Old MacDonald's Farm, EMRBA Rabbit Show, demolition derby, truck pulls and more. For info: Bangor State Fair, 515 Main St, Bangor, ME 04401. Phone: (207) 561-8300. E-mail: fair@bangormaine.gov. Web: www.bangorstatefair.com.

CHANDLER, RAYMOND: BIRTH ANNIVERSARY. July 23, 1888. The American master of postwar hard-boiled crime fiction didn't begin writing until he lost his management job at an oil company in 1933. After publishing short stories in *Black Mask* and other crime magazines, Chandler published his first novel, *The Big Sleep*, in 1939 to popular and critical acclaim. This and subsequent novels featured Philip Marlowe, a Los Angeles private eye who liked "liquor and women and chess and a few other things." Chandler was known for spare prose that featured gripping similes: "The wet air was as cold as the ashes of love" or "She had eyes like strange sins." Chandler also authored or coauthored three Hollywood screenplays, including the searing *Double Indemnity*. Born at Chicago, IL, Chandler died at La Jolla, CA, on Mar 26, 1959.

COMIC-CON INTERNATIONAL. July 23–26. San Diego Convention Center, San Diego, CA. Comic-Con has become ground zero in the world of comics conventions. It offers a giant Exhibit Hall (more than 460,000 square feet); a massive programming schedule (close to 700 separate events), featuring comics and all aspects of the popular arts, including hands-on workshops and educational and academic programming such as the Comics Arts Conference; anime and film screenings (including a separate film festival); games; the Will Eisner Comic Industry Awards; a costume competition with prizes and trophies; an autograph area; an art show; and Portfolio Reviews, bringing together aspiring artists with major companies. Est attendance: 135,000. For info: Comic-Con International. Web: www.comic-con.org/cci.

DELAWARE STATE FAIR. July 23–Aug 1. Harrington, DE. 101st annual fair features major concert and motor events, acres of carnival rides, livestock shows, petting zoos, commercial and competitive events, exotic food and free attractions throughout the grounds. Est attendance: 300,000. For info: Delaware State Fair, PO Box 28, Harrington, DE 19952. Phone: (302) 398-3269. Fax: (302) 398-5030. E-mail: info@thestatefair.net. Web: www.delawarestatefair.com.

DRYSDALE, DON: BIRTH ANNIVERSARY. July 23, 1936. Elected to the Baseball Hall of Fame in 1984, Don Drysdale was a pitcher for the Brooklyn and Los Angeles Dodgers from 1956 to 1969, compiling a win-loss record of 209–166 with a career ERA of 2.95. Following his playing career he became a successful and popular broadcast announcer for the Chicago White Sox and then for the Los Angeles Dodgers. He was born at Van Nuys, CA, and died at Montreal, QC, Canada, July 3, 1993.

EGYPT: REVOLUTION DAY. July 23. National holiday. Anniversary of the revolution in 1952, which was launched by army officers and changed Egypt from a monarchy to a republic led by Nasser.

FIRST US SWIMMING SCHOOL OPENS: ANNIVERSARY. July 23, 1827. The first swimming school in the US opened at Boston, MA. Its pupils included John Quincy Adams and James Audubon.

HOT ENOUGH FOR YA DAY. July 23. We are permitted today to utter the words that suffice when nothing of intelligence comes to mind. "Is it hot enough for ya?" Annually, July 23. (©2006 by WH.) For info: Thomas & Ruth Roy, Wellcat Holidays, 2418 Long Ln, Lebanon, PA 17046-1708. Phone: (717) 279-0184. E-mail: info@wellcat.com. Web: www.wellcat.com.

JAPAN: MARINE DAY. July 23. National holiday also known as Ocean Day. First observed in 1995, but based on an older observance, Marine Memorial Day (originated in 1941). For this island nation, Marine Day is a grateful celebration of the sea and its bounty. Normally observed on the third Monday in July, Marine Day is July 23 in 2020. (In 2019, the Japanese government announced temporary changes to the national holiday schedule as a consequence of the 2020 Olympic Games in Tokyo.)

JAPAN: SOMA NO UMAOI (WILD HORSE CHASING). July 23–25. Hibarigahara, Haramachi, Fukushima Prefecture. A thousand horsemen clad in ancient armor compete for possession of three shrine flags shot aloft on Hibarigahara Plain, and men in white costumes attempt to catch wild horses corralled by the horsemen.

LEO, THE LION. July 23–Aug 22. In the astronomical/astrological zodiac, which divides the sun's apparent orbit into 12 segments, the period July 23–Aug 22 is traditionally identified as the sun sign of Leo, the Lion. The ruling celestial body is the sun.

MAVERICK, SAMUEL: BIRTH ANNIVERSARY. July 23, 1803. The rancher, land baron and politician was born at Pendleton, SC, but spent most of his life in Texas. He was a key figure in the battle for Texas independence from Mexico. As a rancher, Maverick refused to brand his calves—claiming humanitarian reasons, but others saw that habit as a wily way to increase his herd by "adopting" unmarked cattle. Nevertheless, an unbranded or stray calf was remarked as being "Maverick's," and his last name became

a synonym for a stubborn individual. Maverick died Sept 2, 1870, at San Antonio, TX, where he had twice been mayor.

REESE, HAROLD HENRY "PEE WEE": BIRTH ANNIVERSARY. July 23, 1918. Hall of Fame shortstop, born at Ekron, KY. Died Aug 14, 1999, at Louisville, KY.

SAINT APOLLINARIS: FEAST DAY. July 23. First bishop of Ravenna, and a martyr, of unknown date. Observed July 23.

SELASSIE, HAILE: BIRTH ANNIVERSARY. July 23, 1892. Born Ras Tafari Makonnen at Harar, Ethiopia, he adopted the name Haile Selassie when crowned the last emperor of Ethiopia. His 1930–74 rule, interrupted during 1936–41 by Mussolini-led Italian occupation, was one of significant social progress, educational advancements and modernization. He led Ethiopia to the League of Nations and UN membership and made Addis Ababa a pivotal center for the African Union. Famine, rising unemployment and political stagnation resulted in his deposition by the military in 1974. Widely regarded as spiritual leader of African-descended people by Rastafarians since 1930; his status as such has grown since his mysterious death (perhaps by strangulation) on Aug 27, 1975, under house arrest at his palace in Addis Ababa, Ethiopia.

SHARM AL-SHEIKH BOMBINGS: 15th ANNIVERSARY. July 23, 2005. In the worst act of terrorism in Egypt's recent history, the Red Sea resort city of Sharm al-Sheikh was the target of three bomb attacks that killed 88 people and injured more than 200. Various groups claimed responsibility for the attacks, which occurred on Egypt's Revolution Day.

SPACE MILESTONE: FIRST FEMALE COMMANDER: *COLUMBIA* (US). July 23, 1999. Colonel Eileen Collins led a shuttle mission to deploy a $1.5 billion x-ray telescope, the Chandra observatory, into space. It is a sister satellite to the Hubble Space Telescope. The observatory is named after Nobel Prize–winner Subrahmanyan Chandrasekhar.

🎂 BIRTHDAYS TODAY

Ronny Cox, 82, actor (*Deliverance, Bound for Glory, Total Recall*), born Cloudcroft, NM, July 23, 1938.

Omar Epps, 47, actor ("House," *Love & Basketball*), born Brooklyn, NY, July 23, 1973.

Nicholas Gage, 81, journalist, film producer, writer (*Eleni*), born Lia, Greece, July 23, 1939.

Nomar Garciaparra, 47, sportscaster, former baseball player, born Whittier, CA, July 23, 1973.

Woody Harrelson, 59, actor (Emmy for "Cheers"; *The Hunger Games* films, "True Detective," *Lost in London, The Messenger*), born Midland, TX, July 23, 1961.

Don Imus, 80, radio personality, author, born Riverside, CA, July 23, 1940.

Arata Isozaki, 89, architect, born Oita, Japan, July 23, 1931.

Anthony M. Kennedy, 84, former associate justice of the US, born Sacramento, CA, July 23, 1936.

Eriq La Salle, 58, actor ("ER," *Coming to America*), born Hartford, CT, July 23, 1962.

Edie McClurg, 69, actress ("WKRP in Cincinnati," *Eating Raoul, A River Runs Through It*), born Kansas City, MO, July 23, 1951.

Tom Mison, 38, actor ("Sleepy Hollow," *Salmon Fishing in the Yemen*), born London, England, July 23, 1982.

Belinda Montgomery, 70, actress ("Miami Vice," "Doogie Howser, MD"), born Winnipeg, MB, Canada, July 23, 1950.

	S	M	T	W	T	F	S
July				1	2	3	4
	5	6	7	8	9	10	11
	12	13	14	15	16	17	18
2020	19	20	21	22	23	24	25
	26	27	28	29	30	31	

Gary Dwayne Payton, 52, Hall of Fame basketball player, born Oakland, CA, July 23, 1968.

Daniel Radcliffe, 31, actor (Harry Potter films, *The Woman in Black, My Boy Jack*), born London, England, July 23, 1989.

Brandon Roy, 36, baseball player, born Seattle, WA, July 23, 1984.

Marlon Wayans, 48, actor ("In Living Color," *Scary Movie*), born New York, NY, July 23, 1972.

Paul Wesley, 38, actor ("The Vampire Diaries"), born Paul Wasilewski at New Brunswick, NJ, July 23, 1982.

July 24 — Friday

DAY 206   **160 REMAINING**

ANNIE OAKLEY DAYS. July 24–26. Greenville, OH. Since 1963, a festival to keep alive the memory of Annie Oakley—Little Miss Sure Shot (1860–1926). Visitors and locals alike enjoy shooting contests, a car show, fast draw competitions, melodramas, historical tours, a pilgrimage to Annie's grave, special displays at Garst Museum and a Saturday parade. Includes a large antique and collectibles market with crafts and specialty items. Annually, the last full weekend in July. Est attendance: 20,000. For info: Annie Oakley Days Committee, Inc, PO Box 129, Greenville, OH 45331. E-mail: president@annieoakleyfestival.org. Web: www.AnnieOakleyFestival.org.

ARCADIA DAZE. July 24–26. Arcadia, MI. The scenic village of Arcadia is the setting for this midsummer event. Activities include art fair, steak fry, fishing contest, games for the children, pancake breakfast and 5k running race on Saturday, and a street dance on Friday and Saturday. Car show on Saturday. There is a parade on Sunday at 1:30 PM on Lake Street. An old-fashioned good time for the whole family. Sponsor: Arcadia Lions Club. Est attendance: 2,500. For info: Wesley Hull, Arcadia Daze, 3269 Lake St, Arcadia, MI 49613. Phone: (231) 889-5555.

BOLÍVAR, SIMON: BIRTH ANNIVERSARY. July 24, 1783. "The Liberator," born at Caracas, Venezuela. Commemorated in Venezuela and other Latin American countries. Died Dec 17, 1830, at Santa Marta, Colombia. Bolivia is named after him.

COUSINS DAY. July 24. A day to celebrate, honor and appreciate our cousins. For info: Claudia Evart, 30 Park Ave, #2P, New York, NY 10016-0274. E-mail: ms.dia326@gmail.com.

DETROIT FOUNDED: ANNIVERSARY. July 24, 1701. Anniversary of the landing at the site of Detroit by Antoine de la Mothe Cadillac in the service of Louis XIV of France. Fort Pontchartrain du Detroit was the first settlement on site.

DUMAS, ALEXANDRE: BIRTH ANNIVERSARY. July 24, 1802. French playwright and novelist, born at Villers-Cotterêts, France. He is said to have written more than 300 volumes, including *The Count of Monte Cristo* and *The Three Musketeers*. Father of Alexandre Dumas (Dumas fils), also a novelist and playwright (1824–95). Dumas died near Dieppe, France, Dec 5, 1870.

EARHART, AMELIA: BIRTH ANNIVERSARY. July 24, 1897. American aviatrix lost on flight from New Guinea to Howland Island, in the Pacific Ocean, July 2, 1937. First woman to cross the Atlantic solo, second person to cross the Atlantic solo and first person to fly solo across the Pacific from Hawaii to California. Born at Atchison, KS.

GAMES OF THE XXXII OLYMPIAD—TOKYO 2020. July 24–Aug 9. Tokyo, Japan. The world's most prestigious and anticipated sporting event. The games feature 33 sports, broken into 50 disciplines and 339 events. For info: Tokyo 2020. Web: https://tokyo2020.org. Also: International Olympic Committee, Lausanne, Switzerland. Web: www.olympic.org.

JAPAN: SPORTS DAY. July 24. National holiday to encourage physical activity for building a sound body and mind. Created in 1966 to commemorate the day of the opening of the 18th Olympic Games at Tokyo, Oct 10, 1964. Normally, this day is the second Monday in October, but in 2020 it is July 24: in 2019, the Japanese government announced temporary changes to the national holiday schedule as a consequence of the 2020 Olympic Games in Tokyo.

NATCHITOCHES–NORTHWESTERN STATE UNIVERSITY FOLK FESTIVAL AND THE LOUISIANA STATE FIDDLE CHAMPIONSHIP. July 24–25. Prather Coliseum, Northwestern State University, Natchitoches, LA. The festival is a "purist" folk festival in that only folk artists who are reviving a traditional Louisiana folk art or still working a Louisiana tradition are invited. Music, food, crafts and narrative sessions. A four-time winner of the Top Twenty Events in the Southeast, as determined by the Southeast Tourism Society. Annually, the fourth weekend in July. Est attendance: 5,000. For info: Shane Rasmussen, Louisiana Folklife Center, Natchitoches/NSU Folk Festival, NSU Box 3663, Natchitoches, LA 71497. Phone: (318) 357-4332. Fax: (318) 357-4331. E-mail: folklife@nsula.edu. Web: www.nsula.edu/folklife.

NATIONAL DRIVE-THRU DAY. July 24. After WWII, California sunshine and a love affair with automobiles spurred the growth of roadside businesses in the Golden State catering specifically to motorists. As America's first major drive-through hamburger chain, Jack in the Box® restaurants (founded in 1951) helped pave the way for a delicious new dining experience. Annually, on July 24. For info: Brian Luscomb, Jack in the Box, 9330 Balboa Ave, San Diego, CA 92123. Phone: (858) 571-2121. Web: www.jackin-thebox.com.

PIONEER DAY. July 24. Utah. State holiday. Commemorates the day in 1847 when Brigham Young and his followers entered the Salt Lake valley.

🎂 **BIRTHDAYS TODAY**

Barry Bonds, 56, former baseball player, born Riverside, CA, July 24, 1964.

Ruth Buzzi, 84, comedienne, actress ("Rowan & Martin's Laugh-In," "Sesame Street"), born Westerly, RI, July 24, 1936.

Rose Byrne, 41, actress ("Damages," *Bridesmaids, Sunshine*), born Balmain, Sydney, Australia, July 24, 1979.

Lynda Carter, 69, actress ("Wonder Woman," "Partners in Crime"), former Miss World–USA, singer, born Phoenix, AZ, July 24, 1951.

Kristin Chenoweth, 52, actress, singer (stage: *Wicked*, Tony for *You're a Good Man, Charlie Brown*; "The West Wing"), born Broken Arrow, OK, July 24, 1968.

Mitch Grassi, 28, singer (Pentatonix), born Arlington, TX, July 24, 1992.

Kadeem Hardison, 55, actor ("A Different World," "The Sixth Man"), born New York, NY, July 24, 1965.

Robert Hays, 73, actor (*Airplane!*, "Starman"), born Bethesda, MD, July 24, 1947.

Julie A. Krone, 57, former jockey, first woman in National Racing Hall of Fame, born Benton Harbor, MI, July 24, 1963.

Jennifer Lopez, 50, actress (*Maid in Manhattan, The Cell, Out of Sight*), singer, born the Bronx, NY, July 24, 1970.

Karl Malone, 57, Hall of Fame basketball player, born Summerfield, LA, July 24, 1963.

Eugene Mirman, 46, actor ("Bob's Burgers," "Flight of the Conchords"), born Moscow, USSR (now Russia), July 24, 1974.

Elisabeth Moss, 38, actress ("The Handmaid's Tale," "Mad Men," *Top of the Lake*), born Los Angeles, CA, July 24, 1982.

Pat Oliphant, 85, cartoonist, born Adelaide, Australia, July 24, 1935.

Anna Paquin, 38, actress ("True Blood," the X-Men films, *The Piano, Fly Away Home*), born Winnipeg, MB, Canada, July 24, 1982.

Chris Sarandon, 78, actor (*Dog Day Afternoon, The Princess Bride*), born Beckley, WV, July 24, 1942.

Peter Serkin, 73, musician, born New York, NY, July 24, 1947.

July 25 — Saturday

DAY 207   **159 REMAINING**

ALLIES BREAK OUT OF NORMANDY BEACHHEAD: ANNIVERSARY. July 25, 1944. Having made a spectacularly successful landing on D-Day (June 6), Allied forces then secured and extended their position by landing more than a million men and 60,000 tons of supplies. Despite early success with Operation Overlord, the Allies were pinned down, and a breakout was necessary if France was to be retaken. Sustained air bombardment (carpet bombing) created gaps in the German lines, and on this date Allied forces penetrated the lines and outflanked and bypassed the German units. The German forces were incredulous at the speed with which the Allies shook loose from them and advanced over the French countryside.

***ANDREA DORIA* SINKS: ANNIVERSARY.** July 25, 1956. The Italian luxury liner collided with the *Stockholm*, a Swedish liner, on its way to New York. Other ships in the area came to the aid of the *Andrea Doria*. During the ordeal 1,634 people were rescued, including the captain and the crew.

ANTIQUE AND CLASSIC BOAT RENDEZVOUS. July 25–26. Mystic Seaport Museum, Mystic, CT. Pre-1970 power and sailing yachts on view for Mystic Seaport Museum visitors. Mystic River parade on Sunday. Est attendance: 4,000. For info: Mystic Seaport Museum, 75 Greenmanville Ave, Box 6000, Mystic, CT 06355. Phone: (860) 527-0711. Web: www.mysticseaport.org.

BOB DYLAN AT NEWPORT FOLK FESTIVAL: 55th ANNIVERSARY. July 25, 1965. Twenty-four-year-old folk star Bob Dylan rocked the Newport Folk Festival—literally—by playing an electric set on stage. Those in the audience responded with catcalls or silence. Although Dylan had played Newport before, it was as a solo troubadour. On this date, he brought a backing band, the Paul Butterfield Blues Band, and blasted out "Maggie's Farm" and "Like a Rolling Stone." It was a short set—which festival organizers threatened to make shorter by cutting the sound cables—but it went down in music history as a seminal event.

COSTA RICA: GUANACASTE DAY. July 25. National holiday. Commemorates the 1814 transfer of the region of Guanacaste from Nicaragua to Costa Rica by Spain.

FIRST AIRPLANE CROSSING OF ENGLISH CHANNEL: ANNIVERSARY. July 25, 1909. Louis Bleriot—after asking from the cockpit, "Where is England?"—took off from Les Baraques (near Calais), France, and landed on English soil at Northfall Meadow, near Dover, where he was greeted first by English police and customs officers. This, the world's first international overseas airplane flight, was accomplished in a 28-horsepower monoplane with a wingspan of 23 feet. See also: "Bleriot, Louis: Birth Anniversary" (July 1).

GENEVA ARTS FAIR. July 25–26. Geneva, IL. The Geneva Arts Fair transform downtown Geneva into a venue for more than 150 artists. The juried show was voted sixth favorite in artcalendar.com's Best Art Fairs in America, and designated Top 200 Fine Craft Fair by Art Fair Sourcebook. Fair includes a children's art area. Admission is free. Annually, the fourth Saturday and Sunday in July. Est attendance: 20,000. For info: Geneva Chamber of Commerce, PO Box 481, 8 S Third St, Geneva, IL 60134. Phone: (630) 232-6060. E-mail: chamberinfo@genevachamber.com. Web: www.genevachamber.com.

GERMANY: WAGNER FESTIVAL (BAYREUTHER FESTSPIELE). July 25–Aug 28. Bayreuth. Since 1876, the works of Richard Wagner are performed daily at the Festival Theatre, which Wagner had built in 1872–76. For info: Bayreuther Festspiele GmbH, Festspielhügel 1-2, 95445 Bayreuth, Germany. Phone: (49) 921-78-78-0. Web: www.bayreuther-festspiele.de.

HARRISON, ANNA SYMMES: BIRTH ANNIVERSARY. July 25, 1775. Wife of William Henry Harrison, ninth president of the US, born at Morristown, NJ. Died at North Bend, IN, Feb 25, 1864.

NATIONAL DAY OF THE COWBOY. July 25. Annually, the fourth Saturday in July is set aside as a day to pay homage to our cowboy and pioneer heritage, as well as to honor working cowboys and cowgirls, rodeo athletes, Western musicians, cowboy poets, Western artists, ranchers and all others who continue to contribute to the cowboy and pioneer culture. Proclaimed by the US Senate in Resolution 138 for the first time for July 23, 2005. For info: National Day of the Cowboy. Phone: (928) 759-0951. E-mail: info@nationaldayofthecowboy.com. Web: www.nationaldayofthecowboy.com.

PARRISH, MAXFIELD: 150th BIRTH ANNIVERSARY. July 25, 1870. Born at Philadelphia, PA, Frederick Maxfield Parrish become one of the most beloved and popular illustrators of the first half of the twentieth century, creating fantastical dreamscapes for children's books, calendars, magazine covers and bestselling prints and posters. His ethereally cyan blue skies would win such notice that "Maxfield Parrish blue" became a universally recognized color. He illustrated such classic children's books as *Poems of Childhood, The Arabian Nights* and *The Knave of Hearts*. His painting *Daybreak*

July 2020	S	M	T	W	T	F	S
				1	2	3	4
	5	6	7	8	9	10	11
	12	13	14	15	16	17	18
	19	20	21	22	23	24	25
	26	27	28	29	30	31	

(1922) sold more than 200,000 prints and remains his most popular work. Parrish died at Plainfield, NH, on Mar 10, 1966.

PUERTO RICO: CONSTITUTION DAY. July 25. Also called Commonwealth Day or Occupation Day. Commemorates proclamation of constitution in 1952.

PUERTO RICO: LOIZA ALDEA FIESTA. July 25–28. Loiza Aldea. Best known of Puerto Rico's patron saint festivities. Villagers of Loiza Aldea, 20 miles east of San Juan, don devil masks and colorful costumes for a variety of traditional activities.

SPAIN: SAINT JAMES DAY. July 25. Holy day of the patron saint of Spain. When this day falls on a Sunday, it is a Holy Year and pilgrims make the pilgrimage to Santiago de Compostela, the site of the saint's tomb. The next Holy Year is 2021.

THURMOND, NATE: BIRTH ANNIVERSARY. July 25, 1941. Nathaniel "Nate" Thurmond was a double-double center whose 14-year NBA career included seven All-Star appearances and the first-ever recording of a quadruple-double. Thurmond was born at Akron, OH, and starred as a high school player and in college at Bowling Green. Drafted by the San Francisco Warriors in 1963, Thurmond posted strong numbers as Wilt Chamberlain's understudy before blossoming during the 1966–67 and 1967–68 seasons. His 18 rebounds in a single quarter remains an NBA record. He was later a veteran force with the Chicago Bulls and Cleveland Cavaliers, where the remarkable consistency of Thurmond's game became legend. He died at San Francisco, CA, July 16, 2016.

TUNISIA: REPUBLIC DAY. July 25. National holiday. Commemorates the proclamation of the republic in 1957.

🎂 BIRTHDAYS TODAY

Midge Decter, 93, journalist, author, born St. Paul, MN, July 25, 1927.

Illeana Douglas, 55, actress (*Message in a Bottle, Grace of My Heart*), born Boston, MA, July 25, 1965.

Iman, 65, model, actress (*Star Trek VI*), born Iman Mohamed Abdulmajid at Mogadishu, Somalia, July 25, 1955.

James Lafferty, 35, actor ("One Tree Hill," *A Season on the Brink*), born Hemet, CA, July 25, 1985.

Matt LeBlanc, 53, actor ("Man with a Plan," "Episodes," "Friends"), born Newton, MA, July 25, 1967.

Evgeni Nabakov, 45, former hockey player, born Ust-Kamenogorsk, USSR (now Osteman, Kazakhstan), July 25, 1975.

July 26 — Sunday

DAY 208   **158 REMAINING**

AMERICANS WITH DISABILITIES ACT SIGNED: 30th ANNIVERSARY. July 26, 1990. President George H.W. Bush signed the Americans with Disabilities Act, which went into effect two years later. It required that public facilities be made accessible to people with disabilities.

ARMED FORCES UNIFIED: ANNIVERSARY. July 26, 1947. President Truman signed legislation unifying the two branches of the armed forces into the Department of Defense. The branches merged were the War Department (Army) and the Navy. The Air Force was separated from the Army at the same time and made an independent force. Truman nominated James Forrestal to be the first secretary of defense. The legislation also provided for the National Security Council, the Central Intelligence Agency and the Joint Chiefs of Staff.

ATOMIC BOMB DELIVERED: 75th ANNIVERSARY. July 26, 1945. The US cruiser *Indianapolis* arrived at Tinian Island in the Marianas with a deadly cargo. Aboard were the makings of the atomic bomb.

On the island waited scientists prepared to complete the assembly. See also: "*Indianapolis* Sunk: Anniversary" (July 29).

AUNTIE'S DAY®. July 26. 12th annual. This day acknowledges, honors and celebrates the aunt(s) in a child's life, whether she is an Auntie by Relation (ABR), Auntie by Choice (ABC) or godmother, for everything she does for a child not-her-own. The day is especially poignant for 23 million American women who identify as PANK®s, or Professional Aunts No Kids. Annually, the fourth Sunday in July. For info: Melanie Notkin, Savvy Auntie, 200 W 93rd St, Ste 6F, New York, NY 10025. Phone: (917) 449-2917. E-mail: Editor@Savvyauntie.com. Web: www.AuntiesDay.com.

CATLIN, GEORGE: BIRTH ANNIVERSARY. July 26, 1796. American artist famous for his paintings of Native American life, born at Wilkes-Barre, PA. In 1832 he toured North and South American tribes, recording their lives in his work. He died Dec 23, 1872, at Jersey City, NJ.

CLINTON, GEORGE: BIRTH ANNIVERSARY. July 26, 1739. Fourth vice president of the US (1805–12), born at Little Britain, NY. Brigadier general under General George Washington during the American Revolution. Popular governor of New York (1777–95 and 1801–4). Vice president under Thomas Jefferson and James Madison. First vice president to die in office—at Washington, DC, Apr 20, 1812.

CUBA: NATIONAL DAY. July 26. Anniversary of the 1953 beginning of Fidel Castro's revolutionary "26th of July Movement." He launched a failed attack on the Moncada army barracks, and most involved were killed or captured. He was captured and given a trial, during which he made his famous speech, "History will absolve me." Sentenced to 15 years, he was pardoned after just two.

CURAÇAO: CURAÇAO DAY. July 26. Traditional holiday commemorating Columbus's companion Alonso de Ojeda's discovery of the island of Curaçao in 1499, when he sailed into Santa Ana Bay, the entrance of the harbor of Willemstad. Festivities on this day.

EDWARDS, BLAKE: BIRTH ANNIVERSARY. July 26, 1922. American film director, born William Blake Crump at Tulsa, OK. Best known as director of the successful Pink Panther comedies that starred actor Peter Sellers. Other notable films include *Breakfast at Tiffany's*, *Days of Wine and Roses*, *10* and *Victor, Victoria*. He received an honorary Academy Award in 2004 for his career achievements. He was married to actress and singer Julie Andrews for 41 years, and died Dec 15, 2010, at Santa Monica, CA.

HUXLEY, ALDOUS: BIRTH ANNIVERSARY. July 26, 1894. English author, satirist, mystic and philosopher, Aldous Leonard Huxley was born at Godalming, Surrey, England. Best known of his works are *Brave New World* and *Point Counter Point*. Huxley died at Los Angeles, CA, Nov 22, 1963.

KUBRICK, STANLEY: BIRTH ANNIVERSARY. July 26, 1928. American filmmaker, born at the Bronx, NY. Kubrick started out in photography at the age of 16 with *Look* magazine. His first film, *Day of the Fight*, produced in 1950, was a documentary of his photo series about fighter Walter Cartier. His film credits include *Dr. Strangelove*, *Full Metal Jacket* and *2001: A Space Odyssey*. *Eyes Wide Shut*, Kubrick's final film, was released posthumously in the summer of 1999. He died at London, England, Mar 7, 1999.

LIBERIA: INDEPENDENCE DAY. July 26. National holiday. Became republic in 1847, under aegis of the US societies for repatriating former slaves in Africa.

MALDIVES: INDEPENDENCE DAY. July 26. National holiday. Commemorates independence from Britain in 1965.

NEW YORK RATIFICATION DAY. July 26, 1788. Became 11th state to ratify Constitution in 1788.

POTSDAM DECLARATION: 75th ANNIVERSARY. July 26, 1945. As the Potsdam Conference came to a close in Germany, Churchill, Truman and China's representatives fashioned a communiqué to Japan offering it an opportunity to end the war. It demanded that Japan completely disarm; it allowed it sovereignty to the four main islands and to minor islands to be determined by the Allies and it insisted that all Japanese citizens be given immediate and complete freedom of speech, religion and thought. The Japanese would be allowed to continue enough industry to maintain their economy. The communiqué concluded with a demand for unconditional surrender. Unaware these demands were backed up by an atomic bomb, on July 28 Japanese prime minister Admiral Kantaro Suzuki rejected the Potsdam Declaration.

PUBLICATION OF FIRST ESPERANTO BOOK: ANNIVERSARY. July 26, 1887. On this date, Dr. L.L. Zamenhof published *Lingvo internacia* (*International Language*), the first textbook about the universal language Esperanto. Zamenhof used the pen name Doktoro Esperanto (Doctor Hopeful) for the book, and this name was adopted for the language. See also: "Zamenhof, Ludwik Lejzer: Birth Anniversary" (Dec 15).

ROBARDS, JASON: BIRTH ANNIVERSARY. July 26, 1922. A staple on the American stage and screen for six decades, Robards was born at Chicago, IL, and was a decorated WWII veteran. He won the Oscar for Best Supporting Actor two years in a row, for 1976's *All the President's Men* and 1977's *Julia*. His most famous stage roles were in the plays of Eugene O'Neill, including *The Iceman Cometh* and *Long Day's Journey into Night*. He won the Tony Award in 1959 for his portrayal of a fictionalized F. Scott Fitzgerald in *The Disenchanted*. He died at Bridgeport, CT, Dec 26, 2000.

SHAW, GEORGE BERNARD: BIRTH ANNIVERSARY. July 26, 1856. Irish playwright, essayist, vegetarian, socialist, antivivisectionist and, he said, "one of the hundred best playwrights in the world." His major works include *Arms and the Man, Man and Superman, Major Barbara* and *Pygmalion*. Born at Dublin, Ireland. Died at Ayot St. Lawrence, England, Nov 2, 1950.

SPACE MILESTONE: *APOLLO 15* (US). July 26, 1971. Launched this date. Astronauts David R. Scott and James B. Irwin landed on moon (lunar module *Falcon*) while Alfred M. Worden piloted command module *Endeavor*. *Rover 1*, a four-wheel vehicle, was used for further exploration. Departed moon Aug 2, after nearly three days. Pacific landing Aug 7.

US ARMY FIRST DESEGREGATION: ANNIVERSARY. July 26, 1944. During WWII the US Army ordered desegregation of its training camp facilities. Later the same year black platoons were assigned to white companies in a tentative step toward integration of the battlefield. However, it was not until after the war—July 26, 1948— that President Harry Truman signed an order officially integrating the armed forces.

🎂 BIRTHDAYS TODAY

Jacinda Ardern, 40, Prime Minister of New Zealand, born Hamilton, New Zealand, July 26, 1980.

Kate Beckinsale, 47, actress (*Underworld, Pearl Harbor, Van Helsing*), born London, England, July 26, 1973.

Sandra Bullock, 56, actress (Oscar for *The Blind Side*; *Gravity, Crash*), born Arlington, VA, July 26, 1964.

Susan George, 70, actress (*Straw Dogs*), born London, England, July 26, 1950.

Mick Jagger, 77, singer (Rolling Stones), born Michael Philip Jagger at Dartford, England, July 26, 1943.

Helen Mirren, 74, actress (Oscar for *The Queen*; *Gosford Park*, "Prime Suspect," "Elizabeth I"), born London, England, July 26, 1946.

Taylor Momsen, 27, actress (*How the Grinch Stole Christmas, Paranoid Park*, "Gossip Girl"), born St. Louis, MO, July 26, 1993.

Jeremy Piven, 56, actor ("Entourage," "Mr Selfridge," *Grosse Pointe Blank*), born New York, NY, July 26, 1964.

Kevin Spacey, 61, actor (Oscars for *American Beauty* and *The Usual Suspects*; Tony for *Lost in Yonkers*; "House of Cards"), born South Orange, NJ, July 26, 1959.

Cress Williams, 50, actor ("Hart of Dixie," "Friday Night Lights"), born Heidelberg, Germany, July 26, 1970.

July 27 — Monday

DAY 209   **157 REMAINING**

ATLANTIC TELEGRAPH CABLE LAID: ANNIVERSARY. July 27, 1866. Having started from Valentia, Ireland, on July 7, 1866, the *Great Eastern* steamship successfully laid a submarine cable at Heart's Content, Newfoundland, Canada, on this day. This cable provided transatlantic communication and followed almost-successful 1858 and 1865 efforts.

BARBOSA, JOSÉ CELSO: BIRTH ANNIVERSARY. July 27, 1857. Puerto Rican physician and patriot, born at Bayamon, Puerto Rico. His birthday is a holiday in Puerto Rico. He died at San Juan, Puerto Rico, Sept 21, 1921.

CHICAGO RACE RIOTS: ANNIVERSARY. July 27–Aug 3, 1919. On July 27, Eugene Williams, a 17-year-old black youth, crossed an unofficial, invisible segregation barrier on a Chicago, IL, South Side beach. Williams drowned after being stoned by white men. The police refused to arrest the men involved, sparking violence that spread quickly—instigated by members of white, territorial "athletic clubs." An angered black population, many of them WWI veterans, rose against them. By Aug 1, 23 black and 15 white men had died, more than 500 people were injured and more than 1,000 black families had lost their homes to fires.

DUROCHER, LEO: BIRTH ANNIVERSARY. July 27, 1905. Leo Durocher was born at West Springfield, MA. He began his major league baseball career with the New York Yankees in 1925. He also played for the St. Louis Cardinals' "Gashouse Gang" and the Brooklyn Dodgers, where he first served as player-manager in 1939. On July 6, 1946, he used the phrase "Nice guys finish last," which would become his trademark. As a manager, he guided the New York Giants into two World Series. Following a five-year period away from baseball, he resurfaced as a coach with the Los Angeles Dodgers in 1961. In 1966 he signed with the Chicago Cubs as manager. After leaving the Cubs, he spent one season with the Houston Astros and then retired from baseball in 1973. He died Oct 7, 1991, at Palm Springs, CA.

KOREAN WAR ARMISTICE: ANNIVERSARY. July 27, 1953. Armistice agreement ending war that had lasted three years and 32 days was signed at Panmunjom, Korea (July 26, US date), by US and North Korean delegates. Both sides claimed victory at conclusion of two years and 17 days of truce negotiations.

MOON PHASE: FIRST QUARTER. July 27. Moon enters First Quarter phase at 8:32 AM, EDT.

		S	M	T	W	T	F	S
July					1	2	3	4
		5	6	7	8	9	10	11
2020		12	13	14	15	16	17	18
		19	20	21	22	23	24	25
		26	27	28	29	30	31	

MOONDANCE RELEASED: 50th ANNIVERSARY. July 27, 1970. Van Morrison's album *Moondance* was issued in the United Kingdom and was an immediate critical and commercial success. It was rated triple platinum by 1996 and today ranks 65 on *Rolling Stone*'s 500 greatest albums list.

★**NATIONAL KOREAN WAR VETERANS ARMISTICE DAY.** July 27. A special remembrance of the veterans of the Korean War, and especially those of the US and allied combatants who made the ultimate sacrifice in Korea. The display of the US flag is encouraged on this day. Annually, July 27.

TAKE YOUR HOUSEPLANTS FOR A WALK DAY. July 27. Walking your plants around the neighborhood enables them to become familiar with their environment, thereby providing them with a sense of knowing, bringing on wellness. (©2006 by WH.) For info: Thomas & Ruth Roy, Wellcat Holidays, 2418 Long Ln, Lebanon, PA 17046. Phone: (717) 279-0184. E-mail: info@wellcat.com. Web: www.wellcat.com.

TINKER, JOE: BIRTH ANNIVERSARY. July 27, 1880. Born at Muscotah, KS, shortstop Joseph Bert Tinker was part of the Chicago Cubs' famous Tinker-to-Evers-to-Chance double-play combination, which first took the field on Sept 13, 1902. For the next eight years this trio was the soul of the powerhouse Cubs—despite the fact that Tinker and Johnny Evers stopped speaking to each other in September 1905 (they continued the feud for 33 years). Tinker played with the Cincinnati Reds after the Cubs, played and managed in the Federal League and then managed the Cubs. Inducted into the Hall of Fame (with Evers and Chance) in 1946. Died at Orlando, FL, July 27, 1948. See also: "Tinker to Evers to Chance: First Double Play Anniversary" (Sept 15).

US DEPARTMENT OF STATE FOUNDED: ANNIVERSARY. July 27, 1789. The first presidential cabinet department, called the Department of Foreign Affairs, was established by the Congress. Later the name was changed to Department of State.

VIRGIN ISLANDS: HURRICANE SUPPLICATION DAY. July 27. Legal holiday. Population attends churches to pray for protection from hurricanes. Annually, the fourth Monday in July.

WALK ON STILTS DAY. July 27. A day to walk on stilts, providing a chance to develop self-confidence through mastery of balance and coordination. A chance to enjoy the challenge of childhood no matter your age. A celebration of daring accomplishments at homes, circuses and theme parks everywhere. Annually, July 27. For info: Bill "Stretch" Coleman. E-mail: stretch@stiltwalker.com. Web: www.stiltwalker.com.

🎂 BIRTHDAYS TODAY

Cassandra Clare, 47, author (The Mortal Instruments series), born Judith Rumelt at Tehran, Iran, July 27, 1973.

Nikolaj Coster-Waldau, 50, actor ("Game of Thrones," *Mama, Black Hawk Down*), born at Denmark, July 27, 1970.

Peggy Gale Fleming, 72, sportscaster, Olympic figure skater, born San Jose, CA, July 27, 1948.

Bobbie Gentry, 78, singer, songwriter ("Ode to Billie Joe"), born Roberta Streeter at Chickasaw County, MS, July 27, 1942.

Courtney Kupets, 34, gymnast, born Bedford, TX, July 27, 1986.

Norman Lear, 98, television scriptwriter, producer ("All in the Family," "Maude"), born New Haven, CT, July 27, 1922.

Maureen McGovern, 71, singer, actress, born Youngstown, OH, July 27, 1949.

Julian McMahon, 52, actor ("Charmed," "Nip/Tuck"), born Sydney, Australia, July 27, 1968.

Jonathan Rhys-Meyers, 43, actor ("The Tudors," *August Rush, Match Point, Elvis*), born County Dublin, Ireland, July 27, 1977.

Alex Rodriguez, 45, former baseball player, born New York, NY, July 27, 1975.

Maya Rudolph, 48, actress (*Bridesmaids*), comedienne ("Saturday Night Live"), born Gainesville, FL, July 27, 1972.

Taylor Schilling, 36, actress ("Orange Is the New Black"), born Boston, MA, July 27, 1984.

Jordan Spieth, 27, golfer, born Dallas, TX, July 27, 1993.

Betty Thomas, 72, director, actress ("Hill Street Blues"), born St. Louis, MO, July 27, 1948.

Donnie Yen, 57, actor (*Rogue One, Ip Man, Hero*), martial arts champion, producer, action choreographer, born Yen Ji-Dan at Guangzhou, China, July 27, 1963.

July 28 — Tuesday

DAY 210   **156 REMAINING**

FAROE ISLANDS: OLAI FESTIVAL. July 28–29. Torshavn. National festival held in honor of Saint Olav, the patron saint of these small islands of the Norwegian Sea, which are part of the kingdom of Denmark. Begins the eve of St. Olav's Day (July 28) with a procession, sporting events, meetings and concerts. The festival continues on St. Olav's Day itself (July 29) with a ceremonial procession involving political, religious and community leaders to the parliament. After the prime minister's opening speech, the governmental year begins. Ceremonies end at midnight with community singing. Est attendance: 50,000.

FOX, TERRY: BIRTH ANNIVERSARY. July 28, 1958. With cancer requiring amputation of his right leg at age 18, Fox was determined to devote his life to a fight against the disease. His "Marathon of Hope," a planned 5,200-mile run westward across Canada, started Apr 12, 1980, at St. John's, NF, and continued 3,328 miles to Thunder Bay, ON, Sept 1, 1980, when he was forced to stop by spread of the disease. During the run (on an artificial leg) he raised $24 million for cancer research and inspired millions with his courage. Terry Fox was born at Winnipeg, MB, Canada, and died at New Westminster (near Vancouver), BC, Canada, June 28, 1981.

HAMBURG FIRESTORM: ANNIVERSARY. July 28, 1943. More than 42,000 civilians were killed when 2,326 tons of bombs, predominantly incendiaries, were dropped on Hamburg, Germany, by the Allies on this date. At the center of the firestorm the winds uprooted trees, and flames burned eight square miles in the eight

hours the fire lasted. A firestorm occurs when the fires in a given area become so intense that they devour all the oxygen nearby and suck more into themselves, creating hurricane-force winds that feed the fires and move them at great speeds.

HEYWARD, THOMAS: BIRTH ANNIVERSARY. July 28, 1746. American Revolutionary soldier, judge and signer of the Declaration of Independence. Born at St. Luke's Parish, SC, Heyward died at Old House Plantation near Ridgeland, SC, on Mar 6, 1809.

ONASSIS, JACQUELINE LEE BOUVIER KENNEDY: BIRTH ANNIVERSARY. July 28, 1929. Editor, widow of John Fitzgerald Kennedy (35th president of the US), born at Southampton, NY. Later married (Oct 20, 1968) Greek shipping magnate Aristotle Socrates Onassis, who died Mar 15, 1975. The widely admired and respected former first lady died May 19, 1994, at New York City.

PERU: INDEPENDENCE DAY. July 28. San Martin declared independence from Spain on this day in 1821. After the final defeat of Spanish troops by Simon Bolívar in 1824, Spanish rule ended.

PICCARD, JACQUES: BIRTH ANNIVERSARY. July 28, 1922. Oceanographer and explorer, born at Brussels, Belgium. The son of famed hot-air balloon adventurer Auguste Piccard, Jacques worked with his father to develop technology that enabled him to explore the deepest parts of the ocean. Using buoyancy techniques, he created a submersible called a bathyscaphe that he used in 1960 (in conjunction with the US Navy) to explore the Challenger Deep section of the Mariana Trench in the Pacific Ocean. This record-setting dive of nearly seven miles remains the deepest dive ever successfully attempted. He also built the first tourist submarine. He died at Lake Geneva, Switzerland, Nov 1, 2008.

PLANE CRASHES INTO EMPIRE STATE BUILDING: 75th ANNIVERSARY. July 28, 1945. Hampered by a thick fog, a B-25 bomber crashed into the 79th and 80th floors of the Empire State Building, killing 14. Miraculously, Betty Lou Oliver, one of the building's elevator operators, survived a 75-floor plunge in a damaged car.

POTTER, (HELEN) BEATRIX: BIRTH ANNIVERSARY. July 28, 1866. Author, illustrator, naturalist and conservationist born at London, England. She created beloved and bestselling books for children starting with *The Tale of Peter Rabbit* in 1901. Potter died at Sawrey, Lancashire, England, Dec 22, 1943.

SILENT PARADE IN NEW YORK CITY: ANNIVERSARY. July 28, 1917. The NAACP staged the Silent Parade on New York City's Fifth Ave to protest lynchings and the East St. Louis, IL, race riots. Organized by James Weldon Johnson and W.E.B. Du Bois, the parade was composed of more than 10,000 men, women and children. The protesters—mostly from Harlem—were silent. They held signs with messages such as "Mr President, why not make America safe for democracy?" and "The First Blood for American Independence Was Shed by a Negro: Crispus Attucks." Drummers took part but their instruments were muffled.

SPACE MILESTONE: *SKYLAB 3* (US). July 28, 1973. Alan L. Bean, Owen K. Garriott and Jack R. Lousma started 59-day mission in the space station to test human spaceflight endurance. Pacific splashdown Sept 25.

THAILAND: KING'S BIRTHDAY AND NATIONAL DAY. July 28. King Maha Vajiralongkorn's birthday became a public holiday after he took the throne in 2016 following the death of King Bhumibol

Adulyadej. Celebrated throughout the kingdom with colorful pageantry. Stores and houses decorated with spectacular illuminations at night. Public holiday.

TOWNES, CHARLES HARD: BIRTH ANNIVERSARY. July 28, 1915. Born at Greenville, SC, Townes studied at Duke University and the California Institute of Technology, earning a PhD in physics. He worked for Bell Technical Laboratories in the '30s and '40s, designing bombing systems and other wartime uses of radar. In 1948 he moved to Columbia University in New York to teach and research microwave technologies, conceiving of a "maser" that then became a "laser" as his work moved from microwave to light amplification (after he had a famous epiphany on a park bench). His work with his brother-in-law, Dr. A.L. Schawlow, on using lasers in astronomy, earned them the Nobel Prize in Physics in 1964 and led to the discovery of black holes. Future applications of his laser technologies included bar code scanners, CD players, surgical instruments and missile guidance systems. Townes died at Oakland, CA, on Jan 27, 2015.

VALLEE, RUDY: BIRTH ANNIVERSARY. July 28, 1901. American singer, saxophone player and radio idol of millions during the 1930s. Born Hubert Prior Vallee, at Island Pond, VT, the crooner used a megaphone to amplify his voice and introduced his performances with the salutation "Heigh-ho-everybody!" Vallee appeared in a number of movies, including *How to Succeed in Business Without Really Trying*. Among his best-remembered songs are "I'm Just a Vagabond Lover," "Say It Isn't So" and his signature song, "My Time Is Your Time." Vallee died at age 84 at North Hollywood, CA, July 3, 1986.

VETERANS BONUS ARMY EVICTION: ANNIVERSARY. July 28, 1932. Some 15,000 unemployed veterans of WWI marched on Washington, DC, in the summer of 1932, demanding payment of a war bonus. After two months' encampment in Washington's Anacostia Flats, eviction of the bonus marchers by the US Army was ordered by President Herbert Hoover. Under the leadership of General Douglas MacArthur, Major Dwight D. Eisenhower and Major George S. Patton, Jr (among others), cavalry, tanks and infantry attacked. Fixed bayonets, tear gas and the burning of the veterans' tents hastened the end of the confrontation. One death was reported.

WORLD HEPATITIS DAY. July 28. Viral hepatitis—a group of infectious diseases known as hepatitis A, B, C, D and E—affects millions of people worldwide, causing acute and chronic liver disease and killing close to 1.4 million people every year. On this day, the WHO and its partners urge policy makers, health workers and the public to "think again" about this silent killer. Annually, July 28. For info: World Health Organization. Web: www.who.int.

WORLD WAR I BEGINS: ANNIVERSARY. July 28, 1914. Archduke Francis Ferdinand of Austria-Hungary and his wife were assassinated at Sarajevo, Bosnia, by a Serbian nationalist June 28, 1914, touching off the conflict that became WWI. Austria-Hungary declared war on Serbia July 28, the formal beginning of the war. Within weeks, Germany entered the war on the side of Austria-Hungary, and Russia, France and Great Britain entered on the side of Serbia.

🎂 BIRTHDAYS TODAY

William Warren (Bill) Bradley, 77, former US senator (D, New Jersey), Hall of Fame basketball player, born Crystal City, MO, July 28, 1943.

Santiago Calatrava, 69, architect, engineer, born Valencia, Spain, July 28, 1951.

Jim Davis, 75, cartoonist ("Garfield"), born Marion, IN, July 28, 1945.

Manu Ginóbili, 43, basketball player, born Bahai Blanca, Argentina, July 28, 1977.

Darryl Hickman, 89, actor (*The Tingler, The Grapes of Wrath*), born Los Angeles, CA, July 28, 1931.

Linda Kelsey, 74, actress ("Lou Grant"), born Minneapolis, MN, July 28, 1946.

Lori Loughlin, 56, actress ("Full House," *Back to the Beach*), born Long Island, NY, July 28, 1964.

Scott Pelley, 63, journalist, broadcaster ("60 Minutes"), born San Antonio, TX, July 28, 1957.

Sally Struthers, 72, actress ("All in the Family"), born Portland, OR, July 28, 1948.

John David Washington, 36, actor (*BlacKkKlansman*, "Ballers"), born Los Angeles, CA, July 29, 1984.

July 29 — Wednesday

DAY 211 **155 REMAINING**

CHINCOTEAGUE PONY PENNING. July 29–30. Chincoteague Island, VA. To round up the more than 200 wild ponies living on Assateague Island and swim them across the inlet to Chincoteague, where about 60 to 80 of them are sold. Annually, the last Wednesday and Thursday in July. Est attendance: 50,000. For info: Chincoteague Chamber of Commerce, 6733 Maddox Blvd, Chincoteague, VA 23336. Phone: (757) 336-6161. Fax: (757) 336-1242. E-mail: info@chincoteaguechamber.com. Web: www.chincoteaguechamber.com.

GLOBAL TIGER DAY. July 29. International awareness day to celebrate and urge conservation of the endangered tiger, as well as a day to seek preservation and expansion of its natural habitats. This day also promotes the goal of doubling the current tiger population by 2022. Created as a result of the first-ever International Tiger Forum held at Saint Petersburg, Russia, in 2010. There are multiple sponsors of this day. Annually, July 29. For info: World Wildlife Federation. Web: http://tigerday.panda.org.

HIMES, CHESTER: BIRTH ANNIVERSARY. July 29, 1909. Groundbreaking African-American author who accosted American racism in such novels as *If He Hollers Let Him Go* (1945). In the 1950s, after he relocated to a friendlier France, Himes created a series of hard-boiled mystery novels set in Harlem, NY, including *Cotton Comes to Harlem* (1965), that featured black detectives "Coffin Ed" Johnson and "Grave Digger" Jones. Born at Jefferson City, MO, Himes died Nov 12, 1984, at Moraira, Spain.

	S	M	T	W	T	F	S
July				1	2	3	4
	5	6	7	8	9	10	11
2020	12	13	14	15	16	17	18
	19	20	21	22	23	24	25
	26	27	28	29	30	31	

INDIANAPOLIS SUNK: 75th ANNIVERSARY. July 29, 1945. After delivering the atomic bomb to Tinian Island, the American cruiser *Indianapolis* was headed for Okinawa to train for the invasion of Japan when it was torpedoed by a Japanese submarine. Of 1,196 crew members, more than 350 were immediately killed in the explosion or went down with the ship. There were no rescue ships nearby, and those fortunate enough to survive endured the next 84 hours in ocean waters. By the time they were spotted by air on Aug 2, only 318 sailors remained alive, the others having either drowned or been eaten by sharks. This is the US Navy's worst loss at sea.

THE LORD OF THE RINGS: FIRST PART PUBLISHED: ANNIVERSARY. July 29, 1954. *The Fellowship of the Ring*, the first part of J.R.R. Tolkien's epic *The Lord of the Rings*, was published on this date in London, England, by George Allen and Unwin. The publishers chose to publish the novel in three parts because it was so long. *The Two Towers* was published on Nov 11, 1954, and *The Return of the King* was published on Oct 20, 1955.

MUSSOLINI, BENITO: BIRTH ANNIVERSARY. July 29, 1883. Italian Fascist leader, born at Dovia, Italy. Self-styled "Il Duce" (the leader), Mussolini governed Italy, first as prime minister and later as absolute dictator during 1922–43. It was Mussolini who said: "War alone . . . puts the stamp of nobility upon the peoples who have the courage to face it." But military defeat of Italy in WWII was Mussolini's downfall. Repudiated and arrested by the Italian government, he was temporarily rescued by German paratroops in 1943. Later, while attempting to flee in disguise to Switzerland, he and his mistress, Clara Petacci, were killed by Italian partisans near Lake Como, Italy, Apr 28, 1945.

NASA ESTABLISHED: ANNIVERSARY. July 29, 1958. President Eisenhower signed a bill creating the National Aeronautics and Space Administration to direct US space policy.

NORWAY: OLSOK EVE. July 29. Commemorates Norway's Viking king St. Olav, who fell in battle at Stiklestad near Trondheim, Norway, July 29, 1030. Bonfires, historical pageants.

OHIO STATE FAIR. July 29–Aug 9. Columbus, OH. Family fun, amusement rides, games, food booths, parades, entertainment, agriculture exhibits and educational displays. Est attendance: 900,000. For info: Ohio State Fair, 717 E 17th Ave, Columbus, OH 43211. Phone: (614) 644-3247 or (888) OHO-EXPO. Fax: (614) 644-4031. E-mail: info@expo.ohio.gov. Web: www.ohio-statefair.com.

POWELL, WILLIAM: BIRTH ANNIVERSARY. July 29, 1892. Popular actor who entertained audiences in a number of now-iconic roles: the clever sleuth Philo Vance in an early series of "talkies," the slightly inebriated and fun-loving Nick Charles in the hit *Thin Man* films, the "forgotten man" and butler in *My Man Godfrey* (1936) and exasperated father Clarence Day in *Life with Father* (1947). Powell was nominated three times for Best Actor Oscars but failed to win. He was born at Pittsburgh, PA, and died Mar 5, 1984, at Palm Springs, CA.

RAIN DAY AT WAYNESBURG, PENNSYLVANIA. July 29. Legend has it that rain will fall at Waynesburg, PA, on July 29 as it has most years for the last century, according to local records in this community, which was laid out in 1796 and incorporated in 1816.

ROOSEVELT, ALICE HATHAWAY LEE: BIRTH ANNIVERSARY. July 29, 1861. First wife of Theodore Roosevelt, 26th president of the US, whom she married in 1880. Born at Chestnut Hill, MA, she died at New York, NY, Feb 14, 1884.

SPAIN: FIESTA DE SANTA MARTA DE RIBARTEME (FESTIVAL OF NEAR DEATH EXPERIENCES). July 29. As Neves, Pontevedra, Galicia. Religious festival honoring Santa Marta. Those who have been near death and survived are carried in open coffins or march in shrouds to the local church. Est attendance: 5,000.

TARKINGTON, BOOTH: BIRTH ANNIVERSARY. July 29, 1869. American novelist (*The Magnificent Ambersons*), born at Indianapolis, IN. Died there May 19, 1946.

TOCQUEVILLE, ALEXIS DE: BIRTH ANNIVERSARY. July 29, 1805. French politician and author whose 1831 trip to the US inspired *Democracy in America*, one of the most insightful books written on the US. "America is a land of wonders," he wrote, "in which everything is in constant motion and every change seems an improvement." Born at Verneuil, France, Tocqueville died at Cannes, France, on Apr 16, 1859.

🧁 BIRTHDAYS TODAY

Ken Burns, 67, documentary filmmaker (*The Civil War, Baseball, Prohibition*), born New York, NY, July 29, 1953.

Danger Mouse, 43, musician, music producer, born Brian Joseph Burton at White Plains, NY, July 29, 1977.

Elizabeth Hanford Dole, 84, former US senator (R, North Carolina); former president, American Red Cross; former secretary of transportation and secretary of labor; born Salisbury, NC, July 29, 1936.

Fernando González, 40, former tennis player, born Santiago, Chile, July 29, 1980.

Tim Gunn, 67, fashion consultant, television personality ("Project Runway"), born Washington, DC, July 29, 1953.

Martina McBride, 54, country singer, born Sharon, KS, July 29, 1966.

Alexandra Paul, 57, actress ("Baywatch," *Dragnet*), born New York, NY, July 29, 1963.

Rayne Dakota "Dak" Prescott, 27, football player (2016 NFL Offensive Rookie of the Year), born Sulphur, LA, July 29, 1993.

Josh Radnor, 46, actor ("Mercy Street," "How I Met Your Mother"), born Columbus, OH, July 29, 1974.

Patty Scialfa, 64, singer, born Deal, NJ, July 29, 1956.

Paul Taylor, 90, dancer, choreographer, born Allegheny, NY, July 29, 1930.

David Warner, 79, actor (Emmy for *Masada*; *The Omen, Tron, Titanic*), born Manchester, England, July 29, 1941.

Wil Wheaton, 48, actor ("Star Trek: The Next Generation," *Stand by Me*), born Burbank, CA, July 29, 1972.

July 30 — Thursday

DAY 212   **154 REMAINING**

BRONTË, EMILY: BIRTH ANNIVERSARY. July 30, 1818. English novelist and lyric poet, one of the Brontë sisters, best known for her classic novel *Wuthering Heights* (1847). Born at Thornton, Yorkshire, England, she died Dec 19, 1848, at Haworth, Yorkshire.

ELVIS PRESLEY'S FIRST CONCERT APPEARANCE: ANNIVERSARY. July 30, 1954. Elvis Presley appeared in concert for the first time at Overton Park Orchestra Shell in Memphis, TN. He was billed third, and country crooner Slim Whitman was the headliner. Presley, only 19 years old, nervously began gyrating his leg and a

legend was born. See also: "Elvis Presley's First Single Released: Anniversary" (July 19).

FATHER HIDALGO: EXECUTION ANNIVERSARY. July 30, 1811. Miguel Hidalgo y Costilla, fiery leader of revolutionary forces in Mexico seeking independence from Spain, was executed by firing squad in Chihuahua. His head and those of the other executed insurgent leaders were put on public display in Guanajuato, Mexico, for 10 years.

FORD, HENRY: BIRTH ANNIVERSARY. July 30, 1863. Industrialist Henry Ford, whose assembly-line method of automobile production revolutionized the industry, was born at Wayne County, MI, on the family farm. His Model T made up half of the world's output of cars during its years of production. Ford built racing cars until in 1903 he and his partners formed the Ford Motor Company. In 1908 the company presented the Model T, which was produced until 1927, and in 1913 Ford introduced the assembly line and mass production. This innovation reduced the time it took to build each car from 12½ hours to only 1½. This enabled Ford to sell cars for $500, making automobile ownership a possibility for an unprecedented percentage of the population. He is also remembered for introducing a $5-a-day wage for automotive workers and for his statement "History is bunk." Died Apr 7, 1947, at age 83 at Dearborn, MI, where his manufacturing complex was located.

HOFFA, JAMES: DISAPPEARANCE 45th ANNIVERSARY. July 30, 1975. Former Teamsters Union leader, 62-year-old James Riddle Hoffa was last seen on this date outside a restaurant in Bloomfield Township, near Detroit, MI. His 13-year federal prison sentence had been commuted by President Richard M. Nixon in 1971. On Dec 8, 1982, seven years and 131 days after his disappearance, an Oakland County judge declared Hoffa officially dead as of July 30, 1982.

INSULIN FIRST ISOLATED AND EXTRACTED: ANNIVERSARY. July 30, 1921. Dr. Frederick Banting and his assistant at the University of Toronto Medical School, Charles Best, were able to isolate and extract insulin from one dog and inject it into a dog. whose pancreas had been removed. They noted an immediate drop in the injected dog's blood sugar—signaling a promising treatment option. In 1922 insulin was first administered to a diabetic 14-year-old boy.

LOLLAPALOOZA. July 30–Aug 2 (tentative). Grant Park, Chicago, IL. Music festival started in 1991 by Perry Farrell. Today's Lollapalooza spans more than 115 acres, a diverse array of more than 130 artists, multiple stages and lots more. Annually, the last weekend in July or the first weekend in August. For info: Lollapalooza. E-mail: info@lollapalooza.com. Web: www.lollapalooza.com.

MOORE, HENRY: BIRTH ANNIVERSARY. July 30, 1898. English sculptor born at Castleford, Yorkshire, England. Died at Hertfordshire, England, Aug 31, 1986.

July 2020	S	M	T	W	T	F	S
				1	2	3	4
	5	6	7	8	9	10	11
	12	13	14	15	16	17	18
	19	20	21	22	23	24	25
	26	27	28	29	30	31	

NATIONAL CHEESECAKE DAY. July 30. Widely observed celebration of the creamy dessert—by restaurants and bakeries, who usually offer discounts and new flavor introductions. Original sponsor is unknown to date. Annually, July 30.

PAPERBACK BOOKS INTRODUCED: 85th ANNIVERSARY. July 30, 1935. Although books bound in soft covers were first introduced in 1841 at Leipzig, Germany, by Christian Bernhard Tauchnitz, the modern paperback revolution dates to the publication of the first Penguin paperback by Sir Allen Lane at London, England, in 1935. Penguin Number 1 was *Ariel*, a life of Shelley by Andre Maurois.

STENGEL, CHARLES DILLON (CASEY): BIRTH ANNIVERSARY. July 30, 1890. Baseball Hall of Fame outfielder and manager, born at Kansas City, MO. His success as manager of the New York Yankees (10 pennants and 7 World Series titles in 12 years) made him one of the game's enduring stars. Inducted into the Hall of Fame in 1966. Known for his quips, such as "Don't cut my throat, I may want to do that later myself." Stengel died at Glendale, CA, Sept 29, 1975.

TISHA B'AV OR FAST OF AB. July 30. Hebrew calendar date: Ab 9, 5780. Commemorates and mourns the destruction of the First and Second Temples in Jerusalem (586 BC and AD 70). Began at sundown July 29.

UNITED NATIONS: INTERNATIONAL DAY OF FRIENDSHIP. July 30. Proclaimed in 2011. The United Nations recognizes July 30 as International Day of Friendship with the idea that friendship between peoples, countries, cultures and individuals can inspire peace efforts and build bridges between communities. The UN encourages governments, international organizations and civil society groups to hold events, activities and initiatives that contribute to the efforts of the international community toward promoting a dialogue among civilizations, solidarity, mutual understanding and reconciliation. For info: United Nations. Web: www.un.org/en/events/friendshipday/.

UNITED NATIONS: WORLD DAY AGAINST TRAFFICKING IN PERSONS. July 30. In 2013, UN member states designated July 30 as the World Day against Trafficking in Persons: to "raise awareness of the situation of victims of human trafficking and for the promotion and protection of their rights." (Res 68/192.) For info: United Nations, Dept of Public Info, New York, NY 10017. Web: www.un.org.

VANUATU: INDEPENDENCE DAY. July 30. Vanuatu became an independent republic (from France and the United Kingdom) in 1980 and observes its national holiday.

VEBLEN, THORSTEIN: BIRTH ANNIVERSARY. July 30, 1857. American economist, born at Valders, WI, and died at Menlo Park, CA, Aug 3, 1929. "Conspicuous consumption," he wrote in *The Theory of the Leisure Class*, "of valuable goods is a means of reputability to the gentleman of leisure."

YAWM ARAFAT: THE STANDING AT ARAFAT. July 30. Islamic calendar date: Dhu al-Hijjah 9, 1441. The day when people on the hajj (pilgrimage to Mecca) assemble for "the Standing" at the plain of Arafat at Mina, Saudi Arabia, near Mecca. This gathering is a foreshadowing of the Day of Judgment. Different methods for "anticipating" the visibility of the new moon crescent at Mecca are used by different Muslim groups, so date can vary by one to two days. Began at sunset the preceding day.

ZWORYKIN, VLADIMIR: BIRTH ANNIVERSARY. July 30, 1889. Born at Mourom, Russia, scientist Zworykin held more than 120 patents during his life but is best remembered as "the father of television." His inventions of the iconoscope and kinescope laid the foundation for the picture tube television; he was also active in the field of electron microscopy and invented the electron microscope and infrared vision. In 1967 he was awarded the National Medal of Science by the National Academy of Sciences. When asked to comment on the content of American television in a 1981 interview, Zworykin replied, "Awful." Died July 29, 1982, at Princeton, NJ.

🧁 BIRTHDAYS TODAY

Paul Anka, 79, singer, songwriter, born Ottawa, ON, Canada, July 30, 1941.

William Atherton, 73, actor (*The Day of the Locust, Ghostbusters, Die Hard, Die Hard 2*), born New Haven, CT, July 30, 1947.

Simon Baker, 51, actor ("The Mentalist," "The Guardian," *Land of the Dead*), born Launceston, Tasmania, July 30, 1969.

Peter Bogdanovich, 81, producer, director (*The Last Picture Show, Paper Moon*), actor, born Kingston, NY, July 30, 1939.

Alton Brown, 58, chef, television personality ("Good Eats," "Iron Chef America"), born Los Angeles, CA, July 30, 1962.

Delta Burke, 64, actress ("Designing Women"), former Miss Florida, born Orlando, FL, July 30, 1956.

Kate Bush, 62, singer, songwriter, born Lewisham, England, July 30, 1958.

Edd Byrnes, 87, actor ("77 Sunset Strip," *Darby's Rangers*), born New York, NY, July 30, 1933.

James William (Bill) Cartwright, 63, basketball coach and former player, born Lodi, CA, July 30, 1957.

Laurence Fishburne, 59, actor (*Matrix* films, *Akeelah and the Bee, Boyz N the Hood, What's Love Got to Do with It?*, Tony for *Two Trains Running*; "CSI"), born Augusta, GA, July 30, 1961.

Anita Faye Hill, 64, law professor, born Lone Tree, OK, July 30, 1956.

Lisa Kudrow, 57, actress ("Friends," *Romy and Michele's High School Reunion*), born Encino, CA, July 30, 1963.

Misty May-Treanor, 43, Olympic beach volleyball player, born Los Angeles, CA, July 30, 1977.

Patrick Modiano, 75, Nobel Prize–winning author (*Missing Person, Ring Roads*), born Paris, France, July 30, 1945.

Christopher Paul (Chris) Mullin, 57, Hall of Fame basketball player, born New York, NY, July 30, 1963.

Christopher Nolan, 50, filmmaker (*Dunkirk, Inception, Batman* trilogy), born London, England, July 30, 1970.

Ken Olin, 66, actor ("LA Doctors," "thirtysomething"), born Chicago, IL, July 30, 1954.

Jaime Pressly, 43, actress ("My Name Is Earl," *Not Another Teen Movie*), born Kinston, NC, July 30, 1977.

Gina Rodriguez, 36, actress ("Jane the Virgin"), born Chicago, IL, July 30, 1984.

David Sanborn, 75, saxophonist, composer, born Tampa, FL, July 30, 1945.

Arnold Schwarzenegger, 73, former governor of California (R), bodybuilder, actor (*The Terminator, True Lies*), born Graz, Austria, July 30, 1947.

Allan Huber "Bud" Selig, 86, Commissioner Emeritus of Baseball, born Milwaukee, WI, July 30, 1934.

Hope Solo, 39, soccer player, born Richland, WA, July 30, 1981.

Hilary Swank, 46, actress (Oscars for *Boys Don't Cry* and *Million Dollar Baby*), born Lincoln, NE, July 30, 1974.

July 31 — Friday

DAY 213   **153 REMAINING**

BLUEBERRY ARTS FESTIVAL. July 31–Aug 2. State Office Building, Methodist Church and Main Street Gallery, Ketchikan, AK. A street fair featuring arts and crafts, food, games and contests for all ages, performing arts events and poetry and prose readings. Annually, the first weekend in August. Est attendance: 8,000. For info: Ketchikan Area Arts and Humanities Council, 330 Main St, Ketchikan, AK 99901. Phone: (907) 225-2211. E-mail: info@ketchikanarts.org. Web: www.ketchikanarts.org.

EID-AL-ADHA: FEAST OF THE SACRIFICE. July 31. Islamic calendar date: Dhu al-Hijjah 10, 1441. Commemorates Abraham's willingness to sacrifice his son Ishmael in obedience to God. It is part of the hajj (pilgrimage to Mecca). The day begins with the sacrifice of an animal in remembrance of the Angel Gabriel's substitution of a lamb as Abraham's offering. One-third of the meat is given to poor people and the rest is shared with friends and family. Celebrated with gifts and general merrymaking, the festival usually continues for several days. It is celebrated as Tabaski in Benin, Burkina Faso, Guinea, Guinea-Bissau, Ivory Coast, Mali, Niger and Senegal; as Hari Raya Hajj in Southeast Asia and as Kurban Bayram in Turkey and Bosnia. Different methods for "anticipating" the visibility of the new moon crescent at Mecca are used by different Muslim groups, so date can vary by one to two days. Began at sunset the preceding day.

FEAST OF SAINT IGNATIUS OF LOYOLA. July 31. 1491–1556. Founder of the Society of Jesus (Jesuits). Canonized in 1622.

FIRST INDIAN SAINT: ANNIVERSARY. July 31, 2002. In Mexico City, Mexico, Pope John Paul II canonized the Roman Catholic Church's first Indian saint, Juan Diego. In 1531 Diego claimed to have seen the Virgin of Guadalupe, whose rose-framed image later appeared on his cloak. See also: "Day of Our Lady of Guadalupe" (Dec 12).

FIRST US GOVERNMENT BUILDING: ANNIVERSARY. July 31, 1792. The cornerstone of the Philadelphia Mint, the first US government building, was laid on this day.

FRIEDMAN, MILTON: BIRTH ANNIVERSARY. July 31, 1912. A Nobel Prize–winning economist, teacher and author, Friedman was born at Brooklyn, NY. In 1946, he became a professor of economics at the University of Chicago, where he did some of his best-known work. The Chicago School, of which he was a member with like-minded scholars, promulgated influential free-market theories. Died at San Francisco, CA, Nov 16, 2006.

GIGGLEFEET DANCE FESTIVAL. July 31 and Aug 2. Ketchikan, AK. Two evening performances celebrating dance in the community, including jazz, tap, ballet, modern, hip-hop, Native Alaskan,

break-dance and more. Part of the Blueberry Arts Festival. Est attendance: 1,500. For info: Ketchikan Area Arts and Humanities Council, 330 Main St, Ketchikan, AK 99901. Phone: (907) 225-2211. E-mail: info@ketchikanarts.org. Web: www.ketchikanarts.org.

KRESGE, S.S.: BIRTH ANNIVERSARY. July 31, 1867. Retail merchandising innovator Sebastian Spering Kresge was born into a farming family of Swiss heritage near Wilkes-Barre, PA. His S.S. Kresge chain of five-and-dime stores in the Midwest went public in 1912 and expanded across the US—at its prime the chain was second only to Woolworth's. At the time of his death, Oct 18, 1966, at East Stroudsburg, PA, there were 670 Kresge stores and 150 Kmart discount stores. The company was renamed Kmart in 1977.

***MOBY-DICK* MARATHON.** July 31–Aug 1. Mystic Seaport Museum, Mystic, CT. Marathon reading of the classic *Moby-Dick* in celebration of Herman Melville's birthday. Reading takes place on deck of the nation's last wooden whaler, the *Charles W. Morgan*. Annually, 24-hour reading from noon July 31 to noon Aug 1. Est attendance: 6,000. For info: Mystic Seaport Museum, 75 Greenmanville Ave, PO Box 6000, Mystic, CT 06355-0990. Phone: (860) 572-0711. Web: www.mysticseaport.org.

MONTANA STATE FAIR. July 31–Aug 8. Montana Expo Park, Great Falls, MT. 89th annual. Mighty Thomas Carnival, night shows, PRCA rodeo, free acts, food fair, 4-H exhibits and much more. Annually, two weeks beginning on the last Friday in July. Est attendance: 150,000. For info: Montana State Fair, 400 3rd St NW, Great Falls, MT 59404. Phone: (406) 727-8900. E-mail: info@goexpopark.com. Web: www.montanastatefair.com.

MUSIKFEST. July 31–Aug 9. Bethlehem, PA. Showcasing more than 500 musical performances on 15 indoor and outdoor stages throughout Bethlehem. The 10-day event also features delicious foods and desserts, children's activities, visual arts and fine crafts and a closing-night fireworks display. Est attendance: 1,000,000. For info: ArtsQuest, 25 W Third St, Bethlehem, PA 18015-1238. Phone: (610) 332-1300. Fax: (610) 332-1310. E-mail: info@artsquest.org. Web: www.musikfest.org.

NATIONAL CZECH FESTIVAL. July 31–Aug 2. Wilber, NE. 59th annual. Festival to promote preservation of Czech culture, foods and traditions. With accordion, polka and Czech band music; three parades; dancing; national queen contest; art show; Czech dinners; programs; fellowship; reunions. Annually, the first

weekend in August. Est attendance: 50,000. For info: Nebraska Czechs of Wilber, PO Box 652, Wilber, NE 68465. Phone: (402) 821-3233. Web: www.nebraskaczechsofwilber.com.

NATIONAL MUTT DAY—JULY. July 31. This day, founded in 2005 by animal welfare advocate Colleen Paige, celebrates the many wonderful attributes of mixed-breed dogs. It also promotes adoption worldwide. Since shelters are filled to the brim with mixed-breed dogs, we need two dates annually to help these "mutts" find forever homes. Annually, July 31 and Dec 2. For info: The Holiday Guild. Phone: (323) 285-2148. E-mail: k.kelly@theholidayguild.com. Web: www.nationalmuttday.com.

NEW JERSEY STATE FAIR®/SUSSEX COUNTY FARM AND HORSE SHOW. July 31–Aug 9. Sussex County Fairgrounds, Augusta, NJ. The state's largest agricultural fair also includes horse shows, educational exhibits, circus, carnival, vendors, fair food, entertainment and much more. Annually, beginning on the Friday of the first weekend in August. Est attendance: 175,000. For info: New Jersey State Fair, 37 Plains Rd, Augusta, NJ 07822. Phone: (973) 948-5500. E-mail: thefair@njstatefair.org. Web: www.njstatefair.org.

QUANTRILL, WILLIAM: BIRTH ANNIVERSARY. July 31, 1837. Born at Canal Dover, OH, William Quantrill is one of the infamous characters of the American Civil War. He was leader of a guerrilla band ("Quantrill's Raiders") who conducted raids and harassed Union soldiers along the Kansas–Missouri border. Quantrill is most notorious for the violent Aug 21, 1863, raid he led on Lawrence, KS. More than 150 men and boys were killed, and homes and businesses were burned. Quantrill was killed in a Union ambush near Taylorsville, KY, June 6, 1865.

SALVADOR, FRANCIS: DEATH ANNIVERSARY. July 31, 1776. The first Jew to die in the American Revolution, Salvador was also the first Jew elected to office in colonial America. He was voted a member of the South Carolina Provincial Congress in January 1775.

SATCHMO SUMMERFEST. July 31–Aug 2. New Orleans, LA. The spirit of Louis "Satchmo" Armstrong lives with this annual birthday celebration of his music, legacy and cultural contributions. The event includes a jazz-filled music festival, children's activities, seminars and panels, photo exhibits and cultural displays, a jazz mass and Satchmo-inspired New Orleans cuisine. It's all part of New Orleans' ongoing tribute to the "International Ambassador of Jazz" in the birthplace of jazz. Est attendance: 45,000. For info: French Quarter Festivals, Inc, 400 N Peters St, #205, New Orleans, LA 70130. Phone: (800) 673-5725 or (504) 522-5730. E-mail: info@fqfi.org. Web: www.fqfi.org.

"THE SHADOW" RADIO PREMIERE: 90th ANNIVERSARY. July 31, 1930. "Who knows what evil lurks in the hearts of men? The Shadow knows!" This popular crime and suspense program premiered on CBS radio. Originally, the Shadow was just the narrator of the changing stories, but later he became a character with his own adventures—with the alter ego of Lamont Cranston. Orson Welles was the first Shadow.

STURGIS RALLY. July 31–Aug 9. Sturgis, SD. 80th annual. The granddaddy of all motorcycle rallies and races. Since 1938 the

	S	M	T	W	T	F	S
July				1	2	3	4
	5	6	7	8	9	10	11
2020	12	13	14	15	16	17	18
	19	20	21	22	23	24	25
	26	27	28	29	30	31	

small community of Sturgis has welcomed motorcycle enthusiasts from around the world to a week of varied cycle racing, tours of the beautiful Black Hills, trade shows and thousands of bikes on display. Est attendance: 500,000. For info: Sturgis Rally. Web: www.sturgis.com.

TALL TIMBER DAYS FESTIVAL. July 31–Aug 2. Grand Rapids, MN. Festival features the Timberworks Lumberjack Show, chainsaw carvers, bingo, dancing, music, beer garden, arts and crafts and competitions. Ninety-unit parade and children's pet parade. Families welcome. Annually, the first weekend in August. Est attendance: 10,000. For info: Tall Timber Days, PO Box 134, Grand Rapids, MN 55744. E-mail: talltimberdays@gmail.com. Web: www.talltimberdays.com.

US PATENT OFFICE OPENS: ANNIVERSARY. July 31, 1790. The first US Patent Office opened its doors, and the first US patent was issued to Samuel Hopkins of Vermont for a new method of making pearl ash and potash. The patent was signed by George Washington and Thomas Jefferson.

🎂 BIRTHDAYS TODAY

Dean Cain, 54, actor ("Lois & Clark: The New Adventures of Superman"), born Mount Clemens, MI, July 31, 1966.

Geraldine Chaplin, 76, actress (*Nashville, Roseland, Chaplin*), born Santa Monica, CA, July 31, 1944.

Susan Flannery, 77, actress ("The Bold and the Beautiful," "Dallas"), born Jersey City, NJ, July 31, 1943.

Evonne Goolagong, 69, Hall of Fame tennis player, born Griffith, Australia, July 31, 1951.

Gary Lewis, 74, singer, born New York, NY, July 31, 1946.

Evgeni Malkin, 34, hockey player, born Magnitogorsk, Russia, July 31, 1986.

Don Murray, 91, actor (*Bus Stop*, "Twin Peaks," "Knots Landing"), born Hollywood, CA, July 31, 1929.

France Nuyen, 81, actress ("St. Elsewhere"), born Marseilles, France, July 31, 1939.

Jonathan Ogden, 46, former football player, born Washington, DC, July 31, 1974.

Rico Rodriguez, 22, actor ("Modern Family"), born College Station, TX, July 31, 1998.

J.K. Rowling, 55, author (Harry Potter series, Cormoran Strike series, *The Casual Vacancy*), philanthropist, born Joanne Rowling at Bristol, England, July 31, 1965.

Wesley Snipes, 58, actor (*Blade, US Marshals, Jungle Fever, White Men Can't Jump*), born Orlando, FL, July 31, 1962.

◆ August ◆

August 1 — Saturday

AMERICAN ADVENTURES MONTH. Aug 1–31. This month celebrates vacationing in the Americas. Whether traveling in luxury or in primitive conditions, tourists are encouraged to explore South, Central and North America. Experiencing the Americas in a variety of ways unlocks new worlds for all travelers. "Remember to keep adventure in every vacation." For info: Peter Kulkkula, American Adventurer, 381 Billings Rd, Fitchburg, MA 01420-1407. Phone: (978) 343-4009 or (978) 808-6608 (cell phone). E-mail: DebKulkkula@gmail.com. Web: www.AmericanAdventures-Month.com.

BENIN: INDEPENDENCE DAY: 60th ANNIVERSARY OF INDEPEN-DENCE. Aug 1. Public holiday. Commemorates independence from France in 1960. Benin at that time was known as Dahomey.

BLACK BUSINESS MONTH. Aug 1–31. Six months after Black History Month, the focus on and awareness of black-owned and operated enterprises needs a boost. This month is dedicated to starting, maintaining, growing and buying from and committing to black-owned businesses and entrepreneurs. For info: Sylvia Henderson, Springboard Training, 3570 Olney-Laytonsville Rd, Ste 588, Olney, MD 20832. Phone: (301) 260-1538. E-mail: sylvia@spring-boardtraining.com.

BOOMERS MAKING A DIFFERENCE MONTH. Aug 1–31. Since 2010. August celebrates baby boomers who have made a significant contribution to their communities by helping others improve their lives. Each year several boomers are featured for their special efforts, support, skills, products or time in bringing awareness and transformation to people who are in need. Send nominations for impactful baby boomers to the e-mail in the contact info. For info: Amy Sherman. E-mail: amybethsherman@gmail.com. Web: www.yourbabyboomersnetwork.com.

BURK, MARTHA (CALAMITY JANE): DEATH ANNIVERSARY. Aug 1, 1903. Known as a frontierswoman and companion to Wild Bill Hickok, Calamity Jane Burk was born Martha Jane Cannary at Princeton, MO, in May 1852. As a young girl living in Montana, she became an excellent markswoman. She went to the Black Hills of South Dakota as a scout for a geologic expedition in 1875. Several opposing traditions account for her nickname, one springing from her kindness to people who were less fortunate, while another attributes it to the harsh warnings she would give men who offended her. She died at Terry, SD, and was buried at Dead-wood, SD, next to Wild Bill Hickok.

CHILDREN'S EYE HEALTH AND SAFETY MONTH. Aug 1–31. Prevent Blindness provides information about amblyopia, a condition that can affect two to three percent of children and can cause perma-nent vision loss. Additional information includes tips about pre-venting eye injuries in children, signs of possible eye problems and general eye health. For info: Prevent Blindness, 211 W Wacker Dr, Ste 1700, Chicago, IL 60606. Phone: (800) 331-2020. E-mail: info@preventblindness.org. Web: www.preventblindness.org.

CHILDREN'S VISION AND LEARNING MONTH. Aug 1–31. Research-ers estimate that one out of four children has an undiagnosed vision problem that is interfering with the ability to read and learn. Since 80 percent of learning is dependent upon vision, it is vital that parents and educators ensure they understand the signs of vision problems. With children getting ready to go back to school, August is the perfect month for education. For info: College of Optometrists in Vision Development, 215 W Garfield Rd, Ste 200,

Aurora, OH 44202. Phone: (330) 995-0718. E-mail: info@covd.org. Web: www.covd.org.

CLARK, WILLIAM: 250th BIRTH ANNIVERSARY. Aug 1, 1770. The soldier, explorer and public servant was born at Caroline County, VA. He served seven years in the US Army and then gained his lasting fame when Meriwether Lewis asked him to join an expe-dition exploring the Louisiana Territory (1803–06). Clark was an able leader and contributed detailed maps and animal illustrations on the journey. A grateful President Thomas Jefferson made Clark brigadier general of militia for the Louisiana Territory (1807–13) and superintendent of Indian Affairs (1807–38). Clark was also governor of the Missouri Territory (1813–20) and surveyor general for Illinois, Missouri and Arkansas (1824–25). Clark foresaw the tension between US interests and the native peoples of the western US, and he urged that the US treat native tribes with respect. Clark died at St. Louis, MO, on Sept 1, 1838.

COLORADO: ADMISSION DAY: ANNIVERSARY. Aug 1, 1876. Colo-rado admitted to the Union as the 38th state. The first Monday in August is celebrated as Colorado Day.

DIARY OF ANNE FRANK: THE LAST ENTRY: ANNIVERSARY. Aug 1, 1944. To escape deportation to concentration camps, the Jewish family of Otto Frank hid for two years in the warehouse of his food products business at Amsterdam, Netherlands. Gentile friends smuggled in food and other supplies during their confinement. Thirteen-year-old Anne Frank, who kept a journal during the time of their hiding, penned her last entry in the diary Aug 1, 1944: "[I] keep on trying to find a way of becoming what I would like to be, and what I could be, if . . . there weren't any other people living in the world." Three days later (Aug 4, 1944), Grüne Polizei raided the "Secret Annex" where the Frank family was hidden. Anne and her sister were sent to Bergen-Belsen concentration camp, where Anne died at age 15, two months before the liberation of Holland. Young Anne's diary, later found in the family's hiding place, has been translated into 30 languages and has become a symbol of the indomitable strength of the human spirit. See also: "Frank, Anne: Birth Anniversary" (June 12).

EMANCIPATION OF 500: ANNIVERSARY. Aug 1, 1791. Virginia planter Robert Carter III confounded his family and friends by fil-ing a deed of emancipation for his 500 slaves. One of the wealthiest men in the state, Carter owned 60,000 acres over 18 plantations. The deed included the following words: "I have for some time past been convinced that to retain them in Slavery is contrary to the true principles of Religion and Justice and therefore it is my duty to manumit them." The document established a schedule by which 15 slaves would be freed each Jan 1, over a 21-year period, plus slave children would be freed at age 18 for females and 21 for males. It is believed this was the largest act of emancipation in US history and predated the Emancipation Proclamation by 70 years.

FANCY FARM PICNIC. Aug 1. Downtown Fancy Farm, KY. Southern hospitality at its best. The small community volunteers its time to entertain with games, prizes and great fun. Raffle for a brand-new car. Bingo with wonderful prizes. Down-home country dinners including the famous Fancy Farm Picnic Barbecue. Annually, the first Saturday in August. Est attendance: 20,000. For info: Sharon Hayden, c/o Fancy Farm Picnic, 2759 Carrico Rd, Fancy Farm, KY 42039. E-mail: toddhayden@wk.net.

FIRST US CENSUS: ANNIVERSARY. Aug 1, 1790. The first census revealed that there were 3,939,326 citizens in the 16 states and the Ohio Territory. The US has taken a census every 10 years since 1790.

GARCIA, JERRY: BIRTH ANNIVERSARY. Aug 1, 1942. Jerome John Garcia was born at San Francisco, CA. Country, bluegrass and folk musician and a guitar player of remarkable ability, Garcia was the leading force behind the legendary Grateful Dead, the band that sustained a veritable industry for its legion of followers. He died Aug 9, 1995, at Forest Knolls, CA, ending a musical career that spanned more than three decades.

GIRLFRIENDS' DAY. Aug 1. Celebrate this special day by taking your girlfriends shopping, to a play, to the movies, out to eat, to the spa and/or to the park. A fun slumber party is also recommended. Annually, Aug 1. For info: Susan Anne Masters, 931 Monroe Dr NE, Ste A102, #226, Atlanta, GA 30308. Phone: (404) 939-3833. E-mail: susan@MistressSusanTV.com.

HAWAII VOLCANOES NATIONAL PARK ESTABLISHED: ANNIVERSARY. Aug 1, 1916. Area of Hawaii's Hawaii Island, including active volcanoes Kilauea and Mauna Loa, was established as Hawaii National Park in 1916, but its name was changed to Hawaii Volcanoes National Park in 1961.

INTERNATIONAL CLOWN WEEK. Aug 1–7. All over the world, clowns will be clowning around for a good cause this week. Originally proclaimed as a national week by President Richard Nixon in 1971, International Clown Week has blossomed in countries around the world—wherever there's a clown. Clowns have long been known as ambassadors of joy and goodwill, and this is the week we celebrate them and they give back by performing in the community. Annually, Aug 1–7.

INTERNATIONAL PIRATE MONTH. Aug 1–31. 5th annual. During Arrr-gust, those who love the life of the high seas take at least one day in August to bring out their finest pirate gear and celebrate all things pirate-related. But it's more than just dress-up: "pirate" crews hold parties and events to raise money for designated charities. So get your mates together, plan yourselves a to-do and celebrate bein' a pirate. For info: Michael LoPresti, Operator/ Fleet Captain, The Rogues' Armada. E-mail: info@roguesarmada. com. Web: www.roguesarmada.com or www.facebook.com/pg/ InternationalPirateMonth.

JAMAICA: ABOLITION OF SLAVERY. Aug 1, 1834. National day. Spanish settlers introduced the slave trade into Jamaica in 1509 and sugarcane in 1640. Slavery continued until Aug 1, 1834, when it was abolished by the British.

KEY, FRANCIS SCOTT: BIRTH ANNIVERSARY. Aug 1, 1779. American attorney, social worker, poet and author of the US national anthem. While on a legal mission, Key was detained on a ship off Baltimore, MD, during the British bombardment of Fort McHenry on the night of Sept 13–14, 1814. Thrilled to see the American flag still flying over the fort at daybreak, Key wrote the poem "The Star-Spangled Banner." Printed in the *Baltimore American* Sept 21, 1814, it was soon popularly sung to the music of an old English tune, "Anacreon in Heaven." It did not become the official US national anthem until 117 years later when, on Mar 3, 1931, President Herbert Hoover signed into law an act for that purpose. Key was born at Frederick County, MD, and died at Baltimore, Jan 11, 1843.

LEE, SAMMY: 100th BIRTH ANNIVERSARY. Aug 1, 1920. Born to Korean immigrants in Fresno, CA, Lee was the first Asian-American man to win an Olympic gold medal. He competed at the 1948 Olympic games in London, England, winning gold for the 10-meter platform and bronze for the springboard. He also became the first man to grab consecutive golds in diving when he conquered the platform at the 1952 Helsinki Olympics. He was

a medical doctor and served in the Korean War. Later, he was a coach and an ambassador for the United States in the Olympics and for the sport of diving. Lee was elected to the International Swimming Hall of Fame in 1968 and the United States Olympic Hall of Fame in 1990. Lee died Dec 2, 2016, at Newport Beach, CA.

LUGHNASADH. Aug 1. (Also called August Eve, Lammas Eve, Lady Day Eve and Feast of Bread.) One of the "Greater Sabbats" during the Wiccan year, Lughnasadh marks the first harvest. Annually, Aug 1.

MELVILLE, HERMAN: BIRTH ANNIVERSARY. Aug 1, 1819. American author and poet, best known for his epic novel *Moby-Dick*. Its first sentence—"Call me Ishmael"—is one of the most famous in literature. In his Civil War poetry Melville wrote, "All wars are boyish, and are fought by boys." Born at New York, NY, Melville died there Sept 28, 1891.

MITCHELL, MARIA: BIRTH ANNIVERSARY. Aug 1, 1818. An interest in her father's hobby and an ability for mathematics resulted in Maria Mitchell's becoming the first female professional astronomer. In 1847, while assisting her father in a survey of the sky for the US Coast Guard, Mitchell discovered a new comet and determined its orbit. She received many honors for this work, including being elected to the American Academy of Arts and Sciences—its first woman. Mitchell joined the staff at Vassar Female College in 1865—the first US female professor of astronomy—and in 1873 was a cofounder of the Association for the Advancement of Women. Born at Nantucket, MA, Mitchell died June 28, 1889, at Lynn, MA.

MTV PREMIERE: ANNIVERSARY. Aug 1, 1981. The all-music video channel debuted on this date. VH1, another music channel owned by MTV Networks that is aimed at older pop music fans, premiered in 1985.

NATIONAL IMMUNIZATION AWARENESS MONTH. Aug 1–31. Immunization is critical to maintaining health and preventing life-threatening diseases among people of all ages and cultures throughout the US. Each year in the US, tens of thousands of people die because of vaccine-preventable diseases or their complications, and even more experience pain, suffering and disability. This month calls attention to the importance of infant, child, adolescent and adult immunization and seeks to reduce disparities in vaccine use while maintaining public trust in its value and safety. Contact your health provider for more information.

NATIONAL MINORITY DONOR AWARENESS WEEK. Aug 1–7. Intensive awareness campaign focuses on obstacles related to minorities and organ donation, promotes healthy living and disease prevention to decrease the need for transplantation and reaches out to all ethnic groups. Observances have included prayer breakfasts, health walks and donor drives. For info: US Dept of Health and Human Services. Web: www.organdonor.gov.

NATIONAL MUSTARD DAY. Aug 1. Middleton, WI. Mustard lovers across the nation pay tribute to the king of condiments by slathering their favorite mustard on hot dogs, pretzels, circus peanuts and all things edible. The National Mustard Museum holds the world's largest collection of mustards and mustard memorabilia. Activities include the mustard games, live music and lots of great food (with mustard, of course!). Ketchup is not allowed. Join in the mustard college fight song with the "POUPON U" marching band. Annually, the first Saturday in August. Est attendance: 6,000. For info: Barry M. Levenson, Curator, The National Mustard Museum, 7477 Hubbard Ave, Middleton, WI 53562. Phone: (800) 438-6878. E-mail: curator@mustardmuseum.com. Web: www.mustardmuseum.com.

NATIONAL SPINAL MUSCULAR ATROPHY AWARENESS MONTH. Aug 1–31. To promote awareness of this congenital disease that robs people of physical strength by affecting the motor nerve cells in the spinal cord, taking away the ability to walk, eat or breathe. It is the number one genetic cause of death for infants. For info: Cure SMA, 925 Busse Rd, Elk Grove Village, IL 60007. Phone: (800) 886-1762. E-mail: info@curesma.org. Web: www.curesma.org.

READ-A-ROMANCE MONTH. Aug 1–31. First observed in 2013, this monthlong online celebration urges readers to pick a novel to read from the romance genre. Romance novels represent the highest human aspirations: they feature men and women fighting for their best possible lives, against difficult odds and with the universal demand that they change—for the better. This month is a time when romance authors and readers can come together and start conversations. Annually, the month of August. For info: Bobbi Dumas, Read-a-Romance Month. E-mail: bobbiwrites@att.net. Web: www.readaromancemonth.com.

RESPECT FOR PARENTS DAY. Aug 1. A day set aside to think of the positive things parents contribute to society. Annually, Aug 1. For info: Marilyn Dalrymple. E-mail: marilyn160@frontier.com. Web: marilyn_93535.tripod.com.

ROUNDS RESOUNDING DAY. Aug 1. To sing rounds, catches and canons in folk contrapuntal tradition. Motto: "As rounds resound and resound, all the world's joined in a circle of harmony." Annually, Aug 1. (Originated by Gloria Delamar of the Rounds Resounding Society.)

"THE RUSH LIMBAUGH SHOW" NATIONAL RADIO PREMIERE: ANNIVERSARY. Aug 1, 1988. Conservative political commentator and radio personality Rush Limbaugh began his nationally syndicated show on this date with 56 stations. It quickly became the nation's top-rated show and rejuvenated the radio talk format. Today, 590 stations carry the program to an estimated 20 million listeners.

SPIDER-MAN DEBUTS: ANNIVERSARY. Aug 1, 1962. Stan Lee and Steve Ditko introduced a new superhero for Marvel Comics in issue #15 of *Amazing Fantasy*, which hit newsstands in August: Spider-Man. Nerdy teen Peter Parker is bitten by a radioactive spider and soon discovers that he has the proportionate strength and agility of the spider—as well as web-shooting talents and "spidey sense." The arachnid crime fighter got his own comic book in March 1963 and quickly became the center of a multimedia empire.

SWITZERLAND: CONFEDERATION DAY. Aug 1. National holiday. Anniversary of the founding of the Swiss Confederation. Commemorates a pact made in 1291. Parades, patriotic gatherings, bonfires and fireworks. Young citizens' coming-of-age ceremonies. Observed since 600th anniversary of Swiss Confederation was celebrated in 1891.

TRINIDAD AND TOBAGO: EMANCIPATION DAY. Aug 1. Public holiday. Slavery was abolished in all British colonies on this day in 1834. Also called Discovery Day.

UNITED KINGDOM: MINDEN DAY. Aug 1. Day observed by several British army units to commemorate the bravery shown by their regimental predecessors at the Battle of Minden on Aug 1, 1759. The battle, which was part of the Seven Years' War, saw outnumbered allied Anglo and German forces defeat French armies in northern Germany. According to legend, British soldiers picked roses as they advanced to battle, placing them on their uniforms. Today, regiments wear red, white or yellow roses in their caps to remember the men who fought and died.

US CUSTOMS: ANNIVERSARY. Aug 1, 1789. "The first US customs officers began to collect the revenue and enforce the Tariff Act of July 4, 1789, on this date. Since then, the customhouse and the customs officer have stood as symbols of national pride and sovereignty at ports of entry along the land and sea borders of our country." (From Presidential Proclamation 4306.)

WALES: NATIONAL EISTEDDFOD OF WALES. Aug 1–8. Tregaron. In 1880 the National Eisteddfod association was formed and charged with the responsibility of staging an annual festival to be held in North and South Wales alternately, and with the exception of 1914 and 1940, this target has been successfully achieved. The Eisteddfod is the natural showcase for music, dance, visual arts, literature, original performances and much more. Encompassing all aspects of the arts and culture in Wales, it is an inclusive and welcoming festival, which attracts thousands of Welsh learners and those who do not speak the language as well as Welsh speakers every year. Translation services are available in the Pavilion and bilingual information is available. Est attendance: 150,000. For info: Natl Eisteddfod of Wales. E-mail: gwyb@eisteddfod.org.uk. Web: www.eisteddfod.org.uk.

WARSAW UPRISING: ANNIVERSARY. Aug 1, 1944. Having received radio reports from Moscow promising aid from the Red Army, the Polish Home Army rose up against the Nazi oppressors. At 5 PM thousands of windows were thrown open and Polish patriots, 40,000 strong, began shooting at German soldiers in the streets. The Germans responded by throwing eight divisions into the battle. Despite appeals from the London-based Polish government-in-exile, no assistance was forthcoming from the Allies, and after two months of horrific fighting the rebellion was quashed.

WHAT WILL BE YOUR LEGACY MONTH. Aug 1–31. Many people do not realize how their actions affect others. They live their lives selfishly, not realizing the impact of their life choices on present and possibly future generations. What Will Be Your Legacy Month is a time for people to reflect on their past and present actions and vow to make positive changes that will affect generations. The seeds, whether positive or negative, that we plant in our children's lives will grow and reflect our teachings. For info: Martha J. Ross-Rodgers. Phone: (757) 543-9290. E-mail: drmarthajrossrodgers@aol.com.

WORLD BREASTFEEDING WEEK. Aug 1–7. Breast-feeding advocates, healthcare professionals and social service agencies focus attention on the importance and benefits of breast-feeding. Fairs, picnics, fundraising and government proclamations highlight the week. Also, commemorates signing of Innocenti Declaration. Annually, Aug 1–7. For info: World Alliance for Breastfeeding Action. E-mail: wbw@waba.org.my. Web: www.worldbreastfeedingweek.org.

WORLD LUNG CANCER DAY. Aug 1. 9th annual. A day set aside to support, honor, encourage and commemmorate all those affected by lung cancer. Dedicated to the people affected by this disease. This is a nonpolitical and nonorganizational day of recognition and remembrance. In the US, it has been proclaimed in numerous states and cities. Worldwide, it has been recognized and celebrated. Annually, Aug 1. For info: Betsy Thompson, Lung Cancer Survivors Foundation. Web: www.facebook.com/LCSurvivors.

WORLD WIDE WEB: 30th ANNIVERSARY. Aug 1, 1990. The creation of what would become the World Wide Web was suggested this month in 1990 by Tim Berners-Lee and Robert Cailliau at CERN, the European Laboratory for Particle Physics at Switzerland. By October they had designed a prototype Web browser. They also introduced HTML (hypertext markup language) and the URL (universal resource locator). Mosaic, the first graphical Web browser, was designed by Marc Andreessen and released in 1993. By early 1993 there were 50 Web servers worldwide.

ZODIAC KILLER NEWSPAPER LETTERS: ANNIVERSARY. Aug 1, 1969. The California newspapers *San Francisco Chronicle, San Francisco Examiner* and the *Vallejo Times Herald* received letters on this date from a killer claiming credit for three area murders that had occurred Dec 20, 1968, and July 4, 1969. Until these letters arrived, police authorities had not tied the killings together. The letters included a cryptogram claiming (falsely) to reveal the killer's identity. This was the beginning of a public terror campaign from a man calling himself the Zodiac. The Zodiac killed two more people (perhaps more) and sent many letters threatening the schoolchildren of San Francisco, CA. He was never identified.

August 2020	S	M	T	W	T	F	S
							1
	2	3	4	5	6	7	8
	9	10	11	12	13	14	15
	16	17	18	19	20	21	22
	23	24	25	26	27	28	29
	30	31					

🧁 BIRTHDAYS TODAY

Demián Bechir, 57, actor ("The Bridge," "Weeds," *The Hateful Eight, A Better Life*), born Mexico City, Mexico, Aug 1, 1963.

Tempestt Bledsoe, 47, talk show host, actress ("Tempestt," "The Cosby Show"), born Chicago, IL, Aug 1, 1973.

Doug Burgum, 64, Governor of North Dakota (R), born Arthur, ND, Aug 1, 1956.

Chuck D, 60, rapper (Public Enemy), producer, born Carlton Douglas Ridenhour at Roosevelt, Long Island, NY, Aug 1, 1960.

Robert Cray, 67, singer, guitarist, songwriter, born Columbus, GA, Aug 1, 1953.

Giancarlo Giannini, 78, actor (*Swept Away . . ., Seven Beauties*), born La Spezia, Italy, Aug 1, 1942.

James Gleick, 66, author, journalist (*The Information, Chaos, Genius*), born New York, NY, Aug 1, 1954.

Sam Mendes, 55, stage and film director (Oscar for *American Beauty*; *Skyfall, Road to Perdition*), born Reading, England, Aug 1, 1965.

Jason Momoa, 41, actor (*Justice League*, "Frontier," "Game of Thrones," "Stargate: Atlantis"), born Honolulu, HI, Aug 1, 1979.

Jack O'Connell, 30, actor (*Unbroken, '71*), born Alvaston, Derby, England, Aug 1, 1990.

August 2 — Sunday

DAY 215   **151 REMAINING**

AMERICAN FAMILY DAY IN ARIZONA. Aug 2. Observed in Arizona on the first Sunday in August. The observance date is designated by statute.

BALDWIN, JAMES: BIRTH ANNIVERSARY. Aug 2, 1924. Black American author noted for descriptions of black life in the US. Born at New York, NY. His best-known work, *Go Tell It on the Mountain*, was published in 1953. Died at St. Paul-de-Vence, France, Nov 30, 1987.

COSTA RICA: FEAST OF OUR LADY OF ANGELS. Aug 2. National holiday. Celebrates Costa Rica's patron saint, the Virgin of Los Angeles.

DECLARATION OF INDEPENDENCE: OFFICIAL SIGNING: ANNIVERSARY. Aug 2, 1776. Contrary to widespread misconceptions, the 56 signers did not sign as a group and did not do so July 4, 1776. John Hancock and Charles Thomson signed only draft copies that day, the official day the Declaration of Independence was adopted by Congress. The signing of the official declaration occurred Aug 2, 1776, when 50 men probably took part. Later that year, five more apparently signed separately, and one added his name in a subsequent year. (From "Signers of the Declaration . . ." US Department of the Interior, 1975.) See also: "Declaration of Independence Approval and Signing: Anniversary" (July 4).

ENGLAND: INTERNATIONAL SOCIAL MEDIA HOLIDAY. Aug 2. London. Since 2018. Youths are vulnerable when engaging with social media, chat rooms and internet platforms, so this is a day for them to take a holiday from social media. Sponsored by and in support of the not-for-profit organization Purity (Protection under the Real Internet Threats to Youth), which seeks to protect youths from online exploitation. Events to mark this holiday will be held for young people, showcasing local talent and motivational speakers and delivering crucial information to keep young people safe online. For info: Purity. E-mail: Rebecca@purity.org.uk. Web: www.purity.org.uk.

HUNT, LAMAR: BIRTH ANNIVERSARY. Aug 2, 1932. A legend in American professional sports, executive Hunt innovated the NFL, nurtured the growth of professional soccer in the US and cofounded the World Championship Tennis circuit. Hunt cofounded the AFL, which merged with the NFL. The AFL–NFL championship game was coined the "Super Bowl" by Hunt. He owned the Kansas City Chiefs and several soccer teams. Hunt also cofounded the NASL and Major League Soccer, and in recognition for that, America's oldest sporting tournament, the US Open Cup, was renamed for him. Hunt was a hall of famer in football, soccer and tennis. Born in El Dorado, AR, Hunt died in his longtime home of Dallas, TX, on Dec 13, 2006.

IRAQ INVADES KUWAIT: 30th ANNIVERSARY. Aug 2, 1990. On orders of President Saddam Hussein, the Iraqi army invaded Kuwait. Hussein claimed that Kuwait presented a serious threat to Iraq's economic existence by overproducing oil and driving prices down on the world market. After conquering the capital, Kuwait City, Hussein installed a military government in Kuwait, prior to annexing it to Iraq on the claim that Kuwait was historically part of Iraq. This led to the 100-hour war against Iraq, Operation Desert Storm.

ITALY: JOUST OF THE QUINTANA. Aug 2. Ascoli/Piceno. The first Sunday in August is set aside for the Torneo della Quintana, a historical pageant with 15th-century costumes.

L'ENFANT, PIERRE CHARLES: BIRTH ANNIVERSARY. Aug 2, 1754. The architect, engineer and Revolutionary War officer who designed the plan for the city of Washington, DC, L'Enfant was born at Paris, France. He died at Prince Georges County, MD, June 14, 1825.

LOY, MYRNA: BIRTH ANNIVERSARY. Aug 2, 1905. America's favorite leading lady of the 1930s, Loy was born Myrna Adele Williams near Helena, MT. She soared to fame as the madcap New York sophisticate Nora Charles in the Thin Man movies with William Powell (Nick Charles). She also starred in the critically acclaimed *The Best Years of Our Lives* (1946). After a career spanning seven decades, she was awarded an honorary Oscar in 1991 and died at New York, NY, Dec 14, 1993.

MACEDONIA: NATIONAL DAY. Aug 2. Commemorates the nationalist uprising against the Ottoman Empire in 1903. Called Prophet Elias Day or Illinden. (See also: "Saint Elias Day [Illinden]: Macedonian Uprising: Anniversary" below.)

NATIONAL EXERCISE WITH YOUR CHILD WEEK. Aug 2–8. This week encourages parents and guardians to exercise with their children as part of a healthier lifestyle. Exercise enables children to improve their overall well-being, to maintain a healthier weight and to reduce the risk of hypertension and cardiovascular disease. For info: Sheila Madison, PO Box 2733, Washington, DC 20013. Phone: (281) 750-2767. E-mail: info@sheilamadison.com. Web: www.sheilamadison.com.

O'CONNOR, CARROLL: BIRTH ANNIVERSARY. Aug 2, 1924. Television, stage and screen actor born in New York, NY. He was best known for his portrayal of the bigoted, blue-collar Archie Bunker on "All in the Family." He played the role of Bunker from 1971 to 1979 and was nominated for eight Emmy Awards, winning four. He won a fifth Emmy in 1989 for "In the Heat of the Night." He was also inducted into the Television Hall of Fame in 1989. He died at Culver City, CA, on June 21, 2001.

PT 109 AND JOHN F. KENNEDY: ANNIVERSARY. Aug 2, 1943. On the night of Aug 2, 1943, a Japanese destroyer crushed US torpedo boat PT-109 in the Solomon Islands. The 11 survivors swam to the nearest island 3.5 miles away. The 26-year-old commander, Lieutenant John F. Kennedy, towed an injured crewmate by biting into the strap of a life jacket for four hours. Kennedy then swam to other islands looking for food, water and help. The men of PT-109 survived for six days before Solomon Islands scouts found them. The gripping survival tale was turned into song (a hit for Jimmy Dean), a movie starring Cliff Robertson and a book—and helped launch the political career of the heroic Kennedy.

SAINT ELIAS DAY (ILLINDEN): MACEDONIAN UPRISING: ANNIVERSARY. Aug 2, 1903. Most sacred, honored and celebrated day of the Macedonian people. Anniversary of the uprising of Macedonians against the Ottoman Empire. Turkish reprisals against the insurgents were ruthless, including the destruction of 105 villages and the execution of more than 1,700 noncombatants.

SISTERS' DAY®. Aug 2. Celebrating the spirit of sisterhood: sisters nationwide show appreciation and give recognition to one another for the special relationship they share. Send a card, make a phone call or share memories, photos, flowers and candy. Sisters may include biological sisters, sorority sisters, sisterly friends, etc. Annually, the first Sunday in August. For info: Tricia Eleogram, 5112 Normandy Ave, Memphis, TN 38117. Phone: (901) 497-8362. Fax: (901) 754-9923. E-mail: triciaeleogram@gmail.com.

WARNER, JACK: BIRTH ANNIVERSARY. Aug 2, 1892. The tough, cost-conscious film production chief was born at London, ON, Canada. Brothers Harry, Albert, Sam and Jack formed Warner Bros. in 1923 at Burbank, CA. Under Jack Warner's watch, the studio brought out *The Jazz Singer* (1928), the first full-length film with synchronized sound, as well as social dramas and a clutch of gangster films starring Humphrey Bogart and James Cagney. A highlight for the studio was *Casablanca* (1942), which took the Best Picture Oscar. Warner died Sept 9, 1978, at Hollywood, CA.

🎂 BIRTHDAYS TODAY

Isabel Allende, 78, author (*The House of the Spirits, Zorro*), born Isabel Allende Llona at Lima, Peru, Aug 2, 1942.

Joanna Cassidy, 76, actress ("Buffalo Bill," *Under Fire*), born Camden, NJ, Aug 2, 1944.

James Fallows, 71, journalist, former editor (*US News & World Report*), born Philadelphia, PA, Aug 2, 1949.

David Ferrer, 38, tennis player, born Javea, Spain, Aug 2, 1982.

Edward Furlong, 43, actor (*American History X, Before and After, Terminator 2*), born Glendale, CA, Aug 2, 1977.

Kathryn Harrold, 70, actress ("I'll Fly Away," "The Larry Sanders Show," *Modern Romance*), born Tazewell, VA, Aug 2, 1950.

August 2020	S	M	T	W	T	F	S
							1
	2	3	4	5	6	7	8
	9	10	11	12	13	14	15
	16	17	18	19	20	21	22
	23	24	25	26	27	28	29
	30	31					

Victoria Jackson, 61, actress, comedienne ("Saturday Night Live," *I Love You to Death*), born Miami, FL, Aug 2, 1959.

Mary-Louise Parker, 56, actress (Tony for *Proof*; "Weeds," *Fried Green Tomatoes*), born Fort Jackson, SC, Aug 2, 1964.

Jacky Rosen, 63, US Senator (D, Nevada), born Jacklyn Spektor at Chicago, IL, Aug 2, 1957.

Huston Street, 37, baseball player, born Austin, TX, Aug 2, 1983.

Michael Weiss, 44, Olympic figure skater, born Washington, DC, Aug 2, 1976.

Robert Wilkie, 58, US Secretary of Veterans Affairs (Trump administration), born Frankfurt, West Germany (now Germany), Aug 2, 1962.

Sam Worthington, 44, actor (*Avatar, Clash of the Titans*), born Godalming, Surrey, England, Aug 2, 1976.

August 3 — Monday

DAY 216   **150 REMAINING**

ANTIGUA AND BARBUDA: AUGUST MONDAY. Aug 3–4. The first Monday in August and the day following form the August Monday public holiday.

AUSTRALIA: PICNIC DAY. Aug 3. The first Monday in August is a bank holiday in New South Wales and Picnic Day in Northern Territory, Australia.

BAHAMAS: EMANCIPATION DAY. Aug 3. Public holiday in Bahamas. Annually, the first Monday in August. Commemorates the emancipation of slaves by the British in 1834.

BALDWIN, STANLEY: BIRTH ANNIVERSARY. Aug 3, 1867. Born at Bewdley, England, Baldwin was the dominant British interwar political figure, notably as prime minister, a position he held thrice (1923–24, 1924–29, 1935–37). He led the country through various interwar crises, such as the General Strike of May 1926, which initiated with striking coal miners and spread to other trade unions, and King Edward VIII's abdication in 1936, but his reputation was tarnished by his hands-off approach to early regional aggressions of Hitler and Mussolini. Baldwin died Dec 14, 1947, at Astley, England.

CANADA: CIVIC HOLIDAY. Aug 3. The first Monday in August is observed as a holiday in seven of Canada's 10 provinces. Civic holiday in Manitoba, New Brunswick, Northwest Territories, Ontario and Saskatchewan; British Columbia Day in British Columbia and Heritage Day in Alberta.

COLORADO DAY. Aug 3. Colorado. Annually, the first Monday in August. Commemorates Admission Day, Aug 1, 1876, when Colorado became the 38th state.

COLUMBUS SAILS FOR THE NEW WORLD: ANNIVERSARY. Aug 3, 1492. Christopher Columbus, "Admiral of the Ocean Sea," set sail half an hour before sunrise from Palos, Spain, on this date. With three ships, *Niña, Pinta* and *Santa Maria*, and a crew of 90, he sailed "for Cathay" but found instead a New World of the Americas, first landing at Guanahani (San Salvador Island in the Bahamas) on Oct 12. See also: "Columbus Day" (Oct 12).

EQUATORIAL GUINEA: ARMED FORCES DAY. Aug 3. National holiday.

GRENADA: EMANCIPATION DAY. Aug 3. Grenada observes a public holiday annually on the first Monday in August. Commemorates the emancipation of slaves by the British in 1834.

GUINEA-BISSAU: COLONIZATION MARTYRS' DAY. Aug 3. National holiday. Also called Pidjiguiti Martyrs' Day. Commemorates the massacre of 50 striking workers at the Pidjiguiti Docks on Aug 3, 1959, by colonial police.

ICELAND: AUGUST HOLIDAY. Aug 3. National holiday. The first Monday in August. Commemorates Iceland's constitution of 1874.

IRELAND: AUGUST HOLIDAY. Aug 3. National holiday in the Republic of Ireland on the first Monday in August.

JAMAICA: INDEPENDENCE DAY. Aug 3. National holiday observing Jamaica's independence from Britain Aug 6, 1962. Annually, the first Monday in August.

JAMES, P.D.: 100th BIRTH ANNIVERSARY. Aug 3, 1920. Born at Oxford, England, Phyllis Dorothy James is considered one of the best crime novelists of the late 20th century—creating in-depth psychological dramas in such works as *Cover Her Face* and *Original Sin*. Her early career in medical administration and at the Office of Home Affairs lent medical and procedural credence to her novels. Most of her canon features poet and Scotland Yard detective Adam Dalgliesh. James was a member of the Royal Society of Literature (1987) and Royal Society of the Arts (1983). Inducted into the Order of the British Empire (1983) and made a baroness (1991) and Commander of the British Empire (1992), James died Nov 27, 2014, at Oxford.

KUHN, MARGARET (MAGGIE): BIRTH ANNIVERSARY. Aug 3, 1905. When she was forced into retirement because she'd reached the age of 65, Maggie Kuhn founded the Gray Panthers organization to fight age discrimination. Subsequently she waged a battle that resulted in the banning of mandatory retirements. Born at Buffalo, NY, Kuhn died Apr 22, 1995, at Philadelphia, PA.

MOON PHASE: FULL MOON. Aug 3. Moon enters Full Moon phase at 11:59 AM, EDT.

NATIONAL BARGAIN HUNTING WEEK. Aug 3–9. A week encouraging shoppers and businesses to celebrate the thrill of the hunt—for bargains—and the triumph of their finds. Observed since 1996 on the first Monday through Sunday in August. For info: Debbie Keri-Brown, 652 Olde Towne Ave, #V, Columbus, OH 43214. Phone: (614) 226-1397. E-mail: bargainweek@yahoo.com. Web: https://bargainhunting.webs.com.

NATIONAL WATERMELON DAY. Aug 3. A day to enjoy this refreshing melon! A two-cup serving of watermelon contains excellent levels of vitamins A, B6 and C and also serves as a valuable source of potassium. At 92 percent water, watermelon delivers needed fluids and nutrients to the body, including lycopene—which has been studied for its potential role in reducing risk of heart disease, various cancers and protection to skin from harmful UV rays—and citrulline—which can help maintain blood flow within the heart and cardiovascular function. Annually, Aug 3. For info: National Watermelon Promotion Board, 1321 Sundial Point, Winter Springs, FL 32708. Phone: (407) 657-0261. E-mail: info@watermelon.org. Web: www.watermelon.org.

NIGER: INDEPENDENCE DAY: 60th ANNIVERSARY OF INDEPENDENCE. Aug 3. Niger gained its independence from France on this day in 1960.

OLD FIDDLERS' CONVENTION. Aug 3–8. Galax, VA. 85th annual. Event features dance, folk songs and old-time and bluegrass music competition. Est attendance: 35,000. For info: Thomas L. Jones, Jr, Box 655, Galax, VA 24333. Phone: (276) 236-8541. Web: www.oldfiddlersconvention.com.

PSYCHIC WEEK. Aug 3–7. To utilize the power of the psyche to bring peace, find lost individuals and concentrate "psychic power" on beneficial causes. Annually, the first week in August (Monday–Friday). (Created by the late Richard R. Falk.)

PYLE, ERNEST (ERNIE) TAYLOR: BIRTH ANNIVERSARY. Aug 3, 1900. Ernie Pyle was born at Dana, IN, and began his career in journalism in 1923. After serving as managing editor of the *Washington Daily News*, in 1935 he returned to his first journalistic love of working as a roving reporter. His column was syndicated by nearly 200 newspapers and often focused on figures behind the news. His reports of the bombing of London in 1940 and subsequent reports from Africa, Sicily, Italy and France earned him a Pulitzer Prize in 1944. He was killed by machine-gun fire at the Pacific island of Ie Shima, Apr 18, 1945, during the Battle of Okinawa.

SCOPES, JOHN T.: BIRTH ANNIVERSARY. Aug 3, 1900. Central figure in a cause célèbre (the "Scopes Trial" or the "Monkey Trial"), John Thomas Scopes was born at Paducah, KY. An obscure, 24-year-old schoolteacher at the Dayton, TN, high school in 1925, he became the focus of world attention. Scopes never uttered a word at his trial, which was a contest between two of America's best-known lawyers, William Jennings Bryan and Clarence Darrow. The trial, July 10–21, 1925, resulted in Scopes's conviction. He was fined $100 "for teaching evolution" in Tennessee. The verdict was upset on a technicality, and the statute he was accused of breaching was repealed in 1967. Scopes died at Shreveport, LA, Oct 21, 1970.

SCOTLAND: SUMMER BANK HOLIDAY. Aug 3. Bank and public holiday in Scotland. The first Monday in August.

STURGEON MOON. Aug 3. So called by Native American tribes of New England and the Great Lakes because at this time of year this important food fish was most abundant. The August Full Moon.

URIS, LEON: BIRTH ANNIVERSARY. Aug 3, 1924. American novelist born to a family of Russian Jews at Baltimore, MD. His most successful novels were those that chronicled the Holocaust (1960's *Mila 18*) and the founding of Israel (1958's *Exodus*). His novels sold millions and were made into several feature films. Later titles include *QB VII*, a fictionalized account of his own trial for libel, and *Trinity*, which followed the life of three generations of an Irish family. Uris died June 21, 2003, at Shelter Island, NY.

US WOMEN'S AMATEUR (GOLF) CHAMPIONSHIP. Aug 3–9. Woodmont Country Club, Rockville, MD. For info: USGA, Golf House, Championship Dept, PO Box 708, Far Hills, NJ 07931. Phone: (908) 234-2300. E-mail: champs@usga.org. Web: www.usga.org.

ZAMBIA: YOUTH DAY. Aug 3. National holiday. Youth activities are the order of the day. The focal point is Lusaka's Independence Stadium. Annually, the first Monday in August.

🎂 BIRTHDAYS TODAY

Tony Bennett, 94, singer, born Anthony Dominick Benedetto at New York, NY, Aug 3, 1926.

Steven Berkoff, 83, actor, director, writer (*A Clockwork Orange, Beverly Hills Cop*), born London, England, Aug 3, 1937.

Tom Brady, 43, football player, born San Mateo, CA, Aug 3, 1977.

Karlie Kloss, 28, model, born Chicago, IL, Aug 3, 1992.

Evangeline Lilly, 41, actress (*Ant-Man*, The Hobbit films, "Lost"), born Fort Saskatchewan, AB, Canada, Aug 3, 1979.

Ryan Lochte, 36, Olympic swimmer, television personality ("What Would Ryan Lochte Do?"), born Rochester, NY, Aug 3, 1984.

John McGinley, 61, actor (*Platoon, Born on the Fourth of July,* "Scrubs"), born New York, NY, Aug 3, 1959.

Chris Murphy, 47, US Senator (D, Connecticut), born White Plains, NY, Aug 3, 1973.

Martin Sheen, 80, actor (*Apocalypse Now*, "The West Wing"), born Ramon Estevez at Dayton, OH, Aug 3, 1940.

Hannah Simone, 40, model, actress ("The New Girl"), born London, England, Aug 3, 1980.

Martha Stewart, 79, lifestyle consultant, television personality, writer, born Nutley, NJ, Aug 3, 1941.

Isaiah Washington, 57, actor ("Grey's Anatomy," *Romeo Must Die, Exit Wounds*), born Houston, TX, Aug 3, 1963.

Blaine Wilson, 46, former gymnast, born Columbus, OH, Aug 3, 1974.

August 4 — Tuesday

DAY 217   149 REMAINING

ARMSTRONG, LOUIS: BIRTH ANNIVERSARY. Aug 4, 1900 (or 1901). Jazz musician extraordinaire born at New Orleans, LA. Died at New York, NY, July 6, 1971. Armstrong often said he was born on the 4th of July, but documents in the Louis Armstrong Archives of Queens College, Flushing, NY, indicate that he was actually born Aug 4, 1900 or 1901. Asked to define jazz, Armstrong reportedly replied, "Man, if you gotta ask, you'll never know." The trumpet player was also known as Satchmo. He appeared in many films. Popular singles include "What a Wonderful World" and "Hello, Dolly" (with Barbra Streisand).

BORDEN AX MURDERS: ANNIVERSARY. Aug 4, 1892. In a grisly scene, Andrew Jackson Borden, a wealthy area merchant, was found hacked to death in the parlor of his Fall River, MA, home. The body of his second wife, Abby Durfee Borden, lay upstairs. Lizzie Andrew Borden, home at the time, had discovered her father's lifeless form. She was arrested and tried for the murders, but the lack of solid evidence against her led to Borden's eventual acquittal. Debate over her guilt, innocence and motive has raged ever since. See also: "Lizzie Borden Verdict: Anniversary" (June 20).

BURKINA FASO: REVOLUTION DAY. Aug 4. National holiday. Commemorates 1983 coup.

CIVIL RIGHTS WORKERS FOUND SLAIN: ANNIVERSARY. Aug 4, 1964. After disappearing on June 21, three civil rights workers were found murdered and buried in an earthen dam outside Philadelphia, MS. The three young men were workers on the Mississippi Summer Project organized by the Student Nonviolent Coordinating Committee (SNCC) to increase black voter registration. Prior to their disappearance, James Chaney, Andrew Goodman and Michael Schwerner were detained by Neshoba County police on charges of speeding. When their car was found, burned, on June 23, President Lyndon Johnson ordered an FBI search for the men.

COAST GUARD DAY. Aug 4. Celebrates anniversary of founding of the Revenue Cutter Service in 1790, which merged with the Life Saving Service in 1915 to become the US Coast Guard.

CUNNINGHAM, GLENN: BIRTH ANNIVERSARY. Aug 4, 1909. "Kansas Ironman" Glenn Clarence Cunningham—American track athlete, 1934–37 world-record holder for the mile and member of the US Olympic teams in 1932 and 1936—was born at Atlanta, KS. On June 16, 1934, at Princeton, NJ, Cunningham set a world record for the mile (4:06.7) that stood for three years. After WWII, he and his wife opened a youth ranch and cared for more than 10,000 foster children plus 10 of their own. Cunningham died at Menifee, AR, Mar 10, 1988.

NATIONAL NIGHT OUT. Aug 4. Designed to heighten crime prevention awareness and to promote police-community partnerships.

August 2020	S	M	T	W	T	F	S
							1
	2	3	4	5	6	7	8
	9	10	11	12	13	14	15
	16	17	18	19	20	21	22
	23	24	25	26	27	28	29
	30	31					

Annually, the first Tuesday in August. For info: Matt A. Peskin, Dir, Natl Assn of Town Watch, PO Box 303, Wynnewood, PA 19096. Phone: (610) 649-7055 or (800) 648-3688. Fax: (610) 649-5456. E-mail: info@natw.org. Web: www.nationalnightout.org.

OBAMA, BARACK H.: BIRTHDAY. Aug 4, 1961. 44th president of the US (2009–17). Born at Honolulu, HI.

PATER, WALTER: BIRTH ANNIVERSARY. Aug 4, 1839. Critic and essayist who, in such works as *The Renaissance* (1873) and *Marius the Epicurean* (1885), articulated the "arts for arts sake" philosophy that was key to the Pre-Raphaelite and Aestheticism movements. Such late 19th-century aesthetes as Oscar Wilde were influenced by Pater's writings. Pater was born at London, England, and died July 30, 1894, at Oxford, England.

QUEEN ELIZABETH, THE QUEEN MOTHER: BIRTH ANNIVERSARY. Aug 4, 1900. A beloved member of the English royal family, the Queen "Mum" saw England through some of its most trying times in the 20th century. She was born Elizabeth Angela Marguerite Bowes-Lyon at London, England, and married the then Duke of York in 1923. When her husband was unexpectedly crowned King George VI in 1936 (after the abdication of Edward VIII), she became his strong and guiding support. She won the undying gratitude of her subjects, moreover, when she refused to move the royal family to the safety of the countryside during the German bombing of London in WWII. She died Mar 30, 2002.

RICHARD, MAURICE "ROCKET": BIRTH ANNIVERSARY. Aug 4, 1921. Hockey Hall of Fame right wing, born at Montreal, QC, Canada. Died May 27, 2000, at Montreal.

SCALIGER, JOSEPH JUSTUS: BIRTH ANNIVERSARY. Aug 4, 1540. (Old Style date.) French scholar who has been called the founder of scientific chronology. Born at Agen, France, the son of classical scholar Julius Caesar Scaliger. In 1582 he suggested a new system for measuring time and numbering years. His "Julian Period" (named for his father), which consisted of 7,980 consecutive years (beginning Jan 1, 4713 BC), is still in use by astronomers. He died at Leiden, Netherlands, Jan 21, 1609 (OS).

SCHUMAN, WILLIAM HOWARD: BIRTH ANNIVERSARY. Aug 4, 1910. American composer who won the first Pulitzer Prize for Composition and founded the Juilliard School of Music, born at New York City. His compositions include *American Festival Overture, New England Triptych*, the baseball opera *The Mighty Casey* and *On Freedom's Ground*, written for the centennial of the Statue of Liberty in 1986. He was instrumental in the conception of the Lincoln Center for the Performing Arts and served as its first president. In 1985 he was awarded a special Pulitzer Prize for his contributions. He also received a National Medal of Arts in 1985 and a Kennedy Center Honor in 1989. Schuman died at New York City, Feb 15, 1992.

SHELLEY, PERCY BYSSHE: BIRTH ANNIVERSARY. Aug 4, 1792. Poet Percy Bysshe Shelley, one of the leading English Romantic poets, was born near Horsham, Sussex. Self-exiled from England due to the hostile reception of his radical views, he lived in Italy from 1818 until his death at sea off the coast of Viareggio, just a month before his 30th birthday, July 8, 1822. Shelley's important works include "Ozymandias," published in 1818; "Ode to the West Wind," "The Cloud," "To a Skylark" and *Prometheus Unbound* in 1819; and *Adonais* (an elegy for John Keats) in 1821.

WORLD'S FAIR OF MONEY. Aug 4–8. David L. Lawrence Convention Center, Pittsburgh, PA. See coins worth millions! Buy, sell and

trade coins, paper money, medals and tokens. Numismatic education programs, exhibits and family activities. For info: American Numismatic Assn, 818 N Cascade Ave, Colorado Springs, CO 80903. Phone: (800) 367-9723. E-mail: ana@money.org. Web: www.worldsfairofmoney.com.

🎩 BIRTHDAYS TODAY

Richard Belzer, 76, comedian, actor ("Law & Order: SVU," "Homicide: Life on the Street"), born Bridgeport, CT, Aug 4, 1944.

Roger Clemens, 58, former baseball player, born Dayton, OH, Aug 4, 1962.

Greta Gerwig, 37, actress (*20th Century Women, Mistress America, Frances Ha*), director (*Lady Bird*), screenwriter (*Lady Bird*), born Sacramento, CA, Aug 4, 1983.

Jeff Gordon, 49, former race car driver, sportscaster, born Pittsboro, IN, Aug 4, 1971.

Daniel Dae Kim, 52, actor ("Lost," "24," "Hawaii Five-0"), born Pusan, South Korea, Aug 4, 1968.

Lori Lightfoot, 58, Mayor of Chicago, born Massillon, OH, Aug 4, 1962.

Meghan, Duchess of Sussex, 39, former actress (*Horrible Bosses,* "Suits"), born Meghan Markle at Los Angeles, CA, Aug 4, 1981.

Barack Obama, 59, 44th president of the US, former US senator (D, Illinois), born Honolulu, HI, Aug 4, 1961.

Kim Reynolds, 61, Governor of Iowa (R), born Kimberly Strawn at St. Charles, IA, Aug 4, 1959.

Phil Scott, 62, Governor of Vermont (R), born Bar City, VT, Aug 4, 1958.

Cole Sprouse, 28, actor ("Riverdale," "The Suite Life of Zack and Cody"), born Tuscany, Italy, Aug 4, 1992.

Dylan Sprouse, 28, actor ("The Suite Life of Zack and Cody"), born Tuscany, Italy, Aug 4, 1992.

Kristoffer Tabori, 68, actor (*The Hound of the Baskervilles*), voice artist, director, born Christopher Siegel at Los Angeles, CA, Aug 4, 1952.

Billy Bob Thornton, 65, actor ("Fargo," *Friday Night Lights, Bad Santa, Monster's Ball*), director, screenwriter (Oscar for *Sling Blade*), born Hot Springs, AR, Aug 4, 1955.

August 5 — Wednesday

DAY 218   **148 REMAINING**

AIKEN, CONRAD: BIRTH ANNIVERSARY. Aug 5, 1889. Poet, novelist, short-story writer and critic, born at Savannah, GA, and raised in New England. Winner of the Pulitzer Prize (1930), the National Book Award (1954), the Bollingen Prize (1956) and the National Medal for Literature (1969). He was also a consultant in poetry to the Library of Congress (1950–52)—now termed poet laureate. Aiken died at Savannah, GA, Aug 17, 1973.

"AMERICAN BANDSTAND" TV PREMIERE: ANNIVERSARY. Aug 5, 1957. "American Bandstand" and Dick Clark are synonymous; he hosted the show for more than 30 years. "AB" started out as a local show at Philadelphia, PA, in 1952. Clark, then a disk jockey, took over as host at the age of 26. The format was simple: teens dancing, performers doing their latest hits and Clark introducing songs and listing the top 10 songs each week. This hour-long show was not only TV's longest-running musical series but also the first one devoted exclusively to rock and roll. The show was canceled six months after Clark turned over the hosting duties to David Hirsch in 1989.

ARMSTRONG, NEIL: 90th BIRTH ANNIVERSARY. Aug 5, 1930. Astronaut and first man to walk on the moon, born at Wapakoneta, OH. Armstrong first flew in a Tin Goose aircraft at age six and could

fly a plane before he could drive a car. He was a navy fighter pilot during the Korean War and later studied aeronautical engineering. An experimental test pilot for NASA in the 1950s, Armstrong became a candidate for the astronaut program due to his skill at piloting X-15 rocket planes. He flew *Gemini* spacecraft and trained on *Apollo* vehicles as well, and was ultimately chosen by NASA to command the mission to the moon. He took that "small step" on July 20, 1969. A quiet, humble man, he was startled by his own celebrity. He never returned to space but worked as an educator and businessman until his death at Cincinnati, OH, Aug 25, 2012.

BATTLE OF MOBILE BAY: ANNIVERSARY. Aug 5, 1864. A Union fleet under Admiral David Farragut attempted to run past three Confederate forts into Mobile Bay, AL. After coming under fire, the Union fleet headed into a maze of underwater mines, known at that time as torpedoes. The ironclad *Tecumseh* was sunk by a torpedo, after which Farragut is said to have exclaimed, "Damn the torpedoes—full steam ahead!" The Union fleet was successful and Mobile Bay was secured.

BURKINA FASO: REPUBLIC DAY: 60th ANNIVERSARY OF INDEPENDENCE. Aug 5. Burkina Faso (formerly Republic of Upper Volta) gained independence from France in 1960.

CROATIA: HOMELAND THANKSGIVING DAY. Aug 5. National holiday.

ELIOT, JOHN: BIRTH ANNIVERSARY. Aug 5, 1604. (Old Style date.) American "Apostle to the Indians," translator of the Bible into an Indian tongue (the first Bible to be printed in America), was born at Hertfordshire, England. He died at Roxbury, MA, May 21, 1690 (OS).

FIRST ENGLISH COLONY IN NORTH AMERICA: ANNIVERSARY. Aug 5, 1583. Sir Humphrey Gilbert, English navigator and explorer, aboard his sailing ship, the *Squirrel*, sighted the Newfoundland coast and took possession of the area around St. John's harbor in the name of Queen Elizabeth I, thus establishing the first English colony in North America. Gilbert was lost at sea, in a storm off the Azores, on his return trip to England.

HUSTON, JOHN: BIRTH ANNIVERSARY. Aug 5, 1906. This larger-than-life Hollywood figure, son of the actor Walter Huston, spent his whole life before or behind the camera as an actor, writer and director. His first film, 1941's masterpiece of detective-noir, *The Maltese Falcon*, catapulted Humphrey Bogart away from gangster roles into dark, heroic roles. Huston and Bogart collaborated on other great films: *The Treasure of the Sierra Madre* (which featured Huston's father in a Best Supporting Actor role), *Key Largo, The African Queen* and *Beat the Devil*. Born at Nevada, MO, Huston died Aug 28, 1987, at Middletown, RI, not long after completing his final film, *The Dead* (1987).

LYNCH, THOMAS: BIRTH ANNIVERSARY. Aug 5, 1749. Signer, Declaration of Independence. Born Prince George's Parish, SC. Died 1779 (lost at sea, exact date of death unknown).

MERRICK, JOSEPH: BIRTH ANNIVERSARY. Aug 5, 1862. Born at Leicester, England, a young Merrick was forced into work as an itinerant sideshow attraction due to a severe case of what is now believed to have been Proteus syndrome, a condition that causes head, bone and skin deformities. Known as "The Elephant Man," Merrick eventually took up residence at London Hospital in 1886. He died there Apr 11, 1890, of suffocation while he slept.

OMARR, SYDNEY: BIRTH ANNIVERSARY. Aug 5, 1926. Born Sidney Kimmelman at Philadelphia, PA, this world-famous astrologer became fascinated by numerology and astrology and changed his name to Sydney Omarr at age 15. He began contributing to astrology magazines and eventually became well known in Hollywood. He wrote dozens of books, an average of 13 per year, which sold more than 50 million copies. His newspaper astrology column was syndicated in more than 200 newspapers. He died Jan 16, 2003, at Santa Monica, CA.

WALLENBERG, RAOUL: BIRTH ANNIVERSARY. Aug 5, 1912. Swedish architect Raoul Gustaf Wallenberg was born at Stockholm, Sweden. He is credited with saving 100,000 Jews from almost certain death at the hands of the Nazis during WWII. Wallenberg was arrested by Soviet troops at Budapest, Hungary, Jan 17, 1945, and according to the official Soviet press agency, Tass, died in prison at Moscow, July 17, 1947 (although unconfirmed reports claim he died years later). He was the second person in history (Winston Churchill was the first) to be granted honorary American citizenship (US House of Representatives voted 396–2, Sept 22, 1981).

🎂 BIRTHDAYS TODAY

Loni Anderson, 74, actress ("WKRP in Cincinnati," *The Jayne Mansfield Story*), born St. Paul, MN, Aug 5, 1946.

David Baldacci, 60, author (*Absolute Power*), born Richmond, VA, Aug 15, 1960.

Ja'net DuBois, 82, actress ("Good Times," "Beverly Hills 90210"), born Philadelphia, PA, Aug 5, 1938.

Patrick Aloysius Ewing, 58, Hall of Fame basketball player, born Kingston, Jamaica, Aug 5, 1962.

Lorrie Fair, 42, former soccer player, born Los Altos, CA, Aug 5, 1978.

Janet McTeer, 59, actress (*Albert Nobbs, Tumbleweeds*), born Newcastle, Tyne and Wear, England, Aug 5, 1961.

John Olerud, 52, former baseball player, born Seattle, WA, Aug 5, 1968.

Patrick Reed, 30, golfer, born San Antonio, TX, Aug 5, 1990.

John Saxon, 84, actor ("Falcon Crest," *Enter the Dragon, A Nightmare on Elm Street*), born Brooklyn, NY, Aug 5, 1936.

Jonathan Silverman, 54, actor ("The Single Guy," *Weekend at Bernie's*), born Los Angeles, CA, Aug 5, 1966.

Erika Slezak, 74, actress ("One Life to Live"), born Los Angeles, CA, Aug 5, 1946.

Jesse Williams, 39, actor ("Grey's Anatomy"), born Chicago, IL, Aug 5, 1981.

August 6 — Thursday

DAY 219	147 REMAINING

ATOMIC BOMB DROPPED ON HIROSHIMA: 75th ANNIVERSARY. Aug 6, 1945. At 8:15 AM, local time, an American B-29 bomber, the *Enola Gay*, dropped an atomic bomb named "Little Boy" over the center of the city of Hiroshima, Japan. The bomb exploded about 1,800 feet above the ground, killing 80,000 civilians and destroying the city. It is estimated that another 100,000 people were injured and died subsequently as a direct result of the bomb and the radiation it produced. This was the first time in history that such a devastating weapon had been used by any nation.

BALL, LUCILLE: BIRTH ANNIVERSARY. Aug 6, 1911. Film and television pioneer and comedienne born at Jamestown, NY. In addition to her many film and television credits, Lucille Ball will always be remembered for her role in the 1950s CBS sitcom "I Love Lucy." As Lucy Ricardo, the wife of bandleader Ricky Ricardo (her real-life husband, Desi Arnaz), she exhibited a comedic style that became a trademark of early television comedy. She died Apr 26, 1989, at Los Angeles, CA.

BOLIVIA: INDEPENDENCE DAY. Aug 6. National holiday. Gained freedom from Spain in 1825. Named after Simón Bolivar.

August 2020	S	M	T	W	T	F	S
							1
	2	3	4	5	6	7	8
	9	10	11	12	13	14	15
	16	17	18	19	20	21	22
	23	24	25	26	27	28	29
	30	31					

ELECTROCUTION FIRST USED TO CARRY OUT DEATH PENALTY: ANNIVERSARY. Aug 6, 1890. At Auburn Prison, Auburn, NY, William Kemmler of Buffalo, NY, became the first man to be executed by electrocution. He had been convicted of the hatchet murder of his common-law wife, Matilde Ziegler, on Mar 28, 1889. This first attempt at using electrocution to carry out the death penalty was botched. As reported by George Westinghouse, Jr, "It has been a brutal affair. They could have done better with an axe."

FIRST WOMAN SWIMS THE ENGLISH CHANNEL: ANNIVERSARY. Aug 6, 1926. The first woman to swim the English Channel was 19-year-old Gertrude Ederle of New York, NY. Her swim was completed in 14 hours, 31 minutes.

FLEMING, ALEXANDER: BIRTH ANNIVERSARY. Aug 6, 1881. Sir Alexander Fleming, Scottish bacteriologist, discoverer of penicillin and 1945 Nobel Prize recipient, was born at Lochfield, Scotland. He died at London, England, Mar 11, 1955.

***HAMILTON* BROADWAY PREMIERE: 5th ANNIVERSARY.** Aug 6, 2015. This cultural sensation—a hip-hop musical about American Founding Father Alexander Hamilton—opened at the Richard Rodgers Theatre on this date. Lin-Manuel Miranda wrote the book, music and lyrics and starred as Hamilton, with Leslie Odom, Jr, as rival and eventual killer Aaron Burr. Besides winning the Pulitzer Prize for Drama in 2016, *Hamilton* won 11 Tony Awards out of a record-setting 16 nominations, including Best Musical and Best Actor (Odom).

HIROSHIMA DAY. Aug 6. Memorial observances in many places for victims of the first atomic bombing of a populated place, which occurred at Hiroshima, Japan, in 1945, when an American B-29 bomber dropped an atomic bomb over the center of the city. More than 205,000 civilians died either immediately in the explosion or subsequently of radiation.

JAMAICA: INDEPENDENCE ACHIEVED: ANNIVERSARY. Aug 6, 1962. Jamaica attained its independence after centuries of British rule. Sir Alexander Bustamante became the first Jamaican prime minister.

JAPAN: PEACE FESTIVAL. Aug 6. Hiroshima. The festival held annually at Peace Memorial Park is observed in memory of the victims of the Aug 6, 1945, atomic bomb explosion there.

JUDGE CRATER DISAPPEARANCE: 90th ANNIVERSARY. Aug 6, 1930. Anniversary of mysterious disappearance at age 41 of Joseph Force Crater, justice of the New York State Supreme Court. Never seen or heard from after disappearance on this date. Declared legally dead in 1939.

MITCHUM, ROBERT: BIRTH ANNIVERSARY. Aug 6, 1917. The heavy-lidded, chiseled film actor was born at Bridgeport, CT. The hard-working Mitchum had a career that spanned from the 1940s to the 1990s in genres from film noir to Westerns. He is best known for appearing in such film noir classics as *Out of the Past* (1947) and *The Big Steal* (1948), as well as the World War II film *The Story of GI Joe* (which gave the action figure its name) and as a menacing preacher in *The Night of the Hunter* (1955). Mitchum died July 1, 1997, at Santa Barbara County, CA.

NATIONAL HOBO CONVENTION. Aug 6–9. Britt, IA. Held since 1900, the National Hobo Convention celebrates current and retired hoboes and the independent lifestyle they lead. Events include the crowning of the Hobo King and Queen, parade, live entertainment, antique and classic car show and consumption of the traditional mulligan stew. Attractions include Hobo Museum, Hobo Cemetery, Queen's Gardens and Engraved Walkway. Est attendance: 21,000. For info: Britt Hobo Day Assn, PO Box 193,

Britt, IA 50423. Phone: (641) 843-3734. E-mail: britthobodays@ gmail.com. Web: www.britthobodays.com.

O'CONNELL, DANIEL: BIRTH ANNIVERSARY. Aug 6, 1775. Irish Catholic political leader Daniel O'Connell, known as "the Liberator" for his role in achieving the right of Catholics to sit in parliament, was born near Cahirciveen, County Kerry, Ireland. He died May 15, 1847, at Genoa, Italy.

PARSONS, LOUELLA: BIRTH ANNIVERSARY. Aug 6, 1881. A legendary Hollywood gossip columnist, the first of her kind, Parsons was born at Freeport, IL. At the height of her popularity and power— from the 1930s to the 1950s—her column appeared in more than 400 newspapers and was read by approximately 20 million people. She gloried in her power and occasionally used her column in spite, making her a woman feared by many in Hollywood whose careers depended on their reputations and positive publicity. Parsons retired in 1965 and died Dec 9, 1972, at Santa Monica, CA.

ROOSEVELT, EDITH KERMIT CAROW: BIRTH ANNIVERSARY. Aug 6, 1861. Second wife of Theodore Roosevelt, 26th president of the US, whom she married in 1886. Born at Norwich, CT, she died at Long Island, NY, Sept 30, 1948.

SPACE MILESTONE: *VOSTOK 2* (USSR). Aug 6, 1961. Launched on Aug 6, 1961, Gherman Titov orbited Earth 17 times over a period of 25 hours, 18 minutes. Titov broadcast messages in passage over countries and controlled the spaceship manually for two hours.

TENNYSON, ALFRED, LORD: BIRTH ANNIVERSARY. Aug 6, 1809. English poet born at Somersby, Lincolnshire, England. His celebrated works include the poems "The Lady of Shalott" and "Ulysses" and the verse novelettes *Maud, Enoch Arden, In Memoriam, Locksley Hall Sixty Years After* and *The Idylls of the King*. Appointed English poet laureate in 1850 in succession to William Wordsworth and made a peer in 1884. Died at Aldworth, England, Oct 6, 1892.

VOTING RIGHTS ACT OF 1965 SIGNED: 55th ANNIVERSARY. Aug 6, 1965. Signed into law by President Lyndon Johnson, the Voting Rights Act of 1965 was designed to thwart attempts to discriminate against minorities at the polls. The act suspended literacy and other disqualifying tests, authorized appointment of federal voting examiners and provided for judicial relief on the federal level to bar discriminatory poll taxes. Congress amended the act in 1970, 1975, 1982, 1992 and 2006. On June 25, 2013, in *Shelby County, Alabama v Holder,* the Supreme Court found Section 4(b) unconstitutional.

WARHOL, ANDY: BIRTH ANNIVERSARY. Aug 6, 1928. The artist, filmmaker and provocateur was born Andrew Warhola to Czech immigrant parents at Forest City, PA. (Some sources cite his birth year as 1927.) A leader of the Pop Art movement, Warhol challenged the definitions of art. After a stint as a commercial artist, Warhol gained attention in 1962 with paintings of ordinary commercial products—most famously, Campbell's Soup cans—and pop culture figures. He moved on to silk-screen portraits (of subjects such as Marilyn Monroe, Elvis Presley and Mao Tse-tung) and experimental film projects (*Empire* [1964] was a static depiction of the Empire State Building that ran more than eight hours). Warhol was the center of New York's celebrity scene, and in 1968 it was he who claimed, "In the future everyone will be world-famous for 15 minutes." Warhol died Feb 22, 1987, at New York, NY.

WISCONSIN STATE FAIR. Aug 6–16. State Fair Park, West Allis, WI. 169th annual. The Wisconsin State Fair offers a unique experience to all attendees and is also a phenomenal value: 30 free entertainment stages, exciting rides and games in SpinCity, thousands of animals, endless family activities, events, vendors and culinary delights. Est attendance: 1,000,000. For info: Wisconsin State Fair Park, 640 S 84th St, West Allis, WI 53214-0990. Phone: (414) 266-7000. Web: www.WiStateFair.com.

🎂 BIRTHDAYS TODAY

Paolo Bacigalupi, 48, author (Hugo and Nebula awards for *The Windup Girl*; *The Water Knife*), born Colorado Springs, CO, Aug 6, 1972.

Peter Bonerz, 82, actor ("The Bob Newhart Show"), director, born Portsmouth, NH, Aug 6, 1938.

Soleil Moon Frye, 44, actress ("Punky Brewster"), born Glendora, CA, Aug 6, 1976.

Romola Garai, 38, actress (*I Capture the Castle, Atonement*), born Hong Kong, Aug 6, 1982.

Melissa George, 44, actress ("Alias"), born Perth, Australia, Aug 6, 1976.

Dorian Harewood, 70, actor (*The Falcon and the Snowman, Full Metal Jacket*), born Dayton, OH, Aug 6, 1950.

Catherine Hicks, 69, actress ("7th Heaven," *Peggy Sue Got Married*), born Scottsdale, AZ, Aug 6, 1951.

Shirley Ann Jackson, 74, physicist, born Washington, DC, Aug 6, 1946.

David Robinson, 55, Hall of Fame basketball player, born Key West, FL, Aug 6, 1965.

M. Night Shyamalan, 50, filmmaker (*Lady in the Water, Signs, The Sixth Sense*), born Pondicherry, India, Aug 6, 1970.

Robin van Persie, 37, soccer player, born Rotterdam, Netherlands, Aug 6, 1983.

Michelle Yeoh, 58, actress (*Crazy Rich Asians*; *Crouching Tiger, Hidden Dragon*; *Tomorrow Never Dies*), born Yang Zi Chong at Ipoh, Perak, Malaysia, Aug 6, 1962.

August 7 — Friday

DAY 220   **146 REMAINING**

BIKILA, ABEBE: BIRTH ANNIVERSARY. Aug 7, 1932. Ethiopian marathoner and two-time Olympic gold medalist. Born at Jato, Ethiopia, Bikila became the first black African Olympic champion at the 1960 games in Rome. Four years later, he broke his own world record to win gold in the marathon again. In 1969, a car accident left Bikila paralyzed from the waist down. He died of a brain hemorrhage on Oct 25, 1973, in Ethiopia's capital, Addis Ababa. Tens of thousands attended Bikila's funeral, and Ethiopia declared a national day of mourning.

BONDS BREAKS AARON'S CAREER HOME RUN RECORD: ANNIVERSARY. Aug 7, 2007. Barry Bonds of the San Francisco Giants hit his 756th home run to pass Hank Aaron's career record of 755. Bonds's ultimate career home run record was 762.

BRAHAM PIE DAY. Aug 7. Freedom Park, Braham, MN. Celebrate Braham's status as "Homemade Pie Capital of Minnesota" during this one-day festival. Visitors will find homemade pies, craft vendors, pie-eating contests, pie auction, pie trivia contest, pi-cycle show, the "Pie-alluia" chorus and performing artists in Braham's main street park. Also: food vendors, "Sweet as Pie" car show, music and entertainment. Annually, the first Friday in August. Est attendance: 5,000. For info: Braham Pie Day, PO Box 383, Braham, MN 55006. Phone: (320) 396-4956. E-mail: brahampieday@ hotmail.com. Web: www.pieday.com.

BUNCHE, RALPH JOHNSON: BIRTH ANNIVERSARY. Aug 7, 1904. American statesman, UN official, Nobel Peace Prize recipient (the first black to win the award), born at Detroit, MI. Died Dec 9, 1971, at New York, NY. See also: "Ralph Bunche Awarded Nobel Peace Prize: Anniversary" (Dec 10).

COLOMBIA: BATTLE OF BOYACÁ DAY. Aug 7. National holiday. Commemorates victory over Spanish forces in 1819.

CÔTE D'IVOIRE: NATIONAL DAY: 60th ANNIVERSARY OF INDEPENDENCE. Aug 7. Commemorates the independence of the Ivory Coast from France in 1960.

DESERT SHIELD: 30th ANNIVERSARY. Aug 7, 1990. Five days after the Iraqi invasion of Kuwait, US president George H.W. Bush ordered the military buildup that would become known as Desert Shield to prevent further Iraqi advances.

GREENE, NATHANIEL: BIRTH ANNIVERSARY. Aug 7, 1742. (Old Style date.) Born at Patowomut, RI, American Revolutionary War general Nathaniel Greene was described as the "ablest military officer of the Revolution under Washington." Greene died at Savannah, GA, June 19, 1786.

GULF OF TONKIN RESOLUTION: ANNIVERSARY. Aug 7, 1964. Congress approved the "Gulf of Tonkin Resolution," pertaining to the war in Vietnam, which gave President Lyndon Johnson authority "to take all necessary measures to repel any armed attack against the forces of the United States and to prevent further aggression."

HATFIELD-MCCOY FEUD ERUPTS: ANNIVERSARY. Aug 7–9, 1882. The long-simmering tension between two Appalachian families who lived by Tug Fork on the Kentucky–West Virginia border erupted into full-scale violence on Election Day 1882. Brothers Tolbert, Pharmer and Randolph McCoy knifed and shot Ellison Hatfield. The Hatfield family captured the three McCoys. When Ellison Hatfield died on Aug 9, the Hatfields executed the brothers. The feud continued with much loss of life. In 1888, when Kentucky authorities sought to detain the feud murder suspects and West Virginia authorities complained, the dispute went all the way to the Supreme Court, which decided in Kentucky's favor. The feud sputtered out by the end of the century.

INDIANA STATE FAIR. Aug 7–23. Indiana State Fairgrounds, Indianapolis, IN. Top-rated livestock exhibition, top music and entertainment, giant midway and Pioneer Village's world-class harness racing. Est attendance: 900,000. For info: Indiana State Fair, 1202 E 38th St, Indianapolis, IN 46205-2869. Phone: (317) 927-7500. E-mail: pr@indianastatefair.com. Web: www.indianastatefair.com.

ISING, RUDOLF C.: BIRTH ANNIVERSARY. Aug 7, 1903. Rudolf C. Ising, cocreator with Hugh Harmon of "Looney Tunes" and "Merrie Melodies," was born at Kansas City, MO. Ising and Harmon's initial production, "Bosko the Talk-Ink Kid" (1929), was the first talkie cartoon synchronizing dialogue on the soundtrack with the action on screen. Ising received an Academy Award in 1940 for *Milky Way*, a cartoon about three kittens. During WWII he headed the animation division for the Army Air Corps movie unit developing training films. Ising died July 18, 1992, at Newport Beach, CA.

MATA HARI: BIRTH ANNIVERSARY. Aug 7, 1876. Mata Hari (child of the dawn) was born Margaret Gertrude Zelle at Leeuwarden, Netherlands. Her spectacular career as a dancer, courtesan and spy made her known around the world. Probably an ineffective double agent, she nevertheless fascinated royalty and high officials of several countries. Arrested as a German spy (Agent H-21) in a Paris hotel, Feb 13, 1917, she was tried, convicted and sentenced to death. The greatest of her many roles was the final one—when she refused a blindfold and threw a kiss to the firing squad at Vincennes, France, Oct 15, 1917.

NATIONAL LIGHTHOUSE DAY. Aug 7. A day to honor and recognize America's historic lighthouses—on the anniversary of Congress's signing into law on Aug 7, 1789, "An Act for the Establishment and Support of Lighthouses, Beacons, Buoys and Public Piers." On the 200th anniversary of this legislation, in 1989, Congress proclaimed National Lighthouse Day. Many historic US lighthouses still observe this day, opening their grounds to the public. For info: American Lighthouse Foundation, Inc. Web: www.lighthousefoundation.org.

PARTICULARLY PREPOSTEROUS PACKAGING DAY. Aug 7. Buy anything lately? Did you succeed in getting the durn thing open? What do older people do when even younger adults can't open a simple bottle of aspirin, let alone a milk carton? Annually, Aug 7. (©2006 by WH.) For info: Thomas & Ruth Roy, Wellcat Holidays, 2418 Long Ln, Lebanon, PA 17046. Phone: (717) 279-0184. E-mail: info@wellcat.com. Web: www.wellcat.com.

PROFESSIONAL SPEAKERS DAY. Aug 7. A day celebrating the consummate professionals who through their oratorical skills help people. For info: Jim Barber, 1101 Marcano Blvd, Plantation, FL 33322. Phone: (954) 476-9252. E-mail: pro.speaker.day@thebarbershop.com. Web: www.professionalspeakersday.com.

PURPLE HEART: ANNIVERSARY. Aug 7, 1782. At Newburgh, NY, General George Washington ordered the creation of a Badge of Military Merit. The badge consisted of a purple cloth heart with silver braided edge. Only three are known to have been awarded during the Revolutionary War. The award was reinstituted on the bicentennial of Washington's birth, Feb 22, 1932, and recognizes those wounded in action.

SCOTLAND: EDINBURGH FESTIVAL FRINGE. Aug 7–31. Edinburgh. The largest arts festival in the world. Three weeks of nonstop entertainment with more than 53,000 performances of 3,400 different shows in 300 venues around the city, including theater, comedy, dance, music and children's shows. Est attendance: 1,000,000. For info: Edinburgh Festival Fringe, 180 High St, Edinburgh, Scotland EH1 1QS. Phone: (44) (131) 226-0026. E-mail: admin@edfringe.com. Web: www.edfringe.com.

SCOTLAND: EDINBURGH INTERNATIONAL FESTIVAL. Aug 7–31. Edinburgh, Lothian. Since 1947, the festival is one of the most exciting places in the world to experience opera, dance, theater and music. It offers the chance to see and hear some of the world's greatest companies and performers. Est attendance: 440,000. For info: Edinburgh Intl Festival, The Hub, Castlehill, Edinburgh, Scotland EH1 2NE. E-mail: press@eif.co.uk. Web: www.eif.co.uk.

SPACE MILESTONE: FIRST PICTURE OF EARTH FROM SPACE. Aug 7, 1959. US satellite *Explorer VI* transmitted the first picture of Earth from space. For the first time we had a likeness of our planet based on more than projections and conjectures.

US WAR DEPARTMENT ESTABLISHED: ANNIVERSARY. Aug 7, 1789. The second presidential cabinet department, the War Department, was established on this date by Congress.

WORLD TRADE CENTER TIGHTROPE WALK: ANNIVERSARY. Aug 7, 1974. On this date, French juggler and street performer Philippe Petit made an illegal tightrope walk between the twin towers of the World Trade Center, 1,350 feet above the plaza. He and his crew spent months planning the "coup" and smuggling materials into the buildings. Petit crossed eight times in 45 minutes and faced charges of trespassing and disorderly conduct. The 2008 Oscar-winning documentary *Man on Wire* chronicled this "artistic crime of the century."

		S	M	T	W	T	F	S
August								1
		2	3	4	5	6	7	8
2020		9	10	11	12	13	14	15
		16	17	18	19	20	21	22
		23	24	25	26	27	28	29
		30	31					

🧁 BIRTHDAYS TODAY

Sidney Crosby, 33, hockey player, born Cole Harbour, NS, Canada, Aug 7, 1987.

David Duchovny, 60, actor ("The X-Files," "Aquarius," "Californication"), born New York, NY, Aug 7, 1960.

John Glover, 76, actor ("Smallville," *An Early Frost*), born Salisbury, MD, Aug 7, 1944.

Garrison Keillor, 78, humorist, producer, host ("A Prairie Home Companion"), author (*Lake Wobegon Days*), born Anoka, MN, Aug 7, 1942.

DeLane Matthews, 59, actress ("Dave's World"), born Rockledge, FL, Aug 7, 1961.

Kyler Murray, 23, football player (2018 Heisman Trophy winner), born Bedford, TX, Aug 7, 1997.

Harold Parrineau, 57, actor ("Lost," "Oz"), born Brooklyn, NY, Aug 7, 1963.

Alberto Salazar, 63, marathon runner, born Havana, Cuba, Aug 7, 1957.

Michael Shannon, 46, actor ("Waco," "Boardwalk Empire," *The Shape of Water, Revolutionary Road*), born Lexington, KY, Aug 7, 1974.

Charlize Theron, 45, actress (Oscar for *Monster*; *Mad Max: Fury Road, Young Adult, Aeon Flux*), born Benoni, South Africa, Aug 7, 1975.

Billy Joe (B.J.) Thomas, 78, singer, born Houston, TX, Aug 7, 1942.

Mike Trout, 29, baseball player (2012 AL Rookie of the Year), born Vineland, NJ, Aug 7, 1991.

August 8 — Saturday

DAY 221   **145 REMAINING**

BONZA BOTTLER DAY®. Aug 8. To celebrate when the number of the day is the same as the number of the month. Bonza Bottler Day® is an excuse to have a party at least once a month. For more information see Jan 1. For info: Gail Berger, Bonza Bottler Day. Phone: (864) 201-3988. E-mail: bonza@bonzabottlerday.com. Web: www.bonzabottlerday.com.

BUD BILLIKEN PARADE. Aug 8. Chicago, IL. 91st annual parade especially for children begun in 1929 by Robert S. Abbott. The second-largest parade in the United States, it features bands, floats, drill teams and celebrities. There are 65,000 participants and 1.5 million spectators—plus another 25 million watching on TV. Annually, the second Saturday in August. Est attendance: 1,500,000. For info: Robert Sengstacke Abbott Foundation, 3509 S King Dr, Chicago, IL 60653. Phone: (773) 536-3710. E-mail: info@budbillikenparade.org. Web: www.budbillikenparade.org.

DE LAURENTIIS, DINO: BIRTH ANNIVERSARY. Aug 8, 1919. Italian film producer, born at Torre Annunziata, Italy. After spending 30 years producing films in Europe, including several Fellini films, De Laurentiis came to the US in 1976. Over the next 35 years, he produced a diverse assortment of Hollywood projects, including *Serpico, Blue Velvet* and *Manhunter*, as well as several notably unsuccessful films such as *King Kong, Flash Gordon* and *Dune*. He died Nov 10, 2010, at Beverly Hills, CA.

ELVIS WEEK. Aug 8–16. Memphis, TN. Each year Elvis fans from around the world visit Memphis to celebrate the King of Rock and Roll® at his beloved home, Graceland Mansion. Events occur throughout the city with special events sponsored by Graceland. A commemoration of the music, magic and memories associated with the legacy of Elvis Presley. Est attendance: 75,000. For info: Graceland, 3734 Elvis Presley Blvd, Memphis, TN 38116. Phone: (901) 332-3322. E-mail: media@graceland.com. Web: www.elvisweek.com.

ENGLAND: COWES WEEK. Aug 8–15. Cowes, Isle of Wight. Cowes Week is the largest, longest-running (since 1826) and best-known international sailing regatta in the world, with up to 1,000 boats across almost 40 classes of yacht racing. The event is a spectacle to behold. Sponsored by Lendy, Ltd. Est attendance: 100,000. For info: Cowes Week Ltd, Regatta House, 18 Bath Rd, Cowes, Isle of Wight, England PO31 7QN. Phone: (44) (1983) 295-744. E-mail: admin@lendycowesweek.co.uk. Web: www.lendycowesweek.co.uk.

HENSON, MATTHEW A.: BIRTH ANNIVERSARY. Aug 8, 1866. African-American explorer, born at Charles County, MD. He met Robert E. Peary while working in a Washington, DC, store in 1888 and was hired to be Peary's valet. He accompanied Peary on his seven subsequent Arctic expeditions. During the successful 1908–09 expedition to the North Pole, Henson and two of the four Eskimo guides reached their destination Apr 6, 1909. Peary arrived minutes later and verified the location. Henson's account of the expedition, *A Negro Explorer at the North Pole*, was published in 1912. In addition to the Congressional Medal awarded to all members of the North Pole expedition, Henson received the Gold Medal of the Geographical Society of Chicago and, at 81, was made an honorary member of the Explorers Club at New York, NY. Died Mar 9, 1955, at New York.

MARCH, FREDRIC: BIRTH ANNIVERSARY. Aug 8, 1897. Award-winning actor born Frederick McIntyre Bickel at Racine, WI. Over the course of his long and distinguished career, March performed on both the stage and screen. He made more than 65 movies and was nominated for five Academy Awards, winning in 1932 for his role in *Dr. Jekyll and Mr Hyde* and in 1947 for *The Best Years of Our Lives*. In 1956 he appeared on stage in the world premiere of Eugene O'Neill's *Long Day's Journey into Night*. He received the Tony Award for that performance. He died Apr 14, 1975, at Los Angeles, CA.

MARKERT, RUSSELL: BIRTH ANNIVERSARY. Aug 8, 1899. American choreographer Russell Markert was born at Jersey City, NJ. He founded the Radio City Music Hall Rockettes and directed them from 1932 to 1971. He died Dec 1, 1990, at Waterbury, CT.

MIDDLE CHILDREN'S DAY. Aug 8. A day to salute the middle-born children whose youthful activities were limited due to their always being "too young or too old." Today, they are just right! Created in 1986 by Elizabeth Walker. Annually, the second Saturday in August. For info: Litton Walker. E-mail: litton@embarqmail.com.

MORRIS, ESTHER HOBART MCQUIGG: BIRTH ANNIVERSARY. Aug 8, 1814. Esther Hobart McQuigg Morris was born at Tioga County, NY, but eventually moved to the Wyoming Territory, where she worked in the women's rights movement and had a key role in getting a women's suffrage bill passed. Morris became justice of the peace of South Pass City, WY, in 1870, one of the first times a woman held public office in the US. She represented Wyoming at the national suffrage convention in 1895. She died Apr 2, 1902, at Cheyenne, WY.

NATIONAL FRIED CHICKEN AND WAFFLES DAY. Aug 8. Since 2018. Fried chicken and waffles have become an American staple with restaurants across the country featuring the dish on their menus. This day celebrates this sweet and savory dish—enjoy at your

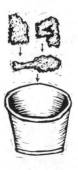

favorite restaurant or prepare it at home. Annually, Aug 8. For info: Metro Diner, 1511 N Westshore Blvd, Tampa, FL 33607. Web: https://metrodiner.com/national-fried-chicken-waffle-day.

NATIONAL GARAGE SALE DAY. Aug 8. A day to turn the nation into a giant shopping mall! Annually, the second Saturday in August. (Copyright © 2001.) For info: C. Daniel Rhodes, 1900 Crossvine Rd, Hoover, AL 35244. Phone: (205) 908-6781. E-mail: rhodan@charter.net.

RAWLINGS, MARJORIE KINNAN: BIRTH ANNIVERSARY. Aug 8, 1896. American short-story writer and novelist (*The Yearling*), born at Washington, DC. Rawlings died at St. Augustine, FL, Dec 14, 1953.

"SÁBADO GIGANTE" TV PREMIERE: ANNIVERSARY. Aug 8, 1962. This popular variety show, originally seven hours long, premiered on Chilean television under the name "Sábados Gigantes." Hosted by the amiable Don Francisco, it was broadcast from Miami, FL, and reached 100 million viewers in 20 countries. The show concluded its run in September 2015.

SECOND BATTLE OF AMIENS: ANNIVERSARY. Aug 8, 1918. Two days after the WWI Battle of Marne ended, the British Fourth Army mounted an offensive at Amiens with the objective of freeing the Amiens–Paris railway from bombardment by the German Second and Eighteenth Armies. More than 16,000 German prisoners were taken in two hours of fighting the first day. The German forces were forced back to the Hindenburg line by Sept 3. This battle is considered a turning point by many historians because of its impact on the psyche of Germany. Aug 8 was described by General Erich Ludendorff as a "Black Day" for Germany.

SNEAK SOME ZUCCHINI ONTO YOUR NEIGHBORS' PORCH NIGHT. Aug 8. Due to overzealous planting of zucchini, citizens are asked to drop off baskets of the squash on neighbors' doorsteps. Annually, Aug 8. (©2006 by WH.) For info: Thomas & Ruth Roy, Wellcat Holidays, 2418 Long Ln, Lebanon, PA 17046. Phone: (717) 279-0184. E-mail: info@wellcat.com. Web: www.wellcat.com.

SOMERSET ANTIQUE AND VINTAGE FAIR. Aug 8. Somerset, PA. 50th annual. More than 100 vendors dealing in quality antiques and collectibles. Est attendance: 5,000. For info: Sandy Berkebile, Somerset County Chamber of Commerce, 601 N Center Ave, Somerset, PA 15501. Phone: (814) 445-6431. E-mail: info@somersetcountychamber.com.

SPACE MILESTONE: *GENESIS* (US). Aug 8, 2001. The robotic explorer *Genesis* was launched on a mission to gather tiny particles of the sun. Its three-year, 20-million-mile, round-trip mission was to shed light on the origin of the solar system. It traveled to a spot where the gravitational pulls of the sun and Earth are equal and gathered atoms from the solar wind hurtling by. But on Sept 8, 2004, the *Genesis* return capsule crashed in a western US desert and most of its solar samples were destroyed.

SPACE MILESTONE: *PIONEER VENUS* MULTIPROBE (US). Aug 8, 1978. Launch of second craft in Pioneer Venus program. Split into five and probed Venus's atmosphere Dec 9.

	S	M	T	W	T	F	S
August							1
	2	3	4	5	6	7	8
2020	9	10	11	12	13	14	15
	16	17	18	19	20	21	22
	23	24	25	26	27	28	29
	30	31					

STREETSCENE. Aug 8. Covington, VA. Car show, open to all types of vehicles. Entertainment throughout the day. Annually, the second Saturday in August. Est attendance: 8,000. For info: Kars Unlimited, Inc, PO Box 851, Covington, VA 24426. Phone: (540) 965-3088. Web: www.commonwealtharms.com/karsunlimited.

TANZANIA: FARMERS' DAY. Aug 8. National holiday. Also called *Nane Nane* ("8–8").

TATE-LABIANCA MURDERS: ANNIVERSARY. Aug 8–9, 1969. In two nights of violence that shocked the nation, members of the Charles Manson commune killed seven people in Los Angeles, CA, including actress Sharon Tate. A sensational trial found Manson and three of his female followers guilty of the murders in 1971.

ZAPATA, EMILIANO: BIRTH ANNIVERSARY. Aug 8, 1879. Hero of the Mexican Revolution (1910–20), commander of the Liberation Army of the South, who advocated agrarian reform and championed the cause of the peasant. Born at Anenecuilco, Mexico, Zapata was ambushed and assassinated at Morelos on Apr 10, 1919.

🎂 BIRTHDAYS TODAY

Keith Carradine, 70, actor (*Nashville, Will Rogers Follies*, "Madam Secretary," "Dexter"), singer, born San Mateo, CA, Aug 8, 1950.

The Edge, 59, musician (U2), born David Evans at East London, England, Aug 8, 1961.

Roger Federer, 39, tennis player, born Basel, Switzerland, Aug 8, 1981.

Dustin Hoffman, 83, actor (Oscars for *Rain Man* and *Kramer vs Kramer*; *The Graduate, Midnight Cowboy*), born Los Angeles, CA, Aug 8, 1937.

Drew Lachey, 44, singer (98 Degrees), television personality ("Dancing with the Stars"), born Cincinnati, OH, Aug 8, 1976.

Shawn Mendes, 22, singer, model, born Toronto, ON, Canada, Aug 8, 1998.

Deborah Norville, 62, television host ("Inside Edition"), born Dalton, GA, Aug 8, 1958.

Roberta Cooper Ramo, 78, first woman president of the American Bar Association, born Denver, CO, Aug 8, 1942.

Connie Stevens, 82, actress ("Hawaiian Eye"), born Brooklyn, NY, Aug 8, 1938.

Michael Urie, 40, actor ("Ugly Betty"), born Dallas, TX, Aug 8, 1980.

August 9 — Sunday

DAY 222   **144 REMAINING**

ASSISTANCE DOG WEEK. Aug 9–15. Assistance dogs transform the lives of their human partners with debilitating physical and mental disabilities by serving as companions, helpers, aides, best friends and close members of the family. Assistance dogs include service dogs, guide dogs, hearing alert dogs and alert/seizure response dogs. They can be from a variety of breeds including, but not limited to, Labrador retrievers, golden retrievers and standard poodles, as well as shelter dogs. Please celebrate the selfless love and devotion these dogs so humbly provide to their disabled partners by observing Assistance Dog Week. For info: Marcie Davis, 59 Wildflower Way, Santa Fe, NM 87506. Phone: (505) 424-6631. Fax: (505) 424-6632. E-mail: mdavis@workinglikedogs.com. Web: www.workinglikedogs.com.

ATOMIC BOMB DROPPED ON NAGASAKI: 75th ANNIVERSARY. Aug 9, 1945. Three days after the atomic bombing of Hiroshima, an American B-29 bomber named *Bock's Car* left its base on Tinian Island carrying a plutonium bomb nicknamed "Fat Man." Its target was the Japanese city of Kokura, but because of clouds and poor visibility, the bomber headed for a secondary target,

Nagasaki, where at 11:02 AM, local time, it dropped the bomb, killing an estimated 70,000 people and destroying about half the city. Memorial services are held annually at Nagasaki and also at Kokura, where those who were spared because of the bad weather also grieve for those at Nagasaki who suffered in their stead.

COCHRAN, JACQUELINE: 40th DEATH ANNIVERSARY. Aug 9, 1980. American pilot Jacqueline Cochran was born at Pensacola, FL, about 1910. She began flying in 1932, and by the time of her death, she had set more distance, speed and altitude records than any other pilot, male or female. She was founder and head of the WASPs (Women's Air Force Service Pilots) during WWII; she won the Distinguished Service Medal in 1945 and the US Air Force Distinguished Flying Cross in 1969. She died at Indio, CA.

HERBERT HOOVER DAY. Aug 9. Iowa. Recognition day issued by proclamation by the state governor. Calls on "the people and officials of the state of Iowa to commemorate the life and principles of Herbert Hoover, to display the American flag and to hold appropriate services and ceremonies." Annually, the Sunday on or nearest Aug 10, the birthday of Herbert Hoover.

HOUSTON, WHITNEY: BIRTH ANNIVERSARY. Aug 9, 1963. Equally adept at danceable pop, stirring gospel and dramatic balladry, Whitney Houston, born at Newark, NJ, was one of the most influential recording artists in music history—and one of the most accomplished: she had a vocal range of three octaves. Early chart success was unprecedented: her 1985 debut, *Whitney Houston*, and *Whitney*, its 1987 follow-up, produced eight number one singles and went on to sell more than 50 million copies combined. "I Will Always Love You," her 1992 single from the film *The Bodyguard*, in which she also starred, topped the Billboard charts for a record 14 weeks and became her signature song. After Houston's accidental death on Feb 11, 2012, at Beverly Hills, CA, it was also the song that came to define her effusive singing style. It reentered the Billboard Hot 100 almost immediately and peaked at number three.

ITALY: PALIO DEL GOLFO. Aug 9. La Spezia. A rowing contest over a 2,000-meter course is held on the second Sunday in August.

JANSSON, TOVE: BIRTH ANNIVERSARY. Aug 9, 1914. Finnish artist, cartoonist, novelist Jansson is best known as the creator of Moomintrolls, loosely based on the trolls of Swedish folklore, which began as children's books and later morphed into the syndicated cartoon strip "Moomins." Born at Helsinki, Finland, she died there June 27, 2001.

JAPAN: MOMENT OF SILENCE. Aug 9. Nagasaki. Memorial observance held at Peace Memorial Park for victims of second atomic bomb, which was dropped on Nagasaki by an American bomber Aug 9, 1945.

JAPANESE REJECT SURRENDER: 75th ANNIVERSARY. Aug 9, 1945. At the same time the atomic bomb was being dropped on the city of Nagasaki, the Japanese Supreme War Direction Council was meeting in Tokyo to discuss the Potsdam Declaration, which called for unconditional surrender. The six generals were evenly divided. Foreign Minister Shigenori Togo and Prime Minister Admiral Suzuki were for surrender. Minister of War General Anami was adamant in his opposition to surrender. An impasse resulted even though news of the devastation at Nagasaki reached the gathering.

NIXON RESIGNS: ANNIVERSARY. Aug 9, 1974. The resignation from the presidency of the US by Richard Milhous Nixon, which had been announced in a speech to the American people the night before, became effective at noon. Nixon, under threat of impeachment as a result of the Watergate scandal, became the first US president to resign.

PERSEID METEOR SHOWERS. Aug 9–13. Among the best-known and most famous meteor showers are the Perseids, peaking about Aug 10–12. As many as 50–100 may be seen in a single night. Wish upon a "falling star"!

ROBERT GRAY BECOMES FIRST AMERICAN TO CIRCUMNAVIGATE EARTH: ANNIVERSARY. Aug 9, 1790. When Robert Gray docked the *Columbia* at Boston Harbor, he became the first American to circumnavigate Earth. He sailed from Boston, MA, in September 1787, to trade with Indians of the Pacific Northwest. From there he sailed to China and then continued around the world. His 42,000-mile journey opened trade between New England and the Pacific Northwest and helped the US establish claims to the Oregon Territory.

SINGAPORE: NATIONAL DAY: 55th ANNIVERSARY OF INDEPENDENCE. Aug 9, 1965. Most festivals in Singapore are Chinese, Indian or Malay, but celebration of National Day is shared by all to commemorate the withdrawal of Singapore from Malaysia and its becoming an independent state in 1965. Music, parades and dancing.

SOUTH AFRICA: NATIONAL WOMEN'S DAY. Aug 9. National holiday. Commemorates the march of women in Pretoria to protest the pass laws in 1956.

UNITED NATIONS: INTERNATIONAL DAY OF THE WORLD'S INDIGENOUS PEOPLE. Aug 9. On Dec 23, 1994, the General Assembly decided that the International Day of the World's Indigenous People be observed Aug 9 every year (Res 59/1740). For info: United Nations, Dept of Public Info, Public Inquiries Unit, Rm GA-57, New York, NY 10017. Phone: (212) 963-4475. E-mail: inquiries@un.org.

VEEP DAY. Aug 9. Commemorates the day in 1974 when Richard Nixon's resignation let Gerald Ford succeed to the presidency of the US. This was the first time the new constitutional provisions for presidential succession took effect. (Created by Robert L. Birch, Pun Corps.)

🎂 BIRTHDAYS TODAY

Gillian Anderson, 52, actress ("The X-Files," *Great Expectations, Bleak House, The House of Mirth*), born Chicago, IL, Aug 9, 1968.

Eric Bana, 52, actor (*Hulk, Munich*), born Melbourne, Australia, Aug 9, 1968.

Amanda Bearse, 62, actress ("Married . . . With Children"), born Winter Park, FL, Aug 9, 1958.

Jessica Capshaw, 44, actress ("Grey's Anatomy," "The Practice"), born Columbia, MO, Aug 9, 1976.

Robert Joseph (Bob) Cousy, 92, Hall of Fame basketball player, former coach, born New York, NY, Aug 9, 1928.

Sam Elliott, 76, actor ("Mission: Impossible," *Gettysburg*), born Sacramento, CA, Aug 9, 1944.

Derek Fisher, 46, basketball player, born Little Rock, AR, Aug 9, 1974.

Melanie Griffith, 63, actress (*Working Girl, Something Wild, Milk Money*), born New York, NY, Aug 9, 1957.

Brett Hull, 56, Hall of Fame hockey player, born Belleville, ON, Canada, Aug 9, 1964.

Anna Kendrick, 35, actress (*Into the Woods, Up in the Air, Pitch Perfect*), born Portland, ME, Aug 9, 1985.

Michael Kors, 61, fashion designer, television personality ("Project Runway"), born Long Island, NY, Aug 9, 1959.

Rodney George (Rod) Laver, 82, Hall of Fame tennis player, born Rockhampton, Australia, Aug 9, 1938.

Kevin McKidd, 47, actor ("Grey's Anatomy," "Rome"), born Elgin, Murray, Scotland, Aug 9, 1973.

Kenneth Howard (Ken) Norton, Sr, 75, former boxer, born Jacksonville, IL, Aug 9, 1945.

Deion Sanders, 53, Hall of Fame football player, former baseball player, born Fort Myers, FL, Aug 9, 1967.

David Steinberg, 78, comedian ("The David Steinberg Show"), born Winnipeg, MB, Canada, Aug 9, 1942.

Audrey Tautou, 44, actress (Amélie, The Da Vinci Code), born Beaumont, Puy-de-Dôme, France, Aug 9, 1976.

August 10 — Monday

DAY 223   **143 REMAINING**

"CANDID CAMERA" TV PREMIERE: ANNIVERSARY. Aug 10, 1948. This show—which appeared at various times on the big three TV networks and in syndication—was created and hosted by Allen Funt. The show was initially an Armed Forces Radio program based on Funt's success in recording and broadcasting soldiers' gripes. The show's modus operandi was to catch people unawares on camera—either as part of a practical joke or just being themselves. It spawned numerous imitators.

"CRAZY BLUES" RECORDED BY MAMIE SMITH: 100th ANNIVERSARY. Aug 10, 1920. On this date Mamie Smith recorded "Crazy Blues" and "It's Right Here for You (If You Don't Get It, 'Tain't No Fault of Mine)" for Okeh Records in New York City—six months after she became the first African-American artist to be recorded. "Crazy Blues" sold one million copies in less than a year.

ECUADOR: INDEPENDENCE DAY. Aug 10. National holiday. Celebrates declaration of independence in 1809. Freedom from Spain was attained May 24, 1822.

HOOVER, HERBERT CLARK: BIRTH ANNIVERSARY. Aug 10, 1874. The 31st president of the US (1929–33) was born at West Branch, IA. Hoover was the first president born west of the Mississippi River and the first to have a telephone on his desk (installed Mar 27, 1929). "Older men declare war. But it is youth that must fight and die," he said at Chicago, IL, at the Republican National Convention, June 27, 1944. Hoover died at New York, NY, Oct 20, 1964. In Iowa, the Sunday nearest Aug 10 is observed as Herbert Hoover Day.

JAPAN: MOUNTAIN DAY (YAMA NO HI). Aug 10. National holiday created in 2014 to give Japanese citizens "opportunities to get familiar with mountains and appreciate blessings from mountains." The first year of observance was 2016. Annually, Aug 11—except this year. In 2019, the Japanese government announced temporary changes to the national holiday schedule as a consequence of the 2020 Olympic Games in Tokyo.

JAPAN'S UNCONDITIONAL SURRENDER: 75th ANNIVERSARY. Aug 10, 1945. A gathering to discuss surrender terms took place in Emperor Hirohito's bomb shelter; the participants were stalemated. Hirohito settled the question, believing continuing the war would only result in further loss of Japanese lives. A message was transmitted to Japanese ambassadors in Switzerland and Sweden to accept the terms issued at Potsdam, July 26, 1945, except that the Japanese emperor's sovereignty must be maintained. The Allies devised a plan in which the emperor and the Japanese government would administer under the rule of the Supreme Commander of the Allied Powers, and the Japanese surrendered.

		S	M	T	W	T	F	S
August								1
		2	3	4	5	6	7	8
2020		9	10	11	12	13	14	15
		16	17	18	19	20	21	22
		23	24	25	26	27	28	29
		30	31					

MISSOURI: ADMISSION DAY: ANNIVERSARY. Aug 10. Became 24th state in 1821.

NATIONAL S'MORES DAY. Aug 10. Every Aug 10, a day to celebrate the gooey, messy, chocolaty campfire treat. Traditionally made with roasted marshmallows, a slab of chocolate and an enclosing sandwich of graham crackers. Girl Scout Loretta Scott Crew is credited with creating the sandwich: her recipe for "Some Mores" was published in Tramping and Trailing with the Girl Scouts in 1927.

NESTLÉ, HENRI: BIRTH ANNIVERSARY. Aug 10, 1814. Inventor of infant formula and entrepreneur, Heinrich Nestlé was born at Frankfurt, Germany, but moved to Vevey, Switzerland, where he trained as a pharmacist. In 1867, perhaps spurred on by the high infant mortality among his siblings, he created farine lactée, a substitute breast milk for infants unable to nurse. By the 1870s he was distributing the formula worldwide. Nestlé sold the Nestlé company in 1875, but the company retained his name, which means "little nest," and only later expanded its business to include chocolate and condensed milk. Died July 7, 1890, at Glion, Switzerland.

SMITHSONIAN INSTITUTION FOUNDED: ANNIVERSARY. Aug 10, 1846. Founding of the Smithsonian Institution at Washington, DC. For info: Smithsonian Institution, 900 Jefferson Dr SW, Washington, DC 20560. Phone: (202) 357-2700.

US AMATEUR (GOLF) CHAMPIONSHIP. Aug 10–16. Bandon Dunes Golf Resort, Bandon, OR. For info: USGA, Golf House, Championship Dept, PO Box 708, Far Hills, NJ 07931. Phone: (908) 234-2300. E-mail: champs@usga.org. Web: www.usga.org.

VICTORY DAY. Aug 10. Rhode Island. State holiday commemorating President Harry Truman's announcement of the surrender of the Japanese to the Allies on Aug 14, 1945. Annually, the second Monday in August.

WORLD LION DAY. Aug 10. Launched in 2013. Guarding our temples, adorning our flags, decorating our coins and capturing our hearts, the lion is beyond doubt the world's most iconic species. On almost every continent and in thousands of cultures, the lion can be found demonstrating humanity's fascination with this magnificent beast. Despite the lions' symbolic importance throughout the ages, they are suffering from a silent extinction across Africa and India. On this day, celebrate the lion, help create conservation awareness and help save them and their kingdom. Annually, Aug 10—a date that falls in the Leo zodiac sign. For info: African Lion and Environmental Research Trust (ALERT). E-mail: info@worldlionday. Web: www.worldlionday.com.

🎂 BIRTHDAYS TODAY

Ian Anderson, 73, musician, lead singer (Jethro Tull), born Blackpool, England, Aug 10, 1947.

Rosanna Arquette, 61, actress (Desperately Seeking Susan, New York Stories), born New York, NY, Aug 10, 1959.

Antonio Banderas, 60, actor (Spy Kids, The Mask of Zorro, Desperado), born Malaga, Spain, Aug 10, 1960.

Riddick Bowe, 53, Hall of Fame boxer, born Brooklyn, NY, Aug 10, 1967.

Angie Harmon, 48, actress ("Rizzoli & Isles," "Law & Order," "Baywatch Nights"), born Dallas, TX, Aug 10, 1972.

Carla Hayden, 68, Librarian of Congress (2016–), born Tallahassee, FL, Aug 10, 1952.

Betsey Johnson, 78, fashion designer, born Wethersfield, CT, Aug 10, 1942.

Juan Manuel Santos, 69, former president of Colombia (2010–18), 2016 Nobel Peace Prize recipient, journalist, born Juan Manuel Santos Calderón at Bogotá, Colombia, Aug 10, 1951.

Ronnie Spector, 77, singer (The Ronettes), born Veronica Yvette Bennett at New York, NY, Aug 10, 1943.

August 11 — Tuesday

DAY 224	142 REMAINING

ATCHISON, DAVID R.: BIRTH ANNIVERSARY. Aug 11, 1807. Missouri legislator who was president of the US for one day. Born at Frogtown, KY. Atchison's strong proslavery opinions made his name prominent in legislative debates. He served as president pro tempore of the Senate a number of times, and he became president of the US for one day—Sunday, Mar 4, 1849—pending the swearing in of President-elect Zachary Taylor on Monday, Mar 5, 1849. The city of Atchison, KS, and the county of Atchison, MO, are named for him. He died at Gower, MO, Jan 26, 1886.

BAHAMAS: FOX HILL DAY. Aug 11. Nassau. Annually, the second Tuesday in August.

BOND, CARRIE JACOBS: BIRTH ANNIVERSARY. Aug 11, 1862. American composer of well-known songs, including "I Love You Truly" and "A Perfect Day," and of scores for motion pictures, Carrie Jacobs Bond was born at Janesville, WI. She died at Hollywood, CA, at age 84, Dec 28, 1946.

CHAD: INDEPENDENCE DAY: 60th ANNIVERSARY OF INDEPENDENCE. Aug 11. National holiday. Commemorates independence from France in 1960.

DOUGLAS, MIKE: 95th BIRTH ANNIVERSARY. Aug 11, 1925. This pioneer of daytime talk shows was born Michael Delaney Dowd, Jr, at Chicago, IL. Douglas hosted his first afternoon talk show in Cleveland in 1961 and within five years was a household name. His nationally syndicated show featured celebrity interviews and topics and remained on the air until 1981. The show received the first Emmy Award for Individual Achievement in Daytime Television. Douglas died Aug 11, 2006, at North Palm Beach, FL.

HALEY, ALEX PALMER: BIRTH ANNIVERSARY. Aug 11, 1921. Born at Ithaca, NY, Alex Palmer Haley was raised by his grandmother at Henning, TN. In 1939 he entered the US Coast Guard and served as a cook, but eventually he became a writer and college professor. His interview with Malcolm X for *Playboy* led to his first book, *The Autobiography of Malcolm X*, which sold 6 million copies and was translated into eight languages. *Roots*, his Pulitzer Prize–winning novel published in 1976, sold millions, was translated into 37 languages and was made into an eight-part TV miniseries in 1977. The story generated an enormous interest in family ancestry. Haley died at Seattle, WA, Feb 13, 1992.

INDIA: KRISHNA JANMASHTAMI. Aug 11. Hindu holiday. Birth anniversary of Lord Vishnu in his human incarnation as Krishna. Because there is no single universally accepted Hindu calendar, this holiday may be celebrated on a different date in some parts of India, but it always falls in August or September.

MOON PHASE: LAST QUARTER. Aug 11. Moon enters Last Quarter phase at 12:45 AM, EDT.

SAINT CLARE OF ASSISI: FEAST DAY. Aug 11. Chiara Favorone di Offreduccio, a religious leader inspired by St. Francis of Assisi, was the first woman to write her own religious order rule. Born at Assisi, Italy, July 16, 1194, she died there Aug 11, 1253. A "Privilege of Poverty" freed her order from any constraint to accept material security, making the "Poor Clares" totally dependent on God.

SPACE MILESTONE: *VOSTOK 3* (USSR). Aug 11, 1962. Launched on this date, Andriyan Nikolayev orbited Earth 64 times over a period of 94 hours, 25 minutes, covering a distance of 1,242,500 miles. Achieved radio communication with *Vostok 4* and telecast from spacecraft.

VERMONT STATE FAIR. Aug 11–16 (tentative). Fairgrounds, Rutland, VT. A family-friendly event since 1846. Live music, demolition derby, culinary and livestock contests, racing pigs and more. Est attendance: 100,000. For info: Vermont State Fair, 175 S Main St, Rutland, VT 05701. Phone: (802) 775-5200. E-mail: VermontStateFair@outlook.com. Web: www.VermontStateFair.org.

WATTS RIOT: 55th ANNIVERSARY. Aug 11, 1965. A minor clash between the California Highway Patrol and two young blacks set off six days of riots in the Watts area of Los Angeles. Thirty-four deaths were reported and more than 3,000 people were arrested. Damage to property was listed at $40 million. The less-immediate cause of the disturbance, and the others that followed, was racial tension between whites and blacks in American society.

WYOMING STATE FAIR AND RODEO. Aug 11–15 (tentative). Douglas, WY. 108th annual. Recognizing the products, achievements and cultural heritage of the people of Wyoming. Bringing together rural and urban citizens for an inexpensive, entertaining and educational experience. Features livestock shows for beef, goats, swine, sheep and horses; youth livestock shows for beef, swine, sheep, horses, goats, dogs, poultry and rabbits; competitions and displays for culinary arts, needlework, visual arts and floriculture; 4-H and FFA County/Chapters State qualification competitions; Demo Derby; live entertainment; carnival; PRCA rodeo and Ranch Rodeo and an antique tractor pull. Est attendance: 58,000. For info: Wyoming State Fair, PO Drawer 10, Douglas, WY 82633. Phone: (307) 358-2398. Fax: (307) 358-6030. E-mail: wystatefair@gmail.com. Web: www.wystatefair.com.

ZIMBABWE: HEROES' DAY. Aug 11. National holiday. Followed by Defense Forces Day on Aug 12.

 BIRTHDAYS TODAY

Jonathan Adler, 54, interior and product designer, ceramicist, author, born in New Jersey, Aug 11, 1966.

David Brooks, 59, journalist, commentator, born Toronto, ON, Canada, Aug 11, 1961.

Arlene Dahl, 92, actress (*Journey to the Center of the Earth,* "One Life to Live"), born Minneapolis, MN, Aug 11, 1928 (some sources say 1925).

Viola Davis, 55, actress (Emmy for "How to Get Away with Murder"; Oscar for *Fences*), born St. Matthews, SC, Aug 11, 1965.

Will Friedle, 44, actor ("Boy Meets World"), born Hartford, CT, Aug 11, 1976.

Chris Hemsworth, 37, actor (*Thor, The Avengers, Rush,* "Home and Away"), born Melbourne, Australia, Aug 11, 1983.

Hulk Hogan, 67, wrestler, actor, born Terry Gene Bollea at Augusta, GA, Aug 11, 1953.

Joe Jackson, 66, musician, songwriter, born Burton-on-Trent, England, Aug 11, 1954.

Ashley Jensen, 51, actress ("Ugly Betty," "Extras"), born Annan, Dumfries and Galloway, Scotland, Aug 11, 1969.

Chris Messina, 46, actor (*Argo,* "The Mindy Project," "The Newsroom"), born New York, NY, Aug 11, 1974.

Carolyn Murphy, 47, model, television personality, born Panama City, FL, Aug 11, 1973.

Marilyn vos Savant, 74, columnist ("Ask Marilyn"), claims world's highest IQ, born St. Louis, MO, Aug 11, 1946.

Stephen Wozniak, 70, Apple computer cofounder, born Sunnyvale, CA, Aug 11, 1950.

August 12 — Wednesday

DAY 225	141 REMAINING

CANTINFLAS: BIRTH ANNIVERSARY. Aug 12, 1911. Mexico's most famous comic actor, Cantinflas, was born at Mexico City as Mario Moreno Reyes. Particularly popular with the poor people of Mexico because he most often portrayed the underdog, Cantinflas got his start in Mexico City *carpas*, the equivalent of vaudeville. He became internationally known for his starring role as Passepartout in *Around the World in 80 Days*. The name *Cantinflas* was invented by the comic to prevent his parents from learning he was in show business, which they considered a shameful endeavor. Died Apr 20, 1993, at Mexico City.

DEMILLE, CECIL B.: BIRTH ANNIVERSARY. Aug 12, 1881. Born at Ashfield, MA, Cecil Blount DeMille was a film showman extraordinaire known for lavish screen spectacles. He produced more than 70 major films, which were noted more for their large scale than for their subtle artistry, including *Cleopatra, The Plainsman, Reap the Wild Wind* and *The Ten Commandments* (in 1923 and 1956). DeMille was awarded an Oscar for *The Greatest Show on Earth* in 1953. He died Jan 21, 1959, at Hollywood, CA.

HAMILTON, EDITH: BIRTH ANNIVERSARY. Aug 12, 1867. Born at Dresden, Germany, classicist Edith Hamilton instilled classical values in students as headmistress of Bryn Mawr School before publishing her own contributions to the discipline upon her retirement. In *Mythology*, a retelling of classical myths, "she [threw] the whole of even familiar Greek and Norse mythology into a fresh and luminous context . . . [and] distilled into incidental observations the whole meaning of mythology itself to the modern scholar." Her translations of Euripides and Aeschylus were regarded as a return to a more accurate reflection of their original Greek austerity. Hamilton died May 31, 1963, at Washington, DC.

HOME SEWING MACHINE PATENTED: ANNIVERSARY. Aug 12, 1851. Isaac Singer developed the sewing machine for use in homes.

IBM PERSONAL COMPUTER INTRODUCED: ANNIVERSARY. Aug 12, 1981. IBM's first personal computer was released. The computer cost the equivalent of $3,000 in today's currency. Although IBM was one of the pioneers in making mainframe and other large computers, this was the company's first foray into the desktop computer market. Eventually, more IBM-compatible computers were manufactured by IBM's competitors than by IBM itself.

KIDD, MICHAEL: BIRTH ANNIVERSARY. Aug 12, 1915. Dancer and choreographer born Milton Greenwald at New York, NY. He was responsible for some of the most memorable Broadway productions of all time, including *Finian's Rainbow, Guys and Dolls* and *Can-Can*. His film choreography includes *Seven Brides for Seven Brothers* and *Hello, Dolly!* He won five Tony Awards for his Broadway productions and an honorary Oscar for "service to the art of dance" in feature films. He died at Los Angeles, CA, Dec 23, 2007.

KING PHILIP ASSASSINATION: ANNIVERSARY. Aug 12, 1676. Philip, a son of Massasoit, chief of the Wampanog tribe, was killed near Mount Hope, RI, by a member of his own tribe, bringing to an end the first and bloodiest war between American Indians and white settlers of New England, a war that had raged for nearly two years and was known as King Philip's War.

MATHEWSON, CHRISTY: BIRTH ANNIVERSARY. Aug 12, 1880. Famed American baseball player Christopher (Christy) Mathewson, one of the first players named to Baseball's Hall of Fame, was born at Factoryville, PA. Died at Saranac Lake, NY, Oct 7, 1925. He pitched three complete games during the 1905 World Series without allowing opponents to score a run. In 17 years he won 372 games while losing 188 and striking out 2,499 players.

MOUNT OGURA PLANE CRASH: 35th ANNIVERSARY. Aug 12, 1985. A Japan Airlines plane crashed into the side of Mount Ogura, Japan, claiming 520 lives. The worst air disaster involving a single plane. See also: "Canary Islands Plane Disaster: Anniversary" (Mar 27).

NIGHT OF THE MURDERED POETS: ANNIVERSARY. Aug 12, 1952. Thirteen prominent Jewish writers and leaders associated with the Jewish Anti-Fascist Committee (JAC) were executed on the orders of Josef Stalin. After WWII, the JAC evolved into an organization promoting the revival of Jewish culture and identity in Russia. Stalin, a rabid anti-Semite, had 15 of the committee's leaders arrested, tried and convicted on trumped-up charges of treason.

OWENS, BUCK: BIRTH ANNIVERSARY. Aug 12, 1929. Country-western star, creator of the "Bakersfield sound" in the 1960s, Alvis Edgar "Buck" Owens was born to a sharecropper outside Sherman, TX. His family moved west with Dust Bowl refugees during the Great Depression, and Owens became a honky-tonk performer in California. He had 19 consecutive number one singles from 1963 to 1967, and his success led him to a cohosting gig on the popular TV variety show "Hee Haw" (1969–86). Inducted into the Country Music Hall of Fame in 1996, Owens died at Bakersfield, CA, Mar 25, 2006.

SHARP, ZERNA ADDIS: BIRTH ANNIVERSARY. Aug 12, 1889. Educator and originator of the "Dick and Jane" readers used for many years in American schools, Sharp collaborated with illustrator Eleanor B. Campbell and others to create the texts while a reading consultant for Scott Foresman. She selected easy-to-read words and patterned the plots from children's interests. Born at Hillisburg, IN, she died June 17, 1981, at Frankfort, IN.

SPACE MILESTONE: *ECHO I* (US): 60th ANNIVERSARY. Aug 12, 1960. First successful communications satellite in Earth's orbit to relay voice and TV signals from one ground station to another was launched.

SPACE MILESTONE: *ENTERPRISE* (US). Aug 12, 1977. Reusable orbiting vehicle (space shuttle) makes first successful flight on its own within Earth's atmosphere. Launched from a Boeing 747 on Aug 12, 1977.

SWEDEN: CRAYFISH PREMIERE. Aug 12. Crayfish may be sold and served in restaurants the day after the season opens. Annually, the second Wednesday in August.

THAILAND: BIRTHDAY OF THE QUEEN. Aug 12. The entire kingdom of Thailand celebrates the birthday of Queen Sirikit.

UNITED NATIONS: INTERNATIONAL YOUTH DAY. Aug 12. Day to increase public awareness of the World Programme of Action for Youth to the Year 2000 and Beyond, which calls for action in 10 priority areas: education, employment, hunger and poverty, health, environment, drug abuse, juvenile delinquency, leisure-time activities, girls and young women, and full and effective participation of youths (15–24 years old) in the life of society and in decision making. For info: United Nations, Dept of Public Info, New York, NY 10017. Web: www.un.org.

VINYL RECORD DAY. Aug 12. We all need a reminder sometimes that life is good, regardless of national news and daily challenges. Favorite songs can bring back fond memories, and Vinyl Record Day encourages celebrating these musical memories with family and friends. The day also seeks to recognize the tremendous cultural influence that vinyl records and album covers have had for

August 2020	S	M	T	W	T	F	S
							1
	2	3	4	5	6	7	8
	9	10	11	12	13	14	15
	16	17	18	19	20	21	22
	23	24	25	26	27	28	29
	30	31					

many years and the need to preserve that audio history. Annually, on Aug 12—the day Thomas Edison invented the phonograph in 1877. (Created by Gary Freiberg.)

WYATT, JANE: BIRTH ANNIVERSARY. Aug 12, 1910. Born at Bergen County, NJ, this Hollywood actress had her big break starring in Frank Capra's *Lost Horizon* in 1937. Other classic performances include her role opposite Gregory Peck in 1947's *Gentlemen's Agreement*. Wyatt's film career suffered when she criticized Senator Joseph McCarthy in the 1950s. She is best remembered for the television show "Father Knows Best," for which she won three consecutive Emmy Awards for her portrayal of Margaret Anderson (1958–61). Wyatt died Aug 20, 2006, at Bel Air, CA.

🎂 BIRTHDAYS TODAY

Casey Affleck, 45, actor (Oscar for *Manchester by the Sea*; *Gone Baby Gone*), born Falmouth, MA, Aug 12, 1975.

Cara Delevingne, 28, model, actress, born London, England, Aug 12, 1992.

George Hamilton, 81, actor (*Love at First Bite*, *Act One*, "The Survivors"), born Memphis, TN, Aug 12, 1939.

François Hollande, 66, former president of France (2012–17), born Rouen, France, Aug 12, 1954.

Sam J. Jones, 66, actor (*Flash Gordon*, *10*), born Chicago, IL, Aug 12, 1954.

Peter Krause, 55, actor ("Parenthood," "Six Feet Under," "Sports Night"), born Minneapolis, MN, Aug 12, 1965.

Ann M. Martin, 65, author (The Baby-Sitters Club series, *A Corner of the Universe*), born Princeton, NJ, Aug 12, 1955.

Pat Metheny, 66, jazz guitarist, born Lee's Summit, MO, Aug 12, 1954.

Pete Sampras, 49, Hall of Fame tennis player, born Washington, DC, Aug 12, 1971.

George Soros, 90, billionaire, financier, philanthropist, born Budapest, Hungary, Aug 12, 1930.

Lakeith Stanfield, 29, actor (*Sorry to Bother You*, *The Girl in the Spider's Web*, *Get Out*, *Straight Outta Compton*, "Atlanta"), rapper, born San Bernardino, CA, Aug 12, 1991.

Antoine Walker, 44, former basketball player, born Chicago, IL, Aug 12, 1976.

August 13 — Thursday

DAY 226	140 REMAINING

ANGSTRÖM, ANDERS JONAS: BIRTH ANNIVERSARY. Aug 13, 1814. Astronomer born at Logdo, Sweden, Angström is noted for founding the science of spectroscopy—the study of light—and in particular, his spectral analyses of the sun and aurora borealis. His studies of the sun's spectra resulted in the discovery of hydrogen in its atmosphere in 1862. Angström deduced the principle of spectrum analysis, and the angstrom unit of length, which measures one ten-billionth of a meter, was named in his honor. Died June 21, 1874, at Uppsala, Sweden.

BAIRD, JOHN LOGIE: BIRTH ANNIVERSARY. Aug 13, 1888. Born at Helensburgh, Scotland, Baird was the first person to demonstrate a working television. For decades scientists had been striving to realize the dream of transmitting images, yet it wasn't until 1924 that Baird first managed to produce a static image across a few feet using a crude mechanical appliance. In two short years he had fine-tuned his invention enough to offer the world a demonstration of moving images, and by 1928, his group, the Baird Television Development Company, achieved the first transatlantic transmission from London to New York. By 1937, however, Guglielmo Marconi's all-electronic television outshone Baird's invention, effectively making it obsolete. Baird died on June 14, 1946, at Bexhill-on-Sea, England.

BERLIN WALL ERECTED: ANNIVERSARY. Aug 13, 1961. Early in the morning, the East German government closed the border between the east and west sectors of Berlin with barbed wire to discourage further population movement to the West. Telephone and postal services were interrupted, and later in the week, a concrete wall was built to strengthen the barrier between official crossing points. The dismantling of the wall began Nov 9, 1989. See also: "Berlin Wall Opened: Anniversary" (Nov 9).

CASTRO, FIDEL: BIRTH ANNIVERSARY. Aug 13, 1926. Revolutionary, dictator, born near Birán, Cuba. Castro embraced revolutionary ideals while studying law at the University of Havana, and in 1953, after leading a failed attempt to overthrow Fulgencio Batista, he made his famous "history will absolve me" speech before his exile to Mexico. Aided by Che Guevara, Castro adopted guerrilla war tactics and succeeded in overthrowing Batista in January 1959. As Cuba's new charismatic leader, Castro nationalized landholdings and health care, severed economic and diplomatic ties with the US, and courted Soviet aid, leading to the Cuban missile crisis of 1962. Hundreds of thousands of refugees fled the country as Castro became a dictator, canceling elections and imprisoning and executing dissenters. Popular for defying world powers, Castro sought to foment revolutions abroad, but his socialist policies at home failed, and Cuba's economy, already suffering from a US embargo, all but collapsed. In failing health, he ceded power to his brother Raul in 2008. Castro died Nov 26, 2016, at Havana, Cuba.

CAXTON, WILLIAM: BIRTH ANNIVERSARY. Aug 13, 1422. First English printer, born at Kent, England. Died at London, England, 1491. Caxton produced his first book printed in English (while he was at Bruges), the *Recuyell of the Histories of Troy*, in 1476, and in the autumn of that year set up a print shop at Westminster, becoming the first printer in England.

CENTRAL AFRICAN REPUBLIC: INDEPENDENCE DAY: 60th ANNIVERSARY OF INDEPENDENCE. Aug 13. Commemorates Proclamation of Independence from France in 1960.

FINLAND: HELSINKI FESTIVAL. Aug 13–30 (tentative). Helsinki. Finland's largest arts festival provides a diverse program of events throughout the city, with experiences ranging from classical to world music and pop, from drama to contemporary dance, and from visual art to film and children's events. Lose yourself in the Night of the Arts or get carried away with our fringe program. This is a festival that brings the arts to everyone! Est attendance: 215,000. For info: Helsinki Festival. Web: www.helsinkifestival.fi.

GREAT RIVER TUG FEST. Aug 13–15. Port Byron, IL, and LeClaire, IA. The Tug is the only tug-of-war across the mighty Mississippi River or any other moving body of water in the world. For two hours barge traffic, pleasure boats and gambling and paddle boats yield the right of way to a 400-foot, 680-pound rope that stretches between Illinois and Iowa. At 1 PM Saturday, the first team of 20 tuggers grip the rope, the crowd counts down and dirt starts flying! Festivals on both sides of the river Friday and Saturday. Fireworks Friday evening. Annually, the second weekend in August (including Thursday). For info: Great River Tug Fest. Phone: (563) 289-4242, ext 61135. Web: www.tugfest.org or www.visitquadcities.com.

HITCHCOCK, ALFRED JOSEPH: BIRTH ANNIVERSARY. Aug 13, 1899. English film director and master of suspense born at London, England. Hitchcock's career as a filmmaker dates back to the silent film era when he made *The Lodger* in 1926, based on the tale of Jack the Ripper. American audiences were introduced to the Hitchcock style in 1935 with *The Thirty-Nine Steps* and *The Lady Vanishes* in 1938, after which he went to Hollywood. There he produced a string of classics including *Rebecca, Suspicion, Notorious, Rear Window, To Catch a Thief, The Birds, Psycho* and *Frenzy,* in addition to his TV series, "Alfred Hitchcock Presents." He died Apr 29, 1980, at Beverly Hills, CA.

HOGAN, BEN: BIRTH ANNIVERSARY. Aug 13, 1912. With Sam Snead and Byron Nelson (all born in 1912), one of the greatest golfers. Born at Stephenville, TX, but later moving to Fort Worth, Hogan caddied with friend and later rival Nelson at the Glen Garden Country Club. He struggled financially until 1938, when he began winning tournaments. His wins were interrupted by three years' military service during WWII. After almost dying in a Feb 2, 1949, auto accident, Hogan was able to recover and win the 1950 US Open. In 1953, Hogan won the Masters, US Open and British Open. New York City gave him a ticker-tape parade to celebrate his British Open win. He is one of only five players to win all four major professional championships, and his 64 career PGA victories rank him fourth after Sam Snead, Jack Nicklaus and Tiger Woods. Hogan died at Fort Worth, TX, July 25, 1997.

ILLINOIS STATE FAIR. Aug 13–23. Springfield, IL. Agricultural exhibits, harness racing, live concerts, amusement rides, Twilight Parade and much more. Features the Butter Cow, which has been an unofficial icon of the fair since the 1920s—500 pounds of unsalted butter are used to sculpt the life-size figure by hand. Lots of great fair food: Illinois-grown sweet corn, watermelon, apple cider slushes and more. Est attendance: 700,000. For info: Illinois State Fair, PO Box 19427, Springfield, IL 62794. Phone: (217) 782-6661. E-mail: agr.StateFair@illinois.gov. Web: www. illinoisstatefair.info.

INTERNATIONAL LEFT-HANDERS DAY. Aug 13. Since 1992, an annual worldwide day when left-handers everywhere can celebrate their sinistrality and increase public awareness of the advantages and disadvantages of being left-handed. There are many ways to mark this day, including left-versus-right sports matches, a left-handed tea party or "Lefty Zones." Right-handers are encouraged to try out everyday left-handed objects to see just how awkward it can feel using the wrong equipment. Annually, Aug 13. For info: Left-Handers Club. Web: www.lefthandersday.com.

IOWA STATE FAIR. Aug 13–23. Iowa State Fairgrounds, Des Moines, IA. One of America's oldest and largest state fairs. A grand showcase of Iowa agriculture, talent and tradition. The fair features the largest foods department of any state fair and one of the largest livestock shows in the world. This annual August extravaganza inspired Phil Stong's acclaimed novel *State Fair,* three motion pictures and a Broadway musical. Est attendance: 1,130,000. For info: Iowa State Fair, PO Box 57130, Des Moines, IA 50317. Phone: 800-545-FAIR. E-mail: info@iowastatefair.org. Web: www. iowastatefair.org.

JERSEY BATTLE OF FLOWERS. Aug 13–14. St. Helier, Jersey, Channel Islands. Colorful parade of floats decorated with hundreds of flowers. First held in 1902 to mark the coronation of Edward VII and Queen Alexandra. Annually, the second Thursday and Friday in August. Est attendance: 27,500. For info: Jersey Battle of Flowers Events Ltd, Meadowbank, La Rue des Pres Sorsoleil, St. Lawrence, Jersey, Channel Islands JE3 1EE. E-mail: events@battleofflowers. com. Web: www.battleofflowers.com.

August 2020	S	M	T	W	T	F	S
							1
	2	3	4	5	6	7	8
	9	10	11	12	13	14	15
	16	17	18	19	20	21	22
	23	24	25	26	27	28	29
	30	31					

KRUPP, ALFRIED VON BOHLEN UND HALBACH: BIRTH ANNIVERSARY. Aug 13, 1907. As sole owner of the massive Krupp industries, Alfried Krupp took over the factories of German-occupied countries and used them for the Nazi war machine. Sometimes he had complete facilities dismantled and reassembled inside Germany. He used prisoners of war, civilians from occupied countries and inmates of concentration camps as forced labor in his factories. Found guilty as a war criminal by the military court at Nuremberg in 1948, he regained his property after serving three years of a 12-year sentence. He was named Alfried von Bohlen und Halbach at birth, but the family was authorized by Emperor Wilhelm II to add the mother's maiden name of Krupp to their own. Born at Essen, Germany, he died there July 30, 1967.

MILWAUKEE IRISH FEST. Aug 13–16. Henry Maier Festival Grounds, Milwaukee, WI. 40th annual. World's largest Irish and Celtic music and cultural event, with the best of Celtic and Irish-American music and dance on 17 stages. Activities include a cultural village, sports, contests, parades, theater shows, marketplace, food and beverages and children's activities. The weeklong Irish Fest Summer School (open to the public) precedes the festival. Annually, the third weekend in August. Est attendance: 100,000. For info: Milwaukee Irish Fest. Phone: (414) 476-3378. E-mail: info@ irishfest.com. Web: www.irishfest.com.

MISSOURI STATE FAIR. Aug 13–23. Sedalia, MO. Livestock shows, commercial and competitive exhibits, horse shows, motor sports, tractor pulls, carnival and headline musical entertainment. Economical family entertainment. Est attendance: 360,000. For info: Missouri State Fair, 2503 W 16th St, Sedalia, MO 65301. Phone: (800) 422-FAIR. E-mail: mostatefair@mda.mo.gov. Web: www. mostatefair.com.

OAKLEY, ANNIE: BIRTH ANNIVERSARY. Aug 13, 1860. Annie Oakley was born at Darke County, OH. She developed an eye as a markswoman early as a child, becoming so proficient that she was able to pay off the mortgage on her family farm by selling the game she killed. A few years after defeating vaudeville marksman Frank Butler in a shooting match, she married him and they toured as a team until joining Buffalo Bill's Wild West Show in 1885. She was one of the star attractions for 17 years. She died Nov 3, 1926, at Greenville, OH.

"SOUTH PARK" TV PREMIERE: ANNIVERSARY. Aug 13, 1997. Comedy Central's irreverent, satiric and often profane animated cartoon for adults features the misadventures of four boys—Stan Marsh, Kyle Broflovski, Eric Cartman and Kenny McCormick—in South Park, CO, as well as a cast of hundreds. Trey Parker and Matt Stone are the creators of the tremendously popular show, which features purposefully crude animation.

SPACE MILESTONE: *HELIOS* SOLAR WING. Aug 13, 2001. The solar-powered plane *Helios* broke the altitude records for propeller-driven aircraft and nonrocket planes on this date, soaring higher than 96,500 feet. The plane has a wingspan longer than a Boeing 747 and uses solar-powered motors to power 14 propellers, flying at speeds as high as 170 mph. NASA plans to develop similar craft for unmanned flights on Mars.

STATE FAIR OF WEST VIRGINIA. Aug 13–22 (tentative). Lewisburg, WV. The state's largest multiday family celebration features thousands of agricultural and livestock displays, dozens of rides at the Reithoffer carnival midway, music and entertainment, spectacular fireworks and more. Annually, usually beginning on the second Thursday in August. Est attendance: 175,000. For info: The State Fair of West Virginia, PO Drawer 986, Lewisburg, WV 24901. Phone: (304) 645-1090. E-mail: events@statefairofwv.com. Web: www.statefairofwv.com.

STONE, LUCY: BIRTH ANNIVERSARY. Aug 13, 1818. American women's rights pioneer, born near West Brookfield, MA, Lucy Stone dedicated her life to the abolition of slavery and the emancipation of women. Although she graduated from Oberlin College, she had to finance her education by teaching for nine years because her father did not favor college education for women. An eloquent speaker for her causes, she headed the list of 89 men and women who signed the call to the first national Woman's Rights Convention, held at Worcester, MA, October 1850. On May 1, 1855, she married Henry Blackwell. They aided in the founding of the American Suffrage Association, taking part in numerous referendum campaigns to win suffrage amendments to state constitutions. She died Oct 18, 1893, at Dorchester, MA.

TUNISIA: WOMEN'S DAY. Aug 13. General holiday. Celebration of independence of women.

🎂 BIRTHDAYS TODAY

Kathleen Battle, 72, opera singer, born Portsmouth, OH, Aug 13, 1948.

Danny Bonaduce, 61, radio personality, actor ("The Partridge Family"), born Broomall, PA, Aug 13, 1959.

DeMarcus Cousins, 30, basketball player, born Birmingham, AL, Aug 13, 1990.

Quinn Cummings, 53, actress (*The Goodbye Girl*, "Family"), born Los Angeles, CA, Aug 13, 1967.

Shani Davis, 38, Olympic speed skater, born Chicago, IL, Aug 13, 1982.

Philippe Petit, 71, high-wire artist, juggler, author, born Nemours, France, Aug 13, 1949.

Sarah Huckabee Sanders, 38, former White House press secretary, political adviser, born Hope, AR, Aug 13, 1982.

Kevin Tighe, 76, actor ("Emergency," *The Graduate, What's Eating Gilbert Grape?*), born Los Angeles, CA, Aug 13, 1944.

Janet Yellen, 74, former chair of the Federal Reserve (2014–18), economist, born Brooklyn, NY, Aug 13, 1946.

August 14 — Friday

DAY 227   **139 REMAINING**

ATLANTIC CHARTER SIGNING: ANNIVERSARY. Aug 14, 1941. The eight-point agreement was signed by US president Franklin D. Roosevelt and British prime minister Winston S. Churchill. The charter grew out of a three-day conference aboard ship in the Atlantic Ocean, off the Newfoundland coast, and stated policies and hopes for the future agreed to by the two nations.

CANADA: ABBOTSFORD INTERNATIONAL AIRSHOW. Aug 14–16. Abbotsford Airport, Abbotsford, BC. "Canada's National Airshow." Leading air show in North America attracts the world's top aeronautical performers. Thrill to the grace of the Canadian Snowbirds and the USAF Thunderbirds, plus the raw power of the international air demonstration squadrons, daring performers and soloists. Ground displays include military and general aviation planes, concessions and trade booths. Air show camping facilities. Annually, the second full weekend in August. Est attendance: 100,000. For info: Abbotsford Intl Airshow, 1464 Tower St, Abbotsford, BC V2T 6H5, Canada. E-mail: info@abbotsfordairshow.com. Web: www.abbotsfordairshow.com.

COLOGNE CATHEDRAL COMPLETION: ANNIVERSARY. Aug 14, 1880. The largest Gothic church in northern Europe, the Cologne Cathedral at Cologne, Germany, was completed on this date, 632 years after rebuilding began on Aug 14, 1248. In fact, there had been a church on its site since 873, but a fire in 1248 made rebuilding necessary. The cathedral was again damaged, by bombing, during WWII.

JAPANESE IMPERIAL PALACE ATTACKED: 75th ANNIVERSARY. Aug 14, 1945. The Japanese news broadcast an overseas radio bulletin that the emperor would soon accept the Potsdam Proclamation. Hirohito, in fact, had already recorded a statement to that effect to be released to the Japanese public. That evening, more than a thousand Japanese soldiers attacked the Imperial Palace with hopes of seizing the recording and preventing the release of the message. Troops faithful to the emperor managed to drive them away, and the message was released the following day.

JUST, ERNEST E.: BIRTH ANNIVERSARY. Aug 14, 1883. American marine biologist Ernest E. Just was born at Charleston, SC. He was the first recipient of the NAACP's Spingarn Medal and was a professor at Howard University from 1907 to 1941, where he was head of physiology at the medical school (1912–20) and head of zoology (1912–41). He died Oct 27, 1941, at Washington, DC.

MACHIAS WILD BLUEBERRY FESTIVAL. Aug 14–16 (tentative). Machias, ME. 45th annual. Harvest festival includes crafts sale, lobster boil, five-mile race, entertainment, children's parade, blueberry foods and a wild blueberry pie-eating contest. Annually, the third weekend in August. Est attendance: 15,000. For info: Machias Wild Blueberry Fest, PO Box 444, Machias, ME 04654. Phone: (207) 255-6665. Web: www.machiasblueberry.com.

NAVAJO NATION: NAVAJO CODE TALKERS DAY. Aug 14. The Navajo Nation Council has established Aug 14 of each year as a tribal holiday recognizing and honoring the distinguished record of the Code Talkers during WWII. The Code Talkers transmitted military messages in the Navajo language during the war, and Axis powers were unable to break the code. For info: Office of the Speaker, Navajo Nation Council, PO Box 3390, Window Rock, AZ 86515. Phone: (928) 871-7160. Web: www.navajonationcouncil.org.

PAKISTAN: INDEPENDENCE DAY. Aug 14, 1947. Gained independence from Britain in 1947.

SOCIAL SECURITY ACT: 85th ANNIVERSARY. Aug 14, 1935. President Franklin D. Roosevelt signed the Social Security Act, which contained provisions for the establishment of a Social Security Board to administer federal old-age and survivors' insurance in the US. By signing the bill into law, Roosevelt was fulfilling a 1932 campaign promise.

SPAIN: VUELTA A ESPAÑA. Aug 14–Sept 5. 75th edition. The third and last of the Grand Tours (along with the Giro d'Italia and the Tour de France) of world cycling. The Vuelta was organized in 1935 as a way to boost circulation of the newspaper *Informaciones*. The race is held over three weeks on an annually changing course and attracts the world's best professional riders. In 2020, the first three days of the race take place in The Netherlands, beginning in Utrecht. For info: Unipublic, SA. E-mail: info@unipublic.es. Web: www.lavuelta.es/en.

THAYER, ERNEST LAWRENCE: BIRTH ANNIVERSARY. Aug 14, 1863. The man who wrote the famous comic baseball ballad "Casey at the Bat" was born at Lawrence, MA. He wrote a series of comic poems for the *San Francisco Examiner*, of which "Casey at the Bat" was the last. It was published Sunday, June 3, 1888, and Thayer received five dollars in payment for it. Thayer, who regarded the poem's fame as a nuisance and whose other writings are largely forgotten, died at Santa Barbara, CA, Aug 21, 1940.

365-INNING SOFTBALL GAME: ANNIVERSARY. Aug 14–15, 1976. The Gager's Diner softball team played the Bend'n Elbow Tavern in a 365-inning softball game. Starting at 10 AM Aug 14, the game was called because of rain and fog at 4 PM, Aug 15. The 70 players, including 20 women, raised $4,000 for construction of a new softball field and for the Monticello, NY, Community General Hospital. The Gagers beat the Elbows 491–467. To date, this remains the longest softball game on record.

V-J DAY: 75th ANNIVERSARY. Aug 14, 1945. Anniversary of President Harry Truman's announcement that Japan had surrendered to the Allies, setting off celebrations across the US. Official ratification of surrender occurred aboard the USS *Missouri* at Tokyo Bay, Sept 2 (Far Eastern time).

🧁 BIRTHDAYS TODAY

Catherine Bell, 52, actress ("Army Wives," "JAG"), born London, England, Aug 14, 1968.

Halle Berry, 52, actress (*Die Another Day, X-Men*, Oscar for *Monster's Ball*), born Cleveland, OH, Aug 14, 1968.

Lynne Cheney, 79, wife of Dick Cheney, 46th vice president of the US, born Casper, WY, Aug 14, 1941.

David Crosby, 79, singer (Crosby, Stills & Nash), songwriter, born Los Angeles, CA, Aug 14, 1941.

Antonio Fargas, 74, actor (*Shaft, I'm Gonna Git You Sucka!, Car Wash*), born the Bronx, NY, Aug 14, 1946.

Marcia Gay Harden, 61, actress (Oscar for *Pollock*; *Into the Wild, Mystic River*), born La Jolla, CA, Aug 14, 1959.

Terin Humphrey, 34, Olympic gymnast, born St. Louis, MO, Aug 14, 1986.

Earvin "Magic" Johnson, Jr, 61, Hall of Fame basketball player, born Lansing, MI, Aug 14, 1959.

Mila Kunis, 37, actress (*Jupiter Ascending, Ted, Black Swan*, "That '70s Show"), born Kiev, Ukraine, Aug 14, 1983.

Arthur Betz Laffer, 80, economist (the Laffer curve), born Youngstown, OH, Aug 14, 1940.

Gary Larson, 70, cartoonist ("The Far Side"), born Tacoma, WA, Aug 14, 1950.

Jay Manuel, 48, photographer, makeup artist, television personality ("America's Next Top Model"), born Toronto, ON, Canada, Aug 14, 1972.

Steve Martin, 75, comedian, actor (*Shopgirl, LA Story, Roxanne, Parenthood*), novelist, musician, born Waco, TX, Aug 14, 1945.

Spencer Pratt, 37, television personality, born Los Angeles, CA, Aug 14, 1983.

Susan Saint James, 74, actress ("McMillan and Wife," "Kate and Allie"), born Long Beach, CA, Aug 14, 1946.

Robin Soderling, 36, tennis player, born Tibro, Sweden, Aug 14, 1984.

Danielle Steel, 73, author (*Vanished, Wanderlust*), born New York, NY, Aug 14, 1947.

Tim Tebow, 33, sportscaster, football player, 2007 Heisman Trophy winner, born Manila, Philippines, Aug 14, 1987.

Rusty Wallace, 64, auto racer, born St. Louis, MO, Aug 14, 1956.

August 15 — Saturday

DAY 228 | **138 REMAINING**

ALLIED LANDINGS IN SOUTH OF FRANCE: ANNIVERSARY. Aug 15, 1944. After several postponements, Allied forces began Operation Dragoon, the landing on the south coast of France during WWII. More than 2,000 transports and landing craft brought 94,000 men to an area between Toulon and Cannes, with only 183 Allied losses. They encountered minimal opposition, and by the end of August, the French coast from the mouth of the Rhône to Nice was in Allied hands.

ANTIQUE MARINE ENGINE EXPOSITION. Aug 15–16. Mystic Seaport Museum, Mystic, CT. Collectors from across the US and Canada gather for an annual exposition of pre-WWII marine engines and engine models. For info: Mystic Seaport Museum, 75

August 2020	S	M	T	W	T	F	S
							1
	2	3	4	5	6	7	8
	9	10	11	12	13	14	15
	16	17	18	19	20	21	22
	23	24	25	26	27	28	29
	30	31					

Greenmanville Ave, PO Box 6000, Mystic, CT 06355-0990. Phone: (860) 572-0711. Web: www.mysticseaport.org.

ASSUMPTION OF THE VIRGIN MARY. Aug 15. Greek and Roman Catholic churches celebrate Mary's ascent to heaven. In Orthodox churches, called the Dormition of Theotokos and commemorated on Aug 15 or 28. A holiday in many Christian countries.

BARRYMORE, ETHEL: BIRTH ANNIVERSARY. Aug 15, 1879. Celebrated award-winning actress of stage, screen and television, born Ethel Blythe at Philadelphia, PA. Sister of John and Lionel Barrymore. Died at Beverly Hills, CA, June 18, 1959.

THE BEATLES AT SHEA STADIUM: 55th ANNIVERSARY. Aug 15, 1965. The global superstars played Shea Stadium at New York, NY—the first time a venue of that size was used for a rock concert. A record-breaking crowd of 55,600 were in attendance overseen by 2,000 police officers. The group took various modes of transportation to reach the stadium: limo, then helicopter, then armored Wells Fargo van. The Fab Four, who opened with "Twist and Shout," grossed $304,000 for the concert—another new record.

BEST FRIEND'S DAY. Aug 15. Celebrate this special day by doing something fun with your best friend. Go shopping, go to the movies, go to a park or restaurant, play a game or just hang out and be together. For info: Susan Anne Masters, 931 Monroe Dr NE, Ste A102, #226, Atlanta, GA 30308. Phone: (404) 939-3833. E-mail: susan@mistresssusantv.com.

BIKE VAN BUREN. Aug 15–16. Van Buren County, IA. A leisurely two-day bicycle tour of the villages, landmarks and landscape of this rural Iowa county. The "red carpet of hospitality" is rolled out for the bikers as they pass through. Annually, the third weekend in August. Est attendance: 500. For info: Villages of Van Buren, Inc, PO Box 9, Keosauqua, IA 52565. Phone: (800) 868-7822. E-mail: info@villagesofvanburen.com. Web: www.villagesofvanburen.com.

BONAPARTE, NAPOLEON: BIRTH ANNIVERSARY. Aug 15, 1769. French emperor, military genius, founder of the Legion of Honor, born in Ajaccio, Corsica. A general at age 24, Napoleon emerged as a leader as the French Revolution ran out of steam. Named emperor in 1804, his empire ranged from the Atlantic to the Russian border. His difficulties enforcing a naval blockade of British goods led him to a war in both Spain and, disastrously, Russia, where his army was forced into a winter retreat that killed all but 40,000 of 500,000 men. After abdicating in 1815, he returned from exile only to be roundly defeated at the Battle of Waterloo. A reformer, Napoleon created a centralized government, a national police force and the foundation for the French legal system, the Napoleonic Code, which he called "the sheet anchor which will save France, and it will entitle me to the benedictions of posterity." Bonaparte died in exile on the island of St. Helena, May 5, 1821.

CHAUVIN DAY. Aug 15. A day named for Nicholas Chauvin, French soldier from Rochefort, France, who idolized Napoleon and who eventually became a subject of ridicule because of his blind loyalty and dedication to anything French. Originally referring to bellicose patriotism, *chauvinism* has come to mean blind or absurdly intense attachment to any cause. Observed on Napoleon's birth anniversary because Chauvin's birth date is unknown.

CHECK THE CHIP DAY. Aug 15. 6th annual. "Check the Chip Day" serves as a reminder to pet owners to have their pets microchipped and to keep their microchip registration information up-to-date. Annually, Aug 15. For info: American Veterinary Medical

Association, 1931 N Meacham Rd, Ste 100, Schaumburg, IL 60173. Phone: (800) 248-2862. Web: www.avma.org.

CHILD, JULIA: BIRTH ANNIVERSARY. Aug 15, 1912. America's beloved food authority, who didn't take a cooking lesson until she was in her 30s, was born at Pasadena, CA. Child's cookbooks and television shows (most famously, "The French Chef") encouraged Americans to cook and eat well and to be skeptical of food fads and diet strictures. "Cooking is not a chore; it is a joy," Child believed. She died at Santa Barbara, CA, Aug 13, 2004.

COMISKEY, CHARLES: BIRTH ANNIVERSARY. Aug 15, 1859. Charles Albert Comiskey, Baseball Hall of Fame first baseman, manager and executive, born at Chicago, IL. Comiskey's career spanned 50 years, 30 of them as founding owner of the Chicago White Sox. But before that, he was an outstanding and innovative player and a tough, successful manager. Inducted into the Hall of Fame in 1939. Died at Eagle River, WI, Oct 26, 1931.

CONGO (BRAZZAVILLE): NATIONAL DAY: 60th ANNIVERSARY OF INDEPENDENCE. Aug 15. National day of the People's Republic of the Congo. Commemorates independence from France in 1960.

DORMITION OF THEOTOKOS. Aug 15. Orthodox observance. According to New Calendar (Gregorian), the Dormition Fast is observed Aug 1–14, followed by Dormition of Theotokos on this day.

EQUATORIAL GUINEA: CONSTITUTION DAY. Aug 15. National holiday. Commemorates the 1982 revision of the original constitution of 1968.

FERBER, EDNA: BIRTH ANNIVERSARY. Aug 15, 1887. Edna Ferber was born at Kalamazoo, MI. She wrote her first novel, *Dawn O'Hara*, in 1911 and became a prolific writer, producing many popular magazine stories. Her novel *So Big* brought her commercial success in 1924 as well as a Pulitzer Prize. Her other novels include *Show Boat, Cimarron, Saratoga Trunk, Giant* and *Ice Palace*, all of which were made into successful films. Ferber collaborated with George Kaufman in writing for the stage on *The Royal Family, Dinner at Eight, Stage Door* and *Bravo*. Ferber died at New York, NY, Apr 16, 1968.

HARDING, FLORENCE KLING DEWOLFE: BIRTH ANNIVERSARY. Aug 15, 1860. Wife of Warren Gamaliel Harding, 29th president of the US, born at Marion, OH. Died there Nov 21, 1924.

HIROHITO'S RADIO ADDRESS: 75th ANNIVERSARY. Aug 15, 1945. At noon Japanese radio broadcast the Japanese national anthem, followed by a prerecorded statement by Emperor Hirohito announcing Japan's decision to surrender, citing the devastating power of the new atomic bomb. This was the first time most Japanese citizens had heard the voice of their emperor.

INDIA: INDEPENDENCE DAY. Aug 15. National holiday. Anniversary of Indian independence from Britain in 1947.

INTERNATIONAL GEOCACHING DAY. Aug 15. A day to celebrate the sport of geocaching: a real-world outdoor treasure-hunting game in which players search for hidden containers, called geocaches, using GPS-enabled devices. Geocaching is enjoyed by people of all ages, and the sport fosters a strong sense of community and support for the environment. Annually, the third Saturday in August. For info: Groundspeak, Inc. E-mail: contact@geocaching.com. Web: www.geocaching.com.

INTERNATIONAL HOMELESS ANIMALS DAY® AND CANDLELIGHT VIGILS. Aug 15. A day to call attention to the fact that millions of healthy dogs and cats are killed each year in US animal shelters because of overpopulation—a problem that has a solution: spaying/neutering. The vigils memorialize the animals killed in the preceding year and sympathize with the caring shelter personnel who must take the lives of the animals. Vigils will be held throughout the US and beyond. Annually, the third Saturday in August. For info: Intl Society for Animal Rights, Inc, Susan Dapsis, Pres, PO Box F, Clarks Summit, PA 18411-0309. Phone: (570) 586-2200. Fax: (570) 586-9580. E-mail: contact@ISARonline.org.

KOREA: INDEPENDENCE DAY: 75th ANNIVERSARY. Aug 15. National holiday commemorates acceptance by Japan of Allied terms of surrender in 1945, thereby freeing Korea from 36 years of Japanese domination. Also marks formal proclamation of Republic of Korea in 1948. Military parades and ceremonies throughout country.

LIECHTENSTEIN: NATIONAL DAY. Aug 15. Public holiday on Assumption Day.

NATIONAL AVIATION WEEK. Aug 15–21. A celebration of flight designed to increase public awareness, knowledge and appreciation of aviation. Annually, the week of Orville Wright's birthday, Aug 19.

NATIONAL RELAXATION DAY. Aug 15. Hold the phones, call in sick or just take a nap. Today is the perfect excuse to reduce stress and improve your lifestyle by relaxing. Spend a few minutes learning or sharing the art of relaxation with family, friends and coworkers. Annually, Aug 15. For info: Sean M. Moeller and A.C. Vierow, PO Box 71, Clio, MI 48420. E-mail: relax15@yahoo.com.

PANAMA CANAL OPENS: ANNIVERSARY. Aug 15, 1914. After 10 years of construction and much multination diplomacy, the Panama Canal opened for operation. A self-propelled crane boat had made the first passage through the canal, a 50-mile waterway connecting the Atlantic and Pacific Oceans, on Jan 7, 1914. The first ocean steamer, the SS *Ancon*, passed through Aug 3, 1914, and the canal officially opened Aug 15, 1914.

PANAMA: PANAMA CITY FOUNDATION DAY. Aug 15. Traditional annual cultural observance recognizes foundation of Panama City.

PETERSON, OSCAR: 95th BIRTH ANNIVERSARY. Aug 15, 1925. Jazz musician born at Montreal, QC, Canada. Also a composer and vocalist, he was considered one of the greatest pianists ever to perform and record in the genre. His recordings won seven Grammy Awards, and he is a member of several music halls of fame. He died at Mississauga, ON, Canada, Dec 23, 2007.

RAND, PAUL: BIRTH ANNIVERSARY. Aug 15, 1914. Designer, considered the father of modern American graphic design, born Peretz Rosenbaum at New York, NY. Rand played an important role in introducing the visual language of cubism, constructivism, de Stijl and the Bauhaus into American design. He designed iconic logos for IBM, UPS, ABC and Westinghouse, among others. Died Nov 26, 1996, at Norwalk, CT.

SCOTT, SIR WALTER: BIRTH ANNIVERSARY. Aug 15, 1771. Born at Edinburgh, Scotland. Famed poet and novelist. Author of the classics *Ivanhoe, Rob Roy, Waverley* and many others. Creator of the historical novel. "But no one shall find me rowing against the stream," he wrote in the introduction to *The Fortunes of Nigel*: "I care not who knows it—I write for the general amusement." Died at Abbotsford, Scotland, Sept 21, 1832.

TRANSCONTINENTAL US RAILWAY COMPLETION: 150th ANNIVERSARY. Aug 15, 1870. The Golden Spike ceremony at Promontory Point, UT, May 10, 1869, was long regarded as the final link in a transcontinental railroad track reaching from an Atlantic port to a Pacific port. In fact, that link occurred unceremoniously on another date in another state. Diaries of engineers working at the site establish "the completion of a transcontinental track at a point 928 feet east of today's milepost 602, or 3,812 feet east of the present Union Pacific depot building at Strasburg (formerly Comanche)," CO. The final link was made at 2:53 PM, Aug 15, 1870. Annual celebration at Strasburg, CO, on a weekend in August. See also: "Golden Spike Driving: Anniversary" (May 10).

WOODSTOCK: ANNIVERSARY. Aug 15, 1969. The Woodstock Music and Art Fair opened on this day in an alfalfa field on or near Yasgur's Farm at Bethel, NY. The three-day rock concert featured 30 acts and drew a crowd of more than 400,000 people.

🧁 BIRTHDAYS TODAY

Ben Affleck, 48, actor (*Batman v Superman, Gone Girl, Argo*), director (*Argo, Gone Baby Gone*), screenwriter (Oscar for *Good Will Hunting*), born Berkeley, CA, Aug 15, 1972.

Anthony Anderson, 50, actor ("Black-ish," "Law & Order"), writer, producer, born Los Angeles, CA, Aug 15, 1970.

Princess Anne, 70, Princess Royal of the UK, equestrian, born London, England, Aug 15, 1950.

Stephen G. Breyer, 82, Associate Justice of the US, born San Francisco, CA, Aug 15, 1938.

Linda Ellerbee, 76, journalist, born Bryan, TX, Aug 15, 1944.

Alejandro Iñárritu, 57, film director (Oscars for *The Revenant* and *Birdman*; *Babel*), screenwriter (Oscar for *Birdman*), born Mexico City, Mexico, Aug 15, 1963.

Zeljko Ivanek, 63, actor ("Heroes," "Damages," "24," *Donnie Brasco*), born Ljubljana, Slovenia, Aug 15, 1957.

Joe Jonas, 31, singer (The Jonas Brothers), actor, born Casa Grande, AZ, Aug 15, 1989.

Vernon Jordan, Jr, 85, civil rights leader, born Atlanta, GA, Aug 15, 1935.

Jennifer Lawrence, 30, actress (Oscar for *Silver Linings Playbook*; *American Hustle,* The Hunger Games films, *X-Men: First Class*), born Louisville, KY, Aug 15, 1990.

Debra Messing, 52, actress ("The Mysteries of Laura," "Will & Grace"), born Brooklyn, NY, Aug 15, 1968.

Kerri Walsh, 42, Olympic beach volleyball player, born Santa Clara, CA, Aug 15, 1978.

Kathryn Whitmire, 74, first woman mayor of Houston, TX, born Houston, TX, Aug 15, 1946.

August 16 — Sunday

DAY 229   **137 REMAINING**

BATTLE OF CAMDEN: ANNIVERSARY. Aug 16, 1780. Revolutionary War battle fought near Camden, SC. American troops led by General Horatio Gates suffered disastrous losses. Nearly 1,000 Americans killed and another 1,000 captured by the British. British losses about 325. One of America's worst defeats in the war.

BEGIN, MENACHEM: BIRTH ANNIVERSARY. Aug 16, 1913. Born at Brest Litovsk, Poland. A militant Zionist and anticommunist, he fled to Russia in 1939 ahead of the advancing Nazis; he was soon arrested and sent to Siberia. Freed in 1941, he went to Palestine and became a leader in the Jewish underground, fighting for Israel's independence; by 1943 he headed the national military organization. Elected prime minister of Israel in 1977, he signed the historic peace treaty between Israel and Egypt with President Anwar el Sadat of Egypt and US president Jimmy Carter at Camp David in 1979. Begin died Mar 9, 1992, at Tel Aviv, Israel.

BENNINGTON BATTLE DAY: ANNIVERSARY. Aug 16, 1777. Anniversary of battle is legal holiday in Vermont.

CHAPMAN KILLED BY PITCH: 100th ANNIVERSARY. Aug 16, 1920. Cleveland Indians shortstop Ray Chapman was hit by a pitch during a game with the New York Yankees. Chapman collapsed with a fractured skull and died the next day. He is the only major league player to have received a fatal injury during play.

August 2020	S	M	T	W	T	F	S
							1
	2	3	4	5	6	7	8
	9	10	11	12	13	14	15
	16	17	18	19	20	21	22
	23	24	25	26	27	28	29
	30	31					

DOMINICAN REPUBLIC: RESTORATION OF THE REPUBLIC. Aug 16. The anniversary of the restoration of the Republic in 1863 is celebrated as an official public holiday.

KLONDIKE GOLD DISCOVERY: ANNIVERSARY. Aug 16, 1896. According to the oral tradition of the Tagish First Nations People, Skookum Jim, Dawson Charlie and George Carmack found gold in Rabbit Creek, a tributary of the Klondike River, lying "thick between the flaky slabs like cheese sandwiches." This event, which led to the great Klondike Gold Rush, is celebrated in the Yukon each year with a public holiday, Discovery Day, observed on the nearest Monday.

LAWRENCE, T.E.: BIRTH ANNIVERSARY. Aug 16, 1888. British soldier, archaeologist and writer, born at Tremadog, North Wales. During WWI, Lawrence, as a British intelligence officer, led the Arab revolt against Turkey, a German ally that had ruled the Arab people for centuries. Lawrence, now hailed as "Lawrence of Arabia," organized successful guerrilla attacks on the Turkish supply chain and captured the essential port of Aqaba. His book *Seven Pillars of Wisdom* is a personal account of the Arab revolt. Lawrence was killed in a motorcycle accident at Dorset, England, May 19, 1935.

MEANY, GEORGE: BIRTH ANNIVERSARY. Aug 16, 1894. American labor leader George Meany was born at New York, NY. A plumber by trade, he became president of the American Federation of Labor (AFL) in 1952, and when he merged the AFL with the Congress of Industrial Organizations (CIO), he became the leading labor spokesperson in the US. In 1957 he expelled Jimmy Hoffa's Teamsters Union from the AFL-CIO, and he lost the United Auto Workers in 1967. His tenure as president lasted until 1979. He died Jan 10, 1980, at Washington, DC.

NATIONAL ROLLER COASTER DAY. Aug 16. On Aug 16, 1878, Richard Knudsen and J.G. Taylor received a U.S. patent for the first wooden roller coaster. The device consisted of two adjacent railway tracks that ran between two towers carrying four-passenger cars: the force of gravity would pull the cars down gently sloping hills. The cars were then hauled upward and into the opposite tower for the return trip. Several years later, a gentleman by the name of LaMarcus Thompson was credited for actually building the first authentic ride of this type at Coney Island, NY. This was the start of something big, and what would eventually become the "king" of thrill rides that millions of thrill seekers know today. Every Aug 16, enthusiasts share their love for the roller coaster at amusement parks everywhere. "May the force of gravity be with you!" For info: Roy J. Brashears, Chairman, National Roller Coaster Day. E-mail: nationalrollercoasterday@yahoo.com. Web: www.nationalrollercoasterday.com.

PARKER, FESS: BIRTH ANNIVERSARY. Aug 16, 1924. American actor, renowned for his portrayals of Davy Crockett and Daniel Boone, born Aug 16, 1924, at Fort Worth, TX. His depiction of Crockett in the Disney television miniseries of 1955–56 made him an overnight sensation. The program's accompanying merchandising blitz evidenced for the first time the power of television. A reported 10 million coonskin caps—the Crockett signature—were sold, along with various other proprietary items. Upon his retirement from acting, Parker spent the remainder of his life managing his real estate developments, which included the Fess Parker Winery and Vineyard. He died Mar 18, 2010, at Santa Ynez, CA.

PETERLOO MASSACRE: ANNIVERSARY. Aug 16, 1819. Anniversary of demonstration by more than 50,000 persons protesting unemployment, starvation wages, overcrowding, high costs and British government policies. The mass meeting was held at St. Peter's Fields, Manchester, England. Police and cavalry charged the unarmed crowd with sabres. Casualty estimates for the 10-minute battle varied widely, but several deaths and up to 500 injuries were claimed. The rest of England was appalled, but the government cracked down on reform, defying the protesters.

PRESLEY, ELVIS: DEATH ANNIVERSARY. Aug 16, 1977. One of America's most popular singers, Elvis Presley was pronounced dead at the Memphis Baptist Hospital at 3:30 PM, Aug 16, 1977, at age 42. The anniversary of his death is an occasion for pilgrimages by admirers to Graceland, his home and gravesite, at Memphis, TN. See also: "Presley, Elvis: Birth Anniversary" (Jan 8).

RUTH, BABE: DEATH ANNIVERSARY. Aug 16, 1948. Baseball fans of all ages and all walks of life mourned when the great "Bambino" died of cancer at New York City at the age of 53. Born Feb 6, 1895, at Baltimore, MD, the left-handed pitcher and "Sultan of Swat" hit 714 home runs in 22 major league seasons of play and played in 10 World Series. His body lay in state at the main entrance of Yankee Stadium, where people waited in line for hours to march past the coffin. On Aug 19 countless people surrounded St. Patrick's Cathedral for the funeral mass and lined the streets along the route to the cemetery as America bade farewell to one of baseball's greatest legends.

STAGG, AMOS ALONZO: BIRTH ANNIVERSARY. Aug 16, 1862. Football player and coach born at West Orange, NJ. Stagg played baseball and football at Yale, where he was a divinity student. He forsook the ministry for physical education. Stagg built the football program at the University of Chicago as an integral part of William Rainey Harper's plan to build a great university. Serving more than 40 years at Chicago, he became the game's greatest innovator and master strategist. When Chicago deemphasized football, he moved to the College of the Pacific, finishing his career with a record of 314–181–15. Died at Stockton, CA, Mar 17, 1965.

SURVEILLANCE DAY. Aug 16. 10th annual. Originally International Wave at Surveillance Day, this day is observed annually Aug 16 to recognize all forms of surveillance worldwide. For info: Zorbitor. E-mail: zorbitor@gmail.com.

🎂 BIRTHDAYS TODAY

Angela Bassett, 62, actress ("9-1-1," *Black Panther, What's Love Got to Do with It, Waiting to Exhale*), born New York, NY, Aug 16, 1958.

James Cameron, 66, director (Oscar for *Titanic; Avatar, True Lies*), born Kapuskasing, ON, Canada, Aug 16, 1954.

Steve Carell, 57, actor, comedian ("The Office" [US]; *The Big Short, Foxcatcher, The 40-Year-Old Virgin*), born Acton, MA, Aug 16, 1963.

Yu Darvish, 34, baseball player, born Farid Yu Darvishsefat at Osaka, Japan, Aug 16, 1986.

Kathie Lee Gifford, 67, television personality, singer, born Paris, France, Aug 16, 1953.

Timothy Hutton, 60, actor ("Leverage," *Sunshine State*, Oscar for *Ordinary People*), born Malibu, CA, Aug 16, 1960.

Laura Innes, 60, actress ("ER," "Wings"), born Pontiac, MI, Aug 16, 1960.

Madonna, 62, singer, actress (*Desperately Seeking Susan, Evita*), born Madonna Louise Veronica Ciccone at Bay City, MI, Aug 16, 1958.

Phil Murphy, 63, Governor of New Jersey (D), born Needham, MA, Aug 16, 1957.

Julie Newmar, 87, actress ("Batman," *Li'l Abner*), born Hollywood, CA, Aug 16, 1933.

Jeff Perry, 65, actor ("Scandal," "Nash Bridges"), founder of Chicago's Steppenwolf Theater, born Highland Park, IL, Aug 16, 1955.

Reginald VelJohnson, 68, actor (*Ghostbusters, Die Hard, Die Hard 2*), born Queens, NY, Aug 16, 1952.

Taika Waititi, 45, actor, comedian (*What We Do in the Shadows, Boy*), director (*Thor: Ragnarok, Hunt for the Wilderpeople*), screenwriter, born Wellington, New Zealand, Aug 16, 1975.

Lesley Ann Warren, 74, actress (*Victor/Victoria, Choose Me,* "Cinderella"), born New York, NY, Aug 16, 1946.

August 17 — Monday

DAY 230   **136 REMAINING**

***ANIMAL FARM* PUBLISHED: 75th ANNIVERSARY.** Aug 17, 1945. In London, England, Secker and Warburg published George Orwell's *Animal Farm*, a dystopian satire of the Russian Revolution and Stalinist USSR.

ARGENTINA: DEATH ANNIVERSARY OF SAN MARTÍN. Aug 17. National holiday. Commemorates the death in 1850 of the hero of Argentina's struggle for independence.

BALLOON CROSSING OF ATLANTIC OCEAN: ANNIVERSARY. Aug 17, 1978. Three Americans—Maxie Anderson, Ben Abruzzo and Larry Newman—all of Albuquerque, NM, became the first to complete a transatlantic trip in a balloon. Starting from Presque Isle, ME, Aug 11, they traveled some 3,200 miles in 137 hours, 18 minutes, landing at Miserey, France (about 60 miles west of Paris), in their craft, named the *Double Eagle II.*

CANADA: YUKON DISCOVERY DAY. Aug 17. In the Klondike region of the Yukon, at Bonanza Creek (formerly known as Rabbit Creek), George Washington Carmack discovered gold Aug 16 or 17, 1896. During the following year, more than 30,000 people joined the gold rush to the area. Anniversary is celebrated as a holiday (Discovery Day) in the Yukon, on nearest Monday.

CHASE, HARRISON V.: BIRTH ANNIVERSARY. Aug 17, 1913. Cofounder and coeditor of *Chase's Annual Events* from 1957 to 1970, Chase was a lifelong teacher. Born at Big Rapids, MI, he had several teaching stints and was a research analyst at the Office of Strategic Services (OSS) from 1943 to 1946 before joining the Department of Geography at Florida State University in 1947. Fondly remembered by colleagues and students (who called him Professor Quark) and awarded the Standard Oil Foundation outstanding teaching award in 1969, Chase retired in 1979. In the summer of 1957, he and brother William brainstormed and created a new reference book that would chronicle the important events and holidays of each year. From its origins as a pamphlet, painstakingly constructed by William and Harrison Chase using index cards, *Chase's Calendar of Events* is now a 752-page tome packed with more than 12,500 events. Harrison Chase died Feb 6, 2000, at Tallahassee, FL.

CLINTON'S "MEANING OF 'IS' IS": ANNIVERSARY. Aug 17, 1998. During grand jury hearings that sought to clarify President Bill Clinton's relationship with Monica Lewinsky, Clinton engaged in some semantic fine-tuning: "It depends on what your meaning of 'is' is. If 'is' means 'is and never has been,' that's one thing—if it means 'there is none,' that was a completely true statement." Clinton also parsed the meanings of "alone," "sexual relations" and "sex." His testimony was later televised to the nation on Sept 21.

CROCKETT, DAVID (DAVY): BIRTH ANNIVERSARY. Aug 17, 1786. American frontiersman, bear hunter, soldier and politician, born at Greene County, TN. After losing a reelection bid to represent Tennessee in Congress, Crockett moved to the colony of Texas and joined the settlers' effort to gain independence from Mexico.

He died during the final heroic defense of the Alamo on Mar 6, 1836, at San Antonio, TX. The larger-than-life figure once boasted: "I can run faster, walk longer, leap higher, speak better and tell more and bigger lies."

FULTON SAILS STEAMBOAT: ANNIVERSARY. Aug 17, 1807. Robert Fulton began the first American steamboat trip, between Albany and New York, NY, on a boat later called the *Clermont*. After years of promoting submarine warfare, Fulton engaged in a partnership with Robert R. Livingston, the US minister to France, allowing Fulton to design and construct a steamboat. His first success came in August 1803 when he launched a steam-powered vessel on the Seine. That same year the US Congress granted Livingston and Fulton exclusive rights to operate steamboats on New York waters during the next 20 years. The first Albany–to–New York trip took 32 hours to travel the 150-mile course. Although his efforts were labeled "Fulton's Folly" by his detractors, his success allowed the partnership to begin commercial service the next year, Sept 4, 1808.

GABON: INDEPENDENCE DAY: 60th ANNIVERSARY OF INDEPENDENCE. Aug 17. National holiday. Commemorates independence from France in 1960.

GARVEY, MARCUS: BIRTH ANNIVERSARY. Aug 17, 1887. Born at St. Ann's Bay, Jamaica, Garvey founded the Universal Negro Improvement Association, through which he sought to organize Jamaicans (and after 1916, Americans) of African descent around principles of racial pride, racial separatism and economic empowerment through black business ownership. He died June 10, 1940, at London, England.

INDONESIA: INDEPENDENCE DAY. Aug 17. National holiday. Republic proclaimed in 1945. It was only after several years of fighting, however, that Indonesia was formally granted its independence by The Netherlands, Dec 27, 1949.

NAIPAUL, V. S.: BIRTH ANNIVERSARY. Aug 17, 1932. Vidiadhar Surajprasad Naipaul, born to Hindu Indian parents in Trinidad, and educated in England, was a prolific writer known for his "suppressed histories," novels set in colonial and post-colonial countries struggling to integrate their native and Western-colonial heritages. These include *A House for Mr. Biswas* (1961), *A Bend in the River* (1979) and *A Way in the World* (1994). *In a Free State* took Britain's Booker Prize in 1971. Naipaul received the Nobel Prize for Literature in 2001. He also received the Trinity Cross in Trinidad and Tobago and was knighted in Britain. He died Aug 11, 2018, in London.

O'HARA, MAUREEN: 100th BIRTH ANNIVERSARY. Aug 17, 1920. The actress with the flaming red hair was born Maureen FitzSimons at Ranelagh, Dublin, Ireland. She appeared—often as an independent, outspoken woman—in countless films over six decades. She appeared in many John Ford films and often with John Wayne—most famously, in *The Quiet Man* (1952). Other famous films include *The Hunchback of Notre Dame, How Green Was My Valley, Miracle on 34th Street* and *The Parent Trap.* Awarded an honorary Oscar in 2014, O'Hara died Oct 24, 2015, at Boise, ID.

POWERS, FRANCIS GARY: BIRTH ANNIVERSARY. Aug 17, 1929. One of America's most famous aviators, Francis Gary Powers was born at Jenkins, KY. The CIA agent, pilot of a U-2 overflight across the Soviet Union, was shot down May 1, 1960, near Sverdlovsk, USSR. He was tried, convicted and sentenced to 10 years' imprisonment, at Moscow, USSR, in August 1960. Returned to the US in 1962, in exchange for an imprisoned Soviet spy (Colonel Rudolf Abel), he found an unwelcoming homeland. Powers died in a helicopter crash near Los Angeles, CA, Aug 2, 1977. On June 15, 2012, Powers was posthumously awarded a Silver Star—the military's third-highest decoration—by the US Air Force.

August 2020	S	M	T	W	T	F	S
							1
	2	3	4	5	6	7	8
	9	10	11	12	13	14	15
	16	17	18	19	20	21	22
	23	24	25	26	27	28	29
	30	31					

SMITH, ELINOR: BIRTH ANNIVERSARY. Aug 17, 1911. The pioneering aviatrix, who made her first solo flight at 15 years of age, was born at Long Island, NY. In 1930, after setting various flight records, Smith was voted best female pilot in America by her colleagues, beating out Amelia Earhart. The "Flying Flapper of Freeport" became the first woman to appear on a Wheaties cereal box in 1934—and she was the first female test pilot for an aircraft company. Smith died Mar 19, 2010, at Palo Alto, CA.

WEST, MAE: BIRTH ANNIVERSARY. Aug 17, 1893 (some sources say 1892). The stage and screen siren, famous for her naughty wisecracks, was born Mary Jane West at Brooklyn, NY. She acted in vaudeville from age five and made her Hollywood debut in 1932. Unique among stars in that she wrote her own plays and film scripts—mostly concerning the joys of men and sex. Her Broadway play *Sex* resulted in her conviction for public obscenity in 1927, and she served time for eight days. Master of the risqué bon mot, West said in *I'm No Angel* (1933), "When I'm good, I'm very, very good, but when I'm bad, I'm better." She died Nov 22, 1980, at Los Angeles, CA.

🎂 BIRTHDAYS TODAY

Belinda Carlisle, 62, singer (Go-Go's), born Hollywood, CA, Aug 17, 1958.

Robert De Niro, 77, actor (Oscars for *Raging Bull* and *The Godfather Part II*; *Taxi Driver, The Deer Hunter*), born New York, NY, Aug 17, 1943.

Julian Fellowes, 71, producer, writer (*Gosford Park*, "Downton Abbey"), born Cairo, Egypt, Aug 17, 1949.

Jonathan Franzen, 61, author (*The Corrections, Freedom*), born Western Springs, IL, Aug 17, 1959.

Thierry Henry, 43, former soccer player, born Paris, France, Aug 17, 1977.

Robert Joy, 69, actor ("CSI: New York," *Atlantic City, Longtime Companion*), born Montreal, QC, Canada, Aug 17, 1951.

Sean Penn, 60, actor (Oscars for *Mystic River* and *Milk*; *Dead Man Walking*), born Santa Monica, CA, Aug 17, 1960.

Nelson Piquet, 68, former auto racer, born Brasília, Brazil, Aug 17, 1952.

Mark Salling, 38, actor ("Glee"), born Dallas, TX, Aug 17, 1982.

Guillermo Vilas, 68, Hall of Fame tennis player, born Mar del Plata, Argentina, Aug 17, 1952.

Donnie Wahlberg, 51, actor ("Blue Bloods," "Band of Brothers"), singer (New Kids on the Block), born Boston, MA, Aug 17, 1969.

August 18 — Tuesday

DAY 231   **135 REMAINING**

BAD POETRY DAY. Aug 18. After all the "good" poetry you were forced to study in school, here's a chance for a payback. Invite some friends over, compose some really rotten verse and send it to your old high school English teacher. (©2006 by WH.) For info: Thomas & Ruth Roy, Wellcat Holidays, 2418 Long Ln, Lebanon, PA 17046. Phone: (717) 279-0184. E-mail: info@wellcat.com. Web: www.wellcat.com.

BIRTH CONTROL PILLS SOLD: 60th ANNIVERSARY. Aug 18, 1960. The first commercially produced oral contraceptives were marketed by the G.D. Searle Company of Illinois. The pill, developed by Gregory Pincus, had been undergoing clinical trials since 1954.

CLEMENTE, ROBERTO: BIRTH ANNIVERSARY. Aug 18, 1934. National League baseball player, born at Carolina, Puerto Rico. Drafted by the Pittsburgh Pirates in 1954, he played his entire major league career with them. Clemente died in a plane crash Dec 31, 1972, while on a mission of mercy to Nicaragua to deliver supplies he had collected for survivors of an earthquake. He was elected to the Baseball Hall of Fame in 1973.

DARE, VIRGINIA: BIRTH ANNIVERSARY. Aug 18, 1587. (Old Style date.) Virginia Dare, the first child of English parents to be born in the New World, was born to Ellinor and Ananias Dare, at Roanoke Island, NC, on this date. When a ship arrived to replenish their supplies in 1591, the settlers (including Virginia Dare) had vanished, without leaving a trace of the settlement.

LEWIS, MERIWETHER: BIRTH ANNIVERSARY. Aug 18, 1774. American explorer (Lewis and Clark expedition), born at Albemarle County, VA. Died Oct 11, 1809, near Nashville, TN.

MAIL-ORDER CATALOG: ANNIVERSARY. Aug 18, 1872. The first mail-order catalog was published by Montgomery Ward. It was only a single sheet of paper. By 1904 the Montgomery Ward catalog weighed four pounds. In 1985 Montgomery Ward closed its catalog operation; in 2000 it announced the closing of its retail stores.

MOON PHASE: NEW MOON. Aug 18. Moon enters New Moon phase at 10:42 PM, EDT.

NATIONAL BADGE RIBBON DAY. Aug 18. 7th annual. The invention of the stackable badge ribbon turned meetings and events on its side when, in 1993, we said goodbye to badges that look straight out of a county fair. On this day we praise the stack-a-ribbon award which has proven to be an easy, inexpensive way to reward, categorize and connect attendees in meetings throughout the world. Many business relationships have this little ribbon to thank for breaking the ice! Annually, Aug 18. For info: pc/nametag, 124 Horizon Dr, Verona, WI 53593. Web: www.pcnametag.com/national-badge-ribbon-day.

NINETEENTH AMENDMENT TO US CONSTITUTION RATIFIED: 100th ANNIVERSARY. Aug 18, 1920. The 19th Amendment extended the right to vote to women.

SERENDIPITY DAY. Aug 18. 9th annual. Serendipity is the faculty of making valuable and wonderful discoveries not sought for. This annual day encourages all people to bring more serendipity into their lives and the lives of others, making the world a happier place one person at a time. Annually, Aug 18. For info: Madeleine Kay. E-mail: mk@madeleinekay.com. Web: www.serendipityday-holiday.com.

WEAVER, BUCK: BIRTH ANNIVERSARY. Aug 18, 1890. George Daniel "Buck" Weaver, baseball player, born at Pottstown, PA. Weaver was one of eight Chicago White Sox players suspended and later banned for life for conspiring to fix the 1919 World Series. He did not participate in the plot but knew of it and declined to report it. Weaver tried six times and failed to get reinstated. He died at Chicago, IL, Jan 31, 1956.

🎂 BIRTHDAYS TODAY

Elayne Boosler, 68, comedienne, born Brooklyn, NY, Aug 18, 1952.

Felipe Calderón Hinojosa, 58, former president of Mexico (2006–12), born Morelia, Michoacán, Mexico, Aug 18, 1962.

Eleanor Rosalynn Smith Carter, 93, former first lady, wife of Jimmy Carter, 38th president of the US, born Plains, GA, Aug 18, 1927.

Bobby Higginson, 50, former baseball player, born Philadelphia, PA, Aug 18, 1970.

Luc Montagnier, 88, virologist, discovered the AIDS virus in 1983, born Chabris, France, Aug 18, 1932.

Martin Mull, 77, actor, comedian ("Sabrina, the Teenage Witch," "Roseanne"), born Chicago, IL, Aug 18, 1943.

Edward Norton, 51, actor (*Birdman, The Grand Budapest Hotel, 25th Hour, Primal Fear*), born Boston, MA, Aug 18, 1969.

Roman Polanski, 87, filmmaker (*The Ghost Writer, The Pianist, Rosemary's Baby, Chinatown*), born Paris, France, Aug 18, 1933.

Robert Redford, 83, actor (*Butch Cassidy and the Sundance Kid, The Sting, The Natural*), director (Oscar for *Ordinary People*), born Santa Monica, CA, Aug 18, 1937.

Andy Samberg, 42, comedian, actor ("Brooklyn Nine-Nine," "Saturday Night Live"), born Mill Valley, CA, Aug 18, 1978.

Christian Slater, 51, actor ("Mr Robot," *Heathers, Broken Arrow, Pump Up the Volume*), born New York, NY, Aug 18, 1969.

Madeleine Stowe, 62, actress (*The Last of the Mohicans, Short Cuts*), born Los Angeles, CA, Aug 18, 1958.

Malcolm-Jamal Warner, 50, actor ("The Cosby Show"), born Jersey City, NJ, Aug 18, 1970.

August 19 — Wednesday

DAY 232   **134 REMAINING**

AFGHANISTAN: INDEPENDENCE DAY. Aug 19. National day. Gained independence from British control, Treaty of Rawalpindi in 1919.

CHANEL, COCO: BIRTH ANNIVERSARY. Aug 19, 1883. The most important fashion designer of the 20th century was born Gabrielle Chanel in rural Saumur, France. After starting out in a millinery shop, she began a fashion revolution when she moved on to couture fashion in the late teens: using men's clothing (pants) for women's wear; creating simple, comfortable clothing that was nonetheless elegant; making dramatic use of costume jewelry (especially ropes of pearls); and popularizing the "little black dress" and sportswear. She was the first couturier to put her name on a signature perfume: Chanel No. 5 (created in 1921, it was an immediate sensation and today sells every 30 seconds around the world). After closing her shop with the outbreak of WWII, Chanel reopened it in 1954 and introduced her signature suit of collarless, bias-trimmed jacket with skirt. "Elegance does not consist in putting on a new dress," she once stated. The fashion icon died on Jan 10, 1971, at Paris, France.

CLINTON, WILLIAM JEFFERSON (BILL): BIRTHDAY. Aug 19, 1946. The 42nd US president (1993–2001), born at Hope, AR.

FARNSWORTH, PHILO: BIRTH ANNIVERSARY. Aug 19, 1906. Farnsworth was a television pioneer who conceived of the idea of television broadcasting while still in high school and realized his dream at 21. His first transmitted image was of a dollar sign. Farnsworth was born at Beaver, UT, and died on Mar 11, 1971, at Salt Lake City, UT.

FORBES, MALCOLM: BIRTH ANNIVERSARY. Aug 19, 1919. Publisher, born at New York, NY. Malcolm Forbes was an unabashed proponent of capitalism, and his beliefs led to his colorful and successful climb to the top of the magazine-publishing industry. Known as much for his lavish lifestyle as his publishing acumen, Forbes was also an avid motorcyclist and hot-air balloonist. He died Feb 24, 1990, at Far Hills, NJ.

GERMAN PLEBISCITE: ANNIVERSARY. Aug 19, 1934. In a plebiscite, 89.9 percent of German voters approved giving Chancellor Adolf Hitler the additional office of president, placing the Führer in uncontestable supreme command of that country's destiny.

HO, DON: 90th BIRTH ANNIVERSARY. Aug 19, 1930. The man who introduced Hawaiian music to the American public was born at Honolulu, HI. A Waikiki nightclub musician who began performing in Hollywood and Las Vegas, he had an unlikely Top 40 hit with "Tiny Bubbles" in 1966. In the 1970s he was a minor television celebrity, hosting his own variety show, but he was always

most comfortable playing for the tourists at various nightclubs in Waikiki. Don Ho continued to entertain until his death at Honolulu on Apr 14, 2007.

LARDNER, RING, JR: BIRTH ANNIVERSARY. Aug 19, 1915. Born at Chicago, IL, son of fabled baseball writer and humorist Ring Lardner. Lardner, Jr, was an Academy Award–winning screenwriter (Oscars for *Woman of the Year* and *M*A*S*H*), and he also wrote for television. He was a member of the Hollywood Ten, a group of film industry executives sent to federal prison in 1950 for their refusal to tell the House Un-American Activities Committee if they were members of the Communist Party. He served nine months and was blacklisted for many years. Died at New York, NY, Oct 31, 2000.

NASH, OGDEN: BIRTH ANNIVERSARY. Aug 19, 1902. American writer, best remembered for his humorous verse. Born at Rye, NY; died May 19, 1971, at Baltimore, MD.

NAT KING COLE RECORDS "THE CHRISTMAS SONG": ANNIVERSARY. Aug 19, 1946. One of the most beloved Christmas songs (often known by its first line: "Chestnuts roasting on an open fire") was recorded this day by the King Cole Trio led by Nat King Cole (vocals and piano), Oscar Moore (guitar) and Johnny Miller (bass) and joined by a small string section at the WMCA studio in New York City. The trio originally made a recording in June, but Cole felt strings were needed. Capitol Records released the 78 rpm disc in late November 1946 and it rose to number three in the pop charts. It became a signature Cole song, and he recorded it again in 1953 and 1961—the 1961 stereo version is the recording most often heard today. "The Christmas Song" was written on a hot July day in 1945 by Mel Tormé and Bob Wells.

RICHARDSON, SAMUEL: BIRTH ANNIVERSARY. Aug 19, 1689. Born at Derbyshire, England, Richardson was an English novelist who founded a new school of writing focused on epistolary novels that juxtaposed inner thoughts and states of the individual with the tempo of outer life. His best-known novel is *Clarissa; or, The History of a Young Lady* (1748). He died July 4, 1761, at London, England.

RODDENBERRY, GENE: BIRTH ANNIVERSARY. Aug 19, 1921. The creator of the popular TV series "Star Trek," Gene Roddenberry was born at El Paso, TX. Turning from his first career as an airline pilot to writing, he created one of the most successful TV science fiction series ever. The original series, which ended its run in 1969, lives on in reruns and led to other popular spin-off series. Numerous films also have been spawned from the original concept. Roddenberry died Oct 24, 1991, at Santa Monica, CA.

SPACE MILESTONE: *SOYUZ T-7* (USSR). Aug 19, 1982. Launched from Tyuratam, USSR, with second woman in space (test pilot Svetlana Savitskaya) and two other cosmonauts. Docked at *Salyut 7* and visited the cosmonauts who had been in residence there for the three previous months before returning to Earth on Aug 27 in the *Soyuz T-5* vehicle, which had been docked there. The *Soyuz T-7* returned to Earth Dec 10.

SPACE MILESTONE: *SPUTNIK 5* (USSR): BELKA AND STRELKA: 60th ANNIVERSARY. Aug 19, 1960. Space menagerie satellite with dogs Belka and Strelka, mice, rats, houseflies and plants launched. These passengers became the first living organisms recovered from orbit when the satellite returned safely to Earth the next day.

TRIAL OF SIXTEEN: ANNIVERSARY. Aug 19–24, 1936. The Trial of Sixteen began in the Soviet Union. This was the first of the Moscow show trials and the defendants included war heroes and long-time Communist functionaries accused of plotting to kill Joseph Stalin. The trial verdicts were predetermined ("guilty") and all were executed. This and later show trials marked the beginning of the Great Purge, which would take 8 to 10 million lives in the next two years.

UNITED NATIONS: WORLD HUMANITARIAN DAY. Aug 19. A day to increase public awareness about humanitarian assistance activities worldwide and the importance of international cooperation in that sphere. It also aims to honor all humanitarian and UN workers in the humanitarian cause, including those who have lost their lives in the cause of duty. (Res 63/139 of Dec 11, 2008.) Annually, Aug 19. For info: United Nations, Dept of Public Info, New York, NY 10017. Web: www.un.org.

WRIGHT, ORVILLE: BIRTH ANNIVERSARY. Aug 19, 1871. Aviation pioneer born at Dayton, OH, and died there Jan 30, 1948. See also: "Wright Brothers First Powered Flight: Anniversary" (Dec 17).

🎂 BIRTHDAYS TODAY

Adam Arkin, 64, actor ("Fargo," "Life," "Chicago Hope"), director, born Brooklyn, NY, Aug 19, 1956.

Jim Carter, 72, actor ("Downton Abbey," "Cranford," *The Golden Compass*), born Harrogate, Yorkshire, England, Aug 19, 1948.

Erika Christensen, 38, actress (*Traffic, Swimfan*, "Parenthood"), born Seattle, WA, Aug 19, 1982.

William Jefferson Clinton, 74, 42nd president of the US, born Hope, AR, Aug 19, 1946.

Kevin Dillon, 55, actor ("Entourage"), born Mamaroneck, NY, Aug 19, 1965.

Peter Gallagher, 65, actor (*sex, lies and videotape; Short Cuts*; "The O.C."), born New York, NY, Aug 19, 1955.

Tipper Gore, 72, wife of Al Gore, 45th vice president of the US, advocate for the homeless, mental health and children's causes, born Mary Elizabeth Aitcheson at Washington, DC, Aug 19, 1948.

Gerald McRaney, 72, actor (*Red Tails*, "Deadwood," "Simon & Simon," "Major Dad"), born Collins, MS, Aug 19, 1948.

Jennifer Morrison, 41, actress ("Once Upon a Time," "House"), born Chicago, IL, Aug 19, 1979.

Diana Muldaur, 82, actress ("Star Trek: The Next Generation," "LA Law," *The Swimmer*), born New York, NY, Aug 19, 1938.

Franklin Story Musgrave, 85, former astronaut, born Boston, MA, Aug 19, 1935.

Cindy Nelson, 65, former alpine skier, born Lutsen, MN, Aug 19, 1955.

Matthew Perry, 51, actor ("The Odd Couple," "Friends," *Fools Rush In*), born Williamstown, MA, Aug 19, 1969.

Pete Ricketts, 56, Governor of Nebraska (R), born Nebraska City, NE, Aug 19, 1964.

Jill St. John, 80, actress (*Diamonds Are Forever*), born Jill Oppenheim at Los Angeles, CA, Aug 19, 1940.

Kyra Sedgwick, 55, actress ("The Closer," *Phenomenon, Born on the Fourth of July*), born New York, NY, Aug 19, 1965.

John Stamos, 57, actor ("Grandfathered," "ER," "Full House"), born Los Angeles, CA, Aug 19, 1963.

August	S	M	T	W	T	F	S
							1
	2	3	4	5	6	7	8
2020	9	10	11	12	13	14	15
	16	17	18	19	20	21	22
	23	24	25	26	27	28	29
	30	31					

August 20 — Thursday

DAY 233 **133 REMAINING**

HARRISON, BENJAMIN: BIRTH ANNIVERSARY. Aug 20, 1833. The 23rd president of the US, born at North Bend, OH. He was the grandson of William Henry Harrison, ninth president of the US. Benjamin Harrison's term of office, Mar 4, 1889–Mar 3, 1893, was preceded and followed by the presidential terms of Grover Cleveland (who thus became the 22nd president and 24th president of the US). Harrison died at Indianapolis, IN, Mar 13, 1901.

HUNGARY: SAINT STEPHEN'S DAY. Aug 20. National holiday. Commemorates the canonization of Saint Stephen, king and founder of the state, in 1083. Under the Communists, commemorated as Constitution Day.

ISLAMIC NEW YEAR. Aug 20. Islamic calendar date: Muharram 1, 1442. The first day of the first month of the Islamic calendar. Different methods for "anticipating" the visibility of the new moon crescent at Mecca are used by different Muslim groups, so date can vary by one to two days. Began at sunset the preceding day.

KENTUCKY STATE FAIR (WITH WORLD'S CHAMPIONSHIP HORSE SHOW). Aug 20–30. Kentucky Fair and Expo Center, Louisville, KY. Since 1902. Midway, concerts by nationally known artists and the World's Championship Horse Show. Est attendance: 650,000. For info: Kentucky Fair and Expo Ctr. Web: www.kystatefair.org.

LOVECRAFT, H.P.: BIRTH ANNIVERSARY. Aug 20, 1890. American writer born at Providence, RI, Howard Phillips Lovecraft was a renowned master of American Gothic literature. His stories emphasize the philosophical—what he termed "weirdness"—over the psychological, a departure from earlier American Gothic authors like Poe, who focused on horrific effects. He wrote, "Memories and possibilities are even more hideous than realities," a theme consistently revisited in his stories, which include *The Case of Charles Dexter Ward*, *The Shadow over Innsmouth* and the Cthulhu series. Lovecraft died Mar 15, 1937, at Providence, RI.

MOROCCO: REVOLUTION OF THE KING AND THE PEOPLE. Aug 20. National holiday. Commemorates the response of the people to Sultan (later King) Sidi Muhammed's being sent into exile in 1953 by the French.

O'HIGGINS, BERNARDO: BIRTH ANNIVERSARY. Aug 20, 1778. First ruler of Chile after its declaration of independence. Called the "Liberator of Chile." Born at Chillan, Chile. Died at Lima, Peru, Oct 24, 1842.

PLUTONIUM FIRST WEIGHED: ANNIVERSARY. Aug 20, 1942. University of Chicago scientist Glen Seaborg and his colleagues first weighed plutonium, the first man-made element.

REEVES, JIM: BIRTH ANNIVERSARY. Aug 20, 1924. Country music star Jim Reeves was born at Galloway, Panola County, TX, and died at Nashville, TN, July 31, 1964, when the single-engine plane in which he was traveling crashed in a dense fog. Reeves's biggest hit was "He'll Have to Go" (1959), and he was inducted into the Country Music Hall of Fame in 1967.

SAARINEN, EERO: BIRTH ANNIVERSARY. Aug 20, 1910. Born at Kirkkonummi, Finland, but raised in the United States by his architect father, Eliel, and sculptor mother. Eero Saarinen was a leading postwar architect and furniture designer whose sculptural designs were in contrast to the reigning International Style. He died Sept 1, 1961, at Ann Arbor, MI.

SAARINEN, ELIEL: BIRTH ANNIVERSARY. Aug 20, 1873. Famed architect. Born at Helsinki, Finland. Died at Bloomfield Hills, MI, July 1, 1950.

SPACE MILESTONE: *VIKING 1* AND *2* (US): 45th ANNIVERSARY. Aug 20 and Sept 9, 1975. Sister ships launched toward Mars from Cape Canaveral, FL, on Aug 20 and Sept 9, 1975. *Viking 1*'s lander touched down on Mars July 20, 1976, and *Viking 2*'s lander on Sept 3, 1976. Sent back to Earth high-quality photographs, analysis of atmosphere, weather information and results of sophisticated experiments intended to determine whether life may be present on Mars.

SPACE MILESTONE: *VOYAGER 2* (US). Aug 20, 1977. This unmanned spacecraft journeyed past Jupiter in 1979, Saturn in 1981, Uranus in 1986 and Neptune in 1989, sending photographs and data back to scientists on Earth.

SUN PRAIRIE'S SWEET CORN FESTIVAL. Aug 20–23. Sun Prairie, WI. Family-oriented fun. Carnival, midget auto races, parade, beer, brats, food, exhibits, entertainment, craft fair and tons of hot, buttered sweet corn. Est attendance: 100,000. For info: Sun Prairie Chamber of Commerce, 109 E Main St, Sun Prairie, WI 53590. Phone: (608) 837-4547. Fax: (608) 837-8765. E-mail: spchamber@frontier.com. Web: www.sunprairiechamber.com.

SWEDEN: SOUR HERRING PREMIERE. Aug 20. By ordinance, the year's supply of sour (fermented) herring may begin to be sold on the third Thursday in August.

🎂 BIRTHDAYS TODAY

Amy Adams, 45, actress (*Arrival, Big Eyes, American Hustle, The Fighter*), born Vicenza, Italy, Aug 20, 1975.

Joan Allen, 64, actress (the Bourne films, *Nixon, The Contender*, Tony for *Burn This*), born Rochelle, IL, Aug 20, 1956.

Andy Benes, 53, former baseball player, born Evansville, IN, Aug 20, 1967.

Connie Chung, 74, journalist, born Constance Yu-Hwa at Washington, DC, Aug 20, 1946.

Steve Daines, 58, US Senator (R, Montana), born Van Nuys, CA, Aug 20, 1962.

Billy Gardell, 51, actor ("Mike & Molly," "My Name Is Earl"), born Pittsburgh, PA, Aug 20, 1969.

Andrew Garfield, 37, actor (Tony for *Angels in America*; *Hacksaw Ridge, The Amazing Spider-Man*), born Los Angeles, CA, Aug 20, 1983.

Todd Helton, 47, former baseball player, born Knoxville, TN, Aug 20, 1973.

Donald (Don) King, 89, boxing promoter, born Cleveland, OH, Aug 20, 1931.

Mark Edward Langston, 60, former baseball player, born San Diego, CA, Aug 20, 1960.

Demi Lovato, 28, singer, actress (*Camp Rock*, "Sonny with a Chance"), born Dallas, TX, Aug 20, 1992.

Ron Paul, 85, former US congressman, physician, Internet broadcaster, born Pittsburgh, PA, Aug 20, 1935.

Robert Plant, 72, singer, born Bromwich, England, Aug 20, 1948.

Al Roker, 66, television personality ("The Today Show"), born Brooklyn, NY, Aug 20, 1954.

August 21 — Friday

DAY 234 **132 REMAINING**

ALEXANDRIA LIBRARY SIT-IN ANNIVERSARY CELEBRATION. Aug 21. Alexandria Library, Alexandria, VA. On Aug 21, 1939, five young African-American men walked into the whites-only Alexandria Library and requested library cards. When refused because they were black, the young men quietly took books off the shelves and sat down to read. Library authorities had them arrested—making this act of civil disobedience one of the earliest of its kind in the modern US civil rights movement. This anniversary observance at Alexandria Library locations focuses on civil rights, human rights and the African-American diaspora. For info: Alexandria Library, 717 Queen St, Alexandria, VA 22314.

Phone: (703) 746-1700. E-mail: pwalker@alexlibraryva.org. Web: www.alexlibraryva.org.

AMERICAN BAR ASSOCIATION FOUNDING: ANNIVERSARY. Aug 21, 1878. Organized at Saratoga Springs, NY.

AQUINO, BENIGNO: ASSASSINATION ANNIVERSARY. Aug 21, 1983. Filipino opposition leader Benigno S. Aquino, Jr, was shot and killed at the Manila airport on his return to the Philippines on this date. The killing precipitated greater anti-Marcos feeling and figured significantly in the Feb 7, 1986, election that brought about the collapse of the government administration of Ferdinand E. Marcos and the inauguration of Corazon C. Aquino, widow of the slain man, as president.

BEARDSLEY, AUBREY VINCENT: BIRTH ANNIVERSARY. Aug 21, 1872. English artist and illustrator born at Brighton, England. Died at Menton, France, Mar 16, 1898.

CAMEROON: LAKE NYOS DISASTER: ANNIVERSARY. Aug 21, 1986. An immense buildup of carbon dioxide in a volcanic crater lake led to tragedy: the deadly gas bubbled to the surface of Lake Nyos in a sudden burst that moved at 45 miles per hour and ranged 14 miles. In the surrounding low-lying areas 1,800 people died immediately as did thousands of domestic and wild animals. The entire village of Lower Nyos (1,000 people) died. After the disaster, venting pipes were installed in the lake to systematically release carbon dioxide to prevent another explosion.

CHAMBERLAIN, WILT: BIRTH ANNIVERSARY. Aug 21, 1936. Basketball Hall of Fame center, considered one of the greatest basketball players of all time. Chamberlain is the only NBA player to score 100 points in a game: on Mar 2, 1962, he achieved that feat with the Philadelphia Warriors against the New York Knicks. Born at Philadelphia, PA, he died Oct 12, 1999, at Los Angeles, CA.

HAWAII: ADMISSION DAY: ANNIVERSARY. Aug 21, 1959. President Dwight Eisenhower signed a proclamation admitting Hawaii to the Union. The statehood bill had passed the previous March with a stipulation that statehood should be approved by a vote of Hawaiian residents. The referendum passed by a huge margin in June, and Eisenhower proclaimed Hawaii the 50th state on Aug 21.

HAWAII ADMISSION DAY HOLIDAY. Aug 21. The third Friday in August is observed as a state holiday each year, recognizing the anniversary of Hawaii's statehood. Hawaii became the 50th state Aug 21, 1959.

LINCOLN-DOUGLAS DEBATES: ANNIVERSARY. Aug 21–Oct 15, 1858. At Ottawa, IL, Abraham Lincoln began a series of debates throughout Illinois with Stephen A. Douglas that would propel Lincoln to national notoriety. Republican Lincoln was challenging Democrat Douglas's bid for reelection to the US Senate. The two men conducted seven spirited public debates that often wrestled with the question of slavery in US territories. Although Douglas won reelection, Lincoln's eloquence gained him acclaim and he was chosen to be the Republican Party's candidate for president in the 1860 elections. In 1860 Lincoln defeated Douglas to become president.

MILNE, CHRISTOPHER ROBIN: 100th BIRTH ANNIVERSARY. Aug 21, 1920. A bookseller by trade, Milne was the inspiration for the character of Christopher Robin in the Winnie-the-Pooh books authored by his father, A.A. Milne. Christopher Milne was enamored of Winnipeg the black bear at the London Zoo, and this "Winnie" along with Milne's stuffed toy animals (including Eeyore, Piglet and Roo) came to life first in a poem in *When We Were Very Young* (1924) and then in a series of beloved books. The stories were set in a fictionalized Ashdown Forest, where A.A. Milne had bought a country retreat in 1925. Christopher Milne was born at London, England, and died Apr 20, 1996, at Totnes, England.

August 2020	S	M	T	W	T	F	S
							1
	2	3	4	5	6	7	8
	9	10	11	12	13	14	15
	16	17	18	19	20	21	22
	23	24	25	26	27	28	29
	30	31					

POET'S DAY. Aug 21. A day for all poets to celebrate their special talents and the vision that makes them so wonderful and dear. Poet's Day is a time to share special thoughts about poets and poetry. (©2001 C. Daniel Rhodes.) For info: C. Daniel Rhodes or Natalie Danielle Rhodes, 1900 Crossvine Rd, Hoover, AL 35244. Phone: (205) 908-6781. E-mail: rhodan@charter.net.

QUANTRILL'S RAID ON LAWRENCE, KANSAS: ANNIVERSARY. Aug 21, 1863. Confederate raider William Clarke Quantrill launched a predawn terrorist raid on Lawrence, KS, leaving 150 civilians dead and much of the town ruined. Quantrill had been denied a commission in the Southern army for his barbaric approach to war.

SEMINOLE TRIBE OF FLORIDA LEGALLY ESTABLISHED: ANNIVERSARY. Aug 21, 1957. In 1953 Congress adopted a proposal to terminate assistance to nonrecognized Indian tribes. Seminole leaders and tribal members began to fight the proposal by drafting a constitution and charter for the Seminole Tribe. These were later approved by the secretary of the interior. On this date a majority of tribal members voted to establish the Seminole Tribe of Florida. Today, 4,000 Seminoles live on six reservations in Florida.

SPACE MILESTONE: *GEMINI 5* **(US): 55th ANNIVERSARY.** Aug 21, 1965. Launched on this date, this craft, carrying astronauts Lieutenant Colonel Gordon Cooper and Lieutenant Commander Pete Conrad, orbited Earth 128 times for a new international record of eight days.

TROTSKY ASSASSINATED: 80th ANNIVERSARY. Aug 21, 1940. Leon Trotsky, Soviet revolutionary in exile, was assassinated in Coyoacán, Mexico, by a Spanish Communist who had infiltrated the Trotsky household. Trotsky had helped lead the October Revolution in Russia in 1917, but after Lenin's death in 1924 he was the loser in the Pyrrhic power struggles that resulted. The USSR disclaimed any responsibility in Trotsky's assassination.

UNITED NATIONS: INTERNATIONAL DAY OF REMEMBRANCE AND TRIBUTE TO THE VICTIMS OF TERRORISM. Aug 21. The United Nations has proclaimed this day to honor and support the victims and survivors of terrorism and to promote and protect the full enjoyment of their human rights and fundamental freedoms (Res 72/165). For info: United Nations. Web: www.un.org.

WESTERN IDAHO FAIR. Aug 21–30. Boise, ID. 122nd annual. Largest fair in the state, including four stages of entertainment on the grounds with local and regional talent, three nights of grandstand concerts, carnival midway and 70 food booths. Annually, starting on the third Friday in August. Est attendance: 254,000. For info: Western Idaho Fair, 5610 Glenwood, Boise, ID 83714. Phone: (208) 287-5650. E-mail: info@idahofair.com. Web: www.idahofair.com.

🎂 BIRTHDAYS TODAY

Usain Bolt, 34, Olympic track athlete, born Trelawny, Jamaica, Aug 21, 1986.

Steve Case, 62, founder of America Online (AOL), born Oahu, HI, Aug 21, 1958.

Kim Cattrall, 64, actress ("Sex and the City," *The Ghost Writer, Mannequin*), born Liverpool, England, Aug 21, 1956.

Jackie DeShannon, 76, singer, songwriter, born Hazel, KY, Aug 21, 1944.

Joanne Froggatt, 40, actress ("Downton Abbey," *In Our Name*), born Littleback, North Hampshire, England, Aug 21, 1980 (some sources say 1979).

Brody Jenner, 37, television personality, born Los Angeles, CA, Aug 21, 1983.

James Robert (Jim) McMahon, 61, former football player, born Jersey City, NJ, Aug 21, 1959.

Kacey Musgraves, 32, singer, songwriter, born Golden, TX, Aug 21, 1988.

Hayden Panettiere, 31, actress ("Nashville," "Heroes," "Guiding Light"), born Palisades, NY, Aug 21, 1989.

Kenny Rogers, 82, singer, born Houston, TX, Aug 21, 1938.

Jon Tester, 64, US Senator (D, Montana), born Havre, MT, Aug 21, 1956.

Melvin Van Peebles, 88, actor, director, playwright (*Ain't Supposed to Die a Natural Death*), born Chicago, IL, Aug 21, 1932.

Peter Weir, 76, director (*Dead Poets Society, Gallipoli, The Truman Show*), born Sydney, Australia, Aug 21, 1944.

Clarence Williams III, 81, actor ("The Mod Squad," *Purple Rain*), born New York, NY, Aug 21, 1939.

Alicia Witt, 45, actress ("Justified," *Fun, Mr Holland's Opus, Dune*), born Worcester, MA, Aug 21, 1975.

August 22 — Saturday

DAY 235   **131 REMAINING**

BATTLE OF STALINGRAD BEGINS: ANNIVERSARY. Aug 22, 1942. Having captured Sevastopol on the Crimea on July 2, after an eight-month siege, the Germans began an offensive to capture Stalingrad. During this five-month-long battle, the city of 500,000 people dwindled to a population of 1,515. In the fighting, Russia lost 750,000 troops, the Germans 400,000, the Romanians nearly 200,000 and the Italians 130,000—a total of 1,480,000. The last German strongholds at Stalingrad surrendered to the Russian army on Feb 2, 1943.

BE AN ANGEL DAY. Aug 22. A day to do one small act of service for someone. Be a blessing in someone's life. Annually, Aug 22. For info: Angel Heights Healing Center, Rev Jayne M. Howard Feldman, PO Box 95, Upperco, MD 21155. Phone: (410) 833-6912. E-mail: earthangel4peace@aol.com.

BELGIUM: WEDDING OF THE GIANTS. Aug 22–23. Ath. Traditional cultural observance marked since 1481 and now recognized by UNESCO as a unique cultural event. Goliath, King of the Festival, marries his fiancée at St. Juliens Church, then battles the shepherd David in the afternoon. A procession of Ath giants courses through the town. Annually, starting the Saturday before the fourth Sunday in August. For info: City of Ath. Web: www.ath.be.

BRADBURY, RAY: 100th BIRTH ANNIVERSARY. Aug 22, 1920. Born at Waukegan, IL, Ray Bradbury was one of the preeminent science fiction/fantasy writers of the 20th century. His body of work, which critiqued social mores and depicted the consequences of unfettered technology, is considered timeless and transcends generations. Notable works include *Something Wicked This Way Comes, The Body Electric* and *Fahrenheit 451*, his most famous novel. Awarded a Special Citation by the Pulitzer Board (2007) for his oeuvre, Bradbury died June 5, 2012, at Los Angeles, CA. He once wrote, "Re-create the world in your own image and make it better for your having been here."

CARTIER-BRESSON, HENRI: BIRTH ANNIVERSARY. Aug 22, 1908. Pioneering photojournalist who cofounded the Magnum photo agency. Probably the most respected 20th-century photographer. Famous for looking for "the decisive moment." Born at Chanteloup, France, he died Aug 2, 2004, at I'lle-sur-Sorgue, France.

DEBUSSY, CLAUDE: BIRTH ANNIVERSARY. Aug 22, 1862. Achille Claude Debussy, French musician and composer, especially remembered for his impressionistic "tone poems," was born at St. Germain-en-Laye, France. He died at Paris, France, Mar 25, 1918.

HERRIMAN, GEORGE: BIRTH ANNIVERSARY. Aug 22, 1880. In 1910 when George Herriman introduced a cat and mouse as subplot characters to his comic strip "The Dingbat Family," their non-sequitur dialogue gained enough attention to result in a spin-off strip of their own. The superbly drafted "Krazy Kat and Ignatz" had as its central theme unrequited love. Kat loved Ignatz, but the malevolent mouse took every opportunity to throw bricks at the devoted cat. "Krazy Kat" was popular with a mass audience as well as artists and intellectuals, and it remained enormously popular after Herriman's death. Born at New Orleans, LA, he died at Hollywood, CA, Apr 25, 1944.

HOOKER, JOHN LEE: BIRTH ANNIVERSARY. Aug 22, 1917. Blues rocker Hooker was born in Coahoma County, MI, the son of a sharecropper. He sang at church, learned some guitar and bounced through a few stops in the South before his career took off in Detroit with his first single, 1948's "Boogie Chillen." An instant classic, the song established Hooker's distinctive guitar work and signature, growling groove, a style that formed the spiritual link between blues and rock and roll. Hooker continued to record and tour until late in life. In 1991, he was inducted into the Rock and Roll Hall of Fame. John Lee Hooker died at Los Altos, CA, June 21, 2001.

INTERNATIONAL YACHT RACE: ANNIVERSARY. Aug 22, 1851. A silver trophy (then known as the "Hundred Guinea Cup" and offered by the Royal Yacht Squadron) was won in a race around the Isle of Wight by the US yacht *America*, which defeated the United Kingdom's *Aurora*. The trophy, later turned over to the New York Yacht Club, became known as the America's Cup and was to be "a perpetual challenge cup for friendly competition between nations." The boat race is the oldest trophy in sports, predating the modern Olympic Games by 45 years.

LANGLEY, SAMUEL PIERPONT: BIRTH ANNIVERSARY. Aug 22, 1834. American astronomer, physicist and aviation pioneer for whom Langley Air Force Base, VA, is named. Born at Roxbury, MA, Langley died at Aiken, SC, Feb 27, 1906.

MINNESOTA RENAISSANCE FESTIVAL. Aug 22–Oct 4 (weekends; Labor Day). Shakopee, MN. A celebration of 16th-century Renaissance Europe with entertainment on 16 lively stages, food, arts and crafts, games and live jousting. Est attendance: 300,000. For info: Minnesota Renaissance Fest, 1244 S Canterbury Rd, Ste 306, Shakopee, MN 55379. Phone: (952) 445-7361. Fax: (952) 445-7380. E-mail: info@renaissancefest.com. Web: www.renaissancefest.com.

MORMON CHOIR FIRST PERFORMANCE: ANNIVERSARY. Aug 22, 1847. What would later become the world-famous Mormon Tabernacle Choir gave its first public performance at Salt Lake City, UT, for an outdoor meeting of the Church of Jesus Christ of Latter-day Saints. Widely known for its concert tours, recordings and weekly radio and television broadcasts from Temple Square. The choir's radio program, "Music and the Spoken Word," is the longest continuously running radio program in network history, dating back to 1929.

NATIONAL BRING YOUR CAT TO THE VET DAY. Aug 22. Don't postpone your cat's trip to the vet: regular exams can help prevent medical emergencies for your cat. Veterinarians can often detect conditions or diseases long before they become significant, painful or more costly to treat. Annually, Aug 22. For info: American Assn of Feline Practitioners, 390 Amwell Rd, Ste 402, Hillsborough, NJ 08844. Phone: (800) 874-0498. Web: https://catvets.com/Cat2VetDay.

PARKER, DOROTHY: BIRTH ANNIVERSARY. Aug 22, 1893. Born Dorothy Rothschild at West End, NJ, the acclaimed poet, critic, author and wit was known as the "wittiest woman in America." She said, "I hate writing, I love having written." During her career, Parker wrote for *Vanity Fair, The New Yorker* (for which she was an original contributor) and other top periodicals, and was one of the founding members of the elite literary group the Algonquin Round Table. Strong, albeit subtle, critiques of sexism were prevailing themes in her works, along with critiques of all other forms of social inequality. Parker was found dead in her New York City residential hotel on June 7, 1967.

RIEFENSTAHL, LENI: BIRTH ANNIVERSARY. Aug 22, 1902. Controversial actress and filmmaker who directed the infamous Nazi propaganda films *Triumph of the Will* (1935) and *Olympia* (1938). Both films are noted for innovative filming techniques. Born at Berlin, Germany, Riefenstahl died at Pöcking, Germany, Sept 8, 2003.

SOUTHERN HEMISPHERE HOODIE-HOO DAY. Aug 22. Long awaited by our "southern-half" friends, this is the day to go outdoors at high noon and yell "Hoodie-Hoo" to chase winter and make ready for spring, only one month away. (©2006 by WH.) For info: Thomas & Ruth Roy, Wellcat Holidays, 2418 Long Ln, Lebanon, PA 17046. Phone: (717) 279-0184. E-mail: info@wellcat.com. Web: www.wellcat.com.

TASTE OF MONTGOMERY COUNTY. Aug 22. General Lew Wallace Study and Museum, Crawfordsville, IN. A panorama of sights, a symphony of sounds and a festival of flavors that represent all that's great about this little corner of the Midwest. Restaurants, caterers and food vendors from throughout Montgomery County gather to showcase a huge variety of their tastiest treats and most mouthwatering morsels. The Taste also features terrific live music to satisfy almost every palate. Annually, the fourth Saturday in August. Est attendance: 3,000. For info: Taste of Montgomery County, PO Box 662, Crawfordsville, IN 47933. Phone: (765) 362-5769. E-mail: study@ben-hur.com. Web: www.tasteofmontgomerycounty.com.

VIETNAM CONFLICT BEGINS: 75th ANNIVERSARY. Aug 22, 1945. Less than a week after the Japanese surrender ended WWII, a team of Free French parachuted into southern Indochina in response to a successful coup by a Communist guerrilla named Ho Chi Minh in the French colony.

🎂 BIRTHDAYS TODAY

Adewale Akinnuoye-Agbaje, 53, actor ("Lost," "Oz"), born London, England, Aug 22, 1967.

Tori Amos, 57, musician, singer, songwriter, born Newton, NC, Aug 22, 1963.

Richard Armitage, 49, actor (The Hobbit trilogy, "Berlin Station," "Spooks" ["MI-5"]), born Huncote, England, Aug 22, 1971.

Ty Burrell, 53, actor ("Modern Family," *Dawn of the Dead*), born Grants Pass, OR, Aug 22, 1967.

Gerald Paul Carr, 88, former astronaut, born Denver, CO, Aug 22, 1932.

James Corden, 42, talk show host, actor (*One Man, Two Guvnors*), born London, England, Aug 22, 1978.

Giada De Laurentiis, 50, chef, cookbook author, television personality ("Everyday Italian"), born Rome, Italy, Aug 22, 1970.

Cory Gardner, 46, US Senator (R, Colorado), born Yuma, CO, Aug 22, 1974.

Valerie Harper, 79, actress ("The Mary Tyler Moore Show," "Rhoda"), born Suffern, NY, Aug 22, 1941.

Steve Kroft, 75, television journalist ("60 Minutes"), born Kokomo, IN, Aug 22, 1945.

Paul Molitor, 64, Hall of Fame baseball player, born St. Paul, MN, Aug 22, 1956.

August 2020	S	M	T	W	T	F	S
							1
	2	3	4	5	6	7	8
	9	10	11	12	13	14	15
	16	17	18	19	20	21	22
	23	24	25	26	27	28	29
	30	31					

Duane Charles (Bill) Parcells, 79, former football coach, born Englewood, NJ, Aug 22, 1941.

E. Annie Proulx, 85, author (*The Shipping News, Accordion Crimes,* "Brokeback Mountain"), born Norwich, CT, Aug 22, 1935.

Kristin Wiig, 47, actress, comedienne ("Saturday Night Live," *Welcome to Me, Bridesmaids*), screenwriter, born Canandaigua, NY, Aug 22, 1973.

Cindy Williams, 72, actress (*American Graffiti*, "Laverne & Shirley"), born Van Nuys, CA, Aug 22, 1948.

Carl Michael Yastrzemski, 81, Hall of Fame baseball player, born Southampton, NY, Aug 22, 1939.

August 23 — Sunday

DAY 236   **130 REMAINING**

BUSHMILLER, ERNIE: BIRTH ANNIVERSARY. Aug 23, 1905. Comic strip artist famous for the "Nancy" strip featuring spiky haired Nancy, her pal Sluggo and glamorous Aunt Fritzi. Born at the Bronx, NY, Bushmiller died Aug 15, 1982, at Stamford, CT.

CUVIER, BARON GEORGES: BIRTH ANNIVERSARY. Aug 23, 1769. Father of paleontology, born at Montbéliard, France. Cuvier created a system of comparative anatomy based on the observation of distinct characteristics through which he defined four main groups of classification: vertebrates, mollusks, radiates and articulates. His study of fossils and their relationship to the strata where they were found provided crucial evidence for the concept of extinction through his careful reassembly of complete skeletons, and he also theorized a series of catastrophic events that might cause a species to cease to exist. Cuvier died at Paris, France, May 13, 1832.

FIRST MAN-POWERED FLIGHT: ANNIVERSARY. Aug 23, 1977. At Schafter, CA, Bryan Allen pedaled the 70-pound *Gossamer Condor* for a mile at a "minimal altitude of two pylons" in a flight certified by the Royal Aeronautical Society of Britain, winning a £50,000 prize offered by British industrialist Henry Kremer. See also: "First Man-Powered Flight Across English Channel: Anniversary" (June 12).

KELLY, GENE: BIRTH ANNIVERSARY. Aug 23, 1912. Actor, dancer, director, choreographer born at Pittsburgh, PA. His movies include the musicals *Singin' in the Rain* and *An American in Paris*. Kelly died at Beverly Hills, CA, Feb 2, 1996.

LUXEMBOURG: SCHUEBERMESS SHEPHERD'S FAIR. Aug 23–Sept 5. Fair dates from 1340. (Two weeks beginning on the next-to-last Sunday in August.)

MASTERS, EDGAR LEE: BIRTH ANNIVERSARY. Aug 23, 1869. American poet and author of the *Spoon River Anthology*. He was born at Garnett, KS, and he died at Melrose Park, PA, Mar 5, 1950.

PERRY, OLIVER HAZARD: BIRTH ANNIVERSARY. Aug 23, 1785. American naval hero, born at South Kingston, RI. Best remembered for his announcement of victory at the Battle of Lake Erie, Sept 10, 1813: "We have met the enemy, and they are ours." Died Aug 23, 1819, at sea.

SACCO-VANZETTI EXECUTION: ANNIVERSARY. Aug 23, 1927. Nicola Sacco and Bartolomeo Vanzetti were electrocuted at the Charlestown, MA, prison on this date. Convicted of a shoe factory payroll robbery during which a guard had been killed, Sacco and Vanzetti maintained their innocence to the end. Six years of appeals marked this American cause célèbre during which substantial evidence was presented to show that both men were elsewhere at the time of the crime. On the 50th anniversary of their execution, Massachusetts governor Michael S. Dukakis proclaimed Aug 23, 1977, a memorial day, noting that the 1921 trial had been "permeated by prejudice."

SPACE MILESTONE: *INTELSAT-4 F-7* (US). Aug 23, 1973. International Communications Satellite Consortium's *Intelsat* launched Aug 23, 1973, to relay communications from North and South America to Europe and Africa.

"STOCKHOLM SYNDROME" BANK ROBBERY: ANNIVERSARY. Aug 23–28, 1973. In a botched bank robbery at Stockholm, Sweden, Jan Erik Olsson took four hostages and barricaded himself with them and a friend, Clark Olofsson, in the vault. After a six-day siege, the police piped in gas and the hostages were freed. Afterward, it emerged that the hostages were more afraid of the police than of their captors, and Swedish professor Nils Bejerot coined the term "Stockholm syndrome" to explain the phenomenon of hostages identifying and sympathizing with their captors.

UNITED NATIONS: INTERNATIONAL DAY FOR THE REMEMBRANCE OF THE SLAVE TRADE AND ITS ABOLITION. Aug 23. For info: United Nations, Dept of Public Info, New York, NY 10017. Web: www.un.org.

VALENTINO MEMORIAL SERVICE. Aug 23. Hollywood Cathedral Mausoleum, Hollywood Forever Cemetery, Los Angeles, CA. Since 1927 annual memorial service celebrating the life of the silent screen's biggest male star, Rudolph Valentino. Held each year on the anniversary of his 1926 death at 12:10 PM—the time he died (in New York City). Attendees include the "Lady in Black." For info: Hollywood Forever Cemetery, 6000 Santa Monica Blvd, Los Angeles, CA, 90038.

VIRGO, THE VIRGIN. Aug 23–Sept 22. In the astronomical/astrological zodiac, which divides the sun's apparent orbit into 12 segments, the period Aug 23–Sept 22 is traditionally identified as the sun sign of Virgo, the Virgin. The ruling planet is Mercury.

🎂 BIRTHDAYS TODAY

Tony Bill, 80, actor (*You're a Big Boy Now*), director (*My Bodyguard*), born San Diego, CA, Aug 23, 1940.

Kobe Bryant, 42, former basketball player, born Philadelphia, PA, Aug 23, 1978.

Scott Caan, 44, actor ("Hawaii Five-0," "Entourage"), born Los Angeles, CA, Aug 23, 1976.

Nelson DeMille, 77, author (*The Cuban Affair, The Gold Coast, The General's Daughter*), born New York, NY, Aug 23, 1943.

Barbara Eden, 86, actress ("I Dream of Jeannie," *Harper Valley P.T.A.*), born Barbara Huffman at Tucson, AZ, Aug 23, 1934.

Sonny Jurgensen, 86, Hall of Fame football player, born Wilmington, NC, Aug 23, 1934.

Jeremy Lin, 32, basketball player, born Los Angeles, CA, Aug 23, 1988.

Shelley Long, 71, actress ("Cheers," *Irreconcilable Differences*), born Fort Wayne, IN, Aug 23, 1949.

Patricia McBride, 78, former dancer (New York City Ballet), born Teaneck, NJ, Aug 23, 1942.

Vera Miles, 90, actress (*The Wrong Man, Psycho*), born Boise City, OK, Aug 23, 1930.

Jay Mohr, 50, actor (*Jerry Maguire, Picture Perfect*, "Action"), comedian, born Verona, NJ, Aug 23, 1970.

Antonia Novello, 76, first woman and first Hispanic US surgeon general (1990–93), born Fajardo, Puerto Rico, Aug 23, 1944.

Mark Russell, 88, political comedian, born Mark Ruslander at Buffalo, NY, Aug 23, 1932.

Richard Sanders, 80, actor ("WKRP in Cincinnati," "Berrenger's"), born Harrisburg, PA, Aug 23, 1940.

Rick Springfield, 71, singer, actor, born Sydney, Australia, Aug 23, 1949.

Gretchen Whitmer, 49, Governor of Michigan (D), born Lansing, MI, Aug 23, 1971.

August 24 — Monday

DAY 237   **129 REMAINING**

ARAFAT, YASSER: BIRTH ANNIVERSARY. Aug 24, 1929. Controversial Middle Eastern leader who for almost 50 years was the face of the Palestinian cause. Reviled by some as a terrorist (as leader of Al-Fatah and the PLO) and cheered by others as a freedom fighter, Arafat shared the 1994 Nobel Peace Prize with Shimon Peres and Yitzhak Rabin. Born Muhammad Abdul Raouf Arafat al-Qudwa al-Husseini at Cairo, Egypt (some sources say Jerusalem or Gaza), Arafat died Nov 11, 2004, in a hospital near Paris, France.

BORGES, JORGE LUIS: BIRTH ANNIVERSARY. Aug 24, 1899. Influential author, critic, poet and librarian, born at Buenos Aires, Argentina. Borges was the director of the National Library of the Argentine Republic from 1955 to 1973. He created intellectually fantastical tales (collected in *Ficciones* and *The Aleph and Other Stories*). "There are so many futures," he said, "[all] quite different from each other." Borges died June 14, 1986, at Geneva, Switzerland.

KAHANAMOKU, DUKE: BIRTH ANNIVERSARY. Aug 24, 1890. Duke Paoa Kahanamoku, Olympic gold medal swimmer and "father of international surfing," was born at Honolulu, HI. Kahanamoku won gold medals in the 100-meter freestyle at the 1912 Olympics and at the 1920 Olympics. In total, he won five medals in four Olympics. Credited with inventing the flutter kick, he enjoyed a long career, not retiring from competition until age 42. Kahanamoku was also Hawaii's ambassador of surfing, popularizing the sport around the world. In 1917, on a 16-foot, 114-pound board, he rode a wave off Waikiki for 1.75 miles. The "Duke" acted in movies and served as sheriff of Honolulu, running alternately on Republican and Democratic tickets. Died at Honolulu, Jan 22, 1968. Hawaii has honored him with a statue on Waikiki Beach, on which fans place leis.

LIBERIA: FLAG DAY. Aug 24. National holiday.

PLUTO DEMOTED: ANNIVERSARY. Aug 24, 2006. On the last day of the annual International Astronomical Union meeting at Prague, Czech Republic, 424 astronomers voted to demote Pluto from planet status. They determined that Pluto is instead a dwarf planet.

REPUBLICAN NATIONAL CONVENTION. Aug 24–27. Spectrum Center, Charlotte, NC. The Republican Party meets to select its nominees for president and vice president in the 2020 election. For info: Republican National Committee, 310 First St SE, Washington, DC 20003. Phone: (202) 863-8500. E-mail: info@gop.com. Web: www.gop.com.

SAINT BARTHOLOMEW'S DAY MASSACRE: ANNIVERSARY. Aug 24, 1572. Anniversary of the massacre in Paris and throughout France of thousands of Protestant Huguenots. The massacre began when the church bells tolled at dawn on Saint Bartholomew's Day, Aug 24, 1572, and continued for several days. Pope Gregory XIII ordered a medal struck to commemorate the event, but Protestant countries abhorred the killings, estimated at 5,000 to 30,000.

SOUTHERN CYCLONE: ANNIVERSARY. Aug 24, 1893. A hurricane hit Savannah, GA, and Charleston, SC, killing 1,000 to 2,000 people.

SPACE MILESTONE: *VOYAGER 2* (US) REACHES NEPTUNE. Aug 24, 1989. Launched in 1977, *Voyager 2* had its first close encounter with Neptune.

UKRAINE: INDEPENDENCE DAY. Aug 24. National day. Commemorates independence from the former Soviet Union in 1991.

VESUVIUS DAY. Aug 24, AD 79. Anniversary of the eruption of Vesuvius, an active volcano in southern Italy, which destroyed the cities of Pompeii, Stabiae and Herculaneum. Pliny the Younger, who escaped the disaster, wrote of it to the historian Tacitus: "[B]lack and horrible clouds, broken by sinuous shapes of flaming winds, were opening with long tongues of fire."

WASHINGTON, DC: INVASION ANNIVERSARY. Aug 24–25, 1814. British forces briefly invaded and raided Washington, DC, burning the Capitol, the president's house and most other public buildings. President James Madison and other high US government officials fled to safety until British troops (not knowing the strength of their position) departed the city two days later.

WILBERFORCE, WILLIAM: BIRTH ANNIVERSARY. Aug 24, 1759. British politician and abolitionist who, as a member in the House of Commons (1780–1825), sponsored legislation that eventually abolished the slave trade (1807) and then slavery (1833) in the British Dominions. Born at Hull, Wilberforce died July 29, 1833, at London, England—three days after passage of the Slavery Abolition Act.

WILLIAM WILBERFORCE DAY. Aug 24. Wilberforce University, Wilberforce, OH. 10th annual. A celebration of the life and legacy of William Wilberforce (1759–1833), inspirational abolitionist who, as a member of the British parliament, sponsored the first bills that helped end the slave trade. Est attendance: 2,500. For info: Dr. Rick Sheridan. Phone: (916) 716-1608. E-mail: sheridanacademics@gmail.com.

🧁 BIRTHDAYS TODAY

Gerry Cooney, 64, former boxer, born New York, NY, Aug 24, 1956.

Ava DuVernay, 48, director and producer (*A Wrinkle in Time, 13th, Selma*), born Los Angeles, CA, Aug 24, 1972.

Stephen Fry, 63, actor (*The Hobbit: The Desolation of Smaug, Gosford Park, Wilde*, "Jeeves and Wooster"), novelist, born Hampstead, London, England, Aug 24, 1957.

Rafael Furcal, 42, former baseball player, born Loma de Cabrera, Dominican Republic, Aug 24, 1978.

John Green, 43, author (*The Fault in Our Stars, Looking for Alaska*), born Indianapolis, IN, Aug 24, 1977.

Rupert Grint, 32, actor (Harry Potter films), born Hertfordshire, England, Aug 24, 1988.

Steve Guttenberg, 62, actor ("Billy," *Three Men and a Baby*), born Brooklyn, NY, Aug 24, 1958.

Mike Huckabee, 65, television host, former governor of Arkansas, born Hope, AR, Aug 24, 1955.

Craig Kilborn, 58, television personality, born Hastings, MN, Aug 24, 1962.

Joe Manchin III, 73, US Senator (D, West Virginia), born Farmington, WV, Aug 24, 1947.

Marlee Matlin, 55, actress (Oscar for *Children of a Lesser God*; *Walker*, "Reasonable Doubts"), born Morton Grove, IL, Aug 24, 1965.

Alexander McCall Smith, 72, author (*The No. 1 Ladies' Detective Agency, The Sunday Philosophy Club*), professor, scholar, born Bulawayo, Southern Rhodesia (now Zimbabwe), Aug 24, 1948.

Reginald Wayne (Reggie) Miller, 55, Hall of Fame basketball player, born Riverside, CA, Aug 24, 1965.

Chad Michael Murray, 39, actor ("One Tree Hill," "Dawson's Creek," *House of Wax*), born Buffalo, NY, Aug 24, 1981.

Alex O'Loughlin, 44, actor ("Hawaii Five-0," "Moonlight"), born Canberra, Australia, Aug 24, 1976.

Michael Richards, 70, actor ("Seinfeld," *Trial and Error*), born Culver City, CA, Aug 24, 1950.

Calvin Edward (Cal) Ripken, Jr, 60, Hall of Fame baseball player, born Havre de Grace, MD, Aug 24, 1960.

Mason Williams, 82, composer, born Abilene, TX, Aug 24, 1938.

Todd Young, 48, US Senator (R, Indiana), born Lancaster, PA, Aug 24, 1972.

August 25 — Tuesday

DAY 238　　　　　　　　　　　　　　　**128 REMAINING**

BE KIND TO HUMANKIND WEEK. Aug 25–31. 32nd annual. All of the negative news that you read and hear about in the media is disheartening—but the truth is the positive stories outweigh the negative stories by a long shot! We just don't hear about them as often. Take heart—most people are caring individuals. Show you care. Decide to be kind. Daily affirmations: Speak Kind Words Saturday, Sacrifice Our Wants for Others' Needs Sunday, Motorist Consideration Monday, Touch a Heart Tuesday, Willing to Lend a Hand Wednesday, Thoughtful Thursday, Forgive Your Foe Friday. For info: Lorraine Jara, 1 Mountain Stream Ct, Barnegat, NJ 08005. E-mail: Lorraine@bekindweek.org. Web: www.bk2hk.org.

BERNSTEIN, LEONARD: BIRTH ANNIVERSARY. Aug 25, 1918. American conductor and composer Leonard Bernstein was born at Lawrence, MA. One of the greatest conductors in American music history, he first conducted the New York Philharmonic Orchestra at age 25 and was its director from 1959 to 1969. His musicals include *West Side Story* and *On the Town*, and his operas and operettas include *Candide*. He died five days after his retirement, Oct 14, 1990, at New York, NY.

CHINA: DOUBLE SEVEN FESTIVAL. Aug 25. Also called Chinese Valentine's Day. Observed on seventh day of seventh lunar month. From a folktale in which two lovers (a cowherd and a weaver) are separated by the Milky Way. They are able to meet once a year when all the world's magpies form a bridge for the lovers.

FOUNDERS DAY. Aug 25. Celebrated within the National Park Service of the US to commemorate its founding on Aug 25, 1916. Founders Day is an opportunity for US parks to show pride, connect with visitors and reflect on the importance of the National Park Service mission. For info: National Park Service. Web: www.nps.gov.

GIBSON, ALTHEA: BIRTH ANNIVERSARY. Aug 25, 1927. Born at Silver, SC, Althea Gibson learned paddle tennis by chance as a child when her block of W 143rd St in New York was designated as a Police Athletic League play street. She overcame great financial and social adversity and eventually won 10 consecutive national titles in the American Tennis Association, a league for

August 2020	S	M	T	W	T	F	S
							1
	2	3	4	5	6	7	8
	9	10	11	12	13	14	15
	16	17	18	19	20	21	22
	23	24	25	26	27	28	29
	30	31					

black players. On Aug 28, 1950, she became the first black player to compete in the national tennis championship at Forest Hills, NY. A few years later, she became the first black woman to win the singles championship at Wimbledon. In her prime, she was ranked as high as seventh in the US, winning titles at the French Open, Wimbledon and US Nationals at Forest Hills. She died at East Orange, NJ, Sept 28, 2003.

HARTE, BRET: BIRTH ANNIVERSARY. Aug 25, 1836. Francis Brett Harte, journalist, poet, printer, teacher and novelist, especially remembered for his early stories of California ("The Luck of Roaring Camp," "The Outcasts of Poker Flat" and "How Santa Claus Came to Simpson's Bar"), was born at Albany, NY. He died at London, England, May 5, 1902.

KELLY, WALT: BIRTH ANNIVERSARY. Aug 25, 1913. Born at Philadelphia, PA, Kelly—creator of "Pogo"—was one of the greatest "funny animal" artists of the postwar golden age in comics. He moved to California in 1935 to work in the animation studio of Walt Disney, but left in 1941 during a labor dispute. Kelly created Pogo Possum and Albert Alligator first for comic books and then in the hugely popular syndicated daily comic strip that ran from 1948 to 1973. The lovable and quirky denizens of Okefenokee Swamp had safe-for-all-ages adventures, but their creator was able nonetheless to inject some political satire during the run of the strip. It was Kelly's character Pogo who paraphrased Oliver Hazard Perry to say, "We has met the enemy, and it is us." Kelly died at Hollywood, CA, Oct 18, 1973.

KISS-AND-MAKE-UP DAY. Aug 25. A day to make amends for relationships that need mending. For info: Jacqueline V. Milgate, 121 Little Tree Ln, Hilton, NY 14468. E-mail: jacqueline825@yahoo.com.

MOON PHASE: FIRST QUARTER. Aug 25. Moon enters First Quarter phase at 1:58 PM, EDT.

NATIONAL PARK SERVICE FOUNDED: ANNIVERSARY. Aug 25, 1916. The Organic Act of 1916 established the National Park Service within the Department of the Interior. The act stated: "The service thus established shall promote and regulate the use of the Federal areas known as national parks, monuments, and reservations . . . , to conserve the scenery and the natural and historic objects and the wildlife therein and to provide for the enjoyment of the same in such manner and by such means as will leave them unimpaired for the enjoyment of future generations."

PARALYMPIC GAMES. Aug 25–Sept 6. Tokyo, Japan. 16th edition. Two weeks following the conclusion of the summer Olympics, disabled athletes will have their chance to compete in the same venues. Highlights include wheelchair basketball, track and field, archery, judo and wheelchair rugby. New events in 2020 are badminton and taekwondo. Some 4,400 athletes from around the world are expected to compete. For info: Tokyo 2020 Paralympic Games. Web: https://tokyo2020.org or www.paralympic.org/tokyo-2020.

PARIS LIBERATED: ANNIVERSARY. Aug 25, 1944. As dawn broke, the men of the Second French Armored Division entered Paris, France, ending the long German occupation of the City of Light. That afternoon General Charles de Gaulle led a parade down the Champs Elysées. Though Hitler had ordered the destruction of Paris, General Dietrich von Choltitz, the German occupying-officer, refused that order and instead surrendered to French Major General Jacques Le Clerc.

PINKERTON, ALLAN: BIRTH ANNIVERSARY. Aug 25, 1819. Scottish-born American detective, founder of detective agency at Chicago, IL, in 1850, first chief of US Army's secret service, remembered now because of his strikebreaking and his lack of sympathy for working people. Pinkerton was born at Glasgow, Scotland, and died at Chicago, July 1, 1884.

RICHARD III'S REMAINS FOUND: ANNIVERSARY. Aug 25–Sept 5, 2012. Excavating a parking lot in Leicester, England, that stood over the ruins of Greyfriars Church, an archaeological team from the University of Leicester found a medieval grave in the choir with the remains of a man—buried without shroud or coffin—who appeared to have scoliosis. During a press conference on Feb 4, 2013, scientists and archaeologists announced that the results of a battery of tests—including DNA testing on a living descendant of Richard III's sister—confirmed that the bones were the infamous king's. King Richard III, the last of the Plantagenets, died at the Battle of Bosworth Field on Aug 22, 1485. He was the last king of England to die in battle. The victor, Henry Tudor, ushered in a new dynasty of royalty as King Henry VII. The dig was conducted by the University of Leicester, with support from Leicester City Council and in association with the Richard III Society. Richard III was reburied with ceremony at Leicester Cathedral on Mar 26, 2015.

URUGUAY: INDEPENDENCE DAY. Aug 25. National holiday. Declared independence from Brazil in 1825. Independence granted in 1828.

WALLACE, GEORGE: BIRTH ANNIVERSARY. Aug 25, 1919. Four-time Democratic governor of Alabama (1962, 1970, 1974, 1982) who campaigned three times for president, Wallace is considered widely influential in the "southernization" of American politics. He gained national notoriety as a symbol of segregation when he defied federal mandates to desegregate schools by blocking enrollment of black students at the University of Alabama in 1963. Shot while campaigning for the Democratic presidential nomination in 1972, Wallace was permanently paralyzed below the waist. Born at Clio, AL, he died Sept 13, 1998, at Montgomery, AL.

***THE WIZARD OF OZ* RELEASED: ANNIVERSARY.** Aug 25, 1939. This motion-picture classic, directed by Victor Fleming, was a musical adaptation of the L. Frank Baum children's book with both black-and-white and color sequences. It starred Judy Garland as Dorothy as well as Frank Morgan as the Wizard (and four other characters), Ray Bolger as the Scarecrow, Bert Lahr as the Lion, Jack Haley as the Tin Man and Margaret Hamilton as the Wicked Witch of the West. Nominated for six Academy Awards, it won two, for Best Original Music Score and Best Song, "Over the Rainbow" (Harold Arlen music and E.Y. Harburg lyrics).

🧁 BIRTHDAYS TODAY

Martin Amis, 71, author (*The Information, London Fields*), critic, born Oxford, England, Aug 25, 1949.

Anne Archer, 73, actress ("Falcon Crest"; stage: *A Couple of White Chicks Sitting Around Talking*), born Los Angeles, CA, Aug 25, 1947.

Albert Belle, 54, former baseball player, born Shreveport, LA, Aug 25, 1966.

Bobby Berk, 39, television personality ("Queer Eye"), interior designer, born Houston, TX, Aug 25, 1981.

Rachel Bilson, 39, actress ("Hart of Dixie," "The O.C."), born Los Angeles, CA, Aug 25, 1981.

Tim Burton, 62, director (*Alice in Wonderland, Sweeney Todd, Edward Scissorhands*), born Burbank, CA, Aug 25, 1958.

Sean Connery, 90, actor (James Bond movies, *Entrapment, The Hunt for Red October, The Name of the Rose*), born Edinburgh, Scotland, Aug 25, 1930.

Elvis Costello, 66, singer, songwriter, born Declan McManus at Paddington, London, England, Aug 25, 1954.

Billy Ray Cyrus, 59, country singer, actor ("Hannah Montana"), born Flatwoods, KY, Aug 25, 1961.

Frederick Forsyth, 82, author (*The Day of the Jackal*), born Ashford, Kent, England, Aug 25, 1938.

Anthony Heald, 76, actor (*The Silence of the Lambs, Searching for Bobby Fischer*), born New Rochelle, NY, Aug 25, 1944.

Blake Lively, 33, actress (*Savages, Green Lantern, The Sisterhood of the Traveling Pants*, "Gossip Girl"), born Tarzana, CA, Aug 25, 1987.

Regis Philbin, 87, television personality ("Live with Regis & Kelly," "Who Wants to Be a Millionaire"), born New York, NY, Aug 25, 1933.

Rachael Ray, 52, chef, cookbook author, television personality ("30 Minute Meals," "$40 a Day"), born Cape Cod, MA, Aug 25, 1968.

John Savage, 71, actor (*The Deer Hunter, Hair*), born Long Island, NY, Aug 25, 1949.

Claudia Schiffer, 50, model, born Rheinberg, Germany, Aug 25, 1970.

Wayne Shorter, 87, jazz musician, born Newark, NJ, Aug 25, 1933.

Gene Simmons, 71, musician (KISS), actor, born Chaim Witz at Haifa, Israel, Aug 25, 1949.

Alexander Skarsgård, 44, actor (*The Legend of Tarzan*, "Big Little Lies," "True Blood"), born Stockholm, Sweden, Aug 25, 1976.

Tom Skerritt, 87, actor ("Picket Fences," *Steel Magnolias*), born Detroit, MI, Aug 25, 1933.

Blair Underwood, 56, actor ("One Life to Live," "LA Law"), born Tacoma, WA, Aug 25, 1964.

Ally Walker, 59, actress ("The Profiler"), born Tullahoma, TN, Aug 25, 1961.

Joanne Whalley, 56, actress ("The Singing Detective"; stage: *What the Butler Saw*), born Manchester, England, Aug 25, 1964.

Charles Wright, 85, former poet laureate of the US (2014–15), born Pickwick Dam, TN, Aug 25, 1935.

Joe Wright, 48, film director (*Darkest Hour, Atonement, Pride and Prejudice*), born London, England, Aug 25, 1972.

August 26 — Wednesday

DAY 239　　　　　　　　　　　　**127 REMAINING**

ALBERT OF SAXE-COBURG-GOTHA: BIRTH ANNIVERSARY. Aug 26, 1819. Born at Rosenau, Germany, Albert is known for his marriage to England's Queen Victoria (1840). Though an arranged marriage, it was one of love and devotion, with Albert serving as Victoria's confidant, chief adviser and personal secretary; he was made Prince Consort in 1857. Her confinement during the births of their nine children necessitated his more active, visible involvement in running the empire and family. At his urging, Victoria transformed the monarchy to a politically neutral constitutional monarchy, and the royal family became a moral force that exemplified Victorian ideals. Albert died of typhoid fever on Dec 14, 1861, at Windsor, England, and Victoria went into prolonged mourning.

BRADLEE, BENJAMIN: BIRTH ANNIVERSARY. Aug 26, 1921. Born at Boston, MA, Bradlee was one of the 20th century's most revered newspaper editors. His early career in journalism included work as US Foreign Service press attaché and *Newsweek*'s European and American correspondent. He is best known for his lengthy tenure as editor of the *Washington Post* (1965–91), where he oversaw Woodward and Bernstein's groundbreaking coverage of the Watergate scandal, the publication of the Pentagon Papers and the paper's receipt of 17 Pulitzer Prizes. In 1991 Bradlee became the paper's vice president, a position in which he remained until his death on Oct 21, 2014, at Washington, DC.

CORTÁZAR, JULIO: BIRTH ANNIVERSARY. Aug 26, 1914. Argentine novelist, short-story writer, translator, born at Brussels, Belgium, most famous for *Hopscotch* (1963), a wildly inventive novel in which readers can piece together their own narrative(s). Author of the short story that served as the basis for the 1966 film *Blow-Up*. "For me, literature is a form of play," he explained in an interview. "It's a game, but it's a game one can put one's life into. One can do everything for that game." He died Feb 12, 1984, at Paris, France, where he had lived many years in exile from Argentina's military dictatorships.

DE FOREST, LEE: BIRTH ANNIVERSARY. Aug 26, 1873. American inventor of the electron tube, the radio knife for surgery and the photoelectric cell; a pioneer in the creation of talking pictures and television. Born at Council Bluffs, IA, De Forest was holder of hundreds of patents but is perhaps best remembered by the moniker he gave himself in the title of his autobiography, *Father of Radio*, published in 1950. So unbelievable was the idea of wireless radio broadcasting that De Forest was accused of fraud and arrested for selling stock to underwrite the invention that later was to become an essential part of daily life. De Forest died at Hollywood, CA, June 30, 1961.

FIRST BASEBALL GAMES TELEVISED: ANNIVERSARY. Aug 26, 1939. WXBS television, New York City, broadcast the first major league baseball games—a doubleheader between the Cincinnati Reds and the Brooklyn Dodgers at Ebbets Field. Announcer Red Barber interviewed Leo Durocher, manager of the Dodgers, and William McKechnie, manager of the Reds, between games.

ISHERWOOD, CHRISTOPHER: BIRTH ANNIVERSARY. Aug 26, 1904. Author of short stories, plays and novels, Christopher William Isherwood was born at High Lane, Cheshire, England. The play and motion picture *I Am a Camera* and the musical *Cabaret* were based on the short story "Sally Bowles" in his collection from the 1930s titled *Goodbye to Berlin*, which contained the line "I am a camera with its shutter open, quite passive, recording, not thinking." Isherwood died at Santa Monica, CA, Jan 4, 1986.

KRAKATOA ERUPTION: ANNIVERSARY. Aug 26, 1883. Anniversary of the biggest explosion in historic times. The eruption of the Indonesian volcanic island Krakatoa (Krakatau) was heard 3,000 miles away, created tidal waves 120 feet high (killing 36,000 people), hurled five cubic miles of earth fragments into the air (some to a height of 50 miles) and affected the oceans and the atmosphere for years.

MONTGOLFIER, JOSEPH MICHEL: BIRTH ANNIVERSARY. Aug 26, 1740. French merchant and inventor, born at Vidalonlez-Annonay, France, who, with his brother Jacques Etienne in November 1782, conducted experiments with paper and fabric bags filled with smoke and hot air, which led to the invention of the hot-air balloon and man's first flight. Died at Balaruc-les-Bains, France, June 26, 1810. See also: "Montgolfier, Jacques Etienne: Birth Anniversary" (Jan 7), "First Balloon Flight: Anniversary" (June 5) and "Aviation History Month" (Nov 1).

NAMIBIA: HEROES' DAY. Aug 26. National holiday. Commemorates beginning of struggle for independence in 1966.

NATIONAL DOG DAY. Aug 26. A day to celebrate dogs for all they do in our lives, the joy they bring us and the unconditional love they give us. It is also a day to highlight the plight of dogs in shelters and the need for adoption as well as spaying and neutering. Annually, Aug 26—the date in 1980 when the founder's father adopted the family's first dog, Sheltie. For info: Colleen Paige. Web: www.nationaldogday.com.

SABIN, ALBERT BRUCE: BIRTH ANNIVERSARY. Aug 26, 1906. American medical researcher Albert Bruce Sabin was born at

	S	M	T	W	T	F	S
August							1
	2	3	4	5	6	7	8
2020	9	10	11	12	13	14	15
	16	17	18	19	20	21	22
	23	24	25	26	27	28	29
	30	31					

Bialystok, Poland. He is most noted for his oral vaccine for polio, which replaced Jonas Salk's injected vaccine because Sabin's provided lifetime protection. He was awarded the US National Medal of Science in 1971. Sabin died Mar 3, 1993, at Washington, DC.

SPAIN: LA TOMATINA. Aug 26. Buñol (near Valencia). The world's biggest food fight takes place today as 35,000 revelers hurl 120 tons of tomatoes at each other (and the town) for two hours. La Tomatina ("Tomato Festival") occurs annually the last Wednesday in August. Festivities kick off with a competition to see who can reach a ham at the top of a greased pole. With the ham secured, the trucks arrive with tomatoes.

★WOMEN'S EQUALITY DAY. Aug 26. Presidential Proclamation issued in 1973 and 1974 at request and since 1975 without request. Annually, Aug 26.

WOMEN'S EQUALITY DAY. Aug 26. Anniversary of certification as part of US Constitution, in 1920, of the 19th Amendment, which prohibits discrimination on the basis of sex with regard to voting. Congresswoman Bella Abzug's bill to designate Aug 26 of each year as "Women's Equality Day" in August 1974 became Public Law 93–382.

🎂 BIRTHDAYS TODAY

Christopher Burke, 55, actor ("Life Goes On"), born New York, NY, Aug 26, 1965.

Mike Colter, 44, actor ("Luke Cage," "Jessica Jones," "The Good Wife," *Million Dollar Baby*), born Columbia, SC, Aug 26, 1976.

Macaulay Culkin, 40, actor (*Home Alone, My Girl*), born New York, NY, Aug 26, 1980.

James Harden, 31, basketball player, born Los Angeles, CA, Aug 26, 1989.

Branford Marsalis, 60, musician, born Beaux Bridge, LA, Aug 26, 1960.

Melissa McCarthy, 50, actress (*Spy, St. Vincent, Bridesmaids*, "Mike & Molly"), born Plainfield, IL, Aug 26, 1970.

Chris Pine, 40, actor (Star Trek films, *Jack Ryan: Shadow Recruit*), born Los Angeles, CA, Aug 26, 1980.

August 27 — Thursday

DAY 240   **126 REMAINING**

ALASKA STATE FAIR. Aug 27–Sept 7. Palmer, AK. Everybody's welcome at the Alaska State Fair, home of record-setting giant vegetables and beautiful flower gardens. Nestled in the heart of the Chugach Mountains, in the fertile Matanuska-Susitna Valley, the fairgrounds are just an hour north of Anchorage. Each fall, the fair provides a setting for Alaska's last blast of summer, a showcase for Alaska's uniqueness and beauty. Visit the fair and enjoy year-round events and services, including horse shows, concerts, trade shows, facility rentals and winter RV and boat storage. Please note that the fairgrounds are now smoke free. Annually, beginning on a Thursday 12 days before and up to Labor Day. Est attendance: 300,000. For info: Alaska State Fair, Inc, 2075 Glenn Hwy, Palmer, AK 99645. Phone: (907) 745-4827 or (800) 850-FAIR. Fax: (907) 746-2699. E-mail: info@alaskastatefair.org. Web: www.alaskastatefair.org.

DAWES, CHARLES GATES: BIRTH ANNIVERSARY. Aug 27, 1865. 30th vice president of the US (1925–29), born at Marietta, OH. Won the Nobel Peace Prize in 1925 for the Dawes Plan for German reparations. Died at Evanston, IL, Apr 23, 1951.

DREISER, THEODORE: BIRTH ANNIVERSARY. Aug 27, 1871. American novelist Theodore Dreiser was born at Terre Haute, IN. He was an exponent of American naturalism in literature. His first novel, *Sister Carrie* (1900), was suppressed by his publisher on moral grounds. Dreiser's finest achievement is widely considered to be his novel *An American Tragedy* (1925). He died Dec 28, 1945, at Hollywood, CA.

"THE DUCHESS" WHO WASN'T DAY. Aug 27. At least once on this day repeat the following now-famous quotation from the novel *Molly Bawn*: "Beauty is in the eye of the beholder." As the author of those words, Margaret Wolfe Hungerford often wrote under the pseudonym "The Duchess," which was the title of her most popular novel—hence the name of this event. A popular romance novelist with about 40 books published, Hungerford was born at Rosscarbery, County Cork, Ireland, on Aug 27, 1850; she died at Bandon, County Cork, in 1897. (Originated by the late Peggy Shirley.)

FIRST COMMERCIAL OIL WELL: ANNIVERSARY. Aug 27, 1859. W.A. "Uncle Billy" Smith discovered oil in a shaft being sunk by Colonel E.L. Drake at Titusville, in western Pennsylvania. Drilling had reached 69 feet 6 inches, when Smith saw a dark film floating on the water below the derrick floor. Soon 20 barrels of crude were being pumped each day. The first oil was refined to make kerosene for lighting, replacing whale oil. Later it was refined to make gasoline for cars. The first gas station opened in 1907.

HAMLIN, HANNIBAL: BIRTH ANNIVERSARY. Aug 27, 1809. 15th vice president of the US (1861–65), born at Paris, ME. Died at Bangor, ME, July 4, 1891.

HEGEL, GEORG WILHELM FRIEDRICH: 150th BIRTH ANNIVERSARY. Aug 27, 1770. Born at Stuttgart, Germany, Hegel was the last of the great German Idealist philosophers. In *Phenomenology of Spirit* (1807), his most discussed work, Hegel develops his eponymous dialectical method. The three editions of *Encyclopedia of Philosophical Sciences* (1817, 1827, 1830) presents his entire mature philosophy. A prolific writer, his oeuvre is widely regarded as one of philosophy's most challenging. A response to Kantian philosophy, Hegelian philosophy influenced Kierkegaard, Sartre and Existentialism, Marxism and the Positivists. Hegel died of cholera Nov 14, 1831, at Berlin, Germany.

HOTTER 'N HELL HUNDRED BIKE RACE. Aug 27–30. Wichita Falls, TX. 39th annual. Cyclists of all ages participate in the largest sanctioned century ride in the US. Treks of 100, 50 or 25 miles. Est attendance: 13,000. For info: Hotter 'N Hell Hundred, PO Box 2096, Wichita Falls, TX 76307. Phone: (940) 322-3223. E-mail: info@hh100.org. Web: www.hh100.org.

JOHNSON, LYNDON BAINES: BIRTH ANNIVERSARY. Aug 27, 1908. The 36th president of the US succeeded to the presidency following the assassination of John F. Kennedy. Johnson's term of office: Nov 22, 1963–Jan 20, 1969. In 1964 he said: "The challenge of the next half century is whether we have the wisdom to use [our] wealth to enrich and elevate our national life—and to advance the quality of American civilization." Johnson was born near Stonewall, TX, and died at San Antonio, TX, Jan 22, 1973. His birthday is observed as a holiday in Texas.

MARYLAND STATE FAIR. Aug 27–Sept 7. Timonium, MD. Home arts, agricultural and livestock presentations, midway rides and games, live entertainment and Thoroughbred horse racing. Est attendance: 500,000. For info: Ms Edie Bernier, Maryland State Fair, PO Box 188, Timonium, MD 21094. Phone: (410) 252-0200,

ext 227. E-mail: msfair@msn.com. Web: www.marylandstatefair.com.

MINNESOTA STATE FAIR. Aug 27–Sept 7. St. Paul, MN. Twelve days of fun ending on Labor Day. Major entertainers, agricultural displays, arts, crafts, food, carnival rides, animal judging and performances. Est attendance: 2,000,000. For info: Minnesota State Fair, 1265 Snelling Ave N, St. Paul, MN 55108-3099. Phone: (651) 288-4400. E-mail: fairinfo@mnstatefair.org. Web: www.mnstatefair.org.

MOLDOVA: INDEPENDENCE DAY. Aug 27. Republic of Moldova. Moldova declared its independence from the Soviet Union in 1991.

MOTHER TERESA: BIRTH ANNIVERSARY. Aug 27, 1910. Albanian Roman Catholic nun born Agnes Gonxha Bojaxhiu at Skopje, Macedonia. She founded the Order of the Missionaries of Charity, which cares for the destitute people of Calcutta, India, and other places. She won the Nobel Peace Prize in 1979. She died at Calcutta, Sept 5, 1997.

MOUNTBATTEN, LOUIS: ASSASSINATION ANNIVERSARY. Aug 27, 1979. Lord Mountbatten (Louis Francis Albert Victor Nicholas Mountbatten), celebrated British war hero, cousin of Queen Elizabeth II, last viceroy of India, was killed by a bomb, along with his 14-year-old grandson and two others, while on his yacht in Donegal Bay off the coast of Ireland, on Aug 27, 1979. Provisional Irish Republican Army claimed responsibility for the explosion and for the killing of 18 British soldiers later the same day, deepening the crisis and conflict between Protestants and Catholics and between England and Ireland. Lord Mountbatten was born at Windsor, England, June 25, 1900.

OREGON STATE FAIR. Aug 27–Sept 7. Salem, OR. 156th annual. Exhibits, products and displays illustrate Oregon's role as one of the nation's major agricultural and recreational states. Floral gardens, sports and recreation activities, sustainable energy displays, carnival, entertainment, horse show and food. Annually, 12 days before and including Labor Day. Est attendance: 360,000. For info: Oregon State Fair, 2330 17th St NE, Salem, OR 97301-0601. Phone: (971) 701-6567. E-mail: info@oregonstatefair.org. Web: www.oregonstatefair.org.

RAYE, MARTHA: BIRTH ANNIVERSARY. Aug 27, 1916. Born at Butte, MT, Martha Raye began singing at age three. Raye performed for American servicemen during three wars and received the Jean Hersholt Humanitarian Award from the Academy of Motion Picture Arts and Sciences (1969) for that service. She appeared in her first film, *Rhythm on the Range*, in 1936. She had several TV shows, including "The Martha Raye Show" (1955–56). In 1993 Raye was awarded the Presidential Medal of Freedom. Martha Raye died Oct 19, 1994, at Los Angeles, CA.

🎂 BIRTHDAYS TODAY

Patrick J. Adams, 39, actor (*Old School*, "Suits," "Luck"), born Toronto, ON, Canada, Aug 27, 1981.

Sarah Chalke, 44, actress ("Roseanne," "Scrubs"), born Ottawa, ON, Canada, Aug 27, 1976.

Tom Ford, 59, fashion designer, filmmaker/screenwriter (*Nocturnal Animals*, *A Single Man*), born Austin, TX, Aug 27, 1961.

Carlos Moya, 44, tennis player, born Palma, Majorca, Spain, Aug 27, 1976.

Aaron Paul, 41, actor ("Big Love," Emmy for "Breaking Bad"), born Aaron Paul Sturtevant at Emmett, ID, Aug 27, 1979.

	S	M	T	W	T	F	S
August							1
	2	3	4	5	6	7	8
2020	9	10	11	12	13	14	15
	16	17	18	19	20	21	22
	23	24	25	26	27	28	29
	30	31					

Paul Reubens, 68, actor, writer ("Pee-Wee's Playhouse," *Pee-Wee's Big Adventure*), born Peekskill, NY, Aug 27, 1952.

Tommy Sands, 83, singer, born Chicago, IL, Aug 27, 1937.

Jim Thome, 50, former baseball player, born Peoria, IL, Aug 27, 1970.

Tuesday Weld, 77, actress ("The Many Loves of Dobie Gillis," *Looking for Mr Goodbar*), born Susan Kerr at New York, NY, Aug 27, 1943.

Chandra Wilson, 51, actress ("Grey's Anatomy"), born Houston, TX, Aug 27, 1969.

Michael Wolff, 67, journalist, author (*Fire and Fury*, *The Man Who Owns the News*), born Paterson, NJ, Aug 27, 1953.

August 28 — Friday

DAY 241   **125 REMAINING**

BOYER, CHARLES: BIRTH ANNIVERSARY. Aug 28, 1897. Film star (*Mayerling*, *Love Affair*, *Conquest*, *Algiers*, *Gaslight*), born at Figeac, France. Boyer was nominated four times for Best Actor Oscars. He died at Phoenix, AZ, Aug 26, 1978.

COLORADO STATE FAIR. Aug 28–Sept 7. State Fairgrounds, Pueblo, CO. First held in 1869 as a horse exhibition, the Colorado State Fair is one of the nation's oldest Western fairs; it is also Colorado's largest summer event. Family fun, top-name entertainment, lots of food and festivities. Annually, beginning the Friday 11 days before and up to Labor Day. Est attendance: 485,000. For info: Colorado State Fair, 1001 Beulah Ave, Pueblo, CO 81004. Phone: (719) 561-8484. Web: www.coloradostatefair.com.

FEAST OF SAINT AUGUSTINE. Aug 28. Bishop of Hippo, author of *Confessions* and *The City of God*, born Nov 13, 354, at Tagaste, in what is now Algeria. Died Aug 28, 430, at Hippo, also in North Africa.

GOETHE, JOHANN WOLFGANG VON: BIRTH ANNIVERSARY. Aug 28, 1749. German author, poet, dramatist and philosopher, born at Frankfurt, Germany. Died Mar 22, 1832, at Weimar, Germany. Best known for the novels *The Sorrows of Young Werther* and *Wilheim Meister* and the play *Faust*.

HAYES, LUCY WARE WEBB: BIRTH ANNIVERSARY. Aug 28, 1831. Wife of Rutherford Birchard Hayes, 19th president of the US, born at Chillicothe, OH. Died at Fremont, OH, June 25, 1889. She was nicknamed "Lemonade Lucy" because she and the president, both abstainers, served no alcoholic beverages at White House receptions.

KIRBY, JACK: BIRTH ANNIVERSARY. Aug 28, 1917. One of the most important, prolific and influential comic book artists/writers of the Golden Age and Silver Age, born Jacob Kurtzberg at New York City. He created or cocreated such famous characters as Captain America, Incredible Hulk, Thor, Iron Man, Fantastic Four, X-Men, New Gods and Kamandi. Kirby died Feb 6, 1994, at Thousand Oaks, CA.

LE FANU, SHERIDAN: BIRTH ANNIVERSARY. Aug 28, 1814. Popular Victorian author of the supernatural and macabre, born at Dublin, Ireland. Best known for the gothic novel *Uncle Silas* (1864) and the novella *Carmilla* (1872), about a female vampire. Le Fanu, who was also a journal editor, died at Dublin on Feb 7, 1873.

MARCH ON WASHINGTON: ANNIVERSARY. Aug 28, 1963. More than 250,000 people attended this civil rights rally at Washington, DC, at which Reverend Dr. Martin Luther King, Jr, made his famous "I Have a Dream" speech.

NATIONAL WEED OUT HATE DAY. Aug 28. This day offers us a chance to tap into the spirit of Dr. Martin Luther King, Jr, on the anniversary of his "I Have a Dream" speech in 1963. Since that day, we have come a long way, but there remain all too many weed seeds of hatred, racism, anti-Semitism and Islamophobia. This day calls for bipartisan action for rooting out such divisive weeds. All 2020 electoral candidates are urged to weed out hate with voters for our communities, our country and our planet. For info: Marc Daniels, Weed Out Hate, 4001 Lavender Ln, Springfield, IL 62711. Phone: (217) 726-5938. Web: www.weedouthate.org.

NEBRASKA STATE FAIR. Aug 28–Sept 7. Grand Island, NE. 151st annual. Showcasing Nebraska pride, people and products. Food booths, variety of entertainment, amusement rides, concerts, livestock shows and tractor pulls. Est attendance: 300,000. For info: Nebraska State Fair, 501 E Fonner Park Rd, Ste 200, Grand Island, NE 68801. Phone: (308) 382-1620. E-mail: contact@statefair.org. Web: www.statefair.org.

NEW YORK STATE FAIR. Aug 28–Sept 7. Syracuse, NY. 175th edition. Agricultural and livestock competitions, top-name entertainment, the International Horse Show, business and industrial exhibits, the midway and ethnic presentations. Annually, beginning the Thursday 12 days before and up to Labor Day. Est attendance: 1,000,000. For info: The Great New York State Fair, 581 State Fair Blvd, Syracuse, NY 13209. Phone: (315) 487-7711 or (800) 475-FAIR. Fax: (315) 487-9260. Web: www.nysfair.org.

O'CONNOR, DONALD: 95th BIRTH ANNIVERSARY. Aug 28, 1925. Singer, dancer and vaudeville performer Donald O'Connor was born into a family of circus performers at Chicago, IL. He starred opposite Francis the Mule in a string of very successful film comedies throughout the 1950s but is best remembered for his role opposite Gene Kelly and Debbie Reynolds in *Singin' in the Rain* (1952). O'Connor died Sept 28, 2003, at Woodland Hills, CA.

OREGON TRAIL RODEO. Aug 28–30. Hastings, NE. PRCA-sponsored rodeo. Est attendance: 6,500. For info: Jolene Laux, Oregon Trail Rodeo, 947 S Baltimore, Hastings, NE 68901. Phone: (402) 462-3247. Fax: (402) 462-4731. Web: www.adamscountyfairgrounds.com.

PETERSON, ROGER TORY: BIRTH ANNIVERSARY. Aug 28, 1908. Naturalist, author of *A Field Guide to Birds*, born at Jamestown, NY. Peterson died at Old Lyme, CT, July 28, 1996.

RACE YOUR MOUSE AROUND THE ICONS DAY. Aug 28. While you're waiting for any number of endless items to finally come up on your screen, don't just sit there. Race your mouse in and around the icons. You'll feel peppy for doing it. (©2006 by WH.) For info: Thomas & Ruth Roy, Wellcat Holidays, 2418 Long Ln, Lebanon, PA 17046. Phone: (717) 279-0184. E-mail: info@wellcat.com. Web: www.wellcat.com.

RADIO COMMERCIALS: ANNIVERSARY. Aug 28, 1922. Broadcasters realized radio could earn profits from the sale of advertising time. WEAF in New York ran a commercial "spot," which was sponsored by the Queensboro Realty Corporation of Jackson Heights to promote Hawthorne Court, a group of apartment buildings at Queens. The commercial rate was $100 for 10 minutes.

SETON, ELIZABETH ANN BAYLEY: BIRTH ANNIVERSARY. Aug 28, 1774. First American-born saint was born at New York, NY. Seton died Jan 4, 1821, at Emmitsburg, MD. See also: "Seton, Elizabeth Ann Bayley: Feast Day" (Jan 4).

TILL, EMMETT: 65th DEATH ANNIVERSARY. Aug 28, 1955. Emmett Till, a 14-year-old African-American teenager from Chicago visiting relatives in Money, MS, was murdered on this date by a group of white men angry at Till's reported flirtation with a white woman. The Till murder and the acquittal of two of the men involved brought the nation's attention to racial tensions in the South and helped spark civil rights protests later—most famously, Rosa Parks's refusal to give up her seat to a white man on a municipal bus in Montgomery, AL, in December of that year.

🎂 BIRTHDAYS TODAY

Ai Weiwei, 63, artist, political activist, born Beijing, China, Aug 28, 1957.

Rita Dove, 68, poet (Pulitzer Prize for *Thomas and Beulah*), former poet laureate of the US (1993–95), dramatist, professor, born Akron, OH, Aug 28, 1952.

Ronald Ames (Ron) Guidry, 70, former baseball player, born Lafayette, LA, Aug 28, 1950.

Scott Hamilton, 62, sportscaster, Olympic figure skater, born Toledo, OH, Aug 28, 1958.

Armie Hammer, 34, actor (*Call Me by Your Name*, *The Man from U.N.C.L.E.*, *The Lone Ranger*, *The Social Network*), born Los Angeles, CA, Aug 28, 1986.

Paul Martin, 82, 21st prime minister of Canada (2003–6), born Windsor, ON, Canada, Aug 28, 1938.

Lou Piniella, 77, former baseball manager, former player, born Tampa, FL, Aug 28, 1943.

Jason Priestley, 51, actor ("Beverly Hills 90210," *Tombstone*), born Vancouver, BC, Canada, Aug 28, 1969.

Carlos Quentin, 38, baseball player, born Bellflower, CA, Aug 28, 1982.

LeAnn Rimes, 38, singer, born Jackson, MS, Aug 28, 1982.

Emma Samms, 60, actress ("General Hospital," "Dynasty"), born Emma Samuelson at London, England, Aug 28, 1960.

David Soul, 74, actor ("Starsky and Hutch," *Salem's Lot*), singer, born David Solberg at Chicago, IL, Aug 28, 1946.

Daniel Stern, 63, actor (*City Slickers*, *Home Alone*), born Bethesda, MD, Aug 28, 1957.

Shania Twain, 55, country singer, born Eileen Twain at Windsor, ON, Canada, Aug 28, 1965.

Quvenzhané Wallis, 17, actress (*Annie*, *Beasts of the Southern Wild*), born Houma, LA, Aug 28, 2003.

August 29 — Saturday

DAY 242   **124 REMAINING**

"ACCORDING TO HOYLE" DAY (EDMOND HOYLE DEATH ANNIVERSARY). Aug 29, 1769. A day to remember Edmond Hoyle and a day for fun and games *according to the rules*. He is believed to have studied law. For many years he lived at London, England, and gave instructions in the playing of games. His "Short Treatise" on the game of whist (published in 1742) became a model guide to the rules of the game. Hoyle's name became synonymous with the idea of correct play according to the rules, and the phrase "according to Hoyle" became a part of the English language. Hoyle was born at London about 1672 and died there.

AMISTAD SEIZED: ANNIVERSARY. Aug 29, 1839. In January 1839, 53 Africans were abducted near modern-day Sierra Leone, taken to Cuba and sold as slaves. While being transferred to another part of the island on the ship *Amistad*, the Africans, led by Cinque, grabbed control of the ship, telling the surviving crew to take them back to Africa. However, the crew secretly changed course, and the ship sailed to Long Island, NY, where it and its "cargo" were seized as salvage. The *Amistad* was towed to New Haven, CT, where the Africans were imprisoned and a lengthy legal battle began to determine if they were property to be returned to Cuba, salvage for the US Coast Guard or free men. John Quincy Adams took their case all the way to the Supreme Court, where on Mar 9, 1841, it was determined that they were free and could return to Africa.

ASHURA: TENTH DAY. Aug 29. Islamic calendar date: Muharram 10, 1442. For Shia Muslims, commemorates death of Muhammad's grandson at the Battle of Karbala. A time of fasting, reflection and meditation. Jews of Medina fasted on the 10th day in remembrance of their salvation from Pharaoh. Different methods for "anticipating" the visibility of the new moon crescent at Mecca are used by different Muslim groups, so date can vary one to two days. Began at sunset the preceding day.

BERGMAN, INGRID: BIRTH ANNIVERSARY. Aug 29, 1915. One of cinema's greatest actresses. Bergman was born at Stockholm, Sweden, and died at London, England, on her 67th birthday, Aug 29, 1982. Three-time Academy Award winner for *Gaslight, Anastasia* and *Murder on the Orient Express*. Controversy over her personal life made her and her films unpopular to American audiences during an interval of several years between periods of awards and adulation.

CORVETTE CROSSROADS AUTO SHOW. Aug 29. Mackinaw City, MI. Show and visitor viewing, awards and parade across the Mackinac Bridge on Saturday at 7 PM. Est attendance: 4,000. For info: Corvette Show, PO Box 856, Mackinaw City, MI 49701. Phone: (231) 436-5574. Web: www.mackinawchamber.com.

DENMARK: HO SHEEP MARKET. Aug 29. Ho. The village of Ho, near Esbjerg, holds its annual sheep market on the last Saturday in August, when some 50,000 people visit the fair.

ENGLAND: NOTTING HILL CARNIVAL. Aug 29–31. London. The biggest street carnival in Europe: annual Caribbean and multicultural celebration on the streets of West London. Three-mile route for spectacular costume bands, steel bands, calypsonians and soca-on-the-move. More than 35 sound systems, live stages featuring top national and international musicians, hundreds of street-trading stalls selling food from all over the world and arts and crafts. Free event. Annually, the Saturday, Sunday and Monday of the August bank holiday weekend. Est attendance: 2,000,000. For info: The Notting Hill Carnival. Web: www.the-londonnottinghillcarnival.com.

"THE FUGITIVE" FINALE: ANNIVERSARY. Aug 29, 1967. David Janssen's Emmy Award–winning adventure series about a wrongly convicted doctor on the run concluded in a two-part episode whose second part was the highest-rated show ever broadcast up to that time. An estimated 78 million people watched "The Judgment": the one-armed man confessed and Dr. Richard Kimble was found innocent of murdering his wife. (The ratings record held until 1980, when "Dallas" revealed who shot J.R.)

HOLMES, OLIVER WENDELL, SR: BIRTH ANNIVERSARY. Aug 29, 1809. Physician and author, father of Supreme Court Justice Oliver Wendell Holmes, Jr. The elder Holmes was born at Cambridge,

MA. Died at Boston, MA, Oct 7, 1894. "A moment's insight," he wrote, "is sometimes worth a life's experience."

HURRICANE KATRINA STRIKES GULF COAST: 15th ANNIVERSARY. Aug 29, 2005. After hitting the southern Florida coast on Aug 25, Hurricane Katrina moved into the Gulf of Mexico and grew into one of the most devastating hurricanes in US history. On this date, as a Category 3 storm, it struck Buras, LA, and surrounding areas, destroying communities up and down the Gulf Coast. Levees in New Orleans were breached, and within two days more than 80 percent of the city was underwater, stranding tens of thousands of people. The death toll in Louisiana, Mississippi, Alabama and Florida was more than 1,300, with more than 1,000 fatalities coming in Louisiana. Thousands remained missing at the end of 2005. The estimated one million people evacuated before and after the storm accounted for the largest movement of people in the US since the Great Depression and the Civil War. And with $100 billion to $200 billion in damage over 90,000 square miles, Hurricane Katrina was the most expensive natural disaster in US history.

INTERNATIONAL BAT NIGHT. Aug 29–30. 24th annual. Originally started by EUROBATS, this special day is now observed in more than 30 countries. Nature conservation agencies pass on information to the public about the way bats live and their needs with presentations, exhibitions and bat walks, often offering the opportunity to listen to bat sounds with the support of ultrasound technology. Annually, the last full weekend in August (although local organizers sometimes choose other dates). For info: UNEP/EUROBATS, United Nations Campus, Platz der Vereinten Nationen 1, D-53113 Bonn, Germany. E-mail: eurobats@eurobats.org. Web: www.eurobats.org.

JACKSON, MICHAEL: BIRTH ANNIVERSARY. Aug 29, 1958. The self-styled "King of Pop," born at Gary, IN. Rising from humble beginnings to become a child star at Motown with his older brothers as the Jackson 5, he later launched a solo career and achieved enormous success as both a singer and dancer/choreographer. He changed the face of music videos with his inventive dance sequences, and his albums *Off the Wall, Bad* and *Thriller* are among the bestselling of all time. His musical legacy was almost overshadowed by his frequent plastic surgeries, eccentric behavior and legal difficulties, but he remained one of the most popular artists in the world and his influence on the musical landscape of the 1970s and '80s was unsurpassed. He died at Los Angeles, CA, June 25, 2009.

LOCKE, JOHN: BIRTH ANNIVERSARY. Aug 29, 1632. (Old Style date.) English philosopher, founder of philosophical liberalism, born at Wrington, England. His ideas influenced the American colonists and were enshrined in the Constitution. Locke died at Essex, England, Oct 28, 1704 (OS).

MARTYRDOM OF SAINT JOHN THE BAPTIST. Aug 29. Commemorates the martyrdom of Saint John the Baptist, beheaded upon order from King Herod, about AD 29.

MARYLAND RENAISSANCE FESTIVAL. Aug 29–Oct 25 (Saturdays, Sundays and Labor Day). Annapolis, MD. A 16th-century English festival with Henry VIII, sword swallowers, magicians, authentic jousting, juggling, music, theater, games, food and crafts. Est attendance: 298,000. For info: Jules Smith, Maryland Renaissance Fest, PO Box 315, Crownsville, MD 21032. Phone: (410) 266-7304. Fax: (410) 573-1508. E-mail: info@rennfest.com. Web: www.MarylandRenaissanceFestival.com.

		S	M	T	W	T	F	S
August								1
		2	3	4	5	6	7	8
2020		9	10	11	12	13	14	15
		16	17	18	19	20	21	22
		23	24	25	26	27	28	29
		30	31					

MORE HERBS, LESS SALT DAY. Aug 29. It's healthier, zestier and lustier! (©2006 by WH.) For info: Thomas & Ruth Roy, Wellcat Holidays, 2418 Long Ln, Lebanon, PA 17046. Phone: (717) 279-0184. E-mail: info@wellcat.com. Web: www.wellcat.com.

NATIONAL CHAMPIONSHIP CHUCKWAGON RACES. Aug 29–Sept 6. Clinton, AR. 35th annual. Five divisions of chuckwagon races, bronc fanning, Snowy River race, live entertainment, trail rides, barn dance, Western show, Western art, saddles and tack-clothing vendors. Est attendance: 25,000. For info: Dan Eoff, 2848 Shake Rag Rd, Clinton, AR 72031. Phone: (501) 745-8407. E-mail: chuckwag@artelco.com. Web: www.chuckwagonraces.com.

PARKER, CHARLIE: 100th BIRTH ANNIVERSARY. Aug 29, 1920. Jazz giant Charlie "Yardbird" Parker was born at Kansas City, KS. The man who later became known simply as "Bird" was mostly self-taught—on an alto saxophone his mother gave him when he was 11. His career took him from jam sessions in Kansas City to New York (in 1939), where he met Dizzy Gillespie and others who were creating an innovative style of jazz that would become known as bop or bebop. Influential to other jazz artists, instrumentalists and the Beat Generation, Parker was a master improviser dubbed "the cool one" by producer Norman Granz. Parker struggled with mental health issues as well as with alcohol and heroin. He died at Rochester, NY, Mar 12, 1955, at age 34.

***ROYAL GEORGE* SINKS: ANNIVERSARY.** Aug 29, 1782. Prized British battleship *Royal George* sank due to fatal human error in one of the worst maritime disasters in history. While the ship was being repaired at Spithead, the port side was tilted too close to the waterline. A gust of wind lowered the ship even farther, allowing tons of water to flood into its open gun ports. The ship sank within minutes before many of the 1,300 people on board realized what was happening, and more than 900 drowned.

SHAYS'S REBELLION: ANNIVERSARY. Aug 29, 1786. Daniel Shays, veteran of the battles of Lexington, Bunker Hill, Ticonderoga and Saratoga, was one of the leaders of more than 1,000 rebels who sought redress of grievances during the depression days of 1786–87. Beginning on Aug 29, they prevented general court sessions, and on Sept 26 they prevented Supreme Court sessions at Springfield, MA. On Jan 25, 1787, they attacked the federal arsenal at Springfield; Feb 2, Shays's troops were routed and fled. Shays was sentenced to death but pardoned June 13, 1788. Later he received a small pension for services in the American Revolution.

SLOVAKIA: NATIONAL UPRISING DAY. Aug 29. National holiday. Commemorates resistance to Nazi occupation in 1944.

UNITED NATIONS: INTERNATIONAL DAY AGAINST NUCLEAR TESTS. Aug 29. Since 2010, a day to galvanize the United Nations, member states, intergovernmental and nongovernmental organizations, academic institutions, youth networks and the media to inform about, educate on and advocate for the necessity of banning nuclear weapon tests as a valuable step toward achieving a safer world. The General Assembly declared this day to be observed annually on Aug 29 (Res 64/35 of Dec 2, 2009)—commemorating the closure of the Semipalatinsk Nuclear Test site on Aug 29, 1991. For info: United Nations, Dept of Public Info, New York, NY 10017. Web: www.un.org.

US SENIOR AMATEUR (GOLF) CHAMPIONSHIP. Aug 24–Sept 3. Country Club of Detroit, Grosse Pointe Farms, MI. For info: USGA, Golf House, Championship Dept, PO Box 708, Far Hills, NJ 07931. Phone: (908) 234-2300. E-mail: champs@usga.org. Web: www.usga.org.

US WOMEN'S MID-AMATEUR (GOLF) CHAMPIONSHIP. Aug 29–Sept 3. Berkeley Hall Club, Bluffton, SC. For info: USGA, Golf House, Championship Dept, PO Box 708, Far Hills, NJ 07931. Phone: (908) 234-2300. E-mail: champs@usga.org. Web: www.usga.org.

🎂 BIRTHDAYS TODAY

Rebecca De Mornay, 58, actress (*Risky Business, The Hand That Rocks the Cradle*), born Santa Rosa, CA, Aug 29, 1962.

William Friedkin, 81, filmmaker (Oscar for *The French Connection*; *The Exorcist*), born Chicago, IL, Aug 29, 1939.

Richard Gere, 71, actor (*Chicago, An Officer and a Gentleman, Pretty Woman*), born Philadelphia, PA, Aug 29, 1949.

Neil Gorsuch, 53, Associate Justice of the US, born Denver, CO, Aug 29, 1967.

Elliott Gould, 82, actor (*M*A*S*H, The Long Goodbye*), born Elliott Goldstein at Brooklyn, NY, Aug 29, 1938.

Pablo Mastroeni, 44, soccer coach and former player, born Mendoza, Argentina, Aug 29, 1976.

Lea Michele, 34, actress ("Glee"; stage: *Spring Awakening*), born the Bronx, NY, Aug 29, 1986.

Mark Morris, 64, choreographer, dancer, born Seattle, WA, Aug 29, 1956.

Roy Oswalt, 43, baseball player, born Kosciusko, MS, Aug 29, 1977.

Liam Payne, 27, singer (One Direction), born Wolverhampton, England, Aug 29, 1993.

William Edward (Will) Perdue III, 55, former basketball player, born Melbourne, FL, Aug 29, 1965.

Jay Ryan, 39, actor ("Beauty and the Beast"), born Auckland, New Zealand, Aug 29, 1981.

Pierre Turgeon, 51, former hockey player, born Rouyn, QC, Canada, Aug 29, 1969.

August 30 — Sunday

DAY 243   **123 REMAINING**

ARTHUR, ELLEN LEWIS HERNDON: BIRTH ANNIVERSARY. Aug 30, 1837. Wife of Chester Alan Arthur, 21st president of the US, born at Fredericksburg, VA. Died at New York, Jan 12, 1880.

BURNING MAN 2020. Aug 30–Sept 7. Black Rock Desert, NV. A temporary art community in the desert. On the Saturday of this annual experiment in radical self-expression, a 50-foot statue will be burned. Participants must bring all the necessities for survival, including food, water and shelter. Must have ticket to participate in this private event. For info: Burning Man. Web: www.burningman.org.

FAMILY DAY IN TENNESSEE. Aug 30. Observed annually on the last Sunday in August.

FIRST WHITE HOUSE PRESIDENTIAL BABY: BIRTH ANNIVERSARY. Aug 30, 1893. Frances Folsom Cleveland (Mrs Grover Cleveland) was the first presidential wife to have a baby at the White House when she gave birth to a baby girl (Esther). The first child ever born in the White House was a grandson to Thomas Jefferson in 1806.

HUEY P. LONG DAY. Aug 30. A legal holiday in Louisiana.

LONG, HUEY PIERCE: BIRTH ANNIVERSARY. Aug 30, 1893. Louisiana politician, known as the "Kingfish," elected governor 1928 and US

senator 1930, born at Winnfield, LA. Dictatorial and flamboyant, Long became a potential contender for the US presidency with his "Share Our Wealth: Every Man a King" plan (which would have guaranteed every family $5,000 a year and confiscated personal annual income over $1 million and inheritances over $5 million). Long was shot (by Dr. Carl Austin Weiss) at the Louisiana State Capitol, Baton Rouge, on Sept 8, 1935, and died two days later, at age 42. Huey P. Long Day is observed as a rotating Louisiana state holiday on his birth anniversary, Aug 30.

MACMURRAY, FRED: BIRTH ANNIVERSARY. Aug 30, 1908. Fred MacMurray was born at Kankakee, IL. His film and television career included a wide variety of roles, ranging from comedy (*The Absent-Minded Professor, Son of Flubber, The Shaggy Dog, The Happiest Millionaire*) to serious drama (*The Caine Mutiny, Fair Wind to Java, Double Indemnity*). During 1960–72 he portrayed the father on "My Three Sons," which is second only to "Ozzie and Harriet" as network TV's longest-running family sitcom. He died Nov 5, 1991, at Santa Monica, CA.

PERU: SAINT ROSE OF LIMA DAY. Aug 30. Saint Rose of Lima was the first saint of the Western Hemisphere. She lived at the time of the colonization by Spain in the 16th century. Patron saint of the Americas and the Philippines. Public holiday in Peru.

RUTHERFORD, ERNEST: BIRTH ANNIVERSARY. Aug 30, 1871. Physicist, born at Nelson, New Zealand. He established the nuclear nature of the atom and the electrical structure of matter and achieved the transmutation of elements, research that later resulted in the atomic bomb. Rutherford died at Cambridge, England, Oct 19, 1937.

SHELLEY, MARY WOLLSTONECRAFT: BIRTH ANNIVERSARY. Aug 30, 1797. English novelist Mary Shelley, daughter of philosopher William Godwin and feminist Mary Wollstonecraft and wife of poet Percy Bysshe Shelley, was born at London, England, and died there Feb 1, 1851. In addition to being the author of the famous novel *Frankenstein*, Shelley is important in literary history for her work in the editing and publishing of her husband's unpublished work after his early death.

STRAITH, CLAIRE, MD: BIRTH ANNIVERSARY. Aug 30, 1891. Innovator in plastic and cosmetic surgery, born at Southfield, MI. After attending an international meeting at Paris, France, at the end of WWI to share information regarding reconstructive surgical techniques used on the battlefield, Straith dedicated his career to the new field of plastic surgery. He developed many of the techniques used in plastic and cosmetic surgery, designed new surgical instruments and led a campaign that persuaded automakers, in 1930, to use safety glass and remove dangerous projections from the interior of cars. Straith died July 13, 1958.

TURKEY: HELLESPONT SWIM. Aug 30. Eceabat and Canakkale. The Hellespont—a narrow channel between Asia and Europe—is undoubtedly one of the most significant open water swims in the world. In 1810, the English poet Lord Byron became the first

known person to swim across the channel. He swam it in honor of Leander, who in Greek mythology would swim nightly across this stretch of water to his lover Hero. The swim is about four miles long and takes place annually on Aug 30, which is Victory Day in Turkey. For info: Canakkale Rotary Club. Web: www.canakkalerotaryclub.org.

TURKEY: VICTORY DAY. Aug 30. Commemorates victory in War of Independence in 1922. Military parades, performance by the Mehtar band (the world's oldest military band), fireworks.

UNITED NATIONS: INTERNATIONAL DAY OF VICTIMS OF ENFORCED DISAPPEARANCES. Aug 30. Enforced disappearance has become a global problem and is not restricted to a specific region of the world. Once largely the product of military dictatorships, enforced disappearances can nowadays be perpetrated in complex situations of internal conflict, especially as a means of political repression of opponents. On Dec 21, 2010, the UN General Assembly declared Aug 30 the International Day of the Victims of Enforced Disappearances, to be observed beginning in 2011 (Res 65/209). For info: United Nations. Web: www.un.org/en/events/disappearancesday.

WELLS, KITTY: BIRTH ANNIVERSARY. Aug 30, 1919. Born Muriel Ellen Deason at Nashville, TN, this country singer was a pioneer in the music industry. One of the first commercially successful women ever signed to a major label, she was about to quit music to raise her family when she scored a surprise hit with 1952's "It Wasn't God Who Made Honky Tonk Angels." That song, the first by a woman to hit number one on the country charts, launched a career ranked the sixth-most-successful in the history of *Billboard*'s country charts. She died at Madison, TN, July 16, 2012.

WILKINS, ROY: BIRTH ANNIVERSARY. Aug 30, 1901. Civil rights leader Roy Wilkins, grandson of a Mississippi slave, was active in the National Association for the Advancement of Colored People (NAACP). He retired as its executive director in 1977. Born at St. Louis, MO. Died at New York, NY, Sept 8, 1981.

WILLIAMS, TED: BIRTH ANNIVERSARY. Aug 30, 1918. Born Theodore Samuel Williams at San Diego, CA, Ted Williams played his first major league baseball game for the Boston Red Sox on Apr 22, 1939. In the years that followed, he became known as perhaps the best hitter ever to play the game. His career batting average was .344, and his record average of .406 set during the 1941 season stands unsurpassed. He played 19 seasons for the Red Sox, but during the prime of his career, he missed three full seasons while serving as a navy pilot in WWII and most of two seasons serving as a marine pilot in the Korean War. He was elected to the Baseball Hall of Fame in 1966. He died July 5, 2002, at Inverness, FL.

🎂 BIRTHDAYS TODAY

Elizabeth Ashley, 81, actress (*Agnes of God, Cat on a Hot Tin Roof*, "Evening Shade"), born Elizabeth Ann Cole at Ocala, FL, Aug 30, 1939.

Lewis Black, 72, comedian ("The Daily Show"), born Silver Spring, MD, Aug 30, 1948.

August	S	M	T	W	T	F	S
							1
	2	3	4	5	6	7	8
2020	9	10	11	12	13	14	15
	16	17	18	19	20	21	22
	23	24	25	26	27	28	29
	30	31					

Timothy Bottoms, 69, actor (*The Last Picture Show, The Paper Chase*), born Santa Barbara, CA, Aug 30, 1951.

Michael Chiklis, 57, actor (Emmy and Golden Globe for "The Shield"), born Lowell, MA, Aug 30, 1963.

Cameron Diaz, 48, actress (*Charlie's Angels, My Best Friend's Wedding, There's Something About Mary*), born San Diego, CA, Aug 30, 1972.

Jean-Claude Killy, 77, Olympic alpine skier, born Saint-Cloud, France, Aug 30, 1943.

Michael Michele, 54, actress ("Homicide: Life on the Street," "ER"), born Evansville, IN, Aug 30, 1966.

David Paymer, 66, actor (*City Slickers, Mr Saturday Night*), born Long Island, NY, Aug 30, 1954.

Andy Roddick, 38, tennis player, born Omaha, NE, Aug 30, 1982.

Thom Tillis, 60, US Senator (R, North Carolina), born Jacksonville, FL, Aug 30, 1960.

August 31 — Monday

DAY 244   **122 REMAINING**

CHARLESTON EARTHQUAKE: ANNIVERSARY. Aug 31, 1886. Charleston, SC. The first major earthquake in the recorded history of the eastern US occurred on this date. It is believed that about 100 persons perished in the quake, centered near Charleston but felt up to 800 miles away. Though a number of smaller eastern US quakes had been described and recorded since 1638, this affected people living in an area of about two million square miles.

COBURN, JAMES: BIRTH ANNIVERSARY. Aug 31, 1928. Academy Award–winning actor born at Laurel, NE. He rose to fame as the knife thrower in *The Magnificent Seven* and became known for his tough-guy roles in films such as *The Great Escape* and *Our Man Flint*. He received an Oscar for his supporting role in *Affliction* (1999). He died at Los Angeles, CA, Nov 18, 2002.

"CRANKSHAFT": ANNIVERSARY. Aug 31, 1987. Celebrating the anniversary of the nationally syndicated comic strip that premiered Aug 31, 1987. For info: Tom Batiuk, 2750 Substation Rd, Medina, OH 44256. Phone: (330) 304-6095.

DIANA, PRINCESS OF WALES: DEATH ANNIVERSARY. Aug 31, 1997. Diana, Princess of Wales, died in a car crash with her companion, Dodi Fayed, on this date, at Paris, France. Although press photographers had been pursuing her car, French courts determined that the paparazzi were not responsible for the crash but rather a driver operating under the influence of alcohol. Diana, a very popular British royal who worked on behalf of many charities, was mourned the world over.

HONG KONG: LIBERATION DAY. Aug 31. Public holiday to celebrate liberation from the Japanese in 1945. Annually, the last Monday in August.

KAZAKHSTAN: CONSTITUTION DAY. Aug 31. National holiday. Commemorates the constitution of 1995.

KLONDIKE ELDORADO GOLD DISCOVERY: ANNIVERSARY. Aug 31, 1896. Two weeks after the Rabbit/Bonanza Creek claim was filed, gold was discovered on Eldorado Creek, a tributary of Bonanza. More than $30 million worth of gold (worth $600–$700 million in today's dollars) was mined from the Eldorado Claim in 1896.

KYRGYZSTAN: INDEPENDENCE DAY. Aug 31. National holiday. Commemorates independence from the former Soviet Union in 1991.

LOVE LITIGATING LAWYERS DAY. Aug 31. Lawyer jokes abound, but when push comes to shove, these are the folks who can end up saving the day. (©2006 by WH.) For info: Thomas & Ruth Roy,

Wellcat Holidays, 2418 Long Ln, Lebanon, PA 17046. Phone: (717) 279-0184. E-mail: info@wellcat.com. Web: www.wellcat.com.

MALAYSIA: FREEDOM DAY. Aug 31. National holiday. Commemorates independence from Britain in 1957.

MOLDOVA: NATIONAL LANGUAGE DAY. Aug 31. National holiday. Also called Mother Tongue Day. Commemorates the replacement of the Cyrillic alphabet with the Latin alphabet in 1991.

MONTESSORI, MARIA: 150th BIRTH ANNIVERSARY. Aug 31, 1870. Physician and educator born at Chiaravalle, Italy. In 1894, Montessori became the first Italian woman in the modern era to get a medical degree. Her areas of specialty were psychiatry and the treatment of children. At the Orthophrenic School in Rome, she experimented with ways of engaging the children and developed what is now called the Montessori method. Montessori died at Noordwijk, Holland, May 6, 1952.

PHILIPPINES: NATIONAL HEROES' DAY. Aug 31. National holiday. The last Monday in August. Commemorates the Aug 26, 1896, beginning of the Philippine fight for independence from Spain.

POLAND: SOLIDARITY FOUNDED: 40th ANNIVERSARY. Aug 31, 1980. The Polish trade union Solidarity was formed at the Baltic Sea port of Gdansk, Poland. It was outlawed by the government, and many of its leaders were arrested. Led by Lech Walesa, Solidarity persisted in its opposition to the Communist-controlled government, and on Aug 19, 1989, Polish president Wojciech Jaruzelski astonished the world by nominating for the post of prime minister Tadeusz Mazowiecki, a deputy in the Polish Assembly, 1961–72, and editor in chief of Solidarity's weekly newspaper, bringing to an end 42 years of Communist Party domination.

SAROYAN, WILLIAM: BIRTH ANNIVERSARY. Aug 31, 1908. American writer of Armenian descent, author of *The Human Comedy* and of the Pulitzer Prize–winning play *The Time of Your Life*, was born at Fresno, CA, and died there May 18, 1981. In April 1981 he gave reporters a final statement for publication after his death: "Everybody has got to die, but I have always believed an exception would be made in my case. Now what?"

SHAWN, WILLIAM: BIRTH ANNIVERSARY. Aug 31, 1907. William Shawn, editor of *The New Yorker* for 35 years, was born at Chicago, IL. He was virtual dictator of editorial policy for the magazine, which in turn had an impact on the literary and reportorial styles of writers throughout the country. Nonfiction pieces in *The New Yorker* contributed to public opinion on important issues during Shawn's tenure. Shawn died Dec 8, 1992, at New York, NY.

TRINIDAD AND TOBAGO: INDEPENDENCE DAY. Aug 31. National holiday. Became an independent nation within the British Commonwealth on this day in 1962. Trinidad became a republic Sept 24, 1976.

UNITED KINGDOM: SUMMER BANK HOLIDAY. Aug 31. Bank and public holiday in England, Wales and Northern Ireland. (Scotland not included.) Annually, the last Monday in August.

US OPEN TENNIS CHAMPIONSHIP. Aug 31–Sept 13. USTA Billie Jean King National Tennis Center, Flushing, NY. Part of the Grand Slam of tennis tournaments. Est attendance: 720,000. For info: United States Tennis Assn, 70 W Red Oak Ln, White Plains, NY

10604. Phone: (914) 696-7000. Web: www.usopen.org or www. usta.com.

WHITECHAPEL MURDERS BEGIN: ANNIVERSARY. Aug 31, 1888. At 3:40 AM, the body of Mary Ann Nichols was found in the impoverished Whitechapel district of London, England. This was (debatably) the first in a series of brutal murders that autumn that claimed the lives of at least five women, perhaps more, by a serial killer who has come to be known as "Jack the Ripper" because of the mutilations he inflicted on his victims. The ferocity of the Whitechapel killings created an "Autumn of Terror" in which the entire populace of London was terrified and where mobs frequently tried to mete out justice to suspects they picked. Mary Kelly, found Nov 9, is considered the last victim. No suspect was ever tried for the murders. See also: "'Jack the Ripper' Letter: Anniversary" (Sept 27).

🎂 BIRTHDAYS TODAY

Jennifer Azzi, 52, basketball coach and former player, born Oak Ridge, TN, Aug 31, 1968.

Marcia Clark, 67, crime reporter/television correspondent ("Marcia Clark Investigates the First 48"), author, former prosecutor, born Marcia Kleks at Alameda, CA, Aug 31, 1953.

Larry Fitzgerald, 37, football player, born Minneapolis, MN, Aug 31, 1983.

Debbie Gibson, 50, singer, born Brooklyn, NY, Aug 31, 1970.

Ted Ligety, 36, Olympic skier, born Salt Lake City, UT, Aug 31, 1984.

Van Morrison, 75, singer, songwriter, born Belfast, Northern Ireland, Aug 31, 1945.

Edwin Corley Moses, 65, Olympic track athlete, born Dayton, OH, Aug 31, 1955.

Hideo Nomo, 52, former baseball player, born Osaka, Japan, Aug 31, 1968.

Itzhak Perlman, 75, violinist, born Tel Aviv, Israel, Aug 31, 1945.

Sara Ramirez, 45, actress ("Grey's Anatomy"; stage: *Spamalot*), born Mazatlan, Mexico, Aug 31, 1975.

Jack Thompson, 80, actor (*The Chant of Jimmie Blacksmith, Breaker Morant*), born Sydney, Australia, Aug 31, 1940.

Glenn Tilbrook, 63, singer, musician (Squeeze), born London, England, Aug 31, 1957.

Chris Tucker, 48, actor (*Silver Linings Playbook, Rush Hour*), born Decatur, GA, Aug 31, 1972.

◆ September ◆

September 1 — Tuesday

DAY 245 **121 REMAINING**

ATRIAL FIBRILLATION AWARENESS MONTH. Sept 1–30. To raise awareness of atrial fibrillation, the most common irregular heartbeat, and to prevent afib-related strokes. For info: Mellanie True Hills, StopAfib.org, PO Box 541, Greenwood, TX 76246. Phone: (940) 466-9898. E-mail: support@stopafib.org. Web: www.Stop Afib.org.

ATTENTION DEFICIT HYPERACTIVITY DISORDER MONTH. Sept 1–30. To educate healthcare groups, children and family organizations, teachers, parents and others interested in childhood health issues by providing information on effective treatments for ADHD. Some treatments have been scientifically validated, tested and proven to reduce the severity of ADHD symptoms and thereby reduce adverse consequences in the child's current and future life. Sponsored by the American College of Apothecaries (ACA)/Pharmacists Planning Service, Inc (PPSI). For info: ACA/PPSI, 2830 Summer Oaks Dr, Bartlett, TN 38134. E-mail: info@ppsinc.org. Web: www.ppsinc.org.

BE KIND TO EDITORS AND WRITERS MONTH. Sept 1–30. A time for editors and writers to show uncommon courtesy toward each other. For info: Lone Star Publications of Humor, 8452 Fredericksburg Rd, PMB 103, San Antonio, TX 78229. E-mail: lspubs@aol.com.

BRAZIL: INDEPENDENCE WEEK. Sept 1–7. Brazil's independence from Portugal in 1822 is commemorated with civic and cultural ceremonies promoted by federal, state and municipal authorities. On Sept 7 a grand military parade takes place and the National Defense League organizes the Running Race in Honor of the Symbolic Torch of the Brazilian Nation.

BURROUGHS, EDGAR RICE: BIRTH ANNIVERSARY. Sept 1, 1875. US novelist (*Tarzan of the Apes*), born at Chicago, IL. Correspondent for the *Los Angeles Times*, died at Encino, CA, Mar 19, 1950.

CARTIER, JACQUES: DEATH ANNIVERSARY. Sept 1, 1557. French navigator and explorer who sailed from St. Malo, France, Apr 20, 1534, in search of a northwest passage to the Orient. Instead, he discovered the St. Lawrence River, explored Canada's coastal regions and took possession of the country for France. Cartier was born at St. Malo, about 1491 (exact date unknown), and died there.

CHICKEN BOY'S BIRTHDAY. Sept 1. Chicken Boy is a 22-foot statue of a boy with a chicken's head, holding a bucket of chicken. Formerly the mascot for the restaurant for which he is named, he was rescued from destruction by Future Studio of Los Angeles, a graphic design studio, when the restaurant went out of business. Chicken Boy has since become a pop culture icon and has been installed on a rooftop in Los Angeles along historic Route 66, so he once again can be seen by the public. For info: Amy Inouye, Future Studio, PO Box 292000, Los Angeles, CA 90029. Phone: (323) 254-4565. E-mail: amy@futurestudio.com. Web: www.chickenboy.com.

CHILDHOOD CANCER AWARENESS MONTH. Sept 1–30. Widely observed month that honors and remembers children and families affected by cancer and that seeks to spread awareness and to support research. Pediatric cancer is the number one cause of death by disease in children.

CHILE: NATIONAL MONTH. Sept 1–30. A month of special significance in Chile: arrival of spring, a Day of Unity on the first Monday in September, Independence of Chile anniversary (proclaimed Sept 18, 1810) and celebration of the 1980 constitution and Army Day, Sept 19.

EMMA M. NUTT DAY. Sept 1. A day to honor the first woman telephone operator, Emma M. Nutt, who reportedly began her professional career at Boston, MA, Sept 1, 1878, and continued working as a telephone operator for 33 years.

FALL HAT MONTH. Sept 1–30. A month of celebration during which the straw hat is put aside by men and women in favor of the felt or fabric hat. Local businesses and the media are encouraged to plan hat-related activities. Originally sponsored by Casey Bush and the Headwear Information Bureau.

GERMANY: CAPITAL RETURNS TO BERLIN: ANNIVERSARY. Sept 1, 1999. In July the monthlong process of moving the German government from Bonn to Berlin began, eight years after parliament had voted to return to its prewar seat. Berlin officially became the capital of Germany on Sept 1, 1999, and parliament reconvened at the newly restored Reichstag on Sept 7, 1999.

GREAT AMERICAN LOW-CHOLESTEROL, LOW-FAT PIZZA BAKE. Sept 1–30. Pizza parlors, restaurants and volunteer agencies nationwide create healthy pizza recipes to increase the public's awareness of the benefits of controlling high cholesterol levels through diet. Sponsored by the American College of Apothecaries (ACA)/Pharmacists Planning Service, Inc (PPSI). For info: ACA/PPSI, 2830 Summer Oaks Dr, Bartlett, TN 38134. E-mail: info@ppsinc.org. Web: www.ppsinc.org.

GYNECOLOGIC CANCER AWARENESS MONTH. Sept 1–30. During September, women are encouraged to learn more about gynecologic cancers—how they can be detected and prevented before they become fatal. For info: Foundation for Women's Cancer. Web: www.foundationforwomenscancer.org.

HAPPY CAT MONTH. Sept 1–30. Cats are America's favorite pets. They outnumber dogs as domestic companions by more than 13 million, yet they are half as likely to visit a veterinarian. And far fewer lost or stray cats in animal shelters are reclaimed by their owners. Time to show some love: Happy Cat Month celebrates cat happiness and the joys of cat ownership. For info: The CATalyst Council, PO Box 3064, Annapolis, MD 21403. E-mail: cats@catalystcouncil.org or jane.brunt@catalystcouncil.org. Web: www.catalystcouncil.org.

HUNGER ACTION MONTH. Sept 1–30. Every September, Feeding America, the nation's leading domestic hunger relief organization, encourages people from all walks of life to raise awareness for hunger relief. Hunger Action Month is an effort to mobilize the public to raise awareness and take action in support of domestic hunger relief. For info: Feeding America. Web: www.feedingamerica.org.

INTERNATIONAL TOY TESTING DAY. Sept 1. New York, NY. Annual event where senior corporate executives test toys and learn how to

use creativity in the workplace. On the same day, children across the world also test and play with toys. Annually, Sept 1. For info: Toy Tips, Inc. E-mail: marianne@toytips.com. Web: www.toytips.com.

INTERNATIONAL WOMEN'S FRIENDSHIP MONTH. Sept 1–30. Every woman has friends she can't live without—those women to whom she tells everything, friends who will always listen and who know just what to say. International Women's Friendship Month provides the perfect opportunity for women to acknowledge the amazing women in their lives and to create new friendships. For info: Heidi Roy, The Confidence Coalition/Kappa Delta Sorority, 3205 Players Ln, Memphis, TN 38125. Phone: (901) 748-1897. E-mail: heidi.roy@kappadelta.org. Web: www.kappadelta.org.

JAPAN: KANTO EARTHQUAKE MEMORIAL DAY. Sept 1. A day to remember the 57,000 people who died during Japan's greatest earthquake in 1923.

KOREAN AIR LINES FLIGHT 007 DISASTER: ANNIVERSARY. Sept 1, 1983. Korean Air Lines Flight 007, en route from New York, NY, to Seoul, South Korea, reportedly strayed more than 100 miles off course, flying over secret Soviet military installations on the Kamchatka Peninsula and Sakhalin Island. Two and one-half hours after it was said to have entered Soviet airspace, a Soviet interceptor plane destroyed the Boeing 747 with 269 persons on board, which then crashed into the Sea of Japan. There were no survivors. President Reagan, in Proclamation 5093, named Sunday, Sept 11, 1983, as a National Day of Mourning as "homage to the memory of those who died."

LIBRARY CARD SIGN-UP MONTH. Sept 1–30. A month when the American Library Association and libraries across the country remind parents that a library card is the most important school supply of all. This observance was launched in 1987 to meet the challenge of then Secretary of Education William J. Bennett, who said, "Let's have a national campaign . . . Every child should obtain a library card—and use it." Since then, thousands of public and school libraries join each fall in a national effort to ensure every child does just that. For info: Megan McFarlane, American Library Assn, Public Information Office, 50 E Huron St, Chicago, IL 60611. E-mail: lsimon@ala.org. Web: http://www.ala.org/conferencesevents/celebrationweeks/card.

MARCIANO, ROCKY: BIRTH ANNIVERSARY. Sept 1, 1923. Rocky Marciano, boxer born Rocco Francis Marchegiano at Brockton, MA. Marciano used superb conditioning to fashion an impressive record that propelled him to fight against Jersey Joe Walcott for the heavyweight title on Sept 23, 1952. Marciano knocked Walcott out, and in 1956 he retired as the only undefeated heavyweight champion. Died in a plane crash at Newton, IA, Aug 31, 1969. The film *Somebody Up There Likes Me* recounts his life story.

MEXICO: PRESIDENT'S STATE OF THE UNION ADDRESS. Sept 1. National holiday.

MISSION SAN LUIS OBISPO DE TOLOSA: FOUNDING ANNIVERSARY. Sept 1, 1772. California mission to the Indians.

MOLD AWARENESS MONTH. Sept 1–30. Mold growth indoors and its negative impact on human health, especially on children and the elderly, is something only recently understood and widely accepted. As we begin to close our doors and our windows for the winter months ahead, take this time to become more aware about mold growth indoors, its causes, cures and prevention. For info: Jason Earle, GOT MOLD?, 71 Broadway, Lobby 2B, Box 256, New York, NY 10006. E-mail: questions@gotmold.com.

NATIONAL BE A FOOD HERO MONTH. Sept 1–30. Since 2009. Food should be fun, tasty, healthful, affordable and enjoyed as a family. As kids go back to school and schedules get busier, we propose that parents don't forget to focus on healthy meals that bring the family together. Anyone is a food hero who brings their family together with healthful food in today's hectic world. For info: Food Hero, USDA Supplemental Nutrition Assistance Program, 106 Ballard Hall, Corvallis, OR 97331. Phone: (541) 737-1017. E-mail: Food.Hero@oregonstate.edu.

NATIONAL CHOLESTEROL EDUCATION MONTH. Sept 1–30. High cholesterol usually doesn't have any symptoms. As a result, many people do not know that their cholesterol levels are too high. However, doctors can do a simple blood test to check your cholesterol. High cholesterol can be controlled through lifestyle changes or if it is not enough, through medications. This month, learn how to prevent high cholesterol and know what your cholesterol levels mean. Annually, September. For info: Natl Heart, Lung and Blood Institute, Natl Cholesterol Education Program, Building 31, 31 Center Dr, Bethesda, MD 20892. Web: www.nhlbi.nih.gov. Or Centers for Disease Control and Prevention. Web: www.cdc.gov/cholesterol/cholesterol_education_month.htm.

NATIONAL DNA, GENOMICS & STEM CELL EDUCATION AND AWARENESS MONTH. Sept 1–30. Sponsored by the American College of Apothecaries (ACA)/Pharmacists Planning Service, Inc (PPSI). For info: ACA/PPSI, 2830 Summer Oaks Dr, Bartlett, TN 38134. E-mail: info@ppsinc.org. Web: www.ppsinc.org.

NATIONAL HEAD LICE PREVENTION MONTH. Sept 1–30. To promote awareness of how to screen and detect pediculosis as easily and as early as possible—as well as to protect against unnecessary and potentially harmful pesticide treatments for children with head lice. For info: Natl Pediculosis Assn, 1005 Boylston St, Ste 343, Newton Highlands, MA 02461. Phone: (617) 905-0176. E-mail: npa@headlice.org. Web: www.headlice.org and www.licemeister.com.

NATIONAL HONEY MONTH. Sept 1–30. To honor US beekeepers and the 2.9 million colonies of honeybees, which produce more than 162 million pounds of honey each year. For info: Natl Honey Board. E-mail: honey@nhb.org or media@nhb.org. Web: www.honey.com.

NATIONAL MUSHROOM MONTH. Sept 1–30. To promote the greater appreciation and use of fresh mushrooms. For info: The Mushroom Council, 303 Twin Dolphin Dr, Ste 600, Redwood Shores, CA 94065. E-mail: info@mushroomcouncil.com. Web: www.mushroominfo.com.

★**NATIONAL PREPAREDNESS MONTH.** Sept 1–30.

NATIONAL RECOVERY MONTH. Sept 1–30. 30th annual. A national observance sponsored by the US Department of Health and Human Services' Substance Abuse and Mental Health Services Administration. Each September, this month highlights the benefits of addiction treatment and mental health services and spreads the positive message that behavioral health is essential to overall health, that prevention works, that treatment is effective and that people can and do recover to live a healthy and rewarding life. This month also lauds the contributions of treatment and recovery service providers. There are more than 1,200

September	S	M	T	W	T	F	S
			1	2	3	4	5
	6	7	8	9	10	11	12
2020	13	14	15	16	17	18	19
	20	21	22	23	24	25	26
	27	28	29	30			

events during this month with more than 400,000 participants. For info: SAMHSA/CSAT, Office of the Director, Natl Recovery Month, 5600 Fishers Ln, 13E-34, Rockville, MD 20857. Phone: (877) SAMHSA-7 or (800) 662-HELP or (800) 487-4889 (TTY). E-mail: media@samhsa.hhs.gov. Web: www.recoverymonth.gov.

NATIONAL RICE MONTH. Sept 1–30. To focus attention on the importance of US-grown rice to the American diet and to salute the US rice industry. For info: USA Rice Federation, 2101 Wilson Blvd, Ste 610, Arlington, VA 22201. Phone: (703) 236-2300. E-mail: riceinfo@usarice.com. Web: www.usarice.com.

NATIONAL SERVICE DOG MONTH. Sept 1–30. A month to honor guide dogs and military service dogs for the inspiring work they do in changing lives. Annually, the month of September. (Originally created by Dick Van Patten as National Guide Dog Month.)

NATIONAL SKIN CARE AWARENESS MONTH. Sept 1–30. A month to focus on achieving healthy, glowing, beautiful skin. Take time to learn about protecting skin from the dangers of the sun, how diet and lifestyle affect skin, developing a proper skin care routine and myths and facts about skin care products. All important knowledge for great-looking skin. Throughout September, the event sponsor posts a *.pdf document with skin tips based on the latest research that anyone can download, copy and distribute. For info: Renee Rouleau, Renee Rouleau Skin Care. Phone: (888) 211-7560. Web: www.reneerouleau.com.

ONE-ON-ONE MONTH. Sept 1–30. This is a month to get to know your coworkers, family members and friends better by meeting one on one. When people spend time together one on one, they are more likely to talk about their lives in a meaningful way. It is easier for them to express their hopes, dreams and ideas and share their interests in ways that they would never do in a group or even a threesome. Annually, every September. For info: Harriet Meyerson, The Confidence Center. E-mail: Harriet@Confidence-Center.com.

ORTHODOX ECCLESIASTICAL NEW YEAR. Sept 1. This beginning of the Eastern Orthodox Church year has been observed on Sept 1 since the early days of Byzantine Christianity and long before the fall of Constantinople in 1453.

OVARIAN CANCER AWARENESS MONTH. Sept 1–30. Ovarian cancer ranks fifth in cancer deaths among women but accounts for more deaths than any other cancer of the female reproductive system. It is estimated that there will be about 15,000 deaths from ovarian cancer in the US annually, a rate that has changed little in the last 50 years. It is estimated that about 22,000 new cases of ovarian cancer will be diagnosed in the US annually. This month promotes awareness and education. Wear teal and create a "teal scene" for ovarian cancer awareness. For info: Natl Ovarian Cancer Coalition, 12221 Merit Dr, Ste 1950, Dallas, TX 75251. Phone: (888) OVARIAN or (214) 273-4200. E-mail: nocc@ovarian.org. Web: www.ovarian.org or www.whyteal.org.

PHILLIS WHEATLEY'S POETRY COLLECTION PUBLISHED: ANNIVERSARY. Sept 1, 1773. On this date the first book of poetry composed by an African American was published. Phillis Wheatley's *Poems on Various Subjects, Religious and Moral* was published at London, England, only 12 years after her arrival in America as a child slave from Senegal. In those 12 years, she learned to read and write English and studied literature in English and Latin. Feted in America and England, Wheatley eventually gained her freedom but died in poverty. See also: "Wheatley, Phillis: Death Anniversary" (Dec 5).

REUTHER, WALTER PHILIP: BIRTH ANNIVERSARY. Sept 1, 1907. American labor leader who began work in a steel factory at age 16 and later became president of the United Automobile Workers (UAW) and the Congress of Industrial Organizations (CIO). Born at Wheeling, WV, Reuther worked for two years in a Russian automobile factory. Often at the center of controversy, he was the target of an assassin in 1948. Reuther and his wife died in an airplane crash May 9, 1970, at Black Lake, MI. The UAW Family

Education Center, a project that he had cherished, was later named for Walter and May Reuther.

SEPTEMBER IS HEALTHY AGING® MONTH. Sept 1–30. Annual health observance designed to focus national attention on the positive aspects of growing older. This month is part of the Healthy Aging® campaign, a national, ongoing health promotion designed to broaden awareness of the positive aspects of aging and to provide inspiration for adults, ages 45+, to improve their physical, mental, social and financial health. The campaign is developed and produced by Educational Television Network, Inc (ETNET), a nonprofit corporation based in Pennsylvania. For info: The Healthy Aging® Campaign, PO Box 442, Unionville, PA 19375. Phone: (610) 793-0979. E-mail: info@healthyaging.net. Web: www.healthyaging.net.

SHAMELESS PROMOTION MONTH. Sept 1–30. This is the month for you to go out and promote yourself, your business, your book or your product shamelessly. For info: Marisa D'Vari, NewOak, 575 5th Ave, 15th Fl, New York, NY 10017. E-mail: mdvari@newoak.com.

SLOVAKIA: CONSTITUTION DAY. Sept 1. Anniversary of the adoption of the Constitution of the Slovak Republic in 1992.

SPORTS EYE SAFETY MONTH. Sept 1–30. There are thousands of eye injuries each year related to sports. Tips on how to protect yourself and your children from such eye injuries will be discussed. For info: Prevent Blindness, 211 W Wacker Dr, Ste 1700, Chicago, IL 60606. Phone: (800) 331-2020. E-mail: info@preventblindness.com. Web: www.preventblindness.org.

SUBLIMINAL COMMUNICATIONS MONTH. Sept 1–30. Not getting the results you want? Make a change for the positive and learn how to maximize your effectiveness. Learn how to put to use your entrepreneurial thinking to achieve your goals and increase your visibility socially or in the corporate world. Recognize and apply prosperity-building opportunities for increasing your networking, marketing and publicity goals through the use of color, scents and language. Finish the last quarter of the year successfully by using the powerful resources you already possess. It's your choice! For info: Lorrie Walters Marsiglio, Lorimar Communications, PO Box 284-CC, Wasco, IL 60183-0284. Phone: (630) 584-9368.

***TITANIC* DISCOVERED: ANNIVERSARY.** Sept 1, 1985. Almost 75 years after the *Titanic* sank in the North Atlantic after striking an iceberg, a joint American-French expedition force led by marine geologist Dr. Robert Ballard located the wreck. The luxury liner was resting on the ocean floor 12,500 feet down—about 350 miles southeast of Newfoundland, Canada. In July 1986 Ballard returned in an expedition aboard the *Atlantis II* to explore the ship with underwater robots. Two memorial bronze plaques were left on the deck. See also: "Sinking of the *Titanic*: Anniversary" (Apr 15).

TWITTY, CONWAY: BIRTH ANNIVERSARY. Sept 1, 1933. Country music star who began his career as a rock-and-roll performer in the style of Elvis Presley, born at Friars Point, MS. Died June 5, 1993, at Springfield, MO.

UPDATE YOUR RÉSUMÉ MONTH. Sept 1–30. This month encourages employed individuals to update and maintain their résumés. For info: Laura DeCarlo, Career Directors International, 1665 Clover Circle, Melbourne, FL 32935. Phone: (321) 752-0442. E-mail: info@careerdirectors.com.

UZBEKISTAN: INDEPENDENCE DAY. Sept 1. National holiday. Commemorates independence upon the dissolution of the Soviet Union in 1991.

WHOLE GRAINS MONTH. Sept 1–30. Eating better is not an all-or-nothing choice; every little improvement you make in what you choose to eat helps. This month is a great time for everyone to get on the whole grains bandwagon. Post a list of "swaps" on your fridge as a reminder and try as many as possible this month. For example, serve bulgur or brown rice instead of potatoes one night in the month, try a new cereal with at least 16 grams of whole grain per serving or try whole-wheat pasta for one meal. Oldways Whole Grains Council offers education and promotions to consumers, retailers and health professionals. For info: Oldways Whole Grains Council, 266 Beacon St, Boston, MA 02116. Phone: (617) 421-5500. Fax: (617) 421-5511. E-mail: media@oldwayspt.org. Web: www.wholegrainscouncil.org.

WORLD BEACH MONTH. Sept 1–30. Since 2018, a time to get out and enjoy the beaches of the world, host clean-up events, play in the sand, go shelling, build a sandcastle, play in the surf and raise awareness about protecting these treasures. For info: Patti Jewel, FloridaSmart.com. E-mail: FloridaSmart1@gmail.com. Web: www.worldbeachmonth.com.

WORLD WAR II BEGINS: GERMANY INVADES POLAND: ANNIVERSARY. Sept 1, 1939. After securing a nonagression pact with the USSR (that secretly allowed for the partition of Poland by the Soviet Union and Germany) on Aug 23, Germany invaded Poland without a declaration of war at 4:45 AM. Two days later, Britain and France declared war, with Canada, Australia, New Zealand and South Africa soon following with their own declarations. Poland, overwhelmed by German air and land power, was in German and Soviet hands before the month concluded.

WORLDWIDE SPEAK OUT MONTH. Sept 1–30. Since 2007, a month to help people face their fear of speaking up at a small gathering or speaking out in public. Annually, in September because, like the school year, this is a great time to begin a new project. "Remember to fight the fear and speak out." For info: Deborah Le Bouf Kulkkula, PhD, 381 Billings Rd, Fitchburg, MA 01420-1407. Phone: (978) 343-4009 or (978) 808-8084 (cell phone). E-mail: DebKulkkula@gmail.com. Web: www.SpeakOutMonth.com.

🎂 BIRTHDAYS TODAY

Zendaya Coleman, 24, actress ("K.C. Undercover," "Shake It Up!"), singer, born Oakland, CA, Sept 1, 1996.

Alan Dershowitz, 82, attorney, author, born Brooklyn, NY, Sept 1, 1938.

Gloria Estefan, 63, singer, born Havana, Cuba, Sept 1, 1957.

Barry Gibb, 74, singer (The Bee Gees), songwriter, born Manchester, England, Sept 1, 1946.

Timothy Duane (Tim) Hardaway, 54, former basketball player, born Chicago, IL, Sept 1, 1966.

Jung Kook, 23, singer (BTS), born Jeon Jung-kook at Busan, South Korea, Sept 1, 1997.

Dr. Phil McGraw, 70, psychologist, author, television personality ("The Oprah Winfrey Show," "Dr. Phil"), born Vinita, OK, Sept 1, 1950.

Seiji Ozawa, 85, conductor, born Hoten, Japan, Sept 1, 1935.

Don Stroud, 83, actor ("Mike Hammer," *The Buddy Holly Story, License to Kill*), born Honolulu, HI, Sept 1, 1937.

September 2020	S	M	T	W	T	F	S
			1	2	3	4	5
	6	7	8	9	10	11	12
	13	14	15	16	17	18	19
	20	21	22	23	24	25	26
	27	28	29	30			

Lily Tomlin, 81, actress, comedienne ("Grace and Frankie," *Nashville*, Tony for *The Search for Signs of Intelligent Life in the Universe*), born Detroit, MI, Sept 1, 1939.

Rachel Zoe, 49, fashion designer, author, television personality, born Rachel Zoe Rosenzweig at New York, NY, Sept 1, 1971.

September 2 — Wednesday

DAY 246   **120 REMAINING**

CALENDAR ADJUSTMENT DAY: ANNIVERSARY. Sept 2, 1752. Pursuant to the British Calendar Act of 1751, Britain (and the American colonies) made the "Gregorian Correction" in 1752. The act proclaimed that the day following Wednesday, Sept 2, should become Thursday, Sept 14, 1752. There was rioting in the streets by those who felt cheated and who demanded the 11 days back. The act also provided that New Year's Day (and the change of year number) should fall Jan 1 (instead of Mar 25) in 1752 and every year thereafter. As a result, 1751 had only 282 days. See also: "Gregorian Calendar Adjustment: Anniversary" (Oct 4).

CHINA AND TAIWAN: FESTIVAL OF HUNGRY GHOSTS. Sept 2. Important Chinese festival, also known as the Chung Yuan Festival. According to Chinese legend, during the seventh lunar month the souls of the dead are released from purgatory to roam the earth. Joss sticks are burned in homes; prayers, food and "ghost money" are offered to appease the ghosts. Market stallholders join together to hold celebrations to ensure that their businesses will prosper in the coming year. Wayang (Chinese street opera) and puppet shows are performed, and fruit and Chinese delicacies are offered to the spirits of the dead. Chung Yuan is observed on the 15th day of the seventh lunar month. Date in other countries may differ from China's.

CORN MOON. Sept 2. The September full moon.

GREAT FIRE OF LONDON: ANNIVERSARY. Sept 2–5, 1666. (Old Style date.) The fire generally credited with bringing about our system of fire insurance started Sept 2, 1666 (OS), in the wooden house of a baker named Farryner, at London's Pudding Lane, near the Tower. During the ensuing three days more than 13,000 houses were destroyed, though it is believed that only six lives were lost in the fire.

HISTORIC MARATHON RUNS: ANNIVERSARY. Sept 2–9, 490 BC. Anniversary of the event during the Persian Wars from which the marathon race is derived. Phidippides, "an Athenian and by profession and practice a trained runner," according to Herodotus, was dispatched from Marathon to Sparta (a distance of 26 miles) on Sept 2 to seek help in repelling the invading Persian army. Help being unavailable by religious law until after the next full moon, Phidippides ran the 26 miles back to Marathon Sept 4. Without Spartan aid, the Athenians defeated the Persians at the Battle of Marathon Sept 9. According to legend Phidippides carried the news of the battle to Athens and died as he spoke the words, "Rejoice, we are victorious." The marathon race was

revived at the 1896 Olympic Games at Athens. Course distance, since 1924, is 26 miles, 385 yards. See also: "Battle of Marathon: Anniversary" (Sept 9).

LILIUOKALANI: BIRTH ANNIVERSARY. Sept 2, 1838. Born Liliu Kamakhea at Honolulu, the island of Hawaii, Liliuokalani was the Kingdom of Hawaii's only female sovereign and its last monarch. She was deposed in 1894 by a group led by Sanford Dole—first president of the Republic of Hawaii. Despite US president Grover Cleveland's insistence that Liliuokalani be restored to the throne, Dole refused. After a failed insurrection in 1895, she spent the remainder of her years leading the Oni pa'a movement, which opposed Hawaii's annexation by the US, until her death on Nov 11, 1917, at Honolulu.

MCAULIFFE, CHRISTA: BIRTH ANNIVERSARY. Sept 2, 1948. Christa McAuliffe, a 37-year-old Concord, NH, high school teacher, was to have been the first "ordinary citizen" in space. Born Sharon Christa Corrigan at Boston, MA, she perished with six crew members in the space shuttle *Challenger* explosion Jan 28, 1986. See also: "Challenger Space Shuttle Explosion: Anniversary" (Jan 28).

MOON PHASE: FULL MOON. Sept 2. Moon enters Full Moon phase at 1:22 AM, EDT.

SHERMAN ENTERS ATLANTA: ANNIVERSARY. Sept 2, 1864. After a four-week siege, Union general William Tecumseh Sherman entered Atlanta, GA. The city had been evacuated on the previous day by Confederate troops under General John B. Hood. Hood had mistakenly assumed Sherman was ending the siege Aug 27, when actually Sherman was beginning the final stages of his attack. Hood then sent troops to attack the Union forces at Jonesboro. Hood's troops were defeated, opening the way for the capture of Atlanta.

US TREASURY DEPARTMENT: ANNIVERSARY. Sept 2, 1789. The third presidential cabinet department, the Treasury Department, was established by Congress.

VIETNAM: INDEPENDENCE DAY. Sept 2. Ho Chi Minh formally proclaimed the independence of Vietnam from France and the establishment of the Democratic Republic of Vietnam on this day in 1945. National holiday.

V-J DAY: 75th ANNIVERSARY. Sept 2, 1945. Official ratification of Japanese surrender to the Allies occurred aboard the USS *Missouri* at Tokyo Bay Sept 2 (Far Eastern time) in 1945, thus prompting President Truman's declaration of this day as Victory-over-Japan Day. Japan's initial, informal agreement of surrender was announced by Truman and celebrated in the US Aug 14.

🎂 BIRTHDAYS TODAY

Nathaniel "Tiny" Archibald, 72, Hall of Fame basketball player, born New York, NY, Sept 2, 1948.

Terry Paxton Bradshaw, 72, sportscaster, Hall of Fame football player, born Shreveport, LA, Sept 2, 1948.

Marge Champion, 101, dancer, actress ("The Marge and Gower Champion Show," *Show Boat*), born Los Angeles, CA, Sept 2, 1919.

Jimmy Connors, 68, Hall of Fame tennis player, born East St. Louis, IL, Sept 2, 1952.

Eric Dickerson, 60, Hall of Fame football player, sportscaster, born Sealy, TX, Sept 2, 1960.

Mark Harmon, 69, actor ("NCIS," "St. Elsewhere," "Chicago Hope"), born Burbank, CA, Sept 2, 1951.

Salma Hayek, 54, actress (*Ask the Dust, Bandidas, Frida*), born Veracruz, Mexico, Sept 2, 1966.

Linda Purl, 65, actress ("Matlock"), born Greenwich, CT, Sept 2, 1955.

Keanu Reeves, 56, actor (*John Wick, The Matrix, Speed*), born Beirut, Lebanon, Sept 2, 1964.

Peter Victor Ueberroth, 83, former commissioner of baseball and Olympic organizer, born Evanston, IL, Sept 2, 1937.

Cynthia Watros, 52, actress ("Lost," "The Drew Carey Show," "Guiding Light"), born Lake Orion, MI, Sept 2, 1968.

September 3 — Thursday

DAY 247   **119 REMAINING**

BEGINNING OF THE PENNY PRESS: ANNIVERSARY. Sept 3, 1833. Benjamin H. Day launched the *New York Sun*, the first truly successful penny newspaper in the US, on this date. The *Sun* was sold on sidewalks by newspaper boys. By 1836 the paper was the largest seller in the country with a circulation of 30,000. It was possibly Day's concentration on human interest stories and sensationalism that made his publication a success while efforts at penny papers at Philadelphia, PA, and Boston, MA, had failed.

BENTON NEIGHBOR DAY. Sept 3–5. Benton, MO. Large festival that includes exhibits, greased pole climb, amusement park, Little Mr and Miss Contest, Queen Contest, Junior Miss Contest, live bands, antique car show, four-wheel-drive mud racing, parade and talent show, cornhole tournament, foodstands and outdoor games for kids and adults. Annually, the Thursday through Saturday before Labor Day. Est attendance: 3,000. For info: Benton Chamber of Commerce, PO Box 477, Benton, MO 63736. Phone: (573) 380-6783.

BLUE HILL FAIR. Sept 3–7. Blue Hill, ME. A "down-to-earth" country fair. Annually, Labor Day weekend. Est attendance: 35,000. For info: Blue Hill Fair, PO Box 390, Blue Hill, ME 04614. Phone: (207) 374-3701. E-mail: bhfair@myfairpoint.net. Web: www.bluehillfair.com.

BRITAIN DECLARES WAR ON GERMANY: ANNIVERSARY. Sept 3, 1939. British ultimatum to Germany, demanding halt to invasion of Poland (which had started at dawn on Sept 1), expired at 11 AM, GMT, Sept 3, 1939. At 11:15 AM, in a radio broadcast, Prime Minister Neville Chamberlain announced the declaration of war against Germany. France, Canada, Australia, New Zealand and South Africa quickly issued separate declarations of war. Winston Churchill was named First Lord of the Admiralty. See also: "World War II Begins: Germany Invades Poland: Anniversary" (Sept 1).

DOUGLASS'S ESCAPE TO FREEDOM: ANNIVERSARY. Sept 3, 1838. Dressed as a sailor and carrying identification papers borrowed from a retired merchant seaman, Frederick Douglass boarded a train at Baltimore, MD, a slave state, and rode to Wilmington, DE, where he caught a steamboat to the free city of Philadelphia, PA. He then transferred to a train headed for New York City, where he entered the protection of the Underground Railway network. Douglass later became a great orator and one of the leaders of the antislavery struggle.

ENGLAND: LAND ROVER BURGHLEY HORSE TRIALS. Sept 3–6. Burghley Park, Stamford, Lincolnshire, England. Major sporting and social event: dressage, cross-country, show jumping, more than 600 shops and renowned food walk. Est attendance: 160,000. For info: Burghley Horse Trials, Barnack Rd, Stamford, Lincolnshire, PE9 3JY England. Phone: (44) (1780) 752-131. E-mail: info@burghley-horse.co.uk. Web: www.burghley-horse.co.uk.

FILENE, EDWARD ALBERT: BIRTH ANNIVERSARY. Sept 3, 1860. American merchant and philanthropist, born at Salem, MA, to German immigrant parents. An innovative retailer and manager, he made the Filene family store into a retail powerhouse that featured the "bargain basement": here, merchandise was automatically discounted as time passed. His Employees Credit Union was the catalyst for the US credit union movement in 1921. Filene died at Paris, France, Sept 26, 1937.

FIRST SECRET SERVICE AGENT TO DIE IN THE LINE OF DUTY: ANNIVERSARY. Sept 3, 1902. While on duty protecting President Theodore Roosevelt, William Craig was killed when a streetcar collided with the carriage carrying the president (who suffered some cuts). The United States Secret Service was founded in 1865 as a branch of the Treasury Department entrusted with foiling counterfeiting but was given the additional role of protecting the US president upon the assassination of William McKinley. Craig, born at Glasgow, Scotland, in 1855, was also a bodyguard for Queen Victoria before moving to Chicago, IL. Roosevelt affectionately called Craig his "shadow."

LAST TRAIN TO AUSCHWITZ: ANNIVERSARY. Sept 3, 1944. A freight train leaving the Nazi Westerbork transit camp in the Netherlands and carrying Dutch Jews to Auschwitz concentration camp was the last such "Holocaust train" of the war. Among others, it carried Anne Frank and her family.

LOUISIANA SHRIMP AND PETROLEUM FESTIVAL AND FAIR. Sept 3-7. Morgan City, LA. Free admission to this event that recognizes and celebrates the importance of the shrimp and petroleum industries to the area. Arts, crafts, water and street parades, Cajun culinary classic, music in the park, unique children's village (a magical adventureland), gospel tent, coronation pageant and ball, carnival, blessing of the fleet. Chosen as the American Bus Association's "Festival of the Year" several times. Voted by the Southeastern Tourism Society as a Top 20 event for several years. Est attendance: 150,000. For info: Darby Ratcliff, Festival Director, Louisiana Shrimp and Petroleum Festival and Fair Assn, PO Box 103, Morgan City, LA 70381. Phone: (985) 385-0703. Fax: (985) 384-4628. E-mail: info@shrimpandpetroleum.org. Web: www.shrimpandpetroleum.org.

MICHIGAN STATE FAIR. Sept 3-7 (tentative). Suburban Collection Showplace, Novi, MI. An annual celebration of the state's grand farming heritage and burgeoning agricultural economy, family entertainment, music, food, contests (baking, home brew and giant pumpkins) and more. The first Michigan State Fair was held in 1849. Est attendance: 350,000. For info: Michigan State Fair, LLC, 46100 Grand River Ave, Novi, MI 48374. Phone: (248) 348-6942. Web: www.michiganstatefairllc.com.

MIDWEST OLD THRESHERS REUNION. Sept 3-7. McMillan Park, Mount Pleasant, IA. The reunion began in 1950. Midwest Old Threshers is a celebration of our rich agricultural heritage. Attractions range from displays of steam engines and agricultural exhibits to turn-of-the-century living and antique cars, tractors and gas engines. There are also steam trains, trolleys, crafts, museums, music and camping. Annually, five days ending on Labor Day. Est attendance: 40,000. For info: Midwest Old Threshers, 405 E Threshers Rd, Mt Pleasant, IA 52641. Phone: (319) 385-8937. Fax: (319) 385-0563. E-mail: info@oldthreshers.org. Web: www.oldthreshers.com.

September 2020	S	M	T	W	T	F	S
			1	2	3	4	5
	6	7	8	9	10	11	12
	13	14	15	16	17	18	19
	20	21	22	23	24	25	26
	27	28	29	30			

NATIONAL SWEETCORN FESTIVAL. Sept 3-7. McFerren Park, Hoopeston, IL. Annual festival includes 50 tons of free corn on the cob, nationally sanctioned beauty pageant, carnival, flea market, horse show, demolition derby, bands and talent shows. Est attendance: 50,000. For info: Danville Area CVB, 100 W Main St, Ste 146, Danville, IL 61832. Phone: (217) 442-2096. Fax: (217) 442-2137. E-mail: info@danvilleareainfo.com.

NOYES, JOHN HUMPHREY: BIRTH ANNIVERSARY. Sept 3, 1811. Born at Brattleboro, VT, Noyes was the founder of one of the most successful and longest-lasting socialist communities in the US: the Oneida Community in New York (1848–79). He also coined the term "free love." Noyes died at Niagara Falls, ON, Canada, on Apr 13, 1886.

PAYSON GOLDEN ONION DAYS. Sept 3-7. Payson, UT. This unique festival includes carnival and amusement rides, a grand parade, arts and crafts booth, entertainment, food booths and much more. Annually, Labor Day weekend. Est attendance: 20,000. For info: Payson Community Coordinator, 439 W Utah Ave, Payson, UT 84651. Phone: (801) 358-3357. E-mail: events@payson.org.

QATAR: INDEPENDENCE DAY. Sept 3. National holiday. Formerly a protectorate of the United Kingdom, Qatar gained its independence on this day in 1971.

SAN MARINO: NATIONAL DAY. Sept 3. Public holiday. Honors St. Marinus, the traditional founder of San Marino.

SOUTH DAKOTA STATE FAIR. Sept 3-7. Huron, SD. 135th annual. Grandstand entertainment nightly, six free stages with multiple shows daily, hundreds of commercial exhibits and thousands of livestock exhibits. Est attendance: 210,000. For info: South Dakota State Fair, 1060 3rd St SW, Huron, SD 57350. Phone: (605) 353-7340 or (800) 529-0900. Web: www.sdstatefair.com.

SULLIVAN, LOUIS: BIRTH ANNIVERSARY. Sept 3, 1856. An American architect responsible for the modern, steel-framed skyscraper, whose designs are characterized by rich ornamentation, plain outer surfaces and cubic forms. His famous motto was "form follows function." Frank Lloyd Wright was a student of Sullivan's before the two quarreled. Born at Boston, MA, Sullivan died Apr 14, 1924, at Chicago, IL.

TREATY OF PARIS ENDS AMERICAN REVOLUTION: ANNIVERSARY. Sept 3, 1783. Treaty between Britain and the US, ending the Revolutionary War, signed at Paris, France. American signatories: John Adams, Benjamin Franklin and John Jay.

🎂 BIRTHDAYS TODAY

Pauline Collins, 80, actress (Tony for *Shirley Valentine*; "Upstairs, Downstairs"), born Exmouth, England, Sept 3, 1940.

Paz de la Huerta, 36, actress ("Boardwalk Empire"), born New York, NY, Sept 3, 1984.

Kiran Desai, 49, author (*The Inheritance of Loss, Hullabaloo in the Guava Orchard*), born New Delhi, India, Sept 3, 1971.

Cristobal Huet, 45, hockey player, born Saint-Martin-d'Héres, France, Sept 3, 1975.

Alison Lurie, 94, author (*Foreign Affairs, The War Between the Tates*), born Chicago, IL, Sept 3, 1926.

Valerie Perrine, 77, actress (*Lenny, W.C. Fields and Me, Superman*), born Galveston, TX, Sept 3, 1943.

Charlie Sheen, 55, actor ("Two and a Half Men," *Wall Street, Platoon*), born Carlos Irwin Estevez at New York, NY, Sept 3, 1965.

Shaun White, 34, Olympic snowboarder, born San Diego, CA, Sept 3, 1986.

September 4 — Friday

DAY 248 **118 REMAINING**

BRING YOUR MANNERS TO WORK DAY. Sept 4. 7th annual. A day to recognize the importance of minding your manners at work and treating others on the job with respect. Celebrated across all industries and professions, the day explores the dos and don'ts for good business behavior: every day, and every week, of the year. Annually, the first Friday in September. For info: The Protocol School of Washington, PO Box 676, Columbia, SC 29202. Phone: (877) 766-3757. E-mail: info@psow.edu. Web: www.psow.edu.

BRITT DRAFT HORSE SHOW. Sept 4–6. Hancock County Fairgrounds, Britt, IA. One of the largest draft horse hitch shows in North America, featuring 18 six-horse hitches from the US and Canada representing the very best of the Belgian, Percheron, Clydesdale and Shire performance horses. Annually, Labor Day weekend. Est attendance: 10,000. For info: Randel or Melodie Hiscocks, Britt Draft Horse Assn, PO Box 312, Britt, IA 50423. Phone: (641) 843-4181.

BRUCKNER, ANTON: BIRTH ANNIVERSARY. Sept 4, 1824. Austrian composer born at Ansfelden, Austria. Died at Vienna, Austria, Oct 11, 1896.

BURNHAM, DANIEL: BIRTH ANNIVERSARY. Sept 4, 1846. American architect and city planner born at Henderson, NY. Daniel Hudson Burnham was an advocate of tall, fireproof buildings, probably the first to be called "sky-scrapers." In 1909 he proposed a long-range city plan for Chicago, IL, that was a key factor in the "forever open, clear and free" policy, which resulted in Chicago's having the most beautiful lakefront of any major city in the US. Died June 1, 1912, at Heidelberg, Germany.

CHATEAUBRIAND, FRANCOIS RENE DE: BIRTH ANNIVERSARY. Sept 4, 1768. French poet, novelist, historian, explorer and statesman, witness to the French Revolution. Inspired the French Romantic movement with his novels set in the American wilderness. His multivolume memoirs (published during his life and posthumously) were tremendously influential to the next generation of French authors. The chateaubriand steak was named in his honor. Born at St. Malo, France, he died at Paris, France, July 4, 1848.

CURAÇAO: ANIMALS' DAY. Sept 4. In Curaçao the Association for the Protection of Animals organizes an animal show for this day, and the best-kept animals are awarded prizes.

EASTERN IDAHO STATE FAIR. Sept 4–12. Blackfoot, ID. Family fun, amusement rides, food booths, entertainment, rodeo, demolition derby, tractor pulls and more. Est attendance: 230,000. For info: Eastern Idaho State Fair, PO Box 250, Blackfoot, ID 83221. Phone: (208) 785-2480. E-mail: thefair@funatthefair.com. Web: www.funatthefair.com.

ENGLAND: BLACKPOOL ILLUMINATIONS. Sept 4–Nov 1. The Promenade, Blackpool, Lancashire. "A five-mile spectacle of lighting" since 1879. More than 400,000 lamps of various types and styles. Annually, from the first Friday after the August bank holiday through the first Sunday in November. Est attendance: 3,500,000. For info: VisitBlackpool. Web: www.visitblackpool.com.

FIRST ELECTRIC LIGHTING: ANNIVERSARY. Sept 4, 1882. Four hundred electric lights came on in offices on Spruce, Wall, Nassau and Pearl streets in lower Manhattan as Thomas Edison hooked up lightbulbs to an underground cable carrying direct current electrical power. Edison had demonstrated his first incandescent lightbulb in 1879. See also: "Incandescent Lamp Demonstrated: Anniversary" (Oct 21).

HARVEY, PAUL: BIRTH ANNIVERSARY. Sept 4, 1918. Legendary radio broadcaster and newsman, born at Tulsa, OK, he is best remembered for his syndicated features that ran twice per day on the ABC Radio Network. "The Rest of the Story" was a behind-the-scenes look at the rise to prominence of famous people from all walks of life, and his morning news program was opinionated, occasionally sarcastic and full of offbeat human interest stories. Harvey died at Phoenix, AZ, Feb 28, 2009.

HOG CAPITAL OF THE WORLD FESTIVAL. Sept 4–7. Kewanee, IL. World's largest outdoor pork barbeque. Also features professional entertainment, carnival, flea market, mud volleyball, Model T races, parade and Hog Stampede (four-mile run). Annually, Labor Day weekend. Est attendance: 20,000. For info: Hog Fest Committee, 306 N Main St, Kewanee, IL 61443. Phone: (309) 852-4644. E-mail: info@kewaneehogdays.com. Web: www.kewaneehogdays.com.

HOPKINTON STATE FAIR. Sept 4–7. Contoocook, NH. Since 1915. "A Labor Day Weekend Tradition." For info: Hopkinton State Fair, 392 Kearsarge Ave, Contoocook, NH 03229-0700. Phone: (603) 746-4191. E-mail: hsfinfo@tds.net. Web: www.hsfair.org.

LITTLE ROCK NINE CRISIS: ANNIVERSARY. Sept 4–25, 1957. On Sept 4, 1957, nine black students were blocked from entering Little Rock Central High School by the Arkansas National Guard, who had been called out two days before by Governor Orval Faubus in order to prevent efforts to desegregate the school. The desegregation crisis continued for that month. The students entered the school Sept 23, but a protesting mob was so unstable that the nine were removed from the building for their own safety. An angry President Eisenhower sent in the 101st Army Airborne to enforce the law allowing the students to integrate the school, and on Sept 25, national troops escorted the nine into the school.

LOS ANGELES, CALIFORNIA, FOUNDED: ANNIVERSARY. Sept 4, 1781. Los Angeles founded by decree and called "El Pueblo de Nuestra Señora La Reina de Los Angeles de Porciuncula." The City of Los Angeles was incorporated on Apr 4, 1850.

NEWSPAPER CARRIER DAY. Sept 4. Anniversary of the hiring of the first "newsboy" in the US, 10-year-old Barney Flaherty, who is said to have answered the following classified advertisement, which appeared in the *New York Sun* in 1833: "To the Unemployed—a number of steady men can find employment by vending this paper. A liberal discount is allowed to those who buy to sell again."

ODYSSEY—A GREEK FESTIVAL. Sept 4–7. Orange, CT. An indoor/outdoor festival celebrating Greek culture, featuring authentic Greek cuisine, live music and marketplace. Est attendance: 15,000. For info: St. Barbara Greek Orthodox Church, 480 Racebrook Rd, Orange, CT 06477. Phone: (203) 795-1347. Web: www.saintbarbara.org. Or: Greater New Haven CVB, One Long Wharf Dr, New Haven, CT 06511. Phone: (203) 777-8550 or (800) 332-STAY. Fax: (203) 782-7755.

POLK, SARAH CHILDRESS: BIRTH ANNIVERSARY. Sept 4, 1803. Wife of James Knox Polk, 11th president of the US. Born at Murfreesboro, TN, and died at Nashville, TN, Aug 14, 1891.

WASHINGTON STATE FAIR. Sept 4–29. Puyallup, WA. Since 1900. One of the top fairs in attendance in the world. Entertainment, rodeo, animals, rides, displays and food. Annually, beginning on the Friday of Labor Day weekend. Est attendance: 1,100,000. For info: Washington State Fair, 110 Ninth Ave SW, Puyallup, WA 98371. Phone: (253) 845-1771. E-mail: info@thefair.com. Web: www.thefair.com.

WISCONSIN STATE COW-CHIP THROW. Sept 4–5. Prairie du Sac, WI. 46th annual. Cow-Chip Throw ("no gloves"), 5k and 10k runs, arts and crafts fair, live music and parade. Annually, the Friday night and Saturday of Labor Day weekend. Est attendance: 50,000. For info: Wisconsin State Cow-Chip Throw. Phone: (608) 643-4317. E-mail: marietta@toolsofmarketing.com. Web: www.wiscowchip.com.

WOODSTOCK FAIR. Sept 4–7. Woodstock, CT. Historic fair whose origins extend back to 1809. Attractions include the Barnyard Babies Birthing Center, 1822 Brunn Barn Museum, livestock and agricultural exhibits, midway, go kart races and more. Annually, Labor Day weekend. Est attendance: 185,000. For info: Woodstock Fair, PO Box 1, South Woodstock, CT 06267. Phone: (860) 928-3246. E-mail: info@woodstockfair.com. Web: www.woodstockfair.com.

WRIGHT, RICHARD: BIRTH ANNIVERSARY. Sept 4, 1908. Novelist and short-story writer whose works include *Native Son, Uncle Tom's Children* and *Black Boy*, born at Natchez, MS. Wright died at Paris, France, Nov 28, 1960.

🧁 BIRTHDAYS TODAY

Wes Bentley, 42, actor (*The Hunger Games, American Beauty*), born Jonesboro, AR, Sept 4, 1978.

Mitzi Gaynor, 89, singer, dancer, actress (*South Pacific*), born Francesca Mitzi Marlene de Charney von Gerber at Chicago, IL, Sept 4, 1931.

Max Greenfield, 40, actor ("New Girl," "Veronica Mars," "Ugly Betty"), born Dobbs Ferry, NY, Sept 4, 1980.

Judith Ivey, 69, actress (*Compromising Positions, Brighton Beach Memoirs*; stage: *Steaming*), born El Paso, TX, Sept 4, 1951.

Beyoncé Knowles, 39, singer, actress (*Dreamgirls*), born Houston, TX, Sept 4, 1981.

Michael Joseph (Mike) Piazza, 52, Hall of Fame baseball player, born Norristown, PA, Sept 4, 1968.

Mark Ronson, 45, singer, musician, music producer, DJ, born London, England, Sept 4, 1975.

Ione Skye, 50, actress (*Say Anything*), born Hertfordshire, England, Sept 4, 1970.

September 2020	S	M	T	W	T	F	S
			1	2	3	4	5
	6	7	8	9	10	11	12
	13	14	15	16	17	18	19
	20	21	22	23	24	25	26
	27	28	29	30			

Thomas Sturges (Tom) Watson, 71, golfer, born Kansas City, MO, Sept 4, 1949.

Damon Wayans, 60, actor, comedian ("In Living Color"), born New York, NY, Sept 4, 1960.

September 5 — Saturday

DAY 249 **117 REMAINING**

BABE RUTH'S FIRST PRO HOMER: ANNIVERSARY. Sept 5, 1914. Babe Ruth hit his first home run as a professional while playing for Providence in the International League, a type of minor league affiliate of the Boston Red Sox. He pitched a one-hit shutout against Toronto.

CAGE, JOHN: BIRTH ANNIVERSARY. Sept 5, 1912. Avant-garde American composer John Cage was born at Los Angeles, CA. He pioneered the experimental music and performance art schools. He used nontraditional instruments such as flowerpots and cowbells in innovative situations, such as performances governed by chance, in which the *I Ching* was consulted to determine the direction of the performance. In 1978 he was elected to the American Academy of Arts and Sciences and in 1982 was awarded France's highest honor for cultural contributions, *Commandeur de l'Ordre des Arts et des Lettres*. He died Aug 12, 1992, at New York, NY.

CAL FARLEY'S BOYS RANCH RODEO AND ADVENTUREFEST. Sept 5. Boys Ranch, TX. Continuing a 75-year tradition, Cal Farley's signature event features family-friendly fun and games, an authentic Western barbecue lunch and impressive rodeo competition including bronc riding, roping and more. Annually, the Saturday of Labor Day weekend. Est attendance: 5,000. For info: Cal Farley's, PO Box 1890, Amarillo, TX 79174-0001. Phone: (800) 687-3722. Fax: (806) 372-6638. E-mail: info@calfarley.org. Web: www.calfarley.org.

CARNOVSKY, MORRIS: BIRTH ANNIVERSARY. Sept 5, 1897. American actor Morris Carnovsky was born at St. Louis, MO. In 1931 with actor Lee Strasberg and others he founded the Group Theater at New York, NY. He was blacklisted in the 1950s by the House Un-American Activities Committee but was still asked by John Houseman to perform in the American Shakespeare Festival in 1956 and began a successful Shakespearean career. He was elected to the Theater Hall of Fame in 1979. Carnovsky died Sept 1, 1992, at Easton, CT.

CLEVELAND NATIONAL AIR SHOW. Sept 5–7. Burke Lakefront Airport, Cleveland, OH. Country's oldest air show, featuring extensive military and foreign aircraft participation. Annually, Labor Day weekend. Est attendance: 80,000. For info: Cleveland Natl Air Show, Burke Lakefront Airport, Cleveland, OH 44114. Phone: (216) 781-0747. Fax: (216) 781-7810. E-mail: info@clevelandairshow.com. Web: www.clevelandairshow.com.

COMMONWHEEL ARTISTS LABOR DAY ART FESTIVAL. Sept 5–7. Memorial Park, Manitou Springs, CO. 46th annual. Juried arts and crafts festival, featuring 120 fine artists and craftspeople and a variety of foods with continuous live entertainment ranging from Celtic harp music to jazz, including original acoustic

songwriters. Est attendance: 15,000. For info: Commonwheel Artists Art Festival, PO Box 42, Manitou Springs, CO 80829. Phone: (719) 577-7700. E-mail: festival@commonwheel.com. Web: www.commonwheel.com/festival.

FIRST CONTINENTAL CONGRESS ASSEMBLY: ANNIVERSARY. Sept 5, 1774. The first assembly of this forerunner of the US Congress took place at Philadelphia, PA. Peyton Randolph, delegate from Virginia, was elected president.

FIRST LABOR DAY OBSERVANCE: ANNIVERSARY. Sept 5, 1882. On this day in New York City, the first observance of Labor Day was held. It was organized by the Central Labor Union. Historians debate whether the inspiration came from Peter McGuire, general secretary of the Brotherhood of Carpenters and Joiners, or Matthew Maguire, secretary of the Central Labor Union. By 1884 other cities were honoring working people. In 1894 it became a federal holiday.

GERALD FORD: ASSASSINATION ATTEMPTS: 45th ANNIVERSARY. Sept 5, 1975. Lynette A. "Squeaky" Fromme, a follower of convicted murderer Charles Manson, attempted to shoot President Gerald Ford. On Sept 22 of the same year, another attempt on Ford's life occurred when Sara Jane Moore shot at him.

ISRAELI OLYMPIAD MASSACRE: ANNIVERSARY. Sept 5–6, 1972. Eleven members of the Israeli Olympic team were killed in an attack on the Olympic Village at Munich, Germany, and attempted kidnapping of team members. Four of seven guerrillas, members of the Black September faction of the Palestinian Liberation Army, were also killed. In retaliation, Israeli jets bombed Palestinian positions at Lebanon and Syria on Sept 8, 1972.

JAMES, JESSE: BIRTH ANNIVERSARY. Sept 5, 1847. Born at Centerville, MO, Jesse Woodson James was a notorious bandit whose gang (including brother Frank) robbed banks, stagecoaches and trains. On Sept 7, 1876, every member of the original gang except for the James brothers was killed or captured while attempting to rob a bank at Northfield, MN. The brothers formed a new gang and resumed their criminal careers in 1879. On Apr 3, 1882, at St. Joseph, MO, Robert Ford, a new gang member, shot James in the back of the head in order to claim a $10,000 reward.

KOESTLER, ARTHUR: BIRTH ANNIVERSARY. Sept 5, 1905. Born at Budapest, Hungary, Koestler is best known for his novel about his disillusionment with communism, *Darkness at Noon*, and for *The God That Failed*. Died at London, England, Mar 3, 1983.

LOUIS XIV: BIRTH ANNIVERSARY. Sept 5, 1638. Born at Saint-Germain-en-Laye, France, Louis the Great, or the Sun King, centralized state power into his person, brilliantly directing able ministers and controlling the nobility. Abroad, he extended the borders of France in a series of wars, but his influence extended beyond politics into all spheres of life. He was a patron of writers, painters and architects, and his court at Versailles is a masterpiece of Baroque architecture. He died Sept 1, 1715, at Versailles.

"THE MACNEIL-LEHRER NEWSHOUR" TV PREMIERE: ANNIVERSARY. Sept 5, 1983. Originally, this PBS news show was entitled "The MacNeil-Lehrer Report" and aired each weeknight for a half hour starting in 1976. Robert MacNeil and Jim Lehrer were joined by Charlayne Hunter-Gault and Judy Woodruff. In 1983 the show was expanded to an hour and became TV's first regularly

scheduled daily hour news show. The show has been praised for its depth and objectivity. Robert MacNeil retired in 1995 and Jim Lehrer retired in 2011. This program is now entitled "PBS Newshour" and is helmed by Judy Woodruff.

MERCURY, FREDDIE: BIRTH ANNIVERSARY. Sept 5, 1946. One of the greatest rock singers of all time was born Farrokh Bulsara at Stone Town, Zanzibar. Boasting a four-octave range, Mercury fronted (and wrote songs for) the English band Queen, leading them to arena rock superstardom. Mercury penned the songs "Bohemian Rhapsody," "Killer Queen" and "Crazy Little Thing Called Love," among others. He died Nov 24, 1991, London, England.

MICHIGAN'S GREAT FIRE OF 1881: ANNIVERSARY. Sept 5, 1881. According to the Michigan Historical Commission, "Small fires were burning in the forests of the 'Thumb area of Michigan,' tinder-dry after a long, hot summer, when a gale swept in from the southwest on Sept 5, 1881. Fanned into an inferno, the fire raged for three days. A million acres were devastated in Sanilac and Huron counties alone. At least 125 persons died, and thousands more were left destitute. The new American Red Cross won support for its prompt aid to the fire victims. This was the first disaster relief furnished by this great organization."

NIELSEN, ARTHUR CHARLES: BIRTH ANNIVERSARY. Sept 5, 1897. Marketing research engineer, founder of AC Nielsen Company, in 1923, known for radio and TV audience surveys, was born at Chicago, IL, and died there June 1, 1980.

SPACE MILESTONE: *VOYAGER 1* (US). Sept 5, 1977. Twin of *Voyager 2*, which was launched Aug 20. On Feb 18, 1998, *Voyager 1* set a new distance record when after more than 20 years in space it reached 6.5 billion miles from Earth.

UNITED NATIONS: INTERNATIONAL DAY OF CHARITY. Sept 5. In recognition of the role of charity in alleviating humanitarian crises and human suffering within and among nations, as well as of the efforts of charitable organizations and individuals, including the work of Mother Teresa, the General Assembly of the United Nations (Res 67/105) designated Sept 5, anniversary of the death of Mother Teresa, as International Day of Charity. For info: United Nations. Web: www.un.org/en/events/charityday.

ZANUCK, DARRYL F.: BIRTH ANNIVERSARY. Sept 5, 1902. Born at Wahoo, NE, Darryl F. Zanuck became a celebrated—and controversial—movie producer. He was also a cofounder of Twentieth Century Studios, which later merged with Fox. His film credits include *The Jazz Singer* (the first full-length sound picture), *Forever Amber*, *The Snake Pit* and *The Grapes of Wrath*. He died Dec 21, 1979, at Palm Springs, CA.

🎂 BIRTHDAYS TODAY

Kristian Alfonso, 56, actress ("Days of Our Lives," "Melrose Place"), born Brockton, MA, Sept 5, 1964.

Elena Delle Donne, 31, basketball player, born Wilmington, DE, Sept 5, 1989.

William Devane, 81, actor ("24," "Knots Landing"), born Albany, NY, Sept 5, 1939.

Dennis Dugan, 74, actor, director (*Big Daddy, Problem Child*), born Wheaton, IL, Sept 5, 1946.

Cathy Lee Guisewite, 70, cartoonist ("Cathy"), born Dayton, OH, Sept 5, 1950.

Michael Keaton, 69, actor (*Birdman, Batman, Beetlejuice*), born Michael Douglas at Pittsburgh, PA, Sept 5, 1951.

Kim Yuna, 30, Olympic figure skater, born Bucheon, South Korea, Sept 5, 1990.

Carol Lawrence, 85, singer, actress (*West Side Story*), born Carol Maria Laraia at Melrose Park, IL, Sept 5, 1935.

Rose McGowan, 47, actress (*Jawbreaker*, "Charmed"), born Florence, Italy, Sept 5, 1973.

Bob Newhart, 91, comedian (*Elf*, "The Bob Newhart Show," "Newhart"), born Chicago, IL, Sept 5, 1929.

Raquel Welch, 78, actress (*The Three Musketeers, Woman of the Year*), model, born Chicago, IL, Sept 5, 1942.

Dweezil Zappa, 51, singer, actor ("Normal Life"), born Hollywood, CA, Sept 5, 1969.

September 6 — Sunday

DAY 250   **116 REMAINING**

ADDAMS, JANE: BIRTH ANNIVERSARY. Sept 6, 1860. American worker for peace, social welfare and rights of women. She cofounded Hull House at Chicago, IL, in 1889, which provided for the needs of the underprivileged community there. Addams was corecipient of the Nobel Peace Prize in 1931—the second woman to receive that honor. Born at Cedarville, IL, she died May 21, 1935, at Chicago.

BALTIC STATES' INDEPENDENCE RECOGNIZED: ANNIVERSARY. Sept 6, 1991. The Soviet government recognized the independence of the Baltic states—Latvia, Estonia and Lithuania. The action came 51 years after the Baltic states were annexed by the Soviet Union. All three Baltic states had earlier declared their independence, and many nations had already recognized them diplomatically, including the US, Sept 2, 1991.

BEECHER, CATHARINE ESTHER: BIRTH ANNIVERSARY. Sept 6, 1800. Catharine Esther Beecher was born at East Hampton, NY. In addition to teaching herself mathematics, philosophy and Latin, Beecher had been formally educated in art and music. An early advocate for equal education for women, she founded the Hartford Female Seminary, which was widely recognized for its advanced curriculum. She was also instrumental in the founding of women's colleges in Iowa, Illinois and Wisconsin. Beecher died May 12, 1878, at Elmira, NY.

BULGARIA: UNIFICATION DAY. Sept 6. National holiday. Commemorates the anniversary of the reunification of the southern part of Bulgaria with the rest of the country in 1885.

FIRST RADIO BROADCAST OF A PRIZEFIGHT: 100th ANNIVERSARY. Sept 6, 1920. In the first boxing match broadcast on radio, Jack Dempsey knocked out Billy Miske in the third round of a scheduled 10-round fight.

ITALY: HISTORICAL REGATTA. Sept 6. Venice. Traditional competition among two-oar racing gondolas, preceded by a procession of Venetian ceremonial boats of the epoch of the Venetian Republic. Annually, the first Sunday in September.

September 2020	S	M	T	W	T	F	S
			1	2	3	4	5
	6	7	8	9	10	11	12
	13	14	15	16	17	18	19
	20	21	22	23	24	25	26
	27	28	29	30			

ITALY: JOUST OF THE SARACEN. Sept 6. Arezzo. The first Sunday in September is set aside for the Giostra del Saracino, a tilting contest of the 13th century, with knights in armor.

KENNEDY, JOSEPH P.: BIRTH ANNIVERSARY. Sept 6, 1888. Prominent businessman, government official and patriarch of the Kennedy dynasty born at Boston, MA. Harvard educated, Kennedy worked as a bank president, movie producer and shipbuilder before retiring as a multimillionaire in 1929. He was the first chairman of both the Securities and Exchange Commission (1934–35) and the US Maritime Commission (1937); his appointment as first Irish-American US ambassador to the United Kingdom marked the pinnacle of his governmental career. Kennedy was instrumental in the advancement of his sons' political careers. He died at his home at Hyannis Port, MA, on Nov 18, 1969.

LAFAYETTE, MARQUIS DE: BIRTH ANNIVERSARY. Sept 6, 1757. The French general and aristocrat, whose full name was Marie-Joseph-Paul-Yves-Roch-Gilbert du Motier, came to America to assist in the Revolutionary cause. Lafayette, who had persuaded Louis XVI to send 6,000 French soldiers to assist the Americans, was given command of an army at Virginia and was instrumental in forcing the surrender of Lord Cornwallis at Yorktown. He was called "The Hero of Two Worlds" and was appointed a brigadier general on his return to France in 1782. He became a leader of the liberal aristocrats during the early days of the French Revolution. As the commander of the newly formed national guard of Paris, he rescued Louis XVI and Marie-Antoinette from a crowd that stormed Versailles Oct 6, 1789. His popularity waned after his guards opened fire on angry demonstrators demanding abdication of the king in 1791. He fled to Austria with the overthrow of the monarchy in 1792, returning when Napoleon Bonaparte came to power. Born at Chavaniac, France, he died at Paris, May 20, 1834.

MUHLENBERG, HENRY MELCHIOR: BIRTH ANNIVERSARY. Sept 6, 1711. Born at Einbeck, Hanover, Germany, Muhlenberg was a Lutheran pastor who immigrated to the US in 1742 to help the nascent Lutheran congregations that needed experienced clergy. Beginning in Pennsylvania and working throughout the eastern seaboard, he organized churches and then convened the first Lutheran synod in the US in 1761. He is thus considered the founder of the US Lutheran Church. Muhlenberg died on Oct 7, 1787, at Trappe, PA.

NATIONAL WAFFLE WEEK. Sept 6–12. A celebration of the wonderful, crispy breakfast orb and its contributions to American society. Annually, the first full week in September. For info: Waffle House, PO Box 6450, Norcross, GA 30091. Phone: (770) 729-5884. E-mail: communications@wafflehouse.com. Web: www.wafflehouse.com.

PAKISTAN: DEFENSE OF PAKISTAN DAY. Sept 6. National holiday. Commemorates the Indo-Pakistan War of 1965.

ROSE, BILLY: BIRTH ANNIVERSARY. Sept 6, 1899. The American theatrical producer, author, songwriter and husband of Fanny Brice was born William S. Rosenberg at New York, NY. His songs include "That Old Gang of Mine," "Me and My Shadow," "Without a Song," "It's Only a Paper Moon" and hundreds of others. Rose died at Montego Bay, Jamaica, Feb 10, 1966.

SCANDINAVIAN FEST. Sept 6. Vasa Park, Budd Lake, NJ. Celebrate and sample the cultures, traditions and contemporary life of the Nordic countries: Denmark, Estonia, Finland, Iceland, Norway and Sweden—through food, entertainment, music, dancing, handicrafts, lectures and special children's activities. Annually, the Sunday before Labor Day. Est attendance: 6,000. For info: Carl Anderson, 5 Christopher Lee Dr, New Oxford, PA 17350. Phone: (610) 417-1483. E-mail: info@ScanFest.org. Web: www.ScanFest.org.

SUBSTITUTE TEACHER APPRECIATION WEEK. Sept 6–12. Although substitute teachers get no sick days or respect, they teach when the regular teacher cannot and continually adjust to different classroom situations. For info: Dorothy Zjawin, 61 W Colfax Ave, Roselle Park, NJ 07204.

SWAZILAND: INDEPENDENCE DAY. Sept 6. National holiday. Commemorates attainment of independence from Britain in 1968. Also called Somhlolo Day in honor of the great 19th-century Swazi leader.

UNITED NATIONS: MILLENNIUM SUMMIT: 20th ANNIVERSARY. Sept 6–8, 2000. More than 150 world leaders met at the United Nations in New York City, the largest gathering of such leaders in history. Among the kings, prime ministers, presidents and generals attending were US president Bill Clinton, Fidel Castro and Yasser Arafat. These leaders adopted a declaration that committed them to promote democracy, strengthen respect for human rights, reverse the spread of AIDS, cut poverty, protect the planet and improve the ability of the UN to keep the peace.

 **BIRTHDAYS TODAY**

Chris Christie, 58, former governor of New Jersey (R), born Newark, NJ, Sept 6, 1962.

Jane Curtin, 73, actress ("3rd Rock from the Sun," "Kate and Allie"), comedienne ("Saturday Night Live"), born Cambridge, MA, Sept 6, 1947.

Jennifer Egan, 58, journalist, author (*A Visit from the Goon Squad*), born Chicago, IL, Sept 6, 1962.

Idris Elba, 48, actor (Golden Globe for "Luther"; *Beasts of No Nation, Mandela: Long Walk to Freedom*, "The Wire"), born London, England, Sept 6, 1972.

Jeff Foxworthy, 62, comedian, actor ("The Jeff Foxworthy Show"), author (*No Shirt, No Shoes . . . No Problem*), born Atlanta, GA, Sept 6, 1958.

Naomie Harris, 44, actress (*Moonlight, Spectre, Mandela: Long Walk to Freedom*), born London, England, Sept 6, 1976.

Tim Henman, 46, sportscaster, former tennis player, born Oxford, England, Sept 6, 1974.

Swoosie Kurtz, 76, actress ("Sisters," *The World According to Garp*, Tony for *The House of Blue Leaves*), born Omaha, NE, Sept 6, 1944.

China Miéville, 48, author (*Kraken, The City & the City, Perdido Street Station*), born Norwich, England, Sept 6, 1972.

Rosie Perez, 56, actress (*King of the Jungle, White Men Can't Jump*), born Brooklyn, NY, Sept 6, 1964.

Sarah Strange, 46, actress ("Men in Trees," "Da Vinci's Inquest"), born Vancouver, BC, Canada, Sept 6, 1974.

Elizabeth Vargas, 58, television journalist, born Paterson, NJ, Sept 6, 1962.

John Wall, 30, basketball player, born Raleigh, NC, Sept 6, 1990.

Justin Whalin, 46, actor ("Charles in Charge," "Lois & Clark"), born San Francisco, CA, Sept 6, 1974.

Jo Anne Worley, 83, comedienne, actress ("Rowan & Martin's Laugh-In"), born Lowell, IA, Sept 6, 1937.

September 7 — Monday

DAY 251   **115 REMAINING**

THE BLITZ BEGINS: 80th ANNIVERSARY. Sept 7, 1940. During WWII, Hitler, who had prohibited attacks on London, England, lifted his ban after an Aug 24–25 RAF attack on Berlin, Germany. So on this date, "The Blitz" began: nighttime bombing raids on London for 57 consecutive nights and then sporadically until May 1941. The Blitz claimed 40,000 lives and left half a million Londoners homeless.

BRAZIL: INDEPENDENCE DAY. Sept 7. Declared independence from Portugal in 1822. National holiday.

CANADA: LABOR DAY. Sept 7. Annually, the first Monday in September.

DEBAKEY, MICHAEL E.: BIRTH ANNIVERSARY. Sept 7, 1908. Heart and vascular surgery pioneer, medical ambassador and inventor, born at Lake Charles, LA. DeBakey invented the roller pump, which helped make open-heart surgery a possibility, and he made the first connection between smoking and cancer. Performed more than 60,000 operations, and cited by the *American Journal of Medicine* as perhaps "the greatest surgeon ever." DeBakey died July 11, 2008, at Houston, TX.

GOOGLE FOUNDED: ANNIVERSARY. Sept 7, 1998. Sergey Brin and Larry Page incorporated the Internet search engine company Google on this date at Menlo Park, CA. Although still in beta, Google.com was receiving 10,000 queries a day at that time. Within a year, the company was doing three million searches a day. Before long, *Google* entered the pop culture zeitgeist by becoming a verb meaning "perform an Internet search."

GRANDMA MOSES DAY. Sept 7. Anna Mary Robertson Moses, modern primitive American painter born at Greenwich, NY, Sept 7, 1860. Started painting at the age of 78. Her 100th birthday was proclaimed Grandma Moses Day in New York state. Died at Hoosick Falls, NY, Dec 13, 1961.

HOLLY, BUDDY: BIRTH ANNIVERSARY. Sept 7, 1936. American music performer, composer and bandleader. Called one of the most innovative and influential musicians of his time, he was a pioneer of rock and roll. His hits include "That'll Be the Day" and "Peggy Sue." Born Charles Harden Holley, at Lubbock, TX, he died at age 22 in an airplane crash near Mason City, IA, Feb 3, 1959.

KAZAN, ELIA: BIRTH ANNIVERSARY. Sept 7, 1909. Born Elia Kazanjoglou at Constantinople (now Istanbul), Turkey, Elia Kazan was one of the most influential directors in the history of American stage and film. He directed the Broadway premieres of Arthur Miller's *Death of a Salesman* and Tennessee Williams's *A Streetcar Named Desire* as well as many other Williams plays. He won directing Oscars for the films *On the Waterfront* and *Gentlemen's Agreement*. He discovered and promoted actors such as Marlon Brando, Warren Beatty and James Dean, whom he directed in *East of Eden*. In 1952 he angered much of Hollywood by testifying before the House Un-American Activities Committee, naming persons he thought to be members of the Communist Party. Kazan died at New York, NY, Sept 7, 2003.

★**LABOR DAY.** Sept 7. There is no greater example of our country's resolve and resilience than that of our workers. As we celebrate Labor Day, we honor those who have advanced our nation's strength and prosperity—American workers.

LABOR DAY. Sept 7. Legal public holiday. Public Law 90–363 sets Labor Day on the first Monday in September. Observed in all states. First observance was a parade on Tuesday, Sept 5, 1882, at New York, NY, probably organized by Peter McGuire, a Brotherhood of Carpenters and Joiners secretary. In 1883 a union resolution declared "the first Monday in September of each year a Labor Day." By 1893 more than half of the states were observing Labor Day on one or another day and a bill to establish Labor Day as a federal holiday was introduced in Congress. On June 28, 1894, President Grover Cleveland signed into law an act making the first Monday in September a legal holiday for federal employees and the District of Columbia. Canada also celebrates Labor Day on the first Monday in September. In most other countries, Labor Day is observed May 1. See also: "First Labor Day Observance: Anniversary" (Sept 5).

LAWRENCE, JACOB: BIRTH ANNIVERSARY. Sept 7, 1917. African-American painter, born at Atlantic City, NJ. Lawrence was best known for his series of historical paintings on John Brown and on the migration of African Americans out of the South. A recipient of the NAACP's Spingarn Medal, he won many other awards during his lifetime. Lawrence died June 9, 2000, at Seattle, WA.

MOUTHGUARD DAY. Sept 7. Founded in 2018 by OPRO Mouthguards, this day seeks to raise awareness of the importance of wearing a mouthguard (aka gum shield) in sport. Wearing a properly fitted mouthguard will do more than just prevent tooth loss from a facial injury, it can also help prevent head injury. Annually, the first Monday in September. For info: Opro Mouthguards, The Willows, Mark Rd, Hemel Hempstead, Hertfordshire HP2 7BN, United Kingdom. Phone: (44) 1442-430-690. E-mail: joel.seshold@oprogroup.com.

NATIONAL PAYROLL WEEK. Sept 7–11. Founded in 1996 by the American Payroll Association to recognize the important partnership of America's workers and the payroll professionals who pay them on time and accurately. Provides an annual opportunity to proudly proclaim "America Works Because We're Working for America!" For info: American Payroll Assn, 660 N Main Ave, Ste 100, San Antonio, TX 78205. Phone: (210) 226-4600. Fax: (210) 224-2028. E-mail: moreinfo@americanpayroll.org. Web: www.nationalpayrollweek.com.

"NEITHER SNOW NOR RAIN" DAY: ANNIVERSARY. Sept 7, 1914. Anniversary of the opening to the public on Labor Day 1914 of the New York Post Office Building at Eighth Avenue between 31st and 33rd streets. On the front of this building was an inscription supplied by William M. Kendall of the architectural firm that planned the building. The inscription, a free translation from Herodotus, reads: "Neither snow nor rain nor heat nor gloom of night stays these couriers from the swift completion of their appointed rounds." This has long been believed to be the motto of the US Post Office and Postal Service. They have, in fact, no motto—but the legend remains.

PRO FOOTBALL HALL OF FAME CHARTER MEMBERS: ANNIVERSARY. Sept 7, 1963. The Pro Football Hall of Fame opened this day in Canton, OH, with the induction of 17 charter members: 11 players and six executives. The players selected were Sammy Baugh, Dutch Clark, Red Grange, Mel Hein, Pete Henry, Cal Hubbard, Don Hutson, Johnny McNally, Bronko Nagurski, Ernie Nevers and Jim Thorpe. They were joined by Bert Bell, Joe Carr, George Halas, Curly Lambeau, Tim Mara and George Preston Marshall.

QUEEN ELIZABETH I: BIRTH ANNIVERSARY. Sept 7, 1533. Queen of England, daughter of Henry VIII and Anne Boleyn, after whom the Elizabethan era was named, was born at Greenwich Palace. She ascended the throne in 1558 at the age of 25. During her reign, the British defeated the Spanish Armada in July 1588, the Anglican Church was essentially established and England became a world power. She died at Richmond, England, Mar 24, 1603.

ROY WEBSTER CROSS CHANNEL SWIM. Sept 7. Hood River, OR. 78th annual. The annual swim across the mighty Columbia River draws 550 contestants each year to swim the approximately one-mile distance for fun. Annually, on Labor Day. Est attendance: 1,000. For info: Roy Webster Cross Channel Swim, Hood River County Chamber of Commerce, 720 E Port Marina Dr, Hood River, OR 97031. Phone: (800) 366-3530 or (541) 386-2000. E-mail: events@hoodriver.org. Web: www.hoodriver.org.

STOCK EXCHANGE HOLIDAY (LABOR DAY). Sept 7. The holiday schedules for the various exchanges are subject to change if relevant rules, regulations or exchange policies are revised. If you have questions, contact: CME Group (CME, CBOT, NYMEX, COMEX) (www.cmegroup.com), Chicago Board Options Exchange (www.cboe.com), NASDAQ (www.nasdaq.com), NYSE (www.nyse.com).

TUPAC SHAKUR SHOT: ANNIVERSARY. Sept 7, 1996. Bestselling rap artist and actor Tupac Shakur was shot multiple times at a Las Vegas, NV, intersection while riding in a car driven by Death Row Records founder Suge Knight. Shakur died of his wounds Sept 13. The murder case has never been closed.

VAN ALLEN, JAMES: BIRTH ANNIVERSARY. Sept 7, 1914. Physicist born at Mt. Pleasant, IA. Van Allen studied Earth's magnetic field; cosmic rays; and Earth's radiation belts, now named the Van Allen belts. The positions of these belts are now taken into consideration when planning spaceflights in order to plot courses that take spacecrafts through the weakest part of the radiation zones. Awarded the National Medal of Science in 1987, Van Allen died Aug 9, 2006, at Iowa City, IA.

WAIKIKI ROUGHWATER SWIM. Sept 7. Waikiki Beach, Honolulu, HI. The 51st annual swim is 2.4 miles, from Sans Souci Beach to Duke Kahanamoku Beach. "The World's Most Prestigious Open Water Swimming Event." Preregistration is required. Online registration at www.pacificsportevents.com. Annually, Labor Day. Est attendance: 1,000. For info: Waikiki Roughwater Swim Committee. Web: www.wrswim.com.

September	S	M	T	W	T	F	S
2020			1	2	3	4	5
	6	7	8	9	10	11	12
	13	14	15	16	17	18	19
	20	21	22	23	24	25	26
	27	28	29	30			

🎂 BIRTHDAYS TODAY

Corbin Bernsen, 66, actor ("LA Law," "Ryan's Hope," *Major League*), born North Hollywood, CA, Sept 7, 1954.

Susan Blakely, 70, actress (*The Way We Were, The Lords of Flatbush, Shampoo*), born Frankfurt, Germany, Sept 7, 1950.

Michael Emerson, 66, actor ("Person of Interest," "Lost"), born Cedar Rapids, IA, Sept 7, 1954.

Michael Feinstein, 64, singer, pianist, born Columbus, OH, Sept 7, 1956.

Angela Gheorghiu, 55, opera singer, born Angela Burlacu at Adjud, Romania, Sept 7, 1965.

Chrissie Hynde, 69, singer, songwriter (Pretenders), born Akron, OH, Sept 7, 1951.

Leslie Jones, 53, comedienne ("Saturday Night Live," *Ghostbusters*), born Memphis, TN, Sept 7, 1967.

Julie Kavner, 69, actress (*Radio Days*, "Rhoda," Marge Simpson's voice on "The Simpsons"), born Los Angeles, CA, Sept 7, 1951.

Devon Sawa, 42, actor ("Nikita," *Final Destination, Wild America*), born Vancouver, BC, Canada, Sept 7, 1978.

Briana Scurry, 49, Hall of Fame soccer player, born Minneapolis, MN, Sept 7, 1971.

Evan Rachel Wood, 33, actress ("Westworld," "True Blood," *Thirteen, Across the Universe*), born Raleigh, NC, Sept 7, 1987.

Vera Zvonareva, 36, tennis player, born Moscow, Russia, Sept 7, 1984.

September 8 — Tuesday

DAY 252   **114 REMAINING**

ANDORRA: NATIONAL HOLIDAY. Sept 8. Honors Our Lady of Meritxell.

CAESAR, SID: BIRTH ANNIVERSARY. Sept 8, 1922. Born at Yonkers, NY, Isaac Sidney Caesar was an intelligent and provocative innovator of the TV comedy-variety show known for his witty monologues, skits and spoofs. His "Your Show of Shows," which launched writers Carl Reiner, Woody Allen and Mel Brooks, established him as a master comedian. Caesar had a decades-long struggle with substance abuse and psychological problems; he was one of the era's first comedians to talk publicly about psychotherapy. Winner of five Emmys, Caesar was inducted into the Television Hall of Fame in 1985. Died Feb 12, 2014, at Beverly Hills, CA.

CLINE, PATSY: BIRTH ANNIVERSARY. Sept 8, 1932. Country singer, born Virginia Patterson Hensley at Winchester, VA. Patsy Cline got her big break in 1957 when she won an Arthur Godfrey Talent Scout show, singing "Walking After Midnight." Her career took off, and she became a featured singer at the Grand Ole Opry, attaining the rank of top female country singer. She died in a plane crash Mar 5, 1963, at Camden, TN, along with singers Hawkshaw Hawkins and Cowboy Copas.

DVOŘÁK, ANTONÍN: BIRTH ANNIVERSARY. Sept 8, 1841. Composer, born at Nelahozeves, Austrian Empire (now Czech Republic), whose work was influenced by the folk music of his native Bohemia. His best-known works include *Symphony Number 9 (From the New World)*, the opera *Rusalka* and the *Cello Concerto*, which is among the most performed pieces for cello and orchestra. Dvořák died on May 1, 1904, at Prague.

GALVESTON HURRICANE: ANNIVERSARY. Sept 8, 1900. The worst national disaster in US history in terms of lives lost. More than 6,000 people were killed when a hurricane struck Galveston, TX, with winds of more than 120 mph, followed by a huge tidal wave. More than 2,500 buildings were destroyed.

HUEY P. LONG SHOT: 85th ANNIVERSARY. Sept 8, 1935. Powerful US senator Huey P. Long was shot on this date at Baton Rouge, LA. The assassin was allegedly Carl Weiss, a political enemy who confronted Long and his bodyguards at the Louisiana State Capitol. The guards opened fire and Weiss was immediately killed. Long was wounded, either by Weiss or by a ricocheting bullet, and died two days later on Sept 10. See also: "Long, Huey Pierce: Birth Anniversary" (Aug 30).

MACEDONIA: INDEPENDENCE DAY. Sept 8. National holiday. Commemorates independence from the Yugoslav Union in 1991.

MALTA: VICTORY DAY. Sept 8. Also known as "Two Sieges and Regatta Day." Festivities commemorate two historical events: victory over the Turks, Sept 8, 1565, when the Great Siege that began in May 1565 was broken by the Maltese and the Knights of St. John after a loss of nearly 10,000 lives; also commemorated is survival of the 1943 siege by the Axis Powers. Parades, fireworks, boat races, etc, especially at the capital, Valleta, and the Grand Harbour.

MCGWIRE BREAKS HOME RUN RECORD: ANNIVERSARY. Sept 8, 1998. Mark McGwire of the St. Louis Cardinals hit his 62nd home run, breaking Roger Maris's 1961 record for the most home runs in a single season. McGwire hit his homer at Busch Stadium at St. Louis against pitcher Steve Trachsel of the Chicago Cubs as the Cardinals won, 6–3. McGwire finished the season with 70 home runs. On Oct 5, 2001, Barry Bonds hit his 71st home run, breaking McGwire's record. Bonds finished the season with 73 homers.

MISS AMERICA FIRST CROWNED: ANNIVERSARY. Sept 8, 1921. Margaret Gorman of Washington, DC, was crowned the first Miss America at the end of a two-day pageant at Atlantic City, NJ.

MISSION SAN GABRIEL ARCHANGEL: FOUNDING ANNIVERSARY. Sept 8, 1771. California mission to the Indians founded on this date.

NIXON PARDONED: ANNIVERSARY. Sept 8, 1974. Anniversary of the "full, free, and absolute pardon unto Richard Nixon, for all offenses against the United States which he, Richard Nixon, has committed or may have committed or taken part in during the period from January 20, 1969, through August 9, 1974." (Presidential Proclamation 4311, Sept 8, 1974, by Gerald R. Ford.)

NORTHERN PACIFIC RAILROAD COMPLETED: ANNIVERSARY. Sept 8, 1883. After 19 years of construction, the Northern Pacific Railroad became the second railroad to link the two coasts. The Union Pacific and Central Pacific lines met at Utah in 1869.

"THE OPRAH WINFREY SHOW" TV PREMIERE: ANNIVERSARY. Sept 8, 1986. This daytime talk show was the top-rated talk show for years and also has the distinction of being the first talk show hosted by an African-American woman, Oprah Winfrey. Her show was taped in front of a studio audience who were solicited for their questions and feedback. In the mid-1990s, fed up with the plethora of trashy talk shows that had sprung up everywhere, Winfrey decided to upgrade the quality of topics that her show presented. Her book club feature was a popular element of her show, and chosen books usually became bestsellers. The show finished its run on May 25, 2011.

PEDIATRIC HEMATOLOGY/ONCOLOGY NURSES DAY. Sept 8. Recognizes those nurses who care for the day-to-day needs of children with cancer and blood disorders, guiding families through the most difficult circumstances anyone can

experience. For info: Stephanie Sayen, Assn of Pediatric Hematology/Oncology Nurses, 8735 W Higgins Rd, Ste 300, Chicago, IL 60631. Phone: (855) 202-9760. E-mail: info@aphon.org. Web: www.aphon.org.

PEPPER, CLAUDE DENSON: BIRTH ANNIVERSARY. Sept 8, 1900. US representative and senator, born near Dudleyville, AL. Pepper's career in politics spanned 53 years and 10 presidents, and he became the champion for America's senior citizens. He was elected to the US Senate in 1936, where he was a principal architect of many of the nation's "safety net" social programs including Social Security, the minimum wage and medical assistance for the elderly and for disabled children. After a 14-year career in the Senate, he returned to Congress in the House of Representatives, where he served 14 terms. He served as chairman of the House Select Committee on Aging, drafted legislation banning forced retirement and fought against cutting Social Security benefits. Pepper died at Washington, DC, May 30, 1989.

PLAY DAYS. Sept 8–12. 43rd annual. In a world filled with downsizing, rightsizing and shaftsizing, we need humor to reaffirm our humanity and sanity. In the week after Labor Day, the HUMOR Project will playfully spread the word on 1,001 ways to add humor to your life and work. Jest for success—the funny line and bottom line intersect! Annually, the Tuesday through Saturday after Labor Day. For info: The HUMOR Project, 10 Madison Ave, Saratoga Springs, NY 12866. Phone: (518) 587-8770. E-mail: info@Humor-Project.com. Web: www.HumorProject.com.

SELLERS, PETER: 95th BIRTH ANNIVERSARY. Sept 8, 1925. Award-winning British comedian and film star, born Richard Henry Sellers at Southsea, Hampshire, England. Sellers is remembered for his multiple roles in *Dr. Strangelove*, his Oscar-nominated role as Chance the Gardener in *Being There* and his role as the bumbling Inspector Clouseau in the Pink Panther films. Died at London, England, July 24, 1980.

"STAR TREK" TV PREMIERE: ANNIVERSARY. Sept 8, 1966. The first of 79 episodes of the TV series "Star Trek" was aired on the NBC network. Although the science fiction show set in the future lasted only a few seasons, it has remained enormously popular through syndication reruns. It has been given new life through many motion pictures, a cartoon TV series and popular spin-off TV series such as "Star Trek: The Next Generation," "Enterprise" and others. It has consistently ranked among the biggest titles in the motion picture, television, home video and licensing divisions of Paramount Pictures.

"TARZAN" TV PREMIERE: ANNIVERSARY. Sept 8, 1966. This adventure series was based on Edgar Rice Burroughs's character, who appeared for the first time on TV. Tarzan, an English lord who preferred the jungle, was played by Ron Ely. Manuel Padilla, Jr, was Jai, a jungle orphan; Alan Caillou was Jason Flood, Jai's tutor; and Rockne Tarkington was Rao, a veterinarian. There was no Jane.

September 2020	S	M	T	W	T	F	S
			1	2	3	4	5
	6	7	8	9	10	11	12
	13	14	15	16	17	18	19
	20	21	22	23	24	25	26
	27	28	29	30			

UNITED NATIONS: INTERNATIONAL LITERACY DAY. Sept 8. An international day observed by the organizations of the United Nations system. For info: United Nations, Dept of Public Info, New York, NY 10017. Web: www.un.org.

🎂 BIRTHDAYS TODAY

David Arquette, 49, actor (*Scream, Muppets from Space*), born Winchester, VA, Sept 8, 1971.

Martin Freeman, 49, actor ("Fargo," "Sherlock," The Hobbit trilogy, "The Office" [UK]), born Aldershot, Hampshire, England, Sept 8, 1971.

Pink, 41, singer, born Alecia Moore at Doylestown, PA, Sept 8, 1979.

Bernie Sanders, 79, US Senator (I, Vermont), born Brooklyn, NY, Sept 8, 1941.

Jonathan Taylor Thomas, 39, actor ("Home Improvement"), born Bethlehem, PA, Sept 8, 1981.

Rogatien (Rogie) Vachon, 75, former hockey executive and player, born Palmarolle, QC, Canada, Sept 8, 1945.

September 9 — Wednesday

DAY 253   **113 REMAINING**

BATTLE OF MARATHON: ANNIVERSARY. Sept 9. On the day of the ninth month's full moon in the year 490 BC, the numerically superior invading army of Persia was met and defeated on the Plain of Marathon by the Athenian army, led by Miltiades. More than 6,000 men died in the day's battle, which drove the Persians to the sea. The mound of earth covering the dead is still visible at the site. This date is in dispute. See also: "Historic Marathon Runs: Anniversary" (Sept 2) for the legendary running of Phidippides and the origin of the marathon race.

BATTLE OF SALERNO: ANNIVERSARY. Sept 9–16, 1943. US general Mark Clark's Fifth Army made an amphibious assault on Salerno, Italy (Operation Avalanche), on Sept 9 at 3:30 AM. The British First Airborne Division seized the southern Italian port of Taranto (Operation Slapstick) without opposition. Initial gains along the western coast of Italy were checked by strong German forces by Sept 12. In some places the Allied forces were pushed back to within two miles of the coast. On Sept 15 the US 82nd Airborne and British Seventh Armoured counterattacked, and on Sept 16 units of the American Fifth Army and the British Eighth Army joined up near Vallo di Lucania.

BONZA BOTTLER DAY®. Sept 9. To celebrate when the number of the day is the same as the number of the month. Bonza Bottler Day® is an excuse to have a party at least once per month. For more information see Jan 1. For info: Gail Berger, Bonza Bottler Day. Phone: (864) 201-3988. E-mail: bonza@bonzabottlerday.com. Web: www.bonzabottlerday.com.

CALIFORNIA: ADMISSION DAY: ANNIVERSARY. Sept 9. Became the 31st state in 1850.

FARMERS AND THRESHERMENS JUBILEE. Sept 9–13. New Centerville, PA. Held since 1953. Many antique steam engines; antique tractors; steam-powered cider mill; threshing demonstrations using manpower, horses and steam; quilt show and crafts; truck and tractor pulls. Home of the Outhouse Dash. Live entertainment, good food. Est attendance: 20,000. For info: Farmers and Threshermens Jubilee, 1428 Casselman Rd, Rockwood, PA 15557. Phone: (814) 926-3142. Web: www.ncrvfc.com.

IRISH FAMINE BEGINS: 175th ANNIVERSARY. Sept 9, 1845. On this day, *The Dublin Evening Post* reported the partial failure of the

potato crop in Ireland. A blight caused by a fungus destroyed 30 percent of the crop; in 1846, 1848 and 1849 nearly the entire potato crop failed. Out of a population of 8 million, about 1 million people died in the resulting famine and 1.5 million emigrated to the US, Canada and Australia. The 1850 US census showed that more than 40 percent of the country's foreign-born population was Irish.

JAPAN: CHRYSANTHEMUM DAY. Sept 9. Traditional chrysanthemum festival.

KOREA, DEMOCRATIC PEOPLE'S REPUBLIC OF: NATIONAL DAY. Sept 9. National holiday in the Democratic People's Republic of [North] Korea.

LUXEMBOURG: LIBERATION CEREMONY. Sept 9. Petánge. Commemoration of liberation of Grand-Duchy by the Allied forces in 1944. Ceremony at monument of the American soldier.

MAO ZEDONG: DEATH ANNIVERSARY. Sept 9, 1976. People's Republic of China pays tribute to memory of the Chinese revolutionary leader, who died at Beijing, China. Memorial Hall, where his flag-draped body lies encased in crystal, was opened at Tiananmen Square at Beijing on the first anniversary of his death. Mao was born Dec 26, 1893, at Hunan Province, China.

NATIONAL SCHOLARSHIP PROVIDERS ASSOCIATION (NSPA) ANNUAL CONFERENCE. Sept 9–11. Chicago Marriott Downtown Magnificent Mile, Chicago, IL. This annual conference, first held in 1999, is the convergence of our profession: the intersection of diverse organizations in the scholarship industry, including foundations, public charities, educational institutions and corporations. Attendees from across North America, US territories and beyond come for two and a half days of learning, networking and sharing. Est attendance: 700. For info: Maggie Brubaker, National Scholarship Providers Association, PO Box 215, Charlottesville, VA 22902. E-mail: mbrubaker@scholarshipproviders.org. Web: www.scholarshipproviders.org.

SANDERS, COLONEL HARLAND DAVID: BIRTH ANNIVERSARY. Sept 9, 1890. Born at Henryville, IN, Sanders was a grade-school dropout and jack-of-all-trades before becoming a pioneer in the fast-food industry at the age of 66 with his creation of one of its most successful franchises, the "finger-lickin' good" Kentucky Fried Chicken. His success was due to his secret spice blend and unique pressure cooker cooking method, as well as catchy marketing and high standards. The savvy "Colonel" (two Kentucky statesmen gave him this honorary title) adopted the signature white suit, black string tie, cane, and white mustache and goatee to appear as an old Southern aristocrat. His likeness, used on KFC promotional materials, made him iconic and one of the most recognizable men in the world even after his death on Dec 16, 1980, at Louisville, KY.

TAJIKISTAN: INDEPENDENCE DAY. Sept 9. National holiday commemorating independence from the Soviet Union in 1991.

TOLSTOY, LEO: BIRTH ANNIVERSARY. Sept 9, 1828. Russian novelist and moral philosopher, born at Tula Province, Russia. Best known for his novels (*War and Peace, Anna Karenina*), Tolstoy also wrote short stories, plays and essays. A member of the nobility, in his moral and religious writings he condemned private property and championed nonviolent protest. Died Nov 20, 1910, at Astapovo, Russia.

"WELCOME BACK, KOTTER" TV PREMIERE: 45th ANNIVERSARY. Sept 9, 1975. In this half-hour sitcom, Gabe Kotter (Gabe Kaplan) returned to James Buchanan High School, his alma mater, to teach the "sweathogs," a group of hopeless underachievers. Other cast members included Marcia Strassman, John Travolta, Robert Hegyes, Ron Palillo, Lawrence Hilton-Jacobs and John Sylvester White. The theme song, "Welcome Back," was sung by John Sebastian. The last telecast was Aug 10, 1979.

WILLIAM, THE CONQUEROR: DEATH ANNIVERSARY. Sept 9, 1087. William I, The Conqueror, King of England and Duke of Normandy, whose image is portrayed in the Bayeux Tapestry, was born about 1028 at Falaise, Normandy. Victorious over Harold at the Battle of Hastings (the Norman Conquest) in 1066, William was crowned King of England at Westminster Abbey on Christmas Day of that year. Later, while waging war in France, William met his death at Rouen, Sept 9, 1087.

WONDERFUL WEIRDOS DAY. Sept 9. All of us are blessed with one or two wonderful weirdos in our lives. These are the folks who remind us to think outside the box, to be a little more true to ourselves. Today's the day to thank them. So give them a hug, and say, "I love you, you weirdo!" (©2006 by WH.) For info: Thomas & Ruth Roy, Wellcat Holidays, 2418 Long Ln, Lebanon, PA 17046. Phone: (717) 279-0184. E-mail: info@wellcat.com. Web: www.wellcat.com.

🎂 BIRTHDAYS TODAY

Mario Batali, 60, chef, author, television personality ("Molto Mario"), born Seattle, WA, Sept 9, 1960.

Shane Battier, 42, former basketball player, born Birmingham, MI, Sept 9, 1978.

Michael Bublé, 45, singer, born Burnaby, BC, Canada, Sept 9, 1975.

Angela Cartwright, 68, actress ("Lost in Space," *The Sound of Music*), born Cheshire, England, Sept 9, 1952.

Christopher Coons, 57, US Senator (D, Delaware), born Greenwich, CT, Sept 9, 1963.

Charles Esten, 55, actor ("Nashville," "Big Love"), born Pittsburgh, PA, Sept 9, 1965.

Hugh Grant, 60, actor (*Notting Hill, About a Boy, Four Weddings and a Funeral*), born London, England, Sept 9, 1960.

Mike Hampton, 48, former baseball player, born Brooksville, FL, Sept 9, 1972.

Rachel Hunter, 51, model, born Glenfield, New Zealand, Sept 9, 1969.

Adam Sandler, 54, actor, comedian (*Happy Gilmore, The Wedding Singer*), born Brooklyn, NY, Sept 9, 1966.

Eric Stonestreet, 49, actor (Emmy for "Modern Family"), born Kansas City, KS, Sept 9, 1971.

Joseph Robert (Joe) Theisman, 71, sportscaster, Hall of Fame football player, born New Brunswick, NJ, Sept 9, 1949.

Henry Thomas, 49, actor (*All the Pretty Horses, E.T. The Extra-Terrestrial*), born San Antonio, TX, Sept 9, 1971.

Goran Visnjic, 48, actor ("Timeless," "ER," *The Girl with the Dragon Tattoo* [US]), born Sibenik, Croatia, Sept 9, 1972.

Michelle Williams, 40, actress (*All the Money in the World, Brokeback Mountain, Blue Valentine*, "Dawson's Creek"), born Kalispell, MT, Sept 9, 1980.

Tom Wopat, 69, actor ("The Dukes of Hazzard," "Cybill," *Annie Get Your Gun*), born Lodi, WI, Sept 9, 1951.

September 10 — Thursday

DAY 254   **112 REMAINING**

BELIZE: SAINT GEORGE'S CAYE DAY. Sept 10. Public holiday celebrated in honor of the 1798 battle between the European Baymen Settlers and the Spaniards for the territory of Belize.

BRAXTON, CARTER: BIRTH ANNIVERSARY. Sept 10, 1736. American Revolutionary statesman and signer of the Declaration of Independence. Born at Newington, VA, he died Oct 10, 1797, at Richmond, VA.

CANADA: TORONTO INTERNATIONAL FILM FESTIVAL. Sept 10–20. Toronto, ON. 45th annual. A 10-day festival of contemporary Canadian and international cinema at various downtown theaters. Call or write for info or to be put on mailing list. Annually, beginning on the Thursday after Labor Day. Est attendance: 250,000. For info: Toronto Intl Film Festival. E-mail: proffice@tiff.net or customerrelations@tiff.net. Web: www.tiff.net.

CHINA: TEACHER'S DAY. Sept 10. Observed since the 1930s as a day to offer gratitude and tokens of appreciation to teachers. Moved to the present fixed date of Sept 10 in 1985. In the future, this day may be moved to Sept 28 in alignment with Taiwan and the traditional celebration of the birthday of Confucious.

"GUNSMOKE" TV PREMIERE: 65th ANNIVERSARY. Sept 10, 1955. "Gunsmoke" was TV's longest-running Western, moving from radio to TV. John Wayne turned down the role of Marshall Matt Dillon but recommended James Arness, who got the role. Other regulars included Amanda Blake as Kitty Russell, saloon owner; Dennis Weaver as Chester B. Goode, Dillon's deputy; and Milburn Stone as Doc Adams. In 1962 Burt Reynolds joined the cast as Quint Asper, followed by Roger Ewing as Thad Greenwood and Buck Taylor as Newly O'Brien. In 1964 Ken Curtis was added as funnyman Festus Haggen, the new deputy. "Gunsmoke" was the number-one rated series for four seasons, and a top 10 hit for six seasons. The last telecast was Sept 1, 1975.

KURALT, CHARLES: BIRTH ANNIVERSARY. Sept 10, 1934. TV journalist ("On the Road with Charles Kuralt") born at Wilmington, NC. Died at New York, NY, July 4, 1997.

LONGS PEAK SCOTTISH/IRISH HIGHLAND FESTIVAL. Sept 10–13. Estes Park, CO. 44th annual Scottish-Irish celebration festival with pipe bands, Highland and Irish dancing, jousting and gathering of the clans. Featuring professional Scottish and Irish entertainers, "Dogs of the British Isles," professional Scottish athletes and vendors with imported and handcrafted merchandise. Annually, the first weekend after Labor Day. For info: Longs Peak Scottish/Irish Highland Festival, Inc, PO Box 1820, Estes Park, CO 80517. Phone: (800) 903-7837. Fax: (970) 586-5328. E-mail: info@scotfest.com. Web: www.scotfest.com.

MARIS, ROGER: BIRTH ANNIVERSARY. Sept 10, 1934. Baseball player born Roger Eugene Maras at Hibbing, MN. In 1961 Maris surpassed the mark set by Babe Ruth in 1927, hitting 61 home runs, a record that wasn't broken until 1998. He won the American League MVP Award in 1960 and 1961 and finished his career with the St. Louis Cardinals. Died at Houston, TX, Dec 14, 1985.

MOON PHASE: LAST QUARTER. Sept 10. Moon enters Last Quarter phase at 5:26 AM, EDT.

NEW MEXICO STATE FAIR. Sept 10–20. EXPO New Mexico, Albuquerque, NM. 82nd annual. "The Biggest Show in New Mexico." Fair features nationally known recording artists on multiple stages, midway, parade, state fair queen contest, PRCA rodeo, exhibits and much more. Est attendance: 504,445. For info: New Mexico State Fair, PO Box 8546, Albuquerque, NM 87198-8546. Phone: (505) 222-9700. E-mail: info@state.nm.us. Web: www.statefair.expoNM.com.

OLIVER, MARY: 85th BIRTH ANNIVERSARY. Sept 10, 1935. Born at Maple Hills Heights, OH, Mary Oliver was a popular and accessible poet beloved for her joyful celebration of nature in poems such as "Wild Geese" and "The Summer Day." Her lifelong exploration of the link between nature and the spiritual world was fueled by her long daily walks in the Ohio woods of her childhood and the Provincetown shoreline of her adulthood. *American Primitive*, her acclaimed fifth book, won the Pulitzer Prize for Poetry. The collection *New and Selected Poems* won a National Book Award. Oliver died Jan 17, 2019, at Hobe Sound, FL.

PALMER, ARNOLD: BIRTH ANNIVERSARY. Sept 10, 1929. Born at Youngstown, OH, Palmer revolutionized golf both as a sport and as a business. Over six decades, the "King of Golf" won 92 tournaments, 62 of them PGA titles between 1955 and 1973, and seven major championships: the Masters Tournament (1958, 1960, 1962, 1964), the US Open (1960) and the British Open (1961, 1962). His energetic style, competitiveness and charm on the links popularized the sport both on TV and for amateurs, even as it made the game lucrative for professionals. His business empire was vast, encompassing the Arnold Palmer drink he loved, golf course design firms, dry cleaners, car dealerships and country clubs. He received the Presidential Medal of Freedom in 2004. Palmer died Sept 25, 2016, at Pittsburgh, PA.

SCHIAPARELLI, ELSA: BIRTH ANNIVERSARY. Sept 10, 1890. Born at Rome, Italy, Elsa Schiaparelli was one of the world's leading fashion designers from the late 1920s through the 1950s. Based in Paris, France, Schiaparelli created striking, often surrealistic designs in collaboration with such artists as Salvador Dali and Jean Cocteau. She introduced the shoulder pad to women's fashion, named "shocking pink" (hot pink) and worked with man-made materials. A white evening dress bedecked with a lobster and a hat that appeared to be a giant shoe were some of her avant-garde looks. "If you define fashion as time moving," she wrote, "then you are not fully alive unless you are moving with it." Schiaparelli died at Paris on Nov 13, 1973.

SWAP IDEAS DAY. Sept 10. To encourage people to explore ways in which their ideas can be put to work for the benefit of humanity, and to encourage development of incentives that will encourage use of creative imagination. (Created by Robert L. Birch, Pun Corps.)

UTAH STATE FAIR. Sept 10–20. Utah State FairPark, Salt Lake City, UT. Exhibits, livestock, family contests, cook-offs, concerts and entertainment. Annually, beginning the first Thursday after Labor Day and lasting 11 days. Est attendance: 314,000. For info: Utah State FairPark, 155 N 1000 W, Salt Lake City, UT 84116. Phone: (801) 538-8400. E-mail: info@utahstatefair.com. Web: www.utah-statefair.com.

WISE, ROBERT: BIRTH ANNIVERSARY. Sept 10, 1914. American film director, born at Winchester, IN. Wise's Hollywood career began in 1933 with a job in the RKO Pictures shipping department. He later worked as a sound effects editor but quickly moved on to directing, working proficiently in numerous genres throughout his career. His credits include the horror film *The Body Snatcher* (1945); a film noir classic, *Born to Kill* (1947); as well as science fiction, melodrama, Westerns and two

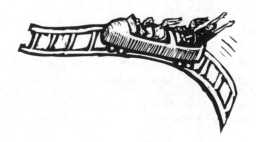

September	S	M	T	W	T	F	S
2020			1	2	3	4	5
	6	7	8	9	10	11	12
	13	14	15	16	17	18	19
	20	21	22	23	24	25	26
	27	28	29	30			

musicals for which he won an Academy Award for Best Director: *West Side Story* (1961) and *The Sound of Music* (1965). Died at Los Angeles, CA, Sept 14, 2005.

WORLD SUICIDE PREVENTION DAY. Sept 10. An opportunity for all sectors of the community—the public, charitable organizations, communities, researchers, clinicians, practitioners, politicians and policy makers, volunteers, those bereaved by suicide, other interested groups and individuals—to join with the International Association for Suicide Prevention and the WHO to focus on the unacceptable burden and costs of suicidal behaviors with diverse activities to promote understanding about suicide and highlight effective prevention activities. Annually, Sept 10. For info: Intl Assn for Suicide Prevention. Web: www.iasp.info/wspd.

"THE X-FILES" TV PREMIERE: ANNIVERSARY. Sept 10, 1993. "The Truth Is Out There" was the mantra of FOX's scary and brainy sci-fi drama. Special FBI agents Fox Mulder (David Duchovny) and Dana Scully (Gillian Anderson) solved the cases too weird for the bureau and also uncovered a vast conspiracy involving aliens and human-alien hybrids. *TV Guide* named "The X-Files" one of the greatest TV shows of all time. Two feature-length films were created as well. The series ended in 2002, but there were limited-series seasons in 2017 and 2018.

 **BIRTHDAYS TODAY**

Misty Copeland, 38, dancer (principal, American Ballet Theatre), born Kansas City, MO, Sept 10, 1982.

José Feliciano, 75, singer, musician, born Lares, Puerto Rico, Sept 10, 1945.

Colin Firth, 60, actor ("Pride and Prejudice," *Bridget Jones's Diary*, Oscar for *The King's Speech*), born Grayshott, Hampshire, England, Sept 10, 1960.

Judy Geeson, 72, actress (*To Sir with Love, The Eagle Has Landed*), born Arundel, Sussex, England, Sept 10, 1948.

Amy Irving, 67, actress (*Carrie, Crossing Delancey*, "Alias"), born Palo Alto, CA, Sept 10, 1953.

Clark Johnson, 56, actor ("Homicide: Life on the Street," "The Wire"), born Philadelphia, PA, Sept 10, 1964.

Randy Johnson, 57, Hall of Fame baseball player, born Walnut Creek, CA, Sept 10, 1963.

Joe Nieuwendyk, 54, Hall of Fame hockey player, born Oshawa, ON, Canada, Sept 10, 1966.

September 11 — Friday

DAY 255   **111 REMAINING**

ATTACK ON AMERICA: ANNIVERSARY. Sept 11, 2001. Terrorists hijacked four planes, piloting two of them into the World Trade Center's twin towers in New York City and one into the Pentagon in Washington, DC. Passengers on the fourth plane attempted to overcome the hijackers, causing the plane to crash in western Pennsylvania instead of reaching its target in Washington. The twin towers at the WTC collapsed about an hour after being hit. More than 3,000 people died as a result of the attacks. The hijackers were agents of the Al Qaeda terrorist group led by Islamic extremist Osama bin Laden, who was headquartered in Afghanistan. In response, the US began unprecedented internal security measures and launched a war on terrorism with the support of many nations.

BATTLE OF BRANDYWINE: ANNIVERSARY. Sept 11, 1777. The largest engagement of the American Revolution, between the Continental Army led by General George Washington and British troops led by General William Howe. General Howe was marching to take Philadelphia when Washington chose to try to stop

the British advance at the Brandywine River near Chadds Ford, PA. The American forces were defeated and the British went on to take Philadelphia Sept 26. They spent the winter in the city while Washington's troops suffered at their encampment at Valley Forge, PA.

BRYANT, BEAR: BIRTH ANNIVERSARY. Sept 11, 1913. Paul William "Bear" Bryant, college football player and legendary coach, born at Moro Bottoms, AR. Bryant earned his nickname by wrestling a bear for money as a young man. He played football at the University of Alabama and began coaching in 1940. After World War II, he was named head coach at Maryland. He later coached at Kentucky, Texas A&M and Alabama (1958–82). His Alabama teams appeared in bowl games 24 consecutive years and won six national championships. He won coach-of-the-year honors three times and finished his career with 325 wins, then a record. Died at Tuscaloosa, AL, Jan 26, 1983.

"THE CAROL BURNETT SHOW" TV PREMIERE: ANNIVERSARY. Sept 11, 1967. This popular comedy-variety show starred comedienne Carol Burnett, who started the show by taking questions from the audience and ended with an ear tug. Sketches and spoofs included recurring characters like "The Family" (later to be spun off as "Mama's Family") and "As the Stomach Turns." Regular cast members included Harvey Korman, Lyle Waggoner and Vicki Lawrence. Later, Tim Conway joined the cast. Dick Van Dyke briefly joined after Korman left in 1977.

CATALONIA: NATIONAL DAY OF CATALONIA. Sept 11. (Festa Nacional de Catalunya.) National day for this autonomous region within Spain composed of the provinces of Barcelona, Tarragona, Girona and Lleida. Observed on the anniversary of the fall of Barcelona to Bourbon forces on Sept 11, 1714, during the War of the Spanish Succession. Often an occasion to demonstrate for independence from Spain.

ENGLAND: JANE AUSTEN FESTIVAL. Sept 11–20. Bath. 20th annual. Festival celebrating the life and works of author Jane Austen (1775–1817) in the city where she lived briefly but which figures prominently in her novels. The festival opens with the spectacular Grand Regency Costumed Promenade and continues with hundreds of participants in authentic period dress and accompanied by a town crier. Other events include readings, film and theatrical presentations, dances, costume workshop, walking tours and music recitals. For info: The Jane Austen Festival, Widcombe Institute, Widcombe Hill, Bath BA2 6AA, England. E-mail: jackie@janeausten.co.uk. Web: www.janeaustenfestival-bath.co.uk.

ETHIOPIA: NEW YEAR'S DAY. Sept 11. In the year 2020, this day will start the year 2013 on the Ethiopian Orthodox calendar. On the Coptic Orthodox calendar, it begins the year 1736.

FESTIVAL OF THE VINE. Sept 11–13. Geneva, IL. Geneva restaurants create an array of specialties under an outdoor tent at the "Flavor Fare"—partnered with wine and live music. An arts and crafts show, flower market, horse-drawn carriage rides and several exceptional wine tastings and dinner events take place around the historic downtown. Est attendance: 75,000. For info: Geneva

Chamber of Commerce, 8 S Third St, Geneva, IL 60134. Phone: (630) 232-6060. E-mail: chamberinfo@genevachamber.com. Web: www.genevachamber.com.

FOOD STAMPS AUTHORIZED: ANNIVERSARY. Sept 11, 1959. Congress passed a bill authorizing food stamps for low-income Americans.

KANSAS STATE FAIR. Sept 11–20. Hutchinson, KS. Commercial and competitive exhibits, entertainment, carnival and other special attractions. Annually, beginning the first Friday after Labor Day. Est attendance: 350,000. For info: Kansas State Fair, 2000 N Poplar St, Hutchinson, KS 67502. Phone: (620) 669-3600. E-mail: info@kansasstatefair.com. Web: www.kansasstatefair.com.

KING TURKEY DAY (WITH TURKEY RACE). Sept 11–12. Worthington, MN. Community celebration that includes live turkey race between Paycheck, Worthington, MN's Paycheck and Cuero, TX's Ruby Begonia. Also included are a grand parade, beer garden, free pancake breakfast and family activities. Est attendance: 10,000. For info: King Turkey Day, Inc, 1121 Third Ave, Worthington, MN 56187. Phone: (507) 372-2919. E-mail: wcofc@worthingtonmn-chamber.com. Web: www.kingturkeyday.net.

LAWRENCE, DAVID HERBERT: BIRTH ANNIVERSARY. Sept 11, 1885. English novelist, critic, playwright and poet, author of *Lady Chatterley's Lover* (1928). Born at Eastwood, Nottinghamshire, England, D.H. Lawrence died Mar 2, 1930, at Vence, France. He said, "The fairest thing in nature, a flower, still has its roots in earth and manure."

LIND, JENNY: US PREMIERE: ANNIVERSARY. Sept 11, 1850. Jenny Lind, the "Swedish Nightingale," gave her first American performance at the Castle Garden Theatre, New York, NY, on this day.

"LITTLE HOUSE ON THE PRAIRIE" TV PREMIERE: ANNIVERSARY. Sept 11, 1974. This hour-long family drama was based on books by Laura Ingalls Wilder. It focused on the Ingalls family and their neighbors living at Walnut Grove, MN: Michael Landon as Charles (Pa), Karen Grassle as Caroline (Ma), Melissa Sue Anderson as daughter Mary, Melissa Gilbert as daughter Laura (from whose point of view the stories were told), Lindsay and Sidney Greenbush as daughter Carrie and Wendi and Brenda Turnbaugh as daughter Grace. In its last season (1982), the show's name was changed to "Little House: A New Beginning." Landon appeared less often and the show centered around Laura and her husband.

MITFORD, JESSICA: BIRTH ANNIVERSARY. Sept 11, 1917. One of the fabled "Mitford Sisters," the journalist, author, civil rights advocate and rebel was born into an aristocratic but eccentric family at Asthall Manor, near Burford, England. Her investigative work led to important and well-received exposés of the US funeral and prison industries: *The American Way of Death* (1963), *Kind and Usual Punishment* (1974) and *The American Prison Business* (1975). She died at Oakland, CA, on July 22, 1996.

MOUNTAIN MEADOWS MASSACRE: ANNIVERSARY. Sept 11, 1857. As tensions grew between the US government and Governor Brigham Young of the Utah Territory, a wagon train of 140 emigrants bound for California from Arkansas was attacked. On this date the emigrants surrendered to local Mormon leader John Doyle Lee but were then massacred. Seventeen small children were parceled out to Mormon families. Despite the ensuing national uproar, federal prosecution didn't happen until 1875. Lee was executed in 1877.

★**NATIONAL DAYS OF PRAYER AND REMEMBRANCE.** Sept 11–13. Proclamation asking that the people of the United States honor and remember the victims of Sept 11, 2001, and their loved ones through prayer, contemplation, memorial services, the visiting of memorials, the ringing of bells, evening candlelight remembrance vigils and other appropriate ceremonies and activities. First proclaimed in 2001 by President George W. Bush for the day of Sept 14, 2001. Annually, the Friday through Sunday nearest to Sept 11.

NATIONAL DOG WALKER APPRECIATION DAY. Sept 11. 5th annual. A day recognizing all the dog walkers who do their best to keep our dogs happy and exercised. In honor of this day, dog walkers (and their clients) wear green. Annually, the Friday after Labor Day. For info: Wag Labs, Inc, 55 Francisco St, Ste 360, San Francisco, CA 94131. E-mail: media@wagwalking.com.

O. HENRY (WILLIAM S. PORTER): BIRTH ANNIVERSARY. Sept 11, 1862. William Sydney Porter, American author, who wrote under the pen name O. Henry. Best known for his short stories, including "The Gift of the Magi." Born at Greensboro, NC, he died at New York, NY, June 5, 1910.

PAKISTAN: FOUNDER'S DEATH ANNIVERSARY. Sept 11. Pakistan observes the anniversary of the death in 1948 of Qaid-e-Azam Mohammed Ali Jinnah (founder of Pakistan) as a national holiday. His birth date, Dec 25, is also a national holiday.

★**PATRIOT DAY AND NATIONAL DAY OF SERVICE AND REMEMBRANCE.** Sept 11. On Dec 18, 2001, a joint resolution of Congress amended Title 36, Chapter 1, Section 144 of the US Code to permit the president to declare Sept 11 of each year as Patriot Day, in commemoration of the terrorist attacks on the United States on Sept 11, 2001. The resolution requests that all state and local governments observe this day "with appropriate programs and activities," that the flag be displayed at half-staff from sunrise till sundown and that a moment of silence be observed in honor of those who lost their lives in the attacks.

1786 ANNAPOLIS CONVENTION: ANNIVERSARY. Sept 11–14, 1786. Twelve delegates from New York, New Jersey, Delaware, Pennsylvania and Virginia met at Annapolis, MD, to discuss commercial matters of mutual interest. The delegates voted, on Sept 14, to adopt a resolution prepared by Alexander Hamilton asking all states to send representatives to a convention at Philadelphia, PA, in May 1787 "to render the constitution of the Federal Government adequate to the exigencies of the Union."

September 2020	S	M	T	W	T	F	S
			1	2	3	4	5
	6	7	8	9	10	11	12
	13	14	15	16	17	18	19
	20	21	22	23	24	25	26
	27	28	29	30			

SPACE MILESTONE: *MARS GLOBAL SURVEYOR* (US). Sept 11, 1997. Launched Nov 7, 1996, this unmanned vehicle was put into orbit around Mars. It was designed to compile global maps of Mars by taking high-resolution photos. This mission inaugurated a new series of Mars expeditions in which NASA launched pairs of orbiters and landers to Mars. *Mars Global Surveyor* was paired with the lander *Mars Pathfinder*. See also: "Space Milestone: *Mars Pathfinder*" (July 4).

TENNESSEE STATE FAIR. Sept 11–20. Nashville, TN. 113th annual. A huge variety of exhibits, carnival midway, animal and variety shows, live stage presentations, livestock, agricultural and craft competitions and food and game booths. Annually, beginning the first Friday after Labor Day. Est attendance: 115,000. For info: Tennessee State Fair Association, PO Box 24747, Nashville, TN 37202. Phone: (615) 800-3675. Web: www.tnstatefair.org.

TYLER'S CABINET RESIGNS: ANNIVERSARY. Sept 11, 1841. In protest of President John Tyler's veto of the Banking Bill, all of his cabinet except Secretary of State Daniel Webster resigned on this day.

🎂 BIRTHDAYS TODAY

Franz Beckenbauer, 75, soccer executive and Hall of Fame player, born Munich, Germany, Sept 11, 1945.

Harry Connick, Jr, 53, singer, pianist, stage and screen actor, born New Orleans, LA, Sept 11, 1967.

Brian De Palma, 80, filmmaker (*Mission: Impossible, The Untouchables, Carrie*), born Newark, NJ, Sept 11, 1940.

Lola Falana, 77, singer, dancer, actress (*The Liberation of L.B. Jones*), born Camden, NJ, Sept 11, 1943.

John Hawkes, 61, actor (*Everest, The Sessions, Winter's Bone*, "Deadwood"), born Alexandria, MN, Sept 11, 1959.

Taraji Henson, 50, actress ("Empire," "Person of Interest," *The Curious Case of Benjamin Button, Hustle & Flow*), born Washington, DC, Sept 11, 1970.

Elizabeth Henstridge, 33, actress ("Agents of S.H.I.E.L.D."), born Sheffield, England, Sept 11, 1987.

Donna Lopiano, 74, women's sports executive and former softball player, born Stamford, CT, Sept 11, 1946.

Ludacris, 43, rapper, actor (*Furious 7, Crash, Hustle & Flow*), born Christopher Bridges at Champaign, IL, Sept 11, 1977.

Amy Madigan, 69, actress (*Places in the Heart, Field of Dreams, Uncle Buck*), born Chicago, IL, Sept 11, 1951.

Virginia Madsen, 57, actress (*Joy, Sideways, Dune*), born Winnetka, IL, Sept 11, 1963.

Kristy McNichol, 58, actress ("Empty Nest," *Little Darlings, Summer of My German Soldier*, Emmys for "Family"), born Los Angeles, CA, Sept 11, 1962.

Moby, 55, rock singer, songwriter, born Richard Melville Hall at New York, NY, Sept 11, 1965.

September 12 — Saturday

DAY 256   **110 REMAINING**

BATTLE OF SAINT-MIHIEL: ANNIVERSARY. Sept 12, 1918. Under the command of General John J. Pershing, the First US Army attacked the Germans at the Saint-Mihiel salient. This was the first major US offensive of WWI. Sixteen army divisions, coupled with French II Colonial Corps tanks and artillery support, forced back the Germans after 36 hours of heavy fighting and reclaimed 200 square miles of French territory that had been in the hands of the Germans since 1914. The First US Army lost about 7,000 soldiers in the Battle of Saint-Mihiel.

CHARLES LEROUX'S LAST JUMP: ANNIVERSARY. Sept 12, 1889. American aeronaut of French extraction, born at New York, NY, about 1857, achieved world fame as a parachutist. After his first public performance (Philadelphia, PA, 1887) he toured European cities, where his parachute jumps attracted wide attention. Credited with 238 successful jumps. On Sept 12, 1889, he jumped from a balloon over Tallinn, Estonia, and perished in the Bay of Reval.

CHEVALIER, MAURICE: BIRTH ANNIVERSARY. Sept 12, 1888. Successful actor-singer born at Paris, France. Nominated for Academy Awards for his roles in *The Love Parade* (1929) and *The Big Pond* (1930), Chevalier was part of a wave of talented actor-singers who popularized the musical as a film genre. He was known for his suave style and signature straw boater, and his most well-known musicals include *Gigi* (1958), *Can-Can* (1960) and *Fanny* (1961). Chevalier won the Cecil B. DeMille Award at the Academy Awards in 1958 and died at Paris, Jan 1, 1972.

DEFENDERS DAY. Sept 12. Maryland. Public holiday. Annual reenactment of bombardment of Fort McHenry in 1814 that inspired Francis Scott Key to write "The Star-Spangled Banner."

GUINEA-BISSAU: NATIONAL HOLIDAY. Sept 12. Amilcar Cabral's birthday, Sept 12, is observed as a national holiday.

ISRAEL COMPLETES GAZA PULLOUT: 15th ANNIVERSARY. Sept 12, 2005. In the early hours of Sept 12, the last of Israel's troops left Gaza, and the withdrawal of settlers and military begun in August 2005 was finished. Israel had occupied Gaza for 38 years. The Palestinian Authority assumed control of Gaza, but Hamas wrested control of the city in 2007.

KNOPF, ALFRED A.: BIRTH ANNIVERSARY. Sept 12, 1892. Distinguished American publisher born at New York City. With his soon-to-be-wife, Blanche Wolf, he started the house that bears his name in 1915 and brought European authors to America. Knopf died Aug 11, 1984, at Purchase, NY. At his memorial service, author John Hersey eulogized Knopf: "When all scores are settled, it will be written that Alfred Knopf was the greatest publisher this country ever had."

"LASSIE" TV PREMIERE: ANNIVERSARY. Sept 12, 1954. This long-running series was originally about a boy and his courageous and intelligent dog, Lassie (played by more than six different dogs, all male). For the first few seasons, Lassie lived on the Miller farm. The family included Jeff (Tommy Rettig); his widowed mother, Ellen (Jan Clayton); and George Cleveland as Gramps. Throughout the years there were many format and cast changes, as Lassie was exchanged from one family to another in order to have a variety of new perils and escapades. Other featured performers included Cloris Leachman, June Lockhart and Larry Wilcox.

LITTLE FALLS ARTS AND CRAFTS FAIR. Sept 12–13. Little Falls, MN. Features 600 artists, craftspeople and hobbyists displaying and selling their items. Est attendance: 125,000. For info: Chamber of Commerce, 200 NW First St, Little Falls, MN 56345. Phone: (320) 632-5155. Fax: (320) 632-2122. E-mail: artsandcrafts@littlefalls-mnchamber.com. Web: www.littlefallsmnchamber.com.

MENCKEN, HENRY LOUIS: BIRTH ANNIVERSARY. Sept 12, 1880. American newspaperman, lexicographer and critic, the "Sage of

Baltimore" was born at Baltimore, MD, and died there Jan 29, 1956. "If, after I depart this vale," he wrote in 1921 (Epitaph, *Smart Set*), "you ever remember me and have thought to please my ghost, forgive some sinner and wink your eye at some homely girl."

"THE MONKEES" TV PREMIERE: ANNIVERSARY. Sept 12, 1966. Featuring a rock group that was supposed to be an American version of The Beatles, this half-hour show featured a blend of comedy and music. Four young actors were chosen from more than 400 to play the group members: Micky Dolenz, Davy Jones, Mike Nesmith and Peter Tork. Dolenz and Jones had acting experience, and Tork and Nesmith had musical experience. The music that they performed on the show proved to be immensely popular; at first they sang with a studio band but later insisted on writing and performing their own music. They released several albums and toured several times. In later years, various members of The Monkees gathered for reunion/anniversary tours.

MUSHROOM FESTIVAL. Sept 12–13. Downtown Kennett Square, PA. 35th annual. A weekend of fun, food and fungi in the Mushroom Capital of the World! Attend cooking or growing demos, mushroom judging, parade, car show and street festival with entertainment. Est attendance: 100,000. For info: Mushroom Festival, PO Box 1000, 114 W State St, Kennett Square, PA 19348. Phone: (610) 925-3373. E-mail: themushroomfestival@gmail.com. Web: www.mushroomfestival.org.

OWENS, JESSE: BIRTH ANNIVERSARY. Sept 12, 1913. James Cleveland (Jesse) Owens, American athlete, winner of four gold medals at the 1936 Olympic Games at Berlin, Germany, was born at Oakville, AL. Owens set 11 world records in track and field. During one track meet, at Ann Arbor, MI, May 25, 1935, Owens, representing Ohio State University, broke three world records and tied a fourth in the space of 45 minutes. Died at Tucson, AZ, Mar 31, 1980.

PRAIRIE DAY. Sept 12. George Washington Carver National Monument, Diamond, MO. Celebrating life on the Missouri prairie during the late 1880s when George Washington Carver was a child, this event includes basket weaving, candle making, Dutch-oven cooking, spinning, weaving, storytelling, musical groups, quilting, a junior ranger station and more events. Annually, the second Saturday in September. For info: George Washington Carver Natl Monument, 5646 Carver Rd, Diamond, MO 64840. Phone: (417) 325-4151. E-mail: gwca_interpretation@nps.gov. Web: www.nps.gov/gwca.

SOUTHEAST MISSOURI DISTRICT FAIR. Sept 12–19. Arena Park Fairgrounds, Cape Girardeau, MO. Oldest outdoor fair in the state. Celebrating its 165th year with beauty pageants, livestock exhibition, horse show, entertainment, carnival, food and 4-H and FFA displays. Annually, starts the Saturday after Labor Day and continues to the next Saturday. Est attendance: 100,000. For info: SEMO District Fair Assn, 410 Kiwanis Dr, Ste 200, Cape Girardeau, MO 63701. Phone: (800) 455-FAIR or

(573) 334-9250. E-mail: info@semofair.com. Web: www.semofair.com.

SPACE MILESTONE: *LUNA 2* (USSR). Sept 12, 1959. First spacecraft to land on moon was launched.

UNITED NATIONS: DAY FOR SOUTH-SOUTH COOPERATION. Sept 12. Formerly observed on Dec 19 (Res 58/220), marking the date when the General Assembly endorsed the Buenos Aires Plan of Action for Promoting and Implementing Technical Cooperation among Developing Countries. Changed on Dec 22, 2011, to be observed annually on Sept 12, to mark the date in 1978 when that same plan was actually adopted. For info: United Nations, Dept of Public Info, New York, NY 10017. Web: www.un.org.

US MID-AMATEUR (GOLF) CHAMPIONSHIP. Sept 12–17. Kinloch Golf Club, Manakin-Sabot, VA. For info: USGA, Golf House, Championship Dept, PO Box 708, Far Hills, NJ 07931. Phone: (908) 234-2300. E-mail: champs@usga.org. Web: www.usga.org.

VIDEO GAMES DAY. Sept 12. A day for kids who love video games to celebrate the fun they have playing them and to thank their parents for all the consoles, games and quarters they have provided to indulge this enthusiasm.

🎂 BIRTHDAYS TODAY

Linda Gray, 79, actress ("Dallas," "Melrose Place"), born Santa Monica, CA, Sept 12, 1941.

Ian Holm, 89, actor (Oscar for *Chariots of Fire*; the Lord of the Rings trilogy, *The Sweet Hereafter*), born Goodmayes, England, Sept 12, 1931.

Jennifer Hudson, 39, singer, actress ("American Idol," Oscar for *Dreamgirls*; *The Secret Life of Bees*), born Chicago, IL, Sept 12, 1981.

Louis C.K., 53, comedian, actor ("Louie," *American Hustle*), born Louis Szekely at Washington, DC, Sept 12, 1967.

Benjamin McKenzie, 42, actor ("Gotham," "Southland," "The O.C."), born Austin, TX, Sept 12, 1978.

Yao Ming, 40, Hall of Fame basketball player, born Shanghai, China, Sept 12, 1980.

Maria Muldaur, 77, singer, born New York, NY, Sept 12, 1943.

Joe Pantoliano, 66, actor ("The Sopranos," *Risky Business, The Fugitive*; stage: *Orphans*), born Jersey City, NJ, Sept 12, 1954.

RM, 26, rapper (BTS), born Kim Nam-joon at Ilsan-gu, South Korea, Sept 12, 1994.

Emmy Rossum, 34, actress ("Shameless," *The Phantom of the Opera*), born New York, NY, Sept 12, 1986.

Peter Scolari, 66, actor ("Bosom Buddies," "Newhart"), born New Rochelle, NY, Sept 12, 1954.

Rachel Ward, 63, actress ("The Thorn Birds," *Against All Odds*), born London, England, Sept 12, 1957.

Amy Yasbeck, 57, actress (*The Mask*, "Wings"), born Cincinnati, OH, Sept 12, 1963.

September 2020	S	M	T	W	T	F	S
			1	2	3	4	5
	6	7	8	9	10	11	12
	13	14	15	16	17	18	19
	20	21	22	23	24	25	26
	27	28	29	30			

September 13 — Sunday

DAY 257 **109 REMAINING**

ANDERSON, SHERWOOD: BIRTH ANNIVERSARY. Sept 13, 1876. American author and newspaper publisher, born at Camden, OH. His best-remembered book is *Winesburg, Ohio.* Anderson died at Colon, Panama, Mar 8, 1941.

BARRY, JOHN: DEATH ANNIVERSARY. Sept 13, 1803. Revolutionary War hero John Barry, first American to hold the rank of commodore, died at Philadelphia, PA. He was born at Tacumshane, County Wexford, Ireland, in 1745. He has been called "the father of the American Navy."

BELGIUM: GREAT PROCESSION OF TOURNAI. Sept 13. Tournai. Religious procession held since 1092 to honor the Virgin Mary delivering the city from the plague. Annually, the second Sunday in September. For info: City of Tournai. Web: www.tournai.be.

COLBERT, CLAUDETTE: BIRTH ANNIVERSARY. Sept 13, 1903. Actress and comedienne Colbert, born Lily Claudette Chauchoin at Paris, France, was a beloved movie star of the '30s. She was best known for her films *Midnight, Cleopatra* and *It Happened One Night,* for which she won an Oscar in 1934. In addition to more than 60 movies, she appeared in Broadway shows and won a Golden Globe Award for her role in the 1986 miniseries "The Two Mrs Grenvilles." She also received a Life Achievement Award from the Kennedy Center for Performing Arts in 1989. She died July 30, 1996, at Bridgetown, Barbados.

DAHL, ROALD: BIRTH ANNIVERSARY. Sept 13, 1916. Author of humorously dark fantasy novels for children, Roald Dahl is often referred to as one of the most significant novelists for children of the 20th century. He was born to a Norwegian family at Llandaff, South Wales. He is best remembered for *Charlie and the Chocolate Factory, James and the Giant Peach, Fantastic Mr Fox, The BFG, Matilda* and many others. Dahl died Nov 23, 1990, at Oxford, England.

ITALY: GIOSTRA DELLA QUINTANA. Sept 13. Foligno. A revival of a 17th-century joust of the Quintana, featuring 600 knights in full costume. Annually, the second Sunday in September.

KIDS TAKE OVER THE KITCHEN DAY. Sept 13. Young Chefs Academy encourages kids and teens across the nation to take over their kitchen. The objective is to empower kids and teens to become more actively involved in the planning, preparation and cooking of meals. In turn, we foster family bonds and actively fight the battle against the many serious health and social issues related to our youths' eating habits in today's time. Annually, Sept 13. For info: Shelly Young, Young Chefs International, 7728 Central Park Dr, Waco, TX 76712. Phone: (254) 751-1040. E-mail: marketing@youngchefsacademy.com. Web: www.youngchefsacademy.com/KTOKDay.

"LAW & ORDER" TV PREMIERE: ANNIVERSARY. Sept 13, 1990. Filmed on location at New York City, "Law & Order" showed the interaction between the police and the district attorney's office in dealing with a crime. Almost the entire cast changed over the life of this program and included Michael Moriarty (Assistant District Attorney Benjamin Stone), Sam Waterston (ADA Jack McCoy), Jerry Orbach (Detective Lennie Briscoe), Christopher Noth (Detective Mike Logan), Jesse L. Martin (Detective Edward Green) and many others. The acclaimed program's final episode aired May 24, 2010. "Law & Order" spun off two other successful series: "Law & Order: Special Victims Unit" and "Law & Order: Criminal Intent."

MONROE, BILL: BIRTH ANNIVERSARY. Sept 13, 1911. The father of bluegrass was born at Rosine, KY. The sound and style Monroe developed in the late 1930s—a furious alchemy of country, folk and blues influences, with four- and five-part harmonies delivered over that driving acoustic rhythm—with his band, the Blue Grass Boys, redefined the genre and made him a star. A true statesman of music, Bill Monroe enjoyed a career that spanned six decades and more than 50 releases. He died on Sept 9, 1996, at Springfield, TN.

"THE MUPPET SHOW" TV PREMIERE: ANNIVERSARY. Sept 13, 1976. This comedy-variety show was hosted by Kermit the Frog of "Sesame Street." The new Jim Henson puppet characters included Miss Piggy, Fozzie Bear and The Great Gonzo. Many celebrities appeared as guests on the show, which was broadcast in more than 100 countries. The show ran until 1981. *The Muppet Movie* (1979) was the first of many films based on "The Muppet Show." In 2015 most of the same characters returned to the small screen in "The Muppets" on ABC.

NATIONAL CELIAC AWARENESS DAY. Sept 13. To raise awareness and to honor Dr. Samuel Gee, who first established the connection between celiac disease and diet. Dr. Gee was born Sept 13, 1839. Recognized by US Senate resolution. For info: National Celiac Assn, 20 Pickering St, Needham, MA 02492. Phone: (888) 4-CELIAC. E-mail: info@nationalceliac.org. Web: https://nationalceliac.org.

NATIONAL GRANDPARENTS' DAY. Sept 13. To honor grandparents, to give grandparents an opportunity to show love for their children's children and to help children become aware of the strength, information and guidance older people can offer. Annually, the first Sunday after Labor Day.

NATIONAL SECURITY OFFICER APPRECIATION WEEK. Sept 13–19. 6th annual. The security professionals who strive to maintain safe and secure workplaces, schools, shopping malls and communities deserve our heartfelt appreciation. Security personnel are hardworking, highly trained men and women who are our country's first responders. These individuals deter crime, lead evacuations, provide information, work closely with local law enforcement and are constantly vigilant in their efforts to keep us safe. This week is an opportunity to say thank you and to recognize security officers' many contributions to our daily lives. Annually, the third week in September. For info: Allied Universal. E-mail: info@aus.com. Web: www.aus.com.

9 × 13 DAY. Sept 13. Since 2017. Something good always comes in a 9 × 13 pan! Today, celebrate the comfort and joy that this treasured pan brings. Create and share a dish served up in a 9 × 13 pan—and maybe a story to tell. Annually, Sept 13. For info: Jacqueline Barnhardt. E-mail: jacquelinebarnhardt@gmail.com.

PERSHING, JOHN J.: BIRTH ANNIVERSARY. Sept 13, 1860. US Army general who commanded the American Expeditionary Force (AEF) during WWI, Pershing was born at Laclede, MO. The AEF, as part of the inter-Allied offensive, successfully assaulted the Saint-Mihiel salient in September 1918 and later that month quickly regrouped for the Meuse-Argonne operation that led to the Armistice of Nov 11, 1918. Pershing died July 15, 1948, at Washington, DC.

REED, WALTER: BIRTH ANNIVERSARY. Sept 13, 1851. American army physician, especially known for his yellow fever research. Born at Gloucester County, VA, he served as an army surgeon for more than 20 years and as a professor at the Army Medical College. He died at Washington, DC, Nov 22, 1902. The US Army's general hospital at Washington, DC, was named in his honor (closed in 2011).

ROALD DAHL DAY. Sept 13. The official Roald Dahl Day takes place every year on Sept 13—the birthday of the world's number

one storyteller. There are many scrumdiddlyumptious ways to celebrate: write a revolting rhyme; give someone a favorite book wrapped in newspaper and tied up in string just as Roald Dahl used to do; make a peach smoothie; read a Dahl book that you've never read before—and if you've read them all, read your favorite again; organize a Dahl quiz; drop "gobblefunk" convincingly into a conversation—and lots more. For info: Roald Dahl Day/Roald Dahl Museum and Story Centre. Web: www.roalddahl.com.

"SCOOBY-DOO, WHERE ARE YOU?" TV PREMIERE: ANNIVERSARY. Sept 13, 1969. A tremendously popular Saturday-morning cartoon, Hanna-Barbera's show featured four wacky kids and lovable Great Dane Scooby-Doo solving spooky (and often hilarious) mysteries. Fred, Daphne and Velma usually do the work, while Shaggy (originally voiced by radio personality Casey Kasem) and Scooby-Doo look for something to eat. A live-action feature film was released in 2002 starring Freddie Prinze, Jr; Sarah Michelle Gellar; Matthew Lillard; Linda Cardellini and a digital Scooby.

"SOAP" TV PREMIERE: ANNIVERSARY. Sept 13, 1977. "Soap" was a prime-time comedy that parodied soap operas. It had plots that were funny (e.g., Corinne's baby is possessed by the devil), controversial (e.g., Billy joins a cult) and downright bizarre (e.g., Burt is abducted by aliens). The show focused on two families, the wealthy Tates and the middle-class Campbells. It starred Katherine Helmond, Robert Mandan, Jennifer Salt, Diana Canova, Jimmy Baio, Robert Guillaume, Cathryn Damon, Richard Mulligan, Ted Wass, Billy Crystal, Richard Libertini, Kathryn Reynolds, Robert Urich, Arthur Peterson, Roscoe Lee Browne and Jay Johnson. Rod Roddy was the announcer who recapped what had happened on the previous episode.

"THE STAR-SPANGLED BANNER" INSPIRED: ANNIVERSARY. Sept 13–14, 1814. On the night of Sept 13, Francis Scott Key was aboard a ship that was delayed in Baltimore harbor by the British attack there on Fort McHenry. Key had no choice but to anxiously watch the battle. That experience and seeing the American flag still flying over the fort the next morning inspired him to pen the verses that, coupled with the tune of a popular drinking song, became America's official national anthem in 1931, 117 years after the words were written.

SUMAC, YMA: BIRTH ANNIVERSARY. Sept 13, 1922. Peruvian singer ("The Nightingale of the Andes") who wowed audiences in the 1940s and '50s with her stunning four-octave vocal range. Born Zoila Augusta Emperatriz Chavarri del Castillo at Ichocan, Peru, Sumac claimed to be a descendant of Incan emperor Atahuallpa—a claim the Peruvian government officially supported in 1946. Sumac's mysterious and exotic persona earned her international acclaim and helped her sell millions of records. She died Nov 1, 2008, at Los Angeles, CA.

UNITED KINGDOM: BATTLE OF BRITAIN WEEK. Sept 13–19. Annually, the week of September containing Battle of Britain Day (Sept 15).

September 2020	S	M	T	W	T	F	S
			1	2	3	4	5
	6	7	8	9	10	11	12
	13	14	15	16	17	18	19
	20	21	22	23	24	25	26
	27	28	29	30			

US CAPITAL ESTABLISHED AT NEW YORK CITY: ANNIVERSARY. Sept 13, 1788. Congress picked New York, NY, as the location of the new US government in place of Philadelphia, PA, which had served as the capital up until this time. In 1790 the capital moved back to Philadelphia for 10 years, before moving permanently to Washington, DC.

🎂 BIRTHDAYS TODAY

Fiona Apple, 43, singer, born New York, NY, Sept 13, 1977.

Jacqueline Bisset, 76, actress (*Dancing on the Edge, Rich and Famous, Bullitt*, "Nip/Tuck"), born Weybridge, England, Sept 13, 1944.

Peter Cetera, 76, singer (former lead singer of Chicago), songwriter, born Chicago, IL, Sept 13, 1944.

Niall Horan, 27, singer (One Direction), born Mullingar, Ireland, Sept 13, 1993.

Michael Johnson, 53, Olympic gold medalist in track, born Dallas, TX, Sept 13, 1967.

Judith Martin, 82, author, journalist ("Miss Manners"), born Washington, DC, Sept 13, 1938.

Daisuke Matsuzake, 40, baseball player, born Tokyo, Japan, Sept 13, 1980.

Stella McCartney, 49, fashion designer, born London, England, Sept 13, 1971.

Thomas Müller, 31, soccer player, born Weilheim, Germany, Sept 13, 1989.

Ralph Northam, 61, Governor of Virginia (D), born Nassawadox, VA, Sept 13, 1959.

Tyler Perry, 51, actor (*Alex Cross, Diary of a Mad Black Woman, Madea's Family Reunion*), director, screenwriter, born Emmitt Perry, Jr, at New Orleans, LA, Sept 13, 1969.

Lili Reinhart, 24, actress ("Riverdale"), born Cleveland, OH, Sept 13, 1996.

Ben Savage, 40, actor ("Boy Meets World"), born Chicago, IL, Sept 13, 1980.

Fred Silverman, 83, television producer, born New York, NY, Sept 13, 1937.

Jean Smart, 61, stage and screen actress ("Legion," "24," "Designing Women"), born Seattle, WA, Sept 13, 1959.

Bernabe (Bernie) Williams, 52, former baseball player, born San Juan, Puerto Rico, Sept 13, 1968.

September 14 — Monday

DAY 258	108 REMAINING

DANTE ALIGHIERI: DEATH ANNIVERSARY. Sept 14, 1321. Medieval poet and magistrate, whose allegorical masterpiece, *The Divine Comedy*, is one of the most influential and revered artistic works in the Western canon. He was born in May 1265 (exact date unknown) at Florence, Italy, but due to political conflicts, was exiled from that city-state beginning in 1301. He died at Ravenna, Italy, shortly after finishing the last volume of the *Divine Comedy*, *Paradiso*.

FIRST VOLUME OF *DAS KAPITAL* PUBLISHED: ANNIVERSARY. Sept 14, 1867. Philosopher and economist Karl Marx published the first volume of his influential book *Das Kapital* on this date. The remaining two volumes were published after his death. Subtitled *Critique of Political Economy*, this first volume discusses the exploitation of the laboring class.

"THE GOLDEN GIRLS" TV PREMIERE: 35th ANNIVERSARY. Sept 14, 1985. This comedy starred Bea Arthur, Betty White, Rue McClanahan and Estelle Getty as four divorced/widowed women sharing

a house in Florida during their golden years. The last episode aired Sept 14, 1992, but the show remains popular in syndication.

GRAVITATIONAL WAVES DETECTED: 5th ANNIVERSARY. Sept 14, 2015. One hundred years after Albert Einstein predicted the existence of gravitational waves, they were detected for the first time. It took two black holes colliding to produce the vibration needed to confirm this key part of Einstein's general theory of relativity. The Laser Interferometer Gravitational-Wave Observatory (LIGO) was created for this sole purpose by scientists from Caltech and MIT. This discovery makes way for direct tests of Einstein's theory, which rests on the concept of space-time and forms the foundation of modern physics.

MCCLOSKEY, ROBERT: BIRTH ANNIVERSARY. Sept 14, 1914. Beloved children's book author and illustrator. Won two Caldecott Awards, for *Make Way for Ducklings* (1941) and *Time of Wonder* (1957). Also wrote and illustrated *Blueberries for Sal* (1948). McCloskey was named a Living Legend by the Library of Congress in 2000. Born at Hamilton, OH, he died June 30, 2003, at Deer Isle, ME.

MCKINLEY, WILLIAM: DEATH ANNIVERSARY. Sept 14, 1901. President William McKinley was shot at Buffalo, NY, Sept 6, 1901. He died eight days later. Assassin Leon Czolgosz was executed Oct 29, 1901.

MOORE, CLAYTON: BIRTH ANNIVERSARY. Sept 14, 1914. Jack Carlton Moore, born at Chicago, IL, was a circus performer before going to Hollywood, where first he was a stuntman. Minor roles in film serials preceded his heroic role on television's hit "The Lone Ranger." Moore, who played the West's masked righter-of-wrongs during 1949–52 and 1954–57, embraced the role and was comfortable with being identified as the Lone Ranger long after he retired from acting. With the backing of the public, he won the right to continue wearing the mask when legally challenged by the copyright owners. Inducted into the Hall of Great Western Performers and an honorary inductee into the Stuntman's Hall of Fame, Moore died Dec 28, 1999, at Los Angeles, CA.

MOTLEY, CONSTANCE BAKER: BIRTH ANNIVERSARY. Sept 14, 1921. New York's first black woman state senator and federal judge, and the first woman elected borough president of Manhattan, Constance Baker Motley became interested in law and civil rights when she was barred from a public beach at age 15. She went on to become one of the top civil rights lawyers of the '50s and '60s. She presented arguments before the US Supreme Court for seven cases and won them all. Motley was born at New Haven, CT, and died at New York, NY, Sept 28, 2005.

NATIONAL BOSS/EMPLOYEE EXCHANGE DAY. Sept 14. To help bosses and employees appreciate each other by sharing each other's point of view for a day. Annually, the first Monday after Labor Day. For info: A.C. Vierow, Box 71, Clio, MI 48420-0071.

NATIONAL LINE DANCE WEEK. Sept 14–19. A week to celebrate the line dance! Line dance is a great way to exercise and to meet people. Annually, the second Monday in September through the following Saturday. For info: Shirley Mitchell, 19769 Murray Hill, Detroit, MI 48235. Phone: (313) 272-7618. E-mail: smitc87213@aol.com.

NICARAGUA: BATTLE OF SAN JACINTO DAY. Sept 14. National holiday. Commemorates the 1856 defeat of US invader William Walker.

SANGER, MARGARET (HIGGINS): BIRTH ANNIVERSARY. Sept 14, 1879. Feminist, nurse and founder of the birth control movement in the US. Born at Corning, NY. (Note: Birth year not entirely certain because, apparently, Sanger often used a later date when obliged to divulge her birthday. Best evidence now points to Sept 14, 1879, rather than the frequently used 1883 date.) She died at Tucson, AZ, Sept 6, 1966.

SETON, ELIZABETH ANN: 45th CANONIZATION ANNIVERSARY. Sept 14, 1975. Elizabeth Ann Seton became the first native-born American to be canonized. She was a converted Catholic who founded the Sisters of Charity and several schools devoted to the Catholic education of young women. She was declared a saint in 1974 by Pope Paul VI.

SOLO TRANSATLANTIC BALLOON CROSSING: ANNIVERSARY. Sept 14–18, 1984. Joe W. Kittinger, 56-year-old balloonist, left Caribou, ME, in a 10-story-tall, helium-filled balloon named *Rosie O'Grady's Balloon of Peace* Sept 14, 1984, crossed the Atlantic Ocean and reached the French coast, above the town of Capbreton, in bad weather Sept 17 at 4:29 PM, EDT. He crash-landed amid wind and rain near Savone, Italy, at 8:08 AM, EDT, Sept 18. Kittinger suffered a broken ankle when he was thrown from the balloon's gondola during the landing. His nearly 84-hour flight, covering about 3,535 miles, was the first solo balloon crossing of the Atlantic Ocean and a record distance for a solo balloon flight.

VON HUMBOLDT, ALEXANDER: BIRTH ANNIVERSARY. Sept 14, 1769. Born at Berlin, Prussia, Von Humboldt was a scientific Renaissance man, with expertise spanning meteorology, botany, geology, geography and oceanography. His explorations and extensive writings greatly expanded Western society's knowledge—his detailed recording of every observation is one of his greatest legacies—along with his influential holistic view of the sciences. During an expedition to South and Central America (1799–1804), Von Humboldt discovered a connection between the Orinoco and Amazon rivers and the eponymous Peru Current, theorized that Ecuadorian volcanoes indicated a flaw in the earth's crust and collected thousands of plant specimens. He also first noted the ability of humans to alter their immediate climate. He created the isothermal map. Von Humboldt said, "I have . . . endeavored to comprehend the phenomena of physical objects in their general connection, and to represent nature as on a great whole, moved and animated by internal forces." Von Humboldt died May 6, 1859, at Berlin, Prussia—by which time he was an international celebrity. His name lives on in scores of named geological features and botanical names.

"THE WALTONS" TV PREMIERE: ANNIVERSARY. Sept 14, 1972. This epitome of the family drama spawned nearly a dozen knockoffs during its nine-year run on CBS. The drama was based on the experiences of creator/writer Earl Hamner, Jr, growing up during the Depression in rural Virginia. It began as the TV movie *The Homecoming*, which was turned into a weekly series covering the years 1933–43. The cast went through numerous changes through the years; the principals were Michael Learned and Ralph Waite as the parents of seven children living on the mountainside, and Richard Thomas, who portrayed John-Boy, the eldest son and narrator. The Walton grandparents were played by Ellen Corby and Will Geer. The last telecast aired Aug 20, 1981.

WILSON, JAMES: BIRTH ANNIVERSARY. Sept 14, 1742. Signer of the Declaration of Independence and one of the first associate justices of the US. Born at Fifeshire, Scotland, he died Aug 21, 1798, at Edenton, NC.

🎂 BIRTHDAYS TODAY

Jessica Brown Findlay, 31, actress ("Harlots," "Downton Abbey"), born Cookham, Berkshire, England, Sept 14, 1989.

Jimmy Butler, 31, basketball player, born Houston, TX, Sept 14, 1989.

Zoe Caldwell, 87, actress (*Medea, The Prime of Miss Jean Brodie*), born Melbourne, Australia, Sept 14, 1933.

Dan Cortese, 53, actor ("Veronica's Closet," *Public Enemies*), born Sewickley, PA, Sept 14, 1967.

Mary Crosby, 61, actress ("Dallas," *Tapeheads*), born Los Angeles, CA, Sept 14, 1959.

Ron DeSantis, 42, Governor of Florida (R), born Jacksonville, FL, Sept 14, 1978.

Faith Ford, 56, actress ("Hope and Faith," "Murphy Brown"), born Alexandria, LA, Sept 14, 1964.

Joey Heatherton, 76, actress (*Cry-Baby, Bluebeard*), born Rockville Centre, NY, Sept 14, 1944.

Walter Koenig, 84, actor, writer, director, producer ("Star Trek" and *Star Trek* movies), born Chicago, IL, Sept 14, 1936.

Melissa Leo, 60, actress ("Treme," *Frozen River*, Oscar for *The Fighter*), born New York, NY, Sept 14, 1960.

Andrew Lincoln, 47, actor ("The Walking Dead," *Love Actually*), born London, England, Sept 14, 1973.

Dmitry Medvedev, 55, Prime Minister of Russia, born Leningrad, USSR (now St. Petersburg, Russia), Sept 14, 1965.

Kate Millett, 86, feminist, writer (*Sexual Politics, Flying*), born St. Paul, MN, Sept 14, 1934.

Sam Neill, 73, actor (*My Brilliant Career, Jurassic Park, The Piano*), born Omagh, County Tyrone, Northern Ireland, Sept 14, 1947.

Deshaun Watson, 25, football player, born Gainesville, GA, Sept 14, 1995.

September 15 — Tuesday

DAY 259   **107 REMAINING**

ACUFF, ROY: BIRTH ANNIVERSARY. Sept 15, 1903. Grand Ole Opry "King of Country Music" Roy Acuff was born at Maynardville, TN. Singer and fiddler Acuff (who was cofounder of Acuff-Rose Publishing Company, the leading publisher of country music) was a regular host on weekly Grand Ole Opry broadcasts. He frequently appeared at the Opry with his group, the Smoky Mountain Boys. In December 1991 Acuff became the first living member elected to the Country Music Hall of Fame. Some of his more famous songs are "The Wabash Cannonball" (his theme song), "Pins and Needles (in My Heart)" and "Night Train to Memphis." Roy Acuff died Nov 23, 1992, at Nashville, TN.

AMERICA'S LARGEST RV SHOW—HERSHEY. Sept 15–20. Hersheypark® Entertainment Complex, Hershey, PA. 52nd annual. America's largest RV show, with more than 1,400 RVs on display. Sept 15 is for the trade only; show is open to the public Sept 16–20. Est attendance: 60,000. For info: PRVCA, 4000 Trindle Rd, Camp Hill, PA 17011. Phone: (888) 303-2887. Fax: (717) 303-0297. E-mail: rvcamping@prvca.org. Web: www.largestrvshow.com.

BENCHLEY, ROBERT: BIRTH ANNIVERSARY. Sept 15, 1889. Popular humorist and comedian of the 1920s and '30s, who, with Dorothy Parker and Robert Sherwood, formed the core of the Algonquin Round Table of wits in New York City. Benchley, born at Worcester, MA, was also an editor and drama critic at such magazines as *Vanity Fair* and *The New Yorker*. He began to present his comedy pieces on stage and eventually made many into short films, beginning a small acting career. His "How to Sleep" (1935) won

the Academy Award for Best Short. Another popular piece was "The Treasurer's Report." Benchley died Nov 21, 1945, at New York, NY.

CHRISTIE, AGATHA: BIRTH ANNIVERSARY. Sept 15, 1890. Nicknamed the "Duchess of Death," Christie is regarded as the creator of the modern detection fiction genre and the world's most popular mystery writer. She is famous for her detective stories, notably those featuring Hercule Poirot (*Murder on the Orient Express*) and Miss Marple (*Murder at the Vicarage*), and her works have been translated into more than 100 languages. Second only to Shakespeare in number of books sold, Christie was named Dame of the British Empire in 1971. Her play *The Mousetrap* set the world's record for longest continuous run. Born at Torquay, England, Christie died Jan 12, 1976, at Wallingford, England.

"COLUMBO" TV PREMIERE: ANNIVERSARY. Sept 15, 1971. "Columbo," based on a 1968 made-for-TV movie, entered the lineup of NBC's "Mystery Movie" series on this date. Peter Falk starred as one of TV's great characters, Lieutenant Columbo, the crime-solving policeman dressed in rumpled raincoat and carrying a chewed-up cigar. In almost every episode, Columbo latches himself onto the main suspect, usually a polished sophisticate in comparison with Columbo's seeming simpleton, and nags him or her to death with questions and comments such as "But one thing bothers me, sir." The series ended in 1978 but reemerged in the form of periodic movies beginning in 1989.

COOPER, JAMES FENIMORE: BIRTH ANNIVERSARY. Sept 15, 1789. American novelist, historian and social critic, born at Burlington, NJ, James Fenimore Cooper was one of the earliest American writers to develop a native American literary tradition. His most popular works are the five novels constituting *The Leatherstocking Tales*, featuring the exploits of one of the truly unique American fictional characters, Natty Bumppo. These novels, *The Deerslayer, The Last of the Mohicans, The Pathfinder, The Pioneers* and *The Prairie*, chronicle Natty Bumppo's continuing flight away from the rapid settlement of America. Other works, including *The Monikins* and *Satanstoe*, reveal Cooper as an astute critic of American life. He died Sept 14, 1851, at Cooperstown, NY, the town founded by his father.

COSTA RICA: INDEPENDENCE DAY. Sept 15. National holiday. Gained independence from Spain in 1821.

EL SALVADOR: INDEPENDENCE DAY. Sept 15. National holiday. Gained independence from Spain in 1821.

FIRST NATIONAL CONVENTION FOR BLACKS: ANNIVERSARY. Sept 15, 1830. The first national convention for blacks was held at Bethel Church, Philadelphia, PA. The convention was called to find ways to better the condition of black people and was attended by delegates from seven states. Bishop Richard Allen was elected as the first convention president.

GREENPEACE FOUNDED: ANNIVERSARY. Sept 15, 1971. The environmental organization Greenpeace, committed to a green and peaceful world, was founded by 12 members of the Don't Make a Wave Committee of Vancouver, BC, Canada, when the boat *Phyllis Cormack* sailed to Amchitka, AK, to protest US nuclear testing. Greenpeace's basic principle is "that determined individuals can alter the actions and purposes of even the overwhelmingly

September	S	M	T	W	T	F	S
2020			1	2	3	4	5
	6	7	8	9	10	11	12
	13	14	15	16	17	18	19
	20	21	22	23	24	25	26
	27	28	29	30			

powerful by 'bearing witness'—drawing attention to an environmental abuse through their mere unwavering presence, whatever the risk."

GUATEMALA: INDEPENDENCE DAY. Sept. 15. National holiday. Gained independence from Spain in 1821.

HONDURAS: INDEPENDENCE DAY. Sept. 15. National holiday. Gained independence from Spain in 1821.

"I SPY" TV PREMIERE: 55th ANNIVERSARY. Sept 15, 1965. Bill Cosby made television history as the first African-American actor starring in a major dramatic role in this spy series. Cosby played Alexander "Scotty" Scott, an intellectual spy with a cover as a tennis trainer. Robert Culp played Kelly Robinson, the "tennis pro" and Scotty's partner in espionage. The series was notable for filming worldwide.

IT PROFESSIONALS DAY. Sept. 15. 6th annual. A day honoring all IT professionals as the unsung heroes of modern business. This observance recognizes their commitment to keeping business technology in the fast lane and ensuring business success. Annually, the third Tuesday in September. For info: SolarWinds, 7171 Southwest Pkwy, Bldg 400, Austin, TX 78735. E-mail: pr@solarwinds.com. Web: www.itproday.org.

LEHMAN BROTHERS COLLAPSES: ANNIVERSARY. Sept 15, 2008. On this date venerable banking giant Lehman Brothers, with debt totaling more than $600 billion, filed for Chapter 11 bankruptcy protection. Prior to 2008, Lehman borrowed heavily to invest in the booming (and historically safe) housing market. However, when home prices plummeted as a result of 2008's "subprime mortgage crisis," Lehman, in its financially vulnerable position, suffered huge losses. The company's bankruptcy was by far the largest in US history, and its collapse caused a ripple effect throughout the global financial system.

"THE LONE RANGER" TV PREMIERE: ANNIVERSARY. Sept 15, 1949. This character was created for a radio serial in 1933 by George W. Trendle. The famous masked man was the alter ego of John Reid, a Texas Ranger who was the only survivor of an ambush. He was nursed back to health by his Native American friend, Tonto. Both men traveled around the West on their trusty steeds, Silver and Scout, fighting injustice. Clayton Moore played the Lone Ranger/John Reid and Jay Silverheels costarred as Tonto. The theme music was Rossini's "William Tell Overture." The last episode aired Sept 12, 1957.

★**NATIONAL HISPANIC HERITAGE MONTH.** Sept 15–Oct 15. Presidential Proclamation. Beginning in 1989, always issued for Sept 15–Oct 15 of each year (PL 100–402 of Aug 17, 1988). Previously issued each year for the week including Sept 15 and 16 since 1968 at request (PL 90–498 of Sept 17, 1968).

NETHERLANDS: PRINSJESDAG. Sept. 15. Official opening of parliament at The Hague. The reigning monarch, by tradition, rides in the Golden Coach to the Ridderzaal for the annual opening of parliament. Annually, on the third Tuesday in September.

NICARAGUA: INDEPENDENCE DAY. Sept. 15. National holiday. Gained independence from Spain in 1821.

QUARTERLY ESTIMATED FEDERAL INCOME TAX PAYERS' DUE DATE. Sept. 15. For those individuals whose fiscal year is the calendar year and who make quarterly estimated federal income tax payments, today is one of the due dates (Jan 15, Apr 15, June 15 and Sept 15, 2020).

16th STREET BAPTIST CHURCH BOMBING: ANNIVERSARY. Sept 15, 1963. In a horrific episode of the civil rights struggle, a bomb blast in the basement of the 16th Street Baptist Church in Birmingham, AL, killed four girls preparing for church: Denise McNair, Carole Robertson, Cynthia Wesley and Addie Mae Collins. Previously, the church had been the center for marches led by Dr. Martin Luther King, Jr. Three suspects were brought to trial in 1977, 2001 and 2002 and found guilty.

SPACE MILESTONE: *ARIANE-3* **(ESA).** Sept 15, 1987. European Space Agency rocket carrying two (Australian and European) communications satellites into Earth's orbit marked the reentry of Western nations into commercial space projects. Launched this date from Kourou, French Guiana, with Arianespace, a private company operating the rocket for the 13-nation European Space Agency.

TAFT, WILLIAM HOWARD: BIRTH ANNIVERSARY. Sept 15, 1857. The 27th president of the US was born at Cincinnati, OH. His term of office was Mar 4, 1909–Mar 3, 1913. Following his presidency he became a law professor at Yale University until his appointment as chief justice of the US in 1921. Died at Washington, DC, Mar 8, 1930, and buried at Arlington National Cemetery.

TINKER TO EVERS TO CHANCE: FIRST DOUBLE PLAY ANNIVERSARY. Sept 15, 1902. Chicago Cubs shortstop Joe Tinker, second baseman Johnny Evers and first baseman Frank Chance recorded their first double play together on this date. This was two days after they took the field for the first time in this configuration, and the Cubs went on to beat the Cincinnati Reds, 6–3. The threesome were later immortalized in Franklin Adams's poem "Baseball's Sad Lexicon." Tinker, Evers and Chance were inducted together into the Baseball Hall of Fame in 1946. See also: "'Baseball's Sad Lexicon' Published: Anniversary" (July 10).

UNITED KINGDOM: BATTLE OF BRITAIN DAY. Sept. 15. Commemorating the day—Sept 15, 1940—that proved the turning point of WWII's Battle of Britain. Prime Minister Winston Churchill called this day "the crux of the Battle of Britain." After this day, the German military saw that the air supremacy needed for an invasion of Britain could not be obtained.

UNITED NATIONS: INTERNATIONAL DAY OF DEMOCRACY. Sept. 15. The General Assembly has declared Sept 15 of each year as the International Day of Democracy (Res 62/7 of Nov 8, 2007) and encourages governments to strengthen national programs devoted to the promotion and consolidation of democracy, in an appropriate manner that contributes to raising public awareness. For info: United Nations, Dept of Public Info, New York, NY, 10017. Web: www.un.org.

UNITED NATIONS: OPENING DAY OF GENERAL ASSEMBLY. Sept. 15. The 75th session. Annually, the Tuesday of the third week in September, counting from the first week that contains at least one working day. For info: United Nations, Dept of Public Info, New York, NY 10017. Web: www.un.org.

USA TODAY **FIRST PUBLISHED: ANNIVERSARY.** Sept. 15, 1982. Media corporation Gannett published a new kind of daily—the "Nation's Newspaper"—that featured general interest articles for a national audience on this date.

WRAY, FAY: BIRTH ANNIVERSARY. Sept 15, 1907. Hollywood's "Scream Queen" was born at Alberta, Canada, on this day. The star of numerous silent films (notably Erich von Stroheim's *The Wedding March*), Wray made her mark in 1930s thrillers—and then became a pop culture icon through her role as Ann Darrow, the giant ape's obsession in the 1933 film *King Kong*. Wray died at New York City, Aug 8, 2004. See also: "*King Kong* Film Premiere: Anniversary" (Mar 2).

🎂 BIRTHDAYS TODAY

Chimamanda Ngozi Adichie, 43, author (*Americanah, Half of a Yellow Sun*), born Enugu, Nigeria, Sept 15, 1977.

Dave Annable, 41, actor ("Brothers & Sisters"), born Suffern, NY, Sept 15, 1979.

Josh Charles, 49, actor ("The Good Wife," "Sports Night"), born Baltimore, MD, Sept 15, 1971.

Norm Crosby, 93, comedian, born Boston, MA, Sept 15, 1927.

Tom Hardy, 43, actor (*Dunkirk, The Revenant, Mad Max: Fury Road, The Dark Knight Rises*, "Taboo"), born Hammersmith, London, England, Sept 15, 1977.

Prince Harry (Henry Charles Albert David), 36, Duke of Sussex, born London, England, Sept 15, 1984.

Tommy Lee Jones, 74, actor (Oscar for *The Fugitive*; *Coal Miner's Daughter, Men in Black, No Country for Old Men*), born San Saba, TX, Sept 15, 1946.

Daniel Constantine (Dan) Marino, Jr, 59, Hall of Fame football player, born Pittsburgh, PA, Sept 15, 1961.

Carmen Maura, 75, actress (*Women on the Verge of a Nervous Breakdown*), born Madrid, Spain, Sept 15, 1945.

Heidi Montag, 34, television personality ("The Hills," "Laguna Beach"), born Crested Butte, CO, Sept 15, 1986.

Jessye Norman, 75, soprano, opera singer, born Augusta, GA, Sept 15, 1945.

Gaylord Jackson Perry, 82, Hall of Fame baseball player, born Williamston, NC, Sept 15, 1938.

Ben Schwartz, 39, actor ("House of Lies," "Parks and Recreation"), born New York, NY, Sept 15, 1981.

Will Shields, 49, Hall of Fame football player, born Fort Riley, KS, Sept 15, 1971.

Oliver Stone, 74, director (*Platoon, JFK, Wall Street*), screenwriter, born New York, NY, Sept 15, 1946.

September 16 — Wednesday

DAY 260   **106 REMAINING**

ANNE DUDLEY BRADSTREET DAY. Sept 16. Aspects of Anne Bradstreet (1612–Sept 16, 1672) remain a mystery; there are no known portraits, and no one thought to describe her appearance. Yet we know Anne more intimately today than most women of her time through her poetry. Anne's 1650 book, *The Tenth Muse Lately Sprung Up in America*, was an immediate success in Britain and the New World. Critics considered poetry an unfit pastime for women and were amazed that Anne wrote with such wit and intelligence. Her book was the first full volume by a single author published from the New World, earning Anne a special place in both American and Women's History. Today, North Andover,

September 2020	S	M	T	W	T	F	S
			1	2	3	4	5
	6	7	8	9	10	11	12
	13	14	15	16	17	18	19
	20	21	22	23	24	25	26
	27	28	29	30			

MA, settled by Anne and her family, holds annual celebrations of her life and accomplishments. For info: Library Director, Stevens Memorial Library, 345 Main St, North Andover, MA 01845. Phone: (978) 688-9505. Fax: (978) 688-9507. E-mail: kkeenan@northandoverma.gov. Web: www.annebradstreet.org or www.stevensmemlib.org.

BACALL, LAUREN: BIRTH ANNIVERSARY. Sept 16, 1924. Born Betty Joan Perske at the Bronx, NY, Bacall was 19 when Howard Hawks cast her opposite future husband Humphrey Bogart in *To Have and Have Not* (1944). The film introduced her husky voice, which she lowered to please Hawks, and "The Look," a sultry downward tilt of the chin with eyes cast upward. The star of film noir classics *The Big Sleep* (1946) and *Key Largo* (1948), Bacall also loved live theater, earning a Tony Award in *Applause* (1970). A memoir, *By Myself*, won a National Book Award in 1978. Bacall died at New York City, Aug 12, 2014.

CHEROKEE STRIP DAY. Sept 16, 1893. Optional school holiday, Oklahoma. Greatest "run" for Oklahoma land in 1893.

"FRASIER" TV PREMIERE: ANNIVERSARY. Sept 16, 1993. In this acclaimed spin-off of "Cheers," psychiatrist Dr. Frasier Crane (Kelsey Grammer) has moved to Seattle, WA, where he dispenses advice on his radio show, produced by Roz Doyle (Peri Gilpin). He lives with his ex-cop father, Martin (John Mahoney), and Martin's physical therapist, Daphne Moon (Jane Leeves). His brother, Dr. Niles Crane (David Hyde Pierce), frequently asks for Frasier's advice about his love life. The show was a five-time Emmy winner for Outstanding Comedy Series, and in total garnered 37 Emmys. It finished its run in 2004.

FUNT, ALLEN: BIRTH ANNIVERSARY. Sept 16, 1914. Creator, producer and host of the first reality television show, Funt orchestrated elaborate hoaxes played on unsuspecting passersby and filmed by a hidden camera. With the catchphrase "Smile, you're on Candid Camera," Funt would reveal he had captured the subjects "in the art of being themselves." Born at New York, NY, Funt worked with concealed wire recorders in the US Army Signal Corps during WWII. Premiering on radio as "Candid Microphone" in 1948, the show quickly moved to TV as "Candid Camera" and aired (later, hosted by Funt's son Peter) until 2004. Funt died Sept 5, 1999, at Pebble Beach, CA.

GENERAL MOTORS: FOUNDING ANNIVERSARY. Sept 16, 1908. The giant automobile manufacturing company was founded by William Crapo "Billy" Durant, a Flint, MI, entrepreneur.

GREAT SEAL OF THE US: ANNIVERSARY. Sept 16, 1782. On this date the Great Seal of the United States was, for the first time, impressed upon an official document. That document authorized George Washington to negotiate a prisoner of war agreement with the British. See also: "Great Seal of the United States: Anniversary" (Jan 28 and July 4).

JIMI HENDRIX LAST PERFORMANCE: 50th ANNIVERSARY. Sept 16, 1970. Rock guitarist Jimi Hendrix performed in public for the last time, appearing with Eric Burdon & War at Ronnie Scott's Jazz Club at London, England. Hendrix died Sept 18 from a drug overdose. He was 27.

KING, B.B.: 95th BIRTH ANNIVERSARY. Sept 16, 1925. The King of the Blues was born on a cotton plantation in Mississippi. King began performing in the late 1940s, and with his trusty black Gibson guitar, Lucille, became a fixture on the R&B charts. He was also a relentless performer, regularly playing over 300 dates

per year. King won a Grammy for his 1969 classic "The Thrill Is Gone" and was inducted into both the Blues and Rock and Roll halls of fame. He is an icon of blues guitar, with an expressive, improvisational style that is instantly recognizable. King died at Las Vegas, NV, May 24, 2015.

MALAYSIA: MALAYSIA DAY (HARI MALAYSIA). Sept 16. Public holiday first observed in 2010. Commemorates the founding of the Malaysian Federation on Sept 16, 1963.

MAYFLOWER DAY: 400th ANNIVERSARY. Sept 16, 1620. Anniversary of the departure of the *Mayflower* from Plymouth, England, with 102 passengers and a small crew. Vicious storms were encountered en route, which caused serious doubt about the wisdom of continuing, but the ship reached Provincetown, MA, Nov 21, and discharged the Pilgrims at Plymouth, MA, December 1620.

MEXICO: INDEPENDENCE DAY. Sept 16. National Day. The official celebration begins at 11 PM, Sept 15 and continues through Sept 16. On the night of the 15th, the president of Mexico steps onto the balcony of the National Palace at Mexico City and voices the same "El Grito" (Cry for Freedom) that Father Hidalgo gave on the night of Sept 15, 1810, which began Mexico's rebellion from Spain.

MIDDLEMARK, MARVIN: BIRTH ANNIVERSARY. Sept 16, 1919. Marvin Middlemark was born at Long Island, NY. His passion for inventing and tinkering led to many inventions, most of which enjoyed little commercial success, like the water-driven automatic potato peeler. But it was as the inventor of a device to improve TV reception, known as "rabbit ears," that he became successful. He died Sept 14, 1989, at Old Westbury, NY.

NATIONAL CHAMPIONSHIP AIR RACES. Sept 16–20. Reno, NV. Experience the heart-pounding excitement of the nation's only head-to-head air racing event. There are six racing classes: Unlimited, Sport, Jet, Formula One, T-6 and Biplane. Bringing the best air show acts to the Biggest Little City, this annual event provides a one-of-a-kind thrill. Plus, enjoy an impressive variety of on-the-ground experiences that honor our military, promote STEM education and celebrate the wonder of aviation. Est attendance: 150,000. For info: Natl Championship Air Races. Phone: (775) 972-6663. Web: www.airrace.org.

NATIONAL GUITAR FLAT-PICKING CHAMPIONSHIPS AND WALNUT VALLEY FESTIVAL. Sept 16–20. Winfield Fairgrounds, Winfield, KS. The Walnut River is the site of this 49th annual family event featuring four stages with eight contests, workshops and many first-class concerts. The Walnut Valley Arts and Crafts Festival features handmade instruments and a large variety of arts and crafts items, both ornamental and functional. All-weather facilities. Est attendance: 13,000. For info: Walnut Valley Assn, PO Box 245, Winfield, KS 67156. Phone: (620) 221-3250. Fax: (620) 221-3109. E-mail: hq@wvfest.com. Web: www. wvfest.com.

NATIONAL SCHOOL BACKPACK AWARENESS DAY. Sept 16. On this day join AOTA and occupational therapy practitioners, educators and students across the country as we help others live life to its fullest by avoiding the pain and injury that can come from heavy backpacks and bags. Students, parents, educators, school administrators and community members can learn how to properly choose, pack, lift and carry various types of bags—including backpacks, purses, briefcases and suitcases. A day to learn safety tips to stay protected from back pain throughout life. Annually,

the third Wednesday in September. For info: American Occupational Therapy Assn, Inc. E-mail: praota@aota.org. Web: www. aota.org/Conference-Events/Backpack-Safety-Awareness-Day. aspx.

OLD IRONSIDES SAVED BY POEM: ANNIVERSARY. Sept 16, 1830. Alarmed by a newspaper report that Congress was to have the USS *Constitution* (popularly known as "Old Ironsides") sent to a scrap yard, law student Oliver Wendell Holmes dashed off a poem in protest. The poem began "Ay, tear her tattered ensign down!/ Long has it waved on high,/And many an eye has danced to see/ That banner in the sky." "Old Ironsides," published anonymously this day in the *Boston Daily Advertisor*, was to stir up national outrage as newspaper after newspaper reprinted it. Congress instead appropriated money for the frigate's reconstruction, and Old Ironsides still floats today. (Some historians think that Holmes never actually saw the ship he saved.) See also: "Old Ironsides Launched: Anniversary" (Oct 21).

PALESTINIAN MASSACRE: ANNIVERSARY. Sept 16, 1982. Christian militiamen (the Phalangists) entered Sabra and Shatila, two Palestinian refugee camps in West Beirut, Lebanon. They began shooting and by Sept 18 hundreds of Palestinians, including elderly men, women and children, were dead. Phalangists had demanded the blood of Palestinians since the assassination of their president, Bashir Gemayel, on Sept 14. Survivors of the massacre said they had not seen Israeli forces inside the camp; however, they claimed Israelis sealed off boundaries to the camps and allowed Christian militiamen to enter.

PANIZZI, ANTHONY: BIRTH ANNIVERSARY. Sept 16, 1797. Sir Anthony Panizzi, the only librarian ever hanged in effigy, was born Antonio Genesio Maria Panizzi at Brescello, Italy. As a young man he joined a forbidden Italian patriotic society that advocated the overthrow of the oppressive Austrians who then controlled most of northern Italy. Tried in absentia by an Austrian court in 1820, he was sentenced to death and all his property was confiscated. He fled to England in 1823, learned the language and by 1831 was employed in the British Museum, where, in 1856, he was named principal librarian. Later described as the "prince of librarians," Panizzi died at London, England, Apr 8, 1879.

PAPUA NEW GUINEA: INDEPENDENCE DAY. Sept 16. National holiday. Commemorates independence from Australian administration in 1975.

PARKMAN, FRANCIS: BIRTH ANNIVERSARY. Sept 16, 1823. The American historian, author of *The Oregon Trail*, was born at Boston, MA, and died there Nov 8, 1893.

UNITED NATIONS: INTERNATIONAL DAY FOR THE PRESERVATION OF THE OZONE LAYER. Sept 16. The ozone layer filters sunlight and prevents the adverse effects of ultraviolet radiation from reaching the earth's surface, thereby preserving life on the planet. On this day UN member states are urged to promote, at the national level, activities in accordance with the objectives of the Montreal Protocol on Substances that Deplete the Ozone Layer. The Montreal Protocol was signed Sept 16, 1987 (Res 49/114 of Dec 19, 1994). Annually, Sept 16.

For info: United Nations, Dept of Public Info, New York, NY 10017. Web: www.un.org.

WALL STREET BOMBING: 100th ANNIVERSARY. Sept 16, 1920. The J.P. Morgan Bank at Wall and Broad streets was bombed by unknown assailants. A horse-drawn cart was filled with dynamite and 500 pounds of iron sash weights. The explosion killed 38 people and injured more than 140 people seriously. Hundreds more were slightly injured. No one was ever caught in the terrorist act, but Italian anarchists were suspected.

WORLD PLAY-DOH DAY. Sept 16. Since 2006, an annual celebration of creatable, colorful, makeable fun! World Play-Doh Day was created by Hasbro to honor the childhood staple that continues to captivate the imaginations of millions of children and artists of all ages across the globe. Open a can of Play-Doh compound and be inspired to squish, mold, roll, cut, extrude or create a favorite character, scene or other imaginative design to commemorate the day. Annually, Sept 16. For info: Hasbro, Inc. E-mail: hasbrobrandpr@hasbro.com. Web: www.playdoh.com.

 BIRTHDAYS TODAY

Marc Anthony, 51, singer, actor (*Bringing Out the Dead*), born New York, NY, Sept 16, 1969.

Elgin Gay Baylor, 86, Hall of Fame basketball player, former coach, born Washington, DC, Sept 16, 1934.

Ed Begley, Jr, 71, actor ("St. Elsewhere"), born Los Angeles, CA, Sept 16, 1949.

Alexis Bledel, 38, actress (*The Sisterhood of the Traveling Pants*, "Gilmore Girls"), born Houston, TX, Sept 16, 1982.

Sabrina Bryan, 36, singer, actress ("The Cheetah Girls," "Dancing with the Stars"), born Yorba Linda, CA, Sept 16, 1984.

David Copperfield, 64, illusionist, born David Kotkin at Metuchen, NJ, Sept 16, 1956.

John Bel Edwards, 54, Governor of Louisiana (D), born Amite, LA, Sept 16, 1966.

Henry Louis Gates, Jr, 70, scholar of African-American studies, author, editor, born Keyser, WV, Sept 16, 1950.

Orel Leonard Hershiser IV, 62, former baseball player, born Buffalo, NY, Sept 16, 1958.

Nick Jonas, 28, singer (The Jonas Brothers), actor, born Dallas, TX, Sept 16, 1992.

Richard Marx, 57, singer, born Chicago, IL, Sept 16, 1963.

Mark McEwen, 66, weatherman, music editor, born San Antonio, TX, Sept 16, 1954.

Janis Paige, 98, singer, actress (stage: *The Pajama Game, Silk Stockings*), born Donna Mae Tjaden at Tacoma, WA, Sept 16, 1922.

Amy Poehler, 49, actress, comedienne (*Sisters, Baby Mama*, "Parks and Recreation"), born Burlington, MA, Sept 16, 1971.

Tim Raines, 61, former baseball player, born Sanford, FL, Sept 16, 1959.

September 2020	S	M	T	W	T	F	S
			1	2	3	4	5
	6	7	8	9	10	11	12
	13	14	15	16	17	18	19
	20	21	22	23	24	25	26
	27	28	29	30			

Mickey Rourke, 64, actor (*The Wrestler, Sin City, Diner*), born Schenectady, NY, Sept 16, 1956.

Susan Ruttan, 70, actress ("LA Law"), born Oregon City, OR, Sept 16, 1950.

Molly Shannon, 56, actress ("Saturday Night Live"), born Shaker Heights, OH, Sept 16, 1964.

Jennifer Tilly, 59, actress (*Johnny Be Good, Made in America*), born Los Angeles, CA, Sept 16, 1961.

Robin R. Yount, 65, Hall of Fame baseball player, born Danville, IL, Sept 16, 1955.

September 17 — Thursday

DAY 261   **105 REMAINING**

ANGOLA: DAY OF THE NATIONAL HERO. Sept 17. National holiday.

BATTLE OF ANTIETAM: ANNIVERSARY. Sept 17, 1862. This date has been called America's bloodiest day in recognition of the high casualties suffered in the Civil War battle between General Robert E. Lee's Confederate forces and General George McClellan's Union army. Estimates vary, but more than 25,000 Union and Confederate soldiers were killed or wounded in this battle on the banks of the Potomac River in Maryland.

"BEWITCHED" TV PREMIERE: ANNIVERSARY. Sept 17, 1964. This sitcom centered around playful blond-haired witch Samantha Stephens (Elizabeth Montgomery). Although she promises not to use her witchcraft in her daily life, Samantha finds herself twitching her nose in many situations. Her husband, Darrin Stephens, was played by Dick York and later Dick Sargent, and her daughter, Tabitha Stephens, was played by Erin and Diane Murphy. The last episode aired July 1, 1972. Other cast members included Agnes Moorehead, David White, Alice Ghostley, Bernard Fox and Paul Lynde.

BURGER, WARREN E.: BIRTH ANNIVERSARY. Sept 17, 1907. Former chief justice of the US, Warren E. Burger was born at St. Paul, MN. A conservative on criminal matters, but a progressive on social issues, he had the longest tenure (1969–86) of any chief justice in the 20th century. Appointed by President Nixon, he voted in the majority on *Roe v Wade* (1973), which upheld a woman's right to an abortion, and on *US v Nixon* (1974), which forced Nixon to surrender audiotapes to the Watergate special prosecutor. He died June 25, 1995, at Washington, DC.

★**CITIZENSHIP DAY.** Sept 17. Presidential Proclamation always issued for Sept 17 at request (PL 82–261 of Feb 29, 1952). Customarily

issued as "Citizenship Day and Constitution Week." Replaces Constitution Day.

CONNOLLY, MAUREEN: BIRTH ANNIVERSARY. Sept 17, 1934. Maureen "Little Mo" Catherine Connolly Brinker, tennis player born at San Diego, CA. Connolly became the second-youngest woman to win the US National championship at Forest Hills, NY, when she captured that title in 1951. She repeated in 1952 and won Wimbledon as well. In 1953 she became the first woman to win the Grand Slam, taking the US, French, Australian and Wimbledon championships. After winning a second straight French title and a third straight Wimbledon, she suffered a crushed leg in a horseback riding accident and never competed again. Died at Dallas, TX, June 21, 1969.

CONSTITUTION COMMEMORATION DAY IN ARIZONA. Sept 17. Arizona. This state holiday commemorates the signing of the US Constitution on Sept 17, 1787.

CONSTITUTION OF THE US: ANNIVERSARY. Sept 17, 1787. Delegations from 12 states (Rhode Island did not send a delegate) at the Constitutional Convention at Philadelphia, PA, voted unanimously to approve the proposed document. Thirty-nine of the 42 delegates present signed it, and the Convention adjourned, after drafting a letter of transmittal to the Congress. The proposed constitution stipulated that it would take effect when ratified by nine states. This day is a legal holiday in Florida.

★**CONSTITUTION WEEK.** Sept 17–23. Presidential Proclamation always issued for the period of Sept 17–23 each year since 1955 (PL 84–915 of Aug 2, 1956).

FOSTER, ANDREW "RUBE": BIRTH ANNIVERSARY. Sept 17, 1879. Rube Foster's efforts in baseball earned him the title of "The Father of Negro Baseball." He was a manager and star pitcher, pitching 51 victories in one year. In 1920 he called a meeting of black baseball owners and organized the first black baseball league, the Negro National League. He served as its president until his death in 1930. Foster was born at Calvert, TX, the son of a minister. He died Dec 9, 1930, at Kankakee, IL.

"THE FUGITIVE" TV PREMIERE: ANNIVERSARY. Sept 17, 1963. A nail-biting adventure series on ABC. Dr. Richard Kimble (David Janssen) was wrongly convicted and sentenced to death for his wife's murder but escaped from his captors in a train wreck. This popular program aired for four years detailing Kimble's search for the one-armed man (Bill Raisch) who had killed his wife, Helen (Diane Brewster). In the meantime, Kimble himself was being pursued by Lieutenant Philip Gerard (Barry Morse). The final episode aired Aug 29, 1967, and featured Kimble extracting a confession from the one-armed man as they struggled from the heights of a water tower in a deserted amusement park. That single episode was the highest-rated show ever broadcast until 1980. The TV series generated a hit movie in 1993 with Harrison Ford as Kimble and Oscar-winner Tommy Lee Jones as Gerard.

HENDRICKS, THOMAS ANDREWS: BIRTH ANNIVERSARY. Sept 17, 1819. Twenty-first vice president of the US (1885) born at Muskingum County, OH. Died at Indianapolis, IN, Nov 25, 1885.

HERZOG, CHAIM: BIRTH ANNIVERSARY. Sept 17, 1918. President of Israel, an ex-general and chief delegate to the UN, author and lawyer, born at Belfast, Northern Ireland. He was a British army officer in WWII. Died at Tel Aviv, Israel, Apr 17, 1997.

"HOME IMPROVEMENT" TV PREMIERE: ANNIVERSARY. Sept 17, 1991. This comedy was a TV program about a TV program. Tim Taylor, played by Tim Allen, was host of the popular fix-it show "Tool Time." His wife, Jill, played by Patricia Richardson, was a housewife going back to school to get a degree in psychology. The couple's three sons were played by Zachery Ty Bryan, Jonathan Taylor Thomas and Taran Noah Smith. Other cast members included Richard Karn as Tim's TV assistant, Earl Hindman, Debbe Dunning and Pamela Anderson. The last episode aired May 25, 1999.

HUMMERBIRD CELEBRATION. Sept 17–20. Rockport and Fulton, TX. To celebrate the spectacular fall migration of the ruby-throated hummingbird and other birds from their summer nesting grounds in the north along the eastern Gulf Coast on the way to their winter grounds in Mexico and Central America and the hummerbirds' 500-mile journey across the Gulf. There are programs, workshops, booths, concessions and bus and boat tours. Est attendance: 6,000. For info: Rockport Fulton Area Chamber of Commerce, HummerBird Celebration, 319 Broadway, Rockport, TX 78382. Phone: (800) 242-0071 or (361) 729-6445. E-mail: tourism@1rockport.org. Web: www.rockporthummingbird.com.

"M*A*S*H" TV PREMIERE: ANNIVERSARY. Sept 17, 1972. This popular, award-winning CBS series was based on the 1970 Robert Altman movie and a book by Richard Hooker. Set during the Korean War, the show aired for 11 years (lasting longer than the war). It followed the lives of doctors and nurses on the war front with both humor and pathos. The cast included Wayne Rogers, McLean Stevenson, Loretta Swit, Larry Linville, Gary Burghoff, William Christopher, Jamie Farr, Harry Morgan, Mike Farrell, David Ogden Stiers and Alan Alda as Captain "Hawkeye" Pierce. The final episode, "Goodbye, Farewell and Amen" in 1983, was the highest-rated program of all time, topping the "Who Shot J.R.?" revelation on "Dallas." The show generated two spin-offs: "Trapper John, MD" and "AfterMASH." See also: "M*A*S*H: The Final Episode: Anniversary" (Feb 28).

"MISSION: IMPOSSIBLE" TV PREMIERE: ANNIVERSARY. Sept 17, 1966. This action-adventure espionage series, which appeared on CBS for seven years, had a simple premise: each week the IMF (Impossible Missions Force) leader would receive instructions on a supersecret mission to be carried out by the crew. Steven Hill played the first IMF leader, Dan Briggs. He was replaced by Peter Graves, who played Jim Phelps. Other cast members included Martin Landau as Rollin Hand, master of disguise; Barbara Bain, real-life wife of Landau, as Cinnamon Carter (three Emmys); Leonard Nimoy as Hand's replacement, Paris; Greg Morris as tech wiz Barney Collier; and Peter Lupus as strongman Willy Armitage. Tom Cruise resurrected the concept for several feature films, beginning in 1996.

MOON PHASE: NEW MOON. Sept 17. Moon enters New Moon phase at 7:00 AM, EDT.

NATIONAL CONSTITUTION CENTER CONSTITUTION DAY. Sept 17. To celebrate and commemorate the signing of the US Constitution Sept 17, 1787. The National Constitution Center hosts special events and activities. Free admission to museum on Sept 17. For info: Natl Constitution Center, Independence Mall, 525 Arch St, Philadelphia, PA 19106. Phone: (215) 409-6600. Web: www.constitutioncenter.org.

NATIONAL FOOTBALL LEAGUE FORMED: 100th ANNIVERSARY. Sept 17, 1920. The National Football League was formed at Canton, OH.

NATIONAL TABLE SHUFFLEBOARD DAY. Sept 17. Since 2017, a day to celebrate a sport that has been played since the 15th century—when English players shoved a groat or penny along a table. On this day, establishments featuring table shuffleboards will host special events and tournaments. Manufacturers will offer special deals. Annually, Sept 17. For info: Charles Ziegler, Chair, National Table Shuffleboard Day, 2540 Nottingham Way, Trenton, NJ 08610. Phone: (609) 947-7884. E-mail: cziegler@zieglerworld.com. Web: www.nationaltableshuffleboardday.com.

OKLAHOMA STATE FAIR. Sept 17–27. State Fair Park, Oklahoma City, OK. One of the top state fairs in North America includes six buildings of commercial exhibits, 10 barns for livestock and horse competitions, Disney on Ice, PRCA championship rodeo, live entertainment and motor sports events. Annually, beginning on the second Thursday after Labor Day. Est attendance: 1,000,000. For info: Oklahoma State Fair, PO Box 74943, Oklahoma City, OK 73147. Phone: (405) 948-6700. Fax: (405) 948-6828. E-mail: news@okstatefair.com. Web: www.okstatefair.com.

SELFRIDGE, THOMAS E.: DEATH ANNIVERSARY. Sept 17, 1908. Lieutenant Thomas E. Selfridge, 26-year-old passenger in 740-pound biplane piloted by Orville Wright, was killed when, after four minutes in the air, the plane fell from a height of 75 feet. Nearly 2,000 spectators witnessed the crash at Fort Myer, VA. The plane was being tested for possible military use by the Army Signal Corps. Orville Wright was seriously injured in the crash. Selfridge Air Force Base, MI, was named after the young lieutenant, a West Point graduate, who was the first fatality of powered airplane travel.

VFW LADIES AUXILIARY ORGANIZED: ANNIVERSARY. Sept 17, 1914. This organization is loyal to the issues and actions affecting America's heroes. Its members offer assistance in addition to supporting veterans' issues in Congress. Part of the organization's mission, according to its charter, is "to assist the Posts and members thereof . . . to foster true patriotism; and to preserve and defend the United States from all her enemies, whomsoever." For info: Veterans of Foreign Wars of the US, Women's Auxiliary. Web: www.ladiesauxvfw.org.

VON STEUBEN, BARON FRIEDRICH: BIRTH ANNIVERSARY. Sept 17, 1730. Prussian-born general who volunteered to serve in the American Revolution. He died at Remsen, NY, Nov 28, 1794. Von Steuben Day is commemorated on this day, on the following Saturday or on the fourth Sunday in September.

WILLIAMS, HANK, SR: BIRTH ANNIVERSARY. Sept 17, 1923. Hiram King Williams, country singer, born at Georgia, AL. He achieved his first hit with "Lovesick Blues," which brought him a contract with the Grand Ole Opry. His hits include "Cold, Cold Heart," "Honky Tonk Blues," "Jambalaya," "Your Cheatin' Heart," "Take These Chains from My Heart" and "I'll Never Get Out of This World Alive," which was released prior to his death Jan 1, 1953, at Oak Hill, VA.

🎂 BIRTHDAYS TODAY

Tomas Berdych, 35, tennis player, born Valasske-Mezirici, Czech Republic, Sept 17, 1985.

Nate Berkus, 49, interior designer, television personality ("The Oprah Winfrey Show"), born Orange County, CA, Sept 17, 1971.

Kyle Chandler, 55, actor ("Friday Night Lights," "Homefront," *Carol, King Kong*), born Buffalo, NY, Sept 17, 1965.

Charles Grassley, 87, US Senator (R, Iowa), born New Hartford, IA, Sept 17, 1933.

Scott Hoying, 29, singer (Pentatonix), born Arlington, TX, Sept 17, 1991.

Philip D. (Phil) Jackson, 75, basketball executive and former coach and player, born Deer Lodge, MT, Sept 17, 1945.

Chuck Liddell, 51, mixed martial artist, born Santa Barbara, CA, Sept 17, 1969.

Baz Luhrmann, 58, director (*The Great Gatsby, Moulin Rouge*), born Mark Anthony Luhrmann at Sydney, Australia, Sept 17, 1962.

Narendra Modi, 70, Prime Minister of India, born Vadnagar, India, Sept 17, 1950.

Alexander Ovechkin, 35, hockey player, born Moscow, Russia, Sept 17, 1985.

Michael L. Parson, 65, Governor of Missouri (R), born Wheatland, MO, Sept 17, 1955.

Cassandra Peterson, 69, actress (movie hostess Elvira), born Manhattan, KS, Sept 17, 1951.

Rita Rudner, 64, comedienne, actress (*Peter's Friends*), born Miami, FL, Sept 17, 1956.

David H. Souter, 81, former associate justice of the US, born Melrose, MA, Sept 17, 1939.

Rasheed Wallace, 46, former basketball player, born Philadelphia, PA, Sept 17, 1974.

September 18 — Friday

DAY 262   **104 REMAINING**

"THE ADDAMS FAMILY" TV PREMIERE: ANNIVERSARY. Sept 18, 1964. Charles Addams's quirky *New Yorker* cartoon creations were brought to life in this ABC sitcom about a family full of oddballs. John Astin played lawyer Gomez Addams, with Carolyn Jones as his morbid wife, Morticia; Ken Weatherwax as son Pugsley; Lisa Loring as daughter Wednesday; Jackie Coogan as Uncle Fester; Ted Cassidy as both Lurch, the butler, and Thing, a disembodied hand; Blossom Rock as Grandmama; and Felix Silla as Cousin Itt. The last episode aired Sept 2, 1966.

THE BIG E. Sept 18–27. West Springfield, MA. Since 1916. New England's autumn tradition and one of the nation's largest fairs. Each September, The Big E features top-name entertainment, a big-top circus and horse show. Also children's attractions, rides, daily parade with custom-built Mardi Gras floats, historic village, Avenue of States, Better Living Center and much more. Annually, beginning the second Friday after Labor Day. Est attendance: 1,500,000. For info: Eastern States Exposition, 1305 Memorial Ave, West Springfield, MA 01089. Phone: (413) 737-2443. Fax: (413) 787-0127. E-mail: info@thebige.com. Web: www.thebige.com.

CHILE: INDEPENDENCE DAY. Sept 18. National holiday. Declared independence from Spain in 1810. Sept 19 is commemorated as Armed Forces Day in Chile.

COLUMBUS'S LAST VOYAGE TO THE NEW WORLD: ANNIVERSARY. Sept 18, 1502. Columbus landed at Costa Rica on his fourth and last voyage to the New World. He returned to Spain in 1504 and died there in 1506.

September 2020	S	M	T	W	T	F	S
			1	2	3	4	5
	6	7	8	9	10	11	12
	13	14	15	16	17	18	19
	20	21	22	23	24	25	26
	27	28	29	30			

DEMILLE, AGNES: BIRTH ANNIVERSARY. Sept 18, 1905. Dancer and choreographer for ballet and Broadway shows such as *Oklahoma!*, born at New York, NY. DeMille died there Oct 7, 1993.

DIEFENBAKER, JOHN: 125th BIRTH ANNIVERSARY. Sept 18, 1895. Canadian lawyer, statesman and Conservative prime minister (1957–63). Born at Normandy Township, ON, Canada, he died at Ottawa, ON, Aug 16, 1979. Diefenbaker was a member of the Canadian parliament from 1940 until his death.

ENGLAND: HARROGATE AUTUMN FLOWER SHOW. Sept 18–20. Great Yorkshire Showground, Harrogate, North Yorkshire. See Britain's finest blooms and talk to the experts. Nearly 100 nurseries plus plant societies and giant vegetable championships. Est attendance: 40,000. For info: Harrogate Flower Shows, North of England Horticultural Society, Regional Agricultural Centre, Great Yorkshire Showground, Harrogate, North Yorkshire, England HG2 8NZ. Phone: (44) (1423) 546-157. E-mail: info@flower-show.org.uk. Web: www.flowershow.org.uk.

FESTIVAL 2020: FESTIVAL OF FINE ARTS AND FINE CRAFTS. Sept 18–20. Dalton, GA. 57th annual. Fine arts and fine crafts festival includes outdoor artist booths, food vendors, children's activities, entertainment for adults and children, cash awards. Est attendance: 5,000. For info: Creative Arts Guild, 520 W Waugh St, Dalton, GA 30720. Phone: (706) 217-6677. E-mail: leanne@creativeartsguild.org. Web: www.creativeartsguild.org/events.

GARBO, GRETA: BIRTH ANNIVERSARY. Sept 18, 1905. International film actress Greta Garbo was born Greta Lovisa Gustafsson at Stockholm, Sweden. A famous recluse, she retired temporarily, then permanently, from films after 19 years and 27 films, which spanned the late silent era and beginning of sound movies. Her on-screen roles were characterized by an image of a seductress involved in tragic love affairs. She died Apr 15, 1990, at New York, NY.

"GET SMART" TV PREMIERE: 55th ANNIVERSARY. Sept 18, 1965. A spy-thriller spoof appearing on both NBC (1965–69) and CBS (1969–70). Don Adams starred as bumbling CONTROL Agent 86, Maxwell Smart. His mission was to thwart the evildoings of the KAOS organization. Agent Smart was usually successful with the help of his friends: Barbara Feldon as Agent 99 (whom Smart eventually married), Edward Platt as the Chief, Robert Karvelas as Agent Larrabee, Dick Gautier as Hymie the Robot and David Ketchum as Agent 13.

HENDRIX, JIMI: 50th DEATH ANNIVERSARY. Sept 18, 1970. Pyrotechnic rock guitarist Jimi Hendrix died in his sleep of a drug overdose in London, England, on this date, stunning the music world. He was buried in Seattle, WA, on Oct 1, 1970. In an interview a year before, Hendrix said, "When I die I want people to play my music, go wild and freak out an' do anything they want to do." See also: "Hendrix, Jimi: Birth Anniversary" (Nov 27).

HULL HOUSE OPENS: ANNIVERSARY. Sept 18, 1889. This settlement house was founded in Chicago, IL, by Jane Addams and Ellen Gates Starr. It soon became the heart of one of the country's most influential social reform movements, offering a mix of cultural and education programs to new immigrants. See also: "Addams, Jane: Birth Anniversary" (Sept 6).

IRON HORSE OUTRACED BY HORSE: ANNIVERSARY. Sept 18, 1830. In a widely celebrated race, the first locomotive built in America, the Tom Thumb, lost to a horse. Mechanical difficulties plagued the steam engine over the nine-mile course between Riley's Tavern and Baltimore, MD, and a boiler leak prevented the locomotive from finishing the race. In the early days of trains, engines were nicknamed "iron horses."

JOHNSON, SAMUEL: BIRTH ANNIVERSARY. Sept 18, 1709. (Old Style date.) English lexicographer and literary lion, creator of the first great dictionary of the English language (1755) and author of poems, novels and essays. Johnson was born at Lichfield, Staffordshire, England, and died at London, England, Dec 13, 1784. Johnson, master of the quip, stated, "Patriotism is the last refuge of a scoundrel."

NATIONAL CHEESEBURGER DAY. Sept 18. A day to celebrate the cheeseburger—at home or in your favorite burger joint. Observed since 2012. Annually, Sept 18.

NATIONAL HIV/AIDS AND AGING AWARENESS DAY. Sept 18. 12th annual. First observed in 2008, this day focuses on the challenging issues facing the aging population with regard to HIV prevention, testing, care and treatment. In addition, there is an increased need for prevention, research, and data targeting the aging population, medical understanding of the aging process and its impact on HIV/AIDS. For info: The AIDS Institute. E-mail: info@TheAIDSInstitute.org. Web: www.TheAIDSInstitute.org.

★**NATIONAL POW/MIA RECOGNITION DAY.** Sept 18. Annually, the third Friday in September.

NATIONAL TRADESMEN DAY. Sept 18. This day focuses on the "Hands That Build America and Keep It Running Strong" and includes celebrations, recognition events and activities throughout the country. Irwin Tools sponsors this day with retailers and community groups and invites the nation to honor the trade professionals whose hard work contributes to our lives in so many meaningful ways. First observed in 2011. Annually, the third Friday in September. For info: Irwin Tools. Web: www.national-tradesmenday.com.

THE *NEW YORK TIMES* FIRST PUBLISHED: ANNIVERSARY. Sept 18, 1851. The *Times* debuted as the *New-York Daily Times*. The name was changed to the current one in 1857.

READ, GEORGE: BIRTH ANNIVERSARY. Sept 18, 1733. Lawyer and signer of the Declaration of Independence, born at Cecil County, MD. Died Sept 21, 1798, at New Castle, DE.

ROSH HASHANAH BEGINS AT SUNDOWN. Sept 18. Jewish New Year. See also: "Rosh Hashanah" (Sept 19).

STORY, JOSEPH: BIRTH ANNIVERSARY. Sept 18, 1779. Associate justice of the US (1811–45), born at Marblehead, MA. "It is astonishing," he wrote a few months before his death, "how easily men satisfy themselves that the Constitution is exactly what they wish it to be." Story died Sept 10, 1845, at Cambridge, MA, having served 33 years on the Supreme Court.

US AIR FORCE ESTABLISHED: ANNIVERSARY. Sept 18, 1947. Although its heritage dates back to 1907 when the army first established military aviation, the US Air Force became a separate military service on this date. Responsible for providing an air force that is capable, in conjunction with the other armed forces, of preserving the peace and security of the US, the department is separately organized under the

secretary of the air force and operates under the authority, direction and control of the secretary of defense.

US CAPITOL CORNERSTONE LAID: ANNIVERSARY. Sept 18, 1793. President George Washington laid the Capitol cornerstone at Washington, DC, in a Masonic ceremony. That event was the first and last recorded occasion at which the stone with its engraved silver plate was seen. In 1958, during the extension of the east front of the Capitol, an unsuccessful effort was made to find it.

US TAKES OUT ITS FIRST LOAN: ANNIVERSARY. Sept 18, 1789. The first loan taken out by the US was negotiated and secured by Alexander Hamilton on Feb 17, 1790. After beginning negotiations with the Bank of New York and the Bank of North America on Sept 18, 1789, Hamilton obtained the sum of $191,608.81 from the two banks in what became known as the Temporary Loan of 1789. The loan was obtained without authority of law and was used to pay the salaries of the president, senators, representatives and officers of the first Congress. Repayment was completed on June 8, 1790.

WHITE WOMAN MADE AMERICAN INDIAN CHIEF: ANNIVERSARY. Sept 18, 1891. Harriet Maxwell Converse was made a chief of the Six Nations Tribe at the Tonawanda Reservation, NY. She was given the name Ga-is-wa-noh, which means "The Watcher." She had been adopted as a member of the Seneca tribe in 1884 in appreciation of her efforts on behalf of the tribe.

🎂 BIRTHDAYS TODAY

Lance Armstrong, 49, retired cyclist, born Plano, TX, Sept 18, 1971.

Frankie Avalon, 81, singer, actor (*Beach Blanket Bingo*), born Philadelphia, PA, Sept 18, 1939.

Robert Blake, 82, actor ("Baretta," *In Cold Blood, Little Rascals*), born Michael Gubitosi at Nutley, NJ, Sept 18, 1938.

Scotty Bowman, 87, Hall of Fame hockey coach, born Montreal, QC, Canada, Sept 18, 1933.

Ben Carson, 69, US Secretary of Housing and Urban Development (Trump administration), neurosurgeon, born Detroit, MI, Sept 18, 1951.

Serge Ibaka, 31, basketball player, born Brazzaville, Zaire, Sept 18, 1989.

James Marsden, 47, actor ("Westworld," X-Men films, *27 Dresses*), born Stillwater, OK, Sept 18, 1973.

Ryne Sandberg, 61, Hall of Fame baseball player, born Spokane, WA, Sept 18, 1959.

Jada Pinkett Smith, 49, actress ("Gotham," *The Nutty Professor, Menace II Society*), born Baltimore, MD, Sept 18, 1971.

Aisha Tyler, 50, television host, actress ("Talk Soup," "24," "CSI"), born San Francisco, CA, Sept 18, 1970.

September 2020	S	M	T	W	T	F	S
			1	2	3	4	5
	6	7	8	9	10	11	12
	13	14	15	16	17	18	19
	20	21	22	23	24	25	26
	27	28	29	30			

September 19 — Saturday

DAY 263　　　　　　　　　　　　**103 REMAINING**

BROUGHAM, HENRY PETER: BIRTH ANNIVERSARY. Sept 19, 1778. Scottish jurist and orator born at Edinburgh, Scotland. Died at Cannes, France, May 7, 1868. The brougham carriage was named after him. "Education," he said, "makes a people easy to lead, but difficult to drive; easy to govern, but impossible to enslave."

CARROLL, CHARLES: BIRTH ANNIVERSARY. Sept 19, 1737. (Old Style date.) American Revolutionary leader and signer of the Declaration of Independence, born at Annapolis, MD. The last surviving signer of the Declaration, he died Nov 14, 1832, at Baltimore, MD.

COVERED BRIDGE FESTIVAL. Sept 19–20. Washington and Greene County, PA. A charming festival featuring the covered bridges and handmade arts and crafts, homestyle food, historical reenactments, demonstrations, children's activities and entertainment. Annually, the third weekend in September. Est attendance: 20,000. For info: Washington County Tourism Promotion Agency, 375 Southpointe Blvd, Ste 240, Canonsburg, PA 15317. Phone: (866) 927-4969 or (724) 225-3010. E-mail: info@visitwashingtoncountypa.com. Web: www.visitwashingtoncountypa.com.

"ER" TV PREMIERE: ANNIVERSARY. Sept 19, 1994. This medical drama took place in the emergency room of the fictional County General Hospital in Chicago, IL. Doctors and nurses cared for life-and-death cases while experiencing their personal traumas as well. The cast included Anthony Edwards, George Clooney, Julianna Margulies, Sherry Stringfield, Noah Wyle, Laura Innes, Gloria Reuben, Eriq La Salle, Maura Tierney, Goran Visnjic, Alex Kingston, John Stamos and many others. On Dec 6, 2007, the 300th episode aired. The final episode aired on Apr 2, 2009.

GERMANY: OKTOBERFEST. Sept 19–Oct 4. Munich. The most famous beer festival in the world takes place in Munich—although many cities in Germany and other nations also hold similar autumn fairs. Not originally a beer festival, the first Oktoberfest was a celebration of the marriage of Bavarian king Ludwig I to Therese von Sachsen-Hildburghausen, which took place on Oct 12, 1810. The festivities gradually grew and shifted to the relatively warmer days of September—but always end the first weekend in October. The event is kicked off when the mayor of Munich taps the first barrel of beer. All beer consumed in the city is actually brewed in the city, and about 1,430,000 gallons are consumed each festival. Annually, beginning on the Saturday in September that is 16 days before the first Sunday in October. Est attendance: 6,200,000. For info: Munich Oktoberfest. Web: www.oktoberfest.de.

GOLDING, WILLIAM: BIRTH ANNIVERSARY. Sept 19, 1911. Born at Columb Minor at Cornwall, England, this celebrated author was recognized for his contributions to literature with a Nobel Prize in 1983. His first and most popular novel was *Lord of the Flies*. He died June 19, 1993, near Truro, Cornwall.

"ICEMAN" MUMMY DISCOVERED: ANNIVERSARY. Sept 19, 1991. At 10,531 feet in the Austrian-Italian Alps, two hikers discovered a 5,300-year-old frozen mummy from late Neolithic times. The man carried a rough bow and arrows as well as a copper ax and wore a grass cloak for warmth. His shoes were made from bearskin, deer hide and tree bark. He now rests as a frozen exhibit at the South Tyrol Museum of Archaeology at Bolzano, Italy. The "Iceman" was gently thawed in September 2000 in order for scientists to conduct valuable DNA analysis and determine his last meal.

INTERNATIONAL COASTAL CLEANUP. Sept 19. 35th annual. Since 1986, 13 million volunteers have collected 249 million pounds of trash from beaches and waterways around the world. Annually, the third Saturday in September. For info: Ocean Conservancy, 1300 19th St NW, 8th Fl, Washington, DC 20036. Phone: (800) 519-1541. E-mail: cleanup@oceanconservancy.org. Web: www.oceanconservancy.org or www.coastalcleanup.org.

INTERNATIONAL RED PANDA DAY. Sept 19. A day to celebrate and learn about the red panda. The red panda, or "firefox," is often referred to as the "lesser panda" in deference to the better-known giant panda. They live in the temperate forests of the Himalayas (in parts of Nepal, China and Myanmar). Zoos throughout the world observe this day and work together to protect this solitary mammal. Annually, the third Saturday in September. For info: Red Panda Network, 494 W 10th Ave, Ste 7, Eugene, OR 97401. Phone: (877) 854-2391. E-mail: info@redpandanetwork.org. Web: www.redpandanetwork.org.

INTERNATIONAL TALK LIKE A PIRATE DAY. Sept 19. A day to release your inner pirate with a hearty "ahoy!" or, if you prefer, a simple "arrrr!" Every man, woman and child on the planet has an opportunity to express their "pirattitude" today. (Dressing up is encouraged, but optional.) The brainchild of John "Ol' Chumbucket" Baur and Mark "Cap'n Slappy" Summers, the celebration has taken on a life of its own and is now celebrated on all seven continents. Yo ho! Annually, Sept 19. For info: Mark "Cap'n Slappy" Summers, 925 1st Ave E, Albany, OR 97321. Phone: (541) 619-9579. E-mail: capnslappy@talklikeapirate.com. Web: www.talklikeapirate.com.

LOCATE AN OLD FRIEND DAY. Sept 19. Everyone has wondered what happened to a childhood friend, an old chum from grade school, a roommate from college or a former neighbor. Today is the day to locate those special people you've lost track of and get reacquainted. It may take some sleuthing on social media, through other acquaintances or in a class yearbook. Reach out to them by calling, sending an e-mail or writing a letter. Annually, the third Saturday in September. For info: Claudia Evart, 30 Park Ave #2P, New York, NY 10016. E-mail: siblingsdayapril10@gmail.com.

LUYTS, JAN: BIRTH ANNIVERSARY. Sept 19, 1655. Dutch scholar, physicist, mathematician and astronomer, Jan Luyts was born at Hoorn in western Netherlands. Little remembered except for his books: *Astronomica Institutio . . .* (1689) and *Introductio ad Geographiam . . .* (1690).

"THE MARY TYLER MOORE SHOW" TV PREMIERE: 50th ANNIVERSARY. Sept 19, 1970. This show—one of the most popular sitcoms of the '70s—combined good writing, an effective supporting cast and contemporary attitudes. The show, starring Mary Tyler Moore, centered around the two most important places in Mary Richards's life—the WJM-TV newsroom and her apartment at Minneapolis, MN. At home she shared the ups and downs of life with her friend Rhoda Morgenstern (Valerie Harper) and the manager of her apartment building, Phyllis Lindstrom (Cloris Leachman). At work, as the associate producer (later producer) of "The Six O'Clock News," Mary struggled to function in a man's world. Figuring in her professional life were her irascible boss, Lou Grant (Ed Asner), levelheaded and softhearted news writer Murray Slaughter (Gavin MacLeod) and narcissistic anchorman Ted Baxter (Ted Knight). In the last of 168 episodes (Mar 19, 1977), the unthinkable happened: everyone in the WJM newsroom except the inept Ted was fired.

MEXICO CITY EARTHQUAKE: 35th ANNIVERSARY. Sept 19–20, 1985. Nearly 10,000 persons perished in the earthquakes (8.1 and 7.5, respectively, on the Richter scale) that devastated Mexico City. Damage to buildings was estimated at more than $1 billion, and 100,000 homes were destroyed or severely damaged.

POWELL, LEWIS F., JR: BIRTH ANNIVERSARY. Sept 19, 1907. Former associate justice of the US, nominated by President Nixon Oct 21, 1971. (Powell took office Jan 7, 1972.) Justice Powell was born at Suffolk, VA. In 1987 he announced his retirement from the Supreme Court. He died Aug 25, 1998, at Richmond, VA.

ROSH HASHANAH OR JEWISH NEW YEAR. Sept 19–20. Jewish holy day observed on two consecutive days. Hebrew calendar dates: Tishri 1–2, 5781. Rosh Hashanah (literally "Head of the Year") is the beginning of 10 days of repentance and spiritual renewal. (Began at sundown Sept 18.)

ROYKO, MIKE: BIRTH ANNIVERSARY. Sept 19, 1932. Syndicated columnist to more than 600 newspapers nationwide, Pulitzer Prize winner and author (*Boss, Slats Grobnick*). Born at Chicago, IL, Royko died there Apr 29, 1997.

SAINT CHRISTOPHER (SAINT KITTS) AND NEVIS: INDEPENDENCE DAY. Sept 19. National holiday. Commemorates independence from Britain in 1983.

SAINT JANUARIUS (GENNARO): FEAST DAY. Sept 19. Fourth-century bishop of Benevento, martyred near Naples, Italy, whose relics in the Naples Cathedral are particularly famous because on his feast days the blood in a glass vial is said to liquefy in response to prayers of the faithful. In September 1979 the Associated Press reported that some 5,000 persons gathered at the cathedral at dawn, and that "the blood liquefied after 63 minutes of prayers." This phenomenon is said to occur also on the first Saturday in May.

TITAN II MISSILE EXPLOSION: 40th ANNIVERSARY. Sept 19, 1980. The third major accident involving America's most powerful single weapon occurred near Damascus, AR. The explosion, at 3 AM, came nearly 11 hours after a fire had started in the missile silo. The multimegaton nuclear warhead (a hydrogen bomb) reportedly was briefly airborne but came to rest a few hundred feet away. One dead, 21 injured in accident. Previous major Titan missile accidents: Aug 9, 1965, near Searcy, AR (53 dead); and Aug 24, 1978, near Rock, KS (2 dead, 29 injured).

TRAIL OF COURAGE LIVING-HISTORY FESTIVAL. Sept 19–20. Rochester, IN. Portrayal of life in frontier Indiana when it was Indian territory. Historic skits and two stages with music and dancing. Historic encampments for Revolutionary War, French and Indian War, Voyageurs, War of 1812, Western Fur Trade and Plains Indians. Re-created 1832 Chippeway Village, Woodland Indian Village, pioneer foods and crafts, muzzle-loading and tomahawk contests, canoe rides. Museum, round barn and Living History Village on grounds. Special honored Potawatomi family from Indiana's history each year. Est attendance: 16,000. For info: Fulton County Historical Society, 37 E 375N, Rochester, IN 46975. Phone: (574) 223-4436. E-mail: fchs@rtcol.com. Web: www.fultoncountyhistory.org or www.potawatomi-tda.org.

🎂 BIRTHDAYS TODAY

James Anthony (Jim) Abbott, 53, former baseball player, born Flint, MI, Sept 19, 1967.

Jimmy Fallon, 46, talk show host ("The Tonight Show Starring Jimmy Fallon"), comedian, actor ("Saturday Night Live"), born Brooklyn, NY, Sept 19, 1974.

Kevin Hooks, 62, actor, director ("The White Shadow," *Sounder*), born Philadelphia, PA, Sept 19, 1958.

Jeremy Irons, 72, actor (Oscar for *Reversal of Fortune*; *Lolita, Dead Ringers*, "The Borgias"), born Cowes, Isle of Wight, England, Sept 19, 1948.

N. K. Jemisin, 48, author (Hugo Awards for *The Fifth Season* and *The Obelisk Gate*; *The Hundred Thousand Kingdoms*), psychologist, born Nora K. Jemisin at Iowa City, IA, Sept 19, 1972.

Joan Lunden, 69, broadcast journalist, born Sacramento, CA, Sept 19, 1951.

Randolph Mantooth, 75, actor ("Emergency"), born Sacramento, CA, Sept 19, 1945.

David McCallum, 87, actor ("NCIS," "The Man from U.N.C.L.E.," *The Great Escape*), born Glasgow, Scotland, Sept 19, 1933.

Joe Morgan, 77, sportscaster, Hall of Fame baseball player, born Bonham, TX, Sept 19, 1943.

Soledad O'Brien, 54, television journalist, born St. James, NY, Sept 19, 1966.

Tim Scott, 55, US Senator (R, South Carolina), born North Charleston, SC, Sept 19, 1965.

Columbus Short, 38, actor, dancer ("Scandal," *Stomp the Yard*), born Kansas City, MO, Sept 19, 1982.

Alison Sweeney, 44, actress ("Days of Our Lives"), television personality ("The Biggest Loser"), born Los Angeles, CA, Sept 19, 1976.

Twiggy, 71, actress (*The Boy Friend, The Blues Brothers*), model, born Leslie Hornby at London, England, Sept 19, 1949.

Paul Williams, 80, singer, composer (Oscar for "Evergreen"), actor, born Omaha, NE, Sept 19, 1940.

Trisha Yearwood, 56, singer, born Monticello, GA, Sept 19, 1964.

September 20 — Sunday

DAY 264 **102 REMAINING**

AUERBACH, RED: BIRTH ANNIVERSARY. Sept 20, 1917. Basketball coach Arnold Jacob Auerbach was born at Brooklyn, NY. As coach of the Boston Celtics from 1950 to 1966, he won nine NBA titles, including eight straight from 1959 to 1966. After retiring from coaching, Auerbach was either general manager or president of the Celtics from 1966 until 1997. He was team president from 2001 until his death at Washington, DC, on Oct 28, 2006. In 1980 he was named the greatest coach in NBA history by the Professional Basketball Writers Association and is widely considered to be the best sports executive in history.

BILLIE JEAN KING WINS THE "BATTLE OF THE SEXES": ANNIVERSARY. Sept 20, 1973. Billie Jean King defeated Bobby Riggs in the nationally televised "Battle of the Sexes" tennis match in three straight sets.

BUILD A BETTER IMAGE WEEK. Sept 20–26. In order to be a success, you need to look like one. This week is set aside for people

	S	**M**	**T**	**W**	**T**	**F**	**S**
September			1	2	3	4	5
2020	6	7	8	9	10	11	12
	13	14	15	16	17	18	19
	20	21	22	23	24	25	26
	27	28	29	30			

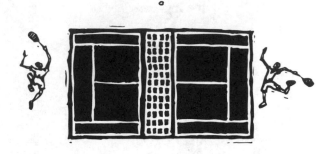

to evaluate their professional image and take the steps necessary to improve on it. "10 Steps to a Better Image" tip sheet available. Annually, the third full week in September. For info: Marlys K. Arnold, ImageSpecialist, PO Box 901808, Kansas City, MO 64190-1808. Phone: (816) 746-7888. E-mail: marnold@imagespecialist.com.

"THE COSBY SHOW" TV PREMIERE: ANNIVERSARY. Sept 20, 1984. This Emmy Award–winning comedy set in New York City revolved around the members of the Huxtable family. Father Dr. Heathcliff Huxtable was played by Bill Cosby; his wife, Clair, an attorney, was played by Phylicia Rashad.

FINANCIAL PANIC OF 1873: ANNIVERSARY. Sept 20, 1873. For the first time in its history, the New York Stock Exchange was forced to close because of a banking crisis. Although the worst of the panic and crisis was over within a week, the psychological effect on businesspeople, investors and the nation at large was more lasting.

FONZIE JUMPS THE SHARK: ANNIVERSARY. Sept 20, 1977. On the popular ABC TV comedy "Happy Days," cool guy Arthur "Fonzie" Fonzarelli goes water skiing in Los Angeles (with trademark leather jacket) and jumps over a shark—a gimmick at odds with the show's normal action. "Jumping the shark" has now become a term to describe engaging in an outlandish stunt in a desperate bid for popularity that signals a creative decline.

INTERNATIONAL GO-KART WEEK. Sept 20–26. The invention of the Go-Kart made it possible for anyone to experience the fun and excitement of racing in a way that is both safe and affordable. This week, reconnect with the thrill of getting behind the wheel of a Go-Kart again. Observed near the September 1956 anniversary of the first public unveiling of the Go-Kart at Pomona Raceway, CA. Annually, the third week in September. For info: David Larson, President, American E-Kart Championship. E-mail: David@AmericanEKart.com. Web: www.AmericanEKart.com.

INTERNATIONAL WOMEN'S ECOMMERCE DAYS. Sept 20–26. This event will celebrate women around the globe and their economic impact and purchasing power. The schedule of events (subject to change) includes encouraging women around the world to make an online purchase today, sending information to the media on all continents, coordinating with more than 290 partnering organizations (made up of 250,000 members) to spread the word and culminating in a World Congress to be held in various locations around the globe. For info: Women in Ecommerce, PO Box 550856, Fort Lauderdale, FL 33355. Phone: (954) 625-6606. E-mail: heidi@wecai.org. Web: www.wecai.org.

MORTON, FERDINAND "JELLY ROLL": BIRTH ANNIVERSARY. Sept 20, 1885. The American jazz pianist, composer and orchestra leader was born at New Orleans, LA (some scholars believe in 1890). Morton, subject of a biography titled *Mr Jelly Roll* by Alan Lomax, died July 10, 1941, at Los Angeles, CA.

NATIONAL EQUAL RIGHTS PARTY FOUNDING: ANNIVERSARY. Sept 20, 1884. The National Equal Rights Party was formed at San Francisco, CA. Its candidate for president in the 1884 election, nominated in convention, was Mrs Belva Lockwood. The vice presidential candidate was Marietta Stow.

★**NATIONAL FARM SAFETY AND HEALTH WEEK.** Sept 20–26. Presidential Proclamation issued since 1982 for the third week in September. Previously, from 1944, for one of the last two weeks in July.

NATIONAL SINGLES WEEK. Sept 20–26. To celebrate single life and to recognize singles and their contributions to society. For info: Rich Gosse, Chairman, American Singles, 205 Mark Twain Ave, San Rafael, CA 94903. Phone: (415) 479-3800. E-mail: rich@rich-gosse.com.

PERKINS, MAXWELL: BIRTH ANNIVERSARY. Sept 20, 1884. The most powerful and influential book editor of the early 20th century, Perkins discovered, nurtured, cajoled, guided and edited such authors as F. Scott Fitzgerald, Ernest Hemingway and Thomas Wolfe at Charles Scribner's Sons. Born at New York, NY, Perkins died June 17, 1947, at Stamford, CT.

SINCLAIR, UPTON BEALL: BIRTH ANNIVERSARY. Sept 20, 1878. American novelist and politician born at Baltimore, MD. He worked for political and social reforms, and his best-known novel, *The Jungle*, prompted one of the nation's first pure food laws. Died at Bound Brook, NJ, Nov 25, 1968.

TOLKIEN WEEK. Sept 20–26. To promote appreciation and enjoyment of the works of J.R.R. Tolkien. Annually, the week that includes Hobbit Day (Sept 22). For info: American Tolkien Society, PO Box 97, Highland, MI 48357-0097. E-mail: americantolkiensociety@yahoo.com. Web: www.americantolkiensociety.org.

UCI ROAD WORLD CHAMPIONSHIPS. Sept 20–27. Aigle-Martigny, Switzerland. Road cycling's premier event, with expected worldwide television audience of 250 million. Sponsored by the Union Cycliste Internationale (UCI), a nonprofit organization founded on Apr 14, 1900. Est attendance: 450,000. For info: Union Cycliste Internationale (UCI), Chemin de la Mêlée 12, 1860 Aigle, Switzerland. E-mail: admin@uci.ch. Web: www.uci.ch.

WORLD REFLEXOLOGY WEEK. Sept 20–26. A week to celebrate this form of therapy and to increase awareness of it. Reflexology is a scientific art based on the premise that there are reflex areas in the feet and hands that correspond to all the body parts. The physical act of applying specific pressure using thumb, finger and hand techniques results in stress reduction—and causes a physiological change in the body. Reflexology groups and associations around the world observe this week and reach out to their communities. Annually, the last full week in September. For info: Assn of Reflexologists or Intl Council of Reflexologists. Web: www.aor.org.uk or www.icr-reflexology.org.

🎂 BIRTHDAYS TODAY

Maggie Cheung, 56, actress (*Clean, In the Mood for Love, Actress*), born Cheung Man Yuk at Hong Kong, Sept 20, 1964.

Dale Chihuly, 79, artist, born Tacoma, WA, Sept 20, 1941.

Gary Cole, 64, actor ("Mercy Street," "Midnight Caller," *Fatal Vision, The Brady Bunch Movie*), born Park Ridge, IL, Sept 20, 1956.

Kristen Johnston, 53, actress ("3rd Rock from the Sun"), born Washington, DC, Sept 20, 1967.

Guy Damien LaFleur, 69, Hall of Fame hockey player, born Thurso, QC, Canada, Sept 20, 1951.

Sophia Loren, 86, actress (Oscar for *Two Women*; *Houseboat, El Cid, Marriage Italian Style, Grumpier Old Men*), born Sofia Scicolone at Rome, Italy, Sept 20, 1934.

George R.R. Martin, 72, author (*A Game of Thrones*), born Bayonne, NJ, Sept 20, 1948.

September 21 — Monday

DAY 265   **101 REMAINING**

ARMENIA: INDEPENDENCE DAY. Sept 21. Public holiday. Commemorates independence from Soviet Union in 1991.

BELIZE: INDEPENDENCE DAY. Sept 21. National holiday. Commemorates independence of the former British Honduras from Britain in 1981.

CANTOR, EDDIE: BIRTH ANNIVERSARY. Sept 21, 1892. The entertainer, who started in vaudeville and ended up on Broadway, radio, film and TV, was born Israel Iskowitz to Belarussian immigrants in New York City (some sources say Jan 31, 1892). Cantor got his big break in the *Ziegfeld Follies of 1917*. A hugely popular comic and singer in the 1930s, he also helped start the March of Dimes fundraising campaign for polio research in 1938. Cantor died Oct 10, 1964, at Beverly Hills, CA.

COHEN, LEONARD: BIRTH ANNIVERSARY. Sept 21, 1934. A vocalist without peer and a songwriter who showed the rest how it's done, Leonard Cohen enchanted the world as a performer for nearly five decades. Born at Westmount, QC, Canada, Cohen was a poet and novelist before turning to music in the late 1960s. With the early support of US folk-scene figures like Judy Collins and James Taylor, Cohen found his footing as a singer and performer, and translated his poetry into song with an unmatched bass voice and distinct nylon string guitar. An influence on countless performers across generations, Cohen's song "Hallelujah" has been performed by more than 200 artists. He continued to write and perform until his death Nov 7, 2016, at Los Angeles, CA.

FAST OF GEDALYA. Sept 21. Jewish holiday. Hebrew calendar date: Tishri 3, 5781. Tzom Gedalya begins at first light of day and commemorates the sixth-century BC assassination of Gedalya Ben Achikam.

***THE HOBBIT* PUBLISHED: ANNIVERSARY.** Sept 21, 1937. University professor J.R.R. Tolkien's fantasy classic featuring Bilbo Baggins was published by George Allen & Unwin in the United Kingdom. Well received by critics and the public, it has never been out of print. Its international success spurred Tolkien to amplify his world of hobbits, dwarves, elves and dragons in *The Lord of the Rings* in the 1950s.

HOPKINSON, FRANCIS: BIRTH ANNIVERSARY. Sept 21, 1737. Signer of the Declaration of Independence. Born at Philadelphia, PA, Hopkinson died there May 9, 1791.

HURRICANE HUGO HITS AMERICAN COAST: ANNIVERSARY. Sept 21, 1989. After ravaging the Virgin Islands, Hurricane Hugo hit the American coast at Charleston, SC. In its wake, Hugo left destruction totaling at least $8 billion.

JAPAN: RESPECT FOR THE AGED DAY. Sept 21. National holiday to honor Japan's senior citizens—especially those who are centenarians. Annually, the third Monday in September.

JONES, CHUCK: BIRTH ANNIVERSARY. Sept 21, 1912. Born at Spokane, WA, Chuck Jones worked as a child extra in Hollywood in the 1920s. After attending art school, he landed a job washing animation cels for famed Disney animator Ub Iwerks. He learned the craft, and by 1962 he headed his own unit at Warner Bros. Animation. He created the characters Road Runner and Wile E. Coyote, Marvin the Martian and Pepe le Pew.

He worked on the development of Bugs Bunny, Elmer Fudd, Daffy Duck and Porky Pig, and also produced, directed and wrote the screenplay for the animated 1966 television classic "Dr. Seuss' How the Grinch Stole Christmas." He won several Academy Awards for his work, and his cartoon "What's Opera, Doc?" is in the National Film Registry. He died on Feb 22, 2002, at Corona del Mar, CA.

MALTA: INDEPENDENCE DAY. Sept 21. National Day. Commemorates independence from Britain in 1964.

"MONDAY NIGHT FOOTBALL" TV PREMIERE: 50th ANNIVERSARY. Sept 21, 1970. Following the complete merger of the American Football League and the National Football League, ABC joined CBS and NBC in televising weekly games with the debut of "Monday Night Football." The show began as an experiment but soon became an institution. Announcers Howard Cosell, Keith Jackson and Don Meredith called the first game, a 31–21 victory by the Cleveland Browns over the New York Jets. On Dec 26, 2005, "Monday Night Football" made its final telecast on ABC. In 2006 it moved to the cable channel ESPN.

NATIONAL SURGICAL TECHNOLOGIST DAY. Sept 21. A day to celebrate the unsung heroes of the operating room. The surgical technologist's motto is *Aeger Primo*: "patient first." Annually, Sept 21. For info: Association of Surgical Technologists. Web: www.ast.org.

"NYPD BLUE" TV PREMIERE: ANNIVERSARY. Sept 21, 1993. This gritty New York City police drama had a large and changing cast. The central characters were partners Detective Bobby Simone (who later died), played by Jimmy Smits, and Detective Andy Sipowicz, played by Dennis Franz. Other cast members included Kim Delaney as Detective Diane Russell, James McDaniel as Lieutenant Arthur Fancy, Gordon Clapp as Detective Gregory Medavoy, Rick Schroder as Detective Danny Sorenson, Nicholas Turturro as Detective James Martinez, Mark-Paul Gosselaar as Detective John Clark and Esai Morales as Lieutenant Tony Rodriguez. The series ended in 2005.

"PERRY MASON" TV PREMIERE: ANNIVERSARY. Sept 21, 1957. Raymond Burr will forever be associated with the character of Perry Mason, a criminal lawyer who won the great majority of his cases. Episodes followed a similar format: the action took place in the first half, with the killer's identity unknown, and the courtroom drama took place in the latter half. Mason was particularly adept at eliciting confessions from the guilty parties. Regulars and semiregulars included Barbara Hale, William Hopper, William Talman and Ray Collins. Following the series' end in 1966, a number of successful "Perry Mason" TV movies aired, and the show remains popular in reruns.

TAYLOR, MARGARET SMITH: BIRTH ANNIVERSARY. Sept 21, 1788. Wife of Zachary Taylor, 12th president of the US, born at Calvert County, MD. She died at Pascagoula, MS, Aug 18, 1852.

"THE TEXACO STAR THEATER" TV PREMIERE: ANNIVERSARY. Sept 21, 1948. Also known as "The Milton Berle Show" and sponsored by Texaco until 1953, this popular variety show was a good sign for the fledgling TV industry. Milton Berle became a superstar. The show featured singing and comedy, especially sight gags and outrageous costumes, and guest stars. Changes were made in the fourth season: Berle cut back his appearances, new writers and a new director were added and the format was changed to a show-within-a-show. Ruth Gilbert, Fred Clark and Arnold Stang were featured, along with the new pitchman, ventriloquist Jimmy Nelson and his dummy, Danny O'Day.

September 2020	S	M	T	W	T	F	S
			1	2	3	4	5
	6	7	8	9	10	11	12
	13	14	15	16	17	18	19
	20	21	22	23	24	25	26
	27	28	29	30			

UNITED NATIONS: INTERNATIONAL DAY OF PEACE. Sept 21. The General Assembly proclaimed this day in 1981, a day "devoted to commemorating and strengthening the ideals of peace both within and among all nations and peoples." In 2001 the assembly decided that, beginning in 2002, the International Day of Peace would be observed on Sept 21 each year (Res 55/282) as a day of global cease-fire and nonviolence, an invitation to all nations and people to honor a cessation of hostilities throughout the day. For info: United Nations, Dept of Public Info, New York, NY 10017. Web: www.un.org.

WELLS, HERBERT GEORGE: BIRTH ANNIVERSARY. Sept 21, 1866. English novelist and historian, born at Bromley, Kent, England. Among his books: *The Time Machine, The Invisible Man, The War of the Worlds* and *The Outline of History*. His contributions to the development of science fiction as a genre were profound, and he was nominated for the Nobel Prize in Literature in 1921, 1932, 1935 and 1946. H.G. Wells died at London, England, Aug 13, 1946. "Human history," he wrote, "becomes more and more a race between education and catastrophe."

🎂 BIRTHDAYS TODAY

Shinzō Abe, 66, Prime Minister of Japan, born Tokyo, Japan, Sept 21, 1954.

Ethan Coen, 63, filmmaker (Oscars for *No Country for Old Men* and *Fargo*), born Minneapolis, MN, Sept 21, 1957.

David James Elliott, 60, actor ("JAG"), born Toronto, ON, Canada, Sept 21, 1960.

Cecil Grant Fielder, 57, former baseball player, born Los Angeles, CA, Sept 21, 1963.

Fannie Flagg, 76, actress, author (*Fried Green Tomatoes*), born Birmingham, AL, Sept 21, 1944.

Artis Gilmore, 71, Hall of Fame basketball player, born Chipley, FL, Sept 21, 1949.

Faith Hill, 53, country singer, born Jackson, MS, Sept 21, 1967.

Stephen King, 73, author (*Christine, Pet Sematary, The Shining, Misery, The Stand*), born Portland, ME, Sept 21, 1947.

Bill Kurtis, 80, television journalist, born Pensacola, FL, Sept 21, 1940.

Ricki Lake, 52, talk show host, actress (*Hairspray, Serial Mom*), born New York, NY, Sept 21, 1968.

Rob Morrow, 58, actor ("Numb3rs," "Northern Exposure," *Quiz Show*), born New Rochelle, NY, Sept 21, 1962.

Bill Murray, 70, comedian, actor (*St. Vincent, Groundhog Day, Caddyshack*), born Evanston, IL, Sept 21, 1950.

Billy Porter, 51, singer, actor (Tony for *Kinky Boots*; "Pose"), born Pittsburgh, PA, Sept 21, 1969.

Nicole Richie, 39, television personality ("The Simple Life"), born Berkeley, CA, Sept 21, 1981.

Kay Ryan, 75, poet, former US poet laureate (2008–10), born San Jose, CA, Sept 21, 1945.

Nancy Travis, 59, actress ("Becker," *Three Men and a Baby*), born New York, NY, Sept 21, 1961.

Luke Wilson, 49, actor (*Old School, The Royal Tenenbaums, Legally Blonde*), born Dallas, TX, Sept 21, 1971.

September 22 — Tuesday

DAY 266   **100 REMAINING**

AMERICAN BUSINESS WOMEN'S DAY. Sept 22. A day set forth by Congress on which all Americans can recognize the important contributions more than 68 million American working women have made and are continuing to make to this nation. Proclaimed by President Ronald Reagan in 1983 and 1986. Annually, Sept 22 (the anniversary of ABWA's founding in 1949). For info: American Business Women's Assn, 9820 Metcalf Ave, Ste 110, Overland Park, KS 66212. Phone: (800) 228-0007. E-mail: webmail@abwa. org. Web: www.abwa.org.

AUTUMN. Sept 22–Dec 21. In the Northern Hemisphere, autumn begins today with the autumnal equinox, at 9:31 AM, EDT. Note that in the Southern Hemisphere today is the beginning of spring. Everywhere on Earth (except near the poles) the sun rises due east and sets due west and daylight length is nearly identical—about 12 hours, 8 minutes.

"CHARLIE'S ANGELS" TV PREMIERE: ANNIVERSARY. Sept 22, 1976. This extremely popular show of the '70s featured three attractive women solving crimes. Sabrina Duncan (Kate Jackson), Jill Munroe (Farrah Fawcett-Majors) and Kelly Garrett (Jaclyn Smith) signed on with detective agency Charles Townsend Associates. Their boss was never seen, only heard (the voice of John Forsythe); messages were communicated to the women by his associate, John Bosley (David Doyle). During the course of the series, Cheryl Ladd replaced Fawcett, and Shelley Hack and Tanya Roberts succeeded Kate Jackson. The show went off the air in 1981, but feature films were made in 2000 and 2003.

DEAR DIARY DAY. Sept 22. Put it on paper. You'll feel better. No need to be a professional writer. (©2006 by WH.) For info: Thomas & Ruth Roy, Wellcat Holidays, 2418 Long Ln, Lebanon, PA 17046. Phone: (717) 279-0184. E-mail: info@wellcat.com. Web: www. wellcat.com.

EMANCIPATION PROCLAMATION: ANNIVERSARY. Sept 22, 1862. One of the most important presidential proclamations of American history is that of Sept 22, 1862, in which Abraham Lincoln, by executive proclamation, freed the slaves in the rebelling states. "That on . . . [Jan 1, 1863] . . . all persons held as slaves within any state or designated part of a state, the people whereof shall then be in rebellion against the United States, shall be then, thenceforward, and forever, free." See also: "Thirteenth Amendment to the US Constitution Ratified: Anniversary" (Dec 6).

"FAMILY TIES" TV PREMIERE: ANNIVERSARY. Sept 22, 1982. This popular '80s sitcom was set at Columbus, OH, and focused on the Keaton family: ex-hippies Elyse (Meredith Baxter-Birney), an architect, and Steven (Michael Gross), a station manager of the local public TV station; Alex (Michael J. Fox), their smart, conservative and financially driven son; Mallory (Justine Bateman), their materialistic, ditzy daughter; and Jennifer (Tina Yothers), their tomboy younger daughter. Later in the series Elyse gave birth to Andrew (Brian Bonsall). Marc Price played Irwin "Skippy" Handleman, the nerdy next-door neighbor who adored the Keatons, and Mallory in particular. The last episode aired Sept 17, 1989.

FARADAY, MICHAEL: BIRTH ANNIVERSARY. Sept 22, 1791. Scientist, born at Newington, Surrey, England. Faraday started his scientific career as an assistant to Humphry Davy. He studied new compounds of chlorine and carbon, discovered benzene and experimented with the liquefaction of gases; he developed new kinds of glass intended for optical purposes. He developed an early prototype of the Bunsen burner and worked extensively with electricity and magnetism. Faraday also established the concept of a magnetic field, groundbreaking research in the early days of the study of electricity. He died at Hampton Court, England, Aug 25, 1867.

FIRST ALL-WOMAN JURY EMPANELED IN COLONIES: ANNIVERSARY. Sept 22, 1656. The General Provincial Court at Patuxent, MD, empaneled the first all-woman jury in the colonies to hear the case of Judith Catchpole, accused of murdering her child. The defendant claimed she had never even been pregnant, and after all the evidence was heard, the jury acquitted her.

"FRIENDS" TV PREMIERE: ANNIVERSARY. Sept 22, 1994. This hugely popular NBC comedy brought together six single friends and the issues in their personal lives, ranging from their jobs to their romances. The cast was Courteney Cox, Lisa Kudrow, Jennifer Aniston, Matthew Perry, David Schwimmer and Matt Le Blanc. The show concluded its run May 6, 2004, with a finale for which 51.1 million viewers tuned in, making that episode the fifth-most-watched TV program finale in history.

HOBBIT DAY. Sept 22. To commemorate the birthdays of Frodo and Bilbo Baggins and their creator, J.R.R. Tolkien. For info: Secretary, American Tolkien Society, PO Box 97, Highland, MI 48357-0097. E-mail: americantolkiensociety@yahoo.com. Web: www.americantolkiensociety.org.

HOUSEMAN, JOHN: BIRTH ANNIVERSARY. Sept 22, 1902. American actor and producer John Houseman was born Jacques Haussmann at Bucharest, Romania. He is best known for his collaboration with Orson Welles on the 1938 radio production of *War of the Worlds* and for his role as Professor Kingsfield in the film and television versions of *The Paper Chase*. He won an Oscar for that film role in 1974 and helped establish the Juilliard drama school and the Acting Company repertory group. He died Oct 30, 1988, at Malibu, CA.

ICE CREAM CONE: ANNIVERSARY. Sept 22, 1903. Italo Marchiony emigrated from Italy in the late 1800s and soon thereafter went into business at New York, NY, with a pushcart dispensing lemon ice. Success soon led to a small fleet of pushcarts, and the inventive Marchiony was inspired to develop a cone, first made of paper, later of pastry, to hold the tasty delicacy. On Sept 22, 1903, his application for a patent for his new mold was filed, and US Patent Number 746971 was issued to him Dec 15, 1903.

INTERNATIONAL DAY OF RADIANT PEACE. Sept 22. Observed since 1999, this day celebrates and commemorates Radiant Peace. Commemorations of the International Day of Radiant Peace range from Walks for Radiant Peace to citywide and statewide proclamations recognizing the International Day of Radiant Peace, special Radiant Peace projects with children, ringing bells for Radiant Peace and Radiant Peace Picnics. Observed annually on Sept 22. For info: The Radiant Peace Foundation

Intl, Inc, PO Box 40822, St. Petersburg, FL 33743. Phone: (727) 343-8212. E-mail: RadiantPeaceIntl@gmail.com. Web: www.radiantpeace.org.

IRAN-IRAQ WAR: 40th ANNIVERSARY. Sept 22, 1980. Iraq invaded western Iran on this date, starting an eight-year war. This deadly war saw one million casualties, the use of chemical weapons and extensive damage to each nation's economy.

JAPAN: AUTUMNAL EQUINOX DAY. Sept 22. National holiday in Japan, first observed in 1945. A day to honor ancestors and the family.

LONG COUNT DAY: ANNIVERSARY. Sept 22, 1927. Anniversary of world championship boxing match between Jack Dempsey and Gene Tunney, at Soldier Field, Chicago, IL. It was the largest fight purse ($990,446) in the history of boxing to that time. Nearly half the population of the US is believed to have listened to the radio broadcast of this fight. In the 7th round of the 10-round fight, Tunney was knocked down. Following the rules, referee Dave Barry interrupted the count when Dempsey failed to go to the farthest corner. The count was resumed and Tunney got to his feet at the count of nine. Stopwatch records of those present claimed the total elapsed time from the beginning of the count until Tunney got to his feet to be 12–15 seconds. Tunney, awarded 7 of the 10 rounds, won the fight and claimed the world championship. Dempsey's appeal was denied and he never fought again. Tunney retired the following year after one more (successful) fight.

MABON. Sept 22. (Also called Alban Elfed.) One of the "Lesser Sabbats" during the Wiccan year, Mabon marks the second harvest as nature prepares for the coming of winter. Annually, on the autumnal equinox.

MALI: INDEPENDENCE DAY: 60th ANNIVERSARY OF INDEPENDENCE. Sept 22. National holiday commemorating independence from France in 1960. Mali, in West Africa, was known as the French Sudan while a colony.

NATIONAL CENTENARIAN'S DAY. Sept 22. A day to recognize and honor individuals who have lived a century or longer. A day not only to recognize these individuals but also to listen to them discuss the memories—filled with historical information—they have of their rich lives. Annually, Sept 22. (Created by the Williamsport Retirement Village.) For info:

NATIONAL WALK 'N' ROLL DOG DAY. Sept 22. 9th annual. A day honoring and celebrating dogs in wheelchairs who teach us to embrace each day with love, hope and joy. Annually, Sept 22. For info: Barbara Techel, 304 Kettleview Ct, Elkhart Lake, WI 53020. Phone: (920) 377-1749. E-mail: barb@joyfulpaws.com. Web: www.joyfulpaws.com/national-walk-n-roll-dog-day.

REMOTE EMPLOYEE APPRECIATION DAY. Sept 22. The landscape for the "typical" employee is constantly changing—and there is an increase in the number of employees who work from home or in cities/states outside of where their hub is. Remote Employee Appreciation Day recognizes those who are not a part of the daily grind; who miss the office birthday cake, the face-to-face social contact and general camaraderie and the other perks of being in an office environment. So show some love today to the remote employee: send some goodies or a card, take them out, take and send a photo with main office employees. Annually, Sept 22. For info: Jill Tobin, Butler/Till, 1565 Jefferson Rd, Bldg 200, Ste 280, Rochester, NY 14623. E-mail: jtobin@butlertill.com.

STANHOPE, PHILIP DORMER: BIRTH ANNIVERSARY. Sept 22, 1694. (Old Style date.) Philip Dormer Stanhope, the Fourth

Earl of Chesterfield, born at London, England. He was a brilliant politician and orator. On Feb 20, 1751, he brought a bill into the House of Lords that caused the "New Style" Gregorian calendar to replace the "Old Style" Julian calendar in 1752. His influential political career was eclipsed by the fame of the letters he wrote to his son Philip, giving shrewd counsel on manners, morals and the ways of the world. Published less than a year after his own death at London, Mar 24, 1773, the *Letters* became immensely popular; they were translated and republished in many editions. The chesterfield, a kind of sofa, is said to be named for him.

TABEI, JUNKO: BIRTH ANNIVERSARY. Sept 22, 1939. Born at Miharu, Japan, mountaineer Tabei challenged Japanese stereotypes about women by becoming the first woman to summit Mount Everest in 1975, leading an all-women (excepting the Sherpa guides) expedition and surviving an avalanche in the process. She later became the first woman to climb the Seven Summits (the highest mountain on each of seven continents) in 1992. In 1969, she had formed the Ladies' Climbing Club, whose motto, "Let's go on an overseas expedition by ourselves," led the women to do just that—they climbed a new route up Nepal's Annapurna III. In later years, she campaigned for greater mountain preservation efforts, criticizing the pollution left by increased numbers of climbers. She died Oct 20, 2016, at Tokyo, Japan.

US POSTMASTER GENERAL ESTABLISHED: ANNIVERSARY. Sept 22, 1789. Congress established office of Postmaster General, following the Departments of State, War and Treasury.

🎂 BIRTHDAYS TODAY

Scott Baio, 59, actor ("Happy Days," "Diagnosis Murder," "Charles in Charge"), born Brooklyn, NY, Sept 22, 1961.

Shari Belafonte-Harper, 66, model, actress, born New York, NY, Sept 22, 1954.

Andrea Bocelli, 62, tenor, born Lajatico, Italy, Sept 22, 1958.

Debbie Boone, 64, singer ("You Light Up My Life"), born Hackensack, NJ, Sept 22, 1956.

Mireille Enos, 45, actress ("Hanna," "The Killing," "Big Love"), born Houston, TX, Sept 22, 1975.

Bonnie Hunt, 56, actress (*Jerry Maguire, Jumanji*), born Chicago, IL, Sept 22, 1964.

Joan Jett, 60, singer, born Philadelphia, PA, Sept 22, 1960.

Thomas Charles (Tommy) Lasorda, 93, Hall of Fame baseball manager and former player, born Norristown, PA, Sept 22, 1927.

Paul Le Mat, 75, actor (*American Graffiti, Melvin and Howard*), born Rahway, NY, Sept 22, 1945.

Tatiana Maslany, 35, actress ("Orphan Black"), born Regina, SK, Canada, Sept 22, 1985.

Catherine Oxenberg, 59, actress ("Dynasty"), born New York, NY, Sept 22, 1961.

Billie Piper, 38, actress ("Doctor Who," "Secret Diary of a Call Girl"), born Swindon, Wiltshire, England, Sept 22, 1982.

Mike Richter, 54, former hockey player, born Philadelphia, PA, Sept 22, 1966.

Ronaldo, 44, former soccer player, born Ronaldo Luiz Nazario de Lima at Rio de Janeiro, Brazil, Sept 22, 1976.

September 2020	S	M	T	W	T	F	S
			1	2	3	4	5
	6	7	8	9	10	11	12
	13	14	15	16	17	18	19
	20	21	22	23	24	25	26
	27	28	29	30			

September 23 — Wednesday

DAY 267   **99 REMAINING**

BASEBALL'S GREATEST DISPUTE: ANNIVERSARY. Sept 23, 1908. In the decisive game between the Chicago Cubs and the New York Giants, the National League pennant race erupted in controversy during the bottom of the ninth with the score tied, 1–1, at the Polo Grounds, New York, NY. New York was at bat with two men on. The batter hit safely to center field, knocking in the winning run. Chicago claimed that the runner on first, Fred Merkle, seeing the winning run scored, headed toward the dugout without advancing to second base, thus invalidating the play. The Chicago second baseman, Johnny Evers, attempted to get the ball and tag Merkle out but was prevented by the fans streaming onto the field. Days later Harry C. Pulliam, head of the National Commission of Organized Baseball, decided to call the game a tie. The teams were forced to play a postseason play-off game, which the Cubs won, 4–2. Fans used the terms "boner" and "bonehead" in reference to the play, and it has gone down in baseball history as "Merkle's Boner."

CELEBRATE BISEXUALITY DAY. Sept 23. Observed internationally by the bisexual community and their supporters. Annually, Sept 23.

CHARLES, RAY: 90th BIRTH ANNIVERSARY. Sept 23, 1930. Born at Albany, GA, Ray Charles Robinson began losing his sight at age five. He began formal music training at the St. Augustine School for the Deaf and Blind, and by age 15 he was earning a living as a musician. He went on to become one of the most influential performers of all time. As a pianist, singer, songwriter, bandleader and producer, he played country, jazz, rock, gospel and standards. His renditions of "Georgia on My Mind," "I Can't Stop Loving You" and "America the Beautiful" are considered true American classics. He died at Beverly Hills, CA, June 10, 2004.

CHECKERS DAY: ANNIVERSARY. Sept 23, 1952. Anniversary of the nationally televised "Checkers Speech" by then vice presidential candidate Richard M. Nixon. Nixon was found "clean as a hound's tooth" in connection with a private fund for political expenses, and he declared he would never give back the cocker spaniel, Checkers, which had been a gift to his daughters.

INNERGIZE DAY. Sept 23. A day set aside for anyone who has said, "I don't have time to do the personal things I want to do for myself." Today is the day to set time aside for yourself to do anything you want to do. Annually, the day after the autumnal equinox. For info: Michelle Porchia, inner dimensions LLC. Phone: (203) 924-1012. E-mail: michelle@innerdimensionsllc.com. Web: www.innerdimensionsllc.com.

"THE JETSONS" TV PREMIERE: ANNIVERSARY. Sept 23, 1962. "Meet George Jetson. His boy Elroy. Daughter Judy. Jane, his wife." These words introduced us to the Jetsons, a cartoon family living in the 21st century, the Flintstones of the Space Age. We followed the exploits of George and his family, as well as his work relationship with his greedy, ruthless boss, Cosmo Spacely. Voices were provided by George O'Hanlon as George, Penny Singleton as Jane, Janet Waldo as Judy, Daws Butler as Elroy, Don Messick as Astro, the family dog, and Mel Blanc as

Spacely. New episodes were created in 1985, which also introduced a new pet, Orbity.

LEWIS & CLARK EXPEDITION RETURNS: ANNIVERSARY. Sept 23, 1806. After more than two years in the American West, the Corps of Discovery returned to St. Louis amid much fanfare. They had traveled—with the assistance of guides Toussaint Charbonneau and his wife, Sacagawea (a member of the Shoshone tribe)—to what is now North Dakota and Montana, over the Continental Divide and to the Columbia River, which took them to the Pacific (November 1805). They lost only one man from the 33-member group. Their valuable findings on western tribes, geography, plants and animals dispelled many long-standing myths about the region.

LIBRA, THE BALANCE. Sept 23–Oct 22. In the astronomical/astrological zodiac that divides the sun's apparent orbit into 12 segments, the period Sept 23–Oct 22 is identified traditionally as the sun sign of Libra, the Balance. The ruling planet is Venus.

LIPPMANN, WALTER: BIRTH ANNIVERSARY. Sept 23, 1889. American journalist, political philosopher and author. Born at New York, NY, he died there Dec 14, 1974. As a syndicated newspaper columnist he was the foremost and perhaps the most influential commentator in the nation. "Without criticism," he said in an address to the International Press Institute in 1965, "and reliable and intelligent reporting, the government cannot govern."

MALLON, MARY ("TYPHOID MARY"): BIRTH ANNIVERSARY. Sept 23, 1869. Known as "Typhoid Mary," Mallon was a cook whose career resulted in lasting infamy. Born at Cookstown, Ireland, Mallon immigrated to the United States as a teenager. Little is known about her life in New York City before epidemiologist George A. Soper took interest in her as a suspected carrier of typhoid during an outbreak investigation in that city. Mallon was confined to Riverside Hospital upon testing positive but promised to change her vocation to obtain her release. She instead assumed an alias and resumed her former occupation, eventually working at Sloane Hospital for Women. A typhoid outbreak soon followed in 1915, resulting in a second arrest on Mar 27, 1915, and confinement at Riverside Hospital on North Brother Island until her death Nov 11, 1938, at New York, NY.

MCGUFFEY, WILLIAM HOLMES: BIRTH ANNIVERSARY. Sept 23, 1800. American educator and author of the famous *McGuffey Readers*, born at Washington County, PA. Died at Charlottesville, VA, May 4, 1873.

MOON PHASE: FIRST QUARTER. Sept 23. Moon enters First Quarter phase at 9:55 PM, EDT.

PAULUS, FRIEDRICH: BIRTH ANNIVERSARY. Sept 23, 1890. The German commander of the Sixth Army who led the advance on Stalingrad in 1942, Friedrich von Paulus was born at Breitenau, Germany. Paulus's troops succeeded in taking most of Stalingrad in November 1942 but eventually were trapped within the city they had captured. Paulus surrendered to the Russians Jan 31, 1943, the same day that Hitler promoted him to field marshal. He appeared as a key witness for the Soviet prosecution at the Nuremberg trials. Paulus died Feb 1, 1957, at Dresden, East Germany (now Germany).

PETIT JEAN FALL ANTIQUE AUTO SWAP MEET. Sept 23–26. Petit Jean Mountain, Morrilton, AR. 23rd annual antique auto swap meet, flea market and open car show. Military vehicle show Friday and Saturday. Open car show on Saturday. More than 600 vendor spaces available. Est attendance: 7,500. For info: Mark Hoelzeman, Museum of Automobiles, 8 Jones Ln, Morrilton, AR 72110. Phone: (501) 727-5427. E-mail: info@museumofautos.com. Web: www.museumofautos.com.

PLANET NEPTUNE DISCOVERY: ANNIVERSARY. Sept 23, 1846. Neptune is 2.796 billion miles from the sun (about 30 times as far from the sun as Earth). Eighth planet from the sun, Neptune takes 164.8 years to revolve around the sun. Diameter is about 31,000

miles, compared with Earth at 7,927 miles. Discovered by German astronomer Johann Galle.

ROONEY, MICKEY: 100th BIRTH ANNIVERSARY. Sept 23, 1920. An outsized personality in a pint-size package, entertainer Mickey Rooney had a career that spanned nine decades in vaudeville, film, television and Broadway. Born Joseph Yule, Jr, at Brooklyn, NY, Rooney became a teen movie idol in the Depression. He was Hollywood's number-one box office star in 1939, 1940 and 1941. Famous for the Andy Hardy films, *Babes in Arms*, *Boys Town* and *National Velvet*. In 1979 he had a career revival in the Broadway show *Sugar Babies*. The recipient of two honorary Oscars (in 1939 and 1983), Rooney died Apr 6, 2014, at Los Angeles, CA.

EL SANTO: BIRTH ANNIVERSARY. Sept 23, 1917. The legendary and beloved Mexican masked wrestler (or *luchador*) was born Rodolfo Guzmán Huerta in Tulancingo, Mexico. Wearing a silver mask (that he only once took off in public), El Santo vanquished foes in a career that spanned from the 1930s to 1982. He also appeared in scores of popular movies. Huerta died Feb 5, 1984, at Mexico City, Mexico, and was buried in his mask.

SAUDI ARABIA: KINGDOM UNIFICATION. Sept 23. National holiday. Commemorates unification in 1932.

UNITED NATIONS: INTERNATIONAL DAY OF SIGN LANGUAGES. Sept 23. First observed in 2018, this day has been proclaimed in order to raise awareness of the importance of sign language in the full realization of the human rights of people who are deaf (Res 72/161). For info: United Nations. Web: www.un.org.

WOODHULL, VICTORIA CLAFLIN: BIRTH ANNIVERSARY. Sept 23, 1838. American feminist, reformer and first female candidate (Equal Rights Party, 1872) for the presidency of the US, born at Homer, OH. A feminist pioneer whose foremost cause was women's suffrage, she was also the first female head of a Wall Street brokerage firm as well as the first female weekly newspaper publisher. Her outspokenness about her beliefs resulted in her eventual rejection by society. She retired to England, where she died at Norton Park, Bremmons, Worcestershire, on June 10, 1927.

🎂 BIRTHDAYS TODAY

Jason Alexander, 61, actor ("Seinfeld," *Bye Bye Birdie*, Tony for *Jerome Robbins' Broadway*), born Jason Greenspan at Newark, NJ, Sept 23, 1959.

Ani DiFranco, 50, singer, songwriter, born Buffalo, NY, Sept 23, 1970.

Julio Iglesias, 77, singer, born Madrid, Spain, Sept 23, 1943.

Rob James-Collier, 44, actor ("Downton Abbey," "Coronation Street"), born Stockport, Greater Manchester, England, Sept 23, 1976.

Anthony Mackie, 41, actor (*All the Way*, *Avengers: Age of Ultron*, *The Hurt Locker*), born New Orleans, LA, Sept 23, 1979.

September 2020	S	M	T	W	T	F	S
			1	2	3	4	5
	6	7	8	9	10	11	12
	13	14	15	16	17	18	19
	20	21	22	23	24	25	26
	27	28	29	30			

Larry Hogan Mize, 62, golfer, born Augusta, GA, Sept 23, 1958.

Paul Petersen, 75, actor ("The Donna Reed Show," *Houseboat*), born Glendale, CA, Sept 23, 1945.

Mary Kay Place, 73, writer, actress ("Mary Hartman, Mary Hartman," *The Big Chill*), born Tulsa, OK, Sept 23, 1947.

Sean Spicer, 49, former White House press secretary (Trump administration), born Manhasset, NY, Sept 23, 1971.

Bruce Springsteen, 71, singer, songwriter, born Freehold, NJ, Sept 23, 1949.

September 24 — Thursday

DAY 268   **98 REMAINING**

BARNESVILLE PUMPKIN FESTIVAL. Sept 24–27. Downtown Barnesville, OH. This 57th annual festival features King Pumpkin contest, Queen Pageant, Giant Pumpkin Parade, classic car show, banjo and fiddle contest and more. Annually, the last full weekend in September. Est attendance: 100,000. For info: Tim Rockwell, President, Barnesville Pumpkin Festival, Inc, PO Box 5, Barnesville, OH 43713. Phone: (740) 425-1114. E-mail: trockwell.bpf09@yahoo.com. Web: www.barnesvillepumpkinfestival.com.

BUFFALO ROUNDUP ARTS FESTIVAL. Sept 24–26. Custer, SD. 26th annual. South Dakota artists and craftsmen display and sell their arts and crafts. Also Western and Native American entertainment, pancake feeds and much more. Est attendance: 21,000. For info: Lydia Austin, Custer State Park, 13329 US Highway 16A, Custer, SD 57730. Phone: (605) 255-4515. Fax: (605) 255-4460. E-mail: custerstatepark@state.sd.us. Web: www.custerstatepark.com.

CAMBODIA: CONSTITUTIONAL DECLARATION DAY. Sept 24. National holiday. Commemorates the new constitution of 1993.

CO-OP AWARENESS MONTH. Sept 24–Oct 31. Co-Op Awareness Month reminds advertisers to take advantage of the vast amounts of co-op funding made available by manufacturers to subsidize the cost of local advertising. Most funds are designed to expire on Dec 31, so advertisers not taking advantage could be throwing money away! For info: Jessica Helinski, AdMall, 600 N Cleveland Ave, Ste 260, Westerville, OH 43082. Phone: (614) 794-0500. E-mail: jessica@salesfuel.com.

"DANIEL BOONE" TV PREMIERE: ANNIVERSARY. Sept 24, 1964. A successful show based loosely on the life of pioneer Daniel Boone, who helped settle Kentucky in the 1770s. Fess Parker starred as the American hero. Ed Ames played Mingo, Boone's Cherokee friend, and Pat Blair played his wife, Rebecca. Also featured were Albert Salmi, Jimmy Dean, Roosevelt Grier, Darby Hinton, Veronica Cartwright and Dallas McKennon.

FANEUIL HALL OPENED TO THE PUBLIC: ANNIVERSARY. Sept 24, 1742. On this date Faneuil Hall at Boston, MA, opened to the public. Designed by painter John Smibiert, it was enlarged in 1805 according to plans by Charles Bulfinch. Today it is on the Freedom Trail, as part of the Boston Historical Park administered by the National Park Service.

FITZGERALD, F. SCOTT: BIRTH ANNIVERSARY. Sept 24, 1896. Short-story writer and novelist; author of *This Side of Paradise, The Great Gatsby* and *Tender Is the Night*. Member of the Lost Generation of American artists and writers. To his daughter, he wrote, "All good writing is swimming under water and holding your breath." Born Francis Scott Key Fitzgerald, at St. Paul, MN, he died at Hollywood, CA, Dec 21, 1940.

GUINEA-BISSAU: INDEPENDENCE DAY. Sept 24. National holiday. Commemorates declaration of independence from Portugal in 1973.

HENSON, JIM: BIRTH ANNIVERSARY. Sept 24, 1936. Puppeteer, born at Greenville, MS. Jim Henson created a unique family of puppets known as the Muppets. Kermit the Frog, Big Bird, Rowlf, Bert and Ernie, Gonzo, Animal, Miss Piggy and Oscar the Grouch are a few of the puppets that captured the hearts of children and adults alike in television and film productions including "Sesame Street," "The Jimmy Dean Show," "The Muppet Show," *The Muppet Movie, The Muppets Take Manhattan, The Great Muppet Caper* and *The Dark Crystal.* Henson began his career in 1954 as producer of the TV show "Sam and Friends" at Washington, DC. He introduced the Muppets in 1956. His creativity was rewarded with 18 Emmy Awards, seven Grammy Awards, four Peabody Awards and five ACE Awards from the National Cable Television Association. Henson died unexpectedly May 16, 1990, at New York, NY.

"THE LOVE BOAT" TV PREMIERE: ANNIVERSARY. Sept 24, 1977. This one-hour comedy-drama featured guest stars aboard a cruise ship, the *Pacific Princess.* All stories had to do with finding or losing love. The ship's crew were the only regulars: Gavin MacLeod as Captain Merrill Stubing, Bernie Kopell as Dr. Adam Bricker, Fred Grandy as assistant purser Burl "Gopher" Smith, Ted Lange as bartender Isaac Washington and Lauren Tewes as cruise director Julie McCoy. The series ended with the last telecast on Sept 5, 1986, but special TV movies were broadcast in later years.

MARSHALL, JOHN: BIRTH ANNIVERSARY. Sept 24, 1755. Fourth chief justice of the US, born at Germantown, VA. Served in House of Representatives and as secretary of state under John Adams. Appointed by President Adams to the position of chief justice in January 1801, he became known as "the Great Chief Justice." Marshall's court was largely responsible for defining the role of the Supreme Court and basic organizing principles of government in the early years after adoption of the Constitution in such cases as *Marbury v Madison, McCulloch v Maryland, Cohens v Virginia* and *Gibbons v Ogden.* He died at Philadelphia, PA, July 6, 1835.

MOZAMBIQUE: ARMED FORCES DAY. Sept 24. National holiday. Commemorates the beginning of the war for independence in 1964.

"THE MUNSTERS" TV PREMIERE: ANNIVERSARY. Sept 24, 1964. "The Munsters" was a half-hour sitcom about an unusual family who thought they were ordinary. Each family member resembled a different type of monster: Herman Munster (Fred Gwynne) was Frankenstein's monster; Lily, his wife (Yvonne DeCarlo), and Grandpa, her father (Al Lewis), were vampires; and his son, Eddie (Butch Patrick), was a werewolf. Only their niece, Marilyn (Beverly Owen and Pat Priest), looked normal, and they considered her the unattractive family member. Most of the show's laughs came from the family's interactions with outsiders. The last telecast was on Sept 1, 1966.

NATIONAL PUNCTUATION DAY. Sept 24. A celebration of the lowly comma, the correctly used quotation mark, and other proper uses of periods, semicolons, and the ever-mysterious ellipsis. For info: Jeff Rubin, Founder, 1517 Buckeye Ct, Pinole, CA 94564. Phone: (510) 724-9507. Fax: (510) 741-8698. E-mail: jeff@nationalpunctuationday.com. Web: www.nationalpunctuationday.com.

NEVERMIND RELEASED: ANNIVERSARY. Sept 24, 1991. The grunge rock group Nirvana released this groundbreaking album—their second—on this date. Riding the popularity of its lead single, "Smells Like Teen Spirit," *Nevermind* became the first alternative rock album to break into mainstream success, unseating Michael Jackson's *Dangerous* as number one album by January 1992. The album has sold more than 26 million copies.

REMEMBER ME THURSDAY®. Sept 24. Since 2013, this day has unified more than 180 countries, 700 animal welfare organizations and scores of celebrities and social media stars to create awareness of homeless pets. In addition to awareness, Remember Me Thursday® grants life-saving funds and food to nominated organizations. On this day, be part of an unstoppable, integrated voice for pets in need of forever homes. Annually, the fourth Thursday in September. For info: Helen Woodward Animal Center, PO Box 64, Rancho Santa Fe, CA 92067. Web: www.remembermethursday.org.

SCHWENKFELDER THANKSGIVING. Sept 24. On this day in 1734, members of the Schwenkfelder Society gave thanks for their deliverance from Old World persecution as they prepared to take up new lives in the Pennsylvania Dutch counties of Pennsylvania. Still celebrated.

"60 MINUTES" TV PREMIERE: ANNIVERSARY. Sept 24, 1968. TV's longest-running prime-time program, and the first news-magazine offering in-depth investigative reports and profiles, was originally hosted by Harry Reasoner and Mike Wallace. The show's correspondents have included Ed Bradley, Steve Kroft, Lesley Stahl, Morley Safer, Andy Rooney, Dan Rather, Diane Sawyer, Bob Simon, Anderson Cooper, Scott Pelley and Oprah Winfrey.

SOUTH AFRICA: HERITAGE DAY. Sept 24. A celebration of South African nationhood, commemorating the multicultural heritage of this rainbow nation.

SPAIN: LA MERCÈ FESTIVAL. Sept 24. Barcelona, Catalonia. Since 1871, annual festival on the feast day of Our Lady of Mercy, which is Sept 24. Events and sights, which take place before and after the 24th, include papier-mâché giants, castells (human towers), fireworks, live music and more.

UNITED NATIONS: WORLD MARITIME DAY. Sept 24. A day to stress the importance of shipping safety and the maritime environment. Annually, the last Thursday in September (although date can vary by nation). For info: United Nations, Dept of Public Info, New York, NY 10017. Web: www.un.org.

🎂 BIRTHDAYS TODAY

Gordon Clapp, 72, actor ("NYPD Blue"), born North Conway, NH, Sept 24, 1948.

Morgan Hamm, 38, Olympic gymnast, born Ashland, WI, Sept 24, 1982.

Paul Hamm, 38, Olympic gymnast, born Ashland, WI, Sept 24, 1982.

Rafael Corrales Palmeiro, 56, former baseball player, born Havana, Cuba, Sept 24, 1964.

Ben Platt, 27, singer, actor (*The Book of Mormon, Pitch Perfect,* Tony Award for *Dear Evan Hansen*), born Los Angeles, CA, Sept 24, 1993.

Kevin Sorbo, 62, actor ("Hercules"), born Mound, MN, Sept 24, 1958.

Nia Vardalos, 58, screenwriter, actress (*My Big Fat Greek Wedding*), born Winnipeg, MB, Canada, Sept 24, 1962.

September 25 — Friday

DAY 269   **97 REMAINING**

BUFFALO ROUNDUP. Sept 25. Custer, SD. 55th annual. To round up, brand and separate 1,300 buffalo before auction in November. Est attendance: 14,000. For info: Lydia Austin, Custer State Park, 13329 US Highway 16A, Custer, SD 57730. Phone: (605) 255-4515. Fax: (605) 255-4460. E-mail: custerstatepark@state.sd.us. Web: www.custerstatepark.com.

DANGER RUN. Sept 25–Oct 31 (Friday and Saturday evenings). Louisville, KY, and Clarksville, IN. This Halloween-themed road rally (ghost run) features participants following a series of rhyming, limerick-style clues that lead to two premier haunted houses. Each of the clues, when solved correctly, will reveal the next turn that participants will make as they attempt to stay on the route. Prizes are awarded to the groups who follow the route most accurately as indicated by their vehicle odometer. A virtual version of the game is also available on the website. For info: Michael Book, Danger Run, PO Box 2070, Clarksville, IN 47131. Phone: (800) 771-9750. E-mail: michael@dangerrun.com. Web: www.dangerrun.com.

FAIRMOUNT MUSEUM DAYS/REMEMBERING JAMES DEAN FESTIVAL. Sept 25–27. Fairmount, IN. The town where James Dean grew up honors Dean and other celebrated former citizens such as Jim Davis, creator of Garfield, journalist Phil Jones and Robert Sheets, retired director of the National Hurricane Center. The Fairmount Museum boasts the Authentic James Dean Exhibit of memorabilia and personal items of Dean's, and it sponsors the festival that also includes a parade, James Dean Look-Alike Contest, custom car show featuring the James Dean Run for pre-1980 autos, Garfield Cat Photo and Art Contest, Garfield Great Run, carnival, booths, live '50s entertainment and more. James Dean Memorial Service is Sept 30. Est attendance: 40,000. For info: Fairmount Historical Museum, Inc, 203 E Washington St, PO Box 92, Fairmount, IN 46928. Phone: (765) 948-4555. Web: www.jamesdeanartifacts.com.

FALL FESTIVAL OF THE ARTS AND CRAFTS. Sept 25–27. Washington, MO. Juried festival featuring the creative talents of artists and crafters from all over the Midwest. Strassenfest, beer and wine, specialty foods and live entertainment. Free. For info: Downtown Washington, Inc, PO Box 144, Washington, MO 63090. Phone: (636) 239-1743. Fax: (636) 239-4832. E-mail: events@downtownwashmo.org. Web: downtownwashmo.org.

FAULKNER, WILLIAM CUTHBERT: BIRTH ANNIVERSARY. Sept 25, 1897. American novelist and short-story writer William Faulkner (born Falkner) was born at New Albany, MS. A Nobel Prize recipient who changed the style and structure of the American novel, he died at Byhalia, MS, on July 6, 1962. Faulkner's first novel, *Soldiers' Pay*, was published in 1926. His best-known book, *The Sound and the Fury*, appeared in 1929. Shunning literary circles, Faulkner moved to a pre–Civil War house on the outskirts of Oxford, MS,

in 1930. From 1930 until the onset of WWII, he published an incredible body of work. In June 1962 Faulkner published his last novel, *The Reivers*.

FIRST AMERICAN NEWSPAPER PUBLISHED: ANNIVERSARY. Sept 25, 1690. The first (and only) edition of *Publick Occurrences Both Foreign and Domestick* was published by Benjamin Harris, at the London-Coffee-House, Boston, MA. Authorities considered this first newspaper published in the US offensive and ordered immediate suppression.

FIRST WOMAN SUPREME COURT JUSTICE: ANNIVERSARY. Sept 25, 1981. Sandra Day O'Connor was sworn in as the first woman associate justice of the US on this date. She had been nominated by President Ronald Reagan in July 1981, and she retired from the court in 2006.

GREENWICH MEAN TIME BEGINS: ANNIVERSARY. Sept 25, 1676. (Old Style date.) Two very accurate clocks were set in motion at the Royal Observatory at Greenwich, England. Greenwich Mean Time (now known as Universal Time) became the standard for England; in 1884 it became the standard for the world.

HUG A VEGAN DAY. Sept 25. Hug all your vegan friends. If you are already vegan, make sure your friends and family show you some love! Annually, the last Friday in September. (Created by peta2.)

LITTLE ROCK NINE ENTER CENTRAL HIGH SCHOOL: ANNIVERSARY. Sept 25, 1957. Three weeks after being barred from Little Rock's all-white Central High School on Sept 4, nine black students finally entered the school with the protective escort of the 101st Army Airborne. The "Little Rock Nine"—Carlotta Walls, Jefferson Thomas, Elizabeth Eckford, Gloria Ray, Ernest Green, Thelma Mothershed, Terrence Roberts, Minnijean Brown and Melba Pattillo—had also attempted to enter the school on Sept 23, but a mob threatened their safety. See also: "Little Rock Nine Crisis: Anniversary" (Sept 4).

MAJOR LEAGUE BASEBALL'S FIRST DOUBLEHEADER: ANNIVERSARY. Sept 25, 1882. The first major league baseball doubleheader was played between the Providence and Worcester teams.

MOUNT PLEASANT GLASS AND ETHNIC FESTIVAL. Sept 25–27. Mount Pleasant, PA. The feel and sense of a "front porch neighborhood" festival in hometown America. Features glass demos, ethnic foods, arts and crafts, Main Street parade, free national and regional entertainment in three areas, Old Town Mount Pleasant area, Sparky's Craft Camp for Kids and more. Also, fireworks, rides, games and nightly Illumination Launch. Free shuttle. Est attendance: 45,000. For info: Jeff Landy, Mount Pleasant Glass and Ethnic Festival, Municipal Bldg, 1 Etze Ave, Mount Pleasant, PA 15666. Phone: (724) 542-4711. Fax: (724) 547-0115. Web: www.mtpleasantglassandethnicfestival.com.

NATIONAL ONE-HIT WONDER DAY. Sept 25. Honors the one-hit wonders of rock and roll. Anyone who ever had a hit single deserves eternal remembrance. For info: Steven Rosen, 550 E Fourth St, #4E, Cincinnati, OH 45202. Phone: (513) 321-1018. E-mail: rosenstevenroy@gmail.com.

NATIONAL PSYCHOTHERAPY DAY. Sept 25. Since 2012. A day for therapists and their clients to educate the public about therapy,

September 2020	S	M	T	W	T	F	S
			1	2	3	4	5
	6	7	8	9	10	11	12
	13	14	15	16	17	18	19
	20	21	22	23	24	25	26
	27	28	29	30			

fight mental health stigma, tell therapy stories and support low-fee counseling centers. Annually, Sept 25. For info: Ryan Howes, PhD, The Psychotherapy Foundation, 595 E Colorado Blvd, Ste 432, Pasadena, CA 91101. Phone: (626) 449-1434. E-mail: ryan@ryanhowes.net. Web: www.nationalpsychotherapyday.com.

PACIFIC OCEAN DISCOVERED: ANNIVERSARY. Sept 25, 1513. Vasco Núñez de Balboa, a Spanish conquistador, stood high atop a peak in the Darien, in present-day Panama, becoming the first European to look upon the Pacific Ocean, claiming it as the South Sea in the name of the king of Spain.

REEVE, CHRISTOPHER: BIRTH ANNIVERSARY. Sept 25, 1952. Born at New York, NY, this actor was best known for his portrayal of the title character in *Superman* (1978) and three sequels during the 1980s. After being paralyzed in a horseback riding accident, he was confined to a wheelchair and became an activist for spinal-cord research and awareness. He died at Mount Kisco, NY, Oct 10, 2004.

RIZZUTO, PHIL: BIRTH ANNIVERSARY. Sept 25, 1917. Hall of Fame baseball player who spent his entire career with the New York Yankees, born at Brooklyn, NY. He played shortstop during 1941–56, winning the league MVP in 1950, and played in nine World Series, winning seven. After his playing career, he became the radio (and later television) broadcaster for the Yankees and remained on the air for more than 40 years. His home run call of "Holy Cow!" is considered legendary. He died at West Orange, NJ, Aug 13, 2007.

RWANDA: REPUBLIC DAY. Sept 25. National holiday. Marks the 1961 abolition of the monarchy.

RYDER CUP 2020. Sept 25–27. Whistling Straits, Haven, WI. Held every two years, this match pits American golfers against a European team. First held in 1927; this is the 43rd edition. Steve Stricker is US captain; Padraig Harrington is Europe's captain. For info: Ryder Cup, Professional Golfers' Assn of America. Web: www.rydercup.com.

SATCHEL PAIGE'S LAST GAME: 55th ANNIVERSARY. Sept 25, 1965. Satchel Paige, the oldest player in major league history at an estimated 59 years, 2 months, 18 days, pitched the last game of his career on this date. He hurled three scoreless innings for the Kansas City Athletics against the Boston Red Sox. Paige gave up only one hit, to Carl Yastrzemski. See also: "Paige, Leroy Robert (Satchel): Birth Anniversary" (July 7).

SEQUOIA AND KINGS CANYON NATIONAL PARK ESTABLISHED: ANNIVERSARY. Sept 25, 1890. Area in central California established as a national park. For further park info: Sequoia Natl Park, Three Rivers, CA 93271.

SHOSTAKOVICH, DMITRI: BIRTH ANNIVERSARY. Sept 25, 1906. Russian composer born at St. Petersburg, Russia. Died at Moscow, USSR, Aug 9, 1975.

SILVERSTEIN, SHEL: 90th BIRTH ANNIVERSARY. Sept 25, 1930. Cartoonist and children's author, best remembered for his poetry, which includes *A Light in the Attic* and *The Giving Tree*. Silverstein won the Michigan Young Reader's Award for *Where the Sidewalk Ends*. Also a songwriter, he wrote "The Unicorn Song" and "A Boy Named Sue." Born at Chicago, IL, he died at Key West, FL, May 9, 1999.

SMITH, WALTER WESLEY "RED": BIRTH ANNIVERSARY. Sept 25, 1905. Pulitzer Prize–winning sports columnist and newspaperman for 54 years, Red Smith was born at Green Bay, WI. Called the "nation's most respected sportswriter." Smith's columns appeared in almost 500 newspapers. He died at Stamford, CT, Jan 15, 1982.

STATE FAIR OF TEXAS. Sept 25–Oct 18. Fair Park, Dallas, TX. The State Fair of Texas is a 501(c)(3) nonprofit organization that celebrates all things Texan by promoting agriculture, education and community involvement through quality entertainment in a family-friendly environment. At 24 consecutive days, the State Fair of Texas is the longest-running fair in the nation, as well as one of the largest. With unlimited shows, live music, exhibits, food, games and rides, the fair is fun for the whole family! For info: State Fair of Texas, PO Box 150009, Dallas, TX 75315. Phone: (214) 565-9931. E-mail: info@bigtex.com. Web: www.bigtex.com.

STATE FAIR OF VIRGINIA. Sept 25–Oct 4. Meadow Event Park, Doswell. It's the Big Red Barn, racing pigs, the State Fair Animal Nursery, the famous State Fair Duck Slide and more! Get up close and personal with more than 5,000 farm animals in Virginia's largest outdoor classroom. Enjoy 10 days of rides, thrills and fun for the whole family with blue ribbon competitions, exhibits, midway rides and shows. It's a Virginia tradition and the only place to get that delicious State Fair food. Est attendance: 300,000. For info: State Fair of Virginia, 13191 Dawn Blvd, Doswell, VA 23047. Phone: (804) 994-2800. Web: www.statefairva.org.

🎂 BIRTHDAYS TODAY

Chauncey Billups, 44, former basketball player, born Denver, CO, Sept 25, 1976.

Tate Donovan, 57, actor ("Damages," *Argo, Love Potion No. 9*), born New York, NY, Sept 25, 1963.

Michael Douglas, 76, actor (Oscar for *Wall Street*; *Behind the Candelabra, Traffic, Fatal Attraction*), director, producer, born New York, NY, Sept 25, 1944.

Jordan Gavaris, 31, actor ("Orphan Black"), born Caledon, ON, Canada, Sept 25, 1989.

Donald Glover, 37, actor (Golden Globe for "Atlanta"; "Community"), writer ("30 Rock," "Atlanta"), producer, comedian, rapper, born Edwards AFB, CA, Sept 25, 1983.

Mark Hamill, 69, actor (Star Wars films), born Oakland, CA, Sept 25, 1951.

Jamie Hyneman, 64, television personality, host ("MythBusters"), born Marshall, MI, Sept 25, 1956.

Heather Locklear, 59, actress ("Spin City," "Melrose Place," "Dynasty"), born Los Angeles, CA, Sept 25, 1961.

Michael Madsen, 61, actor (*The Hateful Eight*, Kill Bill films, *Reservoir Dogs*), born Chicago, IL, Sept 25, 1959.

Lee Norris, 39, actor ("One Tree Hill," "Boy Meets World"), born Greenville, NC, Sept 25, 1981.

Scottie Pippen, 55, sportscaster, Hall of Fame basketball player, born Hamburg, AR, Sept 25, 1965.

Will Smith, 52, actor (*I Am Legend, Ali, Men in Black, Independence Day*), singer, born Philadelphia, PA, Sept 25, 1968.

Robert Walden, 77, actor ("Lou Grant," *All the King's Men*), born New York, NY, Sept 25, 1943.

Barbara Walters, 89, television journalist, interviewer, born Boston, MA, Sept 25, 1931.

Catherine Zeta-Jones, 51, actress (Oscar for *Chicago*; *Traffic, The Mask of Zorro*), born Swansea, Glamorgan, Wales, Sept 25, 1969.

September 26 — Saturday

DAY 270 **96 REMAINING**

APPLESEED, JOHNNY: BIRTH ANNIVERSARY. Sept 26, 1774. John Chapman, better known as Johnny Appleseed, believed to have been born at Leominster, MA. Died at Allen County, IN, Mar 11, 1845. Planter of orchards and friend of wild animals, he was regarded as a great medicine man by native peoples.

BATTLE OF MEUSE–ARGONNE FOREST: ANNIVERSARY. Sept 26, 1918. As part of four major efforts to break the Hindenburg line, a Franco-American offensive began on this date, with the US First Army striking between the Meuse River and the Argonne Forest and with the French Fourth Army to their west. After four taxing weeks of attack, the Germans were gradually pushed back. By Oct 31 the Americans had advanced 10 miles, the French had reached the Aisne River 20 miles away and the Argonne Forest was rid of the Central Powers forces. This was the final great battle of WWI.

"THE BEVERLY HILLBILLIES" TV PREMIERE: ANNIVERSARY. Sept 26, 1962. This half-hour comedy was one of the most successful "rural" comedies on TV; in addition, according to Nielsen, the eight most-watched half-hour shows are episodes of this series. "The Beverly Hillbillies" was about an Appalachian man, Jed Clampett (Buddy Ebsen), who found oil on his property, so he moved his family to a better life in Beverly Hills, CA. Most of its jokes were based on its fish-out-of-water premise. Also in the cast were Irene Ryan as Granny, Jed's mother-in-law; Donna Douglas as his daughter, Elly May; Max Baer, Jr, as his nephew, Jethro Bodine; Raymond Bailey as neurotic Milburn Drysdale, Jed's neighbor and banker; Nancy Kulp as Jane Hathaway, Drysdale's secretary; and Harriet MacGibbon as Margaret Drysdale, Milburn's wife.

"THE BRADY BUNCH" TV PREMIERE: ANNIVERSARY. Sept 26, 1969. This popular sitcom starred Robert Reed as widower Mike Brady, who has three sons and is married to Carol (played by Florence Henderson), who has three daughters. Housekeeper Alice was played by Ann B. Davis. Sons Greg (Barry Williams), Peter (Christopher Knight) and Bobby (Mike Lookinland) and daughters Marcia (Maureen McCormick), Jan (Eve Plumb) and Cindy (Susan Olsen) experienced the typical crises of youth. The program steered clear of social issues and portrayed childhood as a time of innocence. The last episode was telecast on Aug 30, 1974. The program continues to be popular in reruns, and there were also many spin-offs: a cartoon, a variety series, a sitcom, a short-lived dramatic series and films.

DONIZETTI'S *LUCIA DI LAMMERMOOR* PREMIERE: ANNIVERSARY. Sept 26, 1835. *Lucia di Lammermoor*, one of opera's greatest tragic love stories, premiered in Naples, Italy. The opera was composed by Gaetano Donizetti with a libretto by Salvatore Cammarano. The plot was based on Sir Walter Scott's *The Bride of Lammermoor* and unfolds in 17th-century Scotland.

ELIOT, THOMAS STEARNS: BIRTH ANNIVERSARY. Sept 26, 1888. Poet, literary critic, dramatist and editor born at St. Louis, MO. One of the 20th century's preeminent poets, T.S. Eliot—with friend and fellow poet Ezra Pound—worked to modernize contemporary poetic diction to one that reflected the rhythm of educated speech. Eliot's experiments in diction, versification and style are seen throughout the body of his works, which include *The Love Song of J. Alfred Prufrock* (1917), *Four Quartets* (1945) and *The Waste Land* (1922)—his most renowned poem. Awarded the Order of Merit and the Nobel Prize in Literature in 1948, Eliot died at London, England, Jan 24, 1965.

September 2020	S	M	T	W	T	F	S
			1	2	3	4	5
	6	7	8	9	10	11	12
	13	14	15	16	17	18	19
	20	21	22	23	24	25	26
	27	28	29	30			

Fishy Bits

FALL ASTRONOMY DAY. Sept 26. To take astronomy to the people. International Fall Astronomy Day is observed on a Saturday near the first quarter moon between mid-September and mid-October. Cosponsored by 14 astronomical organizations. For info: Gary E. Tomlinson, Coord, Astronomy Day Headquarters, 30 Stargazer Ln, Comstock Park, MI 49321. Phone: (616) 784-9518. E-mail: gtomlins@sbcglobal.net. Web: www.astroleague.org.

FIRST TELEVISED PRESIDENTIAL DEBATE: 60th ANNIVERSARY. Sept 26, 1960. The debate between presidential candidates John F. Kennedy and Richard Nixon was televised from WBBM-TV, a Chicago, IL, TV studio. Howard K. Smith was the moderator.

FISH AMNESTY DAY. Sept 26. Give animals a break by not fishing. Fish are intelligent animals who feel pain just like the dogs and cats who share our homes. Annually, the fourth Saturday in September. For info: PETA, 501 Front St, Norfolk, VA 23510. Phone: (757) 622-7382. Web: www.peta.org.

GENEVA AREA GRAPE JAMBOREE. Sept 26–27. Geneva, OH. 57th annual celebration of grape harvest and products. Wine tasting, free entertainment, food and rides. Annually, the last full weekend in September. Est attendance: 200,000. For info: Geneva Grape Jamboree, Box 92, Geneva, OH 44041. Phone: (440) 466-5262. E-mail: crafts@grapejamboree.com. Web: www.grapejamboree.com.

GERSHWIN, GEORGE: BIRTH ANNIVERSARY. Sept 26, 1898. American composer remembered for his many enduring songs and melodies including "The Man I Love," "Strike Up the Band," "Funny Face," "I Got Rhythm" and the opera *Porgy and Bess*. Many of his works were in collaboration with his brother, Ira. Born at Brooklyn, NY, he died of a brain tumor at Beverly Hills, CA, July 11, 1937. See also: "Gershwin, Ira: Birth Anniversary" (Dec 6).

GETTYSBURG OUTDOOR ANTIQUE SHOW. Sept 26. Gettysburg, PA. More than 150 dealers displaying their wares on the sidewalk. Est attendance: 25,000. For info: Gettysburg Antique Shows, PO Box 4070, Gettysburg, PA 17325. Phone: (717) 253-5750. E-mail: gettysburgantiqueshow@comcast.net. Web: gettysburgretailmerchants.com.

"GILLIGAN'S ISLAND" TV PREMIERE: ANNIVERSARY. Sept 26, 1964. Seven people set sail aboard the *Minnow* for a three-hour tour and became stranded on an island. They used the resources on the island for food, shelter and entertainment. The cast included Bob Denver (Gilligan), Alan Hale, Jr (the Skipper), Jim Backus (Thurston Howell III), Natalie Schafer (Mrs "Lovey" Howell), Russell Johnson (the Professor), Dawn Wells (Mary Ann) and Tina Louise (Ginger Grant, the movie star). The last telecast aired on Sept 4, 1967.

"HAWAII FIVE-O" TV PREMIERE: ANNIVERSARY. Sept 26, 1968. "Book 'em, Dano" became a national catchphrase after this CBS crime series began airing. It starred the granite-jawed Jack Lord as Steve McGarrett, leader of a special Hawaiian state police force that answered only to the governor. His officers included Danny "Dano" Williams (James MacArthur), Chin Ho Kelly (Kam Fong), Duke Lukela (Herman Wedemeyer) and others. Filmed on location at Oahu, HI, and featuring a popular theme song by the Ventures, the show was a huge hit until it

concluded in 1980. (CBS premiered a new version of the show in fall 2010.)

HEIDEGGER, MARTIN: BIRTH ANNIVERSARY. Sept 26, 1889. Widely regarded the most original 20th-century philosopher, Heidegger focused on answering one fundamental question, the meaning of "being," which he explored in his seminal work *Being and Time* (1927), one of the 20th century's most influential books. His analysis revitalized the study of philosophy and strongly influenced Sartre and other existential philosophers. Born at Messkirch, Germany, Heidegger died May 26, 1976, at Freiburg, Germany.

LALANNE, JACK: BIRTH ANNIVERSARY. Sept 26, 1914. The son of French immigrants, born at San Francisco, CA, was to become America's fitness guru through his eponymous TV show and wacky stunts. "The Jack LaLanne Show" went national in 1959, and by the end of its run in the 1980s, it had 3,000 episodes. LaLanne, who kept a 30-inch waist, popularized the benefits of living healthfully with amazing stunts, such as swimming hand-cuffed from Alcatraz Island to Fisherman's Wharf while also towing a 1,000-pound boat (at age 60). LaLanne died Jan 23, 2011, at Morro Bay, CA, at age 96.

★**NATIONAL HUNTING AND FISHING DAY.** Sept 26. Presidential Proclamation 4682, of Sept 11, 1979, covers all succeeding years. Annually, the fourth Saturday in September.

NATIONAL PUBLIC LANDS DAY. Sept 26. 27th annual. The nation's largest hands-on volunteer effort to improve and enhance the public lands that Americans enjoy. Each year volunteers participate in National Public Lands Day in all 50 states, the District of Columbia, Puerto Rico and other US territories. They build trails and bridges, plant trees and plants, remove trash and invasive species and restore historic sites. Sponsored by Toyota Motor Sales. Annually, the fourth Saturday in September. Est attendance: 200,000. For info: Natl Public Lands Day, Natl Environmental Education Foundation. E-mail: npld@neefusa.org. Web: www.neefusa.org/NPLD.

POPE PAUL VI: BIRTH ANNIVERSARY. Sept 26, 1897. Giovanni Battista Montini, 262nd pope of the Roman Catholic Church, born at Concesio, Italy. Elected pope June 21, 1963. Died at Castel Gandolfo, near Rome, Italy, Aug 6, 1978.

UNITED NATIONS: INTERNATIONAL DAY FOR THE TOTAL ELIMINATION OF NUCLEAR WEAPONS. Sept 26. With growing concerns worldwide over the catastrophic humanitarian consequences of the use of even a single nuclear weapon, let alone a regional or global nuclear war, the General Assembly (Res 68/32) created this day to mobilize new international efforts towards achieving the common goal of a nuclear-weapon-free world. Annually, Sept 26. For info: United Nations. Web: www.un.org.

***WEST SIDE STORY* PREMIERE: ANNIVERSARY.** Sept 26, 1957. Composer Leonard Bernstein's updated Romeo and Juliet musical premiered on Broadway and ran until 1960. Stephen Sondheim wrote the lyrics, Arthur Laurents wrote the book and Jerome Robbins created the choreography.

🎂 BIRTHDAYS TODAY

Melissa Sue Anderson, 58, actress ("Little House on the Prairie"), born Berkeley, CA, Sept 26, 1962.

Jim Caviezel, 52, actor ("Person of Interest," *The Passion of the Christ*), born Mount Vernon, WA, Sept 26, 1968.

Bryan Ferry, 75, singer, songwriter, born Durham, England, Sept 26, 1945.

Linda Hamilton, 63, actress (*The Terminator, Terminator 2*, "Beauty and the Beast"), born Salisbury, MD, Sept 26, 1957.

Mary Beth Hurt, 72, actress (*The World According to Garp, Six Degrees of Separation*), born Marshalltown, IA, Sept 26, 1948.

Olivia Newton-John, 72, singer, actress (*Grease*), born Cambridge, England, Sept 26, 1948.

Jane Smiley, 71, author (*A Thousand Acres, Moo*), born Los Angeles, CA, Sept 26, 1949.

Christine T. Whitman, 74, former administrator of the Environmental Protection Agency, former governor of New Jersey (R), born New York, NY, Sept 26, 1946.

Serena Williams, 39, tennis player, born Saginaw, MI, Sept 26, 1981.

September 27 — Sunday

DAY 271   **95 REMAINING**

ADAMS, SAMUEL: BIRTH ANNIVERSARY. Sept 27, 1722. Revolutionary leader and Massachusetts state politician Samuel Adams, cousin to President John Adams (1797–1801), was born at Boston, MA. He died there Oct 2, 1803. As a delegate to the First and Second Continental Congresses, Adams urged a vigorous stand against England. He signed the Declaration of Independence and the Articles of Confederation and supported the War for Independence. Adams served as lieutenant governor of Massachusetts under John Hancock from 1789 to 1793 and then as governor until 1797.

ANCESTOR APPRECIATION DAY. Sept 27. A day to learn about and appreciate one's forebears. (Created by William and Helen Chase.)

BANNED BOOKS WEEK—CELEBRATING THE FREEDOM TO READ. Sept 27–Oct 3. Annual event celebrating the freedom to read and the importance of the First Amendment. Held during the last week of September, Banned Books Week highlights the benefits of free and open access to information while drawing attention to the harms of censorship by spotlighting actual or attempted bannings of books. Sponsors: American Library Association, American Booksellers Association, American Booksellers Foundation for Free Expression, American Society of Journalists and Authors, Association of American Publishers, National Association of College Stores. For info: American Library Assn, Office for Intellectual Freedom. E-mail: bbw@ala.org. Web: www.bannedbooksweek.org.

CONRAD, WILLIAM: 100th BIRTH ANNIVERSARY. Sept 27, 1920. Actor, best known for his roles in the TV series "Cannon" and "Jake and the Fat Man." Also narrated "Rocky and His Friends," the witty cartoon series featuring Rocky and Bullwinkle. Born at Louisville, KY, and died at North Hollywood, CA, Feb 11, 1994.

CORNELIUS, DON: BIRTH ANNIVERSARY. Sept 27, 1936. Born at Chicago, IL, Cornelius was a pioneering and influential television producer and emcee. With his deep, resonant voice, creative drive and keen eye for talent, Don Cornelius created a hit musical variety show that brought black culture into American homes like no syndicated program before it. In 1970 Cornelius debuted "Soul Train" on WCIU-TV, a local Chicago television station. It went national a year later and gave important exposure to now-legendary performers such as James Brown, Michael Jackson and Marvin Gaye at a time when soul and R&B artists had few television outlets and scant access to white audiences. "Soul Train" also acted as a barometer for black youth culture, tracking and shaping the styles, slang and dances of the day. Cornelius remained in a production role on "Soul Train" until 2006. He died at Los Angeles, CA, on Feb 1, 2012.

CRUIKSHANK, GEORGE: BIRTH ANNIVERSARY. Sept 27, 1792. English artist, especially known for caricatures and illustrating of Charles Dickens's books. Born at London, England, and died there Feb 1, 1878.

ETHIOPIA: TRUE CROSS DAY. Sept 27. National holiday. Commemorates the finding of the true cross (*Maskal*). Also a holiday in Eritrea.

GERMANY: BMW BERLIN MARATHON. Sept 27 (subject to change). Berlin. 47th annual. Part of the Abbott World Marathon Majors. The Berlin Marathon—with 40,000 participants—offers fantastic atmosphere with the final meters of the course going through the Brandenburg Gate. Mini-marathon, kids race and inline skating marathon take place Sept 26. Est attendance: 1,000,000. For info: Berlin Marathon, SCC Events GmbH. Web: www.bmw-berlin-marathon.com.

★**GOLD STAR MOTHER'S AND FAMILY'S DAY.** Sept 27. Presidential Proclamation always for last Sunday in each September since 1936. Proclamation 2424, of Sept 14, 1940, covers all succeeding years.

INTERNATIONAL DAY OF THE DEAF. Sept 27. This day draws attention to the achievements of deaf people and to the concerns of the deaf community. Annually, the last Sunday in September. For info: World Federation of the Deaf. E-mail: info@wfdeaf.org. Web: www.wfdeaf.org.

"JACK THE RIPPER" LETTER: ANNIVERSARY. Sept 27, 1888. In the midst of the "Autumn of Terror" in which London, England, was convulsed over the crimes of a brutal serial killer, the city's Central News Agency received a letter in red ink purportedly written by the killer. He dubbed himself "Jack the Ripper" and threatened more killings. Police at the time believed (and most historians today believe) the letter to be a hoax by an irresponsible journalist, but the name took hold in the public imagination and is forever associated with the Whitechapel murders of 1888. See also: "Whitechapel Murders Begin: Anniversary" (Aug 31).

NAST, THOMAS: BIRTH ANNIVERSARY. Sept 27, 1840. American political cartoonist born at Landau, Germany. Abraham Lincoln called Nast "our best recruiting sergeant" for his drawings eliciting support for the Union during the Civil War. He is best known for his successful attack on politically corrupt William "Boss" Tweed and Tammany Hall in New York City, which resulted in the machine's demise and Tweed's incarceration. Nast famously invented the Democratic donkey and Republican elephant before dying of yellow fever Dec 7, 1902, while serving as US consul at Guayaquil, Ecuador.

SAINT VINCENT DE PAUL: FEAST DAY. Sept 27. French priest, patron of charitable organizations, and cofounder of the Sisters of Charity. Canonized 1737 (lived 1581?–1660).

"THE TONIGHT SHOW" TV PREMIERE: ANNIVERSARY. Sept 27, 1954. "The Tonight Show" has gone through numerous changes over the years, yet it has remained a top-rated show that set the standards for all variety/talk shows to come. Steve Allen served as host, 1954–57. He developed the show's format: an opening monologue, games or segments for the studio audience and then celebrity interviews. Jack Paar hosted during 1957–62 and Johnny Carson reigned as the king of comedy during 1962–92. Comedian Jay Leno was the popular host in the years 1992–2009. After a brief period with Conan O'Brien taking over the desk, Leno returned in 2010. Jimmy Fallon became host in 2014.

WARREN COMMISSION REPORT: ANNIVERSARY. Sept 27, 1964. On this day the Warren Commission issued a report stating that Lee Harvey Oswald acted alone in the assassination of President John F. Kennedy on Nov 22, 1963. Congress reopened the investigation, and in 1979 the House Select Committee on Assassinations issued a report stating a conspiracy was most likely involved. See also: "Committee on Assassinations Report: Anniversary" (Mar 29).

WORLD TOURISM DAY. Sept 27. Observed on the anniversary of the adoption of the World Tourism Organization Statutes in 1970. Annually, Sept 27. For info: World Tourism Organization. Web: www.unwto.org.

YOM KIPPUR BEGINS AT SUNDOWN. Sept 27. Jewish Day of Atonement. See "Yom Kippur" (Sept 28).

🧁 BIRTHDAYS TODAY

Wilford Brimley, 86, actor (*Cocoon*, "Our House"), born Salt Lake City, UT, Sept 27, 1934.

Carrie Brownstein, 46, comedienne, actress ("Portlandia"), musician (Sleater-Kinney), born Seattle, WA, Sept 27, 1974.

Shaun Cassidy, 61, television producer, singer, actor ("The Hardy Boys"), born Los Angeles, CA, Sept 27, 1959.

Claude Jarman, Jr, 86, actor (*The Yearling, Rio Grande*), born Nashville, TN, Sept 27, 1934.

Steve Kerr, 55, basketball executive, former player, born Beirut, Lebanon, Sept 27, 1965.

Avril Lavigne, 36, singer, born Belleville, ON, Canada, Sept 27, 1984.

Lil Wayne, 38, rapper, born Dwayne Michael Carter, Jr, at New Orleans, LA, Sept 27, 1982.

Meat Loaf, 73, singer, musician (*The Rocky Horror Picture Show*), born Marvin Lee Aday at Dallas, TX, Sept 27, 1947.

Bello Nock, 52, circus clown, born Demetrius Nock at Sarasota, FL, Sept 27, 1968.

Michael Jack (Mike) Schmidt, 71, Hall of Fame baseball player, born Dayton, OH, Sept 27, 1949.

September	S	M	T	W	T	F	S
2020			1	2	3	4	5
	6	7	8	9	10	11	12
	13	14	15	16	17	18	19
	20	21	22	23	24	25	26
	27	28	29	30			

Cary-Hiroyuki Tagawa, 70, actor ("The Man in the High Castle," *Mortal Kombat*), martial artist, born Tokyo, Japan, Sept 27, 1950.

Delores Taylor, 81, actress, writer, producer (*Billy Jack, The Trial of Billy Jack*), born Winner, SD, Sept 27, 1939.

Francesco Totti, 44, former soccer player, born Rome, Italy, Sept 27, 1976.

September 28 — Monday

DAY 272   **94 REMAINING**

CABRILLO DAY: ANNIVERSARY OF DISCOVERY OF CALIFORNIA.
Sept 28, 1542. California. Commemorates discovery of California by Portuguese navigator Juan Rodríguez Cabrillo, who reached San Diego Bay. Cabrillo died at San Miguel Island, CA, Jan 3, 1543. His birth date is unknown. The Cabrillo National Monument marks his landfall, and Cabrillo Day is still observed in California (in some areas on the Saturday nearest Sept 28).

CAPP, AL: BIRTH ANNIVERSARY. Sept 28, 1909. The creator of the fictitious village of Dogpatch, KY, Al Capp was born Alfred Gerald Caplin at New Haven, CT. The comic strip "Li'l Abner" appeared in daily newspapers from 1934 until its final episode was published Nov 13, 1977. Along with the misadventures of Abner Yokum, Capp lampooned famous public figures. The minor American institution of "Sadie Hawkins Day" made its debut in "Li'l Abner." Al Capp died Nov 5, 1979, at Cambridge, MA.

FIRST NIGHT FOOTBALL GAME: ANNIVERSARY. Sept 28, 1892. The first night football game in America was played between Mansfield State Normal School (now Mansfield University) and Wyoming Seminary at Mansfield, PA.

HARMON, TOM: BIRTH ANNIVERSARY. Sept 28, 1919. Born at Rensselaer, IN, Harmon became a national figure by his exploits in the backfield for the University of Michigan. Known as "Old 98," his uniform number, he won many awards, including the Heisman Trophy in 1940. After service in World War II, during which he bailed out twice from destroyed planes, Harmon played two years with the Los Angeles Rams. Upon retiring from the gridiron, he worked as a sportscaster. Harmon died at Los Angeles, CA, Mar 15, 1990.

MASTROIANNI, MARCELLO: BIRTH ANNIVERSARY. Sept 28, 1924. One of the great international stars of cinema, born at Fontana Liri, Italy. Mastroianni worked with the master directors of the mid-20th century, among them Federico Fellini and Luchino Visconti. Two of his most famous roles were the world-weary journalist of *La Dolce Vita* (1960) and the in-crisis movie director of *8½* (1963)—both films directed by Fellini. He was nominated for Oscars three times and twice won the Best Actor Award at the Cannes Film Festival. Died at Paris, France, Dec 19, 1996.

SCHMELING, MAX: BIRTH ANNIVERSARY. Sept 28, 1905. First European boxer to hold the world heavyweight boxing title (1930–32). Best known for fighting American great Joe Louis twice: the first time defeating him; the second time losing. The Nazi government tried to use Schmeling—to his dismay—as a propaganda tool to demonstrate the superiority of the Aryan race. Schmeling rejected that role, never joined the Nazi Party and was punished by being given dangerous WWII combat duties. Schmeling saved two Jewish boys during the November 1938 Kristallnacht terrors. Schmeling and Louis developed a strong friendship outside the ring, and Schmeling paid for Louis's funeral. Born at Klein Luckow, Germany, Schmeling died Feb 2, 2005, at Hollenstedt, Germany.

SULLIVAN, ED: BIRTH ANNIVERSARY. Sept 28, 1901. Known as the "King of TV Variety," born at New York, NY. Sullivan started his media career in 1932 as a sportswriter for the *Daily News* in New York. His popular variety show, "The Ed Sullivan Show" ("Toast of the Town"), ran from 1948 until 1971. It included such sensational acts as Elvis Presley and The Beatles. He died at New York, NY, Oct 13, 1974.

TAIWAN: CONFUCIUS'S BIRTHDAY AND TEACHERS' DAY. Sept 28. National holiday. Confucius is the Latinized name of K'ung-Fu-tzu, the great philosopher and teacher born at Shantung province on the 27th day of the 10th moon (lunar calendar) in the 22nd year of Kuke Hsiang of Lu (551 BC). This day celebrates Confucius and his contributions to Chinese culture and society. From 1939 to 1951, this day was observed on Aug 27; since 1952, it has been observed on Sept 28 and now is expanded to honor all teachers.

UNITED NATIONS/UNESCO: INTERNATIONAL DAY FOR UNIVERSAL ACCESS TO INFORMATION. Sept 28. First observed in 2016. Universal access to information is bound up with the right to seek and receive information, which is an integral part of the right to freedom of expression. UNESCO has proclaimed this day to encourage more countries to adopt freedom of information (FOI) legislation, develop policies for multilingualism and cultural diversity in the cyberspace and ensure that women and men with disabilities are integrated. Annually, Sept 28. For info: United Nations/UNESCO. Web: https://en.unesco.org.

WIGGIN, KATE DOUGLAS: BIRTH ANNIVERSARY. Sept 28, 1856. Kate Wiggin was born Kate Douglas Smith at Philadelphia, PA. She helped organize the first free kindergarten on the West Coast in 1878 at San Francisco, CA, and in 1880 she and her sister established the California Kindergarten Training School. After moving back East she devoted herself to writing, producing a number of children's books including *The Birds' Christmas Carol, Polly Oliver's Problem* and *Rebecca of Sunnybrook Farm*. She died at Harrow, England, Aug 24, 1923.

WILLARD, FRANCES ELIZABETH CAROLINE: BIRTH ANNIVERSARY. Sept 28, 1839. One of the best-known, most influential women of the late 19th century for her temperance and suffrage work, Willard was also influential in American education. One of the first female administrators of a major coeducational university when made dean of women for Northwestern University's Women's College, she left education to work with the Women's Christian Temperance Union, of which she was president during the years 1879–98. Born at Churchville, NY, she died at New York, NY, Feb 18, 1898; more than 20,000 people paid their last respects at services in New York City and Chicago, IL.

WORLD RABIES DAY. Sept 28. Rabies is the deadliest disease on earth, with a fatality rate approaching 100 percent, but it is also easy to prevent with safe, modern vaccines. Today rabies is overwhelmingly a disease of poverty with more than 95 percent of victims from Asia and Africa. World Rabies Day is a collection of events held worldwide on or near Sept 28 with the express intention of raising awareness of the issues surrounding rabies and its prevention. Get involved, raise funds, raise awareness and end rabies! For info: Global Alliance for Rabies Control, 529 Humboldt St, Ste 1, Manhattan, KS 66502. E-mail: info@rabiesalliance.org. Web: www.rabiesalliance.org/world-rabies-day.

YOM KIPPUR OR DAY OF ATONEMENT. Sept 28. Holiest Jewish observance. A day for fasting, repentance and seeking forgiveness. Hebrew calendar date: Tishri 10, 5781. Began at sundown on Sept 27.

🎂 BIRTHDAYS TODAY

Brigitte Bardot, 86, actress (*And God Created Woman, Viva Maria*), animal rights activist, born Camille Javal at Paris, France, Sept 28, 1934.

Bill Cassidy, 63, US Senator (R, Louisiana), born Highland Park, IL, Sept 28, 1957.

Hilary Duff, 33, actress (*A Cinderella Story*, "Lizzie McGuire"), born Houston, TX, Sept 28, 1987.

Janeane Garofalo, 56, actress (*Reality Bites, The Truth About Cats and Dogs*), born Newton, NJ, Sept 28, 1964.

Frankie Jonas, 20, actor ("Jonas LA"), born Wyckoff, NJ, Sept 28, 2000.

Jeffrey Jones, 73, actor (*Beetlejuice, Stay Tuned*), born Buffalo, NY, Sept 28, 1947.

Steve M. Largent, 66, Hall of Fame football player, born Tulsa, OK, Sept 28, 1954.

Donna Leon, 78, author (Commissario Brunetti mysteries), born Montclair, NJ, Sept 28, 1942.

Robert Manfred, 62, Commissioner of Major League Baseball, born Rome, NY, Sept 28, 1958.

Emeka Okafor, 38, basketball player, born Houston, TX, Sept 28, 1982.

Se Ri Pak, 43, golfer, born Daejeon, South Korea, Sept 28, 1977.

Gwyneth Paltrow, 47, actress (Oscar for *Shakespeare in Love*; *Proof, The Talented Mr Ripley*), born Los Angeles, CA, Sept 28, 1973.

St. Vincent, 38, singer, musician, born Annie Clark at Tulsa, OK, Sept 28, 1982.

Suzanne Whang, 58, comedienne, television personality ("House Hunters"), actress ("Las Vegas"), born Arlington, VA, Sept 28, 1962.

September 29 — Tuesday

DAY 273	93 REMAINING

ANTONIONI, MICHELANGELO: BIRTH ANNIVERSARY. Sept 29, 1912. Groundbreaking Italian filmmaker, born at Ferrara, Italy. His films are known for their experiments with color, cinematography, pacing and narrative structure. He was nominated for two Academy Awards for *Blow-Up* (1966) and was granted a Lifetime Achievement Oscar in 1996. He died at Rome, Italy, July 30, 2007.

AUTRY, GENE: BIRTH ANNIVERSARY. Sept 29, 1907. Born at Tioga, TX, Autry was arguably America's favorite singing cowboy in a career that spanned almost seven decades. He began performing on local radio in his late teens before signing with Columbia Records in 1931 and appearing for a time on the "National Barn Dance" radio show. His film career began soon after, and he starred in nearly 100 films, almost all of which were B-Westerns in which his singing featured prominently. After retiring from acting, Autry became a baseball sports executive. He died at Los Angeles, CA, on Oct 2, 1998.

DOW JONES BIGGEST DROP: ANNIVERSARY. Sept 29, 2008. The Dow Jones Industrial Average plunged 778 points during the worldwide financial crisis of autumn 2008—the biggest one-day drop in its history.

September 2020	S	M	T	W	T	F	S
			1	2	3	4	5
	6	7	8	9	10	11	12
	13	14	15	16	17	18	19
	20	21	22	23	24	25	26
	27	28	29	30			

FERMI, ENRICO: BIRTH ANNIVERSARY. Sept 29, 1901. Nuclear physicist, born at Rome, Italy. Played a prominent role in the splitting of the atom and the construction of the first American nuclear reactor. Died at Chicago, IL, Nov 28, 1954.

HOWARD, TREVOR: BIRTH ANNIVERSARY. Sept 29, 1916. British actor Trevor Howard was born at Cliftonville, England. He appeared in more than 70 films including *The Third Man* (1950) and *Mutiny on the Bounty* (1962). He died Jan 7, 1988, at Bushey, England.

MICHAELMAS. Sept 29. The feast of St. Michael and All Angels in the Greek and Roman Catholic Churches.

NATIONAL ATTEND YOUR GRANDCHILD'S BIRTH DAY. Sept 29. Bonding with your grandchild should begin at birth. This day is set aside to encourage grandparents to participate in their grandchild's birth as well as his or her life. Annually, Sept 29. For info: Carolynn Zorn, PO Box 1424, Novi, MI 48376. E-mail: attendingthebirth@hotmail.com. Web: www.attendingthebirth.com.

NATIONAL BISCOTTI DAY. Sept 29. A day of celebration for the classic dunking cookie. Originating in Italy, biscotti ("twice baked cookies") have been around since the 14th century. Now they are eaten all over the world. While they can be enjoyed with a variety of beverages, they pair best with coffee, which is also celebrated today. Whether you dip, dunk or just snack on biscotti, make sure to have some on National Biscotti Day. Annually, Sept 29. For info: Biscotti Goddess. Phone: (855) 745-9490. E-mail: nationalday@biscotti-goddess.com.

NATIONAL COFFEE DAY. Sept 29. Popular observance for coffee drinkers, celebrated by the coffee industry and coffee shops and houses (often with free cups of joe). Probably first observed in 2005 in the United States. Also a day to learn about fair-trade coffee and practices. Annually, Sept 29.

NELSON, HORATIO: BIRTH ANNIVERSARY. Sept 29, 1758. English naval hero of the Battle of Trafalgar, born at Burnham Thorpe, Norfolk, England. Died during a battle at sea off Cape Trafalgar, Spain, Oct 21, 1805.

PARAGUAY: BOQUERÓN DAY. Sept 29. National holiday. Commemorates a victorious battle over Bolivia during the 1932 Chaco War.

SCOTLAND YARD FIRST APPEARANCE: ANNIVERSARY. Sept 29, 1829. The first public appearance of Greater London's Metropolitan Police occurred amid jeering and abuse from disapproving political opponents. Public sentiment turned to confidence and respect in the ensuing years. The Metropolitan Police had been established by an act of parliament in June 1829, at the request of Home Secretary Sir Robert Peel, after whom the London police officers became more affectionately known as "bobbies." Scotland Yard, the site of their first headquarters near Charing Cross, soon became the official name of the force.

SPACE MILESTONE: *DISCOVERY* (US). Sept 29, 1988. Space shuttle *Discovery*, after numerous reschedulings, launched from Kennedy Space Center, FL, with a five-member crew on board, and

landed Oct 3 at Edwards Air Force Base, CA. It marked the first American manned flight since the *Challenger* tragedy in 1986. See also: "*Challenger* Space Shuttle Explosion: Anniversary" (Jan 28).

SPACE MILESTONE: *SALYUT 6* (USSR). Sept 29, 1977. Soviet space station launched this date. *Salyut* stayed in space for four years, during which 31 spacecraft docked with the space station. Burned up on July 29, 1982, when it reentered Earth's atmosphere after nearly five years.

VETERANS OF FOREIGN WARS ESTABLISHED: ANNIVERSARY. Sept 29, 1899. This organization is loyal to the issues and actions affecting America's heroes. Its members offer assistance in addition to supporting veterans issues in Congress. Part of the organization's mission, according to its charter, is "to preserve and strengthen comradeship among its members; to foster true patriotism; and to preserve and defend the United States from all her enemies, whomsoever." For info: Veterans of Foreign Wars of the United States. Web: www.vfw.org.

🎂 BIRTHDAYS TODAY

Kevin Durant, 32, basketball player, born Washington, DC, Sept 29, 1988.

Bryant Gumbel, 72, television journalist, host, born New Orleans, LA, Sept 29, 1948.

Hersey R. Hawkins, Jr, 54, former basketball player, born Chicago, IL, Sept 29, 1966.

Patricia Hodge, 74, actress ("Rumpole of the Bailey," *The Elephant Man, Betrayal*), born Cleethorpes, Lincolnshire, England, Sept 29, 1946.

Jerry Lee Lewis, 85, singer, musician ("Great Balls of Fire"), born Ferriday, LA, Sept 29, 1935.

Emily Lloyd, 50, actress (*Wish You Were Here, In Country, A River Runs Through It*), born North London, England, Sept 29, 1970.

Ian McShane, 78, actor ("American Gods," "Deadwood," "Lovejoy," *Sexy Beast*; stage: *The Homecoming*), born Blackburn, England, Sept 29, 1942.

Chrissy Metz, 40, actress ("This Is Us," "American Horror Story"), born Homestead, FL, Sept 29, 1980.

John Paxson, 60, basketball executive, former player, born Dayton, OH, Sept 29, 1960.

Lech Walesa, 77, Polish statesman, Solidarity founder, born Popowo, Poland, Sept 29, 1943.

Dave Wilcox, 78, Hall of Fame football player, born Ontario, OR, Sept 29, 1942.

September 30 — Wednesday

DAY 274   **92 REMAINING**

ARCHAEOPTERYX FOSSIL DISCOVERY ANNOUNCED: ANNIVERSARY. Sept 30, 1861. German scientist Hermann von Meyer announced the discovery of an incredible fossil in Bavaria's Solnhofen limestone quarries in a scholarly journal on this date—exciting the world's scientific community. Although a fossilized feather had been discovered a month earlier, this find was a complete skeleton of a "feather-clad" animal that showed both avian and reptilian characteristics. The Jurassic period creature (some 150 million years old) was later named Archaeopteryx, or "ancient wing." It was the size of a pigeon and had teeth as well as grasping claws on its wings.

BABE RUTH SETS HOME RUN RECORD: ANNIVERSARY. Sept 30, 1927. George Herman "Babe" Ruth hit his 60th home run of the season off Tom Zachary of the Washington Senators. Ruth's record for the most homers in a single season stood for 34 years—until Roger Maris hit 61 in 1961. Maris's record was broken in 1998 by Mark McGwire with 62 home runs. Barry Bonds broke McGwire's record on Oct 5, 2001.

BOLAN, MARC: BIRTH ANNIVERSARY. Sept 30, 1947. Influential, flamboyant glam rock star born Marc Feld at London, England. Founder of T. Rex, best known for the hit "Get It On" (1971). Died in a car crash, Sept 16, 1977, at London.

BOTSWANA: INDEPENDENCE DAY. Sept 30. National holiday. The former Bechuanaland protectorate (British colony) became the independent Republic of Botswana in 1966.

CAPOTE, TRUMAN: BIRTH ANNIVERSARY. Sept 30, 1924. American novelist and literary celebrity, born Truman Streckfus Persons at New Orleans, LA. He later took the name of his stepfather to become Truman Capote. Among his best-remembered books: *Other Voices, Other Rooms*; *Breakfast at Tiffany's* and *In Cold Blood*. He was working on a new novel, *Answered Prayers*, at the time of his death at Los Angeles, CA, Aug 25, 1984.

"CHEERS" TV PREMIERE: ANNIVERSARY. Sept 30, 1982. NBC sitcom revolving around the owner, employees and patrons of a Beacon Street bar at Boston, MA. Original cast: Ted Danson as owner Sam Malone, Shelley Long and Rhea Perlman as waitresses Diane Chambers and Carla Tortelli, Nicholas Colasanto as bartender Ernie "Coach" Pantusso, John Ratzenberger as mailman Cliff Clavin and George Wendt as accountant Norm Peterson. Later cast members: Woody Harrelson as bartender Woody Boyd, Kelsey Grammer as Dr. Frasier Crane, Kirstie Alley as Rebecca Howe and Bebe Neuwirth as Dr. Lilith Sternin Crane. The theme song, "Where Everybody Knows Your Name," was sung by Gary Portnoy. The last episode aired Aug 19, 1993.

DEAN, JAMES: 65th DEATH ANNIVERSARY. Sept 30, 1955. Rising young film star James Dean died in an auto accident near Cholame, CA, two hours after getting a speeding ticket. He was 24 years old. His final films, *Rebel Without a Cause* and *Giant*, were released posthumously in 1956. See also: "Dean, James: Birth Anniversary" (Feb 8).

FIRST ANNUAL FAIR IN AMERICA: ANNIVERSARY. Sept 30, 1641. According to the Laws and Ordinances of New Netherlands (now New York and New Jersey), on Sept 30, 1641, authorities declared that "henceforth there shall be held annually at Fort Amsterdam" a Cattle Fair (Oct 15) and a Hog Fair (Nov 1), and that "whosoever hath any things to sell or buy can regulate himself accordingly."

FIRST CRIMINAL EXECUTION IN AMERICAN COLONIES: ANNIVERSARY. Sept 30, 1630. John Billington, one of the first Pilgrims to land in America, was hanged for murder, becoming the first criminal to be executed in the American colonies.

"THE FLINTSTONES" TV PREMIERE: 60th ANNIVERSARY. Sept 30, 1960. This Hanna-Barbera cartoon comedy was set in prehistoric times. Characters included two Stone Age families, Fred and Wilma Flintstone and neighbors Barney and Betty Rubble.

GUADALUPE MOUNTAINS NATIONAL PARK ESTABLISHED: ANNIVERSARY. Sept 30, 1972. Area in western Texas along Texas–New Mexico border, originally authorized Oct 15, 1966, was established as a national park. For further park info: Guadalupe Mountains Natl Park, 400 Pine Canyon, Salt Flat, TX 79847. Web: www.nps.gov/gumo.

GUTENBERG BIBLE PUBLISHED: ANNIVERSARY. Sept 30, 1452. The first section of the Gutenberg Bible, the first book printed from movable type, was published at Mainz, Germany. Johann Gutenberg was the printer. The book was completed by 1456.

INTERNATIONAL TRANSLATION DAY. Sept 30. Sept 30 is the Feast of St. Jerome, the Bible translator who is considered the patron saint of translators. The International Federation of Translators (FIT) has promoted International Translation Day since it was set up in 1953 to show solidarity with the worldwide translation community in an effort to promote the translation profession. Annually, Sept 30.

KERR, DEBORAH: BIRTH ANNIVERSARY. Sept 30, 1921. Film actress born at Helensburgh, Dunbartonshire, Scotland, she starred in such classics as *The King and I, From Here to Eternity* and *An Affair to Remember*. She was nominated for six Oscars, holding the record for most nominations without a win, but she did receive a Lifetime Achievement Award in 1994. She died at Suffolk, England, Oct 16, 2007.

MEREDITH ENROLLS AT OLE MISS: ANNIVERSARY. Sept 30, 1962. Rioting broke out when James Meredith became the first African American to enroll in the all-white University of Mississippi. President Kennedy sent US troops to the area to force compliance with the law. Three people died in the fighting and 50 were injured.

On June 6, 1966, Meredith was shot while participating in a civil rights march at Mississippi. On June 25, Meredith, barely recovered, rejoined the marchers near Jackson, MS.

MERWIN, W.S.: BIRTH ANNIVERSARY. Sept 30, 1927. Born William Stanley Merwin at New York, NY, he was one of his era's most admired poets. Known for his oeuvre's exploration of man's relationship with politics and nature, Merwin is also renowned for his prolific translations, including of Dante's *Purgatorio, Sir Gawain and the Green Knight* and the work of Chilean poet Pablo Neruda. Winner of numerous awards, including two Pulitzers (for *The Carrier of Ladders*, 1971, and *The Shadow of Sirius*, 2009) and the National Book Award, Poetry (2005), and twice named US Poet Laureate (jointly with Rita Dove and Louise Gluck, 1999–2000; 2010–11), he died Mar 15, 2019, at Haiku-Pauwela, HI.

"MURDER, SHE WROTE" TV PREMIERE: ANNIVERSARY. Sept 30, 1984. Angela Lansbury starred as crime novelist Jessica Fletcher from Cabot Cove, Maine, who traveled the country solving murders. This top-rated detective show also featured Tom Bosley as Sheriff Amos Tupper and William Windom as Dr. Seth Hazlett. The program aired for 12 years and is still in syndication.

SAINT JEROME: FEAST DAY. Sept 30. Doctor of the Church, biblical scholar, priest, desert ascetic, born Eusebius Hieronymus at Strido, Dalmatia, around AD 342. Died at Bethlehem, Sept 30, 420. Undertook a revision and translation (from Hebrew and Greek) of the Bible (382–85, 390–404), now known as the Vulgate. Patron saint of librarians, translators and archivists.

WIESEL, ELIEZER "ELIE" WIESEL: BIRTH ANNIVERSARY. Sept 30, 1928. Nobel laureate, Holocaust survivor, born at Sighet, Romania. Wiesel was part of an entire Jewish community taken to Auschwitz in 1943. Transferred to Buchenwald, where his father died, Wiesel was liberated in 1945 and settled in Paris, becoming a journalist. Encouraged by François Mauriac, he jettisoned a voluntary silence about the Holocaust, writing *Night* (1958), a first step in becoming a *force majeure* as a Holocaust witness, through lectures, teaching, journalism, novels and further memoirs. He spoke out against all persecution, calling for aid to Yugoslavian Muslims, Rwandan Tutsis, Cambodians and Kurds. He was honored with a Nobel Peace Prize in 1986. Speaking of all survivors, he said, "Our lives no longer belong to us alone; they belong to all those who need us desperately." Wiesel died July 2, 2016, at New York, NY.

WRIGLEY, WILLIAM, JR: BIRTH ANNIVERSARY. Sept 30, 1861. Born at Philadelphia, PA, Wrigley didn't invent chewing gum, but he did create the business empire that is synonymous with it. In 1892 he was actually selling baking soda and using chewing gum as a promotional giveaway when he realized that gum had more potential. So the Wm. Wrigley Jr Company introduced Juicy Fruit and Spearmint in 1893, and by 1910, Spearmint was the top gum in the country. Wrigley, who also owned the Chicago Cubs and is the namesake for the park where they still play, died on Jan 26, 1932, at Phoenix, AZ.

September	S	M	T	W	T	F	S
			1	2	3	4	5
2020	6	7	8	9	10	11	12
	13	14	15	16	17	18	19
	20	21	22	23	24	25	26
	27	28	29	30			

🧁 BIRTHDAYS TODAY

Deborah Allen, 67, singer, songwriter, born Memphis, TN, Sept 30, 1953.

Crystal Bernard, 56, actress ("Wings"), born Garland, TX, Sept 30, 1964.

Ta-Nehisi Coates, 45, journalist, author (*Between the World and Me*), born Baltimore, MD, Sept 30, 1975.

Marion Cotillard, 45, actress (Oscar for *La Vie en Rose*; *Allied, Midnight in Paris*), born Paris, France, Sept 30, 1975.

Angie Dickinson, 89, actress (Emmy for "Police Woman"; *Dressed to Kill*), born Angeline Brown at Kulm, ND, Sept 30, 1931.

Fran Drescher, 63, actress ("The Nanny," *Jack*), born Flushing, NY, Sept 30, 1957.

Jenna Elfman, 49, actress ("Dharma & Greg," "Townies"), born Los Angeles, CA, Sept 30, 1971.

Martina Hingis, 40, former tennis player, born Kosice, Slovakia, Sept 30, 1980.

Johnny Mathis, 85, singer, born Gilmer, TX, Sept 30, 1935.

Marilyn McCoo, 77, singer (Fifth Dimension), actress, born Jersey City, NJ, Sept 30, 1943.

Dominique Moceanu, 39, Olympic gymnast, born Hollywood, CA, Sept 30, 1981.

Téa Obreht, 35, author (*The Tiger's Wife*), born Belgrade, Yugoslavia (now Serbia), Sept 30, 1985.

Eric Stoltz, 59, actor (*The House of Mirth, Memphis Belle, Fast Times at Ridgemont High*), born Los Angeles, CA, Sept 30, 1961.

Victoria Tennant, 67, actress ("Winds of War," *All of Me, LA Story*), born London, England, Sept 30, 1953.

October 1 — Thursday

DAY 275   **91 REMAINING**

ADOPT-A-SHELTER-DOG MONTH. Oct 1–31. To promote the adoption of dogs from local shelters, the ASPCA sponsors this important observance. "Make Pet Adoption Your First Option®" is a message the organization promotes throughout the year in an effort to end the euthanasia of all adoptable animals. For info: ASPCA, 520 8th Ave, 7th Fl, New York, NY 10018. Phone: (212) 876-7700, ext 4655. E-mail: press@aspca.org. Web: www.aspca.org.

AMERICAN CHEESE MONTH. Oct 1–31. American Cheese Month is a celebration of North American artisan, specialty and farmstead cheeses, held in communities throughout North America. From "Meet the Cheesemaker" and "Farmers Market"–style events, to special cheese tastings and classes at creameries and cheese shops, to cheese-centric menus featured in restaurants and cafés, American Cheese Month is celebrated by cheese lovers in communities large and small. For info: American Cheese Society, 2696 S Colorado Blvd, Ste 570, Denver, CO 80222-5954. Phone: (720) 328-2788. E-mail: info@cheesesociety.org. Web: www.cheesesociety.org and www.americancheesemonth.org.

ANTIDEPRESSANT DEATH AWARENESS MONTH. Oct 1–31. A month to remember those who have been harmed or who have died as a result of taking antidepressants or at the hands of someone who was on antidepressants. An adverse reaction or death while taking any drug should be reported to the Food and Drug Administration at www.fda.gov/Safety/Medwatch or by calling (800) FDA-1088. For info: Ernest and Catherine Ryan, 9138 Legacy Ct, Temperance, MI 48182. Phone: (734) 847-2282.

BABE RUTH CALLS HIS SHOT?: ANNIVERSARY. Oct 1, 1932. In the fifth inning of game three of the 1932 World Series, with a count of two balls and two strikes and with hostile Cubs fans shouting epithets at him, Babe Ruth pointed to the center field bleachers in Chicago's Wrigley Field and followed up by hitting a soaring home run high above the very spot to which he had just gestured. With that homer Ruth squashed the Chicago Cubs' hopes of winning the game, and the Yankees went on to sweep the Series with four straight victories.

BAYOU HURRICANE: ANNIVERSARY. Oct 1–2, 1893. Approximately 2,000 persons died Oct 1–2, 1893, when the Louisiana Bayou country was submerged in a storm that raged from the Gulf of Mexico. The unexpected arrival of this storm caught thousands of residents off guard. The coast was swept by a 10–12-foot tidal wave.

BLACK SOX SCANDAL/1919 WORLD SERIES: ANNIVERSARY. Oct 1–9, 1919. The Cincinnati Reds defeated the Chicago White Sox five games to three in the 1919 World Series. But it was quickly revealed that some White Sox players conspired to lose the series in what became known as the Black Sox Scandal. Ultimately, eight players, including former hero "Shoeless Joe" Jackson, were banned from baseball for life.

BRAZIL: FESTIVAL OF PENHA. Oct 1–31. Rio de Janeiro. Pilgrimages, especially on Saturdays during October, to the Church of Our Lady of Penha, which is built on top of a rock, requiring a climb of 365 steps (representing the days of the year), or a ride in a car on an inclined plane (for children, invalids and aged), for those troubled and sick who seek hope or cure.

BREAST CANCER AWARENESS MONTH. Oct 1–31. Established in 1985 to raise awareness of breast cancer and to encourage early detection practices. The third Friday in October (Oct 16 in 2020)

is National Mammography Day. For info: American Cancer Society. Phone: (800) 227-2345. Web: www.cancer.org. Or Natl Cancer Institute. Phone: (800) 4-CANCER.

CARTER, JIMMY: BIRTHDAY. Oct 1, 1924. 39th president of the US (1977–81), Nobel Peace Prize recipient, born James Earl Carter, Jr, at Plains, GA.

CELEBRATING THE BILINGUAL CHILD MONTH. Oct 1–31. A month to recognize the many children who speak two or more languages and understand multiple cultures. These children connect our communities and can play a big part in improving global communications. For info: Anneke Forzani, Language Lizard, PO Box 421, Basking Ridge, NJ 07920. Phone: (888) 554-9273. Fax: (908) 762-4786. E-mail: info@LanguageLizard.com. Web: www.LanguageLizard.com.

CELIAC DISEASE AWARENESS MONTH. Oct 1–31. Observed since 1987, Celiac Disease Awareness Month is the perfect opportunity to get the word out: share something positive about the disease and the diet with friends and neighbors; meet with the manager of your local grocery store about the importance of the availability of gluten-free options; visit with clergy regarding the strict gluten-free diet, communion and church potlucks; and many more ways. For info: National Celiac Assn, 20 Pickerting St, Needham, MA 02492. Phone: (888) 4-CELIAC. E-mail: info@nationalceliac.org. Web: https://nationalceliac.org.

***CHASE'S CALENDAR OF EVENTS 2021* PUBLISHED.** Oct 1. The 2021 *Chase's* is now available. Buy the book or ebook through your favorite retailer or on our website at www.chases.com.

CHINA: MOON FESTIVAL OR MID-AUTUMN FESTIVAL. Oct 1. According to folk legend this day is the birthday of the earth god T'u-ti Kung. The festival indicates that the year's hard work in the fields will soon end with the harvest. People express gratitude to heaven as represented by the moon and to the earth as symbolized by the earth god for all good things from the preceding year. Special harvest foods are eaten, especially "moon cakes." Observed on the 15th day of the eighth month of the Chinese lunar calendar, this festival is called by different names in different places but is widely recognized throughout Asia, including Taiwan, Korea, Singapore and Hong Kong. Date here is for China; date in other countries may differ.

CHINA, PEOPLE'S REPUBLIC OF: NATIONAL DAY. Oct 1. Commemorates the founding of the People's Republic of China in 1949.

COLLINS, ALBERT: BIRTH ANNIVERSARY. Oct 1, 1932. Blues guitarist Albert Collins was born at Leona, TX. An exciting, improvisational musician, he won a Grammy for *Showdown!* (1985), which was recorded with blues guitarists Robert Cray and Johnny Copeland. He was inducted into the Blues Hall of Fame in 1989. He died Nov 24, 1993, at Las Vegas, NV.

CONTACT LENS SAFETY MONTH. Oct 1–31. Approximately 41 million US residents wear contact lenses. Prevent Blindness provides tips and information on how to obtain, use and care for contact lenses safely. For info: Prevent Blindness, 211 W Wacker Dr, Ste 1700, Chicago, IL 60606. Phone: (800) 331-2020. E-mail: info@preventblindness.org. Web: www.preventblindness.org.

"CYBERSPACE" COINED: *NEUROMANCER* PUBLISHED: ANNIVERSARY. Oct 1, 1984. The groundbreaking science fiction novel *Neuromancer*, by William Gibson, was published on this day and featured a word now commonplace in popular culture: *cyberspace*. The novel won the Hugo, Nebula and Philip K. Dick awards.

CYPRUS: INDEPENDENCE DAY: 60th ANNIVERSARY OF INDEPENDENCE. Oct 1. National holiday. Commemorates independence from Britain in 1960.

DOMESTIC VIOLENCE AWARENESS MONTH. Oct 1–31. Commemorated since 1987, this month attempts to raise awareness of efforts to end violence against women and their children. The Domestic Violence Awareness Month Project is a collaborative effort of the National Resource Center on Domestic Violence, Futures Without Violence, National Coalition Against Domestic Violence, National Domestic Violence Hotline and National Network to End Domestic Violence. For info: NCADV, One Broadway, Ste B210, Denver, CO 80203. Phone: (303) 839-1852. Web: www.ncadv.org.

DYSLEXIA AWARENESS MONTH. Oct 1–31. This month's activities seek to raise public awareness of the signs of dyslexia in adults and children. All across the United States association branches are holding special events ranging from webinars to panel discussions to promote dyslexia awareness. For info: International Dyslexia Assn, 40 York Rd, Ste 400, Baltimore, MD 21204-5202. Phone: (410) 296-0232. E-mail: info@dyslexiaida.org. Web: https://dyslexiaida.org.

EMOTIONAL INTELLIGENCE AWARENESS MONTH. Oct 1–31. Since 2006, a month to increase public awareness and understanding of both the harmful and helpful effects of emotions. During this month the Emotional Intelligence Institute provides a variety of activities for youths and adults and disseminates important knowledge about emotions to local communities. Schools, religious organizations and the media are encouraged to make emotional intelligence a subject of discussion and productive study during October. For info: Emotional Intelligence Institute. Phone: (330) 550-1274. E-mail: guardianship22@gmail.com. Web: www.e-ii.org.

FIREPUP®'S BIRTHDAY. Oct 1. Firepup spends his time teaching fire and burn prevention and life safety awareness to children and their parents in a fun-filled and nonthreatening manner. Materials are available through local fire departments. For info: Natl Fire Safety Council, Inc, PO Box 378, Michigan Center, MI 49254-0378. Phone: (517) 764-2811 or (800) 255-1082. Web: www.nfsc.org.

GAY AND LESBIAN HISTORY MONTH. Oct 1–31. October was selected to commemorate the first two lesbian and gay marches on Washington, DC, in October 1979 and 1987.

GERMAN-AMERICAN HERITAGE MONTH. Oct 1–31. A month celebrating America's German heritage. Numerous historical programs, museum and library exhibits, cultural events, genealogical workshops and more planned. For info: Dr. Don Heinrich Tolzmann, German-American Citizens League, 6829 Westin Ridge, Cleves, OH 45002. Phone: (513) 574-1741. E-mail: dhtolzmann@yahoo.com. Web: www.gacl.org.

GLOBAL DIVERSITY AWARENESS MONTH. Oct 1–31. Celebrating, promoting and appreciating the global diversity of our society. Also, a month to foster and further our understanding of the inherent value of all races, genders, nationalities, age groups, religions, sexual orientations, classes and physical disabilities. Annually, in October. For info: Carole Copeland Thomas, 6 Azel Rd, Lakeville, MA 02347. Phone: (508) 947-5755. E-mail: TellCarole@mac.com. Web: www.tellcarole.com.

GO HOG WILD—EAT COUNTRY HAM MONTH. Oct 1–31. Suuu-eee! It's not just a word; it's a state of mind. For more than 200 years, Americans have been curing and eating country ham. This custom of curing ham, which began in the state of Virginia during the mid-1700s, continues today from Georgia to Missouri and points in between. Discover the difference between "city ham" and "country ham" and get some great recipes to boot during Eat Country Ham Month. For info: Natl Country Ham Assn, PO Box 948, Conover, NC 28613. Phone: (828) 466-2760. E-mail: nationalcurers@bellsouth.net. Web: www.countryham.org.

HARRIS, RICHARD: 90th BIRTH ANNIVERSARY. Oct 1, 1930. Born at Limerick, Ireland, Richard Harris became known as a stage actor on the London theater scene in the 1950s. Although his first love was the stage, it was in films that he earned his highest degree of success. He was King Arthur in the acclaimed film version of *Camelot* (1967) and was twice nominated for Best Actor Oscars: for 1963's *This Sporting Life* and 1991's *The Field*. He portrayed headmaster Albus Dumbledore in the first two Harry Potter films in 2001 and 2002. He died Oct 25, 2002, at London, England.

HARRISON, CAROLINE LAVINIA SCOTT: BIRTH ANNIVERSARY. Oct 1, 1832. First wife of Benjamin Harrison, 23rd president of the US, born at Oxford, OH. Died at Washington, DC, Oct 25, 1892. She was the second first lady to die in the White House.

HARVEST MOON. Oct 1. So called because the full moon nearest the autumnal equinox extends the hours of light into the evening and helps the harvester with the long day's work.

HEALTH LITERACY MONTH. Oct 1–31. Health literacy is about communicating health information in ways others can understand. Join with health literacy advocates worldwide to raise awareness about the importance of understandable health information. For info: The Institute for Healthcare Advancement. E-mail: bscott@iha4health.org. Web: www.healthliteracymonth.org.

HOROWITZ, VLADIMIR: BIRTH ANNIVERSARY. Oct 1, 1904. Virtuoso pianist, born at Berdichev, Russia. Horowitz was widely hailed as one of the world's greatest pianists, renowned for his masterful technique. His debut was at Kiev in 1920, and at the age of 20 he played a series of 23 recitals at Leningrad, performing a total of more than 200 works with no duplications. He made his US debut in 1928 with the New York Philharmonic. He settled in the US in 1940 and became a citizen in 1944. His career swung full circle Apr 20, 1986, when he performed his first concert in his native Russia after a self-imposed absence of 60 years. He died Nov 5, 1989, at New York, NY.

***THE JOY OF SEX* PUBLISHED: ANNIVERSARY.** Oct 1, 1972. English publisher Mitchell Beazley released Dr. Alex Comfort's landmark book on this date. Published in the midst of the Western world's sexual revolution, *The Joy of Sex* was an immediate bestseller and to date has sold 12 million copies.

KENTUCKY APPLE FESTIVAL. Oct 1–3. Paintsville, KY. Apple blossom beauty pageants, country music show, arts and crafts, flea market, antique car show, Corvette show, Terrapin Trot, amusement rides and food booths. Est attendance: 50,000. For info: Kentucky Apple Festival, Inc, PO Box 1245, Paintsville, KY 41240-5245. Phone: (606) 789-4355 or (800) 542-5790. Web: www.kyapplefest.org.

KOREA: CHUSOK. Oct 1. Gala celebration by Koreans everywhere. Autumn harvest thanksgiving moon festival. Observed on 15th day of eighth lunar month (eighth full moon of lunar calendar) each year. Koreans pay homage to ancestors and express gratitude to guarding spirits for another year of rich crops. A time to visit tombs, leave food and prepare for the coming winter season. Traditional food is the "moon cake," made on the eve of Chusok, with rice, chestnuts and jujube fruits. Games, dancing and gift exchanges. Observed since Silla Dynasty (beginning of First Millennium).

LAS VEGAS SHOOTING: ANNIVERSARY. Oct 1, 2017. Late on Oct 1, 2017, a gunman opened fire on 22,000 country music fans at the open-air Route 91 Harvest festival in Las Vegas, NV. For 11 minutes, the 64-year old Nevadan fired two dozen legally obtained AK-15 and AK-10 assault rifles into the dense crowd across Las

Vegas Boulevard from his 32nd-floor suite at the Mandalay Bay Resort and Casino, before taking his own life in a methodically researched and executed mass shooting. The shooter had modified his semiautomatic weapons with unregulated "bump stock" accessories, transforming them into rapid-fire automatic guns able to shoot nine rounds per second. The massacre claimed the lives of 58 people and injured an additional 700—the deadliest in the United States.

LAWRENCE, JAMES: BIRTH ANNIVERSARY. Oct 1, 1781. Brilliant American naval officer, whose last battle was a defeat, but whose dying words became a most honored naval motto. Lawrence, born at Burlington, NJ, was captain of the *Chesapeake* when it engaged in a naval duel with HMS *Shannon* off Boston, MA, June 1, 1813. The *Chesapeake* was captured and towed to Halifax, NS, Canada, as a British prize. Lawrence was mortally wounded by a musket ball during the engagement and uttered his famous last words, "Don't give up the ship," as he was being carried off the ship's deck.

LEVITTOWN OPENS: ANNIVERSARY. Oct 1, 1947. On this date the first residents moved into what would become Levittown at Long Island, NY. The community developed by William Levitt and his brother Alfred with their father, Abraham, started as affordable rental houses built for returning WWII veterans. In 1948 the Levitts began to sell the 800-square-foot homes for less than $8,000. By 1951, when this first community was finished, the Levitts had built 17,447 mass-produced Cape Cod and ranch homes. In 1952 they started construction on a new Levittown at Bucks County, PA, where they built another 17,000 houses, and beginning in 1958, they built 12,000 homes at Willingboro, NJ.

***LITTLE WOMEN* PUBLISHED: ANNIVERSARY.** Oct 1, 1868. Louisa May Alcott's beloved Civil War–era novel of Jo, Meg, Beth and Amy was published on this date to great immediate success. (Some sources say it was published Sept 30, 1868. First reviews appeared on Oct 10, 1868.)

MARIS BREAKS RUTH'S HOME RUN RECORD: ANNIVERSARY. Oct 1, 1961. Roger Maris of the New York Yankees hit his 61st home run, breaking Babe Ruth's record for the most home runs in a season. Maris hit his homer against pitcher Tracy Stallard of the Boston Red Sox as the Yankees won, 1–0. Controversy over the record arose because the American League had adopted a 162-game schedule in 1961, and Maris played in 161 games. In 1927, when Ruth set his record, the schedule called for 154 games, and Ruth played in 151. On Sept 8, 1998, Mark McGwire of the St. Louis Cardinals hit his 62nd home run, breaking Maris's record. On Oct 5, 2001, Barry Bonds of the San Francisco Giants broke McGwire's record.

MATTHAU, WALTER: 100th BIRTH ANNIVERSARY. Oct 1, 1920. The acclaimed actor of stage and screen was born in New York City. He won two Tony Awards—one as best actor in a play for his portrayal of slob Oscar Madison in *The Odd Couple* (1965), a role he repeated in the 1968 film. A frequent film collaborator was Jack Lemmon, first in Billy Wilder's *The Fortune Cookie* (1966), in which Matthau won the Best Supporting Actor Oscar

as "Whiplash Willie" Gingrich. Notable film work for Matthau included *Charade, Cactus Flower, Hello Dolly!, The Front Page, The Sunshine Boys, The Taking of Pelham One Two Three, The Bad News Bears, Grumpy Old Men* and *Kotch.* He died July 1, 2000, at Santa Monica, CA.

MODEL T INTRODUCED: ANNIVERSARY. Oct 1, 1908. Ford introduced the Model T at a price of $850, but by 1924 the basic model sold for as little as $260. Between 1908 and 1927, Ford sold 15,007,033 Model Ts in the US. Although the first Model Ts were not built on an assembly line, the demand for the cars was so high that Ford developed a system in which workers remained at their stations and cars came to them. This enabled Ford to turn out a Model T every 10 seconds.

MOON PHASE: FULL MOON. Oct 1. Moon enters Full Moon phase at 5:05 PM, EDT.

NATIONAL AUDIOLOGY AWARENESS MONTH/PROTECT YOUR HEARING MONTH. Oct 1–31. Nationwide celebration to promote audiology and the importance of hearing protection. More than 36 million American adults have some degree of hearing loss. The statistics are shocking and even more so knowing that more than half of those 36 million Americans are younger than age 65. Hearing loss is an increasing health concern in this nation and is often preventable. Taking time to see an audiologist for regular hearing screenings and knowing the signs of hearing loss can protect your hearing. For info: American Academy of Audiology, 11480 Commerce Park Dr, Ste 220, Reston, VA 20191. Phone: (703) 790-8466. Web: www.howsyourhearing.org/awareness.html.

★**NATIONAL BREAST CANCER AWARENESS MONTH.** Oct 1–31.

NATIONAL BULLYING PREVENTION AWARENESS MONTH. Oct 1–31. A month to observe bullying and cyber-bullying prevention awareness, with activities in schools and communities. Adults must empower the victims and help change the behavior of the bullies. Schools must react swiftly and redirect negative behaviors into positive and productive solutions. Bystanders who witness the assaults, harassment and threats must not remain silent. Parents must teach their kids and teens kindness, compassion and respect, and schools must do the same. Our kids and teens need to know they are valued and protected. For info: STOMP Out Bullying, 220 E 57th St, 9th Fl, Ste G, New York, NY 10022. Phone: (877) NO BULLY. E-mail: info@stompoutbullying.org. Web: www.stompoutbullying.org.

NATIONAL CHIROPRACTIC HEALTH MONTH. Oct 1–31. This annual month helps raise public awareness of the benefits of chiropractic care and its natural, whole-person, patient-centered approach to health and wellness. For info: American Chiropractic Assn, 1701 Clarendon Blvd, Ste 200, Arlington, VA 22209. Phone: (703) 276-8800. E-mail: communications@acatoday.org. Web: www.acatoday.org.

NATIONAL CRIME PREVENTION MONTH. Oct 1–31. During Crime Prevention Month, individuals can commit to working on at least one of three levels—family, neighborhood or community—to drive violence and drugs from our world. It is also a time to honor individuals who have accepted personal responsibility for their neighborhoods and groups who work for the community's common good. Annually, every October. For info: Natl Crime Prevention Council, 2614 Chapel Lake Dr, Ste B, Gambrills, MD 21054. Phone: (443) 292-4565. Web: www.ncpc.org/programs/crime-prevention-month.

★**NATIONAL CYBERSECURITY AWARENESS MONTH.** Oct 1–31. A month proclaimed annually to recognize the role we all play in ensuring our information and communications infrastructure is interoperable, secure, reliable and open to all. This month is observed with activities, events and training that enhance national security and resilience.

NATIONAL CYBERSECURITY AWARENESS MONTH. Oct 1–31. A national campaign focused on educating the American public, businesses, schools and government agencies about ways to secure their part of cyberspace, computers and our nation's critical infrastructure. The goal is to educate the everyday Internet user on

	S	M	T	W	T	F	S
October					1	2	3
	4	5	6	7	8	9	10
2020	11	12	13	14	15	16	17
	18	19	20	21	22	23	24
	25	26	27	28	29	30	31

how to "Protect Yourself Before You Connect Yourself," by taking simple and effective steps to safeguard one's computer from the latest online threats, offer ways to respond to potential cybercrime incidents and link how each person's cybersecurity affects securing our nation's critical infrastructure. For info: Natl Cyber Security Alliance. E-mail: info@staysafeonline.org. Web: www.staysafeonline.org.

NATIONAL DENTAL HYGIENE MONTH. Oct 1–31. To increase public awareness of the importance of preventive oral health care and the dental hygienist's role as the preventive professional. "Brush. Floss. Rinse. Chew." For info: American Dental Hygienists' Assn, 444 N Michigan Ave, Ste 400, Chicago, IL 60611. Phone: (312) 440-8900. E-mail: annl@adha.net. Web: www.adha.org.

NATIONAL DEPRESSION EDUCATION AND AWARENESS MONTH. Oct 1–31. A nonprofit campaign to educate patients, the elderly, consumers and professionals about depression disorders. Annually, the month of October. Sponsored by the American College of Apothecaries (ACA)/Pharmacists Planning Service, Inc (PPSI). For info: ACA/PPSI, 2830 Summer Oaks Dr, Bartlett, TN 38134. E-mail: info@ppsinc.org. Web: www.ppsinc.org.

★**NATIONAL DISABILITY EMPLOYMENT AWARENESS MONTH.** Oct 1–31. Presidential Proclamation issued for the month of October (PL 100–630, Title III, Sec 301a, of Nov 7, 1988). Previously issued as "National Employ the Handicapped Week" for a week beginning during the first week in October since 1945.

NATIONAL DISABILITY EMPLOYMENT AWARENESS MONTH. Oct 1–31. Held each October, National Disability Employment Awareness Month (NDEAM) is a national campaign that raises awareness about disability employment issues and celebrates the many contributions of America's workers with disabilities. NDEAM's roots go back to 1945, when Congress enacted a law declaring the first week in October each year "National Employ the Physically Handicapped Week." In 1962 the word *physically* was removed to acknowledge the employment needs and contributions of individuals with all types of disabilities. In 1988 Congress expanded the week to a month. For info: Office of Disability Employment Policy, US Dept of Labor, 200 Constitution Ave NW, Washington, DC 20210. Phone: (866) 633-7365. E-mail: odep@dol.gov. Web: www.dol.gov/odep/topics/ndeam.

★**NATIONAL DOMESTIC VIOLENCE AWARENESS MONTH.** Oct 1–31.

NATIONAL DOWN SYNDROME AWARENESS MONTH. Oct 1–31. As the national advocate for the value, acceptance and inclusion of people with Down syndrome, NDSS highlights and showcases different ways for the public to get involved in our organization, interact with our talented NDSS staff and support the Down syndrome community through awareness and advocacy. For info: Natl Down Syndrome Society, 8 E 41st St, 8th Fl, New York, NY 10017. Phone: (800) 221-4602. E-mail: info@ndss.org. Web: www.ndss.org.

NATIONAL LIVER AWARENESS MONTH. Oct 1–31. To increase understanding of the importance of liver health and wellness, to promote healthful practices and to encourage research into the causes and cures of liver diseases, including hepatitis. For info: American Liver Foundation, 39 Broadway, Ste 2700, New York, NY 10006. E-mail: info@liverfoundation.org. Web: www.liverfoundation.org.

NATIONAL MEDICAL LIBRARIANS MONTH. Oct 1–31. Recognizes and celebrates the importance and the achievements of health

sciences information professionals. Medical librarians offer efficient access to quality print and online medical and health-related information within a wide variety of healthcare settings. Librarians representing 22 specialty groups and 13 regional chapters of the Medical Library Association (MLA) sponsor several events and educational opportunities throughout the month of October. For info: Medical Library Assn. Phone: (312) 419-9094. E-mail: gunn@mail.mlahq.org. Web: www.mlanet.org.

NATIONAL OLD-TIME MUSIC FESTIVAL & EXPO. Oct 1–4. Christensen Field House, Fremont, NE. 45th annual. Old-time music fans come from around the world to hear their favorites. Also many arts and crafts displays, other musical entertainment and food booths. Est attendance: 50,000. For info: Natl Old-Time Music Festival & Expo, PO Box 492, Anita, IA 50020. Phone: (712) 762-4363. E-mail: bobeverhart@yahoo.com. Web: www.music-savers.com.

NATIONAL PHYSICAL THERAPY MONTH. Oct 1–31. To increase awareness of the role of the physical therapist as the expert in restoring and improving motion in people's lives. Thousands of physical therapists, physical therapist assistants and physical therapy students nationwide celebrate by hosting special activities in their communities. For info: American Physical Therapy Assn. Web: www.MoveForwardPT.com.

NATIONAL POLISH-AMERICAN HERITAGE MONTH. Oct 1–31. A national celebration of Polish history, culture and pride. For info: Michael Blichasz, Chair, Polish American Cultural Center, Natl HQ, 308 Walnut St, Philadelphia, PA 19106. Phone: (215) 922-1700. Fax: (215) 922-1518. E-mail: mail@polishamericancenter.com. Web: www.polishamericancenter.com.

NATIONAL POPCORN POPPIN' MONTH. Oct 1–31. October is National Popcorn Poppin' Month, a harvest-time celebration of one of America's oldest snack foods. As farmers head into the fields to gather crops, families and friends gather to honor this ever popular treat, and with good reason. For info: The Popcorn Board, 330 N Wabash Ave, Ste 2000, Chicago, IL 60611. Phone: (312) 644-6610. E-mail: info@popcorn.org. Web: www.popcorn.org.

NATIONAL READING GROUP MONTH. Oct 1–31. Reading group members celebrate the joy of shared reading and inspire individuals who do not belong to a reading group to join one or start their own. Organizations, bookstores and libraries are encouraged to sponsor reading group events during this month. Signature event hosted by one designated chapter of the Women's National Book Association (11 chapters nationwide). For info: Jill A. Tardiff, Women's Natl Book Assn, 625 Madison St, Ste B, Hoboken, NJ 07030. E-mail: jill.tardiff@gmail.com or nationalreadinggroupmonth@gmail.com. Web: www.nationalreadinggroupmonth.org.

NATIONAL ROLLER SKATING MONTH. Oct 1–31. A monthlong celebration at thousands of roller skating rinks nationwide recognizing the health and fitness benefits, as well as the recreational enjoyment, of the long-loved pastime of roller skating. Parents are encouraged to sign up for the year-round Kids Skate Free program at www.kidsskatefree.com to receive two free passes for up to four children every week at their local participating roller skating rink. Contact the Roller Skating Association International for fitness information, infographics and facts on all things roller skating. For info: Roller Skating Assn International, 6905 Corporate Dr, Indianapolis, IN 46278. Phone: (317) 347-2626. E-mail: pr@rollerskating.com. Web: www.rollerskating.org.

NATIONAL SEAFOOD MONTH. Oct 1–31. To promote the taste, variety and nutrition of fish and shellfish. For info: Natl Fisheries Institute, 7918 Jones Branch Dr, Ste 700, McLean, VA 22102. Web: www.aboutseafood.com.

NATIONAL SPINA BIFIDA AWARENESS MONTH. Oct 1–31. Promoting public awareness of current scientific, medical and educational issues related to spina bifida—the most frequently occurring, permanently disabling birth defect. For info: Spina Bifida Assn, 1600 Wilson Blvd, Ste 800, Arlington, VA 22209. Phone: (800)

621-3141. E-mail: sbaa@sbaa.org. Web: www.spinabifidaassociation.org.

NATIONAL STAMP COLLECTING MONTH. Oct 1–31. Since 1981 the US Postal Service has designated the month of October as National Stamp Collecting Month (NSCM). Developed to introduce children aged 8–12 to this popular and educational hobby, the NSCM program is also intended to raise awareness about the recreational benefits of stamp collecting among all age groups. The Postal Service traditionally kicks off NSCM by issuing new commemorative stamps in late September or early October. For info and educational kits: US Postal Service. Web: www.usps.com.

NATIONAL STOP BULLYING MONTH. Oct 1–31. The bullying and suicide prevention international nonprofit organization Hey U.G.L.Y. (Unique Gifted Lovable You) has designated the month of October as a time for schools across America to conduct bullying prevention classroom activities and school assembly presentations on how to eradicate bullying from schools and neighborhoods. For info: Hey U.G.L.Y., Inc, PO Box 2142, Michigan City, IN 46361. Phone: (219) 814-4224. E-mail: preventbullyingnow@heyugly.org. Web: www.heyugly.org and www.preventbullyingnow.org.

NATIONAL WORK AND FAMILY MONTH. Oct 1–31. On Sept 5, 2003, US Senate Resolution 210 was passed designating October as National Work and Family Month. The resolution expressed "the sense of the Senate that supporting a balance between work and personal life is in the best interest of national worker productivity" and that reducing any conflict between the two "should be a national priority."

NIGERIA: INDEPENDENCE DAY: 60th ANNIVERSARY OF INDEPENDENCE. Oct 1. National holiday. Became independent of Great Britain in 1960 and a republic in 1963.

***NIGHT OF THE LIVING DEAD* RELEASED: ANNIVERSARY.** Oct 1, 1968. George A. Romero's low-budget horror film of rampaging, cannibalistic zombies was released on this date. It quickly became a cult favorite and influenced many other horror filmmakers.

NORWAY: PAGEANTRY IN OSLO. Oct 1. Oslo. The Storting (Norway's parliament) convenes on the first weekday in October, when it decides the date for the ceremonial opening of the Storting—usually the following weekday—and the parliamentary session is then opened by King Harald V in the presence of Corps Diplomatique, preceded and followed by a military procession between the Royal Palace and the Storting.

ORGANIZE YOUR MEDICAL INFORMATION MONTH. Oct 1–31. This month is dedicated to learning how to acquire, understand, utilize and store pertinent medical information and knowledge, enabling each of us to become a more informed and active participant in our own medical care. This organization leads to fewer medical errors, shorter hospital stays, increased positive outcomes, the motivation to seek preventive care and the skills to negotiate the healthcare system. For info: Lynda Shrager. Phone: (518) 368-0322. E-mail: LShrager@otherwisehealthy.com.

POSITIVE ATTITUDE MONTH. Oct 1–31. Sometimes it just comes down to attitude! Zig Ziglar says that attitude, more than aptitude, affects altitude. Keith Harrell says attitude is everything. "Atta-tude" is a self-reflection of your own attitude. This month is dedicated to establishing, boosting or recommitting ourselves to adopting positive attitudes and discovering and/or creating positive self-images. For info: Sylvia Henderson, 3570 Olney-Laytonsville Rd, Ste 588, Olney, MD 20832. Phone: (301) 260-1538. E-mail: sylvia@springboardtraining.com. Web: www.ideasuccess-network.com.

REHNQUIST, WILLIAM HUBBS: BIRTH ANNIVERSARY. Oct 1, 1924. Born at Milwaukee, WI, William Hubbs Rehnquist earned master's degrees in political science and government before finishing Stanford Law School in 1952. He was serving as counsel in the Nixon White House when he was nominated to the US Supreme Court as associate justice in 1971. As the most conservative member of the court, he was a staunch supporter of states' rights and wrote a dissent to 1973's *Roe v Wade* decision. President Reagan nominated him as chief justice upon the retirement of Warren Burger, and he assumed that position on Sept 26, 1986. He presided over the impeachment hearing of President Clinton and ruled on *Bush v Gore* (2000), which awarded the presidential election to George W. Bush following controversial ballot miscounting in Florida. Rehnquist died Sept 3, 2005, at Arlington, VA.

RETT SYNDROME AWARENESS MONTH. Oct 1–31. Rett syndrome is a genetic neurological disorder that occurs almost exclusively in females—occurring worldwide in 1 of every 10,000 female births. Rett syndrome becomes apparent after 6–18 months of early normal development. It results in a regression that leads to lifelong impairments. It is often misdiagnosed as autism or cerebral palsy and has no cure. For info: Intl Rett Syndrome Foundation, 4600 Devitt Dr, Cincinnati, OH 45246. Phone: (800) 818-7388. E-mail: admin@rettsyndrome.org. Web: www.rettsyndrome.org.

SHAW, ROBERT GOULD: BIRTH ANNIVERSARY. Oct 1, 1837. Colonel in the Union army who led the country's first all-black regiment, the Massachusetts 54th. Born in Boston, MA, to prominent abolitionist parents, Shaw studied at Harvard before joining the fight against the Confederacy. He saw action with the Seventh New York Infantry and the Second Massachusetts and was wounded at Antietam before being given command of the 54th and mustering its more than 600 soldiers from free blacks all over the North. Shaw was killed in action on July 18, 1863, during an assault on Confederate positions at Fort Wagner on Morris Island, SC.

SOUTH KOREA: ARMED FORCES DAY. Oct 1. Marked by many colorful military parades, aerial acrobatics and honor guard ceremonies, held around the reviewing plaza at Yoido, an island in the Han River.

SQUIRREL AWARENESS AND APPRECIATION MONTH. Oct 1–31. Set aside to honor one of our friendliest forms of wildlife: squirrels. Annually, the month of October. For info: Janet Allgood, The Squirrel Lover's Club, PO Box 2701, Lower Burrell, PA 15068. Phone: (724) 335-2693. E-mail: squirrelcentralok@gmail.com. Web: www.thesquirreloversclub.com.

STOCKTON, RICHARD: BIRTH ANNIVERSARY. Oct 1, 1730. Lawyer and signer of the Declaration of Independence, born at Princeton, NJ. Died there Feb 8, 1781.

TEEN SERVICES MONTH. Oct 1–31. For 2020, the American Library Association is combining Teen Read Week and Teen Tech Week to create a monthlong celebration of teen programming and teen services in libraries across the country. The celebration includes displays, passive activities, and programming for public libraries, school libraries and beyond. Teen Services Month will be held in October of every year. For info: Young Adult Library Services Assn, American Library Assn, 50 E Huron St, Chicago, IL 60611. Phone: (800) 545-2433, ext 4390. E-mail: yalsa@ala.org.

"THIS IS YOUR LIFE" TV PREMIERE: ANNIVERSARY. Oct 1, 1952. Ralph Edwards hosted this program that lured unsuspecting

	S	M	T	W	T	F	S
October					1	2	3
	4	5	6	7	8	9	10
2020	11	12	13	14	15	16	17
	18	19	20	21	22	23	24
	25	26	27	28	29	30	31

guests onto the show and surprised them by detailing their lives and achievements with their family and friends. It began as a radio show in 1948.

TUVALU: NATIONAL HOLIDAY. Oct 1. Gained independence from Britain on this day in 1978.

UNITED KINGDOM: NATIONAL POETRY DAY. Oct 1. Founded in 1994 by William Sieghart, this annual day is a mass celebration of poetry and all things poetical. Celebrated all over the United Kingdom with readings and special events. Annually, the first Thursday in October. For info: Forward Arts Foundation, c/o The Royal Society of Literature, Somerset House, Strand, London WC2R 1LA, United Kingdom. Web: www.forwardartsfoundation. org/national-poetry-day.

UNITED NATIONS: INTERNATIONAL DAY OF OLDER PERSONS. Oct 1. Designated by the General Assembly on Dec 14, 1990 (originally "International Day for the Elderly," the name was changed on Dec 21, 1995). A day to encourage all societies to better integrate aging issues into the larger context of development. States are encouraged to do everything in their power to enable all men and women to age with security and dignity. For info: United Nations, Dept of Public Info, Public Inquiries Unit, Rm GA-57, New York, NY 10017. Phone: (212) 963-4475. E-mail: inquiries@un.org. Web: www.un.org.

US 2021 FEDERAL FISCAL YEAR BEGINS. Oct 1, 2020–Sept 30, 2021.

VEGETARIAN AWARENESS MONTH. Oct 1–31. A month to advance the awareness of the many surprising ethical, environmental, economic, health, humanitarian and other benefits of the increasingly popular vegetarian lifestyle. Observed by many vegetarian groups.

WORKPLACE POLITICS AWARENESS MONTH. Oct 1–31. Workplace politics may seem to be a moral morass and a colossal waste of time. Many of us try to avoid participating, but too often, we seem to be inevitably drawn in. This month is designed to increase awareness that trying to avoid workplace politics is futile—instead we can learn to deal with the situation. For info: Richard Brenner, Chaco Canyon Consulting, 2455 Eaton Rd, University Heights, OH 44118. Phone: (650) 787-6475. E-mail: rbrenner@ChacoCanyon.com.

WORLD MENOPAUSE MONTH. Oct 1–31. The International Menopause Society, in collaboration with the World Health Organization, has designated Oct 18 as World Menopause Day. In observation of the day, the IMS and the member national societies of the Council of Affiliated Menopause Societies distribute materials and organize activities to inform women about menopause, its management and the impact of estrogen loss. Since it is not always possible for local societies to arrange activities for this specific day, the IMS has also designated October as World Menopause Month. Local societies can also collaborate with other organizations working in the field of adult women's health, such as societies for osteoporosis and breast cancer, to organize joint events. For info: Intl Menopause Society. Web: www.imsociety.org.

WORLD VEGETARIAN DAY. Oct 1. Celebration of vegetarianism's benefits to humans, animals and our planet. In addition to individuals, participants include libraries, schools, colleges, restaurants, food service providers, healthcare centers, health food stores and workplaces. For info: North American Vegetarian Society, PO Box 72, Dolgeville, NY 13329. Phone: (518) 568-7970. Fax: (518) 568-7979. E-mail: navs@telenet.net. Web: www.worldvegetarianday.org.

YOSEMITE NATIONAL PARK ESTABLISHED: ANNIVERSARY. Oct 1, 1890. Yosemite Valley and Mariposa Big Tree Grove, granted to the state of California June 30, 1864, were combined and established as a national park. For info: Yosemite Natl Park, PO Box 577, Yosemite Natl Park, CA 95389.

🎂 BIRTHDAYS TODAY

Julie Andrews, 85, singer, actress (Emmy for "The Julie Andrews Hour"; Oscar for *Mary Poppins*), born Julia Wells at Walton-on-Thames, England, Oct 1, 1935.

Rodney Cline (Rod) Carew, 75, Hall of Fame baseball player, born Gatun, Panama Canal Zone, Oct 1, 1945.

Jimmy Carter, 96, 39th president of the US, born James Earl Carter, Jr, at Plains, GA, Oct 1, 1924.

Stephen Collins, 73, actor ("7th Heaven," *All the President's Men*), born Des Moines, IA, Oct 1, 1947.

Sarah Drew, 40, actress ("Grey's Anatomy," "Everwood"), born Charlottesville, VA, Oct 1, 1980.

Zach Galifianakis, 51, comedian, actor (*The Hangover*, "Bored to Death"), born Wilkesboro, NC, Oct 1, 1969.

Gina Haspel, 64, Director of the Central Intelligence Agency, intelligence officer, born Gina Walker at Ashland, KY, Oct 1, 1956.

Gus Kenworthy, 29, Olympic freestyle skier, born Chelmsford, England, Oct 1, 1991.

Brie Larson, 31, actress (Oscar for *Room*; *Kong*, "United States of Tara"), singer, born Brianne Sidonie Desaulniers at Sacramento, CA, Oct 1, 1989.

Theresa May, 64, former prime minister of the United Kingdom (2016–19), born Theresa Brasier at Eastbourne, England, Oct 1, 1956.

Mark McGwire, 57, former baseball player, born Pomona, CA, Oct 1, 1963.

Esai Morales, 58, actor ("American Family," "NYPD Blue"), born Brooklyn, NY, Oct 1, 1962.

Tim O'Brien, 74, author (*In the Lake of the Woods*, *Going After Cacciato*), born Austin, MN, Oct 1, 1946.

Johnny Oduya, 39, hockey player, born Stockholm, Sweden, Oct 1, 1981.

Randy Quaid, 70, actor (*Brokeback Mountain*, *Independence Day*, *The Last Picture Show*), born Houston, TX, Oct 1, 1950.

Stella Stevens, 84, actress ("Ben Casey," "Flamingo Road"), born Hot Coffee, MS, Oct 1, 1936.

Grete Waitz, 67, marathoner, born Oslo, Norway, Oct 1, 1953.

George Weah, 54, President of Liberia, former soccer player (1995 FIFA World Player of the Year), born Monrovia, Liberia, Oct 1, 1966.

October 2 — Friday

DAY 276   **90 REMAINING**

"ALFRED HITCHCOCK PRESENTS" TV PREMIERE: 65th ANNIVERSARY. Oct 2, 1955. Alfred Hitchcock was already an acclaimed director when he began hosting this mystery anthology series that aired on CBS and NBC for 10 years. Each episode began with an introduction by Hitchcock, the man with the world's most recognized profile. Hitchcock directed about 22 episodes of the series; Robert Altman also directed. Among the many stars who appeared on the show were Barbara Bel Geddes, Brian Keith, Gena Rowlands, Dick York, Cloris Leachman, Joanne Woodward, Steve McQueen, Peter Lorre, Dick Van Dyke, Robert Redford and Katherine Ross.

ARIZONA STATE FAIR. Oct 2–25 (tentative). Phoenix, AZ. Since 1905, the Arizona State Fair has been a gathering place for residents from the far corners of the state. Festival, carnival, concerts, entertainment and food. Closed Mondays and Tuesdays. For info: Arizona State Fair, 1826 W McDowell Rd, Phoenix, AZ 85007. Phone: (602) 252-6771. E-mail: info@azstatefair.com. Web: www.azstatefair.com.

GANDHI, MOHANDAS KARAMCHAND (MAHATMA): BIRTH ANNIVERSARY. Oct 2, 1869. The Indian political and spiritual leader who achieved world honor and fame for his advocacy of nonviolent resistance as a weapon against tyranny was born at Porbandar, India. He was assassinated in the garden of his home at New Delhi, Jan 30, 1948. On the anniversary of Gandhi's birth (Gandhi Jayanti) thousands gather at the park on the Jumna River at Delhi where Gandhi's body was cremated. Hymns are sung; verses from the Gita, the Koran and the Bible are recited; and cotton thread is spun on small spinning wheels (one of Gandhi's favorite activities). Other observances are held at his birthplace and throughout India on this public holiday.

GREENE, GRAHAM: BIRTH ANNIVERSARY. Oct 2, 1904. British author Graham Greene was born at Berkhamsted, Hertfordshire, England. He centered his works around characters facing salvation and damnation in a world of chaos, often with complex Catholic settings. His works include *The Power and the Glory* (1940) and *The Third Man* (1950). He died Apr 3, 1991, at Vevey, Switzerland.

GUARDIAN ANGELS DAY. Oct 2. We all have guardian angels. Now's the time to give them recognition and thanks for being in our lives with their own day. Take the time today to find out how they've played a unique role in our lives, as well as in various cultures, religions and even foods. Celebrate today by doing something special to recognize their qualities. Annually, Oct 2. For info: Lorrie Walters Marsiglio, PO Box 284-CC, Wasco, IL 60183-0284.

GUINEA: INDEPENDENCE DAY. Oct 2. National Day. Guinea gained independence from France in 1958.

GUNN, MOSES: BIRTH ANNIVERSARY. Oct 2, 1929. The 1981 winner of the NAACP Image Award for his performance as Booker T. Washington in the film *Ragtime* was born at St. Louis, MO. His appearances on stage ranged from the title role in *Othello* to Jean Genet's *The Blacks*. He received an Emmy nomination for his role in *Roots* and was awarded several Obies for off-Broadway performances. On film he appeared in *Shaft* and *The Great White Hope*. He died Dec 17, 1993, at Guilford, CT.

HULL, CORDELL: BIRTH ANNIVERSARY. Oct 2, 1871. American statesman who served in both houses of Congress and as secretary of state, born at Pickett County, TN. Noted for his contributions to the "Good Neighbor" policies of the US with regard to countries of the Americas and to the establishment of the United Nations. Recipient of the 1945 Nobel Prize for Peace. Hull died at Bethesda, MD, July 23, 1955.

KIDS MUSIC DAY. Oct 2. 5th annual. Kids Music Day celebrates the importance of including music in every child's education.

October 2020	S	M	T	W	T	F	S
					1	2	3
	4	5	6	7	8	9	10
	11	12	13	14	15	16	17
	18	19	20	21	22	23	24
	25	26	27	28	29	30	31

Keep Music Alive partners with music schools and public/private schools in the US and around the world to hold celebratory events, including open houses, student music performances and instrument donation drives. Annually, the first Friday in October. For info: Vincent James, Keep Music Alive, PO Box 1299, Brookhaven, PA 19015. E-mail: vincent@keepmusicalive.org. Web: www.KidsMusicDay.org.

MARSHALL, THURGOOD: SWORN IN TO SUPREME COURT: ANNIVERSARY. Oct 2, 1967. Thurgood Marshall was sworn in as the first black associate justice to the US Supreme Court. On June 27, 1991, he announced his resignation, effective upon the confirmation of his successor. See also: "Marshall, Thurgood: Birth Anniversary" (July 2).

MARX, GROUCHO: BIRTH ANNIVERSARY. Oct 2, 1890. Born Julius Henry Marx at New York, NY. Comedian who along with his brothers constituted the famous Marx Brothers. The Marx Brothers began as a singing group and then acted in such movies as *Duck Soup* and *Animal Crackers*. During the '40s and '50s, Groucho was the host of the television and radio show "You Bet Your Life." Died at Los Angeles, CA, Aug 19, 1977.

NATIONAL CUSTODIAL WORKERS DAY. Oct 2. A day to honor all janitorial and custodial workers—those who clean up after us. Annually, Oct 2. For info: Bette Tadajewski, All Saints Parish, 817 Sable St, Alpena, MI 49707. Phone: (989) 354-3019.

NATIONAL DIVERSITY DAY. Oct 2. A day to celebrate and embrace who we are, despite our differences, no matter what race, religion, gender, sexual orientation, age, nationality or disability. A day to reflect on and learn about different cultures and ideologies. A day to vow to uphold acceptance and tolerance. A day to consciously address these areas at educational and religious institutions, as well as in the workplace and at home. Our slogan: "Embrace diversity, embrace our world." Annually, the first Friday in October. For info: Dr. Leo Parvis. Phone: (612) 386-7102. E-mail: drparvis@gmail.com. Web: www.nationaldiversityday.com.

"PEANUTS" DEBUTS: 70th ANNIVERSARY. Oct 2, 1950. This comic strip by Charles Schulz featured Charlie Brown, Lucy, Linus, Sally and Charlie's dog, Snoopy. The last new "Peanuts" strip was published Feb 13, 2000.

RAYMOND, ALEX: BIRTH ANNIVERSARY. Oct 2, 1909. This influential comic strip artist, born at New Rochelle, NY, created the science fiction strip "Flash Gordon" (1934). The strip's huge popularity led to Hollywood serials starring Buster Crabbe a few years later. Raymond also created "Secret Agent X-9" and "Rip Kirby," but his career was cut short by a fatal automobile accident on Sept 6, 1956, at Westport, CT.

STREETER, RUTH CHENEY: 125th BIRTH ANNIVERSARY. Oct 2, 1895. Born at Brookline, MA, Ruth Cheney Streeter was the first director of the US Marine Corps Women's Reserve. She was active in unemployment relief, public health, welfare and old-age assistance in New Jersey during the 1930s. A student of aeronautics, she learned to fly while serving as an adjutant of a flight group in the Civil Air Patrol during the early years of WWII. She died Sept 30, 1990, at Morristown, NJ.

SUKKOT BEGINS AT SUNDOWN. Oct 2. Jewish Feast of Tabernacles. See "Sukkot" (Oct 3).

"THE TWILIGHT ZONE" TV PREMIERE: ANNIVERSARY. Oct 2, 1959. "The Twilight Zone" went on the air with these now-familiar words: "There is a fifth dimension, beyond that which is known to man. It is a dimension as vast as space and as timeless as infinity. It is the middle ground between light and shadow, between science and superstition, and it lies between the pit of man's fear and the summit of his knowledge. This is the dimension of imagination. It is an area which we call The Twilight Zone." The anthology program ran five seasons for 154 installments, with a one-year hiatus between the third and fourth seasons. Created and hosted by Rod Serling, it is now considered to have been one of the best dramas to appear on television. The last original episode was telecast June 15, 1964.

UNITED NATIONS: INTERNATIONAL DAY OF NONVIOLENCE. Oct 2. Reaffirming the universal relevance of the principle of nonviolence, and desiring to secure a culture of peace, tolerance, understanding and nonviolence, on June 15, 2007, the General Assembly declared this day to be observed annually on Oct 2 (Res 61/271), the anniversary of Mahatma Gandhi's birth. For info: United Nations, Dept of Public Info, New York, NY, 10017. Web: www.un.org.

WORLD DAY FOR FARMED ANIMALS. Oct 2. Celebrated on Gandhi's birthday. To expose and memorialize the needless suffering and death of billions of innocent, sentient animals in factory farms and slaughterhouses. Local actions include memorial services, vigils, street theater, picketing, leafleting and information tables. For info: Farm Animal Rights Movement, 10101 Ashburton Ln, Bethesda, MD 20817. Phone: (888) FARM-USA. E-mail: info@farmusa.org. Web: www.dayforanimals.org or www.farmusa.org.

WORLD SMILE DAY. Oct 2. A day dedicated to good works and good cheer throughout the world. The official theme for the day is "Do an act of kindness. Help one person smile." The symbol for the day is the world-famous "smiley face" icon, created in 1963 by Harvey Ball of Worcester, MA. This icon is now the international symbol of happiness and goodwill. Annually, the first Friday in October. For info: Charles P. Ball, President, World Smile Corp, 390 Main St, Ste 528, Worcester, MA 01608. Web: www.worldsmileday.com.

BIRTHDAYS TODAY

Lorraine Bracco, 65, actress ("The Sopranos," *Goodfellas*), born Brooklyn, NY, Oct 2, 1955.

Donna Karan, 72, fashion designer, born Forest Hills, NY, Oct 2, 1948.

Annie Leibovitz, 71, photographer, born Waterbury, CT, Oct 2, 1949.

Don McLean, 75, singer, songwriter, born New Rochelle, NY, Oct 2, 1945.

Rex Reed, 81, movie critic, born Fort Worth, TX, Oct 2, 1939.

Kelly Ripa, 50, television host ("Live! with Kelly & Ryan"), actress ("Hope and Faith," "All My Children"), born Stratford, NJ, Oct 2, 1970.

Sting, 69, singer, songwriter, actor (*Dune*), born Gordon Sumner at London, England, Oct 2, 1951.

Paul Teutul, Jr, 46, motorcycle designer, television personality ("American Chopper"), born Oct 2, 1974.

October 3 — Saturday

DAY 277	89 REMAINING

ALBUQUERQUE INTERNATIONAL BALLOON FIESTA. Oct 3–11. Balloon Fiesta Park, Albuquerque, NM. Held since 1972, the largest hot-air balloon gathering in the world features more than 550 hot-air and gas balloons, mass ascensions, balloon glows and specially shaped balloons. The nine-day event includes entries from more than 20 countries. Annually, the first through second weekends in October. For info: Albuquerque International Balloon Fiesta, Inc, 4401 Alameda NE, Albuquerque, NM 87113. Phone: (505) 821-1000 or (888) 422-7277. E-mail: balloons@balloonfiesta.com. Web: www.balloonfiesta.com.

"THE ANDY GRIFFITH SHOW" TV PREMIERE: 60th ANNIVERSARY. Oct 3, 1960. The first of 249 episodes aired on this date. Set in rural Mayberry, NC, the show starred Griffith as Sheriff Andy Taylor; Ron Howard as his son, Opie; Frances Bavier as Aunt Bee Taylor and Don Knotts as Deputy Barney Fife. The last telecast aired Sept 16, 1968.

BANCROFT, GEORGE: BIRTH ANNIVERSARY. Oct 3, 1800. American historian, known as "the father of American History," born at Worcester, MA. Died at Washington, DC, Jan 27, 1891.

BED & BREAKFAST, INN MASCOT DAY. Oct 3. A day to celebrate the furry (or feathery) mascots who support their innkeepers and amuse visitors. This day is observed along with Country Inn, Bed & Breakfast Day on the first Sunday in October to make a weekend celebration. From cozy gatherings to larger affairs, this event may include raffles, discussions, book signings, pet treats and more. (Before visiting, check with participating properties.) This day also celebrates the pets who sometimes lodge at inns. Annually, the first Saturday in October. For info: Dexter the Cat and Tina Czarnota, Country Inn, Bed and Breakfast Day. E-mail: tczarnot@bellsouth.net.

"CAPTAIN KANGAROO" TV PREMIERE: 65th ANNIVERSARY. Oct 3, 1955. On the air until 1985, this was the longest-running children's TV show until it was surpassed by "Sesame Street." Starring Bob Keeshan as Captain Kangaroo, it was broadcast on CBS and PBS. Other characters included Mr Green Jeans, Grandfather Clock, Bunny Rabbit, Mr Moose and Dancing Bear. Keeshan was an advocate for excellence in children's programming and even supervised which commercials would appear on the program. In 1997 "The All New Captain Kangaroo" debuted, starring John McDonough.

CHOWDERFEST. Oct 3–4. Bay Village, Beach Haven, NJ. Fans of Manhattan and New England chowders vote for their favorite recipes after sampling the entries of nearly 20 participating restaurants. The suspense is intense as each chef hopes to win and capture the trophy and bragging rights. Live music, a Merchants Mart featuring blowout bargains and an outdoor food court top off the festivities. For info: Southern Ocean County Chamber of Commerce, Chowderfest, 265 W 9th St, Ship Bottom, NJ 08008. Phone: (800) 292-6372. Web: www.chowderfest.com.

"THE DICK VAN DYKE SHOW" TV PREMIERE: ANNIVERSARY. Oct 3, 1961. This Carl Reiner–created sitcom wasn't an immediate success but soon became a hit. It starred Dick Van Dyke as Rob Petrie, a TV show writer, and Mary Tyler Moore as his wife, Laura, a former dancer. This was one of the first shows revolving around the goings-on at a TV series. Other cast members included Morey Amsterdam, Rose Marie, Richard Deacon, Carl Reiner, Jerry Paris, Ann Morgan Guilbert and Larry Matthews. The last episode aired Sept 7, 1966.

ELECTRA FALL CITYWIDE GARAGE SALE. Oct 3. Electra, TX. Sales throughout the Electra area. Chamber of Commerce will provide free coffee and maps at 7 AM. The Chamber of Commerce office will close at 8 AM so that staff, too, may enjoy all of the bargains. Est attendance: 2,000. For info: Sherry Strange, Electra Chamber of Commerce, 112 W Cleveland, Electra, TX 76360. Phone: (940) 495-3577. E-mail: electracoc@electratel.net. Web: www.electra-texas.org.

FIRST WOMAN US SENATOR: ANNIVERSARY. Oct 3, 1922. On this date Mrs W.H. (Rebecca) Felton, 87, of Cartersville, GA, was appointed by Governor Thomas Hardwick of Georgia to the Senate seat vacated by the death of Thomas E. Watson. It was a two-day ad interim appointment.

FRANCE: QATAR PRIX DE L'ARC TRIOMPHE. Oct 3–4 (subject to change). Longchamp Racecourse, Paris. 99th edition. One of the world's greatest horse races has been held since 1920. Up to 20 of the best entire horses and fillies aged three and above line up each year for the mile-and-a-half contest. Since 2008 and the signature of a five-year partnership with the Qatar Racing and Equestrian

Club, the "Arc" has become the richest thoroughbred race in the world, with a total purse of four million euros. More than one billion viewers in 30 countries. Annually, the first Saturday and Sunday in October. Est attendance: 60,000. For info: France Galop. E-mail: medias@france-galop.com. Web: www.parislongchamp.com/en/qatar-prix-de-larc-triomphe.

GERMAN REUNIFICATION: 30th ANNIVERSARY. Oct 3, 1990. After 45 years of division, East and West Germany reunited just four days short of East Germany's 41st founding anniversary (Oct 7, 1949). The new united Germany took the name the Federal Republic of Germany, the formal name of the former West Germany, and adopted the constitution of the former West Germany. Today is a national holiday in Germany, Tag der Deutschen Einheit (Day of German Unity).

GERMANY: DAY OF GERMAN UNITY. Oct 3. National Day, commemorates the day in 1990 when the German Democratic Republic acceded peacefully to the Federal Republic of Germany. Public holiday.

GORGAS, WILLIAM CRAWFORD: BIRTH ANNIVERSARY. Oct 3, 1854. Physician and sanitary engineer, born at Toulminville, AL. He eradicated yellow fever from Havana, Cuba, and the Panama Canal, allowing the completion of the canal. Gorgas died at London, England, July 4, 1920.

HERRIOT, JAMES: BIRTH ANNIVERSARY. Oct 3, 1916. Author and veterinarian, born James Alfred Wight at Glasgow, Scotland. Under the pen name Herriot he wrote more than 12 books chronicling his life as a veterinarian in northern England. His *All Creatures Great and Small* (1974) was made into a TV series that was an international hit. He was made a member of the Order of the British Empire in 1979. Herriot died Feb 23, 1995, at Yorkshire, England.

HONDURAS: FRANCISCO MORAZÁN HOLIDAY. Oct 3. Public holiday in honor of Francisco Morazán, national hero, who was born in 1799.

KOREA: NATIONAL FOUNDATION DAY. Oct 3. National holiday also called Tangun Day, as it commemorates day when legendary founder of the Korean nation, Tangun, established his kingdom of Chosun in 2333 BC.

KURTZMAN, HARVEY: BIRTH ANNIVERSARY. Oct 3, 1902. Cartoonist and founder of *Mad* magazine, Harvey Kurtzman was born at Brooklyn, NY. At 14 he had his first cartoon published, and he began his career in comic books in 1943. His career led him to EC (Educational Comics), and with the support of William Gaines, he created *Mad* magazine, which first appeared in 1952. He died Feb 21, 1993, at Mount Vernon, NY.

"LA LAW" TV PREMIERE: ANNIVERSARY. Oct 3, 1986. Set in the Los Angeles law firm of McKenzie, Brackman, Chaney and Kuzak, this drama had a large cast. Divorce lawyer Arnie Becker was played by Corbin Bernsen, public defender Victor Sifuentes by Jimmy Smits and managing partner Douglas Brackman by Alan Rachins. Other cast members included Harry Hamlin as Michael Kuzak, Richard Dysart as Leland McKenzie, Susan Dey as Grace Van Owen, Jill Eikenberry as Ann Kelsey, Michael Tucker as Stuart Markowitz and Susan Ruttan as Roxanne Melman. The last telecast was May 19, 1994.

MANSON, PATRICK: BIRTH ANNIVERSARY. Oct 3, 1844. British parasitologist and surgeon sometimes called the father of tropical medicine. Manson's research into insects as carriers of parasites was instrumental in later understanding that mosquitoes transmit malaria. Born at Aberdeen, Scotland, Manson died Apr 9, 1922, at London, England.

October 2020	S	M	T	W	T	F	S
					1	2	3
	4	5	6	7	8	9	10
	11	12	13	14	15	16	17
	18	19	20	21	22	23	24
	25	26	27	28	29	30	31

"MICKEY MOUSE CLUB" TV PREMIERE: 65th ANNIVERSARY. Oct 3, 1955. This afternoon show for children was on ABC. Among its young cast members were Mouseketeers Annette Funicello and Shelley Fabares. A later version, "The New Mickey Mouse Club," starred Keri Russell, Christina Aguilera and Britney Spears.

NETHERLANDS: RELIEF OF LEIDEN DAY. Oct 3. Celebration of the liberation of Leiden in 1574.

"OZZIE AND HARRIET" TV PREMIERE: ANNIVERSARY. Oct 3, 1952. "Ozzie and Harriet" was TV's longest-running sitcom. The successful radio-turned-TV-show about the Nelson family starred the real-life Nelsons—Ozzie; his wife, Harriet; and their sons, David and Ricky. Officially titled "The Adventures of Ozzie and Harriet," this show was set in the family's home. The boys were one reason the show was successful, and Ricky used the advantage to become a pop star. David's and Rick's real-life wives—June Blair and Kris Nelson—also joined the cast. The show was canceled at the end of the 1965–66 season after 435 episodes, 409 of which were in black-and-white and 26 in color. The last episode aired Sept 3, 1966.

ROBINSON NAMED BASEBALL'S FIRST BLACK MAJOR LEAGUE MANAGER: ANNIVERSARY. Oct 3, 1974. The only major league player selected Most Valuable Player in both the American and National leagues, Frank Robinson was hired by the Cleveland Indians as baseball's first black major league manager. During his playing career Robinson represented the American League in four World Series playing for the Baltimore Orioles, led the Cincinnati Reds to a National League pennant and hit 586 home runs in 21 years of play.

SPOON RIVER VALLEY SCENIC DRIVE. Oct 3–4 (also Oct 10–11). Fulton County, IL. 53rd annual. Fall festival in 15 villages with fall foliage, arts and crafts, antiques and collectibles, demonstrations, exhibits, food and the beauty of the 140-mile-long Spoon River Valley. Annually, the first two weekends in October. Est attendance: 100,000. For info: Spoon River Valley Scenic Drive, PO Box 525, Canton, IL 61520. Phone: (309) 647-8980. E-mail: spoonriverdrive@mail.com. Web: www.spoonriverdrive.org.

SUKKOT, SUCCOTH OR FEAST OF TABERNACLES. Oct 3–9. Hebrew calendar date: Tishri 15, 5781, begins seven-day festival in commemoration of Jewish people's 40 years of wandering in the desert and thanksgiving for the fall harvest. This High Holiday season closes with Shemini Atzeret (see entry on Oct 10) and Simchat Torah (see entry on Oct 11). Began at sundown Oct 2.

WOOFSTOCK. Oct 3. Wichita, KS. Fall's fluffiest festival has become the Midwest's largest event of its kind. Woofstock invites dogs and their people to participate in activities catered exclusively to them, including a 2k dog walk and breakfast, agility course, water retrieval, ruff races, doggie musical chairs, furry fashion show and more. Proceeds go directly to help provide care, compassion and a second chance for nearly 16,000 pets in the community each year. Est attendance: 10,000. For info: Kansas Humane Society, 3313 N Hillside, Wichita, KS 67219. Phone: (316) 220-8707. Fax: (316) 554-0356. E-mail: horand@kshumane.org. Web: www.kshumane.org.

🎂 BIRTHDAYS TODAY

Lindsey Buckingham, 73, singer, songwriter (Fleetwood Mac), born Palo Alto, CA, Oct 3, 1947.

Neve Campbell, 47, actress ("Party of Five," *Scream*), born Guelph, ON, Canada, Oct 3, 1973.

Chubby Checker, 79, musician, singer, born Ernest Evans at Philadelphia, PA, Oct 3, 1941.

Fred Couples, 61, golfer, born Seattle, WA, Oct 3, 1959.

Dennis Eckersley, 66, Hall of Fame baseball player, born Oakland, CA, Oct 3, 1954.

Lena Headey, 47, actress ("Game of Thrones," *300*), born Hamilton, Bermuda, Oct 3, 1973.

Zlatan Ibrahimovic, 39, soccer player, born Malmö, Sweden, Oct 3, 1981.

Janel Maloney, 51, actress ("The Leftovers," "The West Wing"), born Woodland Hills, CA, Oct 3, 1969.

Clive Owen, 56, actor (*Children of Men, Elizabeth: The Golden Age, Closer, Sin City*), born Keresley, Coventry, Warwickshire, England, Oct 3, 1964.

Gwen Stefani, 51, singer (No Doubt), designer, born Anaheim, CA, Oct 3, 1969.

Tessa Thompson, 37, actress ("Westworld," *Creed, Men in Black: International, Annihilation, Sorry to Bother You*), born Los Angeles, CA, Oct 3, 1983.

Alicia Vikander, 32, actress (Oscar for *The Danish Girl; Ex Machina, Testament of Youth*), born Gothenburg, Sweden, Oct 3, 1988.

Denis Villeneuve, 53, film director (*Blade Runner 2049, Arrival, Sicario*), born Trois-Rivières, QC, Canada, Oct 3, 1967.

Jack P. Wagner, 61, actor ("Melrose Place," "General Hospital"), born Washington, MO, Oct 3, 1959.

Danny Willett, 33, golfer, born Sheffield, England, Oct 3, 1987.

Dave Winfield, 69, Hall of Fame baseball player, born St. Paul, MN, Oct 3, 1951.

October 4 — Sunday

DAY 278	88 REMAINING

BLESSING OF THE FISHING FLEET. Oct 4. Church of Saints Peter and Paul and Fisherman's Wharf, San Francisco, CA. Annually, the first Sunday in October.

COUNTRY INN, BED-AND-BREAKFAST DAY. Oct 4. Across America and Canada, country inns and bed-and-breakfasts welcome visitors with information and special events. The weekend also introduces people to the world of inns and B&Bs. Inns and their fans around the world are welcome to join the celebration. Annually, the first Sunday in October. For info: Tina Czarnota. E-mail: tczarnot@bellsouth.net.

DICK TRACY DEBUTS: ANNIVERSARY. Oct 4, 1931. Square-jawed detective Dick Tracy made his comic strip debut in the *Detroit Daily Mirror* in "Plainclothes Tracy."

★FIRE PREVENTION WEEK. Oct 4–10. Presidential Proclamation issued annually for the first or second week in October since 1925. For many years prior to 1925, National Fire Prevention Day was observed in October. Sponsored by the National Fire Protection Association. Annually, the Sunday–Saturday during which the Oct 9 anniversary date falls.

FIRE PREVENTION WEEK. Oct 4–10. Since 1922, a week to increase awareness of the dangers of fire and to educate the public on how to stay safe from fire. Fire Prevention Week is observed each year during the week of Oct 9 in commemoration of the Great Chicago Fire, which began on Oct 8, 1871, and caused 250 deaths and devastating damage. For info: Public Affairs Office, Natl Fire Protection Assn, One Batterymarch Park, Quincy, MA 02169. Phone: (800) 344-3555. E-mail: publicaffairs@nfpa.org. Web: www.nfpa.org and www.firepreventionweek.org.

GERMANY: ERNTEDANKFEST. Oct 4. A harvest thanksgiving festival, or potato harvest festival, Erntedankfest (or Erntedanktag) is generally observed on the first Sunday in October.

GETTING THE WORLD TO BEAT A PATH TO YOUR DOOR WEEK. Oct 4–10. To focus attention on improving "public relationships" in order to create success for companies, products and individuals. Free self-evaluation available. For info: Gaughen Global Public Relations, 7456 Evergreen Dr, Santa Barbara, CA 93117. Phone: (805) 680-9445. E-mail: bgaughenmu@aol.com.

GREGORIAN CALENDAR ADJUSTMENT: ANNIVERSARY. Oct 4, 1582. Pope Gregory XIII issued a bulletin that decreed that the day following Thursday, Oct 4, 1582, should be Friday, Oct 15, 1582, thus correcting the Julian calendar, then 10 days out of date relative to the seasons. This reform was effective in most Catholic countries; the Julian calendar continued in use in Britain and the American colonies until 1752, in Russia until 1918 and in Greece until 1923. See also: "Gregorian Calendar Day: Anniversary" (Feb 24) and "Calendar Adjustment Day: Anniversary" (Sept 2).

HAYES, RUTHERFORD BIRCHARD: BIRTH ANNIVERSARY. Oct 4, 1822. Rutherford Birchard Hayes, 19th president of the US (Mar 4, 1877–Mar 3, 1881), was born at Delaware, OH. In his inaugural address, Hayes said: "He serves his party best who serves the country best." He died at Fremont, OH, Jan 17, 1893.

HESTON, CHARLTON: BIRTH ANNIVERSARY. Oct 4, 1923. Born at Evanston, IL, the handsome, resolute Heston won the Best Actor Oscar for his role as Moses in the 1956 Hollywood epic *The Ten Commandments*. Over a career that spanned six decades, his credits included *Ben-Hur, Touch of Evil, Will Penny* and *Planet of the Apes*. Heston died Apr 5, 2008, at Beverly Hills, CA.

INTERNATIONAL SHIPS-IN-BOTTLES DAY. Oct 4. A day commemorating the venerable art of building small ships and other objects to fit and be displayed in a bottle. Builders, who are often referred to as bottle shipwrights, are dedicated men and women who spend long hours researching the subject they wish to bottle and then equally long hours devising ways to place their creation securely and attractively inside a bottle. Annually, Oct 4. For info: David Lavoie, 33 Davis Rd, Methuen, MA 01844. Phone: (603) 930-3071. E-mail: builderofships@gmail.com.

JOHNSON, ELIZA MCCARDLE: BIRTH ANNIVERSARY. Oct 4, 1810. Wife of Andrew Johnson, 17th president of the US, born at Leesburg, TN. Died at Greeneville, TN, Jan 15, 1876.

JOPLIN, JANIS: 50th DEATH ANNIVERSARY. Oct 4, 1970. The biggest female rock star of the 1960s died of a heroin overdose in her Los Angeles hotel room at the age of 27. Joplin was in the midst of recording an album, *Pearl*, with the Full Tilt Boogie Band. *Pearl* was released posthumously and yielded the hit single "Me and Bobby McGee." Joplin was cremated and her ashes were spread along California's coastline. "The more you live, the less you die,"

Joplin told concertgoers. See also: "Joplin, Janis: Birth Anniversary" (Jan 19).

KEATON, BUSTER: 125th BIRTH ANNIVERSARY. Oct 4, 1895. Born Joseph Francis Keaton at Piqua, KS, Buster Keaton (supposedly nicknamed by Harry Houdini) was one of America's greatest filmmakers. He became a star on the vaudeville stage by age six, in a family show with his parents, but moved on to films at age 21, costarring in several comic shorts with Roscoe "Fatty" Arbuckle and then starring in, writing, directing and producing his own shorts—which featured improbable stunts and physical gags along with Keaton's deadpan expression. His full-length silent films are regarded as masterpieces of American comedy, especially *Sherlock, Jr* (1924) and the Civil War epic *The General* (1927)—both of which are on the Library of Congress's National Film Registry. Alcoholism and troubled relations with the MGM studio sidelined his career in the 1930s and '40s, but he later began a quieter career writing gags, making comic cameos in such films as *Around the World in Eighty Days*, appearing on TV's "Candid Camera" and even performing as a clown in Paris's Cirque Medrano. Keaton died on Feb 1, 1966, at Los Angeles, CA.

"LEAVE IT TO BEAVER" TV PREMIERE: ANNIVERSARY. Oct 4, 1957. This family sitcom was a stereotypical portrayal of American family life. It focused on Theodore "Beaver" Cleaver (Jerry Mathers); his patient, understanding and all-knowing father, Ward (Hugh Beaumont); impeccably dressed housewife and mother, June (Barbara Billingsley); and Wally (Tony Dow), Beaver's good-natured, all-American brother. The "perfectness" of the Cleaver family was balanced by other, less-than-perfect characters played by Ken Osmond, Frank Bank, Richard Deacon, Diane Brewster, Sue Randall, Rusty Stevens and Madge Blake. The last episode aired Sept 12, 1963. "Leave It to Beaver" remained popular in reruns.

LESOTHO: INDEPENDENCE DAY. Oct 4. National holiday. Commemorates independence from Britain in 1966. Formerly Basutoland.

MENTAL ILLNESS AWARENESS WEEK. Oct 4–10. To increase public awareness of the causes of, symptoms of and treatments for mental illnesses. Annually, the first full week in October. For info: National Alliance on Mental Illness, 3803 N Fairfax Dr, Ste 100, Arlington, VA 22203-1701. Phone: (703) 524-7600. E-mail: info@nami.org. Web: www.nami.org.

NATIONAL CARRY A TUNE WEEK. Oct 4–10. This week calls for people to celebrate favorite tunes from the past by performing them in a concert, at school, at church or at home. The purpose is to remember tunes from America's past and keep them alive. Annually, the week nearest the birthday of William Billings (born Oct 7, 1746), America's first important tune composer ("Chester"). Sponsor: Tune Lovers Society. For info: Roger Hall, Pine Tree Productions, 235 Prospect St, Stoughton, MA 02072. Phone: (781) 344-6954. E-mail: pinetreepro@aol.com. Web: www.americanmusicpreservation.com/carryatuneweek.htm.

NATIONAL METRIC WEEK. Oct 4–10. Since 1976, a week observing the importance of the metric system as the primary system of measurement for the US. Annually, the week of the 10th month containing the 10th day of the month. For info: US Metric Assn. Web: www.us-metric.org/national-metric-week.

NATIONAL TACO DAY. Oct 4. A day to celebrate the versatile, hand-held favorite: tacos. For millennia, the native people of Central America wrapped meat and toppings in tortillas, setting the framework for our modern-day enchiladas, burritos and tacos. The word *taco* first appeared in a US magazine in 1905. Today's tacos take on a variety of forms but typically include a corn or flour tortilla filled with meat, fish, veggies and spicy sauces. Taco joints often feature taco specials to celebrate National Taco Day. Annually, Oct 4.

PULASKI DAY PARADE. Oct 4. Philadelphia, PA. Parade honoring the Polish patriot known as "the father of the American Cavalry." Begins at 20th and Benjamin Franklin Pkwy and ends at 19th and Benjamin Franklin Pkwy. For info: Polish American Congress, Eastern Pennsylvania District, 308 Walnut St, Philadelphia, PA 19106. Phone: (215) 922-1700. Fax: (215) 922-1518. Web: www.polishamericancongress.com.

REMINGTON, FREDERIC S.: BIRTH ANNIVERSARY. Oct 4, 1861. Born at Canton, NY. Artist and writer Frederic Remington was devoted to the outdoors of New York's North Country and the rugged characters and landscapes of the Old West. He began as an illustrator for popular magazines and worked to become a fine artist and sculptor, capturing images of Native Americans, buffalo soldiers, cowboys, horses and Western adventure. Died Dec 26, 1909, at age 48, at Ridgefield, CT, following an appendectomy.

RUNYAN, DAMON: BIRTH ANNIVERSARY. Oct 4, 1884. American newspaperman and author, born at Manhattan, KS, and died at New York, NY, Dec 10, 1946. The musical *Guys and Dolls* was based on one of his short stories. "Always try to rub up against money," he wrote, "for if you rub up against money long enough, some of it may rub off on you."

SAINT FRANCIS OF ASSISI: FEAST DAY. Oct 4. Giovanni Francesco Bernardone, religious leader, founder of the Friars Minor (Franciscan Order), born at Assisi, Umbria, Italy, in 1181. Died at Porziuncula, Italy, Oct 3, 1226.

SPACE MILESTONE: *SPUTNIK* (USSR). Oct 4, 1957. Anniversary of launching of first successful man-made Earth satellite. *Sputnik I* ("satellite"), weighing 184 pounds, was fired into orbit from the USSR's Tyuratam launch site. Transmitted radio signal for 21 days; decayed Jan 4, 1958. Beginning of the Space Age and humankind's exploration beyond Earth. This first-in-space triumph by the Soviets resulted in a stepped-up emphasis on the teaching of science in American classrooms.

STRATEMEYER, EDWARD L.: BIRTH ANNIVERSARY. Oct 4, 1862. American author of children's books, Stratemeyer was born at Elizabeth, NJ. He created numerous series of popular children's books, including The Bobbsey Twins, The Hardy Boys, Nancy Drew and Tom Swift, hiring ghostwriters to work from his outlines. He and his "Stratemeyer Syndicate," using 60 or more pen names, produced more than 1,300 books, selling more than 200 million copies. Stratemeyer died at Newark, NJ, May 10, 1930, but his daughters continued his legacy of essentially mass-produced literature until 1982.

TEN-FOUR DAY. Oct 4. The fourth day of the 10th month is a day of recognition for radio operators, whose code words "Ten-Four" signal an affirmative reply.

UNITED NATIONS: WORLD SPACE WEEK. Oct 4–10. To celebrate the contributions of space science and technology to the betterment of the human condition. The dates recall the launch, on Oct 4, 1957, of the first artificial satellite, *Sputnik*, and the entry into force, on

October 2020	S	M	T	W	T	F	S
					1	2	3
	4	5	6	7	8	9	10
	11	12	13	14	15	16	17
	18	19	20	21	22	23	24
	25	26	27	28	29	30	31

Oct 10, 1967, of the Treaty on Principles Governing the Activities of States in the Exploration and Use of Outer Space. Annually, Oct 4–10. For info: United Nations, Dept of Public Info, New York, NY 10017. Web: www.un.org.

WORLD CHILD DEVELOPMENT DAY. Oct 4. 7th annual. This day recognizes the importance of the first years of a child's life and the importance of promoting early development by reading to, talking to, holding and interacting with young children. It is also a call to action to learn about and provide/receive developmental screenings so that all children can reach their optimal level at the earliest point possible. Children benefit from early recognition, and with early recognition and treatment if needed, further delay may be prevented. Annually, Oct 4. For info: Darlene Batrowny, 140 Valley Ln, Horseheads, NY 14845. Web: www.liftachild.com.

WORLD COMMUNION SUNDAY. Oct 4. Communion is celebrated by Christians all over the world. Annually, the first Sunday in October.

🎂 BIRTHDAYS TODAY

Armand Assante, 71, actor (*Belizaire the Cajun*, *The Mambo Kings*, *Fatal Instinct*), born New York, NY, Oct 4, 1949.

Caitriona Balfe, 41, actress ("Outlander"), born Monaghan, Ireland, Oct 4, 1979.

Melissa Benoist, 32, actress ("Supergirl," "Glee," *Whiplash*), born Littleton, CO, Oct 4, 1988.

Abraham Benrubi, 51, actor ("ER," "Men in Trees"), born Indianapolis, IN, Oct 4, 1969.

Rachael Leigh Cook, 41, actress (*She's All That*, "The Baby-Sitters Club"), born Minneapolis, MN, Oct 4, 1979.

Clifton Davis, 75, singer, actor ("That's My Mama," "Amen"), composer, born Chicago, IL, Oct 4, 1945.

Anita L. DeFrantz, 68, Olympics executive and former rower, born Philadelphia, PA, Oct 4, 1952.

Charles (Chuck) Hagel, 74, former US secretary of defense (Obama administration), former US senator (R, Nebraska), born North Platte, NE, Oct 4, 1946.

Dakota Johnson, 31, actress (*Fifty Shades of Grey*, *Need for Speed*), born Austin, TX, Oct 4, 1989.

Vicky Krieps, 37, actress (*Phantom Thread*, *The Young Karl Marx*), born Luxembourg, Grand Duchy of Luxembourg, Oct 4, 1983.

Tony La Russa, Jr, 76, former baseball manager and player, born Tampa, FL, Oct 4, 1944.

Anne Rice, 79, novelist (*Interview with the Vampire*), born New Orleans, LA, Oct 4, 1941.

Derrick Rose, 32, basketball player, born Chicago, IL, Oct 4, 1988.

Susan Sarandon, 74, actress (Oscar for *Dead Man Walking*; *Thelma and Louise*), born Susan Tomalin at New York, NY, Oct 4, 1946.

Alicia Silverstone, 44, actress (*Clueless*, *Batman & Robin*), born San Francisco, CA, Oct 4, 1976.

Christoph Waltz, 64, actor (Oscars for *Inglourious Basterds* and *Django Unchained*), born Vienna, Austria, Oct 4, 1956.

Jimy Williams, 77, baseball manager and former player, born Santa Maria, CA, Oct 4, 1943.

October 5 — Monday

DAY 279 **87 REMAINING**

ARTHUR, CHESTER ALAN: BIRTH ANNIVERSARY. Oct 5, 1829. The 21st president of the US, Chester Alan Arthur, was born at Fairfield, VT, and succeeded to the presidency following the death of James A. Garfield. Term of office: Sept 20, 1881–Mar 3, 1885.

Arthur was not successful in obtaining the Republican Party's nomination for the following term. He died at New York, NY, Nov 18, 1886.

BONDS BREAKS SEASON HOME RUN RECORD: ANNIVERSARY. Oct 5, 2001. Barry Bonds of the San Francisco Giants broke Mark McGwire's 1998 season home run record when he hit his 71st homer of the season in a game against the Los Angeles Dodgers at Pacific Bell Park. Later in the game he hit another homer. The Dodgers beat the Giants, 11–10, eliminating them from the playoffs. On Oct 7 Bonds hit one more homer, to finish the season with 73. He also broke Babe Ruth's slugging record of .847 with .863. On Aug 7, 2007, Bonds passed Hank Aaron on the all-time homer list by slugging number 756.

BYRD, RICHARD E.: BIRTH ANNIVERSARY. Oct 5, 1888. Pioneering American aviator and explorer who made the first flight over both polar axes. Born to a prominent family at Winchester, VA, educated at the University of Virginia and the US Naval Academy. Byrd's distinguished naval career included serving as the branch's liaison officer to Congress (1919–21), where he was responsible for the legislation that created the Navy's Bureau of Aeronautics. While he was also credited with the first flight over the North Pole on May 9, 1926, Byrd's primary polar explorations took place in Antarctica. He led the first flight over the South Pole on Nov 28–29, 1929, established the Little America exploration bases on the polar continent and in 1946 commanded Operation Highjump, which mapped 1.5 million square miles of Antarctica by aerial photography. Awarded the Medal of Honor, the Distinguished Service Medal, the Navy Cross, the National Geographic Hubbard Medal and the Department of Defense Medal of Freedom, Byrd died on Mar 11, 1957, at Boston, MA.

CHIEF JOSEPH SURRENDER: ANNIVERSARY. Oct 5, 1877. After a 1,700-mile retreat, Chief Joseph and the Nez Percé Indians surrendered to US Cavalry troops at Bear's Paw near Chinook, MT, Oct 5, 1877. Chief Joseph made his famous speech of surrender, "From where the sun now stands, I will fight no more forever." See also: "Hin-Mah-Too-Yah-Lat-Kekt ("Chief Joseph"): Birth Anniversary" (Mar 3).

★CHILD HEALTH DAY. Oct 5. Presidential Proclamation always issued for the first Monday in October. Proclamation has been issued since 1928. In 1959 Congress changed celebration day from May 1 to the present observance (Public Resolution No. 46 of May 18, 1928, and Public Law 86–352 of Sept 22, 1959).

CIVIL WAR "SUBMARINE" ATTACK: ANNIVERSARY. Oct 5, 1863. In an attempt to disrupt the Union blockade of Charleston Harbor, the Confederate semisubmersible *David* rammed the Union ironclad *New Ironsides* with a spar torpedo. This was the first successful Southern attack using a submersible craft. Although both sides experimented with submarine warfare during the Civil War, the results were far from encouraging as the submarines caused more fatalities to their own crews than to the opposing side.

DUPUYTREN DISEASE AWARENESS DAY. Oct 5. 4th annual. Dupuytren disease cripples hands by making fingers permanently bent and can be associated with other serious health conditions. This day—observed on the birth anniversary of French surgeon Guillaume Dupuytren (1777–1835), whose name identifies this condition—seeks to raise awareness of the plight of millions of people who struggle with Dupuytren disease and of the need for better treatment. Annually, on Oct 5. For info: Charles Eaton, MD, Dupuytren Research Group, 1850 Forest Hill Rd, Ste 201, West Palm Beach, FL 33406. E-mail: c.eaton.md@dupuytrens.org. Web: https://dupuytrens.org/dupuytren-disease-awareness-day.

EDWARDS, JONATHAN: BIRTH ANNIVERSARY. Oct 5, 1703. (Old Style date.) The famed theologian and leader of the "Great Awakening," the religious revival in the colonies, was born at East Windsor, CT. His "Sinners in the Hands of an Angry God" is the most famous sermon in American history. He later became president of the College of New Jersey (now Princeton University). Edwards died at Princeton, NJ, Mar 22, 1758, when he contracted smallpox from an inoculation.

FINE, LARRY: BIRTH ANNIVERSARY. Oct 5, 1902. The fuzzy-haired Stooge, many times a victim of the mean-tempered Moe, was born Louis Feinberg at Philadelphia, PA. He started his show business career in vaudeville with a joke-and-violin act (he was an accomplished musician). Fine was an original member of the Three Stooges, formed in 1925. Fine died Jan 24, 1975, at Woodland Hills, CA.

GODDARD, ROBERT HUTCHINGS: BIRTH ANNIVERSARY. Oct 5, 1882. "The father of the Space Age," born at Worcester, MA. Largely ignored or ridiculed during his lifetime because of his dreams of rocket travel, including travel to other planets. Launched a liquid-fuel-powered rocket Mar 16, 1926, at Auburn, MA. Died Aug 10, 1945, at Baltimore, MD. See also: "Goddard Day" (Mar 16).

HAVEL, VACLAV: BIRTH ANNIVERSARY. Oct 5, 1936. World-renowned poet, playwright, human rights activist and president of Czechoslovakia/Czech Republic, Vaclav Havel was born at Prague, Czechoslovakia (now Czech Republic). His literary works critiqued the dehumanizing effects of totalitarian political regimes, and he was imprisoned for four years (1979–83) for his human rights activism in Communist-controlled Czechoslovakia. After the fall of communism, Havel was the first president of Czechoslovakia and then the Czech Republic (1989–2003); under his leadership, it was one of the first Eastern European countries invited to join NATO. One of the most respected figures of the 20th century, Havel died Dec 18, 2011, at Hradecek, Czech Republic.

JAMES BOND MOVIE SERIES LAUNCHED WITH *DR. NO*: ANNIVERSARY. Oct 5, 1962. Scottish actor Sean Connery played Ian Fleming's super secret agent James Bond, 007, in the first film of a blockbuster franchise.

LUMIÈRE, LOUIS: BIRTH ANNIVERSARY. Oct 5, 1864. Born at Besançon, France, Louis Lumière and brother Auguste were film pioneers who created the first movie, *Workers Leaving the Lumière Factory* (1895). Lumière, considered the father of cinema in France, was inspired by Thomas Edison's Kinetoscope, and he created (with his brother's assistance) the Cinèmatographe, which could project and mechanically move a sprocketed strip of film images. This was patented on Feb 13, 1895. On Dec 28, 1895, the brothers projected short films for paying customers—the first time this had ever been done—at Paris's Grand Café. The Lumières directed or produced thousands of short films of both everyday life and news of the day in what were the first newsreels. The brothers retired from film production in 1901. Louis Lumière spent his later years working on photographic and film innovations, such as an early 3-D system. He died at Bandol, France, on June 6, 1948.

		S	M	T	W	T	F	S
October						1	2	3
		4	5	6	7	8	9	10
2020		11	12	13	14	15	16	17
		18	19	20	21	22	23	24
		25	26	27	28	29	30	31

"MONTY PYTHON'S FLYING CIRCUS" TV PREMIERE: ANNIVERSARY. Oct 5, 1969. This wacky comedy series debuted on BBC-1 in Great Britain and aired until 1974. The cast was made up of Graham Chapman, John Cleese, Eric Idle, Terry Jones, Michael Palin and American Terry Gilliam. John Philip Sousa's "Liberty Bell March" got the show started, and viewers were treated to surreal animation and such skits as "The Spanish Inquisition" and "The Ministry of Silly Walks." On Oct 6, 1974, "Monty Python's Flying Circus" began airing in the US. The cast members also made four films together.

O'BRIEN, FLANN: BIRTH ANNIVERSARY. Oct 5, 1911. Pen name of Brian O'Nolan, born at Strabane, Ireland. O'Nolan, a career civil servant, was incognito a novelist, dramatist and journalist. Best known for *At Swim-Two-Birds* (1939) and *The Third Policeman* (1967). Under the name Myles na gCopaleen, he authored a popular satirical and humorous column for the *Irish Times*. O'Nolan died Apr 1, 1966, at Dublin, Ireland. In keeping with the mordant humor of his works, MylesDay is celebrated on his death day rather than his birthday. See also: "MylesDay" (Apr 1).

PORTUGAL: REPUBLIC DAY. Oct 5. National holiday. Commemorates establishment of the republic in 1910.

SPACE MILESTONE: *CHALLENGER STS 41-G*. Oct 5, 1984. Space shuttle *Challenger*'s sixth mission with crew of seven, including two women. Launched from Kennedy Space Center, FL, on this date and landed there on Oct 13, 1984. Kathryn D. Sullivan became the first American woman to walk in space.

SPAIN: SEMANA CERVANTINA (CERVANTES WEEK). Oct 5–11. Madrid. Festivities saluting the greatest Spanish author, Miguel de Cervantes, actually occur throughout the month of October. But there are intense activities in the week that includes the baptism anniversary (Oct 9) of Cervantes. More than 500 events, including Medieval Market Days, lectures and readings from the work of Cervantes, theatrical pieces, antique book fair, music and more. For info: La Semana Cervantina. Web: www.lacallemayor.net/semana-cervantina.

STONE, THOMAS: DEATH ANNIVERSARY. Oct 5, 1787. Signer of the Declaration of Independence, born 1743 (exact date unknown) at Charles County, MD. Died at Alexandria, VA.

SUPREME COURT 2020–21 TERM BEGINS. Oct 5. Traditionally, the Supreme Court's annual term begins on the first Monday in October and continues with seven two-week sessions of oral arguments. Between the sessions are six recesses during which the opinions are written by the justices. Ordinarily, all cases are decided by the following June or July.

TECUMSEH: DEATH ANNIVERSARY. Oct 5, 1813. Shawnee Indian chief, born at Old Piqua near what is now Oldtown, OH, in March 1768. Tecumseh came to prominence between 1799 and 1804 as a powerful orator, defending his people against whites. He denounced as invalid all treaties by which tribes ceded their lands and condemned the chieftains who had entered into such agreements. With his brother Tenskwatawa, the Prophet, he established a town on the Tippecanoe River near Lafayette, IN, and then embarked on a mission to organize a confederation to stop white encroachment. Although he advocated peaceful methods and negotiation, he did not rule out war as a last resort as he visited tribes throughout the country. While he was away, William Henry Harrison defeated the Prophet at the Battle of Tippecanoe Nov 7, 1811, and burned the town. Tecumseh organized a large force of Indian warriors and assisted the British in the War of 1812. Tecumseh was defeated and killed at the Battle of the Thames.

UNITED NATIONS: WORLD HABITAT DAY. Oct 5. The General Assembly, by a resolution of Dec 17, 1985, has designated the first Monday in October each year as World Habitat Day—a day to reflect on the living conditions of human beings and to take action to address the shortcomings of those conditions. The first observance of this day in 1986 marked the 10th anniversary of the first international conference on the subject. For info: United Nations, Dept of Public Info, Public Inquiries Unit, Rm GA-57, New York, NY 10017. Phone: (212) 963-4475. E-mail: inquiries@un.org. Web: www.un.org.

UNITED NATIONS: WORLD TEACHERS' DAY. Oct 5. A day to honor teachers and their contributions to learning. For info: United Nations, Dept of Public Info, New York, NY 10017. Web: www.un.org.

WORLD DAY OF BULLYING PREVENTION™. Oct 5. "Go Blue!" Kids and adults wear a blue shirt this day to show solidarity against bullying and cyberbullying. Annually, the first Monday in October. For info: STOMP Out Bullying, 220 E 57th St, 9th Fl, Ste G, New York, NY 10022. Phone: (877) NO BULLY. E-mail: info@stompoutbullying.org. Web: www.stompoutbullying.org.

"YOU BET YOUR LIFE" TV PREMIERE: 70th ANNIVERSARY. Oct 5, 1950. This funny game show began on radio in 1947 and moved to TV with Groucho Marx as host and George Fenneman as announcer and scorekeeper. Players tried to answer questions in the category of their choice, but Groucho's improvised interviews stole the show. Many guests appeared who later became famous, including Phyllis Diller and Candice Bergen. Players could also win money by uttering the secret word, an everyday word suspended above the stage on a duck that dropped when the word was spoken. This was one of the few shows to be filmed, because the interviews needed to be edited. Two short-lived revivals of the series aired, with Buddy Hackett as host in 1980, and with Bill Cosby in 1992.

🎂 BIRTHDAYS TODAY

Karen Allen, 69, actress (*The Wanderers, Raiders of the Lost Ark, Starman*), born Carrollton, IL, Oct 5, 1951.

Michael Andretti, 58, race car driver, son of Mario Andretti, born Bethlehem, PA, Oct 5, 1962.

Clive Barker, 68, author, born Liverpool, England, Oct 5, 1952.

Josie Bissett, 50, actress ("Melrose Place"), born Seattle, WA, Oct 5, 1970.

Ben Cardin, 77, US Senator (D, Maryland), born Baltimore, MD, Oct 5, 1943.

Laura Davies, 57, Hall of Fame golfer, born Coventry, England, Oct 5, 1963.

Jesse Eisenberg, 37, actor (*Batman v Superman, The Squid and the Whale, Adventureland, The Social Network*), born New York, NY, Oct 5, 1983.

Bob Geldof, 69, singer (Boomtown Rats), social activist, born Dublin, Ireland, Oct 5, 1951.

Grant Hill, 48, former basketball player, born Dallas, TX, Oct 5, 1972.

Glynis Johns, 97, actress (*Mary Poppins, The Ref, A Little Night Music*), born Pretoria, South Africa, Oct 5, 1923.

Mario Lemieux, 55, Hall of Fame hockey player, hockey executive, born Montreal, QC, Canada, Oct 5, 1965.

Steve Miller, 77, musician, singer (Steve Miller Band), born Dallas, TX, Oct 5, 1943.

Parminder K. Nagra, 45, actress (*Bend It like Beckham*, "ER"), born Leicester, Leicestershire, England, Oct 5, 1975.

Kevin Olusola, 32, singer (Pentatonix), born Owensboro, KY, Oct 5, 1988.

Patrick Roy, 55, hockey manager and former player, born Quebec City, QC, Canada, Oct 5, 1965.

Neil deGrasse Tyson, 62, astrophysicist, television personality ("Cosmos: A Spacetime Odyssey"), born New York, NY, Oct 5, 1958.

Kate Winslet, 45, actress (Oscar for *The Reader*; *Revolutionary Road, Finding Neverland, Titanic*), born Reading, England, Oct 5, 1975.

October 6 — Tuesday

DAY 280 **86 REMAINING**

AMERICAN LIBRARY ASSOCIATION FOUNDING: ANNIVERSARY. Oct 6, 1876. Founded at Philadelphia, PA, by 103 librarians attending the Centennial Exposition.

"CSI: CRIME SCENE INVESTIGATION" TV PREMIERE: 20th ANNIVERSARY. Oct 6, 2000. CBS's consistently top-rated mystery drama focused on a crack Las Vegas police forensics team. "CSI" brought science to the foreground, with close-up looks at technology and lab techniques. The 300th episode aired Oct 23, 2013. The last episode aired Sept 27, 2015. The show spawned spin-offs: "CSI: Miami," "CSI: New York" and (later) "CSI: Cyber."

EGYPT: ARMED FORCES DAY. Oct 6. The Egyptian army celebrates crossing into Sinai in 1973.

GAYNOR, JANET: BIRTH ANNIVERSARY. Oct 6, 1906. Born Laura Gainor at Philadelphia, PA, in 1929, she became the first winner of the Academy Award for Best Actress for her cumulative work in two 1927 films, *Sunrise* and *Seventh Heaven*, and for *Street Angel* (1928). Gaynor died Sept 14, 1984, at Palm Springs, CA.

HEYERDAHL, THOR: BIRTH ANNIVERSARY. Oct 6, 1914. The anthropologist and explorer was born at Larvik, Norway. Seeking to prove the plausibility of South American peoples having settled Polynesia, he embarked on an epic raft ride with five companions in 1947. The *Kon-Tiki* made the 4,300-mile voyage from Peru to Raroia in 101 days. Heyerdahl's book chronicling the adventure became an international bestseller. He continued his travels (including a solo 1970 trip in a reed boat from North Africa to Barbados) and writing until his death. He died at Italy on Apr 18, 2002.

IRELAND: IVY DAY: DEATH ANNIVERSARY OF CHARLES PARNELL. Oct 6. The anniversary of the death in 1891 of Irish nationalist leader and home-rule advocate Charles Stewart Parnell is observed, especially in Ireland, as Ivy Day. A sprig of ivy is worn on the lapel to remember Parnell. James Joyce's short story "Ivy Day in the Committee Room," published in the collection titled *Dubliners*, addresses this event. See also: "Parnell, Charles Stewart: Birth Anniversary" (June 27).

JACKIE MAYER REHAB DAY. Oct 6. Sandusky, OH. Known as Sandusky's "favorite daughter," Jacquelyn Jeanne Mayer, Miss America 1963 and stroke survivor since 1970, is honored on Oct 6, the anniversary of the 1997 renaming of Providence Hospital's rehab and nursing facility as the Jackie Mayer Rehab Center. After seven years of self-directed rehab to regain her speech and mobility, Jackie Mayer has been a motivational speaker and tireless advocate on behalf of stroke survivors across the US and Canada. For info: Dr. Nancy Linenkugel, OSF, 3334 Mowbray Ln, Ste 5, Cincinnati, OH 45226. Phone: (419) 322-1618. Web: www.jackiemayer.com.

LIND, JENNY: 200th BIRTH ANNIVERSARY. Oct 6, 1820. Acclaimed opera singer known as "the Swedish Nightingale." The soprano toured the European continent in the 1840s. Briefly retired at the age of 29, but resumed her career with a popular American concert tour (at the behest of showman P.T. Barnum) in 1850. In later years, she was a professor. Born at Stockholm, Sweden, Lind died at Malvern, England, Nov 2, 1887.

MOODY, HELEN WILLS: BIRTH ANNIVERSARY. Oct 6, 1905. One of the greatest tennis players of the 20th century was born at Centreville, CA. Moody, 1921's US national junior champion, had a phenomenal professional career with a .919 winning average. She won 52 out of 92 tournaments between 1919 and 1938. She won Wimbledon eight out of nine tries, the US Open seven times and the French Open four times. Amazingly, from 1927 to 1932, she did not lose one single set in any singles competition. A 1924 Olympic gold medal winner for singles and doubles, Moody also became the first player to win a grand slam (1928). "Little Miss Poker Face" (as she was nicknamed for her no-nonsense style) was inducted into the International Tennis Hall of Fame in 1969. She died Jan 1, 1998, at Carmel, CA.

★**NATIONAL GERMAN-AMERICAN DAY.** Oct 6. Celebration of German heritage and the contributions German Americans have made to the building of the nation. A Presidential Proclamation has been issued each year since 1987. Annually, Oct 6.

NATIONAL GERMAN-AMERICAN DAY. Oct 6. Observed since the 19th century, this day honors the contributions of German immigrants to US culture and history. Celebrated on the date in 1683 when 13 Mennonite families disembarked near Philadelphia, PA, from Krefeld, Germany. These families later founded Germantown, PA. The day is celebrated by all those who are culturally German from all parts of Europe. This special day had a boost in popularity when President Ronald Reagan became the first US president to proclaim it in 1987.

NATIONAL G.O.E. (GROWTH.OVERCOME.EMPOWER.) DAY. Oct 6. This event connects the varied arts with healing from abuse trauma. Survivors and supporters create safe spaces and link with local resources to promote healing and empowerment. Observed locally in Fitchburg, MA, and nationally through online resources. Annually, the Sunday of the first full weekend in October. For info: My Care Initiative, 19 Pierce Ave, Ste 114, Fitchburg, MA 01420. Phone: (978) 592-2734. E-mail: info@mycareinitiative.org. Web: www.mycareinitiative.org.

NATIONAL NOODLE DAY. Oct 6. A day to celebrate noodles in all shapes and sizes. Noodles, which originated in China, are a staple of many cuisines around the world. The word *noodle* comes from the German word *Nudel*. Observed since 2010. Annually, Oct. 6.

NATIONAL PLUS SIZE APPRECIATION DAY. Oct 6. Since 2017, a day to boost the confidence of plus-size men and women around the world—despite society's strictures on how one is supposed to look or how much one is supposed to weigh. This day provides the opportunity to model empathy and to encourage plus-size individuals to be themselves. For info: Danielle White, 6501 NW 20th Ct, Ste 1, Sunrise, FL 33313. Phone: (786) 518-8804. E-mail: womenrockinc18@gmail.com or plussizeday@mail.com.

SADAT, ANWAR EL-: ASSASSINATION ANNIVERSARY. Oct 6, 1981. Anwar el-Sadat, Egyptian president and Nobel Peace Prize recipient, was killed by assassins at Cairo while he was reviewing a military parade commemorating the 1973 Egyptian-Israeli War. At least eight other persons were reported killed in the attack on Sadat. Anwar el-Sadat was born Dec 25, 1918, at Mit Abu Al-Kom, a village near the Nile River delta.

SEIBERT, FLORENCE: BIRTH ANNIVERSARY. Oct 6, 1897. American physician Florence B. Seibert was born at Easton, PA. She developed the test for tuberculosis that was adopted by the US and used worldwide by the World Health Organization. She died Aug 23, 1991, at St. Petersburg, FL.

UNITED KINGDOM: NATIONAL BADGER DAY. Oct 6. A day to learn about and raise awareness of the United Kingdom's favorite mammal. Badgers often get a bad rap, especially during cull season. So at least for today we are going to change the conversation and show the UK why we love this iconic species. Annually, Oct 6. For info: Badger Trust. Web: www.badger.org.uk.

WESTINGHOUSE, GEORGE: BIRTH ANNIVERSARY. Oct 6, 1846. Engineer and inventor of the air brake for trains, born at Central Bridge, NY. He was the first employer to give his employees paid vacations. Westinghouse died at New York, NY, Mar 12, 1914.

YOM KIPPUR WAR: ANNIVERSARY. Oct 6–25, 1973. A surprise attack by Egypt and Syria pushed Israeli forces several miles behind the 1967 cease-fire lines. Israel was caught off guard, partly because the attack came on the holiest Jewish religious day. After 18 days of fighting, hostilities were halted by the UN Oct 25. Israel partially recovered from the initial setback but failed to regain all the land lost in the fighting.

🎂 BIRTHDAYS TODAY

Britt Ekland, 78, actress (*The Night They Raided Minsky's*), born Stockholm, Sweden, Oct 6, 1942.

Rebecca Lobo, 47, sportscaster, former basketball player, born Southwick, MA, Oct 6, 1973.

Elisabeth Shue, 57, actress (*Adventures in Babysitting, Leaving Las Vegas*), born Wilmington, DE, Oct 6, 1963.

Jeremy Sisto, 46, actor ("Six Feet Under," "Law & Order"), born Green Valley, CA, Oct 6, 1974.

Stephanie Zimbalist, 64, actress ("Remington Steele"), born Encino, CA, Oct 6, 1956.

October 7 — Wednesday

DAY 281   **85 REMAINING**

CATS **PREMIERE: ANNIVERSARY.** Oct 7, 1982. The second-longest-running production in Broadway history (after *The Phantom of the Opera*) opened this day. *Cats* was based on a book of poetry by T.S. Eliot and had a score by Andrew Lloyd Webber. More than 10 million theatergoers saw the New York City production, which closed Sept 10, 2000, after 7,485 performances. *Cats* was also produced in 30 other countries.

GEORGIA TECH BEATS CUMBERLAND 222–0: ANNIVERSARY. Oct 7, 1916. Georgia Tech University defeated Cumberland College, 222–0, in the most lopsided college football game of all time. Cumberland College had ended their football program recently but had to play the previously scheduled game or pay a fine. Consequently, their hastily fielded team were not regular football players. The Georgia Tech Engineers were coached by John Heisman, for whom the prestigious Heisman Trophy is named. Cumberland was led by student manager George Allen, who went on to advise presidents Roosevelt, Truman and Eisenhower.

MISSISSIPPI STATE FAIR. Oct 7–18. Jackson, MS. Features nightly professional entertainment, livestock show, midway carnival, domestic art exhibits. Annually, beginning on the first

October 2020	S	M	T	W	T	F	S
					1	2	3
	4	5	6	7	8	9	10
	11	12	13	14	15	16	17
	18	19	20	21	22	23	24
	25	26	27	28	29	30	31

Wednesday in October. Est attendance: 620,000. For info: Mississippi Fair Commission, PO Box 892, Jackson, MS 39205. Phone: (601) 961-4000. Web: www.mdac.ms.gov/bureaus-departments/state-fair-commission.

RANDOM ACTS OF POETRY DAY. Oct 7. This day is about painting poetry in the public square—either literally or figuratively. Chalk your poem onto the sidewalk (or a blackboard), leave one on a subway seat, pin one onto your local grocery store board. Take poetry action! Annually, the first Wednesday in October. For info: Tweetspeak Poetry. Web: www.tweetspeakpoetry.com/random-acts-of-poetry-day.

RILEY, JAMES WHITCOMB: BIRTH ANNIVERSARY. Oct 7, 1849. One of the most popular of 19th-century American poets, Riley was born at Greenfield, IN. The "Hoosier Poet" created sentimental poetry on rustic subjects. His *Rhymes of Childhood* (1891) was and remains a bestseller. He died at Indianapolis, IN, July 22, 1916.

RODNEY, CAESAR: BIRTH ANNIVERSARY. Oct 7, 1728. (Old Style date.) Signer of the Declaration of Independence who cast a tie-breaking vote. Born near Dover, DE, he died June 26, 1784, at Kent County, DE. Rodney is on the Delaware quarter issued by the US Mint in 1999, the first in a series of quarters that commemorate each of the 50 states.

WALLACE, HENRY AGARD: BIRTH ANNIVERSARY. Oct 7, 1888. 33rd vice president of the US (1941–45), born at Adair County, IA. Died at Danbury, CT, Nov 18, 1965.

🎂 BIRTHDAYS TODAY

Shawn Ashmore, 41, actor (*X-Men: The Last Stand, X2*, "The Following"), born Richmond, BC, Canada, Oct 7, 1979.

Joy Behar, 77, comedienne, television personality, born Brooklyn, NY, Oct 7, 1943.

Matt Bomer, 43, actor ("White Collar," *The Normal Heart, Magic Mike*), born St. Louis, MO, Oct 7, 1977.

Toni Braxton, 53, singer, born Severn, MD, Oct 7, 1967.

Simon Cowell, 61, television producer, personality ("American Idol"), born Brighton, East Sussex, England, Oct 7, 1959.

Charles Dutoit, 84, conductor, born Lausanne, Switzerland, Oct 7, 1936.

Thomas Keneally, 85, novelist (*Schindler's Ark, The Chant of Jimmie Blacksmith*), born Sydney, Australia, Oct 7, 1935.

Yo-Yo Ma, 65, cellist, born Paris, France, Oct 7, 1955.

John Mellencamp, 69, singer, songwriter, born Seymour, IN, Oct 7, 1951.

Tom Perez, 59, Chair of Democratic National Committee, born Buffalo, NY, Oct 7, 1961.

Vladimir Putin, 68, President of Russia, born Leningrad, USSR (now St. Petersburg, Russia), Oct 7, 1952.

Maxim Trankov, 37, Olympic figure skater, born Perm, USSR (now Russia), Oct 7, 1983.

Desmond Tutu, 89, South African archbishop, Nobel Peace Prize recipient, born Klerksdorp, South Africa, Oct 7, 1931.

Thom Yorke, 52, singer, musician (Radiohead), born Wellingborough, England, Oct 7, 1968.

October 8 — Thursday

DAY 282   **84 REMAINING**

ALVIN C. YORK DAY: ANNIVERSARY. Oct 8. While in the Argonne Forest, France, and separated from his patrol, on this day in 1918 during WWI Sergeant Alvin C. York killed 20 enemy soldiers and captured a hill, 132 enemy soldiers and 35 machine guns. He was awarded the US Medal of Honor and French Croix de Guerre. Ironically, York had petitioned for exemption from the draft as a conscientious objector but was turned down by his local draft board.

CROATIA: STATEHOOD DAY. Oct 8. Public holiday. Croatia's National Day.

CURTIS, MARGARET: BIRTH ANNIVERSARY. Oct 8, 1883. Golfer and tennis player born at Boston, MA. Curtis won three women's amateur national golf championships, in 1907, 1911 and 1912. She teamed with Evelyn Sears to win the 1908 women's tennis national doubles title. She played golf well into her 70s. The Curtis Cup, contested biennially between teams of amateur women golfers from the US and Great Britain, was initiated by Curtis and her sister Harriott in 1932. Died at Boston, Dec 25, 1965.

GEORGIA NATIONAL FAIR. Oct 8–18. Georgia National Fairgrounds, Perry, GA. Traditional state agricultural fair features thousands of entries in horse, livestock, horticulture, youth, home and fine arts categories. Family entertainment, education, fun, concerts, fireworks. Sponsored by the State of Georgia. Est attendance: 536,000. For info: Georgia Natl Fair, 401 Larry Walker Pkwy, Perry, GA 31069. Phone: (478) 987-3247. E-mail: kwalker@gnfa.com. Web: www.georgianationalfair.com.

GREAT CHICAGO FIRE: ANNIVERSARY. Oct 8, 1871. Great fire of Chicago began, according to legend, when Mrs O'Leary's cow kicked over the lantern in her barn on DeKoven Street. The fire leveled 3½ square miles, destroying 17,450 buildings and leaving 98,500 people homeless and about 250 people dead. Financially, the loss was $200 million. On the same day, a fire destroyed the entire town of Peshtigo, WI, killing more than 1,100 people.

HERBERT, FRANK: 100th BIRTH ANNIVERSARY. Oct 8, 1920. A writer who started his career as a journalist, Herbert published his first story in 1945 and went on to write the phenomenally successful science-fiction novel *Dune* (1965) and its five sequels. Initially refused by numerous publishers, *Dune* eventually sold more than twelve million copies during Herbert's lifetime; won the Hugo and the Nebula, science fiction's highest awards; and spurred a franchise in screen adaptations, comics, board, video, and role-play games. Born at Tacoma, WA, Herbert died Feb 11, 1986, at Madison, WI.

NATIONAL DEPRESSION SCREENING DAY. Oct 8. Held annually the Thursday of Mental Illness Awareness Week, National Depression Screening Day (NDSD) raises awareness and screens people for depression and related mood and anxiety disorders. NDSD is the nation's oldest voluntary, community-based screening program that provides referral information for treatment. Through the program, more than half a million people each year have been screened for depression since 1990. For info: National Depression Screening Day. Web: www.mentalhealthscreening.org/programs/ndsd.

NATIONAL HYDROGEN AND FUEL CELL DAY. Oct 8. A day to celebrate clean hydrogen and fuel cell energy technologies. Events are held nationwide by fuel cell manufacturers, fuel cell vehicle owners, hydrogen energy suppliers and policymakers. Annually, Oct 8 (10.08)—in reference to the atomic weight of hydrogen (1.008). For info: Fuel Cell and Hydrogen Energy Association, 1211 Connecticut Ave NW, Ste 650, Washington, DC 20036. Phone: (202) 261-1337. E-mail: jlewis@fchea.org. Web: www.hydrogenandfuelcellday.org.

NATIONAL PIEROGY DAY. Oct 8. Celebration of the pierogy! Commemorates the day in 1952 that pierogies were first delivered to a grocery store in Shenandoah, PA—marking the emergence of the traditionally Eastern European food as a mainstream American meal staple. Annually, Oct 8. For info: Mrs T's Pierogies. E-mail: mcass@hunterpr.com. Web: www.pierogies.com.

NATIONAL SALMON DAY. Oct 8. 6th annual. During National Seafood Month, a day to celebrate eating more heart-healthy salmon. Also to honor the many local businesses engaged in salmon-related fishing, packing and distribution. Annually, Oct 8. For info: Chicken of the Sea, 2150 E Grand Ave, El Segundo, CA 90245. Web: www.chickenofthesea.com.

OZZIE AND HARRIET RADIO DEBUT: ANNIVERSARY. Oct 8, 1944. Ozzie and Harriet Nelson made their CBS Radio debut in "The Adventures of Ozzie and Harriet." Although their sons, David and Ricky, were referred to frequently on air and eventually played by others, it was not until Feb 20, 1949, that David (age 12) and Rick (age 8) first appeared playing themselves on the show. "The Adventures of Ozzie and Harriet" hit television airwaves Oct 3, 1952, on ABC.

PEKAR, HARVEY: BIRTH ANNIVERSARY. Oct 8, 1939. Born at Cleveland, OH, this writer changed the face of American comic books with *American Splendor,* a semiautobiographical look at the life of a cranky, depressed file clerk. The comics frankly depicted the mundane issues and irritations of life "off the streets of Cleveland." Pekar worked with many different artists on the series, including R. Crumb, and won an American Book Award in 1987 for his first anthology of collected strips. *American Splendor* was also adapted as a feature film in 2003. Pekar died at Cleveland Heights, OH, July 12, 2010.

PESHTIGO FOREST FIRE: ANNIVERSARY. Oct 8, 1871. One of the most disastrous forest fires in history began at Peshtigo, WI, the same day the Great Chicago Fire began. The Wisconsin fire burned across six counties, killing more than 1,100 people.

RICKENBACKER, EDWARD V.: BIRTH ANNIVERSARY. Oct 8, 1890. American auto racer, war hero and airline executive (Eastern Airlines). Dubbed "America's Ace of Aces" for his victories as a pilot in the 94th Aero Squadron during WWI. Recipient of the Congressional Medal of Honor, the Distinguished Service Medal and the French Croix de Guerre. Born at Columbus, OH, Rickenbacker died July 23, 1973, at Zurich, Switzerland.

ROCKPORT-FULTON SEAFAIR. Oct 8–11. Ski Basin area, Rockport-Fulton, TX. Features fresh-from-the-bay seafood, gumbo cook-off, ongoing live musical entertainment, crab races, arts and crafts booths and land parade on Saturday. Est attendance: 20,000. For info: Rockport-Fulton Seafair, 319 Broadway, Rockport, TX 78382. Phone: (800) 242-0071 or (361) 729-6445. E-mail: tourism@1rockport.org. Web: www.rockportseafair.com.

October 2020	S	M	T	W	T	F	S
					1	2	3
	4	5	6	7	8	9	10
	11	12	13	14	15	16	17
	18	19	20	21	22	23	24
	25	26	27	28	29	30	31

SCHÜTZ, HEINRICH: BIRTH ANNIVERSARY. Oct 8, 1585. German musician and composer sometimes called the father of German music. Born at Kostritz, Saxony, Schütz died at Dresden, Germany, Nov 6, 1672. His works enjoyed renewed attention on the occasions of the bicentennials (1885) and tricentennials (1985) of two of his most devoted followers: George Frederick Handel and Johann Sebastian Bach.

TSVETAEVA, MARINA: BIRTH ANNIVERSARY. Oct 8, 1892. (New Style date.) Important Russian poet of the 20th century, born at Moscow, Russia, into an artistic family. Tsvetaeva was embattled by personal tragedy and the events of the 1917 Russian Revolution—she saw exile, poverty, hunger and the deaths of her husband and daughter. Her passionate and experimental poetry was championed among other poets (notably Boris Pasternak and Rainer Maria Rilke) in her time and grew in stature after her death by suicide at Yelabuga, USSR, on Aug 31, 1941.

🎂 BIRTHDAYS TODAY

Rona Barrett, 84, gossip columnist, born New York, NY, Oct 8, 1936.

Chevy Chase, 77, comedian, actor ("Community," *Caddyshack*), born Cornelius Crane at New York, NY, Oct 8, 1943.

Clodagh, 83, designer, born Clodagh Aubry at Galway, Ireland, Oct 8, 1937.

Matt Damon, 50, actor (*The Martian, The Bourne Identity, Good Will Hunting*), born Cambridge, MA, Oct 8, 1970.

Bill Elliott, 65, race car driver, born Dawsonville, GA, Oct 8, 1955.

Darrell Hammond, 60, comedian, actor ("Saturday Night Live"), born Melbourne, FL, Oct 8, 1960.

Paul Hogan, 81, actor, writer (*Crocodile Dundee*), born Lightning Ridge, Australia, Oct 8, 1939.

Jesse Jackson, 79, clergyman, civil rights leader, born Greenville, NC, Oct 8, 1941.

Sadiq Khan, 50, Mayor of London, politician (Labour), born London, England, Oct 8, 1970.

Bruno Mars, 35, singer, born Peter Gene Hernandez at Honolulu, HI, Oct 8, 1985.

Michael "The Miz" Mizanin, 40, professional wrestler, born Parma, OH, Oct 8, 1980.

Sarah Purcell, 72, television personality ("Real People"), born Richmond, IN, Oct 8, 1948.

Faith Ringgold, 90, artist, writer (*Tar Beach, My Dream of Martin Luther King*), born New York, NY, Oct 8, 1930.

R.L. Stine, 77, author (Goosebumps series), born Columbus, OH, Oct 8, 1943.

Bella Thorne, 23, actress ("Shake It Up!"), born Pembroke Pines, FL, Oct 8, 1997.

Sigourney Weaver, 71, actress (*Ghostbusters, Gorillas in the Mist,* Alien films), born New York, NY, Oct 8, 1949.

October 9 — Friday

DAY 283   **83 REMAINING**

ALABAMA NATIONAL FAIR. Oct 9–18. Garrett Coliseum/Fairgrounds, Montgomery, AL. A midway filled with exciting rides and games, arts and crafts, exhibits, livestock shows, racing pigs, a circus, a petting zoo, food and entertainment. Est attendance: 225,000. For info: Alabama National Fair, PO Box 3304, Montgomery, AL 36109-0304. Phone: (334) 272-6831. E-mail: anf@alnationalfair.org. Web: www.alnationalfair.org.

ALGONQUIN MILL FALL FESTIVAL. Oct 9–11. Five miles south of Carrollton, OH. Presented by the Carroll County Historical

Society. An 1800s pioneer festival featuring steam-powered grist-mill and sawmill in operation. Also featured are antique tools and farm museum; antique cars and tractors; quilting, spinning, dyeing and weaving demonstrations; five log buildings (including a two-story home); musical entertainment and quality craftspeople selling their products. A one-room school and a railroad station are on exhibit. Est attendance: 20,000. For info: Carroll County CVB. Phone: (877) 727-0103. Web: www.carrollcountyohio.com/history.

AMERICA'S FIRST DEPARTMENT STORE: ANNIVERSARY. Oct 9, 1868. Salt Lake City, UT. America's first department store, "ZCMI" (Zion's Co-Operative Mercantile Institution), is still operating at Salt Lake City (although under a new name and new ownership). It was founded under the direction of Brigham Young.

APPLE BUTTER MAKIN' DAYS. Oct 9–11. Mount Vernon, MO. 54th annual. A large festival highlighting the making of apple butter in large copper kettles on the courthouse lawn. Also, 350 craft booths displaying and selling handmade goods, free entertainment, pet parade, wiener dog race and terrapin race. Contests include apple pie baking, apple pie eating, bubble gum blowing, nail driving, peddle tractor pull and queen/princess. Parade Saturday and worship service and Christian music on Sunday. Annually, the second full weekend in October. Est attendance: 100,000. For info: Mount Vernon Chamber of Commerce, PO Box 373, Mount Vernon, MO 65712. Phone: (417) 466-7654. E-mail: chamber@mtvchamber.com. Web: www.mtvchamber.com.

ARKANSAS STATE FAIR AND LIVESTOCK SHOW. Oct 9–18. Barton Coliseum and State Fairground, Little Rock, AR. Showcasing Arkansas with a focus on agriculture, livestock, the arts and technology. Annually, beginning on the second Friday in October. Est attendance: 400,000. For info: Arkansas State Fair, 2600 Howard St, Little Rock, AR 72206. Phone: (501) 372-8341. E-mail: info@arkansasstatefair.com. Web: www.arkansasstatefair.com.

BOK, EDWARD WILLIAM: BIRTH ANNIVERSARY. Oct 9, 1863. Influential magazine executive and editor, born at Den Helder, Netherlands. After immigrating with his family to Brooklyn, NY, Bok worked his way up in the magazine industry, eventually becoming editor of the *Ladies' Home Journal* from 1889 to 1919. He introduced journalistic innovations, championed social reforms (among them women's suffrage) and influenced contemporary culture. His position in society was such that by 1917 readers were sending his office one million letters a year. Bok died Jan 9, 1930, at Lake Wales, FL.

CANADA: KITCHENER-WATERLOO OKTOBERFEST. Oct 9–17. Kitchener and Waterloo, ON. The second-largest Oktoberfest in the world. More than 40 events and festhallen, including one of the premier parades in Canada on Canadian Thanksgiving morning (Oct 12). Annually, beginning on the Friday before Canadian Thanksgiving. Est attendance: 700,000. For info: K-W Oktoberfest Inc, 17 Benton St, Kitchener, ON N2G 3G9, Canada. Phone: (519) 570-4267 or (888) 294-HANS. E-mail: info@oktoberfest.ca. Web: www.oktoberfest.ca.

COLUMBUS DAY FESTIVAL AND HOT-AIR BALLOON REGATTA. Oct 9–11. Columbus, KS. Regatta starts with Balloon Glow on Friday evening; prizes are awarded for both Saturday and Sunday races. Also, car show, arts and crafts fair, entertainment, children's festival and more. Est attendance: 15,000. For info: Columbus Chamber of Commerce, 320 E Maple, Columbus, KS 66725. Phone: (620) 429-1492. E-mail: columbuschamber@columbus-ks.com. Web: www.chamberofcolumbus.com or www.columbusday-balloons.com.

DREYFUS, ALFRED: BIRTH ANNIVERSARY. Oct 9, 1859. This French army officer, born at Mulhouse, France, was the center of a military scandal from 1894 to 1906. From when he was accused of treason (forged documents were used to convict him) in 1894 and sentenced to life in 1895 at Devil's Island, the Dreyfus affair was a lightning rod for rival factions in France and exposed the virulent anti-Semitism in the country (Dreyfus was Jewish). The case was notable for the involvement of France's major literary figures in his defense, most famously Émile Zola, who published "J'Accuse"

in 1898 in a periodical and accused the French army of a massive cover-up. Public outrage ensured two more trials for Dreyfus. He was still found guilty but was pardoned at his last trial in 1899. A 1906 civilian court finally cleared Dreyfus, who eventually returned to the military. He died July 12, 1935, at Paris, France.

FIRST PGA CHAMPIONSHIP: ANNIVERSARY. Oct 9–14, 1916. The then-recently formed Professional Golfers' Association of America held its first championship at Siwanoy Country Club, Bronxville, NY. The trophy and the lion's share of the $2,580 purse were won by British golfer Jim Barnes. Barnes also won the second competition—not held until 1919 because of WWI. In 1921 PGA cofounder Walter Hagen became the first American to win, a feat he accomplished four more times—in 1924, '25, '26 and '27.

ICELAND: LEIF ERIKSON DAY. Oct 9. Celebrates discovery of North America in the year 1000 by the Norse explorer.

KOREA: ALPHABET DAY (HANGUL). Oct 9. Celebrates anniversary of promulgation of Hangul (24-letter phonetic alphabet) by King Sejong of the Yi dynasty in 1446.

★LEIF ERIKSON DAY. Oct 9. Presidential Proclamation always issued for Oct 9 since 1964 at request (PL 88–566 of Sept 2, 1964).

LENNON, JOHN: 80th BIRTH ANNIVERSARY. Oct 9, 1940. John Winston Lennon, English composer, musician and member of The Beatles, the sensationally popular group of musical performers who captivated audiences first in England and Germany, and later throughout the world. A fervent activist for peace. Born at Liverpool, England, Lennon was murdered at New York City, Dec 8, 1980.

MISSION DELORES FOUNDING: ANNIVERSARY. Oct 9, 1776. The oldest building at San Francisco, CA. Formerly known as Mission San Francisco de Asis, the mission survived the great earthquake and fire of 1906.

MOON PHASE: LAST QUARTER. Oct 9. Moon enters Last Quarter phase at 8:39 PM, EDT.

NATIONAL NANOTECHNOLOGY DAY. Oct 9. Since 2016, this day features a series of community-led events and activities to help raise awareness of nanotechnology—how it is currently used in products that enrich our daily lives and the challenges and opportunities it holds for the future. Annually, on or around Oct 9 (10/9 pays homage to the nanometer scale, 10-9 meters). For info: Natl Nanotechnology Coordination Office, 2415 Eisenhower Ave, Alexandria, VA 22314. E-mail: info@nnco.nano.gov. Web: http://nano.gov/nationalnanotechnologyday.

OCEAN COUNTY COLUMBUS DAY PARADE AND ITALIAN FESTIVAL. Oct 9–11. Seaside Heights, NJ. Parade features bands, floats, groups, organizations, antique cars and special performers from Italy. The festival features ethnic and traditional foods, entertainment, exhibits and performances from special guest performers from Italy. Est attendance: 90,000. For info: Ocean County Columbus Day Parade Committee, PO Box 187 (1492), 500 Christopher Columbus Blvd, Seaside Heights, NJ 08751. Phone: (732) 477-6507. E-mail: info@ColumbusNJ.org. Web: www.ColumbusNJ.org.

PERU: DAY OF NATIONAL HONOR. Oct 9. Public holiday. Commemorates nationalization of the oil fields in 1968.

SCENIC DRIVE FESTIVAL. Oct 9–11. Van Buren County, IA. Scenic landscapes, historic architecture, flea market, arts festival, crafts and more. Annually, the second Friday, Saturday and Sunday in October. Est attendance: 18,000. For info: Villages of Van Buren,

Inc, PO Box 9, Keosauqua, IA 52565. Phone: (800) 868-7822. E-mail: info@villagesofvanburen.com. Web: www.villagesofvanburen.com.

SOUTHERN FESTIVAL OF BOOKS: A CELEBRATION OF THE WRITTEN WORD. Oct 9–11 (tentative). War Memorial Plaza, Nashville, TN. 32nd annual. The festival annually welcomes more than 200 authors from throughout the nation and in every genre for readings, panel discussions and book signings. The festival hosts popular book exhibitors and programs and features three performance stages throughout the event. Special events for children are planned throughout the weekend. Annually, the second full weekend in October. Est attendance: 20,000. For info: Southern Festival of Books, Humanities Tennessee, 807 Main St, Ste B, Nashville, TN 37206. Phone: (615) 770-0006. E-mail: info@humanitiestennessee.org. Web: www.humanitiestennessee.org.

SPACE MILESTONE: NASA'S MOON CRASH: ANNIVERSARY. Oct 9, 2009. On this date NASA deliberately crashed two unmanned spacecrafts into the moon in an attempt to confirm the existence of water there. The impact sent a plume of debris more than a mile above the moon's surface, and water particles found in the plume confirmed NASA's suspicions.

TATI, JACQUES: BIRTH ANNIVERSARY. Oct 9, 1908 (some sources say 1907). Born at Le Pecq, France, Tati was a filmmaker and performer who made internationally beloved comic masterpieces—often combining the best of silent comedy in films that depicted the Average Joe's misalliance with modern industrialized society. Tati's filmic alter ego was the pipe-smoking, rumpled hat-wearing Monsieur Hulot, who was always out of step wherever he was. Tati's six films include *Mr Hulot's Holiday* (1953), *Mon oncle* (1958) and *Playtime* (1967). Tati died Nov 5, 1982, at Paris, France.

UGANDA: INDEPENDENCE DAY. Oct 9. National holiday commemorating achievement of autonomy from Britain in 1962.

UNITED NATIONS: WORLD POST DAY. Oct 9. An annual special observance of Postal Administrations of the Universal Postal Union (UPU). Annually, Oct 9. For info: United Nations, Dept of Public Info, New York, NY 10017. Web: www.un.org.

🎂 BIRTHDAYS TODAY

Scott Bakula, 66, actor ("NCIS: New Orleans," "Enterprise," "Quantum Leap"), born St. Louis, MO, Oct 9, 1954.

Jackson Browne, 70, singer, songwriter, born Heidelberg, Germany, Oct 9, 1950.

Zachery Ty Bryan, 39, actor ("Home Improvement"), born Aurora, CO, Oct 9, 1981.

David Cameron, 54, former prime minister of Great Britain (2010–16), born London, England, Oct 9, 1966.

Guillermo del Toro, 56, film director and screenwriter (Oscar for *The Shape of Water*; *Pan's Labyrinth, Hellboy, Cronos*), producer, author, born Guillermo del Toro Gómez at Guadalajara, Mexico, Oct 9, 1964.

Colin Donnell, 38, actor ("Arrow," "Pan Am"), born St. Louis, MO, Oct 9, 1982.

Bella Hadid, 24, model, born Isabella Khair Hadid at Los Angeles, CA, Oct 9, 1996.

Bill Lee, 61, Governor of Tennessee (R), born Franklin, TN, Oct 9, 1959.

Scotty McCreery, 27, country singer, television personality ("American Idol"), born Garner, NC, Oct 9, 1993.

October 2020	S	M	T	W	T	F	S
					1	2	3
	4	5	6	7	8	9	10
	11	12	13	14	15	16	17
	18	19	20	21	22	23	24
	25	26	27	28	29	30	31

Steve McQueen, 51, director (*12 Years a Slave, Shame*), producer (Oscar for *12 Years a Slave*), born London, England, Oct 9, 1969.

Russell Myers, 82, cartoonist ("Broom Hilda"), born Pittsburg, KS, Oct 9, 1938.

Michael Pare, 61, actor (*Streets of Fire, The Philadelphia Experiment*), born Brooklyn, NY, Oct 9, 1959.

Joseph Anthony (Joe) Pepitone, 80, former baseball player, born New York, NY, Oct 9, 1940.

Brandon Routh, 41, actor ("One Life to Live," *Superman Returns*), born Des Moines, IA, Oct 9, 1979.

Tony Shalhoub, 67, actor (Emmys for "Monk"; "The Marvelous Mrs Maisel," "Wings," *Big Night*), born Green Bay, WI, Oct 9, 1953.

Michael (Mike) Singletary, 62, football coach and Hall of Fame player, born Houston, TX, Oct 9, 1958.

Annika Sorenstam, 50, former golfer, born Stockholm, Sweden, Oct 9, 1970.

Robert Wuhl, 69, writer, actor (*Bull Durham, Cobb*), born Union, NJ, Oct 9, 1951.

October 10 — Saturday

DAY 284	82 REMAINING

AGNEW RESIGNATION: ANNIVERSARY. Oct 10, 1973. Spiro Theodore Agnew became the second person to resign the office of vice president of the US. Agnew entered a plea of no contest to a charge of income tax evasion (on contract kickbacks received while he was governor of Maryland and after he became vice president). He was sentenced to pay a $10,000 fine and serve three years' probation. Agnew was elected vice president twice, serving under President Richard M. Nixon. See also: "Agnew, Spiro Theodore: Birth Anniversary" (Nov 9).

AMERICAN INDIAN INTERTRIBAL POWWOW. Oct 10–11. Jamestown Settlement, Williamsburg, VA. Join in a two-day celebration of song, dance and storytelling, featuring American Indian tribes. For info: Jamestown-Yorktown Foundation, PO Box 1607, Williamsburg, VA 23187. Phone: (757) 253-4838 or (888) 593-4682. Fax: (757) 253-5299. Web: www.historyisfun.org.

BONZA BOTTLER DAY®. Oct 10. To celebrate when the number of the day is the same as the number of the month. Bonza Bottler Day® is an excuse to have a party at least once a month. For more information see Jan 1. For info: Gail Berger, Bonza Bottler Day. Phone: (864) 201-3988. E-mail: bonza@bonzabottlerday.com. Web: www.bonzabottlerday.com.

BURGOO FESTIVAL. Oct 10–11. Downtown, North Utica, IL. 51st annual. Only the "Burgoomeister" knows the secret recipe for this pioneer stew, burgoo, served outdoors at this annual Utica festival. Other events include arts and crafts, antiques, food and music. Free admission. Annually, Columbus Day weekend. Est attendance: 45,000. For info: Burgoo Chairman, LaSalle County Historical Museum, 101 Canal St, Utica, IL 61373. Phone: (815) 667-4861. E-mail: events.lchs@gmail.com. Web: www.lasallecountyhistoricalsociety.org.

CHINCOTEAGUE ISLAND OYSTER FESTIVAL. Oct 10. Tom's Cove Park, Chincoteague Island, VA. 48th annual. This festival promotes the seafood industry and marks the arrival of the oyster season. Oysters are prepared just about every way imaginable—and there are clam fritters, clam chowder, hushpuppies, french fries, hot dogs and various beverages. Live entertainment for everyone's enjoyment. Tickets can be obtained in advance by contacting Chincoteague Chamber of Commerce. Tickets will sell out. Est attendance: 3,000. For info: Chincoteague Chamber of Commerce, 6733 Maddox Blvd, Chincoteague Island, VA 23336. Phone: (757) 336-6161. Fax: (757) 336-1242. E-mail: info@chincoteaguechamber.com. Web: www.chincoteaguechamber.com.

CHOWDER DAYS. Oct 10–12. Mystic Seaport Museum, Mystic, CT. A riverfront festival of New England chowders. Annually, Columbus Day weekend. Est attendance: 9,000. For info: Mystic Seaport Museum, 75 Greenmanville Ave, PO Box 6000, Mystic, CT 06355-0990. Phone: (860) 572-0711. Web: www.mysticseaport.org.

CUBA: BEGINNING OF INDEPENDENCE WARS DAY. Oct 10. National holiday. Commemorates the beginning of Cuba's struggle against Spain in 1868.

DOUBLE TENTH DAY (CHINA AND TAIWAN). Oct 10. Double Tenth Day is observed by many Chinese as the anniversary of the outbreak of the revolution against the imperial Manchu dynasty, Oct 10, 1911. Sun Yat-sen and Huan Hsing were among the revolutionary leaders. This is a holiday in Taiwan.

HAYES, HELEN: BIRTH ANNIVERSARY. Oct 10, 1900. Actress Helen Hayes, often called "the First Lady of the American Theater," was born at Washington, DC. Hayes's greatest stage triumph was her role as the long-lived British monarch Queen Victoria in the play *Victoria Regina*. Her first great success was in *Coquette* (1927). She won an Academy Award for Best Actress for her first major film role in *The Sin of Madelon Claudet* (1931) and won Best Supporting Actress for her role in *Airport* (1971). Helen Hayes died Mar 17, 1993, at Nyack, NY.

LEGENDS AND LANTERNS. Oct 10–11 (also Oct 17–18, 23–25). Saint Charles, MO. A Spirited Journey through Halloween History! On Halloween, the city becomes a ghost town—literally. Historic Main Street is invaded by a plethora of playful paranormal poltergeists from parts unknown. These friendly ghouls have more treats to offer than tricks, and they enjoy meeting "little monsters" of all ages. Just look for the lanterns! Enjoy holiday shopping all day and night on Saturdays and Sundays. Annually, the second, third and fourth weekends in October. Est attendance: 50,000. For info: Saint Charles CVB, 230 S Main St, Saint Charles, MO 63301. Phone: (800) 366-2427. Web: www.discoverstcharles.com.

LOUISIANA ART & FOLK FESTIVAL. Oct 10. Columbia, LA. Festival that centers on the rich folklife of Louisiana as well as on the fine arts. Wonderful music all day, antique car show, craft booths, children's art and petting zoo as well as food to please everyone. Est attendance: 3,500. For info: Caldwell Parish Chamber of Commerce, PO Box 1808, Columbia, LA 71418. Phone: (318) 649-0726. E-mail: cpchamber60@yahoo.com.

MONK, THELONIOUS: BIRTH ANNIVERSARY. Oct 10, 1917. Intuitive, innovative and iconoclastic, Thelonious Monk transformed jazz piano. A gifted improviser and composer, Monk's additions to the jazz idiom include "'Round Midnight" and "Straight, No Chaser." His bold compositions often included abrupt percussive moments and sharp silences, and Monk himself was considered an eccentric. Highly regarded by his peers (he recorded with John Coltrane), Monk's work often didn't translate to album sales, though he recorded for Blue Note, Riverside and Columbia throughout the 1950s, 1960s and 1970s. Monk died Feb 17, 1982, at Englewood, NJ. In 2006, he was posthumously awarded a Pulitzer Prize in recognition of his achievements.

MOTORSPORT MEMORIAL DAY. Oct 10. Since 2016, a national day of remembrance paying tribute to motorsport's fallen heroes—all the drivers, marshals, crew members and fans who are no longer with us. Annually, Oct 10. For info: Motorsport Safety Foundation, 2020 Ponce de Leon Blvd, PH2, Coral Gables, FL 33134. Phone: (305) 755-5129. Web: www.motorsport-safety.org.

MOUNTAIN GLORY FESTIVAL. Oct 10. Marion, NC. 37th annual. A celebration of mountain heritage in western North Carolina. Arts, crafts, children's area and continuous entertainment. Annually, the second Saturday in October. Est attendance: 20,000. For info: Mountain Glory Festival, PO Drawer 700, Marion, NC 28752. Phone: (828) 652-2215. Fax: (828) 652-1983. E-mail: info@mntgloryfestival.com. Web: www.mtngloryfestival.com.

NATIONAL CAKE DECORATING DAY. Oct 10. A day to break out your boldest designs and unique techniques. Let your creativity run wild and create your most epic cake design yet. With the right tools, instruction and inspiration, anyone can achieve amazing results in cake decorating and sweet treat making. Annually, Oct 10. For info: Desiree Smith, Wilton Enterprises, 535 E Diehl Rd, Naperville, IL 60563. Phone: (630) 810-2254. E-mail: dsmith@wilton.com. Web: www.wilton.com.

NATIONAL HANDBAG DAY. Oct 10. 8th annual. A day to celebrate the design, craftsmanship and fine materials that go into the thing we carry with us every day: the handbag. Everywhere you look, someone is carrying some kind of handbag—big, small, old, new, cheap or expensive. On the heels of New York Fashion Week, what better way to celebrate what you love to carry and why. Whether you have the newest "It Bag" like an Hermes Birkin or Celine Tote or you carry your mother's vintage Louis Vuitton or you have no idea what kind of bag you carry but you love it, use this day to share pictures and stories with other handbag fanatics. Annually, Oct 10. For info: PurseBlog, 757 SE 17th St, #1177, Ft Lauderdale, FL 33316. E-mail: info@purseblog.com. Web: www.purseblog.com.

OKLAHOMA HISTORICAL DAY. Oct 10. Oklahoma.

PINTER, HAROLD: 90th BIRTH ANNIVERSARY. Oct 10, 1930. British playwright, actor and poet, born at East London, England, eponym of the dramatic term *Pinteresque*. Known for such dark and absurd plays as *The Birthday Party, The Caretaker* and *The Homecoming*, described as "comedies of menace." The 2005 Nobel Prize for Literature went to Pinter, "who in his plays uncovers the precipice under everyday prattle and forces entry into oppression's closed rooms." In 2007 he received the French Legion of Honor. Pinter died Dec 24, 2008, at London.

PRATER'S MILL COUNTRY FAIR. Oct 10–11. Dalton, GA. A Southern festival of artists, craftspeople, music and food. Annually, the second full weekend in October. Est attendance: 18,000. For info: Prater's Mill Country Fair, Prater's Mill Foundation, Inc, PO Drawer H, Varnell, GA 30756. Phone: (706) 694-MILL. E-mail: Fair@PratersMill.org. Web: PratersMill.org/Fair.

SHEMINI ATZERET. Oct 10. Hebrew calendar date: Tishri 22, 5781. The eighth day of Solemn Assembly, part of the Sukkot festival (see entry on Oct 3), with memorial services and cycle of biblical readings in the synagogue. Began at sundown on Oct 9.

TAKE YOUR MEDICINE, AMERICANS WEEK. Oct 10–17. This campaign has been designed to help educate health professionals,

patients and consumers about the problem of not taking prescription drugs or over-the-counter medicines. This is a $290 billion problem that needs a solution. Sponsored by the American College of Apothecaries (ACA)/Pharmacists Planning Service, Inc (PPSI). For info: ACA/PPSI, 2830 Summer Oaks Dr, Bartlett, TN 38134. E-mail: info@ppsinc.org. Web: www.ppsinc.org.

TUXEDO CREATED: ANNIVERSARY. Oct 10, 1886. Griswold Lorillard of Tuxedo Park, NY, fashioned the first tuxedo for men by cutting the tails off a tailcoat.

"UPSTAIRS, DOWNSTAIRS" TV PREMIERE: ANNIVERSARY. Oct 10, 1971. The 52 episodes of this British series covered the years 1903–30 in the life of a wealthy London family ("Upstairs") and their many servants ("Downstairs"). Cast members included Angela Baddeley, Pauline Collins, Gordon Jackson and Jean Marsh. Won a Golden Globe for Best Drama TV Show in 1975 and an Emmy for Outstanding Limited Series in 1976. The last episode aired May 1, 1977. In 2010 the series was revived (without the comma in the title) for episodes set in 1936 with a new family occupying 165 Eaton Place but with Jean Marsh returning as Rose Buck.

US NAVAL ACADEMY FOUNDED: 175th ANNIVERSARY. Oct 10, 1845. A college to train officers for the US Navy was established at Annapolis, MD. Women were admitted in 1976. The academy's motto is "Honor, Courage, Commitment." For info: www.usna.edu.

VERDI, GIUSEPPE: BIRTH ANNIVERSARY. Oct 10, 1813. Italian composer, born at Le Roncole, Italy. His 26 operas, including *Rigoletto*, *Il Trovatore*, *La Traviata* and *Aida*, are among the most popular of all operatic music today. Died at Milan, Italy, Jan 27, 1901.

WORLD DAY AGAINST THE DEATH PENALTY. Oct 10. 18th annual. In 2003 the World Coalition created the first World Day Against the Death Penalty. This initiative was expressed through more than 180 local initiatives across the world. Canada, France, Italy, Mexico, Belgium, the African Commission on Human and Peoples' Rights and the European Union officially supported the World Day. In 2007 the Council of Europe and the European Union officially recognized the World Day as European Day Against the Death Penalty. Each year, the programs expand and a focus is chosen. Annually, Oct 10. For info: World Coalition Against the Death Penalty. Web: www.worldcoalition.org.

WORLD MENTAL HEALTH DAY. Oct 10. This day aims to encourage governments and organizations around the world, in countries at all income levels, to look at mental health issues in their communities and to educate and change prevailing perceptions of mental illness. Annually, Oct 10. For info: World Federation for Mental Health. Web: www.wfmh.com.

October 2020	S	M	T	W	T	F	S
					1	2	3
	4	5	6	7	8	9	10
	11	12	13	14	15	16	17
	18	19	20	21	22	23	24
	25	26	27	28	29	30	31

🎂 BIRTHDAYS TODAY

Bob Burnquist, 44, skateboarder, born Rio de Janeiro, Brazil, Oct 10, 1976.

Charles Dance, 74, actor ("Game of Thrones," *The Jewel in the Crown, White Mischief*), born Worcestershire, England, Oct 10, 1946.

Dale Earnhardt, Jr, 46, sportscaster and former race car driver, born Concord, NC, Oct 10, 1974.

Brett Favre, 51, Hall of Fame football player, born Gulfport, MS, Oct 10, 1969.

Jessica Harper, 71, actress (*Stardust Memories, Pennies from Heaven, My Favorite Year*), born Chicago, IL, Oct 10, 1949.

Mario Lopez, 47, television personality, actor ("Saved by the Bell"), born San Diego, CA, Oct 10, 1973.

Gavin Newsom, 53, Governor of California (D), born San Francisco, CA, Oct 10, 1967.

Chris Pronger, 46, Hall of Fame hockey player, born Dryden, ON, Canada, Oct 10, 1974.

Nora Roberts, 70, author (*Birthright, Hidden Riches, Rising Tides*), born Silver Spring, MD, Oct 10, 1950.

David Lee Roth, 65, singer (Van Halen), born Bloomington, IN, Oct 10, 1955.

Dan Stevens, 38, actor ("Legion," "Downton Abbey," *Beauty and the Beast*), born Croydon, Surrey, England, Oct 10, 1982.

Tanya Tucker, 62, singer, born Seminole, TX, Oct 10, 1958.

Ben Vereen, 74, actor, singer, dancer (Tony for *Pippin*; *Roots, All That Jazz*, "Webster"), born Miami, FL, Oct 10, 1946.

Bradley Whitford, 61, actor (*Get Out, The Post*, "The West Wing," "Transparent"), born Madison, WI, Oct 10, 1959.

October 11 — Sunday

DAY 285　　　　　　　　　　　**81 REMAINING**

BANK OF AMERICA CHICAGO MARATHON. Oct 11. Grant Park, Chicago, IL. Flat, fast 26.2-mile course attracts everyone from elite athletes to novice marathon runners from all 50 states and more than 120 foreign countries. Annually, the Sunday of Columbus Day weekend. Est attendance: 850,000. For info: Bank of America Chicago Marathon. Phone: (312) 904-9800. E-mail: office@chicagomarathon.com. Web: www.chicagomarathon.com.

BLAKEY, ART: BIRTH ANNIVERSARY. Oct 11, 1919. Born at Pittsburgh, PA, Blakey switched from piano to drums while still in his youth and by the late 1930s was gigging with pianist, arranger and fellow Pittsburgh native Mary Lou Williams. The 1940s found Blakey behind the kit for Billy Eckstine's big band, and by 1949 he was recording as a leader for Blue Note. *The Jazz Messengers* (1956, Columbia), with pianist Horace Silver, established him alongside that moniker. The Messengers concentrated on hard bop and jazz traditionalism; with Blakey as its leader, the group was an incubator for numerous jazz luminaries, including Wayne Shorter, Lee Morgan and Wynton Marsalis. "This is the music of my culture good, bad or indifferent," Blakey said of his life's work. "No America—no jazz. It's the only culture America has brought forth." He died Oct 16, 1990, at New York, NY.

BRAZIL: CIRIO DE NAZARE. Oct 11–24. Belem, Para. Greatest festival of northern Brazil, the Feast of Cirio starts on the second Sunday in October in the city of Belem (St. Mary of Bethlehem), capital of the state of Para. Festival lasts two weeks.

CANADA: WINDSOR AND WEST HANTS PUMPKIN REGATTA. Oct 11. Windsor, NS. Held annually since 1999, the regatta is a unique event in which intrepid competitors race giant pumpkin boats (500 to 800 pounds) across Lake Pesaquid. There are three racing divisions: Motor, Paddling and Experimental. The pumpkin boats are referred to as PVCs (personal vegetable crafts). A parade and decoration contest add to the festivities. Annually, the second Sunday in October. Est attendance: 5,000. For info: The Windsor-West Hants Pumpkin Festival Society, 400 College Rd, Windsor, NS, Canada B0N 2T0. Phone: (902) 798-6679. E-mail: vanessa@town.windsor.ns.ca. Web: www.worldsbiggestpumpkins.com.

EARTH SCIENCE WEEK. Oct 11–17. First observed in 1998. A week to help the public gain a better understanding and appreciation of the earth sciences and to encourage stewardship of Earth. Annually, the second full week in October. For info: American Geosciences Institute, 4220 King St, Alexandria, VA 22302. Web: www.earthsciweek.org.

EMERGENCY NURSES WEEK. Oct 11–17. Developed by the Emergency Nurses Association (ENA) in 1989, this weeklong celebration recognizes emergency nurses for standing at the front line of healthcare and for their dedication, service and commitment to patients and communities. The Wednesday of this week is Emergency Nurses Day. For info: Emergency Nurses Assn. E-mail: contact@ena.org. Web: www.ena.org.

★GENERAL PULASKI MEMORIAL DAY. Oct 11. Presidential Proclamation always issued for Oct 11 since 1929. Requested by congressional resolution each year, 1929–46. (Since 1947 has been issued by custom.) Note: Proclamation 4869, of Oct 5, 1981, covers all succeeding years.

GRANDMOTHER'S DAY IN FLORIDA. Oct 11. A ceremonial day on the second Sunday in October.

LEONARD, ELMORE: 95th BIRTH ANNIVERSARY. Oct 11, 1925. Born at New Orleans, LA, prolific author Leonard grew up in Detroit, MI, and earned the nickname "the Dickens of Detroit." Featuring incisive wit, notable works include *Get Shorty, 52 Pick-up, Rum Punch* and the short western "3:10 to Yuma." *Hombre* was named one of the best western novels of all time (1977). Nearly all titles in his canon have been optioned for the big or small screen, and many adaptations (some with his screenplay) became hits. The recipient of numerous awards, including the Edgar Allan Poe Award (1984), PEN USA's Lifetime Achievement Award (2009) and the Western Writers of America's Owen Wister Award (2009), Leonard died Aug 20, 2013, at Bloomfield Village, MI.

NATIONAL COMING OUT DAY. Oct 11. A project of the Human Rights Campaign since 1988. Every Oct 11, thousands of lesbian, gay, bisexual and transgender (LGBT) individuals and their supportive allies celebrate National Coming Out Day, which encourages LGBT individuals to come out and be honest about themselves. Every year workshops, speak-outs, rallies and other kinds of events are held—all aimed at showing the public that LGBT people are everywhere. For info: Human Rights Campaign. Phone: (800) 777-4723. E-mail: feedback@hrc.org or press@hrc.org. Web: www.hrc.org/comingout.

NATIONAL FOOD BANK WEEK. Oct 11–17. Educates and recognizes efforts of food banks, their donors and volunteers to alleviate hunger in the US. Observed at local food banks around the country. Annually, the week encompassing World Food Day (Oct 16). For information on activities or food banks in your area, go to Feeding America's website at www.feedingamerica.org and do a zip code search.

PATENT ISSUED FOR FIRST ADDING MACHINE: ANNIVERSARY. Oct 11, 1887. A patent was granted to Dorr Eugene Felt for the Comptometer, which was the first adding machine known to be absolutely accurate at all times.

REVSON, CHARLES: BIRTH ANNIVERSARY. Oct 11, 1906. Revson, born at Boston, MA, was the colorful and hard-driving force behind Revlon cosmetics, a company he created in 1932. Revson was fond of saying, "Creative people are like a wet towel. You wring them out and pick up another one." By the time of his death, Aug 24, 1975, Revson had an estate valued at $100 million and a cosmetics empire.

ROBBINS, JEROME: BIRTH ANNIVERSARY. Oct 11, 1918. Director, choreographer and ballet dancer, born at New York, NY. Robbins

directed and choreographed many Broadway musicals including *West Side Story, Fiddler on the Roof, The King and I* and *On the Town*. The winner of five Tony Awards and two Oscars, Robbins died at New York, NY, July 29, 1998.

ROBINSON, ROSCOE, JR: BIRTH ANNIVERSARY. Oct 11, 1928. The first black American to achieve the army rank of four-star general. Born at St. Louis, MO, and died at Washington, DC, July 22, 1993.

ROOSEVELT, ANNA ELEANOR: BIRTH ANNIVERSARY. Oct 11, 1884. Wife of Franklin Delano Roosevelt, 32nd president of the US, born at New York, NY. Eleanor Roosevelt led an active and independent life and was the first wife of a president to give her own news conference in the White House (1933). Widely known throughout the world, she was affectionately called "the first lady of the world." She served as US delegate to the United Nations General Assembly for a number of years before her death at New York, NY, Nov 7, 1962. A prolific writer, she wrote in *This Is My Story*, "No one can make you feel inferior without your consent."

SAMOA AND AMERICAN SAMOA: WHITE SUNDAY. Oct 11. The second Sunday in October. For the children of Samoa and American Samoa, this is the biggest day of the year. Traditional roles are reversed, as children lead church services, are served special foods and receive gifts of new church clothes and other special items. All the children dress in white. The following Monday is an official holiday.

"SATURDAY NIGHT LIVE" TV PREMIERE: 45th ANNIVERSARY. Oct 11, 1975. Originally titled "NBC's Saturday Night," this live show features skits, commercial parodies and news satires, with a different guest host and musical guest performing weekly. Its first guest host was comedian George Carlin. Notable cast members have included Chevy Chase, Dan Aykroyd, John Belushi, Jane Curtin, Garrett Morris, Laraine Newman, Gilda Radner, Bill Murray, Joe Piscopo, Eddie Murphy, Billy Crystal, Martin Short, Christopher Guest, Harry Shearer, Joan Cusack, Robert Downey, Jr, Nora Dunn, Jon Lovitz, Dana Carvey, Phil Hartman, Jan Hooks, Dennis Miller, Chris Farley, Mike Myers, Adam Sandler, Will Ferrell, Molly Shannon, Tina Fey, Amy Poehler, Bill Hader, Kristen Wiig, Fred Armisen, Andy Samberg, Kenan Thompson, Will Forte and Kate McKinnon.

SIMCHAT TORAH. Oct 11. Hebrew calendar date: Tishri 23, 5781. Rejoicing in the Torah follows the seven-day Sukkot festival and Shemini Atzeret. Public reading of the Pentateuch is completed and begun again, symbolizing the need for ever-continuing study. Began at sundown on Oct 10.

SIMON, JOE: BIRTH ANNIVERSARY. Oct 11, 1913. Artist Hymie "Joe" Simon was born Oct 11, 1913, at Rochester, NY. Working in New York City as comic books first flourished, Simon met artist Jack Kirby, and in 1941 the duo created superhero Captain America. Simon developed many other characters during this first comics golden Age and stayed active in the industry, serving as the first editor of the company that would become Marvel and creating notable additions to the romance and horror comic genres. In addition to his groundbreaking work in comics, Simon was a talented commercial artist. He died Dec 14, 2011, at New York City.

SOUTHERN FOOD HERITAGE DAY. Oct 11. Join the Southern Food and Beverage Museum in celebrating Southern foods and drinks! Southern Food Heritage Day is the official day to pull out your cast-iron pans and start up the smoker to enjoy your favorite Southern dishes, from cornbread to BBQ, from hoppin' john to shrimp and grits. Annually, Oct 11. For info: Southern Food and Beverage Museum. Web: www.southernfood.org.

SPACE MILESTONE: *DISCOVERY STS-92*: 100th SHUTTLE FLIGHT: 20th ANNIVERSARY. Oct 11, 2000. On this date *Discovery* was launched on its 28th flight, marking the shuttle program's 100th mission. For this mission, the ship headed to the International Space Station, where it docked on Oct 13. On earlier flights, the shuttles *Columbia, Challenger, Endeavour, Atlantis* and *Discovery* had launched the Hubble Space Telescope and Chandra X-Ray Observatory, docked with the *Mir* space station and supported scientific research. The first shuttle flight took place in 1981. See also: "Space Milestone: *Columbia STS-1*" (Apr 12).

STONE, HARLAN FISKE: BIRTH ANNIVERSARY. Oct 11, 1872. Associate justice and later chief justice of the US who wrote more than 600 opinions and dissents for that court. Stone was born at Chesterfield, NH. He served on the Supreme Court from 1925 until his death, at Washington, DC, Apr 22, 1946.

UNITED NATIONS: INTERNATIONAL DAY OF THE GIRL CHILD. Oct 11. The General Assembly has declared this day to recognize girls' rights and the unique challenges girls face around the world (Res 66/170 of Dec 19, 2011). The fulfillment of girls' right to education is first and foremost an obligation and moral imperative. There is overwhelming evidence that girls' education is a powerful, transformative force for societies and girls themselves: it is the one consistent, positive determinant of practically every desired development outcome, from reductions in mortality and fertility, to poverty reduction and equitable growth, to social norm change and democratization. Annually, Oct 11. For info: United Nations, Dept of Public Info, New York, NY 10017. Web: www.un.org.

VATICAN COUNCIL II: ANNIVERSARY. Oct 11, 1962. The 21st ecumenical council of the Roman Catholic Church was convened by Pope John XXIII. It met in four annual sessions, concluding Dec 8, 1965. It dealt with the renewal of the Church and introduced sweeping changes, such as the use of the vernacular rather than Latin in the Mass.

WEEMS, PARSON (MASON LOCKE): BIRTH ANNIVERSARY. Oct 11, 1759. Mason Locke Weems was born at Anne Arundel County, MD. An Episcopal clergyman and traveling bookseller, Weems is remembered for the fictitious stories he presented as historical fact. Best known of his "fables" is the story describing George Washington cutting down his father's cherry tree with a hatchet. Weems's fictionalized histories, however, delighted many readers who accepted them as true. They became immensely popular and were bestsellers for many years. Weems died May 23, 1825, at Beaufort, SC.

WEST, DOTTIE: BIRTH ANNIVERSARY. Oct 11, 1932. American singer Dottie West was born at McMinnville, TN. In 1964 she won the first Grammy ever by a country vocalist for "Here Comes My Baby." She died Sept 4, 1991, at Nashville, TN.

🎂 BIRTHDAYS TODAY

Cardi B, 28, rapper, television personality, born Belcalis Almanzar at the Bronx, NY, Oct 11, 1992.

Mike Conley, 33, basketball player, born Fayetteville, AR, Oct 11, 1987.

Joan Cusack, 58, actress ("Shameless," *In & Out, Working Girl*), born Evanston, IL, Oct 11, 1962.

Emily Deschanel, 44, actress ("Bones"), born Los Angeles, CA, Oct 11, 1976.

Sean Patrick Flanery, 55, actor (*The Boondock Saints*, "Dexter"), born Lake Charles, LA, Oct 11, 1965.

Robert Gale, 75, physician, cofounder of the International Bone Marrow Registry, born Brooklyn Heights, NY, Oct 11, 1945.

Daryl Hall, 72, singer, musician (Hall and Oates), born Pottstown, PA, Oct 11, 1948.

Orlando "El Duque" Hernandez, 55, former baseball player, born Villa Clara, Cuba, Oct 11, 1965.

Jane Krakowski, 52, actress ("Unbreakable Kimmy Schmidt," "30 Rock," "Ally McBeal," Tony for *Nine*), born Parsippany, NJ, Oct 11, 1968.

Ron Leibman, 83, actor (*Norma Rae*, Tony for *Angels in America*), born New York, NY, Oct 11, 1937.

David Morse, 67, actor ("St. Elsewhere," *Proof of Life*), born Beverly, MA, Oct 11, 1953.

Stephen Moyer, 51, actor ("True Blood," "The Starter Wife"), born Brentwood, Essex, England, Oct 11, 1969.

Patty Murray, 70, US Senator (D, Washington), born Seattle, WA, Oct 11, 1950.

Steve Young, 59, Hall of Fame football player, born Salt Lake City, UT, Oct 11, 1961.

October 12 — Monday

DAY 286   **80 REMAINING**

AMERICAN INDIAN HERITAGE DAY (ALABAMA). Oct 12. First declared in 2000, this state holiday is also observed as Columbus Day in Alabama. Annually, the second Monday in October.

BAHAMAS: DISCOVERY DAY. Oct 12. Commemorates the landing of Columbus in the Bahamas in 1492.

BALI TERRORIST BOMBING: ANNIVERSARY. Oct 12, 2002. Two bombs that were detonated in Kuta on the Indonesian island of Bali killed more than 200 people and injured hundreds. The bombs were placed at bars where vacationing tourists were known to gather. Although the terrorist group Al Qaeda claimed responsibility, suspects who later confessed to the crime stated that they were working independently.

BELIZE: COLUMBUS DAY. Oct 12. Public holiday.

BOER WAR: ANNIVERSARY. Oct 12, 1899. The Boers of the Transvaal and Orange Free State in southern Africa declared war on the British. The Boer states were annexed by Britain in 1900, but guerrilla warfare on the part of the Boers caused the war to drag on. It finally ended May 31, 1902, by the Treaty of Vereeniging.

"THE BURNS AND ALLEN SHOW" TV PREMIERE: 70th ANNIVERSARY. Oct 12, 1950. The comedic husband-and-wife duo of George

	S	**M**	**T**	**W**	**T**	**F**	**S**
October					1	2	3
2020	4	5	6	7	8	9	10
	11	12	13	14	15	16	17
	18	19	20	21	22	23	24
	25	26	27	28	29	30	31

Burns and Gracie Allen starred as themselves in this comedy series in which Burns was the straight man and Allen was known for her ditziness. The show employed the technique of speaking directly to the camera ("breaking the fourth wall"); Burns often commented on the plot, told jokes or tried to make sense of Allen's actions and statements. Also on the show were their real-life son, Ronnie Burns; Bea Benaderet; Hal March; John Brown (until blacklisted by McCarthyites in the "red scare"); Fred Clark; Larry Keating; Bill Goodwin and Harry Von Zell. The show was done live for the first two seasons and included vaudeville scenes at the end of each episode.

CANADA: THANKSGIVING DAY. Oct 12. Observed on second Monday in October each year.

★COLUMBUS DAY. Oct 12. Presidential Proclamation always the second Monday in October. Observed on Oct 12 from 1934 to 1970 (Pub Res No. 21 of Apr 30, 1934). Public Law 90–363, of June 28, 1968, required that beginning in 1971 it would be observed on the second Monday in October.

COLUMBUS DAY OBSERVANCE. Oct 12. Public Law 90–363 sets observance of Columbus Day on the second Monday in October. Applicable to federal employees and to the District of Columbia, but observed also in most states. Commemorates the landfall of Columbus in the New World, Oct 12, 1492. See also: "Columbus Day (Traditional)" (Oct 12).

COLUMBUS DAY (TRADITIONAL). Oct 12. Public holiday in most countries in the Americas and in most Spanish-speaking countries. Observed under different names (Día de la Raza or Day of the Race) and on different dates (most often, as in US, on the second Monday in October). Anniversary of Christopher Columbus's arrival, Oct 12, 1492, after a voyage across "shoreless Seas," at the Bahamas (probably the island of Guanahani), which he renamed El Salvador and claimed in the name of the Spanish crown. See also: "Columbus Day Observance" (Oct 12).

DAY OF THE SIX BILLION: ANNIVERSARY. Oct 12, 1999. According to the United Nations, the population of the world reached six billion on this date. More than one-third of the world's people live in China and India. It wasn't until 1804 that the world's population reached one billion; now a billion people are added to the population about every 12 years. See also: "Day of the Five Billion: Anniversary" (July 11).

DISCOVERERS' DAY IN HAWAII. Oct 12. Honors all discoverers, including Pacific and Polynesian navigators. Second Monday in October.

EQUATORIAL GUINEA: INDEPENDENCE DAY. Oct 12. National holiday. Gained independence from Spain in 1968.

FIJI: INDEPENDENCE DAY: 50th ANNIVERSARY OF INDEPENDENCE. Oct 12. National holiday. Observed on the second Monday in October to commemorate Fiji's declaration of independence from Britain on Oct 10, 1970.

GORDONE, CHARLES: 95th BIRTH ANNIVERSARY. Oct 12, 1925. First black playwright to win the Pulitzer Prize for Drama. He won it for his play *No Place to Be Somebody*. Born at Cleveland, OH. Died Nov 17, 1995, at College Station, TX.

INTERNATIONAL MOMENT OF FRUSTRATION SCREAM DAY. Oct 12. To share any or all of our frustrations, all citizens of the world will go outdoors at 1200 hours Greenwich time and scream for 30 seconds. We will all feel better or Earth will go off its orbit. Annually, Oct 12. (©2006 by WH.) For info: Thomas & Ruth Roy, Wellcat Holidays, 2418 Long Ln, Lebanon, PA 17046. Phone: (717) 279-0184. E-mail: info@wellcat.com. Web: www.wellcat.com.

MCNAIR, RONALD E.: 70th BIRTH ANNIVERSARY. Oct 12, 1950. Ronald E. McNair, a 35-year-old physicist, was the second black American astronaut in space (February 1984). He was born at Lake City, SC. As mission specialist for the crew, he perished in the space shuttle *Challenger* explosion Jan 28, 1986. See also: "Challenger Space Shuttle Explosion: Anniversary" (Jan 28).

MEXICO: DIA DE LA RAZA. Oct 12. "Day of the Race" commemorates the discovery of America as well as the common interests and cultural heritage of the Spanish and Indian peoples and the Hispanic nations.

NATIONAL KICK-BUTT DAY. Oct 12. On this day we commit to kicking ourselves in the butt to take action on goals we've set and not achieved, actions we've committed to and not taken, promises we've made and not kept, excuses we've created that have us stalled and difficulties we've faced and not overcome. This is the day we get our butts in gear and move forward in our lives. No butts about it! Annually, the second Monday in October. For info: Sylvia Henderson, 3570 Olney-Laytonsville Rd, Ste 588, Olney, MD 20832. Phone: (301) 260-1538. E-mail: sylvia@springboardtraining.com. Web: www.ideasuccessnetwork.com.

★NATIONAL SCHOOL LUNCH WEEK. Oct 12–16. Presidential Proclamation issued for the Monday through Friday in the week beginning on the second Sunday in October (PL 87–780 of Oct 9, 1962).

NATIONAL SCHOOL LUNCH WEEK. Oct 12–16. To celebrate good nutrition and healthy, safe school lunches. Created in 1962 by President John F. Kennedy. Annually, the Monday through Friday of the week that begins with the second Sunday in October. For info: School Nutrition Assn, 2900 S Quincy St, Ste 700, Arlington, VA 22206. Phone: (703) 824-3000. E-mail: servicecenter@schoolnutrition.org or media@schoolnutrition.org. Web: www.schoolnutrition.org.

NATIVE AMERICANS' DAY (SOUTH DAKOTA). Oct 12. Observed in the state of South Dakota as a legal holiday, dedicated to the remembrance of the great Native American leaders who contributed so much to the history of South Dakota. Annually, the second Monday in October.

PAVAROTTI, LUCIANO: 85th BIRTH ANNIVERSARY. Oct 12, 1935. Born at Modena, Italy, Pavarotti made opera accessible for a wide audience. The most popular tenor of his time, he was known for his perfect tone, especially in the highest ranges. A regular performer at the Metropolitan Opera House in New York City for decades, he brought his music to a wider audience in the 1980s and '90s by performing as one of the "Three Tenors." He, along with Plácido Domingo and José Carreras, crossed into mainstream pop music with television appearances and nationwide tours and sold millions of records. A philanthropist, Pavarotti was active in raising funding and awareness for many humanitarian causes. Widely considered to be the best bel canto singer of the 20th century, he died at Modena Sept 6, 2007.

SPAIN: NATIONAL HOLIDAY. Oct 12. Called Hispanity Day or Day of Spanish Consciousness. Honors Christopher Columbus and the Spanish conquerors of Latin America.

TRUMBULL, JONATHAN: BIRTH ANNIVERSARY. Oct 12, 1710. American patriot, counselor and friend of George Washington, governor of Connecticut Colony, born at Lebanon, CT. He died there Aug 17, 1785.

VAUGHAN WILLIAMS, RALPH: BIRTH ANNIVERSARY. Oct 12, 1872. Composer and conductor Ralph Vaughan Williams was

born at Down Ampney, Gloucestershire, England. He is considered England's first great truly national composer, having rooted "modern" composition techniques in traditional English folk and Tudor music and themes to create a uniquely English style. Among his many works are nine symphonies, church and choral music, film and stage music and several operas. His major compositions include the *Mass in G Minor* and the opera *The Pilgrim's Progress*. He died Aug 26, 1958, at London, England.

VIRGIN ISLANDS–PUERTO RICO FRIENDSHIP DAY. Oct 12. Columbus Day (second Monday in October) also celebrates historical friendship between peoples of Virgin Islands and Puerto Rico.

YORKTOWN VICTORY DAY. Oct 12. Observed as a holiday in Virginia. Annually, the second Monday in October. Commemorates the Revolutionary War battle fought in 1781.

BIRTHDAYS TODAY

Susan Anton, 70, singer, actress (*Goldengirl*), born Yucaipa, CA, Oct 12, 1950.

Carlos Bernard, 58, actor ("24"), born Evanston, IL, Oct 12, 1962.

Kirk Cameron, 50, actor ("Growing Pains," "Kirk"), born Panorama City, CA, Oct 12, 1970.

Josh Hutcherson, 28, actor (The Hunger Games films, *The Kids Are All Right*), born Union, KY, Oct 12, 1992.

Hugh Jackman, 52, actor (*The Greatest Showman, Logan, Les Misérables, The Prestige, X-Men, X2*), born Sydney, Australia, Oct 12, 1968.

Marion Jones, 45, former track athlete, born Los Angeles, CA, Oct 12, 1975.

Anthony Christopher (Tony) Kubek, 84, sportscaster, former baseball player, born Milwaukee, WI, Oct 12, 1936.

Adam Rich, 52, actor ("Eight Is Enough"), born Brooklyn, NY, Oct 12, 1968.

Chris Wallace, 73, broadcaster ("Dateline"), White House correspondent, born Chicago, IL, Oct 12, 1947.

October 13 — Tuesday

DAY 287	**79 REMAINING**

ADA LOVELACE DAY. Oct 13. An international day celebrating the achievements of women in science, technology, engineering and math with a flagship event held in London, England, and grassroots events around the world. Women in tech and science tend to be less well known than their male counterparts despite their valuable contributions. The aim of Ada Lovelace Day is to create new female role models that inspire girls and women alike. Named in honor of Augusta Ada King, Countess of Lovelace (1815–52), who is considered the first computer programmer and was a close friend of Charles Babbage, who conceived a general purpose computing machine called the Analytical Engine. Annually, the second Tuesday in October. For info: Ada Lovelace Day. Web: www.findingada.com.

BROWN, JESSE LEROY: BIRTH ANNIVERSARY. Oct 13, 1926. Born at Hattiesburg, MS, Jesse Leroy Brown was the first black American naval aviator and also the first black naval officer to lose his life

	S	M	T	W	T	F	S
October					1	2	3
2020	4	5	6	7	8	9	10
	11	12	13	14	15	16	17
	18	19	20	21	22	23	24
	25	26	27	28	29	30	31

in combat, when he was shot down over Korea, Dec 4, 1950. He was posthumously awarded the Distinguished Flying Cross. On Mar 18, 1972, USS *Jesse L. Brown* was launched as the first ship to be named in honor of a black naval officer (decommissioned in 1994).

BRUCE, LENNY: 95th BIRTH ANNIVERSARY. Oct 13, 1925. Born Leonard Alfred Schneider at New York, NY, Lenny Bruce was an innovative, hip and searing stand-up comedian whose material touched on adult themes. His satiric and sometimes shocking routines gained him the wrath of public officials, and he was arrested multiple times on obscenity charges. His trials became celebrated calls to arms to protect First Amendment rights. By the time of his death by morphine overdose on Aug 3, 1966, at Hollywood Hills, CA, Bruce was banned in many US cities, Australia and England, and from comedy clubs that feared legal action.

BURUNDI: ASSASSINATION OF THE HERO OF THE NATION DAY. Oct 13. National holiday. Commemorates the assassination of Prince Louis Rwagasore in 1961.

INTERNATIONAL FACE YOUR FEARS DAY. Oct 13. This unique day celebrates people who face and overcome their fears—whether seeking a better job, flying on a plane or pursuing a new relationship. This day is all about going for it and encouraging others to do the same. Annually, the second Tuesday in October. For info: Steve Hughes, 1001 Alsace Ct, St. Louis, MO 63017. Phone: (314) 821-8700. E-mail: Steve@hityourstride.com. Web: www.FaceYourFearsToday.com.

MONTAND, YVES: BIRTH ANNIVERSARY. Oct 13, 1921. French actor Yves Montand was born Ivo Livi at Monsummano Alto, Italy. His career was successful in both France and America, including more than 50 films. He died Nov 9, 1991, at Senlis, France.

NAVY BIRTHDAY. Oct 13. Since 1972, a navywide celebration (for members of the active forces and reserves, as well as retirees and dependents) recognizing the authorization of the Continental Navy on this date in 1775. The celebration is meant "to enhance a greater appreciation of [the] Navy heritage and to provide a positive influence toward pride and professionalism in the naval service." For info: www.history.navy.mil. See also: "US Navy: Authorization Anniversary" (Oct 13).

PITCHER, MOLLY: BIRTH ANNIVERSARY. Oct 13, 1754. "Molly Pitcher," heroine of the American Revolution, was a water carrier at the Battle of Monmouth (June 28, 1778), where she distinguished herself by loading and firing a cannon after her husband, William Hays, was wounded. Affectionately known as "Sergeant Molly" after General Washington issued her a warrant as a noncommissioned officer. Her real name was Mary Hays McCauley (née Ludwig). Born near Trenton, NJ, she died at Carlisle, PA, Jan 22, 1832.

SAINT EDWARD, THE CONFESSOR: FEAST DAY. Oct 13. King of England, 1042–66, Edward was the son of King Ethelred the Unready. Born at Islip, England, in 1003, he died Jan 5, 1066, at London. On Oct 13, 1163, his remains were transported in a ceremony that was of national interest. Since then Oct 13 has been observed as his principal feast day.

THATCHER, MARGARET HILDA ROBERTS: 95th BIRTH ANNIVERSARY. Oct 13, 1925. First woman prime minister in 700 years of English parliamentary history. Election of May 3, 1979, gave the Conservative Party victory, and Thatcher accepted Queen

Elizabeth's appointment as prime minister on May 4. She held the office until forced to resign on Nov 22, 1990. She was given a life peerage as Baroness Thatcher of Kesteven, June 5, 1992, a position that entitled her to a seat in the House of Lords, where she remained an active Tory voice. Born Margaret Hilda Roberts at Grantham, Lincolnshire, England, Thatcher died Apr 8, 2013, at London, England.

UNITED NATIONS: INTERNATIONAL DAY FOR DISASTER REDUCTION. Oct 13. The General Assembly has made this designation for Oct 13 each year as part of its efforts to foster international cooperation in reducing loss of life, property damage and social and economic disruption caused by natural disasters. For info: United Nations, Dept of Public Info, New York, NY 10017. Web: www.un.org.

US NAVY: AUTHORIZATION ANNIVERSARY. Oct 13, 1775. Commemorates legislation passed by Second Continental Congress authorizing the acquisition of ships and establishment of a navy.

WHITE HOUSE CORNERSTONE LAID: ANNIVERSARY. Oct 13, 1792. The presidential residence at 1600 Pennsylvania Ave NW, Washington, DC, designed by James Hoban, observes its birthday Oct 13. The cornerstone was laid; the first presidential family to occupy the building was that of John Adams, in November 1800. With three stories and more than 100 rooms, the White House is the oldest building at Washington. First described as the "presidential palace," it acquired the name "White House" about 10 years after construction was completed. Burned by British troops in 1814, it was reconstructed, refurbished and reoccupied by 1817.

🧁 BIRTHDAYS TODAY

Ashanti, 40, singer, actress (*The Muppets' Wizard of Oz*), born Ashanti Sequoiah Douglas at Long Island, NY, Oct 13, 1980.

William (Billy) Bush, 49, former television host ("Access Hollywood"), radio personality, born New York, NY, Oct 13, 1971.

Maria Cantwell, 62, US Senator (D, Washington), born Indianapolis, IN, Oct 13, 1958.

Chris Carter, 63, producer, screenwriter ("The X-Files"), born Bellflower, CA, Oct 13, 1957.

Sacha Baron Cohen, 49, comedian, actor ("Da Ali G Show," *Borat*), born London, England, Oct 13, 1971.

Melinda Dillon, 81, actress (*Close Encounters of the Third Kind, A Christmas Story*), born Hope, AR, Oct 13, 1939.

Sammy Hagar, 71, singer, musician, born Monterrey, CA, Oct 13, 1949.

Jimin, 25, singer (BTS), born Park Ji-min at Geumjeong District, Busan, South Korea, Oct 13, 1995.

Jerral Wayne "Jerry" Jones, 78, Hall of Fame football executive (Dallas Cowboys), oil industry businessman, born Inglewood, CA, Oct 13, 1942.

Nancy Kerrigan, 51, former figure skater, born Woburn, MA, Oct 13, 1969.

Alexandria Ocasio-Cortez, 31, US Representative (D, New York), born The Bronx, NY, Oct 13, 1989.

Jermaine O'Neal, 42, basketball player, born Columbia, SC, Oct 13, 1978.

Marie Osmond, 61, actress, singer, born Ogden, UT, Oct 13, 1959.

Paul Pierce, 43, basketball player, born Oakland, CA, Oct 13, 1977.

Kelly Preston, 58, actress (*Christine, Twins*), born Honolulu, HI, Oct 13, 1962.

Jerry Rice, 58, Hall of Fame football player, born Starkville, MS, Oct 13, 1962.

Glenn Anton "Doc" Rivers, 59, basketball coach and former player, born Maywood, IL, Oct 13, 1961.

Paul Simon, 79, singer (Simon and Garfunkel), musician, born Newark, NJ, Oct 13, 1941.

Pamela Tiffin, 78, actress (*Harper*; stage: *Dinner at Eight*), born Oklahoma City, OK, Oct 13, 1942.

Kate Walsh, 53, actress ("Grey's Anatomy," "The Drew Carey Show"), born San Jose, CA, Oct 13, 1967.

October 14 — Wednesday

DAY 288   **78 REMAINING**

BATTLE OF HASTINGS: ANNIVERSARY. Oct 14, 1066. The Anglo-Saxon age came to an end with the death of King Harold Godwinson and the defeat of English forces by Norman invaders at Hastings on this day. William, Duke of Normandy, led the daring invasion and was crowned King of England on Dec 25, 1066.

BE BALD AND BE FREE DAY. Oct 14. For those who are bald and who either do wear or do not wear a wig or toupee, this is the day to go "shiny" and be proud. Annually, Oct 14. (©2006 by WH.) For info: Thomas & Ruth Roy, Wellcat Holidays, 2418 Long Ln, Lebanon, PA 17046. Phone: (717) 279-0184. E mail: info@wellcat.com. Web: www.wellcat.com.

DE VALERA, EAMON: BIRTH ANNIVERSARY. Oct 14, 1882. Irish statesman, born at New York, NY. A revolutionary who survived the Easter Rising in 1916, De Valera went on to found the Fianna Fáil political party, which came to power in 1932 and by 1937 was successful in declaring the Free State of Ireland. As leader of Fianna Fáil, De Valera served as Ireland's prime minister three times and as president from 1959 to 1973. He died Aug 29, 1975, at Dublin, Ireland.

EISENHOWER, DWIGHT DAVID: BIRTH ANNIVERSARY. Oct 14, 1890. The 34th president of the US, Dwight David Eisenhower, was born at Denison, TX. Served two terms as president, Jan 20, 1953–Jan 20, 1961. Nicknamed "Ike," he held the rank of five-star general of the US Army (resigned in 1952, and restored by act of Congress in 1961). He served as supreme commander of the Allied forces in western Europe during WWII. Eisenhower's popular presidency coincided with a postwar boom of prosperity and optimism. He promised to seek an end to the Korean War, and he was able to negotiate a truce in 1953. NASA was established under his watch in 1958 in response to the USSR's lead in the space race. He died at Washington, DC, Mar 28, 1969.

EMERGENCY NURSES DAY. Oct 14. Developed by the Emergency Nurses Association (ENA) in 1989, this day recognizes emergency nurses for standing at the front line of health care, and for their dedication, service and commitment to patients and communities. Annually, the second Wednesday in October. For info: Emergency Nurses Assn. E-mail: contact@ena.org. Web: www.ena.org.

FODOR, EUGENE: BIRTH ANNIVERSARY. Oct 14, 1905. Travel writer Eugene Fodor was born at Leva, Hungary. His first travel book was published in 1936, after which he published more than 140,

bringing to them a human element previously lacking in travel books. He died Feb 18, 1991, at Torrington, CT.

GERMANY: FRANKFURTER BUCHMESSE (FRANKFURT BOOK FAIR). Oct 14–18. Messe Frankfurt, Frankfurt. The world's largest international book fair is the best place for international rights and licenses. It also gathers key players from other media, including the film and game industry. Open to trade for three days and to the public for two. Est attendance: 285,000. For info: Frankfurter Buchmesse GmbH, Braubachstrasse 16, 60311 Frankfurt am Main, Germany. Phone: (49) 69-2102-0. E-mail: servicecenter@book-fair. com. Web: www.buchmesse.de/en.

GISH, LILLIAN: BIRTH ANNIVERSARY. Oct 14, 1893. American actress Lillian Diana Gish was born at Springfield, OH. Her film and stage career spanned more than 85 years, 100 films, the silent and sound eras of film and numerous stage productions. She was awarded an honorary Oscar in 1970 and made her last film appearance in *The Whales of August* (1987). She died Feb 27, 1993, at New York, NY.

JAPAN: MEGA KENKA MATSURI OR ROUGHHOUSE FESTIVAL. Oct 14–15. Himeji. Palanquin bearers jostle one another to demonstrate their skill and balance in handling their burdens.

KING AWARDED NOBEL PEACE PRIZE: ANNIVERSARY. Oct 14, 1964. Martin Luther King, Jr, became the youngest recipient of the Nobel Peace Prize up to that time. King donated all of the prize money ($54,000) to furthering the causes of the civil rights movement.

LEE, FRANCIS LIGHTFOOT: BIRTH ANNIVERSARY. Oct 14, 1734. Signer of the Declaration of Independence. Born at Westmoreland County, VA, he died Jan 11, 1797, at Richmond County, VA.

MANSFIELD, KATHERINE: BIRTH ANNIVERSARY. Oct 14, 1888. Influential Modernist author of short stories, born Katherine Mansfield Beauchamp at Wellington, New Zealand. Her collections include *Prelude* (1918), *Bliss* (1920) and *The Garden Party* (1922). Her life was cut short by tuberculosis, and she died at Fontainebleau, France, on Jan 9, 1923, while seeking treatment.

MOORE, ROGER: BIRTH ANNIVERSARY. Oct 14, 1927. Droll quips, a raised eyebrow and so many spread collars: English actor Roger Moore played James Bond seven times, and his films as 007 earned the franchise's most money. Perpetually suave and perhaps a little stiff, Moore was not Sean Connery's superspy of yore. But his work matched the tone of the series as it moved into the 1970s, and *Live and Let Die* (1973) and *Moonraker* (1979) became Bond classics. The singular Moore persona might never have made it to MI6 were it not for the actor's work in "The Saint" (1962–69), a UK-produced TV series based on the novels by Leslie Charteris that featured Moore as Simon Templar, a gallant righter of wrongs with occasional spy-like qualities. "The Saint" was a hit in both England and America, and in 1972 Bond producer Albert R. Broccoli offered the role of a lifetime to Moore. Moore, born at London, England, died May 23, 2017, at Crans-Montana, Switzerland. He

was knighted in 2003 and was a UNICEF Goodwill Ambassador starting in 1991.

NATIONAL BRING YOUR TEDDY BEAR TO WORK DAY. Oct 14. A celebration and observance of the help and joy that teddy bears bring into the lives of people of all ages, at all stages. Annually, the second Wednesday in October. For info: Susan E. Schwartz, Teddies Are the Answer, 454 26th Ave, San Mateo, CA 94403. Phone: (650) 345-4944. E-mail: suwho@astound.net.

NATIONAL BULLYING PREVENTION DAY. Oct 14. Approximately 160,000 teens stay home from school every day because they fear for their safety. The bullying and suicide prevention international nonprofit organization Hey U.G.L.Y. (Unique Gifted Lovable You) has designated the second Wednesday in October (and the entire month of October) as a day and month for schools across America to conduct bullying-prevention classroom activities and school assembly presentations on how to eradicate bullying from schools and neighborhoods. For info and activity plans: Hey U.G.L.Y., Inc, PO Box 2142, Michigan City, IN 46361. Phone: (219) 814-4224. E-mail: preventbullyingnow@heyugly.org. Web: www.heyugly.org and preventbullyingnow.org.

NATIONAL FOSSIL DAY. Oct 14. Since 2010, a celebration organized by the National Park Service to promote public awareness and stewardship of fossils, as well as to foster a greater appreciation of their scientific and educational values. Annually, the Wednesday during Earth Science Week. For info: Natl Park Service. Web: www.nps.gov/subjects/fossilday.

NATIONAL TAKE YOUR PARENTS TO LUNCH DAY. Oct 14. As part of National School Lunch Week, the School Nutrition Association encourages school cafeterias to reach out to parents for the Wednesday of NSLW (or a day of your choosing). Spread the word to parents (or guests like local policy makers) that healthy and tasty options are being served in school cafeterias every day. For info: School Nutrition Assn. Web: www.schoolnutrition.org.

PENN, WILLIAM: BIRTH ANNIVERSARY. Oct 14, 1644. Founder of Pennsylvania, born at London, England. Penn died July 30, 1718, at Buckinghamshire, England. Presidential Proclamation 5284, of Nov 28, 1984, conferred honorary US citizenship on William Penn and his second wife, Hannah Callowhill Penn. They were the third and fourth persons to receive honorary US citizenship (following Winston Churchill and Raoul Wallenberg).

SOUND BARRIER BROKEN: ANNIVERSARY. Oct 14, 1947. Flying a Bell X-1 at Muroc Dry Lake Bed, CA, Air Force pilot Chuck Yeager broke the sound barrier, ushering in the era of supersonic flight.

SOUTH CAROLINA STATE FAIR. Oct 14–25. Columbia, SC. Since 1869! North American Midway Entertainment (NAME), agricultural exhibits, rides, musical entertainment, food booths and children's activities. Est attendance: 500,000. For info: South Carolina State Fair, 1200 Rosewood Dr, Columbia, SC 29201. Phone: (803) 799-3387. E-mail: geninfo@scstatefair.org. Web: www.scstatefair. org.

SUPERSONIC SKYDIVE: ANNIVERSARY. Oct 14, 2012. Austrian daredevil Felix Baumgartner set several records in an incredible jump from a helium balloon in the stratosphere 24 miles above Earth: highest jump, fastest speed attained by a human not traveling in a powered craft and highest manned balloon flight. Baumgartner fell for nine minutes and reached a speed of 844 miles per hour (Mach 1.25) before triggering his parachute and landing safely in the desert near Roswell, NM.

TOMÁS DE TORQUEMADA: 600th BIRTH ANNIVERSARY. Oct 14, 1420. Dominican monk, confessor to Isabella I, who was appointed Grand Inquisitor of Spain in 1483. As Grand Inquisitor, Torquemada expanded the Spanish Inquisition, establishing tribunals all over the country. His remit was to eradicate heresy, and the austere zeal with which he pursued this aim made his name feared at the time and hated throughout the centuries since. Once the Muslims, who supported religious tolerance, left Spain in 1492, Torquemada pushed for expulsion of Jews, which King Ferdinand and Queen Isabella accomplished with their Alhambra Decree

October 2020	S	M	T	W	T	F	S
					1	2	3
	4	5	6	7	8	9	10
	11	12	13	14	15	16	17
	18	19	20	21	22	23	24
	25	26	27	28	29	30	31

on Mar 31, 1492, soon after. Torquemada, who himself was of Jewish background, sought those remaining Jews who had converted to Catholicism he was suspicious of the genuineness of their conversion. Estimates vary of the numbers tortured and/or executed under Torquemada's authority. As many as 2,000 people may have been executed. Torquemada was born at Valladolid, Kingdom of Castile, and died at Ávila, Spain, Sept 16, 1898

WOODEN, JOHN: BIRTH ANNIVERSARY. Oct 14, 1910. One of the most successful basketball coaches in history, born at Hall, IN. Wooden led UCLA to a record-setting 10 NCAA championships in 12 years and is widely considered the most respected coach to ever take the court. His philosophies of leadership were adapted into the business world, and he was a successful author and motivational speaker in his later years. One of only three people inducted into both the collegiate and professional Basketball Halls of Fame, Wooden died at Los Angeles, CA, June 4, 2010.

🎂 BIRTHDAYS TODAY

Steve Coogan, 55, actor (*Philomena, The Trip, 24 Hour Party People*), comedian, screenwriter, born Middleton, Lancashire, England, Oct 14, 1965.

Beth Daniel, 64, Hall of Fame golfer, born Charleston, SC, Oct 14, 1956.

John Dean, 82, lawyer (White House counsel during Watergate), born Akron, OH, Oct 14, 1938.

Greg Evigan, 67, actor ("B.J. and the Bear," "Masquerade"), born South Amboy, NJ, Oct 14, 1953.

Gary Graffman, 92, pianist, born New York, NY, Oct 14, 1928.

Ralph Lauren, 81, designer, born Ralph Lipschitz at the Bronx, NY, Oct 14, 1939.

Natalie Maines, 46, country singer (Dixie Chicks), born Lubbock, TX, Oct 14, 1974.

David Oakes, 37, actor ("The Borgias," *The Pillars of the Earth*), born Hampshire, England, Oct 14, 1983.

Jon Seda, 50, actor ("Chicago P.D.," "Treme," "The Pacific") born New York, NY, Oct 14, 1970.

Usher, 42, singer, actor ("Moesha"), television personality ("The Voice"), born Usher Raymond IV at Chattanooga, TN, Oct 14, 1978.

Mia Wasikowska, 31, actress (*Crimson Peak, Madame Bovary, Jane Eyre, Alice in Wonderland*), born Canberra, Australia, Oct 14, 1989.

October 15 — Thursday

DAY 289	77 REMAINING

AMERICAN DENTAL ASSOCIATION—AMERICA'S DENTAL MEETING. Oct 15–19. Orange County Convention Center, Orlando, FL. 161st session. For info: American Dental Assn, 211 E Chicago Ave, Ste 200, Chicago, IL 60611. Phone: (847) 996-5876 or (800) 974-2925. E-mail: annualmeeting@ada.org. Web: www.ada.org.

★**BLIND AMERICANS EQUALITY DAY.** Oct 15. Presidential Proclamation always issued for Oct 15 since 1964 (PL 88–628 of Oct 6, 1964). Originally proclaimed as White Cane Safety Day.

CHINA: CANTON AUTUMN TRADE FAIR. Oct 15–Nov 15. Canton. The Guangzhou (Canton) Autumn Trade Fair is held during the same dates each year.

FIRST MANNED FLIGHT: ANNIVERSARY. Oct 15, 1783. Jean François Pilatre de Rozier and François Laurent, Marquis d'Arlandes, became the first people to fly when they ascended in a Montgolfier hot-air balloon at Paris, France, less than five months after the first public balloon flight demonstration (June 5, 1783), and less than a year after the first experiments with small paper and

fabric balloons by the Montgolfier brothers, Joseph and Jacques, in November 1782. The first manned free flight lasted about four minutes and carried the passengers at a height of about 84 feet. On Nov 21, 1783, they soared 3,000 feet over Paris for 25 minutes.

GALBRAITH, JOHN KENNETH: BIRTH ANNIVERSARY. Oct 15, 1908. Influential liberal economist, professor, author, diplomat and adviser to presidents Roosevelt, Kennedy and Johnson. Galbraith helped Lyndon Johnson create his Great Society programs. Galbraith's most famous book (out of 33 penned) is *The Affluent Society* (1958), in which he criticized a myopic US consumer culture that ignored community values. Born at Dunwich Township, ON, Canada, Galbraith died Apr 29, 2006, at Cambridge, MA.

GET SMART ABOUT CREDIT DAY. Oct 15. Thousands of bankers visit high schools across America today to teach youth the importance of establishing and maintaining good credit. Annually, the third Thursday in October. For info: American Bankers Assn Community Engagement Foundation, 1120 Connecticut Ave NW, Washington, DC 20036. Phone: (800) BANKERS or (202) 663-5453. E-mail: communityengagement@aba.com. Web: www.aba.com/GetSmart.

"I LOVE LUCY" TV PREMIERE: ANNIVERSARY. Oct 15, 1951. This enormously popular sitcom, TV's first smash hit, starred the real-life husband-and-wife team of Cuban actor/bandleader Desi Arnaz and talented redheaded actress/comedienne Lucille Ball. They played Ricky and Lucy Ricardo, a New York bandleader and his aspiring actress/homemaker wife, who was always scheming to get on stage. Costarring were William Frawley and Vivian Vance as Fred and Ethel Mertz, the Ricardos' landlords and good friends, who participated in the escapades and dealt with the consequences of Lucy's often well-intentioned plans. Famous actors guest-starred on the show, including Harpo Marx, Rock Hudson, William Holden, Hedda Hopper and John Wayne. This was the first sitcom to be filmed live before a studio audience, and it did extremely well in the ratings both the first time around and in reruns. The last telecast ran Sept 24, 1961.

JAPAN: NEWSPAPER WEEK. Oct 15–20. The Nihon Shinbun Kyokai (NSK), or The Japan Newspaper Publishers and Editors Association, sponsors this week to increase public awareness of the significance of "free and responsible newspapers" and, at the same time, to stimulate a sense of responsibility within the press. Originated in 1948. Annually, Oct 15–20. For info: NSK. Web: www.pressnet.or.jp.

MANN, MARTY: BIRTH ANNIVERSARY. Oct 15, 1904. The American social activist and author was born at Chicago, IL. She was founder in 1944 of the National Committee for Education on Alcoholism and author of *A New Primer on Alcoholism*. She died at Bridgeport, CT, July 22, 1980.

MATA HARI EXECUTION: ANNIVERSARY. Oct 15, 1917. Possibly history's most famous spy, Mata Hari refused a blindfold and threw a kiss to the firing squad at her execution. See also: "Mata Hari: Birth Anniversary" (Aug 7).

NATIONAL GROUCH DAY. Oct 15. Honor a grouch; all grouches deserve a day to be recognized. Created for and inspired by Alan Miller, retired teacher and Chairman of the Board, NAG (National

Victor Banerjee, 74, actor (*A Passage to India, The Home and the World*), born Calcutta, India, Oct 15, 1946.

Paige Davis, 51, actress, television personality ("Trading Spaces"), born Philadelphia, PA, Oct 15, 1969.

Sarah Ferguson, 61, Duchess of York, born London, England, Oct 15, 1959.

Kay Ivey, 76, Governor of Alabama (R), born Camden, AL, Oct 15, 1944.

Tito Jackson, 67, singer, musician (Jackson 5), born Toriano Adaryll Jackson at Gary, IN, Oct 15, 1953.

Linda Lavin, 81, actress (Tony for *Broadway Bound*; "Alice"), born Portland, ME, Oct 15, 1939.

James Alvin (Jim) Palmer, 75, Hall of Fame baseball player, sportscaster, born New York, NY, Oct 15, 1945.

Association of Grouches). Annually, Oct 15. For info: Alan R. Miller, NAG, 12281 Alexander St, Clio, MI 48420.

NIETZSCHE, FRIEDRICH WILHELM: BIRTH ANNIVERSARY. Oct 15, 1844. Influential, controversial and often misunderstood philosopher born at Röcken, Prussia. Especially remembered for his declaration that "God is dead." Major works include *Thus Spake Zarathustra, Beyond Good and Evil* and *The Genealogy of Morals.* Nietzsche died at Weimar, Germany, Aug 25, 1900, a decade after suffering a mental breakdown.

NORTH CAROLINA STATE FAIR. Oct 15–25. State Fairgrounds, Raleigh, NC. Agricultural fair with livestock, arts and crafts, home arts, entertainment and carnival. Est attendance: 775,000. For info: North Carolina State Fair, 1010 Mail Service Center, Raleigh, NC 27699-1010. Phone: (919) 821-7400. Web: www.ncstatefair.org.

SPACE MILESTONE: *CASSINI* (US). Oct 15, 1997. The plutonium-powered orbiter was launched on this day and passed between the rings of Saturn on June 30, 2004. It orbits the planet, sending back photographs and information on the planet and its 18 known moons. In 2004 it dispatched the *Huygens* probe to Titan, the largest of these moons.

SULLIVAN, JOHN L.: BIRTH ANNIVERSARY. Oct 15, 1858. Boxer, born at Roxbury, MA. "The Great John L." was one of America's first sports heroes. He captured the world's bare-knuckle heavyweight championship on Feb 7, 1882, and went six years without defending the title. He won the last bare-knuckle fight in 1889 and then lost the title to James J. Corbett in 1892. This was the first fight in which the boxers used gloves and were governed by the Marquess of Queensberry rules. Died at Abingdon, MA, Feb 2, 1918.

UNITED NATIONS: INTERNATIONAL DAY OF RURAL WOMEN. Oct 15. The General Assembly has declared Oct 15 of each year as a day to focus on improving the situation of rural women, including indigenous women, in its national, regional and global development strategies (Res 62/136, Dec 18, 2007). For info: United Nations, Dept of Public Info, New York, NY, 10017. Web: www.un.org.

WILSON, EDITH BOLLING GALT: BIRTH ANNIVERSARY. Oct 15, 1872. Second wife of Woodrow Wilson, 28th president of the US, born at Wytheville, VA. Died at Washington, DC, Dec 28, 1961.

WODEHOUSE, PELHAM GRENVILLE: BIRTH ANNIVERSARY. Oct 15, 1881. English author, lyricist ("Bill") and humorist, creator of Bertie Wooster and Jeeves. Born at Guildford, Surrey, England, P.G. Wodehouse died at Southampton, Long Island, NY, Feb 14, 1975.

October 2020	S	M	T	W	T	F	S
					1	2	3
	4	5	6	7	8	9	10
	11	12	13	14	15	16	17
	18	19	20	21	22	23	24
	25	26	27	28	29	30	31

October 16 — Friday

DAY 290   **76 REMAINING**

APPLE BUTTER STIRRIN'. Oct 16–18. Coshocton, OH. With more than 100 crafters, this invitational craft festival celebrates the sights, sounds and scents of autumn. Smell the fresh apple butter simmering over an open fire; listen to the tunes of bluegrass and old-time music. Living history, quilt raffle, canal boat rides, children's activities and more. Annually, the third weekend in October. Est attendance: 15,000. For info: Roscoe Village Foundation, 600 N Whitewoman St, Coshocton, OH 43812. Phone: (800) 877-1830 or (740) 622-7644. E-mail: ldaniel@roscoevillage.com. Web: www.roscoevillage.com.

BEN-GURION, DAVID: BIRTH ANNIVERSARY. Oct 16, 1886. Born David Gruen at Plonsk, Poland, David Ben-Gurion was the first prime minister of Israel, a post he held for nearly two decades. He is widely credited with having willed Israel into being and setting the country's intellectual course. He died at Tel Aviv, Israel, Dec 1, 1973.

COLLINS, MICHAEL: BIRTH ANNIVERSARY. Oct 16, 1890. Irish revolutionary, born near Clonakilty, Ireland. Collins joined the Irish Republican Brotherhood, took part in Dublin's 1916 Easter Uprising against Britain and was briefly imprisoned. He was named minister of home affairs and of finance for political party Sinn Fein in 1918, but during the subsequent Anglo-Irish War, he masterminded an extensive Irish intelligence network that earned him the moniker "the Man Who Won the War." Calling it "my death warrant," Collins signed the treaty of 1921 that separated Northern Ireland from the Irish Republic and sparked a civil war. Assassinated Aug 22, 1922, at Béal Na mBláth outside Cork.

CRIMEAN WAR: ANNIVERSARY. Oct 16, 1853. The Ottoman Empire declared war on Russia on this day to stem Russian expansionist policies in the empire. Britain, France and parts of Italy allied themselves with the Turks against Russia. A battle in this war was immortalized in Tennyson's poem "The Charge of the Light Brigade." Health conditions for soldiers were scandalous, leading Florence Nightingale to work in the British hospital at Istanbul. This was the first war to be observed firsthand by newspaper reporters and photographers.

DICTIONARY DAY. Oct 16. The birthday of Noah Webster, American teacher and lexicographer, is an occasion to encourage every person to acquire at least one dictionary—and to use it regularly.

DOUGLAS, WILLIAM ORVILLE: BIRTH ANNIVERSARY. Oct 16, 1898. American jurist, world traveler, conservationist, outdoorsman and author. Born at Maine, MN, he served as justice of the US longer than any other (36 years). Died at Washington, DC, Jan 19, 1980.

FALL FESTIVAL OF LEAVES. Oct 16–18. Bainbridge, Ross County, OH. 53rd annual. Celebrating the beauty of the season and region. Folk arts, crafts, music, antique car show, log-sawing contest, flea markets and parades. To obtain a map of self-guided scenic tours, send SASE. For info: Fall Festival of Leaves, Box 571, Bainbridge, Ross County, OH 45612. Phone: (740) 703-8833. Web: www.fall-festivalofleaves.com.

FIRST BIRTH CONTROL CLINIC OPENED: ANNIVERSARY. Oct 16, 1916. The first birth control clinic in the US was opened in New York City by sisters Margaret Sanger and Ethel Byrne, nurses who believed contraception was a vital tool for women's emancipation. Sanger, who coined the term "birth control," modeled the clinic after similar Dutch institutions she visited in 1914 while in Amsterdam. Located at 46 Amboy St in the Brownsville neighborhood of Brooklyn, the clinic was open for only nine days before being raided and shuttered by police, but it nonetheless served 400 women in that brief time.

GLOBAL CAT DAY. Oct 16. This day celebrates the global movement toward a society that values the life of every cat, and empowers and mobilizes the millions of compassionate people worldwide who want to end the killing of cats in shelters. Annually, Oct 16. For info: Alley Cat Allies, 7920 Norfolk Ave, Ste 600, Bethesda, MD 20814-2525. Phone: (240) 482-1980. E-mail: GlobalCatDay@alleycat.org. Web: www.globalcatday.org.

JOHN BROWN'S RAID: ANNIVERSARY. Oct 16, 1859. White abolitionist John Brown, with a band of about 20 men, seized the US Arsenal at Harpers Ferry, WV. Brown was captured and the insurrection put down by Oct 19. Brown was hanged at Charles Town, WV, Dec 2, 1859.

MARIE ANTOINETTE: EXECUTION ANNIVERSARY. Oct 16, 1793. Queen Marie Antoinette of France, whose extravagance and dismissive attitude toward social reform made her a target of the French Revolution, was beheaded on this date in Paris after a show trial for high treason on Oct 14. Her last words were an apology to the executioner (she had stepped on his foot).

MILLION MAN MARCH: 25th ANNIVERSARY. Oct 16, 1995. Hundreds of thousands of black men met at Washington, DC, for a "holy day of atonement and reconciliation" organized by Louis Farrakhan, leader of the Nation of Islam. Marchers pledged to take responsibility for themselves, their families and their communities.

MOON PHASE: NEW MOON. Oct 16. Moon enters New Moon phase at 3:31 PM, EDT.

NATIONAL BOSS DAY. Oct 16. For all employees to honor their bosses. Annually, the weekday on or closest to Oct 16. Patricia Bays Haroski originated this event in 1958 in honor of her own boss, who also happened to be her father.

NATIONAL MAMMOGRAPHY DAY. Oct 16. On this day, or throughout the month of October, participating radiologists provide discounted or free screening mammograms. Annually, the third Friday in October.

O'NEILL, EUGENE GLADSTONE: BIRTH ANNIVERSARY. Oct 16, 1888. American playwright (*Long Day's Journey into Night*, *The Iceman Cometh*, *Ah! Wilderness*), recipient of four Pulitzer Prizes as well as the Nobel Prize in Literature (1936). O'Neill's plays introduced

the technique of realism through his portrayals of characters at society's periphery. Born at New York, NY, he died at Boston, MA, Nov 27, 1953. O'Neill is one of the most widely translated and produced playwrights in history, third only to William Shakespeare and George Bernard Shaw.

PHILIPPINES: MASSKARA FESTIVAL. Oct 16–18. Bacolod City. Vibrant festival—a "festival of smiles"—where colorful and intricately created masks predominate. Features carnival, street dancing competition, drum and bugle corps, pageant, parades, music and more. The name of the festival references the Filipino word for "mask"—*maskara*—as well as *mass* and *cara*, the Spanish word for "face." Annually, the third weekend in October, although festivities occur before and after. Est attendance: 450,000. For info: Bacolod City. Web: www.bacolodcity.gov.ph/masskara_bacolodcity.htm.

STEPHEN FOSTER QUILT SHOW AND SALE. Oct 16–18. Stephen Foster Folk Culture Center State Park, White Springs, FL. As quilters gather to share their work, more than 200 quilts will be exhibited, including traditional bed quilts, art quilts and children's quilts. Workshops, keynote speakers and demonstrations are part of the fun. For info: Quilt Show, Stephen Foster Folk Culture Center State Park, PO Box G, White Springs, FL 32096. Phone: (877) 635-3655. Fax: (386) 397-4262. E-mail: Catherine.Bowron@dep.state.fl.us. Web: www.floridastateparks.org/stephenfoster.

UNITED NATIONS: WORLD FOOD DAY. Oct 16. Annual observance to heighten public awareness of the world food problem and to strengthen solidarity in the struggle against hunger, malnutrition and poverty. Date of observance is anniversary of founding of Food and Agriculture Organization (FAO), Oct 16, 1945, at Quebec, Canada. For info: United Nations, Dept of Public Info, New York, NY 10017. Web: www.un.org.

WAR CRIMINALS (GERMAN) EXECUTION: ANNIVERSARY. Oct 16, 1946. The War Crimes Trials of Berlin and Nuremberg had sentenced 12 of the 22 defendants to death by hanging. They were: Hermann Goering, Joachim von Ribbentrop, Wilhelm Keitel, Ernst Kaltenbrunner, Alfred Rosenberg, Hans Frank, Wilhelm Frick, Julius Streicher, Fritz Sauckel, Alfred Jodl, Martin Bormann and Arthur von Seyss-Inquart. Goering committed suicide a few hours before his scheduled execution, and Martin Bormann had not been found (he was tried in absentia). The remaining 10 were hanged at Nuremberg Prison on this date.

WEBSTER, NOAH: BIRTH ANNIVERSARY. Oct 16, 1758. American teacher and journalist whose name became synonymous with the word *dictionary* after his compilations of the earliest American dictionaries of the English language. Born at West Hartford, CT, he died at New Haven, CT, May 28, 1843.

WILDE, OSCAR: BIRTH ANNIVERSARY. Oct 16, 1854. Irish wit, poet and playwright Oscar Fingal O'Flahertie Wills Wilde was born at Dublin, Ireland. At the height of his career he was imprisoned for two years on a morals offense, during which time he wrote "A Ballad of Reading Gaol." Best known of his plays is *The Importance of Being Earnest*. "We are all in the gutter," he wrote in *Lady Windermere's Fan*, "but some of us are looking at the stars." Wilde died at Paris, France, Nov 30, 1900.

YALE UNIVERSITY FOUNDED: ANNIVERSARY. Oct 16, 1701. (Old Style date.) The Collegiate School was founded at Branford, CT, by Congregationalists dissatisfied with the growing liberalism at Harvard. In 1716 the school was moved to New Haven, CT, where it became Yale College, named after Elihu Yale, a governor of the East India Company. The first degrees were awarded in 1716. Yale became a university in 1887. Founded as a school for men, Yale began admitting women undergraduates in 1969.

🎂 BIRTHDAYS TODAY

Melissa Louise Belote, 64, Olympic swimmer, born Washington, DC, Oct 16, 1956.

Barry Corbin, 80, actor ("Northern Exposure," *Stir Crazy*, *Any Which Way You Can*), born Dawson County, TX, Oct 16, 1940.

Juan Gonzalez, 51, former baseball player, born Vaga Baja, Puerto Rico, Oct 16, 1969.

Bryce Harper, 28, baseball player, born Las Vegas, NV, Oct 16, 1992.

Paul Kariya, 46, former hockey player, born Vancouver, BC, Canada, Oct 16, 1974.

Angela Lansbury, 95, actress ("Murder, She Wrote," *The Manchurian Candidate, Bedknobs and Broomsticks, Gaslight*, five Tony Awards), born London, England, Oct 16, 1925.

Kenneth Lonergan, 58, director (*Manchester by the Sea, You Can Count on Me*), screenwriter (Oscar for *Manchester by the Sea*), born New York, NY, Oct 16, 1962.

Kellie Martin, 45, actress ("Life Goes On," "ER"), born Riverside, CA, Oct 16, 1975.

John Mayer, 43, singer, born Bridgeport, CT, Oct 16, 1977.

Naomi Osaka, 23, tennis player, born Osaka, Japan, Oct 16, 1997.

Tim Robbins, 62, actor (Oscar for *Mystic River*; *The Player*), director, born West Covina, CA, Oct 16, 1958.

Suzanne Somers, 74, actress ("Three's Company," "Step by Step," *American Graffiti*), born San Bruno, CA, Oct 16, 1946.

Bob Weir, 73, musician (The Grateful Dead), born San Francisco, CA, Oct 16, 1947.

David Zucker, 73, writer, producer (*Naked Gun* movies, *Airplane!*), born Milwaukee, WI, Oct 16, 1947.

October 17 — Saturday

DAY 291 **75 REMAINING**

ARTHUR, JEAN: BIRTH ANNIVERSARY. Oct 17, 1900. American actress Jean Arthur was born Gladys Georgianna Greene at Plattsburg, NY. Her films include *Mr Deeds Goes to Town* (1936), *Mr Smith Goes to Washington* (1939) and *Shane* (1953). She died June 19, 1991, at Carmel, CA.

BLACK POETRY DAY. Oct 17. To recognize the contribution of black poets to American life and culture and to honor Jupiter Hammon, first black in America to publish his own verse. Jupiter Hammon of Huntington, Long Island, NY, was born Oct 17, 1711.

BRIDGE DAY. Oct 17. New River Gorge Bridge, Fayetteville, WV. World's biggest extreme sports event and West Virginia's largest festival. Up to 300 BASE jumpers leap off North America's longest single-span bridge at a height of 876 feet. Annually, the third Saturday in October. Est attendance: 80,000. For info: Official Bridge Day Festival, Fayette County Chamber of Commerce, 310 Oyler Av, Oak Hill, WV 25901. Phone: (800) 927-0263. E-mail: bridgeday@officialbridgeday.com. Web: www.officialbridgeday.com.

EWING, BUCK: BIRTH ANNIVERSARY. Oct 17, 1859. William Buckingham (Buck) Ewing, Baseball Hall of Fame catcher, born at Hoagland, OH. Ewing was one of the best catchers of the 19th century and is credited by some with being the first to crouch immediately under the batter. Inducted into the Hall of Fame in 1939. Died at Cincinnati, OH, Oct 20, 1906.

FOOD AND DRUG INTERACTION EDUCATION AND AWARENESS WEEK. Oct 17–24. This campaign has been designed to help educate health professionals, patients and consumers about the problems of certain foods mixed with prescription drugs, over-the-counter drugs and herbal/alternative medicines. Sponsored by the American College of Apothecaries (ACA)/Pharmacists Planning Service, Inc (PPSI). For info: ACA/PPSI, 2830 Summer Oaks Dr, Bartlett, TN 38134. E-mail: info@ppsinc.org. Web: www.ppsinc.org.

HAMMON, JUPITER: BIRTH ANNIVERSARY. Oct 17, 1711. America's first published black poet was born into slavery, probably at Long Island, NY. He was taught to read, however, and as a trusted servant was allowed to use his master's library. On Dec 25, 1760, Jupiter Hammon, then 49, published the 88-line broadside poem "An Evening Thought" and thus became the first black person in America to publish poetry. Hammon died about 1806 (exact date and place of death unknown).

HASSAM, CHILDE: BIRTH ANNIVERSARY. Oct 17, 1859. Artist who brought French Impressionism to America. Hassam's luminous works featured scenes of New York City. Born at Boston, MA, he died Aug 17, 1935, at East Hampton, NY.

HIGH POINT MARKET (FALL). Oct 17–21. High Point, NC. The largest wholesale home furnishings market in the world. (For the trade only: not open to the general public.) Est attendance: 75,000. For info: High Point Market Authority, 164 S Main St, Ste 700, High Point, NC 27260. Phone: (336) 869-1000. E-mail: info@highpointmarket.org. Web: www.highpointmarket.org.

"THE HOLLYWOOD SQUARES" TV PREMIERE: ANNIVERSARY. Oct 17, 1966. On this game show, nine celebrities sat in a giant grid. Two contestants played tic-tac-toe by determining if an answer given by a celebrity was correct. Peter Marshall hosted the show for many years with panelists Paul Lynde, Rose Marie, Cliff Arquette, Wally Cox, John Davidson and George Gobel, among others. John Davidson took over as host in 1986 for a new version of the game show with Joan Rivers and, later, Shadoe Stevens at center square. In 1998 "Hollywood Squares" appeared again with Tom Bergeron as host and Whoopi Goldberg as the center square.

JOHNSON, RICHARD MENTOR: BIRTH ANNIVERSARY. Oct 17, 1780. Ninth vice president of the US (1837–41). Born at Floyd's Station, KY. Died at Frankfort, KY, Nov 19, 1850.

KNIEVEL, ROBERT CRAIG, JR: BIRTH ANNIVERSARY. Oct 17, 1938. Known by his nickname, "Evel," Knievel gained worldwide fame as a stunt performer, conceiving of and executing a series of increasingly outlandish motorcycle jumps throughout the 1970s that often resulted in crashes and broken bones. Born at Butte, MT, he died Nov 30, 2007, at Clearwater, FL.

MILLER, ARTHUR: BIRTH ANNIVERSARY. Oct 17, 1915. Born at New York, NY, Miller began writing plays in college and also published several novels and collections of short stories. He won the Pulitzer Prize in 1949 for *Death of a Salesman*, one of the most significant works in American literature. The play won the Tony Award twice: once in 1949 and again in 1999 when it won for Best Revival. Miller also received a Tony for *The Crucible*, a drama about the Salem witch trials, and a Lifetime Achievement Award in 1999. He was married to actress Marilyn Monroe from 1956 to 1961 and wrote the 1963 play *After the Fall* about their relationship. Miller died at Roxbury, CT, Feb 11, 2005.

MULLIGAN DAY. Oct 17. A day for giving yourself or another a second chance; a day for a "do-over." (© 2001 C. Daniel Rhodes.) For info: C. Daniel Rhodes, 1900 Crossvine Rd, Hoover, AL 65244. Phone: (205) 908-6781. E-mail: rhodan@charter.net.

NATIONAL PLAYING CARD COLLECTION DAY. Oct 17. 5th annual. This day celebrates collecting one of the oldest forms of portable art—playing cards. Playing cards are galleries of art and inspiration and archive the cultural values of their time. Collecting

October 2020	S	M	T	W	T	F	S
					1	2	3
	4	5	6	7	8	9	10
	11	12	13	14	15	16	17
	18	19	20	21	22	23	24
	25	26	27	28	29	30	31

these art pieces allows card enthusiasts to be curators of their own galleries to display. National Playing Card Collection Day is an opportunity to celebrate and share collections to the public and with fellow collectors. Annually, Oct 17. For info: Alexander Chin, Founder, Seasons Playing Cards. E-mail: alex@seasonsplayingcards.com. Web: www.cardcollectionday.com.

POPE JOHN PAUL I: BIRTH ANNIVERSARY. Oct 17, 1912. Albino Luciani, 263rd pope of the Roman Catholic Church. Born at Forno di Canale, Italy, he was elected pope Aug 26, 1978. Died at Rome, Italy, 34 days after his election, Sept 28, 1978. Shortest papacy since Pope Leo XI (Apr 1–27, 1605).

SAN FRANCISCO 1989 EARTHQUAKE: ANNIVERSARY. Oct 17, 1989. The San Francisco Bay area was rocked by an earthquake registering 7.1 on the Richter scale at 5:04 PM, PDT, just as the nation's baseball fans settled in to watch the 1989 World Series at Candlestick Park. A large audience was tuned in to the pregame coverage when the quake hit and knocked the broadcast off the air. The quake caused damage estimated at $10 billion and killed 67 people, many of whom were caught in the collapse of the double-decked Interstate 80, at Oakland, CA.

SIEGEL, JERRY: BIRTH ANNIVERSARY. Oct 17, 1914. Siegel, born at Cleveland, OH, was the writing half of a team that created comic book hero Superman, who debuted in *Action Comics* in June 1938. Siegel, the son of Jewish immigrants, worked with childhood friend Joe Shuster to create the powerful alien trying to find his way in a new world. Superman immediately exploded in popularity, but Siegel and Shuster never profited greatly, having sold the rights to the character in 1938 (although later legal action ensured a modest stipend and creative credit). Siegel died Jan 28, 1996, at Los Angeles, CA.

SWEETEST DAY. Oct 17. Around 1922 a candy company employee named Herbert Birch Kingston decided that it would be a wonderful thing to distribute candy to the sick, shut-ins and orphans of Cleveland, OH. Thus, Sweetest Day was born. Do something nice for someone today, something that will make him or her say, "Oh, that's so sweet!" Annually, the third Saturday in October.

300 MILLIONTH AMERICAN BORN: ANNIVERSARY. Oct 17, 2006. The US Census Bureau reported that the 300 millionth American would be born in the early hours of Oct 17, 2006. A baby girl born at Chicago, IL, at 5:58 AM was probably that American—although there was a margin of error of a few hours. The US population now increases by one every 11 seconds. The 200 millionth American was born Nov 20, 1967.

UNITED NATIONS: INTERNATIONAL DAY FOR THE ERADICATION OF POVERTY. Oct 17. The General Assembly proclaimed this observance (Res 47/196) to promote public awareness of the need to eradicate poverty and destitution in all countries, particularly the developing nations. For info: United Nations, Dept of Public Info, New York, NY 10017. Web: www.un.org.

US OYSTER FESTIVAL. Oct 17–18. Fairgrounds, Leonardtown, MD. Oysters served every style, national oyster-shucking contest and national oyster cook-off. Also featuring lots of other seafood and live entertainment! Est attendance: 18,000. For info: Karen Stone, Administrator, Oyster Fest Office, Box 766, California, MD 20619-0766. Phone: (301) 863-5015. E-mail: usoysterfestival@gmail.com. Web: www.usoysterfest.com.

YORKTOWN VICTORY CELEBRATION. Oct 17–18. American Revolution Museum at Yorktown, Yorktown, VA. Military life and artillery firings mark the 239th anniversary of America's momentous Revolutionary War victory at Yorktown on Oct 19, 1781. Oct 19 commemorative events take place in historic Yorktown and Yorktown Battlefield. For info: Jamestown-Yorktown Foundation, PO Box 1607, Williamsburg, VA 23187. Phone: (757) 253-4838 or toll-free (888) 593-4682. Fax: (757) 253-5299. Web: www.historyisfun.org.

🎂 BIRTHDAYS TODAY

Ernie Els, 51, golfer, born Johannesburg, South Africa, Oct 17, 1969.

Eminem, 48, musician, rapper, actor, born Marshall Bruce Mathers III at Kansas City, MO, Oct 17, 1972.

Martin Heinrich, 49, US Senator (D, New Mexico), born Fallon, NV, Oct 17, 1971.

Mae Jemison, 64, scientist, astronaut, born Decatur, AL, Oct 17, 1956.

Felicity Jones, 37, actress (*Rogue One, The Theory of Everything*), born Birmingham, England, Oct 17, 1983.

Norm Macdonald, 57, comedian, actor ("Saturday Night Live," "Norm"), born Quebec City, QC, Canada, Oct 17, 1963.

Kerry James Marshall, 65, artist, born Birmingham, AL, Oct 17, 1955.

Michael McKean, 73, actor ("Good Omens," "Laverne & Shirley," *This Is Spinal Tap*), born New York, NY, Oct 17, 1947.

Steve McMichael, 63, sportscaster, football coach, former football player, former professional wrestler, born Houston, TX, Oct 17, 1957.

Richard Roeper, 61, newspaper columnist, film reviewer ("Ebert & Roeper and the Movies"), born Chicago, IL, Oct 17, 1959.

George Wendt, 72, actor ("Cheers," "The Naked Truth"), born Chicago, IL, Oct 17, 1948.

October 18 — Sunday

DAY 292   **74 REMAINING**

ANDRÉE, SALOMON AUGUST: BIRTH ANNIVERSARY. Oct 18, 1854. Swedish explorer and balloonist, born at Grenna, Sweden. His North Pole expedition of 1897 attracted world attention but ended tragically. With two companions, Andrée left Spitsbergen, Norway, July 11, 1897, in a balloon, hoping to place the Swedish flag at the North Pole. The last message from Andrée, borne by carrier pigeons, was dated noon, July 13, 1897. The frozen bodies of the explorers were found 33 years later by another polar expedition in the summer of 1930. Diaries, maps and exposed photographic negatives also were found. The photos were developed successfully, providing a pictorial record of the ill-fated expedition.

AZERBAIJAN: INDEPENDENCE DAY. Oct 18. National holiday. Commemorates declaration of independence from the Soviet Union in 1991.

BERGSON, HENRI: BIRTH ANNIVERSARY. Oct 18, 1859. French philosopher, Nobel Prize winner and author of *Creative Evolution*, born at Paris, France. Died there Jan 4, 1941.

BERRY, CHUCK: BIRTH ANNIVERSARY. Oct 18, 1926. Rock and roll pioneer born Charles Edward Anderson Barry at St. Louis, MO. A roustabout from youth, Berry coupled his irascible nature and showman's flair to a distinctive, blues-based guitar sound. A 1955 meeting with Muddy Waters in Chicago led to a Chess Records contract and Berry's first hit, "Maybelline," and he went on to lend rock music its formative voice with cuts like "Johnny B. Goode" and "Sweet Little Sixteen." Legal troubles dogged

Berry throughout his life. After a short prison stay in the early 1960s, Berry increasingly turned to live performance to sustain his career. He also opened a restaurant at Wentzville, MO. Berry entered the Rock & Roll Hall of Fame in 1986. He died at Wentzville, MO, Mar 18, 2017.

BIRTH OF THE BAB. Oct 18. Baha'i observance of anniversary of the birth in 1819 in Shiraz, Persia, of Siyyid Ali Muhammad, who later took the title "the Bab"; the Bab was the prophet-herald of the Baha'i Faith. One of the nine days of the year when Baha'is suspend work. For info: Baha'is of the US, Office of Communications, 1233 Central St, Evanston, IL 60201. Phone: (847) 733-3584. E-mail: ooc@usbnc.org. Web: www.bahai.us.

BROOKS, JAMES DAVID: BIRTH ANNIVERSARY. Oct 18, 1906. Born at St. Louis, MO. During the Depression, Brooks worked as a muralist in the Federal Art Project of the Works Progress Administration. His best-known work of that period is *Flight*, a mural on the rotunda of the Marine Air Terminal at La Guardia National Airport in New York. It was painted over during the 1950s but restored in 1980. Brooks served with the US Army during 1942–45. When he returned to New York, his interest shifted to Abstract Expressionism. His paintings were exhibited in the historic Ninth Street Exhibition as a part of the Museum of Modern Art's exhibits Twelve Americans and New American Painting, among others. He died Mar 8, 1992, at Brookhaven, NY.

BULLYING BYSTANDERS UNITE WEEK. Oct 18–24. Bullying is a serious issue facing youth today. The missing link is the 85 percent who witness bullying. The bullying and suicide prevention international nonprofit organization Hey U.G.L.Y. (Unique Gifted Lovable You) has designated the third week in October a time for schools and law enforcement agencies to launch a pledge drive to educate their communities on how to safely come to the aid of someone being bullied. For info and pledge form: Hey U.G.L.Y., Inc, PO Box 2142, Michigan City, IN 46361. Phone: (219) 814-4224. E-mail: preventbullyingnow@heyugly.org. Web: www.heyugly.org.

CANADA: PERSONS DAY: ANNIVERSARY. Oct 18. A day to commemorate the anniversary of the 1929 ruling that declared women to be persons in Canada. Prior to this ruling English common law prevailed ("Women are persons in matters of pains and penalties, but are not persons in matters of rights and privileges"). The celebrated cause, popularly known as the "Persons Case," was brought by five women of Alberta, Canada; leader of the courageous "Famous Five" was Emily Murphy (1868–1933). This ruling by the Judicial Committee of England's Privy Council, Oct 18, 1929, overturned a 1928 decision of the Supreme Court of Canada. Fifty years after the Persons Case decision, in 1979, the Governor General's Awards in Commemoration of the Persons Case were established to recognize deserving persons who have made outstanding contributions to the quality of life of women in Canada.

CANALETTO, GIOVANNI ANTONIO: BIRTH ANNIVERSARY. Oct 18, 1697. Painter Giovanni Antonio Canaletto (born Canale), best known for his detailed landscapes of Venice and London, was born at Venice, Italy, and died there at age 70, Apr 20, 1768. He was known for his accurate use of perspective, shadow and light. He went to England in 1746 and expanded his range of subjects to include English landscapes and country homes.

FIRST NEWSPAPER COMIC STRIP: ANNIVERSARY. Oct 18, 1896. Although cartoons had appeared in newspapers for many years, the comic strip—a narrative told in cartoons over several panels—took its main form with the appearance of "The Yellow Kid Takes a Hand at Golf" in the *New York Journal*'s weekly supplement,

	S	M	T	W	T	F	S
October					1	2	3
	4	5	6	7	8	9	10
2020	11	12	13	14	15	16	17
	18	19	20	21	22	23	24
	25	26	27	28	29	30	31

American Humorist. The creator was Richard Fenton Outcault. In March 1897 the *Yellow Kid Magazine* gathered the strips and became the first published collection of a comic strip—setting the stage for the first comic books in the late 1920s. See also: "Outcault, Richard Fenton: Birth Anniversary" (Jan 14).

LIEBLING, A.J.: BIRTH ANNIVERSARY. Oct 18, 1904. American journalist and author who said, "Freedom of the press belongs to those who own one." Abbott Joseph Liebling was born at New York, NY, and died there Dec 28, 1963.

MERCOURI, MELINA: 100th BIRTH ANNIVERSARY. Oct 18, 1920. Greek actress and politician Melina Mercouri was born Maria Amalia Mercouri at Athens, Greece, Oct 18, 1920 or 1925 (both reported). Of her more than 70 films and plays, she is best known for her role in *Never on Sunday* (1960). In 1977 she was elected to Greece's parliament; she became the first woman in Greece's senior cabinet when appointed by Premier Andreas Papandreou to the position of minister of culture in 1981. She died Mar 6, 1994, at New York, NY.

★**NATIONAL CHARACTER COUNTS WEEK.** Oct 18–24. One of the greatest building blocks of character is citizen service. The future belongs to those who have the strength of character to live a life of service to others. Annually, the third full week in October.

NATIONAL CHEMISTRY WEEK. Oct 18–24. First observed in 1987. To celebrate the contributions of chemistry to modern life and to help the public understand that chemistry affects every part of our lives. The American Chemical Society provides activities including open houses, contests, workshops, exhibits and classroom visits around the US and Puerto Rico. More than 10 million participants worldwide. Annually, the fourth week in October. For info: Office of Science Outreach, American Chemical Society, 1155 16th St NW, Washington, DC 20036. Phone: (800) 227-5558, ext 7723. E-mail: outreach@acs.org. Web: www.acs.org/ncw.

★**NATIONAL FOREST PRODUCTS WEEK.** Oct 18–24. Presidential Proclamation always issued for the week beginning with the third Sunday in October since 1960 (PL 86–753 of Sept 13, 1960).

RABI' I: THE MONTH OF THE MIGRATION. Oct 18. Begins on Islamic calendar date Rabi al-Awal 1, 1442. The third month of the Islamic calendar, the month of the migration of the Prophet Muhammad from Mecca to Medina in AD 622, the event that was used as the starting year of the Islamic lunar calendar. Different methods for "anticipating" the visibility of the new moon crescent at Mecca are used by different Muslim groups, so date can vary one to two days. Began at sunset the preceding day.

RODENT AWARENESS WEEK. Oct 18–24. Each winter, rodents invade approximately 21 million US homes, through openings as small as a dime, bringing with them a slew of hazards. Rodents contaminate food; spread disease, such as salmonella bacteria; and also carry disease-causing parasites such as fleas and ticks. The deer and white-footed mouse as well as the rice and cotton rat can also transmit hantavirus, a potentially fatal disease. Rodents can chew through wood and electrical wires, putting homes at risk for fires. Since a small rodent infestation can quickly grow into a huge problem, home owners are advised to take measures to prevent rodents from gaining access to homes as they escape the colder temperatures. The National Pest Management Association (NPMA) launched this week to spread awareness and provide essential rodent prevention advice to the American public. For info: Natl Pest Management Assn, 10460 North St, Fairfax, VA 22030. Phone: (703) 352-6762. E-mail: NPMATeam@vaultcommunications.com. Web: www.pestworld.org.

Ne-Yo, 41, singer, actor (*Stomp the Yard*), born Shaffer Chimere Smith, Jr, at Camden, AR, Oct 18, 1979.

Freida Pinto, 36, actress (*Rise of the Planet of the Apes, Slumdog Millionaire*), born Mumbai, India, Oct 18, 1984.

Vincent Spano, 58, actor (*Baby, It's You; Rumblefish*), born New York, NY, Oct 18, 1962.

Jean-Claude Van Damme, 60, actor (*Replicant, Universal Soldier, Kickboxer*), born Brussels, Belgium, Oct 18, 1960.

Lindsey Vonn, 36, Olympic skier, born St. Paul, MN, Oct 18, 1984.

"ROSEANNE" TV PREMIERE: ANNIVERSARY. Oct 18, 1988. This comedy showed the blue-collar Conner family trying to make ends meet. Rosanne Barr played wisecracking Roseanne Conner, John Goodman played her husband, Dan, and Laurie Metcalf played her sister, Jackie. The Conner children were played by Sara Gilbert (Darlene), Alicia Goranson and Sarah Chalke (Becky) and Michael Fishman (D.J.). The last episode aired Nov 14, 1997. (A successful return of the series in summer 2019 was canceled after Barr made racist comments on social media.)

SAINT LUKE: FEAST DAY. Oct 18. Patron saint of doctors and artists, himself a physician and painter; authorship of the third Gospel and Acts of the Apostles is attributed to him. Died about AD 68. Legend says that he painted portraits of Mary and Jesus.

TRUDEAU, PIERRE ELLIOTT: BIRTH ANNIVERSARY. Oct 18, 1919. The youthful, charismatic and "with it" Trudeau caused a sensation when he became the prime minister of Canada in 1968. In fact, the sensation was called "Trudeaumania," and it rivaled reactions to The Beatles earlier in the 1960s. The yoga- and judo-practicing Trudeau (or "PET," as he went by) promised change and new ideas while at the same time dating glamorous women and hobnobbing with John Lennon and Yoko Ono. Trudeau was prime minister from 1968 to 1979 and 1980 to 1984—taken together, the terms equate to 15½ years of service, the third longest by a Canadian prime minister. Born at Montreal, QC, Canada, he died there Sept 28, 2000.

WATER POLLUTION CONTROL ACT: ANNIVERSARY. Oct 18, 1972. Overriding President Nixon's veto, Congress passed a $25 billion Water Pollution Control Act.

WORLD MENOPAUSE DAY. Oct 18. The World Menopause Day challenge calls on every nation to make menopausal health a principal issue in their research and public health agendas in order to help women prevent unpleasant symptoms that can affect productivity and quality of life, as well as reduce rates of osteoporosis, heart disease, colon cancer and other aging- and hormone-related diseases. For info: Intl Menopause Society, PO Box 751, Truro, Cornwall TR2 4WD, United Kingdom. Web: www.imsociety.org.

🎂 BIRTHDAYS TODAY

Pam Dawber, 69, actress ("Mork & Mindy," "My Sister Sam"), born Farmington, MI, Oct 18, 1951.

Mike Ditka, 81, sportscaster, Hall of Fame football player, former coach, born Carnegie, PA, Oct 18, 1939.

Zac Efron, 33, actor (*High School Musical, Hairspray*), born San Luis Obispo, CA, Oct 18, 1987.

Wynton Marsalis, 59, jazz musician, born New Orleans, LA, Oct 18, 1961.

Terry McMillan, 69, author (*How Stella Got Her Groove Back, Waiting to Exhale*), born Port Huron, MI, Oct 18, 1951.

Joe Morton, 73, actor ("Scandal," "Eureka," *Terminator 2, The Brother from Another Planet*), born New York, NY, Oct 18, 1947.

Martina Navratilova, 64, Hall of Fame tennis player, born Martina Subertova at Prague, Czechoslovakia (now the Czech Republic), Oct 18, 1956.

October 19 — Monday

DAY 293   **73 REMAINING**

ALASKA DAY (OBSERVED). Oct 19. Anniversary of transfer of Alaska on Oct 18, 1867, from Russia to the US. The transfer became official on Sitka's Castle Hill. This is a holiday in Alaska; when it falls on a weekend, it is observed on the following Monday.

BIRTH OF BAHA'U'LLAH. Oct 19. Baha'i observance of the anniversary of the birth of Baha'u'llah (born Mirza Husayn Ali) at Nur, Persia, in 1817. Baha'u'llah was prophet-founder of the Baha'i Faith. One of the nine days of the year when Baha'is suspend work. For info: Baha'is of the US, Office of Communications, 1233 Central St, Evanston, IL 60201-1611. Phone: (847) 733-3584. E-mail: ooc@usbnc.org. Web: www.bahai.us.

BROWNE, THOMAS: BIRTH ANNIVERSARY. Oct 19, 1605. (Old Style date.) Physician, scholar and author, Browne was born at London, England. At age 55 he wrote: "The long habit of living indisposeth us for dying." His most famous work, *Religio Medici*, was published in 1642. Browne died at Norwich, England, Oct 19, 1682 (OS).

EVALUATE YOUR LIFE DAY. Oct 19. To encourage people to check and see if they're really headed where they want to be. (©2006 by WH.) For info: Thomas & Ruth Roy, Wellcat Holidays, 2418 Long Ln, Lebanon, PA 17042-0774. Phone: (717) 279-0184. E-mail: info@wellcat.com. Web: www.wellcat.com.

JAMAICA: NATIONAL HEROES DAY. Oct 19. National holiday established in 1969. Always observed on third Monday in October.

JEFFERSON, MARTHA WAYLES SKELTON: BIRTH ANNIVERSARY. Oct 19, 1748. Wife of Thomas Jefferson, third president of the US. Born at Charles City County, VA, she died at Monticello, VA, Sept 6, 1782.

LGBT CENTER AWARENESS DAY. Oct 19. A national day of action focused on awareness around the work of LGBT community centers everywhere. The day was planned to help bring national attention to the Community Center Movement within the LGBT movement, which serves more than 1.7 million people annually, and highlight the ways that people can get involved with or utilize their local centers. For info: Denise Spivak, CenterLink: The Community of LGBT Centers, PO Box 24490, Fort Lauderdale, FL 33307. Phone: (954) 765-6024. Fax: (954) 206-0469. E-mail: denise@lgbtcenters.org. Web: www.lgbtcenters.org.

LUMIÈRE, AUGUSTE: BIRTH ANNIVERSARY. Oct 19, 1862. Born at Besançon, France, Auguste Lumière and brother Louis were film pioneers who created the first movie, *Workers Leaving the Lumière Factory* (1895). He died at Lyon, France, on Apr 10, 1954.

NUCLEAR SCIENCE WEEK. Oct 19–23. Inaugurated in 2010, Nuclear Science Week celebrates and educates about the nuclear advancements to the service of humankind including energy, medicine and scientific research efforts. For info: Natl Museum of Nuclear Science and History, 601 Eubank Blvd SE, Albuquerque, NM 87123. Phone: (505) 245-2137. Web: NuclearScienceWeek.org.

PECK, ANNIE S.: BIRTH ANNIVERSARY. Oct 19, 1850. World-renowned mountain climber Annie S. Peck also won an international following in 1895 when she climbed the Matterhorn in the Swiss Alps. Peck climbed the Peruvian peak Huascaran (21,812 feet), giving her the record for the highest peak climbed in the Western Hemisphere by an American man or woman, and at age 61 she climbed Mount Coropuna (21,250 feet) in Peru and placed a "Votes for Women" banner at its pinnacle. Peck died July 18, 1935, at New York City.

VIRGIN ISLANDS: HURRICANE THANKSGIVING DAY. Oct 19. Third Monday in October is a legal holiday celebrating the end of hurricane season.

YORKTOWN DAY. Oct 19. Yorktown, VA. Representatives of the US, France and other nations involved in the American Revolution gather to celebrate the anniversary of the victory (Oct 19, 1781) that assured American independence. Parade and commemorative ceremonies. Annually, Oct 19. Est attendance: 2,000. For info: Public Affairs Officer, Colonial Natl Historical Park, PO Box 210, Yorktown, VA 23690. Phone: (757) 898-3400. Web: www.nps.gov/colo.

YORKTOWN SURRENDER: ANNIVERSARY. Oct 19, 1781. More than 7,000 English and Hessian troops, led by British general Lord Charles Cornwallis, surrendered to General George Washington at Yorktown, VA, effectively ending the war between Britain and its American colonies. There were no more major battles, but the provisional treaty of peace was not signed until Nov 30, 1782, and the final Treaty of Paris, Sept 3, 1783.

🧁 BIRTHDAYS TODAY

Michael Gambon, 80, actor (Harry Potter films; *The Cook, the Thief, His Wife & Her Lover*; "The Singing Detective"), born Dublin, Ireland, Oct 19, 1940.

Evander Holyfield, 58, boxer, born Atlanta, GA, Oct 19, 1962.

John le Carré, 89, author (*The Spy Who Came in from the Cold, The Constant Gardener*), born David John Moore Cornwell at Poole, Dorset, England, Oct 19, 1931.

John Lithgow, 75, actor (Tonys for *The Sweet Smell of Success* and *The Changing Room*; *Don Quixote*, "3rd Rock from the Sun"), author, born Rochester, NY, Oct 19, 1945.

Peter Max, 83, artist, designer, born Berlin, Germany, Oct 19, 1937.

Ty Pennington, 55, carpenter, television personality ("Trading Spaces," "Extreme Makeover: Home Edition"), born Atlanta, GA, Oct 19, 1965.

Jason Reitman, 43, writer, director (*Thank You for Smoking, Juno, Up in the Air*), born Montreal, QC, Canada, Oct 19, 1977.

Michael Young, 44, former baseball player, born Covina, CA, Oct 19, 1976.

October 20 — Tuesday

DAY 294   **72 REMAINING**

CHADWICK, JAMES: BIRTH ANNIVERSARY. Oct 20, 1891. English physicist, born at Bollington, Cheshire. His study of beta radiation was interrupted by WWI, when he was interned in the Ruhleben camp near Berlin, Germany, from 1913 to 1918. He did have a laboratory in the camp, where he worked with improvised materials like radioactive toothpaste; upon his release, he returned to England to write up his assorted findings and continue his research. In 1932 he published findings on the "Possible Existence of a Neutron," and his continued research in that field earned him the Nobel Prize in Physics (1935). In the 1940s he joined the team on the Manhattan Project in the United States, bringing his work on tube alloys to the endeavor. Chadwick died July 24, 1974, at Cambridge, England; he had been knighted, had received many medals and honors, and had a crater on the moon named in his honor.

DEWEY, JOHN: BIRTH ANNIVERSARY. Oct 20, 1859. American psychologist, philosopher and educational reformer, born at Burlington, VT. His philosophical views of education have been termed pragmatism, instrumentalism and experimentalism. Died at New York, NY, June 1, 1952.

GUATEMALA: REVOLUTION DAY. Oct 20. Public holiday. Commemorates the overthrow of dictator Jorge Ubico Castañada in 1944.

KENYA: MASHUJAA DAY. Oct 20. Public holiday. Oct 20 was originally Kenyatta Day, recognizing nationalist (and later first president) Jomo Kenyatta and five others who were arrested on Oct 20, 1952, by the British colonial government. After 2010, the holiday was expanded to honor all heroes of the independence movement: *mushajaa* is Swahili for "heroes." Festivities center in Nairobi with military parades, speeches and more.

LUGOSI, BELA: BIRTH ANNIVERSARY. Oct 20, 1882. Born Bela Ferenc Denzso Blasko at Lugos, Hungary. Known best for his role as Count Dracula in *Dracula*. Lugosi died of a heart attack at Los Angeles, CA, Aug 16, 1956.

MACARTHUR RETURNS: US LANDINGS ON LEYTE, PHILIPPINES: ANNIVERSARY. Oct 20, 1944. In mid-September 1944 American military leaders made the decision to begin the invasion of the Philippines on Leyte, a small island north of the Surigao Strait. With General Douglas MacArthur in overall command, US aircraft dropped hundreds of tons of bombs in the area of Dulag. Four divisions were landed on the east coast, and after a few hours General MacArthur set foot on Philippine soil for the first time since he was ordered to Australia Mar 11, 1942, thus fulfilling his promise, "I shall return."

MANN, JAMES ROBERT: BIRTH ANNIVERSARY. Oct 20, 1856. American lawyer and legislator, born near Bloomington, IL. Republican member of Congress from Illinois from 1896 until his death, Nov 30, 1922, at Washington, DC. Mann was the author and sponsor of the "White Slave Traffic Act," also known as the "Mann Act," passed by Congress on June 25, 1910. The act prohibited, under heavy penalties, the interstate transportation of women for immoral purposes.

MANTLE, MICKEY: BIRTH ANNIVERSARY. Oct 20, 1931. Baseball Hall of Famer, born at Spavinaw, OK. "The Mick" played his entire career with the New York Yankees (1951–68), who retired his iconic jersey number 7 in 1969. Had a career 536 home runs, was named to 20 American League All-Star teams and was named Most Valuable Player in 1956, 1957 and 1962—among many other triumphs. Mantle died Aug 13, 1995, at Dallas, TX.

MISS AMERICAN ROSE DAY. Oct 20. Miss American Rose is a pageant devoted to high achievement and community service for girls and women of all ages. On this day treat the women in your life like beautiful American roses and/or perform a community service project. For info: Lynanne White, Miss American Rose

October	S	M	T	W	T	F	S
					1	2	3
2020	4	5	6	7	8	9	10
	11	12	13	14	15	16	17
	18	19	20	21	22	23	24
	25	26	27	28	29	30	31

Pageants, 19900 Nilsen Ln, Poulsbo, WA 98370. E-mail: miss@ americanrose.com. Web: www.americanrose.com.

MOSCOW SOCCER TRAGEDY: ANNIVERSARY. Oct 20, 1982. The world's worst soccer disaster occurred at Moscow, USSR, when 340 sports fans were killed during a game between Soviet and Dutch players. Details of the event, blaming police for the tragedy in which spectators were crushed to death in an open staircase, were not published until nearly seven years later (July 1989) in *Sovietsky Sport.*

ORBACH, JERRY: 85th BIRTH ANNIVERSARY. Oct 20, 1935. Actor, born at the Bronx, NY, who starred in the original Broadway productions of *The Fantasticks, 42nd Street* and *Chicago.* He won a Best Actor Tony Award for *Promises, Promises* in 1969. Films include *Dirty Dancing* and the voice of Lumière in Disney's *Beauty and the Beast.* His most popular role was that of wisecracking homicide detective Lennie Briscoe on television's "Law & Order," a role he played from 1992 until his death at New York, NY, on Dec 28, 2004.

***RETURN OF THE KING* PUBLISHED: 65th ANNIVERSARY.** Oct 20, 1955. The final installment of J.R.R. Tolkien's *The Lord of the Rings* was published on this date by George Allen and Unwin at London, England. The previous two parts were published in 1954.

SATURDAY NIGHT MASSACRE: ANNIVERSARY. Oct 20, 1973. Anniversary of dramatic turning point in the Watergate affair. On Oct 20, 1973, the White House announced at 8:24 PM, EDT, that President Richard M. Nixon had discharged Archibald Cox (special Watergate prosecutor) and William B. Ruckelshaus (deputy attorney general) and that Attorney General Elliot L. Richardson had resigned. Immediate and widespread demands for impeachment of the president ensued and were not stilled until President Nixon resigned, Aug 9, 1974.

"THE SIX MILLION DOLLAR MAN" TV PREMIERE: ANNIVERSARY. Oct 20, 1973. This action-adventure series based on the novel *Cyborg* was a monthly feature on "The ABC Suspense Movie" before becoming a regular series in 1974. Lee Majors starred as astronaut Steve Austin, who, after an accident, was "rebuilt" with bionic legs, arms and an eye. He worked for the Office of Strategic Information (OSI) carrying out sensitive missions. Also in the cast were Richard Anderson, Alan Oppenheimer and Martin E. Brooks. "The Bionic Woman," starring Lindsay Wagner, was a spin-off from this show, and the two main characters were paired for several made-for-TV sequels.

SYDNEY OPERA HOUSE OPENS: ANNIVERSARY. Oct 20, 1973. One of the most iconic and dramatic man-made structures of the 20th century, the Sydney Opera House, was opened by Queen Elizabeth II at Sydney, Australia, on this date. Designed by Danish architect Jørn Utzon, the theater is perched on Sydney Harbor and appears to be a ship in full sail. It took 14 years to build, and its roof is covered with more than one million tiles.

UNITED NATIONS: WORLD STATISTICS DAY. Oct 20. Official statistics help decision makers develop informed policies that impact millions of people. Improved data sources, sound statistical methods, new technologies and strengthened statistical systems enable better decisions that eventually result in better lives for all of us. Observed every five years. First observed in 2010. For info: United Nations. Web: www.un.org/en/events/statisticsday or https://worldstatisticsday.org.

WREN, CHRISTOPHER: BIRTH ANNIVERSARY. Oct 20, 1632. (Old Style date.) Sir Christopher Wren, English architect, astronomer and mathematician, was born at East Knoyle, Wiltshire, England. Died Feb 25, 1723 (OS), at London. His epitaph, written by his son, is inscribed over the interior of the north door at St. Paul's Cathedral, London: "Si monumentum requiris, circumspice." ("If you would see his monument, look about you.")

🎂 BIRTHDAYS TODAY

Danny Boyle, 64, filmmaker, director (Oscar for *Slumdog Millionaire; 127 Hours, Trainspotting*), born Radcliffe, Lancashire, England, Oct 20, 1956.

Snoop Dogg, 49, rapper, actor, record producer, born Calvin Cordozar Broadus, Jr, at Long Beach, CA, Oct 20, 1971.

Kamala Harris, 56, US Senator (D, California), born Oakland, CA, Oct 20, 1964.

Keith Hernandez, 67, sportscaster, former baseball player, born San Francisco, CA, Oct 20, 1953.

John Krasinski, 41, actor ("The Office [US]," *A Quiet Place, Away We Go, Leatherheads*), director (*A Quiet Place*), born Boston, MA, Oct 20, 1979.

Melanie Mayron, 68, actress (Emmy for "thirtysomething"; *Car Wash, My Blue Heaven*), born Philadelphia, PA, Oct 20, 1952.

Viggo Mortensen, 62, actor (*The Road, Eastern Promises,* the Lord of the Rings trilogy), poet, born New York, NY, Oct 20, 1958.

Brian Schatz, 48, US Senator (D, Hawaii), born Ann Arbor, MI, Oct 20, 1972.

Sheldon Whitehouse, 65, US Senator (D, Rhode Island), born New York, NY, Oct 20, 1955.

October 21 — Wednesday

DAY 295   **71 REMAINING**

ALDERSON, SAMUEL: BIRTH ANNIVERSARY. Oct 21, 1914. Born at Cleveland, OH, Alderson was a physicist and engineer who invented the crash test dummy, an anthropomorphic data-collecting human body substitute that revolutionized car safety. Alderson died Feb 11, 2005, at Los Angeles, CA.

BATTLE OF TRAFALGAR: ANNIVERSARY. Oct 21, 1805. This famous naval action between the British Royal Navy and the combined French and Spanish fleets removed the threat of Napoleon's invasion of England. The British victory, off Trafalgar on the coast of Spain, guaranteed the fame of Viscount Horatio Nelson, who died in the battle.

CIRCLEVILLE PUMPKIN SHOW. Oct 21–24. Circleville, OH. More than 100,000 pounds of pumpkins, squash and gourds. Annually, starting the third Wednesday in October and running through the following Saturday. Est attendance: 400,000. For info: Pumpkin Show Inc, 159 E Franklin St, Circleville, OH 43113. Phone: (740) 474-7000. Fax: (740) 474-9216. Web: www.pumpkinshow. com.

COLERIDGE, SAMUEL TAYLOR: BIRTH ANNIVERSARY. Oct 21, 1772. English poet ("The Rime of the Ancient Mariner") and essayist born at Ottery St. Mary, Devonshire, England. Died at Highgate, England, July 25, 1834. In *Table Talk,* he wrote: "I wish our clever young poets would remember my homely definitions of prose and poetry; that is, prose = words in their best order; poetry = the *best* words in the best order."

CRUZ, CELIA: BIRTH ANNIVERSARY. Oct 21, 1924. The Grammy Award–winning singer was dubbed "the Queen of Salsa" by her adoring fans. Born as Celia de la Caridad Cruz Alonso at Havana, Cuba (some sources cite her birth year as 1925 or 1929), Cruz had a career spanning six decades and recorded some 70 albums.

Her energetic performances were punctuated by her call of "Azucar!" ("Sugar!") and flamboyant costumes. President Bill Clinton awarded her the National Medal of Arts in 1994. Cruz died at New York, NY, on July 16, 2003.

FILLMORE, CAROLINE CARMICHAEL MCINTOSH: BIRTH ANNIVERSARY. Oct 21, 1813. Second wife of Millard Fillmore, 13th president of the US, born at Morristown, NJ. Died at New York, Aug 11, 1881.

FISHER, CARRIE: BIRTH ANNIVERSARY. Oct 21, 1956. Actress, writer, born at Burbank, CA. She found overnight stardom as the intrepid and wisecracking Princess Leia in the 1977 film *Star Wars*, something that both bemused and irritated her even as she continued the role in later films. As she built an admired body of work with films like *When Harry Met Sally* (1989) and *Hannah and Her Sisters* (1990), she also battled bipolar disorder, substance abuse and a sometimes rocky relationship with mother Debbie Reynolds, all inspirations for later works: her semiautobiographical novel and subsequent film *Postcards from the Edge* (1990) and the memoirs *Wishful Drinking* (2008) and *Shockaholic* (2011). Known for her acerbic wit, Fisher was also a sought-after script doctor. She died Dec 27, 2016, at Los Angeles, CA.

FOR WHOM THE BELL TOLLS PUBLISHED: 80th ANNIVERSARY. Oct 21, 1940. Dedicated to Martha Gellhorn (whom Hemingway married the next month), Ernest Hemingway's novel of love and death in the Spanish Civil War was published by Charles Scribner's Sons. It was an immediate popular and critical success and sold almost 500,000 copies the first six months after publication.

GILLESPIE, JOHN BIRKS "DIZZY": BIRTH ANNIVERSARY. Oct 21, 1917. Dizzy Gillespie, trumpet player, composer, bandleader and one of the founding fathers of modern jazz, was born at Cheraw, SC. In the early 1940s Gillespie and alto saxophonist Charlie Parker created bebop. In the late '40s he created a second music revolution by incorporating Afro-Cuban music into jazz. In 1953 someone fell on Gillespie's trumpet and bent it. Finding he could hear the sound better, he kept it that way; his puffed cheeks and bent trumpet became his trademarks. He won a Grammy in 1975 for *Oscar Peterson and Dizzy Gillespie* and again in 1991 for *Live at the Royal Festival Hall*. He died Jan 6, 1993, at Englewood, NJ.

HAGFISH DAY. Oct 21. Celebrate the beauty of ugly with Hagfish Day. This special day is a fun, somewhat tongue-in-cheek event with an important and serious goal: to raise awareness and understanding of the uniqueness and significance of all sea creatures—even the ugly, slimy, misunderstood or unusual (like the hagfish). Annually, the third Wednesday in October. For info: WhaleTimes, 19190 SW 90th, Ste 2702, Tualatin, OR 97062. E-mail: hagfishday@whaletimes.org. Web: www.whaletimes.org.

INCANDESCENT LAMP DEMONSTRATED: ANNIVERSARY. Oct 21, 1879. Thomas A. Edison demonstrated the first incandescent lamp that could be used economically for domestic purposes. This prototype, developed at his Menlo Park, NJ, laboratory, could burn for 13½ hours.

LE GUIN, URSULA K.: BIRTH ANNIVERSARY. Oct 21, 1929. Born at Berkeley, CA, to an anthropologist and a feminist writer, author Le Guin blended her parents' disciplines in her science fiction/fantasy oeuvre, which portrays strong, feminist protagonists and highly developed descriptions of alien societies. The interplay between individual and society is a central theme in her writing, which is also notable for its significant character development. Works include the Earthsea and Catwings series, *The Left Hand*

of Darkness and *The Dispossessed*. Awarded the National Book Foundation Medal for Distinguished Contribution to American Letters (2014) and the Newbery Silver Medal (1972) and inducted into the American Academy of Arts and Letters (2017), Le Guin died Jan 22, 2018, at Portland, OR.

MISSOURI DAY. Oct 21. Observed by teachers and pupils in schools with appropriate exercises throughout state of Missouri. Annually, the third Wednesday in October.

NOBEL, ALFRED BERNHARD: BIRTH ANNIVERSARY. Oct 21, 1833. Chemist and engineer who invented dynamite, born at Stockholm, Sweden, and died at San Remo, Italy, Dec 10, 1896. His will established the Nobel Prize.

OLD IRONSIDES LAUNCHED: ANNIVERSARY. Oct 21, 1797. The USS *Constitution* was launched and christened by Captain James Sever on this date at Boston, MA, making this frigate the oldest commissioned warship afloat in the world. Congress had commissioned the *Constitution* and five other ships in 1794. The *Constitution* earned its nickname, "Old Ironsides," and place in America's heart through valiant service in the War of 1812. In a fight with Britain's HMS *Guerriere* on Aug 19, 1812, sailors reported a British shot repelled by the side of the ship and declared that its sides were made of iron. No enemy ever boarded the ship in its days of active service. It now rests at Boston Harbor. See also: "Old Ironsides Saved by Poem: Anniversary" (Sept 16).

SHAWN, TED: BIRTH ANNIVERSARY. Oct 21, 1891. Named Edwin Myers Shawn at birth, Ted Shawn was born at Kansas City, MO. Partially paralyzed by diphtheria, Shawn was introduced to ballet for therapeutic purposes and became a professional dancer by the age of 21. The Denishawn School of Dancing was established with the help of his wife, Ruth St. Denis, and became the epicenter of much innovation in 20th-century dance and choreography. Among his many achievements is Jacob's Pillow Dance Festival, which he inaugurated and directed for the remainder of his years, and such modern ballets as *Osage-Pawnee*, *Labor Symphony* and *John Brown*. He died Jan 9, 1972.

SOLTI, GEORG: BIRTH ANNIVERSARY. Oct 21, 1912. Conductor, born at Budapest, Hungary. Sir Georg conducted orchestras at London (for which he was knighted), Paris and Chicago. He died at Antibes, France, Sept 5, 1997.

TAIWAN: OVERSEAS CHINESE DAY. Oct 21. Thousands of overseas Chinese come to Taiwan for this and other occasions that make October a particularly memorable month.

VIETNAM WAR PROTESTERS STORM PENTAGON: ANNIVERSARY. Oct 21, 1967. Some 250 protesters were arrested when thousands of the 50,000 participants in a rally against the Vietnam War at Washington, DC, crossed the Potomac River and stormed the Pentagon. No shots were fired, but many demonstrators were struck with nightsticks and rifle butts.

🎂 BIRTHDAYS TODAY

Elvin Bishop, 78, musician, born Glendale, CA, Oct 21, 1942.
Frances Fitzgerald, 80, journalist, author (*The Fire in the Lake*), born New York, NY, Oct 21, 1940.

	S	M	T	W	T	F	S
October					1	2	3
	4	5	6	7	8	9	10
2020	11	12	13	14	15	16	17
	18	19	20	21	22	23	24
	25	26	27	28	29	30	31

Edward Charles "Whitey" Ford, 92, Hall of Fame baseball player, born New York, NY, Oct 21, 1928.

Kim Kardashian, 40, television personality, born Los Angeles, CA, Oct 21, 1980.

Benjamin Netanyahu, 71, Prime Minister of Israel (2009–), born Tel Aviv, Israel, Oct 21, 1949.

Ken Watanabe, 61, actor (*The King and I, The Last Samurai*), born Kansaku Watanabe at Koide, Niigata, Japan, Oct 21, 1959.

October 22 — Thursday

DAY 296   **70 REMAINING**

BEADLE, GEORGE: BIRTH ANNIVERSARY. Oct 22, 1903. Born on a farm near Wahoo, NE, Beadle began his professional career as a professor of genetics at Harvard, eventually becoming president of the University of Chicago. Dr. Beadle won many international honors, including the Nobel Prize in Medicine in 1958 for his work in genetic research, as well as the National Award of the American Cancer Society in 1959 and the Kimber Genetica Award of the National Academy of Sciences in 1960. Beadle demonstrated how the genes control the basic chemistry of the living cell. Because of his work, he has been described as "the man who did most to put modern genetics on its chemical basis." Beadle died June 9, 1989, at Pomona, CA.

CAPA, ROBERT: BIRTH ANNIVERSARY. Oct 22, 1913. Born Andrei Friedmann at Budapest, Hungary, Capa was one of the great photojournalists in the 20th century, best known for his gritty, close-up battle photography from the five wars he covered in his brief life—most notably the Spanish Civil War, WWII and the early Vietnam War. His handful of images from the midst of the D-Day invasion are legendary, as is his shot of a Spanish loyalist soldier who has just been killed in 1936. Cofounder of the elite Magnum Photos agency, Capa was killed by a land mine on May 25, 1954, at Thai Binh, Vietnam.

CUBAN MISSILE CRISIS: ANNIVERSARY. Oct 22, 1962. President John F. Kennedy, in a nationwide television address on this date, demanded the removal of Soviet missiles from Cuba, launched equipment and bombers and imposed a naval "quarantine" to prevent further weaponry from reaching Cuba. On Oct 28 the USSR announced it would remove the weapons in question. In return, the US removed missiles from Turkey that were aimed at the USSR.

FONTAINE, JOAN: BIRTH ANNIVERSARY. Oct 22, 1917. The Oscar-winning actress was born Joan de Beauvoir de Havilland at Tokyo, Japan, to British parents. Her sister is actress Olivia de Havilland and the two carried on a high-profile feud. Fontaine is best known for her work in 1940s Hollywood: *Rebecca* (1940), *Suspicion* (1941) and *The Constant Nymph* (1943). She was nominated for Best Actress Academy Awards in those three films and won for *Suspicion*. She died at Carmel Highlands, CA, Dec 15, 2013.

FUNICELLO, ANNETTE: BIRTH ANNIVERSARY. Oct 22, 1942. "America's Sweetheart" was born at Utica, NY. Her first big break was as a Mouseketeer on Disney's "Mickey Mouse Club," a role she successfully transitioned into a career as a pop singer, scoring a string of hits in the 1950s. Funicello hit it big again in the early '60s with a series of "beach party" movies (*Bikini Beach, Pajama Party, Beach Blanket Bingo*), most alongside costar Frankie Avalon. Funicello was diagnosed with multiple sclerosis in 1987 and died from complications due to her condition Apr 8, 2013, at Bakersfield, CA.

HOWARD, CURLY: BIRTH ANNIVERSARY. Oct 22, 1903. Howard, born Jerome Lester Horwitz at Brooklyn, NY, was the brother of Stooges Moe and Shemp. The two older brothers groomed Curly for a life in show business, and he got his big break in 1932 when brother Shemp left the Stooges. Curly took his place, and his manic style of slapstick comedy (with trademark "n'yuk-n'yuks") quickly

made him popular. On May 6, 1946, while shooting his 97th Three Stooges film, Howard suffered a stroke and subsequently retired. He died Jan 18, 1952, at San Gabriel, CA.

INTERNATIONAL STUTTERING AWARENESS DAY. Oct 22. Stuttering is a communication disorder in which the flow of speech is broken by repetitions, prolongations or abnormal stoppages of sounds and syllables. More than 70 million people worldwide stutter. For info: Jane Fraser, President, Stuttering Foundation of America, PO Box 11749, Memphis, TN 38111-0749. Phone: (800) 992-9392 or (901) 761-0343. E-mail: info@stutteringhelp.org. Web: www.stutteringhelp.org or www.tartamudez.org in Spanish.

LEARY, TIMOTHY: 100th BIRTH ANNIVERSARY. Oct 22, 1920. Timothy Francis Leary was born at Springfield, MA. Prominent psychologist and professor at Harvard, Leary became an icon of the countercultural movement in the 1960s. He lost his professorship after giving a hallucinogenic drug, psilocybin, to students. Leary was arrested numerous times, and on one occasion, while being held at a California prison, he was forced to submit to a personality test that he had designed himself several years earlier. He continued to advocate the use of LSD in the pursuit of spiritual and political freedom and simply for the fun of it, until his death, of prostate cancer, May 31, 1996, at Beverly Hills, CA.

LESSING, DORIS: BIRTH ANNIVERSARY. Oct 22, 1919. Born at Kermanshah, Persia, British author Doris Lessing created a body of work known for its feminism as well as its explorations of the complex themes of racism in colonial Africa, women's roles in male-dominated spheres, politics and interpersonal relationships. Hailed as "one of the most honest, intelligent, and engaged writers of the day" (Hazelton 1982), she was awarded the Nobel Prize in Literature in 2007. Major works include *The Golden Notebook* and the *Children of Violence* series. She died Nov 17, 2013, at London, England.

LISZT, FRANZ: BIRTH ANNIVERSARY. Oct 22, 1811. The Romantic composer Franz Liszt was born at Raiding, Hungary. He was the most celebrated pianist of the 19th century and taught most of the brilliant musicians of his time. In 1848 he moved to the German duchy of Weimar and began to write music. Liszt was a prolific composer best known for his piano music, but he wrote for many mediums, including a sonata, two orchestral symphonies and choral compositions. He died July 31, 1886, at Bayreuth, Germany.

METROPOLITAN OPERA HOUSE OPENING: ANNIVERSARY. Oct 22, 1883. Grand opening of the original New York Metropolitan Opera House was celebrated with a performance of Gounod's *Faust.*

RANDOLPH, PEYTON: DEATH ANNIVERSARY. Oct 22, 1775. First president of the Continental Congress, died at Philadelphia, PA. Born about 1721 (exact date unknown), at Williamsburg, VA.

REED, JOHN: BIRTH ANNIVERSARY. Oct 22, 1887. Journalist and communist activist, born at Portland, OR. An in-demand reporter and war correspondent, Reed covered the Mexican Revolution and WWI. He married the feminist writer Louise Bryant and traveled with her to Russia in 1917, where they covered the October Revolution. As a supporter of socialism and the rights of the worker,

Reed was sympathetic to the Bolshevik cause. He died of typhus at Moscow on Oct 17, 1920. Reed was buried at the Kremlin Wall Necropolis at Red Square—reserved for heroes of the revolution. His chronicle of the Russian Revolution, *Ten Days That Shook the World* (1919), remains a vital eyewitness account.

SCHOLASTIC ESTABLISHED: 100th ANNIVERSARY. Oct 22, 1920. The *Western Pennsylvania Scholastic* was first published. It was a four-page newspaper for high-school students in the Pittsburgh, PA, area. In 1922, the company became The Scholastic and is today the world's largest provider of children's books and educational media—including 32 classroom magazines.

SMART IS COOL DAY. Oct 22. A day to celebrate the wide range of abilities in young people and to increase appreciation for their unique areas of intelligence. First observed in West Hartford/Hartford, CT. Annually, Oct 22. For info: Signe Rogalski, Smart Is Cool, PO Box 370431, West Hartford, CT 06137. E-mail: sigrogalski@sbcglobal.net.

STATE FAIR OF LOUISIANA. Oct 22–Nov 8 (closed Mondays and Tuesdays). Fairgrounds, Shreveport, LA. Since 1906. Educational, agricultural and commercial exhibits as well as entertainment. Annually, beginning on the fourth Thursday in October. Est attendance: 450,000. For info: Chris Giordano, President, Louisiana State Fairgrounds, 3701 Hudson Ave, Shreveport, LA 71109. Phone: (318) 635-1361. Fax: (318) 631-4909. E-mail: info@statefairoflouisiana.com. Web: www.statefairoflouisiana.com.

TACOMA HOLIDAY FOOD & GIFT FESTIVAL. Oct 22–25. Tacoma Dome, Tacoma, WA. More than 550 booths of arts and crafts, gifts, gourmet foods, entertainment and dining, all under the Tacoma Dome. Take a picture with Santa, learn culinary secrets from top chefs during the Cooking for the Holidays program and enjoy festive entertainment by local schools and studios. Est attendance: 35,000. For info: Lauren Anderson and Paulette Deckers, Showcase Events, Inc, PO Box 2815, Kirkland, WA 98083. Phone: (425) 889-9494 or (800) 521-7469. E-mail: tacoma@showcaseevents.org. Web: www.HolidayGiftShows.com.

WORLD'S END DAY: ANNIVERSARY. Oct 22, 1844. Anniversary of the day set as the one on which the world would end by followers of William Miller, religious leader and creator of a movement known as Millerism. Stories about followers disposing of all earthly possessions and climbing to high places on that date are believed to be apocryphal. (Miller was born at Pittsfield, MA, Feb 15, 1782. Died at Low Hampton, NY, Dec 20, 1849.)

🎂 BIRTHDAYS TODAY

Brian Anthony Boitano, 57, Olympic figure skater, born Mountain View, CA, Oct 22, 1963.

Jan De Bont, 77, director (*Speed, Twister*), born Amsterdam, Netherlands, Oct 22, 1943.

Catherine Deneuve, 77, actress (*Repulsion, The Last Metro, Indochine*), born Catherine Dorleac at Paris, France, Oct 22, 1943.

Jesse Tyler Ferguson, 45, actor ("Modern Family," "The Class"), born Missoula, MT, Oct 22, 1975.

Jeff Goldblum, 68, actor (*The Big Chill, The Fly, Jurassic Park*), born Pittsburgh, PA, Oct 22, 1952.

Valeria Golino, 54, actress (*Big Top Pee-Wee, Hot Shots!*), born Naples, Italy, Oct 22, 1966.

Derek Jacobi, 82, actor (Tony for *Much Ado About Nothing*; "I, Claudius," "Cadfael," *Hamlet, Love Is the Devil*), born London, England, Oct 22, 1938.

October 2020	S	M	T	W	T	F	S
					1	2	3
	4	5	6	7	8	9	10
	11	12	13	14	15	16	17
	18	19	20	21	22	23	24
	25	26	27	28	29	30	31

Christopher Lloyd, 82, actor ("Taxi," Back to the Future films), born Stamford, CT, Oct 22, 1938.

Carlos Mencia, 53, comedian ("Mind of Mencia"), born San Pedro Sula, Honduras, Oct 22, 1967.

Bob Odenkirk, 58, actor ("Better Call Saul," "Breaking Bad," *Nebraska*), born Berwyn, IL, Oct 22, 1962.

Tony Roberts, 81, actor (*Victor/Victoria, Annie Hall*), born New York, NY, Oct 22, 1939.

Ichiro Suzuki, 47, former baseball player, born Kasugai, Japan, Oct 22, 1973.

Arsène Wenger, 71, soccer manager, born Strasbourg, France, Oct 22, 1949.

October 23 — Friday

DAY 297 **69 REMAINING**

APPERT, NICOLAS: BIRTH ANNIVERSARY. Oct 23, 1752. Also known as "Canning Day," this is the anniversary of the birth of French chef, chemist, confectioner, inventor and author Nicolas Appert, at Chalons-sur-Marne, France. Appert, who also invented the bouillon tablet, is best remembered for devising a system of heating foods and sealing them in airtight containers. Known as "the father of canning," Appert won a prize of 12,000 francs from the French government in 1809 and the title "Benefactor of Humanity" in 1812, for his inventions, which revolutionized our previously seasonal diet. Appert died at Massy, France, June 3, 1841.

BATTLE OF LEYTE GULF: ANNIVERSARY. Oct 23–26, 1944. Largest naval battle in history, fought near the Philippine Islands between Japan and the Allies (United States and Australia). First use of kamikaze attacks; last engagement between battleships. Japan suffered serious losses, including three battleships, one of which was the *Musashi*.

BEIRUT TERRORIST ATTACK: ANNIVERSARY. Oct 23, 1983. A suicidal terrorist attack on American forces at Beirut, Lebanon, killed 240 US personnel when a truck loaded with TNT was driven into and exploded at US headquarters there. A similar attack on French forces killed scores more.

CAMBODIA: PEACE TREATY DAY. Oct 23. National holiday. Commemorates peace treaty of 1991.

CARSON, JOHNNY: 95th BIRTH ANNIVERSARY. Oct 23, 1925. Television talk show host, born at Corning, IA. He worked for various radio and TV shows, including "Who Do You Trust?" He first appeared on "The Tonight Show" in 1958 and was named the permanent host in 1962 with the resignation of Jack Paar. He remained on the air for more than 30 years, and, along with sidekick Ed McMahon and bandleader Doc Severinsen, basically invented the TV talk show format as we know it today. When he retired in 1992, he was regarded as a national institution. Carson died at Los Angeles, CA, Jan 23, 2005.

EDERLE, GERTRUDE: BIRTH ANNIVERSARY. Oct 23, 1906. American swimming champion, born at New York City, Gertrude Caroline

Ederle was the first woman to swim the English Channel (from Cape Gris-nez, France, to Dover, England). At age 19 she broke the previous world record by swimming the 35-mile distance in 14 hours, 31 minutes, on Aug 6, 1926. During her swimming career she broke many other records and was a gold medal winner at the 1924 Olympic Games. She died at Wyckoff, NJ, Nov 30, 2003.

HUNGARY: ANNIVERSARY OF 1956 REVOLUTION. Oct 23. National holiday. Also called Uprising Day of Remembrance. Commemorates revolt against Soviet domination, which was crushed on Nov 4, 1956.

HUNGARY: REPUBLIC DAY. Oct 23. Public holiday observing Hungary's creation as an independent republic in 1989.

HUNGARY DECLARES INDEPENDENCE: ANNIVERSARY. Oct 23, 1989. Hungary declared itself an independent republic, 33 years after Russian troops crushed a popular revolt against Soviet rule. The announcement followed a weeklong purge by parliament of the Stalinist elements from Hungary's 1949 constitution, which defined the country as a socialist people's republic. Acting head of state Matyas Szuros made the declaration in front of tens of thousands of Hungarians at Parliament Square, speaking from the same balcony from which Imre Nagy addressed rebels 33 years earlier. Nagy was hanged for treason after Soviet intervention. Free elections held in March 1990 removed the Communist Party to the ranks of the opposition for the first time in four decades.

IPOD UNVEILED: ANNIVERSARY. Oct 23, 2001. The Apple company unveiled its portable MP3 music player to the press on this date. The iPod officially went on sale on Nov 10, 2001, for $399. Critics at the time complained about the cost, but the iPod became incredibly popular. In January 2010 Apple announced that it had sold 250 million iPods.

MOON PHASE: FIRST QUARTER. Oct 23. Moon enters First Quarter phase at 9:23 AM, EDT.

NATIONAL MOLE DAY. Oct 23. Celebrated on Oct 23 each year from 6:02 AM to 6:02 PM in observance of the "mole." The "mole" is a way of counting the Avogadro number, 6.02×10 to the 23rd power, of anything (just as a "dozen" is a way of counting 12 of anything). Mole Day owes its existence to an early 19th-century Italian physics professor named Amedeo Avogadro. He discovered that the number of molecules in a mole is the same for all substances. Because of this, chemists are able to precisely measure quantities of chemicals in the laboratory. Mole Day is celebrated to help all persons, especially chemistry students, become enthused about chemistry, which is the central science. For info: Rebecca Logan, Executive Director, National Mole Day Foundation, 3896 Leaman Ct, Freeland, MI 48623. E-mail: moleday@hotmail.com. Web: www.moleday.org.

SAINT JOHN OF CAPISTRANO: DEATH ANNIVERSARY. Oct 23, 1456. Giovanni da Capistrano, Franciscan lawyer, educator and preacher, was born at Capistrano, Italy, in 1386, and died of the plague. Feast day is Mar 28.

SCORPIO, THE SCORPION. Oct 23–Nov 22. In the astronomical/astrological zodiac that divides the sun's apparent orbit into 12 segments, the period Oct 23–Nov 22 is traditionally identified as the sun sign of Scorpio, the Scorpion. The ruling planet is Pluto or Mars.

STEVENSON, ADLAI EWING: BIRTH ANNIVERSARY. Oct 23, 1835. 23rd vice president of the US (1893–97), born at Christian County, KY. Died at Chicago, IL, June 14, 1914. He was grandfather of Adlai E. Stevenson, the Democratic candidate for president in 1952 and 1956. See also: "Stevenson, Adlai Ewing, II: Birth Anniversary" (Feb 5).

SWALLOWS DEPART FROM SAN JUAN CAPISTRANO. Oct 23. Traditional date for swallows to depart for the winter from old mission of San Juan Capistrano, CA. See also: "Swallows Return to San Juan Capistrano" (Mar 19).

THAILAND: CHULALONGKORN DAY. Oct 23. Annual commemoration of the death of King Chulalongkorn the Great, who died Oct 23, 1910, after a 42-year reign. King Chulalongkorn abolished slavery in Thailand. Special ceremonies with floral tributes and incense at the foot of his equestrian statue in front of Bangkok's National Assembly Hall.

🎂 BIRTHDAYS TODAY

Emilia Clarke, 34, actress ("Game of Thrones," *Me Before You*), born London, England, Oct 23, 1986.

Douglas Richard (Doug) Flutie, 58, sportscaster, former football player, born Manchester, MD, Oct 23, 1962.

Nancy Grace, 62, talk show host, born Macon, GA, Oct 23, 1958.

Sanjay Gupta, 51, neurosurgeon, broadcast journalist, born Novi, MI, Oct 23, 1969.

Ang Lee, 66, director (Oscars for *Brokeback Mountain, Life of Pi* and *Crouching Tiger, Hidden Dragon*), born Taiwan, Oct 23, 1954.

Tiffeny Milbrett, 48, Hall of Fame soccer player, born Portland, OR, Oct 23, 1972.

Pelé, 80, former soccer player, FIFA Player of the Century, born Edson Arantes do Nascimento at Três Corações, Brazil, Oct 23, 1940.

Ryan Reynolds, 44, actor (*Deadpool, Woman in Gold, The Proposal*), born Vancouver, BC, Canada, Oct 23, 1976.

Juan "Chi-Chi" Rodríguez, 86, former golfer, born Río Piedras, Puerto Rico, Oct 23, 1934.

Keith Van Horn, 45, former basketball player, born Fullerton, CA, Oct 23, 1975.

Alfred Matthew "Weird Al" Yankovic, 61, singer, satirist, born Lynwood, CA, Oct 23, 1959.

Dwight Yoakam, 64, country singer, actor (*Sling Blade*), born Pikeville, KY, Oct 23, 1956.

October 24 — Saturday

DAY 298   **68 REMAINING**

BLUE RIDGE FOLKLIFE FESTIVAL. Oct 24. Ferrum College/Blue Ridge Institute and Museum, Ferrum, VA. The largest celebration of authentic folkways in Virginia featuring food, crafts, music and exhibits. Annually, the fourth Saturday in October. Est attendance: 20,000. For info: Ferrum College/BRI, PO Box 1000, Rte 40 W, Ferrum, VA 24088. Phone: (540) 365-4412. Fax: (540) 365-4419. E-mail: bri@ferrum.edu. Web: www.blueridgeinstitute.org.

EMMA CRAWFORD FESTIVAL COFFIN RACES. Oct 24. Manitou Springs, CO. Fun-filled day of artistically created coffins, Emmas, costumes, coffin racing, live music and more. Est attendance: 10,000. For info: Manitou Springs Chamber of Commerce, 354 Manitou Ave, Manitou Springs, CO 80829. Phone: (800) 642-2567. Fax: (719) 685-0355. Web: www.manitousprings.org.

FIRST BARREL JUMP OVER NIAGARA FALLS: ANNIVERSARY. Oct 24, 1901. The spectacle of Niagara Falls attracted no end of daredevils through the centuries, but the first one to go over the falls

and survive in any kind of contraption was the unlikely Annie Edson Taylor, a 63-year-old former dance teacher who was down on her luck and hoping for fame and fortune. On this date she accomplished this feat in a 160-pound barrel. No one repeated her stunt until 1911.

HOGEYE FESTIVAL. Oct 24. Elgin, TX. Day's events include barbecue pork cook-off, Cow Patty Bingo, car show, handmade arts and crafts, kids' activities, Elgin's famous hot sausage and live music. Annually, the fourth Saturday in October. Est attendance: 20,000. For info: Hogeye Festival, PO Box 591, Elgin, TX 78621. Phone: (512) 281-5724. Fax: (512) 285-3016. E-mail: hogeye@ci.elgin.tx.us. Web: www.hogeyefestival.com.

LOCKWOOD, BELVA A. BENNETT: BIRTH ANNIVERSARY. Oct 24, 1830. Belva Lockwood, an educator, lawyer and advocate for women's rights, was born at Royalton, NY. In 1879 she was admitted to practice before the US Supreme Court—the first woman to do so. While practicing law at Washington, DC, she secured equal property rights for women. By adding amendments to statehood bills, Lockwood helped to provide voting rights for women in Oklahoma, New Mexico and Arizona. In 1884 she was the first woman formally nominated for the US presidency. Died May 19, 1917, at Washington, DC.

PRESCRIPTION ERRORS EDUCATION AND AWARENESS WEEK. Oct 24–31. According to a Harvard study, more than 107,000 Americans take their prescription medications incorrectly, resulting in hospitalization or death. This week focuses on educating patients and consumers about serious drug interactions, adverse drug events, allergies and the mixing of prescription drugs with herbals and over-the-counter medications. Sponsored by the American College of Apothecaries (ACA)/Pharmacists Planning Service, Inc (PPSI). For info: ACA/PPSI, 2830 Summer Oaks Dr, Bartlett, TN 38134. E-mail: info@ppsinc.org. Web: www.ppsinc.org.

PURVIS, MELVIN: BIRTH ANNIVERSARY. Oct 24, 1903. Born at Timmonsville, SC, Purvis was America's most famous FBI agent in the 1930s and an early protégé of J. Edgar Hoover, the bureau's influential director. On July 22, 1934, Purvis and his fellow agents cornered John Dillinger outside Chicago's Biograph Theater. The infamous bank robber was shot and killed, and the media hailed Purvis as "the Man Who Got Dillinger." This angered the mercurial and jealous Hoover, who forced him from the FBI for good. Purvis died Feb 29, 1960, at Florence, SC, of a self-inflicted gunshot wound.

RECYCLE YOUR MERCURY THERMOSTAT DAY. Oct 24. Mercury-containing thermostats represent a hazard to the environment. With the growth of programmable and, now, "smart" thermostats, consumers are more likely than ever to confront the question of what to do with the thermostat they are replacing. This day encourages you to replace and safely recycle your mercury thermostat and offers a clear, concise and easy way to safely dispose of old mercury-containing thermostats. Thermostat Recycling Corp, a leader in the field and this day's sponsor, offers information on free recycling locations and events around the nation. For info: Danielle Myers, Operations and Compliance Manager, Thermostat Recycling Corp, 500 Office Center Dr, Ste 400, Fort Washington, PA 19034. Phone: (888) 266-0550. E-mail: trc@thermostat-recycle. org. Web: www.thermostat-recycle.org/thermostatday.

SHERMAN, JAMES SCHOOLCRAFT: BIRTH ANNIVERSARY. Oct 24, 1855. 27th vice president of the US (1909–12), born at Utica, NY. Died there Oct 30, 1912.

SPACE MILESTONE: *CHANG'E-1* (PEOPLE'S REPUBLIC OF CHINA). Oct 24, 2007. China successfully launched its first lunar probe into space. Named *Chang'e-1*, the satellite orbited the moon thousands of times for 16 months before it was deliberately crashed onto the moon's surface in March 2009.

STOCK MARKET PANIC: ANNIVERSARY. Oct 24, 1929. After several weeks of a downward trend in stock prices, investors began panic selling on Black Thursday, Oct 24, 1929. More than 13 million shares were dumped. Desperate attempts to support the market brought a brief rally. See also: "Stock Market Crash of 1929: Anniversary" (Oct 29).

★UNITED NATIONS DAY. Oct 24. Presidential Proclamation. Always issued for Oct 24 since 1948. (By unanimous request of the UN General Assembly.)

UNITED NATIONS DAY: 75th ANNIVERSARY OF FOUNDING. Oct 24, 1945. Official UN holiday commemorates founding of the United Nations and effective date of the UN Charter. In 1971 the General Assembly recommended this day be observed as a public holiday by UN member states (Res 2782/xxvi). For info: United Nations, Dept of Public Info, New York, NY 10017. Web: www.un.org.

UNITED NATIONS: DISARMAMENT WEEK. Oct 24–30. In 1978 the General Assembly called on member states to highlight the danger of the arms race, propagate the need for its cessation and increase public understanding of the urgent task of disarmament. Observed annually, beginning on the anniversary of the founding of the UN. For info: United Nations, Dept of Public Info, New York, NY 10017. Web: www.un.org.

UNITED NATIONS: WORLD DEVELOPMENT INFORMATION DAY. Oct 24. Anniversary of 1970 adoption by General Assembly of the International Development Strategy for the Second United Nations Development Decade. Object is to "draw the attention of the world public opinion each year to development problems and the necessity of strengthening international cooperation to solve them." For info: United Nations, Dept of Public Info, New York, NY 10017. Web: www.un.org.

WORLD ORIGAMI DAYS. Oct 24–Nov 11. Let's get the world to fold! Celebrate origami by spreading the joy of paper folding during World Origami Days, a 2½-week celebration of the international community of origami. Make origami as visible as possible: teach a class, fold on the bus, give your friends origami, exhibit your models. The possibilities are limitless, just as with origami itself. Annually, Oct 24–Nov 11. Oct 24 is the birthday of Lillian Oppenheimer (1898–1992), who founded the first origami group in America and cofounded the British Origami Society and OrigamiUSA. Nov 11 is Origami Day in Japan. For info: OrigamiUSA, 15 W 77th St, New York, NY 10024. Phone: (212) 769-5635. E-mail: wod-info@origamiusa.org or admin@origamiusa.org. Web: origamiusa.org/wod.

🎂 BIRTHDAYS TODAY

F. Murray Abraham, 80, actor (Oscar for *Amadeus*; "Homeland"), born El Paso, TX, Oct 24, 1940.

Drake, 34, singer, born Aubrey Drake Graham at Toronto, ON, Canada, Oct 24, 1986.

Kevin Kline, 73, actor (Oscar for *A Fish Called Wanda*; Tonys for *Present Laughter*, *The Pirates of Penzance* and *On the Twentieth Century*), born St. Louis, MO, Oct 24, 1947.

Michelle Lujan Grisham, 61, Governor of New Mexico (D), born Los Alamos, NM, Oct 24, 1959.

	S	**M**	**T**	**W**	**T**	**F**	**S**
October					1	2	3
	4	5	6	7	8	9	10
2020	11	12	13	14	15	16	17
	18	19	20	21	22	23	24
	25	26	27	28	29	30	31

Jeff Merkley, 64, US Senator (D, Oregon), born Myrtle Creek, OR, Oct 24, 1956.

Kweisi Mfume, 72, former NAACP president, born Baltimore, MD, Oct 24, 1948.

Monica, 40, singer, born Monica Arnold at Atlanta, GA, Oct 24, 1980.

Wayne Rooney, 35, soccer player, born Liverpool, England, Oct 24, 1985.

Kyla Ross, 24, Olympic gymnast, born Honolulu, HI, Oct 24, 1996.

Mike Rounds, 66, US Senator (R, South Dakota), former governor of South Dakota, born Huron, SD, Oct 24, 1954.

Charlie White, 33, Olympic ice dancer, born Dearborn, MI, Oct 24, 1987.

Bill Wyman, 84, musician (Rolling Stones), born William Perks at London, England, Oct 24, 1936.

October 25 — Sunday

DAY 299	67 REMAINING

BERRYMAN, JOHN: BIRTH ANNIVERSARY. Oct 25, 1914. Born at McAlester, OK, Berryman is considered one of the most innovative, important American poets of the 20th century and is best known for bringing idiomatic American English to poetry. Winner of the 1965 Pulitzer Prize for *77 Dream Songs* and, later, the National Book Award for the entire *Dream Songs* collection, Berryman died Jan 7, 1972, at Minneapolis, MN.

BIZET: GEORGES: BIRTH ANNIVERSARY. Oct 25, 1838. Composer, christened Alexandre-César Léopold Bizet, born at Paris, France. His masterpiece, *Carmen* (1875), presaged the work of the verismo school of opera, which emphasized the realistic and gritty. Throughout his career, Bizet struggled to complete pieces and also to gain recognition for his achievements, which did not come until after his death. *Carmen* scandalized audiences when first performed by its representations of a sexually bold, unrepentant fallen woman and the gritty, immoral world she lives in and by its unconventional use of melodies and musical dissonances new to French opera at the time. Its apparent failure may have contributed to Bizet's early and sudden death on June 3, 1875, at Bougival, France.

CHAUCER, GEOFFREY: DEATH ANNIVERSARY. Oct 25, 1400. The best-known English writer and poet of the Middle Ages, Chaucer was born at London, England, probably about 1343. His greatest work, *Canterbury Tales*, consists of some 17,000 poetic lines. Unfinished at his death, it tells the stories of 23 pilgrims. Among his lesser-known prose writings is a treatise on the astrolabe titled *Brede and Milke for Children* (1387), written for "little Lewis, my son." Chaucer died at London and is buried at Westminster Abbey.

CHINA: CHUNG YEUNG FESTIVAL (DOUBLE NINE FESTIVAL). Oct 25. This festival relates to the old story of the Han dynasty, when a soothsayer advised a man to take his family to a high place on the ninth day of the ninth moon for 24 hours in order to avoid disaster. The man obeyed and found, on returning home, that all living things had died a sudden death in his absence. Part of the celebration is climbing to high places. Date in other countries may differ from China's.

EUROPEAN UNION: DAYLIGHT SAVING TIME (SUMMER TIME) ENDS. Oct 25. Member countries of the European Union turn their clocks back one hour at 1 AM on the last Sunday in October.

FIRST FEMALE FBI AGENTS: ANNIVERSARY. Oct 25, 1972. The first women to become FBI agents completed training at Quantico, VA. The new agents, Susan Lynn Roley and Joanne E. Pierce, graduated from the 14-week course with a group of 45 men.

GRENADA INVADED BY US: ANNIVERSARY. Oct 25, 1983. Some 2,000 US Marines and Army Rangers invaded the Caribbean island of Grenada, taking control after a political coup the previous week had made the island a "Soviet-Cuban colony," according to President Reagan. Commemorated as Thanksgiving Day in Grenada, a public holiday.

INDIA: DASARA (DUSSEHRA). Oct 25. Hindu holiday. Marks the triumph of Lord Rama over the demon king, Ravana, or the victory of good over evil. Effigies of Ravana are burned. Because there is no one universally accepted Hindu calendar, this holiday may be celebrated on a different date in some parts of India, but it always occurs in September or October.

INTERNATIONAL MAGIC WEEK. Oct 25–31. A week to celebrate the world of magic and the magicians who create it. Annually, culminates on Oct 31, the anniversary of Harry Houdini's death and Magic Day.

ISRAEL: ALIYAH DAY (YOM HA'ALIYAH). Oct 25. Hebrew calendar date: Heshvan 7, 5781. Commemorates Joshua and the Israelites crossing the River Jordan to the Promised Land. Celebrates those who immigrate to Israel. National Israeli holiday since 2016.

MACAULAY, THOMAS BABINGTON: BIRTH ANNIVERSARY. Oct 25, 1800. English essayist and historian, born at Rothley Temple, Leicestershire, England. "Nothing," he wrote, "is so useless as a general maxim." Died at Campden Hill, London, England, Dec 28, 1859.

MOTHER-IN-LAW DAY. Oct 25. Traditionally, the fourth Sunday in October is occasion to honor mothers-in-law for their contributions to the success of families and for their good humor in enduring bad jokes.

"NEWHART" TV PREMIERE: ANNIVERSARY. Oct 25, 1982. Bob Newhart starred in this sitcom as Dick Loudon, an author of how-to books who moved with his wife, Joanna (Mary Frann), to Vermont to take over the Stratford Inn. Regulars included Tom Poston as George Utley, inn caretaker; Julia Duffy as Stephanie Vanderkellen, the reluctant maid; Peter Scolari as Michael Harris, producer of Dick's talk show and Stephanie's squeeze; and, as the owners of the Minute Man Café, William Sanderson as Larry and Tony Papenfuss and John Volstad as his silent brothers, both named Darryl. The last telecast was Sept 8, 1990.

PEARL, MINNIE: BIRTH ANNIVERSARY. Oct 25, 1912. Comedienne, Grand Ole Opry star, born at Centerville, TN. Pearl died at Nashville, TN, Mar 4, 1996.

PICASSO, PABLO RUIZ: BIRTH ANNIVERSARY. Oct 25, 1881. Called by many the greatest artist of the 20th century, Pablo Picasso excelled as a painter, sculptor and engraver. He is said to have commented once: "I am only a public entertainer who has understood his time." Born at Málaga, Spain, he died Apr 8, 1973, at Mougins, France.

REFORMATION SUNDAY. Oct 25. Many Protestant churches commemorate Reformation Day (Oct 31—anniversary of the day Martin Luther nailed his 95 theses to the door of Wittenberg's Castle Church, protesting the sale of papal indulgences, in 1517) each year on the Sunday preceding Oct 31, or on the 31st, if a Sunday.

SAINT CRISPIN'S DAY. Oct 25. Martyr in the reign of Diocletian. Saint Crispin's Day is famous as the day in 1415 when King Henry V defeated the superior forces of France at the Battle of Agincourt. A passage in Shakespeare's *Henry V* notes this.

SASAKI, SADAKO: 65th DEATH ANNIVERSARY. Oct 25, 1955. Born at Hiroshima, Japan, in 1943, Sadako Sasaki was two years old when her city was hit by an atomic bomb in the closing days of WWII. She was diagnosed with leukemia in January 1955, and, inspired by a folktale in which the gods grant a wish to those who fold 1,000 paper cranes, began the task. She died on this date having folded 644 cranes, and her classmates finished the rest. Students across Japan, moved by her story, collected money to create a monument to her that was erected at Hiroshima Peace Park in 1958. Visitors continue to place folded cranes there.

SOUREST DAY. Oct 25. Since 1969, a day to emphasize the balance of things in nature. A day for sour people. Suck a lemon or drink some lemonade. Annually, Oct 25. Created by Rich "Mirth" Ankli.

TAIWAN EXPELLED FROM UN: ANNIVERSARY. Oct 25, 1971. The United Nations General Assembly voted to admit mainland China and expel Taiwan. This was after many years of debate about which government was the "official" government of China. In 1979 the US accorded diplomatic recognition to mainland China.

TAIWAN: RETROCESSION DAY. Oct 25. Commemorates restoration of Taiwan to Chinese rule in 1945, after a half century of Japanese occupation.

🎂 BIRTHDAYS TODAY

Samantha Bee, 51, comedian, political commentator, television personality ("Full Frontal with Samantha Bee"), born Toronto, ON, Canada, Oct 25, 1969.

Brian Kerwin, 71, actor ("Lobo," "The Blue and the Gray"), born Chicago, IL, Oct 25, 1949.

Robert Montgomery (Bobby) Knight, 80, former college basketball coach and player, born Orrville, OH, Oct 25, 1940.

Pedro Martinez, 49, Hall of Fame baseball player, born Manoquayabo, Dominican Republic, Oct 25, 1971.

Midori, 49, violinist, born Osaka, Japan, Oct 25, 1971.

Katy Perry, 36, singer, born Santa Barbara, CA, Oct 25, 1984.

Helen Reddy, 78, singer, songwriter, born Melbourne, Australia, Oct 25, 1942.

Craig Robinson, 49, actor ("Ghosted," "The Office [US]," *Morris from America, Hot Tub Time Machine*), born Chicago, IL, Oct 25, 1971.

Marion Ross, 84, actress ("Happy Days," *The Evening Star*), born Albert Lea, MN, Oct 25, 1936.

Juan Soto, 22, baseball player, born Santo Domingo, Dominican Republic, Oct 25, 1998.

Anne Tyler, 79, author (*The Accidental Tourist, Breathing Lessons*), born Minneapolis, MN, Oct 25, 1941.

October 2020	S	M	T	W	T	F	S
					1	2	3
	4	5	6	7	8	9	10
	11	12	13	14	15	16	17
	18	19	20	21	22	23	24
	25	26	27	28	29	30	31

October 26 — Monday

DAY 300　　　　　　　　　　　　**66 REMAINING**

AUSTRIA: NATIONAL DAY. Oct 26. National holiday. Commemorates the withdrawal of Soviet troops in 1955.

COOGAN, JACKIE: BIRTH ANNIVERSARY. Oct 26, 1914. Born John Leslie Coogan at Los Angeles, CA, Coogan became a star after appearing as Charlie Chaplin's companion in *The Kid* (1921). Film earnings and merchandise associated with his name brought considerable income, but the money was squandered by his mother and stepfather. Coogan sued them in 1938, and the legal battle resulted in the passage of the protective California Child Actor's Bill, often called the Coogan Act (1939). A glider pilot during WWII, Coogan later returned to film and television, most famously as Uncle Fester in "The Addams Family" (1964–66). He died Mar 1, 1984, at Santa Monica, CA.

DANTON, GEORGES: BIRTH ANNIVERSARY. Oct 26, 1759. Born at Arcis-sur-Aube, France, Danton was a lawyer who gradually emerged as a leader in the French Revolution. Despite his charisma, though, he was unable to rein in the murderous factions swirling in the movement. On Mar 29, 1794, Danton and his moderate followers were arrested. His last words before his execution by guillotine at Paris, France, on Apr 5 were: "Show my head to the people. It is worth the trouble."

ERIE CANAL: ANNIVERSARY. Oct 26, 1825. The Erie Canal, first US major man-made waterway, was opened, providing a water route from Lake Erie to the Hudson River. Construction started July 4, 1817, and the canal cost $7,602,000. Cannons fired and celebrations were held all along the route for the opening.

GUNFIGHT AT THE O.K. CORRAL: ANNIVERSARY. Oct 26, 1881. At 2:30 PM, the Earp brothers and gambler/dentist Doc Holliday confronted the Clanton and McLaury brothers at a vacant lot behind the O.K. Corral at Tombstone, AZ. After 30 seconds of gunfire, three deaths and decades of romanticizing, the incident would become the most notorious of the Old West. Marshal Virgil Earp and Deputy Marshals Wyatt and Morgan Earp attempted to disarm the Clanton faction, when gunfire erupted, although some witnesses claimed that the Clantons and McLaurys threw up their hands when ordered to. Billy Clanton and Frank and Thomas McLaury died. Virgil and Morgan Earp were wounded. After a 30-day murder trial, the presiding judge dismissed the charges, stating that the Earps and Holliday had acted in self-defense.

HANSOM, JOSEPH: BIRTH ANNIVERSARY. Oct 26, 1803. English architect and inventor Joseph Aloysius Hansom registered his "Patent Safety Cab" in 1834. The two-wheeled, one-horse, enclosed cab, with driver seated above and behind the passengers, quickly became a familiar and favorite vehicle for public transportation. Hansom was born at York, England, and died at London, England, June 29, 1882.

IRELAND: OCTOBER BANK HOLIDAY. Oct 26. Bank holiday in the Republic of Ireland. Annually, the last Monday in October. Also called Halloween Holiday.

JACKSON, MAHALIA: BIRTH ANNIVERSARY. Oct 26, 1911. Born at New Orleans, LA, Jackson was the most famous gospel singer of her time. After moving to Chicago, IL, in 1928, Jackson sang with the Johnson Gospel Singers. Thomas A. Dorsey, the father of gospel music, was her adviser and accompanist from 1937 to 1946. By the 1950s Jackson could be heard in concert halls around the world. She sang at the inauguration of President John F. Kennedy and at the 1963 March on Washington rally. Dr. Martin Luther King, Jr, described her voice as "one heard once in a millennium." She died at Chicago, on Jan 27, 1972, and was buried at New Orleans, where her funeral procession was thronged with mourners.

MULE DAY. Oct 26. Anniversary of the first importation of Spanish jacks to the US, a gift from King Charles III of Spain. Mules are said to have been bred first in this country by George Washington from this pair of jacks delivered at Boston, MA, Oct 26, 1785.

NEW ZEALAND: LABOR DAY. Oct 26. National holiday on the fourth Monday in October.

ROCKEFELLER, ABBY GREENE ALDRICH: BIRTH ANNIVERSARY. Oct 26, 1874. A philanthropist and art patron, Abby Rockefeller was one of the three founders of the New York Museum of Modern Art in 1929. Born at Providence, RI, she died Apr 5, 1948, at New York City.

SCARLATTI, DOMENICO: BIRTH ANNIVERSARY. Oct 26, 1685. Italian keyboard composer, born at Naples, Italy. Died July 23, 1757, at Madrid, Spain.

SPACE MILESTONE: *SOYUZ 3* (USSR). Oct 26, 1968. After the crash of *Soyuz 1* and the death of its cosmonaut, *Soyuz 3* was launched this date with Colonel Georgi Beregovoy. It orbited Earth 64 times, rendezvousing but not docking with unmanned *Soyuz 2*, which had been launched the day before. Both vehicles returned to Earth under ground control. *Soyuz* means "union."

ZAMBIA: INDEPENDENCE DAY. Oct 26. National holiday commemorates the independence of what was then Northern Rhodesia from Britain on Oct 24, 1964. Celebrations in all cities, but main parades of military, labor and youth organizations are at the capital, Lusaka. Observed on the fourth Monday in October.

🎂 BIRTHDAYS TODAY

Phillip "CM Punk" Brooks, 42, professional wrestler, born Chicago, IL, Oct 26, 1978.

Tom Cavanagh, 52, actor ("The Flash," "Ed"), born Ottawa, ON, Canada, Oct 26, 1968.

Hillary Rodham Clinton, 73, 2016 Democratic presidential nominee, former US secretary of state; former US senator (D, New York); former first lady, wife of Bill Clinton, 42nd president of the US; born Park Ridge, IL, Oct 26, 1947.

Sasha Cohen, 36, Olympic figure skater, born Westwood, CA, Oct 26, 1984.

Nick Collison, 40, basketball player, born Orange City, IA, Oct 26, 1980.

Cary Elwes, 58, actor (*Saw, Glory, The Princess Bride*), born London, England, Oct 26, 1962.

Dylan McDermott, 58, actor ("The Practice"), born Waterbury, CT, Oct 26, 1962.

Natalie Merchant, 57, singer, born Jamestown, NY, Oct 26, 1963.

James Pickens, Jr, 66, actor ("Grey's Anatomy," "The X-Files," "The Practice"), born Cleveland, OH, Oct 26, 1954.

Jeff Probst, 58, television personality ("Survivor"), born Wichita, KS, Oct 26, 1962.

Ivan Reitman, 74, filmmaker (*Dave, Ghostbusters*), born Komárno, Czechoslovakia (now Slovakia), Oct 26, 1946.

Pat Sajak, 74, game show host ("Wheel of Fortune"), born Chicago, IL, Oct 26, 1946.

Julian Schnabel, 69, artist, filmmaker (*The Diving Bell and the Butterfly*), born New York, NY, Oct 26, 1951.

Jaclyn Smith, 73, actress ("Charlie's Angels"), former Breck Girl, born Houston, TX, Oct 26, 1947.

Keith Urban, 51, country singer, television personality ("American Idol"), born Whangarei, New Zealand, Oct 26, 1969.

October 27 — Tuesday

DAY 301 **65 REMAINING**

COOK, JAMES: BIRTH ANNIVERSARY. Oct 27, 1728. (Old Style date.) English sea captain of the ship *Endeavour* and explorer who brought Australia and New Zealand into the British Empire. Born at Marton-in-Cleveland, Yorkshire, England, he was killed Feb 14, 1779, at the Hawaiian Islands, which he discovered.

CRANKY COWORKERS DAY. Oct 27. Because all of us have bad days (some more than others), here's a day when crankiness at work is actually encouraged. (©2006 by WH.) For info: Thomas & Ruth Roy, Wellcat Holidays, 2418 Long Ln, Lebanon, PA 17046. Phone: (717) 279-0184. E-mail: info@wellcat.com. Web: www.wellcat.com.

DEE, RUBY: BIRTH ANNIVERSARY. Oct 27, 1922. Born Ruby Ann Wallace at Cleveland, OH, Dee pioneered groundbreaking stage and screen roles for African-American women. Her credits include both the stage and film versions of *A Raisin in the Sun* (1959, 1961) and the Broadway productions *Jeb* (1946) and *Zora Is My Name* (1983). Her screen credits include *The Jackie Robinson Story* (1950), *Do the Right Thing* (1989) and *American Gangster* (2007), which earned her an Oscar nomination. Offstage, Dee was a civil rights activist and together with her husband, actor Ossic Davis, led the 1963 March on Washington. Dee died June 11, 2014, at New Rochelle, NY.

***FEDERALIST* PAPERS: ANNIVERSARY.** Oct 27, 1787. The first of the 85 *Federalist* papers appeared in print in a New York City newspaper. These essays, written by Alexander Hamilton, James Madison and John Jay, argued in favor of adoption of the new Constitution and the new form of federal government. The last of the essays was completed Apr 4, 1788.

LICHTENSTEIN, ROY: BIRTH ANNIVERSARY. Oct 27, 1923. Pop artist who used comic strips and other elements of pop culture in his paintings. Born at New York City, he died there Sept 29, 1997.

NAVY DAY. Oct 27. Established in 1922 to honor the "past and present services" of the US Navy to the nation. Also honored Theodore Roosevelt, whose birth date is Oct 27 (and who had been assistant secretary of the Navy early in his public career). Not a national holiday, it was last observed in 1949.

NEW YORK CITY SUBWAY: ANNIVERSARY. Oct 27, 1904. Running from City Hall to W 145th St, the New York City subway began operation. It was privately operated by the Interborough Rapid Transit Company and later became part of the system operated by the New York City Transit Authority.

PAGANINI, NICOLÒ: BIRTH ANNIVERSARY. Oct 27, 1782. Hailed as the greatest violin virtuoso of all time, Paganini was born at Genoa, Italy. Unusually long arms contributed to his legendary Mephistophelian appearance—and probably to his unique skills as a performer. His immensely popular concerts brought him considerable wealth, but his compulsive gambling repeatedly humbled the genius. Paganini died at Nice, France, May 27, 1840.

ROOSEVELT, THEODORE: BIRTH ANNIVERSARY. Oct 27, 1858. 26th president of the US, succeeded to the presidency on the death of William McKinley. His term of office: Sept 14, 1901–Mar 3, 1909. Roosevelt was the first president to ride in an automobile (1902), to submerge in a submarine (1905) and to fly in an airplane (1910). Although his best-remembered quote was perhaps "Speak softly and carry a big stick," he also said: "The first requisite of a good citizen in this Republic of ours is that he shall be able and willing

to pull his weight." Born at New York, NY, Roosevelt died at Oyster Bay, NY, Jan 6, 1919. His last words: "Put out the light."

SAINT VINCENT AND THE GRENADINES: INDEPENDENCE DAY. Oct 27. National Day commemorating independence from Britain in 1979.

THOMAS, DYLAN MARLAIS: BIRTH ANNIVERSARY. Oct 27, 1914. Welsh poet, memoirist and playwright, born at Swansea, Wales. Thomas worked as a BBC broadcaster and poetry commentator in the 1940s and 1950s; his sonorous voice made him famous and contributed to the success of his US tours in the early 1950s. His famous poems include "Do Not Go Gentle into That Good Night" (1951). He died at New York, NY, Nov 9, 1953.

TURKMENISTAN: INDEPENDENCE DAY. Oct 27. National holiday. Commemorates independence from the Soviet Union in 1991.

UNITED NATIONS: WORLD DAY FOR AUDIOVISUAL HERITAGE. Oct 27. A day to recognize that the work of preservation professionals and institutions is needed to safeguard our endangered audiovisual heritage. Audiovisual documents such as films, as well as radio and television programs, contain the primary records of the 20th and 21st centuries. Annually, Oct 27. For info: United Nations/UNESCO. Web: www.un.org.

"WALT DISNEY" TV PREMIERE: ANNIVERSARY. Oct 27, 1954. This highly successful and long-running show appeared on different TV networks under different names but was essentially the same show. It was the first ABC series to break the Nielsen's top 20 and the first prime-time anthology series for kids. "Walt Disney" was originally titled "Disneyland" to promote the park and upcoming Disney releases. When it switched networks, it was called "Walt Disney's Wonderful World of Color" to highlight its being broadcast in color. Presentations featured edited versions of previously released Disney films and original productions (including natural history documentaries, behind-the-scenes peeks at Disney shows and dramatic shows, such as the popular Davy Crockett segments, which were the first TV miniseries). The show went off the air in December 1980 after 25 years, making it one of the longest-running series in prime-time TV history. In 1997 ABC revived the series as "Wonderful World of Disney."

🎂 BIRTHDAYS TODAY

Roberto Benigni, 68, actor, director (Oscar for *Life Is Beautiful*), born Arezzo, Italy, Oct 27, 1952.

John Cleese, 81, actor, writer ("Monty Python's Flying Circus," "Fawlty Towers," *A Fish Called Wanda*), born Weston-Super-Mare, England, Oct 27, 1939.

Matt Drudge, 54, journalist ("The Drudge Report"), born Takoma Park, MD, Oct 27, 1966.

October 2020	S	M	T	W	T	F	S
					1	2	3
	4	5	6	7	8	9	10
	11	12	13	14	15	16	17
	18	19	20	21	22	23	24
	25	26	27	28	29	30	31

Simon Le Bon, 62, singer (Duran Duran), born Bushey, England, Oct 27, 1958.

Fran Lebowitz, 70, essayist, humorist (*Social Studies*), born Morristown, NJ, Oct 27, 1950.

Marla Maples, 57, model, actress, born Dalton, GA, Oct 27, 1963.

Brandon Saad, 28, hockey player, born Pittsburgh, PA, Oct 27, 1992.

Zadie Smith, 45, author (*NW, On Beauty, White Teeth*), born Sadie Smith at Brent, London, England, Oct 27, 1975.

October 28 — Wednesday

DAY 302   **64 REMAINING**

BACON, FRANCIS: BIRTH ANNIVERSARY. Oct 28, 1909. Noted 20th-century artist whose work explored religion, social convention and the self with stark, often gruesome imagery. Born at Dublin, Ireland, Bacon spent much of his adult life in London, England. He died at Madrid, Spain, April 28, 1992.

CZECH REPUBLIC: INDEPENDENCE DAY. Oct 28. National Day. Anniversary of the bloodless revolution at Prague in 1918 resulting in independence from the Austro-Hungarian Empire, after which the Czechs and Slovaks united to form Czechoslovakia (a union they dissolved without bloodshed in 1993).

DICKINSON, ANNA ELIZABETH: BIRTH ANNIVERSARY. Oct 28, 1842. Influential American orator and author of the Civil War era was born at Philadelphia, PA. As an advocate of abstinence, abolition and woman suffrage, she earned the nickname "American Joan of Arc." She died on Oct 22, 1932.

DONNER PARTY FAMINE: ANNIVERSARY. Oct 28, 1846–Apr 21, 1847. The pioneering Donner party, a group of 90 people consisting of immigrants, families and businessmen led by George and Jacob Donner and James F. Reed, headed toward California in 1846 from Springfield, IL, in hopes of beginning a new life. They experienced the normal travails of caravan travel until their trip took several sensational twists. Indian attacks and winter weather forced them to interrupt their journey and led to famine and outright cannibalism, which took their toll on members of the party, whose numbers dwindled to 48 by journey's end.

ERASMUS, DESIDERIUS: BIRTH ANNIVERSARY. Oct 28, 1467. Dutch author and scholar Desiderius Erasmus was born at Rotterdam, Netherlands, probably Oct 28, 1467. Best known of his writings is *Encomium Moriae* (*In Praise of Folly*). Erasmus died at Basel, Switzerland, July 12, 1536.

ESCOFFIER, GEORGES AUGUSTE: BIRTH ANNIVERSARY. Oct 28, 1846. Celebrated French chef and author, inventor of the pêche Melba (honoring the operatic singer Dame Nellie Melba), Escoffier became known as "the king of chefs and the chef of kings." Born at Villeneuve-Loubet, France. He was awarded the Legion d'Honneur in recognition of his contribution to the international reputation of French cuisine, and his service at the Savoy and Carlton hotels at London, England, brought him world fame. He died at Monte Carlo, Monaco, Feb 12, 1935.

FIRST WOMAN US AMBASSADOR APPOINTED: ANNIVERSARY. Oct 28, 1949. Helen Eugenie Moore Anderson became the first woman to hold the post of US ambassador when she was sworn in by President Harry S Truman on this date. She served as ambassador to Denmark.

FRENCH POLYNESIA: HAWAIKI NUI VA'A RACE. Oct 28–30 (tentative). Spectacular, three-day, open-water traditional outrigger canoe race. More than 2,000 racers in more than 100 canoes battle for 78 miles, traveling from Huahine to Raiatea to Tahaa to Bora Bora. *Va'a* is the Tahitian word for canoe. Held annually since 1992. For info: Tahiti Tourisme. E-mail: info@tahititourisme.com. Web: www.tahititourisme.com.

GATEWAY ARCH COMPLETED: 55th ANNIVERSARY. Oct 28, 1965. The steel and concrete, 630-foot-tall Gateway Arch, designed by Eero Saarinen and built as a monument to Thomas Jefferson and the Louisiana Purchase, which made American westward expansion possible, was completed at St. Louis, MO. The Arch was opened to the public in two stages: July 1967 and May 1968.

GERMAN REVOLUTION OF 1918: ANNIVERSARY. Oct 28, 1918. On this date in the final days of WWI, crews of six German battleships protested a series of planned cruiser raids. A mutiny broke out in the fleet at Kiel, Germany. All but one of the ships remaining in port ran up the red flag of revolution: 600 sailors were arrested and imprisoned on shore. The uprising spread to Hamburg, Bremen and Lubeck. On Nov 9 a general strike at Berlin brought the administration to a halt. The abdication of Kaiser Wilhelm began to be seen as the only way to avoid a full-scale revolution.

GREECE: OCHI DAY. Oct 28. National holiday. Commemorates Greek resistance and refusal to open its borders when Mussolini's Italian troops attacked Greece, Oct 28, 1940. *Ochi* means "no." Celebrated with military parades, especially at Athens and Thessaloniki.

HANSON, HOWARD: BIRTH ANNIVERSARY. Oct 28, 1896. Born at Wahoo, NE, Howard Hanson in 1921 became the first American to win the Prix de Rome. In 1924 he became head of the Eastman School of Music at the University of Rochester, NY, where he served for 40 years. Best known for the music he composed, Hanson was awarded the Pulitzer Prize as outstanding contemporary composer in 1944 for his composition *Symphony No. 4*, the George Foster Peabody Award in 1946, the Laurel Leaf of the American Composers Alliance in 1957 and the Huntington Hartford Foundation Award in 1959. He died at Rochester, Feb 26, 1981.

HARVARD UNIVERSITY FOUNDED: ANNIVERSARY. Oct 28, 1636. (Old Style date.) Harvard University was founded at Cambridge, MA, when the Massachusetts General Court voted to provide £400 for a "schoale or colledge."

"THE JACK BENNY PROGRAM" TV PREMIERE: 70th ANNIVERSARY. Oct 28, 1950. One of radio's favorite comedians, Jack Benny made the transition to favorite TV personality with this situation comedy–variety show in 1950. Regulars included Eddie Anderson, Don Wilson, Dennis Day, Mel Blanc, Mary Livingstone (Benny's real-life wife) and Frank Nelson. Benny also had guest stars, including Ken Murray, Frank Sinatra, Claudette Colbert and Basil Rathbone as well as TV newcomers Johnny Carson, Marilyn Monroe and Humphrey Bogart. Famous for his cheapness, Benny had a guard for his vaults, which created many laughs.

SAINT JUDE'S DAY. Oct 28. St. Jude, the saint of hopeless causes, was martyred along with St. Simon at Persia, and their feast is celebrated jointly. St. Jude was supposedly the brother of Jesus and, like his brother, a carpenter by trade. He is most popular with those who attempt the impossible and with students, who often ask for his help on exams.

SALK, JONAS: BIRTH ANNIVERSARY. Oct 28, 1914. Dr. Jonas Salk, developer of the Salk polio vaccine, was born at New York, NY. Salk announced his development of a successful vaccine in 1953, the year after a polio epidemic claimed some 3,300 lives in the US. Polio deaths were reduced by 95 percent after the introduction of the vaccine. Salk spent the last 10 years of his life doing AIDS research. He died June 23, 1995, at La Jolla, CA.

SPACE MILESTONE: INTERNATIONAL SPACE RESCUE AGREEMENT: 50th ANNIVERSARY. Oct 28, 1970. US and USSR officials agreed upon space rescue cooperation.

STATUE OF LIBERTY DEDICATION: ANNIVERSARY. Oct 28, 1886. Frédéric Auguste Bartholdi's famous sculpture, the statue of *Liberty Enlightening the World*, on Bedloe's Island at New York Harbor, was dedicated. Groundbreaking for the structure was in April 1883. A sonnet by Emma Lazarus, inside the pedestal of the statue, contains the words "Give me your tired, your poor, your huddled masses yearning to breathe free, the wretched refuse of your teeming shore. Send these, the homeless, tempest-tossed, to me: I lift my lamp beside the golden door."

VOLSTEAD ACT PASSED: ANNIVERSARY. Oct 28, 1919. The National Prohibition Act, or Volstead Act, the enabling legislation to enforce the 18th Amendment, was passed on this date and went into effect Jan 16, 1920. The law prohibited the manufacture, sale and use of intoxicating beverages (defined as beverages that contain one-half of one percent of alcohol by volume).

🎂 BIRTHDAYS TODAY

Jane Alexander, 81, actress (*The Great White Hope, Kramer vs Kramer*), former chair of the National Endowment for the Arts, born Jane Quigley at Boston, MA, Oct 28, 1939.

Charlie Daniels, 84, musician, singer, songwriter, born Wilmington, NC, Oct 28, 1936.

Jeremy Davies, 51, actor (*Saving Private Ryan*), born Rockford, IA, Oct 28, 1969.

Terrell Davis, 48, former football player, born San Diego, CA, Oct 28, 1972.

Dennis Franz, 76, actor ("Hill Street Blues," "NYPD Blue"), born Maywood, IL, Oct 28, 1944.

Bill Gates, 65, former software executive (Microsoft), philanthropist, born Seattle, WA, Oct 28, 1955.

Jami Gertz, 55, actress ("Still Standing," *Twister*), born Chicago, IL, Oct 28, 1965.

Lauren Holly, 57, actress (*Dumb and Dumber*, "Picket Fences"), born Geneva, NY, Oct 28, 1963.

Telma Hopkins, 72, singer, actress ("Family Matters"), born Louisville, KY, Oct 28, 1948.

Caitlyn Jenner, 71, television personality, Olympic gold medal decathlete, born William Bruce Jenner at Mount Kisco, NY, Oct 28, 1949.

Brad Paisley, 48, country singer, born Glen Dale, WV, Oct 28, 1972.

Annie Potts, 68, actress ("Designing Women," *Ghostbusters, Pretty in Pink*), born Nashville, TN, Oct 28, 1952.

Andy Richter, 54, actor, cohost ("Conan"), born Grand Rapids, MI, Oct 28, 1966.

Julia Roberts, 53, actress (Oscar for *Erin Brockovich*; *August: Osage County, My Best Friend's Wedding, Pretty Woman*), born Smyrna, GA, Oct 28, 1967.

Matt Smith, 38, actor ("The Crown," "Doctor Who"), born Northampton, England, Oct 28, 1982.

October 29 — Thursday

DAY 303   **63 REMAINING**

BOSWELL, JAMES: BIRTH ANNIVERSARY. Oct 29, 1740. (Old Style date.) Lawyer, diarist and biographer, the ninth laird of Auchinleck was born at Edinburgh, Scotland. On May 16, 1763, Boswell met the great man of letters Samuel Johnson. It was a friendship that lasted until Johnson's death and resulted in Boswell's revolutionary and monumental biography, *Life of Johnson* (1791).

Boswell's innovations included sharing the subject's warts as well as accomplishments and sharing actual conversations: "[I am] exceedingly unwilling that any thing, however slight, which my illustrious friend thought it worth his while to express, with any degree of point, should perish." Boswell died at London, England, May 19, 1795.

BRICE, FANNY: BIRTH ANNIVERSARY. Oct 29, 1891. A popular star of vaudeville and early radio, Fania Borach was born to saloon owners in New York City. Dreaming of stardom, she dropped out of school in 1908 to join a burlesque show and was soon discovered by Florenz Ziegfeld, the most significant Broadway and vaudeville producer of his era. She could both sing and be funny, which ensured her success on stage; she headlined the *Ziegfeld Follies* and won a Grammy Award for her signature song, "My Man." At age 45, she began performing on live radio as "Baby Snooks," a precocious toddler with hilarious opinions. The show ran for more than 20 years, ending only with Brice's death on May 29, 1951, at Hollywood, CA. Her life story (and marriages to gambler Nicky Arnstein and Broadway producer Billy Rose) were immortalized in the Broadway musical and later film *Funny Girl*.

DUNNE, DOMINICK: 95th BIRTH ANNIVERSARY. Oct 29, 1925. Born at Hartford, CT, this writer and journalist enjoyed a long career in television production before writing fiction. It was following the brutal murder of his daughter in 1982 that he began chronicling true crime stories, mainly for *Vanity Fair* magazine. He is remembered for his diary-style coverage of assorted celebrity trials, notably those of O.J. Simpson and Claus von Bulow. Equally at home among the Hollywood jet set, he had a unique voice and talent for fictionalizing real-life events and scandals. Dunne died at New York, NY, Aug 26, 2009.

EBBETS, CHARLES: BIRTH ANNIVERSARY. Oct 29, 1859. Charles Hercules Ebbets, baseball executive, born at New York, NY. Ebbets bought into the Brooklyn baseball club in 1890 and became controlling owner in 1898. He sold 50 percent of the team to build Ebbets Field, the park whose enduring reputation has been the model for the new, old-fashioned parks constructed in recent years. Died at New York, Apr 18, 1925.

HURRICANE MITCH: ANNIVERSARY. Oct 29, 1998. Hurricane Mitch made landfall in Honduras on this date as a category four storm. More than 7,000 people were killed at Honduras by flooding. Thousands more were killed in other Central American countries, especially Nicaragua (nearly 4,000), as the hurricane raged until Nov 9.

INTERNET CREATED: ANNIVERSARY. Oct 29, 1969. The first connection on what would become the Internet was made on this day when bits of data flowed between computers at UCLA and the Stanford Research Institute. This was the beginning of ARPANET, the precursor to the Internet developed by the Department of Defense. By the end of 1969 four sites were connected: UCLA, the Stanford Research Institute, the University of California at Santa Barbara and the University of Utah. By the next year there were 10 sites, and soon there were applications like e-mail and file transfer utilities. The @ symbol was adopted in 1972, and a year later 75 percent of ARPANET traffic was e-mail. ARPANET was decommissioned in 1990, and the National Science Foundation's NSFnet took over the role of backbone of the Internet.

MAWLID AL NABI: THE BIRTHDAY OF THE PROPHET MUHAMMAD. Oct 29. Mawlid al Nabi (Birth of the Prophet Muhammad) is observed on Muslim calendar date Rabi al-Awal 12, 1442. Different methods for "anticipating" the visibility of the new moon crescent at Mecca are used by different Muslim groups, so date can vary by one to two days. Began at sunset the preceding day.

NATIONAL CAT DAY. Oct 29. Every year millions of cats enter shelters—and millions are euthanized. Cats lower blood pressure, offer unconditional love and companionship and alert their owners of danger. Cats have so many purr-sonalities and there is so much to love about them! On National Cat Day, celebrate your cats and if you can, please visit a local shelter and offer love and life by adopting a cat. Annually, Oct 29. For info: Colleen Paige. Web: www.nationalcatday.com.

SPACE MILESTONE: OLDEST MAN IN SPACE: *DISCOVERY* (US). Oct 29, 1998. Former astronaut and senator John Glenn became the oldest man in space when he traveled on the space shuttle *Discovery* at the age of 77. In 1962 on *Friendship 7* Glenn had been the first American to orbit Earth. See also: "Space Milestone: *Friendship 7*" (Feb 20).

STOCK MARKET CRASH OF 1929: ANNIVERSARY. Oct 29, 1929. Prices on the New York Stock Exchange plummeted and virtually collapsed four days after President Herbert Hoover had declared, "The fundamental business of the country . . . is on a sound and prosperous basis." More than 16 million shares were dumped, and billions of dollars were lost. The boom was over, and the nation faced nearly a decade of depression. Some analysts had warned that the buying spree, with prices 15 to 150 times above earnings, had to stop at some point. Frightened investors ordered their brokers to sell at whatever price. The resulting Great Depression, which lasted until about 1939, involved North America, Europe and other industrialized countries. In 1932 one out of four US workers was unemployed.

SUPERSTORM SANDY SLAMS INTO US: ANNIVERSARY. Oct 29, 2012. The superstorm—almost 900 miles in diameter at US landfall—hit Atlantic City, NJ, on the evening of Oct 29, 2012, and wreaked havoc across the northeastern United States. As a category 1 hurricane beginning on Oct 24, Sandy had swept through the Caribbean (causing 60 deaths in Haiti). By landfall on Oct 29, it was an extratropical cyclone. The US loss of life was more than 125 people; the damages were estimated at almost $50 billion. More than eight million people were left without power. The storm affected states inland as well, causing three inches of snowfall.

TURKEY: REPUBLIC DAY. Oct 29. Anniversary of the founding of the republic in 1923.

🎂 BIRTHDAYS TODAY

Lee Child, 66, author (Jack Reacher novels), born James Grant at Coventry, England, Oct 29, 1954.

Richard Dreyfuss, 73, actor (*Mr Holland's Opus, Jaws*, Oscar for *The Goodbye Girl*), born Brooklyn, NY, Oct 29, 1947.

Joely Fisher, 55, actress ("'Til Death," "Ellen"), born Los Angeles, CA, Oct 29, 1965.

Finola Hughes, 60, actress ("General Hospital," *Staying Alive*), born London, England, Oct 29, 1960.

Kate Jackson, 72, actress ("Charlie's Angels," "Scarecrow and Mrs King"), born Birmingham, AL, Oct 29, 1948.

Randy Jackson, 59, singer (Jackson 5), born Steven Randall Jackson at Gary, IN, Oct 29, 1961.

Melba Moore, 75, singer, actress, born New York, NY, Oct 29, 1945.

David Remnick, 62, editor in chief (*New Yorker*), author (*Lenin's Tomb, The Bridge*), journalist, born Hackensack, NJ, Oct 29, 1958.

	S	M	T	W	T	F	S
October					1	2	3
	4	5	6	7	8	9	10
2020	11	12	13	14	15	16	17
	18	19	20	21	22	23	24
	25	26	27	28	29	30	31

Tracee Ellis Ross, 48, actress ("Black-ish," "Girlfriends"), born Tracee Joy Silberstein at Los Angeles, CA, Oct 29, 1972.

Winona Ryder, 49, actress ("Stranger Things"; *Girl, Interrupted*; *Little Women*), born Winona Horowitz at Winona, MN, Oct 29, 1971.

Rufus Sewell, 53, actor ("Victoria," "The Man in the High Castle," *Dark City*), born Twickenham, England, Oct 29, 1967.

Ellen Johnson Sirleaf, 82, former president of Liberia (2006–18), women's rights activist, 2016 Nobel Peace Prize recipient, born Monrovia, Liberia, Oct 29, 1938.

Gabrielle Union, 48, actress (*Bring It On, The Honeymooners*), born Omaha, NE, Oct 29, 1972.

October 30 — Friday

DAY 304   **62 REMAINING**

ADAMS, JOHN: BIRTH ANNIVERSARY. Oct 30, 1735. Second president of the US (term of office: Mar 4, 1797–Mar 3, 1801). Adams had been George Washington's vice president and was the father of John Quincy Adams (sixth president of the US). Born at Braintree, MA, he once wrote in a letter to his wife, Abigail: "I must study politics and war that my sons may have liberty to study mathematics and philosophy." Adams and Thomas Jefferson died on the same day, July 4, 1826. Adams died at Quincy, MA. See also: "Adams, John, and Jefferson, Thomas: Death Anniversary" (July 4).

ATLAS, CHARLES: BIRTH ANNIVERSARY. Oct 30, 1892. Charles Atlas (former 97-pound weakling), whose original name was Angelo Siciliano, was born at Acri, Calabria, Italy (some sources say in 1893). A bodybuilder and physical culturist, he created a popular mail-order bodybuilding course. The legendary sand-kicking episode used later in advertising for his course occurred at Coney Island, NY, when a lifeguard kicked sand in Atlas's face and stole his girlfriend. Three generations of comic book fans read his advertisements. He died Dec 24, 1972, at Long Beach, NY.

CHECKLISTS DAY. Oct 30. In recognition of the development of the first well-known checklist, following the crash of a B-17 Flying Fortress prototype caused by pilot error on this date in 1935. Use checklists to help avoid tragedy and disappointment and take advantage of opportunities. For info: Don Parcher, 378 Grouse Ct, Louisville, CO 80027. Phone: (619) 987-5434. E-mail: don@checklists.com. Web: checklists.com/checklists-day.

CLOSING OF COLUMBIAN EXPOSITION: ANNIVERSARY. Oct 30, 1893. After a rousing success, the Columbian Exposition at Chicago, IL, held "American Cities Day" Oct 28, and Chicago mayor Carter Harrison gave a speech before the visiting mayors. After he arrived home, Harrison was shot and killed by Patrick Eugene Prendergast. Instead of the elaborate ceremony that had been planned to close the exposition on Oct 30, a single speech was given and the flags were lowered to half-mast.

CREATE A GREAT FUNERAL DAY. Oct 30. A day to remind people of all the benefits of creating their own unique funerals or memorial services, regardless of age or state of health. For info: Stephanie West Allen, 1376 S Wyandot St, Denver, CO 80223. Phone: (303) 935-8866. E-mail: stephanie@westallen.com.

DEVIL'S NIGHT. Oct 30. Formerly a "Mischief Night" on the evening before Halloween and an occasion for harmless pranks, chiefly observed by children. However, in some areas of the US, the destruction of property and endangering of lives has led to the imposition of dusk-to-dawn curfews during the last two or three days in October. Not to be confused with "Trick or Treat,"

or "Beggar's Night," usually observed on Halloween. See also: "Hallowe'en" (Oct 31).

FRANKENSTEIN FRIDAY. Oct 30. This holiday, founded in 1997, honors and celebrates the "mother" and "father" of Frankenstein, Mary Shelley and Boris Karloff. In years past it has included a torch-lighting ceremony, a film festival and an art display. 2020 marks the 85th anniversary of the film *Bride of Frankenstein* (1935). Annually, the last Friday in October. For info: Ron MacCloskey. E-mail: ronmac55@aol.com.

HALSEY, WILLIAM FREDERICK "BULL": BIRTH ANNIVERSARY. Oct 30, 1882. American admiral and fleet commander who played a leading role in the defeat of the Japanese in the Pacific naval battles of WWII. On Sept 2, 1945, Japan's final instrument of surrender was signed in Tokyo Bay aboard Halsey's flagship, the USS *Missouri*. William Halsey was born at Elizabeth, NJ. He died at Fishers Island, NY, Aug 16, 1959.

HAUNTED REFRIGERATOR NIGHT. Oct 30. Who knows what evil lurks in the refrigerators of men and women? It's time to be afraid, very afraid. Gather friends, open the refrigerator door and venture into the realm of the lower shelf, rear. That "thing" inside that container is much more horrifying than any haunted hayride. Annually, Oct 30. (©2006 by WH.) For info: Thomas & Ruth Roy, Wellcat Holidays, 2418 Long Ln, Lebanon, PA 17046. Phone: (717) 279-0184. E-mail: info@wellcat.com. Web: www.wellcat.com.

MALLE, LOUIS: BIRTH ANNIVERSARY. Oct 30, 1932. Born at Thumeries, France, film director Louis Malle was known for his experimental approach to filmmaking and his investigation of controversial topics. *La Souffle au Coeur* (1971), *Lacombe, Lucien* (1974) and *Pretty Baby* (1978), for instance, dealt with the issues of incest, the collaboration of France with its Nazi occupiers and child prostitution, respectively. Of all his films, Malle wished most to be remembered for *Au Revoir, Les Enfants* (1987). Died Nov 23, 1995, at Beverly Hills, CA.

NATIONAL CANDY CORN DAY. Oct 30. A day to celebrate the sweet, tri-colored treat first created in the 1880s by the Wunderlee Candy Company. About nine billion pieces of candy corn are produced annually. For info: Natl Confectioners Assn. Web: www.candyusa.com.

POST, EMILY: BIRTH ANNIVERSARY. Oct 30, 1872. Emily Post was born at Baltimore, MD. Published in 1922, her book *Etiquette: The Blue Book of Social Usage* instantly became the American bible of manners and social behavior and established Post as a household name in matters of etiquette. It was in its 10th edition at the time of her death Sept 25, 1960, at New York, NY. *Etiquette* inspired a great many letters asking Post for advice on manners in specific situations. She used these letters as the basis for her radio show and her syndicated newspaper column, which eventually appeared in more than 200 papers.

POUND, EZRA LOOMIS: BIRTH ANNIVERSARY. Oct 30, 1885. Modernist poet, editor and critic, born at Hailey, ID. His success as a poet began in 1909 with the publication of *Personae*. In 1912 Pound initiated the Imagist movement; he edited its first anthology in 1914 and collaborated with James Joyce and T.S. Eliot. He moved to Italy in 1924. As a result of his pro-Fascist radio broadcasts from Italy, Pound was indicted for treason July 26, 1943, and arrested near Genoa by the US Army. He was confined to St.

Elizabeth's Hospital, Washington, DC, from 1946 to 1958. Considered mentally unable to stand trial, he was never tried for treason. Pound died at Venice, Italy, Nov 1, 1972.

SHERIDAN, RICHARD BRINSLEY: BIRTH ANNIVERSARY. Oct 30, 1751. Dramatist and member of parliament, born at Dublin, Ireland. Author of *The Rivals* (1775) and *The School for Scandal* (1777). Died at London, England, July 7, 1816. Sheridan is said to have extended the following invitation to a young lady: "Won't you come into the garden? I would like my roses to see you."

"WAR OF THE WORLDS": BROADCAST ANNIVERSARY. Oct 30, 1938. As part of a series of radio dramas based on famous novels, Orson Welles with the Mercury Players produced H.G. Wells's *War of the Worlds*. Near panic resulted when listeners believed the simulated news bulletins, which described a Martian invasion of New Jersey, to be real.

WORLD AUDIO DRAMA DAY. Oct 30. 8th annual. Oct 30 is celebrated each year as the 1938 radio broadcast anniversary of *War of the Worlds*, the most famous audio drama of all time. World Audio Drama Day celebrates the "panic broadcast" as well as the continuing artistry and achievements in American audio drama. From live stage performances to pre-recorded podcasts, there are now more audio dramas produced each year in the US than when Orson Welles and John Houseman's Mercury Theatre first thrilled the nation in 1938. Special events and performances, listening marathons and broadcasts are held throughout late October to celebrate this day. For info: Kettle Falls Media and Audio Drama Network. E-mail: noirdame@gmail.com and audiodramaday@gmail.com. Web: www.audiodramaday.com.

🎂 **BIRTHDAYS TODAY**

Robert A. Caro, 85, author (multivolume biography of Lyndon B. Johnson), born New York, NY, Oct 30, 1935.

Ashley Graham, 33, model, born Lincoln, NE, Oct 30, 1987.

Harry Hamlin, 69, actor ("LA Law," "Studs Lonigan"), born Pasadena, CA, Oct 30, 1951.

Nastia Liukin, 31, Olympic gymnast, born Moscow, Russia, Oct 30, 1989.

Diego Armando Maradona, 60, soccer coach and former player, FIFA Player of the Century, born Lanus, Argentina, Oct 30, 1960.

Marcus Mariota, 27, football player, 2014 Heisman Trophy winner, born Honolulu, HI, Oct 30, 1993.

Andrea Mitchell, 74, news correspondent, born New York, NY, Oct 30, 1946.

Matthew Morrison, 42, actor ("Glee"), born Fort Ord, CA, Oct 30, 1978.

Clémence Poésy, 38, actress ("The Tunnel," "Gunpowder, Treason & Plot," *In Bruges, Birdsong*, Harry Potter films), born Clémence Guichard at Paris, France, Oct 30, 1982.

October 2020	S	M	T	W	T	F	S
					1	2	3
	4	5	6	7	8	9	10
	11	12	13	14	15	16	17
	18	19	20	21	22	23	24
	25	26	27	28	29	30	31

Kevin Pollak, 62, actor (*A Few Good Men, Grumpy Old Men*), born San Francisco, CA, Oct 30, 1958.

Grace Slick, 81, singer (Jefferson Airplane), born Chicago, IL, Oct 30, 1939.

Charles Martin Smith, 67, actor (*American Graffiti, The Untouchables*), director, born Los Angeles, CA, Oct 30, 1953.

Ivanka Trump, 39, fashion executive, presidential adviser, former model, born New York, NY, Oct 30, 1981.

Dick Vermeil, 84, former football coach, born Calistoga, CA, Oct 30, 1936.

Henry Winkler, 75, actor ("Happy Days"), director, children's author, born New York, NY, Oct 30, 1945.

October 31 — Saturday

DAY 305   **61 REMAINING**

BOOKS FOR TREATS DAY. Oct 31. San Jose, CA. The Books for Treats cause gives gently read children's books at Halloween instead of candy. "Feed kids' minds, not their cavities. Give brain candy." Supported by the city of San Jose and numerous community institutions. For info: Rebecca Morgan, Books for Treats, 1440 Newport Ave, San Jose, CA 95125. Phone: (408) 998-7977. E-mail: rebecca@rebeccamorgan.com. Web: www.BooksForTreats.org.

CANDY, JOHN: 70th BIRTH ANNIVERSARY. Oct 31, 1950. Comedic actor who got his start in Second City improvisation at Toronto and graduated to film stardom (*Uncle Buck; Planes, Trains and Automobiles*). Born at Toronto, ON, Canada; died Mar 4, 1994, while on location for a film at Chupederos, Mexico.

"CAR TALK" NATIONAL RADIO PREMIERE: ANNIVERSARY. Oct 31, 1987. "Car Talk," the irreverent talk show that diagnosed auto ills, premiered nationally on National Public Radio on this date. Hosted by brothers Ray and Tom Magliozzi (also known as "Click and Clack, the Tappet Brothers"), "Car Talk" originally debuted at Boston, MA, in 1977. Almost 4.4 million listeners tuned in to the Peabody Award–winning show on 588 NPR stations. In 2012 the brothers announced their retirement from the show, which would continue with re-airings of "best-of" moments. Tom Magliozzi, born June 28, 1937, passed away on Nov 3, 2014.

CHIANG KAI-SHEK: BIRTH ANNIVERSARY. Oct 31, 1887. Chinese soldier and statesman, born at Chekiang, China. Educated at the Whampoa Military Academy, Chiang led the KMT (nationalist) forces in the struggle against the Communist army led by Mao Tse-tung and eventually had to flee mainland China. He died at Taipei, Taiwan, Apr 5, 1975.

FIRST BLACK PLAYER IN NBA GAME: 70th ANNIVERSARY. Oct 31, 1950. Earl Lloyd became the first black athlete ever to play in an NBA game when he took the floor for the Washington Capitols at Rochester, NY. Lloyd was actually one of three black players to become NBA players in the 1950 season, the others being Nat "Sweetwater" Clifton, who was signed by the New York Knicks, and Chuck Cooper, who was drafted by the Boston Celtics (and debuted the night after Lloyd).

HALLOWE'EN OR ALL HALLOWS' EVE. Oct 31. An ancient celebration combining Druid autumn festival and Christian customs. Hallowe'en (All Hallows' Eve) is the beginning of Hallowtide, a season that embraces the Feast of All Saints (Nov 1) and the Feast of All Souls (Nov 2). The observance, dating from the sixth or seventh century, has long been associated with thoughts of the dead, spirits, witches, ghosts and devils. In fact, the ancient Celtic Feast of Samhain, the festival that marked the beginning of winter and of the New Year, was observed Nov 1. See also: "Trick or Treat or Beggar's Night" (Oct 31).

HOUDINI, HARRY: DEATH ANNIVERSARY. Oct 31, 1926. Harry Houdini (whose real name was Ehrich Weisz), magician, illusionist and escape artist, died at Grace Hospital, Detroit, MI, of peritonitis following an Oct 19 blow to the abdomen. Houdini's death anniversary, on Halloween, is occasion for meetings of magicians. See also: "Houdini, Harry: Birth Anniversary" (Mar 24).

HUNTER'S MOON. Oct 31. The full moon following Harvest Moon. So called because the moon's light in evening extends day's length for hunters. The October Full Moon.

KEATS, JOHN: 225th BIRTH ANNIVERSARY. Oct 31, 1795. The great Romantic poet was born at London, England. Famous for "Ode on a Grecian Urn" and "Ode to a Nightingale," among many other poems. Keats wrote to his betrothed, Fanny Brawne, in 1820: "If I should die . . . I have left no immortal work behind me—nothing to make my friends proud of my memory—but I have loved the principle of beauty in all things, and if I had had time I would have made myself remembered." Died at the age of 25 at Rome, Italy, Feb 23, 1821.

LANDON, MICHAEL: BIRTH ANNIVERSARY. Oct 31, 1936. American actor, born Eugene Maurice Orowitz, at Forest Hills, NY. He is best known for his roles in the television series "Bonanza" (1959–73), "Little House on the Prairie" (1974–83) and "Highway to Heaven" (1984–89). He died July 1, 1991, at Malibu, CA.

LOW, JULIETTE GORDON: BIRTH ANNIVERSARY. Oct 31, 1860. Founded Girl Scouts of the USA Mar 12, 1912, at Savannah, GA. Born at Savannah, Low died there Jan 17, 1927.

MAGIC DAY. Oct 31. Traditionally observed on the anniversary of the death of Harry Houdini in 1926.

MOON PHASE: FULL MOON/BLUE MOON. Oct 31. Moon enters Full Moon phase at 10:49 AM, EDT. In recent times, a "blue moon" describes the second full moon falling in the calendar month.

MOUNT RUSHMORE COMPLETION: ANNIVERSARY. Oct 31, 1941. The Mount Rushmore National Memorial was completed after 14 years of work. First suggested by Jonah Robinson of the South Dakota State Historical Society, the memorial was dedicated in 1925, and work began in 1927. The memorial contains sculptures of the heads of four US presidents—George Washington, Thomas Jefferson, Abraham Lincoln and Theodore Roosevelt. The 60-foot-tall sculptures represent, respectively, the nation's founding, political philosophy, preservation and expansion and conservation.

NATIONAL KNOCK-KNOCK DAY. Oct 31. Celebrated in tandem with Halloween, National Knock-Knock Day answers the age-old question "Who's there?" A day for kids of all ages to try out their best knock-knock jokes (Knock Knock/Who's there?/Weirdo/Weirdo who?/Weirdo you keep all your Halloween candy? I'm starving!). For a list of Halloween Knock-Knock Jokes, contact children's joke book authors Matt Rissinger and Philip Yates. Annually, Oct 31. For info: Matt Rissinger/Philip Yates. Phone: (610) 650-9136. E-mail: mrissinger@aol.com or laugharoni@msn.com.

NEVADA: ADMISSION DAY: ANNIVERSARY. Oct 31, 1864. Became 36th state in 1864. Observed as a holiday in Nevada.

PACA, WILLIAM: BIRTH ANNIVERSARY. Oct 31, 1740. Signer of the Declaration of Independence and governor of Maryland. Born near Abingdon, MD, he died Oct 13, 1799, at Talbot County, MD.

REFORMATION DAY/LUTHER'S *95 THESES*: ANNIVERSARY. Oct 31, 1517. Deeply occupied by questions surrounding faith, repentance and salvation, Martin Luther, an Augustinian monk and professor, penned "Disputation on the Power and Efficacy of Indulgences," known as the *95 Theses*. In legend, on Oct 31, 1517, Luther nailed his work to the door of Wittenberg's Castle Church. In reality, he more likely circulated the theses for debate among students, clergy and professors. In either case, his work sparked the beginning of the Reformation in Germany. This 1517 anniversary is observed by many Protestant churches on Reformation Sunday, on Oct 31 if it falls on a Sunday, or on the Sunday before Oct 31.

SAMHAIN. Oct 31. (Also called November Eve, Hallowmas, Hallowe'en, All Hallows' Eve, Feast of Souls, Feast of the Dead, Feast of Apples and Calan Gaeaf.) One of the "Greater Sabbats" during the Wiccan year, Samhain, or "Summer's End," marks the death of the Sun-God, who then awaits his rebirth from the Mother Goddess at Yule (Dec 21 in 2020). In the Celtic tradition, the feast of Samhain was also celebrated as New Year's Eve, as their new year began on Nov 1. Annually, Oct 31.

SLEIDANUS, JOHANNES: DEATH ANNIVERSARY. Oct 31, 1556. German historian, born at Schleiden in 1506. His *Famous Chronicle of Oure Time*, called *Sleidanes Comentaires*, was first translated into English in 1560. The translator spoke thus to the book: "Go forth my painful Boke, Thou art no longer mine. Eche man may on thee loke, The Shame or praise is thine." He died at Strasbourg.

SWEDEN: ALL SAINTS' DAY. Oct 31. Honors the memory of deceased friends and relatives. Annually, the Saturday following Oct 30.

TAIWAN: CHIANG KAI-SHEK DAY. Oct 31. National holiday to honor the memory of Generalissimo Chiang Kai-shek, the first constitutional president of the Republic of China, born Oct 31, 1887.

TRICK OR TREAT OR BEGGAR'S NIGHT. Oct 31. A popular custom on Hallowe'en, in which children wearing costumes visit neighbors' homes, calling out "Trick or treat" and "begging" for candies or gifts to place in their beggars' bags. In recent years there has been increased participation by adults, often parading in elaborate or outrageous costumes and also requesting candy.

UNITED NATIONS: WORLD CITIES DAY. Oct 31. Since 2014, a day to promote planned city extension methodologies to guide the sustainable development of cities experiencing rapid urban growth, in order to prevent slum proliferation, enhance access to urban basic services, support inclusive housing, enhance job opportunities and create a safe and healthy living environment. (Res 68/239.) Annually, Oct 31. For info: United Nations, Dept of Public Info, New York, NY 10017. Web: www.un.org.

WATERS, ETHEL: BIRTH ANNIVERSARY. Oct 31, 1896. Married when she was 13, Ethel Waters began her singing career at the urging of friends. At age 17 she was singing at Baltimore, MD, billing herself as Sweet Mama Stringbean. Her career took her to New York, where she divided her work among the stage, nightclubs and films. She made her Broadway debut in 1927 in the revue *Africana*, and her other stage credits include *Blackbirds* and *Thousands Cheer*. Her memorable stage roles in *Cabin in the Sky* and *A Member of the Wedding* (for which she won the Drama Critics Award) were re-created for film. Born at Chester, PA, she died Sept 1, 1977, at Chatsworth, CA.

🎂 BIRTHDAYS TODAY

Michael Collins, 89, former astronaut, born Rome, Italy, Oct 31, 1931.

Deidre Hall, 72, actress ("Our House," "Days of Our Lives"), born Lake Worth, FL, Oct 31, 1948.

Peter Jackson, 59, director (Lord of the Rings trilogy, The Hobbit trilogy, *King Kong*), born Pukerua Bay, North Island, New Zealand, Oct 31, 1961.

Frederick Stanley (Fred) McGriff, 57, former baseball player, born Tampa, FL, Oct 31, 1963.

Larry Mullen, 59, musician (U2), born Dublin, Ireland, Oct 31, 1961.

Dermot Mulroney, 57, actor (*About Schmidt, My Best Friend's Wedding*), born Alexandria, VA, Oct 31, 1963.

Jane Pauley, 70, journalist, television personality, born Indianapolis, IN, Oct 31, 1950.

Piper Perabo, 44, actress ("Covert Affairs"), born Dallas, TX, Oct 31, 1976.

Dan Rather, 89, journalist (former anchor of "CBS Evening News"), born Wharton, TX, Oct 31, 1931.

Stephen Rea, 74, actor (*The Crying Game, Michael Collins*), born Belfast, Northern Ireland, Oct 31, 1946.

Ron Rifkin, 81, stage and screen actor (Tony for *Cabaret*; *The Substance of Fire*, "Alias"), born New York, NY, Oct 31, 1939.

Rob Schneider, 57, actor, comedian (*Deuce Bigalow: Male Gigolo*, "Saturday Night Live"), born San Francisco, CA, Oct 31, 1963.

Vanilla Ice, 53, rapper, actor, born Robert Van Winkle at Miami, FL, Oct 31, 1967.

Letitia Wright, 27, actress (*Black Panther*, "Humans"), born Georgetown, Guyana, Oct 31, 1993.

◆ November ◆

November 1 — Sunday

DAY 306   **60 REMAINING**

ALGERIA: REVOLUTION DAY. Nov 1. National holiday. Commemorates beginning of revolt against France in 1954.

ALL HALLOWS OR ALL SAINTS' DAY. Nov 1. Roman Catholic holy day of obligation. Commemorates the blessed, especially those who have no special feast days. Observed on Nov 1 since Pope Gregory IV set the date of recognition in AD 835. All Saints' Day is a legal holiday in Louisiana. Halloween is the evening before All Hallows Day.

AMERICAN DIABETES MONTH. Nov 1–30. American Diabetes Month is designed to communicate the seriousness of diabetes and the importance of proper diabetes control and treatment to those diagnosed with the disease and their families. Throughout the month, the American Diabetes Association holds special events and programs on a variety of topics related to diabetes care and treatment. For info: American Diabetes Assn. Phone: (800) DIABETES. Web: www.diabetes.org.

ANTIGUA AND BARBUDA: INDEPENDENCE DAY. Nov 1. National holiday. Commemorates independence from Britain in 1981.

AVIATION HISTORY MONTH. Nov 1–30. Anniversary of aeronautical experiments in November 1782 (exact dates unknown) by Joseph Michel Montgolfier and Jacques Etienne Montgolfier, brothers living at Annonay, France. Inspired by Joseph Priestley's book *Experiments Relating to the Different Kinds of Air*, the brothers experimented with filling paper and fabric bags with smoke and hot air, leading to the invention of the hot-air balloon, man's first flight and the entire science of aviation and flight.

BANANA PUDDING LOVERS MONTH. Nov 1–30. What sweet memories we share of family sitting down together eating their banana pudding dessert. Banana Pudding Lovers Month is a time for families to re-create the memories of their happy childhood. Or start creating memories for your own children! Let's pass the tradition from one generation to another. For info: Rodgers' Puddings, 1410 Poindexter St, Chesapeake, VA 23324. Phone: (757) 543-9290. E-mail: reggie@rodgerspuddings.com. Web: www.rodgerspuddings.com.

CRANE, STEPHEN: BIRTH ANNIVERSARY. Nov 1, 1871. American author (*The Red Badge of Courage*), born at Newark, NJ. Died June 5, 1900, at Badenweiler, Germany.

DAYLIGHT SAVING TIME ENDS; STANDARD TIME RESUMES. Nov 1–Mar 14, 2021. Standard time resumes at 2 AM on the first Sunday in November in each time zone, as provided by the Uniform Time Act of 1966 (as amended in 1986 by Public Law 99–359). The Energy Policy Act of 2005 extended the period of daylight saving time beginning in 2007. Many people use the popular rule "spring forward, fall back" to remember which way to turn their clocks. See also: "Daylight Saving Time" (Mar 8).

DIABETIC EYE DISEASE MONTH. Nov 1–30. Can people with diabetes prevent the onset of diabetic eye disease? During this observance, Prevent Blindness offers information to help the 5.3 million Americans age 18 and older who suffer from diabetic eye disease. For info: Prevent Blindness, 211 W Wacker Dr, Ste 1700, Chicago, IL 60606. Phone: (800) 331-2020. E-mail: info@preventblindness.org. Web: www.preventblindness.org.

EBONY MAGAZINE: 75th ANNIVERSARY. Nov 1, 1945. Black publishing entrepreneur John H. Johnson launched *Ebony* on this date—three years to the day after his first successful African-American lifestyle magazine, *Negro Digest* (1942). By 1946 *Ebony* had a circulation of more than 300,000 copies. On Nov 1, 1951, Johnson launched the equally successful publication *Jet*.

ENGLAND: BONHAMS LONDON TO BRIGHTON VETERAN CAR RUN. Nov 1. London. In 1896, 30 motorists set off to drive the 60 miles from London to Brighton to celebrate the lifting of the Locomotion Act, which required a car to travel at no more than four mph and to be preceded by a man on foot with a red flag. This 60-mile run was known as the Emancipation Run and it formed motoring as we know it today. This celebration continues today as the Bonhams London to Brighton Veteran Car Run, and owners of veteran cars worldwide take part. On Nov 1 around 500 pre-1905 cars take to the start in Hyde Park, London, and set off at sunrise for this "capital-to-coast" challenge to Brighton. An open-top bus follows the route and there are many opportunities for spectators to enjoy the spectacle. A Concours d'Elegance takes place the day before as part of the Regent Street Motor Show. For info: Bonhams London to Brighton Veteran Car Run. E-mail: VCRadmin@goose.co.uk. Web: www.veteran-carrun.com.

EUROPEAN UNION ESTABLISHED: ANNIVERSARY. Nov 1, 1993. The Maastricht Treaty went into effect on this day, formally establishing the European Union. The treaty was drafted in 1991. By 1993, 12 nations had ratified it. In 1995 three more nations ratified the treaty. The European Union grew out of the European Economic Community (also known as the Common Market), which was established in 1958.

EXTRA MILE DAY. Nov 1. Since 2009, a day recognizing the capacity we each have to create positive change in our families, organizations and communities when we go the extra mile. More than 500 cities participate in this event. Annually, Nov 1. For info: Extra Mile America, 13700 Marina Pointe Dr, Ste 606, Marina del Rey, CA 90292. Phone: (310) 402-4826. E-mail: info@ExtraMileAmerica.org. Web: www.ExtraMileAmerica.org.

EYE DONATION MONTH. Nov 1–30. Since 1983, a month to promote awareness of the need to donate eyes, to recognize donors and their families and to celebrate corneal recipients. (Formerly March.) For info: Eye Bank Association of America, 1101 17th St NW, Ste 400, Washington, DC 20036. Phone: (202) 775-4999. Web: www.restoresight.org.

GUATEMALA: KITE FESTIVAL OF SANTIAGO SACATEPÉQUEZ. Nov 1–2. Santiago Sacatepéquez. In folklore, when evil spirits disturbed the good spirits in the cemetery of this village about 20 miles from Guatemala City, a shaman told the townspeople a secret way to get rid of the evil spirits—by flying kites (because the evil spirits were frightened by the noise of wind against paper). Since then, the kite festival has been held at the cemetery each year on All Saints' Day (Nov 1) or All Souls' Day (Nov 2). Village youths work for many weeks to make the giant, elaborate kites of the festival.

HOWL AND OTHER POEMS PUBLISHED: ANNIVERSARY. Nov 1, 1956. Official publication date of poet Allen Ginsberg's epic poem *Howl* by City Lights Books in San Francisco, CA. Once challenged (unsuccessfully) as obscene, *Howl* is now considered one of the most important American poems of the 20th century.

LISBON EARTHQUAKE: ANNIVERSARY. Nov 1, 1755. A powerful earthquake struck Lisbon, Portugal, on this day. The earthquake probably had a Richter scale magnitude of 9 and caused a tsunami to sweep over the capital. In the resulting deluge and fires, more than 75 percent of Lisbon was destroyed. Some 90,000 people died in Portugal, and an additional 10,000 people died in other parts of the Mediterranean.

LUNG CANCER AWARENESS MONTH. Nov 1–30. LCAM is a national campaign dedicated to increasing attention to lung cancer issues—early detection, increased research funding and increased support for those living with lung cancer. Lung Cancer Alliance is the

oldest and leading nonprofit organization dedicated to saving lives and advancing research by empowering those living with and at risk for lung cancer. Support and education resources are available free of charge by phone, by mail, online or via mobile app. For info: The Lung Cancer Alliance, 1700 K St NW, Ste 660, Washington, DC 20006. Phone: (202) 463-2080. E-mail: info@lungcanceralliance.org. Web: www.lungcanceralliance.org.

MEDICAL SCHOOL FOR WOMEN OPENED AT BOSTON: ANNIVERSARY. Nov 1, 1848. Founded at Boston, MA, by Samuel Gregory, a pioneer in medical education for women, the Boston Female Medical School opened as the first medical school exclusively for women. The original enrollment was 12 students. In 1874 the school merged with the Boston University School of Medicine and formed one of the first coed medical schools in the world.

MEXICO: DAY OF THE DEAD. Nov 1–2. Observance begins during last days of October when bakeries sell "dead men's bread"—round loaves decorated with sugar skulls. Departed souls are remembered not in mourning but with a spirit of friendliness and good humor. Cemeteries are visited, and graves are decorated.

MISSION SAN JUAN CAPISTRANO: FOUNDING ANNIVERSARY. Nov 1, 1776. California mission founded on this date, collapsed during the 1812 earthquake. The swallows of Capistrano nest in the ruins of the old mission church, departing each year on Oct 23 and returning the following year on or near St. Joseph's Day (Mar 19).

MOVEMBER. Nov 1–30. Every November, Movember is responsible for the sprouting of mustaches on thousands of men's faces around the world. These men raise vital funds and awareness for men's health, specifically prostate cancer and other cancers that affect men. Once registered at www.movember.com, men start Movember 1 clean-shaven. For the rest of the month, these selfless and generous men, known as Mo Bros, groom, trim and wax their way into the annals of fine mustachery. For info: Movember, PO Box 1595, Culver City, CA 90232. Phone: (310) 450-3399. E-mail: info.us@movember.com. Web: us.movember.com.

★**NATIONAL ADOPTION MONTH.** Nov 1–30.

NATIONAL ADOPTION MONTH. Nov 1–30. To raise awareness of the needs of children waiting to be adopted and to recognize people who have adopted or were adopted. A celebration of adoption! For info: Natl Council for Adoption, 225 N Washington St, Alexandria, VA 22314-2561. Phone: (703) 299-6633. E-mail: ncfa@adoptioncouncil.org. Web: www.adoptioncouncil.org.

NATIONAL AUTHORS' DAY. Nov 1. This observance was adopted by the General Federation of Women's Clubs in 1929 and in 1949 was given a place on the list of special days, weeks and months prepared by the US Department of Commerce. The resolution states in part: "By celebrating an Authors' Day as a nation, we would not only show patriotism, loyalty, and appreciation of the men and women who have made American literature possible, but would also encourage and inspire others to give of themselves in making a better America." It was also resolved "that we commemorate an Authors' Day to be observed on November First each year."

NATIONAL EPILEPSY AWARENESS MONTH. Nov 1–30. Since 1969, a month to increase public awareness about epilepsy, dispel myths about seizures, increase understanding about proper seizure first aid and encourage people living with epilepsy to live to their fullest potential. Annually, the month of November. For info: Epilepsy Foundation, 8301 Professional Pl W, Ste 230, Landover, MD 20785. Phone: (800) 332-1000. E-mail: contactus@efa.org. Web: www.epilepsy.com.

★**NATIONAL FAMILY CAREGIVERS MONTH.** Nov 1–30. To honor family members who care for aging relatives or those with disabilities.

NATIONAL FORGIVENESS AND HAPPINESS DAY. Nov 1. 27th annual. A worldwide celebration in which people take time to share these five wonderful words of wisdom: care, encourage, love, listen, forgive. Annually, Nov 1 (formerly observed on Oct 7). For info: Robert Moyers, Positive People Partners/Followers of Jesus, 4203 County Rd U4, Liberty Center, OH 43532. Phone: (419) 533-4191. E-mail: bobmoy@wcnet.org. Web: www.unconditionallovelive.com.

NATIONAL GEORGIA PECAN MONTH. Nov 1–30. Celebrating Georgia as the number one pecan-producing state as we bring in this year's harvest. For info: Georgia Pecan Commission. Web: www.georgiapecans.org.

NATIONAL INSPIRATIONAL ROLE MODELS MONTH. Nov 1–30. To acknowledge the impact that contemporary and historic role models have on our lives. Individuals chosen for recognition may include celebrities, historic figures, relatives, friends, colleagues, associates, etc. Celebrate with creative projects and activities featuring historic role models and spend time with contemporary role models. Theme for 2020: "Gaining inspiration from sports and the spirit of champions." National Inspirational Role Models Month (NIRMM) is now a signature celebration of National Inspirational Role Models Visionaries (NIRMV), a 501(c)(3) public charity. For info: Darlene House. Phone: (313) 778-1550. Web: nirmv.org.

NATIONAL LONG-TERM CARE AWARENESS MONTH. Nov 1–30. Annual event organized by the American Association for Long-Term Care Insurance (AALTCI) and supported by association members and leading industry organizations. The goal is to create heightened awareness of the need for long-term care and the importance of planning options available to Americans and their families. For info: Jesse Slome, Exec Dir, American Assn for Long-Term Care Insurance, 32504 Carrie Pl, Westlake Village, CA 91361. Phone: (818) 597-3227. Web: www.AALTCI.org.

NATIONAL MARROW AWARENESS MONTH. Nov 1–30. A special nationwide effort to recruit volunteer marrow, blood stem cell and umbilical cord blood donors and to increase patient awareness of the option of unrelated transplantation. For info: US Dept of Health and Human Services. Web: www.organdonor.gov.

NATIONAL MEMOIR WRITING MONTH. Nov 1–30. An opportunity to celebrate ourselves and our families by committing our life stories to writing. Preserving our autobiographies through memoir writing allows us to know ourselves better and to share our stories with future generations. As part of the monthlong celebration, free weekly memoir-writing teleclasses, memoir-writing prompts and community workshops are available. For info: The Memoir Network, 95 Gould Rd, #102, Lisbon Falls, ME 04252. Phone: (207) 353-5454. E-mail: memoirs@TheMemoirNetwork.com. Web: www.TheMemoirNetwork.com.

★**NATIONAL NATIVE-AMERICAN HERITAGE MONTH.** Nov 1–30.

NATIONAL NOVEL WRITING MONTH. Nov 1–30. National Novel Writing Month, or NaNoWriMo, the world's largest writing challenge and nonprofit literary crusade—first observed in 1999. Participants pledge to write 50,000 words in a month, starting from scratch and reaching "The End" by Nov 30. There are no judges, no prizes, and entries are deleted from the server before anyone even reads them. More than 650 regional volunteers in more than 60 countries hold write-ins, hosting writers in coffee shops, bookstores and libraries. Write-ins offer a supportive environment and surprisingly effective peer pressure, turning the usually solitary act of writing into a community experience. For info: Natl Novel Writing Month. Web: www.nanowrimo.org.

		S	M	T	W	T	F	S
November			1	2	3	4	5	6	7
2020		8	9	10	11	12	13	14
		15	16	17	18	19	20	21
		22	23	24	25	26	27	28
		29	30					

NATIONAL RUNAWAY PREVENTION MONTH. Nov 1–30. Since 2002. This annual campaign brings individuals and organizations across the country together to support runaway and homeless youth and to raise awareness of the issues these youth face. This month also seeks to educate the public about the role they can play in ending youth homelessness. In October 2002, President George W. Bush hosted the landmark White House Conference on Exploited and Runaway Children, where leaders from across the country convened to discuss issues and challenges related to the runaway and homeless youth crisis. Originally a week, this event was expanded into a month. Sponsored by the National Runaway Safeline (NRS), Family and Youth Services Bureau (FYSB), Runaway and Homeless Youth Training and Technical Assistance Center (RHYT-TAC) and the National Clearinghouse on Homeless Youth and Families (NCHYF). For info: National Runaway Safeline, 3141B N Lincoln Ave, Chicago, IL 60657. Phone: (773) 880-9860. E-mail: prevention@1800runaway.org. Web: www.1800runaway.org.

NATIONAL SPORTS FAN DAY. Nov 1. Since 2016. Sports are the ultimate unifier and so much fun! This is a day to celebrate your love for your favorite team and everything awesome this passion has brought you. Observed on a "sports equinox"—a day when all the major US sports leagues (NFL, NBA, NHL, MLB and usually the MLS) play at least one game. The rare sports equinox usually occurs in late October, early November. Annually, Nov 1. For info: Shannon Hurd, Founder, Fans Life, 10556 Graymont Ln, Highlands Ranch, CO 80126. Phone: (720) 936-3326. E-mail: shannon@fans.life. Web: www.fans.life.

PEANUT BUTTER LOVERS' MONTH. Nov 1–30. Celebration of America's favorite food and number one sandwich. Whether you prefer creamy or crunchy, find new recipes and fun facts to add flavor to your celebration. For info: Southern Peanut Growers. Web: www.peanutbutterlovers.com.

PICTURE BOOK MONTH. Nov 1–30. This month is an international literacy initiative that celebrates the print picture book during the month of November. Picture books enable even the busiest of us to enjoy a good story in just a few minutes. In a world where so much is rushed, picture books encourage us to slow down and savor. (Created by Dianne de Las Casas.)

POLAR BEAR WEEK. Nov 1–7. This week focuses on the importance of sea ice to polar bears—and why we must take action on climate change to ensure their survival. Polar Bear Week coincides with the fall polar bear migration in Churchill, MB, Canada, where polar bears gather to wait for the freeze-up on Hudson Bay so they can return to hunting seals. Annually, the first full week in November. For info: Polar Bears International, PO Box 3008, Bozeman, MT 59772. Web: www.polarbearsinternational.org.

PPSI/ACA AIDS AWARENESS MONTH. Nov 1–30. To educate consumers, patients, students and professionals on the prevention of AIDS and sexually transmitted diseases. Kit of materials available for $15. Sponsored by the American College of Apothecaries (ACA)/Pharmacists Planning Service, Inc (PPSI). For info: ACA/PPSI, 2830 Summer Oaks Dr, Bartlett, TN 38134. E-mail: info@ppsinc.org. Web: www.ppsinc.org.

PREMATURITY AWARENESS MONTH. Nov 1–30. Sponsored by the March of Dimes to alert Americans to the common, serious and costly problem of premature birth (before 37 weeks). One in eight babies is born prematurely in this country, many without warning and with no known cause. Prematurity is the leading cause of newborn death (before the first month in life), and babies who do survive often face chronic health and developmental disabilities for the rest of their lives. For info: March of Dimes, National Office, 1550 Crystal Dr, Ste 1300, Arlington, VA 22202. Phone: (888) 663-4637. Web: www.marchofdimes.com.

PRESIDENT OCCUPIES THE WHITE HOUSE: ANNIVERSARY. Nov 1, 1800. Philadelphia, PA, had served as the nation's capital from 1790 to 1800. On Nov 1, 1800, President John Adams and his family moved into the newly completed White House, as Washington, DC, became the new capital.

PRIME MERIDIAN SET: ANNIVERSARY. Nov 1, 1884. Delegates from 25 nations met in October at Washington, DC, at the International Meridian Conference to set up time zones for the world. On this day the treaty adopted by the conference took effect, making Greenwich, England, the Prime Meridian (i.e., 0° longitude) and setting the International Date Line at 180° longitude in the Pacific. Every 15° of longitude equals one hour, and there are 24 meridians. While some countries do not strictly observe this system (for example, while China stretches over five time zones, it is the same time everywhere in China), it has brought predictability and logic to time throughout the world.

TCS NEW YORK CITY MARATHON. Nov 1. New York, NY. About 50,000 runners from all over the world gather to compete, with more than two million spectators watching from the sidelines. Annually, the first Sunday in November. Est attendance: 2,000,000. For info: New York Road Runners, NYRR RunCenter, 320 W 57th St, New York, NY 10019. E-mail: help@nyrr.org. Web: www.tcsnycmarathon.org.

US VIRGIN ISLANDS: LIBERTY DAY. Nov 1. Officially "D. Hamilton Jackson Memorial Day," commemorating establishment of the first press in the Virgin Islands in 1915.

WORLD VEGAN MONTH. Nov 1–30. World Vegan Month is celebrated around the world as a time to recognize how far the vegan movement has come, to highlight how accessible and beneficial a vegan lifestyle can be and to encourage the vegan-curious to adopt veganism by sharing advice, recipes and ideas. For info: The Vegan Society. E-mail: info@vegansociety.com. Web: www.vegansociety.com.

WORLDWIDE BEREAVED SIBLINGS AWARENESS MONTH. Nov 1–30. This month promotes support for bereaved siblings. Often people don't know what to say to or do for grieving siblings. So sometimes, they turn away and do nothing. We encourage people to turn back and begin to reach out to bereaved siblings by giving them a listener, a shoulder to cry on or a hug. "Remember to reach out to the bereaved so they won't have to grieve alone." For info: Deborah Le Bouf Kulkkula, PhD, or Jane K. Andrews, B Ed, Worldwide Bereaved Siblings Awareness Month, 381 Billings Rd, Fitchburg, MA 01420-1407. Phone: (978) 343-4009 or (978) 808-8084 (cell). E-mail: DebKulkkula@gmail.com. Web: www.bereavementawareness.com.

ZERO-TASKING DAY. Nov 1. Today is when daylight saving time ends—and we turn our clocks back and "gain" an hour. Instead of filling those extra 60 minutes with more work and stress, use that hour to do nothing more than take a breath, relax, reenergize, refresh and deload (opposite of overload). For info: Nancy Christie. Phone: (330) 793-3675. E-mail: nancy@nancychristie.com.

🎂 BIRTHDAYS TODAY

Penn Badgley, 34, actor ("The Bedford Diaries," "Gossip Girl"), born Baltimore, MD, Nov 1, 1986.

Toni Collette, 48, actress (Emmy and Golden Globe for "United States of Tara," *Hereditary, The Sixth Sense, About a Boy*), born Sydney, Australia, Nov 1, 1972.

Tim Cook, 60, business executive (CEO of Apple), born Mobile, AL, Nov 1, 1960.

Larry Claxton Flynt, 78, publisher, born Magoffin County, KY, Nov 1, 1942.

Lyle Lovett, 63, singer, born Klein, TX, Nov 1, 1957.

Jenny McCarthy, 48, model, actress (*Scary Movie 3*), born Chicago, IL, Nov 1, 1972.

Gary Jim Player, 85, former golfer, born Johannesburg, South Africa, Nov 1, 1935.

Aishwarya Rai, 47, actress (*Enthiran, Bride and Prejudice, Devdas*), Goodwill Ambassador for UNAIDS, born Mangalore, India, Nov 1, 1973.

Rachel Ticotin, 62, actress (*Total Recall, Con Air*), born the Bronx, NY, Nov 1, 1958.

Fernando Anguamea Valenzuela, 60, former baseball player, born Navojoa, Sonora, Mexico, Nov 1, 1960.

November 2 — Monday

DAY 307   **59 REMAINING**

ALL SOULS' DAY. Nov 2. Commemorates the faithful departed. Catholic observance.

AUSTRALIA: RECREATION DAY. Nov 2. The first Monday in November is observed as Recreation Day at Northern Tasmania.

BALFOUR DECLARATION: ANNIVERSARY. Nov 2, 1917. In a letter to the Zionist Federation of Great Britain and Ireland, British Foreign Secretary Arthur James Balfour expressed the support of the British government for the formation of a "national home for the Jewish people." Following World War I, the Ottoman Empire ceded Palestine to Britain, and both the peace treaty and the British Mandate for Palestine expressed the same goals, including the stipulation that the civil and religious rights of non-Jews living in Palestine be respected.

BOONE, DANIEL: BIRTH ANNIVERSARY. Nov 2, 1734. (New Style date.) American frontiersman, explorer and militia officer, born at Berks County, near Reading, PA. In February 1778 he was captured at Blue Licks, KY, by Shawnee Indians, under Chief Blackfish, who adopted Boone when he was inducted into the tribe as "Big Turtle." Boone escaped after five months and in 1781 was captured briefly by the British. He experienced a series of personal and financial disasters during his life but continued a rugged existence, hunting until his 80s. Boone died at St. Charles County, MO, Sept 26, 1820. The bodies of Daniel Boone and his wife, Rebecca, were moved to Frankfort, KY, in 1845.

FIRST SCHEDULED RADIO BROADCAST: 100th ANNIVERSARY. Nov 2, 1920. Station KDKA at Pittsburgh, PA, broadcast the results of the presidential election. The station got its license to broadcast Nov 7, 1921. By 1922 there were about 400 licensed radio stations in the US.

HARDING, WARREN GAMALIEL: BIRTH ANNIVERSARY. Nov 2, 1865. Born at Corsica, Ohio, Harding was 29th president of the US. His term of office: Mar 4, 1921–Aug 2, 1923. He famously stated, "I cannot hope to be one of the great presidents, but perhaps I may be remembered as one of the best loved." Although he won the presidency with the highest popular vote yet, Harding was later regarded as one of the nation's worst presidents. His undistinguished administration was plagued by cronyism and corruption (most famously, the Teapot Dome scandal), the full extent of which wasn't apparent until after his sudden death Aug 2, 1923, at San Francisco, CA.

LANCASTER, BURT: BIRTH ANNIVERSARY. Nov 2, 1913. Distinguished American actor, born Burton Stephen Lancaster, who began his career in show business as a circus acrobat. In a career spanning 45 years, he appeared in nearly 80 films. Some of his more memorable roles are in *From Here to Eternity* (1953), *The Bird Man of Alcatraz* (1962) and *The Leopard* (1963); he received an Academy Award for his performance in the title role of *Elmer Gantry* (1961). His later popular movies include *Atlantic City* (1981), *Local Hero* (1983) and *Field of Dreams* (1989). Born at New York City, he died Oct 20, 1994, at Los Angeles, CA.

NATIONAL PATIENT ACCESSIBILITY WEEK. Nov 2–6. The purpose of this week is to increase awareness among clinicians of the need for accessible healthcare facilities for patients who are disabled, elderly or obese. For info: Tanya Coby, Midmark, 10170 Penny Ln, Ste 300, Miamisburg, OH 45342. Phone: (937) 459-9050. E-mail: tcoby@midmark.com. Web: www.midmark.com.

NATIONAL TRAFFIC PROFESSIONALS DAY. Nov 2. A day honoring radio and TV traffic departments, which schedule programs and announcements on the nation's broadcast stations. Annually, Nov 2 (observed on the following Monday if Nov 2 falls on a Saturday or Sunday). For info: Traffic Directors Guild of America. Web: www.tdga.org.

NEW YORK SUBWAY ACCIDENT: ANNIVERSARY. Nov 2, 1918. The Brighton Beach Express, exceeding its speed limit five times over (going 30 mph) while approaching the station near the Malbone St tunnel at Brooklyn, jumped the tracks, killing 97 people and injuring 100. The supervisor-engineer, taking the place of a striking motorman of the Brotherhood of Locomotive Engineers, was tried and acquitted of charges of negligence.

NORTH DAKOTA: ADMISSION DAY: ANNIVERSARY. Nov 2. Became 39th state in 1889.

POLK, JAMES KNOX: 225th BIRTH ANNIVERSARY. Nov 2, 1795. The 11th president of the United States was born at Mecklenburg County, NC. A compromise candidate at the 1844 Democratic Party convention, Polk was awarded the nomination on the ninth ballot. He served one term of office: Mar 4, 1845–Mar 3, 1849, but those four years were eventful and productive. Controversially, the United States waged war on Mexico from 1846 to 1848 and the victory gained land that would become Nevada, California and Utah with most of Arizona and parts of Colorado and New Mexico. (In 1848, the US House of Representatives formally censured Polk for going to war without congressional approval.) And during his administration the Oregon Territory was established. This expansive growth to the Pacific Ocean is Polk's major legacy. He declined to be a candidate for a second term and declared himself to be "exceedingly relieved" at the completion of his presidency. He died shortly thereafter at Nashville, TN, June 15, 1849.

SENECA FALLS CONVENTION ATTENDEE VOTES: 100th ANNIVERSARY. Nov 2, 1920. The only woman who attended the historic Seneca Falls Women's Rights Convention in 1848 who lived long enough to exercise her right to vote under the 19th Amendment, Charlotte Woodward voted at Philadelphia, PA, in the general election on Nov 2, 1920.

SOUTH DAKOTA: ADMISSION DAY: ANNIVERSARY. Nov 2. Became 40th state in 1889.

SPACE MILESTONE: INTERNATIONAL SPACE STATION INHABITED: 20th ANNIVERSARY. Nov 2, 2000. On Oct 31, 2000, a *Soyuz* shuttle left with the first crew to live in the International Space Station, consisting of American commander Bill Shepherd and two Russian cosmonauts, Sergei Krikalev and Yuri Gidzenko. The flight left from the same site in central Asia where *Sputnik* was launched in 1957, beginning the Space Age. The astronauts stayed on board the International Space Station (ISS) until March 2001, when they were replaced by a crew that arrived on the shuttle *Discovery*. Currently, crew members rotate among astronauts of 16 nations; expanded to a crew of six in 2009.

SPRUCE GOOSE FLIGHT: ANNIVERSARY. Nov 2, 1947. The mammoth flying boat *Hercules*, then the world's largest airplane, was designed, built and flown (once) by Howard Hughes. Its first and only flight was about one mile and at an altitude of 70 feet over Long Beach Harbor, CA. The $25 million, 200-ton plywood craft was nicknamed the "Spruce Goose." It is now displayed at the Evergreen Aviation Museum in McMinnville, OR.

November 2020	S	M	T	W	T	F	S
	1	2	3	4	5	6	7
	8	9	10	11	12	13	14
	15	16	17	18	19	20	21
	22	23	24	25	26	27	28
	29	30					

UNITED NATIONS: INTERNATIONAL DAY TO END IMPUNITY FOR CRIMES AGAINST JOURNALISTS. Nov 2. Over the past decade, more than 700 journalists have been killed for bringing news and information to the public. But on average in the same time frame, only one in 10 murders has successfully been prosecuted to result in a conviction. In Resolution 68/163, the General Assembly proclaimed this day for Nov 2—commemorating the assassination of two French journalists in Mali on Nov 2, 2013. For info: United Nations, Dept of Public Info, New York, NY 10017. Web: www.un.org.

🎂 BIRTHDAYS TODAY

Karamo Brown, 40, television personality ("Queer Eye," "The Real World: Philadelphia"), LGBT activist, born Houston, TX, Nov 2, 1980.

Patrick Buchanan, 82, political commentator, born Washington, DC, Nov 2, 1938.

Shere Hite, 78, researcher on sexual behavior, author (*The Hite Report, Women and Love*), born St. Joseph, MO, Nov 2, 1942.

Brian Kemp, 57, Governor of Georgia (R), born Athens, GA, Nov 2, 1963.

k.d. lang, 59, singer, born Kathryn Dawn Lang at Consort, AB, Canada, Nov 2, 1961.

Stefanie Powers, 78, actress ("Hart to Hart"), born Hollywood, CA, Nov 2, 1942.

David Knapp (Dave) Stockton, 79, golfer, born San Bernardino, CA, Nov 2, 1941.

November 3 — Tuesday

DAY 308   **58 REMAINING**

AUSTIN, STEPHEN FULLER: BIRTH ANNIVERSARY. Nov 3, 1793. A principal founder of Texas, for whom its capital city was named, Austin was born at Wythe County, VA. He first visited Texas in 1821 and established a settlement there the following year, continuing a colonization project started by his father, Moses Austin. Thrown in prison when he advocated formation of a separate state (Texas still belonged to Mexico), he was freed in 1835, lost a campaign for the presidency (of the Republic of Texas) to Sam Houston in 1836 and died (while serving as Texas secretary of state) at Austin, TX, Dec 27, 1836.

AUSTRALIA: LEXUS MELBOURNE CUP. Nov 3. Flemington Racecourse, Melbourne. First run in 1861, the Cup is one of the world's great horse races—celebrated throughout Australia and a public holiday in Melbourne. The handicapped race is 3,200 meters with prize money of AU$6.2 million. Famous winners include Phar Lap (1930) and Makybe Diva (2003, 2004, 2005). Annually, the first Tuesday in November. Est attendance: 100,000. For info: Victoria Racing Club, 448 Epsom Rd, Flemington Victoria 3031, Australia. Web: www.vrc.net.au.

BRONSON, CHARLES: BIRTH ANNIVERSARY. Nov 3, 1921. Movie tough-guy Charles Bronson was born Charles Buchinsky at Ehrenfeld, PA. One of 15 children, he was raised in poverty and was working in the coal mines by age 16. He discovered acting after a stint in the army and was soon making low-budget films, usually violent. His best-known films include *The Magnificent Seven* (1960), *The Great Escape* (1963), *Death Wish* (1974) and four *Death Wish* sequels. He died at Los Angeles, CA, Sept 6, 2003.

BRYANT, WILLIAM CULLEN: BIRTH ANNIVERSARY. Nov 3, 1794. American poet ("Thanatopsis"), born at Cummington, MA. Died at New York, NY, June 12, 1878.

CANADA: NEW INUIT TERRITORY APPROVED: ANNIVERSARY. Nov 3, 1992. Canada's Inuit people voted to accept a federal land-claim package granting them control over a new territory, Nunavut, to be carved out of the existing Northwest Territories by 1999. The voting on Nov 3–5, 1992, indicated that 69 percent of the 9,648 eligible Inuit voters accepted the settlement. In exchange for the new territory, approximately 135,000 square miles, the Inuits gave up their rights to a territory of 775,000 square miles. See also: "Canada: Nunavut Independence: Anniversary" (Apr 1).

CLICHÉ DAY. Nov 3. Use clichés as much as possible today. Hey, why not? Give it a shot! Win some, lose some. You'll never know 'til you try it. Annually, Nov 3. (©2006 by WH.) For info: Thomas & Ruth Roy, Wellcat Holidays, 2418 Long Ln, Lebanon, PA 17046-1708. Phone: (717) 279-0184. E-mail: info@wellcat.com. Web: www.wellcat.com.

"DEWEY DEFEATS TRUMAN" HEADLINE: ANNIVERSARY. Nov 3, 1948. This headline in the *Chicago Tribune* notwithstanding, Harry Truman defeated Republican candidate Thomas E. Dewey for the US presidency.

DOMINICA: NATIONAL DAY. Nov 3. National holiday. Commemorates independence from Britain in 1978.

FELLER, BOB: BIRTH ANNIVERSARY. Nov 3, 1918. Baseball Hall of Fame pitcher Bob Feller was born at Van Meter, IA. In 18 MLB seasons, he played for one squad—the Cleveland Indians (1936–56)—and was an All-Star eight times. Career highlights include pitching triple crown (1940), World Series champion (1948), three no-hitters (including one on Opening Day 1940—the only Opening Day no-hitter to date), MLB strikeout king seven times and much more. He was inducted into the Baseball Hall of Fame in 1962, and the Cleveland Indians retired his jersey number (19) in his honor. Feller died Dec 15, 2010, at Cleveland, OH.

GENERAL ELECTION DAY. Nov 3. Annually, the Tuesday after the first Monday in November. Many state and local government elections are held on this day, as well as presidential and congressional elections in the appropriate years. All US congressional seats and one-third of US senatorial seats are up for election in even-numbered years. Presidential elections are held in even-numbered years that can be divided equally by four. This day is a state holiday in 12 states.

JAPAN: CULTURE DAY. Nov 3. National holiday.

MICRONESIA, FEDERATED STATES OF: INDEPENDENCE DAY. Nov 3. National holiday commemorating independence from US in 1980.

NAGURSKI, BRONKO: BIRTH ANNIVERSARY. Nov 3, 1908. Bronislau "Bronko" Nagurski, College Football Hall of Famer and charter member of the Pro Football Hall of Fame. Born at Rainy River, ON, Canada, he played football at the University of Minnesota, earning All-American honors at both tackle and fullback, and for the Chicago Bears. After retiring from football, Nagurski wrestled professionally. He died at International Falls, MN, Jan 7, 1990.

PANAMA: INDEPENDENCE DAY. Nov 3. Panama declared itself independent of Colombia in 1903.

PUBLIC TELEVISION DEBUTS: ANNIVERSARY. Nov 3, 1969. A string of local educational TV channels united on this day under the Public Broadcasting System banner. Today there are more than 350 PBS stations.

SANDWICH DAY: BIRTH ANNIVERSARY OF JOHN MONTAGUE. Nov 3, 1718. A day to recognize the inventor of the sandwich, John Montague, Fourth Earl of Sandwich, born at London, England. England's first lord of the admiralty, secretary of state for the northern department, postmaster general and the man after whom Captain James Cook named the Sandwich Islands in 1778. A rake and a gambler, he is said to have invented the sandwich as a time-saving nourishment while engaged in a 24-hour-long gambling session in 1762. He died at London, Apr 30, 1792.

SOS ADOPTED: ANNIVERSARY. Nov 3, 1906. On this date the Second International Radio Telegraphic Conference at Berlin, Germany, proposed a new wireless distress signal: SOS. After its use during the sinking of the *Titanic* in 1912, SOS became the standard distress signal at sea. No longer used as a maritime distress signal since 1999, SOS is still a widely recognized code.

SPACE MILESTONE: *SPUTNIK 2* (USSR). Nov 3, 1957. A dog named Laika became the first animal sent into space. Total weight of craft and dog was 1,121 pounds. The satellite was not capable of returning the dog to Earth, and she died when her air supply was gone. Nicknamed "Muttnik" by the American press.

WHITE, EDWARD DOUGLASS: 175th BIRTH ANNIVERSARY. Nov 3, 1845. Ninth chief justice of the US, born at Lafourche Parish, LA. During the Civil War he served in the Confederate army, after which he returned to New Orleans, LA, to practice law. Elected to the US Senate in 1891, he was appointed to the Supreme Court by President Grover Cleveland in 1894. He became chief justice under President William Taft in 1910 and served until 1921. He died at Washington, DC, May 19, 1921.

🧁 BIRTHDAYS TODAY

Adam Ant, 66, singer, born Stewart Goddard at London, England, Nov 3, 1954.

Kate Capshaw, 67, actress (*The Love Letter, How to Make an American Quilt, Indiana Jones and the Temple of Doom*), born Fort Worth, TX, Nov 3, 1953.

Michael S. Dukakis, 87, former governor of Massachusetts (D), 1988 presidential candidate, born Brookline, MA, Nov 3, 1933.

Mazie Hirono, 73, US Senator (D, Hawaii), born Fukushima, Japan, Nov 3, 1947.

Kendall Jenner, 25, model, television personality ("Keeping Up with the Kardashians"), born Los Angeles, CA, Nov 3, 1995.

Colin Kaepernick, 33, football player, born Milwaukee, WI, Nov 3, 1987.

Kathy Kinney, 66, actress ("The Drew Carey Show"), born Stevens Point, WI, Nov 3, 1954.

Dolph Lundgren, 61, actor (*A View to a Kill, Rocky IV*), born Stockholm, Sweden, Nov 3, 1959.

Dennis Miller, 67, comedian, television and radio personality ("Saturday Night Live," "The Dennis Miller Show"), born Pittsburgh, PA, Nov 3, 1953.

Evgeny Plushenko, 38, Olympic figure skater, born Volgograd, Russia, Nov 3, 1982.

Roseanne, 67, comedienne, actress ("Roseanne," *She-Devil*), born Roseanne Barr at Salt Lake City, UT, Nov 3, 1953.

Philip (Phil) Simms, 64, sportscaster, former football player, born Lebanon, KY, Nov 3, 1956.

Monica Vitti, 87, actress (*The Red Desert*), born Monica Luisa Ceciarelli at Rome, Italy, Nov 3, 1933.

Anna Wintour, 71, editor, journalist (*Vogue*), born London, England, Nov 3, 1949.

November 4 — Wednesday

DAY 309	57 REMAINING

CRONKITE, WALTER: BIRTH ANNIVERSARY. Nov 4, 1916. Legendary American broadcast journalist, Walter Leland Cronkite anchored the "CBS Evening News" from 1962 to 1981, covering such monumental events as President John Kennedy's assassination and the *Apollo 11* moon landing. A standard-bearer for exceptional

television journalism; Cronkite's integrity earned him the status as "the most trusted man in America." Born at St. Joseph, MO, Cronkite died at New York, NY, July 17, 2009.

ITALY: VICTORY DAY. Nov 4. Commemorates the signing of a WWI treaty by Austria in 1918, which resulted in the transfer of Trentino and Trieste from Austria to Italy.

KING TUT TOMB DISCOVERY: ANNIVERSARY. Nov 4, 1922. In 1922 one of the most important archaeological discoveries of modern times occurred at Luxor, Egypt. It was the tomb of Egypt's child-king, Tutankhamen, who became pharaoh at the age of nine and died, probably in the year 1352 BC, when he was 19. Perhaps the only ancient Egyptian royal tomb to have escaped plundering by grave robbers, it was discovered more than 3,000 years after Tutankhamen's death by English archaeologist Howard Carter, leader of an expedition financed by Lord Carnarvon. The priceless relics yielded by King Tut's tomb were placed in Egypt's National Museum at Cairo.

MAPPLETHORPE, ROBERT: BIRTH ANNIVERSARY. Nov 4, 1946. Born at Floral Park, NY, Mapplethorpe was one of photography's most controversial artists, known initially for his photographs of sadomasochistic rituals and later for his still lifes, nudes and portraits. Mapplethorpe died at Boston, MA, Mar 9, 1989. Exhibits of his work sparked controversy in 1989 and 1990, leading to intense political debate about the funding practices of the National Endowment for the Arts when its charter was up for renewal by Congress. An exhibition of his work at Cincinnati, OH, led to the arrest of the museum's curator, causing an additional uproar over First Amendment freedoms and obscenity issues.

MISCHIEF NIGHT. Nov 4. Observed in England, Australia and New Zealand. Nov 4, the eve of Guy Fawkes Day, is an occasion for bonfires and firecrackers to commemorate failure of the plot to blow up the Houses of Parliament Nov 5, 1605. See also: "England: Guy Fawkes Day" (Nov 5).

NATIONAL CHICKEN LADY DAY. Nov 4. Miami, FL. The Chicken Lady has helped thousands to learn the art of public speaking through her nonprofit organization the Professional Speakers Network, Inc. Each year as a thank-you, people come out and have a celebration to show their appreciation for what she has done to help them. More than 300 of them, thanks to the Chicken Lady, have published their own books. For info: Dr. Marthenia "Tina" Dupree, The Chicken Lady, PO Box 540821, Opa Locka, FL 33054. Phone: (954) 485-5100. E-mail: chickenlady@prodigy.net.

NATIONAL EASY-BAKE OVEN DAY. Nov 4. The Easy-Bake Oven is a national treasure. As a National Toy Hall of Fame inductee and pop culture icon, the Easy-Bake Oven has earned its place in the hearts of people of all ages since its release on Nov 4, 1963. Memories of the toy hold a special place in the minds of many people and it continues to inspire curiosity and creativity. Annually, Nov 4. For info: Todd Coopee, National Easy-Bake Oven Day, Studio 91, 201-190 Somerset St W, Ottawa, ON, Canada K2P 0J4. Phone: (?(613) 236-9216. E-mail: info@nationaleasybakeovenday.com. Web: https://nationaleasybakeovenday.com.

PANAMA: FLAG DAY. Nov 4. Public holiday.

November 2020	S	M	T	W	T	F	S
	1	2	3	4	5	6	7
	8	9	10	11	12	13	14
	15	16	17	18	19	20	21
	22	23	24	25	26	27	28
	29	30					

ROGERS, WILL: BIRTH ANNIVERSARY. Nov 4, 1879. William Penn Adair Rogers, American writer, actor, humorist and grassroots philosopher, born at Oologah, Indian Territory (now Oklahoma). With aviator Wiley Post, he was killed in an airplane crash near Point Barrow, AK, Aug 15, 1935. "My forefathers," he said, "didn't come over on the *Mayflower,* but they met the boat."

RUSSIA: UNITY DAY. Nov 4. Public holiday created in 2004 to commemorate the liberation of Moscow from occupying Polish troops in 1612. (Replaced Revolution Day, Nov 7, in the civic calendar.) Annually, Nov 4.

SEIZURE OF US EMBASSY IN TEHRAN: ANNIVERSARY. Nov 4, 1979. About 500 Iranians seized the US Embassy in Tehran, taking some 90 hostages, of whom 66 were Americans. They vowed to hold the hostages until the former shah, Mohammad Reza Pahlavi (in the US for medical treatments), was returned to Iran for trial. The shah died July 27, 1980, in an Egyptian military hospital near Cairo. Fourteen Americans were released in 1979 and 1980, but the remaining 52 hostages weren't released until Jan 20, 1981, after 444 days of captivity. The release occurred on America's Presidential Inauguration Day, during the hour in which the American presidency was transferred from Jimmy Carter to Ronald Reagan.

UNESCO: ANNIVERSARY. Nov 4, 1946. The United Nations Educational, Scientific, and Cultural Organization was formed.

WILL ROGERS DAY. Nov 4. Oklahoma.

🎂 BIRTHDAYS TODAY

Laura Bush, 74, former first lady, wife of George W. Bush, 43rd president of the US, born Midland, TX, Nov 4, 1946.

Sean "Diddy" Combs, 50, rapper, music and fashion executive, actor, born New York, NY, Nov 4, 1970.

Kathy Griffin, 54, comedienne, actress ("Kathy Griffin: My Life on the D List"), born Chicago, IL, Nov 4, 1966.

Devin Hester, 38, former football player, born Riviera Beach, FL, Nov 4, 1982.

Ralph Macchio, 58, actor (*The Karate Kid*), born Huntington, NY, Nov 4, 1962.

Andrea McArdle, 57, singer, actress (Tony for *Annie*), born Philadelphia, PA, Nov 4, 1963.

Matthew McConaughey, 51, actor (Oscar for *Dallas Buyers Club*; "True Detective," *The Lincoln Lawyer, A Time to Kill*), born Uvalde, TX, Nov 4, 1969.

Orlando Pace, 45, Hall of Fame football player, born Sandusky, OH, Nov 4, 1975.

Markie Post, 70, actress ("Chicago P.D.," "Night Court," "Hearts Afire"), born Palo Alto, CA, Nov 4, 1950.

Loretta Swit, 83, actress ("M*A*S*H"), born Passaic, NJ, Nov 4, 1937.

November 5 — Thursday

DAY 310	56 REMAINING

DEBS, EUGENE VICTOR: BIRTH ANNIVERSARY. Nov 5, 1855. American politician, first president of the American Railway Union, founder of the Social Democratic Party of America and Socialist Party candidate for president of the US in 1904, 1908, 1912 and 1920; sentenced to 10-year prison term in 1918 (for sedition) and pardoned by President Warren Harding in 1921. Debs was born at Terre Haute, IN, and died at Elmhurst, IL, Oct 20, 1926.

DURANT, WILL: BIRTH ANNIVERSARY. Nov 5, 1885. American author and popularizer of history and philosophy. Among his books: *The Story of Philosophy* and *The Story of Civilization* (a 10-volume series of which the last four were coauthored by his wife, Ariel). Born at North Adams, MA, and died Nov 7, 1981, at Los Angeles, CA.

EL SALVADOR: DAY OF THE FIRST SHOUT FOR INDEPENDENCE. Nov 5. National holiday. Commemorates the first Central American battle for independence in 1811.

ENGLAND: GUY FAWKES DAY. Nov 5. United Kingdom. Anniversary of the "Gunpowder Plot." Conspirators planned to blow up the Houses of Parliament and King James I, Nov 5, 1605. Twenty barrels of gunpowder, which they had secreted in a cellar under Parliament, were discovered on the night of Nov 4, the very eve of the intended explosion, and the conspirators were arrested. They were tried and convicted, and on Jan 31, 1606, eight (including Guy Fawkes) were beheaded and their heads displayed on pikes at London Bridge. Though there were at least 11 conspirators, Guy Fawkes is most remembered. In 1606 the Parliament, which was to have been annihilated, enacted a law establishing Nov 5 as a day of public thanksgiving. It is still observed, and on the night of Nov 5 the whole country lights up with bonfires and celebration. "Guys" are burned in effigy and the old verses repeated: "Remember, remember the fifth of November,/Gunpowder treason and plot;/I see no reason why Gunpowder Treason/Should ever be forgot."

FIRST SHATTERED BACKBOARD: ANNIVERSARY. Nov 5, 1946. Chuck Connors of the Boston Celtics became the first NBA player to shatter a backboard, doing so during the pregame warm-up at Boston Garden. Connors also played major league baseball with the Brooklyn Dodgers and the Chicago Cubs and gained fame as star of the television series "The Rifleman."

FORT HOOD KILLINGS: ANNIVERSARY. Nov 5, 2009. A shooting rampage at Fort Hood, TX, left 13 dead and wounded 30 others. The convicted gunman, Major Nidal Hasan, was a psychiatrist stationed at the army base. Initial reports speculated that the shooting was rooted in radical Islamic beliefs.

LEIGH, VIVIEN: BIRTH ANNIVERSARY. Nov 5, 1913. Born Vivien Mary Hartley at Darjeeling, India, Leigh stunned Hollywood by her brilliant performance as Scarlett O'Hara in *Gone with the Wind* (1939). She received an Academy Award for that role and again for her portrayal of Blanche DuBois in *A Streetcar Named Desire* (1951). Midcareer, Leigh battled an extreme bipolar disorder that affected her ability to work and her marriage to fellow actor Lawrence Olivier; they divorced in 1960. Suffering from tuberculosis since the 1940s, she died from the disease on July 8, 1967, at London, England. George Cukor called her "a consummate actress, hampered by beauty."

LOEWY, RAYMOND: BIRTH ANNIVERSARY. Nov 5, 1893. Raymond Fernand Loewy, the "father of streamlining," an inventor, engineer and industrial designer whose ideas changed the look of 20th-century life, was born at Paris, France. His designs are evident in almost every area of modern life—the US Postal Service logo; the president's airplane, *Air Force One*; and streamlined automobiles, trains, refrigerators and pens. "Between two products equal in price, function and quality," he said, "the better looking will outsell the other." Loewy died at Monte Carlo, Monaco, July 14, 1986.

MAXWELL, ROBERT: DEATH ANNIVERSARY. Nov 5, 1991. Born Jan Ludwig Hoch in 1923 to a poor farm family in the Carpathian Mountains of what was then Czechoslovakia, Maxwell became a billionaire with a media empire that included TV stations in France, the Macmillan Publishing Company in the US, newspapers in Hungary and the former East Germany, MTV Europe, the only official English-language newspaper in China and two of the biggest tabloids in the English-speaking world: New York's *Daily News* and London's *Daily Mirror*. Maxwell died after falling overboard from his yacht near the Canary Islands. After his death, his empire was found to be in significant financial disrepair.

MCCREA, JOEL: BIRTH ANNIVERSARY. Nov 5, 1905. American actor Joel McCrea was born at South Pasadena, CA. His more than 80 films include *Wells Fargo* (1937), *Union Pacific* (1939), *Sullivan's Travels* (1941) and *Foreign Correspondent* (1940). He died Oct 20, 1990, at Los Angeles, CA.

"THE NAT KING COLE SHOW" TV PREMIERE: ANNIVERSARY. Nov 5, 1956. Popular pianist and singer Nat King Cole hosted his own variety show for NBC—the first time an African American had done so. The Nelson Riddle Orchestra and the Randy Van Horne Singers appeared as regulars. Despite its featuring such stars as Tony Bennett, Ella Fitzgerald and Peggy Lee, sponsors refused to back the show, crippling it and prompting Cole to quip, "Madison Avenue is afraid of the dark." The last episode aired Dec 17, 1957.

NATIONAL MEN MAKE DINNER DAY. Nov 5. While 99 percent of men cook on a regular basis, this is one day set aside for men who usually avoid the kitchen. Non-cooking men are encouraged to have some fun and whip up a special meal for the family. In the true spirit of Men Make Dinner Day, barbecues are not allowed. Annually, the first Thursday in November. For info: Sandy Sharkey. E-mail: sandysharkey@rocketmail.com. Web: www.menmakedinnerday.com.

***NEW YORK WEEKLY JOURNAL* FIRST ISSUE: ANNIVERSARY.** Nov 5, 1733. John Peter Zenger, colonial American printer and journalist, published the first issue of the *New York Weekly Journal* newspaper. He was arrested and imprisoned on Nov 17, 1734, for libel. The trial remains an important landmark in the history of the struggle for freedom of the press. See also: "Zenger, John Peter: Arrest Anniversary" (Nov 17).

RETURN DAY. Nov 5. Georgetown, DE. The day when officially tabulated election returns are read from the balcony of Georgetown's redbrick, Greek Revival courthouse to the throngs of voters assembled below. Always the second day after a general election. An official "half-holiday" in Sussex County.

ROGERS, ROY: BIRTH ANNIVERSARY. Nov 5, 1911. Known as the "King of the Cowboys," Rogers was born Leonard Slye at Cincinnati, OH. He made his acting debut in *Under Western Stars* in 1935 and later hosted his own TV series, "The Roy Rogers Show," in 1951; his wife, Dale Evans, was his leading lady. Sitting atop their horses, Trigger and Buttermilk, Rogers and Evans serenaded their audience at the conclusion of each show with "Happy Trails to You." Rogers died at Apple Valley, CA, on July 6, 1998. See also: "'The Roy Rogers Show' TV Premiere: Anniversary" (Dec 30).

TARBELL, IDA M.: BIRTH ANNIVERSARY. Nov 5, 1857. American writer born at Erie County, PA. She edited the muckraking journal *McClure's Magazine*, which exposed the political and industrial corruption of the day and emphasized the need for reform. Died at Bethel, CT, Jan 6, 1944.

UNITED NATIONS: WORLD TSUNAMI AWARENESS DAY. Nov 5. First observed in 2016, this day seeks to acknowledge the destruction of tsunamis and to encourage preparedness and the implementation of early-warning systems. Also seeks to encourage the "Building Back Better" philosophy of reconstruction, which also saves lives. (Res 70/203 of Dec 22, 2015.) Annually, Nov 5. For info: United Nations. Web: www.un.org.

🎂 BIRTHDAYS TODAY

Bryan Adams, 61, singer, songwriter, photographer, born Vancouver, BC, Canada, Nov 5, 1959.

Tony Evers, 69, Governor of Wisconsin (D), born Plymouth, WI, Nov 5, 1951.

Arthur (Art) Garfunkel, 79, singer (Simon and Garfunkel), actor (*Carnal Knowledge*), born Forest Hills, NY, Nov 5, 1941.

Kevin Jonas, 33, singer (The Jonas Brothers), actor, born Teaneck, NJ, Nov 5, 1987.

November 2020	S	M	T	W	T	F	S
	1	2	3	4	5	6	7
	8	9	10	11	12	13	14
	15	16	17	18	19	20	21
	22	23	24	25	26	27	28
	29	30					

Javy Lopez, 50, former baseball player, born Ponce, Puerto Rico, Nov 5, 1970.

Corin Nemec, 49, actor ("Stargate SG-1," "Parker Lewis Can't Lose"), born Little Rock, AR, Nov 5, 1971.

Tatum O'Neal, 57, actress (Oscar for *Paper Moon*; *The Bad News Bears*), born Los Angeles, CA, Nov 5, 1963.

Sam Rockwell, 52, actor (Oscar for *Three Billboards Outside Ebbing, Missouri*; *Moon, Confessions of a Dangerous Mind*), born Daly City, CA, Nov 5, 1968.

Elke Sommer, 79, actress (*A Shot in the Dark*, *The Prize*), born Elke Schletze at Berlin, Germany, Nov 5, 1941.

Jerry Stackhouse, 46, former basketball player, born Kinston, NC, Nov 5, 1974.

Chris Sununu, 46, Governor of New Hampshire (R), born Salem, NH, Nov 5, 1974.

Tilda Swinton, 60, actress (Oscar for *Michael Clayton*; *Only Lovers Left Alive*, *The Deep End*), born London, England, Nov 5, 1960.

Bill Walton, 68, sportscaster, Hall of Fame basketball player, born Mesa, CA, Nov 5, 1952.

Gerry "Bubba" Watson, 42, golfer, born Bagdad, FL, Nov 5, 1978.

Geoffrey Wolff, 83, author (*The Duke of Deception*, *The Age of Consent*), born Los Angeles, CA, Nov 5, 1937.

November 6 — Friday

DAY 311   **55 REMAINING**

COLORADO COUNTRY CHRISTMAS GIFT SHOW. Nov 6–8. Denver Mart, Denver, CO. More than 450 booths of arts, crafts, holiday gifts and specialty foods. Learn culinary secrets from local chefs at the Cooking for the Holidays program. Children enjoy Hammond's Candy Land, Santa Claus and a model train display. Est attendance: 25,000. For info: Kim Peck, PO Box 2815, Kirkland, WA 98083-2815. Phone: (800) 521-7469. E-mail: denver@showcaseevents.org. Web: www.ColoradoCountryChristmas.com.

CONNIFF, RAY: BIRTH ANNIVERSARY. Nov 6, 1916. Born at Attleboro, MA, Conniff was a trombone player who discovered a talent for arranging and worked with many of the greatest names of the 1950s: Mitch Miller, Johnny Mathis, Rosemary Clooney, Frankie Laine and Johnnie Ray. His use of big bands and choirs as background established a uniquely distinctive sound, with the voices "singing" certain instrumentals in parts and harmony. In 1959 his Ray Conniff Singers scored a popular hit with "Somewhere My Love," a lyricized version of the instrumental "Lara's Theme" from the film *Doctor Zhivago*. He died at Escondido, CA, on Oct 12, 2002.

"GOOD MORNING AMERICA" TV PREMIERE: 45th ANNIVERSARY. Nov 6, 1975. This ABC morning program, set in a living room, is a mixture of news reports, features and interviews with news makers and people of interest. It was the first program to compete with NBC's "The Today Show" and initially aired as "A.M. America." Hosts have included David Hartman, Nancy Dussault, Sandy Hill,

Charles Gibson, Joan Lunden, Lisa McRee, Kevin Newman and Diane Sawyer.

LOMBROSO, CESARE: BIRTH ANNIVERSARY. Nov 6, 1835. Italian founder of criminology, born at Verona, Italy. A professor of psychiatry, Lombroso believed that criminality could be identified with certain physical types of people. He died at Turin, Italy, Oct 19, 1909.

"MEET THE PRESS" TV PREMIERE: ANNIVERSARY. Nov 6, 1947. "Meet the Press" holds the distinction of being the oldest program on TV. It originally debuted on radio in 1945. The show has changed its format little since it began: a well-known guest (usually a politician) is questioned on current, relevant issues by a panel of journalists. The moderators have been Martha Rountree, Ned Brooks, Lawrence E. Spivak, Bill Monroe, Roger Mudd, Marvin Kalb, Chris Wallace, Garrick Utley, Tim Russert, Tom Brokaw, David Gregory and Chuck Todd.

MOROCCO: ANNIVERSARY OF THE GREEN MARCH. Nov 6. National holiday. Commemorates the march into the Spanish Sahara in 1975 to claim the land for Morocco.

NAISMITH, JAMES: BIRTH ANNIVERSARY. Nov 6, 1861. Born at Almonte, ON, Canada, Naismith was an athlete who became a physical education instructor and administrator. At a YMCA at Springfield, MA, he invented the game of "basket ball" out of the need for a safe and fun indoor winter sport. Naismith died on Nov 28, 1939, at Lawrence, KS, where he had been a physical education professor from 1917 until 1937. The Naismith Memorial Basketball Hall of Fame was established at Springfield in 1959, and James Naismith was the first inductee.

NATIONAL FARM TOY SHOW. Nov 6–8, Dyersville, IA. The "granddaddy" of farm toy shows, held since 1978. This slice of Americana features farm toys and farm collectibles as far as the eye can see— and much more. Annually, the first full weekend in November. Est attendance: 6,000. For info: National Farm Toy Museum, 1110 16th Ave Ct SE, Dyersville, IA 52040. Phone: (800) 533-8293. Web: www.toyfarmer.com.

NATIONAL MEDICAL SCIENCE LIAISON (MSL) AWARENESS AND APPRECIATION DAY. Nov 6. Created to educate the public on the role of medical science liaisons and what they do across the pharmaceutical, medical device and biotechnology industries. Annually, the first Friday in November. For info: Dr. Erin Albert, Pharm LLC, PO Box 335, Fishers, IN 46038. Phone: (317) 698-3202. E-mail: pharmllc@gmail.com.

NICHOLS, MIKE: BIRTH ANNIVERSARY. Nov 6, 1931. Born Michael Igor Peschkowsky at Berlin, Germany, renowned director/producer Mike Nichols legally changed his surname in 1939 after immigrating to the US from Nazi Germany. Nichols's career began as a comedian with partner Elaine May, but he quickly found his niche directing. One of the few entertainers to ever win an EGOT (at least one Emmy, Grammy, Oscar and Tony Award). Nichols's famous works include the Broadway play *The Odd Couple* and groundbreaking Hollywood films *Who's Afraid of Virginia Woolf?*, *The Graduate* and *The Birdcage*. Nichols died Nov 19, 2014, at New York, NY.

PADEREWSKI, IGNACY JAN: BIRTH ANNIVERSARY. Nov 6, 1860. Polish composer, pianist, patriot born at Kurylowka, Podolia, Poland. He died at New York, NY, June 29, 1941. When Poland fell into the hands of the Soviets after WWII, his family decided he would remain buried in Arlington National Cemetery. In May 1963 President John F. Kennedy dedicated a plaque to Paderewski's memory and declared that the pianist would rest in Arlington until Poland was free. Paderewski's remains were returned to his native country on June 29, 1992, the 51st anniversary of his death, after Poland held its first parliamentary election following its independence from the Soviet Union.

"THE PHIL DONAHUE SHOW" TV PREMIERE: ANNIVERSARY. Nov 6, 1967. The first talk show with audience participation went on the air on this date at Dayton, OH. The first guest interviewed by host Phil Donahue was atheist Madalyn Murray O'Hair. In 1970 the program went national; it moved to Chicago, IL, in 1974 and to New York in 1985. In later years the program was titled "Donahue." After winning 19 Emmy Awards, the show left daytime TV in 1996.

Phil Donahue briefly aired a show on the MSNBC cable network, but it was canceled after six months on Feb 25, 2003.

SAMOA: ARBOR DAY. Nov 6. The first Friday in November is observed as Arbor Day in Samoa (formerly Western Samoa).

SAXOPHONE DAY (ADOLPHE SAX BIRTH ANNIVERSARY). Nov 6. A day to recognize the birth anniversary of Adolphe Sax, Belgian musician and inventor of the saxophone and the saxotromba. Born at Dinant, Belgium, in 1814, Antoine Joseph Sax, later known as Adolphe, was the eldest of 11 children of a musical instrument builder. Sax contributed an entire family of brass wind instruments for band and orchestra use. He was accorded fame and great wealth, but business misfortunes led to bankruptcy. Sax died in poverty at Paris, France, Feb 7, 1894.

SOUSA, JOHN PHILIP: BIRTH ANNIVERSARY. Nov 6, 1854. American composer and band conductor, remembered for stirring marches such as "The Stars and Stripes Forever," "Semper Fidelis" and "El Capitan," born at Washington, DC. Died at Reading, PA, Mar 6, 1932. See also: "'The Stars and Stripes Forever' Day" (May 14).

SWEDEN: GUSTAVUS ADOLPHUS DAY. Nov 6. Honors Sweden's king and military leader killed in 1632.

UNITED NATIONS: INTERNATIONAL DAY FOR PREVENTING THE EXPLOITATION OF THE ENVIRONMENT IN WAR AND ARMED CONFLICT. Nov 6. A day calling attention to the irreparable damage to ecosystems and natural resources caused by armed conflict. For info: United Nations, Dept of Public Info, New York, NY 10017. Web: www.un.org.

🎂 BIRTHDAYS TODAY

Sally Field, 74, actress ("Brothers & Sisters," Oscars for *Norma Rae* and *Places in the Heart*; Emmy for *Sybil*), born Pasadena, CA, Nov 6, 1946.

Nigel Havers, 71, actor (*Chariots of Fire, Empire of the Sun*), born London, England, Nov 6, 1949.

Ethan Hawke, 50, actor (*Boyhood, Training Day, Before Sunrise*), novelist, born Austin, TX, Nov 6, 1970.

Lance Kerwin, 60, actor ("James at 15"), born Newport Beach, CA, Nov 6, 1960.

Zoe McLellan, 46, actress ("NCIS: New Orleans," "JAG"), born La Jolla, CA, Nov 6, 1974.

Thandie Newton, 48, actress ("Westworld," *Crash, Mission: Impossible II*), born London, England, Nov 6, 1972.

Rebecca Romijn, 48, model, actress (*X-Men, Femme Fatale*, "Ugly Betty"), born Berkeley, CA, Nov 6, 1972.

Kelly Rutherford, 52, actress ("Melrose Place," "Gossip Girl"), born Elizabethtown, KY, Nov 6, 1968.

Maria Owings Shriver, 65, broadcast journalist, former first lady of California, born Chicago, IL, Nov 6, 1955.

Emma Stone, 32, actress (Oscar and Golden Globe for *La La Land*; *Birdman, The Amazing Spider-Man*, born Scottsdale, AZ, Nov 6, 1988.

Colson Whitehead, 51, author (Pulitzer Prize and National Book Award for *The Underground Railroad*; *The Intuitionist, John Henry Days*), born New York, NY, Nov 6, 1969.

November 7 — Saturday

DAY 312   **54 REMAINING**

BANGLADESH: SOLIDARITY DAY. Nov 7. National holiday. Commemorates a coup in 1975.

BATTLE OF TIPPECANOE: ANNIVERSARY. Nov 7, 1811. William Henry Harrison, governor of the Indiana Territory, defeated the Shawnee under Tecumseh at the Battle of Tippecanoe and burned their town. Harrison later ran for the presidency under the slogan "Tippecanoe and Tyler, Too." (John Tyler was his vice president.)

BAYOU BACCHANAL. Nov 7. New Orleans, LA. A Caribbean festival on the first Saturday in November, featuring food, steelpan music and a masquerading parade. For info: Bayou Bacchanal, 147 Carondelet St, Box 1091, New Orleans, LA 70130. Phone: (504) 220-8441. E-mail: president@bayoubacchanal.org. Web: www.bayoubacchanal.org.

CAMUS, ALBERT: BIRTH ANNIVERSARY. Nov 7, 1913. The French writer and philosopher, winner of the Nobel Prize in Literature in 1957, was born at Mondavi, Algeria. Camus is renowned for his novels, particularly *The Stranger* (1942), which proffered themes—widely reflective of the feelings of the postwar intellectual—of the isolation of man and the estrangement of the individual from himself. With Jean-Paul Sartre, Camus is seen as the leading existential novelist of the era, although he rejected that or any other label. Camus was killed in an automobile accident at Paris, France, Jan 4, 1960.

CANADIAN PACIFIC RAILWAY: TRANSCONTINENTAL COMPLETION: ANNIVERSARY. Nov 7, 1885. At 9:30 AM the last spike was driven at Craigellachie, British Columbia, completing the Canadian Pacific Railway's 2,980-mile transcontinental railroad track between Montreal, QC, in the east and Port Moody, BC, in the west.

CURIE, MARIE SKLODOWSKA: BIRTH ANNIVERSARY. Nov 7, 1867. Polish chemist and physicist, born at Warsaw, Poland. Curie was the first woman in Europe to receive a doctorate, the first woman to teach and later be appointed a professorship at the Sorbonne, the first woman to receive a Nobel Prize (Physics, 1903—with her husband), and the first person to earn a second Nobel Prize (Chemistry, 1911). Curie remains the only person to have been awarded a Nobel Prize in two separate scientific categories. Curie's work continues to have a lasting impact on nuclear physics and chemistry. She died near Sallanches, France, July 4, 1934.

"FACE THE NATION" TV PREMIERE: ANNIVERSARY. Nov 7, 1954. The CBS counterpart to NBC's "Meet the Press," this show employs a similar format: panelists interview a well-known guest. In 1983 the panel was changed to include experts in addition to journalists. Though usually produced at Washington, DC, the show occasionally interviews people elsewhere (such as Khrushchev in Moscow in 1957).

FIRST BLACK GOVERNOR ELECTED: ANNIVERSARY. Nov 7, 1989. L. Douglas Wilder was elected governor of Virginia, becoming the first elected black governor in US history. Wilder had previously served as lieutenant governor of Virginia, becoming the first black elected to statewide office in the South since Reconstruction.

GREAT OCTOBER SOCIALIST REVOLUTION: ANNIVERSARY. Nov 7, 1917. The Bolshevik Revolution began at Petrograd, Russia, on the evening of Nov 6, 1917. A new government headed by Vladimir Lenin took office the following day under the name Council of People's Commissars. Leon Trotsky was commissar for foreign affairs, and Joseph Stalin became commissar of national minorities. Formerly a holiday until canceled by the Russian Duma in 2004. According to the old Russian calendar, the revolution took place Oct 25, 1917. Soviet calendar reform caused the observance to fall on Nov 7 (Gregorian).

NATIONAL BISON DAY. Nov 7. A celebration of the American bison, the US's official national mammal (per 2016's National Bison Legacy Act). Annually, the first Saturday in November.

NIXON'S "LAST" PRESS CONFERENCE: ANNIVERSARY. Nov 7, 1962. Richard M. Nixon, having been narrowly defeated in his bid for the presidency by John F. Kennedy in the 1960 election, returned to politics two years later as a candidate for governor of California in the election of Nov 6, 1962. Defeated again (this time by incumbent governor Edmund G. Brown), Nixon held his "last" press conference with assembled reporters at Los Angeles, CA, at mid-morning the next day, at which he said: "Just think how much you're going to be missing. You won't have Nixon to kick around anymore, because, gentlemen, this is my last press conference."

ORIGINAL TERLINGUA INTERNATIONAL FRANK X. TOLBERT–WICK FOWLER CHAMPIONSHIP CHILI COOK-OFF. Nov 7. Terlingua, TX. 54th annual. One of two chili cook-offs held in this former mining-ghost town of southwest Texas. More than a bowl of red—includes music, golf, margaritas, Ugly Hat Contest and more. Benefits the South Texas Chapter of the ALS Association. Annually, the first Saturday of November (judging), with preliminary events two days before. For info: Original Terlingua International Championship Chili Cook-Off. Web: www.abowlofred.com.

PUMPKIN DESTRUCTION DAY. Nov 7. The Rock Ranch, The Rock, GA, and nationally. A day to encourage the public to recycle their leftover Halloween jack-o'-lanterns through fun destruction methods. The Rock Ranch takes leftover pumpkins from the public, smashes them in unbelievable ways, then composts them. Thousands of pumpkins are smashed and kept out of landfills. Includes "The Pumpkin Drop" (dropping pumpkins from 40-foot lift cranes), Gallagher-style smashing with wooden mallets, pumpkin bowling, pumpkin reverse darts, bombing them out of airplanes, shooting them out of a giant cannon and crushing them (and cars) with professional monster trucks. Annually, the first Saturday after Halloween. For info: Adam Pugh, The Rock Ranch, 5020 Barnesville Hwy, The Rock, GA 30285. Phone: (770) 633-4105. E-mail: adampugh@therockranch.com. Web: www.therockranch.com.

REPUBLICAN SYMBOL: ANNIVERSARY. Nov 7, 1874. Thomas Nast used an elephant to represent the Republican Party in a satirical cartoon in *Harper's Weekly*. Today the elephant is still a well-recognized symbol for the Republican Party in political cartoons.

ROOSEVELT ELECTED TO FOURTH TERM: ANNIVERSARY. Nov 7, 1944. Defeating Thomas Dewey, Franklin D. Roosevelt became the first, and only, person elected to four terms as president of the US. Roosevelt was inaugurated the following Jan 20 but died in office Apr 12, 1945, serving only 53 days of his fourth term.

RUSSIA: REVOLUTION DAY. Nov 7. Formerly a national holiday in Russia and Ukraine, it was canceled by the Russian Duma in 2004. Still observed unofficially by some of the population. Commemorates the Great Socialist Revolution, which occurred in October 1917 under the Old Style calendar.

SADIE HAWKINS DAY. Nov 7. Old-time observance in the United States, usually on the first Saturday in November. Tradition established in "Li'l Abner" comic strip in 1930s by cartoonist Al Capp: when women and girls are encouraged to take the initiative in inviting the man or boy of their choice for a date. A similar tradition is associated with Feb 29 in leap years.

November 2020	S	M	T	W	T	F	S
	1	2	3	4	5	6	7
	8	9	10	11	12	13	14
	15	16	17	18	19	20	21
	22	23	24	25	26	27	28
	29	30					

SUTHERLAND, DAME JOAN: BIRTH ANNIVERSARY. Nov 7, 1926. Born to Scottish parents at Sydney, Australia, Sutherland began her professional career as a singer at the age of 18. She rose through the ranks of the opera world, gaining a reputation as one of the greatest sopranos of all time, with a range able to reach coloratura with ease. She revitalized the bel canto repertory and style of opera in a career that spanned decades. Sutherland was dubbed "La Stupenda" by the Italian media, and Queen Elizabeth II made her a Dame Commander of the Order of the British Empire in 1978. She died Oct 11, 2010, at Les Avants, Switzerland.

TERLINGUA INTERNATIONAL CHILI CHAMPIONSHIP. Nov 7. Rancho CASI de los Chisos, Terlingua, TX. 54th annual. One of two chili-making championships held in the picturesque former mining town of Terlingua. The granddaddy of all chili cook-offs is the ultimate celebration of chili. The first Saturday in November is the actual day of the Terlingua International Chili Championship Cook-Off, with celebrations starting the Wednesday before. Cooks competing in the championship must have qualified and received an invitation. For info: Chili Appreciation Society International, Inc. Web: www.casichili.net.

USS *NEW YORK* COMMISSIONED: ANNIVERSARY. Nov 7, 2009. On this date Navy Secretary Ray Mabus officially commissioned the state-of-the-art amphibious transport dock. Six thousand spectators turned out for the ceremony at New York City's Intrepid Sea-Air-Space Museum. The bow of the $1 billion warship contains 7¾ short tons of steel salvaged from the World Trade Center after its destruction in the terrorist attack of 9/11.

VERBOORT SAUSAGE AND KRAUT DINNER. Nov 7. Visitation Parish, Forest Grove, OR. 86th annual event features crafts, bingo, raffles, beer garden, local produce, home-baked goods and, of course, famous Verboort sausage and kraut. Annually, the first Saturday in November. Est attendance: 8,000. For info: Visitation B.V.M. Catholic Church, 4285 NW Visitation Rd, Forest Grove, OR 97116. Phone: (503) 357-6990. Web: www.verboort.org/dinner.

🎂 BIRTHDAYS TODAY

José Díaz-Balart, 60, anchor, journalist ("Noticiero Telemundo," "NBC Nightly News"), born Fort Lauderdale, FL, Nov 7, 1960.

Rio Ferdinand, 42, former soccer player, born Peckham, England, Nov 7, 1978.

Keith Lockhart, 61, Boston Pops conductor, born Poughkeepsie, NY, Nov 7, 1959.

Jeremy London, 48, actor ("I'll Fly Away," "Party of Five"), born San Diego, CA, Nov 7, 1972.

Lorde, 24, singer (Grammy for "Royals"), born Ella Marija Lani Yelich-O'Connor at Takapuna, New Zealand, Nov 7, 1996.

Joni Mitchell, 77, singer, songwriter, born Roberta Joan Anderson at McLeod, AB, Canada, Nov 7, 1943.

Lucas Neff, 35, actor ("Raising Hope"), born Chicago, IL, Nov 7, 1985.

Barry Newman, 82, actor ("Petrocelli," *Vanishing Point*), born Boston, MA, Nov 7, 1938.

Johnny Rivers, 78, singer, born John Ramistella at New York, NY, Nov 7, 1942.

Nadezhda Tolokonnikova, 31, political activist, musician (Pussy Riot), born Norilsk, USSR (now Russia), Nov 7, 1989.

November 8 — Sunday

DAY 313   **53 REMAINING**

ABET AND AID PUNSTERS DAY. Nov 8. Laugh instead of groan at incredibly dreadful puns. All-time greatest triple pun: "Though he's not very humble, there's no police like Holmes," from the register of worst puns of Punsters Unlimited. (Originated by Earl Harris and William Rabe.)

BARNARD, CHRISTIAAN: BIRTH ANNIVERSARY. Nov 8, 1922. Pioneering heart surgeon, born at Beaufort West, South Africa. Barnard performed the first human heart transplant on Dec 3, 1967, after years of practicing the procedure, mainly on dogs. The patient, Louis Washkansky, lived for 18 days before dying from an infection. Today heart transplants are performed regularly and with good success. Barnard died at Paphos, Cyprus, Sept 2, 2001, of heart failure.

COOK SOMETHING BOLD AND PUNGENT DAY. Nov 8. Especially for those of us who have tightly closed up the house against chilly weather for the next six months. Now is the time to create the heavenly, homey odor of pungently bold cooking. Don't forget the sauerkraut and garlic! (©2006 by WH.) For info: Thomas & Ruth Roy, Wellcat Holidays, 2418 Long Ln, Lebanon, PA 17046. Phone: (717) 279-0184. E-mail: info@wellcat.com. Web: www.wellcat.com.

CORTÉS MEETS MOCTEZUMA: ANNIVERSARY. Nov 8, 1519. After landing on the Yucatán Peninsula in February, Hernán Cortés led 600 Spanish troops and around 1,000 indigenous enemies of the Aztecs into the interior of Mexico to Tenochtitlan, the Aztec capital. Cortés met Aztec emperor Moctezuma on this date. Moctezuma initially received the Spanish peacefully in hope of buying time to scrutinize and ultimately defeat the invaders. His gamble failed and within two years Cortés had conquered Mexico.

GELLHORN, MARTHA: BIRTH ANNIVERSARY. Nov 8, 1908. Pioneering female war correspondent who covered more than a dozen wars, from the Spanish Civil War to Vietnam. She was the author of numerous nonfiction and fiction works. She was married to Ernest Hemingway from 1940 to 1945 when both were covering WWII. Born at St. Louis, MO, Gellhorn died at London, England, Feb 15, 1998.

HALLEY, EDMUND: BIRTH ANNIVERSARY. Nov 8, 1656. (Old Style date.) Astronomer and mathematician born at London, England. Astronomer Royal, 1721–42. Died at Greenwich, England, Jan 14, 1742 (OS). He observed the great comet of 1682 (now named for him), first conceived its periodicity and wrote in his *Synopsis of Comet Astronomy*: "I may venture to foretell that this Comet will return again in the year 1758." It did, and Edmund Halley's memory is kept alive by the once-every-generation appearance of Halley's comet. There have been 28 recorded appearances of this comet since 240 BC. Average time between appearances is 76 years. Halley's comet is next expected to be visible in 2061.

HOPE DIAMOND MAILED TO SMITHSONIAN: ANNIVERSARY. Nov 8, 1958. The world's most famous blue diamond (at 45.52 carats, the largest dark blue diamond) was donated to the Smithsonian Institution by famed New York jeweler Harry Winston on this date. The priceless gem was sent via registered mail (postage $2.44, but insurance more than $140) after one of Winston's employees rode to the post office with it on the New York subway. The postal carrier delivered it to the Smithsonian on Nov 10 amid great fanfare. The Hope was rumored to be cursed, as it may have originally been part of a diamond stolen during the bloody French Revolution, but the curse has been debunked for the most part.

MITCHELL, MARGARET: BIRTH ANNIVERSARY. Nov 8, 1900. American novelist who won a Pulitzer Prize (1937) for her only book, *Gone with the Wind*, a romantic novel about the Civil War and Reconstruction. *Gone with the Wind* sold about 10 million copies and was translated into 30 languages. Born at Atlanta, GA, Mitchell died there after being struck by an automobile Aug 16, 1949.

MONTANA: ADMISSION DAY: ANNIVERSARY. Nov 8. Became 41st state in 1889.

MOON PHASE: LAST QUARTER. Nov 8. Moon enters Last Quarter phase at 8:46 AM, EST.

MOUNT HOLYOKE COLLEGE FOUNDED: ANNIVERSARY. Nov 8, 1837. The first college for women in the US was founded as Mount Holyoke Seminary in 1837 at South Hadley, MA. While many colleges for women became coeducational institutions in the 1970s and 1980s, Mount Holyoke remains a women's college.

PAGE, PATTI: BIRTH ANNIVERSARY. Nov 8, 1927. Singer Patti Page's sugary, adult pop sound danced effortlessly on the line between traditional vocal country and easy listening, and early hits like "The Tennessee Waltz" (1950) and "(How Much Is That) Doggie in the Window" (1953) became standards of her lengthy career as a performer. Page sold millions of records in the 1950s—she was the top female singer of that decade—and while the explosion of rock and roll slowed her down, she continued to record and perform throughout the next several decades. Born Clara Ann Fowler at Claremore, OK, she died on Jan 1, 2013, at Encinitas, CA.

RORSCHACH, HERMANN: BIRTH ANNIVERSARY. Nov 8, 1884. Psychiatrist born at Zurich, Switzerland, who used his youthful interest in art and sketching to create the unusual and controversial inkblot test that now bears his name. In 1918 Rorschach began showing his patients inkblots on cards—created at random—and asked for their interpretations to gain insight into their unconscious. Rorschach, a psychoanalyst, continued his experimentation before publishing a comprehensive volume of his findings in 1921. He died Apr 2, 1922.

SHAKESPEARE AUTHORSHIP MYSTERY DAY. Nov 8. What's in a name? Maybe a hidden identity. Shakespeare Authorship Mystery Day celebrates the world's greatest literary and historical "whodunit." People have long remarked on the strange disconnect between the life of the provincial grain dealer from Stratford and the supremely literate, courtly, political plays and poetry published under the name William Shakespeare. Join Mark Twain, Charlie Chaplin, Sigmund Freud and former Supreme Court justices Sandra Day O'Connor and John Paul Stevens in wondering who wrote Shakespeare. Annually, Nov 8, the anniversary of the publication of the First Folio. For info: President, Shakespeare Oxford Fellowship, PO Box 66083, Auburndale, MA 02466. E-mail: info@shakespeareauthorshipmysteryday.org. Web: www.shakespeareauthorshipmysteryday.org.

SHAKESPEARE'S FIRST FOLIO PUBLISHED: ANNIVERSARY. Nov 8, 1623. Printer Isaac Jaggard registered the first collected works of William Shakespeare (1564–1616) at Stationer's Hall, St. Paul's Churchyard, London, England. Titled *Mr. William Shakespeares Comedies, Histories & Tragedies*, it was missing two plays, a problem corrected in subsequent editions. Shakespeare's friends and fellow actors, John Heminge and Henry Condell, were the editors. The First Folio is now one of the most valuable books in the world.

TUNISIA: TREE FESTIVAL. Nov 8. National agricultural festival. Annually, the second Sunday in November.

X-RAY DISCOVERY DAY: 125th ANNIVERSARY. Nov 8, 1895. On this day physicist Wilhelm Conrad Röntgen (1845–1923) discovered x-rays, beginning a new era in physics and medicine. Although x-rays had been observed previously, it was Röntgen, a professor at the University of Würzburg (Germany), who successfully repeated x-ray experimentation and who is credited with the discovery.

	S	**M**	**T**	**W**	**T**	**F**	**S**
November	1	2	3	4	5	6	7
	8	9	10	11	12	13	14
2020	15	16	17	18	19	20	21
	22	23	24	25	26	27	28
	29	30					

🎂 BIRTHDAYS TODAY

Edgardo Alfonzo, 47, baseball coach and former player, born St. Teresa, Venezuela, Nov 8, 1973.

Calvin Borel, 54, jockey, born St. Martin Parish, LA, Nov 8, 1966.

Sam Bradford, 33, football player, 2008 Heisman Trophy winner, born Oklahoma City, OK, Nov 8, 1987.

Mary Hart, 69, television host, born Madison, SD, Nov 8, 1951.

Christie Hefner, 68, business executive (*Playboy*), born Chicago, IL, Nov 8, 1952.

Rickie Lee Jones, 66, singer, musician, born Chicago, IL, Nov 8, 1954.

Lourdes "Lou" Leon Guerrero, 70, Governor of Guam (D), born Guam, Nov 8, 1950.

Norman Lloyd, 106, actor (*Trainwreck, Saboteur*, "St. Elsewhere"), director, producer, born Jersey City, NJ, Nov 8, 1914.

David Muir, 47, journalist, anchor ("ABC World News Tonight"), born Syracuse, NY, Nov 8, 1973.

Parker Posey, 52, actress (*Personal Velocity, Best in Show, The House of Yes*), born Baltimore, MD, Nov 8, 1968.

Bonnie Raitt, 71, singer, born Los Angeles, CA, Nov 8, 1949.

Gordon Ramsay, 54, chef, restaurateur, television personality ("Hell's Kitchen"), born Glasgow, Scotland, Nov 8, 1966.

Tara Reid, 45, actress (*American Pie, Josie & the Pussycats*), born Wyckoff, NJ, Nov 8, 1975.

Matthew Rhys, 46, actor ("The Americans," "Brothers & Sisters," *The Edge of Love*), born Matthew Rhys Evans at Cardiff, Wales, Nov 8, 1974 (some sources say Nov 4).

Courtney Thorne-Smith, 53, actress ("According to Jim," "Ally McBeal"), born San Francisco, CA, Nov 8, 1967.

Alfre Woodard, 67, actress ("State of Affairs," *K-Pax, Miss Evers' Boys, How to Make an American Quilt*), born Tulsa, OK, Nov 8, 1953.

Kevin Young, 50, poet (*Jelly Roll, Ardency*), professor, editor, born Lincoln, NE, Nov 8, 1970.

November 9 — Monday

DAY 314   **52 REMAINING**

AGNEW, SPIRO THEODORE: BIRTH ANNIVERSARY. Nov 9, 1918. The 39th vice president of the US, born at Baltimore, MD. Twice elected vice president (1968 and 1972), Agnew became the second person to resign that office, Oct 10, 1973. Agnew entered a plea of no contest to a charge of income tax evasion (on contract kickbacks received while he was governor of Maryland and after he became vice president). He died Sept 17, 1996, at Berlin, MD.

BANNEKER, BENJAMIN: BIRTH ANNIVERSARY. Nov 9, 1731. American astronomer, mathematician, clock maker, surveyor and almanac author, called "first black man of science." Took part in original survey of Washington, DC. Banneker's *Almanac* was published during 1792–97. Born at Elliott's Mills, MD, he died at Baltimore, MD, Oct 9, 1806. A fire that started during his funeral destroyed

his home, library, notebooks, almanac calculations, clocks and virtually all belongings and documents related to his life.

BERLIN WALL OPENED: ANNIVERSARY. Nov 9, 1989. After 28 years as a symbol of the cold war, the Berlin Wall was opened on this evening, and citizens of both sides walked freely through an opening in the barrier as others danced atop the structure to celebrate the end of a historic era. Coming amid the celebration of East Germany's 40-year anniversary, prodemocracy demonstrations led to the resignation of Erich Honecker, East Germany's head of state and party chief. It was Honecker who had supervised the construction of the 27.9-mile wall across the city during the night of Aug 13, 1961, because US president John F. Kennedy had ordered a troop buildup in response to the blockade of West Berlin by the Soviets.

BOSTON FIRE: ANNIVERSARY. Nov 9, 1872. Though Boston, MA, had experienced several damaging fires, the worst one started on this Saturday evening in a dry-goods warehouse. Spreading rapidly in windy weather, it devastated several blocks of the business district, destroying nearly 800 buildings. Damage was estimated at more than $75 million. It was said that the fire caused a bright red glare in the sky that could be seen from nearly 100 miles away. The Boston fire came one year, one month and one day after the Great Chicago Fire of Oct 8, 1871.

CAMBODIA: INDEPENDENCE DAY. Nov 9. National day. Declared independence from France in 1949.

DANDRIDGE, DOROTHY: BIRTH ANNIVERSARY. Nov 9, 1923. Actress and singer Dandridge was a child star, born at Cleveland, OH, who toured with her sisters, Vivian and Etta Jones, as the Dandridge Sisters. They played at the Cotton Club, sharing the stage with artists such as Cab Calloway and W.C. Handy. Dandridge went solo in 1941 to perform in Hollywood movies and on stage with the Desi Arnaz Band. Her big break came with the lead role in Otto Preminger's musical *Carmen Jones*. Dandridge received an Oscar nomination for her performance. Unfortunately, she could not overcome Hollywood's racism and tendency to typecast, and her career foundered. She died at West Hollywood, CA, Sept 8, 1965.

EAST COAST BLACKOUT: 55th ANNIVERSARY. Nov 9, 1965. Massive electric power failure starting in western New York state at 5:16 PM cut electric power to much of northeastern US as well as Ontario and Quebec in Canada. More than 30 million people in an area of 80,000 square miles were affected. The experience provoked studies of the vulnerability of 20th-century technology.

FULBRIGHT, J. WILLIAM: BIRTH ANNIVERSARY. Nov 9, 1905. US senator, born at Sumner, MO. He sponsored the legislation that created the Fulbright scholarships for international study for graduate students, faculty and researchers. Died Feb 9, 1995.

GRIMES, LEONARD ANDREW: BIRTH ANNIVERSARY. Nov 9, 1815. Reverend Leonard Grimes was born at Leesburg, VA, to parents who were free. A free black man living at Washington, DC, he despised slavery and became active in assisting fugitive slaves to escape. He was caught and imprisoned at Richmond, VA. After his release he founded and became the first minister of the Twelfth Street Baptist Church at Boston, MA, where he served until his death Mar 14, 1874.

KRISTALLNACHT (CRYSTAL NIGHT): ANNIVERSARY. Nov 9–10, 1938. During the evening of Nov 9 and into the morning of Nov 10, 1938, mobs in Germany destroyed thousands of shops and homes, carrying out a pogrom against Jews. Synagogues were burned down or demolished. There were bonfires in every Jewish neighborhood, fueled by Jewish prayer books, Torah scrolls and volumes of philosophy, history and poetry. More than 30,000 Jews were arrested and 91 killed. The night got its name from the smashing of glass store windows.

LAMARR, HEDY: BIRTH ANNIVERSARY. Nov 9, 1913. Widely regarded as one of the most beautiful women of her era, actress and inventor Hedy Lamarr was born Hedwig Eva Maria Kiesler at Vienna, Austria. Starring alongside Hollywood legends like Clark Gable, Judy Garland and Spencer Tracy during a career that spanned nearly three decades, she gave her most famous performance in *Samson and Delilah* (1949). Insistent on being esteemed equally for her intelligence, in 1942 Lamarr, with composer George Antheil, patented a frequency hopping device that is now used in satellite and wireless technology. She died Jan 19, 2000, at Casselberry, FL.

THE LINKS, INC: ANNIVERSARY. Nov 9, 1946. At Philadelphia, PA, Margaret Roselle Hawkins and Sarah Strickland Scott founded a nonpartisan, volunteer organization called The Links, "linking" their friendship and resources in an effort to better the lives of disadvantaged African Americans after WWII. From a first group of nine, The Links grew to an incorporated organization of 8,000 women in 240 local chapters in 40 states plus the District of Columbia and two foreign countries. The Links promotes educational, cultural and community activities through a variety of projects domestically and in Africa. In May 1985 The Links became an official nongovernmental organization of the UN.

LOVEJOY, ELIJAH P.: BIRTH ANNIVERSARY. Nov 9, 1802. American newspaper publisher and abolitionist born at Albion, ME. Died Nov 7, 1837, at Alton, IL, in a fire started by a mob angry about his antislavery views.

NATIONAL CHILD SAFETY COUNCIL FOUNDED: 65th ANNIVERSARY. Nov 9, 1955. The National Child Safety Council (NCSC), founded in 1955, is the oldest and largest 501(c)(3) tax-exempt not-for-profit organization dedicated entirely to child safety. In recent years, NCSC has expanded its program to include adults and seniors. NCSC distributes comprehensive safety educational materials through local law enforcement. Many of NCSC's materials feature its mascot, Safetypup®. For info: NCSC. Phone: (517) 764-6070 or (800) 327-5107. Web: www.nationalchildsafetycouncil.org.

NATIONAL YOUNG READERS WEEK. Nov 9–13. Pizza Hut and the Center for the Book in the Library of Congress established National Young Readers Week to remind Americans of the joys and importance of reading for kids. Schools, libraries, families and communities nationwide use this week to celebrate reading in a variety of creative and educational ways. For info: Pizza Hut BOOK IT! Program. Web: www.bookitprogram.com.

"OMNIBUS" TV PREMIERE: ANNIVERSARY. Nov 9, 1952. This eclectic series deserved its name, offering a variety of presentations, including dramas, documentaries and musicals, for more than 10 years. Alistair Cooke hosted the program, which was the first major TV project to be underwritten by the Ford Foundation. Notable presentations included James Agee's "Mr Lincoln"; *Die Fledermaus*, with Eugene Ormandy conducting the Metropolitan Opera Orchestra; Agnes DeMille's ballet *Three Virgins and the Devil* (presented as *Three Maidens and the Devil*); and documentaries from underwater explorer Jacques Cousteau.

SAGAN, CARL: BIRTH ANNIVERSARY. Nov 9, 1934. Astronomer, biologist, author (*Broca's Brain, Cosmos*), born at New York, NY. Died at Seattle, WA, Dec 20, 1996.

VIETNAM VETERANS MEMORIAL STATUE UNVEILING: ANNIVERSARY. Nov 9, 1984. The Vietnam Veterans Memorial was completed by the addition of a statue, *Three Servicemen* (sculpted by Frederick Hart), which was unveiled on this date. The statue faces the black granite wall on which are inscribed the names of more than 58,000 Americans who were killed or missing in action in the Vietnam War.

WHITE, STANFORD: BIRTH ANNIVERSARY. Nov 9, 1853. American architect who designed the old Madison Square Garden, the Washington Square Arch, Players Club, Century Club and Metropolitan Club at New York City. Stanford White was born at New York City and was shot to death on the roof of Madison Square Garden by Harry Thaw, June 25, 1906.

🎂 BIRTHDAYS TODAY

Nikki Blonsky, 32, actress (*Hairspray*), born Great Neck, NY, Nov 9, 1988.

Sherrod Brown, 68, US Senator (D, Ohio), born Mansfield, OH, Nov 9, 1952.

Eric Dane, 48, actor ("Grey's Anatomy," "Charmed," *Marley & Me*), born San Francisco, CA, Nov 9, 1972.

Adam Dunn, 41, baseball player, born Houston, TX, Nov 9, 1979.

David Duval, 49, golfer, born Jacksonville, FL, Nov 9, 1971.

Lou Ferrigno, 69, actor (*Pumping Iron*, "The Incredible Hulk"), former bodybuilder, born Brooklyn, NY, Nov 9, 1951.

Robert (Bob) Gibson, 85, Hall of Fame baseball player, born Omaha, NE, Nov 9, 1935.

Nick Lachey, 47, singer, television personality ("Newlyweds: Nick & Jessica"), born Harlan, KY, Nov 9, 1973.

Thomas Quasthoff, 61, opera singer, born Hanover, Germany, Nov 9, 1959.

Thomas Daniel (Tom) Weiskopf, 78, sportscaster, former golfer, golf course architect, born Massillon, OH, Nov 9, 1942.

November 10 — Tuesday

DAY 315   **51 REMAINING**

AREA CODES INTRODUCED: ANNIVERSARY. Nov 10, 1951. The 10-digit North American Numbering Plan, which provides area codes for Canada, the US and many Caribbean nations, was devised in 1947 by AT&T and Bell Labs. Eighty-four area codes were assigned. However, all long-distance calls at that time were operator-assisted. On this date in 1951, the mayor of Englewood, NJ (area code 201), direct-dialed the mayor of Alameda, CA. By 1960 all telephone customers could dial long-distance calls. The system is administered by the North American Numbering Plan Administration. For info: www.nanpa.com.

BURTON, RICHARD: 95th BIRTH ANNIVERSARY. Nov 10, 1925. Welsh-born stage and film actor who led an intense and tempestuous personal life and career. Richard Burton was never knighted and never won an Oscar, but he was generally regarded as one of the great acting talents of his time. Born Richard Jenkins at Pontrhydyfen, South Wales, the son of a coal miner, he later took the name of his guardian, schoolmaster Philip Burton. Burton played King Arthur in the original production of *Camelot*. His films include *Cleopatra, Becket, Who's Afraid of Virginia Woolf?, Anne of the Thousand Days* and *Equus*. Burton died at Geneva, Switzerland, Aug 5, 1984.

***EDMUND FITZGERALD* MEMORIAL BEACON LIGHTING.** Nov 10. Split Rock Lighthouse, Two Harbors, MN. Includes information on the *Edmund Fitzgerald* and other shipwrecks on Lake Superior; beacon lighting at dusk in memory of the 29 men lost on

the *Edmund Fitzgerald* on Nov 10, 1975, and of all those who lost their lives in other Great Lakes shipwrecks. Lighthouse open. Est attendance: 500. For info: Minnesota Historical Society, 345 W Kellogg Blvd, St. Paul, MN 55102. Phone: (651) 259-3000. E-mail: lauren.peck@mnhs.org. Web: www.mnhs.org/splitrock.

***EDMUND FITZGERALD* SINKING: 45th ANNIVERSARY.** Nov 10, 1975. The ore carrier *Edmund Fitzgerald* broke in two during a heavy storm in Lake Superior (near Whitefish Point). There were no survivors of this, the worst Great Lakes ship disaster of the decade, which took the lives of 29 crew members.

GOLDSMITH, OLIVER: BIRTH ANNIVERSARY. Nov 10, 1728. Irish writer, author of the play *She Stoops to Conquer*. Born at Pallas, County Longford, Ireland, he died Apr 4, 1774, at London, England. "A book may be amusing with numerous errors," he wrote (Advertisement to *The Vicar of Wakefield*), "or it may be very dull without a single absurdity."

HOGARTH, WILLIAM: BIRTH ANNIVERSARY. Nov 10, 1697. English painter and engraver, famed for his satiric series of engravings (*A Harlot's Progress, A Rake's Progress, Four Stages of Cruelty*, etc). Born at London, England, he died there Oct 26, 1764.

LUTHER, MARTIN: BIRTH ANNIVERSARY. Nov 10, 1483. The Augustinian monk who was a founder and leader of the Protestant Reformation was born at Eisleben, Saxony. Luther tacked his 95 Theses "On the Power of Indulgences" on the door of Wittenberg's castle church, on Oct 31, 1517, the eve of All Saints' Day. Luther asserted that the Bible was the sole authority of the church, called for reformation of abuses by the Roman Catholic Church and denied the supremacy of the pope. Tried for heresy by the Roman Church, threatened with excommunication and finally banned by a papal bull (Jan 2, 1521), he responded by burning the bull. In 1525 he married Katherine von Bora, one of nine nuns who had left the convent due to his teaching. Luther died near his birthplace, at Eisleben, Feb 18, 1546.

MARINE CORPS BIRTHDAY: ANNIVERSARY. Nov 10, 1775. Commemorates the Marine Corps's establishment in 1775. Originally part of the navy, it became a separate unit July 11, 1789.

PANAMA: FIRST SHOUT OF INDEPENDENCE. Nov 10. National holiday. Commemorates Panama's first battle for independence from Spain in 1821.

RAINS, CLAUDE: BIRTH ANNIVERSARY. Nov 10, 1889. Stage, film and television actor, born at London, England. Rains trained at the Royal Academy of Dramatic Arts and overcame a speech impediment. Exposed to poison gas during WWI, his vocal chords were damaged, giving his deep voice a raspy quality that he used to great effect in *The Invisible Man* (1933), where he is only a voice until the film's final minutes, and as the corrupt Captain Louis Renault in *Casablanca* (1942). Rains's other notable films include *The Phantom of the Opera* (1943) and *Notorious* (1946). Died May 30, 1967, at Laconia, NH.

"SESAME STREET" TV PREMIERE: ANNIVERSARY. Nov 10, 1969. An important, successful, long-running children's show, "Sesame Street" educates children while they have fun. It takes place along a city street, featuring a diverse cast of humans and puppets. Through singing, puppetry, film clips and skits, children are taught letters, numbers, concepts and other lessons. Shows are "sponsored" by letters and numbers. Human cast members

November	S	M	T	W	T	F	S
2020	1	2	3	4	5	6	7
	8	9	10	11	12	13	14
	15	16	17	18	19	20	21
	22	23	24	25	26	27	28
	29	30					

have included Loretta Long, Matt Robinson, Roscoe Orman, Bob McGrath, Linda Bove, Buffy Sainte-Marie, Ruth Buzzi, Will Lee, Northern J. Calloway, Emilio Delgado and Sonia Manzano. Favorite Jim Henson Muppets include Ernie, Bert, Grover, Oscar the Grouch, the Cookie Monster, Big Bird and Mr Snuffleupagus.

SPACE MILESTONE: *LUNA 17* (USSR): 50th ANNIVERSARY. Nov 10, 1970. Launched in 1970, this unmanned spacecraft landed and released *Lunakhod 1* (eight-wheel, radio-controlled vehicle) on Moon's Sea of Rains Nov 17, which explored lunar surface, sending data back to Earth.

STANLEY FINDS LIVINGSTONE: ANNIVERSARY. Nov 10, 1871. Having begun his search the previous March for the then two-years-missing explorer-missionary David Livingstone, explorer Henry M. Stanley found him on this day at Ujiji (Africa) and uttered those now immortal words, "Dr. Livingstone, I presume?"

UNITED NATIONS: WORLD SCIENCE DAY FOR PEACE AND DEVELOPMENT. Nov 10. By linking science more closely with society, World Science Day for Peace and Development aims to ensure that citizens are kept informed of developments in science. It also underscores the role scientists play in broadening our understanding of the remarkable, fragile planet we call home and in making our societies more sustainable. Annually, Nov 10. For info: UNESCO/United Nations. Web: www.un.org/en/events/scienceday.

VON SCHILLER, FRIEDRICH: BIRTH ANNIVERSARY. Nov 10, 1759. Born at Marbach, Württemberg, Germany, von Schiller was the leading German dramatist of his age. His works include *Don Carlos* (1787), the Wallenstein trilogy (1798–1801) and *Wilhelm Tell* (1804). His "An die Freude" ("Ode to Joy") was used by Beethoven in the choral finale to his Symphony No. 9 in D Minor. Died May 9, 1805, at Weimar, Germany.

🎂 BIRTHDAYS TODAY

Vanessa Angel, 57, actress (*Spies like Us, Kingpin*), born London, England, Nov 10, 1963.

Hugh Bonneville, 57, actor ("Downton Abbey," *Paddington, Notting Hill*), born London, England, Nov 10, 1963.

Isaac Bruce, 48, former football player, born Fort Lauderdale, FL, Nov 10, 1972.

Roland Emmerich, 65, director, producer (*The Day After Tomorrow, Independence Day*), born Stuttgart, Germany, Nov 10, 1955.

Donna Fargo, 71, singer, songwriter, born Yvonne Vaughan at Mount Airy, NC, Nov 10, 1949.

Neil Gaiman, 60, author (*The Graveyard Book, American Gods*), comic book writer (*The Sandman*), born Porchester, England, Nov 10, 1960.

Walton Goggins, 49, actor (*The Hateful Eight,* "Justified," "The Shield"), born Birmingham, AL, Nov 10, 1971.

Miranda Lambert, 37, country singer, born Tyler, TX, Nov 10, 1983.

Tracy Morgan, 52, comedian, actor ("Saturday Night Live," "30 Rock"), born the Bronx, NY, Nov 10, 1968.

Ennio Morricone, 92, composer (Oscar for *The Hateful Eight* score; *Once Upon a Time in America, A Fistful of Dollars*), born Rome, Italy, Nov 10, 1928.

Mackenzie Phillips, 61, actress ("One Day at a Time," *American Graffiti*), born Alexandria, VA, Nov 10, 1959.

Ellen Pompeo, 51, actress ("Grey's Anatomy," *Moonlight Mile*), born Everett, MA, Nov 10, 1969.

Ann Reinking, 71, actress, director and choreographer (*Chicago*), born Seattle, WA, Nov 10, 1949.

Tim Rice, 76, writer, lyricist (Tonys for *Aida* and *Evita; Jesus Christ Superstar, The Lion King*), born Amersham, England, Nov 10, 1944.

Sinbad, 64, comedian, actor (*Jingle All the Way,* "A Different World"), born David Adkins at Benton Harbor, MI, Nov 10, 1956.

November 11 — Wednesday

DAY 316   **50 REMAINING**

ANGOLA: INDEPENDENCE DAY: 45th ANNIVERSARY OF INDEPENDENCE. Nov 11. National holiday. Angola gained its independence from Portugal in 1975.

BONZA BOTTLER DAY®. Nov 11. To celebrate when the number of the day is the same as the number of the month. Bonza Bottler Day® is an excuse to have a party at least once a month. For more information see Jan 1. For info: Gail Berger, Bonza Bottler Day. Phone: (864) 201-3988. E-mail: bonza@bonzabottlerday.com. Web: www.bonzabottlerday.com.

CANADA: REMEMBRANCE DAY. Nov 11. Honors those who died in WWI and WWII. Public holiday.

CHINA: SINGLES' DAY. Nov 11. Also known as Double 11, this is a recent unofficial holiday that sprang up at Nanjing University among students but is now observed in China's largest cities. Originally for bachelors, the day celebrates the single life and/or the ceremonial leaving of singledom for married life. Dating parties are a popular way to celebrate.

COLOMBIA: CARTAGENA INDEPENDENCE DAY. Nov 11. National holiday. Commemorates declaration of independence from Spain of the city of Cartagena in 1811.

DEATH/DUTY DAY. Nov 11. Honoring soldiers on both sides who died on Nov 11, 1918, the day of the armistice that ended the fighting in WWI, 1914–18. The order was to stop fighting at 11 AM, rather than on receipt of the order. (Created by Robert L. Birch, Pun Corps.)

DOSTOYEVSKY, FYODOR MIKHAYLOVICH: BIRTH ANNIVERSARY. Nov 11, 1821. The great novelist, author of *The Brothers Karamazov, Crime and Punishment* and *The Idiot*, was born at Moscow, Russia, and died at St. Petersburg, Russia, Feb 9, 1881. A political revolutionary, he was arrested, tried, convicted and sentenced to death, but instead of execution he served a sentence in a Siberian prison and later served in the army there.

ENGLAND: REMEMBRANCE DAY. Nov 11. Cenotaph, Whitehall, London. Wreath-laying ceremony to commemorate the dead of both World Wars by Her Majesty the Queen, members of the royal family, government and service organizations. Annually, Nov 11. For info: Public Info Office, HQ London District Military, Horse Guards, Whitehall, London, England SW1A 2AX.

FAST, HOWARD: BIRTH ANNIVERSARY. Nov 11, 1914. Prolific novelist, best known for *Spartacus* (1953), born at New York, NY. Was blacklisted in the 1950s for refusing to cooperate with HUAC, and served three months in prison for contempt of Congress. Other key works are *Citizen Tom Paine* (1943), *Freedom Road* (1944) and *The Immigrants* (1977). He died Mar 12, 2003, at Old Greenwich, CT.

FUENTES, CARLOS: BIRTH ANNIVERSARY. Nov 11, 1928. World-renowned Mexican author, born Carlos Fuentes Macías at Panama City, Panama. Fuentes wrote across genres, penning a prolific oeuvre that includes political journalism, screenplays and novels. Combining realism, social protest and psychological insight, his postmodern works, which include *The Death of Artemio Cruz* (1962) and *Christopher Unborn* (1989), add depictions of Mexican

identity previously ignored in the literary canon. He received numerous prestigious awards, notably the Cervantes Prize (1987), the preeminent Spanish-language literary award. Fuentes died May 15, 2012, at Mexico City, Mexico. He wrote, "You start by writing to live. You end by writing so as not to die."

"GOD BLESS AMERICA" FIRST PERFORMED: ANNIVERSARY. Nov 11, 1938. Irving Berlin wrote this song especially for Kate Smith. She first sang it during her regular radio broadcast. It quickly became a great patriotic favorite of the nation and one of Smith's most requested songs.

JAPAN: ORIGAMI DAY. Nov 11. Sponsored by the Nippon Origami Association, an opportunity to learn and celebrate origami. Observed on World Peace Memorial Day/WWI Armistice Day. For info: Nippon Origami Assn. Web: www.origami-noa.jp.

MALDIVES: REPUBLIC DAY. Nov 11. National holiday. Commemorates the abolition of the sultanate in 1968.

MARTINMAS. Nov 11. Feast day of St. Martin of Tours, who lived about AD 316–397. A bishop, he became one of the most popular saints of the Middle Ages. The period of warm weather often occurring about the time of his feast day is sometimes called St. Martin's Summer (especially in England).

PATTON, GEORGE S., JR: BIRTH ANNIVERSARY. Nov 11, 1885. American military officer, graduate of West Point (1909), George Smith Patton, Jr, was born at San Gabriel, CA. Ambitious and flamboyant, he lived for combat. He served in the punitive expedition into Mexico (1916), in Europe in WWI, and in North Africa and Europe in WWII. He received world attention and official censure in 1943 for slapping a hospitalized shell-shocked soldier. While a full general, owing to his critical public statements, he was relieved of his command in 1945. He died at Heidelberg, Germany, Dec 21, 1945, of injuries received in an automobile accident.

POLAND: INDEPENDENCE DAY. Nov 11. Poland regained independence in 1918, after having been partitioned among Austria, Prussia and Russia for more than 120 years.

SPACE MILESTONE: *COLUMBIA STS-5* (US). Nov 11, 1982. Shuttle *Columbia* launched from Kennedy Space Center, FL, with four astronauts Vance Brand, Robert Overmyer, William Lenoir and Joseph Allen. "First operational mission" delivered two satellites into orbit for commercial customers. *Columbia* landed at Edwards Air Force Base, CA, Nov 16, 1982.

SPACE MILESTONE: *GEMINI 12* (US). Nov 11, 1966. Last Project Gemini manned Earth orbit launched. Buzz Aldrin spent five hours on a space walk, setting a new record.

SUFFRAGISTS' VOTING ATTEMPT: ANNIVERSARY. Nov 11, 1868. Testing the wording of the 14th Amendment stipulating that "no State shall make or enforce any law which shall abridge the privileges or immunities of citizens of the United States," 172 New Jersey suffragists, including four black women, attempted to vote in the presidential election. Denied, they cast their votes instead into a women's ballot box overseen by 84-year-old Quaker Margaret Pryer.

SWEDEN: SAINT MARTIN'S DAY. Nov 11. Originally in memory of St. Martin of Tours; also associated with Martin Luther, who is celebrated the day before. Marks the end of the autumn's work and the beginning of winter activities.

SWITZERLAND: MARTINMAS GOOSE (MARTINIGIANS). Nov 11. Sursee, Canton Lucerne. At 3 PM on Martinmas, the "Gansabhauet" is staged in front of Town Hall. Blindfolded participants try to bring down, with a single sword stroke, a dead goose suspended on a wire.

November 2020	S	M	T	W	T	F	S
	1	2	3	4	5	6	7
	8	9	10	11	12	13	14
	15	16	17	18	19	20	21
	22	23	24	25	26	27	28
	29	30					

★VETERANS DAY. Nov 11. Presidential Proclamation. Formerly called Armistice Day and proclaimed each year since 1926 for Nov 11. Public Law 83–380 of June 1, 1954, changed the name to Veterans Day. PL 90–363 of June 28, 1968, required that, beginning in 1971, it would be observed the fourth Monday in October. PL 94–97 of Sept 18, 1975, required that, effective Jan 1, 1978, the observance would revert to Nov 11.

VETERANS DAY. Nov 11. Veterans Day was observed on Nov 11 from 1919 through 1970. Public Law 90–363, the "Monday Holiday Law," provided that, beginning in 1971, Veterans Day would be observed on the fourth Monday in October. This movable observance date, which separated Veterans Day from the Nov 11 anniversary of WWI armistice, proved unpopular. State after state moved its observance back to the traditional Nov 11 date, and finally Public Law 94–97 of Sept 18, 1975, required that, effective Jan 1, 1978, the observance of Veterans Day revert to Nov 11. As Armistice Day this is a holiday in Belgium, France and other European countries. At the 11th hour of the 11th day of the 11th month fighting ceased in WWI.

VONNEGUT, KURT, JR: BIRTH ANNIVERSARY. Nov 11, 1922. Novelist and playwright, born at Indianapolis, IN. His idiosyncratic, semiautobiographical, blackly comic works were campus favorites in the Vietnam-roiled 1960s and '70s, especially *Cat's Cradle* (1963) and *Breakfast of Champions* (1973). *Slaughterhouse-Five* (1969), part of which was based on his WWII experience as a German prisoner of war, is frequently cited as one of the 100 best novels of the 20th century. Vonnegut died Apr 11, 2007, at New York, NY.

WASHINGTON: ADMISSION DAY: ANNIVERSARY. Nov 11. Became 42nd state in 1889.

WORLD WAR I ARMISTICE: ANNIVERSARY. Nov 11, 1918. Anniversary of armistice between Allied forces and Central powers ending WWI, signed at 5 AM, Nov 11, 1918, in Marshal Foch's railway car in the forest of Compiègne, France. Hostilities ceased at 11 AM. Recognized in many countries as Armistice Day, Remembrance Day, Veterans Day, Victory Day or WWI Memorial Day. Many places observe a silent memorial at the 11th hour of the 11th day of the 11th month each year. See also: "Veterans Day" (Nov 11).

🎂 BIRTHDAYS TODAY

Jon Batiste, 34, musician, composer, bandleader (Stay Human), born Kenner, LA, Nov 11, 1986.

Barbara Boxer, 80, former US senator (D, California), born Brooklyn, NY, Nov 11, 1940.

Ashleigh Cummings, 28, actress ("Miss Fisher's Murder Mysteries," "NOS4A2"), born Jeddah, Saudi Arabia, Nov 11, 1992.

Leonardo DiCaprio, 46, actor (Oscar for *The Revenant*; *The Wolf of Wall Street, Titanic*), born Los Angeles, CA, Nov 11, 1974.

Calista Flockhart, 56, actress ("Ally McBeal," "Brothers & Sisters"), born Freeport, IL, Nov 11, 1964.

Rebecca Lowe, 40, sportscaster, born London, England, Nov 11, 1980.

Demi Moore, 58, actress (*Charlie's Angels: Full Throttle, G.I. Jane, Ghost*), born Roswell, NM, Nov 11, 1962.

Frank Urban "Fuzzy" Zoeller, 69, golfer, born New Albany, IN, Nov 11, 1951.

November 12 — Thursday

DAY 317   **49 REMAINING**

BARTHES, ROLAND: BIRTH ANNIVERSARY. Nov 12, 1915. Born at Cherbourg, France, Barthes was a literary critic and writer known for his work in the field of semiotics and critical reading. He helped establish structuralism and poststructuralism as intellectual movements. Barthes died Mar 25, 1980, at Paris, France.

BLACKMUN, HARRY A.: BIRTH ANNIVERSARY. Nov 12, 1908. Former associate justice of the US, nominated by President Richard Nixon Apr 14, 1970. He retired from the Supreme Court Aug 3, 1994. Justice Blackmun was born at Nashville, IL, and died at Arlington, VA, Mar 4, 1999.

KELLY, GRACE PATRICIA: BIRTH ANNIVERSARY. Nov 12, 1929. American award-winning actress (Oscar for *The Country Girl*; *Rear Window, To Catch a Thief*) who became Princess Grace of Monaco when she married that country's ruler, Prince Rainier III, in 1956. Born at Philadelphia, PA, she died of injuries sustained in an automobile accident, Sept 14, 1982, at Monte Carlo, Monaco.

MEXICO: POSTMAN'S DAY. Nov 12. Every year on "Día del cartero," Mexicans show their appreciation for their postal carriers by leaving a little something in their mailboxes.

RODIN, AUGUSTE: BIRTH ANNIVERSARY. Nov 12, 1840. Sculptor born at Paris, France. Rodin's most famous sculptures include *The Thinker* and *The Kiss*, both of which are components of his unfinished Gates of Hell portal created for the Museum of Decorative Arts (Paris). Deemed the "Modern-day Michelangelo," he is considered the greatest portraitist sculptor for his shockingly lifelike pieces. His style, focused on "render[ing] feelings through muscular movement," led the way for 20th-century Expressionism. He stated, "I accentuate the lines which best express the spiritual state that I interpret." Appointed Knight of the French Legion of Honour (1903), he died Nov 17, 1917, at Meudon, France.

SPACE MILESTONE: *COLUMBIA STS-2* (US). Nov 12, 1981. Shuttle *Columbia*, launched from Kennedy Space Center, FL, with Joe Engle and Richard Truly on board, became the first spacecraft launched from Earth for a second orbiting mission. Landed at Edwards Air Force Base, CA, Nov 14, 1981.

SPACE MILESTONE: *PHILAE* (ESA) LANDS ON COMET. Nov 12, 2014. The European Space Agency's *Philae* lander, launched with the *Rosetta* space probe on Mar 2, 2004, made the first-ever landing on a comet nucleus. The robotic craft had a bumpy landing on comet Churyumov–Gerasimenko (67P), bouncing to an unplanned position that blocked the solar light necessary to power it. Even so, *Philae* took photographs of the comet and collected data. After hibernating shortly after landing, *Philae* "woke up" in June 2015 and "communicated" with the ESA.

STANTON, ELIZABETH CADY: BIRTH ANNIVERSARY. Nov 12, 1815. American women's rights activist Stanton was born at Johnstown, NY. Renowned with compatriot Susan B. Anthony as a leader of the American Women's Suffrage Movement, she organized the Seneca Falls Convention (1848)—hailed as the birth of the American women's rights movement—and authored its eponymous Declaration of Sentiments, the first document to call for women's elective franchise. Organizer and president of the leading women's suffrage associations, she also advocated liberal divorce laws. Stanton died Oct 26, 1902, at New York, NY, 18 years before the passage of the 19th Amendment, which she drafted in 1878.

SUN YAT-SEN: BIRTH ANNIVERSARY (TRADITIONAL). Nov 12. Although his actual birth date in 1866 is not known, Dr. Sun Yat-sen's traditional birthday commemoration is held Nov 12. A doctor who gave up his practice to become a revolutionary, he worked behind the scenes in the overthrow of the Qing dynasty and was elected the first president of the newly formed Republic of China. The modern Chinese calendar dates to the first day of his rule: Jan 1, 1912. He died at Beijing, China, Mar 12, 1925. A holiday in Taiwan. His death anniversary is also widely observed. See also: "Sun Yat-sen: Death Anniversary" (Mar 12).

TYLER, LETITIA CHRISTIAN: BIRTH ANNIVERSARY. Nov 12, 1790. First wife of John Tyler, 10th president of the US, born at New Kent County, VA. Died at Washington, DC, Sept 10, 1842.

WORLD PNEUMONIA DAY. Nov 12. Established in 2009, World Pneumonia Day is marked every year on Nov 12 to raise awareness about pneumonia, the world's leading killer of children under the age of five; promote interventions to protect against, prevent and treat pneumonia; and generate action to combat pneumonia. For info: Stop Pneumonia. Web: www.stoppneumonia.org.

🎂 BIRTHDAYS TODAY

Nadia Comaneci, 59, Olympic gymnast, born Onesti, Romania, Nov 12, 1961.

Ryan Gosling, 40, actor (*La La Land, The Big Short, Drive, The Notebook*), born London, ON, Canada, Nov 12, 1980.

Tonya Harding, 50, former figure skater, born Portland, OR, Nov 12, 1970.

Anne Hathaway, 38, actress (Oscar for *Les Misérables*; *The Dark Knight Rises, The Devil Wears Prada, The Princess Diaries*), born Brooklyn, NY, Nov 12, 1982.

Norman Mineta, 89, former US secretary of transportation, born San Jose, CA, Nov 12, 1931.

Megan Mullally, 62, actress ("Will & Grace"), born Los Angeles, CA, Nov 12, 1958.

Jack Reed, 71, US Senator (D, Rhode Island), born Providence, RI, Nov 12, 1949.

David Schwimmer, 54, actor ("Friends"), director, born Queens, NY, Nov 12, 1966.

Sammy Sosa, 52, former baseball player, born San Pedro de Macoris, Dominican Republic, Nov 12, 1968.

Russell Westbrook, 32, basketball player, born Long Beach, CA, Nov 12, 1988.

Neil Young, 75, singer (Buffalo Springfield and Crosby, Stills, Nash & Young), songwriter, born Toronto, ON, Canada, Nov 12, 1945.

November 13 — Friday

DAY 318   **48 REMAINING**

BOOTH, EDWIN (THOMAS): BIRTH ANNIVERSARY. Nov 13, 1833. Famed American actor and founder of the Players Club, born near Bel Air, MD. His brother, John Wilkes Booth, assassinated President Abraham Lincoln. Died at New York, NY, June 7, 1893.

BRANDEIS, LOUIS DEMBITZ: BIRTH ANNIVERSARY. Nov 13, 1856. American jurist, associate justice of the US (1916–39), born at Louisville, KY. Died at Washington, DC, Oct 5, 1941.

FALL OF KABUL: ANNIVERSARY. Nov 13, 2001. Northern Alliance troops opposing the Islamic extremist regime of the Taliban moved into the capital of Afghanistan on this date—the first major victory in the war on terrorism prompted by the Sept 11, 2001,

attacks on America. The Taliban had controlled Kabul since 1996. The US had demanded that the Taliban regime give up Al Qaeda terrorists and their leader, Osama bin Laden, or face reprisals. Upon the Taliban's provocation, the US led a multinational force in support of the Northern Alliance that began with a bombardment and was followed by ground warfare in Afghanistan. The fall of Kabul was the first major step to destroying Al Qaeda's Afghanistan stronghold. See also: "Attack on America: Anniversary" (Sept 11).

FOUR CORNER STATES BLUEGRASS FESTIVAL. Nov 13–15. Everett Bowman Rodeo Grounds, Wickenburg, AZ. 40th annual old-time fiddle, banjo, mandolin, flat-pick guitar championships. Includes gospel music. Special entertainment by nationally known bands as well as 13 competitive events. Est attendance: 5,000. For info: J. Brooks, Exec Dir, Chamber of Commerce, 216 N Frontier St, Wickenburg, AZ 85390. Phone: (928) 684-5479. Fax: (928) 684-5470. E-mail: events@wickenburgchamber.com. Web: www.wickenburgchamber.com.

HOLIDAY LIGHTS ON THE LAKE. Nov 13–Jan 3, 2021. Lakemont Park, Altoona, PA. Drive-through displays of more than 51 acres of animated holiday lights, plus a holiday gift shop, food, model train displays and visits from Santa Claus. Est attendance: 75,000. For info: Lakemont Park, 700 Park Ave, Altoona, PA 16602. Phone: (814) 949-7275 or (800) 434-8006. Fax: (814) 949-9207. E-mail: lakemontparkfun@hotmail.com. Web: www.lakemontparkfun.com.

HOLLAND TUNNEL: ANNIVERSARY. Nov 13, 1927. The Holland Tunnel, running under the Hudson River between New York, NY, and Jersey City, NJ, was opened to traffic. The tunnel was built and operated by the New York–New Jersey Bridge and Tunnel Commission. Comprising two tubes, each large enough for two lanes of traffic, the Holland was the first underwater tunnel built in the US.

MAXWELL, JAMES CLERK: BIRTH ANNIVERSARY. Nov 13, 1831. British physicist noted for his work in the field of electricity and magnetism. Born at Edinburgh, Scotland, he died of cancer Nov 5, 1879, at Cambridge, England.

NATIONAL DONOR SABBATH. Nov 13–15. To increase awareness about the dire need for organs and tissues for transplantation and to dispel fears that tissue and organ donation is incompatible with religion. Annually, the Friday, Saturday and Sunday two weekends before Thanksgiving. For info: US Dept of Health and Human Services. E-mail: donation@hrsa.gov. Web: www.organdonor.gov.

PARIS TERROR ATTACKS: 5th ANNIVERSARY. Nov 13, 2015. A series of coordinated terrorist attacks took place in Paris, France, and its northern suburb of Saint-Denis. Assaults by gunmen and suicide bombers at the Stade De France, the Bataclan theater, and restaurants and cafés culminated in the deaths of 130 people, along with seven of the attackers. The injured numbered 368. The terrorist organization Islamic State (IS) claimed responsibility, and nearly all of the attackers were European nationals. The ensuing weeks and months saw police raids focused in France and Belgium that

led to the discovery of a centralized terror cell based in Brussels, which has been linked to other attacks.

SALT LAKE'S FAMILY CHRISTMAS GIFT SHOW. Nov 13–15. Sandy, UT. A delightful holiday experience where shoppers find gifts, holiday décor, specialty foods and decorations from vendors across the nation. A festive shopping atmosphere with music, entertainment and Santa Claus. Est attendance: 25,000. For info: Showcase Events, Inc, PO Box 2815, Kirkland, WA 98083. Phone: (800) 521-7469. E-mail: saltlake@showcaseevents.org. Web: www.family-christmasgiftshow.com.

STEVENSON, ROBERT LOUIS: BIRTH ANNIVERSARY. Nov 13, 1850. Novelist, poet and travel writer, born at Edinburgh, Scotland, known for his *Child's Garden of Verses* (1885) and classic adventure novels such as *Treasure Island* (1883) and *Kidnapped* (1886). In the influential horror novella "Strange Case of Doctor Jekyll and Mr Hyde" (1886), Stevenson explored the duality of human nature and the interior battle between good and evil. He died at Vailima, Samoa, Dec 3, 1894.

STOKES BECOMES FIRST BLACK MAYOR IN US: ANNIVERSARY. Nov 13, 1967. Carl Burton Stokes became the first black in the US elected mayor when he won the Cleveland, OH, mayoral election Nov 13, 1967. Died Apr 3, 1996.

WORLD ANTIBIOTIC AWARENESS WEEK. Nov 13–19 (tentative). Since 2015, this week aims to increase awareness of global antibiotic resistance and to encourage best practices among the general public, health workers and policy makers to avoid the further emergence and spread of antibiotic resistance. For info: World Health Organization. Web: www.who.int/campaigns/world-antibiotic-awareness-week.

🎂 BIRTHDAYS TODAY

Greg Abbott, 63, Governor of Texas (R), born Wichita Falls, TX, Nov 13, 1957.

Charlie Baker, 64, Governor of Massachusetts (R), born Elmira, NY, Nov 13, 1956.

Gerard Butler, 51, actor (*Olympus Has Fallen, 300, The Phantom of the Opera*), born Glasgow, Scotland, Nov 13, 1969.

Monique Coleman, 40, actress (*High School Musical*), born Orangeburg, SC, Nov 13, 1980.

Sheila E. Frazier, 72, actress (*Super Fly*), born the Bronx, NY, Nov 13, 1948.

Whoopi Goldberg, 71, comedienne, actress (Oscar for *Ghost*; *Sister Act, The Color Purple*), born Caryn Elaine Johnson at New York, NY, Nov 13, 1955.

Jimmy Kimmel, 53, talk show host, comedian ("The Man Show," "Jimmy Kimmel Live"), born Brooklyn, NY, Nov 13, 1967.

Andrés Manuel López Obrador, 67, President of Mexico, born Tepetitlán, Mexico, Nov 13, 1953.

Joe Mantegna, 73, actor (Tony for *Glengarry Glen Ross*; *House of Games, Things Change*, "Criminal Minds"), born Chicago, IL, Nov 13, 1947.

Chris Noth, 63, actor ("Sex and the City," "The Good Wife," "Law & Order"), born Madison, WI, Nov 13, 1957.

Tracy Scoggins, 61, actress ("Babylon 5"), born Galveston, TX, Nov 13, 1959.

Daniel Sullivan, 56, US Senator (R, Alaska), born Fairview Park, OH, Nov 13, 1964.

Vincent Frank (Vinny) Testaverde, 57, former football player, born New York, NY, Nov 13, 1963.

Dana Vollmer, 33, Olympic swimmer, born Syracuse, NY, Nov 13, 1987.

Steve Zahn, 52, actor (*Rescue Dawn, National Security, Sahara*), born Marshall, MN, Nov 13, 1968.

November 2020	S	M	T	W	T	F	S
	1	2	3	4	5	6	7
	8	9	10	11	12	13	14
	15	16	17	18	19	20	21
	22	23	24	25	26	27	28
	29	30					

November 14 — Saturday

DAY 319   **47 REMAINING**

BROOKS, LOUISE: BIRTH ANNIVERSARY. Nov 14, 1906. Born at Cherryvale, KS, Brooks started out as a dancer before finding fame as an actress in 1920s cinema. She is best known for her performances in two 1929 German films: *Pandora's Box* (as Lulu) and *Diary of a Lost Girl*. Would-be flappers the world over copied her trademark hairstyle: a sleek, helmetlike bob. Brooks wrote a well-received book of reminiscences, *Lulu in Hollywood* (1982), before her death on Aug 8, 1985, at Rochester, NY.

COPLAND, AARON: BIRTH ANNIVERSARY. Nov 14, 1900. American composer Aaron Copland was born at Brooklyn, NY. Incorporating American folk music and, later, the 12-tone system, he strove to create an American music style that was both popular and artistic. He composed ballets, film scores and orchestral works including *Fanfare for the Common Man* (1942), *Appalachian Spring* (1944; for which he won the Pulitzer Prize) and the score for *The Heiress* (1948; for which he won an Oscar). He died Dec 2, 1990, at North Tarrytown, NY.

DOW JONES TOPS 1,000: ANNIVERSARY. Nov 14, 1972. The Dow Jones Index of 30 major industrial stocks topped the 1,000 mark for the first time.

EISENHOWER, MAMIE DOUD: BIRTH ANNIVERSARY. Nov 14, 1896. Wife of Dwight David Eisenhower, 34th president of the US, born at Boone, IA. Died Nov 1, 1979, at Gettysburg, PA.

ENGLAND: LORD MAYOR'S SHOW. Nov 14. The City of London. Each year a colorful parade steps off at 11 AM from the Guildhall to the Royal Courts of Justice to mark the inauguration of the new Lord Mayor, who pledges allegiance to the Crown. Annually, the second Saturday in November. Est attendance: 500,000. For info: Pageantmaster, The Lord Mayor's Show, The Barge, Hindringham Rd, Great Walsingham, Norfolk, England NR22 6DR. Web: www.lordmayorsshow.london.

FULTON, ROBERT: BIRTH ANNIVERSARY. Nov 14, 1765. Born at Lancaster County, PA, Fulton was an inventor and engineer noted for his paddlewheel steamboat. Other designs include the steam warship, a submarine and canal waterways. He served on the commission that recommended building the Erie Canal; canals and his steamboat designs, widely employed in the US, subsequently resulted in significant reduction of domestic shipping costs. Initially mocked for his steamboat ventures, dubbed "Fulton's Folly," he famously said, "Patience and perseverance are the friends of science." Fulton died Feb 23, 1815, at New York, NY.

GUINEA-BISSAU: READJUSTMENT MOVEMENT'S DAY. Nov 14. National holiday.

INDIA: CHILDREN'S DAY. Nov 14. Holiday observed throughout India.

INDIA: DIWALI (DEEPAVALI). Nov 14–18. Diwali, the five-day festival of lights that begins today, is the prettiest of all Indian festivals. It celebrates the return of Lord Rama to Ayodhya after a 14-year exile. Thousands of flickering lights illuminate houses and transform urban landscapes while fireworks add color and noise. The goddess of wealth, Lakshmi, is worshipped in Hindu homes on Diwali. Houses are whitewashed and cleaned, and elaborate designs are drawn on thresholds with colored powder to welcome the fastidious goddess. Because there is no one universally accepted Hindu calendar, this holiday may be celebrated on a different date in some parts of India, but it always falls in October or November.

INTERNATIONAL GIRLS DAY. Nov 14. A day to build confidence in girls and celebrate the power of girls to realize their dreams. Girls and their supporters across the country can plan celebrations with the theme "She Can Do Anything!" For info: Heidi Roy, The Confidence Coalition, Kappa Delta Sorority, 3205 Players Ln, Memphis, TN 38125. Phone: (901) 748-1897. E-mail: heidi.roy@kappadelta.org. Web: www.kappadelta.org.

LOOSEN UP, LIGHTEN UP DAY. Nov 14. A day to remind people of all the benefits of joy and laughter. For info: Stephanie West Allen, 1376 S Wyandot St, Denver, CO 80223. Phone: (303) 935-8866. E-mail: stephanie@westallen.com.

MCCARTHY, JOSEPH: BIRTH ANNIVERSARY. Nov 14, 1908. Controversial politician born near Appleton, WI. As a Republican senator, McCarthy became a household name when he began making sweeping statements about the prevalence of secret Communists in the US. In this period of postwar uncertainty and distrust of the Soviets, Americans responded to his claims with fear and indignation. He soon spread his attacks, accusing politicians, State Department employees, journalists and members of the armed forces of being secret Communists. He held congressional hearings to uncover "traitors," using sensational methods that uncovered nothing of substance. After failing to prove any of his allegations, he soon fell out of favor and was censured by Congress for unbecoming conduct in December 1954. He died at Bethesda, MD, May 2, 1957.

MOBY-DICK PUBLISHED: ANNIVERSARY. Nov 14, 1851. Dedicated to friend and fellow author Nathaniel Hawthorne, *Moby-Dick*, by Herman Melville, was published by Harper and Brothers. One of the greatest works of world literature, this enigmatic story of "The Whale" began with the famous sentence "Call me Ishmael." The 2,915-copy printing sold poorly, and a warehouse fire destroyed what hadn't sold. Only in the early 20th century was its genius recognized. (On Oct 18, 1851, the British edition came out, but it was heavily edited and quite a different book.)

MONET, CLAUDE: BIRTH ANNIVERSARY. Nov 14, 1840. Born at Paris, France, Monet is one of the most significant and popular Western artists. He was introduced to the then-uncommon practice of open-air painting by Boudin, and it became his modus operandi. An initiator and leader of Impressionism—the movement's name is derived from his *Impression: Sunrise*—with contemporaries Pissarro and Renoir, Monet is best known for his landscape series, which focused on capturing the changes wrought in color by light and weather. Monet's paintings are renowned for their chromatic vibrancy, one of his most overt stylistic departures from the Old Masters. Died Dec 5, 1926, at Giverny, France.

"MURPHY BROWN" TV PREMIERE: ANNIVERSARY. Nov 14, 1988. This intelligent, often acerbic sitcom set in Washington, DC, starred Candice Bergen as an egotistical, seasoned journalist working for the fictitious TV news show "FYI." Featured were Grant Shaud as the show's high-strung producer, Miles Silverberg (later replaced by Lily Tomlin); Faith Ford as the former Miss America–turned–anchor, Corky Sherwood; Joe Regalbuto as neurotic reporter Frank Fontana; Charles Kimbrough as uptight anchorman Jim Dial; Pat Corley as Phil, owner of the local watering hole; and Robert Pastorelli as Eldin Bernecky, perfectionist housepainter and aspiring artist. The series ended with the May 31, 1998, episode. CBS briefly revived the show in the fall of 2018.

NATIONAL BLOCK IT OUT DAY. Nov 14. Since 2017. The goal of this day is to block negativity from our digital lives and, by doing so, end cruelty, homophobia, LGBTQ discrimination, racism, hatred and online violence. On Block It Out Day, STOMP Out Bullying is encouraging everyone who is being bullied or mistreated online to not only block out their bully on social media, but also go a step

further and encourage and empower their friends to block their own bullies as well. We can all control what we take in, and we can and should refuse to take in negative messages of hate and discrimination! Annually, Nov 14. For info: STOMP Out Bullying, 220 E 57th St, New York, NY 10022. Phone: (877) 602-8559. E-mail: info@stompoutbullying.org. Web: www.stompoutbullying.org.

NEHRU, JAWAHARLAL: BIRTH ANNIVERSARY. Nov 14, 1889. Indian leader who worked for independence and social reform, emphasizing economic welfare. First Indian prime minister after independence in 1947 and architect of India's foreign policy of nonalignment, he was greatly influenced by his friend Mohandas Gandhi. Born at Allahabad, India, Nehru died May 27, 1964, at New Delhi, India.

SALISBURY, HARRISON: BIRTH ANNIVERSARY. Nov 14, 1908. American journalist Harrison Evans Salisbury was born at Minneapolis, MN. *New York Times* Moscow correspondent from 1949 to 1954. Salisbury won the Pulitzer Prize in 1955 for a series of articles on the Soviet Union. He died July 5, 1993, at Providence, RI.

SPACE MILESTONE: *APOLLO 12* (US). Nov 14, 1969. Launched this date. This was the second manned lunar landing—in Ocean of Storms. First pinpoint landing. Astronauts Pete Conrad, Alan Bean and Richard Gordon visited *Surveyor 3* and took samples. Earth splashdown Nov 24.

STEIG, WILLIAM: BIRTH ANNIVERSARY. Nov 14, 1907. Prolific cartoonist, satirist and illustrator, William Steig was born at Brooklyn, NY. *The New Yorker* published more than 1,600 of his drawings, including 117 covers, and he wrote more than 25 books for children. He won the Caldecott Medal in 1970 for *Sylvester and the Magic Pebble* and received two Newbery Honors, for *Abel's Island* and *Dr. De Soto*. Other favorites include *The Amazing Bone, Brave Irene, CDB* and *Shrek*, the basis for a series of animated films. Steig died at Boston, MA, Oct 3, 2003.

UNITED NATIONS: WORLD DIABETES DAY. Nov 14. Welcoming the fact that the International Diabetes Federation has been observing World Diabetes Day globally since 1991, with cosponsorship of the World Health Organization, the UN General Assembly on Dec 20, 2006, designated this day as a United Nations Day, to be observed every year beginning in 2007 (Res 61/225). Annually, Nov 14. For info: United Nations, Dept of Public Info, New York, NY 10017. Web: www.un.org.

🎂 **BIRTHDAYS TODAY**

Prince Charles, 72, Prince of Wales, heir to the British throne, born London, England, Nov 14, 1948.

Josh Duhamel, 48, actor ("Battle Creek," "Las Vegas," *Transformers* films), born Minot, ND, Nov 14, 1972.

	S	M	T	W	T	F	S
November	1	2	3	4	5	6	7
	8	9	10	11	12	13	14
2020	15	16	17	18	19	20	21
	22	23	24	25	26	27	28
	29	30					

Chip Gaines, 46, television personality ("Fixer Upper"), real estate entrepreneur, contractor, carpenter, born Albuquerque, NM, Nov 14, 1974.

Condoleezza Rice, 66, former US secretary of state, former US national security adviser, born Birmingham, AL, Nov 14, 1954.

Laura San Giacomo, 58, actress (*sex, lies and videotape*, "Just Shoot Me"), born Hoboken, NJ, Nov 14, 1962.

Curt Schilling, 54, former baseball player, born Anchorage, AK, Nov 14, 1966.

Joseph "Run" Simmons, 56, rapper (Run DMC), born Queens, NY, Nov 14, 1964.

D.B. Sweeney, 59, actor (*Spawn, The Cutting Edge*), born Shoreham, Long Island, NY, Nov 14, 1961.

Yanni, 66, New Age composer, born Yanni Chrysomalis at Kalamata, Greece, Nov 14, 1954.

November 15 — Sunday

DAY 320   **46 REMAINING**

ALLEN, PHOG: BIRTH ANNIVERSARY. Nov 15, 1885. Forrest Clare "Phog" Allen, basketball player and Basketball Hall of Fame coach, born at Jamesport, MO. Over 46 years, Allen's record as a coach (primarily at University of Kansas, his alma mater) was 771 games won, only 233 lost. He was instrumental in having basketball added to the Olympic program in 1936. Inducted into the Hall of Fame in 1959. Died at Lawrence, KS, Sept 16, 1974.

AMERICA RECYCLES DAY. Nov 15. America Recycles Day, a program of Keep America Beautiful, is a nationally recognized day dedicated to promoting and celebrating recycling in the United States. Every year America Recycles Day event organizers educate neighbors, friends and colleagues through thousands of events. Annually, Nov 15. For info: Programs Director, Attn: America Recycles Day, Keep America Beautiful, 1010 Washington Blvd, Stamford, CT 06901. Phone: (203) 659-3074. Web: www.americarecyclesday.org.

BELGIUM: DYNASTY DAY. Nov 15. National holiday in honor of Belgian monarchy.

BRAZIL: REPUBLIC DAY. Nov 15. Commemorates the proclamation of the republic on Nov 15, 1889.

FIRST BLACK PROFESSIONAL HOCKEY PLAYER: 70th ANNIVERSARY. Nov 15, 1950. When Arthur Dorrington signed a contract to play hockey with the Atlantic City Seagulls of the Eastern Amateur League, he became the first black man to play organized hockey in the United States. He played for the Seagulls during the 1950 and 1951 seasons.

GEORGE SPELVIN DAY. Nov 15. Believed to be the anniversary of George Spelvin's theatrical birth—in Charles A. Gardiner's play *Karl the Peddler* on Nov 15, 1886, in a production at New York, NY. The name (or equivalent—Georgina, Georgetta, etc) is used in play programs to conceal the fact that an actor is performing in more than one role. The fictitious Spelvin is said to have appeared in more than 10,000 Broadway performances. See also: "England: Walter Plinge Day" (Dec 2) for British equivalent.

GERMANY: VOLKSTRAUERTAG. Nov 15. Memorial Day and national day of mourning in all German states for victims of National Socialism and the dead of both World Wars. Observed on the Sunday before Totensonntag. See also: "Germany: Totensonntag" (Nov 22).

HERSCHEL, WILLIAM: BIRTH ANNIVERSARY. Nov 15, 1738. Sir Friedrich Wilhelm (William) Herschel, born at Hanover, Germany, was the most renowned astronomer of his time, discovering the planet Uranus, as well as its two moons, more than 2,000 nebulae and star clusters, and Jupiter's moons. Named the "King's Astronomer" and knighted by King George III, Herschel built a 20-foot reflecting telescope with the king's grant money and systematically began to study the sky. He became the first to observe sunspots and confirm the gaseous nature of the sun, note the movement of the solar system through space and identify the infrared range of sunlight. A member of the Royal Society, he died at Slough, England, on Aug 25, 1822.

JAPAN: SHICHI-GO-SAN (7-5-3 FESTIVAL). Nov 15. Annual children's festival. The *Shichi-Go-San* (Seven-Five-Three) rite is "the most picturesque event in the autumn season." Parents take their three-year-old children of either sex, five-year-old boys and seven-year-old girls to the parish shrines dressed in their best clothes. There the guardian spirits are thanked for the healthy growth of the children, and prayers are offered for their further development.

LEMAY, CURTIS: BIRTH ANNIVERSARY. Nov 15, 1906. Born at Columbus, OH, LeMay was a WWII hero whose bombing strategies for the US helped push the Axis powers toward surrender. He later oversaw the Berlin airlift in 1948 and headed the US Strategic Air Command (1948–57). In 1968 he ran as vice presidential candidate of the American Independent Party, headed by George Wallace. LeMay died Oct 1, 1990, at March AFB, CA.

MOON PHASE: NEW MOON. Nov 15. Moon enters New Moon phase at 12:07 AM, EST.

MOORE, MARIANNE: BIRTH ANNIVERSARY. Nov 15, 1887. Acclaimed poet, critic and editor born at Kirkwood, MO. Her *Collected Poems* (1951) won the National Book Award, the Bollingen Prize and the Pulitzer Prize. She also received the National Medal for Literature—America's highest literary honor. Moore was frequently seen in a tricorn hat and cape—creating an indelible image that outlasted her death on Feb 5, 1972, at New York City.

O'KEEFFE, GEORGIA: BIRTH ANNIVERSARY. Nov 15, 1887. Described as one of the major American artists of the 20th century, Georgia O'Keeffe was born at Sun Prairie, WI. In 1924 she married the famous photographer Alfred Stieglitz. His more than 500 photographs of her have been called "the greatest love poem in the history of photography." She painted desert landscapes and flower studies. She died at Santa Fe, NM, Mar 6, 1986.

ROMMEL, ERWIN: BIRTH ANNIVERSARY. Nov 15, 1891. Field marshal and commander of the German Afrika Korps in WWII, Erwin Rommel was born at Heidenheim, in Württemberg, Germany. Rommel commanded the Seventh Panzer Division in the Battle of France. He was considered an excellent commander, and his early success in Africa made him a legend as the "Desert Fox." But in early 1943 he was outmaneuvered by Field Marshal Bernard Montgomery, and Germany surrendered Tunis in May of that year. Implicated in July 1944 in an attempted assassination of Hitler, he was given the choice of suicide or a trial and chose the former. Rommel died by his own hand at age 52, Oct 14, 1944, near Ulm, Germany.

SPACE MILESTONE: *BURAN* (USSR). Nov 15, 1988. The Soviet Union's first reusable space plane, *Buran*, landed on this date, completing a smooth, unmanned mission at approximately 1:25 AM, EST, after orbiting Earth twice in 3 hours, 25 minutes. Launched at Baikonur, Soviet central Asia. The importance of this mission was in its computer-controlled liftoff and return.

UNITED NATIONS: WORLD DAY OF REMEMBRANCE FOR ROAD TRAFFIC VICTIMS. Nov 15. On Oct 26, 2005, the General Assembly invited member states and the international community to annually recognize the third Sunday in November as the World Day of Remembrance for Road Traffic Victims, as acknowledgment of victims of road traffic crashes and their families (Res 60/5). For info: United Nations, Dept of Public Info, New York, NY 10017. Web: www.un.org.

🎂 BIRTHDAYS TODAY

Ed Asner, 91, actor ("The Mary Tyler Moore Show," "Lou Grant," *Roots*), born Kansas City, MO, Nov 15, 1929.

Daniel Barenboim, 78, musician, conductor, born Buenos Aires, Argentina, Nov 15, 1942.

Joanna Barnes, 86, actress (*The Parent Trap, Spartacus*), author, born Boston, MA, Nov 15, 1934.

Petula Clark, 88, singer, actress, born Ewell, Surrey, England, Nov 15, 1932.

Beverly D'Angelo, 66, actress (*Hair, Coal Miner's Daughter*), born Columbus, OH, Nov 15, 1954.

Winston Duke, 34, actor (*Us, Black Panther*), born Argyle, Trinidad and Tobago, Nov 15, 1986.

Kevin Eubanks, 63, musician, bandleader, born Philadelphia, PA, Nov 15, 1957.

Yaphet Kotto, 83, actor ("Homicide: Life on the Street," *Midnight Run, Blue Collar, Live and Let Die*), born New York, NY, Nov 15, 1937.

Jonny Lee Miller, 48, actor ("Elementary," "Eli Stone," *Trainspotting*), born Kingston-upon-Thames, Surrey, England, Nov 15, 1972.

Liane Moriarty, 54, author (*Big Little Lies*), born Sydney, Australia, Nov 15, 1966.

Karl-Anthony Towns, 25, basketball player, born Edison, NJ, Nov 15, 1995.

Sam Waterston, 80, actor ("Law & Order," "I'll Fly Away," *The Killing Fields, The Great Gatsby*), born Cambridge, MA, Nov 15, 1940.

Shailene Woodley, 29, actress (*The Fault in Our Stars, Divergent*, "The Secret Life of the American Teenager"), born Simi Valley, CA, Nov 15, 1991.

November 16 — Monday

DAY 321   **45 REMAINING**

★**AMERICAN EDUCATION WEEK.** Nov 16–20. Presidential Proclamation 5403, of Oct 30, 1985, covers all succeeding years. Always the week (Monday through Friday) preceding the fourth Thursday in November. Issued during 1921–25 and in 1936, sometimes for a week in December and sometimes as National Education Week. After an absence of a number of years, this proclamation was issued each year during 1955–82 (issued in 1955 as a prelude to the White House Conference on Education). Previously, Proclamation 4967 of Sept 13, 1982, covered all succeeding years as the second week in November.

AMERICAN EDUCATION WEEK. Nov 16–20. 99th annual. This week, observed since 1921, spotlights the importance of providing every child in America with a quality public education from kindergarten through college and the need for everyone to do his or her part in making public schools great. Annually, the week preceding the week of Thanksgiving. For info: Natl Education Assn, 1201 16th St NW, Washington, DC 20036. Phone: (202) 833-4000. Web: www. nea.org.

ESTONIA: DAY OF NATIONAL REBIRTH. Nov 16. National holiday. Commemorates the 1988 Declaration of Sovereignty. Became independent from the Soviet Union in 1991.

HANDY, WILLIAM CHRISTOPHER: BIRTH ANNIVERSARY. Nov 16, 1873. American composer, bandleader, "father of the blues," W.C. Handy was born at Florence, AL. He died at New York, NY, Mar 28, 1958.

ISRAEL: SIGD. Nov 16. Ethiopian Jewish observance 50 days after Yom Kippur. Hebrew calendar date: Heshvan 29, 5781. Etymologically, "prostration" in the Ge'ez language. A day of reaffirmation of faith marked by fasting and revelry. Ethiopian Jews throughout Israel travel to Jerusalem. Became an official Israeli state holiday in 2008.

KAUFMAN, GEORGE S.: BIRTH ANNIVERSARY. Nov 16, 1889. Playwright, director, producer and critic, born at Pittsburgh, PA. Working collaboratively on Broadway and in Hollywood from the 1920s through the 1950s, Kaufman was a theatrical rainmaker; his credits include *The Cocoanuts, Animal Crackers, You Can't Take It with You, The Royal Family* and *Guys and Dolls*. A drama critic for the *New York Times* (1917–30) and a member of the Algonquin Round Table, where his incisive wit and sharp one-liners were legendary: "I saw the play at a disadvantage," he wrote, "the curtain was up." Died June 2, 1961, at New York, NY.

LEWIS AND CLARK EXPEDITION REACHES PACIFIC OCEAN: ANNIVERSARY. Nov 16, 1805. Lewis and Clark's Corps of Discovery reached the Pacific Ocean on this date. They had glimpsed it on Nov 7, moving Clark to write in his journal: "Great joy in camp! We are in view of the Ocean, this great Pacific Ocean which we have been so anxious to see. And the roaring or noise of the waves breaking on the rocky shores . . . may be heard distinctly."

MEREDITH, BURGESS: BIRTH ANNIVERSARY. Nov 16, 1907. Actor (*Of Mice and Men, Rocky*) born at Cleveland, OH. Some sources give his year of birth as 1908 or 1909. Died at Malibu, CA, Sept 9, 1997.

OKLAHOMA: ADMISSION DAY: ANNIVERSARY. Nov 16. Became 46th state in 1907.

RIEL, LOUIS: HANGING: ANNIVERSARY. Nov 16, 1885. Born at Red River Colony, MB, Canada, Oct 22, 1844, Louis Riel, leader of the Metis (French/Indian mixed ancestry), was elected to Canada's House of Commons in 1873 and 1874 but never seated. Having been confined to asylums for madness (feigned or falsely charged, some said), Riel became a US citizen in 1883. In 1885 he returned to western Canada to lead the North West Rebellion. Defeated, he surrendered and was tried for treason, convicted and hanged, at Regina, SK, Canada. Seen as a patriot and protector of French culture in Canada, Riel became a legend and a symbol of the problems between French and English Canadians.

ROMAN CATHOLICS ISSUE NEW CATECHISM: ANNIVERSARY. Nov 16, 1992. For the first time since 1563, the Roman Catholic Church issued a new universal catechism, which addressed modern-day issues.

SAINT EUSTATIUS, WEST INDIES: STATIA AND AMERICA DAY. Nov 16, 1776. St. Eustatius, Leeward Islands. To commemorate the first salute to an American flag by a foreign government, from Fort Oranje in 1776. Festivities include sports events and dancing. During the American Revolution, St. Eustatius was an important trading center and a supply base for the colonies.

SPACE MILESTONE: *SKYLAB 4* (US). Nov 16, 1973. The 30th manned US spaceflight was launched with three astronauts, Gerald P. Carr, William R. Page and Edward G. Gibson, who spent 84 days on the space station. Space walks totaled 22 hours. Returned to Earth on Feb 8, 1974.

SPACE MILESTONE: *VENERA 3* (USSR): 45th ANNIVERSARY. Nov 16, 1965. Launched this date, this unmanned space probe crashed into Venus, Mar 1, 1966. First man-made object on another planet.

UNITED NATIONS: INTERNATIONAL DAY FOR TOLERANCE. Nov 16. On Dec 12, 1996, the General Assembly established the International Day for Tolerance, to commemorate the adoption by UNESCO member states of the Declaration of Principles on Tolerance in 1995. For info: United Nations, Dept of Public Info, New York, NY 10017. Web: www.un.org.

🎂 BIRTHDAYS TODAY

Oksana Baiul, 43, Olympic figure skater, born Dniepropetrovsk, Ukraine, Nov 16, 1977.

Lisa Bonet, 53, actress ("The Cosby Show," "A Different World," *Angel Heart*), born San Francisco, CA, Nov 16, 1967.

Susanna Clarke, 61, author (*Jonathan Strange & Mr Norrell*), born Nottingham, England, Nov 16, 1959.

Elizabeth Drew, 85, journalist, author, born Cincinnati, OH, Nov 16, 1935.

Dwight Eugene Gooden, 56, former baseball player, born Tampa, FL, Nov 16, 1964.

Maggie Gyllenhaal, 43, actress (*Crazy Heart, The Dark Knight, Secretary*), born New York, NY, Nov 16, 1977.

Marg Helgenberger, 62, actress ("CSI," Emmy for "China Beach"), born Fremont, NE, Nov 16, 1958.

Diana Krall, 56, jazz singer, born Nanaimo, BC, Canada, Nov 16, 1964.

Martha Plimpton, 50, actress ("Raising Hope," *Top Girls, The Coast of Utopia*), born New York, NY, Nov 16, 1970.

Amare Stoudemire, 38, basketball player, born Lake Wales, FL, Nov 16, 1982.

November 17 — Tuesday

DAY 322 **44 REMAINING**

HOMEMADE BREAD DAY. Nov 17. A day for the family to remember and enjoy the making, baking and eating of nutritious homemade bread. (Created by William and Helen Chase.)

HONDA, SOICHIRO: BIRTH ANNIVERSARY. Nov 17, 1906. Born at Hamamatsu, Japan, Honda was the enterprising auto racer–turned–businessman who founded the Honda Motor Company, a central part of Japan's postwar emergence as an economic power. Honda retired in 1973 and died Aug 5, 1991, at Tokyo, Japan.

MÖBIUS, AUGUST: BIRTH ANNIVERSARY. Nov 17, 1790. German astronomer, mathematician, teacher and author, August Ferdinand Möbius was born at Schulpforte, Germany. Möbius was a pioneer in the field of topology and first described the Möbius net and the Möbius strip. He died at Leipzig, Germany, Sept 26, 1868.

MONTGOMERY, BERNARD LAW: BIRTH ANNIVERSARY. Nov 17, 1887. Bernard Law Montgomery, who commanded the British Eighth Army to victory at El Alamein in North Africa in 1943, was born at St. Mark's Vicarage, Kennington Oval, London, England. He also led the Eighth Army in the Sicilian and Italian campaigns and commanded all ground forces in the 1944 Normandy landing. Montgomery died Mar 24, 1976, at Alton, Hampshire, England.

NATIONAL UNFRIEND DAY. Nov 17. Inspired by late-night talk show host Jimmy Kimmel, National Unfriend Day is the day on which Facebook users take an honest inventory of their friends list and eliminate all those who aren't true friends. By making

November 2020	S	M	T	W	T	F	S
		1	2	3	4	5	6	7
	8	9	10	11	12	13	14
	15	16	17	18	19	20	21
	22	23	24	25	26	27	28
	29	30					

cuts, they will be able to devote more time and energy to the people who really matter in their lives. Annually, Nov 17. For info: "Jimmy Kimmel Live," 6834 Hollywood Blvd, Hollywood, CA 90028. Phone: (323) 860-5918. Web: www.abc.go.com/shows/jimmy-kimmel-live.

QUEEN ELIZABETH I: ACCESSION ANNIVERSARY. Nov 17, 1558. Anniversary of accession of Elizabeth I to English throne; celebrated as a holiday in England for more than a century after her death in 1603.

SUEZ CANAL FORMAL OPENING: ANNIVERSARY. Nov 17, 1869. It had taken 1.5 million men a decade to dig the 120-mile canal that links the Mediterranean Sea to the Red Sea from Port Said to Port Taufiq (now Suez Port) in Egypt. It shortened the sea route from Europe to India by 4,300 miles. Forced labor hand-dug the canal in the early stages of construction, and it is estimated that 120,000 laborers died. Later, steam- and coal-powered shovels removed sand—75 million cubic meters. The canal was built by the Suez Canal Company (a French enterprise) under the leadership of Ferdinand de Lesseps. The Suez Canal Company ran the canal until 1956, when Egypt's president, Gamal Abdel Nasser, seized it.

WORLD PREMATURITY DAY. Nov 17. Prematurity is the leading killer of America's newborns and affects 15 million babies worldwide each year. Those who survive often have lifelong health problems, including cerebral palsy, intellectual disabilities, chronic lung disease, blindness and hearing loss. This day, part of the monthlong Prematurity Awareness Month, seeks to raise awareness about the seriousness of this problem. For info: March of Dimes, National Office, 1550 Crystal Dr, Ste 1300, Arlington, VA 22202. Phone: (888) 663-4637. Web: www.marchofdimes.org.

ZENGER, JOHN PETER: ARREST ANNIVERSARY. Nov 17, 1734. Colonial printer and journalist who established the *New York Weekly Journal* (first issue, Nov 5, 1733). Zenger was arrested Nov 17, 1734, for libel against the colonial governor but continued to edit his newspaper from jail. Trial was held during August 1735. Zenger's acquittal was an important early step toward freedom of the press in America. Zenger was born at Germany in 1697, came to the US in 1710 and died July 28, 1746, at New York, NY.

🎂 BIRTHDAYS TODAY

Danny DeVito, 76, actor ("It's Always Sunny in Philadelphia," "Taxi," *Twins*), director (*Throw Momma from the Train*), born Neptune, NJ, Nov 17, 1944.

Tom Ellis, 41, actor ("Lucifer," "Miranda"), born Bangor, Wales, Nov 17, 1979.

Daisy Fuentes, 54, actress, television personality, born Havana, Cuba, Nov 17, 1966.

Isaac Hanson, 40, singer (Hanson), born Tulsa, OK, Nov 17, 1980.

Lauren Hutton, 76, model, actress (*American Gigolo*), born Charleston, SC, Nov 17, 1944.

James M. Inhofe, 86, US Senator (R, Oklahoma), born Des Moines, IA, Nov 17, 1934.

Gordon Lightfoot, 82, singer, songwriter, born Orillia, ON, Canada, Nov 17, 1938.

Sophie Marceau, 54, actress (*The World Is Not Enough, Braveheart*), born Paris, France, Nov 17, 1966.

Mary Elizabeth Mastrantonio, 62, actress (*Robin Hood: Prince of Thieves, The Color of Money, Scarface*), born Oak Park, IL, Nov 17, 1958.

Rachel McAdams, 42, actress (*Spotlight, Sherlock Holmes, The Notebook*, "True Detective"), born London, ON, Canada, Nov 17, 1978.

Lorne Michaels, 76, producer ("Saturday Night Live"), born Toronto, ON, Canada, Nov 17, 1944.

Cyril Ramaphosa, 68, President of South Africa, born Soweto, South Africa, Nov 17, 1952.

RuPaul, 60, model, actor, born RuPaul Andre Charles at San Diego, CA, Nov 17, 1960.

Martin Scorsese, 78, director (*Mean Streets, The Color of Money, Raging Bull, Goodfellas*, Oscar for *The Departed*), born Flushing, NY, Nov 17, 1942.

George Thomas (Tom) Seaver, 76, Hall of Fame baseball player, born Fresno, CA, Nov 17, 1944.

Matthew Settle, 51, actor ("Brothers & Sisters," "Gossip Girl"), born Hickory, NC, Nov 17, 1969.

Pat Toomey, 59, US Senator (R, Pennsylvania), born Providence, RI, Nov 17, 1961.

Dylan Walsh, 57, actor ("Nip/Tuck"), born Los Angeles, CA, Nov 17, 1963.

Tom Wolf, 72, Governor of Pennsylvania (D), born York, PA, Nov 17, 1948.

November 18 — Wednesday

DAY 323   **43 REMAINING**

DAGUERRE, LOUIS JACQUES MANDÉ: BIRTH ANNIVERSARY. Nov 18, 1787. French tax collector, theater scene-painter, physicist and inventor, born at Cormeilles-en-Paris, France. Remembered for his invention of the daguerreotype photographic process—one of the earliest to permit a photographic image to be chemically fixed to provide a permanent picture. It wasn't the first photographic process, but it was the most practically viable in that it dramatically reduced the time for an image to appear. The process was presented to the French Academy of Science Jan 7, 1839. In recognition of this accomplishment, Daguerre was admitted to France's Legion of Honour. He died near Paris, France, July 10, 1851.

GALLI-CURCI, AMELITA: BIRTH ANNIVERSARY. Nov 18, 1882. Acclaimed coloratura soprano and popular recording artist, a mainstay of New York City's Metropolitan Opera. Born at Milan, Italy, she made her American debut Nov 18, 1916, at Chicago, IL. Galli-Curci retired in 1937 and died at La Jolla, CA, Nov 26, 1963.

GERMANY: BUSS UND BETTAG. Nov 18. Buss und Bettag (Repentance Day) is observed on the Wednesday before the last Sunday of the church year. Formerly a national holiday, it remains a legal public holiday in the state of Saxony.

GILBERT, SIR WILLIAM SCHWENCK: BIRTH ANNIVERSARY. Nov 18, 1836. English author of librettos for the famed Gilbert and Sullivan comic operas, born at London, England. Died May 29, 1911, at Harrow Weald, Middlesex, England, as a result of a heart attack experienced while saving a woman from drowning.

GRAY, ASA: BIRTH ANNIVERSARY. Nov 18, 1810. Botanist and natural history professor at Harvard, born at Paris, NY. Gray was known as a pioneer in the field of plant geography and a chief advocate of Darwin. Died at Cambridge, MA, Jan 30, 1888.

HAITI: ARMY DAY. Nov 18. Commemorates the Battle of Vertiéres, Nov 18, 1803, in which Haitians defeated the French.

"HOWARD STERN SHOW" RADIO PREMIERE: 35th ANNIVERSARY.
Nov 18, 1985. Radio's pioneering shock jock Howard Stern began broadcasting with sidekick Robin Quivers on New York radio station WXRK-FM. With outrageous humor and a gleeful disregard for taste, Stern quickly became popular nationally, but many remain outraged at his show elements. The FCC frequently fined his broadcasting company. Radio listeners at the show's peak of popularity were about 25 million. On Dec 16, 2005, Stern ended his show on regular radio and moved it to satellite radio beginning in 2006.

JONESTOWN MASSACRE: ANNIVERSARY. Nov 18, 1978. On this date the Indiana-born, 47-year-old Reverend Jim Jones, leader of the "People's Temple," was reported to have directed the suicides of more than 900 persons at Jonestown, Guyana. US Representative Leo J. Ryan of California and four members of his party were killed in an ambush at Port Kaituma airstrip on Nov 18, 1978, when they attempted to leave after an investigative visit to the remote jungle location of the religious cult. On the same day, Jones and his mistress killed themselves after watching the administration of Kool-Aid laced with the deadly poison cyanide to members of the cult. At least 912 persons died in the biggest murder-suicide in history.

LATVIA: INDEPENDENCE DAY. Nov 18. National holiday. Commemorates the declaration of an independent Latvia from Germany and Russia in 1918.

MARRIED TO A SCORPIO SUPPORT DAY. Nov 18. A worldwide day of remembrance to honor all those married to Scorpios and who suffer greatly. Assert yourself today! Hide their household flowcharts. Annually, Nov 18. (©2006 by WH.) For info: Thomas & Ruth Roy, Wellcat Holidays, 2418 Long Ln, Lebanon, PA 17046. Phone: (717) 279-0184. E-mail: info@wellcat.com. Web: www.wellcat.com.

MERCER, JOHN HERNDON (JOHNNY): BIRTH ANNIVERSARY. Nov 18, 1909. American songwriter, singer, radio performer and actor, born at Savannah, GA. Johnny Mercer wrote lyrics (and often the music) for some of the great American popular music from the 1930s through the 1960s, including "Autumn Leaves," "One for My Baby," "Satin Doll," "On the Achison, Topeka, and the Santa Fe," "You Must Have Been a Beautiful Baby," "Come Rain or Come Shine," "Hooray for Hollywood" and "Jeepers Creepers." Mercer died June 25, 1976, at Bel Air, CA.

MICKEY MOUSE'S BIRTHDAY. Nov 18. The comical activities of squeaky-voiced Mickey Mouse first appeared in 1928, on the screen of the Colony Theatre at New York City. The short film, Walt Disney's "Steamboat Willie," was the first animated cartoon talking picture.

NATIONAL BOOK AWARDS ANNOUNCEMENT DAY. Nov 18. New York, NY. Announcement of the winners of the National Book Awards, one of the nation's preeminent literary prizes. For info: National Book Foundation, 90 Broad St, Ste 604, New York, NY 10004. Phone: (212) 685-0261. E-mail: nationalbook@nationalbook.org. Web: www.nationalbook.org.

NATIONAL EDUCATIONAL SUPPORT PROFESSIONALS DAY. Nov 18. A mandate of the delegates to the 1987 National Education Association Representative Assembly called for a special day during American Education Week to honor the contributions of school support employees. Local associations and school districts salute support staff on this annual observance, the Wednesday of American Education Week. For info: Natl Education Assn, 1201 16th St NW, Washington, DC 20036-3290. Phone: (202) 833-4000. Web: www.nea.org.

OMAN: NATIONAL HOLIDAY. Nov 18. Sultanate of Oman celebrates its National Day, the birthday in 1942 of Sultan Qaboos bin Said.

November 2020	S	M	T	W	T	F	S
	1	2	3	4	5	6	7
	8	9	10	11	12	13	14
	15	16	17	18	19	20	21
	22	23	24	25	26	27	28
	29	30					

"SEE IT NOW" TV PREMIERE: ANNIVERSARY. Nov 18, 1951. "See It Now" was a high-quality and significant public affairs show of the 1950s. Known for using its own film footage, unrehearsed interviews and no dubbing, "See It Now" covered many relevant and newsworthy stories of its time, including desegregation, lung cancer and anticommunist fervor. One of the most notable programs focused on Senator Joseph McCarthy, leading to McCarthy's appearance on the show—an appearance that damaged his credibility. "See It Now" was hosted by Edward R. Murrow, who also produced it jointly with Fred W. Friendly. Its premiere was the first live commercial coast-to-coast broadcast. The show had premiered on radio the year before as "Hear It Now."

SHEPARD, ALAN: BIRTH ANNIVERSARY. Nov 18, 1923. Former astronaut and the first American in space (in 1961), Shepard was born at East Derry, NH. He was one of only 12 Americans who have walked on the moon and was America's only lunar golfer, practicing his drive in space with a six iron. He was awarded the Congressional Medal of Honor in 1979. Shepard died near Monterey, CA, July 21, 1998.

SOUTH AFRICA ADOPTS NEW CONSTITUTION: ANNIVERSARY. Nov 18, 1993. After more than 300 years of white majority rule, basic civil rights were finally granted to blacks in South Africa. The constitution providing such rights was approved by representatives of the ruling party, as well as members of 20 other political parties.

SULLIVAN, JAMES: BIRTH ANNIVERSARY. Nov 18, 1860. James Edward Sullivan, amateur sports promoter, born at New York, NY. Sullivan helped to establish the Amateur Athletic Union (AAU) in 1888 to preserve pure amateurism. He also worked as president of the American Sports Publishing Company and edited Spalding's Athletic Library series. The AAU Sullivan Award has been presented annually since 1930 in his honor to the best amateur athlete in the US. Died at New York, Sept 16, 1914.

SUSAN B. ANTHONY ARRESTED FOR VOTING: ANNIVERSARY. Nov 18, 1872. Seeking to test for women the citizenship and voting rights extended to black males under the 14th and 15th Amendments, Susan B. Anthony led a group of women who registered and then voted on Nov 5, 1872, at a Rochester, NY, polling place. She was arrested on Nov 18. In the ensuing federal criminal trial, *United States v Susan B. Anthony*, held June 17–19, 1873, she was found guilty and sentenced to pay a $100 fine. She refused to do so and never did.

US UNIFORM TIME ZONE PLAN: ANNIVERSARY. Nov 18, 1883. Charles Ferdinand Dowd, a college professor and one of the early advocates of uniform time, proposed a time zone plan of the US (four zones of 15 degrees), which he and others persuaded the railroads to adopt and place in operation on this date. Because it didn't involve the enactment of any law, some localities didn't change their clocks. A year later, an international conference applied the same procedure to create time zones for the entire world. US time zones weren't nationally legalized until 1918, with the passage of the Standard Time Act. See also: "Prime Meridian Set: Anniversary" (Nov 1) and "US Standard Time Act: Anniversary" (Mar 19).

🎂 BIRTHDAYS TODAY

Margaret Eleanor Atwood, 81, author (*The Heart Goes Last, The Blind Assassin, The Handmaid's Tale*), born Ottawa, ON, Canada, Nov 18, 1939.

Dante Bichette, 57, former baseball player, born West Palm Beach, FL, Nov 18, 1963.

Linda Evans, 78, actress ("Dynasty," "The Big Valley"), born Hartford, CT, Nov 18, 1942.

Allyson Felix, 35, Olympic track athlete, born Los Angeles, CA, Nov 18, 1985.

Megyn Kelly, 50, journalist, anchor ("The Kelly File"), born Syracuse, NY, Nov 18, 1970.

Andrea Marcovicci, 72, actress ("Trapper John, MD"), singer, born New York, NY, Nov 18, 1948.

Harold Warren Moon, 64, Hall of Fame football player, born Los Angeles, CA, Nov 18, 1956.

Kevin Nealon, 67, comedian, actor ("Weeds," "Saturday Night Live"), born St. Louis, MO, Nov 18, 1953.

Jameson Parker, 73, actor ("Simon & Simon," *A Small Circle of Friends*), born Baltimore, MD, Nov 18, 1947.

Elizabeth Perkins, 60, actress ("Weeds," *Big, The Flintstones*), born Queens, NY, Nov 18, 1960.

Katey Sagal, 64, actress ("Married . . . With Children," "8 Simple Rules," "Futurama"), born Los Angeles, CA, Nov 18, 1956.

Chloë Sevigny, 46, actress ("Big Love," *Boys Don't Cry*), born Darien, CT, Nov 18, 1974.

Gary Sheffield, 52, former baseball player, born Tampa, FL, Nov 18, 1968.

Susan Sullivan, 76, actress ("Falcon Crest," "Dharma & Greg"), born New York, NY, Nov 18, 1944.

Brenda Vaccaro, 81, stage and film actress (*The Goodbye People*), born Brooklyn, NY, Nov 18, 1939.

Owen Wilson, 52, actor (*Midnight in Paris, Wedding Crashers, The Royal Tenenbaums*), screenwriter, born Dallas, TX, Nov 18, 1968.

November 19 — Thursday

DAY 324　　　　　　　　　　**42 REMAINING**

BELIZE: GARIFUNA DAY. Nov 19. Public holiday celebrating the first arrival of black Caribs from St. Vincent and Rotan at southern Belize in 1823.

CAMPANELLA, ROY: BIRTH ANNIVERSARY. Nov 19, 1921. Roy Campanella, one of the first black major leaguers and a star of one of baseball's greatest teams, the Brooklyn Dodgers' "Boys of Summer," was born at Philadelphia, PA. He was named the National League MVP three times in his 10 years of play, in 1951, 1953 and 1955. Campanella had his highest batting average in 1951 (.325), and in 1953 he established three single-season records for a catcher—most putouts (807), most home runs (41) and most runs batted in (142)—as well as having a batting average of .312. His career was cut short on Jan 28, 1958, when an automobile accident left him paralyzed. Campanella gained even more fame after his accident as an inspiration and spokesman for people with disabilities. He was named to the Baseball Hall of Fame in 1969. Roy Campanella died June 26, 1993, at Woodland Hills, CA.

COLD WAR FORMALLY ENDED: 30th ANNIVERSARY. Nov 19–21, 1990. A summit was held at Paris, France, with the leaders of the Conference on Security and Cooperation in Europe (CSCE). The highlight of the summit was the signing of a treaty to dramatically reduce conventional weapons in Europe, thereby ending the cold war.

DEDICATION DAY: 157th ANNIVERSARY OF THE GETTYSBURG ADDRESS. Nov 19. Gettysburg, PA. The anniversary of Lincoln's Gettysburg Address is celebrated with services at Soldiers' National Cemetery in Gettysburg National Military Park. Est attendance: 2,000. For info: Gettysburg Foundation, 1195 Baltimore Pike, Gettysburg, PA 17325. Phone: (717) 338-1243. E-mail: info@gettysburgfoundation.org. Web: www.gettysburgfoundation.org.

DRUCKER, PETER: BIRTH ANNIVERSARY. Nov 19, 1909. Born at Vienna, Austria, Drucker was an economist, theorist, consultant, journalist, professor and author. Arriving in America in 1937 (after leaving his Nazi-overrun homeland), Drucker grew to be one of the most important business thinkers of the century, practically inventing the idea of management as a profession. In 1954 he published his most famous work, *The Practice of Management*—one of almost 40 works. In his long career, he moved from thinking of the corporation as a community builder to being a critical gadfly in the wake of business scandals at the end of the century. He died Nov 11, 2005, at his home in Claremont, CA.

FIRST AUTOMATIC TOLL COLLECTION MACHINE: ANNIVERSARY. Nov 19, 1954. At the Union Toll Plaza on New Jersey's Garden State Parkway, motorists dropped 25 cents into a wire-mesh hopper and a green light would flash. The first modern toll road was the Pennsylvania Turnpike, which opened in 1940.

FIRST PRESIDENTIAL LIBRARY: ANNIVERSARY. Nov 19, 1939. President Franklin D. Roosevelt laid the cornerstone for his presidential library at Hyde Park, NY. He donated the land, but public donations provided funds for the building, which was dedicated on June 30, 1941.

FRANCE: BEAUJOLAIS NOUVEAU RELEASE. Nov 19. By French law, Beaujolais nouveau, a young red wine, can't be released for sale until the third Thursday in November. Once the third Thursday is reached, celebrations abound as the wine travels to markets all over the world.

GANDHI, INDIRA: BIRTH ANNIVERSARY. Nov 19, 1917. Born at Allahabad, India, Gandhi was a member of the dominant Indian political dynasty for the nation's first half-century of independence and arguably the most effective, powerful politician of her time. Daughter of Jawaharlal Nehru, India's first prime minister, Gandhi was an influential leader of the New Congress Party and a four-term Indian prime minister. During her rule, she concluded a treaty of friendship and cooperation with the Soviet Union and backed the Bangladeshi secession movement from Pakistan, exacerbating regional tensions and resulting in the Indo-Pakistan War. Gandhi was assassinated on Oct 31, 1984, at New Delhi by her Sikh bodyguards as revenge for her June 1984 military order removing Sikh separatists from the Golden Temple of Amritsar, which had resulted in at least 450 deaths.

GARFIELD, JAMES ABRAM: BIRTH ANNIVERSARY. Nov 19, 1831. The 20th president of the US (and the first left-handed president) was born at Orange, OH. Term of office: Mar 4–Sept 19, 1881. While walking into the Washington, DC, railway station on the morning of July 2, 1881, Garfield was shot by disappointed office seeker Charles J. Guiteau. Garfield survived, in very weak condition, until Sept 19, 1881, when he succumbed to blood poisoning at Elberon, NJ (where he had been taken for recuperation). Guiteau was tried, convicted and hanged at the jail at Washington, DC, June 30, 1882.

GERMANY: DUISBURG CHRISTMAS MARKET. Nov 19–Dec 30. Duisburg. One of the most beautiful Christmas markets in Germany (North Rhine-Westphalia), the Duisburg market features 750 Christmas trees, more than 100 stalls selling hand-crafted toys and edible delicacies and strings of lights everywhere. A large outdoor ice rink and Ferris wheel complete the winter picture.

GREAT AMERICAN SMOKEOUT. Nov 19. A day observed annually since 1977 to celebrate smoke-free environments. Annually, the third Thursday in November. For info: American Cancer Society. Phone: (800) 227-2345. Web: www.cancer.org/smokeout.

"HAVE A BAD DAY" DAY. Nov 19. For those who are filled with revulsion at being told endlessly to "have a nice day," this day is a brief respite. Store and business owners are to ask workers to tell customers to "have a bad day." Annually, Nov 19. (©2006 by WH.) For info: Thomas & Ruth Roy, Wellcat Holidays, 2418 Long Ln, Lebanon, PA 17046. Phone: (717) 279-0184. E-mail: info@wellcat.com. Web: www.wellcat.com.

LINCOLN'S GETTYSBURG ADDRESS: ANNIVERSARY. Nov 19, 1863. In 1863, 17 acres of the battlefield at Gettysburg, PA, were dedicated as a national cemetery. Noted orator Edward Everett spoke for two hours; the address that Lincoln delivered in less than two minutes was later recognized as one of the most eloquent of the English language. Five manuscript copies in Lincoln's hand survive, including the rough draft begun in ink at the executive mansion at Washington and concluded in pencil at Gettysburg on the morning of the dedication (kept at the Library of Congress).

MONACO: NATIONAL HOLIDAY. Nov 19.

***NATIONAL REVIEW* FIRST PUBLISHED: 65th ANNIVERSARY.** Nov 19, 1955. The leading conservative journal was founded by 29-year-old William F. Buckley, Jr. The cover price on the first issue was 20 cents.

PELÉ SCORES 1,000th GOAL: ANNIVERSARY. Nov 19, 1969. Playing for the Santos team, legendary Brazilian soccer player Pelé scored his 1,000th goal in competition on a penalty kick against the team Vasco de Gama. Pelé dedicated this emotional and tremendous feat to Brazil's poor children and its elderly and suffering people. By the time Pelé retired in 1977, he had scored an astounding 1,281 goals in 1,363 matches—a world record that still stands.

PUERTO RICO: DISCOVERY DAY. Nov 19. Public holiday. Columbus discovered Puerto Rico in 1493 on his second voyage to the New World.

"ROCKY AND HIS FRIENDS" TV PREMIERE: ANNIVERSARY. Nov 19, 1959. This popular cartoon featured the adventures of a talking squirrel, Rocky (Rocket J. Squirrel), and his friend Bullwinkle, a flaky moose. The tongue-in-cheek dialogue contrasted with the simple plots in which Rocky and Bullwinkle tangled with Russian bad guys Boris Badenov and Natasha (who worked for Mr Big). Other popular segments on the show included "Fractured Fairy Tales," "Bullwinkle's Corner" and the adventures of Sherman and Mr Peabody (an intelligent talking dog). In 1961 the show was renamed "The Bullwinkle Show," but the cast of characters remained the same.

SUNDAY, BILLY: BIRTH ANNIVERSARY. Nov 19, 1862. Born William Ashley Sunday at Ames, IA, Sunday rose from poverty to become a professional baseball player with the Chicago White Stockings in 1883. He quit baseball in 1891 to devote himself to evangelism after hearing gospel singers at a Chicago mission. Sunday's fiery, athletic sermons—especially against demon rum—made him a star in the early 1900s, and at each revival he attracted about 100,000 listeners. At a typical revival in Detroit, MI, Sunday exhorted, "Help me, Jesus, help me save all in Detroit who are rushing to hell so fast that you can't see them for the dust." Sunday died Nov 6, 1935, at Chicago, IL.

UNITED NATIONS: WORLD TOILET DAY. Nov 19. Toilets save lives because human waste spreads killer diseases. However, 4.5 billion people live without a household toilet that safely disposes of their waste. World Toilet Day is about inspiring action to tackle the global sanitation crisis. Annually, Nov 19. For info: United Nations. Web: www.un.org/en/events/toiletday.

WOMEN'S CHRISTIAN TEMPERANCE UNION ORGANIZED: ANNIVERSARY. Nov 19, 1874. Developed out of the Women's Temperance Crusade of 1873, the Women's Christian Temperance Union was organized at Cleveland, OH. The crusade had swept through 23 states with women going into saloons to sing hymns, pray and ask saloonkeepers to stop selling liquor. Today the temperance group, headquartered at Evanston, IL, includes more than a million members with chapters in 72 countries and continues to be concerned with educating people on the potential dangers of the use of alcohol, narcotics and tobacco.

WORLD PHILOSOPHY DAY. Nov 19. First observed in 2008, this day celebrates the importance of philosophical reflection and encourages people all over the world to share their philosophical heritage with each other. For UNESCO, philosophy provides the conceptual bases of principles and values on which world peace depends: democracy, human rights, justice and equality. Philosophy helps consolidate these authentic foundations of peaceful coexistence. Annually, the third Thursday in November. For info: UNESCO, Social and Human Sciences. Web: www.unesco.org.

ZION NATIONAL PARK ESTABLISHED: ANNIVERSARY. Nov 19, 1919. Utah's Mukuntuweap National Monument, proclaimed July 31, 1909, and later incorporated in Zion National Monument by proclamation on Mar 18, 1918, was established as Zion National Park in 1919.

🎂 BIRTHDAYS TODAY

Dick Cavett, 84, television pundit ("The Dick Cavett Show"), born Gibbon, NE, Nov 19, 1936.

Eileen Collins, 64, first female space shuttle commander; lieutenant colonel, USAF (retired), born Elmira, NY, Nov 19, 1956.

Ann Curry, 64, television journalist, born at Guam, Nov 19, 1956.

Gail Devers, 54, Olympic sprinter, born Seattle, WA, Nov 19, 1966.

Adam Driver, 37, actor (*BlacKkKlansman, Star Wars: The Force Awakens, Lincoln*, "Girls"), born San Diego, CA, Nov 19, 1983.

Terry Farrell, 57, actress ("Star Trek: Deep Space Nine," "Becker"), born Cedar Rapids, IA, Nov 19, 1963.

Jodie Foster, 58, actress (Oscars for *The Accused* and *The Silence of the Lambs; Taxi Driver*), director (*Home for the Holidays*), born Los Angeles, CA, Nov 19, 1962.

Savion Glover, 47, dancer, choreographer (*Bring in 'Da Noise, Bring in 'Da Funk*), born Newark, NJ, Nov 19, 1973.

Douglas Henshall, 55, actor ("Shetland," "Collision," "Primeval"), born Glasgow, Scotland, Nov 19, 1965.

Ryan Howard, 41, baseball player, born St. Louis, MO, Nov 19, 1979.

Scott Jacoby, 64, actor (*The Little Girl Who Lives Down the Lane, Return to Horror High*), born Chicago, IL, Nov 19, 1956.

Allison Janney, 60, actress (Oscar for *I, Tonya*; Emmys for "Mom" and "The West Wing"), born Dayton, OH, Nov 19, 1960.

Barry Jenkins, 41, director (*If Beale Street Could Talk, Moonlight*), writer (Oscar with Tarell Alvin McCraney for *Moonlight*), born Miami, FL, Nov 19, 1979.

Patrick Kane, 32, hockey player, born Buffalo, NY, Nov 19, 1988.

Larry King, 87, talk show host ("Larry King Now," "Larry King Live"), born Lawrence Zeiger at Brooklyn, NY, Nov 19, 1933.

Calvin Klein, 78, fashion designer, born New York, NY, Nov 19, 1942.

Glynnis O'Connor, 65, actress (*Ode to Billy Joe*), born New York, NY, Nov 19, 1955.

Kathleen Quinlan, 66, actress (*Breakdown, Apollo 13*), born Pasadena, CA, Nov 19, 1954.

Ahmad Rashad, 71, sportscaster, former football player, born Bobby Moore at Portland, OR, Nov 19, 1949.

Meg Ryan, 59, actress (*When Harry Met Sally, Sleepless in Seattle*), born Fairfield, CT, Nov 19, 1961.

Kerri Strug, 43, Olympic gymnast, born Tucson, AZ, Nov 19, 1977.

Ted Turner, 82, baseball, basketball and television executive, born Cincinnati, OH, Nov 19, 1938.

Jack Welch, 85, ex-chairman of GE, born Peabody, MA, Nov 19, 1935.

November 2020	S	M	T	W	T	F	S
	1	2	3	4	5	6	7
	8	9	10	11	12	13	14
	15	16	17	18	19	20	21
	22	23	24	25	26	27	28
	29	30					

November 20 — Friday

DAY 325   **41 REMAINING**

BATTLES OF TARAWA AND MAKIN: ANNIVERSARY. Nov 20–23, 1943. The US began its offensive against Japan in the Central Pacific (Operation Galvanic) by attacking the Gilbert Islands, particularly the islets of Betio and Makin. The Japanese had heavily fortified the Tarawa chain of atolls, especially Tarawa, with pillboxes, blockhouses and ferroconcrete bombproofs. In the days it took the Fifth Amphibious Corps, Second Marine Division and 27th Infantry Division to take the Tarawa and Makin islands, more than 2,000 US soldiers were killed and 2,311 wounded. The Japanese loss was tallied at 5,000 men killed and 17 wounded and captured. The US public, who through censorship previously had been kept in the dark about the human cost of the war, was appalled by casualty figures and photographs from this battle.

BILL OF RIGHTS: ANNIVERSARY OF FIRST STATE RATIFICATION. Nov 20, 1789. New Jersey became the first state to ratify 10 of the 12 amendments to the US Constitution proposed by Congress Sept 25. These 10 amendments came to be known as the Bill of Rights.

BYRD, ROBERT: BIRTH ANNIVERSARY. Nov 20, 1917. The longest-serving senator in US history, born Cornelius Calvin Sale, Jr, at North Wilkesboro, NC. Overcoming early hardships, including the death of his mother and subsequent adoption by an aunt and uncle in coal mining country in West Virginia, Byrd was elected to the West Virginia House of Delegates in 1946 and continued a 64-year political career in which he never lost an election. He authored a four-volume history of the US Senate and was a staunch defender of its pomp, circumstance and traditions. He died at Fairfax, VA, June 28, 2010.

CABARET PREMIERE: ANNIVERSARY. Nov 20, 1966. John Kander and Fred Ebb's musical premiered at the Broadhurst Theatre in New York City. Based on Christopher Isherwood's stories about Weimar Germany before WWII, Cabaret ran until 1969 and later became an acclaimed film. The musical itself was nominated for 11 Tony Awards and won eight, including Best Musical, Best Direction (Harold Prince), Best Composer and Lyricist (Kander and Ebb) and Best Featured Actor (Joel Grey in a legendary turn as the MC). Lotte Lenya received a Best Leading Actress nomination.

CHATTERTON, THOMAS: BIRTH ANNIVERSARY. Nov 20, 1752. English poet Thomas Chatterton was born at Bristol, England, and killed himself at age 17 by taking arsenic at his London garret, Aug 24, 1770. A gifted but lonely child, before he reached his teens, Chatterton had created a fantasy poet-priest, Thomas Rowley, who lived in the 16th century. With his own pen, Chatterton created enough verses "by" Rowley to fill more than 600 printed pages. Chatterton's fantasy-forgery poems attracted little attention during his short life, but they were later admired by Wordsworth, Coleridge, Shelley, Keats and Byron. In addition, he became the subject of at least one play, an opera and a novel.

COOKE, ALISTAIR: BIRTH ANNIVERSARY. Nov 20, 1908. Broadcast journalist and author Alfred Alistair Cooke was born at Salford, England. He came to the US in the 1930s and eventually became an American citizen. His program "Letter from America" was broadcast in more than 50 countries by BBC Radio for an astonishing 58 years. He was the chief American correspondent for the *Guardian* for 26 years, and he hosted PBS's "Masterpiece Theatre" for more than 20 years. Highly regarded for his sophisticated grace and style in both writing and broadcasting, he continued to broadcast "Letter from America" until his death at New York, NY, Mar 30, 2004.

GORDIMER, NADINE: BIRTH ANNIVERSARY. Nov 20, 1923. Born at Spring, South Africa, Nadine Gordimer is one of the world's most revered authors for her vivid, moving depictions of the disintegration of South African society. Antiapartheid and class-conflict themes run throughout her oeuvre, which includes *The Conservationist* (Booker Prize winner), *Burger's Daughter* and *No Time Like the Present*. Recipient of the Nobel Prize for Literature (1991), Fellow of the Royal Society of Literature and member of the Order of the Southern Cross, South Africa, Gordimer was also involved in the African National Congress and helped friend Nelson Mandela edit his famous "I Am Prepared to Die" speech. An ardent HIV/AIDS activist, Gordimer died July 13, 2014, at Johannesburg, South Africa.

GOULD, CHESTER: BIRTH ANNIVERSARY. Nov 20, 1900. In 1931 Chester Gould created comic strip character Dick Tracy, the clean-cut, square-jawed, plainclothed detective who represented the code that "crime doesn't pay." The strip first appeared Oct 4, 1931, in the *Detroit Daily Mirror* and later was syndicated in nearly 1,000 newspapers worldwide. "Dick Tracy" (originally called "Plainclothes Tracy") featured Tess Trueheart (later Mrs Tracy) and a host of bad guys with ugly names and faces to match their ugly ways—Mole, Pruneface, Flat Top, B-B Eyes, Mumbles and others. Closely following actual police methods of crime prevention, it included a "Crimestopper Notebook" with tips on self-protection. More violent than most other comic strips, "Dick Tracy" was a combination of realism and science fiction. Chester Gould was born at Pawnee, OK, and died May 11, 1985, at Woodstock, IL.

HOLIDAY FOLK FAIR INTERNATIONAL. Nov 20–22. Wisconsin State Fair Park, Milwaukee, WI. International festival featuring costumes, dancing, entertainment, exhibits, workshops, folk wares and cuisine from 65 cultures. Also children's activities. Annually, the weekend before Thanksgiving. Est attendance: 50,000. For info: Holiday Folk Fair International, Intl Institute of Wisconsin, 1110 N Old World Third St, Ste 420, Milwaukee, WI 53203. Phone: (414) 225-6220. Fax: (414) 225-6235. E-mail: folkfair@iiwisconsin.org. Web: www.folkfair.org.

HUBBLE, EDWIN POWELL: BIRTH ANNIVERSARY. Nov 20, 1889. American astronomer Edwin Hubble was born at Marshfield, MO. His discovery and development of the concept of an expanding universe has been described as the "most spectacular astronomical discovery" of the 20th century. As a tribute, the Hubble Space Telescope, deployed Apr 25, 1990, from US space shuttle *Discovery*, was named for him. The Hubble Space Telescope, with a 240-centimeter mirror, was to allow astronomers to see farther into space than they had ever seen from telescopes on Earth. Hubble died at San Marino, CA, Sept 28, 1953.

KENNEDY, ROBERT FRANCIS: 95th BIRTH ANNIVERSARY. Nov 20, 1925. The US senator and younger brother of John F. Kennedy, 35th president of the US, was born at Brookline, MA. An assassin shot him at Los Angeles, CA, June 5, 1968, while he was campaigning for the presidential nomination. He died the next day. Sirhan Sirhan was convicted of his murder.

LAGERLOF, SELMA: BIRTH ANNIVERSARY. Nov 20, 1858. The Swedish author, member of the Swedish Academy and the first woman to receive the Nobel Prize in Literature (1909) was born at Sweden's Varmland Province. She died there Mar 16, 1940.

LANDIS, KENESAW MOUNTAIN: BIRTH ANNIVERSARY. Nov 20, 1866. Baseball Hall of Fame executive born at Millville, OH. Landis was a federal judge who was named the first commissioner of baseball in 1920. He rose to public attention with his handling of the "Black Sox" scandal of 1919, in which Chicago White Sox players—angry at being underpaid and mistreated by team owner Charles Comiskey—were accused of throwing the World Series to the Cincinnati Reds. In one of his first acts as commissioner,

Landis banned eight White Sox players for life, even though nothing could be proven and they were acquitted in a trial. Landis ruled with an absolutely firm hand and imposed his view of how baseball should operate upon owners and players alike. Inducted into the Hall of Fame in 1944, he died at Chicago, IL, on Nov 25, 1944.

LAURIER, SIR WILFRED: BIRTH ANNIVERSARY. Nov 20, 1841. Canadian statesman (premier, 1896–1911), born at St. Lin, QC, Canada. Died Feb 17, 1919, at Ottawa, ON, Canada.

MANDELBROT, BENOIT: BIRTH ANNIVERSARY. Nov 20, 1924. Influential mathematician and professor, born at Warsaw, Poland. Mandelbrot was "the father of fractals," and his theories affected economics and finance, computer science, astronomy and other fields of study. He died at Cambridge, MA, on Oct 14, 2010.

MARION, FRANCES: BIRTH ANNIVERSARY. Nov 20, 1888. Screenwriter, author, journalist born at San Francisco, CA. Widely regarded as one of Hollywood's foremost screenwriters, and at one point its highest paid, Marion broke down barriers for women in the film industry. Her screenplays for *The Big House* (1930) and *The Champ* (1931) received Academy Awards. She died at Hollywood, CA, May 12, 1973.

MARRIAGE OF ELIZABETH AND PHILIP: ANNIVERSARY. Nov 20, 1947. The Princess Elizabeth Alexandra Mary was wed to Philip Mountbatten on Nov 20, 1947. Elizabeth was the first child of King George VI and Queen Elizabeth. Philip, the former Prince Philip of Greece, had become a British subject nine months earlier and the title Duke of Edinburgh was bestowed on him. The bride later became Elizabeth II, Queen of the United Kingdom of Great Britain and Northern Ireland and Head of the Commonwealth, upon the death of her father on Feb 6, 1952, her coronation taking place at Westminster Abbey on June 2, 1953.

MEXICO: REVOLUTION DAY. Nov 20. Anniversary of the social revolution launched by Francisco I. Madero in 1910. National holiday.

NAME YOUR PC DAY. Nov 20. Hey, why not? People name their boats! There are a lot more PCs than boats these days. "Binky" is already taken. Annually, Nov 20. (©2006 by WH.) For info: Thomas & Ruth Roy, Wellcat Holidays, 2418 Long Ln, Lebanon, PA 17046. Phone: (717) 279-0184. E-mail: info@wellcat.com. Web: www.wellcat.com.

NCAA DIVISION I FIELD HOCKEY CHAMPIONSHIP. Nov 20–22. LR Hill Sports Complex, Norfolk, VA. 39th annual. For info: NCAA, PO Box 6222, Indianapolis, IN 46206-6222. Phone: (317) 917-6222. Web: www.NCAA.com.

NUREMBERG WAR CRIMES TRIALS: 75th ANNIVERSARY. Nov 20, 1945. The first session of the German war crimes trials started at Berlin, Germany, with indictments against 24 former Nazi leaders. Later sessions were held at Nuremberg, Germany, starting Nov 20, 1945. One defendant committed suicide during his trial, and another was excused because of his physical and mental condition. The trials lasted more than 10 months, and delivery of the judgment was completed on Oct 1, 1946. Twelve were sentenced to death by hanging, three to life imprisonment and four to lesser prison terms; three were acquitted.

***THE SHEIK* FILM RELEASE: ANNIVERSARY.** Nov 20, 1921. The silent film that catapulted Rudolph Valentino into stardom was given a general release on this date after premieres in New York, NY, and Los Angeles, CA. The romantic melodrama, about a prince of the desert's obsession with an Englishwoman, was a hit that actually had women fainting in theaters. The film was scandalously frank for the times about sexual desire. "Sheik" even became slang for a man whom women couldn't resist. While the film made Valentino a reluctant sex symbol, it also typecast him—to his frustration. A sequel, *The Son of the Sheik*, was released in September 1926 a few weeks after Valentino's sudden death.

SUBSTITUTE EDUCATORS DAY. Nov 20. This day honors the educators who are called upon to replace regularly employed teachers. Annually, the Friday of American Education Week. For info: Natl Education Assn, 1201 16th St NW, Washington, DC 20036-3290. Phone: (202) 833-4000. Web: www.nea.org.

SUGARLOAF CRAFTS FESTIVAL. Nov 20–22. Montgomery County Fairgrounds, Gaithersburg, MD. This show features more than 400 nationally recognized craft designers and fine artists displaying and selling their original creations. Includes craft demonstrations, live music, children's entertainment, specialty foods, gift certificate drawings and more. Est attendance: 22,600. For info: Sugarloaf Mountain Works, 13225 Executive Park Terrace, Germantown, MD 20874. Phone: (800) 210-9900. E-mail: sugarloafinfo@sugarloaffest.com. Web: www.sugarloafcrafts.com.

TIERNEY, GENE: 100th BIRTH ANNIVERSARY. Nov 20, 1920. Known best for the title role in the film *Laura*, actress Gene Tierney was born at Brooklyn, NY. Her other films include *Heaven Can Wait, A Bell for Adano, Advise and Consent* and her last film, *The Pleasure Seekers*. She died Nov 6, 1991, at Houston, TX.

TRANSGENDER DAY OF REMEMBRANCE. Nov 20. A day honoring the memory of those murdered because of anti-transgender prejudice. Initially observed to call attention to the murder of Rita Hester on Nov 28, 1998. Annually, Nov 20. For info: Marti Abernathey, Transgender Day of Remembrance. Phone: (888) 206-8009. E-mail: transgenderdor@gmail.com. Web: https://tdor.info.

UNITED NATIONS: AFRICA INDUSTRIALIZATION DAY. Nov 20. The General Assembly proclaimed this day for the purpose of mobilizing the commitment of the international community to the industrialization of the continent (Res 44/237, Dec 22, 1989). Annually, Nov 20. For info: United Nations, Dept of Public Info, New York, NY 10017. Web: www.un.org.

UNITED NATIONS: UNIVERSAL CHILDREN'S DAY. Nov 20. Designated by the General Assembly as Universal Children's Day. First observance was in 1953. A time to honor children with special ceremonies and festivals and to make children's needs known to governments. Observed on different days and in different ways in more than 120 nations. For info: United Nations, Dept of Public Info, New York, NY 10017. Web: www.un.org.

VON FRISCH, KARL: BIRTH ANNIVERSARY. Nov 20, 1886. This Nobel Prize–winning ethologist, born at Vienna, Austria, gave the world astounding new knowledge about bees, his specialty. Von Frisch decoded the "dance" of the honeybee: actually a form of communication in which the dancer describes distance and location of pollen to its hive comrades. He also determined that bees use the sun as a compass and studied bees' sense of taste and smell. Von Frisch was jointly awarded the Nobel Prize in Physiology or Medicine in 1973 along with Konrad Lorenz and Nicholaas Tinbergen for their work on animal behavior. He died at Munich, Germany, on June 12, 1982.

WOLCOTT, OLIVER: BIRTH ANNIVERSARY. Nov 20, 1726. Signer of the Declaration of Independence, governor of Connecticut, born at Windsor, CT. Died Dec 1, 1797, at Litchfield, CT.

November 2020	S	M	T	W	T	F	S
	1	2	3	4	5	6	7
	8	9	10	11	12	13	14
	15	16	17	18	19	20	21
	22	23	24	25	26	27	28
	29	30					

🧁 BIRTHDAYS TODAY

Dierks Bentley, 45, country singer, born Tempe, AZ, Nov 20, 1975.

Joseph Robinette Biden, Jr, 78, former vice president of the US (Obama administration), former US senator (D, Delaware), born Scranton, PA, Nov 20, 1942.

Carlos Boozer, 39, basketball player, born Juneau, AK, Nov 20, 1981.

Steve Dahl, 66, radio personality, born Pasadena, CA, Nov 20, 1954.

Don DeLillo, 84, author (*White Noise, Underworld*), born New York, NY, Nov 20, 1936.

Bo Derek, 64, actress (*10, Bolero, Tarzan, A Change of Seasons*), born Cathleen Collins at Long Beach, CA, Nov 20, 1956.

Veronica Hamel, 77, actress ("Hill Street Blues"), born Philadelphia, PA, Nov 20, 1943.

Sabrina Lloyd, 50, actress ("Sports Night," "Sliders"), born Mount Dora, FL, Nov 20, 1970.

Richard Masur, 72, actor ("One Day at a Time," *Heartburn*), born New York, NY, Nov 20, 1948.

Estelle Parsons, 93, stage and screen actress (Oscar for *Bonnie and Clyde*; *August: Osage County*, "Roseanne"), born Marblehead, MA, Nov 20, 1927.

Dick Smothers, 81, comedian, folksinger (with brother Tom, "The Smothers Brothers Comedy Hour"), born New York, NY, Nov 20, 1939.

Ming-Na Wen, 53, actress ("Agents of S.H.I.E.L.D.," "ER"), born Macau, China, Nov 20, 1967.

Judy Woodruff, 74, journalist, anchor ("PBS NewsHour"), born Tulsa, OK, Nov 20, 1946.

Sean Young, 61, actress (*Blade Runner, No Way Out*), born Louisville, KY, Nov 20, 1959.

November 21 — Saturday

DAY 326   **40 REMAINING**

BARTLETT, JOSIAH: BIRTH ANNIVERSARY. Nov 21, 1729. Signer of the Declaration of Independence. Born at Amesbury, MA, he died at Kingston, NH, May 19, 1795.

CONGRESS FIRST MEETS AT WASHINGTON: ANNIVERSARY. Nov 21, 1800. Congress met at Philadelphia, PA, from 1790 to 1800, when the north wing of the new Capitol at Washington, DC, was completed. The House and the Senate had been scheduled to meet in the new building Nov 17, 1800, but a quorum wasn't achieved until Nov 21.

CUNARD, SAMUEL: BIRTH ANNIVERSARY. Nov 21, 1787. Born at Halifax, NS, Canada, Cunard was already a successful businessman when he contracted with the British government to deliver mail across the Atlantic Ocean on May 4, 1839. With a team of engineers and financiers, Cunard built the steamships necessary for fast, dependable transatlantic mail delivery in a venture called the British and North American Royal Mail Steam Packet Company—later called the Cunard Line. Cunard later expanded into passenger service. He died Apr 28, 1865, at London, England.

DOW JONES TOPS 5,000: 25th ANNIVERSARY. Nov 21, 1995. The Dow Jones Index of 30 major industrial stocks topped the 5,000 mark for the first time.

ELLA FITZGERALD WINS APOLLO AMATEUR NIGHT: ANNIVERSARY. Nov 21, 1934. A shy, impoverished teenager, dressed in borrowed clothes and men's shoes, stepped onto the stage of Harlem, NY's Apollo Theater for Amateur Night on this date. Ella Fitzgerald, in her stage debut, was so nervous that she fumbled her first song, but prompted to restart, she sang "Object of My Affection" and "Judy" to a crowd that exploded with applause. She won the contest. Bandleader Benny Carter, whose orchestra was backing the amateurs that night, helped Fitzgerald make music industry connections, and in 1935 she began to find success as a singer.

FRENCHMAN ROWS ACROSS PACIFIC: ANNIVERSARY. Nov 21, 1991. Gerard d'Aboville completed a four-month solo journey across the Pacific Ocean on this date. D'Aboville began rowing across the Pacific on July 11 when he left Choshi, Japan. His journey ended at Ilwaco, WA.

GREEN, HETTY: BIRTH ANNIVERSARY. Nov 21, 1834. Born at New Bedford, MA, Henrietta Howland Robinson Green was the richest woman in America during her lifetime. Although she hailed from a wealthy mercantile family, her spare Quaker upbringing taught her to live a simple, frugal life. In fact, her miserliness was legendary, and tales of her eccentric behavior were widely circulated at the time. She was a gifted financier, known as the "witch of Wall Street," who grew a substantial inheritance into a formidable fortune, which was estimated to have been in excess of $100 million. She died at New York, NY, July 3, 1916.

LUCKMAN, SID: BIRTH ANNIVERSARY. Nov 21, 1916. Sidney (Sid) Luckman, Pro Football Hall of Fame quarterback, born at New York, NY. Luckman played football at Columbia and then starred as quarterback for the great Chicago Bears teams of the 1940s. Luckman's talents enabled coach George Halas to install a modern version of the T formation, emphasizing speed and deception instead of brute strength. Luckman led the NFL in touchdown passes three times and quarterbacked the Bears to four NFL titles, including their epic 73–0 thrashing of the Washington Redskins in 1940. Inducted into the Hall of Fame in 1965. He died at Aventura, FL, July 5, 1998.

MOON PHASE: FIRST QUARTER. Nov 21. Moon enters First Quarter phase at 11:45 PM, EST.

MUSIAL, STAN: 100th BIRTH ANNIVERSARY. Nov 21, 1920. Legendary left-handed hitter for the St. Louis Cardinals, dubbed "Stan the Man" and famous for his concentration at bat and for his unique "corkscrew" stance. Musial played 22 major league seasons including three World Series championships, won three Most Valuable Player awards and was inducted into the baseball Hall of Fame in 1969. At retirement, Musial held several National League career batting records, including the most hits (3,630) to go with his .331 batting average and 475 home runs. While first in his league to earn a $100,000 salary, Musial was widely held to be the nicest guy in baseball. Musial died Jan 19, 2013, in Ladue, MO.

NCAA DIVISION I CROSS COUNTRY CHAMPIONSHIPS. Nov 21. OSU Cross Country Course, Stillwater, OK. Host is Oklahoma State. For info: NCAA, PO Box 6222, Indianapolis, IN 46206-6222. Phone: (317) 917-6222. Web: www.NCAA.com.

NORTH CAROLINA: RATIFICATION DAY: ANNIVERSARY. Nov 21. Became the 12th state to ratify the Constitution in 1789.

POPE BENEDICT XV: BIRTH ANNIVERSARY. Nov 21, 1854. Giacomo della Chiesa, 258th pope of the Roman Catholic Church, born at Pegli, Italy, and elected pope Sept 3, 1914. Died at Rome, Italy, Jan 22, 1922.

PURCELL, HENRY: 325th DEATH ANNIVERSARY. Nov 21, 1695. (Old Style date.) The great English composer of the early Baroque period, born in 1659 at London, England, had a tragically short life yet was a prolific composer. His fame rests on the proto-operas *Dido and Aeneas* (1689) and *The Fairy Queen* (1692, based on Shakespeare's *A Midsummer-Night's Dream*), ceremonial odes for the court of King Charles II and more than 100 songs. The holder of various court musical positions, Purcell died at London.

REMEMBRANCE DAY PARADE AND CEREMONIES. Nov 21. Gettysburg, PA. An annual event held in conjunction with the Gettysburg Address Anniversary, with a parade of Civil War Living History to the Soldiers' National Cemetery. Remembrance Illumination is at the cemetery from 5:30 to 9:00 PM. Est attendance: 10,000. For info: Destination Gettysburg. E-mail: info@destinationgettysburg.com. Web: www.destinationgettysburg.com.

THAILAND: ELEPHANT ROUNDUP AT SURIN. Nov 21. Surin. Elephant demonstrations in morning, elephant races and tug-of-war between 100 men and one elephant. Observed since 1961 on the third Saturday in November. Special trains from Bangkok on previous day.

UNITED NATIONS: WORLD TELEVISION DAY. Nov 21. On Dec 17, 1996, the General Assembly proclaimed this day as World Television Day, commemorating the date in 1996 on which the first World Television Forum was held at the UN. Annually, Nov 21. For info: United Nations, Dept of Public Info, New York, NY 10017. Web: www.un.org.

VOLTAIRE, JEAN FRANÇOIS MARIE: BIRTH ANNIVERSARY. Nov 21, 1694. French author and philosopher to whom is attributed (perhaps erroneously) the statement: "I disapprove of what you say, but I will defend to the death your right to say it." His most famous work is the novel *Candide*. Born at Paris, France, he died there May 30, 1778.

WHO SHOT J.R.?: 40th ANNIVERSARY. Nov 21, 1980. A record 86.6 million viewers watched CBS's hit drama "Dallas," to see who shot villainous tycoon J.R. Ewing (Larry Hagman). An unseen assailant had gunned him down on the show's season finale Mar 21, 1980, and sparked international curiosity, a ubiquitous catchphrase ("Who shot J.R.?") and Las Vegas bets. (Sue Ellen Ewing's sister, Kristin Shephard, shot J.R.)

WORLD HELLO DAY. Nov 21. 48th annual. Everyone who participates greets 10 people. People in 180 countries have participated in this annual activity for advancing peace through personal communication. Heads of state of 114 countries have expressed approval of the event. For info: The McCormacks, PO Box 641162, Los Angeles, CA 90064. Web: www.worldhelloday.org.

🎂 BIRTHDAYS TODAY

Troy Aikman, 54, sportscaster, Hall of Fame football player, born West Covina, CA, Nov 21, 1966.

Bjork, 55, singer, actress, born Björk Gudmundsdóttir at Reykjavik, Iceland, Nov 21, 1965.

Marcy Carsey, 76, television producer, born South Weymouth, MA, Nov 21, 1944.

James DePreist, 84, conductor, born Philadelphia, PA, Nov 21, 1936.

Richard J. Durbin, 76, US Senator (D, Illinois), born East St. Louis, IL, Nov 21, 1944.

George Kenneth (Ken) Griffey, Jr, 51, former baseball player, born Donora, PA, Nov 21, 1969.

Goldie Hawn, 75, actress (*The Banger Sisters, Private Benjamin*, Oscar for *Cactus Flower*), born Washington, DC, Nov 21, 1945.

November 2020	S	M	T	W	T	F	S
	1	2	3	4	5	6	7
	8	9	10	11	12	13	14
	15	16	17	18	19	20	21
	22	23	24	25	26	27	28
	29	30					

Carly Rae Jepsen, 35, singer, born Mission, BC, Canada, Nov 21, 1985.

John N. Kennedy, 69, US Senator (R, Louisiana), born Centreville, MS, Nov 21, 1951.

Laurence Luckinbill, 86, actor (*Star Trek V*), born Fort Smith, AR, Nov 21, 1934.

Lorna Luft, 68, singer, actress, born Los Angeles, CA, Nov 21, 1952.

Juliet Mills, 79, actress ("Nanny and the Professor," "Passions," *So Well Remembered*), born London, England, Nov 21, 1941.

Sam Palladio, 34, actor ("Nashville," "Episodes"), born Pembury, Kent, England, Nov 21, 1986.

Cynthia Rhodes, 64, actress, dancer (*Flashdance, Dirty Dancing*), born Nashville, TN, Nov 21, 1956.

Tasha Schwikert, 36, gymnast, born Las Vegas, NV, Nov 21, 1984.

Nicollette Sheridan, 57, actress ("Desperate Housewives," "Knots Landing"), born Worthing, Sussex, England, Nov 21, 1963.

Michael Strahan, 49, television personality ("Good Morning America," "FOX NFL Sunday"), Hall of Fame football player, born Houston, TX, Nov 21, 1971.

Marlo Thomas, 82, actress ("That Girl"), author, born Detroit, MI, Nov 21, 1938.

November 22 — Sunday

DAY 327   **39 REMAINING**

ADAMS, ABIGAIL SMITH: BIRTH ANNIVERSARY. Nov 22, 1744. Wife of John Adams, second president of the US, and mother of John Quincy Adams, sixth president of the US. An intelligent woman interested in politics and current affairs, she was a prodigious letter writer and an influence on her husband. Abigail Adams argued to her husband that Congress "should remember the ladies" as the new American government took form. Born at Weymouth, MA, she died Oct 28, 1818, at Quincy, MA.

BRITTEN, EDWARD BENJAMIN: BIRTH ANNIVERSARY. Nov 22, 1913. One of the most important composers of the 20th century was born at Lowestoft, Suffolk, England. In addition to chamber and orchestral works, he was a composer of film scores, song cycles and experimental pieces in collaboration with poets such as W.H. Auden. His best-known and most acclaimed works are the tragic opera *Peter Grimes* (1945)—its success made Britten a celebrity—and *War Requiem* (1962), a moving response to the horror of WWII that premiered in the newly rebuilt Coventry Cathedral. Britten's other operas include *Billy Budd, The Turn of the Screw* and *A Midsummer Night's Dream*. Lord Britten, Baron Britten of Aldeburgh, died at Aldeburgh, England, Dec 4, 1976.

CARMICHAEL, HOAGIE: BIRTH ANNIVERSARY. Nov 22, 1899. Hoagland Howard Carmichael, an attorney who gave up the practice of law to become an actor and songwriter, was born at Bloomington, IN. Among his many popular songs: "Stardust," "Lazybones," "Two Sleepy People" and "Skylark." Carmichael died at Rancho Mirage, CA, Dec 27, 1981.

CHINA CLIPPER: 85th ANNIVERSARY. Nov 22, 1935. A Pan American Martin 130 "flying boat" called the *China Clipper* began regular transpacific mail service on Nov 22, 1935. The plane, powered by four Pratt and Whitney Twin Wasp engines, took off from San Francisco, CA. It reached Manila, Philippines, 59 hours and 48 minutes later. About 20,000 persons watched the historic takeoff. Commercial passenger service was established the following year (Oct 21, 1936).

DE GAULLE, CHARLES ANDRÉ MARIE: BIRTH ANNIVERSARY. Nov 22, 1890. President of France from December 1958 until his resignation in April 1969, Charles de Gaulle was born at Lille, France. A military leader, he wrote *The Army of the Future* (1934), in which he predicted just the type of armored warfare that was used

against his country by Nazi Germany in WWII. After France's defeat at the hands of the Germans, he declared the existence of "Free France" and made himself head of that organization. When the French Vichy government began to collaborate openly with the Germans, the French citizenry looked to de Gaulle for leadership. His greatest moment of triumph was when he entered liberated Paris on Aug 26, 1944. He died at Colombey-les-Deux-Églises, France, Nov 19, 1970.

ELIOT, GEORGE: BIRTH ANNIVERSARY. Nov 22, 1819. Novelist George Eliot, whose real name was Mary Ann Evans, was born at Nuneaton, Warwickshire, England. Her works include *Silas Marner, Adam Bede* and the classic study of marriage *Middlemarch.* Eliot's scandalous relationship with George Henry Lewes initially shocked Victorian society; however, their London home soon became an intellectual and literary mecca. Her literary popularity eventually ended her social isolation, and she discovered that Queen Victoria was a fan of her work. Eliot died at Chelsea, England, Dec 22, 1880.

GARNER, JOHN NANCE: BIRTH ANNIVERSARY. Nov 22, 1868. The 32nd vice president of the US (1933–41). Garner was a congressional representative from 1903 to 1933 and Speaker of the House for two years (1931–33). Garner worked closely with President Franklin D. Roosevelt on New Deal legislation but eventually split with the president over Roosevelt's plan to reorganize the Supreme Court. Garner was born at Red River County, TX; died at Uvalde, TX, Nov 7, 1967.

GERMANY: TOTENSONNTAG. Nov 22. In Germany, Totensonntag is the Protestant population's day for remembrance of the dead. It is celebrated on the last Sunday of the church year (the Sunday before Advent).

KENNEDY, JOHN F.: ASSASSINATION ANNIVERSARY. Nov 22, 1963. President John F. Kennedy was slain by a sniper while riding in an open automobile at Dallas, TX. Accused assassin Lee Harvey Oswald was killed by Jack Ruby while in police custody awaiting trial.

LEBANON: INDEPENDENCE DAY. Nov 22. National day. Gained independence from France in 1943.

MOTHER GOOSE PARADE. Nov 22. El Cajon, CA. 74th annual. "A celebration of children." Floats depict Mother Goose rhymes and fairy tales and/or annual theme. Bands, equestrians and clowns. Traditionally, the Sunday before Thanksgiving. Est attendance: 250,000. For info: Mother Goose Parade Assn. E-mail: info@themothergooseparade.com. Web: www.themothergooseparade.com.

★NATIONAL FAMILY WEEK. Nov 22–28. To celebrate the inclusive spirit of American families and applaud the commitment of those family members who encourage us to reach new heights. Annually, the week that includes Thanksgiving Day.

NATIONAL GAME & PUZZLE WEEK™. Nov 22–28. 26th annual event to increase appreciation of board games and puzzles while preserving the tradition of investing time with family and friends. Special organizer materials and media information available, including press kits, interviews, etc. Annually, the Sunday through Saturday of Thanksgiving week. For info: Beth Muehlenkamp, Natl Game & Puzzle Week, 1400 E Inman Pkwy, Beloit, WI 53511. Phone: (800) 524-4263. Fax: (608) 362-8178. E-mail: bethm@playmonster.com. Web: www.playmonster.com.

***ON THE ORIGIN OF SPECIES* PUBLISHED: ANNIVERSARY.** Nov 22, 1859. Charles Darwin's monumental work, *On the Origin of Species by Means of Natural Selection, or the Preservation of Favoured Races in the Struggle for Life,* was published on this date by London publisher John Murray. The print run of 1,250 (priced at 15 shillings) sold out the same day. A second print run of 3,000 in December also sold quickly. The book immediately generated a firestorm of public and private discussion. The word *evolution* did not appear until the 1872 (last) edition of *Origin.*

POST, WILEY: BIRTH ANNIVERSARY. Nov 22, 1898. Barnstorming aviator, stunt parachutist and adventurer, Wiley Post was born at Grand Plain, TX. Post, who taught himself to fly, and his plane, the *Winnie Mae,* were the center of world attention in the 1930s.

He was coauthor (with his navigator, Harold Gatty) of *Around the World in Eight Days.* In 1935 Post and friend Will Rogers started on a flight to Asia. Their plane crashed near Point Barrow, AK, Aug 15, 1935; both were killed.

PRIME MINISTER THATCHER RESIGNS: 30th ANNIVERSARY. Nov 22, 1990. Margaret Thatcher announced that she would resign from her position as England's prime minister. She had been named prime minister in May 1979 and served until Nov 22, 1990. No other prime minister in the United Kingdom in the 20th century served the post as long as she.

SAGITTARIUS, THE ARCHER. Nov 22–Dec 21. In the astronomical/ astrological zodiac that divides the sun's apparent orbit into 12 segments, the period Nov 22–Dec 21 is traditionally identified as the sun sign of Sagittarius, the Archer. The ruling planet is Jupiter.

SAINT CECILIA: FEAST DAY. Nov 22. The Roman virgin, Christian martyr and patron of music and musicians lived during the second or third century. Survived sentence of suffocation by steam but succumbed to sentence of beheading. Subject of poetry and musical compositions, and her feast day is still an occasion for musical events.

STIR UP SUNDAY. Nov 22. Traditional day in Britain—since before the 19th century—to make the Christmas pudding, when everyone in the household takes a turn stirring up the batter. Each stirrer makes a wish. Often, coins and charms are added to be discovered later. Observed on the Sunday before Advent (five weeks before Christmas). The collect for this day, from *The Book of Common Prayer,* begins, "Stir up, we beseech thee, O Lord."

TEACH, EDWARD "BLACKBEARD": DEATH ANNIVERSARY. Nov 22, 1718. The English pirate of the Caribbean and American Atlantic met his end at Ocracoke Island, NC, in hand-to-hand combat with British naval forces defending coastal cities. Born around 1680 at Bristol, England, Teach had a notorious reputation in a pirate career that spanned the years 1716–18 aboard his ship *Queen Anne's Revenge.* Teach grew his hair and beard to long lengths and plaited them, and set lighted cords about his head to create evil-looking smoke around him.

🎂 BIRTHDAYS TODAY

Boris Becker, 53, Hall of Fame tennis player, born Leimen, Germany, Nov 22, 1967.

Hailey Baldwin Bieber, 24, model, television personality ("Drop the Mic"), born Tucson, AZ, Nov 22, 1996.

Guion S. Bluford, Jr, 78, first black astronaut in space, born West Philadelphia, PA, Nov 22, 1942.

Tom Conti, 79, actor (Tony for *Whose Life Is It Anyway?*), born Paisley, Scotland, Nov 22, 1941.

Jamie Lee Curtis, 62, actress (*True Lies, Halloween, A Fish Called Wanda*), born Los Angeles, CA, Nov 22, 1958.

Harry Edwards, 78, sports sociologist, born St. Louis, MO, Nov 22, 1942.

Terry Gilliam, 80, actor, writer ("Monty Python's Flying Circus," *Life of Brian*), director (*Brazil*), born Minneapolis, MN, Nov 22, 1940.

Mariel Hemingway, 59, actress (*Manhattan, Personal Best, Superman IV*), born Ketchum, ID, Nov 22, 1961.

Scarlett Johansson, 36, actress (*Lucy, The Avengers, Vicky Cristina Barcelona, Lost in Translation*), born New York, NY, Nov 22, 1984.

Richard Kind, 63, actor ("Spin City," "Mad About You"), born Trenton, NJ, Nov 22, 1957.

Billie Jean King, 77, Hall of Fame tennis player, born Long Beach, CA, Nov 22, 1943.

Mads Mikkelsen, 55, actor (*Rogue One, Casino Royale*, "Hannibal"), born Østerbro, Copenhagen, Denmark, Nov 22, 1965.

Mark Ruffalo, 53, actor (*Spotlight, The Avengers, The Kids Are All Right*), born Kenosha, WI, Nov 22, 1967.

November 23 — Monday

DAY 328   **38 REMAINING**

ASHFORD, EMMETT LITTLETON: BIRTH ANNIVERSARY. Nov 23, 1914. Emmett Littleton Ashford, born at Los Angeles, CA, was the first black to officiate at a major league baseball game. Ashford began his pro career calling games in the minors in 1951 and went to the majors in 1966. He was noted for his flamboyant style when calling strikes and outs as well as for his dapper dress, which included cuff links with his uniform. He died Mar 1, 1980, at Marina del Rey, CA.

BETTER CONVERSATION WEEK. Nov 23–28. 20th annual. Have meaningful conversations with friends, family and coworkers during Thanksgiving week. Learn new ways to renew bonds with meaningful, enjoyable talk. Record your elders telling life stories for posterity and make recordings for extended family and friends. For info: Dr. Loren Ekroth, 9030 W Sahara Ave, Ste 430, Las Vegas, NV 89117. E-mail: loren@conversationmatters.com. Web: www.conversationmatters.com.

BILLY THE KID: BIRTH ANNIVERSARY. Nov 23, 1859. Legendary outlaw of western US. Probably named Henry McCarty at birth (New York, NY), he was better known as William H. Bonney. Ruthless killer, a failure at everything legal, he escaped from jail at age 21 while under sentence of hanging. Recaptured at Stinking Springs, NM, and returned to jail, he again escaped, only to be shot through the heart by pursuing Lincoln County sheriff Pat Garrett at Fort Sumner, NM, during the night of July 14, 1881. His last words, answered by two shots, reportedly were, "Who is there?"

"DOCTOR WHO" TV PREMIERE: ANNIVERSARY. Nov 23, 1963. The first episode of "Doctor Who" premiered on British TV with William Hartnell as the first Doctor. Traveling through time and space in the TARDIS (an acronym for Time and Relative Dimensions in Space), the Doctor and his companions found themselves in mortal combat with creatures such as the Daleks. The series aired until 1989, with a special film in 1996. "Doctor Who" didn't air in the US until Sept 29, 1975, but then attracted a huge cult following. A new version of the series began in 2005, with Christopher Eccleston and David Tennant as the 9th and 10th Doctors. Matt Smith made his debut as Doctor number 11 in 2010 and Peter Capaldi began his reign as Doctor number 12 in the 800th episode, which aired Dec 25, 2013. Jodie Whittaker became the first woman to play Doctor Who when she took on the role of number 13 starting in December 2017.

FIBONACCI DAY. Nov 23. Day celebrating the Fibonacci sequence in mathematics: a string of numbers where each number is the sum

of the preceding pair of numbers. In the American shorthand of expressing dates, Nov 23 is 11/23, and 1+1=2; 2+1=3. Fibonacci numbers were named after a medieval Italian mathematician, Leonardo of Pisa, or Leonardo Fibonacci (1170–1240 or later), who described the sequence in his 1202 treatise *Liber abaci*.

FIRST PLAY-BY-PLAY FOOTBALL GAME BROADCAST: ANNIVERSARY. Nov 23, 1919. The first play-by-play football game radio broadcast in the United States took place on this day. Texas A&M blanked the University of Texas, 7–0.

JAPAN: LABOR THANKSGIVING DAY. Nov 23. National holiday.

KARLOFF, BORIS: BIRTH ANNIVERSARY. Nov 23, 1887. Born William Henry Pratt at London, England. An actor known for his portrayal of ghoulish figures; his movies include *Frankenstein, The Body Snatcher* and *The Bride of Frankenstein*. Karloff died Feb 2, 1969, at Sussex, England.

***LIFE* MAGAZINE DEBUTS: ANNIVERSARY.** Nov 23, 1936. The illustrated magazine *Life* debuted on this day. The first cover featured a dramatic photograph by Margaret Bourke-White of Fort Peck Dam.

MARX, HARPO: BIRTH ANNIVERSARY. Nov 23, 1888. Adolph Arthur "Harpo" Marx was born at New York, NY. He was the second-born of the famed Marx Brothers, who were a popular comedy team of stage, screen and radio for 30 years. The silent brother, Harpo wore a red curly wig and communicated by honking a taxi horn at the most inopportune moments. He was a self-taught and expert player of the harp. Marx died Sept 28, 1964, at Hollywood, CA. Other family members who participated in the comedy team were Groucho (Julius), Chico (Leonard) and, briefly, Zeppo (Herbert) and Gummo (Milton).

PIERCE, FRANKLIN: BIRTH ANNIVERSARY. Nov 23, 1804. The 14th president of the US was born at Hillsboro, NH. Term of office: Mar 4, 1853–Mar 3, 1857. Not nominated until the 49th ballot at the Democratic Party Convention in 1852, he was refused his party's nomination in 1856 for a second term. Pierce died at Concord, NH, Oct 8, 1869.

RUTLEDGE, EDWARD: BIRTH ANNIVERSARY. Nov 23, 1749. Signer of the Declaration of Independence, governor of South Carolina, born at Charleston, SC. Died there Jan 23, 1800.

SWITZERLAND: ONION MARKET (ZIBELEMARIT). Nov 23. Berne. Best known and most popular of Switzerland's many autumn markets. Huge heaps of onions in front of Federal Palace. Fourth Monday in November commemorates granting of market right to people after great fire of Berne in 1405.

🎂 BIRTHDAYS TODAY

Viktor Ahn, 35, Olympic speed skater, born Ahn Hyun-soo at Seoul, South Korea, Nov 23, 1985.

Miley Cyrus, 28, actress, singer ("Hannah Montana"), born Destiny Hope Cyrus at Franklin, TN, Nov 23, 1992.

Lucas Grabeel, 36, actor (*High School Musical*), born Springfield, MO, Nov 23, 1984.

Chris Hardwick, 49, comedian, television personality, podcaster ("The Nerdist"), born Louisville, KY, Nov 23, 1971.

Steve Harvey, 64, talk show host ("Steve Harvey"), comedian, actor ("The Steve Harvey Show"), born Welch, WV, Nov 23, 1956.

Krzysztof Penderecki, 87, composer, born Debica, Poland, Nov 23, 1933.

November 2020	S	M	T	W	T	F	S
	1	2	3	4	5	6	7
	8	9	10	11	12	13	14
	15	16	17	18	19	20	21
	22	23	24	25	26	27	28
	29	30					

Nicole "Snooki" Polizzi, 33, television personality ("Jersey Shore"), born Santiago, Chile, Nov 23, 1987.

Charles E. Schumer, 70, US Senator (D, New York), born Brooklyn, NY, Nov 23, 1950.

Richard (Ricky) Whittle, 39, actor ("American Gods," "The 100," "Hollyoaks"), former model, born Oldham, England, Nov 23, 1981.

November 24 — Tuesday

DAY 329   **37 REMAINING**

BARKLEY, ALBEN WILLIAM: BIRTH ANNIVERSARY. Nov 24, 1877. The 35th vice president of the US (1949–53) was born at Graves County, KY. Died at Lexington, VA, Apr 30, 1956.

BATTLE OF CHATTANOOGA: ANNIVERSARY. Nov 24, 1863. After reinforcing the besieged Union army at Chattanooga, TN, General Ulysses S. Grant launched the Battle of Chattanooga on this date. Falsely secure in the belief that his troops were in an impregnable position on Lookout Mountain, Confederate general Braxton Bragg and his army were overrun by the Union forces, Bragg himself barely escaping capture. The battle is famous for the Union army's spectacular advance up a heavily fortified slope into the teeth of the enemy guns.

BUCKLEY, WILLIAM F., JR: 95th BIRTH ANNIVERSARY. Nov 24, 1925. Entertaining and influential postwar conservative standard-bearer as well as author, editor, talk show host and master of polysyllabic parlance. Founded the *National Review* in 1955. Born at New York, NY, Buckley died Feb 24, 2008, at Stamford, CT.

CARNEGIE, DALE: BIRTH ANNIVERSARY. Nov 24, 1888. American inspirational lecturer and author Dale Carnegie was born at Maryville, MO. He was born into poverty and described himself as a "simple country boy." He began teaching public speaking in 1912 and parlayed his success there into his best-known book, *How to Win Friends and Influence People,* published in 1936. The perennial bestseller is still in print and has sold 15 million copies. Carnegie died at New York, NY, Nov 1, 1955.

CELEBRATE YOUR UNIQUE TALENT DAY. Nov 24. We all have at least one extraordinary—and many times weird—ability. Now's the time to get out there and indulge in yours. Enter our unique talent competition in 2020! Annually, Nov 24. For info: Shannon Hurd. Phone: (720) 936-3326. E-mail: info@uniquetalentday.com. Web: www.uniquetalentday.com.

"D.B. COOPER" HIJACKING: ANNIVERSARY. Nov 24, 1971. A middle-aged man whose plane ticket was made out to "D.B. Cooper" parachuted from a Northwest Airlines 727 jetliner, carrying $200,000, which he had collected from the airline as ransom for the plane and passengers as a result of threats made during his earlier flight from Portland, OR, to Seattle, WA. He jumped from the plane over an area of wilderness south of Seattle and was never apprehended. Several thousand dollars of the marked ransom money turned up in February 1980, along the Columbia River, near Vancouver, WA.

DUFF, HOWARD: BIRTH ANNIVERSARY. Nov 24, 1913. American actor Howard Duff was born at Bremerton, WA. He played detective Sam Spade on radio in the 1940s and then went on to films and television ("Knots Landing"). He died July 8, 1990, at Santa Barbara, CA.

JOPLIN, SCOTT: BIRTH ANNIVERSARY. Nov 24, 1868. Influential American musician and composer famed for his ragtime music, born at Texarkana, TX. Composer of the opera *Treemonisha* and best known for "The Maple Leaf Rag" and "The Entertainer." The "King of Ragtime" died at New York, NY, Apr 1, 1917. (Although his tombstone gives his birth date as Nov 24, 1868, Joplin was probably born in 1867 or January 1868.)

SERRA, JUNIPERO: BIRTH ANNIVERSARY. Nov 24, 1713. Priest and pioneer, born Miguel Jose Serra at Petra, Majorca, Spain, whose missionary outposts introduced Catholicism to California and

organized the California frontier for Spain's colonial aims. Serra entered the Franciscan order in 1730 and taught philosophy at Lullian University (Majorca) and also in Mexico City before beginning missionary work in 1750. When Spain began colonizing Alta California, he joined the expedition and founded Mission San Diego in 1769. He founded eight more California missions, converting many Native Americans to Christianity and also teaching them how to farm and raise livestock. Serra died at Mission San Carlos Borromeo on Aug 28, 1784.

SPINOZA, BARUCH: BIRTH ANNIVERSARY. Nov 24, 1632. (Old Style date.) Dutch philosopher, born at Amsterdam, Netherlands. Died at The Hague, Netherlands, Feb 21, 1677 (OS). "Peace is not an absence of war," wrote Spinoza, in 1670, "it is a virtue, a state of mind, a disposition for benevolence, confidence, justice."

STERNE, LAURENCE: BIRTH ANNIVERSARY. Nov 24, 1713. Renowned novelist and humorist, born at Clonmel, Ireland. Sterne's crowning achievement was the comic novel *Tristram Shandy,* published in installments from 1759 to 1767. The novel is notable for its use of unconventional narrative techniques, such as the nonlinear plotline and its demand of interactive participation on the part of the reader, as well as its references to Lockean philosophy. Sterne died of tuberculosis at London, England, Mar 18, 1768.

TAYLOR, ZACHARY: BIRTH ANNIVERSARY. Nov 24, 1784. The Mexican War hero and career soldier who became the 12th president of the US was born at Orange County, VA. Term of office: Mar 4, 1849–July 9, 1850. He was nominated at the Whig Party convention in 1848, but the story goes he did not accept the letter notifying him of his nomination because it had postage due. He had cast his first vote in 1846, when he was 62 years old. Becoming ill July 4, 1850, he died at the White House, July 9. His last words: "I am sorry that I am about to leave my friends."

TOULOUSE-LAUTREC, HENRI DE: BIRTH ANNIVERSARY. Nov 24, 1864. French illustrator, lithographer, post-Impressionist painter. Born at Albi, France, Lautrec, deformed at an early age, found in the bohemian demimonde of Paris, especially the nightclubs and brothels of Montmartre, an outsider atmosphere that enticed him both personally and professionally. His drawings and posters in particular evoke the nightlife and habitués of that world. "Ugliness, everywhere and always, has its enchanting side," Lautrec said. "It is fascinating to discover it where no one else had noticed it." He died Sept 9, 1901, at Château Malromé, Gironde, France.

US MILITARY LEAVES PHILIPPINES: ANNIVERSARY. Nov 24, 1992. The Philippines became a US colony at the turn of the last century when it was taken over from Spain after the Spanish-American War. Though President Franklin D. Roosevelt signed a bill Mar 24, 1934, granting the Philippines independence to be effective July 4, 1946, before that date Manila and Washington signed a treaty allowing the US to lease military bases on the island. In 1991 the Philippine Senate voted to reject a renewal of that lease, and on Nov 24, 1992, after almost 100 years of military presence on the island, the last contingent of US Marines left Subic Base.

🎂 BIRTHDAYS TODAY

Garret Dillahunt, 56, actor ("Raising Hope," *Winter's Bone, No Country for Old Men*), born Castro Valley, CA, Nov 24, 1964.

Katherine Heigl, 42, actress ("Grey's Anatomy," *27 Dresses, Knocked Up*), born Washington, DC, Nov 24, 1978.

Sarah Hyland, 30, actress ("Modern Family," "Lipstick Jungle"), born New York, NY, Nov 24, 1990.

Stanley Livingston, 70, actor ("My Three Sons"), born Los Angeles, CA, Nov 24, 1950.

Keith Primeau, 49, hockey executive and former player, born Toronto, ON, Canada, Nov 24, 1971.

Oscar Palmer Robertson, 82, Hall of Fame basketball player, born Charlotte, TN, Nov 24, 1938.

Dwight Schultz, 73, actor ("Star Trek: The Next Generation," *Fat Man and Little Boy*), born Baltimore, MD, Nov 24, 1947.

Brad Sherwood, 56, comedian, actor ("Whose Line Is It Anyway?"), born Chicago, IL, Nov 24, 1964.

Rudolph (Rudy) Tomjanovich, 72, basketball coach and former player, born Hamtramck, MI, Nov 24, 1948.

November 25 — Wednesday

DAY 330   **36 REMAINING**

BOSNIA AND HERZEGOVINA: NATIONAL DAY. Nov 25. National holiday. Commemorates the declaration of statehood within the federation of Yugoslavia in 1943.

CARNEGIE, ANDREW: BIRTH ANNIVERSARY. Nov 25, 1835. American financier, philanthropist and benefactor of more than 2,500 libraries, born at Dunfermline, Scotland. Carnegie Hall, the Carnegie Foundation and the Carnegie Endowment for International Peace are among his gifts. Carnegie wrote in 1889, "Surplus wealth is a sacred trust which its possessor is bound to administer in his lifetime for the good of the community.... The man who dies ... rich dies disgraced." Carnegie died at his summer estate, Shadowbrook, MA, Aug 11, 1919.

DIMAGGIO, JOSEPH PAUL (JOE): BIRTH ANNIVERSARY. Nov 25, 1914. Baseball Hall of Fame outfielder, born at Martinez, CA. In 1941 he was on "the streak," getting a hit in 56 consecutive games. He was the American League MVP for three years, was the batting champion in 1939 and led the league in RBIs in both 1941 and 1948. DiMaggio was married to actress Marilyn Monroe in 1954, but they later divorced. He died at Harbour Island, FL, Mar 8, 1999.

GERMANY: FRANKFURT CHRISTMAS MARKET. Nov 25–Dec 23. Frankfurt. "Weinachtsmarkt auf dem Romerberg," the Christmas market in Frankfurt, is one of Germany's biggest, best and oldest—with origins dating to mystery plays in 1393. Bells are rung simultaneously from nine downtown churches. Glockenspiels are sounded by hand and trumpets are blown from the old St. Nicolas Church.

KENNEDY, JOHN F., JR: 60th BIRTH ANNIVERSARY. Nov 25, 1960. Lawyer, editor (*George* magazine), born at Washington, DC. Son of John F. Kennedy (35th president of the US) and Jacqueline Bouvier Kennedy. He died along with his wife, Carolyn, and his sister-in-law, Lauren Bessette, when the plane he was piloting crashed off of Cape Cod, MA, July 16, 1999.

MIRABEL SISTERS MURDERED: 60th ANNIVERSARY. Nov 25, 1960. On this date Maria, Teresa and Minerva Mirabel, political activists in the Dominican Republic, were assassinated on orders of dictator Rafael Trujillo. The anniversary of their deaths is now observed by the United Nations as International Day for the Elimination of Violence Against Women.

MONTALBÁN, RICARDO: 100th BIRTH ANNIVERSARY. Nov 25, 1920. Television, stage and film actor Ricardo Gonzalo Pedro Montalbán y Merino was born at Mexico City, Mexico. He was a leading man on the Mexican screen when he moved on to Hollywood, making his debut in 1947's *Fiesta* with Esther Williams. Frustrated with "Latin lover" roles, Montalbán moved to character roles on television, most famously as the mysterious Mr Roarke, resplendent in a crisp, white three-piece suit, in ABC's hit "Fantasy Island." He also reprised his "Star Trek" television role as the villain Khan in the film *Star Trek II: The Wrath of Khan* (1982). Montalbán died at Los Angeles, CA, Jan 14, 2009. The theatre near Hollywood and Vine that was constructed in 1927 was renamed in his honor in 2004.

NATION, CARRY AMELIA MOORE: BIRTH ANNIVERSARY. Nov 25, 1846. American temperance leader, famed as hatchet-wielding smasher of saloons, born at Garrard County, KY. Died at Leavenworth, KS, June 9, 1911.

NEILL, NOEL: 100th BIRTH ANNIVERSARY. Nov 25, 1920. Actress with a career spanning eight decades. Born at Minneapolis, MN, Neill is best known for her portrayal of Lois Lane on the silver screen in 1948 and 1950 and for five seasons on television in "Adventures of Superman" (until its conclusion in 1958 after the unexpected death of lead George Reeves). Neill continued to make supporting appearances in various later Superman films. She died July 3, 2016, at Tucson, AZ.

POPE JOHN XXIII: BIRTH ANNIVERSARY. Nov 25, 1881. Angelo Roncalli, 261st pope of the Roman Catholic Church, born at Sotte il Monte, Italy. Elected pope on Oct 28, 1958. Died June 3, 1963, at Rome, Italy.

SAINT CATHERINE'S DAY. Nov 25. Patron saint of maidens, mechanics and philosophers, as well as of all who work with wheels.

SURINAME: INDEPENDENCE DAY. Nov 25. Holiday. Gained independence from The Netherlands in 1975.

TIE ONE ON DAY. Nov 25. Give from the heart on Wednesday—then give thanks on Thursday. This Thanksgiving Eve, Tie One On (an apron of course!) and bring joy to the life of someone in need. Participation is easy and uplifting: simply wrap a loaf of bread or baked good in an apron and tuck an encouraging note or prayer into the pocket; then present your offering to a neighbor, friend or person in your community who could benefit from a gesture of kindness. Tie One On—and put the "give" back into Thanksgiving. Annually, the Wednesday before Thanksgiving. For info: EllynAnne Geisel, 605 W 17th St, Pueblo, CO 81003. Fax: (719) 542-3947. E-mail: ellynanne@apronmemories.com. Web: www.apronmemories.com.

UNITED NATIONS: INTERNATIONAL DAY FOR THE ELIMINATION OF VIOLENCE AGAINST WOMEN. Nov 25. Observed by the United Nations since 1993 on the anniversary of the 1960 murders of the Mirabel sisters in the Dominican Republic. In 2004 UN Secretary-General Kofi Annan said, "Let us be encouraged that there is a growing understanding of the problem. But let us also pledge to do our utmost to protect women, banish such violence and build a world in which women enjoy their rights and freedoms on an equal basis with men." Annually, Nov 25. For info: www.un.org.

🎂 BIRTHDAYS TODAY

Christina Applegate, 49, actress (*Anchorman*, "Samantha Who?," "Married . . . With Children"), born Hollywood, CA, Nov 25, 1971.

Billy Burke, 54, actor ("Revolution," Twilight Saga films), born Bellingham, WA, Nov 25, 1966.

Cris Carter, 55, sportscaster, former football player, born Troy, OH, Nov 25, 1965.

Katie Cassidy, 34, actress ("Arrow," "Melrose Place," "Gossip Girl"), born Los Angeles, CA, Nov 25, 1986.

Bucky Dent, 69, former baseball player and manager, born Russell Earl O'Dey at Savannah, GA, Nov 25, 1951.

November 2020	S	M	T	W	T	F	S
	1	2	3	4	5	6	7
	8	9	10	11	12	13	14
	15	16	17	18	19	20	21
	22	23	24	25	26	27	28
	29	30					

Jerry Ferrara, 41, actor ("Entourage"), born Brooklyn, NY, Nov 25, 1979.

Joe Jackson Gibbs, 80, Hall of Fame football coach, sportscaster, born Mocksville, NC, Nov 25, 1940.

Amy Grant, 60, singer, born Augusta, GA, Nov 25, 1960.

Charlaine Harris, 69, mystery author (*Dead Until Dark*, "Southern Vampire Mysteries"), born Tunica, MS, Nov 25, 1951.

Jill Hennessy, 51, actress ("Crossing Jordan," "Law & Order"), born Edmonton, AB, Canada, Nov 25, 1969.

Joel Kinnaman, 41, actor ("The Killing," *RoboCop, Suicide Squad, Easy Money*), born Stockholm, Sweden, Nov 25, 1979.

Bernie Joseph Kosar, Jr, 57, former football player, born Boardman, OH, Nov 25, 1963.

John Larroquette, 73, actor (four Emmys for "Night Court"; "Boston Legal"), born New Orleans, LA, Nov 25, 1947.

Lenny Moore, 87, Hall of Fame football player, born Reading, PA, Nov 25, 1933.

Eddie Steeples, 47, actor ("My Name Is Earl"), born Spring, TX, Nov 25, 1973.

Ben Stein, 76, actor, journalist, former speechwriter, born Washington, DC, Nov 25, 1944.

November 26 — Thursday

DAY 331   **35 REMAINING**

ALICE'S ADVENTURES IN WONDERLAND **PUBLISHED: ANNIVERSARY.** Nov 26, 1865. Lewis Carroll's fun-house novel was published on this date. *Through the Looking-Glass, and What Alice Found There* followed in 1871. Lewis Carroll was the pen name of Oxford lecturer in mathematics Charles L. Dodgson.

AMERICA'S THANKSGIVING PARADE®. Nov 26. Detroit, MI. America's Thanksgiving Parade® presented by Art Van is one of the country's largest and most spectacular parades in the United States! Every Thanksgiving morning, hundreds of thousands of parade spectators line historic Woodward Avenue to watch the larger-than-life floats, colorful helium-filled balloons, thunderous marching bands and exciting specialty acts! A holiday tradition since 1924. Named Best Holiday Parade in America by the 2018 *USA TODAY* Readers' Choice Awards. Est attendance: 1,000,000. For info: The Parade Co. Web: www.theparade.org.

CASABLANCA **PREMIERE: ANNIVERSARY.** Nov 26, 1942. Because of the landing of the Allies in North Africa on Nov 8, the premiere and release of the film were moved up from June 1943 to Nov 26, 1942, when it premiered at New York City on Thanksgiving Day. The general nationwide release followed on Jan 23, 1943, during the Roosevelt-Churchill conferences in Casablanca, Morocco.

DALLAS YMCA TURKEY TROT. Nov 26. Dallas, TX. 52nd annual. The Turkey Trot is the largest Thanksgiving Day event of its kind in the country. Starting from humble beginnings in 1967 at White Rock Lake, it has grown into the undisputed "Way to Begin Thanksgiving Day" for thousands of locals as well as those who travel to share in our great event. Includes 5-mile Run/Walk and 8-mile Race. Friendly dogs welcome on leash. Annually, Thanksgiving Day. Est attendance: 40,000. For info: Dallas YMCA Turkey Trot, YMCA of Metropolitan Dallas, 601 N Akard, Dallas, TX 75201. Phone: (214) 954-0500. E-mail: ymcaturkeytrot@ymcadallas.org. Web: www.thetrot.org.

FIRST US HOLIDAY BY PRESIDENTIAL PROCLAMATION: ANNIVERSARY. Nov 26, 1789. President George Washington proclaimed Nov 26, 1789, to be Thanksgiving Day. Both houses of Congress, by their joint committee, had requested him to recommend "a day of public thanksgiving and prayer, to be observed by acknowledging with grateful hearts the many and signal favors of Almighty God, especially by affording them an opportunity to peaceably establish a form of government for their safety and happiness." Proclamation issued Oct 3, 1789. Next proclaimed by President Abraham Lincoln in 1863 for the last Thursday in November. In 1939 President Franklin D. Roosevelt moved Thanksgiving to the fourth Thursday in November.

FOODS AND FEASTS OF COLONIAL VIRGINIA. Nov 26–28. Jamestown Settlement, Williamsburg, VA, and American Revolution Museum at Yorktown, Yorktown, VA. Culinary practices of 17th- and 18th-century Virginia are featured during this three-day event beginning on Thanksgiving Day. For info: Jamestown-Yorktown Foundation, PO Box 1607, Williamsburg, VA 23187. Phone: (757) 253-4838 or (888) 593-4682. Fax: (757) 253-5299. Web: www.historyisfun.org.

GOMEZ, LEFTY: BIRTH ANNIVERSARY. Nov 26, 1908. Vernon Louis "Lefty" Gomez, Baseball Hall of Fame pitcher, born at Rodeo, CA. Gomez was a star pitcher with the New York Yankees from 1930 to 1942. He won six World Series games without a defeat and was the winning pitcher in the first All-Star game. Inducted into the Hall of Fame in 1972. Died at Greenbrae, CA, Feb 17, 1989.

HARVARD, JOHN: BIRTH ANNIVERSARY. Nov 26, 1607. English clergyman and scholar. Born at England, he died Sept 24, 1638, at the Massachusetts Bay Colony. Harvard bequeathed part of his estate to a local college, which renamed itself Harvard in his honor.

MACY'S THANKSGIVING DAY PARADE. Nov 26. New York, NY. 94th annual. Starts at 9 AM, EST, at Central Park West. A part of everyone's Thanksgiving, the parade grows bigger and better each year. Featuring floats, giant balloons, marching bands and famous stars, the parade is televised for the whole country. For info: Macy's. Web: https://macys.com/social/parade.

MONGOLIA: REPUBLIC DAY. Nov 26. National holiday. Commemorates the declaration of the republic in 1924.

MUMBAI TERROR ATTACKS: ANNIVERSARY. Nov 26–29, 2008. Over four days and three nights, 10 young, well-trained Pakistani nationals armed with AK-47s, hand grenades and timer bombs stalked and killed more than 160 people in Mumbai, the financial capital of India. Notable attacks took place in the historic Victoria Terminus train station, a Jewish community center, a hospital and two luxury hotels frequented by foreign dignitaries and tourists.

"THE PRICE IS RIGHT" TV PREMIERE: ANNIVERSARY. Nov 26, 1956. This popular show is also TV's longest-running daily game show, surviving changes in format, networks, time slots and hosts. It began in 1956 with Bill Cullen as host and with Don Pardo as announcer; four contestants bid on an item, and the one who bid closest to the manufacturer's suggested price without going over won the item. In 1972, after a seven-year hiatus, "The Price Is Right" came back in two versions. Bob Barker was the host of the network version until 2007. Drew Carey is the current host.

QUEEN ELIZABETH II AGREES TO PAY TAXES: ANNIVERSARY. Nov 26, 1992. Prime Minister John Major announced that Britain's monarch, Queen Elizabeth, had decided to begin paying taxes on her personal income.

SCHULZ, CHARLES: BIRTH ANNIVERSARY. Nov 26, 1922. Cartoonist, born at Minneapolis, MN. Created the "Peanuts" comic strip, which debuted on Oct 2, 1950. The strip included Charlie Brown; his sister, Sally; his dog, Snoopy; friends Linus and Lucy and a variety of other characters. Schulz's last daily strip was published Jan 3, 2000, and his last Sunday strip was published Feb 13, 2000. The strip ran in more than 2,500 newspapers in many countries. Schulz won the Reuben Award in both 1955 and 1964 and was named International Cartoonist of the Year in 1978. Several TV specials were spin-offs of the strip, including "It's the Great Pumpkin, Charlie Brown" and "You're a Good Man, Charlie Brown." Schulz died at Santa Rosa, CA, Feb 12, 2000. See also: "'Peanuts' Debuts: Anniversary" (Oct 2).

SEVAREID, ERIC: BIRTH ANNIVERSARY. Nov 26, 1912. American journalist Eric Sevareid was born at Velva, ND. He worked for CBS News as a radio reporter during WWII, appeared regularly on "The CBS Evening News" from 1964 to 1977, won the Peabody Award for news interpretations (1950, 1964 and 1967) and earned two Emmys in 1973. He died July 9, 1992, at Washington, DC.

SEX PISTOLS SINGLE, "ANARCHY IN THE UK": ANNIVERSARY. Nov 26, 1976. The first single by the pioneering and profane British punk rock band, the Sex Pistols, was released by EMI. With lead singer Johnny Rotten shout-singing, "I am an Antichrist," the song reached only number 38 on the UK music charts, but it was a storm alert for the growing punk rock movement.

STOCK EXCHANGE HOLIDAY (THANKSGIVING DAY). Nov 26. Also early closure on Nov 27. The holiday schedules for the various exchanges are subject to change if relevant rules, regulations or exchange policies are revised. If you have questions, contact: CME Group (CME, CBOT, NYMEX, COMEX) (www.cmegroup.com), Chicago Board Options Exchange (www.cboe.com), NASDAQ (www.nasdaq.com), NYSE (www.nyse.com).

★**THANKSGIVING DAY.** Nov 26. Presidential Proclamation. Always issued for the fourth Thursday in November.

THANKSGIVING DAY. Nov 26. Legal public holiday. (Public Law 90–363 sets Thanksgiving Day on the fourth Thursday in November.) Observed in all states. In most states, the Friday after Thanksgiving is also a holiday.

TRUTH, SOJOURNER: DEATH ANNIVERSARY. Nov 26, 1883. A former slave who had been sold four times, Sojourner Truth became an evangelist who argued for abolition and women's rights. After a troubled early life, she began her evangelical career in 1843, traveling through New England until she discovered the utopian colony called the Northampton Association of Education and Industry. It was there she was exposed to, and became an advocate for, the cause of abolition, working with Frederick Douglass, Wendell Phillips, William Lloyd Garrison and others. In 1850 she befriended Lucretia Mott, Elizabeth Cady Stanton and other feminist leaders and actively began supporting calls for women's rights. In 1870 she attempted to petition Congress to create a "Negro State" on public lands in the West. Born at Ulster County, NY, about 1797, with the name Isabella Van Wagener, she died Nov 26, 1883, at Battle Creek, MI.

WALKER, MARY EDWARDS: BIRTH ANNIVERSARY. Nov 26, 1832. American physician and women's rights leader, born at Oswego, NY. First female surgeon in US Army (Civil War). Spent four months in Confederate prison. First and only woman ever to receive Medal of Honor (Nov 11, 1865). Two years before her death, on June 3, 1916, a government review board asked that her award be revoked. She continued to wear it, in spite of official revocation, until her death, Feb 21, 1919, at Oswego. On June 11, 1977, the secretary of the army posthumously restored the Medal of Honor to Dr. Walker.

🎂 BIRTHDAYS TODAY

Garcelle Beauvais-Nilon, 54, actress ("NYPD Blue," *Bad Company*), born St. Marc, Haiti, Nov 26, 1966.

Shelley Moore Capito, 67, US Senator (R, West Virginia), born Glen Dale, WV, Nov 26, 1953.

November 2020	S	M	T	W	T	F	S
	1	2	3	4	5	6	7
	8	9	10	11	12	13	14
	15	16	17	18	19	20	21
	22	23	24	25	26	27	28
	29	30					

Shannon Dunn, 48, Olympic snowboarder, born Arlington Heights, IL, Nov 26, 1972.

Dale Jarrett, 64, race car driver, born Conover, NC, Nov 26, 1956.

DJ Khaled, 45, rapper, DJ, producer, radio personality, born Khaled Mohamed Khaled at New Orleans, LA, Nov 26, 1975.

Richard Caruthers (Rich) Little, 82, impressionist, born Ottawa, ON, Canada, Nov 26, 1938.

Tina Turner, 82, singer, born Anna Mae Bullock at Nutbush, TN, Nov 26, 1938.

Kara Walker, 51, artist, born Stockton, CA, Nov 26, 1969.

November 27 — Friday

DAY 332   **34 REMAINING**

AGEE, JAMES: BIRTH ANNIVERSARY. Nov 27, 1909. Poet, critic, novelist (*A Death in the Family*), social historian (*Let Us Now Praise Famous Men*), scriptwriter, born at Knoxville, TN. Died at New York, NY, May 16, 1955.

BELSNICKEL CRAFT SHOW. Nov 27–28. Boyertown High School, Boyertown, PA. 50th annual. Sale of juried fine crafts. Annually, the Friday and Saturday after Thanksgiving. Est attendance: 3,000. For info: Boyertown Area Historical Society, 43 S Chestnut St, Boyertown, PA 19512. Phone: (610) 367-5255. E-mail: boyertown history.office@windstream.net. Web: www.boyertownhistory.org.

BLACK FRIDAY. Nov 27. The traditional beginning of the Christmas shopping season on the Friday after Thanksgiving. Called "Black Friday" because traditionally retailers were in the "black" by this day of the year.

BUY NOTHING DAY. Nov 27–28. A 48-hour moratorium on consumer spending. A celebration of simplicity, about getting our runaway consumer culture back onto a sustainable path. Annually, beginning on the first shopping day after Thanksgiving. For info: Adbusters Media Foundation. E-mail: info@adbusters.org. Web: www.adbusters.org.

CHRISTMAS IN THE VILLAGES. Nov 27–Dec 31. Van Buren County, IA. Event features the Festival of Trees, Santa visits, lighting displays, holiday dinners, bake sales, soup suppers and the natural beauty of the season that is found throughout the county. Est attendance: 5,000. For info: Villages of Van Buren, Inc, PO Box 9, Keosauqua, IA 52565. Phone: (800) 868-7822. Fax: (319) 293-7116. E-mail: info@ villagesofvanburen.com. Web: www.villagesofvanburen.com.

CHRISTMAS TRADITIONS. Nov 27–Dec 24. St. Charles, MO. Holiday festivities include caroling and chestnut roasting, while authentically costumed Santas from around the world walk around. Enjoy old-fashioned holiday shopping all day and night on Wednesdays, Fridays, Saturdays and Sundays. Annually, from the day after Thanksgiving until Christmas. Est attendance: 50,000. For info: St. Charles CVB, 230 S Main St, St. Charles, MO 63301. Phone: (800) 366-2427. Web: www.stcharleschristmas.com.

DINE OVER YOUR KITCHEN SINK DAY. Nov 27. "Sinkies"—people who occasionally dine over the kitchen sink and elsewhere—are encouraged to celebrate this time-honored, casual-yet-tasteful cuisine culture. This is a particularly appropriate day to become acquainted with the sinkie style of dining, since Christmas shopping and Thanksgiving leftovers provide the perfect reasons to enjoy a quick meal. Annually, the day after Thanksgiving. (Formerly, Sinkie Day.) For info: Norm Hankoff, Founder. E-mail: Norm.Hankoff@gmail.com. Web: www.sinkie.com.

FAMILY DAY IN NEVADA. Nov 27. Observed annually on the Friday following the fourth Thursday in November.

FIRST FACE TRANSPLANT: 15th ANNIVERSARY. Nov 27, 2005. In a five-hour operation, French surgeons transplanted the skin, muscles, veins, arteries, nerves and tissues of a brain-dead patient onto the face of a woman who had lost her nose and the bottom part of her face after a dog attack. Doctors said the partial transplant, the first of its kind, created a "hybrid" face—resembling neither the dead donor nor the original face of the recipient.

HENDRIX, JIMI: BIRTH ANNIVERSARY. Nov 27, 1942. American musician and songwriter Jimi Hendrix was born at Seattle, WA. One of the greatest rock guitarists in history, he revolutionized the guitar sound with heavy use of feedback and incredible fretwork. His success first came in England, and then he achieved fame in the US after his appearance at the Monterey Pop Festival (1967). His albums include *Are You Experienced?*, *Electric Ladyland* and *Band of Gypsys*. He died Sept 18, 1970, at London, England.

HOWE GETS 1,000th POINT: 60th ANNIVERSARY. Nov 27, 1960. Right wing Gordie Howe of the Detroit Red Wings became the first player in National Hockey League history to score 1,000 regular-season points by tallying an assist in a 2–0 Red Wings victory over the Toronto Maple Leafs. Howe finished his 26-year career with 1,850 points.

LAERDAL TUNNEL OPENING: 20th ANNIVERSARY. Nov 27, 2000. After five years of construction, the Laerdal Tunnel opened to traffic in Norway. At 24.51 km, it is the world's longest motorway tunnel. It cuts through the mountains of the Filefjell area, linking Aurland and Laerdal near Bergen. Three large "mountain halls" along the way relieve claustrophobia, and special lighting and sound effects were also added to prevent mental fatigue in drivers.

LANTERN LIGHT TOURS. Nov 27–Dec 20 (weekends). Mystic, CT. A New England holiday tradition. Step into Christmas past. During this 70-minute progressive performance, you may find yourself riding in a horse-drawn omnibus, kicking up your heels with revelers in the tavern or spying on silver-haired St. Nick. Est attendance: 7,000. For info: Mystic Seaport Museum, 75 Greenmanville Ave, Box 6000, Mystic, CT 06355. Phone: (860) 572-0711. Web: www.mysticseaport.org.

LEE, BRUCE: 80th BIRTH ANNIVERSARY. Nov 27, 1940. The actor and martial artist was born at San Francisco, CA, but raised in Hong Kong. In 1959 he returned to the US to teach martial arts, opening schools in Seattle, WA, and Oakland, CA. Spotted at a competition by a TV producer, Lee was cast as Kato in TV's *The Green Hornet* in 1966. He moved on to film, where he displayed an intense charisma that would make him a star. Before he could enjoy this new success, Lee died of a cerebral edema on July 20, 1973, at Hong Kong. His films include *Fists of Fury* (1972) and *Enter the Dragon* (1973).

LIVINGSTON, ROBERT R.: BIRTH ANNIVERSARY. Nov 27, 1746. (Old Style date.) Member of the Continental Congress, farmer, diplomat and jurist, born at New York, NY. It was Livingston who administered the oath of office to President George Washington in 1789. He died at Clermont, NY, Feb 26, 1813.

MASTERSON, BAT: BIRTH ANNIVERSARY. Nov 27, 1853. Old American West gambler, saloonkeeper, lawman and newswriter/editor. Born at Henryville, QC, Canada; died Oct 25, 1921, at New York, NY.

NATIONAL FLOSSING DAY. Nov 27. Americans are encouraged to consider the role flossing has played in their lives and make plans to help spread "Peace of Mouth" in their own lives and the lives of others around them, in ways with and without floss. On this day children should also be made aware of the richness and health that flossing can bring to life. For info: National Flossing Council, 533 4th St SE, Washington, DC 20003. Phone: (202) 487-7092. E-mail: nfd@flossing.org. Web: www.flossing.org.

NATIVE AMERICAN HERITAGE DAY. Nov 27. The 111th Congress jointly approved this day June 26, 2009, to honor the achievements of Native Americans and their contributions to the US (Public Law 111-33). This day encourages the people of the US, as well as federal, state and local governments and interested groups and organizations, to honor Native Americans with activities relating to (1) appropriate programs, ceremonies and events to observe Native American Heritage Day; (2) the historical status of Native American tribal governments as well as the present-day status of Native Americans; (3) the cultures, traditions and languages of Native Americans; and (4) the rich Native American cultural legacy that all Americans enjoy today. Annually, the Friday after Thanksgiving Day.

SLINKY® INTRODUCED: 75th ANNIVERSARY. Nov 27, 1945. In 1943 engineer Richard James was working in a Philadelphia shipyard trying to find a way to stabilize a piece of equipment on a ship in heavy seas. One idea was to suspend it on springs. One day a spring tumbled off his desk, giving him the idea for a toy. The accidental plaything was introduced on this date by James and his wife in a Philadelphia Gimbels department store during the 1945 Christmas season. They sold 400 toys in 90 minutes—for one dollar each. Today more than 30 million Slinkys have been sold.

WAIKIKI HOLIDAY PARADE. Nov 27. Waikiki, HI. This holiday parade commemorates Pearl Harbor by honoring survivors and veterans in memory of the attacks from Dec 7, 1941. Local Hawaiian bands, marching bands from the mainland, military units, local officials and dignitaries march down torch-lit Kalakaua Ave along Waikiki Beach. Annually, the Friday following Thanksgiving Day. For info: Waikiki Holiday Parade, Gateway Music Festivals and Tours. E-mail: gmf@musicfestivals.com. Web: www.waikikiholidayparade.com.

WEIZMANN, CHAIM: BIRTH ANNIVERSARY. Nov 27, 1874. Israeli statesman born near Pinsk, Byelorussia. He played an important role in bringing about the British government's Balfour Declaration, calling for the establishment of a national home for Jews at Palestine. He died at Tel Aviv, Israel, Nov 9, 1952.

🎂 BIRTHDAYS TODAY

Kathryn Bigelow, 69, director (Oscar for *The Hurt Locker*; *Zero Dark Thirty, Point Break*), born San Carlos, CA, Nov 27, 1951.

Robin Givens, 56, actress ("Head of the Class," *A Rage in Harlem*), born New York, NY, Nov 27, 1964.

Samantha Harris, 47, television personality ("Dancing with the Stars," "E! News"), born Hopkins, MN, Nov 27, 1973.

Jimmy Rollins, 42, baseball player, born Oakland, CA, Nov 27, 1978.

Gail Henion Sheehy, 83, author (*Passages*), born Mamaroneck, NY, Nov 27, 1937.

Fisher Stevens, 57, actor (*The Brother from Another Planet, Bob Roberts*), born Chicago, IL, Nov 27, 1963.

Nick Van Exel, 49, basketball coach and former player, born Kenosha, WI, Nov 27, 1971.

Jaleel White, 44, actor ("Family Matters"), born Los Angeles, CA, Nov 27, 1976.

November 28 — Saturday

DAY 333   **33 REMAINING**

ALBANIA: INDEPENDENCE DAY. Nov 28. Commemorates independence from the Ottoman Empire in 1912.

ALSTON, CHARLES H.: BIRTH ANNIVERSARY. Nov 28, 1907. African-American painter and sculptor born at Charlotte, NC, and died at New York, NY, Apr 27, 1977. Throughout his career, Alston experimented with styles ranging from realism to abstraction. His realistic WPA murals at Harlem Hospital depict a narrative in the style of Diego Rivera. The Cubist painting *The Family* (1955) is an excellent example of Alston's early work, influenced by Italian artist Amedeo Modigliani. *Black Man, Black Woman USA* has a decidedly Egyptian style of portraiture. *Walking* (1958), which depicts a silent crowd, almost prophesied the turmoil and social agitation of the civil rights movement.

BLAKE, WILLIAM: BIRTH ANNIVERSARY. Nov 28, 1757. English visionary poet and artist born at London, England. Composed "The Tyger," which begins memorably, "Tyger! Tyger! burning bright/In the forests of the night,/What immortal hand or eye/Could frame thy fearful symmetry?" Blake died in poverty at London on Aug 12, 1827.

BUNYAN, JOHN: BIRTH ANNIVERSARY. Nov 28, 1628. (Old Style date.) English cleric and author of *A Pilgrim's Progress*, born at Elstow, Bedfordshire, England. Died at London, England, Aug 31, 1688 (OS).

CHAD: REPUBLIC DAY. Nov 28. National holiday. Commemorates proclamation of the republic in 1958.

COCOANUT GROVE FIRE: ANNIVERSARY. Nov 28, 1942. A fire swept through the popular Cocoanut Grove nightclub in Boston, MA, killing 492 people and injuring hundreds.

ENGELS, FRIEDRICH: 200th BIRTH ANNIVERSARY. Nov 28, 1820. Philosopher and social theorist best known for his lifelong collaboration with Karl Marx, born at Barmen, Prussia (Germany). With Marx, Engels co-founded the German Workers' Society (1847) and co-wrote *The Holy Family* (1845), *The German Ideology* (1846), and, famously, *The Communist Manifesto* (1848); following Marx's death, Engels served as the foremost authority on Marxism, editing the second and third posthumously published volumes of *Das Kapital*. He died Aug 5, 1895, at London, England.

INTERNATIONAL AURA AWARENESS DAY. Nov 28. A day to increase awareness of the human energy body, or aura. Annually, the fourth Saturday in November. For info: Cynthia Larson, PO Box 7393, Berkeley, CA 94707. Phone: (510) 528-2044. E-mail: cynthia@ realityshifters.com. Web: realityshifters.com/pages/auraday.html.

LÉVI-STRAUSS, CLAUDE: BIRTH ANNIVERSARY. Nov 28, 1908. French anthropologist and philosopher best known for advocating the intellectual movement "structuralism." Born at Brussels, Belgium, Lévi-Strauss authored many books, including his acclaimed memoir *Tristes Tropiques*, which recounted his experiences among Brazilian tribes and challenged old ways of thinking about so-called primitive cultures. Lévi-Strauss died at Paris, France, Oct 30, 2009, at the age of 100.

LULLY, JEAN BAPTISTE: BIRTH ANNIVERSARY. Nov 28, 1632. Versatile musician and composer, born at Florence, Italy, who chose France for his homeland. The main influence of French Baroque music. Noted for his quick temper; he struck his own foot with a baton while in a rage. The resulting wound led to blood poisoning, from which he died, at Paris, France, Mar 22, 1687.

MAURITANIA: INDEPENDENCE DAY: 60th ANNIVERSARY OF INDEPENDENCE. Nov 28. National holiday. Attained sovereignty from France in 1960.

MEXICO: GUADALAJARA INTERNATIONAL BOOK FAIR. Nov 28– Dec 6. Guadalajara. Latin America's largest book fair with exhibitors from all over the Spanish-speaking world. Professional days run Nov 30–Dec 2. Est attendance: 800,000. For info: David Unger, Guadalajara Book Fair—US Office, Div of Hum, NAC 5225, City College, New York, NY 10031. Phone: (212) 650-7925. Fax: (212) 650-7912. E-mail: filny@aol.com. Web: www.fil.com.mx.

November 2020	S	M	T	W	T	F	S
	1	2	3	4	5	6	7
	8	9	10	11	12	13	14
	15	16	17	18	19	20	21
	22	23	24	25	26	27	28
	29	30					

PANAMA: INDEPENDENCE FROM SPAIN. Nov 28. Public holiday. Commemorates the independence of Panama (which at the time was part of Colombia) from Spain in 1821.

ROYAL SOCIETY: ANNIVERSARY. Nov 28, 1660. One of the world's oldest scientific academies, the Royal Society, was founded in England on this date at Gresham College, London, with King Charles II as its patron. Scientists, engineers and technologists make up the membership (which has included women since 1945). Prominent fellows past and present include Christopher Wren, Robert Boyle, Isaac Newton, Joseph Banks, Charles Babbage, Charles Darwin, Albert Einstein, Stephen Hawking and Tim Berners-Lee. "If I have seen further," wrote Newton in tribute to his colleagues, "it is because I have stood upon the shoulders of giants."

SMALL BUSINESS SATURDAY. Nov 28. A day to celebrate and support small businesses and all they do for their communities. Originated by American Express in 2010. For info: US Small Business Administration. Web: www.sba.gov.

SPACE MILESTONE: *MARINER 4* (US). Nov 28, 1964. The first successful mission to Mars. Approached within 6,118 miles of Mars on July 14, 1965. Took photographs and instrument readings.

SWITZERLAND: CLAUWAU—SANTA CLAUS WORLD CHAMPIONSHIP. Nov 28. Samnaun. 20th annual. Santa Claus teams compete in various sportive winter disciplines to become world champion. After the finals, everyone celebrates in an open-air concert featuring a famous artist. For info: ClauWau. E-mail: info@samnaun. ch. Web: www.clauwau.ch.

TEHRAN CONFERENCE: ANNIVERSARY. Nov 28–Dec 1, 1943. President Franklin D. Roosevelt, British prime minister Winston Churchill and Soviet premier Joseph Stalin met at Tehran, Iran, to formulate a plan for an Allied assault, a second front, in western Europe. The resulting plan was "Operation Overlord," which commenced with the landing on Normandy's beaches on June 6, 1944 ("D-day").

🎂 BIRTHDAYS TODAY

Michael Bennet, 56, US Senator (D, Colorado), born New Delhi, India, Nov 28, 1964.

Alfonso Cuarón, 59, director (Oscars for *Roma* and *Gravity*; *Children of Men*), screenwriter, born Alfonso Cuarón Orozco at Mexico City, Mexico, Nov 28, 1961.

Berry Gordy, Jr, 91, record and motion picture executive (cofounder of Motown), born Detroit, MI, Nov 28, 1929.

Bryshere Y. Gray, 27, actor ("Empire"), rapper (Yazz the Greatest), born Philadelphia, PA, Nov 28, 1993.

Ed Harris, 70, actor ("Westworld," *The Hours, Pollock, The Right Stuff*), born Englewood, NJ, Nov 28, 1950.

Gary Hart, 82, former US senator (D, Colorado), former presidential candidate, born Gary Hartpence at Ottawa, KS, Nov 28, 1938.

Ryan Kwanten, 44, actor ("True Blood," "Summerland"), born Sydney, Australia, Nov 28, 1976.

S. Epatha Merkerson, 68, actress ("Law & Order," *Lackawanna Blues*), born Detroit, MI, Nov 28, 1952.

Judd Nelson, 61, actor (*The Breakfast Club, St. Elmo's Fire*, "Suddenly Susan"), born Portland, ME, Nov 28, 1959.

Randy Newman, 77, singer, songwriter, composer (film scores for *Ragtime, The Natural*), born New Orleans, LA, Nov 28, 1943.

Wilbur Ross, 83, US Secretary of Commerce (Trump administration), born Weehawken, NJ, Nov 28, 1937.

Paul Shaffer, 71, bandleader ("Late Show with David Letterman"), comedian, born Thunder Bay, ON, Canada, Nov 28, 1949.

Jon Stewart, 58, writer, comedian ("The Daily Show"), filmmaker, born Jonathan Stuart Leibowitz at New York, NY, Nov 28, 1962.

Matt Williams, 55, former baseball player, born Bishop, CA, Nov 28, 1965.

Mary Elizabeth Winstead, 36, actress (*Abraham Lincoln: Vampire Hunter, Scott Pilgrim vs the World*), born Rocky Mount, NC, Nov 28, 1984.

November 29 — Sunday

DAY 334   **32 REMAINING**

ADVENT, FIRST SUNDAY. Nov 29. Advent includes the four Sundays before Christmas, Nov 29, Dec 6, Dec 13 and Dec 20 in 2020.

ALCOTT, LOUISA MAY: BIRTH ANNIVERSARY. Nov 29, 1832. American author, born at Philadelphia, PA. Alcott was the daughter of transcendentalist philosopher Bronson Alcott. She was a regular contributor to the *Atlantic Monthly* and penned (anonymously) lurid thrillers before publishing her most famous novel, *Little Women.* The classic and semiautobiographical story of Meg, Jo, Beth and Amy March was published in 1868 to instant acclaim. Alcott died at Boston, MA, Mar 6, 1888—on the day of her father's funeral.

BERKELEY, BUSBY: 125th BIRTH ANNIVERSARY. Nov 29, 1895. William Berkeley Enos was born at Los Angeles, CA. After serving in WWI as an entertainment officer, he changed his name to Busby Berkeley and began a career as an actor. He turned to directing in 1921, and his lavish Broadway and Hollywood creations include *Forty-Second Street, Gold Diggers of 1933, Footlight Parade, Stage Struck, Babes in Arms, Strike Up the Band, Girl Crazy* and *Take Me Out to the Ball Game.* He retired in 1962 but returned to Broadway in 1970 to supervise a revival of *No, No, Nanette.* He died Mar 14, 1976, at Palm Springs, CA.

CZECHOSLOVAKIA ENDS COMMUNIST RULE: ANNIVERSARY. Nov 29, 1989. Czechoslovakia ended 41 years of one-party Communist rule when the Czechoslovak parliament voted unanimously to repeal the constitutional clauses giving the Communist Party a guaranteed leading role in the country and promoting Marxism-Leninism as the state ideology. The vote came at the end of a 12-day revolution sparked by the beating of protestors Nov 17. Although the Communist Party remained in power, the tide of reform led to its ouster by the Civic Forum, headed by playwright Václav Havel. The Civic Forum demanded free elections with equal rights for all parties, a mixed economy and support for foreign investment. In the first free elections in Czechoslovakia since WWII, Václav Havel was elected president.

ELECTRONIC GREETINGS DAY. Nov 29. Save a letter carrier, save a tree, save a stamp! Today's the day to send your greetings the free, electronic way, via the Internet. (©2006 by WH.) For info: Thomas & Ruth Roy, Wellcat Holidays, 2418 Long Ln, Lebanon, PA 17046. Phone: (717) 279-0184. E-mail: info@wellcat.com. Web: www.wellcat.com.

FIRST ARMY-NAVY GAME: ANNIVERSARY. Nov 29, 1890. Army played Navy for the first time in football, and Navy won, 24–0. Red Emrich scored four touchdowns (worth four points each) and kicked two field goals (worth two points each), and Moulton Johnson added the other touchdown to account for all the scoring.

HANDEL'S MESSIAH SING-ALONG. Nov 29. Richard Nixon Library and Birthplace, Yorba Linda, CA. Audience members are invited to join in singing the choruses of this beloved oratorio in the beautiful East Room of the Nixon Library. Performers include a master choir, orchestra and soloists. Seventeenth-century costumes are encouraged. Free. Annually, the Sunday following Thanksgiving Day. Est attendance: 1,500. For info: Yorba Linda Arts Alliance, PO Box 1037, Yorba Linda, CA 92885. Phone: (714) 996-1960. E-mail: messiahsing@aol.com. Web: www.messiahsing.org.

JOHN F. KENNEDY DAY IN MASSACHUSETTS. Nov 29. Annually, the last Sunday in November.

"KUKLA, FRAN AND OLLIE" TV PREMIERE: ANNIVERSARY. Nov 29, 1948. This popular children's show featured puppets created and handled by Burr Tillstrom and was equally popular with adults. Fran Allison was the only human on the show. Tillstrom's lively and eclectic cast of characters, called the "Kuklapolitans," included the bald, high-voiced Kukla; the big-toothed Oliver J. Dragon (Ollie); Fletcher Rabbit; Cecil Bill; Beulah the Witch; Colonel Crackie; Madame Ooglepuss and Dolores Dragon. Most shows were performed without scripts.

L'ENGLE, MADELEINE: BIRTH ANNIVERSARY. Nov 29, 1918. Prolific author Madeleine L'Engle Camp was born at New York, NY. Her classic novel *A Wrinkle in Time* was famously rejected more than 30 times before being picked up by Farrar, Straus and Giroux in 1962. A groundbreaking work of science fiction for children, the book won the Newbery Medal in 1963 and has gone on to become one of the bestselling children's novels of all time. L'Engle was the writer-in-residence and librarian at the Cathedral of Saint John the Divine in New York City for more than 40 years, until her death at Litchfield, CT, Sept 6, 2007.

LEWIS, C.S. (CLIVE STAPLES): BIRTH ANNIVERSARY. Nov 29, 1898. British scholar, novelist and author (*The Screwtape Letters, Chronicles of Narnia*), born at Belfast, Ireland, died at Oxford, England, Nov 22, 1963.

NETHERLANDS: MIDWINTER HORN BLOWING. Nov 29–Jan 6, 2021. Twente and several other areas in the Netherlands. Midwinter horn blowing, folkloric custom of announcing the birth of Christ, begins with Advent and continues until Epiphany (Jan 6) of the following year.

RADIOLOGICAL SOCIETY OF NORTH AMERICA SCIENTIFIC ASSEMBLY AND ANNUAL MEETING. Nov 29–Dec 4. McCormick Place, Chicago, IL. 106th annual. Every year, radiology's best and brightest convene at the RSNA annual meeting to learn from the specialty's top experts and get an exclusive look at the latest in medical imaging technology. Est attendance: 62,000. For info: Radiological Society of North America, 820 Jorie Blvd, Oak Brook, IL 60523-2251. Phone: (630) 571-2670. Web: www.rsna.org.

ROSS, NELLIE TAYLOE: BIRTH ANNIVERSARY. Nov 29, 1876. Nellie Tayloe Ross became the first female governor in the US when she was chosen to serve out the last month and two days of her husband's term as governor of Wyoming after he died in office. She was elected in her own right in the Nov 4, 1924, election but lost the 1927 race. Ross was appointed vice chairman of the Democratic National Committee in 1926 and named director of the US Mint by President Franklin D. Roosevelt in 1933. She served in that capacity for 20 years. Born at St. Joseph, MO, she died Dec 20, 1977, at Washington, DC.

"TATORT" TV PREMIERE: 50th ANNIVERSARY. Nov 29, 1970. This popular German detective drama ("Crime Scene" in English) is unique in that there are a dozen versions of it produced by regional TV stations. There are different world-weary detective teams for Hamburg, Berlin, Cologne, etc. "Tatort" focuses on characters rather than violence and has been praised for taking on controversial societal issues.

THOMSON, CHARLES: BIRTH ANNIVERSARY. Nov 29, 1729. America's first official record keeper. Chosen secretary of the First Continental Congress Sept 5, 1774, Thomson recorded proceedings for 15 years and delivered his journals together with tens of thousands of records to the federal government in 1789. Born in Ireland, he died Aug 16, 1824. It was Thomson who notified George Washington of his election as president.

UNITED NATIONS: INTERNATIONAL DAY OF SOLIDARITY WITH THE PALESTINIAN PEOPLE. Nov 29. Annual observance proclaimed by General Assembly in 1977. At the request of the Assembly, observance is organized by secretary-general in consultation with Committee on the Exercise of the Inalienable Rights of the Palestinian

People. Recommendations include a plan for return of the Palestinians to their homes and the establishment of an "independent Palestinian entity." For info: United Nations, Dept of Public Info, New York, NY 10017. Web: www.un.org.

WAITE, MORRISON R.: BIRTH ANNIVERSARY. Nov 29, 1816. Seventh chief justice of the US, born at Lyme, CT. Appointed chief justice by President Ulysses S. Grant Jan 19, 1874. The Waite Court is remembered for its controversial rulings that did much to rehabilitate the idea of states' rights after the Civil War and early Reconstruction years. Waite died at Washington, DC, Mar 23, 1888.

🎂 BIRTHDAYS TODAY

Lucas Black, 38, actor (*Friday Night Lights, 42*, "NCIS: New Orleans"), born Speake, AL, Nov 29, 1982.

Chadwick Boseman, 43, actor (*Black Panther, Marshall, 42*), born Anderson, SC, Nov 29, 1977.

Gemma Chan, 38, actress (*Crazy Rich Asians*, "Humans"), born London, England, Nov 29, 1982.

Don Cheadle, 56, actor ("House of Lies," *Talk to Me, Hotel Rwanda, Crash, Ocean's Eleven*), born Kansas City, MO, Nov 29, 1964.

Jacques Rene Chirac, 88, former president of France, born Paris, France, Nov 29, 1932.

Joel Coen, 66, filmmaker (Oscars for *No Country for Old Men* and *Fargo*), born Minneapolis, MN, Nov 29, 1954.

Kim Delaney, 59, actress ("NYPD Blue"), born Philadelphia, PA, Nov 29, 1961.

Rahm Emmanuel, 61, former mayor of Chicago, former White House chief of staff, born Chicago, IL, Nov 29, 1959.

Anna Faris, 44, actress ("Mom," "Entourage," *The House Bunny*), born Baltimore, MD, Nov 29, 1976.

Kasey Keller, 51, Hall of Fame soccer player, born Olympia, WA, Nov 29, 1969.

Diane Ladd, 88, actress (*Alice Doesn't Live Here Anymore, Ramblin' Rose, The Cemetery Club*), born Rose Diane Ladner at Meridian, MS, Nov 29, 1932.

Howie Mandel, 65, comedian, television personality ("America's Got Talent"), actor ("St. Elsewhere"), born Toronto, ON, Canada, Nov 29, 1955.

Chuck Mangione, 80, musician, composer (Grammy for "Bellavia"), born Rochester, NY, Nov 29, 1940.

John Mayall, 87, musician, bandleader (The Bluesbreakers), born Manchester, England, Nov 29, 1933.

Andrew McCarthy, 58, actor (*Pretty in Pink, Weekend at Bernie's*), author, born Westfield, NJ, Nov 29, 1962.

Cathy Moriarty, 60, actress (*Raging Bull, The Mambo Kings*), born the Bronx, NY, Nov 29, 1960.

Janet Napolitano, 63, former US secretary of homeland security (Obama administration), former governor of Arizona (D), born Pittsburgh, PA, Nov 29, 1957.

Mariano Rivera, 51, Hall of Fame baseball player, born Panama City, Panama, Nov 29, 1969.

Vincent Edward (Vin) Scully, 93, sportscaster, born New York, NY, Nov 29, 1927.

Russell Wilson, 32, football player, born Cincinnati, OH, Nov 29, 1988.

November 2020	S	M	T	W	T	F	S
	1	2	3	4	5	6	7
	8	9	10	11	12	13	14
	15	16	17	18	19	20	21
	22	23	24	25	26	27	28
	29	30					

November 30 — Monday

DAY 335　　　　　　　　　　　　　　**31 REMAINING**

ARTICLES OF PEACE BETWEEN GREAT BRITAIN AND THE US: ANNIVERSARY. Nov 30, 1782. These provisional articles of peace, which were to end America's War of Independence, were signed at Paris, France. The refined and definitive treaty of peace between Great Britain and the US was signed at Paris on Sept 3, 1783. In it "His Britannic Majesty acknowledges the said United States . . . to be free, sovereign and independent states; that he treats them as such; and for himself, his heirs and successors, relinquishes all claims to the government, propriety and territorial rights of the same, and every part thereof. . . ."

BARBADOS: INDEPENDENCE DAY. Nov 30. National holiday. Gained independence from Great Britain in 1966.

BEAVER MOON. Nov 30. So called by Native American tribes of New England and the Great Lakes because at this time of year, beavers are industriously preparing themselves for the coming winter. The November Full Moon.

CHISHOLM, SHIRLEY: BIRTH ANNIVERSARY. Nov 30, 1924. Born at Brooklyn, NY, Shirley St. Hill Chisholm was an educator, author and politician who was the first African-American woman elected to the US House of Representatives. A liberal Democrat, she was known for her strong opinions and outspoken nature as she represented the Bedford-Stuyvesant neighborhood of New York City in Congress during 1974–82. She fought against poverty and discrimination and ran for the 1972 Democratic nomination for president just to prove that she could. She retired from politics in the 1980s and died at Ormond Beach, FL, Jan 1, 2005.

CHURCHILL, WINSTON: BIRTH ANNIVERSARY. Nov 30, 1874. Winston Leonard Spencer Churchill, British statesman and the first man to be made an honorary citizen of the US (by an act of Congress, Apr 9, 1963), was born at Blenheim Palace, Oxfordshire, England. Died Jan 24, 1965, at London, England. Dedicated to Britain and total victory over Germany, Churchill as minister of defense and prime minister was a strong leader during WWII. A stirring public speaker, Churchill said upon becoming prime minister in 1940, "I have nothing to offer but blood, toil, tears and sweat."

CIDER MONDAY. Nov 30. Cider Monday is both an invitation to shoppers to visit a real store to see and touch real products and meet real people and an opportunity for the retailers to thank them warmly with a cup of cider and maybe some other delicious treats. Also offers a moment to talk about the effects cyber shopping has on the brick-and-mortar stores in one's community. First observed in 2013 by the Toadstool Bookshop and other New England bookstores and retail establishments. Annually, the Monday after Thanksgiving. For info: The Toadstool Bookshop, 12 Depot Sq, Peterborough, NH 03458. Phone: (603) 924-3543. E-mail: books@ptoad.com. Web: www.toadbooks.com.

CLARK, DICK: BIRTH ANNIVERSARY. Nov 30, 1929. As influential host of television's "American Bandstand" from 1957 to 1987, Dick Clark helped to promote and codify rock and roll and black rhythm and blues to mainstream audiences as those sounds wound their way into the country's psyche. Richard Wagstaff Clark was born at Bronxville, NY. After early stops in New York radio, he moved to Philadelphia, PA, where he became the host of a local music show called "Bandstand." The show went national in 1957, and soon Clark was talking to every teenager in America. His easygoing style and youthful, clean-cut look became a constant in American popular culture. As the entrepreneur of a successful television production company and as the host of innumerable music shows, awards ceremonies and prime-time specials, Clark became the engaging emcee to four decades of entertainment culture. "America's Oldest Teenager" died Apr 18, 2012, at Santa Monica, CA.

CLEMENS, SAMUEL LANGHORNE (MARK TWAIN): BIRTH ANNIVERSARY. Nov 30, 1835. Celebrated American author, whose books include *The Adventures of Tom Sawyer, The Adventures of Huckleberry Finn* and *The Prince and the Pauper.* Born at Florida, MO, Twain is quoted as saying, "I came in with Halley's comet in 1835. It is coming again next year, and I expect to go out with it." He did. Twain died at Redding, CT, Apr 21, 1910 (just one day after Halley's comet perihelion).

COMPUTER SECURITY DAY. Nov 30. The use of computers and the concern for security increase daily. This annual observance, which began in 1988, reminds people to protect their computers, programs and data at home and at work. More than 1,500 companies participate worldwide. For info: Assn for Computer Security Day, 5014 Rodman Rd, Bethesda, MD 20816. Phone: (301) 229-2346. E-mail: computer_security_day@acm.org.

CYBER MONDAY. Nov 30. Traditional beginning of the online Christmas shopping season—when consumers return to work and start ordering online. Annually, the Monday after Thanksgiving.

HOFFMAN, ABBOT (ABBIE): BIRTH ANNIVERSARY. Nov 30, 1936. Political activist, born at Worcester, MA, Abbie Hoffman rose to prominence during the 1968 Democratic National Convention at Chicago, IL, and at his subsequent trial as a member of the Chicago Seven, a group of radicals accused of conspiring to disrupt the convention. Combining politics and street theater was a Hoffman trait. During the 1967 march on the Pentagon, he sought a permit to allow 1,200 demonstrators to encircle and levitate the military headquarters in an attempt to end the war in Vietnam. He, Jerry Rubin and Paul Krassner conceived the Yippie movement as a youth festival of life to run concurrently with the 1968 convention. Hoffman fled underground in 1974 to avoid trial on cocaine-possession charges and remained a fugitive for nearly seven years. Surrendering to authorities in 1980, he served his sentence in a work-release program. Hoffman died Apr 12, 1989, at New Hope, PA.

INDIA: GURU NANAK'S BIRTH ANNIVERSARY. Nov 30. Celebrating the birth of Guru Nanak, the founder of Sikhism. Date can vary depending on whether lunar or solar calendar is used.

THE JOY OF COOKING PUBLISHED: ANNIVERSARY. Nov 30, 1931. America's favorite all-purpose cookbook was self-published on this date by Irma Rombauer (1877–1962). Rombauer was a comforting voice for cooks during the Depression, and the book grew into an institution. The first commercial edition of the book appeared in 1936, and it offered a revolutionary "action format" (chronologically ordered ingredients followed by instructions) now commonplace in cookbooks. The numerous editions overseen by Rombauer and later her daughter and grandson sold more than 14 million copies.

LUNAR ECLIPSE. Nov 30. Partial eclipse of the moon. Visible in the Pacific Ocean and North America.

MOON PHASE: FULL MOON. Nov 30. Moon enters Full Moon phase at 4:30 AM, EST.

PARKS, GORDON: BIRTH ANNIVERSARY. Nov 30, 1912. Award-winning and groundbreaking photojournalist and filmmaker, Parks was born the youngest of 15 children to a poor family at Fort Scott, KS. His photography career encompassed glamorous fashion shoots for *Vogue*, as well as portraits of world leaders and searing photo essays for *Life*, where he was that magazine's first black staff photographer. Parks became the first major black Hollywood film director, with such important works as *The Learning Tree* and *Shaft*. He died Mar 7, 2006, at New York, NY.

PHILIPPINES: BONIFACIO DAY. Nov 30. Also known as National Heroes' Day. Commemorates birth of Andres Bonifacio, leader of the 1896 revolt against Spain. Bonifacio was born in 1863.

SAINT ANDREW'S DAY. Nov 30. Feast day of the apostle and martyr Andrew, who died about AD 60. Patron saint of Scotland.

SIDNEY, SIR PHILIP: BIRTH ANNIVERSARY. Nov 30, 1554. English poet, statesman and soldier born at Penshurst, Kent, England. Best known of his poems is *Arcadia* (1580). Mortally wounded as he led an English detachment aiding the Dutch near Zutphen, Netherlands, Sept 22, 1586, Sidney gave his water bottle to another dying soldier with the words, "Thy necessity is yet greater than mine." He died at Arnhem, Netherlands, Oct 17, 1586, and all England mourned his death.

STAY HOME BECAUSE YOU'RE WELL DAY. Nov 30. So we can call in "well," instead of faking illness, and stay home from work. (©2006 by WH.) For info: Thomas & Ruth Roy, Wellcat Holidays, 2418 Long Ln, Lebanon, PA 17046. Phone: (717) 279-0184. E-mail: info@wellcat.com. Web: www.wellcat.com.

SWIFT, JONATHAN: BIRTH ANNIVERSARY. Nov 30, 1667. (Old Style date.) Considered the world's foremost satirist in English, poet and clergyman Swift was born at Dublin, Ireland. With companions Alexander Pope, John Gay, John Arbuthnut and Thomas Parnell, Swift cofounded the Scriblerus Club in 1713. He is best known for his satirical works *Gulliver's Travels* (1726) and *A Modest Proposal* (1729). Swift's *Drapier's Letters* (1724–25) inflamed anti-English sentiment in his Irish compatriots. The tome was labeled seditious, but Swift was never charged for its defiant pitch, as it was published anonymously. Ireland's patron dean at St. Patrick's until 1742 when he suffered a stroke and aphasia, he died Oct 19, 1745, at Dublin. He famously wrote, "When a true genius appears, you can know him by this sign: that all the dunces are in a confederacy against him."

THRILLER RELEASED: ANNIVERSARY. Nov 30, 1982. Michael Jackson's sixth studio album is one of the most popular and important albums of all time, charting seven songs in the top 10: "Wanna Be Startin' Somethin'," "The Girl Is Mine," "Thriller," "Beat It," "Billie Jean," "Human Nature" and "P.Y.T. (Pretty Young Thing)." It broke the pop charts wide open for black artists, who had often been relegated to R&B charts, and simultaneously gave musical forms like R&B and funk a wider audience while experimenting with bold genre crossovers in its songwriting and production. *Thriller* stayed on the charts for three years and has sold more than 110 million copies. On May 14, 2008, the album was added to the Library of Congress's National Recording Registry.

UNITED NATIONS: DAY OF REMEMBRANCE FOR ALL VICTIMS OF CHEMICAL WARFARE. Nov 30. Since 2005, a day to pay tribute to the victims of chemical warfare, as well as to reaffirm the commitment of the Organization for the Prohibition of Chemical Weapons (OPCW) to the elimination of the threat of chemical weapons. Annually, Nov 30. For info: United Nations, Dept of Public Info, New York, NY 10017. Web: www.un.org.

WINTER WAR: ANNIVERSARY. Nov 30, 1939–Mar 13, 1940. The Soviet Union invaded Finland on Nov 30, 1939, but weakened and demoralized by Stalin's purges, the Red Army was unable to conquer Finland, despite massive numerical superiority. Throughout the bitterly cold winter, the Finns waged a guerrilla-style defense that included the use of Molotov cocktails. The Treaty of Moscow ended hostilities, with the Finns ceding 11 percent of their territory to the Soviets but retaining their sovereignty. The Soviet Union was expelled from the League of Nations over the invasion.

🎂 BIRTHDAYS TODAY

Richard Burr, 65, US Senator (R, North Carolina), born Charlottesville, VA, Nov 30, 1955.

Kaley Cuoco, 35, actress ("The Big Bang Theory," "8 Simple Rules"), born Camarillo, CA, Nov 30, 1985.

Elisha Cuthbert, 38, actress ("24," *The Girl Next Door*), born Calgary, AB, Canada, Nov 30, 1982.

Joan Ganz Cooney, 91, founder of the Children's Television Workshop and creator of "Sesame Street," born Phoenix, AZ, Nov 30, 1929.

Jessalyn Gilsig, 49, actress ("Glee," "Heroes," "Friday Night Lights"), born Montreal, QC, Canada, Nov 30, 1971.

Billy Idol, 65, singer, songwriter, born William Michael Albert Broad at Surrey, England, Nov 30, 1955.

Vincent Edward "Bo" Jackson, 58, former baseball player, former football player, born Bessemer, AL, Nov 30, 1962.

G. Gordon Liddy, 90, convicted Watergate coconspirator, radio talk show host, born New York, NY, Nov 30, 1930.

David Mamet, 73, dramatist (*American Buffalo, Oleanna, Things Change*), born Chicago, IL, Nov 30, 1947.

Colin Mochrie, 63, comedian, actor ("Whose Line Is It Anyway?"), born Ayrshire, Scotland, Nov 30, 1957.

Kristi Noem, 49, Governor of South Dakota (R), born Watertown, SD, Nov 30, 1971.

Sandra Oh, 50, actress (*Under the Tuscan Sun, Sideways*, "Killing Eve," "Grey's Anatomy"), born Nepean, ON, Canada, Nov 30, 1970.

Mandy Patinkin, 68, actor (Tony for *Evita*; "Homeland," "Chicago Hope"), born Chicago, IL, Nov 30, 1952.

Iván "Pudge" Rodríguez, 49, Hall of Fame baseball player, born Vega Baja, Puerto Rico, Nov 30, 1971.

Amy Ryan, 51, actress ("The Wire," *Gone Baby Gone*), born Queens, NY, Nov 30, 1969.

Ridley Scott, 83, director (*Prometheus, Alien, Blade Runner, Gladiator*), born Northumberland, England, Nov 30, 1937.

Ben Stiller, 55, actor (*Greenberg, Zoolander, Starsky & Hutch, Meet the Parents*), director, born New York, NY, Nov 30, 1965.

Noel Paul Stookey, 83, singer, songwriter (Peter, Paul and Mary), born Baltimore, MD, Nov 30, 1937.

Chrissy Teigen, 35, model, television personality, born Delta, UT, Nov 30, 1985.

Allison Williams, 33, actress (*Get Out*, "Girls," "The Mindy Project"), born New Canaan, CT, Nov 30, 1987.

◆ December ◆

December 1 — Tuesday

DAY 336   **30 REMAINING**

ANTARCTICA DAY. Dec 1. The Antarctic Treaty, signed Dec 1, 1959, by 12 nations, continues to shine as a rare beacon of international cooperation. To celebrate this milestone of peace in our civilization with hope and inspiration for future generations, Antarctica Day was established in 2010 as a global initiative to share, interpret and cherish the values associated with Antarctica for the benefit of present and future generations. Annually, Dec 1. For info: Our Spaces—The Foundation for the Good Governance of International Spaces. Web: www.ourspaces.org.uk.

BASKETBALL CREATED: ANNIVERSARY. Dec 1, 1891. James Naismith was a teacher of physical education at the International YMCA Training School at Springfield, MA. To create an indoor sport that could be played during the winter months, he nailed up peach baskets at opposite ends of the gym and gave students soccer balls to toss into them. Thus was born the game of basketball.

BIFOCALS AT THE MONITOR LIBERATION DAY. Dec 1. Our hearts fill with compassion today for coworkers stuck wearing bifocals at the PC. Shed a tear as their heads bob up and down, in and out, trying to read the monitor, trying to decide which set of lenses to use. Annually, Dec 1. (©2006 by WH.) For info: Thomas & Ruth Roy, Wellcat Holidays, 2418 Long Ln, Lebanon, PA 17046. Phone: (717) 279-0184. E-mail: info@wellcat.com. Web: www. wellcat.com.

BINGO'S BIRTHDAY MONTH. Dec 1–31. To celebrate the innovation and manufacture of the game of bingo in 1929 by Edwin S. Lowe. Bingo has grown into a widespread and beloved charitable fund-raiser. For info: Tara Snowden, Pres, Bingo Bugle, Inc, Box 527, Vashon, WA 98070. Phone: (206) 463-5656. E-mail: tara@bingobugle.com.

CANADA: YUKON ORDER OF PIONEERS: ANNIVERSARY. Dec 1, 1894. The Yukon Order of Pioneers held its founding meeting on this date at Fortymile, Yukon. It began as a vigilante police force to deter claim jumping and later inaugurated Discovery Day (Aug 17), a statutory Yukon holiday commemorating the discovery of gold on Bonanza Creek in 1896.

CHRISTMAS NEW ORLEANS STYLE. Dec 1–31. New Orleans, LA. Cathedral Christmas concerts, caroling in Jackson Square, holiday parades with Papa Noel, cooking demonstrations, Celebration in the Oaks, Christmas concerts, Reveillon dinners and Papa Noel hotel rates. For info: French Quarter Festivals, Inc, 400 N Peters St, #205, New Orleans, LA 70130. Phone: (800) 673-5725 or (504) 522-5730. E-mail: info@fqfi.org. Web: www.fqfi.org.

CIVIL AIR PATROL FOUNDED: ANNIVERSARY. Dec 1, 1941. The Director of Civilian Defense, former New York mayor Fiorello H. LaGuardia, signed a formal order creating the Civil Air Patrol (CAP), a US Air Force Auxiliary. The CAP has a three-part mission: to provide an aerospace education program, a CAP cadet program and an emergency services program. For info: Civil Air Patrol Natl Headquarters, 105 S Hansell St, Bldg 714, Maxwell AFB, AL 36112-6332. Phone: (877) 227-9142. E-mail: info@gocivilairpatrol.com. Web: www.gocivilairpatrol.com.

GIVING TUESDAY. Dec 1. 9th annual. A national day of giving to kick off the giving season on the Tuesday following Thanksgiving, Black Friday and Cyber Monday. It celebrates and encourages charitable activities that support nonprofit organizations. Created by 92Y in partnership with the United Nations Foundation. For info: 92Y, 1395 Lexington Ave, New York, NY 10128. E-mail: info@givingtuesday.org. Web: www.givingtuesday.org.

ICELAND: UNIVERSITY STUDENTS' CELEBRATION. Dec 1, 1918. Marks the day in 1918 when Iceland became a state independent from Denmark (but still remained under the king of Denmark).

KIROV ASSASSINATION AND THE GREAT PURGE: ANNIVERSARY. Dec 1, 1934. Sergei Mironovich Kirov, party boss and member of the Politburo, was shot dead at Communist Party headquarters in Leningrad by Leonid Nikolayev, a disgruntled junior party member. Some historians believe the assassination was ordered by Josef Stalin in order to eliminate the powerful and independent Kirov. Stalin publicly blamed the Kirov assassination on a larger anti-Stalinist conspiracy and used the assassination as a pretext to launch what became known as the Great Purge, in which Stalin eliminated virtually all of his political opponents. More than 700,000 people thought to be dangerous to the regime were executed, and hundreds of thousands more were sent to the gulags.

MARTIN, MARY: BIRTH ANNIVERSARY. Dec 1, 1913. Called "America's favorite leading lady of musical comedy," actress Mary Virginia Martin was born at Weatherford, TX. Discovered while singing at the Trocadero club in Los Angeles, CA, Martin immediately triumphed in her first appearance on Broadway, in Cole Porter's *Leave It to Me* (1938). She is best known for her title role in the Broadway (1954–55) and television productions of *Peter Pan*. She won Tony Awards for her starring roles in the stage productions of *South Pacific*, *Peter Pan* and *The Sound of Music* (in which she originated the role of Maria von Trapp). She died Nov 3, 1990, at Rancho Mirage, CA.

MOORE, JULIA A. DAVIS: BIRTH ANNIVERSARY. Dec 1, 1847. Julia Moore, known as the "Sweet Singer of Michigan," was born in a log cabin at Plainfield, MI. A writer of homely verse and ballads, Moore enjoyed remarkable popularity and gave many public readings before realizing that her public appearances were occasions for laughter and ridicule. Her poems were said to be "so bad, her subjects so morbid and her naïveté so genuine" that they were actually gems of humorous genius. At her final public appearance she told her audience: "You people paid 50 cents to see a fool, but I got 50 dollars to look at a house full of fools." Moore died June 17, 1920, near Manton, MI.

★NATIONAL IMPAIRED DRIVING PREVENTION MONTH. Dec 1–31.

NATIONAL WRITE A BUSINESS PLAN MONTH. Dec 1–31. Time to get out of your cubicle and turn your business ideas into reality! Use the last month of the year to craft a business plan—and get a great start in the new year to come. For info: Jocelyn Saccuci, Nationwide Business Plans, LLC, 4718 S Burma Rd, Gilbert, AZ 85297. Phone: (602) 430-3079. E-mail: jocelynsaccuci@yahoo.com.

***PLAYBOY* FIRST PUBLISHED: ANNIVERSARY.** Dec 1, 1953. *Playboy* magazine was launched at Chicago, IL, by publisher Hugh Hefner.

PORTUGAL: INDEPENDENCE DAY. Dec 1. Public holiday. Became independent of Spain in 1640.

PRYOR, RICHARD: 80th BIRTH ANNIVERSARY. Dec 1, 1940. African-American comedian and actor, born at Peoria, IL, who began performing at age seven. He was known for his use of profanity, and his humor was frequently based on racial stereotypes. Extremely successful as a stand-up, Pryor won five Grammy Awards for his comedy albums, and he also wrote or starred in numerous classic comedy films, including *Stir Crazy*, *Silver Streak* and *Car Wash*. His drug problems were well documented in his comedy act, and he struggled with multiple sclerosis late in his life. He died at Encino, CA, Dec 10, 2005.

RAWLS, LOU: BIRTH ANNIVERSARY. Dec 1, 1933. Born at Chicago, IL, Rawls was the popular singer with the unmistakably smooth voice—"sweet as sugar, soft as velvet, strong as steel, smooth as butter"—at home equally in gospel, blues, jazz, soul and pop. The recipient of three Grammys (with 13 nominations) and the creator of 60 albums, later in life Rawls became an indefatigable supporter of humanitarian causes, most famously the United Negro College Fund. Rawls died Jan 6, 2006, at Los Angeles, CA.

ROMANIA: NATIONAL DAY. Dec 1. National holiday. Marks unification of Romania and Transylvania in 1918 and the overthrow of the Communist regime in 1989.

ROSA PARKS DAY: 65th ANNIVERSARY OF ARREST. Dec 1, 1955. Anniversary of the arrest of Rosa Parks, at Montgomery, AL, for refusing to give up her seat and move to the back of a municipal bus. Her arrest triggered a yearlong boycott of the city bus system and led to legal actions that ended racial segregation on municipal buses throughout the southern US. The event has been called the birth of the modern civil rights movement. Rosa McCauley Parks was born at Tuskegee, AL, Feb 4, 1913.

SAFE TOYS AND GIFTS MONTH. Dec 1–31. What are the most dangerous types of toys to children's eyesight? Tips on how to choose age-appropriate, safe toys will be distributed. For info: Prevent Blindness, 211 W Wacker Dr, Ste 1700, Chicago, IL 60606. Phone: (800) 331-2020. E-mail: info@preventblindness.org. Web: www.preventblindness.org.

SPACE MILESTONE: *ATLANTIS* (US). Dec 1, 1988. Launched this date. Mission deployed a new-generation spy satellite able to peer down on the Soviet Union in darkness and through clouds. All-military crew: Navy Commander Robert Gibson, Air Force Colonel Guy Gardner, Air Force Colonel Richard Mullane, Air Force Lieutenant Colonel Jerry Ross and Navy Commander William Shepherd. Landed Dec 6, 1988.

STOUT, REX: BIRTH ANNIVERSARY. Dec 1, 1886. Mystery author Rex Todhunter Stout, born at Noblesville, IN, created two of the most enduring characters in the mystery genre: Nero Wolfe and his feisty sidekick, Archie Goodwin. Stout received the highest honor of the mystery world when the Mystery Writers of America gave him their Grand Master Award in 1959. Stout died Oct 27, 1975, at Danbury, CT.

TUSSAUD, MARIE GROSHOLTZ: BIRTH ANNIVERSARY. Dec 1, 1761. Born Anna Maria Grosholtz at Strasbourg, France, Tussaud was a wax artist who created models of royalty and celebrities. When the French Revolution erupted, she survived by using her craft to satisfy the populace's desire to see likenesses of the executed: she made death masks using corpses as models. Married to François Tussaud in 1795, she went to England in 1802 with her waxworks and relics of the Revolution in a traveling show. In 1835 she established a permanent base at Baker Street, London. Tussaud was a savvy marketer, creating advertising campaigns and innovative exhibits such as the ghoulish Chamber of Horrors, which depicted famous killers. She died at London on Apr 15, 1850, but her wax museum empire—now in many cities around the globe—remains.

UNITED NATIONS: WORLD AIDS DAY. Dec 1. In 1988 the World Health Organization of the UN declared Dec 1 as World AIDS Day, an international day of awareness and education about AIDS. The WHO is the leader in global direction and coordination of AIDS prevention, control, research and education. A program called UN-AIDS was created to bring together the skills and expertise of the World Bank, UNDP, UNESCO, UNICEF, UNFPA and the WHO to strengthen and expand national capacities to respond to the pandemic. For info: United Nations, Dept of Public Info, New York, NY 10017. Web: www.un.org.

★**WORLD AIDS DAY.** Dec 1.

December 2020	S	M	T	W	T	F	S
			1	2	3	4	5
	6	7	8	9	10	11	12
	13	14	15	16	17	18	19
	20	21	22	23	24	25	26
	27	28	29	30	31		

WORLDWIDE FOOD SERVICE SAFETY MONTH. Dec 1–31. This month is geared toward professional food service safety. However, it also reminds cooks in homes all around the world to handle food safely. People working with food need to buy, store, prepare, serve and keep prepared food properly. "Always remember to handle food safely both professionally and at home." For info: Deborah Le Bouf Kulkkula, PhD, or Harold Le Bouf II. Phone: (978) 343-4009 or (978) 808-8084. E-mail: DebKulkkula@gmail.com. Web: www.HaroldLeBouf.com.

🧁 BIRTHDAYS TODAY

Riz Ahmed, 38, actor (*Rogue One, Nightcrawler*, "The Night Of"), rapper, born London, England, Dec 1, 1982.

Woody Allen, 85, filmmaker (Oscar for *Annie Hall*; *Blue Jasmine, Manhattan, Hannah and Her Sisters*), actor, born Allen Stewart Konigsberg at Brooklyn, NY, Dec 1, 1935.

Carol Alt, 60, model, born New York, NY, Dec 1, 1960.

Candace Bushnell, 62, author, journalist (*Sex and the City*), born Glastonbury, CT, Dec 1, 1958.

Nestor Carbonell, 53, actor (*The Dark Knight*, "Lost," "Suddenly Susan," "The Tick"), born New York, NY, Dec 1, 1967.

Bette Midler, 75, singer, actress (*Beaches, For the Boys, Down and Out in Beverly Hills*), born Paterson, NJ, Dec 1, 1945.

Janelle Monáe, 35, singer, actress (*Hidden Figures*), born Janelle Monáe Robinson at Kansas City, KS, Dec 1, 1985.

Emily Mortimer, 49, actress ("The Newsroom," *Lars and the Real Girl, Match Point*), born London, England, Dec 1, 1971.

Gary Peters, 62, US Senator (D, Michigan), born Pontiac, MI, Dec 1, 1958.

Reggie Sanders, 53, former baseball player, born Florence, SC, Dec 1, 1967.

Rick Scott, 68, US Senator (R, Florida), former governor of Florida, born Bloomington, IL, Sept 29, 1942.

Lee Buck Trevino, 81, golfer, born Dallas, TX, Dec 1, 1939.

Larry Walker, 54, former baseball player, born Maple Ridge, BC, Canada, Dec 1, 1966.

Treat Williams, 68, actor ("Everwood," *127 Hours, Hair*), born Rowayton, CT, Dec 1, 1952.

December 2 — Wednesday

DAY 337   **29 REMAINING**

ARTIFICIAL HEART TRANSPLANT: ANNIVERSARY. Dec 2, 1982. Barney C. Clark, 61, became the first recipient of a permanent artificial heart. The operation was performed at the University of Utah Medical Center at Salt Lake City. Near death at the time of the operation, Clark survived almost 112 days after the implantation. He died Mar 23, 1983.

BELL, JOSEPH: BIRTH ANNIVERSARY. Dec 2, 1837. Best known today as the inspiration for the fictional character Sherlock Holmes, Joseph Bell in his time was a well-respected physician and professor at the University of Edinburgh in Scotland. Arthur Conan

Doyle met Bell at the University of Edinburgh's medical school as a student and witnessed Bell's amazing ability to deduce facts about all aspects of a patient's life. Bell was also Queen Victoria's physician whenever she came to Scotland. Bell died at Edinburgh on Oct 4, 1911.

BROWN, JOHN: EXECUTION ANNIVERSARY. Dec 2, 1859. Abolitionist leader who is remembered for his raid on the US Arsenal at Harpers Ferry. Brown was hanged for treason at Charles Town, WV.

CALLAS, MARIA: BIRTH ANNIVERSARY. Dec 2, 1923. Soprano born Maria Anna Sofia Cecilia Kalogeropoulos to Greek immigrant parents at New York, NY. One of the most prominent artists of the 20th century, "La Divina" led the postwar revival of bel canto operas. A dramatic persona on and off the stage, Callas epitomized the diva in popular culture. "To me, the art of music is magnificent, and I cannot bear to see it treated in a shabby way," she once stated. Callas died at Paris, France, Sept 16, 1977.

ENGLAND: WALTER PLINGE DAY. Dec 2. A day to recognize Walter Plinge, said to have been a London pub landlord in 1900. His generosity to actors led to the use of his name as an actor in play programs to conceal the fact that an actor was playing more than one role. See also: "George Spelvin Day" (Nov 15) for US equivalent.

ENRON FILES FOR BANKRUPTCY: ANNIVERSARY. Dec 2, 2001. The once high-flying Houston, TX, energy services company filed for bankruptcy on this date. Subsequent investigations revealed questionable accounting practices and unethical dealings, to the extent that "Enron" became the buzzword for corporate malfeasance of the late 1990s and into the 21st century. Many other corporations were found to have questionable financial statements after the Enron scandal (in which thousands of employees lost their jobs and retirement savings), and investor confidence in the US stock market was shaken. Federal Reserve chairman Alan Greenspan, in a July 16, 2002, report to the Senate Banking Committee, indicted such corporate misbehavior: "An infectious greed seemed to grip much of our business community [in the 1990s]."

FIRST SELF-SUSTAINING NUCLEAR CHAIN REACTION: ANNIVERSARY. Dec 2, 1942. Physicist Enrico Fermi led a team of scientists at the University of Chicago in producing the first controlled, self-sustaining nuclear chain reaction. Their first simple nuclear reactor was built under the stands of the university's football stadium.

HOLIDAY ALE FESTIVAL. Dec 2–6. Pioneer Courthouse Square, Portland, OR. This five-day festival offers a prestigious lineup of winter beers that either have been crafted specifically for the event or are hard-to-find vintages. In addition to beer tasting, the festival features meet-the-brewer events, a craft soda garden, food vendors and a coat check for charity. And despite being outdoors during one of the coldest months of the year, attendees stay warm and dry under clear-topped tents. Gas heaters create a cozy ambience beneath the boughs of the region's largest decorated Christmas tree. Annually, beginning the Wednesday after Thanksgiving. Est attendance: 14,000. For info: Chris Crabb. E-mail: holidayalefestival@gmail.com. Web: www.holidayale.com.

"IMUS IN THE MORNING" RADIO PREMIERE: ANNIVERSARY. Dec 2, 1971. Award-winning radio broadcaster Don Imus signed on to New York City's WNBC on this date. The show offered cantankerous takes on current affairs. On Apr 12, 2007, CBS dropped the show due to racial slurs made by Imus. The show reemerged and is currently broadcast on the Cumulus Media Networks.

LAOS: NATIONAL DAY. Dec 2. National holiday commemorating declaration of the republic in 1975.

MCCARTHY SILENCED BY SENATE: ANNIVERSARY. Dec 2, 1954. On Feb 9, 1950, Joseph McCarthy, a relatively obscure senator from Wisconsin, announced during a speech in Wheeling, WV, that he had a list of Communists in the State Department. Over the next two years he made increasingly sensational charges, and in 1953 McCarthyism reached its height as he held Senate hearings in which he bullied defendants. In 1954 McCarthy's tyranny was exposed in televised hearings during which he took on the army,

and on Dec 2, 1954, the Senate voted to censure him. McCarthy died May 2, 1957.

MONROE DOCTRINE: ANNIVERSARY. Dec 2, 1823. President James Monroe, in his annual message to Congress, enunciated the doctrine that bears his name and that was long hailed as a statement of US policy: "In the wars of the European powers in matters relating to themselves we have never taken any part. . . . We should consider any attempt on their part to extend their system to any portion of this hemisphere as dangerous to our peace and safety."

NATIONAL MUTT DAY—DECEMBER. Dec 2. This day, founded in 2005 by animal welfare advocate Colleen Paige, celebrates the many wonderful attributes of mixed-breed dogs. It also promotes adoption worldwide. Since shelters are filled to the brim with mixed-breed dogs, we need two dates annually to help these "mutts" find forever homes. Annually, July 31 and Dec 2. For info: The Holiday Guild. Phone: (323) 285-2148. E-mail: k.kelly@theholidayguild.com. Web: www.nationalmuttday.com.

NATIONAL PARKS ESTABLISHED IN ALASKA: 40th ANNIVERSARY. Dec 2, 1980. Eight national parks were established in Alaska on this date. Mount McKinley National Park, which was established Feb 26, 1917, and Denali National Monument, which was proclaimed Dec 1, 1978, were combined as Denali National Park and Preserve. Gates of the Arctic National Monument, proclaimed Dec 1, 1978; Glacier Bay National Monument, proclaimed Feb 25, 1925; and Katmai National Monument, proclaimed Sept 24, 1918, were established as national parks and preserves. Kenai Fjords National Monument, proclaimed Dec 1, 1978, and Kobuk Valley National Monument, proclaimed Dec 1, 1978, were established as national parks. Lake Clark National Monument, proclaimed Dec 1, 1978, and Wrangell–St. Elias National Monument, proclaimed Dec 1, 1978, were established as national parks and preserves. For info: www.nps.gov.

ROCKEFELLER CENTER CHRISTMAS TREE: ANNUAL LIGHTING. Dec 2 (tentative). New York, NY. Lighting of the huge Christmas tree in Rockefeller Center signals the opening of the holiday season at New York City. More than 30,000 lights are strung on five miles of electric wire. In 1933 the first formal tree lighting ceremony took place with 700 lights. Date is usually the Tuesday or Wednesday after Thanksgiving.

SAN BERNARDINO TERRORIST ATTACK: 5th ANNIVERSARY. Dec 2, 2015. During a San Bernardino County Department of Public Health employee holiday party, a fellow employee and his wife, both apparently self-radicalized and supporting the Islamic State, gunned down participants—killing 14 people and injuring 22 more. Police later killed the couple.

SEURAT, GEORGES: BIRTH ANNIVERSARY. Dec 2, 1859. French Neo-Impressionist painter born at Paris, France. He died there Mar 29, 1891. Seurat is known for his style of painting with small spots of color, called *pointillism*, as in *Sunday Afternoon on the Island of Grand Jatte*.

SPECIAL EDUCATION DAY. Dec 2. Celebrate the anniversary of the first US special education law—Dec 2, 1975. A time to reflect and move forward. Where were we when President Ford signed the groundbreaking legislation? Where are we now? And where do we need to be tomorrow? A day to honor progress, dialogue about challenges we face and consider reforms for the future of educating

all children. Annually, Dec 2. For info: Special Education Day Committee (SPEDCO). E-mail: info@specialeducationday.com. Web: www.specialeducationday.com.

SPECIAL KIDS DAY. Dec 2. Wilder Mansion, Elmhurst, IL. A day to honor children of all ages with developmental or physical disabilities with an area-wide Christmas celebration. This event builds on UN Resolution 47/3, which sets aside a day to promote the inclusion of those with disabilities into the community. This free, all-volunteer event features a photo session with Santa, gifts for all children with special needs and their siblings, face painters, music, craft projects and other activities. (A 501 C3 not-for-profit organization.) Est attendance: 650. For info: Rich Rosenberg, Special Kids Day, 111 Linden, Elmhurst, IL 60126. E-mail: rich@specialkidsday.org. Web: www.SKD.org.

UNITED ARAB EMIRATES: NATIONAL DAY. Dec 2. Anniversary of the day in 1971 when a federation of seven sheikdoms known as the Trucial States declared independence from the UK and became known as the United Arab Emirates.

UNITED NATIONS: INTERNATIONAL DAY FOR THE ABOLITION OF SLAVERY. Dec 2. Recalls the date of adoption by the General Assembly in 1949 of the Convention for the Suppression of the Traffic in Persons and the Exploitation of Others. For info: United Nations, Dept of Public Info, New York, NY 10017. Web: www.un.org.

WALSTON, RAY: BIRTH ANNIVERSARY. Dec 2, 1914. Comic character actor, born at New Orleans, LA (some sources say in 1919), best known for playing Applegate (the Devil) in the original stage production and later film version of *Damn Yankees* and Uncle Martin O'Hara, the title character in the popular TV series "My Favorite Martian" (1963–66). Walston, who won a Tony Award for Best Actor in *Damn Yankees*, died Jan 1, 2001, at Beverly Hills, CA.

🧁 BIRTHDAYS TODAY

T. Coraghessan Boyle, 72, author (*The Harder They Come, The Tortilla Curtain*), born Peekskill, NY, Dec 2, 1948.

Dan Butler, 66, actor ("Frasier"), born Huntington, IN, Dec 2, 1954.

Dennis Christopher, 65, actor (*Sweet Dreams, Breaking Away*), born Dennis Carrelli at Philadelphia, PA, Dec 2, 1955.

Brendan Coyle, 57, actor ("Downton Abbey," "Lark Rise to Candleford"), born Corby, Northamptonshire, England, Dec 2, 1963.

Cathy Lee Crosby, 72, actress ("That's Incredible," *Coach*), born Los Angeles, CA, Dec 2, 1948.

Nelly Furtado, 42, singer, born Victoria, BC, Canada, Dec 2, 1978.

Randy Gardner, 62, former figure skater, choreographer, born Marina del Rey, CA, Dec 2, 1958.

Lucy Liu, 53, actress ("Elementary," "Ally McBeal," *Charlie's Angels*), born Queens, NY, Dec 2, 1967.

Ann Patchett, 57, author (*Bel Canto, State of Wonder*), born Los Angeles, CA, Dec 2, 1963.

Stone Phillips, 66, anchor ("Dateline," "20/20"), born Texas City, TX, Dec 2, 1954.

Aaron Rodgers, 37, football player, born Chico, CA, Dec 2, 1983.

George Saunders, 62, author (*Lincoln in the Bardo, Tenth of December*), born Amarillo, TX, Dec 2, 1958.

Monica Seles, 47, Hall of Fame tennis player, born Novi Sad, Yugoslavia (now Serbia), Dec 2, 1973.

Britney Spears, 39, singer, born Kentwood, LA, Dec 2, 1981.

William Wegman, 77, artist, photographer, born Holyoke, MA, Dec 2, 1943.

December 2020	S	M	T	W	T	F	S
			1	2	3	4	5
	6	7	8	9	10	11	12
	13	14	15	16	17	18	19
	20	21	22	23	24	25	26
	27	28	29	30	31		

December 3 — Thursday

DAY 338 **28 REMAINING**

BE A BLESSING DAY. Dec 3. Since 2015. Genesis 12:3 lays out a universal human mission: to be a blessing to all the families of the earth—human and otherwise. Taking chapter and verse as a guide, we celebrate Dec 3 (12/3) as Be a Blessing Day: a day for cultivating loving kindness toward person and planet. While we prescribe no set practice, we do encourage people to identify and drop all zero-sum narratives that promote their thriving at the expense of another's suffering, to study ethical teachings rooted in traditions other than their own and to actively engage in acts of loving kindness as individuals, families and communities. Annually, Dec 3. For info: Rabbi Rami Shapiro, One River Foundation, 2441-Q Old Fort Pky, Ste 412, Murfreesboro, TN 37128.

BHOPAL POISON GAS DISASTER: ANNIVERSARY. Dec 3, 1984. At Bhopal, India, a leak of deadly gas (methyl isocyanate) at a Union Carbide Corporation plant killed more than 4,000 persons and injured more than 200,000 in the world's worst industrial accident.

CLERC-GALLAUDET WEEK. Dec 3–10. A week in which to promote awareness and mobilize support of the public for critical issues in the education and human rights of Deaf people. A recognition of the two first visionary leaders in the field of American Deaf education, who were born in December: Laurent Clerc (Dec 26, 1785) and Thomas Hopkins Gallaudet (Dec 10, 1787). Dec 3 is the United Nations International Day of Persons with Disabilities and Dec 10 is United Nations Human Rights Day. For info: Library of Deaf Action, 2930 Craiglawn Rd, Silver Spring, MD 20904-1816. Web: www.foldadeaf.net.

CONRAD, JOSEPH: BIRTH ANNIVERSARY. Dec 3, 1857. English novelist, born Józef Korzeniowski to Polish parents at Berdichev in the Ukraine. He learned English as a sailor on British ships. Author of *Lord Jim* and *Heart of Darkness*, among others. Died Aug 3, 1924, at Bishopsbourne, Kent, England.

E-DISCOVERY DAY. Dec 3. E-Discovery Day was started in 2015 as a way for the e-discovery industry to come together to celebrate the vital and growing role that e-discovery plays in the legal process. It is an industry-wide, vendor-neutral celebration that includes in-person educational and networking events, online webinars, CLE opportunities, white papers, social media conversation and more. For info: Exterro, 4145 SW Watson Ave, Ste 400, Beaverton, OH 97005. Phone: (503) 501-5134. E-mail: media@exterro.com. Web: www.e-discoveryday.com.

FIRST HEART TRANSPLANT: ANNIVERSARY. Dec 3, 1967. Dr. Christiaan Barnard, a South African surgeon, performed the world's first successful heart transplantation at Cape Town, South Africa. See also: "Barnard, Christiaan: Birth Anniversary" (Nov 8).

ILLINOIS: ADMISSION DAY: ANNIVERSARY. Dec 3. Became 21st state in 1818.

MONTOYA, CARLOS: BIRTH ANNIVERSARY. Dec 3, 1903. Guitarist and composer renowned for popularizing flamenco guitar music.

His solo performances of the Spanish folk form lifted flamenco from its traditional accompaniment role. Montoya never learned to read music and relied on the traditional improvisational nature of flamenco rooted in the Andalusian Gypsy form of music that stressed rhythms and harmonic patterns. He was born at Madrid, Spain, and died Mar 3, 1993, at Wainscott, NY.

ROCKY FILM RELEASE: ANNIVERSARY. Dec 3, 1976. After premiering in New York City (Nov 21, 1976), *Rocky* went into general release. Sylvester Stallone wrote the film and starred as Rocky Balboa, the hard-working Philadelphia boxer looking for his big chance. The low-budget and quickly shot film became a sleeper success and won three Oscars, including Best Picture.

ROTA, NINO: BIRTH ANNIVERSARY. Dec 3, 1911. Born at Milan, Italy, Rota was a celebrated composer and conductor, famous for his work with Italian filmmaker Federico Fellini, which included the scores for such classics as *La Dolce Vita* (1960) and *8½* (1963). Other highlights of his lengthy list of opera and film score credits include his love theme for *Romeo and Juliet* (1968) and the theme to *The Godfather* (1972). Rota died at Rome, Italy, on Apr 10, 1979.

A STREETCAR NAMED DESIRE BROADWAY OPENING: ANNIVERSARY. Dec 3, 1947. Tennessee Williams's drama opened on Broadway at the Ethel Barrymore Theatre with Jessica Tandy (as Blanche Du Bois) and newcomer Marlon Brando (as Stanley Kowalski). Williams was already a Broadway star with his first play, *The Glass Menagerie*, and *Streetcar* was to be equally successful: it ran for two years and won the Pulitzer Prize for Drama. Marlon Brando's performance, using his Method style, was a sensation to audience members and critics. Tandy won the Tony Award for Best Actress in a Play.

STUART, GILBERT CHARLES: BIRTH ANNIVERSARY. Dec 3, 1755. American portrait painter whose most famous painting is that of George Washington. He also painted portraits of Madison, Monroe, Jefferson and other important Americans. Stuart was born near Narragansett, RI, and died July 9, 1828, at Boston, MA.

UNITED NATIONS: INTERNATIONAL DAY OF PERSONS WITH DISABILITIES. Dec 3. On Oct 14, 1992 (Res 47/3), at the end of the Decade of Disabled Persons, the General Assembly proclaimed Dec 3 to be an annual observance to promote the continuation of integrating the disabled into general society. Formerly called the International Day of Disabled Persons. For info: United Nations, Dept of Public Info, New York, NY 10017. Web: www.un.org.

WILLIAMS, ANDY: BIRTH ANNIVERSARY. Dec 3, 1927. The embodiment of "easy listening" as both a genre and way of life, Andy Williams made a career out of smooth balladry and clean-cut entertainment. Born at Wall Lake, IA, Williams sang with his brothers—the Williams Brothers—before going it alone and issuing a string of hits in the 1960s. His signature song was the Henry Mancini–Johnny Mercer composition "Moon River." Williams also hosted a popular Emmy Award–winning television variety show from 1962 to 1971 and was well known for his Christmas specials and holiday music showcases. Later in life, Williams had his own theater in the entertainment mecca of Branson, MO. He died there Sept 25, 2012.

🎂 BIRTHDAYS TODAY

Bruno Campos, 46, actor ("Nip/Tuck"), born Rio de Janeiro, Brazil, Dec 3, 1974.

Holly Marie Combs, 47, actress ("Picket Fences," "Charmed"), born San Diego, CA, Dec 3, 1973.

Brendan Fraser, 52, actor (*The Mummy, The Quiet American*), born Indianapolis, IN, Dec 3, 1968.

Jean Luc Godard, 90, filmmaker (*Breathless, Weekend*), born Paris, France, Dec 3, 1930.

Tiffany Haddish, 41, actress (*Girls Trip, Keanu*, "The Carmichael Show"), born Los Angeles, CA, Dec 3, 1979.

Daryl Hannah, 59, actress (*Splash, Grumpy Old Men*), born Chicago, IL, Dec 3, 1961.

Asa Hutchinson, 70, Governor of Arkansas (R), born Bentonville, AR, Dec 3, 1950.

Bucky Lasek, 48, rally cross driver, skateboarder, born Baltimore, MD, Dec 3, 1972.

Rick Ravon Mears, 69, former auto racer, born Wichita, KS, Dec 3, 1951.

Julianne Moore, 59, actress (Oscar for *Still Alice*; *Far from Heaven, The Kids Are All Right*), born Fort Bragg, Fayetteville, NC, Dec 3, 1961.

Jaye P. Morgan, 88, singer, born Mancos, CO, Dec 3, 1932.

Ozzy Osbourne, 72, singer, songwriter (Black Sabbath), born Birmingham, England, Dec 3, 1948.

Alicia Sacramone, 33, Olympic gymnast, born Boston, MA, Dec 3, 1987.

Amanda Seyfried, 35, actress (*Les Misérables, Mamma Mia*, "Big Love"), born Allentown, PA, Dec 3, 1985.

David Villa, 39, soccer player, born David Villa Sánchez at Langreo, Spain, Dec 3, 1981.

Katarina Witt, 55, Olympic figure skater, born Karl-Marx-Stadt, East Germany (now Chemnitz, Germany), Dec 3, 1965.

December 4 — Friday

DAY 339   **27 REMAINING**

BUTLER, SAMUEL: BIRTH ANNIVERSARY. Dec 4, 1835. Victorian author (*Erewhon, The Way of All Flesh*), born at Bingham, Nottinghamshire, England. Died at London, England, June 18, 1902.

CARLYLE, THOMAS: 225th BIRTH ANNIVERSARY. Dec 4, 1795. Scottish essayist and historian, born at Ecclefechan, Scotland. Died at London, England, Feb 4, 1881. "A well-written Life is almost as rare as a well-spent one," Carlyle wrote in his *Critical and Miscellaneous Essays*.

CHASE, HELEN M.: BIRTH ANNIVERSARY. Dec 4, 1924. Longtime chronicler of contemporary civilization as coeditor of *Chase's Annual Events*. Born at Whitehall, MI, Chase died Feb 19, 2009, at Ann Arbor, MI.

CHASE'S CALENDAR OF EVENTS: BIRTHDAY. Dec 4, 1957. Today in 1957 the first copies of the first edition of *Chase's Calendar of Annual Events* (for the year 1958) were delivered by the printer at Flint, MI. Two thousand copies, consisting of 32 pages and listing 364 events, were printed. Now annual editions are more than 750 pages long and list more than 12,500 events.

DICKENS ON THE STRAND. Dec 4–6. Galveston, TX. Victorian Christmas celebration focuses on the 19th-century architecture of Galveston's Strand National Historic Landmark District and ties to Charles Dickens's 19th-century London. Est attendance: 35,000. For info: Galveston Historical Foundation, 2228 Broadway, Galveston, TX 77550. Phone: (409) 765-3404. E-mail: foundation@galvestonhistory.org. Web: www.dickensonthestrand.org.

FRANCO, FRANCISCO: BIRTH ANNIVERSARY. Dec 4, 1892. Spanish military dictator, born Francisco Franco Bahamonde at Ferrol, Galicia, Spain. Led the 1936 coup that toppled the government of the Republic of Spain and led to a three-year-long civil war that took perhaps 500,000 lives. Ruled as *El Caudillo* ("The Chief") until his death at Madrid, Spain, on Nov 20, 1975.

GENEVA'S CHRISTMAS WALK AND HOUSE TOUR. Dec 4–5. Geneva, IL. A special holiday tradition emphasizing the warmth and hospitality of Geneva. On Friday evening, Santa Lucia arrives and Santa makes his debut to open his house. On Friday and Saturday, five distinctive homes festively decorated by local decorators open their doors to visitors for self-guided tours. Enjoy carolers, Great Tree lighting, roasted chestnuts, Swedish cookies, old-fashioned candy cane pull and holiday shopping. Est attendance: 25,000. For info: Geneva Chamber of Commerce, PO Box 481, 8 S Third St, Geneva, IL 60134. Phone: (630) 232-6060. E-mail: chamberinfo@genevachamber.com. Web: www.genevachamber.com.

GHANA: NATIONAL FARMERS' DAY. Dec 4. Public holiday. Honors and celebrates the farmers of Ghana. Observed the first Friday in December.

HOLLY JOLLY WEEKEND. Dec 4–6. ACE Arena, Andrews, TX. Festivities include Holidazzle lighted Christmas parade, synchronized light show, live Nativity and the arrival of Santa at the downtown light display. Other events include the Reds, Whites and Evergreens Wine Tour of Homes and more than 100 vendors at the Holly Jolly Marketplace, the longest-running Christmas market in West Texas. For info: Andrews Chamber of Commerce, 700 W Broadway, Andrews, TX 79714. Phone: (432) 523-2695. E-mail: achamber@andrewstx.com. Web: www.andrewstx.com.

LAST AMERICAN HOSTAGE RELEASED IN LEBANON: ANNIVERSARY. Dec 4, 1991. A sad chapter of US history came to a close when Terry Anderson, an Associated Press correspondent, became the final American hostage held in Lebanon to be freed. Anderson had been held since Mar 16, 1985, one of 15 Americans who were held hostage for from two months to as long as six years and eight months. Three of the hostages, William Buckley, Peter Kilburn and Lieutenant Colonel William Higgins, were killed during their captivity. The other hostages, released previously one or two at a time, were Jeremy Levin, Benjamin Weir, the Reverend Lawrence Martin Jenco, David Jacobsen, Thomas Sutherland, Frank Herbert Reed, Joseph Cicippio, Edward Austin Tracy, Alan Steen, Jesse Turner and Robert Polhill.

***MARY CELESTE* DISCOVERED: ANNIVERSARY.** Dec 4, 1872. The English cargo ship *Dei Gratia* saw a ship under sail apparently out of control near the Azore Islands. After failing to get an answer from the vessel, the American brigantine *Mary Celeste*, members of the *Dei Gratia* boarded the ship and discovered a mystery: despite half a year's supply of food and water, all personal belongings—even pipes—still aboard and with the cargo intact, the ship's captain, his family and the crew had disappeared without a trace. The final entry in the ship's logbook was Nov 24 and recorded a position 700 miles away. Some minor damage and a missing lifeboat suggested a hasty abandonment, but for no clear reason. Numerous investigations and theories abounded, but the nautical mystery has never been solved. A young Scottish doctor, Arthur Conan Doyle, was intrigued enough to write the first (but not last) fictional story on the incident: "J. Habakuk Jephson's Statement" (1884).

MISSION SANTA BARBARA: FOUNDING ANNIVERSARY. Dec 4, 1786. Franciscan mission to Native Americans founded at Santa Barbara, CA. Present structure is the fourth to stand on same site. Last one destroyed by 1812 earthquake.

NATIONAL GRANGE FOUNDING: ANNIVERSARY. Dec 4, 1786. The anniversary of the National Grange, the first organized agricultural movement in the US.

NATIONAL SALESPERSON'S DAY. Dec 4. Salespeople are essential resources for customers today. The talented salesperson filters the vast amount of information that is available to customers and helps businesspeople make the best purchasing decisions. Salespeople also help consumers make better, quicker decisions with the counsel they offer. With the impact of new technologies, the role of the salesperson continually evolves. Annually, the first Friday in December. For info: Maura Schreier-Fleming, Best@Selling, 7028 Judi, Dallas, TX 75252. Phone: (972) 380-0200. E-mail: Maura@BestAtSelling.com.

NCAA DIVISION I WOMEN'S SOCCER CHAMPIONSHIP—THE COLLEGE CUP. Dec 4–6. WakeMed Soccer Park, Cary, NC. Est attendance: 14,000. For info: NCAA, PO Box 6222, Indianapolis, IN 46206-6222. Phone: (317) 917-6222. Web: www.NCAA.com.

RUSSELL, LILLIAN: BIRTH ANNIVERSARY. Dec 4, 1861. Born Helen Louise Leonard at Clinton, IA, Russell was the most popular female entertainer of the 19th century. The zaftig singer and actress specialized in operetta, appearing in several of Gilbert and Sullivan's works before turning to comedy. Considered a great beauty, Russell was also notorious for a wild personal life: four husbands and a long relationship with Diamond Jim Brady, with whom she shared a fondness for expensive baubles and fine food. Russell died on June 6, 1922, at Pittsburgh, PA.

SAINT BARBARA'S DAY. Dec 4. On this day, traditionally the feast day of Saint Barbara, a young girl places a twig from a cherry tree in a glass of water. If it blooms by Christmas Eve, she is certain to marry the following year. Because the narratives of her life and martyrdom are legendary, Saint Barbara was dropped from the Roman Catholic Calendar of Saints in 1970.

SPACE MILESTONE: INTERNATIONAL SPACE STATION LAUNCH (US). Dec 4, 1998. The shuttle *Endeavour* took a US component of the space station named *Unity* into orbit 220 miles from Earth, where spacewalking astronauts fastened it to a component launched by the Russians Nov 20, 1998. On July 25, 2000, the Russian service module *Zvezda* docked with the station. On Oct 31, 2000, NASA launched the first expedition with a three-man crew to stay aloft for four months. Officially completed on May 27, 2011, the space station is 357 feet across and 240 feet long and supports a crew of up to six.

SUGARLOAF CRAFTS FESTIVAL. Dec 4–6. Dulles Expo Center, Chantilly, VA. This show features more than 300 nationally recognized craft designers and fine artists displaying and selling their original creations. Includes craft demonstrations, live music, specialty foods, children's entertainment, gift certificate drawings and more. Est attendance: 22,000. For info: Sugarloaf Mountain Works, 13225 Executive Park Terrace, Germantown, MD 20874. Phone: (800) 210-9900. E-mail: sugarloafinfo@sugarloaffest.com. Web: www.sugarloafcrafts.com.

December	S	M	T	W	T	F	S
			1	2	3	4	5
	6	7	8	9	10	11	12
2020	13	14	15	16	17	18	19
	20	21	22	23	24	25	26
	27	28	29	30	31		

🎂 BIRTHDAYS TODAY

Fred Armisen, 54, comedian, actor ("Portlandia," "Saturday Night Live"), born Valley Stream, NY, Dec 4, 1966.

Max Baer, Jr, 83, actor ("The Beverly Hillbillies"), producer (*Ode to Billy Joe*), born Oakland, CA, Dec 4, 1937.

Tyra Banks, 47, model, actress, talk show host, born Los Angeles, CA, Dec 4, 1973.

Jeff Bridges, 71, actor (Oscar for *Crazy Heart*; *The Big Lebowski, Starman, The Last Picture Show*), born Los Angeles, CA, Dec 4, 1949.

Chris Hillman, 76, singer, musician (The Byrds, The Flying Burrito Brothers, Desert Rose Band), born Los Angeles, CA, Dec 4, 1944.

Jay-Z, 51, rapper, music executive, born Shawn Corey Carter at Brooklyn, NY, Dec 4, 1969.

Jin, 28, singer (BTS), born Kim Seok-jin at Gwacheon, South Korea, Dec 4, 1992.

Marisa Tomei, 56, actress (*In the Bedroom*, Oscar for *My Cousin Vinny*), born Brooklyn, NY, Dec 4, 1964.

Patricia Wettig, 69, actress ("St. Elsewhere," *City Slickers*, Emmys for "thirtysomething"), born Cincinnati, OH, Dec 4, 1951.

Cassandra Wilson, 65, jazz singer, born Jackson, MS, Dec 4, 1955.

December 5 — Saturday

DAY 340   **26 REMAINING**

AFL-CIO FOUNDED: 65th ANNIVERSARY. Dec 5, 1955. The American Federation of Labor and the Congress of Industrial Organizations joined together in 1955, following 20 years of rivalry, to become the nation's leading advocate for trade unions.

AUSTRIA: KRAMPUSLAUF. Dec 5. Salzburg region. On the eve of St. Nicholas's Day, Austrians celebrate the Krampuslauf (Krampus Run). In folklore, the Krampus is a devilish companion of St. Nicholas who punishes bad children just as St. Nicholas rewards good ones. The Krampus, represented by costumed revelers, is usually depicted as a dark, hairy, cloven-hooved beast with red horns, a leering mouth, chains and a switch. Children are invited to throw snowballs at the Krampus. Also known as Krampus Day.

BATHTUB PARTY DAY. Dec 5. Almost everyone nowadays takes showers, so here's a day to recall some of the warm-water luxury of days gone by. Invite a few friends. (©2006 by WH.) For info: Thomas & Ruth Roy, Wellcat Holidays, 2418 Long Ln, Lebanon, PA 17046. Phone: (717) 279-0184. E-mail: info@wellcat.com. Web: www.wellcat.com.

BIKE SHOP DAY. Dec 5. This day, first observed in 2017, serves to connect the independent bike shop and its community. It is about inclusiveness, a healthy lifestyle and sustainable local business practices. Annually, the first Saturday in December. For info: 718 Cyclery, 254 3rd Ave, Brooklyn, NY 11215. Phone: (917) 715-2524. E-mail: info@718c.com. Web: www.bikeshopday.com.

CALDWELL COUNTRY CHRISTMAS PARADE AND FIREWORKS. Dec 5. Columbia, LA. Lighted nighttime parade will roll through

Historic Downtown Columbia. This parade is the highlight of the Christmas season with several bands from the area. Fireworks on the river follow the parade. Est attendance: 8,000. For info: Caldwell Parish Chamber of Commerce, PO Box 726, Columbia, LA 71418. Phone: (318) 649-0726. E-mail: cpchamber60@yahoo.com.

CHESTER GREENWOOD DAY PARADE. Dec 5. Farmington, ME. Celebration of Farmington's famous inventor of the earmuff. An earmuff-themed parade with flag raising. Annually, the first Saturday in December. Est attendance: 2,500. For info: Franklin County Chamber of Commerce, 615 Wilton Rd, Farmington, ME 04938. Phone: (207) 778-4215. E-mail: info@franklincountymaine.org. Web: www.franklincountymaine.org.

CHRISTMAS CANDLELIGHTINGS. Dec 5 (also Dec 12). Roscoe Village, Coshocton, OH. On the first two Saturdays in December, Roscoe Village cheers on the holiday season with its Christmas Candlelighting. Share in the tradition of lighting the Christmas tree and light your own candle as everyone sings "Silent Night." Guests enjoy strolling carolers, roasted chestnuts, candlelight tours, complimentary hot mulled cider and cookies and many other holiday festivities. Est attendance: 2,000. For info: Roscoe Village Foundation, 600 N Whitewoman St, Coshocton, OH 43812. Phone: (740) 622-7644 or (800) 877-1830. E-mail: ldaniel@roscoevillage.com. Web: www.roscoevillage.com.

CHRISTMAS ON THE PRAIRIE. Dec 5–6. Saunders County Museum, Wahoo, NE. Old-fashioned Christmas featuring entertainment by local groups, special postal cancellation, children's activities common to the 1800s and demonstrations in the historical village decorated in the 1800s style. Annually, the first weekend in December. Sponsor: Christmas on the Prairie Steering Committee. Est attendance: 3,000. For info: Curator, Saunders County Museum, 240 N Walnut, Wahoo, NE 68066-1858. Phone: (402) 443-3090. E-mail: saunderscomuseum@hotmail.com. Web: www.saunderscomuseum.com.

CUSTER, GEORGE ARMSTRONG: BIRTH ANNIVERSARY. Dec 5, 1839. Born at New Rumley, OH, Custer was a cavalry officer in the US Civil War whose courage and leadership brought him admiration and fame. He later spent 10 years on the Great Plains fighting in the Indian Wars and leading a successful Black Hills expedition in 1874 to find gold. During a campaign to move the Lakota Sioux onto reservations to make way for the gold rush, Custer attacked an encampment of Sioux and Cheyenne on June 25, 1876. Outnumbered, he and about 215 of his men were quickly killed at the Battle of Little Bighorn—now considered one of the biggest military fiascoes in US history.

DISNEY, WALT: BIRTH ANNIVERSARY. Dec 5, 1901. Innovative animator, filmmaker, producer, studio head, theme park developer, born at Chicago, IL. Cocreator of Mickey Mouse. Recipient of a record 22 Academy Awards in competitive categories as well as three honorary Oscars and the Irving Thalberg Award. Disney died at Los Angeles, CA, Dec 15, 1966.

ENGLAND: ROCHESTER DICKENSIAN CHRISTMAS FESTIVAL. Dec 5–6. Rochester, Kent. Rub shoulders with some of Dickens's most beloved and infamous characters during this enchanting weekend of traditional Victorian Christmas festivities. Charles Dickens's country home was located near Rochester. Street entertainment, song, dance and classic readings. Annually, the first weekend in December. For info: Rochester Dickensian Festival. Web: www.rochesterdickensfestival.org.uk or www.visitmedway.org.

GRANT'S SPEECH OF APOLOGY: ANNIVERSARY. Dec 5, 1876. President Ulysses S. Grant delivered his speech of apology to Congress claiming mistakes he made while he was president were due to his inexperience. His errors, he said, were "errors of judgment, not intent." While Grant's personal integrity was never formally questioned, he was closely associated with many government scandals, which became public during his presidency. He unwittingly aided Jay Gould in an attempt to corner the gold market during his first term. During the second, the Credit Mobilier affair involving many of the president's friends aired, while significant fraud was discovered in the Treasury Department and Indian Service.

HAITI: DISCOVERY DAY. Dec 5. Commemorates the discovery of Haiti by Christopher Columbus in 1492. Public holiday.

"IRRATIONAL EXUBERANCE" ENTERS LEXICON: ANNIVERSARY. Dec 5, 1996. In a speech to the Washington, DC–based American Enterprise Institute for Policy Research, Federal Reserve Chair Alan Greenspan uttered a new catchphrase that the media quickly saw as a warning about the high-flying 1990s stock market. He asked, "How do we know when irrational exuberance has unduly escalated asset values. . . . And how do we factor that assessment into monetary policy?" Those two words, buried in an academic speech, nonetheless sparked panic in markets fearing the Fed would raise interest rates. The Tokyo, Hong Kong, Frankfurt, London and US markets dropped 2 to 4 percent after his speech. Most economists thought Greenspan was simply suggesting that markets needed to slow down a bit. But "irrational exuberance" lives on as Greenspan's most famous quote.

LANG, FRITZ: BIRTH ANNIVERSARY. Dec 5, 1890. Austrian filmmaker, born Friedrich Christian Anton Lang at Vienna, Austria. Working in Germany's Weimar Republic, Lang achieved critical success with his Expressionism-influenced silent film *Metropolis* (1927), and his first sound film, *M* (1931), both of which pit individuals against a corrupt society in a malignant, mechanistic world. Part Jewish, Lang left Germany in 1934 and was invited to Hollywood, where he contributed his dystopic vision of individuals trapped by fate in a hostile world to the genesis of film noir, expressed in works like *You Only Live Once* (1937) and *The Big Heat* (1953). He died at Beverly Hills, CA, Aug 2, 1976.

MONTGOMERY BUS BOYCOTT BEGINS: 65th ANNIVERSARY. Dec 5, 1955. Rosa Parks was arrested Dec 1 at Montgomery, AL, for refusing to give up her seat on a bus to a white man. In support of Parks, and to protest the arrest, the black community of Montgomery organized a boycott of the bus system. The boycott lasted from Dec 5, 1955, to Dec 20, 1956, when a US Supreme Court ruling was implemented at Montgomery, integrating the public transportation system.

NCAA DIVISION I MEN'S WATER POLO CHAMPIONSHIP. Dec 5–6. Avery Aquatic Center, Stanford, CA. Host is Stanford University. For info: NCAA, PO Box 6222, Indianapolis, IN 46206-6222. Web: www.NCAA.com.

PICKETT, BILL: 150th BIRTH ANNIVERSARY. Dec 5, 1870. The great American rodeo cowboy was born in Williamson County, TX, the son of a former slave and one of 13 children. He was the creator of "bulldogging" (an early form of steer wrestling in the modern rodeo) where a cowboy leaps off his mount and wrestles a runaway steer to the ground by grappling its horns. Pickett developed this skill as a ranch hand in the 1890s by watching ranch dogs at work. His own special twist involved biting the lip of the steer. He left ranch work to form the successful touring show The Pickett Brothers Bronco Busters and Rough Riders Association. He then joined the 101 Ranch Wild West Show in 1907, which also featured film star Tom Mix. Pickett himself appeared on film to demonstrate his rodeo skills. He died 11 days after a bronco kicked him in the head at the 101 Ranch on Apr 2, 1932, at Tulsa, OK.

ROSSETTI, CHRISTINA: BIRTH ANNIVERSARY. Dec 5, 1830. English poet of beautiful yet melancholy verses who is best known for her lyrical fable "Goblin Market." Her Christmas poem, "In the Bleak Midwinter," was set to music after her death and is now a beloved carol. Born at London, England, where she died on Dec 29, 1894.

THURMOND, STROM: BIRTH ANNIVERSARY. Dec 5, 1902. One of the longest-serving senators in American history, James Strom Thurmond was born at Edgefield, SC. The first senator ever elected by a write-in vote, he joined the US Senate in 1954. He was elected as both a Democrat and a Republican and is remembered for his record-breaking filibuster protesting pending civil rights legislation. He did not yield the floor for 24 hours, 18 minutes over Aug 28–29, 1957, although the legislation did pass less than two hours later. He served in the Senate until Nov 19, 2002, just a few weeks shy of his 100th birthday. He died at Edgefield on June 26, 2003.

TWENTY-FIRST AMENDMENT TO THE US CONSTITUTION RATIFIED: ANNIVERSARY. Dec 5, 1933. Prohibition ended with the repeal of the 18th Amendment, as the 21st Amendment was ratified. Congress proposed repeal of the 18th Amendment ("the manufacture, sale, or transportation of intoxicating liquors, within, the importation thereof into, or the exportation thereof from the United States and all territory subject to the jurisdiction thereof, for beverage purposes is hereby prohibited") on Feb 20, 1933. By Dec 5, 1933, the repeal amendment had been ratified by the required 36 states and went into effect immediately as the 21st Amendment to the US Constitution.

UNITED NATIONS: INTERNATIONAL VOLUNTEER DAY FOR ECONOMIC AND SOCIAL DEVELOPMENT. Dec 5. In a resolution of Dec 17, 1985, the United Nations General Assembly recognized the desirability of encouraging the work of all volunteers. It invited governments to observe annually on Dec 5 the "International Volunteer Day for Economic and Social Development, urging them to take measures to heighten awareness of the important contribution of volunteer service." A day commemorating the establishment in December 1970 of the UN Volunteers program and inviting world recognition of volunteerism in the international development movement. For info: United Nations, Dept of Public Info, New York, NY 10017. Web: www.un.org.

UNITED NATIONS: WORLD SOIL DAY. Dec 5. Noting that soils constitute the foundation for agricultural development, essential ecosystem functions and food security and hence are key to sustaining life on Earth, the UN General Assembly has declared Dec 5 as World Soil Day. The UN affirms the urgent need to raise awareness and to promote and facilitate national efforts and actions toward sustainable management of the limited world soil resources. For info: United Nations. Web: www.un.org.

VAN BUREN, MARTIN: BIRTH ANNIVERSARY. Dec 5, 1782. The eighth president of the US (term of office: Mar 4, 1837–Mar 3, 1841) was the first to have been born a citizen of the US. His first language was Dutch—he learned English as a second language. Van Buren was a widower for nearly two decades before he entered the White House. His daughter-in-law, Angelica, served as White House hostess during an administration troubled by bank and business failures, depression and unemployment. Van Buren was born at Kinderhook, NY, and died there July 24, 1862.

WHEATLEY, PHILLIS: DEATH ANNIVERSARY. Dec 5, 1784. Born at Senegal, West Africa, about 1753 or 1754, Phillis Wheatley was brought to the US in 1761 and purchased as a slave by a Boston tailor named John Wheatley. She was allotted unusual privileges for a slave, including being allowed to learn to read and write. She

	S	**M**	**T**	**W**	**T**	**F**	**S**
December			1	2	3	4	5
	6	7	8	9	10	11	12
2020	13	14	15	16	17	18	19
	20	21	22	23	24	25	26
	27	28	29	30	31		

wrote her first poetry at age 14, and her first work was published in 1770. Wheatley's fame as a poet spread throughout Europe as well as the US after her *Poems on Various Subjects, Religious and Moral* was published at England in 1773. She was invited to visit George Washington's army headquarters after he read a poem she had written about him in 1776. Phillis Wheatley died at about age 30, at Boston, MA.

🧁 BIRTHDAYS TODAY

Morgan Brittany, 70, actress ("Dallas," "Glitter"), born Suzanne Cupito at Hollywood, CA, Dec 5, 1950.

José Carreras, 74, opera singer, one of the "Three Tenors," born Barcelona, Spain, Dec 5, 1946.

Margaret Cho, 52, actress, comedienne, born San Francisco, CA, Dec 5, 1968.

Joan Didion, 86, author, journalist (*The Year of Magical Thinking, The White Album*), born Sacramento, CA, Dec 5, 1934.

Jeroen Krabbe, 76, actor (*A World Apart, King of the Hill, The Fugitive*), born Amsterdam, Netherlands, Dec 5, 1944.

Little Richard, 85, singer, born Richard Penniman at Macon, GA, Dec 5, 1935.

Jim Messina, 73, singer, songwriter, born Maywood, CA, Dec 5, 1947.

Chad Mitchell, 84, singer, born Spokane, WA, Dec 5, 1936.

Art Monk, 63, Hall of Fame football player, born White Plains, NY, Dec 5, 1957.

Frankie Muniz, 35, actor ("Malcolm in the Middle," *My Dog Skip*), born Ridgewood, NJ, Dec 5, 1985.

Paula Patton, 45, actress (*Mission: Impossible—Ghost Protocol, Precious: Based on the Novel "Push" by Sapphire*), born Los Angeles, CA, Dec 5, 1975.

Calvin Trillin, 85, author (*American Stories, Remembering Denny*), born Kansas City, MO, Dec 5, 1935.

December 6 — Sunday

DAY 341	25 REMAINING

ADORATION PARADE. Dec 6. Branson, MO. The 72nd annual Adoration Celebration Parade will present a celebration of Christmas—the traditional values of faith, family and friendliness. For info: Branson/Lakes Area Chamber of Commerce & CVB, PO Box 1897, Branson, MO 65615. Phone: (417) 334-4084. Fax: (417) 337-5887. E-mail: info@bransonchamber.com. Web: www.bransonchamber.com.

ALTAMONT CONCERT: ANNIVERSARY. Dec 6, 1969. A free concert featuring performances by the Rolling Stones; Jefferson Airplane; Santana; Crosby, Stills, Nash and Young and the Flying Burrito Brothers turned into tragedy. The "thank-you" concert for 300,000 fans was marred by overcrowding, drug overdoses and the fatal stabbing of a spectator by a member of the Hell's Angels motorcycle gang, who had been hired as security guards for the event. The concert was held at the Altamont Speedway, Livermore, CA.

BRUBECK, DAVE: 100th BIRTH ANNIVERSARY. Dec 6, 1920. With his innovative and forever intuitive sound as both a pianist and composer, Dave Brubeck became one of the biggest stars of American jazz in the 1950s and '60s, at a time when rock and roll was the dominant force in popular music. Legendary records like his 1955 Columbia debut, *Brubeck Time*, and the ambitious *Time Out* (1959)—featuring the hit "Take Five" and the first million-selling jazz album—remain as hallmarks of jazz, and document how Brubeck and his collaborators defined the contours of American cool. A recipient of the National Medal of Arts, he was also the first modern jazz musician to be featured on the cover of *Time*

magazine. Born at Concord, CA, Brubeck died Dec 5, 2012, at Norwalk, CT.

CHRISTMAS TO REMEMBER. Dec 6. Laurel, MT. 35th annual. To officially open the Christmas season in Laurel, this daylong celebration includes the arrival of Santa, a community bazaar, tour of Christmas trees, children's craft activities, musical entertainment, lighting ceremony, parade and fireworks. Annually, the first Sunday in December. Est attendance: 5,000. For info: Christmas to Remember Committee, Jean Carroll Thompson, PO Box 463, Laurel, MT 59044. Phone: (406) 248-8557.

ECUADOR: DAY OF QUITO: FOUNDING ANNIVERSARY. Dec 6. Commemorates founding of city of Quito by Spaniards in 1534.

EISENSTAEDT, ALFRED: BIRTH ANNIVERSARY. Dec 6, 1898. American photojournalist Alfred Eisenstaedt was born at Dirschau, Prussia. One of the greatest photojournalists in US history, he is best known for his 86 photos that were used on covers of *Life* magazine, including the iconic image of a sailor kissing a nurse in New York's Times Square at the end of WWII. He died Aug 23, 1995, at Martha's Vineyard, MA.

EVERGLADES NATIONAL PARK ESTABLISHED: ANNIVERSARY. Dec 6, 1947. Part of vast marshland area on southern Florida peninsula, originally authorized May 30, 1934, was established as a national park.

FINLAND: INDEPENDENCE DAY. Dec 6. National holiday. Declaration of independence from Russia in 1917.

GERALD FORD SWEARING IN AS VICE PRESIDENT: ANNIVERSARY. Dec 6, 1973. Gerald Ford was sworn in as vice president under Richard Nixon, following the resignation of Spiro Agnew, who pled no contest to a charge of income tax evasion. See also: "Agnew, Spiro Theodore: Birth Anniversary" (Nov 9) and "Ford, Gerald Rudolph: Birth Anniversary" (July 14).

GERSHWIN, IRA: BIRTH ANNIVERSARY. Dec 6, 1896. Pulitzer Prize–winning American lyricist and author who collaborated with his brother George and with many other composers. Among his Broadway successes: *Lady Be Good, Funny Face, Strike Up the Band* and such songs as "The Man I Love," "Someone to Watch Over Me" and "I Got Rhythm." Born at New York, NY, he died at Beverly Hills, CA, Aug 17, 1983.

HALIFAX, NOVA SCOTIA, DESTROYED: ANNIVERSARY. Dec 6, 1917. More than 1,650 people were killed at Halifax when the Norwegian ship *Imo* plowed into the French munitions ship *Mont Blanc*. *Mont Blanc* was loaded with 4,000 tons of TNT, 2,300 tons of picric acid, 61 tons of other explosives and a deck of highly flammable benzene, which ignited and touched off an explosion. In addition to those killed, 1,028 were injured. A tidal wave caused by the explosion washed much of the city out to sea.

HART, WILLIAM SURREY: BIRTH ANNIVERSARY. Dec 6, 1864. American actor and film director best remembered as the first Western movie star and a top box-office leading man in silent movies from 1914 to 1925. He was one of the rare movie cowboys who had actually worked on a cattle ranch. Roles in *Hell's Hinges* (1916) and *The Narrow Trail* (1917) established Hart as the classic cowboy star whether he was playing the outlaw or the hero. Born in 1864 (or 1870) at Newburgh, NY, he closely identified with the Wild West, even serving as a pallbearer at Wyatt Earp's funeral on Jan 16, 1929. Hart died June 23, 1946, at Newhall, CA.

KILMER, JOYCE ALFRED: BIRTH ANNIVERSARY. Dec 6, 1886. The American poet most famous for his poem "Trees," which was published in 1913, was born at New Brunswick, NJ. Kilmer was killed in action near Seringes-et-Nesles, France, in WWI, July 30, 1918. The army's Camp Kilmer in New Jersey was named for him.

MISSOURI EARTHQUAKES: ANNIVERSARY. Dec 6, 1811. New Madrid, MO. Most prolonged series of earthquakes in US history occurred not in California, but in the Midwest. Lasted until Feb 12, 1812. There were few deaths because of the sparse population. These were the most severe earthquakes in the contiguous US; those higher on the Richter scale have all occurred in Alaska.

NATIONAL MINER'S DAY. Dec 6. In appreciation, honor and remembrance of the accomplishments and sacrifices of miners. A day to provide a sober reminder of the risks that miners are routinely exposed to in their work and to set aside some time on this day for quiet contemplation of those brave miners who have perished in our mines. A National Miner's Day resolution passed in the US Senate on Dec 3, 2009. Observed previously in West Virginia.

NATIONAL PAWNBROKERS DAY. Dec 6. Celebrated on St. Nicholas Day, in honor of the patron saint of pawnbroking. Designed to acknowledge the valuable lending and retail services the pawnbroker provides his or her clientele. (Originally sponsored by Michael Goldstein.)

ROBERT-HOUDIN, JEAN EUGÈNE: BIRTH ANNIVERSARY. Dec 6, 1805. The founder of modern magic who was the first to use electricity in his illusions. Robert-Houdin also popularized wearing evening attire (instead of wizard's robes) on stage. He inspired scores of younger magicians, including Harry Houdini, whose stage name saluted Robert-Houdin's name. Born at Blois, France, Robert-Houdin died at St. Gervais, France, on June 13, 1871.

SAINT NICHOLAS DAY. Dec 6. One of the most venerated saints of both Eastern and Western Christian churches, of whose life little is known, except that he was Bishop of Myra (in what is today's Turkey) in the fourth century, and that from early times he has been especially noted for his charity. Santa Claus and the presentation of gifts is said to derive from St. Nicholas.

SPAIN: CONSTITUTION DAY. Dec 6. National holiday. Commemorates the voters' approval of a new constitution in 1978.

THIRTEENTH AMENDMENT TO THE US CONSTITUTION RATIFIED: ANNIVERSARY. Dec 6, 1865. The 13th Amendment to the Constitution was ratified, abolishing slavery in the US. "Neither slavery nor involuntary servitude, save as a punishment for crime whereof the party shall have been duly convicted, shall exist within the United States, or any place subject to their jurisdiction." This amendment was proclaimed Dec 18, 1865. The 13th, 14th and 15th amendments are considered the Civil War Amendments. See also: "Emancipation Proclamation: Anniversary" (Jan 1) for Lincoln's proclamation freeing slaves in the rebelling states.

🎂 BIRTHDAYS TODAY

Giannis Antetokounmpo, 26, basketball player, born Athens, Greece, Dec 6, 1994.

Andrew Cuomo, 63, Governor of New York (D), born Queens, NY, Dec 6, 1957.

Macy Gray, 51, singer, born Canton, OH, Dec 6, 1969.

Thomas Hulce, 67, actor (*Amadeus, Parenthood*), born Plymouth, MI, Dec 6, 1953.

Johnny Manziel, 28, football player, 2012 Heisman Trophy winner, born Tyler, TX, Dec 6, 1992.

December 2020	S	M	T	W	T	F	S
			1	2	3	4	5
	6	7	8	9	10	11	12
	13	14	15	16	17	18	19
	20	21	22	23	24	25	26
	27	28	29	30	31		

James Naughton, 75, actor (*The Paper Chase, The Good Mother*; stage: *Long Day's Journey into Night*), born Middletown, CT, Dec 6, 1945.

Craig Newmark, 68, founder of craigslist, born Morristown, NJ, Dec 6, 1952.

Sarah Rafferty, 48, actress ("Suits"), born Greenwich, CT, Dec 6, 1972.

Janine Turner, 58, actress ("Northern Exposure," *Cliffhanger*), born Lincoln, NE, Dec 6, 1962.

JoBeth Williams, 67, actress (*The Ponder Heart, The Big Chill*), born Houston, TX, Dec 6, 1953.

Steven Wright, 65, comedian, born New York, NY, Dec 6, 1955.

December 7 — Monday

DAY 342   **24 REMAINING**

ARMENIAN EARTHQUAKE OF 1988: ANNIVERSARY. Dec 7, 1988. An earthquake measuring 6.9 on the Richter scale rocked the Soviet province of Armenia, killing upward of 60,000 people. Many of the deaths were blamed on poor construction practices as many homes had been made of adobe, mud or stones, had unreinforced masonry or were prefabricated structures made of loosely connected concrete slabs. In the quake's aftermath, Soviet president Mikhail Gorbachev cut short his trip to the US to fly home and head the massive worldwide relief efforts.

CATHER, WILLA SIBERT: BIRTH ANNIVERSARY. Dec 7, 1873. American author born at Winchester, VA. Died at New York, NY, Apr 24, 1947. Best known for her novels about the development of early 20th-century American life, such as *O Pioneers!* and *My Ántonia*. She won a Pulitzer Prize in 1922 for her book *One of Ours*.

CENTRAL AFRICAN REPUBLIC: NATIONAL DAY OBSERVED. Dec 7. Commemorates Proclamation of the Republic on Dec 1, 1958. Usually observed on the first Monday in December.

CHAPIN, HARRY: BIRTH ANNIVERSARY. Dec 7, 1942. Folksinger/songwriter Harry Chapin was one of only five songwriters to receive the Special Congressional Gold Medal, for his devotion to the issue of hunger throughout the world. Born at New York, NY, he was killed in a car accident July 16, 1981, at Long Island, NY.

CÔTE D'IVOIRE: COMMEMORATION DAY. Dec 7. National holiday. Commemorates the death of the first president, Félix Houphouët-Boigny, in 1993.

DELAWARE RATIFIES CONSTITUTION: ANNIVERSARY. Dec 7, 1787. Delaware became the first state to ratify the proposed Constitution. It did so by unanimous vote.

IRAN: STUDENTS DAY. Dec 7. Day commemorating the 1953 killing of three university students by the Shah's security forces. The students were among many protesting US vice president Richard Nixon's visit to Iran after the Shah took power.

MOON PHASE: LAST QUARTER. Dec 7. Moon enters Last Quarter phase at 7:36 PM, EST.

NATIONAL FIRE SAFETY COUNCIL: FOUNDING ANNIVERSARY. Dec 7, 1979. Founded to promote fire and burn prevention and life safety awareness. The council distributes comprehensive material to children, adults and seniors through local fire departments and the council's mascot, Firepup®. For info: Natl Fire Safety Council, Inc, PO Box 378, Michigan Center, MI 49254-0378. Phone: (800) 2551082. Web: www.nfsc.org.

NATIONAL OLDER DRIVER SAFETY AWARENESS WEEK. Dec 7-11. Held annually the first week in December, this week seeks to empower older drivers and their families by bringing awareness to the steps between noticing a medical change that can affect driving to completely giving up the keys. Daily themes include Changes That Can Affect Driving, Family Conversations, Screening and Evaluations with an Occupational Therapist, Interventions That Can Empower Drivers and Community Mobility After Driving. For info: The American Occupational Therapy Assn Inc, 4720 Montgomery Ln, Ste 200, Bethesda, MD 20814-3449. Phone: (301) 652-6611. Web: www.aota.org/Conference-Events/Older-Driver-Safety-Awareness-Week.aspx.

★NATIONAL PEARL HARBOR REMEMBRANCE DAY. Dec 7.

PEARL HARBOR DAY: ANNIVERSARY. Dec 7, 1941. At 7:55 AM (local time) Dec 7, 1941, "a date that will live in infamy," nearly 200 Japanese aircraft attacked Pearl Harbor, Hawaii, long considered the US "Gibraltar of the Pacific." The raid, which lasted little more than one hour, left nearly 2,500 dead. Almost the entire US Pacific Fleet was at anchor there, and few ships escaped damage. Several were sunk or disabled, while 188 US aircraft on the ground were destroyed. The attack on Pearl Harbor brought about immediate US entry into WWII, a declaration of war being requested by President Franklin D. Roosevelt and approved by Congress Dec 8, 1941.

SEARS, RICHARD WARREN: BIRTH ANNIVERSARY. Dec 7, 1863. Founder, with Alvah C. Roebuck, and president of the huge retail and mail-order company Sears, Roebuck and Company. Born at Stewartville, MN, Sears died Sept 28, 1914, at Waukesha, WI.

SPACE MILESTONE: *APOLLO 17* **(US).** Dec 7, 1972. Launched this date with three-man crew—Eugene A. Cernan, Harrison H. Schmidt and Ronald E. Evans—who explored the moon, Dec 11-14. Lunar landing module named *Challenger*. Pacific splashdown, Dec 19. This was the last US manned mission to the moon.

SPACE MILESTONE: *GALILEO* **(US): 25th ANNIVERSARY.** Dec 7, 1995. Launched Oct 18, 1989, by the space shuttle *Atlantis*, the spacecraft *Galileo* entered the orbit of Jupiter after a six-year journey. It has been orbiting Jupiter ever since, sending out probes to study three of its moons. Organic compounds, the ingredients of life, were found on them. On May 25, 2001, it passed within 86 miles of Callisto, one of Jupiter's moons.

UNITED NATIONS: INTERNATIONAL CIVIL AVIATION DAY. Dec 7. On Dec 6, 1996, the General Assembly proclaimed Dec 7 as International Civil Aviation Day. On Dec 7, 1944, the Convention on International Civil Aviation, which established the International Civil Aviation Organization, was signed. For info: United Nations, Dept of Public Info, New York, NY 10017. Web: www.un.org.

WALLACH, ELI: BIRTH ANNIVERSARY. Dec 7, 1915. Durable stage, screen and television actor born at Brooklyn, NY. Wallach had memorable roles in such films as *Baby Doll* (his first film, in 1956); *The Magnificent Seven* (1960); *How the West Was Won* (1962); *The Good, the Bad and the Ugly* (1966); *The Godfather: Part III* (1990) and *Wall Street: Money Never Sleeps* (2010). He had scores of television parts, including that of Mr Freeze in the campy "Batman" series. In 2010 he received an honorary Academy Award. Wallach died June 24, 2014, at New York, NY.

🎂 BIRTHDAYS TODAY

Johnny Lee Bench, 73, Hall of Fame baseball player, born Oklahoma City, OK, Dec 7, 1947.

Larry Joe Bird, 64, Hall of Fame basketball player, former coach, born West Baden, IN, Dec 7, 1956.

Ellen Burstyn, 88, actress (Tony for *Same Time, Next Year*; Oscar for *Alice Doesn't Live Here Anymore*), born Edna Rae Gilhooley at Detroit, MI, Dec 7, 1932.

Noam Chomsky, 92, philosopher, linguist, political activist, born Philadelphia, PA, Dec 7, 1928.

Susan M. Collins, 68, US Senator (R, Maine), born Caribou, ME, Dec 7, 1952.

C. Thomas Howell, 54, actor ("Two Marriages," *Soul Man, Tank*), born Los Angeles, CA, Dec 7, 1966.

Tino Martinez, 53, former baseball player, born Tampa, FL, Dec 7, 1967.

John Terry, 40, soccer manager, born Barking, England, Dec 7, 1980.

Tom Waits, 71, singer, songwriter, actor (*Down by Law, Short Cuts*), born Pomona, CA, Dec 7, 1949.

Jeffrey Wright, 55, actor (Tony Award for *Angels in America: Perestroika*; "Westworld," *Hunger Games* films, *Casino Royale, Basquiat*), born Washington, DC, Dec 7, 1965.

December 8 — Tuesday

DAY 343   **23 REMAINING**

AMERICA ENTERS WORLD WAR II: ANNIVERSARY. Dec 8, 1941. One day after the surprise Japanese attack on Pearl Harbor, Congress declared war against Japan and the US entered WWII.

AMERICAN FEDERATION OF LABOR (AFL) FOUNDED: ANNIVERSARY. Dec 8, 1886. Originally founded at Pittsburgh, PA, as the Federation of Organized Trades and Labor Unions of the United States and Canada in 1881, the union was reorganized in 1886 under the name American Federation of Labor (AFL). The AFL was dissolved as a separate entity in 1955 when it merged with the Congress of Industrial Organizations to form the AFL-CIO. See also: "AFL-CIO Founded: Anniversary (Dec 5)."

CHINESE NATIONALISTS MOVE TO FORMOSA: ANNIVERSARY. Dec 8, 1949. The government of Chiang Kai-shek moved to Formosa (Taiwan) after being driven out of Mainland China by the Communists led by Mao Zedong.

DAVIS, SAMMY, JR: 95th BIRTH ANNIVERSARY. Dec 8, 1925. Born at New York, NY, Sammy Davis, Jr, was the son of vaudevillians and first appeared on the stage at the age of four. He made his first film appearance in *Rufus Jones for President* in 1931. He joined the Will Mastin Trio, a song-and-dance team popular on the nightclub circuit; as Davis matured, his singing, dancing and impersonations became the center of the act. Davis began performing on his own in the 1950s, headlining club engagements, appearing on television variety shows and making numerous records. His Broadway debut came in 1956 in the hit musical *Mr Wonderful*, and in the late '50s and early '60s he starred in a number of films, including a series with Frank Sinatra and the Rat Pack. Davis died at Los Angeles, CA, May 16, 1990.

DURANT, WILLIAM CRAPO: BIRTH ANNIVERSARY. Dec 8, 1861. "Billy" Durant, a leading producer of carriages at Flint, MI; promoter of the Buick car; cofounder of Chevrolet and founder, in 1908, of General Motors. He lost, regained and again lost control of GM, after which he founded Durant Motors, went bankrupt in the Depression and operated a Flint bowling alley in his last working years. Durant was born at Boston, MA, and died at New York, NY, Mar 18, 1947.

FEAST OF THE IMMACULATE CONCEPTION. Dec 8. Roman Catholic holy day of obligation. A public holiday in Nicaragua.

GUAM: LADY OF CAMARIN DAY. Dec 8. Declared a legal holiday by Guam legislature, Mar 2, 1971.

HOBAN, JAMES: DEATH ANNIVERSARY. Dec 8, 1831. Irish-born architect who designed the US President's Executive Mansion, later known as the White House. He was born at Callan, County Kilkenny, Ireland, in 1762 (exact date unknown) and died at Washington, DC. The cornerstone for the White House, Washington's oldest public building, was laid in 1792.

INTERMEDIATE-RANGE NUCLEAR FORCES TREATY (INF) SIGNED: ANNIVERSARY. Dec 8, 1987. The USSR and the US signed a treaty at Washington, DC, eliminating medium-range and shorter-range missiles. This was the first treaty completely eliminating two entire classes of nuclear arms. These missiles, with a range of 500 to 5,500 kilometers, were to be scrapped under strict supervision within three years of the signing.

JOHN LENNON SHOT: 40th ANNIVERSARY. Dec 8, 1980. On this date deranged gunman Mark David Chapman shot and killed rock star John Lennon outside his apartment building as he returned from a recording session. The death of the former Beatle, who was an international peace activist, shocked the world. His widow, Yoko Ono, asked for 10 minutes of silence at 2 PM, EST, on the following Sunday, Dec 14, and many US and international radio stations observed it. See also: "Lennon, John: Birth Anniversary" (Oct 9).

MORRISON, JIM: BIRTH ANNIVERSARY. Dec 8, 1943. Songwriter, poet, lead singer of The Doors, Jim Morrison is considered to be one of the fathers of contemporary rock. The bacchic Morrison, known as "the Lizard King," brought avant-garde theatrics to his musical performances and mystical influences to his songs. Born at Melbourne, FL, and died at Paris, France, July 3, 1971.

NAFTA SIGNED: ANNIVERSARY. Dec 8, 1993. President Clinton signed the North American Free Trade Agreement, which cut tariffs and eliminated other trade barriers among the US, Canada and Mexico. The agreement went into effect Jan 1, 1994.

NATIONAL LARD DAY. Dec 8. Today is a celebration of a traditional healthy animal fat—pure lard, derived from pork—that is now enjoying a resurgence within America's food culture, in restaurants (especially those featuring ethnic specialties), fast food operations and home kitchens. Artificial trans fats are out, and minimally processed animal fats like lard—for superior baking, frying and a host of other cooking applications—are making a comeback. The color, texture and flavor that lard imparts make it a vastly superior alternative to heavily processed, industrially produced substitutes. Annually, Dec 8. For info: Healthy Fats Coalition, Ken Greenberg, Edge Communications, Inc, 5417 Hollywood Blvd, C-727, Los Angeles, CA 90027. Web: www.healthy-fatscoalition.org.

RIVERA, DIEGO: BIRTH ANNIVERSARY. Dec 8, 1886. One of the greatest artists of Mexico, Rivera specialized in bold, colorful murals that depicted the struggle of the working classes and/or displayed the grandeur of Mexican history. A commissioned mural at Rockefeller Center in New York City was famously destroyed in 1934 because it contained an image of Lenin. He was twice married to fellow artist Frida Kahlo. Born at Guanajuato, Mexico, Rivera died in his studio at San Angel, near Mexico City, Nov 25, 1957.

SEGAR, ELZIE CRISLER: BIRTH ANNIVERSARY. Dec 8, 1894. Popeye creator Elzie Crisler Segar was born at Chester, IL. Originally called "Thimble Theater," the comic strip that came to be known as "Popeye" had the unusual format of a one-act play in cartoon form. Centered on the Oyl family, especially daughter Olive, the strip introduced a new central character in 1929. A one-eyed sailor with bulging muscles, Popeye became the strip's star attraction almost immediately. Popeye made it to the silver screen in animated form and in 1980 became a movie with Robin Williams playing the lead. Segar died Oct 13, 1938, at Santa Monica, CA.

SIBELIUS, JEAN: BIRTH ANNIVERSARY. Dec 8, 1865. Born at Hämeenlinna, Finland, Sibelius is Finland's greatest musician, regarded by many as the "last master in the Beethoven symphonic tradition." Influenced by Tchaikovsky and Romantic composers, his music conveys mood and atmosphere, although his work is regarded as more classical in nature. His most famous piece, *Finlandia*, exemplary of the presence of Finnish folklore in his music, became synonymous with independence for Finnish patriots. He died Sept 20, 1957, at Järvenpää, Finland, after a lengthy retirement. He famously said, "Music begins where the possibilities of language end."

SOVIET UNION DISSOLVED: ANNIVERSARY. Dec 8, 1991. The Union of Soviet Socialist Republics (USSR) ceased to exist, as the republics of Russia, Byelorussia and Ukraine signed an agreement at Minsk, Byelorussia, creating the Commonwealth of Independent States. The remaining republics, with the exception of Georgia, joined in the new commonwealth as it began the slow and arduous process of removing the yoke of Communism and dealing with strong separatist and nationalistic movements within the various republics.

THURBER, JAMES: BIRTH ANNIVERSARY. Dec 8, 1894. James Grover Thurber, humorist and artist, longtime contributor to the *New Yorker* (starting in 1927), was born at Columbus, OH. He authored the children's books *The 13 Clocks* and *The Wonderful O* and the classic story "The Secret Life of Walter Mitty." He died at New York, NY, Nov 2, 1961.

UZBEKISTAN: CONSTITUTION DAY. Dec 8. National holiday. Commemorates the constitution of 1991.

WHITNEY, ELI: BIRTH ANNIVERSARY. Dec 8, 1765. Inventor of the cotton gin, born at Westborough, MA. Died at New Haven, CT, Jan 8, 1825.

🎂 BIRTHDAYS TODAY

Kim Basinger, 67, actress (Oscar for *LA Confidential*; *Batman, The Natural*), born Athens, GA, Dec 8, 1953.

Gordon Arthur "Red" Berenson, 79, former hockey player and coach, born Regina, SK, Canada, Dec 8, 1941.

Ann Coulter, 59, political commentator, author (*Slander: Liberal Lies About the American Right*), born New Canaan, CT, Dec 8, 1961.

December	S	M	T	W	T	F	S
			1	2	3	4	5
2020	6	7	8	9	10	11	12
	13	14	15	16	17	18	19
	20	21	22	23	24	25	26
	27	28	29	30	31		

James Galway, 81, flutist, born Belfast, Northern Ireland, Dec 8, 1939.

Teri Hatcher, 56, actress ("Desperate Housewives," "Lois & Clark"), born Sunnyvale, CA, Dec 8, 1964.

Dwight Howard, 35, basketball player, born Atlanta, GA, Dec 8, 1985.

Nicki Minaj, 36, singer, rapper, born Onika Tanya Maraj at St. James, Port of Spain, Trinidad and Tobago, Dec 8, 1984.

Dominic Monaghan, 44, actor (Lord of the Rings trilogy, "Lost"), born Berlin, Germany, Dec 8, 1976.

Mike Mussina, 52, Hall of Fame baseball player, born Williamsport, PA, Dec 8, 1968.

Sinead O'Connor, 54, singer, songwriter, born Dublin, Ireland, Dec 8, 1966.

Matthias Schoenaerts, 43, actor (*The Danish Girl, Far from the Madding Crowd, Rust and Bone*), born Antwerp, Belgium, Dec 8, 1977.

Ian Somerhalder, 42, actor ("The Vampire Diaries," "Lost"), born Covington, LA, Dec 8, 1978.

Mary Woronov, 74, actress (*Rock 'n' Roll High School, Eating Raoul*), born Brooklyn, NY, Dec 8, 1946.

December 9 — Wednesday

DAY 344   **22 REMAINING**

BIRDSEYE, CLARENCE: BIRTH ANNIVERSARY. Dec 9, 1886. American industrialist who developed a way of deep-freezing foods. He was marketing frozen fish by 1925 and was one of the founders of General Foods Corporation. Born at Brooklyn, NY, he died at New York City, Oct 7, 1956.

"CORONATION STREET" TV PREMIERE: 60th ANNIVERSARY. Dec 9, 1960. One of the UK's longest-running television series, "Coronation Street" depicts the working-class denizens of a neighborhood in Manchester, England. Created by Tony Warren, this soap is a cultural touchstone, and the show's story lines have been reported on the news. Its 9,000th episode aired Sept 28, 2016.

FOXX, REDD: BIRTH ANNIVERSARY. Dec 9, 1922. Born John Elroy Sanford at St. Louis, MO, Redd Foxx plied his comedic trade on vaudeville stages, in nightclubs, on television, in films and on record albums. His talents reached a national audience with the TV sitcom "Sanford and Son." He died after collapsing during a rehearsal for a new TV sitcom, "The Royal Family," at Los Angeles, CA, Oct 11, 1991.

GENOCIDE CONVENTION: ANNIVERSARY. Dec 9, 1948. The United Nations General Assembly unanimously approved the Convention on Prevention and Punishment of the Crime of Genocide on Dec 9, 1948. It took effect Jan 12, 1951, when ratification by 20 nations had been completed. President Truman sent it to the US Senate for approval on June 16, 1949; it was supported by presidents Kennedy, Johnson, Nixon, Ford, Carter and Reagan. Thirty-seven years after its submission, and after approval by more than 90 nations, the Senate approved it, Feb 19, 1986, by a vote of 83–11.

HARRIS, JOEL CHANDLER: BIRTH ANNIVERSARY. Dec 9, 1848. American author, creator of the "Uncle Remus" stories, born at Eatonton, GA. Died July 3, 1908, at Atlanta, GA.

HOPPER, GRACE: BIRTH ANNIVERSARY. Dec 9, 1906. Born at New York, NY. When she retired from the US Navy at the age of 79, she was the oldest naval officer ever on active duty. She attained the rank of rear admiral and was a leader in the computer revolution, having developed the computer language COBOL. Grace Hopper died Jan 1, 1992, at Arlington, WV.

KELLY, EMMETT: BIRTH ANNIVERSARY. Dec 9, 1898. American circus clown and entertainer, born at Sedan, KS. Kelly was best known for "Weary Willie," a clown dressed in tattered clothes, with a beard and large nose. Died at Sarasota, FL, Mar 28, 1979.

MILTON, JOHN: BIRTH ANNIVERSARY. Dec 9, 1608. English poet, historian, civil servant and defender of freedom of the press; born at Bread Street, Cheapside, London. Considered one of the greatest poets of the English language, second only to William Shakespeare. Author of the great verse epics *Paradise Lost* (1667) and *Paradise Regained* (1671). Died from gout, Nov 8, 1674, at London, England. "No man who knows aught," he wrote, "can be so stupid to deny that all men naturally were born free."

O'NEILL, THOMAS PHILIP, II (TIP): BIRTH ANNIVERSARY. Dec 9, 1912. Democratic congressman from Massachusetts 1953–87, Speaker of the House of Representatives 1977–87, Tip O'Neill was born at Cambridge, MA, and died Jan 5, 1994, at Boston, MA.

PETRIFIED FOREST NATIONAL PARK ESTABLISHED: ANNIVERSARY. Dec 9, 1962. Arizona's Petrified Forest National Monument, proclaimed Dec 8, 1906, was established as a national park.

SANDYS, EDWIN: BIRTH ANNIVERSARY. Dec 9, 1561. Sir Edwin Sandys, English statesman and one of the founders of the Virginia Colony (treasurer, the Virginia Company, 1619–20), born at Worcestershire, England. Died at Kent, England, in October 1629 (exact date unknown).

TANZANIA: INDEPENDENCE AND REPUBLIC DAY. Dec 9. Tanganyika became independent of Britain in 1961. The republics of Tanganyika and Zanzibar joined to become one state (Apr 27, 1964), renamed (Oct 29, 1964) the United Republic of Tanzania.

UNITED NATIONS: INTERNATIONAL ANTI-CORRUPTION DAY. Dec 9. On Oct 31, 2003, the General Assembly adopted the United Nations Convention against Corruption (Res 58/4) and designated Dec 9 as International Anti-Corruption Day, to raise awareness of corruption and of the role of the convention in combating and preventing it. The convention entered into force in December 2005. For info: United Nations, Dept of Public Info, New York, NY, 10017. Web: www.un.org.

UNITED NATIONS: INTERNATIONAL DAY OF COMMEMORATION AND DIGNITY OF THE VICTIMS OF THE CRIME OF GENOCIDE AND OF THE PREVENTION OF THIS CRIME. Dec 9. Established in 2015, this day seeks to raise awareness of the Genocide Convention (adopted on Dec 9, 1948) and its role in combating and preventing the crime of genocide, as defined in the Convention, and to commemorate and honour its victims. For info: United Nations. Web: www.un.org/en/events/genocidepreventionday.

🎂 BIRTHDAYS TODAY

Joan Armatrading, 70, singer, songwriter (*Me, Myself, I*), born St. Kitts, West Indies, Dec 9, 1950.

Reiko Aylesworth, 48, actress ("24," "One Life to Live"), born Chicago, IL, Dec 9, 1972.

Beau Bridges, 79, actor (Emmy for *Without Warning: The James Brady Story*; *The Descendants*, *The Fabulous Baker Boys*), born Los Angeles, CA, Dec 9, 1941.

Phil Bryant, 66, Governor of Mississippi (R), born Moorhead, MS, Dec 9, 1954.

Richard Marvin (Dick) Butkus, 78, Hall of Fame football player, sportscaster, actor, born Chicago, IL, Dec 9, 1942.

Thomas Daschle, 73, former US senator (D, South Dakota), born Aberdeen, SD, Dec 9, 1947.

Judi Dench, 86, actress (*Philomena*, *Mrs Brown*, *Iris*, Oscar for *Shakespeare in Love*), born York, England, Dec 9, 1934.

Kara DioGuardi, 50, songwriter, record producer, television personality ("American Idol"), born Ossining, NY, Dec 9, 1970.

Kirk Douglas, 104, actor (*Champion*, *Lust for Life*), author, born Issur Danielovitch Demsky at Amsterdam, NY, Dec 9, 1916.

Kirsten Gillibrand, 54, US Senator (D, New York), born Albany, NY, Dec 9, 1966.

Simon Helberg, 40, actor ("The Big Bang Theory"), born Los Angeles, CA, Dec 9, 1980.

David Anthony Higgins, 59, actor ("Ellen," "Malcolm in the Middle"), born Des Moines, IA, Dec 9, 1961.

Felicity Huffman, 58, actress (*Transamerica*, "Desperate Housewives," "Sports Night"), born Bedford, NY, Dec 9, 1962.

Jean-Claude Juncker, 66, President of the European Commission, born Redange-sur-Attert, Luxembourg, Dec 9, 1954.

Thomas (Tom) Kite, Jr, 71, golfer, born Austin, TX, Dec 9, 1949.

Joe Lando, 59, actor ("Dr. Quinn, Medicine Woman"), born Chicago, IL, Dec 9, 1961.

John Malkovich, 67, actor (*Eragon*, *Ripley's Game*, *The Killing Fields*), filmmaker, born Christopher, IL, Dec 9, 1953.

McKayla Maroney, 25, Olympic gymnast, born Aliso Viejo, CA, Dec 9, 1995.

Dina Merrill, 95, actress (*Desk Set*, *Operation Petticoat*), born New York, NY, Dec 9, 1925.

Jesse Metcalfe, 42, actor ("Dallas," "Desperate Housewives," "Passions"), born Waterford, CT, Dec 9, 1978.

Michael Nouri, 75, actor ("Search for Tomorrow," *Flashdance*), born Washington, DC, Dec 9, 1945.

Donny Osmond, 63, actor, singer, born Ogden, UT, Dec 9, 1957.

December 10 — Thursday

DAY 345   **21 REMAINING**

CHANUKAH BEGINS AT SUNDOWN. Dec 10. See "Chanukah" (Dec 11).

DEWEY, MELVIL: BIRTH ANNIVERSARY. Dec 10, 1851. The librarian and inventor of the Dewey decimal book classification system was born at Adams Center, NY. Born Melville Louis Kossuth Dewey, he was an advocate of spelling reform, urged use of the metric system and was interested in many other education reforms. Dewey died at Highlands County, FL, Dec 26, 1931.

DICKINSON, EMILY: BIRTH ANNIVERSARY. Dec 10, 1830. One of America's greatest poets, Emily Dickinson was born at Amherst, MA. She was reclusive, mysterious and frail in health. Seven of her poems were published during her life, but after her death on May 15, 1886, at Amherst, her sister, Lavinia, discovered almost 2,000 more poems written on the backs of envelopes and other scraps of paper locked in her bureau. They were published gradually, over 50 years, beginning in 1890. Dickinson now is recognized as one of the most original poets of the English-speaking world.

ENCYCLOPAEDIA BRITANNICA FIRST PUBLISHED: ANNIVERSARY. Dec 10, 1768. The prestigious general encyclopedia was first published in three volumes in Edinburgh, Scotland, by printer Colin Macfarquhar and engraver Andrew Bell. The publisher was identified as "A Society of Gentlemen in Scotland."

FIRST GRAND OLE OPRY BROADCAST: ANNIVERSARY. Dec 10, 1927. Grand Ole Opry made its first radio broadcast from Nashville, TN.

FIRST US HEAVYWEIGHT CHAMP DEFEATED IN ENGLAND: ANNIVERSARY. Dec 10, 1810. Tom Molineaux, the first unofficial heavyweight champion of the US, was a freed slave from Virginia. He was beaten in the 40th round by Tom Cribb, the English champion, in a boxing match at Copthall Common at London.

FIRST US SCIENTIST RECEIVES NOBEL PRIZE: ANNIVERSARY. Dec 10, 1907. University of Chicago professor Albert Michelson, eminent physicist known for his research on the speed of light and optics, became the first US scientist to receive the Nobel Prize.

GALLAUDET, THOMAS HOPKINS: BIRTH ANNIVERSARY. Dec 10, 1787. A hearing educator who, with Laurent Clerc, founded the first public school for deaf people, Connecticut Asylum for the Education and Instruction of Deaf and Dumb Persons (now the American School for the Deaf), at Hartford, CT, Apr 15, 1817. Gallaudet was born at Philadelphia, PA, and died Sept 9, 1851, at Hartford.

★**HUMAN RIGHTS DAY.** Dec 10. Presidential Proclamation 2866, of Dec 6, 1949, covers all succeeding years. Customarily issued as "Bill of Rights Day, Human Rights Day and Week."

★**HUMAN RIGHTS WEEK.** Dec 10–17. Presidential Proclamation issued since 1958 for the week of Dec 10–17, except in 1986. See also: "Human Rights Day" (Dec 10) and "Bill of Rights Day" (Dec 15).

JANE ADDAMS DAY. Dec 10. A day set aside to celebrate Jane Addams's life—on the anniversary of her receiving the first Nobel Peace Prize ever awarded to an American woman (1931). Illinois honors Jane Addams's memory with a commemorative holiday to observe her lifelong commitment to making the city of Chicago, the state of Illinois and the entire world a better place. First observed in 2007. Annually, Dec 10. For info: Jane Addams Hull-House Museum, 800 S Halsted St, Chicago, IL 60607-7017. Phone: (312) 413-5353. E-mail: jahh@uic.edu. Web: www.hullhousemuseum.org.

LAMOUR, DOROTHY: BIRTH ANNIVERSARY. Dec 10, 1914. Popular singer and actress of the 1930s and '40s. Best known for her appearances in the "Road" movies—*Road to Singapore* (1940) and many others—with Bing Crosby and Bob Hope, where she was often clad in a sarong. Other notable films include *The Hurricane* and *My Favorite Brunette*. Born Mary Leta Dorothy Kaumeyer at New Orleans, LA, she died Sept 22, 1996, at Los Angeles, CA.

LOVELACE, ADA: BIRTH ANNIVERSARY. Dec 10, 1815. Born at London, England, the only legitimate child of Romantic poet Lord Byron, Lovelace was an applied mathematician and author of the world's first detailed description of a computer in her work "Notes," which appended an article about friend/mentor Charles Babbage's Analytical Engine. She is hailed as the world's first computer programmer for her work describing how to derive Bernoulli numbers

December	S	M	T	W	T	F	S
			1	2	3	4	5
	6	7	8	9	10	11	12
2020	13	14	15	16	17	18	19
	20	21	22	23	24	25	26
	27	28	29	30	31		

on Babbage's machine. Despite her significant contributions, she signed her work only with her initials so as not to upset societal norms. The contemporary Ada computer language is named for her. Lovelace died Nov 27, 1852, at Marylebone, England.

"THE MIGHTY MOUSE PLAYHOUSE" TV PREMIERE: 65th ANNIVERSARY. Dec 10, 1955. An all-time favorite of the Saturday-morning crowd (including adults). CBS had a hit with its pint-size cartoon character Mighty Mouse, who was a tongue-in-cheek version of Superman. The show had other feature cartoons such as "The Adventures of Gandy Goose."

MISSISSIPPI: ADMISSION DAY: ANNIVERSARY. Dec 10. Became 20th state in 1817.

NIXON, AGNES: BIRTH ANNIVERSARY. Dec 10, 1922. The soap opera maven was born in Chicago, IL. She was mentored by radio drama pioneer Irna Phillips, who hired her in 1948 to write for "Woman in White" and, later, "Guiding Light," teaching her that "real life is more hilarious, more tragic and more incredible than anything we could think up." Nixon went on to create her own groundbreaking soap operas, the almost never-ending *One Life to Live* (1968–2011) and *All My Children* (1970–2012), which introduced daytime television to taboo social issues such as cancer, abortion, interracial relationships and AIDS. The first woman to win a Trustees Award from the National Academy of Television Arts & Sciences in 1981, Nixon also received a lifetime achievement Emmy in 2010. She died Sept 28, 2017, in Rosemont, PA.

NOBEL PRIZE AWARDS CEREMONIES. Dec 10. Oslo, Norway, and Stockholm, Sweden. Alfred Nobel, Swedish chemist and inventor of dynamite who died in 1896, provided in his will that income from his $9 million estate should be used for annual prizes to be awarded to people who are judged to have made the most valuable contributions to the good of humanity. The Nobel Peace Prize is awarded by a committee of the Norwegian parliament and the presentation is made at the Oslo City Hall. Five other prizes, for physics, chemistry, medicine, literature and economics, are presented in a ceremony at Stockholm. Both ceremonies traditionally are held on the anniversary of the death of Alfred Nobel. First awarded in 1901; the current value of each prize is about $1 million. See also: "Nobel, Alfred Bernhard: Birth Anniversary" (Oct 21).

PAN, HERMES: BIRTH ANNIVERSARY. Dec 10, 1909 (some sources say 1905 or 1910). American choreographer born Hermes Panagiotopolous at Memphis, TN. He is best known for choreographing nine of the ten films starring Fred Astaire and Ginger Rogers; he won the Academy Award in choreography for *A Damsel in Distress* (1937). Pan died at Beverly Hills, CA, on Sept 19, 1990.

RALPH BUNCHE AWARDED NOBEL PEACE PRIZE: 70th ANNIVERSARY. Dec 10, 1950. Dr. Ralph Johnson Bunche became the first black man awarded the Nobel Peace Prize. Bunche was awarded the prize for his efforts in mediation between Israel and neighboring Arab states in 1949.

RED CLOUD: DEATH ANNIVERSARY. Dec 10, 1909. Sioux Indian chief Red Cloud was born in 1822 (exact date unknown), near North Platte, NE. A courageous leader and defender of Native American rights, Red Cloud was the son of Lone Man and Walks as She Thinks. His unrelenting determination caused US abandonment of the Bozeman trail and of three forts that interfered with Native American hunting grounds. Red Cloud died at Pine Ridge, SD.

SPACE MILESTONE: *SOYUZ 26* (USSR). Dec 10, 1977. Launched this date with cosmonauts Yuri Romanenko and Georgi Grechko, who

linked it with *Salyut 6* space station on Dec 11, after the unsuccessful attempt by *Soyuz 25* earlier that year. Returned to Earth in *Soyuz 27*, Mar 16, 1978, after record-setting 96 days in space.

THAILAND: CONSTITUTION DAY. Dec 10. National holiday. Commemorates the constitution of 1932, the nation's first.

TREATY OF PARIS ENDS SPANISH-AMERICAN WAR: ANNIVERSARY. Dec 10, 1898. Following the conclusion of the Spanish-American War in 1898, American and Spanish ambassadors met at Paris, France, to negotiate a treaty. Under the terms of this treaty, Spain granted the US the Philippine Islands and the islands of Guam and Puerto Rico and agreed to withdraw from Cuba. Senatorial debate over the treaty centered on the US's move toward imperialism by acquiring the Philippines. A vote was taken Feb 6, 1899, and the treaty passed by a one-vote margin. President William McKinley signed the treaty Feb 10, 1899.

UNITED NATIONS: HUMAN RIGHTS DAY. Dec 10. Official United Nations observance day. Date is the anniversary of adoption of the "Universal Declaration of Human Rights" in 1948. The declaration sets forth basic rights and fundamental freedoms to which all men and women in the world are entitled. For info: United Nations, Dept of Public Info, New York, NY 10017. E-mail: inquiries@un.org. Web: www.un.org.

🎂 BIRTHDAYS TODAY

Rod Blagojevich, 64, former governor of Illinois (D), born Chicago, IL, Dec 10, 1956.

John Boozman, 70, US Senator (R, Arkansas), born Fort Smith, AR, Dec 10, 1950.

Kenneth Branagh, 60, actor ("Wallander," *Shackleton*), director (*Hamlet, Henry V*), born Belfast, Northern Ireland, Dec 10, 1960.

Susan Dey, 68, model, actress ("The Partridge Family," "LA Law,"), born Pekin, IL, Dec 10, 1952.

Bobby Flay, 56, chef, television personality ("Boy Meets Grill," "Iron Chef America"), born New York, NY, Dec 10, 1964.

Gloria Loring, 74, singer, actress ("Days of Our Lives"), born New York, NY, Dec 10, 1946.

David Perdue, 71, US Senator (R, Georgia), born Macon, GA, Dec 10, 1949.

Melissa Roxburgh, 28, actress ("Manifest," *Star Trek Beyond*), born Vancouver, BC, Canada, Dec 10, 1992.

December 11 — Friday

DAY 346   **20 REMAINING**

BUELL, MARJORIE H.: BIRTH ANNIVERSARY. Dec 11, 1904. Cartoonist, creator of comic strip character Little Lulu, Marjorie Buell was considered a pioneer for creating a female character who outsmarted the neighborhood boys. She was born at Philadelphia, PA, and died May 30, 1993, at Elyria, OH.

BURKINA FASO: NATIONAL DAY. Dec 11. Gained independence within the French community, 1958.

CANNON, ANNIE JUMP: BIRTH ANNIVERSARY. Dec 11, 1863. American astronomer and discoverer of five stars, Annie Jump Cannon was born at Dover, DE, and educated at Wellesley College in physics and astronomy before becoming a "Pickering Woman" at the Harvard College Observatory in 1896. She later curated astronomical photographs at the observatory and was a professor of astronomy at Harvard. Cannon, renowned for her cataloging classification system of stars and awarded Oxford University's first honorary doctorate given to a woman (1925) and the National Academy of Sciences Draper Medal (1931), died at Cambridge, MA, Apr 13, 1941.

CHANUKAH. Dec 11–18. Feast of Lights or Feast of Dedication. Festival lasting eight days commemorates victory of Maccabees over

Syrians (165 BC) and rededication of Temple of Jerusalem. Begins on Hebrew calendar date Kislev 25, 5781. Began at sundown on Dec 10.

EDWARD VIII ABDICATION: ANNIVERSARY. Dec 11, 1936. Edward VIII ascended to the English throne upon the death of his father, George V, on Jan 20, 1936, but the coronation never took place. He abdicated on Dec 11, 1936, in order to marry "the woman I love," twice-divorced American Wallis Warfield Simpson. They were married in France, June 3, 1937. Edward was named Duke of Windsor by his brother-successor, George VI. The duke died at Paris, France, May 28, 1972, but was buried in England, near Windsor Castle.

INDIANA: ADMISSION DAY: ANNIVERSARY. Dec 11. Became 19th state in 1816.

KALEIDOSCOPE DAY: DAVID BREWSTER BIRTH ANNIVERSARY. Dec 11. A day to celebrate the kaleidoscope—on the day its inventor, the prominent scientist David Brewster, was born (at Jedburgh, Scotland, Dec 11, 1781). Brewster—physicist, mathematician and astronomer—invented the optical instrument in 1815 to assist him in his study of optics and patented it in 1817. His term *kaleidoscope* comes from the Greek: *kalos*, "beauty"; *eidos*, "form"; and *scopos*, "watcher." Upon its initial manufacture, the kaleidoscope was a roaring success in Europe and the United States. Brewster died Feb 18, 1868, at Jedburgh.

KOCH, ROBERT: BIRTH ANNIVERSARY. Dec 11, 1843. The great German physician and biologist, born at Clausthal, Hannover (now Germany), discovered the bacilli that cause tuberculosis, cholera and anthrax. For his important work on tuberculosis, Koch received the 1905 Nobel Prize in Physiology and Medicine. He died May 27, 1910, at Baden-Baden, Germany.

LA GUARDIA, FIORELLO HENRY: BIRTH ANNIVERSARY. Dec 11, 1882. Popularly known as the "Little Flower," Fiorello H. La Guardia was not too busy as mayor of New York City to read the "funnies" to radio listeners during the New York newspaper strike. He said of himself: "When I make a mistake it's a beaut!" La Guardia was born at New York, NY, and died there Sept 20, 1947.

"MAGNUM, P.I." TV PREMIERE: 40th ANNIVERSARY. Dec 11, 1980. Premiered on CBS television network, starring Tom Selleck, John Hillerman, Roger E. Mosley and Larry Manetti. Each year on this anniversary, "Magnum" fans turn to the international fan organization Magnum Memorabilia by David Romas as the center of observances worldwide. For info: David Romas, Magnum Memorabilia, 438 Leroy St, Ferndale, MI 48220. E-mail: mpifan@yahoo.com.

MAHFOUZ, NAGUIB: BIRTH ANNIVERSARY. Dec 11, 1911. The only author from the Arab world to win the Nobel Prize in Literature (1988), Mahfouz was born at Old Cairo, Egypt. Mahfouz's work depicted a rapidly transforming Egypt. His masterwork is *The Cairo Trilogy* (1956–57), which chronicles three generations of an Egyptian family in the 1920s and 1930s. He wrote scores of novels, short stories and articles—and much of that work was made into films in the Arab world. In 1994 he survived a knife attack that damaged his nerves and slowed his output. Mahfouz died at Cairo on Aug 30, 2006.

NCAA DIVISION I MEN'S SOCCER CHAMPIONSHIP—THE COLLEGE CUP. Dec 11–13. Meredith Field at Harder Stadium, Santa Barbara, CA. For info: NCAA, PO Box 6222, Indianapolis, IN 46206-6222. Phone: (317) 917-6222. Web: www.NCAA.com.

	S	M	T	W	T	F	S
December			1	2	3	4	5
	6	7	8	9	10	11	12
2020	13	14	15	16	17	18	19
	20	21	22	23	24	25	26
	27	28	29	30	31		

OFFICIAL LOST AND FOUND DAY. Dec 11. 9th annual. Today is a day for renewed hope and belief that lost items should never be forgotten or abandoned to lost-and-found limbo. Please take a moment on Official Lost and Found Day to make one more effort, one more leap of faith that what you've lost isn't gone, it's just not conveniently handy. Reach out, make a call, stop by the office, retrace your steps. What was lost can be found. It's up to you. Annually, the second Friday in December. For info: Lance Morgan, Official Lost and Found Day, Chautauqua Elementary, 9309 SW Cemetery Rd, Vashon, WA 98070. Phone: (206) 463-2882. Fax: (206) 463-0937. E-mail: lmorgan@vashonsd.org. Web: www.lostandfoundday.atspace.cc.

SOLZHENITSYN, ALEKSANDR: BIRTH ANNIVERSARY. Dec 11, 1918. Russian author and dissident, born at Kislovodsk, USSR (now Russia). Awarded the 1970 Nobel Prize in Literature in recognition of novels *One Day in the Life of Ivan Denisovich* and *The Gulag Archipelago*, based on his experiences as a prisoner in Soviet forced labor camps (1945–53). Exiled from USSR in 1974; returned in 1994. By the time of his death on Aug 3, 2008, at Troitse-Lykovo, Russia, he had been embraced by his country as an elder statesman and honored author and humanitarian.

UNICEF ESTABLISHED: ANNIVERSARY. Dec 11, 1946. Anniversary of the establishment by the United Nations General Assembly of the United Nations International Children's Emergency Fund (UNICEF).

UNITED NATIONS: INTERNATIONAL MOUNTAIN DAY. Dec 11. With mountains covering one-quarter of Earth's land surface and home to 12 percent of the world's population, mountain people are affected by conflict out of all proportion to their numbers and the land they occupy. The UN General Assembly declared Dec 11 International Mountain Day as a result of the successful observance of the UN International Year of Mountains in 2002, which increased global awareness of the importance of mountains, stimulated the establishment of national committees in 78 countries and strengthened alliances through promoting the creation of the Mountain Partnership. For info: United Nations, Dept of Public Info, New York, NY 10017. Web: www.un.org or www.mountainpartnership.org.

🎂 BIRTHDAYS TODAY

Jay Bell, 55, former baseball player, born Pensacola, FL, Dec 11, 1965.

Gary Dourdan, 54, actor ("CSI," *Alien: Resurrection*), born Philadelphia, PA, Dec 11, 1966.

Teri Garr, 71, actress (*Young Frankenstein, Tootsie, The Black Stallion*), born Lakewood, OH, Dec 11, 1949.

David Gates, 80, singer, songwriter, born Tulsa, OK, Dec 11, 1940.

Jermaine Jackson, 66, singer, musician (Jackson 5), born Gary, IN, Dec 11, 1954.

John F. Kerry, 77, former US secretary of state (Obama administration), former US senator (D, Massachusetts), born Aurora, CO, Dec 11, 1943.

Brenda Lee, 76, singer, born Brenda Mae Tarpley at Atlanta, GA, Dec 11, 1944.

Donna Mills, 77, actress ("Knots Landing," "Melrose Place"), born Chicago, IL, Dec 11, 1943.

Mo'Nique, 53, actress, talk show host (Oscar for *Precious: Based on the Novel "Push" by Sapphire*, "The Parkers"), born Monique Imes at Woodlawn, MD, Dec 11, 1967.

Rita Moreno, 89, singer, actress (Oscar for *West Side Story*; Tony for *The Ritz*), born Hunacao, Puerto Rico, Dec 11, 1931.

Mos Def, 47, rapper, actor (*16 Blocks, The Italian Job*), born Dante Terrell Smith at Brooklyn, NY, Dec 11, 1973.

Susan Seidelman, 68, filmmaker (*Desperately Seeking Susan, Making Mr Right*), born Philadelphia, PA, Dec 11, 1952.

Hailee Steinfeld, 24, actress (*The Edge of Seventeen, True Grit*), born Thousand Oaks, CA, Dec 11, 1996.

Mark Streit, 43, hockey player, born Englisberg, Switzerland, Dec 11, 1977.

Rider Strong, 41, actor ("Boy Meets World"), born San Francisco, CA, Dec 11, 1979.

Ken Wahl, 67, actor ("Wiseguy"; *The Wanderers; Fort Apache, The Bronx*), born Chicago, IL, Dec 11, 1953.

December 12 — Saturday

DAY 347	19 REMAINING

BONZA BOTTLER DAY®. Dec 12. To celebrate when the number of the day is the same as the number of the month. Bonza Bottler Day® is an excuse to have a party at least once a month. For more information see Jan 1. For info: Gail Berger, Bonza Bottler Day. Phone: (864) 201-3988. E-mail: bonza@bonzabottlerday.com. Web: www.bonzabottlerday.com.

DAY OF OUR LADY OF GUADALUPE. Dec 12. The legend of Guadalupe tells how in December 1531, an Indian, Juan Diego, saw the Virgin Mother on a hill near Mexico City. She instructed him to go to the bishop and have him build a shrine to her on the site of the vision. After his request was initially rebuffed, the Virgin Mother appeared to Juan Diego three days later. She instructed him to pick roses growing on a stony and barren hillside nearby and take them to the bishop as proof. Although flowers do not normally bloom in December, Juan Diego found the roses and took them to the bishop. As he opened his mantle to drop the roses on the floor, an image of the Virgin Mary appeared among them. The bishop built the sanctuary as instructed. Our Lady of Guadalupe became the patroness of Mexico City and by 1746 was the patron saint of all New Spain and by 1910 of all Latin America.

FIRST BLACK SERVES IN US HOUSE OF REPRESENTATIVES: 150th ANNIVERSARY. Dec 12, 1870. Joseph Hayne Rainey of Georgetown, SC, was sworn in as the first black to serve in the US House of Representatives. Rainey filled the seat of Benjamin Franklin Whittemore, which had been declared vacant by the House. He served until Mar 3, 1879.

FLAUBERT, GUSTAVE: BIRTH ANNIVERSARY. Dec 12, 1821. Author whose works include one of the greatest 19th-century novels, *Madame Bovary* (serialized 1856, published 1857). Flaubert was born at Rouen, France, and died at Croisset, France, May 8, 1880.

GARRISON, WILLIAM LLOYD: BIRTH ANNIVERSARY. Dec 12, 1805. American antislavery leader, poet and journalist, born at Newburyport, MA. Garrison died at New York, NY, May 24, 1879.

GINGERBREAD HOUSE DECORATING DAY. Dec 12. This very merry day is dedicated to celebrating the family tradition of gingerbread decorating. Surround yourself with family and friends and have fun with ready-to-decorate gingerbread house kits. Kids and adults can have a ton of fun decorating gingerbread. Annually, the second Saturday in December. For info: Desiree Smith, Wilton Enterprises, 535 E Diehl Rd, Naperville, IL 60563. Phone: (630) 810-2254. E-mail: dsmith@wilton.com. Web: www.wilton.com.

JAY, JOHN: 275th BIRTH ANNIVERSARY. Dec 12, 1745. (Old Style date.) The American statesman, diplomat and first chief justice of the US (1789–95), coauthor (with Alexander Hamilton and James Madison) of the influential *Federalist* papers, was born at New York, NY. Jay died at Bedford, NY, May 17, 1829.

KENYA: JAMHURI DAY. Dec 12. Jamhuri Day (Independence Day) is Kenya's official National Day, commemorating proclamation of the republic and independence from Britain in 1963.

KOCH, ED: BIRTH ANNIVERSARY. Dec 12, 1924. Politician born at New York, NY. A congressman during 1969–1977, Koch was elected mayor of New York City in 1977. A colorful figure who rode the subways, Koch reached out to his constituents for advice and commentary. His business acumen brought the city out of dire financial straits, but he weathered many scandals and controversies during his tenure. After leaving office, he practiced law and taught at several universities but was never far from the public eye. He wrote 17 books, including several mysteries, and made scores of cameo appearances in film and television, complete with a brief stint as a judge on "The People's Court." He died Feb 1, 2013, at New York, NY.

MEXICO: GUADALUPE DAY. Dec 12. One of Mexico's major celebrations. Honors the "Dark Virgin of Guadalupe," the republic's patron saint. Parties and pilgrimages, with special ceremonies at the Shrine of Our Lady of Guadalupe at Mexico City.

MUNCH, EDVARD: BIRTH ANNIVERSARY. Dec 12, 1863. Born at Löten, Norway, Munch was a painter and printmaker whose work influenced the development of German Expressionism. Munch's use of bold lines, violent imagery and blunt sexuality shocked conventional society, but he called it "soul painting." His most famous work, *The Scream* (1893), has become an icon of the anxiety inherent in modern consciousness. In 2012, at $120 million, it was the most expensive work of art ever sold at auction. Munch died at Ekely, Norway, on Jan 23, 1944.

NATIONAL DAY OF THE HORSE. Dec 12. The horse is a living link to the heritage and history of our nation and represents a common bond among all peoples who led the way in building our country. Today the horse industry contributes more than $112 billion annually to the American economy. Therefore, the California State Legislature (as well as the US Senate) has declared the second Saturday in December to be the Day of the Horse in honor of these magnificent creatures.

O'BRIAN, PATRICK: BIRTH ANNIVERSARY. Dec 12, 1914. Born Richard Patrick Russ at Chalfont St. Peter, England, O'Brian was a prolific novelist, biographer and translator. His most famous works are the maritime Aubrey-Maturin novels, a 20-volume series set during the Napoleonic wars, which opened with *Master and Commander* (1969). O'Brian died Jan 2, 2000, at Dublin, Ireland.

PENNSYLVANIA RATIFIES CONSTITUTION: ANNIVERSARY. Dec 12, 1787. Pennsylvania became the second state to ratify the US Constitution, by a vote of 46 to 23, in 1787.

POINSETTIA DAY (JOEL ROBERTS POINSETT: DEATH ANNIVERSARY). Dec 12. A day to enjoy poinsettias and to honor Dr. Joel Roberts Poinsett, the American diplomat who introduced into the US the Central American plant that is named for him. Poinsett was born at Charleston, SC, Mar 2, 1799. He also served as a member of Congress and as secretary of war. He died near Statesburg, SC, Dec 12, 1851. The poinsettia has become a favorite Christmas season plant.

POLISH CHRISTMAS OPEN HOUSE. Dec 12. Polish American Cultural Center Museum, Philadelphia, PA. Sw. Mikolaj (Polish St. Nicholas) will greet everyone with gifts for the children. Polish Christmas tree and entertainment. Free admission. For info: Polish American Cultural Center Museum, 308 Walnut St, Philadelphia, PA 19106. Phone: (215) 922-1700. Fax: (215) 922-1518. E-mail: mail@polishamericancenter.com. Web: www.polishamericancenter.com.

PUERTO RICO: LAS MAÑANITAS. Dec 12. Ponce. Procession at 5 AM honoring patron saint, Virgen de la Guadalupe. Mass with music from a mariachi band. Annually, on Dec 12.

SINATRA, FRANK: BIRTH ANNIVERSARY. Dec 12, 1915. Born at Hoboken, NJ, Frank Sinatra matured from a teen idol to the premier singer of American popular music. Known as the "Chairman of the Board" to his fans, he made more than 200 albums. His signature songs include "All the Way," "New York, New York" and "My Way." His film career includes musicals (*On the Town* and *Pal Joey*) and two gritty films: *From Here to Eternity* (Oscar for Best Supporting Actor) and *The Man with the Golden Arm* (Oscar nomination). Died May 14, 1998, at Los Angeles, CA.

SUPREME COURT RULES FOR BUSH: 20th ANNIVERSARY. Dec 12, 2000. The Supreme Court ruled by a vote of 5 to 4 that there could be no further counting of Florida's disputed presidential votes, ending deliberations over the 2000 presidential election. After five weeks of conflict over this pivotal vote count in Florida, Democratic candidate Al Gore conceded the election to George W. Bush. While Bush won the electoral vote to become the nation's 43rd president, Gore won the popular vote. At the time, Bush was only the fourth president in American history to be elected without winning the popular vote.

TURKMENISTAN: NEUTRALITY DAY. Dec 12. National holiday. Commemorates the UN's recognition of Turkmenistan's neutrality in 1995.

UNITED NATIONS: INTERNATIONAL DAY OF NEUTRALITY. Dec 12. The policy of neutrality contributes to the strengthening of peace and security in relevant regions and at the global level and plays an important role in developing peaceful, friendly and mutually beneficial relations between the countries of the world. The General Assembly declared this day to enhance public awareness of the value of neutrality in international relations (Res 71/275). For info: United Nations. Web: www.un.org/en/events/neutralityday.

UNITED NATIONS: INTERNATIONAL UNIVERSAL HEALTH COVERAGE DAY. Dec 12. Per Resolution 72/138, this day aims to raise awareness of the need for strong and resilient health systems and universal health coverage (UHC) with multi-stakeholder partners. On this day, UHC advocates raise their voices to share the stories of the millions of people still waiting for health, champion what we have achieved so far, call on leaders to make bigger and smarter investments in health and encourage diverse groups to make commitments to help move the world closer to UHC by 2030. First proclaimed in 2017. Annually, Dec 12. For info: United Nations. Web: www.un.org/en/events/universal-health-coverage.

WATIE, STAND: BIRTH ANNIVERSARY. Dec 12, 1806. Born at Rome, GA, and died there Sept 9, 1871. Cherokee chief who, by signing the treaty of New Echota, surrendered his people's land in Georgia, forcing relocation to Oklahoma. Though the three other signers were murdered, Watie escaped and went on to initiate the first volunteer Cherokee regiment for the Confederates in the Civil War. Promoted to brigadier general, he was active in destroying the property of other Native Americans who supported the Union.

WILLIAMS, JOE: BIRTH ANNIVERSARY. Dec 12, 1918. Jazz singer born Joseph Goreed at Cordele, GA. By the late 1930s he was on the scene in Chicago, where he hooked up with the Lionel Hampton Orchestra. Count Basie first heard Williams sing in 1950 at Club DeLisa on Chicago's South Side, and numerous successful tours and recordings followed as the singer for Basie's orchestra.

For the next three decades Williams worked regularly as a singer with jazz luminaries like George Shearing and Cannonball Adderley or as a leader of his own combos. He was also an occasional actor and appeared often on "Sesame Street." Williams died Mar 29, 1999, at Las Vegas, NV.

🎂 BIRTHDAYS TODAY

Tracy Ann Austin, 58, Hall of Fame tennis player, born Rolling Hills Estates, CA, Dec 12, 1962.

Bob Barker, 97, television personality, game show host (Emmy for "The Price Is Right"), born Darrington, WA, Dec 12, 1923.

Mayim Bialik, 45, actress ("Blossom," "The Big Bang Theory"), born San Diego, CA, Dec 12, 1975.

Jennifer Connelly, 50, actress (*Reservation Road, Blood Diamond*, Oscar for *A Beautiful Mind*), born Catskill Mountains, NY, Dec 12, 1970.

Sheila E, 61, singer, musician, born Sheila Escovedo at San Francisco, CA, Dec 12, 1959.

Connie Francis, 82, singer, born Constance Franconero at Newark, NJ, Dec 12, 1938.

Lucas Hedges, 24, actor (*Manchester by the Sea*, "The Slap"), born New York, NY, Dec 12, 1996.

Robert Lindsay, 71, actor (*Me and My Girl*), born Derbyshire, England, Dec 12, 1949.

Rey Mysterio, Jr, 46, professional wrestler, born Óscar Gutiérrez Rubio at Washington, DC, Dec 12, 1974.

Robert Lee (Bob) Pettit, Jr, 88, Hall of Fame basketball player, born Baton Rouge, LA, Dec 12, 1932.

Cathy Rigby, 68, Olympic gymnast, born Long Beach, CA, Dec 12, 1952.

Dionne Warwick, 79, singer, born East Orange, NJ, Dec 12, 1941.

Tom Wilkinson, 72, actor (*Denial, In the Bedroom, The Full Monty, Michael Clayton*), born Leeds, West Yorkshire, England, Dec 12, 1948.

December 13 — Sunday

DAY 348   **18 REMAINING**

BATTLE OF FREDERICKSBURG, VIRGINIA: ANNIVERSARY. Dec 13, 1862. Confederate forces were victorious at the Battle of Fredericksburg, VA. Total casualties on both sides estimated at more than 16,000 killed, injured or missing. General Ambrose E. Burnside led Union troops; General Robert E. Lee led the Confederates.

CHINA: NANKING MASSACRE MEMORIAL DAY. Dec 13. Public observance created in 2014 to memorialize the estimated 142,000 victims of the Nanking Massacre, which began on Dec 13, 1937, when Japanese troops invaded that Chinese city and began six weeks of killings and atrocities.

December 2020	S	M	T	W	T	F	S
			1	2	3	4	5
	6	7	8	9	10	11	12
	13	14	15	16	17	18	19
	20	21	22	23	24	25	26
	27	28	29	30	31		

COMMUNITY CAROL SING. Dec 13. Mystic, CT. Lift up your voice in song to celebrate the season. Museum admission is free when you bring a canned good to be donated to charity. A brass quartet and the Mystic Seaport Museum carolers lead an afternoon of joyous musical cheer. Est attendance: 3,000. For info: Mystic Seaport Museum, 75 Greenmanville Ave, Box 6000, Mystic, CT 06355. Phone: (860) 572-0711. Web: www.mysticseaport.org.

HEINE, HEINRICH: BIRTH ANNIVERSARY. Dec 13, 1797. German poet, journalist and critic, born at Dusseldorf, Germany. His lyric poetry was set to music by the major composers of his day, including Robert Schumann and Franz Schubert. Heine died at Paris, France, Feb 17, 1856. Heine wrote, "Where books are burnt, people will eventually burn too."

LINCOLN, MARY TODD: BIRTH ANNIVERSARY. Dec 13, 1818. Wife of Abraham Lincoln, 16th president of the US, born at Lexington, KY. Died at Springfield, IL, July 16, 1882.

MALTA: REPUBLIC DAY. Dec 13. National holiday. Malta became a republic in 1974.

MOORE, ARCHIE: BIRTH ANNIVERSARY. Dec 13, 1913. Born Archibald Lee Wright at Benoit, MS. One of the most colorful fighters ever, Moore boxed from the mid-1930s to 1963, holding the light-heavyweight title for a record nine years. For much of his career, he fought an average of once a month. Moore let an aura of celebrity surround him: he lied about his age, ate an unusual diet, married five times and spoke out on a variety of political and social issues. Died at San Diego, CA, Dec 9, 1998.

NANKING MASSACRE: ANNIVERSARY. Dec 13, 1937–January 1938. "The Rape of Nanking" began after the Japanese took Nanking, China, during the Sino-Japanese War. Hundreds of thousands of Chinese soldiers, civilians and women were murdered or raped.

NEW ZEALAND FIRST SIGHTED BY EUROPEANS: ANNIVERSARY. Dec 13, 1642. Captain Abel Tasman of the Dutch East India Company first sighted New Zealand but was kept from landing by Maori warriors. In 1769 Captain James Cook landed and claimed formal possession for Great Britain.

NORTH AND SOUTH KOREA END WAR: ANNIVERSARY. Dec 13, 1991. North and South Korea signed a treaty of reconciliation and nonaggression, formally ending the Korean War—38 years after fighting ceased in 1953. This agreement was not hailed as a peace treaty, and the armistice that was signed July 27, 1953, between the UN and North Korea, was to remain in effect until it could be transformed into a formal peace.

SWEDEN: SANTA LUCIA DAY. Dec 13. Nationwide celebration of festival of light, honoring St. Lucia. Many hotels have their own Lucia, a young girl attired in a long, flowing white gown, who serves guests coffee and *lussekatter* (saffron buns) in the early morning.

🎂 BIRTHDAYS TODAY

Steve Buscemi, 62, actor ("Boardwalk Empire," *Ghost World, Fargo, Reservoir Dogs*), born Brooklyn, NY, Dec 13, 1958.

John Davidson, 79, singer, actor, former television host, born Pittsburgh, PA, Dec 13, 1941.

Richard Dent, 60, Hall of Fame football player, born Atlanta, GA, Dec 13, 1960.

Sergei Fedorov, 51, hockey manager and former player, born Pskov, Russia, Dec 13, 1969.

Rickie Fowler, 32, golfer, born Murrieta, CA, Dec 13, 1988.

Jamie Foxx, 53, actor (Oscar for *Ray*; *Django Unchained, Jarhead, Collateral*), singer, musician, producer, born Eric Marlon Bishop at Terrell, TX, Dec 13, 1967.

Wendie Malick, 70, actress ("Just Shoot Me," "Hot in Cleveland"), born Buffalo, NY, Dec 13, 1950.

Ted Nugent, 71, singer, born Detroit, MI, Dec 13, 1949.

Christopher Plummer, 91, actor (Oscar for *Beginners*; *All the Money in the World, The Last Station, The Sound of Music*), born Toronto, ON, Canada, Dec 13, 1929.

Taylor Swift, 31, singer, born Reading, PA, Dec 13, 1989.

Mike Tirico, 54, sportscaster ("Thursday Night Football," "Monday Night Football"), born New York, NY, Dec 13, 1966.

Dick Van Dyke, 95, comedian, actor (*Mary Poppins*, "The Dick Van Dyke Show," "Diagnosis Murder"), born West Plains, MO, Dec 13, 1925.

December 14 — Monday

DAY 349   **17 REMAINING**

ALABAMA: ADMISSION DAY: ANNIVERSARY. Dec 14. Became 22nd state in 1819.

CHRISTMAS BIRD COUNT. Dec 14–Jan 5, 2021. In 1900 ornithologist Frank Chapman, an early officer in the then-budding Audubon Society, proposed a new holiday tradition—a "Christmas Bird Census"—that would count birds during the holidays rather than hunt them. Now, tens of thousands of volunteers throughout the Americas take part in an adventure that has become a family tradition among generations. Families and students, birders and scientists, armed with binoculars, bird guides and checklists, go out on an annual mission—often before dawn. Each of the citizen scientists who annually braves snow, wind or rain to take part in the Christmas Bird Count makes an enormous contribution to conservation. Audubon and other organizations use data collected in this longest-running wildlife census to assess the health of bird populations—and to help guide conservation action. Annually, Dec 14 to Jan 5. For info: Natl Audubon Society. Web: www.audubon.org/conservation/science/christmas-bird-count.

DAVIS, ERNIE: BIRTH ANNIVERSARY. Dec 14, 1939. The football running back was born at New Salem, PA, and grew up in Elmira, NY. Playing for Syracuse University, the "Elmira Express" became the first African American to win the Heisman Trophy in 1961. Drafted by the Cleveland Browns, he never played a game as he succumbed to leukemia at age 23. Davis died May 18, 1963, at Cleveland, OH.

DOOLITTLE, JAMES HAROLD: BIRTH ANNIVERSARY. Dec 14, 1896. American aviator and WWII hero General James Doolittle was born at Alameda, CA. A lieutenant general in the US Army Air Force, he was the first person to fly across North America in less than a day. On Apr 18, 1942, Doolittle led a squadron of 16 B-25 bombers, launched from aircraft carriers, on the first US aerial raid on Japan of WWII. He was awarded the Congressional Medal of Honor for this accomplishment. Doolittle also headed the Eighth Air Force during the Normandy invasion. He died Sept 27, 1993, at Pebble Beach, CA.

HALCYON DAYS. Dec 14–28. Traditionally, the seven days before and the seven days after the winter solstice. To the ancients, a time when the fabled bird (called the halcyon) calmed the wind and waves—a time of calm and tranquility.

JACKSON, SHIRLEY: BIRTH ANNIVERSARY. Dec 14, 1916. Author, born at San Francisco, CA, infamous for her 1948 short story "The Lottery," which was published in *The New Yorker*. This story about a sinister force at work in small-town America brought controversy, threats and finally praise—as well as an O. Henry Prize. Jackson also wrote the influential horror novel *The Haunting of Hill House* (1959). She died at North Bennington, VT, Aug 8, 1965.

MEETING OF THE ELECTORS. Dec 14. On the Monday following the second Wednesday in December in presidential election years, the Electors formally cast their ballots for president and vice president of the US, meeting in their respective state capitals. The Electors' ballots will be transmitted "to the Seat of Government of the United States, directed to the President of the Senate," who "in the presence of the Senate and House of Representatives," at 1 PM on Jan 6 following the election, officially counts the electoral votes and announces the result, legally completing the election process if any candidate has received a majority of the electoral votes.

MOON PHASE: NEW MOON. Dec 14. Moon enters New Moon phase at 11:16 AM, EST.

NEWTOWN, CONNECTICUT, SCHOOL SHOOTINGS: ANNIVERSARY. Dec 14, 2012. Twenty-year-old Adam Lanza, a young man with a history of mental illness, fatally shot his mother in the home they shared. Then at approximately 9:30 AM, Lanza shot his way into Sandy Hook Elementary School, Newtown, CT. Carrying an AR-15 assault weapon and two pistols, he killed 20 children and six adults. As police moved in to apprehend him, Lanza turned one of the pistols on himself. The killings shocked the nation and spurred a new national debate over gun control.

NOSTRADAMUS: BIRTH ANNIVERSARY. Dec 14, 1503. The French physician, best remembered for his astrological predictions (written in rhymed quatrains), was born Michel de Notredame, at St. Rémy, Provence, France. Many believed that his book of prophecies actually foretold the future. Nostradamus died at Salon, France, July 2, 1566.

SMITH, MARGARET CHASE: BIRTH ANNIVERSARY. Dec 14, 1897. American politician Margaret Madeline Chase Smith was born at Skowhegan, ME. As the first woman to be elected to both houses of Congress (1941 to the House and 1949 to the Senate), she was also one of seven Republican senators to issue a "declaration of conscience" to denounce Senator Joseph R. McCarthy's Communist witch hunt. She died May 29, 1995, at Skowhegan.

SOLAR ECLIPSE. Dec 14. Total eclipse of the sun. Visible in the Pacific, South America and Antarctica.

December 2020	S	M	T	W	T	F	S
			1	2	3	4	5
	6	7	8	9	10	11	12
	13	14	15	16	17	18	19
	20	21	22	23	24	25	26
	27	28	29	30	31		

SOUTH POLE DISCOVERY: ANNIVERSARY. Dec 14, 1911. The elusive object of many expeditions dating from the 17th century, the South Pole was located and visited by Roald Amundsen with four companions and 52 sled dogs. All five men and 12 of the dogs returned to base camp safely. Next to visit the South Pole, Jan 17, 1912, was a party of five led by Captain Robert F. Scott, all of whom perished during the return trip. A search party found their frozen bodies 11 months later. See also: "Amundsen, Roald: Birth Anniversary" (July 16).

WASHINGTON, GEORGE: DEATH ANNIVERSARY. Dec 14, 1799. The first president of the US died at his home at Mount Vernon, VA, shortly before midnight. He had battled a sudden acute respiratory infection and been bled four times. "I die hard, but I am not afraid to go" were his famous near-dying words. After he confirmed his own burial plans, Washington's actual last words were, "'Tis well." He was mourned throughout the US and in Europe.

🧁 BIRTHDAYS TODAY

Craig Biggio, 55, Hall of Fame baseball player, born Smithtown, NY, Dec 14, 1965.

Jane Birkin, 74, actress (*Blow-Up, Death on the Nile, Evil Under the Sun*), born London, England, Dec 14, 1946.

Leonardo Boff, 82, Catholic theologian, born Concordia, Brazil, Dec 14, 1938.

William Joseph (Bill) Buckner, 71, former baseball player, born Vallejo, CA, Dec 14, 1949.

Vanessa Hudgens, 32, actress (*High School Musical*), born Salinas, CA, Dec 14, 1988.

Natascha McElhone, 51, actress ("Californication," *The Truman Show*), born Surrey, England, Dec 14, 1969.

Samantha Peszek, 29, Olympic gymnast, born McCordsville, IN, Dec 14, 1991.

Dee Wallace Stone, 72, actress (*10, E.T. The Extra-Terrestrial*), born Kansas City, MO, Dec 14, 1948.

December 15 — Tuesday

DAY 350   **16 REMAINING**

BILL OF RIGHTS: ANNIVERSARY. Dec 15, 1791. The first 10 amendments to the US Constitution, known as the Bill of Rights, became effective following ratification by Virginia. The anniversary of ratification and of effect is observed as Bill of Rights Day.

★BILL OF RIGHTS DAY. Dec 15. Presidential Proclamation. Proclaimed each year since 1962, but omitted in 1967 and 1968. (Issued in 1941 and 1946 at congressional request and in 1947 without request.) Since 1968, included in Human Rights Day and Week Proclamation.

CAT HERDERS DAY. Dec 15. If you can say that your job—or even your life—is like trying to herd cats, then this day is for you—with our sympathy. (©2006 by WH.) For info: Thomas & Ruth Roy, Wellcat Holidays, 2418 Long Ln, Lebanon, PA 17046. Phone: (717) 279-0184. E-mail: wellcat@comcast.net. Web: www.wellcat.com.

CURAÇAO: KINGDOM DAY AND ANTILLEAN FLAG DAY. Dec 15. This day commemorates the Charter of Kingdom, signed in 1954 at the Knight's Hall at The Hague, granting the Netherlands Antilles complete autonomy. The Antillean flag was hoisted for the first time on this day in 1959.

"DAVY CROCKETT" TV PREMIERE: ANNIVERSARY. Dec 15, 1954. This show, a series of five segments, can be considered TV's first miniseries. Shown on Walt Disney's "Disneyland" program, it starred Fess Parker as American hero Davy Crockett and was immensely popular. The show spawned Crockett paraphernalia,

including the famous coonskin cap (although the real Crockett never wore one).

EAMES, RAY: BIRTH ANNIVERSARY. Dec 15, 1912. Born Ray Bernice Alexandria Kaiser at Sacramento, CA, designer known for attractive mass-producible furniture cocreated with her husband, Charles Eames. Their use of inexpensive but durable materials such as plywood allowed them to bring fashion into the living rooms of everyday Americans. The couple has also been credited with influencing other visual facets of American life, including architecture, textiles and photography. After Charles Eames died on Aug 21, 1978, Ray Eames continued their design firm's work until she died a decade later—to the day—on Aug 21, 1988, at Los Angeles, CA.

EIFFEL, ALEXANDRE GUSTAVE: BIRTH ANNIVERSARY. Dec 15, 1832. Eiffel, the French engineer who designed the 1,000-foot-high, million-dollar, open-lattice wrought-iron Eiffel Tower and who participated in designing the Statue of Liberty, was born at Dijon, France. The Eiffel Tower, weighing more than 7,000 tons, was built for the Paris International Exposition of 1889. Eiffel died at Paris, France, Dec 23, 1923.

***GONE WITH THE WIND* FILM PREMIERE: ANNIVERSARY.** Dec 15, 1939. One of the 20th century's biggest film blockbusters premiered on this date in Atlanta, GA. Based on Margaret Mitchell's bestselling and Pulitzer Prize–winning novel of Civil War passions, the film starred Vivian Leigh and Clark Gable and was produced by the dynamic David O. Selznick. It won an unprecedented eight Academy Awards, including Best Picture. Hattie McDaniel won a Best Supporting Actress Oscar—the first time an African-American actor had won or been nominated. No film would touch its Oscar achievement or monetary grosses for decades. At the chilly Atlanta premiere, more than 300,000 people lined the streets to catch sight of the film's stars arriving at the Loew's Grand Theater. See also: "*Gone with the Wind* Published: Anniversary" (June 30).

HOFFMANN, JOSEF: 150th BIRTH ANNIVERSARY. Dec 15, 1870. The acclaimed architect and designer was born at Pirnitz, Austria-Hungary. He moved to Vienna, Austria, in 1892 to complete his schooling and in 1899 was appointed professor in that city's school of applied arts—the Kunstgewerbeschule. He was a cofounder of the Vienna Secession and the Wiener Werkstätte. Many Hoffmann designs in furniture and domestic items are still in production. He died May 7, 1956, at Vienna.

PUERTO RICO: NAVIDADES. Dec 15–Jan 6, 2021. Traditional Christmas season begins mid-December and ends on Three Kings Day. Elaborate nativity scenes, carolers, special Christmas foods and trees from Canada and US. Gifts on Christmas Day and on Three Kings Day.

SITTING BULL: DEATH ANNIVERSARY. Dec 15, 1890. Famous Sioux leader, medicine man and warrior of the Hunkpapa Teton band. Known also by his native name, Tatanka-yatanka, Sitting Bull was born at the Grand River, SD. He first accompanied his father on the warpath at the age of 14 against the Crow and thereafter rapidly gained influence within his tribe. In 1866 he launched a raid on Fort Buford. His steadfast refusal to go to a reservation led General Phillip Sheridan to initiate a campaign against him, which led to the massacre of Lieutenant Colonel George Custer's men at the Little Bighorn, after which Sitting Bull fled to Canada, remaining there until 1881. Although many in his tribe surrendered, Sitting Bull remained hostile until his death in a skirmish with US soldiers along the Grand River.

SPACE MILESTONE: *VEGA 1* (USSR). Dec 15, 1984. Craft launched this date to rendezvous with Halley's comet in March 1986. *Vega 2*, launched Dec 21, 1984, was part of same mission, which, in cooperation with the US, carried US-built "comet-dust" detection equipment.

US FORCES LAND IN MINDORO, PHILIPPINES: ANNIVERSARY. Dec 15, 1944. After the usual barrage from naval guns, the US 24th Division landed on Mindoro, the largest of the islands immediately south of Luzon (the most important island of the Philippines). American soldiers easily advanced eight miles inland, took the perimeter of their beachhead and started construction of an airfield. Japanese kamikaze counterattacks, however, sank two motor torpedo boats and damaged the escort carrier *Marcus Island*, two destroyers and a third motor torpedo boat, making Mindoro a more costly conquest than the island of Leyte had been.

ZAMENHOF, LUDWIK LEJZER: BIRTH ANNIVERSARY. Dec 15, 1859. Born at Bialystok in what is now Poland, Zamenhof was an oculist who invented the language Esperanto (first published in 1887) in an effort to find a way to promote international tolerance and expanded communication. Zamenhof, who adopted the pen name Doktoro Esperanto (which means "Doctor Hopeful" in the language), created his vocabulary from the major Western languages—especially Latin. The popularity of the artificial language grew as Zamenhof translated major works of literature and spoke widely about it. The first Esperanto congress took place in 1905 in France. Zamenhof died Apr 14, 1917, at Warsaw, Poland.

🎂 BIRTHDAYS TODAY

Adam Brody, 41, actor ("The O.C.," *Growing Up Brady*), born San Diego, CA, Dec 15, 1979.

Rachel Brosnahan, 30, actress ("The Marvelous Mrs Maisel," "Manhattan," "House of Cards," *Patriots Day*), born Milwaukee, WI, Dec 15, 1990.

Dave Clark, 78, musician (Dave Clark Five), born London, England, Dec 15, 1942.

Charlie Cox, 38, actor ("Daredevil," "Boardwalk Empire," *The Theory of Everything*), born London, England, Dec 15, 1982.

Michelle Dockery, 39, actress ("Downton Abbey," *Non-Stop*), born Essex, England, Dec 15, 1981.

Don Johnson, 71, actor ("Miami Vice," "Nash Bridges"), born Flatt Creek, MO, Dec 15, 1949.

Edna O'Brien, 89, author (*The Country Girls, Saints and Sinners*), born Tuamgraney, Ireland, Dec 15, 1931.

Helen Slater, 57, actress (*City Slickers, The Secret of My Success*), born Long Island, NY, Dec 15, 1963.

Alexandra Stevenson, 40, tennis player, born San Diego, CA, Dec 15, 1980.

Garrett Wang, 52, actor ("Star Trek: Voyager"), born Riverside, CA, Dec 15, 1968.

Mark Warner, 66, US Senator (D, Virginia), former governor of Virginia, born Indianapolis, IN, Dec 15, 1954.

December 16 — Wednesday

DAY 351   **15 REMAINING**

AUSTEN, JANE: BIRTH ANNIVERSARY. Dec 16, 1775. English novelist (*Pride and Prejudice, Sense and Sensibility*), born at Steventon, Hampshire, England. Died July 18, 1817, at Winchester, England.

BAHRAIN: INDEPENDENCE DAY. Dec 16. National holiday. Commemorates independence from British protection in 1971.

BANGLADESH: VICTORY DAY. Dec 16. National holiday. Commemorates victory over Pakistan in 1971. The former East Pakistan became Bangladesh.

BARBIE AND BARNEY BACKLASH DAY. Dec 16. If we have to explain this to you, you don't have kids. It's one day each year when Mom and Dad can tell the kids that Barbie and Barney don't exist. (©2006 by WH.) For info: Thomas & Ruth Roy, Wellcat Holidays, 2418 Long Ln, Lebanon, PA 17046. Phone: (717) 279-0184. E-mail: info@wellcat.com. Web: www.wellcat.com.

BATTLE OF THE BULGE: ANNIVERSARY. Dec 16, 1944–Jan 25, 1945. A German offensive was launched in the Belgian Ardennes Forest, where Hitler had managed to concentrate 250,000 men. The Nazi commanders, hoping to minimize any aerial counterattack by the Allies, chose a time when foggy, rainy weather prevailed and the initial attack by eight armored divisions along a 75-mile front took the Allies by surprise, the Fifth Panzer Army penetrating to within 20 miles of crossings on the Meuse River. US troops were able to hold fast at bottlenecks in the Ardennes, but by the end of December the German push had penetrated 65 miles into the Allied lines (though their line had narrowed from the initial 75 miles to 20 miles). By that time the Allies began to respond, and the Germans were stopped by Montgomery on the Meuse and by Patton at Bastogne. The weather then cleared and Allied aircraft began to bomb the German forces and supply lines by Dec 26. The Allies reestablished their original line by Jan 25, 1945.

BEETHOVEN, LUDWIG VAN: 250th BIRTH ANNIVERSARY. Dec 16, 1770. Regarded by many as the greatest orchestral composer of all time, Ludwig van Beethoven was born at Bonn, Germany. Impairment of his hearing began before he was 30, but even total deafness did not halt his composing and conducting. His last appearance on the concert stage was to conduct the premiere of his *Ninth Symphony*, at Vienna, Austria, May 7, 1824. He was unable to hear either the orchestra or the applause. Often in love, he never married. Of a stormy temperament, he is said to have died during a violent thunderstorm Mar 26, 1827, at Vienna.

BOSTON TEA PARTY: ANNIVERSARY. Dec 16, 1773. Anniversary of the Sons of Liberty's boarding of three British vessels at anchor at Griffin's Wharf, Boston Harbor, Boston Colony. Contents of 342 chests of tea—the entire East India Company shipment—were dumped into the harbor as a protest against the Tea Act of 1773 by the American colonists.

CALABRIA EARTHQUAKE: ANNIVERSARY. Dec 16, 1857. Calabria— an especially quake-prone region near Naples, Italy—experienced a devastating earthquake of great magnitude that left more than 10,000 people dead and entire villages destroyed. Between 1783 (the last big quake) and 1857, about 111,000 people lost their lives in the unstable region.

CLARKE, ARTHUR C.: BIRTH ANNIVERSARY. Dec 16, 1917. Born at Minehead, England, Clarke was a popular writer of science fiction in the 20th century. His short story "The Sentinel" (1951) was the inspiration for the successful film classic *2001: A Space Odyssey*

(1968). Clarke, who was knighted in 2000, worked on sequels to the *2001* story and died Mar 19, 2008, at Colombo, Sri Lanka.

COWARD, NOËL: BIRTH ANNIVERSARY. Dec 16, 1899. English playwright, actor and wit known for his sophisticated comedies *Private Lives* (1930), *Design for Living* (1933), *Blithe Spirit* (1941) and others—many of which were later filmed. He is also known for such songs as "Mad Dogs and Englishmen." He advised actors: "Learn the lines and don't bump into the furniture." Born at Teddington, England, Coward died at St. Mary, Jamaica, on Mar 26, 1973.

"DRAGNET" TV PREMIERE: ANNIVERSARY. Dec 16, 1951. This famous crime show stressed authenticity, and episodes were supposedly based on real cases. It starred Jack Webb as stoic and determined Sergeant Joe Friday, a man whose life was his investigative police work and who was recognized by his recurring line, "Just the facts, ma'am." Friday had many partners: Barton Yarborough played Sergeant Ben Romero for three episodes; for the rest of the season Barney Phillips played Sergeant Ed Jacobs and Ben Alexander played his comedic sidekick, Officer Frank Smith. A new version appeared in 1967 with Webb and his new partner, Officer Bill Gannon (Harry Morgan). "Dragnet" is also known for its theme music and its narrative epilogue describing the fate of the bad guys.

KANDINSKY, VASILY: BIRTH ANNIVERSARY. Dec 16. 1866. Artist, born at Moscow, Russian Empire, whose intensely colorful paintings were a foundation of abstract art. He began painting at the age of 30, compelled by what he called "vibrations in the soul." Kandinsky died at Neuilly-sur-Seine, France, on Dec 13, 1944.

KAZAKHSTAN: INDEPENDENCE DAY. Dec 16. National Day. Commemorates independence from the Soviet Union in 1991.

MEAD, MARGARET: BIRTH ANNIVERSARY. Dec 16, 1901. Influential and at times controversial anthropologist and author, especially known for her studies of peoples of the South Pacific (*Coming of Age in Samoa* was published in 1928). She famously said: "Never doubt that a small group of committed people can change the world. Indeed, it is the only thing that ever has." Born at Philadelphia, PA, Mead died at New York, NY, Nov 15, 1978.

MEXICO: POSADAS. Dec 16–24. A nine-day annual celebration throughout Mexico. Processions of "pilgrims" knock at doors asking for posada (shelter), commemorating the search by Joseph and Mary for a shelter in which the infant Jesus might be born. Pilgrims are invited inside, and fun and merrymaking ensue with blindfolded guests trying to break a piñata filled with gifts and goodies suspended from the ceiling. Once the piñata is broken, the gifts are distributed and the celebration continues.

PHILIPPINES: PHILIPPINE CHRISTMAS OBSERVANCE. Dec 16–Jan 6, 2021. Philippine Islands. Said to be the world's longest Christmas celebration.

PHILIPPINES: SIMBANG GABI. Dec 16–25. Nationwide. A nine-day novena of predawn masses, also called "Misa de Gallo." One of the traditional Filipino celebrations of the holiday season.

SANTAYANA, GEORGE: BIRTH ANNIVERSARY. Dec 16, 1863. Philosopher and author born at Madrid, Spain. Santayana was educated and later tenured at Harvard, where his foundational aesthetic philosophy of naturalism, for which he is most widely known, was first articulated. He left the US—and academia—in 1912 and returned to Europe, where he traveled widely and focused on his writing. In addition to producing philosophical works, he was an accomplished poet and is considered to be influential in the 20th-century transformation of the literary canon. A survivor of both World Wars, Santayana died at Rome, Italy, on Sept 26, 1952. It was Santayana who first wrote, "Those who cannot remember the past are condemned to repeat it."

SOUTH AFRICA: RECONCILIATION DAY. Dec 16. National holiday. Celebrates the spirit of reconciliation, national unity and peace among all citizens.

UNITED NATIONS REVOKES RESOLUTION ON ZIONISM: ANNIVERSARY. Dec 16, 1991. The United Nations voted 111 to 25 to revoke

December	S	M	T	W	T	F	S
			1	2	3	4	5
2020	6	7	8	9	10	11	12
	13	14	15	16	17	18	19
	20	21	22	23	24	25	26
	27	28	29	30	31		

Resolution 3379, which equated Zionism with racism. Resolution 3379 was approved Nov 10, 1975, with 72 countries voting in favor, 35 against and 32 abstentions. The largest bloc of changed votes came from the former Soviet Union and Eastern Europe.

🎂 BIRTHDAYS TODAY

Bruce N. Ames, 92, biochemist, cancer researcher, born New York, NY, Dec 16, 1928.

Benjamin Bratt, 57, actor (*Traffic, Miss Congeniality,* "Law & Order"), born San Francisco, CA, Dec 16, 1963.

Theo James, 36, actor (*Divergent,* "Golden Boy," "Downton Abbey"), born Theo Taptiklis at Oxford, England, Dec 16, 1984.

Alison La Placa, 61, actress ("The John Larroquette Show"), born Lincolnshire, IL, Dec 16, 1959.

William "The Refrigerator" Perry, 58, former football player, born Aiken, SC, Dec 16, 1962.

Krysten Ritter, 39, actress ("Jessica Jones," "Breaking Bad"), born Bloomsburg, PA, Dec 16, 1981.

Edward Ruscha, 83, artist (*Standard Station*), born Omaha, NE, Dec 16, 1937.

Lesley Stahl, 79, journalist ("60 Minutes," former White House correspondent), born Lynn, MA, Dec 16, 1941.

Jon Tenney, 59, actor ("Brooklyn South," "The Closer"), born Princeton, NJ, Dec 16, 1961.

Liv Johanne Ullmann, 81, actress (*Persona, Scenes from a Marriage*), born Tokyo, Japan, Dec 16, 1939.

December 17 — Thursday

DAY 352   **14 REMAINING**

ARAB SPRING BEGINS/BOUAZIZI SELF-IMMOLATION: 10th ANNIVERSARY. Dec 17, 2010. In the town of Sidi Bouzid, Tunisia, street vendor Mohamed Bouazizi, angry at a municipal official's confiscation of his wares and unable to get the local government to hear his case, set himself on fire in protest of the corruption he faced. Demonstrations began almost immediately and grew into the movement now known as the "Arab Spring"—a regionwide revolution of street protests that caused regime change in Tunisia (President Ben Ali stepped down Jan 14, 2011), Egypt, Libya and Yemen; a violent civil war in Syria; and major social and political disruption in the rest of the Arab world. Bouazizi died of his burns Jan 4, 2011.

AZTEC CALENDAR STONE DISCOVERY: ANNIVERSARY. Dec 17, 1790. One of the wonders of the Western Hemisphere—the Aztec Calendar, or Solar Stone—was found beneath the ground by workmen repairing Mexico City's Central Plaza. The centuries-old, intricately carved stone—11 feet, 8 inches in diameter and nearly 25 tons—proved to be a highly developed calendar monument to the sun. Believed to have been carved in the year 1479, this extraordinary time-counting basalt tablet originally stood in the Great Temple of the Aztecs. Buried along with other Aztec idols soon after the Spanish conquest in 1521, it remained hidden until 1790. Its 52-year cycle had regulated many Aztec ceremonies, including grisly human sacrifices, to save the world from destruction by the gods.

BOLÍVAR, SIMÓN: DEATH ANNIVERSARY. Dec 17, 1830. Commemorated in Venezuela and other Latin American countries. Bolívar, called "The Liberator," was born July 24, 1783, at Caracas, Venezuela, and died Dec 17, 1830, at Santa Marta, Colombia.

***A CHRISTMAS CAROL* PUBLISHED: ANNIVERSARY.** Dec 17, 1843. This holiday classic by Charles Dickens was published in a print run of 6,000 copies that sold out in one week. By Jan 6, 1844, an additional 2,000 were sold. The reformation of Ebenezer Scrooge ("Bah humbug!") has remained immensely popular.

CLEAN AIR ACT PASSED BY CONGRESS: ANNIVERSARY. Dec 17, 1967. A sweeping set of laws passed to protect the nation from air pollution. This was the first legislation to place pollution controls on the automobile industry.

FIRST FLIGHT ANNIVERSARY CELEBRATION. Dec 17. Kill Devil Hills, NC. Each year since 1928, on the anniversary of the Wright brothers' first successful heavier-than-air flight at Kitty Hawk, NC, Dec 17, 1903, a celebration has been held at the Wright Brothers National Memorial, with wreaths, flyover and other observances—regardless of weather.

FLOYD, WILLIAM: BIRTH ANNIVERSARY. Dec 17, 1734. Signer of the Declaration of Independence, member of Congress, born at Brookhaven, Long Island. Died at Westernville, NY, Aug 4, 1821.

GERMANY: ODE OF JOY AROUND THE GLOBE (BTHVN 2020). Dec 17. Bonn. Bringing the yearlong celebration of Ludwig van Beethoven's 250th birth anniversary to a close, Daniel Barenboim conducts the Ninth Symphony in a gala concert from the city of Beethoven's birth and youth—a performance live streamed for all the world. For info: Beethoven Jubiläums Gesellschaft, Loggia am Stadthaus, Thomas Mann Str 4, D-53111 Bonn, Germany. E-mail: info@bthvn2020.de. Web: www.bthvn2020.de.

HENRY, JOSEPH: BIRTH ANNIVERSARY. Dec 17, 1797. Scientist Joseph Henry was born at Albany, NY. One of his great discoveries was the principle of self-induction; the unit used in the measure of electrical inductance was named "the henry" in his honor. In 1831 Henry constructed the first model of an electric telegraph with an audible signal. This formed the basis of nearly all later work on commercial wire telegraphy. In 1832 Henry was named professor of natural philosophy at the College of New Jersey, now Princeton University. Henry was involved in the planning of the Smithsonian Institution and became its first secretary in 1846. President Lincoln named Henry as one of the original 50 scientists to make up the National Academy of Sciences in 1863. He served as that organization's president from 1868 until his death May 13, 1878, at Washington, DC.

KING, W.L. MACKENZIE: BIRTH ANNIVERSARY. Dec 17, 1874. Former Canadian prime minister, born at Berlin, ON, Canada. Served 22 years (1921–26, 1926–30, 1935–48), the longest time of any prime minister in Canada. Died at Kingsmere, QC, Canada, July 22, 1950.

LIBBY, WILLARD FRANK: BIRTH ANNIVERSARY. Dec 17, 1908. American educator, chemist, atomic scientist and Nobel Prize winner born at Grand Valley, CO. He was the inventor of the carbon-14 "atomic clock" method for dating ancient and prehistoric plant and animal remains and minerals. Died at Los Angeles, CA, Sept 8, 1980.

NCAA DIVISION I WOMEN'S VOLLEYBALL CHAMPIONSHIP. Dec 17–19. CenturyLink Center, Omaha, NE. For info: NCAA, PO Box 6222, Indianapolis, IN 46206-6222. Phone: (317) 917-6222. Web: www.NCAA.com.

SAMPSON, DEBORAH: BIRTH ANNIVERSARY. Dec 17, 1760. Born at Plympton, MA, Deborah Sampson spent her childhood as an indentured servant. In 1782, wishing to participate in the Revolutionary War, she disguised herself as a man and enlisted in the

Continental Army's Fourth Massachusetts Regiment under the name Robert Shurtleff. Her identity was unmasked, and she was dismissed from the army in 1783. In 1802 Sampson became perhaps the first woman to lecture professionally in the US when she began giving public speeches on her experiences. Deborah Sampson died Apr 29, 1827, at Sharon, MA. Full military pension was provided for her heirs by an act of Congress in 1838.

SATURNALIA. Dec 17–23. Ancient Roman festival honoring Saturnus, the god of agriculture. It was a time of merriment at the end of harvesting and wine making. Presents were exchanged, sacrifices offered, and masters served their slaves. Approximates the winter solstice. Some say that the date for the observance of the nativity of Jesus was selected by the early Christian church leaders to fall on Dec 25 partly to counteract the popular but disapproved-of pre-Christian Roman festival of Saturnalia.

"THE SIMPSONS" TV PREMIERE: ANNIVERSARY. Dec 17, 1989. TV's hottest animated family, "The Simpsons," premiered on this date. The originator of Homer, Marge, Bart, Lisa and Maggie is cartoonist Matt Groening. The show's 400th episode, "You Kent Always Say What You Want," aired May 20, 2007. The 500th episode, "At Long Last Leave," aired Feb 19, 2012. The 600th episode, "Treehouse of Horror XXVII," aired Oct 16, 2016.

TAKE A NEW YEAR'S RESOLUTION TO STOP SMOKING (TANYRSS). Dec 17–Feb 7, 2021. To educate consumers/patients and healthcare professionals to take a New Year's resolution to stop smoking. Final day of observance is on Super Bowl Sunday. Sponsored by the American College of Apothecaries (ACA)/Pharmacists Planning Service, Inc (PPSI). For info: ACA/PPSI, 2830 Summer Oaks Dr, Bartlett, TN 38134. E-mail: info@ppsinc.org. Web: www.ppsinc.org.

TBS DEBUT: ANNIVERSARY. Dec 17, 1976. Media entrepreneur Ted Turner launched Turner Broadcasting System—transforming a local Atlanta, GA, UHF station that he had purchased in 1970 into an influential national cable television network that came to be known as the "Superstation."

WHITTIER, JOHN GREENLEAF: BIRTH ANNIVERSARY. Dec 17, 1807. Poet and abolitionist, born at Haverhill, Essex County, MA. Whittier's books of poetry include *Legends of New England* and *Snowbound*. Died at Hampton Falls, NH, Sept 7, 1892.

★WRIGHT BROTHERS DAY. Dec 17. Presidential Proclamation always issued for Dec 17 since 1963 (PL 88–209 of Dec 17, 1963). Issued twice earlier at congressional request in 1959 and 1961.

WRIGHT BROTHERS FIRST POWERED FLIGHT: ANNIVERSARY. Dec 17, 1903. Orville and Wilbur Wright, brothers, bicycle-shop operators, inventors and aviation pioneers, after three years of experimentation with kites and gliders, achieved the first documented successful powered and controlled flights of an airplane. The flights, near Kitty Hawk, NC, piloted first by Orville and then by Wilbur Wright, were sustained for less than one minute but represented man's first powered airplane flight and the beginning of a new form of transportation. Orville Wright was born at Dayton, OH, Aug 19, 1871, and died there Jan 30, 1948. Wilbur Wright was born at Millville, IN, Apr 16, 1867, and died at Dayton, May 30, 1912.

🎂 BIRTHDAYS TODAY

Pope Francis, 84, leader of the Roman Catholic Church, born Jorge Mario Bergoglio at Buenos Aires, Argentina, Dec 17, 1936.

Bernard Hill, 76, actor (*Titanic*, Lord of the Rings trilogy, "Wolf Hall"), born Manchester, England, Dec 17, 1944.

December 2020	S	M	T	W	T	F	S
			1	2	3	4	5
	6	7	8	9	10	11	12
	13	14	15	16	17	18	19
	20	21	22	23	24	25	26
	27	28	29	30	31		

Laurie Holden, 51, actress ("The Walking Dead," "The Shield"), born Los Angeles, CA, Dec 17, 1969.

Milton "Lil Rel" Howery, 41, actor, comedian (*Get Out*, "The Carmichael Show," "Friends of the People"), born Chicago, IL, Dec 17, 1979.

Ernie Hudson, 75, actor (*Ghostbusters, The Hand That Rocks the Cradle*), born Benton Harbor, MI, Dec 17, 1945.

Eugene Levy, 74, comedian, actor (*American Pie, Best in Show*, "SCTV"), born Hamilton, ON, Canada, Dec 17, 1946.

Manny Pacquiao, 42, boxer, born Kibawe, Bukidnon, Philippines, Dec 17, 1978.

Sarah Paulson, 46, actress ("The People v O.J. Simpson," "American Horror Story," *Carol*), born Tampa, FL, Dec 17, 1974.

Bill Pullman, 66, actor (*Independence Day, While You Were Sleeping*), born Delphi, NY, Dec 17, 1954.

Tommy Steele, 84, actor (*The Happiest Millionaire, Half a Sixpence*), born London, England, Dec 17, 1936.

Sean Patrick Thomas, 50, actor (*Save the Last Dance*, "The District"), born Wilmington, DE, Dec 17, 1970.

Chase Utley, 42, baseball player, born Pasadena, CA, Dec 17, 1978.

Shannon Woodward, 36, actress ("Raising Hope," "The Riches"), born Phoenix, AZ, Dec 17, 1984.

December 18 — Friday

DAY 353   **13 REMAINING**

COBB, TYRUS RAYMOND "TY": BIRTH ANNIVERSARY. Dec 18, 1886. One of the all-time great baseball players. Born at Narrows, GA, Cobb had a lifetime batting average of .367 compiled over 24 years, during which he played in more than 3,000 games—mostly for the Detroit Tigers. His runs scored record was not broken until 2001, and his stolen bases record stood until 1979. Cobb was among the first five players inducted into the National Baseball Hall of Fame in 1936. A savvy businessman who quickly realized the value of using his celebrity for marketing, Cobb died at Atlanta, GA, on July 17, 1961.

DAVIS, BENJAMIN O., JR: BIRTH ANNIVERSARY. Dec 18, 1912. The WWII hero was born at Washington, DC, to the army's first black general. Davis had a distinguished career serving the US: he was the first African American to graduate from West Point in the 20th century; he led the first all-black air unit, the 99th Pursuit Squadron (the Tuskegee Airmen), in WWII; he helped plan the integration of the US Air Force in 1948–49 and he was its first black general (1954). He died at Washington, DC, on July 4, 2002. See also: "Tuskegee Airmen Activated: Anniversary" (Mar 22).

DAVIS, OSSIE: BIRTH ANNIVERSARY. Dec 18, 1917. Born at Cogdell, GA, Davis began his career as an actor with the Rose McClendon Players in Harlem, NY, in the 1940s. He became involved with civil rights, counting among his friends W.E.B. Du Bois, Richard

Wright and Langston Hughes, and worked to promote African Americans in the entertainment industry throughout his life. Often sharing the stage or screen with wife Ruby Dee, he was featured in dozens of stage productions and feature films. He died at Miami Beach, FL, Feb 4, 2005.

GRIMALDI, JOSEPH: BIRTH ANNIVERSARY. Dec 18, 1778. Known as the "greatest clown in history" and the "king of pantomime," Joseph Grimaldi began his stage career at age two. He was an accomplished singer, dancer and acrobat. Born at London, England, he is best remembered as the original "Joey the Clown" and for the innovative humor he brought to the clown's role in theater. Illness forced his early retirement in 1823, and he died at London, May 31, 1837.

MEXICO: FEAST OF OUR LADY OF SOLITUDE. Dec 18. Oaxaca. Pilgrims venerate the patron of the lonely.

NEW JERSEY: RATIFICATION DAY: ANNIVERSARY. Dec 18, 1787. New Jersey became the third state to ratify the Constitution (following Delaware and Pennsylvania). It did so unanimously.

NIGER: REPUBLIC DAY. Dec 18. National holiday. Gained autonomy within the French community in 1958.

STRADIVARI, ANTONIO: DEATH ANNIVERSARY. Dec 18, 1737. Celebrated Italian violin maker was born probably in the year 1644 and died at Cremona, Italy, at about age 93.

"TO TELL THE TRUTH" TV PREMIERE: ANNIVERSARY. Dec 18, 1956. This long-running, popular game show was a production of the Mark Goodson–Bill Todman team. A celebrity panel (and the home audience) tried to guess which of the three guests claiming to be the same person was telling the truth. Panelists took turns questioning the guests, and, at the conclusion, the identity of the person was revealed. Hosts included Bud Collyer, Garry Moore, Joe Garagiola, Robin Ward, Gordon Elliott and Alex Trebek. Celebrity panelists included Dick Van Dyke, Tom Poston, Peggy Cass, Kitty Carlisle and Bill Cullen.

UNDERDOG DAY. Dec 18. To salute, before the year's end, all of the underdogs and unsung heroes—the Number Two people who contribute so much to the Number One people we read about. (Sherlock Holmes's Dr. Watson and Robinson Crusoe's Friday are examples.) Observed annually on the third Friday in December since its founding in 1976 by the late Peter Moeller, THE Chief Underdog. For info: A.C. Vierow, Underdogs Intl, Box 71, Clio, MI 48420-0071.

UNITED NATIONS: ARABIC LANGUAGE DAY. Dec 18. Arabic is one of the United Nations Secretariat's six official and working languages (English, French, Arabic, Chinese, Russian, Spanish). Arabic is of utmost importance to Muslims. It is a sacred language (the language of the Qur'an), and prayer (and other worship) is not practiced in Islam except with the proficiency of some of its words. Arabic is also a major ritual language of a number of Christian churches in the Arab world, as well as many of the most important Jewish religious and intellectual works of the Middle Ages. For info: United Nations. Web: www.un.org/ar/events/arabiclanguageday.

UNITED NATIONS: INTERNATIONAL MIGRANTS DAY. Dec 18. Recognizes the contributions that millions of migrant workers make to the global economy and seeks to draw attention to the precarious state of their rights. For info: United Nations, Dept of Public Info, New York, NY 10017. Web: www.un.org.

BIRTHDAYS TODAY

Ronald Acuña, Jr, 23, baseball player, born La Guaira, Venezuela, Dec 18, 1997.

Christina Aguilera, 40, singer, born Staten Island, NY, Dec 18, 1980.

Josh Dallas, 39, actor ("Manifest," "Once Upon a Time," *Thor*), born Louisville, KY, Dec 18, 1981.

Rachel Griffiths, 52, actress (*Hilary and Jackie*, "Six Feet Under," "Brothers & Sisters"), born Melbourne, Australia, Dec 18, 1968.

Katie Holmes, 42, actress (*Batman Begins, Pieces of April*, "Dawson's Creek"), born Toledo, OH, Dec 18, 1978.

Ray Liotta, 65, actor (*Unforgettable, Goodfellas, Field of Dreams, Something Wild*), born Newark, NJ, Dec 18, 1955.

Leonard Maltin, 70, movie critic, author (*Maltin's Guide*), born New York, NY, Dec 18, 1950.

Michael Moorcock, 81, author (*Mother London, The Warlord of the Air*, Dancers at the End of Time trilogy), born Mitcham, Surrey, England, Dec 18, 1939.

Charles Oakley, 57, former basketball player, born Cleveland, OH, Dec 18, 1963.

Brad Pitt, 56, actor (*The Big Short, Moneyball, Ocean's Eleven*), born Shawnee, OK, Dec 18, 1964.

Keith Richards, 77, musician, singer (Rolling Stones), born Dartford, England, Dec 18, 1943.

Steven Spielberg, 73, filmmaker (Oscars for *Schindler's List* and *Saving Private Ryan*; *War Horse, Jaws*), born Cincinnati, OH, Dec 18, 1947.

Cicely Tyson, 96, actress (Tony for *The Trip to Bountiful*; Emmy for *The Autobiography of Miss Jane Pittman*; *Sounder*), born New York, NY, Dec 18, 1924.

December 19 — Saturday

DAY 354   **12 REMAINING**

BREZHNEV, LEONID: BIRTH ANNIVERSARY. Dec 19, 1906. Leader of the Soviet Union after the overthrow of Nikita Khrushchev in 1964 (which he had a part in). He expanded and modernized Soviet military and nuclear power at the cost of the country's economic health. Born at Kamenskoye, Ukraine, Brezhnev died at Moscow, Russia, Nov 10, 1982.

CHRISTMASTIDE IN VIRGINIA. Dec 19–31. Jamestown Settlement, Williamsburg, VA, and American Revolution Museum at Yorktown, Yorktown, VA. Experience holiday traditions of 17th- and 18th-century Virginia, with musical entertainment of the period and appearances at Jamestown Settlement by the Lord of Misrule. For info: Jamestown-Yorktown Foundation, PO Box 1607, Williamsburg, VA 23187. Phone: (757) 253-4838 or (888) 593-4682. Fax: (757) 253-5299. Web: www.historyisfun.org.

FIRST NHL GAMES: ANNIVERSARY. Dec 19, 1917. The National Hockey League opened its first season of play with two games. The Montreal Canadiens defeated the Ottawa Senators, 7–4, with Joe Malone scoring five goals, and the Montreal Wanderers beat the Toronto Arenas, 10–9, with Harry Hyland scoring five goals. Despite their victory, the Wanderers lasted only six games, withdrawing from the league when the Montreal Arena burned down.

FISKE, MINNIE MADDERN: BIRTH ANNIVERSARY. Dec 19, 1865. American theater actress with a long, distinguished career. First stage appearance at the age of three as "Little Minnie Maddern." Born at New Orleans, LA, she died Feb 15, 1932, at Hollis, NY.

PARRY, WILLIAM: BIRTH ANNIVERSARY. Dec 19, 1790. British explorer Sir William Edward Parry was born at Bath, England. Remembered for his Arctic expeditions and for his search for a Northwest Passage, Parry died at Ems, Germany, July 8, 1855.

SHERMAN, ROBERT B.: 95th BIRTH ANNIVERSARY. Dec 19, 1925. With his brother Richard, Robert B. Sherman formed a successful songwriting partnership that created classics like the Disney anthem "It's a Small World (After All)" as well as "Chim Chim Cheree" and "Supercalifragilisticexpialidocious," both from the film *Mary Poppins* (1964). The Shermans' work for *Mary Poppins* netted them an Academy Award (for "Chim Chim Cheree"), while as staff songwriters at Disney they scored films and shorts like *The Jungle Book*, *The Parent Trap* and "Winnie the Pooh." An expressive writer and thinker, Sherman said that his combat experience in World War II influenced his later songwriting work, which often explored themes of joy, happiness and a generally hopeful outlook for society. Born at Brooklyn, NY, Sherman died at London, England, on Mar 6, 2012.

SPACE MILESTONE: FIRST RADIO BROADCAST FROM SPACE. Dec 19, 1958. At 3:15 PM, EST, the US Earth satellite *Atlas* transmitted the first radio voice broadcast from space, a 58-word recorded Christmas greeting from President Dwight D. Eisenhower that included this message: "To all mankind America's wish for peace on earth and goodwill toward men everywhere." The satellite had been launched from Cape Canaveral Dec 18.

SPACE MILESTONE: *INTELSAT 4 F-3* (US). Dec 19, 1971. Communications satellite launched by NASA on contract with COMSAT. Mission involved intercontinental relay phone and TV communications.

SUSSKIND, DAVID: 100th BIRTH ANNIVERSARY. Dec 19, 1920. American television producer David (Howard) Susskind was born at New York, NY. In 1952 he started his own television production company and soon was producing more live programs than the three networks combined. He began to host talk shows in 1958 and was widely respected for focusing on serious matters. He died Feb 22, 1987, at New York, NY.

***TITANIC* RELEASED: ANNIVERSARY.** Dec 19, 1997. The most expensive film made (up to that time) at $200 million was released in theaters on this date. *Titanic*, written and directed by James Cameron, featured the drama of star-crossed lovers (Leonardo DiCaprio and Kate Winslet) paired with the amazing special-effects re-creation of the doomed 1912 ocean liner's first and last voyage. The film won 11 Academy Awards, including Best Picture, which tied it with 1959's *Ben-Hur*.

WOODSON, CARTER GODWIN: BIRTH ANNIVERSARY. Dec 19, 1875. Historian who introduced black studies to colleges and universities, born at New Canton, VA. His scholarly works include *The Negro in Our History*, *The Education of the Negro Prior to 1861*. Known as the father of black history, he inaugurated Negro History Week. Woodson was working on a six-volume *Encyclopaedia Africana* when he died at Washington, DC, Apr 3, 1950.

🎂 BIRTHDAYS TODAY

Jennifer Beals, 57, actress ("The L Word," *Flashdance*), born Chicago, IL, Dec 19, 1963.

Ronan Farrow, 33, television personality, human rights advocate, journalist, born Satchel Ronan O'Sullivan Farrow at New York, NY, Dec 19, 1987.

Janie Fricke, 68, country singer, born Whitney, IN, Dec 19, 1952.

Jake Gyllenhaal, 40, actor (*Brokeback Mountain, Jarhead, Donnie Darko*), born Los Angeles, CA, Dec 19, 1980.

Richard Hammond, 51, television personality ("The Grand Tour," "Top Gear"), born Solihull, West Midlands, England, Dec 19, 1969.

December 2020	S	M	T	W	T	F	S
			1	2	3	4	5
	6	7	8	9	10	11	12
	13	14	15	16	17	18	19
	20	21	22	23	24	25	26
	27	28	29	30	31		

Richard E. Leakey, 76, anthropologist, born Nairobi, Kenya, Dec 19, 1944.

Kevin Edward McHale, 63, Hall of Fame basketball player, born Hibbing, MN, Dec 19, 1957.

Alyssa Milano, 48, actress ("Charmed," "Melrose Place"), born Brooklyn, NY, Dec 19, 1972.

Rob Portman, 65, US Senator (R, Ohio), born Cincinnati, OH, Dec 19, 1955.

Tim Reid, 76, actor ("Frank's Place," "WKRP in Cincinnati"), born Norfolk, VA, Dec 19, 1944.

Kristy Swanson, 51, actress (*Buffy the Vampire Slayer*), born Mission Viejo, CA, Dec 19, 1969.

December 20 — Sunday

DAY 355   **11 REMAINING**

AMERICAN POET LAUREATE ESTABLISHMENT: 35th ANNIVERSARY. Dec 20, 1985. A bill empowering the Librarian of Congress to name, annually, a poet laureate in poetry was signed into law by President Ronald Reagan. In return for a stipend as poet laureate and a salary as the consultant in poetry, the person named will present at least one major work of poetry and will appear at selected national ceremonies. The first poet laureate of the US was Robert Penn Warren, appointed to that position by the Librarian of Congress Feb 26, 1986. Other poets laureate have included Rita Dove, Robert Pinsky, Billy Collins and W.S. Merwin. Prior to 1985, the Library of Congress named consultants in poetry, and these included Robert Frost, Robert Lowell, Elizabeth Bishop and Gwendolyn Brooks.

CLINTON IMPEACHMENT PROCEEDINGS: ANNIVERSARY. Dec 20, 1998. President William Clinton was impeached by a House of Representatives that was divided along party lines. He was convicted of perjury and obstruction of justice stemming from a sexual relationship with a White House intern. He was then tried by the Senate in January 1999. On Feb 12, 1999, the Senate acquitted him on both charges. Clinton was only the second US president to undergo impeachment proceedings. Andrew Johnson was impeached by the House in 1868, but the Senate voted against impeachment and he finished his term of office. See also: "Johnson Impeachment Proceedings: Anniv" (Feb 24).

"THE DATING GAME" TV PREMIERE: 55th ANNIVERSARY. Dec 20, 1965. Another game show developed by Chuck Barris, it typically featured a "bachelorette" who questioned three men who were hidden from her view and decided, based on their answers, which guy appealed to her the most. The couple was then sent on a date, courtesy of the show. Occasionally, a bachelor would question three women. Jim Lange was the host of the network series and two syndicated ones. Elaine Joyce and Jeff MacGregor hosted one season each on the retitled "The New Dating Game."

DE WOLFE, ELSIE: BIRTH ANNIVERSARY. Dec 20, 1865. Socialite, actress and America's first professional interior decorator, De Wolfe was born at New York City (some sources say in 1870). After a brief stage career, she began helping those in her social class decorate their homes. Working for illustrious clients in Beverly Hills, Newport and New York, De Wolfe made her decorating mark by counteracting the prevailing and dour Victorian trends in decor with pastel colors, lighter woods, mixed styles, mirrors,

chintz—and leopard print fabrics. De Wolfe died July 12, 1950, at Versailles, France.

FIRESTONE, HARVEY S.: BIRTH ANNIVERSARY. Dec 20, 1868. American industrialist, businessman and founder of the Firestone Tire and Rubber Company, Harvey Samuel Firestone was born at Columbiana County, OH. A close friend of Henry Ford, Thomas Edison and John Burroughs, Firestone died at Miami Beach, FL, Feb 7, 1938.

***IT'S A WONDERFUL LIFE* FILM PREMIERE: ANNIVERSARY.** Dec 20, 1946. America's favorite Christmas drama premiered on this date at New York, NY. Directed by Frank Capra and starring James Stewart (George Bailey), Donna Reed (Mary Bailey), Henry Travers (as Clarence Oddbody, trying to earn his angel wings) and Lionel Barrymore (as villainous Mr Potter), the film was nominated for five Academy Awards.

LANGER, SUSANNE K.: 125th BIRTH ANNIVERSARY. Dec 20, 1895. Susanne Langer, a leading American philosopher, author of *Philosophy in a New Key: A Study in the Symbolism of Reason, Rite, and Art*, was born at New York, NY. Her studies of aesthetics and art exerted a profound influence on thinking in the fields of psychology, philosophy and the social sciences. She died at Old Lyme, CT, July 17, 1985.

MENZIES, ROBERT GORDON: BIRTH ANNIVERSARY. Dec 20, 1894. Australian statesman and conservative leader, born at Jeparit, Australia, Sir Robert died at Melbourne, Australia, May 14, 1978, at age 83.

MERKLE, FRED: BIRTH ANNIVERSARY. Dec 20, 1888. Frederick Charles Merkle, born at Watertown, WI, will forever occupy a place in baseball history for his part in the events of Sept 23, 1908, when his team, the New York Giants, played the Chicago Cubs in a crucial game. Merkle was on first in the bottom of the ninth when the winning run apparently scored on a single. As was customary, he did not touch second base. Cubs second baseman Johnny Evers set off baseball's greatest dispute by demanding that Merkle be called out, which he was, in a play dubbed "Merkle's Boner" by baseball historians. Died at Daytona Beach, FL, Mar 2, 1956.

MONTGOMERY BUS BOYCOTT ENDS: ANNIVERSARY. Dec 20, 1956. The US Supreme Court ruling of Nov 13, 1956, calling for integration of the Montgomery, AL, public bus system was implemented. Since Dec 5, 1955, the black community of Montgomery had refused to ride on the segregated buses. The boycott was in reaction to the Dec 1, 1955, arrest of Rosa Parks for refusing to relinquish her seat on a Montgomery bus to a white man.

MUDD, DR. SAMUEL: BIRTH ANNIVERSARY. Dec 20, 1833. Dr. Samuel A. Mudd was born near Bryantown, MD, on Dec 20, 1833. He was convicted of conspiracy in the assassination of President Abraham Lincoln and sentenced to life imprisonment at Fort Jefferson, Dry Tortugas. The basis for his conviction was mainly that he gave medical aid to fleeing Lincoln assassin John Wilkes Booth, who had a broken leg. He was pardoned by President Andrew Johnson in 1869. Mudd and his friends protested his innocence of complicity until his death on Jan 10, 1883, at Waldorf, MD.

RICKEY, BRANCH: BIRTH ANNIVERSARY. Dec 20, 1881. Wesley Branch Rickey, Baseball Hall of Fame player, manager and executive born at Lucasville, OH. Rickey was baseball's most innovative general manager. He invented the farm system, instituted unique training and teaching methods and, most prominently, signed Jackie Robinson to play major league baseball with the Brooklyn Dodgers. Inducted into the Hall of Fame in 1967. Died at Columbia, MO, Dec 9, 1965.

SACAGAWEA: DEATH ANNIVERSARY. Dec 20, 1812. As a young Shoshone Indian woman, Sacagawea in 1805 (with her two-month-old son strapped to her back) traveled with the Lewis and Clark expedition, serving as an interpreter. It is said that the expedition could not have succeeded without her aid. She was born about 1787 and died at Fort Manuel on the Missouri River, Dec 20, 1812. Few other women have been so often honored. There are statues, fountains and memorials of her, and her name has been given to a mountain peak. In 2000 the US Mint issued a $1 coin honoring her.

SOUTH CAROLINA SECESSION: ANNIVERSARY. Dec 20, 1860. South Carolina's legislature voted to secede from the US, the first state to do so. Within six weeks, five more states seceded. On Feb 4, 1861, representatives from the six states met at Montgomery, AL, to establish a government and on Feb 9 Jefferson Davis was elected president of the Confederate States of America. By June 1861, 11 states had seceded.

UNITED NATIONS: INTERNATIONAL HUMAN SOLIDARITY DAY. Dec 20. In connection with its observance of the first UN Decade for the Eradication of Poverty (1997–2006), the UN General Assembly, on Dec 22, 2005, declared this date each year as International Human Solidarity Day (Res 60/209). In taking that action, it recalled that the Millennium Declaration identified solidarity as one of the fundamental and universal values that should underlie relations between peoples in the 21st century. For info: United Nations, Dept of Public Info, New York, NY 10017. Web: www.un.org.

US INVASION OF PANAMA: ANNIVERSARY. Dec 20, 1989. The US launched operation "Just Cause," invading Panama in an attempt to seize Manuel Noriega and bring him to justice for narcotics trafficking. Seven months after Noriega had ruled unfavorable election results null and void, the US toppled the Noriega government and oversaw the installation of Guillermo Endara as president. Although the initial military action was declared a success, Noriega eluded capture. He surrendered to US troops on Jan 4, 1990, and was tried, convicted and imprisoned in the US.

VIRGINIA COMPANY EXPEDITION TO AMERICA: ANNIVERSARY. Dec 20, 1606. Three small ships, the *Susan Constant, Godspeed* and *Discovery*, commanded by Captain Christopher Newport, departed London, England, bound for America, where the royally chartered Virginia Company's approximately 120 persons established the first permanent English settlement in what is now the United States at Jamestown, VA, May 14, 1607.

WIGHTMAN, HAZEL: BIRTH ANNIVERSARY. Dec 20, 1886. Hazel Virginia Hotchkiss Wightman, tennis player, born at Healdsburg, CA. Known as the "Queen Mother of Tennis," Wightman was a championship player, an instructor, a benefactor and the donor of the Wightman Cup, a trophy offered for competition between teams of women players from the US and England. Died at Chestnut Hill, MA, Dec 5, 1974.

🎂 BIRTHDAYS TODAY

Jenny Agutter, 68, actress (Emmy for *The Snow Goose*; "Call the Midwife," *Walkabout, Logan's Run*), born London, England, Dec 20, 1952.

Billy Bragg, 63, singer and activist, born Stephen William Bragg at Barking, Essex, England, Dec 20, 1957.

Sandra Cisneros, 66, author and poet (*The House on Mango Street*), born Chicago, IL, Dec 20, 1954.

Ashley Cole, 40, soccer player, born Stepney, London, England, Dec 20, 1980.

David Cook, 38, singer, television personality ("American Idol"), born Houston, TX, Dec 20, 1982.

Uri Geller, 74, psychic, clairvoyant, born Tel Aviv, Israel, Dec 20, 1946.

Jonah Hill, 37, actor (*War Dogs, The Wolf of Wall Street, Moneyball, Superbad*), born Los Angeles, CA, Dec 20, 1983.

Kylian Mbappé, 22, soccer player, born Paris, France, Dec 20, 1998.

Sonny Perdue, 74, US Secretary of Agriculture (Trump administration), former governor of Georgia (R), born Perry, GA, Dec 20, 1956.

William Julius Wilson, 85, sociologist, educator, writer (*When Work Disappears*), born Derry Township, PA, Dec 20, 1935.

Richard Anthony (Dick) Wolf, 74, television producer ("Law & Order," "Miami Vice"), born New York, NY, Dec 20, 1946.

December 21 — Monday

DAY 356   **10 REMAINING**

BÖLL, HEINRICH: BIRTH ANNIVERSARY. Dec 21, 1917. German novelist, winner of the 1972 Nobel Prize in Literature, author of some 20 books including *Billiards at Half-Past Nine, The Clown* and *Group Portrait with Lady*, born at Cologne, Germany. He died near Bonn, Germany, July 16, 1985.

CELEBRATE SHORT FICTION DAY. Dec 21. 8th annual. Short stories have been around as long as humans have been able to spin tales about people, places and things. So on the first day of winter (i.e., the winter solstice), when we have the least amount of daylight, take advantage of the long winter night and "Celebrate Short Fiction" by reading a short story or two! Annually, on the winter solstice. For info: Nancy Christie. Phone: (330) 793-3675. E-mail: nancy@nancychristie.com. Web: www.nancychristie.com/focusonfiction/celebrate-short-fiction-day.

DISRAELI, BENJAMIN: BIRTH ANNIVERSARY. Dec 21, 1804. British novelist and statesman, born at London, England, and died there Apr 19, 1881. "No government," he wrote, "can be long secure without a formidable opposition."

ELVIS PRESLEY MEETS PRESIDENT NIXON: 50th ANNIVERSARY. Dec 21, 1970. After writing President Richard M. Nixon offering to be a "Federal Agent-at-Large" to fight drug abuse and the drug culture, Elvis Presley met with Nixon at the White House on this date. Presley was not made a federal agent, but the two men had a cordial meeting. The photograph of them shaking hands is the most requested reproduction from the National Archives (more than the Bill of Rights or the US Constitution).

FIRST CROSSWORD PUZZLE: ANNIVERSARY. Dec 21, 1913. The first crossword puzzle was compiled by Arthur Wynne and published in a supplement to the *New York World*.

FOREFATHERS' DAY. Dec 21. Observed mainly in New England in commemoration of landing at Plymouth Rock on this day in 1620.

GIBSON, JOSH: BIRTH ANNIVERSARY. Dec 21, 1911. Joshua (Josh) Gibson, Baseball Hall of Fame catcher born at Buena Vista, GA, is regarded as the greatest slugger to play in the Negro Leagues and perhaps the greatest ballplayer ever. Gibson starred with the Pittsburgh Crawfords. His long home runs are the stuff of legend. Inducted into the Hall of Fame in 1972. Died at Pittsburgh, PA, Jan 20, 1947.

HAGEN, WALTER: BIRTH ANNIVERSARY. Dec 21, 1892. Walter Charles B. Hagen, golfer, born at Rochester, NY. Hagen won two

US Opens, four British Opens and five PGA Championships. He was extraordinary in match play, including the Ryder Cup, because he was a master scrambler and absolutely unflappable. He was also a colorful showman who brought the game to the masses and helped to increase prize money. Died at Traverse City, MI, Oct 5, 1969.

HUMBUG DAY. Dec 21. Allows all those preparing for Christmas to vent their frustrations. Twelve "humbugs" allowed. (©2006 by WH.) For info: Thomas & Ruth Roy, Wellcat Holidays, 2418 Long Ln, Lebanon, PA 17046. Phone: (717) 279-0184. E-mail: info@wellcat.com. Web: www.wellcat.com.

MOON PHASE: FIRST QUARTER. Dec 21. Moon enters First Quarter phase at 6:41 PM, EST.

PAN AMERICAN FLIGHT 103 EXPLOSION: ANNIVERSARY. Dec 21, 1988. Pan Am World Airways Flight 103 exploded in midair and crashed into the heart of Lockerbie, Scotland, the result of a terrorist bombing. The 259 passengers and crew members and 11 persons on the ground were killed in the disaster. The tragedy raised questions about security and the notification of passengers in the event of threatened flights. In the resultant investigation it was revealed that government agencies and the airline had known that the flight was possibly the target of a terrorist attack.

PATERNO, JOE: BIRTH ANNIVERSARY. Dec 21, 1926. Born at Brooklyn, NY, Joe Paterno was head football coach at Pennsylvania State University from 1966 to 2011, leading the program to two national championships and numerous bowl appearances—in front of often 100,000 fans at home games. Paterno led the Nittany Lions to five undefeated seasons and became the winningest coach in NCAA Division I history with a victory over Illinois on Oct 29, 2011. Paterno was admired for his coaching style, which espoused a blend of ethical behavior, concern for academics and respect for the tenets of the game. In 2011, though, he was abruptly fired in the fallout from a child sex-abuse scandal that involved a former staff assistant. In 2012 the NCAA vacated 111 Penn State wins dating back to 1998. But in January 2015, those wins were reinstated, giving Paterno a record 409 wins. He died on Jan 22, 2012, at State College, PA.

PHILEAS FOGG WINS A WAGER DAY. Dec 21. Anniversary, from Jules Verne's *Around the World in Eighty Days*, of the winning of Phileas Fogg's wager, on Dec 21, 1872, when Fogg walked into the saloon of the Reform Club at London, England, announcing, "Here I am, gentlemen!" exactly 79 days, 23 hours, 59 minutes and 59 seconds after starting his trip "around the world in 80 days," to win his £20,000 wager.

PILGRIM LANDING: 400th ANNIVERSARY. Dec 21, 1620. According to Governor William Bradford's *History of Plymouth Plantation*, "On Munday," [Dec 21, 1620, New Style] the Pilgrims, aboard the *Mayflower*, reached Plymouth, MA, "sounded ye harbor, and founde it fitt for shipping; and marched into ye land, & founde diverse cornfields, and ye best they could find, and ye season &

December	S	M	T	W	T	F	S
2020			1	2	3	4	5
	6	7	8	9	10	11	12
	13	14	15	16	17	18	19
	20	21	22	23	24	25	26
	27	28	29	30	31		

their presente necessitie made them glad to accepte of it. . . . And after wards tooke better view of ye place, and resolved wher to pitch their dwelling; and them and their goods." Plymouth Rock, the legendary place of landing since it first was "identified" in 1741, nearly 150 years after the landing, has been a historic shrine since. The landing anniversary is observed in much of New England as Forefathers' Day.

SHERMAN TAKES SAVANNAH: ANNIVERSARY. Dec 21, 1864. Despite efforts by Confederate general William Hardee to defend the city of Savannah, GA, Southern troops were forced to pull out of the city, and on this date Union forces under William Tecumseh Sherman captured the town. By marching from Atlanta to the coast at Savannah, Sherman had cut the lower South off from the center.

SHORTS DAY. Dec 21. Since 1986, a day to celebrate the first day of winter: wear fun, festive shorts on the shortest day of the year (in the Northern Hemisphere)! Annually, on the winter solstice. For info: Jeanne Quinn, B. Able, Inc, 1842 Fox Run Terrace, Warrington, PA 18976. E-mail: kwinzz@yahoo.com. Web: www.shakeandfreeze.com.

***SNOW WHITE AND THE SEVEN DWARFS* FILM PREMIERE: ANNIVERSARY.** Dec 21, 1937. America's first full-length, animated feature film (and also the first Technicolor feature) premiered on this date at the Carthay Circle Theater, Hollywood, CA. The labor of love from Walt Disney—who for years wanted to create a feature-length cartoon—involved more than 750 artists and 1,500 colors in four years of development. The film features the classic songs "Some Day My Prince Will Come" and "Whistle While You Work." Walt Disney received a special Oscar for *Snow White*—along with seven miniature Oscars.

SPACE MILESTONE: *APOLLO 8* (US). Dec 21, 1968. First moon voyage launched, manned by Colonel Frank Borman, Captain James A. Lovell, Jr, and Major William A. Anders. Orbited moon Dec 24, returned to Earth Dec 27. First men to orbit the moon and see the side of the moon away from Earth.

STALIN, JOSEPH: BIRTH ANNIVERSARY. Dec 21, 1879. The Soviet dictator, whose family name was Dzhugashvili, was born at Gori, Georgia. One of the most powerful and feared men of the 20th century, Stalin died (of a stroke) at the Kremlin, at Moscow, USSR, Mar 5, 1953.

SZOLD, HENRIETTA: BIRTH ANNIVERSARY. Dec 21, 1860. Teacher, writer, social worker, organizer and pioneer Zionist, Henrietta Szold is best remembered as founder and first president of Hadassah, the Women's Zionist Organization of America. Born at Baltimore, MD, she was influenced by her father, Rabbi Benjamin Szold, an active and vocal abolitionist. She established the first "night school" at Baltimore, focused on teaching English and job skills to immigrants. Her trip to Palestine in 1910 sparked the genesis of Hadassah. While there, Szold was alarmed by the lack of social, medical and educational services and returned with the idea that a national women's Zionist organization must be formed to carry out practical projects. The "Mother of Social Service in Palestine," Szold died at Jerusalem, Feb 13, 1945. See also: "Hadassah: Anniversary" (Feb 24).

UNITED KINGDOM ALLOWS SAME-SEX CIVIL PARTNERSHIPS: 15th ANNIVERSARY. Dec 21, 2005. On this date a new law took effect legally recognizing same-sex civil unions in the United Kingdom. The law took effect on Dec 19 in Northern Ireland, but on Dec 20 in Scotland and then Dec 21 in England and Wales. Pop star Elton John and his partner, filmmaker David Furnish, were among the first celebrities to wed on the 21st.

WINTER. Dec 21–Mar 20, 2021. In the Northern Hemisphere winter begins today with the winter solstice, at 5:02 AM, EST. Note that in the Southern Hemisphere today is the beginning of summer. Between the equator and Arctic Circle the sunrise and sunset points on the horizon are farthest south for the year and daylight length is minimum (ranging from 12 hours, 8 minutes, at the equator to zero at the Arctic Circle).

YALDA. Dec 21. Yalda, the longest night of the year, is celebrated by Iranians. The ceremony has an Indo-Iranian origin, where Light and Good were considered to struggle against Darkness and Evil. With fires burning and lights lit, family and friends gather to stay up through the night helping the sun in its battle against darkness. They recite poetry, tell stories and eat special fruits and nuts until the sun, triumphant, reappears in the morning.

YULE. Dec 21. (Also called Alban Arthan.) One of the "Lesser Sabbats" during the Wiccan year, Yule marks the death of the Sun-God and his rebirth from the Earth Goddess. Annually, on the winter solstice.

ZAPPA, FRANK: 80th BIRTH ANNIVERSARY. Dec 21, 1940. Rock musician and composer, Zappa was noted for his satire and for being a leading advocate against censorship of contemporary music. He formed the group Mothers of Invention. Born at Baltimore, MD, he died Dec 4, 1993, at Los Angeles, CA, at age 52.

🎂 BIRTHDAYS TODAY

Tina Brown, 67, journalist, editor (*The Daily Beast*), author, born London, England, Dec 21, 1953.

Andy Dick, 55, actor ("NewsRadio"), born Charleston, SC, Dec 21, 1965.

Phil Donahue, 85, former television talk show host ("Donahue"), born Cleveland, OH, Dec 21, 1935.

Christine Marie (Chris) Evert, 66, sportscaster, Hall of Fame tennis player, born Fort Lauderdale, FL, Dec 21, 1954.

Jane Fonda, 83, actress (Oscars for *Klute* and *Coming Home*; *Julia, On Golden Pond*), born New York, NY, Dec 21, 1937.

Mark Ingram, Jr, 31, football player, 2009 Heisman Trophy winner, born Hackensack, NJ, Dec 21, 1989.

Samuel L. Jackson, 72, actor (*The Hateful Eight, Django Unchained, Shaft, Pulp Fiction*), born Washington, DC, Dec 21, 1948.

Jane Kaczmarek, 65, actress ("Malcolm in the Middle"), born Milwaukee, WI, Dec 21, 1955.

Emmanuel Macron, 43, President of France (2017–), born Amiens, France, Dec 21, 1977.

Steven Mnuchin, 58, US Secretary of the Treasury (Trump administration), former hedge fund manager, former investment banker, film producer, born New York, NY, Dec 21, 1962.

Jackson Rathbone, 36, actor (*Twilight*), born at Singapore, Dec 21, 1984.

Ray Romano, 63, comedian, actor ("Men of a Certain Age," "Everybody Loves Raymond"), born Queens, NY, Dec 21, 1957.

Kiefer Sutherland, 54, actor ("24," *Flatliners, A Few Good Men*), born London, England, Dec 21, 1966.

Michael Tilson Thomas, 76, conductor, pianist, organist, born Hollywood, CA, Dec 21, 1944.

Andrew James (Andy) Van Slyke, 60, former baseball player, born Utica, NY, Dec 21, 1960.

Karrie Webb, 46, golfer, born Ayr, Australia, Dec 21, 1974.

Steven Yeun, 37, actor ("The Walking Dead"), born Seoul, South Korea, Dec 21, 1983.

December 22 — Tuesday

DAY 357   **9 REMAINING**

BE A LOVER OF SILENCE DAY. Dec 22. 5th annual. A day to be a lover of silence, quiet, stillness. December is a quiet time of year when we're in the midst of the stillness of winter. Embrace the silence. Annually, Dec 22. For info: Rev Jayne Howard Feldman, PO Box 95, Upperco, MD 21155. Phone: (410) 833-6912. E-mail: earthangel4peace@aol.com.

CAPRICORN, THE GOAT. Dec 22–Jan 19. In the astronomical and astrological zodiac that divides the sun's apparent orbit into 12 segments, the period Dec 22–Jan 19 is traditionally identified as the sun sign of Capricorn, the goat. The ruling planet is Saturn.

ELLERY, WILLIAM: BIRTH ANNIVERSARY. Dec 22, 1727. Signer of the Declaration of Independence, born at Newport, RI, and died there Feb 15, 1820.

FIRST GORILLA BORN IN CAPTIVITY: ANNIVERSARY. Dec 22, 1956. "Colo" was born at the Columbus Zoo and Aquarium, Columbus, OH, weighing in at 3¼ pounds, the first gorilla born in captivity. She died in her sleep Jan 17, 2017, at her birthplace.

JOHNSON, CLAUDIA TAYLOR (LADY BIRD): BIRTH ANNIVERSARY. Dec 22, 1912. Former first lady, born Claudia Alta Taylor at Karnack, TX, this daughter of an East Texas cotton grower married young politician Lyndon Baines Johnson in 1934. She ran his congressional office during his navy stint in WWII and was at his side as his career ran its course from Texas congressman to 36th president of the US. Her personal causes included highway beautification, and she founded the National Wildflower Research Center at Austin, TX, in 1995 (later renamed for her). She died at Austin, July 11, 2007.

OGLETHORPE, JAMES EDWARD: BIRTH ANNIVERSARY. Dec 22, 1696. English general, author and colonizer of Georgia. Founder of the city of Savannah. Oglethorpe was born at London, England. He died June 30, 1785, at Cranham Hall, Essex, England.

PUCCINI, GIACOMO: BIRTH ANNIVERSARY. Dec 22, 1858. Italian composer of such operas as *La Boheme*, *Tosca* and *Madama Butterfly*. Born at Lucca, Tuscany, Italy, he died Nov 29, 1924, at Brussels, Belgium.

RACINE, JEAN-BAPTISTE: BIRTH ANNIVERSARY. Dec 22, 1639. French dramatist and playwright. Working during the reign of Louis XIV, Racine was a contemporary of Molière and ultimately a rival of Corneille. His works include *Andromaque* (1667), *Iphegénie* (1674) and *Phèdre* (1677). He brought to the classical tradition a sublimely refined style, and his plays introduced a new focus—the passions overruling tragic figures—rather than the presentation of a complicated chain of events. Born at La Ferté-Milon, France, he died Apr 22, 1699, at Paris.

ROBINSON, EDWIN ARLINGTON: BIRTH ANNIVERSARY. Dec 22, 1869. Three-time Pulitzer Prize winner best known for his short dramatic poems, including "Richard Cory" and "Miniver Cheevy." Born at Head Tide, ME, and died at Los Angeles, CA, Apr 6, 1935.

🎂 BIRTHDAYS TODAY

Steven Norman (Steve) Carlton, 76, Hall of Fame baseball player, born Miami, FL, Dec 22, 1944.

Ted Cruz, 50, US Senator (R, Texas), born Calgary, AB, Canada, Dec 22, 1970.

Hector Elizondo, 84, actor (*Pretty Woman*, *Frankie and Johnny*, "Chicago Hope"), born New York, NY, Dec 22, 1936.

Ralph Fiennes, 58, actor (Harry Potter films, *Schindler's List*, *The English Patient*), born Suffolk, England, Dec 22, 1962.

Steve Garvey, 72, former baseball player, born Tampa, FL, Dec 22, 1948.

Jerry Pinkney, 81, children's book illustrator, born Philadelphia, PA, Dec 22, 1939.

Diane K. Sawyer, 74, journalist, anchor ("ABC World News"), born Glasgow, KY, Dec 22, 1946.

Jan Stephenson, 69, golfer, born Sydney, Australia, Dec 22, 1951.

December 23 — Wednesday

DAY 358   **8 REMAINING**

FEDERAL RESERVE SYSTEM: ANNIVERSARY. Dec 23, 1913. Established pursuant to authority contained in the Federal Reserve Act of Dec 23, 1913, the system serves as the nation's central bank, with the responsibility for execution of monetary policy. It is called on to contribute to the strength and vitality of the US economy, in part by influencing the lending and investing activities of commercial banks and the cost and availability of money and credit.

FESTIVUS. Dec 23. Tongue-in-cheek secular holiday created by the family of television writer Dan O'Keefe, who introduced it to the rest of the world on the popular sitcom "Seinfeld" on Dec 18, 1997 ("The Strike"). Created as a counter to the excess of the Christmas holidays, Festivus involves a plain aluminum pole, an airing of grievances and wrestling. It has since been embraced by the rest of the world. Annually, Dec 23.

FIRST NONSTOP FLIGHT AROUND THE WORLD WITHOUT REFUELING: ANNIVERSARY. Dec 23, 1987. Dick Rutan and Jeana Yeager set a new world record of 216 hours of continuous flight, breaking their own record of 111 hours set July 15, 1986. The aircraft *Voyager* departed from Edwards Air Force Base in California, Dec 14, 1987, and landed Dec 23, 1987. The journey covered 24,986 miles at an official speed of 115 miles per hour.

METRIC CONVERSION ACT: 45th ANNIVERSARY. Dec 23, 1975. The Congress of the US passed Public Law 94–168, known as the Metric Conversion Act of 1975. This act declares that the SI (International System of Units) will be this country's basic system of measurement and establishes the United States Metric Board, which is responsible for the planning, coordination and implementation of the nation's voluntary conversion to SI. (Congress had authorized the metric system as a legal system of measurement in the US by an act passed July 28, 1866. In 1875 the US became

December 2020	S	M	T	W	T	F	S
			1	2	3	4	5
	6	7	8	9	10	11	12
	13	14	15	16	17	18	19
	20	21	22	23	24	25	26
	27	28	29	30	31		

one of the original signers of the Treaty of the Metre, which established an international metric system.)

MEXICO: FEAST OF THE RADISHES. Dec 23. Oaxaca. Figurines of people and animals cleverly carved out of radishes are sold during festivities.

MONROE, HARRIET: BIRTH ANNIVERSARY. Dec 23, 1860. American poet, editor and founder of *Poetry* magazine. Born at Chicago, IL. Died Sept 26, 1936, at Arequipa, Peru.

SMITH, JOSEPH, JR: BIRTH ANNIVERSARY. Dec 23, 1805. The founding prophet of The Church of Jesus Christ of Latter-day Saints was born at Sharon, VT. He was assassinated by an armed mob on June 27, 1844, at Carthage, IL. See also: "Smith, Joseph, Jr, and Hyrum: Death Anniversary" (June 27).

TRANSISTOR UNVEILED: ANNIVERSARY. Dec 23, 1947. John Bardeen, Walter Brattain and William Shockley of Bell Laboratories shared the 1956 Nobel Prize for their invention of the transistor, which led to a revolution in communications and electronics. It was smaller, lighter, more durable and more reliable and generated less heat than the vacuum tube, which had been used up to that time.

WALKER, MADAM C.J.: BIRTH ANNIVERSARY. Dec 23, 1867. Born Sarah Breedlove at Delta, LA, Walker was a businesswoman, inventor, philanthropist and political activist and the first American woman to be a self-made millionaire. She "revolutionized the personal habits and appearance of millions of human beings" and is renowned for her eponymous manufacturing company that sold African-American hair-care and beauty products. Her products spawned the nationwide growth of African-American beauty shops, spheres of political, social and economic importance for black women. She was one of the first entrepreneurs to employ direct sales marketing and was devoted to helping black women find employment and economic independence. Walker died May 25, 1919, at Irvington-on-Hudson, NY.

🎂 BIRTHDAYS TODAY

Akihito, 87, former emperor of Japan (1989–2019), born Tokyo, Japan, Dec 23, 1933.

Robert Bly, 94, poet, author (*Iron John, What Have I Ever Lost by Dying?*), born Madison, MN, Dec 23, 1926.

Carol Ann Duffy, 65, former poet laureate of the United Kingdom (2009–19), born Glasgow, Scotland, Dec 23, 1955.

Scott Gomez, 41, hockey player, born Anchorage, AK, Dec 23, 1979.

James Joseph (Jim) Harbaugh, 57, football coach and former player, born Toledo, OH, Dec 23, 1963.

Susan Lucci, 71, actress ("All My Children," *Mafia Princess*), born Westchester, NY, Dec 23, 1949.

Hanley Ramirez, 37, baseball player, born Samana, Dominican Republic, Dec 23, 1983.

Donna Tartt, 57, author (*The Goldfinch, The Secret History*), born Greenwood, MS, Dec 23, 1963.

December 24 — Thursday

DAY 359	7 REMAINING

AIDA **PREMIERE: ANNIVERSARY.** Dec 24, 1871. Giuseppe Verdi's opera *Aida* premiered at Cairo, Egypt. It was commissioned by the Khedive of Egypt to celebrate the opening of the Suez Canal.

ARNOLD, MATTHEW: BIRTH ANNIVERSARY. Dec 24, 1822. English poet and essayist, born at Laleham, England. Died Apr 15, 1888, at Liverpool, England. "One has often wondered," he wrote in *Culture and Anarchy*, "whether upon the whole earth there is anything so unintelligent, so unapt to perceive how the world is really going, as an ordinary young Englishman of our upper class."

AUSTRIA: "SILENT NIGHT, HOLY NIGHT" CELEBRATIONS. Dec 24. Oberndorf, Hallein and Wagrain, Salzburg. Commemorating the creation of the Christmas carol by Father Joseph Mohr (lyrics) and Franz Xaver Gruber (music) here in 1818.

CARSON, CHRISTOPHER "KIT": BIRTH ANNIVERSARY. Dec 24, 1809. American frontiersman, soldier, trapper, guide and Indian agent best known as Kit Carson. Born at Madison County, KY, he died at Fort Lyon, CO, May 23, 1868.

CHRISTMAS EVE. Dec 24. In many Christian countries, midnight masses celebrate the birth of Jesus Christ and usher in the Christmas Day festivities. In some traditions, gifts are exchanged on Christmas Eve.

ENGLAND: FESTIVAL OF NINE LESSONS AND CAROLS. Dec 24. King's College Chapel, Cambridge University, Cambridge. Since 1918, a Christmas Eve service of carols and readings from the Bible performed by the Choir of King's College. The carols and readings vary from year to year with the exception of the opening carol, which is always "Once in Royal David's City." Each year the service also includes a new, specially commissioned carol. The service has been broadcast on radio since 1928 and is now broadcast to millions of people around the world. Members of the public who wish to attend must join a queue on the college grounds via the Front Gate from 7:00 AM. For info: King's College, Cambridge University. Web: www.kings.cam.ac.uk.

FIRST SURFACE-TO-SURFACE GUIDED MISSILE: ANNIVERSARY. Dec 24, 1942. German rocket engineer Wernher von Braun launched the first surface-to-surface guided missile. Buzz bombs, a form of guided missile, were used by Germany against Great Britain starting Sept 8, 1944. On Feb 24, 1949, the first rocket to reach outer space (an altitude of 25 miles) was fired. The two-stage rocket, a Wac Corporal set in the nose of a German V-2, was launched from the White Sands Proving Grounds, NM, by a team of scientists headed by von Braun.

GARDNER, AVA: BIRTH ANNIVERSARY. Dec 24, 1922. Actress and leading sex symbol of the 1940s and '50s, Ava Lavinnia Gardner was born at Smithfield, NC. Among Gardner's numerous movies are *The Barefoot Contessa, Bhowani Junction, The Sun Also Rises* and *The Life and Times of Judge Roy Bean*. Gardner was married to Mickey Rooney (1942–43), Artie Shaw (1945–46) and Frank Sinatra (1951–57). Died at London, England, Jan 25, 1990.

HUGHES, HOWARD ROBARD: BIRTH ANNIVERSARY. Dec 24, 1905. Wealthy American industrialist, aviator and movie producer who spent his latter years as a recluse. Born at Houston, TX, he died in an airplane en route from Acapulco, Mexico, to Houston, Apr 5, 1976.

JOULE, JAMES PRESCOTT: BIRTH ANNIVERSARY. Dec 24, 1818. English physicist and inventor after whom Joule's law (the first law of thermodynamics) was named. Born at Salford, Lancashire, England. The unit of measurement of the mechanical equivalent of heat is known as the joule. He died at Cheshire, England, Oct 11, 1889.

LIBYA: INDEPENDENCE DAY. Dec 24. Libya gained its independence from Italy in 1951.

🎂 BIRTHDAYS TODAY

Diedrich Bader, 54, actor ("The Drew Carey Show"), born Alexandria, VA, Dec 24, 1966.

Christopher Buckley, 68, novelist, journalist, satirist, born New York, NY, Dec 24, 1952.

Mary Higgins Clark, 89, author (*Where Are the Children?*, *Silent Night*), born New York, NY, Dec 24, 1931.

Lee Daniels, 61, filmmaker (*Lee Daniels' The Butler, Monster's Ball*), television series creator ("Empire"), born Philadelphia, PA, Dec 24, 1959.

Anil Kapoor, 61, actor (*Slumdog Millionaire, Pukar*), born Mumbai, India, Dec 24, 1959.

Ricky Martin, 49, singer, actor ("General Hospital"), born Enrique José Martín at San Juan, Puerto Rico, Dec 24, 1971.

Stephenie Meyer, 47, author (*Twilight* series), born Hartford, CT, Dec 24, 1973.

Ryan Seacrest, 46, television host ("American Idol"), radio personality ("America's Top 40"), born Atlanta, GA, Dec 24, 1974.

Jeff Sessions, 74, former US attorney general (Trump administration), former US senator (R, Alabama), born Hybart, AL, Dec 24, 1946.

Louis Tomlinson, 29, singer (One Direction), born Louis Austin at Doncaster, England, Dec 24, 1991.

December 25 — Friday

DAY 360　　　　　　　　　　　　　**6 REMAINING**

A'PHABET DAY. Dec 25. Also known as "No-L" Day, this celebration is for people who do not want to send Christmas cards but who want to greet their friends; so they send out cards listing the letters of the alphabet in order, but with a gap where L would be. (Created by Robert L. Birch, Pun Corps.)

ASARAH B'TEVET. Dec 25. Hebrew calendar date: Tevet 10, 5781. The Fast of the 10th of Tevet begins at first morning light and commemorates the beginning of the Babylonian siege of Jerusalem in the sixth century BC.

BARTON, CLARA: BIRTH ANNIVERSARY. Dec 25, 1821. Clarissa Harlowe Barton, American nurse and philanthropist, founder of the American Red Cross, was born at Oxford, MA. In 1881 she became first president of the American Red Cross (founded May 21, 1881). She died at Glen Echo, MD, Apr 12, 1912.

BOGART, HUMPHREY: BIRTH ANNIVERSARY. Dec 25, 1899. American stage and screen actor, Humphrey DeForest Bogart was born at New York, NY. Among his best-remembered films are *The Maltese Falcon, The Big Sleep, Casablanca* and *To Have and Have Not*. He received an Academy Award for Best Actor for his work in *The African Queen*. Bogart died Jan 14, 1957, at Hollywood, CA.

BOOTH, EVANGELINE CORY: BIRTH ANNIVERSARY. Dec 25, 1865. Salvation Army general, active in England, Canada and the US. Author and composer of songs, Booth was born at London, England. She died at Hartsdale, NY, July 17, 1950.

CALLOWAY, CAB: BIRTH ANNIVERSARY. Dec 25, 1907. American singer and bandleader Cabell Calloway was born at Rochester, NY. George Gershwin modeled the part of Sportin' Life in *Porgy and Bess* (1935) after this jazz singer who also played the role across

December 2020	S	M	T	W	T	F	S
			1	2	3	4	5
	6	7	8	9	10	11	12
	13	14	15	16	17	18	19
	20	21	22	23	24	25	26
	27	28	29	30	31		

the US until 1956. He is best known for his song "Minnie the Moocher" (1931). He died Nov 18, 1994, at Hockessin, DE.

CHEVROLET, LOUIS: BIRTH ANNIVERSARY. Dec 25, 1878. Louis Joseph Chevrolet, auto racing driver and engineer, was born at LaChaux-de-Fonds, Switzerland. He immigrated to Montreal, Canada, in 1900 and moved to New York in 1902. He worked on early automobiles, competed in auto races, designed cars and engines and cofounded the company that bore his name with William Durant in 1911. (Chevrolet was folded into General Motors a few years later.) Louis Chevrolet raced in the Indianapolis 400 four times. He died at Detroit, MI, June 6, 1941.

CHRISTMAS. Dec 25. Christian festival commemorating the birth of Jesus of Nazareth. Most popular of Christian observances, Christmas as a Feast of the Nativity dates from the fourth century. Although Jesus's birth date is not known, the Western church selected Dec 25 for the feast, possibly to counteract the non-Christian festivals of that approximate date. Many customs from non-Christian festivals (Roman Saturnalia, Mithraic sun's birthday, Teutonic yule, Druidic and other winter solstice rites) have been adopted as part of the Christmas celebration (lights, mistletoe, holly and ivy, holiday tree, wassailing and gift giving, for example). Some Orthodox churches celebrate Christmas Jan 7 based on the "old calendar" (Julian). Theophany (recognition of the divinity of Jesus) is observed on this date and also on Jan 6, especially by the Eastern Orthodox Church.

CUBA: CHRISTMAS RETURNS: ANNIVERSARY. Dec 25, 1998. Christmas was celebrated in Cuba after Fidel Castro's government announced that it was again a regular holiday in the Cuban calendar. In 1997 the government had granted a Christmas holiday in deference to Pope John Paul II, who was visiting the island the next month. Christmas had been abolished as a holiday in Cuba in 1969.

FARLEY, CAL: 125th BIRTH ANNIVERSARY. Dec 25, 1895. Cal Farley, a retired professional wrestler turned successful businessman, started Cal Farley's Boys Ranch in Amarillo, TX, in 1939. The ranch's aim then and now is to help at-risk youth. Starting with five boys, the ranch has grown into a modern community of around 300 children (girls joined the program in 1992) and has housed and educated more than 4,000 boys and girls over the years. Cal Farley was born at Saxton, IA; he died Feb 19, 1967, at Boys Ranch, TX.

JINNAH, MOHAMMED ALI (QAID-E-AZAM): BIRTH ANNIVERSARY. Dec 25, 1876. The founder of the Islamic Republic of Pakistan, Mohammed Ali Jinnah was born at Karachi, then part of India. When Pakistan became an independent political entity (Aug 15, 1947), Jinnah became its first governor general. He was given the title Qaid-e-Azam (Great Leader) in 1947. He died at Karachi, Sept 11, 1948. Jinnah's birth anniversary is a holiday in Pakistan.

"METROPOLITAN OPERA RADIO BROADCASTS" PREMIERE: ANNIVERSARY. Dec 25, 1931. On Christmas Day 1931, the Metropolitan Opera of New York City broadcast an entire opera, *Hansel and Gretel*, on the NBC radio network—the first time this had ever been done. This broadcast was the first of an ongoing radio series of Saturday matinees. On Dec 7, 1940, Texaco (now ChevronTexaco) became a sponsor and began the longest continuous sponsorship in broadcast history—a sponsorship that ended after the 2003–4 season. For decades, the Metropolitan Opera radio broadcasts have introduced opera to new fans far from New York. Today the broadcasts are heard internationally in 42 countries and are currently sponsored by Toll Brothers.

PATHÉ, CHARLES: BIRTH ANNIVERSARY. Dec 25, 1863. Born at Paris, France, Pathé, with his three brothers, founded the innovative film company Pathé Frères (Pathé Brothers) in 1896. A vertically integrated business, Pathé Frères made film stock, cameras and projectors; the company also produced films and exhibited its works in its own theaters. In 1909 Pathé released its first feature-length film—*Les Misérables*—as well its first newsreel. Soon Pathé Frères had worldwide production facilities and a distribution network that made it dominant in the industry. Charles Pathé retired in 1929 and died Dec 26, 1957, at Monte Carlo, Monaco.

SADAT, ANWAR EL-: BIRTH ANNIVERSARY. Dec 25, 1918. Egyptian president and Nobel Peace Prize recipient, born at Mit Abu Al-Kom, a village near the Nile Delta. Sadat led Egypt through the 1973 Yom Kippur War, and then participated in the groundbreaking negotiation that led to the Egypt-Israel Peace Treaty of 1979, which included the provision of Egypt recognizing Israel. For this peace-making activity, Sadat, along with Israeli prime minister Menachem Begin, received the Nobel Peace Prize (Sadat was the first Muslim recipient of that prize). On Oct 6, 1981, he was killed by assassins from the Egyptian Islamic Jihad at Cairo while he was reviewing a military parade commemorating the 1973 Yom Kippur War.

"THE STEVE ALLEN SHOW" TV PREMIERE: 70th ANNIVERSARY. Dec 25, 1950. Talented actor, comedian, singer and musician, Steve Allen hosted a number of variety shows from 1950 to 1969 (with a few breaks in between to host specials and "The Tonight Show"). For two years, his television show was similar to his radio show and featured singer Peggy Lee, announcer Bern Bennett and Llemuel the llama. His next show competed with Ed Sullivan's show, though Allen's stressed comedy. Some of his "funnymen" were Don Knots; Tom Poston; Louis Nye; Gabe Dell; Pat Harrington, Jr; Dayton Allen and Bill Dana. His other shows included a talk show, a game show, a comedy show, an educational music show and a flashback-comedy show.

STOCK EXCHANGE HOLIDAY (CHRISTMAS DAY). Dec 25. Also early closure Dec 24. The holiday schedules for the various exchanges are subject to change if relevant rules, regulations or exchange policies are revised. If you have questions, contact: CME Group (CME, CBOT, NYMEX, COMEX) (www.cmegroup.com), Chicago Board Options Exchange (www.cboe.com), NASDAQ (www.nasdaq.com), NYSE (www.nyse.com).

TAIWAN: CONSTITUTION DAY. Dec 25. National holiday. Commemorates the adoption of the 1946 constitution.

UNION STOCK YARD AND TRANSIT COMPANY OPENS: ANNIVERSARY. Dec 25, 1865. The Union Stock Yard and Transit Company opened in Chicago, IL, on 320 acres of swampy land and was served by 15 miles of railroad track. This was a perfect storm of the expansion of the railroads, the growth of the meatpacking industry and the establishment of Chicago as a hub between East and West.

UNITED KINGDOM: CHRISTMAS HOLIDAY. Dec 25. Bank and public holiday in England, Wales, Scotland and Northern Ireland.

WASHINGTON CROSSES THE DELAWARE: ANNIVERSARY. Dec 25, 1776. One of the most famous events of the American Revolution happened on a bleak Christmas night, during driving snow. General George Washington led 2,400 men across the Delaware River at McConkey's Ferry, Bucks County, PA, to conduct a surprise attack on Hessian troops at Trenton, NJ. Local fishermen conducted the troops across the river, with the men finally assembling at 3 AM on the other side. Washington achieved victory at Trenton, a key event that changed the course of the war to the rebelling colonists' favor.

WEST, REBECCA: BIRTH ANNIVERSARY. Dec 25, 1892. English author, literary critic, prizewinning journalist and noted feminist, Dame Rebecca West was born Cicily Isabel Fairfield at London, England. She renamed herself after a character in a Henrik Ibsen play. Noted for her first novel, *The Return of the Soldier*, her semiautobiographical novel *The Fountain Overflows* (1956) and the immense socio-historical study of the Balkans, *Black Lamb and Grey Falcon* (1940). She died at London Mar 15, 1983.

🎂 BIRTHDAYS TODAY

Jimmy Buffett, 74, singer ("Margaritaville"), songwriter, born Pascagoula, MS, Dec 25, 1946.

Lawrence Richard (Larry) Csonka, 74, Hall of Fame football player, born Stow, OH, Dec 25, 1946.

Rickey Henderson, 62, Hall of Fame baseball player, born Chicago, IL, Dec 25, 1958.

Rachel Keller, 28, actress ("Legion," "Fargo"), born St. Paul, MN, Dec 25, 1992.

Annie Lennox, 66, singer, born Aberdeen, Scotland, Dec 25, 1954.

Barbara Mandrell, 72, singer, born Houston, TX, Dec 25, 1948.

CCH Pounder, 68, actress ("NCIS: New Orleans," "The Shield," *Bagdad Café*), born Carol Christine Hilaria Pounder at Georgetown, British Guiana (now Guyana), Dec 25, 1952.

Karl Rove, 70, political consultant, former presidential adviser, born Denver, CO, Dec 25, 1950.

Gary Sandy, 75, actor ("All That Glitters," "WKRP in Cincinnati"), born Dayton, OH, Dec 25, 1945.

Hanna Schygulla, 77, actress (*The Marriage of Maria Braun, Berlin Alexanderplatz*), born Kattowitz, Germany, Dec 25, 1943.

Mary Elizabeth (Sissy) Spacek, 71, actress (*In the Bedroom, Crimes of the Heart, Carrie*, Oscar for *Coal Miner's Daughter*), born Quitman, TX, Dec 25, 1949.

Justin Trudeau, 49, 23rd Prime Minister of Canada (2015–), born Ottawa, ON, Canada, Dec 25, 1971.

December 26 — Saturday

DAY 361 **5 REMAINING**

ALLEN, STEVE: BIRTH ANNIVERSARY. Dec 26, 1921. American entertainer and TV pioneer born at New York, NY, Steve Allen created the original "Tonight Show" for NBC in 1953. Also known as a composer and the author of more than 40 books. He died at Encino, CA, Oct 30, 2000.

BABBAGE, CHARLES: BIRTH ANNIVERSARY. Dec 26, 1791. English mathematician, born at Teignmouth, England. He developed the principles on which modern computers are designed. Babbage died at London, England, Oct 18, 1871.

BAHAMAS: JUNKANOO. Dec 26. Kaleidoscope of sound and spectacle combining a bit of Mardi Gras, mummers' parade and ancient African tribal rituals. Revelers in colorful costumes parade through the streets to sounds of cowbells, goatskin drums and many other homemade instruments. Always on Boxing Day.

BOXING DAY. Dec 26. Ordinarily observed on the first day after Christmas. A legal holiday in Canada, the United Kingdom and many other countries. Formerly (according to Robert Chambers) a day when Christmas gift boxes were "regularly expected by a postman, the lamplighter, the dustman and generally by all those functionaries who render services to the public at large, without receiving payment therefore from any individual." When Boxing Day falls on a Saturday or Sunday, the Monday or Tuesday immediately following may be proclaimed or observed as a bank or public holiday.

CLERC, LAURENT: BIRTH ANNIVERSARY. Dec 26, 1785. The first deaf teacher in America, Laurent Clerc assisted Thomas Hopkins Gallaudet in establishing the first public school for the deaf, Connecticut Asylum for the Education and Instruction of Deaf and Dumb Persons (now the American School for the Deaf), at Hartford, CT, in 1817. For 41 years Clerc trained new teachers in the use of sign language and in methods of teaching the deaf. Clerc was born at LaBalme, France, and died July 18, 1869, at Hartford.

DECEMBRIST REVOLT: ANNIVERSARY. Dec 26, 1825–Jan 15, 1826. (New Style.) Following the death of Tsar Alexander I, Russian military officers with 3,000 men occupied the Senate Square in St. Petersburg, demanding reforms, including the abolition of serfdom and the advent of a constitutional monarchy. Once the crowd was dispersed, the leaders were arrested and hanged in Russia's last public executions, but the revolt spurred reform and inspired revolutionaries in Russia.

FIRST BLACK HEAVYWEIGHT CHAMPION: ANNIVERSARY. Dec 26, 1908. Jack Johnson became the first black man to win the heavyweight boxing championship when he knocked out Tommy Burns in the 14th round of a fight at Sydney, Australia.

IRELAND: DAY OF THE WREN. Dec 26. Masked revelers and musicians go from door to door asking for money. Traditional day and night of public merrymaking.

KWANZAA. Dec 26–Jan 1, 2021. African-American family observance created in 1966 by Dr. Maulana Karenga in recognition of traditional African harvest festivals. This seven-day festival stresses unity of the black family, with a harvest feast (karamu) on the first day and a day of meditation on the final one. *Kwanzaa* means "first fruit" in Swahili.

LUXEMBOURG: BLESSING OF THE WINE. Dec 26. Greiveldange. Winemakers parade to the church, where a barrel of wine is blessed.

MAO ZEDONG: BIRTH ANNIVERSARY. Dec 26, 1893. Revolutionary leader and architect of Chinese communism, Mao Zedong is among the 20th century's most influential political leaders. Born at Shoa Shan, Hunan, China, to a prosperous peasant family, Mao was influential in shaping Chinese politics and society, ushering in revolutionary change as founder of the People's Republic of China after his Chinese Communist Party won a decades-long civil war. Universally known as Chairman Mao, his Maoist implementation of Marxist principles resulted in significant humanitarian atrocities, notably the Great Leap Forward and the Cultural Revolution,

earning him a place alongside Stalin and Hitler as one of the 20th century's most notorious despots. Nevertheless, China's unification and emergence as a global power is a direct result of Mao's leadership and policies. He died Sept 9, 1976 at Beijing, China.

MILLER, HENRY VALENTINE: BIRTH ANNIVERSARY. Dec 26, 1891. Controversial novelist born at New York, NY. His first novel, *Tropic of Cancer* (1934), was banned in the US and Great Britain for obscenity, as were his next two novels, *Black Spring* (1936) and *Tropic of Capricorn* (1939). Miller died at Pacific Palisades, CA, June 7, 1980.

NATIONAL CANDY CANE DAY. Dec 26. Honoring the striped, peppermint confection that is such a sweet part of so many holiday celebrations from Thanksgiving to New Year's. Said to have been created in 17th-century Germany for cathedral singers who took part in living nativities—hence the shepherd-crook shape. Annually, Dec 26. For info: National Confectioners Association. Web: www.candyusa.com.

NATIONAL WHINER'S DAY™. Dec 26. A day dedicated to whiners, especially those who return holiday gifts and need lots of attention. People are encouraged to be happy about what they do have, rather than unhappy about what they don't have. The most famous whiner(s) of the year will be announced. Nominations accepted through Dec 15. For info: Kevin C. Zaborney, 2023 Vickory Rd, Caro, MI 48723. Phone: (989) 673-6696. E-mail: kevin@national-huggingday.com. Web: www.nationalwhinersday.com.

NELSON, THOMAS: BIRTH ANNIVERSARY. Dec 26, 1738. Merchant and signer of the Declaration of Independence. Fourth governor of Virginia (after Thomas Jefferson). Born at Yorktown, VA, he died at Hanover County, VA, Jan 4, 1789.

RADIUM DISCOVERED: ANNIVERSARY. Dec 26, 1898. French scientists Pierre and Marie Curie discovered the element radium, for which they later won the Nobel Prize in Physics.

ROLEX SYDNEY HOBART YACHT RACE. Dec 26–Jan 1, 2021. Sydney, Australia, and Hobart, Tasmania. 76th edition. Since it was first held in 1945, the annual Rolex Sydney Hobart has become an icon of Australia's summer sport, ranking in public interest with such national events as the Melbourne Cup horse race, the Australian Open tennis tournament and the cricket tests between Australia and England. The 628-nautical-mile course tracks from Sydney Harbor, into the Tasman Sea, down the southeast coast of mainland Australia, across Bass Strait, then down the east coast of Tasmania, into Storm Bay, up the Derwent River to the port city of Hobart. Annually, starting on Boxing Day. For info: Cruising Yacht Club of Australia and Royal Yacht Club of Tasmania. E-mail: cyca@cyca.com.au. Web: www.rolexsydneyhobart.com.

SAINT STEPHEN'S DAY. Dec 26. One of the seven deacons named by the apostles to distribute alms. Died during first century. Feast day is Dec 26 and is observed as a public holiday in Austria and the Republic of Ireland.

SECOND DAY OF CHRISTMAS. Dec 26. Observed as a holiday in many countries.

December 2020	S	M	T	W	T	F	S
			1	2	3	4	5
	6	7	8	9	10	11	12
	13	14	15	16	17	18	19
	20	21	22	23	24	25	26
	27	28	29	30	31		

SLOVENIA: INDEPENDENCE DAY. Dec 26. National holiday. Commemorates 1990 announcement of separation from the Yugoslav Union.

SOUTH AFRICA: DAY OF GOODWILL. Dec 26. National holiday. Replaces Boxing Day.

SUMATRAN-ANDAMAN EARTHQUAKE AND TSUNAMIS: ANNIVERSARY. Dec 26, 2004. One of the strongest and most lethal earthquakes of modern history unleashed tsunami waves that devastated coasts all around the Indian Ocean, where it was centered. An estimated 250,000 people died, with thousands missing and millions displaced. With a magnitude in the range of 9.3, this was the second-strongest earthquake of all time. The power was the equivalent of a 100-gigaton bomb, and its action vibrated the entire planet. Earth spun faster and the day was fractionally shortened as a result. This was also the longest-lasting earthquake recorded, with a length of about 10 minutes as opposed to the more typical few seconds.

UNITED KINGDOM: BOXING DAY BANK HOLIDAY. Dec 26. Bank and public holiday in England, Wales, Scotland and Northern Ireland.

WIDMARK, RICHARD: BIRTH ANNIVERSARY. Dec 26, 1914. Charismatic actor, born at Sunrise, MN, whose screen debut in 1947 as the giggling psychopathic killer in the film noir *Kiss of Death* made him an instant star. Other notable films are *Panic in the Streets* (1950), *No Way Out* (1950), *Night and the City* (1950), *Judgment at Nuremberg* (1961) and *Madigan* (1968). Widmark died Mar 24, 2008, at Roxbury, CT.

 **BIRTHDAYS TODAY**

Beth Behrs, 35, actress ("Two Broke Girls"), born Lancaster, PA, Dec 26, 1985.

Chris Daughtry, 41, singer, television personality ("American Idol"), born Roanoke Rapids, NC, Dec 26, 1979.

Carlton Ernest Fisk, 73, Hall of Fame baseball player, born Bellows Falls, VT, Dec 26, 1947.

Kit Harington, 34, actor ("Game of Thrones"; stage: *War Horse*), born Christopher Catesby Harington at London, England, Dec 26, 1986.

Marcelo Rios, 45, former tennis player, born Santiago, Chile, Dec 26, 1975.

Steve Sisolak, 67, Governor of Nevada (D), born Milwaukee, WI, Dec 26, 1953.

Osborne Earl (Ozzie) Smith, 66, Hall of Fame baseball player, born Mobile, AL, Dec 26, 1954.

Phil Spector, 80, music producer, born New York, NY, Dec 26, 1940.

December 27 — Sunday

DAY 362   **4 REMAINING**

CAYLEY, GEORGE: BIRTH ANNIVERSARY. Dec 27, 1773. Aviation pioneer Sir George Cayley, English scientist and inventor, a theoretician who designed airplanes, helicopters and gliders. He is credited as the father of aerodynamics, and he was the pilot of the world's first manned glider flight. Born at Scarborough, Yorkshire, England, he died at Brompton Hall, Yorkshire, Dec 15, 1857.

DIETRICH, MARLENE: BIRTH ANNIVERSARY. Dec 27, 1901. Born at Berlin, Germany, Dietrich enrolled in Max Reinhardt's drama school. Her first big break was in 1930 when Josef Von Sternberg cast her in *The Blue Angel*, the first talkie made in Germany. A year later, she and Sternberg moved to Hollywood and began a string of six films together with *Morocco*, the only film for which she received an Academy Award nomination. Some of her other films are *Destry Rides Again*, *Around the World in 80 Days*, *Touch of Evil*, *Judgment at Nuremberg* and *Witness for the*

Prosecution. During the 1950s she was a cabaret singer in a stage revue that toured the globe. Dietrich died May 6, 1992, at Paris, France.

"HOWDY DOODY" TV PREMIERE: ANNIVERSARY. Dec 27, 1947. The first popular children's show was brought to TV by Bob Smith and was one of the first regular NBC shows to be shown in color. It was set in the circus town of Doodyville. Children sat in the bleachers' "Peanut Gallery" and participated in activities such as songs and stories. Human characters were Buffalo Bob (Bob Smith), the silent clown Clarabell (Bob Keeshan, Bobby Nicholson and Lew Anderson), storekeeper Cornelius Cobb (Nicholson), Chief Thunderthud (Bill LeCornec), Princess Summerfall Winterspring (Judy Tyler and Linda Marsh), Bison Bill (Ted Brown) and wrestler Ugly Sam (Dayton Allen). Puppet costars included Howdy Doody, Phineas T. Bluster, Dilly Dally, Flub-a-Dub, Captain Scuttlebutt, Double Doody and Heidi Doody. The filmed adventures of Gumby were also featured. In the final episode, Clarabell broke his long silence to say, "Good-bye, kids."

KEPLER, JOHANNES: BIRTH ANNIVERSARY. Dec 27, 1571. One of the world's greatest astronomers, called "the father of modern astronomy," German mathematician Johannes Kepler was born at Württemberg, Germany; he died at Regensburg, Germany, Nov 15, 1630.

PASTEUR, LOUIS: BIRTH ANNIVERSARY. Dec 27, 1822. French chemist-bacteriologist born at Dole, Jura, France. Died at Villeneuve l'Etang, France, Sept 28, 1895. Discoverer of prophylactic inoculation against rabies. Pasteurization process named for him.

RADIO CITY MUSIC HALL: ANNIVERSARY. Dec 27, 1932. Radio City Music Hall, at New York City, opened on this date. Among the opening-night performers were the "Radio Roxyettes."

SAINT JOHN, APOSTLE-EVANGELIST: FEAST DAY. Dec 27. Son of Zebedee, Galilean fisherman, and Salome. Died about AD 100. Roman Rite feast day is Dec 27. (Observed May 8 by Byzantine Rite.)

SALK, LEE: BIRTH ANNIVERSARY. Dec 27, 1926. American child psychologist Lee Salk was born at New York, NY. He became well known for proving the calming effect of a mother's heartbeat on a newborn infant. Salk's warning during the 1970s that women should not abandon full-time child rearing was met with wide opposition, especially from working mothers. He died May 2, 1992, at New York, NY.

 **BIRTHDAYS TODAY**

Timothée Chalamet, 25, actor (*Call Me by Your Name*, *Lady Bird*), born New York, NY, Dec 27, 1995.

Gerard Depardieu, 72, actor (*The Return of Martin Guerre*, *Cyrano de Bergerac*), born Chateauroux, France, Dec 27, 1948.

Tovah Feldshuh, 68, actress (*Holocaust*), born New York, NY, Dec 27, 1952.

Savannah Guthrie, 49, journalist, anchor ("The Today Show"), born Melbourne, Australia, Dec 27, 1971.

Juan Felipe Herrera, 72, former poet laureate of the US (2015–17), born Fowler, CA, Dec 27, 1948.

Masi Oka, 46, actor ("Heroes," "Hawaii Five-0"), born Tokyo, Japan, Dec 27, 1974.

Carson Palmer, 41, football player, born Fresno, CA, Dec 27, 1979.

Cokie Roberts, 77, news correspondent, born New Orleans, LA, Dec 27, 1943.

Sarah Vowell, 51, journalist, author (*The Wordy Shipmates*), social commentator ("The Daily Show," "This American Life"), born Muskogee, OK, Dec 27, 1969.

December 28 — Monday

DAY 363   **3 REMAINING**

AUSTRALIA: PROCLAMATION DAY. Dec 28. Observed in South Australia.

ENDANGERED SPECIES ACT: ANNIVERSARY. Dec 28, 1973. President Richard Nixon signed the Endangered Species Act into law.

FIRST CINEMA: 125th ANNIVERSARY. Dec 28, 1895. The Lumière brothers—Louis and Auguste—projected short films for paying customers on this date at the Grand Café in Paris, France. This was the first time this had ever been done and is considered a key moment in film history. See also: "First Movie Theater Opens: Anniversary" (Apr 23).

HOLY INNOCENTS DAY (CHILDERMAS). Dec 28. Commemoration of the massacre of children at Bethlehem, ordered by King Herod, who wanted to destroy, among them, the infant Savior. Early and medieval accounts claimed as many as 144,000 victims, but more recent writers, noting that Bethlehem was a very small town, have revised the estimates of the number of children killed to between 6 and 20.

IOWA: ADMISSION DAY: ANNIVERSARY. Dec 28. Became 29th state in 1846.

LEE, STAN: BIRTH ANNIVERSARY. Dec 28, 1922. Stan Lee, born Stanley Martin Lieber at New York City on Dec 28, 1922, was the face of Marvel Comics. Lee elevated and transformed the comic book genre with his dynamic copy, imbuing characters with humanity and tackling real-life social issues. As a Marvel staff writer, he co-created the Fantastic Four with artist Jack Kirby, then subsequently co-launched beloved superheroes like Spider-Man, the Hulk, Black Panther and the X-Men before becoming Marvel's editorial director and publisher. He received the Medal of Arts from President George W. Bush. As Marvel chairman emeritus, Lee shepherded the film franchises *Iron Man, X-Men, Thor* and *The Avengers* in which he made Hitchcock-like cameo appearances. Lee died Nov 12, 2018, at Los Angeles, CA.

MESSINA EARTHQUAKE: ANNIVERSARY. Dec 28, 1908. Messina, Sicily. The ancient town of Messina was struck by an earthquake. Nearly 80,000 persons died in the disaster, and half of the town's buildings were destroyed.

PLEDGE OF ALLEGIANCE RECOGNIZED: 75th ANNIVERSARY. Dec 28, 1945. The US Congress officially recognized the Pledge of Allegiance and urged its frequent recitation in America's schools. The pledge was composed in 1892 by Francis Bellamy, a Baptist minister. At the time, Bellamy was chairman of a committee of state school superintendents of education, and several public schools adopted his pledge as part of the Columbus Day quadricentennial celebration that year. In 1954 the Knights of Columbus persuaded Congress to add the words "under God" to the pledge. In 2002 a federal appeals court found the pledge unconstitutional for use in public schools due to the "under God" phrase, but the Supreme

Court reversed the case for procedural reasons and did not comment on the issue of constitutionality.

POOR RICHARD'S ALMANACK: ANNIVERSARY. Dec 28, 1732. The *Pennsylvania Gazette* carried the first known advertisement for the first issue of *Poor Richard's Almanack* by Richard Saunders (Benjamin Franklin) for the year 1733. The advertisement promised "many pleasant and witty verses, jests and sayings . . . new fashions, games for kisses . . . men and melons . . . breakfast in bed, &c." America's most famous almanac, *Poor Richard's* was published through the year 1758 and has been imitated many times since.

VICE PRESIDENTIAL RESIGNATION: ANNIVERSARY. Dec 28, 1832. John C. Calhoun, who had served as vice president of the US under two presidents (John Quincy Adams and Andrew Jackson), Mar 4, 1825–Dec 28, 1832, finding himself in growing disagreement with President Jackson, resigned the office of vice president, the first to do so. He spent most of his subsequent political life as a US senator from South Carolina.

WILSON, WOODROW: BIRTH ANNIVERSARY. Dec 28, 1856. The 28th president of the US was born Thomas Woodrow Wilson at Staunton, VA. Twice elected president (1912 and 1916), it was Wilson who said, "The world must be made safe for democracy," as he asked the Congress to declare war on Germany, Apr 2, 1917. His first wife, Ellen, died Aug 6, 1914, and he married Edith Bolling Galt, Dec 18, 1915. He suffered a paralytic stroke, Sept 16, 1919, never regaining his health. There were many speculations about who (possibly Mrs Wilson?) was running the government during his illness. His second term of office ended Mar 3, 1921, and he died at Washington, DC, Feb 3, 1924.

🎂 BIRTHDAYS TODAY

David Archuleta, 30, singer, television personality ("American Idol"), born Miami, FL, Dec 28, 1990.

James Blake, 41, tennis player, born Yonkers, NY, Dec 28, 1979.

Ray Bourque, 60, former hockey player, born Montreal, QC, Canada, Dec 28, 1960.

Malcolm Gets, 56, actor ("Caroline in the City"), born near Gainesville, FL, Dec 28, 1964.

Johnny Isakson, 76, US Senator (R, Georgia), born Atlanta, GA, Dec 28, 1944.

Gayle King, 66, broadcast anchor ("CBS This Morning"), journalist, television personality, born New York, NY, Dec 28, 1954.

Mario Kreutzberger (Don Francisco), 80, television host ("Sabado Gigante"), born Talca, Chile, Dec 28, 1940.

John Legend, 42, R&B singer, born John Stephens at Springfield, OH, Dec 28, 1978.

Joe Manganiello, 44, actor ("True Blood," "One Tree Hill," *Magic Mike*), born Pittsburgh, PA, Dec 28, 1976.

Sienna Miller, 39, actress (*Factory Girl, Interview*), born New York, NY, Dec 28, 1981.

Nichelle Nichols, 88, actress (Star Trek films and television series, "Heroes"), singer, born Grace Nichols at Robbins, IL, Dec 28, 1932.

Patrick Rafter, 48, Hall of Fame tennis player, born Mount Isa, Queensland, Australia, Dec 28, 1972.

December 2020	S	M	T	W	T	F	S
			1	2	3	4	5
	6	7	8	9	10	11	12
	13	14	15	16	17	18	19
	20	21	22	23	24	25	26
	27	28	29	30	31		

Todd Richards, 51, Olympic snowboarder, born Worchester, MA, Dec 28, 1969.

Maggie Smith, 86, actress (Oscars for *The Prime of Miss Jean Brodie* and *California Suite*; Harry Potter films; Tony for *Lettice & Lovage*; "Downton Abbey"), born Ilford, England, Dec 28, 1934.

Kevin Stitt, 48, Governor of Oklahoma (R), born Milton, FL, Dec 28, 1972.

Denzel Washington, 66, actor (Oscars for *Training Day* and *Glory*; *Flight, The Hurricane, Malcolm X*), born Mount Vernon, NY, Dec 28, 1954.

Edgar Winter, 74, singer, musician, born Beaumont, TX, Dec 28, 1946.

December 29 — Tuesday

DAY 364   **2 REMAINING**

AMERICAN YMCA ORGANIZED: ANNIVERSARY. Dec 29, 1851. The first US branch of the Young Men's Christian Association was organized at Boston, MA. It was modeled on an organization begun at London, England, in 1844.

CASALS, PABLO: BIRTH ANNIVERSARY. Dec 29, 1876. Lauded cellist and conductor Pablo Carlos Salvador Defillio de Casals was born at El Vendrell, Catalonia, Spain. Noted for his performance and recordings of Bach's Cello Suites (inducted in 2018 into the National Recording Registry of the Library of Congress). Casals died at Rio Pedros, Puerto Rico, Oct 22, 1973.

COLD MOON. Dec 29. So called by Native American tribes of New England and the Great Lakes because the nights have become long at this time of year. Also called the Long Nights Moon. The December Full Moon.

GLADSTONE, WILLIAM EWART: BIRTH ANNIVERSARY. Dec 29, 1809. English statesman and author for whom the gladstone (luggage) bag was named. Inspiring orator, eccentric individual, intensely loved or hated by all who knew him (cheered from the streets and jeered from the balconies), Gladstone is said to have left more writings (letters, diaries, journals, books) than any other major English politician. However, his preoccupation with the charitable rehabilitation of prostitutes was perhaps easily misunderstood. Born at Liverpool, England, he was four times Britain's prime minister. Gladstone died at Hawarden, Wales, May 19, 1898.

JOHNSON, ANDREW: BIRTH ANNIVERSARY. Dec 29, 1808. Seventeenth president of the US, Andrew Johnson, proprietor of a tailor shop at Laurens, SC, before he entered politics, born at Raleigh, NC. Upon Abraham Lincoln's assassination Johnson became president. He was the first president to be impeached by the House and was acquitted Mar 26, 1868, by the Senate. After his term of office as president (Apr 15, 1865–Mar 3, 1869) he made several unsuccessful attempts to win another public office. Finally he was elected to the US Senate from Tennessee and served in the Senate from Mar 4, 1875, until his death at Carter's Station, TN, July 31, 1875.

MOON PHASE: FULL MOON. Dec 29. Moon enters Full Moon phase at 10:28 PM, EST.

MOORE, MARY TYLER: BIRTH ANNIVERSARY. Dec 29, 1936. A native of Brooklyn Heights, NY, Moore was a seven-time Emmy winner and longtime American TV sweetheart, breaking new ground by wearing capris as the stylish, comedic housewife Laura Petrie on "The Dick Van Dyke Show" (1961–66). As Mary Richards on "The Mary Tyler Moore Show" (1970–77), Moore quietly revolutionized TV sitcoms, introducing a single, independent career woman. Her production company, MTM Enterprise, launched numerous hit shows including "The Bob Newhart Show," "WKRP in Cincinnati" and "Hill Street Blues." She received many accolades in the course of her career, including an Oscar nomination and Golden Globe for her role as an angry, grieving mother in *Ordinary People* (1980) and a 2012 Screen Actors Guild lifetime achievement award. A diabetic, she was an active international chair of the Juvenile Diabetes Research Foundation beginning in 2011. She died Jan 25, 2017, in Greenwich, CT.

***A PORTRAIT OF THE ARTIST AS A YOUNG MAN* PUBLISHED: ANNIVERSARY.** Dec 29, 1916. The semiautobiographical novel by Irish modernist author James Joyce, his first, was published in the US by B.W. Huebsch (it was published in the United Kingdom in 1917). The novel had been serialized in a British literary journal, *The Egoist*, from 1914 to 1915 on Ezra Pound's recommendation.

SAINT THOMAS OF CANTERBURY: FEAST DAY. Dec 29. Thomas, Archbishop of Canterbury, was born at London, England, in 1118 and was murdered at the Canterbury Cathedral on this date in 1170.

TEXAS: ADMISSION DAY: 175th ANNIVERSARY. Dec 29. Became 28th state in 1845.

TICK TOCK DAY. Dec 29. Time runs out! All those dreams you've had, all those fantasies? It's time, friend. Do it! Annually, Dec 29. (©2006 by WH.) For info: Thomas & Ruth Roy, Wellcat Holidays, 2418 Long Ln, Lebanon, PA 17046. Phone: (717) 279-0184. E-mail: info@wellcat.com. Web: www.wellcat.com.

WOUNDED KNEE MASSACRE: ANNIVERSARY. Dec 29, 1890. Anniversary of the massacre of more than 200 Native American men, women and children by the US Seventh Cavalry at Wounded Knee Creek, SD. Government efforts to suppress a ceremonial religious practice, the Ghost Dance (which called for a messiah who would restore the bison to the plains, make the white men disappear and bring back the old Native American way of life), had resulted in the death of Sitting Bull, Dec 15, 1890, which further inflamed the disgruntled Native Americans and culminated in the slaughter at Wounded Knee, Dec 29.

🎂 BIRTHDAYS TODAY

Patricia Clarkson, 61, actress (*Married Life, Lars and the Real Girl, The Station Agent, Far from Heaven*), born New Orleans, LA, Dec 29, 1959.

Ted Danson, 73, actor ("CSI," "Cheers," "Becker," *Three Men and a Baby*), born San Diego, CA, Dec 29, 1947.

Iain De Caestecker, 33, actor ("Agents of S.H.I.E.L.D."), born Glasgow, Scotland, Dec 29, 1987.

Marianne Faithfull, 74, singer, actress, born London, England, Dec 29, 1946.

Thomas Edwin (Tom) Jarriel, 86, retired broadcast journalist, born LaGrange, GA, Dec 29, 1934.

Jude Law, 48, actor (*Sherlock Holmes, Closer, Cold Mountain, The Talented Mr Ripley*), born London, England, Dec 29, 1972.

Diego Luna, 41, actor (*Rogue One, Milk, Y tu mamá también*), producer, born Mexico City, Mexico, Dec 29, 1979.

Ross Lynch, 25, singer, actor ("Austin & Ally"), born Littleton, CO, Dec 29, 1995.

Paula Poundstone, 61, comedienne, born Sudbury, MA, Dec 29, 1959.

Jon Voight, 82, actor (*Midnight Cowboy, Deliverance*), born Yonkers, NY, Dec 29, 1938.

Lilly Wachowski, 53, filmmaker (*The Matrix* with sibling Lana Wachowski), born Andrew Wachowski at Chicago, IL, Dec 29, 1967.

December 30 — Wednesday

DAY 365   **1 REMAINING**

FALLING NEEDLES FAMILY FEST. Dec 30. Now that the yuletide tree's been up for weeks and not been watered since a couple of days before Christmas, gather the gang around and watch the needles gently fall one by one. Live it up! Dance barefoot! (©2006 by WH.) For info: Thomas & Ruth Roy, Wellcat Holidays, 2418 Long Ln, Lebanon, PA 17046. Phone: (717) 279-0184. E-mail: info@wellcat.com. Web: www.wellcat.com.

GUGGENHEIM, SIMON: BIRTH ANNIVERSARY. Dec 30, 1867. American capitalist and philanthropist, born at Philadelphia, PA. He established, in memory of his son, the John Simon Guggenheim Memorial Foundation, in 1925. Died Nov 2, 1941, at New York, NY.

JONES, DAVY: 75th BIRTH ANNIVERSARY. Dec 30, 1945. Well known as a member of 1960s pop group The Monkees, Davy Jones was born at Manchester, England. After his big break as the Artful Dodger in a West End, London, production of *Oliver!*, Jones was cast as a member of the fun-loving, made-for-TV combo, singing lead on such hits as "Daydream Believer." Originally airing from 1966 to 1968, "The Monkees" show was also a hit in syndication, and its ubiquity allowed for numerous band reunions and nostalgia tours that kept Jones in the public eye until his death from a heart attack Feb 29, 2012, at Stuart, FL.

KIPLING, RUDYARD: BIRTH ANNIVERSARY. Dec 30, 1865. English poet, novelist and short-story writer, Nobel Prize laureate, Kipling was born at Bombay, India. After working as a journalist at India, he traveled around the world. He married an American and lived in Vermont for several years. Kipling is best known for his children's stories, such as *The Jungle Book* and *Just So Stories*, and poems such as "The Ballad of East and West" and "If." He died at London, England, Jan 18, 1936.

"LET'S MAKE A DEAL" TV PREMIERE: ANNIVERSARY. Dec 30, 1963. Monty Hall hosted this outrageous and no-skill-required game show. Audience members, many of whom wore costumes, were selected to sit in the trading area, and some were picked to "make a deal" with Hall by trading something of their own for something they were offered. Sometimes prizes were worthless ("zonks"). At the end of the show, the two people who had won the most were given the option to trade their winnings for a chance at the "Big Deal," hidden behind one of three doors. A 21st-century revival is hosted by Wayne Brady.

LORD, JACK: 100th BIRTH ANNIVERSARY. Dec 30, 1920. For 12 seasons (1968–80), actor Jack Lord portrayed the tough, pompadoured chief of a special police unit on the hit television series "Hawaii Five-O." As Steve McGarrett, Lord often delivered the show's famous catchphrase, "Book 'em, Danno," when they caught the bad guys. In 1962's *Dr. No*, Lord became the first actor to play the character Felix Leiter in the James Bond franchise. Born John

Joseph Patrick Ryan at Brooklyn, NY, Lord died Jan 21, 1998, at Honolulu, HI.

MONITOR SINKS: ANNIVERSARY. Dec 30, 1862. The Union ironclad ship USS *Monitor* (which achieved fame after its battle with the *Virginia*) sank off Cape Hatteras, NC, during a storm. Sixteen of its crew were lost. See also: "Battle of Hampton Roads: Anniversary" (Mar 9).

PARKS, BERT: BIRTH ANNIVERSARY. Dec 30, 1914. Bert Parks was born at Atlanta, GA. Though he was an actor whose career spanned radio, film, television and Broadway, his name became synonymous with the Miss America pageant, which he emceed for 25 years, ending in 1980. Parks made a special return appearance for the 1990 pageant, once again singing his signature song, "There She Is." He died Feb 2, 1992, at La Jolla, CA.

PHILIPPINES: RIZAL DAY. Dec 30. National holiday. Commemorates martyrdom of Dr. Jose Rizal in 1896.

RASPUTIN, GRIGORI YEFIMOVICH: ASSASSINATION ANNIVERSARY. Dec 30, 1916. In St. Petersburg, Russia, assassins related to the Romanov family killed Grigory Rasputin, the peasant mystic who was a trusted adviser to the imperial couple. Rasputin was born Grigori Yefimovich Novjkh at Siberia about 1871.

"THE ROY ROGERS SHOW" TV PREMIERE: ANNIVERSARY. Dec 30, 1951. This very popular TV Western starred Roy Rogers and his wife, Dale Evans, as themselves. It also featured Pat Brady as Rogers's sidekick who drove a jeep named Nellybelle, the singing group Sons of the Pioneers, Rogers's horse Trigger, Evans's horse Buttermilk and a German shepherd named Bullet. This half-hour show was especially popular with young viewers.

USSR ESTABLISHED: ANNIVERSARY. Dec 30, 1922. After the Russian Revolution of 1917 and the subsequent three-year civil war, the Union of Soviet Socialist Republics (or Soviet Union) was founded, a confederation of Russia, Byelorussia, the Ukraine and the Transcaucasian Federation. It was the first state in the world to be based on Marxist communism. The Soviet Union was dissolved Dec 8, 1991. See also: "Soviet Union Dissolved: Anniversary" (Dec 8).

🎂 BIRTHDAYS TODAY

James Burrows, 80, director ("Cheers," "Taxi"), born Los Angeles, CA, Dec 30, 1940.

Eliza Dushku, 40, actress ("Dollhouse," "Buffy the Vampire Slayer," "Angel"), born Boston, MA, Dec 30, 1980.

Sean Hannity, 59, journalist, radio and television talk show host ("Hannity," "The Sean Hannity Show"), born New York, NY, Dec 30, 1981.

LeBron James, 36, basketball player, born Akron, OH, Dec 30, 1984.

Sanford (Sandy) Koufax, 85, Hall of Fame baseball player, former sportscaster, born Brooklyn, NY, Dec 30, 1935.

Kristin Kreuk, 38, actress ("Beauty and the Beast," "Smallville"), born Vancouver, BC, Canada, Dec 30, 1982.

Matt Lauer, 63, former anchor ("The Today Show"), born New York, NY, Dec 30, 1957.

Kenyon Martin, 43, basketball player, born Saginaw, MI, Dec 30, 1977.

December 2020	S	M	T	W	T	F	S
			1	2	3	4	5
	6	7	8	9	10	11	12
	13	14	15	16	17	18	19
	20	21	22	23	24	25	26
	27	28	29	30	31		

Janet Mills, 73, Governor of Maine (D), born Farmington, ME, Dec 30, 1947.

Michael Nesmith, 78, singer, songwriter (The Monkees), director, born Houston, TX, Dec 30, 1942.

Mike Pompeo, 57, US Secretary of State, former director of the Central Intelligence Agency, born Orange, CA, Dec 30, 1963.

Patti Smith, 74, singer, born Chicago, IL, Dec 30, 1946.

Russ Tamblyn, 85, actor ("Twin Peaks," *Peyton Place, West Side Story*), born Los Angeles, CA, Dec 30, 1935.

Concetta Tomei, 75, actress ("Providence," "China Beach"), born Kenosha, WI, Dec 30, 1945.

Tracey Ullman, 61, actress, singer ("The Tracey Ullman Show," *I Love You to Death*), born Buckinghamshire, England, Dec 30, 1959.

V, 25, singer (BTS), born Kim Tae-hyung at Daegu, South Korea, Dec 30, 1995.

Meredith Vieira, 69, television journalist and personality, born Providence, RI, Dec 30, 1951.

Eldrick "Tiger" Woods, 45, golfer, born Cypress, CA, Dec 30, 1975.

December 31 — Thursday

DAY 366 **0 REMAINING**

BIGGEST FILMED PIE FIGHT—"BATTLE OF THE CENTURY" FILM RELEASE: ANNIVERSARY. Dec 31, 1927. The pie-in-the-face gag, first seen on film screens in 1913, had gotten to be a cliché by 1927, but newly teamed comedians Stan Laurel and Oliver Hardy thought they could overcome that obstacle in their two-reel film short that used 3,000 pies to make a comedy classic of excess. Laurel told a biographer decades later: "Let's give them so many pies that there never will be room for any more pie pictures in the whole history of the movies." (The complete film was lost for decades until a collector found a missing reel in 2015.)

DENVER, JOHN: BIRTH ANNIVERSARY. Dec 31, 1943. Born Henry John Deutschendorf at Roswell, NM, this singer-songwriter ("Rocky Mountain High," "Sunshine on My Shoulders") died in a plane crash off the coast of California, Oct 12, 1997.

FIRST BANK OPENS IN US: ANNIVERSARY. Dec 31, 1781. The first modern bank in the US, the Bank of North America was organized by Robert Morris and received its charter from the Confederation Congress. It began operations Jan 7, 1782, at Philadelphia, PA.

FIRST NIGHTS. Dec 31. Family-oriented, nonalcoholic community celebrations of the New Year—first observed in Boston, MA, in 1976. Observed in scores of American and Canadian cities and communities.

ICE BOWL: THE COLDEST GAME OF PROFESSIONAL FOOTBALL: ANNIVERSARY. Dec 31, 1967. The Green Bay Packers defeated the Dallas Cowboys 21–17 to win the NFL Championship. It was minus-14 (and minus-44 windchill) out there on the frozen tundra of Lambeau Field, Green Bay, WI, making it the coldest game in the history of professional football. Referees were unable to use their metal whistles, as they froze to their lips. (Green Bay, coached by Vince Lombardi, went on to defeat the AFL champion,

the Oakland Raiders, in what is now known as Super Bowl II, on Jan 14, 1968.)

JAPAN: NAMAHAGE. Dec 31. Oga Peninsula, Akita Prefecture. In the evening, groups of "Namahage" men disguised as devils make door-to-door visits, growling, "Any good-for-nothing fellow hereabout?" The object of this annual event is to give sluggards an opportunity to change their minds and become diligent. Otherwise, according to legend, they will be punished by devils.

LEAP SECOND ADJUSTMENT TIME. Dec 31. One of the times that have been favored for the addition or subtraction of a second to or from clock time (to coordinate atomic and astronomical time). The determination to adjust is made by the International Earth Rotation Service of the International Bureau of Weights and Measures, at Paris, France.

MAKE UP YOUR MIND DAY. Dec 31. A day for all those people who have a hard time making up their minds. Make a decision today and follow through with it! Annually, Dec 31. For info: A.C. Vierow and M.A. Dufour, Box 71, Clio, MI 48420-0071.

MARSHALL, GEORGE CATLETT: BIRTH ANNIVERSARY. Dec 31, 1880. Chairman of the newly formed Joint Chiefs of Staff Committee throughout the US's involvement in WWII, General George Marshall was born at Uniontown, PA. He accompanied Roosevelt or represented the US at most Allied war conferences. He served as secretary of state and was designer of the Marshall Plan after the war. Died Oct 16, 1959, at Washington, DC.

NEW YEAR'S EVE. Dec 31. The last evening of the Gregorian calendar year, traditionally a night for merrymaking to welcome in the new year.

NEW YEAR'S EVE BANISHED WORDS LIST. Dec 31. Since 1976 America's dishonorable list of words banished from the Queen's English has been released on New Year's Eve or Day. Overworked words and phrases from 2019 include *wheelhouse, platform, collusion, ghosting, yeet*. Send nominations via e-mail. For info: Lake Superior State University. Phone: (906) 632-6841. E-mail: banish@lssu.edu. Web: www.lssu.edu/banished.

NIXON, JOHN: DEATH ANNIVERSARY. Dec 31, 1808. Revolutionary patriot and businessman, commander of the Philadelphia City Guard, born 1733 (exact date unknown). Appointed to conduct the first public reading of the Declaration of Independence, July 8, 1776. Died at Philadelphia, PA.

NO INTERRUPTIONS DAY. Dec 31. On this day—the last business day of the year—there shall be no interruptions! At work we will minimize or eliminate interruptions to our thought processes or tasks we are performing. At home we will silence and shut down all devices that interrupt us so we can devote ourselves to our families or to ourselves. This is a day for quiet and/or focus. It is a day to renew our energies to prepare ourselves for the new calendar year ahead. For info: Sylvia Henderson, 3570 Olney-Laytonsville Rd, Ste 588, Olney, MD 20832. Phone: (301) 260-1538. E-mail: sylvia@springboardtraining.com.

PANAMA: ASSUMES CONTROL OF CANAL: ANNIVERSARY. Dec 31, 1999. With the expiration of the Panama Canal Treaty of 1979 at noon, the Republic of Panama assumed full responsibility for the canal, and the US Panama Canal Commission ceased to exist.

SAINT SYLVESTER'S DAY. Dec 31. Observed in Belgium, Germany, France and Switzerland. Commemorates death of Pope Sylvester I in AD 335. Feasting, particularly upon "St. Sylvester's Carp."

SAMOA: SAMOAN FIRE DANCE. Dec 31. New Year's Eve is occasion for Samoan bamboo fireworks, singing and traditional performances such as the Samoan Fire Dance.

SCOTLAND: HOGMANAY. Dec 31. The Scottish New Year celebrations date from ancient pagan times. Hogmanay (no one is sure of the origin of the name) traditions include fireworks and torch-lit processions in the cities and bonfires in the rural areas. "First footing" is still observed: it is believed to be good luck for the first foot over the threshold to be that of a dark-haired stranger bearing a piece of coal, shortbread or whiskey. After the midnight chimes, everyone sings "Auld Lang Syne."

SUMMER, DONNA: BIRTH ANNIVERSARY. Dec 31, 1948. Born LaDonna Adrian Gaines at Boston, MA, Summer started her singing career as a child in the church choir. She eventually moved to New York City before joining the Munich production of *Hair* in 1967. Summer's career thrived in Germany, but by 1974 she had returned to the US, where a collaboration with producer Giorgio Moroder led to a string of smash disco singles: "Love to Love You," "I Feel Love" and "Hot Stuff." The "Queen of Disco" continued recording and performing in America and Europe throughout the 1980s and '90s. A recipient of five Grammy Awards, she died May 17, 2012, at Englewood, FL.

VESALIUS, ANDREAS: BIRTH ANNIVERSARY. Dec 31, 1514. Born at Brussels, Belgium, anatomist Vesalius contributed to medicine's inclusion as an empirical science and wrote one of the most important books in medical history, *De Humani Corporis Fabrica* (*On the Fabric of the Human Body*). He broke with medical conventions and dissected cadavers with his students; his subsequent anatomical discoveries overturned the 14-centuries-old Galenic canon and founded modern scientific anatomy. *Fabrica* continues to be renowned for its anatomical accuracy, beauty and aestheticism. He died Oct 15, 1564, in a shipwreck at Zenta, Greece.

WIESENTHAL, SIMON: BIRTH ANNIVERSARY. Dec 31, 1908. Born at Buczacz, Austria-Hungary (now Ukraine), Wiesenthal was a Holocaust survivor who dedicated his postwar life to fighting anti-Semitism and speaking out against racism. For more than 50 years, his Jewish Documentation Center in Vienna, Austria, compiled data about war criminals not yet apprehended as well as information about the six million victims of Nazi persecution. In all, he helped to bring almost 1,100 Nazi war criminals to trial—most famously Adolf Eichmann. In 1977 The Simon Wiesenthal Center, an internationally renowned organization dedicated to remembering the Holocaust, was established in Los Angeles, CA. Wiesenthal died at Vienna, Sept 20, 2005.

🎂 BIRTHDAYS TODAY

Gabrielle Douglas, 25, Olympic gymnast, born Virginia Beach, VA, Dec 31, 1995.

Alex Ferguson, 79, soccer executive, former manager, born Glasgow, Scotland, Dec 31, 1941.

Josh Hawley, 41, US Senator (R, Missouri), born Springdale, AR, Dec 31, 1979.

Sir Anthony Hopkins, 83, actor (Oscar for *The Silence of the Lambs*; *Nixon, The Remains of the Day*), born Port Talbot, Wales, Dec 31, 1937.

Val Kilmer, 61, actor (*Batman Forever, The Doors, Heat*), born Los Angeles, CA, Dec 31, 1959.

Ben Kingsley, 77, actor (Oscar for *Gandhi*; *Sexy Beast, Schindler's List*), born Krishna Bhanji at Yorkshire, England, Dec 31, 1943.

Tim Matheson, 72, actor (*Animal House*, "The Virginian," "Bonanza"), born Los Angeles, CA, Dec 31, 1948.

Sarah Miles, 79, actress (*The Servant, Blow-Up, Hope and Glory*), born Ingatestone, England, Dec 31, 1941.

Bebe Neuwirth, 62, actress ("Cheers," "Frasier"; stage: *Chicago*), born Newark, NJ, Dec 31, 1958.

Psy, 43, singer ("Gangnam Style"), born Park Jae-sang at Seoul, South Korea, Dec 31, 1977.

James Remar, 67, actor ("Dexter," "Sex and the City," *48 Hrs, The Cotton Club*), born Boston, MA, Dec 31, 1953.

Nicholas Sparks, 55, author (*A Walk to Remember, The Notebook, Message in a Bottle*), born Omaha, NE, Dec 31, 1965.

Andy Summers, 78, musician (The Police), born Poulton-le-Fylde, England, Dec 31, 1942.

Diane Halfin von Fürstenberg, 75, fashion designer, author, born Brussels, Belgium, Dec 31, 1945.

Calendar Information for the Year 2020

Time shown is Eastern Standard Time. All dates are given in terms of the Gregorian calendar.

(Based in part on information prepared by the Nautical Almanac Office, US Naval Observatory.)

ERAS	YEAR	BEGINS
Byzantine	7529	Sept 14
Jewish*	5781	Sept 19
Chinese (Year of the Rat)	4718	Jan 25
Roman (AUC)	2773	Jan 14
Nabonassar	2769	Apr 23
Japanese (Reiwa)	2	May 1
Grecian (Seleucidae)	2332	Sept 14 (or Oct 14)
Indian (Saka)	1942	Mar 21
Diocletian	1737	Sept 11
Islamic (Hegira)**	1442	Aug 20

*Year begins the previous day at sunset.
**Year begins the previous evening at moon crescent.

RELIGIOUS CALENDARS

Epiphany .... Jan 6
Shrove Tuesday .... Feb 25
Ash Wednesday .... Feb 26
Lent .... Feb 26–Apr 11
Palm Sunday .... Apr 5
Good Friday .... Apr 10
Easter Day .... Apr 12
Ascension Day .... May 21
Whit Sunday (Pentecost) .... May 31
Trinity Sunday .... June 7
First Sunday in Advent .... Nov 29
Christmas Day (Friday) .... Dec 25

Eastern Orthodox Church Observances

Great Lent begins .... Mar 2
Pascha (Easter) .... Apr 19
Ascension .... May 28
Pentecost .... June 7

Jewish Holy Days*

Purim .... Mar 10
Passover (1st day) .... Apr 9
Shavuot .... May 29–30
Tisha B'av .... July 30
Rosh Hashanah (New Year) .... Sept 19–20
Yom Kippur .... Sept 28
Succoth .... Oct 3–9
Chanukah .... Dec 11–18

*All Jewish holy days begin the previous day at sundown.

Islamic Holy Days**

First Day of Ramadan (1441) .... Apr 24
Eid-Al-Fitr (1441) .... May 24
Islamic New Year (1442) .... Aug 20

**All Islamic holy days begin the previous evening at moon crescent.

CIVIL CALENDAR—USA—2020

New Year's Day .... Jan 1
Martin Luther King's Birthday (obsvd) .... Jan 20
Lincoln's Birthday .... Feb 12
Washington's Birthday (obsvd)/Presidents' Day .... Feb 17
Memorial Day (obsvd) .... May 25
Independence Day .... July 4
Labor Day .... Sept 7
Columbus Day (obsvd) .... Oct 12
General Election Day .... Nov 3
Veterans Day .... Nov 11
Thanksgiving Day .... Nov 26

OTHER DAYS WIDELY OBSERVED IN US—2020

Groundhog Day (Candlemas) .... Feb 2
St. Valentine's Day .... Feb 14
St. Patrick's Day .... Mar 17
Mother's Day .... May 10
Flag Day .... June 14
Father's Day .... June 21
National Grandparents Day .... Sept 13
Hallowe'en .... Oct 31

CIVIL CALENDAR—CANADA—2020

Victoria Day .... May 18
Canada Day .... July 1
Labor Day .... Sept 7
Thanksgiving Day .... Oct 12
Remembrance Day .... Nov 11
Boxing Day .... Dec 26

CIVIL CALENDAR—MEXICO—2020

New Year's Day .... Jan 1
Constitution Day .... Feb 5
Benito Juarez Birthday .... Mar 21
Labor Day .... May 1
Battle of Puebla Day (Cinco de Mayo) .... May 5
Independence Day* .... Sept 16
Dia de La Raza .... Oct 12
Mexican Revolution Day .... Nov 20
Guadalupe Day .... Dec 12

*Celebration begins Sept 15 at 11:00 PM.

CIVIL CALENDAR—UNITED KINGDOM—2020

Accession of Queen Elizabeth II .... Feb 6
St. David (Wales) .... Mar 1
Commonwealth Day .... Mar 9
St. Patrick (Ireland) .... Mar 17
Birthday of Queen Elizabeth II .... Apr 21
St. George (England) .... Apr 23
Coronation Day .... June 2
Birthday of Prince Philip, Duke of Edinburgh .... June 10
The Queen's Official Birthday (tentative) .... June 13
Remembrance Day .... Nov 11
Birthday of the Prince of Wales .... Nov 14
St. Andrew (Scotland) .... Nov 30

BANK AND PUBLIC HOLIDAYS—UNITED KINGDOM—2020

Observed during 2020 in England and Wales, Scotland and Northern Ireland unless otherwise indicated.

New Year .... Jan 1
Bank Holiday (Scotland) .... Jan 2
St. Patrick's Day (Northern Ireland) .... Mar 17
Good Friday .... Apr 10
Easter Monday (except Scotland) .... Apr 13
May Day Bank Holiday .... May 4
Spring Bank Holiday .... May 25
Orangeman's Day (Battle of the Boyne) (Northern Ireland) .... July 12*
Bank Holiday (Scotland) .... Aug 3
Summer Bank Holiday (except Scotland) .... Aug 31
Christmas Day Holiday .... Dec 25
Boxing Day Holiday .... Dec 26

*Observed July 13.

SEASONS

Spring (Vernal Equinox) .... Mar 19, 11:50 PM, EDT
Summer (Summer Solstice) .... June 20, 5:44 PM, EDT
Autumn (Autumnal Equinox) .... Sept 22, 9:31 AM, EDT
Winter (Winter Solstice) .... Dec 21, 5:02 AM, EST

DAYLIGHT SAVING TIME SCHEDULE—2020

Sunday, Mar 8, 2:00 AM–Sunday, Nov 1, 2:00 AM—in all time zones.

CHRONOLOGICAL CYCLES

Dominical Letter .... ED
Epact 5
Golden Number (Lunar Cycle) VII
Julian Period (year of) 6733
Roman Indiction 13
Solar Cycle 13

Calendar Information for the Year 2021

Time shown is Eastern Standard Time. All dates are given in terms of the Gregorian calendar.

(Based in part on information prepared by the Nautical Almanac Office, US Naval Observatory.)

ERAS

	YEAR	BEGINS
Byzantine	7530	Sept 14
Jewish*	5782	Sept 7
Chinese (Year of the Ox)	4719	Feb 12
Roman (AUC)	2774	Jan 14
Nabonassar	2770	Apr 23
Japanese (Reiwa)	3	May 1
Grecian (Seleucidae)	2333	Sept 14 (or Oct 14)
Indian (Saka)	1943	Mar 22
Diocletian	1738	Sept 11
Islamic (Hegira)**	1443	Aug 9

*Year begins the previous day at sunset.
**Year begins the previous evening at moon crescent.

RELIGIOUS CALENDARS

Epiphany	Jan 6
Shrove Tuesday	Feb 16
Ash Wednesday	Feb 17
Lent	Feb 17–Apr 3
Palm Sunday	Mar 28
Good Friday	Apr 2
Easter Day	Apr 4
Ascension Day	May 13
Whit Sunday (Pentecost)	May 23
Trinity Sunday	May 30
First Sunday in Advent	Nov 28
Christmas Day (Saturday)	Dec 25

EASTERN ORTHODOX CHURCH OBSERVANCES

Great Lent begins	Mar 15
Pascha (Easter)	May 2
Ascension	June 10
Pentecost	June 20

JEWISH HOLY DAYS*

Purim	Feb 26
Passover (1st day)	Mar 28
Shavuot	May 17–18
Tisha B'av	July 18
Rosh Hashanah (New Year)	Sept 7–8
Yom Kippur	Sept 16
Succoth	Sept 21–27
Chanukah	Nov 29–Dec 6

*All Jewish holy days begin the previous day at sundown.

ISLAMIC HOLY DAYS**

First Day of Ramadan (1442)	Apr 13
Eid-Al-Fitr (1442)	May 13
Islamic New Year (1443)	Aug 9

**All Islamic holy days begin the previous evening at moon crescent.

CIVIL CALENDAR—USA—2021

New Year's Day	Jan 1
Martin Luther King's Birthday (obsvd)	Jan 18
Lincoln's Birthday	Feb 12
Washington's Birthday (obsvd)/Presidents' Day	Feb 15
Memorial Day (obsvd)	May 31
Independence Day	July 4
Labor Day	Sept 6
Columbus Day (obsvd)	Oct 11
General Election Day	Nov 2
Veterans Day	Nov 11
Thanksgiving Day	Nov 25

OTHER DAYS WIDELY OBSERVED IN US—2021

Groundhog Day (Candlemas)	Feb 2
St. Valentine's Day	Feb 14
St. Patrick's Day	Mar 17
Mother's Day	May 9
Flag Day	June 14
Father's Day	June 20
National Grandparents Day	Sept 12
Hallowe'en	Oct 31

CIVIL CALENDAR—CANADA—2021

Victoria Day	May 24
Canada Day	July 1
Labor Day	Sept 6
Thanksgiving Day	Oct 11
Remembrance Day	Nov 11
Boxing Day	Dec 26

CIVIL CALENDAR—MEXICO—2021

New Year's Day	Jan 1
Constitution Day	Feb 5
Benito Juarez Birthday	Mar 21
Labor Day	May 1
Battle of Puebla Day (Cinco de Mayo)	May 5
Independence Day*	Sept 16
Dia de La Raza	Oct 12
Mexican Revolution Day	Nov 20
Guadalupe Day	Dec 12

*Celebration begins Sept 15 at 11:00 P.M

CIVIL CALENDAR—UNITED KINGDOM—2021

Accession of Queen Elizabeth II	Feb 6
St. David (Wales)	Mar 1
Commonwealth Day	Mar 8
St. Patrick (Ireland)	Mar 17
Birthday of Queen Elizabeth II	Apr 21
St. George (England)	Apr 23
Coronation Day	June 2
Birthday of Prince Philip, Duke of Edinburgh	June 10
The Queen's Official Birthday (tentative)	June 12
Remembrance Day	Nov 11
Birthday of the Prince of Wales	Nov 14
St. Andrew (Scotland)	Nov 30

BANK AND PUBLIC HOLIDAYS—UNITED KINGDOM—2021

Observed during 2020 in England and Wales, Scotland and Northern Ireland unless otherwise indicated.

New Year	Jan 1
Bank Holiday (Scotland)	Jan 4
St. Patrick's Day (Northern Ireland)	Mar 17
Good Friday	Apr 2
Easter Monday (except Scotland)	Apr 5
May Day Bank Holiday	May 3
Spring Bank Holiday	May 31
Orangeman's Day (Battle of the Boyne) (Northern Ireland)	July 12
Bank Holiday (Scotland)	Aug 2
Summer Bank Holiday (except Scotland)	Aug 30
Christmas Day Holiday (observed)	Dec 27
Boxing Day Holiday (observed)	Dec 28

SEASONS

Spring (Vernal Equinox)	Mar 20, 5:37 AM, EDT
Summer (Summer Solstice)	June 20, 11:32 PM, EDT
Autumn (Autumnal Equinox)	Sept 22, 3:21 PM, EDT
Winter (Winter Solstice)	Dec 21, 3:59 PM, EST

DAYLIGHT SAVING TIME SCHEDULE—2021

Sunday, Mar 14, 2:00 AM–Sunday, Nov 7, 2:00 AM—in all time zones.

CHRONOLOGICAL CYCLES

Dominical Letter	C
Epact	16
Golden Number (Lunar Cycle)	VIII
Julian Period (year of)	6734
Roman Indiction	14
Solar Cycle	14

Calendar Information for the Year 2022

Time shown is Eastern Standard Time. All dates are given in terms of the Gregorian calendar.

(Based in part on information prepared by the Nautical Almanac Office, US Naval Observatory.)

ERAS

	YEAR	BEGINS
Byzantine	7531	Sept 14
Jewish*	5783	Sept 26
Chinese (Year of the Tiger)	4720	Feb 1
Roman (AUC)	2775	Jan 14
Nabonassar	2771	Apr 23
Japanese (Reiwa)	4	May 1
Grecian (Seleucidae)	2334	Sept 14
		(or Oct 14)
Indian (Saka)	1944	Mar 22
Diocletian	1739	Sept 11
Islamic (Hegira)**	1444	July 30

*Year begins the previous day at sunset.
**Year begins the previous evening at moon crescent.

RELIGIOUS CALENDARS

Epiphany	Jan 6
Shrove Tuesday	Mar 1
Ash Wednesday	Mar 2
Lent	Mar 2–Apr 16
Palm Sunday	Apr 10
Good Friday	Apr 15
Easter Day	Apr 17
Ascension Day	May 26
Whit Sunday (Pentecost)	June 5
Trinity Sunday	June 12
First Sunday in Advent	Nov 27
Christmas Day (Sunday)	Dec 25

EASTERN ORTHODOX CHURCH OBSERVANCES

Great Lent begins	Mar 7
Pascha (Easter)	Apr 24
Ascension	June 2
Pentecost	June 12

JEWISH HOLY DAYS*

Purim	Mar 17
Passover (1st day)	Apr 16
Shavuot	June 5–6
Tisha B'av	Aug 7
Rosh Hashanah (New Year)	Sept 26–27
Yom Kippur	Oct 5
Succoth	Oct 10–16
Chanukah	Dec 19–26

*All Jewish holy days begin the previous day at sundown.

ISLAMIC HOLY DAYS**

First Day of Ramadan (1443)	Apr 2
Eid-Al-Fitr (1443)	May 1
Islamic New Year (1444)	July 30

**All Islamic holy days begin the previous evening at moon crescent.

CIVIL CALENDAR—USA—2022

New Year's Day	Jan 1
Martin Luther King's Birthday (obsvd)	Jan 17
Lincoln's Birthday	Feb 12
Washington's Birthday (obsvd)/Presidents' Day	Feb 21
Memorial Day (obsvd)	May 30
Independence Day	July 4
Labor Day	Sept 5
Columbus Day (obsvd)	Oct 10
General Election Day	Nov 8
Veterans Day	Nov 11
Thanksgiving Day	Nov 24

OTHER DAYS WIDELY OBSERVED IN US—2022

Groundhog Day (Candlemas)	Feb 2
St. Valentine's Day	Feb 14
St. Patrick's Day	Mar 17
Mother's Day	May 8
Flag Day	June 14
Father's Day	June 19
National Grandparents Day	Sept 11
Hallowe'en	Oct 31

CIVIL CALENDAR—CANADA—2022

Victoria Day	May 23
Canada Day	July 1
Labor Day	Sept 5
Thanksgiving Day	Oct 10
Remembrance Day	Nov 11
Boxing Day	Dec 26

CIVIL CALENDAR—MEXICO—2022

New Year's Day	Jan 1
Constitution Day	Feb 5
Benito Juarez Birthday	Mar 21
Labor Day	May 1
Battle of Puebla Day (Cinco de Mayo)	May 5
Independence Day*	Sept 16
Dia de La Raza	Oct 12
Mexican Revolution Day	Nov 20
Guadalupe Day	Dec 12

*Celebration begins Sept 15 at 11:00 P.M.

CIVIL CALENDAR—UNITED KINGDOM—2022

Accession of Queen Elizabeth II	Feb 6
St. David (Wales)	Mar 1
Commonwealth Day	Mar 14
St. Patrick (Ireland)	Mar 17
Birthday of Queen Elizabeth II	Apr 21
St. George (England)	Apr 23
Coronation Day	June 2
Birthday of Prince Philip, Duke of Edinburgh	June 10
The Queen's Official Birthday (tentative)	June 11
Remembrance Day	Nov 11
Birthday of the Prince of Wales	Nov 14
St. Andrew (Scotland)	Nov 30

BANK AND PUBLIC HOLIDAYS—UNITED KINGDOM—2022

Observed during 2022 in England and Wales, Scotland and Northern Ireland unless otherwise indicated.

New Year	Jan 1
Bank Holiday (Scotland)	Jan 3
St. Patrick's Day (Northern Ireland)	Mar 17
Good Friday	Apr 15
Easter Monday (except Scotland)	Apr 18
May Day Bank Holiday	May 2
Spring Bank Holiday	May 30
Orangeman's Day (Battle of the Boyne) (Northern Ireland)	July 12
Bank Holiday (Scotland)	Aug 1
Summer Bank Holiday (except Scotland)	Aug 29
Christmas Day Holiday (observed)	Dec 26
Boxing Day Holiday (observed)	Dec 27

SEASONS

Spring (Vernal Equinox)	Mar 20, 11:33 AM, EDT
Summer (Summer Solstice)	June 21, 5:14 AM, EDT
Autumn (Autumnal Equinox)	Sept 22, 9:04 PM, EDT
Winter (Winter Solstice)	Dec 21, 4:48 PM, EST

DAYLIGHT SAVING TIME SCHEDULE—2022

Sunday, Mar 6, 2:00 AM–Sunday, Nov 6, 2:00 AM—in all time zones.

CHRONOLOGICAL CYCLES

Dominical Letter	B
Epact	27
Golden Number (Lunar Cycle)	IX
Julian Period (year of)	6735
Roman Indiction	15
Solar Cycle	15

Perpetual Calendar, 1753–2100

A perpetual calendar lets you find the day of the week for any date in any year. Because January 1 may fall on any of the seven days of the week and may be a leap or nonleap year, 14 different calendars are possible. The number next to each year corresponds to one of the 14 calendars. Calendar 11 will be used in 2020; Calendar 6 will be used in 2021; Calendar 7 will be used in 2022.

YEAR/NO		YEAR/NO		YEAR/NO		YEAR/NO		YEAR/NO		YEAR/NO		YEAR/NO		YEAR/NO		YEAR/NO		YEAR/NO		YEAR/NO		YEAR/NO	
1753	2	1782	3	1811	3	1840	11	1869	6	1898	7	1927	7	1956	8	1985	3	2014	4	2043	5	2072	13
1754	3	1783	4	1812	11	1841	6	1870	7	1899	1	1928	8	1957	3	1986	4	2015	5	2044	13	2073	1
1755	4	1784	12	1813	6	1842	7	1871	1	1900	2	1929	3	1958	4	1987	5	2016	13	2045	1	2074	2
1756	12	1785	7	1814	7	1843	1	1872	9	1901	3	1930	4	1959	5	1988	13	2017	1	2046	2	2075	3
1757	7	1786	1	1815	1	1844	9	1873	4	1902	4	1931	5	1960	13	1989	1	2018	2	2047	3	2076	11
1758	1	1787	2	1816	9	1845	4	1874	5	1903	5	1932	13	1961	1	1990	2	2019	3	2048	11	2077	6
1759	2	1788	10	1817	4	1846	5	1875	6	1904	13	1933	1	1962	2	1991	3	2020	11	2049	6	2078	7
1760	10	1789	5	1818	5	1847	6	1876	14	1905	1	1934	3	1963	3	1992	11	2021	6	2050	7	2079	1
1761	5	1790	6	1819	6	1848	14	1877	2	1906	2	1935	3	1964	11	1993	6	2022	7	2051	1	2080	5
1762	6	1791	7	1820	14	1849	2	1878	3	1907	3	1936	11	1965	6	1994	7	2023	1	2052	9	2081	4
1763	7	1792	8	1821	2	1850	3	1879	4	1908	11	1937	6	1966	7	1995	1	2024	9	2053	4	2082	5
1764	8	1793	3	1822	3	1851	4	1880	12	1909	6	1938	7	1967	1	1996	9	2025	4	2054	5	2083	6
1765	3	1794	4	1823	4	1852	12	1881	7	1910	7	1939	1	1968	9	1997	4	2026	5	2055	6	2084	14
1766	4	1795	5	1824	12	1853	7	1882	1	1911	1	1940	9	1969	4	1998	5	2027	6	2056	14	2085	2
1767	5	1796	13	1825	7	1854	1	1883	2	1912	9	1941	4	1970	5	1999	6	2028	14	2057	2	2086	3
1768	13	1797	1	1826	1	1855	2	1884	10	1913	4	1942	5	1971	6	2000	14	2029	2	2058	3	2087	4
1769	1	1798	2	1827	2	1856	10	1885	5	1914	5	1943	6	1972	14	2001	3	2030	3	2059	4	2088	12
1770	2	1799	3	1828	10	1857	5	1886	6	1915	6	1944	14	1973	2	2002	3	2031	4	2060	12	2089	7
1771	3	1800	4	1829	5	1858	6	1887	7	1916	14	1945	2	1974	3	2003	4	2032	12	2061	7	2090	1
1772	11	1801	5	1830	6	1859	7	1888	8	1917	2	1946	3	1975	4	2004	12	2033	7	2062	1	2091	2
1773	6	1802	6	1831	7	1860	8	1889	3	1918	3	1947	4	1976	12	2005	7	2034	1	2063	2	2092	10
1774	7	1803	7	1832	8	1861	3	1890	4	1919	4	1948	12	1977	7	2006	1	2035	2	2064	10	2093	5
1775	1	1804	8	1833	3	1862	4	1891	5	1920	12	1949	7	1978	1	2007	2	2036	10	2065	5	2094	6
1776	9	1805	3	1834	4	1863	5	1892	13	1921	7	1950	1	1979	2	2008	10	2037	5	2066	6	2095	7
1777	4	1806	4	1835	5	1864	13	1893	1	1922	1	1951	2	1980	10	2009	6	2038	5	2067	6	2096	8
1778	5	1807	5	1836	13	1865	1	1894	2	1923	2	1952	10	1981	5	2010	6	2039	7	2068	8	2097	3
1779	6	1808	13	1837	1	1866	2	1895	3	1924	10	1953	5	1982	6	2011	7	2040	8	2069	3	2098	4
1780	14	1809	1	1838	2	1867	3	1896	11	1925	5	1954	6	1983	7	2012	8	2041	3	2070	4	2099	5
1781	2	1810	2	1839	3	1868	11	1897	6	1926	6	1955	7	1984	8	2013	3	2042	4	2071	5	2100	6

Calendar 1

JAN

S	M	T	W	T	F	S
1	2	3	4	5	6	7
8	9	10	11	12	13	14
15	16	17	18	19	20	21
22	23	24	25	26	27	28
29	30	31				

FEB

S	M	T	W	T	F	S
			1	2	3	4
5	6	7	8	9	10	11
12	13	14	15	16	17	18
19	20	21	22	23	24	25
26	27	28				

MAR

S	M	T	W	T	F	S
			1	2	3	4
5	6	7	8	9	10	11
12	13	14	15	16	17	18
19	20	21	22	23	24	25
26	27	28	29	30	31	

APR

S	M	T	W	T	F	S
						1
2	3	4	5	6	7	8
9	10	11	12	13	14	15
16	17	18	19	20	21	22
23	24	25	26	27	28	29
30						

MAY

S	M	T	W	T	F	S
	1	2	3	4	5	6
7	8	9	10	11	12	13
14	15	16	17	18	19	20
21	22	23	24	25	26	27
28	29	30	31			

JUNE

S	M	T	W	T	F	S
				1	2	3
4	5	6	7	8	9	10
11	12	13	14	15	16	17
18	19	20	21	22	23	24
25	26	27	28	29	30	

JULY

S	M	T	W	T	F	S
						1
2	3	4	5	6	7	8
9	10	11	12	13	14	15
16	17	18	19	20	21	22
23	24	25	26	27	28	29
30	31					

AUG

S	M	T	W	T	F	S
		1	2	3	4	5
6	7	8	9	10	11	12
13	14	15	16	17	18	19
20	21	22	23	24	25	26
27	28	29	30	31		

SEPT

S	M	T	W	T	F	S
					1	2
3	4	5	6	7	8	9
10	11	12	13	14	15	16
17	18	19	20	21	22	23
24	25	26	27	28	29	30

OCT

S	M	T	W	T	F	S
1	2	3	4	5	6	7
8	9	10	11	12	13	14
15	16	17	18	19	20	21
22	23	24	25	26	27	28
29	30	31				

NOV

S	M	T	W	T	F	S
			1	2	3	4
5	6	7	8	9	10	11
12	13	14	15	16	17	18
19	20	21	22	23	24	25
26	27	28	29	30		

DEC

S	M	T	W	T	F	S
					1	2
3	4	5	6	7	8	9
10	11	12	13	14	15	16
17	18	19	20	21	22	23
24	25	26	27	28	29	30
31						

Calendar 2

JAN

S	M	T	W	T	F	S
	1	2	3	4	5	6
7	8	9	10	11	12	13
14	15	16	17	18	19	20
21	22	23	24	25	26	27
28	29	30	31			

FEB

S	M	T	W	T	F	S
				1	2	3
4	5	6	7	8	9	10
11	12	13	14	15	16	17
18	19	20	21	22	23	24
25	26	27	28			

MAR

S	M	T	W	T	F	S
				1	2	3
4	5	6	7	8	9	10
11	12	13	14	15	16	17
18	19	20	21	22	23	24
25	26	27	28	29	30	31

APR

S	M	T	W	T	F	S
1	2	3	4	5	6	7
8	9	10	11	12	13	14
15	16	17	18	19	20	21
22	23	24	25	26	27	28
29	30					

MAY

S	M	T	W	T	F	S
		1	2	3	4	5
6	7	8	9	10	11	12
13	14	15	16	17	18	19
20	21	22	23	24	25	26
27	28	29	30	31		

JUNE

S	M	T	W	T	F	S
					1	2
3	4	5	6	7	8	9
10	11	12	13	14	15	16
17	18	19	20	21	22	23
24	25	26	27	28	29	30

JULY

S	M	T	W	T	F	S
1	2	3	4	5	6	7
8	9	10	11	12	13	14
15	16	17	18	19	20	21
22	23	24	25	26	27	28
29	30	31				

AUG

S	M	T	W	T	F	S
			1	2	3	4
5	6	7	8	9	10	11
12	13	14	15	16	17	18
19	20	21	22	23	24	25
26	27	28	29	30	31	

SEPT

S	M	T	W	T	F	S
						1
2	3	4	5	6	7	8
9	10	11	12	13	14	15
16	17	18	19	20	21	22
23	24	25	26	27	28	29
30						

OCT

S	M	T	W	T	F	S
	1	2	3	4	5	6
7	8	9	10	11	12	13
14	15	16	17	18	19	20
21	22	23	24	25	26	27
28	29	30	31			

NOV

S	M	T	W	T	F	S
				1	2	3
4	5	6	7	8	9	10
11	12	13	14	15	16	17
18	19	20	21	22	23	24
25	26	27	28	29	30	

DEC

S	M	T	W	T	F	S
						1
2	3	4	5	6	7	8
9	10	11	12	13	14	15
16	17	18	19	20	21	22
23	24	25	26	27	28	29
30	31					

3

JAN

S	M	T	W	T	F	S
		1	2	3	4	5
6	7	8	9	10	11	12
13	14	15	16	17	18	19
20	21	22	23	24	25	26
27	28	29	30	31		

FEB

S	M	T	W	T	F	S
					1	2
3	4	5	6	7	8	9
10	11	12	13	14	15	16
17	18	19	20	21	22	23
24	25	26	27	28		

MAR

S	M	T	W	T	F	S
					1	2
3	4	5	6	7	8	9
10	11	12	13	14	15	16
17	18	19	20	21	22	23
24	25	26	27	28	29	30
31						

APR

S	M	T	W	T	F	S
	1	2	3	4	5	6
7	8	9	10	11	12	13
14	15	16	17	18	19	20
21	22	23	24	25	26	27
28	29	30				

MAY

S	M	T	W	T	F	S
			1	2	3	4
5	6	7	8	9	10	11
12	13	14	15	16	17	18
19	20	21	22	23	24	25
26	27	28	29	30	31	

JUNE

S	M	T	W	T	F	S
						1
2	3	4	5	6	7	8
9	10	11	12	13	14	15
16	17	18	19	20	21	22
23	24	25	26	27	28	29
30						

JULY

S	M	T	W	T	F	S
	1	2	3	4	5	6
7	8	9	10	11	12	13
14	15	16	17	18	19	20
21	22	23	24	25	26	27
28	29	30	31			

AUG

S	M	T	W	T	F	S
				1	2	3
4	5	6	7	8	9	10
11	12	13	14	15	16	17
18	19	20	21	22	23	24
25	26	27	28	29	30	31

SEPT

S	M	T	W	T	F	S
1	2	3	4	5	6	7
8	9	10	11	12	13	14
15	16	17	18	19	20	21
22	23	24	25	26	27	28
29	30					

OCT

S	M	T	W	T	F	S
		1	2	3	4	5
6	7	8	9	10	11	12
13	14	15	16	17	18	19
20	21	22	23	24	25	26
27	28	29	30	31		

NOV

S	M	T	W	T	F	S
					1	2
3	4	5	6	7	8	9
10	11	12	13	14	15	16
17	18	19	20	21	22	23
24	25	26	27	28	29	30

DEC

S	M	T	W	T	F	S
1	2	3	4	5	6	7
8	9	10	11	12	13	14
15	16	17	18	19	20	21
22	23	24	25	26	27	28
29	30	31				

4

JAN

S	M	T	W	T	F	S
			1	2	3	4
5	6	7	8	9	10	11
12	13	14	15	16	17	18
19	20	21	22	23	24	25
26	27	28	29	30	31	

FEB

S	M	T	W	T	F	S
						1
2	3	4	5	6	7	8
9	10	11	12	13	14	15
16	17	18	19	20	21	22
23	24	25	26	27	28	

MAR

S	M	T	W	T	F	S
						1
2	3	4	5	6	7	8
9	10	11	12	13	14	15
16	17	18	19	20	21	22
23	24	25	26	27	28	29
30	31					

APR

S	M	T	W	T	F	S
		1	2	3	4	5
6	7	8	9	10	11	12
13	14	15	16	17	18	19
20	21	22	23	24	25	26
27	28	29	30			

MAY

S	M	T	W	T	F	S
				1	2	3
4	5	6	7	8	9	10
11	12	13	14	15	16	17
18	19	20	21	22	23	24
25	26	27	28	29	30	31

JUNE

S	M	T	W	T	F	S
1	2	3	4	5	6	7
8	9	10	11	12	13	14
15	16	17	18	19	20	21
22	23	24	25	26	27	28
29	30					

JULY

S	M	T	W	T	F	S
		1	2	3	4	5
6	7	8	9	10	11	12
13	14	15	16	17	18	19
20	21	22	23	24	25	26
27	28	29	30	31		

AUG

S	M	T	W	T	F	S
					1	2
3	4	5	6	7	8	9
10	11	12	13	14	15	16
17	18	19	20	21	22	23
24	25	26	27	28	29	30
31						

SEPT

S	M	T	W	T	F	S
	1	2	3	4	5	6
7	8	9	10	11	12	13
14	15	16	17	18	19	20
21	22	23	24	25	26	27
28	29	30				

OCT

S	M	T	W	T	F	S
			1	2	3	4
5	6	7	8	9	10	11
12	13	14	15	16	17	18
19	20	21	22	23	24	25
26	27	28	29	30	31	

NOV

S	M	T	W	T	F	S
						1
2	3	4	5	6	7	8
9	10	11	12	13	14	15
16	17	18	19	20	21	22
23	24	25	26	27	28	29
30						

DEC

S	M	T	W	T	F	S
	1	2	3	4	5	6
7	8	9	10	11	12	13
14	15	16	17	18	19	20
21	22	23	24	25	26	27
28	29	30	31			

5

JAN

S	M	T	W	T	F	S
				1	2	3
4	5	6	7	8	9	10
11	12	13	14	15	16	17
18	19	20	21	22	23	24
25	26	27	28	29	30	31

FEB

S	M	T	W	T	F	S
1	2	3	4	5	6	7
8	9	10	11	12	13	14
15	16	17	18	19	20	21
22	23	24	25	26	27	28

MAR

S	M	T	W	T	F	S
1	2	3	4	5	6	7
8	9	10	11	12	13	14
15	16	17	18	19	20	21
22	23	24	25	26	27	28
29	30	31				

APR

S	M	T	W	T	F	S
			1	2	3	4
5	6	7	8	9	10	11
12	13	14	15	16	17	18
19	20	21	22	23	24	25
26	27	28	29	30		

MAY

S	M	T	W	T	F	S
					1	2
3	4	5	6	7	8	9
10	11	12	13	14	15	16
17	18	19	20	21	22	23
24	25	26	27	28	29	30
31						

JUNE

S	M	T	W	T	F	S
	1	2	3	4	5	6
7	8	9	10	11	12	13
14	15	16	17	18	19	20
21	22	23	24	25	26	27
28	29	30				

JULY

S	M	T	W	T	F	S
			1	2	3	4
5	6	7	8	9	10	11
12	13	14	15	16	17	18
19	20	21	22	23	24	25
26	27	28	29	30	31	

AUG

S	M	T	W	T	F	S
						1
2	3	4	5	6	7	8
9	10	11	12	13	14	15
16	17	18	19	20	21	22
23	24	25	26	27	28	29
30	31					

SEPT

S	M	T	W	T	F	S
		1	2	3	4	5
6	7	8	9	10	11	12
13	14	15	16	17	18	19
20	21	22	23	24	25	26
27	28	29	30			

OCT

S	M	T	W	T	F	S
				1	2	3
4	5	6	7	8	9	10
11	12	13	14	15	16	17
18	19	20	21	22	23	24
25	26	27	28	29	30	31

NOV

S	M	T	W	T	F	S
1	2	3	4	5	6	7
8	9	10	11	12	13	14
15	16	17	18	19	20	21
22	23	24	25	26	27	28
29	30					

DEC

S	M	T	W	T	F	S
		1	2	3	4	5
6	7	8	9	10	11	12
13	14	15	16	17	18	19
20	21	22	23	24	25	26
27	28	29	30	31		

6

2021

JAN

S	M	T	W	T	F	S
					1	2
3	4	5	6	7	8	9
10	11	12	13	14	15	16
17	18	19	20	21	22	23
24	25	26	27	28	29	30
31						

FEB

S	M	T	W	T	F	S
	1	2	3	4	5	6
7	8	9	10	11	12	13
14	15	16	17	18	19	20
21	22	23	24	25	26	27
28						

MAR

S	M	T	W	T	F	S
	1	2	3	4	5	6
7	8	9	10	11	12	13
14	15	16	17	18	19	20
21	22	23	24	25	26	27
28	29	30	31			

APR

S	M	T	W	T	F	S
				1	2	3
4	5	6	7	8	9	10
11	12	13	14	15	16	17
18	19	20	21	22	23	24
25	26	27	28	29	30	

MAY

S	M	T	W	T	F	S
						1
2	3	4	5	6	7	8
9	10	11	12	13	14	15
16	17	18	19	20	21	22
23	24	25	26	27	28	29
30	31					

JUNE

S	M	T	W	T	F	S
		1	2	3	4	5
6	7	8	9	10	11	12
13	14	15	16	17	18	19
20	21	22	23	24	25	26
27	28	29	30			

JULY

S	M	T	W	T	F	S
				1	2	3
4	5	6	7	8	9	10
11	12	13	14	15	16	17
18	19	20	21	22	23	24
25	26	27	28	29	30	31

AUG

S	M	T	W	T	F	S
1	2	3	4	5	6	7
8	9	10	11	12	13	14
15	16	17	18	19	20	21
22	23	24	25	26	27	28
29	30	31				

SEPT

S	M	T	W	T	F	S
			1	2	3	4
5	6	7	8	9	10	11
12	13	14	15	16	17	18
19	20	21	22	23	24	25
26	27	28	29	30		

OCT

S	M	T	W	T	F	S
					1	2
3	4	5	6	7	8	9
10	11	12	13	14	15	16
17	18	19	20	21	22	23
24	25	26	27	28	29	30
31						

NOV

S	M	T	W	T	F	S
	1	2	3	4	5	6
7	8	9	10	11	12	13
14	15	16	17	18	19	20
21	22	23	24	25	26	27
28	29	30				

DEC

S	M	T	W	T	F	S
			1	2	3	4
5	6	7	8	9	10	11
12	13	14	15	16	17	18
19	20	21	22	23	24	25
26	27	28	29	30	31	

7 — 2022

JAN

S	M	T	W	T	F	S
						1
2	3	4	5	6	7	8
9	10	11	12	13	14	15
16	17	18	19	20	21	22
23	24	25	26	27	28	29
30	31					

FEB

S	M	T	W	T	F	S
		1	2	3	4	5
6	7	8	9	10	11	12
13	14	15	16	17	18	19
20	21	22	23	24	25	26
27	28					

MAR

S	M	T	W	T	F	S
		1	2	3	4	5
6	7	8	9	10	11	12
13	14	15	16	17	18	19
20	21	22	23	24	25	26
27	28	29	30	31		

APR

S	M	T	W	T	F	S
					1	2
3	4	5	6	7	8	9
10	11	12	13	14	15	16
17	18	19	20	21	22	23
24	25	26	27	28	29	30

MAY

S	M	T	W	T	F	S
1	2	3	4	5	6	7
8	9	10	11	12	13	14
15	16	17	18	19	20	21
22	23	24	25	26	27	28
29	30	31				

JUNE

S	M	T	W	T	F	S
			1	2	3	4
5	6	7	8	9	10	11
12	13	14	15	16	17	18
19	20	21	22	23	24	25
26	27	28	29	30		

JULY

S	M	T	W	T	F	S
					1	2
3	4	5	6	7	8	9
10	11	12	13	14	15	16
17	18	19	20	21	22	23
24	25	26	27	28	29	30
31						

AUG

S	M	T	W	T	F	S
	1	2	3	4	5	6
7	8	9	10	11	12	13
14	15	16	17	18	19	20
21	22	23	24	25	26	27
28	29	30	31			

SEPT

S	M	T	W	T	F	S
				1	2	3
4	5	6	7	8	9	10
11	12	13	14	15	16	17
18	19	20	21	22	23	24
25	26	27	28	29	30	

OCT

S	M	T	W	T	F	S
						1
2	3	4	5	6	7	8
9	10	11	12	13	14	15
16	17	18	19	20	21	22
23	24	25	26	27	28	29
30	31					

NOV

S	M	T	W	T	F	S
		1	2	3	4	5
6	7	8	9	10	11	12
13	14	15	16	17	18	19
20	21	22	23	24	25	26
27	28	29	30			

DEC

S	M	T	W	T	F	S
				1	2	3
4	5	6	7	8	9	10
11	12	13	14	15	16	17
18	19	20	21	22	23	24
25	26	27	28	29	30	31

8

JAN

S	M	T	W	T	F	S
1	2	3	4	5	6	7
8	9	10	11	12	13	14
15	16	17	18	19	20	21
22	23	24	25	26	27	28
29	30	31				

FEB

S	M	T	W	T	F	S
			1	2	3	4
5	6	7	8	9	10	11
12	13	14	15	16	17	18
19	20	21	22	23	24	25
26	27	28	29			

MAR

S	M	T	W	T	F	S
				1	2	3
4	5	6	7	8	9	10
11	12	13	14	15	16	17
18	19	20	21	22	23	24
25	26	27	28	29	30	31

APR

S	M	T	W	T	F	S
1	2	3	4	5	6	7
8	9	10	11	12	13	14
15	16	17	18	19	20	21
22	23	24	25	26	27	28
29	30					

MAY

S	M	T	W	T	F	S
		1	2	3	4	5
6	7	8	9	10	11	12
13	14	15	16	17	18	19
20	21	22	23	24	25	26
27	28	29	30	31		

JUNE

S	M	T	W	T	F	S
					1	2
3	4	5	6	7	8	9
10	11	12	13	14	15	16
17	18	19	20	21	22	23
24	25	26	27	28	29	30

JULY

S	M	T	W	T	F	S
1	2	3	4	5	6	7
8	9	10	11	12	13	14
15	16	17	18	19	20	21
22	23	24	25	26	27	28
29	30	31				

AUG

S	M	T	W	T	F	S
			1	2	3	4
5	6	7	8	9	10	11
12	13	14	15	16	17	18
19	20	21	22	23	24	25
26	27	28	29	30	31	

SEPT

S	M	T	W	T	F	S
						1
2	3	4	5	6	7	8
9	10	11	12	13	14	15
16	17	18	19	20	21	22
23	24	25	26	27	28	29
30						

OCT

S	M	T	W	T	F	S
1	2	3	4	5	6	
7	8	9	10	11	12	13
14	15	16	17	18	19	20
21	22	23	24	25	26	27
28	29	30	31			

NOV

S	M	T	W	T	F	S
				1	2	3
4	5	6	7	8	9	10
11	12	13	14	15	16	17
18	19	20	21	22	23	24
25	26	27	28	29	30	

DEC

S	M	T	W	T	F	S
						1
2	3	4	5	6	7	8
9	10	11	12	13	14	15
16	17	18	19	20	21	22
23	24	25	26	27	28	29
30	31					

9

JAN

S	M	T	W	T	F	S
	1	2	3	4	5	6
7	8	9	10	11	12	13
14	15	16	17	18	19	20
21	22	23	24	25	26	27
28	29	30	31			

FEB

S	M	T	W	T	F	S
				1	2	3
4	5	6	7	8	9	10
11	12	13	14	15	16	17
18	19	20	21	22	23	24
25	26	27	28	29		

MAR

S	M	T	W	T	F	S
					1	2
3	4	5	6	7	8	9
10	11	12	13	14	15	16
17	18	19	20	21	22	23
24	25	26	27	28	29	30
31						

APR

S	M	T	W	T	F	S
	1	2	3	4	5	6
7	8	9	10	11	12	13
14	15	16	17	18	19	20
21	22	23	24	25	26	27
28	29	30				

MAY

S	M	T	W	T	F	S
			1	2	3	4
5	6	7	8	9	10	11
12	13	14	15	16	17	18
19	20	21	22	23	24	25
26	27	28	29	30	31	

JUNE

S	M	T	W	T	F	S
						1
2	3	4	5	6	7	8
9	10	11	12	13	14	15
16	17	18	19	20	21	22
23	24	25	26	27	28	29
30						

JULY

S	M	T	W	T	F	S
	1	2	3	4	5	6
7	8	9	10	11	12	13
14	15	16	17	18	19	20
21	22	23	24	25	26	27
28	29	30	31			

AUG

S	M	T	W	T	F	S
				1	2	3
4	5	6	7	8	9	10
11	12	13	14	15	16	17
18	19	20	21	22	23	24
25	26	27	28	29	30	31

SEPT

S	M	T	W	T	F	S
1	2	3	4	5	6	7
8	9	10	11	12	13	14
15	16	17	18	19	20	21
22	23	24	25	26	27	28
29	30					

OCT

S	M	T	W	T	F	S
		1	2	3	4	5
6	7	8	9	10	11	12
13	14	15	16	17	18	19
20	21	22	23	24	25	26
27	28	29	30	31		

NOV

S	M	T	W	T	F	S
					1	2
3	4	5	6	7	8	9
10	11	12	13	14	15	16
17	18	19	20	21	22	23
24	25	26	27	28	29	30

DEC

S	M	T	W	T	F	S
1	2	3	4	5	6	7
8	9	10	11	12	13	14
15	16	17	18	19	20	21
22	23	24	25	26	27	28
29	30	31				

10

JAN

S	M	T	W	T	F	S
		1	2	3	4	5
6	7	8	9	10	11	12
13	14	15	16	17	18	19
20	21	22	23	24	25	26
27	28	29	30	31		

FEB

S	M	T	W	T	F	S
					1	2
3	4	5	6	7	8	9
10	11	12	13	14	15	16
17	18	19	20	21	22	23
24	25	26	27	28	29	

MAR

S	M	T	W	T	F	S
						1
2	3	4	5	6	7	8
9	10	11	12	13	14	15
16	17	18	19	20	21	22
23	24	25	26	27	28	29
30	31					

APR

S	M	T	W	T	F	S
		1	2	3	4	5
6	7	8	9	10	11	12
13	14	15	16	17	18	19
20	21	22	23	24	25	26
27	28	29	30			

MAY

S	M	T	W	T	F	S
				1	2	3
4	5	6	7	8	9	10
11	12	13	14	15	16	17
18	19	20	21	22	23	24
25	26	27	28	29	30	31

JUNE

S	M	T	W	T	F	S
1	2	3	4	5	6	7
8	9	10	11	12	13	14
15	16	17	18	19	20	21
22	23	24	25	26	27	28
29	30					

JULY

S	M	T	W	T	F	S
		1	2	3	4	5
6	7	8	9	10	11	12
13	14	15	16	17	18	19
20	21	22	23	24	25	26
27	28	29	30	31		

AUG

S	M	T	W	T	F	S
					1	2
3	4	5	6	7	8	9
10	11	12	13	14	15	16
17	18	19	20	21	22	23
24	25	26	27	28	29	30
31						

SEPT

S	M	T	W	T	F	S
	1	2	3	4	5	6
7	8	9	10	11	12	13
14	15	16	17	18	19	20
21	22	23	24	25	26	27
28	29	30				

OCT

S	M	T	W	T	F	S
			1	2	3	4
5	6	7	8	9	10	11
12	13	14	15	16	17	18
19	20	21	22	23	24	25
26	27	28	29	30	31	

NOV

S	M	T	W	T	F	S
						1
2	3	4	5	6	7	8
9	10	11	12	13	14	15
16	17	18	19	20	21	22
23	24	25	26	27	28	29
30						

DEC

S	M	T	W	T	F	S
	1	2	3	4	5	6
7	8	9	10	11	12	13
14	15	16	17	18	19	20
21	22	23	24	25	26	27
28	29	30	31			

11

2020

JAN	S	M	T	W	T	F	S
				1	2	3	4
	5	6	7	8	9	10	11
	12	13	14	15	16	17	18
	19	20	21	22	23	24	25
	26	27	28	29	30	31	

FEB	S	M	T	W	T	F	S
							1
	2	3	4	5	6	7	8
	9	10	11	12	13	14	15
	16	17	18	19	20	21	22
	23	24	25	26	27	28	29

MAR	S	M	T	W	T	F	S
	1	2	3	4	5	6	7
	8	9	10	11	12	13	14
	15	16	17	18	19	20	21
	22	23	24	25	26	27	28
	29	30	31				

APR	S	M	T	W	T	F	S
				1	2	3	4
	5	6	7	8	9	10	11
	12	13	14	15	16	17	18
	19	20	21	22	23	24	25
	26	27	28	29	30		

MAY	S	M	T	W	T	F	S
						1	2
	3	4	5	6	7	8	9
	10	11	12	13	14	15	16
	17	18	19	20	21	22	23
	24	25	26	27	28	29	30
	31						

JUNE	S	M	T	W	T	F	S
		1	2	3	4	5	6
	7	8	9	10	11	12	13
	14	15	16	17	18	19	20
	21	22	23	24	25	26	27
	28	29	30				

JULY	S	M	T	W	T	F	S
				1	2	3	4
	5	6	7	8	9	10	11
	12	13	14	15	16	17	18
	19	20	21	22	23	24	25
	26	27	28	29	30	31	

AUG	S	M	T	W	T	F	S
							1
	2	3	4	5	6	7	8
	9	10	11	12	13	14	15
	16	17	18	19	20	21	22
	23	24	25	26	27	28	29
	30	31					

SEPT	S	M	T	W	T	F	S
			1	2	3	4	5
	6	7	8	9	10	11	12
	13	14	15	16	17	18	19
	20	21	22	23	24	25	26
	27	28	29	30			

OCT	S	M	T	W	T	F	S
					1	2	3
	4	5	6	7	8	9	10
	11	12	13	14	15	16	17
	18	19	20	21	22	23	24
	25	26	27	28	29	30	31

NOV	S	M	T	W	T	F	S
	1	2	3	4	5	6	7
	8	9	10	11	12	13	14
	15	16	17	18	19	20	21
	22	23	24	25	26	27	28
	29	30					

DEC	S	M	T	W	T	F	S
			1	2	3	4	5
	6	7	8	9	10	11	12
	13	14	15	16	17	18	19
	20	21	22	23	24	25	26
	27	28	29	30	31		

12

JAN	S	M	T	W	T	F	S
					1	2	3
	4	5	6	7	8	9	10
	11	12	13	14	15	16	17
	18	19	20	21	22	23	24
	25	26	27	28	29	30	31

FEB	S	M	T	W	T	F	S
	1	2	3	4	5	6	7
	8	9	10	11	12	13	14
	15	16	17	18	19	20	21
	22	23	24	25	26	27	28
	29						

MAR	S	M	T	W	T	F	S
		1	2	3	4	5	6
	7	8	9	10	11	12	13
	14	15	16	17	18	19	20
	21	22	23	24	25	26	27
	28	29	30	31			

APR	S	M	T	W	T	F	S
					1	2	3
	4	5	6	7	8	9	10
	11	12	13	14	15	16	17
	18	19	20	21	22	23	24
	25	26	27	28	29	30	

MAY	S	M	T	W	T	F	S
							1
	2	3	4	5	6	7	8
	9	10	11	12	13	14	15
	16	17	18	19	20	21	22
	23	24	25	26	27	28	29
	30	31					

JUNE	S	M	T	W	T	F	S
			1	2	3	4	5
	6	7	8	9	10	11	12
	13	14	15	16	17	18	19
	20	21	22	23	24	25	26
	27	28	29	30			

JULY	S	M	T	W	T	F	S
					1	2	3
	4	5	6	7	8	9	10
	11	12	13	14	15	16	17
	18	19	20	21	22	23	24
	25	26	27	28	29	30	31

AUG	S	M	T	W	T	F	S
	1	2	3	4	5	6	7
	8	9	10	11	12	13	14
	15	16	17	18	19	20	21
	22	23	24	25	26	27	28
	29	30	31				

SEPT	S	M	T	W	T	F	S
				1	2	3	4
	5	6	7	8	9	10	11
	12	13	14	15	16	17	18
	19	20	21	22	23	24	25
	26	27	28	29	30		

OCT	S	M	T	W	T	F	S
						1	2
	3	4	5	6	7	8	9
	10	11	12	13	14	15	16
	17	18	19	20	21	22	23
	24	25	26	27	28	29	30
	31						

NOV	S	M	T	W	T	F	S
		1	2	3	4	5	6
	7	8	9	10	11	12	13
	14	15	16	17	18	19	20
	21	22	23	24	25	26	27
	28	29	30				

DEC	S	M	T	W	T	F	S
				1	2	3	4
	5	6	7	8	9	10	11
	12	13	14	15	16	17	18
	19	20	21	22	23	24	25
	26	27	28	29	30	31	

13

JAN	S	M	T	W	T	F	S
						1	2
	3	4	5	6	7	8	9
	10	11	12	13	14	15	16
	17	18	19	20	21	22	23
	24	25	26	27	28	29	30
	31						

FEB	S	M	T	W	T	F	S
		1	2	3	4	5	6
	7	8	9	10	11	12	13
	14	15	16	17	18	19	20
	21	22	23	24	25	26	27
	28	29					

MAR	S	M	T	W	T	F	S
			1	2	3	4	5
	6	7	8	9	10	11	12
	13	14	15	16	17	18	19
	20	21	22	23	24	25	26
	27	28	29	30	31		

APR	S	M	T	W	T	F	S
						1	2
	3	4	5	6	7	8	9
	10	11	12	13	14	15	16
	17	18	19	20	21	22	23
	24	25	26	27	28	29	30

MAY	S	M	T	W	T	F	S
	1	2	3	4	5	6	7
	8	9	10	11	12	13	14
	15	16	17	18	19	20	21
	22	23	24	25	26	27	28
	29	30	31				

JUNE	S	M	T	W	T	F	S
				1	2	3	4
	5	6	7	8	9	10	11
	12	13	14	15	16	17	18
	19	20	21	22	23	24	25
	26	27	28	29	30		

JULY	S	M	T	W	T	F	S
						1	2
	3	4	5	6	7	8	9
	10	11	12	13	14	15	16
	17	18	19	20	21	22	23
	24	25	26	27	28	29	30
	31						

AUG	S	M	T	W	T	F	S
		1	2	3	4	5	6
	7	8	9	10	11	12	13
	14	15	16	17	18	19	20
	21	22	23	24	25	26	27
	28	29	30	31			

SEPT	S	M	T	W	T	F	S
					1	2	3
	4	5	6	7	8	9	10
	11	12	13	14	15	16	17
	18	19	20	21	22	23	24
	25	26	27	28	29	30	

OCT	S	M	T	W	T	F	S
							1
	2	3	4	5	6	7	8
	9	10	11	12	13	14	15
	16	17	18	19	20	21	22
	23	24	25	26	27	28	29
	30	31					

NOV	S	M	T	W	T	F	S
			1	2	3	4	5
	6	7	8	9	10	11	12
	13	14	15	16	17	18	19
	20	21	22	23	24	25	26
	27	28	29	30			

DEC	S	M	T	W	T	F	S
					1	2	3
	4	5	6	7	8	9	10
	11	12	13	14	15	16	17
	18	19	20	21	22	23	24
	25	26	27	28	29	30	31

14

JAN	S	M	T	W	T	F	S
							1
	2	3	4	5	6	7	8
	9	10	11	12	13	14	15
	16	17	18	19	20	21	22
	23	24	25	26	27	28	29
	30	31					

FEB	S	M	T	W	T	F	S
			1	2	3	4	5
	6	7	8	9	10	11	12
	13	14	15	16	17	18	19
	20	21	22	23	24	25	26
	27	28	29				

MAR	S	M	T	W	T	F	S
				1	2	3	4
	5	6	7	8	9	10	11
	12	13	14	15	16	17	18
	19	20	21	22	23	24	25
	26	27	28	29	30	31	

APR	S	M	T	W	T	F	S
							1
	2	3	4	5	6	7	8
	9	10	11	12	13	14	15
	16	17	18	19	20	21	22
	23	24	25	26	27	28	29
	30						

MAY	S	M	T	W	T	F	S
		1	2	3	4	5	6
	7	8	9	10	11	12	13
	14	15	16	17	18	19	20
	21	22	23	24	25	26	27
	28	29	30	31			

JUNE	S	M	T	W	T	F	S
					1	2	3
	4	5	6	7	8	9	10
	11	12	13	14	15	16	17
	18	19	20	21	22	23	24
	25	26	27	28	29	30	

JULY	S	M	T	W	T	F	S
							1
	2	3	4	5	6	7	8
	9	10	11	12	13	14	15
	16	17	18	19	20	21	22
	23	24	25	26	27	28	29
	30	31					

AUG	S	M	T	W	T	F	S
			1	2	3	4	5
	6	7	8	9	10	11	12
	13	14	15	16	17	18	19
	20	21	22	23	24	25	26
	27	28	29	30	31		

SEPT	S	M	T	W	T	F	S
						1	2
	3	4	5	6	7	8	9
	10	11	12	13	14	15	16
	17	18	19	20	21	22	23
	24	25	26	27	28	29	30

OCT	S	M	T	W	T	F	S
	1	2	3	4	5	6	7
	8	9	10	11	12	13	14
	15	16	17	18	19	20	21
	22	23	24	25	26	27	28
	29	30	31				

NOV	S	M	T	W	T	F	S
				1	2	3	4
	5	6	7	8	9	10	11
	12	13	14	15	16	17	18
	19	20	21	22	23	24	25
	26	27	28	29	30		

DEC	S	M	T	W	T	F	S
						1	2
	3	4	5	6	7	8	9
	10	11	12	13	14	15	16
	17	18	19	20	21	22	23
	24	25	26	27	28	29	30
	31						

National Days of the World for 2020

(Compiled from publications of the U.S. Department of State, the United Nations and from information received from the countries listed.)

Most nations set aside one or more days each year as national public holidays, often recognizing the anniversary of the attainment of independence or the birthday of the country's ruler. It should be noted that in some countries the Gregorian Calendar date of observance varies from year to year. See the Index and the main chronology for further details of observance and for numerous holidays in addition to the national days listed here.

Afghanistan .... Aug 19
Albania .... Nov 28
Algeria .... July 5
Andorra .... Sept 8
Angola .... Nov 11
Antigua and Barbuda .... Nov 1
Argentina .... July 9
Armenia .... Sept 21
Australia .... Jan 26
Austria .... Oct 26
Azerbaijan .... May 28
Bahamas .... July 10
Bahrain .... Dec 16
Bangladesh .... Mar 26
Barbados .... Nov 30
Belarus .... July 3
Belgium .... July 21
Belize .... Sept 21
Benin .... Aug 1
Bhutan .... Dec 17
Bolivia .... Aug 6
Bosnia and Herzegovina .... Mar 1
Botswana .... Sept 30
Brazil .... Sept 7
Brunei Darussalam .... Feb 23
Bulgaria .... Mar 3
Burkina Faso .... Dec 11
Burundi .... July 1
Cambodia .... Nov 9
Cameroon .... May 20
Canada .... July 1
Cape Verde .... July 5
Central African Republic .... Dec 1
Chad .... Aug 11
Chile .... Sept 18
China .... Oct 1
Colombia .... July 20
Comoros .... July 6
Congo .... Aug 15
Congo, Democratic Republic of .... June 30
Costa Rica .... Sept 15
Cote D'Ivoire .... Aug 7
Croatia .... Oct 8
Cuba .... Jan 1
Cyprus .... Oct 1
Czech Republic .... Oct 28
Denmark .... June 5
Djibouti .... June 27
Dominica .... Nov 3
Dominican Republic .... Feb 27
Ecuador .... Aug 10
Egypt .... July 23
El Salvador .... Sept 15
Equatorial Guinea .... Oct 12
Eritrea .... May 24
Estonia .... Feb 24
Ethiopia .... May 28
Fiji .... Oct 14
Finland .... Dec 6
France .... July 14
Gabon .... Aug 17
Gambia .... Feb 18
Georgia .... May 26
Germany .... Oct 3
Ghana .... Mar 6
Greece .... Mar 25
Grenada .... Feb 7
Guatemala .... Sept 15
Guinea .... Oct 2
Guinea-Bissau .... Sept 24
Guyana .... Feb 23
Haiti .... Jan 1
Holy See .... Mar 13
Honduras .... Sept 15
Hungary .... Aug 20
Iceland .... June 17
India .... Jan 26
Indonesia .... Aug 17
Iran .... Apr 1
Iraq .... July 14
Ireland .... Mar 17
Israel .... Apr 29
Italy .... June 2
Jamaica .... Aug 3
Japan .... Dec 23
Jordan .... May 25
Kazakhstan .... Dec 16
Kenya .... Dec 12
Kiribati .... July 12
Korea, Democratic People's Republic of .... Sept 9
Korea, Republic of .... Aug 15
Kosovo, Republic of .... Feb 17
Kuwait .... Feb 25
Kyrgyzstan .... Aug 31
Lao People's Democratic Republic .... Dec 2
Latvia .... Nov 18
Lebanon .... Nov 22
Lesotho .... Oct 4
Liberia .... July 26
Libya .... Oct 23
Liechtenstein .... Aug 15
Lithuania .... Feb 16
Luxembourg .... June 23
Macedonia .... Sept 8
Madagascar .... June 26
Malawi .... July 6
Malaysia .... Aug 31
Maldives .... July 26
Mali .... Sept 22
Malta .... Sept 21
Marshall Islands .... May 1
Mauritania .... Nov 28
Mauritius .... Mar 12
Mexico .... Sept 16
Micronesia (Federated States of) .... May 10
Moldova, Republic of .... Aug 27
Monaco .... Nov 19
Mongolia .... Dec 29
Montenegro, Republic of .... July 13
Morocco .... July 30
Mozambique .... June 25
Myanmar .... Jan 4
Namibia, Republic of .... Mar 21
Nauru .... Jan 31
Nepal .... May 29
Netherlands .... Apr 27
New Zealand .... Feb 6
Nicaragua .... Sept 15
Niger .... Dec 18
Nigeria .... Oct 1
Norway .... May 17
Oman .... Nov 18
Pakistan .... Mar 23
Palau, Republic of .... July 9
Panama .... Nov 3
Papua New Guinea .... Sept 16
Paraguay .... May 15
Peru .... July 28
Philippines .... June 12
Poland .... May 3
Portugal .... June 10
Qatar .... Sept 3
Romania .... Dec 1
Russian Federation .... June 12
Rwanda .... July 1
Saint Christopher (St Kitts) and Nevis .... Sept 19
Saint Lucia .... Feb 22
Saint Vincent and the Grenadines .... Oct 27
Samoa .... June 1
San Marino .... Sept 3
Sao Tome and Principe .... July 12
Saudi Arabia .... Sept 23
Senegal .... Apr 4
Serbia .... Feb 15
Seychelles .... June 18
Sierra Leone .... Apr 27
Singapore .... Aug 9
Slovakia .... Sept 1
Slovenia .... June 25
Solomon Islands .... July 7
Somalia .... July 1
South Africa .... Apr 27
South Sudan .... July 9
Spain .... Oct 12
Sri Lanka .... Feb 4
Sudan .... Jan 1
Suriname .... Nov 25
Swaziland .... Sept 6
Sweden .... June 6
Switzerland .... Aug 1
Syria .... Apr 17
Taiwan .... Oct 10
Tajikistan .... Sept 9
Tanzania, United Republic of .... Apr 26
Thailand .... July 28
Timor-Leste .... May 20
Togo .... Apr 27
Tonga .... June 4
Trinidad and Tobago .... Aug 31
Tunisia .... Mar 20
Turkey .... Oct 29
Turkmenistan .... Oct 27
Tuvalu .... Oct 1
Uganda .... Oct 9
Ukraine .... Aug 24
United Arab Emirates .... Dec 2
United Kingdom .... †
United States of America .... July 4
Uruguay .... Aug 25
Uzbekistan .... Sept 1
Vanuatu .... July 30
Venezuela .... July 5
Vietnam .... Sept 2
Yemen .... May 22
Zambia .... Oct 26
Zimbabwe .... Apr 18

†United Kingdom does not observe a national day.

Selected Special Years: 2000–2020

As sponsored by the United Nations (unless otherwise indicated)

Intl Year for the Culture of Peace: 2000
Intl Year of Thanksgiving: 2000
Intl Year of Volunteers: 2001
Year of Dialogue Among Civilizations: 2001
Intl Year of Mobilization Against Racism: 2001
Intl Year of Mountains: 2002
Intl Year of Ecotourism: 2002
Year for Cultural Heritage: 2002
Intl Year of Freshwater: 2003
Year of Kyrgyz Statehood: 2003
Intl Year to Commemorate the Struggle against Slavery and its Abolition: 2004
Intl Year of Rice: 2004
Intl Year of Microcredit: 2005
Intl Year of Physics: 2005
Intl Year for Sport and Physical Education: 2005
Intl Year of Deserts and Desertification: 2006
Intl Polar Year: 2007
Intl Year of Languages: 2008
Intl Year of the Potato: 2008
Intl Year of Planet Earth: 2008
Intl Year of Sanitation: 2008
Intl Year of Astronomy: 2009
Intl Year of Natural Fibers: 2009
Intl Year of Reconciliation: 2009
Intl Year of Human Rights Learning: 2009
Year of the Gorilla (UNEP and UNESCO): 2009

Intl Year for the Rapprochement of Cultures: 2010
Intl Year of Youth: Aug 12, 2010–Aug 11, 2011
Intl Year of Biodiversity: 2010
Intl Year of the Seafarer: 2010
Intl Year of Forests: 2011
Intl Year of Chemistry: 2011
Intl Year for People of African Descent: 2011
Alan Turing Year (Turing Centenary Advisory Committee): 2012
Intl Year of Cooperatives: 2012
Intl Year of Sustainable Energy for All: 2012
Intl Year of Water Cooperation: 2013
Intl Year of Quinoa: 2013
Intl Year of Solidarity with the Palestinian People: 2014
Intl Year of Crystallography: 2014
Intl Year of Family Farming: 2014
Intl Year of Small Island Developing States: 2014
Intl Year of Light and Light-Based Technologies: 2015
Intl Year of Soils: 2015
Intl Year of Pulses: 2016
Intl Year of Sustainable Tourism for Development: 2017
Intl Year of the Reef (Intl Coral Reef Initiative): 2018
Intl Year of Indigenous Languages: 2019
Intl Year of Moderation: 2019
Intl Year of the Periodic Table of Chemical Elements: 2019
Intl Year of Plant Health: 2020
Year of the Nurse and Midwife: 2020

Chinese Calendar

The Chinese lunar year is divided into 12 months of 29 or 30 days. The calendar is adjusted to the length of the solar year by the addition of extra months at regular intervals. The years are arranged in major cycles of 60 years. Each successive year is named after one of 12 animals. These 12-year cycles are continuously repeated.

2020	Rat	2026	Horse
2021	Ox	2027	Sheep (Goat)
2022	Tiger	2028	Monkey
2023	Hare	2029	Rooster
2024	Dragon	2030	Dog
2025	Snake	2031	Boar (Pig)

World Map of Time Zones

Reprinted courtesy of Her Majesty's Nautical Almanac Office and the UK Hydrographic Office.

Standard Time = Universal Time − value from table
Universal Time = Standard Time + value from table

	h m		h m		h m
Z	0	D*	−4 30	L	−11	Q* +4 30	V +9
A	−1	E	−5	L*	−11 30	R +5	V* +9 30
B	−2	E*	−5 30	M	−12	S +6	W +10
C	−3	F	−6	M*	−13	P* +3 30	T +7	X +11
C*	−3 30	F*	−6 30	M†	−14	Q +4	U +8	Y +12
D	−4	G	−7				

‡ No Standard Time legally adopted

STANDARD TIME ZONES

Corrected to February 2008

Zone boundaries are approximate

Daylight Saving Time (*Summer Time*),
usually one hour in advance of Standard
Time, is kept in some places

Map outline © *Mountain High Maps*
Compiled by HM Nautical Almanac Office

Universal, Standard and Daylight Times

Universal Time (UT) is also known as Greenwich Mean Time (GMT) and is the standard time of the Greenwich meridian (longitude 0°). A time given in UT may be converted to local mean time by the addition of east longitude (or the subtraction of west longitude), where the longitude of the place is expressed in time-measure at the rate of one hour for every 15°. Local clock times may differ from standard times, especially in summer when clocks are often advanced by one hour ("daylight saving" or "summer" time).

The time used in this book is Eastern Standard Time. The following table provides conversion between Universal Time and all time zones in the United States. An asterisk denotes that the time is on the preceding day.

UNIVERSAL TIME	EASTERN DAYLIGHT TIME	EASTERN STANDARD TIME AND CENTRAL DAYLIGHT TIME	CENTRAL STANDARD TIME AND MOUNTAIN DAYLIGHT TIME	MOUNTAIN STANDARD TIME AND PACIFIC DAYLIGHT TIME	PACIFIC STANDARD TIME
0^h	*8 PM	*7 PM	*6 PM	*5 PM	*4 PM
1	*9	*8	*7	*6	*5
2	*10	*9	*8	*7	*6
3	*11 PM	*10	*9	*8	*7
4	0 MIDNIGHT	*11 PM	*10	*9	*8
5	1 AM	0 MIDNIGHT	*11 PM	*10	*9
6	2	1 AM	0 MIDNIGHT	*11 PM	*10
7	3	2	1 AM	0 MIDNIGHT	*11 PM
8	4	3	2	1 AM	0 MIDNIGHT
9	5	4	3	2	1 AM
10	6	5	4	3	2
11	7	6	5	4	3
12	8	7	6	5	4
13	9	8	7	6	5
14	10	9	8	7	6
15	11 AM	10	9	8	7
16	12 NOON	11 AM	10	9	8
17	1 PM	12 NOON	11 AM	10	9
18	2	1 PM	12 NOON	11 AM	10
19	3	2	1 PM	12 NOON	11 AM
20	4	3	2	1 PM	12 NOON
21	5	4	3	2	1 PM
22	6	5	4	3	2
23	7 PM	6 PM	5 PM	4 PM	3 PM

The longitudes of the standard meridians for the standard time zones are:

Eastern . . . . . 75° West Central . . . . . 90° West Mountain . . . . . 105° West Pacific . . . . . 120° West

Leap Seconds

The information below is developed by the editors from data supplied by the US Naval Observatory.

Because of Earth's slightly erratic rotation and the need for greater precision in time measurement, it has become necessary to add a "leap second" from time to time to clocks to coordinate them with astronomical time. Rotation of the Earth has been slowing since 1900, making an astronomical second longer than an atomic second. Since 1972, by international agreement, adjustments have been made to keep astronomical and atomic clocks within 0.9 seconds of each other. The determination to add (or subtract) seconds is made by the Central Bureau of the International Earth Rotation Service, in Paris. Preferred times for adjustment have been June 30 and Dec 31, but any time may be designated by the International Earth Rotation Service. The first such adjustment was made in 1972, and as of July 2019, a total of 27 leap seconds had been added. The additions have been made at 23:59:60 UTC (Coordinated Universal Time), 6:59:60 PM EST (Eastern Standard Time). Leap seconds have been inserted into the UTC time scale on the following dates:

June 30, 1972	Dec 31, 1976	June 30, 1982	Dec 31, 1990	June 30, 1997	June 30, 2015
Dec 31, 1972	Dec 31, 1977	June 30, 1983	June 30, 1992	Dec 31, 1998	Dec 31, 2016
Dec 31, 1973	Dec 31, 1978	June 30, 1985	June 30, 1993	Dec 31, 2005	
Dec 31, 1974	Dec 31, 1979	Dec 31, 1987	June 30, 1994	Dec 31, 2008	
Dec 31, 1975	June 30, 1981	Dec 31, 1989	Dec 31, 1995	June 30, 2012	

Astronomical Phenomena for the Years 2020–2022

All dates are given in terms of Eastern Standard or Daylight Time and the Gregorian calendar.

(Based in part on information prepared by the Nautical Almanac Office, US Naval Observatory.)

2020

PRINCIPAL PHENOMENA, EARTH

Perihelion . . . . Jan 5
Aphelion . . . . .July 4
Equinoxes . . . . Mar 19, Sept 22
Solstices. . . . . June 20, Dec 21

PHASES OF THE MOON

● New Moon	☽ First Quarter	○ Full Moon	☾ Last Quarter
	Jan 2	Jan 10	Jan 17
Jan 24	Feb 1	Feb 9	Feb 15
Feb 23	Mar 2	Mar 9	Mar 16
Mar 24	Apr 1	Apr 7	Apr 14
Apr 22	Apr 30	May 7	May 14
May 22	May 29	June 5	June 13
June 21	June 28	July 5	July 12
July 20	July 27	Aug 3	Aug 11
Aug 18	Aug 25	Sept 2	Sept 10
Sept 17	Sept 23	Oct 1	Oct 9
Oct 16	Oct 23	Oct 31	Nov 8
Nov 15	Nov 21	Nov 30	Dec 7
Dec 14	Dec 21	Dec 29	

ECLIPSES

Penumbral eclipse of the moon. . . . . Jan 10
Penumbral eclipse of the moon. . . . . .June 5
Annular eclipse of the sun . . . . June 21
Partial eclipse of the moon . . . . July 5
Partial eclipse of the moon . . . . Nov 30
Total eclipse of the sun . . . . Dec 14

2021

PRINCIPAL PHENOMENA, EARTH

Perihelion . . . . Jan 2
Aphelion . . . . July 5
Equinoxes . . . . .Mar 20, Sept 22
Solstices . . . . June 20, Dec 21

PHASES OF THE MOON

● New Moon	☽ First Quarter	○ Full Moon	☾ Last Quarter
			Jan 6
Jan 13	Jan 20	Jan 28	Feb 4
Feb 11	Feb 19	Feb 27	Mar 5
Mar 13	Mar 21	Mar 28	Apr 4
Apr 11	Apr 20	Apr 26	May 3
May 11	May 19	May 26	June 2
June 10	June 17	June 24	July 1
July 9	July 17	July 23	July 31
Aug 8	Aug 15	Aug 22	Aug 30
Sept 6	Sept 13	Sept 20	Sept 28
Oct 6	Oct 12	Oct 20	Oct 28
Nov 4	Nov 11	Nov 19	Nov 27
Dec 4	Dec 10	Dec 18	Dec 26

ECLIPSES

Total eclipse of the moon . . . . May 26
Annular eclipse of the sun . . . . .June 10
Partial eclipse of the moon . . . . Nov 19
Total eclipse of the sun . . . . Dec 4

2022

PRINCIPAL PHENOMENA, EARTH

Perihelion . . . . Jan 4
Aphelion . . . . July 4
Equinoxes . . . . .Mar 20, Sept 22
Solstices . . . . June 21, Dec 21

PHASES OF THE MOON

● New Moon	☽ First Quarter	○ Full Moon	☾ Last Quarter
Jan 2	Jan 9	Jan 17	Jan 25
Feb 1	Feb 8	Feb 16	Feb 23
Mar 2	Mar 10	Mar 18	Mar 25
Apr 1	Apr 9	Apr 16	Apr 23
Apr 30	May 8	May 16	May 22
May 30	June 7	June 14	June 20
June 28	July 6	July 13	July 20
July 28	Aug 5	Aug 11	Aug 19
Aug 27	Sept 3	Sept 10	Sept 17
Sept 25	Oct 2	Oct 9	Oct 17
Oct 25	Nov 1	Nov 8	Nov 16
Nov 23	Nov 30	Dec 7	Dec 16
Dec 23	Dec 29		

ECLIPSES

Partial eclipse of the sun . . . . Apr 30
Total eclipse of the moon . . . . May 16
Partial eclipse of the sun . . . . .Oct 25
Total eclipse of the moon . . . . Nov 8

The Naming of Hurricanes

Why are hurricanes named? Experience shows that the use of short, distinctive names greatly reduces confusion when two or more tropical storms occur at the same time. The use of easily remembered names in written and spoken communication is quicker and less subject to error than the older, more cumbersome latitude-longitude identification methods, advantages which are especially important in exchanging detailed storm information between hundreds of widely scattered stations, airports, coastal bases and ships at sea.

During World War II forecasters and meteorologists began using female names for storms in weather map discussions, and in 1953 the US weather services adopted the practice, creating a new international phonetic alphabet of women's names from A–W to name hurricanes. In 1978 men's names were also introduced into the storm lists.

Because hurricanes affect other nations and are tracked by their weather services, the lists have an international flavor. Names are agreed upon during international meetings of the World Meteorological Organization by the nations involved, and can be retired and replaced with new names in the event of particularly severe storms. For example, Iniki—the name of the hurricane that devastated Hawaii—has been replaced with Iolana on List 2.

The National Hurricane Center near Miami, FL, keeps a constant watch on oceanic storm-breeding areas for tropical disturbances that may herald the formation of a hurricane. If a disturbance intensifies into a tropical storm—with rotary circulation and wind speeds above 39 miles per hour—the Center will give the storm a name from one of six lists. The Atlantic and Eastern Pacific lists are rotated year by year so that the 2020 set, for example, will be used again to name storms in 2026.

The lists of names for Central Pacific and Western Pacific hurricanes (tropical cyclones) are not rotated on a yearly basis. Meteorologists follow each list until all those names have been used, then go on to the next list.

ATLANTIC HURRICANE NAMES

2020	2021	2022
Arthur	Ana	Alex
Bertha	Bill	Bonnie
Cristobal	Claudette	Colin
Dolly	Danny	Danielle
Edouard	Elsa	Earl
Fay	Fred	Fiona
Gonzalo	Grace	Gaston
Hanna	Henri	Hermine
Isaias	Ida	Ian
Josephine	Julian	Julia
Kyle	Kate	Karl
Laura	Larry	Lisa
Marco	Mindy	Martin
Nana	Nicholas	Nicole
Omar	Odette	Owen
Paulette	Peter	Paula
Rene	Rose	Richard
Sally	Sam	Shary
Teddy	Teresa	Tobias
Vicky	Victor	Virginie
Wilfred	Wanda	Walter

EASTERN PACIFIC HURRICANE NAMES

2020	2021	2022
Amanda	Andres	Agatha
Boris	Blanca	Blas
Cristina	Carlos	Celia
Douglas	Dolores	Darby
Elida	Enrique	Estelle
Fausto	Felicia	Frank
Genevieve	Guillermo	Georgette
Hernan	Hilda	Howard
Iselle	Ignacio	Ivette
Julio	Jimena	Javier
Karina	Kevin	Kay
Lowell	Linda	Lester
Marie	Marty	Madeline
Norbert	Nora	Newton
Odalys	Olaf	Orlene
Polo	Pamela	Paine
Rachel	Rick	Roslyn
Simon	Sandra	Seymour
Trudy	Terry	Tina
Vance	Vivian	Virgil
Winnie	Waldo	Winifred
Xavier	Xina	Xavier
Yolanda	York	Yolanda
Zeke	Zelda	Zeke

If more than 24 tropical cyclones occur in a year, then the Greek alphabet will be used following Zelda or Zeke.

CENTRAL PACIFIC TROPICAL CYCLONE NAMES

LIST 1	LIST 2	LIST 3	LIST 4
Akoni	Aka	Alika	Ana
Ema	Ekeka	Ele	Ela
Hone	Hene	Huko	Halola
Iona	Iolana	Iopa	Iune
Keli	Keoni	Kika	Kilo
Lala	Lino	Lana	Loke
Moke	Mele	Maka	Malia
Nolo	Nona	Neki	Niala
Olana	Oliwa	Omeka	Oho
Pena	Pama	Pewa	Pali
Ulana	Upana	Unala	Ulika
Wale	Wene	Wali	Walaka

WESTERN PACIFIC TROPICAL CYCLONE NAMES

LIST 1	LIST 2	LIST 3	LIST 4	LIST 5
Damrey	Kong-rey	Nakri	Krovanh	Trases
Haikui	Yutu	Fengshen	Dujuan	Mulan
Kirogi	Toraji	Kalmaegi	Surigae	Meari
Yun-Yeung	Man-yi	Fung-wong	Choi-wan	Ma-on
Koinu	Usagi	Kanmuri	Koguma	Tokage
Bolaven	Pabuk	Phanfone	Champi	Hinnamnor
Sanba	Wutip	Vongfong	In-fa	Muifa
Jelawat	Sepat	Nuri	Cempaka	Merbok
Ewiniar	Mun	Sinlaku	Nepartak	Nanmadol
Maliksi	Danas	Hagupit	Lupit	Talas
Gaemi	Nari	Jangmi	Mirinae	Noru
Prapiroon	Wipha	Mekkhala	Nida	Kulap
Maria	Francisco	Higos	Omais	Roke
Son-Tinh	Lekima	Bavi	Conson	Sonca
Ampil	Krosa	Maysak	Chanthu	Nesat
Wukong	Bailu	Haishen	Dianmu	Haitang
Jongdari	Podul	Noul	Mindulle	Nalgae
Shanshan	Lingling	Dolphin	Lionrock	Banyan
Yagi	Kajiki	Kujira	Kompasu	Yamaneko
Leepi	Faxai	Chan-hom	Namtheun	Pakhar
Bebinca	Peipah	Linfa	Malou	Sanvu
Rumbia	Tapah	Nangka	Nyatoh	Mawar
Soulik	Mitag	Saudel	Rai	Guchol
Cimaron	Hagibis	Molave	Malakas	Talim
Jebi	Neoguri	Goni	Megi	Doksuri
Mangkhut	Bualoi	Atsani	Chaba	Khanun
Barijat	Matmo	Etau	Aere	Lan
Trami	Halong	Vamco	Songda	Saola

Some Facts About the US Presidents

	NAME	BIRTHDATE, PLACE	PARTY	TENURE	DIED	FIRST LADY	VICE PRESIDENT
1.	George Washington	2/22/1732, Westmoreland Cnty, VA	Federalist	1789–1797	12/14/1799	Martha Dandridge Custis	John Adams
2.	John Adams	10/30/1735, Braintree (Quincy), MA	Federalist	1797–1801	7/4/1826	Abigail Smith	Thomas Jefferson
3.	Thomas Jefferson	4/13/1743, Shadwell, VA	Democratic-Republican	1801–1809	7/4/1826	Martha Wayles Skelton	Aaron Burr, 1801–05 George Clinton, 1805–09
4.	James Madison	3/16/1751, Port Conway, VA	Democratic-Republican	1809–1817	6/28/1836	Dolley Payne Todd	George Clinton, 1809–12 Elbridge Gerry, 1813–14
5.	James Monroe	4/28/1758, Westmoreland Cnty, VA	Democratic-Republican	1817–1825	7/4/1831	Elizabeth Kortright	Daniel D. Tompkins
6.	John Q. Adams	7/11/1767, Braintree (Quincy), MA	Democratic-Republican	1825–1829	2/23/1848	Louisa Catherine Johnson	John C. Calhoun
7.	Andrew Jackson	3/15/1767, Waxhaw Settlement, SC	Democrat	1829–1837	6/8/1845	Mrs. Rachel Donelson Robards	John C. Calhoun, 1829–32 Martin Van Buren, 1833–37
8.	Martin Van Buren	12/5/1782, Kinderhook, NY	Democrat	1837–1841	7/24/1862	Hannah Hoes	Richard M. Johnson
9.	William H. Harrison	2/9/1773, Charles City Cnty, VA	Whig	1841	4/4/1841†	Anna Symmes	John Tyler
10.	John Tyler	3/29/1790, Charles City Cnty, VA	Whig	1841–1845	1/18/1862	Letitia Christian Julia Gardiner	
11.	James K. Polk	11/2/1795, near Pineville, NC	Democrat	1845–1849	6/15/1849	Sarah Childress	George M. Dallas
12.	Zachary Taylor	11/24/1784, Barboursville, VA	Whig	1849–1850	7/9/1850†	Margaret Mackall Smith	Millard Fillmore
13.	Millard Fillmore	1/7/1800, Locke, NY	Whig	1850–1853	3/8/1874	Abigail Powers Mrs. Caroline Carmichael McIntosh	
14.	Franklin Pierce	11/23/1804, Hillsborough, NH	Democrat	1853–1857	10/8/1869	Jane Means Appleton	William R. D. King
15.	James Buchanan	4/23/1791, near Mercersburg, PA	Democrat	1857–1861	6/1/1868		John C. Breckinridge
16.	Abraham Lincoln	2/12/1809, near Hodgenville, KY	Republican	1861–1865	4/15/1865*	Mary Todd	Hannibal Hamlin, 1861–65 Andrew Johnson, 1865
17.	Andrew Johnson	12/29/1808, Raleigh, NC	Democrat	1865–1869	7/31/1875	Eliza McCardle	
18.	Ulysses S. Grant	4/27/1822, Point Pleasant, OH	Republican	1869–1877	7/23/1885	Julia Boggs Dent	Schuyler Colfax, 1869–73 Henry Wilson, 1873–75
19.	Rutherford B. Hayes	10/4/1822, Delaware, OH	Republican	1877–1881	1/17/1893	Lucy Ware Webb	William A. Wheeler
20.	James A. Garfield	11/19/1831, Orange, OH	Republican	1881	9/19/1881*	Lucretia Rudolph	Chester A. Arthur

NAME	BIRTHDATE, PLACE	PARTY	TENURE	DIED	FIRST LADY	VICE PRESIDENT
21. Chester A. Arthur	10/5/1829, Fairfield, VT	Republican	1881–1885	11/18/1886	Ellen Lewis Herndon	
22. Grover Cleveland	3/18/1837, Caldwell, NJ	Democrat	1885–1889	6/24/1908	Frances Folsom	Thomas A. Hendricks, 1885
23. Benjamin Harrison	8/20/1833, North Bend, OH	Republican	1889–1893	3/13/1901	Caroline Lavinia Scott Mrs. Mary Dimmick	Levi P. Morton
24. Grover Cleveland	3/18/1837, Caldwell, NJ	Democrat	1893–1897	6/24/1908	Frances Folsom	Adlai Stevenson, 1893–97
25. William McKinley	1/29/1843, Niles, OH	Republican	1897–1901	9/14/1901*	Ida Saxton	Garret A. Hobart, 1897–99 Theodore Roosevelt, 1901
26. Theodore Roosevelt	10/27/1858, New York, NY	Republican	1901–1909	1/6/1919	Alice Hathaway Lee Edith Kermit Carow	Charles W. Fairbanks
27. William H. Taft	9/15/1857, Cincinnati, OH	Republican	1909–1913	3/8/1930	Helen Herron	James S. Sherman
28. Woodrow Wilson	12/28/1856, Staunton, VA	Democrat	1913–1921	2/3/1924	Ellen Louise Axson Edith Bolling Galt	Thomas R. Marshall
29. Warren G. Harding	11/2/1865, near Corsica, OH	Republican	1921–1923	8/2/1923†	Florence Kling DeWolfe	Calvin Coolidge
30. Calvin Coolidge	7/4/1872, Plymouth Notch, VT	Republican	1923–1929	1/5/1933	Grace Anna Goodhue	Charles G. Dawes
31. Herbert C. Hoover	8/10/1874, West Branch, IA	Republican	1929–1933	10/20/1964	Lou Henry	Charles Curtis
32. Franklin D. Roosevelt	1/30/1882, Hyde Park, NY	Democrat	1933–1945	4/12/1945†	Eleanor Roosevelt	John N. Garner, 1933–41 Henry A. Wallace, 1941–45 Harry S. Truman, 1945
33. Harry S. Truman	5/8/1884, Lamar, MO	Democrat	1945–1953	12/26/1972	Elizabeth Virginia (Bess) Wallace	Alben W. Barkley
34. Dwight D. Eisenhower	10/14/1890, Denison, TX	Republican	1953–1961	3/28/1969	Mamie Geneva Doud	Richard M. Nixon
35. John F. Kennedy	5/29/1917, Brookline, MA	Democrat	1961–1963	11/22/1963*	Jacqueline Lee Bouvier	Lyndon B. Johnson
36. Lyndon B. Johnson	8/27/1908, near Stonewall, TX	Democrat	1963–1969	1/22/1973	Claudia Alta (Lady Bird) Taylor	Hubert H. Humphrey
37. Richard M. Nixon	1/9/1913, Yorba Linda, CA	Republican	1969–1974**	4/22/1994	Thelma Catherine (Pat) Ryan	Spiro T. Agnew, 1969–73 Gerald R. Ford, 1973–74
38. Gerald R. Ford	7/14/1913, Omaha, NE	Republican	1974–1977	12/26/2006	Elizabeth (Betty) Bloomer	Nelson A. Rockefeller
39. James E. Carter, Jr	10/1/1924, Plains, GA	Democrat	1977–1981		Rosalynn Smith	Walter F. Mondale
40. Ronald W. Reagan	2/6/1911, Tampico, IL	Republican	1981–1989	6/5/2004	Nancy Davis	George H. W. Bush
41. George H. W. Bush	6/12/1924, Milton, MA	Republican	1989–1993		Barbara Pierce	J. Danforth Quayle
42. William J. Clinton	8/19/1946, Hope, AR	Democrat	1993–2001		Hillary Rodham	Albert Gore Jr.
43. George W. Bush	7/6/1946, New Haven, CT	Republican	2001–2009		Laura Welch	Richard Cheney
44. Barack H. Obama	8/4/1961, Honolulu, HI	Democrat	2009–2017		Michelle Robinson	Joe Biden
45. Donald J. Trump	6/14/1946, New York, NY	Republican	2017–		Melania Knauss	Mike Pence

*assassinated while in office
**resigned Aug 9, 1974
†died while in office—nonviolently

Some Facts About the United States

STATE	CAPITAL	POPULAR NAME	AREA (SQ. MI.)	STATE BIRD	STATE FLOWER	STATE TREE	ADMITTED TO THE UNION	ORDER OF ADMISSION
Alabama	Montgomery	Cotton or Yellowhammer State; or Heart of Dixie	51,609	Yellowhammer	Camellia	Southern pine (Longleaf pine)	1819	22
Alaska	Juneau	Last Frontier	591,004	Willow ptarmigan	Forget-me-not	Sitka spruce	1959	49
Arizona	Phoenix	Grand Canyon State	114,000	Cactus wren	Saguaro (giant cactus)	Palo Verde	1912	48
Arkansas	Little Rock	The Natural State	53,187	Mockingbird	Apple blossom	Pine	1836	25
California	Sacramento	Golden State	158,706	California valley quail	Golden poppy	California redwood	1850	31
Colorado	Denver	Centennial State	104,091	Lark bunting	Rocky Mountain columbine	Blue spruce	1876	38
Connecticut	Hartford	Constitution State	5,018	Robin	Mountain laurel	White oak	1788	5
Delaware	Dover	First State	2,044	Blue hen chicken	Peach blossom	American holly	1787	1
Florida	Tallahassee	Sunshine State	58,664	Mockingbird	Orange blossom	Cabbage (sabal) palm	1845	27
Georgia	Atlanta	Empire State of the South	58,910	Brown thrasher	Cherokee rose	Live oak	1788	4
Hawaii	Honolulu	Aloha State	6,471	Nene (Hawaiian goose)	Hibiscus	Kukui	1959	50
Idaho	Boise	Gem State	83,564	Mountain bluebird	Syringa (mock orange)	Western white pine	1890	43
Illinois	Springfield	Prairie State	56,345	Cardinal	Native violet	White oak	1818	21
Indiana	Indianapolis	Hoosier State	36,185	Cardinal	Peony	Tulip tree or yellow poplar	1816	19
Iowa	Des Moines	Hawkeye State	56,275	Eastern goldfinch	Wild rose	Oak	1846	29
Kansas	Topeka	Sunflower State	82,277	Western meadowlark	Sunflower	Cottonwood	1861	34
Kentucky	Frankfort	Bluegrass State	40,409	Kentucky cardinal	Goldenrod	Kentucky coffeetree	1792	15
Louisiana	Baton Rouge	Pelican State	47,752	Pelican	Magnolia	Bald cypress	1812	18
Maine	Augusta	Pine Tree State	33,265	Chickadee	White pine cone and tassel	White pine	1820	23
Maryland	Annapolis	Old Line State	10,577	Baltimore oriole	Black-eyed Susan	White oak	1788	7
Massachusetts	Boston	Bay State	8,284	Chickadee	Mayflower	American elm	1788	6
Michigan	Lansing	Wolverine State	58,527	Robin	Apple blossom	White pine	1837	26
Minnesota	St. Paul	North Star State	84,402	Common loon	Pink and white lady's slipper	Norway, or red, pine	1858	32
Mississippi	Jackson	Magnolia State	47,689	Mockingbird	Magnolia	Magnolia	1817	20
Missouri	Jefferson City	Show Me State	69,697	Bluebird	Hawthorn	Flowering dogwood	1821	24
Montana	Helena	Treasure State	147,046	Western meadowlark	Bitterroot	Ponderosa pine	1889	41
Nebraska	Lincoln	Cornhusker State	77,355	Western meadowlark	Goldenrod	Cottonwood	1867	37
Nevada	Carson City	Silver State	110,540	Mountain bluebird	Sagebrush	Single-leaf piñon	1864	36

STATE	CAPITAL	POPULAR NAME	AREA (SQ. MI.)	STATE BIRD	STATE FLOWER	STATE TREE	ADMITTED TO THE UNION	ORDER OF ADMISSION
New Hampshire	Concord	Granite State	9,304	Purple finch	Purple lilac	White birch	1788	9
New Jersey	Trenton	Garden State	7,787	Eastern goldfinch	Purple violet	Red oak	1787	3
New Mexico	Santa Fe	Land of Enchantment	121,593	Roadrunner	Yucca flower	Piñon, or nut pine	1912	47
New York	Albany	Empire State	49,108	Bluebird	Rose	Sugar maple	1788	11
North Carolina	Raleigh	Tar Heel State or Old North State	52,669	Cardinal	Dogwood	Pine	1789	12
North Dakota	Bismarck	Peace Garden State	70,702	Western meadowlark	Wild prairie rose	American elm	1889	39
Ohio	Columbus	Buckeye State	41,330	Cardinal	Scarlet carnation	Buckeye	1803	17
Oklahoma	Oklahoma City	Sooner State	69,956	Scissortail flycatcher	Mistletoe	Redbud	1907	46
Oregon	Salem	Beaver State	97,073	Western meadowlark	Oregon grape	Douglas fir	1859	33
Pennsylvania	Harrisburg	Keystone State	45,308	Ruffed grouse	Mountain laurel	Hemlock	1787	2
Rhode Island	Providence	Ocean State	1,212	Rhode Island Red	Violet	Red maple	1790	13
South Carolina	Columbia	Palmetto State	31,113	Carolina wren	Carolina jessamine	Palmetto	1788	8
South Dakota	Pierre	Sunshine State	77,116	Ring-necked pheasant	American pasqueflower	Black Hills spruce	1889	40
Tennessee	Nashville	Volunteer State	42,114	Mockingbird	Iris	Tulip poplar	1796	16
Texas	Austin	Lone Star State	266,807	Mockingbird	Bluebonnet	Pecan	1845	28
Utah	Salt Lake City	Beehive State	84,899	Seagull	Sego lily	Blue spruce	1896	45
Vermont	Montpelier	Green Mountain State	9,614	Hermit thrush	Red clover	Sugar maple	1791	14
Virginia	Richmond	Old Dominion	40,767	Cardinal	Dogwood	Dogwood	1788	10
Washington	Olympia	Evergreen State	68,139	Willow goldfinch	Coast rhododendron	Western hemlock	1889	42
West Virginia	Charleston	Mountain State	24,231	Cardinal	Rhododendron	Sugar maple	1863	35
Wisconsin	Madison	Badger State	56,153	Robin	Wood violet	Sugar maple	1848	30
Wyoming	Cheyenne	Equality State	97,809	Meadowlark	Indian paintbrush	Cottonwood	1890	44

State & Territory Abbreviations: United States

Alabama . . . . AL	Kansas . . . . KS	Ohio . . . . OH
Alaska . . . . AK	Kentucky . . . . KY	Oklahoma . . . . OK
American Samoa . . . . AS	Louisiana . . . . LA	Oregon . . . . OR
Arizona . . . . AZ	Maine . . . . ME	Pennsylvania . . . . PA
Arkansas . . . . AR	Maryland . . . . MD	Puerto Rico . . . . PR
California . . . . CA	Massachusetts . . . . MA	Rhode Island . . . . RI
Colorado . . . . CO	Michigan . . . . MI	South Carolina . . . . SC
Connecticut . . . . CT	Minnesota . . . . MN	South Dakota . . . . SD
Delaware . . . . DE	Mississippi . . . . MS	Tennessee . . . . TN
District of Columbia . . . . DC	Missouri . . . . MO	Texas . . . . TX
Florida . . . . FL	Montana . . . . MT	Utah . . . . UT
Georgia . . . . GA	Nebraska . . . . NE	Vermont . . . . VT
Guam . . . . GU	Nevada . . . . NV	Virginia . . . . VA
Hawaii . . . . HI	New Hampshire . . . . NH	Virgin Islands VI
Idaho . . . . ID	New Jersey . . . . NJ	Washington . . . . WA
Illinois IL	New Mexico . . . . NM	West Virginia . . . . WV
Indiana . . . . IN	New York . . . . NY	Wisconsin . . . . WI
Iowa . . . . IA	North Carolina . . . . NC	Wyoming . . . . WY
	North Dakota . . . . ND	

State Governors/US Senators/US Supreme Court

Office holders current as of July 2019.

GOVERNORS
Name (Party, State)

Kay Ivey (R, AL)
Mike Dunleavy (R, AK)
Doug Ducey (R, AZ)
Asa Hutchinson (R, AR)
Gavin Newsom (D, CA)
Jared Polis (D, CO)
Ned Lamont (D, CT)
John Carney (D, DE)
Ron DeSantis (R, FL)
Brian Kemp (R, GA)
David Ige (D, HI)
Brad Little (R, ID)
J.B. Pritzker (D, IL)
Eric Holcomb (R, IN)
Kim Reynolds (R, IA)
Laura Kelly (D, KS)
Matt Bevin (R, KY)
John Bel Edwards (D, LA)
Janet Mills (D, ME)
Larry Hogan (R, MD)
Charlie Baker (R, MA)
Gretchen Whitmer (D, MI)
Tim Walz (DFL, MN)
Phil Bryant (R, MS)
Mike Parson (R, MO)
Steve Bullock (D, MT)
Pete Ricketts (R, NE)
Steve Sisolak (D, NV)
Chris Sununu (R, NH)
Phil Murphy (D, NJ)
Michele Lujan Grisham (D, NM)
Andrew M. Cuomo (D, NY)
Roy Cooper (D, NC)
Doug Burgum (R, ND)
Mike DeWine (R, OH)
Kevin Stitt (R, OK)
Kate Brown (D, OR)
Tom Wolf (D, PA)
Gina Raimondo (D, RI)
Henry McMaster (R, SC)
Kristi Noem (R, SD)
Bill Lee (R, TN)
Greg Abbott (R, TX)
Gary R. Herbert (R, UT)
Phil Scott (R, VT)
Ralph Northam (D, VA)
Jay Inslee (D, WA)
Jim Justice (R, WV)
Tony Evers (D, WI)
Mark Gordon (R, WY)

SENATORS
Name (Party, State)

Richard Shelby (R, AL)
Doug Jones (D, AL)
Daniel Sullivan (R, AK)
Lisa Murkowski (R, AK)
Kyrsten Sinema (D, AZ)
Martha McSally (R, AZ)
John Boozman (R, AR)
Tom Cotton (R, AR)
Dianne Feinstein (D, CA)
Kamala Harris (D, CA)
Cory Gardner (R, CO)
Michael Bennet (D, CO)
Richard Blumenthal (D, CT)
Chris Murphy (D, CT)
Christopher Coons (D, DE)
Thomas R. Carper (D, DE)
Rick Scott (R, FL)
Marco Rubio (R, FL)
David Perdue (R, GA)
Johnny Isakson (R, GA)
Mazie Hirono (D, HI)
Brian Schatz (D, HI)
Jim Risch (R, ID)
Michael Crapo (R, ID)
Richard J. Durbin (D, IL)
Tammy Duckworth (D, IL)
Mike Braun (R, IN)
Todd Young (R, IN)
Charles E. Grassley (R, IA)
Joni Ernst (R, IA)
Jerry Moran (R, KS)
Pat Roberts (R, KS)
Mitch McConnell (R, KY)
Rand Paul (R, KY)
Bill Cassidy (R, LA)
John N. Kennedy (R, LA)
Angus King (I, ME)
Susan M. Collins (R, ME)
Chris Van Hollen (D, MD)
Benjamin Cardin (D, MD)
Ed Markey (D, MA)
Elizabeth Warren (D, MA)
Gary Peters (D, MI)
Debbie A. Stabenow (D, MI)
Tina Smith (D, MN)
Amy Klobuchar (D, MN)
Cindy Hyde-Smith (R, MS)
Roger Wicker (R, MS)
Roy Blunt (R, MO)
Josh Hawley (R, MO)
Steve Daines (R, MT)
Jon Tester (D, MT)
Ben Sasse (R, NE)
Deb Fischer (R, NE)
Catherine Cortez Masto (D, NV)
Jacky Rosen (D, NV)
Maggie Hassan (D, NH)
Jeanne Shaheen (D, NH)
Cory Booker (D, NJ)
Robert Menendez (D, NJ)
Tom Udall (D, NM)
Martin Heinrich (D, NM)
Charles E. Schumer (D, NY)
Kirsten Gillibrand (D, NY)
Thom Tillis (R, NC)
Richard Burr (R, NC)
Kevin Cramer (R, ND)
John Hoeven (R, ND)
Rob Portman (R, OH)
Sherrod Brown (D, OH)
James N. Inhofe (R, OK)
James Lankford (R, OK)
Ron Wyden (D, OR)
Jeff Merkley (D, OR)
Pat Toomey (R, PA)
Robert P. Casey Jr (D, PA)
Jack Reed (D, RI)
Sheldon Whitehouse (D, RI)
Lindsey Graham (R, SC)
Tim Scott (R, SC)
Mike Rounds (R, SD)
John R. Thune (R, SD)
Lamar Alexander (R, TN)
Marsha Blackburn (R, TN)
Ted Cruz (R, TX)
John Cornyn (R, TX)
Mitt Romney (R, UT)
Mike Lee (R, UT)
Patrick J. Leahy (D, VT)
Bernard Sanders (I, VT)
Mark Warner (D, VA)
Tim Kaine (D, VA)
Patty Murray (D, WA)
Maria Cantwell (D, WA)
Joe Manchin III (D, WV)
Shelley Moore Capito (R, WV)
Tammy Baldwin (D, WI)
Ron Johnson (R, WI)
John Barrasso (R, WY)
Michael B. Enzi (R, WY)

SUPREME COURT JUSTICES
Name (Appointed by, Year)

John G. Roberts Jr, Chief Justice (G.W. Bush, 2005)
Clarence Thomas (G.H.W. Bush, 1991)
Ruth Bader Ginsburg (Clinton, 1993)
Stephen G. Breyer (Clinton, 1994)
Samuel A. Alito Jr (G.W. Bush, 2006)
Sonia Sotomayor (Obama, 2009)
Elena Kagan (Obama, 2010)
Neil Gorsuch (Trump, 2017)
Brett Kavanaugh (Trump, 2018)

Some Facts About Canada

PROVINCE/TERRITORY	CAPITAL	POPULATION*	FLOWER	LAND/FRESH WATER (SQ. MI.)	TOTAL AREA
Alberta	Edmonton	4,067,175	Wild rose	248,000/7,541	255,541
British Columbia	Victoria	4,648,055	Pacific dogwood	357,216/7,548	364,764
Manitoba	Winnipeg	1,278,365	Prairie crocus	213,729/36,387	250,116
New Brunswick	Fredericton	747,101	Purple violet	27,587/563	28,150
Newfoundland & Labrador	St. John's	519,716	Pitcher plant	144,343/12,100	156,543
Northwest Territories	Yellowknife	41,786	Mountain avens	456,791/62,943	519,734
Nova Scotia	Halifax	923,598	Mayflower	20,593/752	21,345
Nunavut	Iqaluit	35,944	Purple saxifrage	747,537/60,648	808,185
Ontario	Toronto	13,448,494	White trillium	354,341/61,256	415,599
Prince Edward Island	Charlottetown	142,907	Lady's slipper	2,185/0	2,185
Quebec	Quebec City	8,164,361	White garden lily	527,079/68,313	595,391
Saskatchewan	Regina	1,098,352	Western red lily	228,445/22,921	251,366
Yukon Territory	Whitehorse	35,874	Fireweed	183,163/3,109	186,272

*Based on the 2016 Canadian Census

Province & Territory Abbreviations: Canada

Alberta.........................AB
British Columbia..................BC
Manitoba........................MB
New Brunswick...................NB
Newfoundland & Labrador..........NL

Northwest Territories...............NT
Nova Scotia.......................NS
Nunavut.........................NU
Ontario...........................ON
Prince Edward Island...............PE

Quebec...........................QC
Saskatchewan.....................SK
Yukon Territory....................YT

Some Facts About Mexico

STATE	ABBREVIATION	CAPITAL	POPULATION*	AREA (SQ. MI.)
Aguascalientes	Ags.	Aguascalientes	1,184,924	2,156
Baja California	B.C.	Mexicali	3,154,174	27,655
Baja California Sur	B.C.S.	La Paz	637,065	27,979
Campeche	Camp.	Campeche	822,001	19,672
Chiapas	Chis.	Tuxtla Gutiérrez	4,793,406	28,732
Chihuahua	Chih.	Chihuahua	3,401,140	94,831
Coahuila	Coah.	Saltillo	2,748,366	58,067
Colima	Col.	Colima	650,129	2,010
Distrito Federal	D.F.	Mexico City	8,873,017	573
Durango	Dgo.	Durango	1,632,860	47,691
Guanajuato	Gto.	Guanajuato	5,485,971	11,805
Guerrero	Gro.	Chilpancingo	3,386,706	24,887
Hidalgo	Hgo.	Pachuca	2,664,969	8,058
Jalisco	Jal.	Guadalajara	7,350,355	31,152
México	Mex.	Toluca	15,174,272	8,268
Michoacán	Mich.	Morelia	4,348,485	23,202
Morelos	Mor.	Cuernavaca	1,776,727	1,917
Nayarit	Nay.	Tepic	1,084,957	10,547
Nuevo León	N.L.	Monterrey	4,643,321	25,136
Oaxaca	Oax.	Oaxaca	3,801,871	36,375
Puebla	Pue.	Puebla	5,779,007	13,126
Querétaro	Qro.	Querétaro	1,827,985	4,432
Quintana Roo	Q.R.	Chetumal	1,324,257	19,630
San Luis Potosí	S.L.P.	San Luis Potosí	2,585,942	24,417
Sinaloa	Sin.	Culiacán	2,767,552	22,582
Sonora	Son.	Hermosillo	2,662,432	70,484
Tabasco	Tab.	Villahermosa	2,238,818	9,783
Tamaulipas	Tamps.	Ciudad Victoria	3,270,268	30,734
Tlaxcala	Tlax.	Tlaxcala	1,169,825	1,555
Veracruz	Ver.	Jalapa	7,638,378	27,759
Yucatán	Yuc.	Mérida	1,953,027	14,868
Zacatecas	Zac.	Zacatecas	1,490,550	28,125

*Based on the 2010 Mexican Census

Presidential Proclamations
Issued, Jan 1, 2018–June 15, 2019

2018

9689 Martin Luther King, Jr., Federal Holiday, 2018: Jan 15, 2018 (Jan 12, 2018)

9690 Religious Freedom Day, 2018: Jan 16, 2018 (Jan 16, 2018)

9691 National Sanctity of Human Life Day, 2018: Jan 22, 2018 (Jan 19, 2018)

9692 National School Choice Week, 2018: Jan 21–27, 2018 (Jan 22, 2018)

9693 To Facilitate Positive Adjustment to Competition from Imports of Certain Crystalline Silicon Photovoltaic Cells (Whether or Not Partially or Fully Assembled into Other Products) and for Other Purposes (Jan 23, 2018)

9694 To Facilitate Positive Adjustment to Competition from Imports of Large Residential Washers (Jan 23, 2018)

9695 American Heart Month, 2018: February (Jan 31, 2018)

9696 National African American History Month, 2018: February (Jan 31, 2018)

9697 Honoring the Victims of the Tragedy in Parkland, FL (Feb 15, 2018)

9698 Death of Billy Graham (Feb 21, 2018)

9699 Modifying and Continuing the National Emergency with Respect to Cuba and Continuing To Authorize the Regulation of the Anchorage and Movement of Vessels (Feb 22, 2018)

9700 American Red Cross Month, 2018: March (Feb 28, 2018)

9701 Irish-American Heritage Month, 2018: March (Feb 28, 2018)

9702 Women's History Month, 2018: March (Feb 28, 2018)

9703 National Consumer Protection Week, 2018: Mar 4–10, 2018 (Mar 2, 2018)

9704 Adjusting Imports of Aluminum into the United States (Mar 8, 2018)

9705 Adjusting Imports of Steel into the United States (Mar 8, 2018)

9706 National Poison Prevention Week, 2018: Mar 18–24, 2018 (Mar 16, 2018)

9707 Vocational-Technical Education Week, 2018: Mar 18–24, 2018 (Mar 16, 2018)

9708 National Agriculture Day, 2018: Mar 20, 2018 (Mar 19, 2018)

9709 Greek Independence Day: A National Day of Celebration of Greek and American Democracy, 2018: Mar 25, 2018 (Mar 22, 2018)

9710 Adjusting Imports of Aluminum into the United States (Mar 22, 2018)

9711 Adjusting Imports of Steel into the United States (Mar 22, 2018)

9712 Education and Sharing Day, USA, 2018: Mar 27, 2018 (Mar 27, 2018)

9713 Cancer Control Month, 2018: April (Mar 29, 2018)

9714 National Child Abuse Prevention Month, 2018: April (Mar 29, 2018)

9715 National Donate Life Month, 2018: April (Mar 29, 2018)

9716 National Fair Housing Month, 2018: April (Mar 30, 2018)

9717 National Sexual Assault Awareness and Prevention Month, 2018: April (Mar 30, 2018)

9718 Second Chance Month, 2018: April (Mar 30, 2018)

9719 World Autism Awareness Day, 2018: Apr 2, 2018 (Apr 2, 2018)

9720 50th Anniversary of the Assassination of Dr. Martin Luther King, Jr (Apr 3, 2018)

9721 National Crime Victims' Rights Week, 2018: Apr 8–14, 2018 (Apr 6, 2018)

9722 National Former Prisoner of War Recognition Day, 2018: Apr 9, 2018 (Apr 6, 2018)

9723 Maintaining Enhanced Vetting Capabilities and Processes for Detecting Attempted Entry Into the United States by Terrorists or Other Public-Safety Threats (Apr 10, 2018)

9724 Days of Remembrance of Victims of the Holocaust, 2018: Apr 12–19, 2018 (Apr 11, 2018)

9725 Pan American Day and Pan American Week, 2018: Apr 14 and Apr 8–14, 2018 (Apr 12, 2018)

9726 National Volunteer Week, 2018: Apr 15–21, 2018 (Apr 16, 2018)

9727 Death of Barbara Bush (Apr 17, 2018)

9728 National Park Week, 2018: Apr 21–29, 2018 (Apr 20, 2018)

9729 World Intellectual Property Day, 2018: Apr 26, 2018 (Apr 26, 2018)

9730 National Small Business Week, 2018: Apr 29–May 5, 2018 (Apr 27, 2018)

9731 Jewish American Heritage Month, 2018: May (Apr 30, 2018)

9732 Law Day, USA, 2018: May 1, 2018 (Apr 30, 2018)

9733 Asian-American and Pacific Islander Heritage Month, 2018: May (Apr 30, 2018)

9734 National Foster Care Month, 2018: May (Apr 30, 2018)

9735 National Mental Health Awareness Month, 2018: May (Apr 30, 2018)

9736 Older Americans Month, 2018: May (Apr 30, 2018)

9737 National Physical Fitness and Sports Month, 2018: May (Apr 30, 2018)

9738 Loyalty Day, 2018: May 1, 2018 (Apr 30, 2018)

9739 Adjusting Imports of Aluminum into the United States (Apr 30, 2018)

9740 Adjusting Imports of Steel into the United States (Apr 30, 2018)

9741 National Day of Prayer, 2018: May 3, 2018 (May 3, 2018)

9742 National Charter Schools Week, 2018: May 6–12, 2018 (May 4, 2018)

9743 National Hurricane Preparedness Week, 2018: May 6–12, 2018 (May 4, 2018)

9744 Public Service Recognition Week, 2018: May 6–12, 2018 (May 4, 2018)

9745 Be Best Day, 2018: May 7, 2018 (May 7, 2018)

9746 Military Spouse Day, 2018: May 11, 2018 (May 11, 2018)

9747 National Defense Transportation Day and National Transportation Week, 2018: May 18 and May 13–19, 2018 (May 11, 2018)

9748 Peace Officers Memorial Day and Police Week, 2018: May 15 and May 13–19, 2018 (May 11, 2018)

9749 Mother's Day, 2018: May 13, 2018 (May 11, 2018)

9750 National Safe Boating Week, 2018: May 19–25, 2018 (May 18, 2018)

9751 Emergency Medical Services Week, 2018: May 20–26, 2018 (May 18, 2018)

9752 World Trade Week, 2018: May 20–26, 2018 (May 18, 2018)

9753 Armed Forces Day, 2018: May 19, 2018 (May 18, 2018)

9754 Honoring the Victims of the Tragedy in Santa Fe, Texas (May 18, 2018)

9755 National Maritime Day, 2018: May 22, 2018 (May 21, 2018)

9756 Prayer for Peace, Memorial Day, 2018: May 28, 2018 (May 25, 2018)

9757 Great Outdoors Month, 2018: June (May 30, 2018)

9758 Adjusting Imports of Aluminum into the United States (May 31, 2018)

9759 Adjusting Imports of Steel into the United States (May 31, 2018)

9760 National Caribbean-American Heritage Month, 2018: June (May 31, 2018)

9761 National Homeownership Month, 2018: June (May 31, 2018)

9762 National Ocean Month, 2018: June (May 31, 2018)

9763 African-American Music Appreciation Month, 2018: June (June 1, 2018)

9764 Flag Day and National Flag Week, 2018: June 14 and June 10–16, 2018 (June 8, 2018)

9765 Father's Day, 2018: June 17, 2018 (June 15, 2018)

9766 Honoring the Victims of the Tragedy in Annapolis, Maryland (July 3, 2018)

9767 Captive Nations Week, 2018: July 15–21, 2018 (July 13, 2018)

9768 Made in America Day and Made in America Week, 2018: July 17 and July 15–21, 2018 (July 13, 2018)

9769 Americans with Disabilities Act of 1990 (July 25, 2018)

9770 National Korean War Veterans Armistice Day: July 27, 2018 (July 26, 2018)

9771 To Take Certain Actions under the African Growth and Opportunity Act and for Other Purposes (July 30, 2018)

9772 Adjusting Imports of Steel into the United States (Aug 10, 2018)

9773 National Employer Support of the Guard and Reserve Week, 2018: Aug 19–25, 2018 (Aug 17, 2018)

9774 Women's Equality Day, 2018: Aug 26, 2018 (Aug 24, 2018)

9775 Death of Senator John Sidney McCain III (Aug 27, 2018)

9776 Adjusting Imports of Aluminum into the United States (Aug 29, 2018)

9777 Adjusting Imports of Steel into the United States (Aug 29, 2018)

9778 National Alcohol and Drug Addiction Recovery Month, 2018: September (Aug 31, 2018)

9779 National Preparedness Month, 2018: September (Aug 31, 2018)

9780 Labor Day, 2018: Sept 3, 2018 (Aug 31, 2018)

9781 National Days of Prayer and Remembrance, 2018: Sept 7–9, 2018 (Sept 7, 2018)

9782 Patriot Day, 2018: Sept 11, 2018 (Sept 10, 2018)

9783 National Hispanic Heritage Month, 2018: Sept 15–Oct 15, 2018 (Sept 13, 2018)

9784 National Farm Safety and Health Week, 2018: Sept 16–22, 2018 (Sept 13, 2018)

9785 National Gang Violence Prevention Week, 2018: Sept 16–22, 2018 (Sept 14, 2018)

9786 National Historically Black Colleges and Universities Week, 2018: Sept 16–22, 2018 (Sept 14, 2018)

9787 Prescription Opioid and Heroin Epidemic Awareness Week, 2018: Sept 16–22, 2018 (Sept 14, 2018)

9788 Constitution Day, Citizenship Day, and Constitution Week, 2018: Sept 17 and Sept 17–23, 2018 (Sept 14, 2018)

9789 National POW/MIA Recognition Day, 2018: Sept 21, 2018 (Sept 20, 2018)

9790 National Hunting and Fishing Day, 2018: Sept 22, 2018 (Sept 21, 2018)

9791 National Breast Cancer Awareness Month, 2018: October (Sept 28, 2018)

9792 National Cybersecurity Awareness Month, 2018: October (Sept 28, 2018)

9793 National Disability Employment Awareness Month, 2018: October (Sept 28, 2018)

9794 National Energy Awareness Month, 2018: October (Sept 28, 2018)

9795 National Substance Abuse Prevention Month, 2018: October (Sept 28, 2018)

9796 Gold Star Mother's and Family's Day, 2018: Sept 30, 2018 (Sept 28, 2018)

9797 Child Health Day, 2018: Oct 1, 2018 (Sept 28, 2018)

9798 National Manufacturing Day, 2018: Oct 5, 2018 (Oct 4, 2018)

9799 German-American Day, 2018: Oct 6, 2018 (Oct 5, 2018)

9800 Fire Prevention Week, 2018: Oct 7–13, 2018 (Oct 5, 2018)

9801 Columbus Day, 2018: Oct 8, 2018 (Oct 5, 2018)

9802 Leif Erikson Day, 2018: Oct 9, 2018 (Oct 8, 2018)

9803 National Domestic Violence Awareness Month, 2018: October (Oct 9, 2018)

9804 General Pulaski Memorial Day, 2018: Oct 11, 2018 (Oct 10, 2018)

9805 Minority Enterprise Development Week, 2018: Oct 14–20, 2018 (Oct 12, 2018)

9806 National School Lunch Week, 2018: Oct 14–20, 2018 (Oct 12, 2018)

9807 Blind Americans Equality Day, 2018: Oct 15, 2018 (Oct 12, 2018)

9808 National Character Counts Week, 2018: Oct 21–27, 2018 (Oct 19, 2018)

9809 National Forest Products Week, 2018: Oct 21–27, 2018 (Oct 19, 2018)

9810 United Nations Day, 2018: Oct 24, 2018 (Oct 23, 2018)

9811 Establishment of the Camp Nelson Heritage National Monument (Oct 26, 2018)

9812 Honoring the Victims of the Tragedy in Pittsburgh, Pennsylvania (Oct 27, 2018)

9813 To Modify the List of Products Eligible for Duty- Free Treatment under the Generalized System of Preferences (Oct 30, 2018)

9814 Critical Infrastructure Security and Resilience Month, 2018: November (Oct 31, 2018)

9815 National Adoption Month, 2018: November (Oct 31, 2018)

9816 National Entrepreneurship Month, 2018: November (Oct 31, 2018)

9817 National Family Caregivers Month, 2018: November (Oct 31, 2018)

9818 National Native American Heritage Month, 2018: November (Oct 31, 2018)

9819 National Veterans and Military Families Month, 2018: November (Oct 31, 2018)

9820 Honoring the Victims of the Tragedy in Thousand Oaks, California (Nov 8, 2018)

9821 World Freedom Day, 2018: Nov 9, 2018 (Nov 8, 2018)

9822 Addressing Mass Migration through the Southern Border of the United States (Nov 9, 2018)

9823 American Education Week, 2018: Nov 11–17, 2018 (Nov 9, 2018)

9824 National Apprenticeship Week, 2018: Nov 12–18, 2018 (Nov 9, 2018)

9825 Veterans Day, 2018: Nov 11, 2018 (Nov 9, 2018)

9826 National Family Week, 2018: Nov 18–24, 2018 (Nov 16, 2018)

9827 Thanksgiving Day, 2018: Nov 22, 2018 (Nov 20, 2018)

9828 National Impaired Driving Prevention Month, 2018: December (Nov 30, 2018)

9829 World AIDS Day, 2018: Dec 1, 2018 (Nov 30, 2018)

9830 Announcing the Death of George Herbert Walker Bush (Dec 1, 2018)

9831 National Pearl Harbor Remembrance Day, 2018: Dec 7, 2018 (Dec 6, 2018)

9832 Human Rights Day, Bill of Rights Day, and Human Rights Week, 2018: Dec 10, Dec 15 and Dec 9–15, 2018 (Dec 7, 2018)

9833 Wright Brothers Day, 2018: Dec 17, 2018 (Dec 14, 2018)

9834 To Take Certain Actions under the African Growth and Opportunity Act and for Other Purposes (Dec 21, 2018)

9835 National Slavery and Human Trafficking Prevention Month, 2019: January (Dec 31, 2018)

2019

9836 Religious Freedom Day, 2019: Jan 16, 2019 (Jan 15, 2018)

9837 National School Choice Week, 2019: Jan 20–26, 2019 (Jan 18, 2019)

9838 National Sanctity of Human Life Day, 2019: Jan 20, 2019 (Jan 18, 2019)

9839 Martin Luther King, Jr., Federal Holiday, 2019: Jan 21, 2019 (Jan 18, 2019)

9840 American Heart Month, 2019: February (Jan 31, 2019)

9841 National African American History Month, 2019: February (Jan 31, 2019)

9842 Addressing Mass Migration through the Southern Border of the United States (Feb 7, 2019)

9843 Death of John David Dingell, Jr (Feb 8, 2019)

9844 Declaring a National Emergency Concerning the Southern Border of the United States (Feb 15, 2019)

9845 American Red Cross Month, 2019: March (Mar 1, 2019)

9846 Irish-American Heritage Month, 2019: March (Mar 1, 2019)

9847 Women's History Month, 2019: March (Mar 1, 2019)

9848 National Consumer Protection Week, 2019: Mar 3–9, 2019 (Mar 1, 2019)

9849 National Agriculture Day, 2019: Mar 14, 2019 (Mar 13, 2019)

9850 National Poison Prevention Week, 2019: Mar 17–23, 2019 (Mar 15, 2019)

9851 Greek Independence Day: A National Day of Celebration of Greek and American Democracy, 2019: Mar 25, 2019 (Mar 18, 2019)

9852 Recognizing the Golan Heights as the Part of the State of Israel (Mar 25, 2019)

9853 Cancer Control Month, 2019: April (Mar 29, 2019)

9854 National Child Abuse Prevention Month, 2019: April (Mar 29, 2019)

9855 National Donate Life Month, 2019: April (Mar 29, 2019)

9856 National Sexual Assault Awareness and Prevention Month, 2019: April (Mar 29, 2019)

9857 Second Chance Month, 2019: April (Mar 29, 2019)

9858 World Autism Awareness Day, 2019: Apr 2, 2019 (Apr 1, 2019)

9859 National Crime Victims' Rights Week, 2019: Apr 7–13, 2019 (Apr 5, 2019)

9860 National Volunteer Week, 2019: Apr 7–13, 2019 (Apr 5, 2019)

9861 National Former Prisoner of War Recognition Day, 2019: Apr 9, 2019 (Apr 8, 2019)

9862 Pan American Day and Pan American Week, 2019: Apr 14 and Apr 14–20, 2019 (Apr 15, 2019)

9863 Education and Sharing Day, USA, 2019: Apr 16, 2019 (Apr 16, 2019)

9864 National Park Week, 2019: Apr 20–28, 2019 (Apr 19, 2019)

9865 World Intellectual Property Day, 2019: Apr 26, 2019 (Apr 25, 2019)

9866 Days of Remembrance of Victims of the Holocaust, 2019: Apr 28–May 5, 2019 (Apr 26, 2019)

9867 Asian-American and Pacific Islander Heritage Month, 2019: May (Apr 30, 2019)

9868 Jewish American Heritage Month, 2019: May (Apr 30, 2019)

9869 National Foster Care Month, 2019: May (Apr 30, 2019)

9870 National Physical Fitness and Sports Month, 2019: May (Apr 30, 2019)

9871 Law Day, USA, 2019: May 1, 2019 (Apr 30, 2019)

9872 Older Americans Month, 2019: May (Apr 30, 2019)

9873 National Day of Prayer, 2019: May 2, 2018 (Apr 30, 2019)

9874 Loyalty Day, 2019: May 1, 2019 (Apr 30, 2019)

9875 National Mental Health Awareness Month, 2019: May (May 1, 2019)

9876 Missing and Murdered American Indians and Alaska Natives Awareness Day, 2019: May 5, 2019 (May 3, 2019)

9877 National Hurricane Preparedness Week, 2019: May 5–11, 2019 (May 3, 2019)

9878 National Small Business Week, 2019: May 5–11, 2019 (May 3, 2019)

9879 Public Service Recognition Week, 2019: May 5–11, 2019 (May 3, 2019)

9880 Addressing Mass Migration through the Southern Border of the United States (May 8, 2019)

9881 Military Spouse Day, 2019: May 10, 2019 (May 9, 2019)

9882 Mother's Day, 2019: May 12, 2019 (May 10, 2019)

9883 National Charter Schools Week, 2019: May 12–18, 2019 (May 10, 2019)

9884 National Defense Transportation Day and National Transportation Week, 2019: May 17 and May 12–18, 2019 (May 10, 2019)

9885 Peace Officers Memorial Day and Police Week, 2019: May 15 and May 12–18, 2019 (May 10, 2019)

9886 Proclamation to Modify the List of Beneficiary Developing Countries under the Trade Act of 1974 (May 16, 2019)

9887 Adjusting Imports of Steel into the United States (May 16, 2019)

9888 Adjusting Imports of Automobiles and Automobile Parts into the United States (May 17, 2019)

9889 National Safe Boating Week, 2019: May 18–24, 2019 (May 17, 2019)

9890 Emergency Medical Services Week, 2019: May 19–25, 2019 (May 17, 2019)

9891 World Trade Week, 2019: May 19–25, 2019 (May 17, 2019)

9892 Armed Forces Day, 2019: May 18, 2019 (May 17, 2019)

9893 Adjusting Imports of Aluminum into the United States (May 19, 2019)

9894 Adjusting Imports of Steel into the United States (May 19, 2019)

9895 National Maritime Day, 2019: May 22, 2019 (May 20, 2019)

9896 Prayer for Peace, Memorial Day, 2019: May 27, 2019 (May 24, 2019)

9897 African-American Music Appreciation Month, 2019: June (May 31, 2019)

9898 Great Outdoors Month, 2019: June (May 31, 2019)

9899 National Caribbean-American Heritage Month, 2019: June (May 31, 2019)

9900 National Homeownership Month, 2019: June (May 31, 2019)

9901 National Ocean Month, 2019: June (May 31, 2019)

9902 Proclamation to Modify the List of Beneficiary Developing Countries under the Trade Act of 1974 (May 31, 2019)

9903 Honoring the Victims of the Tragedy in Virginia Beach, Virginia (June 1, 2019)

9904 National Day of Remembrance of the 75th Anniversary of D-Day (June 6, 2019)

9905 Flag Day and National Flag Week, 2019: June 14 and June 9–15, 2019 (June 7, 2019)

9906 Father's Day, 2019: June 16, 2019 (June 15, 2019)

2020 Special Months

For more information on these special months, see the listing on the first day of the month (unless specified otherwise).

January
Be Kind to Food Servers Month
Book Blitz Month
Child-Centered Divorce Month, Intl
Children Impacted by a Parent's Cancer Month
Clean Up Your Computer Month, Natl
Creativity Month, Intl
Get Organized Month
Glaucoma Awareness Month, Natl
Hot Tea Month, Natl
Mentoring Month, Natl
Oatmeal Month
Personal Self-Defense Awareness Month, Natl
Poverty in America Awareness Month, Natl
Radon Action Month, Natl
Rising Star Month, Worldwide
Skating Month, Natl
Slavery and Human Trafficking Prevention Month, Natl
Volunteer Blood Donor Month, Natl

February
AMD/Low Vision Awareness Month
American Heart Month
Bird-Feeding Month, Natl
Black History Month, Natl
Cherry Month, Natl
Condom Month, Natl
Feline Fix by Five Month
Goat Yoga Month, Natl
Library Lovers' Month
Marfan Syndrome Awareness Month
Parent Leadership Month, Natl
Pet Dental Health Month, Natl
Plant the Seeds of Greatness Month
Renaissance of the Heart Month, Worldwide
Return Shopping Carts to the Supermarket Month
Spay/Neuter Awareness Month
Spunky Old Broads Month
Time Management Month, Natl
Wise Health Care Consumer Month
Youth Leadership Month

March
Alport Syndrome Awareness Month
Black Women in Jazz Month, Intl
Clap 4 Health Month
Clean Up Your IRS Act Month, Natl
Colorectal Cancer Education and Awareness Month, Natl
Credit Education Month
Employee Spirit Month
Home Schooling Awareness Month, Worldwide
Humorists Are Artists Month
Ideas Month, Intl
Irish-American Heritage Month
Kidney Month, Natl
Mirth Month, Intl
Multiple Sclerosis Education and Awareness Month, Natl
Music in Our Schools Month
Nutrition Month, Natl
Optimism Month
Paws To Read Month

Peanut Month, Natl
Play-the-Recorder Month
Poison Prevention Awareness Month
Red Cross Month
Save the Vaquita Month
Save Your Vision Month
Social Work Month
Umbrella Month, Natl
Women's History Month, Natl
Workplace Eye Wellness Month
Youth Art Month

March–April
Deaf History Month (Mar 13–Apr 15)

April
Adopt a Ferret Month
African-American Women's Fitness Month, Natl
Alcohol Awareness Month
Astronomy Month, Global
Autism Awareness Month, Natl
Bereaved Spouses Awareness Month, Worldwide
Black Women's History Month, Intl
Cancer Control Month, Natl
Child Abuse Prevention Month, Natl
Customer Loyalty Month, Intl
Distracted Driving Awareness Month
Donate Life Month, Natl
Frog Month, Natl
Grange Month
Heartworm Awareness Month, Natl
Holy Humor Month
Humor Month, Natl
Informed Woman Month
Jazz Appreciation Month
Landscape Architecture Month, World
Lawn Care Month, Natl
Mathematics and Statistics Awareness Month
Medical Cannabis Education and Awareness Month
9-1-1 Education Month, Natl
Occupational Therapy Month, Natl
Pecan Month, Natl
Pest Management Month, Natl
Pet First Aid Awareness Month
Pharmacists' War on Diabetes
Poetry Month, Natl
Prevention of Animal Cruelty Month
Rebuilding Month, Natl
Rosacea Awareness Month
School Library Month
Sexual Assault Awareness and Prevention Month, Natl
Sexually Transmitted Diseases (STDs) Education and Awareness Month, Natl
Straw Hat Month
Stress Awareness Month
Twit Award Month, Intl
Women's Eye Health and Safety Month
Workplace Conflict Awareness Month
Youth Sports Safety Month, Natl

April–May
Card and Letter Writing Month, Natl (Apr 1–May 10)

May
Allergy/Asthma Awareness Month, Natl
Arthritis Awareness Month, Natl
Asian-American and Pacific Islander Heritage Month
Asthma Awareness Month
Barbecue Month, Natl
Bike Month, Natl
Civility Awareness Month, Global
Fibromyalgia Education and Awareness Month
Foster Care Month, Natl
Gardening for Wildlife Month
Get Caught Reading Month
Gifts From the Garden Month
Good Car-Keeping Month, Natl
Hamburger Month, Natl
Hepatitis Awareness Month, Natl
Huntington's Disease Awareness Month
Jewish-American Heritage Month
Meditation Month, Natl
Mediterranean Diet Month, Intl
Mental Health Month, Natl
Military Appreciation Month, Natl
Motorcycle Safety Month
Mystery Month
Older Americans Month
Osteoporosis Month, Natl
Physical Fitness and Sports Month, Natl
Preservation Month, Natl
REACT Month
Read to Your Baby Bump Month, Natl
Salad Month, Natl
Save Your Tooth Month
Skin Cancer Awareness Month
Spiritual Literacy Month
Strike Out Strokes Month
Ultraviolet Awareness Month
Victorious Woman Month, Intl
Vinegar Month, Natl
Women's Health Care Month
Young Achievers/Leaders of Tomorrow Month

June
Adopt-A-Shelter-Cat Month
African-American Music Appreciation Month
Alzheimer's and Brain Awareness Month
Aphasia Awareness Month, Natl
Audiobook Appreciation Month
Bathroom Reading Month, Natl
Cancer from the Sun Month
Candy Month, Natl
Caribbean-American Heritage Month, Natl
Cataract Awareness Month
Child Vision Awareness Month
Dementia Care Professionals Month
Effective Communications Month
Entrepreneurs "Do It Yourself" Marketing Month
Foster a Pet Month, Natl
GLBT Book Month, Natl
Great Outdoors Month
Iced Tea Month, Natl
Indigenous History Month, Natl (Canada)
June Dairy Month
Lesbian, Gay, Bisexual and Transgender Pride Month

Men's Health Education and Awareness
   Month
Men's Month, Intl
Migraine and Headache Awareness Month
Oceans Month, Natl
Outdoor Marketing Month
Perennial Gardening Month
Pharmacists Declare War on Alcoholism
Pollinator Month, Natl
PTSD Awareness Month
Rivers Month, Natl
Rose Month, Natl
Safety Month, Natl
Skyscraper Month
Soul Food Month, Natl
Student Safety Month
Surf Music Month, Intl
Zoo and Aquarium Month, Natl

June–July
Fireworks Safety Months (June 1–July 31)

July
Alopecia Month for Women, Intl
Bereaved Parents Awareness Month,
   Worldwide
Bioterrorism/Disaster Education and
   Awareness Month
Cell Phone Courtesy Month
Deli Salad Month, Natl
"Doghouse Repairs" Month, Natl
Grilling Month, Natl
Herbal/Prescription Interaction Awareness
   Month
Horseradish Month, Natl
Hot Dog Month, Natl
Ice Cream Month, Natl
Make a Difference to Children Month, Natl
Minority Mental Health Awareness Month,
   Natl
Park and Recreation Month, Natl
Smart Irrigation Month
Watermelon Month, Natl
Women's Motorcycle Month

August
American Adventures Month
Black Business Month
Boomers Making a Difference Month
Children's Eye Health and Safety Month
Children's Vision and Learning Month
Immunization Awareness Month, Natl
Pirate Month, Intl
Read-a-Romance Month
Spinal Muscular Atrophy Awareness Month,
   Natl
What Will Be Your Legacy Month

September
Atrial Fibrillation Awareness Month
Attention Deficit Hyperactivity Disorder
   Month
Be a Food Hero Month, Natl
Be Kind to Editors and Writers Month
Beach Month, World
Childhood Cancer Awareness Month
Cholesterol Education Month, Natl
DNA, Genomics and Stem Cell Education
   and Awareness Month, Natl
Fall Hat Month
Gynecologic Cancer Awareness Month

Happy Cat Month
Head Lice Prevention Month, Natl
Honey Month, Natl
Hunger Action Month
Library Card Sign-Up Month
Mold Awareness Month
Mushroom Month, Natl
One-on-One Month
Ovarian Cancer Awareness Month, Natl
Preparedness Month, Natl
Prostate Cancer Awareness Month, Natl
Recovery Month, Natl
Rice Month, Natl
September Is Healthy Aging Month
Service Dog Month, Natl
Shameless Promotion Month
Skin Care Awareness Month, Natl
Speak Out Month, Worldwide
Sports Eye Safety Month
Subliminal Communications Month
Update Your Resume Month
Whole Grains Month
Women's Friendship Month, Intl

September–October
Hispanic Heritage Month, Natl (Sept 15–Oct
   15)
Co-op Awareness Month (Sept 24-Oct 31)

October
Adopt-A-Shelter-Dog Month
American Cheese Month
Antidepressant Death Awareness Month
Audiology Awareness Month/Protect Your
   Hearing Month, Natl
Breast Cancer Awareness Month, Natl
Bullying Prevention Awareness Month, Natl
Celebrating the Bilingual Child Month
Celiac Disease Awareness Month
Chiropractic Health Month, Natl
Contact Lens Safety Month
Crime Prevention Month, Natl
Cybersecurity Awareness Month, Natl
Dental Hygiene Month, Natl
Depression Education and Awareness
   Month, Natl
Disability Employment Awareness Month,
   Natl
Domestic Violence Awareness Month
Down Syndrome Awareness Month, Natl
Dyslexia Awareness Month
Emotional Intelligence Awareness Month
Gay and Lesbian History Month
German-American Heritage Month
Global Diversity Awareness Month
Go Hog Wild—Eat Country Ham Month
Health Literacy Month
Liver Awareness Month, Natl
Medical Librarians Month, Natl
Menopause Month, World
Organize Your Medical Information Month
Orthodontic Health Month, Natl
Physical Therapy Month, Natl
Polish-American Heritage Month
Popcorn Poppin' Month, Natl
Positive Attitude Month
Reading Group Month, Natl
Rett Syndrome Awareness Month
Roller Skating Month, Natl
Seafood Month, Natl
Spina Bifida Awareness Month, Natl

Squirrel Awareness and Appreciation Month
Stamp Collecting Month, Natl
Stop Bullying Month, Natl
Teen Services Month
Vegetarian Awareness Month
Work and Family Month, Natl
Workplace Politics Awareness Month

November
Adoption Month, Natl
American Diabetes Month
Aviation History Month
Banana Pudding Lovers Month
Bereaved Siblings Month, Worldwide
Diabetic Eye Disease Month
Epilepsy Awareness Month, Natl
Eye Donation Month
Family Caregivers Month, Natl
Georgia Pecan Month, Natl
Inspirational Role Models Month, Natl
Long-Term Care Awareness Month, Natl
Lung Cancer Awareness Month
Marrow Awareness Month, Natl
Movember
Memoir Writing Month, Natl
Native-American Heritage Month, Natl
Novel Writing Month, Natl
Peanut Butter Lovers' Month
Picture Book Month
PPSI/ACA AIDS Awareness Month
Prematurity Awareness Month
Runaway Prevention Month, Natl
Vegan Month, World

December
Bingo's Birthday Month
Food Service Safety Month, Worldwide
Impaired Driving Prevention Month, Natl
Safe Toys and Gifts Month
Write a Business Plan Month, Natl

Looking Forward

2021

Total solar eclipse
Magellan's Discovery of Guam, 500th anniversary
Plymouth Pilgrims celebrate their first harvest with
    local Native Americans, 400th anniversary
Central American nations declare independence
    from Spain, 200th anniversary
Missouri Statehood Bicentennial
Great Chicago Fire/Peshtigo Forest Fire, 150th anniversary
Elizabeth Ann Seton's death, 200th anniversary
Clara Barton's birth, 200th anniversary
Miss America Pageant created, 100th anniversary
NPR's first broadcast, 50th anniversary

2022

Susan B. Anthony arrested for voting, 150th anniversary
USSR established, 100th anniversary
King Tut's tomb discovered, 100th anniversary
Watergate arrests, 50th anniversary
Molière's birth, 400th anniversary
Louis Pasteur's birth, 200th anniversary
Ulysses S. Grant's birth, 200th anniversary
Rutherford B. Hayes' birth, 200th anniversary
Jack Kerouac's birth, 100th anniversary
Charles Schulz's birth, 100th anniversary

2023

William Shakespeare's First Folio published, 400th
    anniversary

Boston Tea Party, 250th anniversary
Vietnam Peace Agreement signed, 50th anniversary
Skylab launched, 50th anniversary
Nicolaus Copernicus' birth, 550th anniversary
Adam Smith's birth, 300th anniversary
William Henry Harrison's birth, 250th anniversary
Alan Shepard's birth, 100th anniversary

2024

Leap Year
Total solar eclipse
Games of the XXXIII Olympiad, Paris, France
Ludwig van Beethoven's Symphony No. 9 first
    performed, 200th anniversary
Herbert Hoover's birth, 150th anniversary
Harry Houdini's birth, 150th anniversary
Winston Churchill's birth, 150th anniversary
George H. W. Bush's birth, 100th anniversary
Jimmy Carter's birth, 100th anniversary
Richard Nixon resignation, 50th anniversary

2025

First Council of Nicaea, 1,700th anniversary
Spanish conquistador Hernán Cortés executes the last
    Aztec emperor, Cuauhtémoc, 500th anniversary
American Revolutionary War begins, 250th
    anniversary
Library of Congress founded, 225th anniversary
The Great Gatsby published, 100th anniversary
Mary McLeod Bethune's birth, 150th anniversary
Malcolm X's birth, 100th anniversary
Scott Carpenter's birth, 100th anniversary
B.B. King's birth, 100th anniversary

2026

Antoni Gaudí's La Sagrada Família completed

2050

World population predicted to be 9 billion

2061

Halley's Comet returns

Major Awards Presented in 2018–2019

AWARDS FOR FILM, STAGE AND TELEVISION

2019 ACADEMY AWARDS

91st Annual, for 2018 Achievement

Picture: *Green Book*
Directing: Alfonso Cuarón, *Roma*
Actor: Rami Malek, *Bohemian Rhapsody*
Actress: Olivia Colman, *The Favourite*
Supporting Actor: Mahershala Ali, *Green Book*
Supporting Actress: Regina King, *If Beale Street Could Talk*
Original Screenplay: Brian Currie, Nick Vallelonga and Peter Farrelly, *Green Book*
Adapted Screenplay: Spike Lee, Kevin Willmott, Charlie Wachtel, David Rabinowitz, *BlacKkKlansman*
Foreign Language Film: *Roma*
Animated Feature: *Spider-Man: Into the Spider-Verse*
Animated Short Film: *Bao*
Live Action Short Film: *Skin*
Documentary Feature: *Free Solo*
Documentary Short Subject: *Period. End of Sentence.*
Film Editing: John Ottman, *Bohemian Rhapsody*
Production Design: Hannah Beachler, set decoration: Jay Hart, *Black Panther*
Costume Design: Ruth Carter, *Black Panther*
Cinematography: Alfonso Cuarón, *Roma*
Visual Effects: Paul Lambert, Ian Hunter, Tristan Myles and J.D. Schwalm, *First Man*
Makeup and Hairstyling: Greg Cannom, Kate Biscoe and Patricia Dehaney, *Vice*
Sound Mixing: Paul Massey, Tim Cavagin and John Casali, *Bohemian Rhapsody*
Sound Editing: John Warhurst and Nina Hartstone, *Bohemian Rhapsody*
Original Score: Ludwig Göransson, *Black Panther*
Original Song: Lady Gaga, Mark Ronson, Anthony Rossomando and Andrew Wyatt, "Shallow" from *A Star Is Born*

2019 GOLDEN GLOBE AWARDS

76th Annual, for 2018 Achievement

MOVIES

Drama: *Bohemian Rhapsody*
Musical or Comedy: *Green Book*
Director: Alfonso Cuarón, *Roma*
Actor, Drama: Rami Malek, *Bohemian Rhapsody*
Actress, Drama: Glenn Close, *The Wife*
Actor, Musical or Comedy: Christian Bale, *Vice*
Actress, Musical or Comedy: Olivia Colman, *The Favourite*
Supporting Actor: Mahershala Ali, *Green Book*
Supporting Actress: Regina King, *If Beale Street Could Talk*
Screenplay: Brian Currie, Nick Vallelonga and Peter Farrelly, *Green Book*
Animated Film: *Spider-Man: Into the Spider-Verse*
Foreign Language Film: *Roma*
Original Score: Justin Hurwitz, *First Man*
Original Song: Lady Gaga, Mark Ronson, Anthony Rossomando and Andrew Wyatt, "Shallow" from *A Star Is Born*

TELEVISION

Series, Drama: "The Americans"
Series, Musical or Comedy: "The Kominsky Method"
Miniseries or TV Movie: *The Assassination of Gianni Versace: American Crime Story*
Actor, Series, Drama: Richard Madden, "Bodyguard"
Actress, Series, Drama: Sandra Oh, "Killing Eve"

Actor, Series, Musical or Comedy: Michael Douglas, "The Kominsky Method"
Actress, Series, Musical or Comedy: Rachel Brosnahan, "The Marvelous Mrs. Maisel"
Actor, Miniseries or TV Movie: Darren Criss, *The Assassination of Gianni Versace: American Crime Story*
Actress, Miniseries or TV Movie: Patricia Arquette, *Escape at Dannemora*
Actor, Supporting Role: Ben Whishaw, *A Very English Scandal*
Actress, Supporting Role: Patricia Clarkson, *Sharp Objects*

2019 SUNDANCE FILM FESTIVAL AWARDS

38th Annual

Grand Jury Prize, Dramatic: *Clemency*
Grand Jury Prize, Documentary: *One Child Nation*
World Cinema Grand Jury Prize, Dramatic: *The Souvenir*
World Cinema Grand Jury Prize, Documentary: *Honeyland*
Audience Award, Dramatic: *Brittany Runs A Marathon*
Audience Award, Documentary: *Knock Down the House*
Audience Award, World Cinema Dramatic: *Queen of Hearts*
Audience Award, World Cinema Documentary: *Sea of Shadows*
NEXT Audience Award: *The Infiltrators*
NEXT Innovator Award: Alex Rivera and Cristina Ibarra, *The Infiltrators*
Directing Award, Dramatic: Joe Talbot, *The Last Black Man in San Francisco*
Directing Award, Documentary: Steven Bognar and Julia Reichert, *American Factory*
Directing Award, World Cinema Dramatic: Lucía Garibaldi, *The Sharks*
Directing Award, World Cinema Documentary: Mads Brügger, *Cold Case Hammarskjöld*
Waldo Salt Screenwriting Award: Pippa Bianco, *Share*
Documentary Special Jury Award for Moral Urgency: Jacqueline Olive, *Always in Season*
Documentary Special Jury Award for Emerging Filmmaker: Liza Mandelup, *Jawline*
Documentary Special Jury Award for Cinematography: Luke Lorentzen, *Midnight Family*
Dramatic Special Jury Award for Creative Collaboration: Joe Talbot, *The Last Black Man in San Francisco*
Dramatic Special Jury Award for Vision and Craft: Alma Har'el, *Honey Boy*
Dramatic Special Jury Award for Achievement in Acting: Rhianne Barreto, *Share*
Dramatic Special Jury Award for Editing: Todd Douglas Miller, *APOLLO 11*
World Cinema Documentary Special Jury Award for No Borders: Hassan Fazzili, *Midnight Traveler*
World Cinema Documentary Special Jury Award for Impact for Change: Tamara Kotevska and Ljubomir Stefanov, *Honeyland*

World Cinema Documentary Special Jury Award for Cinematography: Fejmi Daut and Samir Ljuma, *Honeyland*
World Cinema Dramatic Special Jury Award for Originality: *We Are Little Zombies*
World Cinema Dramatic Special Jury Award: Alejandro Landes, *Monos*
World Cinema Dramatic Special Jury Award for Acting: Krystyna Janda, *Dolce Fine Giornata*

2019 CANNES FILM FESTIVAL
72nd Annual
Palme d'Or (Golden Palm): *Parasite*, Bong Joon-ho
Grand Prix: *Atlantique*, Mati Diop
Jury Prize (TIE): *Les Misérables* and *Bacurau*
Best Actress: Emily Beecham, *Little Joe*
Best Actor: Antonio Banderas, *Dolor y Gloria (Pain and Glory)*
Best Director: Luc Dardenne and Jean-Pierre Dardenne, *Le Jeune Ahmed (Young Ahmed)*
Best Screenplay: Céline Sciamma, *Portrait de la Jeune Fille en Feu (Portrait of a Lady on Fire)*
Camera d'Or: *Our Mothers*, César Diaz
Special Mention: Elia Suleiman, *It Must Be Heaven*
Honorary Palme d'Or: Alain Delon
Short Film Palme d'Or: "The Distance Between Us and the Sky"
Short Film Special Distinction by the Jury: "Monstruo Dios" ("Monster God")

TONY AWARDS
73rd Annual, for 2018–2019 Achievement
Play: *The Ferryman*
Musical: *Hadestown*
Revival of a Play: *The Boys in the Band*
Revival of a Musical: *Rodgers and Hammerstein's Oklahoma!*
Director of a Play: Sam Mendes, *The Ferryman*
Director of a Musical: Rachel Chavkin, *Hadestown*
Leading Actor in a Play: Bryan Cranston, *Network*
Leading Actress in a Play: Elaine May, *The Waverly Gallery*
Leading Actor in a Musical: Santino Fontana, *Tootsie*
Leading Actress in a Musical: Stephanie J. Block, *The Cher Show*
Featured Actor in a Play: Bertie Carvel, *Ink*
Featured Actress in a Play: Celia Keenan-Bolger, *To Kill a Mockingbird*
Featured Actor in a Musical: André De Shields, *Hadestown*

Featured Actress in a Musical: Ali Stroker, *Rodgers and Hammerstein's Oklahoma!*
Book of a Musical: *Tootsie*, Robert Horn
Original Musical Score: *Hadestown*, music and lyrics: Anaïs Mitchell
Scenic Design of a Play: Rob Howell, *The Ferryman*
Scenic Design of a Musical: Rachel Hauck, *Hadestown*
Costume Design of a Play: Rob Howell, *The Ferryman*
Costume Design of a Musical: Bob Mackie, *The Cher Show*
Lighting Design of a Play: Neil Austin, *Ink*
Lighting Design of a Musical: Bradley King, *Hadestown*
Sound Design of a Play: Fitz Patton, *Choir Boy*
Sound Design of a Musical: Nevin Steinberg and Jessica Paz, *Hadestown*
Choreography: Sergio Trujillo, *Ain't Too Proud: The Life and Times of the Temptations*
Orchestrations: Michael Chorney and Todd Sickafoose, *Hadestown*
Lifetime Achievement in the Theater: Rosemary Harris, Terrence McNally, Harold Wheeler
Special Tony Awards: Marin Mazzie, Jason Michael Webb, Sonny Tilders and Creature Technology Company
Regional Theater Award: TheatreWorks Silicon Valley
Isabelle Stevenson Award: Judith Light
Tony Honors for Excellence in the Theater: Broadway Inspirational Voices — Michael McElroy, Founder; Peter Entin; FDNY Engine 54, Ladder 4, Battalion 9; Joseph Blakely Forbes

2018 PRIMETIME EMMY AWARDS
Major Categories—70th Annual
Drama: "Game of Thrones," HBO
Comedy: "The Marvelous Mrs. Maisel," Amazon
Limited Series: "The Assassination of Gianni Versace: American Crime Story," FX
Television Movie: *Black Mirror: USS Callister*, Netflix
Lead Actress in a Drama Series: Claire Foy, "The Crown," Netflix
Lead Actor in a Drama Series: Matthew Rhys, "The Americans," FX
Lead Actress in a Comedy Series: Rachel Brosnahan, "The Marvelous Mrs. Maisel," Amazon
Lead Actor in a Comedy Series: Bill Hader, "Barry," HBO
Lead Actress in a Limited Series: Regina King, "Seven Seconds," Netflix
Lead Actor in a Limited Series: Darren Criss, "The Assassination of Gianni Versace: American Crime Story," FX
Supporting Actress in a Drama Series: Thandie Newton, "Westworld," HBO
Supporting Actor in a Drama Series: Peter Dinklage, "Game of Thrones," HBO
Supporting Actress in a Comedy Series: Alex Borstein, "The Marvelous Mrs. Maisel," Amazon
Supporting Actor in a Comedy Series: Henry Winkler, "Barry," HBO
Supporting Actress in a Limited Series or TV Movie: Merritt Wever, "Godless," Netflix
Supporting Actor in a Limited Series or TV Movie: Jeff Daniels, "Godless," Netflix
Variety Talk Series: "Last Week Tonight With John Oliver," HBO
Variety Sketch Series: "Saturday Night Live," NBC
Variety Special (Pre-Recorded): "Dave Chappelle: Equanimity," Netflix
Animated Program: "Rick And Morty," Adult Swim
Animated Program (Short Format): "Robot Chicken," Adult Swim

Reality Program—Competition: "RuPaul's Drag Race," VH1

Reality Program—Structured: "Queer Eye," Netflix

Reality Program—Unstructured: "United Shades of America with W. Kamau Bell," CNN

Host for a Reality or Reality/Competition Program: RuPaul, "RuPaul's Drag Race," VH1

Informational Series or Special: "Anthony Bourdain: Parts Unknown," CNN

Documentary or Nonfiction Series: "Wild Wild Country," Netflix

Documentary or Nonfiction Special: "The Zen Diaries of Garry Shandling," HBO

Children's Program: "The Magical Wand Chase: A Sesame Street Special," HBO

Drama Series Directing: Stephen Daldry, "Paterfamilias," "The Crown," Netflix

Comedy Series Directing: Amy Sherman-Palladino, "Pilot," "The Marvelous Mrs. Maisel," Amazon

Nonfiction Program Directing: Brett Morgan, "Jane," National Geographic

Variety, Music or Comedy Series Directing: Don Roy King, "Saturday Night Live," NBC

Variety Special Directing: Glenn Weiss, "The Oscars," ABC

Limited Series, TV Movie or Dramatic Special Directing: Ryan Murphy, "The Man Who Would Be Vogue," "The Assassination of Gianni Versace: American Crime Story," FX

Drama Series Writing: Joel Fields and Joe Weisberg, "Start," "The Americans," FX

Comedy Series Writing: Amy Sherman-Palladino, "Pilot," "The Marvelous Mrs. Maisel," Amazon

Variety, Music or Comedy Series Writing: "Last Week Tonight With John Oliver," HBO

Variety Special Writing: John Mulaney, "John Mulaney: Kid Gorgeous At Radio City," Netflix

Limited Series, TV Movie or Dramatic Special Writing: William Bridges and Charlie Brooker, *Black Mirror: USS Callister,* Netflix

AWARDS FOR ARTS, HUMANITIES AND JOURNALISM

NOBEL PRIZES

Highly prestigious international awards given yearly since 1901. Details can be found at www.nobelprize.org.

2018 Recipients:

Peace: Denis Mukwege and Nadia Murad

Physics: Arthur Ashkin, Gérard Mourou and Donna Strickland

Chemistry: Frances H. Arnold, George P. Smith and Sir Gregory P. Winter

Physiology or Medicine: James P. Allison and Tasuku Honjo

Literature: *(No prize awarded.)*

Economics: William D. Nordhaus and Paul M. Romer

MACARTHUR FELLOWS 2018

Named by the MacArthur Foundation recognizing exceptionally creative individuals with a track record of achievement and the potential for even more significant contributions in the future.

Matthew Aucoin, composer and conductor

Julie Ault, artist and curator

William J. Barber II, pastor and social justice advocate

Clifford Brangwynne, biophysical engineer

Natalie Diaz, poet

Livia S. Eberlin, analytical chemist

Deborah Estrin, computer scientist

Amy Finkelstein, health economist

Gregg Gonsalves, epidemiologist and global health advocate

Vijay Gupta, violinist and social justice advocate

Becca Heller, human rights lawyer

Raj Jayadev, community organizer

Titus Kaphar, painter

John Keene, writer

Kelly Link, fiction writer

Dominique Morisseau, playwright

Okwui Okpokwasili, choreographer and performer

Kristina Olson, psychologist

Lisa Parks, media scholar

Rebecca Sandefur, sociologist and legal scholar

Allan Sly, mathematician

Sarah T. Stewart, planetary scientist

Wu Tsang, filmmaker and performance artist

Doris Tsao, neuroscientist

Ken Ward, Jr., investigative journalist

2019 PULITZER PRIZES

Honoring excellence in journalism and the arts. First awarded in 1917.

LETTERS, DRAMA AND MUSIC

Fiction: *The Overstory,* Richard Powers

Drama: *Fairview,* Jackie Sibblies Drury

History: *Frederick Douglass: Prophet of Freedom,* David W. Blight

Biography: *The New Negro: The Life of Alain Locke,* Jeffrey C. Stewart

Poetry: *Be With,* Forrest Gander

General Nonfiction: *Amity and Prosperity: One Family and the Fracturing of America,* Eliza Griswold

Music: *p r i s m,* Ellen Reid

JOURNALISM

Public Service: *South Florida Sun Sentinel* staff

Breaking News Reporting: *Pittsburgh Post-Gazette* staff

Investigative Reporting: Matt Hamilton, Harriet Ryan and Paul Pringle, *Los Angeles Times*

Explanatory Reporting: David Barstow, Susanne Craig and Russ Buettner, *The New York Times*

Local Reporting: *The Advocate* staff

National Reporting: *The Wall Street Journal* staff

International Reporting: Maggie Michael, Maad al-Zikry and Nariman El-Mofty, Associated Press, and Reuters staff with notable contributions from Wa Lone and Kyaw Soe Oo

Feature Writing: Hannah Dreier, *ProPublica*

Commentary: Tony Messenger, *St. Louis Post-Dispatch*

Criticism: Carlos Lozada, *The Washington Post*

Editorial Writing: Brent Staples, *The New York Times*

Editorial Cartooning: Darrin Bell, freelance cartoonist

Breaking News Photography: Reuters photography staff

Feature Photography: Lorenzo Tugnoli, *The Washington Post*

Special Citations: Aretha Franklin and *Capital Gazette* staff

2018 GEORGE POLK AWARDS
70th Annual

Awarded for special achievement in journalism.

Special Award: David Ignatius and Karen Attiah, *The Washington Post*

Special Award: Madeleine Baran and Samara Freemark, APM Reports

National Reporting: *The New York Times* staff

Foreign Reporting: Wa Lone and Kyaw Soe Oo, Reuters

State Reporting: Jeff Adelson, Gordon Russell, John Simerman and *The Advocate* staff (New Orleans)

Local Reporting: Kathleen McGrory and Neil Bedi, *Tampa Bay Times*

Immigration Reporting: *ProPublica* staff

Political Reporting: David Barstow, Susanne Craig and Russ Buettner, *The New York* Times

Environmental Reporting: Larry C. Price and reporters for *Undark Magazine*

Medical Reporting: Kirby Dick, Amy Ziering and Amy Herdy, Netflix

Magazine Reporting: Ben Taub, *The New Yorker*

Education Reporting: Craig Harris, Anne Ryman, Alden Woods and Justin Price, *The Arizona Republic*

Justice Reporting: Julie K. Brown, *Miami Herald*

Local Television Reporting: Joe Bruno, WSOC-TV

Foreign Television Reporting: Jane Ferguson, "PBS NewsHour"

Career Award: Bill Siemering, NPR

2018 PEABODY AWARDS
78th Annual Awards

Entertainment

"Barry" (HBO)

"Hannah Gadsby: Nanette" (Netflix)

"Killing Eve" (BBC America)

"Patriot Act with Hasan Minhaj" (Netflix)

"Pose" (FX)

"Random Acts of Flyness" (HBO)

"The Americans" (FX)

"The End of the F***ing World" (Netflix)

"The Good Place" (NBC)

Children/Youth

"Steven Universe" (Cartoon Network)

Documentary

A Dangerous Son (HBO)

Dolores (PBS)

The Judge (PBS)

Lorraine Hansberry: Sighted Eyes/Feeling Heart (PBS)

Minding the Gap (Hulu/PBS)

POV: The Apology (PBS)

"The Facebook Dilemma" (PBS)

The Jazz Ambassadors (**PBS**)

Career Achievement Award

Rita Moreno

Institutional Awards

Kartemquin Films

"Sesame Street"

Catalyst Award

ProPublica

News

Anatomy of a Killing (BBC)

"Back of the Class" (NBC affiliate/KING-TV)

"Cambridge Analytica" (Channel 4 News)

"**Separated:** Children at the Border" (PBS)

"**Spartan Silence:** Crisis at Michigan State" (ESPN)

"The Plastic Problem" (PBS)

"**$2 Tests:** Bad Arrests" (WAGA-TV)

Radio/Podcast

"Believed" (NPR)

"Buried Truths" (WABE)

"Caliphate" (*The New York Times*)

"Kept Out" (Public radio stations nationwide)

"Monumental Lies" (Public radio stations nationwide)

AWARDS FOR LITERATURE

NATIONAL BOOK AWARDS 2018
69th Annual

Given annually by the National Book Foundation.

Fiction: *The Friend,* Sigrid Nunez

Nonfiction: *The New Negro: The Life of Alain Locke,* Jeffrey C. Stewart

Poetry: *Indecency,* Justin Phillip Reed

Young People's Literature: *The Poet X,* Elizabeth Acevedo

Translated Literature: *The Emissary;* Margaret Mitsutani, translator; Yoko Tawada, author

THE NATIONAL BOOK CRITICS CIRCLE AWARDS 2018

Fiction: *Milkman,* Anna Burns

General Nonfiction: *Directorate S: The C.I.A. and America's Secret Wars in Afghanistan,* Steve Coll

Biography: *Flash: The Making of Weegee the Famous,* Christopher Bonanos

Autobiography: *Belonging: A German Reckons with History and Home,* Nora Krug

Poetry: *The Carrying,* Ada Limón

Criticism: *Feel Free: Essays,* Zadie Smith

John Leonard Prize (Outstanding first book in any genre): *There There,* Tommy Orange

Nona Balakian Citation for Excellence in Reviewing: Maureen Corrigan

Ivan Sandrof Lifetime Achievement Award: Arte Público Press

PEN/FAULKNER AWARD FOR FICTION 2019

An award given by an organization of writers to honor their peers.

Call Me Zebra, Azareen Van der Vliet Oloomi

Finalists

Tomb of the Unknown Racist, Blanche McCrary Boyd

The Overstory, Richard Powers

Love War Stories, Ivelisse Rodriguez

Don't Skip Out on Me, Willy Vlautin

THE INDIES CHOICE BOOK AWARD WINNERS 2019

Given annually by the American Booksellers Association.

Adult Fiction: *Circe: A Novel,* Madeline Miller
Adult Nonfiction: *Educated: A Memoir,* Tara Westover
Adult Debut: *There There: A Novel,* Tommy Orange
Audiobook: *Circe: A Novel,* by Madeline Miller, read by Perdita Weeks
Young Adult: *The Poet X,* Elizabeth Acevedo
E.B. White Read-Aloud Award—Middle Reader: *Ghost Boys,* Jewell Parker Rhodes
E.B. White Read-Aloud Award—Picture Book: *We Don't Eat Our Classmates,* Ryan T. Higgins
Indie Champion: Jacqueline Woodson
Picture Book Hall of Fame: *The Circus Ship,* Chris Van Dusen; *Grandfather's Journey,* Allen Say; *Why Mosquitoes Buzz in People's Ears,* Verna Aardema, Leo and Diane Dillon, illustrators

2019 AMERICAN LIBRARY ASSOCIATION AWARDS FOR CHILDREN'S BOOKS

The Newbery Medal has been awarded since 1922 and the Randolph Caldecott Medal since 1938. These and other ALA Awards are listed below. When not listed, honor books can be found at www.ala.org. The Alex Awards can be found at www.ala.org/yalsa/alex-awards.

NEWBERY MEDAL

For most distinguished contribution to American literature for children published in 2018.

Merci Suárez Changes Gears, Meg Medina

Honor Books

The Night Diary, Veera Hiranandani
The Book of Boy, Catherine Gilbert Murdock, author, and Ian Schoenherr, illustrator

CALDECOTT MEDAL

For most distinguished American picture book for children published in 2018.

Hello Lighthouse, Sophie Blackall, author and illustrator

Honor Books

Alma and How She Got Her Name, Juana Martinez-Neal, author and illustrator
A Big Mooncake for Little Star, Grace Lin, author and illustrator
The Rough Patch, Brian Lies, author and illustrator
Thank You, Omu! Oge Mora, author and illustrator

MICHAEL L. PRINTZ AWARD

For excellence in writing literature for young adults.

The Poet X, Elizabeth Acevedo

CORETTA SCOTT KING AWARD

For outstanding books by African-American authors and illustrators.

Author Award: Claire Hartfield, *A Few Red Drops: The Chicago Race Riot of 1919*

Illustrator Award: Ekua Holmes, *The Stuff of Stars*

CORETTA SCOTT KING/JOHN STEPTOE NEW TALENT AWARD

Author Award: Tiffany D. Jackson, *Monday's Not Coming*
Illustrator Award: Oge Mora, *Thank You, Omu!*

CORETTA SCOTT KING–VIRGINIA HAMILTON AWARD FOR LIFETIME ACHIEVEMENT

Dr. Pauletta Brown Bracy

ROBERT F. SIBERT AWARD

For most distinguished informational book for children published in 2018.

The Girl Who Drew Butterflies: How Maria Merian's Art Changed Science, Joyce Sidman

PURA BELPRÉ AWARDS

For the Latino author whose work best portrays, celebrates and affirms Latino culture in a children's book.

Author Award: Elizabeth Acevedo, *The Poet X*
Illustrator Award: Yuyi Morales, *Dreamers*

THEODOR SEUSS GEISEL MEDAL

For the author and illustrator of the most distinguished contribution to the body of American children's literature known as beginning reader books published in 2018.

Corey R. Tabor, *Fox the Tiger*

MILDRED L. BATCHELDER AWARD

For the best children's book in a language other than English and first published in a country other than the United States.

The Fox on the Swing, Evelina Daciūtė

MAY HILL ARBUTHNOT LECTURE AWARD

Neil Gaiman, recipient

CHILDREN'S LITERATURE LEGACY AWARD

For an author or illustrator whose books (published in the United States) have made a substantial and lasting contribution to literature for children.

Walter Dean Myers

WILLIAM C. MORRIS AWARD

For a debut book published by a first-time author writing for teens.

Darius the Great Is Not Okay, Adib Khorram

MARGARET A. EDWARDS AWARD

For lifetime achievement in writing for young adults.

M. T. Anderson

SCHNEIDER FAMILY BOOK AWARD

For books that embody an artistic expression of the disability experience.

Teen: *Anger Is a Gift,* Mark Oshiro
Middle School: *The Truth as Told by Mason Buttle,* Leslie Connor
Young Children: *Rescue & Jessica: A Life-Changing Friendship,* Jessica Kensky and Patrick Downes, authors; Scott Magoon, illustrator

STONEWALL BOOK AWARDS/MIKE MORGAN AND LARRY ROMANS CHILDREN'S AND YOUNG ADULT LITERATURE AWARD

For children's and young adult books of exceptional merit relating to the gay, lesbian, bisexual and transgender experience.

Julián Is a Mermaid, Jessica Love
Hurricane Child, Kheryn Callender

ASIAN/PACIFIC AMERICAN AWARD FOR LITERATURE

For a book that promotes Asian/Pacific American culture and heritage.

Picture Book: *Drawn Together,* Minh Lê, author, Dan Santat, illustrator
Children's Literature: *Front Desk,* Kelly Yang

Young Adult Literature: *Darius the Great Is Not Okay*, Adib Khorram

SYDNEY TAYLOR BOOK AWARD

For outstanding books for children and teens that authentically portray the Jewish experience.

Younger Readers: *All-of-a-Kind Family Hanukkah*, Emily Jenkins, author, Paul Zelinsky, illustrator

Older Readers: *Sweep: The Story of a Girl and Her Monster*, Jonathan Auxier

Teen Readers: *What the Night Sings*, Vesper Stamper

YALSA AWARD FOR EXCELLENCE IN NONFICTION FOR YOUNG ADULTS

The Unwanted: Stories of the Syrian Refugees, Don Brown, author and illustrator

WILLIAM C. MORRIS AWARD

For a debut book published by a first-time author writing for teens.

Darius the Great Is Not Okay, Adib Khorram

ODYSSEY AWARD

For the best audiobook produced for children and/or young adults.

Sadie, produced by Macmillan Audio, written by Courtney Summers, narrated by Rebecca Soler, Fred Berman, Dan Bittner, Gabra Zackman and more.

EXCELLENCE IN EARLY LEARNING DIGITAL MEDIA AWARD

Play and Learn Science, PBS Kids

THE NATIONAL JEWISH BOOK AWARDS 2018

Given annually by the Jewish Book Council, to the most outstanding books on aspects of Jewish life. 68th annual.

Jewish Book of the Year: *Hunting the Truth: Memoirs of Beate and Serge Klarsfeld*, Beate and Serge Klarsfeld

Carolyn Starman Hessel Mentorship Award: Susan Shapiro

American Jewish Studies: *The New American Judaism: How Jews Practice Their Religion Today*, Jack Wertheimer

Biography: *Witness: Lessons from Elie Wiesel's Classrooms*, Ariel Burger

Autobiography and Memoir: *My Country, My Life: Fighting for Israel, Searching for Peace*, Ehud Barak

Book Club: *The Girl from Berlin*, Ronald Balson

Children's Literature: *All Three Stooges*, Erica Perl

Contemporary Jewish Life and Practice: *The Going: A Meditation on Jewish Law*, Leon Wiener Dow

Debut Fiction: *The Book of Dirt*, Bram Presser

Jewish Education and Identity: *The Talmud: A Biography*, Barry Scott Wimpfheimer

Fiction: *The Last Watchman of Old Cairo*, Michael David Lukas

Poetry: *Holy Moly Carry Me: Poems*, Erika Meitner

History: *Rise and Kill First: The Secret History of Israel's Targeted Assassinations*, Ronen Bergman

Holocaust: *Anatomy of a Genocide: The Life and Death of a Town Called Buczacz*, Omer Bartov

Modern Jewish Thought and Experience: *Does Judaism Condone Violence? Holiness and Ethics in the Jewish Tradition*, Alan L. Mittleman

Scholarship: *Historical Atlas of Hasidism*, Marcin Wodziński

Sephardic Culture: *Dominion Built of Praise: Panegyric and Legitimacy Among Jews in the Medieval Mediterranean*, Jonathan Decter

Women's Studies: *Never a Native*, Alice Shalvi

Writing Based on Archival Material: *Rescue Board: The Untold Story of America's Efforts to Save the Jews of Europe*, Rebecca Erbelding

Young Adult: *Refugee*, Alan Gratz

THE MAN BOOKER INTERNATIONAL PRIZE 2019

Celebrates the finest in global fiction.

Celestial Bodies, Jokha Alharthi

Shortlisted Titles

The Years, Annie Ernaux

The Pine Islands, Marion Poschmann

Drive Your Plow Over the Bones of the Dead, Olga Tokarczuk

The Shape of the Ruins, Juan Gabriel Vásquez

The Remainder, Alia Trabucco Zerán

THE MAN BOOKER PRIZE 2018

Given annually to the best full-length novel written in English and published in the United Kingdom.

Milkman, Anna Burns

Shortlisted titles

Washington Black, Esi Edugyan

Everything Under, Daisy Johnson

The Mars Room, Rachel Kushner

The Overstory, Richard Powers

The Long Take, Robin Robertson

COSTA BOOK AWARDS 2018

An award given to celebrate the most enjoyable British writing of the previous year.

Book of the Year: *The Cut Out Girl*, Bart van Es

Novel: *Normal People*, Sally Rooney

First Novel: *The Seven Deaths of Evelyn Hardcastle*, Stuart Turton

Poetry: *Assurances*, J.O. Morgan

Biography: *The Cut Out Girl*, Bart van Es

Children's Book: *The Skylark's War*, Hilary McKay

Short Story: "Breathing Water," Caroline Ward Vine

2019 WOMEN'S PRIZE FOR FICTION

A British award celebrating the excellence of women's writing.

An American Marriage, Tayari Jones

Shortlisted titles

The Silence of the Girls, Pat Barker

My Sister, the Serial Killer, Oyinkan Braithwaite

Milkman, Anna Burns

Ordinary People, Diana Evans

Circe, Madeline Miller

THE EDGAR AWARDS 2019

The Mystery Writers of America honor the best in mystery writing produced in the previous year. Named in honor of Edgar Allan Poe.

Best Novel: *Down the River Unto the Sea*, Walter Mosley

Best First Novel by an American Author: *Bearskin*, James A. McLaughlin

Best Paperback Original: *If I Die Tonight*, Alison Gaylin

Best Fact Crime: *Tinderbox: The Untold Story of the Up Stairs Lounge Fire and the Rise of Gay Liberation*, Robert W. Fieseler

Best Critical/Biographical Work: *Classic American Crime Fiction of the 1920s*, Leslie S. Klinger

Best Short Story: "English 398: Fiction Workshop" (*Ellery Queen Mystery Magazine*), Art Taylor

Best Juvenile: *Otherwood*, Pete Hautman

Best Young Adult: *Sadie*, Courtney Summers

Best Television Episode Teleplay: "The One That Holds Everything" – "The Romanoffs," Teleplay by Matthew Weiner and Donald Joh

Robert L. Fish Award: "How Does He Die This Time?" (*Ellery Queen Mystery Magazine*), Nancy Novick

Grand Master: Martin Cruz Smith

Raven Award: Marilyn Stasio, *New York Times*

Ellery Queen Award: Linda Landrigan, *Alfred Hitchcock Mystery Magazine*

Mary Higgins Clark Award: *The Widows of Malabar Hill*, Sujata Massey

Sue Grafton Memorial Award: *Shell Game*, Sara Paretsky

THE HUGO AWARDS 2018

Also known as the Science Fiction Achievement Award, given annually by the World Science Fiction Society. 63rd annual awards.

Best Novel: *The Stone Sky*, N.K. Jemisin

Best Novella: *All Systems Red*, Martha Wells

Best Novelette: "The Secret Life of Bots," Suzanne Palmer

Best Related Work: *No Time to Spare: Thinking About What Matters*, Ursula K. Le Guin

Best Short Story: "Welcome to your Authentic Indian Experience™," Rebecca Roanhorse

Best Graphic Story: *Monstress, Volume 2: The Blood*, Marjorie M. Liu, author; Sana Takeda, illustrator

Best Dramatic Presentation, Long Form: *Wonder Woman*, screenplay by Allan Heinberg, story by Zack Snyder and Allan Heinberg and Jason Fuchs, directed by Patty Jenkins

Best Dramatic Presentation, Short Form: "The Good Place: The Trolley Problem," written by Josh Siegal and Dylan Morgan, directed by Dean Holland

Best Editor, Short Form: Lynne M. Thomas and Michael Damian Thomas

Best Editor, Long Form: Sheila E. Gilbert

Best Professional Artist: Sana Takeda

Best Semiprozine: *Uncanny Magazine*, edited by Lynne M. Thomas and Michael Damian Thomas, Michi Trota and Julia Rios; podcast produced by Erika Ensign and Steven Schapansky

Best Fanzine: *File 770*, edited by Mike Glyer

Best Fancast: "Ditch Diggers," presented by Mur Lafferty and Matt Wallace

Best Fan Writer: Sarah Gailey

Best Fan Artist: Geneva Benton

Best Series: *World of the Five Gods*, by Lois McMaster Bujold

John W. Campbell Award for Best New Writer (Dell Magazines): Rebecca Roanhorse

THE NEBULA AWARDS 2018

53rd annual awards given by Science Fiction and Fantasy Writers of America, Inc.

Novel: *The Calculating Stars*, Mary Robinette Kowal

Novella: "The Tea Master and the Detective," Aliette de Bodard

Novelette: "The Only Harmless Great Thing," Brooke Bolander

Short Story: "The Secret Lives of the Nine Negro Teeth of George Washington," P. Djèlí Clark

Ray Bradbury Award for Outstanding Dramatic Production: Spider-Man: Into the Spider-Verse written by Phil Lord and Rodney Rothman

Andre Norton Award: *Children of Blood and Bone*, Tomi Adeyemi

Game Writing: Black Mirror: Bandersnatch, Charlie Brooker

Solstice Award: Nisi Shawl, Neil Clarke

Damon Knight Grand Master Award: William Gibson

Service to SFWA Award: Lee Martindale

THE LAMBDA LITERARY AWARDS 2019

31st annual, to recognize excellence in lesbian/gay/bisexual/transgender/queer (LGBTQ) literature, for works published in 2018.

Lesbian Fiction: *The Tiger Flu*, Larissa Lai

Gay Fiction: *Jonny Appleseed*, Joshua Whitehead

Bisexual Fiction: *Disoriental*, Négar Djavadi

Transgender Fiction: *Little Fish*, Casey Plett

Bisexual Nonfiction: *Out of Step: A Memoir*, Anthony Moll

LGBTQ Nonfiction: *Looking for Lorraine: The Radiant and Radical Life of Lorraine Hansberry*, Imani Perry

Transgender Nonfiction: *Histories of the Transgender Child*, Julian Gill-Peterson

Lesbian Poetry: *Each Tree Could Hold a Noose or a House*, Ru Puro

Gay Poetry: *Indecency*, Justin Phillip Reed

Bisexual Poetry: *We Play a Game*, Duy Doan

Transgender Poetry: *lo tercario / the tertiary*, Raquel Salas Rivera

Lesbian Mystery: *A Study in Honor: A Novel*, Claire O'Dell

Gay Mystery: *Late Fees: A Pinx Video Mystery*, Marshall Thornton

Lesbian Memoir/Biography: *Chronology*, Zahra Patterson

Gay Memoir/Biography: *No Ashes in the Fire: Coming of Age Black and Free in America*, Darnell L. Moore

Lesbian Romance: *Beowulf for Cretins: A Love Story*, Ann McMan

Gay Romance: *Crashing Upwards*, S.C. Wynne

LGBTQ Erotica: *Miles & Honesty in SCFSX!*, Blue Delliquanti and Kazimir Lee

LGBTQ Anthology: *As You Like It: The Gerald Kraak Anthology, Volume II*, The Other Foundation

LGBTQ Children's/Young Adult: *Hurricane Child*, Kacen Callender

LGBTQ Drama: *Draw the Circle*, Mashuq Mushtaq Deen

LGBTQ Graphic Novel: *The Lie and How We Told It*, Tommi Parrish

LGBTQ SF/F/Horror: *The Breath of the Sun*, Isaac R. Fellman

LGBTQ Studies: *Toxic Silence: Race, Black Gender Identity and Addressing the Violence Against Black Transgender Women in Houston*, William T. Hoston

Trustee Award: Alexander Chee

Visionary Award: Masha Gessen

THE JAMES BEARD FOUNDATION BOOK AWARDS 2019
Given annually to the best original, English-language books on culinary topics published in the previous year.

Book of the Year: *Cocktail Codex*, Alex Day, Nick Fauchald, and David Kaplan, with Devon Tarby
Cookbook Hall of Fame: Jessica B. Harris
American Cooking: *Between Harlem and Heaven: Afro-Asian-American Cooking for Big Nights, Weeknights, and Every Day*, JJ Johnson and Alexander Smalls with Veronica Chambers
Baking and Dessert: *SUQAR: Desserts and Sweets from the Modern Middle East*, Greg Malouf and Lucy Malouf
Beverage: *Wine Folly: Magnum Edition*, Madeline Puckette and Justin Hammack
Restaurant and Professional: *Chicken and Charcoal: Yakitori, Yardbird, Hong Kong*, Matt Abergel
General Cooking: *Milk Street: Tuesday Nights*, Christopher Kimball
Health and Special Diets: *Eat a Little Better*, Sam Kass
International: *Feast: Food of the Islamic World*, Anissa Helou
Photography: *Tokyo New Wave*, Andrea Fazzari
Reference, History and Scholarship: *Canned: The Rise and Fall of Consumer Confidence in the American Food Industry*, Anna Zeide
Single Subject: *Goat: Cooking and Eating*, James Whetlor
Vegetable-focused Cooking: *Saladish*, Ilene Rosen
Writing: *Buttermilk Graffiti: A Chef's Journey to Discover America's New Melting-Pot Cuisine*, Edward Lee

AWARDS FOR MUSIC

2018 AMERICAN MUSIC AWARDS
46th Annual
Artist of the Year: Taylor Swift
New Artist of the Year: Camila Cabello
Collaboration of the Year: "Havana," Camila Cabello featuring Young Thug
Tour of the Year: Taylor Swift
Video of the Year: "Havana," Camila Cabello featuring Young Thug
Social Artist: BTS
Soundtrack: *Black Panther: The Album, Music From And Inspired By*

Pop/Rock
Male Artist: Post Malone
Female Artist: Taylor Swift
Band, Duo or Group: Migos
Album: *reputation*, Taylor Swift
Song: "Havana," Camila Cabello featuring Young Thug

Soul/Rhythm and Blues
Male: Khalid
Female Artist: Rihanna
Album: *17*, XXXTENTACION
Song: "Finesse," Bruno Mars and Cardi B

Country
Male Artist: Kane Brown
Female Artist: Carrie Underwood
Band, Duo or Group: Florida Georgia Line
Album: *Kane Brown*, Kane Brown
Song: "Heaven," Kane Brown

Rap/Hip-Hop
Artist: Cardi B
Album: *beerbongs & bentleys*, Post Malone
Song: "Bodak Yellow (Money Moves)," Cardi B

Latin Artist: Daddy Yankee
Electronic Dance Music Artist: Marshmello
Contemporary Inspirational Artist: Lauren Daigle
Alternative Artist: Panic! At The Disco
Adult Contemporary Artist: Shawn Mendes

2018 COUNTRY MUSIC ASSOCIATION AWARDS
52nd Annual
Entertainer of the Year: Keith Urban
Male Vocalist of the Year: Chris Stapleton
Female Vocalist of the Year: Carrie Underwood
Vocal Group of the Year: Old Dominion
Vocal Duo of the Year: Brothers Osborne
New Artist of the Year: Luke Combs
Single of the Year: "Broken Halos," Chris Stapleton
Album of the Year: *Golden Hour*, Kacey Musgraves
Song of the Year: "Broken Halos," Mike Henderson, Chris Stapleton
Musician of the Year: Mac McAnally
Musical Event of the Year: "Everything's Gonna Be Alright," David Lee Murphy (with Kenny Chesney)
Music Video of the Year: "Marry Me," Thomas Rhett

2019 ACADEMY OF COUNTRY MUSIC AWARDS
54th Annual
Entertainer of the Year: Keith Urban
Male Vocalist of the Year: Thomas Rhett
Female Vocalist of the Year: Kacey Musgraves
Vocal Group of the Year: Old Dominion
Vocal Duo of the Year: Dan + Shay
New Female Artist of the Year: Ashley McBride
New Male Artist of the Year: Luke Combs
New Vocal Duo or Group of the Year: Lanco
Single of the Year: "Tequila," Dan + Shay
Album of the Year: *Golden Hour*, Kacey Musgraves

Song of the Year: "Tequila," Dan + Shay (Nicolle Galyon, Jordan Reynolds, and Dan Smyers, songwriters)

Songwriter of the Year: Shane McAnally

Video of the Year: "Drunk Girl," Chris Janson (Producer: Ben Skipworth, Director: Jeff Venable)

Music Event of the Year: "Burning Man," Dierks Bentley featuring Brothers Osborne

Artist of the Decade: Jason Aldean

2019 GRAMMY AWARDS

61st Annual

Record of the Year: "This Is America" by Childish Gambino

Album of the Year: *Golden Hour* by Kacey Musgraves

Song of the Year: "This is America" Donald Glover, Ludwig Göransson and Jeffery Lamar Williams, songwriters (Childish Gambino)

Best New Artist: Dua Lipa

Best Pop Solo Performance: "Joanne (Where Do You Think You're Goin'?)" by Lady Gaga

Best Pop Duo/Group Performance: "Shallow" by Lady Gaga and Bradley Cooper

Best Traditional Pop Vocal Album: *My Way,* Willie Nelson

Best Pop Vocal Album: *Sweetener,* Ariana Grande

Best Rock Performance: "When Bad Does Good" by Chris Cornell

Best Rock Song: "Masseduction" Jack Antonoff and Annie Clark, songwriters (St. Vincent)

Best Rock Album: *From The Fires,* Greta Van Fleet

Best Metal Performance: "Electric Messiah" by High On Fire

Best Alternative Music Album: *Colors,* Beck

Best Contemporary Instrumental Album: *Steve Gadd Band,* Steve Gadd Band

Best Urban Contemporary Album: *Everything Is Love,* The Carters

Best R&B Album: *H.E.R.,* H.E.R.

Best R&B Song: "Boo'd Up" Larrance Dopson, Joelle James, Ella Mai and Dijon McFarlane, songwriters (Ella Mai)

Best Traditional R&B Performance (TIE): "Bet Ain't Worth The Hand" by Leon Bridges and "How Deep Is Your Love" by PJ Morton featuring Yebba

Best R&B Performance: "Best Part," H.E.R. featuring Daniel Caesar

Best Rap/Sung Performance: "This Is America," Childish Gambino

Best Rap Song: "God's Plan," Aubrey Graham, Daveon Jackson, Brock Korsan, Ron LaTour, Matthew Samuels and Noah Shebib, songwriters (Drake)

Best Rap Performance (TIE): "King's Dead" by Kendrick Lamar, Jay Rock, Future and James Blake and "Bubblin" by Anderson .Paak

Best Rap Album: *Invasion of Privacy* by Cardi B

Best Country Solo Performance: "Butterflies" by Kacey Musgraves

Best Country Duo/Group Performance: "Tequila" by Dan + Shay

Best Country Song: "Space Cowboy" Luke Laird, Shane McAnally and Kacey Musgraves, songwriters (Kacey Musgraves)

Best Country Album: *Golden Hour,* Kacey Musgraves

Best Americana Album: *By The Way, I Forgive You,* Brandi Carlile

Best Bluegrass Album: *The Travelin' McCourys,* The Travelin' McCourys

Best Contemporary Blues Album: *Please Don't Be Dead,* Fantastic Negrito

Best Traditional Blues Album: *The Blues Is Alive and Well,* Buddy Guy

Best Folk Album: *All Ashore,* Punch Brothers

Best Regional Roots Music Album: *No 'Ane'i,* Kalani Pe'a

Best American Roots Performance: "The Joke," Brandi Carlile

Best American Roots Song: "The Joke," Brandi Carlile, Dave Cobb, Phil Hanseroth and Tim Hanseroth, songwriters (Brandi Carlile)

Best Jazz Vocal Album: *The Window,* Cécile McLorin Salvant

Best Improvised Jazz Solo: "Don't Fence Me In," John Daversa, soloist

Best Jazz Instrumental Album: *Emanon,* The Wayne Shorter Quartet

Best Large Jazz Ensemble Album: *American Dreamers: Voices of Hope, Music of Freedom,* John Daversa Big Band featuring DACA Artists

Best Latin Jazz Album: *Back to the Sunset,* Dafnis Prieto Big Band

Best Gospel Performance/Song: "Never Alone," Tori Kelly featuring Kirk Franklin

Best Contemporary Christian Music Performance/Song: "You Say," Lauren Daigle; Lauren Daigle, Jason Ingram and Paul Mabury, songwriters

Best Gospel Album: *Hiding Place,* Tori Kelly

Best Contemporary Christian Music Album: *Look Up Child,* Lauren Daigle

Best Roots Gospel Album: *Unexpected,* Jason Crabb

Best Latin Pop Album: *Sincera,* Claudia Brant

Best Latin Rock, Urban or Alternative Album: *Aztlán,* Zoé

Best Tropical Latin Album: *Anniversary,* Spanish Harlem Orchestra

Best Regional Mexican Music Album (Including Tejano): *¡México Por Siempre!,* Luis Miguel

Best Dance Recording: "Electricity," Silk City and Dua Lipa featuring Diplo and Mark Ronson

Best Dance/Electronic Album: *Woman Worldwide,* Justice

Best Reggae Album: *44/876,* Sting and Shaggy

Best World Music Album: *Freedom,* Soweto Gospel Choir

Best New Age Album: *Opium Moon,* Opium Moon

Best Instrumental Composition: "Blut und Boden (Blood and Soil)," Terence Blanchard

Best Arrangement, Instrumental or A Cappella: "Stars and Stripes Forever," John Daversa, arranger (John Daversa Big Band featuring DACA Artists)

Best Arrangement, Instruments and Vocals: "Spiderman Theme," Mark Kibble, Randy Waldman and Justin Wilson, arrangers (Randy Waldman Featuring Take 6 and Chris Potter)

Best Historical Album: *Voices of Mississippi: Artists and Musicians Documented by William Ferris,* William Ferris, April Ledbetter and Steven Lance Ledbetter, compilation producers; Michael Graves, mastering engineer (Various Artists)

Best Engineered Album, Non-Classical: *Colors,* Julian Burg, Serban Ghenea, David "Elevator" Greenbaum, John Hanes, Beck Hansen, Greg Kurstin, Florian Lagatta, Cole M.G.N., Alex Pasco, Jesse Shatkin, Darrell Thorp and Cassidy Turbin, engineers; Chris Bellman, Tom Coyne, Emily Lazar and Randy Merrill, mastering engineers (Beck)

Producer of the Year, Non-Classical: Pharrell Williams

Best Remixed Recording, Non-Classical: "Walking Away (Mura Masa Remix)," Alex Crossan, remixer (Haim)

Best Immersive Audio Album: *Eye in the Sky—35th Anniversary Edition,* Alan Parsons, surround mix engineer; Dave Donnelly, PJ Olsson and Alan Parsons, surround mastering engineers; Alan Parsons, surround producer (The Alan Parsons Project)

Best Engineered Album, Classical: *Shostakovich: Symphonies Nos. 4 and 11,* Shawn Murphy and Nick Squire, engineers; Tim Martyn, mastering engineer (Andris Nelsons and Boston Symphony Orchestra)

Producer of the Year, Classical: Blanton Alspaugh

Best Orchestral Performance: *Shostakovich: Symphonies Nos. 4 and 11,* Andris Nelsons, conductor (Boston Symphony Orchestra)

Best Opera Recording: *Bates: The (R)evolution of Steve Jobs,* Michael Christie, conductor; Sasha Cooke, Jessica E. Jones, Edward Parks, Garrett Sorenson and Wei Wu; Elizabeth Ostrow, producer (The Santa Fe Opera Orchestra)

Best Choral Performance: *McLoskey: Zealot Canticles,* Donald Nally, conductor (Doris Hall-Gulati, Rebecca Harris, Arlen Hlusko, Lorenzo Raval and Mandy Wolman; The Crossing)

Best Chamber Music/Small Ensemble Performance: *Anderson, Laurie: Landfall,* Laurie Anderson and Kronos Quartet

Best Classical Instrumental Solo: *Kernis: Violin Concerto,* James Ehnes; Ludovic Morlot, conductor (Seattle Symphony)

Best Classical Solo Vocal Album: *Songs of Orpheus—Monteverdi, Caccini, D'India and Landi,* Karim Sulayman; Jeannette Sorrell, conductor; Apollo's Fire, ensembles

Best Contemporary Classical Composition: *Kernis: Violin Concerto,* Aaron Jay Kernis, composer (James Ehnes, Ludovic Morlot and Seattle Symphony)

Best Classical Compendium: *Fuchs: Piano Concerto 'Spiritualist'; Poems of Life; Glacier; Rush,* JoAnn Falletta, conductor; Tim Handley, producer

Best Comedy Album: *Equanimity and The Bird Revelation,* Dave Chappelle

Best Children's Album: *All the Sounds,* Lucy Kalantari and The Jazz Cats

Best Spoken Word Album (Includes Poetry, Audio Books and Storytelling): *Faith—A Journey For All,* Jimmy Carter

Best Musical Theater Album: *The Band's Visit,* Etai Benson, Adam Kantor, Katrina Lenk and Ari'el Stachel, principal soloists; Dean Sharenow and David Yazbek, producers; David Yazbek, composer and lyricist (Original Broadway Cast)

Best Compilation Soundtrack for Visual Media: *The Greatest Showman,* Hugh Jackman (and Various Artists); Alex Lacamoire, Benj Pasek, Justin Paul and Greg Wells, compilation producers

Best Score Soundtrack for Visual Media: *Black Panther,* Ludwig Göransson, composer

Best Song Written for Visual Media: "Shallow," Lady Gaga, Mark Ronson, Anthony Rossomando and Andrew Wyatt, songwriters (Lady Gaga and Bradley Cooper)

Best Music Video: "This Is America," Childish Gambino; Hiro Murai, video director; Ibra Ake, Jason Cole and Fam Rothstein, video producers

Best Music Film: *Quincy,* Quincy Jones; Alan Hicks and Rashida Jones, video directors; Paula DuPré Pesmen, video producer

Best Recording Package: *MASSEDUCTION,* Willo Perron, art director (St. Vincent)

Best Boxed or Special Limited Edition Package: *Squeeze Box: The Complete Works of "Weird Al" Yankovic,* Meghan Foley, Annie Stoll and Al Yankovic, art directors ("Weird Al" Yankovic)

Best Album Notes: *Voices of Mississippi: Artists and Musicians Documented by William Ferris,* David Evans, album notes writer (Various Artists)

◆ Index ◆

Montgomery Boycott Arrests: Anniv, Feb 22

Montgomery Bus Boycott Begins: Anniv, Dec 5

Montgomery Bus Boycott Ends: Anniv, Dec 20

NAACP Founded: Anniv, Feb 12

New York Slave Revolt: Anniv, Apr 7

Niagara Movement Founded: Anniv, Jul 11

Parks, Rosa: Birth Anniv, Feb 4

Ralph Bunche Awarded Nobel Peace Prize: Anniv, Dec 10

Robinson Named Baseball's First Black Manager: Anniv, Oct 3

Rosa Parks Day, Dec 1

Saint Louis Race Riots: Anniv, Jul 2

Scottsboro Trial: Anniv, Apr 6

Silent Parade in New York City: Anniv, Jul 28

16th Street Baptist Church Bombing: Anniv, Sep 15

Soul Food Month, Natl, Jun 1

Spelman College Established: Anniv, Apr 11

Stokes Becomes First Black Mayor in US: Anniv, Nov 13

Trayvon Martin Shooting: Anniv, Feb 26

Truth, Sojourner: Death Anniv, Nov 26

Tubman, Harriet: Death Anniv, Mar 10

Tuskegee Airmen Activated: Anniv, Mar 22

Tuskegee Institute Opening: Anniv, Jul 4

US Colored Troops Founders Day (Washington, DC), May 22

Waco Horror: Jesse Washington Lynching: Anniv, May 15

Wheatley, Phillis: Poetry Collection Published: Anniv, Sep 1

With All Deliberate Speed: Anniv, May 31

African Freedom Day, May 25

African Violet Week, Natl (Little Rock, AR), May 24

Agassi, Andre: Birth, Apr 29

Agassiz, Louis: Birth Anniv, May 28

Agee, James: Birth Anniv, Nov 27

Aggie Muster, Apr 21

Agnew Resignation: Anniv, Oct 10

Agnew, Spiro: Birth Anniv, Nov 9

Agriculture (including state and county fairs),

Agriculture Day, Natl, Mar 24

Alabama Natl Fair (Montgomery, AL), Oct 9

Alaska State Fair (Palmer, AK), Aug 27

Arizona State Fair (Phoenix, AZ), Oct 2

Arkansas State Fair (Little Rock, AR), Oct 9

Bangor State Fair (Bangor, ME), Jul 23

Big E (West Springfield, MA), Sep 18

Blue Hill Fair (Blue Hill, ME), Sep 3

Calgary Stampede (Calgary, AB, Canada), Jul 3

California State Fair (Sacramento, CA), Jul 10

Colorado State Fair (Pueblo, CO), Aug 28

Delaware State Fair (Harrington, DE), Jul 23

Eastern Idaho State Fair (Blackfoot, ID), Sep 4

Fairfest (Hastings, NE), Jul 15

Farm Safety and Health Week, Natl (Pres Proc), Sep 20

Florida State Fair (Tampa, FL), Feb 6

Georgia Natl Fair (Perry, GA), Oct 8

Grange Month, Apr 1

Harvard Milk Days Fest (Harvard, IL), Jun 5

Hood River County Fair (Hood River, OR), Jul 22

Hopkinton State Fair (Contoocook, NH), Sep 4

Illinois State Fair (Springfield, IL), Aug 13

Indiana State Fair (Indianapolis, IN), Aug 7

Iowa State Fair (Des Moines, IA), Aug 13

Kansas State Fair (Hutchinson, KS), Sep 11

Kentucky State Fair (Louisville, KY), Aug 20

Livestock Show, Rio Grande Valley (Mercedes, TX), Mar 12

Louisiana, State Fair of (Shreveport, LA), Oct 22

Maryland State Fair (Timonium, MD), Aug 27

Michigan State Fair (Novi, MI), Sep 3

Minnesota State Fair (St. Paul, MN), Aug 27

Mississippi State Fair (Jackson, MS), Oct 7

Missouri State Fair (Sedalia, MO), Aug 13

Montana State Fair (Great Falls, MT), Jul 31

Morrill Land Grant Act Passed: Anniv, Jul 1

Nebraska State Fair (Grand Island, NE), Aug 28

Nevada State Fair (Carson City, NV), Jun 4

New Jersey State Fair/Sussex Farm and Horse Show (Augusta, NJ), Jul 31

New Mexico State Fair (Albuquerque, NM), Sep 10

New York State Fair (Syracuse, NY), Aug 28

North Carolina State Fair (Raleigh, NC), Oct 15

North Dakota State Fair (Minot, ND), Jul 17

No-Tillage Conference, Natl (St. Louis, MO), Jan 7

Nottingham Goose Fair (Nottingham, England), Sep 30

Ohio State Fair (Columbus, OH), Jul 29

Oklahoma State Fair (Oklahoma City, OK), Sep 17

Oregon State Fair (Salem, OR), Aug 27

Purplehull Pea Fest/Rotary Tiller Race, World Chmpshp (Emerson, AR), Jun 26

Ruffin, Edmund: Birth Anniv, Jan 5

Rural Life Sunday, May 17

Rural Women, Intl Day of (UN), Oct 15

Soil Day, World (UN), Dec 5

South Carolina State Fair (Columbia, SC), Oct 14

South Dakota State Fair (Huron, SD), Sep 3

Southeast Missouri District Fair (Cape Girardeau, MO), Sep 12

State Fair of Texas (Dallas, TX), Sep 25

State Fair of West Virginia (Lewisburg, WV), Aug 13

Stewardship Week, Apr 26

Tennessee State Fair (Nashville, TN), Sep 11

Utah State Fair (Salt Lake City, UT), Sep 10

Vermont State Fair (Rutland, VT), Aug 11

Virginia, State Fair of (Doswell, VA), Sep 25

Washington State Fair (Puyallup, WA), Sep 4

Wayne Chicken Show (Wayne, NE), Jul 10

Western Idaho Fair (Boise, ID), Aug 21

Wisconsin State Fair (West Allis, WI), Aug 6

World Ag Expo (Tulare, CA), Feb 11

World Day for Farmed Animals, Oct 2

Wyoming State Fair & Rodeo (Douglas, WY), Aug 11

Agron, Dianna: Birth, Apr 30

Aguilera, Christina: Birth, Dec 18

Agutter, Jenny: Birth, Dec 20

Ahmed, Riz: Birth, Dec 1

Ahn, Viktor: Birth, Nov 23

Ai Weiwei: Birth, Aug 28

AiArthritis Day, World, May 20

Aida Premieres: Anniv, Dec 24

AIDS,

AIDS Day, World (UN), Dec 1

AIDS Day, World (Pres Proc), Dec 1

Awareness Month, PPSI/ACA, Nov 1

Black HIV/AIDS Awareness Day, Natl, Feb 7

Condom Month, Natl, Feb 1

First Noted: Anniv, Jun 5

HIV Long-Term Survivors Awareness Day, Jun 5

HIV Testing Day, Natl, Jun 27

HIV/AIDS and Aging Awareness Day, Natl, Sep 18

Women and Girls HIV/AIDS Awareness Day, Natl, Mar 10

Zero Discrimination Day (UNAIDS), Mar 1

Aiello, Danny, Jr: Birth, Jun 20

Aiken, Conrad: Birth Anniv, Aug 5

Aikman, Troy: Birth, Nov 21

Ailey, Alvin: Birth Anniv, Jan 5

Aimee, Anouk: Birth, Apr 27

Ainge, Danny: Birth, Mar 17

Air Force Academy, US, Established: Anniv, Apr 1

Air-Conditioning Appreciation Days, Jul 3

Ajaye, Franklyn: Birth, May 13

Ajayi, Jay: Birth, Jun 15

Akeley, Carl: Birth Anniv, May 19

Akers, Michelle: Birth, Feb 1

Akhmatova, Anna: Birth Anniv, Jun 23

Akihito: Birth, Dec 23

Akinnuoye-Agbaje, Adewale: Birth, Aug 22

Akon: Birth, Apr 16

Al Qaeda,

Attack on America: Anniv, Sep 11

Fall of Kabul: Anniv, Nov 13

London Terrorist Bombings: Anniv, Jul 7

Madrid Train Bombings: Anniv, Mar 11

Osama Bin Laden Killed: Anniv, May 2

Alabama,

Admission Day, Dec 14

American Indian Heritage Day, Oct 12

Battle of Mobile Bay: Anniv, Aug 5

Confederate Memorial Day, Apr 27

Helen Keller Fest (Tuscumbia), Jun 25

Ivey, Kay: Birth, Oct 15

Jones, Doug: Birth, May 4

Natl Fair (Montgomery), Oct 9

Shelby, Richard C.: Birth, May 6

Bicycle,
Bicycle Day, World (UN), Jun 3
Bike Month, Natl, May 1
Bike Shop Day, Dec 5
Bike To School Day, Natl, May 6
Bike to Work Day, Natl, May 15
Bike Van Buren (Van Buren County, IA), Aug 15
Five Boro Bike Tour (New York, NY), May 3
Giro d'Italia (Italy), May 9
Hotter 'n Hell Hundred Bike Race (Wichita Falls, TX), Aug 27
Learn To Ride a Bike Day, May 2
RAGBRAI—Register's Bicycle Ride Across Iowa (Des Moines, IA), Jul 19
Tour de France, Jun 27
Tour Down Under, Santos (Australia), Jan 16
UCI Road World Chmpshps (Aigle-Martigny, Switzerland), Sep 20
UCI Track Cycling World Chmpshps (Berlin, Germany), Feb 26
Vuelta a Espana (Spain), Aug 14
Biden, Jill: Birth, Jun 5
Biden, Joe: Birth, Nov 20
Bieber, Hailey Baldwin: Birth, Nov 22
Bieber, Justin: Birth, Mar 1
Biel, Jessica: Birth, Mar 3
Biennale Architettura (Venice, Italy), May 23
Bierce, Ambrose: Birth Anniv, Jun 24
Bifocals at the Monitor Liberation Day, Dec 1
Big Bang Coined: Anniv, Mar 28
Big Bend Natl Park Established: Anniv, Jun 12
Big Bertha Paris Gun: Anniv, Mar 23
Big Boi: Birth, Feb 1
Big E, The (West Springfield, MA), Sep 18
Big Sky State Games (Billings, MT), Jul 17
Big Wind: Anniv, Apr 12
Bigelow, Kathryn: Birth, Nov 27
Biggio, Craig: Birth, Dec 14
Biggs, Jason: Birth, May 12
Bikila, Abebe: Birth Anniv, Aug 7
Bikini Debut: Anniv, Jul 5
Biles, Simone: Birth, Mar 14
Bilingual Child Month, Celebrating the, Oct 1
Bill of Rights Day (Pres Proc), Dec 15
Bill of Rights Proposed: Anniv, Jun 8
Bill of Rights: Anniv, Dec 15
Bill of Rights: Anniv of First State Ratification, Nov 20
Bill, Tony: Birth, Aug 23
Billups, Chauncey: Birth, Sep 25
Billy the Kid: Birth Anniv, Nov 23
Bilson, Rachel: Birth, Aug 25
Bin Laden, Osama, Killed: Anniv, May 2
Bingo's Birthday Month, Dec 1
Binoche, Juliette: Birth, Mar 9
Biodiesel Day, Natl (Rudolph Diesel Birth Anniv), Mar 18
Biographers Day, May 16
Biological Clock Gene Discovered: Anniv, Apr 28
Biological Diversity, Intl Day for (UN), May 22
Bioterrorism/Disaster Education and Awareness Month, Jul 1
Bipolar Day, World, Mar 30
Bird, Larry: Birth, Dec 7

Birds,
Bald Eagle Appreciation Days (Keokuk, IA), Jan 18
Bird Day, Natl, Jan 5
Bird-Feeding Month, Natl, Feb 1
Christmas Bird Count, Dec 14
Curlew Day, Mar 16
Fest of Owls, Intl (Houston, MN), Mar 6
Great Backyard Bird Count, Feb 14
HummerBird Celebration (Rockport, Fulton, TX), Sep 17
Migratory Bird Day, Intl, May 9
Respect for Chickens Day, Intl, May 4
Swallows Depart from San Juan Capistrano (CA), Oct 23
Swallows Return to San Juan Capistrano (CA), Mar 19
Birdseye, Clarence: Birth Anniv, Dec 9
Birkebeinerrennet (Rena and Lillehammer, Norway), Mar 21
Birkin, Jane: Birth, Dec 14
Birmingham (AL) Resistance: Anniv, Apr 3
Birmingham Riots: Anniv (England), Jul 14
Birney, David: Birth, Apr 23
Birth Control Clinic Opened, First: Anniv, Oct 16
Birth Control Pills Sold: Anniv, Aug 18
Birth Defects Day, World, Mar 3
Biscotti Day, Natl, Sep 29
Bisexuality Day, Celebrate, Sep 23
Bishop, Elizabeth: Birth Anniv, Feb 8
Bishop, Elvin: Birth, Oct 21
Bismarck, Otto von: Birth Anniv, Apr 1
Bison Day, Natl, Nov 7
Bisset, Jacqueline: Birth, Sep 13
Bissett, Josie: Birth, Oct 5
Bizet, Georges: Birth Anniv, Oct 25
Bjorgen, Marit: Birth, Mar 21
Bjork: Birth, Nov 21
Black Dahlia Murder: Anniv, Jan 15
Black Friday, Nov 27
Black Hills Stock Show and Rodeo (Rapid City, SD), Jan 24
Black History Month, Natl, Feb 1
Black Nazarene Fiesta (Philippines), Jan 1
Black Nazarene, Feast of the (Philippines), Jan 9
Black Poetry Day, Oct 17
Black Press Day: Anniv of the First Black Newspaper, Mar 16
Black Sox Scandal/1919 World Series: Anniv, Oct 1
Black Women's History Month, Intl, Apr 1
Black, Clint: Birth, Feb 4
Black, Hugo La Fayette: Birth Anniv, Feb 27
Black, Lewis: Birth, Aug 30
Black, Lisa Hartman: Birth, Jun 1
Black, Lucas: Birth, Nov 29
Black, Shirley Temple: Birth Anniv, Apr 23
Blackbeard the Pirate (Edward Teach): Death Anniv, Nov 22
Blackburn, Marsha: Birth, Jun 6
Blackmun, Harry A.: Birth Anniv, Nov 12
Blackout, East Coast: Anniv, Nov 9
Blackpool Illuminations (Blackpool, England), Sep 4
Blackwell, Elizabeth, Awarded MD: Anniv, Jan 23
Blackwell, Elizabeth: Birth Anniv, Feb 3
Blades, Ruben: Birth, Jul 16
Blagojevich, Rod: Birth, Dec 10
Blah Blah Blah Day, Apr 17

Blaine, David: Birth, Apr 4
Blair, Bonnie: Birth, Mar 18
Blair, Linda: Birth, Jan 22
Blair, Tony: Birth, May 6
Blake, Eubie: Birth Anniv, Feb 7
Blake, James: Birth, Dec 28
Blake, Robert: Birth, Sep 18
Blake, William: Birth Anniv, Nov 28
Blakely, Susan: Birth, Sep 7
Blakey, Art: Birth Anniv, Oct 11
Blame Someone Else Day, Mar 13
Blanc, Mel: Birth Anniv, May 30
Blanchett, Cate: Birth, May 14
Blanco, Cuauhtemoc: Birth, Jan 17
Blass, Bill: Birth Anniv, Jun 22
Blatter, Sepp: Birth, Mar 10
Bledel, Alexis: Birth, Sep 16
Bledsoe, Drew: Birth, Feb 14
Bledsoe, Tempestt: Birth, Aug 1
Bleeth, Yasmine: Birth, Jun 14
Bleriot, Louis: Birth Anniv, Jul 1
Blessing of Animals at the Cathedral (Mexico), Jan 17
Blethyn, Brenda: Birth, Feb 20
Bleu, Corbin: Birth, Feb 21
Blige, Mary J.: Birth, Jan 11
Blind Americans Equality Day (Pres Proc), Oct 15
Blitz Begins: Anniv, Sep 7
Blizzard of '88, Great: Anniv, Mar 12
Block It Out Day, Natl, Nov 14
Blondin, Charles: Birth Anniv, Feb 28
Blondin, Charles: Conquest of Niagara Falls: Anniv, Jun 30
Blonsky, Nikki: Birth, Nov 9
Blood Donor Day, World, Jun 14
Bloodworth-Thomason, Linda: Birth, Apr 15
Bloody Sunday (Northern Ireland): Anniv, Jan 30
Bloom, Claire: Birth, Feb 15
Bloom, Harold: Birth, Jul 11
Bloom, Orlando: Birth, Jan 13
Bloom, Rachel: Birth, Apr 3
Bloomberg, Michael: Birth, Feb 14
Bloomer, Amelia Jenks: Birth Anniv, May 27
Bloomsday: Anniv, Jun 16
Blue Ridge Folklife Fest (Ferrum, VA), Oct 24
Blueberry Arts Fest (Ketchikan, AK), Jul 31
Blueberry Fest, Machias Wild (Machias, ME), Aug 14
Bluegrass. See also Fiddlers,
Four Corner States Bluegrass Fest (Wickenburg, AZ), Nov 13
Old Fiddlers' Conv (Galax, VA), Aug 3
Blues. See Jazz and Blues,
Chicago Blues Fest (Chicago, IL), Jun 12
New Orleans Jazz/Heritage Fest (New Orleans, LA), Apr 23
Bluford, Guion S., Jr: Birth, Nov 22
Blume, Judy: Birth, Feb 12
Blumenthal, Richard: Birth, Feb 13
Blunt, Emily: Birth, Feb 23
Blunt, James: Birth, Feb 22
Blunt, Roy: Birth, Jan 10
Bly, Nellie: Around the World in 72 Days: Anniv, Jan 25
Bly, Nellie: Birth Anniv, May 5
Bly, Robert: Birth, Dec 23
Blyleven, Bert: Birth, Apr 6

Brittany, Morgan: Birth, Dec 5
Britten, Benjamin: Birth Anniv, Nov 22
Britton, Connie: Birth, Mar 6
Broadbent, Jim: Birth, May 24
Broccoli, Barbara: Birth, Jun 18
Brock, Lou: Birth, Jun 18
Broderick, Matthew: Birth, Mar 21
Brodeur, Martin: Birth, May 6
Brody, Adam: Birth, Dec 15
Brody, Adrien: Birth, Apr 14
Brokaw, Tom: Birth, Feb 6
Brolin, James: Birth, Jul 18
Brolin, Josh: Birth, Feb 12
Bronco Chase: Anniv, Jun 17
Bronson, Charles: Birth Anniv, Nov 3
Bronte, Anne: Birth Anniv, Jan 17
Bronte, Charlotte: Birth Anniv, Apr 21
Bronte, Emily: Birth Anniv, Jul 30
Bronte200 (Haworth, England), Jan 17
Brook, Peter: Birth, Mar 21
Brooklyn Bridge Opened: Anniv, May 24
Brooks, Albert: Birth, Jul 22
Brooks, David: Birth, Aug 11
Brooks, Garth: Birth, Feb 7
Brooks, Gwendolyn: Birth Anniv, Jun 7
Brooks, James David: Birth Anniv, Oct 18
Brooks, James L.: Birth, May 9
Brooks, Jason: Birth, May 10
Brooks, Louise: Birth Anniv, Nov 14
Brooks, Mel: Birth, Jun 28
Brooks, Phillip "CM Punk": Birth, Oct 26
Brosnahan, Rachel: Birth, Dec 15
Brosnan, Pierce: Birth, May 16
Brother's Day, May 24
Brothers: Siblings Day, Natl, Apr 10
Brougham, Henry P.: Birth Anniv, Sep 19
Brown Findlay, Jessica: Birth, Sep 14
Brown v Board of Education: Anniv,
    May 17
Brown, Alton: Birth, Jul 30
Brown, Bobby: Birth, Feb 5
Brown, Bryan: Birth, Jun 23
Brown, Chris: Birth, May 5
Brown, Curtis, Jr: Birth, Mar 11
Brown, Dan: Birth, Jun 22
Brown, Gordon: Birth, Feb 20
Brown, Helen Gurley: Birth Anniv,
    Feb 18
Brown, James: Birth Anniv, May 3
Brown, Jesse Leroy: Birth Anniv, Oct 13
Brown, Jim: Birth, Feb 17
Brown, John: Birth Anniv, May 9
Brown, John: Execution Anniv, Dec 2
Brown, John: Raid Anniv, Oct 16
Brown, Karamo: Birth, Nov 2
Brown, Kate: Birth, Jun 21
Brown, Millie Bobby: Birth, Feb 19
Brown, Sherrod: Birth, Nov 9
Brown, Sterling K.: Birth, Apr 5
Brown, Tim: Birth, Jul 22
Brown, Tina: Birth, Dec 21
Brown, Tony: Birth, Apr 11
Browne, Jackson: Birth, Oct 9
Browne, Thomas: Birth Anniv, Oct 19
Browning, Elizabeth Barrett: Birth Anniv,
    Mar 6
Browning, John Moses: Birth Anniv,
    Jan 21
Browning, Robert: Birth Anniv, May 7
Brownmiller, Susan: Birth, Feb 15
Brownstein, Carrie: Birth, Sep 27
Broz, Josip "Tito": Birth Anniv, May 25
Brubeck, Dave: Birth Anniv, Dec 6
Bruce, Dylan: Birth, Apr 21

Bruce, Isaac: Birth, Nov 10
Bruce, Lenny: Birth Anniv, Oct 13
Bruckner, Anton: Birth Anniv, Sep 4
Bruhl, Daniel: Birth, Jun 16
Brunei: National Day, Feb 23
Bruschi, Tedy: Birth, Jun 9
Brussels Terrorist Attack: Anniv, Mar 22
Brutus Day, Mar 15
Bryan, Bob: Birth, Apr 29
Bryan, Luke: Birth, Jul 17
Bryan, Mike: Birth, Apr 29
Bryan, Sabrina: Birth, Sep 16
Bryan, William Jennings: Birth Anniv,
    Mar 19
Bryan, Zachery Ty: Birth, Oct 9
Bryant, Anita: Birth, Mar 25
Bryant, Bear: Birth Anniv, Sep 11
Bryant, Kobe: Birth, Aug 23
Bryant, Kris: Birth, Jan 4
Bryant, Phil: Birth, Dec 9
Bryant, William C.: Birth Anniv, Nov 3
Brynner, Yul: Birth Anniv, Jul 11
Bryson, Peabo: Birth, Apr 13
Bubba Day, Natl, May 1
Bubble Gum Day, Feb 7
Bubble Wrap Appreciation Day, Jan 27
Buble, Michael: Birth, Sep 9
Buchanan, James: Birth Anniv, Apr 23
Buchanan, Patrick: Birth, Nov 2
Buchenwald, Liberation of: Anniv, Apr 11
Buck Moon, Jul 5
Buck, Pearl S.: Birth Anniv, Jun 26
Buckingham, Lindsey: Birth, Oct 3
Buckley, Betty: Birth, Jul 3
Buckley, Christopher: Birth, Dec 24
Buckley, William F., Jr.: National Review
    First Published: Anniv, Nov 19
Buckley, William F.: Birth Anniv,
    Nov 24
Buckner, Bill: Birth, Dec 14
Buddha, Birthday of (Taiwan), May 10
Buddha: Birthday (China), Apr 30
Buddha: Birthday of the Buddha (Vesak),
    May 7
Buell, Marjorie H.: Birth Anniv, Dec 11
Buffalo Bill (William F. Cody): Birth Anniv,
    Feb 26
Buffalo Roundup (Custer, SD), Sep 25
Buffett, Jimmy: Birth, Dec 25
Buffy the Vampire Slayer TV Premiere:
    Anniv, Mar 10
Bugs Bunny's Debut: Anniv, Apr 30
Bujold, Genevieve: Birth, Jul 1
Bulgakov, Mikhail: Birth Anniv, May 15
Bulgaria,
    Babin Den (Day of the Midwives), Jan 23
    Culture Day, May 24
    Hristo Botev Day, Jun 2
    Liberation Day, Mar 3
    Saint Lasarus's Day, Apr 1
    Unification Day, Sep 6
    Viticulturists' Day, Feb 14
Bulldogs Are Beautiful Day, Natl, Apr 21
Bullfinch Exchange Fest (Japan), Jan 7
Bullock, Sandra: Birth, Jul 26
Bullock, Steve: Birth, Apr 11
Bullwinkle Show: Rocky and His Friends
    TV Premiere: Anniv, Nov 19
Bullying,
    Block It Out Day, Natl, Nov 14
    Bullying Bystanders Unite Week, Oct 18
    Bullying Prevention Awareness Month,
    Natl, Oct 1
    Bullying Prevention Day, Natl, Oct 14

Bullying Prevention, World Day of,
    Oct 5
    Making the First Move Day, Natl, Apr 7
    Stop Bullying Month, Natl, Oct 1
    Weed Out Hate Day, Natl, Aug 28
Bun Day (Iceland), Feb 24
Bunche, Ralph: Awarded Nobel Peace Prize:
    Anniv, Dec 10
Bunche, Ralph: Birth Anniv, Aug 7
Bundchen, Gisele: Birth, Jul 20
Bunker Hill Day (Suffolk County, MA),
    Jun 17
Bunker, Chang and Eng: Birth Anniv,
    May 11
Bunsen Burner Day, Mar 31
Bunsen, Robert: Birth Anniv, Mar 31
Bunyan, John: Birth Anniv, Nov 28
Buonarroti, Michelangelo: Birth Anniv,
    Mar 6
Burbank, Luther: Birth Anniv, Mar 7
Burch, Tory: Birth, Jun 17
Bure, Candace Cameron: Birth, Apr 6
Bure, Pavel: Birth, Mar 31
Bureau of Indian Affairs Established:
    Anniv, Mar 11
Bureau of Internal Revenue Established:
    Anniv, Jul 1
Burger, Warren E.: Birth Anniv, Sep 17
Burgess, Anthony: Birth Anniv, Feb 25
Burgess, Tituss: Birth, Feb 21
Burghoff, Gary: Birth, May 24
Burgoo Fest (North Utica, IL), Oct 10
Burgum, Doug: Birth, Aug 1
Burj Khalifa: World's Tallest Building:
    Anniv, Jan 4
Burk, Martha (Calamity Jane): Death
    Anniv, Aug 1
Burke, Billy: Birth, Nov 25
Burke, Cheryl: Birth, May 12
Burke, Christopher: Birth, Aug 26
Burke, Delta: Birth, Jul 30
Burke, Edmund: Birth Anniv, Jan 12
Burke, Solomon: Birth Anniv, Mar 21
Burkina Faso,
    National Day, Dec 11
    Republic Day, Aug 5
    Revolution Day, Aug 4
Burnett, Carol: Birth, Apr 26
Burnham, Daniel: Birth Anniv, Sep 4
Burning Man (Black Rock Desert, NV),
    Aug 30
Burnquist, Bob: Birth, Oct 10
Burns and Allen Show TV Premiere: Anniv,
    Oct 12
Burns, George: Birth Anniv, Jan 20
Burns, Ken: Birth, Jul 29
Burns, Robert: Birth Anniv, Jan 25
Burr, Aaron: Birth Anniv, Feb 6
Burr, Aaron: Duel with Alexander
    Hamilton: Anniv, Jul 11
Burr, Raymond: Birth Anniv, May 21
Burr, Richard: Birth, Nov 30
Burrell, Ty: Birth, Aug 22
Burroughs, Edgar Rice: Birth Anniv,
    Sep 1
Burroughs, John: Birth Anniv, Apr 3
Burroughs, William S.: Birth Anniv,
    Feb 5
Burrows, James: Birth, Dec 30
Bursting Day (Iceland), Feb 25
Burstyn, Ellen: Birth, Dec 7
Burton, Hilarie: Birth, Jul 1
Burton, LeVar: Birth, Feb 16
Burton, Richard: Birth Anniv, Nov 10

Burton, Tim: Birth, Aug 25
Burundi,
   Assassination of the Hero of the Nation
      Day, Oct 13
   Independence Day, Jul 1
Buscemi, Steve: Birth, Dec 13
Busey, Gary: Birth, Jun 29
Busfield, Timothy: Birth, Jun 12
Bush, Barbara: Birth Anniv, Jun 8
Bush, Billy: Birth, Oct 13
Bush, George H.W. and Barbara, Wedding:
   Anniv, Jan 6
Bush, George H.W.: Birth Anniv, Jun 12
Bush, George W.: Birthday, Jul 6
Bush, George W.: Supreme Court Rules for
   Bush: Anniv, Dec 12
Bush, Kate: Birth, Jul 30
Bush, Laura: Birth, Nov 4
Bush, Reggie: Birth, Mar 2
Bush, Sophia: Birth, Jul 8
Bushmiller, Ernie: Birth Anniv, Aug 23
Bushnell, Candace: Birth, Dec 1
Business (including business history,
   skills, workplace life, types of). See also
   Careers, Labor,
   Amazon Incorporated: Anniv, Jul 16
   American Business Women's Day, Sep 22
   America's First Department Store: Anniv,
      Oct 9
   AT&T Divestiture: Anniv, Jan 8
   Badge Ribbon Day, Natl, Aug 18
   Bike Shop Day, Dec 5
   Black Business Month, Aug 1
   Bookstore Day, Independent, Apr 25
   Boss/Employee Exchange Day, Natl, Sep 14
   Bridal Sale Day, Natl, Jul 18
   Bring Your Manners to Work Day, Sep 4
   Bring Your Teddy Bear to Work Day, Natl,
      Oct 14
   Build a Better Trade Show Image Week,
      Feb 16
   Business Etiquette Week, Natl, Jun 7
   Business of America Quotation: Anniv,
      Jan 17
   Cider Monday, Nov 30
   Clean Out Your Inbox Week, Jan 26
   Clean-Off-Your-Desk Day, Natl, Jan 13
   Computer Security Day, Nov 30
   Consumer Protection Week, Natl (Pres
      Proc), Mar 1
   Co-Op Awareness Month, Sep 24
   Customer Loyalty Month, Intl, Apr 1
   Cyber Monday, Nov 30
   Eat at a Food Truck Day, Natl, Jun 26
   E-discovery Day, Dec 3
   Employee Legal Awareness Day, Feb 13
   Employee Spirit Month, Mar 1
   Enron Files for Bankruptcy: Anniv, Dec 2
   Entrepreneurs Do It Yourself Marketing
      Month, Jun 1
   Fair Trade Day, World, May 9
   Federal Government Seizure of Steel Mills:
      Anniv, Apr 8
   First US Chamber of Commerce Founded:
      Anniv, Apr 5
   Five-Dollar-a-Day Minimum Wage: Anniv,
      Jan 5
   General Motors Bankruptcy: Anniv, Jun 1
   Get to Know Your Customer Day, Jan 16
   Getting the World to Beat a Path to Your
      Door Week, Oct 4
   Google Founded: Anniv, Sep 7
   Handshake Day, Natl, Jun 25
   Intellectual Property Day, World (UN),
      Apr 26

   Irrational Exuberance Enters Lexicon:
      Anniv, Dec 5
   Laugh at Work Week, Apr 1
   Lehman Brothers Collapses: Anniv, Sep 15
   Local Quilt Shop Day, Jan 25
   Ludlow Mine Incident: Anniv, Apr 20
   Mail-Order Catalog: Anniv, Aug 18
   Micro-, Small and Medium-Sized
      Enterprises Day (UN), Jun 27
   Mom and Pop Business Owners Day, Natl,
      Mar 29
   Montgomery Ward Seized: Anniv, Apr 26
   Napping Day, Natl, Mar 9
   New York Stock Exchange Established:
      Anniv, May 17
   Outdoor Marketing Month, Jun 1
   Payroll Week, Natl, Sep 7
   Recess at Work Day, Jun 18
   Record Store Day, Apr 18
   Remote Employee Appreciation Day,
      Sep 22
   Safety and Health at Work, World Day for
      (UN), Apr 28
   Scholastic Established: Anniv, Oct 22
   Shameless Promotion Month, Sep 1
   Small Business Saturday, Nov 28
   Small Business Week (Pres Proc), May 3
   Small Business Week, Natl, May 3
   Stay Home Because You're Well Day,
      Nov 30
   Stock Market Crash of 1893: Anniv, May 5
   Stock Market Crash of 1929: Anniv, Oct 29
   Subliminal Communications Month, Sep 1
   Supply Chain Professionals Day, May 18
   Take Your Dog to Work Day, Jun 26
   Take Your Poet to Work Day, Jul 15
   Telecommuter Appreciation Week, Mar 1
   Triangle Shirtwaist Fire: Anniv, Mar 25
   Union Stock Yard and Transit Co Opens:
      Anniv, Dec 25
   Use Your Gift Card Day, Natl, Jan 18
   Wall Street Bombing: Anniv, Sep 16
   Women's Ecommerce Days, Intl, Sep 20
   Work and Family Month, Natl, Oct 1
   Workplace Conflict Awareness Month,
      Apr 1
   Workplace Eye Wellness Month, Mar 1
   Workplace Politics Awareness Month,
      Oct 1
   Write a Business Plan Month, Natl, Dec 1
Butkus, Dick: Birth, Dec 9
Butler, Benjamin: Farragut Captures New
   Orleans: Anniv, Apr 25
Butler, Brett: Birth, Jan 30
Butler, Caron: Birth, Mar 13
Butler, Dan: Birth, Dec 2
Butler, Gerard: Birth, Nov 13
Butler, Jimmy: Birth, Sep 14
Butler, Octavia: Birth Anniv, Jun 22
Butler, Samuel: Birth Anniv, Dec 4
Butterfield, Asa: Birth, Apr 1
Button, Dick: Birth, Jul 18
Buy Nothing Day, Nov 27
Buzzi, Ruth: Birth, Jul 24
Byers, Trai: Birth, Jul 19
Bynes, Amanda: Birth, Apr 3
Byrd, Richard E.: Birth Anniv, Oct 5
Byrd, Robert: Birth Anniv, Nov 20
Byrne, David: Birth, May 14
Byrne, Gabriel: Birth, May 12
Byrne, Rose: Birth, Jul 24
Byrnes, Edd: Birth, Jul 30
Byron, George Gordon: Birth Anniv, Jan 22

C2E2 (Chicago Comic & Entertainment
   Expo, Chicago, IL), Feb 28

Caan, James: Birth, Mar 26
Caan, Scott: Birth, Aug 23
Cabaret Premiere: Anniv, Nov 20
Cabinet, US: Perkins, Frances (First
   Woman Appointed), Mar 4
Cable Car Patent: Anniv, Jan 17
Cabrillo Day (CA), Sep 28
Cabrini, Mother Frances Xavier:
   Canonized: Anniv, Jul 7
Caesar, Sid: Birth Anniv, Sep 8
Caesarean Section, First: Anniv, Jan 14
Cage, John: Birth Anniv, Sep 5
Cage, Nicolas: Birth, Jan 7
Cagney & Lacey TV Premiere: Anniv,
   Mar 25
Cahn, Sammy: Birth Anniv, Jun 18
Cain, Dean: Birth, Jul 31
Cain, James M.: Birth Anniv, Jul 1
Caine, Michael: Birth, Mar 14
Cake Decorating Day, Natl, Oct 10
Cal Farley's Boys Ranch Rodeo and
   Adventurefest (Boys Ranch, TX),
   Sep 5
Calabro, Thomas: Birth, Feb 3
Calamity Jane (Martha Burk): Death Anniv,
   Aug 1
Calatrava, Santiago: Birth, Jul 28
Calder, Alexander: Birth Anniv, Jul 22
Calderon, Felipe: Birth, Aug 18
Caldwell, Zoe: Birth, Sep 14
Calendar Adjustment Day: Anniv (British
   Gregorian change), Sep 2
Calendar Day, Gregorian, Feb 24
Calendar Stone, Aztec, Discovery: Anniv,
   Dec 17
Calhoun, John C.: Birth Anniv, Mar 18
Calhoun, John C.: Vice Presidential
   Resignation: Anniv, Dec 28
Caliendo, Frank: Birth, Jan 19
California,
   Admission Day, Sep 9
   AFRMA Display at America's Family Pet
      Expo (Costa Mesa), Apr 24
   Bay to Breakers Race (San Francisco),
      May 31
   Blessing of the Fishing Fleet (San
      Francisco), Oct 4
   Books for Treats Day (San Jose), Oct 31
   Cabrillo Day, Sep 28
   California Gold Discovery: Anniv, Jan 24
   California State Fair (Sacramento), Jul 10
   Castroville Artichoke Fest (Monterey),
      Jun 6
   Celebration of the Arts (Yorba Linda),
      Jun 7
   Cesar Chavez Day, Mar 31
   Chinese New Year Parade (San Francisco),
      Feb 8
   Coachella Valley Music and Arts Fest
      (Indio), Apr 10
   Comic-Con Intl (San Diego), Jul 23
   Date Fest, Natl (Indio), Feb 14
   Desert Classic Golf Tournament (La
      Quinta), Jan 15
   Disneyland Opened: Anniv, Jul 17
   Feinstein, Dianne: Birth, Jun 22
   Golden Gate Bridge Opened: Anniv,
      May 27
   Grammy Awards (Los Angeles), Jan 26
   Handel's Messiah Sing-Along (Yorba
      Linda), Nov 29
   Harris, Kamala: Birth, Oct 20
   Los Angeles Founded: Anniv, Sep 4
   Los Angeles Riots: Anniv, Apr 29

Clark, Dave: Birth, Dec 15
Clark, Dick: American Bandstand TV Premiere: Anniv, Aug 5
Clark, Dick: Birth Anniv, Nov 30
Clark, Marcia: Birth, Aug 31
Clark, Mark: Birth Anniv, May 1
Clark, Mary Higgins: Birth, Dec 24
Clark, Petula: Birth, Nov 15
Clark, Susan: Birth, Mar 8
Clark, William: Birth Anniv, Aug 1
Clarke, Arthur C.: Birth Anniv, Dec 16
Clarke, Emilia: Birth, Oct 23
Clarke, Susanna: Birth, Nov 16
Clarke: Jason: Birth, Jul 17
Clarkson, Jeremy: Birth, Apr 11
Clarkson, Kelly: Birth, Apr 24
Clarkson, Patricia: Birth, Dec 29
ClauWau—Santa Claus World Chmpshp (Samnaun, Switzerland), Nov 28
Clay (Muhammad Ali) Becomes Heavyweight Champ: Anniv, Feb 25
Clay, Henry: Birth Anniv, Apr 12
Clayton, Adam: Birth, Mar 13
Clean Air Act Passed by Congress: Anniv, Dec 17
Clean Out Your Inbox Week, Jan 26
Clean Up Your Computer Month, Natl, Jan 1
Clean-Off-Your-Desk Day, Natl, Jan 13
Cleary, Beverly: Birth, Apr 12
Cleary, Beverly: DEAR Day, Natl, Apr 12
Cleese, John: Birth, Oct 27
Clemens, Roger: Birth, Aug 4
Clemens, Samuel (Mark Twain): Birth Anniv, Nov 30
Clement, Jemaine: Birth, Jan 10
Clemente, Roberto: Birth Anniv, Aug 18
Clements, George Harold: Birth, Jan 26
Clerc, Laurent: Birth Anniv, Dec 26
Clerc-Gallaudet Week, Dec 3
Clerihew Day (Edmund Clerihew Bentley Birth Anniv), Jul 10
Cleveland Natl Air Show (Cleveland, OH), Sep 5
Cleveland, Esther: First White House Presidential Baby, Aug 30
Cleveland, Frances: Birth Anniv, Jul 21
Cleveland, Grover,
   Birth Anniv, Mar 18
   Second Inauguration: Anniv, Mar 4
   Secret Surgery: Anniv, Jul 1
Cliburn, Van, Conquers Moscow: Anniv, Apr 14
Cliburn, Van: Birth Anniv, Jul 12
Cliche Day, Nov 3
Cliche Week, Sports, Jul 12
Clijsters, Kim: Birth, Jun 8
Cline, Ernest: Birth, Mar 29
Cline, Patsy: Birth Anniv, Sep 8
Clinton, Chelsea: Birth, Feb 27
Clinton, George: Birth Anniv, Jul 26
Clinton, Hillary Rodham: Birth, Oct 26
Clinton, William Jefferson,
   Birthday, Aug 19
   Impeachment Proceedings: Anniv, Dec 20
   "Meaning of 'Is' Is": Anniv, Aug 17
   Senate Acquits: Anniv, Feb 12
Clodagh: Birth, Oct 8
Cloning of an Adult Animal, First: Anniv, Feb 23
Clooney, George: Birth, May 6
Clooney, Rosemary: Birth Anniv, May 23
Close, Eric: Birth, May 24

Close, Glenn: Birth, Mar 19
Closer TV Premiere: Anniv, Jun 13
Clothesline Week, Intl, Jun 6
Clown Church Service (London, England), Feb 2
Clown Week, Intl, Aug 1
Clowney, Jadeveon: Birth, Feb 14
Clowns: Grimaldi, Joseph: Birth Anniv, Dec 18
Clowns: Kelly, Emmett: Birth Anniv, Dec 9
Clymer, George: Birth Anniv, Mar 16
CN Tower Opened: Anniv, Jun 26
CNN Debut: Anniv, Jun 1
Coachella Valley Music and Arts Fest (Indio, CA), Apr 10
Coaching; Coaching Events,
   African-American Coaches Day, Feb 4
   Dating and Life Coach Recognition Week, Jan 5
Coast Guard Day, Aug 4
Coast Guard, US: Fleet Week New York (New York, NY), May 20
Coastal Cleanup, Intl, Sep 19
Coates, Ta-Nehisi: Birth, Sep 30
Cobb, Ty: Birth Anniv, Dec 18
Coben, Harlan: Birth, Jan 4
Coburn, James: Birth Anniv, Aug 31
Cochise: Death Anniv, Jun 8
Cochran, Jacqueline: Death Anniv, Aug 9
Cockroach Races, Australia Day (Brisbane, Australia), Jan 26
Cocoanut Grove Fire: Anniv, Nov 28
Cocteau, Jean: Birth Anniv, Jul 5
Cody, Diablo: Birth, Jun 14
Cody, William F. "Buffalo Bill": Birth Anniv, Feb 26
Coen, Ethan: Birth, Sep 21
Coen, Joel: Birth, Nov 29
Coffee Day, Natl, Sep 29
Cohen, Leonard: Birth Anniv, Sep 21
Cohen, Rob: Birth, Mar 12
Cohen, Sacha Baron: Birth, Oct 13
Cohen, Sasha: Birth, Oct 26
Coin Week, Natl, Apr 19
Coins Stamped "In God We Trust": Anniv, Apr 22
Colantoni, Enrico: Birth, Feb 14
Colbert, Claudette: Birth Anniv, Sep 13
Colbert, Claudette: It Happened One Night Film Release: Anniv, Feb 22
Colbert, Stephen: Birth, May 13
Cold Moon, Dec 29
Cold War: Treaty Signed to Mark End: Anniv, Nov 19
Coldest Game of Pro Football (Ice Bowl): Anniv, Dec 31
Cole, Ashley: Birth, Dec 20
Cole, Gary: Birth, Sep 20
Cole, Nat King: Birth Anniv, Mar 17
Cole, Nat King: Records the Christmas Song: Anniv, Aug 19
Coleman, Bessie: Birth Anniv, Jan 26
Coleman, Dabney: Birth, Jan 3
Coleman, Jack: Birth, Feb 21
Coleman, Jenna: Birth, Apr 27
Coleman, Monique: Birth, Nov 13
Coleman, Signy: Birth, Jul 4
Coleman, Zendaya: Birth, Sep 1
Coleridge, Samuel: Birth Anniv, Oct 21
Colfax, Schuyler: Birth Anniv, Mar 23
Colfer, Chris: Birth, May 27
College Football Playoff Natl Chmpshp Game (New Orleans, LA), Jan 13

Collette, Toni: Birth, Nov 1
Collins, Albert: Birth Anniv, Oct 1
Collins, Eileen: Birth, Nov 19
Collins, Joan: Birth, May 23
Collins, Judy: Birth, May 1
Collins, Lily: Birth, Mar 18
Collins, Michael: Birth, Oct 31
Collins, Michael: Birth Anniv, Oct 16
Collins, Pauline: Birth, Sep 3
Collins, Phil: Birth, Jan 30
Collins, Stephen: Birth, Oct 1
Collins, Susan M.: Birth, Dec 7
Collins, Wilkie: Birth Anniv, Jan 8
Collinsworth, Cris: Birth, Jan 27
Collison, Nick: Birth, Oct 26
Colman, Olivia: Birth, Jan 30
Cologne Cathedral Completion: Anniv, Aug 14
Colombia,
   Battle of Boyaca Day, Aug 7
   Carnival of Blacks and Whites (Pasto), Jan 4
   Cartagena Independence Day, Nov 11
   Copa America, Jun 12
   Independence Day, Jul 20
Color TV Broadcast (CBS), First: Anniv, Jun 25
Colorado,
   Admission Day, Aug 1
   Bennet, Michael: Birth, Nov 28
   Colorado Country Christmas Gift Show (Denver), Nov 6
   Colorado Day, Aug 3
   Commonwheel Artists Labor Day Art Fest (Manitou Springs), Sep 5
   Emma Crawford Fest Coffin Races (Manitou Springs), Oct 24
   Gardner, Cory: Birth, Aug 22
   Geographers Annual Mtg, Assn of American (Denver), Apr 6
   Longs Peak Scottish/Irish Highland Fest (Estes Park), Sep 10
   Polis, Jared: Birth, May 12
   Rocky Mountain Natl Park Established: Anniv, Jan 26
   State Fair (Pueblo), Aug 28
   US Girls' Junior (Golf) Chmpshp (Colorado Springs), Jul 13
Colorectal Cancer Awareness Month, Natl, Mar 1
Colorectal Cancer Education and Awareness Month, Mar 1
Colt, Samuel: Birth Anniv, Jul 19
Colter, Jessi: Birth, May 25
Colter, Mike: Birth, Aug 26
Coltrane, Robbie: Birth, Mar 30
Columbia River Cross Channel Swim, Roy Webster (Hood River, OR), Sep 7
Columbia Space Shuttle Disaster: Anniv, Feb 1
Columbian Exposition Closing: Anniv, Oct 30
Columbian Exposition Opening: Anniv, May 1
Columbine High School Killings: Anniv, Apr 20
Columbo TV Premiere: Anniv, Sep 15
Columbus Day Parade and Italian Fest, Ocean County (Seaside Heights, NJ), Oct 9
Columbus, Christopher,
   Columbus Day (Observed), Oct 12
   Columbus Day (Pres Proc), Oct 12
   Columbus Day (Traditional), Oct 12

Delaware,
  Carney, John: Birth, May 20
  Carper, Tom: Birth, Jan 23
  Coons, Christopher: Birth, Sep 9
  Delaware State Fair (Harrington),
    Jul 23
  Ratification Day, Dec 7
  Return Day (Georgetown), Nov 5
Delevingne, Cara: Birth, Aug 12
Delgado, Carlos: Birth, Jun 25
Deli Salad Month, Natl, Jul 1
DeLillo, Don: Birth, Nov 20
Delle Donne, Elena: Birth, Sep 5
Delmonico, Lorenzo: Birth Anniv, Mar 13
Dementia Care Professionals Month, Jun 1
DeMille, Agnes: Birth Anniv, Sep 18
DeMille, Cecil B.: Birth Anniv, Aug 12
DeMille, Nelson: Birth, Aug 23
Democracy, Intl Day of (UN), Sep 15
Democratic National Convention
    (Milwaukee, WI), Jul 13
Dempsey, Jack: Birth Anniv, Jun 24
Dempsey, Jack: Long Count Day: Anniv,
    Sep 22
Dempsey, Patrick: Birth, Jan 13
DeMunn, Jeffrey: Birth, Apr 25
Denali Natl Park: Anniv, Dec 2
Dench, Judi: Birth, Dec 9
Deneuve, Catherine: Birth, Oct 22
Deng, Luol: Birth, Apr 16
Denmark,
  Common Prayer Day, May 8
  Constitution Day, Jun 5
  Eel Fest (Jyllinge), Jun 6
  Frederikssund Viking Games
    (Frederikssund), Jun 19
  Ho Sheep Market, Aug 29
  Midsummer Eve, Jun 23
  Observation of 1945 Liberation, May 5
  Observation of Nazi Occupation, Apr 9
  Queen Margrethe's Birthday, Apr 16
Dennehy, Brian: Birth, Jul 9
Dennings, Kat: Birth, Jun 13
Dennis, Sandy: Birth Anniv, Apr 27
Dent, Bucky: Birth, Nov 25
Dent, Richard: Birth, Dec 13
Dental. See also Health,
  Dental Assn Annual Session, American
    (Orlando, FL), Oct 15
  Dental Drill Patent: Anniv, Jan 26
  Dental Hygiene Month, Natl, Oct 1
  Flossing Day, Natl, Nov 27
  Pet Dental Health Month, Natl, Feb 1
  Save Your Tooth Month, May 1
Denton, James: Birth, Jan 20
Denver, Bob: Birth Anniv, Jan 9
Denver, John: Birth Anniv, Dec 31
Depardieu, Gerard: Birth, Dec 27
Depp, Johnny: Birth, Jun 9
DePreist, James: Birth, Nov 21
Depression Education and Awareness
    Month, Natl, Oct 1
Depression Screening Day, Natl, Oct 8
Derby Fest (Epsom Downs, Surrey,
    England), Jun 5
Derek, Bo: Birth, Nov 20
Dern, Bruce: Birth, Jun 4
Dern, Laura: Birth, Feb 10
Derrida, Jacques: Birth Anniv, Jul 15
Dershowitz, Alan: Birth, Sep 1
Desai, Kiran: Birth, Sep 3
DeSantis, Ron: Birth, Sep 14
Descartes, Rene: Birth Anniv, Mar 31
Deschanel, Emily: Birth, Oct 11
Deschanel, Zooey: Birth, Jan 17

Desegregation, US Army First: Anniv,
  Jul 26
Desert Classic Golf Tournament (La
    Quinta, CA), Jan 15
Desert Shield: Anniv, Aug 7
Desert Storm,
  Ground War Begins: Anniv, Feb 23
  Gulf War Begins: Anniv, Jan 16
  Kuwait Liberated: Anniv, Feb 27
DeShannon, Jackie: Birth, Aug 21
Detroit Auto Show: North American Intl
    Auto Show (Detroit, MI), Jun 9
Detroit Founded: Anniv, Jul 24
Devane, William: Birth, Sep 5
Development Information Day, World
    (UN), Oct 24
Devers, Gail: Birth, Nov 19
Devil's Night, Oct 30
DeVito, Danny: Birth, Nov 17
Devlin, Bernadette: Birth, Apr 23
DeVoe, Ronald: Birth, Feb 17
DeVos, Betsy: Birth, Jan 8
Dewey Defeats Truman Headline: Anniv,
    Nov 3
Dewey, John: Birth Anniv, Oct 20
Dewey, Melvil: Birth Anniv, Dec 10
Dewhurst, Colleen: Birth Anniv, Jun 3
DeWine, Mike: Birth, Jan 5
Dewitt, Joyce: Birth, Apr 23
Dey, Susan: Birth, Dec 10
Dia de la Raza (Mexico), Oct 12
Dia de la Raza: See Columbus Day, Oct 12
Diabetes Assn Alert Day, American, Mar 24
Diabetes Day, World (UN), Nov 14
Diabetes Month, American, Nov 1
Diabetic Eye Disease Month, Nov 1
Diamond, Hope, Mailed to Smithsonian:
    Anniv, Nov 8
Diamond, Neil: Birth, Jan 24
Diana, Princess of Wales: Birth Anniv, Jul 1
Diana, Princess of Wales: Death Anniv,
    Aug 31
Diary Day, Dear, Sep 22
Diaz, Cameron: Birth, Aug 30
Diaz-Balart, Jose: Birth, Nov 7
Diaz-Canel, Miguel: Birth, Apr 20
DiCaprio, Leonardo: Birth, Nov 11
Dicing for Bibles (Huntingdonshire,
    England), Jun 1
Dick Tracy Debuts: Anniv, Oct 4
Dick Van Dyke Show TV Premiere: Anniv,
    Oct 3
Dick, Andy: Birth, Dec 21
Dickens on the Strand (Galveston, TX),
    Dec 4
Dickens, Charles: Birth Anniv, Feb 7
Dickens, Charles: Christmas Carol
    Published: Anniv, Dec 17
Dickensian Christmas Fest, Rochester
    (Rochester, England), Dec 5
Dickerson, Eric: Birth, Sep 2
Dickinson, Angie: Birth, Sep 30
Dickinson, Anna: Birth Anniv, Oct 28
Dickinson, Emily: Birth Anniv, Dec 10
Dictionary Day, Oct 16
Dictionary of American English Published,
    First: Anniv, Apr 14
Didion, Joan: Birth, Dec 5
Didrikson, Babe: See under Zaharias,
    Jun 26
Diefenbaker, John: Birth Anniv, Sep 18
Diego, Jose de: Birth Anniv, Apr 16
Dien Bien Phu Falls: Anniv, May 7
Diesel Engine Patented: Anniv, Feb 23

Diesel, Rudolph: Birth Anniv, Mar 18
Diesel, Rudolph: Natl Biodiesel Day,
    Mar 18
Diesel, Vin: Birth, Jul 18
Dietrich, Marlene: Birth Anniv,
    Dec 27
Diets, Dieting (including weight loss and
    weight issues). See also Health,
  No Diet Day, May 6
Different Colored Eyes Day, Jul 12
DiFranco, Ani: Birth, Sep 23
Diggs, Taye: Birth, Jan 2
Dillahunt, Garret: Birth, Nov 24
Dillane, Stephen: Birth, Mar 27
Diller, Phyllis: Birth Anniv, Jul 17
Dillinger, John: Death Anniv, Jul 22
Dillon, Kevin: Birth, Aug 19
Dillon, Matt: Birth, Feb 18
Dillon, Melinda: Birth, Oct 13
DiMaggio, Joe: Birth Anniv, Nov 25
Dimpled Chad Day, Jan 4
DiMucci, Dion: Birth, Jul 18
Dine Over Your Kitchen Sink Day,
    Nov 27
Dinkins, David: Birth, Jul 10
Dinklage, Peter: Birth, Jun 11
DioGuardi, Kara: Birth, Dec 9
Dion, Celine: Birth, Mar 30
Dionne Quintuplets: Birthday, May 28
Dior, Christian: Birth Anniv, Jan 21
Disabled,
  Americans with Disabilities Act: Anniv,
    Jul 26
  Bell, Alexander Graham: Birth Anniv,
    Mar 3
  Blind Americans Equality Day (Pres Proc),
    Oct 15
  Clerc-Gallaudet Week, Dec 3
  Day of the Deaf, Intl, Sep 27
  Deaf History Month, Mar 13
  Disability Employment Awareness Month,
    Natl, Oct 1
  Disability Employment Awareness Month,
    Natl (Pres Proc), Oct 1
  First School for Deaf Founded: Anniv,
    Apr 15
  Fishing Has No Boundaries (Hayward,
    WI), May 15
  Fishing Has No Boundaries (Monticello,
    IN), May 16
  Helen Keller's Miracle: Anniv, Apr 5
  Persons with Disabilities, Intl Day of (UN),
    Dec 3
  Seeing Eye Established: Anniv, Jan 29
  Special Olympics: Anniv, Jul 20
Disarmament Week (UN), Oct 24
Discoverers' Day (Hawaii), Oct 12
Discovery Day (Newfoundland and
    Labrador, Canada), Jun 22
Disney, Walt: Birth Anniv, Dec 5
Disneyland Opened: Anniv, Jul 17
Disraeli, Benjamin: Birth Anniv, Dec 21
Distinguished Service Medal: Anniv, Jan 2
Distracted Driving Awareness Month,
    Apr 1
Ditka, Mike: Birth, Oct 18
Divac, Vlade: Birth, Feb 3
Diversity Awareness Month, Global, Oct 1
Diversity Day, Natl, Oct 2
Diversity: Two Different Colored Shoes Day,
    Natl, May 3
Divorce: Child-Centered Divorce Month,
    Intl, Jan 1
Diwali (India), Nov 14
Dix, Dorothea L.: Birth Anniv, Apr 4

Best Friend-in-Law Day, Natl, May 23
Fil-American Friendship Day, Jul 4
Friendship, Intl Day of (UN), Jul 30
Girlfriends' Day, Aug 1
Locate an Old Friend Day, Sep 19
New Friends, Old Friends Week, Intl, May 17
Unfriend Day, Natl, Nov 17
Virgin Islands-Puerto Rico Friendship Day, Oct 12
Wingman's Day, Natl, Feb 13
Women's Friendship Month, Intl, Sep 1
Froebel, Friedrich: Birth Anniv, Apr 21
Frog Month, Natl, Apr 1
Froggatt, Joanne: Birth, Aug 21
Frontline TV Premiere: Anniv, Jan 17
Froome, Chris: Birth, May 20
Frost, Robert: Birth Anniv, Mar 26
Fruits and Vegetables Day, Natl Eat More, May 21
Fry, Stephen: Birth, Aug 24
Frye, Soleil Moon: Birth, Aug 6
Fuentes, Carlos: Birth Anniv, Nov 11
Fuentes, Daisy: Birth, Nov 17
Fugitive Finale: Anniv, Aug 29
Fugitive TV Premiere: Anniv, Sep 17
Fukudome, Kosuke: Birth, Apr 26
Fukunaga, Cary Joji: Birth, Jul 10
Fulbright, J. William: Birth Anniv, Nov 9
Fuller, Alfred Carl: Birth Anniv, Jan 13
Fuller, Buckminster: Birth Anniv, Jul 12
Fuller, Margaret: Birth Anniv, May 23
Fuller, Melville Weston: Birth Anniv, Feb 11
Fulton, Robert: Birth Anniv, Nov 14
Fulton, Robert: Sails Steamboat: Anniv, Aug 17
Fun Facts About Names Day, Mar 2
Funeral Day, Create a Great, Oct 30
Funicello, Annette: Birth Anniv, Oct 22
Funky Winkerbean: Anniv, Mar 27
Funt, Allen: Birth Anniv, Sep 16
Furcal, Rafael: Birth, Aug 24
Furlong, Edward: Birth, Aug 2
Furtado, Nelly: Birth, Dec 2

G, Kenny: Birth, Jun 6
G.I. Joe Introduced: Anniv, Feb 1
G.O.E. Day, Natl, Oct 6
Gabel, Elyes: Birth, May 8
Gable, Clark: Birth Anniv, Feb 1
Gable, Clark: Gone with the Wind Film Premiere: Anniv, Dec 15
Gable, Clark: It Happened One Night Film Release: Anniv, Feb 22
Gabon,
  Independence Day, Aug 17
  National Day, Mar 12
Gabriel, Peter: Birth, Feb 13
Gad, Josh: Birth, Feb 23
Gadot, Gal: Birth, Apr 30
Gagarin, Yuri A.: Birth Anniv, Mar 9
Gage, Nicholas: Birth, Jul 23
Gagne, Eric: Birth, Jan 7
Gagne, Simon: Birth, Feb 29
Gail, Max: Birth, Apr 5
Gaiman, Neil: Birth, Nov 10
Gaines, Boyd: Birth, May 11
Gaines, Chip: Birth, Nov 14
Gaines, Ernest J.: Birth, Jan 15
Gaines, Joanna: Birth, Apr 19
Gaines, William M.: Birth Anniv, Mar 1

Gainsborough, Thomas: Baptism Anniv, May 14
Galbraith, John Kenneth: Birth Anniv, Oct 15
Gale, Robert: Birth, Oct 11
Galecki, Johnny: Birth, Apr 30
Galifianakis, Zach: Birth, Oct 1
Galilei, Galileo: Birth Anniv, Feb 15
Gallagher, Peter: Birth, Aug 19
Gallaudet, Thomas Hopkins: Birth Anniv, Dec 10
Galli-Curci, Amelita: Birth Anniv, Nov 18
Galligan, Zach: Birth, Feb 14
Gallipoli, Battle of: Anniv, Apr 25
Gallo, Frank: Birth, Jan 13
Gallo, Julio: Anniv, Mar 21
Galveston Historic Homes Tour (Galveston, TX), May 2
Galveston, TX, Hurricane: Anniv, Sep 8
Galway, James: Birth, Dec 8
Gambia: Independence Day, Feb 18
Gambon, Michael: Birth, Oct 19
Game & Puzzle Week, Natl, Nov 22
Games, Multisport Competitions,
  Backyard Games Week, Natl, May 25
  Big Sky State Games (Billings, MT), Jul 17
  Games of the XXXII Olympiad (Tokyo, Japan), Jul 24
  Invictus Games (The Hague, Netherlands), May 9
  Winter Youth Olympic Games (Lausanne, Switzerland), Jan 9
Gandhi, Indira: Birth Anniv, Nov 19
Gandhi, Mohandas,
  Assassinated: Anniv, Jan 30
  Birth Anniv, Oct 2
  Makes Salt: Anniv, Apr 6
  Nonviolence, Intl Day of (UN), Oct 2
Ganz Cooney, Joan: Birth, Nov 30
Garage Sale Day, Natl, Aug 8
Garai, Romola: Birth, Aug 6
Garber, Victor: Birth, Mar 16
Garbo, Greta: Birth Anniv, Sep 18
Garcia Marquez, Gabriel: Birth Anniv, Mar 6
Garcia Marquez, Gabriel: One Hundred Years of Solitude Published: Anniv, May 30
Garcia, Andy: Birth, Apr 12
Garcia, Jeff: Birth, Feb 24
Garcia, Jerry: Birth Anniv, Aug 1
Garcia, Jorge: Birth, Apr 28
Garcia, Sergio: Birth, Jan 9
Garciaparra, Nomar: Birth, Jul 23
Gardell, Billy: Birth, Aug 20
Garden; Gardening. See also Flowers, Flower Shows,
  Garden Meditation Day, May 3
  Gardening for Wildlife Month, May 1
  Gifts from the Garden Month, May 1
  Historic Garden Week (VA), Apr 18
  Landscape Architecture Month, World, Apr 1
  Lawn Care Month, Natl, Apr 1
  Perennial Gardening Month, Jun 1
  Pollinator Month, Natl, Jun 1
  Pollinator Week, Natl, Jun 22
  Seed Swap Day, Natl, Jan 25
Gardner, Ava: Birth Anniv, Dec 24
Gardner, Cory: Birth, Aug 22
Gardner, Erle Stanley: Birth Anniv, Jul 17
Gardner, Randy: Birth, Dec 2
Garfield, Andrew: Birth, Aug 20

Garfield, James A.: Assassination Anniv, Jul 2
Garfield, James A.: Birth Anniv, Nov 19
Garfield, Lucretia R.: Birth Anniv, Apr 19
Garfunkel, Art: Birth, Nov 5
Garland, Alex: Birth, May 26
Garland, Judy: Birth Anniv, Jun 10
Garland, Judy: Wizard of Oz Released: Anniv, Aug 25
Garner, Jennifer: Birth, Apr 17
Garner, John Nance: Birth Anniv, Nov 22
Garnett, Kevin: Birth, May 19
Garofalo, Janeane: Birth, Sep 28
Garr, Teri: Birth, Dec 11
Garrett, Brad: Birth, Apr 14
Garrick, David: Birth Anniv, Feb 19
Garrison, William Lloyd: Birth Anniv, Dec 12
Garten, Ina: Birth, Feb 2
Garth, Jennie: Birth, Apr 3
Garvey, Marcus: Birth Anniv, Aug 17
Garvey, Steve: Birth, Dec 22
Gasol, Marc: Birth, Jan 29
Gasol, Pau: Birth, Jul 6
Gasoline Alley Creator: King, Frank: Birth Anniv, Apr 9
Gastronomy Day, Sustainable (UN), Jun 18
Gates of the Arctic Natl Park: Anniv, Dec 2
Gates, Bill: Birth, Oct 28
Gates, David: Birth, Dec 11
Gates, Henry Louis, Jr: Birth, Sep 16
Gatlin, Justin: Birth, Feb 10
Gatlin, Larry: Birth, May 2
Gauguin, Paul: Birth Anniv, Jun 7
Gaultier, Jean-Paul: Birth, Apr 24
Gaumont, Leon: Birth Anniv, May 10
Gavaris, Jordan: Birth, Sep 25
Gay, Lesbian, Bisexual, Transgender,
  Celebrate Bisexuality Day, Sep 23
  Coming Out Day, Natl, Oct 11
  First US Same-Sex Marriages: Anniv, May 17
  Gay and Lesbian History Month, Oct 1
  Gay and Lesbian Pride Month, Jun 1
  Gay/Lesbian/Bi/Trans Pride Parade (Chicago, IL), Jun 28
  GLBT Book Month, Natl, Jun 1
  LGBT Center Awareness Day, Oct 19
  Saints and Sinners Literary Fest (New Orleans, LA), Mar 27
  San Francisco Pride Celebration and Parade (San Francisco, CA), Jun 27
  Stonewall Riot: Anniv, Jun 28
  Supreme Court Strikes Down Defense of Marriage Act: Anniv, Jun 26
  Transgender Day of Remembrance, Nov 20
  UK Allows Same-Sex Civil Partnerships: Anniv, Dec 21
Gayle, Crystal: Birth, Jan 9
Gaynor, Janet: Birth Anniv, Oct 6
Gaynor, Mitzi: Birth, Sep 4
Gaza: Israel Completes Pullout: Anniv, Sep 12
Gbowee, Leymah: Birth, Feb 1
Geary, Anthony: Birth, May 29
Gedalya, Fast of, Sep 21
Geeson, Judy: Birth, Sep 10
Geffen, David: Birth, Feb 21
Gehrig, Lou: Birth Anniv, Jun 19
Gehry, Frank: Birth, Feb 28

Geisel, Theodor "Dr. Seuss": Birth Anniv, Mar 2
Geldof, Bob: Birth, Oct 5
Gellar, Sarah Michelle: Birth, Apr 14
Geller, Uri: Birth, Dec 20
Gellhorn, Martha: Birth Anniv, Nov 8
Gemini Begins, May 21
Genealogy Day, Mar 7
Genealogy: Family History Day, Jun 14
General Election Day (US), Nov 3
General Hospital TV Premiere: Anniv, Apr 1
General Motors Bankruptcy: Anniv, Jun 1
General Motors: Founding Anniv, Sep 16
Geneva Accords: Anniv, Jul 20
Genital Mutilation, Intl Day of Zero Tolerance for Female (UN), Feb 6
Genocide Convention: Anniv, Dec 9
Genocide: Day of Commemoration and Dignity of the Victims of the Crime of Genocide and of the Prevention of this Crime, Intl, Dec 9
Genovese Murder: Anniv, Mar 13
Gentry, Bobbie: Birth, Jul 27
Geocaching Day, Intl, Aug 15
Geographers Annual Mtg, Assn of American (Denver, CO), Apr 6
Geographic Bee Finals, Natl (Washington, DC), May 10
Geographic Bee, State Level, Natl, Mar 27
George III: Birth Anniv, Jun 4
George Spelvin Day, Nov 15
George VI's Coronation: Anniv, May 12
George, Elizabeth: Birth, Feb 26
George, Melissa: Birth, Aug 6
George, Paul: Birth, May 2
George, Phyllis: Birth, Jun 24
George, Susan: Birth, Jul 26
Georgia,
　Confederate Memorial Day, Apr 26
　Cotton Pickin' Fair (Gay), May 2
　FDR Commemorative Ceremony (Warm Springs), Apr 12
　Fest 2018: Fest of Fine Arts and Fine Crafts (Dalton), Sep 18
　Final Four: NCAA Div I Men's Basketball Chmpshp (Atlanta), Apr 4
　Georgia Pecan Month, Natl, Nov 1
　Isakson, Johnny: Birth, Dec 28
　Jefferson Davis Captured: Anniv, May 10
　Kemp, Brian: Birth, Nov 2
　Masters Tournament (Augusta), Apr 6
　Memorial Day Ceremonies (Andersonville), May 24
　Money Show, Natl (Atlanta), Feb 27
　Natl Fair (Perry), Oct 8
　NCAA Women's Div I Swimming/Diving Chmpshps (Athens), Mar 18
　Peachtree Road Race, AJC (Atlanta), Jul 4
　Perdue, David: Birth, Dec 10
　Prater's Mill Country Fair (Dalton), Oct 10
　Pumpkin Destruction Day (The Rock), Nov 7
　Ratification Day, Jan 2
　Sherman Enters Atlanta: Anniv, Sep 2
　Sherman Takes Savannah: Anniv, Dec 21
　Southern Cyclone: Anniv, Aug 24
Georgia (Europe): Independence Day, May 26
Georgia (Europe): Soviet Georgia Votes Independence: Anniv, Mar 31
Georgia Tech Beats Cumberland 222-0: Anniv, Oct 7

Gerard, Gil: Birth, Jan 23
Gere, Richard: Birth, Aug 29
German-American Day, Natl, Oct 6
German-American Day, Natl (Pres Proc), Oct 6
German-American Heritage Month, Oct 1
Germany,
　Berlin Airlift: Anniv, Jun 24
　Berlin Intl Film Fest (Berlin), Feb 20
　Berlin Marathon (Berlin), Sep 27
　Berlin Wall Opened: Anniv, Nov 9
　Buss und Bettag, Nov 18
　Capital Returns to Berlin: Anniv, Sep 1
　Day of German Unity, Oct 3
　Day of Remembrance for Victims of Nazism, Jan 27
　Dresden Firebombing: Anniv, Feb 13
　Duisburg Christmas Market (Duisburg), Nov 19
　Erntedankfest, Oct 4
　Fasching, Feb 24
　Fasching Sunday, Feb 23
　Frankfurt Christmas Market (Frankfurt), Nov 25
　Frankfurter Buchmesse (Frankfurt), Oct 14
　German Plebiscite: Anniv, Aug 19
　German Surrender at Stalingrad: Anniv, Feb 2
　Hamburg Harbor Birthday, May 7
　Invades Poland: Anniv, Sep 1
　Kristallnacht: Anniv, Nov 9
　Leipzig Bach Fest (Leipzig), Jun 11
　Munich Fasching Carnival, Jan 7
　Munich Founded: Anniv, Jun 14
　Nuremberg War Crimes Trials: Anniv, Nov 20
　Ode of Joy around the World (Bonn), Dec 17
　Oktoberfest (Munich), Sep 19
　Red Army Departs Berlin: Anniv, Jun 11
　Reunification: Anniv, Oct 3
　Tatort TV Premiere: Anniv, Nov 29
　Totensonntag, Nov 22
　UCI Track Cycling World Chmpshps (Berlin), Feb 26
　Volkstrauertag, Nov 15
　Wagner Fest (Bayreuth), Jul 25
　Waldchestag (Frankfurt), Jun 2
Geronimo: Death Anniv, Feb 17
Gerrard, Steven: Birth, May 30
Gerry, Elbridge: Birth Anniv, Jul 17
Gershwin, George: Birth Anniv, Sep 26
Gershwin, Ira: Birth Anniv, Dec 6
Gertz, Jami: Birth, Oct 28
Gervais, Ricky: Birth, Jun 25
Gerwig, Greta: Birth, Aug 4
Get Caught Reading Month, May 1
Get Smart TV Premiere: Anniv, Sep 18
Gets, Malcolm: Birth, Dec 28
Getty, Balthazar: Birth, Jan 22
Gettysburg Address, Lincoln's: Anniv, Nov 19
Gettysburg Address: Dedication Day Memorial Ceremony (Gettysburg, PA), Nov 19
Gettysburg Outdoor Antique Show (Gettysburg, PA), May 16
Getz, Stan: Birth Anniv, Feb 2
Ghana,
　Farmers' Day, Natl, Dec 4
　Independence Day, Mar 6
　Republic Day, Jul 1
Gheorghiu, Angela: Birth, Sep 7
Ghesquiere, Nicolas: Birth, May 9

Ghosts, Fest of Hungry (China and Taiwan), Sep 2
Giamatti, Paul: Birth, Jun 6
Giambi, Jason: Birth, Jan 8
Giannini, Giancarlo: Birth, Aug 1
Gibb, Barry: Birth, Sep 1
Gibbon, Edward: Birth Anniv, Apr 27
Gibbons, Leeza: Birth, Mar 26
Gibbs, Joe: Birth, Nov 25
Gibbs, Marla: Birth, Jun 14
Gibbs, Mifflin Wistar: Birth Anniv, Apr 17
Gibran, Kahlil: Birth Anniv, Jan 6
Gibson, Althea, Wins Wimbledon: Anniv, Jul 6
Gibson, Althea: Birth Anniv, Aug 25
Gibson, Bob: Birth, Nov 9
Gibson, Debbie: Birth, Aug 31
Gibson, Josh: Birth Anniv, Dec 21
Gibson, Kirk: Birth, May 28
Gibson, Mel: Birth, Jan 3
Gibson, Thomas: Birth, Jul 3
Gibson, William: Cyberspace Coined: Anniv, Oct 1
Gielgud, Sir John: Birth Anniv, Apr 14
Gies, Miep: Birth Anniv, Feb 15
Gifford, Kathie Lee: Birth, Aug 16
Giffords, Gabrielle: Birth, Jun 8
Gift Card: Use Your Gift Card Day, Natl, Jan 18
Giguere, Jean-Sebastien: Birth, May 16
Gilbert, John: Birth Anniv, Jul 10
Gilbert, Melissa: Birth, May 8
Gilbert, Sara: Birth, Jan 29
Gilbert, Sir William: Birth Anniv, Nov 18
Gillespie, Dizzy: Birth Anniv, Oct 21
Gilley, Mickey: Birth, Mar 9
Gilliam, Terry: Birth, Nov 22
Gillibrand, Kirsten: Birth, Dec 9
Gilligan's Island TV Premiere: Anniv, Sep 26
Gillis, Margaret: Birth, Jul 9
Gilmore, Artis: Birth, Sep 21
Gilmore, Jared: Birth, May 30
Gilmour, Dave: Birth, Mar 6
Gilpin, Peri: Birth, May 27
Gilsig, Jessalyn: Birth, Nov 30
Gingerbread Decorating Day, Dec 12
Gingrich, Newt: Birth, Jun 17
Ginobili, Manu: Birth, Jul 28
Ginsberg, Allen: Birth Anniv, Jun 3
Ginsberg, Allen: Howl and Other Poems Published: Anniv, Nov 1
Ginsburg, Ruth Bader: Birth, Mar 15
Girl Child, Intl Day of the (UN), Oct 11
Girl Scouts Founding: Anniv, Mar 12
Girlfriends' Day, Aug 1
Girls and Women in Sports Day, Natl, Feb 5
Girls Day, Intl, Nov 14
Giro d'Italia (Italy), May 9
Gish, Lillian: Birth Anniv, Oct 14
Giuliani, Rudolph: Birth, May 28
Giuntoli, David: Birth, Jun 18
Givens, Robin: Birth, Nov 27
Giving Tuesday, Dec 1
Giving: Bubble Gum Day, Feb 7
Giving: Tie One On Day, Nov 25
Glacier Bay Natl Park: Anniv, Dec 2
Gladstone, William: Birth Anniv, Dec 29
Glaser, Paul Michael: Birth, Mar 25
Glass, Ira: Birth, Mar 3
Glass, Philip: Birth, Jan 31
Glastonbury Fest (Pilton, England), Jun 24

Glaucoma Awareness Month, Natl, Jan 1
Glavine, Tom: Birth, Mar 25
Gleason, Jackie: Birth Anniv, Feb 26
Gleeson, Domhnall: Birth, May 12
Gleick, James: Birth, Aug 1
Glenn, John: Birth Anniv, Jul 18
Glenn, Scott: Birth, Jan 26
Gless, Sharon: Birth, May 31
Glor, Jeff: Birth, Jul 12
Glover, Crispin: Birth, Apr 20
Glover, Danny: Birth, Jul 22
Glover, Donald: Birth, Sep 25
Glover, John: Birth, Aug 7
Glover, Savion: Birth, Nov 19
Go Hog Wild—Eat Country Ham Month, Oct 1
Go-Kart Week, Intl, Sep 20
Goals, Goal Setting (personal and professional growth),
    Build a Better Image Week, Sep 20
    Clean Out Your Inbox Week, Jan 26
    Evaluate Your Life Day, Oct 19
    Kick-Butt Day, Natl, Oct 12
    Make Up Your Mind Day, Dec 31
    May One Day, May 1
    No Interruptions Day, Dec 31
    Plant the Seeds of Greatness Month, Feb 1
    Resolution Renewal Day, Jul 1
    Rising Star Month, Worldwide, Jan 1
    Single-Tasking Day, Feb 23
    Take a New Year's Resolution to Stop Smoking, Dec 17
    Tick Tock Day, Dec 29
    Time Management Month, Natl, Feb 1
    Toss Away the "Could Haves" and "Should Haves" Day, Jul 18
Goat Yoga Month, Natl, Feb 1
Gobert, Rudy: Birth, Jun 26
God Bless America First Performed: Anniv, Nov 11
Godard, Jean Luc: Birth, Dec 3
Goddard Day: Launch of First Liquid-Fueled Rocket: Anniv, Mar 16
Goddard, Robert H.: Birth Anniv, Oct 5
Godfather Film Premiere: Anniv, Mar 15
Godwin, Mary. See Wollstonecraft, Mary: Birth Anniv, Apr 27
Goeppert-Mayer, Maria: Birth Anniv, Jun 28
Goethals, George W.: Birth Anniv, Jun 29
Goethe, Johann W.: Birth Anniv, Aug 28
Goggins, Walton: Birth, Nov 10
Gogol, Nikolai: Birth Anniv, Mar 31
Gold Discovery, California: Anniv, Jan 24
Gold Discovery, Klondike Eldorado: Anniv, Aug 31
Gold Discovery, Klondike: Anniv, Aug 16
Gold Star Mother's and Family's Day (Pres Proc), Sep 27
Gold Star Spouses Day, Apr 5
Gold, Missy: Birth, Jul 14
Gold, Tracey: Birth, May 16
Goldberg, Rube: Birth Anniv, Jul 4
Goldberg, Whoopi: Birth, Nov 13
Goldbergs TV Premiere: Anniv, Jan 17
Goldblum, Jeff: Birth, Oct 22
Golden Gate Bridge Opened: Anniv, May 27
Golden Girls TV Premiere: Anniv, Sep 14
Golden Globe Awards, Jan 5
Golden Spike Driving: Anniv, May 10
Golding, William: Birth Anniv, Sep 19
Goldsmith, Oliver: Birth Anniv, Nov 10
Goldwyn, Samuel: Birth Anniv, Jan 31

Goldwyn, Tony: Birth, May 20
Golf,
    Curtis Cup (Caernarvonshire, Wales), Jun 12
    Desert Classic (La Quinta, CA), Jan 15
    First PGA Chmpshp: Anniv, Oct 9
    Hogan, Ben: Birth Anniv, Aug 13
    Jones Wins First Grand Slam: Anniv, Jul 12
    Jones, Bobby: Birth Anniv, Mar 17
    Masters Tournament (Augusta, GA), Apr 6
    Open, The (British Open) (Sandwich, England), Jul 12
    Ouimet, Francis DeSales: Birth Anniv, May 8
    PGA Chmpshp (San Francisco, CA), May 11
    PGA Founded: Anniv, Jan 17
    Ryder Cup (Haven, WI), Sep 25
    Sarazen, Gene: Birth Anniv, Feb 27
    Snead, Sam: Birth Anniv, May 27
    US Amateur Chmpshp (Bandon, OR), Aug 10
    US Amateur Four-Ball Chmpshp (Philadelphia, PA), May 23
    US Girls' Junior Chmpshp (Colorado Springs, CO), Jul 13
    US Junior Amateur Chmpshp (Chaska, MN), Jul 20
    US Mid-Amateur Chmpshp (Manakin-Sabot, VA), Sep 12
    US Open Chmpshp (Mamaroneck, NY), Jun 18
    US Senior Amateur Chmpshp (Grosse Pointe Farms, MI), Aug 29
    US Senior Open Chmpshp (Newport, RI), Jun 25
    US Senior Women's Open Chmpshp (Fairfield, CT), Jul 9
    US Women's Amateur Chmpshp (Rockville, MD), Aug 3
    US Women's Amateur Four-Ball Chmpshp (Naples, FL), Apr 25
    US Women's Mid Amateur Chmpshp (Blufton, SC), Aug 29
    US Women's Open Chmpshp (Houston, TX), Jun 4
    Zaharias, Mildred Babe Didrikson: Birth Anniv, Jun 26
Golino, Valeria: Birth, Oct 22
Gomez, Lefty: Birth Anniv, Nov 26
Gomez, Scott: Birth, Dec 23
Gomez, Selena: Birth, Jul 22
Gompers, Samuel: Birth Anniv, Jan 27
Gonchar, Sergei: Birth, Apr 13
Gone with the Wind Film Premiere: Anniv, Dec 15
Gone with the Wind Published: Anniv, Jun 30
Gonzales, Pancho: Birth Anniv, May 9
Gonzalez, Fernando: Birth, Jul 29
Gonzalez, Juan: Birth, Oct 16
Good Friday, Apr 10
Good Friday Bank Holiday (United Kingdom), Apr 10
Good Friday Peace Agreement in Northern Ireland: Anniv, Apr 10
Good Morning America TV Premiere: Anniv, Nov 6
Good Samaritan Involvement Day, Mar 13
Good Times TV Premiere: Anniv, Feb 1
Goodall, Jane: Birth, Apr 3
Goode, Matthew: Birth, Apr 3
Goodell, Roger: Birth, Feb 19

Gooden, Dwight: Birth, Nov 16
Goodeve, Grant: Birth, Jul 6
Gooding, Cuba, Jr: Birth, Jan 2
Goodman, Benny: Birth Anniv, May 30
Goodman, Ellen: Birth, Apr 11
Goodman, John: Birth, Jun 20
Goodwill: Helms, Edgar J.: Birth Anniv, Jan 19
Goodwin, Doris Kearns: Birth, Jan 4
Goodwin, Ginnifer: Birth, May 22
Goof-Off Day, Natl, Mar 22
Google Founded: Anniv, Sep 7
Goolagong, Evonne: Birth, Jul 31
Gorbachev, Mikhail: Birth, Mar 2
Gordimer, Nadine: Birth Anniv, Nov 20
Gordon, Jeff: Birth, Aug 4
Gordon, Keith: Birth, Feb 3
Gordon, Mark: Birth, Mar 14
Gordone, Charles: Birth Anniv, Oct 12
Gordon-Levitt, Joseph: Birth, Feb 17
Gordy, Berry, Jr: Birth, Nov 28
Gore, Al: Birth, Mar 31
Gore, Tipper: Birth, Aug 19
Gorgas, William Crawford: Birth Anniv, Oct 3
Gorilla Born in Captivity, First: Anniv, Dec 22
Gorillas: Koko: Birth Anniv, Jul 4
Gorky, Maxim: Birth Anniv, Mar 28
Gorsuch, Neil: Birth, Aug 29
Gosling, Ryan: Birth, Nov 12
Gospel. See also Music,
    Dorsey, Thomas A.: Birth Anniv, Jul 1
    Jackson, Mahalia: Birth Anniv, Oct 26
    Singing on the Mountain (Linville, NC), Jun 28
Gossage, Goose: Birth, Jul 5
Gosselaar, Mark-Paul: Birth, Mar 1
Gosselin, Kate: Birth, Mar 28
Gossett, Louis, Jr: Birth, May 27
Goth Day, World, May 22
Gottlieb, Robert: Birth, Apr 29
Gottschalk, Louis Moreau: Birth Anniv, May 8
Gotye: Birth, May 21
Gould, Chester: Birth Anniv, Nov 20
Gould, Elliott: Birth, Aug 29
Gould, Jay: Birth Anniv, May 26
Goya, Francisco Jose de: Birth Anniv, Mar 30
Grabeel, Lucas: Birth, Nov 23
Grace, Mark: Birth, Jun 28
Grace, Nancy: Birth, Oct 23
Grace, Topher: Birth, Jul 19
Graf, Steffi: Birth, Jun 14
Graffman, Gary: Birth, Oct 14
Graham, Ashley: Birth, Oct 30
Graham, Calvin "Baby Vet": Birth Anniv, Apr 3
Graham, David: Birth, May 23
Graham, Heather: Birth, Jan 29
Graham, Katharine: Birth Anniv, Jun 16
Graham, Lauren: Birth, Mar 16
Graham, Lindsey: Birth, Jul 9
Graham, Martha: Birth Anniv, May 11
Grahame, Kenneth: Birth Anniv, Mar 8
Grainger, Holliday: Birth, Jan 1
Grains Month, Whole, Sep 1
Grammar Day, Natl, Mar 4
Grammer, Kelsey: Birth, Feb 21
Grammy Awards (Los Angeles, CA), Jan 26
Granato, Cammi: Birth, Mar 25
Grand Canyon Natl Park Established: Anniv, Feb 26

Hashoah/Holocaust Day, Apr 21
Hebron Massacre: Anniv, Feb 25
Independence Day (Yom Ha'atzma'ut),
    Apr 29
Israeli Siege of Suez City Ends: Anniv,
    Jan 28
Jerusalem Day (Yom Yerushalayim),
    May 22
Remembrance Day (Yom Ha'zikkaron),
    Apr 28
Sigd, Nov 16
Israeli Olympiad Massacre: Anniv, Sep 5
It Happened One Night Film Release:
    Anniv, Feb 22
IT Professionals Day, Sep 15
Italy,
    Biennale Architettura (Venice), May 23
    Bologna Children's Book Fair (Bologna),
        Mar 30
    Calabria Earthquake: Anniv, Dec 16
    Calcio Fiorentino (Florence), Jun 24
    Carnival Week (Milan), Feb 23
    Epiphany Fair (Rome), Jan 5
    Explosion of the Cart (Florence), Apr 12
    Feast of the Incappucciati (Gradoli), Feb 20
    Feast of the Redeemer (Venice), Jul 19
    Fest of St. Efisio (Cagliari), May 1
    Gioco Del Ponte (Pisa), Jun 7
    Giostra della Quintana (Foligno), Sep 13
    Giro d'Italia, May 9
    Historical Regatta (Venice), Sep 6
    Joust of the Quintana (Ascoli/Piceno),
        Aug 2
    Joust of the Saracen (Arezzo), Sep 6
    La Befana, Jan 6
    Liberation Day, Apr 25
    Palio (Siena), Jul 2
    Palio dei Balestrieri (Gubbio), May 31
    Palio del Golfo (La Spezia), Aug 9
    Procession of Addolorata and Mysteries
        (Taranto), Apr 9
    Purgatory Banquet (Gradoli), Feb 26
    Republic Day, Jun 2
    Victory Day, Nov 4
    Wedding of the Sea (Venice), May 24
It's a Wonderful Life Film Premiere: Anniv,
    Dec 20
Ivanek, Zeljko: Birth, Aug 15
Iverson, Allen: Birth, Jun 7
Iverson, Johnathan Lee: Birth, Jan 30
Ives, Burl: Birth Anniv, Jun 14
Ivey, Judith: Birth, Sep 4
Ivey, Kay: Birth, Oct 15
Ivory, James: Birth, Jun 7
Ivy Day (Ireland), Oct 6
Iwo Jima Day: Anniv, Feb 23
Izzard, Eddie: Birth, Feb 7

Jack Benny Program TV Premiere: Anniv,
    Oct 28
Jack Johnson v Jim Jeffries: Anniv, Jul 4
Jack the Ripper Letter: Anniv, Sep 27
Jackman, Hugh: Birth, Oct 12
Jackon, Stonewall: Lee-Jackson Day, Jan 17
Jackson, Andrew: Battle of New Orleans:
    Anniv, Jan 8
Jackson, Andrew: Birth Anniv, Mar 15
Jackson, Bo: Birth, Nov 30
Jackson, Glenda: Birth, May 9
Jackson, Jackie: Birth, May 4
Jackson, Janet: Birth, May 16
Jackson, Jesse: Birth, Oct 8
Jackson, Joe: Birth, Aug 11
Jackson, Jonathan: Birth, May 11

Jackson, Joshua: Birth, Jun 11
Jackson, Kate: Birth, Oct 29
Jackson, Lamar: Birth, Jan 7
Jackson, Mahalia: Birth Anniv, Oct 26
Jackson, Marlon: Birth, Mar 12
Jackson, Michael: Birth Anniv, Aug 29
Jackson, Michael: Thriller Released: Anniv,
    Nov 30
Jackson, Peter: Birth, Oct 31
Jackson, Phil: Birth, Sep 17
Jackson, Rachel D.: Birth Anniv, Jun 15
Jackson, Randy: Birth, Oct 29
Jackson, Randy: Birth, Jun 23
Jackson, Reggie: Birth, May 18
Jackson, Samuel L.: Birth, Dec 21
Jackson, Shirley Ann: Birth, Aug 6
Jackson, Shirley: Birth Anniv, Dec 14
Jackson, Shirley: Lottery Published: Anniv,
    Jun 26
Jackson, Thomas J. "Stonewall": Birth
    Anniv, Jan 21
Jackson, Tito: Birth, Oct 15
Jackson, Victoria: Birth, Aug 2
Jacob, Irene: Birth, Jul 15
Jacobi, Derek: Birth, Oct 22
Jacobs, Marc: Birth, Apr 9
Jacoby, Scott: Birth, Nov 19
Jaeger, Andrea: Birth, Jun 4
Jaeger, Sam: Birth, Jan 29
Jagger, Bianca: Birth, May 2
Jagger, Mick: Birth, Jul 26
Jagr, Jaromir: Birth, Feb 15
Jahn, Helmut: Birth, Jan 1
Jain: Mahavir Jayanti, Apr 6
Jakes, John: Birth, Mar 31
Jamaica,
    Abolition of Slavery, Aug 1
    Discovery by Columbus: Anniv, May 4
    Independence Achieved: Anniv, Aug 6
    Independence Day, Aug 3
    Maroon Fest, Jan 6
    Natl Heroes Day, Oct 19
James Bond Series Launched with Dr. No:
    Anniv, Oct 5
James, Etta: Birth Anniv, Jan 25
James, Henry: Birth Anniv, Apr 15
James, Jesse: Birth Anniv, Sep 5
James, John: Birth, Apr 18
James, Kevin: Birth, Apr 26
James, LeBron: Birth, Dec 30
James, Lily: Birth, Apr 5
James, P.D.: Birth Anniv, Aug 3
James, Theo: Birth, Dec 16
James, William: Birth Anniv, Jan 11
James-Collier, Rob: Birth, Sep 23
Jamestown Day (Williamsburg, VA),
    May 9
Jamestown, VA: Founding Anniv, May 14
Jane Austen Fest (Bath, England), Sep 11
Janis, Byron: Birth, Mar 24
Janitors: Custodial Workers Day, Natl,
    Oct 2
Jankovic, Jelena: Birth, Feb 28
Janney, Allison: Birth, Nov 19
Jansen, Dan: Birth, Jun 17
Jansson, Tove: Birth Anniv, Aug 9
Japan,
    Autumnal Equinox Day, Sep 22
    Bean-Throwing Fest (Setsubun), Feb 3
    Birthday of the Emperor, Feb 23
    Bon Fest (Feast of Lanterns), Jul 15
    Children's Day, May 5
    Chrysanthemum Day, Sep 9
    Coming-of-Age Day, Jan 13

    Constitution Memorial Day, May 6
    Cormorant Fishing Fest (Gifu), May 11
    Culture Day, Nov 3
    Day of the Rice God (Chiyoda), Jun 7
    Doll Fest (Hina Matsuri), Mar 3
    Earthquake and Tsunami of 2011: Anniv,
        Mar 11
    Flower Fest (Hana Matsuri), Apr 8
    Foundation Day, Natl, Feb 11
    Games of the XXXII Olympiad (Tokyo),
        Jul 24
    Golden Week Holidays, Apr 29
    Greenery Day, May 4
    Hari-Kuyo (Fest of Broken Needles),
        Feb 8
    Haru-No-Yabuiri, Jan 16
    Hiroshima Day, Aug 6
    Hollyhock Fest (Kyoto), May 15
    Kakizome, Jan 2
    Kanto Earthquake Memorial Day, Sep 1
    Labor Thanksgiving Day, Nov 23
    Marine Day, Jul 23
    Mega Kenka Matsuri (Himeji), Oct 14
    Moment of Silence (Nagasaki), Aug 9
    Mount Ogura Plane Crash: Anniv,
        Aug 12
    Mountain Day, Aug 10
    Namahage (Akita), Dec 31
    Nanakusa, Jan 7
    Newspaper Week, Oct 15
    Origami Day, Nov 11
    Paralympic Games 2020 (Tokyo),
        Aug 25
    Peace Fest (Hiroshima), Aug 6
    Reiwa Era Begins: Anniv, May 1
    Respect for the Aged Day, Sep 21
    Rice Planting Fest (Osaka), Jun 14
    Roughhouse Fest (Himeji), Oct 14
    Sapporo Snow Fest (Sapporo), Jan 31
    Sasaki, Sadako: Death Anniv, Oct 25
    Shichi-Go-San (Seven-Five-Three Fest),
        Nov 15
    Showa Day, Apr 29
    Soma No Umaoi (Wild Horse Chasing),
        Jul 23
    Sports Day, Jul 24
    Suffers Major Earthquake: Anniv, Jan 17
    Tanabata (Star Fest), Jul 7
    Tokyo Raid: Anniv, Apr 18
    Usokae (Bullfinch Exchange Fest), Jan 7
    Vernal Equinox Day, Mar 19
    Water-Drawing Fest (Omizutori), Mar 1
Japanese Attack US Mainland: Anniv,
    Feb 23
Japanese Internment (WWII): Anniv,
    Feb 19
Jarman, Claude, Jr: Birth, Sep 27
Jarrell, Randall: Birth Anniv, May 6
Jarrett, Dale: Birth, Nov 26
Jarriel, Tom: Birth, Dec 29
Jarvik, Robert: Birth, May 11
Jaws Film Release: Anniv, Jun 20
Jay, John: Birth Anniv, Dec 12
Jay-Z: Birth, Dec 4
Jazz and Blues,
    Appreciation Month, Apr 1
    Black Women in Jazz Month, Intl,
        Mar 1
    Davis, Miles: Birth Anniv, May 25
    Jazz Day, Intl, Apr 30
    New Orleans Jazz/Heritage Fest (New
        Orleans, LA), Apr 23
    Parker, Charlie: Birth Anniv, Aug 29
    Ra, Sun: Birth Anniv, May 22
    Satchmo Summerfest (New Orleans, LA),
        Jul 31

Essence Fest (New Orleans, LA), Jul 2
Glastonbury Fest (Pilton, England), Jun 24
Grammy Awards (Los Angeles, CA), Jan 26
Guitar Flat-Picking Chmpshps, Natl (Winfield, KS), Sep 16
Helsinki Fest (Helsinki, Finland), Aug 13
Jazz Appreciation Month, Apr 1
Jazz Day, Intl, Apr 30
Joseph Brackett Day, May 6
Kids Music Day, Oct 2
King's College Fest of Nine Lessons and Carols (Cambridge, England), Dec 24
Leipzig Bach Fest (Leipzig, Germany), Jun 11
Lollapalooza (Chicago, IL), Jul 30
Louie Louie Day, Intl, Apr 11
Music Day, World, Jun 21
Music in Our Schools Month, Mar 1
Musikfest (Bethlehem, PA), Jul 31
Natl Eisteddfod of Wales (Tregaron, Wales), Aug 1
Ode of Joy around the World (Bonn, Germany), Dec 17
Old-Time Music Fest & Expo, Natl (Fremont, NE), Oct 1
One-Hit Wonder Day, Natl, Sep 25
Play-the-Recorder Day, Mar 21
Play-the-Recorder Month, Mar 1
Quirky Country Music Song Titles Day, Mar 27
Record Store Day, Apr 18
Rounds Resounding Day, Aug 1
Saxophone Day, Nov 6
South by Southwest (Austin, TX), Mar 13
Spirit of the Woods Folk Fest (Brethren, MI), Jun 20
Spoleto Fest USA (Charleston, SC), May 22
Stars and Stripes Forever Day, May 14
Summer Music Fest (Sitka, AK), Jun 9
Summerfest (Milwaukee, WI), Jun 24
Surf Music Month, Intl, Jun 1
Teach Music Week, Intl, Mar 16
Tomorrowland (Boom, Belgium), Jul 17
Vinyl Record Day, Aug 12
Wagner Fest (Bayreuth, Germany), Jul 25
Musical Anniversaries. See also Beatles; Presley, Elvis; Opera,
Altamont Concert: Anniv, Dec 6
America the Beautiful Published: Anniv, Jul 4
American Top 40 Radio Premiere: Anniv, Jul 4
Anderson, Marian: Easter Concert: Anniv, Apr 9
Beatles' Last Concert: Anniv, Jan 30
Beethoven's Ninth Symphony Premiere: Anniv, May 7
Bowie, David: Rise and Fall of Ziggy Stardust Released: Anniv, Jun 16
Capitol Records Building Opens: Anniv, Apr 6
Crazy Blues Recorded by Mamie Smith: Anniv, Aug 10
Day the Music Died (Holly, Richardson, Valens: Death Anniv), Feb 3
Dylan, Bob, at Newport Folk Fest: Anniv, Jul 25
Ella Fitzgerald Wins Apollo Amateur Night: Anniv, Nov 21
First African American to be Recorded: Anniv, Feb 14
God Bless America First Performed: Anniv, Nov 11

Grapes of Wrath Evening: Guthrie Meets Seeger: Anniv, Mar 3
Happy Birthday to "Happy Birthday to You", Jun 27
Jimi Hendrix Last Performance: Anniv, Sep 16
Live Aid Concerts: Anniv, Jul 13
Monterey Intl Pop Fest: Anniv, Jun 16
Moondance Released: Anniv, Jul 27
Mormon Choir First Performs: Anniv, Aug 22
Nat King Cole Records The Christmas Song: Anniv, Aug 19
Nevermind Released: Anniv, Sep 24
Pop Music Chart Introduced: Anniv, Jan 4
Premiere of Handel's Messiah: Anniv, Apr 13
Rite of Spring Premiere and Riot: Anniv, May 29
Sex Pistols Single, "Anarchy in the UK": Anniv, Nov 26
Shakur, Tupac, Shot: Anniv, Sep 7
Thriller Released: Anniv, Nov 30
Van Cliburn Conquers Moscow: Anniv, Apr 14
Vietnam Moratorium Concert: Anniv, Mar 28
Musk, Elon: Birth, Jun 28
Muslim Observances,
Ashura: Tenth Day, Aug 29
Eid-al-Adha: Feast of the Sacrifice, Jul 31
Eid-al-Fitr: Celebrating the Fast, May 24
Isra al Mi'raj: Ascent of Prophet Muhammad, Mar 22
Mawlid al Nabi: Birthday of the Prophet Muhammad, Oct 29
Muharram (New Year), Aug 20
Rabi' I: Month of the Migration, Oct 18
Ramadan: Islamic Month of Fasting, Apr 24
Yawm Arafat: The Standing at Arafat, Jul 30
Mussina, Mike: Birth, Dec 8
Mussolini, Benito: Birth Anniv, Jul 29
Mussorgsky, Modest: Birth Anniv, Mar 21
Mustaches: Movember, Nov 1
Mustard Day, Natl, Aug 1
Mutiny on the Bounty: Anniv, Apr 28
Mutombo, Dikembe: Birth, Jun 25
Mutt Day, Natl, Dec 2
Muybridge, Eadweard: Birth Anniv, Apr 9
My Lai Massacre: Anniv, Mar 16
My Way Day, Feb 17
Myanmar,
Independence Day, Jan 4
Resistance Day, Mar 27
Union Day, Feb 12
Myers, Mike: Birth, May 25
Myers, Russell: Birth, Oct 9
MylesDay (Flann O'Brien Death Day), Apr 1
Mysterio, Rey, Jr: Birth, Dec 12
Mystery Month, May 1

NAACP Founded: Anniv, Feb 12
Nabakov, Evgeni: Birth, Jul 25
Nadal, Rafael: Birth, Jun 3
Nader, Ralph: Birth, Feb 27
Nafels Pilgrimage (Canton Glarus, Switzerland), Apr 2
NAFTA Signed: Anniv, Dec 8
Nagra, Parminder K.: Birth, Oct 5
Nagurski, Bronko: Birth Anniv, Nov 3
Naipaul, V.S.: Birth Anniv, Aug 17

Naismith, James: Birth Anniv, Nov 6
Najimy, Kathy: Birth, Feb 6
Nakba Day, May 15
Namath, Joe: Birth, May 31
Names,
Bubba Day, Natl, May 1
Celebrate Your Name Week, Mar 1
Discover What Your Name Means Day, Mar 4
Fun Facts About Names Day, Mar 2
Get a Different Name Day, Feb 13
Mario Day, Mar 10
Middle Name Pride Day, Mar 6
Name Your PC Day, Nov 20
Namesake Day, Mar 1
Nametag Day, Mar 5
Unique Names Day, Mar 3
Z Day, Jan 1
Nametag Day, Mar 5
Namibia,
Heroes' Day, Aug 26
Independence Day, Mar 21
Nanak, Guru: Birth Anniv, Nov 30
Nanakusa (Japan), Jan 7
Nanjiani, Kumail: Birth, Feb 21
Nanking Massacre Memoral Day (China), Dec 13
Nanking Massacre: Anniv, Dec 13
Nanotechnology Day, Natl, Oct 9
Napolitano, Janet: Birth, Nov 29
Napping Day, Natl, Mar 9
Naruhito: Birth, Feb 23
NASA Established: Anniv, Jul 29
Nash, Graham: Birth, Feb 2
Nash, Niecy: Birth, Feb 23
Nash, Ogden: Birth Anniv, Aug 19
Nash, Steve: Birth, Feb 7
Nast, Thomas: Birth Anniv, Sep 27
Nastase, Ilie: Birth, Jul 19
Nat King Cole Show TV Premiere: Anniv, Nov 5
Natchitoches-NW State Univ Folk Fest (Natchitoches, LA), Jul 24
Nation, Carry: Birth Anniv, Nov 25
National Bank, First Chartered by Congress: Anniv, Feb 25
National Broadcasters Convention (Las Vegas, NV), Apr 18
National Review First Published: Anniv, Nov 19
Native American Heritage Day, Nov 27
Native-American,
American Indian Heritage Day (AL), Oct 12
American Indian Intertribal Powwow (Williamsburg, VA), Oct 10
Apache Wars Begin: Anniv, Feb 4
Battle of Little Bighorn: Anniv, Jun 25
Bureau of Indian Affairs Established: Anniv, Mar 11
Chief Joseph Surrender: Anniv, Oct 5
Cochise: Death Anniv, Jun 8
Hayes, Ira Hamilton: Birth Anniv, Jan 12
Hin-mah-too-yah-lat-kekt (Chief Joseph): Birth Anniv, Mar 3
Last Formal Surrender of Confederate Troops: Anniv, Jun 23
Loloma, Charles: Birth Anniv, Jun 9
Native American Citizenship Day, Jun 15
Native Americans' Day (SD), Oct 12
Native-American Heritage Month, Natl (Pres Proc), Nov 1

Oklahoma! Broadway Premiere: Anniv, Mar 31
Oktoberfest (Munich, Germany), Sep 19
Olajuwon, Hakeem: Birth, Jan 21
Olbermann, Keith: Birth, Jan 27
Old Inauguration Day, Mar 4
Old Ironsides Launched: Anniv, Oct 21
Old Ironsides Saved by Poem: Anniv, Sep 16
Old New Year's Day, Mar 25
Oldenburg, Claes: Birth, Jan 28
Older Americans Month (Pres Proc), May 1
Oldest Man in Space: Discovery, Oct 29
Oldman, Gary: Birth, Mar 21
Olds, Ransom: Birth Anniv, Jun 3
Olerud, John: Birth, Aug 5
Olin, Ken: Birth, Jul 30
Oliphant, Pat: Birth, Jul 24
Olive Branch Petition: Anniv, Jul 8
Oliver, Jamie: Birth, May 27
Oliver, John: Birth, Apr 23
Oliver, Mary: Birth Anniv, Sep 10
Oliver, Pam: Birth, Mar 10
Olivier, Laurence: Birth Anniv, May 22
Olivieri, Dawn: Birth, Feb 8
Olmos, Edward James: Birth, Feb 24
Olmsted, Frederick L.: Birth Anniv, Apr 26
O'Loughlin, Alex: Birth, Aug 24
Olsen, Ashley: Birth, Jun 13
Olsen, Mary-Kate: Birth, Jun 13
Olusola, Kevin: Birth, Oct 5
Olympic Games,
    First Modern Olympics: Anniv, Apr 6
    First Perfect Score: Anniv, Jul 18
    First Winter Olympics: Anniv, Jan 25
    Games of the XXXII Olympiad (Tokyo, Japan), Jul 24
    Israeli Olympiad Massacre: Anniv, Sep 5
    Paralympic Games 2020 (Tokyo, Japan), Aug 25
    Special Olympics: Anniv, Jul 20
    Winter Youth Olympic Games (Lausanne, Switzerland), Jan 9
Olyphant, Timothy: Birth, May 20
Oman: Natl Holiday, Nov 18
Omarr, Sydney: Birth Anniv, Aug 5
O'Meara, Mark: Birth, Jan 13
Omizutori Water-Drawing Fest (Japan), Mar 1
Omnibus TV Premiere: Anniv, Nov 9
On the Origin of Species Published: Anniv, Nov 22
Onassis, Jacqueline Kennedy: Birth Anniv, Jul 28
One Hundred Years of Solitude Published: Anniv, May 30
One Life to Live TV Premiere: Anniv, Jul 15
O'Neal, Jermaine: Birth, Oct 13
O'Neal, Ryan: Birth, Apr 20
O'Neal, Shaquille: Birth, Mar 6
O'Neal, Tatum: Birth, Nov 5
One-Hit Wonder Day, Natl, Sep 25
O'Neill, Ed: Birth, Apr 12
O'Neill, Eugene: Birth Anniv, Oct 16
O'Neill, Jennifer: Birth, Feb 20
O'Neill, Rose Cecil: Birth Anniv, Jun 25
O'Neill, Thomas (Tip): Birth Anniv, Dec 9
One-on-One Month, Sep 1
Ono, Yoko: Bed-in for Peace: Anniv, Mar 25
Ono, Yoko: Birth, Feb 18
O'Nolan, Brian (Flann O'Brien): Birth Anniv, Oct 5
Ontkean, Michael: Birth, Jan 24

Open That Bottle Night, Feb 1
Open-Heart Surgery, First: Anniv, Jul 9
Opera,
    Aida Premieres: Anniv, Dec 24
    Donizetti's Lucia di Lammermoor Premiere: Anniv, Sep 26
    Madama Butterfly Premiere: Anniv, Feb 17
    Marian Anderson Performs with Metropolitan Opera: Anniv, Jan 7
    Metropolitan Opera House: Opening Anniv, Oct 22
    Metropolitan Opera Radio Broadcasts Premiere: Anniv, Dec 25
    Opera Debut in the Colonies: Anniv, Feb 8
    Ponselle, Rosa: Birth Anniv, Jan 22
    Verdi, Giuseppe Birth Anniv, Oct 10
    Wagner, Richard: Birth Anniv, May 22
Operation Argo: Anniv, Jan 27
Operation Iraqi Freedom: Anniv, Mar 19
Oprah Winfrey Show TV Premiere: Anniv, Sep 8
Optimism Month, Mar 1
O'Quinn, Terry: Birth, Jul 15
Orange Bowl, Capital One (Miami, FL), Jan 1
Orangemen's Day (Northern Ireland), Jul 13
Orbach, Jerry: Birth Anniv, Oct 20
Oregon,
    Admission Day, Feb 14
    Brown, Kate: Birth, Jun 21
    Concours d'Elegance (Forest Grove), Jul 19
    Hangover Handicap Run (Klamath Falls), Jan 1
    Holiday Ale Fest (Portland), Dec 2
    Hood River County Fair (Hood River), Jul 22
    Lincoln, Abraham: Birthday Observance, Feb 3
    Merkley, Jeff: Birth, Oct 24
    Oregon Brewers Fest (Portland), Jul 22
    Oregon State Fair (Salem), Aug 27
    Portland Rose Fest (Portland), May 22
    Portland's Birthday, Feb 8
    Roy Webster Cross Channel Swim (Hood River), Sep 7
    Sherwood Robin Hood Fest (Sherwood), Jul 17
    US Amateur (Golf) Chmpshp (Bandon), Aug 10
    Verboort Sausage and Kraut Dinner (Forest Grove), Nov 7
    Wyden, Ron: Birth, May 3
Organic Act Day (US Virgin Islands), Jun 15
Organization of American States Founded: Anniv, Apr 30
Organization, Organizing,
    Checklists Day, Oct 30
    Clean Out Your Inbox Week, Jan 26
    Clean-Off-Your-Desk Day, Natl, Jan 13
    Garage Sale Day, Natl, Aug 8
    Get Organized Month, Jan 1
    Organize Your Medical Information Month, Oct 1
    Single-Tasking Day, Feb 23
    Simplify-Your-Life Day, Mar 3
Origami Day (Japan), Nov 11
Origami Days, World, Oct 24
Orlando Nightclub Massacre: Anniv, Jun 12
Orlando, Tony: Birth, Apr 3
Orman, Suze: Birth, Sep 5
Ormond, Julia: Birth, Jan 4
Orr, Bobby: Birth, Mar 20
Orthodox Christian Observances (Eastern),
    Ascension Day, May 28
    Dormition of Theotokos, Aug 15

    Dumb Week (Greece), Apr 5
    Easter Sunday, Apr 19
    Ecclesiastical New Year, Sep 1
    Festival of All Saints, Jun 14
    Forgiveness/Cheesefare Sunday, Mar 1
    Green Monday, Mar 2
    Holy Week, Apr 12
    Lazarus Saturday, Apr 11
    Lent, Mar 2
    Meatfare Sunday, Feb 23
    Orthodox Christmas, Jan 7
    Palm Sunday, Apr 12
    Pentecost, Jun 7
    Roman Catholic/Eastern Orthodox Meeting: Anniv, Jan 5
Ortiz, Ana: Birth, Jan 25
Ortiz, Tito: Birth, Jan 23
Orton, Randy: Birth, Apr 1
Orwell, George: Animal Farm Published: Anniv, Aug 17
Orwell, George: Birth Anniv, Jun 25
Osaka, Naomi: Birth, Oct 16
Osborne, Jeffrey: Birth, Mar 9
Osbourne, Ozzy: Birth, Dec 3
Oscars (Academy Awards) Presentation, Feb 9
Osceola: Death Anniv, Jan 30
Osgood, Charles: Birth, Jan 8
Osment, Haley Joel: Birth, Apr 10
Osmond, Donny: Birth, Dec 9
Osmond, Marie: Birth, Oct 13
Ostara, Mar 19
Osteen, Joel: Birth, Mar 5
Osteoporosis Month, Natl, May 1
O'Sullivan, Maureen: Birth Anniv, May 17
Oswalt, Patton: Birth, Jan 27
Oswalt, Roy: Birth, Aug 29
O'Toole, Annette: Birth, Apr 1
Ott, Mel: Birth Anniv, Mar 2
Otter Day, World, May 27
Ouimet, Francis DeSales: Birth Anniv, May 8
Outback Bowl (Tampa, FL), Jan 1
Outcault, Richard Felton: Birth Anniv, Jan 14
Outdoor Marketing Month, Jun 1
Outdoors Month, Great (Pres Proc), Jun 1
Outrigger Canoes: Hawaiki Nui Va'a Race (French Polynesia), Oct 28
Ovarian Cancer Awareness Month, Sep 1
Ovechkin, Alexander: Birth, Sep 17
Overall, Park: Birth, Mar 15
Overseas Chinese Day (Taiwan), Oct 21
Owen, Clive: Birth, Oct 3
Owen, Robert: Birth Anniv, May 14
Owens, Buck: Birth Anniv, Aug 12
Owens, Jesse: Birth Anniv, Sep 12
Owens, Jesse: Greatest Day in Track and Field: Anniv, May 25
Oxenberg, Catherine: Birth, Sep 22
Oyelowo, David: Birth, Apr 1
Oyster Fest, US (Leonardtown, MD), Oct 17
Oz, Frank: Birth, May 24
Oz, Mehmet: Birth, Jun 11
Ozawa, Seiji: Birth, Sep 1
Ozick, Cynthia: Birth, Apr 17
Ozone Layer, Intl Day for Preservation of the (UN), Sep 16

Rifle Chmpshps, NCAA Div I (Lexington, KY), Mar 13
Rigby, Cathy: Birth, Dec 12
Rigg, Diana: Birth, Jul 20
Riggs, Bobby: Billie Jean King Wins: Anniv, Sep 20
Riggs, Chandler: Birth, Jun 27
Rihanna: Birth, Feb 20
Riley, Amber: Birth, Feb 15
Riley, James Whitcomb: Birth Anniv, Oct 7
Riley, Pat: Birth, Mar 20
Rimes, LeAnn: Birth, Aug 28
Ringgold, Faith: Birth, Oct 8
Ringwald, Molly: Birth, Feb 18
Riordan, Rick: Birth, Jun 5
Rios, Marcelo: Birth, Dec 26
Riot Act: Anniv, Jul 20
Riot, Watts: Anniv, Aug 11
Ripa, Kelly: Birth, Oct 2
Ripken Streak Begins: Anniv, May 30
Ripken, Cal, Jr: Birth, Aug 24
Ripper, Jack the: Letter: Anniv, Sep 27
Ripper, Jack the: Whitechapel Murders Begin: Anniv, Aug 31
Risch, Jim: Birth, May 3
Rising Star Month, Worldwide, Jan 1
Rite of Spring Premiere and Riot: Anniv, May 29
Ritter, Jason: Birth, Feb 17
Ritter, Krysten: Birth, Dec 16
Rivera, Chita: Birth, Jan 23
Rivera, Diego: Birth Anniv, Dec 8
Rivera, Geraldo: Birth, Jul 4
Rivera, Mariano: Birth, Nov 29
Riverfest (La Crosse, WI), Jul 1
Rivers Month, Natl, Jun 1
Rivers, Doc: Birth, Oct 13
Rivers, Johnny: Birth, Nov 7
Rizzuto, Phil: Birth Anniv, Sep 25
RM: Birth, Sep 12
Roach, Hal: Birth Anniv, Jan 14
Roach, Mary: Birth, Mar 20
Road Traffic Victims, World Day of Remembrance for (UN), Nov 15
Roald Dahl Day, Sep 13
Robards, Jason: Birth Anniv, Jul 26
Robbie, Margot: Birth, Jul 2
Robbins, Jerome: Birth Anniv, Oct 11
Robbins, Tim: Birth, Oct 16
Robert the Hermit: Death Anniv, Apr 1
Robert-Houdin, Jean Eugene: Birth Anniv, Dec 6
Robert's Rules Day, May 2
Roberts, Cokie: Birth, Dec 27
Roberts, Eric: Birth, Apr 18
Roberts, John: Birth, Jan 27
Roberts, Julia: Birth, Oct 28
Roberts, Nora: Birth, Oct 10
Roberts, Pat: Birth, Apr 20
Roberts, Tony: Birth, Oct 22
Robertson, Oscar: Birth, Nov 24
Robertson, Pat: Birth, Mar 22
Robertson, Robbie: Birth, Jul 5
Robeson, Paul: Birth Anniv, Apr 9
Robin Hood Fest, Sherwood (Sherwood, OR), Jul 17
Robinson Crusoe Day, Feb 1
Robinson, Bill "Bojangles": Birth Anniv, May 25
Robinson, Brooks: Birth, May 18
Robinson, Craig: Birth, Oct 25
Robinson, David: Birth, Aug 6
Robinson, Eddie: Birth Anniv, Feb 13

Robinson, Edwin Arlington: Birth Anniv, Dec 22
Robinson, Frank: Named Baseball's First Black Manager: Anniv, Oct 3
Robinson, Jackie: Birth Anniv, Jan 31
Robinson, Jackie: Breaks Baseball Color Line: Anniv, Apr 15
Robinson, Roscoe, Jr: Birth Anniv, Oct 11
Robinson, Smokey: Birth, Feb 19
Robinson, Sugar Ray: Birth Anniv, May 3
Robot Enters World Lexicon: Anniv, Jan 25
Robot Killing, First: Anniv, Jul 21
Robotics Week, Natl, Apr 4
Rochester Lilac Fest (Rochester, NY), May 8
Rochesterfest (Rochester, MN), Jun 20
Rochette, Joannie: Birth, Jan 13
Rochon, Lela: Birth, Apr 17
Rock, Chris: Birth, Feb 7
Rockefeller, Abby Greene Aldrich: Birth Anniv, Oct 26
Rockefeller, John D.: Birth Anniv, Jul 8
Rockefeller, Nelson: Birth Anniv, Jul 8
Rocket: Launch of First Liquid-Fueled (Goddard Day): Anniv, Mar 16
Rockne, Knute: Birth Anniv, Mar 4
Rockwell, Norman: Birth Anniv, Feb 3
Rockwell, Sam: Birth, Nov 5
Rocky and His Friends TV Premiere: Anniv, Nov 19
Rocky Film Release: Anniv, Dec 3
Rocky Mountain Natl Park Established: Anniv, Jan 26
Roddenberry, Gene: Birth Anniv, Aug 19
Roddick, Andy: Birth, Aug 30
Rodent Awareness Week, Oct 18
Rodeo,
    Black Hills Stock Show and Rodeo (Rapid City, SD), Jan 24
    Cal Farley's Boys Ranch Rodeo and Adventurefest (Boys Ranch, TX), Sep 5
    Calgary Stampede (Calgary, AB, Canada), Jul 3
    Ennis Rodeo & Parade (Ennis, MT), Jul 3
    Fiesta De Los Vaqueros/Tucson Rodeo (Tucson, AZ), Feb 15
    Fort Worth Stock Show and Rodeo (Fort Worth, TX), Jan 17
    Houston Livestock Show/Rodeo (Houston, TX), Mar 3
    Oregon Trail Rodeo (Hastings, NE), Aug 28
Rodgers, Aaron: Birth, Dec 2
Rodgers, Richard: Oklahoma! Broadway Premiere: Anniv, Mar 31
Rodin, Auguste: Birth Anniv, Nov 12
Rodman, Dennis: Birth, May 13
Rodney, Caesar: Birth Anniv, Oct 7
Rodriguez, Alex: Birth, Jul 27
Rodriguez, Chi-Chi: Birth, Oct 23
Rodriguez, Gina: Birth, Jul 30
Rodriguez, Ivan "Pudge": Birth, Nov 30
Rodriguez, Rico: Birth, Jul 31
Rodriguez, Robert: Birth, Jun 20
Roe v Wade Decision: Anniv, Jan 22
Roeper, Richard: Birth, Oct 17
Rogation Sunday, May 17
Rogen, Seth: Birth, Apr 15
Rogers, Edith Nourse: Birth Anniv, Mar 19
Rogers, Fred: Birth Anniv, Mar 20
Rogers, Ginger: Birth Anniv, Jul 16
Rogers, Kenny: Birth, Aug 21
Rogers, Mimi: Birth, Jan 27
Rogers, Roy: Birth Anniv, Nov 5
Rogers, Will: Birth Anniv, Nov 4

Roget, Peter Mark: Birth Anniv, Jan 18
Roker, Al: Birth, Aug 20
Role Models Month, Natl Inspirational, Nov 1
Rolen, Scott: Birth, Apr 4
Rolfe, Lilian: Birth Anniv, Apr 26
Roller Coaster Day, Natl, Aug 16
Roller Coaster, First, Opens: Anniv, Jun 13
Roller Skating Month, Natl, Oct 1
Rolling Stones: Altamont Concert: Anniv, Dec 6
Rollins, Jimmy: Birth, Nov 27
Roma Day, Intl, Apr 8
Roman Catholic/Eastern Orthodox Meeting: Anniv, Jan 5
Roman Catholic: New Catechism: Anniv, Nov 16
Romance (including dating, love, relationships),
    Dating and Life Coach Recognition Week, Jan 5
    Decide to Be Married Day, Jun 27
    Dump Your "Significant Jerk" Week, Feb 2
    Flirting Week, Intl, Feb 9
    Kiss-and-Make-Up Day, Aug 25
    Love a Mensch Week, Feb 9
    Love Reset Day, Feb 15
    Meet a Mate Week, Jun 15
    Proposal Day!, Mar 19
    Read-a-Romance Month, Aug 1
    Sadie Hawkins Day, Nov 7
    Saint Valentine's Day, Feb 14
    Singles' Day (China), Nov 11
    Wingman's Day, Natl, Feb 13
Romania,
    National Day, Dec 1
Romano, Ray: Birth, Dec 21
Rombauer, Irma: Joy of Cooking Published: Anniv, Nov 30
Rome Executions: Anniv, Mar 25
Rome Liberated: Anniv, Jun 4
Rome, Sack of: Anniv, May 6
Rome: Birthday (Italy), Apr 21
Romijn, Rebecca: Birth, Nov 6
Rommel, Erwin: Birth Anniv, Nov 15
Romney, Mitt: Birth, Mar 12
Romo, Tony: Birth, Apr 21
Ronaldinho: Birth, Mar 21
Ronaldo, Cristiano: Birth, Feb 5
Ronaldo: Birth, Sep 22
Ronan, Saoirse: Birth, Apr 12
Rondo, Rajon: Birth, Feb 22
Ronson, Mark: Birth, Sep 4
Ronstadt, Linda: Birth, Jul 15
Rontgen, Wilhelm K.: Birth Anniv, Mar 27
Rontgen, Wilhelm: X-Ray Discovery Day: Anniv, Nov 8
Room of One's Own Day, Jan 25
Rooney, Mickey: Birth Anniv, Sep 23
Rooney, Wayne: Birth, Oct 24
Roosevelt, Alice: Birth Anniv, Jul 29
Roosevelt, Edith: Birth Anniv, Aug 6
Roosevelt, Eleanor: Birth Anniv, Oct 11
Roosevelt, Franklin Delano,
    Birth Anniv, Jan 30
    Commemorative Ceremony (Warm Springs, GA), Apr 12
    Death Anniv, Apr 12
    Elected to Fourth Term: Anniv, Nov 7
    First Fireside Chat: Anniv, Mar 12
    First Presidential Telecast: Anniv, Apr 30

Unconditional Surrender Statement: Anniv, Jan 24
US Bank Holiday: Anniv, Mar 5
Roosevelt, Theodore: Birth Anniv, Oct 27
Roosevelt, Theodore: First Secret Service Agent to Die in the Line of Duty: Anniv, Sep 3
Roosevelt, Theodore: Wrestling: Anniv, Apr 9
Rorschach, Hermann: Birth Anniv, Nov 8
Rosacea Awareness Month, Apr 1
Rose Bowl Game (Pasadena, CA), Jan 1
Rose Fest, Portland (Portland, OR), May 22
Rose Month, Natl, Jun 1
Rose Parade (Pasadena, CA), Jan 1
Rose, Billy: Birth Anniv, Sep 6
Rose, Charlie: Birth, Jan 5
Rose, Derrick: Birth, Oct 4
Rose, Jalen: Birth, Jan 30
Rose, Peace: Introduced to World: Anniv, Apr 29
Rose, Pete: Birth, Apr 14
Roseanne TV Premiere: Anniv, Oct 18
Roseanne: Birth, Nov 3
Rosen, Jacky: Birth, Aug 2
Rosenbaum, Michael: Birth, Jul 11
Rosenberg Execution: Anniv, Jun 19
Roses, Orangeburg Fest of (Orangeburg, SC), May 1
Rosh Hashanah, Sep 19
Rosh Hashanah Begins, Sep 18
Ross, Betsy: Birth Anniv, Jan 1
Ross, Diana: Birth, Mar 26
Ross, George: Birth Anniv, May 10
Ross, Katharine: Birth, Jan 29
Ross, Kyla: Birth, Oct 24
Ross, Marion: Birth, Oct 25
Ross, Nellie Tayloe: Birth Anniv, Nov 29
Ross, Nellie Tayloe: Wyoming Inaugurates First US Woman Gov: Anniv, Jan 5
Ross, Rick: Birth, Jan 28
Ross, Tracee Ellis: Birth, Oct 29
Ross, Wilbur: Birth, Nov 28
Rossellini, Isabella: Birth, Jun 18
Rossetti, Christina: Birth Anniv, Dec 5
Rossum, Emmy: Birth, Sep 12
Rostropovich, Mstislav: Birth Anniv, Mar 27
Rota, Nino: Birth Anniv, Dec 3
Rotary Tiller Race, World Chmpshp/ Purplehull Pea Fest (Emerson, AR), Jun 26
Roth, David Lee: Birth, Oct 10
Roth, Eli: Birth, Apr 18
Roth, Philip: Birth Anniv, Mar 19
Roth, Tim: Birth, May 14
Roughhouse Fest (Himeji, Japan), Oct 14
Rounds Resounding Day, Aug 1
Rounds, Mike: Birth, Oct 24
Roundtree, Richard: Birth, Jul 9
Rourke, Mickey: Birth, Sep 16
Rousey, Ronda: Birth, Feb 1
Rousseau, Henri: Birth Anniv, May 20
Rousseau, Jean J.: Birth Anniv, Jun 28
Routh, Brandon: Birth, Oct 9
Rove, Karl: Birth, Dec 25
Rowing: NCAA Div I Women's Chmpshp (Oak Ridge, TN), May 29
Rowlands, Gena: Birth, Jun 19
Rowling, J.K.: Birth, Jul 31
Roxburgh, Melissa: Birth, Dec 10
Roy Rogers Show TV Premiere: Anniv, Dec 30

Roy, Brandon: Birth, Jul 23
Roy, Patrick: Birth, Oct 5
Royal Society: Anniv, Nov 28
Royall, Anne: Birth Anniv, Jun 11
Royce, Henry: Birth Anniv, Mar 27
Royko, Mike: Birth Anniv, Sep 19
Rozelle, Pete: Birth Anniv, Mar 1
Rozier, Jean Francois Pilatre de: First Fatal Aviation Accident: Anniv, Jun 15
Rubens, Peter P.: Birth Anniv, Jun 28
Rubik, Erno: Birth, Jul 13
Rubio, Marco: Birth, May 28
Ruck, Alan: Birth, Jul 1
Rucker, Darius: Birth, May 13
Rudd, Paul: Birth, Apr 6
Rudner, Rita: Birth, Sep 17
Rudolph, Maya: Birth, Jul 27
Rudolph, Wilma: Birth Anniv, Jun 23
Ruffalo, Mark: Birth, Nov 22
Ruffin, Davis Eli (David): Birth Anniv, Jan 18
Ruffin, Edmund: Birth Anniv, Jan 5
Rugby,
    Six Nations Chmpshp, Feb 1
Runaway Prevention Month, Natl, Nov 1
Rundgren, Todd: Birth, Jun 22
Running,
    Anvil Mountain Run (Nome, AK), Jul 4
    Bank of America Chicago Marathon (Chicago, IL), Oct 11
    Bay to Breakers Race (San Francisco, CA), May 31
    Berlin Marathon (Berlin, Germany), Sep 27
    Boston Marathon (Boston, MA), Apr 20
    Dallas YMCA Turkey Trot (Dallas, TX), Nov 26
    Egg Races (Switzerland), Apr 13
    Hangover Handicap Run (Klamath Falls, OR), Jan 1
    Historic Marathon Runs: Anniv, Sep 2
    Houston Marathon (Houston, TX), Jan 19
    London Marathon (London, England), Apr 26
    Longest Dam Race (Fort Peck, MT), Jun 20
    New York City Marathon (New York, NY), Nov 1
    Oklahoma City Memorial Marathon (Oklahoma City, OK), Apr 26
    Peachtree Road Race, AJC (Atlanta, GA), Jul 4
    Runner's Selfie Day, Jun 23
    Running Day, Global, Jun 3
Runyan, Damon: Birth Anniv, Oct 4
RuPaul: Birth, Nov 17
Rural Life Sunday, May 17
Ruscha, Edward: Birth, Dec 16
Rush, Barbara: Birth, Jan 4
Rush, Benjamin: Birth Anniv, Jan 4
Rush, Geoffrey: Birth, Jul 6
Rush, William: Death Anniv, Jan 17
Rushdie, Salman, Death Sentence: Anniv, Feb 14
Rushdie, Salman: Birth, Jun 19
Rusk, (David) Dean: Birth Anniv, Feb 9
Russell, Bill: Birth, Feb 12
Russell, Charles M.: Birth Anniv, Mar 19
Russell, Karen: Birth, Jul 10
Russell, Keri: Birth, Mar 23
Russell, Kurt: Birth, Mar 17
Russell, Lillian: Birth Anniv, Dec 4
Russell, Mark: Birth, Aug 23
Russell, Theresa: Birth, Mar 20
Russell-Einstein Manifesto: Anniv, Jul 9

Russia (including USSR),
    Baltic States' Independence Recognized: Anniv, Sep 6
    Battle of Stalingrad Begins: Anniv, Aug 22
    Boris Yeltsin Inaugurated as President: Anniv, Jul 10
    Chelyabinsk Meteor Explosion: Anniv, Feb 15
    Christmas Day, Jan 7
    COMECON and Warsaw Pact Disband: Anniv, Jun 28
    Corridor of Death: Anniv (Leningrad), Jan 18
    Czar Nicholas II and Family Executed: Anniv, Jul 17
    Decembrist Revolt: Anniv, Dec 26
    Defender of the Fatherland Day, Feb 23
    Emancipation of the Serfs: Anniv, Mar 3
    German Surrender at Stalingrad: Anniv, Feb 2
    Great October Socialist Revolution: Anniv, Nov 7
    Intl Labor Day, May 1
    Katyn Forest Massacre Ordered: Anniv, Mar 5
    New Year's Day Observance, Jan 1
    Night of the Murdered Poets: Anniv, Aug 12
    Old New Year's Eve, Jan 13
    Revolution Day, Nov 7
    Russia Day, Jun 12
    Saint Petersburg Founded: Anniv, May 27
    Saint Petersburg Massacre: Anniv, Jan 9
    Soviet Cosmonaut Returns to New Country: Anniv, Mar 26
    Soviet Union Dissolved: Anniv, Dec 8
    Soviet Union Invaded: Anniv, Jun 22
    Trial of Sixteen: Anniv, Aug 19
    Trial of the Twenty-One: Anniv, Mar 2
    Unity Day, Nov 4
    USSR Established: Anniv, Dec 30
    Victory Day, May 9
    Winter War: Anniv, Nov 30
    Women's Day, Intl, Mar 8
Russian Language Day (UN), Jun 6
Russo, Rene: Birth, Feb 17
Russo, Richard: Birth, Jul 15
Rustin, Bayard: Birth Anniv, Mar 17
Ruth, George Herman,
    Babe Ruth Day: Anniv, Apr 27
    Baseball Hall of Fame's Charter Members: Anniv, Feb 2
    Birth Anniv, Feb 6
    Calls His Shot?: Anniv, Oct 1
    Curse of the Bambino Begins: Anniv, Jan 3
    Death Anniv, Aug 16
    First Pro Homer: Anniv, Sep 5
    Pitching Debut: Anniv, Apr 22
    Ruth Retires: Anniv, Jun 2
    Sets Home Run Record: Anniv, Sep 30
Rutherford, Ernest: Birth Anniv, Aug 30
Rutherford, Kelly: Birth, Nov 6
Rutledge, Edward: Birth Anniv, Nov 23
Rutledge, John: Death Anniv, Jul 18
Ruttan, Susan: Birth, Sep 16
Rwanda,
    Genocide Remembrance Day, Apr 7
    Independence Day, Jul 1
    Reflection on the Genocide in Rwanda, Intl Day of (UN), Apr 7

Republic Day, Sep 25
Tragedy in Rwanda: Anniv, Apr 6
Ryan, Amy: Birth, Nov 30
Ryan, Jay: Birth, Aug 29
Ryan, Jeri: Birth, Feb 22
Ryan, Kay: Birth, Sep 21
Ryan, Matt: Birth, May 16
Ryan, Meg: Birth, Nov 19
Ryan, Nolan: Birth, Jan 31
Ryan's Hope TV Premiere: Anniv, Jul 7
Rydell, Bobby: Birth, Apr 26
Ryder Cup (Haven, WI), Sep 25
Ryder, Winona: Birth, Oct 29
Rylance, Mark: Birth, Jan 18

Saad, Brandon: Birth, Oct 27
Saarinen, Eero: Birth Anniv, Aug 20
Saarinen, Eero: Gateway Arch Completed:
    Anniv, Oct 28
Saarinen, Eliel: Birth Anniv, Aug 20
Sabado Gigante TV Premiere: Anniv,
    Aug 8
Sabathia, C.C.: Birth, Jul 21
Sabatini, Gabriela: Birth, May 16
Sabato, Antonio, Jr: Birth, Feb 29
Saberhagen, Bret: Birth, Apr 11
Sabin, Albert Bruce: Birth Anniv, Aug 26
Sacagawea: Death Anniv, Dec 20
Sacco-Vanzetti Execution: Anniv, Aug 23
Sackhoff, Katee: Birth, Apr 8
Sackville-West, Vita: Birth Anniv, Mar 9
Sacramone, Alicia: Birth, Dec 3
Sadat, Anwar el-: Assassination Anniv,
    Oct 6
Sadat, Anwar el-: Birth Anniv, Dec 25
Sadie Hawkins Day, Nov 7
Safe Boating Week, Natl, May 16
Safety. See also Crime,
    Bullying Bystanders Unite Week, Oct 18
    Bullying Prevention Awareness Month,
        Natl, Oct 1
    Bullying Prevention Day, Natl, Oct 14
    Bullying Prevention, World Day of,
        Oct 5
    Check Your Batteries Day, Mar 8
    Child Safety Council Founded, Natl:
        Anniv, Nov 9
    Crime Prevention Month, Natl, Oct 1
    Distracted Driving Awareness Month,
        Apr 1
    Dog Bite Prevention Week, Natl, Apr 12
    Drowsy Driver Awareness Day, Apr 6
    Farm Safety and Health Week, Natl (Pres
        Proc), Sep 20
    Fire Prevention Week, Oct 4
    Fire Prevention Week (Pres Proc), Oct 4
    Fire Safety Council, Natl: Anniv, Dec 7
    Firepup's Birthday, Oct 1
    Fireworks Safety Months, Jun 1
    Heimlich Maneuver Introduced: Anniv,
        Jun 1
    Hurricane Preparedness Week, Natl (Pres
        Proc), May 3
    Impaired Driving Prevention Month, Natl
        (Pres Proc), Dec 1
    Keep Kids Alive—Drive 25 Day, May 1
    Lightning Safety Awareness Week, Jun 21
    Missing Children's Day, Natl, May 25
    Motorcycle Safety Month, May 1
    Night Out, Natl, Aug 4
    9-1-1 Education Month, Natl, Apr 1
    Older Driver Safety Awareness Week, Natl,
        Dec 7
    Personal Self-Defense Awareness Month,
        Natl, Jan 1

Poison Prevention Week, Natl, Mar 15
Poison Prevention Week, Natl (Pres Proc),
    Mar 15
Rabies Day, World, Sep 28
REACT Month, May 1
Recycle Your Mercury Thermostat Day,
    Oct 24
Rodent Awareness Week, Oct 18
Safe Boating Week, Natl, May 16
Safe Boating Week, Natl (Pres Proc),
    May 16
Safe Toys and Gifts Month, Dec 1
Safety and Health at Work, World Day for
    (UN), Apr 28
Safety Month, Natl, Jun 1
Safetypup's Birthday, Feb 12
Security Officer Appreciation Week, Natl,
    Sep 13
Sexual Assault Awareness and Prevention
    Month, Natl (Pres Proc), Apr 1
Sexual Assault Awareness Month, Natl,
    Apr 1
SOS Adopted: Anniv, Nov 3
Sports Eye Safety Month, Sep 1
Stop Bullying Month, Natl, Oct 1
Student Safety Month, Jun 1
Workers Memorial Day, Apr 28
Worldwide Food Service Safety Month,
    Dec 1
Youth Sports Safety Month, Natl, Apr 1
Sagal, Katey: Birth, Nov 18
Sagan, Carl: Birth Anniv, Nov 9
Sager, Carole Bayer: Birth, Mar 8
Saget, Bob: Birth, May 17
Sagittarius Begins, Nov 22
Sahl, Mort: Birth, May 11
Sailors: Day of the Seafarer (UN), Jun 25
Saint Aubin, Helen "Callaghan": Birth
    Anniv, Mar 13
Saint Bartholomew's Day Massacre: Anniv,
    Aug 24
Saint Christopher: Independence Day,
    Sep 19
Saint Elias Day: Macedonian Uprising:
    Anniv, Aug 2
Saint Eustatius, West Indies: Statia and
    America Day, Nov 16
Saint George's Day (Newfoundland,
    Canada), Apr 23
Saint James, Susan: Birth, Aug 14
Saint Lasarus's Day (Bulgaria), Apr 1
Saint Lawrence Seaway Act: Anniv, May 13
Saint Lawrence Seaway: Dedication Anniv,
    Jun 26
Saint Lucia: Independence Day, Feb 22
Saint Patrick's Day (Northern Ireland),
    Mar 17
Saint Patrick's Day Parade (Baton Rouge,
    LA), Mar 14
Saint Patrick's Day Parade (Hornell, NY),
    Mar 14
Saint Patrick's Day Parade (New York, NY),
    Mar 17
Saint Petersburg Founded: Anniv, May 27
Saint Petersburg Massacre: Anniv, Jan 9
Saint Vincent and the Grenadines:
    Independence Day, Oct 27
Saint, Eva Marie: Birth, Jul 4
Sainte-Marie, Buffy: Birth, Feb 20
Saint-Gaudens, Augustus: Birth Anniv,
    Mar 1
Saints and Sinners Literary Fest (New
    Orleans, LA), Mar 27
Saints, Saints' Days,
    Andrew's Day, Nov 30

Anthony of Padua: Feast Day (Portugal),
    Jun 13
Anthony's Day, Jan 17
Apollinaris: Feast Day, Jul 23
Augustine of Canterbury, Feast of, May 26
Augustine, Feast of, Aug 28
Barbara's Day, Dec 4
Basil's Day, Jan 1
Bernard of Montjoux: Feast Day, May 28
Cabrini, Mother Frances Xavier:
    Canonized: Anniv, Jul 7
Catherine of Siena: Feast Day, Apr 29
Catherine's Day, Nov 25
Cecilia: Feast Day, Nov 22
Clare of Assisi: Feast Day, Aug 11
Crispin's Day, Oct 25
David's Day (Wales), Mar 1
Dwynwen's Day, Jan 25
Edward, the Confessor: Feast Day, Oct 13
Erasmus (Elmo) Day, Jun 2
Fiesta de Santa Marta de Ribarteme (As
    Neves, Galicia, Spain), Jul 29
Frances of Rome: Feast Day, Mar 9
Frances Xavier Cabrini: Birth Anniv,
    Jul 15
Francis of Assisi: Feast Day, Oct 4
Gabriel: Feast Day, Mar 24
Genevieve: Feast Day, Jan 3
George: Feast Day (England), Apr 23
Gudula: Feast Day, Jan 8
Ignatius of Loyola, Feast of, Jul 31
Isidro Day (Mexico), May 15
James Day (Spain), Jul 25
Januarius: Feast Day, Sep 19
Jerome: Feast Day, Sep 30
Joan of Arc: Feast Day, May 30
John Nepomucene Neumann: Birth Anniv,
    Mar 28
John of Capistrano: Death Anniv,
    Oct 23
John the Baptist Day, Jun 24
John, Apostle-Evangelist: Feast Day,
    Dec 27
Joseph's Day, Mar 19
Juan Diego: First Indian Saint: Anniv,
    Jul 31
Jude's Day, Oct 28
Knut's Day, Jan 13
Lucia Day (Sweden), Dec 13
Luke: Feast Day, Oct 18
Maron's Day (Lebanon), Feb 9
Martin's Day (Sweden), Nov 11
Martyrdom of John the Baptist, Aug 29
Nicholas Day, Dec 6
Oswald of Worcester: Feast Day, Feb 1
Patrick's Day, Mar 17
Peter and Paul Day, Jun 29
Peter's Day (Turkey), Jun 29
Piran's Day, Mar 5
Pius X: Birth Anniv, Jun 2
Rose of Lima Day, Aug 30
Saint Paul's Feast (Kato Paphos, Cyprus),
    Jun 28
Sebastian's Day (Brazil), Jan 20
Seton, Elizabeth Ann Bayley: Feast Day,
    Jan 4
Stephen's Day, Dec 26
Swithin's Day, Jul 15
Sylvester's Day, Dec 31
Teresa of Avila: Birth Anniv, Mar 28
Thomas of Canterbury: Feast Day,
    Dec 29
Valentine's Day, Feb 14
Vincent De Paul: Feast Day, Sep 27
Vincent De Paul: Old Feast Day, Jul 19
Vincent: Feast Day, Jan 22

Sajak, Pat: Birth, Oct 26
Sakharov, Andrei Dmitriyevich: Birth
    Anniv, May 21
Sakic, Joe: Birth, Jul 7
Salad Month, Natl, May 1
Salah, Mohamed: Birth, Jun 15
Salazar, Alberto: Birth, Aug 7
Saldana, Zoe: Birth, Jun 19
Salem Witch Hysteria Begins: Anniv,
    Mar 1
Salem Witch Trials Begin: Anniv, Jun 2
Salesperson's Day, Natl, Dec 4
Salinger, J.D.: Birth Anniv, Jan 1
Salisbury, Harrison: Birth Anniv, Nov 14
Salk, Jonas: Birth Anniv, Oct 28
Salk, Lee: Birth Anniv, Dec 27
Salling, Mark: Birth, Aug 17
Salmon Day, Natl, Oct 8
Salomon, Haym: Death Anniv, Jan 6
Salter, Susanna: Elected First Woman
    Mayor in US: Anniv, Apr 4
Salto del Colacho (Baby Jumping Fest,
    Castrillo de Murcia, Spain), Jun 14
Salute to 35-Plus Moms Week, May 10
Salvador, Francis: Death Anniv, Jul 31
Salvation Army Founder's Day, Apr 10
Salvation Army in US: Anniv, Mar 10
Salvation Army: Booth, William: Birth
    Anniv, Apr 10
Salvation Army: Donut Day, Natl, Jun 5
Samberg, Andy: Birth, Aug 18
Sambora, Richie: Birth, Jul 11
Same-Sex Marriages, First US: Anniv,
    May 17
Samhain, Oct 31
Samms, Emma: Birth, Aug 28
Samoa,
    ANZAC Day, Apr 25
    Arbor Day, Nov 6
    Independence Day, Jun 1
    Samoan Fire Dance, Dec 31
    White Sunday, Oct 11
Samoa, American: Flag Day, Apr 17
Sampras, Pete: Birth, Aug 12
Sampson, Deborah: Birth Anniv, Dec 17
Sampson, Ralph: Birth, Jul 7
Samuelson, Joan Benoit: Birth, May 16
San Bernardino Terrorist Attack: Anniv,
    Dec 2
San Francisco 1906 Earthquake: Anniv,
    Apr 18
San Francisco 1989 Earthquake: Anniv,
    Oct 17
San Francisco Chinese New Year Parade,
    Feb 8
San Giacomo, Laura: Birth, Nov 14
San Isidro Day (Mexico), May 15
San Jacinto Day (TX), Apr 21
San Marino: National Day, Sep 3
San Sebastian's Day (Brazil), Jan 20
Sanborn, David: Birth, Jul 30
Sand, George: Birth Anniv, Jul 1
Sand, Paul: Birth, Mar 5
Sandberg, Ryne: Birth, Sep 18
Sandburg, Carl: Birth Anniv, Jan 6
Sande, Emeli: Birth, Mar 10
Sanders, Barry: Birth, Jul 16
Sanders, Bernie: Birth, Sep 8
Sanders, Bob: Birth, Feb 24
Sanders, Colonel Harland: Birth Anniv,
    Sep 9
Sanders, Deion: Birth, Aug 9
Sanders, Jay O.: Birth, Apr 16
Sanders, Reggie: Birth, Dec 1

Sanders, Richard: Birth, Aug 23
Sanders, Sarah Huckabee: Birth,
    Aug 13
Sandino, Cesar: Assassination Anniv,
    Feb 21
Sandler, Adam: Birth, Sep 9
Sands, Tommy: Birth, Aug 27
Sandwich Day: John Montague Birth Anniv,
    Nov 3
Sandy Hook Elementary School Shootings
    (Newton, CT): Anniv, Dec 14
Sandy, Gary: Birth, Dec 25
Sandys, Edwin: Birth Anniv, Dec 9
Sanger, Margaret (Higgins): Birth Anniv,
    Sep 14
Sanger, Margaret: First Birth Control Clinic
    Opened: Anniv, Oct 16
Santa Lucia Day (Sweden), Dec 13
Santana, Carlos: Birth, Jul 20
Santayana, George: Birth Anniv, Dec 16
Santiago, Benito: Birth, Mar 9
Santiago, Saundra: Birth, Apr 13
Santo: Birth Anniversary, Sep 23
Santos, Juan Manuel: Birth, Aug 10
Sao Tome and Principe: Independence Day,
    Jul 12
Saperstein, Abe: Birth Anniv, Jul 4
Sapporo Snow Fest (Sapporo, Japan), Jan 31
Sarandon, Chris: Birth, Jul 24
Sarandon, Susan: Birth, Oct 4
Sarazen, Gene: Birth Anniv, Feb 27
Sargent, John Singer: Birth Anniv, Jan 12
Sarkozy, Nicolas: Birth, Jan 28
Sarnoff, David: Birth Anniv, Feb 27
Saroyan, William: Birth Anniv, Aug 31
Sartre, Jean-Paul: Birth Anniv, Jun 21
Sasaki, Sadako: Death Anniv, Oct 25
Sasse, Ben: Birth, Feb 22
Sassoon, Vidal: Birth Anniv, Jan 17
Satchmo Summerfest (New Orleans, LA),
    Jul 31
Satisfied Staying Single Day, Feb 11
Saturday Night Live TV Premiere: Anniv,
    Oct 11
Saturday Night Massacre: Anniv, Oct 20
Saturn: Cassini-Huygens Reaches, Jul 1
Saturnalia, Dec 17
Satyarthi, Kailash: Birth, Jan 11
Saudi Arabia: Dakar Rally (Jeddah, Riyadh,
    Al Qiddiya), Jan 5
Saudi Arabia: Kingdom Unification, Sep 23
Saunders, George: Birth, Dec 2
Sauntering Day, World, Jun 19
Savage, Adam: Birth, Jul 15
Savage, Ben: Birth, Sep 13
Savage, Fred: Birth, Jul 9
Savage, John: Birth, Aug 25
Savant, Doug: Birth, Jun 21
Save Your Vision Month, Mar 1
Sawa, Devon: Birth, Sep 7
Sawyer, Diane: Birth, Dec 22
Sax, Adolphe: Birth Anniv (Saxophone
    Day), Nov 6
Saxon, John: Birth, Aug 5
Saxophone Day, Nov 6
Say Something Nice Day, Jun 1
Sayer, Leo: Birth, May 21
Sayers, Dorothy: Birth Anniv, Jun 13
Sayers, Gale: Birth, May 30
Scacchi, Greta: Birth, Feb 18
Scaggs, Boz: Birth, Jun 8
Scalia, Antonin: Birth Anniv, Mar 11
Scaliger, Joseph J.: Birth Anniv, Aug 4
Scarlatti, Domenico: Birth Anniv, Oct 26

Scarry, Richard M.: Birth Anniv, Jun 5
Scenic Drive Fest (Van Buren County, IA),
    Oct 9
Schaal, Kristen: Birth, Jan 24
Schatz, Brian: Birth, Oct 20
Schiaparelli, Elsa: Birth Anniv, Sep 10
Schieffer, Bob: Birth, Feb 25
Schiff, Richard: Birth, May 27
Schiffer, Claudia: Birth, Aug 25
Schilling, Curt: Birth, Nov 14
Schilling, Taylor: Birth, Jul 27
Schindler, Oskar: Birth Anniv, Apr 28
Schirra, Wally: Birth Anniv, Mar 12
Schlatter, Charlie: Birth, May 1
Schmeling, Max: Birth Anniv, Sep 28
Schmidt, Mike: Birth, Sep 27
Schnabel, Julian: Birth, Oct 26
Schneider, John: Birth, Apr 8
Schneider, Rob: Birth, Oct 31
Schneiderman, Rose: Birth Anniv,
    Apr 6
Schoenaerts, Matthias: Birth, Dec 8
Scholarship Providers Assn, Natl, Annual
    Conf (Chicago, IL), Sep 9
Scholastic Established: Anniv, Oct 22
School. See also Education,
    Breakfast Week, Natl, Mar 2
    Library Month, Apr 1
    Lunch Week, Natl, Oct 12
    Lunch Week, Natl (Pres Proc), Oct 12
    Nurse Day, Natl, May 6
    Pizza Party Day, Natl, May 15
    Principals' Day, May 1
Schopenhauer, Arthur: Birth Anniv,
    Feb 22
Schroder, Gerhard: Birth, Apr 7
Schroder, Rick: Birth, Apr 13
Schroeder, Patricia: Birth, Jun 30
Schubert, Franz: Birth Anniv, Jan 31
Schuck, John: Birth, Feb 4
Schultz, Dwight: Birth, Nov 24
Schulz, Charles: Birth Anniv, Nov 26
Schuman Plan Anniv: European Union,
    May 9
Schuman, William Howard: Birth Anniv,
    Aug 4
Schumer, Amy: Birth, Jun 1
Schumer, Charles E.: Birth, Nov 23
Schurz, Carl: Birth Anniv, Mar 2
Schutz, Heinrich: Birth Anniv, Oct 8
Schwartz, Ben: Birth, Sep 15
Schwartzman, Jason: Birth, Jun 26
Schwarzenegger, Arnold: Birth, Jul 30
Schweitzer, Albert: Birth Anniv, Jan 14
Schwenkfelder Thanksgiving, Sep 24
Schwikert, Tasha: Birth, Nov 21
Schwimmer, David: Birth, Nov 12
Schygulla, Hanna: Birth, Dec 25
Scialfa, Patty: Birth, Jul 29
Science,
    American Assn for the Advancement
        of Science Annual Mtg (Seattle, WA),
        Feb 13
    Asteroid Day, Jun 30
    Astronomy Day, Fall, Sep 26
    Astronomy Day, Spring, May 2
    Big Bang Coined: Anniv, Mar 28
    Biological Clock Gene Discovered: Anniv,
        Apr 28
    Brain Awareness Week, Mar 16
    Bunsen Burner Day, Mar 31
    Cellophane Tape Patented: Anniv, May 27
    Chemistry Week, Natl, Oct 18
    Cloning of an Adult Animal, First: Anniv,
        Feb 23

Minnesota State Fair (St. Paul, MN), Aug 27

Mississippi State Fair (Jackson, MS), Oct 7

Missouri State Fair (Sedalia, MO), Aug 13

Montana State Fair (Great Falls, MT), Jul 31

Nebraska State Fair (Grand Island, NE), Aug 28

Nevada State Fair (Carson City, NV), Jun 4

New Jersey State Fair/Sussex Farm and Horse Show (Augusta, NJ), Jul 31

New Mexico State Fair (Albuquerque, NM), Sep 10

New York State Fair (Syracuse, NY), Aug 28

North Carolina State Fair (Raleigh, NC), Oct 15

North Dakota State Fair (Minot, ND), Jul 17

Ohio State Fair (Columbus, OH), Jul 29

Oklahoma State Fair (Oklahoma City, OK), Sep 17

Oregon State Fair (Salem, OR), Aug 27

South Carolina State Fair (Columbia, SC), Oct 14

South Dakota State Fair (Huron, SD), Sep 3

State Fair of Texas (Dallas, TX), Sep 25

State Fair of West Virginia (Lewisburg, WV), Aug 13

Tennessee State Fair (Nashville, TN), Sep 11

Utah State Fair (Salt Lake City, UT), Sep 10

Vermont State Fair (Rutland, VT), Aug 11

Virginia, State Fair of (Doswell, VA), Sep 25

Washington State Fair (Puyallup, WA), Sep 4

Western Idaho Fair (Boise, ID), Aug 21

Wisconsin State Fair (West Allis, WI), Aug 6

Wyoming State Fair & Rodeo (Douglas, WY), Aug 11

Statistics Day, World (UN), Oct 20

Statistics: Mathematics and Statistics Awareness Month, Apr 1

Statue of Liberty: Dedication Anniv, Oct 28

Staub, Rusty: Birth, Apr 1

Staubach, Roger: Birth, Feb 5

Staunton, Imelda: Birth, Jan 9

Stay Home Because You're Well Day, Nov 30

Stay Out of the Sun Day, Jul 3

Stay Up All Night Night, May 9

Stealth Bomber Flight: Anniv, Jul 17

Steel Mills, Federal Government Seizure: Anniv, Apr 8

Steel, Danielle: Birth, Aug 14

Steele, Tommy: Birth, Dec 17

Steenburgen, Mary: Birth, Feb 8

Steeples, Eddie: Birth, Nov 25

Stefani, Gwen: Birth, Oct 3

Steichen, Edward: Birth Anniv, Mar 27

Steig, William: Birth Anniv, Nov 14

Steiger, Rod: Birth Anniv, Apr 17

Stein, Ben: Birth, Nov 25

Stein, Gertrude: Birth Anniv, Feb 3

Steinbeck, John: Birth Anniv, Feb 27

Steinberg, David: Birth, Aug 9

Steinberg, Saul: Birth Anniv, Jun 15

Steinbrenner, George: Birth Anniv, Jul 4

Steinem, Gloria: Birth, Mar 25

Steiner, Max: Birth Anniv, May 10

Steinfeld, Hailee: Birth, Dec 11

Stella, Frank: Birth, May 12

Stendhal: Birth Anniv, Jan 23

Stengel, Casey: Birth Anniv, Jul 30

Stephens, James: Birth, May 18

Stephenson, George: Birth Anniv, Jun 9

Stephenson, Jan: Birth, Dec 22

Stern, Daniel: Birth, Aug 28

Stern, Howard: Birth, Jan 12

Stern, Howard: Radio Show Premiere: Anniv, Nov 18

Stern, Itzhak: Birth Anniv, Jan 25

Stern, Robert A.M.: Birth, May 23

Sterne, Laurence: Birth Anniv, Nov 24

Sternhagen, Frances: Birth, Jan 13

Steve Allen Show TV Premiere: Anniv, Dec 25

Stevens, Cat: Birth, Jul 21

Stevens, Connie: Birth, Aug 8

Stevens, Dan: Birth, Oct 10

Stevens, Fisher: Birth, Nov 27

Stevens, Stella: Birth, Oct 1

Stevenson, Adlai, II: Birth Anniv, Feb 5

Stevenson, Adlai: Birth Anniv, Oct 23

Stevenson, Alexandra: Birth, Dec 15

Stevenson, Parker: Birth, Jun 4

Stevenson, Robert Louis: Birth Anniv, Nov 13

Stewardship Week, Apr 26

Stewart, French: Birth, Feb 20

Stewart, Jackie: Birth, Jun 11

Stewart, James: Birth Anniv, May 20

Stewart, Jon: Birth, Nov 28

Stewart, Kristen: Birth, Apr 9

Stewart, Martha: Birth, Aug 3

Stewart, Patrick: Birth, Jul 13

Stewart, Potter: Birth Anniv, Jan 23

Stewart, Rod: Birth, Jan 10

Stieglitz, Alfred: Birth Anniv, Jan 1

Stiles, Julia: Birth, Mar 28

Stiles, Ryan: Birth, Apr 22

Stiller, Ben: Birth, Nov 30

Stiller, Jerry: Birth, Jun 8

Stills, Stephen: Birth, Jan 3

Stilts: Walk on Stilts Day, Jul 27

Stine, R.L.: Birth, Oct 8

Sting (Gordon Sumner): Birth, Oct 2

Stipe, Michael: Birth, Jan 4

Stir Up Sunday, Nov 22

Stitt, Kevin: Birth, Dec 28

Stock Exchange Holiday, Jan 1

Stock Exchange Holiday, Jan 20

Stock Exchange Holiday, Feb 17

Stock Exchange Holiday, Apr 10

Stock Exchange Holiday, May 25

Stock Exchange Holiday, Jul 3

Stock Exchange Holiday, Sep 7

Stock Exchange Holiday, Nov 26

Stock Exchange Holiday, Dec 25

Stock Exchange, NY, Established: Anniv, May 17

Stock Market Crash of 1893: Anniv, May 5

Stock Market Crash of 1929: Anniv, Oct 29

Stock Market Panic: Anniv, Oct 24

Stockholm Syndrome Bank Robbery: Anniv, Aug 23

Stockings, Nylon: Anniv, May 15

Stocks: Dow Jones Biggest Drop: Anniv, Sep 29

Stocks: Dow Jones Tops 1,000: Anniv, Nov 14

Stocks: Dow Jones Tops 5,000: Anniv, Nov 21

Stocks: Dow Jones Tops 10,000: Anniv, Mar 29

Stocks: Dow Jones Tops 11,000: Anniv, May 3

Stocks: Dow Jones Tops 15,000: Anniv, May 7

Stocks: Dow Jones Tops 25,000: Anniv, Jan 4

Stockton, Dave: Birth, Nov 2

Stockton, John: Birth, Mar 26

Stockton, Richard: Birth Anniv, Oct 1

Stockwell, Dean: Birth, Mar 5

Stockwell, John: Birth, Mar 25

Stojakovic, Peja: Birth, Jun 9

Stojko, Elvis: Birth, Mar 22

Stokes, Carl: Becomes First Black Mayor in US: Anniv, Nov 13

Stoltz, Eric: Birth, Sep 30

Stone, Dee Wallace: Birth, Dec 14

Stone, Emma: Birth, Nov 6

Stone, Harlan Fiske: Birth Anniv, Oct 11

Stone, Lucy: Birth Anniv, Aug 13

Stone, Oliver: Birth, Sep 15

Stone, Sharon: Birth, Mar 10

Stone, Sly: Birth, Mar 15

Stone, Steve: Birth, Jul 14

Stone, Thomas: Death Anniv, Oct 5

Stonestreet, Eric: Birth, Sep 9

Stonewall Riot: Anniv, Jun 28

Stookey, Paul: Birth, Nov 30

Stoppard, Tom: Birth, Jul 3

Storey, David: Birth, Jul 13

Story, Joseph: Birth Anniv, Sep 18

Stotz, Carl E.: Birth Anniv, Feb 20

Stoudemire, Amare: Birth, Nov 16

Stout, Rex: Birth Anniv, Dec 1

Stover, Russell: Birth Anniv, May 6

Stowe, Harriet Beecher: Birth Anniv, Jun 14

Stowe, Madeleine: Birth, Aug 18

Stradivari, Antonio: Death Anniv, Dec 18

Strahan, Michael: Birth, Nov 21

Strait, George: Birth, May 18

Straith, Claire: Birth Anniv, Aug 30

Strang, James Jesse: Birth Anniv, Mar 21

Strange, Curtis: Birth, Jan 30

Strange, Sarah: Birth, Sep 6

Strassman, Marcia: Birth, Apr 28

Stratemeyer, Edward L.: Birth Anniv, Oct 4

Strathairn, David: Birth, Jan 26

Stratton, Dorothy C.: Birth Anniv, Mar 24

Strauss, Levi: Birth Anniv, Feb 26

Strauss, Peter: Birth, Feb 20

Strauss, Richard G.: Birth Anniv, Jun 11

Stravinsky, Igor F.: Birth Anniv, Jun 17

Stravinsky, Igor: Rite of Spring Premiere and Riot: Anniv, May 29

Straw Hat Month, Apr 1

Strawberry Moon, Jun 5

Strawberry, Darryl: Birth, Mar 12

Streep, Meryl: Birth, Jun 22

Street, Huston: Birth, Aug 2

Street, Picabo: Birth, Apr 3

Streetcar Named Desire Broadway Opening: Anniv, Dec 3

Streeter, Ruth Cheney: Birth Anniv, Oct 2

Streisand, Barbra: Birth, Apr 24

Streit, Mark: Birth, Dec 11

Stress Awareness Day, Natl, Apr 16

Stress Awareness Month, Apr 1

Stress Management: Zero-Tasking Day, Nov 1

Strindberg, August: Birth Anniv, Jan 22

Stringfield, Sherry: Birth, Jun 24

Stritch, Elaine: Birth Anniv, Feb 2

Strokes Month, Strike Out, May 1

Strong, Rider: Birth, Dec 11

Stroud, Don: Birth, Sep 1

Villa, David: Birth, Dec 3
Villeneueve, Jacques: Birth, Apr 9
Villeneuve, Denis: Birth, Oct 3
Vincent, Fay: Birth, May 29
Vinegar Month, Natl, May 1
Vinson, Fred M.: Birth Anniv, Jan 22
Vinton, Bobby: Birth, Apr 16
Vinyl Record Day, Aug 12
Virgen de la Guadalupe: Las Mananitas
   (Ponce, Puerto Rico), Dec 12
Virgin Islands,
   Hurricane Supplication Day, Jul 27
   Hurricane Thanksgiving Day, Oct 19
   Virgin Islands-Puerto Rico Friendship
      Day, Oct 12
Virginia,
   African-American Cultural Heritage
      Month (Williamsburg and Yorktown),
      Feb 1
   Alexandria Library Sit-In Anniv
      Celebration (Alexandria), Aug 21
   American Indian Intertribal Powwow
      (Williamsburg), Oct 10
   Battle of Bull Run: Anniv, Jul 21
   Battle of Cold Harbor: Anniv, Jun 3
   Battle of Hampton Roads: Anniv, Mar 9
   Battle of Spotsylvania: Anniv, May 12
   Battle of the Wilderness: Anniv, May 5
   Blue Ridge Folklife Fest (Ferrum), Oct 24
   Chincoteague Island Easter Decoy Show
      (Chincoteague Island), Apr 10
   Chincoteague Island Oyster Fest
      (Chincoteague Island), Oct 10
   Chincoteague Pony Penning
      (Chincoteague Island), Jul 29
   Chincoteague Seafood Fest
      (Chincoteague), May 2
   Christmastide in Virginia (Williamsburg
      and Yorktown), Dec 19
   Defeat at Five Forks: Anniv, Apr 1
   Fall of Richmond: Anniv, Apr 3
   First US Breach of Promise Suit: Anniv,
      Jun 14
   Foods/Feasts of Colonial Virginia
      (Williamsburg), Nov 26
   Foxfield Races (Charlottesville), Apr 25
   George Washington Birthday Parade
      (Alexandria), Feb 17
   Highland County Maple Fest (Highland
      County), Mar 14
   Historic Garden Week, Apr 18
   James Monroe Birthday Celebration
      (Charlottesville), Apr 28
   Jamestown Day (Williamsburg), May 9
   Kaine, Tim: Birth, Feb 26
   Lee-Jackson Day, Jan 17
   Liberty Celebration (Yorktown), Jul 4
   Military Through the Ages
      (Williamsburg), Mar 21
   NCAA Div I Field Hockey Chmpshp
      (Norfolk), Nov 20
   NCAA Div I Men's Volleyball Chmpshp
      (Fairfax), May 7
   Northam, Ralph: Birth, Sep 13
   Old Fiddlers' Conv (Galax), Aug 3
   Ratification Day, Jun 25
   Seven Days Campaign: Anniv, Jun 25
   State Fair (Doswell), Sep 25
   Streetscene (Covington), Aug 8
   Sugarloaf Crafts Fest (Chantilly), Mar 27
   Sugarloaf Crafts Fest (Chantilly), Dec 4
   Union Officers Escape Libby Prison:
      Anniv, Feb 9
   US Mid-Amateur (Golf) Chmpshp
      (Manakin-Sabot), Sep 12
   Warner, Mark: Birth, Dec 15

Washington's Birthday at Mount Vernon
   (Mount Vernon), Feb 14
Yorktown Day (Yorktown), Oct 19
Yorktown Victory Celebration (Yorktown),
   Oct 17
Yorktown Victory Day, Oct 12
Virginia Company Expedition to America:
   Anniv, Dec 20
Virginia Plan Proposed: Anniv, May 29
Virginia Tech Shootings: Anniv, Apr 16
Virgo Begins, Aug 23
Vision and Learning Month, Children's,
   Aug 1
Vision: AMD/Low Vision Awareness
   Month, Feb 1
Visit Your Relatives Day, May 18
Visnjic, Goran: Birth, Sep 9
Vitale, Dick: Birth, Jun 9
Vitamin C Isolated: Anniv, Apr 4
Viticulturists' Day (Bulgaria), Feb 14
Vito, Louie: Birth, Mar 20
Vitti, Monica: Birth, Nov 3
V-J Day (Announcement): Anniv, Aug 14
V-J Day (Ratification), Sep 2
Voiceover Day, Natl, Mar 15
Voight, Jon: Birth, Dec 29
Volcanoes,
   Cameroon: Lake Nyos Disaster: Anniv,
      Aug 21
   Krakatoa Eruption: Anniv, Aug 26
   Laki Volcano Eruption: Anniv, Jun 8
   Montserrat: Volcano Erupts: Anniv, Jun 25
   Mount Pelee Eruption: Anniv, May 8
   Mount Pinatubo Erupts: Anniv, Jun 15
   Mount Saint Helens Eruption: Anniv,
      May 18
   Vesuvius Day (Pompeii Destroyed: Anniv),
      Aug 24
Volleyball,
   NCAA Div I Men's Chmpshp (Fairfax,
      VA), May 7
   NCAA Div I Women's Chmpshp (Omaha,
      NE), Dec 17
Vollmer, Dana: Birth, Nov 13
Volosozhar, Tatiana: Birth, May 22
Volstead Act Passed: Anniv, Oct 28
Voltaire: Birth Anniv, Nov 21
Volunteer Blood Donor Month, Natl, Jan 1
Volunteers, Volunteering,
   Community Spirit Days, Apr 1
   Greencare for Troops Awareness Week,
      Jun 14
   Mandela Day, Jul 18
   Rebuilding Day, Natl, Apr 25
   Rebuilding Month, Natl, Apr 1
   SnowCare for Troops Awareness Week,
      Jan 19
   Volunteer Day for Economic/Social
      Development, Intl (UN), Dec 5
   Volunteer Week, Natl, Apr 19
   Volunteer Week, Natl (Pres Proc), Apr 19
von Braun, Wernher: First Surface-to-
   Surface Guided Missile: Anniv, Dec 24
Von Frisch, Karl: Birth Anniv, Nov 20
von Furstenberg, Diane: Birth, Dec 31
Von Humboldt, Alexander: Birth Anniv,
   Sep 14
Von Oy, Jenna: Birth, May 2
von Richthofen, Manfred (Red Baron):
   Birth Anniv, May 2
von Richthofen: Red Baron Shot Down:
   Anniv, Apr 21
Von Sacher-Masoch, Leopold: Birth Anniv,
   Jan 27
von Schiller, Friedrich: Birth Anniv, Nov 10

von Stade, Frederica: Birth, Jun 1
Von Steuben, Baron Friedrich: Birth Anniv,
   Sep 17
Von Sydow, Max: Birth, Apr 10
Vonn, Lindsey: Birth, Oct 18
Vonnegut, Kurt, Jr: Birth Anniv, Nov 11
vos Savant, Marilyn: Birth, Aug 11
Voting,
   Blacks Ruled Eligible to Vote: Anniv, Apr 3
   League of Women Voters Formed: Anniv,
      Feb 14
   Seneca Falls Convention Attendee Votes:
      Anniv, Nov 2
   Suffragists' Voting Attempt: Anniv, Nov 11
   Susan B. Anthony Arrested for Voting:
      Anniv, Nov 18
   Voting Age Changed (26th Amendment):
      Anniv, Jul 1
   Voting Rights Act Signed: Anniv, Aug 6
   Women's Rights Convention at Seneca
      Falls: Anniv, Jul 19
   Women's Suffrage Amendment
      Introduced: Anniv, Jan 10
Vowell, Sarah: Birth, Dec 27
Vuelta a Espana (Spain), Aug 14

Wachowski, Lana: Birth, Jun 21
Wachowski, Lilly: Birth, Dec 29
Waco Horror: Jesse Washington Lynching:
   Anniv, May 15
Wade, Dwyane: Birth, Jan 17
Wade, Virginia: Birth, Jul 10
Wadlow, Robert Pershing: Birth Anniv,
   Feb 22
Waffle Week, Natl, Sep 6
Waggoner, Lyle: Birth, Apr 13
Wagner Fest (Bayreuth, Germany), Jul 25
Wagner, Billy: Birth, Jun 25
Wagner, Honus: Birth Anniv, Feb 24
Wagner, Jack: Birth, Oct 3
Wagner, Kurt: Birth, Jun 22
Wagner, Lindsay: Birth, Jun 22
Wagner, Richard: Birth Anniv, May 22
Wagner, Robert: Birth, Feb 10
Wagon Day, Little Red, Mar 25
Wahl, Ken: Birth, Dec 11
Wahlberg, Donnie: Birth, Aug 17
Wahlberg, Mark: Birth, Jun 5
Waikiki Holiday Parade (Waikiki, HI),
   Nov 27
Waikiki Roughwater Swim (Honolulu, HI),
   Sep 7
Waitangi Day (New Zealand), Feb 6
Waite, Morrison R.: Birth Anniv, Nov 29
Waite, Terry: Birth, May 31
Waititi, Taika: Birth, Aug 16
Waits, Tom: Birth, Dec 7
Waitstaff Day, Natl, May 21
Waitz, Grete: Birth, Oct 1
Walcott, Derek: Birth Anniv, Jan 23
Walden, Robert: Birth, Sep 25
Waldseemuller, Martin: Cosmographiae
   Introductio Published: Anniv, Apr 25
Wales,
   Christmas Holiday, Dec 25
   Curtis Cup (Caernarvonshire), Jun 12
   Natl Eisteddfod of Wales (Tregaron), Aug 1
   Saint David's Day, Mar 1
   Saint Dwynwen's Day, Jan 25
Walesa, Lech: Birth, Sep 29
Walesa, Lech: Solidarity Founded: Anniv,
   Aug 31

Accessing the Exclusive
Chase's Calendar of Events Website!

The power of *Chase's* is now at your fingertips with an exclusive online companion website for purchasers of the 2020 edition! With this website, you can access all of the 12,500 events, holidays, birthdays and special observances of the main calendar; perform simple or advanced searches in a variety of ways and print out the results.

Simply go to **www.2020ChasesCalendarofEvents.com** and enter the password **Fidelio1770SusanB19th20** to discover all the content of the 2019 edition and much more!

At **www.2020ChasesCalendarofEvents.com**, you'll find these features:

- **An advanced Search page** that allows customized searches of *Chase's* content by keyword, location, category, attendance and more

- **What's on Today?** Holidays, anniversaries, astronomical phenomena for the current day

- **Birthdays Today:** Birthdays of note for the current day

- **Around Your World:** Search an interactive map of the world to find unique and colorful festivals

- **Calendar and Day Counter:** Plan your month—or next month—and count down the days of the year

- **Link to *Chase's* Twitterfeed**

- Plus pages for **Major Awards, About the Holidays, Glossary of Calendar Terms** and **Special Months for the Year**

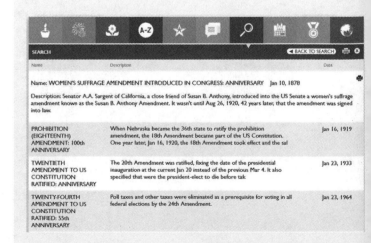

The *Chase's* online companion site is for purchasers only and can be accessed by Macs, PCs, laptops and tablets (7" to 10") from Oct 14, 2019 to Dec 31, 2020.